Contents

Collins

BRADFORD'S
CROSSWORD
SOLVER'S
DICTIONARY

ANNE R. BRADFORD

HarperCollins Publishers
Westerhill Road
Bishopbriggs
Glasgow
G64 2QT
Great Britain

Ninth Edition 2013

First edition published by Longman;
second, third and fourth editions
published by Peter Collin Publishing
Ltd

ISBN 978-0-00-752339-9

www.collinsdictionary.com
www.collins.co.uk

A catalogue record for this book is
available from the British Library

Technical support and typesetting by
Thomas Callan

Printed in Italy by Lego SpA,
Lavis (Trento)

Note

Author's Preface

Word puzzles have existed nearly as long as words themselves with examples being found during archaeological excavations. In his book, *The Anatomy of the Crossword*, D.St.P. Barnard describes letter patterns in triangular or diamantine form and an ingenious word square discovered at a Roman site at Cirencester.

Word puzzles are a source of pleasure even to quite young children. I myself remember playing a game where we each had a square grid – 5×5 or 6×6 – and we took turns choosing a letter to insert in it until all the squares were occupied, scoring points for any proper words that appeared either across the grid or down.

The Victorians were fond of acrostics, usually in verse form with the initial letters of each line giving the solution. Double acrostics went a step further with both initial and last letters of each line being employed. At first these tended to be tributes of a sort. They became quite difficult puzzles when the initial verse was turned into a definition of the answer, and the subsequent lines became clues to the acrostic part.

> We shun the light and fly by night (BAT (initial letter) OWL (final))
> 1. An interjection that may make you start   BoO
> 2. A feathered foe may pierce you to the heart   ArroW
> 3. A tax oft levied on a horse and cart   ToLL

Many years later we were playing a simpler version (BAT is the only answer),
> My first is in cable, but not in wire,
> My second in arson, but not in fire
> My last is in lettuce, though not in bean
> My whole in daylight is rarely seen.

Spoken word games were equally popular before the age of electronics. 'I-spy' is still with us and repetitive round games are very good for the memory. For example, 'I love my love with an A because she is – adorable', to be repeated by the next player who adds 'I love my love with a B because she is – beautiful' and on through the alphabet, but ignoring X and Z for the most part.

Acrostics were followed by the earliest form of the crossword as we know it, consisting of simple grids which allowed for both across and down answers, hence 'cross' words. The USA was the first country to provide this exercise in regular print when the *New York World* introduced it in 1913. More than a decade passed before such puzzles appeared in Britain, with *The Sunday Times* being the first to publish one, in 1925. People soon became addicted and the popular postcard manufacturers were quick to bring out postcards with a crossword theme, as in this illustration:

One of the thirty seven comic crossword designs by Donald McGill. Reproduced with consent from the Donald McGill Archive & Museum, Ryde.

My mother and at least one of her sisters loved crosswords, so I was introduced to them at an early age. She had taught me to read and write long before I started school – entry in those days being after the 5th birthday – but although I had a passion for words I did no regular crossword puzzles until my late teens, and it was a few years more before I really took them seriously. I struggled with the weekly Ximenes puzzle in the weekend paper, learning many new words. He was particularly fond of 'lat' a form of pillar, so I started to write down a sort of memorandum. It was then that the idea came to me of a 'reverse dictionary' where headword and definition would change place. Full of enthusiasm, and by this time staying at home raising a family, I wrote to several leading dictionary publishers, none of whom were interested – possibly rightly so because when I pressed ahead with the project regardless, it was over 20 years before I had anything like enough material for a book. I analysed each crossword I completed (as I do still), selecting synonym, cross references, familiar adjectives and also anagram indicators. These were entered into alphabetical files and each week I worked out the percentage already included, having a target of 70% in mind in order to make a book worthy of publication. It was quite a few years before I converted to an alphabetical main file, my back up ones being indexed by page numbers. Besides analysing puzzles I was also working my way through English dictionaries and other word books in search of further material, and barely arriving at the end of one before a new edition of another reached the market.

It was about 25 years before my labours bore fruit with the eventual appearance of *Longman's Crossword Solver's Dictionary* in 1986, but the firm was taken over by Penguin around 1990 and the reference section closed down, so I was once again seeking a publisher. A year or so later I was lucky to find Peter Collin, who published only reference works. The name *Collin's Crossword Solver's Dictionary* was unsuitable for obvious reasons, and so it became Bradford's, but might well have been Collins when this company took it on in 2002. Happily they decided my surname was sufficiently established and should remain.

Who knows how long crosswords will survive, given our present electronic age and the advance of numerical puzzles. I am delighted to have been involved with them for most of my life, and to have made so many friends along the way. My sincere thanks to you all for your encouragement and for keeping me on my toes, and to the team at Collins who are so supportive.

Anne R. Bradford *2012*

Solving Crossword Clues

Crossword puzzles tend to be basically 'quick' or 'cryptic'. A 'quick' crossword usually relies on a one- or two-word clue which is a simple definition of the answer required. Many words have different meanings, so that the clue 'ball' could equally well lead to the answer 'sphere', 'orb', or 'dance'. The way to solve 'quick' crosswords is to press on until probable answers begin to interlink, which is a good sign that you are on the right track.

'Cryptic' crosswords are another matter. Here the clue usually consists of a basic definition, given at either the beginning or end of the clue, together with one or more definitions of parts of the answer. Here are some examples taken from all-time favourites recorded over the years:

1. *'Tradesman who bursts into tears'* (**Stationer**)

   Tradesman is a definition of stationer. *Bursts* is cleverly used as an indication of an anagram, which *into tears* is of stationer.

2. *'Sunday school tune'* (**Strain**)

   Here *Sunday* is used to define its abbreviation S, *school* is a synonym for train, and put together they give strain, which is a synonym of *tune*.

3. *'Result for everyone when head gets at bottom'* (**Ache**)
   (used as a 'down' clue)

   This is what is known as an '& lit' clue, meaning that the setter has hit on a happy composition which could literally be true. *Everyone* here is a synonym for each, move the *head* (first letter) of the word to the *bottom*, and the answer is revealed, the whole clue being the definition of the answer in this case.

4. *'Tin out East'* (**Sen**)

   In this example, *tin*, implying 'money', requires its chemical symbol Sn to go *out*(side) *East*, or its abbreviation, E, the whole clue being a definition of a currency (sen) used in the East.

5. *'Information given to communist in return for sex'* (**Gender**)

Information can be defined as gen; *communist* is almost always red, *in return* indicates 'reversed', leading to gen-der, a synonym for *sex*.

6. *'Row about no enclosure of this with sardines'* (**Tin-opener**)

Row is a synonym for tier, *about* indicates 'surrounding', *no enclosure* can be no pen, leading to ti-no pen-er, and another '& lit' clue.

7. *'Cake-sandwiches-meat, at Uncle Sam's party'* (**Clambake**)

Meat here is lamb, *sandwiches* is used as a verb, so we have C-lamb-ake, which is a kind of party in America. *Uncle Sam* or US is often used to indicate America.

8. *'Initially passionate meeting of boy and girl could result in it'* (**Pregnancy**)

Initially is usually a sign of a first letter, in this case 'p' for *passionate* + Reg (a *boy*) and Nancy (a *girl*), and another clever '& lit'.

With 'cryptic' clues the solver needs to try to analyse the parts to see what he or she is looking for – which word or words can be the straight definition, and which refer to the parts or hint at anagrams or other subterfuges. Whilst it would be unrealistic to claim total infallibility, practice has shown that in most crosswords some 90% of the answers are to be found in this work.

Anne R. Bradford

How to use the Dictionary

This dictionary is the result of over fifty-five years' analysis of some 325,000 crossword clues, ranging from plain 'quick' crosswords requiring only synonyms to the different level of cryptic puzzles. Therefore the words listed at each entry may be connected to the keyword in various ways, such as:

- a straightforward synonym

- a commonly-associated adjective

- an associated or proper noun

- a pun or other devious play on words

Keywords are listed alphabetically; in cases where the heading consists of more than one word, the first of these words is taken to be the keyword, and in cases where the end of a word is bracketed, the material up to the opening bracket is taken to be the keyword. Keywords marked with the symbol ▶ refer the user to other entries where additional information may be found. Keywords marked with the symbol ▷ give leads to anagrams and other ploys used by crossword setters. If the keywords found in the clue do not lead directly to the required answer, the solver should look under words given as cross-references to other entries. These are indicated by the symbol →, with the cross-referenced word shown in capitals.

Some additional entries have been divided into two parts – a general entry similar to the standard entries which appear elsewhere, and a panel entry which contains a list of more specific or encyclopedic material. So, for example, the entry 'Artist(ic)' includes not only a list of general words connected with 'Artist' or 'Artistic' in some way, such as 'Bohemian', 'Cubist', 'Fine' and 'Virtuoso', but also a panel with the heading 'Artists' containing a list of the names of specific artists, such as 'Bellini', 'Constable', and 'Rembrandt'. For added help, the words in these panels are arranged by length, with all three-letter words grouped together in alphabetical order, then all four-letter words, then all five-letter words, and so on.

The Crossword Club

If you are interested in crosswords, you might like to consider joining the Crossword Club. Membership is open to all who enjoy tackling challenging crosswords and who appreciate the finer points of clue-writing and grid-construction. The Club's magazine, Crossword, contains two prize puzzles each month. A sample issue and full details are available on request.

The Crossword Club
Coombe Farm
Awbridge
Romsey, Hants.
SO51 0HN
UK

email: bh@thecrosswordclub.co.uk
website address: www.thecrosswordclub.co.uk

About the Author

Anne Bradford's love of words began to make itself evident even in her schooldays, when, as Head Girl of her school, she instituted a novel punishment – instead of making rulebreakers write lines, she had them write out pages from a dictionary, on the grounds that this was a more useful exercise. Little did she know this was soon to be her own daily routine!

As Anne tells in her preface to this edition, she conceived the idea for the dictionary pretty well along with her first child. Over the space of 25 years, Anne continued to build on her collection of solutions, analysing every crossword clue as she solved it and adding it to her steadily growing bank of entries. This unique body of material eventually reached such proportions that she had the idea of offering it to her fellow crossword solvers as a reference book, and since then, the book has gone from strength to strength, providing valuable help to countless cruciverbalists over a number of editions.

Anne Bradford continues to devote time each day to solving crosswords, averaging some 20 a week – both quick and cryptic – and still avidly collects new solutions for her *Crossword Solver's Dictionary* at a rate of around 150 a week, compiling each solution by hand (without the use of a computer!). This latest edition therefore includes much new material, gleaned by a true crossword lover who not only solves crosswords but, as an active member of the Crossword Club, can offer the user an insight into the mind of a cunning crossword compiler.

Aa

A, An Ack, Adult, Ae, Alpha, Angstrom, Are, Argon, D, Ein, Her, If, L, One, Per, They

A1 Tiptop

AA Milne

Aardvark Ant-bear, Ant-eater, Earth-hog, Ground-hog

Aaron's Rod Hagtaper

Aba, Abba Patriarch

Abacus Counter, Soroban

Abaft Astern, Sternson

Abalone Ormer, Paua, Perlemoen

Abandon(ed), Abandonment Abdicate, Abnegate, Abort, Adrift, Aguna(h), Amoral, Apostasy, Back down, Cade, Cancel, Castaway, Chuck, Corrupt, Decommission, Defect, Derelict, → **DESERT**, Desuetude, Dice, Discard, Disown, Dissolute, Disuse, Ditch, Drop, Dump, Elan, Evacuate, Expose, Flagrant, Forhoo(ie), Forhow, Forlend, Forsake, Gomorra, Gretel, Hansel, Immoral, Jack(-in), Jettison, Jilt, Leave, Loose, Louche, Mad, Maroon, Old, Orgiastic, Profligate, Quit, Rakish, Rat, Relinquish, Renounce, Reprobate, Scrap, Shed, Sink, Strand, Vacate, Waive, Wanton, Wild, Yield

Abase Degrade, Demean, Disgrace, Eat crow, Embrute, Grovel, → **HUMBLE**, Kowtow, Lessen

Abash Daunt, Discountenance, Mortify

Abate(ment) Allay, Appal, Decrescent, Deduction, Defervescence, Diminish, Let up, Lyse, Lysis, Moderate, Reduce, Remit, → **SUBSIDE**

▷ **Abate** *may indicate* a contention

Abattoir Knackery, Slaughterhouse

Abbey Abbacy, Ampleforth, Bath, Buckfast, Cloister, Downside, Fonthill, Fountains, Glastonbury, Györ, Je(r)vaulx, Medmenham, Melrose, Minster, Nightmare, Northanger, Priory, Rievaulx, Tintern, Westminster, Whitby, Woburn

Abbot Aelfric, Archimandrite, Brother, Eutyches, Friar

Abbreviate, Abbreviation Abridge, Ampersand, Compendium, Condense, Curtail, → **SHORTEN**, Sigla

ABC Absey

Abdicate, Abdication Cede, Demission, Disclaim, Disown, Resign

Abdomen Belly, C(o)eliac, Epigastrium, Gaster, Hypochondrium, Opisthosoma, Paunch, Pleon, → **STOMACH**, Tummy, Venter, Ventral

Abduct(ed), Abduction Asport, Enlèvement, Kidnap, Rapt, Ravish, Shanghai, Steal

Aberdeen Granite City

Aberrant, Aberration Abnormal, Aye-aye, Chromatic, Deviant, Idolon, Perverse, Spherical

Abet(tor) Aid, Back, Candle-holder, Second

Abeyance, Abeyant Dormant, Shelved, Sleeping, Store

Abhor(rent) → **DETEST**, Execrable, → **HATE**, Loathe, Odious, Shun

Abide Adhere, Dwell, Inhere, → **LAST**, Lie, Live, Observe, Remain, Stand, Tarry

Abigail Maid, Masham

Ability Acumen, Aptitude, Calibre, Capacity, Cocum, → **COMPETENCE**, Efficacy, ESP, Facility, Faculty, Ingine, Initiative, Instinct, Lights, Potential, Power, Prowess, Savey, Savoir-faire, Savv(e)y, Skill, Talent

Abject Base, Craven, Grovel, Humble, Servile, Slave

Abjure Eschew, Forswear, Recant, Renege, Reny

Ablaze Afire, Alow, Ardent

Able Ablins, Accomplished, → **ADEPT**, Aiblins, Apt, Capable, → **COMPETENT**, Fere, Fit, Idiot savant, Literate, Proficient, Seaman, Yibbles

Abnormal(ity) Anomalous, Aplasia, Atypical, Autism, → **DEVIANT**, Dysfunction, Ectopic, Erratic, Etypical, Exceptional, Freakish, Hare-lip, Malocclusion, Odd, Peloria, Phenocopy, Preternatural, → **QUEER**, Sport, Teras, Trisome, Unconventional, Unnatural, Varus

Aboard On

Abode Domicile, Dwelling, Habitat, → **HOME**, In(n), Lain, Libken, Limbo, Midgard, Remain, Seat

Abolish, Abolition(ist) Abrogate, Annihilate, Annul, Axe, → **BAN**, D, Delete, Destroy, Eradicate, Erase, Extirpate, John Brown, Nullify, Remove, Repeal, Rescind, Scrap, Tubman, Wilberforce

Abomasum Read

Abominable, Abominate, Abomination Anathema, Bane, Cursed, → **HATE**, Nefandous, Nefast, Revolting, Snowman, Vile, Yeti

Aboriginal, Aborigine Adivasi, Ainu, Aranda, Autochthon, Awakabai, Binghi, Black-fellow, Boong, Buck, Bushmen, Carib, Devil's Marbles, Dharuk, Dhurga, Dieri, Diyari, Evolué, Fringe-dweller, Gin, Gurindji, Indigenous, Inuit, Jacky(-Jacky), Kamilaroi, Kipper, Koori, Lubra, Maori, Mary, Motu, Myall, Negro, Nisga'a, Nyunga(r), Pintubi, Pitjant(j)ara, Pre-Dravidian, Sakai, San, Sican, Siwash, Truganini, Vedda(h), Warlpiri, Wemba, Weniba, Wergaia, Wiradhui, Wiradjai, Yagara, Yupik

Abort(ion), Abortive Apiol, Back-street, Cancel, Contagious, Ecbolic, Foeticide, Induced, Misbirth, Miscarry, Moon-calf, Slip, Sooterkin, Spontaneous, Teras, Termination

Abound(ing) Bristle, Copious, Enorm, Flush, Overflow, Rife, Swarm, Teem

About A, Almost, Anent, Around, C, Ca, Cir(c), Circa, Circiter, Concerning, Encompass, Environs, Going, Near, Of, On, Over, Re, Regarding, Soon at

▷ **About** *may indicate* one word around another

Above Abune, Aforementioned, Aloft, Over, Overhead, Overtop, Owre, Sopra, Superior, Supra-, Suspicion, Upon

Abracadabra Cantrip, Heypass

Abrade, Abrasive Alumina, Carbanado, Carborundum®, Chafe, Emery, Erode, File, Garnet paper, → **GRATE**, Rub, Sand, Scrape, Scrat, Scuff

Abraham Father of the faithful, Lincoln, Patriarch, Urite

Abreast Afront, Alongside, Au courant, Au fait, Beside, Level, Up

Abridge(ment) Audley, Compress, Condense, Contract, Cut, Digest, Dock, Edit, Epitome, Pot, Shorten, Trim

Abroad Afield, Away, Distant, Elsewhere, Forth, Offshore, Out, Overseas

▷ **Abroad** *may indicate* an anagram

Abrogate Abolish, Repeal, Replace

Abrupt(ly) Bold, Brusque, Curt, Gruff, Jerky, Offhand, Premorse, Prerupt, Short, Staccato, Terse

▷ **Abrupt** *may indicate* a shortened word

Abscess Gumboil, Impost(h)ume, Ulcer, Warble

Abscond Absquatulate, Decamp, Desert, Elope, Escape, Flee, Jump ship, Leg-bail, Levant, Run away, Skase, Welch

Abseil(ing) Dulfer, Rappel, Roping-down

Absence, Absent(ee), Absent-minded(ness) A, Abs, Abstracted, Away, Distant, Distracted, Distrait, Dreamy, Exeat, Exile, Gone, Hookey, Malingerer, Missing, Mitch, No show, Oblivious, Sabbatical, Scatty, Skip, Truant, Vacuity, Void, Wanting, Wool-gathering

Absinthe Wormwood

Absolute(ly) Bang, Complete, Dead, Deep-dyed, Downright, Fairly, Flat, Heartily, Implicit, Ipso facto, Just, Literally, Meer, Mere, Mondo, Nominative, Outright, Plenary, Plumb, Quite, Real, Sheer, Simply, Thorough, Total, Truly, Unadulterated, Unconditional, Unmitigated, Unqualified, Utter, Veritable, Very, Yeah

Absolve, Absolution Acquit, Assoil, Assoilzie, Clear, Exculpate, Excuse, Pardon, Redeem, Shrift, Shrive

Absorb(ed), Absorbent, Absorbing, Absorption Assimilate, Autism, Blot, Consume, Desiccant, Devour, Digest, Dope, Drink, Eat, → **ENGROSS**, Enrapt, Imbibe, Immerse, Ingest, Inhaust, Intent, Merge(r), Occlude, Occupy, Osmosis, Permeable, Porous, Preoccupation, Preoccupied, Rapt, Sorbefacient, Spongy, Subsume, Unputdownable, Yrapt

Absquatulate Skedaddle

Abstain(er), Abstemious, Abstention, Abstinence, Abstinent Band of Hope, Celibacy, Chastity, Continent, Desist, Eschew, Fast, Forbear, Forgo, Maigre, Nazarite, Nephalism, Pioneer, Rechab(ite), Refrain, Resist, Sober, Teetotaller, Temperate, TT, Virtue

Abstract(ed), Abstraction Abrege, Abridge, Academic, Appropriate, Brief, Compendium, Deduct, Digest, Discrete, Distrait, Epitome, Essence, Inconscient, Metaphysical, Musing, Notional, Précis, Preoccupied, Prepossessed, Prescind, Remove, Resumé, Reverie, Scatty, Stable, Steal, Subduct, Summary, Syllabus, Tachism

Abstruse Arcane, Deep, Esoteric, Impenetrable, Obscure, Recondite

Absurd(ity) Alician, Apagoge, Fantastic, Farcical, Folly, Inept, Irrational, Laputan, Ludicrous, Madness, Nonsense, Paradox, Preposterous, Ridiculous, Silly, Solecism, Stupid, Toshy, Whim-wham

Abundance, Abundant A-gogo, Ample, Aplenty, Bounty, Copious, Corn in Egypt, Cornucopia, Cosmic, Excess, Flood, Flush, Fouth, Fowth, Fruitful, Galore, Lashings, Lavish, Luxuriance, Mickle, Mine, Mint, Muckle, Natural, Oodles, Oodlins, Opulent, Over, Plenitude, Plenteous, → **PLENTIFUL**, Plenty, Pleroma, Plethora, Plurisie, Profusion, Prolific, Relative, Replete, Rich, Rife, Rock and manger, Routh, Rowth, Sonce, Sonse, Store, Stouth and routh, Superabound, Surfeit, Tallents, Teeming, Tons, Uberous

Abuse, Abusive Assail, Becall, Billingsgate, Blackguard, Chemical, Cruelty, Diatribe, Ear-bashing, Flak, Fustilarian, Fustil(l)irian, Hail, Hate mail, Ill-treat, Insolent, Insult, Invective, Jobbery, Limehouse, Malpractice, Maltreat, Miscall, → **MISTREAT**, Misuse, Mofo, Molest, Mud, Obloquy, Oppress, Opprobrium, Philippic, Rail, Rampallian, Rate, Rayle, Revile, Ritual, Satanic, Satire, Scarab(ee), Scurrilous, Serve, Sexual, Slang, Slate, Sledging, Snash, Solvent, Strap, Substance, Thersitical, Tirade, Torture, Verbal, Vilify, Violate, Vituperation, Wosbird

Abut Adjoin, Border, Touch

Abysm(al), Abyss Avernus, Barathrum, Barranca, Chasm, Deep, Gulf, Swallet, Tartarean, Tartarus

AC Current, Erk

Acacia Bablah, Boree, Brigalow, Eumong, Eumung, Fever tree, Gidgee, Gidjee, Koa, Mimosa, Mulga, Myall, Sallee, Shittim, Wattle

Academic(ian) A, Acca, Acker, Della-Cruscan, Don, Erudite, Fellow, Hypothetic(al), Immortals, Literati, Master, Pedantic, PRA, Prof(essor), RA, Reader, Rector

Academy, Academic A, Athenaeum, Dollar, Donnish, Forty, French, Learned, Loretto, Lyceum, Military, Naval, Plantilla, RA, Royal, St Cyr, Sandhurst, School, Seminary, Studious, The Shop, West Point

Acanthus Brankursine, Ruellia

Accelerate, Acceleration, Accelerator Antedate, Betatron, Bevatron, Collider, Cosmotron, Cyclotron, Festinate, G, Gal, Grav, Gun, Hasten, Increase, Linac, Linear, Rev, Signatron, Speed, Stringendo, Supercollider, Synchrotron, Throttle

Accent(ed), Accentuate Acute, Beat, Breve, Brogue, Bur(r), Circumflex, Cut-glass, Doric, Drawl, Enclitic, Enhance, Gammat, Grave, Hacek, Intonation, Kelvinside, Long,

Macron, Marcato, Martelé, Mockney, Morningside, Mummerset, Nasal, Orthotone, Oxford, Oxytone, Paroxytone, Perispomenon, Pitch, Primary, Proparoxytone, Rhotic, Rhythm, Rinforzando, Secondary, Sforzando, Stress, Tittle, Tone, Tonic, Twang

Accentor Dunnock

Accept(able), Acceptance, Accepted A, Accede, Adequate, Admit, Adopt, Agree, Allow, Alright, Approbate, Bar, Believe, Buy, Can-do, Common, Consent, Cool, Cosher, Decent, Done, Embrace, Going, Grant, Idee recue, Include, Kosher, Meet, Nod, Obey, On, Pocket, Putative, Receive, Resipiscence, Satisfactory, Settle, Stand, Street cred, Suppose, Swallow, Take (on board), Tolerate, U, Valid, Wear, Widespread

Access(ible), Accessibility Avenue, Blue-jacking, Card, Come-at-able, Conditional, Credit, Direct, Door, Entrée, → **ENTRY**, Fit, Gateway, Get-at-able, Hack, Ingo, Key, Log in, Log on, Manhole, Near, Passe-partout, Passkey, Password, Phreaking, Ping, Random, Recourse, Remote, Sequential, Spasm, Telnet, Wayleave

Accessory, Accessories Abettor, Addition, Aide, Ally, Ancillary, Appendage, Appurtenance, Attachment, Attribute, Bandanna, Bells and whistles, Cribellum, Cuff-links, Findings, Fitment, Staffage, Trappings, Trimming

Accident(al) Adventitious, Arbitrary, Bechance, Blowdown, Blunder, Calamity, → **CHANCE**, Circumstance, Contingency, Contretemps, Crash, Criticality, Dent, Disaster, Double flat, Fall, Fluke, Fortuitous, Hap, Hit and run, Inadvertent, Meltdown, Mischance, Mishap, Note, Promiscuous, Random, Rear-ender, Shunt, Smash, Smash-up, Spill, Stramash, Unmeant, Wreck

Accidie Acedia, Sloth, Torpor

Acclaim Accolade, Applaud, Brava, Bravo, Cheer, Eclat, Fame, Fanfare, Hail, Kudos, Ovation, Praise, Salute, Zindabad

Acclimatize Attune

Accolade Award, Brace, Dubbing, Honour, Palm, Token, Tribute

Accommodate, Accommodating, Accommodation Adapt, Almshouse, B and B, Bedsit, Berth, Billet, Board, Botel, Bunkhouse, Camp, Chalet, Chambers, Compromise, Crashpad, Digs, Flotel, Gaff, Gite, Grace and favour, Homestay, Hostel, Hotel, House, Lend, Loan, Lodge, Lodgement, Minshuku, Motel, → **OBLIGE**, Parador, Pension, Pliant, Prefab, Quarters, Rapprochement, Recurve, Room, Sheltered, Single-end, Sorehon, Stabling, Stateroom, Steerage, Storage, Tent, Timeshare, Wharepuni, Xenodochium

▷ **Accommodating** *may indicate* one word inside another

Accompany(ing), Accompanied (by), Accompaniment, Accompanist Accessory, Alberti, And, Attach, Attend, Backing, Chaperone, Chum, Concomitant, Consort, Continuo, Descant, → **ESCORT**, Fixings, Harmonise, Herewith, Obbligato, Obligate, Obligato, Repetiteur, Soundtrack, Trimmings, Vamp

Accomplice Abettor, Aide, → **ALLY**, Bagman, Bonnet, Collaborator, Confederate, Federarie, Federary, Partner, Shill, Stale, Swagsman

Accomplish(ed), Accomplishment Able, → **ACHIEVE**, Arch, Attain, Clever, Complete, Consummate, Done, Doss, Effect, Galant, Master, Over, Perform, Polished, Prowess, Put through, Realise, Ripe, Savant, Success, Tour de force

Accord, According(ly), According to After, Agree, Ala, Allow, As per, Attune, Chime, Congree, Consensus, Give, Grant, Harmony, Jibe, Meech Lake, Meet, Per, So, Sort, Thus

According to nature SN

Accordion Bandoneary, Button, Concertina, Flutina, Piano, Squeeze-box

Accost Abord, Approach, Greet, Hail, Importune, Molest, Solicit, Tackle

Account(s) AC, Anecdote, Appropriation, Audit, Battels, Behalf, Bill, Books, Budget, Cause, Charge, Checking, Chequing, Chronicle, Control, Current, Deposit, Discretionary, Drawing, Enarration, Expense, Explain, Exposition, ISA, Joint, Lawin, Ledger, Log, Long, Memoir, Narration, Nominal, Nostro, Numbered, Procès-verbal, Real, Reason, Recital, Regest, Register, → **REPORT**, Repute, Resumé, Sake, Short, Suspense, Swindlesheet, Tab, Tale, TESSA, Thesis, Trust, Version, Vostro

Accountable Responsible

Accountant Auditor, Bean counter, Bookkeeper, CA, Cost, Forensic, Hyde, Liquidator, Reckoner, Vestry-clerk

Accredit Attribute

Accrue Earn, Grow

Accumulate, Accumulation Accrue, Adsorb, Aggregate, → **AMASS**, Augment, Backlog, Build, Collect, Gather, Hoard, Lodg(e)ment, Oedema, Pile, Pool, Rack up, Run up, Save, Stockpile, Uplay

Accuracy, Accurate(ly) Bang-on, Cocker, → **CORRECT**, Dead-on, Exact, Fair, Fidelity, Griff, Minute, Precise, Realistic, Right, Spot-on, To scale, True, Unerring, Veracious, Word-perfect

Accursed Argued, Blest, Blist, Damned, Sacred

Accusation, Accuse(d) Allege, Arraign, Asperse, Attaint, Bill, Blame, Calumny, Censure, Challenge, Charge, Criminate, Denounce, Dite, Gravamen, Impeach, Incriminate, Indictment, Information, Name, Panel, Plaint, Prosecute, Suspect, Tax, Threap, Threep, Traduce, Wight, Wite, Wyte

Accustom(ed) Acquaint, Attune, Enure, General, Habituate, Harden, Inure, Teach, Wont, Woon

Ace(s) Basto, Blackjack, Crabs, Dinger, → **EXPERT**, Jot, Master, Mega, Mournival, One, Quatorze, Smashing, Spadille, Spadill(i)o, Spot, Tib, Virtuoso, Whizz, Wonderful

Acerbate Intensify

Acetylene Ethyne

Ache, Aching Aitch, Die, Hunger, Long, Mulligrubs, Nag, Otalgia, Pain, Sore, Stitch, Stound, Stownd, Work, Yearn, Yen

Achieve(ment) Accomplish, Acquisition, Attain, Big League, Come, Compass, Coup, Cum laude, → **EFFECT**, Enacture, Exploit, Feat, Fulfil, Gain, Hatchment, Masterpiece, Realise, Res gestae, Satisfice, Satisfy, Stroke, Succeed, Threepeat, Triumph, Trock, Troke, Truck

Achilles Heel, Tendon

Acid(ity) Acrimony, Corrosive, Drop, Etchant, Hydroxy, Reaction, Ribosomal, Ribozyme, Sharp, Solvent, Sour, Tart, Vinegar, Vitriol

---

ACIDS

2 letters:	Amide	Bromic	Phenol
PH	Amino	Capric	Picric
	Auric	Cholic	Quinic
3 letters:	Boric	Citric	Serine
DNA	Caro's	Cyanic	Sialic
EPA	Eisel	Domoic	Sorbic
HCL	Fatty	Erucic	Tannic
LSD	Folic	Formic	Tiglic
Oxo	Iodic	Gallic	Toluic
RNA	L-dopa	Lactic	Valine
	Lewis	Lauric	
4 letters:	Malic	Leucin	**7 letters:**
Acyl	Mucic	Lipoic	Abietic
Dopa	Oleic	Lysine	Acrylic
PABA	Orcin	Maleic	Alanine
Pyro	Osmic	Marine	Alginic
Uric	Trona	Niacin	Benzoic
Wood		Nitric	Butyric
	6 letters:	Oxalic	Caproic
5 letters:	Acetic	Oxygen	Cerotic
Algin	Adipic	Pectic	Chloric

Chromic
Creatin
Cystine
Ellagic
Eugenic
Ferulic
Folacin
Fumaric
Fusidic
Glycine
Guanine
Leucine
Malonic
Meconic
Melanic
Muramic
Nitrous
Nucleic
Orcinol
Peracid
Plumbic
Proline
Prussic
Pteroic
Pyruvic
Racemic
Sebacic
Selenic
Silicic
Stannic
Stearic
Suberic
Terebic
Titanic
Valeric
Vanadic
Xanthic
Xylonic

8 letters:
Abscisic
Adenylic
Arginine
Ascorbic
Aspartic
Butanoic
Caprylic
Carbamic
Carbolic
Carbonic
Chlorous
Cinnamic
Creatine
Cresylic

Crotonic
Cyclamic
Cysteine
Decanoic
Ethanoic
Fulminic
Glutamic
Glyceric
Glycolic
Guanylic
Hippuric
Hydracid
Iopanoic
Itaconic
Linoleic
Lysergic
Manganic
Margaric
Molybdic
Muriatic
Myristic
Nonanoic
Palmitic
Periodic
Phthalic
Retinoic
Rhodanic
Succinic
Sulfonic
Tantalic
Tartaric
Telluric
Tungstic
Tyrosine
Uridylic
Valproic

9 letters:
Aqua-regia
Carnitine
Cevitamic
Citydylic
Dichromic
Glutamine
Histidine
Hydrazoic
Hydriodic
Isocyanic
Linolenic
Mefenanic
Methanoic
Nalidixic
Nicotinic
Ornithine

Panthenic
Pentanoic
Polybasic
Propanoic
Propenoic
Propionic
Saccharic
Salicylic
Sassolite
Selenious
Sulphonic
Sulphuric
Tellurous
Threonine

10 letters:
Aquafortis
Asparagine
Barbituric
Carboxylic
Citrulline
Dithionous
Dodecanoic
Glucuronic
Glutamatic
Glutaminic
Hyaluronic
Isoleucine
Margaritic
Methionine
Neuraminic
Orthoboric
Pelargonic
Perchloric
Phosphonic
Phosphoric
Proprionic
Pyrogallic
Ricinoleic
Thiocyanic
Thymidylic
Trans-fatty
Tryptophan

11 letters:
Arachidonic
Butanedioic
Decanedioic
Ethanedioic
Ferricyanic
Ferrocyanic
Gibberellic
Hydnocarpic
Hydrobromic

Hydrocyanic
Hyponitrous
Methacrylic
Octanedioic
Pantothenic
Permanganic
Phosphorous
Ribonucleic
Sarcolactic
Taurocholic
Tryptophane

12 letters:
Dicraboxylic
Hydrochloric
Hydrofluoric
Hypochlorous
Indoleacetic
Orthosilicic
Persulphuric
Phenylalanin
Polyadenalic
Propanedioic
Prostacyclin
Pyroligneous
Terephthalic

13 letters:
Galactosamine
Heptadecanoic
Indolebutyric
Phenylalanine
Prostaglandin
Pyrosulphuric
Thiosulphuric
Transbutadoic

14 letters:
Metaphosphoric
Polyphosphoric
Pyrophosphoric

15 letters:
Orthophosphoric
Paramenobenzone
Pteroylglutamic
Trichloroacetic

16 letters:
Deoxyribonucleic
Triiodothyronine

Acknowledge(ment) Accept, Admit, Agnise, Allow, Answer, Avow, Con, Confess, Credit, Grant, Greet, Mea culpa, Nod, Own, Receipt, Recognise, Resipiscence, Respect, Righto, Roger, Salute, Ta, Thank you, Touché, Wilco, Yo

Acme Apex, Apogee, Climax, Comble, Crest, Peak, Summit, Top, Zenith

Acolyte Nethinim, Novice, Server, Thurifer

Acorn(s), Acorn-shell Balanus, Glans, Mast, Rac(c)ahout, Valonia

Acoustic(s) Harmonics, Phenocamptics, Phonics, Sonics

Acquaint(ance), Acquainted Advise, Cognisant, Enlighten, Familiar, → INFORM, Knowledge, Nodding, Notify, Tell, Versed

Acquiesce(nce), Acquiescent Accede, Accept, Bow, Conform, Resigned, Righto, Roger, Wilco, Yield

Acquire, Acquisition, Acquisitive Acquest, Adsorb, Cop, Earn, Ern, Gain, → GET, Glom, Irredentist, Land, Learn, Obtain, Procure, Purchase, Rapacity, Secure, Steal, Take-over, Target, Usucap(t)ion

Acquit(tal) Absolve, Assoil, Cleanse, Clear, Exonerate, Free, Loose, Loste, Pardon, Vindicate

Acre(s) A, Area, Bigha, Hide, Rival, Rood

Acrid, Acrimony Bitter(ness), Empyreuma, Pungent, Resentment, Rough, Sour, Surly

Acrobat(s), Acrobatics Equilibrist, Gymnast, Hot dog, Jerry-come-tumble, Ropedancer, Rope-walker, Speeler, Splits, Trampoline, Trick cyclist, Tumbler, Wing-walker

Acropolis Citadel, Parthenon

Across A, Ac, Athwart, Betwixt, O'ed, Opposite, Over, Through

Act(ing), Action, Active, Acts A, Actus reus, Affirmative, Afoot, Antic, Assist, Assumpsit, Atonement, Auto, Barnstorm, Barrier, Behave, Bit, Business, Camp, Campaign, Capillary, Caretaker, Case, Caster, Cause, Charade, Class, Come, Conduct, Consolation, COPPA, Coup, Daff, Deal, Declaratory, → DEED, Delaying, Deputise, Detinue, Dido, Direct, Do, DORA, Double, Enabling, Enclosure, Epitasis, Excitement, Exert, Exploit, Factory, Feat, Feign, Forthcoming, Forth-putting, Function, Habeas corpus, Histrionic, Homestead, Identic, Impersonate, Impro(visation), Improbation, Incident, Industrial, Juristic, Lance-jack, Law, Litigate, Lock-out, Locutionary, Masterstroke, Measure, Method, Mime, Movement, Mum, Mutiny, Navigation, Onstage, Overt, Partypiece, Pas, Perform(ance), Perlocutionary, Personate, Play, Positive, Pp, Practice, Pretence, Private, Procedure, Process, Public, Qua, Quia timet, Qui tam, Quiver, Reflex, Reform bill, Replevin, Represent, Riot, Rising, Roleplay, Routine, Sasine, Scenery, Secondary, Septennial, Serve, Settlement, Showdown, Shtick, Sick-out, Simulate, Speech, Sprightly, Stamp, Stanislavski, Statute, Steps, Suit, Synergy, Terminer, Test, Theatricise, Thellusson, Thing, Transitory, Treat, Trover, Truck, Turn, Twig, Uniformity, Union, Vicegerent, War, Windlass

Actinium Ac

Actinon An

Activate Arm, Engage, Goad, Spark, Spur, Stur, Styre, Trigger

Active, Activist, Activity A, Agile, Alert, At, Athletic, Brisk, Busy, Cadre, Deedy, DIY, Do(ing), Dynamited, Dynamo, Ecowarrior, Effectual, Energetic, Energic, Erupting, Exercise, Extra-curricular, Floruit, Fluster, Game, Go-go, Goings-on, Hum, Hyper, Leish, Licht, Live, Mobile, Motile, Nimble, Nippy, Ongo, On the go, Op, Operant, Optical, Play, Rambunctious, Residual, Shenanigan, Sideline, Sprightly, Springe, Spry, Sthenic, Stir, Surge, Third house, Vacuum, Voice, Wick, Wimble, Working, Ya(u)ld, Zionist

Actor(s), Actor-like Agent, Alleyn, Artist, Ashe, Barnstormer, Benson, Betterton, Bit player, Burbage, Cast, Character, Company, Diseur, Donat, Equity, Gable, Garrick, Gielgud, Guiser, Ham, Hamfatter, Heavy, Histrio(n), Impersonator, Jay, Juve(nile), Kean, Keaton, Luvvie, MacReady, Mime, Mummer, Olivier, O'Toole, Pantomimist, Performer, Player, Playfair, Protagonist, RADA, Roscian, Roscius, Savoyard, Scofield, Sim, Spear-carrier, Stager, Strolling, Super, Theatrical, Thespian, Tragedian, Tree, Tritagonist, Trouper, Understudy, Utility man, Wolfit

Actress Bankhead, Bow, Buffa, Duse, Figurant, Garbo, Harlow, Ingenue, Loren, Pierrette, Siddons, Soubrette, Swanson, Terry, West

Actual(ity), Actually De facto, Entelechy, Literal, Live, Material, Real, Real-life, Tangible, True, Very

Actuate, Actuator Suppository

Acumen Insight, Sense

Acupressure Jin shin do, Shiatsu

Acupuncture Moxa, Stylostixis

Acute Astute, Dire, Fitché, Incisive, → **INTENSE**, Keen, Quick-witted, Sharp

▶ **Ad** *see* **ADVERT(ISE)**

Adage Aphorism, Gnome, Maxim, Motto, Paroemia, Proverb, Saw, Saying, Truism

Adam Bede, Delved, Jailer

Adamant Firm, Inexorable, Insistent, Obdurate, Rigid, Unbending

Adapt(er), Adaptable, Adaptation, Adaptor Adjust, Bushing, Ecad, Flexible, Naturalise, Persona, Pliant, Refashion, Reorient, Resilient, Tailor, Timeserver, Transform, Versatile

Add(ed), Addendum, Adder Accrue, Adscititious, Annex, → **APPENDIX**, Attach, Cast, Coopt, Death, Dub, Ech(e), Eik, Eke, Elaborate, Embroider, Enhance, Fortify, Insert, Lace, Puff, Reckon, Retrofit, Score, Spike, Sum, Summate, Tack on, Top up, Tot(e), Total, Viper

Addict(ion), Addicted, Addictive Abuser, Acid freak, Acidhead, A colt's tooth, Alcoholic, Base head, Blunthead, Buff, Chocoholic, Couch potato, Dependency, Devotee, Dope-fiend, Dopehead, Etheromaniac, Fan, Fiend, Freak, Given, Glue-sniffing, Habit-forming, Hophead, Hound, Hype, Jones, Joypopper, Junkie, Lover, Mainliner, Mania, Narcotist, Need, Opiate, Opioid, Opium, Pillhead, Pillpopper, Pothead, Shithead, Shooter, Shopaholic, Slave, Snowbird, Space-cadet, Speedfreak, Sybaritism, Theism, User, Vinolent, Wino, Workaholic

Addison Spectator

Addition(al), Additive Accession, Addend, Additive, Adscititious, Adulterant, Advene, Also, And, Annexure, Antiknock, Appendage, (As an) in, Bolt-on, Braata, Carrag(h)anin, Carrageenan, Codicil, Corollary, Dextran, Eik, Eke, Encore, Epexegesis, Epithesis, Etc, Extender, Extension, → **EXTRA**, Extramural, Footnote, → **IN ADDITION**, Increment, Mae, Makeweight, Mo, Monkey, New, Odd, On, On top, Other, Padding, Paragog(u)e, Parergon, Plus, PS, Rider, Ripieno, Spare, Suffect, Suffix, Supplementary, Surcharge, Thereto, Top-up, Verandah

Address, Address system Accommodation, Accost, Adroit, Allocution, Apostrophe, Apostrophise, Appellation, Art, → **ATLAS**, Ave, Bub, Buster, Call, Cariad, Chuck, Compellation, Cousin, Dedication, Delivery, Den, Diatribe, Direction, Discourse, Election, Epilogue, Epirrhema, Esquire, Gettysburg, Gospodin, Hail, Home, Homily, Inaugural, IP, Jimmy, Kiddo, Lala, Lecture, Mac, Mester, Mister, Mush, Mynheer, Nkosi, Ode, Orate, Parabasis, Past master, Pastoral, Poste-restante, Prelection, Rig, Salute, Sermon, Sir(ree), Speech, Squire, Stance, Tact, Tannoy®, → **TITLE**, Towkay, Tuan, URL, Valedictory, Wambenger, Web, Wus, Y'all, You-all

Adduce Cite

Adelphic Adam

Adept Able, Adroit, Buff, Dab, Deacon, Don, → **EXPERT**, Fit, Handy, Mahatma, Past master

Adequate Condign, Does, Due, Egal, Equal, Ere-now, Passable, Proper, → **SUFFICIENT**, Tolerable, Valid

Adhere(nt), Adherence, Adhesive Allegiance, Ally, Araldite®, Blutack®, Bond, Burr, Child, Cling, Conform, Cow Gum®, Dextrin, Disciple, Emplastic, Epoxy, Fidelity, Follower, Glair, Glue, Goldsize, Guebre, Gum, Hot-melt, Impact, Jain(a), Loyalist, Mucilage, Nomism, Partisan, Resin, Sectator, Servitor, Stand pat, Sticker, Supporter, Synechia, Votary, Waterglass

Adjacent, Adjoining Bordering, Conterminous, Contiguous, Handy, Neighbouring, Nigh

Adjective Adnoun, Epithet, Gerundive

Adjourn(ment) Abeyance, Defer, Delay, → **POSTPONE**, Prorogate, Recess, Rise, Suspend

Adjudicate, Adjudication, Adjudicator Arbiter, Decide, Judge, Jury, Referee, Try, Umpire

Adjunct Addition, Aid, Ancillary, Rider

Adjust(able), Adjustment, Adjuster Accommodate, Adapt, Attune, Coapt, Dress, Ease, Fine-tune, Fit, Focus, Gang, Gauge, Gerrymander, J'adoube, Modify, Modulate, Orientate, Prepare, Primp, Redo, Reduce, Regulate, Reorientate, Reset, Resize, Retrofit, Scantle, Scotopia, Sliding, Suit, Tailor, Temper, Toe-in, Tram, Trim, True, Tune, Tweak, Vernier

▷ **Adjust** *may indicate* an anagram

Adjutant Aide, Argala, Officer, Stork

Adler Irene

Ad-lib Ex tempore, Improvise, Wing it

Administer, Administration, Administrator Adhibit, Anele, Apply, Arrondissement, Bairiki, Bureaucrat, Control, Corridors of power, Curia, → **DIRECT**, Dispence, Dispense, Executive, Front office, Intendant, Intinction, → **MANAGE**, MBA, Penpusher, Pepys, Raj, Regime, Registrar, Run, Secretariat, Soke, Steward, Sysop, Trustee

Admirable, Admiration, Admire(d), Admirer Clinker, Clipper, Conquest, Crichton, Esteem, Estimable, → **EXCELLENT**, Fine, Flame, Fureur, Gaze, Gem, Ho, Iconise, Idolater, Laudable, Lionise, Partisan, Rate, Regard, Respect, Ripping, Rocking, Splendid, Stotter, Toast, Tribute, Venerate, Wonder, Wow

Admiral Adm, AF, Anson, Beatty, Beaufort, Benbow, Blake, Bligh, Boscawen, Butterfly, Byng, Byrd, Capitan, Drake, Effingham, Fisher, Hood, Hornblower, Howard, Jellicoe, Keyes, Marrowfat, Mountbatten, Navarch, Nelson, Old Grog, Raeder, Red, Rodney, Spee, Sturdee, Togo, Vanessa, Van Nieman, Van Tromp, White

Admission, Admit(ting), Admitted, Admittance Accept, Access, Agree, Allow, Avow, Cognovit, Concede, → **CONFESS**, Enter, Entrée, Entry, Estoppel, Give, Grant, Induct, Ingress, Initiate, Intromit, Ordain, Ordination, Owe, Own, Privy, Recognise, Shrift, Take, Tho(ugh), Yield

Admonish, Admonition Caution, Chide, Lecture, Moralise, Pi-jaw, Rebuke, Reprimand, → **SCOLD**, Tip, Warn

Ado Bother, Bustle, Fuss, Lather

Adolescent Bodgie, Developer, Grower, Halflin, Immature, Juvenile, Neanic, Teenager, Tweenager, Veal, Widgie, Youth

Adonais Keats

Adonis Pheasant's Eye

Adopt(ed) Accept, Affect, Affiliate, Allonym, Assume, Dalt, Embrace, Espouse, Father, Foster, Mother

Adoration, Adore(r), Adoring Doat, Dote, Goo-goo, Homage, Idolise, Latria, Love, Pooja(h), Puja, Revere, Venerate, Worship, Zoolater

Adorn(ed), Adornment Aplustre, Attrap, Banderol, Bedeck, Bedight, Begem, Bejewel, Caparison, Clinquant, Deck, Dight, Drape, Embellish, Emblaze, Emblazon, Embroider, Enchase, Equip, Festoon, Flourish, Furnish, Garnish, Grace, Graste, Ornament, Riband, Story, Tattoo, Tatu, Tinsel, Trappings

Adrenaline Epinephrin(e)

Adroit Adept, Clever, Dextrous, Expert, Neat, Skilful

Adulate, Adulation Flatter(y), Praise, → **WORSHIP**

Adullam Cave

Adult Amadoda, Consenting, Grown-up, Imago, Man, Mature, Upgrown, X

Adulterant, Adulterate Cut, Debase, Impurify, Lime, Load, Mix, Multum, → **POLLUTE**, Sophisticate, Weaken

Adulterer, Adultery Avoutery, Co-respondent, Cuckold, Fornication, Francesca, Lenocinium, Two-timer

Advance(d), Advancement A, Abord, Accelerate, Anabasis, Ante, Approach, Ascend, Assert, Better(ment), Breakthrough, Bring on, Charge, Develop, Elevation, Evolué, Extreme, Far, Fast-forward, Fore, Forge, Forward, Further, Gain, Get on, Grubstake, Haut(e), Hi-tec(h), Impress, Imprest, Incede, Late, Lend, → **LOAN**, March, Mortgage, On(ward), Outcome, Overture, Pass, Piaffe, Posit, Postulate, Precocious, Prefer, Prepone, Prest, Process, Progress, → **PROMOTE**, Propose, Propound, Retainer, Ripe, Rise, Scoop, Sub, Submit, Tiptoe, Top end, Ultramodern, Upfront, Upgang, Voorskot

Advantage(ous) Accrual, Ad, Aid, → **ASSET**, Avail, Batten, Benefit, Bisque, Boot, Bright, Edge, Emolument, Expedient, Exploit, Favour, Fruit, Gain, Grouter, Handicap, Handle, Head-start, Help, Inside (track), Interess, Interest, Lever(age), Mess of pottage, Nonmonetary, Obvention, Odds, One-up, Oneupmanship, Oyster, Pecuniary, Percentage, Plus, Privilege, Prize, Pro, Pull, Purchase, Salutary, Serviceable, Start, Stead, Strength, Toe-hold, Trump card, Upper-hand, Upside, Use, Van, Whiphand, Whipsaw

Advent(ist) Coming, Shaker

Adventure(r), Adventuress, Adventurous Argonaut, Assay, Aunter, Bandeirante, Buccaneer, Casanova, Conquistador, Dareful, Daring, Emprise, Enterprise, Escapade, → **EXPLOIT**, Filibuster, Gest, Lark, Mata Hari, Mercenary, Merchant, Picaresque, Picaro, Picaroon, Risk, Routier, Rutter, Swashbuckler, Vamp, Viking, Voyage

Adversary Antagonist, Cope(s)mate, Enemy, Foe, Opponent

Adverse, Adversity Calamity, Cross, Down, Downside, Harrow, Misery, Reversal, Setback, Unfavourable, Untoward, Woe

Advert(ise), Advertisement, Advertiser, Advertising Above the line, Ad, Air, Allude, Attack, Banner, Bark, Bill, Blipvert, Circular, Classified, Coign(e), Coin, Commercial, Copy, Display, Dodger, Earpiece, Flier, Flyer, Flyposting, Flysheet, Hard sell, Hype, Infomercial, Jingle, Knocking copy, Madison Avenue, Mailshot, Market, Niche, Noise, → **NOTICE**, Out, Packshot, Parade, Personnel, Placard, Playbill, Plug, → **POSTER**, Proclaim, Promo, Promote, Promulgate, Prospectus, Puff, Quoin, Refer, Semisolus, Shoutline, Showbill, Skyscraper, Sky-write, Splash, Sponsor, Spot, Stunt, Subliminal, Teaser, Tele-, Throwaway, Tout, Trailer, Trawl, Want(s) (ad), Wrap around

Advice Conseil, Counsel, → **GUIDANCE**, Guideline, Information, Invoice, Opinion, Read, Recommendation, Re(e)de, Reed, Tip

Advise(d), Adviser, Advisable Acquaint, Assessor, Avise(ment), Back-seat driver, Brains trust, CAB, Cabal, Camarilla, Consultant, Cornerman, Counsel, Egeria, Enlighten, Expedient, Genro, Induna, Inform, Instruct, Mentor, Oracle, Peritus, Politic, Prudent, Ralph, → **RECOMMEND**, Starets, Staretz, Tutor, Urge, Wise

Advocate(d) Agent, Argue, Attorney, Back, Counsel, Devil's, Endorse, Exponent, Gospel, Intercede, Lawyer, Move, Paraclete, Peat, Peddle, Pleader, Pragmatist, Preach, Proponent, Silk, Statist, Syndic, Urge

Aeon Hadean, Phanerozoic

Aerial Aeolian, Aery, Antenna, Beam, Clover, Clover leaf, Communal, Dipole, Directional, Dish, Ethereal, Ferrite-rod, Folded dipole, Frame, Ground-plane, Long-wire, Loop, Minidish, Parabolic, Rhombic, Satellite dish, Slot, Yagi

Aerobatics Stunt

Aerobics Pilates, Step

Aerodrome → **AIRPORT**, Landing field, Rotor-station

Aerodynamics Slipstream

Aerofoil Spoiler, Trimtab

▶ **Aeroplane** *see* **AIRCRAFT**

Aerosol Atomiser, Ioniser, Mace®

Aesir Loki

Aesthete, Aesthetic Arty, Beautiful, Essene, Poseur, Tasteful

Affable, Affability Amiable, Avuncular, Benign, Bonhomie, Cordial, Gracious, Hearty, Suave, Urbane

Affair(s) Amour, Business, Concern, Current, Effeir, Effere, Event, External, Fight, Fling, Foreign, Go, Indaba, Internal, Intrigue, Liaison, Matter, Pash, Pidgin, Pi(d)geon, Ploy, Relationship, Res, Romance, Shebang, Subject, Thing

Affect(ed), Affectation, Affection(ate), Affecting Air, Airtsy-mairtsy, Alter, Arty, Breast, Camp, Chi-chi, Concern, Cordial, Crachach, Crazy, Distress, Effete, Endearment, Euphuism, Foppery, Frappant, Grip, Heartstrings, High-sounding, Hit, Impress, Ladida, Lovey-dovey, Mimmick, Minauderie, Mincing, Minnick, Minnock, Mouth-made, Mwah, Phoney, → **POSE**, Poseur, Precieuse, Preciosity, Pretence, Prick-me-dainty, Smitten, Spoilt, Stag(e)y, Storge, Stricken, Strike, Supervene, Susceptible, Sway, Sympathetic, Tender, Topophilia, Touched, Touchy-feely, Twee, Unction, Unnatural, Upend, Warm, Yah

Affiliate, Affiliation Adopt, Associate, Merge, Unite

Affinity Bro, Kin(ship), Penchant, Rapport, Tie

Affirm(ative), Affirmation Assert, Attest, Avow, Maintain, Positive, Predicate, Profess, Protestation, State, Uh-huh, → **VERIFY**, Yebo

Affix(ed) Append, Ascribe, → **ATTACH**, Connect, Fasten, On

Afflict(ed), Affliction Aggrieve, Ail, Asthma, Cross, Cup, Curse, Dead leg, Disease, Furnace, Harass, Hurt, Lacerate, Lumbago, Molest, Nosology, Palsy, Persecute, Pester, Plague, Scourge, Smit, Sore, → **SORROW**, Stricken, Teen, Tene, Tic, Tine, Tribulation, → **TROUBLE**, Try, Unweal, Visitation, Woe

Affluence, Affluent Abundance, Dinky, Ease, Fortune, Grey panther, Inflow, Opulence, Upmarket, Wealth

Afford Allow, Bear, Give, Manage, Offer, Provide, Run to, Spare, Yield

Affray Brawl, Fight, Fracas, Mêlée, Scuffle, Skirmish

Affront Assault, Defy, Facer, → **INSULT**, → **OFFEND**, Outrage, Scandal, Slight, Slur

Afghan(istan) Bactria, Dard, Hound, Kaf(f)ir, Pakhto, Pakhtu, Pashto, Pashtu, Pathan, Pushto(o), Pushtu, Taliban

Afloat Aboard, Abroach, Adrift, Natant

Afoot Astir, Up

Aforesaid Above, Same

Afraid Adrad, Alarmed, Chicken, Fearful, Funk, Nesh, Rad, Regretful, Scared, Timorous, Windy, Yellow

Afresh De novo

Africa(n) Abyssinian, Adamawa, Akan, Algerian, Amakwerekwere, Angolan, Ashanti, Baganda, Bambara, Bantu, Barbary, Barotse, Basotho, Basuto, Bechuana, Beento, Bemba, Beninese, Berber, Biafran, Bintu, Black, Boer, Botswana, Bushman, Caffre, Cairene, Carthaginian, Chewa, Chichewa, Ciskei, Congo(l)ese, Cushitic, Dagomba, Damara, Dark continent, Dinka, Duala, Dyula, Efik, Eritrean, Ethiopian, Eve, Fang, Fantee, Fanti, Fingo, Flytaal, Fula(h), Gabonese, Galla, Gambian, Ganda, Gazankulu, Grikwa, Griqua, Guinean, Gullah, Hamite, Hausa, Herero, Hottentot, Hutu, Ibibio, Ibo, Igbo, Impi, Ivorian, Kabyle, Kaffer, Kaf(f)ir, Kenyan, Khoikhoi, Khoisan, Kikuyu, Kongo, Lango, Lesotho, Liberian, Libyan, Lowveld, Lozi, Luba, Luo, Maghreb, Maghrib, Malagasy, Malawi, Malian, Malinke, Mande, Mandingo, Mandinka, Masai, Mashona, Matabele, Mende, Moor, Moroccan, Mossi, Mozambican, Mswahili, Munt(u), Mzee, Nama(qua), Namibian, Ndebele, Negrillo, → **NEGRO**, Ngoni, Nguni, Nilot(e), Nubian, Nuer, Numidian, Nyanja, Oromo, Ovambo, Pedi, Pied noir, Pondo, Qwaqwa, Rastafarian, Rhodesian, Rwandan, Sahelian, San, Senegalese, Shilluk, Shluh, Shona, Somali, Songhai, Songhay, Sotho, Soweto, Sudanese, Susu, Swahili, Swazi, Tanzanian, Temne, Tiv, Togolese, Tonga, Transkei, Transvaal, Tshi, Tsonga, Tswana, Tuareg, Tutsi, Twi, Ugandan, Uhuru, Venda, Voltaic, Waswahili, Watu(t)si, Wolof, X(h)osa, Yoruban, Zairean, Zulu

Afrikaan(s), Afrikaner Cape Dutch, Crunchie, Hairyback, Mynheer, Taal, Volk, Voortrekker

After(wards) About, A la, At, Behind, Beyond, Eft, Epi-, → **LATER**, On, Once, Past, Post hoc, Rear, Since, Sine, Subsequent, Syne

Afterbirth Secundines, Sooterkin

Afterimage Photogene

▷ **After injury** *may indicate* an anagram

Afterlife Other world, The Great Beyond

Aftermath Consequence, Fall out, Legacy, Mow(ing), Rawing, Rawn, Rowan, Rowen, Rowing, Sequel(a)

Afternoon A, Arvo, Ex-am, PM, Postmeridian, Undern

Afterpiece, Afterthought Addendum, Codicil, Epimetheus, Exode, Footnote, Note, PS, Supplement

Aftertaste T(w)ang

Again Afresh, Agen, Ancora, Anew, Back, Bis, De novo, Ditto, Do, Eft, Eftsoons, Encore, Iterum, More, Moreover, O(v)er, Re-, Recurrence, Reprise, Than, Then

Against A, Anti, Beside, Con, Counter, For, Gainsayer, Into, Nigh, On, One-to-one, Opposing, To, V, Versus

Agape Feast, Hiant, Ringent, Yawning

Agate Chalcedonyx, Moss, Murr(h)a, Onyx, Ruin

Agave Century plant, Henequen, Lily, Maenad, Maguey

Age(d), Ages, Aging Absolute, Achievement, Ae, Aeon, Aet, Alcheringa, Anno domini, Antique, Archaise, Atomic, Augustan, Azilian, Bronze, Calpa, Century, Chair-days, Chellean, Coon's, Copper, Cycle, Dark, Date, Day, Discretion, Distress, Doddery, Eld, Elizabethan, Eon, Epact, Epoch(a), Era, Eternity, Generation, Gerontic, Golden, Grey, Heroic, Hoar, Hore, Ice, Information, Iron, Jazz, Jurassic, Kaliyuga, Kalpa, La Tene, Lias, Magdalenian, Maglemosian, Mature, Mental, Mesolithic, Middle, Millennium, Neolithic, New, New Stone, Of, Old, Oligocene, Paleolithic, Passé, Periclean, Period, Phanerozoic, Progeria, Radiometric, Reindeer, Saros, S(a)eculum, Senescence, Senility, Silver, Solera, Space, Stone, Third, Villanovan, Wrinkly, Yellow, Yonks, Yug(a)

Ageless Evergreen

Agency, Agent Agitator, Alkylating, Ambassador, Antistatic, Art, Autolysin, Bailiff, Bargaining, Barm, Bicarb(onate), Bond, Broker, BSI, Bureau, Catalyst, Cat's paw, Cause, Chelating, Child support, Commis, Commission, Complexone, Comprador(e), Confidential, Consul, Consular, Counter, Countryside, Crown, Customs, Dating, Defoaming, Del credere, Developing, Dicumaral, Disclosing, Distributor, Doer, Double, Emissary, Environment, Envoy, Enzyme, -er, Escort, Estate, Exciseman, Executant, Executor, Factor, Fed, Finger, Flack, Forwarding, Free, Galactagogue, G-man, Go-between, Good offices, Hand, Hirudin, House, Implement, Indian, Influence, Institorial, Instrument, Intermediary, Itar Tass, Kinase, Law, Leavening, Legate, Literary, Magic bullet, Man, Masking, Means, Medium, Melanin, Mercantile, Mitogen, Mole, Moral, Mutagen, Narc, Narco, Nerve, Ninja, Nucleating, OO, Operation, -or, Orange, Order paper, Oxidizing, Parliamentaire, Parliamentary, Patent, Pathogen, Pawn, Peace corps, Penetration, Pinkerton, Press, Procurator, Proxy, Realtor, Reducing, Rep(resentative), Resident, Reuters, Riot, Road, Runner, Salesman, Secret (service), Setter, Shipping, Ship's husband, SIS, Sleeper, Solvent, Soman, Spook, Spy, Stock, Surfactant, Syndic, Tass, Teratogen, Third party, Ticket, Tiger team, Training, Travel, UNESCO, Vakeel, Vakil, Virino, Voice, Welfare, Wetting, Wire service

Agenda Business, Hidden, Order paper, Programme, Remit, Schedule

Aggie Agnes, Ines, Nessa, Nesta

Aggravate Annoy, Exacerbate, Exasperate, Inflame, Irk, Needle, Nettle, Provoke, Rankle, Try, Vex

Aggregate, Aggregation Ballast, Congeries, Detritus, Etaerio, Granulite, Gravel, Hard core, Manifold, Number, Omnium, Ore, Ped, Sum, Total

Aggression, Aggressive(ly), Aggressor, Aggro Anti-Imperialism, Arsey, Attack, Ballbreaker, Bare-knuckle, Bellicose, Belligerent, Biffo, Bovver, Bullish, Butch, Defiant, Enemy, Feisty, Foe, Go-getter, Gungho, Hard-hitting, Hawk, Invader, In-your-face, Laddish, Lairy, Macho, Militant, Nasty, On-setter, Pushing, Rambo, Rampant, Road rage, Sabre-rattling, Shirty, Tooth and nail, Truculent, Wild

Aggrieve(d) Sore

Agile Acrobatic, Deft, Lissom(e), Nifty, Nimble, Quick, Spry, Supple, Swank, Twinkletoes, Wiry

Agitate(d), Agitation, Agitator Acathisia, Activist, Ado, Agitprop, Akathisia, Alarm, Betoss, Boil, Bolshie, Bother, Chartist, Churn, Commotion, Commove, Convulse, Demagogue, Discompose, Distraught, → **DISTURB**, Doodah, Ebullient, Emotion, Euoi, Euouae, Evovae, Excite, Extremist, Fan, Fantad, Fanteeg, Fantigue, Fantod, Ferment, Firebrand, Flap, Flurry, Fluster, Flutter, Fraught, Frenzy, Fuss, Fusspot, Goad, Heat, Hectic, Impatience, Jabble, Khilafat, Lather, Militant, Overwrought, Panicky, Pedetic, Perturb, Poss, Pother, Protest, Rabble-rouser, Rattle, Restless, Rouse, Ruffle, Seethed, Shake, Sod, Stir(-up), Swivet, Tailspin, Taking, Tempest, Tew, Thermal, Tizzy, Toss, Tremor, Trepidation, Trouble, Turmoil, Tweak, Twitchy, Twittery, Unrest, Upset, Welter, Whisk, Wrought up, Ytost

▷ **Agitate** *may indicate* an anagram

Agley Awry, Unevenly

Aglow Alight, Fervid, Tipsy

▶ **Agnes** *see* **AGGIE**

Agnostic Laodicean

Ago Lang syne, → **SINCE**

Agog Astir, Athirst, Eager, Excited, Keen, Pop-eyed

Agonise, Agony Ache, Anguish, Brood, Dread, Ecstasy, Heartache, → **PAIN**, Throe(s), Torment, Torture

Agree(ing), Agreed, Agreement Accede, Accept, Accord, Acquiescence, Adhere, Agt, Aline, Allow, Amen, Analog(ue), Analogy, Apply, As one, Assent, Assort, Atone, Ausgleich, Aye, Bilateral, Bipartite, Bond, Camp David, Cartel, Champerty, Charterparty, Chime, Closing, Coincide, Collective, Comart, Community, Compact, Comply, Comport, Concert, Concord(at), Concur, Condone, Conform, Congree, Congruent, Consension, Consensus, → **CONSENT**, Consist, Consonant, Contract, Contrahent, Convention, Correspond, Cotton, Covenant, Covin, Covyne, Cushty, Dayton Accords, Deal, Deffo, Deign, Done, Embrace, Entente, Equate, Escrow, Fadge, Finalise, Gatt, Gentleman's, Handfast, Harmony, Homologous, Indenture, Jibe, Knock-for-knock, League, Like-minded, Mercosur, Munich, National, Net Book, Nod, Nudum pactum, Okay, On, Pact(um), Pair, Placet, Plant, Plea bargaining, Prenuptial, Procedural, Productivity, Protocol, Rabat(te), Recognise, Repo, Repurchase, Right(o), Right on, Roger, Sanction, Schengen, Service, Settlement, Side, Sort(ance), Specialty, Sponsion, Square, Standstill, Substantive, Suit, Sweetheart, Sympathy, Synastry, Sync(hronise), Synesis, Syntony, Tally, Technology, Threshold, Trade, Treaty, Trucial, Uh-huh, Union, Unison, Unity, Unspoken, Wilco, Wukkas, Yalta, Yea, Yea-say, Yes

Agreeable Amene, Harmonious, Pleasant, Sapid, Sweet, Well-disposed, Willing, Winsome

Agriculture, Agricultural(ist) Arval, Ceres, Farming, Geoponic, Georgic, Inari, Moshav, Permaculture, Slash and burn, Smallholding, Tull

Aground Ashore, Beached, Sew, Stranded

Ague Dumb

▷ **Ague(ish)** *may indicate* an anagram

Ah Ach, Ay

Ahead Anterior, Before, Foreship, Forward, Frontwards, In store, Onward, Precocious, Up

Aiblins Perhap, Perhaps, Yibbles

Aid(s), Aide Accessory, ADC, Adjutant, Artificial, Assist, Audiovisual, Audiphone,

Decca, → **DEPUTY**, First, Foreign, Galloper, Gift, Grant, Hearing, Help(line), Key, Legal, Lend-lease, Life-saver, Monitor, Optophone, Orthosis, PA, Realia, Relief, Satnav, Seamark, Serve, Sex, Sherpa, Subsidy, Subvention, Succour, Support, Teaching, Visual, Yeoman('s) service, Zimmer®

AIDS Slim

Ail(ment) Affect, Afflict(ion), Complaint, Croup, Disease, Disorder, Malady, Misorder, Narks, Occupational, Pink-eye, Pip, Sickness, Suffer, TB

Aim Approach, Aspire, Bead, Bend, End, Ettle, Eye, Goal, Hub, Intent, Level, Mark, Mint, Mission, Object, Peg, Plan, Plank, Point, Point blank, Purpose, Quest, Reason, Sake, Seek, Sight(s), Target, Tee, Telos, Train, Try, View, Visie, Vizy, Vizzie, Zero-in

Aimless Adrift, Drifting, Erratic, Haphazard, Random, Unmotivated

Air(s), Airer, Air-space, Airy Aerate, Aerial, Aero, Affectation, Allure, Ambiance, Ambience, Anthem, Appearance, Aquarius, Arietta, Arioso, Arpeggio, Attitude, Aura, Bearing, Breath, Calypso, Canzona, Canzone, Cavatina, Compressed, Dead, Demaine, Descant, Ditty, Draught, Dry, Emphysema, Ether(eal), Expose, Fan, Filmy, Front, Gemini, Heat-island, Heaven, Horse, Inflate, Libra, Lift, Light, Liquid, Look, Lullaby, Madrigal, Manner, Melody, Microburst, Mien, Night, Nitre, Oat, Open, Ozone, Parade, Periptery, Pneumatic, Poseur, Radio, Screen, Scuba, Serenade, Serenata, Serene, Shanty, Side, Sinus, Sky, Slipstream, Solo, Song, Strain, Swank, Thin, Tidal, Trigon, → **TUNE**, Vent, Ventilate, Vital, Wake, Wind

Airborne Ab

Air Chief Marshal Dowding

Air-conditioning Plenum system

Aircraft, Airship Aerodyne, Aerostat, Angels, AST, Auster, Autoflare, Autogiro, Autogyro, Aviette, Avion, Biplane, Blimp, Brabazon, Bronco, Camel, Canard, Canberra, Chaser, Chopper, Coleopter, Comet, Concorde, Convertiplane, Corsair, Crate, Cropduster, Cyclogiro, Delta-wing, Dirigible, Dive-bomber, Doodlebug, Drone, Eagle, Enola Gay, Eurofighter, F, Ferret, Fixed-wing, Flivver, Flying fortress, Flying wing, Fokker, Freedom-fighter, Freighter, Galaxy, Glider, Gotha, Gyrodyne, Gyroplane, Hang-glider, Harrier, Hawkeeze, Heinkel, Helicopter, Helo, Hercules, Hunter, Hurricane, Interceptor, Intruder, Jet star, Jumbo, Jump-jet, Kite, Lancaster, Liberator, Lifting-body, Lysander, Messerschmitt, Microjet, Microlight, Microlite, MIG, Mirage, Monoplane, Mosquito, Moth, Multiplane, Nightfighter, Nightfinder, Nimrod, Oerlikon, Orion, Ornithopter, Orthopter, Parasol, Penguin, Phantom, → **PLANE**, Provider, Prowler, Pusher, Ramjet, Rigid, Rotaplane, Runabout, Scout, Scramjet, Semi-rigid, Skiplane, Skyhawk, Sopwith, Sopwith Camel, Spitfire, SST, Stack, Starfighter, Starlifter, Stealth bomber, STOL, Stratocruiser, Stratotanker, Stuka, Super Sabre, Sweptwing, Swing-wing, Tankbuster, Taube, Taxiplane, Thunderbolt, Thunderchief, Tomcat, Tornado, Torpedo bomber, Towplane, Tracker, Trident, Tri-jet, Triplane, Tube, Turbofan, Turbo-jet, Turbo-prop, Turboramjet, Variable geometry, Vessel, Vigilante, Viking, Viscount, Vomit comet, Voodoo, VTOL, War bird, Widebody, Wild weasel, Zeppelin

Aircraftsman, Airman AC, Aeronaut, AR, Bleriot, Co-pilot, Erk, Fokker, Kiwi, LAC, Observer, RAF

Aircraftswoman Penguin, Pinguin

▶ **Airfield** *see* **AIRPORT**

Air force Luftwaffe

Airless Close, Stuffy

Airlift Thermal

Airline, Airway Aeroflot, Anthem, BAC, BEA, Bronchus, Duct, El Al, JAL, Larynx, Lot, Lyric, Purple, Qantas, SAS, S(ch)norkel, TWA, Upcast, Vent, Weasand(-pipe), Windpipe

▶ **Airman** *see* **AIRCRAFTSMAN, FLIER**

Airport Chiang Kai Shek, Drome, Entebbe, Faro, Gander, Gatwick, Heliport, Idlewild, John Lennon, Kennedy, La Guardia, Landing strip, Le Bourget, Lod, Luton, Lydda, Lympne, O'Hare, Orly, Prestwick, Runway, Shannon, Stansted, Stolport, Terminal,

Vertiport, Wick

Air-raid Blitz, Mission

Air-tight Hermetic, Indisputable, Sealed

Aisle Gangway

Aitch Ache, Aspirate, H

Ajar Agee

Ajax Lav, Loo

Aka Alias

Akin Alike, Cognate, Congener, Kindred, Sib

Alabaster Oriental

Alarm(ed), Alarming Affright, Agitation, Alert, Arouse, Bell, Bleep, Bugaboo, Caution, Concern, Dismay, Eek, False, Fire, Flap, Fricht, Fright, Frit, Ghast, Hairy, Larum, Panic, Perturb, Radio, Rock, Rouse, Siren, Smoke, Startle, Tirrit, Tocsin, Unease, Warn, Yike(s)

Alas Ah, Alack, Ay, Eheu, Ha, Haro, Harrow, Io, Lackadaisy, Lackaday, O, Oh, Ohone, O me, Ou, Sadly, Waesucks, Waly, Well-a-day, Wel(l)away, Wellanear, Woe

Alaskan AK, Sourdough, Tlingit, Yupik

Alb Sticharion

Alban Berg

Albanian Arna(o)ut

Albatross Alcatras, Black-footed, Golf, Gooney(-bird), Millstone, Omen, Onus, Quaker-bird, Wandering

Albeit Tho(ugh)

Albert Chain, Chevalier, Consort, Hall, Herring, Slang

Albion Perfidious

Album Autograph, Looseleaf, Photo, Record, Stamp

Albumen, Albumin Chalaza, Glair, Leucosin, Mucin, Myogen, Protein, Ricin, Serum, Treadle, Treddle, White

Alchemic, Alchemist, Alchemy Adept, Arch-chimic, Brimstone, Cagliostro, Faust(us), Hermetic(s), Multiplier, Orpiment, Paracelsus, Quicksilver, Sal ammoniac, Sorcery, Spagyric, Spagyrist, Witchcraft

Alcides Hercules

Alcohol(ic) Absolute, Acrolein, Aldehyde, Amyl, Bibulous, Blue ruin, Booze, Borneol, Catechol, Cetyl, Chaptalise, Cholesterol, Choline, Citronellol, Cresol, Denatured, Diol, Dipsomaniac, Drinker, Ethal, Ethanol, Ethyl, Farnesol, Feni, Fenny, Firewater, Fusel-oil, Geraniol, Glycerin(e), Grain, Grog, Gut-rot, Hard, Hard stuff, Inebriate, Inositol, Isopropyl, Jakey, Jungle juice, Lauryl, Linalool, Lush, Mahua, Mahwa, Malt, Mannite, Mannitol, Mercaptan, Mescal, Mescalin(e), Methanol, Meths, Methyl, Mow(r)a, Nerol, Phytol, Pisco, Plonko, Polyol, Potato spirit, Propyl, Pyroligneous, Rotgut, Rubbing, Rubby, Scrumpy, Secondary, Snake juice, Sorbitol, Sphingosine, Spirits, Spirits of wine, Spirituous, Sterol, Taplash, Terpineol, Thiol, Tincture, Tocopherol, Triol, Wash, White lightning, Wino, Witblits, Wood, Xylitol

Alcove Apse, Bay, Bole, Carrel(l), Dinette, Inglenook, Lunette, Niche, Nook, Recess, Reveal, Tokonoma

Alcyonarian Sea-feather

Aldehyde Acrolein, Aldol, Vanillin

Alder Fothergilla

Alderman Bail(l)ie, CA

Alderney CI, Cow

Ale, Alehouse Audit, Barleybree, Barley-broo, Barley-broth, Barley wine, Beer, Brown, Bummock, CAMRA, Church, Feast, Four, Heather, Humming, Humpty-dumpty, Keg, Lager, Lamb's wool, Light, Mild, Morocco, Nappy, Nog, Nogg, October, Pale, Plain, Porter, Purl, Real, Small, Stout, Swats, Tiddleywink, Tipper, White, Whitsun, Wort, Yard, Yill, Yorkshire stingo

Alert Agog, Amber, Arrect, Astir, Attentive, Aware, Conscious, Gleg, Gogo, Intelligent,

Open-eyed, Presential, Qui vive, Red, Scramble, Sharp, Sprack, Sprag, Stand-to, Tentie, Up and coming, Vigilant, Volable, Wary, Watchful, Wide-awake, Yellow

Alewife Barkeeper, Gaspereau

Alexander, Alexandrine Alex, Arius, Macedonian, Pope, Sandy, Sasha, Sawn(e)y, Selkirk, Senarius

Alfalfa Lucern(e), Luzern

Alfred Dreyfus, Garnet, Jingle

Alfresco Barbecue, Plein-air

Alga(e) Anabaena, Blanketweed, Chlorella, Chlorophyte, Conferva, Desmid, Diatom, Dulse, Heterocontae, Isokont, Jelly, Nostoc, Periphyton, Phycology, Pleuston, Pond scum, Prokaryon, Protococcus, Red, Rhodophyte, Seaweed, Spirogyra, Star-jelly, Stonewort, Ulothrix, Ulotrichales, Valonia, Volvox, Witches' butter, Yellow-green, Zooxanthella

Algebra Boolean, Linear, Quadratics

Algeria(n) .dz, Kabyle, Nimidian, Pied noir

Algonquin Innu, Wampanoag

Alias Aka, Byname, Epithet, Moni(c)ker, Nick(name), Pen-name, Pseudonym

Alibi Excuse, Watertight

Alien(ate), Alienation A-effect, Amortise, Devest, Disaffect, Ecstasy, Erotic, Estrange, ET, Exotic, External, Foreign, Forinsecal, Fremd, Hostile, Little green man, Martian, Metic, Outlandish, Outsider, Philistine, Repugnant, Strange(r)

Alight Alowe, Avail(e), Avale, Detrain, Disembark, Dismount, Flambe, In, Lambent, Land, Lit, Perch, Pitch, Rest, Settle

Align Arrange, Associate, Collimate, Dress, Juxtapose, Marshal, Orient, Straighten, Synchronize

▸ **Alike** *see* **LIKE(NESS)**

Alimentary Oesophagus, Pharynx

Aliquot Submultiple

Alive Alert, Animated, Breathing, Extant, Quick, Teeming

Alkali(ne), Alkaloid Antacid, Apomorphine, Atropine, Base, Bebeerine, Berberine, Betaine, Borax, Brak, Brucine, Caffein(e), Capsaicin, Chaconine, Choline, Cinchon(id)ine, Codeine, Colchicine, Corydaline, Curarine, Emetin(e), Ephedrine, Ergotamine, Gelsemin(in)e, Guanidine, Harmalin(e), Harmin(e), Hydrastine, Hyoscine, Hyoscyamine, Ibogaine, Kali, Limewater, Lixivium, Lobeline, Lye, Mescalin, Narceen, Narceine, Nicotine, Papaverine, Physostigmine, Pilocarpin(e), Piperine, Potash, Potass, Quinine, Reserpine, Rhoeadine, Scopaline, Scopolamine, Soda, Solanine, Sparteine, Stramonium, Thebaine, Theine, Theobromine, Theophylline, Totaquine, Tropine, Tubocurarine, Veratridine, Veratrin(e), Vinblastine, Vinca, Vincristine, Volatile, White, Yohimbine

Alkane Hexane

All A, En bloc, → **ENTIRE**, Entity, Every man Jack, Finis, Omni, Pan, Quite, Sum, → **TOTAL**, Toto, Tutti, Whole

Allah Bismillah, God

All at once Holus-bolus, Per saltum, Suddenly

Allay Alleviate, Calm, Disarm, Lessen, Quieten, Soothe

Allegation, Allege(d) Accuse, Assert, Aver, Claim, Mud, Obtend, Plead, Purport, Represent, Smear, So-called

Allegiance Faith, Foy, Loyalty, Tribalism

Allegory, Allegorical Apologue, Fable, Mystic, Myth, Parable

Allergy Atopy, Aversion, Bagassosis, Hay fever, Hives

Alleviate Allay, Alleg(g)e, Calm, Mitigate, Mollify, Palliate, → **RELIEVE**, Temper

Alley Aisle, Blind, Bonce, Bowling, Corridor, Ennog, Ginnel, Lane, Laura, Marble, Passage, Rope-walk, Silicon, Tin Pan, Twitten, Vennel, Walk, Wynd

Alliance Agnation, Axis, Bloc, Cartel, Coalition, Combine, Compact, Confederation, Dreibund, Dual, Entente, Federacy, → **LEAGUE**, Marriage, NATO, Quadruple, Syndicate,

Triple, Union

Alligator Al(l)igarta, Avocado, Caiman, Cayman

Alliteration Cynghanedd, Head-rhyme

Allocate, Allocation Allot, Apportion(ment), Assign, Designate, Distribute, Earmark, Placement, Priorate, Ration, Share, Soum, Zone

Allot(ment), Allow(ance), Allowed, Allowing Admit, Affect, Alimony, Allocation, Although, Aret(t), Assign, Attendance, Award, Batta, Beteem(e), Brook, Budget, Bug, Cater, Charter, Cloff, Confess, Cor(r)ody, Diet, Discount, Dole, Draft, Enable, Entitle, Excuse, Expenses, Feod, Give, Grant, House-bote, Husbandage, Indulge, Jobseekers', Latitude, Legit(imate), Let, License, Licit, Luit(en), Machining, Mag, Mete, Mobility, Okay, Palimony, Parcel, Pension, Percentage, → **PERMIT**, Personal, Pittance, Plot, Portion, Prebend, Quarterage, Quota, Ratio, Ration, Rebate, Rood, Salt-money, Sanction, Separation, Sequel, Share(-out), Shrinkage, Sizings, Stint, Stipend, Subsistence, Suffer, Tare, Tax, Teene, Though, Tolerance, Tolerate, Tret, Viaticum, Weighting, Whack, Yield

Allotment-holder Cleruch

▶ **Allow** *see* **ALLOT(MENT)**

Allow(ance) Brook, Cap, Field, Fya, Privy purse, Table money

Alloy Albata, Alnico®, Amalgam, Babbitt, Bell-metal, Billon, Brass, Britannia metal, Bronze, Cermet, Chrome(l), Compound, Constantan, Cupronickel, Duralumin®, Dutch leaf, Electron, Electrum, Eutectoid, Ferrochrome, Ferrosilicon, Gunmetal, Invar®, Iridosmine, Kamacite, Latten, Magnalium, Magnox, Manganin®, Marmem, Mischmetal, Mix, Monel®, Nichrome®, Nickel-silver, Nicrosilal, Nimonic, Nitinol, Occamy, Oreide, Orichalc, Ormolu, Oroide, Osmiridium, Paktong, Pewter, Pinchbeck, Platinoid, Porous, Potin, Pot metal, Prince's metal, Shakudo, Shibuichi, Similor, Solder, Speculum, Spelter, Steel, Stellite®, Tambac, Terne, Tombac, Tombak, Tutenag, White metal, Y, Zircal(l)oy, Zircoloy

▷ **Alloy** *may indicate* an anagram

Allright A1, Assuredly, Fit, Hale, Hunky(-dory), Jake, OK, Safe, Tickety-boo, Well

All-round(er) Generalist, Overhead, Versatile

All-seeing Panoptic

Allspice Jamaica pepper, Pim(i)ento

All the same Even so, Nath(e)less, Nevertheless

Allude, Allusion Hint, Imply, Innuendo, Mention, Refer, Reference, Suggest

Allure, Alluring Agaçant(e), Charm, Circe, Decoy, Delilah, Entice, Femme fatale, Glam, Glamour, Inviting, It, Magnet(ic), SA, Seduce, Seductive, Siren, Tempt, Trap, Trepan, Vamp

Alluvium Carse

Ally, Allied Accomplice, Agnate, Aide, Alley, Alliance, Ami, Backer, Belamy, Co-belligerent, Cognate, Colleague, Dual, Foederatus, German(e), Holy, Marble, Marmoreal, Pal, Partner, Plonker, Related, Taw, Unholy, Unite

Almanac Calendar, Clog, Ephemeris, Morrison, Nautical, Nostradamus, Whitaker's, Wisden, Zadkiel

Almighty Creator, Deity, Dollar, God, Jehovah, Omnipotent

Almond Amygdal, Burnt, Emulsion, Jordan, Marchpane, Marzipan, Orgeat, Praline, Ratafia, Sugared, Valencia

Almost Anear, Anigh, Close on, Most, Near(ly), Nigh(ly), Practically, Ripe, Une(a)th, Virtually, Well-nigh, Welly

Alms Awmous, Charity, Dole, Handout, Zakat

Aloe Agave, Pita

Aloft Aheight

Alone Hat, Jack, Lee-lane, Onely, Pat, Secco, Separate, Single, Singly, Sola, Solo, Solus, Tod, Unaccompanied, Unaided, Unattended, Unholpen

Along, Alongside Abeam, Aboard, Abreast, Apposed, Beside, By, Parallel

Aloof Abeigh, Apart, Asocial, Chilly, Cool, Detached, Distant, Hou inch, Indrawn,

Mugwump, Offish, Remote, Reserved, Reticent, Skeigh, Snooty, Stand-offish, Toffee-nosed, Unapproachable

Alpaca Paco

Alpha A, Male

Alphabet ABC, Absey, Augmented Roman, Black-out, Brahmi, Braille, Chalcidian, Christcross, Cyrillic, Deaf, Devanagari, Estrang(h)elo, Finger, Futhark, Futhorc, Futhork, Glagol, Glagolitic, Glossic, Grantha, Hangul, Horn-book, International, IPA, ITA, Kana, Kanji, Katakana, Kufic, Latin, Manual, Nagari, Og(h)am, Pangram, Phonetic, Pinyin, Romaji, Roman, Runic, Signary, Slavonic, Syllabary

Alpine, Alps Australian, Bernese, Cottian, Dinaric, Eiger, Gentian, Graian, Julian, Laburnum, Lepontine, Maritime, Matterhorn, Ortles, Pennine, Rhaetian, Rock plant, Savoy, Southern, Transylvanian, Tyrol, Western

Also Add, And, Eke, Item, Likewise, Moreover, Plus, Too, Und, Withal

Altar, Altar-cloth, Altarpiece Butsudan, Diptych, Dossal, Dossel, High, Polyptych, Retable, Shrine, Tabula, Triptych

Alter, Alteration Adapt, Adjust, Bushel, Change, Changeover, Chop and change, Convert, Cook, Correct, Customise, Distort, Evolve, Falsify, Lib, Material, Modify, Modulate, Munge, Mutate, Recast, Revise, Transient, Transmogrify, Transpose, Up-end, Variance, → **VARY**

▷ **Alter(native)** *may indicate* an anagram

Altercation Barney, Brawl, Fracas, Quarrel, Row, Words, Wrangle

Alternate, Alternating, Alternation, Alternative Aka, Boustrophedon, Bypass, Exchange, Instead, Metagenesis, → **OPTION**, Or else, Ossia, Other, Rotate, Second string, Solidus, Staggered, Stop-go, Systaltic, Tertian, Variant, Vicissitude

▷ **Alternately** *may indicate* every other letter

Althaea Mallow, Malva

Although Admitting, Albe(e), All-be, But, Even, Howsoever, Howsomever, Whereas, While

Altitude Elevation, Height, Meridian, Pressure, Rated, Snowline

Alto Countertenor

Altogether Algate(s), All-to-one, Bare, Completely, Entirely, Holus-bolus, Idea, In all, Lock, stock and barrel, Naked, Nude, Nudity, Purely, Slick, Tout (ensemble), Uncut, Wholly

▷ **Altogether** *may indicate* words to be joined

Altruistic, Altruism Heroic, Humane, Philanthropic, Selfless(ness), Unselfish

Alum Potash

Aluminium, Alumino-silicate Al, Allanite, Bauxite, Euclase, Gibbsite, Sillimanite, Stilbite, Tinfoil

Alumnus Graduate, OB

Always Algate(s), Ay(e), Constant, E'er, Eternal, Ever(more), Forever, For keeps, I, Immer, Semper, Sempre, Still

Amalgamate Coalesce, Consolidate, Fuse, Merge, Unite

Amalthea Cornucopia

Amanuensis Tironian

Amarylli(d)s Leocojum, Lily, Polianthes

Amass Accumulate, Assemble, Collect, Gather, Heap, Hoard, Pile, Upheap

Amateur(s) A, AA, Armchair, Beginner, Corinthian, Dabbler, Dilettante, DIY, Enthusiast, Hacker, Ham, Inexpert, L, Laic, Lay, Neophyte, Novice, Prosumer, Sunday painter, Tiro, Tyro

Amatory Eros, Erotic, Fervent

Amaze(d), Amazement, Amazing Agape, Astonish, Astound, Awe, Awhape, Bewilder, Cor, Criv(v)ens, Dum(b)found, Far out, Flabbergast, Gee-whiz, Gobsmack, Goodnow, Grace, Incredible, Jesus wept, Magical, Monumental, O, Open-eyed, Open-mouthed, Perplex, Poleaxe, Pop-eyed, Prodigious, Stagger, Strewth, Stupefaction,

Stupendous, Thunderstruck, Unreal, Wow

Amazon(ian) Ant, ATS, Brimstone, Britannia, Dragon, Hippolyta, Hoyden, Jivaro, Orellana, Penthesilea, Shield-maid, Shield-may, Thalestris, Tupi, Virago

Ambassador At-large, Diplomat, Elchee, Elchi, Eltchi, Envoy, Extraordinary, Fetial, HE, Internuncio, Leaguer, Ledger, Legate, Leidger, Leiger, Lieger, Minister, Nuncio, Plenipo, Plenipotentiary, Pronuncio

Amber Colophony, Electric, Lammer, Ligure, Resin, Retinite, Succinum

Ambience Atmosphere, Aura, Milieu, Setting

Ambiguous, Ambiguity Amphibology, Cryptic, Delphic, Double, Double entendre, Enigmatic, Epicene, Equivocal, Gnomic, Inexactness, Loophole, Oracular, Weasel words

Ambit Scope

Ambition, Ambitious Adventurer, Aim, Arrivisme, Aspiring, Careerism, Drive, Emulate, Go-ahead, Goal, Go-getter, Grail, High-flier, Keen, Office-hunter, Purpose, Pushy, Rome-runner, Thrusting, Type A

Amble Meander, Mosey, Pace, Poddle, Pootle, Saunter, Single-foot, Stroll

Ambrose Emrys

Ambrosia(l) Amreeta, Amrita, Beebread, Fragrant, Odorant, Ragweed, Savoury

Ambulance, Ambulanceman Badger, Blood-wagon, Field, Meat wagon, Pannier, Paramedic, Van, Yellow-flag, Zambu(c)k

Ambulatory Stoa

Ambush(ed) Ambuscade, Belay, Bushwhack, Emboscata, Embusque, Forestall, Latitant, Lurch, Perdu(e), Trap, Watch, Waylay

Amelia Bloomer

Ameliorate Amend, Ease, Improve, Lenify, Remedy

Amen Ammon, Approval, Inshallah, Verify

Amenable Putty

Amend(ment) Alter, Change, Correct, Edit, Expiate, Expurgate, Fifth, Protocol, Redress, Reform, Repair, Restore, → **REVISE**, Satisfy

▷ **Amend** *may indicate* an anagram

Ament Catkin, Idiot

America(n) A, Algonki(a)n, Algonqu(i)an, Am, Angeleno, Basket Maker, Caddo, Cajun, Canadian, Carib, Chicano, Chickasaw, Chinook, Copperskin, Digger, Doughface, Down-easter, Federalist, Flathead, Fox, Geechee, Gringo, Guyanese, Huron, Interior, Joe, Jonathan, Latino, Miskito, Mission Indian, Mistec, Mixtec, Mound builder, Native, New World, Norteno, Olmec, Paisano, Salish, Stateside, Statesman, Statist, Tar-heel, Tico, Tupi, Uncle Sam, US(A), WASP, Yankee (Doodle), Yanqui

Americium Am

Amethyst Oriental

Amiable, Amicable Friendly, Genial, Gentle, Inquiline, Mungo, Peaceful, Sweet, Warm

Amid(st) Among, Atween, Between, Inter, Twixt

Amide Asparagine

Amine Putrescine, Spermine

Amino-acid Dopa, Tyrosine, Valine

Amiss Awry, Ill, Up, Wrong

Ammonia(c) Amide, Amine, Choline, Ethylamine, Hartshorn, Imide, Oshac

Ammonite Serpent-stone

Ammunition Ammo, Bandoleer, Bandolier, Birdshot, Buckshot, Bullets, Chain-shot, Dum-dum, Grape(shot), Grenade, Round, Shot, Slug, Tracer

Amnesia Anterograde, Fugal, Fugue, Lethe, Retrograde

Amnesty Oblivion, Pardon

Amoeba Melboean

Amok Rampaging

Among Amid(st), In, Inter al, Within

Amorous(ly) Casanova, Erotic, Fervent, Lustful, Nutty, Romantic, Smickly, Spoony, Warm

Amorphous Formless, Guanine, Nuclein, Shapeless, Vague

Amount Come, Degree, Dose, Element, Figure, Glob, Gobbet, Handful, Lashings, Levy, Lot, Measure, Nip, Number, Ocean, Offset, Outage, Plethora, Pot(s), Premium, Price, Quantity, Quantum, Shedload, Span, Stint, Sum, Throughput, Volume, Whale, Wheel

Amour Affair(e), Intrigue, Love

Ampersand Tironian sign

Amphetamine Benny, Benzedrine, Speed

Amphibian(s), Amphibious Amb(l)ystoma, Amtrack, Anura, Axolotl, Batrachian, Caecilia, Caecilian, Desman, Eft, Frog, Guana, Hassar, Herpetology, Labyrinthodont, Mermaid, Mudpuppy, Newt, Olm, Ophiomorph, Proteus, Rana, Salamander, Salientia, Seal, Siren, Tadpole, Toad, Tree frog, Urodela(n), Urodele, Weasel

Amphipod Sand-screw, Shrimp

Amphitheatre Arena, Bowl, Circus Maximus, Coliseum, Colosseum, Ring, Stage

Ample, Amplitude Bellyful, Copious, Enough, Generous, Good, Large, Much, Opulent, Profuse, Rich, Roomy, Round, Sawtooth, Spacious, Uberous, Voluminous

Amplifier, Amplify Booster, Double, Eke, Enlarge, Hailer, Laser, Loud hailer, Maser, Megaphone, Push-pull, Solion, Soundboard, Tannoy®, Transistor, Treble

Amputate Sever, Transfix

Amulet Abraxas, Charm, Churinga, Fetish, Greegree, Grigri, Grisgris, Haemon, Pentacle, Periapt, Phylactery, Sea-bean, Talisman, Tiki, Toadstone, Token

Amuse(ment), Amusing(ly) Account, Caution, Cottabus, Disport, Diversion, Divert, Divertimento, Divertissement, Drole, Droll, Entertain, Game, Gas, Giocoso, Glee, Hoke, Hoot, Jocular, Killing, Levity, Light, Occupy, Pleasure, Popjoy, Priceless, Regale, Rich, Riot, Scream, Slay, Solace, → **SPORT**, Tickle, Titillate, Wacky

Amy Johnson, Robsart

▸ **An** see **A**

Ana(s) Story, Teal

Anabaptist Abecedarian, Dipper, Dopper, Hutterite, Knipperdolling

Anableps Four-eyes

Anachronism, Anachronistic Archaism, Solecism, Unhistorical

Anaconda Water boa

Anacreon Te(i)an

Anaemia, Anaemic Aplastic, Cooley's, Diamond-blackfan, Fanconi's, Favism, Haemolytic, Megaloblastic, Miner's, Pernicious, Sallow, Sickle-cell, Sicklemia, Thalassaemia

Anaesthetic, Anaesthetise(d), Anaesthetist Analgesic, Apgar, Avertin®, Basal, Benzocaine, Bupivacaine, Caudal, Chloralose, Chloroform, Cocaine, Endotracheal, Epidural, Ether, Eucain(e), Freeze, Gas, General, Halothane, Hibernation, Infiltrate, Intravenous, Jabber, Ketamine, Lidocaine, Lignocaine, Local, Metopryl, Morphia, Novocaine, Number, Opium, Orthocaine, Pentothal, Phenacaine, Phencyclidine, Procaine, Rhigolene, Special K, Spinal, Stovaine, Topical, Trike, Twilight sleep, Under, Urethan(e)

Anagram Jumble

Anal, Anus Back passage, Poepol, Proctal, Ring, Tewel

Analgesic Aspirin, Bute, Codeine, Diclofenac, Disprin, Fentanyl, Ketamine, Menthol, Meperidine, Methadone, Morphia, Moxa, Opium, Painkiller, Paracetamol, Pethidine, Phenacetin, Phencyclidine, Quina, Salicin(e), Sedative

Analogous, Analogy Akin, Corresponding, Like, Parallel, Similar

Analyse(r), Analysis Alligate, Anagoge, Anatomy, Assess, Blot, Breakdown, Combinatorial, Conformational, Construe, Critique, Diagnosis, Dimensional, Discourse, Dissect, Emic, Esda, Eudiometer, Examine, Explication, Factor, Force-field, Fourier, Gap, Gravimetric, Harmonic, Input-output, Job, Kicksorter, Lexical, Linguistic, Logical, Miscue, Numerical, Parse, Pollen, Post-mortem, Process, Psych out, Qualitative, Quant,

Quantitative, Reductionism, Risk, Rundown, Sabermetrics, Scan(sion), Semantics, Sift, Spectral, Spectroscopic, Spectrum, Statistician, → **swot**, Systems, Test, Transactional, Unpick, Volumetric

▷ **Analysis** *may indicate* an anagram

Analyst Alienist, Investment, Jung, Lay, Psychiatrist, Quant(ative), Shrink, Trick cyclist

Anarchist, Anarchy Black Bloc(k), Black Hand, Bolshevist, Chaos, Kropotkin, Nihilism, Provo, Rebel, Revolutionary, Trotskyite, Unrule

Anathema Ban, Curse, Execration, Maranatha, Oath, Warling

Anatole, Anatolia(n) Asia minor, France, Hittite, Ionian, Turk

Anatomy, Anatomist Bones, Cuvier, De Graaf, Dubois, Framework, Henle, Herophilus, Histology, Hunter, Malpighi, Morbid, Osteology, Pacini, Prosector, Puccini, Schneider, Spiegel, Topology, Worm

Ancestor, Ancestral, Ancestry Adam, Avital, Dawn man, Descent, Extraction, For(e)bear, Forefather, Gastraea, Hereditary, Humanoid, Kachina, Lin(e)age, Parent, Parentage, Pedigree, Predecessor, Primogenitor, Proband, Profectitious, Progenitor, Propositus, Roots, Sire, Tipuna, Tree, Tupina

Anchor(age) Atrip, Berth, Bower, Cell, Deadman, Drag, Drift, Drogue, Eremite, Grapnel, Hawse, Hermit, Host, Kedge, Kedger, Killick, Killock, Laura, Moor, Mud-hook, Mushroom, Nail, Ride, Roads(tead), Rode, Root, Scapa Flow, Sea, Sheet, Spithead, Stock, Stream, Toehold, Waist, Weather

Anchorite Recluse

Anchovy Fish, Pear

Ancient Antediluvian, Archaic, Auld-warld, Bygone, Early, Gonfanoner, Historic, Hoary, Iago, Immemorial, Lights, Neolithic, Ogygian, → **older)**, Old-world, Primeval, Primitive, Pristine, Ur, Veteran

Ancient city Carthage, Ur

Ancillary Adjunct, Secondary, Subservient

And Als(o), Ampassy, Ampersand, Amperzand, Ampussyand, Besides, Et, Furthermore, Item, 'n', Plus, Tironian sign, Und

Andalusite Macle

Andiron Chenet, Dog, Firedog

Andrew(es) Aguecheek, Lancelot, Merry

Androgynous Epicene

Android Automaton, Golem, Replicant, Robot

Anecdote(s) Ana, Exemplum, Story, Tale, Yarn

Anemometer Wind-sleeve, Windsock

Anemone Actinia, Pasque-flower, Windflower

Anew De integro, De novo

Angel(s) Abdiel, Adramelech, Apollyon, Archangel, Ariel, Arioch, Asmadai, Azrael, Backer, Banker, Beelzebub, Belial, Benefactor, Cake, Cherub, Clare, Destroying, Deva, Dominion, Dust, Eblis, Fallen, Falls, Fuzzy-wuzzy, Gabriel, Guardian, Heavenly host, Hierarchy, Host, Iblis, Investor, Israfel, Ithuriel, Lucifer, Michael, Nurse, Power, Principality, Raphael, Recording, Rimmon, Saint, St, Seraph, Spirit, Throne, Uriel, Uzziel, Virtue, Watcher, Zadkiel, Zephiel

Angela Brazil

Angelica Archangel

Angel's wings Begonia

Anger, Angry → **annoy**, Apeshit, Bate, Bile, Black, Bristle, Choler(ic), Conniption, Cross, Dander, Displeased, Dudgeon, Enrage, Exasperation, Face, Fired up, Fuff, Fury, Gram, Heat, Het up, Horn-mad, Huff, Incense, Inflame, Infuriate, Iracund, Irascible, Ire, Kippage, Livid, Mad, Monkey, Moody, Nettle, Pique, Provoke, Radge, Rage, Rampant, Ratty, Renfierst, Rile, Roil, Rouse, Sore, Spleen, Steam, Stroppy, Tamping, Tantrum, Tarnation, Teed off, Teen(e), Temper, Tene, Tooshie, Vex, Vies, Warm, Waspish, Waxy, Worked-up, Wound up, Wrath, Wroth, Yond

Angina Sternalgia, Vincent's

Angle(d), Angler, Angular, Angles, Angling Acute, Argument, Aspect, Attitude, Axil, Azimuthal, Baiter, Canthus, Cast, Catch, Chiliagon, Coign, Complementary, Conjugate, Contrapposto, Corner, Cos, Critical, Diedral, Diedre, Dihedral, Elbow, Elevation, Ell, Exterior, Facial, Fish, Fish-hook, Fork, Geometry, Gonion, Hade, Hip, Hour, Hyzer, In, Incidence, Interior, L, Laggen, Laggin, Latitude, Loft, Longitude, Mitre, Mung, Negative, Oblique, Obtuse, Parallax, Pediculate, Perigon, Peterman, Phase, Piend, Piscator, Pitch, Pitch-cone, Plane, Polyhedral, Position, Positive, Quoin, Radian, Rake, Re-entrant, Reflex, Right, Rod(ster), Rod(s)man, Round, Salient, Sally, Saltchucker, Sine, Sinical, Slip, Solid, Spherical, Stalling, Steeve, Steradian, Straight, Supplementary, Sweepback, The gentle craft, Trotline, Vertical, Viewpoint, Visual, Walton, Waltonian, Washin, Weather, Wide-gab

Anglesey Mona

Anglican(s) CE-men, Conformist, Episcopal

Anglo-Catholic High-church, Spire

Anglo-Indian Qui-hi, Qui-hye, Topi-wallah

Angora Goat, Mohair, Rabbit

Angostura Cusparia bark

Angst Dread

Anguish(ed) Agony, Distress, Gip, Grief, Gyp, Hag-ridden, Heartache, Misery, → **PAIN**, Pang, Sorrow, Throes, → **TORMENT**, Torture, Woe

Angus Aberdeen

Animal(s) Acrita, Anoa, Armadillo, Atoc, Bag, Bandog, Barbastel, Beast, Bestial, Brute, Cariacou, Carnal, Chalicothere, Cleanskin, Coati, Creature, Criollo, Critter, Ethology, Fauna, Felis, Feral, Gerbil, Guanaco, Herd, Huanaco, Ichneumon, Jacchus, Jerboa, Kinkajou, Klipdas, Mammal, Marmoset, Marmot, Menagerie, Moose, Noctule, Oribi, Pack, Parazoon, Party, Pet, Political, Protozoa, Pudu, Pygarg, Quadruped, Quagga, Rac(c)oon, Rhesus, Rotifer, Sensual, Sloth, Stud, Symphile, Tarsier, Teledu, Urson, Waler, Xenurus, Yale, Yapock, Zerda, Zoo

Animal-catcher Utricularia

Animate(d), Animation Activate, Actuate, Alive, Arouse, Biophor, Cartoon, Ensoul, Excite, Fire, Frankenstein, Heat, Hortatory, Hot, Inspire, Lit, Live, Morph, Mosso, Perky, Pixil(l)ation, Rouse, Spark, Spiritoso, Spritely, Stop-motion, Suspended, Toon, Verve, Vivacity, Vivify

Animosity Enmity, Friction, Hostility, Ill-will, Malice, Pique, Rancour

Ankle Coot, Cuit, Cute, Hock, Hucklebone, Knee, Malleolus, Talus

Ankle(t), Ankle covering Cootikin, Cuitikin, Cutikin, Gaiter, Jess

Anna, Anne, Annie Boleyn, Hathaway, Laurie, Oakley, Page, Pavlova, Pice, Sewell, Sister

Annal(s) Acta, Archives, Chronicles, Register

Annatto Roucou

Annex(e) Acquire, Add, Affiliate, Attach, Codicil, Extension, Lean-to, Subjoin

Annihilate Destroy, Erase, Exterminate, Obliterate, Slay, Unbe

Anniversary Birthday, Feast, Jubilee, Obit, Triennial, Wedding, Yahrzeit

Annotate, Annotator Comment, Interpret, Note, Postil, Scholiast

Announce(r), Announcement Banns, Bellman, Bill(ing), Blazon, Bulletin, Communiqué, Declare, Decree, Disclose, Divulgate, Flash, Gazette, Herald, Hermes, Inform, Intimate, Meld, Name and shame, Newsflash, Noise, Post, Preconise, Proclaim, Profess, Promulgate, Pronunciamento, Publish, Release, → **REPORT**, Rescript, Speaker(ine), State, Tannoy, Toastmaster, Town crier, Trumpet

Annoy(ance), Annoyed, Annoying Aggravate, Aggrieve, Anger, Antagonise, Badger, Bane, Blight, Bother, Bug, Bugbear, Chagrin, Choleric, Contrary, Cross, Deuce(d), Disturb, Doggone, Doh, Drat, Fash, Fleabite, Frab, Fumed, Gall, Gatvol, Hack off, Hang, Harass, Hatter, Hector, Hip, Hoots, Huff, Hump, Humph, Incense, Irk, → **IRRITATE**,

Mickey-taking, Miff, Mischief, Molest, Moryah, Nag, Nark, Needle, Nettle, Niggle, Noisome, Noy(ance), Peeve, Pesky, Pester, Pipsqueak, Pique, Plague, Provoke, Rankle, Rats, Ratty, Resentful, Ride, Rile, Roil, Rub, Shirty, Sting, Testy, Tiresome, Tracasserie, Try, Vex, Wazzock

Annual, Annuity Bedder, Book, Consolidated, Contingent, Deferred, Etesian, → **FLOWER**, Half-hardy, Hardy, Immediate, Life, Pension, Perpetuity, → **PLANT**, Rente, Tontine, Yearbook, Yearly

Annul(ment) Abolish, Abrogate, Cashier, Cassation, Dissolution, Invalidate, Irritate, Negate, Recision, Repeal, Rescind, Reversal, Revoke, Vacate, Vacatur, Vacuate, → **VOID**

Annular Toric

Anodyne Balm, Narcotic, Paregoric, Sedative

Anoint(ing) Anele, Cerate, Chris(o)m, Consecrate, Embrocate, Grease, Hallow, Nard, Smear

Anomaly Eccentric, Gravity, Magnetic, Mean, True

▷ **Anomaly** *may indicate* an anagram

Anon Again, Anew, Erelong, Later, Soon

Anonymous Adespota, Anon, A.N.Other, Faceless, Grey, Impersonal, Nameless, Somebody, Unnamed, Valentine

Anorak Geek, Nerd, Trainspotter, Wonk

Another Extra, Per pro

Answer(ing), Answer(s) Account, Acknowledge, Amoebaean, Ans, Antiphon, Because, Comeback, Crib (sheet), Defence, Dusty, Echo, Key, Lemon, Light, No, Oracle, Rebuttal, Rebutter, Rein, Rejoin(der), Repartee, Reply, Rescript, Respond, Response, Responsum, Retort, Return, Riposte, Serve, Sol, Solution, Solve, Verdict, Yes

Ant(s), Anthill Amazon, Army, Bull(dog), Carpenter, Colony, Driver, Dulosis, Emmet, Ergataner, Ergates, Ergatogyne, Ergatomorph, Fire, Formic, Formicary, Leafcutter, Legionary, Myrmecoid, Myrmidon, Nasute, Neuter, Pharaoh, Pismire, Red, Sauba, Slave, Slave-maker, Soldier, Termite, Thief, Umbrella, Velvet, White, Wood

Antacid Limewater, Magnesia, Peptic

Antagonist(ic), Antagonise Adverse, Estrange, Hostile, Oppugnant, Peare, Peer

Antarctica Adelie Land, Byrd Land, Graham Land, Marie Byrd Land, Wilkes Land

Ant-bear Tamanoir

Ante Bet, Punt, Stake

Ant-eater Aardvark, Banded, Echidna, Edental, Giant, Manis, Numbat, Pangolin, Scaly, S(e)ladang, Spiny, Tamandu, Tamandua, Tapir

Antelope Addax, Antilope, Blackbuck, Blaubok, Blesbok, Bloubok, Bluebuck, Bongo, Bontebok, Bubal(is), Bushbuck, Cabric, Chamois, Chikara, Chiru, Dikdik, Duiker, Duyker, Dzeren, Eland, Elk, Gazelle, Gemsbok, Gerenuk, Gnu, Goa, Goral, Grysbok, Harnessed, Hartbees, Hartebeest, Impala, Inyala, Kaama, Kid, Klipspringer, Kob, Kongoni, Koodoo, Kudu, Lechwe, Madoqua, Marshbuck, Mhorr, Mohr, Nagor, Nilgai, Nilgau, Nyala, Nylghau, Oribi, Oryx, Ourebi, Ox, Pale-buck, Pallah, Prongbuck, Pronghorn, Pronk, Puku, Pygarg, Reebok, Reedbuck, Rhebok, Sable, Saiga, Sasin, Sassaby, Serow, Sitatunga, Situtunga, Springbok, Steenbok, Steinbock, Stemback, Stembok, Suni, Takin, Thar, Topi, Tragelaph, Tsessebe, Waterbuck, Wildebeest

Antenatal Labour

Antenna Aerial, Dipole, Dish, Feeler, Horn, Rabbit's ears, Sensillum, TVRO

Anterior Anticous, Earlier, Front, Prior

Anteroom Voiding-lobby

Anthelmintic Worm

Anthem Chant, Die Stem, Hymn, Introit, Isodica, Marseillaise, Motet(t), National, Offertory, Psalm, Red Flag, Responsory, Song, Star Spangled Banner, Stem, Theme, Tract, Troparion

Anthology Album, Ana, Chrestomathy, Digest, Divan, Florilegium, Garland, Pick, Spicilege

Anthony Absolute, Adverse, Runt, Trollope
Anthracite Blind-coal
Anthrax Sang, Splenic fever, Woolsorter's disease
Anthropo(i)d Peripatus, Sivapithecus
Anthropologist, Anthropology Ethnography, Heyerdahl, Levi-Strauss, Mead, Somatology, Strathern, Strehlow, Verchow
Anti Against, Agin, Averse, Con, Hostile
Anti-abortion Right to life
Anti-aircraft AA
Anti-bacterial, Antibiotic Aclarubicin, Actinomycin, Allicin, Amoxicillin, Ampicillin, Aureomycin®, Avoparcin, Bacitracin, Bacteriostat, Carbenicillin, Cecropin, Cephalosporin, Cipro®, Ciprofloxacin, Cloxacillin, Colistin, Cortisone, Co-trimoxazole, Cycloserine, Doxorubicin, Doxycycline, Drug, Erythromycin, Gentamicin, Gramicidin, Griseofulvin, Interferon, Interleukin, Kanamycin, Lincomycin, Macrolide, Magainin, Methicillin, Mitomycin, Neomycin, Nystatin, Opsonin, Oxacillin, Oxytetracycline, Penicillin, Polymyxin, Puromycin, Quinolone, Rifampicin, Rifamycin, Spectinomycin, Streptokinase, Streptomycin, Streptothricin, Terramycin®, Tetracycline, Tyrocidine, Tyrothricin, Vancomycin, Virginiamycin, Wide-spectrum
Antibody Agglutinin, Alemtuzumab, Amboceptor, Antitoxin, Blocker, Catuximab, H(a)emolysin, Hybroid, IgA/E/G/M/O, Isoagglutinin, Lysin, Monoclonal, Opsonin, Precipitin, Reagin, Retuximab, Trastuzumab
Antic(s) Caper, Dido, Frolic, Gambado, Hay, Prank, Shenanigan, Stunt
Anti-carlist Queenite
Antichrist The Man of Sin
Anticipate, Anticipation Against, Antedate, Augur, Await, Drool, → **EXPECT**, Forecast, Foresee, Foresight, Forestall, Foretaste, Forethought, Hope, Intuition, Pre-empt, Preparation, Prevenancy, Prolepsis, Prospect, Second-guess, Type
Anticlimax Bathos, Comedown, Damp squib, Deflation, Disappointment, Letdown
Anticline Upwrap
Anticlockwise Dextrorse, Laevorotatory, Widdershins, Withershins
Anticoagulant C(o)umarin, Heparin, Hirudin, Prostacyclin, Warfarin
Anticommunist John Birch(er), McCarthyism
Anticyclone High
Antidepressant Prozac
Antidote Adder's wort, Alexipharmic, Angelica, Antivenin, Arrowroot, Bezoar, Contrayerva, Cure, Dimercaprol, Emetic, Guaco, Interleukin, Mithridate, Nostrum, Orvietan, Picrotoxin, Remedy, Ribavirin, Senega, Theriac(a), (Venice-)Treacle
Anti-freeze Glycerol, Lagging
Antigen Agglutinogen, Hapten(e)
Antihistamine Dimenhydrinate, Quercetin
Anti-imperialist Guelf, Guelph
Antimacassar Tidy
Antimonopoly Trust buster
Antimony Kohl, Sb, Speiss, Stibium, Tartar emetic
Antinuclear CND
Antioxidant Lycopene
Anti-parliamentarian Poujadist
Antipasto Caponata
Antipathy Allergy, Animosity, Aversion, Detest, → **DISLIKE**, Enmity, Intolerance, Repugnance
Anti-perfectionist Cobden
Antiphon The Reproaches
Antipodean Abo, Antarctic, Antichthon, Aussie, Enzed, Underworld
Antipope Novatian(us)

Anti-protectionist Cobden
Antiquated, Antique, Antiquarian Ancient, Archaic, A(u)stringer, Bibelot, Curio, Dryasdust, Egyptian, FAS, Fogram(ite), Fog(e)y, Fossil, Moth-eaten, Old-fangled, Ostreger, Relic
Anti-reformer Obscurant
Anti-revolutionary Vendean, White
Anti-Roman Ghibel(l)ine
Anti-royalist Puritan, Whig
Anti-Semitic Pamyat
Antiseptic Acriflavine, Carbolic, Cassareep, Creosote, Cresol, Disinfectant, Eupad, Eusol, Formaldehyde, Formalin, Formol, Germicide, Guaiacol, Iodine, Lister, Lysol®, Merbromin, Phenol, Sterile, Tar, Thymol, Tutty
Anti-slavery Free-soil, Wilberforce
Anti-smoker ASH, Misocapnic
Antisocial Hoodie, Hostile, Ishmaelitish, Litterbug, Loner, Misanthropic, Oik, Psychopath
Antithesis Contrary, Converse, Opposite
Anti-three Noetian
Antitoxin Antibody, Antivenin, Guaco, Serum, Vaccine
Anti-union Secesher
Antiviral Rebavirin
Antivitamin Pyrithiamine
Antler(s) Bosset, Crown, Horn, Palm, Rights, Staghorn, Surroyal, Tine
Ant-proof Bilian
▶ **Anus** *see* ANAL
Anvil Bick-iron, Block, Incus, Stiddie, Stithy
Anxiety, Anxious Angst, Brood, Care(ful), Cark, Concern, Disquiet, Dysthymia, Edgy, Fanteeg, Fantigue, Fantod, Fear, Fraught, Grave, Habdabs, Heebie-jeebies, Hung-up, Hypochondria, Impatient, Inquietude, Itching, Jimjams, Jumpy, Keen, Nerviness, Reck, Restless, Scruple, Separation, Shpilkes, Solicitous, Stewing, Stress, Suspense, Sweat, Tension, Toey, Trepidation, Twitchy, Unease, Unquiet, Upset, Uptight, White-knuckle, Willies, Worriment, Worryguts, Worrywort
Any Arrow, Ary, Some
Anybody, Anyone Everyman, One, Whoso, You
Anyhow, Anyway Anyroad(s), However, Leastways, Regardless
Anything Aught, Diddly-squat, Oucht, Ought, Owt, Whatnot
▷ **Anyway** *may indicate* an anagram
Apache Arizona, AZ, Geronimo
Apart Aloof, Aside, Asunder, Atwain, Beside, Separate
Apartheid Racism, Segregation, Verkrampte
Apartment Atrium, Ben, Condominium, Digs, Duplex, Efficiency, Flat, Insula, Mansion, Pad, Paradise, Penthouse, Pied-a-terre, Quarters, Room, Simplex, Solitude, Suite, Tenement, Unit, Walk-up
Apathetic, Apathy Accidie, Acedia, Incurious, Indifferent, Languid, Lethargic, Listless, Lobotomized, Lukewarm, Mopish, Pococurante, Stoical, Torpid, Unenthusiastic
Ape(-like), Apeman Anthropoid, Barbary, Big-foot, Bonobo, Catarrhine, Copy, Dryopithecine, Gelada, Gibbon, Gorilla, → IMITATE, Magot, Mimic, → MONKEY, Naked, Orang, Paranthropus, Parrot, Pithecoid, Pongid, Pongo, → PRIMATE, Proconsul, Sacred, Simian, Simulate, Troglodyte, Yowie
Aperient Cascara, Laxative, Senna
Aperitif Campari, → DRINK, Pernod®
Aperture Balistraria, Chink, Fenestella, Hole, Keyhole, Opening, Orifice, Osculum, Peephole, Pinhole, Porta, Punctum, Relative, Spiracle, Swallow, Window
Apex Acme, Culmen, Gonion, Keystone, Knoll, Knowe, Solar, Summit, Vortex

Aphid Ant-cow, Blackfly, Greenfly, Phylloxera
Aphorism Adage, Epigram, Gnome, Pensée, Proverb, Sutra
Aphrodisiac, Aphrodite Cytherean, Erotic, Idalian, Paphian, Philter, Philtre, Spanish fly, Urania, Yohimbine
Aplomb Assurance, Cool, Equanimity, Poise, Sangfroid, Serenity
Apocryphal Spurious, Tobit
Apograph Roneo®
Apollo Belvedere, Pythian, Sun
Apologetic, Apology Ashamed, Excuse, Justifier, Mockery, My bad, Oops, Pardon, Scuse, Sir-reverence
Apostate Citer, → **HERETIC**, Pervert, Rat, Recreant, Renegade, Runagate, Turncoat
Apostle, Apostolic Cuthbert, → **DISCIPLE**, Evangelist, Johannine, Jude, Matthew, Pauline, Spoon, Thad(d)eus, Thomas, Twelve
Apostrophe, Apostrophise Elision, O(h), Soliloquy, Tuism
Apothecary Chemist, Dispenser, Druggist, LSA, Pharmacist, Pottingar
Apothegm Dictum, Maxim, Motto
Appal(ling) Abysmal, Affear(e), Aghast, Dire, Dismay, Egregious, Execrable, Frighten, Horrify, Piacular, Shock, Tragic
▷ **Appallingly** *may indicate* an anagram
Apparatus Absorptiometer, Alembic, Alkalimeter, Appliance, Aqualung, Aspirator, Autoclave, Breeches buoy, Bridgerama, Caisson, Calorimeter, Chemostat, Churn, Clinostat, Codec, Coherer, Colorimeter, Commutator, Condenser, Converter, Convertor, Cosmotron, Critical, Cryostat, Davis, Decoy, Defibrillator, Desiccator, → **DEVICE**, Digester, Ebullioscope, Effusiometer, Egg, Electrograph, Electrophorus, Electroscope, Elutriator, Enlarger, Eprouvette, Equipment, Eudiometer, Exciter, Fixings, Gadget, Gasogene, Gazogene, Generator, Giant('s) stride, Golgi, Graith, Gyroscope, Heater, Heliograph, Helioscope, Hemocytometer, Hodoscope, Holophote, Horse, Hydrophone, Hygrostat, Incubator, Inhalator, Injector, Inspirator, Installation, Instrument, Iron lung, Jacquard, Kipp's, Kymograph, Langmuir-trough, Lease-rod, Life-preserver, Loom, Masora(h), Microreader, Mimeograph, Mine-detector, Multi-gym, Nephoscope, Nitrometer, Oscillator, Oscillograph, Oxygenator, Pasteuriser, Peat-seeker, Percolator, Phon(o)meter, Photophone, Photostat®, Phytotron, Plate-warmer, Plethysmograph, Plumber's snake, Pommel horse, Potometer, Projector, Proto®, Pulmotor®, Push-pull, Radiator, Radiosonde, Rattlebag, Rattletrap, Rectifier, Replenisher, Resistor, Respirator, Respirometer, Resuscitator, Retort, Rotisserie, Rounce, Scintiscanner, Scrubber, Scuba, Searchlight, Seeder, Semaphore, Set, Skimmer, Slide rest, Smoker, Snake, Sniffer, Snorkel, Snowbox, Soundboard, Sphygmograph, Spirophore, Starter, Stellarator, Steriliser, Still, Substage, Switchgear, Tackle, Tackling, Talk-you-down, Telecine, Teleprinter, Teleseme, Tellurian, Thermopile, Tokamak, Transformer, Transmitter, Tribometer, Tromp(e), Tuner, Ventouse, Wheatstone's bridge, Whip-and-derry, ZETA
Apparel Attire, Besee, → **COSTUME**, Garb, Raiment, Wardrobe, Wardrop
Apparent(ly) Ap, Clear, Detectable, Manifest, Ostensible, Outward, Overt, Plain, Prima facie, Seeming, Semblance, Visible
▷ **Apparent** *may indicate* a hidden word
Apparition Dream, Eidolon, Fetch, Ghost, → **ILLUSION**, Phantom, Shade, Spectre, Vision, Visitant, Wraith
Appeal(ing) Ad, Beg, Cachet, Catchpenny, Charisma, Charm, Cri de coeur, Cry, Dreamy, Entreat, Entreaty, Epirrhema, Exhort, Eye-catching, Fetching, Glamorous, Howzat, Invocation, It, Mediagenic, Miserere, O, Oath, Oomph, Plead, SA, Screeve, Sex(iness), Solicit, SOS, Suit, Yummy
Appear(ance) Advent, Air, Apport, Arise, Arrival, Aspect, Broo, Brow, Burst, Cast, Colour, Compear, Debut, Effeir, Effere, Emerge, Enter, Exterior, Eye, Facade, Fa(s)cia, Facies, Far(r)and, Farrant, Feature, Format, Garb, Guise, Habitus, Hue, Image, Kithe, Kythe, Looks, Loom, Manifestation, → **MANNER**, Mien, Occur, Ostensibly, Ostent,

Outward, Person, Phase, Phenomenon, Physiognomy, Presence, Prosopon, Represent, Rig, Rise, Seem, Semblance, Show, Species, Spring, Superficies, Theophany, View, Visitation, Vraisemblance, Whistle-stop, Wraith

Appease(ment) Allay, Alleviate, Atone, Calm, Conciliation, Danegeld, Mitigate, → **MOLLIFY**, Munichism, Pacify, Placate, Propitiate, Satisfy, Soothe, Sop

Appellant Roe

Append(age) Adjunct, Affix, Aglet, Allantois, Annex, Antennule, Aril, Arista, Cercus, Chelicera, Codpiece, Ctene, Fang, Flagellum, Hanger-on, Lobe, Lug, Palp(us), Paraglossa, Parapodium, Pedipalp, Pendicle, Postfix, Proboscis, Stipel, Stipule, Suffix, Swimmeret, Tail, Tailpiece, Tentacle, Ugly, Uropod, Uvula

Appendix Addendum, Apocrypha, Codicil, Grumbling, Label, Pendant, Pendent, Rider, Schedule, Vermiform

Appetite, Appetitive, Appetise(r), Appetize(r) Amuse-bouche, Amuse-gueule, Antepast, Antipasto, Aperitif, Appestat, Bhagee, Bhajee, Bulimia, Bulimy, Canapé, Concupiscence, Concupy, Crudités, Desire, Dim-sum, Entremes(se), Entremets, Flesh, Hunger, Inner man, Limosis, Malacia, Meze, Mezze, Nacho, Orectic, Orexis, Passion, Pica, Polyphagia, Relish, Tapa(s), Titillate, Twist, Ventripotent, Whet, Yerd-hunger, Yird-hunger

Applaud, Applause Acclaim, Bravo, → **CHEER**, Clap, Claque, Eclat, Encore, Extol, Hum, Kentish fire, Olé, Ovation, Praise, Root, Ruff, Tribute

Apple Adam's, Alligator, Bad, Baldwin, Balsam, Biffin, Blenheim orange, Braeburn, Bramley, Cashew, Charlotte, Codlin(g), Cooker, Costard, Crab, Custard, Dead Sea, Discord, Eater, Granny Smith, Greening, Jenneting, John, Jonathan, Kangaroo, Leather-coat, Love, Mammee, May, McIntosh (red), Medlar, Nonpareil, Oak, Pacific Rose, Pearmain, Pippin, Pomace, Pome(roy), Pomroy, Pom(e)water, Potato, Punic, Pupil, Pyrus, Quarantine, Quarenden, Quar(r)ender, Quarrington, Queening, Quodlin, Redstreak, Reinette, Rennet, Ribston(e), Ripstone, Rotten, Royal gala, Ruddock, Russet, Seek-no-further, Snow, Sops-in-wine, Sorb, Sturmer (Pippin), Sugar, Sweeting, Thorn, Toffee, Windfall, Winesap

Apple juice Malic

Apple-picker Atalanta

Applicant Ordinand, Postulant

Application, Applicable, Apply, Appliance(s) Address, Adhibit, Appeal, Appose, Assiduity, Barrage, Blender, Concentration, Devote, Diligence, Dressing, Exercise, Exert, Foment, Germane, Give, Implement, Inlay, Juicer, Lay, Liquidiser, Lotion, Mixer, Ointment, Opodeldoc, Pertinent, Petition, Plaster, Poultice, Put, Request, Resort, Respirator, Rub, Sinapism, Stupe, Talon, Toggle, Truss, → **USE**, Vice, White goods

Appliqué Hawaiian

Appoint(ee), Appointment Advowson, Assign, Berth, Co-opt, Date, Delegate, Depute, Designate, Dew, Due, Executor, Induction, Installation, Make, Name, → **NOMINATE**, Nominee, Office, Ordain, Place, Position, Post, Posting, Rendezvous, Room, Set, Tryst

▷ **Appointed** *may indicate* an anagram

Apportion(ment) Allocate, Allot, Entail, Mete, Parcel, Ration, Share, Weigh

Apposite Apt, Cogent, Germane, Pat, Pertinent, Relevant, Suitable

Appraise, Appraisal Analyse, → **EVALUATE**, Gauge, Guesstimate, Judge, Once-over, Tape, → **VALUE**, Vet

Appreciate, Appreciation Acknowledgement, Cherish, Clap, Comprehensible, Dig, Empathy, Endear, Esteem, Gratefulness, Increase, Phwoar, Prize, Realise, Recognise, Regard, Relish, Rise, Sense, Stock, Taste, Thank you, Treasure, → **VALUE**, Welcome

Apprehend(ing), Apprehension Afears, Alarm, Arrest, Attuent, → **CATCH**, Collar, Fear, Grasp, Insight, Intuit, Perceive, Quailing, See, Suspense, Take, Toey, Trepidation, Uh-oh, Unease, Uptake

Apprehensive Jumpy, Nervous, Uneasy

Apprentice(ship) Article, Commis, Cub, Devil, Garzone, Improver, Indent(ure), Jockey, L, Learner, Lehrjahre, Novice, Noviciate, Novitiate, Printer's devil, Pupillage, Snob, Tiro, Trainee, Turnover, Tyro(ne)

Approach(ing), Approachable Abord, Access, Accost, Advance, Affable, Anear, Angle, Anigh, Appropinquate, Appulse, Asymptotic, Avenue, Close, Coast, Come, Converge, Cost(e), Draw nigh, Drive, Driveway, Fairway, Feeler, Gate, Imminent, Ingoing, Line, Near, Nie, Open, Overture, Pitch, Procedure, Road, Run-in, Run-up, Stealth, Strategy, Towards, Verge, Warm

Appropriate(ly), Appropriateness Abduct, Abstract, Annex, Applicable, Apposite, Apt, Aright, Asport, Assign, Bag, Befitting, Borrow, Collar, Commandeer, Commensurate, Condign, Confiscate, Congruous, Convenient, Due, Element, Eligible, Embezzle, Expedient, Fit, Germane, Good, Happy, Hijack, Hog, Impound, Jump, Just, Meet, Nick, Pertinent, Pilfer, Plagiarise, Pocket, Pre-empt, Proper, Propriety, Purloin, Right, Seise, Seize, Sequester, Sink, Snaffle, Steal, Suit, Swipe, Take, Timely, Trouser, Usurp

Approval, Approve(d), Approbation Accolade, Admire, Adopt, Allow, Amen, Applaud, Assent, Attaboy, Aye, Blessing, Bravo, Brownie points, Change, Clap, → COUNTENANCE, Credit, Cushty, Dig, Endorse, Favour, For, Green light, Hear hear, Homologate, Hubba-hubba, Hurra(h), Imprimatur, Initial, Kitemark, Know, Laud, Nod, Okay, Olé, Orthodox, Pass, Plaudit, Rah, Ratify, Recommend, Right-on, Rubber-stamp, Sanction, Stotter, Thumbs-up, Tick, Tribute, Vivat, Voice, Warm to, Yay, Yes, Zindabad

Approximate(ly), Approximation Almost, Around, Ballpark, Circa, Close, Coarse, Estimate, Guess, Imprecise, Near, Rough and ready, Roughly

Apricot Mebos

April, April fool Apr, Huntiegowk, Hunt-the-gowk

Apron Airside, Barm-cloth, Bib, Blacktop, Brat, Bunt, Canvas, Dick(e)y, Ephod, Fig-leaf, Gremial, Ice, Napron, Pinafore, Pinner, Pinny, Placket, Rim, Stage, Tablier, Tier, Waist

Apse Concha, Exedra, Niche, Recess, Tribune

Apt(ly) Apposite, Appropriate, Apropos, Ben trovato, Capable, Evincive, Fit, Gleg, Happy, Liable, Pat, Prone, Suitable, Tends

Aptitude Ability, Bent, Ear, Eye, Faculty, Feel, Flair, Gift, Knack, Nose, Skill, Talent, Taste, Tendency, Touch, Viability

Aqua(tic) Euglena, Flustra, Lentic, Lotic, Regia, Zizania

Aqualung Rebreather, Scuba

Aquamarine Madagascar

Aquarium Oceanarium

Aqueduct Canal, Channel, Conduit, Hadrome, Xylem

Arab(ian), Arabia, Arabic Abdul, Adeni, Adnan, Algorism, Ali, Baathist, Bahraini, Bahrein, Bedouin, Bedu, Druse, Druz(e), Effendi, Fedayee(n), Gamin, Geber, Hani, Hashemite, Hassaniya, Himyarite, Horse, Iraqi, Jawi, Kuwaiti, Lawrence, Moor, Mudlark, Nabat(a)ean, Nas(s)eem, Nes(h)ki, Omani, Omar, PLO, Qatari, Rag(head), Saba, Sab(a)ean, Saracen, Saudi, Seleucid, Semitic, Sheikh, Street, Syrian, UAR, Urchin, Yemen

Arabis Cress

Arachnid Mite, Podogona, Ricinulei, Solpuga, → SPIDER

Arbitrary Despotic, Haphazard, Peculiar, Random, Wanton, Whim

Arbitrate, Arbitration, Arbitrator, Arbiter ACAS, Censor, Daysman, Judge, Negotiator, Ombudsman, Pendulum, Prud'homme, Ref(eree), Umpire

Arboreal, Arbour Bower, Dendroid, Pergola, Trellis

Arc Azimuth, Bow, Carbon, → CURVE, Flashover, Fogbow, Foil, Halo, Hance, Haunch, Island, Limb, Mercury, Octant, Quadrant, Rainbow, Reflex, Seadog, Trajectory, White rainbow

Arcade Amusement, Burlington, Cloister, Gallery, Loggia, Mall, Penny, Triforium, Video

Arcadia(n) Idyllic, Nemoral, Sylvan

Arcane Esoteric, Mystic, Obscure, Occult, Orphism, Recherché, Rune, Secret

Arch(ed), Arching Acute, Admiralty, Alveolar, Arblaster, Arcade, Arcature, Archivolt,

Arcuate, Camber, Chief, Coom, Counterfort, Crafty, Cross-rib, Crown-green, Ctesiphon, → **CUNNING**, Curve, Discharging, Elfin, Embow, Espiegle, Eyebrow, Fallen, Flying buttress, Fog-bow, Fornicate, Fornix, Gill, Gothic, Hance, Haunch, Hog, Horseshoe, Instep, Intrados, Inverted, Keel, Keystone, Lancet, Leery, Lierne, Limb-girdle, Marble, Neural, Norman, Ogee, Ogive, Opistholomos, Order, Parthian, Pectoral, Pelvic, Plantar, Pointed, Portal, Proscenium, Recessed, Relieving, Roach, Roguish, Roman, Safety, Saucy, Segmental, Shouldered, Skew, Sly, Soffit, Span, Squinch, Stilted, Trajan, Triumphal, Vault, Zygoma

Archaeological, Archaeologist, Archaeology Bell, Carter, Childe, Dater, Dig, Evans, Industrial, Layard, Leakey, Mallowan, Mycenae, Petrie, Pothunter, Qumran, Schliemann, Sutton Hoo, Type-site, Wheeler, Winckelmann, Woolley

Archangel Azrael, Gabriel, Israfeel, Israfel, Israfil, Jerahmeel, Michael, Raguel, Raphael, Sariel, Satan, Uriel, Yellow

Arch-binder Voussoir

Archbishop Anselm, Augustine, Cosmo, Cranmer, Davidson, Dunstan, Ebor, Elector, Hatto, Lambeth, Lanfranc, Lang, Langton, Laud, Metropolitan, Morton, Primate, Scroop, Temple, Trench, Tutu, Whitgift

Archdeacon Rev, Ven(erable)

Archduke Trio

Archer(y) Acestes, Bow-boy, → **BOWMAN**, Cupid, Eros, Hood, Petticoat, Philoctetes, Sagittary, Tell, Toxophilite

Archetype Avatar, Form, Model, Pattern

Archibald, Archie, Archy Ack-ack, Cockroach, Oerlikon, Rice, Roach

Archilochian Epode

Archimandrite Eutyches

Archimedes Screw

Archipelago Alexander, Antarctic, Azores, Bismarck, Camaguey, Dhivehi, East Indian, Fiji, Franz Josef Land, Gulag, Japan, Kerguelen, Malay, Maldives, Marquesas, Mergui, Novaya Zemlya, Palmer, Paumotu, St Pierre and Miquelon, Severnaya Zemlya, Spitsbergen, Sulu, Svalbard, Tierra del Fuego, Tonga, Tuamoto, West Indies

Architect(ure), Architectural Arcology, Baroque, Bauhaus, Bricolage, Brutalism, Byzantine, Cartouche, Churrigueresque, Community, Composite, Computer, Corinthian, Creator, Data-flow, Decorated, Decorated style, Designer, Domestic, Doric, Early English, Elizabethan, Entablature, Federation, Flamboyant, Georgian, Gothic, Greek Revival, Ionic, Italian, Jacobean, Landscape, Listed, Lombard, Maker, Mission, Moderne, Moorish, Moresque, Mudejar, Naval, Neoclassical, Neo-gothic, Norman, Palladian, Pelasgian, Perpendicular, Picnostyle, Planner, Plateresque, Prostyle, Queen Anne, Romanesque, Saracenic, Saxon, Spandrel, Spandril, Tectonic, Tudor, Tudorbethan, Tuscan, Vitruvian

ARCHITECTS

3 letters:	Wren	Utzon	Street
Cox		Wyatt	Voysey
Pei	5 letters:		Wright
	Barry	6 letters:	
4 letters:	Gaudi	Breuer	7 letters:
Adam	Hooke	Casson	Alberti
Kent	Horta	Foster	Behrens
Loos	Inigo	Lasdun	Bernini
Nash	Nervi	Nissen	Blacket
Shaw	Pugin	Repton	Columbo
Webb	Scott	Romano	Erskine
Wood	Soane	Spence	Griffin

Gropius	Greenway	Macquarie	**11 letters:**
Lutyens	Niemeyer	Vitruvius	Abercrombie
Neumann	Palladio		Butterfield
Percier	Piranesi	**10 letters:**	Churrighera
Seidler	Saarinen	Inigo Jones	Le Corbusier
Venturi	Stirling	Mackintosh	
Vignola	Vanbrugh	Tange Kenzo	**12 letters:**
		Trophonius	Brunelleschi
8 letters:	**9 letters:**	Van der Rohe	
Bramante	Borromini	Waterhouse	**15 letters:**
Chalgrin	Hawksmoor		Vitruvius Pollio
Fontaine	Mackmurdo		

Architrave Epistyle, Platband

Archive(s) Backfile, Morgue, Muniment, PRO, Records, Register

Archon Draco

Arch-villain Ringleader

Arctic Estotiland, Frigid, Hyperborean, In(n)uit, Inupiat, Polar, Tundra

Ardent, Ardour Aflame, Aglow, Boil, Broiling, Burning, Enthusiasm, Fervent, Fervid, Fiery, Fire, Flagrant, Flaming, Gusto, Heat, Het, → **HOT**, Hot-brained, In, Mettled, Mettlesome, Passion(ate), Perfervid, Rage, Spiritous, Vehement, Warm-blooded, Zealous, Zeloso

Arduous Laborious, Steep, Uphill

Are A, Exist, 're

Area Acre, Aleolar, Apron, Arctogaea, Are, Assisted, Bailiwick, Beat, Belt, Bovate, Broca's, Built-up, Carucate, Catchment, Centare, Centiare, Centre, Chill-out, Clearing, Conurbation, Courtyard, Craton, Curtilage, Dec(i)are, Dedans, Depressed, Dessiatine, Development, Disaster, District, Docklands, Domain, Downtown, Endemic, Eruv, Extent, Farthingland, Forecourt, Gau, Goal, Grey, Growth, Heartland, Hectare, Henge, Hide, Hinterland, Hotspot, Husbandland, Imperium, Input, Karst, Landmass, Lathe, Latitude, Lek, Locality, Lodg(e)ment, Manor, Metroplex, Milieu, Mofussil, Morgen, Mush, Neogaea, Nidderdale, No-go, No-man's-land, Notogaea, Orb, Oxgang, Oxgate, Oxland, Pale, Parish, Patch, Penalty, Place, Pleasance, Plot, Precinct, Province, Purlieu, Quad, Quadrat, Quarter (section), Range, Redevelopment, Refugium, → **REGION**, Renosterveld, Res(ervation), Reserve, Rest, Restricted, Retrochoir, Rood, Rule, Sector, Service, Shire, Site, Slurb, Special, Staging, Sterling, Subtopia, Support, Surface, Target, Tartary, Technical, Terra, Terrain, Territory, Theatre, Tie, Tract, Tundra, Tye, Uptown, Urban, Ure, Weald, White, Wilderness, Work station, Yard, Zone

Arena Battleground, Circus, Cockpit, Dohyo, Field, Lists, Maidan, Olympia, → **RING**, Rink, Snowdome, Stadium, Tiltyard, Velodrome, Venue

Argal Ergo

Argent Ag, Silver

Argentina RA

Argon Ar

Argonaut Acastus, Jason, Lynceus, Meleager, Nautilus, Paper-sailor

Argot Flash, Idiom, Jargon, Lingo, Scamto, Shelta

Argue, Argument(ative) Altercation, Antistrophon, Argie-bargie, Argle-bargle, Argy-bargy, Bandy, Beef, Blue, Brush, Cangle, Case, Casuism, Choplogic, Conflict, Contend, Contest, Contra, Cosmological, Debate, Deprecate, Diallage, Difference, Dilemma, Ding-dong, Dispute, Dissent, Elenchus, Elenctic, Enthusiasm, Enthymeme, Eristic, Exchange, Expostulate, Forensic, Fray, Free-for-all, Generalisation, Hysteron proteron, Logic, Logomachy, Mexican standoff, Moot, Ob and soller, Object, Ontological, Paralogism, Patter, Pettifog, Plead, Polemic, Polylemma, Premiss, Propound, Pros and cons, Quarrel, Quibble, Quodlibet, Rammy, Ratiocinate, → **REASON**, Remonstrate, Row,

Run-in, Scene, Sequacious, Socratise, Sophism, Sophistry, Sorites, Spar, Stickle, Straw man, Stroppy, Stushie, Summation, Syllogism, Teleological, Theme, Thetic, Third man, Tiff, Transcendental, Trilemma, Verbal, Vociferate, Words, Yike

Argyle Argathelian, Gravy-boat, Sock

Aria Ballad, Cabaletta, Cantata, Meiody, Song

Arid Dry, Parched, Sere

Ariel Pen

Aris Arse, → **BOTTOM**, Can

Arise Appear, Be, Develop, Emanate, Emerge, Upgo, Wax

Aristocracy, Aristocrat(ic) Blood, Boyar, Buckeen, Classy, Debrett, Duc, Elite, Eupatrid, Gentle, Gentry, Grandee, High-hat, Junker, Nob, Noble, Optimate, Passage, Patrician, Thane, Toff, Tony, U-men, Upper-crust, Well-born

Aristotle Peripatetic, Stagirite, Stagyrite

Arithmetic(ian) Algorism, Algorith, Arsmetrick, Cocker, Euclid, Logistic, Modular, Quadrivium, Sums

Ark(wright) Chest, Noah, Zoo

Arly Thicket

Arm(ed), Arms Akimbo, Arsenal, Bearing, Brachial, Branch, Bundooks, Canting, Cove, Crest, Cross bow, Embattle, Equip, Escutcheon, Estoc, Fin, Firth, Frith, Gnomon, Halbert, Hatchment, Heel, Heraldic, Inlet, Jib, Krupp, Limb, Loch, Long, Member, Olecranon, Pick-up, Quillon, Radius, Rail, Ramous, Rocker, Rotor, SAA, Secular, Shield, Shotgun, Side, Small, Smooth-bore, Spiral, Tappet, Tentacle, Timer, Tone, Tooled-up, Transept, Tremolo, Ulnar, Water pistol, → **WEAPON**, Whip

▷ **Arm** *may indicate* an army regiment, etc.

Armada Spanish

Armadillo Dasypod, Dasypus, Fairy, Giant, Pangolin, Peba, Pichiciego, Tatou(ay), Xenurus

Armature Keeper, Shuttle

Armband Torc, Torque

Armenian Haikh, Yezedi

Armhole Scye

Armistice Still-stand, Truce

Armless Inermous

Armour(ed), Armoury Ailette, Armature, Armet, Barbette, Beaver, Besagew, Bevor, Brasset, Breastplate, Brigandine, Buckler, Byrnie, Camail, Cannon, Casspir, Cataphract, Chaffron, Chain, Chamfrain, Chamfron, Character, Chausses, Corium, Cors(e)let, Couter, Cuirass, Cuish, Cuisse, Culet, Curat, Curiet, Cush, Defence, Fauld, Garderobe, Garniture, Gear, Genouillère, Gere, Gorget, Greave, Habergeon, Hauberk, Hoplology, Jack, Jambe, Jambeau, Jazerant, Jesserant, Lamboys, Loricate, Mail, Male, Mentonnière, Mesail, Mezail, Nasal, Nosepiece, Palette, Panoply, Panzer, Pauldron, Petta, Placcat, Placket, Plastron, Plate, Poitrel, Poleyn, Pouldron, Rerebrace, Rest, Roundel, Sabaton, Scale, Secret, → **SHIELD**, Solleret, Spaudler, Splint, Stand, Tace, Tank, Taslet, Tasse(t), Thorax, Tonlet, Tuille, Vambrace, Vantbrass, Ventail, Visor, Voider, Weed

Armpit Axilla, Oxter

Armstrong Louis, Satchmo

Army Arrière-ban, BEF, Blue Ribbon, Church, Colours, Confederate, Crowd, Federal, Field, Fyrd, Golden (Horde), Horde, Host, IRA, Junior Service, Land, Landwehr, Lashkar, Legion, Line, Military, Militia, Mobile Command, Multitude, New Model, Para-military, Red, SA, Sabaoth, Salvation, SAS, Sena, Service, Soldiers, Squad, Standing, Stratonic, Swarm, TA, Tartan, Terracotta, Territorial, Thin red line, Volunteer, War, Wehrmacht

▷ **Army** *may indicate* having arms

Aroma(tic) Allspice, Aniseed, Aryl, Balmy, Coriander, Fenugreek, Fragrant, Nose, Odorous, Pomander, Spicy, Stilbene, Vanillin, Wintergreen

Around About, Ambient, Circa, Near, Peri-, Skirt, Tour

▷ **Around** *may indicate* one word around another

Arouse, Arousal Alarm, → **EXCITE**, Fan, Fire, Incite, Inflame, Inspire, Must(h), Needle, Provoke, Stimulate, Stole, Suscitate, Touch up, Urolagnia, Waken, Whet

Arpad ELO

Arrange(r), Arrangement Adjust, Array, Attune, Ausgleich, Bandobast, Bank, Bundobust, Concert, Concinnity, Configuration, Coordinate, Design, Display, Dispose, Do, Dress, Echelon, Edit, Engineer, Finger, Fix, Foreordain, Format, Formation, Formwork, Grade, Ikebana, Layout, Lineation, Marshal, Modus vivendi, Neaten, Orchestrate, Orchestration, Ordain, → **ORDER**, Ordonnance, Organise, Pack, Pattern, Perm, Permutation, Plan, Position, Prepare, Prepense, Quincunx, Redactor, Regulate, Run, Rustle up, Schedule, Schema, Scheme, Score, Set, Settle, Sort, Spacing, Stack, Stage-manage, Stereoisomerism, Stow, Straighten, Structure, Style, System, Tabulate, Tactic, Taxis, Tidy, Transcribe, Vertical

▷ **Arrange** *may indicate* an anagram

Arras Tapestry

Array(ed) Attire, Bedight, Deck, Herse, Logic, Marshal, Muster, Panoply, Phased, Seismic

Arrear(s) Aft, Ahint, Backlog, Behind, Debt, Owing

Arrest(ed), Arresting Abort, Alguacil, Alguazil, Ament, Apprehend, Attach, Attract, Blin, Book, Bust, Caption, Capture, Cardiac, Catch, Check, Citizen's, Collar, Detain, False, Furthcoming, Hold, House, Knock, Lag, Lift, Lightning, Nab, Nail, Nick, Nip, Nobble, Pinch, Pull, Restrain, Retard, Riveting, Round-up, Run-in, Salient, Sease, Seize, Snaffle, Snatch, Stasis, Stop, Sus(s)

Arris Groin

Arrival, Arrive, Arriving Accede, Advent, Attain, Come, Entrance, Get, Happen, Hit, Inbound, Influx, Johnny-come-lately, Land, Latecomer, Natal, Nativity, Newcomer, Pitch up, Reach, Roll up, Show, Strike

Arrogance, Arrogant Assumption, Bold, Bravado, Bumptious, Cavalier, Cocksure, Cocky, Contemptuous, Disdain, Dogmatic, Effrontery, Haughty, Haut(eur), High, High and mighty, High-handed, High-hat, Hogen-mogen, Hoity-toity, Hubris, Imperious, Jumped up, Lordly, Morgue, Overweening, Presumption, Pretentious, Proud, Proud-stomached, Prussianism, Side, Snobbish, Stuck-up, Surquedry, Surquedy, Toploftical, Topping, Turkeycock, Uppish, Uppity, Upstart

Arrogate Appropriate, Assume, Claim, Impute, Usurp

Arrow, Arrow-head Acestes, Any, Ary, Blunt, Bolt, Broad(head), Cloth-yard shaft, Dart, Dogbolt, Filter, Flechette, Flight, Missile, Pheon, Pointer, Quarrel, Reed, Sagittate, Shaft, Sheaf, Straight

Arrowroot Kuzu, Maranta, Pia

Arsenal Ammo, Armo(u)ry, Depot, Fire-arms, Magazine, Side, Toulon

Arsenate, Arsenic(al), Arsenide As, Erythrite, Realgar, Resalgar, Rosaker, Salvarsan, Scorodite, Skutterudite, Smaltite, Speiss, Zarnich

Arson(ist) Firebug, Pyromania, Torching

Art(s), Arty, Art movement, Art school, Art style Abstract, Alla prima, Applied, Ars, Arte Povera, Bauhaus, Bloomsbury, Bonsai, Britart, Brut, Chiaroscuro, Clair-obscure, Clare-obscure, Click, Clip, Cobra, Collage, Commercial, Conceptual, Constructivism, Contrapposto, Craft, Cubism, Culture vulture, Cunning, Curious, Dada, Daedal(e), Deco, Decorative, Dedal, De Stijl, Die Brucke, Diptych, Divisionism, Earth, Ekphrasis, Enamel(ling), Environmental, Es, Expressionism, Fauvism, Feat, Fine, Finesse, Flemish, Folk, Fugue, Futurism, Genre, Graphic, Guile, High Renaissance, Humanities, Ikebana, Impressionist, Jugendstil, Kakemono, Kano, Ka pai, Kinetic, Kirigami, Kitsch, Knack, Lacquerware, Land, Liberal, Mandorla, Mannerism, Martial, Masterwork, Mehndi, Minimal, Modern(e), Montage, Motivated, Music, Mystery, Nabis, Nazarene, Neoclassical, Neo-impressionism, New Wave, Noli-me-tangere, Norwich, Nouveau, Optical, Origami, Orphic Cubism, Orphism, Outsider, Pastiche, Performance, Performing, Perigordian, Plastic, Pointillism, Pop, Postimpressionism, Postmodern,

Practical, Pre-Raphaelite, Primitive, Psychedelic, Public, Purism, Quadratura, Quadrivium, Relievo, Sienese, → **SKILL**, Social realism, Stained glass, Still-life, Suprematism, Surrealism, Synchronism, Tachism(e), Tactics, Tatum, Tenebrism, Toreutics, Trecento, Triptych, Trivium, Trompe l'oeil, Trouvé, Tsutsumu, Useful, Verism, Virtu, Visual, Vorticism

▷ **Art** *may indicate an -est ending*

Artefact(s) Neolith, Palaeolith, Tartanalia, Tartanry, Xoanon

▷ **Artefact** *may indicate an anagram*

Artemis Selene

Artemus Ward

Artery Aorta, Brachial, Carotid, Coronary, Duct, Femoral, Frontal, Iliac, Innominate, M1, Maxillary, Phrenic, Pulmonary, Radial, Route, Spermatic, Temporal

Artful Cute, Dodger, Foxy, Ingenious, Quirky, Shifty, Sly, Subtle, Tactician, Wily

Arthropod Insecta, Limulus, Peripatus, Prototracheata, Sea-slater, Tardigrade, Trilobite, Water-bear

Artichoke Cardoon, Jerusalem

Article(s) A, An, Apprentice, Clause, Column, Commodity, Cutting, Definite, Feature, Feuilleton, Five, Gadget, Indefinite, Indenture, Item, Leader, Leading, Op-ed, Paper, Part, Piece, Pot-boiler, Shipping, Sidebar, Specify, The, Thing, Thinkpiece, Thirty-nine, Treatise, Turnover, Ware

Articulation, Articulate(d) Clear, Coherent, Coudé, Diarthrosis, Distinct, Eloquent, Enounce, Express, Fluent, Fortis, Gimmal, Gomphosis, Hinged, Intonate, Jointed, Jymold, Lenis, Limbed, Lisp, Pretty-spoken, Pronounce, Schindylesis, Single-tongue, Tipping, Trapezial, Utter, Vertebrae, Voice

Artifice(r), Artificial Bogus, Chouse, Contrived, Davenport-trick, Dodge, Ersatz, Factitious, False, Finesse, Guile, Hoax, In vitro, Logodaedaly, Made, Man-made, Mannered, Opificer, Phoney, Postiche, Pretence, Prosthetic, Pseudo, Reach, Ruse, Sell, Set, Sham, Spurious, Stratagem, → **STRATEGY**, Synthetic, Theatric, → **TRICK**, Unnatural, Wile, Wright

Artificial respiration Kiss of life, Schafer's method

Artillery Battery, Cannon, Cohorn(e), Field, Fougade, Fougasse, Guns, Mortar, Ordnance, Pyroballogy, RA, Rafale, Ramose, Ramus, Train

Artiodactyl Camel, Chevrotain, Deerlet

Artisan Craftsman, Decorator, Joiner, Journeyman, Mechanic, Peon, Pioneer, Pioner, Pyoner, Shipwright, Workman

Artist(e), Artistic Aesthetic, Animator, Blaue Reiter, Bohemian, Cartoonist, Colourist, Cubist, Dadaist, Daedal(e), Deccie, Decorator, Die Brucke, Enameller, Escape, Etcher, Fauve, Fine, Foley, Gentle, Gilder, Graffiti, ICA, Illustrator, Impressionist, Landscapist, Left Bank, Limner, Linear, Maestro, Master, Mime, Miniaturist, → **MUSICIAN**, Nabis, Nazarene, Oeuvre, Orphism, → **PAINTER**, Pavement, Paysagist, Perspectivist, Piss, Plein-airist, Pre-Raphaelite, Primitive, Quick-change, RA, Rap, Screever, → **SCULPTOR**, Sideman, Sien(n)ese, Surrealist, Tachisme, Tagger, Tap dancer, Touch, Trapeze, Trecentist, Virtuose, Virtuoso

ARTISTS

3 letters:	Chia	Emin	Long
Arp	Cole	Etty	Miró
Cox	Cuyp	Goya	Nash
Dix	Dadd	Gris	Opie
Ono	Dali	Hals	Phiz
	Done	John	Rees
4 letters:	Doré	Klee	West
Bell	Dufy	Lely	

5 letters:
Aiken
Appel
Bacon
Bakst
Balla
Blake
Bosch
Brown
Buren
Burra
Corot
Crane
Crome
Dürer
Danby
David
Degas
Dulac
Ensor
Ernst
Gelée
Grosz
Hirst
Hoare
Hooch
Johns
Klimt
Kline
Léger
Leech
Lippi
Lotto
Lowry
Makar
Manet
Monet
Moses
Munch
Olley
Olsen
Orpen
Poons
Redon
Riley
Rodin
Seago
Steen
Steer
Tatum
Watts

6 letters:
Albers
Boudin
Braque
Bratby
Brucke
Calder
Callot
Claude
Clouet
Cotman
Derain
De Wint
Dobell
D'Orsay
Eakins
Escher
Fabrio
Fuseli
Gilles
Giotto
Greuze
Guardi
Haydon
Herman
Hopper
Ingres
Knight
Le Nain
Man Ray
Millet
Moreau
Morris
Newman
Oliver
Renoir
Ribera
Rivera
Romano
Romney
Rothko
Rubens
Sendak
Seurat
Signac
Sisley
Strang
Stubbs
Tissot
Titian
Turner
Vasari
Warhol
Zeuxis

7 letters:
Acconci
Allston
Apelles
Audubon
Bellini
Bernini
Bonnard
Borduas
Boucher
Bruegel
Cassall
Cézanne
Cellini
Chagall
Chardin
Chirico
Christo
Cimabue
Collier
Courbet
Cranach
Daumier
Da Vinci
Duchamp
El Greco
Epstein
Gauguin
Hobbema
Hockney
Hogarth
Hokusai
Holbein
Hoppner
Kneller
Lepicie
Lorrain
Martens
Martini
Matisse
Meldrum
Memling
Millais
Morisot
Morland
Murillo
Nattier
O'Keeffe
Parrish
Picabia
Picasso
Popover
Poussin
Preston

Prudhon
Pucelle
Rackham
Raeburn
Raphael
Rouault
Russolo
Sargent
Schiele
Sickert
Spencer
Tiepolo
Uccello
Utamaro
Utrillo
Van Dyke
Van Eyck
Van Gogh
Vermeer
Watteau
Zeuxian
Zoffany

8 letters:
Annigoni
Auerbach
Barbizon
Baselitz
Beckmann
Boccioni
Bronzino
Carracci
Clemente
Daguerre
Daubigny
Drysdale
Eastlake
Giordana
Kauffman
Kaufmann
Kirchner
Landseer
Leonardo
Magritte
Mantegna
Masaccio
Mondrian
Munnings
Nevinson
Passmore
Perceval
Perugino
Piranesi
Pissarro

Pontormo
Reynolds
Rockwell
Rossetti
Rousseau
Severini
Thorburn
Topolski
Veronese
Whistler
Whiteley

9 letters:
Beardsley
Bonington
Canaletto
Carpaccio
Constable
Correggio
De Chirico

De Kooning
Delacroix
Delaroche
Delauncey
Donatello
Fragonard
Francesca
Gericault
Giorgione
Grunewald
Hiroshige
Kandinsky
Kokoschka
Le Lorrain
Mitsunobo
Nicholson
Oldenburg
Rembrandt
Thornhill
Velasquez

10 letters:
Alma-Tadema
Botticelli
Burne-Jones
Caravaggio
Fiorentino
Guillaumin
Holman Hunt
Madox Brown
Modigliani
Motherwell
Rowlandson
Schwitters
Signorelli
Sutherland
Tintoretto
Van der Goes
Waterhouse

11 letters:
Fairweather
Fra Angelico
Gentileschi

12 letters:
Fantin-Latour
Gainsborough
Lichtenstein
Michelangelo
Rauschenberg
Winterhalter

14 letters:
Jackson Pollock

15 letters:
Hieronymus Bosch
Toulouse-Lautrec

Artless Candid, Homespun, Ingenuous, Innocent, Naive, Open, Seely, Simple

Art nouveau Jugendstil

Arturo Toscanini

Arum Acorus, Green-dragon, Lily, Taro

As Aesir, Als, Arsenic, Coin, Eg, Forasmuch, Kame, Qua, Ridge, 's, Since, So, Thus, Ut, While

As above US, Ut supra

Asafoetida Hing

As before Anew, Ditto, Do, Stet

Asbestos Amiant(h)us, Amosite, Chrysolite, Crocidolite, Earthflax, Fireproof, Rockwood

Ascend(ant), Ascent, Ascension Anabasis, Climb, Dominant, Escalate, Gradient, Lift, Pull, Ramp, Right, Rise, Sclim, Sklim, Slope, Up, Upgang, Uphill, Uprise, Zoom

Ascertain Determine, Discover, → **ESTABLISH**, Prove

Ascetic Agapetae, Anchor(et), Anchorite, Ancress, Ashramite, Austere, Dervish, Diogenes, Encratite, Eremital, Essene, Fakir, Faquir, Gymnosophist, Hermit, Jain(ite), Monk, Nazarite, Nazirite, Nun's flesh, Sad(d)hu, Simeon Stylites, Stylite, Sufic, Therapeutae, Yogi(n)

Ascidian Chordate, Urochordate

Asclepiad Stapelia

Ascribe Assign, → **ATTRIBUTE**, Blame, Imply, Impute

Asdic Sonar

As far as Quoad

As good as Equal, Tantamount

Ash(es), Ashen, Ashy Aesc, Aizle, Bone, Breeze, Cinders, Cinereal, Clinker(s), Easle, Embers, Fly, Fraxinas, Griseous, Kali, Lahar, Pallor, Pearl, Pozz(u)olana, Prickly, Rowan, Ruins, Soda, Sorb, Spodo-, Stinking, Tephra, Urn, Varec, Volcanic, Wednesday, Weeping, White, Witchen, Yg(g)drasil(l)

Ashamed Abashed, Embarrassed, Hangdog, Mortified, Repentant, Sheepish, Shent

Ashore Aland, Beached, Grounded, Stranded

Ash-pan Backet

Ashram Haven

Asia(n), Asiatic Afghan, Altaic, Angaraland, Armenian, Azari, Balinese, Bangladeshi, Bengali, Bithynia, Cambodian, Cantonese, Desi, E, Evenki, Ewenki, Gook, Harijan,

Harsha, Hun, Hyksos, Indian, Indonesian, Jordanian, Karen(ni), Kashmir, Kazakh, Kirghiz, Korean, Kurd, Kyrgyz, Lao, Lydian, Malay, Medea, Media, Mongol, Naga, Negrito, Nepalese, Pasht(o)um, Phrygian, Pushtu, Samo(y)ed, Shan, Siamese, Sindi, Sogdian, Tamil, Tartar, Tatar, Tibetan, Tocharian, Tokharian, Turanian, Turk(o)man, Uzbeg, Uzbek, Vietnamese

Asia Minor Anatolia, Ionic

Aside Apart, By, Despite, Private, Separate, Shelved, Sotto voce

Asinine Crass, Dull, Idiotic, Puerile, Stupid

Ask Bed, Beg, Beseech, Bid, Cadge, Charge, Demand, Desire, Enquire, Entreat, Evet, Implore, Intreat, Invite, Lobby, Newt, Petition, Pray, Prithee, Pump, Quiz, Request, Require, Rogation, Seek, Solicit, Speer, Speir, Touch

Askance Asconce, Askew, Oblique, Sideways

Askew Agee, Aglee, Agley, Ajee, Aslant, Awry, Crooked, Skivie

Aslant Skew

Asleep Dormant, Dove, Inactive, Napping

As needed Ad hoc

As often as Toties quoties

Asparagus Asperge, Sparrow-grass, Spear, Sprew, Sprue

Aspect Angle, Bearing, Brow, Face, Facet, Facies, Feature, Look, Mien, Nature, Outlook, Perfective, Perspective, Sextile, Side, → **VIEW**, Visage, Vista

Aspen Trembling poplar

Aspersion, Asperse Calumny, Defame, Innuendo, Libel, Slander, Slur, Smear

Asphalt Bitumen, Blacktop, Gilsonite®, Jew's pitch, Pitch, Pitch Lake, Uinta(h)ite

Asphyxia Apn(o)ea

Aspirant, Aspirate, Aspiration, Aspire Ambition, Breath, Buckeen, Challenger, Desire, Dream, Endeavour, Ettle, Goal, H, Hope(ful), Pretend, Pursue, Rough, Spiritus, Wannabe(e), Would be, Yearn

Ass(es) Buridan's, Burnell, Burro, Cardophagus, Chigetai, Clot, Couscous, Cuddie, Denarius, Dick(e)y, Donkey, Dziggetai, Funnel, Golden, Hemione, Hemionus, Hinny, Jack, Jenny, Jerusalem pony, Kiang, Kourbash, Kourmiss, Kouskous, K(o)ulan, Kumiss, Kurbash, Kyang, Liripipe, Liripoop, Moke, Neddy, Nitwit, Onager, Quagga, Sesterce, Simp, → **STUPID PERSON**

Assail(ant) Afflict, Assault, Attack, Batter, Bego, Belabour, Bepelt, Beset, Bombard, Harry, Impugn, Onsetter, Oppugn, Pillory, Ply, Revile

Assassin(ate), Assassination Attentat, Booth, Brave, Bravo, Brutus, Casca, Cassius, Character, Corday, Cut-throat, Frag, Gunman, Highbinder, Hitman, Killer, Ninja, Oswald, Sword, Sworder, Thuggee, Tyrannicide

Assault ABH, Assail, Assay, Attack, Battery, Bombard, GBH, Hamesucken, Head-butt, Indecent, Invasion, Knee, Maul, Molest, Mug, Push, → **RAID**, Scalade, Stoor, Storm, Stour, Stowre

Assay Cupel, Examine, Proof, Test, Wet

As seen Voetstoots

Assemble(d), Assembly Agora, Audience, Ball, Band, Bottom-hole, Bundestag, Chapter, Chatuaqua, Cho(u)ltry, Church, Co, Collation, → **COLLECTION**, Comitia, Company, Conclave, Concourse, Congeries, Congregate, Congress, Consistory, Constituent, Convene, Conventicle, Convention, Convocation, Convoke, Corroboree, Cortes, Council, Court, Curia, Dail Eireann, Dewain, Diet, Divan, Donnybrook, Ecclesia, Eisteddfod, Erect, Feis(anna), Fit, Folkmoot, Folkmote, Force, Forgather, Fuel, Gather(ing), Gemot(e), General, Gorsedd, Group, Headstock, Hoi polloi, House, Jirga, Kgotla, Knesset, Landtag, Legislative, Lekgotla, Levee, Loya jirga, Majlis, Make, Mass, Meet, → **MEETING**, Mejlis, Moot, Muster, National, Oireachtas, Panegyry, Panoply, Parishad, Parliament, Patron, Pattern, Plenum, Pnyx, Powwow, Prefabrication, Presence, Primary, Quorum, Rally, Rallying-point, Rechate, Recheate, Reichstag, Relie, Repair, Resort, Riksdag, Roll up, Sanghat, Sanhedrin, Sanhedron, Sejm, Senate, Senedd, Skupshtina, Sobranje, Soc,

Society, Stort(h)ing, Synagogue, Synedrion, Synod, T(h)ing, Tribunal, Troop, Turn out, Unlawful, Vidhan Sabha, Volksraad, Wapens(c)haw, Wapins(c)haw, Wappens(c)haw, Wardmote, Weapon-s(c)haw, Witan, Witenagemot, Zemstvo

Assent Accede, Acquiesce, Agree, Amen, Aye, Comply, Concur, Jokol, Nod, Placet, Royal, Sanction, Viceregal, Yea, Yield

Assert(ing), Assertion, Assertive Affirm, Allege, Bumptious, Constate, Contend, → DECLARE, Dogmatic, Forceful, Ipse-dixit, → MAINTAIN, Pose, Predicate, Proclaim, Pronounce, Protest, Pushing, Pushy, Rumour, Swear (blind), Thetical

Assess(ment) Affeer, Appraise, Audition, Cense, Consider, Critique, Eleven-plus, Estimate, Evaluate, Formative, Gauge, Guesstimate, Inspect, → JUDGE, Levy, Means test, Measure, Perspective, Rating, Referee, Report, Risk, Scot and lot, Size up, Special, Stent, Stocktake, Summative, Tax, Value, Weigh

Asset(s) Advantage, Capital, Chargeable, Chattel, Current, Fixed, Floating, Goodwill, Intangible, Inventory, Liquid, Net, Plant, Property, Resource, Seed corn, Talent, Virtue, Wasting

Assiduous Attentive, Busy, Constant, Diligent, Studious, Thorough

Assign(ation), Assignment Allocate, → ALLOT, Apply, Appoint, Aret, Ascribe, Attentat, Attribute, Award, Date, Dedicate, Detail, Duty, Entrust, Errand, Fix, Give, Grant, Impute, Ordain, Point, Quota, Refer, Sort, Tak(e), Tryst

Assimilate(d) Absorb, Blend, Digest, Esculent, Fuse, Imbibe, Incorporate, Merge, Osmose

Assist(ance), Assistant Acolyte, Adjunct, Adviser, Aid(e), Aide-de-camp, Ally, Alms, Attaché, Au pair, Batman, Best boy, Busboy, Cad, Chainman, Collaborate, Counterhand, Counter-jumper, Dresser, Ex parte, Facilitate, Factotum, Famulus, Feldschar, Felds(c)her, Gofer, → HAND, Handlanger, Help, Henchman, Legal aid, Matross, Mentor, National, Nipper, Number two, Offsider, Omnibus, Proproctor, Public, Reinforce, Relief, Second, Server, Service, Servitor, Shill, Sidekick, Sidesman, Smallboy, Social, Stead, Subeditor, Subsidiary, Subsidy, Suffragan, Supernumerary, → SUPPORT, Tawny Owl, Usher

Assize Botley, Circuit, Court, Maiden, Oyer

Associate(d), Association Accomplice, Affiliate, Alliance, Amphictyony, Ass, Attach, Bedfellow, Brotherhood, Cartel, Chapel, Chum, Clang, Club, Cohort, Combine, Comecon, Community, Company, Compeer, Complice, Comrade, Concomitant, Confrère, → CONNECT, Consort(ium), Co-partner, Correlate, Crony, Enclisis, Fellow, Fraternise, Free, Gesellschaft, Goose club, Guild, Hobnob, Housing, Inquiline, Intime, Join, Kabele, Kebele, League, Liaison, Link, Lloyds, Mell, Member, Mess, Mix, Moshav, Oddfellows, Pal, Parent teacher, Partner(ship), Phoresy, Press, Probus, Professional, Relate, Residents', Ring, Round Table, Samit(h)i, Sangh(at), Sidekick, Sodality, Stablemate, Staff, Symbiosis, Syndicate, Synonymous, Tenants', Toc H, Toenadering, Trade, UN(A), Union, Verein, Whiteboy, Wiener Werkstatte, Word, Yoke-mate

Assort(ed), Assortment Choice, Congeries, Etc, Medley, Paraphernalia, Pick-'n'-mix, Various

▷ **Assorted** *may indicate* an anagram

Assuage Allay, Appease, Beet, Calm, Ease, Mease, Mitigate, Mollify, Relieve, Slake, Soften, Soothe

As such Qua

Assume(d), Assuming, Assumption Adopt, Affect, Arrogate, Artificial, Attire, Axiom, Believe, Don, Donné(e), Feign, Hypothesis, Lemma, Occam's Razor, Posit, Postulate, Preconception, Premise, Premiss, Presuppose, Pretentious, Principle, Putative, Saltus, Say, Suppose, Surmise, Take

▷ **Assumption** *may indicate* 'attire'

Assure(d), Assurance Aplomb, Aver, Avouch, Belief, Calm, → CERTAIN, Comfort, Confidence, Confirm, Earnest, Gall, Guarantee, Knowing, Life, Pledge, Poise, Secure, Self-confidence, Term, Warranty

Assuredly Indeed, Perdie, Verily, Yea

Astatine At

Aster Starwort

Astern Abaft, Apoop, Rear

Asteroid Ceres, Eros, Eros 433, Hermes, Hygiea, Icarus, Juno, Pallas, Phaethon, Pholus, Planetoid, Sea-star, Star, Starfish, Trojan, Vesta

Astir Afoot, Agate, Agog

Astonish(ed), Astonishing, Astonishment, Astound Abash, Admiraunce, Amaze, Banjax, Bewilder, Bowl over, Confound, Corker, Crikey, Daze, Donnert, Dumbstruck, Dum(b)found, Eye-popping, Flabbergast, Gobsmack, Heavens, Mind-boggling, Open-eyed, Open-mouthed, Phew, Pop-eyed, Prodigious, Rouse, Shake, Singular, Stagger, Startle, Stun, Stupefaction, Stupefy, Stupendous, Surprise, Thunderstruck, Wide-eyed, Wow

Astray Abord, Amiss, Errant, Lost, Will, Wull

Astride Athwart, En cavalier, Spanning, Straddle-back

Astringent Acerbic, Alum, Catechu, Dhak, Gambi(e)r, Harsh, Kino, Krameria, Myrobalan, Obstruent, Puckery, Rhatany, Sept-foil, Severe, Sour, Stypsis, Styptic, Tormentil, Witch-hazel

Astrologer, Astrology, Astrological Archgenethliac, Chaldean, Culpeper, Faust, Figure-caster, Genethliac, Judicial, Lilly, Magus, Midheaven, Moore, Nostradamus, Soothsayer, Starmonger, Zadkiel

Astronaut Aldrin, Cosmonaut, Gagarin, Glenn, Lunarnaut, Spaceman, Spacer, Taikonaut

Astronomer, Astronomy, Astronomical Airy, Almagest, Aristarchus, Azimuth, Barnard, Bessel, Bliss, Bradley, Brahe, Callipic, Cassini, Celsius, Christie, Coal sack, Copernicus, Dyson, Eddington, Encke, Eratosthenes, Eudoxus, Flamsteed, Galileo, Gamma-ray, Graham-Smith, Hale, Halley, Herschel, Hertzsprung, Hewish, Hipparchus, Hoyle, Hubble, Huggins, Infra red, Jeans, Kepler, Lagrange, Laplace, Leverrier, Lockyer, Lovell, Maskelyne, Meton, Moore, Neutrino, Olbers, Omar Khayyam, Oort, Physical, Planetesimal, Planetology, Pond, Ptolemy, Quadrivium, Radar, Radio, Reber, Rees, Roche, Roemer, Russell, Ryle, Schwarzschild, Selenography, Selenology, Seyfert, Sosigenes, Spencer-Jones, Stargazer, Star read, Telescopy, Tycho Brahe, Ultraviolet, Urania, Uranic, Uranography, Wolfendale, Woolley, X-ray, Zwicky

Astrophel Penthia

Astrophysicist Seifert

Astute Acute, Canny, Crafty, Cunning, Downy, Perspicacious, Shrewd, Subtle, Wide, Wily

As usual Solito

As well Additionally, Also, Both, Even, Forby, Too

Asylum Bedlam, Bin, Bughouse, Frithsoken, Funny-farm, Girth, Grith, Haven, Institution, Loony bin, Lunatic, Madhouse, Magdalene, Nuthouse, Political, Rathouse, Refuge, Retreat, Sanctuary, Shelter, Snake-pit

Asymmetric(al) Contrapposto, Lopsided, Skew

At Astatine, In, Kip, To, Up-bye

Atahualpa Inca

At all Ava, Ever, Oughtlings

At all events Algate

Atavistic Reversion, Throw-back

At first Erst

Atheist Doubter, Godless, Infidel, Irreligious, Sceptic

Athenian, Athene Attic, Cleruch, Pallas, Pericles, Solon, Timon

Athlete, Athletic(s) Agile, Agonist, Blue, Coe, Discobolus, Field, Gymnast, Hurdler, Jock, Leish, Miler, Milo, Nurmi, Olympian, Owens, Pacemaker, Quarter-miler, Runner, Sexual, Shamateur, Sportsman, Sprinter, Track, Track and field, Triple jump

Athodyd Ram-jet

Athwart Across, Awry, Oblique, Traverse

Atlantic Millpond, Pond

Atlas Dialect, Linguistic, Maps, Range, Silk, Telamon

▷ **At last** *may indicate* a cobbler

Atmosphere Aeropause, Afterdamp, Air, Ambience, Aura, Chemosphere, Climate, Elements, Epedaphic, Ether, Exosphere, F-layer, Geocorona, Ionosphere, Lid, Magnetosphere, Mesosphere, Meteorology, Miasma, Mood, Ozone, Standard, Stratosphere, Thermosphere, Tropopause, Troposphere, Upper, Vibe(s), Vibrations

At most Al piu

Atoll Bikini, Enewetak, Eniwetok, Funafuti, Kwajalein, Male, Motu, Tarawa

Atom(ic), Atoms, Atomism Boson, Chromophore, Dimer, Electron, Excimer, Free, Gram, Ion, Iota, Isobare, Isotone, Isotope, Labelled, Ligand, Logical, Molecule, Monad, Monovalent, Muonic, Nematic, Nuclide, Odoriphore, Particle, Pile, Primeval, Radionuclide, Recoil, Sellafield, Side-chain, Species, Steric, Stripped, Substituent, Tagged, Windscale, Xylyl

Atomiser Airbrush, Nebuliser

At once Directly, Ek dum, Holus-bolus, Immediate, Instanter, Presto, Statim, Straight away, Swith, Tight, Tit(e), Titely, Tout de suite, Tyte

Atone(ment) Aby(e), Acceptilation, Appease, Assoil, Expiate, Penance, Purge, Redeem, Redemption, Yom Kippur

Atop Upon

▷ **At random** *may indicate* an anagram

Atrocious, Atrocity Abominable, Brutal, Diabolical, Enorm, Flagitious, Heinous, Horrible, Massacre, Monstrous, Outrage, Piacular, Terrible, Vile

Atrophy Degeneration, Marasmus, Sudeck's, Sweeny, Wasting

▷ **At sea** *may indicate* an anagram

Attach(ed), Attachment Accessory, Accrete, Adhesion, Adhibition, Adnate, Adnation, Adscript, Affix, Allonge, Annexe, Bolt, Bro, Byssus, Cleat, Covermount, Curtilage, Devotement, Devotion, Distrain, Dobby, Eyehook, Feller, Garnish, Glom, → JOIN, Netsuke, Obconic, Piggyback, Pin, Reticle, Sew, Snell, Stick, Tendon, Tie, Weld

Attack(ing), Attacker Access, Affect, Aggression, Airstrike, Alert, Anti, Apoplexy, Asperse, Assail, Assault, Assiege, At, Banzai, Batter, Bego, Belabour, Beset, Bestorm, Blitz(krieg), Bodrag(ing), Bombard, Bordraging, Bout, Broadside, Bushwhack, Calumny, Camisade, Camisado, Campaign, Cannonade, Carte, Charge, Clobber, Club, Counteroffensive, Coup de main, Denounce, Depredation, Descent, Diatribe, Discomfit, Excoriate, Feint, Fit, Flèche, Foray, Fork, Forward, Gas, Get, Glass, Handbag, Happy-slapping, Harry, Hatchet job, Headbutt, Heart, Heckle, Iconoclast, Ictus, Impingement, Impugn, Incursion, Inroad, Invade, Inveigh, Knee, Lampoon, Lash out, Lese-majesty, Let fly, Maraud, Molest, Mug, Offence, Offensive, Onding, Onfall, Onrush, Onset, Onslaught, Oppugn, Outflank, Panic, Philippic, Pillage, Pin, Poke, Polemic, Pounce, Predacious, Pre-emptive, Push, Quart(e), Raid, Rally, Rough, Sail, Sandbag, Savage, Second strike, Seizure, Sic(k), Siege, Skitch, Slam, Snipe, Sortie, Storm, Strafe, Straff, Strike, Swoop, Thrust, Tilt, Vilify, Vituperate, Wage, Warison, Wolf-pack, Zap

Attain(ment) Accomplish, Arrive, Earn, Fruition, Get, Land, Reach

Attempt Attentat, Bash, Bid, Burl, Crack, Debut, Effort, Egma, Endeavour, Essay, Go, Mint, Nisus, Potshot, Seek, Shot, Show, Shy, Spell baker, Stab, Strive, → TRY, Venture, Whack, Whirl

Attend(ance), Attendant Accompany, Acolyte, Aide, Apple-squire, Await, Batman, Bearer, Be at, Behold, Bell-hop, Bulldog, Caddy, Cavass, Chaperone, Chasseur, Checker, Commissionaire, Corybant, Courtier, Cuadrilla, Cupbearer, Custrel, Doula, Dresser, Entourage, Equerry, Escort, Esquire, Famulus, Footman, Gate, G(h)illie, Gilly, Hand-maiden, Harken, Hear, → HEED, Hello, Holla, Iras, Janitor, Kavass, Keeper, Led captain, → LISTEN, Loblolly-boy, Maenad, Marshal, Mute, Note, Orderly, Outrider, Outrunner, Page, Panisc, Panisk, Paranymph, People, Pew-opener, Presence, Pursuivant, Respect, Roll-up, Satellite, Second, Server, S(a)ice, Sort, Sowar, Steward, Syce,

Therapeutic, Trainbearer, Trolleydolly, Turn-out, Up at, Valet, Varlet, Visit, Wait, Watch, Whiffler, Zambuck

Attention, Attentive Achtung, Alert, Assiduity, Care(ful), Court, Coverage, Dutiful, Ear, Gallant, Gaum, Gorm, Hark, Heed, Interest, Mind, Note, Notice, Observant, Present, Ps(s)t, Punctilious, Qui vive, → **REGARD**, Selective, Solicitous, Spellbound, Spotlight, Tenty, Thorough, Thought, Uxorious, Voila

Attenuate, Attenuation Lessen, Neper, Rarefy, Thin, Weaken

Attest Affirm, Certify, Depose, Guarantee, Notarise, Swear, → **WITNESS**

Attic Bee-bird, Cockloft, Garret, Greek, Koine, Loft, Mansard, Muse, Salt, Sky parlour, Solar, Soler, Sollar, Soller, Tallat, Tallet, Tallot

Attila Etzel, Hun

Attire Accoutre, Adorn, Apparel, Clobber, Clothe, Clothing, → **DRESS**, Garb, Habit

Attitude Air, Aspect, Behaviour, Demeanour, Light, → **MANNER**, Mindset, Nimby, Outlook, Pose, Position, Possie, Posture, Propositional, Scalogram, Sense, Song, Spirit, Stance, Tone, Uppity, Viewpoint

Attorney Advocate, Counsellor, DA, District, Lawyer, Private, Proctor, Prosecutor, Public

Attract(ion), Attractive(ness), Attractor Attrahent, Bait, Barrie, Beauté du diable, Becoming, Bedworthy, Bewitch, Bonnie, Bonny, Bootylicious, Catchy, Charisma, → **CHARM**, Cheesecake, Clou, Comely, Crowd puller, Cute, Cynosure, Dinky, Dipolar, Dish(y), Draught, → **DRAW**, Dreamboat, Duende, Engaging, Entice, Epigamic, Eye candy, Eye-catching, Eyeful, Fanciable, Fascinate, Feature, Fetching, Fox(y), Goodly, Gravity, Great, Groovy, Heartthrob, Himbo, Hot, Hot stuff, Hotty, Hunky, Inducement, Inviting, It, Jolie laide, Loadstone, Lodestone, Looker, Lovable, Lovely, Lure, Luscious, Magnes, Magnet(ism), Mecca, Mediagenic, Meretricious, Nubile, Pack in, Personable, Pheromone, Photogenic, Picture postcard, Picturesque, Popsy, Pretty, Pull, Sematic, Sexpot, Shagtastic, Sideshow, Sightly, Slick, Smasher, Snazzy, Soote, Speciosity, Spunk, Stotter, Striking, Studmuffin, Stunner, Taking, Taky, Tasteful, Tasty, Tempt, Theme-park, Toothsome, Tottie, Totty, Triff(ic), Va-va-voom, Weber, Winning, Winsome, Zaftig, Zoftig, Zoophilia

Attribute, Attribution Accredit, Allot, Ap(p)anage, Ascribe, Asset, By, Credit, Gift, Impute, Lay, Metonym, Owe, Proprium, Quality, Refer, Resource, Shtick, Strength

Attune Accord, Adapt, Temper

Atypical Aberrant, Anomalous

Aubergine Brinjal, Brown jolly, Egg-plant, Mad-apple

Aubrey Beardsley

Auburn Abram, Chestnut, Copper, Titian, Vill(age)

Auction(eer) Barter, Bridge, Cant, Dutch, Hammer, Knock out, Outcry, Outro(o)per, Roup, Sale, Subhastation, Tattersall, Trade sale, Vendue, Warrant sale

Audacious, Audacity Bald-headed, Bold, Brash, Cheek, Chutspah, Cool, Der-doing, Devil-may-care, Effrontery, Face, Hardihood, Indiscreet, Insolence, Intrepid, Neck, Nerve, Rash, Sauce

Audible Out loud

Audience, Auditorium Assembly, Court, Durbar, Gate, Hearing, House, Interview, Pit, Sphendone, Theatre, Tribunal

Audiovisual AV

Audit(or) Accountant, Check, Ear, Environmental, Examine, Green, Inspect, Listener, Medical, Position, Vet

Audition Apply, Cattle-call, Hearing, Screen-test

Auditory Acoustic, Oral

Audrey Hoyden

Auger Miser

Augment(ed) Boost, Eche, Eke, Grow, Ich, Increase, Pad, Supplement, Swell, Tritone

Augury → **DIVINATION**, Ornithoscopy

August Awe-inspiring, Grand, Imperial, Imposing, Lammas, Majestic, Noble, Royal,

Solemn, Stately, Stern, Strindberg

Augustine, Augustus Austin, Hippo, John

Auk Guillemot, Ice-bird, Puffin, Roch, Rotch(e)

Aunt(ie) Agony, Augusta, Beeb, Giddy, Maiden, Naunt, Sainted, Tia

Aura Aroma, Emanation, Halo, Mystique, Nimbus, Odour, Vibe(s), Vibrations

Aureole Coronary, Halo, Nimbus

Auricle Ear, Otic

Aurora Australis, Borealis, Eos, Leigh, Matutinal, Merry dancers, Northern lights, Southern (lights)

Auspice(s) Aegis, Patronage

Auster S-wind

Austere, Austerity Ascetic, Astringent, Bleak, Dantean, Dervish, Hard, → **HARSH**, Moral, Plain, Rigour, Severe, Spartan, Stern, Stoic, Stoor, Strict, Vaudois, Waldensian

Austin Friar

Australia(n) A, Alf, Antichthone, Antipodean, .au, Aussie, Balt, Banana-bender, Bananalander, Billjim, Bodgie, Canecutter, Cobber, Coon, Currency, Current, Darwinian, Digger, Gin, Godzone, Gumsucker, Gurindji, Jackie, Jacky, Koori, Larrikin, Lucky Country, Murree, Murri, Myall, Norm, Ocker, Ossie, Outbacker, Oz(zie), Pintupi, Roy, Sandgroper, Strine, Sydneysider, Wallaby, Yarra-yabbies

Austrian Cisleithan, Tyrolean

Authentic(ate), Authentication Certify, Des(h)i, Echt, Genuine, Honest, Notarise, Official, Probate, Real, Sign, Simon-pure, Test, True, Validate

Author(ess) Anarch, Architect, Auctorial, Hand, Inventor, Me, Parent, Scenarist, Volumist, Wordsmith, → **WRITER**

▷ **Author** *may refer to* author of puzzle

Authorise(d), Authorisation Accredit, Clearance, Countersign, Delegate, Depute, Empower, Enable, Entitle, Exequatur, Imprimatur, Legal, Legit, → **LICENCE**, Mandate, Official, OK, Passport, → **PERMIT**, Plenipotentiary, Retainer, Sanction, Sign, Stamp, Warrant

Authority, Authoritarian, Authoritative Ascetic, Canon, Charter, Circar, Cocker, Commission, Commune, Crisp, Definitive, Domineering, Dominion, Establishment, Ex cathedra, Expert, Fascist, Free hand, Gravitas, Hegemony, Inquirendo, Jackboot, Leadership, Licence, Light, Local, Magisterial, Mana, Mandate, Mantle, Mastery, Name, Oracle, Permit, PLA, Potency, → **POWER**, Prefect, Prestige, Pundit, Regime, Remit, Right, Rod, Say-so, Sceptre, Sircar, Sirkar, Source, Supremacy, Supremo, Tyrannous, Unitary, Warrant

Autobiography Memoir

Autochthonous Aboriginal

Autocrat(ic) Absolute, Caesar, Cham, Despot, Khan, Neronian, Tenno, Tsar, Tyrant

Autograph Signature

Autolycus Scrapman

Automatic, Automaton Android, Aut, Browning, Deskill, Instinctive, Knee-jerk, Machine, Mechanical, Pistol, Quarter-boy, Quarter-jack, Reflex, Robot, RUR, Zombi

Auto-pilot George

Autopsy Necropsy

Auto-suggestion Coueism

Autumn(al) Fall, Filemot, Leaf-fall, Libra, Philamot

Auxiliary Adjunct, Adjuvant, Adminicle, Aide, Ancillary, Be, Feldsher, Foederatus, Have, Helper, Ido, Modal, Subsidiary

Avail(able) Benefit, Dow, Eligible, Going, Handy, In season, Off-the-shelf, On, On call, On hand, On tap, Open, Out, Pickings, Potluck, → **READY**, Serve, To hand, Up for grabs, Use, Utilise

Avalanche Bergfall, Deluge, Icefall, Landfall, Landslide, Landslip, Lauwine, Slide, Slip, Snowdrop

Avant-garde Modernistic, Spearhead, Ultramodern

Avarice, Avaricious Cupidity, Gimmes, Golddigger, Greed, Money-grubbing, Pleonexia, Predatory, Shylock, Sordid

Avatar Epiphany, Incarnation, Rama

Avaunt Away, Go

Avenge(r) Alecta, Eriny(e)s, Eumenides, Goel, Kuraitcha, Megaera, Nightrider, Punish, Redress, Requite, → **REVENGE**, Steed, Tisiphone, Wreak

Avenue Allee, Alley, Approach, Arcade, Boulevard, Channel, Corso, Cradle-walk, Hall, Madison, Mall, Midway, Passage, Vista, Way, Xyst(us)

Aver Affirm, Assert, Asseverate, Declare, Depose, State, Swear, Vouch

Average Adjustment, Av, Batting, Dow Jones, Fair, Mean, Mediocre, Middle-brow, Middling, Moderate, Moving, Norm, Par, Particular, Run, Run-of-the-mill, Soso, Standard, Weighted

Averse, Aversion, Avert Against, Antipathy, Apositia, Disgust, Dislike, Distaste, Hatred, Horror, Opposed, Pet, Phengephobia, Phobic, Photophobia, Risk, Scunner, Sit(i)ophobia, Stave off

Avert Avoid, → **DEFLECT**, Forfend, Parry, Ward

Aviary Volary, Volery

Aviator Airman, Alcock, Bleriot, Brown, Byrd, Co-pilot, De Havilland, Earhart, Flier, Hinkler, Icarus, Johnson, Lindbergh, Pilot, Red Baron, Richthofen, Yeager

Avid Agog, Athirst, → **EAGER**, Greedy, Keen

Avifauna Ornis

Avignon Pont

Avocado Aguacate, Guac(h)amole, Pear

Avocet Scooper

Avoid(er), Avoidance Abstain, Ba(u)lk, Boycott, Bypass, Cop-out, Cut, Dodge, Duck, Elude, Escape, Eschew, Evade, Evitate, Evite, Fly, Forbear, Gallio, Hedge, Miss, Obviate, Parry, Prevaricate, Scape, Scutage, Secede, Shelve, Shirk, Shun, Sidestep, Skirt, Skive, Spare, Spurn, Tergiversate, Waive

Avoirdupois Size, Weight

Avow(ed) Acknowledged, Affirm, Declare, Own, Swear

Await(ed) Abide, Bide, Expect, Godot, Tarry

Awake(ning) Aware, Conscious, Conversion, Fly, Rouse, Vigilant

Award Academy, Accolade, Acquisitive, Addeem, Addoom, Allot, Alpha, Apple, Arbitrament, Aret(t), Bafta, Bar, Bestow, Bursary, Cap, Charter Mark, Clasp, Clio, Compensation, Crown, Degree, Emmy, Exhibition, Genie, Golden handshake, Golden Raspberry, Golden Starfish, Grammy, Grant, Honours, Juno, Logie, Lourie, Medal, Meed, Mete, MOBO, Oscar, Padma Shri, Palatinate, Palme d'Or, Premium, Present(ation), Prix Goncourt, → **PRIZE**, Queen's, Razzie, Rosette, Scholarship, Tony, Trophy, Vir Chakra, Yuko

Aware(ness) Alert, Aware, C(o)enesthesis, Coconscious, Cognisant, Conscious, Conversant, ESP, Est, Hep, Hip, Informed, Knowing, Liminal, Mindshare, Onto, Panaesthesia, Prajna, Presentiment, Samadhi, Scienter, Sensible, Sensile, Sensitive, Sentience, Streetwise, Switched on, Vigilant, Weet, Wit, Wot

Away Abaxial, Absent, Afield, Apage, Avaunt, By, For-, Forth, Fro(m), Go, Hence, Off, Out, Past

▷ **Away** *may indicate* a word to be omitted

Awe(d) Dread, D(o)ulia, Fear, Intimidate, Loch, Overcome, Popeyed, Regard, Respect, Reverent, Scare, Solemn, Wonderment

Awe-inspiring, Awesome Mega, Numinous

Awful(ly) Alas, Appalling, Deare, Dere, Dire, Fearful, Horrendous, Lamentable, Nasty, O so, Piacular, Rotten, Terrible, Third rate

▷ **Awfully** *may indicate* an anagram

Awkward All thumbs, Angular, Blate, Bolshy, Bumpkin, Clumble-fisted, Clumsy,

Complicated, Contrary, Corner, Crabby, Cubbish, Cumbersome, Cussed, Dub, Embarrassing, Farouche, Fiddly, Fix, Gangly, Gauche, Gawky, Handless, Howdy-do, Inconvenient, Inelegant, Inept, Kittle-cattle, Knotty, Lanky, Loutish, Lurdan(e), Lurden, Maladdress, Mauther, Mawr, Naff, Nasty, Nonconformist, Ornery, Perverse, Refractory, Slouch, Slummock, So-and-so, Spot, Sticky, Stiff, Stroppy, Stumblebum, Swainish, Ticklish, Uncoordinated, Uncouth, Uneasy, Ungainly, Unhandy, Unwieldy, Wooden, Wry

Awl(-shaped) Brog, Els(h)in, Nail, Stob, Subulate

Awn(ing) Barb, Beard, Canopy, Ear, Shade, Shamiana(h), Sunblind, Velarium

Awry Agley, Amiss, Askent, Askew, Athwart, Cam, Haywire, Kam(me), Pear-shaped, Wonky

Axe(s) Abolish, Adz(e), Bardiche, Bill, Celt, Chop(per), Cleaver, Curtal, Eatche, Gisarme, Gurlet, Halberd, Halbert, Hatchet, Hew, Holing, Ice, Jeddart staff, Jethart-staff, Labrys, Lochaber, Mattock, Palstaff, Palstave, Partisan, Piolet, Retrench, Sax, Scrub, Slate, Sparth(e), Sperthe, Spontoon, Stone, Thunderbolt, Tomahawk, Twibill, X, Y, Z

Axeman Bassist, Guitarist, Hendrix

Axe-shaped Securiform

Axiom Adage, Motto, Peano's, Proverb, Saw, Saying

Axis Alliance, Anorthic, Anticous, Axle, Caulome, Chital, Cob, Columella, Deer, Epaxial, Henge, Hinge, Major, Minor, Modiolus, Myelon, Neutral, Optic, Pivot, Polar, Precess, Principal, Rachis, Radical, Spindle, Sympodium, Visual, X, Y, Z, Zone

Axle, Axle-shoulder Arbor, Axis, Driving, Fulcrum, Hurter, Journal, Live, Mandrel, Mandril, Pivot, Spindle, Stub

Ay Ever, I, Indeed

Aye Always, Eer, Ever, Yea, Yes

Ayesha She

Azo-dye Para-red

Aztec Nahuatl

Bb

B Bachelor, Black, Book, Born, Boron, Bowled, Bravo, Flipside

Babble(r) Blather, Brook, Chatter, Gibber, Haver, Lallation, Lurry, Prate, Prattle, Runnel, Tonguester, Tonguework, Twattle, Waffle, Witer

Babel Charivari, Confusion, Din, Dovercourt, Medley

Baboon Ape, Bobbejaan, Chacma, Cynocephalus, Dog-ape, Drill, Gelada, Hamadryas, Mandrill, Sphinx

Baby Bairn, Band-Aid®, Blue, Bub, Bunting, Changeling, Coddle, Designer, Duck, Grand, Infant, Jelly, Litter, Neonate, Nursling, Pamper, Papoose, Plunket, Preverbal, Rhesus, Sis, Small, Sook, Spoil, Suckling, Tar, Test tube, Thalidomide, Tot, War, Wean

Babylonian Mandaean, Semiramis, Sumerian

Bacchanalian, Bacchus Ivied, Upsee, Ups(e)y

Bacchantes Maenads

Bachelor BA, Bach, Benedict, Budge, Celibate, En garçon, Knight, Pantagamy, Parti, Seal, Single, Stag, Wifeless

Bacillus Comma, Germ, Klebs-Loffler, Micrococcus, Tubercle, Virus

Back(er), Backing, Back out, Back up, Backward Abet, Accompany, Addorse, Aft, Again, Ago, Aid, Anticlockwise, Antimacassar, Arear, Arrear, Arrière, Assist, Baccare, Backare, Bankroll, Buckram, Champion, Chorus, Consent, Cry off, Culet, Defender, Dorsal, Dorse, Dorsum, Dos, Ebb, Empatron, Encourage, Endorse, Fakie, Finance, Frae, Fro, Full, Fund(er), Gaff, Half, Help, Hind, Historic, Incremental, La-la, Late, Notaeum, Notal, Notum, On, Patronise, Pendu, Poop, Pronotum, Punt, Rear(most), Retral, Retro(grade), Retrogress, Retrorse, Retrospective, Return, Rev, Reverse, Ridge, Root, Running, Scenery, Shy, Spinal, Sponsor, Standby, Stern, Sternboard, Sternway, → **SUPPORT**, Sweeper, Syndicate, Tail, Telson, Tergum, Third, Thrae, Three-quarter, Tonneau, Ulu, Uphold, Verso, Vie, Vo, Wager, Watteau

▷ **Back(ing)** *may indicate* a word spelt backwards

Back and forth Boustrophedon

Backbiter, Backbiting Catty, Defame, Detract, Libel, Molar, Slander

Backbone Atlas, Chine, Grit, Guts, Mettle, Spina, Spine

Backchat Lip, Mouth, Sass

Backcloth, Backdrop Cyclorama, Scenery

Backer Angel, Benefactor, Funder, Patron, Punter, Seconder, Sponsor

Backfire Boomerang

Backgammon Acey-deucy, Blot, Lurch, Tick-tack, Trick-track, Tric-trac, Verquere

Background Antecedence, Chromakey, Cyclorama, Field, Fond, History, Horizon, Microwave, Muzak, Natural, Retrally, Setting, Ulterior

Backhander Bribe, Payola, Reverso, Sweetener

Back problem Kyphosis, Lumbago, Osteoporosis, Scolioma, Scoliosis

Backroom Boffin, Boy, Moor

Backslide(r), Backsliding Apostate, Lapse, Regress, Relapse, Revert

Backwash Rift

Backwater Bogan, Ebb, Logan, Retreat, Slough, Wake

Backwoods(man) Boondocks, Boonies, Hinterland, Rowdy

Backyard Court, Patio

Bacon Bard, Canadian, Collar, Danish, Essayist, Flitch, Francis, Gammon, Lardo(o)n, Pancetta, Pig(meat), Pork, Rasher, Roger, Spec(k), Streaky, Verulam

Bacteria, Bacteriologist, Bacterium Acidophilus, Actinomycete, Aerobe, Amphitricha, Bacilli, Bacteriological, Baregin, Botulinum, → **BUG**, Campylobacter, Chlamydia, Clostridia, Cocci, Coliform, Culture, Detritivore, Diplococcus, Escherichia, Foul-brood, → **GERM**, Gonococcus, Gram-negative, Gram-positive, Hib, Intestinal flora, Klebsiella, Koch, Legionella, Listeria, Lysogen, Meningococcus, Microbe, Micrococcus, Microphyte, Mother, MRSA, Mycoplasma, Nitrifying, Nitrite, Nitrous, Nostoc, Operon, Packet, Pasteurella, Pathogen, Peritrich(a), Petri, Pneumococcus, Probiotic, Prokaryote, Proteus, Pseudomonas, Pus, Ray-fungus, Rhizobium, Rickettsia, Salmonella, Schizomycete, Septic, Serogroup, Serotype, Serum, Shigella, Spirilla, Spirochaete, Spirulina, Spore, Staph, Staphylococcus, Strep(tococcus), Streptobacillus, Streptomyces, Sulphur, Superbug, Thermophil(e), Treponemata, Vibrio, Vincent's angina, Vinegar-plant, Yersinia, Zoogloea

Bad, Badness Abysmal, Addled, Chronic, Crook, Defective, Diabolic, Drastic, Dud, Duff, Dystopia, Egregious, Execrable, Faulty, Fearful, Fourth-rate, God-awful, Half-pie, Heinous, Ill, Immoral, Inferior, Injurious, Lither, Lulu, Mal(vu), Naughty, Nefandrous, Nefarious, Nice, Off, Ominous, Oncus, Onkus, Parlous, Piacular, Poor, Rancid, Rank, Reprobate, Ropy, Scampish, Scoundrel, Sinful, Spoiled, The pits, Turpitude, Undesirable, Unspeakable, Useless, Wack, Wick, → **WICKED**

▷ **Bad(ly)** *may indicate* an anagram

Badge Brassard, Brooch, Button, Chevron, Cockade, Cockleshell, Comm, Cordon, Crest, Eagle, Emblem, Ensign, Epaulet, Episemon, Fáinne, Film, Flash, Garter, Gorget, ID, Insigne, Insignia, Kikumon, Mark, Mon, Numerals, Orange, Pilgrim's sign, Pin, Rondel, Rosette, Scallop, Scallop-shell, Shield, Shouldermark, → **SIGN**, Symbol, Tiger, Token, Vernicle, Vine branch, Vine-rod, Wings

Badger → **ANNOY**, Bait, Bedevil, Beset, Brock, Browbeat, Bug, Bullyrag, Cete, Dassi(e), Ferret, Gray, Grey, → **HARASS**, Hassle, Heckle, Hog, Honey, Hound, Nag, Pester, Plague, Provoke, Ratel, Ride, Roil, Sand, Sow, Stinking, Teledu, Wisconsin

Bad habit Cacoethes, Vice

Badinage Banter, Chaff, Raillery

Bad luck Ambs-ace, Ames-ace, Deuce-ace, Hard cheese, Hard lines, Hoodoo, Jinx, Jonah, Shame, Voodoo

Bad-tempered Carnaptious, Curmudgeon, Curnaptious, Curst, Grouchy, Grum(py), Irritable, Marabunta, Moody, Nowty, Patch, Scratchy, Shirty, Splenetic, Stroppy

Bad woman Harridan, Loose, Mort

Baffle(d), Baffling Anan, Balk, Bemuse, Bewilder, Confound, Confuse, Elude, Evade, Floor, Flummox, Foil, Fox, Get, Hush-kit, Mate, Muse, Mystify, Nark, Nonplus, Perplex, Pose, Puzzle, Stump, Throw, Thwart

Bag(gage), Bags Acquire, Air, Alforja, Allantois, Amaut, Amowt, Ascus, Ballonet, Bedroll, Besom, Bladder, Blue, Body, Bounty, Bulse, Bum, Buoyancy, Caba(s), Caecum, Callet, Capture, Carpet, Carrier, Carryall, Case, Cecum, Clutch, Cly, Cod, Colostomy, Cool, Corduroy, Crone, Crumenal, Cyst, Daypack, Dilli, Dilly, Dime, Diplomatic, Ditty, Doggy, Dorothy, Douche, Duffel, Dunnage, → **EFFECTS**, Emery, Excess, Fanny pack, Flannels, Flotation, Follicle, Galligaskins, Game, → **GEAR**, Gladstone, Goody, Grab, Grip, Gripsack, Grow, Holdall, Ice, Impedimenta, Jelly, Jiffy®, Kill, Knapsack, Ladies' companion, Lavender, Lithocyst, Marsupium, Materiel, Meal-poke, Messenger, Minx, Mixed, Money, Monkey, Moon, Mummy, Musette, Musk, Muzzle, Mystery, Nap, Necessaire, Net, Nunny, Organiser, Overnight, Overnighter, Oxford, Packsack, Pantaloons, Plastic, Plus fours, Pochette, Pock(et), Pocketbook, Pockmanky, Pockmantie, Poke, Politzer's, Poly(thene), Port(manteau), Portmantle, Portmantua, Post, Pot, Pouch, Pounce, Pudding, Punch, Purse, Rake, Red, Reticule, Ridicule, Rucksack, Sabretache, Sac(cule), Sachet, Sack, Saddle, Sag, Satchel, Scent, School, Scrip, Scrotum, Sea, Shopper, Sick, Slattern, Sleeping, Specialty, Sponge, Sporran, Stacks, Strossers, Sugar, Survival, Tea, Tote, → **TRAP**, Trews, Trollop, Trouse(r), Tucker (box), Udder, Unmentionables, Utricle, Valise, Vanity, Viaticals, Waist, Wallet, Water, Weekend, Win, Woolpack, Work, Wrap, Wrapping, Ziplock

Bagatelle Bauble, Fico, Trifle, Trinket

Bagpipe Biniou, Chorus, Cornemuse, Drone, Gaita, Musette, Pibroch, Piffero, Skirl, Sourdeline, Uillean, Zampogna

Bahama(s), Bahamian BS, Conch

Bail(er), Bailment Bond, Ladle, Mainpernor, Mainprise, Mutuum, Replevin, Replevy, Scoop

Bailey Bridge, Castle wall, Ward

Bailiff Adam, Bandog, Beagle, Bum, Factor, Foud, Grieve, Huissier, Hundreder, Hundredor, Land-agent, Nuthook, Philistine, Reeve, Shoulder-clapper, Shoulder-knot, Steward, Tipstaff, Water

Bairn Baby, → CHILD, Infant, Wean

Bait Angleworm, Badger, Berley, Brandling, Burley, Capelin, Chum, Dap, Decoy, Entice, Gentle, Gudgeon, Harass, Hellgram(m)ite, Incentive, Lobworm, Lug(worm), Lure, Mawk, → RAG, Ragworm, Sandworm, Sledge, Teagle, Tease, Tempt, Tole, Toll

Bake(r), Baked, Baking Alaska, Batch, Baxter, Coctile, → COOK, Fire, Icer, Kiln-dry, Oven, Pieman, Roast, Scorch, Shir(r)

Baker's daughter Own

Baker Street Irregular

Bakery Patisserie

Balance(d) Account, Beam, Compensation, Counterpoise, Countervail, Counterweight, Equate, Equilibrium, Equipoise, Equiponderate, Even, Fixed, Funambulate, Gyroscope, Gyrostat, Horn, Hydrostatic, Invisible, Isostasy, Launce, Libra, Librate, Meet, Otocyst, Otolith, Pease, Peise, Perch, Peyse, Poise, → REMAINDER, Remnant, Residual, Rest, Running, Scale, Sea-legs, Spring, Stability, Stand, Steelyard, Symmetry, Together, Torsion, → TOTAL, Trial, Trim, Tron(e), Unicycle, Visible

Balcony Circle, Gallery, Loggia, Mirador, Moucharaby, Pew, Porch, Quarter-gallery, Sundeck, Tarras, Terrace, Veranda(h)

Bald, Baldness Alopecia, Apterium, Awnless, Barren, Calvities, Coot, Crude, Egghead, Fox-evil, Glabrous, Hairless, Madarosis, Open, Peelgarlic, Pilgarlic(k), Pollard, Psilosis, Slaphead, Smoothpate, Stark, Tonsured

Balderdash Drivel, Flapdoodle, Nonsense, Rot

Baldmoney Emeu, Meu, Spignel

Bale Bl, Bundle, Evil, Lave, Pack, Sero(o)n, Truss

Baleful Evil, Malefic, Malignant

▶ **Balk** *see* **BAULK**

Balkan Albanian, Bosnian, Bulgarian, Macedon, Rumanian, Serb, Vlach

Ball(s) Aelopile, Aelopyle, Aeolipile, Aeolipyle, Agglomerate, Alley, Ally, Ammo, Aniseed, Apple, Beach, Bead, Beamer, Bearings, Birthing, Bobble, Boll, Bolus, Bosey, Bosie, Bouncer, Break, Buckshot, Buzzer, Caltrap, Caltrop, Camphor, Cap, Cherry, Chin, Chinaman, Chopper, Clew, Clue, Condylar, Condyle, Cotill(i)on, Cramp, Creeper, Croquette, Crystal, Cue, Curve, Daisy-cutter, → DANCE, Delivery, Dink, Dodge, Dollydrop, Doosra, Dot, Dribbler, Eight, Ensphere, Eolipile, Eolipyle, Eolopile, Eolopyle, Falafel, Felafel, Full-pitch, Full-toss, Fungo, Gazunder, → GLOBE, Glomerate, Gobstopper, Googly, Goolies, Gool(e)ys, Grounder, Grub, Grubhunter, Gutta, Gutter, Gutty, Hank, Hop, Hummer, Hunt, Inswinger, Ivory, Jinglet, Jump, Knob, Knur(r), Leather, Leg-break, Leg-cutter, Lob, Long-hop, Marble, Masked, Masque(rade), Matzo, Medicine, Minié, Mirror, Moth, Nur(r), O, Object, Off-break, Off-cutter, Off-spin, Orb, Outswinger, Over, Overarm, Pakora, Parrel truck, Pea, Pellet, Pill, Poi, Pomander, Pompom, Pompon, Prom, Puck, Punch, Quenelle, Rabbit, Rissole, Root, Round, Rover, Rundle, Seamer, Shooter, Shot, Sliotar, Sneak, Sphere, Spinner, Stress, Strike, Swinger, Swiss, Taw, Tea, Testes, Thenar, Three, Tice, Time, Track(er), Witches, Wood, Wrecker's, Wrecking, Yorker, Zorb®

Ballad Bab, Bothy, Broadside, Bush, Calypso, Carol, Fanzone, Folk-song, Forebitter, Lay, Lillibullero, Lilliburlero, Mento, Reading Gaol, Singsong, → SONG, Torch-song

Ballast Kentledge, Makeweight, Stabiliser, Trim, Weight

Ball-boy Dry-bob

Ballerina Coryphee, Dancer, Pavlova, Prima

Ballet, Ballet movement, Ballet-system Arabesque, Assemblé, Balancé, Ballon, Battement, Bharat Natyam, Bolshoi, Brisé, Cabriole, Cambré, Chainé, Changement, Checkmate, Daphnis and Chloe, Développé, Don Pasquale, Écarté, Echappé, Enchainement, Entrechat, Firebird, Fouette, Giselle, Jeté, Kirov, Laban, Labanotation, Leg business, Mayerling, Nutcracker, Pas de basque, Pas de bourrée, Pas de chat, Petit battement, Pirouette, Plastique, Plie, Pointe, Pointer, Port de bras, Relevé, Saut, Swan Lake

Ballet-interlude Divertimento

Ballista Scorpion

Ballistic Wildfire

Balloon(ist) Aeronaut, Aerostat, Airship, Bag, Barrage, Billow, Blimp, Bloat, Dirigible, Distend, Dumont, Enlarge, Fumetto, Hot air, Lead, Montgolfier, Pilot, Rawinsonde, Sonde, Trial, Weather, Zeppelin

Ballot Butterfly, Election, Mulligan, → **POLL**, Referendum, Second, Suffrage, Ticket, Vote

Ballot-box Urn

Ballpoint Bic®, Biro®

Balm(y) Anetic, Arnica, Balsam, Calamint, Emollient, Fragrant, Garjan, Gilead, Gurjan, Lemon, Lenitive, Lotion, → **MILD**, Mirbane, Myrbane, Nard, Oil, Opobalsam, Ottar, Redolent, Remedy, Soothe, Spikenard, Tiger, Tolu, Unguent

Balmoral Bonnet, Cap, Castle

Baloney Bunk, Hooey, Nonsense

Balsam Canada, Copaiba, Copaiva, Friar's, Nard, Noli-me-tangere, Peruvian, Resin, Spikenard, Tamanu, Tolu(ic), Touch-me-not, Tous-les-mois, Turpentine

Balt Esth, Lett

Baltic Estonian, Lettic

Bamboo Cane, Kendo, Split cane, Tabasheer, Whangee

Bamboozle(d) Cheat, Dupe, Flummox, Hoodwink, Mystify, Nose-led, Perplex, Trick

Ban(ned) Abolish, Accurse, Anathema, Black(ing), Censor, Curfew, Debar, D-notice, Embargo, Estop, Excommunicate, Forbid, For(e)say, For(e)speak, Gag, Gate, Green, Moratorium, No, Outlaw, Prohibit, Proscribe, Suppress, Taboo, Tabu, Test, Verboten, Veto

Banal Corny, Dreary, Flat, Hackneyed, Jejune, Mundane, Platitudinous, → **TRITE**, Trivial

Banana(s) Abaca, Hand, Loco, → **MAD**, Matoke, Musa, Plantain, Scitamineae, Split, Strelitzia, Top, Zany

Band(ed), Bands Absorption, Alice, Ambulacrum, Anadem, Anklet, Armlet, Barrulet, Belt, Border, Braid, Brake, Brass, Brassard, Brassart, Caravan, CB, Channel, Chinstrap, Chromosome, Cingulum, Circlet, Citizens', Clarain, Closet, Cohort, Collar, Collet, Combo, Company, Conduction, Corslet, Coterie, Crape, Crew, Deely boppers, Elastic, ELO, Endorse, Energy, Enomoty, Facia, Falling, Fascia, Fasciole, Ferret, Ferrule, Fess, Filament, Fillet, Fourchette, Fraternity, Frequency, Frieze, Frog, Frontlet, Galloon, Gamelan, → **GANG**, Garage, Garland, Garter, Gasket, Gaskin, Geneva, German, Gird, Girr, Girth, Group, Guard, → **HOOP**, Hope, Iron, Jazz, Jug, Kara, Kitchen, Label, Laticlave, Lytta, Macnamara's, Maniple, Mariachi, Massed, Military, Mourning, Myrmidon, Noise, Obi, One-man, Orchestra, Orchestrina, Pack, Parral, Parrel, Parsal, Parsel, Pass, Patte, Pipe, Plinth, Property, Purfle, Puttee, Retinaculum, Rib, Ribbon, Rigwiddie, Rigwoodie, Rim, Ring, Robbers, Round, Rubber, Rymme, Sash, Scarf, Screed, Scrunchie, Scrunchy, Sect, Shadow, Shallal, Shash, Sheet, Shoe, Snood, Speckled, Steel, Strake, Strand, Strap, Stratum, String, Stripe, Succinctory, Swath(e), Sweat, Tambu-bambu, Tape, Tendon, Thecla, Thoroughbrace, Throat-latch, Tie, Tippet, Torques, Tourniquet, Train, Trangle, Tribute, Troop, Troupe, Tumpline, Turm, Tyre, Unite, Valence, Vinculum, Virl, Vitrain,

Vitta, Wanty, Wedding, Weed, Weeper, Welt, Wings, With(e), Wristlet, Zona, Zone, Zonule

Bandage Bind, Blindfold, Capeline, Dressing, Fillet, Ligature, Lint, Living, Pledget, Roller, Scapular, Sling, Spica, Suspensor, Swaddle, Swathe, T, Tape, Truss, Tubigrip®, Wadding

Bandicoot Bilby, Pig-rat

Bandit Apache, Bravo, Brigand, Desperado, Fruit-machine, Gunslinger, Klepht, Moss-trooper, Outlaw, Pirate, Rapparee, → **ROBBER**, Squeegee, Turpin

Bandsman, Band-leader Alexander, Bugler, Conductor, Maestro, Miller, Wait

Bandstand Kiosk, Stage

Bandy Bow, Exchange, Revie, Toss, Vie

Bane Curse, Dioxin, Evil, Harm, Poison

Bang(er) Amorce, Andouillette, Beat, Big, Cap, Chipolata, Clap, Cracker, Crock, Explode, Firecracker, Flivver, Fringe, Haircut, Heap, Implode, Jalopy, Jammy, Maroon, Pep(p)eroni, Rattletrap, Report, Sausage, Sizzler, Slam, Sonic, Thrill, → **TNT**, Wurst

Bangladesh .bd

Bangle Anklet, Armlet, Bracelet, Kara

Banish(ment) Ban, Deport, Depose, Dispel, Exile, Expatriate, Expel, Extradition, Forsay, Maroon, Ostracise, → **OUTLAW**, Relegate, Rusticate

Banjo Ukulele

Bank(ing), Bank on An(n)icut, Asar, Backs, Bar, Bay, Beneficiary, Bet, Bk, Blood, Bluff, Bottle, Brae, Brim, Bund, Camber, Cay, Central, Chesil, Clearing (house), Cloud, Commercial, Cooperative, Data, Depend, Deposit, Dogger, Down, Drawee, Dune, Dyke, Earthwork, Escarp, Fog, Gene, Giro, Glacis, Gradient, Gradin(e), Hack, Hele, Hill, Home, Incline, Jodrell, Kaim, Kame, Land, Left, Lender, Levee, Link, Lombard Street, Memory, Merchant, Mound, Nap, National, Needle, Nore, Overslaugh, Oyster, Parapet, Penny, Piggy, Pot, Private, Rake, Ramp, Rampart, Reef, → **RELY**, Reserve, Retail, Ridge, Rivage, Riverside, Rodham, Row, Sandbar, Savings, Seed, Shallow, Shelf, Side, Slope, Soil, Sperm, Staithe, State, Sunk, Telephone, Terrace, Terreplein, Tier, Trust, Vault, West, World

Banker Agent, Cert(ainty), Financial, Fugger, Gnome, Lombard, Medici, → **RIVER**, Rothschild, Shroff, Teller

▷ **Banker** *may indicate* a river

Banknote(s) Flimsy, Greenback, Snuff-paper

Bankrupt(cy) Break, Broke, Bung, Bust, Cadaver, Carey Street, Chapter-eleven, Crash, Debtor, Deplete, Duck, Dyvour, Fail, Fold, Insolvent, Lame duck, Notour, Penniless, Receivership, Ruin, Rump, Scat, Sequestration, Skatt, Smash

▷ **Bankrupt** *may indicate* 'red' around another word

Bank system Giro

Bann(s) Out-ask

Banner Banderol(e), Bandrol, Bannerol, Blue blanket, → **FLAG**, Gumphion, Labarum, Oriflamme, Sign, Standard, Streamer

Banquet Beanfeast, Dine, Feast, Junket, Nosh-up, Spread

Banquette Firestep

Bant Diet, Reduce

Bantam Dandy-cock, Dandy-hen

Banter Backchat, Badinage, Borak, Borax, Chaff, Dicacity, Dieter, Jest, → **JOKE**, Persiflage, Picong, Rag, → **RAILLERY**, Rally, Repartee, Ribaldry, Roast, Rot, Tease

Bantu Bosotho, Gazankulu, Herero, Kaffir, Lebowa, Qwaqwa, Shangaan, Sotho, Transkei, Tutsi, X(h)osa

Bap Bread, Roll, Tommy

Baptise(d), Baptism, Baptist Affusion, Amrit, Christen, Clinical, Conditional, Dip, Dipper, Dopper, Dunker, Hypothetical, Illuminati, Immersion, John, Mandaean, Mersion, Palingenesis, Private, Sabbatarian, Sprinkle, Tinker

Bar(s) Address, Angle-iron, Anti-roll, Astragal, Asymmetric, Axletree, Bail, Ban, Barrelhouse, Baulk, Beam, Bierkeller, Bilboes, Billet, Bistro, Blackball, Blacklist,

Block(ade), Bloom, Bolt, Boom, Bottega, Brasserie, Buffet, Bull, Bumper, But, Buvette, Café(-chantant), Café-concert, → CAGE, Cake, Came, Cantina, Capo, Capstan, Channel, Clasp, Clip joint, Cocktail, Coffee, Colour, Counter, Cramp(on), Cross(head), Crow, Crush, Currency, Dive, Doggery, Double, Double-tree, Draw, Drift, Dumbbell, Efficiency, Espresso, Estaminet, Estop(pel), Except, Exclude, Fern, Fid, Flinders, Fonda, Forbid, Foreclose, Forestall, Fret, Gad, Gastropub, Gemel, Glazing, Grate, Grid, Grog-shop, Gunshop, Hame, Handrail, Handspike, Heck, → HINDRANCE, Horizontal, Hound, Hyphen, Impediment, Ingoes, Ingot, Ingowes, Inn, Inner, Judder, Juice, Karaoke, Keeper, Kickstand, Knuckleduster, Latch, Let, Lever, Limbo, Line, Lingot, Local, Lock out, Lounge, Macron, Mandrel, Mandril, Measure, Menu, Merchant, Milk, Mousing, Muesli, Mullion, Nail, Nanaimo, Navigation, Nineteenth hole, No-go, Norman, Obstacle, Omerta, Onely, Orgue, Outer, Overslaugh, Oxygen, Parallel, Perch, Pile, Pinch, Pole, Posada, Prescription, Private, Prohibit, Pub, Public, Putlog, Rack, Raddle, Rail, Ramrod, Rance, Randle-balk, Randle-perch, Randle-tree, Raw, Reach, Restrict, Rib, Risp, Rod, Roll, Roo, Rung, Saddle, Salad, Saloon, Sand, Sans, Save, Saving, Scroll, Semantron, Shaft, Shanty, Shet, Shut, Singles, Skewer, Slice, Slot, Snack, Snug, Spacer, Spar, Speakeasy, Sperre, Spina, Spit, Splinter, Sprag, Stancher, Stanchion, Status, Stave, Stemmer, Sternson, Stick, Stirre, Stretcher, Stripe, Strut, Suspend, Sway, Swee, T, Tael, Tap(-room), Tapas, Taphouse, Task, Tavern(a), Temple, Tiki, Title, Toll, Tombolo, Tommy, Tool, Torsion, Tow, Trace, Trangle, Transom, Trapeze, Triblet, Trundle, Type, U-bolt, Vinculum, Wall, Ward, Wet, Whisker, Window, Wine, Wire, Wrecking, Z, Zed, Zygon

Barabbas Robber

Barb(ed) Bur(r), Fluke, Harl, Herl, → HOOK, Jag(g), Jibe, Pheon, Prickle, Ramus, Tang, Thorn, Vexillum

Barbados, Barbadian Bajan, Bim(m)

Barbara Allen, Major

Barbarian, Barbaric Boor, Crude, Fifteen, Foreigner, Goth, Heathen, Hottentot, Hun, Inhuman, Lowbrow, Outlandish, Philistine, Rude, Savage, Tartar, Tatar(ic)

Barbary Ape, Roan

Barbecue Braai(vleis), Chargrill, Cook-out, Flame-grill, Grill, Hangi, Hibachi, Roast, Spit

Barbel Beard

Barber Epilate, Figaro, Scrape(r), Shaver, Strap, Todd, Tonsor, Trimmer

Barbiturate Goofball

Bard(ic) Ariosto, Druid, Gorsedd, Griot, Heine, Meat, Minstrel, Muse, Ossian, Ovate, Scald, Scop, Skald, Taliesin

Bare, Bare-headed Adamic, Aphyllous, Bald, Barren, Blank, Bodkin, Cere, Décolleté, Denude, Hush, Lewd, Marginal, Mere, Moon, → NAKED, Nude, Open, Plain, Scablands, Scant, Sear, Stark, Timber line, Topless, Uncase, Uncover, Unveil

Bareback Godiva

Barefoot Discalced, Unshod

Barely At a pinch, At a stretch, Hand-to-mouth, Hardly, Just, Merely, Scarcely, Scrimp

Bargain(ing) Agreement, Bargoon, Barter, Braata, Chaffer, Champerty, → CHEAP, Cheapo, Collective, Compact, Contract, Coup, Deal, Dicker, Distributive, Effort, Find, Go, Haggle, Higgle, Horse-trade, Huckster, Indent, Integrative, Negotiate, Option, → PACT, Plea, Productivity, Scoop, Snip, Steal, Supersaver, Time, Trade, Trock, Troke, Truck, Wanworth, Wheeler-dealing

Barge Birlinn, Bucentaur, Budgero(w), Butty, Casco, Elbow, Gabbard, Gabbart, Galley-foist, Hopper, Intrude, Jostle, Keel, Lighter, Nudge, Obtrude, Pra(a)m, Ram, Scow, → SHIP, Trow, Wherry

▷ **Barge** *may indicate* an anagram

Bargee, Bargeman Hobbler, Keeler, Keelman, Legger, Lighterman, Ram, Trow

Barium Ba, Witherite

Bark Angostura, Ayelp, Azedarach, Bass, Bast, Bay, Bowwow, Calisaya, Cambium,

Canella, Caribbee, Cascara, Cascara sagrada, Cascarilla, Cassia, China, Cinchona, Cinnamon, Cork, Cortex, Cusparia, Honduras, Jamaica, Jesuits', Kina, Kinakina, Latration, Liber, Mezereon, Mezereum, Myrica, Parchment, Peel, Pereira, Peruvian, Phloem, Quebracho, Quest, Quill, Quillai, Quina, Quinquina, Red, Rind, Sagrada, Salian, Sassafras, Scrape, Scurf, Shag, → **SHIP**, Skin, Slippery elm, Tan, Tap(p)a, Totaquine, Waff, Waugh, Winter's, Woof, Wow, Yaff, → **YAP**, Yellow, Yelp, Yip

Bar-keep(er), Barmaid, Barman, Bartender Advocate, Ale-wife, Barista, Bencher, Curate, Hebe, Luckie, Lucky, Tapster, Underskinker

Barley (water) Awn, Bear, Bere, Bigg, Hordeum, Malt, Orgeat, Pearl, Pot, Scotch, Truce, Tsamba

Barm(y) Yeast

Barmecide, Barmecidal Imaginary

Barn Bank, Byre, Cowshed, Dutch, Farm, Grange, Mow, Perchery, Skipper, Tithe

Barnaby Rudge

Barnacle Acorn, Cirriped(e), Cypris, Goose(neck), Limpet

Barometer Aneroid, Glass, Orometer, Statoscope, Sympiesometer, Torricellian tube, Weatherglass

Baron B, Corvo, Drug, Munchausen, Noble, Robber, Thyssen, Tycoon

Baronet Bart

Baronne Dudevant Sand

Baroque Fancy, Gothic, Ornate, Rococo

▷ **Baroque** *may indicate* an anagram

Barrack(s), Barracking Asteism, Boo, Cantonment, Casern(e), Cat-call, Garrison, Heckle, Irony, Jeer, Quarters

Barrage Balloon, Fusillade, Heat, Salvo, Shellfire

Barred Banned, Edh, Trabeculated

Barrel Bbl, Bl, Butt, Cade, Capstan, Cascabel, Cask, Clavie, Croze, Cylinder, Drum, Hogshead, Keg, Kibble, Morris-tube, Oildrum, Organ, Pièce, Pork, Run(d)let, Tan-vat, Thrall, Tierce, Tun, Vat, Water, Wood

Barrel-organ Apollonicon, Hurdy-gurdy, Street piano

Barren Addle, Arid, Badlands, Blind, Blunt, Clear, Dry, Eild, → **EMPTY**, Farrow, Hardscrabble, Hi(r)stie, Jejune, Sterile, Unbearing, Waste, Wasteland, Wilderness, Yeld, Yell

Barrier Bail, Barrage, Barricade, Bayle, Block, Boom, Breakwater, Cauld, Checkrail, Cheval de frise, Chicane, Cordon (sanitaire), Crash, Crush, → **DAM**, Defence, Deterrent, Drawgate, Dyke, Fence, Fraise, Gate, Guard rail, Ha-ha, Handicap, Heat, Hedge, Hurdle, Mach, Obstruct, Pain, Paling, Potential, Rail(-fence), Rampart, Restraint, Revetment, Ring fence, Roadblock, Rope, Screen, Skreen, Sonic, Sound, Spina, Stockade, Thames, Thermal, Tollgate, Trade, Transonic, Traverse, Turnpike, Turnstile, Vapour, → **WALL**

Barrister Advocate, Attorney, Counsel, Devil, Lawyer, Revising, Rumpole, Sergeant (at law), Serjeant(-at-law), Silk, Templar, Utter

Barrow Applecart, Clyde, Dolly, Handcart, Henge, How, Hurley, Kurgan, Molehill, Mound, Pushcart, Tram, Trolley, Truck, Tumulus

Barrow-boy Coster, Trader

Bar-tail Scamel, Staniel, Stannel

Barter Chaffer, Chop, Coup, Dicker, → **EXCHANGE**, Haggle, Hawk, Niffer, Permutate, Sco(u)rse, Swap, → **TRADE**, Traffic, Truck

Basalt Diabase, Melaphyre, Tachylite, Tephrite, Toadstone, Trap(pean), Traprock, Wacke

Base Adenine, Air, Airhead, Alkali, Bag, Bed, Beggarly, Billon, Board, Bottom, Brest, Caitiff, Camp, Choline, Codon, Cytosine, Degenerate, Degraded, Dog, Down, E, Erinite, → **ESTABLISH**, First, Floor, Fond, Foot, Foothold, Footstall, Fort Knox, Found, Foundation, Fundus, Guanine, Harlot, Histamine, Hydroxide, Ignoble, Ignominious, Imidazole, Indamine, Infamous, Iniquitous, Install, Knowledge, La Spezia, Leuco, Lewis, → **LOW**, → **MEAN**, Nefarious, Nook, Oasis®, Octal, Parasaniline, Partite, Patten,

Platform, Plinth, Podium, Predella, Premise, Ptomaine, Purin(e), Pyrimidine, Pyrrolidine, Raca, Radix, Rascally, Ratty, Rests, Ribald, Root, Rosaniline, Rude, Scapa Flow, Schiff, Servile, Shameful, Shand, Sheeny, Snide, Socle, Soda, Sordid, Spaceport, Springing, Staddle, → **STAND**, Station, Substrate, Ten, Tetracid, Thymine, Torus, Triacid, Turpitude, Unworthy, Uracil, Vile

Baseball Apple, Nine, Twi-night

Baseless Idle, Unfounded, Ungrounded

Base-line Datum

Basement Bargain, Below stairs, Crypt

Bash Attempt, Belt, Bonk, Clout, Dint, Go, Hit, Rave, Shot, Slog, Strike, Swat, Swipe

Bashful Awed, Blate, Coy, Diffident, Modest, Retiring, Shamefast, Sheep-faced, Sheepish, → **SHY**

Basic(s), Basically, Basis ABC, Abcee, Alkaline, Aquamanale, Aquamanile, At heart, Brass tacks, Cardinal, Crude, Elemental, → **ESSENTIAL**, Fiducial, Fond, Fundamental, Ground(work), Gut, In essence, Integral, Intrinsic, Logic, Meat and potatoes, Nitty-gritty, No-frills, No-nonsense, Nuts and bolts, One-horse, Pou sto, Presumption, Primordial, Principle, Protoplasm, Radical, Rudimentary, Spit-and-sawdust, Staple, Substance, Substratum, Underlying, Unsophisticated, Uracil

Basilica St Peter's

Basilisk Cannon, Lizard

Basin Aquamanale, Aquamanile, Artesian, Aspergillum, Aspersorium, Benitier, Bidet, Bowl, Brazil, Canning, Catch, Catchment, Chott, Cirque, Corrie, Cwm, Dish, Dock, Doline, Donets, Drainage, Foxe, Geosyncline, Great, Impluvium, Kuzbass, Kuznetsk, Lavabo, Laver, Minas, Monteith, Ocean, Okavango, Pan, Park, Piscina, Playa, Porringer, Pudding, Reservoir, River, Scapa Flow, Sink, Slop, Stoop, Stoup, Sugar, Tank, Tarim, Tidal, Washhand

Bask Apricate, Revel, Sun, Sunbathe, → **WALLOW**

Basket, Basket-work Baalam, Bass, Bassinet, Bread, Buck, Cabas, Calathus, Canephorus, Car, Cesta, Chip, Cob, Coop, Corbeil(le), Corbicula, Corf, Creel, Cresset, Dosser, Fan, Flasket, Flax kit, Frail, Gabian, Goal, Hamper, Hask, Junket, Kago, Kajawah, Kipe, Kit, Kite, Leap, Litter, Maund, Mocock, Mocuck, Moses, Murlain, Murlan, Murlin, Osiery, Pannier, Ped, Petara, Pitara(h), Plate, Pollen, Pottle, Punnet, Rip, Round file, Scull, Scuttle, Seed-lip, Skep, Skull, Trolley, Trout, Trug, Van, Wagger-pagger(-bagger), Waste(-paper), Wattlework, Whisket, Wicker(-work), Will(e), Wisket, Work

Basketball Tip-off

Basket-bearer Canephor(a), Canephore, Canephorus

Basket-maker Alfa, Cane, Halfa, Wicker

Basque Biscayan, Bodice, Euskarian, Jacket

Bass Alberti, Ale, Alfie, B, Black, Continuo, Deep, Double, El-a-mi, Figured, Fish, Ground, Largemouth, Low, Ostinato, Serran, Smallmouth, String, Thorough, Walking

Bassoon Fagotto, Sausage

Bast Liber

Bastard, Bastard-wing Alula, Base, Basket, By-blow, Filius nullius, Git, Haram(za)da, Illegitimate, Mamzer, Misborn, Momzer, Mongrel, Sassaby, Side-slip, Slink, Spuriae, Spurious, Whoreson

▷ **Bastard** *may indicate* an anagram

Baste Enlard, Sew, Stitch, Tack

Bastion Citadel, Lunette, Moineau

Bat(sman), Bat's wing, Batter, Batting, Batty Aliped, Ames, Assail, Barbastelle, Baton, Belfry, Blink, Chiroptera, Close, Club, Cosh, Crackers, Crease, Cudgel, Dad, Die Fledermaus, Eyelid, False vampire, Flittermouse, Flying fox, Fruit, Fungo, Grace, Hammerhead, Hatter, Haywire, Hit, Hobbs, Hook, Horseshoe, In, Ink mouse, Insectivorous, Kalong, Knock, Language, Lara, Leisler, Man, Mastiff, Maul, May, Mormops, Mouse-eared, Myopic, Nictate, Nictitate, Night, Nightwatchman, Noctilio,

Nora, Nurdle, Opener, Paddle, Patagium, Pinch-hit, Pipistrel(le), Poke, Pummel, Rabbit, Racket, Racquet, Ram, Rearmouse, Reremice, Reremouse, Roussette, Ruin, Sauch, Saugh, Scorer, Scotch hand, Serotine, Sledge, Spectre, Stick, Stonewall, Straight, Striker, Swat, Switch hitter, Tail(ender), Trap-stick, Trunnion, Vampire, Vespertilionid, Viv, Whacky, Willow, Wood

Batch Bake, Bunch, Clutch, Crop, Tranche

Bath(room) Aerotone, Aeson's, Aquae sulis, Bagnio, Bain-marie, Balneotherapy, Banya, Bed, Bidet, Blanket, Blood, Bubble, Caldarium, Cor, Dip, En suite, Epha, Foam, Hammam, Hip, Hummaum, Hummum, Jacuzzi®, Laver, Mik vah, Mud, Mustard, Oil, Piscina, Plunge, Salt, Sauna, Shower, Sitz, Slipper, Soak, Spa, Sponge, Steam, Stew, Stop, Tepidarium, Therm, Tub, Turkish, Tye, Vapour, Whirlpool, Wife

Bathe(r), Bathing Archimedes, Balneal, Balneation, Balneology, Balneotherapy, Bay(e), Beath, Bogey, Bogie, Dip, Dook, Douk, Embay, Foment, Immerse, Lave, Lip, Skinny-dip, Souse, Splash, Stupe, → **SWIM**, Tub, → **WASH**

Bathos Anticlimax

Bathrobe Peignoir

Batman Valet

Baton Mace, Rod, Sceptre, Staff, Truncheon, Wand

Batrachian Frog, Toad

▷ **Bats, Batting** *may indicate an anagram*

Battalion Bn, Corps, Troop

Batten Dropper, Fasten, Tie

Batter(ed) Bombard, Bruise, Buffet, Decrepit, Pound, Thump

Battery Accumulator, Artillery, Button-cell, Cannonade, Drycell, Field, Galvanic, Heliac, Henhouse, Li(thium)-ion, Masked, Nicad, Nickel cadmium, NIMH, Penlight, Pra(a)m, Primary, Solar, Storage, Troop, Voltaic, Waffle, Water

Battle(s), Battleground Action, Affair, Ben, Clash, Cockpit, Combat, → **CONFLICT**, Encounter, Engagement, Field, → **FIGHT**, Fray, Front, Hosting, Joust, Maiden, Pitched, Royal, Running, Sarah, Sciamachy, Skiamachy, Spurs, Stoor, Stour, Stowre, Theatre, Theomachy, Wage, → **WAR**, Wargame

---

BATTLES

3 letters:	Arras	*6 letters:*	Shiloh
Kut	Boyne	Actium	Tobruk
Ulm	Bulge	Arbela	Towton
	Crecy	Arcola	Varese
4 letters:	Ipsus	Argyle	Verdun
Alma	Issus	Arnhem	Vigrid
Chad	Lewes	Barnet	Wagram
Ivry	Lissa	Camlan	Wipers
Jena	Marne	Cannae	
Laon	Mylae	Cressy	*7 letters:*
Lodi	Nancy	Crimea	Aboukir
Loos	Parma	Imphal	Alamein
Mons	Pavia	Kosovo	Almanza
Nile	Pydna	Lutzen	Argonne
Zama	Sedan	Maldon	Bautzen
	Somme	Midway	Beaches
5 letters:	Tours	Mohacs	Britain
Accra	Valmy	Mycale	Bull Run
Alamo	Ypres	Naseby	Cambrai
Allia		Sadowa	Carrhae
Arcot		Senlac	Chalons

Colenso
Coronel
Corunna
Deorham
Dunkirk
Evesham
Flodden
Flowers
Glencoe
Iwo Jima
Jericho
Jutland
Legnano
Lepanto
Leuctra
Magenta
Marengo
Nations
Newbury
Nineveh
Okinawa
Orleans
Panipat
Picardy
Plassey
Plataea
Poltava
Pultowa
Salamis
Sempach
Vimelro
Vitoria
Warburg

8 letters:
Antietam
Ardennes
Ayacucho
Blenheim
Borodino
Bosworth
Chioggia
Clontarf

Culloden
Custozza
Edgehill
Erzurium
Flanders
Fontenay
Hastings
Hydaspes
Inkerman
Jemappes
Kulikova
Le Cateau
Lechfeld
Manassas
Marathon
Mehawand
Metaurus
Montreal
Naumachy
Navarino
Normandy
Omdurman
Palo Alto
Philippi
Poitiers
Ragnarok
Rossbach
Saratoga
Solomons
Spion Kop
St Albans
Syracuse
Talavera
Toulouse
Waterloo
Yorktown

9 letters:
Agincourt
Balaclava
Caporetto
Castilion
Chaeronea

El Alamein
Gallipoli
Ladysmith
Moerkirch
Nicopolis
Otterburn
Oudenarde
Pharsalus
Princeton
Ramillies
Sedgemoor
Solferino
St Vincent
The Saints
Trafalgar
Vercellae
Wandewash
Worcester

10 letters:
Adrianople
Armageddon
Austerlitz
Beneventum
Bennington
Brunanburh
Bunker Hill
Camperdown
Ferhbellin
Gettysburg
Lundy's Lane
Majuba Hill
Malplaquet
Mount Badon
Petersburg
Quatre Bras
River Plate
Shipka Pass
Stalingrad
Steenkerke
Tannenberg
Tewkesbury

11 letters:
Aegospotami
Aljubarrota
Armentières
Aubers Ridge
Bannockburn
Belleau Wood
Bismarck Sea
Chapultepec
Chattanooga
Hohenlinden
Marston Moor
Philiphaugh
Prestonpans
Thermopylae
Wounded Knee

12 letters:
Flodden Field
Mons Graupius
Monte Cassino
Roncesvalles

13 letters:
Alcazar-Quivir
Bosworth Field
Little Bighorn
Neuve-Chapelle
Neville's Cross
Passchendaele
Spanish Armada

14 letters:
Castlebar Races
Stamford Bridge

15 letters:
Missionary Ridge
Plains of Abraham
Teutoberger Wald

16 letters:
Las Navas de Tolosa

Battle-axe Amazon, Bill, Gorgon, Halberd, Ogress, Sparth(e), Termagant, Termagent, Turmagant, Turmagent
Battlement Barmkin, Crenellate, Merlon, Rampart
Battle-order Phalanx
Battleship Carrier, Destroyer, Dreadnought, Gunboat, Man-o'-war, Pocket, Potemkin
Bauble Bagatelle, Gaud, Gewgaw, Trifle
Bauhaus Gropius
Baulk Demur, Gib, Hen, Impede, Jib, Reest, Reist, Shy, Thwart
Bavardage Fadaise
Bawd(y) Hare, Raunchy, Risque, Sculdudd(e)ry, Skulduddery

Bawl Bellow, Gollar, Howl, Weep

Bay Ab(o)ukir, Aere, Arm, Baffin, Bantry, Bark, Bell, Bengal, Bez, Bight, Biscay, Bonny, Botany, Broken, Byron, Cape Cod, Cardigan, Chesapeake, Cienfuegos, Classis, Cleveland, Colwyn, Corpus Christi, Cove, Covelet, Creek, Daphne, Delagoa, Delaware, Discovery, Dublin, Dundalk, Dvina, False, Famagusta, Fleet, Frobisher, Fundy, Galway, Gdansk, Georgian, Gibraltar, Glace, Golden, Great Australian Bight, Green, Guanabara, Guantanamo, Gulf, Hangzhou, Harbour, Hawke's, Herne, Hervey, Horse, → **HOWL**, Hudson, Inhambane, Inlet, Ise, Islands, James, Jervis, Jiazhou, Kavalla, Kuskokwim, Laura, Laurel, Layby, Loading, Lobito, Loblolly, Lutzow-Holm, MA, Magdalena, Manila, Massachusetts, Montego, Moreton, Narragansett, New York, Niche, Oleander, Omaha, Oriel, Passamaquoddy, Pegasus, Pigs, Plenty, Plymouth, Port Phillip, Poverty, Recess, Red, Roan, St Austell, St Michel, San Francisco, San Pedro, Santiago, Scene, Setubal, Shark, Sick, Sligo, Stall, Suvla, Swansea, Table, Tampa, Tasman, Thunder, Tor, Toyama, Tralee, Trincomalee, Ungava, Vae, Vigo, Vlore, Voe, Vyborg, Waff, Walfish, Walvis, Wash, Whitley, Wick, Yowl

Bayonet Jab, Skewer, Stab, Sword

Bazaar Alcaiceria, Emporium, Fair, Fete, Market, Pantechnicon, Sale, Sook, Souk

BBC Auntie

Be Exist, Live, Occur

Beach(head) Anzio, Bondi, Chesil, Coast, Daytona, Ground, Hard, Lido, Littoral, Machair, Miami, Myrtle, Omaha, Palm, Plage, Raised, Sand, Sea-coast, Seashore, Seaside, Shingle, Shore, Storm, Strand, Waikiki

Beachcomber Arenaria

Beachwear Thong

Beacon Belisha, Brecon, Fanal, Landing, Lantern, Lightship, Need-fire, Pharos, Racon, Radar, Radio, Robot, Signal

Bead(s), Beaded Adderstone, Aggri, Aggry, Astragal, Baily's, Ballotini, Bauble, Blob, Bugle, Cabling, Chaplet, Crab's-eyes, Crab-stones, Dewdrop, Drop, Droplet, Gadroon, Gaud, Job's tears, Kumbaloi, Love, Mala, Moniliform, Nurl, Ojime, Passament, Passement, Paternoster, Poppet, Poppit, Prayer, Rosary, Sabha, St Cuthbert's, Se(a)wan, Spacer, Spacer plate, Subha, Sweat, Tear, Wampum(peag), Worry

Beadle Apparitor, Bederal, Bedral, Bumble, Herald, Paritor, Shammash, Shammes, Verger

Beagle Snoopy, Spy

Beak AMA, Bailie, Bill, Cad, Cere, Coronoid, Egg-tooth, Gar, JP, Kip(p), Magistrate, Master, Metagnathous, Mittimus, Nasute, Neb, Nose, Pecker, Prow, Ram, Rostellum, Rostrum, Shovel

Beaker Bell, Cup, Goblet

Beakless Erostrate

Beak-shaped Coracoid

Beam(ing) Arbor, Balance, Ba(u)lk, Bar, Binder, Boom, Bowstring, Box, Breastsummer, Bressummer, Broadcast, Bum(p)kin, Cantilever, Carline, Carling, Cathead, Collar, Crossbar, Crosshead, Crosspiece, Deck, Effulge, Electron, Girder, Grin, Hammer, Hatch, Herisson, Holophote, I, Irradiate, Joist, Ke(e)lson, Landing, Laser, Lentel, Lintel, Manteltree, Maser, Molecular, Moonlight, Needle, Outrigger, Particle, Pencil, Principal, Proton, Purlin, Putlock, Putlog, Radio, → **RAFTER**, → **RAY**, Rayon, Refulgent, Rident, Ridgepole, Rood, Roof-tree, Sandwich, Scale, Scantling, Sealed, Searchlight, Shaft, Shine, Shore, Sleeper, Smile, Soffit, Solive, Spar, Stanchion, Stemson, Sternpost, Straining, Streamer, Stringer, Stringpiece, Summer, Support, Tailing, Tie, Timber, Trabeate, Trabecula, Transom, Trave, Trimmer, Truss, Universal, Viga, Walking, Weigh-bauk, Yard, Yardarm

Beamish Galumphing, Nephew

Bean Abrus, Adsuki, Aduki, Adzuki, Arabica, Asparagus pea, Baked, Berry, Black, Black-eye, Borlotti, Broad, Bush, Butter, Cacao, Calabar, Castor, Cluster, Cocoa, Coffee,

Cow-pea, Dwarf, Edamame, Fabaceous, Fava, Flageolet, French, Frijol(e), Garbanzo, Goa, Gram, Green, Haricot, Harmala, Head, Horse, Hyacinth, Jack, Jelly, Jequirity, Jumping, Kachang putch, Kidney, Lablab, Legume, Lentil, Lima, Locust, Molucca, Moong, Moth, Mung, Nelumbo, Nib, Noddle, Ordeal, Pichurim, Pinto, Pulse, Runner, St Ignatius's, Scarlet, Scarlet runner, Shell, Silverskin, Snap, Snuffbox, Soy(a), String, Sugar, Sword, Tepary, Tonga, Tonka, Tonquin, Urd, Wax, Winged, Yard-long

Beanfeast → **PARTY**, Spree, Wayzgoose

Bear(er), Bear lover Abide, Abrooke, Andean, Arctic, Arctophile, Baloo, Balu, Beer, Bigg, Breed, Brook, Brown, Bruin, Brunt, → **CARRY**, Cave, Churl, Cinnamon, Coati-mondi, Coati-mundi, Cub, Demean, Dree, Ean, → **ENDURE**, Engender, Exert, Fur-seal, Gest(e), Gonfalonier, Great, Grizzly, Hack, Ham(m)al, Harbinger, Have, Hod, Hold, Honey, Humf, Hump(h), Jampanee, Jampani, Keb, Kinkajou, Koala, Kodiak, Koolah, Lioncel(le), Lionel, Lug, Mother, Nandi, Nanook, Owe, Paddington, Panda, Pertain, Polar, Pooh, Rac(c)oon, Roller, Rupert, Russia, Sackerson, Seller, Shoulder, Sit, Sloth, Spectacled, Stand, Stay, Stomach, → **SUFFER**, Sun, Sunbear, Sustain, Targeteer, Teddy, Teem, Thole, Throw, Tolerate, Tote, Transport, Undergo, Upstay, Ursine, Water, Whelp, White, Wield, Withstand, Woolly, Yean, Yield

Bearberry Manzanita, Uva-ursi

Beard(ed) Aaron, Alfalfa, Anchor, Arista, Assyrian, Aureole, Awn, Balaclava, Barb, Barbiche, Beaver, Belgrave, Cadiz, Cathedral, Charley, Charlie, Confront, Defy, Ducktail, Escort, Face, Five o'clock shadow, Forked, Fungus, Goatee, Hair(ie), Hairy, Hear(ie), Imperial, Jewish, Kesh, Lincolnesque, Mephistopheles, Newgate frill, Newgate fringe, Old Dutch, Olympian, Outface, Peak, Pencil, Raleigh, Rivet, Roman T, Screw, Shenandoah, Spade, Stibble, Stiletto, Stubble, Swallowtail, Tackle, Tile, Trojan, Tuft, Uncle Sam, Vandyke, Whiskerando, Whiskery, Ziff

Beardless Callow, Clean, Tahr, Tehr

▷ **Bearhug** *may indicate* Teddy or similar around a word

Bearing(s) Air, Allure, Amenaunce, Armorial, Aspect, Azimuth, Babbitt, Ball, Behaviour, Bush, Carriage, Deportment, Direction, E, Endurance, Gait, Germane, Gest, Gudgeon, Hatchment, Haviour, Heading, → **HERALDIC**, Hugger-mugger, Lioncel(le), Lionel, Manner, Martlet, Mascle, Middy, Mien, N, Needle, Nor, Pall, Pheon, Port, Presence, Reference, Relevant, Roller, S, Seme(e), Subordinary, Teeming, Tenue, Thrust, W, Yielding

▷ **Bearing** *may indicate* compass points

Beast(ly) → **ANIMAL**, Arna, Behemoth, Brute, Caliban, Caribou, Chimera, → **CREATURE**, Dieb, Dragon, Dzeren, Fatstock, Gargoyle, Gayal, Genet, Godzilla, Grampus, Hippogriff, Hodog, Hog, Hydra, Hy(a)ena, Jumart, Kinkajou, Lion, Mammoth, Marmot, Mastodon, Mhorr, Monoceros, Narwhal, Ogre, Oliphant, Opinicus, Oryx, Panda, Potto, Quagga, Queen's, Rac(c)oon, Rhytina, Rother, Rumptifusel, Sassaby, Steer, Sumpter, Swinish, Tarand, Teg, Theroid, Triceratops, Triton, Wart-hog, Whangam, Yahoo, Yak, Yale, Zizel

Beat(ing), Beaten, Beater(er) Anoint, Arsis, Athrob, Bandy, Bang, Baste, Bastinado, Batter, Battue, Beetle, Belabour, Belt, Bepat, Best, Blatter, Bless, Bo Diddley, Bubble, Cadence, Cane, Cat, Chastise, Clobber, Club, Clump, Cob, Conquer, Cream, Cudgel, Cuff, Curry, Debel, → **DEFEAT**, Ding, Donder, Dress, Drub, Duff up, Dunt, Elude, Excel, Fatigue, Faze, Feague, Feeze, Fibbed, Firk, Flagellate, Flail, Flam, Float, Flog, Floor, Flush, Fly, Fustigate, Hipster, Hollow, Horsewhip, Ictus, Inteneration, Jole, Joll, Joule, Jowl, Knock, Knubble, Lace, Laidie, Laidy, Lambast(e), Larrup, Lash, Lather, Latin, Laveer, Lay, Lick, Lilt, Lounder, Mall, Malleate, Manor, Mell, Mersey, Mullah, Muller, Nubble, Onceover, Outclass, Outdo, Outflank, Outstrip, Outstroke, Paik, Palpitate, Pandy, Paradiddle, Pash, Paste, Pip, Ploat, Pommel, Pound, Prat, Pug, Pulsate, Pulsatile, Pulse, Pulsedge, Pummel, Pun, Quop, Raddle, Ram, Ratten, Resolve, Retreat, Rhythm, Ribroast, Rope's end, Round, Rout, Rowstow, Ruff(le), Scourge, Scutch, Slat, Smight, Smite, Soak, Sock, Sort, Strap, Strap-oil, Strike, Swinge, Swingle, Syncopation, Systole, Taber, Tabor, Tabrere, Tachycardia, Tact, Tala, Tan, Tattoo, Thesis, Thrash, Thresh,

Throb, Thud, Thump, Thwack, Tick, Time, Tired, Top, Torture, Tricrotic, Trounce, Tuck, Tund, Verberate, Vibrate, Wallop, Wappend, Weary, Welt, Wham, Whip, Whisk, Whitewash, Whup, Wraught, Ybet, Yerk, Yirk

▷ **Beaten-up** *may indicate* an anagram

Beat it Skedaddle, Vamo(o)se

Beatitude Macarism

Beau Admirer, Blade, Brummel, Cat, Damoiseau, Dandy, Flame, Geste, Lair, Lover, Masher, Nash, Spark, Tibbs

Beaufort Scale, Windscale

Beaut(y) Advantage, Bathing, Belle, Bellibone, Bombshell, Camberwell, Charmer, Colleen, Comeliness, Corker, Dish, Doll, Glamour, Glory, Grace, Helen, Houri, Hyperion, Kanta, Lana, Looks, Monism, Peri, Picture, Pride, Pulchritude, Purler, Sheen, Smasher(oo), Stunner

Beautician Glamoriser

Beautiful, Beautify Angelic, Astrid, Bonny, Bright, Embellish, Enhance, Exquisite, Fair, Fine, Gorgeous, Junoesque, Ornament, Pink, Radiant, Scenic, Smicker, Specious, Sublime, To kalon

Beauty spot Patch, Tempe, Tika

Beaver Beard, Castor, Eager, Grind, Mountain, Oregon, Rodent, Sewellel

Because (of) As, Forasmuch, Forwhy, Hence, In (that), Inasmuch, Ipso facto, Sens, Since

Beckon Gesture, Nod, Summons, Waft, Wave, Wheft

Become, Becoming Apt, Besort, Decent, Decorous, Enter, Fall, Fit, Flatter, Get, Go, Grow, Happen, Occur, Seemly, Suit, Wax, Worth

Bed(s), Bedding, Bedstead Air, Allotment, Amenity, Apple-pie, Arroyo, Bacteria, Base, Bassinet, → **BEDCOVER**, Berth, Border, Bottom, Bottomset, Box, Bundle, Bunk, Caliche, Camp, Capillary, Carrycot, Channel, Charpoy, Cill, Cot(t), Couch(ette), Counterpane, Couvade, Coverlet, Cradle, Crib, Cross, Cul(t)ch, Day, Divan, Doona, Doss, Duvet, Erf, False, Feather, Filter, Fluidized, Flying, Form, Four-poster, Futon, Gault, Greensand, Hammock, Inlay, Kago, Kang, Kingsize, Kip, Knot, Knot garden, Lay(er), Lazy, Lilo®, Litter, Marriage, Mat, Matrix, Mattress, Murphy, Naked, Nap, Nest, Nookie, Oyster, Pad, Paillasse, Pallet, Palliasse, Pan, Parterre, Passage, Patch, Pavement, Pay, Pig, Pit, Plank, Plant, Plot, Procrustean, Puff, Queensize, Quilt, Retire, River, Rollaway, Roost, Rota, Sack, Scalp, Settle, Shakedown, Sill, Sitter, Sleep, Sofa, Standing, Stratum, Stretcher, Sun, T(h)alweg, Tanning, Test, The downy, Thill, Trough, Truckle, Trundle, Twin, Wadi, Wady, Ware, Water, Wealden, Wedding

Bedaub Cake, Deck, Smear

Bed-bug B, B flat, Chinch, Flea, Louse, Vermin

Bedchamber, Bedroom Boudoir, Bower, Br, Chamber, Cubicle, Dorm(itory), Dormer, Dorter, Ruelle, Ward

Bedcover Palampore, Palempore, Puff

Bedeck Adonise, Adorn, Array, Festoon

▷ **Bedevilled** *may indicate* an anagram

Bedjacket Nightingale

Bedlam Chaos, Furore, Madness, Nuthouse, Tumult, Uproar

Bed-rest Dutch-wife

Bedrock Costean

Bedsit Pad

Bedwetting Enuresis

Bee Afrikanised, Athenia, Bike, Bumble, Carpenter, Cuckoo, Deborah, Debra, Deseret, Dog, Drone, Drumbledor, Dumbledore, Group, Hiver, Honey, Humble, Husking, Killer, King, Lapidary, Leaf-cutter, Mason, Melissa, Mining, Nurse, Pollinator, Queen, Quilting, Raising, Solitary, Spell, Spell-down, Spelling, Swarm, Trixie, Worker, Working

Beech Antarctic, Copper, Fagus, Hornbeam, Mast, Taw(h)ai, Tree

Bee-eater Merops, Rainbow-bird

Beef(y) Aitchbone, Baron, Bleat, Brawny, Bresaola, Bull(y), Bullock, Carp, Carpaccio, Charqui, Chateaubriand, Chuck, Clod, Complain, Corned, Filet mignon, Flank, Groan, Grouch, Grouse, Hough, Jerk, Kobe, Liebig, Mart, Mice, Moan, Mousepiece, Muscle, Neat, Ox, Pastrami, Peeve, Plate, Porterhouse, Rother, Salt-horse, Salt-junk, Sauerbraten, Sey, Shin, Silverside, Sirloin, Stolid, Stroganoff, Topside, Tournedos, Tranche, Undercut, Vaccine, Wagyu, Wellington

Beefeater Billman, Exon, Gin, Oxpecker, Warder, Yeoman

Bee-glue Propolis

Beehive Alveary, Apiary, Ball, Dioptric, Gum, Skep

Beelzebub Devil

Been Bin

Beer Ale, Alegar, Amber fluid, Amber liquid, Bantu, Barley sandwich, Bitter, Black, Bock, Chaser, Coldie, Draught, Drink, Dry, Entire, Export, Gill, Ginger, Granny, Grog, Guest, Heavy, Herb, Home-brew, Kaffir, Keg, Kvass, Lager, Lambic, Lite, Lush, Malt, March, Middy, Mild, Milk stout, Mum, Near, Nog, October, Pils(e)ner, Pint, Pony, Porter, Real, Real ale, Rice, Root, Saki, Scoobs, Sherbet, Six-pack, Skeechan, Small, Spruce, Stingo, Stout, Stubby, Suds, Swankie, Swanky, Swats, Swipes, Switchel, Table, Taplash, Tinnie, Tipper, Tshwala, Tube, Turps, Wallop, Wheat, Zythum

Beer garden Brasserie

Bee's nest Bink

Beet Blite, Chard, Fat-hen, Goosefoot, Mangel(wurzel), Seakale, Silver, Spinach, Sugar

Beethoven WoO

Beetle Ambrosia, Anobiid, Argos tortoise, Asiatic, Bacon, Bark, Batler, Bee, Blister, Bloody-nosed, Boll weevil, Bombardier, Bruchid, Bug, Bum-clock, Buprestidae, Buprestus, Burying, Bustle, Buzzard-clock, Cabinet, Cadelle, Cane, Cantharis, Carabid, Cardinal, Carpet, Carrion, Chafer, Christmas, Churchyard, Cicindela, Click, Clock, Cockchafer, Cockroach, Coleoptera, Coleopterous, Colorado, Coprophagan, Curculio, Darkling, Deathwatch, Dermestid, Devil's coach-horse, Diamond, Diving, Dor(r), Dor-fly, Dumbledore, Dung, Dyticus, Dytiscus, Elater, Elmbark, Elytron, Elytrum, Firefly, Flea, Furniture, Glow-worm, Gold(smith), Goliath, Gregor, Ground, Hammer, Hangover, Hercules, Hop-flea, Hornbug, Huhu, Humbuzz, Impend, Japanese, Jewel, June, Khapra, Ladybird, Ladybug, Lamellicorn, Larder, Leaf, Leather, Longhorned, Longicorn, Mall(et), Maul, May-bug, Meloid, Minotaur, Museum, Musk, Oakpruner, Oil, Overhang, Pill, Pinchbuck, Pine, Pine-chafer, Potato, Project, Protrude, Race(-bug), Rhinoceros, Rhynchophora, Roach, Rosechafer, Rove, Sacred, Saw palmetto, Scamper, Scarab(ee), Scavenger, Scolytus, Scurry, Sexton, Shard, Skelter, Sledge(-hammer), Snapping, Snout, Soldier, Spanish fly, Spider, Spring, Squirr, Stag, Tenebrio, Tiger, Toktokkie, Tortoise, Tumble-bug, Tumble-dung, Turnip-flea, Typographer, Vedalia, VW, Water, Weevil, Whirligig, Wireworm, Woodborer, Wood-engraver

Beetle-crushers Cops

Befall Happen, Occur

Before(hand) A, Advance, Already, An, Ante, Avant, By, Coram, Earlier, Early, Ere, Erst(while), First, → **FORMER**, Or (e'er), Parava(u)nt, Pre, Previously, Prior, Pro, Sooner, Till, To, Until, Van, Zeroth

Before food Ac

Befriend Assist, Cotton, Fraternise, Support

Befuddle(ment) Bemuse, Dwaal, Inebriate, Stupefy

Beg(gar), Beggarly, Begging Abr(ah)am-man, Ask, Badgeman, Beseech, Besognio, Bey, Bezonian, Blighter, Blue-gown, Cadge, Calendar, Clapper-dudgeon, Crave, → **ENTREAT**, Exoration, Flagitate, Fleech, Gaberlunzie, Gangrel, Hallan-shaker, Implore, Impoverish, Irus, Jarkman, Lackall, Lazar(us), Lazzarone, Limitary, Lumpenproletariat, Maund, Mendicant, Montem, Mooch, Mouch, Mump, Niggardly, Obtest, Palliard, Panhandle, Pauper, Penelophon, Penniless, → **PLEAD**, Pled, Pray, Prig, Prog, Ptochocracy, Rag, Randie, Randy, Ruffler, Ruin(ate), Sadhu, Schnorr(er),

Screeve, Scrounge, Shool(e), Skelder, Skell, Solicit, Standpad, Sue, Suppliant, Supplicate, Thig(ger), Toe-rag, Touch, Undo, Uprightman, Whipjack

Beget Gender, Kind

Beggar rule Ptochocracy

Begging bowl Clackdish, Clapdish

Begin(ner), Beginning Ab initio, Ab ovo, Alpha, Alphabetarian, Author, B, Babyhood, Black, Cause, Che(e)chako, Clapdash, Commence, Daw, Dawn, Deb, Debut, Embryo, Enter, Exordium, Fall-to, Fledgling, Found, Fountainhead, Genesis, Germ, Go, Greenhorn, Inaugural, Inception, Inchoate, Incipient, Incipit, Initial, Initiate, Intro, Johnny-raw, L, Launch, Lead, Learn, Learner, Logos, Nascent, Neophyte, Noob, → **NOVICE**, Oncome, Onset, Ope(n), Ord, → **ORIGIN**, Outbreak, Pose, Prelim(inary), Presidium, Primer, Rookie, Seed, Set, Shoot, → **START**, Startup, Strike up, Takeoff, Tenderfoot, Threshold, Tiro, To-fall, Tyro(ne), Yearn

Begone Aroint, Aroynt, Avaunt, Scram, Shoo, Vamo(o)se

Begonia Elephant's-ear(s)

Begorrah Bedad, Musha

Begrudge Envy, Resent

Beguile(r) Bewitch, Charm, Coax, Distract, Divert, Enchant, Ensnare, Entice, Flatter, Gull, Intrigue, Jack-a-lantern, Tice, Trick, Wile

Behalf Ex parte, For, Part, Sake

Behave, Behaviour, Behaving Abear, Accepted, Acquired, Act, Appeasement, Attitude, Carriage, Conduct, Consummatory, Convenance, Decorum, Demean, Deportment, Do, Effrontery, Epimeletic, Etepimeletic, Ethics, Ethology, Form, Freak out, Goings-on, Guise, Horme, Life style, → **MANNER**, Meme, Nature, Netiquette, Noblesse oblige, Obey, Orientation, Practice, Praxeology, Quit, React, Response, Satisficing, Strong meat, Tribalism, Unreasonable

Behead Decapitate, Decollate, Guillotine

Behind(hand) Abaft, Aft(er), Ahind, Ahint, Apoop, Arear, Arere, Arrear, Arse, Astern, Backside, Beneath, Bottom, Bum, Buttocks, Can, Croup, Derrière, Fud, Late, Overdue, Post, Prat, → **REAR**, Rump, Slow, Tushie

Behold(en) Affine, Ecce, Eye, Grateful, Here's, Indebted, La, Lo, Look, Observe, See, View, Voilà

Beige Buff, Greige, Neutral, Suede, Tan

Being Cratur, Creature, Critter, Ens, Entia, Entity, Esse, Essence, Existence, Human, Man, Metaphysics, Mode, Nature, Omneity, Ontology, → **PERSON**, Saul, Soul, Subsistent, Substance, Supreme, Ubiety, Wight

Bejabers Arrah

Belch Boak, Boke, Brash, Burp, Emit, Eruct, Erupt, Rift, Spew, Toby, Yex

Belcher Foulard, Handkerchief, Hanky, Toby

Beldam(e) Crone, Hag, Harridan, Scold

Belfry Campanile, Tower

Belgian Flemish, Walloon

Belief, Believe, Believed, Believer, Believing Accredit, Adam and eve, Anata, Ativism, Bigot, Buy, Capernaite, Catechism, Chiliasm, Christian, Conviction, Creationism, Credence, Credit, Creed, Cult, Culture, Deem, Deist, Di(o)physite, Doctrine, Doxastic, Doxy, Dukkha, Dyophysite, Evangelical, Faith, Formulism, Gnostic, Guess, Heresy, Heterodoxy, Hold, Holist, Idea, Ideology, Idolater, Imagine, Islam, Ism, Latitudinarian, Ludism, Manichaeism, Mechanist, Meme, Messianist, Methink, Mysticism, Notion, → **OPINION**, Orthopraxy, Ovist, Pacifism, Pantheism, Pelagianism, Persuasion, Physicism, Pluralism, Postmillenarian, Presumption, Religion, Reputed, Revelationist, S(h)aivism, Second Coming, Secularism, Seeing, Shema, Solfidian, Solipsism, Superstition, Supremacist, Suspect, Swallow, Tenet, Test, Tetratheism, Thanatism, Theist, Theosophy, Think, Threap, Threep, Traducianism, Transcendentalism, Trinitarian, Triphysite, Trow, Trust, Ubiquitarianism, Umma(h),

Unitarian, Universalism, Wear, Ween, Wis(t)

Belittle Cheapen, Cry down, Decry, Demean, Depreciate, Derogate, Detract, Diminish, Discredit, Disparage, Downgrade, Humble, Pooh-pooh, Slight

Bell(s) Acton, Agogo, Angelus, Ben, Big Ben, Bob, Bow, Bronte, Cachecope, Canterbury, Carillon, Chime, Chinese pavilion, Clanger, Crotal, Curfew, Currer, Daisy, Diving, Division, Ellis, Gong, Grandsire, Jar, Liberty, Low, Lutine, Market, Mass, Minute, Mort, Muffin, Pancake, Passing, Pavilion, Peal, Peter, Pinger, Pudding, Ring, Roar, Sacring, Sanctus, Shark, Sleigh, Tailor, Tantony, Tenor, Tent, Tintinnabulum, Tocsin, Toll, Tom, Triple, Tubular, Vair, Vaire, Verry, Vesper, Wind

Bell-bird Arapunga, Campanero

Belle Beauty, Starr, Toast, Venus

Bell-founder Belleter

Bellicose, Belligerent Chippy, Combatant, Gung-ho, Hostile, Jingoist, Martial, Militant, Truculent, Warmonger

Bellow(s) Buller, Holla, Holler, Moo, Rant, Rave, Roar, Rout, Saul, Thunder, Troat, Tromp(e), Trumpet, Windbag

Bell-ringer, Bell-ringing Bob, Campanology, Changes, Clapper, Course, Grandsire, Handstroke, Hunting, Maximus, Quasimodo, Rope, Sally, Tintinnabulation, Tocsin, Toller

Belly Abdomen, Alvine, Bag, Beer, Beer-gut, Boep, Bunt, Calipee, Celiac, Coeliac, Gut, Kite, Kyte, Paunch, Pod, → **STOMACH**, Swell, Tum(my), Venter, Wame, Weamb, Wem(b), Womb

Belong, Belonging(s) Appertain, Apply, Appurtenant, Chattels, Effects, Incident, Inhere, Intrinsic, Our, Paraphernalia, Pertain, → **PROPERTY**, Relate, Roots, Things, Traps

Beloved Acushla, Alder-lief(est), Amy, Boyfriend, David, Dear, Doy, Esme, Inamorata, Joy, Leve, Lief, Loor, Morna, Pet, Popular, Precious

Below Beneath, Inf(erior), Infra, Nether, Sub, Subjacent, Under, Unneath

Belt(ed) Baldric(k), Band, Bandoleer, Bandolier, Baudric(k), Bible, Black, Cartridge, Chastity, Cholera, Clitellum, Clobber, Clock, Commuter, Conveyor, Copper, Cotton, Crios, Demolition, Equator, Fan, Flog, Fold and thrust, Galvanic, Garter, Gird(le), Girt, Great, Green, Hip, Hydraulic, Inertial, Judoka, Kuiper, Lap, Larrup, Life, Lonsdale, Mitre, Money, Muesli, Orion's, Orogenic, Polt, Pound, Radiation, Roller, Roll-on, Rust, Safety, Sahel, Sam Browne, Sanitary, Sash, Seat, Speed, Stockbroker, Storm, Strap, Stratosphere, Sun, Surcingle, Suspender, Swipe, Sword, Taiga, Tawse, Tear, Thump, Tore, Tract, Van Allen, Wampum, Wanty, Webbing, Wing, Zodiac, Zone, Zoster

Belt up Sh

Belvedere Gazebo, Mirador

Bemoan → **LAMENT**, Mourn, Sigh, Wail

Bemuse Infatuate, Stonn(e), Stun, Stupefy, Throw

Ben Battle, Hur, Jonson, Mountain, Nevis, Spence

Bench Banc, Banker, Bink, Bleachers, Counter, Court, Cross, Exedra, Form, Front, King's, Knifeboard, Magistrates, Optical, Pew, Queen's, Rout seat, Rusbank, → **SEAT**, Settle, Siege, Stillage, Thoft, Thwart, Treasury, Trestle, Widow's

Benchmark Criteria, Standard, Yardstick

Bend(er), Bending, Bends Angle, Arc, Arch, Articular, Becket, Bight, Binge, Bow, Buck(le), Bust, Camber, Carrick, Chicane, Circumflect, Contort, Corner, Crank(le), Cringe, → **CROOK**, Crouch, Curl, Curve, Diffraction, Dog-leg, Double up, Elbow, Engouled, Epinasty, Es(s), Expansion, Falcate, Fawn, Flex(ural), Flexion, Flexure, Fold, Geller, Geniculate, Genu, Genuflect, Grecian, Hairpin, Hinge, Hook, Horseshoe, Hunch, Incline, Inflect, Jag, Kink, Knee(cap), Kneel, Knot, Kowtow, Meander, Mould, Nutant, Ox-bow, Pitch, Plash, Plié, Ply, Recline, Reflex, Retorsion, Retortion, Retroflex, Riband, S, Scarp, Sheet, Souse, Spree, Spring, Stave, Stoop, Swan-neck, Trend, Twist, U, Ups(e)y, Uri, Wale, Warp, → **YIELD**, Z

▷ **Bendy** *may indicate* an anagram

Beneath Below, Sub, Under, Unworthy

Benedict(ine) Black Monk, Cluniac, Cluny, Dom, Eggs, Maurist, Olivetan, OSB, Tironensian, Tyronensian

Benediction Ben(t)sh, Blessing, God-speed

Benefactor Angel, Backer, Barmecide, Carnegie, Donor, Maecenas, → **PATRON**, Philanthropist, Promoter

Beneficial, Beneficiary, Benefit, Benefice Advantage, → **AID**, Alms, Ameliorate, Asset, Avail, Behalf, Behoof, Behove, Bespeak, Bonus, Boon, Boot, Charity, Collature, Commendam, Commensal, Devisee, Disablement, Dole, Donee, Endorsee, Enjoy, Enure, FIS, For, Fringe, Grantee, Housing, Incapacity, Incumbent, Inheritor, Injury, Interest, Inure, Invalidity, Legal aid, Living, Manna, Maternity, Ménage, Mileage, Neckverse, Pay, Perk, Perquisite, Plenarty, Plus, Portioner, Postulate, Prebend, Profit, Sake, Salutary, Sanative, Sickness, Sinecure, Spin-off, Stipend, Supplementary, Symbiotic, Trickle down, UB40, Unemployment, Use, Usufruct, Va(u)ntage, Wholesome, Wonderful, Workfare

Benevolence, Benevolent Charitable, Clement, Dobbie, Dobby, Goodwill, Humanitarian, Kind, Liberal, Nis(se), Pecksniffian, Philanthropy, Pickwickian, Sprite

Bengali Oriya

Benighted Ignorant

Benign Affable, Altruistic, Gracious, Innocuous, Kindly, Trinal

Benin DY

Benito Duce, Mussolini

Benjamin Franklin

Bennett Alan, Phil

Bent Akimbo, Bowed, Brae, Coudé, Courb, Crooked, Curb, Determined, Dorsiflex, Falcate, Fiorin, Flair, Geniculate, Habit, Heath, Inclination, Ingenium, Intent, Inverted, Leant, Out, Peccant, Penchant, Ply, Predisposition, Reclinate, Redtop, Round-shouldered, Scoliotic, Stooped, Swayed, Talent, Taste, Twisted

▷ **Bent** *may indicate* an anagram

Bent grass Fiorin, Redtop

Bentham Utilitarian

Benzine Kinone, Phene, Toluene, Toluol

Bequeath, Bequest Bestow, Chantr(e)y, Demise, Endow, Heirloom, → **LEAVE**, Legacy, Mortification, Pass down, Pittance, Testament, Transmit, Will

Berate(d) Censure, Chastise, Chide, Jaw, Reproach, Scold, Shent, Slate, Vilify

Berber Almoravide, Kabyle, Moor, Rif(i), Riff, Shluh, Tuareg

Bereave(d), Bereavement Deprive, Loss, Mourning, Orb, Sorrow, Strip, Widow

Beret Green

Berg Alban, Floe, Kopje

Berk Clot

Bermuda Shorts

Bernard Levin, Shaw

Bernini Baroque

Berry Acai, Allspice, Bacca, Blackcurrant, Cubeb, Fruit, Goosegog, Haw, Konini, Miracle, Mistletoe, Pepo, Peppercorn, Persian, Pigeon, Pimento, Poke, Pottage, Raccoon, Rhein, Rhine, Sal(l)al, Salmonberry, Slae, Sloe, Sop, Tomatillo

Berserk Amok, Ape-shit, Baresark, Frenzy, Gungho, Rage

Berth Anchorage, Bunk, Cabin, Couchette, Dock, Moor, Seat, Space

Beryl Aquamarine, Emerald, Heliodor, Morganite, Silica

Beryllium Be

Beseech Beg, Crave, Entreat, Implore, Invoke, Obsecrate

Beset Amidst, Assail, Assiege, Badger, Bego, Embattled, Environ, Harry, Obsess, Perplex, Scabrid, Siege

Beside(s) Adjacent, Alone, And, At, Au reste, By, Else, Forby(e), Further(more), Moreover, Next, On, To, Withal, Yet

Besiege(d) Beset, Best(ed), Blockade, Gherao, Girt, Invest, Obsess, Plague, Poliorcetic, Surround

▷ **Besiege** *may indicate* one word around another

Besmirch(ed) Bloody, Bludie, Smear, Soil, Spoil, Sully

Besom Cow, Kow

Besot(ted) Dotard, Infatuate, Intoxicate, Lovesick, Stupefy

Bespangle Adorn, Gem

Bespeak, Bespoken Address, Bee, Beta, Engage, Hint

Best A1, Ace, All-time, Aristocrat, Beat, Bonzer, Cap, Cat's whiskers, Choice, Conquer, Cream, Creme, Damnedest, Deluxe, Elite, Eximious, Finest, First, Flagship, Flower, Foremost, Greatest, Highlight, Ideal, Nicest, Optima, Outdo, Outwit, Overcome, Peak, Peerless, Pick, Pièce de résistance, Pink, Plum, Purler, Quintessence, Ream, Sunday, Super, Supreme, The, The tops, Tiptop, Top, Topper, Transcend, Vanquish, Wale

Bestiality Zoophalia

Bestiary Physiologus

Best man Paranymph

Bestow(al) Accord, Bequeath, Confer, Donate, Endow, → **GIVE**, Grant, Impart, Investiture, Present

Bestride Cross

Bet(ting), Betting System A cheval, Ante, Antepost, Back, Banco, Banker, Chance, Daily double, Double, Each way, Flutter, Gaff, Gamble, Go, Hedge, Impone, Lay, Long shot, Martingale, Mise, Note, Pari-mutuel, Parlay, Perfecta, Pip, Place, Pot, Punt, Quadrella, Quinella, Ring, Risk, Roll up, Roulette, Saver, Set, Spec, Sport, Spread, Stake, Superfecta, Tattersalls, Tatts, Totalisator, Totalise, Tote, Treble, Treble chance, Triella, Trifecta, → **WAGER**, Win, Yankee

Betel Catechu, Paan, Pan, Pawn, Siri(h)

Betimes Anon, Early, Soon

Betise Solecism

Betray(al), Betrayer Abandon, Abuse, Belewe, Bewray, Cornuto, Desert, Disclose, Divulge, Dob, Dobbin, Double-cross, Gethsemane, Giveaway, Grass, Judas, Proditor, Renegade, Renege, Rumble, Sell, Sellout, Shop, Sing, Sinon, Split on, Stab, Telltale, Traditor, Traitor, Treachery, Treason, Turncoat

Betroth(ed), Betrothal Affiance, Affy, Assure, Engage, Ensure, Espouse, Fiancé(e), Handfasting, Pledge, Promise, Sponsalia, Subarr(h)ation

Better Abler, Amend, Apter, Bigger, Buck, Cap, Comparative, Convalescent, Fairer, Finer, Gambler, Gamester, Imponent, Improve, Meliorate, Mend, Mitigate, Outdo, Outpeer, Outpoint, Outshine, Outsmart, Outstrip, Outwit, Piker, Preponderate, Punter, Race-goer, Reform, Score off, Superior, Surpass, Throw, Top, Turfite, Work, Worst

Between Amid, Bet, Betwixt, Inter, Interjacent, Linking, Mesne, Twixt

Bevel Angle, Cant, Oblique, Slope, Splay

Beverage Ale, Cocoa, Coffee, Cordial, Cup, → **DRINK**, Hydromel, Nectar, Tea

Bevy Flock, Group, Herd, Host

Beware Cave, Fore, Heed, Look out, Mind, Mistrust, Pas op, Tut

Bewilder(ed), Bewildering, Bewilderment Amaze, At sea, Baffle, Buffalo, Confuse, Consternation, Daze, Distract, Flummox, Mate, Maze, Mind-boggling, Mystify, Obfuscate, Perplex, Stun, Taivert, Tutulbay, Wander, Will, Wull

Bewitch(ed), Bewitching Charm, Delight, Elf-shot, Enchant, Ensorcell, Enthral, Glam(orous), Hex, Hoodoo, Jinx, Obeah, Obiah, Strike

Beyond Above, Ayont, Besides, Farther, Outwith, Over, Past, Thule, Trans, Ulterior, Ultra

Bezique Royal marriage

Bias(ed) Angle, Aslant, Bent, Chauvinism, Colour, Discriminatory, Forward, Grid,

Imbalance, Loaded, One-sided, Partial, Parti pris, Partisan, Penchant, Preconception, Predilection, → **PREJUDICE**, Prepossess, Set, Sexism, Skew, Slant, Slope, Spin, Tendency, Unjust, Warp

Bib, Bibulous Apron, Beery, Feeder, Pout, Tope, Tucker

Bibelot Objet d'art

Bible, Biblical Adulterous, Alcoran, Alkoran, Antilegomena, Apocrypha, ASV, Authority, AV, Avesta, Bamberg, Book, Breeches, Bug, Coverdale, Cranmer, Cromwell, Douai, Douay, Family, Ferrara, Fool, Forgotten sins, Gemara, Geneva, Gideon, Good book, Goose, Gospel, Gutenberg, Haggada, Hagiographa, Helachah, Heptateuch, Hermeneutic, Hexapla, Hexateuch, Holy, Idle, Isagogic, Itala, Italic, King James (version), Leda, Matthew Parker, Mazarin(e), Midrash, Missal, Murderer, New English, NT, Omasum, Ostrog, OT, Pentateuch, Peshito, Peshitta, Peshitto, Polyglot, Psalter, Revised Version, RSV, RV, Scriptures, Septuagint, Stomach, Talmud, Tanach, Tantra, Targum, Taverner, Taverners, Text, Thirty-six-line, Treacle, Tyndale, Unrighteous, Vinegar, Vulgate, Whig, Wicked, Wife-hater, Wyclif(fe), Zurich

Biblical scholar Rechabite, USPG, Wycliffe

Bibliophagist, Bibliophile Bookworm

Bicarb Saleratus

Bicker Argue, Bowl, Brawl, Coggie, Dispute, Tiff, Wrangle

Bicycle, Bike(r) All-terrain, Bambi, Bee, Bone-shaker, Chopper, Coaster, Crog(gy), Dandy-horse, Dirt, Draisene, Draisine, Exercise, Fixed-wheel, Hell's angels, Hobby, Hobbyhorse, Kangaroo, Mixte, Moped, Mount, Mountain, Multicycle, Ordinary, Pedal, Penny-farthing, Quad, Raleigh®, Recumbent, Roadster, Rocker, Safety, Scooter, Ski-bob, Solo, Spin, Stationary, Tandem, Trail, Tree, UCI, Velocipede

Bid(der), Bidding (system) Abundance, Acol, Apply, Blackwood, Call, Canape, Command, Contract, Cue, Declare, Double, Forcing, Gone, Hostile, INT, Invite, Jump, Misère, Nod, NT, → **OFFER**, Order, Pass, → **PRE-EMPT(IVE)**, Proposal, Psychic, Puffer, Redouble, Rescue, Shut-out, Summon, Take-out, Take-over, Tell, Tender, Vied, White bonnet

Biddy Crone, Gammer, Hen

Biennial Trieteric

Bier Hearse, Litter

Big Altruistic, Beamy, Bulky, Bumper, Burly, Cob, Enormous, Fat, Ginormous, Gross, → **LARGE**, Loud, Mansize, Massive, Mighty, Obese, Roomy, Skookum, Slockdoliger, Slockdologer, Soc(k)dologer, Sogdolager, Sogdoliger, Stonker, Strapping, Substantial, Swopper, Thumping, Tidy, Vast, Whacker, Whopper

Bigamy, Bigamist, Bigamous Bluebeard, Diandrous

Bighead Besserwisser, Ego

Bight Canterbury, Great Australian, Heligoland, Karamea, South Taranaki

Bigot(ed) Chauvinist, Dogmatist, Fanatic, Hide-bound, Intolerant, Narrow-minded, Racialist, Racist, Sexist, Wowser, Zealot

Bigshot, Bigwig Cheese, Law lord, Nib, Nob, Oner, Oneyer, Oneyre, Swell, Titan, Toff, → **VIP**

Bijou Doll-like

▶ **Bike** *see* **BICYCLE**

Bikini Atoll, Tanga

Bile, Bilious(ness) Cholaemia, Choler, Gall, Icteric, Melancholy, Scholaemia, Venom, Yellow

Bilge Leak, Pump, Rhubarb, Rot, Waste

Bilingual Diglot

Bilk Default

Bill(ed), Billy Ac(c), Accommodation, Accompt, Account, Act, Ad, Addition, Allonge, Appropriation, Barnacle, Beak, Becke, Budd, Buffalo, Can, Caress, Carte, Charge, Chit(ty), Cody, Coo, Coronoid, Cross(-bencher), Demand, Dixy, Docket, Double, Due,

Egg-tooth, Exactment, Fee, Fin, Finance, Foreign, Gates, Goat, Hybrid, Inland, Invoice, Kaiser, → LAW, Lawin(g), Legislation, Liam, Liar, Line-up, List, Measure, Menu, Nail, Neb, Ness, Nib, → NOTE, Notice, Paper, Petition, Platypus, Pork barrel, Portland, Poster, Private, Programme, Pruning, Public, Puffing, Reckoning, Reform, Remanet, Rhamphotheca, Rostral, Rostrum, Score, Short, Shot, Show, Sickle, Silly, Sparth(e), Sperthe, Spoon, Sticker, Tab, Tenner, Tomium, Trade, Treasury, True, Twin, Victualling, Watch, Willy

Billet Berth, Casern, Cess, Chit, Coupon, Note, Quarter

Billet doux Capon, Valentine

Billiards, Billiards player, Billiards stroke Bar, Cannon-game, Cueist, Jenny, Lagging, Long jenny, Massé, Pills, Pocket, Pool, Potter, Pyramids, Short jenny, Snooker, String, Whitechapel

Billion Gillion, Milliard, Tera

Bill of sale Bs

Billow Roil, Roller, Rule, Surge, Swell, Wave

▶ **Billy** *see* BILL(ED)

Bimbo Twinkle

Bin Bing, Box, Chilly, Container, Crib, Dump, Hell, Litter, Loony, Receptacle, Sin, Snake-pit, Stall, Throw away, Wagger-pagger, Wheelie, Wheely

Binary ASCII, Contact, Semidetached

Bind(er), Binding Adherent, Adhesive, Akedah, Alligate, Apprentice, Astrict, Astringent, Bale, Bandage, Bandeau, Bandster, Bias, Bibliopegist, Boyer, Brail, Burst, Calf, Cement, Cerlox®, Chain, Cinch, Circuit, Clamp, Colligate, Complain, Cord, Cummerbund, Dam, Deligation, De Vigneaud, Drag, Edge, Embale, Enchain, Engage, Enslave, Enwind, → FASTEN, Fetter, Final, Galloon, Gird, Girdle, Grolier, Half-leather, Haworth, Hay-wire, Hold, Hole, Hopkins, Incumbent, Indenture, Iron, Keckle, Krebs, Lash(er), Law-calf, Leash, Ligament, Ligature, Mail, Marl, Martin, Meyerhof, Morocco, Muslin, Obi, Obligate, Oblige, Oop, Organdie, Oup, Parpen, Paste grain, Perfect, Pinion, Porter, Raffia, Red Tape, Restrict, Ring, → ROPE, Roxburghe, Seize, Sheaf, Spiral, Strap, Stringent, Stygian, Swathe, Syndesis, Tape, Tether, Thirl, Thong, Three-quarter, Tie, Tree-calf, Truss, Twine, Unsewn, Valid, Whip, Withe, Yapp, Yerk, Yoke

Bindweed Bearbine, Convolvulus, With(y)wind

Bing Crosby, Go, Heap

Binge, Binging Bat, Beano, Bend(er), Blind, Carouse, Dipsomania, → DRINK, Drinking-bout, Engorge, Gorge, Party, Pig out, Riot, Soak, Souse, Splore, Spree, Toot, Tout

Bingo Beano, Housey-housey, Keno, Lotto, Tombola

Binocular(s) Glasses, Jumelle, OO, Stereoscope

Biochemical, Biochemist(ry) Ames, Boyer, Chain, Dam, De Vigneaud, DNA, Haworth, Hopkins, Krebs, Martin, Meyerhof, Porter, Proteomics

Biographer, Biography Boswell, CV, Hagiography, History, Life, Memoir, Plutarch, Potted, Prosopography, Suetonius, Vita

Biology, Biologist Algology, Berg, Bordet, Carrel, Cladistics, Cohen, Dawkins, Delbruck, Genetics, Haller, Kendrew, Kinsey, Mendel, Molecular, Morphology, Phenetics, Photodynamics, Shatten, Somatology, Stoechiology, Stoich(e)iology, Taxonomy, Teratology, Transgenics, Weismann

Bioscope Kinema

Biped Man, Yahoo

Birch Betula, Birk, Cane, Cow, Flog, Hazel, Kow, Larch, Larrup, Reis, Rice, Rod, Silver, Swish, Twig, Weeping, Whip, White, Withe

Bird(s) Al(l)erion, Altricial, Aves, Avian, Bertram, Brood, Damsel, Doll, Early, Flier, Fowl, Gal, → GIRL, Grip, Hen, Jail, Layer, Left, Limicoline, Nestling, Ornis, Ornithology, Pecker, Pen, Perching, Poultry, Praecoces, Prison, Quod, Raptor, Rare, Roaster, Sentence, Sis, Skirt, Time, Visitant, Warbler

BIRDS

2 letters:
Ka
Oi

3 letters:
Ani
Auk
Boo
Cob
Emu
Fum
Jay
Kae
Kea
Mag
Maw
Mew
Moa
Nun
Owl
Pea
Pie
Ree
Roc
Ruc
Tit
Tui

4 letters:
Barb
Chat
Cirl
Cobb
Cock
Coly
Coot
Crax
Crow
Dodo
Dove
→ DUCK
Emeu
Erne
Eyas
Fung
Gled
Gnow
Guan
Guga
Gull
Hawk
Hern

Huia
Huma
Ibis
Iynx
Jynx
Kagu
Kaka
Kite
Kiwi
Knot
Koel
Kora
Lark
Loom
Loon
Lory
Mina
Monk
Myna
Nene
Otis
Pavo
Pawn
Pern
Piet
Pink
Pown
Pyot
Rail
Rhea
Roch
Rook
Ruff
Ruru
Rype
Shag
Skua
Smee
Sora
Swan
Taha
Tara
Teal
Tern
Tick
Tody
Tuli
Weka
Wren
Xema
Yale
Yite

5 letters:
Agami
Ardea
Ariel
Bennu
Booby
Bosun
Buteo
Cahow
Capon
Colin
Colly
Crake
Crane
Diver
Eagle
Egret
Finch
Fleet
Galah
Glede
Goose
Goura
Grebe
Heron
Hobby
Homer
Isaac
Junco
Kawau
Kight
Liver
Lowan
Macaw
Madge
Manch
Mavis
Merle
Mimus
Mohua
Monal
Murre
Mynah
Nandu
Nelly
Noddy
Ousel
Ox-eye
Peggy
Pekan
Pewit
Picus

Pilot
Piper
Pipit
Pitta
Poaka
Poker
Potoo
Prion
Quail
Quest
Quist
Raven
Reeve
Robin
Rotch
Ryper
Saker
Satin
Scape
Scart
Scaup
Scops
Scray
Scrub
Serin
Shama
Sitta
Skart
Snipe
Solan
Soree
Spink
Sprug
Squab
Stare
Stilt
Stint
Stork
Swift
Sylph
Terek
Tewit
Topaz
Twite
Umber
Umbre
Urubu
Veery
Vireo
Wader
Whaup
Widow

Wonga
Yaffa

6 letters:
Aquila
Avocet
Avoset
Bantam
Barbet
Bishop
Bittor
Bittur
Bonxie
Boubou
Brolga
Bulbul
Canary
Chough
Chukar
Condor
Corbie
Coucal
Cuckoo
Curlew
Cushat
Darter
Dikkop
Dipper
Drongo
Duiker
Dunlin
Duyker
Elanet
Evejar
Falcon
Fulmar
Gambet
Gander
Gannet
Garuda
Gentle
Gentoo
Go-away
Godwit
Gooney
Goslet
Grakle
Grouse
Hagden
Hagdon
Haglet
Hermit
Hoopoe
Houdan

Jabiru
Jacana
Jaeger
Jubjub
Kakapo
Kotare
Kotuku
Lanner
Leipoa
Linnet
Lintie
Loerie
Loriot
Lourie
Lungie
Magpie
Martin
Matata
Menura
Merlin
Merops
Missel
Mistle
Monaul
Mopoke
Mossie
Motmot
Musket
Mutton
Nandoo
Nhandu
Oriole
Oscine
Osprey
Oxbird
Parrot
Parson
Pavone
Peahen
Peeper
Peewee
Peewit
Pernis
Petrel
Phoebe
Pigeon
Piopio
Plover
Pouter
Progne
Puffin
Pukeko
Pullet
Queest

Quelea
Quoist
Redcap
Redleg
Reeler
Roller
Rotche
Scamel
Scarth
Scaury
Scoter
Scraye
Sea-cob
Sea-mew
Seapie
Shrike
Simara
Simorg
Simurg
Siskin
Skarth
Smeath
Soland
Sorage
Strich
Sultan
Sylvia
Tailor
Takahe
Tarcel
Tassel
Tewhit
Thrush
Tom-tit
Toucan
Towhee
Trogon
Turaco
Turbit
Turkey
Tyrant
Tystie
Verdin
Walker
Waxeye
Weaver
Whidah
Whydah
Willet
Woosel
Yaffle
Ynambu
Yucker
Zoozoo

7 letters:
Amokura
Anhinga
Antbird
Apteryx
Axebird
Babbler
Bécasse
Bee-kite
Bittern
Bittour
Bluecap
Blue-eye
Blue jay
Bluetit
Boobook
Bullbat
Bunting
Buphaga
Bush-tit
Bustard
Buzzard
Cacique
Cariama
Cheeper
Chewink
Chicken
Coal-tit
Cole-tit
Colibri
Corella
Cotinga
Courlan
Courser
Cow-bird
Creeper
Crombec
Cropper
Diamond
Dinorus
Dottrel
Dovekie
Dunnock
Emu-wren
Fantail
Fern-owl
Figbird
Finfoot
Flicker
Frigate
Gleerie
Gobbler
Goburra
Gorcrow

Goshawk
Grackle
Grallae
Grey jay
Hacklet
Hadedah
Hagbolt
Hagdown
Halcyon
Harrier
Hemipod
Hoatzin
Horn owl
Humming
Ice-bird
Jacamar
Jackdaw
Kahawai
Kamichi
Kestrel
Killdee
Kinglet
Koekoea
Lapwing
Leghorn
Limpkin
Manakin
Marabou
Martlet
Mesites
Minivet
Mudlark
Oilbird
Ortolan
Oscines
Ostrich
Oven-tit
Pandion
Peacock
Peafowl
Pelican
Penguin
Phoenix
Pickmaw
Piculet
Pinnock
Pintado
Pintail
Pochard
Pockard
Poe-bird
Poussin
Poy-bird
Quetzal

Rainbow
Rasores
Ratitae
Redpoll
Redwing
Regulus
Rooster
Rosella
Rotchie
Ruddock
Sakeret
Sawbill
Scooper
Scourie
Seaduck
Seagull
Sea-lark
Sea-mell
Seriema
Simurgh
Sirgang
Sitella
Skimmer
Skylark
Snow-cap
Spadger
Sparrow
Squacco
Staniel
Stinker
Sturnus
Sunbird
Swallow
Tanager
Tanagra
Tarrock
Tattler
Teacher
Teuchat
Tiercel
Tinamou
Titanis
Titlark
Titling
Tokahea
Totanus
Touraco
Tumbler
Tweeter
Vulture
Vulturn
Wagtail
Waxbill
Waxwing

Whooper
Widgeon
Wimbrel
Witwall
Woosell
Wren-tit
Wrybill
Wryneck
Yang-win

8 letters:
Aasvogel
Accentor
Adjutant
Aigrette
Alcatras
Altrices
Amadavat
Aquiline
Araponga
Arapunga
Arenaria
Avadavat
Barnacle
Bee-eater
Bellbird
Blackcap
Bluebird
Blue-wing
Boatbill
Boattail
Bobolink
Bob-white
Buln-buln
Caracara
Cardinal
Cargoose
Cheewink
Chirn-owl
Cockatoo
Cockerel
Coquette
Curassow
Dabchick
Didapper
Dip-chick
Dobchick
Dotterel
Estridge
Fauvette
Fernbird
Fish-hawk
Flamingo
Gambetta

Gang-gang
Garefowl
Garganey
Gnatwren
Greenlet
Grosbeak
Guacharo
Hackbolt
Hangbird
Hangnest
Hawfinch
Hazelhen
Heath-hen
Hemipode
Hernshaw
Hickwall
Hoactzin
Hornbill
Killdeer
Kingbird
Kiskadee
Landrail
Lanneret
Laverock
Longspur
Lorikeet
Lyrebird
Macaroni
Magotpie
Man-of-war
Marabout
Marsh-tit
Megapode
Mire-drum
Miromiro
Morepork
Murrelet
Nightjar
Notornis
Nuthatch
Ovenbird
Oxpecker
Paradise
Parakeet
Peesweep
Peetweet
Percolin
Petchary
Phaethon
Pheasant
Philomel
Pihoihoi
Podargus
Poorwill

Prunella
Puffbird
Quarrian
Quarrion
Rainbird
Rallidae
Redshank
Redstart
Reedling
Reed-wren
Rice-bird
Ringtail
Riroriro
Rocketer
Rock-lark
Sandlark
Sandpeep
Scolopar
Screamer
Sea-eagle
Shake-bag
Shelduck
Shoebill
Silktail
Sittella
Skua-gull
Snowbird
Snowy owl
Stanniel
Starling
Struthio
Surfbird
Swiftlet
Tantalus
Tapacolo
Tapaculo
Teru-tero
Thrasher
Thresher
Throstle
Tickbird
Ticklace
Titmouse
Tom-noddy
Toucanet
Tragopan
Trembler
Troopial
Troupial
Tubenose
Umbrella
Umbrette
Waldropp
Water-hen

Wheatear
Whimbrel
Whinchat
Whipbird
Whitecap
White-eye
Wildfowl
Wirebird
Woodchat
Woodcock
Woodlark
Woodwale
Wood wren
Xanthura
Yoldring
Zopilote

9 letters:

Accipiter
Aepyornis
Albatross
Aylesbury
Bald Eagle
Baldicoot
Baltimore
Beccaccia
Beccafico
Beefeater
Bergander
Blackbird
Blackhead
Blackpoll
Blood bird
Bower-bird
Brambling
Broadbill
Bullfinch
Campanero
Cassowary
Chaffinch
Chatterer
Chickadee
Coachwhip
Cockatiel
Cormorant
Corncrake
Crocodile
Cross-bill
Currawong
Dove prion
Dowitcher
Eider duck
Estreldid
Fieldfare

Fig-pecker
Fire-crest
Fledgling
Francolin
Friarbird
Frogmouth
Gallinule
Gerfalcon
Gier-eagle
Goldcrest
Goldfinch
Goosander
Grassquit
Grenadier
Guillemot
Hammerkop
Happy Jack
Helldiver
Heronshaw
Hornywink
Icteridae
Impundulu
Jack-snipe
Kittiwake
Lintwhite
Little auk
Little owl
Mallemuck
Merganser
Mistletoe
Mollymawk
Mousebird
Night-hawk
Nutjobber
Nutpecker
Olive-back
Organ-bird
Ossifraga
Ossifrage
Paddy bird
Pardalote
Partridge
Peaseweep
Peregrine
Phalarope
Pictarnie
Pine finch
Porphyrio
Ptarmigan
Razorbill
Redbreast
Red siskin
Riflebird
Rosy-finch

Sabrewing
Salangane
Sandpiper
Sapsucker
Satinbird
Scansores
Sea-turtle
Secretary
Sedge-wren
Seedeater
Sheldrake
Shoveller
Silver eye
Skunk-bird
Solitaire
Sooty tern
Spoonbill
Standgale
Stonechat
Stormbird
Storm-cock
Sugarbird
Swart-back
Sword-bill
Talegalla
Thickhead
Thick-knee
Thornbill
Trochilus
Trumpeter
Turnstone
Volucrine
Water cock
Water-rail
Willowtit
Wind-hover
Woodshock
Woodspite
Xanthoura

10 letters:

Aberdevine
Arctic tern
Bananaquit
Bearded tit
Bluebreast
Bluethroat
Brain-fever
Bubbly-jock
Budgerigar
Butter-bump
Cape pigeon
Chiff-chaff
Crested tit

Demoiselle
Dickcissel
Didunculus
Dive-dapper
Dollarbird
Dung-hunter
Ember-goose
Eyas-musket
Fallow-chat
Fly-catcher
Four o'clock
Fringillid
Goatsucker
Gobemouche
Grassfinch
Greenfinch
Greenshank
Guinea fowl
Hen-harrier
Herald-duck
Honey-eater
Honey guide
Kingfisher
Kookaburra
Locust-bird
Mallee fowl
Marsh-robin
Meadowlark
Night-churr
Night heron
Noisy miner
Nutcracker
Peckerwood
Pettichaps
Pettychaps
Pick-cheese
Pratincole
Quaker-bird
Racket-tail
Rafter-bird
Rain-plover
Ramphastos
Regent-bird
Rhinoceros
Roadrunner
Ruby-throat
Saddleback
Saddlebill
Sanderling
Sandgrouse
Sea swallow
Shearwater
Sheathbill
Sicklebill

Silverbill
Silver gull
Snowy egret
Spatchcock
Stone-snipe
Sun bittern
Tanagridae
Tropicbird
Turtledove
Wattlebird
Weasel coot
Weaver bird
Whisky-jack
Whisky-john
Wonga-wonga
Woodpecker
Woodpigeon
Wood shrike
Wood thrush
Yaffingale
Yellowbird
Yellowhead
Yellowlegs
Yellowyite

11 letters:
Apostlebird
Bokmakierie
Bristlebird
Butcherbird
Canada goose
Cape sparrow
Cooper's hawk
Coppersmith
Fallow-finch
Fringilline
Gnatcatcher
Golden eagle
Grallatores
Happy-family
Honey-sucker
House martin
Humming-bird
Ichthyornis
Java sparrow
Leatherhead
Little grebe
Mockingbird
Moss-bluiter
Moss-cheeper
Nightingale
Pied wagtail
Plantcutter
Purple finch

Pyrrhuloxia
Reed bunting
Reed-warbler
Scissorbill
Scissortail
Snowbunting
Sparrow-hawk
Stilt-plover
Stone-curlew
Storm petrel
Stymphalian
Thunderbird
Tree-creeper
Tree-sparrow
Wall creeper
Water-thrush
Weaver-finch
Whitethroat
Wishtonwish
Woodcreeper
Woodswallow
Woodwarbler
Yellow-ammer

12 letters:
Bronze-pigeon
Collared dove
Drongo-cuckoo
Drongo-shrike
Flowerpecker
Hedge-warbler
Honey creeper
Missel-thrush
Mosquito-hawk
Peppershrike
Ring-dotterel
Sage-thrasher
Sandwich tern
Sedge-warbler
Serpent-eater
Spotted crake
Standard-wing
Stonechatter
Stormy petrel
Tangle-picker
Throstle-cock
Water-wagtail
Whippoorwill
Willy wagtail
Yellow-hammer
Yellowthroat
Yellow-yowley

13 letters:
Archaeopteryx

Babblingbrook
Bermuda petrel
Cetti's warbler
Chaparral cock
Cock-of-the-rock
Indigo bunting
Mocking thrush
Owlet nightjar
Oyster-catcher
Pintado petrel
Pipiwharauroa
Plantain-eater
Whistling duck
Willow-wagtail
Willow warbler
Wilson's petrel

14 letters:
Manx shearwater
Tawny frogmouth
Welcome swallow
Woodchat shrike

15 letters:
Baltimore oriole
Chipping sparrow
Chuck-will's widow
Montagu's harrier
Purple gallinule
Rainbow lorikeet
Rough-legged hawk

16 letters:
Loggerhead shrike
Roseate spoonbill
Tyrant flycatcher
White-fronted tern

17 letters:
Pectoral sandpiper
Spotted flycatcher

18 letters:
Paradise flycatcher
Rough-legged
  buzzard

19 letters:
White-crowned
  sparrow

20 letters:
Mother Carey's
  chickens
Rose-breasted
  grosbeak

▷ **Bird** *may indicate* a prison sentence
Bird-catcher Avicularia, Fowler, Papageno
Bird-like Hirundine, Sturnine
Bird's nest(ing) Caliology, Monotropa, Soup
Bird-watcher Augur, Twitcher
Birkenhead F.E.Smith
Birmingham Brum(magem)
Birth Burden, Congenital, Delivery, Drop, Extraction, Genesis, Geniture, Happy event,
   Jataka, Lineage, Multiple, Nativity, Natural, Origin, Parage, Parity, Parthenogenesis,
   Parturition, Virgin, Water, Whelp(ing)
Birthday Anniversary, Genethliac, Prophet's
Birthmark Blemish, Mole, Mother-spot, Naevus, Port wine stain, Stigmata, Strawberry
Birthright Heritage, Mess, Patrimony
Birthwort Aristolochia
Bis Again, Anew
Biscuit Abernethy, Amaretto, Bake, Bath-oliver, Biscotto, Bourbon, Brandysnap,
   Brown George, Butterbake, Captain's, Charcoal, Cookie, Cracker, Cracknel, Crispbread,
   Dandyfunk, Digestive, Dog, Dunderfunk, Fairing, Flapjack, Florentine, Fly cemetery,
   Fortune cookie, Four-by-two, Garibaldi, Ginger nut, Gingersnap, Hardtack, Jumbal, Kiss,
   Langue de chat, Lavash, Lebkuchen, Macaroon, Marie, Mattress, Matza(h), Matzo(h),
   Nut, Oatcake, Oliver, Osborne, Parkin, Perkin, Petit four, Petticoat tail, Pig's ear,
   Pilot, Poppadom, Poppadum, Pretzel, Puff, Ratafia, Rice, Rusk, Rye-roll, Sea, Ship's,
   Shortbread, Snap, Soda, Sweetmeal, Tack, Tan, Tararua, Tea, Teiglach, Tollhouse cookie,
   Wafer, Water, Wine, Zwieback
Bisexual AC/DC, Freemartin, Switch-hitter
Bishop(ric) Aaronic, Abba, Aberdeen, Aidan, Ambrose, Apollinaris, Bench, Berkeley, Bp,
   Cambrensis, Cantuar, Chad, Chorepiscopal, Coadjutor, Coverdale, Cranmer, Diocesan,
   Dunelm, Ebor, Ely, Eparch, Episcopate, Eusebian, Exarch, Exon, Golias, Hatto, Henson,
   Jansen, Latimer, Lord, Magpie, Man, Metropolitan, Missionary, Norvic, Odo, Ordainer,
   Patriarch, Peter, Petriburg, Piece, Polycarp, Pontiff, Prelate, Priest, Primate, Primus,
   Proudie, Ridley, Roffen, RR, St Swithin, Sarum, Sleeve, Sodor and Man, Suffragan,
   The purple, Titular, Tulchan, Weaver, Weed, Winton, Wrexham
Bismarck Otto
Bismuth Bi
Bison Bonas(s)us, Buffalo, Ox, Wisent
Bit Ate, Baud, Byte, Cantle(t), Centre, Chad, Cheesecake, Chip, Coin, Crumb, Curb, Curn,
   Dash, Degree, Drib, Excerpt, Flibbert, Fraction, Fraise, Gag, Haet, Hait, Hate, Ion, Iota,
   Jaw, Jot, Leptum, Mite, Modicum, Morsel, Mote, Mu, Nit, Ort, Ounce, Pelham, Peni,
   Penny, → **PIECE**, Pinch, Port, Rap, Rare, Ratherish, Rowel, Scintilla, Scrap, Section,
   Shaving, Shiver, Shred, Smattering, Smidgen, Smidgeon, Smidgin, Snaffle, Snatch,
   Snippet, Some, Soupcon, Spale, Speck, Splinter, Spot, Spudding, Stop, Suspicion, Tad,
   Tait, Tate, Threepenny, Trace, Unce, Vestige, What, Whit
Bite(r), Biting, Bitten Astringent, Begnaw, Canapé, Caustic, Chelicera, Chew, Cold,
   Eat, Engouled, Erose, Etch, Gnash, Gnat, Gnaw, Hickey, Hickie, Incisor, Knap, Masticate,
   Midge, Molar, Mordacious, Mordant, Morsel, Morsure, Nacho, Nibble, Nip(py), Occlude,
   Peck, Pium, Pointed, Premorse, Rabid, Sarcastic, Sharp, Shrewd, Snack, Snap, Sound,
   Spammie, Tart
Bitter(ness) Absinth, Acerb, Acid, Acrid, Acrimonious, Ale, Aloe, Angostura, Bile,
   Cassareep, Caustic, Eager, Edge, Envenomed, Ers, Fell, Gall, Heated, Jaundiced, Keen,
   Keg, Marah, Maror, Myrrh, Picamar, Pique, Rancorous, Rankle, Resentful, Sarcastic,
   Sardonic, Snell, Sore, Spleen, Tannin, Tart(aric), Venom, Verjuice, Virulent, Vitriolic,
   Wersh, Wormwood, Wry
Bittern Boomer, Bull-of the-bog, Butterbump, Heron, Mossbluiter, Sedge, Siege
Bittersweet Dulcamara, Poignant, Staff-tree

Bitumen Albertite, Asphalt, Blacktop, Elaterite, Gilsonite®, Maltha, Mineral tar, Pissasphalt, Pitch, Tar, Tarseal, Uintaite

Bivalve Clam, Cockle, Lamellibranch, Mollusc, Muscle, Mussel, Oyster, Pelecypod, Piddock, Razorshell, Scallop, Tuatua, Whelk

Bivouac Camp

Bizarre Antic, Curious, Eccentric, Exotic, Fantastic, Far-out, Freaky, Gonzo, Grotesque, Odd, Offbeat, Off-the-wall, Outlandish, Outré, Pythonesque, Queer, Strange, Surreal, Weird

▷ **Bizarre** *may indicate* an anagram

Blab Babble, Gossip, Prate, Squeal

Black(en), Blackness, Black-out Afro-American, Amadoda, Atramental, B, Ban, BB, Bess, Blae, Boong, Cape Coloured, Carbon, Char, Charcoal, Cilla, Coal, Coloured, Coon, Cypress, Darkie, Darky, Death, Debar, Denigrate, Dinge, Dwale, Ebon(y), Eclipse, Ethiop, Evil, Fuzzy-wuzzy, Geechee, Gladwellise, Graphite, Grime, Heben, Hole, Ink(y), Ivory, Japan, Jeat, Jet, Jim Crow, Kohl, Lepidomelane, Malign, Market, Melanic, Melano, Moke, Moor, Muntu, Myall, Negritude, Negro, Niello, Niger, Nigrescent, Nigritude, Obliterate, Obscure, Outage, Oxford, Piceous, Pitch, Platinum, Pongo, Prince, Pudding, Puke, Quashee, Quashie, Raven, Sable, Sambo, Scab, School, Sericon, Sheep, Slae, Sloe, Snowball, Sodium, Solvent, Sombre, Soot, Sooterkin, Soul brother, Soul sister, Spade, Spook, Starless, Stygian, Swart(y), Swarth(y), Tar, Thick-lips, Uncle Tom, Weeds

Black art Necromancy, Nigromancy

Blackball Ban, Exclude, Ostracise, Pill, Pip, Reject

Blackberry Acini, Bramble, Mooch, Mouch

Blackbird Collybird, Crow, Jackdaw, Merl(e), Ousel, Raven, Woosel

Blackcurrant Quinsy-berry

Black eye(d) Half-mourning, Keeker, Mouse, Shiner, Susan

Blackguard Leg, Nithing, Raff, Revile, Rotter, Scoundrel, Sweep

Blackhead Comedo

Black hole Collapsar

Blackjack Billie, Billy, Cosh, Flag, Sphalerite, Tankard, Truncheon, Vingt(-et)-un

Blackleg Fink, Rat, Scab, Snob

Black-letter Gothic

Black magic Goety

Blackmail(er) Bleed, Chantage, Chout, Exact, Extort, Greenmail, Honey-trap, Ransom, Shakedown, Strike, Vampire

Blackout ARP, Eclipse, Faint, Shallow water, Swoon, Syncope

Black Sea Pontic, Pontus Euxinus

Black sheep Neer-do-well, Reprobate

Blacksmith Brontes, Burn-the-wind, Farrier, Forger, Harmonious, Plater, Shoer, Vulcan

Blackthorn Sloe

Bladder(wort) Air, Balloon, Blister, Cholecyst, Cyst, Gall, Hydatid, Isinglass, Popweed, Sac, Sound, Swim, Urinary, Utricle, Varec(h), Vesica, Vesicle

Blade(s) Acrospire, Andrew Ferrara, Bilbo, Brand, Brown Bill, Cleaver, Co(u)lter, Cutlass, Dandy, Espada, Faible, Foible, Forte, Gleave, Gouge, Guillotine, Hydrofoil, Knife, Kris, Lance, Lawnmower, Leaf, Man, Mouldboard, Oar, Omoplate, Paddle, Palmetto, Peel, Propeller, Rachilla, Rapier, Razor, Rip, Rotor, Scalpel, Scimitar, Scull, Scythe, Skate, Spade-, Spatula, Spatule, Spear, Spoon, Stiletto, Stock, Strigil, Sweep, → **SWORD**, Symitar, Toledo, Turbine, Vane, Vorpal, Wash, Web

Blair Eric, Lionel, Orwell, Tony

Blame(worthy) Accuse, Censure, Condemn, Confound, Culpable, Decry, Dirdam, Dirdum, Dispraise, Fault, Guilt, Incriminate, Inculpate, Odium, Rap, Reprehensible, Reproach, Reprove, Stick, Thank, Twit, Wight, Wite, Wyte

Blameless Innocent, Irreproachable, Lily-white, Unimpeachable

Blanch Bleach, Etiolate, Scaud, Whiten

Blancmange Carrageen, Flummery, Mould, Shape, Timbale

Bland Anodyne, Glop, Insipid, Mild, Neutral, Pigling, Sleek, Smooth, Spammy, Suave, Tame, Tasteless, Unctuous

Blandish(ment) Agremens, Agrement, Cajole, → COAX, Flatter, Treacle, Wheedle

Blank Burr, Cartridge, Deadpan, Empty, Erase, Flan, Ignore, Lacuna, Mistigris, Planchet, Shot, Space, Tabula rasa, → VACANT

Blanket Afghan, All-over, Bluey, Chilkat, Counterpane, Cover, Electric, Fire, General, Hudson's Bay, Kaross, Mackinaw, Manta, Obscure, Overall, Overlay, Poncho, Quilt, Rug, Saddle, Sarape, Security, Serape, Shabrack, Smog, Space, Stroud, Umbrella, Wagga, Wet, Whittle

Blare Horn, Trumpet

Blarney Cajolery, Flattery, Nonsense, Sawder, Sleeveen, Taffy

Blasé Bored, Worldly

Blaspheme, Blasphemous Abuse, → CURSE, Defame, Profanity, Revile

Blast(ed), Blasting Blight, Blore, Blow, Bombard, Dang, Darn, Dee, Drat, Dynamite, Explode, Fanfare, Flaming, Flurry, Fo(e)hn, Gale, Grit, Gust, Hell, Noser, Oath, Pan, Parp, Planet-struck, Pryse, Rats, Ruddy, Scarth, Scath(e), Sere, Shot, Sideration, Skarth, Stormer, Tantara, Toot, Tout, Tromp(e), Trump(et), Volley

Blatant Flagrant, Hard-core, Noticeable, Open, Strident, Unashamed, Vulgar

Blather Baloney, Gabble, Gibber

Blaze(r), Blazing Afire, Beacon, Bonfire, Burn, Cannel, Conflagration, Firestorm, → FLAME, Flare, Glare, Jacket, Low(e), Lunt, Palatinate, Race, Ratch, Sati, Star, Sun, Tead(e)

Bleach(er) Agene, Blanch, Chemic, Chloride, Decolorate, Etiolate, Fade, Frost, Janola®, Keir, Kier, Peroxide, Whiten, Whitster

Bleak Ablet, Bare, Barren, Blay, Bley, Cheerless, Dour, Dreary, Dreich, Gaunt, Midwinter, Raw, Soulless, Wintry

Bleary Blurred, Smudged

Bleat Baa, Blat, Bluster, Maa

Bleed(er), Bleeding Breakthrough, Cup, Diapedesis, Ecchymosis, Emulge, Epistaxis, Extort, Extravasate, Fleam, Haemorrhage, Leech, Menorrhagia, Menorrh(o)ea, Metrorrhagia, Milk, Purpura, Rhinorrhagia, Root-pressure

Bleep Earcon, Pager

Blefuscudian Big-endian, Little-endian

Blemish Birthmark, Blot, Blotch, Blur, Botch, Defect, Eyesore, Flaw, Lepra, Mackle, Mark, Milium, Mote, Naevus, Scar, Smirch, Spot, Stain, Sully, Taint, Tash, Verruca, Vice, Wart, Wen

Blench Flinch, Recoil, Wince

Blend(ing) Amalgam, Coalesce, Commix, Contemper, Contrapuntal, Counterpoint, Electrum, Fit, Fuse, Go, Harmonize, Hydrate, Interfuse, Interlace, Intermix, Liquidise, Meld, Melt, → MERGE, Mingle, Mix, Osmose, Portmanteau, Scumble, Sfumato, Synalepha

▷ **Blend** *may indicate* an anagram

Blenny Eel-pout, Gunnel, Shanny

Bless(ing), Blessed(ness) Amen, Anoint, Approval, Asset, Beatitude, Benedicite, Benediction, Benison, Benitier, Bensh, Bismillah, Boon, Brachah, Brocho, Charmed, Consecrate, Cup, Damosel, Darshan, Elysium, Ethereal, Felicity, Gesundheit, Godsend, Grace, Gwyneth, Holy (dam), Kiddush, Luck, Macarise, Mercy, Mixed, Sain, Saint, Sanctify, Sanctity, Sheva Brachoth, Sheva Brochos, Sneeze, Toronto, Urbi et orbi, Xenium

Bless me Lawk(s)

Blight Afflict, Ague, American, Apple, Bespot, Blast, Destroy, Early, Eyesore, Fire, Late, Planning, Potato, Rot, → RUIN, Rust, Sandy, Shadow, Viticide, Waldersterben, Wither

Blighter Cuss, Perisher, Varment, Varmint

Blimey Coo, Cor, Crimini, O'Riley, Strewth

Blimp Airship, Colonel

Blind(ness), Blind spot Amaurosis, Amblyopia, Artifice, Austrian, Bedazzle, Beesome, Binge, Bisson, Blend, Blotto, Camouflage, Carousal, Cecity, Chi(c)k, Cog, Concealed, Dazzle, Drop serene, Drunk, Eyeless, Feint, Festoon, Flash, Gravel, Hemeralopia, Homer, Hood, Jalousie, Legless, Meropia, Mole, Night, Nyctalopia, Onchocerciasis, Persian, Persiennes, Pew, Pickled, Prestriction, Rash, River, Roller, Roman, Scotoma, Seel, Shade, Shutter, Sightless, Snow, Stimie, Stimy, Stymie, Sun, Swear, Teichopsia, Typhlology, Venetian, Visually challenged, Window, Word, Yblent

Blindfish Amblyopsis

Blindfold Bandage, Hoodwink, Muffle, Seal, Wimple

Blindworm Anguis

Bling Tsatske

Blink, Blinker(s), Blinkered, Blinking Bat, Blepharism, Blinders, Bluff, Broken, Eye-flap, Flash, Haw, Idiot, Insular, Nictate, Owl-eyed, Owly, Twink, Wapper, Water, Wink

Bliss(ful) Beatitude, Bouyan, Cheer, Composer, Delight, → **ECSTASY**, Eden, Elysium, Glee, Happy, Heaven, Idyll, Ignorance, Joy, Married, Millenium, Nirvana, Paradise, Rapture, Sion, Tir-na-nog, Valhalla, Walhalla, Wedded

Blister(ed), Blistering Blab, Blain, Bleb, Bubble, Bullate, Cantharidine, Cold sore, Epispastic, Fever, Herpes, Overgall, Pemphigus, Phlyct(a)ena, Scorching, Tetter, Vesicant, Vesicle, Visicate, Water

Blitz Attack, Bombard, Onslaught, Raid

Blizzard Buran, Gale, Snowstorm, Whiteout

Bloat(ed), Bloater Buckling, Gross, Puff, Strout, Swell, Tumefy, Two-eyed steak, Yarmouth

Blob Bead, Bioblast, Dollop, Drop, Globule, O, Pick, Spot, Tear

Bloc Alliance, Cabal, Cartel, Party

Block(er), Blockage, Blocked, Blocking Altar, Anvil, Ashlar, Atresia, → **BAR**, Barber's, Barricade, Barrier, Battle-axe, Brake, Breeze, Brick, Briquet(te), Building, Bung, Bunt, Capital, Cavity, Chinese, Choke, Chunk, Cinder, Cleat, Clint, Clog, Clot, Cloy, Compass, Congest, Constipated, Cut-off, Cyclopean, Cylinder, Dado, → **DAM**, Dead-eye, Debar, Defect, Delete, Dentel, Dentil, Die, Dit, Domino, Electrotint, Embolism, Emphractic, Encompass, Erratic, Euphroe, Fiddle, Fipple, Frog, Gypsum, Hack-log, Heart, High-rise, Hunk, Ice, Ileus, Impasse, Impede, Impost, Ingot, Input, Insula, Interclude, Interrupt, Investment, Ischaemia, Jam, Licence, Lifestyle, Line, Lingot, Lodgment, Log-jam, Lump, Mental, Ministroke, Mitre, Monkey, Mounting, Mutule, Nerve, Nifedipine, Nog, Notepad, Oasis®, Obstacle, → **OBSTRUCT**, Occlude, Office, Opossum, Oppilate, Pad, Page, Parry, Perched, Pile-cap, Pile-up, Pillow, Planer, Plinth, Plummer, Power, Pre-empt, Prevent, Process, Psychological, Quad, Ram, Saddle, Scotch, Seal, Sett, Siege, Snatch, Stalemate, Stap, Starting, Stenosis, Stimie, Stimy, Stone, Stonewall, Stop, Stumbling, Stymie, Sun, Swage, Tamp, Tetrapod, Thwart, Tint, Tower, Tranche, Trig, Triglyph, Truck, Uphroe, Upping-stock, Veto, Vibropac®, Wedge, Wig, Wood(cut), Wrest, Writer's, Zinco, Zugzwang

Blockbuster Epic

Blockhead Jolterhead, Mome, Nitwit, Noodle, Pig sconce, Stupid

Blockhouse Igloo

Bloke Beggar, Chap, Codger, Cove, Fellow, Gent, Man, Oik

Blond(e) Ash, Bombshell, Cendré, Fair, Flaxen, Goldilocks, Peroxide, Platinised, Platinum, Strawberry, Tallent, Tow-haired, Towhead

Blood(y), Blood-letter, Blood-letting A, Ancestry, B, Bad, Bally, Blue, Bluggy, Blut, Buck, Butchery, Claret, Clot, Cold, Cruor, Cup, Dutch pink, Ecchymosis, Ensanguine, Epigons, Factor, First, Full, → **GORE**, Haemal, Haematoma, Haemorrhage, Ichor, Internecine, Introduce, Kin, Kinship, Knut, Leech, Menses, Microcyte, New, Nut, O, Opsonin, Parentage, Penny dreadful, Persue, Phlebotomist, Pigeon's, Plasma, Platelet, Plurry, Properdin, Pup, Purple, Race, Rare, Red, Rh negative, Rh positive, Ruby, Sang,

Sangrado, Schistosoma, Serum, Show, Stroma, Thrombin, Toff, Venisection, Welter, Whole, Young

Blood disease, Blood disorder, Blood-poisoning Haematuria, Hypinosis, Isch(a)emia, Leukemia, Lipaemia, Oligaemia, Purpura, Pyaemia, Sapraemia, Septicemia, Spanaemia, Thalassemia, Thrombocytopenia, Toxaemia, Uraemia

Bloodhound Lime, Lyam, Lym, Rach(e), Ratch, Sleuth, Spartan

Bloodless Anaemic, Isch(a)emic, Wan, White

Blood money Eric

▸ **Blood-poisoning** *see* **BLOOD DISEASE**

Blood-pressure Hypertension, Hypotension, Normotensive

Bloodshot Red-eyed

Blood-sport Hunting, Shooting, Venery

Blood-sucker Anoplura, Asp, Bed bug, Dracula, Flea, Gnat, Ked, Leech, Louse, Mosquito, Parasite, Reduviid, Soucouyant, Sponger, Tick, Vampire(-bat)

Bloodthirsty Tiger

Bloom(er), Blooming Anthesis, Bally, Blossom, Blow, Blush, Boner, Bread, Cobalt, Dew, Dratted, Effloresce, Error, Film, Florence, Florescent, Flourish, Flowery, Flush, Gaffe, Glaucous, Heyday, Knickers, Loaf, Miscalculation, Nickel, Out, Peach, Pruina, Rationals, Reh, Remontant, Rosy, Ruddy, Thrive, Underwear

▹ **Bloomer** *may indicate* a flower

Blossom Blow, Burgeon, Catkin, Develop, Festoon, Flourish, Flower, Marybud, May, Orange, Pip, Springtime

Blot Atomy, Blob, Cartel, Delete, Disgrace, Dry, Eyesore, Obscure, Smear, Smudge, Southern, Splodge, Splotch

Blotch(y) Blemish, Giraffe, Monk, Mottle(d), Spot, Stain

Blotto Legless

Blouse Choli, Garibaldi, Gimp, Guimpe, Kerbaya, Middy, Pneumonia, Sailor, Shell, Shirtwaist, Smock, Tunic, Waist(er), Windjammer

Blow(er) Appel, Bang, Bash, Bat, Bellows, Biff, Billow, Blip, Bloom, Box, Brag, Breeze, Buckhorse, Buffet, Bump, Burst, Calamity, Clap, Clat, Claut, Clip, Clout, Clump, Conk, Coup, Cuff, Dad, Daud, Dawd, Dev(v)el, Dinnyhayser, Dint, Dod, Douse, Dowse, Estramacon, Etesian, Exsufflate, Facer, Fan, Fillip, Finisher, Fisticuffs, Fuse, Gale, Grampus, Gust, Hammer, Hander, Haymaker, Hit, Hook, Ictus, Impact, Insufflate, Karate, Kibosh, Knuckle sandwich, KO, Lame, Lander, Left-hander, Lick, Lounder, Muff, Muzzler, Neck-herring, Northerly, Noser, Oner, One-two, Paddywhack, Paik, Pash, Peise, Phone, Piledriver, Plague, Plug, Plump(er), Polt, Pow, Puff, Punch, Purler, Raft, Rats, Rattler, Rib-roaster, Roundhouse, Sas(s)arara, Scat, Settler, Short, Sideswipe, Side-winder, Sis(s)erary, Skiff, Skite, Skyte, Slat, Slog, Slug, Snell, Snot, Sock, Sockdolager, Sockdologer, Southwester, Spanking, Spat, Spout, Squall, Squander, Squelcher, Stripe, Stroke, Strooke, Stunning, Sufflate, Supercharger, Swash, Swat, Swinger, Telephone, Thump, Thwack, Tingler, Tootle, Triple whammy, Trump(et), Tuck, Undercut, Upper-cut, Waft, Wallop, Wap, Waste, Welt, Whammy, Whample, Whang, Whap, Wheeze, Wherret, Whiffle, Whirret, Whistle, → **WIND**, Winder, Wipe, Wuther

Blown-up Elated, Enlarged, Exploded

Blow-out Binge, Bloat, Exhale, Feast, Feed, Flat, Fulminate, Lava, Nosh-up, Snuff, Spiracle, → **SPREAD**

Blowpipe Hod, Peashooter, Sarbacane, Sumpit(an)

Blub(ber) Cry, Fat, Snotter, Sob, Speck, → **WEEP**, Whimper

Bludge Sinecure

Bludgeon Bulldoze, Bully, Club, Cosh, Cudgel, Sap

Blue(s), Bluesman Abattu, Accablé, Adult, Anil, Aqua, Aquamarine, Azure, Azurn, Beard, Berlin, Bice, Bleuâtre, Blow, Bottle, Butterfly, C, Caesious, Cafard, Cambridge, Cantab, Celeste, Cerulean, City, Clair de lune, Classic, Cobalt, Coomassie, Copenhagen, Cornflower, Country, Coventry, Cyan, Danish, Danube, Dejected, Dirty, Disconsolate,

Doldrums, → **DOWN**, Duck-egg, Eatanswill, Eggshell, Electric, Erotica, Facetiae, Firmament, Fritter, Gentian, Germander, Glaucous, Glum, Hauyne, Heliotrope, Hump, Indecent, Indigo, Indol(e), Iron, Isatin(e), Lapis lazuli, Lavender, Leadbelly, Lewd, Lionel, Low, Mazarine, Methylene, Midnight, Monastral®, Mope, Morose, Murder, Nattier, Naughty, Navy, Nile, Obscene, Ocean, Off-colour, Oxford, Peacock, Periwinkle, Perse, Petrol, Phycocyan, Porn, Powder, Prussian, Rabbi, Racy, Ribald, Riband, Right, Ripe, Robin's egg, Royal, Sad, Sapphire, Saxe, Saxon(y), Scurrilous, → **SEA**, Shocking, → **SKY-TINCTURED**, Slate, Smalt(o), Smutty, Sordid, Spirit, Splurge, Squander, Stafford, Steel, Stocking, Teal, Thenard's, Tony, Top shelf, Tory, Trist, True, Trypan, Turnbull's, Turquoise, Ultramarine, Unhappy, Urban, Verditer, Washing, Watchet, Wedgwood®, Welkin, Woad, Zaffer, Zaffre

▷ **Blue** *may indicate* an anagram

Bluebell Blawort, Blewart, Campanula, Harebell

Bluebottle Blawort, Blewart, Blowfly, Blowie, Brommer, Brummer, Cop, Cornflower, Fly, Officer, Policeman

▸ **Blue-legged** *See* **BLUESTOCKING**

Blueprint Cyanotype, Design, Draft, Drawing, Plan, Recipe

Bluestocking, Blue-legged Basbleu, Carter, Erudite, Femme savante, Hamburg(h), Mrs Montagu, Précieuse, Sheba

Bluff(ing) Blunt, Cle(e)ve, Cliff, Clift, Crag, Double, Escarpment, Fake, Flannel, Four-flush, Frank, Hal, Headland, Height, Hoodwink, Kidology, Pose, Precipice, Scarp, Steep, Trick

Blunder(er), Blundering Barry (Crocker), Betise, Bévue, Bish, Bloomer, Blooper, Boner, Boob, Break, Bull, Bumble, Bungle, Clanger, Clinker, Cock-up, Crass, Err, Fault, Faux pas, Floater, Flub, Fluff, Gaff(e), Goof, Howler, Inexactitude, Irish, Josser, Malapropism, → **MISTAKE**, Muddle, Mumpsimus, Ricket, Slip, Slip up, Solecism, Stumble, Trip

Blunt(ed), Bluntly Abrupt, Alleviate, Bald, Bate, Bayt, Brash, Brusque, Candid, Deaden, Disedge, Downright, Dull, Forthright, Frank, Hebetate, Mole, Morned, Obtund, Obtuse, Outspoken, Pointblank, Rebate, Retund, Retuse, Roundly, Snub, Straight-out, Stubby

Blur(red), Blurring, Blurry Cloud, Confuse, Daze, Fog, Fuzz, Halation, Mackle, Macule, Muzzy, Pixilation, → **SMUDGE**, Stump, Tortillon, Unfocussed

Blurb Ad, Puff

Blush(ing) Colour, Cramoisy, Crimson, Erubescent, Erythema, Incarnadine, Mantle, → **REDDEN**, Rosy, Rouge, Rubescent, Ruby, Rufescent, Rutilant

Bluster(ing), Blusterer, Blustery Arrogance, Bellow, Blore, Brag, Fanfaronade, Hector, Huff-cap, Rage, Rant, Rodomontade, Roister, Sabre-rattler, Squash, Swagger, Vapour, Windbag, Wuthering

Boar Barrow, Calydonian, Erymanthian, Hog, Pentheus, Sanglier, Sounder, Tusker, Wild

Board(s), Boarding Abat-voix, Admiralty, Aquaplane, Baffle, Banker, Barge, Bd, Beaver, Billet, Bristol, Bulletin, Catchment, Centre, Cheese, Chevron, Circuit, Collegium, Committee, Contignation, Counter, Cribbage, Dagger, Dam, Dart, Daughter, Deal, Directors, Diving, Draft, Draining, Drawing, Embark, Embus, Emery, Enter, Entrain, Expansion, Fa(s)cia, Fare, Farm out, Featheredge, Fibro, Fibrolite®, Flannelgraph, Full, Gib(raltar), Groaning, Gunwale, Gutter, Hack, Half, Half-royal, Hawk, Hoarding, Idiot, Instrument, Insulating, Ironing, Kip, Lag, Lap, Leader, Ledger, Lee, Lodge, Magnetic, Malibu, Marketing, Masonite®, Match, Message, Mill, Monkey, Mortar, Moulding, Notch, Notice, Otter, Ouija, Paddle, Palette, Pallet, Panel, Paper, Parochial, Particle, Patch, Pedal, Peg(board), Pension, Planch(ette), Plank, Plug, Ply(wood), Punch, Quango, Ribbon-strip, Roof, Running, Sandwich, Sarking, Scale, Scaleboard, School, Score, Scraper, Scratch, Screen, Sheathing, Shelf, Shifting, Shingle, Shooting, Side-table, Sign, Skim, Skirting, Sleeve, SMART®, Smoke, Snow, Sounding, Splasher, Spring, Stage, Stretcher, Strickle, Stringboard, Supervisory, Surf, Switch, → **TABLE**, Telegraph, Thatch, Theatre, Trencher, Verge, Wainscot, Wobble, Wokka, Wood chip

▷ **Board** *may refer to* chess or draughts

Boarder Interne, Pensioner, PG, Roomer
Boarding house Digs, Kip, Lodgings, Pension
Boast(er), Boastful, Boasting Bigmouth, Big-note, Blew, Blow, Blowhard, Bluster,
Bobadil, Bounce, Brag, Braggadocio, Bravado, Breeze, Bull, Cock-a-hoop, Crake,
Crow, Fanfaronade, Gas, Gascon(nade), Glory, Hot air, Jact(it)ation, Line, Loudmouth,
Ostent(atious), Prate, Rodomontade, Scaramouch, Self-glorious, Show-off, Skite,
Spread-eagle, Swagger, Swank, Tall, Thrasonic, Vainglory, Vapour, Vaunt, Yelp
Boat → SHIP, → VESSEL

BOATS

1 letter:	Jolly	Tender	Mosquito
Q	Kaiak	Torpid	Pleasure
	Kayak	Trek-ox	Skipjack
2 letters:	Motor	Wangan	Surfboat
PT	Power	Wangun	
	Pucan	Wherry	9 letters:
3 letters:	Sauce		Destroyer
Ark	Skiff	7 letters:	Lapstrake
Cat	Sloop	Coaster	Lap streak
Fly	Smack	Cruiser	Outrigger
Kit	Stake	Curragh	Oysterman
She	Swing	Drifter	Privateer
	Wager	Foyboat	Vaporetto
4 letters:	Waist	Galliot	Weekender
Bark	Whiff	Liberty	Whaleback
Cock		Lighter	Whaleboat
Cott	6 letters:	Lymphad	
Four	Advice	Pair-oar	10 letters:
Isis	Bawley	Pearler	Hydroplane
Keel	Caique	Scooter	Purse seine
Lake	Cobble	Sculler	Track-scout
Long	Codder	Shallop	Trekschuit
Pont	Cutter	Sharpie	
Proa	Dragon	Slogger	11 letters:
Scow	Flying	Sounder	Cockleshell
Tilt	Galiot	Vedette	Double scull
Trow	Galley	Vidette	Sidewheeler
Yawl	Goldie	Wanigan	
	Hooker		12 letters:
5 letters:	Launch	8 letters:	Clinker-built
Barge	Monkey	Billyboy	Fore-and-after
Canal	Narrow	Corvette	Paddle steamer
Coble	Packet	Faltboat	Sternwheeler
Eight	Pedalo	Flagship	Tangle-netter
Ferry	Puffer	Flatboat	
Funny	Pulwar	Foldboat	13 letters:
Gravy	Sailer	Gallivat	Black skipjack
Gulet	Sea Dog®	Mackinaw	Revenue cutter
Hatch	Tanker	Monohull	

Boater → HAT, Punter, Straw
Boatman Bargee, Charon, Cockswain, Coxswain, George, Gondolier, Harris, Hoveller,
Legger, Noah, Phaon, Voyageur, Waterman, Wet-bob

Boat population Tank(i)a
Boat-shaped Carina, Scaphoid
Boatswain Bosun, Serang, Smee
Bob Acres, Beck, Curtsey, Deaner, Dip, Dock, Dop, Duck, Dylan, Eton crop, Float, Hod, Hog, Jerk, Major, Maximus, Minor, Page-boy, Peal, Plain, Plumb, Plummet, Popple, Rob, Royal, S, Shingle, Skeleton, Skip, Sled(ge), Sleigh
Bobbin Quill, Reel, Shuttle, Spindle, Spool
Bobble Pompom
Bobby Bluebottle, Busy, Copper, Flatfoot, Patrolman, Peeler, Pig, → **POLICEMAN**
Bobby-dazzler Dinger, Stunner
Bock Stein
Bode Augur
Bodgie Aussie, Ted
Bodice Basque, Bolero, Bustier, Chemise, Chemisette, Choli, Corsage, Gilet, Halter, Jirkinet, Liberty, Plastron, Polonie, Polony, Spencer, Tucker, Waist, Watteau
Bodkin Eyeleteer, Needle, Poniard, Stilet(to)
Body, Bodies, Bodily Administration, Amount, Anatomic, Astral, Barr, Board, Bouk, Buik, Buke, Bulk, Cadaver, Cadre, Carcase, Carcass, Carnal, Caucas, Centrosome, Chapel, Chapter, Chassis, Chondriosome, Ciliary, Clay, Coachwork, Coccolite, Cohort, Column, Comet, Committee, Contingent, Cormus, Corpora, Corpor(e)al, Corps, Corpse, Corpus, Corse, Cytode, Detail, Earth, Elaiosome, Flesh, Food, Frame, Fuselage, Gazo(o)n, Golgi, Goner, Grey, → **GROUP**, Heavenly, Hull, Immune, Incarnate, Inclusion, Kenning, Ketone, Lewy, Lich, Lifting, Like, Lithites, Malpighian, → **MASS**, Militia, Mitochondrion, Moit, Mote, Mummy, Nacelle, Nave, Nucleole, Nucleolus, Olivary, Orb, Order, Pack, Personal, Phalanx, Pineal, Plant, Platelet, Platoon, Polar, Politic, Posse, Purview, Quango, Relic(t), Remains, Review, Ruck, Satellite, Senate, Shaft, Solid, Soma(tic), Soredium, Sound-box, Soyle, Spinar, Spore, Squadron, Square, Staff, Statoblast, Stiff, Strobila, Syndicate, Systemic, Tagma, Testis, Thallus, Torse, Torso, Trunk, Turm, Ulema, Uvula, Vase, Vitreous, Wolffian, X
▷ **Body** *may indicate* an anagram
Body builder Expander, He-man, Muscleman, Steroid
Bodyguard Amulet, Beefeater, → **ESCORT**, Gentleman-at-arms, House-carl, Minder, Praetorian, Protector, Retinue, Schutzstaffel, → **SHIELD**, SS, Switzer, Triggerman, Varangian, Yeomen
Body segment Arthromere, Genome, Metamere
Boer Afrikaner, Kruger, Van der Merwe
Boffin Brain, Egghead, Expert
Bog(gy) Allen, Blanket, Can, Carr, Clabber, Fen, Gents, Glaur, Hag, Lair, Latrine, Lerna, Lerne, Letch, Loo, Machair, Marish, Marsh, Merse, Mire, Moory, Morass, Moss(-flow), Mud, Muskeg, Peat, Petary, Quag, Raised, Serbonian, Slack, Slade, Slough, Spew, Spouty, Stodge, Sump, Urinal, Vlei, Washroom, WC, Yarfa, Yarpha
Bog(e)y Boggart, Bug(aboo), Bugbear, Chimera, Colonel, Eagle, Gremlin, Mumbo jumbo, Nis(se), Par, Poker, Rawhead, Scarer, Siege, Spectre, Troll
Boggle Astonish, Bungle, Demur, Hesitate, Perplex, Shy
Bogie Trolley
Bog-trotter Tory
Bogus Assumed, Counterfeit, Fake, False, Histrionic, Phoney, → **SHAM**, Snide, Snobbish, Spoof, Spurious
Bohemian Arty, Beatnik, Boho, Calixtin(e), Demi-monde, Gypsy, Hippy, Hussite, Mimi, Offbeat, Taborite, Trustafarian
Boil(er), Boiled, Boiling (point) Aleppo, Angry, Anthrax, Blain, Botch, Brew, Bubble, C, Carbuncle, Coction, Cook, Copper, Cree, Dartre, Decoct, Ebullient, Foam, Furuncle, Gathering, Hen, Herpes, Kettle, Leep, Ligroin, Pimple, Pinswell, Poach, Poule, Rage, Reflux, Samovar, Seethe, Set pot, Simmer, Sod, Sore, Steam, Stew, Stye, Tea-kettle, Water tube

Boisterous(ly) Ariot, Gilp(e)y, Goustrous, Gusty, Hoo, Knockabout, Ladette, Noisy, Rambunctious, Randy, Riotous, Rollicking, Rorty, Rough, Rounceval, Splurge, Stormy, Strepitoso, Tearer, Termagant, Tomboy, Turbulent, Wild

Bold(ly), Boldness Assumptive, Audacious, Brash, Brass, Bravado, Bravery, Bravura, Brazen, Brussen, Caleb, Crust, Daredevil, Dauntless, Defiant, Derring-do, Diastaltic, Familiar, Free, Gallus, Gutsy, Hard-edge, Hardihood, Heroics, High-spirited, Impudent, Intrepid, Malapert, Mature, Minx, Outspoken, Parrhesia, Pert, Plucky, Presumptive, Rash, Risoluto, Sassy, Temerity, Unshrinking

Bole Niche, Stem, Trunk

Bolivar Liberator

Bollard Cone, Kevel

Bolshevik, Bolshie Agitator, Communist, Maximalist, Rebel, Soviet, Stroppy

Bolster Cushion, Dutch wife, Pillow, → **PROP**

Bolt Arrow, Captive, Carriage, Coach, Cuphead, Dash, Dead, Do a runner, Eat, Elope, Expansion, Explosive, Fasten, Fish, Flee, Gobble, Gollop, Gorge, Gulp, Latch, Levant, Levin, Lightning, Lock, Machine, Missile, Panic, Pig, Pintle, Ragbolt, Rivet, Roll, Scoff, Slot, Snib, Sperre, Stud, Tap, Through, Thunder, Toggle, U, Wing, Wolf, Wring

Bolus Ball

Bomb(ed), Bomber, Bombing Atom, Attack, B, Benny, Blast, Blitz, Blockbuster, Borer, Bunkerbuster, Buzz, Candle, Car, Carpet, Cluster, Cobalt, Daisycutter, Depth charge, Deterrent, Dirty, Doodlebug, Drogue, Egg, Fission, Flop, Flying, Flying Fortress, Fragmentation, Fusion, Glide, Greek fire, Grenade, H, Harris, Homicide, Hydrogen, Lancaster, Land-mine, Letter, Liberator, Loft, Logic, Mail, Megaton, Millennium, Mills, Minnie, Mint, Molotov cocktail, Mortar, Nail, Napalm, Necklace, Neutron, Nuclear, Nuke, Packet, Parcel, Petar, Petard, Petrol, Pineapple, Pipe, Plaster, Plastic, Prang, Precision, Radium, Ransom, Robot, Sex, Shell, Skip, Smart, Smoke, Sneak-raid, Stealth, Stick, Stink, Stratofortress, Stuka, Suicide, Tactical, Terrorist, Thermonuclear, Time, Torpedo, Turkey, V1, Volcanic, Vulcan, Walleye

Bombard(ment) Attack, Battery, Blitz, Cannonade, Drum-fire, Mortar, Pelt, Shell, Stone, Stonk, Strafe, Straff

Bombardon Tuba

Bombast(ic) Ampullosity, Euphuism, Fustian, Grandiloquent, Grandiose, Hot air, Magniloquence, Orotund, Pomp, Rant, Swol(le)n, Timid, Tumid, Turgent

Bombay Nasik

Bombay duck Bum(m)alo

▶ **Bomber** *see* **BOMB(ED)**

Bona fide Echt, Genuine

Bonanza Luck, Windfall

Bonaparte Boney, → **NAPOLEON**, Plon-plon

Bond(s), Bondage, Bonding, Bondsman Adhesive, Affinity, Afrikander, Agent, Assignat, Baby, Bail, Bearer, Cedula, Cement, Chain, Chemical, Compact, Connect, Consols, Coordinate, Copula, Corporate, Covalent, Covenant, Daimyo, Dative, Debenture, Deep-discount, Double, Duty, Electrovalent, English, Ernie, Escrow, Esne, Fetter, Fleming, Flemish, Geasa, Gilt, Glue, Granny, Heart, Herringbone, Hydrogen, Hyphen, Income, Investment, Ionic, James, Junk, Knot, Liaise, Ligament, Ligature, Link(age), Long, Manacle, Managed, Metallic, Mortar, Multicentre, Municipal, Nexus, Noose, Obligation, Pair, Peptide, Performance, → **PLEDGE**, Post-obit, Premium, Property, Rapport, Recognisance, Relationship, Revenue, Running, Samurai, Savings, Security, Semipolar, Serf, Servitude, Shackle, Shogun, Single, Singlet, Sinter, Slave, Solder, Stacked, Starr, Superglue, Surety, Thete, Thral(l)dom, Three-per-cent, → **TIE**, Tiger, TIGR, Treasury, Triple, Trivalent, Tusking, Valence, Valency, Vassal, Vinculum, Yearling, Yoke, Zebra

Bone(s), Bony Acromion, Anableps, Angular, Apatite, Astragalus, Atlas, Axis, Baculum, Busk, Calcaneus, Caluarium, Cannon, Capitate, Capitellum, Carina, Carpal, Carpus, Cartilage, Catacomb, Centrum, Chine, Chordate, Clavicle, Cly, Coccyx,

Coffin, Columella, Concha, Condyle, Coracoid, Coral, Costa, Coxa, Crane, Cranium, Cuboid, Cuneiform, Cuttlefish, Dentary, Diaphysis, Dib, Dice, Diploe, Doctor, Dolos, Endosteal, Ethmoid, Femur, Fetter, Fibula, Fillet, Frontal, Funny, Ganoid, Gaunt, Hamate, Haunch, Hause-bane, Horn, Humerus, Hyoid, Ilium, Incus, Innominate, Interclavicle, Involucrum, Ischium, Ivory, Jugal, Kneecap, Knuckle, Lacrimal, Lamella, Long, Luez, Lunate, Luz, Malar, Malleolus, Malleus, Mandible, Manubrium, Marrow, Mastoid, Maxilla, Medulla, Membrane, Metacarpal, Metatarsal, Napier's, Nasal, Navicular, Occipital, Olecranon, Omoplate, Orthopaedics, Os, Ossicle, Osteo-, Palatine, Parasphenoid, Parietal, Patella, Pecten, Pectoral, Pedal, Pelvis, Pen, Percoid, Perone, Petrous, Phalanx, Pisiform, Ploughshare, Premaxilla, Prenasal, Pterygoid, Pubis, Pygostyle, Quadrate, Rack, Radiale, Radialia, Radius, Relic, Rib, Rump-post, Sacrum, Scaphoid, Scapula, Sclere, Sepium, Sequestrum, Sesamoid, Share, Skeleton, Skull, Spade, Sphenoid, Splint, Splinter, Spur, Squamosal, Stapes, → **STEAL**, Sternebra, Sternum, Stifle, Stirrup, Suboperculum, T, Talus, Tarsometatarsus, Tarsus, Temporal, Tibia, Tibiotarsus, Tot, Trapezium, Triquetral, Trochanter, Trochlea, True-rib, Turbinate, Tympanic, Ulna, Vertebrae, Vomer, Whirl, Wish, Wormian, Zygomatic

Bonehead(ed) Capitellum, Capitulum, Obtuse

Bonehouse Charnel house, Ossuary

Boneshaker Dandy-horse, Draisene, Draisine

Bonfire Bale-fire, Beltane, Blaze, Chumping, Clavie, Feu de joie, Pyre

Boniface Inn-keeper, Landlord, Taverner

Bonne-bouche Cate

Bonnet Balmoral, Bongrace, Cap, Cornette, Cowl, Easter, Glengarry, Hood, Hummel, Hummle, Kiss-me(-quick), Mobcap, Mutch, Poke, Scotch, Sun, Toorie, Tourie, War

Bonny Blithe, Gay, Merry, Sonsy, Weelfar'd

Bonsai Saikei

Bonus Bisque, Bounty, Braata, Bye, Christmas box, Danger money, Dividend, Escalator, Extra, Hand-out, Lagniappe, No-claim, → **PREMIUM**, Reversionary, Reward, Scrip, Signing, Spin-off, Windfall

Boo Explode

Boob Gaffe, Nork, Simpleton, Stumer

Booby Dunce, Gremial, Hick, Patch, Patchcocke, Patchoke, → **STUPID**

Boojum Snark

Book(s), Bookish, Bookwork Abcee, Absey, Academic, Album, Antilegomena, Antiphonary, Appointment, Audio, B, Backlist, Bedside, Bestiary, Bestseller, Black, Block, Blockbuster, Blotter, Blue, Cash, Chick, Chrestomathy, Classic, Closed, Coffee-table, Diary, Digest, Directory, Diurnal, Eightvo, Ench(e)iridion, Engage(ment), Enter, Erudite, Exercise, Facetiae, Folio, Fortune, Good, Gradual, Gradus, Guide, Hardback, Hymnal, Imprint, Index, Issue, Lectionary, Ledger, Lib, Liber, Literary, Livraison, Manual, Memorandum, Missal, Monograph, Muster, Octavo, Octodecimo, Office, Open, Order, Page-turner, Paperback, Pass, Pedantic, Peerage, Phrase, Pica, Plug, Polyglot, Potboiler, Pseudepigrapha, Publication, Puzzle prize, Quair, Quarto, Quire, → **RESERVE**, Road, Roman-a-clef, Script, Sealed, Sext, Sexto, Sextodecimo, Sixmo, Sixteenmo, Sketch, Softback, Source, Spelling, Spine-chiller, Statute, Studious, Study, Style, Swatch, Symbolical, Table, Tablet, Talking, Tall copy, Te igitur, Text(ual), Thirty-twomo, Thriller, Title, Titule, Tome, Trade, Transfer, Twelvemo, Twenty-fourmo, Unputdownable, Visiting, Visitor's, Vol(ume), Waste, White, Work, Year

BOOKS

2 letters:	*3 letters:*	Hab	Log
NT	Dan	Hag	Rag
OT	Eph	Jud	Red
	Gal	Lam	Rom

Sir
Sus
Tit

4 letters:
Acts
Amos
Blad
Edda
Ezek
Ezra
Joel
John
Jude
Luke
Macc
Mark
Mook
Obad
Ruth
Veda

5 letters:
Atlas
Bible
Chron
Hosea
James
Kells
Kings
Manga
Micah
Nahum
Pop-up
Snobs
Sutra
Titus
To-bit

6 letters:
Aeneid
Baruch
Caxton
Course

Daniel
Eccles
Esdras
Esther
Exeter
Exodus
Haggai
Herbal
I Ching
Isaiah
Jashar
Jasher
Joshua
Judges
Prayer
Primer
Prompt
Psalms
Ration
Reader
Romans
Scroll
Tanach
Tanack

7 letters:
Chumash
Cookery
Ezekiel
Genesis
Grolier
Malachi
Martyrs
Matthew
Numbers
Obadiah
Octapla
Omnibus
Orarium
Ordinal
Psalter
Susanna
Timothy

8 letters:
Breviary
Clarissa
Domesday
Doomsday
Georgics
Grimoire
Habakkuk
Haggadah
Haggadoh
Hermetic
Libretto
Megillah
Nehemiah
Ordinary
Philemon
Porteous
Portesse
Prophets
Proverbs
Triodion
Vercelli
Vesperal

9 letters:
Apocrypha
Ephesians
Formulary
Galatians
Gazetteer
Kama Sutra
Leviticus
Maccabees
Portolano
Reference
Remainder
Satyricon
Sibylline
Sybilline
Telephone
Tripitaka
Vade-mecum
Zephadiah

10 letters:
Apocalypse
Chronicles
Colossians
Compendium
Cyclopedia
Dictionary
Heptameron
Heptateuch
Hitopadesa
Incunabula
Passionary
Persuasion
Teratology

11 letters:
Commonplace
Concordance
Corinthians
Deuteronomy
Evangeliary
Hagiographa
Nomenclator
Philippians
Revelations

12 letters:
Bodice-ripper
Ecclesiastes
Encyclopedia
Lamentations
Panchatantra
Paralipomena
Processional
Responsorial
Twelve Tables

13 letters:
Penny dreadful
Pharmacopoeia
Thessalonians

Bookbinder, Bookbinding Fanfare, Grolier, Mutton-thumper, Organdie
Book-case Credenza, Press, Satchel
Bookie(s), Bookmaker Binder, John, Layer, Librettist, Luke, Mark, Matthew, Printer, Ringman, To-bit, Turf accountant
Booking Reservation
Bookkeeper, Bookkeeping Clerk, Double entry, Librarian, Posting, Recorder, Satchel, Single-entry
Booklet B, Brochure, Folder, Inlay
Book-like Solander

Book-lover Incunabulist
Bookmark Flag, Tassel
Book-scorpion Chelifer
Bookseller Bibliopole, Colporteur, Conger, Sibyl, Stallman
Bookworm Sap, Scholar
Boom(ing) Baby, Beam, Boost, Bowsprit, Bump, Fishpole, Gaff, Increase, Jib, Loud, Orotund, Plangent, Prosper, Resound, Roar, Sonic, Spar, Supersonic, Swinging, Thrive, Torpedo, Wishbone
Boomer Bittern, Bull-of the-bog, Butter-bump, Kangaroo, Mire-drum
Boomerang Backfire, Kiley, Kyley, Kylie, Recoil, Ricochet, Throwstick, Woomera
Boon Bene, Benefit, Blessing, Bounty, Cumshaw, Gift, Godsend, Mills, Mitzvah, Prayer, Windfall
Boor(ish) Borel, Bosthoon, Chuffy, Churl, Clodhopper, Crass, Curmudgeon, Goth, Grobian, Hog, Ill-bred, Jack, Keelie, Kern(e), Kernish, Kill-courtesy, Lob, Lout, Lumpen, Lumpkin, Ocker, Peasant, Philistine, Pleb, Trog, Uncouth, Unmannerly, Yahoo, Yob, Yokel
Boost(er) Adrenalin, Afterburner, Bolster, Ego, Eik, Eke, Encourage, Fillip, Help, Hoist, Impetus, Increase, Injection, Invigorate, Lift, Promote, Raise, Rap, Reheat, Reinforce, Reinvigorate, Spike, Steal, Step up, Supercharge, Tonic, Wrap
Boot(s) Addition, Adelaide, Ankle-jack, Avail, Balmoral, Beetle-crushers, Benefit, Blucher, Bottine, Bovver, Brogan, Brogue, Buskin, Cerne, Chelsea, Chukka, Cockers, Cold, Combat, Concern, Cothurn(us), Cowboy, Cracowe, Crowboot, Denver, Derby, Desert, Dismiss, Field, Finn(e)sko, Finsko, Fire, Football, Galage, Galosh, Gambado, Go-go, Granny, Gum, Heave-ho, Hessian, High shoe, Hip, Jack, Jemima, Jodhpur, Kamik, Kinky, Kletterschuh, Lace-up, Larrigan, Last, Mitten, Moon, Muchie, Muc(k)luc(k), Mukluk, Pac, Para, Profit, Riding, Rock, Russian, Sabot, → **SACK**, Seven league, → **SHOE**, Shoepac(k), Skivvy, Stogy, Surgical, Tackety, Thigh, Toe, Tonneau, Tops, Trunk, Ugg, Vibram®, Vibs, Wader, Walking, Warm, Weller, Wellie, Wellington, Welly
Booth Assassin, Crame, Cubicle, Kiosk, Polling, Stall, Stand, Telephone, Tolsel, Tolsey, Voting
Bootleg(ger) Cooper, Coper, Pirate, Runner
Bootless Futile, Idle, Unprofitable, Vain
Booty Creach, Creagh, Haul, Loot, Prey, Prize, Spoil(s), Spolia optima, Swag
Booze(r) → **DRINK**, Inn, Liquor, Pub, Spree, Tipple
Bora Rite, Wind
Borage Bugloss, Comfrey, Gromwell, Myosote
Borax Tincal
Bordeaux Claret
Border(s), Borderland, Borderline Abut, Adjoin, Apron, Bed, Bind, Bound, Boundary, Braid, Brush, Checkpoint, Coast, Cot(t)ise, Dado, Dentelle, → **EDGE**, Engrail, Fimbria, Frieze, Fringe, Frontier, Furbelow, Guilloche, Head-rig, Hedgerow, Hem, Herbaceous, Impale, Kerb, Lambrequin, Limb, Limbate, Limbo, Limen, Limes, Limit, Limitrophe, Lip, List, March, Marchland, → **MARGIN**, Mat, Mattoid, Meith, Mete, Mount, Neighbour, Orle, Pand, Pelmet, Penumbra, Perimeter, Purfle, Purlieu, Rand, Rim, Rio Grande, Roadside, Roon, Royne, Rubicon, Rund, Rymme, Scottish, Screed, Selvage, Selvedge, Side, Skirt, Skirting, Splenium, Strand, Strip, Surround, Swage, T(h)alweg, The Marches, Trench, Tressure, Valance, Valence, → **VERGE**
▷ **Borders** *may indicate* first and last letters
Bore(d), Boredom, Borer, Boring Aiguille, Airshaft, Anobium, Anorak, Apathy, Aspergillum, Aspergillus, Aspersoir, Auger, Awl, Beetle, Bind, Bit, Blasé, Broach, Brog, Bromide, Calibre, Cataclysm, Chokebore, Deadly, Drag, → **DRILL**, Dry, Dullsville, Dusty, Dweeb, Eagre, Eat, Eger, Elshin, Elsin, Endured, Ennui, Ennuye, Fag, Flat, Foozle, Gim(b)let, Gouge, Gribble, Grind, Had, Heigh-ho, Ho-hum, Irk, Jack, Jumper, Land, Listless, Longicorn, Longueur, Miser, Mole, Motormouth, Nerd, Noyance, Nudni(c)k,

Nuisance, Nyaff, Operose, Pain, Pall, Penetrate, Perforate, Pest, Pholas, Pierce, Pill, Platitude, Probe, Prosaic, Prosy, Punch, Ream(ingbit), Rime, Saddo, Sat, Schmoe, Scolytus, Screw, Severn, Shothole, Snooze, Snore, Sondage, Spleen, Spod, Spudding-un, Sting, Stob, Stupid, Tediosity, Tedious, Tedisome, Tedium, Tedy, Terebra, Teredo, Termes, Termite, Thirl, Tire, Trepan, Trocar, Tunnel, Turn-off, Vapid, → **WEARY**, Well, Wimble, Windbag, Wonk, Woodworm, Workaday, Worldweary, Xylophaga, Yawn

Borgia Cesare, Lucretia

Boric Sassolin, Sassolite

Born B, Free, Great, Nascent, Nat(us), Né(e)

Borneo Kalimantan, Sabahan

Boron B

Borough Borgo, Close, Pocket, Port, Quarter, Queens, Rotten, Township, Wick

Borrow(ed), Borrowing Adopt, Appropriate, Cadge, Copy, Derivative, Eclectic, George, Hum, Leverage, Scunge, Stooze, Straunge, → **TAKE**, Touch

Bosh Humbug, Nonsense, Rot

Bosom Abraham's, Breast, Bristols, Close, Gremial, Heart, Inarm, Intimate, Poitrine

Boson Gauge, Squark

Boss(ed), Bossy Big White Chief, Blooper, Burr, Cacique, Capo, Cow, Director, Dominate, Domineer, Gadroon, Gaffer, Governor, Headman, Honcho, Hump, Inian, Inion, Jewel, Knob, Knop, Knot, Leader, Maestro, → **MANAGER**, Massa, MD, → **MISTAKE**, Mistress, Netsuke, Noop, Nose-led, Omphalos, Oubaas, Overlord, Overseer, Owner, Padrone, Pannikin, Pellet, Protuberance, Ruler, Run, Sherang, Straw, Stud, Superintendent, Superior, Supervisor, Supremo, Taskmaster, Top banana, Umbo(nate)

Boston Hub

Bot Oestrus

Botany, Botanist Banks, Bryology, Candolle, Carpology, Cockayne, Dendrologist, Frees, Garden, Godet, Graminology, Herbist, Jungermann, Linnaeus, Marchant, Mendel, Mycology, Phytogenesis, Phytology, Pteridology, Tradescant, Weigel

Botch(ed) Bungle, Clamper, Cock-up, Flub, Fudge, Mismanage, Pig's ear, Spoil, Tink

Both Together, Two

Bother(some) Ado, Aggro, Annoy, Brush, Care, Deave, Deeve, Disturb, Drat, Fash, Fluster, Fuss, Get, Harassment, Harry, Hassle, Hector, Hoot-toot, Incommode, Irk, Irritate, Moither, Nag, Nark, Nuisance, Palaver, Perturb, Pesky, Pest(er), Pickle, Reke, Todo, → **TROUBLE**, Vex

Bottle(s) Ampul(la), Bacbuc, Balthasar, Balthazar, Belshazzar, Blackjack, Borachio, Bravado, Bundle, Carafe, Carboy, Case, Chapine, Cock, Cork, Costrel, Courage, Cruet, Cruse, Cucurbital, Cutter, Dead-man, Decanter, Demijohn, Fearlessness, Feeding, Fiasco, Filette, Flacket, Flacon, Flagon, Flask, Glass can, Goatskin, Gourd, Grit, Guts, Half-jack, Hen, Imperial, Jeroboam, Junk, Klein, Lachrymal, Lagena, Magnetic, Magnum, Marie-Jeanne, Matrass, Medicine, Melchior, Methuselah, Mettle, Mickey, Middy, Nansen, Nebuchadnezzar, → **NERVE**, Nursing, Phial, Pig, Pilgrim, Pitcher, Pooter, Pycnometer, Rehoboam, Resource, Retort, Salmanaser, Salmanazar, Scent, Screwtop, Siphon, Smelling, Split, Squeeze, Squeezy, Stubby, Sucking, Tear, Tube, Twenty-sixer, Vial, Vinaigret(te), Wad, Water, Water bouget, Weighing, Winchester, Wine, Woulfe

▷ **Bottle(d)** *may indicate* an anagram or a hidden word

Bottom Anus, Aris, Arse, Ass, Base, Batty, Beauty, Bed, Benthos, Bilge, Booty, Breech, Bum, Butt, Buttocks, Coit, Croup(e), Croupon, Demersal, Derrière, Doup, Dowp, End, Fanny, Floor, Foot, Foundation, Fud, Fundus, Haunches, Hunkers, Hurdies, Jacksy, Keel(son), Kick, Lumbar, Nadir, Nates, Planning, Podex, Posterior, Pottle-deep, Prat, Pyramus, Quark, Rear, Rock, Root, Rump, Seat, Ship, Sill, Sole, Staddle, Tail, Tush, Weaver

Bottom drawer Glory box

Bottomless Subjacent

Botulism Limberneck

Boudoir Bower, Room
Bouffant Pouf
Bough Branch, Limb, Roughie, Roughy
Bought Coft
Boulder Erratic, Gibber, Niggerhead, Rock, Sarsen, → **STONE**
Boule Senate
Bounce(r), Bouncing, Bouncy Ananias, Ball, Bang, Blague, Bound, Caper, Convention, Dandle, Dap, Dead-cat, Doorman, Dop, Dud, Eject, Evict, Fib, Jounce, Keepy-uppy, Kite, Lie, Lilt, Muscleman, Resilient, Ricochet, Spiccato, Spring, Stot, Tale, Tamp, Tigger, Valve, Verve, Vitality, Yorker, Yump
▷ **Bouncing** *may indicate* an anagram
Bound(er), Boundary Adipose, Apprenticed, Articled, Bad, Barrier, Beholden, Border, Bourn(e), Bubalis, Cad, Cavort, Certain, Circumference, Curvet, Decreed, Demarcation, Demarkation, Divide, Dool, Dule, Duty, End, Engirt, Entrechat, Erub, Eruv, Event horizon, Exciton, Fence, Finite, Four, Frape, Frontier, Galumph, Gambado, Gambol, Girt, Harestane, Hedge, Heel, Held, Hoarstone, Hops, Hourstone, Ibex, Interface, Izard, Jump, Kangaroo, K/T, → **LEAP**, Limes, Limit, Linch, Lollop, Lope, March-stone, Mason-Dixon line, Meare, Meer, Meith, Mere, Merestone, Mete, Moho, Muscle, Obliged, Ourebi, Outedge, Outward, Pale, Parameter, Perimeter, Periphery, Plate, Prance, Precinct, Prometheus, Purlieu, Quickset, Redound, Ring-fence, Roller, Roo, Roped, Rubicon, Scoundrel, Scoup, Scowp, Serf, Side, Sideline, Six(er), Skelp, Skip, Spang, Spring, Sten(d), Stoit, Stylolite, Sure, T(h)alweg, Terminator, Tide, Tied, Touchline, Upstart, Vault, Verge, Wallaby
Boundless Illimited, Unlimited
▷ **Bounds** *may indicate* outside letters
Bounty, Bountiful Aid, Bligh, Boon, Christian, Generosity, → **GIFT**, Goodness, Grant, Head money, Honorarium, Largess(e), Lavish, Queen Anne's, Queen's
Bouquet Aroma, Attar, Aura, Compliment, Corsage, Fragrancy, Garni, Nose, Nosegay, Odour, Perfume, Plaudit, Posy, Pot pourri, Scent, Spiritual, Spray
Bourbon Alfonso
Bourgeois(ie) Biedermeier, Common, Middle class, Pleb(eian), Pooter(ish)
Bout Bender, Bust, Contest, Dose, Go, Jag, Match, Spell, Spree, Turn, Venery, Venewe, Venue
Boutique Shop
Bovine Stolid
Bow(ing), Bower, Bowman Accede, Alcove, Arbour, Arc, Arch, → **ARCHER**, Arco, Arson, Bandy, Beck, Bend, Boudoir, Butterfly, Clara, Congé(e), Crescent, Crook, Cupid, → **CURVE**, Defer, Dicky, Drail, Droop, Duck, Echelles, Eros, Eugh, Eyes, Fiddle(r), Fiddlestick, Foredeck, Halse, Hawse, Headgear, Honour, Incline, Inswing(er), Jook, Jouk, Kneel, Kotow, Laval(l)ière, Lean, Londoner, Long, Loof, Lout, Lowt, Luff, Martellato, Moulinet, Namaste, Nameste, Nock, Nod, Nutate, Oar, Obeisance, Obtemper, Outswing, Paganini, Pergola, Prore, Quarrel, Reverence, Salaam, Seamer, Shelter, Slope, Sound, Spiccato, Staccato, Stick, → **SUBMIT**, Swing, Throw, Tie, Torrent, Tureen, Weather, Yew, Yield
Bowdler(ize) Comstockery, Edit(or), Water
Bowels Entrails, Guts, Innards, Melaena, Viscera
▷ **Bower** *may indicate* using a bow
Bowl(ing), Bowler, Bowl over, Bowls B, Basin, Begging, Bicker, Bocce, Bocci(a), Boccie, Bodyline, Bool, Bosey, Bouncer, Cage-cup, Calabash, Candlepins, Cap, Carpet, Caup, Chalice, Cheese, Chinaman, Christie, Christy, Cog(g)ie, Concave, Coolamon, Crater, Cup, Deliver, Derby, → **DISH**, Dismiss, Dome, Doosra, Drake, Dumbfound, Dust, Ecuelle, End, Finger, Fivepin, Goblet, Goldfish, Googly, Grub, Headgear, Hog, Hoop, Inswing(er), Jack, Jeroboam, Jorum, Kegler, Krater, Lavabo, Laver, Leg-spin, Lightweight, Lob, Locke, Mazer, Monteith, Night, Offbreak, Off-cutter, Old, Outswing, Over-arm, Overpitch,

Pace(man), Pan, Pétanque, Piggin, Pitch, Porringer, Pot-hat, Pottinger, Punch, Raku, Rice, Rink, Roll, Roundarm, Seam(er), Skip, Skittle(s), Spare, Speed, Spinner, Spofforth, Stadium, Stagger, Stummel, Sucrier, Super, Swing, Ten-pin, Throw, Tom, Tureen, Underarm, Underhand, Underwood, Voce, Wassail, Wood, York(er)

Box(ing) Baignoire, Ballot, Bandbox, Bareknuckle, Bento, Bijou, Bimble, Binnacle, Black, Blow, Blue, Bonk, Booth, Buist, Bunk, Bush, Caddy, Call, Camera, Canister, Case, Cash, Casket, Cassolette, Chest, Chinese, Christmas, Ciborium, Clog, Coach, Coffer, Coffin, Coffret, Coin, Commentary, Confessional, Cool, Crash, Crate, Cuff, Dabba, Dead-letter, Deed, Dialog(ue), Dispatch, Ditty, Dog, Drawer, Egg, Encase, Enclose, Etui, → **FIGHT**, File, Fist, Fund, Fuse, Fuzz, Gear, Glory, Glove, Go-kart, Grass, Hat, Hay, Hedge, Hive, Honesty, Horse, Humidor, Hutch, Ice, Idiot, Inherce, Inro, Inter, Jewel, Journal, Juke, Junction, Jury, Keister, Kick, Kiosk, Kite, Knevell, Knowledge, Ladle, Letter, Light, Live, Locker, Lodge, Loge, Loose, Lug, Lunch, Match, Message, Mill, Mitre, Mocock, Mocuck, Money, Musical, Nest(ing), Noble art, Noble science, Omnibus, Orgone, Out, Package, Packing, Paint, Pandora's, Papeterie, Patch, Pattress, Peepshow, Peg, Penalty, Petara, Pew, Phylactery, Piggybank, Pill, Pillar, Pitara, Pix, Poor, Post, Pounce(t), Powder, Press, Prize fight, Prompt, Protector, Puff, Pugilism, Pyxis, Register, Resonance, Ring, Rope-a-dope, Royal, Safe-deposit, Saggar(d), Sagger, Sand, Savate, Scent, Scrap, Seggar, Sentry, Set-top, Shadow, Shoe, Shooting, Side, Signal, Skinner, Skip(pet), Slipcase, Smudge, Sneeshin-mull, Sneeze, Soap, Solander, Sound, Sound body, → **SPAR**, Spice, Spit, Spring, Squawk, Squeeze, Strong, Stuffing, Swell, Tabernacle, Tee, Tefillin, Telephone, Telly, Thai, Tick, Tin, Tinder, Tool, Touch, Trunk, Tube, Tuck, TV, TiVo, Urn, Vanity, Vasculum, Vinaigrette, Voice, Weather, Window, Wine, Witness, Yakhdan

Boxer Ali, Amycus, Babyweight, Bantamweight, Bruiser, Bruno, Canine, Carnera, Carpentier, Carthorse, Chinaman, Cooper, Corbett, Crater, Cruiserweight, Darcy, Dempsey, Dog, Eryx, Farr, Featherweight, Flyweight, Foreman, Ham, Heavyweight, Lightweight, McCoy, Middleweight, Mosquito-weight, Pandora, Pollux, Pug, Pugil(ist), Rebellion, Rocky, Shadow, Southpaw, Sparrer, Strawweight, Sugar Ray Robinson, Welterweight, Wilde

Boxing-glove Hurlbat, Muffle, Whirlbat, Whorlbat

Boy(s) Amoretto, Anchor, Apprentice, Ball, Bevin, Blue-eyed, Bovver, Bub(by), Cabin, Callant, Catamite, Champagne, Chiel(d), → **CHILD**, Chokra, Chummy, Cub, Cupid, Dandiprat, Errant, Galopin, Garçon, Gorsoon, Gossoon, Green Mountain, Groom, Grummet, Ha, Hansel, Jack, Kid, Klonkie, Knave, Knave-bairn, Kwedien, Lackbeard, → **LAD**, Loblolly, Loon(ie), Minstrel, Nibs, Nipper, Office, Page, Poster, Pot, Prentice, Principal, Putto, Rent, Roaring, Rude, Shaver, Ship's, Son, Spalpeen, Sprig, Stripling, Swain, Tad, Tar, Ted(dy), Tiger, Toxic, Toy, Urchin, Whipping, Wide, → **YOUTH**

▷ **Boy** *may indicate* an abbreviated name

Boycott Avoid, Ban, Bat, Black, Blacklist, Exclude, Geoff(rey), Hartal, Isolate, Ostracise, Shun, Swadeshi

Boyfriend Beau, Date, Fella, Fellow, Squeeze, Steady

Boyle Juno

Bp Bishop, DD, RR

Brace(s), Bracing Accolade, Couple, Crosstree, Fortify, Gallace, Gallows, Gallus(es), Gird, Hound, Invigorate, Ozone, Pair, Pr, Rear-arch, Rere-arch, Sea air, Skeg, Spider, Splint, Stage, Steady, Stiffener, Strut, → **SUPPORT**, Suspenders, Tauten, Thorough, Tone, Tonic, Two

Bracelet Armil(la), Armlet, Bangle, Cuff, Darbies, Handcuff, Identity, Manacle, Manilla

Brachiopod Ecardines, Lamp-shell, Spirifer

Bracken Brake, Fern, Pteridium, Tara

Bracket Ancon, Angle-iron, Bibb, Brace, Cantilever, Console, Corbel, Couple, Cripple, Gusset, Hanger, Lance rest, Misericord(e), Modillion, Mutule, Parenthesis, Potence, Pylon, Rigger, Round, Sconce, Square, Straddle, Strata, → **STRUT**, Trivet, Truss

Bract Glume(lla), Hypsophyll, Involucel, Involucre, Job's tears, Leaf, Lemma, Palea, Palet, Phyllary, Spathe

Brad Nail, Pin, Rivet, Sprig

Brag(gart), Bragging Basilisco, Birkie, Bluster, Boast, Bobadil, Boister, Braggadocio, Bull, Cockalorum, Crow, Falstaff, Fanfaronade, Gab, Gascon, Hot-air, Loudmouth, Mouth off, Parolles, Puckfist, Puff, Rodomontader, Skite, Slam, Swagger, Thrason, Thrasonic, Tongue-doubtie, Tongue-doughty, Upstart, Vainglorious, Vapour, Vaunt

Brahma(n) San(n)yasi(n)

Braid A(i)glet, Aiguillette, Fishbone, French, Frog, Galloon, Lacet, Plait, Plat, Rickrack, Ricrac, Scrambled eggs, Seaming-lace, Sennet, Sennit, Sinnet, Soutache, Tress, Trim, Twist, Weave

Braille (system) Moon

Brain(box), Brain disease, Brain-power, Brain problem, Brains, Brainstorm, Brainy Amygdala, Appestat, Bean, Boffin, Bright, Cerebellum, Cerebrum, Contravene, Cortex, Crane, Cranium, Diencephalon, Dura mater, Encephalon, Epencephalon, Fornix, Genius, Gliosis, Gyrus, Harn(s), Head, Headpiece, Hippocampus, Hydrocephalus, Hypothalamus, Inspiration, Insula, Intelligence, IQ, Kuru, Left, Limbic, Loaf, Lobe, Mastermind, Mater, Medulla, Medulla oblongata, Metencephalon, Mind, Noddle, Noesis, Nous, Peduncle, Pericranium, Pia mater, Pons, Pontile, Prosencephalon, Quick, Rhinencephalon, Rhombencephalon, Ringleader, Sconce, Sense, Sensorium, Smarty pants, Striatum, Subcortex, Sulcus, Tapagnosia, Tectum, Telencephalon, Thalamencephalon, Thalamus, Upper stor(e)y, Vermis, Vortex, Wetware

▷ **Brain(s)** *may indicate* an anagram

Brainless Anencephaly, Bimbo, Stupid, Thick

Brainwash(ing) Indoctrinate, Menticide, Persuade, Propaganda

Brake, Braking ABS, Adiantum, Aerodynamic, Air, Anchors, Antilock, Bracken, Centrifugal, Curb, Disc, Dive, Drag, Drum, Estate car, Fern, Fly, Foot, Grove, Hand, Hub, Hydraulic, Nemoral, Overrun, Ratchet, Rein, Rim, Shoe, Shooting, → **SLOW**, Spinney, Sprag, Tara, Thicket, Vacuum, Westinghouse

Bramble, Brambly Batology, Blackberry, Boysenberry, Brier, Cloudberry, Rubus, Thorn, Wait-a-bit, Youngberry

Bran Cereal, Chesil, Chisel, Oats, Pollard

Branch(ed), Branches, Branching, Branch office Affiliate, Antler, Arm, BO, Bough, Chapel, Cladode, Cow, Dendron, Dept, Diversify, Diverticulum, Divide, Filiate, Fork, Grain, Jump, Kow, Lateral, Leaf-trace, Limb, Lobe, Lobus, Loop, Lye, Lylum, Offshoot, Olive, Patulous, Phylloclade, Rachilla, Raguly, Ramate, Ramulus, Reis, Rice, Shroud, Special, Spray(ey), Sprig, Spur, Stirpes, Tributary, Turning, Turn-off, Twig, Wattle, Whip, Yard

Branch-rib Lierne

Brand Broadsword, Buist, Burn, Cauterise, Chop, Class, Dealer, Denounce, Earmark, Ember, Excalibur, Falchion, Faulchin, Faulchion, Flambeau, Home, Idiograph, Inust, Iron, Label, Line, → **MARK**, Marque, Name, Own, Power, Sear, Sere, Stigma, Sweard, Sword, Torch, Wipe

Brandish Bless, Flaunt, Flourish, Hurtle, Waffle, Wampish, Wave

Brandy Aguardiente, Applejack, Apricot, Aqua vitae, Armagnac, Bingo, Calvados, Cape smoke, Cherry bounce, Cognac, Cold without, Dop, Eau de vie, Fine, Fine champagne, Framboise, Grappa, Kirsch, Mampoer, Marc, Mirabelle, Mobbie, Mobby, Nantes, Nantz, Napoleon, Palinka, Peach, Quetsch, Slivovic(a), Slivovitz, Smoke

Bras Arms

Brash Cocky, Flashy, Impudent, Jack-the-lad, Jumped-up, Pushy, Rain, Rash, Uppity

Brass(y), Brassware Alpha-beta, Benares, Brazen, Cheek, Club, Corinthian, Cornet, Dinanderie, Effrontery, Face, Front, Harsh, High, Horn, Horse, Latten, Lip, Lolly, Loot, Lota(h), Loud, Matrix, → **MONEY**, Moola(h), Oof, Oricalche, Orichalc, Palimpsest, Pyrites, Sass, Snash, Sopranino, Talus, Top, Trombone, White, Wood, Yellow metal

Brassard Armlet
Brass hat Brig
Brassica Brussels (sprout), → **CABBAGE**, Colza, Turnip
Brassière Gay deceiver
Brat Bairn, Bra(t)chet, Enfant terrible, Gait(t), Gamin, Geit, Get, Git, Gyte, Imp, Lad, Terror, Urchin
Braun Eva
Bravado, Brave(ry) Amerind, Apache, Bold, Conan, Corragio, Courage, Creek, Dare, → **DEFY**, Derring-do, Doughty, Dress, Face, Fearless, Gallant, Game, Gamy, Gutsy, Hardy, Heroism, Indian, Injun, Intrepid, → **LION**, Lion-hearted, Lionly, Manful, Manly, → **MEXICAN**, Nannup, → **NORTH AMERICAN**, Plucky, Prow(ess), Redskin, Russian roulette, Sannup, Skookum, → **SOUTH AMERICAN**, Spunk, Stout, Uncas, Valiant, Valour, Wight, Withstand, Yeoman
Bravo Acclaim, B, Bandit, Bully, Desperado, Euge, Murderer, Olé, Shabash, Spadassin, Villain
Brawl(er) Affray, Bagarre, Bicker, Brabble, Donnybrook, Dust, Dust-up, Fight, Flite, Flyte, Fracas, Fratch, Fray, Melee, Prawl, Punch up, Rammy, Roarer, Roughhouse, Row, Ruck, Scold, Scuffle, Set-to, Shindig, Slugfest, Stoush, Tar, Wrangle
Brawn Beef, Burliness, Headcheese, He-man, Might, Muscle, Power, Rillettes, Sinew
Bray Cry, Heehaw, Stamp, Vicar, Whinny
Brazen Blatant, Bold, Brassy, Flagrant, Forward, Impudent, Shameless, Unabashed
Brazier Brasero, Fire, Hibachi, Mangal, Scaldino
Brazil(ian) Caboclo, Carioca, Cream-nut, Para, Yanomami, Yanomamo
Breach Assault, Break, Chasm, Cleft, Foul, Gap(e), Great schism, Infraction, Redan, Rift, Rupture, Saltus, Schism, Solecism, Solution, Trespass, Violate
Bread, Bread crumbs Afikomen, Azym(e), Bagel, Baguette, Bannock, Bap, Barmbrack, Barm cake, Batch, Baton, Brewis, Brioche, Brownie, Bun, Cash, Chal(l)ah, Chametz, Chapati, Cheat, Ciabatta, Cob, Coburg, Compone, Corn (pone), Corsned, Croissant, Crostini, Croute, Crouton, Crumpet, Crust, Currency, Damper, Dibs, Dika, Doorstep, Elephant's-foot, Eulogia, Fancy, Flatbread, Focaccia, Fougasse, French (stick), Funds, Garlic, Gluten, Graham, Granary, Grissini, Guarana, Hallah, Hametz, Hometz, Horse, Host, Indian, Injera, Jannock, Johnny-cake, Kaffir, Lavash, Laver, Leavened, Loaf, Long tin, Manchet, Maori, Milk loaf, Milk-sop, → **MONEY**, Monkey, Na(a)n, Pain, Panada, Panary, Pane, Paneity, Panko, Paratha, Pay, Petit pain, Pikelet, Pit(t)a, Pone, Poori, Popover, Poppadom, Poultice, Prozymite, Pumpernickel, Puree, Puri, Quick, Raspings, Ravel, Roll, Rooty, Roti, Round, Rusk, Rye, Sally Lunn, Schnecken, Shewbread, Shive, Simnel, Sippet, Smor(re)brod, Soda, Soft-tommy, Sop, Sourdough, Split tin, Staff of life, Standard, Stollen, Stottie, Sugar, Sweet, Tartine, Tea, Tommy, Tortoise-plant, Twist, Wastel, Wrap, Zakuski, Zwieback
Breadfruit Ja(c)k
Breadwinner Earner, Pa
Break, Break-down, Break down, Break-in, Break-up, Break up, Broken
Adjourn, Analyse, Apn(o)ea, Aposiopesis, Bait, Breach, Breather, Bust, Caesura, Caesure, Cantle, Career, Cark, Cesure, Chinaman, Chip, Cleave, Coffee, Comb, Comma, Commercial, Comminute, Compost, Compurgatory, Conk, Contravene, Crack, Crock, Crumble, Dash, Deave, Debacle, Decompose, Deeve, Demob, Destroy, Diffract, Disband, Disintegrate, Disperse, Disrupt, Erumpent, Erupt, Exeat, Fast, Fault, Flaw, Four, → **FRACTURE**, Fragment, Fritter, Frush, Gaffe, Gap, Give, Greenstick, Half-term, Half-time, Harm, Hernia, Hiatus, Holiday, Infringe, Interim, Interlude, Intermission, Interrupt, → **INTERVAL**, Irrupt, Kark, Knap, Knickpoint, Lacuna, Lapse, Layover, Leave, Lysis, Moratorium, Nickpoint, Nooner, Outage, Parse, Part, Pause, Phreak, Playtime, Poach, Polarise, Price, Reave, Recess, Recrudescent, Relief, Rend, Resolve, Resorption, Respite, Rest, Rift, Rise, Ruin, Rupture, Saltus, Schism(a), Secede, Service, Shatter, Shear, Shiver, Smash, Smokeho, Smoko, Snap, Split, Stave, Stop, Stop-over, Stove, Sunder,

Take five, Take ten, Tame, Tea-ho, Tear, Tenderise, Time-out, Torn, Transgress, Truce, Twist, Vacation, Violate, Watergate, Weekend

Breakable Brittle, Delicate, Fissile, Fragile, Frail, Friable

Breakdown Abruption, Analyse, Autolysis, Cataclasm, Collapse, Conk, Crack-up, Glitch, Glycolosis, Glycolysis, Histolysis, Hydrolysis, Lyse, Lysis, Nervous, Ruin

Breaker Billow, Circuit, Comber, Ice, Roller, Smasher, Surf

Breakfast B, Brunch, Chota-hazri, Continental, Deskfast, Disjune, English, Kipper, Petit déjeuner, Power, Wedding

Breakneck Headlong

Breakthrough Discovery, Quantum leap

Breakwater Groyne, Jetty, Mole, Pier, Tetrapod

Bream Fish, Porgy, Sar(gus), Sea, Silver, Tai, White

Breast(s), Breastbone, Breastwork Bazuma, Boob, Bosom, Brave, Brisket, Bristols, Bust, Chimney, Clean, Counter, Diddy, Duddy, Dug, Falsies, Garbonza, Gazunga, Heart-spoon, Jubbies, Jugs, Knockers, Norg, Nork, Pigeon, Rampart, Redan, Sangar, Stem, Sternum, Stroke, Sungar, Supreme, Tit, Xiphisternum

Breastplate Armour, Byrnie, Curat, Curiet, Pectoral, Plastron, Rational, Rest, Shield, Thorax, Xiphiplastron

Breath(e), Breathing, Breather Aerobe, Air-sac, Apneusis, Aqualung, Aspirate, Bated, Branchia, Buteyko method, Caesural, Cheyne-Stokes, Circular, Cypress-knee, Eupnoea, Exhalation, Expiration, Flatus, Gasp, Gill, H, Halitosis, Hauriant, Haurient, Hobday, Hypernoea, Hyperventilation, Hypopnoea, Inhale, Inspiration, Knee, Lung, Nares, Nostril, Orthopnoea, Oxygenator, Pant, Plosion, Pneuma, Prana, Pulmo, Rale, Respire, Respite, Rest, Rhonchus, Rough, Scuba, Sigh, Smooth, Snore, Snorkel, Snortmast, Snotter, Snuffle, Souffle, Spiracle, Spirit, Spiritus, Stertor, Stridor, Tachypnoea, Trachea, Vent, Wheeze, Whiff, Whift, Whisper, Whist, Wind, Windpipe

Breathless(ness) Anhelation, Apnoea, Asthma, Dyspnoea, Emphysema, Orthopnoea, Puffed-out, Tachypnoea, Wheezing

Breathtaking Amazing, Asphyxia

Breech(es) Bible, Buckskin, Chaps, Chausses, Flog, Galligaskins, Hose, Jodhpurs, Kneecords, Knickerbockers, Pantaloons, Petticoat, Plushes, Riding, Smallclothes, Smalls, Trews, Trouse(rs), Trunk hose, Trusses

Breed(er), Breeding(-place) Bear, Beget, Cleck, Endogamous, Engender, Engend(r)ure, Eugenics, Fancier, Fast, Generation, Gentilesse, Gentility, Gentrice, Hetero, Hotbed, In-and-in, Line, Lineage, → **MANNERS**, Origin, Panmixia, Procreate, Propagate, Pullulate, Race, Raise, Rear, Savoir vivre, Seminary, Sire, Species, Stirpiculture, Stock, Strain, Stud, Telegony, Thremmatology, Tribe, Voltinism

Breeze, Breezy Air, Breath, Brisk, Cakewalk, Catspaw, Chipper, Doctor, Draught, Fresh, Gentle, Gust, Land, Light, Mackerel, Moderate, Pushover, Sea, Slant, Sniffler, Snifter, Strong, Tiff, Zephyr

Brethren Bohemian, Close, Darbyite, Elder, Exclusive, Herrnhuter, Ignorantine, Kin, Open, Plymouth, Trinity

Breton Armoric, Brezonek

Breve Minim, Note, O

Breviary Portesse, Portous

▸ **Brevity** *see* **BRIEF(S)**

Brew(ery), Brewer, Brewing Afoot, Ale, Billycan, Boutique, Brose, Browst, Bummock, → **CONCOCT**, Contrive, Dictionary, Distillery, Elixir, Ferment, Infusion, Liquor, Malt, Percolate, Perk, Potion, Scald, Steep, Witches', Yeast, Yill, Zymurgy

Briar Bramble, Canker, Lawyer

Bribe(ry) Backhander, Barratry, Barretry, Bonus, Boodle, Bung, Carrot, Dash, Douceur, Embracery, Get at, Graft, Grease, Hamper, Hush-money, Insult, Kickback, Lubricate, Oil, Palm, Palm-grease, Palm-oil, Payola, Schmear, Slush, Soap, Sop, Square, Straightener, Suborn, Sweeten(er), Tamper, Tempt, Tenderloin, Vail, Vales

Bric-a-brac Bibelot, Curio, Rattle-trap, Smytrie, Tatt, Virtu
Brick(s), Brickwork Adobe, Air, Bat, Bath, Bonder, Bondstone, Boob, Breeze, Bristol, Bullnose, Bur(r), Clanger, Clinker, Closer, Course, Dutch clinker, Fletton, Gaffe, Gault, Gold, Hard stocks, Header, Ingot, Klinker, Lateritious, Lego®, Malm, Nog(ging), Opus latericium, Red, Rubber, Soldier, Spawn, Sport, Stalwart, Stretcher, Terra-cotta, Testaceous, Tile, Trojan, Trump
Brickbat Flak, Missile
Bricklayer Churchill
Bride(s) Bartered, Danaides, Ellen, Hen, Mail-order, Newlywed, Spouse, War, Wife, Ximena
Bridesmaid Paranymph
Bridge(head), Bridge player Acol, Air, Al Sirat, Aqueduct, Auction, Australian, Avignon, Ba(u)ck, Bailey, Balance, Barre, Bascule, Bestride, Bifrost, Biritch, Board, Bridle-chord, Brig, Brooklyn, Cable-stayed, Cantilever, Capo, Capodastro, Capotasto, Catwalk, Chevalet, Chicago, Chicane, Clapper, Clifton, Contract, Counterpoise, Cross, Cut-throat, Deck, Declarer, Drawbridge, Duplicate, Flying, Flyover, Foot, Four-deal, Gangplank, Gangway, Gantry, Girder, Golden Gate, Hog's back, Humber, Humpback, Humpbacked, Ice, Irish, Jigger, Land, Lattice, Leaf, Lifting, Ligger, Link, London, Menai, Millau, Millennium, Murray, Nasion, Overpass, Pivot, Plafond, Ponceau, Pons, Ponticello, Pontifice, Pont levis, Pontoon, Raft, Rainbow, Rialto, Rubber, Severn, Sighs, Sinvat, Skew, Snow, → **SPAN**, Spanner, Stamford, Straddle, Suspension, Swing, Tay, Temper, Tête-de-pont, Through, Tide over, Transporter, Traversing, Trestle, Truss, Turn, Vertical lift, Viaduct, Vint, Waterloo, Weigh, Wheatstone, Wire
Bridge pair EW, NS, SN, WE
Bridge protector Ice-apron
Bridge system Acol
Bridle Bit, Branks, Bridoon, Bristle, Browband, Crownpiece, Curb, Double, Hackamore, Halter, Headstall, Musrol, Noseband, Rein, Scold's
Bridle path Orbit, Track
Brief(s), Briefing, Briefly, Brevity Acquaint, Advocate, Attorney, Awhile, Barristerial, Bluette, Brachyology, Breviate, Cape, Compact, → **CONCISE**, Conspectus, Counsel, Crisp, Curt, Dossier, Ephemeral, Fill in, Fleeting, Instruct, King's, Laconic, Lawyer, Nearly, Pants, Papal, Pennorth, Pithy, Prime, Scant, → **SHORT(EN)**, Short-term, Short-winded, Sitrep, Sparse, Succinct, Summing, Tanga, Terse, Transient, Undershorts, Undies, Update, Watching
Brig Br, Hermaphrodite, Jail, Nancy Bell, → **SHIP**, Snow
Brigade Anchor Boys, Boys', Corps, Fire, Fur, Girls', Green-ink, International, Naval, Red, Troop
Brigand Bandit, Bandolero, Cateran, Haidu(c)k, Heiduc, Heyduck, Klepht, Pillager, Pirate, → **ROBBER**, Rob Roy, Trailbaston
Bright, Brightness Afterglow, Alert, Ashine, Bertha, Brainbox, Brainy, Breezy, Brilliant, Brisk, Cheery, Chiarezza, Clara, Cla(i)re, Clear, Clever, Cuthbert, Danio, Effulgent, Eileen, Elaine, Ellie, Facula, Fair, Floodlit, Florid, Garish, Gay, Glad, Glary, Glow, Helen, Hono(u)r, Hubert, Light, Lit, Loud, Lucent, Lucid, Luculent, Luminous, Lustre, Net(t), Nit, Nitid, Radiant, Roarie, Rorie, Ro(a)ry, Rosy, Scintillating, Sematic, Sharp, Sheeny, Sheer, Shere, Skyre, Smart, Spark(y), Stilb, Sunlit, Sunny, Vive, Vivid, White, Zara
Bright spot Facula
Brilliant, Brilliance Ace, Aine, Blaze, Brainy, Bravura, Bright, Def, Effulgent, Eurian, Flashy, Galaxy, Gay, Gemmy, Gifted, Glitter, Glossy, High flyer, Humdinger, Inspired, Irradiance, Lambent, Leam, Lucent, Lustre, Mega-, Meteoric, Nitid, Pear, → **RADIANT**, Refulgent, Resplendent, Shiny, Spangle, Splendid, Splendour, Star, Superb, Virtuoso, → **VIVID**, Water
Brim Edge, Lip, Rim, Ugly
Brimstone Hellfire, S, Sulphur

Brindisi Skolion, Toast
Brindled Piebald, Tabby, Tawny
Brine Muriatic, Ozone, Pickle, Saline, Salt
Bring Afferent, Bear, Carry, Cause, Conduct, Convey, Earn, Evoke, Fet, Fetch, Foist, Hatch, Induce, Land, Precipitate, Produce, Wreak
Bring up Breed, Educate, Exhume, Foster, Nurture, Raise, → REAR
Brink → EDGE, Lip, Rim, Shore, → VERGE
Brio Elan
Brisk(ly), Briskness Active, Alacrity, Alert, Allegro, Breezy, Busy, Cant, Chipper, Con moto, Crank, Crisp, Crouse, Fresh, Gaillard, Galliard, Jaunty, Kedge, Kedgy, Kidge, Lively, Nippy, Peart, Perk, Pert, Rattling, Roaring, Scherzo, Sharp, Smacking, Smart, Snappy, Spanking, Spirited, Sprightly, Vivace, Yare, Zippy
Bristle, Bristling, Bristly Aciculum, Arista, Awn, Barb, Bewhiskered, Birse, Bridle, Campodeiform, Chaeta, Flurry, Fraught, Frenulum, Glochidium, Gooseflesh, Hackles, Hair, Hérissé, Hispid, Horrent, Horripilation, Nereid, Polychaete, Seta, Setose, Striga, Strigose, Stubble, Styloid, Vibraculum, Villus, Whisker
Bristle-tail Campodea
Brit(ish), Briton(s) All-red, Anglo, Herring, Iceni, Insular, Isles, Kipper, Limey, Pict, Pom, Rooinek, Saxon, Silt, Silurian, UK
Britain Alban(y), Albion, GB, Old Dart
Britannia, Britannia metal Tutania
Brittany Armorica
Brittle Bruckle, Crackly, Crimp, Crisp, Delicate, Edgy, → FRAGILE, Frush, Hot-short, Redsear, Red-share, Red-shire, Redshort, Shivery, Spall, Spalt
▷ **Brittle** *may indicate* an anagram
Broach Approach, Open, Raise, Spit, Suggest, Tap, Widen
Broad(ly) Cheesy, Crumpet, Dame, Doll, Doxy, Drab, Eclectic, General, Generic, Hippy, Largo, Latitudinous, Loose, Outspoken, Ovate, Pro, Roomy, Spatulate, Tart, Thick, Tolerant, Wide, Woman
Broad-beaked Latirostrate
Broadcast(er), Broadcasting Ad(vertise), Air, Announce, Beam, Breaker, Broadband, CB, Disperse, Disseminate, Downlink, Emission, Ham, IBA, Monophonic, Multicast, Narrowband, Network, Newscast, OB, On, Outside, Pirate, Programme, Promulgate, Public address, Put out, Radiate, Radio, Reith, Relay, RTE, Run, Satellite, → SCATTER, Scattershot, Screen(ed), SECAM, Seed, Simulcast, Sky, Sow, Sperse, Sportscast, Spread, Sprinkle, Stereophonic, Telebridge, Telethon, Transmission, Veejay, Ventilate, Wavelength, Wireless
Broad-nosed Platyrrhine
Broadside Barrage, Criticism, Salvo, Tire
Broadway Boulevard, Esplanade, Great White Way, Motorway
Brocade Arrasene, Baldachin, Baldaquin, Baudekin, Bawdkin, Kincob, Zari
Brochure Booklet, Leaflet, Pamphlet, Programme, Throwaway, Tract
Brogue Accent, → SHOE
Broke(n) Bankrupt, Boracic, Bust(ed), Duff, Evans, Fritz, Impoverished, Insolvent, Kaput, On the rocks, Puckeroo, Shattered, Skint, Stony, Stove, Strapped
▷ **Broken** *may indicate* an anagram
Broken off Prerupt
Broker Agent, Banian, Banyan, Discount, Go-between, Government, Jobber, Mediator, → MERCHANT, Power, Shadchan, Uncle
Bromide Halide, Haloid, Platitude, Truism
Bromine Br
Bronchitis, Bronchitic Chesty, Husk
Bronte(s) Bell, Cyclops
Brontosaurus Apatosaurus

Bronze, Bronze age Aeneous, Aluminium, Bell, Bras(s), Brown, Corinthian, Eugubine, Gunmetal, Hallstatt(ian), Helladic, Kamakura, Manganese, Minoan, Mycenean, Ormolu, Phosphor, Schillerspar, Sextans, Talos, Tan, Third, Torso

Brooch Breastpin, Cameo, Clasp, Fibula, Luckenbooth, Ouch, Owche, Pin, Plaque, Preen, Prop, Spang, Sunburst

Brood(y) Clecking, Clock, Clucky, Clutch, Cogitate, Cour, Cover, Covey, Eye, Eyrie, Hatch, Hover, Incubate, Introspect, Kindle, Litter, Meditate, Mill, Mope, Mull, Nest, Nid, Perch, Pet, → **PONDER**, Repine, Roost, Sit, Sulk, Team

Brook Abide, Babbling, Becher's, Beck, Branch, Burn, Countenance, Creek, Endure, Ghyll, Gill, Kerith, Kill, Pirl, Purl, Rill(et), River, Rivulet, Runlet, Runnel, Springlet, Stand, Stomach, Stream, Suffer, Thole, Tolerate

Broom Besom, Brush, Butcher's, Cow, Cytisus, Genista, Gorse, Greenweed, Hog, Knee-holly, Kow, New, Orobranche, Plantagenet, Retama, Spart, Sweeper, Whisk

Brose Atholl, Pease

Broth Bouillon, Bree, Brew(is), Court bouillon, Cullis, Dashi, Kail, Kale, Muslin-kale, Pot liquor, Pottage, Ramen, Scotch, Skilly, → **SOUP**, Stock

Brothel Bagnio, Bawdy-house, Bordel(lo), Cathouse, Corinth, Crib, Den, Flash-house, Honkytonk, Hothouse, Kip, Knocking shop, Leaping-house, Red-light, Seraglio, Sporting house, Stew, Vaulting-house

Brother(s), Brotherhood Ally, Bhai, Billie, Billy, Blood, Boet, Brethren, Bro, Bud, Comrade, Félibre, Fellow, Fra, Freemason, Grimm, Guild, Lay, Marx, → **MONK**, Moose, Plymouth, Pre-Raphaelite, Sib(ling), Theatine, Trappist, Worker

Brought (back) Redux

Brow Crest, Forehead, Glabella, Ridge, Sinciput, Superciliary, Tump-line

Browbeat(en) Badger, Bully, Butt, Cow, Hangdog, Hector, Nut

Brown(ed) Abram, Adust, Amber, Apricate, Auburn, Au gratin, Bay, Biscuit, Bisque, Bister, Bistre, Bole, Br, Braise, Brindle, Bronzed, Brunette, Bruno, Burnet, Burnt umber, Camel, Capability, Caramel, Caromel, Centennial, Chamois, Cinnamon, Cook, Coromandel, Drab, Dun, Duncan, Fallow, Filemot, Fulvous, Fusc(ous), Grill, Hazel, Infuscate, Ivor, John, Khaki, Liver, March, Meadow, Mocha, Mousy, Mulatto, Mushroom, Nut, Ochre, Olive, Oxblood, Philamot, Pygmalion, Rufous, Rugbeian, Russet, Rust, Sallow, Scorch, Seal, Sepia, Sienna, Snuff, Soare, Sore, Sorrel, Spadiceous, Tan, Tawny, Tenné, Tenny, Terracotta, Testaceous, Toast, Tom, Umber, Vandyke, Wallflower, Walnut, Wholemeal, Windsor

Browne Sam

Brownian movement Agitation, Pedesis

Brownie Dobbie, Dobby, Dobie, Goblin, Hob, Kobold, Leprechaun, Nis(se), Rosebud, Sprite

Browse(r) Eland, Graze, Mouch, Netscape®, Pasture, Read, Scan, Stall-read, Surf

Bruce Robert

Bruise Black eye, Clour, Contund, Contuse, Crush, Damage, Ding, Ecchymosis, Frush, Golp(e), Haematoma, Hurt, Intuse, Livedo, Lividity, Mark, Mouse, Pound, Purpure, Rainbow, Shiner, Ston(n), Stun, Surbate, Vibex

Brummagem Tatty

Brunette Dark, Latin

Brush (off), Brushwood Bavin, Bottle, Brake, Broom, Carbon, Chaparral, Clash, Clothes, Dandy, Dismiss, Dust, Encounter, Fan, Filbert, Filecard, Firth, Fitch, Foxtail, Frith, Grainer, Hag, Hagg, Hair-pencil, Hog, Kiss, Liner, Lip, Loofa(h), Mop, Paint, Pallet, Pig, Pope's head, Putois, Rebuff, Rice, Rigger, Sable, Scrap, Scrub, Scuff, Shaving, Skim, Striper, Sweep, Tail, Thicket, Touch, Undergrowth, Whisk, Wire

Brusque Abrupt, Blunt, Brief, Curt, Downright, Offhand, Pithy, Short

Brussels Carpet, Lace

Brutal(ity), Brute Animal, Atrocity, Barbaric, Beast, Bête, Caesar, Caliban, Cruel, Down and dirty, Hun, Iguanodon, Inhuman, Nazi, Nero, Ostrogoth, Pitiless, Quagga, Rambo, Rottweiler, Roughshod, Ruffian, Thresher-whale, Yahoo

Brutus Wig
Bryophyte Moss, Tree-moss
Bubble(s), Bubbly Aeration, Air-bell, Air-lock, Barmy, Bead(ed), Bell, Bleb, Blister, Boil, Buller, Cavitate, Champagne, Cissing, Ebullition, Effervesce, Embolus, Enthuse, Espumoso, Foam, → **FROTH**, Gassy, Globule, Gurgle, Head, Magnetic, Mantle, Mississippi, Moet, Popple, Rale, Reputation, Roundel, Rowndell, Seed, Seethe, Simmer, Soap, South Sea, Vesicle, Widow
Bubble and squeak Colcannon
Buccaneer Corsair, Dampier, Drake, Freebooter, Morgan, Picaroon, Pirate
Buck (up) Bongo, Brace, Cheer, Dandy, Deer, Dollar, Elate, Encheer, Hart, Jerk, Leash, Male, Ourebi, Pitch, Pricket, Ram, Rusa, Sore, Sorel(l), Sorrel, Spade, Spay(a)d, → **STAG**, Staggard, Stud, Water, Wheel
Buckaroo Cowboy, Cowpoke
Bucket(s) Bail, Bale, Clamshell, Ice, Jacob's ladder, Kibble, Ladle, Noria, Pail, Piggin, Rain, Rust, Scuttle, Situla, Slop, Stoop(e), Stope, Stoup, Tub
Buckeye Ohio
Buckle Artois, Bend, Clasp, Contort, Crumple, Deform, Dent, Fasten, Warp
▷ **Buckle** *may indicate* an anagram
Buckle-beggar Patrico
Buckler Ancile, Rondache, → **SHIELD**, Targe
▷ **Bucks** *may indicate* an anagram
Buckshee Free
Buckthorn Cascara, Rhineberry, Wahoo
Buckwheat Brank, Sarrasin, Sarrazin
Bucolic Aeglogue, Eglogue, Idyllic, Pastoral, Rural, Rustic
Bud(ding), Buddy Botoné, Bottony, Bulbil, Burgeon, Cacotopia, Clove, Cobber, Deb, Eye, Gem(ma), Germinate, Hibernaculum, Holly, Knop, Knosp, Knot, Nascent, Pal, Scion, Serial, Shoot, Sprout, Statoblast, Taste, Turion
Buddha, Buddhism, Buddhist Abhidhamma, Ahimsa, Amitabha, Anata, Anatta, Anicca, Arhat, Asoka, Bardo, Bodhisattva, Dalai Lama, Dukkha, Esoteric, Foism, Gautama, Hinayana, Jain, Jataka, Jodo, Kagyu, Mahatma, Mahayana, Maitreya, Maya, Nichiren, Pali, Pitaka, Pure Land, Rinzai, Ryobu, Sakya-muni, Sangha, Shinto, Siddhartha Gautama, Sila, Sima, Soka Gakkai, Soto, Sutra, Tantric, Theravada, Tripitaka, Triratna, Vajrayana, Zen(o)
Budge Jee, Move, Stir, Submit
Budgerigar Shell parrakeet, Shell parrot
Budget Allocation, Allot, Cheap, Estimate, Operating, Plan, Programme, Rudder, Save, Shoestring
Buff Altogether, Beige, Birthday suit, Blind man's, Cineaste, Eatanswill, Expert, Fan, Fawn, Maven, Mavin, Nankeen, Natural, Nude, Nut, Polish, → **RUB**, Streak
Buffalo African, Anoa, Arna, Asiatic, Bison, Bonasus, Bugle, Cap, Cape, Carabao, Ox, Perplex, Takin, Tamarao, Tamarau, Timarau, Water, Zamouse
Buffer Bootblack, Cofferdam, Cutwater, Fender, Sleek-stone
Buffet Bang, Blow, Box, Carvery, Counter, Cuff, Finger-food, Fork luncheon, Fork-supper, Hit, Lam, Maltreat, Meal, Perpendicular, Shove, Sideboard, Smorgasborg, Strike, Strook(e)
Buffoon(ery) Antic, Clown, Droll, Fool, Goliard, Harlequin, Horseplay, Iniquity, Jack pudding, Jester, Mime(r), Mome, Mountebank, Mummer, Nutter, Pantagruel, Pantaloon(ery), Pickle-herring, Pierrot, Punchinello, Scaramouch, Scogan, Scoggin, Scurrile, Slouch, Tomfool, Vice, Wag, Zany
Bug(s) Ambush, Annoy, Anoplura, Antagonise, Arthropod, Assassin, Bacteria, Bedevil, Beetle, Berry, Bishop's mitre, Bunny, Cabbage, Capsid, Chinch, Cimex, Coccidae, Cockchafer, Corixid, Creepy-crawly, Croton, Damsel, Debris, Demon, Dictograph®, Eavesdrop, E-coli, Error, Exasperate, Germ, Get at, Ground, Harlequin, Hassle,

Hemiptera, → **INSECT**, Irritate, Jitter, June, Kissing, Lace, Lightning, Listeria, Maori, May, Mealy, Micrococcus, Microphone, Mike, Milkweed, Millennium, Mite, Nark, Nettle, Pest(er), Pill, Reduviid, Rhododendron, Rile, Shield, Skeeter, Sow, Squash, Tap, Vex, Water-measurer, Wheel, Wiretap

Bugbear Anathema, Bargest, Bête noire, Bogey, Bogle, Bogy, Eten, Ettin, Poker, Rawhead

Buggy Beach, Car, Cart, Inside-car, Pushchair, Shay, Tipcart, Trap

Bughouse Fleapit, Loco

Bugle, Bugle call Boots and saddles, Chamade, Clarion, Cornet, Flugelhorn, Hallali, Kent, Last post, Ox, Reveille, Taps, → **TRUMPET**, Urus

Build, Building(s), Building site, Build-up Accrue, Aggrade, Anabolism, Ar(a)eostyle, Assemble, Barn, Basilica, Bhavan, Big, Boathouse, Bricks and mortar, Capitol, Chapterhouse, Cob, Colosseum, Commons, Construction, Containment, Corncrib, Cot, → **CREATE**, Cruck, Curia, Days' house, Develop, Dipteros, Dome, Drystone, Duplex, Ectomorph, Edifice, Edify, Endomorph, Erect, Exchange, Fabric, Gatehouse, Hangar, Heapstead, High-rise, Hut, Infill, Insula, Kaaba, Ken, Linhay, Listed, Low-rise, Lyceum, Mesomorph, Minaret, Monopteron, Mosque, Mould, Observatory, Odeon, Odeum, Outhouse, Palace, Palazzo, Pataka, Pavilion, Pentagon, Pentastyle, Phalanstery, Phalanx, Physique, Pile, Portakabin®, Premises, Prytaneum, Quonset®, Raise, Ribbon, Rotunda, Shippen, Skyscraper, Somatotype, Squat, Stance, Statehouse, Structure, Summerhouse, Suspension, Synthesis, System, Systyle, Tectonic, Telecottage, Temple, Tenement, Tholos, Tower, Tower block, Town hall, Triplex®, Whata

Builder Bob, Brick, Cheops, Constructor, Engineer, Entrepreneur, Mason, Millwright, Spiderman, Stonemason, Waller

▷ **Building** *may indicate* an anagram

Built-up Urban

Bulb Camas(h), Camass, Chive, Cive, Corm, Flash, Globe, Lamp, Light, Olfactory, Pearl, Rupert's drop, Scallion, Set, Shallot, Squill

Bulgaria BG

Bulge, Bulging Astrut, Bag, Bias, Biconvex, Bug, Bulbous, Bunchy, Cockle, Entasis, Expand, Exsert, Inion, Prolate, Protrude, Protuberant, Relievo, Rotund, Shoulder, Strout, Strut, → **SWELL**, Torose, Tumid

Bulk(y) Aggregate, Ample, Big, Body, Bouk, Corpulent, Density, Extent, Gross, Hull, Immensity, Lofty, Massive, Preponderance, Roughage, Scalar, → **SIZE**, Stout, Vol(ume), Voluminous, Weight

Bull(s), Bullock, Bully(ing) Abuser, Anoa, Apis, Bakha, Beef, Blarney, Bludgeon, Bluster, Bouncer, Bovine, Brag, Brave, Browbeat, Buchis, Bucko, Centre, Cuttle, Despot, Dragoon, Drawcansir, Encierro, Englishman, Eretrian, Fancyman, Farnese, Flashman, Flatter, Gold, Gosh, Hapi, Harass, Hawcubite, Haze(r), Hector, Hibernicism, Hogwash, Hoodlum, Huff, Intimidate, Investor, Iricism, Irish(ism), John, Killcow, Lambast, Maltreat, Menace, Merwer, Mick(e)(y), Mistake, Mithraism, Mohock, Nandi, Neat, Oppressor, Ox, Pamplona, Papal, Pennalism, Piker, Pistol, Placet, Poler, Pussy-whip, Railroad, Rhodian, Roarer, Rot, Ruffian, Sitting, Souteneur, Stag, Stale, Strong-arm, Swash-buckler, Taurine, Taurus, Toitoi, Tommy-rot, Tosh, Trash, Tripe, Twaddle, Tyran(ne), Tyrannise, Tyrant, Unigenitus, Victimise, Winged, Zo(bo)

Bulldog Marshal, Tenacious

Bulldoze(r) Angledozer, Coerce, Earthmover, Leveller, Overturn, Raze

Bullet Ammo, Balata, Ball, Baton round, Biscayan, Blank, Dumdum, Fusillade, Lead towel, Magic, Minié, Minié ball, Missile, Pellet, Percussio, Plastic, Round, Rubber, Shot, Slug, Soft-nosed, Tracer

Bulletin All points, Memo, Message, Newscast, Newsletter, Report, Summary

Bull-fight(er), Bull-fighting Banderillero, Banderillo, Corrida, Cuadrilla, Encierro, Escamillo, Faena, Mano a mano, Matador, Picador, Rejoneador, Tauromachy, Toreador, Torero

Bullfinch Monk

Bull-head Cottoid, Father-lasher, Pogge, Sea-poacher
Bull-rider Europa
Bull-roarer Rhombos, Tu(r)ndun
Bull's eye Carton, Gold, Humbug, Prick, Target
Bullshit BS
▶ **Bully** *see* **BULL(S)**
Bulrush Pandanaceous, Raupo, Reed, Reed-mace, Tule
Bulwark Bastion, Defence, Rampart, Resistor
Bum Ass, Beg, Beggar, Deadbeat, Prat, Scrounge, Sponge, Thumb, Tramp, Vagabond
Bumble Beadle, Bedel(l)
▷ **Bumble** *may indicate* an anagram
Bumboat woman Buttercup
Bumf Spam
Bump(er), Bumps, Bumpy Big, Blow, Bouncer, Bradyseism, Bucket, Bustle, Clour, Collide, Dunch, Encephalocele, Fender, Hillock, Immense, Inian, Inion, Jo(u)le, Joll, Jolt, Jowl, Keltie, Kelty, Knar, Knock, Mamilla, Mogul, Organ, Overrider®, Phrenology, Reveille, Rouse, Speed, Thump, Uneven
Bumph Loo-roll
Bumpkin Bucolic, Bushwhacker, Clodhopper, Hawbuck, Hayseed, Hick, Jock, Lout, Oaf, Peasant, Put(t), Rube, Rustic, Yokel, Zany
Bumptious Arrogant, Brash, Randie, Randy, Uppity
Bun Barmbrack, Bath, Black, Chelsea, Chignon, Chou, Cookie, Currant, Devonshire split, Hot-cross, Huffkin, Mosbolletjie, Roll, Teacake, Toorie, Wad
Bunch Acinus, Anthology, Bob, Botryoid, Bouquet, Byndle, Cluster, Fascicle, Finial, Flock, Gang, → **GROUP**, Hand, Handful, Ilk, Lot, Lump, Nosegay, Panicle, Raceme, Spray, Staphyline, Tassel, Tee, Truss, Tuft, Tussie-mussie
Bundle(d) Axoneme, Bale, Bavin, Bluey, Bottle, Byssus, Desmoid, Dorlach, Drum, Fag(g)ot, Fascicle, Fasciculate, Fascine, Fibre, Fibrovascular, Kemple, Knitch, Lemniscus, Matilda, → **PACK(AGE)**, Parcel, Sack, Sheaf, Shiralee, Shock, Shook, Stela, Stook, Swag, Tie, Top, Trousseau, Truss, Vascular, Wad, Wadge, Wap, Yealm
Bung Cork, Dook, Obturate, Plug, Stopgap, Stopper
Bungalow Dak
Bungle(r), Bungled, Bungling Blunder, Blunk, Bodge, Boob, Boss shot, Botch, Bumble, Bummle, Dub, Duff, Fluff, Foozle, Foul, Foul up, Goof, Gum up, Maladroit, Mash, Mess, Mis(h)guggle, Muddle, Muff, Mull, Prat, Screw, Spoil, Tinker
Bunk(er), Bunk off, Bunkum Abscond, Absquatulate, Balderdash, Baloney, Berth, Blah, Bolt, Casemate, Claptrap, Clio, Entrap, Guff, Guy, Hazard, History, Hokum, Hooey, Humbug, Malarky, Moonshine, Nonsense, Rot, Sandtrap, Scuttle, Skive, Stokehold, Tommy-rot, Tosh, Trap, Tripe, Truant, Twaddle
Bunter Billy, Owl
Bunthorne Aesthete, Poet
Bunting Bird, Cirl, Flag, Fringilline, Ortolan, Pennant, Snow, Streamer, Tanager, Towhee, Yellow-hammer, Yowley
Buoy (up) Bell, Breeches, Can, Dan, Daymark, Dolphin, Float, Life, Marker, Nun, Raft, Reassure, Ring, Seamark, Sonar, Sonobuoy, Spar, Sustain, Wreck
Buoyant Afloat, Blithe, Floaty, Resilient
Burble Blat, Gibber
Burden Albatross, Beare, Bob, Cargo, Cark, Chant, Chorus, Cross, Cumber, Deadweight, Drone, Droore, Encumber, Encumbrance, Fa-la, Fardel, Folderol, Fraught, Freight, Gist, Handicap, Hum, Lade, → **LOAD**, Lumber, Millstone, Monkey, Oercome, Onus, Oppress, Payload, Put-upon, Refrain, Rumbelow, Saddle, Servitude, Shanty, Substance, Task, Tax, Tenor, Torch, Trouble, Weight, White man's, Woe, Yoke
Burdensome Irksome, Onerous, Oppressive, Weighty
Burdock Clote(-bar), Clothur, Cockle-bar, Gobo, Hardoke, Weed

Bureau Agency, Agitprop, Breakfront, Cominform, Davenport, Desk, Interpol, Kominform, Marriage, → **OFFICE**, Volunteer, Weather

Bureaucracy, Bureaucrat(ic) Bean-counter, CS, Functionary, Impersonal, Jack-in-office, Mandarin, Red tape, Tapist, Technocrat, Wallah

Burgeon(ing) Asprout, Blossom, Bud, Grow, Sprout

Burgess, Burgher Citizen, Freeman, Portman

Burgh Burrowstown, Parliamentary, Police, Royal

Burglar(y), Burgle Aggravated, Area-sneak, Break-in, Cat, Crack(sman), House-breaker, Intruder, Peterman, Picklock, Raffles, Robber, Screw, Thief, Yegg

Burgundy Macon, Vin

Burial(place) Catacomb, Charnel, Committal, Crypt, Cubiculum, Darga, Funeral, God's acre, Golgotha, Grave, Green, Interment, Kurgan, Lair, Last rites, Pyramid, Sepulchre, Sepulture, Speos, Tomb, Tumulus, Vault, Vivisepulture, Zoothapsis

Burin Graver

Burlesque Caricatura, Caricature, Comedy, Farce, Heroicomical, Hudibrastic(s), Hurlo-thrumbo, Lampoon, Macaronic, Parody, Satire, Skimmington, Skit, Spoof, Travesty

Burlington RA

Burly Bluff, Stout, Strapping

Burma, Burmese Karen(ni), Mon(-Khmer), Myanmar, Naga, Shan

Burn(ed), Burner, Burning, Burnt Ablaze, Adust, Afire, Alow(e), Ardent, Argand, Arson, Ash, Auto-da-fé, Back, Bake, Bats-wing, Beck, Bishop, Blaze, Blister, Blowtorch, Blush, Brand, Bren(ne), Brent, Brook, Bunsen, Causalgia, Caustic, Cauterise, Char, Chark, Chinese, Cinder, Clavie, Coal, Coke, Combust, Conflagration, Cremate, Crozzled, Crucial, Deflagrate, Destruct, Effigy, Eilding, Ember, Emboil, Empyreuma, Fervid, Fircone, → **FIRE**, First degree, Fishtail, Flagrant, Flare, Flash, Fresh(et), Gleed, Gut, Holocaust, Ignite, In, Incendiary, Incense, Incinerate, Inure, Inust(ion), Itch, Kill, Lean, Live, Lunt, Moorburn, Muirburn, Offering, On, Oxidise, Oxyacetylene, Phlogiston, Pilot, Plo(a)t, Powder, Pyric, Pyromania, Raster, Rill, Sati, Scald, Scaud, Scorch, Scouther, Scowder, Scowther, Sear, Sienna, Sike, Singe, Sizzle, Smart, Smoulder, Stake, Suttee, Swale, Third-degree, Thurible, Torch, Umber, Urent, Ustion, Ustulation, Weeke, Welsbach, Wick, Ybrent

Burp Belch, Eruct

Burr(ing) Brei, Brey, Clote, Croup, Dialect, Knob, Rhotacism

Burrow(er), Burrowing Dig, Earth, Fossorial, Gopher, Groundhog, Hole, How, Howk, Mine, Mole, Nuzzle, Root, Sett, Terricole, Tunnel, Viscacha, Warren, Wombat, Worm

Bursar(y) Camerlengo, Camerlingo, Coffers, Grant, Purser, Scholarship, Tertiary, Treasurer

Bursitis Beat

Burst(ing), Bursts Blowout, Bout, Brast, Break, Dehisce, Disrupt, Dissilient, Ebullient, Erumpent, Erupt, → **EXPLODE**, Fits and starts, Flare-up, Fly, Gust, Implode, Pop, Salvo, Sforzato, Shatter, Spasm, Spirt, Split, Sprint, Spurt, Stave, Tetterous

Burundi RU

Bury Cover, Eard, Earth, Embowel, Engrave, Enhearse, Entomb, Graff, Graft, Imbed, Inearth, Inhearse, Inherce, Inhume, Inter, Inurn, Landfill, Repress, Sepulture, Sink, Ye(a)rd, Yird

Bus Aero, Bandwagon, Car, Charabanc, Coach, Crew, Double-decker, Greyhound, Highway, Hondey, Hopper, ISA, Jitney, Mammy-wagon, Purdah, Rattletrap, Single-decker, Tramcar, Trolley, Trunk, Walking

Bus conductor Cad, Clippy

Bush(es), Bush-man, Bushy Bitou, Bramble, Brier, Bullace, Busket, Calico, Clump, Cotton, Creosote, Dumose, Firethorn, Greasewood, Hawthorn, Hedge, Hibiscus, Ivy-tod, Jaborandi, Kapok, Kiekie, Mallee, Matagouri, Mulberry, Outback, Pachysandra, Poinsettia, Poly-poly, President, Prostanthera, Sallee, San, Scrog, Shepherd, Shrub, Sloe, Sloethorn, Sugar, Thicket, Tire, Tod(de), Tumatakuru

Bush-baby Durukuli, Galago, Nagapie, Night-ape
Bushel Ardeb, Bu, Co(o)mb, Cor, Ephah, Fou, Homer, Peck, Weight, Wey
Bushwalker Hoon
Business Affair, Agency, Biz, Bricks and clicks, Brokerage, Bus, Cahoot, Cartel, Cerne, Chaebol(s), Co, Commerce, Company, Concern, Conglomerate, Corporate, Craft, Custom, Dealership, Duty, Enterprise, Ergon, Establishment, Exchange, Fasti, Field, Firm, Funny, Game, Gear, Hong, Industry, Kaizen, Lifestyle, Line, Métier, Monkey, Office, Palaver, Pidgin, Pi(d)geon, Practice, Professional, Racket, Shebang, Shop, Show, To-do, Trade, Traffic, Transaction, Tread, Turnover, Unincorporated, Vocation, Zaibatsu, Zaikai
Businessman Babbitt, Capitalist, City, Dealer, Entrepreneur, Fat-cat, Financier, Realtor, Taipan, Trader, Tycoon
Busk(er) Bodice, Corset, Entertainer, German-band
Buskin(s) Brod(e)kin, Cothurn(us), Shoe
Buss Kiss, Osculate, Smack
Bussu Troelie, Troely, Troolie
Bust Beano, Boob, Brast, Break, Chest, Dollarless, Falsies, Figurehead, Herm(a), Insolvent, Kaput, Mamma, Raid, Rupture, Sculp, Shatter(ed), Spree, Statue, Term(inus), To-tear, To-torne, Ups(e)y
▷ **Bust** *may indicate* an anagram
Bustard Bird, Otis, Turkey
Buster Keaton
Bustle Ado, Beetle, Do, Dress-improver, Flap, Fuss, Pad, Scurry, → **STIR**, Swarm, To-do, Tournure, Whew
Busy Active, At (it), Deedy, → **DETECTIVE**, Dick, Doing, Eident, Employ, Engaged, Ergate, Eye, Goer, Hectic, Hive, Hot spot, Humming, Manic, Occupied, Operose, Ornate, Prodnose, Stir, Stirabout, Tec, Throng, Worksome
Busybody Bee, Bustler, Meddler, Noser, Pantopragmatic, Pragmatic, Snooper, Trout, Yenta
But Aber, Algates, Bar, Except, However, Keg, Merely, Nay, Only, Save, Sed, Simply, Tun, Without, Yet
Butch He-man, Macho
Butcher(s), Butchery Cumberland, Decko, Dekko, Eyeful, Flesher, Gander, Ice, Kill, Killcow, Look, Looksee, Mangle, Massacre, Ovicide, Peek, Sever, Shambles, Shochet, Shufti, Slaughter, Slay, Slink
Butler Bedivere, Bread-chipper, Jeeves, Khansama(h), Major-domo, RAB, Rhett, Samuel, Servant, Sewer, Sommelier, Steward
Butt (in) Aris, Arse, Ass, Barrel, Bumper, Buns, Bunt, Clara, Dimp, Dout, Dowt, Dunch, Enter, Geck, Glasgow kiss, Goat, Header, Horn, Jesting-stock, Laughing-stock, Mark, Nut, Outspeckle, Pantaloon, Pipe, Push, Ram, Roach, Scapegoat, Snipe, Stompie, → **STOOGE**, Straight man, Stump, Target, Tun, Ups
Butter Adulation, Apple, Beurre, Billy, Blandish, Brandy, Butyric, Cacao, Cocoa, Coconut, Drawn, Flatter, Galam, Garcinia, Ghee, Ghi, Goa, Goat, Illipi, Illupi, Kokum, Mahua, Mahwa, Maitre d'hotel, Mow(r)a, Nut, Nutter, Palm, Pat, Peanut, Print, Ram, Rum, Scrape, Shea, Spread, Vegetable
▷ **Butter** *may indicate* a goat or such
Buttercup Bumboat woman, Crowfoot, Crow-toe, Goldilocks, Ranunculus, Reate, Thalictrum
Butterfingers Muff
Butterfish Nine-eyes
Butterflies, Butterfly Apollo, Argus, Birdwing, Blue, Brimstone, Brown, Cabbage white, Camberwell beauty, Cardinal, Chequered skipper, Cleopatra, Clouded yellow, Collywobbles, Comma, Common blue, Copper, Dilettante, Eclosion, Elfin, Emperor, Fritillary, Gate-keeper, Grayling, Hair-streak, Heath, Hesperid, Imaginal, Kallima, Large copper, Large white, Leaf, Lycaena, Marbled-white, Meadow brown, Metalmark,

Milk-weed, Monarch, Morpho, Mountain ringlet, Mourning-cloak, Nerves, Nymphalid, Nymphean, Orange-tip, Owl, Painted lady, Papilionidae, Peacock, Pieris, Psyche, Purple emperor, Red admiral, Rhopalocera, Ringlet, Satyr(idae), Satyrinae, Scotch argus, Silverspot, Skipper, Small white, Snake's head, Speckled wood, Stamper, Stroke, Sulphur, Swallow-tail, Thecla, Thistle, Tiger swallowtail, Tortoiseshell, Two-tailed pasha, Vanessa, Wall brown, White admiral

Buttermilk Bland, Lassi

Butternut Souari

Butter-tree Mahua, Mahwa, Mow(r)a

Buttocks Aristotle, Arse, Ass, Bahookie, Booty, Bottom, Buns, Can, Cheeks, Coit, Derrière, Doup, Duff, Fanny, Fud, Fundament, Gluteus maximus, Heinie, Hinder-end, Hinderlan(d)s, Hunkers, Hurdies, Jacksie, Jacksy, Keester, Keister, Mooning, Nache, Nates, Posterior, Prat, Quatch, Quoit, Seat, Tush

Button(s) Barrel, Bellboy, Fastener, Frog, Hold, Hot, Knob, Mescal, Mouse, Mute, Netsuke, Olivet, Page(boy), Panic, Pause, Pearl, Press, Push, Snooze, Stud, Switch, Toggle, Toolbar

Buttonhole Accost, Boutonniere, Detain, Doorstep, Eye, Flower

Buttress Brace, Counterfort, Flying, Hanging, Pier, Prop, Stay, Support, Tambour

Butty Chum, Oppo

Buxom Bonnie, Busty, Plump, Sonsy, Well-endowed, Wench

Buy(ing), Buyer Believe, Bribe, Coemption, Coff, Corner, Customer, Emption, Engross, Impulse, Monopsonist, Oligopsony, Panic, Purchase, Redeem, Regrate, Shop, Shout, Spend, Take, Trade, Treat, Vendee

▷ **Buyer** *may indicate* money

Buzz(er) Bee, Birr, Bombilate, Bombinate, Button, Drone, Fly, Hum, Kazoo, Rumour, Scram, Whirr, Whisper, Zed, Zing, Zoom

Buzzard Bee-kite, Bird, Buteo, Hawk, Honey, Pern, Puttock, Turkey, Vulture

By Alongside, At, Beside, Gin, Gone, In, Near, Neighbouring, Nigh, Of, On, Past, Per, Through, With, X

Bye Extra

Bye-bye Adieu, Farewell, Tata

By far Out and away

Bygone B.C., Dead, Departed, Past, Yore

By Jove Egad

Bypass Avoid, Beltway, Circuit, Coronary, → **DETOUR**, Dodge, Evade, Ignore, Omit, Shunt, Skirt

By-product Epiphenomenon, Spill-over, Spin-off

Byre Cowshed, Manger, Stable, Trough

By so much The

Byte Nybble

By the way Apropos, Incidentally, Ob(iter)

Byway Alley, Lane, Path

Byword Ayword, Nayword, Phrase, Proverb, Slogan

Byzantine Catapan, Comnenus, Complicated, Exarch, Intricate, Intrince, Theme

C Around, Caught, Celsius, Cent, Centigrade, Charlie, Conservative, San

Cab Boneshaker, Crawler, Drosky, Fiacre, Four-wheeler, Growler, Gurney, Hackney, Hansom, Mini, Noddy, Taxi, Vettura

Cabal(ler) Arlington, Ashley, Buckingham, Clifford, Clique, Conspiracy, Coterie, Faction, Junto, Lauderdale, Party, Plot

Cab(b)alistic Abraxis, Mystic, Notarikon, Occult

Cabaret Burlesque, Floorshow

Cabbage(-head), Cabbage soup Black, Bok choy, Borecole, Brassica, Castock, Cauliflower, Cavalo nero, Chinese, Chou, Choucroute, Cole, Collard, Crout, Custock, Drumhead, Gobi, Kerguelen, Kohlrabi, Kraut, Loaf, Loave, Mibuna, Mizuna, Pak-choi, Pamphrey, Pe-tsai, St Patrick's, Sauerkraut, Savoy, Sea-kale, Shchi, Shtchi, Skunk, Thieve, Turnip, Wild, Wort

Caber Fir, Janker, Log, Sting

Cabin Berth, Bibby, Bothy, Box, Cabana, Caboose, Camboose, Coach, Cottage, Crannog, Crib, Cuddy, Den, Gondola, Hovel, Hut, Izba, Lodge, Loghouse, Long-house, Pod, Pressure, Room, Roundhouse, Saloon, Shack, Shanty, Signal box, Stateroom, Trunk

Cabin-boy Grummet

Cabinet Armoire, Bahut, Cabale, Case, Cellaret, Chiffonier, Chill, Closet, Commode, Console, Cupboard, Display, Filing, Kitchen, Ministry, Nest, Official family, Repository, Secretaire, Shadow, Shrinal, Unit, Vitrine

Cabinet maker Banting, Chippendale, Ebeniste, Hepplewhite, Joiner, PM

Cable(way), Cable-car Arrester, Choucroute, Coax(ial), Extension, Flex, Halser, Hawser, Jumper, Jump leads, Junk, Kissagram, Landline, Lead, Lead-in, Lifeline, Null-modern, Oil-filled, Outhaul, Outhauler, Rope, Shroud, Slatch, Snake, Téléférique, → **TELEGRAM**, Telegraph, Telepherique, Telpher(age), Topping lift, Trunking, Wire, Yoke

Cache Deposit, Hidlin(g)s, → **HOARD**, Inter, Stash, Store, Treasure

Cachet Prestige

Cackle Cluck, Gaggle, Gas, Haw, Horse laugh, Snicker, Titter

Cacography Scrawl

Cacophony Babel, Caterwaul, Charivari, Discord, Jangle

Cactus, Cactus-like Alhagi, Barel, Cereus, Cholla, Christmas, Dildo, Easter, Echino-, Hedgehog, Jointed, Jojoba, Maguey, Mescal, Mistletoe, Nopal, Ocotillo, Ombrophobe, Opuntia, Organ-pipe, Peyote, Pita(ha)ya, Prickly pear, Retama, Saguaro, Schlumbergera, Stapelia, Star, Strawberry, Torch-thistle, Tuna, Xerophytic

Cad Base, Boor, Bounder, Churl, Cocoa, Heel, Oik, Rascal, Rotter, Skunk, Varlet

Cadaver(ous) Body, Corpse, Deathly, Ghastly, Goner, Haggard, Stiff

Caddy Porter, Tea, Teapoy

Cadence Authentic, Beat, Close, Euouae, Evovae, Fa-do, Flow, Interrupted, Lilt, Meter, Perfect, Plagal, Rhythm

Cadenza Fireworks

Cadet(s) Junior, OTC, Plebe, Recruit, Rookie, Scion, Snooker, Space, Syen, Trainee, Younger

Cadge(r) Beg, Bludge, Bot, Bum, Impose, Mutch, Ponce, → **SCROUNGE**, Sponge

Cadmium Cd

Caesar Despot, Nero

Caesium Cs

Café, Cafeteria Automat, Bistro, Brasserie, Buvette, Canteen, Carvery, Commissary, Cybercafe, Diner, Dinette, Donko, Eatery, Estaminet, Filtré, Greasy spoon, Hashhouse, Internet, Juke joint, Netcafé, Noshery, Pizzeria, Pull-in, Snackbar, Tearoom, Tea-shop, Transport, Truckstop
Cage Bar, Battery, Box, Cavie, Confine, Coop, Corf, Dray, Drey, Enmew, Faraday, Fold, Frame, Grate, Hutch, Keavie, Mew, Mortsafe, Pen, → **PRISON**, Roll, Safety, Squirrel, Trave
Cag(e)y Chary
Cahoots Hugger-mugger
Cairn Barp, Clearance, Dog, Horned, Man, Mound, Raise
Caisson Bends
Caitiff Meanie
Cajole(ry) Beflum, Beguile, Blandish, Blarney, Carn(e)y, → **COAX**, Cuittle, Humbug, Inveigle, Jolly, Persuade, Wheedle, Whillywha(w), Wiles
Cake Clot, → **HARDEN**, Mud, Pat, → **PLASTER**, Set, Tablet, Wad

---

CAKES

3 letters:	Latke	Pepper	Saffron
Bam	Layer	Potato	Savarin
Bun	Patty	Simnel	Stollen
Hoe	Poori	Sponge	Stottie
Nut	Pound	Waffle	Twelfth
Oil	Rosti	Wonder	Vetkoek
Pan	Scone		Wedding
Tea	Spawn	7 letters:	Yule log
	Spice	Baklava	
4 letters:	Sushi	Banbury	8 letters:
Baba	Tansy	Bannock	Agnus dei
Farl	Tipsy	Brioche	Barmbrack
Fish	Torte	Brownie	Birthday
Idli	Wafer	Carcake	Black bun
Kueh	Yeast	Chapati	Chillada
Pone		Chupati	Chapatti
Puff	6 letters:	Cruller	Chupatty
Puri	Biffin	Crumpet	Flapjack
Rice	Cattle	Currant	Macaroon
Rock	Coburg	Drizzle	Meringue
Roti	Cookie	Fritter	Mooncake
Rout	Cotton	Galette	Napoleon
Rusk	Dainty	Gateaux	Ready-mix
Salt	Dundee	Jannock	Sandwich
Seed	Eccles	Jumbles	Slapjack
Slab	Eclair	Kruller	Teabread
Soul	Filter	Linseed	Tortilla
	Girdle	Madeira	
5 letters:	Hockey	Oatmeal	9 letters:
Angel	Johnny	Paratha	Bara brith
Babka	Jumbal	Pavlova	Buckwheat
Bhaji	Kuchen	Pikelet	Chupattie
Fancy	Marble	Pomfret	Clapbread
Farle	Muffin	Popover	Croquante
Genoa	Parkin	Ratafia	Croquette
Lardy	Pastry	Rum baba	Lamington

Madeleine	**10 letters:**	Parliament	Lady's finger
Panettone	Battenberg	Pontefract	Profiterole
Petit four	Brandy snap	Puftaloona	Sachertorte
Puftaloon	Corn dodger	Religieuse	
Queencake	Devil's food	Upside down	**12 letters:**
Sally Lunn	Frangipane		Maid of honour
Swiss roll	Frangipani	**11 letters:**	Millefeuille
	Koeksister	Gingerbread	Singing-hinny

▷ **Cake** *may indicate* an anagram
Cake-shaped Placentiform
Cakestand Curate
Cakewalk Doddle
Calaboose Jail, Loghouse
Calamitous, Calamity Blow, Catastrophe, Dire, → **DISASTER**, Distress, Fatal, Ill, Jane, Ruth, Storm, Tragic, Unlucky, Visitation, Woe
Calcareous Ganoin, Lithite
Calcium Ca, Colemanite, Dogger, Dripstone, Flowstone, Otolith, Quicklime, Scawtite, Whewellite, Wollastonite
Calculate(d), Calculation, Calculator Abacus, Actuary, Comptometer, Compute(r), Cost, Design, Estimate, Extrapolate, Four-function, Log, Napier's bones, Number-crunch, Prorate, Quip(p)u, Rate, → **RECKON**, Slide-rule, Sofar, Soroban, Tactical, Tell
Calculus Cholelith, Differential, Functional, Infinitesimal, Integral, Lambda, Lith, Lithiasis, Predicate, Propositional, Science, Sentential, Sialolith, Stone, Tartar, Urolith
Caledonian Kanak
Calendar Advent, Agenda, Almanac, Chinese, Diary, Dies fasti, Fasti, Gregorian, Hebrew, Intercalary, Jewish, Journal, Julian, Luach, Lunisolar, Menology, Newgate, New Style, Ordo, Perpetual, Planner, Revolutionary, Roman, Sothic
Calender(ing) Dervish, Mangle, Swissing
Calf Ass, Bobby, Box, Cf, Deacon, Divinity, Dogie, Dogy, Fatted, Freemartin, Golden, Law, Leg, Maverick, Mottled, Poddy, Sleeper, Slink, Smooth, Stirk, Sural, Tollie, Tolly, Tree, Veal, Vitular
Caliban Moon-calf
Calibrate, Calibre Bore, Capacity, Graduate, Mark, → **QUALITY**, Text
California(n) Fresno, Golden State
Californium Cf
Caliph Abbasid(e), Omar, Vathek
Call(ed), Call (for), Calling, Call on, Call up Adhan, Ahoy, Appeal, Arraign, Art, Awaken, Azan, Banco, Bawl, Beck, Behote, Bevy, Bid, Boots and saddles, Bugle, Business, Buzz, Career, Chamade, Cite, Claim, Clang, Clarion, Cleep, Clepe, Close, Cold, Conference, Conscript, Convene, Convoke, Coo, Cooee, Cry, Curtain, Dial, Drift, Dub, Effectual, Entail, Evoke, First post, Game, Go, Hail, Hallali, Halloa, Haro, Heads, Heave-ho, Hech, Hete, Hey, Hight, Ho, Hot(e), Howzat, Huddup, Hurra(h), Invocation, Job, Junk, Last (post), Levy, Line, Local, Look in, Margin, Métier, Misère, Mobilise, Mot, Name, Nap, Need, Nemn, Nempt, Nominate, No trumps, Nuisance, Olé, Page, Peter, Phone, Photo, Pop in, Post, Proo, Pruh, Pursuit, Rechate, Recheat, Retreat, Reveille, Ring, Roll, Rort, Rouse, Route, Sa-sa, See, Sennet, → **SHOUT**, Shut-out, Slam, Slander, Slogan, Soho, Sola, SOS, STD, Style, Subpoena, Summon(s), Tails, Tally ho, Tantivy, Taps, Telephone, Term, Toho, Toll, Trumpet, Trunk, Turn, Tweet, Visit, Vocation, Waken, Wake-up, Whoa-ho-ho, Wo ha ho, Yell, Yo, Yodel, Yodle, Yo-ho(-ho), Yoicks, Yoo-hoo
Calla(s) Aroid, Lily, Maria
Caller Fresh, Guest, Herring, Inspector, Muezzin, Rep, Traveller, → **VISITOR**
Calligraphy Grass style, Kakemono

Callipers Odd legs

Callisthenics T'ai chi (ch'uan)

Call off Abort

Callosity, Call(o)us Bunion, Cold, Corn, Hard, Horny, Obtuse, Ringbone, Seg, Thylose, Tough, Tylosis, Unfeeling

Callow Crude, Green, Immature, Jejune

Calm Abate, Alegge, Aleye, Allay, Allege, Appease, Ataraxy, Composed, Cool, Dead-wind, Dispassionate, Doldrums, Easy, Easy-osy, Eevn, Equable, Equanimity, Even, Eye, Flat, Glassy, Halcyon, Level, Loun(d), Lown(d), Lull, Mellow, Mild, Milden, Millpond, Nonchalant, Pacify, Patient, Peaceable, Peaceful, Philosophical, Phlegmatic, Placate, Placid, Quell, Quiet, Raise, Relax(ed), Repose, Restful, Restrained, Sedate, Self-possessed, Seraphic, Serena, Serene, Settle, Simmer down, Sleek, → **SOOTHE**, Sopite, Steady, Still, Stilly, Subside, Supercool, Tranquil(lise), Unruffled, Unturbid, Windless

Calorie Gram, Kilogram

Calumniate, Calumny Aspersion, Backbite, Defame, Libel, Malign, Sclaunder, Slander, Slur

Calvary Golgotha

Calvin(ist), Calvinism Accusative, Coolidge, Genevan, Hopkins, Huguenot, Infralapsarian, Perseverance of saints, Predestination, Sublapsarian, Supralapsarian

Calydonian Boar

Calypso Ogygia, Siren, Soca, Sokah, → **SONG**

Cam Cog, Dwell, River, Snail, Tappet

Camaraderie Fellowship, Rapport, Team spirit

Camber Hog, Slope

Cambium Phellogen

Cambodia(n) K, Kampuchean, Khmer (Rouge), Montagnard, Pol Pot

Cambria(n) Menevian, Wales

Cambric Lawn

Cambridge Blue, Cantab, Squat, Uni

Came Arrived

Camel, Camel train Aeroplane, Arabian, Artiodactyla, Bactrian, Beige, Caisson, Colt, Dromedary, Kafila, Llama, Oont, Sopwith, Tulu

Camelopard Giraffe

Cameo Anaglyph, Camaieu, Carving

Camera, Camera man All-round, Box, Brownie®, Camcorder, Candid, Chambers, Cine, Compact, Digicam, Digital, Disc, Dolly, Electron, Flash, Gamma, Gatso®, Grip(s), Iconoscope, Image orthicon, Imager, Instant, Kodak®, Lucida, Miniature, Minicam, Movie, Nannycam, Obscura, Orthicon, Palmcorder, Panoramic, Pantoscope, Periphery, Phone-cam, Pinhole, Point and shoot, Polaroid®, Process, Programmed, Projectionist, Reflex, Retina, Schmidt, SLR, Somascope, Speed, Spycam, Steadicam®, Stop-frame, Subminiature, Swing-back, Video, Vidicon, Viewfinder, Webcam

Camouflage Conceal, → **DISGUISE**, Mark, Maskirovka, War-dress

▷ **Camouflaged** *may indicate* an anagram

Camp(er) Affectation, Aldershot, Auschwitz, Banal, Base, Belsen, Bivouac, Boma, Boot, Buchenwald, Caerleon, Cantonment, Castral, Colditz, Concentration, Dachau, David, Death, Depot, D(o)uar, Dumdum, Epicene, Faction, Fat, Flaunt, Gulag, Happy, Health, High, Holiday, Labour, Laer, La(a)ger, Lashkar, Leaguer, Low, Manyat(t)a, Motor, Oflag, Outlie, Peace, Prison, Side, Siwash, Stagey, Stalag, Stative, Summer, Swagman, Tent, Theatrical, Transit, Treblinka, Valley Forge, Work, Zare(e)ba, Zariba, Zereba, Zeriba

Campaign(er) Activist, Agitate, Barnstorm, Battle, Blitz, Blitzkrieg, Canvass, Crusade, Doorknock, Drive, Enterprise, Field, Gallipoli, Hustings, Jihad, Lobby, Mission, Offensive, Pankhurst, Promotion, Roadshow, Run, Satyagraha, Smear, Stint, Stopes, Strategist, The stump, Tree-hugger, Venture, Veteran, War, Warray, Warrey, Whispering, Whistle-stop, Witchhunt

Campanula Rampion
Campeador Chief, Cid
Camp-follower Lascar, Leaguer-lady, Leaguer-lass, Sutler
Camphor Carvacrol, Menthol
Campion Knap-bottle, Lychnis, Ragged robin, Silene
▷ **Camptown** *may indicate* de-
Can(s) Able, Aerosol, Billy, Bog, Capable, Churn, Cooler, Dow, Dyke, Gaol, Garbage, Gents, Headphones, Is able, Jerry, John, Jug, Karsy, Kazi, Lav(atory), Loo, May, Nick, Pail, Pitcher, Pot, Preserve, → **PRISON**, Privy, Six-pack, Stir, Tank, Tin, Trash, Tube, Watering
Canada, Canadian Abenaki, Acadian, Bella Bella, Bella Coola, Beothuk, Bois-brûlé, .ca, Canuck, Comox, Coureur de bois, Dakotan, Dene, Dogrib, Habitans, Hare, Heiltsuk, Herring choker, Inuit, Johnny Canuck, Joual, Maliseet, Manitoban, Metis, Montagnais, Naskapi, Nuxalk, Péquiste, Quebeccer, Quebecker, Québecois, Salishan, Salteaux, Saulteaux, Slavey, Stoney, Tsimshian, Ungava, Yukon
Canal Alimentary, Ampul, Anal, Birth, Caledonian, Channel, Conduit, Corinth, Cruiseway, Da Yunhe, Duct, Duodenum, Ea, Ear, Enteron, Erie, Foss(e), Gota, Grand (Trunk), Grande Terre, Grand Union, Groove, Gut, Haversian, Houston Ship, Kiel, Klong, Labyrinth, Lode, Manchester Ship, Meatus, Midi, Mittelland, Moscow, Navigation, New York State Barge, Oesophagus, Panama, Pharynx, Pipe, Pound, Regent's, Resin, Rhine-Herne, Ring, Root, Sault Sainte Marie, Scala, Schlemm's, Semi-circular, Ship, Shipway, Soo, Spinal, Stone, Suez, Suo, Urethra, Vagina, Vertebral, Waterway, Welland, Zanja
Canal-boat Barge, Fly-boat, Gondola, Vaporetto
Canapé Cate, Chesterfield, Crostini, Snack, → **SOFA**, Titbit
Canary Bird, Grass, Prisoner, Roller, Serin, Singer, Yellow
Cancel(led) Abrogate, Adeem, Annul, Counteract, Countermand, Cross, Delete, Destroy, Erase, Kill, Negate, Nullify, Obliterate, Override, Rained off, Red line, Remit, Repeal, Rescind, Retract, Retrait, Revoke, Scrub, Undo, Unmake, Void, Wipe, Write off
Cancer(ian), Cancerous Big C, Carcinoma, Crab, Curse, Hepatoma, Kaposi's sarcoma, Leukaemia, Lymphoma, Marek's disease, Moon child, Oat-cell, Oncogenic, Tropic, Tumour, Wolf
Candela Cd
▶ **Candelabra** *see* **CANDLESTICK**
Candid, Candour Albedo, Blunt, Camera, Forthright, Franchise, Frank, Honesty, Ingenuous, Man-to-man, Open, Outspoken, Plain(-spoken), Round, Upfront
Candida Fungus
Candidate(s) Agrege, Applicant, Aspirant, Contestant, Entrant, Field, Literate, Nomenklatura, Nominee, Office-seeker, Ordinand, Postulant, Running mate, Short list, Slate, Spoiler, Stalking horse, Testee
Candied, Candy Angelica, Caramel, Cotton, Eryngo, Eye, Glace, Maple, Rock, Snow, Succade, Sucket, Sugar, → **SWEET**
Candle(stick), Candelabra Amandine, Bougie, C(i)erge, Chanukiah, Corpse, Dip, Fetch, Girandole, Hanukiah, International, Jesse, Lampadary, Light, Long-sixes, Menorah, Mould, New, Padella, Paschal, Pricket, Roman, Rushlight, Sconce, Serge, Shammash, Shammes, Shortsix, Slut, Sperm, Standard, Tace, Tallow, Tallow-dip, Taper, Tea-light, Torchère, Tricerion, Vigil light, Wax, Waxlight
Candlefish Eulachon, Oolakon, Oulachon, Oulakon, Ulic(h)an, Ulic(h)on, Ulikon
▶ **Candy** *see* **CANDIED**
Cane, Caning Arrow, Baculine, Bamboo, Baste, Beat, Birk, Crabstick, Dari, Dhurra, Doura, Dur(r)a, Ferula, Ferule, Goor, Gur, Jambee, Malacca, Narthex, Penang-lawyer, Pointer, Raspberry, Rat(t)an, Rod, Six of the best, Split, Stick, Sugar, Swagger-stick, Swish, Switch, Sword, Swordstick, Tan, Tickler, Vare, Wand, Whangee, Wicker(-work)
Canine Biter, C, Dhole, Dog, Eye-tooth
Canker Corrosion, Curse, Lesion, Ulcer

Cannabis Benj, Bhang, Bifter, Blow, Boneset, Durban poison, Ganja, Ganny, Grass, Hash, Hemp, Henry, Louie, Number, Pot, Skunk, Wacky baccy, Zol

Cannibal Anthropophagus, Heathen, Long pig, Man-eater, Ogre, Thyestean, Wendigo

Cannon Amusette, Barrage, Basilisk, Bombard, Breechloader, Carom, Carronade, Chaser, Collide, Criterion, Culverin, Drake, Drop, Falcon, Gun, Howitzer, Kiss, Long-tom, Loose, Monkey, Mons Meg, Nursery, Oerlikon, Saker, Stern-chaser, Water, Zamboorak, Zomboruk, Zumbooru(c)k

Cannot Canna, Cant, Downa(e), Downay

Canny Careful, Frugal, Prudent, Scot, Shrewd, Slee, Sly, Thrifty, Wice, Wily, Wise

Canoe(ist) Bidarka, Bidarkee, Canader, Canadian, Dugout, Faltboat, Kayak, Log, Mokoro, Monoxylon, Montaria, Oomiack, Paddler, Peterborough, Piragua, Pirogue, Rob Roy, Surf, Waka, Woodskin

Canon(ise) Austin, Besaint, Brocard, Camera, Cancrizens, Chapter, Chasuble, Code, Crab, Decree, Honorary, Infinite, Isidorian, → **LAW**, Line, Mathurin(e), Minor, Nocturn, Norbertine, Nursery, Pitaka, Polyphony, Prebendary, Precept, Premonstrant, Premonstratensian, Regular, Residential, Retrograde, Rota, Round, Rule, Secular, Square, Squier, Squire, Standard, Tenet, Unity, Vice-dean, White

Canopy Awning, Baldachin, Baldaquin, Chuppah, Ciborium, Clamshell, Dais, Gore, He(a)rse, Huppah, Majesty, Marquee, Marquise, Parapente, Pavilion, Shamiana(h), State, Tabernacle, Tent, Tester, Veranda(h)

Cant Argot, Bevel, Doublespeak, Heel, Incline, Jargon, Mummery, Outrope, Patois, Patter, Rogue's Latin, Shelta, Slang, Slope, Snivel, Snuffle, Tip

Cantankerous Cussed, Fire-eater, Ornery, Querulous, Testy, Tetchy

Cantata Kinderspiel, Motet, Tobacco

Canteen Chuck-wagon, Cutlery, Dry, Mess, Munga, Naafi, Wet

Canter Amble, Hypocrite, Jog, Lope, Run, Tit(t)up, Tripple

Canticle Benedictus, Nunc dimittis

Canto Air, Fit(te), Fitt, Fytte, Melody, Verse

Canton(ese) Aargau, Appenzell, Basil, Basle, District, Eyalet, Fribourg, Glarus, Graubunden, Jura, Lucerne, Neuchatel, Quarter, St Gall, Schaffhausen, Schwyz, Solothurn, Tanka, Thurgau, Ticino, Unterwalden, Uri, Valais, Vaud, Zug, Zurich

Cantor Haz(z)an

Cantred Commot(e)

Canvas Awning, Binca®, Burlap, Drab(b)ler, Fly-sheet, Lug-sail, Mainsail, Maintopsail, Marquee, Oil-cloth, Paint, Raven's-duck, Reef, → **SAIL**, Square-sail, Staysail, Stuns(ai)l, Tent, Trysail, Wigan, Woolpack

Canvass(er), Canvassing Agent, Doorstep, Drum, Mainstreeting, Poll, Press flesh, Solicit

▷ **Canvasser** *may indicate* a painter or a camper

Canyon Box, Canada, Coprates, Defile, Grand, Grand Coulee, Kings, Nal(l)a, Nallah, Ravine, Submarine

Cap(ped) Call, Crest, → **CROWN**, → **HAT**, Knee, Legal, Maintenance, Outdo, Patella(r), Perplex, Polar, → **SURPASS**

CAPS

3 letters:	4 letters:	Pile	Cloth
Lid	Blue	Root	Dutch
Mob	Caul		Fool's
Taj	Coif	5 letters:	Gimme
Tam	Cope	Beret	Kippa
Toe	Cowl	Black	Mutch
Top	Flat	Chaco	Night
Toy	Kepi	Chape	Pagri

Quoif
Shako
Thrum
Toque
Truck
Tuque
Turk's
Watch

6 letters:
Abacot
Amorce
Barret
Berret
Better
Biggin
Blakey
Calpac
Chapka
Charge
Cornet
Cradle
Czapka
Dunce's
Filler
Forage
Gandhi
Granny
Jockey
Juliet
Kalpak

Kipput
Morion
Muffin
Petrol
Pileus
Pinner
Square
Summit
Toorie

7 letters:
Bathing
Bellhop
Bendigo
Biretta
Bycoket
Calotte
Calpack
Chapeau
Chechia
College
Fatigue
Ferrule
Grannie
Hunting
Iceberg
Kippoth
Kiss-me
Liberty
Monteer
Montero

Morrion
Newsboy
Old wife
Statute
Thimble
Wishing

8 letters:
Balmoral
Baseball
Capeline
Chaperon
Coonskin
Garrison
Gorblimy
Havelock
Monmouth
Phrygian
Puggaree
Schapska
Skullcap
Stocking
Thinking
Trencher
Yarmulka
Yarmulke
Zuchetto

9 letters:
Balaclava
Glengarry

Gorblimey
Trenchard

10 letters:
Blue-bonnet
Calyptrate
Cockernony
Kilmarnock
Percussion

11 letters:
Bonnet-rouge
Deerstalker
Kiss-me-quick
Mortar-board
Tam-o'-shanter

12 letters:
Cheese-cutter
Davy Crockett
Hummel bonnet
Squirrel-tail

13 letters:
International

14 letters:
Kilmarnock cowl

Capable, Capability Able, Brown, Capacity, Competent, Deft, Effectual, Efficient, Firepower, Intelligent, Qualified, Skilled, Susceptible, Up to, Viable

Capacitance, Capacity Ability, Aptitude, C, Cab, Calibre, Carrying, Co(o)mb, Competence, Content, Cor, Cubic, Endowment, Full, Function, Gift, Legal, Limit, Log, Mneme, Potency, Potential, Power, Qua, Rated, Receipt, Scope, Size, Skinful, Tankage, Thermal, Tonnage, Valence, Vital, Volume

Caparison Robe, Trap(pings)

Cape(s) Agulhas, Almuce, Athlete, Beachy Head, Blanc(o), Bon, Burnouse, Byron, C, Calimere Point, Canaveral, Canso, Cardinal, Chelyuskin, Cloak, Cod, Comorin, Delgado, Dezhnev, Domino, Dungeness, East(ern), Fairweather, Faldetta, Fanion, Fanon, Farewell, Fear, Fichu, Finisterre, Flattery, Gallinas Point, Good Hope, Guardafui, Harp, Hatteras, Head(land), Helles, Hoe, Hogh, Hook of Holland, Horn, Inverness, Kennedy, Leeuwin, Lindesnes, Lizard, Manteel, Mantilla, Mantle, Mant(e)let, Mantua, Matapan, May, Miseno, Moz(z)etta, Muleta, Naze, Ness, Nordkyn, North, Northern, Ortegal, Palatine, Palliser, Parry, Pelerine, Peninsula, Point, Poncho, Promontory, Race, Ras, Ray, Reinga, Roca, Ruana, Runaway, Sable, St Vincent, Sandy, Scaw, Skagen, Skaw, Sontag, Southwest, Talma, Tippet, Trafalgar, Ushant, Verde, Vert, Waterproof, Western, Wrath, York

Cape of Good Hope Stellenbosch

Caper(ing) Antic, Bean, Boer, Capparis, Capriole, Cavort, Dance, Dido, Flisk, Frisk, Frolic, Gambado, Gambol, Harmala, Harmalin(e), Harmel, Harmin(e), Jaunce, Jaunse, Prance, Prank, Romp, Saltant, Sault, Scoup, Scowp, Skip, Tit(t)up

Capet Marie Antoinette

Cape Town SA
Capital(s) A1, Assets, Block, Boodle, Bravo, Bully, Cap, Chapiter, Chaptrel, Circulating, Doric, Equity, Euge, Excellent, Fixed, Flight, Float, Floating, Fonds, Great, Helix, Human, Initial, Ionic, Lethal, Lulu, Metropolis, Principal, Refugee, Risk, Rustic, Seat, Seed, Share, Social, Splendid, Sport, Stellar, Stock, Super, Topping, UC, Upper case, Venture, Wealth, Working

CAPITALS

3 letters:	Leon	Chiba	Melun
Fes	Lima	Colon	Meroe
Fez	Linz	Cuzco	Minna
Gap	Lomé	Cuzev	Minsk
Jos	Male	Dacca	Monza
Ray	Metz	Dakar	Namur
Rio	Nara	Delhi	Nancy
Ude	Nuuk	Dhaka	Natal
Ufa	Oslo	Dijon	Nimes
Van	Pegu	Dilli	Nukus
Zug	Pune	Dover	Oskub
	Riga	Dutse	Palma
4 letters:	Rome	Emisa	Paris
Aden	Safi	Enugu	Parma
Agra	San'a	Goias	Patna
Albi	Sian	Gotha	Pella
Apia	Sion	Guaco	Perth
Auch	Susa	Hanoi	Petra
Baki	Suva	Harar	Pinsk
Baku	Vila	Hefei	Poona
Bari	Xian	Hofei	Praha
Bern		Hsian	Praia
Bida	*5 letters:*	Ikeja	Quito
Boac	Aarau	Jambi	Rabat
Bonn	Abiya	Jammu	Rouen
Brno	Abuja	Jinan	Salem
Caen	Adana	Kabul	Sanaa
Cali	Agana	Kandy	Scone
Chur	Aijal	Karor	Segou
Cluj	Akita	Kazan	Seoul
Cork	Akure	Kizyl	Siena
Dili	Amman	Konia	Simla
Doha	Aosta	Konya	Sofia
Faro	Arlon	Koror	Stans
Graz	Assen	Kyoto	Sucré
Homs	Batum	Lagos	Tepic
Hums	Beira	Lassa	Terni
Ipoh	Belém	Laval	Tokyo
Jaen	Berne	Le Paz	Trier
Jolo	Bisho	Le Puy	Tunis
Kiel	Blois	Lhasa	Turin
Kiev	Boise	Liege	Uxmal
Kobe	Bourg	Lille	Vaasa
Laon	Braga	Lyons	Vadso
Laos	Cairo	Macao	Vaduz

Wuhan
Yanan
Yenan
Zomba

6 letters:
Abakan
Albany
Almaty
Andros
Angkor
Ankara
Annecy
Anyang
Asmara
Astana
Athens
Austin
Bagdad
Baguio
Bamako
Bangui
Banjul
Bassau
Bastia
Batumi
Bauchi
Beirut
Berlin
Bhopal
Bogota
Bruges
Brunei
Cahors
Canton
Chonju
Colima
Colmar
Cracow
Cucuta
Cuenca
Cuiaba
Darwin
Denver
Dessau
Dispur
Dodoma
Dublin
Edessa
Erfurt
Fuchou
Geneva
Giyani
Gondar

Grozny
Habana
Haikou
Harare
Harbin
Havana
Helena
Hobart
Hohhot
Ibadan
Iloilo
Ilorin
Imphal
Jaffna
Jaipur
Jalapa
Johore
Juneau
Kaduna
Kaunas
Kerman
Kigali
Kisumu
Kohima
Kuwait
Lahore
Lisbon
Loanda
Lokoja
London
Luanda
Lusaka
Macapá
Maceió
Madrid
Maikop
Majuro
Malabo
Manama
Manaus
Manila
Maputo
Marsan
Maseru
Mekele
Merano
Merida
Moroni
Moscow
Mumbai
Munich
Murcia
Muscat
Mutare

Nagpur
Nakuru
Namibe
Nassau
Nevers
Niamey
Nouméa
Oaxaca
Orense
Ottawa
Oviedo
Owerri
Palmas
Panaji
Panjim
Peking
Pierre
Prague
Puebla
Punaka
Quebec
Quetta
Ranchi
Recife
Regina
Rennes
Riyadh
Roseau
Ryazan
Saigon
Sardes
Sardis
Sarnen
Sendai
Skopje
Sokoto
Sparta
St Gall
St Paul
Sydney
Tabora
Taipei
Tallin
Tarawa
Tarbes
Tarsus
Tehran
Tetuan
Thebes
Thimbu
Tirana
Tobruk
Toledo
Toluca

Topeka
Ulundi
Umtata
Urumqi
Vesoul
Vienna
Warsaw
Xining
Yangon
Yaunde
Zagreb
Zurich
Zwolle

7 letters:
Abidjan
Ajaccio
Alençon
Algiers
Altdorf
Antioch
Atlanta
Augusta
Auxerre
Baghdad
Bangkok
Barnaul
Begawan
Beijing
Belfast
Belfort
Bien Hoa
Bijapur
Bikaner
Bishkek
Bobigny
Bologna
Calabar
Caracas
Cardiff
Cayenne
Cesenza
Cetinje
Chengdu
Chennai
Coblenz
Coimbra
Colombo
Conakry
Concord
Cordoba
Cotonou
Cremona
Cuttack

Douglas
Durango
Foochow
Funchal
Gangtok
Goiania
Guiyang
Haarlem
Halifax
Hanover
Hassett
Herisau
Honiara
Huhehot
Iqaluit
Iquique
Isfahan
Izhevsk
Jackson
Jakarta
Kaesong
Kaifeng
Kampala
Karachi
Kashmir
Katsina
Kayseri
Kharkov
Khartum
Koblenz
Konakri
Kuching
Kunming
Kwangju
Lansing
Lanzhou
Lashkar
Legaspi
Liestal
Limoges
Lincoln
Louvain
Lucerne
Lucknow
Madison
Malacca
Managua
Masbate
Mathura
Mbabane
Memphis
Messene
Morelia
Munster

Nairobi
Nalchik
Nanjing
Nanking
Nanning
Nicosia
Nineveh
Novi Sad
Olomouc
Orleans
Oshogbo
Pachuca
Palermo
Palikit
Papeete
Perugia
Phoenix
Pishpek
Plovdiv
Potenza
Potsdam
Punakha
Quimper
Raleigh
Rangoon
San José
San Juan
Santa Fe
Sao Tomé
Sapporo
Saransk
Segovia
Seville
Stanley
St John's
Taiyuan
Tallinn
Tangier
Tbilisi
Teheran
Tel Aviv
Thimphu
Tiemcen
Toronto
Trenton
Trieste
Tripoli
Umuahia
Urumshi
Valetta
Vicenza
Vilnius
Vilnyus
Vitoria

Xanthus
Yakutsk
Yaounde
Yerevan

8 letters:
Abeokuta
Abu Dhabi
Adelaide
Agartala
Ashgabet
Asuncion
Auckland
Bar-le-Duc
Belgrade
Belmopan
Besancon
Beyrouth
Boa Vista
Brasilia
Brisbane
Brussels
Budapest
Cagliari
Calcutta
Campeche
Canberra
Cape Town
Castries
Chambéry
Changsha
Chaumont
Cheyenne
Chisinau
Coahuila
Columbia
Columbus
Culiacan
Curitiba
Damascus
Debrecen
Dehra Dun
Denpasar
Djibouti
Dushanbe
Ecbatana
Edmonton
Eraklion
Florence
Freetown
Fribourg
Funafuti
Gaborone
Godthaab

Golconda
Hamilton
Hangzhou
Hannover
Hargeisa
Hartford
Helsinki
Honolulu
Istanbul
Jayapura
Kandahar
Katmandu
Khartoum
Kilkenny
Kinshasa
Kirkwall
Kishinev
La Spezia
Lausanne
Liaoyand
Lilongwe
Luneburg
Mandalay
Mechelen
Mexicali
Monrovia
Monterey
Nanchang
Nanching
Nanterre
Narbonne
Ndjamena
New Delhi
Pago Pago
Pamplona
Pergamum
Peshawar
Pnom-Penh
Port Said
Port-Vila
Pretoria
Pristina
Roskilde
Saltillo
Salvador
Salzburg
Santiago
Sao Paulo
Sarajevo
Seremban
Shah Alam
Shanghai
Shenyang
Shillong

Silvassa
Srinagar
Sterling
St Helier
Szczecin
Tashkent
The Hague
Thonburi
Tiaxcala
Torshavn
Toulouse
Usumbura
Valencia
Valletta
Victoria
Vladimir
Warangai
Windhoek
Winnipeg
Yinchuan
Zaragoza

9 letters:
Amsterdam
Annapolis
Ashkhabad
Ayutthaya
Banda Aceh
Bandar Ser
Bangalore
Benin City
Birobijan
Bucharest
Bujumbura
Cartagena
Changchun
Changshar
Chengchow
Cherkessk
Chihuahua
Darmstadt
Des Moines
Edinburgh
Fongafale
Fortaleza
Frankfort
Grand Turk
Guangzhou
Heraklion
Hyderabad
Innsbruck
Islamabad
Jalalabad
Jerusalem

Karlsruhe
Kathmandu
Kingstown
Kisangani
Knoxville
Kuch Bihar
Lamberene
Leningrad
Ljubljana
Magdeburg
Maiduguri
Marrakesh
Melbourne
Mogadishu
Montauban
Monterrey
Nashville
Nelspriut
Nuku'alofa
Perigueux
Perpignan
Phnom Penh
Podgorica
Polokwane
Port Blair
Port Louis
Porto Novo
Port Royal
Putrajaya
Pyongyang
Reykjavik
Rio Branco
Samarkand
San Merino
Singapore
Solothurn
St George's
Stockholm
Stuttgart
Thorshavn
Trebizond
Ulan Bator
Vientiane
Wad Medani
Wiesbaden
Zhengzhou

10 letters:
Addis Ababa
Basse-terre
Baton Rouge
Bellinzona
Birobidzan
Bratislava

Bridgetown
Campobosso
Carson City
Chandigarh
Charleston
Cienfuegos
Cochabamba
Concepcion
Cooch Behar
Copenhagen
Cuernavaca
Diyarbakir
Eisenstadt
Frauenfeld
Georgetown
Harrisburg
Heidelberg
Hermosillo
Joao Pessoa
Klagenfurt
Kota Baharu
Kragujevac
Launceston
Leeuwarden
Libreville
Little Rock
Maastricht
Mexico City
Middelburg
Mogadiscio
Montevideo
Montgomery
Montpelier
Nouakchott
Panama City
Paramaribo
Persepolis
Podgoritsa
Porto Velho
Providence
Rawalpindi
Sacramento
Trivandrum
Tskhinvali
Valladolid
Valparaiso
Washington
Wellington
Whitehorse
Willemstad
Winchester
Yashkar-Ola

11 letters:
Bhubaneswar
Brazzaville
Buenos Aires
Campo Grande
Carcassonne
Charlestown
Dares Salaam
Fredericton
Gandhinagar
Guadalajara
Hermoupolis
Johore Bahru
Kuala Lumpur
Montbeliard
Nakhichevan
Ouagadougou
Pandemonium
Pondicherry
Port Moresby
Porto Alegre
Port of Spain
Rio Gallegas
Saarbrucken
San Salvador
Springfield
St Peter Port
Tallahassee
Tegucigalpa
Thohoyandou
Ulaanbaatar
Vatican City
Vladikavkaz
Yellowknife

12 letters:
Antananarivo
Anuradhapura
Barquisimeto
Barranquilla
Bloemfontein
Chilpancingo
Fort-de-France
Indianapolis
Johannesburg
Kota Kinabalu
Mont-de-Marsan
Muzzafarabad
Pandaemonium
Petrozavodsk
Ponta Delgada
Port-au-Prince
Port Harcourt
Rio de Janeiro

Salt Lake City	Williamsburg	Udjung Pandang	**15 letters:**
San Cristobal	Yamoussoukro	Yaren District	Chalons-sur-Marne
Santo Domingo			Charlotte Amalie
Schaffhausen	**13 letters:**	**14 letters:**	Clermont-Ferrand
Schoemansdal	Belo Horizonte	Andorra la Vella	Sekondi-Takoradi
Seringapatam	Charlottetown	Constantinople	
Shijiazhuang	Florianopolis	Kuala Trengganu	**16 letters:**
Sidi-bel-Abbes	Funafuti Atoll	Oaxaca de Juarez	Pietermaritzburg
Tenochtitian	Guatemala City	Puerto Princesa	Trixtia Gutiérrez
Ujungpandang	Hertogenbosch	's-Hertogenbosch	
Villahermosa	Jefferson City		

Capitalise Carpe diem
Capitalist Bloated, Financier, Moneyer, Sloane
▷ **Capitalist** *may indicate* a citizen of a capital
Capitulate Acquiesce, Comply, Defer, → SURRENDER
Capless Bare
▷ **Capless** *may indicate* first letter missing
Capone Al, Scarface
▷ **Capriccioso** *may indicate* an anagram
Caprice, Capricious Arbitrary, Boutade, Capernoitie, Cap(p)ernoity, Conceit, Desultory, Eccentric, Erratic, Fancy, Fickle, Fitful, Freak, Humoresk, Humoresque, Irony, Megrim, Migraine, Mood, Perverse, Quirk, Vagary, Wayward, Whim(sy)
Capsize Crank, Keel, Overbalance, Purl, Tip, Turn turtle, Upset, Whemmle, Whomble
▷ **Capsized** *may indicate* a word upside down
Capstan Sprocket, Windlass
Capsule Amp(o)ule, Boll, Bowman's, Cachet, Habitat, Internal, Nidamentum, Ootheca, Orbiter, Ovisac, Pill, Pyxidium, Space, Spacecraft, Spansule, Spermatophore, Suppository, Time, Urn
Captain Ahab, Bligh, Bobadil, Bones, Bossyboots, Brassbound, Capt, Channel, Chief, Cid, Commander, Condottiere, Cook, Copper, Cuttle, Flint, Group, Hook, Hornblower, Kettle, Kidd, Leader, Macheath, Master, Nemo, Oates, Old man, Owner, Patron, Patroon, Post, Privateer, Protospatharius, Rittmaster, Skip(per), Standish, Subah(dar), Subedar, Swing, Trierarch
Caption Cutline, Heading, Headline, Inscription, Masthead, Roller, Sub-title, Title
Captious Critical, Peevish
Captivate(d), Captivating Beguile, Bewitch, Charm, Enamour, Enthrall, Epris(e), Rapt, Take, Winsome
Captive, Captivity Bonds, Duress, Hostage, POW, Prisoner, Slave, Thrall
Capture Abduct, Annex, Bag, Catch, Collar, Cop, Data, Electron, Enchain, Enthral(l), Entrance, Grab, Land, Motion, Nail, Net, Prize, Rush, Seize, Snabble, Snaffle, Snare, → TAKE
Capuchin Cebus, Monkey, Sajou
Car Alvis, Astra, Audi, Austin, Auto, Banger, Beemer, Beetle, Berlin, Biza, BL, Bluebird, Bomb, Boneshaker, Brake, Bubble, Buffet, Bugatti, Buick, Bumper, Bus, Cab(riolet), Cadillac, Catafalco, Catafalque, Chariot, Chorrie, Citroen, Classic, Clunker, Coach, Compact, Company, Concept, Convertible, Cortina, Coupé, Courtesy, Crate, Daimler, Diesel, Diner, Dodgem®, Drag(ster), Drophead, Dunger, Elf, Estate, E-type, Fastback, Ferrari, Fiat, Flivver, Ford, Formula, Freight, Friday, Gas guzzler, Ghost, Gondola, Griddle, GT, Gyrocar, Hardtop, Hatchback, Heap, Hearse, Hillman, Horseless carriage, Hot hatch, Hot-rod, Irish, Jaguar, Jalop(p)y, Jamjar, Jammy, Jam sandwich, Jaunting, Jim Crow, Kart, Kit, Knockabout, Lada, Lagonda, Lancia, Landaulet, Landrover, Lift-back, Limo, Limousine, Lincoln, Merc(edes), MG, Mini, Model T, Morgan, Morris, Motor, Muscle, Nacelle, Notchback, Observation, Opel, Pace, Palace, Panda, Parlo(u)r, Patrol,

Pimpmobile, Popemobile, Production, Prowl, Pullman, Racer, Ragtop, Railroad,
Rattletrap, Restaurant, Roadster, Roller, Rolls (Royce), Rover, RR, Runabout, Runaround,
Rust bucket, Saloon, Scout, Sedan, Service, Shooting-brake, Skoda, Sleeper, Sleeping,
Soft-top, Speedster, Sports, Squad, Station wagon, Steam, Stock, Stretch-limo,
Subcompact, Sunbeam, Supermini, SUV, Tank, Telepherique, Telpher, Three-wheeler,
Tin Lizzie, Tonneau, Tourer, Touring, Tram, Triumph, Trolley, Tumble, Turbo,
Two-seater, Vehicle, Veteran, Vintage, Voiture, VW, Wheeler, Wheels

Caramel Brûlé

Carat Point

Caravan(ner) Caf(f)ila, Convoy, Fleet, Kafila, Motor home, Safari, Trailer, Trailer trash,
Winnebago®

Caravanserai Choltry, Choutry, Inn, Khan

Caraway Aj(o)wan, Carvy, Seed

Car-back Boot, Dick(e)y, Tonneau

Carbamide Urea

Carbide Silicon

Carbine Escopette, Gun, Musket

Carbohydrate Agar, Agarose, Callose, Carrageenan, Cellulose, Chitin, Dextran,
Disaccharide, Glycogen, Heptose, Hexose, Inulin, Ketose, Laminarin, Mannan, Mucilage,
Pectin, Pectose, Pentene, Pentose, Pentylene, Polysaccharide, Saccharide, Sorbitol,
Starch, Sucrose, Sugar

Carbolic Orcin

Carbon(ate) Activated, Ankerite, Austenite, Buckminsterfullerene, Buckyball, C,
Charcoal, Coke, Dialogite, Diamond, Drice, Dry ice, Flame, Flimsy, Fullerene, Gas black,
Graphite, Lampblack, Martensite, Natron, Petroleum coke, Scawtite, Soot, Spode,
Spodium, Urao, Witherite, Zaratite

Carbon deficiency Acapnia

Carboy Demijohn

Carbuncle Anthrax, Eyesore, Ruby

Carcase, Carcass Body, Cadaver, Carrion, Corpse, Cutter, Krang, Kreng, Morkin,
Mor(t)ling

Card(s), Cardboard, Carding Accelerator, Ace, Affinity, Amex®, Arcana, Baccarat,
Basto, Bill, Birthday, Blue Peter, Bower, Business, Calling, Canasta, Cartes, Cash,
Caution, Charge, Cheque, Chicane, Cigarette, Club, Comb, Communion, Community,
Compass, Court(esy), Credit, Cue, Curse of Scotland, Dance, Debit, Deck, Deuce, Devil's
(picture) books, Diamond, Doffer, Donor, Drawing, Ecarté, Eccentric, Euchre, Expansion,
Face, False, Flash, Flaught, Flush, Fourchette, → **GAME**, Gold, Goulash, Graphics, Green,
Guide, Hand, Hard, Health, Heart, Hole, Honour, ID, Identification, Identity, Idiot,
Intelligent, Jack, Jambone, Jamboree, Joker, Kanban, Key, King, Knowing, Laser, Leading,
Letter, Loo, Loyalty, Magnetic, Manille, Master, Matador, Maximum, Meishi, Meld,
Memory, Menu, Mise, Mistigris, Mogul, Mournival, Natural, Notelet, Oddity, Ombre,
Pack, Past, Pasteboard, Payment, PC, Phone, Picture, Piquet, Placard, Place, Plastic,
Playing, Postal, Proximity, Punch(ed), Quatorze, Quatre, Queen, Queer, Quiz, Race, Rail,
Ration, Red, Rippler, Rove, Royal marriage, Score, Scraperboard, Scratch, Screwball,
Scribble, Shade, Show, SIM, Singleton, Smart, Soda, Solo, Sound, Spade, Spadille,
Squeezer, Stiffener, Store, Strawboard, Sure, Swab, Swipe, Swish, Switch, Swob, Swot,
Talon, Tarok, Tarot, Tease(r), Tenace, Test, Thaumatrope, Ticket, Tiddy, Time, Top-up,
Tose, Toze, Trading, Trey, Trump, Two-spot, Union, Valentine, Visa, Visiting, Wag,
Warrant, Weirdie, Whitechapel, Wild, Wit, Yellow, Zener

Cardigan Ballet-wrap, Jacket, Wampus, Wam(m)us, Woolly

Cardinal Apostolic vicar, Camerlingo, Chief, College, Eight, Eminence, Eminent,
Grosbeak, Hat, HE, Hume, Legate, Manning, Mazarin, Medici, Newman, Nine, Number,
Pivotal, Polar, Prefect, Prelate, Radical, Red, Red-hat, Richelieu, Sacred college, Seven,
Sin, Spellman, Ten, Virtue, Vital, Wolsey, Ximenes

Card-player Dealer, Pone

Care(r), Caring Attention, Befriend, Burden, Cark, Caution, Cerne, Cherish, Community, → CONCERN, Cosset, Doula, Grief, Guard, Heed, Intensive, Kaugh, Keep, Kiaugh, Maternal, Mind, Pains, Palliative, Parabolanus, Primary, Providence, Reck(e), Reke, Residential, Respite, Retch, Shared, Solicitude, → TEND, Tenty, Ward, Worry

Careen(ing) Parliament-heel

Career Course, Hurtle, Life, Line, Profession, Run, Rush, Scorch, Speed, Start, Tear, Vocation

▷ **Career** *may indicate* an anagram

Carefree Blithe, → CARELESS(LY), Dozy, Happy-go-lucky, Irresponsible, → NEGLIGENT, Oops, Perfunctory, Rollicking, Thoughtless, Tinker's cuss, Tinker's damn

Careful(ly) Canny, Chary, Discreet, Gentle, Hooly, Leery, Meticulous, Mindful, Painstaking, Penny-pinching, Penny-wise, Pernickety, Provident, Prudent, Scrimp, Scrupulous, Softly-softly, Studious, Tentie, Tenty, Thorough, Vigilant, Ware, Wary

Careless(ness), Careless(ly) Anyhow, Casual, Cheery, Debonair, Easy, Free-minded, Gallio, Improvident, Imprudent, Inadvertent, Inattention, Insouciance, Irresponsible, Lax, Lighthearted, Négligé, → NEGLIGENT, Nonchalant, Oops, Oversight, Perfunctory, Raffish, Rash, Remiss, Resigned, Riley, Rollicking, Slam-bang, Slapdash, Slaphappy, Slipshod, Sloppy, Sloven(ly), Slubber, Taupie, Tawpie, Thoughtless, Unguarded, Unmindful, Untenty, Unwary

▷ **Carelessly** *may indicate* an anagram

Caress Bill, Coy, Embrace, Feel, Fondle, Kiss, Lallygag, Lollygag, Noursle, Nursle, Pet, Straik, Stroke, Touch

Caretaker Acting, Concierge, Curator, Custodian, Dvornik, Granthi, Guardian, Interim, Janitor, Nightwatchman, Sexton, Shammash, Shammes, Superintendent, Verger, Warden

Careworn Haggard, Lined, Tired, Weary

Cargo Boatload, Bulk, Burden, Fraught, Freight, Lading, Last, → LOAD, Navicert, Payload, Shipload, Shipment

Caribbean Belonger, Puerto Rican, Soca, Sokah, Spanish Main, Taino, WI

Caribou Tuktoo, Tuktu

Caricature, Caricaturist Ape, Beerbohm, Burlesque, Caran d'Ache, Cartoon, Cruikshank, Doyle, Farce, Gillray, Mimicry, Rowlandson, Scarfe, Skit, Spy, Tenniel, Toon, Travesty

Carlin Pug

Carmelite Barefoot, White (Friar)

Carmen AA, BL, Chai, RAC

Carnage Bloodshed, Butchery, Massacre, Slaughter

Carnal Bestial, Lewd, Outward, Sensual, Sexual, Worldly

Carnation Clove pink, Dianthus, Gillyflower, Malmaison, Picotee, Pink

Carnival Fair, Fasching, Festival, Fete, Mardi Gras, Mas, Moomba, Rag, Revelry, Surf

Carnivore, Carnivorous Cacomistle, Cacomixl, Coati, Creodont, Ermelin, Fennec, Fo(u)ssa, Genet, Glutton, Grison, Hyena, Meerkat, Otter, Ratel, Stoat, Sundew, Suricate, Viverridae, Wolverine, Zoophagan

Carob Algar(r)oba, Locust, St John's bread

Carol(ler) Noel, Sing, Song, Wait, Wassail, Yodel

Carousal, Carouse Bend, Birl(e), Bouse, Bride-ale, Compotation, Drink, Mallemaroking, Mollie, Orge, Orgy, → REVEL, Roist, Screed, Spree, Upsee, Upsey, Upsy, Wassail

Carp(er) Beef, Cavil, Censure, Complain, Crab, Critic, Crucian, Crusian, Gibel, Goldfish, Id(e), Koi, Kvetch, Mirror, Mome, Nag, Nibble, Nitpick, Roach, Roundfish, Scold, Twitch, Whine, Yerk, Yirk

Carpenter Beveller, Bush, Cabinet-maker, Carfindo, Chips, Fitter, Joiner, Joseph, Menuisier, Quince, Tenoner, Woodworker, Wright

▷ **Carpenter** *may indicate* an anagram

Carpet(ing) Aubusson, Axminster, Beetle, Berate, Bessarabian, Body, Broadloom, Brussels, Castigate, Chide, Dhurrie, Drugget, Durrie, Dutch, Kali, Kelim, Khilim, Kidderminster, Kilim, Kirman, Lecture, Lino, Magic, Mat, Moquette, Persian, Rate, Red, Reprimand, Reproach, Roast, Rug, Runner, Shagpile, Shark, Shiraz, Stair, Turkey, Wall-to-wall, What for, Wig, Wilton

Carrageen Sea-moss

Carriage Air, Ar(a)ba, Aroba, Bandy, Barouche, Bearing, Berlin(e), Bier, Brake, Brit(sch)ka, Britska, Britzka, Brougham, Buckboard, Buggy, Cab, Calash, Calèche, Car, Cariole, Caroche, Carriole, Carryall, Cartage, Chaise, Charabanc, Charet, Chariot, Chassis, Chay, Clarence, Coach, Coch, Composite, Conveyance, Coupé, Curricle, Demeanour, Dennet, Deportment, Désobligeante, Diner, Dormeuse, Dormitory-car, Dos-a-dos, Do-si-do, Drag, Dros(h)ky, Ekka, Equipage, Fiacre, Fly, Four-in-hand, Gait, Gig, Gladstone, Go-cart, Growler, Gun, Haulage, Herdic, Horseless, Howdah, Hurley-hacket, Jampan, Job, Landau(let), Landing, Limber, Mien, Non-smoker, Norimon, Observation-car, Phaeton, Pick-a-back, Pochaise, Pochay, Poise, Port(age), Portance, Postchaise, Posture, Poyse, Pram, Pullman, Purdah, Railcar, Railway, Random, Rath(a), Remise, Ricksha(w), Rig, Rockaway, Set-up, Shay, Sled, Sleeper, Smoker, Sociable, Spider, Spider phaeton, Stanhope, Sulky, Surrey, Tarantas(s), Taxi, T-cart, Tender, Tenue, Tilbury, Tim-whiskey, Tonga, Trail, Trap, Van, Vetture, Victoria, Voiture, Wagonette, Waterage, Whirligig, Whisk(e)y, Whisky gig

Carrier Aircraft, Airline, Arm, Baldric, Barkis, Barrow, Bomb-ketch, Bulk, Cacolet, Caddy, Cadge, Camel, Coaster, Common, Conveyor, Donkey, Escort, Fomes, Fomites, Frog, Grid, Hamper, Haversack, Hod, Janker, Jill, Majority, Minority, Nosebag, Noyade, Obo, Packhorse, Personnel, Pigeon, Porter, Rucksack, Satchel, Schistosoma, Semantide, Sling, Straddle, Stretcher, Tiffin, Tranter, → **TRAY**, TWA, Vector, Wave

Carrion Cadaver, Carcase, Carcass, Flesh, Ket, Stapelia

Carrot(s) Lure, Seseli, Titian

Carry(ing), Carry over Asport, Bear, Chair, Convey, Enlevé, Escort, Ferry, Frogmarch, Hawk, Hent, Humf, Hump, Humph, Kurvey, Land, Move, Pack, Pickaback, Port, Reappropriate, Stock, Sustain, Tide over, Tote, → **TRANSPORT**, Trant, Wage, With, Yank

Carry on Continue, Create, Wage

Carry out Execute, Implement, Mastermind, Pursue

Cart(er) Bandy, Barrow, Bogey, Buck, Cape, Car(r)iole, Chapel, Dandy, Democrat, Democrat wagon, Dog, Dolly, Dray, Egyptologist, Float, Furphy, Gambo, Gill, Golf, Governess, Gurney, Hackery, Jag, Jill, Lead, Mail(-gig), Night, Pie, Pram, Rickshaw, Scot, Scotch, Shandry, T, Tax(ed), Telega, Trolley, Tumbrel, Tumbril, Village, Wag(g)on, Wain, Water, Wheelbarrow, Whitechapel

Cartel Duopoly, Ring, Syndicate, Zaibatsu

Carthaginian Punic

Carthorse Aver, Shire

Carthusian Bruno

Cartilage Antitragus, Arytenoid, Chondral, Chondrin, Chondrus, Cricoid, Darwin's tubercle, Disc, Ensiform, Epiglottis, Gristle, Hyaline, Lytta, Meniscus, Semilunar, Tendrons, Thyroid, Tragus, Worm, Xiphoid

Cartload Fother, Seam

Cartographer Cabot, Chartist, Kremer, Mercator, OS, Speed

Carton Box, Case, Crate, Sydney, Tub

Cartoon(ist) Andy Capp, Animated, Bairnsfather, Caricature, Comic, Comic strip, Disney, Drawn, Emmet, Fougasse, Fumetto, Garland, Goldberg, Lancaster, Leech, Low, Manga, Mel, Partridge, Popeye, Robinson, Schulz, Short, Shrek, Spy, Strip, Superman, Tenniel, Thurber, Tidy, Tintin, Trog

Cartridge Ball, Blank, Bullet, Cartouche, Cassette, Crystal, Doppie, Live, Magazine, Magnetic, Magnum, QIC, Rim-free, Shell, Spent

Cart-track Rut

Cartwheel Handspring
Caruncle Aril, Carnosity, Strophiole
Carve(d), Carver, Carving Abated, Alcimedon, Armchair, Bas relief, Camaieu, Cameo, Chair, Chisel, Cilery, Crocket, Cut, Dismember, Doone, Enchase, Engrave, Entail, Entayle, Fiddlehead, Gibbons, Glyphic, Glyptic, Hew, Incise, Inscribe, Insculp, Intaglio, Knotwork, Netsuke, Nick, Petroglyph, Scrimshaw, Sculp(t), Slice, Tondo, Trophy, Truncheon, Tympanum, Whakairo, Whittle
Caryatid Column, Telamon
Casanova Heartbreaker, Leman, Playboy, Womaniser
Cascade Cataract, Fall, Lin(n), Stream, Waterfall
Cascara Amarga, Buckthorn, Honduras bark, Rhamnus, Sagrada, Wahoo
Case(s), Casing Abessive, Ablative, Accusative, Action, Adessive, Allative, Altered, Appeal, Aril, Ascus, Assumpsit, Attaché, Basket, Beer, Bere, Bin, Bittacle, Blimp, Box, Brief, Bundwall, Burse, C, Ca, Cabinet, Cachet, Calyx, Canister, Canterbury, Capsule, Cartouch(e), Cartridge, Cask, Cause celebre, Cellaret, Chase, Chitin, Chrysalis, Cocoon, Coffin, Comitative, Compact, Crate, Croustade, Crust, Cyst, Dative, Declension, Detinue, Dispatch, Dossier, Dressing, Elative, Elytron, Enallage, Enclose, Ensheath, Ergative, Essive, Etui, Etwee, Event, Example, Flan, Flapjack, Flask, Frame, Genitive, Grip, Hanaper, Hard, Hatbox, Hold-all, Housewife, Hull, Humidor, Husk, Illative, Imperial, → **IN CASE**, Index, Indusium, Inessive, Instance, Kalamdan, Keg, Keister, Locative, Locket, Lorica, Manche, Matter, Mermaid's purse, Mezuzah, Music, Nacelle, Nominative, Non-suit, Nutshell, Objective, Oblique, Ochrea, Ocrea, Outpatient, Packing, Pair, Papeterie, Patient, Pencil, Penner, Phylactery, Plight, Plummer-block, Pod, Port, Portfolio, Possessive, Prima facie, Puparium, Quiver, Recce, Reconnoitre, Red box, Sabretache, Sad, Scabbard, Seashell, Sheath(e), Shell, Situation, Six-pack, Sleeve, Sporocyst, Sporran, Stead, Sted, Subjective, Suit, Tantalus, Tea-chest, Telium, Test, Theca, Tichborne, Toolbox, Trial, Trunk, Valise, Vanity bag, Vasculum, Vitrine, Vocative, Volva, Walise, Walking, Wallet, Wardian, Wing, Worst, Writing
Case-harden Nitrode
Casein Curd
Casement Frame, Roger, Sash, Window
Cash Blunt, Bonus, Bounty, Change, Coin, Digital, Dosh, Dot, Float, Funds, Hard, Idle money, Imprest, Liquid, Lolly, → **MONEY**, Needful, Ochre, Oof, Oscar, Pence, Petty, Ready, Realise, Redeem, Rhino, Spondulicks, Spot, Stumpy, Tender, Tin, Wampum, Wherewithal
Cashew Hog-plum
Cashier, Cash machine Annul, ATM, Break, Depose, Disbar, Dismiss, Oust, Teller, Treasurer
Cashmere Circassienne
Casino Monte Carlo
Cask(et) Armet, Barrel, Barrico, Bas(i)net, Box, Breaker, Butt, Cade, Casque, Cassette, Drum, Firkin, Galeate, Harness, Heaume, Hogshead, Keg, Leaguer, Octave, Pin, Pipe, Puncheon, Pyxis, Run(d)let, Salade, Sallet, Sarcophagus, Scuttlebutt, Shook, Shrine, Solera, Tierce, Tun, Wine
Cask-stand Stillion
Cassava Manioc, Tapioca, Yucca
Casserole Diable, Hotpot, Osso bucco, Pot, Salmi, Terrine, Tzimmes
Cassette Cartridge, Tape, Video
Cassia Cleanser, Senna
Cassio Lieutenant
Cassiterite Needle-tin, Tinstone
Cassock Gown, Soutane, Subucula
Cast (down, off, out), Casting Abattu, Actors, Add, Angle, Appearance, Bung, Cire perdue, Dash, Death mask, Die, Discard, Ecdysis, Ectype, Eject, Emit, Endocranial,

Exorcise, Exuviae, Exuvial, Fling, Found, Fusil, Grape, Hawk, Heave, Hob, Hue, Hurl, Impression, Ingo(w)es, Keb, Look, Lose, Lost wax, Mew, Molt, Moulage, Mould, Pick, Plaster(stone), Plastisol®, Players, Print, Put, Reject, Sand, Shed, Shoot, Sling, Slive, Slough, Spoil, Stamp, Stookie, Swarm, Tailstock, → **THROW**, Toss, Tot, Warp, Wax, Ytost

▷ **Cast** *may indicate* an anagram or a piece of a word missing

Castanet Crotal(um), Knackers

Castaway Adrift, Crusoe, Gunn, Left, Man Friday, Outcast, Robinson, Selkirk, Stranded, Weft

▷ **Cast by** *may indicate* surrounded by

Caste Brahmin, Burakumin, Class, Dalit, Group, Harijan, Hova, Kshatriya, Rajpoot, Rajpout, Rajput, Rank, Scheduled, Sect, Shudra, Sudra, Untouchable, Vaisya, Varna

Caster Truckle

Castigate Berate, Chasten, Chastise, Criticise, Denounce, Keelhaul, Lash, Punish, Rate, Scold

Cast-iron Spiegeleisen

Castle(d) Barbara, Bouncy, Broch, C, Casbah, Chateau, Citadel, Fastness, Fort, Kasba(h), Maiden, Man, Mot(t)e, Move, Palace, Rook, Stronghold, Villa

CASTLES

4 letters:	Belvoir	Doubting	Trausnitz
Sand	Blarney	Egremont	
Trim	Braemar	Elephant	*10 letters:*
	Calzean	Elsinore	Caerphilly
5 letters:	Canossa	Inverary	Kenilworth
Blois	Chillon	Kronberg	Pontefract
Conwy	Colditz	Malperdy	
Corfe	Cooling	Pembroke	*11 letters:*
Hever	Culzean	Perilous	Carisbrooke
Leeds	Despair	Rackrent	Chateauroux
Spain	Harlech	Reculver	Eilean Donan
Upnor	Lincoln	Richmond	Gormenghast
	Otranto	Stirling	
6 letters:	Schloss	Stokesay	*12 letters:*
Cawdor	Skipton	Stormont	Fotheringhay
Forfar	Warwick	Tintagel	Herstmonceux
Glamis	Windsor	Urquhart	Sissinghurst
Howard		Wartburg	
Ludlow	*8 letters:*		*13 letters:*
Raglan	Balmoral	*9 letters:*	Carrickfergus
Wemyss	Bamburgh	Dangerous	
	Bastille	Dunsinane	*14 letters:*
7 letters:	Berkeley	Edinburgh	Motte and bailey
Adamant	Carbonek	Lancaster	
Amboise	Chepstow	Rochester	
Arundel	Crotchet	Sherborne	

Castor Muffineer

Castor-oil Ricinus

Castrate(d), Castrato Alter, Cut, Doctor, Emasculate, Eunuch, Evirate, Farinelli, Geld, Glib, Lib, Manzuoli, Moreschi, Mutilate, Neuter, Senesino, Spado, Spay, Swig, Wethers

Castro Fidel

Casual(ly) Accidental, Adventitious, Airy(-fairy), Blasé, Chance, Chav(ette), Flippant, Grass, Haphazard, Idle, Incidental, Informal, Jaunty, Lackadaisical, Nonchalant,

Odd(ment), Odd-jobber, Offhand, Off-the-cuff, Orra, Overly, Passing, Promiscuous, Random, Scratch, Slaphappy, Slipshod, Sporadic, Stray, Temp, Throwaway

Casualty Blue on blue, Caduac, Chance-medley, ER, → VICTIM

Casuist Jesuit

Cat Ailuro-, Barf, Boat, Boke, Bush, Catamount, Dandy, Domestic, Egurgitate, Fat, Felid, Feline, Flog, Foss, Gossip, Hipster, Jazzer, Lair, Lash, Mewer, Mog, Native, Neuter, Nib, Oriental, Painter, Palm, Pardal, Practical, Puss, Regurgitate, Sacred, Scourge, Sick, Singed, Spew, Spue, Swinger, Top, Vomit, Whip

---

CATS

3 letters:	Foussa	Viverra	Jaguarondi
Gib	Jaguar		Jaguarundi
Gus	La Perm	*8 letters:*	Ring-tailed
Kit	Malkin	Balinese	Selkirk Rex
Rex	Margay	Baudrons	Turkish Van
Tom	Mouser	Cacomixl	
	Musang	Cheshire	*11 letters:*
4 letters:	Ocelot	Devon Rex	Colourpoint
Eyra	Ocicat	Kilkenny	Egyptian Mau
Lion	Serval	Long-hair	Havana Brown
Lynx	Somali	Mountain	Russian Blue
Manx	Sphynx	Munchkin	Tongkingese
Musk	Tibert	Ringtail	
Pard	Tybalt	Snowshoe	*12 letters:*
Puma	Weasel	Tiffanie	American Curl
	Zibeth		Scottish Fold
5 letters:		*9 letters:*	
Alley	*7 letters:*	Asparagus	*13 letters:*
Civet	Burmese	Binturong	Tortoise-shell
Felix	Caracal	Bluepoint	Turkish Angora
Fossa	Cheetah	Chantilly	
Genet	Clowder	Chartreux	*14 letters:*
Hodge	Dasyure	Delundung	Asian Shorthair
Korat	Foumart	Grimalkin	Australian Mist
Manul	Genette	Himalayan	Siberian Forest
Ounce	Leopard	Lioncelle	
Quoll	Linsang	Maine Coon	*15 letters:*
Rasse	Lioncel	Marmalade	Norwegian Forest
Rumpy	Maltese	Mehitabel	
Tabby	Nandine	Niebelung	*16 letters:*
Tiger	Pallas's	Sealpoint	American Wirehair
Tigon	Panther	Shorthair	
Zibet	Persian	Tobermory	*17 letters:*
	Pharaoh	Tonkinese	American Shorthair
6 letters:	Polecat		
Angora	Ragdoll	*10 letters:*	*19 letters:*
Birman	Siamese	Abyssinian	Californian Spangled
Bobcat	Tiffany	Cacomistle	
Cougar	Tigress	Cornish Rex	

Cataclysm Apocalypse

Catacomb Cemetery, Crypt, Hypogeum, Vault

Catalepsy Catatony, Trance

Catalogue(r) Categorise, Cattle dog, Dewey, Dictionary, Durchkomponi(e)rt, Index, Inventory, Itemise, K(ochel), List, Litany, Magalog, MARC, Messier, Ragman, Ragment, Raisonné, Record, Register, Specialogue, Star, Subject, Table, Tabulate, Thematic, Union

Catalyst Accelerator, Agent, Aldol, Chemical, Enzyme, Erepsin, Influence, Kryptonite, Stereospecific, Unicase, Ziegler

Catamite Gunsel, Ingle, Pathic

Catapult Ballista, Ging, Launch, Mangon(el), Perrier, Petrary, Propel, Scorpion, Shanghai, Sling, Slingshot, Stone-bow, Tormentum, Trebuchet, Wye, Y

Cataract Cascade, Film, Overfall, Pearl, Pearl-eye, Torrent, Waterfall, Web and pin

Catarrh Coryza, Rheum

Catastrophe, Catastrophic Apocalypse, Calamity, Damoclean, → **DISASTER**, Doom, Epitasis, Fiasco, Meltdown, Ruinous, Tragedy

Catatonia Stupor

Cat-call Boo, Jeer, Mew, Miaow, Miaul, Razz, Wawl, Whistle, Wrawl

Catch(y), Caught Air, Apprehend, Arrest, Attract, Bag, Benet, Bone, C, Capture, Chape, Clasp, Cog, Collar, Contract, Cop, Corner, Cotton on, Ct, Deprehend, Detent, Dolly, Engage, Enmesh, Ensnare, Entoil, Entrap, Fang, Field, Fumble, Gaper, Get, Glee(some), Grasp, Had, Hank, Haud, Haul, Hear, Hitch, Hold, Hook, Inmesh, Keddah, Keight, Kep(pit), Kheda, Kill, Land, Lapse, Lasso, Latch, Lazo, Lime, Lock, Morse, Nab, Nail, Net, Nick, Nim, Nobble, Noose, Overhear, Overhent, Overtake, Parti, Pawl, Rap, Release, Rope, Round, Rub, Safety, Save, Sean, Sear, See(n), Seize, → **SNAG**, Snap, Snare, Snib, Snig, → **SONG**, Stop, Surprise, Swindle, Tack, Taen, Take, Tane, Tickle, Trammel, Trap, Trawl, Trick, Tripwire, Troll, Twenty two, Twig, Understand, Wrestle

Catchword Motto, Shibboleth, Slogan, Tag

Catechism Carritch, Shorter, Test

Categorise, Category → **CLASS**, Classify, Etic, Genre, Genus, Infraclass, Infraorder, Label, Order, Pigeonhole, Range, Stereotype, Taxon, Triage, Type

Cater(er) Acatour, Cellarer, Feed, Manciple, → **PROVIDE**, Purveyor, Serve, Steward, Supply, Victualler, Vivandière

Caterpillar Army worm, Aweto, Boll worm, Cabbageworm, Cotton-worm, Cutworm, Eruciform, Geometer, Gooseberry, Grub, Hop-dog, Hornworm, Inchworm, Larva, Looper, Osmeterium, Palmer, Silkworm, Tent, Webworm, Woolly-bear

Catfish Hassar, Woof

Cathartic Turbeth

Cathedral Amiens, Basilica, Birmingham, Burgos, Chartres, Chester, → **CHURCH**, Cologne, Cortona, Dome, Duomo, Durham, Ely, Evreux, Exeter, Gloucester, Guildford, Hereford, Hertford, Huesca, Kirkwall, Lateran, Lichfield, Lincoln, Lugo, Minster, Mullingar, Notre Dame, Rheims, Ripon, Rochester, St Albans, St Davids, St Paul's, Salisbury, Santiago de Compostela, Sens, Teruel, Up(p)sala, Viseu, Wakefield, Wells, Westminster, Winchester, Worcester, York

Catherine Braganza, Parr

Catherine-wheel Girandole

Cathode Electrode, Filament, Ray

Catholic Assumptionist, Broad, Christian Socialism, Defenders, Doolan, Eclectic, Ecumenical, Fenian, General, German, Irvingism, Jebusite, Latin, Lazarist, Left-footer, Liberal, Marian, Old, Opus Dei, Ostiary, Papalist, Papaprelatist, Papist, Passionist, Recusant, Redemptionist, Roman, Romish, Salesian, Spike, Taig, Te(a)gue, Teigue, Theatine, Thomist, Tike, Tory, Tridentine, Tyke, Universal, Ursuline, Waldenses, Wide

Catkin Amentum, Chat, Lamb's tail, Pussy-willow, Salicaceous

Cat-lover Ailurophile

Catmint Nep, Nepeta, Nip

Cato Porcian, Uticensis

Cats-eye Chatoyant, Cymophane

Catsmeat Lights

Catspaw Pawn, Property, Tool

Cat's tail Reed-mace, Typha

Cat's whiskers Vibrissa

Cattle(pen) Aberdeen Angus, Africander, Ankole, Aver, Ayrshire, Beefalo, Belgian Blue, Belted Galloway, Bestial, Black, Brahman, British White, Buffalo, Carabao, Charbray, Charolais, Chillingham, Dexter, Drove, Durham, Fee, Friesian, Friesland, Galloway, Gaur, Gayal, Guernsey, Gyal, Heard, Herd, Hereford, Highland, Holstein (Friesian), Illawarra, Jersey, Kerry, Kine, Kouprey, Kraal, Ky(e), Kyloe, Lairage, Limousin, Lincoln, Longhorn, Luing, Neat, Nout, Nowt, Owsen, Oxen, Piemontese, Rabble, Redpoll, Rother, Santa Gertrudis, Shorthorn, Simment(h)al, Soum, South Devon, Sowm, Steer, Stock, Store, Stot, Sussex, Tamarao, Tamarau, Teeswater, Wagyu, Welsh Black

Cattle disease Actinobacillosis, Actinomycosis, Anthrax, Black water, Dry-bible, Footrot, Gallsickness, Heart-water, Hoove, Johne's, Listeriosis, Lumpy jaw, Mange, Mastitis, Milk lameness, Moorill, New Forest, Quarter-ill, Red-water, Rinderpest, Scours, Scrapie, Texas fever, Wire-heel, Woody-tongue

Cattle food Fodder, Poonac, Silage

Cattleman Cowboy, Herder, Maverick, Rancher, Ringer, Stock-rider

Catty Kin, Spiteful

Caucasian Aryan, Azabaijani, Azeri, Cherkess, European, Georgian, Iberian, Kabardian, Melanochroi, Paleface, Semite, Shemite, White, Yezdi, Yezidee, Zezidee

Caucus Assembly, Cell, Gathering, Race

▸ **Caught** *see* CATCH(Y)

Caul Baby-hood, Kell, Membrane, Sillyhow

Cauldron Kettle, Pot

Cauliflower Curd, Ear, Floret, Gobi

Caulk Fill, Pay, Pitch, Snooze

Causation, Cause(d), Causes Aetiology, Agent, Bandwagon, Beget, Breed, Bring, Célèbre, Common, Compel, Create, Crusade, Determinant, Due, Effect, Efficient, Encheason, Engender, Entail, Evoke, Expedite, Factor, Final, First, Flag-day, Formal, Gar(re), Generate, Ideal, Induce, Inspire, Lead, Lost, Make, Material, Motive, Movement, Natural, → OCCASION, Parent, Pathogen, Probable, Prompt, Provoke, Proximate, Reason, Root, Sake, Secondary, Show, Source, Teleology, Topic, Ultimate, Wreak

Causeway Giant's, Tombolo

Caustic Acid, Acrimonious, Alkaline, Burning, Common, Erodent, Escharotic, Lime, Lunar, Moxa, Pungent, Sarcastic, Scathing, Seare, Soda, Tart, Vitriol, Waspish, Withering

Cauterise, Cauterisation Brand, Burn, Disinfect, Inustion, Moxibustion, Sear

Caution, Cautious (person) Achitophel, Admonish, Ahithophel, Alert, Amber, Awarn, Beware, Cagey, Card, Care, Cave, Caveat, Chary, Circumspect, Credence, Cure, Defensive, Deliberate, Discretion, Fabian, Forewarn, Gingerly, Guard(ed), Heedful, Leery, Prudent, Rum, Scream, Skite, Tentative, Timorous, Vigilant, Ware, → WARN, Wary, Yellow card

Cavalcade Pageant, Parade, Procession, Sowarree, Sowarry

Cavalier Brusque, Careless, Cicisbeo, Devil-may-care, Gallant, Lively, Malignant, Offhand, Peart, Rider, Royalist

▷ **Cavalier** *may indicate* an anagram

Cavalry(man) Blues, Car(a)bineer, Car(a)binier, Cornet, Cossack, Dragoon, Equites, Heavies, Horse, Horse Guards, Household, Hussar, Ironsides, Knights, Lancers, Life Guards, Light-horse, Plunger, Ressaldar, Risaldar, Rough-rider, Rutter, Sabres, Sabreur, Silladar, Spahee, Spahi, Uhlan, Yeomanry

Cave(rn), Caves, Cave-dwelling, Cave in Acherusia, Aladdin's, Alert, Altamira, Antar, Antre, Beware, Bone, Capitulate, Cellar, Cheddar, Collapse, Corycian, Den, Domdaniel, Erebus, Fingal's, Fore, Grot(to), Hollow, Jenolan, Lascaux, Look-out, Lupercal, Mammoth, Mind out, Nix, Pot-hole, Proteus, Sepulchre, Snow, Spel(a)ean,

Speleology, Spelunker, Speos, Tassili, Trophonian, Vault, Waitomo, Ware, Weem, Wookey Hole

Cave-dweller Pict, Troglodyte, Troll

Caveman Adullam, Aladdin, Fingal, Neanderthal, Primitive, Troglodyte, Troll

Caviare Beluga, Osietra, Roe, Sevruga, Sturgeon

Cavil Carp, Haggle, Quibble

Cavity Acetabulum, Amygdale, Amygdule, Androclinium, Antrum, Archenteron, Atrial, Atrium, Body, Camera, Camouflet, Celom, Chamber, Cisterna, Clinandrium, Coelenteron, Coelom(e), Conceptacle, Concha, Countermark, Crater, Crypt, Dent, Domatium, Druse, Enteron, Follicle, Foss, Gap, Geode, Glenoid, Gloryhole, Hold, Hole, Lacuna, Locule, Mediastinum, Mialoritic, Orbita, Orifice, Pelvis, Pleural, Pocket, Pulp, Resonant, Segmentation, Sinus, Stomod(a)eum, Tartarus, Tear, Thunderegg, Tympanum, Vacuole, Vein, Ventricle, Vesicle, Vitta, Vomica, Vug, Vugg, Vugh, Well

Cavort(ing) Dance, Gambol, Jag

Cavy Agouti, Capybara, Hograt, Paca

Cayman Islands Tax haven

Cease(fire) Abate, Blin, Cut, Desist, Devall, Die, Disappear, Halt, Ho, Intermit, Lin, Lose, Pass, Refrain, Remit, Sessa, → **STOP**, Truce

Ceaseless Eternal, Incessant

Cecil Rhodes

Cedar(wood) Arolla, Atlas, Barbados, Cryptomeria, Deodar, Incense, Jamaica, Japanese, Toon

Cede Grant, Yield

Ceiling Absolute, Barrel, Coffered, Cove, Cupola, Dome, Glass, Lacunar, Laquearia, Limit, Plafond, Roof, Service, Silver, Soffit, Stained glass

Celebrate(d), Celebration, Celebrity Ale, A-list, Beanfeast, Besung, Big name, Bigwig, Binge, B-list, Brat-packer, Carnival, Cel, Chant, Commemorate, Distinguished, Do, Emblazon, Encaenia, Epithalamion, Epithalamium, Fame, Feast, Fest(al), Festivity, Fete, Fiesta, First-footing, Gala, Gaudeamus, Gaudy, Glitterati, Glorify, Grog-up, Harvest home, Headliner, Hold, Holiday, Honour, Hoop-la, Jamboree, Jol, Jollifications, Jollities, Jubilee, Keep, Large it, Laud, Legend, Limelight, Lion, Loosing, Lowsening, Maffick, Mardi Gras, Mass, Mawlid al-Nabi, Megastar, Monstre sacre, Name, Noted, Nuptials, Observe, Occasion, Orgy, Panathenaea, Party, Pinata, Praise, Randan, Rave-up, Record, Rejoice, Renown, Repute, Revel, Rite, Roister, Sangeet, Saturnalia, See in, Sex symbol, Shindig, Sing, Spree, Star, Storied, Sung, Superstar, Tet, Treat, Triumph, Wassail, Wet, Whoopee

Celerity Dispatch, Haste, Speed, Velocity

Celery Alexanders, Smallage, Stick

Celestial Chinese, Cosmic, Divine, Ethereal, Heavenly, Supernal, Uranic

Celibate, Celibacy Bachelor, Chaste, Paterin(e), Rappist, Rappite, Shakers, Single, Spinster

Cell(s), Cellular Battery, Black hole, Bullpen, Cadre, Chamber, Chapel, Condemned, Crypt, Cubicle, Death, Dungeon, Group, Laura, Lock up, Padded, Peter, → **PRISON**, Safety, Strip, Tank, Unit

---

CELLS

1 letter:		Cyte	Soma
T	Sex	Fuel	Stem
	Wet	Germ	Zeta
3 letters:	4 letters:	Hair	
Dry	Axon	HeLa	5 letters:
Egg	Comb	Mast	Ascus
Pec	Cone	Oxum	Basal

Canal
Clark
Cyton
Flame
Giant
Gland
Guard
Islet
Linin
Lymph
Nerve
Nicad
Solar
Sperm
Spore
Stone
Swarm
Water
White
X-body

6 letters:
Button
Censor
Collar
Cybrid
Cytoid
Diaxon
Gamete
Goblet
Hadley
Helper
Killer
Morula
Mother
Neuron
Oocyte
Plasma
Sensor
Sickle
Somite
Target
Thread
Zygote

7 letters:
Bimorph
Cadmium
Cambium
Cathode
Conical
Daniell
Energid
Euploid

Gemmule
Gravity
Helper T
Initial
Lithite
Myotome
Myotube
Neurite
Neurone
Neutron
Plastid
Primary
Purinje
Schwann
Sertoli
Sleeper
Somatic
Spindle
Spireme
Sporule
Storage
Tapetum
Vesicle
Voltaic

8 letters:
Akaryote
Auxocyte
Basidium
Basophil
Blasteme
Blastula
Congenic
Cytology
Daughter
Defensin
Ectomere
Endoderm
Endosarc
Ependyma
Epiblast
Eukaryon
Galvanic
Gonidium
Gonocyte
Hapteron
Hemocyte
Meiocyte
Meristem
Monocyte
Myoblast
Neoblast
Palisade
Parietal

Platelet
Purkinje
Receptor
Retinula
Schizont
Selenium
Seredium
Squamous
Standard
Sweatbox
Symplast
Synergid
Tracheid
Unipolar
Zoosperm
Zoospore

9 letters:
Adipocyte
Antipodal
Astrocyte
Athrocyte
Auxospore
Basophile
Coenocyte
Companion
Corpuscle
Desmosome
Ectoplasm
Embryo-sac
Fibrocyte
Haemocyte
Honeycomb
Hybridoma
Idioblast
Internode
Iridocyte
Karyology
Laticifer
Leclanché
Leucocyte
Leukocyte
Macromere
Merozoite
Microcyte
Micromere
Myelocyte
Myofibril
Notochord
Organelle
Periplasm
Periplast
Phagocyte
Phellogen

Proembryo
Satellite
Secondary
Spermatid
Sporocyte
Suspensor
Syncytium
Synkaryon
Thymocyte
Trabecula
Tracheide

10 letters:
Ameloblast
Archespore
Blastoderm
Blastomere
Centrosome
Choanocyte
Chromaffin
Chromosome
Cnidoblast
Eosinophil
Epithelium
Fibroblast
Gametocyte
Histiocyte
Leucoblast
Leukoblast
Lymphocyte
Macrophage
Melanocyte
Mesenchyme
Microphage
Multipolar
Myeloblast
Neuroblast
Neutrophil
Normoblast
Osteoblast
Osteoclast
Perikaryon
Phelloderm
Protoplast
Spermatium
Spherocyte
Suppressor
Totipotent
White-blood

11 letters:
Aplanospore
Arthrospore
Calyptrogen

Endothelium	Poikilocyte	Erythroblast	*13 letters:*
Erythrocyte	Propoceptor	Gametrangium	Chromatophore
Granulocyte	Schistocyte	Haematoblast	Mitochondroin
Interneuron	Spheroplast	Interstitial	Photoelectric
Kinetoplast	Suppressor T	Paraphysisis	Photoreceptor
Lymphoblast	Trophoblast	Photovoltaic	Sustentacular
Megaloblast		Reticulocyte	
Melanoblast	*12 letters:*	Spermatocyte	*14 letters:*
Microgamete	Aplanogamete	Spermatozoid	Spermatogonium
Microvillus	Chondroblast	Spermatozoon	Weston standard
Motor neuron	Cytogenetics	Spongioblast	
Odontoblast	Electrolytic		

Cellar Basement, Bodega, Coalhole, Dunny, Hypogeum, Ratskeller, Salt, Shaker, Storm, Vault, Vaultage, Vaut, Wine

Cell division Amitosis

Cellist, Cello Casals, Du Pré, Hermit, Prisoner, Tortelier

Celluloid, Cellulose Acetate, Cel, Viscose, Xylonite

Celt(ic) Belgic, Breton, Brython, Cornish, Druid, Gadhel, Gael(dom), Goidel, Helvetii, Kelt, La Tène, P, Q, Taffy, Welsh

Cement Araldite®, Asbestos, Blast-furnace, Compo, Concrete, Fix, Flaunch, Glue, Grout, Gunite, High-alumina, Hydraulic, Lute, Maltha, Mastic, Mastich, Mortar, Paste, Pointing, Porcelain, Portland, Putty, Rice-glue, Roman, Rubber, Slurry, → STICK, Trass, Water

Cemetery Aceldama, Arenarium, Arlington, Boneyard, Boot Hill, Campo santo, Catacomb, Churchyard, God's Acre, Golgotha, Graveyard, Musall, Necropolis, Père Lachaise, Potter's field, Saqqara, Urnfield

Censer Cassolette, Navicula, Thurible

Censor(ious), Censorship, Censure Accuse, Admonition, AD notice, Airbrush, Animadvert, Appeach, Ban, Banner, Berate, Blame, Blue-pencil, Bowdler, Braid, Cato, Chasten, Comstockery, → CONDEMN, Critical, Criticise, Cut, Damn, Dang, Decry, Dispraise, Edit, Excommunicate, Excoriate, Expurgate, Gag, Obloquy, Opprobrium, Rap, Rebuke, Repress, Reprimand, Reproach, Reprobate, Reprove, Satirise, Scold, Scrub, Slam, Slate, Stricture, Suppress, Tax, Tear into, Tirade, Traduce, Wig

Census, Census taker Count, Numerator, Poll

Cent(s) Bean, Coin, Ct, Penny, Red, Zack

Centaur Ch(e)iron, Horseman, Nessus, Sagittary, Therianthropic

Centenary, Centennial Anniversary, Colorado

Centipede Chilopoda, Earwig, Pauropod, Polypod, Scolopendra, Scutiger

Central(ly), Centre Active, Amid, Assessment, Attendance, Axis, Broca's, Bunt, Call, Cardinal, Chakra, Civic, Community, Contact, Core, Cost, Crisis, Day, Daycare, Dead, Detention, Detoxification, Deuteron, Deuton, Downtown, Drop-in, Epergne, Eye, Field, Focus, Foyer, Frontal, Garden, Health, Heart, Heritage, Hotbed, Hothouse, Hub, Incident, Inmost, Internal, Interpretive, Juvenile, Juvie, Kernel, Kingpin, Law, Leisure, Lincoln, Live, Main, Mecca, Median, Medulla, Mid(st), Midpoint, Midway, Mission, Music, Nave, Nerve, Nucleus, Omphalus, Pompidou, Profit, Property, Reception, Rehabilitation, Remand, Respiratory, Service, Shopping, Social Education, Storm, Teachers', Trauma, Visitor, Waist, Weather, Youth custody

Central American Mangue, Miskito, Olmec, Otomi, Pueblo, Totomac, Zapotec

Central heating Cen, CH

▷ **Centre** *may indicate* middle letters

Centrepiece Epergne

Century Age, C, Era, Magdeburg, Period, Siècle, Ton

Cephalopod Ammonite, Calamary, Cuttle, Loligo, Nautilus, Octopus, Sepia, Squid

Ceramic(s) Agateware, Arcanist, China, Earthen, Ferrite, Ferronneries, Porcelain,

Pottery, Sialon, Syalon®, Tiles

Cereal Amelcorn, Barley, Blé, Bran, Bread-basket, Buckwheat, Bulgar, Bulg(h)ur, Cassava, Corn, Cornflakes, Couscous, Emmer, Farina, Gnocchi, Grain, Granola, Groats, Hominy, Maize, Mandioc(a), Mandiocca, Manihot, Mani(h)oc, Mealie, Millet, Muesli, Oats, Paddy, Popcorn, Rye(corn), Sago, Samp, Sarassin, Seed, Semolina, Sorghum, Spelt, Tapioca, Tef(f), Triticale, Triticum, Wheat, Zea

Cerebral Sensoria

Cerebrate, Cerebration Pore, Thought

Ceremonial, Ceremony Aarti, Amrit, Asperges, Baptism, Barmitzvah, Chado, Chanoyu, Commemoration, Common Riding, Coronation, Doseh, Durbar, Encaenia, Enthronement, Etiquette, Eucharist, Flypast, Form(al), Formality, Gongyo, Habdalah, Havdalah, Havdoloh, Heraldry, Investiture, Koto(w), Matsuri, Maundy, Mummery, Observance, Occasion, Ordination, Pageantry, Parade, Pomp, Powwow, Protocol, Rite, Rite of passage, Ritual, Sacrament, Sado, Seder, Service, State, Sun dance, Tea, Topping-out, Trooping (the Colour), Unveiling, Usage

Cerium Ce

Cert(ain), Certainty Absolute, Actual, Assured, Banker, Bound, Cast-iron, Cinch, Cocksure, Confident, Conviction, Convinced, Decided, Definite, Doubtless, Exact, Fact, Fate, Indubitable, Inevitable, Infallible, Keen, Lock, Monte, Moral, Nap, Needly, One, Positive, Poz, Precise, Racing, Red-hot, Shoo-in, Siccar, Sicker, Snip, Some, Stiff, → **SURE**, Sure-fire, Truth, Type, Unerring, Yes

Certainly Agreed, And how, Ay, Aye-aye, Certes, Fegs, Forsooth, Indeed, Iwis, Jokol, OK, Oke, Pardi(e), Pardy, Perdie, Siccar, Sicker, → **SURE**, Truly, Verily, Well, Yea, Yes, Yokul, Ywis

Certificate, Certified, Certify Accredit, Affirm, Assure, Attest, Bene decessit, Birth, Bond, Chit, Cocket, Confirm, Credential, Death, Debenture, Depose, Diploma, Docket, Document, End-user, Enseal, Gold, Guarantee, Landscrip, Licence, Lines, Medical, MOT, Notarise, Paper, Patent, Proven, Savings, School, Scrip, Scripophily, Security, Share, Smart-ticket, Stamp note, Stock, Sworn, Talon, Testamur, Testimonial, Treasury, U, Unruly, Voucher, Warrant

Cesspit Bog, Dungmere, Jawhole, Sinkhole, Slurry

Cetacean Dolphin, Porpoise, Whale

Cete(acean) Badger

Ceylon(ese) Serendip, Vedda(h)

Chad Dimpled, Swinging

Chafe(r), Chafing Chunter, Fray, Fret, Gall, Harass, Intertrigo, Irritate, Pan, → **RUB**, Seethe, Worry

Chaff(y) Badinage, Banter, Bran, Chip, Cornhusk, Dross, Have on, Hay, Husk, Rag, Raillery, Rally, Ramentum, Refuse, Roast, Rot, Tease, Twit

Chaffer(ing) Bandy, Bargain, Haggle, Higgle, Hucksterage, Traffic

Chaffinch Wheatbird, Whitewing

Chagrin Annoyance, Envy, Mortify, Spite, Vexation

Chain(s), Chained Acre's-breadth, Albert, Anklet, Band, Bicycle, Bind, Bond, Bracelet, Branched, Bucket, Cable, Catena, Chatelaine, Choke, Cistron, Closed, Cordillera, Cyclic, Daisy, Decca, Dixie, Drive, Duplex, Dynasty, Engineer's, Esses, Fanfarona, Fetter, Fob, Food, Furlong, Gleipnir, Golden, Grand, Gunter's, Gyve, Heavy, Human, Learner's, Light, Line, Lockaway, Markov, Mayor, Micella(r), Micelle, → **MOUNTAIN**, Noria, Open, Pennine, Pitch, Range, Rockies, Rode, Roller, Safety, Seal, → **SERIES**, Shackle, Side, Slang, Snigging, Snow, Span, Sprocket, Straight, String, Strobila, Supply, Surveyor's, Suspensor, Team, Tug, Voluntary, Watch

Chain-gang Coffle

Chair Balloon-back, Basket, Bath, Bench, Bentwood, Berbice, Bergère, Birthing, Bosun's, Butterfly, Camp, Cane, Captain's, Carver, Club, Cromwellian, Curule, Deck, Dining, Director's, Easy, Elbow, Electric, Emeritus, Estate, Fauteuil, Fiddle-back, Folding,

Frithstool, Garden, Gestatorial, Guérite, High, Jampan, Jampanee, Jampani, Ladder-back, Lounger, Love-seat, Lug, Merlin, Morris, Musical, Nursing, Personal, Pew, Preside, Professorate, Recliner, Rocker, Ruckseat, Rush-bottomed, → **SEAT**, Sedan, Settee, Steamer, Stool, Straight, Sugan, Swivel, Throne, Wainscot, Wheel, Windsor, Wing

Chair-back Ladder, Splat

Chairman Convener, Emeritus, Humph, Landammann, Mao, MC, Pr(a)eses, Prof, Prolocutor, Sheraton, Speaker

Chalaza Albumen, Treadle, Treddle

Chalcedony Enhydros

Chaldean Babylonian, Ur

Chalet Cabana, Cot, Skio

Chalice Poisoned

Chalk(y) Black, Calcareous, Cauk, Cawk, Crayon, Credit, Cretaceous, Dentin, French, Senonian, Soapstone, Spanish, Steatite, Tailor's, White(n), Whit(en)ing

Challenge(r), Challenging Acock, Assay, Call, Cartel, Champion, Charge, Confront, Contest, Dare, Defy, Dispute, Face, Gage, Gainsay, Gauntlet, Glove, Hazard, Hen(ner), Iconoclasm, Impugn, Insubordinate, Oppugn, Provoke, Query, Question, Recuse, Sconce, Shuttle, Tackle, Taker, Tall order, Tank, Threat, Tongue-twister, Vie, Wero, Whynot

Chamber(s) Airlock, Anteroom, Atrium, Auricle, Bladder, Bubble, Camarilla, Camera, Casemate, Cavern, Cavitation, Cavity, Cell(a), Chanty, Close-stool, Cloud, Cofferdam, Columbarian, Combustion, Cubicle, Decompression, Dene-hole, Dolmen, Echo, Float, Fogou, Fumatorium, Fume, Gas, Gazunder, Gilded, Hall, Horrors, Hyperbaric, Hypogea, Inspection, Ionization, Jerry, Jordan, Kiva, Lavatory, Lethal, Locule, Lok Sabha, Lower, Magma, Manhole, Manifold, Mattamore, Mesoscaphe, Plenum, Po(t), Presence, Priest('s)-hole, Privy, Reaction, Resonance-box, Roum, Second, Serdab, Silo, Spark, Star, Stateroom, Steam-chest, Swell-box, Synod, Thalamus, Undercroft, Upper, Utricle, Vault, Ventricle, Wilson cloud, Zeta

Chamberlain Camerlengo, Camerlingo, Censor

Chameleon Adaptor, American, Anole, Ethiopian, Floating voter, Lizard, Tarand

Chamfer Bevel, Groove

Chamois Ibex, Izard, Shammy

Champ(er), Champers Bite, Chafe, Chew, Chomp, Eat, Gnash, Gnaw, Hero, Ivories, Mash, Morsure, Munch

Champagne Boy, Bubbly, Charlie, Fizz, Gigglewater, Krug, Mumm, Pop, Sillery, Simkin, Simpkin, Stillery, Troyes, Widow

Champion(s) Ace, Adopt, Ali, Apostle, Artegal, Assert, Back, Belt, Brill(iant), Campeador, Cid, Cock, Crusader, Cupholder, Defend, Don Quixote, Doucepere, Douzeper, Dymoke, Endorse, Enoch, Espouse, Gladiator, Gun, Harry, → **HERO**, Herodotus, Horse, Kemp, Kemper(yman), King, Knight, Maintain, Matchless, Messiah, Messias, Neil, Paladin, Palmerin, Peerless, Perseus, Promachos, Proponent, Protagonist, Roland, St Anthony, St David, St Denis, St George, St James, St Patrick, Seven, Spiffing, Spokesman, Star, Support, Title-holder, Tribune, Upholder, Victor, Wardog, → **WINNER**, World-beater, Yokozuna

Championship Five Nations, Open, Seven, Six Nations, Super Bowl, Title, Tri-nations

Chance (upon), Chancy Accident, Adventitious, Aleatory, Aunter, Bet, Break, Buckley's, Cast, Casual, Cavel, Coincidence, Contingent, Dice, Earthly, Even, Fat, → **FATE**, Fighting, First refusal, Fluke, Fortuitous, Fortuity, Fortune, → **GAMBLE**, Game, Hap, Happenstance, Hobnob, Iffy, Kevel, Light, Loaves and fishes, Look-in, Lot, → **LOTTERY**, Luck, Main, Meet, Mercy, Occasion, Occur, Odds, Odds-on, Opening, Opportunity, Outside, Peradventure, Posse, Potluck, Prayer, Probability, Prospect, Random, Rise, Risk, Run into, Russian roulette, Serendipity, Shot, Slant, Snip, Spec, Sporting, Stake, Stochastic, Stray, Sweep, Toss-up, Treble, Turn, Tychism, Ventre, Venture, Wager, Wild card

Chancel Adytum, Bema, Nave

Chancellor Adolf, Bismarck, Dollfuss, Kohl, Logothete, Minister, More, Schmidt, Vicar-general, Wolsey

Chancery Court, Hanaper

Chandelier Candlestick, Corona, Drop, Electrolier, Gasolier, Girandole, Lustre, Pendant

Chandler Acater, Acatour, Raymond

Chaney Lon

Change(able), Changes, Changing About-face, Adapt, Adjust, Agio, Aleatoric, → **ALTER**, Amendment, Amoeba, Attorn, Backtrack, Barter, Become, Bob-major, Capricious, Cash, Catalysis, Cent, Chameleon, Channel-hop, Chop, Chump, Climacteric, Cline, Commute, Convert, Coppers, Covary, Cut, Denature, Departure, Development, Diachrony, Dissolve, Diversion, Ectopia, Edit, Enallage, Esterify, Eustatic, Evolution, Evolve, Exchange, Fickle, Find, Flighty, Float, Fluctuate, Flux, Grandsire, Guard, Gybe, Histogen, Inflect, Innovate, Instead, Kaleidoscope, Kembla, Killcrop, Labile, Loose, Make-over, Menopause, Mercurial, Metabolic, Metabolise, Metamorphose, Metamorphosis, Metathesise, Mew, Mobile, Modify, Morph, Mutable, Mutalis mutandis, Mutanda, Mutation, Ontogeny, Parallax, Paraphrase, Peal, Pejoration, Peripet(e)ia, Permute, Port, Prisere, Prophase, Protean, Quantum leap, Quarter, Rat, Realise, Recant, Rectify, Redo, Reform, Refraction, Regime, Rejig, Reshuffle, Resipiscence, Rest, Reverse, Revise, Revolutionise, Rework, Sandhi, Scourse, Sd, Sea, Seasonal, Seesaw, Sere, Sex, Shake-out, Shake-up, Shift, Silver, Small, Sublimation, Substitute, Swap, Swing, Switch, Tempolabile, Tolsel, Tolsey, Tolzey, Transfer, Transfiguration, Transform, Transition, Transmogrify, Transmute, Transpose, Transubstantial, Triple, Turn, Tweak, Uncertain, Upheaval, U-turn, Vagary, Variant, Variation, Vary, Veer, Versatile, Vicissitude, Volatile, Volte-face, Wankle, Washers, Waver, Weathercock, Wheel, Wow

▷ **Change(d)** *may indicate* an anagram

Changeling Auf, Killcrop, Oaf, Turncoat

Channel Access, Aflaj, Airwave, Al Jazeera, Aqueduct, Artery, Beagle, Bed, Billabong, Binaural, Bristol, Canal, Canaliculus, Chimb, Chime, Chine, Chute, Conduit, Course, Creek, Culvert, Cut, Cutting, Datagram, Distribution, Ditch, Drain, Duct, Dyke, Ea, Eau, English, Estuary, Euripus, Fairway, Falaj, Feeder, Floodway, Flume, Foss, Funnel, Furrow, Gat, Gate, Geo, Gio, Glyph, Grough, Gully, Gut, Gutter, Head-race, Ingate, Katabothron, Katavothron, Khor, Kill, Kos, Kyle, Lake, La Manche, Lane, Latch, Leat, Lee-lane, Leet, Limber, Major, Meatus, Medium, Minch, Moat, Mozambique, Multiplex, Narrows, North, Offtake, Penstock, Pentland Firth, Pescadores, Pipeline, Qanat, Race, Raceway, Rean, Rebate, Rigol(l), Rigolets, Rivulet, Run, St George's, Sea-gate, Seaway, Sewer, Shatt-el-Arab, Shunt, Sinus, Sky, Sloot, Sluice, Sluit, Sny(e), Solent, Solway Firth, Sound, Sow, Spillway, Sprue, Strait, Suez, Sure, Swash, Tailrace, Tideway, Tracheole, Trough, Ureter, Vallecula, Vein, Wasteweir, Watercourse, Waterspout, Wireway, Yucatan

Chant Anthem, Antiphon, Canticle, Cantillate, Cantus, Chaunt, Daimoku, Decantate, Euouae, Evovae, Gregorian, Haka, Harambee, Hymn, Incantation, Intone, Introit, Mantra(m), Motet, Pennillion-singing, Plainsong, Proper, Psalm, Sing, Slogan, Te Deum, The Reproaches, Yell

Chantilly Cream, Lace

Chaos, Chaotic Abyss, Anarchy, Confusion, Disorder, Fitna, Fractal, Goat fuck, Havoc, Hun-tun, Jumble, Maelstrom, Mayhem, Mess, Mixter-maxter, Muddle, Muss, Shambles, Shambolic, Snafu, Tohu bohu, Turmoil

▷ **Chaotic** *may indicate* an anagram

Chap(s) Beezer, Bloke, Bo, Bod, Bor, Buffer, Cat, Chafe, Cheek, Chilblain, Chop, Cleft, Cod, Codger, Cove, Crack, Customer, Dog, Fella, Feller, Fellow, Flews, Genal, Gent, Gink, Guy, Hack, Joll, Jowl, Kibe, Lad, → **MAN**, Maxilla, Mouth, Mum, Ocker, Person, Rent, Rime, Spray, Spreathe, Spreaze, Spreethe, Spreeze, Wang

Chapel Alamo, Bethel, Bethesda, Beulah, Cha(u)ntry, Chevet, Ebenezer, Feretory, Galilee, Lady, Oratory, Parabema, Proprietary, Prothesis, Sacellum, Sistine

Chaperon(e) Beard, Cap, Duenna, Escort, Gooseberry, Griffin, Griffon, Gryphon, Muffin

Chaplain(cy) CF, Ordinary, Padre, Priest, Scarf, Skypilot, Slope

Chaplet Anadem, Coronet, Fillet, Garland, Wreath

▷ **Chaps** *may indicate* an anagram

Chapter Accidents, C, Canon, Cap, Capitular, Ch, Chap, Cr, Division, Episode, Lodge, Phase, Section, Social, Sura(h), Verse

Char(woman) Adust, Burn, Cleaner, Coal, Daily, Duster, Mop(p), Mrs Mop(p), Rosie Lee, Scorch, Sear, Singe, Smoulder, Toast, Togue, Torgoch

Charabanc Bus, Chara, Coach

Character(s) Aesc, Alphabet, Ampersand, Ampussyand, Atmosphere, Aura, Backslash, Brand, Calibre, Case, Cipher, Clef, Cliff, Climate, Coloration, Complexion, Contour, Credit, Delimiter, Deuteragonist, Devanagari, Digamma, Digit, Dramatis personae, Emoticon, Ess, Essence, Eta, Ethos, → **FEATURE**, Fish, Fist, Form, Grain, Graphics, Grass, Grit, Hair, Hieroglyphic, Homophone, Hue, Ideogram, Ideograph, Italic, Kanji, Kern, Kind, La(m)bda, Letter, Logogram, Make-up, Mark, Mu, Nagari, → **NATURE**, Non-person, Nu, Ogam, Ogham, Pahlavi, Pantaloon, Part, Pehlevi, Person(a), Personage, → **PERSONALITY**, Phonogram, Physiognomy, Pi, Polyphone, Protagonist, Psi, Raisonneur, Reference, Reference-mark, Repute, Rho, Role, Rune, Runic, Sampi, San, Sel(f), Sigma, Sirvente, Slash, Sonancy, Sort, Space, Sphenogram, Stamp, Subscript, Superhero, Superscript(ion), Swung dash, Syllabary, Symbol, Tab, Testimonial, Ton(e), Trait, Uncial, Unit, Vav, Vee, Waw, Wen, Wild card, Wyn(n), Yogh, Zeta

Characterise(d), Characterism, Characteristic(s) Acquired, Attribute, Aura, Cast, Colour, Distinctive, Earmark, Ethos, Example, Facies, Feature, Hair, Hallmark, Has, Headmark, Idiomatic, Idiosyncrasy, Jizz, Keystroke, Lineament, Mark, Mien, Nature, Notate, Peculiar, Persona, Phenotype, Point, Property, Quality, Signature, Stigma, Strangeness, Streak, Style, → **TRAIT**, Transfer, Typical, Vein, Way

Characterless Anon, Impersonal, Inane, Wet

Charade Enigma, Pretence, Riddle

Charcoal Activated, Carbon, Coke, Fusain, Sugar

Charge(s), Charged, Charger Access, Accusal, Accuse, Aerate, Agist, Allege, Anion, Annulet, Arraign, Ascribe, Assault, Baton, Battery, Bear, Behest, Blame, Brassage, Brush, Buckshot, Bum rap, Burden, Care, Carrying, Cathexis, Cellarage, Commission, Community, Complaint, Congestion, Corkage, Cost, Count, Cover, Criminate, Damage, Debit, Delate, Delf, Delph, Demurrage, Depth, Depute, Directive, Dittay, Dockage, Due, Duty, Dynamise, Electric, Electron, Entrust, Entry, Exit, Expense, Fare, Fee, Fill, Fixed, Flag fall, Fleur-de-lis, Floating, Flock, Freight, Fullage, Fuse, Fusil, Fuze, Gazump, Giron, Gravamen, Gyron, → **HERALDIC**, Horse, Hot, Hypothec, Impeach, Impute, Indict, Inescutcheon, Inform, Instinct, Ion, Isoelectric, Last, Levy, Lien, Lioncel(le), Lionel, Live, Load, Mandate, Mine, Mount, Nuclear, Objure, Obtest, Onrush, Onslaught, Onus, Ordinary, Orle, Overhead, Pastoral, Pervade, Pew-rent, Plaint, Positive, Premium, Prime, Prix fixe, Q, Quayage, Rack-rent, Rap, Rate, Recrimination, Red-dog, Rent, Report, Reprise, Reverse, Roundel, Run, → **RUSH**, Saddle, Service, Specific, Stampede, Steed, Storm, Supplement, Tariff, Tax, Tear, Terms, Tilt, Toll, → **TRAY**, Tressure, Trickle, Trust, Tutorage, Upfill, Vaire, Vairy, Verdoy, Vigorish, Ward, Warhead, Warhorse, Wharfage, Yardage

Chariot(eer) Auriga, Automedon, Biga, Cart, Charet, Curricle, Hur, Phaethon, Quadriga, Rath(a), Vimana, Wagon, Wain

Charisma Oomph, Personality

Charitable, Charity Aid, Alms, Alms-deed, Awmous, Benign, Breadline, Caritas, Cause, Chugger, Dole, Dorcas, Eleemosynary, Good works, Kiwanis, Largesse, Leniency, Liberal, Lion, Love, Mercy, Oddfellow, Openhanded, Oxfam, Pelican, Philanthropic, Samaritan, Zakat

Charivari Rough music, Uproar

Charlatan Cheat, Crocus, Empiric, Escroc, Faker, Imposter, Katerfelto, Mountebank, Poseur, Quack(salver), Saltimbanco

Charlemagne Carlovingian

Charles, Charley, Charlie(s) Beard, C, Car, Champagne, Chan, Chaplin, Checkpoint, Elia, Fox, Half-wit, Lamb, Mug, (Old) Rowley, Pretender, Ray, Reynard, Rug-gown, Sap, Schmoe, Snow, Tail-end, Watchman

Charles de Gaulle Airport

Charlock Runch

Charlotte Bronte, Russe, Yonge

Charm(er), Charmed, Charming Abracadabra, Abrasax, Abraxas, Agacerie, Allure, Amulet, Appeal, Aroma, Attraction, Bangle, Beguile, Bewitch, Captivate, Charisma, Chocolate box, Circe, Comether, Cramp-bone, Cute, Cutie, Debonair, Delectable, Delight(ful), Emerods, Enamour, Enchant, Engaging, → ENTRANCE, Fascinate, Fay, Fetching, Fetish, Grace, Greegree, Gri(s)gris, Hand of glory, Horseshoe, Houri, Incantation, Juju, Magnetic, Mascot, Mojo, Nice, Obeah, Obi(a), Periapt, Phylactery, Porte-bonheur, Pretty, Prince, Pull, Quaint, Quark, Ravish, Siren, Smoothie, Spellbind, Suave, Sweetness, Taking, Talisman, Tefillah, Telesm, Tephillah, Tiki, Trinket, Unction, Voodoo, Winning, Winsome

▷ **Charming** *may indicate* an anagram

Chart(ed), Charting Abac, Alignment, Bar, Breakeven, Card, Control, Diagram, Eye, Flip, Flow, Gantt, Graph, Histogram, Horoscope, Hydrography, Isogram, Isopleth, List, Magna Carta, → MAP, Mappemond, Movement, Nomogram, Organisation, Pie, Plane, Plot, Portolano, Ringelmann, Run, Snellen, Social, Sociogram, Table, Test, Timetable, Waggoner, Weather, Z

Charta, Charter Atlantic, Book, Citizen's, Covenant, Freedom, Hire, Lease, Let, Novodamus, Rent, Social (Chapter), Tenants', Time, Voyage

Chary Cagey, Careful, Cautious, Frugal, Shy, Wary

Charybdis Maelstrom, Whirlpool

Chase(d), Chaser, Chasing Cannock, Chace, Chevy, Chivy, Ciseleur, Ciselure, Course, Cranbome, Decorate, Drink, Game, Harass, Hound, → HUNT, Inlaid, Jumper, Oxo, Pursuit, Race, Scorse, Sic(k), Snag, Steeple, Sue, Suit, Wild-goose

Chasm Abyss, Crevasse, Fissure, Gap, Gorge, Gulf, Rent, Schism, Yawn

Chaste, Chastity Aggie, Agnes, Attic, Celibate, Classic, Clean, Continent, Fatima, Florimell, Ines, Innocent, Modesty, Nessa, Platonic, → PURE, Vestal, Virginal, Virtue

Chasten, Chastise(d), Chastisement Beat, Correct, Discipline, Disple, Lash, Punish, Rib-roast, Rollicking, Scold, Scourge, Shame-faced, Spank, Strap, Whip

Chat, Chatter(box), Chatterer Babble, Bavardage, Bird, Blab(ber), Blatherskite, Blether, Campanero, Causerie, Chelp, Chew the fat, Chinwag, Clack, Clishmaclaver, Confab(ulate), Converse, Cosher, Coze, Crack, Dialogue, Froth, Gab(ble), Gas, Gibble-gabble, Gossip, Gup, Hobnob, Jabber, Jargon, Jaw, Kilfud, Liaise, Madge, Mag(pie), Nashgab, Natter, Patter, Pie, Pourparler, Prate, Prattle, Rabbit, Rabble, Rap, Rattle, Scuttlebutt, Shmoose, Shoot the breeze, Stone, Talk, Talkee-talkee, Tattle, Tongue-work, Twattle, Waffle, Whin, Windbag, Witter, Wongi, Yacketyyak, Yad(d)a-yad(d)a-yad(d)a, Yak, Yap, Yarn, Yatter, Yellow-breasted, Yoking

Chateau Castle, Cru, Fontainebleau, Malmaison, Rambouillet, Schloss

Chateaubriand René

Chattel Asset, Chose, Deodand, Effects

Chaucer(ian) Dan, OE

Chauffeur Cabby, Coachy, Driver, Sice, Syce

Chauvinist Alf, Bigot, Jingo, MCP, Partisan, Patriot, Racist, Sexist

Cheap A bon marché, Bargain, Base, Catchpenny, Cheesy, Chintzy, Cut-price, Downmarket, Gimcrack, Giveaway, Ignoble, Knockdown, Low, Off-peak, Poor, Sacrifice, Shoddy, Steerage, Stingy, Tatty, Tawdry, Ticky-tacky, Tinhorn, Tinpot, Tinselly, Trashy, Trivial, Tuppenny, Two-bit, Twopenny, Twopenny-halfpenny, Undear, Vile

▷ **Cheap** *may indicate* a d- or p- start to a word

Cheapside Bow

Cheat(ers), Cheating Bam, Bamboozle, Beguile, Bilk, Bite(r), Bob, Bonnet, Bubble, Bucket, Bullock, Bunce, Burn, Cabbage, Cardsharp(er), Charlatan, Chiaus, Chicane(ry), Chisel, Chouse, Clip, Cod, Cog(ger), Colt, Con, Cony-catcher, Cozen, Crib, Cross, Cross-bite(r), Cuckold, Cully, Defraud, Delude, Diddle, Dingo, Dish, Do, Doublecross, Double-dealer, Duckshove, Dupe, Escroc, Faitor, Fiddle, Finagle, Fix, Flam, Flanker, Fleece, Fob, Foister, Fox, Fraud, Gaff, Gip, Glasses, Gudgeon, Gull-catcher, Gum, Gyp, Hoax, Hocus, Hoodwink, Hornswoggle, Horse, Intake, Jockey, Leg, Magsman, Mulct, Mump, Nick, Pasteboard, Picaro(on), Poop, Queer, Rib, Rig, Rogue, Rook, Rush, Scam, Screw, Screw over, Sell, Shaft, Sharper, Sharpie, Short-change, Slur, Smouch, Snap, Stack, Stiff, Sting, Swindle, Thimble-rigging, Trepan, Trick(ster), Trim, Twister, Two-time, Welch, Welsh, Wheedle

Check Abort, Arrest, Audit, Ba(u)lk, Bauk, Bill, Block, Bridle, Collate, Compesce, Confirm, Control, Count, Cramp, Cross-index, Curb, Dam, Damp, Detain, Detent, Discovered, Dogs-tooth, Examine, Foil, Forestall, Frustrate, Halt, Hamper, Hobble, Houndstooth, Inhibit, Inspect, Jerk, Jerque, Let, Limit, Mate, Medical, Meter, Monitor, Observe, Overhaul, Parity, Perpetual, Prevent, Rain, Reality, Rebuff, Rebuke, Rein, Repress, Reprime, Repulse, Reread, → **RESTRAIN**, Revoke, Saccade, Screen, Service, Setback, Shepherd's, Shorten, Sit-upon, Sneap, Sneb, Snib, Snub, Sound, Spot, Standard, Std, → **STEM**, Stent, Stint, Stocktake, Stop, Stunt, Suppress, Tab, Tally, Tartan, Tattersall, Test, Thwart, Tick, Trash, Verify, Vet

Checkers Chinese, Piece

Check-out Till

Cheddar Cheese, Gorge

Cheek(y) Alforja, Audacity, Brass-neck, Buccal, Chap, Chit, Chollers, Chutzpah, Cool, Crust, Cub, Flippant, Fresh, Gall, Gena(l), Gobby, Gum, Hard-faced, Hussy, Impertinent, Impudent, Joll, Jowl, Lip, Malapert, Malar, Masseter, Neck, Nerve, Noma, Pert, Presumption, Quean, Sass, Sauce, Sideburns, Uppity, Wang, Yankie, Zygoma

Cheep Chirp, Chirrup, Peep

Cheer(s), Cheerful(ness), Cheering Acclaim, Agrin, Applaud, Arrivederci, Banzai, Barrack, Blithe, Bonnie, Bravo, Bright, Bronx, Bubbly, Buck, Buoy, Cadgy, Canty, Carefree, Cherry, Chin-chin, Chipper, Chirpy, Chirrupy, → **COMFORT**, Crouse, Debonair, Drink, Ease, Elate, Elevate, Encourage, Enliven, Exhilarate, Exuberant, Festive, Genial, Gladden, Happy-go-lucky, Hearten, Hilarity, Holiday, Hooch, Hoorah, Hurra(h), Huzzah, Insouciance, Jocund, Jovial, Kia-ora, L'allegro, Light-hearted, Lightsome, Lively, Meal, Olé, Optimistic, Ovate, Peart, Perky, Please, Praise, Prosit, Rah, Riant, Rivo, Roar, Root, Rosy, Rumbustious, Shout, Sko(a)l, Slainte, Sonsie, Sunny, Ta, Tata, Thanks, Three, Tiger, Tiggerish, Toodle-oo, Up, Upbeat, Warm, Winsome, Yell

Cheerless Bleak, Dismal, Drab, Drear, Gloomy, Glum, Wint(e)ry

Cheese, Cheesy Grand Panjandrum, Macaroni, Numero uno, VIP

CHEESES

3 letters:			6 letters:
Ewe	Goat	Dutch	Asiago
Fet	Hard	Esrom	Cantal
Oka	Skyr	Fynbo	Casein
Pot	Tofu	Gouda	Chèvre
	Whey	Green	Damson
	Yarg	Islay	Dunlop
4 letters:		Kenno	Ermite
Blue	5 letters:	Lemon	Junket
Brie	Caboc	Quark	Orkney
Curd	Colby	Samso	Paneer
Edam	Cream	Stone	Rennet
Feta	Derby	Swiss	

Romano
Tilsit

7 letters:
Boursin
Caseous
Cheddar
Chessel
Cottage
Crowdie
Fontina
Gruyère
Havarti
Kebbock
Kebbuck
Limburg
Munster
Mycella
Rarebit
Ricotta
Sapsago
Stilton®

Truckle

8 letters:
American
Bel Paese
Blue vein
Cheshire
Emmental
Halloumi
Huntsman
Manchego
Muenster
Parmesan
Pecorino
Raclette
Taleggio
Vacherin

9 letters:
Amsterdam
Appenzell
Boconcini

Cambazola
Camembert
Emmenthal
Ilchester
Jarlsberg®
Killarney
Leicester
Limburger
Lymeswold®
Mousetrap
Port Salut
Provolone
Reblochon
Roquefort
Sage Derby

10 letters:
Bocconcini
Caerphilly
Danish blue
Dolcelatte
Emmentaler

Gloucester
Gorgonzola
Lancashire
Mascarpone
Mozzarella
Neufchatel
Stracchino

11 letters:
Coulommiers
Emmenthaler
Grana Padano
Pont l'Eveque
Wensleydale

12 letters:
Fromage frais
Monterey Jack
Red Leicester

16 letters:
Double Gloucester

Cheesecake Pin-up, Talmouse
Cheese-scoop Pale
Chef Commis, Escoffier, Oliver, Ramsay
Chekhov Anton
Chemical Acanthin, Acid, Acrolein, Adrenalin®, Agent Orange, Alar, Aldehyde, Alkali, Allomone, Alum(ina), Amide, Anabolic, Avertin, Barilla, Bradykinin, Bute, Camphene, Camphor, Carbide, Carnallite, Caseose, Catalyst, Cephalin, Cerebroside, Coal tar, Depside, Developer, Dopamine, Encephalin, Enkephalin(e), Enol, Ethanal, Ethoxy, Ethyl, Fixer, Fluoride, Formyl, Freon, Fungicide, Furosemide, Gamone, Gibbsite, Glutamine, Glycol, Halon, Harmin, Heavy, Hecogenin, Heptane, Hexylene, Hexylresorcinol, Histamine, Hormone, Hypo, ICI, Imine, Imipramine, Indican, Inositol, Interleukin, Larvicide, Lewisite, Lipid, Masking-agent, Massicot, Morphactin, Naioxone, Napalm, Naphtha, Natron, Neurotransmitter, Nitre, Nonylphenol, Oestrogen, Olefin, Olein, Oxide, Oxysalt, Paraben, Pentane, Pentene, Pentyl, Peptide, Periclase, Phenol, Phenyl, Pheromone, Potash, Potassa, Psoralen, Ptomaine, Reagent, Resorcin, Resorcinol, Restrainer, Sequestrant, Serotonin, Soman, Soup, Stearate, Strontia, Styrene, Sulphide, Terpene, Thio-salt, Toluol, Toner, Trimer, Tritide, Weedicide, Weedkiller, Xylol
Chemise Cymar, Sark, Serk, Shift, Shirt, Simar(re), Smock, Symar
Chemist Analyst, Apothecary, Dispenser, Druggist, Drugstore, FCS, LSA, MPS, Pharmacist, Pothecary, RIC

CHEMISTS

4 letters:
Bohn
Curl
Davy
Gahn
Hahn
Todd
Urey

5 letters:
Curie
Debye
Dewar
Haber
Kroto
Nobel
Prout

Soddy

6 letters:
Baeyer
Bunsen
Hevesy
Liebig
Muller

Nernst
Proust
Sanger
Schiff
Wohler

7 letters:
Buchner

	8 letters:	**9 letters:**	Strassman
Faraday	Lipscomb	Arrhenius	
Fischer	Mulliken	Backeland	**10 letters:**
Helmont	Newlands	Berzelius	Mendeleyer
Hodgkin	Sabatier	Butenandt	Paracelsus
Macadam	Smithson	Cavendish	
Pasteur	Weizmann	Lavoisier	**11 letters:**
Pauling	Welsbach	Leclanche	Hinshelwood
Smalley		Pelletier	Le Chatelier
Ziegler		Priestley	

Chemistry Alchemy, Alchymy, Chemurgy, Iatrochemistry, Inorganic, Nuclear, Organic, Physical, Radiation, Spageric, Spagiric, Spagyric, Stinks, Stoecheometry, Stoechiometry, Stoich(e)iometry, Technical, Zymurgy

Cheops Khufu

Cheque Blank, Bouncer, Giro, Gregory, Open, Rubber, Stumer, Tab, Traveller's

Chequer Dice

Cherish(ed) Dear, Dote, Enshrine, Entertain, Esteem, Foment, Foster, Harbour, Inshrine, Nestle, Nurse, Pamper, Pet, Precious, Refocillate, Treasure

Cheroot Cigar, Manil(l)a

Cherry (tree) Amarelle, Amazon, Ball, Barbados, Bigaroon, Bigarreau, Bird, Blackheart, Bladder, Cerise, Choke, Cornelian, Gean, Ground, Heart, Jerusalem, Kearton, Kermes, Kermesite, Malpighia, Marasca, Maraschino, May-duke, Maz(z)ard, Merry, Morel(lo), Prunus, Red, Sweet, Whiteheart

Cherry-pie Heliotrope

Cherub Angel, Putto, Seraph

Chervil Cow-parsley

Chess (move), Chess player, Chess term Andersson, Black, Blindfold, Endgame, Euwe, Fianchetto, FIDE, Hexagonal, J'adoube, Karpov, Kasparov, Lightning, Mate, Miranda, Patzer, Plank, Rapid transit, Shogi, Speed, White, Zugzwang, Zwischenzug

Chessman Bishop, Black, Castle, Cheque, Horse, King, Knight, Pawn, Pin, Queen, Rook, White

Chest(y) Ark, Bahut, Bosom, Box, Breast, Buist, Bunker, Bureau, Bust, Caisson, Cap-case, Case, Cassone, Chapel, Charter, Chiffonier, Coffer, Coffin, Coffret, Commode, Community, Cub, Dresser, Girnel, Hope, Hutch, Inro, Kist, Larnax, Locker, Lowboy, Meal-ark, Medicine, Ottoman, Pectoral, Pereion, Pigeon, Pleural, Ribcage, Safe, Scrine, Scryne, Sea, Shrine, Slop, Steam, Sternum, Tallboy, Tea, Thorax, Toolbox, Treasure, Trunk, Wangan, Wangun, Wanigan, War, Wind

Chester Deva

Chestnut Auburn, Badious, Ch, Chincapin, Chinese, Chinkapin, Chinquapin, Cliché, Conker, Dwarf, Favel(l), Hoary, Horse, Marron, Marron glacé, Moreton Bay, Roan, Russet, Saligot, Soare, Sorrel, Spanish, Sweet, Water

Chest protector → ARMOUR, Bib

Chevalier Bayard, Knight, Pretender

Chevron Dancette, Stripe, V-shape

Chew(ing) Bite, Champ, Chaw, Crunch, Cud, Eat, Fletcherism, Gnaw, Gum, Manducate, Masticate, Maul, Meditate, Moop, Mou(p), Munch, Ruminate, Siri(h), Spearmint

Chewink Ground-robin

Chiastolite Macle

Chic Dapper, Debonair, Elegant, Heroin, In, Kick, Modish, Posh, Radical, Smart, Soigné, Stylish, Swish, Tonish, Trim

Chicago Windy City

Chicane(ry) Artifice, Deception, Fraud, Wile

Chichester Yachtsman

Chichi Precious
Chick(en) Australorp, Battery, Biddy, Boiler, Broiler, Capon, Cheeper, Chittagong, Chuckie, Clutch, Cochin(-China), Coronation, Coward, Cowherd, Craven, Drumstick, Eirack, Gutless, Hen, Howtowdie, Kiev, Layer, Marengo, Minorca, Mother Carey's, Niderling, Pavid, Poltroon, Poot, Pope's nose, Poult, Pout, Prairie, Precocial, Pullus, Quitter, Roaster, Scaredy-cat, Spatchcock, Spring, Squab, Supreme, Sussex, Timorous, Unheroic, Wimp, Windy, Wishbone, Wyandotte, Yellow
Chickenfeed Maize, Peanuts
Chickenpox Varicella
Chickpea Chana, Felafel, Garbanzo
Chickweed Snow-in-summer
Chicory Endive, Radiccio, Succory, Witloof
Chide Admonish, Berate, Dress, Objurgate, Rate, Rebuke, Reprove, Row, Scold, Tick off, Twit, Upbraid
Chief(tain) Ag(h)a, Arch, Ardrigh, Ariki, Boss, Caboceer, Cacique, Calif, Caliph, Capital, Capitan, Capitayn, Capo, Caradoc, Cazique, Ch, Chagan, Dat(t)o, DG, Dominant, Duke, Emir, Finn (MacCool), First, Foremost, Geronimo, Grand, Haggis, → **HEAD**, Hereward, Jarl, Kaid, Keystone, King, Leader, → **MAIN**, Mass, Mocuddum, Mokaddam, Mugwump, Muqaddam, Nawab, Nizam, Nkosi, Oba, Overlord, Paramount, Pendragon, Premier, Primal, Prime, Principal, Quanah, Raja(h), Rajpramukh, Rangatira, Rangatiratanga, Ratoo, Ratu, Sachem, Sagamore, Sardar, Sarpanch, Sea-king, Sheikh, Sirdar, Staple, Sudder, Supreme, Tanist, Tank, Taxiarch, Thane, Top
Chiffonier Cabinet, Commode
Chilblain Kibe
Child(ren), Childhood, Childish Aerie, Alannah, Ankle biter, Auf, Babe, Baby, Bach(ch)a, Badger, Bairn, Bambino, Bantling, Boy, Brat, Brood, Butter-print, Ch, Changeling, Cherub, Chick, Chickabiddy, Chit, Collop, Cub, Dream, Duddie weans, Elfin, Eyas, Feral, Foster, Foundling, Gait, Gangrel, Ge(i)t, Girl, Gyte, Heir, Hellion, Hurcheon, Imp, Infancy, Infant, Inner, Issue, It, Jailbait, Jejune, Juvenile, Kid, Kiddie(wink), Kiddy, Kidult, Kinder, Lad, Latchkey, Limb, Litter, Littlie, Littling, Love, Mamzer, Mardy, Minion, Minor, Mite, Moppet, Munchkin, Naive, Nipper, Nursling, Offspring, Pantywaist, Papoose, Piccaninny, Pickin, Problem, Progeny, Puerile, Puss, Putto, Ragamuffin, Rip, Romper, Rug rat, Scion, Second, Seed, Siblings, Small fry, Smout, Smowt, Sprog, Street arab, Subteen, Tacker, Ted, Teeny-bopper, Tike, Toddle(r), Tot(tie), Totty, Trot, Tweenager, Tweenie, Tyke, Urchin, Waif, Wean, Weanel, Weanling, Weeny-bopper, Whelp, Young, Youngster, Younker, Youth
Childbearing, Childbirth Couvade, Dystocia, Intrapartum, Lamaze, Obstetrics, Parity, Puerperal, Tocology, Tokology
Child-eater, Child-killer Herod, Thyestes
Childless Atocous, Atokous, Barren, Nullipara, Sp
Chile(an) CH, Mapuche
Chill(er), Chilly Bleak, Cauldrife, → **COLD**, Cool, Cryogen, Frappé, Freeze, Freon®, Frigid, Frosty, Gelid, Ice, Iciness, Laze, Mimi, Oorie, Ourie, Owrie, Parky, Raw, Refrigerate, Rigor, Scare
Chilli Bird's eye, Cayenne, → **PEPPER**, Pimentón
Chime(s) Bell, Clam, Cymar, Jingle, Peal, Rhime, Semantron, Tink, → **TOLL**, Wind
Chimera Graft
Chimney (pot), Chimney corner Can, Cow(l), Femerall, Flare stack, Flue, Funnel, Lamp, Lug, Lum, Smokestack, Stack, Stalk, Steeplejack, Tallboy, Tunnel
Chimney-sweep Chummy
Chimp(anzee) Ape, Bonobo, Jocko, Pygmy
Chin, Chinwag Chitchat, Double, Genial, Hill-man, Jaw, Jowl, Mentum
China(man), Chinese Ami, Amoy, Bone, Boxer, Bud(dy), Cameoware, Cantonese, Catayan, Cathay, Celestial, Ch, Chelsea, Chink(y), Chow, Coalport, Cochin, Cock,

Colleague, Communist, Confucius, Crackle, Crockery, Delft, Derby, Dresden, Eggshell, Etrurian, Flowery land, Friend, Fukien, Google, Googly, Goss, Hakka, Han, Hizen, Hmong, Imari, Ironstone, Kanji, Kaolin, Kuo-yu, Limoges, Macanese, Manchu, Manchurian, Mandarin, Mangi, Maoist, Mate, Meissen, Middle kingdom, Min, Ming, Minton, National, Oppo, Pal, Pareoean, Pekingese, Pe-tsai, Pinyin, Porcelain, → **POTTERY**, Putonghua, Queensware, Quina, Red, Rockingham, Royal Worcester, Rusticware, Semiporcelain, Seric, Sèvres, Shanghai, Sinaean, Sinic, Sino-, Spode®, Sun Yat-sen, Tai-ping, Taoist, Teng, Tocharian, Tungus, Uigur, Wal(l)y, Ware, Wedgwood®, Whiteware, Willow pattern, Willowware, Worcester, Wu, Yao, Yellow peril

Chine Chink, Chynd, Ridge

Chink(y) Chinaman, Chop, Cleft, Clink, Cloff, Crack, Cranny, Crevice, Gap, Rent, Rift, Rima, Rimose, Sinic, Window

Chintz Kalamkari

Chip(s) Blitter, Blue, Bo(a)st, Carpenter, Counter, Cut, Deep-fried, EPROM, EROM, Fish, Flake, Fragment, Game, Hack, Knap, Log, Micro, Nacho(s), Neural, Nick, Pin, Potato, Shaving, Silicon, Spale, Spall, Span, Splinter, Tease, Teraflop, Tortilla, Transputer, Virus

▷ **Chip** *may indicate* an anagram

Chipmunk Gopher, Hackee, Suslik, Zizel

Chippendale Chinese

Chipper Jaunty, Spry, Wedge

Chiron Centaur

Chiropody Pedicure, Podiatry

Chiropractic McTimoney

Chirp(y), Chirrup Cheep, Cherup, Chirm, Chirr, Cicada, Peep, Pip, Pipe, Pitter, Stridulate, Trill, Tweet, Twitter

Chisel(ler), Chisel-like Bam, Boaster, Bolster, Bur, Burin, Carve, Cheat, Clip, Drove, Firmer, Gad, → **GOUGE**, Half-round, Mason, Paring, Scalpriform, Scauper, Scorper, Sculpt, Slick, Socket, Sting

Chit Docket, Girl, Memo, Note, Voucher

Chivalry, Chivalrous Brave, Bushido, Courtly, Datin, Gallant, Gent, Grandisonian, Quixotic

Chivvy Badger, Harass, Pursue

Chloride, Chlorine Calomel, Muriate

Chlorophyll Granum, Leaf-green

Chock Trig

Chocolate Aero, Brown, Cacao, Carob, Cocoa, Dragee, Ganache, Milk, Neapolitan, Noisette, Pinole, Plain, Praline, Rolo®, Theobroma, Truffle, Vegelate, Vermicelli

Choice, Choose, Choosy, Chosen Adopt, Anthology, Appoint, Aryan, Cherry-pick, Cull, Dainty, Decide, Druthers, Eclectic, Elect, Elite, Esnecy, Fine, Fork, Free will, Hercules, Hobson's, Leet, Leve, Lief, List, Multiple, Opt, Option, Or, Ossian, Peach, Peacherino, Peculiar, → **PICK**, Picking, Plum(p), Precious, Predilect, Prefer, Proairesis, Rare, Recherché, → **SELECT**, Superb, Try(e), Via media, Volition, Wale

Choiceless Beggar

Choir, Choral, Chorister, Chorus Antiphony, Antistrophe, Anvil, Apse, Burden, Choragus, Choregus, Chorister, Choryphaeus, Dawn, Decani, Faburden, Fauxbourdon, Group, Hallelujah, Harmony, Hymeneal, Motet, Ninth, Parabasis, Precentor, Quirister, → **REFRAIN**, Reprise, Ritual, Schola cantorum, Serenata, Singing, Stop, Strophe, Treble, Triad, → **UNISON**

Choir-master Choragus, Choregus, Precentor

Choke(r) Accloy, Block, Clog, Die, Gag, Garotte, Glut, Silence, Smoor, Smore, Smother, Stap, Stifle, Stop, Strangle(hold), Strangulate, → **THROTTLE**, Warp

Choky Can, Prison

Choler Irascibility, Yellow bile

Cholera Asiatic, British, Hog

Cholesterol Spinacene, Squalene
Choliamb Scazon
▸ **Choose** *see* CHOICE
Chop, Chops, Chopper(s), Choppy Adze, Air tax, Ax(e), Cakehole, Celt, Charge, Cheek, Chump, Cleave, Côtelette, Cuff, Cutlet, Dice, Fell(er), Flew, Hack, Hash, Helicopter, Hew, Ivory, Karate, Lop, Mince, Mouth, Rotaplane, Rough, Split, Standing, Suey, Teeth, To-rend, Underhand, Wang
Chopin Pantoufle, Shoe
Chopstick(s) Waribashi
Chord(s) Altered, Arpeggio, Barré, Broken, Common, Diameter, Eleventh, Harmony, Intonator, Latus rectum, Neapolitan sixth, Nerve, Ninth, Picardy third, Riff, Seventh, Sixth, Submediant, Thirteenth, Triad, Vocal
Chore Darg, Duty, Fag, Task
Chorea Sydenham's
Choreographer Arranger, Ashton, Balanchine, Bourne, Cecchetti, Cranko, Cunningham, Dolin, Fokine, Laban, Lifar, Massine, Murphy, Tetley, Tharp
▸ **Chorus** *see* CHOIR
Chosen Elite, Korea
Chough Chewet
Chow Nosh
Chowder Bouillabaisse, Clam, Skink, Soup
Christ Ecce homo, Lamb of God, Logos, Messiah, Pantocrator, Paschal Lamb, Prince of Peace, Saviour, Son (of God), Son of man, The Good Shepherd, The Redeemer, X, Xt
Christen(ing) Baptise, Launch, Name-day
Christian(ity) Abcee, Abecedarian, Absey, Adventist, Albigenses, Anabaptist, Antioch, Beghard, Believer, Cathar(ist), Charismatic, Colossian, Coptic, Dior, Donatist, D(o)ukhobor, Ebionite, Fletcher, Galilean, Giaour, Gilbertine, Gnostic, Godsquad, Goy, Heteroousian, Holy roller, Homo(i)ousian, Hutterite, Jehovah's Witness, Lutheran, Maronite, Marrano, Melchite, Melkite, Methodist, Molinism, Monarchian, Monophysite, Moral, Mozarab, Muscular, Mutineer, Nazarene, Nestorian, Phalange, Pilgrim, Presbyterian, Protestant, Quaker, Quartodeciman, RC, Sabotier, Scientist, SCM, Shambe, Solifidian, Traditor, Uniat(e), Unitarian, Valdenses, Waldensian, Wesleyan, Xian, Zwinglian
Christian Scientist Eddy
Christmas(time) Beetle, Box, Cactus, Card, Carol, Chrissie, C(h)rimbo, Day, Dec, Island, Nativity, Noel, Nowel(l), Pudding, Stocking, Xmas, Yuletide
Christopher Kit, Robin, Sly, Wren
Chromatin Karyotin
Chromium Cr
Chromosome Aneuploid, Autosome, Barr body, Centromere, Cistron, Euchromatin, Genome, Haploid, Homologous, Id(ant), Karyotype, Lampbrush, Operon, Philadelphia, Ploid(y), Polytene, Prophage, Satellite, Sex, Telomere, Trisomy, X, Y
Chronicle(r) Anglo-Saxon, Annal, Brut, Calendar, Diary, Froissart, Hall, Historiographer, History, Holinshed, Logographer, Moblog, Narrative, Paralipomena, Parian, Paris, → RECORD, Register, Stow
Chrysalis Nymph, Pupa
Chrysanthemum Corn-marigold, Feverfew, Korean
Chrysolite Olivine, Peridot
Chub Chavender, Cheven, Chevin, Fish
Chubby Butterball, Plump
Chuck (out) Berry, Buzz, Chook(ie), Discard, Eject, Food, Four-jaw, Grub, Independent-jaw, Pat, Pitch, Scroll, Shy, Sling, Three-jaw, Toss, Turf
Chuckle Chortle, Giggle, Gurgle
Chukka Polo

Chum(my) Ally, Associate, Boet, Buddy, Cobber, Cock, Companion, Comrade, Crony, Mate, Pal, Playmate, Sociable, Sodality

Chump Cretin, Fool, Mug(gins), Noddle, Sap, → **STUPID PERSON**

Chunk(y) Boxy, Chubby, Gob, Piece, Slab, Squat, Wad

Church Abbey, Armenian, Auld Licht, Autocephalous, Basilica, Bethel, Bethesda, Broad, Brood, Byzantine, → **CATHEDRAL**, CE, Ch, Chapel, Chevet, Classis, Clergy, Collegiate, Congregational, Coptic, Delubrum, Easter (Orthodox), Eastern, EC, Ecumenical, Episcopal, Episcopalian, Established, Faith, Fold, Free, Greek, High, House, Institutional, Kirk, Lateran, Latin, Low, Lutheran, Maronite, Melchite, Methodist, Minster, Moonie, Moravian, Mormon, Mother, National, Nazarene, New, New Jerusalem, Old Light, Oratory, Orthodox, Parish, Peculiar, Pentecostal, Preaching-house, Prebendal, Presbyterian, Ratana, RC, Reformed, Relief, Rome, Russian Orthodox, Schism house, Schism shop, Secession, Shrine, Smyrna, Station, Stave, Steeple, Steeplehouse, Tabernacle, Temple, Title, Titular, Transept, Triumphant, Unification, Unitarian, United Free, United Reformed, Visible, Wee Free, Western, Wool

Churchgoer, Churchman, Churchwarden Anglican, Antiburgher, Azymite, Baptist, Barnabite, Believer, Cameronian, Cantor, Classis, Clay, Cleric, Clerk, Congregation, Deacon, Dom, Dopper, Elder, Evangelist, Hatto, Ignorantine, Incumbent, Invisible, Knox, Lector, Lutheran, Marrowman, Methodist, Militant, Moderator, Moonie, Mormon, MU, Newman, Oncer, Parson, PE, Pew-opener, Pipe, Pontiff, Prebendary, Precentor, Predicant, Predikant, Prelate, Presbyterian, Priest, Protestant, Puritan, Racovian, Rector, Romanist, Ruridecanal, Sacristan, Sidesman, Sim, Simeonite, Socinian, Spike, Subchanter, Subdeacon, Succentor, Swedenborgian, Tantivy, Triumphant, Ubiquitarian, Unitarian, Verger, Vestryman, Visible, Wesleyan, Worshipper, Wren

Church house Deanery, Manse, Parsonage, Presbytery, Rectory, Vicarage

Churchill Tank, Winston

Churchyard God's acre, Stoke Poges

Churl(ish) Attercop, Boor, Crabby, Curmudgeonly, Cynical, Ethercap, Ettercap, Gruff, Ill-natured, Nabal, Peasant, Rustic, Serf, Surly

Churn Bubble, Kirn, Seethe, Sicken

Chute Flume, Runway

Ciao Adieu, Adios, Aloha

CIC Shogun, Sirdar

Cicada Greengrocer, Locust, Periodical, Tettix

Cicatrix Scar

Cicely Myrrh, Seseli, Sweet

Cicero Cic, Orator, Tully

Cicerone Guide

CID Sûreté

Cid Campeador, Chief, Hero

Cider Drink, Hard, Perry, Scrumpy, Sweet

Ci-devant Ex

Cigar(ette), Cigarette cards Beedi(e), Bidi, Biftah, Bifter, Bumper, Burn, Camberwell carrot, Cancer stick, Caporal, Cartophily, Cheroot, Cigarillo, Claro, Coffin nail, Conch, Concha, Corona, Dog-end, Doob, Durry, Fag, Filter-tip, Gasper, Giggle(-stick), Havana, Joint, Locofoco, Long-nine, Loosies, Maduro, Manilla, Number, Panatella, Paper-cigar, Perfecto, Puritano, Reefer, Regalia, Roach, Roll-up, Segar, Smoke, Snout, Splif(f), Stogie, Stog(e)y, Stompie, Tab, Twist, Weed, Whiff, Woodbine, Zol

Cinch Belt, Certainty, Duck soup, Easy, Girth, Stroll

Cinchona Kina, Quina

Cinder(s) Ash, Breeze, Clinker, Dander, Embers, Slag

Cinderella Drudge, Stepdaughter

Cinema(s) Art house, Big screen, Biograph, Bioscope, Circuit, Drive-in, Films, Fleapit, Flicks, Grindhouse, IMAX®, Megaplex, Movies, Multiplex, Multiscreen, Mutoscope,

New Wave, Nickelodeon, Nouvelle Vague, Odeon, Picture palace, Pictures, Plaza, Scope, Theatre, Tivoli

Cinnabar Vermilion

Cinnamon, Cinnamon stone Canella, Cassia (bark), Essonite, Hessonite, Saigon, Spice

Cipher Chi-rho, Code, Cryptogram, Enigma, Nihil, Nobody, → **NOTHING**, Number, O, Steganogram, Zero

Circle Almacantar, Almucantar, Annulet, Antarctic, Arctic, Circassian, Co, Colure, Company, Compass, Corn, Corolla, Coterie, Cromlech, Crop, Cycloid, Cyclolith, Dip, Disc, Dress, Druidical, Eccentric, Ecliptic, Embail, Enclose, Engird, Epicyclic, Equant, Equator, Equinoctial, Euler's, Fairy ring, Family, Fraternity, Full, Galactic, Girdle, Gloriole, Great, Gyrate, Gyre, Halo, Henge, Hoop, Horizon, Hour, Hut, Inner, Inorb, Lap, Longitude, Loop, Magic, Malebolge, Mandala, Meridian, Mohr's, Mural, Nimbus, O, Orb, Orbit, Parhelic, Parquet, Parterre, Penannular, Peristalith, Pitch, Polar, Quality, Red-line, Rigol, → **RING**, Rondure, Rotate, Roundlet, Seahenge, Sentencing, Set, Setting, Small, Sphere, Stemme, Stone, Stonehenge, Striking, Surround, Tinchel, Tondino, Traffic, Transit, Tropic, Turning, Umbel, Upper, Vertical, Vicious, Vienna, Virtuous, Volt, Wheel, Whorl

Circuit(-board), Circuitous Ambit, AND, Autodyne, Bridge, Bus, Bypass, Chipset, Closed, Comparator, Daughterboard, Diocese, Discriminator, Dolby®, Equivalent, Eyre, Feedback, Gate, Gyrator, Half-adder, Highway, IC, Integrated, Interface, Lap, Le Mans, Limiter, Live, Logic, Loop, Microchip, Microprocessor, Monza, Motherboard, NAND, NOR, NOT, Open, OR, Perimeter, Phantom, Phase, Printed, Push-pull, Quadripole, Reactance, Ring, Round, Roundure, Rubber-chicken, Scaler, Series, Short, Smoothing, Sound card, Squelch, Stage, Three-phase, Tour, Trunk, Windlass, XNOR, XOR

Circuit-breaker Air gap, Fuse

Circular Annular, Court, Disc(al), Endless, Flysheet, Folder, Leaflet, Mailshot, Orby, Round, Spiral, Unending, Vertical, Wheely

Circulate, Circulation Ambient, Astir, Bandy, Bloodstream, Cyclosis, Disseminate, Flow, Gross, Gyre, Issue, Mingle, Mix, Orbit, Pass, Publish, Report, Revolve, Rotate, Scope, Send round, Spread, Stir, Troll, Utter

▷ **Circulating** *may indicate* an anagram

Circumcise(r), Circumcision Bris, Brith, Brit milah, Infibulate, Milah, Mohel, Pharaonic, Sandek

Circumference Boundary, Girth, Perimeter, Size

Circumflex Perispomenon

Circumlocution Bafflegab, Periphrasis, Tautology

Circumnavigation Periplus

Circumscribe(d) Define, Demarcate, Enclose, Eruv, Restrain

Circumspect Canny, Chary, Discreet, Guarded, Prudential, Wary, Watchful

Circumstance(s), Circumstantial Case, Detail, Event, Fact, Formal, → **INCIDENT**, Mitigating, Precise, Shebang, Situation, Stede

Circumvent Bypass, Dish, Evade, Negotiate, Outflank, Outwit, Usurp

Circus, Circus boy Arena, Big top, Eros, Flea, Flying, Harrier, Hippodrome, Marquee, Maximus, Media, Monty Python, Ring, Sanger, Slang, Three-ring

Cissy Nelly

Cistercian Trappist

Cistern Feed-head, Flush-box, Sump, Tank, Tub, Vat

Citadel Acropolis, Alhambra, Castle, Fort(ress), Keep, Kremlin, Sea-girt

Citation, Cite Adduce, Allegation, Instance, Mensh, Mention, Name, Quote, Recall, Reference, Repeat, Sist, Summon

Citizen(s), Citizenship Burgess, Burgher, Civism, Cleruch, Denizen, Dicast, Ephebe, Franchise, Freeman, Jus sanguinis, Jus soli, Kane, Keelie, National, Oppidan, Patrial, People, Proletarian, Propr(a)etor, Quirites, Resident, Roman, Second-class, Senior, Snob, Subject, Trainband, Trierarch, Venireman, Vigilante, Voter

Citroen DS

Citron, Citrous Bergamot

Citrus Acid, Calamondin, Cedrate, Hesperidium, Lemon, Lime, Mandarin, Min(n)eola, Orange, Pomelo, Tangerine, Ugli

City Agra, Astrakhan, Athens, Atlantis, Babylon, Burgh, Cardboard, Carthage, Cosmopolis, Ctesiphon, Dodge, EC, Empire, Eternal, Forbidden, Free, Garden, Gath, Heavenly, Hilversum, Holy, Imperial, Inner, LA, Leonine, Medina, Megalopolis, Metropolis, Micropolis, Mother, Municipal, Mycenae, Ninevah, NY, Persepolis, Petra, Pompeii, Rhodes, Salem, See, Smoke, Sparta, Square mile, Tech, Teheran, The Big Smoke, Town, Ur, Vatican, Weltstadt, Wen

Civet Binturong, Cat, Fo(u)ssa, Genet(te), Herpestes, Linsang, Musang, Nandine, Palm, Paradoxine, Paradoxure, Rasse, Suricate, Toddy-cat, Viverra, Zibet

Civil(ian), Civilisation, Civilised, Civility Amenity, Amicable, Christian, Cit, Citizen, Civ(vy), Comity, Courtesy, Culture, Fertile crescent, Humane, Indus Valley, Kultur, Maya, Mufti, Municipal, Nok, Non-combatant, Plain clothes, Polite, Politesse, Push-button, Secular, Temporal, Urbane

Civil Service CS

Clad(ding) Sarking, Weatherboard

Clag(gy) Stickjaw

Claim(s) Allege, Appeal, Arrogate, Assert, Asseverate, Bag, Challenge, Charge, Crave, Darraign(e), Darrain(e), Darrayn, Demand, Deraign, Droit, Encumbrance, Exact, Haro, Harrow, Insist, Lien, List, Maintain, Nochel, Plea, Pose, Posit, Postulate, Predicate, Pretence, Pretend, Profess, Pulture, Purport, Puture, Rank, Revendicate, Right, Set-off, Small, Sue, Title

Claimant Irredentist, Petitioner, Pot-waller, Pretender, Prospector, Tichborne, Usurper

Clairvoyance, Clairvoyancy, Clairvoyant ESP, Extrasensory, Fey, Insight, Lucidity, Psiphenomena, Psychic, Second sight, Taisch, Taish, Telegnosis, Telepathic, Tel(a)esthesia

Clam Bivalve, Chowder, Cohog, Geoduck, Giant, Gweduc, Hardshell, Littleneck, Mollusc, Mya, Quahang, Quahog, Razor(-shell), Round, Soft-shell, Steamer, Tridacna, Venus, Vongole

Clamant Vociferous

Clamber Climb, Crawl, Scramble, Spra(i)ckle, Sprauchle

Clammy Algid, Damp, Dank, Moist, Sticky, Sweaty

Clamour(ing), Clamorous Blatant, Brouhaha, Din, Forensis strepitus, Hubbub, Hue, Katzenjammer, Noise, Outcry, Racket, Raird, Reird, Rout, Shout, Strepitant, Uproar, Utis, Vociferate

Clamp(er) Beartrap, Chuck, Clinch, Coupler, Denver boot, Fasten, Grip, Haemostat, Holdfast, Jumar, Pinchcock, Potato-pit, Serrefine, Stirrup, Tread, Vice, Wheel

Clan(sman) Brood, Cameron, Campbell, Clique, Gens, Gentile, Group, Horde, Kiltie, Kindred, Name, Ngati, Phratry, Phyle, Sect, Sept, Society, Stewart, Stuart, Tribe

Clandestine Covert, Furtive, Secret, Surreptitious, Underhand

Clang(er), Clanging, Clank Bell, Belleter, Boob, Boo-boo, Clash, Gong, Jangle, Plangent, Ring

Clap(per), Clapping Applaud, Blow, Castanet, Chop, Crotal, Dose, Jinglet, Peal, Plaudite, Stroke hands, Thunder, Tonant

Claptrap Bilge, Blab, Bombast, Bunkum, Eyewash, Hokum, Rot, Tripe, Twaddle

Claque(ur) Fans, Hat, Laudator, Sycophant

Clara Bow, Butt

Clare Nun, Sister

Claret Blood, Loll-shraub, Loll-shrob, Vin

Clarify, Clarified, Clarifier Clear, Despumate, Dilucidate, Explain, Explicate, Fine, Finings, Ghee, Purge, Refine, Render, Simplify, Tease out

Clarinet Chalumeau, Reed

Clarion Brassy, Clear, Trumpet

Clary Orval, Sage

Clash(ing) Bang, Clangour, Clank, Claver, Coincide, Collide, Conflict, Dissonant, Friction, Gossip, → **IMPACT**, Incident, Irreconcilable, Jar, Loud, Missuit, Riot, Shock, Showdown, Strike, Swash

Clasp(ing) Adpress, Agraffe, Amplexus, Barrette, Brooch, Button, Catch, Chape, Clip, Embrace, Fibula, Grasp, Hasp, Hesp, Hook, Hug, Inarm, Interdigitate, Link, Morse, Ochreate, Ouch, Peace, Press, Slide, Tach(e), Tie, Unite

Class(ification), Classify, Classified, Classy Acorn, Arrange, Assort, Bourgeois(ie), Bracket, Brand, Breed, Business, Cabin, Canaille, Caste, → **CATEGORY**, Chattering, Cheder, Cl, Cladistics, Clan, Clerisy, Clinic, Club, Composite, Course, Criminal, Dalit, Dewey, Digest, Division, Economy, Estate, Evening, Faction, First, Form, Genera, Gentry, Genus, → **GRADE**, Group, Harvard, Haryan, Heder, Hubble, Ilk, Keep-fit, Kidney, Kohanga reo, League, Lesson, Life, Linn(a)ean, List, Lower, Mammal, Master, Meritocracy, Middle, Night, Number, Nursery, Order, Peasantry, Phenetics, Phylum, Pigeon-hole, Pleb(eian), Posh, Proper, Race, Range, Rank, Rate, Rating, Raypoot, Raypout, Reception, Remove, Ruling, Salariat, Second, Secret, Seminar, Shell, Siege, Social, Sort(ation), Spectral, Sphere, Standard, Steerage, Stratum, Stream, Syntax, Taxonomy, Teach-in, Third, Tony, Tourist, Tribe, Tutorial, → **TYPE**, U, Universal, Upper, Varna, Water, Working, World, Year

Classic(al), Classics, Classicist Ageless, Ancient, Basic, Derby, Elzevir, Grecian, Greek, Humane, Leger, Literature, Oldie, Pliny, Purist, Roman, Standard, Traditional, Vintage

Clatch Blunk, Smear, Spoil

Clatter Bicker, Charivari, Clack, Din, Noise, Rattle

Clause Acceleration, Adjunct, Apodosis, Article, Basket, Complement, Condition, Conscience, Coordinate, Dependent, Disability, Endorsement, Escalator, Escape, Exclusion, Exemption, Filioque, Four, Golden parachute, Grandfather, Independent, Main, Member, Noun, Novodamus, Object, Omnibus, Option, Poison-pill, Predicator, Principal, Protasis, Proviso, Reddendum, Relative, Reported, Reservation, Reserve, Rider, Salvo, Saving, Sentence, Subject, Subordinate, Sunset, Tenendum, Testatum, Testing, Warrandice

Claw Chela, Claut, Cloye, Crab, Dewclaw, Edate, Falcula, Grapple, Griff(e), Hook, Insessorial, Nail, Nipper, Pounce, Scrab, Scramb, Sere, Talent, → **TALON**, Tear, Telson, Tokay, Unguis

Clay Allophane, Argil, Argillite, Barbotine, B(e)auxite, Bentonite, Blaes, Blaise, Blaize, Blunge, Bole, Boulder, Calm, Cam, Cassius, Caum, Ceramic, Charoset(h), China, Cimolite, Cloam, Clunch, Cob, Cornish, Earth, Engobe, Fango, Figuline, Fire, Fuller's earth, Gault, Glei, Gley, Gumbotil, Hardpan, Haroset(h), Illite, Kaolin, Kokowai, Laterite, Lithomarge, Loam, London, Lute, Malm, Marl, Meerschaum, Mire, Mortal, Mud, Oxford, Papa, Pipeclay, Pipestone, Pise, Plastic, Plastilina, Porcelain, Potter's, Pottery, Puddle, Pug, Saggar(d), Sagger, Scroddle(d), Seggar, Sepiolite, Slip, Slurry, Smectite, Terra sigillata, Thill, Till(ite), Tumphy, Varve, Warrant, Warren, Wax

Clean(er), Cleaning, Cleanse Absterge, Ammonia, Bathbrick, Besom, Bidet, Blanco, Bleach, Blue flag, Bream, Broom, Careen, Catharise, Catharsis, Chamois leather, Char(e), Chaste, Clear, Cottonbud, Daily, Debride, Decontaminate, Dentifrice, Depurate, Deterge(nt), Dhobi, Dialysis, Dicht, Disinfect, Do, Douche, Dredge, Dust(er), Dyson®, Eluant, Emunge, Enema, Epurate, Erase, Ethnic, Evacuant, Evacuate, Expurgate, Fay, Fettle, Fey, Floss, Flush, Full, Grave, Groom, Gut, Heels, Hoover®, House-trained, Hygienic, Immaculate, Innocent, Kosher, Launder, Lave, Linish, Lustrum, Lye, Mouthwash, Mrs Mop(p), Mundify, Net, Nipter, Overhaul, Porge, Prophylaxis, Pull-through, Pumice, Pure, Purgative, Purge, Ramrod, Rebite, Rub, Rump, Sandblast, Sanitize, Scaffie, Scavenge, Scour, Scrub, Shampoo, Shot-blast, Snow-white, Soap, Soogee, Soogie, Soojey, Sponge, Spotless, Square, Squeaky, Squeegee, Squilgee, Sterile,

Sujee, Swab, Sweep, Syringe, Tidy, Toothpick, Ultrasonic, Uproot, Vac(uum), Valet, → **WASH**, Whistle, Whiter, Wipe, Zamboni

Clear(ance), Cleared, Clearly Absolve, Acquit, Allow, Aloof, Apparent, Articulate, Assart, Bald, Bell, Berth, Bold, Bore, Brighten, Bus, Categorical, Clarify, Cloudless, Cogent, Concise, Consomme, Crystal, Daylight, Decode, Definite, Delouse, Demist, Diaphanous, Dispel, Distinct, Downright, Earn, Eidetic, Evacuate, Evident, Exculpate, Exonerate, Explicit, Fair, Five-by-five, Flagrant, Gain, Get over, Headroom, Highland, Hyaline, Intelligible, Iron, Laund, Leap, Legible, Limpid, Lucid, Luculent, Manifest, Mop, Neat, Negotiate, Net(t), → **NOT CLEAR**, Observable, Obvious, Ope(n), Overleap, Overt, Palpable, Patent, Pay, Pellucid, Perspicuous, Plain, Play, Pratique, Predy, Pure, Purge, Quit, Rack, Realise, Reap, Remble, Rid, Ripple, Serene, Sheer, Shere, Silvery, Slum, Specific, Stark, Straight, Strip, Succinct, Sweep, Swidden, Thro(ugh), Thwaite, Transire, Translucent, Transparent, Unblock, Unclog, Uncork(ed), Unequivocal, Unstop, Vault, Vindicate, Vivid, Void, Well, Whiten, Windage, Wipe

Clearing Assart, Glade, Opening, Shire, Slash

Cleat Bitt, Wedge

Cleave, Cleavage, Cleft Adhere, Bisulcate, Builder's bottom, Builder's bum, Chimney, Chine, Chink, Cling, Cloff, Cohere, Cut, Divide, Division, Divorce(ment), Fissure, Gap, Ghaut, Goose-grass, Grike, Gryke, Harelip, Meroblastic, Notch, Pharynx, Rift, Riva, Scissure, Severance, Slack, Slaty, Space, Spathose, Split, Sulcus

Clef Soprano, Treble

Cleft Notch

Clematis Montana, Old man's beard, Traveller's joy, Virgin's-bower

Clemenceau Tiger

Clemency, Clement Ahimsa, Grace, Lenience, Lenity, Mercy, Mildness, Quarter, Temperate

Cleopatra Needle

Clergy(man), Cleric(al) Abbé, Canon, Cantor, Cardinal, Chancellor, Chaplain, Chapter, Circuit rider, Cleric, Clerk, Cloth, Curate, Curé, Deacon, Dean, Ecclesiast(ic), God-botherer, Goliard, Holy Joe, Incumbent, Josser, Levite, Ministerial, Ministry, Minor canon, Non-juror, Non-usager, Notarial, Paperwork, Parson, Pastor, Pontifex, Pontiff, Preacher, Prebendary, Precentor, Prelate, Presbyter, Presenter, Priest, Primate, Prior, Proctor, Rabbi, Rector, Red-hat, Reverend, Rome-runner, Scribal, Secretarial, Secular, Shaveling, Shepherd, Sky pilot, Slope, Spin-text, Spirituality, Squarson, Subdeacon, Theologian, Vartabed, Vicar

Clergy-hater Misoclere

Clerk(s) Actuary, Articled, Baboo, Babu, Basoche, Circar, Cleric, Cratchit, Cursitor, Enumerator, Filing, Heep, Lay, Limb, Notary, Paper-pusher, Parish, Pen-driver, Penman, Penpusher, Petty Bag, Poster, Protocolist, Prot(h)onotary, Recorder, St Nicholas's, Salaryman, Scribe, Secretariat, Shipping, Sircar, Sirkar, Tally, Town, Vestry, Vicar, Writer

Clever(ness) Able, Adroit, Astute, Brainy, Bright, Canny, Cool, Cunning, Cute, Daedal(e), Deep-browed, Deft, Genius, Gleg, Habile, Ingenious, Intellectual, Jackeen, Know-all, Natty, Nimblewit, Resourceful, Sage(ness), Shrewd, Skilful, Smart(y), Smarty-pants, Souple, Subtle

Clevis Becket

Cliché Banality, Boilerplate, Commonplace, Corn, Journalese, Platitude, Saying, Tag

Click(er), Clicking Castanet, Catch, Forge, Implosive, Pawl, Rale, Ratch(et), Snick, Succeed, Tchick, Ticktack

Client Account, Customer, End-user, Fat, Gonk, John, Patron, Thin, Trick

Cliff(s) Beachy Head, Bluff, Cleve, Corniche, Crag, Craig, Escarp, Lorelei, Palisade(s), Precipice, Sca(u)r

Cliffhanger Samphire, Serial, Thriller

Climate Ambience, Atmosphere, Attitude, Continental, Mood, Sun, Temperament, Temperature, Weather

Climax Apex, Apogee, Catastasis, Come, Crescendo, Crest, Crisis, Culminate, Edaphic, End, Head, Height, Heyday, Moment of truth, Orgasm, Payoff, Selling, Top, Zenith

Climb(er), Climbing Aid, Alpinist, Aralia, Aristolochia, Artificial, Ascend, Bignonian, Breast, Briony, Bryony, Clamber, Clematis, Clusia, Cowage, Cowhage, Cowitch, Crampon, Creeper, Cubeb, Cucumber, Dodder, Ers, Heart-pea, Hedera, Ivy, Jamming, Kie-kie, Kudzu, Lawyer, Layback, Liana, Liane, → **MOUNT**, Munro-bagger, Pareira, Parvenu, Pea, Peg, Poison oak, Prusik, Rat(t)an, Rhoicissus, Rise, Root, Rope, Scale, Scan, Scandent, Scansores, Sclim, Scramble, Shin, Shinny, Sklim, Smilax, Social, Speel, Steeplejack, Stegophilist, Sty(e), Swarm, Timbo, Tuft-hunter, Udo, Up(hill), Uprun, Vetch, Vine, Vitaceae, Wistaria, With(y)wind, Woodbine, Zoom

Clinch Attach, Carriwitchet, Determine, Ensure, Fix, Quibble, Rivet, Secure, Settle

Cling(er), Clinging Adhere, Bur(r), Cherish, Cleave, Embrace, Hold, Hug, Limpet, Ring, Suctorial, Tendril

Clinic Abortuary, Antenatal, Dental, Dispensary, Hospital, Hospitium, Mayo, Well-woman

Clink Gingle, Jail, Jingle, Lock up, Prison, Stir, Ting, Tinkle

Clinker Ash, Slag

Clint Limestone

Clip(ped), Clipper, Clipping Alberta, Banana, Barrette, Bicycle, Brash, Bulldog, Butterfly, Cartridge, Chelsea, Clasp, Crocodile, Crop-ear, Crutch, Curt, Curtail, Cut, Cutty Sark, Dag, Dock, Dod, Excerpt, Film, Fleece, Hairslide, Jubilee, Jumar, Krab, Lop, Money, Nail, Outtake, Pace, Paper, Pare, Pedicure, Peg, Prerupt, Prune, Roach, Scissel, Secateur, Shear, Ship, Shore, Shorn, Snip, Spring, Staccato, Tie, Tie-tack, Tinsnips, Toe, Tonsure, Topiarist, Trim, Trot

Clippy Cad, Conductor

Clique Cabal, Clan, Club, Coterie, Faction, Four Hundred, Gang, Junta, Ring, Set

Clive Arcot

Cloak(room), Cloaks Aba, Abaya, Abba, Abolla, Amice, Anonymity, Bathroom, Buffalo-robe, Burnous, Capa, Cape, Capote, Caracalla, Cardinal, Cassock, Chasuble, Chimer(e), Chlamydes, Chlamys, Chuddah, Chuddar, Cocoon, Conceal, Cope, Cover, Disguise, Dissemble, Djellaba(h), Domino, Gabardine, Gaberdine, Gal(l)abea(h), Gal(l)abi(y)a(h), Gal(l)abi(y)eh, Gentlemen, Gents, Grego, Hall-robe, Heal, Hele, Himation, Hood, Inverness, Jelab, Jellaba, Joseph, Kaross, Korowai, Manta, Manteau, Manteel, Mantle, Mant(e)let, → **MASK**, Mourning, Mousquetaire, Mozetta, Opera, Paenula, Paletot, Pallium, Paludamentum, Pelisse, Pilch, Poncho, Powder-room, Rail, Revestry, Rocklay, Rokelay, Roquelaure, Sagum, Sarafan, Scapular, → **SCREEN**, Shroud, Swathe, Talma, Toga, Vestiary, Vestry, Visite

Clobber Anoint, Apparel, Attire, Do, Dress, Garb, Habiliments, Lam, Tack

Clock Alarm, Ammonia, Analogue, Astronomical, Atomic, Beetle, Big Ben, Biological, Blowball, Body, Bracket, Bundy, Caesium, Carriage, Cartel, Clepsydra, Cuckoo, Dandelion, Digital, Doomsday, Dutch, Floral, Grandfather, Grandmother, Hit, Knock, Long case, Meter, Paenula, Parliament, Quartz, Repeater, Sandglass, Settler's, Solarium, Speaking, Speedo, Strike, Sundial, Taximeter, Tell-tale, Time(r), Turret, Wag at the wa', Water

Clockmaker Fromanteel, Graham, Harrison, Knibb, Mudge, Tompion

Clockwise Deasil, Deasiul, Deasoil, Deiseal, Deisheal

Clockwork Precision, Regular

Clod Clumsy, Divot, Glebe, Lump, Mool, Mould, Mug, Put(t), Scraw, Sod, Stupid, Turf

Clog Accloy, Ball, Block, Clam, Crowd, Dance, Fur, Galosh, Golosh, Hamper, Jam, Lump, Mire, Obstruct, Overshoe, Patten, Sabot

Cloisonné Shippo

Cloister Arcade, Confine, Cortile, Immure, Monastery, Mure, Refuge, Seclude

Clone, Cloning Mini-me, Ramet, Replicant, Reproduce, Therapeutic

Cloots Worricow

Close(d), Closing, Closure Adjourn, Agree, Airless, Alongside, Anigh, Atresia, Block,

Boon, By, Cadence, Clammy, Clap, Clench, Collapse, Compact, Complete, Concentration, Cone off, Court, Dear, Debar, Dense, Dissolve, → **END**, Epilogue, Ewest, Eye to eye, Finale, Forby, Gare, Grapple, Handy, Hard, Hard by, Hot, Humid, Imminent, Inbye, Infibulate, Intent, Intimate, Local, Lock, Lucken, Marginal, Mean, Miserly, Muggy, Mure, Narre, Narrow, Near, Nearhand, Neck and neck, Neist, Next, Nie, Niggardly, Nigh, Nip and tuck, Obturate, Occlude, Occlusion, Oppressive, Parochial, Penny-pinching, Placket, Precinct, Reserved, Reticent, Seal, Secret, Serre, Serried, Serry, Shet, Shut(ter), Shutdown, Silly, Slam, Snug, Stap, Sticky, Stifling, Stuffy, Sultry, Tailgate, Temenos, Terminate, Tight, Uproll, Wafer, Wanr, Warm, Yard

Close-cropped Crewcut, Not-pated

Close-fitting Skintight, Slinky, Tight

Closet Cabinet, Confine, Cubicle, Cupboard, Dooket, Earth, Locker, Safe, Wardrobe, WC, Zeta

Close-up Detail, Fill, Shut, Stop, Zoom

Closing-time Eleven, End

Clot(ting) Agglutinate, Ass, Bozo, Clag, Clump, Coagulate, Congeal, Crassamentum, Cruor, Curdle, Dag, Duffer, Embolism, Embolus, Gel, Globule, Gob, Gout, Grume, Incrassate, Incrust, Jell, Lapper, Lopper, → **LUMP**, Mass, Prothrombin, Splatch, Stupid, Thicken, Thrombosis, Thrombus

Clotbuster Heparin

Cloth Aba, Abaya, Abba, Antependium, Bearing, Bib, Bribe, Carmelite, Clergy, Cloot, Clout, Communion, Corporal(e), Dishrag, Duster, → **FABRIC**, → **FELT**, Frocking, Frontal, Gremial, G-string, Interfacing, Jharan, Loin, Lungi, Manta, → **MATERIAL**, Mercery, Meshing, Nap, Napery, Napje, Napkin, Nappie, Neckerchief, Needlework, Netting, Pack, Painted, Pall, Pane, Pilch, Priesthood, Pull-through, Purificator, Puttee, Putty, Rag, Raiment, Roll, Roon, Runner, Sashing, Scarlet, Serviette, Sheet, Sheeting, Shirting, Shoddy, Stock, Stripe, Stuff, Stupe, Sudarium, Supper, Sweatband, Tapestry, Tea, → **TEXTILE**, Throw, Tissue, Toilet, Vernicle, Veronica, Washrag, Whole

CLOTH

1 letter:	Gair	Tick	Grass
J®	Haik	Wire	Gunny
T	Harn	Wool	Haick
	Hyke		Honan
3 letters:	Ikat	*5 letters:*	Jaspe
Abb	Kelt	Atlas	Kanga
Lap®	Knit	Baize	Kente
Rep	Lace	Beige	Khadi
Say	Lamé	Binca	Khaki
Web	Lawn	Budge	Kikoi
	Leno	Chino	Linen
4 letters:	Line	Crape	Lisle
Aida	Lint	Crash	Llama
Amis	Mull	Crepe	Loden
Baft	Nude	Denim	Lurex®
Bark	Pina	Dobby	Lycra®
Ciré	Puke	Drill	Moiré
Doek	Repp	Duroy	Mongo
Drab	Rund	Fanon	Monk's
Duck	Shag	Foulé	Mummy
Felt	Slop	Frisé	Mungo
Fent	Sulu	Gauze	Ninon
Flax	Tapa	Gazar	Nylon

Orlon®
Panel
Panne
Paper
Perse
Pilot
Piqué
Plaid
Plush
Poult
Print
Rayon
Satin
Scrim
Serge
Slops
Surah
Surat
Surge
Tabby
Tamin
Tammy
Tappa
Terry
Tibet
Toile
Towel
Tulle
Tweed
Tweel
Twill
Union
Voile
Wigan

6 letters:
Aertex®
Alpaca
Angora
Armure
Barège
Beaver
Bouclé
Broche
Burlap
Burnet
Burrel
Byssus
Caddis
Calico
Camlet
Camlot
Canvas
Chintz

Cilice
Cloqué
Coburg
Coutil
Covert
Crepon
Cubica
Cyprus
Dacron®
Damask
Dévoré
Dimity
Domett
Dossal
Dossel
Dowlas
Dralon®
Drapet
Duffel
Duffle
Dupion
Durrie
Etamin
Faille
Fannel
Frieze
Gloria
Greige
Gurrah
Haique
Harden
Herden
Hodden
Hoddin
Humhum
Hurden
Jersey
Kersey
Khanga
Kincob
Lampas
Madras
Medley
Melton
Merino
Mohair
Mongoe
Moreen
Muleta
Muslin
Mutton
Nankin
Nettle
Oxford

Pongee
Poplin
Rateen
Ratine
Russel
Samite
Satara
Sateen
Saxony
Sendal
Shalli
Sherpa
Sindon
Soneri
Stroud
Tactel®
Tamine
Tartan
Tencel®
Thibet
Tricot
Vellet
Velour
Velure
Velvet
Vicuna
Wadmal
Wincey
Winsey

7 letters:
Abattre
Acrylic
Alamode
Alepine
Baracan
Batiste
Bolting
Brocade
Cabbage
Cambric
Camelot
Challie
Challis
Cheviot
Chiffon
Crombie
Cypress
Delaine
Dhurrie
Doeskin
Domette
Dorneck
Dornick

Drabbet
Drapery
Droguet
Drugget
Duvetyn
Etamine
Faconné
Fannell
Fishnet
Flannel
Foulard
Fustian
Galatea
Genappe
Gingham
Gore-tex®
Grogram
Hessian
Holland
Hopsack
Jaconet
Jamdani
Khaddar
Kitenge
Leather
Lockram
Mockado
Nacarat
Nankeen
Oil-silk
Oilskin
Organza
Orleans
Ottoman
Paisley
Percale
Printer
Rabanna
Raploch
Raschel
Ratteen
Rattine
Ripstop
Sacking
Sagathy
Satinet
Schappe
Silesia
Sinamay
Spandex®
Stammel
Supplex®
Tabaret
Tabinet

Taffeta
Ticking
Tiffany
Trolley
Tussore
Viscose
Viyella®
Wadmaal
Webbing
Woolsey
Worsted
Zanella

8 letters:
Aircraft
Algerine
American
Armozeen
Armozine
Arresine
Bagheera
Barathea
Barracan
Bayadere
Bearskin
Bobbinet
Boulting
Brocatel
Cameline
Casement
Cashmere
Casimere
Celanese
Chambray
Chamelot
Chenille
Ciclaton
Corduroy
Coteline
Coutille
Cretonne
Drabette
Duchesse
Dungaree
Duvetine
Duvetyne
Eolienne
Florence
Gambroon
Gossamer
Homespun
Jacquard
Jeanette
Lava-lava

Lustring
Mackinaw
Mantling
Marcella
Marocain
Mazarine
Moleskin
Moquette
Nainsook
Organdie
Osnaburg
Pashmina
Plaiding
Pleather
Prunella
Rodevore
Sarcenet
Sarsenet
Sealskin
Shabrack
Shalloon
Shantung
Sicilian
Suedette
Swanskin
Tabbinet
Tarlatan
Toilinet
Velveret
Whipcord
Wild silk
Zibeline

9 letters:
Aeroplane
Alcantara
Baldachin
Balzarine
Bengaline
Bombasine
Calamanco
Cassimere
Cerecloth
Charmeuse®
Ciclatoun
Cottonade
Courtelle®
Crepoline
Crimplene®
Crinoline
Evenweave
Fabrikoid®
Farandine
Filoselle

Folk-weave
Gaberdine
Georgette
Grenadine
Grosgrain
Haircloth
Horsehair
Indiennes
Interlock
Kalamkari
Levantine
Longcloth
Mandilion
Mandylion
Marseille
Matelassé
Messaline
Moygashel
Nitro-silk
Open-weave
Organzine
Overcheck
Paramatta
Penistone
Percaline
Persienne
Petersham
Pinstripe
Polyester
Ravenduck
Sackcloth
Sailcloth
Satin jean
Sharkskin
Silkalene
Silkaline
Stockinet
Strouding
Swansdown
Tarpaulin
Tricotine
Veloutine
Velveteen
Wire gauze
Worcester
Zibelline

10 letters:
Balbriggan
Baldachino
Book muslin
Broadcloth
Brocatelle
Candlewick

Farrandine
Fearnought
Ferrandine
Florentine
Geotextile
Kerseymere
Lutestring
Matellasse
Mousseline
Needlecord
Parramatta
Polycotton
Ravensduck
Russel-cord
Seersucker
Shabracque
Shiveshive
Sicilienne
Tattersall
Toilinette
Tuftaffeta
Tuftaffety
Winceyette

11 letters:
Abercrombie
Bedford cord
Canton crepe
Cheesecloth
Cloth of gold
Dotted Swiss
Drap-de-berry
Dreadnought
Flannelette
Hammercloth
Kendal green
Marquisette
Nun's veiling
Sempiternum
Stockinette
Stretch knit
Swiss muslin

12 letters:
Brilliantine
Cavalry twill
Crepe de chine
Elephant cord
Leather-cloth

13 letters:
Gros de Londres
Linsey-woolsey

Cloth-designing Batik

Clothe(s), Clothing, Clothed Accoutrements, Ao dai, Apparel, Array, Attire, Baggies, Battledress, Besee, Bib and tucker, Cape, Casuals, Chasuble, Choli, Cits, Clad, Clericals, Clobber, Coat, Combinations, Confection, Coordinates, Costume, Cour, Cover, Croptop, Cruisewear, Culottes, Deck, Diffusion line, Dight, Don, Drag, → **DRESS**, Duds, Emboss, Endue, Fig leaf, Finery, Foot muff, Frippery, Garb, Garments, Gear, Gere, Get-up, Glad rags, Grave, Gymslip, Gyves, Habit, Haute couture, Hejab, Innerwear, Judogi, Jumps, Kimono, Layette, Leathers, Lederhosen, Long-togs, Mitumba, Mocker, Muff, Outfit, Pannicle, Pantsuit, Pareu, Pea-coat, Pea-jacket, Pin-striped, Plain, Playsuit, Plus fours, Raggery, Rag trade, Raiment, Rami, Rigout, Robes, Samfoo, Samfu, Scapulary, Schmutter, Scrubs, Scungies, Shell suit, Shirtwaister, Shmatte, Shroud, Slops, Stomacher, Sunday best, Sundress, Sunsuit, Swaddling, Swathe, Swothling, Tackle, Things, Toggery, Togs, Tracksuit, Trappings, Trews, Trousseau, Tube top, Tweeds, Two-piece, Veiling, Vernicle, Vestiary, Vestiture, Vestment, Wardrobe, Watteau, Weeds, Wetsuit, Widow's weeds, Workwear, Yclad, Ycled, Y-fronts

Clothes basket, Clothes horse Airer, Petara, Winterhedge

Cloud(ing), Clouded, Cloudiness, Cloudy Altocumulus, Altostratus, Banner, Benight, C, Cataract, Cirrocumulus, Cirrostratus, Cirrus, Coalsack, Coma, Contrail, Crab Nebula, Cumulonimbus, Cumulus, Dim, Dull, Emission nebula, Fog, Fractocumulus, Fractostratus, Funnel, Goat's hair, Haze, Horsehead Nebula, Infuscate, Magellanic, Mammatus, Mare's tail, Milky, Mist, Molecular, Mushroom, Nacreous, Nephele, Nephelometer, Nepho-, Nimbostratus, Nimbus, Nubecula, Nubilous, Nuée ardente, Obnubilation, Obscure, Octa, Okta, Oort, Overcast, Pall, Pother, Protostar, Rack, Roily, Smoor, Stain, Storm, Stratocumulus, Strat(o)us, Thunder(head), Turbid, Virga, War, Water-dog, Weft, Woolpack, Zero-zero

Cloudberry Mountain bramble

Cloudless Serene

Clough Dale, Gorge, Ravine

Clout Belt, Cloth, Crown, Hit, Influence, Lap(pie), Lapje, Power, Pull, Raddle

Clove Chive, Eugenia, Garlic, Rose-apple, Split, Yrent

Clover Alfalfa, Alsike, Berseem, Calvary, Cinque, Cow-grass, Four-leaf, Hare's-foot, Hop, Hop-trefoil, Japan, Ladino, Lespedeza, Medic(k), Melilot, Owl's, Pin, Rabbit-foot, Red, Serradella, Serradilla, Shamrock, Souple, Sucklers, Suckling, Sweet, Trefoil, Trilobe, Truelove, White

Clown(ish) Airhead, Antic, Antick, August(e), Boor, Bor(r)el, Buffoon, Carl, Chough, Chuff, Clout-shoe, Coco, → **COMEDIAN**, Comic, Costard, Daff, Feste, Froth, Girner, Gobbo, Goon, Gracioso, Grimaldi, Harlequin, Hob, Idiot, Jack-pudding, Jester, Joey, Joker, Joskin, Leno, Merry Andrew, Mountebank, Nedda, Nervo, Patch(c)ocke, Peasant, Pickle-herring, Pierrot, Put, Rustic, Slouch, Thalian, Touchstone, Trinculo, Wag, Zany

Cloy(ing) Choke, Clog, Glut, Pall, Satiate, Surfeit, Sweet

Club(s), Club-like Adelphi, Airn, Alloa, Almack's, Alpeen, Apex, Army and Navy, Arsenal, Artel, Association, Athen(a)eum, Baffy, Band(y), Basto, Bat, Bath, Beefsteak, Blackjack, Blaster, Bludgeon, Boodles, Bourdon, Brassie, Breakfast, Brook's, Bulger, C, Caman, Card, Carlton, Caterpillar, Cavalry, Chapter, Chartered, Chigiriki, Clavate, Cleek, Clip-joint, Combine, Compassion, Conservative, Constitutional, Cordeliers, Cosh, Cotton, Country, Crockford's, Cudgel, Devonshire, Disco(theque), Driver, Driving iron, Drones, Fan, Farm team, Fascio, Fellowship, Feuillant, Fleshpot, Fustigate, Garrick, Glee, Golf, Guards, Guild, Hampden, Health, Hell-fire, Hercules', Hetairia, Honky-tonk, Indian, Investment, Iron, Jacobin, Jigger, Job, Jockey, Junior Carlton, Kennel, Kierie, Kiri, Kitcat, Kiwanis, Knobkerrie, Landsowne, Lathi, Laughter, League, Leander, Lions, Lofter, Luncheon, Mace, Mallet, Mashie, Maul, Mell, Mere, Meri, Mess, Midiron, Monday, National Liberal, Niblick, Night(stick), Nightspot, Nitery, Nulla(-nulla), Oddfellows, Paris, Patu, Pitching wedge, Polt, Pregnant, Priest, Provident, Pudding, Putter, Putting-cleek, Quarterstaff, RAC, R & A, Reform, Ring, Rota, Rotarian, Rotary,

Round Table, Sand wedge, Savage, Savile, Shillelagh, Slate, Society, Soroptimist, Sorority, Sorosis, Spoon, Spot, Spurs, Strike, Strip, Stunner, Supper, Texas wedge, Thatched House, Tong, Travellers, Trefoil, Truncheon, Trunnion, Union, United Services, Variety, Waddy, Warehouse, Wedge, White's, Wood, Yacht, Youth

Club-foot Kyllosis, Po(u)lt-foot, Talipes, Varus

Clubman Member

Club-rush Deer-hair, Scirpus, Sedge

Cluck Cherup, Chirrup, Dent

Clue 1ac, Across, Anagram, Aradne, Ball, Charade, Clavis, Dabs, Down, → **HINT**, Inkling, Key, Lead, Light, Rebus, Scent, Scooby(doo), Signpost, Thread, Tip

Clueless Ignorant

Clump Cluster, Finial, Knot, Mass, Mot(te), Patch, Plump, Tread, Tuft, Tump, Tussock

▷ **Clumsily** *may indicate* an anagram

Clumsy Artless, Awkward, Bauchle, Bungling, Butterfingers, Cack-handed, Calf, Chuckle, Clatch, Clodhopper, Cumbersome, Dub, Dutch, Galoot, Gauche, Gimp, Gink, Ham(-fisted), Heavy-handed, Horse-godmother, Hulk, Inapt, Inelegant, Inept, Inexpert, Klutz, Lob, Loutish, Lubbard, Lubber, Lumbering, Lummox, Lumpish, Maladdress, Maladroit, Mauther, Mawr, Mawther, Messy, Mor, Nerd, Nurd, Oafish, Off-ox, Overhasty, Palooka, Plonking, Rough, Schlemihl, S(c)hlemiel, Spastic, Spaz(zy), Squab, Stot, Stumbledom, Swab, Swob, Taupie, Tawpie, Two-fisted, Unco, Ungain, Unskilful, Unsubtle, Unwieldy

Cluster Acervate, Ament, Assemble, Asterism, Bunch, Clump, Collection, Concentre, Constellate, Conurbation, Corymb, Cyme, Galactic, Gather, Gear, Globular, Glomeration, Group, Knot, Oakleaf, Packet, Plump, Raceme, Rhipidium, Sheaf, Sorus, Strap, Thyrse, Tone, Truss, Tuffe, Tuft, Umbel, Verticillaster

Clutch(es) Battery, Brood, Chickens, Clasp, Cling, Eggs, Friction, Glaum, Grab, → **GRASP**, Gripe, Hold, Nest, Net, Seize, Sitting, Squeeze

Clutter Confusion, Litter, Mess, Rummage

Coach Autodidact, Battlebus, Berlin, Bogie, Bus, Car, Carriage, Chara, Clerestory, Crammer, Diligence, Dilly, Double-decker, Drag, Edifier, Fiacre, Fly, Four-in-hand, Gig, Griddle car, Hackney, Handler, Landau(let), Life, Microbus, Mourning, Phaeton, Post chaise, Pullman, Railcar, Rattler, Repetiteur, Saloon, Shay, Sleeper, Slip, Sobriety, Stage, Surrey, Tally(-ho), Teach(er), Thoroughbrace, Train(er), Transport, Tutor, Voiture

Coach-horse Rove-beetle

Coachman Automedon, Bunene, Coachy, Dragsman, Jarvey, Jehu, John

Coagulant, Coagulate, Coagulation Cautery, Clot, Congeal, Curds, Jell, Rennet, Run, Runnet, Set, Solidify, Thicken

Coal Anthracite, Bituminous, Black diamonds, Block, Brown, Burgee, Cannel, Char, Cherry, Clinker, Coking, Coom, Crow, Culm, Day, Dice, Edge, Eldin, Ember, Fusain, Gas, Gathering, Hard, Indene, Jud, Knob, Lignite, Maceral, Mineral, Nut, Open-cast, Paper, Parrot, Pea, Purse, Sapropelite, Score, Sea, Slack, Soft, Splint, Steam, Stone, Surtarbrand, Surturbrand, Vitrain, Wallsend, White, Wood

Coalesce(nce) Amalgamate, Concrete, Fuse, Merge, Sintery, Synaloepha, Unite

Coalfish Saith

Coalition Alliance, Bloc, Fusion, Janata, Merger, Rainbow, Tie, Union

Coal-tar Aniline, Cresol, Indene

Coal-tub Corf, Dan, Scuttle

Coarse(ness) Base, Bawdy, Blowzy, Bran, Broad, Chav, Common, Crude, Dowlas, Earthy, Fisherman, Foul, Gneissose, Grained, Grobian, Gross, Grossièreté, Haggery, Ham, Illbred, Indelicate, Low-bred, Plebeian, Rabelaisian, Rank, Rappee, Raunchy, Ribald, Rough, Rudas, Rude, Russet, Sackcloth, Schlub, Semple, Slob, Sotadic, Unrefined, Vulgar

Coast(al) Barbary, Beach, Bight, Caird, Cape, Causeway, Coromandel, Costa, Dalmatian, Drift, Freewheel, Glide, Gold, Hard, Heritage, Ivory, Littoral, Longshore, Malabar,

Maritime, Murman(sk), Orarian, Riviera, Scrieve, Seaboard, Seafront, Seashore, Seaside, → **SHORE**, Slave, Sledge, Strand, Sunshine, Toboggan, Trucial

Coaster Beermat, Drog(h)er, Mat, Roller, Ship

Coastguard CG, Gobby

Coastline Watermark

Coast-road Corniche

Coat(ed), Coating Ab(b)a, Abaya, Achkan, Acton, Admiral, Afghan, Anarak, Anodise, Anorak, Balmacaan, Barathea, Basan, Bathrobe, Belton, Benjamin, Blazer, Bloomed, Box, British warm, Buff, Buff-jerkin, Calcimine, Car, Chesterfield, Cladding, Claw-hammer, Clearcole, Cloak, Clutch, Cocoon, Coolie, Cover, Covert, Creosote, Crust(a), Cutaway, Dip, Doggett's, Drape, Dress, Duffel, Duster, Electroplate, Enamel, Encrust, Envelope, Ermelin, Ermine, Exine, Extine, Fearnought, Film, Fleece, Frock, Fur, Gabardine, Galvanise, Gambeson, Ganoin, Glaze, Grego, Ground, Hair, Happi, Ha(c)queton, Impasto, Integument, Inverness, Iridise, Jack(et), Jemmy, Jerkin, Jodhpuri, Joseph, Jump, Jupon, Lacquer, Lammie, Lammy, Lanugo, Layer, Laying, Limewash, Loden, Lounge, Mac, Mackinaw, Matinee, Metallise, Mink, Morning, Newmarket, → **OVERCOAT**, Paint, Paletot, Palla, Paper, Parka, Parkee, Passivate, Patina(te), Pebbledash, Pelage, Pelisse, Perfuse, Peridium, Petersham, Pitch, Pla(i)ster, Plate, Polo, Pos(h)teen, Primer, Primine, Prince Albert, Raglan, Redingote, Resin, Resist, Riding, Roquelaure, Sable, Sack, Salband, Saque, Sclera, Sclerotic, Scratch, Seal, Sheepskin, Shellac, Sherardise, Sherwani, Silver, Skinwork, Spencer, Sports, Stadium, Surtout, Swagger, Swallowtail(ed), Tabard, Taglioni, Tail, Tar, Teflon, Tent, Top, Trench, Truss, Trusty, Tunic, Tuxedo, Ulster(ette), Underseal, Veneer, Verdigris, Warm, Wash, Whitewash, Windjammer, Wool, Wrap-rascal, Zamarra, Zamarro, Zinc

Coat of arms Crest, Hatchment

Coat-tail Flap

Coax Blandish, Blarney, Cajole, Carn(e)y, Collogue, Cuittle, Entice, Flatter, Lure, Persuade, Wheedle, Whillywha(w)

Cob Hazel(nut), Horse

Cobalt Co, Zaffer, Zaffre

Cobble(s), Cobbled, Cobbler(s), Cobblestone Bunkum, Claptrap, Clicker, Coggle, Cosier, Cozier, Dessert, Mend, Patch, Pie, Rot, Snob, Soutar, Souter, Sowter, Stone, Sutor, Twaddle, Vamp

Cobra King, Spitting

Cobweb(by) Arachnoid, Araneous, Gossamer, Snare, Trap

Cocaine Basuco, C, Charlie, Coke, Crystal, Freebase, Moonrock, Nose candy, Number, Ready-wash, Snow

Coccid Wax-insect

Cochlear Scala

Cock(y), Cockerell Alectryon, Ball, Brash, Capon, Chanticleer, Chaparral, Confident, Erect, Escape, Fighting, Flip, Fowl, France, Fugie, Half, Hay, Heath, Henny, Jack-the-lad, Jaunty, Midden, Penis, Perk, Roadrunner, Robin, Rooster, Shake-bag, Snook, Strut, Sunshine, Swaggering, Tap, Tilt, Turkey, Twaddle, Vain, Valve, Vane, Weather-vane

Cock-a-hoop Crowing, Elated, Jubilant

Cockatoo Bird, Corella, Galah, Leadbeater's, Major Mitchell, Parrot

Cockboat Cog

Cockchafer Humbuzz, May beetle, Maybug

Cock crow Skreigh of the day

Cocker Blenheim, Cuiter, Spaniel

Cockeyed Agee, Askew, Skewwhiff

Cockfight(ing) By(e), Main

Cockle Bulge, Crease, Wrinkle

▷ **Cockle(s)** *may indicate* an anagram

Cockney 'Arriet, 'Arry, Bow, Eastender, Londoner, Londonese

▷ **Cockney** *may indicate* a missing h
Cockpit Greenhouse, Office, Well
Cockroach Archy, Beetle, Black beetle, Croton bug, German, Oriental, Orthoptera
▶ **Cockscomb** *see* COXCOMB
Cocktail → DRINK, → HORSE, Melange, Mix, Prawn

COCKTAILS

4 letters:
Sour

5 letters:
Bumbo
Fruit
Julep
Punch
Twist

6 letters:
Atomic
Crusta
Gibson
Gimlet
Mai-Tai
Mojito
Rickey

7 letters:
Bellini
Cobbler
Egg-flip
Fustian

Martini®
Molotov
Negroni
Sangria
Sazerac®
Side-car
Slammer
Stengah
Stinger
Swizzle

8 letters:
Aperitif
Bullshot
Cold duck
Daiquiri
Highball
Pink lady
Sangaree
Snowball
Spritzer

9 letters:
Alexander

Buck's fizz
Kir Royale
Manhattan
Margarita
Pisco Sour
Rusty nail
Sea Breeze
Snakebite
White-lady

10 letters:
Bloody Mary
Calpirinha
Dry Martini
Horse's neck
Moscow mule
Piña colada
Tom Collins

11 letters:
Grasshopper
Screwdriver
Whiskey Sour

12 letters:
Black Russian
Old-fashioned
White Russian

13 letters:
Planter's punch

14 letters:
Sherry cobbler
Singapore sling
Tequila sunrise

15 letters:
Brandy Alexander

16 letters:
Between the sheets
Harvey Wallbanger

17 letters:
Champagne cocktail

Cocoa Criollo, Nib(s)
Coconut Coco-de-mer, Coir, Copra, Head, Madafu, Poonac, Toddy-palm
Cocoon Dupion, Mother, Pod, Swathe, Trehala
Cocotte Strumpet
Cod Bag, Cape, Coalfish, Fish, Gade, Gadus, Haberdine, Hoax, Keeling, Kid, Lob, Man, Morrhua, Murray, Red, Saith, Saltfish, Spoof, Stockfish, Tease, Torsk, Tusk, Whiting
Coda End(ing), Epilogue, Rondo, Tail(piece)
Coddle Cosset, Molly, Nancy, Pamper, Pet, Poach, Wet-nurse
Code, Coding, Codification Access, Alphanumeric, Amalfitan, Area, Bar, Barred, Binary, Brevity, Bushido, Canon, Character, Cheat, Cipher, City, Civil, Clarendon, Codex, Colour, Computing, Condition, Cookie, Country, Cryptogram, Cryptograph, Da Vinci, Dialling, Disciplinary, Dogma, Dress, DX, Easter egg, EBCDIC, Enigma, Error, Escape, Ethics, Etiquette, Fuero, Genetic, Gray, Green Cross, Hammurabic, Highway, Hollerith, Iddy-umpty, Justinian, MAC, Machine, Morse, Napoleon(ic), National, Netiquette, Object, Omerta, Opcode, Penal, PGP, Pindaric, Postal, Price, Protocol, Reflective binary, Rulebook, Scytale, Sharia, Shulchan Aruch, Signal, Sort, Source, STD, Talmud, Time, Twelve Tables, Zip
Code-breaker, Code-breaking Bletchley Park, Malpractitioner, Turing
Codger Buffer, Fellow
Codicil Addition, Label, PS, Rider, Supp(lement)
Codon Initiator

Coefficient Absorption, Correlation, Differential, Diffusion, Distribution, Modulus, Partition, Pearson's correlation, Permeability, Saturation, Spearman's rank-order, Transmission, Young's modulus

Coelacanth Latimeria

Coerce, Coercion Big stick, Bully, Compel, Dragoon, Duress, Gherao, Pressure, Railroad, Restrain, Threaten

Coffee, Coffee beans, Coffee pot Americano, Arabica, Bean, Brazil, Cafetiere, Cappuccino, Decaff, Demi-tasse, Espresso, Expresso, Filter, Frappuccino, Gaelic, Gloria, Granules, Instant, Irish, Java, Latte, Macchiato, Mocha, Peaberry, Percolator, Robusta, Rye, Skinny latte, Tan, Triage, Turkish

Coffee-house Lloyd's

Coffer Ark, Box, Casket, Cassone, Chest, Lacunar, Locker

Coffin Bier, Box, Casket, Hearse, Kist, Larnax, Sarcophagus, Shell, Wooden kimono, Wooden overcoat

Cog(ged) Contrate, Mitre-wheel, Nog, Pinion, Tooth

Cogent Compelling, Forceful, Good, Sound, Telling

Cogitate Deliberate, Mull, Muse, Ponder

Cognate Paronym

Cohabit(ant) Bed, Indwell, Room-mate, Share

Co-heir Parcener

Cohere(nt) Agglutinate, Clear, Cleave, Cling, Logical, Stick

Cohort Colleague, Crony, Soldier

Coif Calotte, Cap, Hood

Coiffure Hairdo, Pompadour, Tête

Coil(s), Coiled Armature, Bight, Bought, Choke, Choking, Circinate, Clew, Clue, Convolute(d), Convolve, Curl, Current, Fake, Fank, Field, Flemish, Furl, Hank, Helix, Ignition, Induction, Loading, Loop, Mortal, Mosquito, Moving, Primary, Resistance, Rouleau, Scorpioid, Solenoid, Spark, Spiral, Spiraster, Spire, Tesla, Tickler, Toroid, Twine, Twirl, → **WIND**, Wound, Wreath, Writhe, Yoke

Coin Base, Bean, Broad(piece), Cash, Change, Coign(e), Contomiate, Copper, Create, Doctor, Dosh, Double-header, Dump(s), Fiddler's money, Fiver, Han(d)sel, Imperial, Invent, Lucky piece, Make, Mill, Mint, Mintage, → **MONEY**, Neoterise, Numismatic, Nummary, Piece, Plate, Pocket-piece, Proof, Shiner, Slip, Specie, Stamp, Sterling, Strike, Subsidiary, Sum, Tenner, Thin'un, Token, Touchpiece, Unity

COINS

1 letter:	Dam	Moy	Bani
D	Ecu	Ore	Birr
	Fen	Pul	Buck
2 letters:	Fil	Pya	Cedi
As	Fin	Red	Cent
DM	Flu	Sen	Chon
Kr	Hao	Sol	Dibs
Rd	Jun	Som	Dime
Xu	Kip	Sou	Doit
	Lat	Won	Dong
3 letters:	Lei	Yen	Dram
Avo	Lek	Zuz	Duro
Ban	Leu		Euro
Bar	Lev	*4 letters:*	Fiat
Bit	Lew	Anna	Fils
Bob	Mil	Aora	Inti
Cob	Mna	Baht	Jack

Jane
Jiao
Kina
Kobo
Kuna
Kyat
Lari
Lion
Lipa
Lira
Loti
Luma
Lwei
Maik
Mark
Merk
Mina
Mite
Mule
Obol
Para
Paul
Peag
Peni
Peso
Pice
Posh
Pula
Puli
Punt
Rand
Real
Reis
Rial
Riel
Rock
Ryal
Sene
Sent
Slog
Tael
Taka
Tala
Tein
Toea
Tray
Trey
Vatu
Yuan
Zack

5 letters:
Agora
Angel

Asper
Aurar
Baiza
Bekah
Belga
Bodle
Brown
Butat
Butut
Chiao
Colon
Conto
Crore
Cross
Crown
Daric
Dibbs
Dinar
Diram
Dobra
Ducat
Eagle
Eyrir
Franc
Fugio
Gazet
Gerah
Gopik
Groat
Grosz
Haler
Hauer
Khoum
Krona
Krone
Kroon
Kurus
Laari
Laree
Leone
Liard
Litai
Litas
Livre
Louis
Lumma
Lyart
Maile
Manat
Maneh
Marka
Mohur
Mongo
Mopus

Naira
Nakfa
Ngwee
Noble
Obang
Oscar
Paisa
Paolo
Pence
Pengo
Penie
Penni
Penny
Plack
Pound
Razoo
Rider
Royal
Rubel
Ruble
Rupee
Sceat
Scudo
Scute
Semis
Sente
Shand
Smelt
Soldo
Souon
Sucre
Sycee
Tenge
Tetri
Thebe
Tical
Ticky
Tiyin
Tolar
Toman
Tyiyn
Unite
Zaire
Zimbi
Zloty

6 letters:
Agorol
Ariary
Aureus
Balboa
Bawbee
Bender
Bezant

Boddle
Byzant
Canary
Centas
Colone
Copeck
Couter
Décime
Dalasi
Danace
Deaner
Denier
Derham
Dirham
Dirhem
Dodkin
Dollar
Double
Drachm
Ekuele
Escudo
Filler
Florin
Forint
Gilder
Gourde
Guinea
Gulden
Halala
Haleru
Heller
Hryvna
Jitney
Kobang
Koruna
Kroner
Kroona
Kruger
Kwacha
Kwanza
Lepton
Likuta
Loonie
Makuta
Mancus
Markka
Mawpus
Mongoe
Pa'anga
Paduan
Pagoda
Pataca
Pennia
Peseta

Pesewa
Poisha
Qintar
Rappen
Rouble
Rupiah
Santim
Satang
Sceatt
Seniti
Sequin
Shekel
Sickle
Siglos
Somoni
Stater
Stiver
Stotin
Talent
Tanner
Tester
Teston
Thaler
Tickey
Toonie
Tugrik
Turner
Vellon
Wakiki

7 letters:
Afghani
Austral
Bolivar
Cardecu
Carolus
Centavo
Chetrum
Cordoba
Crusado
Drachma
Ekpwele
Guarani

Guilder
Hryvnya
Jacobus
Joannes
Kopiyka
Kreuzer
Lempira
Lisente
Metical
Millime
Milreis
Moidore
Ostmark
Ouguiya
Patrick
Piastre
Piefort
Pistole
Pollard
Quarter
Quetzal
Ringgit
Ruddock
Rufiyaa
Sextans
Solidus
Spanker
Tambala
Testoon
Testril
Thick'un
Thrimsa
Thrymsa
Tughrik
Unicorn
Xerafin

8 letters:
Brockage
Cardecue
Cruzeiro
Denarius
Doubloon

Ducatoon
Emalengi
Farthing
Groschen
Johannes
Kreutzer
Louis d'or
Maravedi
Millieme
Napoleon
Ngultrum
Nuevo sol
Picayune
Pistolet
Planchet
Portague
Portigue
Quadrans
Rigmarie
Semuncia
Sesterce
Shilling
Skilling
Solidare
Spur-rial
Spur-ryal
Stotinka
Twopence
Xeraphin
Zecchino

9 letters:
Boliviano
Britannia
Centesimo
Dandiprat
Dandyprat
Didrachma
Dupondius
Fourpence
Half-eagle
Half-tiger
Lilangeni

Luckpenny
Maple leaf
Ninepence
Pistareen
Rennminbi
Rix-dollar
Rose noble
Schilling
Sou marque
Sovereign
Spur-royal
Yellowboy
Zwanziger

10 letters:
Chervonets
Krugerrand
Portcullis
Reichsmark
Siege-piece

11 letters:
Bonnet-piece
Deutschmark
Double eagle
Sword-dollar
Tetradrachm

12 letters:
Antoninianus
Iraimbilanja

13 letters:
Half-sovereign
Rennminbi yuan

14 letters:
Three-farthings

18 letters:
Maria Theresa dollar

Coinage Currency, Invention, Nonce-word, Symmetallism
Coincide(nt), Coincidence Accident, Chance, Consilience, Conterminous, Fit, Fluke, Homotaxis, Overlap, Rabat(to), Simultaneous, Synastry, Synchronise, Tally
Coke Chark, Coal, Cocaine, Kola
Col Pass, Poort, Saddle
Cold(-blooded), Cold(ness) Ague, Algid, Aloof, Apathetic, Arctic, Asperity, Austere, Biting, Bitter, Bleak, Blue, Brr(r), C, Catarrh, Cauld(rife), Charity, Chill(y), Colubrine, Common, Coryza, Coy, Dead, Distant, Ectotherm, Emotionless, Fish, Frappé, Frem(d), Fremit, Frigid, Frost(y), Gelid, Glacial, Hiemal, Icy, Impersonal, Jeel, Nippy, Nirlit, Parky, Passionless, Perishing, Piercing, Poikilotherm(ic), Polar, Psychro-, Remote, Rheumy,

Rigor, Rume, Siberia, Snap, Snell, Sniffles, Sour, Standoffish, Starving, Streamer, Subzero, Taters, Unmoved, Weed, Wintry

Cold sore Herpes, Shiver

Coldstream Borderer, Guard

Cole Colza, King, Nat, Porter

Colic Batts, Bots, Botts, Gripe, Lead, Painter's, Sand, Upset, Zinc

Collaborate, Collaborator, Collaboration Assist, Combine, Comply, → **COOPERATE**, Keiretsu, Milice, Quisling, Synergy, Team spirit, Vichy, Vichyite, Vichyssois(e)

Collage Cut up, Paste up

Collapse, Collapsing Apoplexy, Breakdown, Buckle, Burn out, Cave, Conk, Crash, Crumble, Crumple, Debacle, Downfall, Fail(ure), Fall, Flake out, Fold, Founder, Give, Go phut, Implode, Inburst, Landslide, Meltdown, Phut, Purler, Rack, Rickety, Rockfall, Rot, Ruin, Scat(ter), Sink, Slump, Snap, Stroke, Subside, Sunstroke, Swoon, Telescope, Tumble, → **TUMBLEDOWN**, Wilt, Wrack, Zonk

▷ **Collapsing** *may indicate* an anagram

Collar(ed) Arrest, Astrakhan, Band, Bermuda, Bertha, Berthe, Bib, Bishop, Blue, Brecham, Buster, Butterfly, Button-down, Buttonhole, Capture, Carcanet, Chevesaile, Choke(r), Clerical, Collet, Dog, Esses, Eton, Falling-band, Flea, Gorget, Grandad, Hame, Head(stall), Holderbat, Horse, Jabot, Jampot, Karenni, Mandarin, Moran, Mousquetaire, Nab, Nail, Neckband, Necklet, Ox-bow, Peter Pan, Piccadell, Piccadillo, Piccadilly, Pikadell, Pink, Polo, Puritan, Rabaline, Rabato, Rebater, Rebato, Revers, Rollneck, Roman, Romance, Ruff, Sailor, Seize, Shawl, Steel, Storm, Tackle, Tappet, Tie-neck, Torque, Turndown, Turtleneck, Vandyke, Whisk, White, Wing, Yoke

Collation Comparison, Meal, Repast

Colleague(s) Accomplice, Ally, Associate, Bedfellow, Co-host, Confrère, Mate, Mentor, Oppo, Partner, Sociate, Team, Workmate

Collect(ion), Collectable, Collected, Collective(ly), Collectivism, Collector Accrue, Agglomerate, Aggregate, Album, Alms, Amass, Amildar, Ana, Anthology, Arcana, Artel, Assemble, Aumil, Bank, Bow, Budget, Bunch, Bundle, Burrell, Bygones, Caboodle, Calm, Cap, Cete, Clan, Clowder, Compendium, Compile, Congeries, Conglomerate, Covey, Cull, Dossier, Dustman, Earn, Egger, Exaltation, Exordial, Fest, (Fest)schrift, Fetch, Fleet, Florilegium, Gaggle, Garbo, Garner, Gather, Get, Gilbert, Glean, Glossary, Grice, Harvest, Heap, Herd, Hive, Idant, In all, Jingbang, Job lot, Kit, Kitty, Levy, Library, Loan, Magpie, Meal, Meet, Meinie, Mein(e)y, Menagerie, Menyie, Miscellany, Mish-mash, Montem, Munro-bagger, Murmuration, Museum, Muster, Nide, Offertory, Olio, Omnibus, Omnium-gatherum, Pack, Paddling, Pile, Plate, Pod, Poor box, Post, Poste restante, Prayer, Quest, Raft, Raise, Rammle, Recheat, Rhapsody, Rouleau, Sangfroid, Scramble, Sedge, Self-possessed, Serene, Set, Shoe, Siege, Skein, Smytrie, Sord, Sottisier, Sounder, Spring, Stand, Tahsildar, Team, Toolkit, Tronc, Troop, Ujamaa, Unkindness, Uplift, Watch, Wernher, Whipround, Wisp

▷ **Collection** *may indicate* an anagram

Collection-box Brod, Ladle, Rammle

Collectorate Taluk

College(s) Academy, All Souls, Alma mater, Ampleforth, Balliol, Brasenose, Business, C, Caius, Campus, CAT, Cheltenham, Clare, Classical, Coed, Commercial, Community, Conservatoire, Corpus (Christi), Cow, Cranwell, Downing, Dulwich, Electoral, Emmanuel, Eton, Exeter, Foundation, Freshwater, Girton, Grande école, Hall, Heralds', Jail, Junior, Keble, King's, Lancing, Linacre, Lincoln, LSE, Lycée, Lyceum, Madras(s)a(h), Madressah, Magdalen(e), Marlborough, Medrese, Medresseh, Merton, Newnham, Nuffield, Open, Oriel, Pembroke, Poly, Polytechnic, Pontifical, Protonotariat, Queen's, Ruskin, Sacred, St Johns, Saliens, Sandhurst, Selwyn, Seminary, Sixth-form, Somerville, Sorbonne, Staff, Tech(nical), Technikon, Tertiary, Theologate, Training, Trinity, Tug, UMIST, Up, Village, Wadham, Winchester, Yeshiva(h)

Collide, Collision Afoul, Barge, Bird-strike, Bump, Cannon, Carom(bole), Clash, Conflict, Dash, Elastic, Fender-bender, Foul, Head-on, Hurtle, Impact, Inelastic, Into, Kiss, Meet, Pile-up, Prang, Ram, Rencounter, Smash-up, Strike, Thwack

Collie Bearded, Border, Dog, Kelpie, Kelpy, Rough, Sheepdog

Collier Geordie, Hoastman, Miner, Necklace, Patience, Ship

Colloid Aerogel, Gel, Lyophil(e), Sol

Collude, Collusive Abet, Cahoots, Conspire, Deceive

Colon Aspinwall, C(a)ecum, Sigmoid, Spastic, Transverse

Colonel Bird, Blimp, Bogey, Chinstrap, Col, Everard, Goldstick, Newcome, Nissen, Pride

Colonial(ist), Colonist Ant, Antenatal, Bee, Boer, Creole, Emigré, Goan, Oecist, Oikist, Overseas, Phoenician, Pioneer, Planter, Polyp(e), Settler, Sicel(iot), Sikel(ian), Sikeliot, Stuyvesant, Swarm, Territorial, Voter, Wasp

Colonnade Ar(a)eostyle, Eustyle, File, Gallery, Peristyle, Porch, Portico, Stoa

Colony Acadia, Aden, Burkina Faso, Cape, Charter, Cleruchy, Crown, Dependency, Elea, Gibraltar, Halicarnassian, Hive, Hongkong, Kaffraria, Nudist, Penal, Plymouth, Presidio, Proprietary, Rookery, Senegal, Settlement, Swarm, Termitarium, Warren, Zambia, Zimbabwe

Colophony Roset, Rosin

Colossal → ENORMOUS, Epochal, Gigantic, Huge, Vast

Colosseum Amphitheatre

Colossus Eten, Ettin

Colour(ed), Colouring, Colours Achromatic, Bedye, Blanco, Blee, Blush, C, Cap, Chromatic, Chrome, Complementary, Complexion, Crayon, Criant, Cross, Distort, Dye, False, Film, Flag, Florid, Flying, Gouache, Haem, → HUE, Imbue, Ink, Irised, Kalamkari, Leer, Local, Lutein, Metif, Nankeen, Orpiment, Palette, Pantone®, Pastel, Pied, Pigment, Pochoir, Polychrome, Primary, Prism, Prismatic, Process, Queen's, Raddle, Reddle, Regimental, Rinse, Riot, Ruddle, Secondary, Sematic, Shade, Shot, Solid, Spectrum, Stain, Startle, Tertiary, Tie-dye, Tinc(ture), Tinctorial, Tinge, Tint, Tone, Uvea, Wash

COLOURS

2 letters:	Navy	Gules	Auburn
Or	Pink	Ivory	Bisque
	Plum	Khaki	Bister
3 letters:	Puce	Lemon	Bistre
Bay	Puke	Lilac	Cerise
Dun	Roan	Lovat	Day-Glo®
Jet	Rose	Mauve	Isabel
Red	Ruby	Ocher	Maroon
Tan	Sand	Ochre	Orange
	Sloe	Olive	Reseda
4 letters:	Teal	Peach	Roucou
Anil	Vert	Pearl	Sienna
Bice	Woad	Rouge	Sludge
Blue		Sepia	Titian
Buff	5 letters:	Slate	Tusser
Cyan	Beige	Taupe	
Ecru	Camel	Tenné	7 letters:
Fawn	Chica	Tenny	Annatta
Gold	Coral	Umber	Annatto
Grey	Cream		Apricot
Jade	Eosin	6 letters:	Arnotto
Lake	Flame	Anatta	Caramel
Lime	Green	Anatto	Crimson

	8 letters:	**9 letters:**	French navy
Emerald	Alizarin	Alizarine	Tartrazine
Filemot	Burgundy	Anthocyan	Vermillion
Gamboge	Cardinal	Carnation	
Indulin	Chestnut	Chocolate	**11 letters:**
Magenta	Cinnamon	Indigotin	Ultramarine
Melanin	Eau de nil	Olive drab	
Oatmeal	Gunmetal	Royal blue	**12 letters:**
Old gold	Lavender	Solferino	Cappagh-brown
Old rose	Off-white	Turquoise	Dragon's blood
Oxblood	Pea-green	Vermilion	
Saffron	Philamot		**19 letters:**
Scarlet	Philomot	**10 letters:**	Thunder and
Umbrage	Raw umber	Aquamarine	Lightning
Vermeil	Santalin	Burnt umber	

Colour blindness Daltonism, Deuteranopia, Dichrom(at)ism, Monochromatic, Protanomaly, Protanopia, Protanopic, Tritanopia

▷ **Coloured** *may indicate* an anagram

Colourful Abloom, Brave, Exotic, Flamboyant, Flowery, Gay, Iridescent, Kaleidoscope, Opalescent, Showy, Splashy, Vivid

Colourless Albino, Bleak, Drab, Dull, Faded, Flat, Hyalite, Pallid, Pallor, Wan, White

Colour-spot Gutta

Colt C, Cade, Foal, Gun, Hogget, Sta(i)g, Teenager, Two-year-old

Columbine Aquilegia

Column(s), Column foot Agony, Anta, Atlantes, Clustered, Commentary, Control, Corinthian, Correspondence, Cylinder, Decastyle, Diastyle, Distillation, Doric, Editorial, Eustyle, Fifth, File, Flying, Fractionating, Geological, Gossip, Hypostyle, Impost, Lat, Lonelyhearts, Monolith, Nelson's, Newel, Notochord, Obelisk, Pericycle, Peripteral, Peristyle, Persian, Personal, Pilaster, → **PILLAR**, Pilotis, Plume, Prostyle, Pycnostyle, Rouleau, Row, Sheet pile, Short, Spina, Spinal, Spine, Stalactite, Stalagmite, Steering, Stylobate, Systyle, Tabulate, Telamone, Third, Tige, Tore, Torus, Trajan's, Vertebral

Columnist Advertiser, Agony aunt, Caryatid, Newsman, Stylite, Telamon, Writer

Coma(tose) Apoplexy, Crown, Sedated, Sleep, Torpor, Trance

Comb(er), Combed, Combing Afro, Alveolate, Beehive, Breaker, Card, Copple, Crest, Curry, Dredge, Fine-tooth, Hackle, Heckle, Hot, Kaim, Kame, Kangha, Kemb, Noils, Pecten, Pectinal, Rake, Rat-tail, Red(d), Ripple(r), Rose, Scribble, Search, Side, Small tooth, Smooth, Tease(l), Toaze, Tooth, Tose, Toze, Trawl, Tuft, Wave

Combat(ant), Combative Argument, Batteilant, → **BATTLE**, Bolshie, Bolshy, Competitor, Conflict, Contest, Dispute, Duel, → **FIGHT**, Gladiator, Joust, Judicial, Jujitsu, Just, Karate, Kendo, Krav mega, List, Mêlée, Militant, Oppose, Paintball, Protagonist, Spear-running, Unarmed, Veteran, War

Combe Hope

Combination, Combine(d), Combining Accrete, Aggregate, Alligate, Ally, Amalgam, Associate, Axis, Bloc, Cartel, Cleave, Clique, Coalesce, Coalition, Composite, Concoction, Conflated, Conglomerate, Consolidate, Consortium, Coordinate, Crasis, Fuse, Group, Harvester, Incorporate, Integration, Interfile, Join, Junta, Kartell, League, Meld, Merge(r), Mingle, Mixture, Monogram, Motor cycle, One, Perm(utation), Piece, Pool, Quill, Ring, Solvate, Splice, Syncretize, Synthesis, Terrace, Trivalent, Trona, Unite, Valency, Wed, Zaibatsu

Comb-like Ctenoid, Pecten

Combustible, Combustion Air-gas, Ardent, Fiery, Inflammable, Phlogistic, Phlogiston, Spontaneous, Wildfire

▷ **Combustible** *may indicate* an anagram

Come, Coming (back), Coming out Accrue, Advent, Anear, Anon, Appear, Approach, Ar(r), Arise, Arrive, Attend, Debouch, Derive, Emerge, Future, Happen, Iceman, Issue, Millenarian, Orgasm, Parousia, Pass, Pop, Reach, Respond, Second, Via

Come again Eh

Comeback Boomerang, Bounce, Echo, Homer, Quip, Rally, Rearise, Rebound, Recovery, Repartee, Reply, Reprisal, Retort, Retour, Return, Reversion, Riposte

Come by Obtain

Comedian Benny, Buffoon, Chaplin, → CLOWN, Comic, Durante, Emery, Farceur, Gagman, Goon, Groucho, Hardy, Hope, Joe Miller, Joker, Jokesmith, Karno, Keaton, Laurel, Leno, Punster, Quipster, Robey, Scream, Screwball, Stand-up, Starr, Tate, Tati, Tummler, Wag, Wise, Witcracker, Yell

Comedo Blackhead

Comedown Avale, Bathetic, Bathos, Crash landing, Disappointment, Drop, Letdown, Shower

Comedy Alternative, Black, Blackadder, Com, Custard-pie, Drama, Ealing, Errors, Farce, High, Humour, Improv(ised), Keystone, Knockabout, Lazzo, Low, Millamant, Musical, Romantic, Romcom, Screwball, Situation, Slapstick, Stand-up, Thalia, Travesty

Comely, Comeliness Beseen, Bonny, Fair, Goodly, Graceful, Jolly, Likely, Looks, Pleasing, Pretty, Proper

Comestible(s) Cate, Eats, Fare

Comet Chiron, Geminid, Halley's, Kohoutek, Meteor, Oort cloud, Reindeer, Shoemaker-Levy 9, Vomet, Xiphias

Come through Weather

Come to Cost, Wake(n)

Comfort(able), Comforter, Comforting, Comfy Affluent, Amenity, Analeptic, Armchair, Balm, Bein, Bildad, Calm, Canny, Cheer, Cherish, Cherry, Clover, Cold, Consolation, Console, Convenience, Cose, Cosh, Cosy, Couthie, Couthy, Creature, Crumb, Cushy, Dummy, Dutch, Ease, Easy, Eliphaz, Featherbed, Gemutlich, Heeled, Homely, Homy, Job's, Mumsy, Noah, Plum, Plushy, Reassure, Relaxed, Relief, Relieve, Rosewater, Rug, Scarf, Sinecure, Snug, Solace, Soothe, Succour, There, Tosh, Trig, Warm, Wealthy, Well, Well-to-do, Zofar, Zophar

Comic(al) Beano, Buff, Buffo(on), Bumpkin, Buster, Chaplin, Clown, → COMEDIAN, Dandy, Drag, Droll, Eagle, Facetious, Fields, → FUNNY, Gagster, Hardy, Horror, Jester, Knock-about, Laurel, Leno, Mag, Manga, Quizzical, Rich, Robey, Stand up, Strip, Tati, Trial, Wag, Zany

Comma Inverted, Oxford

Command(eer), Commanding, Commandment(s) Behest, Bid, Categorical imperative, Charge, Coerce, Control, Decalogue, Direct, Direction, Dominate, Domineer, Easy, Edict, Fiat, Fiaunt, Fighter, Firman, Grip, Haw, Hest, High, Hijack, Imperious, Impress, Injunction, Instruction, Jussive, Magisterial, Mandate, Maritime, Mastery, Mitzvah, Mobile, → ORDER, Peremptory, Precept, Press, Query language, Requisition, Rule, Seize, Ukase, Warn, Warrant, Will, Wish, Writ

Commander Admiral, Ag(h)a, Agamemnon, Ameer, Barleycorn, Bey, Bloke, Blucher, Boss, Brennus, Brig, Caliph, Centurion, Cid, Decurion, Dreyfus, Emir, Emperor, Encomendero, Field cornet, Generalissimo, Hetman, Hipparch, Imperator, Killadar, Kitchener, Leader, Manager, Marshal, Master, Meer, Mir, Moore, Officer, Overlord, Pendragon, Polemarch, Pr(a)efect, Raglan, Seraskier, Shogun, Sirdar, Supreme, Taxiarch, Trierarch, Turcopolier, Vaivode, Voivode, Waivode, Warlord, Wing

Commando Chindit(s), Fedayee(n), Green Beret, Raider, Ranger, SAS

Commemorate, Commemoration Encaenia, Epitaph, Eulogy, Keep, Memorial, Month's mind, Monument, Plaque, Remember, Saint's day, Trophy, Year's mind

Commence Begin, Initiate, Open, Start

Commend(ation) Applaud, Belaud, Bestow, Cite, Encomium, Entrust, Laud, Mooi, Panegyric, → PRAISE, Roose, Tribute

Commensal Epizoon, Messmate
Commensurate Adequate, Enough, Equivalent, Relevant
Comment(ary), Commentator Analyst, Animadvert, Annotate, Apercu, Comm, Coryphaeus, Coverage, Critic, Critique, Descant, Discuss, Editorial, Essay, Exegete, Explain, Exposition, Expound, Fair, Footnote, Gemara, Gloss(ographer), Glosser, Hakam, Kibitz, Margin, Marginalia, Midrash(im), Note, Obiter dictum, Observation, Par, Platitude, Play-by-play, Postil, Remark, Rider, Running, Scholiast, Scholion, Scholium, Sidenote, Voice-over, Zohar
Commerce, Commercial Ad, Adland, Barter, Business, Cabotage, Jingle, Marketable, Mercantile, Mercenary, Merchant, Retail, Shoppy, Simony, Trade, Traffic, Wholesale
Commercial traveller Drummer, Rep
Commiserate, Commiseration Compassion, Pity, Sympathise
Commissar People's, Political
Commission(er), Commissioned Agio, Audit, Authorise, Bonus, Boundary, Brevet, Brokage, Brokerage, Charge, Charity, Competition, Contango, Countryside, Delegation, Depute, ECE, Employ, Engage, Envoy, Errand, European, Factor, Gosplan, High, Husbandage, Job, Kickback, Law, Magistrate, Mandate, Office(r), Official, Ombudsman, Order, Oyer and terminer, Percentage, Perpetration, Place, Poundage, Price, Rake-off, Resident, Roskill, Roving, Royal, Shroffage, Task, Task force, Trust, Wreck
Commit(tal), Committed, Commitment Allegiance, Aret(t), Consign, Contract, Decision, Dedication, Delegate, Devotion, Devout, Do, Engage, Entrust, Enure, Impeachment, Paid up, Perpetrate, Pledge, Position, Rubicon
Committee ACRE, Audit, Board, Body, Collegium, Commission, Commune, Council, Delegacy, Group, Hanging, Joint, Junta, Politburo, Presidium, Propaganda, Review body, Riding, Samiti, School, Select, Standing, Steering, Syndicate, Table, Think tank, Vigilance, Watch, Ways and means, Works
Commode, Commodious Ample, Closestool, Roomy, Spacious
Commodities, Commodity Article, Futures, Gapeseed, Item, Physicals, Soft, Staple, Ware
Common(ly), Commoner, Commons Alike, As per usual, Average, Cad, Conventional, Diet, Dirt, Doctor's, Ealing, Eatables, Enclosure, Endemic, Epicene, Everyday, Familiar, Fare, Folk, General, Green, Greenham, Gutterblood, House, Law, Lay, Low, Lower House, Mark, Mere, MP, Mutual, Naff, Non-U, Normal, People, Pleb, Plebe(i)an, Prevalent, Prole, Public, Related, Rife, Roturier, Ryfe, Scran, Sense, Shared, Stock, Stray, Tarty, The mob, Tie, Tiers d'état, Trite, Tritical, Tuft, Two-a-penny, Tye, Use, → **USUAL**, Vile, Vul(gar), Vulgo, Vulgus, Widespread, Wimbledon, Working-class
Commonplace Adversarian, Banal, Copybook, Dime-a-dozen, Everyday, Hackneyed, Homely, Humdrum, Idée reçue, Mot, Ordinary, Pedestrian, Philistine, Plain, Platitude, Prosaic, Quotidian, Trite, Workaday
Commonsense Gumption, Nous, Savoir-faire, Smeddum, Wit
Commonwealth Protectorate, Puerto Rico, Res publica
Commotion Babel, Bluster, Brouhaha, Bustle, Carfuffle, Clangour, Clatter, Curfuffle, Dirdam, Dirdum, Do, Dust, Ferment, Flap, Flurry, Fraise, Furore, Fuss, Hell, Hoo-ha(h), Hurly-burly, Hurry, Kerfuffle, Pother, Pudder, Racket, Romage, Rort, Ruckus, Ruction, Rumpus, Shemozzle, Shindig, Shindy, Shivaree, Steer(y), Stir, Stirabout, Storm, Stushie, Tirrivee, Tirrivie, To-do, Toss, Tumult, Turmoil, Upheaval, Uproar, Whirl, Wroth
Communal, Commune Agapemone, Collective, Com, Meditate, Mir, Paris, Phalanstery, Public, Talk, Township
Communicate, Communication Ampex, Anastomosis, Announce, Appui, Baud, Bluetooth, Boyau, Braille, Cable, Cellnet, Channelling, Citizen's band, Conversation, Convey, Cybernetic, E-mail, Expansive, Exude, Impart, Infobahn, Inform, Infrastructure, Intelpost, Intelsat, Internet, Liaison, Lifeline, Memoranda, Message, Multichannel, Multimedia, Nonverbal, Note, Oracy, Paralanguage, Prestel®, Proxemics, Put across, Reach, Reportage, Revelation, Road, Semiotics, Signal, Sitrep, Syncom, Talkback,

Tannoy®, Telecom, Telepathy, Telephony, Teletex, Telex, Telstar, Tieline, Transmit, Utraquist, Viewdata, Webmail, Word of mouth

Communion Creed, Fellowship, Host, Housel, Intinction, Lord's Supper, Species, Viaticum

Communiqué Announcement, Statement

Communism, Communist Apparat(chik), Aspheterism, Bolshevist, Brook Farm, Castroism, Com, Comecon, Cominform, Comintern, Commo, Comsomol, Deviationist, Engels, Essene, Fourier, Fraction, Khmer Rouge, Komsomol, Leninite, Maoist, Marxist, Menshevist, Nomenklatura, Perfectionist, Pinko, Politburo, Populist, Red (Guard), Revisionism, Second World, Soviet, Spartacist, Stalinism, Tanky, Titoist, Trot, Vietcong, Vietminh

Communities, Community Agapemone, Alterne, Ashram, Association, Biome, Body, Brook Farm, Brotherhood, Clachan, Climax, Closed, Coenobitism, Coenobium, Colonia, Colony, Consocies, District, EC, Ecosystem, EEC, Enclave, Etat, European, Faith, Frat(e)ry, Gated, Global, Hamlet, Kahal, Kibbutz, Mesarch, Mir, Neighbourhood, Pantisocracy, People, Phalanx, Phyle, Preceptory, Public, Pueblo, Republic, Sarvodaya, Seral, Sere, Settlement, Shtetl, Sisterhood, Sociation, Society, Speech, Street, Toon, Town, Tribe, Ujamaa, Ummah, Village, Virtual, Volost, Zupa

Commute(r) Change, Convert, Reduce, Shuttle, Standee, Straphanger, Travel

Como Lake, Perry

Compact Agreement, Cement, Concise, Conglobe, Covenant, Covin, Coyne, Dense, Entente, Fast, Firm, Flapjack, Hard, Knit, League, Match, Neat, Pledge, Powder, Solid, Tamp, Terse, Tight, Treaty, Well-knit

Companion(able) Achates, Arm candy, Associate, Attender, Barnacle, Bedfellow, Bonhomie, Brolga, Bud(dy), Butty, CH, China, Comate, Compeer, Compotator, Comrade, Consort, Contubernal, Crony, Cupman, Duenna, Ephesian, Escort, Feare, Felibre, → **FELLOW**, Fere, Franion, Furked, Handbook, Helpmate, Man Friday, Mate, Native, Oliver, Pal, Pard, Pheer(e), Playmate, Pot, Roland, Shadow, Sidekick, Skaines mate, Stable, Stablemate, Thane, Thegn, Trojan, Vade-mecum, Wag, Walker

Company, Companies Actors, Along, Artel, Ass, Assembly, Band, Bank, Battalion, Bevy, Brigade, → **BUSINESS**, Bv, Cahoot, Cartel, Cast, Cavalcade, Chartered, CIA, Circle, City, Close, Club, Co, Conger, Consort, Cordwainers, Core, Corporation, Corps, Coy, Crew, Crowd, Crue, Decury, Dotcom, East India, Enterprise, Entourage, Faction, Finance, Fire, → **FIRM**, Flock, Free, Gang, Garrison, Ging, Guild, Haberdashers, Heap, Holding, Hudson's Bay, ICI, Inc, Indie, In-house, Intercourse, Investment, Jingbang, Joint-stock, Limited, Listed, Livery, Management, Maniple, Muster, Order, Organisation, Parent, Plc, Present, Pride, Private, Public, Public limited, Push, Quoted, Rep(ertory), Room, SA, Sedge, Set, Set out, Shell, Siege, Sort, SpA, Stationers', Stock, Subsidiary, Syndicate, Table, Team, Thiasus, Touring, Troop, Troupe, Trust, Twa, Two(some), Visitor, White, Yfere

Compare(d), Comparison Analogy, Balance, Beside, Bracket, Collate, Confront, Contrast, Correspond, Cp, Equate, Liken, Match, Odious, Parallel, Relation, Simile, Weigh

Compartment Ballonet, Bay, Booth, Box, Cab, Carriage, Casemate, Cell, Chamber, Cockpit, Cofferdam, Cubbyhole, Cubicle, Dog box, Glove, Locellate, Locker, Loculament, Loculus, Panel, Partition, Pigeonhole, Pocket, Pod, Room(ette), Severy, Smoker, Stall, Till, Trunk, Watertight, Wind chest

Compass Ambit, Area, Beam, Binnacle, Bounds, Bow, Dividers, Extent, Gamut, Goniometer, Gyro, Gyromagnetic, Gyroscope, Infold, Magnetic, Mariner's, Needle, Orbit, Pelorus, Pencil, Perimeter, Prismatic, Radio, → **RANGE**, Reach, Rhumb, Room, Scale, Sweep, Tessitura, Trammel, Width

Compassion(ate) Aroha, Bleed(ing), Clemency, Commiseration, Empathy, Goodwill, Heart, Humane, Kuan Yin, Kwan Yin, Loving kindness, Mercy, Pity, Remorse, Samaritan, Sympathy, Ubuntu

Compatible Consistent, Fit, Harmonious
Compatriot National
Compel(ling), Compelled, Compulsion, Compulsive, Compulsory Addiction, Coact, Coerce, Cogent, Command, Constrain, Dragoon, Duress, Enforce, Extort, Fain, → **FORCE**, Force majeure, Gar, Make, Mandatory, Obligate, Oblige, Pathological, Steamroller, Strongarm, Tyrannise, Urge, Walk Spanish
Compendium Breviate
Compensate, Compensation Amend(s), Balance, Boot, Bote, Comp, Counterbalance, Counterpoise, Damages, Demurrage, Guerdon, Indemnity, Offset, Payment, Recoup, Redeem, Redress, Reparation, Reprisal, Requital, Restitution, Restore, Retaliation, Salvage, Satisfaction, Solatium, Wergild, X-factor
Compère Emcee, Host, MC, Presenter
Compete Contend, Dog eat dog, Emulate, Enter, Match, Outvie, Play, Rival, Run, Vie
Competence, Competent Ability, Able, Adequate, Can, Capable, Capacity, Dab, Dow, Efficient, Fit, Proficient, Responsible, Sui juris, Worthy
Competition, Competitive, Competitor Agonist, Backmarker, Battle, Bee, Biathlon, Buckjumping, Candidate, Checks and balances, Comper, Concours, Contender, Contention, Contest, Cook off, Cup, Dog eat dog, Drive, Entrant, Event, Field, Finals, Freestyle, Gamesman, Grand prix, Gymkhana, Head over heels, Head-to-head, Heptathlon, Imperfect, Iron woman, Judoka, Jump off, Karateka, Keen, Knockout, Match, Match-play, Monopolistic, Olympiad, Open, Opponent, Outsider, Pairs, Panellist, Pentathlon, Perfect, Player, Pools, Premiership, Pro-am, Puissance, Race, Rally, Rat race, Regatta, Repechage, Rival(ise), Rodeo, Run, Runner-up, Show-jumping, Slam, Spelldown, Stableford, Starter, Super G, Tenson, Test, Three-day event, Tiger, Tournament, Tourney, Track meet, Trial, Triallist, Wap(p)enshaw, Wild card
Compile(r), Compilation Anthology, Arrange, Collect, Cross, Doxographer, Edit, Prepare, Segue, Synthesis, Zadkiel
Complacent Babbitt, Fatuous, Joco, Pleasant, Self-satisfied, Smug
Complain(t), Complainer Adenoids, Affection, Affliction, Alas, Alastrim, Alopecia, Anaemia, Angashore, Angina, Arthritis, Asthma, Barrack, Beef, Bellyache, Bitch, Bleat, BSE, Carp, Cavil, Charge, Chorea, Colic, Crab, Cramp, Criticise, Diatribe, Disorder, Dropsy, Epidemic, Ergot, Exanthema, Girn, Gout, Gravamen, Grievance, Gripe, Groan, Grouch, Grouse, Growl, Grudge, Grumble, Grutch, Harangue, Hives, Hone, Hypochondria, Ileitis, → **ILLNESS**, Jeremiad, Kvetch, Lament, Lumbago, Lupus, Malady, Mange, Mean(e), Mein, Mene, Moan, Morphew, Mump(s), Murmur, Nag, Natter, Neuralgia, Ologoan, Pertussis, Plica, Poor-mouth, Protest, Pule, Pyelitis, Querimony, Rail, Remonstrate, Repine, Report, Rhinitis, Rickets, Sapego, Sciatica, Scold, Sequacious, Sigh, Silicosis, Squawk, Staggers, Thrush, Tic, Tinea, Upset, Wheenge, Whimper, Whine, Whinge, Yammer, Yaup, Yawp
Complaisant Agreeable, Flexible, Suave, Supple
Complement(ary) Alexin, Amount, Balance, Biota, Esteemed, Finish, Freebie, Gang, Glowing, Lot, Reciprocate
▷ **Complement** *may indicate* a hidden word
Complete(d), Completely, Completion Absolute, Accomplish, Achieve, All, Altogether, Arrant, Attain, Clean, Congenital, Consummate, Crashing, Crown, Dead, Do, Downright, End, Entire, Finalise, Finish, Flat, Follow through, Foregone, Fruition, Fulfil, Full, Full-blown, Head over heels, Hollow, Incept, Integral, In toto, Neck and crop, One, Ouroboros, Out, Out and out, Perfect, Plenary, Plum, Prolative, Pure, Quite, Rank, Ready, Root and branch, Rounded, Self-contained, Sew-up, Sheer, Spang, Sum, Teetotal, Thorough(going), Total, Unanimous, Unbroken, Uncensored, Uncut, Unequivocal, Unmitigated, Utter, Whole (hog), Wrap
Complex(ity) Abstruse, Advanced, Arcane, Castration, Compound, Daedal, Difficult, Electra, Golgi, Hard, Heath Robinson, Immune, Inferiority, Intricate, Intrince, Involute, Knot, Manifold, MHC, Military-industrial, Mixed, Multinucleate, Nest, Network,

Obsession, Oedipus, Overwrought, Paranoid, Persecution, Phaedra, Plexiform, Ramification, Subtle, Superiority, Syndrome, System, Tangle, Web

Complexion Aspect, Blee, Hue, Leer, Permatan, Temper, Tint, View

Compliance, Compliant, Comply Abet, Agree, Amenable, Assent, Conform, Deference, Docile, Follow, Hand-in-glove, Obedience, Obey, Observe, Obtemper, Sequacious, Surrender, Wilco, Yield

Complicate(d), Complication Bewilder, Complex, Deep, Elaborate, Embroil, Implex, Intricate, Involution, Involve, Inweave, Node, Nodus, Perplex, Ramification, Rigmarole, Sequela, Snarl, Tangle, Tirlie-wirlie

▷ **Complicated** *may indicate* an anagram

Compliment(s), Complimentary Backhanded, Baisemain, Bouquet, Congratulate, Devoirs, Douceur, Encomium, Esteemed, Flatter, Flummery, Freebie, Glowing, Greetings, Praise, Soap, Trade-last, Tribute

Component(s) Base, Capacitor, Coherer, Con-rod, Constituent, Contact, CRT, Daisy-wheel, Element, Factor, Formant, Guidance, Hygristor, Impedor, Inductor, Ingredient, Longeron, Member, Module, → **PART**, Partial, Piece, Pre-amp, Profile, Reactance, Resistor, Subunit, Tensor, Touchstone

Compose(d), Composure Aplomb, Arrange, Calm, Choreograph, Consist, Cool, → **CREATE**, Equable, Equanimity, Equilibrium, Even, Face, Improvise, Indite, Level-headed, Lull, Notate, Orchestrate, Patience, Pen, Phlegm, Placid, Poise, Produce, Reconcile, Sangfroid, Sedate, Serenity, Settle, Soothe, Tranquil, Unruffled, Write

Composer Contrapunt(al)ist, Hymnist, Inditer, Inventor, Maker, Melodist, Minimalist, Musician, Musicker, → **POET**, Serialist, Six, Songsmith, Songwriter, Symphonist, Triadist, Tunesmith, Writer

COMPOSERS

3 letters:
Bax

4 letters:
Adam
Arne
Bach
Berg
Blow
Brel
Bull
Byrd
Cage
Dima
Graf
Ives
Kern
Lalo
Monk
Nono
Orff
Peri
Raff
Wolf

5 letters:
Alwyn
Auber
Auric
Balfe
Berio
Bizet
Bliss
Bloch
Boito
Boyce
Brian
Bruch
Crumb
D'Indy
Dukas
Dupre
Elgar
Falla
Fauré
Field
Finzi
Glass
Gluck
Grieg
Harty
Haydn
Henze
Holst

Ibert
Lasso
Lehar
Liszt
Loewe
Lully
Nyman
Ogdon
Parry
Prout
Ravel
Reger
Rossi
Satie
Sousa
Spohr
Suppe
Tosti
Verdi
Watts
Weber
Weill
Zappa

6 letters:
Alfven
Arnold

Azione
Barber
Bartók
Bennet
Berlin
Boulez
Brahms
Bridge
Burney
Busoni
Chopin
Coates
Czerny
Delius
Duparc
Dvorák
Flotow
Franck
German
Glière
Glinka
Gounod
Handel
Hummel
Joplin
Kodaly
Lassus

Ligeti
Mahler
Martin
Mingus
Morley
Mozart
Ogolon
Parker
Pierne
Porter
Rameau
Rubbra
Schutz
Tallis
Varese
Wagner
Waller
Walton
Webern

7 letters:
Albeniz
Alberti
Allegri
Amadeus
Babbitt
Bantock
Bellini
Bennett
Berlioz
Berners
Borodin
Britten
Brubeck
Christy
Copland
Corelli
Debussy
De Falla
Delibes
Dohnany
Dowland
Gibbons
Ireland
Janácek
Lambert
Lilburn

Mancini
Martinu
Menotti
Milhaud
Nielsen
Novello
Ormandy
Poulenc
Puccini
Purcell
Purnell
Quilter
Rodgers
Rodrigo
Romberg
Rossini
Roussel
Salieri
Smetana
Stainer
Strauss
Tartini
Tippett
Vivaldi
Warlock
Xenakis
Youmans

8 letters:
Alaleona
Albinoni
Anderson
Boughton
Bruckner
Chabrier
Chausson
Cimarosa
Coltrane
Couperin
Gabrieli
Gershwin
Gesualdo
Glazunov
Grainger
Granados
Honegger
Korngold

Kreutzer
Marcello
Mascagni
Massenet
Messager
Messiaen
Paganini
Respighi
Schnabel
Schubert
Schumann
Scriabin
Sessions
Sibelius
Sondheim
Stamford
Stanford
Sullivan
Taverner
Telemann
Vangelis

9 letters:
Bacharach
Balakirev
Beethoven
Bernstein
Boulanger
Broughton
Buxtehude
Chaminade
Cherubini
Donizetti
Dunstable
Hindemith
Meyerbeer
Offenbach
Pachelbel
Pergolesi
Prokofiev
Scarlatti
Schnittke
Schonberg
Zemlinsky

10 letters:
Birtwistle

Boccherini
Buxterhude
Canteloube
Carmichael
Cole Porter
Monteverdi
Mussorgsky
Palestrina
Penderecki
Ponchielli
Rawsthorne
Saint-Saëns
Schoenberg
Stravinsky
Villa-Lobos
Waldteufel
Williamson

11 letters:
Charpentier
Frescobaldi
Humperdinck
Leoncavallo
Lloyd Webber
Mendelssohn
Stockhausen
Tchaikovsky
Theodorakis
Wolf Ferrari

12 letters:
Dallapiccola
Khachaturian
Rachmaninoff
Shostakovich

13 letters:
Havergal Brian
Maxwell Davies

14 letters:
Rimsky-Korsakov

15 letters:
Vaughan Williams

▷ **Composing** *may indicate* an anagram

Composite Aster, Costmary, Foalfoot, Gerbera, Groundsel, Hawkweed, Hybrid, Integral, Metal, Motley, Opinicus, Rag(weed), Sphinx, Synthesized, Thistle

Composition, Compositor Albumblatt, Aleatory, Azione, Bagatelle, Beaumontage, Beaumontague, Canon, Capriccio, Caprice, Cob, Concerto, Concertstuck, Concetto, Creation, Dite, Essay, Etude, Exaration, Fantasia, Inditement, Ingredient, Line,

Literature, Loam, Met, Montage, Morceau, Nonet(te), Nonetto, Opus, Oratorio, Organum, Part-writing, Pastiche, Piece, Pieta, Poem, Polyphony, Polyrhythm, Port, Printer, Quartette, Raga, Repoussage, Rhapsody, Round, Setting, Ship, Sing, Smoot, Smout, Sonata, Sonatina, Structure, Study, Suite, Symphony, Synthesis, Terracotta, Texture, Toccata, Treatise, Trio, Typesetter, Verismo, Voluntary, Work

Compost Digestate, Dressing, Fertilizer, Humus, Vraic, Zoo doo

Compound (stop), Compound word Addition, Admixture, Aggravate, Amalgam, Anti-inflammatory, Anti-knock, Blend, → **CAMP**, Composite, Constitute, Coordination, Cpd, Cutting, Derivative, Ethiops, Mix, Mixture, Multiply, Rooting, Synthesise, Tatpurusha, Type

COMPOUNDS

3 letters:
Azo
Hex
TBT

4 letters:
Alum
Clay
Deet
Dopa
EDTA
Enol
Haem
Heme
Tepa
TEPP
Urea

5 letters:
Algin
Allyl
Aloin
Amide
Amino
Azide
Azine
Azole
Caria
Diazo
Diene
Dimer
Diode
Erbia
Ester
Furan
Halon
Imide
Imine
Lipid
Nitro
Olein

Oxide
Oxime
Potin
Pyran
Salol
Sarin
Soman
Tabun
Thiol
Trona
Vinyl

6 letters:
Acetal
Alkane
Alkene
Alkyne
Ammine
Arsine
Baryta
Borane
Calque
Cetane
Chrome
Cresol
Diazin
Diquat
Epimer
Fluate
Glycol
Halide
Haloid
Hexene
Isatin
Isomer
Ketone
Kinone
Lichen
Lithia
Malate
Niello

Octane
Phenol
Pinene
Potash
Purine
Pyrene
Rennet
Retene
Silane
Speiss
Tannin
Tartar
Tetryl
Thymol
Triene
Trimer
Uranyl

7 letters:
Acetone
Acridin
Aglycon
Ammonia
Argyrol®
Aspirin
Barilla
Bauxite
Benzene
Betaine
Borazon
Bromide
Caliche
Calomel
Camphor
Caprate
Carbide
Cellose
Chelate
Choline
Cinerin
Creatin

Cumarin
Cyanide
Diamine
Diazine
Diazole
Dioxide
Dvandva
Epoxide
Erinite
Ethanol
Eugenol
Excimer
Fenuron
Ferrite
Flavone
Hormone
Hydrate
Hydride
Indican
Indoxyl
Inosine
Lactate
Lactone
Menthol
Metamer
Monomer
Niobite
Nitride
Nitrile
Nitrite
Oxazine
Oxonium
Pentane
Peptide
Peptone
Polyene
Polymer
Prodrug
Protein
Quassia
Quinoid

Quinone
Realgar
Skatole
Steroid
Sulfide
Syncarp
Taurine
Terpene
Toluene
Tritide
Urethan
Uridine
Vanadic
Wolfram
Zymogen

8 letters:
Acridine
Aglycone
Aldehyde
Alizarin
Arginine
Asbestos
Astatide
Butyrate
Caffeine
Carbaryl
Catenane
Cephalin
Ceramide
Chloride
Chromene
Coenzyme
Coumarin
Creatine
Cyanogen
Datolite
Dieldrin
Dopamine
Ethoxide
Farnesol
Fluoride
Furfuran
Glycogen
Haloform
Hydroxyl
Iodoform
Isologue
Ketoxime
Lecithin
Luteolin
Massicot
Melamine
Monoxide

Oligomer
Pentosan
Peroxide
Phthalin
Piperine
Psilocin
Ptomaine
Purpurin
Pyrazole
Pyruvate
Racemate
Retinoid
Rock-alum
Rotenone
Selenate
Silicide
Siloxane
Sodamide
Stilbene
Sulphide
Sulphone
Tautomer
Tetroxid
Thiazide
Thiazine
Thiazole
Thiophen
Thiotepa
Thiourea
Thyroxin
Titanate
Tolidine
Triazine
Triazole
Trilling
Trioxide
Tyramine
Urethane
Xanthate
Xanthine
Ytterbia
Zirconia

9 letters:
Aflatoxin
Alicyclic
Aliphatic
Anhydride
Auranofin
Bahuvrihi
Biguanide
Capsaicin
Carbazole
Carnitine

Caseinate
Celloidin
Cellulose
Cementite
Cetrimide
Chromogen
Copolymer
Cortisone
Deuteride
Dibromide
Dipeptide
Disulfram
Endorshin
Ferrocene
Flavanone
Fool's gold
Fulleride
Glycoside
Greek fire
Guanosine
Haematein
Histamine
Hydantoin
Hydrazide
Hydroxide
Imidazole
Impsonite
Ionophore
Isoniazid
Jasmonate
Limestone
Menadione
Mepacrine
Merbromin
Methoxide
Monoamine
Organotin
Pentoxide
Perborate
Phenazine
Phenoxide
Pheromone
Phosphide
Phthalate
Piperonal
Polyamine
Porphyrin
Prussiate
Pyrethrin
Qinghaosu
Quercetus
Quercitin
Quinidine
Quinoline

Saltpetre
Salvarsan
Sapogenin
Serotonin
Sidenafil
Telluride
Tetroxide
Thiophene
Thyroxine
Valproate
Verapamil
Veratrine

10 letters:
Adrenaline
Agglutinin
Amphoteric
Argyrodite
Azobenzene
Bradykinin
Cellosolve®
Cytochroma
Dichloride
Dimethoate
Disulphide
Endosulfan
Enkephalin
Ethambutol
Halocarbon
Indophenon
Isocyanate
Lumisterol
Mercaptide
Nitrazepam
Nucleoside
Nucleotide
Phenacaine
Phenformin
Picrotoxin
Piperazine
Piperidine
Propionate
Putrescine
Pyrethroid
Pyrimidine
Pyrogallol
Sildenafil
Sulphonium
Tetracaine
Thimerosal
Tocopherol

11 letters:
Acetanilide

Amphetamine
Coprosterol
Dimercaprol
Diphosphate
Electrolyte
Fluorescein
Galantamina
Ghitathione
Hydrocarbon
Neostigmine
Nitrosamine
Resveratrol
Sesquioxide
Sphingosine
Tributyltin
Trichlorfon
Trichloride

12 letters:
Arsphenamine
Carbohydrate
Formaldehyde
Haematoxylin
Hydrastinine
Hydroquinone
Mifepristone
Permanganate
Phenanthrine
Polyurethane
Quinalizarin
Sulphonamide
Testosterone
Thiosinamine
Triglyceride
Trimethadine

13 letters:
Catecholamine
Cycloheximide
Diphenylamine
Isoproterenol
Mercurochrome
Metronidazole
Nitroglycerin
Nortriptyline
Phenothiazine
Physostigmine
Plastoquinone
Sulphonylurea
Trinucleotide

14 letters:
Cyanocobalamin

Oxyhaemoglobin
Phenolphthalin
Polycarboxylic
Polyunsaturate
Sulphonmethane
Trihalomethane

15 letters:
Perfluorocarbon
Succinylcholine
Tribromoethanol

17 letters:
Pentachlorophenol

▷ **Compound(ed)** *may indicate* an anagram

Comprehend, Comprehensive All-in, Broad-brush, Catch-all, Catholic, Compass, Compendious, Contain, Exhaustive, Fathom, Follow, Full-scale, General, Global, Grand, Grasp, Include, Indepth, Ken, Large, Omnibus, Overall, Panoptic, Panoramic, Perceive, School, Sweeping, Thoroughgoing, Tumble, → **UNDERSTAND**, Wide

Compress(ed), Compression, Compressor Astrict, Astringe, Axial-flow, Bale, Coarctate, Contract, Pack, Pump, Shoehorn, Solidify, Squeeze, Stupe, Thlipsis, Turbocharger

Comprise Contain, Embody, Embrace, Include

Compromise, Compromising Avoision, Brule, Commit, Concession, Endanger, Fudge, Give and take, Golden mean, Halfway house, Happy medium, Honeytrap, Involve, Middleground, Modus vivendi, Negotiate, Settlement, Time-server, Trade off, Via media

▶ **Compulsion** *see* **COMPEL(LING)**

Compunction Hesitation, Regret, Remorse, Scruple, Sorrow

Computation, Compute(r) Analog(ue), Apple (Mac)®, Calcular, Desknote, Desktop, Digital, Eniac, Fifth generation, Front-end, Host, IALI, Laptop, Mainframe, Micro, Multiuser, Network, Notebook, Number-cruncher, Palmtop, PC, Personal, Proxy server, Reckon, TALISMAN, Turing machine, Voice response, WIMP

Computer hardware, Computer memory Busbar, Chip, Dataglove®, Docking station, DRAM, EAROM, EPROM, Floptical, IDE, Modem, Neurochip, Pentium®, Platform, Plug'n'play, Processor, PROM, RAM, ROM, Router, Tower, Track(er)ball

Computer language ADA, ALGOL, APL, ASCII, Assembly, AWK, Basic, C, COBOL, COL, Computerese, CORAL, Fortran, High-level, ICL, Java®, Java script®, LISP, LOGO, Low-level, OCCAM, PASCAL, Perl, PROLOG, Python, Scratchpad, Scripting, Small-talk, SNOBOL, SQL, Visual Basic, Weblish

Computer network, Computer systems Arpa, ARPANET, BIOS, Cambridge ring, ERNIE, Ethernet, Evernet, Executive, Extranet, Fileserver, Freenet, HOLMES, Hypermedia, Internet, Intranet, JANET, LAN, Linux, MARC, MIDI, Multipoint, Neural, Peer-to-peer, Stand-alone, TALISMAN, Tally, TAURUS, Telnet, Token ring, Unix, Usenet, VAN, WAN, Web, Wide-area, WIMP

Computer programs, Computer software Abandonware, Acrobat, ActiveX, Address harvester, Adware, Agent, Antivirus, App(let), Application, Assembler, Auto-responder, Autotune, Bloatware, Bootstrap, Bot, Browse, CADMAT, Cancelbot, Careware, Case, Casemix, Chatbot, Checksum, Choiceboard, Client, Closed-loop, Columbus, Courseware, Crippleware, CU See Me, Datel®, Debugger, Demo, Device-driver, Diagnostic, Dictionary, Disassembler, Emacs, Enterprise, ERP, Est,

E-wallet, Extreme, Facemail, Firewall, Firmware, Flash, Formatter, Free-to-air, Freeware, Groupware, HAL, Hard card, Heuristic, Hypermedia, iTunes®, Linker, Loader, Logic bomb, Macro, Mail-merge, Malware, Middleware, Mmorpg, Module, Neural net, Object, OCR, Parser, Payware, Plug-in, Powerpoint, Relocator, Ripper, RISC, Rootkit, Screensaver, Servlet, Shareware, Shell, Shopping agent, Shovelware, Spam killer, Spellchecker, Spider, Spreadsheet, Spyware, Stiffware, Systems, TELNET, Text editor, Translator, Trialware, Utility, Vaccine, Vaporware, Virus, Warez, Web browser, Webcast, Web crawler, Wiki, Windows®, Word processor, Worm

Computer terms Address bus, Alert box, Algorism, Authoring, Autosave, Backslash, Bank-switching, Bitmap, Blog(ging), Blogroll, Bookmark, Boot, Boot-virus, Bot army, Breakpoint, Broadband, Calculate, Calculus, Cascade, Chatroom, Choke route, Clickstream, Client-server, Clipboard, Cobweb site, Coder, Cold boot, Conf, Core(dump), Counter, Cron, Cuspy, Cyber(netics), Cybercafe, Cyberslacking, Dataglove, Defrag(ment), Dial-up, DIF, Disk drive, Domain name, Dotcom, Earcon, Enqueue, Estimate, FAT, Figure, Flash ROM, Floptical, GIGO, Gopher, Greybarland, Half-adder, Hardwire, Hashing, High-end, Hotlist, Hybrid, Hypertext, Inbox, Inputter, Integrator, Interface, IT, Joypad, Kludge, Linear, List serv, Logic, Mail merge, Measure, Meatspace, Memory stick, Moblog, Morphing, Motherboard, Mouseover, Mouse potato, Mung, Network, Neural, Non-volatile, Notwork, Numlock, Nybble, Nyetwork, Object, On-line, Outbox, Package, Packet sniffer, Pageview, Patch, Path name, Peer-to-peer, Pel, Permalink, Pharming, Phishing, Phreak, Pixel, Platform, Plug and play, Podcast, Podcatcher, Point and click, Poke, Popunder, Pop-up, Pseudocode, Pseudorandom, Public-key, Pushdown, Reader farm, README file, Read-out, Realtime, Reboot, Reckoner, Report program, Rogue dialler, Rogue site, Rootserver, Screensaver, Screen turtle, Scriptkiddie, Search engine, Serial port, Server, Server farm, Shared logic, Shell, Shovelware, Sim, Smart, Smurfing, Soft return, Source, Spigot, Spim, Splog, Spreadsheet, Sprite, String, Style sheet, Subroutine, Superserver, Systems, Tape streamer, Telecottage, Thick client, Thin client, Time slice, Toggle, Token ring, Triple, Turnkey, Turtle graphics, Unicode, Username, Utility program, Vaccine, Vlog, Vodcast, Voice response, Voxel, Wave file, Webbie, WebBoard, Webfarm, Wideband, Wi-fi, Wiki, WIMAX, Wordwrap, WORM, Wysiwyg, Yottabyte, Zettabyte, Zmodem

Computer user(s) Alpha geek, Anorak, Brain, Browser, Cast(er), Chiphead, Cyberpunk, Cybersurfer, Digerati, Hacker, Liveware, Luser, Mouse potato, Nerd, Nethead, Netizen, Nettie, Onliner, Otaku, Pumpking, Surfer, Tiger team, Troll, Webhead, White hat

Comrade Achates, Ally, Buddy, Bully-rook, Butty, China, Fellow, Frater, Friend, Kamerad, Mate, Oliver, Pal, Pard, Roland, Tovarich, Tovaris(c)h

Con(man) Against, Anti, Bunco, Defraudment, Diddle, Dupe, Fleece, Gyp, Hornswoggle, Inveigle, Jacob, Lag, Learn, Peruse, Pretence, Read, Scam, Scan, Steer, Sucker, Swindle, Tweedler

Concave Dished, Invexed

Conceal(ed), Concealment Blanket, Blind, Closet, Clothe, Cover, Curtain, Disguise, Dissemble, Doggo, Drown, Feal, Harbour, Heal, Heel, Hele, → **HIDE**, Latent, Latescent, Misprision, Occult, Palm, Paper over, Perdu(e), Recondite, Screen, Scriene, Secrete, Shroud, Sleeve, Smokescreen, Smother, Snow job, Stash, Subreption, Ulterior, Veil, Whitewash, Wrap

Concede, Concession Acknowledge, Admit, Allow, Appeasement, Budge, Carta, Charter, Compromise, Confess, Favour, Forfeit, Franchise, Grant, Munich, Ou, Ow, Owe, Own, Privilege, Ship, Sop, Synchoresis, Yield

Conceit(ed) Bumptious, Caprice, Carriwitchet, Cat-witted, Cocky, Concetto, Crank, Crotchet, Device, Dicty, Egoist, Egomania, Fancy, Fastuous, Figjam, Flory, Fop, Fume, Hauteur, Idea, Mugwump, Notion, Podsnappery, Popinjay, Prig, Princock, Princox, Puppyism, Quiblin, Self-assumption, Side, Snotty, Stuck-up, Swellhead, Swollenhead, Toffee-nose, Vain(glory), Wind

Conceive, Conceivable Beget, Create, Credible, Imagine, Possible, Surmise

Concentrate(d), Concentration Aim, Apozem, Application, Attend, Bunch, Cathexis, Centre, Collect, Condense, Dephlegmate, Distil, Elliptical, Essence, Extract, Focalise, Focus, Geographical, Intense, Kurtosis, Listen, Major, Mantra, Mass, Molality, Molarity, Navel-gazing, Potted, Reduce, Rivet, Samadhi, Strong, Titrate, Titre, Undivided

Concept(ion) Alethic, Brain, Hent, Ideal, Ideation, Image, Immaculate, K(h)arma, Mooncalf, Myth, Notion, Onomascology, Sortal, Stereotype, Theurgy, Weltanschauung

Concern(ed), Concerning About, Affair, After, Ail, Altruism, Anent, As to, Bother, Business, Care, Cerne, Company, Disturb, Dot com, Firm, Going, Heed, House, Humanitarian, In re, Intéressé, Interest, Into, Lookout, → **MATTER**, Mell, Misease, Over, Part, Pidgin, Pigeon, Re, Reck, Regard, Reke, Relevant, Respect, Retch, Shake, Solicitude, Touch, Trouble, Versant, Wirra, Worry

▷ **Concerned** *may indicate* an anagram

Concert (place) Agreement, Ballad, Benefit, Chamber, Charivari, Cooperation, Device, Dutch, Gig, Hootanannie, Hootananny, Hootenanny, Hootnannie, Hootnanny, Odeon, Odeum, Pop, Prom(enade), Recital, Singsong, Smoker, Smoking, Subscription, Symphony, The Proms, Together, Unison, Unity, Wit

Concertina Bandoneon, Pleat, Squeezebox, Squiffer

Concerto Brandenburg, Emperor, Grosso

▶ **Concession** *see* **CONCEDE**

Conch Shell, Strombus

Conchie CO

Concierge Housekeeper, Porter

Conciliate, Conciliator Allay, Bridge builder, Calm, Disarm, Dove, Ease, Mollify, Placate, Reconcile

Concise Compact, Curt, Encapsulated, Laconic, Short, Succinct, Telegraphic, Terse, Tight

Conclave Assembly, Caucus, Confab, Meeting

Conclude(d), Conclusion, Conclusive Achieve, A fortiori, Afterword, Amen, Binding, Button-up, Cease, Clinch, Close, Complete, Consectary, Dead, Decide, Deduce, Demise, Diagnosis, → **END**, End-all, Endwise, Envoi, Epilogue, Explicit, Finding, Fine, Finis, → **FINISH**, Foregone, Gather, Illation, Infer, Lastly, Limit, Non sequitur, Omega, Over, Peroration, Point, Postlude, Punchline, Reason, Resolve, Settle, Showdown, Summary, Terminate, Upshot, Uptie

Conclusive Cogent, Convincing, Estoppel, Final

Concoct(ion) Brew, Compound, Creation, Hydromal, Plan, Tisane, Trump (up)

Concord Concent, Consonance, Harmony, Peace, Plane, Sympathy, Treaty, Unity

Concorde SST

Concourse Assembly, Confluence, Esplanade, Throng

Concrete, Concretion Actual, Aggregate, Beton, Bezoar, Breeze, Cake, Calculus, Caprolite, Clot, Dogger, Gunite, Hard, Laitance, Lean, Mass, Minkstone, No-fines, Pile-cap, Positive, Prestressed, Real, Reify, Reinforced, Siporex, Solid, Tangible, Tremie, Vacuum

Concubine Apple-squire, Campaspe, Harem, Hetaera, Hetaira, Madam, Mistress, Odalisk, Sultana

Concur Accord, Agree, Coincide, Comply, → **CONSENT**, Gree

Concurrent(ly) Meantime

Concuss(ion) Clash, Shock, Stun

Condemn(ation) Abominate, Accuse, Beknave, Blame, Blast, Cast, Censor, Censure, Convict, Damn, Decry, Denounce, Deprecate, Doom, Judge, Kest, Obelise, Proscribe, Reprove, Revile, Sentence, Theta, Upbraid

Condense(d), Condenser Abbe, Abbreviate, Abridge, Brief, Capacitator, Compress, Contract, Distil, Encapsulate, Epitomise, Jet, Liebig, Précis, Rectifier, Reduce, Shorten, Shrink, Summarise, Surface, Vernier, Vinificator

Condescend(ing) De haut en bas, Deign, Patronise, Snobbish, Stoop, Superior, Vouchsafe

Condiment Caraway, Catsup, Cayenne, Chutney, Cum(m)in, Flavour, Horse radish, Kava, Ketchup, Mustard, Pepper, Relish, Salt, Sambal, Sauce, Spice, Tracklement, Turmeric, Vinegar, Zedoary

Condition(al), Conditioning Autism, Case, Cense, Cinchonism, Circ(s), Circumstance, Classical, Congenital, Connote, Contingent, Disease, Disomy, Dropsy, Experimental, Feather, Fettle, Finite, Going, Hammertoe, Health, Hood, Hunk, If, → **IN GOOD CONDITION**, Kelter, Kernicterus, Kilter, Latah, Necessary, Nick, Order, Pass, Pavlovian, Plight, Pliskie, Ply, Point, Position, Predicament, Premise, Premiss, Prepare, Prerequisite, Presupposition, Protasis, Proviso, Provisory, Repair, Reservation, Reserve, Rider, Ropes, Sine qua non, Sis, Spina bifida, Standing, State (of play), Status quo, Sted, Stipulation, String, Sufficient, Term, Tid, Tox(a)emia, Trim, Trisomy, Understanding, Unless, Vir(a)emia, White finger

Condom(s) Blob, Cap, Franger, French letter, Gumboot, Johnny, Letter, Prophylactic, Rubber, Rubber goods, Safe, Scumbag, Sheath

Condone Absolve, Excuse, Forgive, Overlook

Conduct(or), Conductress Abbado, Accompany, Administer, Anode, Ansermet, Arm, Arrester, Barbirolli, Barenboim, Bearing, Beecham, Behaviour, Bohm, Boult, Bulow, Bus-bar, Cad, Chobdar, Clippie, Coil, Comport, Demean(our), Deportment, Direct, Disorderly, Drive, Editor, Electrode, Escort, Feedthrough, Fetch, Goings-on, Guide, Haitink, Hallé, Ignitron, Karajan, Kempe, Klemperer, Lark, Lead, Liber, Lightning, Mackerras, Maestro, Mantovani, Mho, Microchip, Nerve, N-type, Officiate, Ormandy, Outer, Ozawa, Parts, Photodiode, → **PILOT**, Previn, Probe, Prosecute, Protocol, Psychagogue, Psychopomp, P-type, Rattle, Safe, Sargent, Scudaller, Scudler, Shunt, Silicon, Skudler, Solicit, Solti, Stokowski, Strauss, Szell, Tao, Thermal, Thermistor, Thyristor, Toscanini, Transact, → **USHER**, Varactor, Varistor, Walter, Wave guide, Wire, Wood, Zener diode

▷ **Conducting** may indicate an '-ic' ending

Conduit Aqueduct, Canal, Carrier, Channel, Duct, Main, Penstock, Pipe, Tube, Utilidor, Wireway

Cone(s), Conical, Cone-shaped Alluvial, Cappie, Circular, Conoidal, Egmont, Ellipse, Female, Fir, Fusion, Monticule, Moxa, Nose, Pastille, Peeoy, Pineal, Pingo, Pioy(e), Pottle, Puy, Pyramid, Pyrometric, Retinal, Seger, Shatter, Spire, Storm, Strobilus, Taper, Tee, Traffic, Volcanic, Wind, Windsock

Coney Daman, Doe, Hyrax

Confection(er), Confectionery Bonbon, Candy, Candyfloss, Caramel, Chocolate, Concoction, Conserve, Countline, Halva, Ice, Kiss, Marzipan, Meringue, Noisette, Nougat, Quiddery, Rock, Sweet, Sweetmeat, Tablet

Confederal, Confederacy, Confederate, Confederation Accessory, Alliance, Ally, Association, Body, Bund, Bunkosteerer, Cover, Creek, F(o)edarie, Gueux, Illinois, League, Partner, Senegambia, Union

Confer(ence) Bestow, Bretton Woods, Cf, Collogue, Colloqium, Colloquy, Congress, Council, Diet, Do, Dub, Fest, Forum, Grant, Huddle, Hui, Imparlance, Imperial, Indaba, Intercommune, Lambeth, Meeting, Munich, Negotiate, News, Palaver, Parley, Pawaw, Pear, Potsdam, Pourparler, Powwow, Press, Pugwash, Quadrant, Seminar, Settle, Summit, Symposium, Synod, → **TALK**, Teach-in, Video, Vouchsafe, Yalta

Confess(ion), Confessor Acknowledge, Admit, Agnise, Avowal, Concede, Confiteor, Cough up, Declare, Disclose, Edward, Helvetic, Own, Peccavi, Recant, Shema, Shrift, Shriver, Sing, Tetrapolitan, Verbal, Whittle

Confide(nce), Confident(ial), Confidant Aplomb, Aside, Assertive, Assured, Authoritative, Bedpost, Belief, Bottle, Bouncy, Brash, Can do, Certitude, Chutzpah, Cocksure, Cocky, Cred, Crouse, Entre nous, Entrust, Extravert, Extrovert, Faith, Favourite, Fearless, Feisty, Gatepost, Hardy, Hope, Hubris, Hush-hush, Intimate, Morale, Nerve, Pack, Positive, Private, Privy, QT, Sanguine, Secret, Secure, Self-assured, Self-possessed, Self-trust, Suavity, Sub rosa, Sure, Sure-footed, Tell, Together, Trust, Unbosom, Under the rose, Vaulting

Confine(d), Confines, Confinement Ambit, Bail, Bale, Cage, CB, Chain, Closet, Constrain, Contain, Coop, Cramp, Crib, Detain, Emmew, Encase, Enclose, Endemic, Enmew, Ensheath, Gaol, Gate, Gender-moon, House arrest, Immanacle, Immew, Immure, Impound, → IMPRISON, Incage, Incarcerate, Incommunicado, Inertial, Inhoop, Intern, Limit, Local, Mail, March, Mew, Mure, Narrow, Pen, Pent, Pinion, Poky, Quarantine, Restrict, Rule 43, Rules, Section, Solitary, Tether, Thirl, Trammel

Confirm(ed), Confirmation Addict, Approve, Ascertain, Assure, Attest, Bear, Certify, Chris(o)m, Christen, Chronic, Clinch, Corroborate, Dyed-in-the-wool, Endorse, Homologate, Ink in, Obsign, Official, OK, Qualify, Ratify, Reassure, Sacrament, Sanction, Seal, Strengthen, Substantiate, Ten-four, Tie, Validate, Vouch

Confiscate, Confiscation Attainder, Deprive, Dispossess, Distrain, Escheat, Garnishee, Impound, Infangenethef, Raupatu, Seize, Sequestrate

Conflagration Blaze, Holocaust, Inferno, Wildfire

Conflict(ing) Agon, Antinomy, Armageddon, At odds, Battle, Boilover, Camp, Casus belli, Clash, Close, Contend, Contravene, Controversy, Disharmony, Diverge, Encounter, Feud, Fray, Inconsistent, Internecine, Jar, Lists, Mêlée, Muss, Off-key, Oppose, Psychomachia, Rift, Scrape, Strife, → STRUGGLE, Tergiversate, War

Conform(ist), Conformity Accord, Adjust, Comply, Conservative, Consistence, Correspond, Normalise, Obey, Observe, Procrustean, Propriety, Quadrate, Standardize, Stereotype(d), Suit, Time-server, Trimmer, Yield

Confound(ed) Abash, Amaze, Astound, Awhape, Baffle, Bewilder, Blamed, Blasted, Blest, Blinking, Bumbaze, Contradict, Darn, Dismay, Drat, Dumbfound, Elude, Floor, Jigger, Mate, Murrain, Nonplus, Perishing, Perplex, Rabbit, Spif(f)licate, Stump, Throw

▷ **Confound** *may indicate* an anagram

Confrère Ally

Confront(ation) Appose, Beard, Breast, Brush, Cross, Eyeball, Face, Face down, Head-to-head, Incident, Loggerheads, Mau-Mau, Meet, Militance, Nose, Oppose, Outface, Showdown, Smackdown, Tackle, Toe-to-toe, War

Confuse(d), Confusedly, Confusion Addle, Adrift, Anarchy, Astonishment, At sea, Babel, Baffle, Bazodee, Bedevil, Befog, Befuddle, Bemuse, Bewilder, Blur, Bobby-die, Burble, Bustle, Callaloo, Chaos, Cloud, Clutter, Complicate, Consternation, Debacle, Desorienté, Didder, Disarray, Discombobulate, Disconcert, Disorient, Distract, Dither, Dizzy, Dudder, Dust, Dwaal, Egarement, Embrangle, Embroglio, Embroil, Entanglement, Farrago, Flap, Flat spin, Flummox, Flurry, Fluster, Fog, Fox, Fubar, Fuddle, Gaggle, Galley-west, Garble, Guddle, Hash, Havoc, Hazy, Helter-skelter, Hirdy-girdy, Hubble-bubble, Huddle, Hugger-mugger, Hurly-burly, Hurry-scurry, Hurry-skurry, Imbrangle, Imbroglio, Inchoate, Incoherent, → IN CONFUSION, Indistinct, Litter, Lost, Lurry, Maelstrom, Maffled, Maving, Mayhem, Maze, Melange, Melee, Mess, Mingle, Mish-mash, Misorder, Mither, Mixter-maxter, Mixtie-maxtie, Mix-up, Mizzle, Mizzy maze, Moider, Moither, Moonstruck, Morass, → MUDDLE, Mudge, Muss(e), Muzzy, Obfuscate, Overset, Pellmell, Perplex, Pi(e), Pose, Puzzle head, Ravel, Razzle-dazzle, Razzmatazz, Rout, Rummage, Scramble, S(c)hemozzle, Skimble-skamble, Snafu, Spaced out, Spin, Stump, Stupefy, Surprise, Swivet, Synchysis, Tangle, Tapsalteerie, Throw, Tizzy, Topsy-turvy, Toss, Turbulence, Turmoil, Tzimmes, Upside down, Welter, Whemmle, Whomble, Whummle, Woolly, Woozy

▷ **Confuse(d)** *may indicate* an anagram

Confute Confound, Contradict, Deny, Disprove, Infringe, Redargue, Refel

Congeal Coagulate, Freeze, Gel, Gunge, Pectise, Set, Solidify

Congenial Agreeable, Amiable, Compatible, Connate, Couthie, Couthy, Happy, Kindred, Simpatico, Sympathique

Congenital Connate, Inborn, Innate, Inveterate

Conger Sea-eel

Congest(ed), Congestion Choke, Coryza, Cram, Crowd, Engorge, Impact, Jam, Logjam, Nasal, (O)edema, Turgid

Conglomerate, Conglomeration Aggregate, Banket, Chaebois, Chaebol, Empire, Gather, Heap, Mass, Pudding-stone

Congo(u) Shaba, Tea

Congratulate, Congratulation Applaud, Felicitate, Laud, Mazeltov, Preen, Salute

Congregate, Congregation(alist) Assembly, Barnabite, Body, Brownist, Class, Community, Conclave, Ecclesia, Flock, Fold, Gathering, Host, Laity, Oratory, Propaganda, Synagogue

Congress(man) ANC, Assembly, Capitol, Conclave, Continental, Council, Eisteddfod, Intercourse, Legislature, Pan-Africanist, Rally, Senator, Solon, Synod, Vienna

Conifer(ous) Araucaria, Cedar, Cypress, Cyrus, Evergreen, Larch, Macrocarpa, Picea, Pine, Redwood, Retinispora, Rimu, Spruce, Taiga, Taxus, Thuja, Yew

Conject(ure) Augur, Fancy, Goldbach's, Guess, Guesswork, Speculate, Surmise, Theory, View

Conjoin Alligate, Ally, Connect, Knit

Conjugate, Conjugation Couple, Hermitian, Join, Nuptial, Synopsis, Typto, Zygosis

Conjunction Alligation, Ampersand, And, Combination, Consort, Coordinating, Inferior, Nor, Polysyndeton, Subordinating, Superior, Synod, Syzygy, Together, Union, Unition, Unless

Conjure(r), Conjuror Angekkok, Charm, Contrive, Cooper, Heypass, Heypresto, Hocus-pocus, Illusionist, Imagine, Invoke, Mage, Magic, Mystery-man, Palmer, Prestidigitator, Prestigiator, Thaumaturgus

Conk Nose

Connect(ed), Connection, Connector About, Accolade, Adaptor, Affiliate, Affinity, Agnate, Anastomosis, And, Associate, Attach, Band, Bind, Bridge, Bridle, Cable, Chiasm, Clientele, Cognate, Coherent, Colligate, Conjugate, Correlate, Couple, Cross-link, Delta, DIN, Dovetail, Downlink, Drawbar, Earth, Fishplate, Fistula, Hook-up, → **IN CONNECTION WITH**, Interlink, Interlock, Interrelation, Join, Jumper, Kinship, Liaison, Lifeline, Link, Linkup, Marry, Merge, Mesh, Neck, Network, Nexus, On, Online, Patch, Pons, Raphe, Rapport, Relate, Relative, Respect, Sentence, Shank, Splice, S-R, Synapse, Syntenosis, Syssarcosis, Tendon, Through, Tie, Tie-in, Union, Y, Yoke, Zygon

Connecticut Ct

Connive, Connivance Abet, Cahoots, Collude, Condone, Conspire, Lenocinium, Plot

Connoisseur Aesthete, Barista, Cognoscente, Epicure, Expert, Fancier, Gourmet, Judge, Maven, Mavin, Oenophil(e)

Connotate, Connotation Imply, Infer, Intent, Meaning, Overtone

Conquer(or), Conquering, Conquest Alexander, Beat, Conquistador, Cortes, Crush, Debel, Defeat, Genghis Khan, Hereward, → **MASTER**, Moor, Norman, Ostrogoth, Overcome, Overpower, Overrun, Pizarro, Saladin, Subjugate, Tame, Tamerlane, Vanquish, Victor, Vincent, Win

Conquistador Cortes, Cortez, Pizarro

Conscience, Conscientious Casuistic, Duteous, Heart, Inwit, Morals, Painstaking, Pang, Remorse, Scruple(s), Scrupulous, Sense, Superego, Syneidesis, Synteresis, Thorough, Twinge

Conscious(ness) Awake, Aware, Black, Chit, Deliberate, Limen, Mindful, On to, Persona, Sensible, Sentient, Witting

Conscript(ion) Blood-tax, Choco, Commandeer, Draft(ee), Impress, Inductee, Landsturm, Levy, Nasho, National Service, → **RECRUIT**, Register

Consecrate(d), Consecration Bless, Enoch, Hallow, Noint, Oint, Sacring, Sanctify, Venerate

Consecutive Sequential, Successive

Consensus Agreement, Harmony, Unanimity

Consent Accord, Acquiesce, Affo(o)rd, Agree, Approbate, Comply, Concur, Grant, Informed, Permit, Ratify, Submit, Una voce, Volens, Yes-but, Yield

Consequence, Consequent(ial), Consequently Aftermath, Consectaneous,

Corollary, Effect, End, Implication, Importance, Issue, Karma, Knock-on, Logical, Moment, Outcome, Out-turn, Ramification, Repercussion, → **RESULT**, Sequel, Thence, Thereat, Thus, Upshot

Conservative Blimpish, Blue, C, Cautious, Diehard, Disraeli, Fabian, Hard-hat, Hidebound, Hunker, Neanderthal, New Right, Old guard, Old-line, Old School, Preppy, Progressive, Rearguard, Redneck, Right(-wing), Safe, Square, Thrifty, Tory, True blue, Unionist, Verkramp, Verkrampte, Young Fogey

Conservatory Hothouse, Lean-to, Orangery, Solarium

Conserve, Conservation(ist) Can, Comfiture, Husband(ry), Jam, Jelly, Maintain, Maintenance, Noah, NT, Protect, Save

Consider(able), Considerate, Consideration Ad referendum, Animadvert, Attention, Avizandum, By-end, Case, Cerebrate, Chew over, Cogitate, Contemplate, Count, Courtesy, Debate, Deem, Deliberate, Entertain, Envisage, Factor, Fair, Feel, Forethought, Gay, Gey, Heed, Importance, Inasmuch, Judge, Kind, Many, Materially, Measure, Meditate, Muse, Pay, Perpend, Poise, Ponder, Premeditate, Pretty, Pro and con, Rate, Reck, Reckon, Reflect, Regard, Respect, Scruple, See, Sensitive, Several, Shortlist, Solicitous, Song, Speculate, Steem, Study, Substantial, Think, Tidy, Vast, View, Ween, Weigh

Consign(ment) Allot, Award, Batch, Bequeath, Delegate, Deliver, Drop shipment, Entrust, Lading, Ship, Shipment, Transfer

Consist(ent), Consistency Agree, Changeless, Coherent, Comprise, Concordant, Enduring, Even, Liaison, Rely, Sound, Steady, Texture

Consolation, Console Ancon, Appease, Balm, Cheer, Comfort, Games, Panel, Play, Reassure, Relief, Solace, Sop, Station

Consolidate Coalesce, Combine, Compact, Gel, Merge, Pun, Unify

Consommé Julienne, Soup

Consonant(s) Affricate, Agma, Agreeing, Alveolar, Cacuminal, Cerebral, Explosive, Fortis, Fricative, Harmonious, Implosive, Labial, Lateral, Lenis, Media, Mouillé, Plosive, Sonorant, Spirant, Surd, Tenuis, Velar

Consort Ally, Associate, Maik, Mate, Moop, Moup, Partner, Spouse

Consortium Coalition, Combine, Ring

Conspicuous Arresting, Blatant, Bold, Clear, Eminent, Glaring, Kenspeck(le), Landmark, Light, Manifest, Patent, Radiant, Salient, Shining, Showy, Signal, Striking

Conspiracy, Conspirator, Conspire, Conspiring Brutus, Cabal, Cartel, Casca, Cassius, Catiline, Cato St, Champerty, Cinna, Collaborate, Colleague, Collogue, Collude, Complot, Connive, Covin, Covyne, Guy, Highbinder, In cahoots, Intrigue, Oates, Omerta, → **PLOT**, Practisant, Ring, Scheme

Constable Beck, Catchpole, Cop, Dogberry, Dull, Elbow, Harman(-beck), Headborough, High, Hog, John, Lord High, Officer, Painter, Petty, Pointsman, → **POLICEMAN**, Posse, Special, Thirdborough, Tipstaff, Uniformed, Verges

Constancy, Constant Abiding, Boltzmann, C, Changeless, Chronic, Coefficient, Cosmic, Cosmological, Decay, Devotion, Dielectric, Diffusion, Dilys, Dirac, Eccentricity, Equilibrium, Eternal, Faith, Firm, Fixed, Fundamental, G, Gas, Gravitational, H, Honesty, Hubble's, K, Lambert, Leal(ty), Logical, Loyal, Magnetic, Nonstop, Often, Parameter, → **PERPETUAL**, Pi, Planck's, Pole star, Rate, Regular, Relentless, Resolute, Sad, Solar, Staunch, Steadfast, Steady, Time, True, Unceasing, Unfailing, Uniform, Usual

Constellation Crater, Galaxy, → **PLANET**, → **STAR**

CONSTELLATIONS

3 letters:	4 letters:		5 letters:
Ara	Apus	Lynx	Aries
Leo	Argo	Lyra	Cetus
	Grus	Pavo	Delta
		Vela	

Draco
Gruis
Hydra
Indus
Lepus
Libra
Lupus
Mensa
Musca
Norma
Orion
Pyxis
Spica
Twins
Virgo
Whale

6 letters:
Antlia
Aquila
Auriga
Bootes
Caelum
Carina
Corvus
Cygnus
Dorado
Fornax

Gemini
Hydrus
Octans
Pictor
Puppis
Scutum
Tucana
Virgin
Volans

7 letters:
Cepheus
Columba
Dolphin
Lacerta
Pegasus
Perseus
Phoenix
Sagitta
Serpens
Sextans
The Rule
Unicorn
Wagoner

8 letters:
Aquarius
Circinus

Cynosure
Equuleus
Eridanus
Hercules
Leo Minor
Scorpius
Sculptor
Waggoner
Zodiacal

9 letters:
Andromeda
Centaurus
Chameleon
Delphinus
Great Bear
Monoceros
Ophiuchus
Reticulum
Vilpecula
Vulpecula

10 letters:
Canis Major
Canis Minor
Cassiopeia
Chamaeleon
Horologium

Little Bear
Triangulum

11 letters:
Coma Cluster
Sagittarius
Telescopium

12 letters:
Camelopardus
Little Dipper
Microscopium

13 letters:
Canes Venatici
Coma Berenices
Southern Cross

14 letters:
Camelopardalis

15 letters:
Piscis Austrinus

18 letters:
Triangulum Australe

Consternation Alarm, Dismay, Doodah, Fear, Horror, Panic

Constipate(d), Constipation Astrict, Bind, Block, Costive, Mawbound, Stegnotic, Stenosis

Constituency, Constituent Borough, Component, Element, Immediate, Part, Principle, Seat, Staple, Ultimate, Voter

▷ **Constituents** *may indicate* an anagram

Constitute, Constitution(al) Appoint, Character, Charter, Clarendon, Compose, Comprise, Congenital, Creature, Establishment, Form, Fuero, Health, Physique, Policy, Polity, Seat, State, Stroll, Synthesis, Upmake, Walk

Constrain(ed), Constraint Bind, Bondage, Boundary, Coerce, Confine, Coop, Curb, Duress(e), Force, Hard, Localise, Oblige, Pressure, Repress, Stenosis, Taboo, Tie, Trammel

Constrict(ed), Constriction Bottleneck, Cage, Choke, Coarctate, Contract, Cramp, Hour-glass, Impede, Isthmus, Limit, Narrow, Phimosis, Squeeze, Stegnosis, Stenosis, Strangle, Strangulate, Thlipsis, Tighten, Venturi

Construct(ion), Constructor, Constructive Build, Cast, Compile, Engineer, Erect, Fabricate, Facture, Fashion, Form, Frame, Idolum, Make, Manufacture, Meccano, Partners, Seabee, Stressed-skin, Tectonic, Weave

Construe Deduce, Explain, Expound, Infer

Consul Ambassador, Attaché, Cicero, Horse, Lucullus, Praetor

Consult(ant), Consultation Avisement, Confer, Deliberate, Discuss, Emparl, Imparl, Joint, Peritus, See, Sexpert, Shark watcher, Surgery, Vide

Consume(r), Consumption, Consumptive Bolt, Burn, Caterpillar®, Conspicuous, Decay, Devour, Diner, Eat, End-user, Engross, Exhaust, Expend, Feed, Glutton, Hectic, Mainline, Scoff, Spend, Swallow, TB, Use, Waste, Wear

Consummate, Consummation Achieve, Crown, Keystone, Seal

Contact Abut, Adpress, Contingence, Electrode, Eye, Fax, Hook-up, Lens, Liaise, Liaison, Meet, Outreach, Radio, Reach, Shoe, Taction, → **TOUCH**, Touchy-feely, Wiper

Contagious, Contagion Infection, Noxious, Poison, Taint, Variola, Viral

Contain(er) Amphora, Ampulla, Aquafer, Aquifer, Ashcan, Barrel, Basket, Bass, Beaker, Bidon, Billy(-can), Bin, Boat, Bottle, Box, Brazier, Buddle, Bunker, Butt, Butter-boat, Cachepot, Can, Canakin, Canikin, Canister, Cannikin, Cantharus, Capsule, Carafe, Carboy, Carry, Carton, Case, Cask, Cassette, Censer, Chase, Chest, Chilly bin, Churn, Clip, Coffer, Comprise, Coolamon, Crate, Crater, Crucible, Cup, Cupel, Cuvette, Decanter, Dracone, Dredger, Encircle, Enclose, Encompass, Enseam, Esky®, Feretory, Flagon, Flask, Flat, Gabion, Gallipot, Gourd, Growler, → **HOLD**, House, Humidor, Igloo, Include, Incubator, Intray, Jar, Jeroboam, Jerrican, Jerrycan, Jug, Keg, Kirbeh, Leaguer, Lekythos, Locker, Magnox, Melting-pot, Monkey, Monstrance, Mould, Muffineer, Nosebag, Olpe, Ostensorium, Out-tray, Pail, Percolator, Pinata, Piscina, Pitcher, Pithos, Pod, Pottle, Punnet, Pyxis, Receptacle, Reliquary, Repository, Restrain, Sac(k), Safe, Saggar, Scyphus, Shaker, Situla, Skin, Skip, Snaptin, Solander, Spittoon, Stamnos, Stillage, Tank, Tantalus, Terrarium, Tinaja, Trough, Tub, Tun, Tupperware®, Urn, Valise, Vase, Vessel, Vinaigrette, Wardian case, Wineskin, Woolpack, Workbag

Contaminate(d), Contamination Adulterate, Corrupt, Defile, Denature, Flyblown, Impure, Infect, Moit, Mysophobia, Pollute, Soil, Spike, Stain, Tarnish

Contemplate, Contemplation Consider, Ecce, Envisage, Hesychasm, Meditate, Muse, Ponder, Reflect, Retrospection, Rue, Samadhi, Spell, Study, Think, Watch

Contemporary AD, Coetaneous, Concomitant, Current, Equal, Fellow, Modern, Modish, Present, Verism

Contempt(ible), Contemptuous Abject, Ageism, Aha, Arsehole, Bah, BEF, Blithering, Cheap, Contumely, Crud, Crumb, Crummy, Cullion, Cur, Cynical, Derision, Despisal, Diddy, Dis(s), Disdain, Dismissive, Disparaging, Disrespect, Dog-bolt, Dusty, Fico, Fig, Figo, Git, Hangdog, Ignominious, Insect, Jive-ass, Lousy, Low, Mean, Measly, Misprision, Och, Odious, Paltry, Pelting, Pfui, Phooey, Pipsqueak, Pish, Poof, Poxy, Pshaw, Ratfink, Rats, Razoo, Scabby, Scarab, Schlub, Scofflaw, → **SCORN**, Scumbag, Scurvy, Sdeign, Sexism, Shabby, Shitface, Shithead, Slimeball, Sneer, Sneeze, Sniffy, Snook, Snooty, Snot, Snotty, Soldier, Sorry, Sprat, Squirt, Squit, Supercilious, Toad, Toerag, Tossy, Turd, Tush, Vilipend, Weed, Whipster, Wretched

Contend(er) Allege, Argue, Candidate, Claim, Clash, Compete, Cope, Debate, Dispute, Fight, Grapple, Oppose, Rival, Stickle, → **STRIVE**, Struggle, Submit, Tussle, → **VIE**, Wrestle

Content(ed) Apaid, Apay, Appay, Blissful, Happy, Inside, Please, Raza, Reza, Satisfy, Subject matter, Volume

▷ **Content** *may indicate* a hidden word

Contention, Contentious Argument, Bellicose, Cantankerous, Case, Combat, Competitive, Logomachy, Perverse, Polemical, Rivalry, Strife, Struggle, Sturt

Contest(ant) Agon, Battle, Beauty, Beetle drive, Biathlon, Bout, Catchweight, Challenge, Championship, Combat, Competition, Concours, Darraign, Decathlon, Defend, Deraign, Dogfight, Duathlon, Duel(lo), Entrant, Eurovision, Event, Examinee, Finalist, Free-for-all, Fronde, Handicap, Heptathlon, Kemp, Kriegspiel, Lampadephoria, Match, Matchplay, Olympiad, Pancratium, Par, Paralympics, Pentathlon, Pingle, Play-off, Prizer, Race, Rat race, Rival, Roadeo, Rodeo, Scrap, Scrum, Set-to, Skirmish, Slam, Slugfest, Strife, Struggle, Tenson, Tetrathlon, Tournament, Triathlon, Tug-of-war, Vie, War, With

Context Intentional, Opaque, Transparent

Continent(al) Abstinent, Asia, Atlantis, Austere, Chaste, Dark, Epeirogeny, Euro, European, Gallic, Gondwanaland, Greek, Landmass, Laurasia, Lemuria, Mainland, Moderate, NA, Pang(a)ea, Shelf, Teetotal, Temperate, Walloon

Contingency, Contingent Accident, Arm, Casual, Chance, Conditional, Dependent, Event, Fluke, Group, Possibility, Prospect

Continual(ly), Continuous Adjoining, At a stretch, Away, Ceaseless, Chronic, Connected, Eer, Endlong, Eternal, Eterne, Ever, Forever, Frequent, Incessant, Non-stop, On(going), Unbroken, Unceasing

Continue, Continuation, Continuing, Continuity Abye, Duration, Dure, During, Enduring, Enjamb(e)ment, Follow-on, Go on, Hold, Keep, Last, Link, Ongoing, Onward, Perpetuate, Persevere, Persist, Proceed, Prolong, Push on, Remain, Resume, Sequel, Sequence, Stand, Subsist, Survive, Sustain, Synaphe(i)a, Tenor

▷ **Continuously** *may indicate* previous words to be linked

Contort(ion) Deform, Gnarl, Jib, Twist, Warp, Wreathe, Wry

Contour Curve, Graph, Isallobar, Isobase, Isocheim, Isochime, Isogeothermal, Isohel, Isohyet, Line, Profile, Silhouette, Streamline, Tournure

Contraband Hot, Illicit, Prohibited, Smuggled

Contraception, Contraceptive Billings method, Cap, Coil, Condom, Depo-Provera®, Diaphragm, Dutch cap, Etonogestrol, IU(C)D, Legonorgestrel, Lippes loop, Loop, Minipill, Oral, Pessary, Pill, Precautions, Prophylactic, Rubber(s), Sheath, Spermicide, Vimule®

Contract(ion), Contractor Abbreviate, Abridge, Affreightment, Agreement, Appalto, Astringency, Bargain, Biceps, Binding, Bottomry, Braxton-Hicks, Bridge, Builder, Catch, Champerty, Charter (party), Clench, Clonus, Concordat, Condense, Consensual, Constringe, Contrahent, Convulsion, Covenant, Cramp, Crasis, Curtail, Debt, Develop, Diastalsis, Dupuytren's, Dwindle, Engage, Entrepreneur, Escrow, Extrasystole, Fibrillation, Fitzgerald-Lorentz, Flex, Forward, Gainsay, Gooseflesh, Guarantee, Hand-promise, Hire, Incur, Indenture, Jerk, Ketubah, Knit, Labour, Lease, Lessen, Levator, Lorentz-Fitzgerald, Make, Mandate, Miosis, Myosis, Narrow, Obligee, Outsource, Party, Peristalsis, Privilege, Promise, Pucker, Purse, Restriction, Risus (sardonicus), Service, Shrink, Shrivel, Sign, Slam, Slim, Social, Spasm, Specialty, Squinch, Steelbow, Stenosis, Stipulation, Straddle, Supplier, Swap, Sweetheart, Synaloepha, Syngraph, Systole, Telescope, Tender, Tetanise, Tetanus, Tic, Tighten, Time bargain, Tittle, Tonicity, Tontine, Treaty, Triceps, Trigger-finger, Trismus cynicus, Undertaker, Wrinkle, Yellow-dog, Z

▷ **Contract** *may indicate* a bridge call, e.g. 1S, 1C, 1D

Contradict(ion), Contradictory Ambivalent, Antilogy, Antinomy, Belie, Bull, Contrary, Counter, Dementi, Deny, Disaffirm, Disprove, Dissent, → **GAINSAY**, Negate, Oxymoron, Paradox, Sot, Stultify, Sublate, Threap, Threep, Traverse

Contralto Clara Butt

Contraption Contrivance, Scorpion

Contrapuntal Fugue

Contrarily, Contrary Adverse, A rebours, Arsy-versy, But, Captious, Converse, Counter, Counterfleury, Crosscurrent, Cross-grained, Cross-purpose, Froward, Hostile, Inverse, Mary, Opposite, Oppugnant, Ornery, Perverse, Rebuttal, Retrograde, Wayward, Withershins

Contrast Chiaroscuro, Clash, Colour, Compare, Differ, Foil, Relief

Contravene Infringe, Oppose, Thwart, Violate

Contribute, Contribution Abet, Add, Assist, Chip in, Conduce, Donate, Dub, Furnish, Go, Help, Input, Kick in, Mite, Offering, Share, Sub, Subscribe, Whack, Widow's mite

▷ **Contributing to** *may indicate* a hidden word

Contrite, Contrition Apologetic, Penance, Penitent, Remorse, Repentant, Rue, Sackcloth, → **SORRY**

Contrivance, Contrive(r), Contrived Art, Artificial, Cam, Chicaner, Contraption, Cook, Deckle, Deus ex machina, Device, Devise, Dodge, Engine, Engineer, Finesse, Frame, Gadget, Gimmick, Gin, Hatch, Hokey, Intrigue, Invention, Machinate, Manage, Manoeuvre, Page, Plan, Plot, Procure, Rest, Rowlock, Scheme, Secure, Shift, Stage, Trump, Wangle, Weave

Control(ler), Controllable, Controlled Ada, Aircon, Appestat, Autopilot, Big

Brother, Birth, Boss, Boundary layer, Bridle, Cabotage, Camshaft, Chair, Check, Chokehold, Christmas tree, Contain, Corner, Corset, Curb, Cybernetics, Damage, Descendeur, Dirigible, Dirigism(e), Dominate, Dominion, Driving seat, Duopsony, Dynamic, Elevon, Etatiste, Fader, Fast-forward, Fet(ch), Finger, Flood, Fly-by-wire, Gain, Gar, George, Gerent, Govern, Ground, Gubernation, Hae, Harness, Have, Heck, Helm, Hog, Influence, Influx, Inhibitor, Interchange, Joystick, Keypad, Knee-swell, Lead, Lever, Limit, Line, → **MANAGE**, Martinet, Mastery, Moderate, Mouse, Nipple, Noise, Nozzled, Numerical, Operate, Override, Pilot, Placebo, Police, Population, Possess, Power, Preside, Price, Process, Puppeteer, Quality, Radio, Referee, Regulate, Regulo®, Rein, Remote, Rent, Repress, Restrain, Restrict, Rheostat, Ride, Ripple, Rule, Run, School, Servo, Slide(r), Snail, Solion, Spoiler, Stage-manage, Steady, Steer, Stop, Stranglehold, Stringent, Subdue, Subject, Subjugate, Supervise, Suzerain, Svengali, Sway, Switch, Takeover, Tame, Temperate, Thermostat, Throttle, Tie, Tiller, Tone, Traction, Umpire, Upper hand, Valve, Weld, Wield, Zapper

Controversial, Controversy Argument, Contention, Debate, Dispute, Emotive, Eristic(al), Furore, Heretical, Hot potato, Polemic(al), Tendentious, Troll

▷ **Contuse** *may indicate* an anagram

Conundrum Acrostic, Egma, Enigma, Puzzle, Riddle, Teaser

Convalesce(nt), Convalescence Anastatic, Mend, Rally, Recover, Recuperate, Rest-cure

▶ **Convene** *see* **CONVOKE(R)**

Convenience, Convenient Behoof, Commode, Cosy, Easy, Eft, Ethe, Expedient, Facility, Gain, Gents, Handsome, → **HANDY**, Hend, Lav, Leisure, Near, Opportune, Pat, Privy, Public, Suitable, Toilet, Use, Well

Convent Abbatial, Cloister, Fratry, Friary, House, → **MONASTERY**, Motherhouse, Nunnery, Port-royal, Priory, Retreat

Convention(al) Academic, Accepted, Babbitt, Blackwood, Bourgeois, Caucus, Code, Conclave, Conformity, → **CUSTOMARY**, Diet, Done, Formal, Geneva, Habitude, Hidebound, Iconic, Lame, Lingua franca, Mainstream, Meeting, Middlebrow, Middle-of-the-road, More, National, Nomic, Orthodox, Ossified, Pompier, Proper, Propriety, Readymade, Schengen, Staid, Starchy, Stereotyped, Stock, Straight, Stylebook, Synod, The thing, Uptight, Usage, Warsaw

Converge(nce) Approach, Focus, Inrush, Meet, Toe-in

Conversation(alist), Converse, Conversant Abreast, Antithesis, Antitype, Board, Buck, Cackle, Causerie, Chat, Chitchat, Colloquy, Commune, Confab, Convo, Crack, Crossfire, Crosstalk, Deipnosophist, Dialogue, Discourse, Eutrapelia, Eutrapely, Exchange, Facemail, Hobnob, Interlocution, In tune with, Jaw-jaw, Natter, Opposite, Palaver, Parley, Persiflage, Rap, Rhubarb, Shop, Shoptalk, Sidebar, Small talk, Socialise, → **TALK**, Transpose, Trialogue, Wongi, Word

Conversion, Converter, Convert(ible) Adapt, Alter, Assimilate, Azotobacter, Bessemer, Cabriolet, Cash, Catalytic, Catechumen, Change, Commutate, Commute, Cyanise, Damascene, Diagenesis, Disciple, Encash, Etherify, Evangelize, Exchange, Expropriate, Fixation, Gummosis, Hodja, Ismalise, Kho(d)ja, Landau, L-D, Liquid, Marrano, Metamorphosis, Metanoia, Missionary, Neophyte, Noviciate, Novitiate, Persuade, Prill, Proselyte, Put, Ragtop, Realise, Rebirth, Reclamation, Recycle, Revamp, Romanise, Sheik(h), Soft-top, Souper, Tablet, Taw, Torque, Transduce, Transform, Transmute, Try, Vert

▷ **Conversion, Converted** *may indicate* an anagram

Convex(ity) Arched, Bowed, Camber, Curved, Entasis, Extrados, Gibbous, Lenticle, Nowy

Convey(ance) Assign, BS, Carousel, Carriage, Carry, Carrycot, Cart, Charter, Coach, Conduct, Cycle, Deed, Deliver, Eloi(g)n, Enfeoffment, Esloyne, Exeme, Giggit, Grant, Guide, Lease, Litter, Lorry, Mailcar(t), Pirogue, Pneumatic, Re-lease, Sac, Screw, Sled, Soc, Tip, Title deed, Tote, Tram, Transfer, Transit, Transmit, Transport, Trolley, Vehicle

Convict(ion) Attaint, Belief, Botany Bay, Bushranger, Canary, Certitude, Cockatoo, Cogence, Crawler, Credo, Creed, Crime, Criminal, Demon, Dogma, Emancipist, Faith, Felon, Forçat, Gaolbird, Government man, Jailbird, Lag, Magwitch, Old chum, → **PERSUASION**, Plerophory, Previous, Prisoner, Record, Ring, Trusty, Vehemence, Yardbird

Convince(d), Convincing Assure, Certain, Cogent, Credible, Doubtless, Luculent, Persuade, Plausible, Satisfy, Sold, Sure

Convivial(ity) Boon, Bowl, Festive, Gay, Genial, Jovial, Social

Convoke(r) Assemble, Call, Chairman, Convene, Summon

Convolute(d), Convolution Coiled, Gyrus, Helical, Intricate, Maze, Spiral, Tortuous, Twisty, Whorl, Writhen

Convolvulus Bindweed, Dodder

Convoy Caravan, Column, Conduct, Escort, Fur brigade, Pilot, Train, Wagon-train

Convulse, Convulsion(s), Convulsive Agitate, Clonic, Clonus, Commotion, Disturb, DT, Eclampsia, → **FIT**, Galvanic, Paroxysm, Spasm, Throe, Tic

Cook(s), Cooker(y), Cooking Aga®, Babbler, Babbling brook, Bake, Balti, Beeton, Benghazi, Bhindi, Bouche, Braise, Broil, Cacciatore, Calabash, Captain, Charbroil, Chargrill, Chef, Coction, Coddle, Concoct, Cordon bleu, Creole, Cuisine, Cuisinier, Deep-fry, Delia, Devil, Do, Doctor, Dumple, Easy over, Edit, En papillote, Escoffier, Explorer, Fake, Falsify, Fiddle, Fireless, Fix, Flambé, Forge, Fricassee, Fry, Fudge, Fusion, Gastronomy, Gratinate, Greasy, Griddle, Grill, Haute cuisine, Haybox, Hibachi, Jackaroo, Kiln, Lyonnaise, Marengo, Marinière, Meunière, Microwave, Mount, Nouvelle cuisine, Poach, Prepare, Pressure, Provencale, Range, Ribroast, Rig, Ring, Roast, Roger, Sauté, Short-order, Silver, Sous-chef, Spit, Steam, Stew, Stir-fry, Stove, Tandoori, Tikka, Tire, Toast

▷ **Cook** *may indicate* an anagram

Cool(er), Coolant, Cooling, Coolness Ace, Aloof, Aplomb, Calm, Can, Chill, Chokey, Collected, Composed, Cryogen, Cryostat, Defervescence, Desert, Dignified, Dispassionate, Distant, Esky®, Fan, Frappé, Fridge, Frigid, Frosty, Gaol, Goglet, Hip, Ice(box), Imperturbable, In, Jail, Jug, Keel, La Nina, Lubricating oil, Maraging, Nervy, Nonchalant, Offish, Phlegm, Poise, Prison, Quad, Quod, Reefer, Refresh, Regenerative, Reserved, Sangfroid, Serene, Shady, Skeigh, Splat, Stir, Super-duper, Sweat, Temper(ate), Thou(sand), Trendy, Unruffled, Wint(e)ry

Coop Cage, Cavie, Confine, Gaol, Hutch, Mew, Pen, Rip

Cooper Gary, Henry, Tubman

Cooperate, Cooperation, Cooperative Ally, Artel, Bipartisan, Collaborate, Combine, Conspire, Contribute, Coop, Credit union, Give and take, Liaise, Pitch in, Play, Synergy, Tame, Teamwork, Together, Worker's

Coordinate(s), Coordinated, Coordination Abscissa, Abscisse, Agile, Arrange, Cartesian, Del, Ensemble, Harmony, Nabla, Orchestrate, Ordonnance, Peer, Polar, Right ascension, Spherical, Synergy, Teamwork, Tight, Twistor, Waypoint, X, Y, Z

Coot Stupid, Sultan

Cop(s) Bag, Bull, Catch, Copper, Dick, Flic, Keystone, Peeler, Peon, → **POLICEMAN**, Silent

Copal Dammar, Resin

Cope Chlamys, Deal, Face, Fare, Handle, Make do, → **MANAGE**, Mantle, Meet, Negotiate, Pallium, Poncho

Coping (stone) Balustrade, Capstone, Skew

Copious Abundant, Affluent, Ample, Fecund, Fluent, Fruitful, Fulsome, Plentiful, Profuse

Copper As, Atacamite, Beast, Blister, Bluebottle, Bobby, Bornite, Busy, Cash, Cent, Chessylite, → **COIN**, Cu, D, Dam, Double, Erinite, Flatfoot, Lawman, Lota(h), Malachite, Mountain-blue, Ormolu, Peacock, Pence, Penny, Pfennig, Pie, Pig, Plack, Policeman, Red, Rosser, Rozzer, S, Sen(s), Slop, Special, Traybit, Venus, Verdet, Verditer, Washer, Washtub, Wire bar

Coppice, Copse Thicket, Underwood

Copulate Boff, Intercourse, Line, Mate, Roger, Serve, Tread, Tup

Copy(ing), Copier, Copyist, Copywriter Adman, Aemule, Ape, Apograph, Association, Autotype, Calk, Calque, Camera-ready, Carbon, Clerk, Clone, Counterpart, Crib, Cyclostyle, Diazo, Ditto, Download, Dyeline, Echo, Echopraxia, Ectype, Edition, Eidograph, Electro, Emulate, Engross, Estreat, Example, Facsimile, Fair, Fax, Flimsy, Forge, Hard, Hectograph, → **IMITATE**, Issue, Jellygraph, Knocking, Knockoff, Manifold, Manuscript, Match, Me-tooer, Microdot, Milline, Mimeograph®, Mimic, Mirror, MS, Offprint, Ozalid, Pantograph, Parrot, Photostat®, Plagiarism, Polygraph, Read-out, Repeat, Replica, Reprint, Repro, Reproduce, Review, Rip, Roneo®, Scanner, Scribe, Script, Scrivener, Sedulous, Show, Simulate, Skim, Soft, Spit, Stat, Stencil, Stuff, Tall, Telautograph®, Telefax, Tenor, Tenure, Trace, Transcribe, Transume, Transumpt, Vidimus, Xerox®

Copyright C, Landgrab

Coquette Agacerie, Flirt, Rosina, Tease, Vamp

Cor Bath, Crumbs, Ephah, Gosh, Homer

Coracle Currach, Curragh

Coral (reef) Alcyonaria, Aldabra, Atoll, Brain, Cup, Deadmen's fingers, Gorgonia(n), Laccadives, Madrepore, Millepore, Organ-pipe, Pink, Precious, Red, Reef, Sea fan, Sea ginger, Sea-pen, Sea whip, Seed, Staghorn, Stony, Zoothome

Cord, Cord-like Aiguillette, Band, Bedford, Bind, Boondoggle, Cat-gut, Chenille, Communication, Creance, Cybernaculum, Drawstring, Elephant, Flex, Fourragère, Funicle, Gasket, Heddle, Lace, Laniard, Lanyard, Ligature, Line, Moreen, Myelon, Nerve, Net, Ocnus, Picture, Piping, Quipo, Quipu, Rep(s), Restiform, Rip, Rope, Sash, Sennit, Service, Shroudline, Sinew, Sinnet, Spermatic, Spinal, → **STRING**, Tendon, Tie, Tieback, Torsade, Twine, Twitch, Umbilical, Vocal, Wick

Cordial Amicable, Anise(ed), Anisette, Benedictine, Cassis, Drink, Elderflower, Gracious, Grenadine, Hearty, Hippocras, Kind, Neighbourly, Oporice, Orangeade, Persico(t), Pleasant, Ratafia, Rosa-solis, Roso(g)lio, Shrub, Tar-water, Warm

Cordon Band, Beltcourse, Picket, Ring, Sanitaire, Surround

Corduroy Rep(p)

Cordyline Ti-tree

Core Barysphere, Calandria, Campana, Centre, Chog, Essence, Filament, Hard, Heart, Hub, Kernel, Magnetic, Nife, Nitty-gritty, Plerome, Quintessence, Runt, Slug

Co-religionist Brother

Corfu Corfiot(e)

Coriander Cilantro

Corinthian(s) Casuals, Caulis, Epistolaters

Cork(ed), Corker Balsa, Bouché, Bung, Float(er), Humdinger, Mountain, Oner, Periderm, Phellem, Phellogen, Plug, Seal, Shive, Stopper, Suber(ate)

Corkscrew Bore, Opening, Spiral, Twine

Cormorant Duiker, Duyker, Scart(h), Shag, Skart(h)

Corn(y) Bajr(a), Banal, Blé, Callus, Cereal, Cob, Dolly, Durra, Emmer, Epha, Flint, Gait, Graddan, Grain, Green, Grist, Guinea, Hokey, Icker, Indian, Kaffir, Kanga pirau, Mabela, Maize, Mealie, Muid, Negro, Nubbin, Pickle, Pinole, Posho, Rabi, Rye, Seed, Shock, Stitch, Straw, Sugar, Sweet, Tail ends, Thrave, Trite, Zea

Corncrake Landrail

Cornel Dogberry, Tree

Corner Amen, Angle, Bend, Canthus, Cantle, Canton, Chamfer, Cranny, Dangerous, Diêdre, Elbow, Entrap, Hog, Hole, Hospital, Long, Lug, Monopoly, NE, Niche, Nook, NW, Penalty, Predicament, Quoin, SE, Short, Speakers', Spot, SW, Tack, Tattenham, Tight, Trap, Tree, Vertex

Cornerstone Coi(g)n, Encoignure, Skew-corbel, Skew-put, Skew-table

Cornet Cone, Cornopean, Field, Horn

Cornice Surbase
Cornish(man) Cousin Jack
Cornstalks Strammel, Straw, Strummel, Stubble
Cornucopia Amalthea, Horn
Cornwall SW
Corollary Conclusion, Dogma, Porism, Rider, Theory, Truism
Corona Aureole, Cigar, Halo, Larmier, Nimbus, Wreath
Coronation Enthronement
Coroner Procurator fiscal
Corporal Bardolph, Bodily, Bombardier, Brig(adier), Lance-pesade, Lance-prisade, Lance-prisado, Lance-speisade, Master, Naik, NCO, Nym, Pall, Physical, Trim
Corporation Belly, Body, Breadbasket, Closed, Commune, Company, Conglomerate, Guild, Kite, Kyte, Paunch, Pot, Public, Public service, Stomach, Swag-belly, Tum, Wame, Wem
Corps Body, C, Crew, Diplomatic, Marine, Peace, RAC, RE, REME, Unit
Corpse(s) Blob, Body, Cadaver, Carcass, Carrion, Deader, Dust, Goner, Like, Mort, Quarry, Relic, Remains, Stiff, Zombi(e)
Corpulence, Corpulent Adipose, Fat, Fleshy, Gross, Obese, Poddy, Stout, Thickset, Tubby
Corpuscle Cell, Erythrocyte, Malpighian, Meissner's, Microcyte, Neutrophil, Pacinian, Phagocyte, Porkilocyte, Tactile
Corral Kraal, OK
Correct(ive), Correcting, Correctly, Correctness, Correction, Corrector About east, Accepted, Accurate, Alexander, Align, Amend, Aright, Blue-pencil, Bodkin, Castigate, Chasten, Chastise, Check, Cheese, Decorous, Diorthortic, Edit, Emend, Epanorthosis, Ethical, Exact, Fair, Fix, Grammatical, Legit, Mend, Orthopaedic, Politically, Preterition, Probity, Proofread, Proper, Propriety, Punctilious, Punish, Purism, Rebuke, Rectify, Rectitude, Red pencil, Redress, Remedial, Reprove, Revise, Right(en), Scold, Spinning-house, Spot-on, Straighten, Sumpsimus, Tickety-boo, Tippex®, Trew, True, Twink, U, Yep, Yes
▷ **Corrected** *may indicate* an anagram
Correspond(ence), Correspondent, Corresponding Accord, Agree, Analogy, Assonance, Coincident, Communicate, Congruence, Counterpart, Cynghanedd, Epistolist, Equate, Equivalence, Eye-rhyme, Fit, Foreign, Hate mail, Homolog(ue), Identical, Isomorph, Lobby, Match, On all fours, One-one, One to one, Par, Parallel, Parity, Penpal, Post(bag), Relate, Snail mail, Symmetry, Sync, Tally, Veridical, War, Write
Corridor Air, Aisle, Berlin, Entry, Gallery, Greenway, Lobby, Passage, Penthouse, Polish, Re-entry
Corroborate Confirm, Support, Underpin, Verify
Corrode(d), Corrosion, Corrosive Acid, Acid rain, Brinelling, Burn, Canker, Decay, Eat, Erode, Etch, Fret, Gnaw, Hydrazine, Mordant, → **ROT**, Rubiginous, Rust, Waste
Corrugate Gimp
Corrupt(er), Corrupting, Corruption Abuse, Adulterate, Bastardise, Bent, Bobol, Bribable, Canker, Cesspit, Debase, Debauch, Debosh, Decadent, Defile, Degenerate, Depravity, Dissolute, Dry rot, Emancipate, Embrace(o)r, Embrasor, Empoison, Enseam, Etch, Evil, Fester, Gangrene, Graft(er), Immoral, Impaired, Impure, Infect, Inquinate, Jobbery, Leprosy, Malversation, Nefarious, Obelus, Payola, Perverse, Poison, Pollute, Power, Putrefaction, Putrid, Rakery, Ret(t), Rigged, Rot, Scrofulous, Seduce, Sepsis, Septic, Sleaze, Sodom, Sophisticate, Spoil, Suborn, Taint, Tammany, Twist, Ulcered, Venal, Vice, Vitiate
Corsage Buttonhole, Pompadour, Posy, Spray
Corsair Barbary, Picaroon, Pirate, Privateer, Robber, Rover
Corset, Corslet Belt, Bodice, Busk, Featherbone, Girdle, Lorica, Roll-on, Stays, Thorax, Waspie, Whalebone
Corsican Napoleon

Cortege Parade, Retinue, Train
Cortex Cerebral, Renal
Cortisone Hecogenin
Corundum Emery, Sapphire
Corvo Rolfe
Corybant Roisterer
Cosh Life preserver, Sap
Cosmetic Aloe vera, Beautifier, Blusher, Bronzer, Chapstick, Conditioner, Detangler, Eye-black, Eyeliner, Eye-shadow, Face-pack, Foundation, Fucus, Highlighter, Kohl, Lightener, Liner, Lip gloss, Lip liner, Lipstick, Lotion, Maquillage, Mascara, Moisturizer, Mousse, Mudpack, Nail polish, Paint, Panstick, Pearl-powder, Pearl-white, Powder, Q-tip, Reface, Rouge, Talcum, Toner
▶ **Cosmic** *see* **COSMOS**
Cosmonaut Gagarin, Spaceman, Tereshkova
Cosmopolitan International, Urban
Cosmos, Cosmic Globe, Heaven, Infinite, Mundane, Nature, Universe, World
Cossack Ataman, Hetman, Kazak(h), Mazeppa, Russian, Tartar, Zaporogian
Cosset Caress, Coddle, Fondle, Nanny, Pamper
Cost(s), Costly Be, Bomb, Carriage, Charge, Current, Damage, Direct, Disadvantage, Earth, Escuage, Estimate, Exes, → **EXPENSE**, Factor, Fetched, Fixed, Hire, Historic(al), Indirect, Loss, Marginal, Opportunity, Outlay, Overhead, Precious, Price, Prime, Quotation, Rate, Rent, Running, Sacrifice, Standard, Storage, Sumptuous, Tab, Toll, Unit, Upkeep, Usurious, Variable
Costa Rica(n) Tico
Costermonger Barrow-boy, Kerb-merchant, Pearly, Pearly king, Pearly queen
Costume(s) Apparel, Attire, Camagnole, Cossie, Dress, Ensemble, Get-up, Gi(e), Guise, Judogi, Livery, Maillot, Motley, Nebris, Polonaise, Rig, Ruana, Surcoat, Tanga, Togs, Trollopee, Tutu, Uniform, Wardrobe, Wear
Cosy Cosh, Gemutlich, Intime, Snug
Cot Cotangent, Dovehouse, Moses basket
Coterie Camarilla, Cell, Cenacle, Circle, Clan, Clique, Club, Ring, Set, Society
Cottage(r) Bach, Batch, Bordar, Bothie, Bothy, Bower, Box, Bungalow, Cabin, Cape Cod, Chalet, Cot, Crib, Dacha, Home-croft, Hut, Lodge, Mailer, Thatched
Cotton Absorbent, Agree, AL, Alabama, Balbriggan, Batiste, Batting, Bengal, Calico, Candlewick, Ceiba, Chambray, Chino, Chintz, Collodion, Coutil(le), Cretonne, Denim, Dho(o)ti, Dimity, Ducks, Fustian, Galatea, Gossypine, Gossypium, Humhum, Ihram, Jaconet, Lavender, Lawn, Lea, Lille, Lint, Lisle, Longcloth, Madras, Manchester, Marcella, Muslin, Nainsook, Nankeen, Nankin, Osnaburg, Percale, Pongee, Sateen, Sea-island, Seersucker, Silesia, Stranded, Surat, T-cloth, Thread, Twig, Upland, Velveteen
Cotton soil Regar, Regur
Cotyledon Seed-leaf
Couch Bed, Casting, Davenport, Daybed, → **DIVAN**, Express, Grass, Lurk, Palanquin, Palkee, Palki, Quick, Recamier, Sedan, Settee, Sofa, Studio, Triclinium, Vis-à-vis, Winnipeg, Word
Coué Auto-suggestion
Cougar Cat, Painter, Puma
Cough(ing) Bark, Chin, Croup, Expectorate, Hack, Harrumph, Hawk, Hem, Hoast, Hooping, Kink, Pertussis, Phthisis, Rale, Tisick, Tussis, Ugh, Whooping
Could Couth
Council (meeting), Councillor, Counsel(lor) Achitophel, Admonish, Admonitor, Advice, Advocate, Ahithophel, Alderman, Alfred, Amphictryon, Anziani, Aread, Ar(r)e(e)de, Assembly, Attorney, Aulic, Aunt, Ayuntamiento, Board, Body, Boule, Bundesrat, Burgess, Cabal, Cabinet, Casemate, Committee, Consistory, Corporation, County, Cr, Decurion, Dergue, Devil, Dietine, Divan, Douma, Duma, Ecofin, Ecumenical,

Egeria, Europe, European, Executive, Exhort, General, Great, Greenbag, Hebdomadal, Indaba, Induna, Industrial, Info, Islands, Jirga, Junta, Kabele, Kebele, King's, Kite, Landst(h)ing, Lateran, Leader, Legislative, Loan, Majlis, Mentor, Nestor, Nicaean, Nicene, Panchayat, Paraclete, Parish, Powwow, Press, Privy, Provincial, Queen's, Rede, Regional, Reichsrat, Robber, Runanga, Samaritan, Sanhedrim, Sanhedrin, Security, Senate, Shoora, Shura, Sobranje, Sobranye, Soviet, States, Syndicate, Synedrion, Synod, Thing, Town, Tradeboard, Trades, Trent, Tridentine, Trullan, Unitary, Vatican, Volost, Wages, Whitley, Witan, Witenagemot, Works, Zemstvo, Zila, Zila parishad, Zillah

Count(ed), Counter(balance), Counting Abacus, Add, Algoriam, Anti, Aristo, Balance, Bar, Basie, Blood, Buck, Buffet, Calculate, Calorie, Cavour, Census, Check, Chip, Compute, Coost, Crystal, Cuisenaire rods, Desk, Disc, Dracula, Dump, Earl, Enumerate, Fish, Geiger, Geiger-Muller, Graf(in), Grave, Itemise, Jet(t)on, Landgrave, Margrave, Marker, Matter, Meet, Merel(l), Meril, Milton work, Nobleman, Number, Numerate, Obviate, Olivia, Oppose, Outtell, Palatine, Palsgrave, Paris, Pollen, Presume, Proportional, Rebut, → **RECKON**, Refute, Rejoinder, Rely, Resist, Retaliate, Retort, Rhinegrave, Scaler, Scintillation, Score, Shopboard, Sperm, Squail, Statistician, Stop, Sum, Table, Tally, Tell, Tiddleywink, Tolstoy, Ugolino, Weigh, Zeppelin

Countenance Approve, Brow, Endorse, Face, Favour, Mug, Sanction, Support, Visage

Counteract(ing) Ant-, Antidote, Cancel, Correct, Frustrate, Neutralise, Offset, Talion

Counterbalance Bascule, Offset, Undo, Weigh

Counter-charge Recrimination

Counterclockwise L(a)evorotatory

Counterfeit(er) Bastard, Belie, Bogus, Boodle, Brum, Coiner, Doctor, Duffer, Dummy, Fain, Fantasm, Fayne, Flash, Forge, Fraudster, Imitant, Paperhanger, Phantasm, Phoney, Pinchbeck, Postiche, Pseudo, Queer, Rap, Schlenter, Sham, Shan(d), Simular, Simulate, Skim, Slang, Slip, Smasher, Snide, Spurious, Stumer

Counterfoil Stub

Counterglow Gegenschein

Counter-irritant Seton

Countermand Abrogate, Annul, Cancel, Override, Rescind, Retract, Revoke, Unorder

Counterpart Copy, Double, Obverse, Oppo, Parallel, Shadow, Similar, Spit(ting), Tally, Twin

Counterpoint Contrapuntal, Descant

Countersign Endorse, Password

Counterthrust Riposte

Counties, County Co, Comital, Comitatus, District, Hundred, Metropolitan, Palatine, Parish, Seat, Shire, Six

---

COUNTIES

2 letters:	Kent	Gwent	Worcs
NI	Mayo	Herts	
Sy	Ross	Hunts	6 letters:
		Kerry	Antrim
3 letters:	5 letters:	Laois	Armagh
Ely	Angus	Louth	Barset
Som	Cavan	Meath	Carlow
	Clare	Moray	Dorset
4 letters:	Clwyd	Notts	Dublin
Avon	Derry	Omagh	Durham
Beds	Devon	Perth	Galway
Cork	Dyfed	Powys	Offaly
Down	Essex	Sligo	Surrey
Fife	Flint	Wilts	Sussex

Tyrone

7 letters:
Cumbria
Donegal
Gwynedd
Kildare
Leitrim
Norfolk
Rutland
Suffolk
Torfaen
Wexford
Wicklow

8 letters:
Cheshire
Cornwall
Finnmark
Kesteven
Kilkenny
Limerick
Longford
Lothians
Monaghan
Somerset

9 letters:
Berkshire
Buteshire
Caithness

Champagne
Cleveland
Fermanagh
Hampshire
Loamshire
Roscommon
The Mearns
Tipperary
Waterford
Westmeath
Yorkshire

10 letters:
Banffshire
Ceredigion
Derbyshire
Devonshire
Humberside
Lancashire
Merseyside
Midlothian
Nairnshire
Perthshire
Shropshire
Sutherland
West Sussex

11 letters:
Breconshire
East Lothian
Lanarkshire

Londonderry
Oxfordshire
Radnorshire
Tyne and Wear
West Lothian

12 letters:
Berwickshire
Denbighshire
Kinrossshire
Lincolnshire
Mid-Glamorgan
Peeblesshire
Renfrewshire
Selkirkshire
Warwickshire
West Midlands
Westmoreland
Wigtownshire

13 letters:
Dumfriesshire
Herefordshire
Monmouthshire
Pembrokeshire
Roxburghshire
Staffordshire
Stirlingshire
West Glamorgan
West Yorkshire

14 letters:
Brecknockshire
Dumbartonshire
Glamorganshire
Invernessshire
Leicestershire
Merionethshire
Northumberland
North Yorkshire
South Glamorgan
South Yorkshire

15 letters:
Caernarvonshire
Carmarthenshire
Gloucestershire
Kincardineshire
Montgomeryshire
Neath Port Talbot
Ross and Cromarty
Vale of Glamorgan

16 letters:
Clackmannanshire
Northamptonshire

18 letters:
Kirkcudbrightshire

Countless Infinite, Innumerable, Myriad, Umpteen, Unending, Untold
Country(side), Countrified Annam, Arcadia, Bangladesh, Bolivia, Boondocks, Bucolic, Champaign, Clime, Colchis, Edom, Enchorial, Farmland, Fatherland, Greenwood, High, Jordan, Karoo, Karroo, → **LAND**, Lea, Lee, Low, Mongolia, Motherland, Nation, Nature, Parish, Paysage, People, Province, Rangeland, Realm, Region, Republic, Rural, Rustic, Satellite, Scenery, Scythia, Soil, State, Sultanate, The sticks, Thrace, Tundra, Tweedy, Veld, Venezuela, Weald, Wold, Yemen
Country girl Amaryllis
Country house Hall, Manor, Quinta
Countryman Arcadian, Bacon, Boor, Culchie, Hayseed, Hick, Hillbilly, Hodge, National, Native, Peasant, Ruralist, Un, Yokel
Coup Blow, Deal, KO, Move, Putsch, Scoop, Stroke, Treason
Coup d'etat Putsch
Coupé Cabriolet, Landaulet
Couple(r), Coupling Acoustic, Ally, Attach, Band, Brace, Bracket, Connect, Direct, Duet, Duo, Dyad, Enlink, Fishplate, Flange, Galvanic, Gemini, Geminy, Hitch, Interlock, Item, → **JOIN**, Marrow, Marry, Mate, Meng(e), Ment, Ming, Octave, Pair, Pr, Relate, Shackle, Tenace, Tie, Tirasse, Turnbuckle, Tway, Union, Unite, Universal, Voltaic, Wed, Yoke
Couple of ducks Spectacles
Couplet Distich, Heroic, Riding-rhyme
Coupon(s) Ration, Ticket, Voucher

Courage(ous) Balls, Ballsy, Bottle, Bravado, Bravery, Bulldog, Cojones, Daring, Derring-do, Dutch, Fortitude, Gallantry, Game, Gimp, Grit, Gumption, Guts, Hardihood, Hardy, Heart, Heroism, Indomitable, Lion-heart, Macho, Manful, Mettle, Moral, Moxie, Nerve, Pluck, Prowess, Rum, Spirit, Spunk, Stalwart, Steel, Stomach, Valiant, Valour, Wight

Courgette Zucchini

Courier Deliveryman, Estafette, Fed-EX, Guide, Harbinger, Herald, → **MESSENGER**, Postillion, Postman

Course(s) Access, Afters, Aim, Aintree, Antipasto, Appetiser, Arroyo, Ascot, Assault, Atlantic, Back straight, Barge, Bearing, Beat, Belt, Canal, Career, Channel, Chantilly, Chase, Circuit, Civics, Collision, Consommé, Conversion, Correspondence, Crash, Current, Curriculum, Cursus, Daltonism, Damp(-proof), Dessert, Diadrom, Dish, Dromic, Easting, Entrée, Epsom, Fish, Food, Foundation, Going, Golf, Goodwood, Greats, Gut, Heat, Hippodrome, Induction, Isodomon, Lacing, Lane, Lap, Layer, Leat, Leet, Line, Lingfield, Links, Longchamp, Magnetic, Main, Meal, Meat, Mess, Mizzen, Newbury, Newmarket, Nine-hole, Northing, Nulla, Obstacle, → **OF COURSE**, Orbit, Orthodromic, Period, Policy, PPE, Practicum, Procedure, Process, Programme, Progress, Pursue, Quadrivium, Race, → **RACETRACK**, Raik, Ravioli, Refresher, Regimen, Rhumb, Ride, Ring, Rink, Road, Rota, Route, Routine, Run, Rut, Sandown, Sandwich, Semester, Seminar, Series, Slalom, Sorbet, Soup, Southing, Stadium, Starter, Stearage, Steerage, Step(s), Straight, Stratum, Streak, Stream, Stretch, Stretching, String, Syllabus, Tack, Tanride, Tenor, Track, Trade, Trail, Trend, Troon, Vector, Via media, Water table, Way, Wearing, Wentworth, Westing

Court(ier), Courtship, Courtyard Ad(vantage), Address, Admiralty, Appellate, Arbitration, Arches, Areopagus, Atrium, Attention, Audience, Audiencia, Aula, Banc, Bar, Basecourt, Bench, Beth Din, Bishop's, Boondock, Caerleon, Camelot, Canoodle, Caravanserai, Cassation, Centre, Chancery, Chase, Clay, Cloister-garth, Commercial, Commissary, Commission, Conscience, Conservancy, Consistory, County, Criminal, Crown, CS, Ct, Curia, Curia Regis, Curtilage, Cutcher(r)y, Date, Dedans, Deuce, Dicastery, Diplock, District, Divisional, Doctor's Commons, Domestic, Duchy, Durbar, Dusty Feet, En tout cas, Evora, Eyre, Faculties, Federal, Fehm(gericht), Fehmgerichte, Fiars, Fifteen, Forensic, Forest, Forum, Fronton, Galleria, Garth, Go steady, Grass, Guildenstern, Halimot(e), Hampton, Hard, High, High Commission, Hof, Holy See, Hustings, Hypaethron, Inferior, Innyadr, Intermediate, Invite, Jack, Judicatory, Justice, Juvenile, Kachahri, Kacheri, Kangaroo, Keys, King, King's Bench, Kirk Session, Knave, Law, Leet, Lobby, Lyon, Magistrate's, Majlis, Marshalsea, Mash, Moot, Old Bailey, Open, Osric, Palace, Parvis, Patio, Peristyle, Petty Sessions, Philander, Piepowder, Police, Porte, Praetorium, Prerogative, Presbytery, Prize, Probate, Provincial, Provost, Quad, Quarter Sessions, Queen, Queen's Bench, Racket, Request, Retinue, Romance, Rosenkrantz, Royal, St James's, Sanhedrim, Sanhedrin, Scottishland, See, Service, Session, Sheriff, Shire-moot, Small-claims, Spoon, Stannary, Star Chamber, Sudder, Sue, Suitor, Superior, Supreme, Swanimote, Sweetheart, Synod, Thane, Thegn, Traffic, Trial, Tribunal, Vehm, Vehmgericht(e), Vestibulum, Walk out, Ward, Wardmote, Wench, Woo, World, Wow, Yard, Youth

Courteous, Courtesy Affable, Agreement, Bow, Chivalry, Civil, Comity, Devoir, Etiquette, Fair, Genteel, Gentilesse, Gentility, Gracious, Hend, Polite, Politesse, Refined, Strain, Urbanity, Well-mannered

Courtesan Anonyma, Aspasia, Bianca, Bona-roba, Delilah, Demi-monde, Demi-rep, Geisha, Hetaera, Lais, Lampadion, Lorette, Madam, Phryne, Plover, Pornocracy, Prostitute, Stallion, Thais

Courtly Aulic, Chivalrous, Cringing, Dignified, Flattering, Refined

Court-martial Drumhead

Courtyard Area, Atrium, Close, Cortile, Enceinte, Garth, Marae, Patio, Quad

Cousin(s) Bette, Cater, Country, Coz, Cross, First, German, Kin, Kissing, Parallel, Robin, Second, Skater

Couthy Bien, Nice

Couturier Designer, Dior, Dressmaker, Hartnell

Cove Abraham's, Arm, Bay, Bight, Buffer, Creek, Cure, Gink, Grot, Guy, Hithe, Hythe, Inlet, Lulworth, Nook

Covenant(er) Abrahamic, Alliance, Appurtenant, Bond, Contract, Hillmen, Pledge, Restrictive, Testament, Warranty, Whiggamore

Coventry Isolation

Cover(ed), Covering Adventitia, Air, A l'abri, Amnion, Antependium, Antimacassar, Apron, Aril, Armour, Attire, Awning, Barb, Bard(s), Bark, Bathrobe, Bedspread, Bestrew, Bind, Blanket, Bodice, Bonnet, Brood, Bubblewrap, Bury, Cache-sex, Camouflage, Canopy, Cap, Caparison, Cape, Capsule, Cartonnage, Casing, Casque, Catch-all, Caul, Ceil, Ciborium, Cladding, Clapboard, Cleithral, Clithral, Coat, Cocoon, Coleorhiza, Conceal, Cope, Copyright, Cosy, Cot, Counterpane, Cour, Covert, Cowl, Crust, Curtain, Deadlight, Debruised, Deck, Deputise, Dividend, Dome, Drape(t), Dripstone, Duchesse, Dusting, Dust-sheet, Duvet, Eiderdown, Encase, Endue, Enguard, Enlace, Ensheathe, Enshroud, Envelop(e), Enwrap, Exoderm(is), Exoskeleton, Extra, Eyelid, Face, Falx, Fanfare, Felting, Fielder, Figleaf, Fingerstall, First-day, Flashing, Flown, Fother, Front, Gaiter, Gambado, Glove, Gobo, Grolier, Ground, Groundsheet, Hap, Harl, Hat, Hatch, Havelock, Heal, Heel, Hejab, Hele, Hell, Helmet, Hide, Hijab, Hood, Housing, Hubcap, Immerse, Incase, Include, Indument, Indusium, Inmask, Insulate, Insurance, Insure, Jacket, Lag, Lambrequin, Lay, Leap, Leep, Legging, Legwarmer, Lid, Ligger, Liner, Loose, Manche, Mantle, Mask, Mat, Metal, Mort-cloth, Mount, Muffle, Mulch, Notum, Numnah, Obscure, OC, Occlude, On, Oose, Operculum, Orillion, Orlop, Overlap, Overlay, Overnet, Overwrap, Pad, Palampore, Palempore, Pall, Pand, Panoply, Parcel, Partlet, Pasties, Patch, Patent, Pavilion, Pebbledash, Pelmet, Periderm, Perigone, Pillow sham, Plaster, Plate, Pleura, Point, Pseudonym, Pullover, Quilt, Radome, Redingote, Regolith, Riza, Robe, Roof, Roughcast, Rug, Run, Sally, Screen, Serviette, Setting, Sheath, Sheet, Shell, Shelter, Shield, Shower, Shrink-wrap, Shroud, Shuck, Skin, Slipcase, Smokescreen, Solleret, Span, Spat, Splashback, Stand-by, Stifle, Stomacher, Strew, Strow, Superfrontal, Superimpose, Swathe, Tampian, Tampion, Tapadera, Tapis, Tarpaulin, Teacosy, Tectorial, Tectum, Tegmen, Tegument, Tent, Test(a), Tester, Thatch, Thimble, Thumbstall, Tick(ing), Tidy, Tile, Tilt, Tonneau, Top, Trapper, Trench, Trip, Turtleback, Twill, Twilt, Umbrella, Up, Upholster, Valance, Veale, Veil, Vele, Veneer, Ventail, Vert, Vesperal, Vest, Vestiture, Visor, Volva, Wainscot, Warrant, Waterdeck, Whelm, Whemmle, Whitewash, Whomble, Whommle, Whummle, Wrap, Wrappage, Wrapper, Wreathe, Yapp, Yashmak

Covert(ly) Clandestine, Copse, Privy, → **SECRET**, Shy, Sidelong, Sub rosa, Surreptitious, Tectrix, Ulterior

Covet(ed), Covetous Avaricious, Crave, Desiderata, Desire, Eager, Envy, Greedy, Hanker, Yearn

Cow(s) Adaw, Alderney, Amate, Appal, Awe, Ayrshire, Belted Galloway, Boss(y), Bovine, Brahmin, Browbeat, Cash, Cattle, Charolais, Colly, Crummy, Dant(on), Daunt, Dexter, Dsomo, Dun, Friesian, Galloway, Gally, Goujal, Guernsey, Hawkey, Hawkie, Heifer, Hereford, Intimidate, Jersey, Kouprey, Kyloe, Lea(h), Mart, Milch, Milker, Mog(gie), Moggy, Mooly, Muley, Mulley, Neat, Oppress, Overawe, Redpoll, Red Sindhi, Rother(-beast), Runt, Sacred, Santa Gertrudis, Scare, Simmental, Slattern, Springing, Steer, Step on, Stirk, Subact, Subjugate, Teeswater, Threaten, Unnerve, Vaccine, Zebu, Z(h)o

Coward(ice), Cowardly Bessus, Cat, Chicken, Cocoa, Craven, Cuthbert, Dastard, Dingo, Dunghill, Fraidy-cat, Fugie, Funk, Gutless, Hen, Hilding, Jessie, Lily-livered, Mangy, Meacock, Milk-livered, Nesh, Niddering, Nidderling, Nidering, Niderling, Niding, Nithing, Noel, Panty-waist, Poltroon, Pusillanimous, Recreant, Scaramouch(e), Scaredy cat, Sganarelle, Sissy, Slag, Sook, Squib, Viliaco, Viliago, Villagio, Villiago, Weak-spirited, White feather, Yellow, Yellow-belly

Cowboy, Cowgirl Broncobuster, Buckaroo, Cowpoke, Cowpuncher, Gaucho, Inexpert, Io, Jerrybuilder, Leger, Llanero, Neatherd, Puncher, Ranchero, Ritter, Roper, Shoddy, Vaquero, Waddie, Waddy, Wrangler

Cow-catcher Fender, Reata

Cower Cringe, Croodle, Crouch, Fawn, Quail, Ruck, Skulk, Wince

Cowl Bonnet, Capuchin, Granny, Hood, Kilmarnock

Cowpat Dung, Tath

Cowpox Vaccinia

Cowshed, Cowstall Byre, Crib, Shippen, Shippon, Stable, Stall, Staw

Cowslip Culver-key, Herb Peter, Pa(i)gle

Cox Helmsman, Steerer

Coxcomb Aril, Caruncle, Copple, Crest, Dandy, Dude, Fop, Jackanapes, Popinjay, Yellow-rattle

Coy Arch, Coquettish, Demure, Laithfu', Mim, Modest, Nice, Shamefast, → **SHY**, Skeigh, Skittish

Coyote Prairie-wolf, SD

CPRS Think tank

Crab(by), Crablike Apple, Attercop, Blue swimmer, Boston, Calling, Cancer, Cancroid, Cantankerous, Capernoity, Cock, Coconut, Daddy, Decapoda, Diogenes, Dog, Ethercap, Ettercap, Fiddler, Ghost, Grouch, Hard-shell, Hermit, Horseman, Horseshoe, King, Land, Limulus, Mantis, Mitten, Mud, Nebula, Ochidore, Oyster, Pagurian, Partan, Pea, Perverse, Podite, Roast, Robber, Rock, Sand, Saucepan-fish, Scrawl, Sentinel, Sidle, Soft-shell, Soldier, Spectre, Spider, Std, Stone, Velvet, Velvet-fiddler, Woolly-hand, Xiphosura, Zoea

▷ **Crab** *may indicate* an anagram

Crab-apple Scrog-bush, Scrog-buss

Crab-eater Urva

Crabs-eye Abrus

Crack(ed), Cracker(s), Cracking Ace, Ad-lib, Admirable, Bananas, Beaut, Biscuit, Bonbon, Break, Cat, Catalytic, Chap, Chasm, Chat, Chink, Chip, Chop, Clap, Cleave, Cleft, Cloff, Confab, Cranny, Craquelure, Craqueture, Craze, Cream, Crepitate, Crevasse, Crevice, Crispbread, Dawn, Decipher, Decode, Def, Doom, Dunt, Elite, Excellent, Fab, Fatiscent, Fent, Firework, First-rate, Fisgig, Fissure, Fizgig, Flaw, Flip-flop, Fracture, Gem, Go, Graham, Grike, Gryke, Gully, Hairline, Hit, Insane, Jibe, Joint, Knacker, Leak, Liar, Little-endian, Lulu, Matzo, Mot, Moulin, Oner, Peterman, Pleasantry, Pore, Praise, Prawn, Quarter, Quip, Rap, Report, Rhagades, Rictus, Rift, Rille, Rima, Rime, Rimous, Rive, Rock, Saltine, Sand, Seam, Shake, Shatter, Snap, Soda, Solve, Split, Spring, Squib, Sulcus, Toe, Top, Try, Waterloo, Wind shake, Yegg

Crackerjack Ace, Nailer, Trump

Crackle, Crackling Craze, Crepitation, Crepitus, Crinkle, Decrepitate, Fizz, Glaze, Rale, Skin, Static

Crackpot Nutter

Cracksman Burglar, Peterman, Raffles

Cradle Bassinet, Berceau, Book rest, Cat's, Cot, Crib, Cunabula, Hammock, Knife, Nestle, Newton's, Rocker

Craft(y) Aerostat, Arch, Art, Aviette, Barbola, Batik, Boat, Canal boat, Cautel, Cunning, Disingenuous, Finesse, Fly, Guile, Hydroplane, Ice-breaker, Insidious, Knack, Kontiki, Landing, Loopy, Machiavellian, Mister, Mystery, Oomiack, Pedalo, Powerboat, Reynard, Saic, Shallop, Ship, Shuttle, → **SKILL**, Slee, Sleeveen, Slim, Slippy, Sly, Slyboots, Sneaky, State, Subdolous, Subtil(e), Subtle, Suttle, Tender, Trade, Triphibian, Umiak, Underhand, Versute, → **VESSEL**, Wile, Workmanship

▷ **Craft** *may indicate* an anagram

Craftsman AB, Artificer, Artisan, Artist, Chippy, Coppersmith, Cutler, Ebonist, Fabergé, Finisher, Gondolier, Guild, Hand, Joiner, Journeyman, Mason, Mechanic, Morris,

Opificer, Potter, Tinsmith, Wainwright, Wright

Crag(gy) Coralline, Eyrie, Height, Heuch, Heugh, Krantz, Noup, Rock

Craig Ailsa

Cram(mer) Bag, Bone up, Candle-waster, Cluster, Craig, Fill, Gag, Gavage, Mug up, Neck, Pang, Prime, Revise, Rugged, Scar(p), Shoehorn, Spur, Stap, Stodge, Stow, Swat, Tuck

Cramp(ed) Agraffe, Charleyhorse, Claudication, Confine, Constrict, Crick, Hamper, Hamstring, Incommodious, Musician's, Myalgia, Narrow, Pinch, Poky, Potbound, Restrict, Rigor, Sardines, Scrivener's palsy, Squeeze, Stunt, Tenesmus, Tetany, Writer's

Crane, Crane-driver Adjutant-bird, Australian, Brolga, Cherry picker, Container, Davit, Deck, Demoiselle, Derrick, Dogman, Dragline, Gantry, Gooseneck, Grabbing, Herd, Heron, Hooper, Ichabod, Jenny, Jib, Jigger, Kenworthy, Luffing-jib, Native companion, Numidian, Rail, Sandhill, Sarus, Sedge, Seriema, Shears, Sheer, Siege, Stork, Stretch, Tower, Tulip, Whooper, Whooping, Winch

Crane-fly Daddy-long-legs, Leatherjacket, Tipulidae

Cranium Harnpan

Crank(y) Bell, Eccentric, Grouch, Handle, Lever, Mot, Perverse, Whim, Wince, Winch, Wind

Crap Feculence

Crash Accident, Bingle, Collapse, Disk, Ditch, Dush, Fail, Fall, Fragor, Frush, Intrude, Linen, Nosedive, Pile up, Plough into, Prang, Rack, Ram, Rote, Shock, Shunt, Slam, Smash, South Sea Bubble, Thunderclap, Topple, Wham, Wrap

▷ **Crashes** *may indicate* an anagram

Crass Coarse, Crude, Naff, Rough, Rude

Crate Banger, Biplane, Box, Case, Ceroon, Crib, Hamper, Jalopy, Langrenus, Petavius, Purbach, Sero(o)n, Soapbox, Tube

Crater Alphonsus, Aniakchak, Aristarchus, Aristotle, Askja, Autolycus, Bail(l)y, Blowhole, Caldera, Cavity, Cissing, Clavius, Copernicus, Fra Mauro, Grimaldi, Hipparchus, Hole, Hollow, Kepler, Kilauea, Maar, Meteor, Newton, Pit, Plato, Ptolemaeus, Pythagoras, Schickard, Sinus iridum, Theophilus, Tycho

Cravat Ascot, Neckatee, Neck-cloth, Oerlay, Overlay, Scarf, Soubise, Steenkirk, Steinkirk, Tie

Crave, Craving Appetent, Appetite, Aspire, Beg, Beseech, Covet, Desire, Entreat, Gasp, Greed, Hanker, Hunger, Itch, Libido, Long, Lust, Malacia, Methomania, Munchies, Opsomania, Orexis, Pica, Polyphagia, Sitomania, The munchies, Thirst, Yearn, Yen

Craven Abject, Coward, Dastard, Hen, Recreant

Crawl(er) All fours, Aswarm, Australian, Back, Clamber, Creep, Cringe, Drag, Front, Grovel, Inchworm, Isopod, Jenkins, Lag, Lickspittle, Pub, Reptile, Scramble, Scrome, Side, Skulk, Slither, Snail, Swim, Sycophant, Tantony, Trail, Truckle, Trudge(o)n, Yes-man

Crayfish Astacology, Gilgie, Jilgie, Marron, Yabbie, Yabby

Crayon Chalk, Colour, Conté®, Pastel, Pencil, Sauce

Craze(d), Crazy Absurd, Ape, Apeshit, Avid, Barmy, Bats, Batty, Berserk, Bonkers, Break, Cornflake, Crack(ers), Crackpot, Cult, Daffy, Dement, Derange, Dingbats, Dippy, Distraught, Doiled, Doilt, Doolally, Doolally tap, Dottle, Dotty, Fad, Flaky, Flaw, Folie, Frantic, Furious, Furore, Furshlugginer, Gaga, Geld, Gonzo, Gyte, Haywire, Headbanger, Insane, Loco, Loony, Loopy, Lunatic, Madden, Maenad(ic), Mania, Manic, Mattoid, Melomania, Meshug(g)a, Moonstruck, Nuts, Out to lunch, Porangi, Potty, Psycho(path), Rage, Rave, Round the bend, Round the twist, Scatty, Screwball, Skivie, Slatey, Stunt, Thing, Troppo, Typomania, Unhinge, Wacko, W(h)acky, Wet, Whim, Wowf, Zany

▷ **Crazy** *may indicate* an anagram

Creak(y) Cry, Grate, Grind, Rheumatic, Scraich, Scraigh, Scroop, Seam, Squeak

Cream(y) Barrier, Bavarian, Best, Chantilly, Cherry-pick, Cleansing, Clotted, Cold, Cornish, Crème fraîche, Devonshire, Double, Elite, Foundation, Frangipane, Glacier, Heavy, Ivory, Jollop, Lanolin, Liniment, Lotion, Mousse, Off-white, Ointment, Opal,

Paragon, Pastry, Pick, Ream, Rich, Salad, Salve, Sillabub, Single, Skim, Smitane, Sour, Sun(screen), Syllabub, Vanishing, Whipped, Whipping

Crease Bowling, Crinkle, Crumple, → **FOLD**, Goal, Lirk, Pitch, Pleat, Popping, Return, Ridge, Ruck(le), Ruga, Rugose, Wreathe, Wrinkle

Create, Creation, Creative Arty, Brainstorm, Build, Cause, Coin, Compose, Continuous, Craft, Devise, Dreamtime, Engender, Establish, Fabricate, Forgetive, Form, Found, Generate, Genesis, Godhead, Hexa(h)emeron, Ideate, Imaginative, → **INVENT**, Kittle, Knit, Omnific, Oratorio, Originate, Produce, Promethean, Shape, Synthesis, Universe

Creator Ahura Mazda, Author, Demiurge, Demiurgus, God, Inventor, Maker, Ormazd, Ormuzd

Creature Animal, Ankole, Basilisk, Beast, Being, Bigfoot, Chevrotain, Cratur, Critter, Crittur, Indri, Man, Moner(on), Nekton, Saprobe, Sasquatch, Sphinx, Whiskey, Wight, Zoon

Credence, Credential(s) Certificate, Document, Papers, Qualifications, Shelf, Testimonial

Credibility, Credible, Credit(or), Credits Ascribe, Attribute, Belief, Billboard, Brownie points, Byline, Carbon, Catholic, Crawl, Easy terms, Esteem, Extended, Family, Ghetto, Honour, HP, Kite, Kudos, LC, Lender, Mense, On the nod, Post-war, Probable, Reliable, Renown, Repute, Revolving, Shylock, Social, Strap, Street, Tally, Tax, Tick, Title, Trust, Weight, Youth

Credulous Charlie, Gobe-mouches, Green, Gullible, Naive, Simple, Superstitious, Trusting

Creed Apostles', Athanasian, Belief, Doctrine, Faith, Ideology, Ism, Nicene, Ophism, Outworn, Persuasion, Sect, Tenet

Creek Antietam, Bay, Breaches, Cooper, Cove, Crick, Dawson, Estuary, Fleet, Geo, Gio, Goe, Indian, Inlet, Kill, Pow, Slough, Vae, Voe, Wick

Creel Basket, Hask, Scull, Skull

Creep(er), Creeping, Creeps, Creepy Ai, Ampelopsis, Arbutus, Aseismic, Boston ivy, Cleavers, Crawl, Eery, Function, Grew, Grovel, Grue, Heebie-jeebies, Heeby-jeebies, Herpetic, Honey, Inch, Insect, Ivy, Mission, Nerd, Nuthatch, Periwinkle, Pussyfoot, Repent, Reptant, Sarmentous, Sidle, Silverweed, Sittine, Skulk, Slink, Snake, Sneak(sby), Sobole(s), Soil, Steal, Toad, Tropaeolum, Truckle, Vinca, Vine, Virginia, Wickthing, Willies

Creeping Jenny Moneywort

Cremate, Cremation, Crematorium Burn, Char, Cinerarium, Ghat, Ghaut, Incinerate, Pyre, Sati, Suttee, Ustrinium

Creole Gullah, Haitian, Kriol, Papiamento, Tok Pisin

Crepe Blini, Blintz(e), Canton, Pancake

Crescent Barchan(e), Bark(h)an, Fertile, Growing, Lune(tte), Lunulate, Lunule, Meniscus, Moon, Red, Sickle, Waxing

Cress Cardamine, Garden, Hoary, Isatis, Pepperwort, Swine's, Thale, Wart, Water, Yellow

Crest(ed) Acme, Brow, Chine, Cimier, Cockscomb, Comb, Copple, Crista, Height, Kirimon, Knap, Mon, Peak, Pileate, Pinnacle, Plume, Ridge, Rig, Summit, Tappit, Tee, → **TOP**, Tufty, Wreath

Cretaceous Chalky, Senonian, The Chalk

Cretan Candiot(e), Minoan, Teucer

Crevasse Bergschrund, Chasm, Gorge, Rimaye

Crevice Chine, Cranny, Fissure, Interstice, Ravine, Vallecula

Crew Boasted, Company, Complement, Co-pilot, Core, Deckhand, Eight, Equipage, Four, Ground, Lot, Manners, Men, Oars, Prize, Sailors, Salts, Seamen, Ship men, Team, Teme, Torpid

Crew-cut Not(t)

Crib Cheat, Cot, Cowhouse, Cradle, Cratch, Filch, Horse, → **KEY**, Manger, Pony, Purloin,

Putz, Shack, Stall, Steal, Trot

Crick Cramp, Kink, Spasm

Cricket(er) Balm, Bat, Bosanquet, Botham, Bowler, Bradman, CC, Cicada, Dry-bob, Fly slip, French, Grade, Grasshopper, Grig, Hobbs, Hopper, Jerusalem, Katydid, Keeper, Knott, Lara, Leg, Long-leg, Long-off, Long-on, Longstop, March, May, Mid-on, Mole, Muggleton, Nightwatchman, Nurdle, Opener, Overs, Packer, Point, Pyjama, Shield, Single-wicket, Slip, Sobers, Stool, Stridulate, Tate, Test, Tettix, Tip and run, Vigoro, Warner, Wart-biter, Windball, Windies, Wisden, XI (gent), Yahoo

Crier Bellman, Herald, Muezzin, Niobe, Outrooper

Crikey Argh, Gosh

Crime Attentat, Barratry, Bias, Caper, Car jack, Chantage, Chaud-mellé, Computer, Corpus delicti, Ecocide, Embracery, Fact, Felony, Fraud, GBH, Graft, Hate, Heist, Iniquity, Inside job, Insider trading, Malefaction, Mayhem, Misdeed, Misdemeanour, → **OFFENCE**, Organised, Ovicide, Peccadillo, Perjury, Pilferage, Public wrong, Ram raid, Rap, Rape, Rebellion, → **SIN**, Stranger, Theft, Tort, Transgression, Treason, Victimless, Villa(i)ny, War, White-collar, Wrong

Crimea Balaclava

Criminal Accessory, Arsonist, Bandit, Bent, Bigamist, Bushranger, Chain gang, Chummy, Con, Cosa Nostra, Counterfeiter, Crack-rope, → **CROOK**, Culpable, Culprit, Delinquent, Desperado, Escroc, Fagin, Felon, Flagitious, Forensic, Gangster, Goombah, Hard men, Heavy, Heinous, Highbinder, Hitman, Hood(lum), Jailbird, Ladrone, Lag, Larcener, Lifer, Looter, Lowlife, Maf(f)ia, Malefactor, Maleficent, Malfeasant, Mens rea, Miscreant, Mob(ster), Molester, Ndrangheta, Nefarious, Nefast, Offender, Outlaw, Peculator, Pentito, Perp(etrator), Peterman, Prohibited, Racketeer, Ram raider, Receiver, Recidivist, Reprehensible, Rustler, Safe blower, Sinner, Snakehead, Thug, Triad, Triggerman, Underworld, Villain, Wicked, Wire, Yakuza, Yardie, Yegg

▷ **Criminal** *may indicate an anagram*

Criminologist Lombroso

Crimp Pleat, Quill

Crimson Carmine, Incarnadine, Modena, Red, Scarlet

Cringe, Cringing Cower, Creep, Crouch, Cultural, Fawn, Grovel, Recoil, Shrink, Sneaksby, Sycophantic, Truckle

Crinkle, Crinkly Rugate, Rugose

Crinoline Farthingale, Hoop

Cripple(d) Damage, Debilitate, Disable, Game, Hamstring, Handicap, Injure, → **LAME**, Lameter, Lamiter, Maim, Paralyse, Polio, Scotch, Spoil

Crisis Acme, Crunch, Drama, Emergency, Exigency, Fastigium, Fit, Flap, Head, Identity, Make or break, Midlife, Panic, Pass, Quarterlife, Shake-out, Solution, Suez, Test, Turn

Crisp(ness) Brisk, Clear, Crimp, Crunchy, Fire-edge, Fresh, Potato, Sharp, Short, Succinct, Terse

Crispin Sutor(ial)

Criss-cross Alternate, Fret, Interchange, Vein

Criteria, Criterion Benchmark, Gauge, Koch's postulates, Measure, Precedent, Proof, Rayleigh, Rule, Shibboleth, → **STANDARD**, Test, Touchstone

Critic(al), Criticise, Criticism Acute, Agate, Agee, Animadversion, Archer, Aristarch, Armchair, Arnold, Attack, Backbite, Badmouth, Bagehot, Barrack, Bellettrist, Berate, Bird, Blame, Boileau, Boo, Brickbat, Bucket, Captious, Carp, Castigate, Cavil, Censor(ious), → **CENSURE**, Climacteric, Clobber, Comment, Condemn, Connoisseur, Crab, Criticaster, → **CRUCIAL**, Crunch, Dangle, Decisive, Denigrate, Denounce, Deprecate, Desperate, Diatribe, Do down, Dutch uncle, Earful, Etain, Exacting, Excoriate, Exegesis, Fastidious, Fateful, Feuilleton, Flak, Flay, Fulminous, Gosse, Hammer, Harrumph, Higher, Important, Impugn, Inge, Inveigh, Judge, Judgemental, Knife-edge, Knock(er), Lambast, Lash, Leavis, Life and death, Literary, Lower, Masora(h), Mas(s)orete, Mordacious, Nag, Nasute, Nibble, Nice, Niggle, Nitpicker, Obloquy, Overseer, Pan, Pater, Peck, Puff,

Pundit, Quibble, Rap, Rebuke, Reprehend, Reproach, Review(er), Rip, Roast, Ruskin, Scalp, Scarify, Scathe, Scorn, Second guess, Serious, Severe, Sharp-tongued, Shaw, Sideswipe, Slag, Slam, Slashing, Slate, Sneer, Snipe, Spray, Stick, Stricture, Strop, Swipe, Tense, Textual, Thersitic, Threap, Tipping-point, Touch and go, Trash, Ultracrepidate, Upbraid, Urgent, Vet, Vitriol, Vituperation, Vivisect, Watershed, Zoilism

Croak(er) Creak, Crow, Die, Grumble, Gutturalise, Perish, Sciaena

Croatia(n) Cravates, Glagolitic, HR, Serb

Crochet Lace, Weave

Crock Chorrie, Crate, Jar, Mug, Pig, Pitcher, Pot, Potshard, Potshare, Potsherd, Stean(e)

Crockery Ceramics, China, Dishes, Earthenware, Oddment, Service, Sunbeam, Ware

▷ **Crocks** *may indicate* an anagram

Crocodile Cayman, File, Flat dog, Garial, Gavial, Gharial, Gotcha lizard, Line, Mud gecko, Mugger, River-dragon, Saltie, Saltwater, Sebek, Teleosaur(ian)

Crocus Autumn, Meadow saffron, Naked lady, Prairie, Saffron

Croesus Lydia

Croft Bareland, Pightle

Cromwell Antimonarchist, Ironside, Lord Protector, Noll, Oliver, Protector, Richard, Roundhead

Crone(s) Beldam(e), Ewe, Graeae, Hag, Mawkin, Ribibe, Rudas, Sibyl, Sybil, Trot, Trout, → **WITCH**

Crony Anile, Chum, Intimate, Mate, Pal, Sidekick

Crook(ed), Crookedness Adunc, Ajee, Aslant, Asymmetric, Awry, Bad, Bend, Bow, Cam, Camsheugh, Camsho(ch), Cock-eyed, Criminal, Cromb, Crome, Crosier, Crummack, Crummock, Crump, Curve, Dishonest, Elbow, Fraud, Heister, Hook, Ill, Indirect, Kam(me), Kebbie, Lituus, Malpractitioner, Obliquity, Operator, Shank, Sheep-hook, Shyster, Sick, Skew(whiff), Slick(er), Squint, Staff, Swindler, Thraward, Thrawart, Thrawn, Twister, Wonky, Wrong'un, Wry, Yeggman

▷ **Crooked** *may indicate* an anagram

Croon(er), Crooning Bing, Como, Lament, Lull, Monody, Murmur, Sing

Crop(ped), Cropping, Crops, Crop up Basset, Browse, Cash, Catch, Cereal, Clip, Cover, Craw, Cut, Distress, Dock, Emblements, Emerge, Energy, Epilate, Eton, Foison, Forage, → **HAIRCUT**, Harvest, Hog, Ingluvies, Kharif, Ladino, Lop, Milo, Not(t), Plant, Poll, Produce, Prune, Rabi, Rawn, Riding, Rod, Root, Scythe, Shear, Shingle, Silage, Sithe, Standing, Stow, Strip, Subsistence, Succession, Top, Truncate, White

Cropper Downfall, Header, Purler

Croquet (term) Peel, Rover, Wire

Croquette Kromesky, Quenelle, Rissole

Cross(ing), Crossbred Angry, Ankh, Ansate, Archiepiscopal, Banbury, Bandog, Basta(a)rd, Baster, Beefalo, Bestride, Bois-brule, Boton(n)e, Brent, Bridge, Bristling, Buddhist, Burden, Calvary, Cancel, Cantankerous, Canterbury, Capital, Capuchin, Cat(t) alo, Cattabus, Celtic, Channel, Charing, Chi, Chiasm(a), Choleric, Cleche, Clover-leaf, Compital, Constantine, Crosslet, Crosswalk, Crotchety, Crucifix, Crux, Cut, Decussate, Demi-wolf, Dihybrid, Double, Dso(mo), Dzobo, Eleanor, Encolpion, Faun, Fiery, Fitché, Fleury, Foil, Footbridge, Ford, Frabbit, Fractious, Frampold, Franzy, Funnel, Fylfot, Geneva, George, Grade, Greek, Hinny, Holy rood, Humette, Hybrid, Ill, Imp, Indignant, Interbreed, Intersect, Intervein, Iona, Iracund, Irascible, Irate, Irked, Iron, Jersian, Jerusalem, Jomo, Jumart, King's, Kiss, Krest, Ladino, Latin, Level, Liger, Lorraine, Lurcher, Maltese, Mameluco, Market, Mermaid, Military, Misfortune, Mix, Moline, Mongrel, Mule, Narky, Nattery, Node, Norman, Northern, Nuisance, Oblique, Obverse, Ordinary, Orthodox, Overpass, Overthwart, Papal, Patonce, Patriarchal, Pattée, Pectoral, Pedestrian, Pelican, Percolin, Plumcot, Plus, Pommé, Potence, Potent, Preaching, Puffin, Quadrate, Railway, Ratty, Reciprocal, Red, Roman, Rood, Rose, Rosy, Rouen, Rouge, Rubicon, Ruthwell, Sain, St Andrew's, St Anthony's, St George's, St Patrick's, St Peter's, Saltier, Saltire, Sambo, Satyr, Shirty, Sign, Snappy, Southern, Span, Splenetic, Strid,

Svastika, Swastika, T, Tangelo, Tau, Tayberry, Ten, Testy, Thraw, Thwart, Tiglon, Tigon, Times, Toucan, Transit, Transom, Transverse, Traverse, Tree, Unknown, Urdé, Vexed, Vext, Victoria, → **VOTE**, Weeping, Whippet, Wholphin, Wry, X, Yakow, Zambo, Zebra(ss), Zebrinny, Zebroid, Zebrula, Zebrule, Zedonk, Zhomo, Z(h)o, Zobu

▷ **Cross** *may indicate* an anagram

▶ **Cross-bar** *see* CROSSPIECE

▶ **Crossbeam** *see* CROSSPIECE

Cross-bearer Crucifer

Cross-bill Metagnathous

Cross-bones Marrowbones

Cross-bow Arbalest, Bal(l)ista

Cross-country Langlauf, Overland

Cross-dress(er), Cross-dressing En travesti, Eonism, Gender-bender

Cross-examination, Cross-examine Elenctic, Grill, Interrogate, Question, Targe

Cross-eyed Skelly(-eyed), Squint

Crossfertilisation Allogamy, Heterosis, Hybrid vigour, Xenogamy

Cross-grained Ill-haired, Mashlam, Mashlim, Mashlock, Mashlum, Mas(h)lin, Stubborn

Crosspiece, Cross-bar, Cross beam, Cross-timber Bar, Cancelli, Fingerground, Footrail, Inter-tie, Lierne, Phillipsite, Putlock, Putlog, Quillon, Serif, Seriph, Stempel, Stemple, Stretcher, Stull, Swingle-tree, Toggle, Transom, Trave, Whiffle-tree, Whipple-tree, Yoke

Crossroads Carfax, Carfox, Carrefour, Compital, Junction, Soap

Crossword Cryptic, Grid, Puzzle, Quickie

Crotchet(y) Eccentric, Fad, Fancy, Grouch, Kink, Liverish, Quarter-note, Toy

Crouch Bend, Cringe, Falcade, Fancy, Lordosis, Ruck, Set, Squat, Squinch

Croup Angina, Cough, Kink, Rump

Crow Big-note, Bluster, Boast, Brag, Carrion, Chewet, Chough, Corbie, Corvus, Crake, Currawong, Daw, Flute-bird, Gab, Gloat, Gorcrow, Hooded, Hoodie, Huia, Jackdaw, Jim(my), Murder, Piping, Raven, Rook, Saddleback, Scald, Skite, Squawk, Swagger, Vaunt

Crowbar Gavelock, James, Jemmy, Lever

Crowd(ed) Abound, Army, Bike, Boodle, Bumper, Bunch, Byke, Caboodle, Clutter, Concourse, Congest(ed), Cram, Crush, Crwth, Dedans, Dense, Doughnut, Drove, Fill, Flock, Galere, Gang, Gate, Gathering, Herd, Horde, → **HOST**, Huddle, Hustle, Jam, Jam-packed, Lot, Many, Meinie, Mein(e)y, Menyie, Mob, Mong, Multitude, Ochlo-, Pack, Pang, Populace, Press, Rabble, Raft, Ragtag, Ram, Ratpack, Ring, Ruck, Scrooge, Scrouge, Scrowdge, Scrum, Serr(é), Shoal, Shove, Slew, Slue, Squash, Squeeze, Stuff, Swarm, Swell, Thick, Thrang, Three, Throng, Trinity, Varletry

Crowfoot Gilcup, Reate

Crown Acme, Apex, Bays, Bull, Camp, Cantle, Cap, Capernoity, Cidaris, Civic, Coma, Corona, Cr, Diadem, Ecu, Engarland, Enthrone, Fillet, Garland, Gloria, Haku, Head, Headdress, Instal, Iron, Ivy, Krantz, Laurel, Monarch, Mural, Naval, Nole, Noll, Northern, Noul(e), Nowl, Olive, Optical, Ore, Ovation, Pate, Peak, Pediment, Pschent, Sconce, Stephen's, Taj, Thick'un, Tiar(a), → **TOP**, Triple, Triumphal, Trophy, Vallary, Vertex

Crucial Acute, Critical, Essential, Key, Paramount, Pivotal, Quintessential, Vital, Watershed

Crucible Cruset, Melting-pot, Vessel

Crucifix(ion), Crucify Calvary, Cross, Golgotha, Mortify, Rood, Torment, Torture

Crud Red snow

Crude(ness) Bald, Brash, Brute, Coarse, Earthy, Halfbaked, Immature, Incondite, No tech, Primitive, Raunch, Raw, Rough, Rough and ready, Rough-hewn, Rough-wrought, Tutty, Uncouth, Unrefined, Vulgar, Yahoo

Cruel(ty) Barbarous, Bloody, Brutal, Cut-throat, Dastardly, De Sade, Draconian, Fell,

Fiendish, Flinty, Hard, Heartless, Immane, Inhuman(e), Machiavellian, Mental, Neronic, Pitiless, Raw, Remorseless, Sadistic, Stern, Tiger, Tormentor, Tyranny, Unmerciful, Vicious, Wanton

▷ **Cruel** *may indicate* an anagram

Cruet Ampulla, Condiments, Decanter

Cruise(r) Booze, Busk, Cabin, Coast, Nuke, Orientation, Prowl, Rove, Sail, Sashay, Ship, Tom, Travel, Trip, Voyager

Crumb(le), Crumbly, Crumbs Coo, Cor, Decay, Disintegrate, Ee, Fragment, Friable, Golly, Law, Leavings, Moulder, Mull, Murl, Nesh, Nirl, Ort, Panko, Particle, Ped, Pulverise, Raspings, Rot, Rotter

Crumpet Dish, Girl, Muffin, Nooky, Pash, Pikelet

Crumple Collapse, Crunkle, Crush, Raffle, Scrunch, Wrinkle

Crunch(y) Abdominal, Acid test, Chew, Craunch, Crisp, Gnash, Graunch, Grind, Munch, Occlude, Scranch

Crusade(r) Baldwin, Campaign, Cause, Lionheart, Pilgrim, Tancred, Templar

Crush(ed), Crusher, Crushing Acis, Anaconda, Annihilate, Beetle, Bow, Breakback, Champ, Comminute, Conquer, Contuse, Cranch, Crunch, Defeat, Destroy, Graunch, Grind, Hug, Humble, Jam, Knapper, Levigate, Litholapaxy, Mangle, Mash, Mill, Molar, Mortify, Nib, Oppress, Overcome, Overwhelm, Pash, Policeman, Pound, Press, Pulp, Pulverise, Quash, Quell, Ruin, Schwarmerei, Scotch, Scrum, Scrumple, Scrunch, Smash, Squabash, Squash, Squeeze, Squelch, Squish, Stamp, Stave, Steam-roll, Stove, Stramp, Suppress, Telescope, Trample, Tread, Vanquish

Crusoe Robinson, Selkirk

Crust(y) Argol, Beeswing, Cake, Coating, Coffin, Continental, Cover, Crabby, Craton, Fur, Gratin, Heel, Horst, Ice fern, Kissing, Kraton, Lithosphere, Oceanic, Orogen, Osteocolla, Pie, Reh, Rind, Rine, Sal, Salband, Scab, Scale, Shell, Sial, Sima, Sinter, Sordes, Surly, Tartar, Teachie, Tectonics, Terrane, Tetchy, Upper, Wine-stone

Crustacea(n) Amphipod, Barnacle, Brachyuran, Branchiopoda, Camaron, Cirriped, Cirripede, Cirripid, Cladoceran, Copepod, Crab, Crayfish, Cumacean, Cyclops, Cyprid, Cypris, Daphnia, Decapod(a), Entomostraca, Euphausia, Fishlouse, Foot-jaw, Gribble, Isopod, Krill, Langoustine, Limulus, Lobster, Macrura, Malacostracan, Marine borer, Maron, Nauplius, Nephrops, Ostracoda, Pagurian, Phyllopod, Prawn, Red seed, Rhizocephalan, Sand-hopper, Sand-skipper, Scampi, Scampo, Schizopod, Sea slater, Shellfish, Shrimp, Slater, Squilla, Stomatopod, Woodlouse, Yabbie, Yabby

Crutch Morton's, Potent

Crux Essence, Nub

Cry(ing) Aha, Alalagmus, Alew, Baa, Banzai, Bark, Battle, Bawl, Bay, Bell, Bemoan, Bill, Blat, Bleat, Bleb, Blub(ber), Boo, Boohoo, Boom, Bray, Bump, Caramba, Caw, Cheer, Chevy, Chirm, Chivy, Clang, Cooee, Crake, Croak, Crow, Dire, Euoi, Eureka, Evoe, Evoke, Exclaim, Eye-water, Fall, Field-holler, Gardyloo, Gathering, Geronimo, Gowl, Greet, Halloo, Harambee, Haro, Harrow, Havoc, Heigh, Hemitrope, Herald, Hinny, Hoicks, Holler, Honk, Hoo, Hoop, Hosanna, Hout(s)-tout(s), Howl, Humph, Io, Kaw, Low, Mewl, Miaou, Miau(l), Miserere, Mourn, Night-shriek, Nix, O(c)hone, Oi, Olé, Ow, Pugh, Rabbito(h), Rallying, Rivo, Sab, Scape, Scream, Screech, Sell, Sese(y), Sessa, → **SHOUT**, Shriek, Slogan, Snivel, Snotter, Sob, Soho, Sola, Squall, Squawk, Street, Sursum corda, Tally-ho, Tantivy, Umph, Vagitus, View-halloo, Vivat, Vociferate, Wail, War, War whoop, Watchword, Waterworks, Waul, Wawl, Weep, Westward ho, Whammo, Whee(ple), Whimper, Whine, Whinny, Whoa, Whoop, Winge, Wolf, Yammer, Yawl, Yelp, Yicker, Yikker, Yip, Yippee, Yodel, Yo-heave-ho, Yo-ho-ho, Yoick, Yoop, Yowl

Crypt(ic) Catacomb, Cavern, Chamber, Crowde, Encoded, Enigmatic, Esoteric, Favissa, Grotto, Hidden, Obscure, Occult, Secret, Sepulchre, Short, Steganographic, Tomb, Unclear, Undercroft, Vault

Cryptaesthesia ESP

Cryptogam Acotyledon, Acrogen, Fern(-ally), Moss, Pteridophyte, Steganograph

Cryptogram, Cryptographer, Cryptography Decoder, Public-key, Steganograph, Ventris

Crystal(s), Crystal-gazer, Crystalline, Crystallise Allotriomorphic, Axinite, Baccara(t), Beryl, Candy, Citrine, Clathrate, Clear, Cleveite, Copperas, Coumarin, Cumarin, Cut-glass, Dendrite, Druse, Effloresce, Elaterin, Enantiomorph, Epitaxy, Erionite, Form, Fuchsin(e), Geode, Glass, Hemihedron, Hemimorphic, Hemitrope, Ice-stone, Ideal, Imazadole, Jarosite, Lase, Lead, Liquid, Lithium, Love-arrow, Macle, Macro-axis, Melamine, Mixed, Needle, Nematic, Nicol, Orthogonal, Orthorhombic, Pellucid, Penninite, Pericline, Phenocryst, Piezo, Piezoelectric, Pinacoid, Pinakoid, Prism, Pseudomorph, Purin(e), Quartz, R(h)aphide, R(h)aphis, Rhinestone, Rock, Rotenone, Rubicelle, Scryer, Shoot, Silica, Skatole, Skryer, Smectic, Snowflake, Sorbitol, Spar, Spherulite, Spicule, Table, Tina, Tolan(e), Trichite, Triclinic, Trilling, Twin(ned), Wafer, Watch-glass, Xanthene, Xenocryst, Yag

Cub(s) Baby, Kit, Lionet, Novice, Pup, Sic, Whelp, Wolf, Youth

Cuba C

Cube, Cubic, Cubist Bath, Braque, Cu, Dice, Die, Magic, Necker, Nosean, Quadrate, Rubik's®, Serac, Smalto, Snub, Solid, Stere, Stock, Tesseract

Cubicle Alcove, Booth, Carrel(l), Stall

Cuckold Actaeon, Cornute, Graft, Homer, Lenocinium, Two-time, Vulcan's badge, Wittol

Cuckoo Ament, Ani, April fool, Bird, Brain-fever bird, Chaparral cock, Dotty, Gouk, Gowk, Inquiline, Insane, Koekoea, Koel, → **MAD**, Mental, Piet-my-vrou, Rabid, Stupid

▷ **Cuckoo** *may indicate* an anagram

Cuckoopint Arum

Cucumber Bitter-apple, Choko, Colocynth, Coloquintida, Dill, Elaterium, Gherkin, Pickle, Sea-slug, Squirting, Trepang, Wolly

Cuddle, Cuddly Canoodle, Caress, Clinch, Embrace, Fondle, Hug, Inarm, Nooky, Smooch, Smuggle, Snog, Snuggle, Zaftig

Cudgel Alpeen, Ballow, Bludgeon, Brain, Club, Cosh, Drub, Fustigate, Oaken towel, Plant, Rack, Rung, Shillelagh, Souple, Stick, Swipple, Tan, Towel, Truncheon

Cue Billiard, Cannonade, Catchword, Feed, Feed-line, Half-butt, Hint, Mace, → **PROMPT**, Reminder, Rod, Sign, Signal, Wink

Cuff Box, Buffet, Clout, French, Gauntlet, Iron, Muffettee, Rotator, Storm, Strike, Swat

Cuirass Armour, Corselet, Lorica

Cuisine Balti, Bourgeoise, Cookery, Food, Lean, Menu, Minceur, Nouvelle

Cul-de-sac Blind (alley), Dead-end, Impasse, Loke

Cull Gather, Pick, Reap, Select, Thin, Weed

Culminate, Culmination Apogean, Apogee, Climax, Conclusion, Crest, End, Head, Orgasm

Culpable Blameworthy, Guilty

Cult Aum Shinrikyo, Cabiri, Candomble, Cargo, Creed, Fertility, Flower power, Macumba, New Age, Personality, Rastafarian, Sect, Shango, Shinto, Snake, Voodoo, Wicca, Worship

Cultivate(d), Cultivation, Cultivator Agronomy, Arty, Breed, Civilise, Developed, Dig, Dress, Ear, Ere, Farm, Garden, Genteel, Grow, Hoe, Hydroponics, Improve, Labour, Plough, Polytunnel, Pursue, Raise, Reclaim, Refine, Sative, Sophisticated, Tame, Tasteful, Till, Tilth, Wainage, Woo, Work

Culture(d), Cultural Abbevillean, Acheulean, Acheulian, Agar, Art(y), Aurignacian, Azilian, Bacterian, Bel esprit, Brahmin, Broth, Canteen, Capsian, Civil(isation), Clactonian, Club, Compensation, Corporate, Dependency, Enterprise, Ethnic, Experiment, Explant, Fine arts, Folsom, Gel, Gravettian, Grecian, Halafian, Hallstatt, Hip-hop, Humanism, Intelligentsia, Kultur(kreis), La Tène, Learning, Levallois, Madelenian, Magdalenian, Maglemosean, Maglemosian, Meristem, Minoan, Monolayer, Mousterian, New Age, Organisational, Perigordian, Polish, Polite, Pure, Refinement, Solutrean, Sophisticated, Starter, Strepyan, Suspension, Tardenoisian, Tissue, Villanovan, Water

Cumbersome Clumsy, Heavy, Lumbering, → **UNWIELDY**
Cunctator Dilatory
Cuneiform Wedge(d)
Cunning Arch, Art, Artifice, Astute, Cautel, Craft(y), Deceit, Deep, Devious, Down,
Finesse, Foxy, Guile, Insidious, Leary, Leery, Machiavellian, Quaint, Skill, Slee(kit),
Sleight, Slim, Sly(boots), Smart, Sneaky, Stratagem, Subtle, Vulpine, Wheeze, Wile, Wily
Cup(s), Cupped Aecidium, America's, Beaker, Bledisloe, Calcutta, Calix, Calyculus,
Cantharus, Ca(u)p, Chalice, Claret, Communion, Cotyle, Cruse, Cupule, Cyathus, Cylix,
Davis, Demitasse, Deoch-an-doruis, Deuch-an-doris, Dish, Doch-an-dorach, Dop, Egg,
European, Eyebath, FA, Fairs, Final, Fingan, Finjan, Fruit, Gemma, Glenoid, Goblet,
Grace, Grease, Gripe's egg, Hanap, Horn, Kylix, Loving, Melbourne, Merry, Monstrance,
Moustache, Mug, Noggin, Nut, Optic, Pannikin, Paper, Parting, Planchet, Plate, Poley,
Posset, Pot, Procoelous, Quaff, Quaich, Quaigh, Rhyton, Rider, Ryder, Sangrado,
Scyphus, Sippy, Stem, Stirrup, Suction, Tantalus, Tass(ie), Tastevin, Tazza, Tea-dish, Tig,
Tot, → **TROPHY**, Tyg, UEFA, Volva, Waterloo, World
▷ **Cup** *may indicate* a bra size
Cup-bearer Ganymede, Hebe
Cupboard Airing, Almery, Almirah, A(u)mbry, Armoire, Beauf(f)et, Cabinet, Chiffonier,
Chiff(o)robe, Closet, Coolgardie safe, Court, Credenza, Dresser, Encoignure, Fume,
Livery, Locker, Meat-safe, Press, Walk-in
Cup-holder Hanaper, Hebe, Plinth, Saucer, Zarf, Zurf
Cupid Amoretto, Amorino, Archer, Blind, Bow-boy, Cherub, Dan, Eros, Love, Putto
Cupola Belfry, Dome, Tholos
Cup-shaped Glenoid, Poculiform
Cur Dog, Hound, Messan, Mongrel, Mutt, Pi-dog, Scab, Scoundrel, Whelp, Wretch, Yap
Curare, Curari Ourali, Poison, Wourali
Curassow Crax
Curate Barman, Minister, Nathaniel, Padré, Perpetual, Priest
Curator Aquarist
Curb Bit, Brake, Bridle, Check, Clamp, Coaming, Dam, Edge, Puteal, Rein, Restrain,
Restringe, Rim, Snub, Well
Curd(s) Bean, Cheese, Junket, Lapper(ed)-milk, Lemon, Skyr, Tofu
Curdle Clot, Congeal, Earn, Erne, Grue, Lopper, Posset, Ren, Rennet, Run, Set, Sour,
→ **TURN**, Whig, Yearn
Cure(d), Curative Ameliorate, Amend, Antidote, Antirachitic, Bloater, Cold turkey,
Dry-salt, Dun, Euphrasy, Faith, Fix, Flue, Ginseng, Heal, Heal-all, Heat treatment,
Hobday, Hydropathy, Jadeite, Jerk, Kipper, Laetrile, Magic bullet, Medicinal, Nature,
Nostrum, Panacea, Park-leaves, Prairie oyster, → **PRESERVE**, Reast, Recover, Recower,
Reest, Relief, Remede, Remedy, Re(i)st, Restore, Salt, Salve, Save, Serum, Smoke,
Smoke-dry, Snakeroot, Tan, → **TREATMENT**, Tutsan, Water
▷ **Cure** *may indicate* an anagram
Curfew Bell, Gate, Prohibit, Proscribe
Curie Ci
Curio, Curiosity, Curious Agog, Bibelot, Bric a brac, Ferly, Freak, Inquisitive,
Interesting, Into, Meddlesome, Nos(e)y, Objet d'art, Objet de vertu, Odd, Peculiar,
Prurience, Quaint, Rarity, Rum, Spectacle, → **STRANGE**, Wondering
▷ **Curious(ly)** *may indicate* an anagram
Curium Cm
Curl(s), Curler, Curling, Curly Ailes de pigeon, Bev, Bonspiel, Cirrus, Coil, Crimp,
Crimple, Crinkle, Crisp, Crocket, Dildo, Earlock, Eddy, Favourite, Frisette, Friz(z),
Frizzle, Heart-breaker, Hog, Inwick, Kiss, Leaf, Loop, Love-lock, Outwick, Perm, Pin,
Quiff, Repenter, Ringlet, Roll, Roulette, Scroll, Shaving, Spiral, Spit, Tong, Tress, Trunk,
Twiddle, → **TWIST**, Ulotrichous, Undée, Wave, Wind
Curlew Bird, Whaup, Whimbrel

Curmudgeon Boor, Churl, Grouch, Route, Runt

Currant Berry, Flowering, Raisin, Rizard, Rizzar(t), Rizzer

Currency Cash, Circulation, → **COIN**, Coinage, Decimal, Euro(sterling), Finance, Fractional, Jiao, Kip, Koruna, Managed, Monetary, → **MONEY**, Prevalence, Reserve, Soft

▷ **Currency** *may indicate* a river

Current Abroad, AC, Actual, Alternating, Amp(ere), Amperage, California, Canary, Contemporaneous, Cromwell, Dark, DC, Direct, Draught, Drift, Dynamo, Ebbtide, Eddy, Electric, El Nino, Emission, Equatorial, Euripus, Existent, Faradic, Flow, Foucault, Galvanic(al), Going, Gyre, Headstream, Hot button, Humboldt, Hummock, I, Immediate, Inst, Intermittent, In vogue, Japan, Kuroshio, Labrador, Live, Maelstrom, Millrace, Modern, Newsy, North Atlantic, Now, Ongoing, Output, Peru, Present, Present day, Prevalent, Pulsating, Race, Rapid, Rife, Rip, Roost, Running, Ryfe, Stream, Thames, Thermal, Thermionic, Tide, Tideway, Topical, Torrent, Turbidity, Underset, Undertow, Updraught, Up-to-date

Curriculum Core, Cursal, National, Programme

Curry Bhuna, Brush, Comb, Cuittle, Dhansak, Fawn, Groom, Ingratiate, Korma, Madras, Ruby (Murray), Skater, Spice, Tan, Tandoori, Turmeric, Vindaloo

Curse Abuse, Anathema, Badmouth, Ban, Bane, Beshrew, → **BLASPHEME**, Blast, Chide, Dam(me), Damn, Dee, Drat, Ecod, Egad, Evil, Excommunicate, Execrate, Heck, Hex, Hoodoo, Imprecate, Jinx, Malediction, Malgre, Malison, Maranatha, Mau(l)gré, Mockers, Moz(z), Mozzle, Nine (of diamonds), Oath, Paterson's, Pize, Plague, Rant, Rats, Scourge, Snails, Spell, Swear, Tarnation, Upbraid, Vengeance, Vituperate, Wanion, Weary, Winze, Wo(e)

Cursive Estrang(h)elo, Run

Cursor Mouse, Turtle

Cursorily, Cursory Casual, Hasty, Lax, Obiter, Passing, Perfunctory, Sketchy, Speedy, Superficial

Curt Abrupt, Blunt, Crusty, Laconic, Offhand, Short, Snappy, Stern

Curtail(ment) Abate, Apocope, Crop, Cut, Reduce, Shorten

Curtain(s), Curtain raiser, Curtain-rod Air, Arras, Backdrop, Bamboo, Café, Canopy, Casement, Caudle, Cloth, Cyclorama, Death, Demise, Drape, Drop, Dropcloth, Dropscene, Fatal, Hanging, Iron, Lever de rideau, Louvre, Net, Pall, Portière, Purdah, Rag, Safety, Scene, Screen, Scrim, Shower, Swag, Tab, Tableau, Tormentor, Tringle, Upholstery, Vail, Valance, Veil, Vitrage, Window

Curtsey Bob, Bow, Dip, Dop, Honour

Curve(d), Curvaceous, Curvature, Curving, Curvy Adiabatic, Aduncate, Anticlastic, Apophyge, Arc, Arch, Archivolt, Assurgent, Axoid, Bend, Bezier, Bight, Bow, Brachistochrone, Camber, Cardioid, Catacaustic, Catenary, Caustic, Characteristic, Chordee, Cissoid, Conchoid, Contrapposto, Crescent, Cycloid, Demand, Diacaustic, Dogleg, Dowager's hump, Ellipse, Entasis, Epicycloid, Epinastic, Epitrochoid, Ess, Evolute, Exponential, Extrados, Felloe, Felly, Folium, Freezing point, French, Gaussian, Geodesic, Gooseneck, Growth, Hance, Harmonogram, Helix, Hodograph, Hollow-back, Hook, Hyperbola, Hypocycloid, Inswing, Intrados, Invected, Isochor, J, Jordan, Kyphosis, Laffer, Learning, Lemniscate, Limacon, Linkage, Liquidus, Lissajous figure, Lituus, Lordosis, Loxodrome, Meniscus, Normal, Nowy, Ogee, Parabola, Phillips, Pothook, Pott's disease, Pulvinate, Reclinate, Record, Rhumb, RIAA, Roach, Rondure, Rotundate, Scolioma, Scoliosis, Sheer, Sigmoid flexure, Sinuate, Sinusoid, Slice, Sonsie, Spiral, Spiric, Strophoid, Supply, Survival, Swayback, Synclastic, Tautochrone, Tie, Tractrix, Trajectory, Trisectrix, Trochoid, Tumble-home, Twist, Undulose, U-turn, Volute, Witch (of Agnesi)

Cushion(s) Air, Allege, Bank, Beanbag, Bolster, Buffer, Bustle, Frog, Ham, Hassock, Kneeler, → **PAD**, Pillow, Pin, Pouf(fe), Pulvinus, Scatter, Soften, Squab, Tyre, Upholster, Whoopee

Cusp Horn, Spinode, Tine

Custard (apple) Crème caramel, Flam(m), Flan, Flaune, Flawn, Flummery, Pa(w)paw, Pastry, Zabaglione

Custodial, Custodian, Custody Care, Claviger, Curator, Guard, Hold, Incarceration, Janitor, Keeping, Protective, Retention, Sacrist, Steward, Trust, Ward, Wardship

Custom(ised), Customs (officer), Customs house, Customary Agriology, Chophouse, Coast-waiters, Cocket, Consuetude, Conventional, Couvade, Dedicated, De règle, Dhamma, Dharma, Douane, Exciseman, Familiar, Fashion, Folklore, → **HABIT**, Land-waiter, Lore, Manner, Montem, Mores, Nomic, Obsequy, Octroi, Ordinary, Perfunctory, Practice, Praxis, Protocol, Relic, Rite, Routine, Rule, Set, Sororate, Spanish, Sunna, Tax, Thew, Tidesman, Tide-waiter, Tikanga, Time-honoured, Tradition, Trait, Unwritten, Usance, Used, Usual, Won, Wont, Woon, Zollverein

Customer(s) Client, Cove, End user, Footfall, Gate, Patron, Prospect, Punter, Purchaser, Shillaber, Shopper, Smooth, Stiff, Trade, Trick, Ugly, Vendee

Cut(ter), Cutdown, Cutting Abate, Abbreviate, Abjoint, Ablate, Abridge, Abscission, Abscond, Acute, Adeem, Adze, Aftermath, Ali Baba, Amputate, Apocopate, Apocope, Axe, Bang, Bisect, Bit, Bite, Bowdlerise, Boycott, Brilliant, Broach, Caesarean, Caique, Canal, Cantle, Caper, Carver, Castrate, Caustic, Censor, Chap, Cheese, Chisel, Chopper, Chynd, Circumscribe, Cleaver, Clinker-built, Clip, Colter, Commission, Concise, Coppice, Coulter, Coupé, Crew, Crop, Cruel, Cube, Culebra, Curtail, Deadhead, Decrease, Dedekind, Dicer, Die, Director's, Discide, Discount, Disengage, Dismember, Dissect, Division, Divorce, Dock, Dod, Edge, Edit, Emarginate, Embankment, Engraver, Entail, Entayle, Epistolary, Epitomise, Escalope, Eschew, Estrepe, Etch, Excalibur, Excide, Excise, Exscind, Exsect, Exude, Fashion, Fell, Filet mignon, Fillet, Flench, Flense, Flinch, Flymo®, Form, Framp, Froe, Frow, Gaillard, Garb, Gash, Go-down, Grater, Graven, Gride, Groove, Gryde, Hack, Hairdo, Handsaw, Hew(er), Ignore, Incision, Incisor, Indent, Insult, Intersect, Jigsaw, Joint, Junk, Kerf, Kern, Kirn, Lacerate, Lance, Leat, Lesion, Limit, Lin, Lop, Math, Medaillon, Medallion, Microtome, Milling, Minimise, Mohel, Mortice, Mortise, Mower, Nache, Nick, Not, Notch, Nott, Occlude, Omit, Open, Operate, Osteotome, Oxyacetylene, Padsaw, Pare, Pink, Plant, Pliers, Ploughshare, Poll, Pollard, Pone, Power, Precisive, Press, Proin, Quota, Race, Rake off, Rase, Razee, Razor, Reap, Rebate, Reduction, Re-enter, Resect, Retrench, Revenue, Ring, Ripsaw, Roach, Rose, Rout, Saddle, Sarcastic, Sarky, Saw(n), Saw-tooth, Scaloppine, Scarf, Scathing, Scion, Scission, Scissor, Score, Scrap, Sculpt, Scye, Scythe, Secant, Secateurs, Sect, Section, Sever, Sey, Share (out), Shaver, Shears, Shingle, Ship, Shive, Shorn, Short, Shred, Shun, Sickle, Side, Sirloin, Skin, Skip, Slane, Slash, Slice(r), Slip, Slit, Sloop, Sned, Snee, Snib, Snick, Snip, Snippet, Snub, Spade, Speedy, Spin, Spud, Stall, Steak, Stencil, Stereotomy, Stir, Stramac, Stramazon, Strimmer®, Style, Surgeon, Swath(e), Tailor(ess), Tap, Tart, Tenderloin, Tenotomy, Tomial, Tomium, Tonsure, Tooth, Topside, Transect, Trash, Trench, Trenchant, Trepan, Trim, Truant, Truncate, Urchin, Vivisection, Whang, Whittle, Winey

▷ **Cut** *may indicate* an anagram
▷ **Cutback** *may indicate* a reversed word

Cute Ankle, Perspicacious, Pert, Pretty, Taking

Cuticle Epidermis, Eponychium, Periplast, Pleuron, Skin

Cut in Interpose, Interrupt

Cutlass Machete, Sword

Cutlery Canteen, Eating irons, Flatware, Fork, Knife, Service, Setting, Silver, Spoon, Spork, Sunbeam, Tableware, Trifid

Cutlet Chop, Schnitzel

Cut off Elide, Enisle, Estrange, Inisle, Insulate, Intercept, → **ISOLATE**, Lop, Prune

Cut-throat Razor, Ruinous, Sweeney Todd

Cuttlebone, Cuttlefish Octopus, Pen, Polyp(e)s, Polypus, Sea-grape, Sea-sleeve, Sepia, Sepiost(aire), Sepium, Squid

CV Biodata

Cyanide Acrylonitrile, Nitrile, Potassium, Prussiate

Cyborg Replicant

Cycad Coontie, Coonty

Cyclamen Sow-bread

Cycle, Cyclist, Cycling Anicca, Arthurian, Bike, Biorhythm, Biospheric, Born-Haber, Business, Cal(l)ippic, Calvin, Carbon, Carnot, Cell, Circadian, Citric acid, Closed, Daisy, Diesel, Eon, Era, Fairy, Four-stroke, Freewheel, Frequency, Geological, Gigahertz, Heterogony, Hydrologic, Indiction, Keirin, Ko, Krebs, Life, Light-year, Lunar, Lytic, Madison, Metonic, Moped, Natural, Nitrogen, Oestrus, Operating, Orb, Otto, Pedal, Peloton, Period, Product life, Rankine, Repulp, Revolution, Ride, Roadman, Roadster, Rock, Rota, Round, Samsara, Saros, Scorch, Series, Sheng, Solar, Song, Sonnet, Sothic, Spin, Sunspot, TCA, Trade, Trick, Trike, Turn, UCI, Urea, Vicious, Water, Wheeler, Wheelman, Wu

Cyclone Cockeye(d) bob, Storm, Tornado, Tropical, Typhoon, Willy-willy

Cyclops Arges, Arimasp(i), Brontes, Polyphemus, Steropes

Cylinder, Cylindrical Air, Capstan, Clave, Column, Dandy-roll, Drum, Licker-in, Magic, Master, Nanotube, Pipe, Pitch, Roll, Rotor, Siphonostele, Slave, Spool, Steal, Stele, Swift, Terete, Torose, Treadmill, Tube, Vascular

Cymbal(s) High-hat, Hi-hat, Zel, Zill

Cynic(al) Crab, Diogenes, Doubter, Hard-bitten, Hard-boiled, Menippus, Misanthropist, Pessimist, Sardonic, Sceptic, Thersites, Timon, Worldly-wise, World-weary

Cynosure Centre, Focus

Cynthia Artemis, Moon

Cypress Bald, Lawson's, Leyland(ii), Monterey, Retinospora, Swamp, Tree

Cypriot Enosis, Eoka

Cyst Atheroma, Bag, Blister, Chalazion, Dermoid, Hydatid, Impost(h)ume, Meibomian, Ranula, Sac, Sebaceous, Vesicle, Wen

Cytogenesis Amoebic

Czar Despot, Nicholas

Czech(oslovakia), Czechoslovakian CZ, Moravian, Ruthenian, Sudetenland

Dd

D Daughter, Delta, Died, Edh, Eth, Penny

Dab(s) Bit, Daub, Fish, Flounder, Lemon, Pat, Print, Ringer, Smear, Smooth, Spot, Stupe, Whorl

Dabble(r) Amateur, Clatch, Dally, Dilettante, Plouter, Plowter, Potter, Smatter, Splash, Stipple, Trifle

Dachshund Teckel

Dactyl Anapaest

Dad(dy) Blow, Dev(v)el, Father, Generator, Hit, Male, Pa(pa), Pater, Polt, Pop, Slam, Sugar, Thump

Daddy-longlegs Crane-fly, Jennyspinner, Leather-jacket, Spinning-jenny, Tipula

Daffodil Asphodel, Jonquil, Lent-lily, Narcissus

Daft Absurd, Crazy, Potty, Ridiculous, Silly, Simple, Stupid

Dag Jag, Pierce, Pistol, Prick, Stab, Tag, Wool

Dagga Cape, Red, True

Dagger(s) An(e)lace, Ataghan, Baselard, Bayonet, Bodkin, Crease, Creese, Da(h), Diesis, Dirk, Double, Dudgeon, Hanger, Han(d)jar, Jambiya(h), Katar, Khanjar, Kindjahl, Kirpan, Kreese, Kris, Lath, Misericord(e), Obelisk, Obelus, Poi(g)nado, Poniard, Pugio, Puncheon, Pusser's, Quillon, Rondel, Sgian-dubh, Shank, Skean, Skene(-occle), Spanish, Stiletto, Swordbreaker, Whiniard, Whinyard, W(h)inger, Yatag(h)an, Yuc(c)a

Dahlia Cosmea, Pompom

Daily Adays, Broadsheet, Char(lady), Circadian, Cleaner, Diurnal, Domestic, Guardian, Help, Journal, Mail, Mirror, Mrs Mopp, Paper, Per diem, Quotidian, Rag, Regular, Scotsman, Sun, Tabloid

Dainty, Daintiness Cate(s), Cute, Delicacy, Dinky, Elegant, Elfin, Entremesse, Entremets, Exquisite, Genty, Junket, Lickerish, Liquorish, Mignon(ne), Minikin, → **MORSEL**, Neat, Nice, Particular, Petite, Precious, Prettyism, Pussy, Sunket, Twee

Dairy Creamery, Days' house, Loan, Parlour, Springhouse

Dairymaid, Dairyman Cowfeeder, Dey, Patience

Dais Estate, Machan, Platform, Podium, Pulpit, Rostrum, Stage, Tribune

Daisy African, Aster, Barberton, Bell, Boneset, Felicia, Gerbera, Gowan, Groundsel, Hardheads, Hen and chickens, Livingstone, Marguerite, Marigold, Michaelmas, Moon, Ox-eye, Ragweed, Saw-wort, Shasta, Transvaal, Vegetable sheep

Dale(s) Dell, Dene, Diarist, Dingle, Glen, Nidder, Ribbles, Swale, Vale, Valley, Wensley, Wharfe, Yorkshire

Dally Coquet(te), Dawdle, Dilatory, Finger, Flirt, Philander, Play, Spoon, Sport, Tick and toy, Toy, Trifle, Wait

Dalmatian Spotted dog

Dam An(n)icut, Arch, Aswan, Aswan High, Bar, Barrage, Barrier, Block, Boulder, Bund, Cabora Bassa, Cauld, Check, Dental, Grand Coulee, Grande Dixence, Gravity, Hoover, Kariba, Kielder, Ma, Mangla, Mater, Obstacle, Obstruct, Pen, Sennar, Stank, → **STEM**, Sudd, Tank, Three Gorges, Turkey nest, Volta River, Weir, Yangtze

Damage(d), Damages, Damaging Accidental, Appair, Bane, Banjax, Bloody, Blunk, Bruise, Buckle, Charge, Chip, Collateral, Contuse, Cost, Cripple, Dent, Desecrate, Detriment, Devastate, Devastavit, Discredit, Distress, Estrepe, Exemplary, Expense, Fault, Flea-bite, Foobar, Fubar, Fuck up, Harm, Havoc, Hedonic, Hit, Hole, Hurt, Impair, Injury, Insidious, Lesion, Loss, Mar, Mayhem, Moth-eaten, Mutilate, Nobble, Opgefok,

Pair(e), Prang, Price, Punitive, Ratten, Ravage, Reparation, Retree, Ruin, Sabotage, Scaith, Scath(e), Scotch, Scratch, Skaith, Smirch, Solatium, → **SPOIL**, Tangle, Tear, Tigger, Toll, Value, Vandalise, Violate, Wear and tear, Wing, Wound, Wreak, Wreck, Write off

▷ **Damage(d)** *may indicate* an anagram

Dambuster Ondatra

Dame Crone, Dowager, Edna (Everage), Gammer, Lady, Matron, Nature, Naunt, Partlet, Peacherino, Sis, Title(d), Trot, Woman

Damn(ation), Damned Accurst, Attack, Blame, Blast, Blinking, Condemn, Curse, Cuss, D, Darn, Dee, Doggone, Drat, Execrate, Faust, Heck, Hell, Hoot, Jigger, Malgre, Perdition, Predoom, Sink, Swear, Tarnal, Tarnation, Tinker's, Very

Damp(en), Damping, Dampness Aslake, Black, Blight, Blunt, Check, Clam(my), Dank, Dewy, Fousty, Fusty, Humid, Mesarch, Moch, Moist, Muggy, Raw, Retund, Rheumy, Rising, Roric, Soggy, Sordo, Sultry, Unaired, Viscous, → **WET**, White

Damper Barrier, Check, Dashpot, Killjoy, Mute, Register-plate, Sordino, Sourdine

Damsel Girl, Lass, Maiden, Wench

Damson Plumdamas

Dan Box, Cupid, Dare, Leno, Olivetan, Scuttle, Tribe

Dance(r), Dancing Alma(in), Astaire, Baladin(e), Balanchine, Ballabile, Ballant, Ballerina, Ballroom, Baryshnikov, Bayadère, Bob, Body-popping, Caper, Ceili(dh), Chorus-girl, Comprimario, Contredanse, Corp de ballet, Corybant, Coryphee, Dervish, De Valois, Diaghilev, Dinner, Dolin, Exotic, Figurant, Figure, Fooling, Foot, Foot-it, Gandy, Gigolo, Groove, Hetaera, Hetaira, Hoofer, Isadora Duncan, Kick-up, Knees-up, Leap, Maenad, Majorette, Markova, Modern, Nautch-girl, Night, Nijinsky, Nod, Nureyev, Oberek, Old-time, Orchesis, Partner, Pavlova, Peeler, Petipa, Pierette, Prom(enade), Pyrrhic, Rambert, Raver, Reindeer, Ring, St Vitus, Salome, Saltant, Saltatorious, Shearer, Skank, Skipper, Slammer, Spring, Step, Strut, Table, Tea, Terpsichore, Thé dansant, Tread, Trip(pant), Vogue(ing), Whirl, Wire-walker

---

DANCES

3 letters:	Folk	Sand	Gigue
Bop	Fris	Shag	Glide
Fan	Frug	Slam	Gopak
Gig	Giga	Spin	Horah
Hay	Go-go	Spot	Limbo
Hey	Haka	Stag	Loure
Hop	Hora	Taxi	Mambo
Ice	Hula	Wire	Mooch
Jig	Jive		Natch
Lap	Jota	*5 letters:*	Paspy
Pas	Juba	Bamba	Pavan
Poi	Juke	B and S	Paven
Sun	Kolo	Belly	Pavin
Tap	Line	Bogle	Polka
Toe	Lion	Brawl	Ragga
War	Loup	Break	Robot
	Mosh	Carol	Round
4 letters:	Nach	Ceroc®	Rueda
Ball	Pogo	Conga	Rumba
Barn	Polo	Disco	Salsa
Bull	Punk	Fling	Samba
Clog	Rain	Furry	Shake
Dump	Reel	Galop	Skirt
Fado	Rope	Ghost	Snake

Stomp
Sword
Tango
Torch
Truck
Twist
Valse
Volta
Waltz

6 letters:
Apache
Ballet
Bolero
Boogie
Boston
Branle
Bubble
Canary
Can-can
Cha-cha
Fading
Floral
Friska
German
Hustle
Jump-up
Kathak
Lavolt
Maxixe
Minuet
Morris
Pavane
Redowa
Shadow
Shimmy
Smooch
Square
Trophe
Valeta
Veleta
Waggle
Watusi

7 letters:
Bambuca
Beguine
Bourrée
Bransle
Brantle
Cantico
Capuera
Carioca
Coranto

Cossack
Country
Courant
Csardas
Farruca
Forlana
Foxtrot
Furlana
Gavotte
Halling
Hoe-down
Lambada
Lancers
Landler
Lavolta
Macabre
Maypole
Mazurka
Measure
Moresco
Morisco
Morrice
Moshing
Musette
One-step
Pericon
Planxty
Polacca
Ridotto
Ringlet
Romaika
Roundel
Roundle
Routine
Sardana
Sashaya
Shuffle
Tanagra
Tordion
Toyi-toy
Trenise
Trip-hop
Two-step
Watutsi
Ziganka

8 letters:
Alegrias
Boogaloo
Bunnyhop
Bunnyhug
Cachucha
Cakewalk
Canticoy

Capoeira
Chaconne
Cotillon
Courante
Egg-dance
Excuse-me
Fandango
Flamenco
Flip-flop
Galliard
Guimbard
Habanera
Hay-de-guy
Haymaker
Headbang
Hey-de-guy
Heythrop
Hoolican
Hornpipe
Hula-hula
Irish jig
Joncanoe
Junkanoo
Kantikoy
Kapa haka
Kazachok
Kazatzka
Krumping
Lindy hop
Macarena
Marinera
Matachin
Matelote
Medicine
Merengue
Murciana
Rigadoon
Robotics
Ronggeng
Saraband
Snowball
Soft-shoe
Taglioni
Toyi-toyi
Trucking

9 letters:
Allemande
Bergamask
Bergomask
Bossanova
Caballero
Cha-cha-cha
Chipaneca

Cotillion
Ecossaise
Eightsome
Farandole
Formation
Gallopade
Hoolachan
Jitterbug
Kathakali
Malaguena
Pas de deux
Paso doble
Passepied
Paul Jones
Polonaise
Poussette
Quadrille
Quickstep
Ring-shout
Roundelay
Sarabande
Siciliana
Siciliano
Sink-a-pace
Sugarfoot
Tambourin
Tripudium
Variation
Zapateado

10 letters:
Antimasque
Breakdance
Carmagnole
Charleston
Cinderella
Cinque-pace
Corroboree
Gay Gordon's
Hay-de-guise
Hay-de-guyes
Hey-de-guise
Hey-de-guyes
Hokey-cokey
Passamezzo
Petronella
Rug-cutting
Saltarello
Seguidilla
Sicilienne
Sinke-a-pace
Strathspey
Tarantella
Tripudiate

Turkey trot	Palais glide	Passemeasure	**15 letters:**
Tyrolienne	Passacaglia	Passy-measure	Soft shoe shuffle
Walk-around	Pastourelle	Virginia reel	
	Progressive		**16 letters:**
11 letters:	Schottische	**13 letters:**	Circassian circle
Antistrophe	Shimmy-shake	Highland fling	
Black bottom	Varsovienne	Virginian reel	**18 letters:**
Buck and wing			Sir Roger de Coverley
Cracovienne	**12 letters:**	**14 letters:**	
Eurhythmics	Bharat Natyam	Divertissement	
Lambeth walk	Labanotation	Jack-in-the-green	

Dance hall Disco, Juke-joint, Palais

Dance movement Arabesque, Balancé, Battement, Batterie, Benesh, Bourree, Brisé, Chaine, Chassé, Dos-à-dos, Dosido, Entrechat, Fishtail, Fouetté, Glissade, Jeté, Lassu, Pantalon, Pas de basque, Pas de chat, Pas seul, Pigeonwing, Pirouette, Plastique, Plié, Poule, Poussette, Promenade, Routine, Sauté, Step, Telemark, Twinkle

Dance tune Toy

▷ **Dancing** *may indicate* an anagram

Dancing party Ball, Ridotto

Dandelion Hawkbit, Kok-saghyz, Piss-a-bed, Scorzonera, Taraxacum

Dander Anger, Gee, Passion, Saunter, Temper

Dandle Dance, Doodle, Fondle, Pet

Dandruff Furfur, Scurf

Dandy Adonis, Beau, Beau Brummell, Blood, Boulevardier, Buck(een), Cat, Cockscomb, Coxcomb, Dapper, → **DUDE**, Exquisite, Fantastico, Fop, Gem, Jay, Jessamy, Johnny, Kiddy, Knut, Lair, Macaroni, Masher, Modist, Monarcho, Muscadin, Nash, Nut, Posh, Puss-gentleman, Roy, Smart, Spark, Spiff, Swell, Ted, Toff, U, Yankee-doodle

Dandy-horse Draisene, Draisine

Dane(s) Clemence, Dansker, Ogier, Ostmen

Danger(ous) Apperil, Breakneck, Chancy, Crisis, Critical, Dic(e)y, Dire, Dodgy, Emprise, Fear, Hairy, Hazard, Hearie, Hero, High-risk, Hot, Hotspot, Insecure, Jeopardy, Lethal, Menace, Mine, Minefield, Nettle, Nocuous, Objective, Parlous, Periculous, → **PERIL**, Pitfall, Plight, Precarious, Quicksand, Risk, Rock, Serious, Severe, Sicko, Snag, Snare, Tight, Tight spot, Trap, Treacherous, Ugly, Wonchancy

Dangle A(i)glet, Aiguillette, Critic, Flourish, Hang, Loll, Swing

Daniel Dan, Defoe, Deronda, Lion-tamer, Portia, Quilp

Dank Clammy, Damp, Humid, Moist, Wet, Wormy

Daphne Agalloch, Agila, Eaglewood, Lace-bark, Laura, Laurel, Mezereon

Dapper Dressy, Natty, Neat, Smart, Spiff, Sprauncy, Spruce, Sprush, Spry, → **TRIM**

Darbies Cuffs, Irons, Snaps

Dare, Dare-devil, Daring Adventure, Audacious, Aweless, Bold, Brave, Bravura, Challenge, Courage, Dan, Da(u)nton, Defy, Durst, Emprise, Face, Gallant, Gallus, Groundbreaking, Hardihood, Hazard, Hen, Intrepid, Moxie, Neck, Prowess, Racy, Risk, Stuntman, Swashbuckler, Taunt, Venture

Dark(en), Darkie, Darkness Aphelia, Aphotic, Apophis, Black(out), Blind, Byronic, Caliginous, Cimmerian, Cloud, Colly, Crepuscular, Depth, Dim, Dingy, Dirk(e), Dusky, Eclipse, Egyptian, Erebus, Evil, Gloom, Glum, Grim, Inky, Inumbrate, Jet, Kieran, Low-key, Mare, Maria, Melanous, Mulatto, Murk(y), Negro, Night, Obfuscate, Obnubilation, Obscure, Obsidian, Ominous, Ousel, Ouzel, Overcast, Pall, Phaeic, Pitch-black, Pit-mirk, Rooky, Sable, Sad, Secret, Shades, Shady, Shuttered, Sinister, Solein, Sombre, Sooty, Sphacelate, Stygian, Sullen, Sunless, Swarthy, Tar, Tenebrose, Tenebr(i)ous, Unfair, Unlit, Wog, Woosel, Yellowboy, Yellowgirl

Darling Acushla, Alannah, Asthore, Beloved, Charlie, Cher, Chéri(e), Chick-a-biddy,

Chick-a-diddle, Chuck-a-diddle, Dear, Dilling, Do(a)ting-piece, Duck(s), Favourite, Grace, Honey, Idol, Jarta, Jo(e), Lal, Love, Luv, Mavourneen, Mavournin, Minikin, Minion, Oarswoman, Own, Peat, Pet, Poppet, Precious, Squeeze, Sugar, Sweetheart, Sweeting, Yarta, Yarto

Darn Begorra, Blow, Doggone, Hang, Mend, Repair, Sew

Dart(s), Darter Abaris, Arrow, Banderilla, Beetle, Dace, Dash, Deadener, Dodge, Fleat, Fléchette, Flirt, Flit, Harpoon, Javelin, Launch, Leap, Lunger, Pheon, Scoot, Shanghai, Skrim, Speck, Spiculum, Sprint, Strike, Thrust, Wheech

Dash(ing), Dashed Backhander, Bally, Blade, Blight, Blow, Bribe, Buck, Charge, Collide, Cut, Dad, Dah, Damn, Dapper, Dart(le), Daud, Dawd, Debonair, Ding, Dod, Elan, Em, En, Fa(s)cia, Flair, Fly, Go-ahead, Hang, Hurl, → **HURRY**, Hustle, Hyphen, Impetuous, Jabble, Jaw, Jigger, Lace, Leg it, Line, Minus, Modicum, Morse, Natty, Nip, Panache, Pebble, Race, Raffish, Rakish, Ramp, Rash, Rule, Run, Rush, Sally, Scamp(er), Scapa, Scarper, Scart, Scoot, Scrattle, Scurry, Scuttle, Shatter, Showy, Skitter, Soupçon, Souse, Spang, Speed, Splash, Splatter, Sprint, Strack, Streak, Stroke, → **STYLE**, Swashbuckling, Swung, Throw, Tinge, Touch, Treacherous, Ugly, Viretot

Dashboard Fascia, Panel

Dashwood Hell-fire club

Dastard(ly) Base, Coward, Craven, Nid(d)erling, Poltroon

Data(base), Datum Archie, Cyberspace, Donne(e), Evidence, Factoid, Facts, Fiche, File, Floating-point, Garbage, Gen, Hard copy, HOLMES, Info, Input, IT, Material, Matrix, Newlyn, News, Ordnance, Read-out, Soft copy, Statistic, Table, Triple

Date(d), Dates, Dating AD, Age, AH, Almanac, Appointment, Blind, Boyfriend, Calendar, Carbon, Carbon-14, Computer, Court, Deadline, Engagement, Epoch, Equinox, Era, Escort, Exergue, Expiry, Fission-track, Fixture, Gig, Girlfriend, Ides, Julian, Meet, Outmoded, → **OUT OF DATE**, Passé, Past, Radioactive, Radio-carbon, Radiometric, Rubidium-strontium, See, System, Target, → **TRYST**, Ult(imo), Uranium-lead, Value

Daub Begrime, Blob, Dab, Gaum, Mess, Moil, Noint, Plaister, Plaster, → **SMEAR**, Smudge, Splodge, Teer, Wattle

Daughter (in law) Child, D, Elect, Girl, Imogen, Jephthah's, Niece, Offspring, Skevington's

Daunt Adaw, Amate, Awe, Deter, Dishearten, Intimidate, Overawe, Quail, Stun, Stupefy, Subdue

Dauphin Delphin

David Dai, Psalmist

Davit Crane, Derrick, Hoist

Davy Crockett, Jones

Daw Bird, Magpie, Margery

Dawdle(r) Dally, Draggle, Drawl, Idle, Lag(gard), → **LOITER**, Malinger, Potter, Shirk, Slowcoach, Snail, Tarry, Troke, Truck

Dawn(ing) Aurora, Cockcrow, Daw, Daybreak, Daylight, Day-peep, Dayspring, Enlightenment, Eoan, Eos, False, French, Light, Morning, Morrow, Occur, Prime, Roxane, Sparrowfart, Spring, Start, Sunrise, Sun up, Ushas

Day(s) Account, Ahemeral, All Fools', All Hallows', All Saints', All Souls', Anniversary, Annunciation, Anzac, April Fool's, Arbor, Armistice, Ascension, Australia, Bad hair, Baker, Banian, Banyan, Barnaby, Bastille, Borrowing, Box, Boxing, Broad, Calendar, Calends, Calpa, Canada, Canicular, Childermas, Civil, Columbus, Commonwealth, Contango, Continental, Continuation, D, Daft, Date, Decoration, Degree, Derby, Der Tag, Dismal, Distaff, Dog, Dominion, Double, Dress down, Dressed, Duvet, Early, Ember, Empire, Epact, Fast, Fasti, Father's, Feast, Ferial, Field, Fiesta, Flag, Fri, Gang, Gaudy, Glory, Groundhog, Guy Fawkes', Halcyon, Hey, High, Hogmanay, Holocaust, Holy, Holy Innocents', Holy-rood, Hundred, Ides, Inauguration, Independence, Intercalary, Judgment, Juridical, Kalends, Kalpa, Labo(u)r, Lady, Laetare, Lammas, Last, Law(ful), Lay, Leap, Mardi, Market, May, Memorial, Michaelmas, Midsummer, Mon,

Morrow, Mother's, Muck-up, Mufti, Mumping, Name, Ne'erday, New Year's, Nones, Nychthemeron, Oak-apple, Octave, Off, Open, Orangeman's, Pancake, Paper, Pay, Poppy, Post, Pound, Present, Press(ed), Primrose, Pulvering, Quarter, Rag, Rainy, Red-letter, Remembrance, Rent, Rest, Robin, Rock, Rogation, Rood(-mas), Rosh Chodesh, Sabbath, St John's, Saint's, St Swithin's, St Thomas's, St Valentine's, Salad, Sansculotterie, Sat, Scambling, Settling, Sexagesima, Shick-shack, Show, Sidereal, Snow, Solar, Solstice, Speech, Sports, Station, Sun, Supply, Tag, Term, Thanksgiving, Thurs, Ticket, Time, Transfer, Trial, Triduum, Tues, Twelfth, Utas, Valentine's, Varnishing, VE, Vernissage, Veterans', Victoria, Visiting, VJ, Waitangi, Wash, Wed, Wedding, Working

Daybreak Cockcrow, Cockleert, Skreigh of day

Daydream(er), Daydreaming Brown study, Castle(s) in the air, Dwam, Dwaum, Fancy, Imagine, Muse, Reverie, Rêveur, Walter Mitty, Woolgathering

Daylight Artificial, Dawn, Living, Space, Sun

Daze(d) Amaze, Bemuse, Confuse, Dwaal, Gally, Muddle, Muzzy, Petrify, Punch drunk, Reeling, Spaced out, → **STUN**, Stupefy, Stupor, Trance

Dazzle(d), Dazzler, Dazzling Bewilder, Blend, Blind, Bobby, Eclipse, Foudroyant, Glare, Larking glass, Meteoric, Outshine, Radiance, Resplendent, Splendour, Yblent

Deacon Cleric, Doctor, Minister, Permanent

Deactivate Unarm

Dead(en) Abrupt, Accurate, Alamort, Asgard, Asleep, Bang, Blunt, Brown bread, Bung, Cert, Cold, Complete, D, Deceased, Defunct, Dodo, Doggo, Expired, Extinct, Flatliner, Gone(r), Inert, Infarct, Late, Lifeless, Morkin, Muffle, Mute, Napoo, Niflheim, Numb, Obsolete, Obtund, Ringer, Sequestrum, She'ol, Slain, Smother, Stillborn, True, Under hatches, Utter, Waned

Dead end, Deadlock Blind alley, Cut-off, Dilemma, Impasse, Logjam, Stalemate, Stoppage

Dead-leaf colour Filemot, Philamot, Philomot

Deadline Date, Epitaph, Limit

Deadlock Stand-off, Sticking-point

Deadly Baleful, Dull, Fell, Funest, Internecine, → **LETHAL**, Malign, Mortal, Mortific, Pestilent, Thanatoid, Unerring, Venomous

Deadly nightshade Belladonna, Dwale

Deadpan Expressionless

Dead reckoning Dr

Dead tree Rampick, Rampike

Deaf(en), Deafening, Deafness Adder, Asonia, Deave, Deeve, Dunny, Heedless, Paracusis, Presbyac(o)usis, Presbyc(o)usis, Surd(ity)

Deal(er), Dealership, Dealing(s), Deal with Address, Agent, Agreement, Allot(ment), Arb, Arbitrageur, Bargain, Biz, Breadhead, Brinjarry, Broker, Bulk, Business, Cambist, Candyman, Chandler, Chapman, Clocker, Commerce, Connection, Cope, Coup, Cover, Croupier, Dispense, Distributor, Do, Dole, East, Eggler, Exchange, Fir, Franchise, Fripper, Front-running, Goulash, Hack, Hand(le), Help, Inflict, Insider, Interbroker, Jiggery-pokery, Jobber, Lashing, Lay on, Lay out, Loads, Lot, Manage, Mercer, Merchandise, Merchant, Mickle, Middleman, Monger, Mort, Negotiate, New, North, Operator, Package, Pine, Plain, Post, Productivity, Pusher, Raft, Raw, Red, Sale, Serve, Side, Sight, Simoniac, Slanger, Sort, South, Spicer, Square, Stapler, Stockist, Stockjobber, Takeover, Tape, Timber, Totter, Tout(er), → **TRADE**, Traffic, Traffick, Transaction, Treat, Truck, West, Wheeler, White, Wholesaler, Wield, Woolstapler, Yarborough, Yardie

Dean Acheson, Arabin, Colet, Decani, Den, Doyen, Forest, Head, Inge, Nellie, Provost, RD, Rural, Rusk, Skater, Slade, Spooner, Swift, Vale, Vicar-forane, V rev

Dear(er), Dearest, Dear me Ay, Bach, Beloved, Cara, Caro, Cher(e), Cherie, Chou, Chuckie, Darling, Duck(s), Expensive, High, Honey(bun), Joy, Lamb, Leve, Lief, Lieve, Loor, Love, Machree, Mouse, My, Pet, Pigsney, Pigsnie, Pigsny, Soote, Steep, Sugar, Sweet, Sweetie, Sweeting, Toots(ie), Unreasonable, Up

Dearth Famine, Lack, Paucity, Scantity, Scarcity, → **SHORTAGE**
Deaspiration Psilosis
Death(ly) Abraham's bosom, Auto-da-fe, Bane, Bargaist, Barg(h)est, Biolysis, Black, Carnage, Cataplexis, Charnel, Clinical, Commorientes, Cot, Curtains, Cypress, Demise, Deodand, Departure, Dormition, End, Eschatology, Euthanasia, Exit, Extinction, Fatality, Fey, Funeral, Fusillation, Gangrene, Grim Reaper, Hallal, Heat, Infarction, Jordan, Karoshi, King of Terrors, Lead colic, Lethee, Leveller, Living, Loss, Mors, Mortality, Napoo, Necrosis, Nemesis, Night, Obit, Passing, Quietus, Reaper, Sati, Sergeant, SIDS, Small-back, Strae, Sudden, Suttee, Terminal, Thanatism, Thanatology, Thanatopsis, Thanatos, Yama
Death-flood Styx
Deathless(ness) Athanasy, Eternal, Eterne, Immortal, Struldberg, Timeless, Undying
Debacle Cataclysm, Collapse, Disaster, Fiasco
Debag Dack, Unbreech
Debar Black, Deny, Exclude, Forbid, → **PREVENT**, Prohibit
Debase(d) Adulterate, Allay, Bemean, Cheapen, Corrupt, Demean, Depreciate, Dialectician, Dirty, Grotesque, Hedge, Lower, Pervert, Traduce, Vitiate
Debate(r) Adjournment, Argue, Casuist, Combat, Contention, Contest, Deliberate, Dialectic, Discept, Discourse, Discuss(ion), → **DISPUTE**, Flyte, Forensics, Full-dress, Moot, Paving, Polemics, Powwow, Reason, Teach-in, Warsle, Wrangle, Wrestle
Debauch(ed), Debauchee, Debauchery Corrupt, Decadent, Defile, Degenerate, Dissipate, Dissolute, Heliogabalus, Libertine, Licence, Orgy, Profligate, Raddled, Rake-hell, Riot, Roist, Roué, Royst, Seduce, Spree, Stuprate, Wet, Whore
Debenture Bond, Security
Debilitate(d), Debility Asthenia, Atonic, Cachexia, Feeble, Languid, Weak
Debit Charge, Debt, Direct
Debonair Cavalier, Chipper, Gay, Gracious, Jaunty
Debrief Wash up, Wind up
Debris Bahada, Bajada, Detritus, Eluvium, Flotsam, Jetsam, Moraine, Moslings, Pyroclastics, Refuse, → **RUBBLE**, Ruins, Shrapnel, Tel, Tephra, Waste, Wreckage
▷ **Debris** *may indicate* an anagram
Debt(or) Abbey-laird, Alsatia, Arrears, Arrestee, Bankrupt, Bonded, Dr, Due, Floating, Funded, Insolvent, IOU, Liability, Moratoria, National, Obligation, Oxygen, Poultice, Public, Queer Street, Score, Senior, Subordinated, Tick, Tie, Unfunded
Debt-collector Bailiff, Forfaiter, Remembrancer
Debut Launch, Opening, Outset, Presentation
Debutante Bud, Deb
Decade Rosary, Ten
Decadence, Decadent Babylonian, Decaying, Degeneration, Dissolute, Effete, Fin-de-siècle, Libertine
Decamp Abscond, Absquatulate, Bolt, Bunk, Depart, Flee, Guy, Levant, Mizzle, Slide, Slope, Vamoose
Decant Pour, Unload
Decapitate, Decapitation Aphesis, → **BEHEAD**, Guillotine
▷ **Decapitated** *may indicate* first letter removed
Decay(ed), Decaying Alpha, Appair, Beta, Biodegrade, Blet, Canker, Caries, Caseation, Consenescence, Crumble, Decadent, Declension, Decline, Decompose, Decrepit, Dieback, Disintegrate, Dissolution, Doat, Doddard, Doddered, Dote, Dricksie, Druxy, Dry rot, Ebb, Fail, F(o)etid, Forfair, Gamma, Gangrene, Heart-rot, Impair, Moulder, Pair(e), Perish, Plaque, Ptomaine, Putrefy, Radioactive, Ret, Rot, Rust, Saprogenic, Sap-rot, Seedy, Sepsis, Spoil, Tabes, Thoron, Time-worn, Wet-rot
Decease(d) Death, Decedent, Demise, Die, Stiff
Deceit(ful), Deceive(r) Abuse, Ananias, Artifice, Bamboozle, Barrat, Befool, Bitten, Blag, Blind, Bluff, Braide, → **CHEAT**, Chicane, Chouse, Con, Cozen, Cuckold, Defraud,

Deke (out), Delude, Diddle, Dissemble, Do brown, Double-cross, Double-dealing, Double-tongued, Dupe, Duplicity, False(r), Fastie, Fast-talk, Fiddle, Fineer, Flam, Fool, Four-flusher, Fox, Fraud, Gag, Gerrymander, Gloze, Guile, Gull, Hoax, Hoodwink, Hornswoggle, Humbug, Hype, Hypocritical, Illusion, Imposition, Inveigle, Invention, Jacob, Jiggery-pokery, Kid, Lead on, Liar, Malengine, Mamaguy, Mata Hari, Mendacious, Misinform, Mislead, Mislippen, Patter, Perfidy, Phenakism, Poop, Poupe, Pretence, Prevaricate, Punic, Rig, Ruse, Sell, Sham, Sinon, Sleekit, Snow job, Spruce, Stratagem, Subreption, Swindle, Swizzle, Take in, Tregetour, Trick, Trump, Two-faced, Two-time, Weasel, Wile

Decency, Decent Chaste, Decorum, Fitting, Godly, Healsome, Honest, Kind, Mensch, Modest, Moral, Passable, Salubrious, Seemly, Sporting, Wholesome, Wise-like

Decentralise Disperse

Deception, Deceptive Abusion, Artifice, Bluff, Catchpenny, Catchy, Cheat, Chicanery, Codology, → **DECEIT**, Disguise, Dupe, Duplicity, Elusive, Eyewash, Fallacious, False, Feigned, Fineer, Flam, Fraud, Fubbery, Gag, Gammon, Guile, Gullery, Have-on, Hocus-pocus, Hokey-pokey, Hum, Hunt-the-gowks, Hype, Ignes-fatui, Ignis-fatuus, Illusion, Insidious, Jiggery-pokery, Kidology, Lie, Mamaguy, Moodies, Phantasmal, Runaround, Ruse, Sciolism, Sell, Sleight, Smoke and mirrors, Specious, Sting, The moodies, Thimblerig, → **TRICK**, Trompe l'oeil, Two-timing, Underhand

Decide(r), Decided, Decisive Addeem, Adjudge, Agree, Ar(r)e(e)de, Ballot, Barrage, Bottom-line, Call, Cast, Clinch, Conclude, Conclusive, → **DECISION**, Deem, Definite, Determine, Distinct, Effectual, Engrenage, Fatal, Firm, Fix, Foregone, Jump-off, Mediate, Opt, Parti, Predestination, Pronounced, Rescript, Resolute, → **RESOLVE**, Result, Rule, Run-off, See, Settle, Split, Sudden death, Sure, Tiebreaker, Try

Decimal Mantissa, Recurring, Repeating, Terminating

Decimate Destroy, Lessen, Tithe, Weaken

Decipher(ing) Cryptanalysis, Decode, Decrypt, Descramble, Discover, Interpret

▷ **Decipher(ed)** *may indicate* an 'o' removed

Decision Arbitrium, Arrêt, Bottom line, Crossroads, Crunch, Crux, Decree, Engrenage, Fatwa, Fetwa, Firman, Judg(e)ment, Parti, Placit(um), Referendum, Resolution, Resolve, Responsa, Ruling, Sentence, Split, Sudden death, Verdict

Decisive Climactic, Clincher, Critical, Crux, Definite, Final, Pivotal

Deck Adonise, Adorn, Angled, Array, Attrap, Bejewel, Boat, Canted, Cards, Clad, Daiker, Daub, Decorate, Dizen, Embellish, Equip, Flight, Focsle, Forecastle, Garland, Hang, Helideck, Hurricane, Lower, Main, Mess, Monkey poop, Orlop, Ornament, Pack, Pedestrian, Platform, Poop, Prim, Promenade, Quarter, Saloon, Spar, Sun, Tape, Upper, Void, Weather, Well

Declare, Declaration, Declaim, Decree Absolute, A(r)e(e)de, Affidavit, Affirm, Air, Allege, Announce, Annunciate, Aread, Assert, Asseverate, Aver, Avow, Balfour, Bann(s), Bayyan, Breda, Dictum, Diktat, Doom, Edict, Elocute, Emit, Enact, Fatwa(h), Fiat, Firman, Go, Grace, Harangue, Hatti-sherif, Independence, Indiction, Indulgence, Insist, Interlocutory, Irade, Law, Mandate, Manifesto, Mecklenburg, Meld, Motu proprio, Mou(th), Nisi, Noncupate, Novel(la), Nullity, Nuncupate, Orate, Ordain, Order, Ordinance, Parlando, Petition of Right, Pontificate, Predicate, Present, Proclaim, Profess, Promulgate, Pronounce, Protest, Psephism, Publish, Rant, Read, Recite, Rescript, Resolve, Restatement, Rights, Rule, Ruling, Saw, SC, Sed, Senatus consultum, Senecan, Shahada, Signify, Speak, Spout, State, Statutory, Swear, Testament-dative, Testify, Testimony, UDI, Ukase, Ultimatum, Unilateral, Vie, Voice, Vouch, Will, Word

▷ **Declaring** *may indicate* a word beginning 'Im'

Decline, Declination, Declining Age, Ail, Atrophy, Catabasis, Comedown, Decadent, Degeneration, Degringoler, Deny, Descend, Deteriorate, Devall, Die, Diminish, Dip, Dissent, Downhill, Downtrend, Downturn, Droop, Drop, Dwindle, Ebb, Escarpment, Fade, Fall, Flag, Forbear, Lapse, Magnetic, Opt out, Paracme, Pejoration, Peter, Plummet, Quail, Recede, Recession, Reflow, Refuse, Retrogression, Rot, Ruin, Rust, Sag, Senile,

Set, Sink, Slide, Slump, Slumpflation, Stoop, Tumble, Twilight, Wane, Welke, → **WILT**, Withdraw, Wither

Decoct(ion) Apozem, Cook, Devise, Ptisan, Tisane

Decode(d) En clair

Decolleté Low, Neckline

Decompose, Decomposition Biodegradable, Crumble, Decay, Degrade, Disintegrate, Electrolysis, Fermentation, Hydrolysis, Mor, Pyrolysis, Rot, Wither

Decompression Bends

Decor Background, Scenery

Decorate(d), Decoration, Decorative Adorn, Aiguilette, Angelica, Aogai, Arpillera, Attrap, Award, Bard, Bargeboard, Baroque, Bauble, Beaux-arts, Bedizen, Bells and whistles, Biedermeier, Bordure, Braid, Brattishing, Braze, Breastpin, Brooch, Cartouche, Centrepiece, Chain, Chambranle, Champlevé, Chinoiserie, Christingle, Cinquefoil, Cloissoné, Coffer, Cresting, Crocket, Croix de guerre, Cul-de-lampe, Daiker, Decoupage, Dentelle, Dentil, Diamante, Doodad, Doodah, Do over, Dragée, Dragging, Emblazon, Emboss, Embrave, Engrail, Enrich, Epaulet, Epergne, Etch, Fancy, Festoon, Filigree, Finery, Finial, Fleuret(te), Fleuron, Floriated, Flushwork, Fluting, Fob, Fourragère, Frieze, Frill, Frog, Frost, Furbish, Gammadion, Garniture, Gaud, Gild, Gilt, Glitter, Goffer, Gradino, Grecque key, Grotesque, Guilloche, Historiated, Ice, Illuminate, Impearl, Inlay, Intarsia, Intarsio, Interior, Jabot, Jari, Knotwork, Leglet, Linen-fold, Linen-scroll, Marquetry, MC, Medal(lion), Mola, Motif, Moulding, Oath, OBE, Openwork, Order, → **ORNAMENT**, Ornate, Orphrey, Overglaze, Ovolo, Paint, Paper, Parament, Pâté-sur-pâté, Photomural, Pinata, Pipe, Pokerwork, Polychromy, Pompom, Prettify, Prink, Purfle, Purple heart, Quilling, Rag-rolling, Rangoli, Repoussé, Ribbon, Rich, Ric(k)-rac(k), Rosemaling, Ruche, Scallop, Schwarzlot, Scrimshander, Scrimshaw, Serif, Set-off, Sgraffito, Skeuomorph, Soutache, Spangle, Staffage, Stomacher, Storiated, Strapwork, Stucco, Studwork, Tailpiece, Tart up, Tattoo, TD, Titivate, Tool, Topiary, Tracery, Trim, Veneer, Vergeboard, Wallpaper, Well-dressing, Wirework, Zari

Decorous, Decorum Becoming, Demure, Etiquette, Fitness, Modest, Parliamentary, Prim, → **PROPER**, Propriety, Sedate, Seemlihe(a)d, → **SEEMLY**, Staid, Tasteful

Decoy Allure, Bait, Bonnet, Button, Call-bird, Coach, Crimp, Entice, Lure, Piper, Roper, Ruse, Shill, Stale, Stalking-horse, Stall, Stool-pigeon, Tame cheater, Tice, Tole, Toll, Trap, Trepan

Decrease Cut back, Decrew, Diminish, Dwindle, Iron, Lessen, Press, Ramp down, Reduce, Rollback, Slim, Step-down, Subside, Wane, Wanze

▸ **Decree** *see* **DECLARE**

Decrepit Dilapidated, Doddery, Doitit, Failing, Feeble, Frail, Moth-eaten, Spavined, Time-worn, Tumbledown, Warby, Weak

Decriminalise Launder

Decry Condemn, Crab, Denounce, Derogate, Detract, Downgrade

Dedicate(d), Dedication Corban, Determination, Devote, Dinah, Endoss, Hallow, Inscribe, Oblate, Pious, Sacred, Single-minded, Votive, Work ethic

Deduce, Deduction, Deductive A priori, Assume, Conclude, Consectary, Corollary, Derive, Discount, Dockage, Gather, Illation, Infer(ence), Natural, Obvert, Off-reckoning, Reason, Rebate, Recoup, Reprise, Stoppage, Surmise, Syllogism

Deed(s) Achievement, Act(ion), Atweel, Backbond, Back letter, Charta, Charter, Defeasance, Derring-do, Disposition, Escrol(l), Escrow, Exploit, Fact(um), Feat, Indeed, Indenture, Manoeuvre, Mitzvah, Muniments, Premises, Settlement, Specialty, Starr, → **TITLE**, Trust, Work

Deem Consider, Judge, Opine, Ordain, Proclaim, Repute, Think

Deep(en), Deeply Abstruse, Bass(o), Brine, Briny, Enhance, Excavate, Grum, Gulf, Hadal, Intense, Low, Mindanao, Mysterious, → **OCEAN**, Profound, Re-enter, Rich, Sea, Sonorous, Sunk(en), Throaty, Upsee, Ups(e)y

Deep-rooted Inveterate

Deer(-like) Axis, Bambi, Barasing(h)a, Barking, Blacktail, Brocket, Buck, Cariacou, Caribou, Carjacou, Cervine, Chevrotain, Chital, Doe, Elaphine, Elk, Fallow, Gazelle, Hart, Hog, Irish elk, Jumping, Moose, Mouse, Mule, Muntjac, Muntjak, Musk, Père David's, Pricket, Pudu, Pygarg, Red, Rein, Roe, Rusa, Sambar, Sambur, Selenodont, Sika, Sorel(l), Spade, Spay(d), Spayad, Spitter, Spottie, Stag(gard), Tragule, Ungulate, Virginia, Wapiti, Water, White-tailed

Deer-hunter Tinchel

Deface Disfigure, Spoil

▷ **Defaced** *may indicate* first letter missing

Defame, Defamatory, Defamation Abase, Bad mouth, Blacken, Calumny, Cloud, Denigrate, Detract, Dishonour, Impugn, In rixa, Libel, Malign, Mud, Mudslinging, Obloquy, Sclaunder, Scurrilous, Slander, Smear, Stigmatise, Traduce, Vilify

Default(er) Absentee, Bilk, Dando, Delinquent, Flit, Levant, Neglect, Omission, Waddle, Welsh

Defeat(ed), Defeatist Beat, Best, Bowed, Caning, Capot, Cast, Codille, Conquer, Counteract, Cream, Debel, Defeasance, Demolish, Destroy, Discomfit, Dish, Ditch, Donkey-lick, Drub, Fatalist, Floor, Foil, Foyle, Hammer, Hiding, Kippered, Laipse, Lick, Loss, Lurch, Marmelize, Master, Mate, Moral, Negative, Out, Outclass, Outdo, Outfox, Outgeneral, Outgun, Outplay, Outvote, Outwit, → **OVERCOME**, Overmarch, Overpower, Overreach, Overthrow, Overwhelm, Pip, Plaster, Pulverise, Quitter, Rebuff, Reverse, Rout, Rubicon, Scupper, Set, Shellacking, Sisera, Skunk, Squabash, Stump, Tank, Thrash, Thwart, Toast, Tonk, Trounce, Undo, Vanquish, War, Waterloo, Whap, Whip, Whitewash, Whop, Whup, Wipe-out, Worst

Defecate, Defecation Encopresis, Horse, Mute, Poop, Scumber, Shit, Skummer, Tenesmus

Defect(ion), Defective, Defector Abandon, Amateur, Apostasy, Bug, Coma, Crack, Crawling, Deficient, Desert, Failing, Faulty, Flaw, → **FORSAKE**, Frenkel, Halt, Hamartia, Hiatus, Kink, Low, Manky, Mass, Mote, Natural, Paralexia, Point, Psellism, Rachischisis, Renegade, Renegate, Ridgel, Ridgil, Rig, Rogue, Runagate, Schottky, Shortcoming, Spina bifida, Stammer, Substandard, Terrace, Treason, Trick, Want, Wanting, Weakness, Wreath

Defence, Defend(er), Defensible, Defensive Abat(t)is, Alexander, Alibi, Antibody, Antidote, Antigenic, Antihistamine, Apologia, Arm, Back, Back four, Bailey, Barbican, Barmkin, Barricade, Bastion, Battery, Battlement, Berm, Bestride, Bridgehead, Bulwark, Calt(h)rop, Catenaccio, CD, Champion, Chapparal, Civil, Curtain, Demibastion, Ditch, Embrasure, Estacade, Goalie, Hedgehog, Herisson, Hold, Immunity, J(i)u-jitsu, Justify, Kaim, Keeper, Kraal, Laager, Laer, Last-ditch, Libero, Linebacker, Maginot-minded, Maintain, Martello tower, MIDAS, Moat, Motte and bailey, Muniment, Outwork, Palisade, Parapet, Pentagon, Perceptual, Propugnation, Protect, Rampart, Redan, Redoubt, Refute, Resist, Ringwall, Sangar, Seawall, → **SHELTER**, Shield(wall), Stonewall, Strategic, Support, Sweeper, Tenable, Tenail(le), Testudo, Tower, Trench, Trou-de-loup, Uphold, Vallation, Vallum, Vindicate, Wall, Warran(t), Zonal

Defenceless Helpless, Inerm, Naked, Sitting duck, Vulnerable

Defendant Accused, Apologist, Respondent, Richard Roe

Defer(ence), Deferential, Deferring Bow, Complaisance, Curtsey, Delay, Dutiful, Homage, Moratory, Morigerous, Obeisant, Pace, Polite, Postpone, Procrastinate, Protocol, Respect, Roll over, Shelve, Stay, Submit, Suspend, Waive, Yield

Defiance, Defiant, Defy Acock, Bite the thumb, Bold, Brave, Cock a snook, Contumacy, Dare, Daring, Disregard, Do or die, Flaunt, Insubordinate, Outbrave, Outdare, Rebellion, Recalcitrant, Recusant, Resist, Scab, Stubborn, Titanism, Truculent, Unruly, Yahboo

Deficiency, Deficient Absence, Acapnia, ADA, Anaemia, Anoxia, Aplasia, Beriberi, Defect, Failing, Hypinosis, Inadequate, Incomplete, Kwashiorkor, Lack, Osteomalacia, Scant, Scarcity, SCID, Shortage, Shortfall, Spanaemia, Want

▷ **Deficient** *may indicate* an anagram

Deficit Anaplerotic, Arrears, Defective, Ischemia, Loss, Poor, Shortfall

Defile(ment) Abuse, Array, Barranca, Barranco, Besmear, Col, Conspurcation, Desecrate, Dishonour, Donga, Enseam, → **FOUL**, Gate, Gorge, Gully, Inquinate, Inseem, Kloof, Moil, Pass, Pollute, Poort, Ravine, Ray, Roncesvalles, Smear, Spoil, → **SULLY**

Define(d), Definition, Definitive Classic, Clear-cut, Decide, Demarcate, Determine, Diorism, Distinct, Explain, Fix, Limit, Parameter, Set, Sharp, Specific, Tangible, Term

Definite(ly) Categorically, Classic, Clear, Concrete, Deffo, Emphatic, Firm, Hard, Indeed, Pos, Positive, Precise, Sans-appel, Specific, Sure, Yes

Deflate Burst, Collapse, Flatten, Lower, Prick, Puncture, Squeeze

Deflect(or), Deflection Avert, Back-scatter, Bend, Detour, Diverge, Divert, Glance, Holophote, Otter, Paravane, Refract, Snick, Swerve, Throw, Trochotron, Veer, Windage

Deform(ed), Deformity Anamorphosis, Blemish, Boutonniere, Contracture, Crooked, Disfigure, Distort, Gammy, Hammer-toe, Harelip, Misborn, Miscreated, Misfeature, Mishapt, Mooncalf, Mutilate, Phocomelia, Phocomely, Polt-foot, Saddle-nose, Stenosed, Talipes, Valgus, Varus, Warp

▷ **Deformed** *may indicate* an anagram

Defraud Bilk, Cheat, Cozen, Gull, Gyp, Lurch, Mulct, Shoulder, Skin, Sting, Swindle, Trick

Defray Bear, Cover, Meet

Defrost Thaw

Deft Adept, Agile, Dab, Dexterous, Elegant, Handy, Nimble

Defunct Deceased, Extinct, Obsolete

▶ **Defy** *see* **DEFIANCE**

Degenerate, Degeneration, Degenerative Acorn-shell, Ascidian, Atrophy, Backslide, Balanus, Base, Cirrhipedia, Cirrhipedia, Cirrhipod(a), Cirripedia, Cirripedia, Decadent, Deprave, Descend, Deteriorate, Eburnation, Effete, Fatty, Kaliyuga, Necrobiosis, Pejorate, Pervert, Rakehell, Relapse, Retrogress, Salp, Stentosis, Tunicate

Degrade, Degradation Abase, Cheapen, Culvertage, Debase, Demission, Demote, Depose, Diminish, Disennoble, Embase, Humble, Imbase, Imbrute, Lessen, Lower, → **SHAME**, Sink, Waterloo

Degree(s) Aegrotat, As, Attila (the Hun), Azimuthal, BA, Baccalaureate, BCom, BD, B es S, C, Class, D, Desmond (Tutu), Doctoral, Double first, Douglas (Hurd), Engler, Extent, External, F, First, Forbidden, Foundation, Geoff (Hurst), German, Gradation, Grade, Grece, Gree(s), Greece, Gre(e)se, Grice, Griece, Grize, → **IN A HIGH DEGREE**, Incept, Incidence, K, Lambeth, Latitude, Letters, Level, Levitical, Licentiate, Longitude, MA, Measure, Mediant, Nth, Nuance, Order, Ordinary, Pass, Peg, PhD, Pin, Poll, Rate, Reaumur, Remove, Second, Stage, Status, Step, Submediant, Subtonic, Supertonic, Third, Trevor (Nunn), Water

Dehiscence Suture

Dehydrate(d) Exsiccate, Thirsty

Deification, Deify Apotheosis

Deign Condescend, Stoop

Deity Avatar, Cabiri, Demogorgon, Divine, Faun, → **GOD**, → **GODDESS**, Idolise, Immortalise, Krishna, Numen, Pan, Satyr, Zombi(e)

Deject(ed), Dejection Abase, Abattu, Alamort, Amort, Blue, Chap-fallen, Crab, Crestfallen, Despondent, Dismay, Dispirited, Down, Downcast, Gloomy, Hangdog, Humble, Low, Melancholy, Spiritless, Wae

Delaware DE(L)

Delay(ed), Delaying Adjourn(ment), Ambage, Avizandum, Backlog, Behindhand, Check, Cunctator, Dawdle, Defer, Demurrage, Detention, Dilatory, Fabian, Filibuster, Forsloe, For(e)slow, Frist, Hangfire, Hesitate, Hinder, Hitch, Hold up, Hysteresis, Impede, Laches, Lag, Late, Laten, Let, Linger, Loiter, Mora(torium), Obstruct, Pause, Procrastinate, Prolong, Prorogue, Remanet, Reprieve, Respite, Retard, Rollover, Setback,

Slippage, Sloth, Slow, → **STALL**, Stand-over, Stay, Stonewall, Suspend, Temporise, Wait

Delectable Delicious, Luscious, Tasty

Delegate, Delegation Agent, Amphictyon, Apostolic, Appoint, Assign, Commissary, Decentralise, Depute, Devolution, Mission, Nuncio, Offload, Representative, Secondary, Transfer, Vicarial, Walking

Delete Adeem, Annul, Cancel, Cut, Erase, Excise, Expunge, Purge, Rase, Scratch, Scrub, Strike, Twink out

Deliberate(ly), Deliberation Adagio, Calculated, Consider, Debate, Intentional, Meditate, Moderate, Muse, On purpose, Overt, Plonking, Pointedly, Ponder, Prepensely, Purposely, Ruminate, Studied, Thought, Voulu, Weigh, Witting

Delicacy, Delicate Airy-fairy, Beccafico, Blini, Canape, Cate, Caviare, Dainty, Difficult, Discreet, Dorty, Ectomorph, Eggshell, Elfin, Ethereal, Fastidious, Filigree, Fine, Finespun, Finesse, Flimsy, Fragile, → **FRAIL**, Friand, Gentle, Goody, Gossamer, Guga, Hothouse, Inconie, Incony, Kickshaw, Kidglove, Lac(e)y, Ladylike, Light, Lobster, Morbidezza, Nesh, Nicety, Niminy-piminy, Ortolan, Oyster, Pastel, Reedy, Roe, Sensitive, Soft(ly-softly), Subtle(ty), Sunket, Sweetmeat, Tactful, Taste, Tender, Tenuous, Ticklish, Tidbit, Titbit, Trotter, Truffle, Wispy

Delicatessen Charcuterie

Delicious Ambrosia, Delectable, Exquisite, Fragrant, Goloptious, Goluptious, Gorgeous, Lekker, Lip-smacking, Mor(e)ish, Mouthwatering, Savoury, Scrummy, Scrumptious, Tasty, Toothsome, Yummo, Yummy, Yum-yum

Delight(ed), Delightful Bewitch, Bliss, Charm, Chuff, Coo, Delice, Dreamy, Edna, Elated, Elysian, Enamour, Enjoyable, Enrapture, Exhilarate, Exuberant, Felicity, Fetching, Frabjous, Gas, Glad, Glee, Gratify, Honey, Joy, Lap up, Nice, Overjoy, Over the moon, Please, Pleasure, Precious, → **RAPTURE**, Regale, Rejoice, Revel, Scrummy, Super, Sweet, Taking, Tickle, Turkish, Whacko, Whee, Whoopee, Wizard, Yippee, Yum-yum

▷ **Delight** *may indicate* 'darken'

Delineate Draft, Outline, Prosciutto, Sketch, Trace

Delinquent Bodgie, Criminal, Halbstarker, Hoody, Juvenile, Negligent, Offender, Ted

Delirious, Delirium Deranged, DT, Fever, Frenetic, Frenzy, Insanity, Mania, Phrenetic, Phrenitis, Spaced out, Spazz, Wild

Deliver(ance), Delivered, Deliverer, Delivery(man) Accouchement, Air-lift, Bailment, Ball, Birth, Born, Bowl, Breech, Caesarean, Consign, Convey, Courier, Deal, Doosra, Drop, Elocution, Escape, Express, Extradition, Give, Googly, Jail, Lead, Liberate, Lob, Mail drop, Orate, Over, Pronounce, Receipt, Recorded, Redeem, Refer, Release, Relieve, Render, Rendition, → **RESCUE**, Rid, Round(sman), Salvation, Save, Say, Seamer, Sell, Shipment, Soliloquy, Speak, Special, Tice, Transfer, Underarm, Underhand, Ventouse extraction, Wide, Yorker

Dell Dale, Dargle, Dene, Dimble, Dingle, Dingl(e)y, Glen, Valley

Delphic Pythian

Delphinium Larkspur

Delta Camargue, D, Del, Flood-plain, Kronecker, Nabla, Nile, Oil Rivers, Triangle

Delude, Delusion Bilk, Cheat, Deceive, Fallacy, Fool, Hoax, Megalomania, → **MISLEAD**, Paranoia, Schizothymia, Trick, Zoanthropy

Deluge Avalanche, Cascade, Flood, Ogygian, Saturate, Submerge, → **SWAMP**

De luxe Extra, Plush, Special

Delve Burrow, Dig, Excavate, Exhume, Explore, Probe, Search

Demagogue Agitator, Fanariot, Leader, Mobsman, Phanariot, Speaker, Tribune

Demand(ing) Appetite, Ball-buster, Call, Claim, Cry, Derived, Dun, Exact, Excess, Exigent, Fastidious, Final, Heavy, Hest, → **INSIST**, Mandate, Market, Necessitate, Need, Order, Postulate, Pressure, Request, Requisition, Rigorous, Rush, Sale, Severe, Stern, Stipulate, Stringent, Summon, Tax, Ultimatum, Want

Demean(ing) Belittle, Comport, Debase, Degrade, Humble, Infra dig, Lower, Maltreat

Demeanour Air, Bearing, Conduct, Expression, Front, Gravitas, Mien, Port, Presence

Dement(ed) Crazy, Frenetic, Hysterical, Insane, Mad, Possessed, Wacko
Demi-god Aitu, Daemon, Garuda, Hero
Demi-mondaine Cocotte, → LOOSE WOMAN, Prostitute
Demise Death(-damp), Decease, Finish
Demo March, Parade, Protest, Rally, Sit-in
Democracy, Democrat, Democratic D, Hunker, Industrial, Liberal, Locofoco,
Menshevik, Montagnard, People's, Popular, Republic, Sansculotte, Social, Tammany
Demoiselle Crane, Damselfish, Odonata
Demolish, Demolition Bulldoze, Devastate, Devour, Dismantle, Floor, KO, Level,
Rack, → RAZE, Smash, Tear down, Wreck
▶ **Demon** *see* DEVIL(ISH)
Demoness Lilith
Demonstrate, Demonstration, Demonstrator Agitate, Barrack, Dharma, Display,
Endeictic, Évènement, Evince, Explain, Hunger march, Maffick, Manifest, March,
Morcha, Ostensive, Peterloo, Portray, Proof, Protest, Prove, Provo, Send-off, → SHOW,
Sit-in, Touchy-feely, Verify, Vigil
Demoralise, Demoralisation Bewilder, Corrupt, Depths, Destroy, Dishearten,
Shatter, Unman, Weaken
Demos, Demotic Greek
Demote, Demotion Comedown, Degrade, Disbench, Disrate, Embace, Embase,
Reduce, Relegate, Stellenbosch
Demotic Enchorial
Demur Hesitate, Jib, Object
Demure Coy, Mim, Modest, Prenzie, Primsie, Sedate, Shy
Den Dive, Domdaniel, Earth, Hell, Hide-away, Holt, Home, Lair, Lie, Lodge, Opium,
Room, Shebeen, Spieler, Study, Sty, Wurley
Denial, Deny, Denier Abnegate, Antinomian, Aspheterism, Bar, Belie, Contradict,
Controvert, Démenti, Disavow, Disenfranchise, Disown, Forswear, → GAINSAY, Nay,
Negate, Nick, Nihilism, Protest, Refuse, Refute, Renague, Renay, Reneg(e), Renegue,
Reney, Renig, Renounce, Reny, Repudiate, Sublate, Traverse, Withhold
Denigrate Besmirch, Blacken, Defame, Tar
Denim Jeans
Denizen Diehard, Inhabitant, Resident
Denomination Category, Cult, Sect, Variety
Denote Import, Indicate, Mean, Signify
Denouement Anagnorisis, Catastrophe, Climax, Coda, Exposure, Outcome, Showdown
Denounce, Denunciation Ban, Commination, Condemn, Criticise, Decry, Delate,
Diatribe, Fulminate, Hatchet job, Hereticate, Proclaim, Proscribe, Shop, Stigmatise,
Thunder, Upbraid
Denry Card
Dense, Density B, Buoyant, Charge, Compact, Critical, Current, D, Double, Firm, Flux,
Intense, Neutral, Opaque, Optical, Packing, Rank, Reflection, Relative, Single, Solid,
Spissitude, Tesla, Thick, Transmission, Vapour, Woofy
Dent(ed) Batter, Concave, Dancette, Depress, Dimple, Dinge, Dint, Nock, Punctate, Punt, V
Dental (problem), Dentist(ry) DDS, Entodontics, Extractor, Kindhart, LDS,
Malocclusion, Odontic, Paedodontics, Periodontic, Toothy
Dentures Biteplate, Bridge, Bridgework, False teeth, Plate, Prosthodontia, Store teeth,
Wallies
Denude Strip
▶ **Deny** *see* DENIAL
Deodorant Anti-perspirant, Cachou, Roll-on
Deoxidise Outgas, Reduce
Depart(ed), Departing, Departure Abscond, Absquatulate, Apage, Bunk, D, Dead,
Decamp, Decession, Defunct, Demise, Die, Digress, Divergence, Egress, Exception, Exit,

Exodus, Flight, French leave, → **GO**, Imshi, Late, Leave, Lucky, Moonlight flit, Outbound, Rack off, Remue, Send-off, Vacate, Vade, Vamoose, Walkout

Department Achaea, Ain, Aisne, Allier, Alpes de Provence, Alpes-Maritimes, Angers, Arcadia, Ardeche, Ardennes, Argo, Argolis, Ariege, Arrondissement, Arta, Attica, Aube, Aude, Aveyron, Bas-Rhin, Belfort, Bell-chamber, Beziers, Bouches-du-Rhône, Branch, Bureau, Calvados, Cantal, Charente, Charente-Maritime, Cher, Cleansing, Commissariat, Corrèze, Cote d'Or, Cotes d'Armor, Cotes du Nord, Creuse, DEFRA, Deme, Deuxième Bureau, Deux-Sevres, Division, Domain, Dordogne, Doubs, Drôme, El(e)ia, Essonne, Eure, Eure-et-Loir, Extramural, Faculty, Finistere, Fire, FO, Foggy Bottom, Gard, Gers, Gironde, Greencloth, Guadeloupe, Gulag, Hanaper, Haute-Garonne, Haute-Loire, Haute-Marne, Haute-Normandie, Hautes-Alpes, Haute-Saône, Haute Savoie, Hautes-Pyrenees, Haute-Vienne, Haut-Rhin, Hauts-de-Seine, Helpdesk, Herault, Home, Ille-et-Vilaine, Indre, Indre-et-Loire, Inspectorate, Isere, Jura, Landes, Loire, Loiret, Loir-et-Cher, Lot, Lot-et-Garonne, Lozere, Maine-et-Loire, Manche, Marne, Martinique, Mayenne, Meurthe-et-Moselle, Meuse, Ministry, Morbihan, Moselle, Nièvre, Nome, Nomos, Nord, Office, Oise, Ordnance, Orne, Pas-de-Calais, Portfolio, Province, Puy de Dôme, Pyrénées(-Atlantique), Pyrénées-Orientales, Region, Rehabilitation, Rhône, Sanjak, Saône-et-Loire, Sarthe, Savoie, Secretariat(e), Section, Seine-et-Marne, Seine Maritime, Seine St Denis, Somme, Sphere, State, Tarn(-et-Garonne), Treasury, Tuscany, Unit, Val de Marne, Val d'Oise, Var, Vaucluse, Vendée, Vienne, Voiotia, War, Wardrobe, Yonne, Yvelines

Depend(ant), Dependence, Dependency, Dependent Addicted, Child, Client, Colony, Conditional, Contingent, Count, Dangle, E, Fief, Habit, Hang, Hinge, Icicle, Lean, Lie, Lippen, Minion, Pensioner, Relier, Rely, Retainer, Ross, Sponge, Stalactite, Statistical, Subject, Subordinate, Trust, Turn on, Vassal, Virgin Islands

Dependable Reliable, Reliant, Rock, Safe, Secure, Sheet-anchor, Solid, Sound, Staunch, Sure, → **TRUSTWORTHY**

Depict Delineate, Describe, Display, Draw, Limn, Paint, Portray, Present, Represent

Depilate, Depilation, Depilatory Electrolysis, Grain, Rusma, Slate

Deplete Depauperate, Diminish, Drain, Exhaust, Reduce, Sap

Deplorable, Deplore Base, Bemoan, Chronic, Complain, Deprecate, Dolorous, Execrate, Grieve, Lament, Mourn, Pathetic, Piteous, Regret, Rue, Shocking, Woeful

Deploy(ment) Extend, Field, Herse, Unfold, Use

▷ **Deploy(ment)** *may indicate* an anagram

Depopulate Deracinate

Deport(ation), Deportment Address, Air, Banish, → **BEARING**, Carriage, Demeanour, Exile, Extradite, Mien, Renvoi, Renvoy, Repatriation

Depose, Deposition Affirm, Banish, Dethrone(ment), Displace, Dispossess, Hoard, Overthrow, Pieta, Testify

Deposit(s), Depository Aeolian, Alluvial, Alluvium, Aquifer, Arcus, Argol, Arles, Atheroma, Bank, Bathybius, Bergmehl, Calc-sinter, Calc-tuff, Caliche, Cave-earth, Coral, Crag, Crystolith, Delta, Depone, Diatomite, Diluvium, Drift, Dust, Evaporite, Fan, File, Firn, Fort Knox, Fur, Glacial, Gyttja, Hoard, Illuvium, Kieselguhr, Land, Laterite, Lay, Lay away, Lay-by, Laydown, Lead tree, Limescale, Lodge(ment), Loess, Löss, Measure, Moraine, Natron, Outwatch, Park, Pay dirt, Pay in, Phosphorite, Placer, Plank, Plaque, Precipitate, Put, Repose, Residuum, Saburra, Salamander, Sandbank, Saprolite, Saturn's tree, Scale, Sea dust, → **SEDIMENT**, Silt, Sinter, Sludge, Soot, Speleothem, Stockwork, Storeroom, Stratum, Surety, Tartar, Terramara, Terramare, Till, Time, Tophus, Tripoli, Turbidite

Depot Barracoon, Base, Camp, Depository, Etape, Station, Terminus, Treasure-city, Warehouse

Deprave(d), Depravity Bestial, Cachexia, Cachexy, Caligulism, → **CORRUPT**, Dissolute, Evil, Immoral, Low, Outrage, Reprobate, Rotten, Sodom, Total, Turpitude, Ugly, Unholy, Vice, Vicious, Vile

Deprecate Censure, Deplore, Expostulate, Reproach

Depreciate Abase, Belittle, Derogate, Detract, Discount

Depredate, Depredation Pillage, Plunder, Rob

Depress(ed), Depressing, Depression Accablé, Agitated, Alamort, Alveolus, Amort, Astrobleme, Attrist, Black dog, Blight, Blue devils, Blues, Cafard, Caldron, Canada, Canyon, Chill, Col, Combe, Couch, Crab, Crush, Cyclone, Dampen, Deject, Dell, Demission, Dene, Dent, Despair, → **DIMPLE**, Dip, Dismal, Dispirit, Ditch, Dolina, Doline, Doomy, Downlifting, Drear, Drere, Dumpish, Endogenous, Exanimate, Flatten, Fonticulus, Foss(ula), Fossa, Fovea, Frog, Geosyncline, Ghilgai, Gilgai, Gilgie, Glen, Gloom, Graben, Grinch, Ha-ha, Hammer, Heart-spoon, Hilar, Hilum, Hilus, Hollow, Howe, Hyp, Hypothymia, Indentation, Joes, Kettle, Kick(-up), Lacuna, Leaden, Low(ness), Low-spirited, Megrims, Moping, Morose, Neck, Ocean basin, Pan, Pit, Polje, Postnatal, Postpartum, Prostrate, Punt, Qattara, Recession, Re-entrant, Retuse, Sad, Saddle, Sag, Salt-cellar, Salt-pan, Scrobicule, Sink, Sinkhole, Sinus, Sitzmark, Slot, → **SLUMP**, Slumpflation, Soakaway, Spiritless, Stomodaeum, Sump, Swag, Swale, Swallowhole, Trench, Trough, Umbilication, Vale, Vallecula, Valley, Wallow, Weigh down, Wet blanket

Deprivation, Deprive(d) Amerce, Bereft, Deny, Disenfranchise, Disfrock, Disseise, Disseize, Expropriate, Famine, Foreclose, Geld, Ghetto, Have-not, Hunger, Reduce, Remove, Rob, Sensory, Starve, Strip, Withhold

Depth Draught, Draw, F, Fathom, Gravity, Intensity, Isobath, Pit, Profundity

Deputise, Deputy Act, Agent, Aide, Assistant, Commis(sary), Delegate, Legate, Lieutenant, Locum, Loot, Mate, Number two, Prior, Pro-chancellor, Proxy, Represent, Secondary, Sidekick, Standby, Sub, Subchanter, Substitute, Succentor, Surmistress, Surrogate, Tanaiste, Vicar, Vice, Viceregent, Vidame

Derange(d), Derangement Craze, Détraqué, Disturb, Insane, Loopy, Manic, Trophesy, Troppo, Unhinge, Unsettle

Derby Boot, Demolition, Donkey, Eponym, Hat, Kentucky, Kiplingcotes, Race, Roller

Derek Bo

Derelict Abandoned, → **DECREPIT**, Deserted, Negligent, Outcast, Ramshackle, Tramp

Deride, Derision, Derisive Contempt, Gup, Guy, Hiss, Hoot, Jeer, Mock, Nominal, Pigs, Raspberry, → **RIDICULE**, Sardonic, Scoff, Scorn, Sneer, Snifty, Snort, Ya(h)boo (sucks), Yah

Derive, Derivation, Derivative Amine, Ancestry, Apiol, Creosote, Deduce, Descend, Extract, Get, Kinone, Of, Offshoot, Origin, Pedigree, Picoline, Secondary, Taurine, Tyramine

▸ **Dermatitis** *see* **SKIN DISEASE**

Derogate, Derogatory Aspersion, Belittle, Decry, Defamatory, Demeaning, Detract, Discredit, Libellous, Pejorative, Personal, Slanderous, Slighting, Snide, Tushing

Deronda Daniel

Derrick Crane, Davit, Hoist, Jib, Spar, Steeve

Dervish Calender, Doseh, Mawlawi, Mevlevi, Revolver, Santon, Whirling

Descant Comment, Discourse, Faburden, Melody, Song

Descartes René

Descend(ant), Descent Ancestry, Avail, Avale, Bathos, Blood, Cadency, Catabasis, Chute, Cion, Decline, Degenerate, Dégringoler, Derive, Dismount, Dive, Drop, Epigon, Extraction, Heir, Heraclid, → **LINEAGE**, Offspring, Pedigree, Posterity, Progeny, Prone, Purler, Rappel, Said, Say(y)id, Scarp, Scion, Seed, Shelve, Sien(t), Sink, Spearside, Stock, Syen, Vest, Volplane

Describe, Describing, Description, Descriptive Blurb, Define, Delineate, Depict, Designate, Draw, Epithet, Exposition, Expound, Graphic, Job, Label, Narrate, Outline, Paint, Portray, Rapportage, Recount, Relate, Report, Sea-letter, Semantic, Signalment, Sketch, Specification, Synopsis, Term, Trace, Vignette, Write-up

▷ **Describing** *may indicate* 'around'

Descry Behold, Discern, Get, Notice, Perceive

Desecrate, Desecration Abuse, Defile, Dishallow, Profane, Sacrilege, Unhallow

▷ **Desecrated** *may indicate* an anagram

Desert(er), Deserted, Deserts Abandon, Absquatulate, Apostasy, Arabian, Arid, Ar Rimal, Arunta, Atacama, AWOL, Badland, Barren, Bledowska, Bug, Bunk, Colorado, Come-uppance, D, Dahna, Defect, Desolate, Dissident, Due, Empty, Eremic, Etosha Pan, Factious, Fail, Fezzan, Foresay, Forhoo, Forhow, Forlorn, Forsake, Forsay, Frondeur, Garagum, Gibson, Gila, Gobi, Great Basin, Great Indian, Great Sandy, Great Victoria, Heterodox, Indian, Jump ship, Kalahari, Kara Kum, Karma, Kavir, Kyzyl Kum, Libyan, Lurch, Meeds, Merit, Mohave, Mojave, Nafud, Namib, Negev, Nubian, Ogaden, Painted, Patagonian, Pindan, Rat, Refus(e)nik, Reg, → **RENEGADE**, Reward, Rub'al-Khali, Run, Runaway, Sahara, Sahel, Sands, Secede, Sertao, Shamo, Simpson, Sinai, Sonoran, Sturt, Syrian, Tacna-Arica, Tergiversate, Thar, Turncoat, Ust(y)urt, Victoria, Void, Wadi, Waste(land), Western Sahara, Wild, Wilderness, Worthiness

Deserve(d) Condign, Earn, → **MERIT**, Rate, Well-earned, Worthy

Desiccate(d) Dry, Sere

Design(er) Adam, Aim, Amies, Arabesque, Architect, Argyle, Armani, Ashley, Batik, Between-subjects, Broider, Cable stitch, Calligram(me), Cardin, Cartoon, Castrametation, Chop, Cloisonné, Courreges, Couturier, Create, Cul de lampe, Damascene, Decal(comania), Decor, Deep, Depict, Devise, Dévoré, Dior, Draft, Embroidery, End, Engender, Engine(r), Engineer, Erté, Etch, Fashion, Feng-shui, Flanch, Format, Former, Hepplewhite, Hitech, Iconic, Imagineer, Impresa, Imprese, Industrial, Inlay, Intend(ment), Intent(ion), Interior, Issigonis, Layout, Le Corbusier, Limit-state, Linocut, Logo, Marquetry, Mascle, Matched pairs, Mean, Meander, Mehndi, Millefleurs, Modiste, Monogram, Morris, Mosaic, Motif, Multifoil, Nailhead, Nissen, Paisley, Pattern, → **PLAN**, Plot, Propose, Pyrography, Quant, Retro, Ruse, Schema, Scheme, Schiaparelli, Seal, Sheraton, Sketch, Sopwith, Spatterwork, Specification, Sprig, Stencil, Stubble, Stylist, Sunburst, Tatow, Tattoo, Tattow, Tatu, Think, Tooling, Townscape, Trigram, Versace, Vignette, Watermark, Weiner, Werkstalte, Whittle, Within-subjects

Designate Destine, Earmark, List, Mark, Name, Note, Style, Title

Desirable, Desire, Desirous Ambition, Aphrodisia, Appetite, Aspire, Avid, Best, Cama, Conation, Concupiscence, Covet, Crave, Cupidity, Des, Dreamboat, Earn, Eligible, Epithymetic, Fancy, Gasp, Greed, Hanker, Hope, Hots, Hunger, Itch, Kama(deva), Le(t)ch, Libido, List, Long, Luscious, Lust, Mania, Notion, Nymphomania, Orectic, Owlcar, Pica, Plum, Reak, Reck, Request, Residence, Salt, Slaver, Spiffing, Streetcar, Thirst, Urge, Velleity, Vote, Wanderlust, Want, Whim, Will, Wish, Yearn, Yen

Desist Abandon, Cease, Curb, Pretermit, Quit, Stop

Desk Almemar, Ambo, Bonheur-du-jour, Bureau, Carrel(l), Cash, Check-in, Cheveret, City, Copy, Davenport, Desse, Devonport, E(s)critoire, Enquiry, Faldstool, Lectern, Lettern, Litany, Pay, Pedestal, Prie-dieu, Pulpit, Reading, Roll-top, Scrutoire, Secretaire, Vargueno, Writing

Desman Pyrenean

Desolate, Desolation Bare, Barren, Desert, Devastate, Disconsolate, Forlorn, Gaunt, Godforsaken, Gousty, Moonscape, Waste, Woebegone

Despair, Desperate, Desperation Acharne, Anomy, Dan, De profundis, Despond, Dire, Dismay, Extreme, Frantic, Gagging, Giant, Gloom, Hairless, Headlong, Hopelessness, Last-ditch, Last-gasp, Life and death, Reckless, Unhopeful, Urgent, Wanhope

▶ **Despatch** *see* **DISPATCH**

Desperado Bandit, Bravo, Ruffian, Terrorist

Despicable Abject, Base, Bleeder, Caitiff, Cheap, Churl, Contemptible, Heel, Heinous, Ignoble, Ignominious, Low-down, Mean, Moer, Poep(ol), Puke, Ratbag, Ratfink, Scumbag, Shabby, Snip, Toerag, Vermin(ous), Vile, Wretched

Despise(d) Condemn, Conspire, Contemn, Forhow, Futz, Hate, Ignore, Scorn, Spurn, Vilify, Vilipend

Despite For, Malgré, Notwithstanding, Pace, Though, Venom

Despoil Mar, Rape, Ravage, Vandalise

Despondent Dejected, Downcast, Forlorn, Gloomy, Lacklustre, Sad

Despot(ism) Autarchy, Autocrat, Bonaparte, Caesar, Darius, Dictator, Little Hitler, Martinet, Napoleon, Nero, Satrap, Stratocrat, Tsar, Tyrant, Tzar

Dessert Afters, Baked Alaska, Baklava, Banana split, Bavarian cream, Bavarois, Blancmange, Bombe, Cannoli, Charlotte, Charlotte russe, Cheesecake, Clafoutis, Cobbler, Compote, Coupe, Cranachan, Cream, Crème brulée, Crème caramel, Crepe Suzette, Dulce de leche, Entremets, Eve's pudding, Floating Island, Flummery, Fool, Granita, Junket, Kissel, Knickerbocker glory, Kulfi, Marquise, Mousse, Mud pie, Nesselrode, Pannacotta, Parfait, Pashka, Pavlova, Peach Melba, → **PUDDING**, Rasmalai, Roulade, Sabayon, Sawine, Semifreddo, Shoofly pie, Split, Spumone, Strudel, Sundae, Syllabub, Tart, Tarte tatin, Tartufo, Tiramisu, Tortoni, Trifle, Vacherin, Whip, Zabaglione

Destine(d), Destination Born, Design, End, Fate, Foredoom, Goal, Gole, Home, Intend, Joss, Meant, Port, Purpose, Vector, Weird

Destiny Doom, → **FATE**, Karma, Kismet, Lot, Manifest, Moira, Portion, Yang, Yin

Destitute Bankrupt, Bare, Broke, Devoid, Dirt-poor, Down and out, Helpless, Impoverished, Indigent, Necessitous, Needy, Penniless, Poor, Sterile, Void, Waif and stray

Destress Anneal

Destroy(er) Annihilate, Antineutrino, Antineutron, Antiparticle, Apollyon, Atomise, Blight, Bulldoze, Can, Crush, D, Decimate, Deep-six, Deface, Delete, Demolish, Demyelinate, Denature, Destruct, Dish, Dismember, Dissolve, Eat, Efface, End, Eradicate, Erase, Estrepe, Exterminate, Extirpate, Flivver, Fordo, Graunch, Harry, Iconoclast, Incinerate, Invalidate, → **KILL**, KO, Locust, Murder, Obliterate, Overkill, Perish, Predator, Pulverize, Q-ship, Ravage, Raze, Ruin, Saboteur, Sack, Scuttle, Slash, Smash, Spif(f)licate, Spoil, Sterilize, Stew-can, Stonker, Stultify, Subvert, Trash, Undo, Uproot, Vandal, Vitiate, Waste, Whelm, Wreck, Zap

Destruction, Destructive Adverse, Autolysis, Bane, Can, Catabolism, Collapse, Deathblow, Deleterious, Devastation, Doom, Downfall, Ecocide, End, Götterdämmerung, Grave, Havoc, Holocaust, Hunnish, Iconoclasm, Insidious, Internecine, Kali, Lethal, Loss, Maelstrom, Maleficent, Moorburn, Nihilistic, Pernicious, Pestilential, Pogrom, Quelea, Rack, Ragnarok, Ravage, Ruination, Sabotage, Speciocide, Stroy, Wrack, Wreckage

Desultory Aimless, Cursory, Fitful, Idle

Detach(ed), Detachment Abeigh, Abstract, Alienate, Aloof, Apart, Body, Calve, Clinical, Cut, Detail, Discrete, Dispassionate, Distinct, Insular, Isle, Isolate, Loose, Outlying, Outpost, Patrol, Picket, Picquet, Separate, Sever, Staccato, Stoic, Unfasten, Unhinge, Unit

Detached work Ravelin

Detail(s), Detailed Annotate, Circumstances, Dock, Elaborate, Embroider, Expatiate, Explicit, Exploded, Expound, Instance, → **ITEM**, Itemise, Minutiae, Nicety, Nuts and bolts, Particular(ise), Pedantry, Point, Recite, Recount, Relate, Respect, Send, Spec, Special, Specific, Specification, Technicality, Touch

▷ **Detailed** *may indicate* last letter missing

Detain(ee), Detention (centre) Arrest, Buttonhole, Collar, Custody, Delay, Demurrage, Detinue, Gate, Glasshouse, Hinder, Intern, Juvie, Keep, POW, Preventive, Retard, Sin bin, Stay, → **WITHHOLD**

Detect(or), Detective Agent, Arsène, Asdic, Bloodhound, Brown, Bucket, Busy, Catch, Chan, CID, Cuff, Det, Dick, Discover, Divine, Doodlebug, Dupin, Espy, Eye, Fed, Find, Flambeau, Flic, Fortune, French, Geigercounter, Geophone, G-man, Gumshoe, Hanaud, Hercule, Holmes, Interpol, Investigator, Jack, Lecoq, Lupin, Maigret, Metal, Methanometer, Microwave, Mine, Minitrack®, Morse, Nail, Nose, Peeper, PI, Pinkerton, Plant, Poirot, Private, Private eye, Prodnose, Radar, Reagent, Retinula, Rumble, Scent, Scerne, Sense, Sensor, Shadow, Shamus, Sherlock, → **SLEUTH**, Sleuth-hound, Sofar, Solver, Sonar, Sonobuoy, Spot, Tabaret, Take, Tec, Thorndyke, Toff, Trace, Trent, Vance, Wimsey, Yard(man)

Detent Pawl, Trigger

Deter(rent) Block, Check, Daunt, Dehort, Delay, Disincentive, Dissuade, Prevent, Restrain, Turn-off, Ultimate

Detergent Cationic, Clean(s)er, Non-ionizing, Solvent, Surfactant, Syndet, Tepol, Whitener

Deteriorate, Deterioration Decadence, Degenerate, Derogate, Entropy, Pejoration, Relapse, Rust, Worsen

▷ **Deterioration** *may indicate* an anagram

▷ **Determination** *may indicate* 'last letter'

Determine(d), Determination All-out, Appoint, Arbitrament, Ardent, Ascertain, Assign, Assoil, Bent, Causal, Condition, Dead-set, → **DECIDE**, Define, Dictate, Doctrinaire, Dogged, Do-or-die, Dour, Drive, Earnest, Fix, Govern, Granite, Grim, Grit(ty), Headstrong, Hell-bent, Indomitable, Influence, Intent, Ironclad, Judgement, Law, Liquidate, Orient, Out, Point, Pre-ordain, Purpose, Quantify, → **RESOLUTE**, Resolve, Rigwiddie, Rigwoodie, Self-will, Set, Settle, Set upon, Shape, Soum, Sowm, Stalwart, Steely, Tenacious, Type, Valiant, Weigh

Detest(able), Detested Abhor, Anathema, Despise, Execrable, Execrate, Hate, Loathsome, Pestful, Vile

Detonate, Detonator Blast, Explode, Fire, Fuse, Fuze, Ignite, Kindle, Plunger, Primer, Saucisse, Saucisson, Spring, Tetryl, Trip-wire

Detour Bypass, Deviate, Divert

Detract Belittle, Decry, Diminish, Discount, Disparage

Detriment(al) Adverse, Damage, Harm, Injury, Loss, Mischief

Detroit Motown

Deuce Dickens, Old Harry, Twoer

Deuteron Diplon

Devalue Cheapen, Debase, Impair, Reduce, Undermine

Devastate, Devastation Demolish, Destroy, Gut, Lay waste, Overwhelm, Ravage, Ruin, Sack, Traumatise, Waste, Wrack, Wreck

Develop(er), Developed, Developing, Development Advance, Age, Agile, Amidol®, Aplasia, Apotheosis, Breakthrough, Breed, Bud, Build, Burgeon, Catechol, Creep, Cutting edge, Dark room, Educe, Elaborate, Enlarge, Epigenetic, Escalate, Evolve, Expand, Expatriate, Foetus, Full-fledged, Fulminant, Genesis, Germinate, Gestate, Grow, Hatch, Hothouse, Hydroquinone, Hypo, Imago, Improve, Incipient, Incubate, Lamarckism, Larva, Mature, Metamorphose, Metol, Morphogenesis, Morphosis, Mushroom, Nascent, Nurture, Offshoot, Oidium, Ongoing, Ontogenesis, Pathogeny, Pullulate, Pupa, Pyro, Pyrogallol, Quinol, Ribbon, Ripe(n), Sarvodaya, Sensorimeter, Separate, Shape, Soup, Speciation, Sprawl, Subtopia, Technography, Teens, Tone, Unfold, Upgrow

▷ **Develop** *may indicate* an anagram

Deviant, Deviate, Deviation Aberrance, Abnormal, Anomaly, Average, Brisure, Deflect, Deflexure, Depart, Derogate, Detour, Digress, Discrepant, Diverge, Divert, Drift, Error, Kinky, Kurtosis, List, Mean, Pervert, Quartile, Sheer, Solecism, Sport, Standard, Stray, Swerve, Transvestite, → **TURN**, Valgus, Varus, Veer, Wander, Wend

Device Allegory, → **APPARATUS**, Appliance, Artifice, Bush, Contraption, Contrivance, Deus ex machina, Dodge, Emblem, Expedient, Gadget, Gimmick, Gismo, Gubbins, Instrument, Logo, Mnemonic, Motto, Plan, Pointing, Ruse, Safeguard, → **STRATAGEM**, Subterfuge, Tactic, Tag, Thing, Tool, Trademark, Trick, Wile

---

DEVICES

3 letters:	Mux	Set	*4 letters:*
Bug	Pad	Van	Capo
FET	Pig	Zip	Drag
LED	POP		Fret

Fuse
Gobo
Grab
Head
Orle
Plug
Rest
Shoe
Skid
Spur
Stop
Tram
Trap

5 letters:
Audio
Balun
Chaff
Choke
Chuck
Clamp
Cleat
Combi
Conch
Cramp
Crank
Diode
E-nose
Frame
Gatso®
Gizmo
Gland
Input
Lidar
Maser
Meter
Mixer
Modem
Mouli
Mouse
Optic®
Otter
Pager
Petar
Prism
Probe
Quipu
Relay
Rotor
Saser
Scale
Scart
Servo
Shear

Sieve
Siren
Snare
Sonde
Spool
Sprag
SQUID
Stent
Timer
Tromp
Truss
Turbo
Valve
V-chip
Waldo
Winch

6 letters:
Analog
Atlatl
Balise
Beeper
Biodot
Blower
Bungee
Buzzer
Charge
Chowri
Chowry
Clevis
Cotter
Cursor
Cut-out
Dasher
Deckle
De-icer
Detent
Dimmer
Dongle
Elevon
Engine
Etalon
Euouae
Evovae
Faller
Feeder
Filter
Friend®
Grater
Heddle
Imager
Jigger
Joypad
Keeper

Kludge
Logger
Masker
Nanite
Packer
Peeler
Petard
Pick-up
Pinger®
Possum
Preset
Quippu
Rabble
Reverb
Rocker
Roller
Router
Selsyn
Sensor
Server
Shaker
Shower
Socket
Stocks
Stoner
Switch
Swivel
Tablet
Tamper
Temple
Tipple
Tracer
Tremie
Triode
Trompe
Turtle
Tympan
Viewer
Wafter
Walker
Widget
Zapper

7 letters:
Air-trap
Bearing
Bendlet
Bleeper
Charger
Chopper
Clapper
Cleaver
Clicker
Coherer

Compass
Counter
Coupler
Crampon
Dashpot
Denture
Digibox®
Divider
Doubler
Flip-top
Fuzzbox
Gas mask
Genlock
Gimbals
Grapnel
Hushkit
Imprese
Inhaler
Isotron
Jetpack
Krytron
Lighter
Limiter
Machine
Minicom
Monitor
Padlock
Pelorus
Pessary
Pickoff
Pillory
Plunger
Ratchet
Reactor
Roll-bar
Rotator
Rowlock
Scanner
Shopbot
Shut-off
Shutter
Shuttle
Simcard
Slipper
Sniffer
Snorkel
Snubber
Snuffer
Sordino
Sounder
Spoiler
Stapler
Starter
Stinger

Storage
Sundial
Swatter
Synchro
Toaster
Tokamak
Tonepad
Vernier
Vocoder

8 letters:
Airscoop
Alcolock
Analogue
Anti-icer
Atomiser
Autodial
Ballcock
Barostat
Betatron
Bootjack
Calutron
Commutor
Conveyor
Coupling
Cryostat
Demister
Detector
Diagraph
Diestock
Earphone
Ecraseur
Eggtimer
Enlarger
Episcope
Episemon
Expander
Fairlead
Firework
Flashgun
Flywheel
Forklift
Geophone
Gunsight
Heat pump
Holdback
Hotplate
Ignitron
Launcher
Light-pen
Monogram
Nailhead
Occluder
Odograph

Odometer
Orthosis
Ozoniser
Paravane
Playback
Plectrum
Pullback
Pulsator
Pushback
Push-pull
Pyrostat
Radar gun
Radiator
Resister
Robotics
Shoehorn
Shredder
Silencer
Slip ring
Snow-eyes
Snowshoe
Solenoid
Splitter
Spray gun
Spreader
Squeegee
Sweatbox
Swellbox
Terminal
Thin-film
Trembler
Varactor
Varistor
Vibrator

9 letters:
Aspirator
Autometer
Autotimer
Capacitor
Compasses
Convector
Converter
Corkscrew
Decoherer
Deflector
Defroster
Delayline
Detonator
Dispenser
Dynamotor
Eccentric
Equalizer
Excelsior

Exerciser
Extractor
Fetoscope
Gear-lever
Gear-shift
Gearstick
Generator
Gyroscope
Headstock
Hendiadys
Hodoscope
Hydrofoil
Hydrostat
Hygrostat
Indicator
Insulator
Jack screw
Keylogger
Konimeter
Kymograph
Megaphone
Mekometer
Metronome
Milometer
Modulator
Nebuliser
Octophone
Optophone
Overdrive
Pacemaker
Parachute
Patent log
Pedometer
Periscope
Phonopore
Photocell
Pitchbend
Polariser
Polygraph
Powerpack
Propeller
Rectifier
Regulator
Remontoir
Resonator
Responsor
Retractor
Rheotrope
Rotachute
Rotameter®
Satellite
Scrambler
Separator
Sequencer

Simulator
Smokejack
Sonograph
Spaceband
Spindryer
Spinhaler
Sprinkler
Stairlift
Steadicam
Stretcher
Tabulator
Tape drive
Tape punch
Tasimeter
Telegraph
Telemeter
Telepoint
Thermette
Thyristor
Tonometer
Tormentor
Trackball
Tremulant
Well sweep

10 letters:
Acetometer
Anemoscope
Applicator
Attenuator
Autowinder
Blackberry®
Calculator
Ceilometer
Centrifuge
Chaingrate
Chronotron
Clapometer
Commutator
Comparator
Compressor
Copyholder
Cyclometer
Cyclostyle
Daisy-wheel
Databogger
Derailleur
Descendeur
Eprouvette
Fairleader
Foetoscope
Groundprox
Humidistat
Hygroscope

Integrator
Jawbreaker
Jaws of Life
Jellygraph
Kicksorter
Lactometer
Mason's mark
Metrostyle
Microphone
Microprobe
Microscope
Mileometer
Moulinette
Nephograph
Nightscope
Noisemaker
Otter-board
Peripheral
Phonoscope
Planometer
Radiometer
Remontoire
Respirator
Self-feeder
Siderostat
Snowplough
Spirograph
Stabiliser
Stimpmeter
Suppressor
Switchgear
Tachograph
Tachometer
Tape reader
Telewriter
Thermistor
Thermopile
Thermostat
Tourniquet
Transducer

Transistor
Turbulator
Turnbuckle
Ventilator
Vertoscope®
Videophone
Viewfinder
Viscometer
Zener diode

11 letters:
Afterburner
Annunciator
Answerphone
Autochanger
Baffle-plate
Carburettor
Collet chuck
Compass rose
Distributor
Epidiascope
Floor turtle
Fluoroscope
Helping hand
Immobilizer
Insufflator
Intoximeter
Lie detector
Link trainer
Manipulator
Microfitter
Microreader
Microwriter
Moving-coils
Multiplexer
Paper cutter
Recuperator
Self-starter
Smokerlyzer
Snickometer

Solarimeter
Space heater
Spectograph
Speedometer
Stuffing-box
Swingometer
Telestrator
Thermoscope
Trackerball
Transceiver
Transformer
Transmitter
Transponder
Weather vane

12 letters:
Breathalyser
Concentrator
Desert cooler
Ebulliometer
Effusiometer
Electrometer
Evaporograph
Extensometer
Extinguisher
Galvanometer
Intrauterine
Lithotripter
Magnetometer
Make and break
Object finder
Oscillograph
Oscilloscope
Picturephone
Sensitometer
Snooperscope
Speaking tube
Spectrometer
Spectroscope
Supercharger

Tape streamer
Telautograph
Teleprompter
Tellurometer
Thermocouple
Turbidimeter
Viscosimeter

13 letters:
Accelerometer
Baton-sinister
Contraceptive
Dead man's pedal
Electromagnet
Electrophorus
Metal detector
Phonendoscope
Potentiometer
Rack and pinion
Read-write head
Scintiscanner
Shock-absorber
Smoke detector

14 letters:
Anamorphoscope
Dead man's handle
Interferometer
Intervalometer
Peltier element
Plethysmograph
Retroreflector
Scintillometer
Spinthariscope
Surge protector
Trickle charger

15 letters:
Radiogoniometer

Devil(ish), Demon Abaddon, Afreet, Afrit, Ahriman, Amaimon, Apollyon, Asmodeus, Atua, Auld Hornie, Azazel, Barbason, Beelzebub, Belial, Buckra, Cacodemon, Cartesian, Clootie, Cloots, Dasyure, Davy Jones, Deev, Deil, Demogorgon, Demon, Deuce, Devling, Diable, Diabolic, Dickens, Div, Drudge, Dust, Eblis, Falin, Familiar, Fend, Fiend, Fient, Ghoul, Goodman, Goodyear, Grill, Hangie, Hornie, Iblis, Imp, Incubus, Infernal, Knave, Lamia, Legion, Lilith, Lord of the Flies, Lori, Lucifer, Mahoun(d), Man of Sin, Manta, Mara, Maxwell's, Mazikeen, Mephisto(pheles), Mischief, Nick, Nickie-ben, Old Bendy, Old Nick, Old One, Old Pandemonium, Old Poker, Old Roger, Old Split-foot, Old Toast, Printer's, Ragamuffin, Ragman, Rahu, Ralph, Satan, Satan(h)as, Satyr, Scour, Scratch, Screwtape, Season, Setebos, Shaitan, Shedeem, Snow, Sorra, Succubine, Succubus, Tailard, Tasmanian, Tempter, Titivil, Tutivillus, Wendigo, Wicked, Wicked One, Wirricow, Worricow, Worrycow, Zernebock
Devious Braide, Cunning, Deep, Eel(y), Erroneous, Evasive, Heel, Implex, Indirect,

Scheming, Shifty, Sly, Sneaky, Stealthy, Subtle, Tortuous, Tricky

Devise(d) Arrange, Coin, Comment, Concoct, Contrive, Decoct, Hatch, Hit-on, Imagine, Invenit, Invent, Plan, Plot, Thermette

Devitrified Ambitty

Devoid Barren, Destitute, Empty, Vacant, Wanting

Devolution West Lothian question

Devolve Occur, Result, Transmit

Devote(e), Devotion(al), Devoted Addiction, Aficionado, Âme damnée, Angelus, Attached, Bhakti, Buff, Bunny, Commitment, Consecrate, Corban, Dedicate, Employ, Enthusiast, Fan, Fervid, Fetishism, Fidelity, Fiend, Grebo, Holy, Hound, Loyalty, Mariolate, Novena, Nut, Ophism, Partisan, Passion, Pious, Puja, Religioso, Sacred, Saivite, S(h)akta, Savoyard, Sea-green incorruptible, Sivaite, Solemn, Sworn, True, Voteen, Zealous

Devour(ing) Consume, Eat, Engorge, Engulf, Manducate, Moth-eat, Scarf, Scoff, Snarf, → SWALLOW, Vorant

▷ **Devour** *may indicate* one word inside another

Devout Holy, Pia, Pious, Religiose, Reverent, Sant, Sincere, Solemn

Dew(y) Bloom, Gory, Moist, Mountain, Rime, Roral, Roric, Rorid, Roscid, Serein, Serene, Tranter

Dexterity, Dexterous Adept, Adroit, Aptitude, Cleverness, Craft, Deft, Feat(e)ous, Featuous, → HANDY, Knack, Shrewd, Sleight, Slick

Diabolic(al) Cruel, → DEVILISH, Infernal, Satanic

Diacritic (mark) Acute, Angstrom, Cedilla, Circumflex, Diaresis, Eth, Grave, Háček, Thorn, Tilde, Umlaut

Diadem Coronet, Fillet, Garland, Tiara

Diagnose, Diagnosis, Diagnostic Amniocentesis, Fetal, Findings, Identify, Iridology, Pulse, Radionics, Scan, Scintigraphy, X-ray

Diagonal(ly) Bend(wise), Bias, Cater(-corner), Catty-cornered, Counter, Oblique, Principal, Slant, Solidus, Speed, Twill

Diagram Argand, Block, Butterfly, Chart, Chromaticity, Cladogram, Compass rose, Decision tree, Dendrogram, Drawing, Fault-tree, Feynman, Figure, Flow, Graph, Graphics, Grid, Hertzsprung-Russell, Indicator, Logic, Map, Phase, Plan, Plat, Run-chart, Scatter, Schema, Schematic, Scintigram, Stem-and-leaf, Stemma, Stereogram, Tephigram, Topo, Tree, Venn, Wind rose

Dial(ling) Card, Face, Mug, Phiz, Phone, Pulse, Ring, Speed, STD, Visage

Dialect Acadian, Accent, Aeolic, Alemannic, Amoy, Anglican, Arcadic, Attic, Basuto, Burr, Castilian, Damara, Doric, Eldin, Eolic, Epic, Erse, Eye, Franconian, Friulian, Gallo-Romance, Gascon, Geechee, Geordie, Greenlander, Hassaniya, Hegelian, Idiom, Ionic, Isogloss, Jargon, Jockney, Joual, Khalka, Koine, Konkani, Ladin, Lallans, Landsmaal, Langobardic, Langue d'oc, Langue d'oil, Langue d'oui, Ledden, Lingo, Low German, Mackem, Min, Norman, Norn, Occitan, Old Icelandic, Old North French, Parsee, Parsi, Patavinity, Patois, Pedi, Picard, Prakrit, Rhaeto-Romance, Rhotic, Riffian, Rock English, Romans(c)h, Ruthenian, Salish, Savoyard, Scouse, Sesotho, Syriac, Taal, Tadzhik, Ta(d)jik, Talkee-talkee, Talky-talky, Tongue, Tshi, Tuscan, Twi, Tyrolese, Umbrian, Vaudois, Vernacular, Walloon, West Saxon, Wu, Yealdon, Yenglish, Yinglish

Dialogue Colloquy, Conversation, Critias, Discussion, Exchange, Interlocution, Lazzo, Pastourelle, Speech, Stichomythia, Talk, Upspeak

Dialysis Kidney, Peritoneal

Diameter Breadth, Calibre, Gauge, Systyle, Tactical, Width

Diamond(s), Diamond-shaped Adamant, Black, Boart, Brilliant, Bristol, Carbon, Carbonado, Cullinan, D, DE, Delaware, Eustace, False, Florentine, Hope, Ice, Industrial, Isomer, Jim, Koh-i-Noor, Lasque, Lattice, Lozenge, Paragon, Pick, Pitch, Pitt, Quarry, Reef, Rhinestone, Rhomb, Rock, Rose-cut, Rosser, Rough, Rustre, Sancy, Solitaire, Spark, Sparklers, Squarial, Suit

Diana Artemis, Di, Dorse
Diapason Normal, Open, Ottava, Stopped
Diaphanous Clear, Sheer, Translucent
Diaphoretic Sweater
Diaphragm Cap, Iris, Mid-riff, Phrenic, Stop
Diaresis Trema
▶ **Diarist** *see* **DIARY**
Diarrhoea Collywobbles, Delhi belly, Gippy tummy, Lientery, Montezuma's revenge, Runs, Scours, Squitters, The shits, Trots, Verbal, Weaning-brash, Wood-evil
Diary, Diarist Adrian Mole, Blogger, Burney, Chronicle, Dale, Day-book, Evelyn, Frank, Hickey, Journal, Journal intime, Kilvert, Log, Nobody, Noctuary, Pepys, Personal organiser, Planner, Pooter, Record, Video
Diaspora Exodus, Galuth
Diatribe Harangue, Invective, Philippic, Tirade
Dibble(r) Marsupial, Theria
Dice(r), Dicey Aleatory, Astragals, Bale, Bones, Chop, Craps, Cube, Doctor, Dodgy, Fulham, Fullams, Fullans, Gourd(s), Hash, Highman, Jeff, Mandoline, Novum, Poker, Shoot, Smalto, Snake-eyes, Tallmen
Dichotomy Split
Dick(y), Dickey Clever, Deadeye, Front, Ill, Laid up, Moby, OED, Policeman, Rumble, Shaky, Shirt, Spotted, Tec, Tonneau, Tucker, Tumbledown, Unstable, Wankle, Weak, Whittington
▷ **Dick** *may indicate* a dictionary
Dickens Boz, Deuce, Devil, Mephistopheles
Dicker Bargain, Barter, Haggle, Trade
▷ **Dicky** *may indicate* an anagram
Dictate, Dictator(ial) Amin, Authoritarian, Autocrat, Big Brother, Caesar, Castro, Cham, Command, Czar, Decree, Demagogue, Despot, Duce, Franco, Fu(e)hrer, Gaddafi, Gauleiter, Hitler, Impose, Indite, Lenin, Mussolini, Ordain, Overbearing, Peremptory, Peron, Pol Pot, Salazar, Shogun, Stalin, Tell, Tito, Totalitarian, Trujillo, Tsar, Tyrant, Tzar
Diction Language, Lexis, Palavinity, Speech, Style
Dictionary Alveary, Calepin, Chambers, Data, Etymologicon, Fowler, Gazetteer, Glossary, Gradus, Hobson-Jobson, Idioticon, Johnson's, Larousse, Lexicon, Lexis, OED, Onomasticon, Thesaurus, Vocabulary, Webster, Wordbook
Dictum Obiter, Saw, Say-so
Did Began, Couth, Fec(it), Gan
Didactic Sermonical
Diddle Cheat, Con, Hoax
Dido Antic, Caper, Carthaginian, Elissa
Die(d), Dying Ache, Buy the farm, Cark, Choke, Conk out, Crater, Croak, Cube, D, Decadent, Desire, End, Evanish, Exit, Expire, Fade, Fail, Flatline, Forfair, Fulham, Fulhan, Fullam, Go, Go west, Hallmark, Hang, Highman, Hop, Hop the twig, Infarct, Kark, Long, Morendo, Moribund, Ob(iit), Orb, Pass, Peg out, Perdendosi, Perish, Peter, Pop off, Pop one's clogs, Slip the cable, Snuff, Snuff it, Solidum, Sphacelation, Stagheaded, Stamp, Sterve, Succumb, Suffer, Swage, Swelt, Terminal, Tine, Touch, Wane
Diehard Blimp, Fanatic, Intransigent, Reactionary, Standpatter, Zealot
Diesel Red
Diet(er), Dieting Assembly, Atkins, Augsburg, Bant(ing), Cacotrophy, Council, Dail, Eat, Fare, Feed, Hay, Intake, Kashrut(h), Ketogenic, Landtag, Lent, Macrobiotic, Parliament, Pleading, Reduce, Regimen, Reichstag, Short commons, Slim, Solid, Sprat, Staple, Strict, Tynwald, Vegan, Vegetarian, Weightwatcher, Worms, Yo-yo
Dietetics Sit(i)ology
Differ(ence), Differing, Different(ly) Afresh, Allo, Alterity, Barney, Change, Cline,

Contrast, Contretemps, Deviant, Diesis, Disagree, Discord, Discrepant, Disparate, Dispute, Dissent, Dissimilitude, Distinct, Diverge, Diverse, Else, Elsewise, Epact, Exotic, Gulf, Heterodox, Nuance, Omnifarious, Other, Othergates, Otherguess, Otherness, Otherwise, Poles apart, Potential, Quantum, Separate, Several, Special, Symmetric, Tiff, Unlike, Variform, Various, Vary

Differential, Differentiate, Differentiation Calculus, Del, Distinguish, Nabla, Product, Secern, Segregate, Taxeme, Wage

Difficult(y), Difficult person Abstruseness, Ado, Aporia, Arduous, Augean, Badass, Balky, Ballbuster, Bitter, Block, Bolshie, Bother, Cantankerous, Catch, Choosy, Complex, Complication, Corner, Cough drop, Crisis, Crotchety, Deep, Delphic, Depth, Dysphagia, Embarrassment, Extreme, Fiddly, Formidable, Gnomic, Gordian, → **HARD**, Hassle, Hazard, Hiccough, Hiccup, Hobble, Hole, Hoor, Hump, Ill, Impasse, Indocile, Inscrutable, Intractable, Intransigent, Jam, Kink, Kittle, Knot, Lob's pound, Lurch, Mulish, Net, Nodus, Obstacle, Parlous, Pig, Pitfall, Plight, Predicament, Quandary, Queer St, Recalcitrant, Rough, Rub, Scabrous, Scrape, Scrub, Setaceous, Shlep, Snag, Soup, Steep, Stey, Stick, Sticky, Stiff, Stinker, Strait, Stubborn, Stymie, Swine, Tall order, Testing, Thorny, Ticklish, Tight spot, Tough, Trial, Tricky, Troublous, Trying, Une(a)th, Uphill, Via dolorosa, Woe

Diffident Bashful, Meek, Modest, Reserved, Retiring, Shy

Diffuse, Diffusion Barophoresis, Disperse, Disseminate, Endosmosis, Exude, Osmosis, Permeate, Pervade, Radiate, Run, Sperse, Spread, Thermal

Dig(s), Digger, Digging, Dig up Antipodean, Australian, Backhoe, Barb, Beadle, Bed(e)ral, Bedsit, Billet, Bot, Burrow, Costean, Delve, Deracinate, Enjoy, Excavate, Flea-bag, Flophouse, Fork, Fossorial, Gaulter, Get, Gibe, Gird, Graft, Graip, Grub, Hoe, Howk, Into, Jab, Kip, Lair, Like, Lodgings, Luxor, Mine, Navvy, Nervy, Nudge, Pad, Pioneer, Probe, Prod, Raddleman, Resurrect, Root(le), Ruddleman, Sap, See, Sneer, Spade, Spit, Spud, Star-nose, Taunt, Till, Tonnell, Trench, Tunnel, Undermine, Unearth

Digest(ible), Digestion, Digestive Abridgement, Absorb, Abstract, Aperçu, Archenteron, Assimilate, Beeda, Codify, Concoct, Endue, Epitome, Eupepsia, Eupepsy, Fletcherism, Gastric, Indew, Indue, Light, Pandect, Pem(m)ican, Pepsin(e), Peptic, Précis, Salt-cat, Steatolysis, → **SUMMARY**

Digit(s) Binary, Bit, Byte, Check, Dactyl, Figure, Finger, Hallux, Mantissa, Number, Pollex, Prehallux, Thumb, Toe

Dignified, Dignify August, Elevate, Ennoble, Exalt, Grace, Handsome, Honour, Imposing, Lordly, Maestoso, Majestic, Manly, Proud, Solemn, Stately, Statuesque

Dignitary Bigwig, Dean, Eminence, Name, Personage, Provost, → **VIP**

Dignity Aplomb, Bearing, Cathedra, Decorum, Face, Glory, Grandeur, Gravitas, High horse, Maestoso, Majesty, Nobility, Poise, Pontificate, Presence, Scarf, Tiara

Digraph Ash, Eng, Ng

Digress(ion) Apostrophe, Deviate, Diverge, Ecbole, Episode, Excurse, Excursus, Maunder, Vagary, Veer, Wander

Dike Bank, Channel, Cludgie, Dam, Ditch, → **DYKE**, Embank(ment), Estacade, Lav(atory), Levee, Wall

Dilapidated, Dilapidation Clapped out, Clunker, Decrepit, Derelict, Desolate, Disrepair, Eroded, Rickle, Ruined, Rust bucket, Shoddy, Tumbledown

Dilate, Dilation, Dilatation Amplify, Develop, Diastole, Ecstasis, Enlarge, Expand, Increase, Mydriasis, Sinus, Swell, Telangiectasia, Tent, Varix

Dilatory Protracting, Slow, Sluggish, Tardy

Dilemma Casuistry, Choice, Cleft (stick), Dulcarnon, Fix, Horn, Jam, Predicament, Quandary, Why-not

Dilettante Aesthete, Amateur, Butterfly, Dabbler, Playboy

Diligence, Diligent Active, Application, Assiduous, Coach, Conscience, Eident, Hard-working, Industry, Intent, Painstaking, Sedulous, Studious

Dill Anise, Pickle

Dilute(d), Dilution Adulterate, Allay, Deglaze, Delay, Diluent, Lavage, Qualify, Simpson, Thin, Water, Weaken, Wishy-washy

Dim(ness), Dimming, Dimwit(ted) Becloud, Blear, Blur, Brownout, Caligo, Clueless, Crepuscular, Dense, Dusk, Eclipse, Fade, Faint, Feint, Fozy, Gormless, Ill-lit, Indefinable, Indistinct, Mist, Nebulous, Ninny, Obscure, Overcast, Owl, Pale, Purblind, Shadow, Unsmart

Dimension(s) Area, Breadth, Extent, Fourth, Height, Length, Linear, Measure, New, Scantling, Size, Space, Third, Volume, Width

Dimer Cystine

Diminish(ed), Diminishing, Diminuendo, Diminution, Diminutive Abatement, Assuage, Baby, Bate, Calando, Contract, Cot(t)ise, Deactivate, Decline, Decrease, Détente, Detract, Disparage, Dissipate, Dwarf, Dwindle, Erode, Fourth, Hypocorism(a), Lessen, Lilliputian, Minify, Minus, Mitigate, Petite, Pigmy, Ritardando, Scarp, Small, Stultify, Subside, Taper, Toy, Trangle, Wane, Whittle

Dimple(d) Dent, Depression, Hollow, Orange-peel

Din Babel, Charivary, Chirm, Commotion, Deen, Discord, Gunga, Hubbub, → **NOISE**, Racket, Raird, Randan, Reel, Reird, Uproar, Utis

Dine(r), Dining Aristology, Café, Eat, Feast, Mess, Refect, Sup, Trat(toria)

Dingbat Doodad, Weirdo

Dingo Warrigal

Ding(h)y Cott, Inflatable, Pram, Shallop, Ship, Skiff

Dingy Crummy, Dark, Dirty, Drear, Dun, Fleapit, Fusc(ous), Grimy, Isabel(la), Isabelline, Lurid, Oorie, Ourie, Owrie, Shabby, Smoky

Dining-room Cafeteria, Cenacle, Commons, Frater, Hall, Langar, Mess hall, Refectory, Restaurant, Triclinium

Dinky Twee

Dinner Banquet, Collation, Feast, Hall, Kail, Kale, Meal, Prandial, Progressive, Repast, Spread

Dinner jacket Penguin suit

Dinosaur Aepyornis, Allosaurus, Ankylosaur, Apatosaurus, Archosaur, Atlantosaurus, Baryonyx, Brachiosaurus, Brontosaurus, Ceratopsian, Ceratosaurus, Ceteosaurus, Chalicothere, Coelurosaur, Compsognathus, Cotylosaur, Cynodont, Dinothere, Diplodocus, Dolichosaurus, Duck-billed, Elasmosaur, Galeopithecus, Glyptodon, Hadrosaur, Ichthyosaur(us), Iguanodon, Megalosaur, Microraptor, Mosasaur, Odontornithes, Ornithischian, Ornithopod, Ornithosaur, Oviraptor, Pachycephalosaur, Pelycosaur, Perissodactyl, Placoderm, Plesiosaur, Pliosaur, Prehistoric, Prosauropod, Pteranodon, Pterodactyl, Pterosaur, Pythonomorpha, Raptor, Rhynchocephalian, Saurischian, Sauropod, Saaeropterygian, Smilodon, Square, Stegodon(t), Stegosaur, Teleosaurus, Theropod, Titanosaurus, Titanothere, Triceratops, Tyrannosaurus, Uintothere, Velociraptor

Dint Brunt, Dent, Depression, Force, Means, Power

Diocese Bishopric, District, Eparchate, Eparchy, See

Diode Esaki, Tunnel, Zener

Diogenes Cynic

Dioxide Cassiterite, Needle-tin

Dip(per), Dippy Bagna cauda, Baptise, Basin, Bathe, Bob, Brantub, Dabble, Dap, Dean, Dib, Diver, Dop, Double, Duck, Dunk, Fatuous, Foveola, Geosyncline, Guacomole, Houmous, H(o)ummus, Humus, Immerge, Immerse, Intinction, Ladle, Lucky, Magnetic, Ousel, Ouzel, Paddle, Plough, Rinse, Rollercoaster, Sag, Salute, Sheep-wash, Star, Submerge, Tapenade, Taramasalata, Tzatziki, Ursa

Diphthong Crasis, Synaeresis, Synaloepha, Synizesis

Diploma Bac, Charter, Parchment, Qualification, Scroll, Sheepskin

Diplomacy, Diplomat(ic) Alternat, Ambassador, Attaché, Career, CD, Chargé d'affaires, Chateaubriand, Cheque-book, Consul, DA, Dean, Discretion, Dollar, Doyen,

El(t)chi, Emissary, Envoy, Fanariot, Fetial, Finesse, Gunboat, Legation, Lei(d)ger, Megaphone, Metternich, Phanariot, Plenipotentiary, Shuttle, Suave, → **TACT**
▷ **Dippy** *may indicate* a bather
Dipsomania Lush, Oenomania
Dire Dreadful, Fatal, Fell, Grim, Hateful, Ominous, Urgent
Direct(or), Directed, Directly Ad hominem, Administer, Advert, Aim, Airt, Air-to-air, Auteur, Aventre, Beeline, Board, Boss, Cann, Cast, Chairperson, Channel, Charge, Chorus-master, Command, Compere, Con(n), Conduct, Control, Cox, Dead, Due, Dunstable road, Enjoin, Executive, Explicit, Fair, Fast-track, Fellini, First-hand, Forthright, Frontal, Guide, Helm, Immediate, Impresario, Instruct, Intendant, Kapellmeister, Lead, Manager, Mastermind, Navigate, Nonexecutive, Outright, Oversee, Pilot, Play, Point-blank, Ready, Refer, Régisseur, Rudder, Send, Set, Signpost, Slap-bang, Stear, → **STEER**, Straight, Teach, Telic, Tell, Train, Unvarnished, Vector

---

DIRECTORS

3 letters:
Ray

4 letters:
Coen
Ford
Hall
Lang
Lean
Meno
Reed
Roeg
Tati
Weir

5 letters:
Brook
Clair
Fosse
Hawks
Joffe
Kazan
Korda
Losey

Lucas
Mamet
Noyce
Orson
Parer
Vidor
Wajda

6 letters:
Brooks
Bunuel
Curtiz
De Sica
De Vito
Dreyer
Herzog
Huston
Jarman
Ophuls
Pagnol
Powell
Welles
Wilder

7 letters:
Berkoff
Bresson
Campion
Chabrol
Coppola
Guthrie
Kaufman
Kubrick
Rivette
Russell
Sennett

8 letters:
Cousteau
Griffith
Merchant
Pasolini
Scorsese
Truffaut
Visconti

9 letters:
Antonioni

Hitchcock
Preminger
Spielberg
Tarantino
Tarkovsky

10 letters:
Eisenstein
Littlewood
Passbinder
Rossellini
Zeffirelli

11 letters:
Orson Welles
Pressburger
Riefenstahl
Von Stroheim

12 letters:
Stanislavski
Van Sternberg

Direction Aim, Airt, Arrow, Astern, Bearings, Course, Cross-reference, E, End-on, Guidance, Guide, Heading, Keblah, L, Line, N, Orders, Orientation, Passim, Quarter, R, Recipe, Route, Rubric, S, Sanction, Send, Sense, Side, Slap, Tacet, Tack, Tenor, Thataway, Tre corde, Trend, W, Way, Wedelns
Direction-finder Asdic, Compass, Decca, Quadrant, Radar, Sextant, Sonar
Directory Crockford, Data, Debrett, Encyclop(a)edia, Folder, French, Kelly, List, Red book, Register, Root, Search, Web, Yellow Pages®
Dirge Ballant, Coronach, Dirige, Epicedium, Knell, Monody, Requiem, Song, Threnody
Dirigible Airship, Balloon, Blimp, Zeppelin
Dirk Anelace, Dagger, Skean, Whinger, Whiniard, Whinyard
Dirt(y) Augean, Bed(r)aggled, Begrime, Bemoil, Cacky, Chatty, Clag, Clarty, Colly, Contaminate, Coom, Crock, Crud, Defile, Distain, Draggle, Dung, Dust, Earth, Festy, Filth, Foul, Gore, Grime, Grubby, Grufted, Grungy, Impure, Manky, Moit, Mote, Muck,

Obscene, Ordure, Pay, Pick, Pollute, Ray, Scandal, Scody, Sculdudd(e)ry, Scum, Scungy, Scuttlebutt, Scuzzy, Skanky, Skulduddery, Slattery, Smirch, Smut(ch), Soil, Sooty, Sordes, Sordor, Squalid, Squalor, Stain, Sully, Trash, Unclean, Unsatisfactory, Unwashed, Warb, Yucky, Yukky

Dis Hades, Hell

Disability, Disable(d) Cripple, Crock, Gimp, Handicapped, Hors de combat, Incapacitate, Kayo, Lame, Maim, Paralyse, Scissor-leg, Scotch, Supercrip, Wreck

Disabuse Unteach

Disadvantage Detriment, Disamenity, Downside, Drawback, Flipside, Handicap, Mischief, Out, Penalise, Penalty, Prejudice, Supercherie, Upstage, Wrongfoot, Zugswang

Disaffected Malcontent

Disagree(ing), Disagreeable, Disagreement Altercation, Argue, Argy-bargy, Bad, Clash, Conflict, Contest, Debate, Differ, Discrepant, Dispute, Dissent, Dissonant, Evil, Fiddlesticks, Friction, Heterodoxy, Pace, Plagu(e)y, Rift, Troll, Uh-uh, Unpleasing, Vary

Disallow Forbid, Overrule, Surcharge

Disappear(ing) Cook, Dispel, Evanesce, Evanish, Evaporate, Fade, Kook, Latescent, Melt, Occult, Pass, Skedaddle, Slope, → **VANISH**

Disappoint(ment), Disappointed, Disappointing Anticlimax, Balk, Baulk, Bombshell, Bummer, Chagrin, Comedown, Crestfallen, Delude, Disgruntle, Fizzer, Frustrate, Gutted, Heartsick, Lemon, Letdown, Mislippen, Off, Regret, Sell, Setback, Shucks, Sick, Suck-in, Sucks, Swiz(zle), Thwart, Tsk, Underwhelm

Disapproval, Disapprove(d) Ach, Animadvert, Boo, Catcall, Censure, Condemn, Deplore, Deprecate, Discountenance, Expostulate, Fie, Frown, Harrumph, Hiss, Mal vu, Napoo, Object, Pejorative, Po-faced, Pshaw, Raspberry, Razz, Reject, Reproach, Reprobate, Squint, Tush, Tut, Tut-tut, Umph, Veto, Whiss

Disarm(ament), Disarming Bluff, Defuse, Demobilise, Nuclear, Winsome

Disarrange Disturb, Muddle, Ruffle, Tousle, Unsettle

Disarray Disorder, Mess, Rifle, Tash, Undress

Disaster, Disastrous Accident, Adversity, Apocalypse, Bale, Calamity, Cataclysm(ic), Catastrophe, Crash, Crisis, Debacle, Dire, Doom, Evil, Fatal, Fiasco, Flop, Impostor, Meltdown, Mishap, Pitfall, Providence, Quake, Rout, Ruin, Screw-up, Seism, Shipwreck, Titanic, Tragedy, Wipeout

Disavow Abjure, Deny, Disclaim, Recant, Retract

Disbelief, Disbelieve(r) Acosmism, Anythingarian, Atheism, Cor, Doubt, Gawp, Incredulity, Mistrust, Nothingarianism, Occamist, Pfui, Phew, Phooey, Puh-lease, Puh-leeze, Question, Sceptic, Shoot, Stroll on, Voetsak

Disburse Distribute, Expend, Outlay, Spend

Disc, Disk Accretion, Bursting, Button, CD, Cheese, Clay pigeon, Compact, Coulter, Counter, Diaphragm, Dogtag, EP, Epiphragm, Fla(w)n, Flexible, Floppy, Frisbee®, Gold, Gong, Granum, Grindstone, Hard, Hard card, Harrow, Impeller, Intervertebral, Laser, LP, Magnetic, Mono, O, Optic(al), Parking, Paten, Patin, Planchet, Plate, Platinum, Platter, Puck, RAID, RAM, Rayleigh, Record, Reflector, Rosette, Roundel, Roundlet, Rowel, Rundle, Sealed unit, Silver, Slipped, Slug, Stereo, Stylopodium, Sun, Swash plate, System, Tax, Thylacoid, Token, Video, Wafer, Wharve, Whorl, Winchester, Wink, WORM, Zip®

Discard(ed) Abandon, Burn, Crib, Defy, Dele, Jettison, Kill, Leave, Obsolete, Off, Offload, Oust, Outtake, → **REJECT**, Scrap, Shed, Shuck, Slough, Sluff, Supersede, Throw over, Trash

Discern(ing), Discernment Acumen, Acute, Clear-eyed, Descry, Detect, Discrimination, Eagle-eyed, Flair, Insight, Perceive, Percipient, Perspicacity, Quick-sighted, Realise, Sapient, Scry, See, Skry, → **TASTE**, Tell, Wate

Discharge Absolve, Acquit, Arc, Assoil, Blennorrhoea, Blow off, Boot, Brush, Cashier, Catamenia, Catarrh, Conditional, Corona, Corposant, Dejecta, Deliver, Demob, Depose, Disembogue, Disgorge, Dishono(u)rable, Dismiss, Disruptive, Dump, Efflux, Effusion, Egest, Ejaculate, Eject, Embogue, Emission, Emit, Encopresis, Enfilade, Evacuate, Excrete, Execute, Exemption, Expulsion, Exude, Fire, Flashover, Flower, Flux, Frass,

Free, Fusillade, Gleet, Glow, Honourable, Issue, Jaculatory, Lava, Lay off, Leak, Let off, Leucorrhoea, Liberate, Lochia, Loose, Maturate, Menses, Mitimus, Muster out, Mute, Offload, Otorrhoea, Oust, Ozaena, Pass, Pay, Perform, Period, Planuria, Pour, Purulence, Pus, Pyorrhoea, Quietus, Redeem, Release, Rheum, Rhinorrhoeal, Run, Sack, Salvo, Sanies, Secretion, Seepage, Show, Shrive, Snarler, Spark, Spill, Static, Suppurate, Teem, Unload, Unloose, Vent, Void, Water, Whites

Disciple(s) Adherent, Apostle, Babi, Baruch, Catechumen, Chela, Dorcas, Follower, John, Judas, Luke, Mark, Matthew, Peter, Simon, Son, Student, The Seventy, Thomist, Votary

Disciplinarian, Discipline(d) Apollonian, Ascesis, Chasten, Chastise, Constrain, Correct, Despot, Drill, Exercise, Feng shui, Inure, Judo, Martinet, Mathesis, Penal, Punish, Ramrod, Regimentation, Regulate, Sadhana, School, Science, Spartan, Stickler, Subject, Taskmaster, Train, Tutor

▶ **Disc jockey** *see* **DJ**

Disclaim(er) Deny, Disown, No(t)chel, Recant, Renounce, → **REPUDIATE**, Voetstoots

Disclose, Disclosure Apocalypse, Confess, Divulge, Expose, Impart, Leak, Manifest, Propale, → **PUBLISH**, Report, Reveal, Spill, Tell, Unheal, Unhele, Unrip, Unveil

Discoloration, Discolour(ed) Acrocyanosis, Bloodstain, Bruise, Cyanosis, Dyschroa, Ecchymosis, Fox, Livedo, Livid, Livor, Stain, Streak, Tarnish, Tinge, Weather

Discomfit(ure) Abash, Confuse, Disconcert, Disturb, Frustrate, Lurch, Shend

Discomfort(ed) Ache, All-overish, Angst, Dysphoria, Gyp, Heartburn, Pain, Unease

Disconcert(ing) Abash, Astound, Confuse, Disturb, Embarrass, Faze, Feeze, Flurry, Fluster, Nonplus, Off-putting, Phase, Pheese, Pheeze, Phese, Put off, → **RATTLE**, Shatter, Startle, Tease, Throw, Unnerve, Upset, Wrong-foot

▷ **Disconcert(ed)** *may indicate* an anagram

Disconnect(ed) Asynartete, Decouple, Detach, Disassociate, Disjointed, Off-line, Segregate, Sever, Staccato, Trip, Uncouple, Undo, Ungear, Unplug

Disconsolate Desolate, Doleful, Downcast, → **GLOOMY**

Discontent(ed) Disquiet, Dissatisfied, Humph, Repined, Sour, Umph, Unrest

Discontinue, Discontinuance, Discontinuity Abandon, Break off, Cease, Desist, Desuetude, Drop, Moho, Prorogue, Stop, Terminate

Discord(ant) Absonant, Ajar, Charivari, Conflict, Din, Dispute, Division, Eris, Faction, Hoarse, Jangle, Jar(ring), Raucous, Ruction, Strife

▷ **Discord(ant)** *may indicate* an anagram

Discount Agio, Cashback, Deduct, Disregard, Forfaiting, Invalidate, Quantity, → **REBATE**, Trade

Discountenance Disfavour, Efface, Embarrass

Discourage(ment) Caution, Chill, Dampen, Dash, Daunt, Deject, Demoralise, Deter, Dishearten, Disincentive, Dismay, Dispirit, Dissuade, Enervate, Frustrate, Intimidate, Opposition, Stifle, Unman

Discourse Address, Argument, Colloquy, Conversation, Descant, Diatribe, Dissertate, Eulogy, Expound, Homily, Lecture, Lucubrate, Orate, Philippic, Preach, Recount, Relate, Rigmarole, Sermon, Wash

Discourteous, Discourtesy Disrespect, Impolite, Insult, Rude, Slight, Uncivil, Unmannerly

Discover(y), Discoverer Amundsen, Anagnorisis, Ascertain, Betray, Breakthrough, Columbus, Cook, Descry, Detect, Determine, Discern, Discure, Esery, Eureka, → **FIND**, Heurema, Heuristic, Hit on, Learn, Locate, Manifest, Moresby, Protegé, Rumble, Serendip, Serendipity, Spy, Tasman, Trace, Treasure trove, Trouvaille, Unearth, Unhale, Unmask, Unveil

▷ **Discovered in** *may indicate* an anagram or a hidden word

Discredit(able) Debunk, Decry, Disbelieve, Disgrace, Explode, Infamy, Scandal, Slur, Smear, Unworthy

Discreet, Discretion Cautious, Circumspect, Finesse, Freedom, Judicious, Option, Polite, Politic, Prudence, Prudent, Trait, Unobtrusive, Wise

Discrepancy Difference, Gap, Lack, Shortfall, Variance
Discrete Distinct, Separate, Unrelated
Discriminate, Discriminating, Discrimination Ag(e)ism, Colour bar, Diacritic, Differentiate, Discern, Distinguish, Elitism, Fastidious, Handism, Invidious, Lookism, Nasute, Racism, Rankism, Reverse, Secern, Segregate, Select, Sexism, Siz(e)ism, Speciesism, Subtle, Taste
Discursive Roving
Discuss(ed), Discussion Agitate, Air, Bat around, Canvass, Commune, Confer(ence), Consult, Corridor work, Debate, Deliberate, Dialectic, Dialogue, Dicker, Disquisition, Emparl, En l'air, Examine, Excursus, Expatiate, Gabfest, Handle, Heart-to-heart, Hob and nob, Imparl, Interlocution, Issue, Kick-about, Korero, Moot, Negotiation, Over, Palaver, Parley, Pourparler, Prolegomenon, Quodlibet, Rap, Re, Symposium, Talk, Talkathon, Talkboard, Tapis, Treatment, Trialogue, Ventilate, Vex, Words
Disdain(ful) Belittle, Contempt, Coy, Deride, Despise, Geck, Poof, Pooh-pooh, Pugh, Puh, Rats, Sassy, Scoffer, → **SCORN**, Scout, Sdei(g)n, Sneering, Sniffy, Spurn, Stuffy, Supercilious, Ugh
Disease(d) Affection, Ailment, Bug, Communicable, Comorbid, Complaint, Deficiency, Defluxion, Epidemic, Fever, Functional, Industrial, Infection, Malady, Noso-, Nosocomial, Notifiable, Occupational, Organic, Pest(ilence), Rot, Scourge, Sickness

DISEASES

2 letters:	Lyme	Sprue	Morbus
CD	Roup	Surra	Mosaic
MD	Wind	Tinea	Nagana
ME	Yaws	Virus	Oedema
MS		Weil's	Paget's
TB	**5 letters:**	Worms	Parrot
VD	Bang's		Rabies
	Black	**6 letters:**	Sapego
3 letters:	Borna	Anbury	Scurvy
ALS	Brand	Aphtha	Social
BSE	Dread	Blight	Still's
Flu	Dutch	Blotch	Thrush
Haw	Ebola	Border	Tunnel
MND	Edema	Cancer	Typhus
Pip	Ergot	Canker	Ulitis
Pox	Favus	Chagas'	Urosis
Sod	Fifth	Chorea	Yuppie
→ **STD**	Gapes	Cowpox	Zoster
TSE	Hoove	Crohn's	
Wog	Kwok's	Cruels	**7 letters:**
	Lupus	Dartre	Ascites
4 letters:	Lurgi	Dengue	Batten's
Aids	Lurgy	Eczema	Blue-ear
Boba	Mesel	Farcin	Bright's
Bunt	Mumps	Graves'	British
Clap	Ngana	Herpes	Caisson
Conk	Palsy	Income	Cholera
Gout	Pinta	Johne's	Coeliac
Keel	Polio	Mad cow	Crewels
Kuru	Pott's	Marek's	Crinkle
Loco	Rabid	Meazel	Dieback
Lues	Scall	Mildew	Dourine

Endemic
English
Eyespot
Frogeye
Frounce
Gum rash
Hansen's
Hardpad
Hydatid
Icterus
Kissing
Leprosy
Lockjaw
Maidism
Malaria
Marburg
Miller's
Mimesis
Mooneye
Moor-ill
Murrain
Mycosis
Myiasis
Pébrine
Podagra
Purples
Pyaemia
Quittor
Redfoot
Rickets
Ring rot
Rosette
Scabies
Scrapie
Sequela
Serpigo
Tetanus
Tetters
Typhoid
Variola
Wilson's
Zymosis

8 letters:
Addison's
Alastrim
Aujesky's
Basedow's
Beri-beri
Blackleg
Black-rot
Bornholm
Bullnose
Club root

Crown rot
Curly top
Cushing's
Cynanche
Diabetes
Dutch elm
Economo's
Epilepsy
Fishskin
Fowl pest
Gape-worm
Gaucher's
Glanders
Glaucoma
Goujeers
Gummosis
Hodgkin's
Hookworm
Impetigo
Jaundice
Kala-azar
Kawasaki
Leaf-roll
Leaf-spot
Liver-rot
Loose-cut
Menière's
Minamata
Mycetoma
Myopathy
Myxedema
Nosology
Pandemic
Pathogen
Pellagra
Phthisis
Phytosis
Porrigro
Progeria
Pullorum
Rachitis
Raynaud's
Red water
Rose-rash
Scaly leg
Scrofula
Shingles
Slimmers'
Smallpox
Soft sore
Suppeago
Swayback
Swinepox
Syphilis

Tay-Sachs
The bends
Time-zone
Trembles
Uteritis
Venereal
Vincent's
Zoonosis

9 letters:
Arthrosis
Bilharzia
Blackhead
Black knot
Black-lung
Brown lung
Chancroid
Chlorosis
Christmas
Cirrhosis
Contagion
Cytopathy
Diathesis
Distemper
Dysentery
Ear-cockle
Enteritis
Exanthema
Filanders
Gonorrhea
Idiopathy
Ixodiasis
Kawasaki's
King's evil
Lathyrism
Leucaemia
Leukaemia
Loose smut
Myxoedema
Navicular
Nephritis
Nephrosis
Newcastle
New Forest
Pellagrin
Pemphigus
Phossy-jaw
Porphyria
Seborrhea
Siderosis
Silicosis
Toxicosis
Trichosis
Tularemia

Tulip root
Yuppie flu

10 letters:
Acromegaly
Alzheimer's
Amoebiasis
Asbestosis
Autoimmune
Babesiosis
Bagassosis
Black death
Bluetongue
Byssinosis
Chickenpox
Dandy-fever
Diphtheria
Erysipelas
Filariasis
Fire-blight
Fowl plague
Framboesia
Giardiasis
Gonorrhoea
Heartwater
Hemophilia
Iatrogenic
Ichthyosis
Impaludism
Lassa fever
Leuchaemia
Limber-neck
Lou Gehrig's
Louping ill
Moniliasis
Muscardine
Myasthenia
Neuropathy
Nosography
Nosophobia
Ornithosis
Parkinson's
Quarter-ill
Scarlatina
Seborrhoea
Texas fever
Topagnosia
Tularaemia

11 letters:
Anthracosis
Berylliosis
Brittle-bone
Cardiopathy

Coccidiosis
Consumption
Farmer's lung
Green monkey
Haemophilia
Hebephrenia
Huntington's
Isle of Wight
Kwashiorkor
Listeriosis
Myxomatosis
Parasitosis
Paratyphoid
Psittacosis
Rickettsial
Sarcoidosis
Scleroderma
Scrub typhus
Septicaemia
Thalassemia
Tonsillitis
Trench mouth
Trichinosis
Waldsterben

Woolsorter's
Yellow-fever

12 letters:
Alkaptonuria
Avitaminosis
Black quarter
Cor Pulmonate
Ehrlichiosis
Enterobiasis
Fascioliasis
Finger and toe
Foot and mouth
Furunculosis
Hoof and mouth
Legionnaires'
Molybdenosis
Motor neurone
Osteomalacia
Osteoporosis
Scheuermann's
Shaking palsy
Slapped cheek
Thalassaemia

Tuberculosis
Uncinariasis

13 letters:
Elephantiasis
Leichmaniasis
Leptospirosis
Osteomyelitis
Panleucopenia
Poliomyelitis
Salmonellosis
Sclerodermata
Syringomyelia
Toxoplasmosis
Tsutsugamushi

14 letters:
Coalminer's lung
Cystic fibrosis
Histoplasmosis
Leucodystrophy
Onchocerciasis
Pasteurellosis
Pneumoconiosis

Psillid yellows
River blindness
Sporotrichosis
St Anthony's Fire
Trichomoniasis
Trichophytosis
Vincent's angina

15 letters:
Graft-versus-host
Schistosomiasis
Sydenham's chorea
Trypanosomiasis

16 letters:
Pneumonoconiosis
Sleeping sickness
Strongyloidiasis
Sweating sickness

17 letters:
Friedreich's ataxia
Multiple sclerosis

▷ **Diseased** *may indicate* an anagram

Disembark Alight, Detrain, Land

Disembarrass Extricate, Rid, Unthread

Disembowel Eviscerate, Exenterate, Gralloch, Gut, Viscerate

Disenchant Disabuse, Disillusion, Dismay, Embitter

Disencumber Free, Rid, Unburden

Disengage(d), Disengagement Clear, Detach, Divorce, Liberate, Loosen, Neutral, Release, Untie

Disentangle Debarrass, Extricate, Red(d), Solve, Unravel, Unsnarl

Disestablishmentarian Cosmist

Disfavour Doghouse, Maugre

Disfigure(ment), Disfigured Agrise, Agryze, Camsho, Club-foot, Deface, Deform, Goitre, Mangle, Mutilate, Scar, Spoil, Tash, Ugly

▷ **Disfigured** *may indicate* an anagram

Disgorge Discharge, Eject, Spew, Spill, Vent, Void

Disgrace, Disgraceful Atimy, Attaint, Baffle, Blot, Contempt, Contumely, Degrade, Diabolical, Discredit, Dishonour, Dog-house, Fie, Ignoble, Ignominious, Ignominy, Indign, Indignity, Infamous, Infamy, Mean, Notorious, Obloquy, Opprobrium, Pity, Reprehensible, Scandal, Scandalous, Shame, Shameful, Shend, Slur, Soil, Stain, Stigma, Turpitude, Yshend

Disgruntled Brassed off, Hacked off, Malcontent, Narked, Resentful, Sore

▷ **Disgruntled** *may indicate* an anagram

Disguise(d) Alias, Blessing, Camouflage, Cloak, Colour, Conceal, Cover, Covert, Dissemble, Hide, Hood, Incog(nito), Mantle, Mask, Masquerade, Obscure, Peruke, Pretence, Pseudonym, Ring, Shades, Stalking horse, Travesty, Veil, Vele, Veneer, Visagiste, Visor, Vizard

▷ **Disguised** *may indicate* an anagram

Disgust(ing) Ach-y-fi, Ad nauseam, Aversion, Aw, Bah, Cloy, Discomfort, Execrable, Faugh, Fie, Foh, Fulsome, Grisly, Grody, Icky, Irk, Loathsome, Manky, Mawkish, Minging,

Nauseous, Noisome, Obscene, Odium, Oughly, Ouglie, Pah, Pho(h), Pish, Pshaw, Pugh, Repel, Repugnant, Repulse, → **REVOLT**, Revulsion, Scomfish, Scumfish, Scunner, Scuzz, → **SICKEN**, Sir-reverence, Si(e)s, Slimeball, Slimy, Squalid, Turn off, Tush, Ugh, Ugly, Ugsome, Vile, Yech, Yucko, Yu(c)k, Yukky

Dish(y) Adonis, Allot, Apollo, Ashet, Basin, Belle, Bowl, Chafing, Charger, Cocotte, Compotier, Concoction, Cook-up, Cutie, Dent, Diable, Dole, Dreamboat, Epergne, Flasket, Flatware, Grail, Kitchen, Laggen, Laggin, Lanx, Luggie, Menu, Muffineer, Ovenware, Pan, Pannikin, Paten, Patera, Patin(e), Petri, Plate, Platter, Popsy, Porringer, Ramekin, Ramequin, Receptacle, Rechauffé, Remove, Rout, Sangraal, Sangrail, Sangreal, Satellite, Saucer, Scorifier, Scupper, Serve, Service, Side (order), Smasher, Special, Stunner, Toll, Watchglass, Woodenware

---

DISHES

3 letters:
Poi

4 letters:
Flan
Fool
Kiev
Melt
Mess
Milt
Olla
Puri
Sate
Soss
Taco
Tian

5 letters:
Adobo
Balti
Bhaji
Bhuna
Bitok
Boxty
Brose
Champ
Crepe
Curry
Dolma
Gomer
Gruel
Kasha
Keema
Kibbe
Kofta
Korma
Laksa
Maror
Perog
Pilaf

Pilau
Pilow
Poori
Raita
Ramen
Rosti
Sabji
Salad
Salmi
Satay
Split
Sushi
Tamal
Tikka
Tripe

6 letters:
Bhagee
Bharta
Bhoona
Bridie
Chilli
Cou-cou
Cuscus
Entrée
Fondue
Haggis
Hotpot
Kimchi
Kishke
Kissel
Masale
Mornay
Mousse
Muesli
Nachos
Paella
Pakora
Panada
Pirogi

Quiche
Ragout
Regale
Roesti
Salmis
Sea-pie
Sowans
Sowens
Subgum
Surimi
Tamale
Tsamba

7 letters:
Biriani
Bobotie
Burrito
Calzone
Cannoli
Cassava
Ceviche
Chowder
Comport
Compote
Crowdie
Crubeen
Crumble
Custard
Cuvette
Dariole
Dhansak
Dopiaza
Egg roll
Fajitas
Fal-a-fel
Fel-a-fel
Foo yung
Friture
Grav lax
Haroset

Marengo
Mousaka
Padella
Pad thai
Piccata
Pierogi
Poutine
Rarebit
Ravioli
Risotto
Sasatie
Sashimi
Scallop
Seviche
Sosatie
Soufflé
Spag bol
Stir-fry
Stovies
Supreme
Tartare
Tempura
Terrine
Timbale
Tostada
Zampone

8 letters:
Bhelpuri
Brandade
Bresaola
Calabash
Caponata
Chasseur
Chop suey
Chow mein
Coolamon
Coq au vin
Coquille
Couscous

Crostini
Dog's-body
Dolmades
Entremes
Feijoada
Flummery
Frittata
Furmenty
Gado-gado
Grillade
Halloumi
Handroll
Haroseth
Jalfrezi
Kedgeree
Keftedes
Kickshaw
Kouskous
Kreplach
Linguini
Mahi-mahi
Matelote
Mazarine
McCallum
Meat loaf
Meunière
Moussaka
Pandowdy
Pastrami
Porridge
Pot-au-feu
Pot-roast
Raclette
Scrapple
Shashlik
Sillabub
Souvlaki
Squarial
Sukiyaki
Syllabub
Teriyaki

Tzatziki
Vindaloo
White-pot
Yakimono
Yakitori

9 letters:
Carbonara
Carpaccio
Cevapcici
Clafoutis
Egg-fo-yang
Enchilada
Entremets
Escabeche
Fricassee
Galantine
Gravad lax
Guacamole
Howtowdie
Jambalaya
Lobscouse
Lyonnaise
Manicotti
Marinière
Matelotte
Pastitsio
Pepper-pot
Reistafel
Rijstafel
Rillettes
Rogan josh
Scotch egg
Shashlick
Souvlakia
Succotash
Surf n' turf
Turducken

10 letters:
Blanquette

Bombay duck
Cacciatore
Cottage pie
Coulibiaca
Couscousou
Doner kebab
Egg custard
Egg-foo-yung
Jugged hare
Koulibiaca
Mousseline
Nasi goreng
Parmigiana
Pease brose
Plat du jour
Provençale
Quesadilla
Rijsttafel
Salmagundi
Sauerkraut
Scaloppine
Shish kebab
Spankopita
Spitchcock
Spring roll
Steak diane
Stroganoff
Teppan-yaki
Zabaglione

11 letters:
Banana split
Buck-rarebit
Chimichanga
Crappit-head
French toast
Fritto misto
Saltimbocca
Sauerbraten
Smorgasbord
Spanakopita

Surf and turf
Welsh rabbit

12 letters:
Buffalo wings
Eggs Benedict
Parmigianino
Shepherd's pie
Solomon Gundy
Steak tartare
Sweet and sour
Taramasalata
Welsh rarebit

13 letters:
Fish and brewis
Rumbledethump
Salade nicoise
Skirl in the pan
Toad-in-the-hole

14 letters:
Beef stroganoff
Beef Wellington
Chilli con carne
Rumbledethumps
Scotch woodcock

15 letters:
Bubble and squeak
Eggs in moonshine

16 letters:
Moules marinieres
Potatoes and point

17 letters:
Cauliflower cheese

Dishabille Disarray, Négligé, Undress
Dishearten Appal, Core(r), Cow, Daunt, Depress, Deter, Discourage, Dispirit, Ettle
Dishevel(led) Bedraggled, Blowsy, Blowzy, Daggy, Mess, Rumpled, Scraggly, Touse, Tousle, Touzle, Towse, Tumble, Uncombed, Unkempt, Untidy, Windswept
Dishonest(y) Bent, Crooked, Cross, Dodgy, False, Fraud, Graft, Hooky, Hot, Improbity, Jiggery-pokery, Knavery, Light-fingered, Malpractice, Malversation, Maverick, Rort, Shonky, Sleazy, Snide, Stink, Twister, Underhand, Venal, Wrong'un
Dishonour Abatement, Defile, Disgrace, Disparage, Ignominy, Indignity, Seduce, → SHAME, Violate, Wrong
Disillusion(ment) Awakening, Disenchant, Sour
Disincline(d), Disinclination Apathy, Averse, Loth, Off, Reluctant
Disinfect(ant) Acriflavin(e), Carbolic, Carvacrol, Cineol(e), Cleanse, Dip, Eucalyptole,

Formalin, Formol, Fuchsine, Fumigate, Lysol®, Orcein, Phenol, Purify, Sheep-dip, Sheep-wash, TCP, Terebene

Disingenuous Insincere, Mask, Oblique, Two-faced

Disinherit Deprive, Dispossess

Disintegrate, Disintegration Break, Collapse, Crumble, Decay, Dialysis, Erode, Fragment, Lyse, Lysis, Osteoclasis, Rd, Rutherford

Disinter Exhume, Unearth

Disinterested Apathetic, Impartial, Incurious, Mugwump, Unbiased

Disjoint(ed) Bitty, Dismember, Incoherent, Rambling, Scrappy

Disjunction Exclusive, Inclusive

▶ **Disk** *see* DISC

Dislike(d) Abhor, Allergy, Animosity, Animus, Antipathy, Aversion, Bete noire, Derry, Disesteem, Displeasure, Distaste, Gross out, Hate, Lump, Mind, Needle, Resent, Scunner, Ug, Warling

Dislocate, Dislocation Break, Diastasis, Displace, Fault, Luxate, Slip, Subluxate

Dislodge Budge, Displace, Expel, Luxate, Oust, Rear, Tuft, Unship, Uproot

Disloyal(ty) Blue, False, Recreant, Treason, Unfaithful, Untrue

Dismal Black, Bleak, Blue, Cheerless, Dark, Dowie, Dowly, Drack, Dreary, Funereal, → GLOOMY, Grey, Long-faced, Morne, Obital, Sepulchral, Sombre, Sullen, Trist(e), Wae, Woebegone, Wormy

Dismantle(d), Dismantling Decommission, Derig, Divest, Get-out, Sheer-hulk, Strike, Strip, Unrig

Dismast Unstep

Dismay(ed) Aghast, Alarm, Amate, Appal, Confound, Consternation, Coo, Criv(v)ens, Daunt, Dispirit, Dread, Fie, Ha, Hah, Horrify, Lordy, Lumme, Qualms, Strewth, Uh-oh

Dismember Quarter

Dismiss(al), Dismissive Airy, Annul, Ax, Boot, Bounce, Bowl(er), Brush off, Bum's rush, Can, Cancel, Cashier, Catch, Chuck, Congé, Constructive, Daff, Discard, Discharge, Dooced, Expulsion, Fire, Forget, Golden bowler, Heave-ho, Kiss-off, Lay off, License, Marching orders, Mitten, Och, Pink-slip, Prorogue, Push, Recall, Reform, Reject, Remove, R.O., Road, Sack, Scout, Send, Shoo, Shrug off, Skittle out, Spit, Spurn, Stump, Suka wena, Via, Voetsak, Walking papers, Wicket, York

Dismount Alight, Hecht

Disobedience, Disobedient, Disobey Contumacy, Defy, Flout, Insubordination, Rebel, Sit-in, Unruly, Wayward

Disorder(ly), Disordered Affective, Ague, Ailment, Anarchy, Ariot, Asthma, Ataxia, Betumbler, Catatonia, Chaos, Chlorosis, Clutter, Collywobbles, Conduct, Confuse, Consumption, Contracture, Conversion, Defuse, Derange, Deray, Diabetes, Dishevel, Dissociative, DT's, Dyslexia, Dysthymic, Dystrophy, Echolalia, Entropy, Epilepsy, Farrago, Folie a deux, Greensickness, Grippe, Haemophilia, Hallucinosis, Heartburn, Huntingdon's chorea, Hypallage, Inordinate, Irregular, Mange, Mare's nest, ME, Mental, Mess, Misrule, Mistemper, → MUDDLE, Muss(y), Neurosis, Oncus, Onkus, Overset, Pandemonium, Panic, Para-, Pell-mell, Personality, Phenylketonuria, Porphyria, Priapus, Psychomatic, Psychoneurosis, Psychopathic, Psychosis, Ragmatical, Rile, Roughhouse, Rowdy, Rumple, SAD, St Vitus' Dance, Schizophrenia, Schizothymia, Seborrh(o)ea, Shell-shock, Slovenly, Snafu, Sydenham's chorea, Tarantism, Thalass(a)emia, Thought, Tousle, Turbulence, Turmoil, Unhinge, Unruly, Upheaval, Upset, Virilism

▷ **Disorder(ed)** *may indicate* an anagram

Disorganise(d) At sea, Deranged, Disorderly, Haphazard, Haywire, Higgledy-piggledy, Ragtag, Ramshackle, Scatterbrain, Scatty, Shambolic, Structureless

Disorientation Jet lag

Disown Deny, Disclaim, Disinherit, Renig, Renounce, Repudiate, Unget

Disparage, Disparaging Abuse, Belittle, Decry, Defame, Denigrate, Depreciate,

Derogate, Detract, Discredit, Lessen, Pejorative, Poor mouth, Racist, Run down,
→ **SLANDER**, Slur, Snide, Traduce, Vilify

Disparate Motley

Dispassionate Calm, Clinical, Composed, Cool, Impartial, Objective, Serene

Dispatch Bowl, Celerity, Consign, Destroy, Dismiss, Epistle, Expede, Expedite, Express,
Gazette, Kibosh, Kill, Letter, Message, Missive, Note, Post, Pronto, Remit, Report,
→ **SEND**, Shank, Ship, Slaughter, Slay, Special

Dispel Disperse, Scatter

Dispensation, Dispense(r), Dispense with Absolve, Administer, Aerosol,
Apothecary, Automat, Ax(e), Cashpoint, Chemist, Chop, Container, Distribute, Dose,
Dropper, Exempt, Fountain, Handout, Hole in the wall, Indult, Optic, Pour, Scrap,
Siphon, Soda fountain, Spinneret, Vendor, Visitation

Disperse, Dispersible, Dispersion Deflocculate, Diaspora, Diffract, Diffuse,
Disband, Dissolve, Distribute, Evaporate, Lyophil(e), Mode, Scail, Scale, → **SCATTER**,
Skail, Sow, Spread, Strew

Dispirit(ed), Dispiriting Chapfallen, Crestfallen, Dampen, Dash, Daunt, Discourage,
Dishearten, Exorcism, Gloomy, Listless, Sackless

Displace(ment), Displaced Antevert, Blueshift, Chandler's wobble, Depose,
Dethrone, Disturb, Ectopia, Ectopy, Fault, Heterotopia, Lateroversion, Load, Luxate,
Move, Oust, Proptosis, Ptosis, Reffo, Shift, Stir, Subluxation, Unseat, Unsettle, Uproot,
Upthrow, Valgus, Varus, Volumetric

Display, Display ground Air, Array, Blaze, Blazon, Brandish, Bravura, Depict,
Eclat, Epideictic, Etalage, Evidence, Evince, Exhibition, Exposition, Express, Extend,
Extravaganza, Exude, Fireworks, Flash, Flaunt, Float, Gala, Gondola, Hang, Head-down,
Head-up, Heroics, Iconic, Lay out, LCD, LED, Lek, Liquid crystal, Manifest, Motorcade,
Mount, Muster, Ostentation, Outlay, Overdress, Pageant, Parade, Paraf(f)le, Peepshow,
Pixel, Pomp, Present(ation), Propale, Pyrotechnics, Rode, Rodeo, Roll-out, Scene, Scroll,
Set piece, Shaw, → **SHOW**, Showcase, Sight, Spectacle, Splash, Splurge, Sport, Spree,
State, Stunt, Tableau, Tattoo, Tournament, Turn out, Up, Vaunt, Wear, Window dressing

Displease(d), Displeasure Anger, Dischuffed, Humph, Irritate, Provoke, Umbrage

Disport Amuse, Divert, Play

Dispose(d), Disposal, Disposition Apt, Arrange, Bestow, Bin, Cast, Despatch,
Dump, Eighty-six, Kibosh, Kybosh, Lay(-out), Mood, Ordonnance, Prone, Riddance, Sale,
Sell, Service, Settle, Spirit, Stagger, Throwaway

▷ **Disposed, Disposition** *may indicate* an anagram

Disposition Affectation, Attitude, Bent, Bias, Humour, Inclination, Kidney, Lie, Nature,
Penchant, Propensity, Talent, Temper(ament), Trim

Dispossess(ed) Abate, Attaint, Bereft, Depose, Deprive, Disseise, Evict, Oust

Disproportion(ate) Asymmetric, Extreme, Imbalance, Incommensurate, Unequal

Disprove, Disproof, Disproval Debunk, Discredit, Invalidate, Negate, Rebut,
Rebuttal, Redargue, Reductio ad absurdum, Refel, Refute

Dispute(d), Disputant Argue, Argy-bargy, At odds, Barney, Brangle, Cangle, Case,
Chaffer, Challenge, Chorizont(ist), Contend, Contest, Contravene, Contretemps,
Controversy, Debate, Demarcation, Deny, Differ, Discept, Discuss, Eristic, Feud,
Fracas, Fray, Haggle, Kilfud-yoking, Lock-out, Loggerheads, Militate, Ob and soller,
Odds, Oppugn, Plea, Polemic, Pro-and-con, Quarrel, → **QUESTION**, Quibble, Rag,
Resist, Slanging-match, Spar, Spat, Stickle, Stoush, Threap(it), Threep(it), Tiff, Tissue,
Tug-of-love, Variance, Wrangle

Disqualify Debar, Incapacitate, Recuse, Reject, Unfit

Disquiet(ed) Agitate, Concern, Discomboberate, Discombobulate, → **DISTURB**, Pain,
Perturb(ation), Solicit, Turmoil, Uneasy, Unnerve, Unrest, Vex

Disraeli Dizzy, Tancred

Disregard(ed) Anomie, Anomy, Contempt, Defy, Disfavour, Flout, Forget, Ignore,
Neglect, Oblivion, Omit, Overlook, Oversee, Pass, Pretermit, Slight, Spare, Violate, Waive

Disrepair Dilapidation, Fritz, Ruin

Disreputable, Disrepute Base, Black sheep, Bowsie, Disgrace, Grubby, Ken, Louche, Low, Lowlife, Notorious, Raffish, Ragamuffin, Reprobate, Rip, Scuzz(ball), Scuzzbag, Scuzzbucket, Seamy, Seamy side, Shady, Shameful, Shy, Shyster, Sleazy

Disrespect(ful) Contempt, Derogatory, Discourtesy, Flip(pant), Impiety, Impolite, Irreverent, Levity, Profane, Slight, Uncivil, Violate

Disrupt(ion) Breach, Cataclasm, Dislocate, Disorder, Distract, Hamper, Hiatus, Interrupt, Jetlag, Mayhem, Perturb, Quonk, Ruffle, Screw, Upheaval

▷ **Disruption** *may indicate* an anagram

Dissatisfaction Displeasure, Distaste, Humph, Umph

Dissect(ion) Analyse, Dismember, Examine, Necrotomy, Zootomy

Dissemble(r) Conceal, Feign, Fox, Hypocrite, Impostor, Misinform

Dissent(er), Dissension, Dissenting Contend, Differ, Disagree, Discord, Dissident, Divisiveness, Faction, Flak, Heretic, Holmes, Jain, Leveller, Lollard, Maverick, Noes, Non-CE, Non-con(formist), Occasional conformist, Old Believer, Pantile, Protest, Raskolnik, Recusant, Remonstrant, Sectary, Separat(ion)ist, Splinter group, → **STRIFE**, Vary

Dissertation Essay, Excursus, Lecture, Paper, Thesis, Treatise

Dissidence → **DESERTER**, Schism

▸ **Dissident** *see* **DESERTER**

Dissimilar Different, Diverse, Heterogeneous, Unlike

Dissipate(d) Debauch, Decadent, Diffuse, Disperse, Dissolute, Gay, Revel, Scatter, Shatter, Squander, Waste

▷ **Dissipated** *may indicate* an anagram

Dissociate Separate, Sever, Withdraw

Dissolute Decadent, Degenerate, Demirep, Falstaffian, Hell, Lax, Libertine, Licentious, Loose, Rake-helly, Rakish, Rip, Roué, Wanton

▷ **Dissolute** *may indicate* an anagram

Dissolution Dismissal, Divorce, End, Repeal, Separation

Dissolve Deliquesce, Digest, Disband, Disunite, Lap, Liquesce, Melt, Repeal, Terminate, Thaw

Dissonance Wolf

Dissuade Dehort, Deter, Discourage

Distaff Clotho, Female, Lady, Rock, Stick

Distance Absciss(a), Afield, Apothem, Breadth, Coss, Declination, Eloi(g)n, Elongation, Farness, Focal, Foot, Headreach, Height, Hyperfocal, Ice, Intercalumniation, Interval, Klick, Kos(s), Latitude, League, Length, Long-haul, Maintenance, Mean, Mean free path, Middle, Mileage, Northing, Ordinate, Outland, Parasang, Parsec, Range, Reserve, Rod, Skip, Span, Spitting, Stade, Striking, Way, Yojan, Zenith

Distant Aloof, Chilly, Cold, Far, Frosty, Hyperfocal, Icy, Long, Northing, Offish, Outland, Outremer, Polar, Remote, Tele-, Timbuctoo, Timbuktu, Unfriendly, Yonder

Distaste(ful) Dégoût, Gory, Grimace, Gross-out, Repellent, Repugnant, Ropy, Scunner, Unpalatable, Unpleasant, Unsavoury

Distemper Ailment, Colourwash, Equine, Hard-pad, Paint, Panleucopenia, Pip, Tempera

Distend(ed), Distension Bloat, Dilate, Ectasia, Emphysema, Expand, Hoove, Inflate, Meteorism, → **STRETCH**, Swell, Turgid, Tympanites, Varicocele, Varicose

Distil(late), Distillation, Distiller, Distilling Alcohol, Alembic, Anthracine, Azeotrope, Brew, Cohobate, Condense, Destructive, Drip, Ethanol, Fractional, Naphtha, Pelican, Pyrene, Pyroligneous, Rosin, Turps, Vacuum, Vapour

▷ **Distillation** *may indicate* an anagram

Distinct(ive) Apparent, Characteristic, Clear, Determinate, Different, Discrete, Evident, Grand, Idiosyncratic, Individual, Peculiar, Plain, Separate, Several, Signal, → **SPECIAL**, Stylistic, Trenchant, Vivid

Distinction Beaut(y), Blue, Cachet, Credit, Diacritic, Difference, Dignity, Diorism,

Disparity, Division, Eclat, Eminence, Honour, Lustre, Mark, Mystique, Nicety, Note, Nuance, OM, Prominence, Quiddity, Rank, Renown, Speciality, Style, Title

Distinguish(ed), Distinguishing Classify, Contrast, Demarcate, Denote, Diacritic, Different(iate), Discern, Discriminate, Divide, Elevate, Eminent, Eximious, Mark, Nameworthy, Notable, Perceive, Pick out, Prestigious, Prominent, Rare, Renowned, Scerne, Secern, Signal, Special, Stamp, Tell

Distort(ion), Distorted Anamorphosis, Bend, Bias, Caricature, Colour, Contort, Deface, Deform, Dent, Fudge, Garble, Harmonic, Helium speech, Jaundiced, Mangle, Misshapen, Pervert, Rubato, Skew, Stretch, Thraw, Time-warp, Travesty, Twist, → **WARP**, Wow, Wrest, Wring, Writhe, Wry

▷ **Distort(ed)** *may indicate* an anagram

Distract(ed), Distraction Absent, Agitate, Amuse, Avocation, Bewilder, Divert, Embroil, Éperdu, Forhaile, Frenetic, Lost, Madden, Mental, Nepenthe, Perplex, Scatty, Sidetrack, Sledge, Upstage

▷ **Distract(ed)** *may indicate* an anagram

Distrain(t) Na(a)m, Poind, Sequestrate, Stress

Distraught Deranged, Elfish, Elvan, Frantic, Mad, Troubled, Unstrung

Distress(ed), Distressing Afflict, Aggrieve, Agony, Ail, Alack, Alopecia, Anger, Anguish, Antique, Crise, Distraint, Dolour, Exigence, Extremity, Gnaw, Grieve, Harass, Harrow, Heartbreak, Hurt, Ill, → **IN DISTRESS**, Irk, Misease, Misfortune, Need, Oppress, Pain, Poignant, Prey, Privation, Sad, Shorn, Sore, SOS, Straiten, Straits, Suffering, Tole, Torment, Tragic, Traumatic, Tribulation, → **TROUBLE**, Une(a)th, Unstrung, Upset, Wound

Distribute(d), Distribution, Distributor Allocate, Allot, Binomial, Busbar, Carve, Chi-square, Colportage, Deal, Deliver(y), Deploy, Dish, Dispense, Dispose, Dissemination, Exponential, F, Frequency, Gamma, Gaussian, Geographical, Geometric, Issue, Ladle out, Lie, Lot, Mete, Normal, Out, Pattern, Poisson, Prorate, Renter, Repartition, Send out, Serve, Share, Strew

▷ **Distributed** *may indicate* an anagram

District Alsatia, Amhara, Arcadia, Ards, Area, Arrondissement, Attica, Bail(l)iwick, Banat, Banate, Bannat, Barrio, Belt, Canton, Cantred, Circar, Classis, Community, Congressional, Diocese, Encomienda, End, Exurb, Falernian, Federal, Fitzrovia, Gau, Ghetto, Hundred, Land, Lathe, Liberty, Locality, Loin, Manor, Metropolitan, Nasik, → **NEIGHBOURHOOD**, Oblast, Pachalic, Pale, Pargana, Parish(en), Paroch, Pashalik, Patch, Peak, Pergunnah, Phocis, Precinct, Province, Quarter, Quartier, Rape, → **REGION**, Reserve, Ride, Riding, Ruhr, Rural, Sanjak, Section, Sheading, Sircar, Sirkar, Soc, Soke(n), Stake, Stannary, Suburb, Sucken, Talooka, Taluk, Tenderloin, Township, Urban, Venue, Vicinage, Walk, Wapentake, Way, Wealden, Zila, Zillah, Zone

Distrust(ful) Caution, Doubt, Misanthropic, Misfaith, Suspect, Wariness

Disturb(ance), Disturbed, Disturbing Ado, Aerate, Affray, Aggrieve, Agitate, Atmospherics, Autism, Betoss, Brabble, Brainstorm, Brash, Brawl, Broil, Carfuffle, Collieshangie, Concuss, Delirium, Dementia, Derange, Desecrate, Disquiet, Dust, Dysfunction, Feeze, Firestorm, Fracas, Fray, Fret, Harass, Hoopla, Incident, Incommode, Infest, Interference, Interrupt, Intrude, Jee, Kerfuffle, Kick-up, Kurfuffle, Macabre, Muss, Neurosis, Outbreak, Perturb(ation), Prabble, Rammy, Ramp, Riot, Ripple, Romage, Rook, Roughhouse, Rouse, Ruckus, Ruction, Ruffle, Rumpus, Shake, Shellshock, Shindig, Shindy, Shook-up, Stashie, Static, Steer, Stir, Sturt, Tremor, Troppo, Trouble, Turbulent, Turmoil, Unquiet, Unrest, Unsettle, Upheaval, Uproot, → **UPSET**, Vex, Whistler

▷ **Disturb(ed)** *may indicate* an anagram

Disunite Alienate, Dissever, Divide, Divorce, Split

Disuse Abandon, Abeyance, Atrophy, Desuetude, Discard, Lapse

Ditch Abolish, Barathron, Barathrum, Channel, Chuck, Crash-land, Cunette, Delf, Delph, Dike, Discard, Donga, Drainage, Drop, Dyke, Euripus, Foss(e), Graft, Grip, Gully, Ha(w)-ha(w), Jettison, Khor, Level, Lode, Moat, Nal(l)a(h), Nulla(h), Rean, Reen, Rhine, Rid, Sea, Sheuch, Sheugh, Sike, Sloot, Sluit, Spruit, Stank, Sunk-fence, Syke, Trench

Dither(ing) Agitato, Bother, Dally, Dicker, Faff, Flap, Hesitate, Indecisive, Pusillanimous, Pussyfoot, Twitter, Vacillate

Dittany Gas-plant

Ditty, Ditties Air, Arietta, Canzonet, Departmental, Jingle, Lay, Song

Diuretic Frusemide, Furosemide, Pipsissewa, Spironolactone, Theobromine

Diva Callas, Patti, Singer

Divan Compilement, Congress, Couch, Council, Settee, Sofa

Dive, Diver(s), Diving Armstand, Backflip, Belly-flop, Crash, Dart, Den, Didapper, Duck, Embergoose, File, Flop, Free-fall, Frogman, Full-gainer, Gainer, Grebe, Guillemot, Half-gainer, Header, Honkytonk, Jackknife, Joint, Ken, Loom, Loon, Lungie, Merganser, Nitery, Nose, Pass, Pearl, Pickpocket, Pike, Plong(e), Plummet, Plunge, Plutocrat, Pochard, Poker, Power, Puffin, Saturation, Sawbill, Scoter, Scuba, Skin, Snake-bird, Sound, Speakeasy, Stage, Step-to, Stoop, Submerge, Swallow, Swan, Swoop, Tailspin, Urinant, Urinator , Zoom

Diverge(nce) Branch, Deviate, Divaricate, Spread, Swerve, Variant, Veer

Divers(e), Diversify Alter, Branch out, Chequer, Dapple, Different, Eclectic, Interlard, Intersperse, Manifold, Many, Miscellaneous, Motley, Multifarious, Separate, Some, Sundry, Variegate, Various, Vary

Diversion, Divert(ing) Amuse, Avocation, Beguile, Cone, Deflect, Detour, Disport, Dissuade, Distract, Entertain, Game, Hare, Hijack, Hive off, Hobby, Interlude, Pastime, Pleasure, Prolepsis, Ramp, Red-herring, Refract, Reroute, Ruse, Shunt, Sideshow, Sidetrack, Siphon, Smokescreen, Sport, Stalking-horse, Steer, Stratagem, Sublimation, Sway, Switch, Syphon, Tickle, Upstage, Yaw

▷ **Diverting** *may indicate* an anagram

Divest Denude, Rid, Strip, Undeck, Undress

Divide(d), Divider, Division Abkhazia, Adzharia, Apportion, Balk, Balkanise, Band, Bifurcate, Bipartite, Bisect, Branch, Cantle, Chancery, Cleave, Cleft, Comminute, Commot(e), Continental, Counter-pale, Cut, Deal, Demerge, Digital, Dimidiate, Dissever, Estrange, Fork, Great, Indent, Parcel, Part, Partite, Partitive, Party wall, Pentomic, Plebs, Polarise, Potantial, Ramify, Rend, Rift, Sectionalise, Separate, Sever, Share, → **SPLIT**, Stanza, Sunder, Transect, Tribalism, Trisect, Twixt, Utgard, Voltage, Watershed, Zone

Dividend Bonus, Div, Interim, Into, Numerator, Peace, Share

Divination, Diviner Anthroposcopy, Arithmancy, Augury, Auspices, Axinomancy, Belomancy, Bibliomancy, Botanomancy, Capnomancy, Cartomancy, Ceromancy, Chiromancy, Cleromancy, Coscinomancy, Crithomancy, Crystal-gazing, Crystallomancy, Doodlebug, Dowser, Empyromancy, Gastromancy, Geloscopy, Geomancy, Gyromancy, Hariolation, Haruspex, Hepatoscopy, Hieromancy, Hieroscopy, Hydromancy, I Ching, Intuition, Lampadomancy, Leconomancy, Lithomancy, Magic, Mantic, Myomancy, Omphalomancy, Oneiromancy, Onphalomancy, Onychomancy, Ornithomancy, Ornithoscopy, Osteomancy, Palmistry, Pegomancy, Pessomancy, Pyromancy, Radiesthesia, Rhabdomancy, Scapulimancy, Scapulomancy, Sciomancy, Seer, Sibyl, Sideromancy, Sortes, Sortilege, Spae(man), Spodomancy, Taghairm, Tais(c)h, Tephromancy, Theomancy, Tripudiary, Vaticanator, Xylomancy, Zoomancy

Divine, Divine presence, Divinity Acoemeti, Aitu, Ambrose, Atman, Avatar, Beatific, Blessed, Celestial, Clergyman, Conjecture, Curate, DD, Deduce, Deity, Douse, Dowse, Ecclesiastic, Empyreal, Forecast, Foretell, Fuller, → **GOD**, → **GODDESS**, Godhead, Godlike, Guess, Hallowed, Hariolate, Heavenly, Holy, Hulse, Immortal, Inge, Isiac, Kami, Mantic, Numen, Numinous, Olympian, Pontiff, Predestinate, Predict, Presage, Priest, Prophesy, RE, Rector, RI, Rimmon, Scry, Sense, Seraphic, Shechinah, Shekinah, Spae, Superhuman, Supernal, Theandric, Theanthropic, Theologise, Theology, Triune

Division, Divisible Amitosis, Angiosperm, Arcana, Arm, Arrondissement, Bajocian, Banat(e), Bannet, Bar, Bizone, Branch, Brome, Caesura, Canto, Canton, Cantred, Cantref, Cassini's, Caste, Category, Cell, Champart, Chapter, Classification, Cleft, Cloison, Clove, Comitatus, Commot(e), Commune, Compartment, Coralline Crag, Corps,

County, Crevasse, Curia, Department, Dichotomy, Disagreement, Disunity, Div, Duan, Eyalet, Family, Farren, Fissile, Fork, Fragmentation, Glires, Grisons, Guberniya, Gulf, Gulph, Hapu, Hedge, Hide, Holland, Hotchpot, Hundred, Inning, Isogloss, Keuper, Kim(m)eridgian, Lathe, Leet, Legion, Lindsey, List, Lobe, Long, Mannion, Maturation, M(e)iosis, Mitosis, Mofussil, Nome, Oblast, Over, Pachytene, Pargana, Part, Partition, Passus, Pergunnah, Period, Phratry, Phyle, Phylum, Pipe, Pitaka, Platoon, Polarisation, Presidency, Province, Quartering, Queen's Bench, Quotition, Rape, Red Crag, Reduction, Region, Replum, Reservation, Riding, Sanjak, Schism, Section, Sector, Segment, Semeion, Sept(ate), Sever, Share, Sheading, Shed, Shire, Short, Stage, Stake, Subheading, Suborder, Tahsil, Tanach, Taxis, Telophase, Tepal, Thanet, Theme, Trichotomy, Trio, Trivium, Troop, Tuath, Unit, Vilayet, Volost, Wapentake, Ward, Watershed

Divisor Aliquant, Aliquot

Divorce(d) Alienate, Diffarreation, Disaffiliate, Dissolve, Disunion, Div, Estrange, Get(t), Part, Put away, Separate, Sequester, → **SUNDER**, Talak, Talaq

Divot Clod, Sod, Turf

Divulge Confess, Disclose, Expose, Publish, Reveal, Split, Tell, Unveil, Utter

DIY Flatpack

Dizziness, Dizzy Beaconsfield, Ben, Capricious, Dinic, Disraeli, Giddy, Giglot, Lightheaded, Mazey, Mirligoes, Scotodinia, Scotomania, Swimming, Vertiginous, → **VERTIGO**, Woozy

DJ Deejay, Jock, Mixmaster, Monkey-suit, Penguin suit, Presenter, Selecta, Shockjock, Tuxedo, Veejay

DNA Adenine, Antisense, Centromere, Chromatin, Cistron, Codon, Complementary, Cytosine, Double helix, Exon, Gene, Heteroduplex, Homopolymer, Intron, Junk, Microsatellite, Mitochondrial, Muton, Nucleosome, Operator, Palindrome, Papovavirus, Plasmid, Polyoma, Poxvirus, Procaryote, Profiling, Prokaryote, Pseudogene, Purine, Recombinant, Replication fork, Replicon, Retrotransposon, Ribosome, RNA, Satellite, Selfish, Southern blot, Synthetic, Telomere, Thymidine, Transcript(ion), Transfection, Transfer, Translation, Transposon, Vector, Watson-Crick model

Do(es), Doing Accomplish, Achieve, Act, Anent, Banquet, Barbecue, Bash, Beano, Begin, Blow-out, Char, Cheat, Chisel, Cod, Con, Cozen, Deed, Dich, Diddle, Dish, Div, Doth, Dupe, Effectuate, Enact, Execute, Fare, Fleece, Function, Fuss, Gull, Handiwork, Hoax, Imitate, Measure up, Mill, Occasion, Perform, Perpetrate, Provide, Rip off, Same, Serve, Settle, Shindig, Spif(f)licate, Suffice, Swindle, Thrash, Thrive, Tonic, Up to, Ut

▷ **Do** *may indicate* an anagram

Do away Abolish, Banish, Demolish, Kill

Dobbie Elf, Fairy

Docile Agreeable, Amenable, Biddable, Dutiful, Facile, Meek, Obedient, Submissive, Tame, Tractable, Yielding

Dock(er), Docked, Docks Abridge, Barber, Basin, Bistort, Bob, Camber, Canaigre, Clip, Crop, Curta(i)l, Cut, Deduct, De-tail, Dry, Floating, Grapetree, Graving, Knotweed, Lay-up, Longshoreman, Lop, Lumper, Marina, Monk's rhubarb, Moor, Off-end, Pare, Patience, Pen, Pier, Quay, Rhubarb, Rumex, Rump, Scene, Seagull, Shorten, Snakeweed, Sorrel, Sourock, Stevedore, Tilbury, Watersider, Wet, Wharf, Wharfie, Yard

Docket Bordereau, Invoice, Label, Tag

Dockyard Arsenal, Chatham, Naval, Rosyth, Sheerness

Doctor(s) Allopath, Alter, Arnold, Asclepiad, Barefoot, Barnardo, Bleeder, BMA, Bones, Breeze, Bright, Brighton, Brown, Caius, Castrate, Chapitalize, Clinician, Cook, Crocus, Cup(per), Cure(r), Dale, Diagnose, Dr, Dryasdust, Erasmus, Extern(e), Fake, Falsify, Family, Faustus, Feldsher, Fell, Fiddle, Finlay, Flying, Foster, Fu manchu, Fundholder, Galen, Geriatrician, Geropiga, GP, Hakeem, Hakim, Healer, Homeopath, Houseman, Hyde, Imhotep, Intern, Internist, Jekyll, Jenner, Johnson, Kildare, Lace, Leach, Leech, Linacre, Load, Locum, Luke, Manette, Manipulate, Massage, MB, MD, Medicate, Medico, Mganga, Middleton, Mindererus, Minister, Misrepresent, MO, MOH, Molla(h), Moreau,

Mulla(h), Myologist, Neuter, No, Ollamh, Ollav, Paean, Paediatrician, Panel, Pangloss, Paracelsus, Paramedic, Pedro, PhD, Physician, Pill(s), Practitioner, Quack, Quacksalver, Rabbi, RAMC, Registrar, Resident, Rig, Rorschach, Salk, Sangrado, Saw, Sawbones, School, Script, Seraphic, Seuss, Shaman, Slammer, Slop, Spay, Spin, Stum, Surgeon, Syn, Syntax, Thorne, Treat, Vaidya, Vet, Water, Watson, Who, Wind, Witch

▷ **Doctor(ed)** *may indicate* an anagram

Doctrine Adamitism, Adoptianism, Adoptionism, Antinomian, Apollinarian, Archology, Arianism, Averr(h)oism, Blairism, Bonism, Brezhnev, Cab(b)ala, Cacodoxy, Calvanism, Catastrophism, Chiliasm, Consubstantiation, Credo, Creed, Determinism, Diabology, Ditheism, Ditheletism, Divine right, Docetism, Dogma, Doxie, Doxy, Dualism, Dysteleology, Encratism, Eschatology, Esotery, Evangel, Febronianism, Federalism, Fideism, Finalism, Functionalism, Gnosticism, Gospel, Henotheism, Hesychasm, Holism, Idealism, Illuminism, Immaterialism, Immersionism, Indeterminism, Infralapsarianism, Islam, Ism, Jansenism, Krypsis, Laches, Lore, Machtpolitik, Malthusian, Manich(a)eism, Materialism, Metempsychosis, Modalism, Molinism, Monadism, Monergism, Monism, Monothel(et)ism, Monroe, Neomonianism, Nestorianism, Neutral monism, Nihilism, Panentheism, Pantheism, Pelagianism, Physiocracy, Pluralism, Pragmatism, Predestination, Premillennialism, Preterition, Probabilism, Psilanthropism, Pythagorean(ism), Quietism, Real presence, Reformism, Satyagrahi, Scotism, Secularism, Sharia, Sheria, Shibboleth, Solidism, Soteriology, Strong meat, Subjectivism, Sublapsarianism, Subpanation, Substantialism, Swedenborgianism, Syndicalism, Synergism, System, Teleology, → **TENET**, Terminism, Theory, Theravada, Thomism, Transubstantiation, Trialism, Tridentine, Tutiorism, Universalism, Utilitarianism, Voluntarism, Wasm, Weismannism, Whiteboyism, Zoism, Zwinglian

Document(s), Documentary Blog, Brevet, Bumf, Bumph, Carta, Certificate, Charge sheet, Charter, Chop, Contract, Conveyance, Copy, Covenant, Daftar, Deed, Diploma, Docket, Doco, Dompass, Dossier, Elegit, Escrow, Fiat, Fieri Facias, Fly-on-the-wall, Form, Grand Remonstrance, Holograph, Latitat, Logbook, Mandamus, Offer, Papers, Permit, Policy, Precept, Production, Pro forma, Public, Ragman, Ragment, Record, Resort, Roll, Roul(e), Screed, Scroll, Sea brief, Source, Stamp note, Voucher, Warrant, Waybill, Weblog, Webpage, Writ, Write up

Dod Pet, Poll

Dodder(y) Old, Shake, Stagger, Strangleweed, Totter, Tremble

Doddle Easy

Dodge, Dodgy Artful, Avoid, Bell-ringing, Column, Elude, Evade, Evasion, Evite, Iffy, Jink, Jook, Jouk, Malinger, Racket, Ruse, Scam, Shirk, Sidestep, Skip, Slalom, Slinter, Tip, Trick, Twist, Urchin, Weave, Welsh, Wheeze, Wire, Wrinkle

Doe(s) Deer, Faun, Hind

Doff Avail(e), Avale, Remove, Rouse, Shed, Tip

Dog(s), Doglike Assistance, Attack, Bowwow, Canes, Canidae, Canine, Cynic, Feet, Fire, Fog, Hearing, Hot, Huntaway, Hunter, Isle, Kennel, Leading, Native, Nodding, Pursue, Ranger, Ratter, Sea, Search, Seeing-eye, Shadow, Sleeve, Sleuthhound, Sniffer, Spotted, Stalk, Strong-eye, Sun, Tag, Tail, Therapy, Top, Toto, Tracker, Trail, Truffle, Tumbler, Wammul, Water, Water dog, Working, Yellow

DOGS

3 letters:	Rab	Bran	Iron
Cur	Yap	Bush	Kuri
Eye		Cant	Kuta
Gun	4 letters:	Chow	Kuti
Pig	Barb	Dane	Leam
Pom	Bird	Fido	Lyam
Pug	Brak	Heel	Mutt

Oath
Peke
Puli
Rach
Sled
Stag
Tike
Toby
Tosa
Tray
Tyke
Wolf

5 letters:
Akita
Alans
Apsos
Argos
Boots
Boxer
Brach
Cairn
Coach
Corgi
Dhole
Dingo
Guard
Guide
Haunt
Hound
Husky
Hyena
Kurre
Laika
Lorel
Luath
Merle
Moera
Pidog
Pluto
Pooch
Rache
Ratch
Rover
Shock
Spitz
Spoor
Whelp
Zorro

6 letters:
Afghan
Bandog
Barbet

Barker
Basset
Beagle
Bitser
Blanch
Borzoi
Bounce
Bowler
Briard
Caesar
Canaan
Chenet
Cocker
Collie
Coyote
Dangle
Eskimo
Gelert
Goorie
Heeler
Jackal
Katmir
Kelpie
Kennet
Ketmir
Kratim
Lassie
Mauthe
Messan
Moppet
Pariah
Piedog
Police
Poodle
Pye-dog
Saluki
Setter
Shaggy
Shough
Sirius
Sothic
Talbot
Teckel
Touser
Towser
Vizsla
Westie
Yapper
Yorkie

7 letters:
Andiron
Basenji
Bobbery

Boerbul
Bouvier
Brachet
Bulldog
Coondog
Courser
Griffon
Harrier
Iceland
Lowchen
Lurcher
Maltese
Maremma
Mastiff
Mongrel
Orthrus
Pointer
Prairie
Raccoon
Reynard
Samoyed
Sapling
Sausage
Shar-Pei
Sheltie
Shih tzu
Showghe
Sloughi
Spaniel
Starter
→ **TERRIER**
Volpino
Whiffet
Whippet
Yapster

8 letters:
Aardwolf
Aberdeen
Airedale
Alsatian
Blenheim
Bouvrier
Bratchet
Brittany
Carriage
Cerberus
Chow-chow
Doberman
Elkhound
Hovawart
Kangaroo
Keeshond
Komondor

Labrador
Landseer
Malamute
Malemute
Papillon
Pekinese
Pembroke
Pinscher
Samoyede
Sealyham
Sheepdog
Springer
Turnspit
Warragal
Warrigal

9 letters:
Blue merle
Buckhound
Chihuahua
Coonhound
Dachshund
Dalmatian
Deerhound
Dobermann
Draghound
Gazehound
Great Dane
Greyhound
Harlequin
Kerry blue
Lhasa apso
Molossian
Pekingese
Retriever
Rin-tin-tin
Schnauzer
Staghound
Wolfhound

10 letters:
Bedlington
Bloodhound
Blueheeler
Fox terrier
Otterhound
Pomeranian
Rottweiler
Schipperke
Shin-barker
Tripehound
Weimaraner

11 letters:
Bichon frise
Irish setter
Jack Russell
Labradoodle
Montmorency
Skye terrier
Tibetan apso
Trendle-tail
Trindle-tail
Trundle-tail
Wishtonwish

12 letters:
Border collie
Gazelle hound
Japanese chin
Newfoundland
Saint Bernard

Water spaniel
Welsh terrier
West Highland

13 letters:
Affenpinscher
Cocker spaniel
Dandie Dinmont
English setter
Scotch terrier
Sussex spaniel

14 letters:
German shepherd
Italian spinone
Norwich terrier
Pit bull terrier
Tibetan mastiff
Tibetan spaniel

Tibetan terrier

15 letters:
Bernese mountain
Brussels griffon
Estreia mountain
Golden retriever
Hamilton stovare
Mexican hairless
Norwegian buhund
Portuguese water
Swedish vallhund

16 letters:
Australian cattle
Doberman-pinscher
Lancashire heeler
Pyrenean mountain
Russian wolfhound

Shetland sheepdog

17 letters:
Anatolian Shepherd
Dobermann-pinscher
Labrador retriever

18 letters:
Large Munsterlander
Old English sheepdog
Rhodesian ridgeback

20 letters:
Landseer
Newfoundland

21 letters:
Polish Lowland
sheepdog

Dog-bane Apocynum
Doge Dandolo
Dogfish Huss, Rigg, Rock salmon
Dogged Determined, Die-hard, Dour, Indefatigable, Pertinacious, Relentless, Stubborn, Sullen, Tenacious
Doggerel Cramboclink, Crambo-jingle, Laisse, Rat-rhyme
Dog letter R
Dogma(tic) Assertive, Belief, Bigotry, Conviction, Creed, Doctrinal, En têté, Ewe, Ideology, Ipse dixit, Opinionative, Pedagogic, Peremptory, Pontifical, Positive, → **TENET**
Do-gooder Lady Bountiful, Piarist, Reformer, Salvationist, Samaritan, Scout
Dogsbody Bottle-washer, Gofer, Skivvy
Dog star Canicula, Lassie, Sirius, Sothic
Do it Dich
Dolce Stop, Sweet
Dole Alms, Batta, B(u)roo, Give, Grief, Maundy, Mete, Payment, Pittance, Pog(e)y, Ration, → **SHARE**, Tichborne, Vail, Vales
Doleful Sombre
Doll(y) Barbie®, Bimbo, Bobblehead, Common, Corn, Creeper, Crumpet, Dress, Dutch, Ewe, Golliwog, Kachina, Kewpie®, Maiden, Marionette, Matryoshka, Maumet, Mommet, Moppet, Mummet, Ookpik®, Ornament, Paris, Parton, Pean, Peen, Peggy, Pein, Pene, Poppet, Puppet, Ragdoll, Russian, Sindy®, Sis(ter), Sitter, Tearsheet, Toy, Trolley, Varden, Washboard, Wax
Dollar(s) Balboa, Boliviano, Buck, Cob, Cob money, Euro, Fin, Greenback, Iron man, Peso, Petrol, Piastre, Pink, S, Sand, Sawbuck, Sawhorse, Scrip, Smacker, Spin, Sword, Top, Wheel
Dollop Glob, Helping, Share
▷ **Dolly** *may indicate* an anagram
Dolly-bird Dish
Dolly Varden Hat
Dolour, Dolorous Anguished, Grief, Pain, Sorrow
Dolphin Amazon, Arion, Beluga, Bottlenose, Cetacean, Coryphene, Delphinus, Grampus, Lampuka, Lampuki, Mahi-mahi, Meer-swine, Porpes(e), Risso's, River, Sea-pig
Dolt Ass, Blockhead, Clodhopper, Mooncalf, Noodle, Oaf, Ouph(e), Owl, → **STUPID**
DOM Lewdsby

Domain Archaea, Archduchy, Bacteria, Bourn(e), Demain, Demesne, Eminent, Emirate, Empire, Estate, Eukarya, Kingdom, Manor, Net, Predicant, Public, Rain, Realm, Region, Reign, Starosty

Dome(-shaped) Al-Aqsa, Bubble, Cap, Cupola, Cupula, Dagoba, Geodesic, Head, Imperial, Louvre, Millennium, Onion, Periclinal, Rotunda, Salt, Stupa, Tee, Tholobate, Tholos, Tholus, Tope, Vault, Xanadu

Domestic(ate) Char, Cinderella, Cleaner, Dom, Esne, Familiar, Homebody, Home-keeping, Homely, House, Housetrain, Humanise, Interior, Internal, Intestine, Maid, Menial, → **SERVANT**, Swadeshi, Tame, Woman

Domicile Abode, Dwelling, Hearth, Home, Ménage

Dominate, Dominance, Dominant, Domination Alpha, Ascendancy, Baasskap, Ballbreaker, Bethrall, Boss, Clou, Coerce, Control, Enslave, Hegemony, Henpeck, Maisterdome, Master, Mesmerise, Momism, Monopolise, O(v)ergang, Overmaster, Override, Overshadow, Power, Preponderant, Preside, Rule, Soh, → **SUBDUE**, Subjugate, Top dog, Tower

Domineer(ing) Authoritarian, Autocratic, Boss, Henpeck, Lord, Ride, Swagger, Tyrannize

Dominica(n) Jacobite, Monk, OP, Preaching friar, Predicant, Savonarola, WD

Dominie Maister, Master, Pastor, Sampson, Schoolmaster

Dominion Dom, Empire, Khanate, NZ, Realm, Reame, Reign, → **RULE**, Supremacy, Sway, Territory

Domino(es) Card, Fats, Mask, Matador

Don Academic, Address, Assume, Caballero, Camorrist, Endue, Fellow, Garb, Giovanni, Grandee, Indew, Juan, Lecturer, Mafia, Prof, Quixote, Reader, Señor, Spaniard, Tutor, Wear

Dona(h) Duckie, Love

Donate, Donation Aid, Bestow, Contribution, Gift, Give, Peter's pence, Present, Wakf, Waqf

Done Achieved, Complete, Crisp, Ended, Executed, Had, Over, Spitcher, Tired, Weary

Donjon Dungeon, Keep

Donkey Ass, Burro, Cardophagus, Cuddie, Cuddy, Dapple, Dick(e)y, Dunce, Eeyore, Engine, Funnel, Fussock, Genet(te), Ignoramus, Jackass, Jacket, Jennet, Jenny, Jerusalem pony, Kulan, Modestine, Moke, Mule, Neddy, Nodding, Onager, Stupid, Years

Donor Benefactor, Bestower, Settlor, Universal

Doo Dove

Doodle(r) Scribble, Yankee

Doodlebug Antlion, Larva, V1

Doofer Thingumabob

Doom(ed) Condemned, Damnation, Date, Destine, Destiny, → **FATE**, Fay, Fey, Fie, Goner, Ill-omened, Ill-starred, Lot, Predestine, Preordain, Ragnarok, Ruined, Sentence, Spitcher, Star-crossed, Weird

Doone Carver, Lorna

Door(s), Doorstep, Doorway Aperture, Communicating, Damnation, Drecksill, Dutch, Elephant, Entry, Exit, Fire, Folding, Front, Gull-wing, Haik, Hake, Hatch, Heck, Ingress, Jib, Lintel, Louver, Louvre, Muntin, Oak, Open, Overhead, Patio, Portal, Postern, Revolving, Rory, Screen, Sliding, Stable, Stage, Storm, Street, Swing, Tailgate, Trap, Up and over, Vomitory, Wicket, Yett

Doorkeeper, Doorman Bouncer, Commissionaire, Concierge, Guardian, Janitor, Nab, Ostiary, Porter, Tiler, Tyler, Usher

Doormat Subservient, Weakling, Wuss

Doorpost Architrave, Dern, Durn, Jamb, Yate, Yett

Dope Acid, Amulet, Bang, Coke, Crack, → **DRUG**, Facts, Fuss, Gen, Goose, Info, Lowdown, Narcotic, Nitwit, Nobble, Rutin, Sedate, Soup, → **STUPID PERSON**, Tea

Doppelganger Double, Look-alike, Ringer

Dorcas Gazelle, Needle, Shepherdess

Dorian, Doric Metope, Mutule

Doris Day, Lessing, Mollusc

Dormant Abed, Comatose, Hibernating, Idle, Inactive, Inert, Joist, Latent, Latitant, Quiescent, Resting, → **SLEEPING**, Torpescent

Dormer Luthern

Dormitory Barrack, Bunkhouse, Dorter, Dortour, Hall, Hostel, Quarters

Dormouse Loir

Dorothy Bag, Dot, Sayers

Dorsal Back, Neural, Notal

Dory Fish, John

Dosage, Dose Absorbed, Acute, Administer, Aperient, Booster, Cascara, Cumulative, Drachm, Draught, Drench, Drug, Fix, Hit, Kilogray, Lethal, → **MEASURE**, Permissible, Physic, Posology, Potion, Powder, Rem, Standing off, Threshold, Tolerance

Doss (house) Dharmsala, Dharmshala, Kip, Padding-ken, Spike

Dossier File, Record

Dot(s), Dotted, Dotty Absurd, Bind(h)i, Bullet (point), Centred, Criblé, Dieresis, Dit, Dower, Dowry, Ellipsis, Engrailed, Leader, Lentiginous, Limp, Micro, Morse, Occult, Or, Particle, Pinpoint, Pixel, → **POINT**, Pointillé, Polka, Precise, Punctuate, Punctulate, Punctum, Schwa, Semé(e), Set, Speck, Spot, Sprinkle, Stigme, Stipple, Stud, Tap, Tittle, Trema, Umlaut

Dote, Dotage, Doting, Dotard Adore, Anile, Anility, Cocker, Dobbie, Idolise, Imbecile, Pet, Prize, Senile, Spoon(e)y, Tendre, Twichild

Double(s) Amphibious, Ancipital, Bi-, Bifold, Binate, Clone, Counterpart, Crease, Dimeric, Doppel-ganger, Doppio, Dual, Duo, Duple(x), Duplicate, Equivocal, Fetch, Fold, Foursome, Geminate, Gimp, Image, Ingeminate, Ka, Look-alike, Loop, Martingale, Pair, Parlay, Polyseme, Reflex, Replica, Ringer, Run, Similitude, Spit, Stuntman, Trot, Turnback, Twae, → **TWIN**, Two(fold), Two-ply

Double-barrelled Tautonym

Double-cross, Double dealing Ambidext(e)rous, Two-time

Double-entendre Polyseme, Polysemy

Doublet Peascod, Pourpoint, TT

Doubt(s), Doubter, Doubtful Agnostic, Ambiguous, Aporia, Askance, But, Debatable, Discredit, Distrust, Dubiety, Dubitate, Erm, Hesitate, Hum, Iffy, Incertitude, Misgiving, Mistrust, → **NO DOUBT**, Or, Precarious, Qualm, Query, → **QUESTION**, Rack, Scepsis, Sceptic, Scruple, Second thoughts, Shady, Shy, Sic, Skepsis, Sus, Suspect, Suspicious, Suss, Thomas, Thos, Umph, Uncertain, Unsure, Waver

Doubtless Certain, Iwis, Probably, Sure, Truly, Ywis

Douceur Bonus, Sop, Sweetener

Douche Bath, Gush, Rinse, Shower, Wash

Dough(y) Boodle, Cake, Calzone, Cash, Duff, Gnocchi, Hush-puppy, Knish, Loot, Magma, Masa, Money, Paste, Pop(p)adum, Ready, Sad, Sour, Spondulicks, Strudel

Doughboy Dumpling, Soldier

Doughnut Bagel, Beavertail®, Cruller, Fried cake, Knish, Koeksister, Olycook, Olykoek, Sinker, Torus

Doughty Brave, Intrepid, Resolute, Stalwart, Valiant

Dour Glum, Hard, Mirthless, Morose, Reest, Reist, Sinister, Sullen, Taciturn

Douse Dip, Drench, Extinguish, Snuff, Splash

Dove Collared, Columbine, Culver, Cushat, Diamond, Doo, Ground, Ice-bird, Mourning, Pacifist, → **PIGEON**, Queest, Quoist, Ring, Rock, Stock, Turtle

Dove-cot(e) Columbarium, Columbary, Louver, Louvre, Lover

Dovetail Fit, Interosculate, Lewis(son), Mortise, Tally, Tenon

Dowager Elder, Widow

Dowdy Frumpish, Mopsy, Mums(e)y, Plain Jane, Shabby, Sloppy, Slovenly

Dowel Peg, Pin

Down(s), Downbeat, Downsize, Downward, Downy A bas, Abase, Abattu, Alow, Amort, Bank, Below, Berkshire, Blue, Cast, Catabasis, Chapfallen, Comous, Cottony, Crouch, Darling, Dejected, Descent, Disconsolate, Dowl(e), Drink, Epsom, Feather, Fledge, Floccus, Flue, Fluff, Fly, Fuzz, Glum, Goonhilly, Ground, Hair, Hill, Humble, Humiliate, Jeff, Kennet, Lanate, Lanugo, Latitant, Losing, Low, Lower, Miserable, Moxa, Nap, Neck, North Wessex, Oose, Ooze, Owing, Pappus, Pennae, Pile, Plumage, Powder, Quark, Quash, Repress, Scuttle, Sebum, Slim, Sussex, Thesis, Thistle, Tomentum, Under, Unserviceable, Urinant, Vail, Watership, Wold, Wretched

Downcast Abject, Chapfallen, Dejected, Despondent, Disconsolate, Dumpish, Hangdog, Hopeless, Melancholy, Woebegone

Downfall, Downpour Brash, Cataract, Collapse, Deluge, Fate, Flood, Hail, Onding, Overthrow, Plash, Rain, Rainstorm, Ruin, Shower, Thunder-plump, Torrent, Undoing, Waterspout

Downgrade(d) Déclassé, Deskill, Disrate, Relegate

Downmarket Naff

Downright Absolute, Arrant, Bluff, Candid, Clear, Complete, Flat, Plumb, Plump, Pure, Rank, Sheer, Stark, Utter

Downstairs Below

Downstream Tail

Downturn Recession, Slump

Downwind Leeward

Dowry Dot, Dower, Lobola, Lobolo, Merchet, Portion, Settlement, Tocher

Dowse(r), Dowsing Divine, Enew, Fireman, Radionics, Rhabdomancy, Water-witch

Doxology Gloria, Glory

Doxy Harlot, Loose woman, Opinion, Wench

Doyen Dean, Senior

Doze Ca(u)lk, Catnap, Dove(r), Nap, Nod, Semi-coma, Sleep, Slip, Slumber

Dozen(s) Baker's, Daily, Dz, Long, Round, Thr(e)ave, Twal, Twelve

Dr Debtor, Doctor, Dram

Drab Ash-grey, Cloth, Dell, Dingy, Dowdy, Dreary, Dull, Dun, Ecru, Hussy, Isabel(line), Lifeless, Livor, Mumsy, Olive, Prosaic, Pussel, Quaker-colour, Rig, Road, Scarlet woman, Slattern, Sloven, Strumpet, Subfusc, Tart, Taupe, Trull, Wanton, Whore

Drabble Bemoil, Draggle

Dracula Bat, Count, Vampire

Draft Bank, Bill, Cheque, Draw, Ebauche, Essay, Landsturm, Minute, MS, Outline, Paste up, Plan, Press, Project, Protocol, Rough, Scheme, Scroll, Scrowle, → **SKETCH**

Drag Car, Clothing, Drail, Dredge, Drogue, Elicit, Eonism, Epicene, Extort, Fiscal, Form, Gender-bender, Hale, Hang, Harl, → **HAUL**, Induced, Keelhaul, La Rue, Lug, Nuisance, Parasite, Pressure, Profile, Puff, Pull, Rash, Sag, Schlep, Shockstall, Shoe, Skidpan, Sled, Snake, Snig, Sweep, Toke, Tote, Tow, Trail, Trailing vortex, Train, Travail, Travois, Trawl, Treck, Trek, Tug, Tump, Vortex

Draggle Drail, Lag, Straggle

Dragon Aroid, Basilisk, Bel, Bellemère, Chaperon(e), Chindit, Draco, Drake, Fafnir, Fire-drake, Gargouille, Komodo, Kung-kung, Ladon, Lindworm, Opinicus, Peist, Puk, Python, Rouge, Safat, Serpent, Shrew, Typhoeus, Wantley, Wivern, Worm, Wyvern, Yacht

Dragonfly Aeschna, Demoiselle, Devil's darning needle, Nymph, Odonata

Dragon's teeth Cadmus, Spartae, Sparti

Dragoon Coerce, Force, Press, Rope-in, Trooper

Drain(ed), Drainage, Draining, Drainpipe Bleed, Brain, Buzz, Can(n)ula, Catchment, Catchwater, Channel, Cloaca, Condie, Culvert, Cundy, Cunette, Delf, Delph, Dewater, Ditch, Dry, Ea(u), → **EMPTY**, Emulge(nt), Exhaust, Field, Fleet, Grating, Grip, Gully, Gutter, Ketavothron, Kotabothron, Lade, Leach, Leech, Limber, Lose, Lymphatic,

Milk, Mole, Nala, Nalla(h), Nulla(h), Penrose, Pump, Rack, Rone, Sanitation, Sap, Scalpins, Scupper, Seton, Sew(er), Sheuch, Sheugh, Shore, Silver, Sink, Siver, Sluice, Sluse, Small-trap, Soakaway, Sough, Spend, Stank, Storm, Suck, Sump, Sure, Syver, Tile, Trench, Trocar, Unwater, Ureter, U-trap, Weary, Well

Drainpipe(s) Downspout, → **TROUSERS**

Dram Drink, Drop, Nipperkin, Nobbler, Portion, Snifter, Tickler, Tiff, Tot, Wet

Drama(tic), Drama school Auto, Azione, Catastasis, Charade, Closet, Comedy, Costume, Drastic, Epic, ER, Eumenides, Farce, Heroic, Histrionic, Kabuki, Kathakali, Kitchen sink, Legit, Legitimate, Mask, Masque, Mime, Moralities, Music, No, Nogaku, Noh, Oresteia, Piece, Play, RADA, Sangeet, Scenic, Sensational, Singspiel, Soap, Spinto, Stagy, Striking, Sudser, Tetralogy, Theatric, The Birds, Thespian, Tragedy, Unities, Wagnerian, Wild

Dramatist Adamov, Aeschylus, Albee, Anouilh, Aristophanes, Arrabal, Beaumarchais, Beaumont, Beddoes, Bleasdale, Brecht, Bridie, Calderon, Centlivre, Chapman, Congreve, Corneille, Coward, Dekker, Drinkwater, Ennius, Euripides, Farquhar, Fletcher, Frisch, Fry, Gay, Genet, Gogol, Goldoni, Havel, Heywood, Ibsen, Ionesco, Jarry, Kyd, Lorca, Lyly, Mamet, Marlowe, Massinger, Menander, Middleton, Molière, Odets, O'Neill, Orton, Osborne, Otway, Pinero, Pirandello, Plautus, → **PLAYWRIGHT**, Racine, Rostand, Rowe, Rowley, Schiller, Seneca, Shadwell, Shaffer, Sherriff, Sophocles, Stoppard, Strindberg, Synge, Terence, Udall, Vanbrugh, Voltaire, Von Klinger, Webster, Wedekind, Wesker, Wilde, Wilder, Will, → **WRITER**, Yeats

Dram-shop Bar, Boozingken, Bousingken

Drape(ry) Adorn, Coverlet, Coverlid, Curtain, Festoon, Fold, Hang, Lambrequin, Mantling, Swag, Swathe, Valance, Veil, Vest

Draper Clothier, Gilpin, Haberdasher, Hosier, Mercer, Outfitter, Ruth, Scotch cuddy, Tailor

Drastic Dire, Dramatic, Extreme, Harsh, Purge, Senna, → **SEVERE**, Swingeing, Violent

Drat Bother, Dang, Darn

Draught(s), Draughtsman(ship) Aloetic, Apozem, Aver, Breeze, Dam, Dams, Design, Dose, Drench, Drink, Fish, Gulp, Gust, Haal, Hippocrene, King, Line, Men, Nightcap, Outline, Plan, Potation, Potion, Pull, Quaff, Sketch, Sleeping, Slug, Swig, Tracer, Up-current, Veronal, Waft, Waucht, Waught, Williewaught

▷ **Draught** *may refer to* fishing

Draught-board Dam-board, Dambrod

Dravidian Tamil

Draw (off), Drawer(s), Drawing, Drawn Adduct, Allure, Attract, Bleed, Blueprint, Bottom, Cartoon, Charcoal, Cityscape, Cock, Crayon, Dead-heat, Delineate, Dentistry, Derivation, Describe, Detail, Diagram, Dis(em)bowel, Doodle, Dr, Draft, Drag, Dress, Educe, Elevation, Elicit, Elongate, Entice, Equalise, Escribe, Evaginate, Extract, Fet(ch), Freehand, Fusain, Gather, Gaunt, Glorybox, Goalless, Graphics, Gut, Haggard, Hale, Halve, Haul, Identikit, Indraft, Induce, Indue, Inhale, Isometric, Lead, Lengthen, Limn, Line, Longbow, Lots, Lottery, Mechanical, Monotint, No-score, Orthograph, Pantalet(te)s, Panty, Pastel(list), Pen and ink, Perpetual check, Petroglyph, Profile, Protract, Pull, RA, Rack, Raffle, Realize, Reel, Remark, Scenography, Scent, Score, Seductive, Sepia, Sesquipedalian, Shottle, Shuttle, Silverpoint, Siphon, Sketch, Slub, Snig, Spin, Stalemate, Stretch, Study, Stumps, Sweepstake, Syphon, Tap, Taut, Technical, Tempera, Tempt, Tenniel, Tie, Till, Toke, Tole, Tombola, Top, Tose, Tow(age), Toze, Trace, Traction, Trice, Troll, Tug, Unsheathe, Uplift, Visual, Wash, Working

▷ **Draw** *may indicate* something to smoke

Drawback Catch, Downside, Ebb, Handicap, Impediment, → **OBSTACLE**, Rebate, Retraction, Shrink, Snag

Drawbridge Bascule, Pontlevis

Drawl Dra(u)nt, Haw, Slur, Twang

▷ **Drawn** *may indicate* an anagram

Drawn up Atrip, Drafted
Dray Cart, Lorry, Wagon
Dread(ed), Dreadful Angst, Anxiety, Awe, Awful, Chronic, Dearn, Dern, Dire, Fear, Formidable, Funk, Ghastly, Horrendous, → **HORROR**, Nosophobia, Penny, Rasta, Redoubt, Sorry, Terrible, Thing, Tragic, Unholy, Willies
Dream(er), Dream home, Dream state, Dreamy Aisling, Alchera, Alcheringa, American, Aspire, Castle, Desire, Drowsy, Dwalm, Dwa(u)m, Fantast, Fantasy, Faraway, Gerontius, Idealise, Illusion, Imagine, Languor, Long, Mare, Mirth, Moon, Morpheus, Muse, Nightmare, On(e)iric, Pensive, Phantasmagoria, Phantom, Pipe, → **REVERIE**, Rêveur, Romantic, Somniate, Spac(e)y, Stargazer, Surreal, Sweven, Trance, Trauma, Vague, Vision, Walter Mitty, Wet, Wool-gathering
Dreary Bleak, Desolate, Dismal, Doleful, Dreich, Dull, Gloom, Gousty, Gray, Grey, Oorie, Ourie, Owrie, Sad
Dredge(r) Caster, Scoop, Unearth
Dreg(s) Bottom, Draff, Dunder, F(a)eces, Fecula, Gr(e)aves, Grounds, Lag(s), Lees, Legge, Mother, Mud, Residue, Riffraff, Scaff, Sediment, Settlings, Silt, Snuff, Ullage
Dreikanter Ventifact
Drench Dowse, Sluice, Sluse, Soak, Souse, Steep, Submerge
Dress(ing), Dressed Accoutre, Adjust, Adorn, Aguise, Align, Apparel, Array, Attire, Attrap, Bandage, Bandoline, Bedizen, Boast, Boun, Bowne, Brilliantine, Busk, Cataplasm, Charpie, Clad, → **CLOTHING**, Comb, Compost, Compress, Curry, Dandify, Deck, Deshabille, Dight, Dink, Dizen, Doll, Don, Dub, Dubbin, Elastoplast®, Endue, Enrobe, Fertiliser, French, Full, Gamgee tissue, Garnish, Gauze, Girt, Graith, Guise, Gussy up, → **HABIT**, Italian, Jaconet, Ketchup, Line, Lint, Marie Rose, Mayonnaise, Mineral, Mulch, Oil, Ore, Pad, Patch, Plaster, Pledget, Pomade, Potash, Poultice, Prank, Preen, Prepare, Ranch, Rational, Ray, Rehearsal, Rémoulade, Rig, Russian, Rybat, Salad, Salad cream, Sartorial, Sauce, Scutch, Seloso, Sterile, Stupe, Tartare, Taw, Tenue, Tew, Thousand Island, Tiff, Tire, Toilet, Tonic, Treat, Trick, Trim, Vinaigrette, Wear, Well, Wig, Window, Ycled, Ycled

---

DRESSES

3 letters:	Vest	Tunic	Tartan
Fig			Tussah
Mob	5 letters:	6 letters:	Tusser
Rag	Ao dai	Bodice	Tuxedo
Tog	Brale	Caftan	
Top	Cimar	Chimer	7 letters:
	Court	Corset	Bloomer
4 letters:	Cymar	Dirndl	Blouson
Coat	Fancy	Dolman	Corsage
Drag	Frock	Empire	Costume
Garb	Ihram	Finery	Dashiki
Gown	Kanga	Kaftan	Evening
Kilt	Mufti	Khanga	Gymslip
Maxi	Power	Kimono	Kitenge
Midi	Samfu	Kirtle	Lounger
Robe	Shift	Muu-muu	Morning
Sack	Shirt	Peplos	Plumage
Sari	Simar	Russet	Raiment
Suit	Smock	Sacque	Simarre
Tent	Stole	Samfoo	Subfusc
Toga	Symar	Sarong	Subfusk
Tuck	Tasar	Sheath	Tussore

			12 *letters:*
Uniform	Pantsuit	Separates	Merveilleuse
Wedding	Pinafore	Trollopee	Princess line
	Princess		Shirtwaister
8 *letters:*	Sundress	10 *letters:*	
Academic	White-tie	Farrandine	13 *letters:*
Black-tie		Ferrandine	Mother Hubbard
Cocktail	9 *letters:*	Shirtwaist	
Fatigues	Cheongsam		
Flamenco	Clericals	11 *letters:*	
Highland	Farandine	Dolly Varden	
National	Polonaise	Farthingale	

Dressage Caracol(e), Demivolt(e), Manège, Passade, Passage, Pesade, Piaffe
▷ **Dressed up, Dressing** *may indicate* an anagram
Dresser Adze, Almery, Bureau, Chest, Couturier, Deuddarn, Dior, Lair, Lowboy, Sideboard, Transvestite, Tridarn, Welsh
Dressing-gown Bathrobe, Negligée, Peignoir
Dressing-room Apodyterium, Vestiary, Vestry
Dressmaker Costumier, Dorcas, Modiste, Seamstress, Tailor
Drew Steeld, Stelled
Dribble Drip, Drivel, Drop, Seep, Slaver, Slobber, Slop, Trickle
Dried fish Bum(m)alo, Bummaloti, Haberdine, Speld(r)in(g), Stockfish
▶ **Dried fruit** *see* DRY FRUIT
Drift(ing), Drifter Becalmed, Continental, Crab, Cruise, Current, Digress, Diluvium, Drumlin, Float, Flow, Genetic, Heap, Impulse, Longshore, Maunder, Natant, Nomad, North Atlantic, Plankton, Purport, Rorke, Slide, Tendence, Tendency, → TENOR, Tramp, Waft, Wander, Zooplankton
Drill(ing) Appraisal, Archimedean, Auger, Bore, Burr, Close order, Directional, Educate, Exercise, Fire, Form, Hammer, Jackhammer, Jerks, Kerb, Monkey, Pack, PE, Pierce, Pneumatic, Power, PT, Radial, Reamer, Ridge, Rimer, Rock, Rope, Seeder, Sow, Square-bashing, Teach, Train, Twill, Twist, Usage, Wildcat
Drink(er), Drunk(enness) AA, Absorb, Adrian Quist, Alkie, Alky, A pip out, Babalas, Bacchian, Barfly, Bender, Beverage, Bev(v)y, Bezzle, Bib(ite), Bibber, Binge, Birl(e), Bladdered, Bland, Blatted, Blind, Blitzed, Bloat, Blootered, Blotto, Bombed, Boose, Booze, Borachio, Bosky, Bottled, Bouse, Bowl, Bowsey, Bowsie, Bracer, Brahms and Liszt, Brandy, Brew, Bucket, Bumper, Burst, Capernoitie, Cap(p)ernoity, Carafe, Carousal, Cat-lap, Chaser, Chota peg, Compotation, → CORDIAL, Corked, Cot case, Crapulent, Crapulous, Cratur, Crocked, Cuppa, Cut, Demitasse, Digestif, Dipsomaniac, Discombobulated, Double, Down, Drain, Draught, Drop, Ebriate, Ebriose, Elixir, Energy, Entire, Eye-opener, Feni, Feny, Finger, Fleein', Flush, Flying, Fou, Fuddle-cap, Fuddled, Full, Glug, Gnat's piss, Grog, Half-cut, Half-seas-over, Happy, Heart-starter, Heavy wet, High, Hobnob, Hogshead, Honkers, Hooker, Hophead, Imbibe, In-cups, Indulge, Inhaust, Inked, In liquor, Intemperate, Irrigate, Ivresse, Jag, Jakey, Jar, Juice, Juicehead, Kaylied, Knock back, Lager lout, Langered, Lap, Legless, Lethean, Libation, → LIQUOR, Lit, Loaded, Lord, Lower, Lush(y), Maggoty, Maltworm, Maudlin, Mellow, Merry, Methomania, Methysis, Mixer, Moon-eyed, Moony, Mops and brooms, Mortal, Mug, Mullered, Neck, Nog(gin), Obfuscated, Ocean, Oenomania, Oiled, On, One, Oppignorate, Overshot, Paid, Paint, Paralytic, Partake, Particular, Peg, Pickled, Pick-me-up, Pie-eyed, Pint(a), Piss-artist, Pissed, Pisshead, Pisspot, Piss-up, Pixil(l)ated, Pledge, Plonk(o), Potation, Poteen, Potion, Primed, Quaff, Quencher, Quickie, Rat-arsed, Ratted, Roaring, Rolling, Rotten, Round, Rouse, Rumfustian, Rummer, St Martin's evil, Screamer, Screwed, Sea, Shebeen, Shicker, Shotover, Silenus, Sink, Sip(ple), Skinned, Slake, Slewed, Sloshed, Slued, Slug, Slurp, Smashed, Smoothie, Snort, Soak, Soused, Sozzled, Sponge, Spongy, Spunge, Squiffy, Steaming, Stewed, Stimulant, Stinko,

Stocious, Stoned, Stonkered, Stotious, Stukkend, Stuporous, Sucker, Suckle, Suiplap, Sup, Swacked, Swallow, Swig, Swill, Tank, Tanked up, Tape, Temulence, Tiddl(e)y, Tiff, Tift, Tight, Tincture, Tipper, Tipple, Tipsy, Tope, Toss, Tossicated, Tost, Tot, Two-pot, Two-pot screamer, Under the weather, Up the pole, Usual, Wash, Wat, Wauch, Waught, Well away, Well-oiled, Wet, Whiffled, Williewaught, Winebag, Wine bibber, Wino, Wish-wash, Woozy, Wrecked, Zonked

DRINKS

2 letters:
It

3 letters:
Ale
Ava
Bub
Cha
Cup
Dop
Fap
G&T
Hom
Kir
L&P
Mum
Pop
Red
Rum
Rye
Sec
Tea
Vin

4 letters:
Arak
Asti
Beer
Bock
Bull
Cava
Chug
Coke®
Flip
Half
Hock
Homa
Kava
Kola
Malt
Marc
Mate
Mead
Mild
Nipa

Ouzo
Port
Purl
Rack
Raki
Rosé
Sack
Sake
Saki
Soda
Soft
Soma
Sour
Sura
Tass
Tent
Yill

5 letters:
Assai
Bingo
Bombo
Bumbo
Cider
Cocoa
Copus
Crush
Doris
Float
Glogg
Haoma
Hogan
Hooch
Joram
Jorum
Julep
Kefir
Kelty
Kvass
Lager
Lassi
Mâcon
Malwa
Mauby
Meath

Medoc
Meths
Mobby
Morat
Mosel
Mulse
Nappy
Negus
Pekoe
Pepsi®
Perry
Pimms
Polly
Pombe
Punch
Rakee
Rumbo
Rummy
Sarsa
Sarza
Shake
Short
Shrub
Skink
Sling
Smile
Stout
Toddy
Tonic
Totty
Turps
Twist
Vodka
White
Xeres

6 letters:
Amrita
Apozem
Arrack
Bishop
Bitter
Burton
Busera
Cassis

Caudle
Cauker
Chasse
Claret
Coffee
Cognac
Cooler
Cooper
Doctor
Eggnog
Enzian
Frappe
Geneva
Gimlet
Grappa
Graves
Gutrot
Hootch
Kümmel
Kalied
Keltie
Kephir
Kirsch
Kumiss
Maotai
Meathe
Mescal
Mickey
Mobbie
Nectar
Obarni
Old Tom
Oolong
Orgeat
Oulong
Oxymel
Pastis
Pernod®
Plotty
Porter
Posset
Pulque
Red-eye
Rickey
Rotgut

Saloop
Samshu
Scoosh
Shandy
Sherry
Skoosh
Smiler
Squash
Stingo
Strega
Strunt
Taffia
Tisane
Waragi
Whisky
Yaqona
Zythum

7 letters:
Absinth
Akvavit
Alcopop
Amoroso
Aniseed
Aquavit
Bacardi®
Bastard
Bitters
Cachaca
Campari®
Caribou
Catawba
Chablis
Chianti
Cobbler
Curaçao
Curaçoa
Daquiri
Eggflip
Fairish
Fustian
Gin fizz
Guarana
Instant
Italian
Koumiss
Limeade
Madeira
Malmsey
Marsala
Martini
Mineral
Nobbler
Oenomel

Oloroso
Orvieto
Persico
Philter
Philtre
Pilsner
Pink gin
Plottie
Quetsch
Ratafia
Reviver
Rosiner
Rosolio
Samshoo
Sangria
Sazerac
Screech
Scrumpy
Sherbet
Sherris
Sloe gin
Snifter
Soda pop
Stengah
Swizzle
Tequila
Tio Pepe®
Wassail
Whiskey

8 letters:
Absinthe
Aleberry
Ambrosia
Anisette
Aperitif
Armagnac
Babbelas
Bordeaux
Brown cow
Burgundy
Calvados
Champers
Charneco
Ciderkin
Club soda
Coca-cola®
Cocktail
Cold duck
Daiquiri
Dog's nose
Dubonnet®
Eau de vie
Geropiga

Gin sling
Gluhwein
Highball
Hollands
Homebrew
Hydromel
Lemonade
Light ale
Log juice
Mahogany
Nepenthe
Nightcap
Persicot
Pilsener
Pinotage
Ragmaker
Red biddy
Regmaker
Resinata
Resinate
Rice beer
Riesling
Root beer
Rosoglio
Saketini
Sangaree
Schnapps
Skokiaan
Snowball
Spritzer
Spumante
Switchel
Tequilla
Vermouth
Witblits

9 letters:
Applejack
Aqua libra®
Aqua vitae
Ayahuasca
Ayahuasco
Badminton
Buck's fizz
Burnt sack
Calabogus
Champagne
Chocolate
Claret cup
Cream soda
Cuba libre
Eccoccino
Febrifuge
Firewater

Gingerade
Ginger pop
Grenadine
Hippocras
Lambswool
Manhattan
Metheglin
Milk punch
Milkshake
Mint julep
Mirabelle
Moonshine
Moose milk
Nipperkin
Orangeade
Refresher
Rosa-solis
Sauternes
Slivovica
Slivovitz
Snakebite
Soda water
Stiffener
Sundowner
The cratur
Whisky mac

10 letters:
Blackstone
Bloody Mary
Buttermilk
Chartreuse®
Ginger beer
Ginger wine
Hippomanes
Hop bitters
Lolly water
Maraschino
Mickey Finn
Mochaccino
Piña colada
Poppy water
Pousse-café
Shandygaff
Tanglefoot
Tom Collins

11 letters:
Aguardiente
Amontillado
Athole Brose
Benedictine
Bitter lemon
Black and tan

Black velvet	Whiskey sour	Humpty-dumpty	Ginger cordial
Boiler-maker	Whisky toddy	Jimmy Woodser	Liebfraumilch
Doch-an-doris		Marcobrunner	Mild and bitter
Frappuccino	*12 letters:*	Old-fashioned	Planter's punch
Half-and-half	Bloody Caesar	Sarsaparilla	Prairie oyster
Niersteiner	Brandy pawnee		
Screwdriver	Deoch-an-doris	*13 letters:*	*14 letters:*
Soapolallie	Doch-an-dorach	Cobbler's punch	John Barleycorn
Tom and Jerry	Doch-an-doruis	Deoch-an-doruis	

Drink store Cellar, Grog shop

Drip Bore, Dew-drop, Dribble, Drop, Gloop, Gutter, IV, Leak, Milksop, Post-nasal, Saline, Seep, Splatter, Stillicide, Trickle, Wimp

Dripstone Label, Larmier

Drive(r), Driving, Drive out AA, Acquired, Actuate, Amber gambler, Ambition, Automatic, Backseat, Banish, Battue, Beetle, Belt, Bullocky, Ca', Cabby, Campaign, Carman, Chain, Charioteer, Chauffeur, Coachee, Coachy, Coact, Coerce, Crankshaft, Crew, Crowd, Designated, Disk, Dislodge, Dr, Drover, Drum, Dynamic, Economy, Eject, Emboss, Energy, Enew, Enforce, Engine, Exorcise, Expatriate, Faze, Feeze, Ferret, Fire, Firk, Flash, Flexible, Fluid, Force, Four-stroke, Four-wheel, Front-wheel, Fuel, Gadsman, Goad, Hack, Hammer, Haste, Heard, Helmsman, Herd, Hie, Hish, Hiss, Hoon, Hoosh, Hot-rod, Hoy, Hunt, Hurl, Hydrostatic, Impact, Impel, Impetus, Impinge, Impulse, Instinct, Jarvey, Jehu, Jockey, Juggernaut, Key(ring), Lash, Libido, Locoman, Lunge, Mahout, Make, Mall, M(a)cGuffin, Micro, Miz(z)en, Motor, Motorman, Muleteer, Offensive, Overland, Peg, Penetrate, Phase, Piston, Pocket, Power, Powertrain, P-plater, Propel, Puncher, Push, Put, Quill, RAC, Rack, Rally(e), Ram, Rear-wheel, Rebut, Reinsman, Ride, Road, Roadhog, Run, Sales, Scorch, Screw, Scud, Senna, Sex, Shepherd, Shoo, Shover, Spank, Spin, Spur, Start, Steer, Stroke, Sumpter-horse, Sunday, Sweep, Swift, Tape, Task-master, Teamster, Tee, Test, Testosterone, Thrust, Thumb, Toad, Toe and heel, Tool, Tootle, Torrential, Trot, Trucker, Truckie, Truckman, Tup, Turn, Twoccer, Two-stroke, Urge, Urgence, USB, Vetturino, Wagoner, Warp, Whist, Wood, Wreak, Zest

Drivel Balderdash, Blether(skate), Drip, Drool, Humbug, Maunder, Nonsense, Pabulum, Pap, Rot, Salivate, Slabber, Slaver

Driving club AA, Iron, RAC

Drizzle Drow, Haze, Mist, Mizzle, Roke, Scotch mist, Scouther, Scowther, Serein, Skiffle, Smir(r), Smur, Spit

Droll Amusing, Bizarre, Comic, Funny, Jocular, Queer, Waggish

Drone Bee, Buzz, Dog-bee, Doodle, Dor(r), Drant, Draunt, Drawl, Grind, Hanger-on, Hum, Idler, Parasite, Reedy, Tamboura, Thrum, Windbag

Drool Dribble, Drivel, Gibber, Salivate, Slaver

Droop(y), Drooping Cernuous, Decline, Epinasty, Flaccid, Flag, Languish, Lill, Limp, Lob, Loll, Lop, Nutate, Oorie, Ourie, Owrie, Peak, Pendulous, Ptosis, → **SAG**, Slink, Slouch, Slump, Weeping, Welk(e), Wilt, Wither

Drop(s), Dropping Acid, Airlift, Apraxia, Bag, Bead, Beres, Blob, Cadence, Calve, Cascade, Cast, Chocolate, Cowpat, Dap, Decrease, Delayed, Descent, Deselect, Dew, Dink, Dip, Downturn, Drappie, Drib(let), Ean, Ease, Ebb, Escarp(ment), Fall, Floor, Flop, Fruit, Fumet, Gallows, Glob(ule), Gout(te), Guano, Gutta, Guttate, Ha-ha, Instil, Knockout, Land, Lapse, Minim, Modicum, Muff, Mute, Omit, Pilot, Plap, Plonk, Plop, Plummet, Plump, Plunge, Plunk, Precepit, Precipice, (Prince) Rupert's, Rain, Scat, Scrap, Shed, Sip, Skat, Slurry, Spat, Spill, Splash, Spraint, Stilliform, Tass, Taste, Tear, Thud, Trapdoor, Turd, Virga, Wrist

Drop-out Beatnik, Hippie, Hippy

Drop-shot Dink

Dropsy Anasarca, Ascites, Edema, Oedema

Dross Chaff, Dirt, Dregs, Recrement, Scoria, Scorious, Scum, Sinter, Slack, Slag, Waste
Drought Dearth, Drouth, Lack, Thirst
Drove(r) Band, Crowd, Flock, Herd, Host, Masses, Mob, Overlander, Puncher
Drown(ed), Drowning Drench, Drent, Drook, Drouk, Engulf, Inundate, Noyade, Overcome, Sorrows, Submerge
Drowse, Drowsiness, Drowsy Blet, Comatose, Doze, Hypnagogic, Hypnopompic, Lethargic, Nap, Narcolepsy, Narcosis, Nod, Snooze, Somnolent
Drub Anoint, Thrash
Drudge(ry) Boswell, Devil, Dogsbody, Donkey-work, Fag, Grind, Hack, Hackwork, Jackal, Johnson, Menial, Plod, Scrub, Slave(y), Snake, Spadework, Stooge, Sweat, Swink, Thraldom, Toil, Trauchle, Treadmill
Drug(ged) Acaricide, ACE inhibitor, Anorectic, Antabuse®, Antarthritic, Anti-depressant, Antimetabolite, Antipyrine, Bag, Barbiturate, Base, Blow, Blue devil, Bolus, Bomber, Boo, Botanical, Chalybeate, Cholagogue, Clofibrate, Clot buster, Contraceptive, Corrigent, Custom, Dadah, Deck, Depot, Depressant, Designer, DET, Diuretic, Dope, Downer, E, Ecbolic, Ecphractic, Elixir, Emmenagogue, Errhine, Euphoriant, Fantasy, Fertility, Fig, Galenical, Gateway, Gear, Generic, Hallucinogen, Hard, High, Hocus, Homeopathy, Hypnotic, Immunosuppressant, Indinavir, Joint, Knockout drops, Largactic, Lifestyle, Line, Load, Mainline, Medicine, Mercurial, Mind-expanding, Miracle, Modified release, Monged, Nervine, Nobble, Nootropic, Obstruent, OD, Opiate, Orlistat, Orphan, Painkiller, Paregoric, Parenteral, Peace, Pharmaceutics, Pharmacology, Pharmacopoeia, Poison, Popper, Prophylactic, Psychedelic, Psychoactive, Psychodelic, Purgative, Recreational, Scag, Sedate, Sedative, Shit, Shot, Sialogogue, Skin-pop, Smart, Snort, Soft, Soporific, Sorbefacient, Speedball, Spermicide, Spike, Stimulant, Stone(d), Street name, Stupefacient, Stupefy, Styptic, Substance, Sudorific, Suppressant, Synthetic, Toot, Tout, Tranquiliser, Truth, Upper, Vasoconstrictor, Vasodilator, Vermicide, Vermifuge, Weed, White stuff, Wonder, Wrap, Zeolitic

---

DRUGS

1 letter:	Adam	Coxib	Zyban®
H	Aloe	Crank	
Q	Ara-A	Dagga	*6 letters:*
	Bang	Dexie	Amulet
3 letters:	Bute	Ganja	Amytal®
AZT	Coca	Grass	Ativan®
Dex	Dopa	Hop-up	Basuco
EPO	Hash	Intal®	Bindle
Eve	Hemp	L-dopa	Charas
GHB	Junk	Meths	Curare
Hop	Khat	Mummy	Dragée
Ice	Sida	Opium	Heroin
INH	Snow	Picra	Inulin
Kat	Soma	Quina	Joypop
Kif	SSRI	Rutin	Lariam®
LSD	Tina	Salep	Mescla
PCP®	Trip	Salop	Mummia
Qat	Whiz	Senna	Nubain®
STP		Speed	Peyote
Tab	*5 letters:*	Splay	Pituri
Tea	Aloes	Sugar	Prozac®
	Benny	Sulfa	Roofie
4 letters:	Bhang	Taxol	Saloop
Acid	Candy	Whizz	Statin

Sulpha
Valium®
Viagra®
Zantac®

7 letters:
Alcohol
Aricept®
Atabrin
Atebrin®
Botanic
Cascara
Charlie
Churrus
Cocaine
Codeine
Damiana
Dapsone
Diconal®
Ecstasy
Eserine
Eucaine
Guarana
Hashish
Henbane
Hypnone
Insulin
Jellies
Librium®
Metopon
Miltown®
Mogadon®
Morphia
Nurofen®
Pareira
Patulin
Quinine
Relenza®
Ritalin®
Seconal®
Septrin®
Seroxat®
Steroid
Suramin
Tacrine
Tamiflu
Trional
Triptan
Turpeth
Veronal®
Xenical®

8 letters:
Adjuvant

Ataraxic
Atenolol
Banthine
Benadryl®
Curarine
Diazepam
Doxapram
Fentanyl
Goofball
Hyoscine
Ketamine
Laetrile
Laudanum
Mersalyl
Mescalin
Methadon
Miticide
Moonrock
Morphine
Naloxone
Naproxen
Narcotic
Nembutal
Nepenthe
Nystatin
Orlistat
Oxytocic
Procaine
Psilocin
Quaalude®
Retrovir®
Rifampin
Roborant
Rohypnol®
Scopolia
Serevent®
Snowball
Special K
Tetronal
Thiazide
Varidase®
Veratrin
Viricide
Zerumbet
Zolpidem

9 letters:
Acyclovir
Analeptic
Angel-dust
Anovulant
Antrycide
Augmentin
Barbitone

Biguanide
Bupropion
Busulphan
Captopril
Carbachol
Celecoxib
Cisplatin
Clonidine
Clozapine
Compound Q
Corticoid
Cyclizine
Cytotoxin
Dexedrine®
Digitalis
Dramamine®
Electuary
Ephedrine
Foscarnet
Frusemide
Herceptin®
Ibuprofen
Iprindole
Isoniazid
Jaborandi
Largactil®
Lidocaine
Lorazepam
Marijuana
Meloxicam
Mepacrine
Methadone
Minoxidil
Modafinil
Mydriasis
Naltrexol
Novocaine
Nux vomica
Oxycodone
Oxycontin®
Paludrine®
Pethidine
Phenytoin
Practolol
Quinidine
Quinquina
Reserpine
Ritonavir
Synergist
Tamoxifen
Temazepam
Teniacide
Totaquine
Tretinoin

Trinitrum
Verapamil
Veratrine
Wobbly egg
Zanamivir

10 letters:
Acedapsone
Amantadine
Ampicillin
Antagonist
Anxiolytic
Atracurium
Belladonna
Benzedrine
Bufotenine
Cimetidine
Clomiphene
Clonazepam
Colestipol
Disulfiram
Endostatin®
Ergotamine
Etanercept
Ethambutol
Fluoxetine
Formestane
Furosemide
Gabapentim
Hiera-picra
Imipramine
Indapamide
Iproniazid
Irinotecan
Isoaminile
Isoniazide
Ivermectin
Ketoprofen
Lofexidine
Mandragora
Mefloquine
Methidrine
Methyldopa
Mickey Finn
Nalbuphine
Natorphine
Nifedipine
Nitrazepam
Olanzapine
Omeprazole®
Papaverine
Paroxetine
Penicillin
Pentaquine

Phenacetin
Prednisone
Primaquine
Probenecid
Psilocybin
Quinacrine
Raloxifine
Rifampicin
Salbutamol
Saquinavir
Selegiline
Stramonium
Sucralfate
Tacrolimus
Taeniacide
Taeniafuge
Vagotropic
Vancomycin
Worm-powder
Zidovudine

11 letters:
Acamprosate
Aldesleukin
Alendronate
Allopurinol
Aminobutene
Amoxycillin
Amphetamine
Anastrozole
Beta-blocker
Butazolidin®
Carbimazole
Carminative
Chloroquine
Ciclosporin
Cinnarizine
Clenbuterol
Clindamycin
Clopidogrel
Cyclosporin
Deserpidine
Distalgesic

Finasteride
Fluconazole
Fluvoxamine
Galantamine
Ganciclovir
Gemcitabene
Gemfibrozil
Haloperidol
Hydralazine
Idoxuridine
Indometacin
Ipratropium
Isoxsuprine
Magic bullet
Meprobamate
Methicillin
Neostigmine
Nikethamide
Ondansetron
Oseltamivir
Paracetamol
Pentamidine
Pentazocine
Phentermine
Pravastatin
Propranolol
Purple heart
Risperidone
Simvastatin
Succedaneum
Sulfadoxine
Terfenadine
Thalidomide
Theobromine
Tolbutamide
Tous-les-mois
Tropomyosin
Tumorigenic
Varenicline
Varicomycin
Vinblastine
Vincristine

12 letters:
Alpha-blocker
Anistreplace
Anthelmintic
Antiperiodic
Arsphenamine
Atorvastatin
Azathioprine
Capecitabine
Chlorambucil
Clomipramine
Clotrimazole
Cyclandelate
Dipyridamole
Eflornithine
Fenfluramine
Fluorouracil
Fluphenazine
Glanciclover
Gonadotropin
Guanethidine
Indomethacin
Isoprenaline
Isotretinoin
Lansoprazole
Mecamylamine
Methaqualone
Methotrexate
Mifepristone
Noradrenalin
Perphenazine
Physotigmine
Promethazine
Revastigmine
Salicylamide
Streptomycin
Sulfadiazine
Temozolomide
Trimethoprim

13 letters:
Amitriptyline
Anthelminthic

Antihistamine
Carbamazepine
Depressometer
Flunitrazepam
Materia medica
Metronidazole
Nitroglycerin
Nortriptyline
Penicillamine
Phencyclidine
Pyrimethamine
Spectinomycin
Sulfadimidine
Sulfathiazole
Sulphadiazine
Suxamethonium
Thiabendazole
Triamcinolone

14 letters:
Bendrofluozide
Bisphosphonate
Butyrhophenone
Combretastatin
Cyclobarbitone
Cyclopentolate
Cyproheptadine
Discodermolide
Flucloxacillin
Norethisterone
Pentobarbitone
Phenacyclidine
Phenobarbitone
Phenylbutazone
Spironolactone
Sulphanilamide

15 letters:
Sympathomimetic

17 letters:
Sildenafil citrate

Druid Gorsedd

Drum(mer), Drumming, Drumbeat Arête, Atabal, Barrel, Bass, Beatbox, Bodhran, Bongo, Brake, Carousel, Chamade, Conga, Cylinder, Cymograph, Daiko, Dash-wheel, Devil's tattoo, Dhol, Djembe, Dr, Drub, Ear, Flam, Gran cassa, Kettle, Kymograph, Lambeg, Mridamgam, Mridang(a), Mridangam, Myringa, Naker, Ngoma, Oil, Pan, Paradiddle, Percussion, Rappel, Rataplan, Reel, Rep, Ridge, Rigger, Ringo, Roll, Ruff, Ruffle, Salesman, Side, Skin, Snare, Steel, Tabla, Tabour, Tabret, Taiko, Tambour, Tambourine, Tam-tam, Tap, Tattoo, Tenor, Thrum, Timbal, Timp(ano), Tom-tom, Touk, Traps, Traveller, Tuck, Tymbal, Tympanist, Tympano, Whim, Winding, Work

Drum-belly Hoven

Drumstick Attorney, Leg, Rute, Tampon
▶ **Drunk(ard)** *see* **DRINK(ER)**
▷ **Drunken** *may indicate* an anagram
Drupe(l) Etaerio, Tryma
Druse Crystal
Dry(ing), Drier, Dryness Air, Anhydrous, Arefaction, Arefy, Arid, Blot, Bone, Brut,
  Corpse, Crine, Dehydrate, Desiccate, Detox, Drain, Droll, Dull, Eild, Ensear, Evaporate,
  Exsiccator, Firlot, Fork, Harmattan, Hasky, Hi(r)stie, Humidor, Hydrate, Jejune, Jerk,
  Khor, Kiln, Mummify, Oast, → **PARCH**, Prosaic, Reast, Rehab, Reist, Rizzar, Rizzer,
  Rizzor, Scarious, Sciroc, Scorch, Sear, Season, Sec(co), Seco, Sere, Shrivel, Siccative,
  Silical gel, Siroc(co), Sober, Sponge, Squeegee, Squeeze, Steme, Stove, Ted, Thirsty,
  Thristy, Toasted, Torrefy, Torrid, Towel, Tribble, Trocken, TT, Tumbler, Unwatery,
  Watertight, Welt, Wilt, Win(n), Windrow, Wipe, Wither, Wizened, Wry, Xeransis,
  Xerasia, Xero(sis), Xeroderma, Xerophthalmia, Xerostomia
Dryad Eurydice, Nymph
Dry fruit, Dried fruit Achene, Akene, Cubeb, Currant, Mebos, Prune, Raisin, Samara,
  Silicula, Siliqua, Silique, Sultana
Dry mouth Xerostoma
DT's Dingbats, Hallucinations, Zooscopic
Dual Double, Twin, Twofold
Dub Array, → **CALL**, Ennoble, Entitle, Hete, Knight, Name
Dubious Arguable, Backscratching, Doubtful, Elliptic, Equivocal, Fishy, Fly-by-night,
  Hesitant, Iffy, Improbable, Left-handed, Questionable, Scepsis, Sceptical, Sesey, Sessa,
  → **SHADY**, Shonky, Suspect, Touch and go, Unclear, Unlikely
▷ **Dubious** *may indicate* an anagram
Dubliner Jackeen
Duce Leader, Musso(lini)
Duchess Anastasia, Camilla, Malfi, Peeress, Titled
Duchy Anhalt, Brabant, Brunswick, Cornwall, Dukedom, Franconia, Grand, Hesse,
  Holstein, Limburg, Luxembourg, Nassu, Normandy, Omnium, Realm, Savoy, Swabia,
  Valois, Westphalian
Duck(ling), Ducked Amphibian, Avoid, Aylesbury, Bald-pate, Bargander, Bathe,
  Bergander, Blob, Blue, Bluebill, Bob, Bombay, Broadbill, Bufflehead, Bum(m)alo, Burrow,
  Butterball, Canard, Canvasback, → **COUPLE OF DUCKS**, Dead, Dearie, Decoy, Dip,
  Diving, Dodge, Dodo, Douse, Drook, Drouk, Dunk(er), Eider, Elude, Enew, Escape,
  Evade, Ferruginous, Flapper, Gadwall, Garganey, Garrot, Golden-eye, Goosander,
  Greenhead, Hareld, Harlequin, Heads, Herald, Immerse, Indian runner, Jook, Jouk,
  King-pair, Lame, Long-tailed, Mallard, Mandarin, Muscovy, Musk, Nil, Nodding, Nun,
  O, Oldsquaw, Old Tom, Orpington, Paddling, Pair of spectacles, Palmated, Paradise,
  Pekin(g), Pintail, Plunge, Pochard, Poker, Putangitangi, Redhead, Ring-bill, Ruddy,
  Runner, Rush, St Cuthbert's, Scaup, Scoter, Sheld(d)uck, Shieldrake, Shirk, Shovel(l)er,
  Shun, Sitting, Smeath, Smee(th), Smew, Sord, Souse, Sowse, Spatula, Spirit, Sprigtail,
  Steamer, Surf(scoter), Teal, Team, Tufted, Tunker, Ugly, Velvet scoter, Whio, Whistling,
  Whitewing, Widgeon, Wigeon, Wild, Wood, Zero
Duckbill Ornithorhynchus, Platypus
Duckwalk Waddle
Duckweed Lemna
Ducky Sweet, Twee
Duct Bile, Canal(iculus), Channel, Conduit, Diffuser, Diffusor, Emunctory, Epididymus,
  Fistula, Gland, Lachrymal, Lacrimal, Laticifer, Lumen, Mesonephric, Pancreatic, Parotid,
  Passage, Pipe, Tear, Thoracic, Tube, Ureter, Vas deferens, Wolffian
Dud Bouncer, Failure, Flop, Shan(d), Stumer
Dude Cat, Clothes horse, Coxcomb, Dandy, Fop, Lair, Macaroni, Popinjay, Roy
Dudgeon Anger, Hilt, Huff, Pique

Due(s) Accrued, Adequate, Annates, Arrearage, Claim, Debt, Deserts, Expected, Fit(ment), Forinsec, Geld, Heriot, Inheritance, Just, Lot, Mature, Needful, Offerings, Offload, Owing, Reddendo, Rent, Right, → **SUITABLE**, Thereanent, Toll, Tribute, Worthy

Duel(list) Delope, Mensur, Monomachy, Principal, Tilt

Duenna Chaperone, Dragon

Duff Bum, Bungle, Dough, Nelly, NG, Plum, Pudding, Rustle

Duffer Bungler, Rabbit, Useless

Dug Ploughed, Teat, Titty, Udder

Dugong Halicore, Sea-cow, Sea-pig, Sirenian

Dug-out Abri, Canoe, Piragua, Pirogue, Shelter, Trench, Trough

Duke(dom) Albany, Alva, Chandos, Clarence, D, Duc, Ellington, Fist, Iron, Milan, Orsino, Peer, Prospero, Rohan, Wellington

Dulcimer Cembalo, Citole, Cymbalo, Santir, Sant(o)ur

Dull(ard), Dullness Anodyne, Anorak, Bald, Banal, Barren, Besot, Bland, Blear, Blockish, Blunt, Boeotian, Boring, Cloudy, Colourless, Commonplace, Dead (and alive), Deadhead, Dense, Dim, Dinge, Dingy, Ditchwater, Doldrums, Dowf, Dowie, Drab, Drear, Dreich, Dry, Dunce, Faded, Flat, Fozy, Gray, Grey, Heavy, Hebetate, Himbo, Ho-hum, Humdrum, Illustrious, Insipid, Jejune, Lacklustre, Lifeless, Log(y), Lowlight, Mat(t), Matte, Monotonous, Mopish, Mull, Mundane, Obtund, Obtuse, Opacity, Opiate, Ordinary, Overcast, Owlish, Pall, Pedestrian, Perstringe, Plodder, Podunk, Prosaic, Prose, Prosy, Rebate, Rust, Saddo, Slow, Solein, Sopite, Staid, Stick, Stodger, Stodgy, Stolid, Stuffy, Stultify, → **STUPID**, Sunless, Tame, Tarnish, Tedious, Ticky-tacky, Toneless, Torpor, Treadmill, Trite, Tubby, Unimaginative, Unresponsive, Vapid, Wonk, Wooden, Zoid

Dumb(ness) Alalia, Aphonic, Blonde, Crambo, Hobbididance, Inarticulate, Mute, Mutism, Shtum, Silent, Stumm, Stupid, Thunderstruck

Dumbfound(ed) Amaze, Astound, Flabbergast, Stun, Stupefy, Stupent

Dumb ox Aquinas

Dummy Clot, Comforter, Copy, Effigy, Fathead, Flathead, Lummox, Mannequin, Mannikin, Mock-up, Model, Pacifier, Quintain, Soother, Table, Teat, Waxwork

Dump(ing), Dumps Abandon, Blue, Core, Dejection, Dispirited, Doldrums, Empty, Eyesore, Fly-tipping, Hole, Jettison, Jilt, Junk, Laystall, Mine, Offload, Scrap, Screen, Shoot, Store(house), Tip, Toom, Unlade, Unload

Dumpling Clootie, Dim sum, Dough(boy), Gnocchi, Gyoza, Knaidel, Knaidloch, Kneidlach, Knish, Kreplach, Matzoball, Norfolk, Perogi, Pi(e)rogi, Quenelle, Ribaude, Suet, Won ton

Dumpy Pudgy, Squat

Dun Annoy, Cow, Importune, Pester, → **SUE**, Tan

Duncan Isadora

Dunce Analphabet, Booby, Clod, Dolt, Donkey, Dullard, Fathead, Schmo, Schmuck, Schnook, Stupid

Dune Areg, Bar, Barchan(e), Bark(h)an, Erg, Sandbank, Seif, Star, Whaleback

Dung(hill) Argol, Buffalo chips, Buttons, Chip, Cock, Coprolite, Cowpat, Droppings, Fewmet, Fumet, Fumiculous, Guano, Hing, Manure, Midden, Mixen, Mute, Night soil, Ordure, Puer, Pure, Scat, Scumber, Shairn, Shard, Sharn, Siege, Skat, Skummer, Sombrerite, Sombrero, Spawn brick, Spraint, Stercoraceous, Tath

Dungarees Overalls

Dung-eating Merdiverous

Dungeon Bastille, Cell, Confine, Donjon, Durance, Oubliette, Souterrain

Dunk Immerse, Sop, Steep, Submerge

Dunnock Accentor

Duo Couple, Pair, Twosome

Dupe Catspaw, Chiaus, Chouse, Cony, Cull(y), Delude, Easy game, Easy mark, Easy meat, Geck, Gull, Hoax, Hoodwink, Mug, Pawn, Pigeon, Plover, Sitter, Soft mark, Sucker, Swindle, → **TRICK**, Victim

Duplex Twofold

Duplicate, Duplication, Duplicator Clone, Copy, Counterpart, Cyclostyle, Double, Echo, Facsimile, Match, Ozalid®, Paginal, Replica, Reproduce, Roneo®, Spare, Spit(ting)

Durable Enduring, Eternal, Eterne, Hardy, Lasting, Permanent, Stout, Tough

Duralumin® Y-alloy

Duration Extent, Limit, Period, Span, Timescale

Duress Coercion, Pressure, Restraint

Durham Palatine

During Amid, Dia-, For, In, Live, Over, Throughout, While, Whilst

Dusk(y) Dark, Dewfall, Dun, Eve, Eventide, Gloaming, Gloom, Half-light, Owl-light, Phaeic, Twilight, Umbrose

Dust(y) Arid, Ash, Bo(a)rt, Calima, Clean, Coom, Cosmic, Culm, Derris, Devil, Dicht, Duff, Earth, Fuss, Gold, Khak(i), Lemel, Limail, Limit, Lo(e)ss, Miller, Nebula, Pellum, Pollen, Pother, Pouder, Poudre, Powder, Pozz(u)olana, Pudder, Rouge, Sea, Seed, Shaitan, Slack, Springfield, Stour, Talc, Timescale, Volcanic, Wipe

▷ **Dusted** *may indicate* an anagram

Duster Cloth, Feather, Red, Talcum, Torchon

Dustman Doolittle, Garbo(logist), Refuse collector, Scaffie, Trashman

Dust measure Konimeter, Koniscope

Dutch(man), Dutchwoman Batavian, Boor, Butterbox, Cape, Courage, D(u), Double, Elm, Erasmus, Flying, Fri(e)sian, Frow, German, Kitchen, Knickerbocker, Middle, Missis, Missus, Mynheer, Parnell shout, Patron, Pennsylvania, Sooterkin, Taal, Vrouw, Wife

Dutiful, Duty Active, Ahimsa, Allegiance, Attentive, Average, Blench, Bond, Charge, Corvee, Countervailing, Customs, Death, Debt, Deontology, Detail, Devoir, Docile, Drow, Due, Duplicand, End, Estate, Excise, Export, Fatigue, Feu, Filial, Function, Heriot, Homage, Import, Imposition, Impost, Incumbent, Lastage, Legacy, Likin, Mission, Mistery, Mystery, Obedient, Obligation, Octroi, Office, Onus, Pia, Picket, Pious, Point, Preferential, Prisage, Probate, Rota, Sentry-go, Shift, Stamp, Stillicide, Stint, Succession, Tariff, → **TASK**, Tax, Toll, Transit, Trap, Trow, Watch, Zabeta

Duvet Doona, Quilt

Dwarf(ism) Achondroplasia, Agate, Alberich, Andvari, Ateleiosis, Bashful, Belittle, Bes, Black, Bonsai, Brown, Doc, Dopey, Droich, Drow, Durgan, Elf, Gnome, Grumpy, Happy, Hobbit, Homuncule, Hop o' my thumb, Knurl, Laurin, Leetle, Little man, Man(n)ikin, → **MIDGET**, Mime, Minikin, Minim, Nanism, Nectabanus, Ni(e)belung, Nurl, Outshine, Overshadow, Pacolet, Pigmy, Pygmy, Red, Regin, Ront, Rumpelstiltskin, Runt, Skrimp, Sleepy, Sneezy, → **STUNT**, Tiddler, Titch, Tokoloshe, Tom Thumb, Toy, Troll, Trow, White

Dwell(er), Dwelling Abide, Aweto, Be, Bungalow, Cabin, Cell, Cot(tage), Descant, Discourse, Domicile, Habitation, Harp, Heteroscian, Hogan, House, Hut, Ice colours, Igloo, Laura, Lavra, Live, Lodge, Longhouse, Maison(n)ette, Mansion, Messuage, Midgard, Midgarth, Mithgarthr, Palafitte, Pied-à-terre, Place, Pueblo, Reside, Roof, Single-end, Stress, Sty, Tenement, Tepee, Terramara, Tipi, Two-by-four, Weem, Wigwam, Won(ing), Wonning, Woon

Dwindle Decline, Diminish, Fade, Lessen, Peter, Shrink, Wane

Dye(ing), Dyestuff, Dye-seller Acid, Alkanet, Amaranth, Anil, Anthracene, Anthraquinone, Archil, Aweto, Azo(benzine), Azurine, Bat(t)ik, Benzidine, Brazil(e)in, Burnt umber, Camwood, Canthaxanthin, Carthamine, Catechin, Chay(a), Chica, Chicha, Chico, Choy, Cinnabar, Cobalt, Cochineal, Colour, Congo, Coomassie blue, Corkir, Crocein, Crotal, Crottle, Cudbear, Dinitrobenzene, Direct, Embrue, Engrain, Envermeil, Eosin, Flavin(e), Fluoxene, Fuchsin(e), Fustet, Fustic, Fustoc, Gambi(e)r, Gentian violet, Grain, Haematoxylin, Henna, Hue, Ice colours, Ikat, Imbrue, Imbue, Incarnadine, Indamine, Indican, Indigo, Indigocarmine, Indigotin, Indirubin, Indoxyl, Indulin(e), Ingrain, Kalamkari, Kamala, Kermes, Kohl, Korkir, Lightfast, Madder, Magenta, Mauvein(e), Mauvin(e), Methyl violet, Murex, Myrobalan, Nigrosin(e), Orcein, Orchel(la),

Orchil, Para-red, Phenolphthalein, Phthalein, → **PIGMENT**, Ponceau, Primuline, Puccoon, Purple, Purpurin, Pyronine, Quercitron, Quinoline, Raddle, Resorcinol, Rhodamine, Rosanilin(e), Safranin(e), Salter, Shaya, → **STAIN**, Stilbene, Stone-rag, Stone-raw, Sumac(h), Sunfast, Tannin, Tartrazine, Tie-dye, Tinct, Tint, Tropaeolin, Trypan blue, Turmeric, Turnsole, Ultramarine, Valonia, Vat, Wald, Weld, Woad, Woald, Wold, Xanthium, Xylidine

▶ **Dying** *see* **DIE(D)**

Dyke Aboideau, Aboiteau, Bund, Devil's, → **DIKE**, Ditch, Gall, Offa's, Ring, Sea-wall

Dynamic(s) Ballistics, Ball of fire, Driving, Energetic, Forceful, Gogo, High-powered, Kinetics, Potent

Dynamite Blast, Explode, Gelignite, Giant powder, TNT, Trotyl

Dynamo Alternator, Armature, Tiger

Dynasty Abbasid(e), Angevin, Bourbon, Capetian, Carolingian, Chen, Chin(g), Ch'ing, Chou, Era, Fatimid, Frankish, Gupta, Habsburg, Han, Hanoverian, Hapsburg, Holkar, Honan, House(hold), Hyksos, Khan, Manchu, Maurya, Merovingian, Ming, Omayyad, Osman, Pahlavi, Plantagenet, Ptolemy, Qajar, Q'in(g), Rameses, Romanov, Rule, Safavid, Saga, Sassanid, Seleucid, Seljuk, Shang, Song, Sui, Sung, Tai-ping, Tang, Tudor, Umayyad, Wei, Yi, Yuan, Zhou

Dysentery Amoebic, Bloody flux, Shigellosis

Dysfunction Kernicterus

Dyslexia Strephosymbolia

Dyspeptic Cacogastric

Dysprosium Dy

Dystrophy Duchenne's, Muscular

Ee

E Boat, East, Echo, Energy, English, Spain

Each All, Apiece, A pop, Ea, → **EVERY**, Ilka, Per, Respective, Severally

Eager(ly) Agog, Antsy, Ardent, Avid, Beaver, Bore, Bright-eyed, Dying, Earnest, Enthusiastic, Fain, Fervent, Fervid, Fidge, Frack, Game, Greedy, Gung-ho, Hot, Intent, → **KEEN**, Perfervid, Prone, Race, Raring, Rath(e), Ready, Roost, Sharp-set, Sore, Spoiling, Thirsty, Toey, Wishing, Yare, Zealous

Eagle Al(l)erion, Altair, American, Aquila, Bald, Bateleur, Berghaan, Bird, Double, Eddy, Ensign, Erne, Ethon, Fish, Gier, Golden, Harpy, Hawk, Legal, Lettern, Nisus, Ossifrage, Sea, Spread, Tawny, Wedge-tailed

Ear(drum), Ear problem Ant(i)helix, Attention, Audience, Auricle, Barotitis, Cauliflower, Cochlea, Concha, Conchitis, Deafness, Dionysius, Dolichotus, External, Glue, Hearing, Helix, Icker, Incus, Inner, Internal, Jenkins, Kieselguhr, Labyrinth, Labyrinthitis, Listen, Locusta, Lop, Lug, Malleus, Middle, Modiolus, Myringa, Myringitis, Nubbin, Otalgia, Otalgy, Otic, Otocyst, Paracusis, Paramastoid, Parotic, Pavilion, Periotic, Petrosal, Phonic, Pinna, Presby(a)c(o)usis, Prootic, Souse, Spike, Spikelet, Stapes, Thick, Tin, Tragus, Tympanitis, Utricle

Earl(dom) Belted, Leofric, Mar, Peer, Sandwich

Earlier, Early Above, Ago, Ahead, Alsoon, AM, Antelucan, Auld, Betimes, Cockcrow, Daybreak, Ere-now, Ex, Germinal, Incipient, Matin, Or, Precocious, Precursor, Prehistoric, Premature, Premie, Prevernal, Previous, Primeur, Primeval, Primordial, Prior, Rath(e), Rath(e)ripe, Rear, Rough, Rudimentary, Small hours, Soon, Timely, Tim(e)ous

▷ **Early** *may indicate* belonging to an earl

Early man Eoanthropus, Flat-earther

▷ **Early stages of** *may indicate* first one or two letters of the words following

Earmark Allocate, Bag, Book, Characteristic, Flag, → **RESERVE**, Tag, Target, Ticket

Earn(er), Earning(s) Achieve, Addle, Breadwinner, Curdle, Deserve, Digerati, Ern, Gain, Income, Invisible, Make, Merit, O.T.E., Pay packet, Reap, Rennet, Runnet, Win, Yearn

Earnest(ly) Agood, Ardent, Arle(s)(-penny), Deposit, Devout, Fervent, Imprest, Intent, Promise, Serious, Sincere, Token, Wistly, Zealous

Earring Drop, Ear bob, Hoop, Keeper, Pendant, Sleeper, Snap, Stud

Earshot Hail, Hearing

Earth(y), Earthling Alkaline, Antichthon, Art, Asthenosphere, Barbados, Brown, Bury, Capricorn, Carnal, Clay, Cloam, Clod, Cologne, Craton, Den, Diatomite, Dirt, Drey, Dust, E, Eard, Edaphic, Epigene, Foxhole, Friable, Fuller's, Gaea, Gaia, Gault, Ge, Globe, Green, Ground, Heavy, Horst, Infusiorial, Kadi, Lair, Leaf-mould, Lemnian, Lithosphere, Loam, Malm, Mankind, Mantle, Mools, Mould, Mouls, Papa, Pise, Planet, Podsol, Rabelaisian, Racy, Rare, Raunchy, Red, Samian, Seat, Sett, Sod, → **SOIL**, Subsoil, Surcharge, Taurus, Telluric, Tellus, Terra, Terrain, Terramara, Terran, Terrene, Topsoil, Tripoli, Virgo, Wad, Yellow, Ye(a)rd, Yird

Earth-bound Chthonian, Mundane

Earthenware Arretine, Biscuit, Ceramic, Creamware, Crock(ery), Delf(t), Della-robbia, Delph, Faience, Figuline, Graniteware, Maiolica, Majolica, Pig, Pot, Queen's ware, Raku, Samian, Sanitary, Terracotta, Terra sigillata

Earthquake Aftershock, Aseismic, Bradyseism, Foreshock, Mercalli, Richter, Seism,

Shake, Shock, Temblor, Trembler, Tremor

Earth's surface Sal, Sial

Earthwork Agger, Bank, Cursus, Gazon, Parados, Rampart, Remblai, Vallum

Earthworm Angledug, Angletwitch, Angleworm, Annelid, Bait, Night-crawler

Earwig Clipshear(s), Eavesdrop, Forkit-tail, Forky-tail

Ease, Easing, Easygoing Alleviate, Carefree, Clear, Clover, Comfort, Content, Defuse, Deregulate, Détente, Easy-osy, Facility, Genial, Hands down, Informal, Lax, Mellow, Mid(dy), Mitigate, Otiosity, Palliate, Peace, Pococurante, Quiet, Relieve, Reposal, Repose, Soothe

East(erly), Eastward Anglia, Asia, Chevet, E, Eassel, Eassil, Eothen, Eurus, Far, Levant, Middle, Morning-land, Near, Orient, Ost, Sunrise

Easter Festival, Island, Pace, Pasch(al), Pasque

Eastern(er), Eastern language Asian, Kolarian, Oriental, Ostman, Virginian

East European Lettic, Slovene

East German Ossi

Easy, Easily ABC, Breeze, Cakewalk, Carefree, Child's play, Cinch, Comfy, Cushy, Degage, Doddle, Doss, Duck soup, Eath(e), Ethe, Facile, Free, Gift, Glib, Gravy train, Hands down, Independent, Jammy, Kid's stuff, Lax, Light, Midshipman, Natural, Nimps, No-brainer, Oldster, Picnic, Pie, Plain sailing, Pushover, Romp, Scoosh, Simple, Sitter, Skoosh, Snap, Snotty, Soft, Spoon fed, Tolerant, Turkey shoot, User-friendly, Walk-over, Well, Yare

▷ **Easy** *may indicate* an anagram

Easy-care Non-iron

Eat(able), Eater, Eating Bite, Bolt, Break bread, Champ, Chop, Commensal, Consume, Corrode, Cram, Devour, Dig in, Dine, Edible, Edite, Endew, Endue, Erode, Esculent, Etch, Fare, Feast, → **FEED**, Fret, Gastronome, Gnaw, Go, Gobble, Gourmand, Gourmet, Graze, Grub, Have, Hoe into, Hog, Hyperorexia, Hyperphagia, Ingest, Manducate, Mess, Muckamuck, Munch, Nosh, Nutritive, Omnivore, Partake, Phagomania, Phagophobia, Predate, Refect, Scoff, Snack, Stuff, Sup, Swallow, Syssitia, Take, Taste, Trencherman, Trophesy, Tuck away, Tuck into, Twist, Whale

Eating problem Anorexia, Bulimia, Cachexia

Eavesdrop(per) Cowan, Detectophone, Earwig, Icicle, Listen, Overhear, Pry, Snoop, Stillicide, Tab-hang, Tap, Wiretap

Ebb(ing) Abate, Decline, Recede, Refluent, Sink, → **WANE**

Ebonite Hard rubber

Ebony Black, Cocus-wood, Coromandel, Hebenon, Jamaican

Ebullient Brash, Effervescent, Exuberant, Fervid

Eccentric Abnormal, Antic, Atypical, Cam, Card, Character, Crackpot, Crank, Curious, Daffy, Dag, Deviant, Dingbat, Ditsy, Ditzy, E, Farouche, Fay, Fey, Fie, Freak, Fruitcake, Geek, Gonzo, Iffish, Irregular, Kinky, Kook(y), Madcap, Mattoid, Monstre sacré, Nutcase, Nutter, Odd(ball), Offbeat, Off-centre, Off the wall, Original, Outré, → **PECULIAR**, Phantasime, Pixil(l)ated, Queer, Quirky, Quiz, Rake, Raky, Recondite, Rum, Scatty, Screwball, Screwy, Spac(e)y, Squirrelly, Wack(y), W(h)acko, Way-out, Weird(o), Weirdie

▷ **Eccentric** *may indicate* an anagram

Ecclesiast(es), Ecclesiasticus, Ecclesiastical Abbé, Clergyman, Clerical, Lector, Secular, Sir(ach), Theologian, The Preacher, Vatican

Echelon Formation

Echinoderm Asteroidea, Basket-star, Brittle-star, Comatulid, Crinoid, Heart-urchin, Ophiurid, Sea-egg, Sea-lily, Sea-urchin, Starfish

Echo, Echoing, Echo-sounder Angel, Answer, Ditto, E, Fathometer®, Imitate, Iterate, Phonocamptic, Rebound, Repeat, Repercussion, Reply, Resemble, Resonant, → **RESOUND**, Respeak, Reverb(erate), Revoice, Ring, Rote, Sonar, Tape

Eclat Flourish, Glory, Prestige, Renown

Eclectic Babist, Broad, Complex, Diverse, Liberal

Eclipse Annular, Block, Cloud, Deliquium, Excel, Hide, Lunar, Obscure, Occultation, Outmatch, Outshine, Outweigh, Overshadow, Partial, Penumbra, Rahu, Solar, Total, Transcend, Upstage

Eclogue Bucolic, Idyll, Pastoral

Eco-community Seral

Eco-friendly Biodegradable

Ecology Bionomics

Economise Budget, Conserve, Eke, Entrench, Finance, Husband, Intrench, Pinch, Retrench, Scrimp, Skimp, Spare, → **STINT**, Whip the cat

Economist Angell, Bentham, Chrematist, Cole, Coombs, Friedman, Galbraith, Giffen, Keynes, Laffer, Malthus, Marginalist, Meade, Mill, Monetarist, Nugget, Pareto, Physiocrat, Rathenau, Ricardo, Schumacher, Schumpeter, Singh, Smith, Tinbergen, Tobin, Toynbee, Veblen, Webb, Weber

Economy, Economic(al), Economics Agronomy, Autarky, Black, Brevity, Careful, Chrematistics, Cliometrics, Command, Conversation, Cut, Dismal science, Domestic, Frugal, Hidden, Home, Informal, Knowledge, LSE, Market, Mitumba, Mixed, Neat, New, Parsimony, Planned, Political, Provident, Pusser's logic, Retrenchment, Shadow, Shoestring, Siege, Sparing, Stagflation, Stakeholder, Stumpflation, Supply-side, Thrift, Tiger, Token, Welfare

Ecstasy, Ecstatic Bliss, Delight, Delirious, Dove, E, Exultant, Joy, Liquid, Lyrical, Nympholepsy, Pythic, Rapture, Rhapsodic, Sent, Trance, Transport

Ecumenical Catholic, Lateran

Eczema Pompholyx, Salt rheum, Tetter

Edda Elder, Prose, Younger

Eddy Backset, Curl, Duane, Gurge, Maelstrom, Nelson, Pirl, Purl, Rotor, Sousehole, Swelchie, Swirl, Vortex, Weel, Well, Whirlpool, Wiel

Eden Bliss, Fall, Heaven, Paradise, PM, Utopia

Edentate Ant-eater, Armadillo, Peba, Sloth, Tatou, Xenarthra

Edge, Edging, Edgy Advantage, Arris, Bleeding, Border, Bordure, Brim, Brink, Brittle, Brown, Burr, Chamfer, Chimb, Chime, Chine, Coaming, Costa, Creston, Cutting, Dag, Deckle, Ease, End, Flange, Flounce, Frill, Fringe, Frontier, Furbelow, Gunnel, Gunwale, Hem, Hone, Inch, Inside, Kerb, Knife, Leading, Leech, Limb(ate), Limbus, Limit, Lip, List, Lute, Marge(nt), Margin, Neckline, Nosing, Orle, Outside, Parapet, Periphery, Picot, Pikadell, Piping, Rand, Reeding, Rim, Rund, Rymme, Selvage, Selvedge, Side, Sidle, Skirt, Strand, Surbed, Tense, Tomium, Trailing, Trim, Tyre, Uptight, Verge, Wear, Whet

▸ **Edible** *see* **EATABLE**

Edict(s) Ban, Bull, Clementines, Decree, Decretal, Extravagantes, Fatwa, Firman, Interim, Irade, Nantes, Notice, Order, Pragmatic, Proclamation, Pronouncement, Pronunciamento, Rescript, Sext, Ukase

Edifice Booth, Building, Structure, Stupa, Superstructure

Edify Instruct, Teach

Edinburgh Auld Reekie

Edit(or), Editorial Abridge, Amend, Article, City, Copy (read), Cut, Dele, Desk, Dramaturg(e), Ed, Emend, Expurgate, Footsteps, Garble, Leader, Manipulate, Overseer, Prepare, Recense, Redact, Revise, Seaman, Tweak

▹ **Edited** *may indicate* an anagram

Edith Sitwell

Edition Aldine, Bulldog, Bullpup, Ed, Extra, Facsimile, Ghost, Hexapla(r), Impression, Issue, Library, Limited, Number, Omnibus, Trade, Variorum, Version

Edmond, Edmund Burke, Gosse, Ironside(s), Rostand, Spenser

Educate(d) Academic, Baboo, Babu, Enlighten, Evolué, Informed, Instruct, Learned, Lettered, Noursle, Nousell, Nousle, Nurture, Nuzzle, Polymath, Preppy, Progressive, Scholarly, School, → **TEACH**, Train, Yuppie

Education(alist) Adult, Basic, B.Ed, Classical, Conductive, D.Ed, Didactics, Estyn,

Further, Heurism, Learning, Literate, Mainstream, Montessori, Paedotrophy, Pedagogue, Pestalozzi, Physical, Piarist, Primary, Schooling, Special, Steiner, Teacher, Tertiary, Upbringing

Educe Elicit, Evoke, Extract, Infer

Edward Confessor, Ed, Elder, Lear, Longshanks, Martyr, Ned, Ted

Eel Conger, Congo, Electric, Elver, Glass, Grig, Gulper, Gunnel, Hagfish, Kingklip, Lamper, Lamprey, Lant, Launce, Leptocephalus, Moray, Murray, Murr(e)y, Olm, Paste, Salt, Sand(ling), Silver belly, Snake, Snig, Spitchcock, Tuna, Vinegar, Wheat, Wolf

Eerie Creepy, Spooky, Uncanny, Unked, Weird

Efface Cancel, Delete, Dislimn, → **ERASE**, Expunge, Obliterate

Effect(s), Effective(ness), Effectual Able, Achieve, Acting, Alienation, Auger, Babinski, Bags, Barkhausen, Belongings, Binaural, Bit, Bite, Bohr, Border, Border edge, Bricolage, Butterfly, Bystander, Causal, C(h)erenkov, Chromakey, Coanda, Coastline, Competent, Compton, Consequence, Coriolis, Do, Domino, Doppler, Dr(y)ice, Eclat, Edge, Efficacious, Electro-optical, Enact, End, Estate, Execute, Experimenter, Fet, Foley, Fringe, Functional, Fungibles, Gangbuster, Gear, General, Goods, Greenhouse, Ground, Gunn, Hall, Halo, Hangover, Hawthorne, Home, Horns and halo, Impact, Implement(al), Impression, Influence, Introgenic, Josephson, Joule(-Thomson), Kerr, Keystone, Knock-on, Magneto-optical, Magnus, Meissner, Militate, Moire, Mossbauer, Mutual, Neat, Net, Nisi, Notch, Operant, Optical, Outcome, Ovshinsky, Oxygen, Parallax, Peltier, Perficient, Personal, Phi, Photoelectric, Photovoltaic, Piezoelectric, Piezomagnetic, Pinch, Placebo, Pogo, Position, Potent, Practical, Primary, Promulgate, Punchy, Raman, Ratchet, Reaction, Recency, Redound, Repercussion, → **RESULT**, Ripple, Schottky, Seebeck, Shadow, Shore, Side, Skin, Slash-dot, Sound, Sovereign, Special, Spectrum, Spin-off, Stage, Stark, Striking, Stroop, Submarine, Subsidiary, Tableau, Teeth, Telling, Thermoelectric, Thomson, Toxic, Tunnel, Tyndall, Upshot, Valid, Viable, Virtual, Well, Win, Withdrawal, Work, Zeeman

Effeminate Airtsy-mairtsy, Camp, Carpet-knight, Carpet-monger, Cissy, Coddle, Cookie-pusher, Dildo, Epicene, Female, Gussie, Jessie, Milksop, Minty, (Miss) Nancy, Molly(coddle), Nellie, Nelly, Pansy, Panty-waist, Poovy, Pretty, Prissy, Punce, Queenie, Sissy, Swish, Tender, Tenderling, Tonk, Unman, Wuss(y)

Effervescence, Effervescent Bubbling, Ebullient, Fizz, Frizzante, Pétillant, Soda

▷ **Effervescent** *may indicate* an anagram

Effete Camp, Epicene, Epigon(e)

Efficacious, Efficacy Effective, Operative, Potent, Sovereign, Valid, Value

Efficiency, Efficient Able, Businesslike, Capable, Competent, Current, Despatch, Ecological, Electrode, Ergonomics, High-powered, Luminous, Productivity, Quantum, Smart, Spectral luminous, Streamlined, Strong, Thermal, Volumetric

Effigy Buddha, Figure, Guy, Idol, Image, Statua, Statue

Efflorescence Bloom, Blossom, Reh

Effluence, Effluent, Effluvia Air, Aura, Billabong, Discharge, Fume, Gas, Halitus, Miasma, Odour, Outflow, Outrush

Effort Achievement, All-out, Attempt, Best, Conatus, Concerted, Damnedest, Drive, Endeavour, Essay, Exertion, Fit, Frame, Hardscrabble, Herculean, Labour, Molimen, Nisus, Pains, Pull, Rally, Shy, Spurt, Stab, Strain, Struggle, Team, → **TRY**, Work, Yo

Effortless Lenis, Low-impact, Low maintenance, Spoonfed

Effrontery Audacity, Brass, Cheek, Face, Gall, Neck, Nerve, Temerity

Effulgent Bright, Radiant, Shining

Effuse, Effusion, Effusive Emanate, Exuberant, Exude, Gush, Lyric, Ode, Outburst, Prattle, Rhapsody, Sanies, Screed, Spill

Eft After

Eg As, Example

Egest Eliminate, Evacuate, Excrete, Void

Egg(s), Egg on Abet, Addled, Benedict, Berry, Blow, Bomb, Caviar(e), Cavier, Chalaza,

Cheer, Cleidoic, Clutch, Cockney, Collop, Coral, Curate's, Darning, Easter, Edge, Encourage, Fabergé, Fetus, Flyblow, Foetus, Free-range, Glair(e), Goad, Goog, Graine, Hoy, Incite, Instigate, Isolecithal, Layings, Mine, Nest, Nidamentum, Nit, Oocyte, Oophoron, Ostrich, Ova, Ovum, Pace, Pasch, Plover's, Prairie oyster, Press, Prod, Raun, Roe, Rumble-tumble, Scotch, Scrambled, Seed, Setting, Spat, Spawn, Spur(ne), Tar(re), Thunder, Tooth, Tread(le), Urge, Whore's, Wind, Yelk, Yolk, Zygote

Egg-case Pod, Shell

Egghead Brainbox, Don, Highbrow, Intellectual, Mensa, Pedant

Eggnog Flip

Egg-plant Aubergine, Brinjal

Egg-producer Gametophyte, Hen, Ovipositor

Egg-shaped Obovate, Oval, Ovate

Egg-white Albumen, Glair

Ego(ism), Egoist, Egotist(ical) Che, Conceit, I, Narcissism, Not-I, Pride, Self, Self-seeker, Solipsism, Tin god, Ubu, Vanity

Egocentric Solipsistic

Egregious Eminent, Flagrant, Glaring, Shocking

Egret Snowy

Egypt(ian), Egyptologist Arab, Cairene, Carter, Cheops, Chephren, Cleopatra, Copt(ic), ET, Gippo, Goshen, Gyppo, Imhotep, Nasser, Nefertiti, Nilote, Nitrian, Old Kingdom, Osiris, Ptolemy, Rameses, Syene, UAR, Wafd, Wog

Eiderdown Bedspread, Duvet, Quilt

Eight(h), Eighth day Acht, Byte, Crew, Cube, Middle, Nundine, Oars, Octa, Octad, Octal, Octastrophic, Octave, Octet, Octonary, Octuor, Ogdoad, Okta, Ottava, Ure, Utas

Eighteen Majority

Eighty Fourscore, R

Einsteinium Es

Either Also, Both, O(u)ther, Such

Ejaculate Blurt, Discharge, Emit, Exclaim

Eject Belch, Bounce, Defenestrate, Disgorge, Dismiss, Emit, Erupt, Evict, Expel, Oust, Propel, Spew, Spit, Spue, Turf out, Vent, Void

Eke Augment, Eche, Enlarge, Husband, Supplement

Elaborate Creation, Detail, Develop, Dressy, Enlarge, Evolve, Fancy, Flesh out, Florid, Imago, Improve, Intricate, Magnificent, Opulent, Ornate, Rich, Spectacular, Stretch

Elan Dash, Drive, Esprit, → **FLAIR**, Gusto, Lotus, Panache, Spirit, Style, Vigour

Elapse Glide, Intervene, Overpass, Pass

Elastic(ity) Adaptable, Bungee, Buoyant, Dopplerite, Elater, Flexible, Give, Resilient, Rubber, Scrunchie, Scrunchy, Spandex®, Springy, Stretchy, Tone, Tonus

Elastomer Adiprene®

Elate(d), Elation Cheer, Euphoric, Exalt, Exhilarate, Gladden, Hault, High, Lift, Rapture, Ruff(e), Uplift

Elbow, Elbow tip Akimbo, Ancon, Angle, Bender, Cubital, Hustle, Joint, Jolt, Jostle, Justle, Kimbo, Noop, Nudge, Olecranon, Tennis

El Cid Diaz

Elder(ly), Eldest Ainé(e), Ancestor, Ancient, Bourtree, Chief, Classis, Coffin dodger, Eigne, Geriatric, Greying, Guru, Kaumatua, Kuia, OAP, Presbyter, → **SENIOR**, Sire, Susanna, Wallwort

Eldorado Ophir

Eleanor(a) Bron, Duse, Nora(h)

Elect(ed), Election(eer), Elective, Electoral Ballot, Choice, Choose, Chosen, Co-opt, Eatanswill, Elite, General, Gerrymander, Hustings, In, Israelite, Khaki, Off-year, Opt, Optional, Pick, PR, Predetermine, Primary, Psephology, Rectorial, Return, Select, Stump

Electrical discharge Corposant, Ion, Zwitterion

Electrical instrument Battery, Charger, Galvaniser, Mains, Resistor, Rheostat, Shoe
Electrical unit Amp(ere), Coulomb, Farad, Kilowatt, Ohm, Volt, Watt
Electric eye Pec
Electrician Gaffer, Lineman, Ohm, Siemens, Sparks, Tesla
Electricity Galvanism, Grid, HT, Inductance, Juice, Mains, Negative, Positive, Power, Static, Utility, Vitreous
Electrify Astonish, Galvanise, Startle, Stir, Thrill
Electrode Anode, Cathode, Dynode, Element, Photocathode
Electrolyte Ampholyte
Electromagnet(ic) Abampere, Armature, Oersted, Solenoid, Weber
Electron(ic), Electronics, Electronic device Cooper pairs, Exciton, FET, Fly-by-wire, Linac, Lone pair, Martenot, Mole(cular), Polaron, Possum®, Quantum, Smart, Tetrode, Thermionics, Valence, Valency
Elegance, Elegant Artistic, Bijou, Chic, Classy, Concinnity, Dainty, Daynt, Debonair, Dressy, Fancy, Feat, Finesse, Gainly, Galant, Grace, Jimp, Luxurious, Neat, Polished, Recherché, Refined, Ritzy, → **SMART**, Soigné(e), Style, Suave, Svelte, Swish, Tall, Urbane
Elegy Dirge, Lament, Poem
Element(s), Elementary Abcee, Abecedarian, Absey, Barebones, → **COMPONENT**, Detail, → **ESSENCE**, Essential, Factor, Feature, Fuel, Heating, Hot-plate, Ideal, Identity, Insertion, Logical, M(a)cGuffin, Milieu, Non-metal, Peltier, Pixel, Primary, Principle, Rare earth, Rudimental, Sieve, Simple, Simplex, Strand, Superheavy, Trace(r), Tramp, Transition, Transuranic, Weather

ELEMENTS

3 letters:
Air
Tin (Sn)

4 letters:
Atom
Fire
Gold (Au)
Iron (Fe)
Lead (Pb)
Neon (Ne)
Ylem
Zinc (Zn)

5 letters:
Alloy
Argon (Ar)
Boron (B)
Earth
Morph(eme)
Niton
Radon (Rn)
Terra
Water
Xenon (Xe)

6 letters:
Barium (Ba)
Carbon (C)

Cerium (Ce)
Cesium
Cobalt (Co)
Copper (Cu)
Curium (Cm)
Erbium (Er)
Helium (He)
Indium (In)
Iodine (I)
Nickel (Ni)
Osmium (Os)
Oxygen (O)
Radium (Ra)
Silver (Ag)
Sodium (Na)

7 letters:
Arsenic (As)
Bismuth (Bi)
Bromine (Br)
Cadmium (Cd)
Caesium (Cs)
Calcium (Ca)
Dubnium (Db)
Fermium (Fm)
Gallium (Ga)
Hafnium (Hf)
Hahnium (Hn)
Halogen

Hassium (Hs)
Holmium (Ho)
Iridium (Ir)
Isotope
Krypton (Kr)
Lithium (Li)
Mercury (Hg)
Natrium
Niobium (Nb)
Rhenium (Re)
Rhodium (Rh)
Silicon (Si)
Sulphur (S)
Terbium (Tb)
Thorium (Th)
Thulium (Tm)
Uranide
Uranium (U)
Wolfram
Yttrium (Y)

8 letters:
Actinide
Actinium (Ac)
Antimony (Sb)
Astatine (At)
Chlorine (Cl)
Chromium (Cr)
Columbic

Didymium
Europium (Eu)
Fluorine (F)
Francium (Fr)
Hydrogen (H)
Illinium
Inchoate
Lutetium (Lu)
Masurium
Nebulium
Nitrogen (N)
Nobelium (No)
Platinum (Pt)
Polonium (Po)
Rubidium (Rb)
Samarium (Sm)
Scandium (Sc)
Selenium (Se)
Tantalum (Ta)
Thallium (Tl)
Titanium (Ti)
Tungsten (W)
Vanadium (V)

9 letters:
Alabamine
Aluminium (Al)
Americium (Am)
Berkelium (Bk)

Beryllium (Be)
Brimstone
Columbium (Cb)
Germanium (Ge)
Jollotium
Lanthanum (La)
Magnesium (Mg)
Manganese (Mn)
Metalloid
Neodymium (Nd)
Neptunium (Np)
Palladium (Pd)
Plutonium (Pu)
Potassium (K)
Ruthenium (Ru)

Strontian
Strontium (Sr)
Tellurium (Te)
Virginium
Ytterbium (Yb)
Zirconium (Zr)

10 letters:
Dysprosium (D)
Gadolinium (Gd)
Lanthanide
Lawrencium (Lr)
Meitnerium (Mt)
Molybdenum (Mo)
Phlogiston

Phosphorus (P)
Promethium (Pm)
Seaborgium (Sg)
Technetium (Tc)

11 letters:
Californium (Cf)
Einsteinium (Es)
Mendelevium (Md)
Unnilennium (Une)
Unnilhexium (Unh)
Unniloctium (Uno)
Ununquadium (Uuq)

12 letters:
Darmstadtium
Kurchatovium
Nielsbohrium
Praseodymium (Pr)
Protactinium (Pa)
Unnilpentium (Unp)
Unnilseptium (Uns)

13 letters:
Rutherfordium (Rf)
Transactinide
Unniliquadium (Unq)

Elephant(ine) African, Babar, Hathi, Indian, Jumbo, Kheda, Mammoth, Mastodon, Oliphant, Pachyderm, Pad, Pink, Proboscidean, Rogue, Stegodon, Subungulata, Trumpeter, Tusker, White

Elephant-headed Ganesa

Elephant's ears Begonia

Elevate(d), Elevation, Elevator Agger, Attitude, Bank, Cheer, Colliculus, El, Eminence, Ennoble, Foothill, Glabella, Grain, Haute, Heighten, Hoist, Jack, Lift, Machan, Montic(u)le, Monticulus, Pitch, Promote, → **RAISE**, Random, Relievo, Ridge, Rise, Steeve, Sublimate, Up(lift), Uplying, Upraise, Wallclimber

Eleven Elf, Hendeca-, Legs, O, Side, Tail-ender, Team, XI

Elf(in), Elves Alfar, Chiricaune, Dobbie, Dobby, Fairy, Fey, Fie, Goblin, Imp, Kobold, Ouph, Pigwiggen, Pixie, Ribhus, Sprite, Urchin

Elicit Evoke, Extract, Toase, Toaze, Tose, Toze

Eligible Available, Catch, Fit, Nubile, Parti, Qualified, Worthy

Eliminate, Elimination Cull, Cure, Deep-six, Delete, Discard, Exclude, Execute, Extirpate, Heat, Knock out, Liquidate, Omit, Preclude, Purge, Red-line, Rid, Separate, Slay, Void, Zap

Elision Apocope, Synal(o)epha, Syncope

Elite Best, Choice, Crachach, Crack, → **CREAM**, Crème, Egalitarian, Elect, Flower, Liberal, Meritocracy, Ton, Top drawer, Twelve pitch, U, Zaibatsu

Elixir Amrita, Arcanum, Bufo, Cordial, Daffy, Essence, Medicine, Panacea, Quintessence, Tinct

Elizabeth Bess(ie), Gloriana, Oriano

Elk Deer, Gang, Irish, Moose

Elkoshite Nahum

Ellipse, Elliptic Conic, Oblong, Oval

Elm Dutch, Rock, Slippery, Wahoo, Weeping, Wich, Winged, Wych

Elmer Gantry

Elongate Extend, Lengthen, Protract, Stretch

Elope Abscond, Decamp

Eloquence, Eloquent Articulate, Demosthenic, Facundity, Fluent, Honey-tongued, Oracy, Rhetoric, Speaking, Vocal

Else(where) Absent, Alibi, Aliunde, Et al, Other

Elucidate Explain, Expose, Interpret, Simplify

Elude, Elusion, Elusive Avoid, Dodge, Eel, Escape, → **EVADE**, Evasive, Foil, Intangible, Jink, Pimpernel, Sliddery, Slippy, Subt(i)le, Will o' the wisp

▶ **Elves** see **ELF(IN)**

Elysium Tir-nan-Og

Em Mut(ton), Pica

Emaciated, Emaciation Atrophy, Erasmus, Gaunt, Haggard, Lean, Skeleton, Skinny, Sweeny, Tabid, Thin, Wanthriven, Wasted

Email Flame, Spam, Spim

Emanate, Emanation Arise, Aura, Discharge, Exude, Issue, Miasma, Radiate, Spring

Emancipate(d), Emancipation Catholic, Deliver, Forisfamiliate, Free, → LIBERATE, Manumission, Uhuru

Emasculate Bobbitt, Castrate, Debilitate, Evirate, Geld, Unsex

Embalm Anele, Anoint, Cere, Mummify, Preserve

Embankment Berm, Bund, Causeway, Dam, Dyke, Earthwork, Levee, Mattress, Mound, Rampart, Remblai, Sconce, Staith(e), Stopbank, Terreplein

Embargo → BAN, Blockade, Boycott, Edict, Restraint

Embark Begin, Board, Enter, Inship, Launch, Sail

Embarrass(ed), Embarrassing, Embarrassment Abash, Ablush, Awkward, Barro, Besti, Buttock-clenching, Chagrin, Cheap, Colour, Cringe-making, Cringe-worthy, Disconcert, Discountenance, Encumber, Gêne, Haw, Mess, Mortify, Plethora, Pose, Predicament, Scundered, Scunnered, Shame, Sheepish, Squirming, Straitened, Toe-curling, Tongue-tied, Upset, Whoopsie, Writhing

▷ **Embarrassed** *may indicate* an anagram

Embassy Chancery, Consulate, Embassade, Legation, Mission

Embed(ded) Fix, Immerse, Implant, Inlaid, Set

Embellish(ed), Embellishment Adorn, Beautify, Bedeck, Curlicue, Deck, Decor(ate), Décor, Dress, Embroider, Enrich, Fioritura, Frill, Garnish, Garniture, Melisma, Mordent, → ORNAMENT, Ornate, Overwrought, Prank, Prettify, Rel(l)ish, Roulade, Story, Turn, Twist

Ember(s) Ash, Cinder, Clinker, Gleed

Embezzle(ment) Defalcate, Malversation, Peculate, Purloin, Shoulder, → STEAL

Embitter(ed) Acerbate, Aggravate, Enfested, Exacerbate, Rankle, Sour

Emblem(atic) Badge, Bear, Colophon, Daffodil, Device, Figure, Hammer and sickle, Ichthys, Impresa, Insignia, Kikumon, Leek, Lis, Maple leaf, Oak, Pip, Rose, Roundel, Shamrock, Sign, Spear-thistle, → SYMBOL, Tau-cross, Thistle, Token, Totem(ic), Triskelion, Wheel

Embody, Embodied, Embodiment Epitome, Fuse, Impanation, Incarnation, Incorporate, Personify, Quintessence, Version

Embolism Clot, Infarct

Emboss(ed) Adorn, Chase, Cloqué, Engrave, Matelassé, Pounce, Raise, Repoussé, Toreutic

Embrace(d) Abrazo, Accolade, Arm, Bear hug, Canoodle, Clasp, Clinch, Clip, Coll, Complect, Comprise, Cuddle, Embosom, Encircle, Enclasp, Enclose, Enfold, Enlacement, Envelop, Espouse, Fold, Grab, Halse, Haulst, Hause, Hesp, Hug, Imbrast, Inarm, Inclasp, Inclip, Include, Inlace, Kiss, Lasso, Neck, Overarch, Press, Snog, Snug(gle), Stemme, Twine, Welcome, Wrap

▷ **Embraces, Embracing** *may indicate* a hidden word

Embrocate, Embrocation Anoint, Arnica, Liniment

Embroider(y) Add, Appliqué, Arpillera, Arrasene, Assisi, Battalia-pie, Braid, Brede, Colour, Couching, Crewellery, Crewel-work, Cross-stitch, Cutwork, Drawn threadwork, Embellish, Exaggerate, Eyelet, Fag(g)oting, Fancywork, Featherstitch, Filet, Framework, Gros point, Handiwork, Knotting, Lace(t), Laid work, Mola, Needlepoint, Needlework, Open-work, Opus anglicanum, Orfray, Ornament, Orphrey, Orris, Petit point, Pinwork, Pulled threadwork, Purl, Queen-stitch, Sampler, Sew, Smocking, Spider-wheel, Stitch, Stitchery, Stumpwork, Tambour, Tent, Wrap, Zari

Embroideress Mimi

Embroil Confuse, Entangle, Involve, Trouble

Embryo(nic), Embryologist Archenteron, Blastocyst, Blastospore, Blastula,

Conceptus, Epicotyl, Fo(e)tus, Gastrula, Germ, Mesoblast, Morula, Nepionic, Neurula, Origin, Rudiment, Undeveloped, Wolff

Emend Adjust, Alter, Edit, Reform

Emerald Beryl, Gem, Green, Oriental, Smaragd, Uralian

Emerge(ncy), Emerging Anadyomene, Arise, Craunch, Crise, Crisis, Crunch, Debouch, Eclose, Emanate, Enation, Erupt, Exigency, Flashpoint, Hard-shoulder, Issue, Lash-up, Last-ditch, Loom, Need, Outcrop, Pinch, SOS, Spare, Spring, Stand-by, Stand-in, Strait, Surface

▷ **Emerge from** *may indicate* an anagram or a hidden word

Emerson Waldo

Emetic Apomorphine, Cacoon, Evacuant, Ipecac(uanha), Puke, Sanguinaria, Stavesacre, Tartar, Vomitory

Emigrant, Emigration, Émigré Chozrim, Colonist, Exile, Italiot, Jordim, Redemptioner, Settler, When-we, Yordim

Emile Zola

Emily Ellis

Eminence, Eminent Alp, Altitude, Cardinal, Distinguished, Eximious, Grand, Height, Hill, Hywel, Illustrious, Inselberg, Knoll, Light, Lion, Lofty, Luminary, Noble, → **NOTABLE**, Note, Palatine, Prominence, Red hat, Renown, Repute, Stature, Tor, Trochanter, → **VIP**, Wallah

Emirate Abu Dhabi, Dubai, Qatar, Sharjah

Emissary Agent, Envoy, Legate, Marco Polo

Emission, Emit Discharge, Emanate, Field, Give, Issue, Radiate, Spallation, Thermionic, Utter, Vent

Emmer Amelcorn, Wheat

Emollient Paregoric

Emolument Income, Perk, Remuneration, Salary, Stipend, Tip, Wages

Emotion(s), Emotional Affection, Anger, Anoesis, Atmosphere, Breast, Cathartic, Chord, Ecstasy, Empathy, Excitable, Feeling, Flare up, Freak-out, Gushing, Gusty, Gut-wrenching, Hate, Heartstrings, Hippocampus, Histrionics, Hoo, Hysteria, Intense, Joy, Limbic, Maenad, Nympholepsy, Passion, Poignant, Reins, Rhapsodic, Roar, Sensibility, Sensitive, Sentiment, Spirit, Stormy, Theopathy, Torrid, Transport, Weepy, Wigged out

Emotionless Deadpan, Glassy

Empathy Identifying, Rapport, Rapprochement, Sympathy

Emperor Agramant(e), Akbar, Akihito, Antoninus, Augustus, Aurelian, Babur, Bao Dai, Barbarossa, Bonaparte, Caesar, Caligula, Caracalla, Charlemagne, Claudius, Commodus, Concerto, Constantine, Diocletian, Domitian, Ferdinand, Flavian, Gaius, Galba, Genghis Khan, Gratian, Great Mogul, Hadrian, Haile Selassie, Heraclius, Hirohito, HRE, Imp, Imperator, Inca, Jimmu, Justinian, Kaiser, Keasar, Kesar, King, Manuel I Comnenus, Maximilian, Meiji, Menelik, Mikado, Ming, Mogul, Montezuma, Mpret, Napoleon, Negus, Nero, Nerva, Otho, Otto, Penguin, Peter the Great, Purple, Pu-yi, Rex, Rosco, Ruler, Severus, Shah Jahan, Shang, Sovereign, Sultan, Tenno, Theodore, Theodosius, Tiberius, Titus, Trajan, Tsar, Valens, Valentinian, Valerian, Vespasian, Vitellius, Wenceslaus

Emphasis(e), Emphasize, Emphatic Accent, Birr, Bold, Dramatise, Ek se, Forcible, Foreground, Forzando, Forzato, Hendiadys, Highlight, Italic, Marcato, Point up, Positive, Resounding, Risoluto, Sforzando, Sforzato, → **STRESS**, Underline, Underscore, Vehement

Empire Assyria, British, Byzantine, Celestial, Chain, Chinese, Domain, Empery, First, French, Georgia, Holy Roman, Indian, Kingdom, Latin, NY, Ottoman, Parthia, Persian, Principate, Realm, Reich, Roman, Russian, Second, Turkish, Western

Empiricism Positivism

Emplacement Battery, Platform

Employ(ment) Bestow, Business, Calling, Designated, Engage, Exercitation, Hire, Occupy, Pay, Place, Portfolio, Post, Practice, Pursuit, Retain, Service, Shiftwork, Trade, Use, Using, Utilise, Vocation

Employee(s) Barista, Casual, Clock-watcher, Factotum, Hand, Help, Hireling, Intrapreneur, Minion, Munchkin, Networker, Payroll, Pennyboy, Personnel, Rainmaker, Salariat, Servant, Staff, Staffer, Valet, Walla(h), Worker, Workforce, Workpeople

Employer Baas, Boss, Malik, Master, Melik, Padrone, Taskmaster, User

▷ **Employs** *may indicate* an anagram

Emporium Bazaar, Shop, Store

Empower Authorise, Enable, Entitle, Permit

Empress Eugenie, Josephine, Matilda, Messalina, Queen, Sultana, Tsarina, VIR

Empty Addle, Bare, Barren, Blank, Boss, Buzz, Claptrap, Clear, Deplete, Deserted, Devoid, Disembowel, Drain, Exhaust, Expel, Forsaken, Futile, Gousty, Gut, Hent, Hollow, Inane, Jejune, Lade, Lave, Meaningless, Null, Phrasy, Pump, Shallow, Teem, Toom, Tum(e), Unfurnished, Uninhabited, Unoccupied, Unpeople, Vacant, Vacate, Vacuous, Vain, Viduous, → **VOID**

▷ **Empty** *may indicate* an 'o' in the word or an anagram

Empty-headed Vain

Emulate Ape, Copy, Envy, Equal, Imitate, Match

Emulsion Nuclear, Pseudosolution, Tempera

Enable Authorise, Capacitate, Empower, Permit, Potentiate, Qualify, Sanction

Enact Adopt, Effect, Ordain, Personate, Portray

Enamel(led), Enamel work Aumail, Champlevé, Cloisonné, Della-robbia, Dentine, Fabergé, Ganoin(e), Lacquer, Mottled, Nail, Polish, Porcelain, Schwarzlot, Shippo, Smalto, Stoved, Vitreous

Encampment Bivouac, Castrametation, Douar, Dowar, Duar, Laager, Laer, Settlement

Encase(d), Encasement Box, Crate, Emboîtement, Encapsulate, Enclose, Obtect, Sheathe

Enchant(ing), Enchanted, Enchantment Bewitch, Captivate, Charm, Delight, Gramary(e), Incantation, Magic, Necromancy, Orphean, Rapt, Sirenize, Sorcery, Spellbind, Thrill

Enchanter, Enchantress Archimage, Archimago, Armida, Circe, Comus, Faerie, Fairy, Houri, Lorelei, Magician, Medea, Mermaid, Prospero, Reim-kennar, Sorcerer, Vivien, Witch

Encircle(d), Encirclement Belt, Besiege, Enclose, Encompass, Enlace, Entrold, Gird, Hoop, Inorb, Introld, Orbit, Pale, Ring, Siege, Stemme, → **SURROUND**, Wreathe

Enclave Cabinda, Ceuta, → **ENCLOSURE**, Melilla, Pocket, San Marino

Enclose(d), Enclosing, Enclosure Bawn, Beset, Boma, Box, Bullring, Cage, Carol, Carrel, Case, Circumscribe, Common, Compound, Corral, Court, Embale, Embowel, Embower, Enceinte, Enchase, Encircle, Enclave, Engirt, Enhearse, Enlock, Enshrine, Fence, Fold, Forecourt, Garth, Haggard, Haining, Haw, Hem, Henge, Hope, Impound, In, Incapsulate, Inchase, Infibulate, Inlock, Insert, Interclude, Lairage, Obvolute, Paddock, Pale, Parrock, Peel, Pele, Pen(t), Petavius, Pightle, Pin, Pinfold, Pit, Playpen, Plenum, Pocket, Radome, Rail, Rath, Recluse, Ree(d), Ring, Run, Saddling, Saleyard, Seal, Sekos, Sept, Seraglio, Serail, Several, Sin bin, Steeld, Stell, Stive, Stockade, Sty, → **SURROUND**, Tatt(ersall)s, Terrarium, Tine, Unsaddling, Vibarium, Ward, Winner's, Wrap, Yard, Zareba

Encode Cipher, Scramble

Encomium Eulogy, Praise, Sanction, Tribute

Encompass Bathe, Begird, Beset, Environ, Include, Surround

Encore Again, Agen, Ancora, Bis, Ditto, Do, Iterum, Leitmotiv, Recall, Repeat, Reprise

Encounter Battle, Brush, Close, Combat, Contend, Cope, Dogfight, Experience, Face, Hit, Incur, Intersect, Interview, → **MEET**, One-one, Rencontre, Ruffle, Skirmish, Tilt

Encourage(ment), Encouraging Abet, Acco(u)rage, Alley-oop, Animate, Attaboy, Barrack, Bolster, Boost, Brighten, Buck, Cheer, Chivy, Cohortative, Come-on, Comfort,

Commend, Dangle, Egg, Elate, Embolden, Empatron, Exhort, Fillip, Fire, Fortify, Foster, Fuel, Gee, Hearten, Heigh, Help, Heuristic, Hope, Hortatory, Incite, Inspire, Inspirit, Invite, Lift, Nourish, Nurture, Pat, Patronise, Pep talk, Proceleusmatic, Prod, Promote, Protreptic, Push, Reassure, Root, Seed, Spur, Stimulate, Support, Tally-ho, Train, Upcheer, Uplift, Urge, Wean, Yay, Yo, Yoicks

Encroach(ment) Eat out, Impinge, Infringe, Inroad, Intrude, Invade, Overlap, Overstep, Poach, Purpresture, Trespass, Usurp

Encrypt(ion) Coding, Public key

Encumber, Encumbrance Accloy, Burden, Charge, Clog, Dead weight, Deadwood, Dependent, → **HANDICAP**, Impede, Load, Obstruct, Saddle

Encyclopaedia, Encyclopaedic Compendium, Comprehensive, Diderot, Extensive, Universal, Vast

End(ing) Abolish, Abort, Abut, Aim, Ambition, Amen, Anus, Arse, Big, Bitter, Bourn(e), Butt, Cease, Cessation, Cesser, Climax, Close, Closure, Cloture, Coda, Conclude, Crust, Culminate, Curtain, Curtains, Cut off, Dead, Death, Decease, Denouement, Desinence, Desistance, Destroy, Determine, Dissolve, Domino, Effect, Envoi, Envoy, Epilogue, Exigent, Expire, Explicit, Extremity, Fade, Fatal, Fattrels, Feminine, Fin, Final(e), Fine, Finis, → **FINISH**, Finite, Gable, Grave, Heel, Ice, Ish, Izzard, Izzet, Kill, Kybosh, Lapse, Last, Let up, Limit, Little, Loose, Masculine, Mill, Nirvana, No side, Ort, Out, Outrance, Outro, Period, Peter, Pine, Point, Purpose, Quench, Receiving, Remnant, Rescind, Result, Roach, Round off, Runback, Scotch, Scrag, Shank, Slaughter, Sopite, Split, Sticky, Stub, Supernaculum, Surcease, Swansong, Tag, Tail, Tailpiece, Telesis, Telic, Telos, Term, Terminal, Terminate, Terminus, Thrum, Tip, Toe, Top, Ultimate, Up, Upshot, Utterance, West, Z

Endanger Hazard, Imperil, Periclitate, Risk, Threaten

Endear(ing), Endearment Adorable, Affection, Asthore, Bach, Caress, Cariad, Chuck, Cute, Darling, Dear, Ducks, Ducky, Enamour, Hinny, Honey(-bunch), Honey-chile, Ingratiate, Jarta, Lovey, Luv, Machree, Mavourneen, Peat, Pet, Pigsnie, Pigsn(e)y, Sweetie, Sweet nothings

Endeavour Aim, Attempt, Effort, Enterprise, Essay, Morse, Strain, Strive, Struggle, Try, Venture

Endemic Local, Prevalent

Endive Escarole

Endless Aeonian, Continuous, Ecaudate, Eternal, Eterne, Infinite, Interminable, Perpetual, Undated

▷ **Endlessly** *may indicate* a last letter missing

End of the world Doomsday, Ragnarok

Endorse(ment) Adopt, Affirm, Allonge, Approve, Assurance, Back, Certify, Confirmation, Docket, Initial, Okay, Oke, Ratify, Rubber stamp, Sanction, Second, Sign, Subscript, → **SUPPORT**, Underwrite, Visa

Endow(ment) Assign, Bequeath, Bestow, Bless, Cha(u)ntry, Dot, Dotation, Enrich, Foundation, Gift, Leave, Patrimony, State, Vest, Wakf, Waqf

Endurance, Endure(d), Enduring Abide, Abought, Aby(e), Bear, Bide, Brook, Dree, Dure, Face, Fortitude, Granite, Have, Hold, → **LAST**, Livelong, Lump, Marathon, Patience, Perseverance, Persist, Pluck, Ride, Stamina, Stand, Stay, Stomach, Stout, Substantial, Support, Sustain, Swallow, Tether, Thole, Timeless, Tolerance, Undergo, Wear, Weather

Endymion Bluebell

Enema Barium, Catharsis, Clyster, Purge

Enemy Adversary, Antagonist, Boer, Devil, Fifth column, Foe(n), Fone, Opponent, Public, Time

Energetic, Energise, Energy Active, Alternative, Amp, Animation, Arduous, Atomic, Barnstorming, Binding, Bond, Brisk, Cathexis, Chakra, Chi, Dash, Doer, Drive, Dynamic, Dynamo, E, Enthalpy, Entropy, EV, Fermi, Fireball, Firebrand, Firecracker, Force, Fossil, Free, Fructan, Fusion, Geothermal, Gism, Go, Go ahead, Graviton, Hartree, H.D.R.,

Horme, Hustle, Hyper, Input, Instress, Internal, Isotonic, → **JET**, Jism, Jissom, Joie de vivre, Joule, Kerma, Kinetic, Kundalini, Lattice, Libido, Life, Lossy, Luminous, Magnon, Moxie, Nuclear, Orgone, Pep, Phonon, Pithy, Potency, Potential, → **POWER**, Powerhouse, Prana, QI, Quantum, Quasar, Rad, Radiant, Radiatory, Renewable, Roton, Rydberg, S(h)akti, Sappy, Second-wind, Solar, Stamina, Steam, Sthenic, Stingo, Tidal, Trans-uranic, Vehement, Verve, Vibrational, Vigour, Vim, Vital, Vivo, Wave, Whammo, Whirlwind, Wind(-farm), Zappy, Zealous, Zero point, Zing, Zip

Enervate Exhaust

Enfold Clasp, Embrace, Envelop, Hug, Stemme, Swathe, Wrap

Enforce(ment) Administer, Coerce, Control, Exact, Implement, Impose

Eng Agma

Engage(d), Engagement, Engaging Absorb, Accept, Adorable, Appointment, At, Attach, Bespoken, Betrothal, Bind, Book, Busy, Contract, Date, Embark, Employ, Engross, Enlist, Enmesh, Enter, Fascinate, Fiance(e), Fight, Gear, Gig, Hire, Hold, In gear, Interest, Interlock, Lock, Mesh, Met, Occupy, Pledge, Promise, Prosecute, Rapt, Reserve, Residency, Sapid, Skirmish, Sponsal, Sponsion, Spousal, Sprocket, Trip, Wage, Winsome

▷ **Engagement** *may indicate* a battle

Engender Beget, Breed, Cause, Occasion, Produce, Spawn

Engine, Engine part Air, Analytical, Athodyd, Atmospheric, Banker, Banking, Beam, Booster, Bricole, Bypass, Carburettor, Catapult, Compound, Dashpot, Diesel, Dividing, Donkey, Dynamo, Fan-jet, Fire, Four-cycle, Four-stroke, Gas, Gin, Heat, Humdinger, ICE, Internal combustion, Ion, Iron horse, Jet, Lean-burn, Light, Little-end, Loco(motive), Machine, Mangonel, Mogul, → **MOTOR**, Nacelle, Oil, Onager, Orbital, Otto, Outboard, Overhead valve, Petard, Petrary, Petrol, Petter, Pilot, Plasma, Podded, Pony, Puffer, Pug, Pulp, Pulsejet, Push-pull, Put-put, Radial, Ramjet, Reaction, Reciprocating, Retrorocket, Rocket, Rose, Rotary, Scorpion, Scramjet, Search, Side-valve, Sleeve valve, Stationary, Steam, Stirling, Sustainer, Tank, Terebra, Testudo, Thermometer, Thruster, Top-end, Traction, Trompe, Turbine, Turbofan, Turbojet, Turboprop, Turbo-ram-jet, Two-handed, Two-stroke, V, Vernier, V-type, Wankel, Warwolf, Water, Wildcat, Winch, Winding

Engineer(ing), Engineer(s) Aeronautical, AEU, Arrange, Badge, BE, CE, Chartered, Concurrent, Contrive, Genetic, Greaser, Ground, Human, Interactive, Knowledge, Liability, Manhattan District, Manoeuvre, Marine, Mastermind, Mechanical, Mechatronics, Military, Mime, Operator, Organise, Paper, Planner, Process, RE, Repairman, Reverse, Rig, Sales, Sanitary, Sapper, Scheme, Social, Software, Sound, Stage, Systems, Traffic, Usability, Wangle

ENGINEERS

4 letters:	Eiffel	Smeaton	9 letters:
Ader	Fokker	Strauss	Armstrong
Arup	McAdam	Telford	Cockerell
Otto	Savery	Whittle	De Lessops
Watt	Wankel		Whitworth
		8 letters:	
5 letters:	7 letters:	Bessemer	10 letters:
Baird	Brinell	Brindley	Stephenson
Royce	Heinkel	Kennelly	Trevithick
Tesla	Junkers	Samarski	
	Marconi	Sikorsky	12 letters:
6 letters:	Parsons	Sinclair	Barnes Wallis
Austin	Porsche	Stirling	
Brunel	Rogallo	Von Braun	
Diesel	Siemens		

▷ **Engineer** *may indicate* an anagram

England Albany, Albion, Blighty, Demi-paradise, Eden, John Bull, Merrie, Merry, Middle, The Old Dart

English(man) Angle, Anglican, Anglice, Baboo, Babu, Basic, Brit, Bro talk, Canajan, Choom, E, Ebonics, Eng, Estuary, Gringo, Hawaiian, Hiberno, Hong Kong, Indian, Irish, Jackeroo, John Bull, King's, Kipper, Limey, Middle, Mister, Modern, Morningside, Newspeak, New Zealand, Nigerian, Norman, Officialese, Old, Oxford, Philippine, Pidgin, Plain, Pom(my), Pommie, Pongo, Pork-pudding, Queen's, Qui-hi, Qui-hye, Rock, Rooinek, Rosbif, Sassenach, Saxon, Scotic, Scottish, Seaspeak, Shopkeeper, Side, Singapore, Singlish, South African, South Asian, Southron, Southroun, Spanglish, Standard, Strine, Wardour Street, Whingeing Pom, Woodbine, World, Yanqui, Yinglish

Engorge Devour, Glut, Swallow

Engraft Inset

Engrave(r), Engraving Aquatint, Blake, Bury, Carve, Cerography, Cerotype, Chalcography, Character, Chase, Cut, Die-sinker, Dry-point, Durer, Enchase, Eng, Etch, Glyptic, Glyptograph, Heliogravure, Hogarth, Impress, Inchase, Inciser, Inscribe, Insculp, Intagliate, Inter, Lapidary, Line, Mezzotint, Niello, Photoglyphic, Photogravure, Plate, Scalp, Scrimshander, Scrimshandy, Scrimshaw, Steel, Stillet, Stipple, Stylet, Stylography, Toreutics, Turn, Wood, Xylographer

Engross(ed) Absorb, Engage, Enwrap, Immerse, Inwrap, Monopolise, → **OCCUPY**, Preoccupy, Prepossess, Rapt, Rivet, Sink, Writ large

Engulf Overwhelm, Swamp, Whelm

Enhance(r) Add, Augment, Better, Catalyst, Elevate, Embellish, Exalt, Heighten, Improve, Intensify, Supplement

Enigma(tic) Charade, Conundrum, Dilemma, Gioconda, Gnomic, Mystery, Oracle, Poser, Problem, → **PUZZLE**, Quandary, Question, Rebus, Recondite, Riddle, Secret, Sphinxlike, Teaser

Enjoin Command, Direct, Impose, Prohibit, Require

Enjoy(able), Enjoyment Apolaustic, Appreciate, Ball, Brook, Delectation, Fruition, Glee, Groove, Gusto, Have, High jinks, Lap up, Lekker, Like, Own, Palate, Pleasing, Possess, Relish, Ripping, Sair, Savour, Stonking, Taste, Wallow

Enlarge(ment), Enlarger Accrue, Acromegaly, Add, Aneurism, Aneurysm, Augment, Blow-up, Diagraph, Dilate, Exostosis, Expand, Expatiate, Explain, Increase, → **MAGNIFY**, Pan, Piece, Ream, Rebore, Sensationalize, Spavin, Swell, Telescope, Tumefy, Upbuild, Varicosity, Zoom

Enlighten(ed), Enlightenment Aufklarung, Awareness, Bodhisattva, Dewali, Disabuse, Divali, Edify, Educate, Explain, Haskalah, Illumine, Instruct, Liberal, Luce, Nirvana, Relume, Revelation, Satori, Verlig(te)

Enlist Attest, Conscript, Draft, Engage, Enrol, Induct, Join, Levy, Muster, Prest, Recruit, Rope in, Roster, Sign on, Volunteer

Enliven(ed) Animate, Arouse, Brighten, Cheer, Comfort, Exhilarate, Ginger, Invigorate, Juice, Merry, Pep, Refresh, Warm

Enmity Animosity, Aversion, Bad blood, Hatred, Malice, Nee(d)le, Rancour, Spite

Ennoble(ment) Dub, Elevate, Ermine, Exalt, Honour, Raise

Ennui Boredom, Tedium

Enormous Colossal, Exorbitant, Gargantuan, Giant, Gigantic, Googol, Hellacious, Huge, Humongous, Humungous, → **IMMENSE**, Jumbo, Mammoth, Mega, Plonking, Vast, Walloper, Walloping

Enough Adequate, → **AMPLE**, Anow, Basta, Belay, Enow, Fill, Geyan, Nuff, Pax, Plenty, Qs, Sate, Satis, Sese, Sessa, Suffice, Sufficient, Via, When

Enounce Affirm, Declare, State

Enquire, Enquiring, Enquiry Ask, Case, Check, Curious, Eh, Examine, Inquest, Inquire, Organon, Public, Request, Research, Scan, See, Steward's, Trial

Enrage(d) Bemad, Emboss, Enfelon, Imboss, → **INCENSE**, Inflame, Infuriate, Irate, Livid, Madden, Wild

Enrapture(d) Enchant, Eprise, Ravish, Sent, Transport

Enrich Adorn, Endow, Enhance, Fortify, Fructify, Oxygenate

Enrol(ment) Attest, Conscribe, Conscript, Empanel, Enlist, Enter, Incept, → **JOIN**, List, Matriculate, Muster, Register

Ensconce(d) Establish, Niche, Settle, Shelter, Snug

Ensemble Band, Gamelan, Octet(te), Orchestra, Outfit, Ripieno, Set, Tout, Whole

Enshrine Cherish, Sanctify

Ensign Ancient, Badge, Banner, Duster, Ens, → **FLAG**, Gonfalon, Officer, Pennon, Red, White

Enslave(ment) Addiction, Bondage, Captivate, Chain, Enthral, Thrall, Yoke

Ensnare Illaqueate, → **TRAP**

Ensue, Ensuing Et sequens, Follow, Result, Succeed, Supervene, Transpire

Ensure Check

Entail Involve, Necessitate, Require

Entangle(ment) Amour, Ball, Cot, Elf, Embrangle, Embroil, Encumber, Ensnarl, Entrail, Fankle, Implicate, → **KNOT**, Liaison, Mat, Ravel, Retiarius, Taigle, Trammel

Enter, Entry Admit, Board, Broach, Come, Enrol, Field, Infiltrate, Ingo, Inscribe, Insert, Intromit, Invade, Item, Key in, Lodge, Log, Penetrate, Pierce, Post, Record, Run, Slate, Submit, Table, Wild card

Enterprise, Enterprising Adventure, Ambition, Aunter, Cash cow, Dash, Emprise, Forlorn hope, Free, Go ahead, Goey, Go-getter, Gumption, Indie, Industry, Initiative, Minefield, Plan, Private, Project, Public, Push, Spirit, Starship, Stunt, Up and coming, Venture

Entertain(er), Entertaining, Entertainment Accourt, Acrobat, Afterpiece, All-dayer, All-nighter, Amphitryon, Amuse, Apres ski, Balladeer, Ballet, Barnum, Beguile, Bread and circuses, Bright lights, Burlesque, Busk, Cabaret, Carnival, Cater, Charade, Cheer, Chout, Circus, Comedian, Comic, Concert (party), Conjure, Consider, Cottabus, Crack, Craic, Cuddy, Diseur, Diseuse, Distract, Divert, Divertissement, ENSA, Extravaganza, Fete (champetre), Fleshpots, Floorshow, Foy, Friendly lead, Fun, Gaff, Gala, Gas, Gaudy, Geisha, Gig, Harbour, Harlequin, Have, Hospitality, Host(ess), Impresario, Impressionist, Infotainment, Interest, Interlude, Intermezzo, Jester, Juggler, Karaoke, Kidult, Kursaal, Lap-dancer, Lauder, Leg-show, Levee, Liberace, Light, Masque, Melodrama, Mind candy, Minstrel, Movieoke, Musical, Music hall, Olio, Opera, Palladium, Panto, Pap, Party, Peepshow, Performer, Piece, Pierrot, Play, Pop singer, Raree-show, Reception, Recreation, Regale, Review, Revue, Rice, Ridotto, Rinky-dink, Roadshow, Rodeo, Rush, Serenade, Showbiz, Showgirl, Sideshow, Simulcast, Singer, Sitcom, Slapstick, Snake-charmer, Soirée, Son et lumière, Street theatre, Striptease, Table, Tamasha, Tattoo, Treat, Tumbler, Tummler, Variety, Vaudeville, Ventriloquist, Wattle

Enthral(l) Agog, Bewitch, Charm, Enchant, Enslave, Spellbind

Enthuse, Enthusiasm, Enthusiast(ic) Acclamatory, Addict, Aficionado, Amateur, Ardent, Ardour, Boy, Buff, Bug, Buzz, Cat, Cheerleader, Crazy, Crusader, Delirium, Demon, Devotee, Eager, Ebullience, Ecstatic, Effusive, Empresse, Energy, Estro, Exuberant, Fanatic, Fandom, Fashionista, Fervid, Fiend, Fire, Flame, Freak, Furor(e), Geek, Get-up-and-go, Glowing, Gung-ho, Gusto, Hacker, Hearty, Hype, Into, Keen, Live wire, Lyrical, Mad, Mane, Mania, Motivated, Muso, Nethead, Nut, Nympholept, Oomph, Outpour, Overboard, Passion, Perfervid, Petrolhead, Preoccupation, Rah-rah, Raring, Rave, Relish, Rhapsodise, Schwärmerei, Sold, Spirit, Teeny-bopper, Thing, Verve, Warmth, Whacko, Whole-hearted, Wonk, Young gun, Zealot, Zest

Entice(ment), Enticing Allure, Angle, Cajole, Carrot, Dangle, Decoy, Draw, Lure, Persuade, Seductive, → **TEMPT**, Tole, Toll, Trap, Trepan

Entire(ly), Entirety Absolute, All, Bag and baggage, Clean, Complete, Full Monty,

Genuine, Holistic, Inly, Intact, Integral, In toto, Jingbang, Livelong, Lot, Purely, Root and branch, Systemic, Thorough, Total, Tout, → **WHOLE**

Entitle(ment) Birthright, Empower, Enable, Folk-right, Legitim, Name, Peerage, Right

Entity Being, Body, Existence, Holon, Monad, Tao, Tensor, Thing, Transfinite, Virino

Entomologist Fabré

Entourage Cortège

Entrail(s) Bowels, Chawdron, Giblets, Gralloch, Guts, Ha(r)slet, Humbles, Lights, Numbles, Offal, Quarry, Tripe, Umbles, Viscera

Entrance(d), Entrant, Entry Access, Adit, Admission, Anteroom, Arch, Atrium, Attract, Avernus, Bewitch, Charm, Closehead, Contestant, Door, Doorstop, Double, Dromos, Eye, Fascinate, Foyer, Gate, Ghat, Hypnotise, In-door, Infare, Inflow, Ingate, Ingress, Inlet, Introitus, Item, Jawhole, Jaws, Jib-door, Mesmerise, Mouth, Narthex, Pend, Porch, Porogamy, Portal, Porte-cochère, Postern, Propylaeum, Propylon, Ravish, Reception, Record, Regest, Registration, Single, Spellbound, Starter, Stem, Stoa, Stoma, Stulm, Throat, Torii

Entreat(y) Appeal, Ask, Beg, Beseech, Flagitate, Impetrate, → **IMPLORE**, Orison, Petition, Plead, Pray, Precatory, Prevail, Prig, Rogation, Solicit, Sue, Supplicate

Entrée Access, Dish, Entry, Ingate

Entrench(ment) Coupure, Encroach, Fortify, Trespass

Entrepreneur Branson, Businessman, E-tailer, Executor, Impresario, Wheeler-dealer, Yettie

Entropy S

Entrust Aret(t), Charge, Confide, Consign, Delegate, Give

▶ **Entry** see **ENTRANCE(D)**

Entwine Complect, Impleach, Intervolve, Lace, Twist, Weave

Enumerate, Enumeration Catalogue, Count, Detail, Fansi, List, Tell

Enunciate, Enunciation Articulate, Declare, Deliver, Diction, Elocution, Proclaim

Envelop(e) Arachnoid, Bangtail, Chorion, Corolla, Corona, Cover(ing), Cuma, Enclose, Enshroud, Entire, First day cover, Flight, Floral, Flown cover, Invest, Involucre, Jiffy(bag)®, Muffle, Mulready, Nuclear, Perianth, Sachet, Sae, Serosa, Shroud, Skin, Smother, Surround, Swathe, Window, Wrap

Environment(s), Environmental(ist) ACRE, Ambience, Cyberspace, Druid, Ecofreak, Econut, Eco-warrior, Element, Entourage, Ergonomics, F of E, Green(ie), Greenpeace, Habitat, Hotbed, Milieu, Realo, SEPA, Setting, Sphere, Surroundings, Umwelt, Vicinity

Envisage Contemplate, Imagine, Suppose

Envoi Farewell, RIP

Envoy Agent, Diplomat, Elchee, El(t)chi, Hermes, Legate, Plenipotentiary

Envy, Enviable, Envious Begrudge, Covet, Jaundiced, Jealousy, Penis, Plum, Resentful

---

ENZYMES

3 letters:	DNAase	Caspase	Plasmin
ACE	Kinase	Cyclase	Ptyalin
PSA	Ligase	Emulsin	Sirtuin
	Lipase	Enolase	Sucrase
5 letters:	Mutase	Erepsin	Trypsin
DNase	Papain	Guanase	Uricase
ELISA	Pepsin	Hydrase	
Lyase	Rennin	Inulase	*8 letters:*
Lysin	Zymase	Lactase	Aldolase
Renin		Maltase	Allozyme
	7 letters:	Oxidase	Arginase
6 letters:	Amylase	Pectase	Bromelin
Cytase	Apyrase	Pepsine	Catalase

Diastase
Elastase
Esterase
Lysozyme
Nuclease
Permease
Protease
Steapsin
Synthase
Thrombin

9 letters:
Amylopsin
Autolysin
Bromelain
Cathepsin
Cellulase
Coagulase
Deaminase
DNAligase
Hydrolase
Inducible
Invertase
Isomerase

Oxygenase
Peptidase
Reductase
Sulfatase
Synaptase
Trehalase
Urokinase

10 letters:
Allosteric
Hexokinase
Kallikrein
Luciferase
Peroxidase
Peroxisome
Polymerase
Proteinase
Rancreatin
Saccharase
Subtilisin
Sulphatase
Telomerase
Tyrosinase

11 letters:
Carboxylase
Chymopapain
Collagenase
Dipeptidase
Glucosidase
Histaminase
Lecithinase
Phosphatase
Restriction
Transferase
Transposase

12 letters:
Asparaginase
Carbohydrase
Chymotrypsin
Constitutive
Enterokinase
Fibrinolysin
Flavoprotein
Ribonuclease
Transaminase

13 letters:
Decarboxylase
Dehydrogenase
DNApolymerase
Galactosidase
Hyaluronidase
Neuraminidase
Oxdoreductase
Penicillinase
Phosphorylase
Streptokinase
Thrombokinase
Topoisomerase
Transcriptase

14 letters:
Cholinesterase
Creatine kinase
Pectinesterase
Streptodornase
Thromboplastin

17 letters:
Carbonic anhydrase

Eon Arch(a)ean, Cenozoic, Epoch, Mesozoic, Phanerozoic, Proterozoic
Epaminondas Theban
Epaulette Swab
Ephemera(l) Brief, Day, Drake, Fungous, Mayfly, Momentary, Passing, Transient, Transitory, Trappings
Epic Aeneid, Ben Hur, Beowulf, Calliope, Colossal, Dunciad, Edda, Epopee, Epyllion, Gilgamesh, Heroic, Homeric, Iliad, Kalevala, Lusiad(s), Mahabharata, Nibelungenlied, Odyssey, Ramayana, Rhapsody, Saga
Epicene Hermaphrodite
Epicure(an) Apicius, Apolaustic, Connoisseur, Friand(e), Gastronome, Gastrosopher, Glutton, → **GOURMAND**, Gourmet, Hedonist, Sybarite
Epidemic Enzootic, Outbreak, Pandemic, Pestilence, Plague, Prevalent, Rampant, Rash, Rife
Epigram Adage, Apophthegm, Gnomic, Mot, Proverb
Epigraph Citation, Inscription, RIP
Epilepsy, Epileptic Clonic, Eclampsia, Falling evil, Falling sickness, Fit, Grand mal, Petit mal, Turn
Epilogue Appendix, Coda, End, Postlude, Postscript
Epiphany Twelfthtide
Epiphenomenon ESP
Epiphyte Air-plant
Episcopalian PE, Prelatic
Episode(s), Episodic Bipolar, Chapter, Incident, Microsleep, Page, Picaresque, Scene, Serial
Epistle(s) Catholic, Dispatch, General, Lesson, Letter, Missive, Pastoral, Titus
Epitaph Ci-git, Hic jacet, Inscription, RIP
Epithet Adj(ective), Antonomasia, Apathaton, Byword, Curse, Expletive, Panomphaean, → **TERM**, Title
Epitome, Epitomise Abridge, Abstract, Avowal, Digest, Image, Model, Summary, Typify

Epoch Age, Eocene, Era, Holocene, Magnetic, Miocene, Neogene, Oligocene, Palaeocene, Palaeolithic, Perigordian, Period , Pleistocene, Pl(e)iocene

Epsom salts Kieserite

Equable, Equably Calm, Just, Pari passu, Placid, Smooth, Tranquil

Equal(ly), Equality, Equal quantities A(n)a, Across the board, Alike, All square, As, Balanced, Commensurate, Compeer, Co-partner, Egal(ity), Emulate, Equinox, Equiparate, Equity, Even, Even-steven, Ex aequo, Feer, Fe(a)re, Fiere, Fifty-fifty, For, Identical, Identity, Is, Iso-, Isocracy, Isonomy, Level, Level-pegging, Maik, Make, Match, Mate, Owelty, Par, Parage, Parametric, Pari passu, → **PEER**, Peregal, Pheer(e), Rise, Rival, → **SO**, Square, Upsides, Wyoming, Ylike

Equanimity Aplomb, Balance, Poise, Serenity

Equate, Equation(s) Arrhenius, Balance, Chemical, Cubic, Defective, Differential, Diophantine, Dirac, Exponential, Gas, Identity, Linear, Logistic, Maxwell, Nernst, Parametric, Personal, Polar, Quadratic, Reduce, Relate, Rhizic, Schrödinger, Simultaneous, Van der Waals', Wave

Equator(ial) Celestial, Galactic, Line, Magnetic, Thermal, Tropical

Equerry Courtier, Officer, Page

Equestrian Dressage, Eventer, Turfite

Equilibrium Balance, Composure, Homeostasis, Instable, Isostasy, Poise, Punctuated, Stable, Stasis, Steady state, Tautomerism, Thermodynamic

Equine Hinny

Equinox Autumnal, Vernal

Equip(ment), Equipage Accoutrement, Accustrement, Adorn, Aguise, Aguize, Apparatus, Apparel, Appliance, Armament, Array, Attire, Carriage, Clobber, Clothe, Codec, Deadstock, Deck, Dight, Expertise, → **FURNISH**, Gear, Gere, Get-up, Graith, Habilitate, Hand-me-up, Hardware, Headset, Hi-tech, Incubator, iPod®, Kit, Lie-detector, Material, Matériel, Mechanise, Monitor, Muniments, Outfit, Paraphernalia, Pile-driver, Plant, Receiver, Refit, Retinue, Rig, Sonar, Sonobuoy, Spikes, Stapler, Stereo, Stock, Stuff, Tabulator, Tack(le), Tool, Trampet(te), Trampoline, Turn-out, Vision-mixer, Webcam

Equitable Fair, Just

Equity Actors, Equality, Justice, Law, Negative, Owner's, Union

Equivalence, Equivalent Akin, Amounting to, Correspondent, Dose, Equal, Equipollent, Ewe, Formal, In-kind, Same, Tantamount, Version

Equivocal Ambiguous, Dubious, Evasive, Fishy, Oracular, Vague

Equivocate Flannel, Lie, Palter, Prevaricate, Quibble, Tergiversate, Waffle, Weasel

Er Um

Era Age, Archaean, C(a)enozoic, Christian, Common, Cretaceous, Cryptozoic, Decade, Dynasty, Ediocaron, Eozoic, Epoch, Hadean, Hegira, Hej(i)ra, Hijra, Jurassic, Lias, Mesozoic, Palaeozoic, Period, Precambrian, Proterozoic, Republican, Torridonian, Vulgar

Eradicate, Erase Abolish, Delete, Demolish, Destroy, Dislimn, Efface, Expunge, Exterminate, Extirp, Obliterate, Purge, Root, Scrat, Scratch, Stamp-out, Strike off, Strike out, Uproot, Uptear

Erasmus Humanist

Eratosthenes Sieve

Erbium Er

Erect(ion), Erector Attolent, Boner, Build, Construct(ion), Elevate, Hard-on, Henge, Horn, Perpendicular, Priapism, Prick, Rear, Rigger, Stiffy, Straight-pight, Tentigo, Upend, Upright, Vertical

Ergo Argal, Hence, Therefore

Erica Heather, Ling

Ermine Fur, Minever, Miniver, Stoat

Ernie Bondsman

Erode, Erosion Abrade, Corrasion, Degrade, Denude, Destroy, Deteriorate, Detrition, Etch, Fret, Hush, Planation, Spark, Wash, Wear, Yardang

Eros, Erotic(a) Amatory, Amorino, Amorous, Aphrodisiac, Carnal, Cupid, Curiosa, Lascivious, Philtre, Prurient, Salacious, Steamy

Err(or) Aliasing, Anachronism, Bish, Blip, Blooper, Blunder, Boner, Boob(oo), Bug, Clanger, Comedy, Corrigendum, EE, Execution, Fat-finger, Fault, Fluff, Glaring, Heresy, Hickey, Human, Inaccuracy, Inherited, Jeofail, K'thibh, Lapse, Lapsus, Literal, Mackle, Mesprise, Mesprize, Misgo, Misprint, Misprise, Misprize, Misstep, → **MISTAKE**, Mumpsimus, Out, Parachronism, Probable, Recoverable, Rounding, Rove, Runtime, Sampling, Semantic, Sin, Slip, Slip-up, Solecism, Standard, Stray, Trip, Truncation, Type I, Type II, Typo, Typographical, Unforced, Wander

Errand Ance, Chore, Commission, Fool's, Message, Mission, Once, Sleeveless, Task, Yince

Errand-boy Cad, Galopin, Page

Erratic Haywire, Planetary, Spasmodic, Temperamental, Unstable, Vagary, Vagrant, Wayward, Whimsical

Erroneous False, Inaccurate, Mistaken, Non-sequitur

Ersatz Artificial, Synthetic

Erudite, Erudition Academic, Didactic, Learned, Savant, Scholar, Well-bred, Well-read, Wisdom

Erupt(ion), Erupture Belch, Brash, Burst, Ecthyma, Eject, Emit, Emphlysis, Exanthem(a), Exanthemata, → **EXPLODE**, Fissure, Flare, Fumarole, Hives, Hornito, Lichen, Mal(l)ander, Mallender, Morphew, Outbreak, Outburst, Papilla, Paroxysm, Plinian, Pompholyx, Pustule, Rash, Rose-drop, Scissure

Escalate, Escalator Accrescence, Expand, Granary, Grow, Lift, Snowball, Travolator

Escape(e), Escapade, Escapist Abscond, Adventure, Atride, Avoid, Bale out, Bolt, Bolthole, Breakout, Caper, Close call, Eject, Elope, Elude, Elusion, Esc, Eschewal, Evade, Exit, Fire, Flee, Flight, Fredaine, Frolic, Fugacity, Gaolbreak, Get-out, Hole, Hoot, Houdini, Houdini act, Hout, Lam, Lark, Leakage, Leg-it, Let-off, Levant, Lifeline, Loop(-hole), Meuse, Mews, Miss, Muse, Narrow, Near thing, Outlet, Prank, Refuge, Rollick, Runaway, Sauve qui peut, Scapa, Scarper, Seep(age), Shave, Slip, Splore, Squeak, Vent, Walter Mitty, Wilding, Wriggle

Escapement Anchor, Dead-beat, Foliot, Recoil

Eschew Abandon, Avoid, For(e)go, Ignore, → **SHUN**

Escort Accompany, Arm candy, Attend, Beard, Bodyguard, Bring, Chaperone, Comitatus, Conduct, Convoy, Cortège, Corvette, Date, Destroyer, Entourage, Frigate, Gallant, Gigolo, Guard, Guide, Lead, Outrider, Protector, Retinue, See, Send, Set, Squire, Take, Tend, Usher, Walker

Escutcheon Achievement, Crest, Shield

Esker OS

Eskimo Aleut, Caribou, Husky, In(n)uit, Inuk, Inukitut, Thule, Yupik

Esoteric Abstruse, Acroamatic, Arcane, Inner, Mystic, Occult, Orphic, Private, Rarefied, Recondite, Secret

ESP Psi, Retrocognition

Especial(ly) Chiefly, Esp, Espec, Outstanding, Particular

Esperanto Ido, Zamenhof

Espionage Industrial, Spying, Surveillance

Esplanade Promenade, Walk

Esprit Insight, Spirit, Understanding, Wit

Esquire Armiger(o), Esq, Gent

Essay(s) Article, Attempt, Causerie, Critique, Dabble, Disquisition, Dissertation, Endeavour, Festschrift, Go, Paper, Prolusion, Sketch, Stab, Study, Theme, Thesis, Tractate, Treatise, Try

Essayist Addison, Bacon, Carlyle, Columnist, Elia, Ellis, Emerson, Hazlitt, Holmes,

Hunt, Huxley, Lamb, Locke, Montaigne, Pater, Prolusion, Ruskin, Scribe, Steele, Tzara, → **WRITER**

Essence Alma, Atman, Attar, Aura, Being, Core, Crux, Element, Entia, Esse, Extract, Fizzen, Flavouring, Flower, Foison, Gist, Heart, Hom(e)ousian, Inbeing, Inscape, Kernel, Marrow, Mauri, Mirbane, Myrbane, Nub, Nutshell, Oil, Ottar, Otto, Perfume, Per-se, Pith, Quiddity, Ratafia, Saul, Soul, Substance, Sum, Ylang-ylang

Essential(ly) Arabin, At heart, Basic, Central, Crucial, Entia, Formal, Fundamental, Imperative, In, Indispensable, Inherent, In se, Integral, Intrinsic, Kernel, Key, Lifeblood, Linch-pin, Marrow, Material, Mun, Must, Necessary, Need, Nitty-gritty, Nuts and bolts, Part-parcel, Per-se, Prana, Prerequisite, Quintessence, Radical, Requisite, Sine qua non, Soul, Vital, Whatness

Essex Roseland

Establish(ed) Abide, Anchor, Ascertain, Base, Bred-in-the-bone, Build, Chronic, Create, Deep-seated, Deploy, Embed, Enact, Endemic, Engrain, Ensconce, Entrench, Erect, Evidence, Evince, Fix, → **FOUND**, Haft, Honoured, Imbed, Ingrain, Instal(l), Instate, Instil, Institute, Inveterate, Ordain, Pitch, Pre-set, Prove, Radicate, Raise, Redintegrate, Root(ed), Secure, Set, Stable, Standing, State, Stell, Substantiate, Trad, Trite, Valorise, Verify

Establishment Building, Business, CE, Church, Co, Concern, Creation, Hacienda, Household, Instauration, Institution, Lodge, Proving ground, Salon, School, Seat, Succursal, System, Traditional

Estate, Estate-holder Allod(ium), Alod, Assets, Campus, Car, Commons, Dais, Demesne, Domain, Dominant, Dowry, Est, Estancia, Fazenda, Fee-simple, Fee-tail, Fen, First, Fourth, General, Hacienda, Hagh, Haugh, Having, Hay, Housing, Industrial, Jointure, Land-living, Latifundium, Legitim, Life, Manor, Messuage, Odal, Patrimony, Pen, Personal(ity), Plantation, Press, Princedom, → **PROPERTY**, Real, Runrig, Second, Situation, Spiritual, Standing, Talooka, Taluk(a), Temporal, Termer, Termor, Thanage, Third, Trading, Trust, Udal, Zamindari, Zemindari

Estate agent Realtor

Esteem(ed), Estimable Account, Admiration, Appreciation, Count, Credited, Have, Honour, Izzat, Los, Precious, Prestige, Price, Pride, Prize, Rate, → **REGARD**, Reputation, Respect, Revere, Store, Value, Venerate, Wonder, Worthy

Ester Benzocaine, C(o)umarin, Depside, Glyceride, Lactone, Olein, Palmitin, Phthalate, Psilocybin, Succinate, Triglyceride, Urethan(e)

▶ **Estimable** see **ESTEEM(ED)**

Estimate, Estimation Appraise, Assess, Calculate, Carat, Conceit, Cost, Esteem, Extrapolation, Forecast, Gauge, Guess(timate), Inexact, Interval, Opinion, Point, Projection, Quotation, Rate, Rating, Reckon, Regard, Sight, Value, Weigh

Estrange Alienate, Disunite, Wean

Estuary Bay, Clyde, Creek, Dee, Delta, Firth, Gironde, Humber, Inlet, Mouth, Orwell, Ostial, Para, Rio de la Plata, Tay

Esurient Arid, Insatiable

Etc(etera) Et al(ia), So on

Etch(ing) Aquafortis, Aquatint(a), Bite, → **ENGRAVE**, Incise, Inscribe

Eternal(ly), Eternity Aeonian, Ageless, All-time, Amarantine, Endless, Everlasting, Evermore, Eviternal, Ewigkeit, Forever, Immortal, Infinity, Never-ending, Perdurable, Perpetual, Sempiternal, Tarnal, Timeless, Triangle

Ether Atmosphere, Ch'i, Crown, Gas, Petroleum, Sky, Yang, Yin

Ethereal Airy, Delicate, Fragile, Heavenly, Nymph

Ethic(al), Ethics Deontics, Ideals, Marcionite, Moral, Principles, Situation, Work

Ethiopia(n) African, Amharic, Asmara, Cushitic, Falasha, Galla, Geez, Kabele, Kebele, Ogaden

Ethnic Racial, Roots

Ethyl ET

Etiquette Code, Conduct, Decorum, Kawa, → **MANNERS**, Politesse, Propriety, Protocol, Ps and Qs, Punctilious

Etna Empedocles, Vessel, Volcano

Etonian Oppidan, Victim

Etruscan Tyrrhenian

Etymologist, Etymology Hobson-Jobson, Isodore

Eucalyptus Blackbutt, Bloodwood, Cadaga, Cadagi, Coolabah, Gum-tree, Ironbark, Jarrah, Mallee, Marri, Morrell, Red gum, Sallee, Sally, Stringybark, Sugar gum, Tallow wood, Tewart, Tooart, Tuart, Wandoo, White gum, Woolly butt, Yate

Eucharist Azymite, Communion, Housel, Mass, Prozymite, Supper, Viaticum

Euchre Jambone

Eugene Aram, Onegin

Eugenia Jambal, Jambolan(a), Jambu(l)

Eulogistic, Eulogy Encomium, Epaenetic, Epainetic, Laudatory, Panegyric, Praise, Tribute

Eunuch Ridg(e)ling, Rig

Euphausia Krill, Shrimp

Euphemism Fib, Gosh, Gracious, Heck, Hypocorism

Euphonic Huge

Euphoria, Euphoric Buzz, Cock-a-hoop, Ecstasy, Elation, High, Jubilation, Mindfuck, Nirvana, Rapture, Rush

Euphrasia Eyebright

Eurasian Chee-chee, Chi-chi

Europe(an) Andorran, Balt, Bohunk, Bosnian, Catalan, Community, Continent, Croat, E, Esth, Estonian, Faringee, Faringhi, Feringhee, Fleming, Hungarian, Hunky, Icelander, Japhetic, Lapp, Lett, Lithuanian, Magyar, Palagi, Polack, Ruthene, Ruthenian, Serb, Slavonian, Slovak, Slovene, Topi-wallah, Transleithan, Tyrolean, Vlach, Yugoslav

Europium Eu

Eustace Diamonds

Euthanasia Exit

Evacuate, Evacuation Dunkirk, Excrete, Expel, Getter, Medevac, Movement, Planuria, Planury, Retreat, Scramble, Stercorate, Stool, Vent, Void, Withdraw

Evade, Evasion, Evasive Ambages, Avoid, Circumvent, Cop-out, Coy, Dodge, Duck, Elude, Equivocate, Escape, Fence, Fudge, Hedge, Jink, Loophole, Mealymouthed, Parry, Prevaricate, Quibble, Quillet, Quirk, Salvo, Scrimshank, Shack, Shifty, Shirk, Shuffling, Sidestep, Skive, Skrimshank, Slippy, Stall, Subterfuge, Tergiversate, Waive, Weasel, Weasel out, Whiffler

Evaluate, Evaluation Appraise, Assess, Estimate, Gauge, Job, Measure, Ponder, Rate, Review, Waid(e), Weigh

Evanescent Cursory, Fleeting, Fugacious

Evangelical, Evangelist(ical) Buchman, Clappy-doo, Converter, Crusader, Fisher, Godsquad, Gospeller, Graham, Happy-clappy, Hot gospeller, Jansen, Jesus freak, John, Luke, Marist, Mark, Matthew, Missioner, Moody, Morisonian, Peculiar, Preacher, Propagandist, Revivalist, Salvationist, Salvo, Sankey, Sim(eonite), Stundist, Wild

Evaporate, Evaporation Condense, Dehydrate, Desorb, Disappear, Dry, Exhale, Steam, Steme, Ullage, Vaporise

Eve(ning) All Hallow's, Nightfall, Postmeridian, St Agnes's, Soirée, Subfusk, Sunset, Tib(b)s, Twilight, Vesperal, Vespertinal, Vigil, Watch night, Yester

Evelyn Diarist, Hope

Even(ly), Evenness Aid, Albe(e), Albeit, All, Average, Balanced, Clean, Drawn, Dusk, Een, Ene, Equable, Equal, Erev, Fair, Fair play, Flush, Forenight, Iron, J'ouvert, Level, Level-pegging, Meet, Pair, Par, Plain, Plane, Plateau, Quits, Rib, Smooth, Square, Standardise, Temperate, Tie(d), Toss-up, Uniform, Yet

Even-handed Ambidextrous

Evening flight Ro(a)ding

Evensong Vespers

Event(ing) Bash, Case, Circumstance, Contingency, Cross-country, Discus, Dressage, Encaenia, Episode, Fest, Field, Fiesta, Function, Gymkhana, Happening, Happy, Heat, Incident, Iron man, Landmark, Leg, Liquidity, Media, Meeting, Milestone, Occasion, Occurrence, Ongoing, Outcome, Pass, Rag-day, Regatta, Result, Show-jumping, Soirée, Stick-on, Three-day, Three-ring circus, Time trial, Track, Triple

Even-toed Artiodactyl

Eventual(ity), Eventually Case, Contingent, Finally, Future, In time, Later, Nd, Sooner or later, Ultimate

Ever Always, Ay(e), Constantly, Eternal, Eviternity

Everglade Vlei

Evergreen Abies, Ageless, Arbutus, Cembra, Cypress, Gaultheria, Golden lie, Holly, Ivy, Myrtle, Olearia, Periwinkle, Pinaster, Privet, Thuja, Thuya, Washington, Winterberry, Yacca

Everlasting Cat's ear, Changeless, Enduring, Eternal, Immortal, Immortelle, Perdurable, Recurrent, Tarnal

Every(one), Everything All, A'thing, Catch-all, Complete, Each, Et al, Existence, Full Monty, Ilk(a), In toto, Monty, Sub chiz, Sum, The full monty, The works, To a man, Tout, Tout le monde, Universal, Varsal

Everyday Banal, Informal, Mundane, Natural, Ordinary, Plain, Routine

Everywhere Ambient, Omnipresent, Passim, Rife, Throughout, Ubique, Ubiquity, World

Evict(ion), Evict(or) Clearance, Disnest, Disseisor, Eject, Expel, Oust

Evidence, Evident Adminicle, Apparent, Argument, Axiomatic, Circumstantial, Clear, Compurgation, Confessed, Credentials, Deposition, Direct, Distinct, DNA, Document, Empirical, Exemplar, Flagrant, Hearsay, Indicate, Internal, King's, Manifest, Marked, Material, Naked, Obvious, Overt, → **PATENT**, Plain, Premise, Prima facie, Probable, Proof, Queen's, Record, Sign, Smoking gun, State's, Surrebuttal, Testimony, Understandable

Evil Ahriman, Alastor, Amiss, Bad, Badmash, Bale, Beelzebub, Budmash, Corrupt, Curse, Depraved, Eale, Falling, Guilty, Harm, Heinous, Hydra, Ill, Immoral, Iniquity, King's, Loki, Malefic, Malign, Mare, Mischief, Monstrous, Nasty, Necessary, Night, Perfidious, Rakshas(a), Satanic, Shrewd, Sin, → **SINISTER**, Theodicy, Turpitude, Vice, Villainy, Wicked

Evil eye Jettatura

Evince Disclose, Exhibit, Indicate, → **MANIFEST**, Show

Eviscerate(d) Debilitate, Disembowel, Drawn, Gralloch

Evoke Arouse, Awaken, Elicit, Move, Stir

Evolution(ary) Convergent, Countermarch, Development, Emergent, Growth, Holism, Lamarck, Lysenkoism, Moner(on), Neo-Lamarckism, Orthogenesis, Phylogeny, Social, Spencerman, Stellar, Transformism, Turning

▷ **Evolution** *may indicate* an anagram

Evolve Speciate

Ewe Crone, Gimmer, Keb, Rachel, Sheep, Teg, Theave

Ewer Aquamanale, Aquamanile, → **JUG**

Ex Former, Late, Quondam, Ten

Exacerbate Aggravate, Embitter, Exasperate, Inflame, Irritate, Needle

Exact(ing), Exactitude, Exactly Accurate, Authentic, Bang on, Careful, Dead, Definite, Due, Elicit, Estreat, Even, Exigent, Extort, Fine, Formal, It, Jump, Literal, Literatim, Mathematical, Meticulous, Nice(ty), On the nail, Pat, Point-device, → **PRECISE**, Require, Slap-bang, Spang, Specific, Spot-on, Strict, Stringent, T, To a 't', Verbatim

Exaction Blackmail, Extortion, Impost, Montem, Sorelion, Tax

Exaggerate(d), Exaggeration Agonistic, Amplify, Ballyhoo, Boast, Brag, Camp, Colour, Distend, Dramatise, → **EMBROIDER**, Exalted, Goliathise, Hoke, Hype,

Hyperbole, Inflate, Lie, Line-shoot, Magnify, Munch(h)ausen, Mythomania, Overdo, Overdraw, Overegg, Overpaint, Overpitch, Overplay, Overrate, Overstate, Overstretch, Over-the-top, Play up, Romance, Shoot a line, Steep, Stretch, Tall, Theatrical, Writ large

Exalt(ed), Exaltation Attitudes, Deify, Dignify, Elation, Enhance, Ennoble, Ensky, Enthrone, Erect, Extol, Glorify, High, Jubilance, Larks, Lofty, Magnific, → **PRAISE**, Raise, Rapture, Ruff(e), Sama, Sublime, Supernal, Throne

Exam(ination), Examine, Examinee, Examiner Agrégé, A-level, Alnage, Analyse, Analyst, Appose, Assess, Audit, Auscultation, Autopsy, Baccalauréat, Biopsy, Case, Check-out, Check-up, Cognosce, Collate, Comb, Common Entrance, Concours, Consideration, Cross-question, CSE, Deposal, Depose, Disquisition, Dissect, Docimasy, Edexcel, Eleven plus, Endoscopy, Entrance, Expiscate, Explore, Eyeball, Finals, GCE, GCSE, Going-over, Grade(s), Great-go, Greats, Gulf, Haruspex, Hearing, Higher, Inspect, Inter, Interrogate, Interview, Introspection, Jerque, Jury, Laparoscopy, Little-go, Local, Look, Mark, Matriculation, Medical, Mocks, Moderator, Mods, Mug, O-level, Once-over, Oral, Ordalian, Ordeal, Overhaul, Palp(ate), Paper, Peruse, Physical, Post-mortem, Prelims, Probe, Professional, Pry, Psychoanalyse, Pump, → **QUESTION**, Quiz, Ransack, Recce, Reconnaissance, Resit, Responsions, Review, Sayer, Scan, Schools, Scope, Screen, Scrutator, Scrutineer, Scrutinise, Search, Seek, Shroff, Sift, Sit, Smalls, Study, Survey, Sus(s), Test, Trial, Tripos, Try, Unseen, Vet, Viva, Vivisection, Voir dire

Example Apotheosis, Assay-piece, Byword, Epitome, Erotema, Foretaste, → **FOR EXAMPLE**, Illustration, Instance, Lead, Lesson, Model, Monument, Paradigm, Paragon, → **PATTERN**, Praxis, Precedent, Prototype, Quintessence, Role model, Say, Shining, Showpiece, Specimen, Standard, Stormer, Such as, Touchstone, Type, Typify

Exasperate, Exasperating, Exasperation Anger, Embitter, Galling, Irk, Irritate, Nettle, Provoke

Excavate, Excavation, Excavator Armadillo, Burrow, Catacomb, Crater, Cutting, Delf, Delph, → **DIG**, Dike, Disinter, Ditch, Dragline, Dredge, Drift, Drive, Earthwork, Gaulter, Graft, Heuch, Heush, Hollow, JCB, Mine, Pichiciago, Pioneer, Pioner, Power shovel, Pyoner, Quarry, Shaft, Sink, Sondage, Spade, Steam-shovel, Stope, Well

Exceed, Exceeding(ly) Amain, Not half, Outdo, Outnumber, Outstrip, Overstep, Preponderate, Surpass, Transcend, Very

Excel(lence), Excellency, Excellent A1, Ace, Admirable, A-per-se, Assay-piece, Awesome, Bangin(g), Bang on, Beat, Beaut, Beezer, Better, Bitchin', Blinder, Bodacious, Boffo, Bonzer, Booshit, Boss, Bottler, Bravo, Brill, Bully, Capital, Castor, Champion, Cheese, Choice, Class(y), Classical, Cool, Copacetic, Copesettic, Copybook, Corking, Crack, Crackajack, Crackerjack, Crucial, Cushty, Daisy, Def, Dic(k)ty, Dilly, Dominate, Doozy, Dope, Elegant, Excelsior, Exemplary, Eximious, Exo, Extraordinaire, Fab, Fabulous, Fantastic, First rate, Five-star, Goodly, Goodness, Great, Grit, Grouse, HE, Hellacious, High, Humdinger, Hunky(-dory), Inimitable, Jake, Jammy, Jim-dandy, Kiff, Knockout, Lal(l)a palooza, Laudable, Lollapalooza, Lummy, Matchless, Mean, Mega-, Merit, Neat, Noble, Nonesuch, Olé, Out and outer, Outbrag, Outdo, Outstanding, Outstrip, Outtop, Overdo, Overpeer, Overtop, Paragon, Peachy, Peerless, Perfection, Phat, Prime, Pure, Quality, Rad, Rare, Rattling, Ring, Rinsin', Ripping, Ripsnorter, Say-piece, Shagtastic, → **SHINE**, Shit-hot, Sick-dog, Sik, Slammin(g), Socko, Sound, Spanking, Spiffing, Stellar, Stonking, Stupendous, Sublime, Superb, Super-duper, Superior, Supernal, Supreme, Surpass, Swell, Terrific, Tip-top, Top flight, Top-hole, Topnotch, Topping, Tops, Transcend, Transcendent, Triff, Virtue, Virtuoso, Wal(l)y, War, Way-out, Whizzo, Whizzy, Wicked, Worth

Except(ion) Bar, But, Else, Exc, Nobbut, Omit, Save, Than, Then, Unless

Exceptional Abnormal, Anomaly, Cracker, Doozy, Egregious, Especial, Extraordinary, Extreme, Gas, Inimitable, Rare, Ripsnorter, Select, Singular, Spanking, Special, Super, Unco(mmon), Unusual, Zinger

Excerpt(s) Digest, Extract, Passage, Scrap

Excess(ive), Excessively All-fired, Almighty, Basinful, Binge, De trop, Epact,

Exaggeration, Exorbitant, Extortionate, Extravagant, Flood, Fulsome, Glut, Hard, Inordinate, Lake, → **LAVISH**, Mountain, Needless, Nimiety, OD, Old, OTT, Outrage, Over, Overage, Overblown, Overcome, Overdose, Overkill, Overmuch, Overspill, Over-the-top, Owercome, Plethora, Preponderance, Profuse, Salt, Satiety, Spate, Spilth, Staw, Steep, Superabundant, Superfluity, Surplus, Surfeit, Surplus, Terrific, Thundering, Too, Troppo, Ultra, Undue, Unequal, Woundily

Exchange Baltic, Bandy, Banter, Barter, Bourse, Cambist, Cash, Catallactic, Change, Chop, Commodity, Commute, Confab, Contango, Convert, Cope, Corn, Ding-dong, Employment, Enallage, Excambion, Foreign, Global, Inosculate, Intercooler, Interplay, Ion, Labour, Logroll, → **MARKET**, Mart, Needle, Niffer, Paraphrase, PBX, Post, Quid pro quo, Rally, Rate, RE, Recourse, Redeem, Rialto, Royal, Scorse, Scourse, Sister-chromated, Stock, Swap, Switch, Swop, Telephone, Tolsel, Tolsey, Tolzey, → **TRADE**, Traffic, Transfusion, Transpose, Trophallaxis, Truck

Exchequer Remembrancer

Excise(man), Excise district Ablate, Bobbitt, Crop, Expunge, Gauger, Resect, Ride, Tax

Excite(ment), Excitable, Excitability, Excited, Exciting Ablaze, Aboil, Abuzz, Aerate, Aflutter, Agitate, Agog, Amove, Amp, Animate, Apeshit, Aphrodisiac, Arouse, Athrill, Atwitter, Awaken, Brouhaha, Buck-fever, Climactic, Combustible, Commotion, Delirium, Dither, Electrify, Emove, Enthuse, Erethism, Eventful, Feisty, Fever, Fire, Flap, Flat spin, Frantic, Frenzy, Frisson, Furore, Fuss, Galvanise, Gas, Grip, Headiness, Heat, Hectic, Het, Hey-go-mad, Highly-strung, Hilarity, Hobson-Jobson, Hoopla, Hothead, Hyped, Hyper, Hypomania, Hysterical, Impel, Incite, Inebriate, Inflame, Intoxicate, Jimjams, Kick, Kindle, Liven, Maenad, Mania, Metastable, Must, Nappy, Neurotic, Oestrus, On fire, Orgasm, Overheat, Overwrought, Panic, Passion, Pride, Prime, Provoke, Racy, Radge, Red-hot, Rile, Roil, → **ROUSE**, Rousement, Ruff(e), Rut, Salutation, Send, Sexy, Shivering, Spin, Splash, Spur, Startle, Stimulate, Stir(e), Suscitate, Suspense, Swashbuckling, Temperamental, Tense, Tetanoid, Tetany, Tew, Thrill, Tickle, Titillate, Turn-on, Twitter, Upraise, Va-va-voom, Waken, Whee, Whet, Whoopee, Work up, Yahoo, Yerk, Yippee, Yirk, Yoicks

▷ **Excite(d)** *may indicate* an anagram

Exclaim, Exclamation (mark) Ahem, Arrah, Aue, Begorra, Bliksem, Blurt, Bo, Ceas(e), Crikey, Criv(v)ens, Dammit, Ecphonesis, Eina, Eish, Ejaculate, Epiphonema, Eureka, Expletive, Fen(s), Good-now, Hadaway, Haith, Halleluiah, Hallelujah, Heigh-ho, Hem, Hip, Hookey Walker, Hosanna, Inshallah, Interjection, Moryah, Omigod, Oof, Oops, Phew, Pish, Pling, Pow, Protest, Pshaw, Push, Sasa, Screamer, Sese(y), Sessa, Uh-oh, Uh-uh, Unberufen, Vociferate, Walker, Whau, Whoops, Wirra, Wow, Yay, Yeehaw, Yippee, Yo-ho-ho, Yummy, Zounds

Exclave Cabinda

Exclude, Excluding, Exclusion Ban, Banish, Bar, Berufsverbot, Block, Competitive, Corner, Debar, Deforcement, Disbar, Drop, Eliminate, Ex, Except, Excommunicate, Freeze out, Ice out, Omit, Ostracise, Outbar, Outwith, Pauli, Proscribe, Rule out, Shut out, Social, Upmarket

Exclusive Cliquish, Closed-shop, Complete, Debarment, Elect, Esoteric, Monopoly, Particular, Pure, Rare, Scoop, Select, Single, Sole

Excommunicate Curse

Excoriate Flay, Slam

Excrement, Excretion, Excretory Cystinuria, Dirt, Doo-doo, Dung, Emunctory, Faeces, Fecula, Flyspeck, Frass, Jobbie, Keech, Meconium, Oliguria, Ordure, Poo(p), Poo-poo, Puer, Pure, Refuse, Scatology, Shit(e), Sir-reverence, Stercoraceous, Stool, Strangury, Turd, Urea, Waste, Whoopsie

Excrescence Aril, Carnosity, Caruncle, Enate, Gall, Growth, Knob, Knurl, Lump, Nurl, Pimple, Pin, Spavin(e), Strophiole, Talpa, Twitter(-bone), Wart

Excruciate, Excruciating Agonising, Rack, Torment, Torture

Exculpate Acquit, Clear, Forgive

Excursion Airing, Cruise, Dart, Digression, Jaunt, Junket, Outing, Pleasure-trip, Railtour, Road, Sally, Sashay, Sortie, Tour, Trip

Excuse, Excusable Absolve, Alibi, Amnesty, Bunbury, Condone, Cop-out, Essoin, Essoyne, Evasion, Exempt, Exonerate, Explain, Faik, Forgive, Gold brick, Hook, Let off, Mitigate, Occasion, Off come, Out, Overlook, Palliate, → **PARDON**, Plea, Pretext, Release, Salvo, Venial, Viable, Whitewash

Execrate Abhor, Ban, Boo, Curse

Execute(d), Executioner, Executive, Executor Abhorson, Accomplish, Account, Administrate, Behead, Carnifex, Deathsman, Despatch, Discharge, Dispatch, Exor, Finish, Fry, Gan, Gar(r)otte, Gin, Guardian, Hang, Headsman, Implement, Ketch, Kill, Koko, Literary, Lynch, Management, Martyr, Monsieur de Paris, Noyade, Official, Perform, Perpetrate, Pierrepoint, Politburo, Scamp, Top, Tower Hill, Trustee, Tyburn

Exemplar(y) Byword, Classic, Impeccable, Laudable, Model, Paragon, Perfect, St, Warning

Exemplify Cite, Epitomise, Illustrate, Instantiate, Satisfy

Exempt(ion) Dispensation, Exclude, Exeem, Fainites, Fains, Free, Immune, Impunity, Indemnity, Indulgence, Overslaugh, Privilege, Quarter, Spare, Tyburn ticket, Vains

Exercise(s) Aerobics, Air, Antic, Apply, Bench press, Burpee, Buteyko method, Cal(l)isthenics, Callanetics®, Chi kung, Chin-up, Circuit training, Cloze, Constitutional, Dancercise, Drill, Employ, Enure, Eurhythmics, Exert, Falun dafa, Falun gong, Fartlek, Five-finger, Floor, Gradus, Hatha yoga, Inure, Isometrics, Kata, Keepy-uppy, Kegel, Krav Maga, Lat spread, Lesson, Limber, Manual, Medau, Op, Operation, PE, Physical jerks, Pilates, Ply, Plyometrics, Popmobility, Practice, Practise, Preacher curl, Press-up, Prolusion, PT, Pull-up, Pump iron, Push-up, Qigong, Sadhana, Shintaido, Sit-up, Solfege, Solfeggi(o), Step (aerobics), Stretch, Tae-Bo®, Tai chi (ch'uan), Thema, Theme, Thesis, Train, Trampoline, Trunk curl, Use, Vocalism, Warm-down, Warm-up, Wield, Work, Work-out, Xyst(us), Yogalates, Yomp

▷ **Exercise(d)** *may indicate* an anagram

Exert(ion) Conatus, → **EFFORT**, Exercise, Labour, Operate, Strain, Strive, Struggle, Trouble, Wield

Ex-European Japhetic

Exhalation, Exhale Breath, Fume, Miasma, Reek, Sigh, Smell, Steam, Transpire, Vapour

Exhaust(ed), Exhausting, Exhaustion, Exhaustive All-in, Backbreaking, Beaten, Beggar, Bugger(ed), Burn, Burn-out, Bushed, Clapped out, Collapse, Consume, Deadbeat, Debility, Deplete, Detailed, Dissipate, Do, Done, Drain, Eduction, Effete, Emission, Empty, End, Enervate, Euchred, Fatigue, Flue, Fordo, Forfeuchen, Forfochen, Forfoughen, Forfoughten, Forjaskit, Forjeskit, Forspent, Forswink, Frazzle, Gruelling, Heat, Heatstroke, Inanition, Jet-lagged, Jet-stream, Jiggered, Knacker, Mate, Milk, Out, Outwear, Overtax, Peter, Play out, Poop, Powfagged, Prostrate, Puckerood, Puggled, Rag, Ramfeezle, Rundown, Sap, Shatter, Shot, Shotten, Spend, Spent, Stonkered, Tailpipe, Tax, Tire, Trauchled, Use, Used up, Wabbit, Wappend, Warby, Washed-up, Wasted, Waygone, → **WEARY**, Wind, Worn, Zonked

Exhibition (centre), Exhibit(ing), Exhibitionist, Exhibitioner Aquashow, Bench, Circus, Concours, Demo, Demonstrate, Demy, Diorama, Discover, Display, ENC, Endeictic, Evince, Expo, Expose, Extrovert, Fair, Hang, Indicate, Installation, Lady Godiva, → **MANIFEST**, NEC, Olympia, Pageant, Panopticon, Parade, Present, Retrospective, Rodeo, Salon, Scene, Set forth, Show(piece), Showcase, Show-off, Showplace, Sideshow, Stand, Viewing, Waxworks, Zoo

Exhilarate(d) Bubble, Cheer, Elate, Enliven

Exhort(ation) Admonish, Allocution, Caution, Counsel, Incite, Lecture, Par(a)enesis, Persuade, Protreptic, Urge

Exhume Delve, Disinter, Resurrect, Unearth

Exigency, Exigent Demanding, Emergency, Pressing, Taxing, Urgent, Vital

Exile Adam, Babylon, Ban, Banish, Deport, Deportee, Eject, Emigré, Eve, Expatriate, Exul, Galut(h), Ostracise, Outlaw, Relegate, Tax, Wretch

Exist(ence), Existing Be(ing), Corporeity, Dwell, Enhypostasia, Entelechy, Esse, Extant, Haeccity, Identity, Inbeing, In esse, Inherent, Life, Lifespan, Live, Ontology, Perseity, Solipsism, Status quo, Substantial, Ubiety

Existentialist Camus, Sartre

Exit Débouché, Door, Egress, Emergency, Exhaust, Gate, Leave, Log off, Log out, Outgate, Outlet, Swansong, Vent, Vomitory

Exodus Book, Departure, Flight, Hegira, Hejira, Passover

Ex-official Outler

Exogamous Outbred

Exonerate(d) Absolve, Acquit, Clear, Excuse, Exempt, Shriven

Exorbitant Excessive, Expensive, Slug, Steep, Tall, Undue

Exorcise, Exorcist Benet, Lay

Exordium Opening, Preface, Prelude

Exotic Alien, Chinoiserie, Ethnic, Fancy, Foreign, Free, Outlandish, Strange

Expand(able), Expanse, Expansion Amplify, Boom, Branch out, Bulking, Develop, Diastole, Dilate, Distend, Ectasis, Elaborate, → ENLARGE, Escalate, Flesh out, Grow, Increase, Magnify, Ocean, Outspread, Outstretch, Snowball, Sprawl, Spread, Stretch, Swell, Tensite, Vastitude, Wax, Wire-draw

Expatiate Amplify, Descant, Dwell, Enlarge, Perorate

Expatriate Banish, Colonial, Emigrate, Émigré, Exile, Outcast

Expect(ant), Expectation, Expected, Expecting Agog, Anticipate, Ask, Await, Due, Foresee, Gravid, Hope, Imminent, Lippen, Look, Natural, On cue, Par, Pip, Predict, Pregnant, Presume, Prim, Probable, Prognosis, Prospect, Require, → SUPPOSE, Tendance, Think, Thought, Usual, Ween

Expectorant, Expectorate Expel, Guaiacol, Hawk, Spit

Expedient Advisable, Artifice, Contrivance, Dodge, Fend, Make-do, Makeshift, Measure, Politic, Resort, Resource, Salvo, Shift, Stopgap, Suitable, Wise

Expedite, Expedition, Expeditious Advance, Alacrity, Anabasis, Celerity, Crusade, Dispatch, Excursion, Fastness, Field trip, Hasten, Hurry, Kon-Tiki, Mission, Pilgrimage, Post-haste, Quest, Rapidity, Safari, Short cut, Speed, Trek, Trip, Turn out, Voyage, Warpath

Expel Amove, Deport, Dispossess, Drum out, Egest, Evacuate, Evict, Excommunicate, Excrete, Exile, Exorcize, Hoof, Oust, Out(cast), Read out, Spit, Turn forth, Void

Expend(iture) Budget, Consume, Cost, Dues, Gavel, Goings-out, Mise, Occupy, Oncost, Outgo(ing), Outlay, Poll, Squander, Tithe, Toll, Use, Waste

Expendable Cannon-fodder

Expense(s) Boodle, Charge, Cost, Current, Exes, Fee, Housekeeping, Law, Oncost, Outgoing, Outlay, Overhead, Price, Sumptuary

Expensive Chargeful, Costly, Dear, Executive, High, Ruinous, Salt, Steep, Top dollar, Upmarket, Valuable

Experience(d) Accomplished, A posteriori, Assay, Blasé, Come up, Discovery, Empiric, Encounter, Expert, → FEEL, Felt, Find, Foretaste, Freak-out, Gust, Hands-on, Hard way, Have, Incur, Know, Learn, Live, Mature, Meet, Mneme, Near-death, Old hand, Old-stager, Ordeal, Out-of-body, Pass, Plumb, Seasoned, See, Senior, Sense, Sensory, Spin, Stager, Stand, Street-smart, Streetwise, Taste, Transference, Trial, Trip, Trocinium, Try, Undergo, Versed, Veteran, Work, Worldly wise

Experiment(al) Attempt, Aufgabe, Avant-garde, Ballon d'assai, Control, Empirical, Essay, Gedanken, → JET, Michelson-Morley, Peirastic, Pilot, Sample, Shy, Single-blind, Taste, Tentative, → TRIAL, Trial balloon, Try, Venture, Vivisection

Expert(ise) Able, Accomplished, Ace, Adept, Adroit, Arch, Astacologist, Au fait, Authority, Boffin, Buff, Cambist, Cocker, Cognoscente, Competent, Connoisseur, Crack,

Craft, Dab(ster), Dab hand, Dan, Deft, Demon, Diagnostician, Digerati, Don, Egghead, Fancier, Finesse, Fundi, Gourmet, Gun, Hotshot, Karateka, Know-all, Know-how, Learned, Luminary, Maestro, Masterly, Mastery, Maven, Mavin, Meister, Nark, Old hand, Oner, Oneyer, Oneyre, Oracle, Peritus, Practised, Pro, Proficient, Pundit, Ringer, Rubrician, Savvy, Science, Shroff, Skill(y), Sly, Specialist, Techie, Technique, Technocrat, Technofreak, Technophile, Tipster, Troubleshooter, Ulema, Used, Whizz, Wireman, Wisard, W(h)iz, Wizard, Wonk

Expiate, Expiation, Expiatory Amends, Atone, Penance, Piacular

Expire(d), Expiry Blow, Collapse, Croak, → DIE, End, Exhale, Go, Invalid, Ish, Lapse, Neese, Pant, → PERISH, Sneeze, Terminate

Explain(able), Explanation Account, Annotate, Aperçu, Appendix, Aread, Arede, Arreede, Clarify, Conster, Construe, Decline, Define, Describe, Eclaircissement, Elucidate, Epexegesis, Explicate, Exponible, Expose, Expound, Extenuate, Gloss, Glossary, Gloze, Justify, Outline, Parabolize, Salve, Solve, Tell, Upknit, Why

Explanation, Explanatory Apology, Commentary, Exegesis, Exegetic, Exposition, Farse, Gloss, Gloze, Hypothesis, Key, Note, Preface, Reading, Rigmarole, Solution, Theory

Expletive Arrah, Darn, Exclamation, Oath, Ruddy, Sapperment

Explicit Clean-cut, Clear(-cut), Definite, Express, Frank, Full-on, Graphic, Outspoken, → PRECISE, Specific, Unequivocal

Explode, Explosion, Explosive Agene, Airburst, Amatol, Ammonal, ANFO, Antimatter, Aquafortis, Backfire, Bang, Bangalore torpedo, Big bang, Blast, Blow-out, Booby-trap, Burst, C4, Cap, Cheddite, Chug, Controlled, Cordite, Cramp, Crump, Cyclonite, Debunk, Demolitions, Depth bomb, Detonate, Dualin, Dunnite, Dust, Egg, Erupt, Euchloric, Euchlorine, Fiery, Fireball, Firecracker, Firedamp, Firework, Flip, Fulminant, Fulminate, Gasohol, Gelatine, Gelignite, Glottal stop, Grenade, Guncotton, Gunpaper, Gunpowder, HE, High, Initiator, Iracund, Jelly, Landmine, Low, Lyddite, Megaton, Melinite, Mine, Nail-bomb, Napalm, Nitre, Nitro(glycerine), Nitrobenzene, Nitrocotton, Outburst, Ozonide, Paravane, Payload, Petar(d), Petre, Phreatic, Phut, Plastic, Plastique, Pluff, Pop, Population, Pow, Priming, Propellant, Ptarmic, Pustular, Report, Roburite, SAM, Saucisse, Semtex®, Sheet, Shrapnel, Snake, Sneeze, Soup, Squib, Supernova, TATP, Tetryl, Thermite, Thunderflash, Tinderbox, TNT, Tonite, Trinitrobenzene, Trotyl, Volatile, Volcanic, Warhead, Xyloidin(e)

Exploit(ation), Exploiter, Exploiting, Exploits Act, Adventure, Arbitrage, Coup, Coyote, Deed, Develop, Escapade, Feat, Freeloader, Gest, Geste, Harness, Ill-use, Impose, Kulak, Manoeuvre, Milk, Mine, Mission, Misuse, Parlay, Play on, Predatory, Profit, Rachmanism, Ramp, Res gestae, Rip-off, Shark, Stunt, Sweat, Tap, Use, Utilise

Explore(r), Exploration Bandeirante, Chart, Discover, Dredge, Examine, Feel, Field trip, Investigate, Map, Navigator, Pathfinder, Pioneer, Potholer, Probe, Research, Scout, Search, Spaceship, Voyageur

EXPLORERS

3 letters:		Drake	6 letters:
Fox	Park	Fuchs	Baffin
	Ross	Giles	Balboa
4 letters:		Oates	Bering
Byrd	5 letters:	Parry	Burton
Cook	Baker	Peary	Cabral
Dias	Banks	Ponce	Cortes
Diaz	Boone	Scott	Da Gama
Eric	Burke	Speke	Darwin
Eyre	Cabot	Sturt	De Soto
Grey	Clark	Wills	Lawson
	David		

Nansen	Fiennes	Humboldt	*10 letters:*
Ralegh	Hillary	Magellan	Przewalski
Rhodes	Raleigh	Mitchell	Shackleton
Sabine	Stanley	Vespucci	
Stuart			*11 letters:*
Tasman	*8 letters:*	*9 letters:*	Leif Ericson
	Amundsen	Champlain	Livingstone
7 letters:	Columbus	Frobisher	Vasco da Gama
Amerigo	Cousteau	Mackenzie	
Barents	Eriksson	Marco Polo	*14 letters:*
Cartier	Flinders	Mungo Park	Bellingshausen
Cordoba	Franklin	Vancouver	
Dampier	Hargrave	Wentworth	

▷ **Explosive** *may indicate* an anagram

Exponent Advocate, Example, Index, Interpreter, Logarithm

Export(s) Despatch, Frustrated, Invisible, Klondike, Klondyke, Ship, Visible

Expose(d), Exposure Adamic, Air, Anagogic, Bare, Bleak, Blot, Blow, Burn, Crucify, Debag, Debunk, Denude, Desert, Disclose, Double, Endanger, En prise, Exhibit, Flashing, Glareal, Indecent, Insolate, Liable, Moon, Nail, Nude, Object, Open, Out, Over, Paramo, Propale, Reveal, Showdown, Snapshot, Starkers, Streak, Strip, Subject, Sun, Time, Uncover, Unmask, Unrip, Unshroud, Windburn, Windswept

Exposition Aperçu

Expostulate, Expostulation Argue, Arrah, Protest, Remonstrate

Expound(er) Discourse, Discuss, Exegete, Explain, Open, Prelict, Red, Scribe, Ulema

Express(ed), Expression, Expressionism, Expressive Abstract, Air, APT, Arrah, Aspect, Breathe, Cacophemism, Circumbendibus, Cliché, Colloquialism, Conceive, Concetto, Couch, Countenance, Crumbs, Declare, Denote, Eloquent, Embodiment, Epithet, Estafette, Explicit, Face, Fargo, Flying Scotsman, Formulate, Function, Godspeed, Good-luck, Gotcha, Gup, Hang-dog, Hech, Heck, Hell's bells, Idiom, Isit, Limited, Locution, Lyrical, Manifest, Metonym, Mien, Mot (juste), Neologism, Non-stop, Orient, Paraphrase, Phrase, Pleonasm, Pony, Precise, Pronouncement, Pronto, Put, Quep, Rapid, Register, Say(ne), Shade, Show, Soulful, → **SPEAK**, State, Strain, Succus, Sumpsimus, Taxeme, Term, Token, Tone, Topos, Trope, Utterance, Vent, → **VOICE**

Expressionless Aphasia, Blank, Boot-faced, Deadpan, Glassy, Impassive, Inscrutable, Po(ker)-faced, Vacant, Wooden

Expressman Fargo

Expropriate Dispossess, Pirate, Seize, Usurp

Expulsion Abjection, Discharge, Eccrisis, Ejection, Eviction, Exile, Pride's Purge, Removal, Sacking, Synaeresis

Expunge Cancel, Delete, Efface, Erase, Obliterate

Expurgate Bowdlerize, Castrate, Censor, Purge

Exquisite Beautiful, Choice, Ethereal, Fine, Intense, Lair, Macaroni, Pink, Princox, Refined, Soigné(e), Too-too

Ex-serviceman Vet

Extempore, Extemporise(d) Ad lib, Autoschediasm, Improvise, Pong

Extend(ed), Extension Add, Aggrandise, Aspread, Augment, Conservative, Cremaster, Dendrite, Draw, Drop-leaf, Ecarté, Eke, Elapse, Ell, Elongate, Enlarge, Escalate, Expand, Exsert, Extrapolation, Fermata, Grow, Increase, Jumboise, Lanai, Leaf, Length, Long, Long-range, Long-stay, Long-term, Offer, Outgrowth, Overbite, Overlap, Pong, Porrect, Proffer, Prolong, Propagate, Protract, Reach, Renew, Retrochoir, Span, Spread, Steso, → **STRETCH**, Substantial, Vert, Widen

Extensive, Extent Acre, Ambit, Area, Capacious, Catch-all, Compass, Comprehensive, Degree, Distance, Duration, Far-reaching, Large, Latitude, Length, Limit,

→ **MAGNITUDE**, Outspread, Panoramic, Range, Reach, Scale, Scope, Size, Spacious, Span, Spread-eagle, Sweeping, Wholesale, Wide, Widespread

Extenuate Diminish, Lessen, Mitigate, Palliate

Exterior Aspect, Crust, Derm, Exoteric, Facade, Outer, → **OUTSIDE**, Shell, Surface, Veneer

Exterminate, Extermination Abolish, Annihilate, Destroy, Ethnocide, Holocaust, The final solution, Uproot

External Exoteric, Exterior, Extraneous, Foreign, Outer

Extinct(ion) Archaeopteryx, Bucardo, Bygone, Chalicothere, Creodont, Dead, Death, Defunct, D(e)inothere, Dodo, Oblivion, Obsolete, Ostracoderm, Placoderm, Quagga, Quietus, Rasure, Rhytina, Saururae, Theodont

Extinguish Douse, Dout, Dowse, Dowt, Extirpate, Obscure, Quash, Quell, Quench, Slake, Slo(c)ken, Smother, Snuff, Stamp out, Stifle, Suppress

Extirpate End, Erase, Excise, Obliterate, Root, Uproot

Extol Commend, Enhance, Eulogise, Exalt, Laud, Praise, Puff

Extort(ion), Extortionate, Extortioner Barathrum, Blackmail, Bleed, Bloodsucker, Chantage, Chout, Churn, Compel, Exact, Force, Gombeen, Malversation, Montem, Outwrest, Rachman, Rack, Racketeer, Ransom, Rapacious, Screw, Shank, Sokaiya, Squeeze, Sweat, Urge, Vampire, Wrest, Wring

Extra Accessory, Additament, Addition(al), Additive, Adjunct, And, Annexe, Attachment, Bisque, Bonus, By(e), Codicil, Debauchery, Encore, Etcetera, Frill, Further, Gash, Lagniappe, Left-over, Leg bye, Make-weight, Mo, More, Nimiety, No ball, Odd, Optional, Out, Over, Overtime, Perk, Plus, Plusage, Reserve, Ripieno, → **SPARE**, Spilth, Staffage, Sundry, Super, Superadd, Supernumerary, Supplementary, Suppletive, Surplus, Top up, Trop, Undue, Walking-gentleman, Walking-lady, Wide, Woundy

Extract(ion), Extractor Apozem, Bleed, Breeding, Catechu, Clip, Corkscrew, Decoction, Descent, Distil, Draw, Educe, Elicit, Emulsin, Enucleate, Essence, Estreat, Excerpt, Exodontics, Extort, Gist, Gobbet, Insulin, Kino, Liebig, Liver, Malta, Milk, Mine, Oust, Parentage, Passage, Pericope, Pick, Piece, Pituitary, Prize, Pry, Pyrene, Pyrethrin, Quintessence, Quotation, Render, Retour, Smelt, Snippet, Soundbite, Squeeze, Stope, Succus, Suck, Summary, Tap, Tincture, Trie, Try, Vanilla, Vegemite®, Ventouse, Winkle, Worm, Wring, Yohimbine

Extradition Renvoi

Extraneous Extrinsic, Foreign, Irrelevant, Outlying, Spurious

Extraordinary Amazing, By-ordinar, Case, Curious, Egregious, Humdinger, Important, Nonesuch, Phenomenal, Preternatural, Rare, Signal, Singular, Sorter, Startling, Strange, Unusual

Extrasensory Clairaudience, Clairvoyance, → **ESP**

Extra time Lean

Extravagance, Extravagant, Extravaganza Bizarre, Bombastic, Dissipation, Elaborate, Enthusiasm, Excessive, Fancy, Feerie, Flamboyant, Glitzy, Heroic, High-flown, High roller, Hyperbole, Immoderate, Lavish, Luxury, Outré, Prodigal, Profligate, Profuse, Rampant, Reckless, Riotise, Romantic, Splash, Splurge, Squander, Sumptuous, Superfluous, Waste

Extreme(s), Extremely, Extremist, Extremity Acute, All-fired, Almighty, Bourn(e), Butt, Crisis, Deep-dyed, Desperate, Die-hard, Digit, Drastic, Edge, Ending, Exceptional, Farthermost, Finger(-tip), Gross, In spades, → **INTENSE**, Jacobin, Limb, Limit, Major, Maximum, Mega-, Merveilleux, Militant, Minimum, Mondo, National Front, Nazi, Opposite, OTT, Outrance, Over the top, Parlous, Pole, Pretty, Radical, Remote, Root and branch, Solstice, Steep, Sublime, Tendency, Terminal, The last cast, Thule, Tip, Toe, Too, Tremendous, Ultimate, Ultima thule, Ultra, Unco, Utmost, Utter(ance), → **VERY**, Violent, Vitally, Wing

▷ **Extreme** *may indicate* a first or last letter

Extricate Liberate, Loose, Outwind, Rescue, Untangle

Extrinsic Aliunde, External, Irrelevant, Outward

Extrovert Lad, Outgoing

Extrude Debar, Eject, Project

Exuberance, Exuberant Brio, Copious, Ebullient, Effusive, Feisty, Flamboyant, Gleeful, Gusto, Hearty, Joie de vivre, Lavish, Mad, Overflowing, Profuse, Rambunctious, Rumbustious, Skippy, Streamered

Exudation, Exude Bleed, Ectoplasm, Emit, Extravasate, Guttate, Ooze, Secrete, Still, Sweat, Swelter, Ulmin, Weep

Exult(ant) Crow, Elated, → **GLOAT**, Glorify, Jubilant, Paeonic, Rejoice, Tripudiate, Triumphant, Whoop

Eye(d), Eyes, Eye-ball, Eyeful, Eye movement, Eyepiece Aperture, Beady, Canthus, Compound, Cringle, Deepset, Eagle, Ee, Eine, Electric, Emmetropia, Evil, Glad, Glass, Glim, Glom, Goggles, Hurricane, Huygen's, Iridal, Iris, Jack, Keek, Klieg, Lamp, Lazy, Leer, Lens, London, Magic, Many, Mincepie, Mind's, Mongoloid, Naked, → **OBSERVE**, Ocellar, Ocular, Ogle, Ommateum, Ommatidium, Optic, Orb, Pedicel, Peeper, PI, Pigsnie, Pigsn(e)y, Pineal, Private, Public, Pupil, Regard, Retina, Rhabdom, Roving, Saccade, Saucer, Sclera, Screw, Seeing, Sheep's, Shufti, Shufty, Sight, Spy, Stemma, Storm-centre, Tec, Third, Uvea, Watch, Water-pump, Weather, Whally, Windows, Winker

Eyebright Euphrasy

Eyebrow Bree, Brent-hill, Glib, Penthouse, Superciliary

Eyeglass Loupe

Eyelash Cilium, Winker

Eyelet Cringle, Grommet, Hole

Eyelid Canthus, Ectropion, Haw, Palpebral, Winker

Eye-opener, Eye-opening Revelatory

Eye-rod Rhabdom

Eye-shadow Kohl

Eyesore Blot, Carbuncle, Disfigurement, Sty(e)

Eye-stalk Ommatophore, Stipes

Eye trouble Albugo, Amblyopia, Ametropia, Anirida, Aniseikonia, Anisomatropia, Aphakia, Asthenopia, Astigmatism, Caligo, Cataract, Ceratitis, Coloboma, Cycloplegia, Detached retina, Diplopia, Ectropion, Ectropium, Entropion, Erythropsia, Exophthalmus, Glaucoma, Gravel-blind, Hemeralopia, Hemi(an)op(s)ia, Heterotropia, Hypermetropia, Hyperopia, Iritis, Keratitis, Lazy eye, Leucoma, Lippitude, Micropsia, Miosis, Monoblepsis, Muscae volitantes, Mydriasis, Myosis, Nebula, Nyctalopia, Nystagmus, Ommateum, Palinop(s)ia, Pearl eye, Photophobia, Photopsia, Pin and web, Pink-eye, Presbyopia, Proptosis, Ptosis, Retinitis, Retinoblastoma, Sandy blight, Scotoma(ta), Shiner, Stigmatism, Strabismus, Strephosymbolia, Strong, Stye, Synechia, Teichopsia, Thylose, Thylosis, Trachoma, Trichiasis, Tritanopia, Tylosis, Wall-eye, Xeroma, Xerophthalmia

Eye-wash Collyrium

Eyrie Nest

Ezra Pound

Ff

F Fahrenheit, Fellow, Feminine, Fluorine, Following, Force, Foxtrot
Fab Super
Fabian, Fabius Dilatory, Washington, Webb
Fable(s) Aesop, Allegory, Apologue, Exemplum, Fiction, Hitopadesa, La Fontaine, Legend, Lie, Marchen, Milesian, Myth, Panchatantra, Parable, Romance, Tale, Tarand
Fabric Acetate, → CLOTH, Contexture, Dévoré, Evenweave, Framework, Interfacing, Interlining, Orlon®, Plissé, Ripstop, Spandex, Stretch-knit, Textile, Velour
Fabricate, Fabrication Artefact, Concoct, Construct, Contrive, Cook, Fake, Fangle, Figment, Forge, → INVENT, Lie, Make up, Porky, Trump, Weave, Web
Fabulous (beast), Fabulous place Ace, Apocryphal, Apologue, Atlantis, Chichevache, Chimera, Cockatrice, Eldorado, Fictitious, Fung, Gear, Griffin, Hippogriff, Hippogryph, Huma, Incredible, Jabberwock(y), Kylin, Legendary, Magic, Manticora, Manticore, Merman, Monoceros, Mythical, Opinicus, Orc, Phoenix, Roc, Romantic, Simorg, Simurg(h), Snark, Sphinx, Tarand, Tragelaph, Unicorn, Unreal, Utopia, Wivern, Wyvern, Yale
Facade Front(age), Frontal, Mask, Persona, Pretence
Face, Facing Abide, Affront, Ashlar, Ashler, Aspect, Audacity, Bide, Bold, Brave, Brazen, Caboched, Caboshed, Cheek, Chiv(v)y, Cliff, Coal, Confront, Countenance, Culet, Dalle, Dare, Dartle, Deadpan, Dial, Eek, Elevation, Encounter, Facade, Fat, Favour, Features, Fineer, Fortune, → FRONT, Gardant, Girn, Gonium, Grid, Groof, Groue, Grouf, Grufe, Gurn, Hatchet, Head-on, Jib, Kisser, Light, Lining, Look, Lore, Mascaron, Meet, Metope, Moe, Mug, Mush, Obverse, Oppose, Opposite, Outstare, Outward, Pan, Paper tiger, Pavilion, Phisnomy, Phiz(og), Physiognomy, Poker, Puss, Revet, Revetment, Roughcast, Rud, Rybat, Side, Snoot, Socle, Straight, Stucco, Tallow, Three-quarter, Type, Veneer, Vis(age), Visnomy, Wall, Withstand, Zocco(lo)
Face-ache Noli-me-tangere
Face-lift Rhytidectomy
Face-saving Redeeming, Salvo
Facet(ed) Angle, Aspect, Bezel, Culet, Face, Pavilion, Polyhedron
Facetious Frivolous, Jocose, Jocular, Waggish, Witty
Facile Able, Adept, Complaisant, Ductile, Easy, Fluent, Glib
Facilitate, Facilities, Facility Amenity, Assist, Benefit, Bent, Capability, Committed, → EASE, Expedite, Fluency, Gift, ISO, Knack, Lavatory, Loo, Provision, Skill
Facsimile Copy, Electro, Electrotype, Photostat®, Replica, Repro
Fact(s), Factual Actual, Brass tacks, Case, Corpus delicti, Correct, Data, Datum, Detail, Eo ipso, French, Gospel, Griff, In esse, Info, Information, Literal, Mainor, Material, Nay, Poop, Really, Stat, Statistics, Truism, Truth, Veridical, Yes
Faction Bloc, Cabal, Camp, Caucus, Clique, Contingent, Ghibelline, Group, Guelph, Junto, Party, Red Army, Schism, Sect, Tendency, Wing
Factor(s) Agent, Aliquot, Broker, Cause, Chill, Clotting, Coagulation, Co-efficient, Common, → COMPONENT, Divisor, Edaphic, Element, F, Feedback, Feel-bad, Feel-good, Fertility, Growth, House, Imponderabilia, Institorial, Intrinsic, Judicial, Load, Modulus, Multiple, Power, Pull, Q, Quality, Reflection, Representative, Rh, Rhesus, Risk, Safety, Sex, Steward, Transfer, Unit, Utilization, Wind chill, X
Factory Ashery, Bakery, Brickworks, Cannery, Etruria, Gasworks, Glassworks, Hacienda, Ironworks, Maquiladora, Mill, Plant, Refinery, Sawmill, Shot tower, Steelworks, Sugarhouse, Sweatshop, Tanyard, Tinworks, Wireworks, Works, Workshop

Factotum Circar, Handyman, Servant, Sircar, Sirkar
Faculty Aptitude, Arts, Capacity, Department, Ear, Ease, Indult, Knack, Lavatory, Loo, Moral, Power, School, Sense, Speech, → **TALENT**, Teachers, Uni(versity), Wits
Fad(dish) Crank, Craze, Cult, Fashion, Foible, Ismy, Thing, Vogue, Whim
Fade(d), Fading Blanch, Die, Diminuendo, Dinge, Disperse, Elapsion, Etiolate, Evanescent, Fall, Filemot, Lessen, Mancando, Miffy, Pale, Passé, Perdendo(si), Peter, Smorzando, Smorzato, Stonewashed, Vade, Vanish, Wallow, Wilt, Wither
Faeces Cesspit, Dingleberry, Dung, Kak, Meconium, Motion, Mute, Number two, Scybalum, Skatole, Stercoraceous, Stools
Fag(ging) Chore, Cigarette, Drag, Drudge, Fatigue, Gasper, Homosexual, Menial, Pennalism, Quean, Reefer, Snout, Tire, Toil, Weary
Fag-end Ash, Butt, Dout, Lag, Snipe, Stub
Fag(g)ot(s) Bavin, Bundle, Fascine, Firewood, Homosexual, Kid, Knitch, Twigs
Fail(ing), Failure Achalasia, Ademption, Anile, Anuria, Awry, Backfire, Blemish, Blow, Bomb, Bummer, Burst-up, Cark, Chicken, → **COLLAPSE**, Common-mode, Conk, Crack up, Crash, Cropper, Debacle, Decline, Defalcation, Default, Defeat, Defect, Demerit, Demise, Die, Dog, Down the tubes, Dry, Dud, Fatigue, Fault, Feal, Fiasco, Fink out, Flame out, Flivver, Flop, Flow, Flunk, Fold, Founder, Frost, Glitch, Goner, Go phut, Gutser, Impotent, Infraction, Isn't, Lapse, Lemon, Lose, Lossage, Malfunction, Manqué, Meltdown, Mis-, Miscarry, Misfire, Misprision, Miss, Muff, Nerd, No-hoper, No-no, No-show, Omission, Omit, Outage, Oversight, Pip, Plough, Plow, Pluck, Pratfall, Reciprocity, Refer, Refusal, Respiratory, Shambles, Short(coming), Short circuit, Shortfall, Sink, Slippage, Smash, Spin, Stumer, Tank, Turkey, Vice, Wash-out, Waterloo, Weakness, White elephant, Wipeout
Fain Lief
Faineant Gallio
Faint(ness) Black-out, Conk, Darkle, Dim, Dizzy, Dwalm, Fade, Giddy, Lassitude, Pale, Stanck, Swarf, Swarve, Swelt, Swerf, Swerve, Swoon, Swound, Syncope, Unclear, Wan, Whitish
Faint-heart Boneless, Coward, Craven, Eery, Hen, Timid, Wet
Fair Adequate, Aefauld, Aefwld, A(e)fald, Barnet, Bartholomew, Bazaar, Beauteous, Beautiful, Belle, Blond, Bon(n)ie, Bonny, Brigg, Clement, Decent, Dishy, Donnybrook, Eirian, Equal, Equitable, Evenhanded, Exhibition, Expo(sition), Fancy, Feeing-market, → **FESTIVAL**, Fête, Fine, Fiona, Funfair, Gaff, Gala, Gay, Gey, Goose, Gwyn, Hiring, Honest, Hopping, Isle, Isold(e), → **JUST**, Kermesse, Kermis, Kirmess, Light, Market, Mart, Mediocre, Mela, Mop, Nundinal, Objective, OK, Paddington, Passable, Play, Pro rata, Rosamond, Sabrina, So-so, Sporting, Sportsmanlike, Square, Statute, Steeple, Straight, Tavistock, Tidy, Tolerable, Tow-headed, Trade, Tryst, Unbias(s)ed, Vanity, Wake, Widdicombe, Xanthe
Fair-buttocked Callipygean
Fairing Ornament, Spat
Fairly Clearly, Enough, Evenly, Midway, Moderately, Pari passu, Pretty, Properly, Quite, Ratherish, So-so
Fairway Dog-leg, Pretties
Fairy, Fairies Banshee, Befana, Brownie, Cobweb, Dobbie, Dobby, Elf(in), Fay, Gloriana, Good neighbour, Good people, Hob, Hop o' my thumb, Leprechaun, Lilian, Little people, Mab, Morgane(tta), Morgan le Fay, Moth, Mustardseed, Nis, Oberon, Peri, Pigwidgin, Pigwiggen, Pisky, Pixie, Pouf, Puck, Punce, Queen Mab, Sandman, Seelie, Sidhe, Spirit, Sprite, Sugar-plum, Tink(erbell), Titania, Tooth, Unseelie, Urchin-shows
Faith(ful) Accurate, Achates, Belief, Constant, Creed, Cupboard, Devoted, Doctrine, Faix, Fay, Feal, Fegs, Fideism, Fiducial, Haith, Implicit, Islam, Lay, Liege, Loyal, Pantheism, Plerophory, Punic, Puritanism, Quaker, Reliance, Religion, Shahada, Shema, Solifidian, Staunch, Strict, Troth, → **TRUE**, True-blue, Trust, Truth, Umma(h), Vera
Faithless Atheist, Disloyal, False, Giaour, Hollow, Infidel, Nullifidian, Perfidious, Punic

Fake(d), Faker, Faking Bodgie, Bogus, Charlatan, Cod, Copy, Counterfeit, Duff(er), Ersatz, False, Fold, Forgery, Fraud, Fudge, Imitation, Imposter, Impostor, Paste, Phoney, Pirate(d), Postiche, Pretend, Pseudo, Sham, Spurious, Straw man, Toy, Trucage, Trumped up, Truquage, Truqueur, Unreal

Falcon Cast, Gentle, Hawk, Hobby, Iceland, Kestrel, Lanner(et), Merlin, Nankeen kestrel, Nyas, Peregrine, Prairie, Saker, Sakeret, Spar-hawk, Sparrow-hawk, Stallion, Staniel, Stannel, Stanyel, Stone, Tassel-gentle, Tassell-gent, Tercel-gentle, Tercel-jerkin

Falklander Kelper

Fall(s), Fallen, Falling, Fall out Abate, Accrue, Alopecia, Angel, Anticlimax, Arches, Astart, Autumn, Boyoma, Cadence, Caducous, Cascade, Cataract, Churchill, Chute, Collapse, Crash, Cropper, Cross press, Declension, Decrease, Degenerate, Descent, Dip, Domino effect, Douse, Downswing, Dowse, → **DROP**, Ebb, Firn, Flag, Flop, Flump, Folding press, Free, Grabble, Grand, Gutser, Gutzer, Horseshoe, Idaho, Iguaçu, Incidence, Kabalega, Kaieteur, Keel over, Lag, Landslide, Lapse, Lin(n), Montmorency, Mtarazi, Niagara, Oct(ober), Onding, Overbalance, Owen, Perish, Plonk, Plummet, Plump, Plunge, Precipitance, Prolapse, Ptosis, Purl(er), Rain, Reaction, Relapse, Ruin, Season, Sheet, Sin, Sleet, Slide, Slip, Snow, Soss, Spill, Stanley, Sutherland, Swallow, Tailor, Takakkau, Topple, Toss, Trip, Tugela, Tumble, Victoria, Voluntary, Wipeout, Yellowstone, Yosemite

Fallacious, Fallacy Elench(us), Error, Gamblers', Idolon, Idolum, Ignoratio elenchi, Illogical, Illusion, Material, Naturalistic, Pathetic, Sophism, Specious, Unsound

Fallible Human, Imperfect

▷ **Falling** *may indicate* an anagram or a word backwards

Fallow Barren, Lea, Tan, Uncared, Uncultivated, Untilled

False, Falsify, Falsification, Falsehood Adulterate, Assumed, Bastard, Bodgie, Bogus, Braide, Bricking, Bum, Calumny, Canard, Cavil, Charlatan, Cook, Counterfeit, Deceitful, Disloyal, Dissemble, Doctor, Façade, Fake, Feigned, Fiddle, Forge, Illusory, Knave, Lying, Meretricious, Misconception, Mock, Mooncalf, Myth, Obreption, Perjury, Pinchbeck, Postiche, Pretence, Pseudo, Rap, Refute, Roorback, Sham, Specious, Spoof, Spurious, Strumpet, Treacherous, Trumped-up, Two-faced, Untrue, Veneer

False notions Idola

Falter Hesitate, Limp, Lurch, Stoiter, Totter, Waver

Fame, Famous A-list, All-star, Bruit, Cause célèbre, Celebrity, Distinguished, Eminent, Five, Glitterati, Gloire, Glory, Greatness, History, Humour, Illustrious, Known, Kudos, Legendary, Luminary, Luminous, Megastar, Mononym, Name, Noted, Notorious, Prestige, Reclamé, Renown, Repute, Robert, Rumour, Splendent, Spotlight, Spur, Stardom, Word

Familiar(ise), Familiarity Accustom, Acquaint, Assuefaction, Au fait, Auld, Chummy, Comrade, Consuetude, Conversant, Couth, Crony, Dear, Demon, Easy, Free, Fresh, Friend, Habitual, Homely, Homey, Incubus, Intimate, Known, Liberty, Maty, Old, Old-hat, Privy, Python, Streetwise, Used, Versant, Versed, Warhorse

Family Ainga, Ancestry, Bairn-team, Blood, Breed, Brood, Clan, Class, Close-knit, Cognate, Consanguine, County, Descent, Dynasty, Extended, Eye, Hapsburg, House(hold), Issue, Kin, Kind, Kindred, Line, Mafia, Medici, Name, Nuclear, One-parent, Orange, People, Phratry, Progeny, Quiverful, Race, Roots, Sept, Sib(b), Sibship, Single-parent, Stem, Stirps, Storge, Strain, Sub-order, Syndyasmian, Taffy, Talbot, Totem, Tribe, Whanau

Family tree Pedigree, Stemma

Famine Dearth, Lack, Scarcity

Famish(ed) Esurient, Hungry, Ravenous, Starving

▷ **Famished** *may indicate* an 'o' in the middle of a word

Fan(s), Fan-like Adherent, Admirer, Aficionado, Alligator, Alluvial, Arouse, Bajada, Barmy-army, B-boy, Blow, Cat, Clapper, Claque, Colmar, Cone, Cool, Cuscus, Devotee, Diadrom, Dryer, Ducted, Enthusiast, Extractor, Fiend, Flabellum, Following, Goth, Grebo, Groupie, Groupy, Headbanger, Hepcat, Khuskhus, Muso, Nut, Outspread,

Partisan, Popette, Propellor, Public, Punka(h), Rhipidate, Ringsider, Rooter, Sail, Spectator, Spread, Supporter, Tail, Tartan army, Tifosi, Trekkie, Ventilate, Votary, Voteen, Washingtonia, Wind machine, Wing, Winnow, Zealot, Zelant

▷ **Fan** *may indicate* an anagram

Fanatic(al) Bigot, Boatie, Devotee, Energumen, Enthusiastic, Extremist, Fiend, Frenetic, Glutton, Mad, Maniac, Nut, Partisan, Phrenetic, Picard, Rabid, Santon, Ultra, Workaholic, Wowser, Zealot

Fancy, Fancies, Fanciful Caprice, Chim(a)era, Conceit, Concetto, Crotchet, Daydream, Dream, Dudish, Elaborate, Fangle, Fantasy, Fit, Flam, Florid, Flowery, Frilly, Frothy, Guess, Hallo, Idea(te), Idolon, → **IMAGINE**, Inclination, I say, Itch, Lacy, Liking, Maggot, Maya, Mind, My, Nap, Notion, Opine, Ornamental, Ornate, Petit four, Picture, Pipe dream, Predilection, Preference, Reverie, Rococo, Suppose, Thought, Unreal, Urge, Vagary, Visionary, Ween, Whigmaleerie, Whigmaleery, Whim(sy), Woolgather

▷ **Fancy** *may indicate* an anagram

Fane Banner, Pronaos

Fanfare Flourish, Sennet, Show, Tantara, Trump, Tucket

Fang Tooth, Tusk

Fanny Adams, Bottom, Gas-lit, Price

Fantasist, Fantasy, Fantastic Absurd, Amazing, Antic, Bizarre, Brilliant, Caprice, Centaur, Chimera, Cloud-cuckoo land, Cockaigne, Cockayne, Escapism, Fab, Fanciful, First class, Grotesque, Hallucination, Idol, Idola, Illusion, Kickshaw(s), Lucio, Make believe, Mega, Myth, Outré, Phantasmagoria, Pipe-dream, Queer, Reverie, Romance, Schizoid, Transcendent, Unreal, Untrue, Walter Mitty, Wannabe(e), → **WHIM**, Whimsical, Wild, Wishful thinking, Wuxia

Far Apogean, Away, Distal, Distant, Eloi(g)n, Extreme, Outlying, Remote, Thether, Thither

Farce(ur), Farcical Burletta, Charade, Comedy, Exode, Feydeau, Lazzo, Mime, Mockery, Pantomime, Risible, Rix, Screaming, Sham, Travesty

Fare Apex, Charge, Cheer, Commons, Do, Eat, Excess, Excursion, → **FOOD**, Go, Passage, Passage money, Passenger, Rate, Saver, Table, Traveller

Farewell Adieu, Adios, Aloha, Apopemptic, Bye, Cheerio, Departure, Godspeed, → **GOODBYE**, Leave, Prosper, Sayonara, Send off, So long, Toodle-oo, Toodle-pip, Totsiens, Vale, Valediction

Far-fetched Fanciful, Improbable, Recherché

Farm(ing), Farmhouse Agronomy, Arable, Bender, Bocage, Bowery, City, Cold Comfort, Collective, Cooperative, Croft, Cultivate, Dairy, Deep-litter, Dry, Emmerdale, Estancia, Extensive, Factory, Fat, Fish(ery), Funny, Geoponical, Grange, Hacienda, Health, Home, Homestead, Husbandry, Intensive, Kibbutz, Kolkhoz, Land, Ley, Loaf, Location, Mailing, Mains, Mas, Mixed, No-tillage, Onstead, Orley, Oyster, Pen, Plaas, Plough, Poultry, Ranch, Render, Rent, Set-aside, Sewage, Shamba, Sheep station, Smallholding, Sovkhoz, Station, Stead(ing), Sted(d), Stedde, Steed, Stock, Store, Stump, Subsistence, Tank, Till, Toon, Toun, Town, Trash, Tree, Trout, Truck, Wick, Wind

Farmer Blockie, Boer, Campesino, Carl, Cockatoo, Cocklaird, Cocky, Collins Street, Colon, Cow cocky, Crofter, Estanciero, Gebur, Gentleman, George, Giles, Hick, Hobby, Husbandman, Macdonald, Metayer, Nester, NFU, Peasant, Pitt Street, Publican, Queen St, Rancher, Reaper, Ryot, Share-cropper, Smallholder, Sodbuster, Squatter, Stubble-jumper, Tax, Tenant, Tiller, Whiteboy, Yeoman, Zeminda(r)

Farmhand Cadet, Churl, Cottar, Cotter, Cottier, Cowman, Ditcher, Hand, He(a)rdsman, Hind, Land girl, Orraman, Peon, Ploughman, Redneck, Rouseabout, Roustabout, Shearer, Sheepo, Stockman, Swineherd, Thresher

▶ **Farmhouse** *see* **FARM(ING)**

Farmyard Barton, Homestall, Villatic

Faroe Islands FO

Farouche Awkward, Shy, Sullen

Farrago Hotch-potch, Jumble, Medley, Mélange

Farrier Marshal, Smith

Farrow Litter, Mia, Sow

Far-sighted Presbyte

Fart Poep, Trump

Farthing Brass, F, Fadge, Har(r)ington, Mite, Q, Quadragesimal, Rag

Fascia Band, Fillet, Platband

Fascinate(d), Fascinating, Fascinator Allure, Attract, Bewitch, → CHARM, Dare, Enchant, Engross, Enrapt, Enthral(l), Fetching, Inthral, Into, Intrigue, Jolie laide, Kill, Mesmeric, Rivet, Sexy, Siren, Witch

Fascist Blackshirt, Blue shirt, Brownshirt, Dictator, Falange, Falangist, Iron Guard, Lictor, Nazi, Neo-Nazi, NF, Phalangist, Rexist, Sinarchist, Sinarquist

Fashion(able), Fashioned, Fashion house Aguise, À la (mode), Alta moda, Armani, Bristol, Build, Chic, Construct, Convention, Cool, Corinthian, Craze, Create, Cult, Custom, Cut, Dernier cri, Design, Directoire, Du jour, Elegant, Entail, Fabricate, Fad, Feat, Feign, Fly, Forge, Form, Garb, Genteel, Go, Hew, High, Hip, Hot, In, Invent, Kitsch, Look, → MAKE, Man-about-town, Manière, Manners, Method, Mode, Mondain(e), Mould, Newgate, Pink, Prada, Preppy, Rage, Rag trade, Rate, Roy, Sc, Shape, Smart, Smith, Snappy, Snazzy, Stile, Stylar, Style, Swish, Tailor, Ton, Tonish, Ton(e)y, → TREND(Y), Turn, Twig, Vogue, Waif, Way, Wear, Wise, With-it, Work, Wrought

Fast(ing), Faster Abstain, Apace, Ashura, Breakneck, Brisk, Citigrade, Clappers, Clem, Clinging, Cracking, Daring, Dharna, Dhurna, Double-quick, Elaphine, Express, Fizzer, Fleet, Hypersonic, Immobile, Lent, Lightning, Loyal, Maigre, Meteoric, Moharram, Muharram, Muharrem, Pac(e)y, Posthaste, Presto, Promiscuous, Pronto, Quadragesimal, Quick, Raffish, Raking, Ramadan, Ramadhan, Rash, Rathe, Relay, Sehri, Siyam, Spanking, Speedy, Stretta, Stretto, Stuck, Supersonic, Sure, Swift, Tachyon, Thick, Tight, Tisha b'Av, TishaBov, Tishah-Baav, Tishah-b(e)Ab, Tishah-b(e)Av, Whistle-stop, Xerophagy, Yarer, Yom Kippur

Fast and loose Fickle, Prick-the-garter, Strap-game

Fasten(er), Fastening Anchor, Attach, Bar, Belay, Belt, Bind, Bolt, Buckle, Button, Chain, Clamp, Clasp, Click, Clinch, Clip, Cramp, Cufflink, Dead-eye, Diamond-hitch, Dome, Espagnolette, Eye-bolt, Frog, Gammon, Hasp, Hesp, Hitch, Hook, Infibulation, Lace, Latch, Lock, Moor, Morse, Nail, Netsuke, Nip, Nut, Padlock, Parral, Patent, Pectoral, Pin, Preen, Press stud, Reeve, Rivet, Rope, Rove, Safety pin, Screw, Seal, → SECURE, Sew up, Shut, Spar, Sprig, Staple, Steek, Stitch, Strap, Suspender, Swift(er), Tach(e), Tag, Tape, Tassel, Tether, Thong, Tintack, Toggle, Twist-tie, U-bolt, Velcro®, Wedge, Zip

Fastidious Chary, Critical, Dainty, Fusspot, Fussy, Neat, Nice, Overnice, Particular, Picky, Precieuse, Precious, Purism, Quaint, Queasy, Quiddler, Rosewater, Squeamish

Fastness Bastille

Fat(s), Fatted, Fatten, Fatty Adipic, Adipocere, Adipose, Aldermanly, Aliphatic, Arcus, Atheroma, Bard, Batten, Battle, Blubber, Brown, Butter, Calf, Calipash, Calipee, Cellulite, Cholesterol, Chubbed, Chubby, Corpulent, Creesh, Curd, Degras, Deutoplasm, Dika-oil, Dosh, Dripping, Embonpoint, Enarm, Endomorph, Ester, Flab, Flesh, Flick, Fozy, Frank, Fubsy, Galam-butter, Grease, Gross, Keech, Kitchen-fee, Lanolin, Lard, Lard-ass, Leaf, Lipaemia, Lipid, Lipoma, Love handles, Margarine, Marge, Marrow, Mart, Moti, Motu, Obese, Oil, Olein, Oleomargarine, Olestra, OS, Palmitin, Pinguid, Plump, Poddy, Podgy, Polyunsaturated, Portly, Pudgy, Puppy, Pursy, Rich, Rolypoly, Rotund, Saddlebags, Saginate, Saim, Saturated, Schmal(t)z, Seam(e), Sebacic, Sebum, Shortening, Soil, Spare tyre, Spe(c)k, Squab, Stearic, Steatopygia, Steatorrhea, Steatosis, Suberin, Suet, Tallow, Tin, Tomalley, Trans, Triglyceride, Tub, Unsaturated, Vanaspati, Waller, Well-padded, Wool

Fatal(ism), Fatality, Fate(s), Fated, Fateful Apnoea, Atropos, Cavel, Chance, Clotho, Deadly, Death, Decuma, Destiny, Doom, End, Fay, Fell, Joss, Karma, Kismet, Lachesis, Lethal, Lethiferous, Loss, Lot, Meant, Moera(e), Moira, Morta, Mortal,

Mortiferous, Nemesis, Nona, Norn(a), Parca, Pernicious, Portion, Predestination, Skuld, Urd, Verdande, Waterloo, Weird, Weird sisters

Father(s), Fatherly Abba, Abbot, Abuna, Adopt, Agnation, Apostolic, Bapu, Begetter, Breadwinner, Brown, City, Conscript, Curé, Da, Dad, Engender, Foster, Founding, Fr, Generator, Genitor, Getter, Gov, Governor, Guv, Male, NASCAR dad, Pa, Padre, Papa, Pappy, Parent, Pater(nal), Paterfamilias, Patriarch, Patroclinic, Père, Pilgrim, Pop(pa), Popper, Priest, Rev, Seraphic, Sire, Stud, Thames, Tiber, William

Father-lasher Sea-scorpion

Fathom Delve, Depth, Dig, F, Plumb, Plummet, Understand

Fatigue(d) Battle, Bonk, Combat, Compassion, Exhaust, Fag, Jade, Jet lag, ME, Metal, Neurasthenia, Overdo, Overwatch, Swinked, Time-zone, Tire, Weariness, Weary

Fatuous Gaga, Idiotic, Inane, Silly, Stupid

Faucet Cock, Spigot, Tap

Fault(y), Fault-finding Arraign, Bad, Beam, Blame(worthy), Blunder, Bug, Cacology, Captious, Carp, Compound, Culpa, Culpable, Defect, Demerit, Dip, Dip-slip, Drop-out, Dud, Duff, → **ERROR**, Failing, Flaw, Foot, Frailty, Gall, Glitch, Gravity, Henpeck, Hitch, Impeach, Imperfect, Knock, Literal, Massif, → **MISTAKE**, Mortal sin, Nag, Nibble, Niggle, Nit-pick, Oblique, Oblique-slip, Out, Outcrop, Overthrust, Pan, Para, Peccadillo, Pre-echo, Quibble, Rate, Reprehend, Rift, Rupes Recta, San Andreas, Sclaff, Set-off, Short, Slip, Snag, Step, Strike, Strike-slip, Technical, Thrust, Trap, Trough, Underthrust, Upbraid, Vice

Faultless Immaculate, Impeccable, Lily-white, Perfect

Fauna Benthos, Mesobenthos, Wild life

Fauvist Matisse

Faux pas Blunder, Boner, Gaffe, Leglen-girth, Solecism

Favour(able), Favoured, Favourite Advance, Advantage(ous), Aggrace, Agraste, Alder-liefest, Anne, Approval, Auspicious, Aye, Back, Befriend, Behalf, Benign, Bless, Boon, Bribe, Cert, Chosen, Cockade, Condescend, Conducive, Countenance, Curry, Darling, Ewe lamb, Ex gratia, Fancy, Favonian, Form horse, Good turn, Grace, Gracioso, Graste, Gratify, Gree, Hackle, Hot, In, Indulge, Kickback, Minion, Nod, Odour, Optimal, Particular, Peat, Persona grata, Pet, Pettle, Popular, → **PREFER**, Promising, Propitious, Resemble, Rib(b)and, Roseate, Rose-knot, Rosette, Side, Smile, Toast, Token, White boy, White-headed, Win-win

Fawn(er), Fawning Adulate, Bambi, Beige, Blandish, Brown-nose, Camel, Crawl, Creep, Cringe, Deer, Ecru, Elaine, Flatter, Fleech, Footlick, Grovel, Ko(w)tow, Lickspittle, Obsequious, Servile, Slavish, Smarm, Smoo(d)ge, Subservient, Sycophant, Tasar, Toady, Truckle, Tussah, Tusseh, Tusser, Tussore

Fax Replica

Fay Fairy, Korrigan, Peri

Faze Unnerve

FBI G-men

Fear Aichmophobia, Angst, Apprehension, Astra(po)phobia, Awe, Bathophobia, Bête noire, Bugbear, Claustrophobia, Cold sweat, Crap, Creeps, Cyberphobia, Dismay, Doubt, Drad, Dread, Dromophobia, Ecophobia, Foreboding, → **FOR FEAR**, Fright, Funk, Genophobia, Hang-up, Horripilation, Horror, Kenophobia, Monophobia, Mysophobia, Nostopathy, Nyctophobia, Ochlophobia, Panic, → **PHOBIA**, Photophobia, Redoubt, Revere, Taphephobia, Taphophobia, Terror, Thalassophobia, Trepidation, Willies

Fearful Afraid, Cowardly, Dire, Horrific, Nervous, Pavid, Rad, Redoubtable, Timorous, Tremulous, Windy

Fearless Bold, Brave, Courageous, Daring, Gallant, Impavid, Intrepid, Proud, Unafraid

Fearsome Alarming, Dire, Formidable

Feasible Goer, Likely, On, Possible, Practical, Probable, Viable

Feast(s) Adonia, Agape, Assumption, Banquet, Barmecide, Beano, Belshazzar's, Blow-out, Candlemas, Carousal, Celebration, Convive, Dine, Do, Double, Eat, Encaenia,

Epiphany, Epulation, Festival, Fleshpots, Fool's, Gaudeamus, Gaudy, Hakari, Halloween, Hallowmas, Heortology, Hockey, Hogmanay, Holy Innocents, Id-al-Adha, Id-al-Fitr, Immaculate Conception, Ingathering, Isodia, Junket, Kai-kai, Lady Day, Lamb-ale, Lammas, Love, Luau, Luau, Lucullus, Martinmas, Michaelmas, Midnight, Movable, Noel, Passover, Pentecost, Pesach, Pig, Potlatch, Purim, Regale, Repast, Revel, Roodmas, Seder, Shindig, Spread, Succoth, Sukkot(h), Tabernacles, Trumpets, Tuck-in, Wake, Wayzgoose, Weeks, Yule, Zagmuk

Feast-day Mass

Feat Achievement, Deed, Effort, Exploit, Gambado, Handspring, Stunt, Trick

Feather(s), Feathered, Feather-star Aigrette, Alula, Barbicel, Boa, Braccate, Cock, Contour, Covert, Crinoid, Crissum, Down, Duster, Egret, Filoplume, Flags, Fledged, Fletch, Flight, Gemmule, Hackle, Harl, Hatchel, Herl, Lei, Lure, Macaroni, Manual, Oar, Ostrich, Pen(na), Pin, Pinna, Pith, Plumage, Plume, Plumule, Prince's, Pteryla, Ptilosis, → **QUILL**, Rectrix, Remex, Remiges, Rocket-tail, Saddle-hackle, Scapular, Scapus, Secondary, Semiplume, Shaft, Shag, Sickle, Standard, Stipa, Swansdown, Tail covert, Tectrix, Tertial, Tippet, Vibrissa, White, Wing covert

Feather-pate Man-milliner

Feather-worker Plumassier

Feature(s) Acoustic, Amenity, Appurtenance, Article, Aspect, Attribute, Brow, Character, Chin, Depict, Double, Eye, Eyebrow, Face, Facet, Figure, Fronton, Hallmark, Highlight, Item, Jizz, Landmark, Lineament, Neotery, Nose, Nucleus, Overfold, Phiz(og), Physiognomy, Signature, Snoot, Spandrel, Star, Temple, Topography, Touch, Trait, Underlip

Featureless Flat

Febrifuge Atabrin, Atebrin®, Mepacrine, Quina

February Fill-dyke

Fecund(ity) Fertile, Fruitful, Prolific, Uberty

Fed Agent, G-man

Federal, Federation Alliance, Axis, Bund, Commonwealth, Interstate, League, Russian, Solidarity, Statal, Union

Fee(s) Base, Bench, Capitation, Charge, Chummage, Commitment, Common, Conditional, Consideration, Consultation, Contingency, Corkage, Corporation, Drop-dead, Dues, Duty, Emolument, Entrance, Entry, Faldage, Fine, Great, Groundage, Hire, Honorarium, Interchange, Kill, Mortuary, Mouter, Obvention, Pay, Pierage, Premium, Ransom, Refresher, Retainer, Sub, Subscription, Transfer, Tribute

Feeble Banal, Characterless, Daidling, Debile, Decrepit, Droob, Effete, Feckless, Fizzenless, Flabby, Flaccid, Foisonless, Footling, Fragile, Fus(h)ionless, Geld, Ineffective, Infirm, Jessie, Limp, Mimsy, Namby-pamby, Pale, Puny, Rickety, Sassy, Sickly, Silly, Slender, Slight, Soppy, Tailor, Tame, Thin, Tootle, Unmanly, Wallydrag, Wallydraigle, Washy, Wastrel, Weak, Weak-kneed, Weak-minded, Weed, Weedy, Wersh, Wet, Wimpish, Worn

Feed(er), Feeding Battle, Bib, Break, Browse, Cake, Cater, Cibation, Clover, Cowfeteria, Cram, Cue, Demand, Diet, Dine, Dressing, Drip, → **EAT**, Fatten, Filter, Fire, Fishmeal, Flushing, Fodder, Food, Force, Gavage, Graze, Hay, Input, Intravenous, Line, Lunch, Meal, Nourish, Nurse, Paid, Pecten, Provender, Refect, Repast, Sate, Soil, Stoke, Stooge, Storer, Stover, Stuff, Suckle, Sustain, Tire, Tractor, Wean, Wet nurse

Feedback Negative, Positive

Feel(ingly), Feeling(s) Aesthesia, Affetuoso, Algesis, Angst, Animus, Artificial, À tâtons, Atmosphere, Ballottement, Compassion, Darshan, Déjà vu, → **EMOTION**, Empathy, Empfindung, Euphoria, → **EXPERIENCE**, Fellow, Finger, Flaw, Frisk, Grope, Groundswell, Handle, Hard, Heart, Heartstrings, Hunch, Intuit, Knock, Know, Palp, Passible, Passion, Phatic, Pity, Premonition, Presentiment, Probe, Realise, Sensate, Sensation, → **SENSE**, Sensitive, Sentiency, Sentiment, Somesthesis, Spirit, Sprachgefühl, Tactual, Tingle, Touch, Turn, Undercurrent, Vehemence, Vibes, Vibrations, Zeal

Feeler Antenna, Ballon d'essai, Barbel, Exploratory, Overture, Palp, Sensillum, Tentacle, Trial balloon

▶ **Feet** *see* **FOOT(ING)**

Feign Act, Affect, Assume, Colour, Fake, Malinger, Mime, Mock, → **PRETEND**, Sham, Simulate

Feint Deke, Disguise, Dodge, Faint, Fake, Spoof, Trick

Felicity Bliss, Happiness, Joy, Relevance

▶ **Feline** *see* **CAT**

Fell Axe, Chop, Cruel, Cut down, Deadly, Dire, Dread, Fierce, Floor, Heath, Hew, Hide, Hill, Inhuman, Knock-down, KO, Lethal, Lit, Log, Malign, Moor, Pelt, Poleaxe, Ruthless, Sca, Shap, Skittle

Fellow(s), Fellowship Academic, Associate, Bawcock, Birkie, Bloke, Bo, Bro, Bucko, Buffer, Callan(t), Carlot, Cat, Chal, Chap(pie), Chi, China, Chum, Co, Cock, Cod(ger), Collaborator, Co-mate, Communion, Companion, Comrade, Confrère, Cove, Cully, Cuss, Dandy, Dean, Dog, Don, Dude, Equal, F, Fogey, Fop, Gadgie, Gadje, Gaudgie, Gauje, Gink, Guy, Joe, Joker, Josser, Kerel, Lad, Like, M, Mall, Man, Match, Mate, Member, Mister, Mun, Odd, Partner, Peer, Professor, Rival, Seniority, Sister, Skate, Sociate, Society, Sodality, Stablemate, Swab, Teaching, Twin, Waghalter, Wallah

Felon(y) Baddy, Bandit, Convict, Crime, Gangster, Offence, Villain

Fel(d)spar Adularia, Albite, Anorthite, Bytownite, Gneiss, Hyalophane, Labradorite, Moonstone, Orthoclase, Peristerite, Petuntse, Petuntze, Plagioclase, Sanidine, Saussurite, Sun-stone

Felt Baize, Bat(t), Drugget, Knew, Met, Numdah, Numnah, Pannose, Roofing, Sensed, Tactile, Underlay, Velour

Female (bodies), Feminine, Feminist Anima, Bint, Bit, Dame, Distaff, Doe, F, Fair sex, Filly, Girl, Greer, Harem, Hen, Her, Kermes, Lady, Libber, Maiden, Muliebrity, Pen, Petticoate, Pistillate, Riot girl, Sakti, Shakti, She, Sheila, Shidder, Soft, Spindle, Thelytoky, -trix, → **WOMAN**, Womens' libber, Yin

▷ **Female, Feminine** *may indicate* an -ess ending

Fen Bog, Carr, Chiao, Coin, Ea, Jiao, Marsh, Morass, Silicon, Swamp, Wash, Yuan

Fence(r), Fencing (position) Appel, Balestra, Bar, Barrier, Botte, Carte, Croisé, Cyclone®, Deer, Derobement, Dogleg, Electric, Enclose, Épée, Feint, Fight, Flanconade, Flèche, Foils, Fraise, Froissement, Haha, Hay, Hedge, Hot, Hurdle, Iaido, Imbroccata, Inquartata, Kendo, Kittle, Line, Link, Mensur, Molinello, Montant, Netting, Obstacle, Ox, Oxer, Pale, Paling, Palisade, Palisado, Parry, Passado, Pen, Picket, Post and rail, Quart(e), Quinte, Rabbit-fence, Rabbit-proof, Raddle, Rail, Rasper, Receiver, Reset, Ring, Scrimure, Seconde, Sepiment, Sept(um), Septime, Singlestick, Sixte, Snake, Snow, Stacket, Stockade, Stramac, Stramazon, Sunk, Swordplay, Tac-au-tac, Tierce, Touché, Trellis, Virginia, Wattle, Wear, Weir, Weldmesh®, Wire, Worm, Zigzag

Fend(er), Fend off Buffer, Bumper, Cowcatcher, Curb, Mudguard, Parry, Provide, Resist, Skid, Stiff-arm, Ward, Wing

Fennel Finnochio, Finoc(c)hio, Florence, Herb, Love-in-a-mist, Narthex, Ragged lady

Fent Offcut, Remnant, Slit

Feral Brutal, Fierce, Savage, Wild

Ferdinand Archduke, Bull

Ferment(ation) Barm, Brew, Enzym(e), Leaven, Mowburn, Protease, Ptyalin, Seethe, Solera, Storm, Stum, Trypsin, Turn, Vinify, Working, Ye(a)st, Zyme, Zymo-, Zymology, Zymosis, Zymotic, Zymurgy

Fermium Fm

Fern Acrogenous, Adder's-tongue, Adiantum, Archegonial, Asparagus, Aspidium, Asplenium, Azolla, Barometz, Beech, Bird's nest, Bladder, Bracken, Brake, Bristle, Buckler, Bungwall, Ceterach, Cinnamon, Coral, Cryptogam, Cyathea, Cycad, Dicksonia, Door, Elkhorn, Fairy moss, Filicales, Filices, Filmy, Fishbone, Grape, Hard, Hart's-tongue, Holly, Ice, Isoetes, Lady, Maidenhair, Male, Man, Mangemange, Marattia,

Marsh, Marsilea, Marsilia, Meadow, Miha, Moonwort, Mosquito, Mulewort, Nardoo, Nephrolepis, Northern, Oak, Ophioglossum, Osmunda, Para, Parsley, Peppergrass, Pepperwort, Pig, Pillwort, Polypody, Polystichum, Ponga, Pteridology, Pteris, Punga, Rachilla, Rhizocarp, Rockbrake, Royal, Rusty-back, Salvinia, Scale, Schizaea, Scolopendrium, Seed, Shield, Silver, Snowbrake, Soft tree, Spleenwort, Staghorn, Sweet, Sword, Tara, Tree, Venus's hair, Walking, Wall rue, Water, Whisk, Woodsia

Ferocious Brutal, Cruel, Fell, Predatory, Rambunctious, Savage, Tiger, Violent, Wild

Ferret Albin, Black-footed, Business, Fesnyng, Gill, Hob, Jill, Nose, Polecat, Ribbon, Rootle, Snoop, Trace, Unearth

Ferry(man) Charon, Convey, Flying bridge, Harper's, Hovercraft, Passage, Plier, Pont, Roll-on, RORO, Sea-cat, Sealink, Shuttle, Soyuz, Train, Traject, Tranect

Fertile, Fertility (symbol), Fertilisation Arable, Ashtoreth, Battle, Cleistogamy, Fat, Fecund, Fruitful, Green, Linga, Priapus, Productive, Prolific, Rhiannon, Rich, Uberous

Fertilise(r), Fertilisation Ammonia, Auxin, Bee, Bone-ash, Bone-earth, Bone-meal, Caliche, Caprify, Compost, Cross, Fishmeal, Guano, Heterosis, Humogen, Humus, In-vitro, IVF, Kainite, Krilium®, Manure, Marl, Night soil, Nitrate, Nitre, Nitro-chalk, Pearl-ash, Phallus, Phosphate, Pollen, Pollinator, Potash, Potassa, Seaware, Self, Sham, Side dressing, Stamen, Superfetation, Superphosphate, Tankage, Top dressing

Fervent, Fervid, Fervour Ardent, Burning, Earnest, Heartfelt, Heat, Hot, Hwyl, Intense, Into, Keen, Passionate, White-hot, Zeal, Zeloso

Fester Beal, Putrefy, Rankle, Rot, Suppurate

Festival, Festive, Festivity Anniversary, Beano, Carnival, Celebration, Commemoration, Convivial, En fête, → **FAIR**, Feast, Feis, Fête, Fête-champêtre, Gaff, → **GALA**, Gaudy, High day, → **HOLIDAY**, Lemural, Let-off, Play, Revel, Rush-bearing, Semi-double, Wake

---

FESTIVALS

3 letters:
Ale
Bon
Mod
Pop
Tet

4 letters:
Holi
Lent
Mela
Noel
Obon
Puja
Tide
Utas
Yule

5 letters:
Doseh
Druid
Hosay
Miraj
Pasch
Pesah

Pooja
Purim
Seder
Vesak
Wesak

6 letters:
Adonia
Ashura
Bairam
Dewali
Divali
Diwali
Easter
Fiesta
Fleadh
Fringe
Hosein
Lammas
Mawlid
Mayday
Moomba
Pardon
Pesach
Pongal

Poojah
Shrove
Yom Tob
Yomtov

7 letters:
Al Hijra
Baisaki
Beltane
Greater
Harvest
Holy-ale
J'ouvert
Kermess
Kermiss
Kirmess
Kwanzaa
Lady-Day
Lemuria
Matsuri
Palilia
Potlach
Samhain
Vinalia
Yuan Tan

8 letters:
Al Hijrah
Baisakhi
Bayreuth
Biennale
Cerealia
Chanukah
Dassehra
Day of awe
Dionysia
Encaenia
Epiphany
Fête-Dieu
Hanukkah
Hock-tide
Hogmanay
Id-al-fitr
Lag b'Omer
Passover
Salzburg
Shabuath
Shavuath
Slugfest
Tanabata
Yuletide

9 letters:
Aldeburgh
Candlemas
Chanukkah
Church-ale
Crouchmas
Hallowmas
Kumbh Mela
Martinmas
Navaratra
Navaratri
Pentecost
Thargelia
Up-Helly-Aa
Woodstock
Yom Arafat

10 letters:
Ambarvalia
Assumption
Childermas
Corroboree
Eisteddfod
Lughnasadh
Lupercalia
Merry-night
Michaelmas
Quirinalia
Saturnalia
Shrovetide
Terminalia
Visitation
Vulcanalia

11 letters:
Anthesteria
Fête-galante
Glastonbury
Harvest home

12 letters:
All Saints' Day
Circumcision
Feast of weeks
Glyndebourne
Lailat-ul-Qadr
Lesser Bairam
Panathenaean
Plough Monday
Rosh Hashanah

Simchas Torah
Simchat Torah
Thesmophoria

13 letters:
Corpus Christi
Greater Bairam
Laylat-al-Miraj
Simchath Torah

14 letters:
Shemini Atseres

15 letters:
Transfiguration

Festoon Deck, Decorate, Encarpus, Garland, Swag, Wreathe

Fetch(ing), Fetch up Arrive, Attract, Bring, Charming, Fet(t), Get, Gofer, Realise, Spew

Fête Bazaar, Champêtre, Entertain, → **FESTIVITY**, Gala, Honour, Tattoo

Fetish(ist) Charm, Compulsion, Gimp, Idol, Ju-ju, Obeah, Obi(a), Talisman, Totem, Voodoo

Fetter Anklet, Basil, Bilboes, Chain, Gyve, Hamshackle, Hopple, Iron, Leg-iron, Manacle, Shackle

Fettle Arrange, Condition, Frig, Potter, Repair

Feu Tenure

Feud Affray, Blood, Clash, Dissidence, Feoff, Fief, Quarrel, Strife, → **VENDETTA**

Feudal (service), Feudalism Arriage, Auld-farrant, Fief, Forinsec, Old, Vassalage

Fever(ish) African coast, Ague, Beaver, Biliary, Blackwater, Brain, Breakbone, Buck, Cabin, Calenture, Camp, Cat-scratch, Cerebrospinal, Childbed, Dandy, Dengue, East coast, Enteric, Febrile, Ferment, Fog, Frenetic, Gastric, Gate, Glandular, Haemorrhagic, Hay, Heatstroke, Hectic, Hyperpyretic, Insolation, Intense, Intermittent, Jail, Japanese river, Jungle, Kala-azar, Kissing disease, Lassa, Malaria, Malta, Marsh, Mediterranean, Miliary, Milk, Mono, Mud, Paratyphoid, Parrot, Parturient, Passion, Phrenitis, Puerperal, Putrid, Pyretic, Pyrexia, Pyrogenic, Q, Quartan, Quintan, Quotidian, Rabbit, Ratbite, Recurrent, Relapsing, Remittent, Rheumatic, Rift Valley, Rock, Rocky Mountain spotted, Roseola, Sandfly, Scarlatina, Scarlet, Sextan, Ship, Splenic, Spotted, Spring, Stage, Sunstroke, Swamp, Swine, Tap, Temperature, Tertian, Texas, Tick, Trench, Typhoid, Typhus, Undulant, Valley, Verruga, Vomito, Weed, West Nile, Whot, Worm, Yellow(jack)

Few(er) Handful, Infrequent, → **LESS**, Limited, Scarce, Some, Wheen

Fey Clairvoyant, Eccentric, Elfin, Weird

Fez Tarboosh, Tarboush, Tarbush

Fiancé(e) Betrothed, Intended, Promised

Fiasco Bomb, Debacle, Disaster, Failure, Flask, Flop, Lash-up, Wash-out

Fiat Command, Decree, Edict, Order, Ukase

Fib Gag, → **LIE**, Prevaricate, Story, Taradiddle, Untruth

Fibre, Fibrous Abaca, Acrilan®, Acrylic, Aramid, Arghan, Backbone, Bass, Bast, Beta, Buaze, Bwazi, Cantala, Carbon, Coir, Constitution, Corpus Callosum, Cotton, Courtelle®, Cuscus, Desmosome, Dietary, Dralon®, Elastane, Elastin, Filament, Filasse, Flax, Funicle, Giant, Glass, Gore-Tex®, Graded-index, Hair, Harl, Hemp, Henequen, Henequin, Herl, Hypha, Ispaghula, Istle, Ixtle, Jipyapa, Jute, Kapok, Kenaf, Kevlar®, Kittul, Lemniscus, Maguey, Manilla, Monkey-grass, Monofil, Monomode, Moorva, Moral, Multimode, Mungo, Murva, Muscle, Myotube, Nap, Natural, Nerve, Noil(s), Nylon, Oakum, Olefin(e), Optic(al), Orlon®, Peduncle, Piassaba, Piassava, Pina,

Pine-wool, Pita, Polyarch, Pons, Pontine, Pulu, Raffia, Ramee, Rami, Ramie, Rayon, Rhea, Rock-cork, Roughage, Rove, Shoddy, Sida, Silk, Sinew, Sisal, Slagwool, Sleave, Slub(b), Spandex, Spherulite, Splenium, Staple, Stepped-index, Sterculia, Strand, Strick, Sunn-hemp, Tampico, Tencel®, Toquilla, Tow, Towy, Uralite, Viver, Vulcanized, Wallboard, Watap, Whisker, Wood pulp

Fibula Bone, Brooch, Perone

Fickle(ness) Capricious, Change, False, Flibbertigibbet, Inconsistent, Inconstant, Kittle, Light, Mutable, Protean, Shifty, Varying, Volage, Volatile, Wind-changing

Fiction(al), Fictitious Airport, Bogus, Chick-lit, Cyberpunk, Fable, Fabrication, Legal, Myth, Pap, Phoney, Picaresque, Pulp, Romance, Science, Sex and shopping, Slash, Speculative, Splatterpunk, → **STORY**, Sword and sorcery, Transgressive, Whole cloth

Fiddle(r), Fiddling, Fiddlestring Amati, Bow, Calling-crab, Cello, Cheat, Crab, Cremona, Croud, Crouth, Crowd, Crwth, Do, Fidget, Fix, Gju, Ground, Gu(e), Gut-scraper, Jerrymander, Kit, Launder, Nero, Peculate, Petty, Potter, Racket, Rebec(k), Rig, Rote, Sarangi, Saw, Sawah, Scam, Scotch, Scrape, Scrapegut, Second, Sharp practice, Short change, Spiel, Strad, Sultana, → **TAMPER**, Tinker, Toy, Trifle, Tweedle(-dee), Twiddle, Viola, → **VIOLIN**, Wangle

Fiddle-faddle Nipperty-tipperty

Fidelity Accuracy, Faith, Fealty, Loyalty, Troth, Trust

Fidget(y) Fantad, Fanteeg, Fantigue, Fantod, Fike, Fuss, Fyke, Hirsle, Hotch, Impatient, Jimjams, Jittery, Niggle, Restive, Trifle, Twiddle, Twitch, Uneasy

Fiduciary Trustee

Fief Benefice, Fee

Field(er), Fielding, Fields(man) Aalu, Aaru, Abroad, Aceldama, Aerodrome, Area, Arena, Arish, Arpent, Arrish, Baseman, Bocage, Campestral, Campestrian, Catch, Champ(s), Chief, Close, Colour, Coulomb, Cover, Cover-point, Diamond, Domain, Electric, Electromagnetic, Electrostatic, Elysian, Entry, Extra cover, Fid, Fine leg, Flodden, Flying, Force, Forte, Fylde, Glebe, Gracie, Gravitational, Grid(iron), Gull(e)y, Hop-yard, Ice, Keep wicket, Killing, Land, Landing, Lare, Lay, Lea(-rig), Leg slip, Ley, Line, Long leg, Long-off, Long-on, Longstop, Lords, Magnetic, Mead(ow), Mid-off, Mid-on, Mid-wicket, Mine, Oil, Padang, Paddock, Paddy, Parrock, Pasture, Peloton, Pitch, Playing, Point, Potter's, Province, Quintessence, Realm, Reame, Runners, Salting, Sawah, Scarecrow, Scope, Scout, Shamba, Short leg, Short stop, Silly, Slip, Sphere, Square leg, Stage, Stray, Stubble, Territory, Third man, Tract, Unified, Vector, Visual, W.C., World

▷ **Field** *may indicate* cricket

Field marshal Allenby, Bulow, French, Haig, Ironside, Kesselring, Kitchener, Montgomery, Roberts, Robertson, Rommel, Slim, Wavell

Fieldwork Lunette, Ravelin, Redan, Redoubt, Tenaillon

Fiend Barbason, Buff, Demon, → **DEVIL**, Enthusiast, Flibbertigibbet, Fraretetto, Hellhound, Hellion, Hobbididance, Mahn, Modo, Obidicut, Smulkin, Succubus

Fierce(ly) Amain, Billyo, Breem, Breme, Cruel, Draconic, Dragon, Grim, Hard-fought, Intense, Lorcan, Ogreish, Rampant, Renfierst, → **SAVAGE**, Severe, Tigerish, Tigrish, Violent, Wild, Wood, Wrathy, Wud

Fiery Abednego, Ardent, Argand, Aries, Con fuoco, Dry, Eithna, Fervent, Hot, Hotspur, Idris, Igneous, Impassioned, Leo, Mettlesome, Phlogiston, Piri-piri, Sagittarius, Salamander, Zealous

Fiesta Festival, Fête, Gala, Holiday

Fife Piffero

Fifth Column, Diapente, Hemiol(i)a, Nones, Perfect, Quentin, Quint(ile), Sesquialtera, Sextans

Fifty Bull, Demi-c, Jubilee, L

Fig Bania, Banyan, Benjamin-tree, Caprifig, Fico, Figo, Footra, Fouter, Foutra, Foutre, Hottentot, Indian, Moreton Bay, Mouldy, Sycamore, Sycomium, Sycomore, Trifle

Fight(er), Fighting Achilles, Action, Affray, Agonistics, Aikido, Alpino, Altercate,

Arms, Bandy, Bare-knuckle, Barney, → **BATTLE**, Bicker, Biffo, Blue, Bout, Box, Brave, Brawl, Bruiser, Bundeswehr, Bush-whack, Camp, Campaign, Chaud-mellé, Chetnik, Chindit, Combat, Compete, Conflict, Contest, Contra, Crusader, Cuirassier, Defender, Digladiation, Ding-dong, Dog, Donnybrook, Dreadnought, Duel, Ecowarrior, Encounter, Engagement, Extremes, F, Faction, Fecht, Fence, Fisticuffs, Flyting, Fray, Freedom, Free-for-all, Fund, Gamecock, Garibaldi, Ghazi, Gladiator, Grap(p)le, Green beret, Grudge, Guerilla, Gunslinger, Gurkha, Handicuffs, Hurricane, J(o)ust, Karate, Kendo, Kite, Kumite, Lapith, Maquis, Marine, Med(d)le, Medley, Mêlée, Mercenary, MIG, Militate, Mill, Mujahed(d)in, Mujahidin, Naumachy, Night, Partisan, Pellmell, Pillow, PLO, Prawle, Press, Pugilist, Pugnacity, Punch up, Rammy, Rapparee, Rejoneo, Repugn, Resist, Ring, Rough and tumble, Ruck, Ruction, Rumble, Run-in, Running, Savate, Sciamachy, Scold, Scrap, Scrape, Scrimmage, Scuffle, Set-to, Shadow, Shine, Shoot-out, Skiamachy, Skirmish, Slam, Slugger, Soldier, Spar, Spat, Spitfire, Squabble, Stealth, Stoush, Straight, Strife, Struggle, Sumo, Swordsman, Tar, Tatar, Thersites, Tilt, Toreador, Tuilyie, Tuilzie, Tussle, Ultimate, Umbrella, War(-dog), War-horse, War-man, Warplane, Warrior, Wraxle, Wrestle, Yike, Zero

Figment Delusion, Fiction, Invention

Figure(d), Figures, Figurine, Figurative Action, Allegoric, Arabic, Aumail, Bas-relief, Body, Build, Caganer, Canephorus, Cartouche, Caryatid, Cast, Chladni, Cinque, Cipher, Cone, Cube, Cypher, Decahedron, Digit, Ecorché, Effigy, Eight, Ellipse, Enneagon, Enneahedron, Epanadiplosis, Equiangular, Escher, → **FORM**, Fret, Fusil, Gammadion, Giosphinx, Girth, Gnomon, Graph, Heptagon, Hexagon, Hour-glass, Icon, Icosahedron, Idol, Ikon, Image, Impossible, Insect, Intaglio, Integer, Interference, Lay, Lissajous, Magot, Manaia, Mandala, Matchstick, Moai, Monogram, Motif, Nonagon, Number, Numeral, Numerator, Numeric, Octagon, Octahedron, Orant, Ornate, Outline, Ovoid, Parallelepiped, Parallelogram, Pentacle, Pentalpha, Plane, Polygon, Polyhedron, Poussette, Prism, Puppet, Pyramid, Reckon, Repetend, Repoussoir, Rhomboid, Sector, See, → **SHAPE**, Sheela-na-gig, Significant, Simplex, Solid, Sonorous, Stat(istic)s, Statue(tte), Stick, String, Tableau, Tanagra, Telamon, Tetragon, Tetrahedron, Torus, Triangle, Trigon, Trihedron, Triskele, Triskelion, Trisoctahedron, Tropology, Undecagon, Ushabti, Waxwork

Figure of speech Abscission, Allegory, Alliteration, Analogy, Antimask, Antimasque, Antimetabole, Antithesis, Antonomasia, Assonance, Asyndeton, Catachresis, Cataphora, Chiasmus, Deixis, Diallage, Ellipsis, Euphemism, Hendiadys, Hypallage, Hyperbaton, Hyperbole, Hysteron proteron, Irony, Litotes, Meiosis, Metalepsis, Metaphor, Metonymy, Onomatopoeia, Oxymoron, Paral(e)ipsis, Prolepsis, Prosopopoeia, Siddhuism, Simile, Solecism, Syllepsis, Synecdoche, Taxeme, Tmesis, Trope, Tropology, Zeugma

Figure study Arithmetic, Mathematics, Numeration

Figure-weaver Draw-boy

Filament Barbule, Byssus, Cirrus, Fibre, Fimbria, Floss, Gossamer, Hair, Hormogonium, Hypha, Mycor(r)hiza, Myofibril, Paraphysis, Protonema, → **THREAD**, Whisker, Wreath

Filch Appropriate, Drib, Pilfer, Pinch, Prig, Purloin, Smouch, → **STEAL**

File, Filing(s) Abrade, Archive, Back up, Bastard, Batch, Binary, Binder, Box, Burr, Circular, Clyfaker, Coffle, Croc(odile), Crosscut, Database, Data set, Dead-smooth, Disc, Disk, Dossier, Download, Enter, Floatcut, Folder, Generation, Half-round, In-box, Index, Indian, Lemel, Lever-arch, Limail, Limation, Line, Lodge, Nail, Out-box, Packed, Pickpocket, Pigeon-hole, Podcast, Pollute, Quannet, Rank, Rasp, Rat-tail, README, Riffler, Risp, Rolodex®, Row, Scalprum, Scratch, Signature, Single, Single-cut, String, Swap, Swarf, Text, Tickler, TIF(F)

Filial generation F₁

Filibuster Freebooter, Hinder, Obstruct, Pirate, Run on, Stonewall

Filigree Delicate, Fretwork, Sheer

Filipino Igorot, Moro, → **PHILIPPINE(S)**

Fill(ing), Filler Anaplerosis, Balaam, Banoffee, Banoffi, Beaumontag(u)e, Beaumontique, Billow, Bishop, Bloat, Brick-nog, Brim, Bump, Centre, Charge, Cram, Fat-lute, Ganache,

Gather, Gorge, Heart, Imbue, Implete, Impregn(ate), Inlay, Instill, Jampack, Line, Load, Mastic, Mincemeat, Nagging, Occupy, Pabulous, Packing, Permeate, Plug, Replenish, Repletive, Salpicon, Sate, Satisfy, Sealant, Shim, Slush, Stack, Stocking, Stopgap, Stopping, → **STUFF**, Tales, Tampon, Tank-up, Teem, Top up, Ullage

Fillet(s) Anadem, Annulet, Band, Bandeau, Bandelet, Bone, Cloisonné, Flaunching, Fret, Goujons, Grenadine, Headband, Infula, Label, Lemniscus, List(el), Mitre, Moulding, Reglet, Regula, Ribbon, Rollmop, Slice, Snood, Sphendone, Stria, Striga, Taeniate, Tape, Teniate, Tilting, Tournedos, Vitta

Fillip Boost, Kick, Snap, Stimulus, Tonic

Filly Colt, Foal, She

Film(s), Filmmaker, Filmy, Filming Acetate, Actioner, Amnion, Animatronics, Anime, Biopic, Blaxploitation, Blockbuster, Bollywood, Buddy, Carry On, Cartoon, Casablanca, Caul, Cel, Chick-flick, Chiller, Chopsocky, Cine, Cinéma vérité, Cinerama®, Circlorama®, Cliffhanger, Cling, Clip, Coat, Colour, Compilation, Creature feature, Deepie, Dew, Diorama, Docudrama, Documentary, Dogme, Dramedy, Dust, Epic, ET, Exposure, Fantasia, Feature, Featurette, Fiche, Flick, Floaty, Footage, Genevieve, Gigi, Gossamer, Hammer, Haze, Hollywood, Horror, Horse opera, Ident, Infomercial, Jaws, Kell, Kidult, Lacquer, Lamella, Layer, Limelight, Loid, Machinima, Mask, Membrane, Microfiche, Mist, Molecular, Monochrome, Montage, Movie, Mylar®, Neo-noir, Newsreel, Noddy, Noir, Non-flam, Oater, Omnimax®, Outtake, Ozacling®, Panchromatic, Pathé, Patina, Pellicle, Photo, Pilot, Plaque, Prequel, Projection, Psycho, Quickie, Quota-quickie, Reel, Release, Reversal, Rockumentary, Roll, Romcom, Rush, Safety, Scale, Scenario, Scent-scale, Screen, Scum, Sepmag, Sheet, Shoot-'em-up, Short, Shot, Silent, Skin, Skin flick, Slasher-movie, Slashfest, Slick, Slo-mo, Snuff, Spaghetti western, Splatter, Star Wars, Studio, Super 8, Suspensor, Sword and sandal, Take, Talkie, Tear-jerker, Technicolor, Technothriller, Titanic, Toon, Trailer, Travelogue, Trippy, Two-shot, Ultrafiche, Ultra-rapid, Varnish, Vertigo, Vicenzi, Video, Videogram, Video-nasty, Vitaphone®, Wardour St, Web, Weepie, Weepy, Weft, Western, Wuxia

Filmgoer Cineaste

Film star Extra, Monroe, Vedette

Filter(ing) Band-pass, Bo(u)lt, Clarify, Colour, Dialysis, Dichroic, High-pass, Leach, Low-pass, Percolate, Perk, Polarizing, Refine, Seep, Sieve, → **SIFT**, Sile, Skylight, Strain

Filth(y) Addle, Augean, Bilge, Bogging, Colluvies, Crock, Crud, Defile, Dirt, Dung, Feculent, Foul, Grime, Hard core, Litter, Lucre, Mire, Muck, Obscene, Pythogenic, Refuse, Slime, Smut(ch), Soil, Squalor, Stercoral, Sullage, Yuck

Fin Adipose, Anal, Caudal, Crack, Ctene, Dollars, Dorsal, Fiver, Fluke, Pectoral, Pelvic, Pinna, Pinnule, Rib, Skeg, Skegg, Stabiliser, Ventral

Final(e), Finalise, Finally Absolute, Apogee, At last, Closing, Coda, Conclusive, Cup, Decider, Denouement, End, End-all, Epilogue, Eventual, Exam, Extreme, Grand, Last, Last gap, Net(t), Peremptory, Sew up, Swansong, Terminal, Ultimate, Utter

Finance, Financial, Financier Ad crumenam, Angel, Back, Banian, Banker, Bankroll, Banyan, Bay Street, Bottomry, Cambism, Chrematistic, City (man), Equity, Exchequer, Fiscal, Forfaiting, Gnome, Grubstake, Mezzanine, Monetary, Moneyman, Patronise, Revenue, Sponsor, Subsidise, Treasurer, Underwrite, Wall Street

Finch Bird, Brambling, Bunting, Canary, Charm, Chewink, Conirostral, Crossbill, Darwin's, Fringillid, Gouldian, Grosbeak, Linnet, Marsh-robin, Peter, Redpoll, Rosy, Serin, Siskin, Spink, Twite, Zebra

Find(er), Finding Ascertain, Come across, Detect, Dig up, Direction, Discover(y), Get, Gobind, Govind, Hit, Inquest, → **LOCATE**, Meet, Minitrack®, Provide, Rake up, Rarity, Rumble, Trace, Track down, Trouvaille, Unearth, Verdict

Fine, Fine words A1, Admirable, Amende, Amerce, Amerciament, Arts, Assess, Beau(t), Bender, Blood-wit(e), Bonny, Boshta, Boshter, Boss, Brandy, Brave, Braw, Bully, Buttock-mail, Champion, Cobweb(by), Dainty, Dandy, Dick, Dry, End, Eriach, Eric(k), Estreat, F, Fair, Famous, Forfeit, Gate, Godly, Good(ly), Gossamer, Gradely, Graithly,

Grand, Grassum, Hair, Hairline, Handsome, Heriot, Hunkydory, Idle, Immense, Impalpable, Inconie, Incony, Infangthief, Issue, Keen, Leirwite, Log, Maritage, Merchet, Mooi, Mulct, Nice, Nifty, Niminy-piminy, Noble, OK, Oke, Okey-doke(y), Outfangthief, → **PENALTY**, Phat, Precise, Pretty, Pure, Relief, Righto, Safe, Sconce, Scratch, Sheer, Sicker, Slender, Smart, Spanking, Subtle, Summery, Super, Sure, Tax, Thin, Ticket(t)y-boo, Tiptop, Topping, Transmission, Unlaw, Wally, Waly, Well, Wer(e)gild, Wispy

Fine-collector Cheater

Finery Braws, Fallal, Frills, Frippery, Gaudery, Ornament, Trinket, Wally, Warpaint

Finesse Artifice, Artistry, Delicacy, Skill, Strategy

Fine-weather All-hallond, All-hallow(e)n, All-hollown

Finger(s), Fingernail Annular, Dactyl, Digit, Fork, Green, Handle, Idle worms, Index, Lunula, Medius, Name, Nip, Piggy, Pinky, Pointer, Potato, Prepollex, Pusher, Ring(man), Shop, Sponge, Talaunt, Talon, Tot, Trigger, White

Finger-hole Lill, Ring

Fingerprint(ing) Arch, Dabs, Dactylogram, DNA, Genetic, Loop, Whorl

Fingerstall Hutkin

Finial Bunch, Knob, Ornament, Tee

Finical, Finicky Faddy, Fastidious, Fussy, Particular, Pernickety, Precise

Finish(ed), Finishing (touch) Arch, Blanket, Calendar, Close, Coating, Coda, Complete, → **CONCLUDE**, Crown, Dénouement, Die, Dish, Do, Dope, Dress, Eggshell, → **END**, Epilog(ue), Epiphenomena, Exact, Fine, Full, Gloss, Grandstand, Ice, Intonaco, Kibosh, Lacquer, Log off, Mat(t), Mirror, Neat, Outgo, Outwork, Pebbledash, Peg out, Perfect, Photo, Picking, Polish off, Refine, Ripe, Round, Satin, Settle, Shellac, Shot, Spitcher, Surface, Terminate, Through, Top out, Up (tie), Varnish, Veneer, Washed-up, Wau(l)k, Wind-up, Wrap

Finite Bounded, Limited

Finland, Finn(ish) Esth, Esthonian, Huck(leberry), Karelian, Lapp, Mickey, Mordvin, Suomic, Udmurt, Votyak

Fiord Bay, Hardanger, Inlet, Oslo, Randers, Trondheim

Fir Abies, Balsam, Douglas, Larch, Oregon, Scotch, Scots, Silver, Spruce, Umbrella

Fire(side), Firing Accend, Agni, Aidan, Aiden, Animate, Anneal, Ardour, Arouse, Arson, Atar, Awaken, Axe, Bake, Bale, Barbecue, Barrage, Beacon, Behram, Biscuit, Blaze, Boot, Brand, Brazier, Brush, Burn, Bush, Cashier, Central, Chassé, Conflagration, Corposant, Counterbattery, Covering, Delope, Discharge, Dismiss, Élan, Electric, Element, Embolden, Ena, Energy, Enfilade, Enkindle, Enthuse, Flak, Flame, Friendly, Furnace, Glost, Greek, Gun, Hearth, Heater, Hob, Ignite, Inferno, Ingle, Inspire, Kentish, Kiln, Kindle, Launch, Let off, Light, Liquid, Lowe, Oust, Pop, Prime, Prometheus, Pull, Pyre, Quick, Radiator, Rake, Rapid, Red, Red cock, Sack, St Anthony's, St Elmo's, Scorch, Shell, Shoot, Smudge, Spark, Spirit, Spunk, Stoke, Stove, Strafe, Torch, Tracer, Trial, Trigger, Wake, Watch, Wisp, Zeal, Zip

▸ **Firearm** *see* **GUN(FIRE)**

Fireback Reredos

Fireball Bolide

Firebird Phoenix

Fire-break Epaulement, Greenstrip

Firedamp Blower

Fire-dog Andiron

Fire engine Green Goddess

Fire-extinguisher Halon, Hell-bender, Salamander

Firefly Glow-worm, Lightning-bug, Luciferin, Pyrophorus

Fire-guard Fender

Fireman Abednego, Brigade, Deputy, Prometheus, Stoker, Visiting

Fire-opal Girasol

Fireplace Camboose, Chiminea, Chimney, Grate, Hearth, Hob, Ingle, Loop-hole, Range

Fireplug H, Hydrant
Fireproof Abednego, Asbestos, Incombustible, Inflammable, Meshach, Salamander, Shadrach, Uralite
Firewalker Abednego, Salamander
Firewood Billet, Faggot, Knitch, Tinder
Firework(s) Banger, Bengal-light, Bunger, Catherine wheel, Cherry bomb, Cracker, Devil, Feu d'artifice, Firedrake, Fisgig, Fizgig, Flip-flop, Fountain, Gerbe, Girandole, Golden rain, Indian fire, Iron sand, Jumping jack, Maroon, Pastille, Peeoy, Petard, Pharaoh's serpent, Pinwheel, Pioy(e), Pyrotechnics, Realgar, Rocket, Roman candle, Serpent, Set piece, Skyrocket, Slap-bang, Sparkler, Squib, Tantrum, Throwdown, Tourbill(i)on, Volcano, Waterloo cracker, Wheel, Whizzbang
Fire-worshipper Parsee
Firing Baking, Counterbattery, Fusillade, Mitten, Salvo, Touchpaper, Trigger
Firm, Firmness Adamant, Agency, Al dente, Binding, Business, Collected, Compact, Company, Concern, Concrete, Conglomerate, Consistency, Constant, Crisp, Decided, Definite, Determined, Duro, Establishment, Faithful, Fast, Fixed, Hard, House, Inc, Insistent, Loyal, Marginal, Oaky, Obdurate, Obstinate, Partnership, Persistent, → **RESOLUTE**, Sclerotal, Secure, Set, Siccar, Sicker, → **SOLID**, Sound, Stable, Stalwart, Staunch, Steady, Ste(a)dfast, Steely, Steeve, Stern, Stieve, Stiff, Strict, Sturdy, Sure, Tight, Tough, Unflinching, Unshakeable, Well-knit
Firmament Canopy, Empyrean, Heaven, Sky
First 1st, Ab initio, Alpha, Arch, Archetype, Best, Calends, Champion, Chief, Earliest, Eldest, E(a)rst, Foremost, Former, Front, Head, I, Ideal, Imprimis, Initial, Kalends, Led, Maiden, No 1, One, Opener, Or, Original, Pioneer, Pole, Pole position, Premier, Première, Prima, Primal, Prime, Primo, Primordial, Principal, Prototype, Rudimentary, Senior, Starters, Top, Uppermost, Victor, Yama
First-aid(ers) Zambu(c)k
First born Ariki, Cain, Eigne, Eldest, Heir, Major, Primogeniture, Senior
First class, First rate A1, Crack, Plump, Prime, Pukka, Slap up, Super-duper, Supreme, Tiptop, Top(notch)
First day Calends
First fruits Annat, Arles, Primitiae, Windfalls
First man Adam, Ask, Gayomart, Premier, President, Yama, Ymer, Ymir
First offender Eve, Probationer
▶ **First rate** *see* **FIRST CLASS**
First woman Embla, Eve, Pandora, Premier
Firth Dornoch, Estuary, Forth, Inlet, Moray, Pentland, Solway, Tay
Fish(ing) Angle, Bob, Bottom, Cast, Catch, Chowder, Coarse, Counter, Cran, Creel, Deep-sea, Dib, Dredge, Dry, Dry-fly, Episcate, Fly, Flying, Frozen, Fry, Game, Gefilte, Gefulte, Goujons, Guddle, Halieutics, Haul, Hen, Inshore, Ledger, Mess, Net, Odd, Offshore, Oily, Otterboard, Overnet, Piscary, Piscine, Poisson, Queer, Roe, Rough, Runner, Sacred, Sashimi, Shoal, Skitter, Sleeper, Snigger, Sniggle, Spin, Spot, Surfcasting, Surimi, Trawl, Troll, Trotline, Tub, Walking, Wet, Whiff, White

---

FISH

2 letters:	Bar	Dog	Lob
Ai	Bib	Eel	Mud
Id	But	Gar	Par
	Cat	Ged	Pod
3 letters:	Cod	Hag	Ray
Ahi	Cow	Ide	Rig
Aua	Dab	Koi	Sar
Ayu	Dap	Lax	Tai

Top

4 letters:
Barb
Bass
Blay
Bley
Brit
Butt
Carp
Cero
Chad
Char
Chub
Chum
Coho
Cray
Cusk
Dace
Dare
Dart
Dory
Drum
Fugu
Gade
Goby
Gump
Hake
Harl
Hoka
Hoki
Huso
Huss
Ikan
Jack
Kelt
Keta
Lant
Leaf
Ling
Luce
Lump
Lung
Maid
Masu
Maze
Moki
Mola
Mort
Opah
Orfe
Parr
Peal
Peel

Penk
Pike
Pink
Poll
Pope
Pout
Raun
Rawn
Rigg
Rudd
Ruff
Scad
Scar
Scat
Scup
Seer
Seir
Shad
Sild
Slip
Snig
Sole
Star
Tope
Trot
Tuna
Tusk
Wels
Woof

5 letters:
Ablet
Ahuru
Allis
Angel
Apode
Aspro-
Basse
Belta
Blain
Bleak
Bream
Brill
Bully
Capon
Charr
Cisco
Clown
Cobia
Cohoe
Coley
Cuddy
Danio
Dorad

Doras
Doree
Dorse
Elops
Elver
Fluke
Gadus
Gibel
Grunt
Jewie
Jurel
Koura
Laker
Lance
Loach
Lythe
Maise
Maize
Manta
Masus
Mease
Molly
Murre
Murry
Nerka
Nurse
Padle
Perai
Perca
Perch
Pilot
Piper
Pirai
Platy
Pogge
Powan
Prawn
Roach
Roker
Royal
Ruffe
Saith
Sargo
Saury
Scrod
Sewen
Sewin
Shark
Sheat
Skate
Slope
Smelt
Smolt
Snoek

Snook
Solen
Speck
Sprat
Sprod
Squid
Tench
Tetra
Tiger
Togue
Torsk
Trout
Tunny
Umber
Wahoo
Wirra
Witch
Yabby
Zebra

6 letters:
Alevin
Allice
Anabas
Angler
Archer
Ballan
Barbel
Belone
Beluga
Bichir
Big-eye
Blenny
Bonito
Bounce
Bowfin
Braise
Braize
Bumalo
Burbot
Callop
Caplin
Caranx
Caribe
Cheven
Clupea
Cockle
Comber
Conger
Conner
Cottus
Cudden
Cuddie
Cuddin

Cunner
Cuttle
Darter
Dentex
Diodon
Dipnoi
Discus
Doctor
Dorado
Dun-cow
Ellops
Espada
Finnac
Finnan
Fogash
Fumado
Gadoid
Garvie
Gilgie
Goboid
Goramy
Grilse
Groper
Gulper
Gunnel
Gurami
Gurnet
Haddie
Hapuka
Hassar
Inanga
Jerker
Jilgie
Kipper
Kokiri
Labrus
Lancet
Launce
Lizard
Louvar
Lunker
Mad Tom
Mahsir
Maigre
Marari
Marlin
Matjes
Meagre
Medaka
Medusa
Megrim
Milter
Minnow
Morgay

Mudcat
Mullet
Murena
Nerite
Oyster
Paddle
Paidle
Pakoko
Parore
Parrot
Patiki
Pholas
Piraya
Plaice
Podley
Pollan
Porgie
Puffer
Redfin
Remora
Rewaru
Robalo
Roughy
Saithe
Salmon
Samlet
Sander
Sardel
Sargus
Sauger
Saurel
Scampi
Sea-bat
Sea-owl
Seeder
Serran
Shanny
Sheath
Shiner
Skelly
Sparid
Splake
Sucker
Tailor
Tarpon
Tautog
Tinker
Toitoi
Tomcod
Trygon
Turbot
Twaite
Ulicon
Ulikon

Vendis
Weever
Wirrah
Wrasse
Yabbie
Zander
Zingel

7 letters:
Ale-wife
Anchovy
Anemone
Anhinga
Asterid
Azurine
Batfish
Bellows
Bergylt
Birchir
Bloater
Bluecap
Boxfish
Brassie
Buffalo
Bumallo
Bummalo
Cabezon
Candiru
Capelin
Catfish
Cavalla
Cavally
Ceviche
Cichlid
Codfish
Copepod
Corvina
Cottoid
Crappie
Croaker
Crucian
Crusian
Cutlass
Dipnoan
Dogfish
Eelfare
Eel-pout
Escolar
Fantail
Findram
Finnack
Finnock
Flattie
Garfish

Garoupa
Garpike
Garvock
Geelbek
Gemfish
Goldeye
Gourami
Grouper
Growler
Grunion
Gudgeon
Gurnard
Gwiniad
Gwyniad
Haddock
Hagdown
Hagfish
Halibut
Herling
Herring
Hirling
Hogfish
Homelyn
Houting
Ichthys
Inconnu
Jewfish
Kahawai
Keeling
Koi carp
Kokanee
Lampern
Lamprey
Lampuki
Lantern
Lingcod
Lobster
Lubfish
Lyomeri
Maatjes
Mahseer
Matelot
Medacca
Merling
Mojarra
Moon-eye
Morwong
Muraena
Oarfish
Old-wife
Oolakan
Opaleye
Osseter
Oulakan

Oulicon
Panchax
Pandora
Peacock
Pegasus
Pigfish
Pinfish
Piranha
Pollack
Pomfret
Pompano
Pupfish
Ragfish
Rasbora
Ratfish
Rat-tail
Redfish
Rorqual
Roughie
Sand dab
Sand-eel
Sardine
Scalare
Scallop
Schelly
Sculpin
Sea-bass
Sea-cock
Sea-dace
Sea-moth
Sea-pike
Sea-star
Sea-wife
Sevruga
Sillock
Silurid
Skegger
Skipper
Snapper
Sock-eye
Sparoid
Speldin
Sterlet
Sunfish
Sunstar
Surgeon
Teleost
Tiddler
Tilapia
Titling
Torgoch
Torpedo
Tubfish
Ulichon

Vendace
Vendiss
Wall-eye
Whipray
Whistle
Whiting
Wide-gab

8 letters:
Albacore
Albicore
Anableps
Arapaima
Asteroid
Atherine
Billfish
Blennius
Bloodfin
Blowfish
Blueback
Bluefish
Bluegill
Boarfish
Brisling
Bullhead
Bullhorn
Bummallo
Cabezone
Cabrilla
Carangid
Cardinal
Cavefish
Characid
Characin
Chimaera
Coalfish
Corkwing
Cow-pilot
Cucumber
Cyprinid
Dealfish
Dragonet
Drumfish
Eagle-ray
Elephant
Escallop
Eulachon
Fallfish
Fighting
Filefish
Flathead
Flounder
Four-eyes
Frogfish

Gambusia
Ganoidei
Gillaroo
Gilthead
Goatfish
Gobiidae
Graining
Grayling
Greeneye
Hackbolt
Hair-tail
Half-beak
Hard-head
Holostei
Hornbeak
Hornpout
Jackfish
Kabeljou
Killfish
Kingfish
Kingklip
Kukukuma
Lionfish
Luderick
Lumpfish
Lungfish
Mackerel
Mahi-mahi
Mata Hari
Menhaden
Milkfish
Millions
Monkfish
Moonfish
Moray eel
Mosquito
Mulloway
Nannygai
Nennigai
Nine-eyes
Oulachon
Paradise
Patutuki
Pickerel
Pilchard
Pipefish
Pirarucu
Poor-john
Rascasse
Redbelly
Red roman
Reperepe
Rock-cook
Rockfish

Rockling
Roncador
Rosefish
Saibling
Sailfish
Saltfish
Sardelle
Scabbard
Scaridae
Sciaenid
Scorpion
Scuppaug
Sea-bream
Sea-devil
Seahorse
Sea-lemon
Sea-raven
Sea-robin
Sergeant
Serranus
Skipjack
Smear-dab
Snake-eel
Sparidae
Sparling
Spelding
Speldrin
Stenlock
Sting-ray
Stonecat
Sturgeon
Surffish
Tarakihi
Tarwhine
Teraglin
Terakihi
Tile-fish
Toadfish
Trevally
Tropical
Tubenose
Tullibee
Weakfish
Whitling
Wolffish

9 letters:
Ahuruhuru
Amberjack
Anabantid
Anchoveta
Argentine
Barracuda
Blackfish

Bummaloti
Butterfly
Carangoid
Cascadura
Ceratodus
Chaetodon
Chavender
Clingfish
Clupeidae
Coregonus
Coryphene
Cyprinoid
Devilfish
Gaspereau
Glassfish
Globefish
Goldfinny
Goldsinny
Golomynka
Goosefish
Grass carp
Greenbone
Greenling
Grenadier
Haberdine
Hornyhead
Hottentot
Houndfish
Ichthyoid
Jacksmelt
Jewelfish
Kabeljouw
Killifish
Labyrinth
Latimeria
Matelotte
Menominee
Mudhopper
Neon tetra
Pikeperch
Porbeagle
Porcupine
Queenfish
Quillback
Roussette
Scaldfish
Scalefish
Schnapper
Scorpaena
Selachian
Shubunkin
Siluridae
Slickhead
Snailfish

Snakefish
Snakehead
Snipefish
Solenette
Spadefish
Spearfish
Speldring
Stargazer
Steenbras
Stingaree
Stockfish
Stonefish
Surfperch
Surmullet
Sweetfish
Sweetlips
Swellfish
Swinefish
Swordfish
Sword-tail
Thornback
Threadfin
Tittlebat
Tommy ruff
Topminnow
Trachinus
Troutfish
Troutling
Trumpeter
Trunkfish
Whitebait
White-bass
Wreckfish
Yellowfin

10 letters:
Amblyopsis
Barracoota
Barracouta
Barramundi
Bitterling
Bombay duck
Bottlehead
Butterfish
Candlefish
Cockabully
Cofferfish
Cornetfish
Cyclostome
Damselfish
Demoiselle
Dollarfish
Etheostoma
Fingerling

Flutemouth
Groundling
Guitarfish
Horned pout
Lake-lawyer
Largemouth
Lumpsucker
Maskalonge
Maskanonge
Maskinonge
Midshipman
Mossbunker
Mudskipper
Needlefish
Nurse-hound
Paddlefish
Pakirikiri
Rabbitfish
Red emperor
Red-snapper
Ribbonfish
Rudderfish
Sandsucker
Scopelidae
Sea-poacher
Sea-surgeon
Serrasalmo
Sheepshead
Ship-holder
Shovelnose
Silverside
Small mouth
Springfish
Squeteague
Teleostome
Titarakura
Tommy rough
Trailperch
Tripletail
White cloud
White perch
Yellowtail

11 letters:
Cephalis pie
Chondrostei
Cyprinodont
Dolly Varden
Istiophorus
Lapidosteus
Lepidosiren
Lophobranch
Maskallonge
Moorish idol

Muskellunge
Ostracoderm
Oxyrhynchus
Plagiostome
Plectognath
Pumpkinseed
Scolopendra
Seventy-four
Snail darter
Soldierfish
Stickleback
Stoneroller
Surgeonfish
Triggerfish
Trumpetfish
Water souchy
White martin
Yellowbelly

12 letters:
Ballan-wrasse
Elasmobranch
Father-lasher
Heterosomata
Histiophorus
Jack crevalle
Mangrove Jack
Miller's thumb
Mouthbreeder
Mouthbrooder
Orange roughy
Plectognathi
Rainbow-trout
Silver dollar
Squirrelfish

13 letters:
Burnett salmon
Leatherjacket
Musselcracker
Rainbow runner
Sailor's choice
Sergeant Baker

14 letters:
Smallmouth-bass
Snaggle-toothed
Walking catfish
Winter flounder

15 letters:
Crossopterygian

Fish and chips Greasies
Fish-basket Creel, Hask, Kipe
Fish disease Argulus
Fisher(man) Ahab, Andrew, Angler, Black cat, Caper, Codder, Dragman, Heron, Herringer, High-liner, Liner, Pedro, Peter (Grimes), Piscator, Rodster, Sharesman, Walton
▸ **Fisherwoman** *see* **FISH-SELLER**
Fish-hawk Osprey
Fishing-ground Haaf
Fishing-line G(u)imp, Gymp, Paternoster
Fishpond Ocean, Stew, Vivarium
Fish-seller, Fisherwoman Fishwife, Molly Malone, Ripp(i)er, Shawley, Shawlie
Fishy Botargo, Suspicious, Vacant
Fission Multiple, Nuclear
Fissure Chasm, Cleft, Crack, Crevasse, Crevice, Gap, Grike, Gryke, Lode, Rent, Rift, Rolando, Sand-crack, Scam, Sylvian, Sylvius, Vallecula, Vein, Zygon
Fist Clench, Dukes, Hand, Iron, Join-hand, Mailed, Neaf(f)e, Neif, Neive, Nief, Nieve, Pud, Punch, Thump, Writing
Fit(s), Fitful, Fitter, Fitting(s), Fitness Able, Access, Adapt, Ague, Align, Aline, Apoplexy, Appointment, Appropriate, Apropos, Apt, A salti, Babbitt, Bayonet, Beseemly, Bout, Canto, Capable, Cataleptic, Cataplexy, Click, Competent, Concinnous, Condign, Congruous, Conniption, Convulsion, Culver-tail, Darwinian, Decent, Decorous, Desultory, Dod, Dove-tail, Due, Eclampsia, Egal, Eligible, Ensconce, Epilepsy, Equip, Exies, Expedient, Fairing, Fay, Fiddle, Form, Furniment, Furnishing, Fytte, Gee, Germane, Gusty, Habile, Hale, Handsome, Hang, Health, Hinge, Hissy, Huff, Hysterics, Ictus, Inclusive, In-form, Interference, Intermittent, In trim, Jactitation, Jag, Just, Kashrut(h), Like, Lune, Marry, Mate, Meet, Mood, Nest, Opportune, Paroxysm, Passus, Pertinent, Pet, Prepared, Press, → **PROPER**, Queme, Ready, Rig, Rightful, Rind, Ripe, Roadworthy, Rynd, Seemly, Seizure, Serving, Set, Shrink, Sit, Sliding, Slot, Snit, Snotter, Sort, Sound, Spasm, Spell, Start, Suit(able), Syncope, Tailor, Tantrum, Tenoner, Throe, Tide, To prepon, Tref(a), Treif, Trim, Turn, Up to, Well, Wobbler, Wobbly, Worthy, Wrath
▷ **Fit(ting)** *may indicate* a 't'
Fitment Adaptor, Unit
Fitzgerald Edward, Ella, Scott
Fitzwilliam Darcy
Five(s), Fiver Cinque, Flim, Mashie, Pallone, Pedro, Pentad, Quinary, Quincunx, Quintet, Sextan, Towns, V
Five hundred D, Monkey
Five years Lustre, Lustrum
Fix(ation), Fixed, Fixer, Fixative Affeer, Anchor, Appoint, Appraise, → **ARRANGE**, Assess, Assign, Attach, Bind, Brand, Cement, Clamp, Clew, Clue, Constant, Corking-pin, Cure, Decide, Destinate, Destine, Determine, Do, Embed, Empight, Encastré, Engrain, Establish, Fast, Fasten, Fiddle, Firm, Fit, Freeze, Gammon, Hard and fast, Hold, Hypo(sulphite), Immutable, Impaction, Impasse, Imprint, Inculcate, Ingrain, Iron on, Jag, Jam, Locate, Lodge, Mend, Nail, Name, Narcotic, Nitrogen, Nobble, Odd-job man, Orientate, Peen, Peg, Persistent, Pin, Place, Point, Quantify, Repair, Resolute, Rig, Rigid, Rivet, Rove, Rut, Scrape, Screw, Seat, Seize, Set, Settle, Ship, Shoo, Skatole, Skewer, Splice, Square, Stable, Stage, Staple, Static, Steady, Stell, Step, Stereotype, Stew, Stuck, Swig, Swing, Tie, Toe, Unchangeable, Valorize, Weld
Fixture Attachment, Away, Event, Home, Match, Permanence, Rawlplug®, Unit
Fizz(ed), Fizzy Bubbles, Buck's, Effervesce, Gas, Hiss, Pop, Sherbet, Sod, Soda
Fizzle Failure, Flop, Hiss, Washout
▸ **Fjord** *see* **FIORD**
Flab(by) Flaccid, Lank, Lax, Limp, Pendulous, Saggy, Tubby
Flabbergast(ed) Amaze, Astound, Floor, Thunderstruck

Flaccid Flabby, Lank, Limp, Soft

Flag(gy), Flags Acorus, Ancient, Ashlar, Banderol, Banner, Black, Blackjack, Blue (Ensign), Blue Peter, Bunting, Burgee, Calamus, Chequered, Colour(s), Dan(n)ebrog, Decline, Droop, Duster, Ensign, Fail, Faint, Falter, Fane, Fanion, Field colours, Gladdon, Gonfalon, Green, Guidon, Hail, Hoist, House, Irideal, Iris, Jack, Jade, Jolly Roger, Kerbstone, Languish, Lis, Maple leaf, Old Glory, Orris, Pave(ment), Pavilion, Paviour, Pencel, Pennant, Pennon, Penoncel(le), Pensel, Pensil, Peter, Pilot, Pin, Prayer, Quarantine, Rag, Rainbow, Red, Red Duster, Red Ensign, Repeater, Royal standard, Sag, Sedge, Semaphore, Sett, Sick, Sink, Slab(stone), Slack, Stand, Standard, Stars and Bars, Stars and Stripes, Streamer, Substitute, Sweet, Tire, Tricolour, Union (Jack), Vane, Vexillology, Waft, Weaken, Whiff, Whift, White (ensign), Wilt, Wither, Yellow (Jack)

Flagday Tagday

Flagellate Beat, Euglena, Mastigophora, Scourge, Trypanosome, Whip

Flagon Bottle, Carafe, Ewer, Jug, Pitcher, Stoop, Stoup, Vessel

Flagpole Pin, Staff

Flagrant Blatant, Egregious, Glaring, Heinous, Patent, Rank, Wanton

Flagship Admiral, Barge, Victory

Flag-waving Jingoism

Flail Beat, Drub, Swingle, Swip(p)le, Threshel

Flair Art, Bent, Élan, Gift, Instinct, Knack, Nose, Panache, Style, → **TALENT**

Flak AA, Attack, Criticism

Flake Chip, Flame, Flaught, Flaw, Floccule, Flocculus, Fragment, Peel, Scale, Smut, Snow, Spark

Flam Impose

Flamboyant Baroque, Brilliant, Florid, Garish, Grandiose, Jazzy, Loud, Ornate, Ostentatious, Paz(z)azz, Piz(z)azz, Pzazz, Showoff, Swash-buckler

Flame, Flaming Ardent, Blaze, Fire, Flake, Flambé, Flammule, Flareback, Glow, Kindle, Leman, Lover, Lowe, Musical, Olympic, Oxyacetylene, Reducing, Sensitive, Sweetheart

Flan Pastry, Quiche, Tart

Flanders Mare, Moll

Flange Border, Collar, Collet, Lip, Rim

Flank(s) Accompany, Anta, Flange, Flitch, Ilia, Lisk, Loin, Side, Spur

Flannel Blather, Canton, Cloth, Cotton, Face, Flatter, Outing, Soft-soap, Waffle, Washrag, Zephyr

Flap(ped), Flapper, Flapping Ado, Agnail, Aileron, Alar, Alarm(ist), Aventail(e), Bate, Beat, Bird, Bobbysoxer, Bustle, Chit, Dither, Earcap, Elevon, Epiglottis, Fipple, Flacker, Flaff, Flag, Flaught, Flutter, Fly, Fuss, Giglet, Giglot, Hover, → **IN A FLAP**, Labium, Labrum, Lapel, Loma, Louvre, Luff, Lug, Omentum, Operculum, Panic, Spin, Spoiler, State, Tab, Tag, Tailboard, Tailgate, Tiswas, To-do, Tongue, TRAM, Volucrine, Wave, Whisk

Flare(d), Flares, Flare up Bell, Bell-bottoms, Fishtail, Flame, Flanch, Flaunch, Godet, Magnesium, Scene, Signal, Skymarker, Solar, Spread, Spunk, Ver(e)y, Widen

Flash(y), Flasher, Flashpoint Bling, Bluette, Brainstorm, Brash, Coruscate, Cursor, Electronic, Emicant, Essex Man, Exposure, Fire-flag, Flare, Flaught, Fulgid, Fulgural, Garish, Gaudy, Glaik, Gleam, Glent, Glint, Glisten, Glitzy, Green, Green ray, Helium, Indicate, Instant, Jay, Lairy, Levin, Lightning, Loud, Magnesium, Meretricious, Mo, Moment, Ostentatious, Photopsy, Raffish, Ribbon, Ring, Roary, Scintillation, Second, Sequin, Showboater, Showy, Sluice, Snazzy, Spark, Sparkle, Sport, Streak, Strobe, Swank(e)y, Tick, Tigrish, Trice, Tulip, Twinkle, Vivid, Wink, Wire

▷ **Flashing** *may indicate* an anagram

Flask(-shaped) Ampulla, Aryballos, Bottle, Canteen, Carafe, Cask, Coffin, Conceptacle, Costrel, Cucurbit, Dewar, Erlenmeyer, Fiasco, Flacket, Flacon, Florence, Goatskin, Hip, Lekythos, Livery pot, Matrass, Mick(e)y, Moon, Pocket-pistol, Powder, Pycnidium, Reform, Retort, Thermos®, Vacuum, Vial

Flat(s), Flatness, Flatten(ed), Flattener Adobe, Alkali, Amaze, Ancipital, Apartment, Bachelor, Bald, Banal, Beat, Bed-sit, Blow-out, Bulldoze, Callow, Cape, Complanate, Compress, Condominium, Corymb(ose), Cottage, Coulisse, Court, Dead, Demolish, Dorsiventral, Double, Dress, Dry, Dull, Even, Feeble, Flew, Floor, Flue, Fool, Gaff, Garden, Granny, Guyot, Haugh, High-rise, Homaloid, Home-unit, Horizontal, Insipid, Ironed, Jacent, Key, KO, Law, Lay, Level, Lifeless, Llano, Lodge, Maderised, Marsh, Monotonous, Mud, Nitwit, Norfolk, Obcompressed, Oblate, Ownership, Pad, Pancake, Pedestrian, Peneplain, Peneplane, Penthouse, Pentice, Pied-à-terre, Plain, Planar, Plane, Planish, Plap, Plat, Plateau, Platitude, Press, Prone, Prostrate, Recumbent, Rooms, Salt, Scenery, Service, Smooth, Splayfoot, Spread-edged, Squash, Studio, Tableland, Tabular, Tame, Tasteless, Tenement, True, Uniform, Unsensational, Vapid, Walk-up

Flat-chested Cithara

Flat-faced Socle

Flat-foot(ed) Policeman, Splay

Flat-nosed Camus

Flatter(er), Flattering, Flattery Adulate, Becoming, Beslaver, Blandish, Blarney, Bootlick, Butter, Cajole, Candied, Carn(e)y, Claw(back), Complimentary, Comprabatio, Court-dresser, Damocles, Earwiggy, En beau, Eyewash, Fawn, Fillibrush, Flannel, Flannen, Fleech, Flummery, Foot-licker, Fulsome, Gloze, Gnathonic(al), Grease, Honey, Imitation, Lip-salve, Moody, Palp, Phrase, Poodle-faker, Proneur, Puffery, Sawder, Smarm, Snow job, Soap, Soft soap, Soother, Souk, Spaniel, Stroke, Sugar, Sweet talk, Sycophant, Taffy, Toady, Treacle, Unction, Wheedle, Word

Flatulence, Flatulent Belch, Borborygmus, Burp, Carminative, Colic, Gas, Tympanites, Ventose, Wind, Wind dropsy

Flaunt Brandish, Flourish, Gibe, Parade, Skyre, Sport, Strout, Strut, Wave

Flavour(ed), Flavouring, Flavoursome Absinth(e), Alecost, Amaracus, Anethole, Angostura, Anise, Aniseed, Aroma, Benne, Bergamot, Bold, Borage, Bouquet garni, Clove, Coriander, Cumin, Dill, Essence, Eucalyptol, Fenugreek, Flor, Garlic, Garni, Gingili, Marinate, Mint, Orgeat, Piperonal, Quark, Race, Ratafia, Relish, Rocambole, Sair, Sapor, Sassafras, Season, Sesame, Spearmint, Tack, Tang, Tarragon, → **TASTE**, Til, Tincture, Twang, Umami, Vanilla, Yummy

Flaw Blemish, Brack, Bug, Chip, Crack, Defect, Fallacy, → **FAULT**, Gall, Hamartia, Imperfection, Infirmity, Kink, Knothole, Lophole, Nick, Red-eye, Rima, Spot, Stain, Taint, Tear, Thief, Tragic, Windshake

Flawless Impeccable, Intact, Perfect

Flax(en) Aleseed, Blonde, Codilla, Harakeke, Harden, Hards, Herden, Herl, Hurden, Line, Linseed, Lint, Lint-white, Linum, Mill-mountain, Poi, Tow

Flay Excoriate, Fleece, Flense, Scourge, Skin, Strip, Uncase, Whip

Flea Aphaniptera, Chigger, Chigoe, Chigre, Daphnid, Hopper, Itch-mite, Lop, Pulex, Sand, Turnip, Water

Flea-bane Erigeron

Fleabite Denier

Fleck Dash, Freak, Spot, Streak

Fledgling Aerie, Eyas, Sorage

Flee(ing) Abscond, Bolt, Decamp, Escape, Eschew, Fly, Fugacity, Lam, Loup, Run, Scapa, Scarper, Scram

Fleece, Fleecy Bilk, Bleed, Coat, Despoil, Flocculent, Golden, Jib, Lambskin, Lanose, Nubia, Pash(i)m, Pashmina, Plo(a)t, Pluck, Rifte, Ring, Rob, Rook, Shave, Shear, Sheepskin, Skin, Skirtings, → **SWINDLE**, Toison

Fleer Ogle

Fleet(ing) Armada, Brief, Camilla, Caravan, Convoy, Ephemeral, Evanescent, Fast, First, Flit, Flota, Flotilla, Fugacious, Fugitive, Glimpse, Hasty, Hollow, Lightfoot, Navy, Pacy, Passing, Prison, Spry, Street, Swift, Transient, Velocipede, Volatile

Flemish Flamingant

Flesh(y) Beefy, Body, Carneous, Carrion, Corporeal, Corpulent, Creatic, Dead-meat, Digastric, Finish, Goose, Gum, Hypersarcoma, Joint, Jowl, Ket, Longpig, Love handles, Lush, Meat, Mole, Mons, Muffin top, Mummy, Muscle, Mutton, Proud, Pulp, Quick, Sarcous, Spare tyre, Succulent, Tissue, Wattle

Flesh-eating Cannibalism, Carnassial, Creophagus, Omophagic

Fleshless Dry, Maigre, Pem(m)ican

Flex(ible), Flexibility Adaptable, Bend(y), Compliant, Double-jointed, Elastic, Genu, Leeway, Limber, Lissom(e), Lithe, Pliant, → **RESILIENT**, Rubato, Rubbery, Squeezy, Supple, Tensile, Tonus, Tractile, Versatile, Wieldy, Willing, Willowy, Wiry

▷ **Flexible, Flexuous** *may indicate* an anagram

Flick(er), Flicks Bioscope, Cinema, Fillip, Film, Flip, Flirt, Flutter, Glimmer, Gutter, Movie, Movy, Riffle, Snap, Snow, Spang-cockle, Spark, Switch, Talkie, Twinkle, Waver, Wink, Zap

Flickertail ND

Flier Aerostat, Airman, Alcock, Amy, Aviator, → **BIRD**, Bleriot, Blimp, Brown, Crow, Daedalus, Erk, Fur, George, Gotha, Handout, Icarus, Insert, Leaflet, Lindbergh, Montgolfier, Pilot, RAF, Scotsman, Spec, Speedy

Flight(y), Flight-path Air corridor, Backfisch, Birdbrain, Bolt, Bubble-headed, Capricious, Charter, Contact, Dart, Dash, Departure, Escalier, Escape, Exaltation, Exodus, Fast, Fickle, Flapper, Flaught, Flibbertigibbet, Flip, Flock, Flyby, Fly-past, Free, Fugue, Getaway, Giddy, Grece, Grese, Gris(e), Guy, Hegira, Hejira, Hejra, Hellicat, Hijra, Lam, Loup-the-dyke, Mercy, Milk-run, Mission, Open-jaw, Pair, Proving, Redeye, R(a)iser, Rode, Ro(a)ding, Rout, Runaway, Skein, Sortie, Stairs, → **STAMPEDE**, Stayre, Steps, Swarm, Test, Top, Tower, Trap, Vol(age), Volageous, Volatile, Volley, Whisky-frisky, Wing

Flightless Kakapo, Nandoo, Ostrich, Rhea, Struthious

▷ **Flighty** *may indicate* an anagram

Flimsy Finespun, Fragile, Gimcrack, Gossamer, Jimcrack, Lacy, Paper thin, Sleazy, Sleezy, Tenuous, Thin, Weak, Wispy

Flinch Blench, Cringe, Funk, Quail, Recoil, Shrink, Shudder, Start, Wince

Fling Affair, Dance, Flounce, Heave, Highland, Hurl, Lance, Pitch, Shy, Slat, Slug, Slump, Spanghew, Spree, Throw, → **TOSS**

Flint Chert, Firestone, Granite, Hag-stone, Hornstone, Microlith, Mischmetal, Optical, Pirate, Rock, Silex, Silica, Stone, Touchstone, Tranchet

Flip(pant), Flippancy, Flipping Airy, Bally, Brash, Cocky, Facetious, Flick, Frivolous, Impudent, Jerk, Nog, Overturn, Persiflage, Pert, Purl, Ruddy, Sassy, Saucy, Toss, Turn, Upend

Flipper(s) Fin-toed, Paddle, Pinniped(e)

Flirt(ation), Flirtatious, Flirting Bill, Buaya, Carve, Chippy, Cockteaser, Come-hither, Come-on, Coquet(te), Dalliance, Demivierge, Fizgig, Footsie, Gallivant, Heart-breaker, Kittenish, Lumber, Mash, Minx, Neck, Philander(er), Pickeer, Prick-teaser, Prink, Rig, Spark, Toy, Trifle, Vamp, Wow

Flit Dart, Decamp, Flicker, Flutter, Moonlight, Scoot

Float(er), Floating, Flotation Balsa, Bob, Bubble, Buoy, Caisson, Camel, Carley, Clanger, Drift, Fleet, Flotsam, Flutterboard, Froth, Fucus, Jetsam, Jetson, Levitate, Lifebuoy, Milk, Natant, Neuston, Oropesa, Outrigger, Paddle, Planula, Pontoon, Pram, Quill, Raft, Ride, Sail, Skim, Sponson, Stick, Trimmer, Vacillate, Waft, Waggler, Waterwings, Weightless

Floating garden Chinampa

Flock(s) Assemble, Bevy, Charm, Chirm, Company, Congregation, Dopping, Drove, Flight, Fold, Forgather, Gaggle, Gather, Gregatim, Herd, Mob, Paddling, Rally, Rout, School, Sedge, Sord, Spring, Trip, Troop, Tuft, Vulgar, Walk, Wing, Wisp, Wool

Flog(ger), Flogging Beat, Birch, Breech, Cane, Cat, Clobber, Exert, Flay, Hawk, Hide, Knout, Lace, Lambast, Larrup, Lash, Lather, Lick, Orbilius, Rope's end, Scourge, Sell, Strap, Tat, Taw, → **THRASH**, Thwack, Tout, Vapulate, Welt, Whip, Whipping-cheer

Flood(ed) Avalanche, Awash, Bore, Cataclysm, Deluge, Deucalion's, Diffuse, Diluvium, Drown, Dump, Eger, Flash, Freshet, Gush, Inundate, Irrigate, Noachic, Ogygian deluge, Outpouring, Overflow, Overswell, Overwhelm, Pour, Rage, Smurf, Spate, Speat, Suffuse, Swamp, Tide, → **TORRENT**, Undam, Washland

Floodgate St(a)unch

Floodlight Ashcan, Blond(e), One-key

Floor(ing) Area, Astonish, Astound, Baffle, Barbecue, Beat, Bemuse, Benthos, Chess, Deck(ing), Dev(v)el, Down, Entresol, Étage, Fell, Flags(tone), Flatten, Flight, Gravel, Ground, Kayo, KO, Mezzanine, Mould loft, Paralimnion, Parquet, Pelvic, Piano nobile, Pit, Planch, Platform, Puncheon, Screed, Shop, Siege, Sole, Stage, Stagger, Story, Stump, Terrazzo, Tessella, Tessera, Thill, Throw, Trading, Woodblock

Flop Belly-landing, Bomb, Collapse, Dud, Failure, Fizzer, Fosbury, Lollop, Mare's-nest, Misgo, Phut, Plump, Purler, Washout, Whap, Whitewash

Flora Benthos, Biota, Cybele, Flowers, Intestinal

Florence, Florentine Medici, Tuscan

Florid Baroque, Coloratura, Cultism, Flamboyant, Fresh, Gongorism, High, Red, Rococo, Rubicund, Ruddy, Taffeta

Florida Fa

Florin Scotchman

Florist Spry

Floss(y) Dental, Flashy, Florence, Ornate, Silk

▶ **Flotation** *see* **FLOAT(ER)**

Flotilla Armada, Escadrille

Flotsam Detritus, Driftwood, Flotage, Waift, Waveson, Weft

Flounce Falbala, Frill, Furbelow, Huff, Prance, Ruffle, Sashay, Toss

Flounder Blunder, Fluke, Reel, Sandsucker, Slosh, Struggle, Stumble, Tolter, Toss, Wallop, Wallow

Flour Buckwheat, Cassava, Couscous(ou), Cribble, Crible, Farina, Graham, Gram, Kouskous, Meal, Middlings, Pinole, Plain, Powder, Red-dog, Rice, Rock, Rye, Self-raising, Soy(a), Strong, Wheatmeal, White, Wholegrain, Wholemeal, Wholewheat, Wood

Flourish(ed), Flourishing Blague, Bless, Bloom, Blossom, Boast, Brandish, Bravura, Burgeon, Cadenza, Epiphonema, Fanfare, Fiorita, Fl, Flare, Floreat, Florescent, Green, Grow, Kicking, Lick, Lush, Melisma, Mort, Omar, Palmy, Paraph, Pert, Prosper, Rubric, Scroll, Swash, Tantara, Thrive, Tucket, Veronica, Vigorous, Wampish, Wave, Welfare

Flout Disdain, Disobey, Insult, Malign, Mock, Profane, Scorn, Scout

Flow(ing) Abound, Afflux, Cantabile, Cantilena, Cash, Circumference, Current, Cursive, Cusec, Data, Distil, Ebb, Emanate, Estrang(h)elo, Fleet, Fluent, Fluid, Flush, Flux, Freeform, Gene, Gush, Issue, Knickpoint, Lahar, Laminar, Liquid, Loose-bodied, Nappe, Nickpoint, Obsequent, Onrush, Ooze, Popple, Pour, Purl, Rail(e), Rayle, Rill, Rin, Run, Rush, Scapa, Seamless, Seep, Seton, Setter, Slip, Slur, Spate, Spurt, Stream, Streamline, Teem, Tidal, Torrent, Trickle, Turbulent, Viscous

Flower (part), Flowering, Flowers, Flower bed Best, Bloom, Bloosme, Blossom, Composite, Cream, Develop, Disc, Efflorescence, Elite, Fiori, Inflorescence, Parterre, Passion, Plant, Pre-vernal, Prime, Quatrefeuille, Quatrefoil, Remontant, → **RIVER**, Rogation, Serotine, Spray, Square, Stalked, Stream, Thyrse, Trefoil, Trumpet, Tyrse, Verdoy, Vernal, Wreath

---

FLOWERS

3 *letters:*	4 *letters:*		
May	Aloe	Gold	Lily
Mum	Arum	Gool	Pink
Rue	Cyme	Gule	Rose
	Disa	Irid	Wald
	Flag	Iris	Weld
		Knot	

5 letters:
Agave
Aster
Brook
Bugle
Camas
Canna
Daisy
Enemy
Erica
Hosta
Lotus
Lupin
Orris
Oxlip
Padma
Pansy
Phlox
Poppy
Spink
Stock
Tansy
Toran
Tulip
Umbel
Viola
Yulan

6 letters:
Adonis
Annona
Arabis
Camash
Camass
Corymb
Cosmos
Crants
Dahlia
Gollan
Henbit
Lupine
Madder
Maguey
Mallow
Mimosa
Nuphar
Onagra
Orchid
Oxslip
Paeony

Pompom
Pompon
Protea
Scilla
Sesame
Silene
Smilax
Spadix
Tassel
Thrift
Torana
Wasabi
Yarrow

7 letters:
Aconite
Alyssum
Amarant
Anemone
Astilbe
Bugloss
Campion
Cowslip
Freesia
Fuchsia
Fumaria
Gentian
Gilt-cup
Glacier
Gladdon
Godetia
Golland
Gowland
Hawkbit
Ipomoea
Jonquil
Kikumon
Lobelia
Melilot
Mimulus
Nosegay
Petunia
Picotee
Primula
Quamash
Rampion
Statice
Sulphur
Tellima
Verbena

8 letters:
Abutilon
Amaranth
Argemone
Asphodel
Bindi-eye
Bluebell
Bullhoof
Carolina
Clematis
Cyclamen
Daffodil
Floscule
Foxglove
Gardenia
Geranium
Gillyvor
Gladioli
Glory-pea
Hepatica
Hesperis
Hibiscus
Kok-sagyz
Larkspur
Leucojum
Magnolia
Marigold
Myosotis
Oleander
Primrose
Scabious
Stapelia
Trollius
Tuberose
Turnsole
Valerian

9 letters:
Bald-money
Belamoure
Buttercup
Cineraria
Columbine
Edelweiss
Eglantine
Galingale
Gessamine
Hellebore
Hollyhock
Hydrangea

Jessamine
Melampode
Pimpernel
Pyrethrum
Rudbeckia
Santonica
Saxifrage
Speedwell
Strobilus
Tiger lily

10 letters:
Bellamoure
Buttonhole
Coronation
Granadilla
Heliotrope
Immortelle
Nasturtium
Pentstemon
Poached egg
Poinsettia
Polyanthus
Pulsatilla
Quinsy-wort
Snapdragon
Stavesacre
Tibouchine
Touch-me-not

11 letters:
Boutonniere
Bur-marigold
Gillyflower
Loose-strife
Meadow-sweet
Saintpaulia

12 letters:
Hortus siccus
None-so-pretty
Pasqueflower
Pheasant's eye
Tradescantia

13 letters:
Flannelflower

14 letters:
Transvaal daisy

▷ **Flower** *may indicate* a river
Flower arrangement, Flower work Barbola, Ikebana, Lei
Flowery Anthea, Anthemia, Damassin, Orchideous, → **ORNATE**, Pseudocarp, Verbose

Flu Bird, Fujian, Gastric, → **INFLUENZA**, ME, Wog

Fluctuate(r), Fluctuation Ambivalence, Balance, Seasonal, Seiche, Trimmer, Unsteady, Vacillate, Vary, Waver, Yo-yo

Flue Chimney, Duct, Funnel, Pipe, Recuperator, Tewel, Uptake, Vent

Fluent(ly) Eloquent, Facile, Flowing, Glib, Liquid, Oracy, Verbose, Voluble

Fluff(y) Bungle, Candyfloss, Dowl(e), Down, Dust, Dust bunny, Feathery, Fleecy, Flocculent, Floss, Flue, Fug, Fuzz, Girl, Lint, Mess-up, Muff, Noil, Oose, Ooze, Plot, Thistledown

Fluid Aldehyde, Amniotic, Anasarca, Ascites, Bile, Broo, Chyle, Cisterna, Colostrum, Condy's, Coolant, Correcting, Dewdrop, Edema, Enema, Erf, Fixative, Fl, Glycerin, Humour, Joint-oil, Juice, Latex, → **LIQUID**, Lymph, Movable, Mucus, Oedema, Perfect, Perilymph, Plasma, Pus, Sap, Seminal, Serous, Serum, Shifting, Spermatic, Spittle, Succus, Synovia, Transudate, Vitreum, Vril, Water

▷ **Fluid** *may indicate* an anagram

Fluke Accident, Anchor, Chance, Fan, Flounder, Ga(u)nch, Grapnel, Killock, Liver, Lobe, Redia, Schistosome, Scratch, Spud, Upcast

Flummery BS, Pudding

Flummox Baffle, Bamboozle, Floor, Nonplus

Flunk Fail

Flunkey Chasseur, Clawback, Haiduck, Heyduck, Jeames, Lackey, Servant, Toady

Fluorescence, Fluorescent Bloom, Day-glo, Epipolism, Glow, Phosphorescence, Uranin

Fluorine F

Flurry Bustle, Fluster, Haste, Hoo-ha, Shower

Flush(ed) Affluent, Beat, Busted, Even, Ferret, Florid, Flow, Gild, Hectic, Heyday, Hot, Level, Red, Rolling, Rose, Royal, Rud, Scour, Sluice, Spaniel, Start, Straight, Sypher, Thrill, Tierce, Vigour, Wash, Well-heeled

Fluster(ed) Befuddle, Confuse, Disconcert, Faze, Flap, Jittery, Pother, Pudder, Rattle, Shake

Flute (player) Bellows-maker, Bohm, Channel, Claribel(la), Crimp, English, Fife, Fipple, Flageolet, German, Glass, Glyph, Groove, Marsyas, Nose, Ocarina, Piccolo, Pipe, Poogye(e), Quena, Shakuhachi, Sulcus, Thisbe, Tibia, Toot, Transverse, Whistle, Wineglass, Zuf(f)olo

Flutter Bat, Bet, Fan, Fibrillate, Flacker, Flaffer, Flaught, Flichter, Flicker, Flitter, Fly, → **GAMBLE**, Hover, Palpitate, Pitapat, Play, Pulse, Sensation, Twitter, Waft, Winnow

Flux B, D, Electric, Flow, Fusion, Luminous, Magnetic, Maxwell, Melt, Neutron, Panta rhei, Radiant, Tesla, Weber

Fly(ing), Flies Abscond, Agaric, Airborne, Alder, Alert, Antlion, Arch, Assassin, Astute, Aviation, Awake, Aware, A-wing, Baker, Bedstead, Bee, Black, Blister, Blowfly, Blue-arsed, Bluebottle, Bolt, Bot, Breese, Breeze, Brize, Brommer, Bulb, Bush, Cab, Caddis, Canny, Carriage, Carrot, Cecidomyia, Chalcid, Cheesehopper, Cheese skipper, Cleg, Cluster, Cock-a-bondy, Crane, Cuckoo, → **CUNNING**, Damsel, Dash, Decamp, Deer, Diptera, Dobson, Doctor, Dolphin, Doodlebug, Dragon, Drake, Drone, Drosophila, Dry, Dung, Dutchman, Escape, Face, Fiacre, Flee, Flesh, Flit, Fox, Frit, Fruit, Gad, Glide, Glossina, Gnat, Goutfly, Grannom, Greenbottle, Greenhead, Hackle, Hairy Mary, Harl, Harvest, Hedge-hop, Herl, Hessian, Homoptera, Hop, Horn, Horse, Hover, Hurtle, Ichneumon, Instrument, Jenny-spinner, Jock Scott, Lace-wing, Lamp, Lantern, Laputan, March brown, Midge, Mosquito, Mossie, Moth, Motuca, Murragh, Musca, Mutuca, Namu, Needle, New Forest, Nymph, Onion, Opening, Ox-warble, Palmer, Para, Pilot, Pium, Plecopteran, Pomace, Rapid, Robber, Sacrifice, Saucer, Sciaridae, Scorpion, Scotsman, Screwworm, Scud, Sedge, Sheep ked, Silverhorn, Simulium, Smart, Smother, Snake, Snipe, Soar, Spanish, Speed, Spinner, Stable, Stream, Syrphidae, Tabanid, Tachina, Tail, Tear, Thrips, Tipula, Trichopteran, Tsetse, Tube, Turkey brown, Turnip, Vamoose, Vinegar, Volatic, Volitate, Warble, Watchet, Water, Welshman's button, Wet,

Wheat, Wide-awake, Willow, Wily, Wing, Yellow Sally, Yogic, Zebub, Zimb, Zipper, Zoom

Fly-catcher Attercop, Clamatorial, Cobweb, Darlingtonia, Dionaea, King-bird, Phoebe, Spider, Tanrec, Tentacle, Tyrant, Yellowhead

Flying-fox Fruit-bat, Kalong

Flying saucer UFO

Fly-killer Chowri, Chowry, DDT, Swat

Flyover Overpass

Foam(ing) Aerogel, Barm, Bubble, Froth, Head, Lather, Mousse, Oasis®, Polystyrene, Ream, Scum, Seethe, Spindrift, Spooming, Spume, Sud(s), Surf, Wake, Wild water, Yeast, Yest

Fob Chain, Defer, Fub, Pocket, Slang

Focal, Focus Centre, Centrepiece, Clou, Concentrate, Converge, Fix, Hinge, Hub, Narrow, Nub, Pinpoint, Point, Prime, Principal, Real, Spotlight, Train, Zoom

Fodder Alfalfa, Browsing, Buckwheat, Cannon, Clover, Eatage, Emmer, Ensilage, Foon, Forage, Gama-grass, Grama, Guar, Hay, Lucerne, Mangle, Mangold, Oats, Oilcake, Pasture, Provender, Rye-grass, Sainfoin, Silage, Soilage, Stover, Straw, Ti-tree, Vetch, Yarran

Foe Anti, Arch, Contender, → **ENEMY**, Opponent, Rival

Foetus Embryo

Fog Aerosol, Brume, Cloud, Damp, Fret, Haar, (London) Particular, Miasm(a), Mist, Murk, Obscure, Pea-soup(er), Roke, Sea-fret, Sea-haar, Smog, Smoke, Soup, Thick, Vapour, Yorkshire

Fogg Phileas, Solicitor

Fog(e)y Die-hard, Square

Foible Failing, Flaw, Idiosyncrasy, Quirk, Weakness

Foil(ed) Ba(u)lk, Chaff, Cross, Dupe, Epée, Fleuret(te), Frustrate, Gold, Gold leaf, Lametta, Leaf, Offset, Paillon, Pip, Scotch, Scupper, Silver, Stime, Stooge, Stump, Stymie, Sword, Tain, Thwart, Tinsel, Touché

Foist Fob, Insert, Insinuate, Suborn, Wish

Fold(er), Folding, Folded, Folds Anticline, Bend, Binder, Close, Collapse, Concertina, Convolution, Corrugate, Cote, Crash, Crease, Crimp, Crinkle, Crunkle, Diapir, Diptych, Dog-ear, Double, Duo-tang®, Epicanthus, Epiploon, Fake, Fan, File, Fourchette, Fr(a) enum, Frill, Furl, Gather, Geanticline, Groin, Gyrus, Inflexure, Intussuscept, Jacket, Jack-knife, Lap, Lapel, Lap(p)et, Lirk, Mantle, Mesentery, Mitre, Monocline, Nappe, Nympha, Obvolute, Octuple, Omentum, Origami, Pastigium, Pen, Pericline, Pintuck, Pleach, → **PLEAT**, Plica, Plunging, Ply, Pound, Prancke, Pran(c)k, Ptyxis, Recumbent, Ruck(le), Ruga, Sheep-pen, Syncline, Triptych, Tuck, Vocal, Wrap

Foliage Coma, Finial, Frond, Frondescence, Greenery, Leafage, Leaves

Folio(s) Crown, Elephant, F(f), File, Foolscap, Imperial, Percy, Royal

Folk(sy) Beaker, Homespun, Kin, People, Public

Follicle Graafian

Follow(er), Following Acolyte, Acolyth, Adhere, Admirer, After, Agree, Amoret, And, Anthony, Attend(ant), Believer, Chase, Clientele, Consequence, Copy, Dangle, Disciple, Dog, Echo, Ensew, Ensue, Entourage, Epigon(e), Equipage, F, Fan, Groupie, Heel(er), Henchman, Hereon, Hunt, Imitate, Jacob, Man, Merry men, Mimic, Minion, Muggletonian, Myrmidon, Neist, Next, Obey, Pan, Post, Pursue, Rake, Road, Run, Satellite, School, Sectary, Secundum, Seewing, Segue, Sequel, Seriation, Servitor, Shadow, Sheep, Sidekick, S(h)ivaite, Stag, Stalk, Stear, Steer, Subsequent, Succeed, Sue, Suivez, Supervene, Tag, Tail, Tantony, Trace, Track, Trail, Train, Use, Vocation, Votary

▷ **Follower** *may indicate* B

Folly Absurd, Antic, Bêtise, Idiocy, Idiotcy, Imprudence, Lunacy, Madness, Mistake, Moria, Stupidity, Unwisdom, Vanity

Foment(ation) Arouse, Brew, Embrocation, Excite, Incite, Poultice, Stupe

Fond(ness) Amatory, Ardour, Attachment, Dote, Keen, Loving, Partial, Penchant, Tender, Tendre

Fondant Ice, Sweet

Fondle Canoodle, Caress, Dandle, Grope, Hug, Nurse, Pet, Snuggle, Stroke

Font Aspersorium, Bénitier, Bitmap, Delubrum, Ennage, Outline, Proportional, Raster, Scalable, Source, True-type, Vector

Food Aliment, Ambrosia, Bakemeat, Balti, Batten, Battill, Battle, Bellytimber, Bento, Board, Bolus, Bord, Broth, Browse, Bully, Burger, Bush-tucker, Carry-out, Cate, Cereal, Chametz, Cheer, Cheese, Chop, Chow, Chuck, Chyme, Cocoyam, Collation, Comestible, Comfort, Commons, Convenience, Cook-chill, Course, Cud, Curd, Deutoplasm, Dietetics, → **DISH**, Dodger, Dog's body, Doner kebab, Dunderfunk, Eatage, Eats, Esculents, Eutrophy, Falafel, Famine, Fare, Fast, Fast casual, Felafel, Fodder, Forage, Formula, Franken(stein), Freedom, Fuel, Functional, Giffengood, Grub, Gruel, Hamburger, Hangi, Hometz, Incaparina, Ingesta, Jootha, Jorts, Junk, Kai, Keep, Langar, Leben, Lerp, Long-pig, Maigre, Makan, Maki, Manna, Mato(o)ke, Matzoon, Meal, Meat, Muckamuck, Nacho, Nardoo, Nosebag, Nosh, Nourishment, Nourriture, Obento, Opsonium, Ort, Oven-ready, Pabulum, Pannage, Pap, Parev(e), Parve, Pasta, Pasture, Peck, Pemmican, Pizza, Prog, Provand, Provender, Provision, Pu(l)ture, Ration(s), Real, Refreshment, Risotto, Roughage, Rysttafel, Sambal, Samosa, Sap, Sashimi, Scaff, Schri, Scoff, Scran, Scroggin, Sitology, Sizings, Skin, Skran, Slow, Snack, Soft meat, Soil, Soul, Square meal, Staple, Stir fry, Stodge, Sushi, Table, Tack, Takeaway, Tamale, Taro, Tempeh, Tempura, Teriyake, Tex-Mex, Tofu, Trimmings, Tripe, Trophallaxis, Tsamba, Tuck(er), Vegeburger, Veggie-burger, Viand, Victuals, Vivers, Vivres, Waffle, Yantia, Yittles, Yog(h)urt

Food-plant Laser, Silphium

Foodstore Delicatessen, Grocery, Larder, Pantry, Silo

Fool(hardy), Foolish(ness) Air-head, Anserine, April, Asinico, Asinine, Assot, Berk, BF, Blithering, Bob, Booby, Bottom, Brainless, Brash, Buffoon, Cake, Capocchia, Chump, Clot, Clown, Cockeyed, Coney, Coof, Coxcomb, Cuif, Cully, Daft, Dagonet, Daw, Delude, Desipience, Dessert, Dilly, Divvy, Doat, Doilt, Dote, Dummy, Dunce, Dweeb, Empty, Etourdi, Fatuous, Feste, Flannel(led), Folly, Fon, Fond, Fox, Gaby, Gaga, Galah, Git, Glaikit, Goat, Gobbo, Goon, Goose, Gooseberry, Groserts, Gubbins, Gull, Gullible, Halfwit, Hanky-panky, Hare-brained, Have, Haverel, Highland, Hoax, Huntiegowk, Hunt-the-gowk, Idiotic, Imbecile, Inane, Ineptitude, Injudicious, Insensate, Jest, Jester, Joke, Kid, Kissel, Lark, Loon, Madcap, Mamba, Misguide, Mislead, Mome, Moron, Muggins, Nerk, Niaiserie, Ni(n)compoop, Nignog, Ninny, Nong, Noodle, Nose-led, Nut, Oanshagh, Omadhaun, Patch, Pea-brained, Poop, Poupe, Prat, Punk, Rash, Sawney, Scogan, Scoggin, Senseless, Shallow, Shmo, Simpleton, Snipe, Soft, Sot, Spoony, Stultify, → **STUPID**, Sucker, Sweet, Tom (noddy), Trifle, Turkey, Unwitty, Vice, Wantwit, Yap, Yorick, Yoyo, Zany

Foolproof Fail-safe

Fool's gold Mundic, Pyrites

Foot(ing), Footwork, Feet Amphibrach, Amphimacer, Anap(a)est, Antibacchius, Antispast, Athlete's, Bacchius, Ball, Base, Board, Choliamb, Choree, Choreus, Choriamb, Club, Cold, Cretic, Dactyl, Dance, Dipody, Dochmii, Dochmius, Epitrite, F, Flat, Ft, Hephthemimer, Hoof, Hoppus, Iamb(us), Immersion, Infantry, Ionic, Molossus, Ockodols, Pad, Paeon, Palama, Pastern, Paw, Pay, Pedal, Pedate, Pedicure, Penthemimer, Pes, Pettitoes, Plates, Podiatry, Podium, Proceleusmatic, Pyrrhic, Roothold, Scazon, Semeia, Serif, Shanks's mare, Shanks's pony, Spade, Splay, Spondee, Standing, Syzygy, Tarsus, Terms, Tootsie, Tootsy, Tootsy-wootsy, Tread, Trench, Tribrach, Trilbies, Triseme, Trochee, Trotter, Tube, Ungula, Verse, Wrong

Football(er) Aerial pingpong, American, Association, Australian Rules, Back, Banyana-banyana, Barbarian, Ba'spiel, Best, Camp, Canadian, Centre, Double header, Fantasy, FIFA, Five-a-side, Flanker(back), Fly-half, Futsal, Gaelic, Gazza, Goalie, Gridder, Half, Hooker, Keeper, Kicker, League, Libero, Linebacker, Lineman, Lock, Midfield, Moore,

National code, Nickelback, Pack, Pele, Pigskin, Ranger, RU, Rugby, Rugger, Rules, Safety, Seven-a-side, Sevens, Soccer(oos), Sport, Stand-off, Striker, Subbuteo®, Superbowl, Sweeper, Table, Tight-end, Togger, Total, Touch(back), Wallgame, Wing, Wingman

Footboard Stretcher

Foot-fault Bunion, Corn, Hammer-toe, Talipes, Verruca

Foothills Submontane

Foothold Lodgement, Purchase, Stirrup

Footlights Floats

Footling Trivial

Footloose Peripatetic

Footman Attendant, Flunkey, Hiker, Lackey, Ped(estrian), Pompey, Valet de chambre, Yellowplush

Footnote Addendum, Passim, PS

Footpad Land-rat, Mugger, Robber

Footpath, Footway Banquette, Catwalk, Clapper, Track

Footplate Horseshoe

Footprint Carbon, Ecological, Electronic, Ichnite, Ichnolite, Ornithichnite, Pad, Prick, Pug, Seal, Slot, Trace, Track, Tread, Vestige

Footrest, Footstool Coaster, Cricket, Hassock, Pouffe, Stirrup, Stool, Tramp

Footrot, Footsore Blister, Bunion, Corn, Halt, Surbate, Surbet, Weary, Wire-heel

Footslogger Infantryman

Footwashing Maundy, Nipter

Footwear Gumboot, Jackboot, → **SHOE**, Slipper, Sock, Spats, Stocking

Fop(pish) Apery, Barbermonger, Beau, Buck, Cat, Coxcomb, Dandy, Dude, Exquisite, Fallal, Fangled, Fantastico, Finical, La-di-da, Macaroni, Monarcho, Muscadin, Petit maître, Popinjay, Skipjack, Toff

For Ayes, Because, Concerning, Cos, Pro, Since, To

Forage Alfalfa, Fodder, Graze, Greenfeed, Ladino, Lucern(e), Pickeer, Prog, Raid, Rummage, Sainfoin, Search

Foray Attack, Creach, Creagh, Raid, Sortie, Spreagh

Forbear(ance), Forbearing Abstain, Clement, Endure, Indulgent, Lenience, Lineage, Longanimity, Mercy, Overgo, Pardon, Parent, Patient, Quarter, → **REFRAIN**, Suffer, Tolerant, Withhold

Forbid(den), Forbidding Ban, Bar, City, Denied, Don't, Dour, Enjoin, For(e)speak, Gaunt, Grim, Haram, Hostile, Loury, NL, Prohibit, Proscribe, Sinister, Stern, Taboo, Tabu, Tapu, Tref(a), Verboten, Veto

Force(d), Forceful, Forces, Forcible, Forcing Activist, Agency, Air-arm, Army, Assertive, Back emf, Barge, Bind, Birr, Bludgeon, Body, Bounce, Brigade, Bring, Brunt, Bulldoze, Cadre, Capillary, Cascade, Centrifugal, Centripetal, Chi, Coerce, Coercive, Cogency, Commando, Compel, Constrain, Cops, Coriolis, Cram, Delta, Detachment, Dint, Domineer, Downflow, Dragoon, Drive, Duress(e), Dynamic, Dyne, E, Edge, Electromotive, Emphatic, Energetic, Equilibrant, Erdgeist, Erg, Exact, Exchange, Expeditionary, Extort, Extrude, F, Farci, Fifth, Fire brigade, Foot-pound, Foot-ton, Foss, Frogmarch, Full-line, G, Gar, Gendarmerie, Gilbert, Gism, Gouge, Gravitational, Great Attractor, Hale, High-powered, Host, Hunter-killer, Hurricane, Impetus, Impose, Impress, Impulsion, Inertial, Instress, Intense, Interpol, Irgun, Irrupt, Jism, Juggernaut, Kinetic, Kundalini, Labour, Land, Landsturm, Landwehr, Lashkar, Legion, Leverage, Life, Lift, Lin(n), Live load, Lorentz, Magnetomotive, Magnus, Make, Mana, Manpower, Market, Met, Militia, Moment, Momentum, Muscle, Nature-god, Navy, Newton, Numen, Oblige, Od, Odyl(e), OGPU, Old Contemptibles, Orgone, Orotund, Personnel, Phrenism, Physical, Pigs, Pion, Pithy, Plastic, Police, Polis, Posse, Potent, Pound, Poundal, Power, Prana, Press(gang), Pressure, Prise, Procrustean, Psyche, Psychic, Pull, Punchy, Pushy, Put, Qi, Railroad, Ram, Rape, Ravish, Reave, Red Army, Regular, Require, Restem, Route, Rush, SAS, Sforzando, Shear, Shoehorn, Snorting, Spent, Spetsnaz, Squad, Squeeze,

Squirt, Steam(roller), Steem, Stick, Stiction, Sting and ling, Strained, Strength, → **STRESS**, Strong-arm, Subject, Sword, TA, Task, Teeth, Telergy, Telling, Territorial, The Bill, The Great Attractor, Thrust, Torque, Tractive, Troops, Upthrust, Van der Waals', Vehement, Vigorous, Vim, Violence, Vires, Vis, Vis visa, Vital, Vively, Vociferous, Vril, Weak, Wedge, Wrench, Wrest, Wring, Zap

▷ **Force(d)** *may indicate* an anagram

Forced labour Begar

Force-feeding Gavage

Forceps Bulldog, Capsule, Crow(s)bill, Hemostatic, Mosquito, Obstetrical, Pedicellaria, Pincers, Rongeur, Tenaculum, Thumb, Vulsella

Ford Anglia, Anna, Capri, Car, Crossing, Drift, Escort, Industrialist, Irish bridge, Sierra, Strid, Tin Lizzy, Wade

Forearm Cubital, Radius, Ulna

▶ **Forebear** *see* **FORBEAR(ANCE)**

Foreboding Anxiety, Augury, Cloudage, Croak, Feeling, Freet, Hoodoo, → **OMEN**, Ominous, Premonition, Presage, Presentient, Presentiment, Sinister, Zoomantic

Forecast(er), Forecasting Augury, Auspice, Divine, Extrapolation, Glass, Horoscope, Long-range, Metcast, Metman, Numerical, Omen, Perm, Portend, Precurse, Predicate, Predict, Presage, Prescience, Prevision, Prognosis, Prognosticate, Projection, Prophesy, Quant, Rainbird, Scry, Shipping, Skry, Soothsay, Spae, Tip, Weather

Foreclose Bar, Block, Obstruct, Preclude

Forefather(s) Ancestor, Elder, Forebear, Parent, Rude

Forefront Van, Vaward

Foreground Repoussage, Repoussoir

Forehead Brow, Front(let), Frontal, Glabella(r), Nasion, Sincipitum, Temple

Foreign(er) Adventitious, Alien, Amakwerekwere, Arab, Auslander, Barbarian, Easterling, Ecdemic, Eleanor, Ethnic, Étranger, Exclave, Exotic, External, Extraneous, Extrinsic, Forane, Forinsecal, Forren, Fraim, Fremit, Gaijin, German, Gringo, Gweilo, Malihini, Metic, Moit, Mote, Outlander, Outside, Oversea, Peregrine, Remote, → **STRANGE**, Stranger, Taipan, Tramontane, Uitlander, Unfamiliar, Wog

▷ **Foreign** *may indicate* an anagram

Foreign Office FO, Quai d'Orsay

Foreknowledge Prescience

Foreman Baas, Boss, Bosun, Chancellor, Clicker, Gaffer, Ganger, Manager, Overseer, Steward, Straw boss, Superintendent, Tool pusher, Topsman, Walla(h)

Foremost First, Front, Leading, Primary, Prime, Salient, Supreme, Upfront, Van

▷ **Foremost** *may indicate* first letters of words following

Forenoon Undern

Forepart Cutwater, Front

Forerunner Augury, Harbinger, Herald, Messenger, Omen, Pioneer, Precurrer, Precursor, Prequel, Trailer, Vaunt-courier

Foresee Anticipate, Divine, Preview, Prophesy, Scry

Foreshadow Adumbrate, Augur, Bode, Forebode, Hint, Portend, Pre-echo, Prefigure, Presage, Type

Foreshow Betoken, Bode, Signify

Foresight Ganesa, Prescience, Prophecy, Prospect, Providence, Prudence, Taish, Vision

Foreskin Prepuce

Forest(ry), Forested Arden, Ardennes, Argonne, Ashdown, Black, Bohemian, Bracknell, Brush, Bush, Caatinga, Charnwood, Chase, Cloud, Cranborne Chase, Dean, Deer, Elfin, Epping, Firth, Fontainebleau, Gallery, Gapo, Glade, Greenwood, Igapo, Jungle, Katyn, Managed, Monte, Nandi, Nemoral, New, Nottingham, Petrified, Rain, Savernake, Selva, Sherwood, Silviculture, Taiga, Teutoburg, Thuringian, Urman, Virgin, Waltham, Wealden, → **WOOD**, Woodcraft, Woodland

Forestall Anticipate, Head-off, Obviate, Pip, Pre-empt, Prevent, Queer, Scoop

Forester Foster, Kangaroo, Lumberjack, Verderer, Waldgrave, Walker, Woodman, Woodward

Foretaste Antepast, Antipasto, Appetiser, Avant-goût, Pregustation, Prelibation, Preview, Sample, Trailer

Foretell(ing), Forewarn Augur, Bode, Caution, Divine, Fatidic, Forecast, Portend, Predict, Premonish, Presage, Previse, Prognosticate, Prophecy, Soothsay, Spae, Weird

Forethought Anticipation, Caution, Prometheus, Provision, Prudence

Forever All-time, Always, Amber, Ay(e), Constant, Eternal, Evermore, Keeps

▶ **Forewarn** *see* **FORETELL(ING)**

Foreword Introduction, Preamble, Preface, Proem, Prologue

For example Eg, Say, Vg, ZB

For fear Lest

Forfeit(ed) Confiscated, Deodand, Fine, Forgo, → **PENALTY**, Phillepina, Phillepine, Philop(o)ena, Relinquish, Rue-bargain, Sconce

Forge(d), Forger(y) Blacksmith, Copy, Counterfeisance, Counterfeit, Drop, Dud, Fabricate, Fake, Falsify, Fashion, Foundry, Hammer, Heater, Horseshoe, Ireland, Ironsmith, Lauder, Mint, Nailery, Paper-hanger, Pigott, Progress, Rivet head, Rivet-hearth, Smith(y), Smithery, Spurious, Stiddie, Stiff, Stithy, Stumer, Tilt, Trucage, Truquage, Utter, Valley, Vermeer, Vulcan, Weld

Forget(ful), Forget-me-not, Forgetting Amnesia, Dry, Fluff, Infonesia, Lethe, Lotus, Myosotis, Neglect, Oblivious, Omit, Overlook, Senior moment, Unlearn, Wipe

Forgive(ness), Forgiving Absolution, Amnesty, Clement, Condone, Divine, Excuse, Lenity, Merciful, Overlook, Pardon, Placable, Remission, Remittal, Tolerant

Forgo(ne) Abstain, Expected, Refrain, Renounce, Waive

Forgotten Bygone, Lost, Missed, Sad

For instance As

Forjeskit Overscutched

Fork(ed), Fork out Bifurcate, Biramous, Branch, Caudine, Cleft, Crotch, Crutch, Divaricate, Forficate, Fourchette, Grain, Graip, Morton's, Osmeterium, Pastry, Pay, Pickle, Prong, Replication, Runcible, Slave, Sucket, Tine, Toaster, Toasting, Tormenter, Tormentor, Trident, Trifid, Tuner, Tuning, Y

Forlorn(ness) Abject, Aidless, Desolate, Destitute, Drearisome, Godforsaken, Lonely, Miserable, Nightingale, Sad, Woebegone

Form(s) Allotropic, Alumni, Bench, Bumf, Cast, Ceremonial, Charterparty, Class, Clipped, Constitute, Coupon, Create, Document, Draw up, Dress, Experience, Fashion, Feature, Fig, → **FIGURE**, Formula, Frame, Free, Game, Generate, Gestalt, Hare, Idea, Image, Inscape, Keto, Lexicalise, Life, Logical, Mode, Mood, Morph(ic), Morphology, Mould, Order, Originate, → **OUT OF FORM**, P45, Penitent, Physique, Protocol, Questionnaire, Redia, Remove, Rite, Ritual, Schedule, Shape, Shell, Sonata, Song, Stage, Stamp, State, Stem, Stereotype, Structure, Style, Symmetry, Talon, Ternary, Version

▷ **Form** *may indicate* a hare's bed

Formal, Formality Amylum, Black tie, Ceremonious, Ceremony, Conventional, Dry, Exact, Fit, Ice, Literal, Methodic, Official, Pedantic, Pedantry, Perfunctory, Pomp, Precise, Prim, Protocol, Punctilio, Reserved, Routine, Set, Solemn, Starch, Starched, Stiff, Stiff-necked, Stodgy, Stuffed shirt, Tails

Formation Battalion, Brown, Catenaccio, Configuration, Diapyesis, Echelon, Eocene, Fours, Growth, Layout, Line, Manufacture, Origin, Pattern, Phalanx, Potence, Prophase, Reaction, Reticular, Riss, Series, Serried, Shotgun, Testudo, Wedge

Former(ly) Ance, Auld, Before, Ci-devant, Earlier, Ere-now, Erst(while), Ex, Late, Maker, Matrix, Old, Once, One-time, Past, Previous, Prior, Pristine, Quondam, Sometime, Then, Umquhile, Umwhile, Whilom, Yesterday

▷ **Former** *may indicate* something that forms

Formidable Alarming, Armipotent, Battleaxe, Fearful, Forbidding, Gorgon, Powerful, Redoubtable, Shrewd, Stoor, Stour, Stowre, Sture, Tiger

Formless Amorphous, Invertebrate, Nebulous, Shapeless
▷ **Form of, Forming** *may indicate* an anagram
Formosan Tai
Formula(te) Define, Devise, Doctrine, Empirical, Equation, Frame, Graphic, Incantation, Invent, Kekule, Lurry, Molecular, Paternoster, Prescription, Protocol, Prunes and prisms, → **RECIPE**, Reduction, Rite, Ritual, Stirling's, Structural
For now Interim, Meanwhile
Forsake Abandon, Desert, Quit, Renounce
Forsooth Certes, Certy, Even, Marry, Quotha
For sure Pukka
Forswear Abandon, Abjure, Disavow, Renounce, Reny
Forsyte Fleur, Saga, Soames
Fort(ification), Fortress Abatis, Acropolis, Alamo, Alhambra, Balclutha, Bastel-house, Bastide, Bastille, Bastion, Battlement, Bawn, Berchtesgaden, Blockhouse, Bonnet, Breastwork, Bridgehead, Burg, Casbah, Castellated, Castellum, Castle, Citadel, Contravallation, Counterscarp, Crémaillère, Demilune, Deva, Dun, Earthwork, Edinburgh, Enceinte, Epaule, Escarpment, Fastness, Fieldwork, Flanker, Flèche, Fortalice, Fortilage, Fortlet, Fraise, Ft, Gabion(ade), Garrison, Gatehouse, Golconda, Haven, Hedgehog, Hill, Hornwork, Kaim, Kame, Kasba(h), Keep, Knox, La(a)ger, Lauderdale, Legnaga, Line, Louisbourg, Maiden, Malakoff, Mantua, Martello tower, Masada, Merlon, Mile-castle, Moat, Moineau, Motte and bailey, Orillion, Pa(h), Peel, Pele, Pentagon, Peschiera, Place, Przernysl, Rampart, Rath, Ravelin, Redan, Redoubt, Reduit, Ring, Salient, Sallyport, Sangar, Sconce, Stavropol, Stockade, Stronghold, Sumter, Talus, Tenaille, Terreplein, Tête-de-pont, Ticonderoga, Tower, Tower of London, Trench, Vallation, Vallum, Verona, Vitrified, William, Worth
Forte F, Métier, Specialty, Strength
Forth Away, From, Hence, Out
Forthright(ness) Blunt, Candid, Direct, Four-square, Frank, Glasnost, Outspoken, Prompt, Vocal
Forthwith Anon, Directly, Eft(soons), Immediately
Fortify Arm, Augment, Brace, Casemate, Embattle, Lace, Munify, Soup up, Steel, → **STRENGTHEN**
Fortitude Endurance, Grit, Guts, Mettle, Patience, Pluck, → **STAMINA**
Fortune, Fortunate, Fortuitous Auspicious, Blessed, Blest, Bomb, Chance, Coincident, Godsend, Happy, Killing, → **LUCKY**, Madoc, Opportune, Pile, Providential, Sonce, Tyche, Up, Well, Well off
Fortune teller, Fortune-telling Auspicious, Bonanza, Bumby, Cartomancy, Chaldee, Cha(u)nce, Chiromancy, Destiny, Dukkeripen, Fame, Fate, Felicity, Forecast, Genethliac, Geomancy, Hap, Hydromancy, I Ching, Lot, Luck, Mint, Motser, Motza, Oracle, Packet, Palmist, Peripety, Pile, Prescience, Pyromancy, Sibyl, Soothsayer, Sortilege, Spaewife, Success, Taroc, Tarok, Tarot, Tyche, Wealth, Windfall
Forty, Forties Capot, F, Hungry, Kemple, Roaring
Forty-ninth Parallel
Forum Arena, Assembly, Debate, Platform, Synod, Tribunal
Forward (looking), Forward(s) Accede, Advanced, Ahead, Along, Anterior, Arch, Assertive, Assuming, Avanti, Bright, Cheeky, Early, Flanker, Forrad, Forrit, Forth, Fresh, Future, Hasten, Hooker, Immodest, Impudent, Insolent, Lock, Malapert, Minx, Number eight, On(wards), Pack, Pert, Petulant, Porrect, Precocious, Prescient, → **PROGRESS**, Promote, Prop, Readdress, Redirect, Saucy, Scrum, Send, Stem, Striker, To(ward), Van, Wing
Fossil(ised), Fossils Amber, Ammonite, Baculite, Belemnite, Blastoid(ea), Calamite, Ceratodus, Chondrite, Conodont, Corallian, Cordaites, Creodont, Crinite, Derived, Dolichosauria, Encrinite, Eohippus, Eozoon, Eurypterus, Exuviae, Fairy stone, Florula, Florule, Fogy, Goniatite, Graptolite, Hipparion, Hippurite, Hominid, Ichnite,

Ichnolite, Ichnology, Ichthyodurolite, Ichthyolite, Index, Jew's stone, Kenyapithecus, Lepidostrobus, Lingulella, Living, Mosasauros, Nummulite, Odontolite, Olenellus, Olenus, Oligocene, Orthoceras, Osteolepis, Ostracoderm, Oxfordian, Pal(a)eo-, Pentacrinus, Petrifaction, Phytolite, Plesiosaur, Pliohippus, Pliosaur, Psilophyton, Pteridosperm, Pterodactyl(e), Pterygotus, Pythonomorph, Relics, Reliquiae, Remanié, Reworked, Sigillaria, Sinanthropus, Sivatherium, Snakestone, Stigmaria, Stromatolite, Taphonomy, Teleosaurus, Tentaculite, Thunderegg, Titanotherium, Trace, Trilobite, Uintatherium, Wood-opal, Zinganthropus, Zone, Zoolite

Foster (child, mother), Fostering Adopt, Cherish, Da(u)lt, Develop, Farm out, Feed, Fornent, Further, Harbour, Incubation, Metapelet, Metaplot, Nourish, Nourse(l), Noursle, Nousell, Nurse, Nurture, Nuzzle, → **REAR**

Foul, Foul-smelling Base, Bastardise, Bedung, Beray, Besmirch, Besmutch, Bewray, Bungle, → **DEFILE**, Dreggy, Drevill, Dunghole, Enseam, Evil, Feculent, Funky, Gross, Hassle, Hing, In-off, Mephitic, Mud, Noisome, Olid, Osmeterium, Paw(paw), Personal, Professional, Putid, Putrid, → **RANK**, Reekie, Reeky, Rotten, Sewage, Soiled, Squalid, Stagnant, Stain, Stapelia, Technical, Unclean, Unfair, Vilde, Vile, Violation, Virose

▷ **Foul** *may indicate* an anagram

Found(ation), Foundations Base, Basis, Bedrock, Corset, Cribwork, Establishment, Fond, Footing, Girdle, Grillage, Ground, Grounding, Groundwork, Hard-core, Hypostasis, Infrastructure, Initiate, Institution, Matrix, Mattress, Panty girdle, Pile, Pitching, Roadbed, Rockefeller, Root, Scholarship, Stays, Stereobate, Subjacent, Substrata, Substructure, Trackbed, Underlie, Underlinen

Found (in) Among, Base, Bed, Bottom, Build, Cast, Caught, Emong, Endow, → **ESTABLISH**, Eureka, Institute, Introduce, Met, Occur, Plant, Recovered, Rest, Stablish, Start, Table

▷ **Foundations** *may indicate* last letters

Founder Author, Bell, Collapse, Crumple, Fail, Inventor, Iron-master, Miscarry, Oecist, Oekist, Patriarch, Perish, Progenitor, Settle, Sink, Steelman, Stumble

Fount Aonian, Digital, Source, Springlet, Wrong

Fountain Acadine, Aganippe, Arethusa, Bubbler, Castalian, Cause, Conduit, Drinking, Fauwara, Forts, Gerbe, Head, Hippocrene, Jet, Pant, Pirene, Salmacis, Scuttlebutt, Soda, Spring, Trevi, Well-spring, Youth

Fountain basin Laver

Four(times), Foursome, Four-yearly Cater, Georges, Horsemen, IV, Mess, Mournival, Penteteric, Qid, Quartet, Quaternary, Quaternion, Reel, Tessara, Tessera, Tetrad, Tetralogy, Tiddy, Warp

Fourpence Groat

Fourteenth Bastille, Trecento, Valentine

Fourth Deltaic, Estate, Fardel, Farl(e), Firlot, Forpet, Forpit, July, Martlet, Perfect, Quarter, Quartet, Quaternary, Quintan, Sesquitertia, Tritone

Fowl Barnyard, Biddy, Boiler, Brahma, Brissle-cock, Burrow-duck, Capon, Chicken, Chittagong, Cob, Cock, Coot, Domestic, Dorking, Duck, Ember, Gallinaceous, Gallinule, Game, Gleenie, Guinea, Hamburg(h), Heather-bleat(er), → **HEN**, Houdan, Jungle, Knob, Kora, Leghorn, Mallee, Moorhen, Orpington, Papageno, Partridge, Pheasant, Pintado, Plymouth Rock, Poultry, Quail, Rooster, Rumkin, Rumpy, Scrub, Solan, Spanish, Spatchcock, Spitchcock, Sultan, Sussex, Teal, Turkey, Wyandotte

Fox(y) Alopecoid, Arctic, Baffle, Bat-eared, Bewilder, Blue, Charley, Charlie, Corsac, Crafty, Cunning, Desert, Fennec, Floor, Flying, Fool, Friend, Fur, Grey, Kit, Lowrie(-tod), Outwit, Pug, Puzzle, Quaker, Red, Reynard, Rommel, Russel, Silver, Skulk, → **SLY**, Stump, Swift, Tod, Uffa, Uneatable, Vixen, White, Zerda, Zoril(le), Zorro

Foxglove Cowflop, Deadmen's bells, Digitalis, Witches'-thimble

Foxhole Earth

Foxtrot Dance, F

Foyer Hall, Lobby, Reception

Fracas Brawl, Dispute, Mêlée, Prawle, Riot, Rumpus, Scrum, Shindig, Uproar

Fraction Common, Complex, Compound, Continued, Decimal, Improper, Ligroin, Mantissa, Mixed, Mole, Packing, Part, Partial, Piece, Proper, Scrap, Simple, Some, Tithe, Vulgar

Fracture Break, Colles, Comminuted, Complicated, Compound, Crack, Fatigue, Fault, Fissure, Gap, Greenstick, Hairline, Impacted, Incomplete, Oblique, Pathological, Platy, Pott's, Rupture, Shear, Simple, Spiral, Splintery, Split, Stress, Transverse

Fragile Brittle, Crisp, Delicate, Flimsy, Frail, Frangible, Nesh, Slender, Tender, Vulnerable, Weak

Fragment(s) Agglomerate, Atom, Bit, Bla(u)d, Brash, Breccia, Brockage, Brockram, Cantlet, Clastic, Crumb, Disjecta membra, End, Flinder, Fritter, Frust, Graile, Lapilli, Mammock, Mite, Morceau, Morsel, Ort, → **PARTICLE**, Piece, Piecemeal, Potshard, Potsherd, Relic, Restriction, Rift, Rubble, Scrap, Segment, Shard, Shatter, Sheave, Shiver, Shrapnel, Shred, Skerrick, Sliver, Smithereens, Smithers, Snatch, Splinter

▷ **Fragment of** *may indicate* a hidden word

Fragrance, Fragrant Aromatic, Attar, Balsam, Bouquet, Conima, Nosy, Odiferous, Odour, Olent, → **PERFUME**, Pot-pourri, Redolent, → **SCENT**, Sent, Spicy, Suaveolent

Frail Brittle, Creaky, Delicate, Feeble, Flimsy, → **FRAGILE**, Puny, Rushen, Slight, Slimsy, Tottery, Weak

Framboesia Morula, Yaws

Frame(work) A, Adjust, Airer, Angle, Armature, Bail, Bayle, Bier, Body, Bow, Brickbat, Build, Bustle, Cadge, Cadre, Cage, Case, Casement, Casing, Centreing, Cent(e)ring, Chase, Chassis, Clamper, Climbing, Coaming, Cold, Compages, Companion, Cowcatcher, Cradle, Cratch, Cribwork, Deckel, Deckle, Draw, Dutchwife, Entablature, Everest pack, Fabric, Falsework, Fender, Fiddley, Fit-up, Flake, Form, Frisket, Gallows, Gambrel, Gantry, Garden, Gate, Gauntry, Grid-iron, Haik, Hake, Heck, Horse, Hovel, Hull, Incriminate, Jungle gym, Lattice, Limit, Louvre, Mantel, Mixte, Monture, Mood, Mount, Mullion, Muntin(g), Newsreel, Ossature, Outrigger, Oxford, Pack, Pannier, Pantograph, Parameter, Partners, Passe-partout, Pergola, Physique, Pillory, Plant, Plot, Plummer-block, Poppet head, Portal, Pumphead, Punchboard, Puncheon, Quilting, Rack, Rave, Reading, Redact, Retable, Rib(bing), Rim, Roof rack, Sampling, Sash, Scaffold, Screen, Scuncheon, Sect(ion), Set, Setting, Skeleton, Spider, Spring-box, Stanchion, Stand, Stern, Still(age), Stitch up, Stocking, Stocks, Straddle, Stretcher, Stretching, Stroma, → **STRUCTURE**, Studwork, Surround, Swift, Tabernacle, Taboret, Tabouret, Tambour, Tent(er), Tepee, Time, Timeline, Trave, Trellis, Tress, Tressel, Trestle, Tribble, Trussing, Vacuum, Victimize, Walking, Wattle, Ways, Window, Yoke, Zarf, Zimmer®

Framley Parsonage

Franc Fr, Leu, Lev, Lew

France Anatole, Marianne, RF, Thibault

Franchise Charter, Concession, Contract, Liberty, Pot-wall(op)er, Privilege, Right, Suffrage, Vote, Warrant

Franciscan Conventional, Custos, Greyfriars, Minorite, Observant, Salesian, Scotist, Tertiaries

Francium Fr

Franck Cesar

Frank(ish) Artless, Austrasia, Bluff, Blunt, → **CANDID**, Direct, Easy, Four square, Free, Free-spoken, Guileless, Honest, Ingenuous, Man-to-man, Merovingian, Natural, Open, Outspoken, Overt, Postage, Postmark, Raw, Ripuarian, Salian, Sincere, Squareshooter, Stamp, Straight, Straightforward, Sty, Upfront

Frankincense Laser, Olibanum, Thus

Frans, Franz Hals, Lehar

Frantic Demoniac, Deranged, Distraught, Drissy, Frenzied, Hectic, Mad, Overwrought, Phrenetic, Rabid, Violent, Whirl(ing)

▷ **Frantic** *may indicate* an anagram

Frappé Iced

Fraternise, Fraternity Affiliate, Brotherhood, Burschenschaft, Consort, Elk, Fellowship, Lodge, Mingle, Moose, Order, Shriner, Sodality

Fratricide Cain

Fraud(ulent) Barratry, Bobol, Bogus, Bubble, Chain-letter, Charlatan, Cheat, Chisel, Collusion, Covin, Cronk, Deceit, Diddle, Do, Fineer, Grift, Gyp, Humbug, Hypocrite, → IMPOSTOR, Imposture, Jiggery-pokery, Jobbery, Kite, Knavery, Liar, Peculator, Phishing, Phon(e)y, Piltdown, Pious, Pseud(o), Put-up, Quack, Ringer, Rip-off, Roguery, Rort, Salami technique, Scam, Shoulder surfing, South Sea Bubble, Stellionate, Sting, Stumer, Supercherie, Swindle, Swiz(z), Swizzle, Tartuffe, Trick, Vishing, Wire

Fraught Perilous

Fray(ed) Bagarre, Brawl, Contest, Feaze, Frazzle, Fret, Fridge, Ravel, Riot, Scrimmage, Wigs on the green

Frazzle Wear down

Freak(ish) Bizarre, Cantrip, Caprice, Chimera, Control, Deviant, Geek, Jesus, Lusus naturae, Mooncalf, Sport, Teras, Vagary, Weirdo, Whim, Whimsy

Freckle Ephelis, Fern(i)tickle, Fern(i)ticle, Heatspot, Lentigines, Lentigo, Spot, Sunspot

Frederick Barbarossa, Carno, Great

Free(d), Freely Abstrict, Acquit, Assoil, At large, Buckshee, Candid, Canny, Church, Clear, Complimentary, Cuffo, Dead-head, Deliver, Deregulate, Detach, Devoid, Disburden, Disburthen, Disembarrass, Disembroil, Disengage, Disentangle, Eleutherian, Emancipate, Enfranchise, Enlarge, Excuse, Exeem, Exeme, Exempt, Exonerate, Extricate, Familiar, Footloose, Frank, French, Gratis, House, Idle, Immune, Indemnify, Independent, Kick, Large, Lavish, Lax, Leisure, Let, Liberate, Loose, Manumit, Open, Parole, Pro bono, Pure, Quit(e), Range, Ransom, Redeem, → RELEASE, Relieve, Requiteless, Rescue, Reskew, Rick, Rid, Sciolto, Scot, Solute, Spare, Spring, Stald, Stall, Trade, Unbowed, Unlace, Unlock, Unloosen, Unmew, Unmuzzle, Unshackle, Unsnarl, Unstick, Untangle, Untie, Untwist, Vacant, Verse, Voluntary

▷ **Free** *may indicate* an anagram

Freebooter Cateran, Corsair, Franklin, Marauder, Moss-trooper, Pad, Pindaree, Pindari, Pirate, Rapparee, Rider, Snapha(u)nce, Snaphaunch, Thief, Viking

Freedom Abandon, Autonomy, Breadth, Carte blanche, Eleutherian, Exemption, Fear, Fling, Four, Immunity, Impunity, Independence, Laisser aller, Laisser faire, Laissez aller, Laissez faire, Latitude, Leeway, Leisure, Liberty, Licence, Moksha, Play, Range, Releasement, Speech, Uhuru, UNITA, Want, Wiggle room, Worship

Free gift Bonus, Charism, Perk

Freehold(er) Enfeoff, Franklin, Frank tenement, Odal(l)er, Seisin, Udal(ler), Yeoman

Freelance Eclectic, Independent, Mercenary, Stringer

Freeload(er) Scrounge, Sponge

▷ **Freely** *may indicate* an anagram

Freeman Burgess, Ceorl, Churl, Franklin, Liveryman, Thegn, Thete, Villein

Freemason(ry), Freemason's son Craft, Lewis, Lodge, Moose, Templar

Free-range Eggs, Outler

Free State Orange

Freethinker Agnostic, Bradlaugh, Cynic, Libertine, Sceptic

Free-trade(r) Cobdenism, Wright

Free-wheel Coast, Idle

Freeze(s), Freezer, Freezing Alcarrazo, Arctic, Benumb, Congeal, Cool, Cryogenic, Cryonics, Eutectic, Freon®, Frost, Geal, Harden, Ice, Ice cold, Lyophilize, Moratoria, Nip, Numb, Paralyse, Regelate, Riss, Stiffen, Wage

Freight(liner) Cargo, Carriage, Fraught, Goods, Goods train, Load

French(man), Frenchwoman Alain, Alsatian, Anton, Aristo, Basque, Breton, Cajun, Crapaud, Creole, Dawn, Dreyfus, Emil(e), Frog, Gallic(e), Gaston, Gaul, Gombo, Grisette,

Gumbo, Homme, Huguenot, Joual, Jules, M, Mamselle, Marianne, Midi, Monsieur, Mounseer, Neo-Latin, Norman, Parleyvoo, Pierre, René, Rhemish, Savoyard, Yves

Frenetic Deranged, Frantic, Manic, Overwrought

Frenzied, Frenzy Amok, Berserk, Corybantic, Deliration, Delirium, Demoniac, Enrage, Enrapt, Euhoe, Euoi, Evoe, Feeding, Fever, Fit, Fury, Hectic, Hysteric, Lune, Maenad, Mania, Must, Nympholepsy, Oestrus, Phrenetic, Rage, Tantrum

Frequency, Frequent(er), Frequently Angular, Attend, Audio, Bandwidth, Channel, Common, Constant, Expected, Familiar, Forcing, Formant, FR, Fresnel, Gene, Habitué, Hang-out, Haunt, Hertz, High, Incidence, Intermediate, Kilocycle, L-band, Low, Medium, Megahertz, Mode, Natural, Often, Passband, Penetrance, Pulsatance, Radio, Recurrent, Regular, Relative, Resort, Spatial, Spectrum, Superhigh, Terahertz, Thick, Ultrahigh, Video, Waveband

Fresco Intonaco, Sinopia, Tempera

Fresh(en), Freshness Airy, Anew, Aurorean, Brash, Caller, Chilly, Clean, Crisp, Deodorise, Dewy, Entire, Evergreen, Fire-new, Forward, Green, Hot, Insolent, Live(ly), Maiden, Nas(s)eem, New, Novel, Quick, Rebite, Recent, Roral, Roric, Rorid, Smart, Span-new, Spic(k), Sweet, Tangy, Uncured, Verdure, Vernal, Virent, Virescent

Freshman, Fresher Bajan, Beginner, Bejan(t), Fresher, Frosh, Pennal, Plebe, Recruit, Student

Fret(ful) Chafe, Filigree, Fray, Gnaw, Grate, Grecque, Haze, Impatient, Irritate, Key, Mist, Ornament, Peevish, Repine, Rile, Ripple, Roil, Rub, Stop, Tetchy, Tracery, Whittle, Worry

Friable Crisp, Crumbling, Powdery

Friar(s) Augustinian, Austin, Bacon, Barefoot, Black, Bonaventura, Bonaventure, Brother, Bungay, Capuchin, Carmelite, Conventual, Cordelier, Crutched, Curtal, Dervish, Dominican, Fra(ter), Franciscan, Frate, Grey, Jacobin, Laurence, Limiter, Lymiter, Minim, Minor, Minorite, → **MONK**, Observant, Observantine, Preaching, Predicant, Recollect, Recollet, Redemptionist, Rush, Tuck, White

Fricative Rill

Friction Attrition, Conflict, Detrition, Dissent, Drag, Massage, Rift, Rub, Skin, Sliding, Stiction, Stridulation, Tribology, Tripsis, Wear, Windblast, Xerotripsis

Friday Black, Casual, Girl, Golden, Good, Holy, Man, Person, Savage

Fridge Esky®, Freezer, Icebox, Minibar, Rub

Fried cake Croquette, Cruller

Friend(ly), Friends Achates, Affable, Ally, Alter ego, Ami(cable), Amigo, Approachable, Associate, Avuncular, Bach, Belamy, Benign, Boet(ie), Bosom, Bra, Bro, Bru, Bud(dy), Buster, Butty, Cackermander, Cater-cousin, China, Choma, Chommie, Chum, Circle, Cobber, Cock, Cohort, Compadre, Companion, Companionable, Comrade, Confidant, Cordial, Cotton, Couthie, Couthy, Crony, Cully, Damon, Downhome, Edwin, Ehoa, En ami, Fairweather, False, Familiar, Feare, Feathered, Feer, Fere, Fiere, Folksy, Gemütlich, Gossib, Gossip, Gregarious, Hail-fellow-well-met, Homeboy, Ingle, Intimate, Inward, Jong, Kidgie, Kith, Litigation, Lover, Marrow, Mate, McKenzie, Mentor, Mucker, Mutual, Near, Next, Oppo, Outgoing, Paisano, Pal, Paranymph, Pen, Penn, Pheere, Playmate, Privado, Prochain ami, Prochein ami, Pythias, Quaker, Sidekick, Sociable, Societal, Sport, Steady, Thawing, Thick, Tillicum, Tonga, Tosh, Type B, User, Wack(er), Warm, Well-disposed, Well-wisher, Wus(s), Yaar

Friendliness, Friendship Amity, Bonhomie, Camaraderie, Contesseration, Entente, Platonic, Rapprochement, Sodality

Frieze Dado, Metope, Penistone, Zoophorus

Fright(en), Frightened, Frightening, Frightful Afear, Affear(e), Agrise, Agrize, Agryze, Alarm, Aroint, Aroynt, Ashake, Chilling, Cow, Da(u)nt, Dare, Deter, Eek, Eerie, Eery, Faceache, Fear(some), Flay, Fleg, Fleme, Fley, Flush, Gallow, Gally, Ghast, Gliff, Glift, Grim, Grisly, Hairy, Horrid, Horrific, Intimidate, Ordeal, Panic, Petrify, Scar, → **SCARE**, Scarre, Scaur, Schrecklich, Shocking, Sight, Skear, Skeer, Skrik, Spine-chilling, Spook, Stage, Startle, Terrible, Terrify, Terror, Tirrit, Unco, Unman, White-knuckle,

Windy, Yitten

Frigid Bleak, Cold, Dry, Frory, Frosty, Ice, Indifferent, Serac, Stiff

Frill(y) Armil, Armilla, Bavolet, Falbala, Flounce, Furbelow, Jabot, Lingerie, Newgate, Oriental, Ornament, Papillote, Ruche, Ruff(le), Shirt, Tucker, Valance

▷ **Frilly** *may indicate* an anagram

Fringe(s), Fringed Bang, Border, Bullion, Celtic, Ciliated, Ciliolate, Edge, Fall, Fimbria, Frisette, Interference, Laciniate, Loma, Lunatic, Macramé, Macrami, Newgate, Pelmet, Peripheral, Robin, Ruff, Run, Thrum, Toupee, Toupit, Tsitsith, Tzitzit(h), Valance, Verge, Zizith

Frisian Holstein

Frisk(y) Caper, Cavort, Curvet, Fisk, Flimp, Frolic, Gambol, Search, Skip, Wanton

Fritillary Snake's-head

Fritter Batter, Beignet, Dribble, Dwindle, Fragment, Fribble, Pakora, Piddle, Potter, Puf(f)taloon, Squander, Waste, Wonder

Frivolity, Frivolous Butterfly, Empty(-headed), Etourdi(e), Facetious, Featherbrain, Flighty, Flippant, Frippet, Frothy, Futile, Giddy, Idle, Inane, Levity, Light, Light-minded, Lightweight, Moth, Persiflage, Playboy, Skittish, Trifling, Trivial

Frizz(le), Frizzly Afro, Crape, Crimp, Crinkle, Curly, Fry, Fuzz, Hiss

Frock Dress, Gown, Ordain, Robe, Smock

Frog Anoura, Anura, Arrow poison, Batrachia(n), Braid, Breton, Bullfrog, Cape nightingale, Crapaud, Depression, Flying, Fourchette, Frenchman, Frush, Goliath, Hairy, Hyla, Leopard, Marsupial, Mounseer, Nic, Nototrema, Paddock, Paradoxical, Peeper, Pelobatid, Platanna, Puddock, Puttock, Rana, Ranidae, Spring peeper, Tree, Wood, Xenopus

Frogman Diver

Frogmouth Mo(re)poke, Podargus

Frog spawn Redd, Tadpole

Frolic(some) Bender, Bust(er), Cabriole, Caper, Cavort, Curvet, Disport, Escapade, → FRISK(Y), Fun, Galravage, Galravitch, Gambol, Gammock, Gil(l)ravage, How's your father, Jink, Kittenish, Lark, Play, Pollick, Prank, Rag, Rand, Rant, Rig, Romp, Scamper, Skylark, Splore, Sport, Spree, Stooshie, Tittup, Wanton

From A, Against, Ex, For, Frae, Off, Thrae

Frond Fern, Leaf, Tendril

Front(al), Frontman Antependium, Anterior, Bow, Brass, Brow, Cold, Cover, Dead, Dickey, Dicky, Esplanade, Facade, Face, Fore(head), Forecourt, Fore end, Foreground, Groof, Grouf, Grufe, Head, Home, Insolence, Metope, National, Newscaster, Nose, Occluded, Paravant, People's, Plastron, Polar, Popular, Pose, Preface, Presenter, Pro, Prom, Prow, Rhodesian, Sector, Sinciput, Stationary, Tabula, Temerity, Van, Vaward, Ventral, Warm, Western

Frontier(sman) Afghan, Barrier, Border, Boundary, Calamity Jane, Checkpoint, Crockett, Earp, Limit, Limitrophe, List, March, North-west, Outpost, Pathan, Wild West

Front page P1

Front-ranker Pawn

Frost(ing), Frosty, Frostbite Air, Alcorza, Black, Chill, Cranreuch, Cryo-, Freon®, Frigid, Frore(n), Frorne, Glacé, Ground, Hoar, Hore, Ice, Icing, Jack, Mat, Nip, Rime, Silver, Trench foot, White

Froth(y) Barm, Bubble, Chiffon, Cuckoospit(tle), Despumate, Foam, Frogspit, Gas, Head, Lather, Mantle, Nappy, Off-scum, Ream, Saponin, Scum, Seethe, Shallow, Spoom, Spoon, Spume, Sud, Toadspit, Yeasty, Yest, Zephir

Frown Glower, Knit, Lour, Lower, Scowl

Froze(n) Congealed, Froren, Frorn(e), Frory, Gealed, Gelid, Glacé, Graupel, Ice-bound, Spellbound, Static, Tundra

Fructification, Fructify, Fructose Aeci(di)um, Basidium, Fertilise, Flower, Fruit, Inulin

Frugal Meagre, Parsimonious, Provident, Prudent, Scant, Skimpy, Spare, Spartan, Thrifty
Fruit(ing), Fruit tree, Fruity Accessory, Achaenocarp, Achene, Acinus, Akene, Allocarpy, Apothecium, Autocarp, Bacciform, Catapult, Cedrate, Coccus, Compot(e), Confect, Conserve, Cremocarp, Crop, Dessert, Drupe, Eater, Encarpus, Etaerio, First, Follicle, Forbidden, Fritter, Harvest, Issue, Multiple, Orchard, Poof, Primeur, Primitiae, Product(ion), Pseudocarp, Regma(ta), Replum, Result, Return, Rich, Ripe, Schizocarp, Seed, Silicle, Siliqua, Silique, Soft, Sorosis, Stoneless, Succade, Sweetie, Sweety, Syconium, Syncarp, Utricle, Valve, Wall, Xylocarp, Yield

FRUITS

3 letters:
Fig
Haw
Hep
Hip
Hop
Jak
Key
Nut

4 letters:
Acai
Akee
Bael
Bito
Cone
Date
Gage
Gean
Jack
Kaki
Kiwi
Lime
Noni
Pear
Pepo
Plum
Pome
Sloe
Sorb
Star
Tuna
Ugli®
Yuzu

5 letters:
Ackee
Anana
Anona
Apple
Assai
Berry
Bread

Carob
Choko
Genip
Gourd
Grape
Guava
Jaffa
Lemon
Lichi
Lotus
Mamey
Mango
Melon
Nancy
Naras
Nashi
Nelis
Olive
Papaw
Prune
Rowan
Whort

6 letters:
Almond
Ananas
Babaco
Banana
Banian
Banyan
Carica
Cherry
Chocho
Citron
Citrus
Comice
Damson
Durian
Durion
Emblic
Feijoa
Lichee
Litchi

Longan
Lychee
Mammee
Medlar
Narras
Nelies
Oilnut
Orange
Papaya
Pawpaw
Pepino
Pomace
Pomelo
Pruine
Punica
Quince
Raisin
Rennet
Russet
Samara
Sapota
Seckel
Sharon
Squash
Tomato
Wampee

7 letters:
Apricot
Avocado
Bullace
Chayote
Crab-nut
Currant
Cypsela
Geebung
Genipap
Gherkin
Kumquat
Leechee
Litchee
Manjack
Morello

Passion
Pimento
Pinguin
Poperin
Pumpkin
Pupunha
Rosehip
Ruddock
Satsuma
Soursop
Tangelo
Winesap

8 letters:
Abricock
Aguacate
Apricock
Bergamot
Bilberry
Blimbing
Calabash
Caprifig
Dewberry
Fraughan
Goosegog
Hagberry
Hastings
Hedgehog
Kalumpit
Minneola
Mirliton
Mulberry
Physalis
Plantain
Prunello
Rambutan
Rathripe
Sebesten
Shaddock
Silicula
Sunberry
Sweeting
Sweetsop

Tamarind
Tayberry
Teaberry
Waxberry

9 letters:
Algarroba
Apple-john
Aubergine
Bakeapple
Blueberry
Butternut
Cantaloup
Carambola
Caryopsis
Cherimoya
Colocynth
Crab apple
Cranberry
Deerberry
Freestone
Haanepoot
Hackberry
Juneberry
Manzanita
Melon-pear

Mirabelle
Musk melon
Myrobalan
Naseberry
Nectarine
Neesberry
Ortanique
Persimmon
Pinot noir
Plumdamas
Poppering
Raspberry
Ratheripe
Sapodilla
Saskatoon
Shadberry
Sorb-apple
Star-apple
Tangerine
Tomatillo
Victorine
Whimberry
Whinberry

10 letters:
Blackberry

Cantaloupe
Cherimoyer
Chinaberry
Chokeberry
Clementine
Clingstone
Elderberry
Granadilla
Grenadilla
Jargonelle
Loganberry
Mangosteen
Paddymelon
Pick-cheese
Punicaceae
Redcurrant
Scaldberry
Strawberry
Watermelon
Youngberry

11 letters:
Boysenberry
Chokecherry
Granny Smith
Hesperidium

Huckleberry
Lingonberry
Marionberry
Pampelmoose
Pampelmouse
Pomegranate
Pompelmoose
Pompelmouse
Salmonberry

12 letters:
Blackcurrant
Checkerberry
Custard-apple
Service-berry
Thimbleberry
Whortleberry

13 letters:
Bullock's heart
Sapodilla plum

14 letters:
Worcesterberry

Fruitcake Dundee, Madman, Nutter
Fruitful(ness) Calathus, Ephraim, Fat, Fecund, Feracious, Fertile, Productive, Prolific, Teeming, Uberty, Worthwhile
Fruitless Bare, Fool's errand, Futile, Sisyphean, Sooterkin, Sterile, Useless, Vain
Frump(ish) Dowdy, Judy, Shabby, Unkempt
Frustrate(d), Frustration Baffle, Ba(u)lk, Beat, Blight, Bugger, Check, Cheesed off, Confound, Countermine, Dash, Disappoint, Discomfit, Dish, Disillusionment, Foil, Hogtie, Outwit, Scotch, Spike, Stymie, Tantalise, Thwart
Fry, Fried Blot, Brit, Christopher, Elizabeth, Fricassee, Fritter, Frizzle, Parr, Sauté, Sizzle, Skirl-in-the-pan, Small, Spawn, Whippersnapper, Whitebait
Fuddle(d) Drunk, Fluster, Fuzzle, Maudlin, Ta(i)vert, Tosticated, Woozy
▷ **Fuddle(d)** *may indicate* an anagram
Fudge Cook, Doctor, Dodge, Drivel, Evade, Fiddlesticks, Nonsense, Rot, Stop-press, Sweet(meat)
Fuel Anthracite, Argol, Astatki, Atomic, Avgas, Benzine, Benzol, Biodiesel, Biogas, Borane, Briquet(te), Brown coal, Bunker, Butane, Candle-coal, Cannel, Carbonette, Charcoal, Coal, Coalite®, Coke, Derv, Diesel, Eilding, Eldin(g), Ethane, Faggot, Feed, Fire(wood), Fossil, Gasahol, Gasohol, Gasoline, Go-juice, Hexamine, Hydrazine, Hydyne, Ignite, Jud, Kerosene, Kerosine, Kindling, Knitch, Lead-free, Lignite, Lox, Mox, Napalm, Naphtha, Nuclear, Oilgas, Orimulsion, Outage, Paraffin, Peat, Propane, Propellant, Smokeless, Smudge, Solid, Sterno®, Stoke, SURF, Synfuel, Tan balls, Triptane, Unleaded, Yealdon
Fug Frowst
Fugitive Absconder, Ephemeral, Escapee, Fleeting, Hideaway, Lot, Outlaw, Refugee, Runagate, Runaway, Runner, Transient, Vagabond
Fugue Ricercar(e), Ricercata, Stretto
Fulcrum Key-pin, Pivot

Fulfil(ment) Accomplish, Complete, Consummate, Fruition, Honour, Implementation, Meet, Pass, Realise, → **SATISFY**, Steed, Subrogation

Fulgent Bright, Shining

Full(est), Fullness, Fully Abrim, Ample, Arrant, Bouffant, Capacity, Chock-a-block, Chocker, Complete, Copious, Embonpoint, Engorged, Entire, Fairly, Fat, Fed, Flush, Fou, Frontal, German, High, Hoatching, Hotch, Mill, Orotund, Plein, Plenary, Plenitude, Pleroma, Plethora, Plump, Replete, Rich, Rotund, Sated, Satiated, Thorough, Torose, Torous, Toss, Turgid, Turgor, Ullage, Uncut, Up, Wau(l)k, Whole hog, Wholly

Full-bodied Amoroso

Full-faced Caboched, Caboshed

Full-grown Seeded

Full-throated Goitred

Fulminate, Fulmination Detonate, Explode, Levin, Lightning, Rail, Renounce, Thunder

Fumarole Hornito, Mofette

Fumble Blunder, Faff, Grope, Misfield, Muff

Fume(s) Bluster, Gas, Halitus, Incense, Nidor, Rage, Reech, Reek, Settle, Smoke, Stum, Vapours

Fumigate, Fumigator Disinfect, Pastil(le), Smoke, Smudge

Fun(ny), Funny bone Amusing, Antic, Boat, Buffo, Caper, Clownery, Comedy, Comic(al), Crack, Craic, Delight, Droll, Frolic, Gammock, Gas, Gig, Giocoso, Glaik, Guy, Hilarity, Humerus, Humorous, Hysterical, Ill, Ironic, Jest, Jouisance, Jouysaunce, Killing, Kinky, Lark, Music, Play, Pleasure, Priceless, Rag, Rib-tickling, Rich, Rummy, Scream, Sidesplitting, Skylark, Slap and tickle, Sport, Suspect, Uproarious, Weird(o), Wisecrack, Wit, Yell

Funambulist Blondin, Equilibrist, Tight-rope

Function(al), Functioning, Functions Act, Algebraic, Antilog, Apparatchik, Arccos, Arcsin(e), Arctan, Assignment, Behave, Bodily, Bunfight, Business, Ceremony, Characteristic, Circular, Cosec, Cosh, Cot(h), Cotangent, Dance, Density, Discriminant, Distribution, Do, Dynamic, Exponential, Gamma, Gibbs, Hamilton(ian), Helmholtz, Hyperbolic, Integral, Integrand, Inverse, Jacobian, Job, Logarithm, Map(ping), → **OPERATE**, Periodic, Polymorphic, Practicable, Probability, Propositional, Quadric, Quantical, Quartic, Reception, Recursive, Role, Run, Sec(h), Secant, Sensation, Sentential, Service, Sine, Sinh, State, Ste(a)d, Step, Surjection, Tan(h), Tangent, Tick, Tool bar, Transcendental, Trigonometric, Truth, Up and running, Use, Utensil, Utility, Versin, Vital, Wave, Wingding, → **WORK**

Functionary Official

Functionless Otiose

Fund(ing), Fund raiser, Fundraising, Funds -(a)thon, Bank, Bankroll, Barrel, Capital, Chest, Consolidated, Emendals, Endow, Evergreen, Finance, Fisc, Fisk, Focus, Gap, Gild, Green, Hedge, Imprest, Index, Jackpot, Kitty, Maestro®, Managed, Mutual, Nest-egg, Pension, Pool, Pork-barrel, Prebend, Private, Public, Purse, Rest, Revolving, Roll-up, Sinking, Slush, Social, Sou-sou, Stabilisation, Stock, Store, Subsidise, Sustentation, Susu, Telethon, -thon, Tracker, Treasury, Trust, Vulture, Wage(s), War chest, Wherewithal

Fundamental(ist) Basic(s), Bedrock, Cardinal, Essence, Grass-roots, Hamas, Integral, Missing, Nitty-gritty, Organic, Prime, Principle, Radical, Rudimentary, Taleban, Taliba(a)n, Ultimate

Fund-holder Rentier

Funeral, Funereal Charnel, Cortege, Dismal, Exequy, Feral, Hearse, Interment, Obit, Obital, Obsequy, Sad-coloured, Solemn, Tangi

Fungicide Benomyl, Biphenyl, Bordeaux mixture, Burgundy mixture, Captan, Diphenyl, Ferbam, Menadione, PCP, Pentachlorophenol, Resveratrol, Thiram, Zineb

Fungoid, Fungus Endophyte, Pest

FUNGI

3 letters:
Cup
Ray

4 letters:
Asci
Barm
Bunt
Ceps
Conk
Gall
Gill
Pore
Rust
Scab
Smut

5 letters:
Black
Brand
Ergot
Favus
Honey
Hypha
Jelly
Morel
Mould
Mucor
Shelf
Slime
Spunk
Stipe
Tuber
Yeast

6 letters:
Aecium
Agaric
Amadou
Ascius
Elf-cup
Empusa
Ink-cap
Lichen
Mildew
Oidium
Peziza
Pileum
Torula

Wax cap
Xyloma

7 letters:
Amanita
Blewitsa
Blue-rot
Boletus
Bracket
Candida
Chytrid
Fission
Jew's ear
Milk cap
Monilia
Mycetes
Oak-wilt
Phallus
Porcino
Pythium
Russula
Tarspot
Truffle
Uredine
Yellows

8 letters:
Ambrosia
Basidium
Bootlace
Botrytis
Clubroot
Corn smut
Death-cap
Death-cup
Dutch elm
Erumpent
Fusarium
Fuss-ball
Fuzz-ball
Merulius
Mushroom
Mycelium
Mycology
Noble rot
Oomycete
Puccinia
Puckfist
Puffball

Rhizopus
Rhytisma
Sariodes
Stromata
Thalline
Tremella
Tuckahoe
Ustilago

9 letters:
Beefsteak
Bird's nest
Blackknot
Blue-mould
Coral spot
Cramp-ball
Earth-star
Eumycetes
Funnel-cap
Horsehair
Imperfect
Mucorales
Polyporus
Shaggy cap
Stinkhorn
Toadstool
Wheat rust
Zygospore

10 letters:
Anthersmut
Apothecium
Armillaria
Ascomycete
Bread-mould
Death angel
Gibberella
Lawyer's wig
Liberty cap
Oak-leather
Orange-peel
Prototroph
Rhizomorph
Saprophyte
Shaggy mane
Shoestring
Sooty mould
Water mould
Yellow rust

Zygomycete

11 letters:
Anthracnose
Aspergillus
Chantarelle
Chanterelle
Condiophore
Craterellus
Fairy butter
Ithyphallus
Penicillium
Phycomycete
Saprolegnia
Sulphur tuft
Thallophyte
Velvet shank
Witches' meat
Yellow brain

12 letters:
Cladosporium
Conidiophore
Cryptococcus
Discomycetes
Flowers of tan
Hypersarcoma
Shaggy ink cap
Trichophyton
Verticillium
Wood hedgehog

13 letters:
Jupiter's beard
Magic mushroom
Plica polonica
Powdery mildew
Saccharomyces
Witches' butter

14 letters:
Wood woollyfoot

15 letters:
Dermatophytosis
Destroying angel

19 letters:
Fairy ring
  champignon

Fungus-eater Mycophagist
Funicular Cable-car

Funk(y) Blue, Dodge, Dread, Fear, Scared, Spark, Stylish

Funnel Buchner, Chimney, Choana, Drogue, Flue, Hopper, Infundibulum, Separating, Smokestack, Stack, Stovepipe, Tun-dish, Tunnel, Wine

Fur(ry) Astrakhan, Astrex, Atoc, Beaver(skin), Boa, Broadtail, Budge, Calabre, Caracul, Castor, Chinchilla, Civet, Coati, Cony-wool, Coonskin, Crimmer, Deposit, Ermelin, Ermine, Fitchew, Flix, Flue, Fun, Galyac, Galyak, Genet, Genette, Kolinsky, Krimmer, Lettice, Marten, Minever, Miniver, Mink, Mouton, Musquash, Ocelot, Otter, Palatine, Pane, Pashm, Pean, Pekan, Rac(c)oon, Roskyn, Sable, Sealskin, Sea-otter, Stole, Stone-marten, Tincture, Tippet, Vair(e), Victorine, Wolverine, Zibeline, Zorino

Furbish Polish, Renovate, Spruce, Vamp

Furl Clew up, Fold, Roll, Stow, Wrap

Furlough Congé, Leave

Furnace Arc, Athanor, Blast, Bloomery, Bosh, Breeze, Calcar, Cockle, Cremator, Cupola, Destructor, Devil, Electric, Finery, Firebox, Forge, Gas, Glory-hole, Incinerator, Kiln, Lear, Lehr, Lime-kiln, Oast, Oon, Open-hearth, Oven, Pot, Producer, Reverberatory, Scaldino, Solar, Stokehold, Stokehole, Tank, Wind

Furnish(ing) Appoint, Array, Deck, Decorate, Endow, Endue, Equip, Feed, Fledge, Gird, Lend, Nourish, Produce, Provision, Purvey, Soft, Stock, Suit, Supply, Tabaret, Upholster

Furniture, Furniture designer Armoire, Biedermeier, Bombe, Chattels, Chippendale, Duncan Phyfe, Encoignure, Escritoire, Etagère, Flatpack, Fyfe, Hallstand, Hatstand, Hepplewhite, Highboy, Insight, Lowboy, Lumber, Moveable, Queen Anne, Screen, Sheraton, Sideboard, Sticks, Stoutherie, Street, Tire, Unit, Washstand, Whatnot

Furore Brouhaha, Commotion, Outburst, Outcry, Stink, Storm, Uproar

Furrier Trapper

Furrow(ed) Crease, Feer, Feerin(g), Furr, Groove, Gutter, Plough, Pucker, Rabbet, Ridge, Rill(e), Rugose, Rut, Stria, Sulcus, Vallecula, Wrinkle

Fur-seal Seecatch(ie)

Further(est), Furthermore, Furthest Additional, Advance, Again, Aid, Also, Apolune, Besides, Deeper, Else, Expedite, Extend, Extra, Extreme, Fresh, Infra, Longer, Mo(e), Mow, Onwards, Other, Promote, Serve, Speed, Subserve, Then, To boot

Furtive(ly) Clandestine, Covert, Cunning, Hole and corner, Secret, Shifty, Sly, Sneaky, Stealthy, Stowlins, Stownlins

Fury, Furies, Furious Acharné, Agitato, Alecto, → **ANGER**, Apoplexy, Atropos, Avenger, Eriny(e)s, Eumenides, Exasperation, Frantic, Frenzied, Furor, Hairless, Hectic, Hot, Incandescent, Incensed, → **IRE**, Livid, Maenad, Manic, Megaera, Paddy, Rabid, Rage, Red, Ripsnorter, Savage, Seething, Tisiphone, Virago, Wood, Wrath, Yond

Furze Gorse, Whin

Fuse(d), Fusion Anchylosis, Ankylosis, Arthrodesis, Blend, Coalesce, Cohere, Colliquate, Conflate, Converge, Encaustic, Endosmosis, Flow, Flux, Igniter, Integrate, Knit, Match, Melt, Merge, Merit, Nuclear, Percussion, Plasmogamy, Portfire, Proximity, Rigelation, Run, Sacralization, Safety, Saucisse, Saucisson, Short, Slow-match, Solder, Symphytic, Syncretism, Syngamy, Time, Tokamak, Unite, Weld

Fuselage Body, Monocoque, Structure

Fuss(y) Ado, Agitation, Anile, Ballyho, Bobsie-die, Bother, Br(o)uhaha, Bustle, Carfuffle, Carry on, Chichi, Coil, Commotion, Complain, Cosset, Create, Cu(r)fuffle, Dust, Elaborate, Faddy, Faff, Fantad, Fantod, Fiddle-faddle, Finical, Finikin, Futz, Hairsplitter, Hoohah, Hoopla, Mither, Mother, Niggle, Nit-pick, Noise, Old-womanish, Overexact, Overnice, Overwrought, Palaver, Particular, Pedantic, Perjink, Pernickety, Picky, Pother, Precise, Prejink, Primp, Prissy, Pudder, Racket, Raise cain, Razzmatazz, Rout, Song, Song and dance, Spoffish, Spoffy, Spruce, Stashie, Stickler, Stink, → **STIR**, Stishie, Stooshie, Stushie, Tamasha, To-do, Tracasserie

Fustian Bombast, Gas, Pompous, Rant

Futile Empty, Feckless, Idle, Inept, No-go, Nugatory, Null, Otiose, Pointless, Sleeveless, Stultified, Trivial, Useless, → **VAIN**

Future(s), Futurist Again, Avenir, Be-all, By and by, Coming, Demain, Financial, Hence, Horoscope, Index, Interest-rate, Later, Long-range, Offing, Ovist, Paragogic, Posterity, Prospect, To-be, To come, Tomorrow, Vista

Fuzz(y) Blur, Crepe, Down, Fluff, Foggy, Lint, Pig, Policeman

Gg

G George, Golf, Gravity

Gab(ble), Gabbler Chatter, Dovercourt, Jabber, Pie, Prattle, Talkative, Yabber

Gable Clark, Corbie, Jerkinhead, Pediment, Pine end

Gabriel Angel, Walter

Gad(about), Gadzooks Gallivant, Lud, Rover, Sbuddikins, Sdeath, Traipse, Trape(s), Viretot

Gadfly Breese, Breeze, Brize

Gadget Adaptor, Appliance, Artifice, Device, Dingbat, Dingus, Doodad, Doodah, Doofer, Doohickey, Gismo, Gizmo, Gubbins, Hickey, Jiggumbob, Jimjam, Notion, Possum, Tool, Toy, Utility, Waldo, Widget

Gadolinium Gd

Gadzooks Odsbobs

Gaekwar Baroda

Gael(ic) Celt, Erse, Goidel, Irish, Scottish, Teague

Gaff(e), Gaffer Bêtise, Blague, Bloomer, Error, Floater, Foreman, Gamble, Game, Old man, Overseer, Solecism, Spar, Throat, Trysail, Yokel

Gag Brank, Choke, Estoppel, Joke, Pong, Prank, Retch, Silence(r), Smother, Wheeze, Wisecrack

Gage Challenge, Pawn, Pledge, Plum

▸ **Gaiety** *see* **GAY**

Gain(s), Gained Acquire, Appreciate, Attain, Avail, Boodle, Boot, Bunce, Capital, Carry, Catch, Chevisance, Clean-up, Derive, Earn, Edge, Fruit, → **GET**, Good, Gravy, Ill-gotten, Land, Lucre, Obtain, Plus, Profit, Purchase, Rake-off, Reap, Thrift, Unremittable, Use, Velvet, Wan, Win, Windfall, Winnings

Gainsay Contradict, Deny

Gait Bearing, Canter, → **CHILD**, Pace, Piaffer, Rack, Trot, Volt(e)

Gaiter(s) Cootikin, Cu(i)tikin, Gambado, Hogger, Legging(s), Puttee, Spat(s), Spattee, Spatterdash, Vamp

Gala Banquet, Festival, Regatta

Galaxy, Galaxies Active, Andromeda, Blazar, Elliptical, Great Attractor, Heaven, Irregular, Local group, Magellanic cloud, Milky Way, Radio, Regular, Seyfert, Spiral, Stars

Galbanum Ferula

Gale(s) Backfielder, Equinoctial, Fresh, Moderate, Near, Peal, Ripsnorter, Sea turn, Snorter, Squall, Storm, Strong, Tempest, Whole, Winder

Gall, Gall bladder Aleppo, Bedeguar, Bile, Bitterness, Brass, Canker, Cholecyst, Crown, Ellagic, Enrage, Fell, Fungus, Ink, Irritate, Mad-apple, Malice, Maugre, Maulgre, Oak(nut), Oak apple, Saddle, Sage-apple, Sandiver, → **SAUCE**, Tacahout, Vine

Gallant(ry) Admirer, Amorist, Beau, Blade, Buck, Cavalier, Chevalier, Cicisbeo, Courtliness, Lover, Prow, Romeo, Sigisbeo, Spark, Valiance

Galleon Galloon, Ghostly, Ship

Gallery Accademia, Alure, Amphitheatre, Arcade, Assommoir, Balcony, Belvedere, Brattice, Bretasche, Bretesse, Brettice, Brow, Burrell (Collection), Catacomb, Celestials, Cupola, Dedans, Fly, Gods, Hayward, Hermitage, Jube, Ladies', Loft, Loggia, Louvre, Machicolation, Mine, Minstrel, National, Organ, Pawn, Picture, Pinacotheca, Pinakothek, Pitti, Prado, Press, Public, Rogues', Scaffolding, Serpentine, Shooting, Singing, Strangers', Tate, Terrace, Traverse, Tribune, Triforium, Uffizi, Veranda(h), Whispering,

Whitechapel, Winning

Galley Bireme, Bucentaur, Caboose, Drake, Galliot, Kitchen, Lymphad, Penteconter, Proof

Gallimaufry Macedoine, Mishmash, Stew

Gallium Ga

Gallon(s) Bushel, Cong(ius), Cran, Hin, Imperial, Pottle, Rundlet, Tierce

Galloon Lace, Orris

Gallop(er) Aide, Canter, Canterbury, Career, Lope, Trot, Wallop

Gallows Bough, Cheat, Drop, Dule-tree, Forks, Gibbet, Nub, Nubbing-cheat, Patibulary, Stifler, Three-legged mare, Tree, Tyburn, Tyburn-tree, Widow, Woodie

Gallows-bird Crack-halter, Crack-hemp, Crack-rope

Gall-stone Cholelith

Galore Abundance, À gogo, Plenty, Whisky

Galosh Overshoe, Rubber

Galvanise Activate, Buck up, Ginger, Rouse, Zinc

Galvanometer Tangent

Gam Pod

Gambia WAG

Gambit Manoeuvre, Ploy, Stratagem

Gamble(r), Gambling(-house), Gambling place Adventure, Amber, Ante, Back, Bet, Bouillotte, Casino, Chance, Dice(-play), Double or quits, Flutter, Gaff, Hell, High-roller, Jeff, Lotto, Martingale, Mise, Pari-mutuel, Parlay, Partingale, Piker, Plunge, Policy, Punt(er), Raffle, Reno, Risk, Roulette, School, Spec, Speculate, Speculator, Sweep(stake), Throw(ster), Tinhorn, Tombola, Tontine, Treble chance, Two-up, → **WAGER**, Wheeze

Gambol Frisk, Frolic

Game (birds) Bag, Covey, Fowl, Grouse, Guan, Hare, Meat, Partridge, Pheasant, Prairie chicken, Ptarmigan, Quail, → **QUARRY**, Rype(r), Snipe, Spatchcock, Venery, Wildfowl, Woodcock

Game(s) Away, Caper, Circensian, Closed, Commonwealth, Computer, Console, Decider, Easy, Electronic, Elis, Exhibition, Fair, Frame, Gallant, Gammy, Ground, Gutsy, High-jinks, Highland, Home, Intrepid, Isthmian, Jeu, → **LAME**, Match, Middle, Mind, MUD, Needle, Nemean, Numbers, Olympic, On, Open, Panel, Paralympic, Parlour, Perfect, Platform, Play, Plaything, Preference, Pythian, Raffle, Ready, Road, Role-playing, Round, Rubber, Saving, Scholar's, Secular, Sport, Square, Strategy, String, Table, Test, Tie-break, Tournament, Video, Vie, Waiting, Willing

GAMES

2 letters:	Put	Faro	Putt
Eo	Sim	Goff	Ruff
Go	Swy	Golf	Scat
PE	Tag	Grab	Skat
RU	Tig	I-spy	Slam
	Top	Keno	Snap
3 letters:	War	Kino	Solo
Cat		Laik	Taws
Hob	**4 letters:**	Loto	Vint
Loo	Base	Ludo	Wall
Maw	Brag	Main	Word
Nap	Bull	Mora	
Nim	Crap	Palm	**5 letters:**
Pam	Dibs	Polo	Bingo
Pit	Fa-fi	Pool	Bocce

Bowls
Cards
Cardy
Catch
Chess
Cinch
Cloak
Craps
Darts
Fives
Gleek
Goose
Halma
House
Jacks
Keeno
Lotto
Lurch
Manty
Merel
Meril
Monte
Morra
Noddy
Novum
Omber
Ombre
Pairs
Pareo
Pareu
Poker
Prime
Quino
Roque
Rummy
Shell
Shogi
Spoof
Stops
Tarok
Tarot
Touch
Trugo
Trump
Two-up
Ulama
Whisk
Whist

6 letters:
Ballon
Basset
Beetle
Boccia

Bo-peep
Boston
Boules
Bounce
Bridge
Casino
Chemmy
Cluedo
Clumps
Crambo
Ecarté
Euchre
Fantan
Footer
Gammon
Gobang
Gomoku
Hazard
Hearts
Hockey
Hoopla
Hurley
Kaluki
Kitcat
Merell
Peepbo
Pelota
Piquet
Quinze
Quoits
Shinny
Shinty
Sindon
Soccer
Socker
Squail
Squash
Sudoku
Tenpin
Tipcat
Trunks
T-shirt
Uckers
Vigoro

7 letters:
Balloon
Ba'spiel
Bezique
Braemar
Bunting
Camogie
Canasta
Cassino

Charade
Chicken
Codille
Conkers
Coon-can
Croquet
Curling
Diabolo
Doubles
Frisbee
Fusball
God game
Hangman
Hurling
Iceball
In-and-in
Jai alai
Jukskei
Kabaddi
Kalooki
Lottery
Mahjong
Mancala
Marbles
Matador
Muggins
Murphy's
Netball
Old maid
Pachisi
Paddler
Pallone
Passage
Patball
Peekabo
Peevers
Pharaoh
Pinball
Plafond
Pontoon
Primero
Push-pin
Pyramid
Rackets
Reversi
Ring-taw
Seven-up
Singles
Snooker
Squails
Tag ends
Tenpins
Vingt-un
Wet suit

Zero-sum

8 letters:
All-fives
All-fours
Baccarat
Baseball
Beat 'em up
Bob-apple
Bumpball
Buzkashi
Canfield
Cardigan
Charades
Chequers
Chouette
Conquian
Cottabus
Coverall
Cribbage
Dominoes
Draughts
Fivepins
Foosball
Football
Forfeits
Four-ball
Foursome
Fussball
Gallabea
Gin rummy
Goalball
Handball
Handicap
Hardball
Honeypot
Kalookie
Kickball
Klondike
Klondyke
Korfball
Lacrosse
Leapfrog
Mahjongg
Michigan
Monopoly®
Napoleon
Ninepins
Nintendo®
Octopush
Pachinko
Pall-mall
Parchesi
Pastance

Patience
Peekaboo
Pegboard
Penneech
Penneeck
Penuchle
Petanque
Ping-pong
Pinochle
Pintable
Pope Joan
Push-ball
Pyramids
Reversis
Rolypoly
Roulette
Rounders
Sardines
Scrabble®
Scroller
Septleva
Showdown
Skittles
Slapjack
Softball
Sphairee
Subbuteo®
Teetotum
Trap-ball
Tray-trip
Tredille
Tric-trac
Verquere
Verquire

9 letters:
Acey-deucy
Aunt Sally
Badminton
Bagatelle
Billiards
Black-cock
Black-jack
Bob-cherry
Broomball
Crazy golf
Crokinole
Cutthroat
Dodgeball
Duplicate
Fillipeen
Hacky Sack®
Hopscotch
Jackstraw

Jingo-ring
Lanterloo
Level-coil
Long-whist
Matrimony
Minidress
Mistigris
Mournival
Mumchance
Newmarket
Nineholes
Paintball
Parcheesi®
Pelmanism
Punchball
Quadrille
Quidditch®
Shell game
Shoot'em-up
Simon says
Solitaire
Solo whist
Speedball
Spoilfive
Stoolball
Strap-game
Stud poker
Tip-and-run
Tredrille
Trick-trac
Tric-track
Twenty-one
Vingt-et-un
Water polo

10 letters:
Angel-beast
Backgammon
Basketball
Battledore
Boiler suit
Bouillotte
Candlepins
Cat's cradle
Cup and ball
Deck tennis
Dumb crambo
Five-stones
Flapdragon
Geocaching
Handy-dandy
Horseshoes
Hot cockles
Jackstones

Jackstraws
Knurr-spell
Kriegspiel
Lansquenet
Paddleball
Paper chase
Phillipina
Phillipine
Philopoena
Pooh sticks
Punto-banco
Put and take
Short whist
Shuffle-cap
Snapdragon
Spillikins
Strip poker
Tablanette
Tchoukball
Thimblerig
Trick-track
Troll-madam
Trou-madame
Volley-ball

11 letters:
Barley-brake
Barley-break
Bumble-puppy
Catch-the-ten
Chemin de fer
Family coach
Fox and geese
General post
Gerrymander
Hide and seek
Knucklebone
Kriegsspiel
Mumbletypeg
PlayStation®
Post and pair
Puncto-banco
Racquetball
Rouge et noir
Sancho-pedro
Shovelboard
Span-counter
Speculation
Table-tennis
Tick-tack-toe
Tiddlywinks
Troll-my-dame

12 letters:
Bar billiards
Consequences
Fast and loose
Hoodman-blind
Housey-housey
Knucklebones
Minister's cat
One-and-thirty
Pitch and putt
Pitch and toss
Shuffleboard
Span-farthing
Squash-tennis
Troll-my-dames

13 letters:
Blind man's buff
Chicken-hazard
Chuck-farthing
Double or quits
French cricket
Jingling match
Kiss-in-the-ring
Musical chairs
Pass the parcel
Pitch-farthing
Postman's knock
Prisoner's base
Scavenger hunt
Space Invaders®
Spin-the-bottle
Squash rackets
Table football
Table-skittles
Tenpin bowling
Tickly-benders

14 letters:
British bulldog
Crown and anchor
Ducks and drakes
Fives and threes
Follow-my-leader
Hunt-the-slipper
Nievie-nick-nack
Nine men's morris
Pig-in-the-middle
Prick-the-garter
Shove-halfpenny
Snip-snap-snorum
Tenpins bowling
Three-card monte

15 letters:
Chinese checkers
Chinese whispers
Fivepenny morris
King-of-the-castle
Laugh and lay down
Laugh and lie down

Ninepenny morris
Puss-in-the-corner
Russian roulette

16 letters:
Piggy-in-the-middle
Scotch and English

Snakes and ladders
Trente-et-quarante

17 letters:
Noughts and crosses
Tom Tiddler's ground

20 letters:
Kiss-me-quick-in-
    the-ring
Nievie-nievie-nick-
    nack

Gamekeeper Mellors, Velveteen, Venerer, Warrener

Gamete Ootid

Gamin(e) Hoyden

Gaming place Bucket-shop, Casino, Saloon, Table

Gammerstang Taupie, Tawpie

Gammon Baloney, Bilge, Hokum, Tosh

Gamut Compass, Range

Gander Airport, Glimpse, Look-see

Gandhi Mahatma

Gang Baader-Meinhof, Band(itti), Bevy, Bikers, Bing, Bunch, Canaille, Chain, Coffle, Core, Crew, Crue, Droog, Elk, Go, Group, Hell's Angels, Horde, Massive, Mob, Mods, Nest, Outfit, Pack, Posse, Press, Push, Ratpack, Rent-a-mob, Ring, Rockers, Shearing, Triad, Tribulation, Troop, Tsotsi, Yardie

Ganglia Basal

Gangrene Canker, Gas, Mortified, Necrose, Noma, Phaged(a)ena, Sphacelate, Thanatosis

Gangster Al, Bandit, Capone, Crook, Dacoit, Dakoit, Goodfella, Hatchet-man, Highbinder, Home boy, Homey, Homie, Hood, Mafioso, Mobster, Ochlocrat, Scarface, Skinhead, Skollie, Skolly, Tsotsi, Yakuza, Yardie

Gangway Brow, Catwalk, Road

Gannet Alcatras, Booby, Guga, Solan(d)

Gantry Elmer

Ganymede Cupper

▶ **Gaol(er)** *see* JAILER

Gap Aperture, Belfort, Breach, Chasm, Chink, Credibility, Cumberland, Day, Deflationary, Diastema, Dollar, Embrasure, Energy, F-hole, Financing, Flaw, Fontanel(le), Gender, Generation, Gulf, Gulph, Hair-space, Hiatus, Hole, Inflationary, Interlude, Interstice, Kirkwood, Lacunae, Leaf, Leap, Lin(n), Loophole, Mews, M(e)use, Muset, Musit, Node of Ranvier, Opening, Ostiole, Outage, Pass, Rest, Rift, Rima, Shard, Sherd, Skills, Slap, → SPACE, Spark, Spread, Street, Synapse, Trade, Truth-value, Vacancy, Vent, Water, Wind, Window

Gape(r), Gaping Comber, Dehisce, Fatiscent, Gant, Ga(u)p, Gerne, Hiant, Mya, Outstare, Rictal, Rictus, Ringent, Rubberneck, Stare, Yawn, Yawp

Garage Barn, Carport, Chopshop, Hangar, Lock-up, Muffler shop

Garb Apparel, Costume, Gear, Gere, Guise, Ihram, Invest, Leotard, Raiment, Toilet, Uniform

Garbage Bunkum, Junk, Refuse, Rubbish, Trash

Garble Edit, Jumble, Muddle

▷ **Garble** *may indicate* an anagram

Garcon Waiter

Garden(ing), Gardens Arboretum, Arbour, Area, Babylon(ian), Bagh, Bear, Beer, Botanic, Chinampa, Colegarth, Container, Cottage, Covent, Cremorne, Dig, Eden, Erf, Floriculture, Garth, Gethsemane, Hanging, Herb(ar), Hesperides, Hoe, Horticulture, Italian, Japanese, Kailyard, Kew, Kitchen, Knot, Landscape, Lyceum, Market, Monastery, NJ, Olitory, Orchard, Orchat, Paradise, Parterre, Physic, Plantie-cruive, Pleasance, Plot, Potager, Ranelagh, Rockery, Roji, Roof, Rosarium, Rosary, Rosery, Stourhead, Tea, Tilth, Topiary, Truck-farm, Tuileries, Vauxhall, Walled, Welwyn,

Window, Winter, Yard, Zoological

Gardener Adam, Capability Brown, Fuchs, Hoer, Hoy, Jekyll, Landscape, Mali, Mallee, Mary, Nurseryman, Topiarist, Tradescant, Trucker

Gargantuan Enormous, Huge, Pantagruel, Vast

Gargle Gargarism, Mouthwash

Gargoyle Magot, Waterspout

Garibaldi Biscuit, Blouse, Red Shirt

Garish Criant, Flashy, Gaudy, Glitzy, Jazzy, Kitsch, Painty, Roary, Rorie, Rory, Technicolour

Garland Anadem, Anthology, Chaplet, Coronal, Crants, Festoon, Lei, Stemma, Toran(a), Vallar(y), Wreath

Garlic Cepaceous, Clove, Elephant, Hedge, Rams(on), Rocambole

Garment → DRESS, Habit, Vestment, Vesture

GARMENTS

3 letters:
Aba
Alb
Top

4 letters:
Abba
Bubu
Gown
Izar
Kilt
Rail
Rami
Sari
Slop
Sulu
Toga
Togs
Weed
Wrap

5 letters:
Abaya
Ao dai
Boubu
Bubou
Burka
Burqa
Cardy
Cimar
Cloak
Clout
Cotta
Ephod
Fanon
Gilet
Gipon
G-suit

Ihram
Jupon
Kanga
Kanzu
Levis
Manty
Pareo
Pareu
Pilch
Ramée
Ramie
Ruana
Shrug
Skirt
Smock
Stola
Stole
Tanga
Thong
Tunic

6 letters:
Blouse
Bodice
Bolero
Boubou
Bourka
Burkha
Breeks
Caftan
Chador
Chimer
Cilice
Dirndl
Exomis
Fleece
Jibbah
Jilbab

Jubbah
Jumper
Kaftan
Kaross
Khanga
Kittel
Mantle
Mantua
Nebris
Nighty
Peplos
Polony
Poncho
Rochet
Sarong
Shroud
Sindon
Skivvy
Step-in
Sweats
Tabard
Trunks
T-shirt
Woolly
Yukata
Zephyr

7 letters:
Blouson
Bourkha
Burnous
Busuuti
Catsuit
Crop top
Dashiki
Djibbah
Doublet
Exomion

Jilabib
Leotard
Nightie
Paddler
Pallium
Partlet
Pelisse
Polonie
Popover
Rompers
Singlet
Soutane
Surcoat
Tankini
Tank-top
Tunicle
Unitard
Wet suit
Woollen
Wrapper

8 letters:
Body suit
Cardigan
Chasuble
Chausses
Coverall
Dalmatic
Gallabea
Gambeson
Himation
Jumpsuit
Leggings
Lingerie
Monokini
Negligée
One-piece
Pannicle

Pelerine
Scapular
Slipover
Surplice
Swimsuit
Two-piece

9 letters:
Brassière
Cerements
Cothurnis
Cover-slut
Dishdasha

Housecoat
Mandilion
Mandylion
Minidress
Nightgown
Nightrobe
Nightwear
Outerwear
Pantihose
Pantyhose
Polonaise
Sackcloth
Sanbenito

Sweatsuit
Waistcoat

10 letters:
Body warmer
Boiler suit
Cote-hardie
Foundation
Habiliment
Hand-me-down
Hug-me-tight
Jeistiecor
Legwarmers

Nightdress
Salopettes
Sticharion
Sweatpants
Sweatshirt

11 letters:
Dreadnought
Penitential
Reach-me-down

Garnet Alabandine, Almandine, Andradite, Carbuncle, Demantoid, Essonite, Grossular(ite), Hessonite, Melanite, Pyrenite, Pyrope, Rhodolite, Spessartite, Topazine, Topazolite, Uvarovite

Garnish Adorn, Attach, Cress, Crouton, Decorate, Engild, Gremolata, Lard, Parsley, Sippet, Staffage

Garotte(r) Thug(gee), Ugly man

Garret Attic, Loft, Sol(l)ar, Sol(l)er

Garrison Fort, Man, Presidial

Garrulity, Garrulous Babbling, Gas, Gushy, Sweetiewife, Windbag

Garter Bowyang, Crewel, Flash, G(r)amash, Gramosh, Nicky-tam

Gary Glitter, Player

Gas(sy) Blah(-blah), Blather, Blether, Blow off, Bottle(d), Chat, Emanation, Fizz, Flatulence, Gabnash, Jaw, Meteorism, Prate, → **TALK**, Waffle, → **WIND**, Yackety-yak

GASES

1 letter:
H
O

2 letters:
BZ
CN
CS
He
Kr
Ne
RN
VX

3 letters:
Air
Nox
Oil
War

4 letters:
Coal
Damp
Flue

Mace®
Neon
Rare
Sour
Tear
Town

5 letters:
Argon
Azote
Bloat
Calor®
Ether
Ideal
Inert
Lurgi
Marsh
Nerve
Noble
Ozone
Radon
Sarin
Sewer
Soman

Swamp
Sweet
Tabun
Therm
Water
Xenon

6 letters:
Allene
Arsine
Butane
Butene
Ethane
Ethene
Ethine
Ethyne
Flatus
Helium
Hot-air
Ketene
Napalm
Olefin
Oxygen
Petrol

Plasma
Poison
Sewage
Silane
Thoron
V-agent
Vapour

7 letters:
Ammonia
Argonon
Carrier
Coal-oil
Crypton
Fluorin
Halitus
Krypton
Methane
Mofette
Mustard
Natural
Olefine
Perfect
Propane

Propene
Stibine
Utility

8 letters:
Chlorine
Cyanogen
Etherion
Ethylene
Firedamp
Fluorine
Fugacity
Hydrogen
Laughing
Lewisite
Nitrogen
North Sea

Phosgene
Producer

9 letters:
Acetylene
Afterdamp
Blue water
Butadiene
Chokedamp
Flocculus
Phosphine
Propylene
Protostar
Semiwater
Solfatara
Synthesis
Whitedamp

10 letters:
Crab nebula
Diphosgene
Dispersant
Euchlorine
Greenhouse
Propellant

11 letters:
Carburetted
Methylamine
Nitric oxide
Non-metallic
Protogalaxy

12 letters:
Carbonic acid

Chromosphere
Cyclopropane
Electrolytic
Formaldehyde
Nitrous oxide
Oxyacetylene
Taraniki wind

14 letters:
Chromatosphere
Sulphur dioxide

17 letters:
Tetrafluoroethene

19 letters:
Tetrafluoroethylene

Gasbag Airship, Blimp, Envelope, Prattler
Gascon(ade) Boast, Braggart, Skite
Gash Incise, Rift, Rip, Score, Scotch, → **SLASH**
Gasket Seal
Gas-mask Inhaler
Gasp(ing) Anhelation, Apn(o)ea, Breath, Chink, Exhale, Kink, Oh, Pant, Puff, Singult, Sob
Gast(e)ropod Ataata, Conch, Cowrie, Cowry, Dog-whelk, Dorididae, Doris, Euthyneura, Fusus, Glaucus, Haliotis, Harp-shell, Helmet-shell, Limpet, Mitre, Mollusc, Money cowry, Murex, Nerita, Nerite, Nudibranch, Opisthobranch, Ormer, Pelican's foot, Pennywinkle, Periwinkle, Pteropod, Purpura, Sea-ear, Sea-hare, Slug, Snail, Spindle-shell, Streptoneura, Stromb, Top, Top shell, Triton, Turbo, Turritella, Unicorn, Wentletrap, Whelk, Winkle
Gate(s), Gateway Alley, Attendance, Bill, Brandenburg, Caisson, Cilician, Corpse, Crowd, Decuman, Entry, Erpingham, Golden, Head, Iron, Ivory, Kissing, Lock, Lych, Mallee, Menin, Moon, Moravian, NOR, Payment, Pearly, Port, Portal, Portcullis, Postern, Praetorian, Propylaeum, Propylon, Pylon, Sallyport, Silver, Starting, Tail, Taranaki, Toran(a), Torii, Traitor's, Turnout, Turnstile, Vimana, Waste, Water, Wicket, Yate, Yet(t)
Gateau Black Forest
Gatecrash(er) Interloper, Intrude, Ligger, Sorn, Unasked
Gatepost Sconcheon, Scontion, Scuncheon
▷ **Gateshead** *may indicate 'g'*
Gather(ed), Gatherer, Gathering Accrue, AGM, Amass, Army, Assemble, Bee, Braemar, Clambake, Cluster, Collate, → **COLLECT**, Colloquium, Concentration, Concourse, Conglomerate, Congregate, Conventicle, Conversazione, Corral, Corroboree, Crop, Crowd, Cull, Derive, Eve, Fest, Frill, Function, Gabfest, Galaxy, Get together, Glean, Glomerate, Hangi, Harvest, Hear, Hive, Hootenanny, Hotchpot, Hui, Hunter, Husking, In, Infer, Jamboree, Kommers, Learn, Lek, Lirk, Love-in, Meinie, Menyie, Multitude, Pleat, Plica, Plissé, Pluck, Pucker, Purse, Raft, Raising-bee, Rake, Rally, Rave, Reap, Reef, Reunion, Round-up, Rout, Ruche, Ruck, Ruff(le), Salon, Scrump, Sheave, Shindig, Shir(r), Shoal, Shovel, Singsong, Social, Spree, Suppurate, Swapmeet, Take, Tuck, Vindemiate, Vintage, Wappensc(h)aw, Witches' sabbath
Gauche Awkward, Clumsy, Farouche, Graceless, Tactless
Gaudy Classy, Criant, Fantoosh, Flash, Garish, Glitz(y), Meretricious, Tacky, Tawdry, Tinsel
Gauge Absolute, Alidad(e), Anemometer, → **ASSESS**, Block, Bourdon, Broad, Calibre,

Denier, Depth, Dial, Estimate, Etalon, Evaluate, Feeler, Judge, Lee, Limit, Loading, Manometer, Marigraph, Measure, Meter, Narrow, Nilometer, Oil, Ombrometer, Oncometer, Perforation, Plug, Pressure, Rain, Rate, Ring, Scantle, Size, Slip, Standard, Steam, Strain, Tape, Template, Tonometer, Tram, Tread, Tyre, Udometer, Vacuum, Water, Weather, Wind, Wire

Gauguin Paul

Gaul Asterix, Cisalpine, Transalpine, Vercingetorix

Gaunt Cadaverous, Haggard, Lancaster, Lean, Peaked, Randletree, Rannetree, Rannletree, Rantletree, Rawbone, → **THIN**, Wasted

Gauntlet C(a)estus, Gantlope

Gauss G

Gautama Buddha

Gauze, Gauzy Dandy-roll, Gas mantle, Gossamer, Illusion, Muslin, Sheer, Tiffany, Wire

Gawky Clumsy, Cow, Gammerstang, Sloucher

Gawp Rubberneck

Gay, Gaiety Blithe, Bonny, Boon, Buxom, Camp, Canty, Daffing, Debonair, Festal, Frolic, Gallant, Gaudy, Gladsome, Glee, Gordon, Grisette, Inverted, Jolly, Lightsome, May, Merry, Nitid, Out, Rackety, Riant, Rorty, Tit(t)upy, Volatile

Gaze Moon, Pore, Regard, Stare

Gazelle Ariel, Gerenuk, Goa, Mhorr, Mohr, Tabitha, Thomson's

Gazette London, Paper

Gear(ing), Gearbox Alighting, Angel, Apparatus, Arrester, Attire, Bags, Bevel, Capital, Clobber, Dérailleur, Differential, Draw, Duds, Engrenage, Epicyclic, Fab, Finery, Granny, G-suit, Harness, Helical, Herringbone, High, Hypoid, Idle wheel, Involute, Kit, Landing, Lay-shaft, Low, Mesh, Mess, Mitre, Neutral, Notchy, Overdrive, Planetary, Ratio, Reduction, Reverse, Rig, Riot, Rudder, Running, Spur, Steering, Stickshift, Straight, Sun and planet, Switch, Synchromesh, → **TACKLE**, Timing, Tiptronic®, Top, Trim, Tumbler, Valve, Variable, Worm(-wheel)

Gecko Tokay

Gee Horse, Hump, My, Reist, Sulk, Tout, Towt, Urge

Geek Creep, Nerd, Nurd, Uncool

Geiger-counter Scintillator

Geisha Maiko

Gel Hair, Pectin, Pectise, Silica

Gelatin(e), Gelatinous Blasting, Calipash, Coenchyma, Collagen, Glutinous, Isinglass, Size, Tunicin

Geld(ing) Castrate, Lib, Neuter, Sort, Spado

Gelignite Jelly

Geller Uri

Gem Intaglio, → **JEWEL**, Stone

GEMS

2 letters:	5 letters:		
ID	Agate	Jaspis	Asteria
	Boule	Ligure	Callais
4 letters:	Idaho	Morion	Cat's eye
Jade	Pearl	Plasma	Diamond
Onyx	Prase	Pyrope	Emerald
Opal		Rubine	Girasol
Pear	6 letters:	Scarab	Girosol
Ruby	Iolite	Zircon	Jacinth
Sard	Jargon		Jargoon
	Jasper	7 letters:	Kunzite
		Abraxas	Peridot

Rose-cut	Wood opal	Pleonaste	Topazolite
Sardius		Rhodolite	Tourmaline
Smaragd	**9 letters:**	Rubellite	
	Almandine	Rubicelle	**11 letters:**
8 letters:	Amazonite	Solitaire	Alexandrite
Baguette	Andradite	Starstone	Amazon stone
Cabochon	Brilliant	Tiger's eye	Chrysoberyl
Diamante	Briolette	Turquoise	Chrysoprase
Emeraude	Cacholong	Uvarovite	Lapis lazuli
Girasole	Cairngorm		Rose-diamond
Hawk's eye	Carbuncle	**10 letters:**	Scarabaeoid
Heliodor	Carnelian	Alabandine	Spessartite
Hyacinth	Cornelian	Birthstone	Spleenstone
Marquise	Cymophane	Bloodstone	Verd-antique
Melanite	Demantoid	Chalcedony	Vesuvianite
Menilite	Grossular	Chrysolite	
Peridote	Hessonite	Draconites	**12 letters:**
Pleonast	Hiddenite	Heliotrope	Dumortierite
Sapphire	Marcasite	Indicolite	Grossularite
Sardonyx	Moonstone	Lherzolite	
Sparkler	Morganite	Mocha stone	
Sunstone	Moss agate	Rhinestone	

Gemination, Gemini Diplogenesis, Twins
Gemma Bud, Knosp
Gen Info
Gendarme Flic
Gender Form, Natural, Sex
Gene(tics) Allel(e), Allelomorph, Anticodon, Codominant, Codon, Complementary, Control, Creation, Designer, Disomic, Dysbindin, Episome, Exon, Factor, Gay, Genome, Hereditary, Heterogamy, Holandric, Hologynic, Homeobox, Homeotic, Intron, Jumping, Lysenkoism, Mendel, Michurinism, Molecular, Muton, Oncogene, Operon, Orthologue, Paralogue, Plasmon, Promoter, Proteome, Regulatory, Reporter, Reverse, Selfish, STR, Structural, Suppressor, Synteny, Telegony, Terminator, Testcross, Transposon, Weismannism
Genealogist, Genealogy Armory, Cadency, Family, Heraldry, Line, Pedigree, Seannachie, Seannachy, Sennachie, Whakapapa
General(ly) At large, Broad, Common, Communal, Current, Eclectic, Ecumenical, Election, Five-star, Gen, Inspector, In the main, In the mass, Main, Omnify, Overall, Overhead, Prevailing, Public, Rife, Rough, Strategist, Structural, Sweeping, Tactician, → **UNIVERSAL**, Usual, Vague, Wide

GENERALS

3 letters:	**5 letters:**	Sulla	Franco
GOC	Barca	Wolfe	Gordon
Ike	Booth		Joffre
Lee	Botha	**6 letters:**	Joshua
	Cleon	Antony	Leslie
4 letters:	Clive	Ataman	Marius
Cato	De Wet	Banquo	Napier
C in C	Grant	Brutus	Patton
Slim	Monty	Caesar	Pompey
	Smuts	Custer	Powell

Raglan	Massena	Montcalm	Lafayette
Rommel	Othello	Napoleon	Macarthur
Scipio	Sherman	Pershing	
	Turenne	Shrapnel	*10 letters:*
7 letters:		Stilwell	Alcibiades
Agrippa	*8 letters:*	Tom Thumb	Clausewitz
Allenby	Agricola		Coriolanus
Blucher	Burgoyne	*9 letters:*	Cornwallis
Cassius	De Gaulle	Agamemnon	Holofernes
Crassus	Diadochi	Antigonus	Montgomery
Fairfax	Galtieri	Antipater	
Gamelin	Hannibal	Boulanger	*16 letters:*
Hadrian	Marshall	Kitchener	Stonewall Jackson

Generate, Generation, Generator Abiogenetic, Age, Beat, Beget, Boomerang, Breeder, Charger, Cottonwool, Create, Dynamo, Electrostatic, Epigon, Father, Fuel-cell, House, Kipp, Loin, Lost, Magneto, Me, Motor, Noise, Olds, Powerhouse, Signal, Sire, Spawn, Spontaneous, Stallion, Stonewall, Turbine, Van de Graaff, Windmill, X, Yield

Generosity, Generous Ample, Bounty, Charitable, Expansive, Free-handed, Free-hearted, Handsome, Kind, Largess(e), → **LAVISH**, Liberal, Magnanimous, Munificent, Noble(-minded), Open, Open-handed, Open-hearted, Philanthropic, Plump, Profuse, Round, Selfless, Sporting, Tidy, Unstinting

Genesis Episome

▶ **Genetic** *see* **GENE(TICS)**

Geneva(n) Calvinist, Gin, Hollands

Genial(ity) Affable, Amiable, Benign, Bluff, Bonhomie, Chin, Convivial, Cordial, Expansive, Human, Kindly, Mellow

Genie Djinn, Mazikeen, Shedeem

Genipap Lana

Genital(s) Ballocks, Bol(l)ix, Bollocks, Box, Cooze, Crack, Crotch, Cunt, Fanny, Fourchette, Front bottom, Labia, Lunchbox, Minge, Muff, Naff, Nympha, Private parts, Privates, Pubes, Pudendum, Puna(a)ni, Puna(a)ny, Pussy, Quim, Secrets, Snatch, Tackle, Tail, Twat, Vagina, Vulva, Wedding tackle, Yoni

Genitive Ethical

Genius Agathodaimon, Brain, Daemon, Einstein, Engine, Flash, Ingine, Inspiration, Ka, Mastermind, Michaelangelo, Numen, Prodigy

Genome Prophage

Genre Splatterpunk, Tragedy, Variety

Gent(leman), Gentlemanly, Gentlemen Amateur, Baboo, Babu, Beau, Caballero, Cavalier, Dandy, Duni(e)wassal, Dunniewassal, Esq(uire), Gemman, Gemmen, Hidalgo, Ja(u)nty, Knight, Messrs, Milord, Mister, Mr, Nob, Proteus, Ritter, Runner, Rye, Sahib, Senor, Signor, Sir, Sirra(h), Smuggler, Squire, Sri, Stalko, Stir(rah), Swell, Tea, Toff, Tuan, Valet, Von, Yeoman, Younker

Genteel Conish, Polite, Proper, Refined

Gentian European, Felwort, Violet, Yellow

Gentile(s) Aryan, Ethnic, Goy, Nations, Shi(c)ksa, Uncircumcised

Gentle(ness) Amenable, Amenage, Bland, Clement, Delicate, Gradual, Grub, Kind, Lamb, Light, Linda, Lynda, Maggot, Mansuete, Mansuetude, Mild, Soft, Sordamente, Tame, Tender

Gentry County, Landed, Quality, Squir(e)age

Gents Bog, John, Lav, Loo, WC

Genuflexion Bend, Curts(e)y, Knee, Kowtow, Salaam

Genuine Authentic, Bona-fide, Dinkum, Dinky-di, Echt, Entire, Fair dinkum, Frank, Heartfelt, Honest, Intrinsic, Jannock, Jonnock, Kosher, Legit(imate), McCoy, Nain,

Proper, Pucka, Pukka, Pure, Pusser, → **REAL**, Real McCoy, Right, Simon-pure, Sincere, Square, Sterling, True, Unfeigned, Unsophisticated, Veritable

Genus Class, Form, -ia, Mustela

Geode Druse

Geographer, Geography Chorography, Dialect, Economic, Hakluyt, Linguistic, Mercator, Pausanias, Physical, Political, Strabo

Geological, Geologist, Geology Buckland, Dynamic(al), Economic, Erathem, Geodynamics, Hard-rock, Historical, Hutton, Isotope, Mineralogy, Phanerozoic, Sedgwick, Seismology, Self-rock, Structural, Tectonics, Werner

Geometry, Geometrician, Geometer Affine, Analytical, Conics, Coordinate, Descriptive, Differential, Elliptic, Euclid(ean), Hyperbolic, Moth, Non-Euclidean, Parabolic, Plane, Porism, Projective, Quadrivium, Riemannian, Solid, Spherics, Topologist

Geordie Guinea, Tynesider

George(s) Autopilot, Best, Borrow, Eliot, Farmer, Lloyd, Orwell, Pilot, Sand

Georgia(n) Abkhaz, Ga, Hanover, Iberian, Mingrel(ian)

Geraint Knight

Geranium Dove's foot, Rose, Stork's bill, Yellow

Gerbil Jird

Germ(s) Bacteria, Bug, Culture, Klebsiella, Seed, Sperm, Spirilla, Staph(ylococcus), Strep, Virus, Wheat, Wog, Zyme

German(y), Germanic Alemannic, Al(e)main(e), Angle, Anglo-Saxon, Bavarian, Berliner, Blood-brother, Boche, Cimbri, Composer, Cousin, Denglish, Franconian, Frank, Fritz, G, Goth, Habsburg, Hans, Hapsburg, Herr, Hessian, High, Hun, Jerry, Jute, Kaiser, Kraut, Landgrave, Low, Ludwig, Lusatian, Neanderthal, Ossi, Ostrogoth, Otto, Palsgrave, Pennsylvania, Plattdeutsch, Pruce, Prussian, Rolf, Salic, Saxon, Squarehead, Tedesco, Teuton(ic), Vandal, Visigoth, Volsungs, Wessi, Wolfgang

Germane Apt, → **PERTINENT**, Relevant

Germanium Ge

Germ-free Aseptic

Germinate Grow, Pullulate, Sprout

Gesticulate, Gesticulation, Gesture(s) Air quotes, Ameslan, Beck(on), Ch(e)ironomy, Fico, Fig, Gest(e), Harvey Smith, Mannerism, Mime, Motion, Mudra, Nod, Pass, Salaam, Salute, → **SIGN**, Signal, Snook, Token, Wink

Get(ting), Get back, Get off, Get(ting) by, Get(ting) on, Get out Acquire, Advance, Aggravate, Annoy, Attain, Bag, Become, Becoming, Brat, Bring, Capture, Click, Come by, Cop, Cope, Debark, Derive, Draw, Escape, Fathom, Fet(ch), Fette, Gain, Gee, Land, Learn, Make, Manage, Milk, Net, Niggle, Noy, → **OBTAIN**, Pass, Peeve, Procure, Progress, Reach, Realise, Recure, Rile, Roil, Secure, See, Shift, Sire, Twig, Understand, Win

Getaway Disappearance, Escape, Vamoose

▷ **Getting** *may indicate* an anagram

Getting better Convalescing, Improving, Lysis

Get-up Tog(s)

Geum Avens

Gewgaw Bagatelle, Bauble, Doit, Tat, Trifle

Geyser Soffioni, Therm

Ghana .gh

Ghanaian Ashanti, Fantee, Fanti, Tshi, Twi

Ghastly Charnel, Gash, Grim, Gruesome, Hideous, Lurid, Macabre, Pallid, Spectral, Ugsome, Welladay, White

Gherkin Cornichon

Ghetto Barrio, Slum

Ghost(ly) Acheri, Apparition, Apport, Banquo, Caddy, Chthonic, Duende, Duppy, Eerie,

Eery, Fantasm, Fetch, Gytrash, Haunt, Hint, Holy, Jumbie, Jumby, Larva(e), Lemur, Malmag, Masca, No'canny, Paraclete, Pepper's, Phantasm(agoria), Phantom, Poe, Revenant, Sampford, Shade, Shadow, Spectre, Spectrology, → **SPIRIT**, Spook, Trace, Truepenny, Umbra, Unearthly, Vision, Visitant, Waff, Wraith

Ghoul(ish) Fiend, Macabre

GI Joe, Yankee

Giant(ess) Alcyoneus, Alifanfaron, Anak, Antaeus, Archiloro, Argus, Ascapart, Atlas, Balan, Balor, Bellerus, Blunderbore, Bran, Briareus, Brobdingnagian, Cacus, Colbrand, Colbronde, Colossus, Coltys, Cormoran, Cottus, Cyclop(e)s, Despair, Drow, Enceladus, Ephialtes, Eten, Ettin, Ferragus, Gabbara, Galligantus, Gargantua, Géant, Gefion, Geirred, Gigantic, Gog, Goliath, Great, Grim, Harapha, Heimdal(l), Hrungnir, Hymir, Idris, Irus, Jotun(n), Jumbo, Krasir, Large, Lestrigon, Leviathan, Magog, Mammoth, Mimir, Monster, Oak, Og, Ogre, Orion, Otus, Pallas, Pantagruel, Patagonian, Polyphemus, Pope, Red, Rounceval, Skrymir, Slaygood, Talos, Talus, Thrym, Titan, Tityus, Tregeagle, Triton, Troll, Tryphoeus, Typhon, Urizen, Utgard, Ymir, Yowie

Gibberish Claptrap, Double Dutch, Drivel, Greek, Jargon, Mumbo-jumbo

Gibbet Gallows, Patibulary, Potence, Ravenstone, Tree

Gibbon(s) Hoolock, Hylobate, Orlando, Siamang, Stanley, Wou-wou, Wow-wow

Gibe Barb, Brocard, Chaff, Fleer, Glike, Jeer, Jibe, Quip, Shy, Slant, Wisecrack

Gibraltar Calpe

Giddy (girl), Giddiness Capernoitie, Cap(p)ernoity, Dinic, Dizzy, Fisgig, Fishgig, Fizgig, Giglet, Giglot, Glaikit, Glaky, Haverel, Hellicat, Hoity-toity, Jillet, Light, Light-headed, Skipping, Staggers, Sturdy, Turn, Vertigo, Volage(ous), Wheel, Woozy

Gift(s), Gifted Ability, Alms, Aptitude, Bef(f)ana, Bequest, Blessing, Blest, Bonbon, Bonsel(l)a, Boon, Bounty, Charism(a), Congiary, Corban, Covermount, Cumshaw, Dash, Deodate, → **DONATION**, Etrenne, Fairing, Fidecommissum, Flair, Foy, Free, Freebie, Frumentation, Gab, Garnish, Give, Godsend, Goody-bag, Grant, Greek, Handout, Han(d)sel, Hogmanay, Indian, Knack, Koha, Kula, Lagniappe, Largesse, Legacy, Manna, Ne'erday, Nuzzer, Offering, Parting, Peace-offering, PET, Potlatch, → **PRESENT**, Presentation, Prezzie, Propine, Reward, Sop, Talent, Tongues, Treat, Tribute, Wakf, Waqf, Windfall, Xenium

Gig Cart, Dennet, Flapper, Hurly-hacket, Moze, Whisk(e)y

Gigantic Atlantean, Briarean, Colossal, Goliath, → **HUGE**, Immense, Mammoth, Monster, Patagonian, Rounceval, Titan, Vast

Giggle, Giggling Cackle, Fou rire, Ha, Ha-ha, He-he, Keckle, Simper, Snicker, Snigger, Tehee, Titter

Gigolo Gallant, Ladykiller, Pimp, Romeo

Gilbert Bab, Gb, White, WS

Gild(ed), Gilding Checklaton, Embellish, Enhance, Inaurate, Ormolu, S(c)hecklaton, Vermeil

Gill(s) Beard, Branchia, Cart, Ctenidium, Dibranchiate, Jill, Noggin, Spiracle, Trematic

Gillman's Aqualung

Gilpin Draper, John, Renowned

Gilt Elt, Glamour, Ormolu, Parcel, Sow

Gimcrack Gewgaw, Tawdry, Trangam

Gimmick Doodad, Doodah, Hype, Novelty, Ploy, Ruse, Stunt

Gin Bathtub, Blue ruin, Geneva, Genever, Hollands, Illaqueable, Juniper, Lubra, Max, Mother's ruin, Noose, Old Tom, Pink, Ruin, Schiedam, Schnapp(s), Sloe, Snare, Springe, Square-face, Toil, Trap, Trepan, Twankay

Ginger, Ginger beer Activist, Amomum, Asarum, Californian bees, Cassumunar, Costus, Curcuma, Enliven, Galanga(l), Galengale, Galingale, Gari, Malaguetta, Nut, Pachak, Pep, Pop, Putchock, Putchuk, Race, Rase, Red(head), Root, Spice, Stem, Turmeric, Wild, Zedoary, Zingiber

Gingerbread D(o)um-palm, Lebkuchen, Parkin, Parliament(-cake), Pepper-cake

Gingivitis Ulitis

▶ **Gipsy** *see* **GYPSY**

Giraffe Camelopard, Okapi

Gird Accinge, Belt, Equip, Gibe, Jibe, Quip

Girder Beam, Binder, Box, H-beam, I-beam, Lattice, Loincloth, Spar

Girdle Baldric, Center, Cestus, Chastity, Cincture, Cingulum, Corset, Enzone, Equator, Hippolyte, Hoop, Mitre, Panty, Pectoral, Pelvic, Ring, Sash, Shoulder, Surcingle, Surround, Zona, Zone, Zonulet

▷ **Girl** *may indicate* a female name

Girl(s) Backfisch, Ball, Bimbo, Bint, Bird, Bit, Bobby-dazzler, Bobby-soxer, Bohemian, Bondmaid, Broad, Burd, Call, Charlie, Chick, Chit, Chorus, Coed, Colleen, Cover, Crumpet, Cummer, Cutey, Cutie, Cutty, Dam(o)sel, Deb, Dell, Demoiselle, Dish, Doll, Dollybird, Essex, Filly, Fisgig, Fizgig, Flapper, Flower, Fluff, Fraulein, Frippet, Gaiety, Gal, Gammerstang, Geisha, Gibson, Gill(et), Gilp(e)y, Giselle, Good-time, Gouge, Gretel, Grisette, Hen, Hoiden, Hoyden, Hussy, It, Italian, Judy, Kimmer, Kinchinmort, Ladette, Land, Lass(ock), Lorette, Maid(en), Mauther, Mawr, Mawther, May, Miss(y), Moppet, Mor, Mot, Mousmé, Mousmee, Muchacha, Mystery, Nautch, Number, Nymph(et), Nymphette, Oanshagh, Peach, Peacherino, Petticoat, Piece, Pigeon, Popsy, Poster, Principal, Puss, Quean, Queyn, Quin(i)e, Randy, Riot, Señorita, Sheila, Shi(c)ksa, Sis(s), Smock, Sweater, Tabby, Taupie, Tawpie, Teddy, Teenybopper, Tiller, Tit, Tootsie, Totty, Trull, Vi, Weeny-bopper, Wench, Widgie, Wimp

Girlfriend Baby, Chérie, Confidante, Date, Flame, Hinny, Lady, Leman, Moll, Peat, Squeeze, Steady, Wag

Girth Cinch, Compass, Exploitable, Size, Surcingle

Gist Drift, Essence, Kernel, → **NUB**, Pith, Substance

Give(r), Give up, Giving Abandon, Abstain, Accede, Accord, Administer, Afford, Award, Bend, Bestow, Buckle, Cede, Confiscate, Consign, Contribute, Dative, Dispense, Dole, → **DONATE**, Duck, Elasticity, Enable, Endow, Enfeoff, Forswear, Gie, Grant, Hand, Impart, Indian, Jack, Largition, Present, Provide, Render, Resign, Sacrifice, Sag, Spring, Stop, Tip, Vacate, Vouchsafe, Yeve, Yield

Give-away Freebie, Gift-horse

Given If

Give out Belch, Bestow, Dispense, Emit, Exude, Peter

Give over Cease, Lin

Glace Candied

Glacial, Glaciation Gunz, Mindel, Riss, Wurm

Glacier Aletsch, Crevasse, Drumline, Fox, Franz-Josef, Hanging, Iceberg, Ice-cap, Icefall, Moraine, Moulin, Muir, Rhône, Riss, Serac, Stadial, Stoss, Stoss and lee, Tasman

Glad(ly), Gladden, Gladness Cheer, Fain, → **HAPPY**, Lettice, Lief, Willing

Glade La(u)nd

Gladiator Retiarius, Samnite, Spartacus

Glamour, Glamorise, Glamorous Charm, Glitter(ati), Glitz, Halo, It, Prestige, SA, Sex up, Sexy, Spell, Swanky, Tinseltown

Glamour girl Cheesecake, Odalisk, Odalisque, Pin-up

Glance Allusion, Amoret, Argentite, Blink, Browse, Carom(bole), Copper-head, Coup d'oeil, Dekko, Draw, Eld, Eliad, Eye-beam, Galena, Glad eye, Glimpse, Illiad, Inwick, Lustre, Oeillade, Once-over, Peek, → **PEEP**, Ray, Redruthite, Ricochet, Scan, Sheep's eyes, Shufti, Shufty, Side, Silver, Skellie, Skelly, Slant, Snick, Squint, Squiz, Tip, Twire, Vision, Waff

Gland(s) Acinus, Adenoid, Adenoma, Adrenal, Apocrine, Bartholin's, Bulbourethral, Clitellum, Colleterial, Conarium, Cowper's, Crypt, Dart-sac, Digestive, Ductless, Duodenal, Eccrine, Endocrine, Epiphysis, Exocrine, Goitre, Green, Holocrine, Hypophysis, Hypothalamus, Ink-sac, Lachrymal, Lacrimal, Liver, Lymph, Mammary, Melbomian, Musk-sac, Nectary, Oil, Osmeterium, Ovary, Pancreas, Paranephros,

Parathyroid, Parotid, Parotis, Parotoid, Perineal, Pineal, Pituitary, Pope's eye, Preen, Prostate, Prothoracic, Racemose, Salivary, Salt, Scent, Sebaceous, Sericterium, Shell, Silk, Sublingual, Submaxillary, Suprarenal, Sweat, Sweetbread, Tarsel, Tear, Testicle, Testis, Third eye, Thymus, Thyroid, Tonsil, Uropygial, Vesicle, Vulvovaginal, Zeiss

Glanders Farcy

Glandular (trouble) Adenitis

Glare, Glaring Astare, Blare, Blaze, Dazzle, Egregious, Flagrant, Garish, Gleam, Glower, Gross, Holophotal, Iceblink, Lour, Low(e), Naked, Shine, Vivid, Whally

Glass(es), Glassware, Glassy Amen, Ampul(la), Aneroid, Avanturine, Aventurine, Aviator, Baccara(t), Balloon, Barometer, Bell, Bifocals, Bins, Borosilicate, Bottle, Brimmer, Bumper, Burmese, Burning, Calcedonio, Case, Cheval, Claude Lorraine, Cloche, Cocktail, Cooler, Copita, Cordial, Coupe, Cover, Crookes, Crown, Crystal, Cullet, Cupping, Cut, Dark, Delmonico, Dildo, Diminishing, Eden, Euphon, Favrile, Fibre, Field, Flint, Float, Flute, Foam, Frigger, Frit, Fulgurite, Gauge, Glare, Goblet, Goggles, Granny, Green, Ground, Hand, Handblown, Highball, Horn-rims, Humpen, Hyaline, Iceland agate, Jar, Jena, Jigger, Keltie, Kelty, Lace, Lacy, Lalique, Laminated, Lanthanum, Larking, Latticinio, Lead, Lead crystal, Lens, Liqueur, Liquid, Log, Lorgnette, Loupe, Lozen(ge), Lunette, Magma, Magnifying, Metal, Mica, Middy, Milk, Millefiori, Minimizing, Mirror, Moldavite, Monocle, Mousseline, Multiplying, Murr(h)ine, Muscovy, Musical, Nitreous, Object, Obsidian, One-way, Opal(ine), Opera, Optical, Ovonic, Pane, Parison, Paste, Pearlite, Pebble, Peeper, Pele, Pele's hair, Perlite, Perspective, Pier, Pince-nez, Pinhole, Pitchstone, Plate, Pocket, Pon(e)y, Pressed, Prism, Prospective, Prunt, Psyche, Pyrex®, Quarrel-pane, Quarry, Quartz, Reducing, Roemer, Ruby, Rummer, Safety, Schmelz, Schooner, Seam, Seidel, Shard, Sheet, Silex, Silica, Sleever, Slide, Sliver, Smalt(o), Snifter, Soluble, Specs, → **SPECTACLES**, Spun, Stained, Stein, Stem, Stemware, Stone, Storm, Strass, Straw, Sun, Supernaculum, Tachilite, Tachylite, Tachylyte, Tektite, Telescope, Tiffany, Tiring, Toilet, Trifocals, Triplex®, Tumbler, Uranium, Varifocals, Venetian, Venice, Vernal, Vita, Vitrail, Vitreous, Vitreous silica, Vitrescent, Vitro-di-trina, Volcanic, Watch, Water, Waterford, Weather, Window (pane), Wine, Wire, Yard of ale

Glass-gall Sandiver

Glass-house Conservatory, Orangery

Glassite Sandemania

Glass-maker Annealer, Blower, Glazier, Lalique, Pontie, Pontil, Ponty, Puntee, Punty

Glaze(d), Glazing Aspic, Ciré, Clair de lune, Coat, Double, Eggwash, Film, Flambé, Frit, Glost, Ice, Majolica, Peach-blow, Salt, Sancai, Slip, Tammy, Temmoku, Velatura, Vitreous

Gleam(ing) Aglow, Blink, Flash, Glint, Glisten, Glitter, Gloss, Leme, Light, Lustre, Ray, Relucent, Sheen, Shimmer, → **SHINE**

Glean(er) Gather, Harvest, Lease, Stibbler

Glee Delight, Exuberance, Hysterics, Joy, Madrigal, Mirth, Song

Glen Affric, Ghyll, Gill, Rushy, Silicon, Vale

Glib Flip, Pat, Slick, Smooth

Glide(r), Glideaway, Gliding Aquaplane, Aviette, Chassé, Coast, Elapse, Float, Illapse, Lapse, Luge, Microlight, Monoplane, Off, On, Parascend, Portamento, Rogallo, Sail, Sailplane, Sashay, Scorrendo, Scrieve, Skate, Ski, Skim, Skite, Skyte, Sleek, Slide, Slip, Slur, Swim, Volplane

Glimmer(ing) Gleam, Glent, Glint, Glow, Inkling, Light, Stime, Styme, Twinkle, Wink

Glimpse Aperçu, Flash, Glance, Gledge, Glisk, Peep, Stime, Styme, Waff, Whiff

Glint Flash, Shimmer, → **SPARKLE**, Trace, Twinkle

Glisten(ing) Ganoid, Glint, Sheen, Shimmer, → **SHINE**, Sparkle

Glitter(ing) Asterism, Clinquant, Garish, Gemmeous, Glee, Paillon, Scintillate, Sequin, Spang(le), Sparkle, Tinsel

Gloat(ing) Crow, Drool, Enjoy, Exult, Schadenfreude

Globe, Globule Artichoke, Ball, Bead, Celestial, Drop, Earth, Orb, Pearl, Planet, Shot, Sphear, Sphere, Territorial, World

Globulin Legumin, Protein

Gloom(y) Atrabilious, Benight, Blues, Cheerless, Cimmerian, Cloud, Crepuscular, Damp, Dark, → **DESPAIR**, Dingy, Disconsolate, Dismal, Dool(e), Downbeat, Drab, Drear, Drumly, Dump(s), Dyspeptic, Feral, Funereal, Glum, Grey, Grim, Louring, Lowery, Mirk, Misery, Mopish, Morbid, Morne, Morose, Mumps, Murk, Obscurity, Overcast, Sable, Sad, Saturnine, Sepulchral, Shadow, Solein, Solemn, → **SOMBRE**, Sourpuss, Stygian, Subfusc, Sullen, Tenebrious, Tenebrose, Tenebrous, Unlit, Wan

Glorification, Glorify Aggrandise, Apotheosis, Avatar, Bless, → **EXALT**, Extol, Halo, Laud, Lionise, Praise, Radiance, Roose, Splendour

Glorious, Gloria, Glory Chorale, Grand, Halo, Hosanna, Ichabod, Knickerbocker, Kudos, Lustre, Magnificent, Nimbus, Strut, Sublime, Twelfth

Glory-pea Kaka-beak, Kaka-bill, Kowhai

Gloss(y) Ciré, Enamel, Gild, Glacé, Interpret, Japan, Lip, Lustre, Mag, Patina, → **POLISH**, Postillate, Sheen, Sleek, Sleekit, Slick, Slide, Slur, Supercalendered, Veneer, Wetlook, Whitewash

Glossary Catalogue, Clavis, Index, K'thibh

Gloucester Cheese

Glove Boxing, Cestus, Dannock, Gage, Gauntlet, Kid, Mermaid's, Mitten, Mousquetaire, Muffle, Oven, Rubber, Velvet

Glow(er), Glowing, Glowworm Aflame, Ashine, Aura, Bloom, Burn, Calescence, Candent, Candescence, Emanate, Fire, Firefly, Flush, Foxfire, Gegenschein, Gleam, Glimmer, Halation, Iceblink, Incandescence, Lambent, Lamp-fly, Leam, Leme, Luculent, Luminesce, Lustre, Perspire, Phosphorescence, Radiant, Reflet, Ruddy, Rushlight, Rutilant, Shine, Snowblink, Sullen, Translucent, → **WARMTH**

Glucin(i)um Gl

Glucose, Glucoside Aesculin, Amygdalin, Dextrose, Digitalin, Indican, Maltose, Salicin(e), Saponin, Solanine

Glue(y) Alkyd, Araldite®, Bee, Cement, Colloidal, Epoxy, Fish, Gelatin(e), Gunk, Hot-melt, Ichthyocolla, Isinglass, Marine, Paste, Propolis, Rice, Size, Solvent, Spetch, Uhu®

Glum Dour, Livery, Lugubrious, Moody, Morose, Ron, Sombre

Glut Choke, Gorge, Plethora, Sate, Satiate, Saturate, Surfeit

Gluten, Glutinous Goo, Ropy, Seiten, Sticky, Tar, Viscid, Zymome

Glutton(ous), Gluttony Bellygod, Carcajou, Cormorant, Edacity, Feaster, Free-liver, Gannet, Gorb, Gourmand, Greedyguts, Gulosity, Gutser, Gutsy, Gutzer, Hog, Lurcher, Pig, Ratel, Scoffer, Sin, Trencherman, Trimalchio, Wolverine

Glyceride, Glycerine Ester, Olein, Palmitin

Glycoside Hesperidin

Gnarl(ed) Knot, Knuckly, Knur, Nob

Gnash(ing) Bruxism, Champ, Grate

Gnat Culex, Culicidae, Midge, Mosquito

Gnaw(ing) Corrode, Erode, Fret, Lagomorph, Rodent

Gnome Adage, Bank-man, Chad, Cobalt, Epigram, Europe, Financier, Garden, Hobbit, Kobold, Maxim, Motto, Proverb, Saw, Sprite, Zurich

Gnostic(ism) (A)eon, Archontic, Cainite, Mand(a)ean, Marcionism, Ophite, Sabian, Tsabian, Zabian

Gnu Brindled, Horned horse, White-tailed, Wildebeest

Go, Going (after, ahead, back, for, off, on, through, up, etc) Advance, Afoot, Anabasis, Animation, Ascent, Assail, Attempt, Attend, Bash, Betake, Bing, Bout, Brio, Choof, Clamber, Comb, Continuance, Crack, Deal, Depart, Die, Do, Energy, Fare, Function, Gae, Gang, Gaun, Gee, Gonna, Green, Hamba, Hark, Heavy, Hence, Hie, Hup, Imshi, Imshy, Ish, Kick, → **LEAVE**, March, Match, Move, Off, OK, Path, Pee, Pep, Perpetual, Ply, Quit, Raik, Repair, Resort, Resume, Run, Scat, Scram, Segue, Shoo, Shot, Skedaddle, Snick-up, Sour, Spank, Spell, Square, Stab, Success, Transitory, Trine, Try, Turn, Vamo(o)se, Vanish, Verve, Via, Viable, Vim, Wend, Work, Yead, Yede, Yeed, Zap, Zest, Zing, Zip

Goad Ankus, Brod, Gad, Impel, Incite, → **NEEDLE**, Prod, Provoke, Rowel, Spur, Stimulate, Stimulus, Taunt

Goal(posts) Ambition, Basket, Bourn(e), Cage, Destination, Dool, Dream, Drop, Dule, End, Ettle, Field, Golden, Grail, Hail, Home, Horme, Hunk, Intent, Limit, Mark, Mission, Moksha, Net, Own, Score, Silver, Tap-in, Target, Tip-in, Touch-in, Ultima Thule, Uprights

Goalless Idle

Goat(-like) Alpine, Amalthea, Angora, Antelope, Antilope, Billy, Bok, Bucardo, Buck, Caprine, Cashmere, Cilician, Gait, Gate, Giddy, Goral, Hircine, Ibex, Izard, Kashmir, Kid, Libido, Markhor, Mountain, Nan(ny), Nubian, Rocky Mountain, Roue, Ruminant, Saanen, Sassaby, Serow, Serpent-eater, Steenbok, Steinbock, Tahr, Takin, Tehr, Thar, Toggenburg

Goatsucker Fern-owl, Nightjar

Gob(bet) Bespit, Clot, Dollop, Mouth, Sailor, Spit, Tar, Yap

Gobble Bolt, Devour, Gorge, Gulp, Scarf, Slubber, Wolf

Gobelin Tapestry

Go-between Broker, Factor, Intermediate, Link, Mediate, Middleman, Pandarus, Pander, Shuttle

Goblet Chalice, Hanap

Goblin Banshee, Bargaist, Barg(h)est, Bodach, Bogey, Bogle, Bogy, Brownie, Bucca, Bull-beggar, Croquemitaine, Empusa, Erl-king, Esprit follet, Genie, Gnome, Gremlin, Knocker, Kobold, Lob-lie-by-the-fire, Lubberfiend, Lutin, Nis(se), Phooka, Phynnodderree, Pooka, Pouke, Puca, Puck, Pug, Red-cap, Red-cowl, Shellycoat, → **SPRITE**, Troll, Trow

Gobstopper Everlasting

Goby Dragonet

God(s) All-seer, Amen, Ancient of Days, → **DEITY**, Deus, Di, Divine, First Cause, Gallery, Gracious, Holy One, Household, Immortals, Inner Light, Light, Maker, Od(d), Olympian, Prime Mover, Principle, Providence, Serpent, Shechina, Soul, Supreme Being, The Creator, Tin, Trinity, Truth, Unknown, Vanir, War, Water

GODS

1 letter:	Seb	Eros	5 letters:
D	Set	Faun	Aegir
	Sol	Frey	Aesir
2 letters:	Tiu	Joss	Allah
An	Tiw	Kama	Ammon
As	Tum	Kami	Brage
Ra	Tyr	Llyr	Bragi
Re		Loki	Comus
	4 letters:	Lugh	Cupid
3 letters:	Abba	Mars	Dagan
Anu	Agni	Mors	Dagon
Bel	Aitu	Nebo	Donar
Bes	Amun	Odin	Freyr
Dis	Apis	Ptah	Haoma
Gad	Ares	Rama	Horus
Geb	Asur	Seth	Hymen
Jah	Aten	Siva	Indra
Keb	Atum	Soma	Janus
Lar	Baal	Thor	Khnum
Lir	Brag	Tyrr	Liber
Lug	Bran	Yama	Lludd
Mab	Cama	Zeus	Mimir
Mot	Deva		Momus
Pan	Dieu		Njord

Numen
Orcus
Orixa
Pales
Picus
Pluto
Rudra
Satyr
Sebek
Shiva
Sinis
Surya
Thoth
Titan
Wodan
Woden
Wotan
Yahve
Yahwe

6 letters:
Adonai
Adonis
Aeolus
Amen-ra
Amon-ra
Anubis
Apollo
Ashtar
Asshur
Avatar
Balder
Boreas
Brahma
Cabiri
Chemos
Clotho
Cronus
Delian
Elohim
Faunus
Ganesa
Ganesh
Garuda
HaShem

Helios
Hermes
Hughie
Hypnos
Kronos
Mahoun
Mammon
Marduk
Mexitl
Mextli
Mithra
Moerae
Molech
Moloch
Nereus
Njorth
Oannes
Orisha
Ormazd
Ormuzd
Osiris
Panisc
Panisk
Plutus
Rimmon
Saturn
Somnus
Tammuz
Teraph
Teshup
Thamiz
Thunor
Triton
Uranus
Varuna
Vishnu
Vulcan
Yahweh
Zombie

7 letters:
Alastor
Alpheus
Angus Og
Anteros

Bacchus
Bhagwan
Chemosh
Daikoku
Ganesha
Goddess
Hanuman
Heimdal
Jehovah
Jupiter
Krishna
Kuan Yin
Kwan Yin
Mahound
Mercury
Mithras
Neptune
Nisroch
Oceanus
Penates
Phoebus
Priapus
Proteus
Rameses
Sarapis
Sat Guru
Serapis
Setebos
Shamash
Silenus
Thammuz
Zagreus

8 letters:
Achelous
Dionysus
Heimdall
Hyperion
Kamadeva
Mahadeva
Morpheus
Mulciber
Nataraja
Pantheon
Poseidon

Quirinus
Silvanus
Sylvanus
Terminus
Thanatos
Trimurti
Wahiguru
Zephyrus

9 letters:
All-father
Asclepius
Fabulinus
Heimdallr
Jagganath
Promachos
Tetragram
Thunderer
Vertumnus
Zernebock

10 letters:
Ahura Mazda
Demogorgon
Elegabalus
Hephaestus
Hephaistos
Juggernaut
Karttikaya
Mumbo-jumbo
Prometheus
Trophonius

11 letters:
Adrammelech
Aesculapius
Bodhisattva

12 letters:
Quetzalcoati
Trismegistus

14 letters:
Tetragrammaton

God-bearing Deiparous
Goddess(es) Divine, Green, Muse, Sea nymph

GODDESSES

2 letters:
Ge

3 letters:
Ate
Eos

Hel
Mut
Nox

Nut
Nyx
Ops

Pax

4 letters:
Dian
Eris
Gaea
Gaia
Hera
Idun
Iris
Isis
Juno
Kali
Leda
Leto
Luna
Maat
Maut
Mors
Nike
Norn
Pele
Rhea
Sita
Thea

5 letters:
Aruru
Ceres
Diana
Dione
Durga
Erato

Flora
Freya
Grace
Horae
Houri
Hulda
Iduna
Irene
Kotys
Moera
Moira
Pales
Tanit
Terra
Tyche
Ushas
Venus
Vesta

6 letters:
Aglaia
Ashnan
Athene
Aurora
Bastet
Clotho
Cybele
Cyrene
Eastre
Freyja
Frigga
Graeae
Graiae

Hathor
Hecate
Hertha
Hestia
Huldar
Hyaeia
Idalia
Ishtar
Ithunn
Lucina
Pallas
Parcae
Phoebe
Pomona
Satyra
Selene
Semele
Tellus
Tethys
Themis
Thetis

7 letters:
Artemis
Astarte
Astraea
Bellona
Cotytto
Cynthia
Demeter
Fortuna
Kotytto
Lakshmi

Megaera
Minerva
Nemesis
Nephthys
Parvati
Sabrina
Strenia
Victory

8 letters:
Cloacina
Cytherea
Libitina
Rhiannon
Thanatas
Valkyrie
Victoria
Walkyrie

9 letters:
Aphrodite
Ashtaroth
Ashtoreth
Eumenides
Mnemosyne
Sarasvati

10 letters:
Amphitrite
Proserpina
Proserpine

Godfather, Godmother Capo, Cummer, Fairy, Gossip, Kimmer, Rama, Sponsor, Woden

Godless Agnostic, Atheistic, Atheous, Impious, Profane

Godly Deist, Devine, Devout, Holy, Pious

Godown Hong

God-willing Deo volente, DV, Inshallah, Mashallah

Go-getter Arriviste, Hustler

Goggle(s) Gaze, Snow-eyes, Stare

Go-go Alert

Going wrong Aglee, Agley, Misfiring

▷ **Going wrong** *may indicate* an anagram

Goitre Derbyshire neck, Exophthalmic, Graves' disease, Struma

Gold(en) Age, Amber, Apple, Ass, Au, Aureate, Auriel, Auriferous, Auriol, Aurum, Bendigo, Bough, Bull, Bullion, Bull's eye, California, Chryselephantine, Doubloon, Dutch, Eagle, Electron, Electrum, Emerods, Fairy, Filigree, Filled, Fleece, Fool's, Free, Fulminating, Gate, Gilden, Gule, Handshake, Hind, Horde, Horn, Ingot, Kolar, Leaf, Lingot, Moidore, Mosaic, Muck, Nugget, Oaker, Obang, Ochre, Ophir, Or, Oreide, Ormolu, Oroide, Pistole, Placer, Pyrites, Red, Reef, Rolled, Silence, Silver-gilt, Sol, Standard, Stream, Stubborn, Taelbar, Talmi, Thrimsa, Tolosa, Treasury, Venice, Virgin, Wash-up, White, Witwatersrand, Xanthe, Yellow

Gold-digger Forty-niner, Prospector

Golden fleece Phrixus

Goldfield Rand

Goldfinch Charm, Chirm, Redcap

Gold leaf Ormolu

Gold rush Kalgoorlie, Klondike

Goldsmith Cellini, Fabergé, Hilliard, Oliver

Golf (ball) Best ball, Better-ball, Clock, Crazy, Foursome, G, Gutta, Matchplay, Medal play, Miniature, Repaint, Round, Stableford, Texas scramble

Golfer Alliss, Braid, Cotton, Els, Faldo, Hogan, Lyle, Pivoter, Rees, Roundsman, Seve, Snead, Teer, Texas scramble, Tiger Woods, Trevino, Wolstenholme, Yipper

Goliath Giant

Golly Cor, Crumbs, Gosh

Gondolier Balloonist, Bargee, Marco

Gone Ago, Dead, Defunct, Deid, Napoo, Out, Past, Ygo(e), Yod

▷ **Gone off** *may indicate* an anagram

Gone west Had it

Gong Bell, DSO, → **MEDAL**, Tam-tam, VC

Gonorrhoea Clap

Goo Gleet, Gloop, Gum, Gunge, Poise, Treacle, Ulmin

Goober Monkey nut

Good(ness), Goody-goody Agatha, Agathodaimon, Altruism, Angelic, Ascertained, Bad, Bein, Benefit, Blesses, Bon, Bonzer, Bosker, Bounty, Braw, Brod, Budgeree, Canny, Castor, Civil, Classy, Clinker, Common, Coo, Cool, Crack(ing), Credit, Crikey, Dab, Dandy, Def, Divine, Dow, Enid, Estimable, Fancy that, Fantabulous, Finger lickin', First-class, G, Gear, Giffen, Glenda, Gold, Gosh, Guid, Hooray, Humdinger, Lekker, Lois, Lor, Ma foi, Mega, Merchandise, Moral, Neat, Nobility, → **NO GOOD**, Pi, Plum, Prime, Proper, Pucka, Pukka, Purler, Rattling, Rectitude, Riddance, Right(eous), Rum, Sake, Salutary, Samaritan, Sanctity, Slap-up, Smashing, Spiffing, Splendid, St, Suitable, Super, Taut, Tollol, Topping, Valid, Virtue, Virtuous, Weal, Welfare, Whacko, Wholesome, Worthy

Goodbye Addio, Adieu, Adios, Aloha, Apopemptic, Arrivederci, Cheerio, Cheers, Ciao, Congé, Farewell, Haere ra, Hamba kahle, Hooray, Hooroo, Later, Sayonara, See-you, So long, Tata, Toodle-oo, Toodle-pip, Vale

Good evening Den

Goodfellow Brick, Puck, Robin, Samaritan, Worthy

Good-for-nothing Bum, Donnat, Donnot, Dud, Idler, Layabout, Lorel, Lorrell, Losel, Napoo, Naught, Scal(l)awag, Scallywag, Scant o'grace, Sculpin, Shot-clog, Stiff, Useless, Vaurien, Waff, Waster, Wastrel

Good Friday Parasceve, Pasch of the Cross

Good-humour(ed), Good-natured Amiable, Bonhomie, Clever, Gruntled, Kind, Mellow

Good-looking Bon(n)ie, Bonny, Bonwie, Comely, Fair, Handsome, Personable, Pretty, Wally, Weel-fa(u)st

Good news Evangel

Good number Thr(e)ave

Good order Eutaxy, Shipshape

Goods Bona, Brown, Cargo, Commodities, Consumer, Disposable, Durable, Durables, Fancy, Flotsam, Freight, Futures, Gear, Hardware, Insight, Ironware, Lagan, Lay-away, Line, Luxury, Piece, Products, Property, Schlock, Soft, Sparterie, Truck, Wares, White

Goodwill Amity, Bonhom(m)ie, Favour, Gree

Goody, Goody-goody Teacher's pet, Wrong'un

Goofy Simple-minded

Goon Bentine, Bluebottle, Eccles, Milligan, Secombe, Sellers

Goop Ooze

Goose, Geese Anserine, Barnacle, Bernicle, Blue, Brent, Canada, Cape Barren, Colonial, Daftie, Ember, Gaggle, Gander, Gannet, Golden, Greylag, Grope, Harvest, Hawaiian, Idiot, Juggins, MacFarlane's, Magpie, Michaelmas, Mother, Nana, Nene, Pink-footed, Pygmy, Quink, Roger, Saddleback, Silly, Simpleton, Skein, Snow, Solan, Strasbourg, Stubble, → **STUPID PERSON**, Swan, Team, Wav(e)y, Wawa, Wedge, Whitehead

Gooseberry Cape, Chaperon(e), Chinese, Coromandel, Detrop, Fool, Gog, Groser(t), Groset, Grossart, Grozer, Honey blob, Kiwi, Physalis, Tomato

Gooseflesh Horripilation

Goosefoot Allgood, Amarantaceae, Beet, Blite, Fat-hen, Mercury, Orache, Saltbush

Gooseherd Quill-driver

Gopher Camass-rat, Minnesota, Pocket

Gordian Knot

Gordon Chinese, Flash, Rioter

Gore, Gory Blood, Cloy, Danse macabre, Gair, Horn, Inset, Toss

Gorge(s) Abyss, Arroyo, Barranca, Barranco, Canyon, Carnarvon, Chasm, Cheddar, Cleft, Couloir, Cram, Defile, Donga, Flume, Gap, Ghyll, Glut, Grand Canyon, Gulch, Ironbridge, Iron Gate, Katherine, Khor, Kloof, Lin(n), Nala, Nalla(h), Nulla(h), Olduvai, Overeat, Overfeed, Pass, Pig, Ravine, Snarf, Staw, → **STUFF**, Throat, Tire, Tums, Valley, Valley of the Kings, Yosemite

Gorgeous Delectable, Dreamboat, Grand, Splendid, Superb

Gorgon Euryale, Medusa, Ogress, Stheno

Gorilla Heavy, → **MONKEY**, Silverback

Gorse Broom, Furze, Gosse, Ulex, Whin

Gosh Begad, Begorra, Blimey, Coo, Cor, Crumbs, Ecod, Gadzooks, Gee, Golly, Gracious, Gum, Heavens, Lor, My, Och, Odsbobs, Odso, Really, Shucks

Gospel(s), Gospeller Apocryphal, Creed, Diatessaron, Evangel, Fact, John, Kerygma, Luke, Mark, Matthew, Nicodemus, Prosperity, Protevangelium, Synoptic, Truth, Waldensian

Gossamer(y) Araneous, Byssoid, Cobwebby, Gauzy

Gossip Ana(s), Aunt, Backbite, Blether, Cackle, Cat, Causerie, Chat, Chin, Chitchat, Clash, Clash-me-clavers, Claver, Cleck, Clish-clash, Clishmaclaver, Confab, Cosher, Coze, Crack, Cummer, Dirt, Flibbertigibbet, Furphy, Gab(nash), Gabfest, Gas, Gash, Goster, Gup, Hearsay, Hen, Jaw, Loose-tongued, Maundrel, Moccasin telegraph, Nashgab, Natter, Newsmonger, Noise, On dit, Pal, Personalist, Prattle, Prose, Quidnunc, Reportage, Rumour, Scandal(monger), Schmooze, Scuttlebutt, Shmoose, Shmooze, Sweetie-wife, Tabby(cat), Talk(er), Tattle, Tattletale, Tibby, Tittle(-tattle), Twattle, Whisper, Yak, Yatter, Yenta

Got Gat, Obtained, Won

Goth(ic) Alaric, American, International, Lurid, Moesia

Gothamite Abderian, New Yorker

Gouge Chisel, Groove, Scoop

Gourd Bottle, Calabash, Courgette, Dishcloth, Guiro, Hercules' club, Loofa, Maraca, Marrow, Melon, Monkeybread, Pumpkin, Squash, Zucchini

Gourmand, Gourmet Aesthete, Apicius, Chowhound, → **EPICURE**, Free-liver, Gastronome, Gastrosopher, Lickerish, Table, Trencherman, Ventripotent

Gout(y) Chalkstone, Chiragra, Hamarthritis, Podagra, Taste, Tophus

Govern(or), Government Adelantado, Administer, Ag(h)a, Agricola, Alderman, Amban, Amman, Amtman, ANC, Andocracy, Archology, Aristocracy, Autarchy, Autocrat, Autonomy, Bahram, Ban, Bashaw, Beehive, Beg, Beglerbeg, Bencher, Bey, Bridler, Bureaucracy, Burgrave, Cabinet, Caciquism, Caliphate, Caretaker, Cassio, Castellan, Catapan, Cham, Circar, Classis, Coalition, Command, Commonwealth, Condominium, Congress, Constable, Constitution, Consulate, Cybernetic, Darogha, Democracy, Dergue, Despotism, Despotocracy, Dey, Diarchy, Dictatorship, Dinarchy, Directoire, Directory, Domain, Dominate, Downing St, Duarchy, Dulocracy, Duumvirate, Dyarchy, Dynast, Earl,

Ecclesiarchy, Eminent domain, Empery, Eparch, Ergatocracy, Escapement, Ethnarch, Exarch, Fascism, Federal, G, Gauleiter, Gerontocracy, Gov, Grieve, Gubernator, Guv, Gynarchy, Hagiarchy, Hagiocracy, Hague, Hajjaz, Hakim, Harmost, HE, Helm, Heptarchy, Hexarchy, Hierocracy, Honcho, Hospodar, Imperialism, Ins, Inspector, Isocracy, Junta, Kaimakam, Kakistocracy, Kawanatanga, Kebele, Kemalism, Khalifate, Khan, Kremlin, Legate, Local, Majlis, Majorism, Matriarchy, Monarchy, Monocracy, Mudir, Nabob, Naik, Nomarch, Nomocracy, Ochlocracy, Oireachtas, Oligarchy, Optic®, Pa, Pacha, Padishah, Pasha, Pater, Patriarchism, Pentarch, Père, Petticoat, Physiocracy, Pilate, Placemen, Plutocracy, Podesta, Polity, Polyarchy, Porte, Power, Priest-king, Proconsul, Propraetor, Proveditor, Provedor(e), Providor, Ptochocracy, Quadrumvirate, Quirinal, Raj, Realpolitik, Rection, Rector, Rectrix, Regency, Regié, Regime(n), Regulator, Reign, Rein, Republican, Ride, → **RULE**, Satrap, Senate, Serkali, Shogun, Signoria, Sircar, Sirkar, Stad(t)holder, Stakhanovism, Statecraft, Stear, Steer, Stratocracy, Subadar, Subah(dar), Sway, Technocracy, Tetrarchy, Thalassocracy, Thalattocracy, Thatcherism, Thearchy, Theocracy, Theonomy, Third Republic, Timocracy, Totalitarianism, Triarchy, Triumvirate, Tuchun, Tyranny, Vaivode, Vali, Viceregal, Viceroy, Vichy, Vichyssois(e), Voivode, Wali, Warden, Wealsman, Whitehall, White House, Witan, Woiwode

Governess Duenna, Eyre, Fraulein, Griffin, Mademoiselle, Prism, Vicereine

Government revenue Jaghir(e), Jagir

Gown Banian, Banyan, Dressing, Empire, Geneva, Green, Johnny, Kimono, Kirtle, Manteau, Manto, Mantua, Manty, Mazarine, Morning, Mother Hubbard, Negligee, Peignoir, Polonaise, Robe, Sack, Silk, Slammakin, Slammerkin, Slop, Stola, Stuff, Tea, Wrap(per)

Grab Accost, Annexe, Areach, Bag, Clutch, Cly, Collar, Glaum, Grapnel, Hold, Holt, Nab, Rap, Reach, Seise, Seize, Snaffle, → **SNATCH**, Steal, Swipe

Gracchi Jewels

Grace(s), Graceful Aglaia, Airy, Amazing, Amnesty, Anna, Bad, Beauty, Become, Benediction, Ben(t)sh, Bethankit, Blessing, Charis(ma), Charites, Charity, Cooperating, Darling, Dr, Elegance, Eloquent, Euphrosyne, Fluent, Gainly, Genteel, Genty, Godliness, Grazioso, Handsome, Honour, Light, Mense, Mercy, Molinism, Mordent, Omnium, Ornament, Plastique, Polish, Pralltriller, Prayer, Sacrament, Saving, Spirituelle, Streamlined, Style, Svelte, Thalia, Thanks, Thanksgiving, Tuesday, WG, Willowy

Grace note Nachschlag

Gracious Benign, By George, Charismatic, Generous, Good, Handsome, Hend, Mamma mia, Merciful, Polite

Gradation Ablaut, Cline, Degree, Nuance, Stage

Grade, Gradient Alpha, Analyse, Angle, Assort, Beta, Bubs, Class(ify), Conservation, Dan, Degree, Delta, Echelon, Gamma, Geothermal, Gon, Gride, Hierarchy, Inclination, Kyu, Lapse, Measure, Order, Ordinary, Pressure, Rank, Reserve, Score, Seed, Slope, Stage, Standard, Status, Temperature, Thermocline, Tier

Gradual Gentle, Grail, Imperceptible, Inchmeal, Piecemeal, Slow

Graduate, Graduation Alumnus, BA, Bachelor, Calibrate, Capping, Classman, Incept, Laureateship, Licentiate, LlB, MA, Master, Nuance, Optime, Ovate

Graffiti Bomb, Doodle, Tag, Tagger

Graft Anaplasty, Autoplasty, Boodle, Bribery, Bud, Bypass, Cion, Cluster, Crown, Dishonesty, Dub, Enarch, Enrace, Flap, Hard, Heteroplasty, Imp, Implant, Inarch, Inoculate, Payola, Pomato, Racket, Scion, Shoot, Sien(t), Skin, Slip, Syen, Transplant, Whip, Ympe

Grail Chalice, Cup, Sangraal, Sangrail, Sangreal

Grain(y) Bajra, Bajree, Bajri, Barley(corn), Bear, Bere, Boll, Bran, Cereal, Corn, Couscous, Crop, Curn, Curn(e)y, Cuscus, Distillers', D(o)urra, Dye, Extine, Floor, Frumentation, Gr, Graddan, Granule, Grit(s), Groats, Grout, Grumose, Intine, Kaoliang, Knaveship, Malt, Mashlam, Mashlin, Mashloch, Mashlum, Maslin, Mealie, Millet, Milo, Minim, Mongcorn, Oats, Panic(k), Pannick, Pickle, Pinole, Pollen, Polynology, Popcorn, Proso,

Psyllium, Puckle, Quarter, Quinoa, Rabi, Raggee, Raggy, Ragi, Rhy, Rye, Sand, Scruple, Seed, Semsem, Sorghum, Tef(f), Thirlage, Tola, Touch, Wheat, Wholemeal

Gram Black, Chich, Chick-pea, Green, Teen, Tene, Urd

Grammar(ian), Grammatical Ablative absolute, Accidence, Amphibology, Anacoluthia, Anacoluthon, Anaphora, Anastrophe, Case, Cataphora, Categorical, Causative, Deixis, Donat, Donet, Generative, Gr, Inessive, Linguistics, Montague, Paradigm, Parataxis, Paucal, Pivot, Primer, Priscianist, Priscianus, Protasis, Relational, Scholiast, Stratificational, Syndetic, Syndeton, Synectics, Synesis, Syntax, Systemics, Tagmeme, Transformational, Trivium, Typto, Universal, Valency

Gramophone Record player, Victrolla®

Grampus Orc(a), Risso's dolphin, Thresher-whale, Whale

Granary Barn, Girnel, Silo

Grand(eur), Grandiose Big, Canyon, Epical, Flugel, G, Gorgeous, Guignol, High-faluting, Hotel, Imposing, La(h)-di-da(h), Long, Lordly, Magnificent, Majestic, Megalomania, Noble, Overblown, Palatial, Piano(forte), Pompous, Regal, Splendid, Stately, Stoor, Stour, Stowre, Sture, Sublime, Swell, Tour

Grandchild Mokopuna, Niece, Oe, Oy(e)

Grandee Adelantado, Aristo, Don, Magnifico

Grandfather Ancient, Avital, Clock, Goodsire, Gramps, Gudesire, Gutcher, Luckie-dad, Oldster, Old-timer, Oupa

Grandmother Babushka, Beldam, Gran(nie), Granny, Luckie, Moses, Nan(a), Nokomis, Ouma

Grandparent(al) Aval, Avital

Grand Prix Race(-cup)

Grandsire Peal

Grange Moated

Granite Aberdeen, Chinastone, Graphic, Greisen, Luxul(l)ianite, Luxulyanite, NH, Pegmatite, Protogine

Grannie, Granny Cowl, Forebear, Knot, Nan(a)

Grant(ed) Accord, Aid, Allot, Allow, Award, Benefaction, Bestow, Beteem(e), Block, Bounty, Bursary, Carta, Cary, Cede, Charta, Charter, Concession, → **CONFER**, Cy, Datum, Endow, Enfranchise, Exhibition, Feoff, Give, Hugh, Land, Lend, Let, License, Munich, Obreption, Patent, President, Regium donum, Scholarship, Send, Sop, Subsidy, Subvention, Supply, Teene, Ulysses, Ure, Vouchsafe, Yeven, Yield

Granule, Granulate(d) Kern, Otolith, Pearl, Plastid, Pound, Prill, Saburra, Statolith, Volutin

Grape(s) Aligoté, Botros, Botryoid, Bullace, Cabernet, Cabernet Sauvignon, Carmenère, Catawba, Cépage, Chardonnay, Chenin blanc, Colombard, Concord, Cot, Delaware, Diamond, Fox, Gamay, Garnacha, Gewurztraminer, Grenache, Haanepoot, Hamburg(h), Hanepoot, Honeypot, Hyacinth, Lambrusco, Malbec, Malmsey, Malvasia, Malvesie, Malvoisie, Marsanne, Merlot, Montepulciano, Muscadel, Muscadine, Muscat(el), Nebbiolo, Noble rot, Oregon, Petite Syrah, Pinot, Pinotage, Pinot blanc, Pinot Chardonnay, Primitivo, Ptisan, Racemose, Raisin, Rape, Riesling, Sangiovese, Sauvignon, Scuppernong, Sémillon, Sercial, Shiraz, Sour, Staphyline, Steen, Sultana, Sweet-water, Sylvaner, Syrah, Tokay, Uva, Verdelho, Véronique, Vino, Vognier, Wineberry, Zinfandel

Grapefruit Pampelmoose, Pomelo, Pompelmouse, Pompelo, Pumple-nose, Shaddock, Ugli®

Grape-grower Vigneron, Vine-dresser

Grapeshot Mitraille

Grape-sugar Glucose

Grapevine Gossip, Hearsay, Mocassin telegraph, Moccasin telegraph

Graph, Graphic(s) Bar, Chart, Clip art, Computer, Contour, Diagram, Histogram, Learning curve, Nomograph, Ogive, Picturesque, Pie (chart), Plot, Profile, Raster, Sine curve, Sonogram, Table, Turtle, Vivid, Waveform, Waveshape

Graphite Kish, Plumbago

Grapple Clinch, Close, Hook, Lock, Struggle, Wrestle

Grasp(ing) Apprehend, Catch, Clat, Claut, Claw, Clench, Clinch, → **CLUTCH**, Compass, Comprehend, Fathom, Get, Go-getting, Grab, Grapple, Greedy, Grip(e), Hend, Hold, Hug, Knowledge, Prehend, Prehensile, Raptorial, Realise, Rumble, Seize, Sense, Snap, Snatch, Twig, Uptak(e)

Grass(land), Grass roots, Grassy Agrostology, Alang, Alfa(lfa), Arrow, Avena, Bahia, Bamboo, Bang, Barbed wire, Barley, Barnyard, Beard, Bennet, Bent, Bermuda, Bhang, Blade, Blady, Blue(-eyed), Blue moor, Bristle, Brome-grass, Bromus, Buffalo, Buffel, Bunch, Bush, Campo, Canary, Cane, Canna, Cannach, Carpet, Cat's tail, Cheat, Chess, China, Citronella, Cleavers, Clivers, Clover, Cochlearia, Cocksfoot, Cockspur, Cogon, Cord, Cortaderia, Cotton, Couch, Cow, Crab, Culm, Cuscus, Cutty, Dactylis, Danthonia, Dari, Darnel, Deergrass, Dhur(r)a, Diss, Divot, Dogstail, Dog's tooth, Dogwheat, Doob, Doura, Dura, Durra, Eddish, Eel, Eelwrack, Elephant, Emmer, Ers, Esparto, Feather, Fescue, Finger, Fiorin, Flinders, Floating, Flote, Fog, Foggage, Foxtail, Gage, Gama-grass, Ganja, Gardener's garters, Glume, Glumella, Goose, Grama, Gramineae, Green(sward), Hair, Halfa, Harestail, Hashish, Hassock, Haulm, Hay, Haycock, Heath(er), Hemp, Herbage, High veld, Holy, Indian corn, → **INFORM**, Jawar(i), Job's tears, Johnson, Jowar(i), Kangaroo, Kans, Kentucky blue, Khuskhus, Kikuyu, Knoll, Knot, Lalang, Laund, Lawn, Lay, Lea, Lee, Lemon, Locusta, Lolium, Lop, Lucern(e), Lyme, Mabela, Machair, Maize, Manna, Marram, Marrum, Mary Jane, Mat, Materass, Matweed, Mead, Meadow(-fescue), Meadow foxtail, Mealies, Melic, Melick, Millet, Milo, Miscanthus, Monkey, Moor, Moss-crop, Nark, Nassella tussock, Nature strip, Negro-corn, Nit, Nose, Nut, Oat, Orange, Orchard, Oryza, Painted, Palet, Pamir, Pampas, Panic, Paspalum, Pasturage, Peach, Pennisetum, Pepper, Persicaria, Phleum, Pilcorn, Plume, Poa, Porcupine, Pot, Purple moor, Puszta, Quack, Quaking, Quick, Quitch, Ramee, Rami(e), Rat, Rat on, Redtop, Reed, Rescue, Rhodes, Rib, Ribbon, Rice, Rips, Roosa, Rotgrass, Rough, Rumble(r), Rusa, Rush, Rye(-brome), Sacaton, Sago, Salt, Sand, Savanna(h), Saw, Scorpion, Scraw, Scurvy, Scutch, Sea-reed, Sedge, Seg, Sesame, Shave, Sheep's fescue, Shop, Sing, Sinsemilla, Sisal, Sneak(er), Snitch, Snout, Snow, Sorghum, Sour-gourd, Sourveld, Spanish, Spear, Spelt, Spike, Spinifex, Splay, Split, Squeal, Squirrel-tail, Squitch, Stag, Star(r), Stipa, Stool-pigeon, Storm, Sudan, Sugar, Sward, Swath(e), Sword, Tape, Taramea, Tath, Tea, Tef(f), Tell, Teosinte, Timothy, Toad, Toetoe, Toitoi, Triticale, Triticum, True-love, Tuffet, Turf, Tussac, Tussock, Twitch, Veld(t), Vernal, Vetiver, Viper's, Whangee, Wheat, Wheatgrass, Whistleblower, Whitlow, Wild oats, Windlestraw, Wire, Witch, Wood melick, Worm, Yard, Yellow-eyed, Yorkshire fog, Zizania, Zostera, Zoysia

Grasshopper Cicada, Cricket, Grig, Katydid, Locust, Long-horned, Meadow, Reeler, Short-horned, Tettix, Wart-biter, Weta

Grate(r), Grating Abrade, Burr, Cancelli, Chafe, Chain, Chirk, Crepitus, Diffraction, Erosure, → **FRET**, Graticule, Gravelly, Grid, Grill, Guichet, Guttural, Hack, Haik, Hake, Harsh, Hearth, Heck, Hoarse, Ingle, Iron, Jar, Mort-safe, Nag, Portcullis, Rasp, Risp, Rub, Ruling, Scrannel, → **SCRAPE**, Scrat, Scroop, Shred, Siver, Strident, Syver

Grateful Beholden, Cinders, Indebted, Obliged

Gratification, Gratify(ing) Aggrate, Indulge, Kick, Masochism, Narcissism, Oblige, Pleasure, Regale, Reward, Sadism, Satisfaction, Sensuous, Venery, Yummy

Gratin Tian

Gratitude Debt, God 'a mercy, Ta, Thanks

Gratuitous, Gratuity Baksheesh, Beer-money, Bonsella, Bonus, Bounty, Cumshaw, Dash, Free, Glove-money, Gratis, Lagn(i)appe, Mag(g)s, Tip

Grave(yard) Accent, Arlington, Barrow, Bass, Bier, Burial, Charnel, Chase, Critical, Darga, Demure, Dust, God's acre, Heavy, Heinous, Important, Ingroove, Kistvaen, Kurgan, Long home, Mool, Mould, Mound, Passage, Pit, Sad, Saturnine, Serious, Sober, Solemn, Sombre, Speos, Staid, Stern, Tomb, Watery

Grave-digger Bederal, Fossor, Inhumer, Sexton

Gravel(ly) Calculus, Channel, Chesil, Chisel, Eskar, Esker, Glareous, Grail(e), Grit, Hard, Hoggin(g), Murram, Nonplus, Pay, Pea, Pingo, Shingle

Gravity Barycentric, G, Geotaxis, Geotropism, Great Attraction, Magnitude, Mascon, Quantum, Specific, Weight, Zero

Gravy Baster, Bisto®, Browning, Coin, Jus, Milk, Sauce

Gravy-boat Argyle, Argyll

▸ **Gray** *see* **GREY(ING)**

Grayling Umber

Graze, Grazing, Grazier Abrade, Agist, Bark, Brush, Crease, Crop, Feed, Glance, Gride, Gryde, Heft, Herdwick, Leasow(e), Machair, Moorburn, Muirburn, Pascual, Pastoralist, Pasture, Rake, Rangeland, Scrape, Scrawn, Shave, Sheepwalk, Shieling, Transhumance, Zero

Grease, Greasy Bribe, Creesh, Dope, Dubbing, Elaeolite, Elbow, Enlard, Enseam, Glit, Lanolin, Lard, Lubricate, Oil, Ointment, Pinguid, Saim, Seam(e), Shearer, Sheep-shearer, Smarm, Smear, Suint, Unctuous

Great deal Mort

Greater, Greatest, Great(ly), Greats Alfred, Ali, A majori, Astronomical, Brilliant, Bully, Capital, Classical, Colossus, Cosmic, Enorm(ous), Ever so, Excellent, Extreme, Fantastic, Gargantuan, Gatsby, Gay, Gey, Gran(d), Grit, Gt, Guns, Hellova, Helluva, Immense, Immortal, Important, Intense, Large, Lion, Macro, Magic, Magnus, Main, Major, Massive, Mega, Mickle, Mochell, Modern, Much, Muchel(l), Muckle, No end, OS, Preponderant, Profound, Rousing, Splendiferous, Stoor, Stour, Stupendous, Sture, Sublime, Super, Superb, Superduper, Swingeing, Synergy, Tall, Thrice, Titan(ic), Top notch, Tremendous, Unco, Untold, Utmost, Vast, Voluminous, Wide, Zenith

Grebe Cargoose

Grecian Bend, Nose

Greed(y) Avarice, Avid, Bulimia, Bulimy, Cupidity, Edacious, Esurient, Gannet, Gare, Grabby, Grip(ple), Gulosity, Guts(e)y, Harpy, Insatiable, Killcrop, Lickerish, Liquorish, Mercenary, Money-grubbing, Piggery, Pleonexia, Rapacity, Selfish, Shark's manners, Solan, Voracity, Wolfish

Greek(s) Achaean, Achaian, Achilles, Aeolic, Agamemnon, Ajax, Ancient, Aonian, Arcadia, Archimedes, Argive, Aristides, Athenian, Attic, Boeotian, Byzantine, Cadmean, Cleruch, Corinthian, Cretan, Cumae, Cyzicus, Delphian, Demotic, Demotike, Ding, Diomedes, Dorian, Doric, Elea, Eoka, Eolic, Epaminondas, Ephebe, Epirus, Euclid, Evzone, Fanariot, Gr, Helladic, Hellene, Hellenic, Hesychast, Homer, Hoplite, Ionian, Isocrates, Italiot(e), Javan, Katharev(o)usa, Klepht, Koine, Laconian, Lapith, Late, Leonidas, Linear B, Locrian, Lucian, Lysander, Macedonia, Medieval, Middle, Milesian, Modern, Molossian, Momus, Nestor, Nike, Nostos, Orestes, Paestum, Patroclus, Pelasgic, Pelopid, Perseus, Phanariot, Pythagoras, Romaic, Samiot, Seminole, Spartacus, Spartan, Stagirite, Strabo, Sybarite, Tean, Teian, Theban, Thersites, Theseus, Thessal(on)ian, Thracian, Timon, Typto, Uniat, Xenophon, Zorba

Green(ery) Almond, Apple, Avocado, Baggy, Bice, Biliverdin, Bleaching, Bottle, Bowling, Caesious, Callow, Celadon, Cerulein, Chard, Chartreuse, Chlorophyll, Chrome, Citron, Cole, Collard, Common, Copper, Corbeau, Crown, Cyan, Dioptase, Eau de nil, Eco-, Ecofriendly, Ecologic, Econut, Emerald, Emerande, Envious, Environmentalist, Erin, Fingers, Foliage, Forest, Fuchsin, Fundie, Fundy, Gaudy, Glaucous, Go, Goddess, Grass, Gretna, Gull, Immature, Inexpert, Jade, Jungle, Kendal, Kensal, Khaki, L, Lawn, Leafage, Lime, Lincoln, Loden, Lovat, Mead, Monastral®, Moss, Moulding, Naive, New, Nile, Oasis, Olive, Paris, Pea, Peridot, Pistachio, Porraceous, Putting, Raw, Realo, Reseda, Rifle, Rink, Sage, Sap, Scheele's, Sea, Seasick, Shaw, Sludge, Smaragdine, Sward, Teal, Tender, Terre-vert, Tiro, Turacoverdin, Tyro, Unfledged, Uninitiated, Unripe, Unsophisticated, Untrained, Uranite, Verdant, Verd antique, Verdigris, Verdure, Vert, Virent, Vir(id)escent, Virid, Viridian, Yearn, Young

Greenheart Bebeeru

Greenhorn Baby, Dupe, Ingenue, Put(t), Rookie, Sucker

Greenhouse Conservatory, Cooohouse, Orangery, Phytotron, Polytunnel

Greenland(er) Inuit

Greens Broccoli, Cabbage, Calabrese, Cash, Castor, Mangetout, Sprout, Vegetable(s)

Greet, Greeting(s) Abrazo, Accost, Air-kiss, All hail, Aloha, Arvo, Banzai, Benedicite, Bid, Blubber, Bonsoir, Chimo, Ciao, Den, G'day, Glad hand, Gorillagram, Hail, Hallo, Halse, Handclasp, Handshake, Haway, Heil, Heita, Hello, Herald, Hi, High-five, Hiya, Hongi, How, How d'ye do, Howsit, Jai Hind, Jambo, Kia ora, Kiss, Kissagram, Mihi, Namaskar, Namaste, Respects, Salaam, Salam alaikum, Salue, Salute, Salve, Save you, Sd, Shalom, Shalom aleichem, Sorry, Strippagram, Strippergram, Tena koe, Tena korua, Tena koutou, Wave, Weep, → **WELCOME**, Wellmet, Wotcha, Wotcher, Yo

Gregarious Outgoing, Social

Gregorian Chant, NS, Plagal

▸ **Gremlin** *see* **GOBLIN**

Grenade, Grenadier Bomb, Egg, Fragmentation, Hand, Pineapple, Rat-tail, Rifle, Stun

Grenadine(s) Bequia, Canounan, Mustique, Union Island

Greta Garbo

Grey(ing), Gray, Greybeard Age, Agnes, Argent, Ashen, Ashy, Battleship, Beige, Bloncket, C(a)esius, Charcoal, Cinereous, Clair de lune, Dapple, Dorian, Dove, Drab, Earl, Ecru, Feldgrau, Field, Glaucous, Gloomy, Gr, Gridelin, Griesie, Gries(l)y, Grise, Grisy, Grizzled, Gunmetal, Gy, Hoary, Hodden, Hore, Inn, Iron, Leaden, Liard, Lipizzaner, Livid, Lloyd, Lucia, Lyart, Mouse-coloured, Neutral, Oldster, Olive drab, Oyster, Pearl, Perse, Pewter, Poliosis, Putty, Sclate, Slaty, Steel, Taupe, Zane

Greyfriars Bunter, Magnet

Greyhound Grew, Italian, Lapdog, Longtail, Ocean, Persian, Saluki, Sapling, Whippet

Grey matter Cinerea

Grid(dle), Gridiron Bar, Barbecue, Brandreth, Cattle, Control, Dot matrix, Grate, Graticule, Grating, Lattice, National, Network, Reseau, Reticle, Roo-bar, Schema, Screen, Starting, Suppressor, Tava(h), Tawa, Windscale

Gride Creak, Grate

Grief, Grievance, Grieve, Grievous Axe, Bemoan, Bitter, Complaint, Condole, Cry, Dear(e), Deere, Distress, Dole, Dolour, Eyedrop, Gram(e), Gravamen, Grudge, Heartbreak, Hone, Illy, Io, → **MISERY**, Monody, Noyous, O(c)hone, Overset, Pain, Pathetic, Plaint, Plangent, Rue, Score, Sore, Sorrow, Tears, Teen, Tene, Tragic, Wayment, Weeping, Woe, Wrong

Griffin Gripe, Grype, Novice, Pony

Grill(er), Grilling Braai, Brander, Broil, Carbonado, Crisp, Cross-examine, Devil, Gridiron, Inquisition, Interrogate, Kebab, Mixed, Pump, Question, Rack, Radiator, Reja, Yakimona

Grim Austere, Dire, Dour, Forbidding, Gaunt, Glum, Gurly, Hard, Macabre, Reaper, Stern

▹ **Grim** *may indicate* an anagram

Grimace Face, Girn, Moe, Mop, Moue, Mouth, Mow, Murgeon, Pout, Wince

Grime(s), Grimy Colly, Coom, Dirt, Grunge, Peter, Rechie, Reechie, Reechy, Soil, Sweep, Tash

Grin Fleer, Girn, Risus, Simper, Smirk, Sneer

Grind(er), Grinding Bray, Bruxism, Chew, Crunch, → **CRUSH**, Droil, Drudgery, Gnash, Grate, Graunch, Grit, Home, Kern, Kibble, Labour, Levigate, Mano, Metate, Mill, Mince, Molar, Muller, Offhand, Pug, Pulpstone, Pulverise, Slog, Stamp, Triturate

Grip(ping), Gripper Absorb, Arm lock, Ascendeur, Bite, Chuck, Clam, Clamp, Cleat, Clip, Clutch, Craple, Dog, Embrace, Engrasp, Enthral, Get, Grapple, → **GRASP**, Haft, Hair, Hairpin, Hand(fast), Handhold, Headlock, Hend, Hold, Hug, Interesting, Jaw, Key, Kirby®, Lewis, Obsess, Pincer, Pinion, Pistol, Prehensile, Purchase, Raven, Rhine, Sally, Setscrew, Sipe, Strain, Streigne, Thrill, Traction, Twist, Valise, Vice, Walise, Wrestle

Gripe(s) Colic, Complain, Ditch, Grasp, Griffin, Ileus, Pain, Tormina, Whine
Grisly Gory, Macabre
Grist Burden
Gristle, Gristly Cartilage, Chondroid, Lytta, Proteoglycan, Raven's bone
Grit(s), Gritty Blinding, Clench, Gnash, Granular, Grate, Guts, Hominy, Mattress, Millstone, Nerve, Pennant, Pluck, Resolution, Sabulose, Sand, Shingle, Swarf, Toughness, Valour, Yorkshire
Gritty Tacky, Ugly
Grizzle(d) Grey
Groan(er), Groaning Bewail, Bing, Moan, Overladen, Sigh, Titus
Grocer(y) Dairy, Epicier, Grasshopper, Jorrocks, Pepperer, Symbol
Grog(gy) Dazed, Queasy, Shaky
Groin Gnarr, Inguinal, Lisk
Groom(ed) Brush, Coistrel, Coistril, Comb, Curry, Dress, Fettler, Kempt, Neaten, Ostler, Palfrenier, Paranymph, Preen, Primp, Prink, S(a)ice, Smarten, Spouse, Strapper, Syce, Tiger, Tracer, Train, Wrangler
▷ **Groom** *may indicate* an anagram
Groove(d), Grooves, Groovy Bezel, Canal, Cannelure, Chamfer, Channel, Chase, Clevis, Cool, Coulisse, Croze, Dièdre, Exarate, Fissure, Flute, Fuller, Furr, Furrow, Glyph, Gouge, Hill and dale, Kerf, Key-seat, Keyway, Lead-in, Lead-out, Nock, Oche, Pod, Quirk, Rabbet, Race(way), Raggle, Raphe, Rare, Rebate, Rif(f)le, Rifling, Rigol(l), Rout, → **RUT**, Scrobe, Scrobiculate, Sipe, Slot, Sulcus, Throat, Track, Trough, Vallecula
Grope(r) A tatons, Feel, Fumble, Grabble, Hapuka, Ripe, Scrabble
Gross All-up, Coarse, Coarse-grained, Complete, Crass, Dense, Earn, Earthy, Flagrant, Frankish, Fustilugs, Giant, Gr, Loathsome, Material, Obese, Obscene, Outsize, Overweight, Pre-tax, Rank, Ribald, Rough, Stupid, Sum, Whole
▷ **Gross** *may indicate* an anagram
Grotesque Antic, Bizarre, Fantastic, Fright, Gargoyle, Macaroni, Magot, Outlandish, Rabelaisian, Rococo, Teras
Grotto Cave, Lupercal
Grotty Tacky, Ugly
Ground(ed), Grounds Abthane, Acreage, Arena, Astroturf, A terre, Basis, Bottom, Breeding, Campus, Cause, Common, Criterion, Crushed, Deck, Dregs, Eard, Earth, Edgbaston, Epig(a)eal, Epig(a)ean, Epigene, Epig(a)eous, Etching, Floor, Footing, Forbidden, Gathering, Grated, Grist, Grouts, Happy hunting, Headingley, High, Home, Hunting, Justification, Lees, Leeway, Lek, Lords, Lot, Marl, Meadow, Mealed, Middle, Motive, Occasion, Oval, Parade, Piste, Pitch, Plat, Pleasure, Plot, Policy, Proving, Quad, → **REASON**, Rec(reation), Réseau, Ring, Sandlot, Sediment, Slade, Soil, Solum, Sports, Stadium, Stamping, Strand, Terra, Terrain, Tiltyard, Tom Tiddler's, Touch, Tract, Turf, Udal, Vantage, Venue, Waste(land), Yard, Yird
▷ **Ground** *may indicate* an anagram
Groundbait Chum
Ground-breaker Pioneer
Ground-crew Erk
Ground-rent Crevasse
Groundsheet Hutchie
Groundsman Greenkeeper
Group(ie), Grouping Abelian, Acyl, Affinity, Al Fatah, 'A'list, Bananarama, Band, Batch, Battle, Beatles, Bee, Bevy, Bloc(k), Blood, Bloomsbury, Board, Body, Bracket, Bratpack, Break-out, Bruges, Bunch, Caboodle, Cadre, Camarilla, Camp, Cartel, Category, Caucus, Cave, Cell, Chain, Choir, Chordata, Circle, Clade, Clan, Class(is), Clique, Clump, Cluster, Clutch, Coachload, Cohort, Colony, Combo, Commune, Community, Complex, Concertino, Confraternity, Conglomerate, Congregation, Consort(ium), Constellation, Contact, Contingent, Control, Convoy, Coterie, Covey, Crew, Decile, Dectet, Deme,

Demi-monde, Denomination, Department, Detachment, Detail, Drove, Enclave, Encounter, Ensemble, Faction, Family, Fascio, Fauna, Fleet, Flora, Focus, Fold, Follower, Fraternity, Front, Functional, Gaggle, Galère, Gang, Gemeinschaft, Gender, Generation, Genotype, Genus, Gesellschaft, Ginger, Globe, Guild, Hapu, Heading, Herd, Hexad, Hirsel, House, Household, Income, In-crowd, Interest, Keiretsu, Ketone, Kit, Knob, Knot, League, Led Zeppelin, Lichfield, Linkage, Local, Lot, Lumpenproletariat, Marathon, Marshal, Minority, Minyan, Network, Nexus, Oasis, Order, Outfit, Oxford, Pack(et), Panel, Parti, Party, Passel, Peer, Phalange, Phalanx, Phratry, Phylum, Platoon, Pleiad, PLO, Plump, Pocket, Pod, Point, Pool, Pop, Posse, Powerbase, Pressure, Prosthetic, Push, Quincunx, Raceme, Racemose, Rap, Reading, Retinue, Ring, Rush, Salon, School, Sector, Seminar, Senate, Series, Set, Several, Sex, Shoal, Shower, Society, Sort, Sorus, Species, Splinter, Squad(ron), Stick, Strain, Stream, String, Study, Subclass, Subfamily, Sub-general, Sub-order, Subset, Subspecies, Support, Symbol, Syndicate, Synectics, Syntagm, System, T, Tales, Taxon, Team, Tetrad, The few, Tithing, Topological, Trainband, T-Rex, Tribe, Tribune, Trilogy, Trio, Troika, Troop, Troupe, TU, Umbrella, Undecimole, Unit, Usenet®, User, Vertical, Vigilante, Wing, Workshop, Zaibatsu, Zupa

Grouse Bellyache, Black, Blackcock, Bleat, Blue, Caper(caillie), Capercailzie, Covey, Game, Gorcock, Greyhen, Gripe, Growl, Grumble, Hazel-hen, Heath-cock, Heathfowl, Heath-hen, Jeremiad, Kvetch, Moan, Moorcock, Moorfowl, Moor-pout, Muir-poot, Muir-pout, Mutter, Natter, Peeve, Pintail, Prairie chicken, Prairie-hen, Ptarmigan, Red, Red game, Resent, Ruffed, Rype(r), Sage, Sharp-tailed, Snarl, Spruce, Squawk, Twelfth, Wheenge, Willow, W(h)inge

Grout Cement, Lees

Grove Academy, Arboretum, Bosk, Bosquet, Copse, Glade, Hurst, Lyceum, Motte, Nemoral, Orchard, Orchat, Silva, Tope

Grovel Cheese, Crawl, Creep, Fawn, Ko(w)tow, Worm

Grow(ing), Grow out, Growth Accrete, Accrue, Acromegaly, Adenoma, Aggrandisement, Angioma, Apophysis, Arborescence, Auxesis, Bedeguar, Boom, Braird, Breer, Burgeon, Carcinoma, Car(b)uncle, Chancre, Cholelith, Chondroma, Compensatory, Condyloma, Corn, Crescendo, Crop, Culture, Cyst, Down, Ectopia, Edema, Ellagic, Enate, Enchondroma, Enlarge, Epiboly, Epinasty, Epitaxy, Excrescence, Exostosis, Expansion, Fibroid, Flor, Flourish, Flush, Gain, Gall, Germinate, Get, Glareal, Goitre, Hepatocele, Hummie, Hyperostosis, Hypertrophy, Hyponasty, Increase, Involucrum, Keloidal, Keratosis, Knur(r), Lichen, Lipoma, Mole, Monopodial, Moss, Mushroom, Myoma, Neoplasia, Nur(r), Oak-nut, Oedema, Oncology, Osselet, Osteoma, Osteophyte, Pharming, Polyp, Polypus, Proleg, Proliferate, Rampant, Rank, Scirrhus, Scopa, Septal, Snowball, Spavin, → **SPROUT**, Stalagmite, Stand, Stipule, Sympodial, Tariff, Thigmotropism, Thrive, Trichome, → **TUMOUR**, Tylosis, Vegetable, Wart, Wax, Weed, Witches'-broom, Wox, Zeatin

▷ **Grow(n)** *may indicate* an anagram

Growl(er), Growling Fremescent, Gnar, Groin, Grr, Gurl, Iceberg, Knar, Roar(e), Roin, Royne, Snar(l)

Grown up Adult, Mature, Risen

Groyne Breakwater

Grub(by) Assart, Aweto, Bardie, Bardy, Bookworm, Caddis, Caterpillar, Cheer, Chow, Chrysalis, Deracinate, Dig, Eats, Fare, Fodder, → **FOOD**, Gentle, Groo-groo, Gru-gru, Larva, Leatherjacket, Maggot, Mawk, Mess, Nosh, Palmerworm, Peck, Pupa, Root(le), Rout, Rowt, Sap, Slave, Stub, Tired, Wireworm, Witchetty, Wog, Worm

Grudge, Grudging Chip, Derry, Envy, Grievance, Grutch, Resent, Score, Sparse, Spite, Spleen, Sting

Gruel Brochan, Bross, Loblolly, Skilligalee, Skilligolee, Skilly

Gruesome Ghastly, Grisly, Grooly, Horror, Livid, Macaberesque, Macabre, → **MORBID**, Sick

Gruff Guttural, Hoarse, Surly

Grumble Beef, Bellyache, Bitch, Bleat, Chunter, Crab, Croak, Girn, Gripe, Grizzle, Groin, Growl, Moan, Mump, Murmur, Mutter, Nark, Natter, Repine, Rumble, Whinge, Yammer

Grump(y) Attercop, Bearish, Cross, Curmudgeon, Ettercap, Grouchy, Moody, Ogre(ish), Sore-headed, Surly, Testy

Grunt Groin, Grumph, Humph, Oink, Pigfish, Spanish, Ugh, Wheugh

Guano Dung, Sombrerite

Guanoco Llama

Guarantee(d) Accredit, Assure, Avouch, Certify, Collateral, Ensure, Fail-safe, Gage, Hallmark, Insure, Mainprise, Money-back, Pignerate, Pignorate, → **PLEDGE**, Plight, Promise, Seal, Secure, Sponsion, Surety, Underwrite, → **VOUCHSAFE**, Warn, Warrandice, Warrant(y)

Guard(ed), Guards Acolouthos, Advance, Apron, Beefeaters, Blues, Bostangi, Bouncer, Bracer, Cabiri, Cage, Cag(e)y, Centinel(l), Centry, Cerberus, Chamfrain, Chaperon(e), Chary, Cheesemongers, Cherry-pickers, Coast, Coldstream, Colour, Conductor, Cordon, Crinoline, Curator, Custodian, Custos, Defend, Diehards, Dragoons, Duenna, Equerry, Escort, Eunuch, Excubant, Exon, Fence, Fender, Gaoler, Gateman, Gauntlet, Grenadiers, Greys, Hedge, Home, Horse, INS, Insure, Irish, Iron, Jaga, Jailer, Keep, Lancers, Life, Lilywhites, Look out, Mask, Militia, Mort-safe, Muzzle, National, Nightwatch(man), Noncommital, Nutcrackers, Old, Out-rider, Out-sentry, Pad, Palace, Patrol, Picket, Point, Policeman, Praetorian, → **PROTECT**, Provost, Quillon, Rail, Red, Ride, Roof, Scots, Screw, Secure, Security, Sentinel, Sentry, Shadow, Shield, Shin, Shopping, Shotgun, Splashback, Splashboard, Splasher, SS, Strelitz, Streltzi, Swiss, Switzer, Tapadera, Tapadero, Tile, Toecap, Tsuba, Turnkey, Vambrace, Vamplate, Varangian, Vigilante, Visor, Wage, Wait(e), Ward, Warder, Wary, Watch (and ward), Watchdog, Watchman, Wear, Weir, Wire, Yeoman

Guardian(ship) Agathodaimon, Altair, Argus, Caretaker, Chaperone, Curator, Custodian, Custos, Dragon, Gemini, Granthi, Hafiz, Janus, Julius, Miminger, Patron, Protector, Templar, Trustee, Tutelage, Tutelar(y), Tutor, Warder, Watchdog, Xerxes

Guatemala(n) Mam

Gudgeon Fish, Pin, Trunnion

Guenon Grivet, Vervet

Guer(r)illa Bushwhacker, Chetnik, Comitadji, Contra, ETA, Fedayee, Gook, Haiduk, Heyduck, Irregular, Khmer Rouge, Komitaji, Maquis, Mujahadeen, Mujahedeen, Mujahed(d)in, Mujahideen, Partisan, Phalanx, Red Brigade, Tamil Tiger, Terrorist, Tupamaro, Urban, Viet Cong, Zapata, Zapatista

Guess Aim, Aread, Arede, Arreede, Assume, Augur, Conjecture, Divine, Educated, Estimate, Harp, Hazard, Hunch, Imagine, Infer, Inspired, Level, Mor(r)a, Mull, Psych out, Reckon, Shot, Speculate, Stab, Suppose, Surmise, Theorise, Venture

Guessing game Handy-dandy, Mor(r)a, Quiz

Guest(s) Caller, Company, House-party, Inquiline, Invitee, Parasite, Paying, PG, Symbion(t), Symphile, Synoecete, Umbra, Visitant, → **VISITOR**, Xenial

Guesthouse B & B, Minshuku, Taverna, Xenodochium

Guff Bosh, Gas

Guianian S(a)ouari

Guidance, Guide, Guiding, Guideline Advice, Antibarbus, Aunt, Auspice, Baedeker, Bradshaw, Cicerone, Clue, Command, Concordance, Conduct, Counsel, Courier, Cox, Curb, Cursor, Cybrary, Director(y), Docent, Dragoman, Drive, Engineer, → **ESCORT**, Field, Gillie, Graticule, Helm, Heuristic, Homing, Index, Inertial, Inspire, Itinerary, Jig, Key, Lad, Landmark, Lead, Lodestar, Mahatma, Manoeuvre, Map, Mark, Marriage, Mentor, Michelin, Missile, Model, Navaid, Navigate, Nose, Pelorus, Pilot, Pointer, Postil(l)ion, Principle, Providence, Queen's, Rainbow, Range, Ranger, Reference, Rein, Relate, Rudder, Sabot, Sea Ranger, Shepherd, Sherpa, Shikaree, Shikari, Sight, Sign, Sixer, Standard, Stear, Steer, Stire, Target, Template, Templet, Terminal, Terrestrial, Tiller, Train, Travelogue, Tutelage, Usher(ette), Vocational,

Voyageur, Waymark, Weise, Weize, Wise

Guild Artel, Basoche, Company, Freemason, Gyeld, Hanse, Hoastman, League, Mistery, Mystery, Society, Tong, Union

Guile Art, Cunning, Deceit, Dole, Malengine

Guillotine Closure, Decapitate, Louisiette, Maiden, Marianne

Guilt(y) Affluenza, Angst, Blame, Cognovit, Flagitious, Hangdog, Mea culpa, Nocent, Peccavi, Remorse, Wicked

Guinea(s) Canary, Geordie, Gns, Job, Ls, Meg, Spade

Guinea-fowl Pintado

Guinea-pig Abyssinian, Agoute, Agouti, Cavie, Cavy, Paca, Subject

Guinea-worm Dracunculus

Guise Form, Manner, Shape

Guitar(ist) Acoustic, Axe(man), Bass, Bottleneck, Cithern, Cittern, Dobro®, Electric, Fender®, Fretman, Gittarone, Gittern, Hawaiian, Humbucker, Lute, Lyre, Pedal steel, Plankspanker, Samisen, Sancho, Sanko, Shamisen, Sitar, Slide, Spanish, Steel, Uke, Ukulele

Gulf Aden, Anadyr, Aqaba, Bay, Bothnia, California, Cambay, Campeche, Carpentaria, Chasm, Chihli, Corinth, Cutch, Darien, Dvina, Exmouth, Finland, Fonseca, G, Genoa, Gonaives, Hauraki, Honduras, Iskenderun, Isthmus, Izmit, Joseph Bonaparte, Kutch, Lepanto, Leyte, Lingayen, Lions, Mannar, Martaban, Maw, Mexico, Ob, Oman, Patras, Persian, Pozzuoli, Queen Maud, Rapallo, Riga, St Lawrence, St Vincent, Salerno, Salonika, Saronic, Saros, Siam, Sidra, Spencer, Taganrog, Taranto, Thailand, Tongking, Tonkin, Trieste, Tunis, Van Diemen, Venice, Vorago

Gull(s) Bamboozle, Black-backed, Bonxie, Cheat, Cob(b), Cod, Cony, Cozen, Cull(y), Dupe, Fool, Geck, Glaucous, Haglet, Have, Hoodwink, Hum, Ivory, Kittiwake, Laridae, Larus, Lie to, Maw, Mew, Mollyhawk, Pickmaw, Pigeon, Queer, Ring-billed, Rook, Sabine's, Saddleback, Scaury, Scourie, Scowrie, Sea-cob, Sea-mew, Sell, Simp, Skua, Sucker, Swart-back, Tern, Tystie, Xema

Gullet Crop, Enterate, Maw, Oesophagus, Throat, Weasand-pipe

Gullible Credulous, Green, Mug punter, Naive, Starry-eyed, Sucker

Gulliver Lemuel

Gully Couloir, Donga, Fielder, Geo, Gio, Goe, Grough, Gulch, Infielder, Pit, Rake, Ravine, Sloot, Sluit, Wadi

Gulp Bolt, Draught, Gollop, Quaff, Slug, Sob, → **SWALLOW**, Swig, Swipe, Wolf

Gum (tree) Acacia, Acajou, Acaroid, Agar, Algin, Angico, Arabic, Arabin, Arar, Arctic, Asafoetida, Bablah, Balata, Balm, Bandoline, Bdellium, Benjamin, Benzoin, Bloodwood, Blue, Boot, Bubble, Cerasin, Chicle, Chuddy, Chutty, Coolabah, Courbaril, Cow®, Dextrin(e), Dragon's-blood, Ee-by, Eucalyptus, Euphorbium, Flooded, Frankincense, Galbanum, Gamboge, Ghost, Gingival, → **GLUE**, Goat's-thorn, Gosh, Grey, Guar, Ironbark, Juniper, Karri, Kauri, Lac, La(b)danum, Lentisk, Mastic(h), Mucilage, Myrrh, Nicotine, Olibanum, Opopanax, Oshac, Red, River red, Sagapenum, Sarcocolla, Scribbly, Size, Sleep, Snow, Spearmint, Spirit, Starch, Sterculia, Stringybark, Sugar, Sweet, Tacamahac, Tragacanth, Tupelo, Ulmin, Water, White, Xanthan

Gumbo Okra

Gumboil Parulis

Gumption Nous, Spirit

Gun(fire), Guns, Gunfight Amusette, Archibald, Archie, Arquebus, Automatic, Barker, Baton, Bazooka, Beanbag, Beretta, Big Bertha, Biscayan, Blunderbuss, Bofors, Bombard, Breech(-loader), Bren, Broadside, Brown Bess, Browning, Bulldog, Bullpup, Bundook, Burp, Caliver, Cannonade, Carbine, Carronade, Cement, Chokebore, Chopper, Coehorn, Colt®, Dag, Derringer, Electron, Elephant, Escopette, Falcon(et), Field, Fieldpiece, Firearm, Fire lock, Flame, Flash, Flintlock, Four-pounder, Fowler, Fowlingpiece, Full-bore, Garand, Gas, Gat(ling), Gingal(l), Grease, HA, Hackbut, Half-cock, Harquebus, Heater, Hired, Howitzer, Jezail, Jingal, Kalashnikov, Lewis, Long

Tom, Luger®, Machine, Magazine, Magnum, Maroon, Martini-Henry®, Matchlock, Mauser®, Maxim, Metal, Minnie, Minute, Mitrailleuse, Mons Meg, Mortar, Musket(oon), Muzzle-loader, Nail, Needle, Neutron, Noonday, Oerlikon, Ordnance, Over and under, Owen, Paderero, Paterero, Ped(e)rero, Pelican, Perrier, Petronel, Piece, Pistol(et), Pompom, Pump (action), Punt, Purdey®, Quaker, Radar, Ray, Repeater, Rev, Revolver, Riot, Rod, Roscoe, Saker, Sarbacane, Saturday night special, Scatter, Self-cocker, Shooter, Shooting iron, Shoot-out, Sidearm, Siege, Smoothbore, Snapha(u)nce, Spear, Speed, Spray, Squirt, Staple, Starting, Sten, Sterculia, Sterling, Stern-cannon, Stern-chaser, Stun, Swivel, Taser®, Tea, Thirty eight, Thompson, Three-pounder, Tier, Time, Tire, Tommy, Tool, Tupelo, Turret, Uzi, Walther, Wesson, Wheel-lock, Young, Zip

Gunge Gowl, Paste

Gunman Ace, Assassin, Bandit, Earp, Greaser, Pistoleer, Sniper, Starter

Gunner, Gunner's assistant Arquebusier, Arsenal, Artillerist, Cannoneer, Cannonier, Culverineer, Gr, Matross, RA

Gunpowder Charcoal, Pebble-powder, Saucisse, Saucisson

Gunwale Gunnel, Portland, Portlast, Portoise

Guppy Million

Gurgle Burble, Clunk, Glug, Gobble, Gollar, Goller, Guggle, Ruckle, Squelch

Gurnard Tubfish

Guru Bhagwan, Lifestyle, Sadhu, Teacher

Gush(er), Gushing Blether, Effusive, → **FLOOD**, Flow, Fountain, Jet, Outpour, Rail, Raile, Regurgitate, Rhapsodize, Scaturient, Spirt, Spout, Spurt, Surge, Too-too

Gusset Godet, Gore, Insert, Inset, Mitre

Gust Blast, Blore, Flaught, Flaw, Flurry, Puff, Sar, Squall, Waff

Gusto Élan, Relish, Verve, Zest

Gut(s), Gutty Abdomen, Archenteron, Balls, Beer, Bowel(s), Chitterlings, Cloaca, Disembowel, Draw, Duodenum, Enteral, Enteron, Entrails, Fore, Gill, Hind, Ileum, Insides, Kyle, Mesenteron, Mid, Minikin, Omental, Omentum, Purtenance, Remake, Sack, Sand, Snell, Stamina, Staying-power, Strip, Thairm, Tripe, Ventriculus, Viscera

Gutta-percha Jelutong, Pontianac, Pontianak

Gutter(ing) Arris, Channel, Conduit, Coulisse, Cullis, Grip, Gully, Kennel, Rhone, Rigol(l), Roan, Rone, Runlet, Runnel, Sough, Spout, Strand, Swale, Swayl, Sweal, Sweel

Guttersnipe Arab, Gamin, Thief

Guttural Faucal, Throaty

Guy Backstay, Bo, Burgess, Buster, Cat, Chaff, Clewline, Decamp, Deride, Dude, Effigy, Fall, Fawkes, Fellow, Gink, Josh, Mainstay, Mannering, Parody, Rag, Rib, Ridicule, Rope, Scarecrow, Stay, Taunt, Tease, Vang, Wise

Guzzle(d) Gannet, Gorge, Go(u)rmandize, Overeat, Snarf

Gwyn Nell

Gym(nasium), Gymnast(ic) Acrobat, Akhara, Arena, Contortionist, Dojo, Exercise, Jungle, Lyceum, Palaestra, PE, PT, Real, Rhythmic, Sokol, Tumbler, Turner

Gymnosophist Yogi

Gypsum Alabaster, Gesso, Plaster, Satin spar, Satin-stone, Selenite, Terra alba

Gypsy, Gipsy Bohemian, Cagot, Caird, Caqueux, Chai, Chal, Chi, Collibert, Egyptian, Esmeralda, Faw, Gipsen, Gitano, Hayraddin, Lavengro, Meg, Pikey, Rom(any), Rye, Scholar, Siwash, Tinker, Traveller, Travelling folk, Tsigane, Tzigane, Tzigany, Vagabond, Vlach, Walach, Wanderer, Zigan, Zigeuner, Zincala, Zincalo, Zingaro

Gyrate Revolve, Rotate, → **SPIN**, Twirl

Hh

H Ache, Aitch, Aspirate, Height, Hospital, Hotel, Hydrant, Hydrogen, Zygal

Haberdasher(y) Clothier, Ferret, Hosier, Notions

Habit(s), Habitual, Habituate, Habitué Accustom, Addiction, Apparel, Assuefaction, Assuetude, Bent, Cacoethes, Chronic, Clothes, Coat, Consuetude, Cowl, Crystal, Custom, Diathesis, Dress, Ephod, Frequenter, Garb, Hand-me-down, Inure, Inveterate, Motley, Mufti, Nature, Outfit, Pathological, Practice, Quirk, Raiment, Regular, Riding, Robe, Rochet, Routine, Scapular, Schema, Season, Second nature, Set, Soutane, Suit, Surplice, Toge, Trait, Trick, Tway, Usual, Way, Won, Wont, Xerotes

Habitable, Habitat(ion) Element, Environment, Haunt, Home, Locality, Pueblo, Refugium, Station, Tel

Hacienda Ranch

Hack(er), Hacking Blackhat, Chip, Chop, Cough, Cut, Cypherpunk, Drudge, Garble, Gash, Ghost, Grub-Street, Hag, Hash, Hedge-writer, Heel, Hew, Horse, Journo, Mangle, Mutilate, Nag, Nerd, Notch, Pad, Paper-strainer, Penny-a-liner, Phreak, Pick, Plater, Pot-boiler, Rosinante, Script kiddie, Slash, Spurn, Steed, Tadpole, Taper, Tap into, Tiger team, Tussis, Unseam, Warchalking, White hat

Hackle(s) Comb, Rough

Hackney(ed) Banal, Cab, Cliché, Corny, Percoct, Stale, Threadbare, Tired, Trite, Twice-told, Worn

Had (to) Ate, Moten, Must, Obliged, Threw

Haddock Arbroath smokie, Findram, Finnan, Fish, Norway, Rizzered, Smoky, Speldin(g), Speldrin(g), Whitefish

Hades Dis, Hell, Orcus, Pit, Tartarus

Haematite Oligist

Haemoglobin Chelate, Hb

Haemorrhoids Farmer Giles, Piles

Hafnium Hf

Hag(-like) Anile, Beldame, Besom, Carlin(e), Crone, Harpy, Harridan, Hell-cat, Hex, Moss, Nickneven, Occasion, Rudas, Runnion, Sibyl, Trot, Underwood, Witch

Haggard Drawn, → **GAUNT**, Pale, Rider

Haggis Kishke

Haggle Argue, Badger, → **BARGAIN**, Barter, Chaffer, Dicker, Horse-trade, Niffer, Palter, Prig

Ha-ha Dike, So there, Sunk-fence

Hahnium Hn

Hail(er) Acclaim, Ahoy, Ave, Bull-horn, Cheer, Fusillade, Graupel, Greet, Gunfire, Hi, Ho, Megaphone, Salue, Salute, Shower, Signal, Skoal, Skol, Sola, Stentor, Storm, Trumpet, What ho, Whoa-ho-ho

Hair(y), Haircut, Hairlike, Hair problem/condition, Hair style Afro, Ailes de pigeon, Ainu, Alopecia, Backcomb, Baldy, Bang, Barnet, Beard, Beehive, Bingle, Bob, Bouffant, Braid, Brede, Bristle, Brutus, Bumfluff, Bun, Bunches, Bush, Butch, Cadogan, Camel, Capillary, Catogan, Chignon, Cilia, Cleopatra, Coat, Cockernony, Coif, Coiffure, Comal, Comate, Combings, Comb-over, Comose, Cornrow, Corymbus, Cowlick, Crepe, Crew-cut, Crinal, Crinigerous, Cronet, Crop, Cue, Curlicue, DA, Dangerous, Dicey, Dreadlocks, Dubbing, Duck's arse, Ducktail, Earmuffs, Elf locks, En brosse, Esau, Excrement, Eyelash, Feather, Feather-cut, Fetlock, Fibril, Filament, Flat-top, Floccus,

Forelock, French pleat, French roll, Frenulum, Fringe, Fur, Garconne, Glib(s), Glochidium, Goatee, Guard, Hackles, Heare, Heer(i)e, Hispid, Hog, Indumentum, Kemp, Kesh, Lanugo, Lash, List, Lock, Lovelock, Lowlights, Madarosis, Mane, Marcel, Mohawk, Mohican, Mop, Mophead, Mullet, Muttonchops, Not(t), Number two, Pageboy, Pappus, Pashm, Peekabo(o), Pele(s), Pelt, Perm(anent), Pigtail, Pika, Pile, Pilus, Pincurl, Plait, Plica, Plica Polonica, Pompadour, Ponytail, Poodle cut, Porcupine, Pouf(fe), Pow, Prison crop, Psilosis, Puberulent, Pubescent, Pudding basin, Punk, Queue, Quiff, Radicle, Rat-tail, Red mullet, Rhizoid, Roach, Root, Rug, Rush, Scaldhead, Scalp lock, Scopate, Scopula, Sericeous, Set, Shag, Shingle, Shock, Sideburns, Sidelock, Snell, Spikes, Stinging, Strammel, Strand, Strigose, Strummel, Switch, Sycosis, Tache, Tête, Thatch, Tomentose, Tonsure, Toorie, Topknot, Tour(ie), Tragus, Tress, Trichoid, Trichology, Trichome, Trichosis, Trim, Ulotrichous, Updo, Velutinous, Vibrissi, Villi, Villosity, Villus, Wedge, Whisker, Widow's peak, Wig, Wiglet, Wisp, → **WOOL**, Xerasia

Hair-cream, Hair-oil Conditioner, Pomade

Hairdresser Barber, Coiffeur, Comb, Crimper, Friseur, Marcel, Salon, Stylist, Trichologist

Hairless Bald, Callow, Glabrate, Glabrescent, Glabrous, Irate

Hairline Brow, Nape

Hairnet Kell, Snood

Hairpiece Frisette, Merkin, Postiche, Strand, Toupee, → **WIG**

Hairpin Barrette, Bobbypin, Bodkin, Slide, U, U-turn

Hair-shirt Ab(b)a, Cilice

Haiti RH

Hal Prince

Halberd Spontoon

Halcyon Calm, Kingfisher, Mild

Hale(r) Drag, Healthy, Koruna, Raucle, Robust, Well

Half, Halved Bifid, Demi, Dimidiate, Dirempt, Divide, Hemi, Moiety, Semi, Share, Split, Stand-off, Term

Half-a-dozen Six, VI

Half-asleep, Half-conscious Dove, Dozy

Half-baked Foolish, Mediocre, Samel, Slack-bake

Half-breed, Half-caste Bastard, Baster, Creole, Eurasian, Griqua, Mameluco, Mestee, Mestiza, Mestizo, Metif, Métis(se), Miscegen, Mongrel, Mulatto, Mustee, Octaroon, Quadroon, Quarteroon, Quintero, Quintroon, Sambo, Yellow-boy, Yellow-girl, Zambo

Half-dead Alamort

Half-guinea Smelt

Half-hearted Reluctant, Tepid

Half-hour Bell

Half-pence, Half-penny Mag, Magpie, Maik, Mail(e), Make, Obolus, Patrick, Portcullis, Posh, Rap, Wood's

Half-time Midhour

Half-turn Caracol(e), Demivolt

Half-wit Changeling, Mome, Simpleton, → **STUPID**

Hall Anteroom, Apadana, Assembly, Atrium, Auditorium, Aula, Bachelor's, Basilica, Bingo, Carnegie, Casino, Chamber, Citadel, City, Concert, Concourse, Corridor, Dance, Divinity, Dojo, Domdaniel, Dome, Dotheboys, Ex(h)edra, Festival, Foyer, Gallen, Guild, Hardwick, Holkham, Hostel, Ivied, Judgement, Kedleston, Liberty, Lobby, Locksley, Megaron, Mess, Moot, Music, Narthex, Newby, Odeon, Palais, Palais de danse, Passage, Prytaneum, Rathaus, Rideau, Salle, Saloon, Stationer's, Study, Tammany, Tara, Tolsel, Town, Trullen, Valhalla, Vestibule, Walhall(a), Wildfell

Hallmark(ed) Brand, Contrôlé, Logo, Platemark, Seal, Stamp

Hallow Consecrate, Revere, Worship

Halloween Guiser

Hallucinate, Hallucinating, Hallucination, Hallucinogen Autoscopy, DT's, Fantasy, Formication, Freak, Freak out, Illusion, Image, Mirage, Negative, Photism, Psilocin, Psilocybin, Psychedelic, Psychotic, Trip

Halo Antheolion, Areola, Aura, Aureola, Corona, Galactic, Gloria, Gloriole, Mandorla, Nimbus, Rim, Vesica, Vesica piscis

Halogen Iodine

Halt(er) Abort, Arrest, Block, Brake, Bridle, Cavesson, Cease, Cesse, Check, End, Full stop, Game, Hackamore, Heave-to, Hilch, Lame(d), Limp, Noose, Prorogue, Rope, Stall, Standstill, Staw, → **STOP**, Stopover, Toho, Tyburn-tippet, Whoa, Widdy

Ham(s) Amateur, Barnstormer, Flitch, Gammon, Haunch, Hock, Hoke, Hough, Hunker, Jambon, Jay, Mutton, Nates, Overact, Overplay, Parma, Pigmeat, Prat, Prosciutto, Radio, Serrano, Spe(c)k, Tiro, Westphalian, York

Hamburger Sloppy joe

Hamfisted Maladroit, Unheppen

Hamite Berber, Nilot(e)

Hamlet(s) Aldea, Auburn, Cigar, Clachan, Dane, Dorp, Hero, Kraal, Stead, Thorp(e), Tower, Vill(age), Wick

Hammer(ed), Hammerhead, Hammering About-sledge, Atmospheric, Ballpeen, Ballpein, Beetle, Bully, Bush, Celt, Claw, Dolly, Drop, Excudit, Flatten, Fore, Fuller, Gavel, Hack, Incuse, Jack, Kevel, Knap, Knapping, Kusarigama, Lump, Madge, Mall(et), Malleate, Martel, Maul, Mjol(l)nir, Monkey, Nevel, Oliver, Ossicle, Pane, Pean, Peen, Pein, Pene, Percussion, Percussor, Piledriver, Planish, Plessor, Plexor, Pneumatic, Rawhide, Repoussé, Rip, Rout, Sheep's-foot, Shingle, Sledge, Steam, Stone, Strike, Tack, Tenderizer, Tendon, Tilt, Trip, Trounce, Umbre, Water, Wippen

▷ **Hammered** *may indicate* an anagram

Hammerthrower Thor

Hammock Cott

▷ **Hammy** *may indicate* an anagram

Hamper Basket, Cabin, Ceroon, Cramp, Cumber, Delay, Encumber, Entrammel, Hamstring, Handicap, Hobble, Hog-tie, Impede, Obstruct, Pad, Pannier, Ped, Pinch, Restrict, Rub, Sero(o)n, Shackle, Tangle, Trammel, Tuck

Hamster Cricetus, Idea

Hamstring, Hamstrung Cramp, Hock, Hox, Lame, Popliteal, Powerless, Thwart

Hand(s), Hand over, Hand down, Hand-like, Handwriting Applause, Assist(ance), Bananas, Bequeath, Cacography, Calligraphy, Charge, Chicane, Chirography, Clap(ping), Claque, Club, Clutch, Copperplate, Court, Crabbed, Crew, Cursive, Dab, Daddle, Danny, Dawk, Dead, Deal, Deck, Deliver, Devolve, Donny, Dukes, Dummy, Extradition, Famble, Fin, Fist, Flipper, Flush, Free, Full (house), Glad, Graphology, Half-text, Help, Helping, Hidden, Hond, Hour, Impart, Iron, Israel, Italian, Jambone, Jamboree, Jemmy, Kana, L, Laydown, Lone, Loof, Man, Manual, Manus, Maulers, Medieval, Minute, Mitt(en), Mutton-fist, Nes(h)ki, Niggle, Operative, Orthography, Pad, Palaeography, Palm(atifid), Part, Pass, Paw, Podium, Post, Pud, R, Referral, Rein (arm), Round, Running, Script, Second, Secretary, Signature, Span, Spencerian, Stage, Station, Straight, Sweep, Text, Tiger, Uncial, Upper, Whip, Widow, Worker, Yarborough

Handbag Caba(s), Grip, Indispensable, Pochette, Purse, Reticule, Valise

Handbook Baedeker, Companion, Enchiridion, Guide, Manual, Vade-mecum

Handcuff(s) Bracelet, Darbies, Golden, Irons, Manacle, Mittens, Nippers, Shackle, Snaps, Wristlet

Handful Few, Gowpen, Grip, Hank, Problem, Pugil, Rip(p), V

Handicap Bisque, Burden, Cambridgeshire, Disable, Ebor, Encumber, Half-one, Hamper, Impede, Impost, Lame, Liability, Lincolnshire, Mental, → **OBSTACLE**, Off, Physical, Restrict, Scratch, Weigh(t), Welter-race

Handicraft Marquetry

Handkerchief, Hanky Bandan(n)a, Belcher, Billy, Buffon, Clout, Curch, Fogle, Foulard, Kleenex®, Madam, Madras, Monteith, Mouchoir, Muckender, Napkin, Nose-rag, Orarium, Romal, Rumal, Sudary, Tissue, Wipe(r)

Handle(d), Handler Ansate, Bail, Bale, Behave, Bitstock, Brake, Broomstick, Cope, Crank, Dead man's, Deal, Doorknob, Dudgeon, Ear, Feel, Field, Finger, Forename, Gaum, Gorm, Grab, Grip, Gunstock, Haft, Helve, Hilt, Hold, Knob, Knub, Lug, → **MANAGE,** Manipulate, Manubrium, Maul, Moniker, Name, Nib, Palp, Paw, Pistol-grip, Pommel, Port-crayon, Process, Roadie, Rounce, Shaft, Snath(e), Snead, Sneath, Sned, Staff, Staghorn, Stale, Starting, Steal(e), Steel, Steil, Stele, Stilt, Stock, Sweep, Tiller, Title, To-name, Touch, Transact, Treat, Use, Whipstock, Wield, Winder, With(e)

Handmaid(en) Iras, Manicurist, Valkyrie

Hand-out Alms, Charity, Dole, Gift, Issue, Release, Sample

Handshake Golden

Hand-signal Beck(on), Point, Wave

Handsome Adonis, Apollo, Attractive, Bonny, Brave, Comely, Dashing, Dishy, Featuous, Fine, Gracious, Kenneth, Liberal, Lush, Resplendent, Seemly

Handspring, Handstand Cartwheel, Diamodov

Hand-warmer Muff, Pome

Hand-washer Pilate

▸ **Handwriting** *see* **HAND(S)**

Handy(man) Accessible, Close, Convenient, Deft, Dext(e)rous, Digit, Factotum, Gemmy, Get-at-able, Jack(-of-all-trades), Jemmy, Near, Nigh, Palmate, Palmist, Ready, Skilful, Spartan, Useful

Hang, Hanger, Hanging(s) Append, Arras, Aweigh, Chick, Chik, Coat, Curtain, Dangle, Darn, Depend, Dewitt, Dorser, Dossal, Dossel, Dosser, Drape, Droop, Execute, Exhibit, Frontal, Gobelin, Hinge, Hoove, Hove(r), Icicle, Kakemono, Kilt, Lime, Lobed, Loll, Lop, Lynch, Mooch, Noose, Nub, Oudenarde, Pend(ant), Sag, Scenery, Scrag, Set, Sit, Sling, String up, Suspend, Suspercollate, Swag, Swing, Tapestry, Tapet, Tapis, The rope, Toran(a)

Hanger-on Bur, Lackey, Leech, Limpet, Liripoop, Parasite, Satellite, Sycophant, Tassel, Toady

Hangman, Hangmen Bull, Calcraft, Dennis, Derrick, Executer, Gregory, Ketch, Lockman, Marwood, Nubbing-cove, Pierrepoint, Topsman

Hangnail Agnail

Hangover Canopy, Cornice, Crapulence, Drape, DT's, Executer, Head, Hot coppers, Katzenjammer, Mistletoe, Relic, Remnant, Tester, Valance

Hank Bobbin, Coil, Fake, Lock, Skein

Hanker(ing) Desire, Envy, Hunger, Itch, Long, Yearn, Yen

Hannibal Lecter, Punic

Hansard Minutes

Haphazard Anyhow, Casual, Chance, Helter-skelter, Higgledy-piggledy, Hit and miss, Hitty-missy, Promiscuous, → **RANDOM,** Rough and tumble, Scattershot, Slapdash, Willy-nilly

Happen(ing), Happen to Afoot, Are, Be, Befall, Befortune, Betide, Come, Crop up, Event(uate), Fall-out, Materialise, → **OCCUR,** Pan, Pass, Prove, Subvene, Thing, Tide, Transpire, Worth

Happiness, Happy Apposite, Ave, Beatific, Beatitude, Blessed, Bliss, Bluebird, Bonny, Carefree, Cheery, Chirpy, Chuffed, Cloud nine, Cock-a-hoop, Dwarf, Ecstatic, Elated, Eud(a)emony, Exhilarated, Felicity, Felix, Fool's paradise, Fortunate, Glad(some), Gleeful, Golden, Goshen, Gruntled, Halcyon, Half-cut, Hedonism, High-feather, Inebriated, Jovial, Joy, Jubilant, Kvell, Larry, Light-hearted, Mellow, Merry, Opportune, Radiant, Rapture, Sandboy, Seal, Seel, Sele, Serene, Slap, Sunny, Tipsy, Trigger, Warrior

Happy medium Juste milieu

Hara-kiri Eventration, Seppuku, Suicide

Harangue Declaim, Diatribe, Earwigging, Laisse, Lecture, Oration, Perorate, Philippic, Sermon, Speech, Spruik, Tirade

Harass(ed) Afflict, Annoy, Badger, Bait, Beleaguer, Beset, Bother, Chivvy, Distract, Dun, Gall, Grill, Grind, Grounden, Hassle, Haze, Heckle, Hector, Henpeck, Hound, Importune, Irritate, Molest, Needle, Nettle, Overdo, Persecute, Pester, Pingle, Plague, Press, Sekuhara, Stalk, Tailgate, Thwart, Trash, Vex

Harbinger Herald, Omen, Precursor, Usher

Harbour(ed) Alee, Anchorage, Basin, Brest, Cherish, Deep water, Dock, Entertain, Foster, Heard, Herd, Hide, Hythe, Incubate, Kaipara, Lodge, Macquarie, Manukau, Marina, Mulberry, Nurse, Pearl, PLA, Poole, Port, Quay, Reset, Scapa Flow, Seaport, → **SHELTER**, Waitemata, Waterfront, Wellington

Hard(en), Hardened, Hardness Abstruse, Adamant(ine), Adularia, Augean, Austere, Billy-o, Bony, Brindell, Brinell, Brittle, Bronze, Cake, Calcify, Callous, Caramel, Cast-iron, Chitin, Concrete, Cornute, Crusty, Dentin(e), Difficult, Dour, Draconian, Ebonite, Emery, Endure, Enure, Exacting, Fiery, Firm, Flint(y), Geal, Granite, Gruelling, H, Hawkish, Hellish, Herculean, HH, Horny, Indurate, Inure, Inveterate, Iron(y), Jasper, Knotty, Liparite, Lithoid, Metallic, Metally, Mohs, Mohs' scale, Murder, Nails, Obdurate, Obdure, Osseous, Ossify, Permafrost, Permanent, Petrify, Picrite, Raw, Rugged, Ruthless, Schist, Scirrhus, Scleral, Set, Severe, Solid, Sore, Steel(y), Steep, Stereo, Stern, Sticky, Stiff, Stoic, Stony, Strongly, Teak, Temper, Temporary, Tough, Uneasy, Unyielding, Wooden

Hardback Case-bound

Hardboard Masonite®

Hard-core Riprap, Scalpins

Hard-headed Stegochepalian

Harding Warden

Hardliner Hawk

Hardly Borderline, Ill, Just, Scarcely, Uneath(es), Unnethes

Hard-pressed Strait, Taxed

Hardship Affliction, Austerity, Grief, Mill, Mishap, Ordeal, Penance, Privation, Rigour, Trial, Trouble

Hardware → **COMPUTER HARDWARE**, Gear, Ironmongery

Hardy Brave, Dour, Durable, Gritty, Manful, Oliver, Ollie, Rugged, Spartan, Sturdy, Thomas

Hare Arctic, Baud(rons), Bawd, Belgian, Doe, Dolicholis, Down, Electric, Husk, Jack-rabbit, Jugged, Jumping, Lam, Leporine, Malkin, Mara, March, Mawkin, Mountain, Mouse, Ochotona, Pika, Piping, Puss, Scut, Snowshoe, Spring, Wat

Harebell Blawort

Hare-brained Giddy, Madcap, Scatty

Harem, Harem lady Gynaeceum, Gynoecium, Odalisque, Seraglio, Serai(l), Zenana

Hark(en) Ear, Hear, List(en)

Harlequin Chequered, Columbine, Pantaloon

Harlot Blue gown, Drab, Hussy, Loon, Loose, Lown, Paramour, Plover, Pusle, Pussel, Quail, Rahab, Scrubber, Slut, Strumpet, Whore

Harm(ed), Harmful Aggrieve, Bane, Blight, Damage, Deleterious, Dere, Detriment, Discredit, Endamage, Evil, Hurt, Inimical, Injury, Insidious, Maim, Maleficent, Malignant, Maltreat, Mischief, Nocuous, Noisome, Noxious, Pernicious, Sinister, Spoil, Wroken, Wrong

Harmless Benign, Canny, Drudge, Informidable, Innocent, Innocuous, Innoxious, Inoffensive

Harmonica Harp, Orpheus

Harmonious, Harmonise, Harmonist, Harmony Accord, Agree(ment), Alan, Allan, Allen, Alternation, Assort, Atone, Attune, Balanced, Barbershop, Blend, Chord, Close, Community, Concent, Concentus, Concert, Concinnity, Concord, Congruous,

Consonant, Consort, Coordinate, Correspondence, Counterpoint, Descant, Diapason, Diatessaron, Doo-wop, Euphony, Eur(h)ythmy, Faburden, Feng-shui, Go, Jibe, Keeping, Match, Melody, Mesh, Musical, Overblow, Overtone, Rappite, Rapport, Salve, Solidarity, Suit, Symmetry, Sympathy, Symphonious, Sync, Thorough-bass, Tone, Tune, Unanimity, Unison, Unity

Harmotome Cross-stone

Harness(maker) Breeching, Bricole, Bridle, Cinch, D-ring, Equipage, Frenum, Gear, Gere, Girth, Hitch, Inspan, Lorimer, Loriner, Pad-tree, Partnership, Swingletree, Tack(le), Throat-stop, Tie, Trace, Trappings, Whippletree, Yoke

Harp(sichord) Aeolian, Cembalo, Clairschach, Clarsach, Clavier, Drone, Dwell, Irish, Jew's, Kora, Lyre, Nebel, Trigon, Triple, Virginal, Welsh, Wind, Zither

Harpagon L'avare, Miser

Harpoon(er) Bart, Fis(h)gig, Fizgig, Grain, Iron, Lily iron, Peg, Spear, Specktioneer, Toggle iron, Toggler, Tow-iron, Trident

Harpy Aello, Celeno, Eagle, Ocypete

Harridan Hag, Harpy, Shrew, Termagant, Xantippe, Zantippe, Zentippe

Harrier Hen, Montagu's

Harriet Hetty, Martineau

Harris Boatman, Cloth, Island, Isle, Rolf

Harrow(ing) Alas, Appal, Brake, Disc, Drag, Frighten, Herse, Lacerant, Pitch-pole, Plough, Rake, Rend, Shock, Welaway, Welladay, Wellanear, Wellaway

Harry Aggravate, Badger, Bother, Champion, Chase, Chivvy, Coppernose, Dog, Dragoon, Flash, Fret, Hal, Harass, Hassle, Hector, Herry, Houdini, Hound, Lauder, Lime, Maraud, Molest, Nag, Pester, Plague, Rag, Ravage, Reave, Reive, Rieve, Rile, Tate, Tchick, Torment

▷ **Harry** *may indicate* an anagram

Harsh(ness) Abrasive, Acerbic, Asperity, Austere, Barbaric, Brassy, Cacophonous, Coarse, Cruel, Desolate, Discordant, Draconian, Extreme, Glary, Grating, Gravelly, Grim, Gruff, Guttural, Hard, Hoarse, Inclement, Oppressive, Raucid, Raucle, Raucous, Raw, Rigour, Risp, Rude, Ruthless, Scabrid, Scrannel, Screechy, → **SEVERE**, Sharp, Spartan, Stark, Stern, Stoor, Stour, Stowre, Strict, Strident, Unkind

Hart Deer, Spade, Spay, Spay(a)d, Venison

Harte Bret

Hartebeest Bubal, Kaama, Kongoni, Sassaby, Tsessebe

Harum-scarum Bayard, Chaotic, Madcap, Rantipole

Harvest(er), Harvest home Combine, Crop, Cull, Fruit, → **GATHER**, Hairst, Hawkey, Hay(sel), Hockey, Horkey, In(ning), Ingather, Kirn, Lease, Nutting, Pick, Produce, Rabi, Random, Reap, Seed-time, Shock, Spatlese, Spider, Tattie-howking, Thresh, Vendage, Vendange

Has Habet, Hath, Owns, 's

Has-been Effete, Ex, Outmoded

Hash(ish) Benj, Bungle, Charas, Discuss, Garble, Garboil, Hachis, Lobscouse, Mince, Pi(e), Ragout

▷ **Hashed** *may indicate* an anagram

Hasn't Hant, Nas

Hassle Aggro, Bother, Harry, M(o)ither, Moider, Strife

Hassock Kneeler, Pouf(fe), Stool, Tuffet

Haste(n), Hastening, Hastily, Hasty Amain, Cursory, Despatch, Elan, Expedite, Express, Festinately, Fly, Hare, Headlong, Hie, Hotfoot, → **HURRY**, Hurry-scurry, Impetuous, Precipitant, Race, Ramstam, Rash, Run, Rush, Scuttle, Speed, Spur, Stringendo, Subitaneous, Sudden, Tear, Tilt, Urge, Whistle-stop

Hastings Banda, Bustles, Senlac, Warren

Hat Broad-brim, Bronx, → **CAP**, Cocked, Crush, Hard, → **HEADDRESS**, Head-rig, Lid, Lum, Nab, Red, Scarlet, Silk, Straw, Tit(fer)

HATS

3 letters:	Basher	Homburg	9 letters:
Fez	Beanie	Leghorn	Astrakhan
Tam	Beaver	Matador	Billycock
Tin	Bicorn	Petasus	Cartwheel
Top	Boater	Picture	Cockle-hat
	Bobble	Pill-box	Dunstable
4 letters:	Bonnet	Plateau	Glengarry
Kepi	Bowler	Pork-pie	Lamington
Pith	Breton	Puritan	Ramillies
Plug	Castor	Skimmer	Souwester
Poke	Claque	Stetson®	Stovepipe
Sola	Cloche	Sundown	Sugarloaf
Tile	Coolie	Tarbush	Sunbonnet
Topi	Cowboy	Tricorn	Tarpaulin
Ugly	Fedora		Ten-gallon
	Gaucho	8 letters:	Wide-awake
5 letters:	Hennin	Balmoral	
Ascot	Mob-cap	Bearskin	10 letters:
Beany	Panama	Bongrace	Balibuntal
Beret	Safari	Capotain	Bluebonnet
Brass	Sailor	Christie	Chimneypot
Busby	Shacko	Mountie's	Poke-bonnet
Chaco	Shovel	Mushroom	Sola-helmet
Derby	Slouch	Planter's	
Gibus	Sunhat	Puggaree	11 letters:
Gimme	Toorie	Ramilies	Cabbage tree
Mitre	Topper	Runcible	Deerstalker
Opera	Trilby	Skull-cap	Dolly Varden
Pagri	Turban	Snap-brim	Kamelaukion
Pixie	Witch's	Sola-topi	Mortarboard
Shako		Sombrero	Tam o'Shanter
Solah	7 letters:	Tarboosh	
Terai	Biretta	Tarboush	12 letters:
Topee	Chapeau	Thrummed	Cheese-cutter
Toque	Christy	Tricorne	Fore-and-after
	Cossack	Tyrolean	Steeple-crown
6 letters:	Flat-cap		
Akubra®	Hattock		

Hat-band Weeper
Hatch(ment), Hatching Achievement, Altricial, Booby, Breed, Brew, Brood, Cleck, Clutch, Companion, Concoct, Cover, Devise, Eclosion, Emerge, Escape, Incubate, Serving, Set, Trap-door
Hatchet(-shaped) Axe, Bill, Chopper, Claw, Cleaver, Dolabriform, Tomahawk
▷ **Hatching** *may indicate* an anagram
Hatchway (surround) Companionway, Fiddley, Guichet, Porthole, Scuttle, Service
Hate(d), Hateful, Hatred Abhor, Abominable, Abominate, Anims, Antipathetic, Aversion, Bugbear, Detest, Enmity, Haterent, Loathe, Misogyny, Odium, Pet, Phobia, Racism, Resent, Sacred, Spite, Toad, Ug(h), Vitriol
Hatless Bareheaded, Unbeavered
Hat-plant S(h)ola
Hatter Mad

Hat-trick Threepeat

Hatty Etta

Haughty, Haughtiness Aloof, Aristocratic, Arrogant, Bashaw, Cavalier, Disdainful, Dorty, Fastuous, High, Hogen-mogen, Hoity-toity, Hye, Imperious, Lofty, Morgue, Orgillous, Orgulous, Paughty, → **PROUD**, Scornful, Sdeignful, Sniffy, Stiff-necked, Toffee-nosed, Toplofty, Upstage

Haul(age), Haulier Bag, Bouse, Bowse, Brail, Carry, Cart, Catch, Drag, Heave, Hove, Kedge, Long, Loot, Plunder, Pull, Rug, Sally, Scoop, Snake, Snig, TIR, Touse, Touze, Tow(se), Towze, Transporter, Trice, Winch, Yank

Haunch Hance, Hip, Huckle, Hunkers, Quarter

Haunt(s) Catchy, Den, Dive, Frequent, Ghost, Hang-out, Honky-tonk, Houf(f), Howf(f), Infest, Obsess, Purlieu, Resort, Spot, Spright

Hauteur Bashawism, Height, Morgue, Vanity

Havana Cigar

Have, Having Bear, Ha(e), Han, Hoax, Hold, Hoodwink, Know, Of, → **OWN**, Possess, Sell, With

Haven Asylum, Harbour, Hithe, Hythe, Oasis, Port, Refuge, Refugium, Retreat, Safe, Sekos, Shelter, Tax

Haver(s) Blether, Clanjamfray, Dither, Gibber, Nigel, Owner

▶ **Haversack** *see* **RUCKSACK**

Havoc Desolation, Devastation, Hell, Ravage, Waste

▷ **Havoc** *may indicate* an anagram

Haw Drawl, Hip, Sloe

Hawaiian Kanaka

Hawk(er), Hawkish Accipitrine, Auceps, Austringer, Badger, Bastard, Buzzard, Cadger, Camelot, Caracara, Cast, Cheapjack, Cooper's, Cry, Duck, Eagle, Elanet, Eyas, Falcon, Fish, Gerfalcon, Goshawk, Haggard, Hardliner, Harrier, Harrumph, Hobby, Honey-buzzard, Keelie, Kestrel, Kight, Kite, Lammergeier, Lanner(et), Marsh, Merlin, Molla(h), Monger, Moolah, Mosquito, Mullah, Musket, Night, Nyas, Osprey, Ossifrage, Passage(r), Pearlie, Pearly, Peddle, Pedlar, Peregrine, Pigeon, Privet, Ringtail, Sacre(t), Sell, Slab, Slanger, Soar(e), Sorage, Sore(-eagle), Sparrow, Spiv, Staniel, Stone, Sutler, Tallyman, Tarsal, Tarsel(l), Tassel, Tercel(et), Tiercel, Tote, Tout, Trant(er), Trucker, Warlike

Hawkeye IA, Iowa

Hawk-keeper Austringer, Ostreger

Hawser Line, Rope

Hawthorn Albespine, Albespyne, May(flower), Quickset, Quickthorn

Hay(cock), Hey, Haybox Antic, Bale, Cock, Contra-dance, Fodder, Goaf, Hi, Kemple, Math, Mow, Norwegian nest, Norwegian oven, Pleach, Pook, Salt, Stack, Straw, Truss, Windrow

Hayfever Pollenosis, Pollinosis

Haymaker Blow, Slog

Hayseed Chaw-bacon, Hodge, Joskin, Rustic

Hazard(ous) Bet, Breakneck, Bunker, Chance, Danger, Dare, Die, Dye, Game, Gremlin, Guess, Hero, Ice, Imperil, In-off, Jeopardy, Losing, Main, Minefield, Mist, Moral, Nice, Niffer, Occupational, Perdu(e), Peril, Pitfall, Play, Pothole, Queasy, → **RISK**, Risque, Stake, Trap, Venture, Vigia, Wage, Winning

Haze, Hazy Blear, Cloud, Filmy, Fog, → **MIST**, Mock, Muzzy, Nebulous, Smaze, Smog, Tease

▷ **Haze** *may indicate* an anagram

Hazel(wort) Amenta, Asarabacca, Catkin, Cob, Corylus, Filbert, Lambs' tails

HC Encomia, Encomium

He, HE A, Helium, Tag, Tig, → **TNT**, Tom

Head(s), Heading, Headman, Head shaped, Heady Aim, Apex, Ard-ri(gh),

Beachy, Bean, Behead, Bill, Block, Bonce, Boss, Bound, Brain, Brainpan, Bregma, Brow, But(t), Cabbage, Caboceer, Cape, Capitani, Capitate, Capitulum, Capo, Captain, Caption, Caput, Caudillo, Cauliflower, Cephalic, Chaton, Chief, Chump, Coarb, Coconut, Coma, Comarb, Commander, Conk, Cop, Coppin, Costard, Cranium, Crest, Crisis, Crown, Crumpet, Crust, Cylinder, Dateline, Dean, Director, Dome, Dummy, Each, Ear, Exarch, Figure, Flamborough, Foam, Foreland, Froth, General, Glomerate, Grand Mufti, Hegumen(os), Herm(a), Hoe, Hogh, Huff-cap, Inion, Jowl, Karmapa, Keyword, Knob, Knowledge-box, Lead(er), Lemma, Lid, Lizard, Loaf, Loave, Loo, Lore, Malik, Manager, Mayor, Maz(z)ard, Melik, Mocuddum, Mogul, Mokaddam, Morne, Mr Big, Mull, Muqaddam, Nab, Nana, Napper, Nappy, Ness, Nob, Noddle, Noggin, Noll, Noup, Nowl, Nut, Obverse, Occiput, Onion, Panicle, Panorama, Parietal, Pash, Pate, Pater(familias), Patriarch, Pick-up, Point, Poll, Pow, Prefect, President, Pressure, Principal, Promontory, Provost, Ras, Read-write, Ream, Rector, Rubric, Sarpanch, Scalp, Scaup, Scaw, Scholarch, Scolex, Sconce, Short, Sinciput, Skaw, Skull, Sound, Source, Spume, Squeers, Stad(t)holder, Starosta, Strapline, Subject, Superior, Taipan, Talking, Tanadar, Tete, Thanadar, Throne, Tight, Tintagel, Tip, Title, Toilet, Top, Topic, Tsantsa, Twopenny, Upperworks, Vaivode, Velocity, Voivode, Yorick, Zupan

▷ **Head** *may indicate* the first letter of a word

Headache Cephalalgia, Encephalalgia, Hangover, Hemicrania, Megrim, Migraine, Neuralgia, Red out, Scotodinia, Splitter

Headband Blindfold, Fillet, Garland, Infula, Sphendone, T(a)enia

Headbanger Grebo, Nutcase

Head cover, Headdress Aigrette, Alice band, Ampyx, Balaclava, Bandeau, Bas(i)net, Bonnet, Burnous(e), Busby, Calotte, Caul, Chaplet, Circlet, Comb, Commode, Cor(o)net, Cowl, Coxcomb, Crownet, Curch, Diadem, Doek, Dopatta, Dupatta, Fascinator, Feather bonnet, Fontange, Fool's cap, Frontlet, Hat(tock), Helm(et), Joncanoe, Juliet cap, Kaffiyeh, Kell, Kerchief, Kuffiyeh, Kufiah, Kufiya(h), Madras, Mantilla, Mitre, Mobcap, Modius, Mortarboard, Nubia, Periwig, Pill-box, Plug-hat, Porrenger, Porringer, Quoif, Romal, Rumal, Sakkos, Ship-tire, Silly-how, Skullcap, Sphendone, Stephane, Taj, Tarbush, Tiara, Tire-vallant, Topi, Tower, Tulban, Turban, War bonnet, Wig, Wimple, Wreath

Header Bonder, Brick, Dive, Fall, Rowlock

Headhunter Naga

Headland Beachy Head, Bill, Cape, Cape Horn, Dungeness, Finisterre, Foreland, Head-rig, Hoe, Hogh, Land's End, Morro, Naze, Ness, Noup, Point, → **PROMONTORY**, Ras, Ross, St Vincent, Scaw, Skaw

Headless Acephalous

Headlight(s) Beam, Brights, Dip, Halo, Sealed-beam

Headline Banner, Caption, Drophead, Frown, Kicker, Ribbon, Scare-head, Screamer, Splash, Strapline, Streamer, Title

Headlock Chancery

Headlong Breakneck, Helter-skelter, Pell-mell, Plummet, Precipitate, Ramstam, Reckless, Steep, Sudden, Tantivy, Tearaway

▶ **Headman** *see* **HEAD(S)**

Headmaster Principal, Squeers

Headphone(s) Cans, Earpiece, Walkman®

Headquarters Base, Command, Command post, Depot, Guardhouse, Guildhall, Pentagon, Praetorium, SHAEF, SHAPE, Station, Torshavn, Valley Forge

▷ **Heads** *may indicate* a lavatory

Headsman Executioner

Headstrong Obstinate, Rash, Stubborn, Unruly, Wayward, Wilful

Head-to-tail Tête-bêche

Headway Advancement, Headroom, Progress

▶ **Headwear** *see* **HEAD COVER**

Head-word Lemma

Heal(ing) Absent, Aesculapian, Ayurveda, Balsam, Chiropractic, Cicatrise, Cleanse, Curative, Cure, Distant, Esculapian, G(u)arish, Hele, Hippocratise, Intention, Knit, Mend, Mental, Naturopathy, New Thought, Olosis, Osteopathy, Recuperation, Restore, Sain, Salve, Sanative, Sanitary, Spiritual, Styptic, Therapeutic, Time, Vulnerary

Healer Althea, Asa, Doctor, Homeopath, Naturopath, Osteopath, Sangoma, Shaman, Time

Health(y) Aglow, Bouncing, Bracing, Cheerio, Chin-chin, Constitution, Cosy, Doer, Environmental, Fat-free, Fit, Flourishing, Gesundheit, Hail, Hale, Hartie-hale, Heart, Holism, Kia-ora, L'chaim, Lustique, Lusty, Medicaid, Medicare, Piert, Pink, Prosit, Public, Robust, Rosy, Ruddy, Salubrious, Sane, Slainte, Sound, Toast, Tope, Valentine, Valetudinarian, Vigour, Welfare, Well, WHO, Wholesome

Heap(ed), Heaps Acervate, Agglomerate, Amass, Bing, Boneshaker, Bulk, Car, Clamp, Coacervate, Cock, Compost, Congeries, Cumulus, Drift, Hog, Jalopy, Lot, Molehill, Pile, Raff, Raft, Rick(le), Ruck, Scads, Scrap, Shell, Slag, Stash, Tass, Toorie, Up-piled

Hear(ing), Hearing problem Acoustic, Attend, Audience, Audile, Avizandum, Captain's mast, Catch, Clairaudience, Dirdum, Ear, Glue ear, Harken, Learn, List(en), Oyer, Oyez, Panel, Paracusis, Pick up, Session, Subpoena, Tin ear, Tinnitus, Try

▷ **Hear(say)** *may indicate* a word sounding like one given

Hearsay Account, Gossip, Report, Rumour, Second-hand, Surmise

Hearse Bier, Catafalco, Catafalque, Meat wagon, Shillibeer

Heart(en), Heartily, Hearty, Heart-shaped AB, Agood, Auricle, Backslapping, Beater, Bleeding, Bluff, Bosom, Bradycardia, Buoy, Cant, Cardiac, Centre, Cheer, Cockles, Columella, Cordate, Cordial, Core, Courage, Crossed, Daddock, Embolden, Encourage, Essence, Fatty, Floating, Gist, H, Hale, Herz, Hub, Inmost, Jarta, Kernel, Lepid, Lonely, Lusty, Memoriter, Mesial, Mid(st), Middle, Nub, Nucleus, Obcordate, Pericardium, Pith, Purple, Reassure, Robust, Root, Sacred, Sailor, Seafarer, Seaman, Sinoatrial, Staunch, Tachycardia, Tar, Ticker, Yarta, Yarto

Heart-break Crève-coeur, Grief, Sorrow

Heartfelt Deep, Genuine, Real, Sincere, Soulful, Triste

Hearth Cupel, Finery, Fireside, Home, Ingle, Killogie

Heartless Callous, Cored, Cruel, Inhumane, Three-suited

Heart's ease Pansy

Heart-throb Valentino

Heart trouble, Heartburn Bradycardia, Brash, Cardialgia, Fallot's tetralogy, Fibrillation, Murmur, Pyrosis, Tachycardia

Heat(ed), Heater, Heating Anneal, Ardour, Arousal, Atomic, Background, Bainite, Barrage, Beath, Blood, Brazier, Calcine, Calescence, Califont, Caloric, Calorifier, Central, Chafe, Convector, Dead, Decay, Dielectric, Dudgeon, Eccaleobion, Element, Eliminator, Endothermic, Enthalpy, Estrus, Etna, Excite, Exothermic, Fan, Ferment, Fever, Fire, Fluster, Fug, Furnace, Gat, Gun, Het, Hibachi, Hyperthermia, Hypocaust, Immersion, Incalescence, Induction, J, Kettle, Kindle, Latent, Liquate, Lust, Mowburn, Moxibustion, Normalise, Oestrus, Panel, Passion, Prelim, Prickly, Q, Quartz, Radiant, Radiator, Rankine, Recalescence, Red, Render, Repechage, Rut, Salt, Scald, Sinter, Sizzle, Smelt, Solar, Space, Specific, Spice, Stew, Storage, Stove, Swelter, Teend, Temperature, Thermotics, Tind, Tine, Torrefy, Total, Tynd(e), Underfloor, Warming-pan, Warmth, White, Zip®

Heath(land) Bearberry, Bent, Briar, Brier, Egdon, Epacrid, Erica, Geest, Lande, Manoao, Manzanita, Moor, Muir, Stead, Ted

Heathen(s) Ethnic, Gentile, Godless, Idolator, Infidel, Litholatrous, Nations, Pagan, Pa(i)nim, Paynim, Philistine, Primitive, Profane, Proselyte of the gate

Heather(y) Bell, Broom, Calluna, Epacrid, Erica, Ericoid, Foxberry, Ling, Rhodora, Sprig

▷ **Heating** *may indicate* an anagram

Heave(d), Heaving Cast, Emesis, Fling, Frost, Heeze, Hoise, Hoist, Hump, Hurl, Popple, Retch, Shy, Sigh, Vomit

▷ **Heave** *may indicate* 'discard'

Heaven(s), Heavenly Air, Aloft, Ama, Ambrosial, Arcady, Asgard, Bliss, Celestial, Celia, Divine, Ecstasy, Elysian, Elysium, Empyrean, Ethereal, Fiddler's Green, Firmament, Hereafter, Himmel, Hog, Holy, Hookey Walker, Land o' the Leal, Leal, Lift, Mackerel, New Jerusalem, Olympus, Paradise, Pole, Rapture, Seventh, Shangri-la, Sion, Sky, Sublime, Supernal, Svarga, Swarga, Swerga, Tir na n'Og, Uranian, Utopia, Welkin, Zion

Heavy(weight), Heavily, Heaviness Ali, Bodyguard, Bouncer, Clumpy, Dutch, Elephantine, Embonpoint, Endomorph, Gorilla, Grave, Hefty, Last, Leaden, Lumpish, Onerous, Osmium, Pesante, Ponderous, Roughneck, Sad, Scelerate, Stodgy, Stout, Top, Torrential, Upsee, Ups(e)y, Weighty, Wicked

Hebe Barmaid

Hebrew Aramaic, Eli, Heb, Jesse, Karaism, Levi, Mishnayoth, Modern, Rabbinical, Yid

Hebrides, Hebridean Harris, Western Isles

Heckle Badger, Gibe, Harass, Hatchel, Jeer, Needle, Spruik

Hectic Ding-dong, Feverish, Frenetic, Rat race

Hector Badger, Bluster, Browbeat, Bully, → **HARASS**, Nag

Hedge, Hedging Box, Bullfinch, Enclosure, Equivocate, Evade, Haw, Hay, Lay off, Meuse, Mews, Muse, Pleach, Prevaricate, Privet, Pussyfoot, Quickset, Raddle, Sepiment, Shield, Stall, Stonewall, Temporise, Texas, Thicket, Waffle

Hedgehog Gymnure, Hérisson, Tenrec, Tiggywinkle, Urchin

Hedge-hop Fly low

Hedge-parson Bucklebeggar, Patercove

Hedge-sparrow Accentor

Hedonist Cyreniac, Epicurean, Playboy, Sybarite

Heed(ed), Heedful Attend, Cavendo tutus, Gaum, Gorm, Listen, → **MIND**, Notice, Obey, Observe, Rear, Reck, Regard(ant), Reke, Respect, Rought, Tent, Tinker's cuss

Heedless Blithe, Careless, Inattentive, Incautious, Rash, Scapegrace, Scatterbrain

Heel Achilles, Cad, Calcaneum, Cant, Careen, Cuban, Dogbolt, Foot, French, Kitten, List, Louse, Parliament, Rat, Rogue, Seel, Spike, Stacked, Stiletto, Tilt, Wedge, Wedgie

Heel-tap Snuff

Hefty Brawny, Heavy, Solid, Weighty

Heifer Freemartin, Io, Quey, Stirk

Height(en), Heights Abraham, Altitude, Cairngorm, Ceiling, Dimension, Elevation, Embroider, Eminence, Enhance, Golan, H, Hill, Hypsometry, Level, Might, Mount, Peak, Procerity, Roof, Spot, Stature, Stud, Sum, → **SUMMIT**, Tallness, Tor, X

Heinous Abominable, Atrocious, Flagrant

Heir Alienee, Claimant, Coparcener, Dauphin, Devisee, Distributee, Eigne, H(a)eres, Institute, Intitule, Legatee, Parcener, Scion, Sprig, Successor, Tanist

Heirless Escheat, Intestate

Held Captive, Hostage, Sostenuto, Ten(uto)

▷ **Held by** *may indicate* a hidden word

Helen Elaine, Nell(y)

Helicopter (crew), Heliport Airstop, Chopper, Egg-beater, Gunship, Hover, Iroquois, Medevac, Rotodyne, Sea Cobra, Sea King, Sea Knight, Sea Sprite, Sea Stallion, Sikorsky, Sky-hook, Whirlybird, Winchman

Helios Hyperion

Heliotrope Cherry-pie

Helium He

Helix Alpha, Coil, Double, Parastichy, Spiral

Hell(ish) Abaddon, Abyss, Ades, Agony, Amenthes, Annw(yf)n, Avernus, Below, Blazes, Bottomless pit, Chthonic, Dis, Erebus, Furnace, Gehenna, Hades, Heck, Inferno, Jahannam, Lower regions, Malebolge, Naraka, Netherworld, Orcus, Pandemonium, Perditious, Pit, Ruin, Sheol, Stygian, Tartar(ean), Tartarus, Tophet, Torment

Hellbender Menopome, Mud-puppy

Hellebore Bear's foot, Itchweed, Melampode, Setterwort

Hellenic Dorian

Hellespont Dardanelles

Hello, Hallo, Hullo Aloha, Chin-chin, Ciao, Dumela, Golden, Hi, Ho(a), Hoh, Howdy, Howzit, Wotcha, Yoo-hoo

Helm(sman) Cox, Navigator, Pilot, Steer, Tiller, Timon(eer)

Helmet Armet, Balaclava, Basinet, Bearskin, Beaver, Brain bucket, Burganet, Burgonet, Cask, Casque, Comb, Crash, Galea, Gas, Heaume, Knapscal, Knapscull, Knapskull, Montero, Mor(r)ion, Nasal, Pickelhaube, Pith, Plumed, Pot, Pressure, Salade, Sal(l)et, Shako, Skid-lid, Smoke, Tin hat, Topee, Topi

Helot Esne, Slave

Help(er), Helping, Helpful Abet, Accomplice, Adjuvant, Advantage, Aid(ance), Aidant, Aide, Alexis, Alleviate, Ally, Asset, → **ASSIST**, Avail, Back, Beet-master, Beet-mister, Befriend, Benefit, Bestead, Boon, Brownie, Char(woman), Coadjutor, Collaborate, Complice, Conducive, Daily, Dollop, Dose, Ezra, Forward, Further(some), Go, Hand, Handyman, Henchman, Hint, Home, Hyphen, Instrumental, Intercede, Kind, Leg-up, Life-saver, Maid, Mayday, Monitor, Obliging, Ophelia, Order, Patronage, Pitch in, Quantity, Ration, Recourse, Relieve, Samaritan, Servant, Serve, Slice, SOS, Stead, Sted, Subserve, Subvention, Succour, Taste, Therapeutic, Use

Helpless(ness) Adynamia, Anomie, Downa-do, Feeble, High and dry, Impotent, Incapable, Paralytic, Prostrate, Useless

Helpmate Consort

Hem Border, Fringe, Hoop, List

He-man Adonis, Hunk, Jock, Macho

Hemisphere, Hemispherical Antichthon, Cupular, Dominant, Magdeburg, Rose-cut, Western

Hemlock Conia, Cowbane, Insane root, Tsuga

Hemp Abaca, Bhang, Boneset, Bowstring, Carl(ot), Choke-weed, Codilla, Crotalaria, Dagga, Fimble, Ganja, Hards, Henequen, Hiniquin, Indian, Kef, K(a)if, Love-drug, Manil(l)a, Mauritius, Moorva, Murva, Neckweed, Pita, Sida, Sisal, Sunn, Tat, Tow

Hen(s) Ancona, Andalusian, Australorp, Biddy, Buff Orpington, Chock, Clocker, Cochin, Deep litter, Dorking, Eirack, Fowl, Grig, Houdan, Langshan, Layer, Leghorn, Maori, Marsh, Mother, Mud, Orpington, Partlet, Pertelote, Plymouth Rock, Poulard, Poultry, Pullet, Ree(ve), Rhode Island red, Sitter, Spanish fowl, Speckled, Sultan, Tappit, Welsummer, Wyandotte

Hence Apage, Avaunt, Ergo, Go, Hinc, Scram, So, Therefore, Thus

Henchman Attendant, Follower, Myrmidon, Satellite

Hen-house Battery, Eggery

Henna Camphire

Hennery Run

Hen-party Kitchen tea

Hen-pecked Pussy-whipped, Spineless, Woman-tired

Henry Eighth, H, Hal, Hank, Hooray, Hy, James, Navigator, O

Hep Bacca, Berry, Hip, Wise

Hepatic Scale-moss

Hepatitis Favism, Jaundice

Herald(ic), Heraldry Crier, Hermes, Messenger

HERALDRIES

2 letters:	Vol	Coue	Nowy
Or		Fess	Pale
	4 letters:	File	Paly
3 letters:	Bars	Golp	Pile
Lis	Bend	Lyon	Posé

Vair
Vert
Yale

5 letters:
Azure
Cabré
Chief
Crest
Fesse
Flory
Golpe
Gules
Morné
Nowed
Pheon
Sable
Scarp
Scrog
Tenné
Trick
Usher
Vairé

6 letters:
Albany
Argent
Armory
Bagwyn
Billet
Checky
Cleché
Coupee
Erased
Fecial
Fetial
Flanch
Garter
Lionel
Lodged
Mullet
Naiant

Nebulé
Nebuly
Norroy
Pallet
Potent
Sea dog
Sejant
Verdoy
Verrey
Voided
Volant
Vorant
Wivern
Wreath
Wyvern

7 letters:
Alerion
Armiger
Bearing
Bordure
Chevron
Compone
Compony
Dormant
Endorse
Enfiled
Fracted
Gardant
Gironny
Gyronny
Herissé
Issuant
Manchet
Martlet
Nascent
Nombril
Passant
Portate
Portend
Purpure
Rampant

Red Hand
Roundel
Roundle
Rousant
Salient
Sea lion
Sejeant
Statant
Stentor
Trangle
Trundle
Urinant

8 letters:
Allerion
Bendwise
Blazonry
Caboched
Cicerone
Couchant
Degraded
Dragonné
Emblazon
Hauriant
Herisson
Naissant
Opinicus
Ordinary
Proclaim
Segreant
Tressure
Trippant
Umbrated
Woodwose

9 letters:
Abatement
Debruised
Dimidiate
Displayed
Eightfoil
Precursor

Regardant
Supporter
Woodhouse

10 letters:
Bloody Hand
Blue Mantle
Cinquefoil
Clarenceux
Cockatrice
Difference
Fetterlock
Forerunner
King-of-arms
Portcullis
Pursuivant
Quartering
Rouge Croix
Sans nombre

11 letters:
Clarencieux
Honour-point
Rouge Dragon
Subordinary

12 letters:
Bend sinister
Interfretted
Vaunt-courier

13 letters:
Baton sinister
Calygreyhound
Undifferenced

14 letters:
Counter-passant
Lyon King of Arms

Herb(aceous), Herbs Garnish, Maror, Salad, Simple, Suffruticose, Weed

---

HERBS

3 letters:
Bay
Oca
Pia
Rue

4 letters:
Aloe
Cive
Dill
Forb
Mint
Moly

Sage
Wort

5 letters:
Anise
Avens
Basil

Chive
Clary
Cumin
Eruca
Fitch
Inula
Medic

Orval
Senna
Tansy
Thyme
Typha
Vetch
Yerba

6 letters:
Ajowan
Bennet
Betony
Borage
Capers
Cicely
Cohosh
Cummin
Fennel
Ferula
Garlic
Hyssop
Lovage
Madder
Orache
Origan
Purpie
Saloop
Savory
Sesame
Sorrel
Willow
Yarrow
Za'atar

7 letters:
Aconite
Alecost
Aniseed
Arugula
Boneset
Caraway
Catmint
Chervil
Chicory
Comfrey
Dittany
Felicia
Fuller's
Gentian
Gunnera
Lewisia
Madwort
Mustard
Oregano
Origane
Paprika
Parsley
Phlomis
Saffron
Salsify
Vervain

8 letters:
Agrimony
Allspice
Angelica
Bergamot

Cardamom
Centaury
Cilantro
Costmary
Estragon
Feverfew
Fireweed
Fluellin
Knapweed
Mandrake
Marjoram
Origanum
Plantain
Purslane
Reed-mace
Rosemary
Soapwort
Staragen
Tarragon
Turmeric
Valerian
Veronica
Wormwood

9 letters:
Chamomile
Colic root
Coriander
Echinacea
Eyebright
Fenugreek
Germander
Haworthia

Kalanchoe
Lamb's ears
Laserwort
Parakelia
Pussytoes
Rhizocarp
Rodgersia
Spearmint
Tormentil

10 letters:
Oleraceous
Parakeelya
Pipsissewa
Rest-harrow

11 letters:
Laserpicium
Rupturewort
Sweet cicely

12 letters:
Aristolochia
Mountain flax
Ornithogalum
Skunk cabbage
Southernwood

13 letters:
Good-King-Henry

14 letters:
Paterson's curse

Herbalist Simplist

Herbarium Hortus siccus

Herbert Alan, AP(H), Lom, Spencer

Herbicide Agent Orange, Atrazine, Defoliant, Diquat, Glufosinate, Picloram, Simazine

Herbivore Iguanodon, Sauropod

Hercules Alcides, Huge, Rustam, Rustem

Herd(er), Herding, Herdsman Band, Buffalo, Byreman, Corral, Cowpuncher, Drive, Drover, Flock, Gang, Marshal, Meinie, Mein(e)y, Menyie, Mob, Pod, Rabble, Raggle-taggle, Round-up, Shepherd, Tail, Tinchel, Vaquero, Wrangling

Here Adsum, Hi, Hic, Hither, Kilroy, Local, Now, Oy, Present

Hereafter Eternity, Other world

Hereditary, Heredity Ancestry, Blood, Breeding, Codon, Dynastic, Eugenics, Exon, Genetics, Id(ant), Idioplasm, Inborn, Mendelism, Panagenesis

▷ **Herein** *may indicate* a hidden word

Here is laid HS

Heresiarch Nestor

Heresy, Heretic(al) Agnoitae, Albi, Albigensian, Apollinaris, Apostasy, Arian, Arius, Bab, Bogomil, Bugger, Cathar, Cerinthus, Docete, Donatist, Dulcinist, Encratite, Eudoxian, Giaour, Gnosticism, Heresearch, Heterodoxy, Lollard, Manichaean, Montanism, Nestorian, Non-believer, Nonconformist, Origen, Patarin(e), Pelagius,

Phrygian, Racovian, Rebel, Unitarian, Zendik
Heritage Birthright, Due, NT, Odette, Ottilie, Patrimony
Hermaphrodite Androgynous, Bi-, Gynandromorph, Monochinous, Monoecious, Prot(er)andry, Protogyny
Hermes (rod) Caduceus, Mercury
Hermetic Alchemist, Sealed
Hermit(age), Hermit-like Anchoret, Anchorite, Ascetic, Ashram(a), Augustinian, Austin, Cell, Cloister, Crab, Eremite, Grandmontine, Hieronymite, Loner, Marabout, Monk, Museum, Nitrian, Pagurid, Peter, Recluse, Retreat, Robber-crab, Sannyasi, Soldier-crab, Solitary, Troglodyte
Hernia Bubonocele, Cystocoele, Diverticulum, Enterocele, Eventration, Hiatal, Hiatus, Inguinal, Rectocele, Rupture
Hero(es), Heroic Asgard, Brave, Champ(ion), Couplet, Derring-do, Eidola, Epic, Eponym, Folk, God, Goody, Great, Icon, Ideal, Idol, Lion, Noble, Olitory, Priestess, Principal, Resolute, Tragic, Valiant, VC, White knight

HEROES

3 letters:
Cid

4 letters:
Aitu
Ajax
Eric
Finn
Kami
Tell

5 letters:
Bader
Drake
El Cid
Faust
Jason
Orfeo
Orion
Rambo
Raven
Sheik
Zorro

6 letters:
Aeneas
Amadis
Bunyan
Cyrano
Fingal

Gideon
Hector
Kaleva
Nestor
Oliver
Onegin
Ossian
Revere
Roland
Rustem
Rustum
Samson
Shandy
Sigurd
Tarzan
Virago

7 letters:
Alcides
Asterix
Beowulf
Dan Dare
Demigod
Gluscap
Gluskap
Ivanhoe
Lothair
Marmion
Oedipus
Paladin

Perseus
Rinaldo
Saladin
Tancred
Theseus
Tristam
Tristan
Ulysses
Volsung
Werther

8 letters:
Achilles
Balarama
Cisco Kid
Crockett
Everyman
Glooscap
Heracles
Hercules
Hiawatha
Leonidas
Meleager
Odysseus
Owlglass
Parsifal
Pericles
Roderego
Roderick
Superman

Tristram

9 letters:
Agamemnon
Cuchulain
Dambuster
Garibaldi
John Henry
Lochinvar
Lord Byron
Owleglass
Owspiegle
Siegfried
Spiderman

10 letters:
Cuchullain
Howleglass
Owlspiegle

11 letters:
Bellerophon
Finn MacCool
Hudibrastic
Philoctetes
Ramachandra
Tam o' Shanter

13 letters:
Vercingetorix

Herod Agrippa, Antipas
Heroin Chase-the-dragon, Diamorphine, Dogfood, Doojie, Dynamite, Gumball, H, Harry, Henry, Horse, Jack, Junk, Scag, Schmeck, Shit, Skag, Smack, Snow, Snowball, Speedball, Sugar, White stuff
Heroine Andromeda, Ariadne, Candida, Cleopatra, Darling, Demigoddess, Eurydice,

Hedda, Imogen, Isolde, Judith, Juliet, Leda, Leonora, Lulu, Manon, Mimi, Nana, Norma, Pamela, Star, Tess, Tosca, Una

Heron(s) Ardea, Bird, Bittern, Boat-billed, Butter-bump, Egret, Green, Handsaw, Kotuko, Screamer, Sedge, Siege, Squacco, Winnard

Herpes Cold sore, Dartre, Shingles, Shiver

Herring Bismarck, Bloater, Brisling, Brit, Buckling, Caller, Cisco, Clupea, Digby chick(en), Gaspereau, Glasgow magistrate, Kipper, Lake, Maise, Maize, Ma(a)tjes, Mattie, Maze, Mease, Menhaden, Norfolk capon, Ox eye, Rabbitfish, Red, Rollmop, Sea-stick, Shotten, Sild, Silt, Sparling, Teleost, Whitebait

Herringbone Sloping

Hesitant, Hesitate, Hesitation Balance, Boggle, Cunctation, Delay, Demur, Dicker, Dither, Doubtful, Dubitate, Dwell, Er, Erm, Falter, Halting, Haver, Haw, Irresolute, Mammer, Mealy-mouthed, → **PAUSE**, Qualm, Scruple, Shillyshally, Shrink, Stagger, Stammer, Stutter, Swither, Tarrow, Teeter, Tentative, Think twice, Um, Um and ah, Ur, Vacillate, Wait, Waver

Hesperus Vesper

Hessian Burlap, Hireling

Heterodoxy Heresy

Heterogeneous Diverse, Motley, Piebald

Heterosexual Hasbian, Straight

Hew(er) Ax, Chop, Cut, Gideon, Hack, Sever

Hex Bewitch, Jinx, Voodoo

Hexameter Dolichurus, Miurus

▸ **Hey** *see* **HAY(COCK)**

Heyday Prime, Summer

Hi Cooee, Hello, Howdie

Hiatus Caesura, Entr'acte, Gap, Hernia, Interact, Interregnum, Interval, Lacuna, Lull

Hibernal, Hibernate, Hibernating Estivate, Hiemal, Hole up, Latitant, Sleep, Winter

Hibernian Irish

Hibiscus Okra, Roselle, Rozelle

Hiccup Blip, Glitch, Hitch, Singultus, Snag, Spasm, Yex

Hick Jake, Oaf, Podunk, Rube, Yokel

Hickory Black, Jackson, Mockernut, Pecan, Scaly-bark, Shagbark

Hidden Buried, Cabalistic, Covert, Cryptic, Delitescent, De(a)rn, Doggo, Healed, Hooded, Latent, Obscure, Occult, Pentimento, Recondite, Screened, Secret, Shuttered, Sly, Ulterior, Unseen, Veiled, Wrapped

▷ **Hidden** *may indicate* a concealed word

Hide, Hiding (place) Abscond, Babiche, Basan, Befog, Bield(y), Blind, Box-calf, Burrow, Bury, Butt, Cache, Camouflage, Cane, Ceroon, Coat, → **CONCEAL**, Coonskin, Cootch, Cordwain, Couch, Cour, Crop, Curtain, Cwtch, Dea(r)n, Deerskin, Derm, Doggo, Earth, Eclipse, Encave, Ensconce, Enshroud, Envelop, Epidermis, Fell, Flaught, Flay, Fur, Gloss over, Harbour, Heal, Heel, Hele, Hell, Hole-up, Hoodwink, Incave, Inter, Kip, Kipskin, Lair, Leather, Mai-mai, Mask, Mew, Mobble, Morocco, Nebris, → **OBSCURE**, Paper over, Parfleche, Pell, Pelt, Plank, Plant, Priest's hole, Repress, Robe, Saffian, Screen, Secrete, Shadow, Shellac(k), Shroud, Skin, Spetch, Squirrel, Stash, Strap-oil, Tappice, Thong, Thrashing, Trove, Veil, Wallop, Whang, Wrap

Hideous(ness) Deform(ed), Enormity, Gash, Ghastly, Grotesque, Horrible, Monstrous, Odious, Ugly, Ugsome

Hierarchic, Hierarchy Byzantine, Elite, Theocracy

Hieroglyph Cipher, Pictogram

Hi-fi, High-fidelity Ambisonics®, Ghetto blaster

Higgledy-piggledy Mixtie-maxtie

▷ **High** *may indicate* an anagram

High(er), Highly, Highness Alt(a), Altesse, Alteza, Altissimo, Apogee, Atop, Brent, Climax, Culminant, Doped, Drugged, E-la, Elation, Elevated, Eminent, Euphoria, Exalted, Excelsior, Exhilarated, Five, Frequency, Gamy, Haut(e), Intoxicated, Jinks, Lofty, Maggotty, Mind-blowing, Orthian, Prime, Rancid, Ripe, School, Senior, Sent, Shrill, So, Steep, Stenchy, Stoned, Stratospheric, String-out, Strong, Superior, Swollen, Tall, Tension, Tipsy, Top-lofty, Topmost, Treble, Turned on, Ultrasonic, Up(per), Very, Wired, Zonked

High and mighty, High-handed Haughty, Hogen-mogen, Lordly

Highball Drink, Lob, Loft

Highbrow Brain, Egghead, Intelligentsia, Long-hair, Third programme

High-class Best, Pedigree, Superior, U

High-crowned Copataine

Highest Best, Climax, Culminant, Mostwhat, Ne plus ultra, Progressive, Supreme

Highest note E-la

High-flier, High-flown Bombastic, Euphuism, Icarus

Highland(er), Highlands Black Forest, Blue-bonnet, Blue-cap, Cameron, Cat(h)eran, Down, Dun(n)iewassal, Duniwassal, Gael, Gaelic, Irish Scot, Karoo, Kiltie, Masai, Nainsel(l), Plaid(man), Redshank, Riff, Scot, Seaforth, Shire, Teuchter

Highlight Accent, Feature, Focus, Heighten, Stress

▸ **High-pitched** *see* **HIGH(ER)**

High-spirited Extravert, Extrovert

High tension HT

Highway Alaska, Alcan, Autobahn, Autopista, Autostrada, Bus, Camino Real, Divided, Flyover, Freeway, Information, Interstate, King's, Motorway, Overpass, Parkway, Pass, Queen's, Road, Rode, Tarseal, Thoroughfare, Tightrope, Tollway, Watling St

Highwayman, Highway robber(y) Bandit, Bandolero, Duval, Footpad, Fraternity, Gilderoy, Jack Sheppard, Land-pirate, Land-rat, Latrocinium, MacHeath, Motorist, Rank-rider, Road-agent, Scamp, Skyjacker, Toby, Tobyman, Turpin, Twitcher, Wheel

Hijack(er) Abduct, Pirate

Hike(r) Backpack, Bushbash, Bushwalk, Raise, Rambler, Ramp, Rise, Traipse, Tramp, Trape(s), Up(raise)

Hilarious, Hilarity Gaiety, Hoot, Hysterical, Jollity, Mirth, Riot, Side-splitting

Hilary Term

Hill(ock), Hills, Hillside Ant, Antidine, Arafar, Areopagus, Aventine, Barrow, Beacon, Ben, Bent, Berg, Beverly, Black, Blackdown, Bluff, Bombay, Brae, Breed's, Brew, Broken, Bunker, Butte, Caelian, Calvan, Capitol(ine), Cheviots, Chiltern, Chin, Cleve, Coast, Cone, Coolin, Coteau, Crag-and-tail, Crest, Cuillin, Damon, Djebel, Drumlin, Dun(e), Dunsinane, Eminence, Esquiline, Fell, Flodden, Gebel, Golan Heights, Golgotha, Gradient, Grampians, Hammock, Height, Helvellyn, Highgate, Holt, Horst, How, Howe, Hummock, Incline, Inselberg, Janiculum, Jebel, Kip(p), Knap, Knoll, Knot, Kop(je), Koppie, Lammermuir, Lavender, Law, Loma, Low, Ludgate, Majubar, Malvern, Mamelon, Man, Marilyn, Matopo, Mendip, Merrick, Mesa, Monadnock, Monte Cassino, Monticule, Morro, Mound, Mount Lofty Ranges, Nab, Naga, Nanatak, Nilgiri(s), North Downs, Otway Ranges, Palatine, Pap, Pennines, Pike, Pingo, Pnyx, Quantocks, Quirinal, Rand, Range, Saddleback, Savoy, Scaur, Seven, Silbury, Sion, Steep, Stoss, Strawberry, Tara, Tel(l), Toft, Toot, Tor, Toss, Tump, Tweedsmuir, Valdai, Vatican, Viminal, Wolds, Wrekin, Zion

Hillbilly Yap

Hill-dweller Ant

Hillman Areopagite, Nepalese

Hilltop Crest, Knoll, Nab

Hilt Basket, Coquille, Haft, Handle, Hasp, Shaft

Him(self) He, Ipse, Un

Himalaya(n) Nepali, Panda, Sherpa, Tibetan

Hind(er), Hindering, Hindrance, Hindsight Back, Bar, Block, Check, Counteract,

Cramp, Crimp, Cumber, Debar, → **DELAY**, Deter, Encumber, Estop, Hamper, Handicap, Harass, Holdback, Imbar, Impeach, Impede, Inconvenience, Inhibit, Obstacle, Overslaugh, Porlock, Posterior, Preclusion, Pull-back, Rear, Rein, Remora, Retard, Retrospect, Rump, Rumple, Set back, Shackle, Slow, Stop, Stunt, Stymie, Taigle, Thwart, Trammel

Hind(most) Back, Deer, Lag, Rear, Starn, Stern

Hindi, Hindu(ism) Arya Samaj, Babu, Bania(n), Banyan, Brahman, Brahmin, Dalit, Gentoo, Gurkha, Harijan, Jaina, Kshatriya, Maharishi, Nagari, Pundit, Rajpoot, Rajput, Rama, Sad(d)hu, Saiva, S(h)akta, Saktas, Sanatana Dharma, Sankhya, Shaiva, Sheik(h), Shiv Sena, Shudra, Smriti, Sudra, Swami, Swinger, Trimurti, Untouchable, Urdu, Vaishnava, Vais(h)ya, Varna, Vedanta, Vedism

Hindquarters Backside, Crupper, Haunches

Hinge(d) Butt, Cardinal, Cross-garnet, Drop-leaf, Garnet, Gemel, Gimmer, Ginglymus, Gullwing, Joint, Knee, Mount, Parliament, Piano, Pivot, Stamp, Strap

▷ **Hinge(s)** *may indicate* a word reversal

Hingeless Ecardinate

Hinny Ass, Donkey, Joe

Hint Allude, Clew, Clue, Cue, Echo, Element, Gleam, Hunch, Idea, Imply, Inkle, Inkling, Innuendo, Insinuate, Intimate, Key, Mint, Nod, Nuance, Office, Overtone, Pointer, Preview, Ray, Reminder, Scintilla, Shadow, Soupçon, → **SUGGEST**, Tang, Tip, Touch, Trace, Trick, Wind, Wink, Wisp, Word, Wrinkle

▷ **Hint** *may indicate* a first letter

Hip(pie), Hippy, Hips Cafard, Cheer, Coxa(l), Drop-out, Huck(le), Hucklebone, Hunkers, Ilium, Informed, Ischium, Pubis, Sciatic, Tonish

Hippopotamus Behemoth, River-horse, Sea-cow, Sea horse

Hire(d), Hiring Affreightment, Charter, Employ, Engage, Fee, Freightage, Job, Lease, Merc(enary), Never-never, Pensionary, Rent, Shape-up, Ticca, Wage

Hirsute Hairy, Pilose, Shaggy

▷ **His** *may indicate* greetings

Hispanic Latino

Hiss(ing) Boo, Fizzle, Goose, Hish, Sibilant, Siffle, Sizzle, Static, Swish

Historian Acton, Adams, Antiquary, Archivist, Arrian, Asellio, Bede, Biographer, Bryant, Buckle, Camden, Carlyle, Centuriator, Chronicler, Du Bois, Etain, Eusebius, Froude, Gibbon, Gildas, Green, Griot, Herodotus, Knickerbocker, Livy, Macaulay, Oman, Paris, Pliny, Plutarch, Ponsonby, Procopius, Read, Renan, Roper, Sallust, Spengler, Starkey, Strabo, Strachey, Suetonius, Tacitus, Taylor, Thiers, Thucydides, Toynbee, Trevelyan, Wells, Xenophon

History, Historic(al) Account, Age, Anamnesis, Ancient, Annal, Bunk, Case, Chronicle, Clio, Diachronic, Epoch(a), Epoch-making, Ere-now, Ever, Heritage, Legend, Life, Living, Mesolithic, Modern, Natural, Ontogency, Oral, Past, Record, Renaissance, Story

Histrionic Operatic, Theatrical

Hit Bang, Bash, Baste, Bat, Bean, Belt, Bepat, Blip, Blockbuster, Bloop, Blow, Bludgeon, Boast, Bolo, Bonk, Bunt, Catch, Chip, Clip, Clobber, Clock, Clout, Club, Collide, Cuff, Dot, Flail, Flick, Flip, Foul, Fourpenny-one, Fungo, Fustigate, Get, Hay, Head-butt, Home(-thrust), Ice-man, Impact, Knock, Lam, Lob, Magpie, Mug, Pandy, Paste, Pepper, Pistol-whip, Polt, Prang, Punto dritto, Ram, Roundhouse, Sacrifice, Score, Sensation, Six, Skier, Sky, Slam, Slap, Slosh, Smash(eroo), Smit(e), Sock, Spank, Spike, Stoush, Straik, Stricken, Strike, Strook, Struck, → **SUCCESS**, Swat, Switch, Thwack, Time-thrust, Tip, Tonk, Touché, Twat, Undercut, Venewe, Venue, Volley, Wallop, Whack, Wham, Wing, Ythundered, Zap, Zonk

Hitch(ed) Catch, Cat's paw, Contretemps, Edge, Espouse, Harness, Hike, Hirsle, Hoi(c)k, Hotch, Jerk, Kink, Lorry-hop, Rub, Setback, Sheepshank, Sheet bend, Shrug, Snag, Technical, Thumb, Wed

Hitherto Before, Yet

Hitman Gun

Hittite Uriah

HIV Viral load

Hive(s) Colony, Nettlerash, Skep, Spread, Swarm, Wheal

Hoar(y) Ashen(-grey), Canescent, Froren, Frost, Gaudy-day, Grizzled, Rime

Hoard(ing) Accumulate, Amass, Bill, Billboard, Cache, Coffer, Eke, Heap, Hog, Hoord, Husband, Hutch, Mucker, Plant, Pose, Salt away, Save, Sciurine, Snudge, Squirrel, Stash, Stock, Stockpile, Store, Stow, Treasure

Hoarse(ness) Croupy, Frog, Grating, Gruff, Husky, Raucous, Roar(er), Roopit, Roopy, Roup, Throaty

Hoax April-fish, Bam, Canard, Cod, Do, Doff, Fub, Fun, Gag, Gammon, Gowk, Gull, Have on, Hum, Huntie-gowk, Kid, Leg-pull, Piltdown, Put-on, Quiz, Sell, Sham, Skit, Spoof, String, Stuff, Supercherie, → **TRICK**

Hob Ceramic, Cooktop, Ferret, Goblin, Lout

Hobble, Hobbling Enfetter, Game, Hamshackle, Hilch, Hitch, Lame, Limp, Pastern, Picket, Shackle, Spancel, Stagger, Tether

Hobby Avocation, Fad, Falcon, Interest, Pastance, → **PASTIME**, Predator, Pursuit, Recreation, Scrimshaw

Hobby-horse Dada, Obsession, Play-mare

Hobgoblin Bog(e)y, Bull-beggar, Puck, Worriecow

Hobnail Clinker, Tacket

Hobnob Chat, Mingle

Hobo Bum, Drifter, → **TRAMP**, Vagrant

Hock Cambrel, Dip, Gambrel, Gambril, Gammon, Ham, Heel, Hough, Hypothecate, Pawn, Pledge, Rhenish, Wine

Hockey Field, Goal, Grass, Hurling, Ice, Pond, Shinny, Shinty, Street

Hod Carrier, Tray

Hodge Peasant, Rustic, Yokel

Hoe Claut, Draw, Dutch, Grub, Grubbing, Jembe, Nab, Pecker, Prong, Rake, Scuffle, Thrust, Weed

Hog Babiroussa, Babirussa, Boar, Glutton, Guttle, Peccary, Pig, Porker, Puck, Road, Shoat, Shott, Whole

Hogmanay Ne'erday

Hog-rat Hutia

Hogshead Butt, Cask, Muid

Hogwash Bull, Nonsense, Swill, Twaddle

Hoi-polloi Prole(tariat), Rabble

Hoist Boom, Bouse, Bunk-up, Crane, Davit, Derrick, Garnet, Gin, Heft, Hills, Jack, Lewis, Lift, Raise, Shearlegs, Shears, Sheerlegs, Sheers, Sway, Teagle, Trice, Whip-and-derry, Wince, Winch, Windas, Windlass

Hold(er), Holding, Hold back, out, up, etc Absorb, Allege, Alow, Anchor, Apply, Argue, Backbreaker, Belay, Believe, Boston crab, Caesura, Canister, Cease, Cement, Cinch, Clamp, Clasp, Cling, Clip, Clutch, Contain, Cotland, Cresset, Defer, Delay, Detain, Display, Document, Dog, Embrace, Engage, Engross, Er, Facebar, Farm, Fast, Fief, Fistful, Frog, Full nelson, Garter, → **GRASP**, Grip, Grovet, Half-nelson, Hammerlock, Handle, Haud, Have, Headlock, Heft, Heist, Hiccup, Hinder, Hitch, Ho(a), Hoh, Hoy, Hug, Impedance, Impede, Impediment, Impound, In chancery, Incumbent, Inhibit, Intern, Intray, Japanese stranglehold, Keep, Keepnet, Lease, Maintain, Manure, Nef, Nelson, Nurse, Oasis, Obstacle, Occupant, Own, Port, Proffer, Purchase, Rack, Reach, Reluct, Reserve, Restrain, Retain, Rivet, Rob, Rundale, Runrig, Save, Scissors, Shelve, Shore, Sleeve, Sostenuto, Stand, Stock, Suplex, Suspend, Take, Tenancy, Tenement, Tenure, Toehold, Toft, Tray, Tripod, Trivet, Wait, → **WRESTLING**, Wristlock, Zarf, Zurf

Hole(s), Holed, Holey Ace, Agloo, Aglu, Albatross, Antrum, Aubrey, Beam, Birdie, Black, Bogey, Bolt, Burrow, Cat, Cave, Cavity, Cenote, Cissing, Coal, Coalsack, Collapsar,

Crater, Cubby, Cup, Dell, Den, Dene, Dog-leg, Dolina, Doline, Dormie, Dormy, Dreamhole, Dry, Dugout, Eagle, Earth, Ethmoid, Eye(let), Faveolate, Finger, Foramen, Funk, Gap, Geat, Glory, Gnamma, Gutta, Hag(g), Hideout, Kettle, Knot, Lenticel, Lill, Limber, Loop, Loup, Lubber's, Lumina, Maar, Mortise, Moulin, Namma, Nineteenth, Oillet, → **OPENING**, Orifex, Orifice, Ozone, Perforate, Pierce, Pigeon, Pinprick, Pit, Pocket, Pore, Port, Pot, Potato, Priest's, Punctuate, Punctum, Puncture, Rabbet, Rivet, Rowport, Sallyport, Scupper, Scuttle, Scye, Sinus, Situation, Slot, Snag, Snow, Soakaway, Socket, Sound, Spandrel, Spider, Spiraculum, Starting, Stead, Stew, Stop, Stove, Swallow, Tear, Thirl, Thumb, Tight spot, Touch, Trema, Vent, Ventage, Ventige, Voided, Vug, Watering, Weep(er), Well, White, Wookey

Holiday(s), Holiday maker Away, Bank, Benjo, Break, Busman's, Camper, Carnival, Childermas, Days of Awe, Ferial, Festa, → **FESTIVAL**, Fête, Fiesta, Fly-drive, Furlough, Gala, Half(term), High, Honeymoon, Kwanzaa, Lag b'Omer, Laik, Leasure, Leave, Legal, Leisure, Long, Minibreak, Off-day, Off-time, Outing, Pace, Packaged, Pink-eye, Play-day, Playtime, Public, Purim, Recess, Repose, Rest, Roman, Schoolie, Seaside, Shabuoth, Shavuot, Sojourn, Statutory, Stay, Sunday, Tax, Trip, → **VACATION**, Villeggiatura, Wake(s), Whitsun

Holinshed Chronicler

Holland(s) Batavia, Genevese, Gin, Hogen-mogen, Netherlands, NL

Hollow(ed) Acetabulum, Aeolipile, Alveary, Antar, Antre, Antrum, Armpit, Axilla, Blastula, Boss, Bowl, Cave(rn), Cavity, Chasm, Chott, Cirque, Cleché, Comb(e), Concave, Coomb, Corrie, Crater, Cup(mark), Cwm, Deaf, Dean, Dell, Delve, Den(e), Dent, Dimple, Dingle, Dip, Dish(ing), Dolina, Doline, Empty, Fossette, Frost, Gilgai, Glenoid, Gnamma-hole, Gowpen, Groove, Grot(to), Hole, How, Howe, Igloo, Incavo, Insincere, Intaglio, Keck(sy), Kettle(hole), Kex, Khud, Lap, Lip-deep, Mortise, Namma-hole, Niche, Omphaloid, Orbita, Pan, Philtrum, Pit, Punt, Redd, Rout, Rut, Scoop, Shott, Sinus, Slade, Sleepy, Slot, Slough, Socket, Swire, Thank-you-ma'am, Trematic, Trough, Vacuous, Vesicle, Vlei, Vola, Wame, Wem

Holly Aquifoliaceae, Eryngo, Ilex, Mate, Winterberry, Yaupon

Hollyhock Althaea, Malva, Rose mallow

Hollywood Bowl, Tinseltown

Holm Isle

Holmes Sherlock, Wendell

Holmium Ho

Holocaust Churban, Shoah

Hologram, Holograph Laser, MS

Holothurian Trepang

Holster Sheath

Holy (man), Holiness Adytum, Alliance, Ariadne, Blessed, → **DIVINE**, Godly, Grail, Halidom, Hallowed, Helga, Hery, Khalif, Loch, Mountain, Olga, Orders, Pan(h)agia, Pious, Sacred, Sacrosanct, Sad(d)hu, Saintly, Sanctitude, Sannayasi(n), Santon, Sekos, Sepulchre, Shrine, Starets, Staretz, SV, Tirthankara, War

Holy books, Holy writing Adigranth, Atharvaveda, Bible, Gemara, Granth, Hadith, Hagiographa, Koran, Mishnah, NT, OT, Pia, Purana, Rigveda, Sama-Veda, → **SCRIPTURE**, Shaster, Shastra, Smriti, Sura(h), Tanach, Writ, Yajur-Veda

Holy building, Holy city, Holy place Chapel, Church, Kaaba, Mashhad, Mecca, Medina, Meshed, Najaf, Penetralia, Sanctum, Station, Synagogue, Temenos, Temple

Holy Ghost Paraclete

Holy water Amrit

Homage Bow, Cense, Honour, Kneel, Manred, Obeisance, Tribute, Vail

Home(land), Homeward Abode, Apartment, Base, Blighty, Bro, Broken, Burrow, Cheshire, Chez, Clinic, Community, Convalescent, Domal, Domicile, Earth, Eventide, Family, Fireside, Flat, Funeral, Gaff, Goal, Habitat, Harvest, Heame, Hearth, Heme, Hospice, House, In, Lair, Libken, Lockwood, Lodge, Maisonette, Mental, Mobile,

Montacute, Motor, Nest, Nursing, Old sod, Orphanage, Pad, Penny-gaff, Pied à terre, Pile, Pit dwelling, Plas Newydd, Remand, Res(idence), Rest, Starter, Stately, Tepee, Turangawaewae, Up-along, Villa, Warren

Homecoming Nostos

Home counties SE

Homeless Arab, Bag lady, Evicted, Gangrel, Outler, Rootless, Skell

Homer(ic) Comatose, Cor, Epic(ist), Maeonides, Nod, Pigeon, Somnolent

Home-rule Parnellism, Swaraj

Homesick(ness) Heimweh, Mal du pays

Homespun Cracker-barrel, Plain, Raploch, Russet, Simple

Homestead Ranch, Toft

Homework → DIY, Prep, Preparation

Homicidal, Homicide Chance-medley, Justifiable, Killing, Manslaughter

Homily Lecture, Midrash, Pi, Postil, Prone, Sermon, Tract

▷ **Homing** *may indicate* coming back

Hominid Oreopitheous

Homogeneous Indiscrete

Homogram, Homograph Abac, Heteronym

Homosexual(ity) Arse bandit, Auntie man, Bardash, Batty boy, Bender, Bent, Buftie, Bufty, Camp, Cat, Catamite, Closet queen, Cocksucker, Cottaging, Dike, Dyke, Fag(got), Fairy, Friend of Dorothy, Fruit, Gay, Gaydar, Ginger, Homophile, Invert, Lesbian, Meatrack, Minty, Moffie, Muscle Mary, Pederast, Ponce, Poof(tah), Poofter, Poove, Pouf(fe), Poufter, Puff, Punk, Quean, Queer, Queercore, Quiff, Rough trade, Shirt-lifter, Slash, Swish(y), Tonk, Tribade, Twinkle, Uranism, Urning, Woofter

Hone Grind, → SHARPEN, Whet

Honest(y), Honestly Aboveboard, Afauld, Afawld, Amin, Candour, Clean, Fair dinkum, Genuine, Incorruptible, Injun, Jake, Jannock, Jonnock, Legitimate, Lunaria, Lunary, Mensch, Open-faced, Penny, Probity, Realtie, Rectitude, Reputable, Righteous, Round, Sincere, Soothfast, Square, Squareshooter, Straight, Straight-arrow, Straight-out, Trojan, → TRUE, Truepenny, Upfront, Upright, Upstanding

Honey Comb, Flattery, Hybla(ean), Hymettus, Mel, Melliferous, Nectar, Oenomel, Oxymel, Palm, Peach, Popsy-wopsy, Sis, Sugar, Sweetheart, Sweetie, Virgin, Wild, Wood

Honeycomb(ed) Cellular, Faveolate, Favose, Favous, Smock, Waxwork

Honeydew Mildew

Honey-eater Bear, Blue-eye, Pooh

Honeypot Haanepoot

Honeysuckle Abelia, Anthemion, Caprifoil, Caprifole, Lonicera, Rewa rewa, Suckling, Twinflower, Woodbind, Woodbine

Hong Kong .hk

Honour(able), Honorary, Honoured, Honorific, Honours A, Accolade, Ace, Adore, Adward, Birthday, Blue, Bow, CBE, Commemorate, Credit, Crown, Curtsey, Dan, Elate, Emeritus, Ennoble, → ESTEEM, Ethic, Face-card, Fame, Fête, Gloire, Glory, Grace, Greats, Homage, Insignia, Invest, Izzat, J, Jack, K, King, Knave, Knight, Kudos, Laudation, Laureate, Laurels, MBE, Mensch, Mention, Military, OBE, Optime, Pundonor, Q, Queen, Regius, Remember, Repute, Respect, Revere, Reward, Salute, Straight, Ten, Tenace, Titular, Tripos, Venerate, White, Worship, Wranglers

Honourable companion CH

Honourless Yarborough

Hooch Hogan, Hogen, Moonshine

Hood(ed) Almuce, Amaut, Amice, Amowt, Apache, Balaclava, Bashlik, Biggin, Blindfold, Calash, Calèche, Calyptra, Capeline, Capuccio, Capuche, Chaperon(e), Coif, Cope, Cowl, Cucullate(d), Faldetta, Fume, Gangster, Jacobin, Kennel, Lens, Liripipe, Liripoop, Mantle, Mazarine, Nithsdale, Pixie, Robin, Rowdy, Snood, Trot-cosey, Trot-cozy, Visor

Hoodlum Gangster, Roughneck, Thug, Wanksta

Hoodoo Jonah, Moz(z)

Hoodwink(ed) Blear, Bluff, Cheat, → DECEIVE, Gull, Mislead, Nose-led, Seel

Hoof(ed) Artiodactyla, Cloot, Coffin, Frog, Trotter, Ungula

Hoohah Humdudgeon

Hook(ed), Hooker, Hooks Addict, Adunc, Aduncous, Arrester, Barb(icel), Barbule, Becket, Butcher's, Cant(dog), Catch, Chape, Claw, Cleek, Clip, Clove, Cocotte, Corvus, Crampon, Cromb, Crome, Crook, Crotchet, Cup, Drail, Duck, Fifi, Fish, Floozy, Fluke, Fly, Gab, Gaff, Gig, Grap(p)le, Grapnel, Grappling, Gripple, Hamate, Hamose, Hamulus, Heel, Hitch, Inveigle, Kype, Meat, Picture, Pot, Prostitute, Pruning, Retinaculum, Sister, Snare, Snell, Sniggle, Swivel, Tala(u)nt, Tart, Tenaculum, Tenter, Tie, Trip, Uncus, Wanton, Welsh

Hookah Bong, Chillum, Hubble-bubble, Kalian, Narghil(l)y, Narg(h)ile, Nargileh, Nargil(l)y, Pipe

Hooligan Apache, Bogan, Casual, Desperado, Droog, Goonda, Hobbledehoy, Hoon, Keelie, Larrikin, Lout, Ned, Rough(neck), Ruffian, Skollie, Skolly, Tearaway, Ted, Tityre-tu, Tough, Tsotsi, Vandal, Yahoo, Yob(bo)

Hoop(s) Bail, Band, Circle, Farthingale, Garth, Gird, Girr, Hula®, O, Pannier, → RING, Sleeper, Tire, Trochus, Trundle

Hooray Whoopee, Yippee

Hoot(er) Conk, Deride, Honk, Madge, Nose, Owl, Riot, Screech-owl, Siren, Ululate

Hoover Consume, Dam, Vacuum

Hop(per) An(o)ura, Ball, Bin, Cuscus, Dance, Flight, Jeté, Jump, Kangaroo, Leap, Lilt, Long, Opium, Pogo, Roo, Saltate, Scotch, Skip, Spring, Tremié, Vine

Hope(ful) Anticipate, Aspirant, Combe, Comer, Contender, Daydream, Desire, Dream, Esperance, Evelyn, Expectancy, Forlorn, Gleam, Good, Inshallah, Pipe-dream, Promising, Roseate, Rosy, Sanguine, Trust, Valley, Wannabe, White, Wish

Hopeless(ness), Hopeless quest Abattu, Anomie, Anomy, Black, Buckley's chance, Dead duck, Despair, Despondent, Forlorn, Gloom, Goner, Non-starter, Perdu, Pessimist

Hophead Drinker, Lush, Sot

Hopscotch Peevers

Horace Flaccus, Ode, Satirist

Horatio Nelson

Horatius Cocles

Horde Crowd, Golden, Many, Mass, Mob, Swarm

Horizon A, Apparent, Artificial, B, C, Celestial, Event, Gyro, Rational, Scope, Sea-line, Sensible, Skyline, Visible

Horizontal Advection, Flat, Level, Prone, Supine, Tabular

Hormone Growth, Plant, Sex

HORMONES

3 letters:	7 letters:	Bursicon	9 letters:
FSH	Gastrin	Ecdysone	Adrenalin®
IAA	Ghrelin	Estrogen	Corticoid
TSH	Inhibin	Florigen	Cortisone
	Insulin	Glucagon	Cytokinin
4 letters:	Relaxin	Juvenile	Endocrine
ACTH	Steroid	Oestriol	Melatonin
	Thyroid	Oestrone	Oestrogen
5 letters:		Oxytocin	Pituitrin
Auxin	8 letters:	Resistin	Progestin
Kinin	Abscisin	Secretin	Prolactin
	Androgen	Thymosin	Secretion
	Autacoid		Serotonin

Thyroxine

10 letters:
Adrenaline
Calcitonin
Folliculin
Intermedin
Lipotropin
Oestradiol

11 letters:
Aldosterone
Angiotensin
Gibberellin
Luteinizing
Parathyroid

Progestogen
Somatomedin
Thyrotropin
Vasopressin

12 letters:
Androsterone
Antidiuretic
Biosynthesis
Gonadotropin
Luteotrophic
Noradrenalin
Pancreozymin
Progesterone
Secretagogue
Somatostatin

Somatotropin
Stilboestrol
Testosterone
Thyrotrophin

13 letters:
Catecholamine
Gonadotrophic
Gonadotrophin
Melanotropine
Noradrenaline
Prostaglandin
Somatotrophin

14 letters:
Corticosteroid

Corticosterone
Erythropoietin
Hydrocortisone
Levonorgestral
Norepinephrine

15 letters:
Cholecystokinin

16 letters:
Triiodothyronine

17 letters:
Mineralocorticoid

Horn(s), Horny Acoustic, Advancer, Amalthea, Antenna(e), Antler, Baleen, Basset, Beeper, Bez, Brass, Buck, Bugle, Bur(r), Cape, Ceratoid, Cor, Cornet, Cornett, Cornopean, Cornu(a), Cornucopia, Cromorna, Cromorne, Cusp, Dilemma, English, Exponential, Flugel-horn, French, Frog, Gemshorn, Golden, Gore, Hooter, → **HORNBLOWER**, Hunting, Ivory, Keratin, Klaxon, Lur, Morsing, Mot, Oliphant, Parp, Periostracum, Plenty, Post, Powder, Pryse, Ram's, Saddle, Scur, Shofar, Shophor, Spongin, Tenderling, Trey, Trez, Trumpet, Tusk, Vulcan's badge, Waldhorn

Hornblende Syntagmatite

Hornblower Brain, Horatio, Peel, Triton, Trumpeter

Hornbook Battledoor, Battledore

Horned (sheep) Cabrié, Cabrit, Cornute, Hamate, Lunate, Mouflon, Muflon

Hornet Stinger

Hornless Doddy, Humbel, Humlie, Hummel, Mooly, Mul(l)ey, Poley, Polled

Hornpipe Matelote

Horoscope Figure, Future, Prophecy, Star-map

Horrible, Horror Appalling, Aw(e)some, Beastly, Brat, Creepy, Dire, Distaste, Dread(ful), Execrable, Gashful, Ghastly, Grand Guignol, Grisly, Grooly, Gruesome, Grysie, Hideous, Loathsome, Minging, Nightmare, Odious, Panic, Rascal, Shock, Stupefaction, Terror, Ugh, Vile

Horrid, Horrific, Horrify(ing) Agrise, Appal, Dire, Dismay, Dreadful, Frightful, Ghastly, Gothic, Grim, Grisly, H, Loathy, Odious, Spine-chilling, Spiteful, Ugly

Hors d'oeuvres Antipasto, Canapé, Carpaccio, Ceviche, Hoummos, Houmus, Hummus, Mez(z)e, Pâté, Smor(re)brod, Smør(re)brød, Smorgasbord, Starter, Zak(o)uski

Horse Airer, Bidet, Bloodstock, Carriage, Cut, Cutting, Dark, Doer, Dray, Drier, Drug, Equine, Form, H, → **HEROIN**, High, Hobby, Iron, Knight, Kt, Light, Lot, Maiden, Malt, Non-starter, Outsider, Pack, Pantomime, Plug, Ride, Rocking, Sawbuck, Scag, Screen, Selling-plater, Sense, Snow, Stalking, Standard-bred, Starter, Stayer, Steeplechaser, Stiff, Stock, Teaser, Trestle, Vanner, Vaulting, White, Willing, Wooden

HORSES

2 letters:
GG

3 letters:
Ass
Bay

Cob
Dun
Gee
Nag
Pad
Pot

Rip
Tit

4 letters:
Arab
Aver

Barb
Buck
Cert
Colt
Crib
Dale

Fell
Foal
Hack
Jade
Mare
Pole
Pony
Post
Prad
Roan
Span
Stud
Taki
Trot
Yale
Yaud

5 letters:
Arion
Arkle
Bevis
Borer
Caple
Capul
Favel
Filly
Genet
Morel
Mount
Neddy
Pacer
Paint
Pinto
Poler
Punch
Rogue
Screw
Seian
Shire
Stage
Steed
Tacky
Takhi
Trace
Troop
Waler
Wheel
Zebra

6 letters:
Ambler
Bayard
Bronco
Brumby

Calico
Canuck
Cayuse
Chaser
Cooser
Crollo
Curtal
Cusser
Dobbin
Entire
Exmoor
Favell
Ganger
Garran
Garron
Gennet
Hogget
Hunter
Jennet
Kanuck
Keffel
Lampos
Livery
Morgan
Mudder
Novice
Pad-nag
Plater
Pommel
Poster
Quagga
Randem
Remuda
Roarer
Rouncy
Runner
Sabino
Saddle
Shoo-in
Sorrel
String
Stumer
Summer
Tandem
Tarpan
Tracer
Trojan

7 letters:
Bobtail
Breaker
Caballo
Cavalry
Centaur

Charger
Clipper
Coacher
Courser
Cuisser
Dappled
Draught
Eclipse
Eventer
Gelding
Hackney
Hobbler
Liberty
Marengo
Marocco
Morocco
Mustang
Palfrey
Pegasus
Piebald
Pointer
Quarter
Remount
Saddler
Sheltie
Spanker
Sumpter
Swallow
Swinger
Trigger
Trooper
Trotter
Walking
Wheeler
Xanthos
Xanthus

8 letters:
Aquiline
Bangtail
Bathorse
Boerperd
Buckskin
Camargue
Chestnut
Clay-bank
Cocktail
Dartmoor
Destrier
Eohippus
Friesian
Galloway
Highland
Holstein

Hyperion
Kochlani
Lusitano
Palomino
Schimmel
Shetland
Skewbald
Sleipnir
Springer
Stallion
Stibbler
Trippler
Warragal
Warragle
Warragul
Warrigal
Welsh cob
Whistler
Yarraman
Yearling

9 letters:
Appaloosa
Black Bess
Caballine
Clavileno
Coldblood
Connemara
Dapple bay
Gringolet
Houyhnhnm
Icelandic
Incitatus
Knabstrup
Percheron
Rosinante
Rozinante
Warmblood

10 letters:
Andalusian
Bucephalus
Buckjumper
Buttermilk
Clydesdale
Copenhagen
Dapple-grey
Lipizzaner
Lippizaner
Pliohippus
Przewalski
Showjumper
Stagecoach
Svadilfari

Wheelhorse	Przewalski's	Suffolk Punch	**16 letters:**
		Thoroughbred	Tennessee Walking
11 letters:	**12 letters:**		
Daisy-cutter	Cleveland Bay	**13 letters:**	
High-stepper	Hambletonian	Perissodactyl	

Horseback Croup
Horse-box Stable, Stall
Horse-chestnut Aesculus, Conker
Horse collar Brecham, Hame
Horse complaint, Horse disease, Horse problem, Horse trouble Blind staggers, Blood spavin, Bogspavin, Bot(t)s, Broken wind, Canker, Capel(l)et, Cracked heels, Cratches, Curb, Dourine, Drepance, Equinia, Eweneck, Farcin, Farcy, Fives, Founder, Frush, Glanders, Gourdy, Grape, Grass-sickness, Head staggers, Heaves, Hippiatric, Knee spavin, Laminitis, Lampas, Lampers, Malander, Mallander, Mallender, Megrims, Miller's disease, Moon Blindness, Mooneye, Mud fever, N(a)gana, Parrot mouth, Poll-evil, Quartercrack, Quitter, Quittor, Ringbone, Roaring, Sallenders, Sand crack, Scratches, Seedy-toe, Shaft, Spavie, Spavin, Springhalt, Staggers, Strangles, Stringhalt, Summer sores, Surra, Sway-back, Sween(e)y, Thorough-pin, Thrush, Toe-crack, Tread, Vives, Weed, Weid, Whistling, Windgall, Wind-sucking, Wire-heel, Yellows
Horse-dealer Buster, Coper
Horse-lover Philip
Horseman Ataman, Caballero, Cavalry, Centaur, Conquest, Cossack, Cowboy, Death, Dragman, Famine, Farrier, Hobbler, Hussar, Knight, Lancer, Nessus, Ostler, Parthian, Picador, Pricker, Quadrille, Revere, → **RIDER**, Slaughter, Spahi, Stradiot, Tracer, Wrangler
Horsemanship Manège
Horseplay Caper, Chukka, Knockabout, Polo, Rag, Rant, Romp
Horsepower Hp, Indicated, Ps
Horseradish Ben, Moringa
Horseshoe(-shaped) Henge, Hippocrepian, King-crab, Lophophorate, Lunette, Manilla, Oxbow, Plate
Horsetail Equisetum
Horse thief Blanco, Rustler
Horticultural, Horticulture, Horticulturist Grower, Pomology, RHS
Hose Chausses, Fishnet, Galligaskins, Gaskins, Lisle, Netherstock(ing), Nylons, Panty, Sock, Stockings, Tabi, Tights, Trunk, Tube
Hospice, Hospital Ambulance, Asylum, Barts, Base, Bedlam, Booby hatch, Bughouse, Clinic, Cottage, Day, Dressing station, ENT, Field, Foundation, General, Guest-house, Guys, H, Home, Hospice, Hôtel dieu, Imaret, Infirmary, Isolation, Karitane, Lambarene, Lazaretto, Leprosarium, Leprosery, Lock, Loony bin, Lying-in, MASH, Mental, Nosocomial, Nuthouse, Nuttery, Ozzie, Pest-house, Polyclinic, Rathouse, San, Scutari, Sick bay, Snake-pit, Special, Spital, Spittle, Teaching, Trauma centre, Trust, UCH
Hospitable, Hospitality Cadgy, Convivial, Corporate, Entertainment, Euxine, Kidgie, Lucullan, Open house, Philoxenia, Social, Xenial
Host(s), Hostess Alternate, Amphitryon, Army, Barmecide, Bunny girl, Chatelaine, Compere, Crowd, Definitive, Emcee, Entertainer, Eucharist, Geisha, Heavenly, Hirsel, Hotelier, Innkeeper, Intermediate, Inviter, Laban, Landlady, Landlord, Legend, Legion, Licensee, Lion-hunter, Lot, Mass, Mavin, MC, Number, Presenter, Publican, Quickly, Sabaoth, Speakerine, Swarm, Taverner, Throng, Torrent, Trimalchio, Wafer
Hostage Gherao, Pawn, Pledge, POW
Hostel(ry) Asylum, Auberge, Dharms(h)ala, Dorm, Dormitory, Entry, Halfway house, Inn, Y(MCA), YHA, Youth

Hostile, Hostility Adverse, Aggressive, Alien, Anger, Animus, Anti, Arms, Aversion, Bellicose, Bitter, Chilly, Currish, Diatribe, Feud, Forbidding, Hating, Icy, Ill, Ill-will, Inimical, Inveterate, Oppugnant, Pugnacity, Unfriendly, Virulent, Vitriolic, War

Hot(spot), Hot (tempered) Aboil, Ardent, Big, Blistering, Breem, Breme, Cajun, Calid, Candent, Dog days, Enthusiastic, Erotic(al), Facula, Fervid, Feverish, Fiery, Fuggy, Gospeller, Het, In, Incandescent, Irascible, Latest, Lewd, Live, Mafted, Mirchi, Mustard, Nightclub, Pepper, Piping, Potato, Quick, Randy, Red, Roaster, Scalding, Scorcher, Sexpot, Sexy, Sizzling, Spicy, Spitfire, Steamy, Stewy, Stifling, Stolen, Sultry, Sweaty, Sweltering, Sweltry, Tabasco®, Thermidor, Torrid, Toustie, Tropical, Zealful

Hotchpotch Bricolage, Farrago, Mish-mash, Powsowdy, Welter

Hotel, Hotelkeeper Bo(a)tel, Boutique, Commercial, Fleabag, Flophouse, Gasthaus, Gasthof, H, Hilton, Host, Hydro, Inn, Internet, Military, Motel, Parador, Patron(ne), Pension, Posada, Private, Ritz, Roadhouse, Savoy, Tavern, Telco, Temperance, Trust, Waldorf, Watergate

Hothead(ed) Impetuous, Rash, Spitfire, Volcano

Hot-house Conservatory, Forcing-house, Nursery, Orangery, Vinery

Hot plate Griddle, Salamander

Hot rod Dragster

Hotshot Whiz

Hotspot Bricolage, Farrago, Mish-mash, Powsowdy, Welter

Hotspur Harry, Hothead, Percy, Rantipole

Hottentot Griqua, Khoikhoi, Strandloper

Hot water Soup, Therm

Hound(s) Afghan, Badger, Basset, Beagle, Bellman, Brach, Cad, Canine, Cry, → **DOG**, Entry, Gabriel's, Gaze, Hamiltonstovare, Harass, Harrier, Hen-harrier, Ibizan, Javel, Kennet, Lyam, Lym(e), Mute, Otter, Pack, Persecute, Pharaoh, Pursue, Rache, Ranter, Reporter, Saluki, Talbot, True, Tufter

Hound's bane Palay

Hour(s) Canonical, Complin(e), Daylight, Elders', Eleventh, Flexitime, Golden, H, Happy, Holy, Hr, Literacy, Little, Lunch, None(s), Office, Orthros, Peak, Prime, Rush, Sext, Sidereal, Small, Staggered, Terce, Tide, Time, Undern, Unsocial, Vespers, Visiting, Witching, Working, Zero

Hourglass Meniscoid

House(s), Housing, Household(er) Abode, Accepting, Adobe, Aerie, Aery, Astrology, Audience, Auditorium, B, Bach, Bastide, Beehive, Beth, Bhavan, Bhawan, Biggin, Billet, Bingo, Black, Block, Boarding, Bondage, Brick veneer, Broadcasting, Broiler, Brownstone, Bundestag, Casa, Chalet, Chamber, Chapter, Charnel, Château, Chattel, Chez, Clan, Clapboard, Clearing, Coffee, Commercial, Concern, Convent, Cote, Cottage (orné), Council, Counting, Country, Crankcase, Crib, Custom(s), Dacha, Dail, Death, Demain, Demesne, Derry, Des res, Discount, Disorderly, Domal, Domestic, Domicile, Donga, Door, Dower, Drostdy, Drum, Duplex, Dwelling, Dynasty, Edifice, Entertain, Establishment, Este, Eyrie, Familial, Fashion, Fibro(cement), Finance, Firm, Forcing, Frame, Fraternity, Free, Frontager, Full, Gaff, Gambling, Garage, Gite, Government, Grace and favour, Habitat, Habitation, Hacienda, Halfway, Hall, Harbour, Hearth, HK, Ho, Home, Homestead, Ice, Igloo, Infill, Inn, Inner, Insula, Issuing, Joss, Ken, Lodge, Lofted, Loose, Lot(t)o, Maison(ette), Malting, Manor, Manse, Mansion, Mas, Meeting, Meiney, Meinie, Meiny, Ménage, Menyie, Messuage, Mobility, Monastery, Montagne, Nacelle, Node, Open(-plan), Opera, Outer, Pad, Parliament, Pent, Picts, Picture, Pilot, Pleasure, Pole, Pondokkie, Post, Prefab, Printing, Public, Quinta, Radome, Ranch, Ratepayer, Register, Residence, Rooming, Root, Rough, Sacrament, Safe, Saltbox, Satis, Schloss, School, Seat, Semi, Shanty, Sheltered, Show, Sign, Social, Software, Spec-built, Sporting, Stable, State, Station, Steeple, Storey, Succession, Tavern, Tea, Tenement, Terrace, Theatre, Third, Tied, Toft, Tombola, Tower, Town, Tract, Treasure, Tree, Trust, Try, Upby, Vaulting, Vicarage, Villa(-home),

Wash, Watch, Weather, Weatherboard, Weigh, Wendy, Whare, Wheel, Work, Zero, Zodiac

---

HOUSES

3 letters:	Orange	*8 letters:*	*10 letters:*
Leo	Queen's	Burghley	Chatsworth
	Seanad	Chequers	Heartbreak
4 letters:	Stuart	Hapsburg	Kirribilli
Bush	Wilton	Harewood	Odelsthing
Keys		Hatfield	
Riad	*7 letters:*	Holyrood	*11 letters:*
Syon	Althing	Lagthing	Plantagenet
York	Althorp	Longleat	Russborough
	Bourbon	Petworth	Sandringham
5 letters:	Commons	Somerset	
Lords	Hanover		*12 letters:*
Scala	Kenwood	*9 letters:*	Lockwood Home
Tudor	Knesset	Admiralty	
Upper	Lodging	Chartwell	*13 letters:*
Usher	Osborne	Knebworth	Seanad Eireann
White	Stewart	Lancaster	
	Trinity	Number Ten	*15 letters:*
6 letters:	Windsor	Odelsting	Representatives
Grange			

House-boat Wan(i)gan, Wangun
House-builder Jack
House-keeper Chatelaine, Go(u)vernante, Matron, Publican
House-leek Sengreen
Housemaid's knee Bursa
Houseman Betty, Doctor, Intern, Peer
Housemate Co-tenant
House-warming Infare
Housewife Etui, Needlecase, WI
Housework Chore, DIY
Housing Case, Crankcase, Shabrack, Shelter, Slum, Tenement
Hova Malagash
Hove Plim, Swell
Hovel Cru(i)ve, Den, Pigsty, Shack, Shanty
Hover Hang, Levitate, Lurk, Poise
Hovercraft Air-car
How Hill, Hollow, What
How'dyedo, How d'ye do Hallo, Pass, Salve
However Although, As, But, Even-so, Leastwise, Sed, Still, Though, Yet
Howitzer Gun
Howl(er) Banshee, Bawl, Bay, Bloop, Clanger, Hue, Mycetes, Slip up, Squawk, Ululate, War whoop, Wow, Yawl, Yowl
How much The
Hoy Bilander, Ship
HP Never-never
HQ Centre, Headquarters, SHAPE
Hub Boss, Boston, Centre, Focus, Hob, Nave, Nucleus, Pivot, Tee
Hubbub Charivari, Chirm, Coil, Din, Level-coil, Palaver, Racket, Row, Stir

Hubris Pride
Huckster Hawker, Kidd(i)er, Pedlar
Huddle Cringe, Gather, Hunch, Ruck, Shrink
Hudson River, Rock
Hue Chrome, Colour, Dye, Outcry, Proscription, Steven, Tincture, Tinge, Umbrage, Utis
Huff Dudgeon, Hector, Pant, Pet, Pique, Snuff, Strunt, Umbrage, Vex
Hug Bear, Caress, Coll, Cuddle, Embosom, → **EMBRACE**, Snuggle, Squeeze
Huge (number) Astronomical, Brobdingnag, Colossal, Enorm(ous), Gargantuan, Giant,
   → **GIGANTIC**, Gillion, Ginormous, Humongous, Humungous, Immane, Immense,
   Leviathan, Lulu, Mega-, Milliard, Monolithic, Monster, Monumental, Octillion,
   Prodigious, Socking, Stupendous, Tall, Thumping, Titanian, Tremendous, Vast,
   Voluminous, Whacking
Hugo Victor
Huguenot Camisard
Hulk Lout, Ruin, Shale, Shell, Ship
Hull Bottom, Framework, Husk, Inboard, Monocoque, Pod, Sheal, Sheel, Shell, Shiel,
   Shill, Shiplap
Hullabaloo Outcry, Raz(z)mataz(z), Razzamatazz
▶ **Hullo** *see* **HELLO**
Hum(ming) BO, Bombilate, Bombinate, Bum, Buzz, Chirm, Chirr, Drone, Eident, Lilt,
   Moan, Murmur, Nos(e)y, Odorate, Odorous, Pong, Ponk, Rank, Reek, Sough, Sowf(f),
   Sowth, Stench, Stink, Stir, Whir(r), Zing
Human(e), Humanist, Humanity Anthropoid, Anthropology, Bang, Colet, Earthling,
   Earthman, Erasmus, Incarnate, Kindness, Mandom, Meatbot, Merciful, Mortal,
   Philanthropic, Species, Sympathy, Ubuntu, Virtual, Wight
Humble Abase, Abash, Afflict, Baseborn, Chasten, Conquer, Cow, Degrade, Demean,
   Demiss(ly), Lower, Lowly, Mean, Mean-born, → **MEEK**, Modest, Morigerate, Obscure,
   Poor, Rude, Small, Truckle
Humbug Berley, Blague, Blarney, Buncombe, Bunk(um), Burley, Cant, Claptrap, Con,
   Delude, Eyewash, Flam, Flummery, Fraud, Fudge, Gaff, Gammon, Gas, Guff, Gum, Hoax,
   Hoodwink, Hookey-walker, Kibosh, Liar, Maw-worm, Nonsense, Prig, Shenanigan,
   Tosh, Wind
Humdinger Cracker, Lulu
Humdrum Banal, Boredom, Bourgeois, Monotonous, Mundane, Ordinary, Prosaic,
   Routine, Tedious
Humid(ity) Clammy, Damp, Dank, Hydrometry, Machie, Machy, Moch, Muggy,
   Saturation, Steam, Sticky, Sultry, Tropical
Humiliate(d), Humiliation, Humility Abase, Abash, Baseness, Comedown,
   Degrade, Disbench, Eating crow, Fast, Indignity, Laughing stock, Lose face, Lowlihead,
   Mortify, Put-down, → **SHAME**, Skeleton, Take-down, Wither
Humming-bird Colibri, Hermit, Racket-tail, Rainbow, Rubythroat, Sabre-wing,
   Sapphire-wing, Sappho, Sawbill, Sylph, Thornbill, Topaz, Trochilus
Hummock Tump
Humorist Cartoonist, Comedian, Jester, Leacock, Lear, Punster, Thurber, Twain,
   Wodehouse
Humour, Humorous Aqueous, Bile, Blood, Caprice, Cardinal, Chaff, Choler, Coax,
   Cocker, Coddle, Cosher, Cuiter, Cuittle, Daut, Dawt, Droll, Dry, Facetious, Fun, Gallows,
   Ichor, Indulge, Irony, Jocose, Jocular, Juice, Kidney, Lavatorial, Levity, Light, Melancholy,
   → **MOOD**, Observe, One-liner, Pamper, Phlegm, Pun, Pythonesque, Ribaldry, Salt, Serum,
   Sick, Temper, Trim, Vein, Vitreous, Vitreum, Wetness, Whim, Whimsy, Wit
Humourless Dry, Po(-faced)
Hump(ed), Humping Boy, Bulge, Dorts, Dowager's, Gibbose, Gibbous, Hog, Huff,
   Hummock, Hunch, Middelmannetjie, Pip, Ramp, Road, Sex, Sleeping policeman, Speed
   bump, Tussock

▶ **Humpback** *see* HUNCH(ED)

Humphrey Bogart

Humus Compost, Leafmould, Moder, Mor, Mull

Hun Alaric, Atli, Attila, Fritz, German

Hunch(ed), Hunchback Camel, Chum, Crookback, Gobbo, Hump, Intuition, Kyphosis, Premonition, Quasimodo, Roundback, Sense, Squat, Urchin

Hundred(s), Hundredth Burnham, C, Cantred, Cantref, Cent, Centesimal, Centum, Century, Chiltern, Commot, Days, Desborough, Great, Host, → IN A HUNDRED, Long, Northstead, Old, Shire, Stoke, Tiyin, Ton, Tyiyn, Wapentake

Hundred and fifty CL, Y

Hundred and sixty T

Hundred thousand C

Hundredweight Centner, Long, Metric, Quintal, Short

Hung Displayed, Executed, Framed, High

Hungarian, Hungary Bohunk, Cheremis(s), Csardas, Magyar, Nagy, Szekely, Tzigane, Ugric, Vogul

Hunger (strike), Hungry Appestat, Appetite, Bulimia, Bulimy, Clem, → CRAVE, Desire, Edacity, Empty, Esurient, Famine, Famish, Fast, Hanker, Hunter, Insatiate, Itch, Orectic, Pant, Peckish, Pine, Pyne, Rapacious, Raven, Ravin, Sharp-set, Starve, Unfed, Unfuelled, Yaup, Yearn

▷ **Hungry** *may indicate* an 'o' in another word

Hunk(s) Beefcake, Chunk, Dry-fist, He-man, Miser(ly), Slab, Wedge

Hunker Squat

Hunt(er), Hunting, Huntress, Huntsman Actaeon, Alew, Archer, Artemis, Atalanta, Battue, Beagle, Bellman, Bounty, Bushman, Calydon, Chace, Chase(r), Chasseur, Chevy, Cool, Coursing, Crockett, Cynegetic, Dog, Drag(net), Esau, Ferret, Fox, Free-shot, Gun, Halloo, Herne, Hound, Jager, Kennet, Lamping, Leigh, Letterbox, Lurcher, Montero, National, Nimrod, Orion, Peel, Pig-sticking, Poacher, Poot, Pout, Predator, Pursue, Quest, Quorn, Rabbit, Rach(e), Rake, Ran, Rancel, Ranzel, Ride, Rummage, Run, San, Scavenge(r), Scorse, Scout, → SEARCH, Seek, Shikar(ee), Shikari, Skirter, Slipper, Stag, Stalk, Sticker, Still, Swiler, Terrier, Thimble, Ticker, Tinchel, Tower, Trail, Trap, Treasure, Venatic, Venator, Venerer, Venery, → WATCH, Whip, Whipper-in, Witch, Wolfer, Woodman, Woodsman, Yager

Hunting-call Rechate, Recheat, Tally-ho, View-halloo

Hunting-ground Forestation, Walk

Hurdle(r) Barrier, Doll, Fence, Flake, Gate, Hemery, Obstacle, Raddle, Sticks, Wattle

Hurdy (gurdy) Barrel-organ, Hainch, Haunch, Vielle

Hurl(ing) Camogie, Cast, Dash, → FLING, Heave, Put(t), Sling, Throw, → TOSS

Hurly-burly Furore, Noise

Hurrah Bravo, Cheers, Huzza, Io, Whee

Hurricane Baguio, Tornade, Tornado, Typhoon, → WIND

Hurry Belt, Bustle, Chivvy, Chop-chop, Dart, Dash, Drive, Expedite, Festinate, Fisk, Frisk, Gad, Gallop, Giddap, Giddup, Giddy-up, Hadaway, Hare, Haste, Hie, Hightail, Induce, Mosey, Post-haste, Press, Push, Race, Railroad, → RUSH, Scamper, Scoot, Scramble, Scur(ry), Scutter, Scuttle, Skelter, Skurry, Spank, Speed, Streak, Tear, Whirr

Hurt(ful) Abuse, Ache, Aggrieve, Ake, Bruise, Cutting, Damage, De(a)re, Detriment, Disservice, Harm, Harrow, Hit, → INJURE, Lesion, Maim, Nocent, Nocuous, Noisome, Noxious, Noyous, Offend, Pain, Pang, Prick(le), Scaith, Sting, Trauma, Wound, Wring

Hurtle Rush, Spin, Streak, Streek

Husband(ry), Husbands Add, Baron, Betty, Breadwinner, Consort, Darby, Ear, Eche, Economy, Eke, Ere, Farm, Gander-mooner, Georgic, Goodman, Groom, H, Hoddy-doddy, Hodmandod, Hubby, Ideal, Lord and master, Man, Manage, Mate, Partner, Polyandry, Reserve, Retrench, Save, Scrape, Scrimp, Spouse, Squirrel, → STORE, Tillage

Hush(-hush) Bestill, Gag, Sh, Silent, Smug, St, Tace, Wheesh(t), Whisht

Husk(s), Husky Acerose, Bran, Draff, Eskimo, Hoarse, Hull, Malemute, Seed, Sheal, Shiel, Shuck

Hussar Cherry-picker, Cherubim

Hussite Calixtin(e), Taborite

Hussy Besom, Hen, Jezebel, Limmer, Loose, Minx, Vamp

Hustle(r) Fast talk, Frogmarch, Jostle, Pro, Push, Railroad, Shoulder, Shove, Skelp

Hut(s) Banda, Booth, Bothie, Bothy, Bustee, Cabin, Caboose, Chalet, Choltry, Gunyah, Hogan, Humpy, Igloo, Mia-mia, Nissen, Pondok(kie), Quonset®, Rancheria, Rancho, Rondavel, Shack, Shanty, Sheal(ing), Shebang, Shed, Shiel(ing), Skeo, Skio, Succah, Sukkah, Tilt, Tolsel, Tolsey, Tolzey, Tramping, Wan(n)igan, Whare, Wigwam, Wi(c)kiup, Wil(t)ja, Wurley, Wurlie

Hutch Buddle, Crate, Pen, Rabbit

Hyacinth Cape, Grape, Starch, Wild

Hybrid Bigener, Bois-brûlé, Cama, Catalo, Centaur, Chamois, Chichi, Chimera, Citrange, Cockatrice, Cross, Dso, Funnel, Geep, Graft, Hippogriff, Hircocervus, Incross, Interbred, Jersian, Jomo, Jumart, Lurcher, Mameluco, Mermaid, Merman, Metif, Métis, Mongrel, Mule, Mutation, Noisette, Onocentaur, Opinicus, Ortanique, Ox(s)lip, Percolin, Plumcot, Pomato, Ringed, Single-cross, Tangelo, Tiglon, Tigon, Topaz, Ugli, Werewolf, Zedonk, Zho(mo)

▷ **Hybrid** *may indicate* an anagram

Hydra Polyp

Hydrant Fireplug, H

Hydrocarbon Acetylene, Aldrin, Alkane, Alkene, Alkyl, Alkyne, Amylene, Arene, Asphaltite, Benzene, Butadiene, Butane, Butene, Camphane, Camphene, Carotene, Cetane, Cubane, Cumene, Cycloalkane, Cyclohexane, Cyclopropane, Cymogene, Decane, Diene, Dioxin, Diphenyl, Ethane, Ethylene, Gutta, Halon, Hatchettite, Heavy oil, Hemiterpene, Heptane, Hexane, Hexene, Hexyl(ene), Indene, Isobutane, Isoprene, Ligroin, Limonene, Mesitylene, Methane, Naphtha, Naphthalene, Naphthalin(e), Nonane, Octane, Olefin(e), Paraffin, Pentane, Pentene, Pentylene, Phenanthrene, Phene, Picene, Pinene, Polyene, Propane, Pyrene, Pyridine, Pyrimidine, Retene, Squalene, Stilbene, Styrene, Terpene, Toluene, Triptane, Wax, Xylene, Xylol

Hydrogen Deut(er)on, Diplon, Ethene, H, Heavy, Muonium, Protium, Replaceable, Tritium

Hydroid Sea-fir

Hydrolysis Saponification

Hydrometer Salinometer

Hydrophobia, Hydrophobic Rabid, St Hubert's disease

Hydroplane Skid

Hydroponic Soil

Hydrozoa(n) Campanularia, Millepore, Physalia, Portuguese man-of-war, Siphonophore

Hyena Aard-wolf, Earthwolf, Laughing, Nandi bear, Spotted, Strand-wolf, Tiger-wolf

Hygiene, Hygienic Aseptic, Clean, Dental, Godly, Oral, Sanitary, Sepsis, Sleep

Hymen Maidenhead

Hymn(s) Amazing Grace, Anthem, Benedictine, Bhajan, Canticle, Carol, Cathisma, Choral(e), Coronach, Dies Irae, Dithyramb, Doxology, Epithalamia, Gloria, Hallel, Introit(us), Ithyphallic, Lay, Magnificat, Mantra, Marseillaise, Nunc Dimittis, Ode, P(a)ean, Psalm, Psalmody, Recessional, Rigveda, Sanctus, Secular, Sequence, Stabat Mater, Sticheron, Tantum Ergo, Te Deum, Trisagion, Troparion, Veda

Hymnographer, Hymnologist David, Faber, Heber, Moody, Neale, Parry, Sankey, Watts

Hype(d) Aflutter, Ballyhoo

Hyperbola Rectangular

Hyperbole, Hyperbolic Auxesis, Exaggeration, Sech

Hypercritical Fastidious
Hyperion Titan
Hypersensitive, Hypersensitivity Allergic, Atopy, Idiosyncratic
Hypha(e) Conidiophore, Stroma
Hyphen(ated) Dash, Parasyntheton, Soft
Hypnosis, Hypnotise, Hypnotic, Hypnotism, Hypnotist Braidism, Chloral,
 Codeine, Enthral, Entrance, Fluence, Hypotonia, Magnetic, Magnetise, Meprobamate,
 Mesmerism, Psychognosis, Svengali
Hypochondria(c) Atrabilious, Hyp, Nosophobia, Phrenesiac, Valetudinarian
Hypocrisy, Hypocrite, Hypocritical Archimago, Bigot, Byends, Cant, Carper,
 Chadband, Creeping Jesus, Deceit, Dissembler, Dissimulating, False-faced, Heep,
 Holy Willie, Humbug, Insincere, Janus-faced, Mucker, Nitouche, Pecksniff, Pharisaic,
 Pharisee, Piety, Plaster saint, Prig, Sanctimony, Self-pious, Sepulchre, Tartuf(f)e,
 Two-faced, Whited sepulchre
Hypothesis, Hypothetical Avogadro, Biophor, Conditional, Continuum, Gaia, Gluon,
 Graviton, Micella, Nebular, Notional, Null, Planetesimal, Sapir-Whorf, Suppositious,
 Theory, Virtual, Whorf, Working
Hyrax Cony, Daman, Dassie, Klipdas, Rock rabbit
Hysteria, Hysteric(al) Achiria, Astasia, Conniption, Crazy, Delirium, Frenzy, Meemie,
 Mother

Ii

I A, Ch, Cham, Che, Dotted, Ego, Ich, Indeed, India, Iodine, Italy, J, Je, Me, Muggins, Myself, One, Self, Yours truly

Iambus Scazon

Ian Scot

Iberian Celtiberian

Ibex Izard

Ibis Hadedah, Sacred, Waldrapp

Ice(d), Ice-cream, Icing, Icy A la mode, Alcorza, Anchor, Arctic, Ballicatter, Banana split, Berg, Black, Brainstorm, Brash, Camphor, Cassata, Coconut, Cone, Cool, Cornet, Coupe, Cream, Crystal, Diamonds, Drift, Dry, Field, Floe, Frappé, Frazil, Freeze, Frigid, Frore, Frosting, Frosty, Gelato, Gelid, Gems, Glacé, Glacial, Glacier, Glare, Glaze, Glib, Granita, Graupel, Ground, Growler, Hailstone, Hok(e)y-pok(e)y, Hommock, Hummock, Intention, Kitty-benders, Knickerbocker glory, Kulfi, Lolly, Macallum, Marzipan, Neapolitan, Neve, Oaky, Pack, Pancake, Pingo, Polar, Popsicle®, Rime, Rink, Rivière, Ross, Royal, Sconce, Serac, Shelf, Sherbet, Slay, Slider, Slob, Sludge, Slush, Sorbet, Spumone, Spumoni, Stream, Sugar, Sundae, Theme, Tickly-benders, Topping, Tortoni, Tutti-frutti, Verglas, Virga, Wafer, Water, Wintry

Ice-axe Piolet

Iceberg Calf, Floe, Growler

Ice-box Cooler, Freezer, Fridge, Frig, Yakhdan

▶ **Ice-cream** *see* ICE(D)

Iceland IS

Ice-skating Choctaw, Figure, Glide

Icicle Tangle

Icon Fashion, Idol, Image, Madonna, Shrine, Sprite, Toolbar

Icterus Jaundice

ID PIN

Id(e) Ego, Fish, Orfe

Idea(s) Archetype, Brainchild, Brainstorm, Brainwave, Clou, Clue, Conceit, Concept, Fancy, Figment, Fixed, Germ, Hunch, Idée fixe, Idolum, Image, Inkling, Inspiration, Intention, Interpretation, Keynote, Light, Meme, → NOTION, Obsession, Plan, Plank, Rationale, Recept, Theme, Theory, Thought, Whimsy, Zeitgeist

Ideal(ise) A1, Abstract, Apotheosis, At best, Bee's knees, Cat's whiskers, Dream, Eden, Ego, Erewhon, Goal, Halo, Hero, Model, Monist, Mr Right, Nirvana, Notional, Paragon, Pattern, → PERFECT, Prince Charming, Role-model, Romantic, Rose, Siddhi, Sidha, Sublimate, Transcendental, Utopian, Vision

Idealism, Idealist(ic) Dreamer, More, Perfectionist, Quixotic, Romantic, Transcendental, Utopian, Visionary

Identical Alike, Clone, Congruent, Equal, Indistinguishable, Menechmian, One, Same, Selfsame, Verbatim, Very

Identification, Identify Bertillonage, Codeword, Cookie, Credentials, Designate, Diagnosis, Differentiate, Discern, Document, Dog-tag, Earmark, E-fit, Empathy, Espy, Finger(print), ID, Identikit®, Label, Mark, Monomark, Name, Name-tape, Password, Photofit®, Pin, Pinpoint, Place, Point up, Recognise, Registration, Reg(g)o, Secern, Specify, Spot, Swan-hopping, Swan-upping, Verify

Identikit® E-fit, Videokit

Identity Alias, Appearance, Corporate, Credentials, Equalness, Likeness, Mistaken, Numerical, Oneness, Personal, Qualitative, Seity, Self, Selfhood

Ideology, Ideologue Credo, Hard-liner, Ism, Stalinism

Idiom Americanism, Argot, Britishism, Cant, Dialect, Expression, Idioticon, Jargon, Language, Pahlavi, Parlance, Pehlevi, Persism, Scotticism, Slavism, Syri(a)cism, Syrism

Idiosyncrasy, Idiosyncratic Foible, Mannerism, Nature, Quirk, Way, Zany

Idiot(ic), Idiocy Airhead, Congenital, Dingbat, Dipstick, Dolt, Dumbo, Eejit, Fatuity, Fool, Goose, Half-wit, Headbanger, Imbecile, Inane, Maniac, Moron, Nana, Natural, Nerk, Nidget, Noncom, Numpty, Oaf, Ouph(e), Stupe, → **STUPID**, Tony, Twit, Village, Whacko, Zany

Idle(ness), Idler Beachcomber, Bludger, Boondoggle, Bum, Bumble, Bummle, Cockaigne, Couch potato, Dally, Deadbeat, Diddle, Dilly-dally, Dole-bludger, Donnat, Donnot, Do-nothingism, Drone, Eric, Fainéant, Fallow, Farnarkel, Fester, Flaneur, Flim-flam, Footle, Frivolous, Gold brick, Groundless, Hawm, Inaction, Indolent, Inert, Lackadaisical, Laesie, Lallygag, Layabout, Laze, Lazy, Lead-swinger, Lie, Lig, Light, Limer, Loaf, Loll, Lollop, Lollygag, Lotophagus, Lounge, Lusk, Micawber, Mike, Mollusc, Mooch, Mouch, Otiose, Otium, Patagonian, Piddle, Potato, Ride, Scapegrace, Shiftless, Skive, Slob, Sloth, Sluggard, Spiv, Stalko, Stock-still, Stooge, Stroam, Sweirt, Tarry, Tick over, Transcendental, Trifle, Trock, Troke, Truant, Truck, Twiddle, Unbusy, Unoccupied, Vacuity, Vain, Vegetate, Veg out, Waste, Whip the cat, Workshy

Idol(ise) Adore, Adulate, Baal(im), Baphomet, Bel, Crush, Eikon, E(i)luned, Fetich(e), Fetish, God, Heartthrob, Hero, Icon, Image, Joss, Juggernaut, Lion, Mammet, Manito, Manitou, Matinee, Maumet, Mawmet, Molech, Moloch, Mommet, Moorish, Mumbo-jumbo, Pagoda, Stotter, Swami, Teraph(im), Termagant, Vision, Wood, Worship

Idyll(ic) Arcady, Eclogue, Eden, Paradise, Pastoral, Peneian

Ie Sc

If, If it All-be, An('t), Condition, Gif, Gin, In case, Kipling, Pot, Provided, Sobeit, Whether

Igloo Snowden

Igneous Pyrogenic

Ignis-fatuus Elf-fire, Fire-dragon, Fire-drake, Friar's lanthorn, Wildfire

Ignite, Ignition Coil, Electronic, Flare, Kindle, Lightning, Spark, Spontaneous, Starter

Ignoble Base, Inferior, Mean, Vile

Ignominious, Ignominy Base, Dishonour, Fiasco, Humiliation, Infamous, Scandal, → **SHAME**

Ignorance, Ignorant 404, Agnoiology, Analphabet, Anan, Artless, Benighted, Blind, Clueless, Darkness, Green, Hick, Illiterate, Inerudite, Ingram, Ingrum, Inscient, Irony, Know-nothing, Lewd, Lumpen, Misken, Nescience, Night, Oblivious, Oik, Philistine, Purblind, Red-neck, Unaware, Uneducated, Unlessoned, Unlettered, Unread, Unschooled, Untold, Unversed, Unwist

Ignore(d) Alienate, Ba(u)lk, Blink, Bypass, Connive, Cut, Discount, Disregard, Forget, Leave, Neglect, Omit, Overlook, Override, Overslaugh, Pass, Pass up, Rump, Scrub round, Slight, Snub, Tune out, Unheeded

Igor Prince

Iguana Chuckwalla

I know Iwis, Ywis

Iliad Homeric

Ill(ness) Adverse, All-overish, Bad, Bilious, Cronk, Crook, Disorder, Evil, Gout, Grotty, Inauspicious, Income, Indisposed, Labyrinthitis, Misorder, Off-colour, Poorly, Queer, Ropy, Rough, SARS, Schistosomiasis, Scrofula, Sea-sick, → **SICK**, Strongylosis, Strung out, Unpropitious, Unweal, Unwell, Valetudinarian, Vomito, Wog, Wrong

▷ **Ill** *may indicate* an anagram

Ill-adjusted Sad sack

Ill-balanced Lop-sided

Ill-bred Carl, Churlish, Plebeian, Uncouth, Unmannerly

▷ **Ill-composed** *may indicate* an anagram

Ill-defined Diagnosis, Grey, Hazy, Unclear, Vague

Ill-disposed Baleful

Ill-dressed Frumpish

Illegal, Illicit Adulterine, Black, Bootleg, Breach, Contraband, Furtive, Ill-gotten, Malfeasance, Misbegotten, Pirated, Shonky, Unlawful, Wrong(ous)

Illegitimate Baseborn, Bastard, By-blow, Come-o'-will, Fitz, Irregular, Love-child, Lucky-piece, Mamzer, Misbegotten, Misborn, Misfortunate, Momzer, Natural, Scarp, Slink, Spurious, Unlawful, Unlineal

Ill-fated Inauspicious

Ill-favoured Lean, Offensive, Thin, Ugly

Ill-feeling, Ill-humour Bad blood, Bile, Complaint, Curt, Dudgeon, Glum, Hate, Miff, Peevish, Pique, Rheumatic

Illiberal Insular, Redneck, Skinflint, Strict

▶ **Illicit** *see* **ILLEGAL**

Illiterate Analphabet, Ignoramus, Letterless, Unlettered, Unread

Ill-looking Peaky, Poorly

Ill-luck Ambs-ace, Ames-ace, Bad trot, Deuce-ace, Fate, Misfortune

Ill-mannered, Ill-natured, Ill-tempered Attercop, Bitchy, Coarse, Crabby, Crotchety, Curst, Ethercap, Ettercap, Gnarly, Goop, Gurrier, Guttersnipe, Huffy, Stingy, Sullen, Surly, Ugly, Uncouth, Unkind

Illness Aids, Ailment, Attack, Autism, Brucellosis, Chill, Complaint, Croup, Death-bed, Diabetes, Disease, DS, Dwalm, Dwaum, Dyscrasia, Eale, Eclampsia, Grippe, Hangover, Hypochondria, Lockjaw, Malady, ME, SAD, Scarlatina, Sickness, Terminal, Toxaemia, Urosis, Weed, Weid, Wog

Ill-nourished Emaciated

Illogical Absurd, Inconsequent, Non-sequitur

Ill-sighted Owl, Purblind

Ill-smelling F(o)etid, High, Hing, Miasmic, Stinking

▶ **Ill-tempered** *see* **ILL-MANNERED**

Ill-timed Inopportune, Unseasonable

Ill-treat Harm, Hurt, Shaft

Illuminate(d), Illumination, Illuminating Ambient, Aperçu, Brighten, Bright-field, Clarify, Cul-de-lampe, Daylight, Decorate, Enlighten, Floodlit, Lamplight, Langley, Light, Limbourg, Limelight, Limn, Miniate, Moonlight, Nernst, Phot, Pixel, Radiate, Rushlight, Starlight

Illusion(ary), Illusionist, Illusory, Illusive Air, Apparition, Barmecide, Chimera, Deception, Déjà vu, Escher, Fallacy, Fancy, Fantasy, Fata morgana, Hallucination, Ignis-fatuus, Indian rope trick, Mare's-nest, Maya, Mirage, Muller-Lyer, Optical, Phantasmal, Phantom, Phi-phenomenon, Size-weight, Specious, Transcendental, Trompe l'oeil, Unreality, Will o'the wisp

Illustrate(d), Illustration, Illustrator Artwork, Attwell, Bleed, Case, Centrefold, Collotype, Demonstrate, Dore, Drawing, Eg, Elucidate, Epitomise, Exemplify, Explain, Figure, Frontispiece, Grangerize, Graphic, Half-tone, Heath Robinson, Hors texte, Illume, Illumin(at)e, Instance, Instantiate, Keyline, Limner, Lithograph, Pictorial, Plate, Rockwell, Show, Sidelight, Spotlight, Tenniel, Vignette, Visual, Woodcut

Illustrious Bright, Celebrated, Distinguished, Famous, Legendary, Noble, Renowned, Roshan

Ill-will Animosity, Enmity, Grudge, Hostility, Malice, Maltalent, Mau(l)gre, Spite

I'm I'se

Image(s), Imaging Atman, Blip, Brand, Corporate, Discus, Effigy, Eidetic, Eidolon, Eikon, Eiluned, Emotion, Enantiomorph, Favicon, Fine-grain, Graphic, Graven, Hologram, Hypnagogic, Icon, Iconograph, Ident, Idol, Invultuation, Joss, Latent, Likeness, Matte, Mirror, Morph, Murti, Paranthelium, Paraselene, Pentimento, Persona,

Phantasmagoria, Photogram, Photograph, Pic(ture), Pieta, Pixel(l)ated, Pixil(l)ated, Poetic, Profile, Public, Radionuclide, Real, Recept, Reflectogram, Reflectograph, Representation, Scintigram, Search, Shadowgraph, Shrine, Simulacrum, Sonogram, Species, Spectrum, Spitting, Split, Stereotype, Symbol, Teraph(im), Thermal, Thermogram, Thumbnail, Tiki, Tomogram, Totem, Vectograph, Venogram, Video, Virtual, Waxwork, Xoanon

Imagine(d), Imaginary (land), Imagination, Imaginative Assume, Bandywallop, Believe, Boojum, Bullamakanka, Cloud-cuckoo-land, Cockaigne, Cockayne, Conceive, Conjure, Create, Cyborg, Dystopia, Envisage, Erewhon, Esemplasy, Faery, Faine, Fancy, Feign, Fictional, Fictitious, Fictor, Figment, Figure, Hallucinate, Hobbit, Ideate, Invent, Mind's eye, Moral, Narnia, Never-never-land, Notional, Otherworldly, Oz, Picture, Poetical, Prefigure, Pretend, Propose, Recapture, Replicant, Scotch mist, Snark, Straw, → **SUPPOSE**, Surmise, Think, Tulpa, Vicarious, Visualise, Whangam, Wonderland

Imam Ismail

Imbecile Anile, Fool, Idiot, → **STUPID**

▷ **Imbecile** *may indicate* an anagram

Imbibe Absorb, Drink, Lap, Quaff, Suck, Swallow

Imbricate Overlie

Imbroglio Complication, Maze

Imbrue, Imbue Colour, Impregnate, Indoctrinate, Infuse, Inoculate, Permeate, Revitalise, Soak, Steep

Imitate, Imitation, Imitator Act, Ape, Burlesque, Caricature, Clone, Copy(cat), Counterfeit, Crib, Dud, Echo, Echopraxia, Emulate, Epigon(e), Ersatz, Facsimile, Fake, False, Faux, Follow, Hit off, Marinist, Me-too, Mime, Mimesis, Mimetic, Mimic(ry), Mini-me, Mockery, Monkey, Onomatopoeia, Parody, Parrot, Paste, Paste grain, Pastiche, Pinchbeck, Potichomania, Repro, Rhinestone, Rip-off, Sham, Simulate, Stumer, Take-off, Travesty

Immaculate Conception, Flawless, Lily-white, Perfect, Pristine, Spotless, Virgin

Immanentist Pantheist

Immaterial Insignificant, Spiritual, Trifling

▷ **Immature** *may indicate* a word not completed

Immature(ly), Immaturity Adolescent, Beardless, Callow, Childish, Crude, Embryo, Ergate(s), Green, Inchoate, Larval, Neotenic, Non-age, Nymph, Puberal, Puberulent, Pupa, Raw, Rudimentary, Sophomoric, Tender, Unbaked, Underage, Unformed, Unripe, Young

Immediate(ly) Alsoon, Anon, At once, B(e)live, Direct, Eftsoons, Ekdum, First-time, Forthwith, Imminent, Incontinent, Instantaneous, Instanter, Lickety-split, Near, Next, → **NOW**, Now-now, On the knocker, Outright, Posthaste, Present, Pronto, Right-off, Short-term, Slapbang, Spontaneous, Stat, Statim, Straight, Straight off, Sudden, Then, Tout de suite

Immense Astronomical, Brobdingnag, Cosmic, Enormous, → **GIGANTIC**, Huge, Vast, Wide

Immerse Baptise, Demerge, Demerse, Drench, Embathe, Emplonge, Enew, Engage, Imbathe, Plunge, Soak, Steep, Submerge

Immigrant, Immigration, Immigrate Aliya(h), Aussiedler, Brain gain, Carpet-bagger, Cayun, Chalutz, Freshie, Gastarbeiter, Greener, Greenhorn, Halutz, Illegal, Incomer, Issei, Jimmy Grant, Merino, Metic, New chum, Nisei, Non-quota, Olim, Outsider, Overstayer, Pilgrim, Pommy, Quota, Redemption(er), Reffo, Sanei, Sansei, Settler, Wetback, Whenwe

Imminent Approaching, Close, Immediate, Pending

Immobility, Immobile, Immobilise(r) Akinesia, Cataplexy, Catatonia, Hamstring, Hog-tie, Inertia, Pinion, Rigidity, Taser, Tether

Immoderate Excessive, Extreme, Inordinate, Intemperate, Lavish, Undue, Unreasonable

Immodest(y) Brash, Brazen, Forward, Impudicity, Indelicate, Unchaste

Immolation Sacrifice, Sati, Suttee

Immoral(ity) Corrupt, Degenerate, Dissolute, Evil, Lax, Libertine, Licentious, Loose, Nefarious, Peccable, Reprobate, Scarlet, Sleazebag, Sleazeball, Sleazy, Turpitude, Unchaste, Unclean, Unholy, Unsavoury, Vice, Vicious, Wanton

Immortal(ity) Agelong, Amarant(h), Amarantin, Amritattva, Athanasy, Deathless, → **DIVINE**, Endless, Enoch, Eternal, Ever-living, Famous, Godlike, Memory, Sin, Struldbrug, Timeless, Undying

Immovable Fast, Firm, Gomphosis, Obdurate, Rigid, Stable, Stubborn

Immune, Immunisation, Immunise(r), Immunity Acquired, Active, Amboceptor, Anamnestic, Anergy, Antiserum, Bar, Cree, Diplomatic, Dispensation, Free, Humoral, Inoculate, Klendusic, Natural, Non-specific, Passive, Pasteurism, Pax, Premunition, Properdin, Serum, Tachyphylaxis, Vaccine

Immure Confine, Encloister, Imprison

Imp(ish) Devilet, Elf, Flibbertigibbet, Gamin(e), Gremlin, Hobgoblin, Limb, Lincoln, Litherly, Monkey, Nickum, Nis(se), Puck, Ralph, Rascal, Spright, Sprite

Impact Astrobleme, Bearing, Bump, Chase, Clash, Collision, Feeze, Glance, Head-on, High, Impinge, Imprint, Jar, Jolt, Pack, Percuss, Pow, Slam, Souse, Strike home, Wham, Whammo

Impair(ed), Impairment Appair, Cripple, Damage, Disease, Enfeeble, → **HARM**, Injure, Lame, Mar, Mental, Odd, Pair(e), Paralogia, Stale, Vitiate

Impala Pallah

Impale Elance, Ga(u)nch, Skewer, Spike, Transfix

Impart Bestow, Convey, Divulge, Impute, Infect, Shed, Tell

Impartial(ity) Candid, Detached, Disinterest, Dispassionate, Equitable, Equity, Even-handed, Fair, Just, Neutral, Unbiased

Impasse, Impassable Deadlock, Dilemma, Invious, Jam, Log jam, Mexican standoff, Snooker, Stalemate, Zugzwang

Impassioned Earnest, Emotional, Fervid, Fiery, Heated, Zealous

Impassive Apathetic, Deadpan, Stoical, Stolid, Unemotional

Impatience, Impatient Chafing, Chut, Dysphoria, Dysthesia, Eager, Fiddle-de-dee, Fiddlesticks, Fidgety, Fretful, Hasty, Hoot(s), Irritable, Och, Peevish, Peremptory, Petulant, Pish, Pshaw, Restless, Tilly-fally, Till(e)y-vall(e)y, Tut

Impeach Accuse, Challenge, Charge, Delate, Indict

Impeccable Faultless, Novice

Impecunious Land-poor, Penniless, Poor, Short

Impedance, Impede, Impediment Burr, Clog, Dam, Diriment, Encumber, Halt, Hamper, Hamstring, Handicap, → **HINDER**, Hog-tie, Let, Log, Obstacle, Obstruct, Reactance, Rub, Shackle, Snag, Speed bump, Stammer, Stymie, Tongue-tie, Trammel, Veto, Z

Impel(led), Impelling Actuate, Coerce, Drave, Drive, Drove, Goad, Inspire, Projectile, → **URGE**

Impend(ing) Imminent, Looming, Toward

Impenetrable Adamantine, Air-tight, Dense, Hard, Impervious, Proof, Watertight

Imperative Categorical, Dire, Hypothetical, Jussive, Mood, Need-be, Pressing, Vital

Imperceptible, Imperceptive Blind Freddie, Intangible, Invisible, Latent, Minimal, Subtle

Imperfect(ion) Aplasia, Aplastic, Blotch, Defect, Deficient, Faulty, Feathering, Flawed, Half-pie, Kink, Kinkle, Lame, Poor, Rough, Second, Unideal

Imperial(ist), Imperious Beard, C(a)esarian, Commanding, Dictatorial, Flag-waver, Haughty, Lordly, Majestic, Masterful, Mint, Peremptory, Regal, Rhodes, Royal, Tuft

Imperil Endanger, Risk

Imperishable Eternal, Immarcescible, Immortal, Indestructible

Impermeable Airtight, Athermanous, Proof, Resistant

Impersonal Abstract, Cold, Detached, Inhuman, Institutional

Impersonate(d), Impersonation, Impersonator Amphitryon, Ape, As, Double, Drag queen, Echo, Imitate, Imposter, Impostor, Impression, Mimic, Pose, Spoof

Impertinence, Impertinent Backchat, Crust, Flip(pant), Fresh, Impudent, Irrelevant, Rude, Sass, Sauce

Imperturbable Cool, Placid, Stoic, Tranquil, Unruffable

Impervious(ness) Athermancy, Callous, Hardened, Obdurate, Proof, Tight

Impetigo Scrumpox

Impetuous, Impetuosity Birr, Brash, Bullheaded, Élan, Harum-scarum, → **HASTY**, Headstrong, Heady, Hothead, Impulsive, Rash, Rees, Rhys, Tearaway, Vehement, Violent, Young Turk

Impetus Birr, Drift, Drive, Incentive, MacGuffin, Momentum, Propulsion, Slancio, Steam, Swing

Impious Blasphemous, Godless, Irreverent, Unholy

Implacable Deadly

Implant(ation) AID, Cochlear, Embed, Engraft, Enrace, Enroot, Graft, Inset, Instil, Nidation, Silicone, Sow

Implausible Far-fetched, Lame, Off-the-wall

Implement Agent, Apply, Backscratcher, Biffer, Celt, Cultivator, Curette, Disgorger, Do, Eolith, Execute, Flail, Follow out, Fork, Fulfil, Grater, Grubber, Hacksaw, Harrow, Hayfork, Mezzaluna, Mop, Muller, Neolith, Pin, Pitchfork, Plectrum, Plough, Pruning-bill, Pusher, Rest, Ricker, Ripple, Scarifier, Scuffler, Scythe, Seed drill, Shoehorn, Sickle, Snuffer, Spatula, Splayd®, Spork, Squeegee, Strickle, Sucket fork, Sucket spoon, Tongs, → **TOOL**, Toothpick, Tribrach, Utensil, Wheelbrace

Implicate, Implication Accuse, Concern, Connotation, Embroil, Incriminate, Innuendo, → **INVOLVE**, Material, Overtone

Implore Beg, Beseech, Crave, → **ENTREAT**, Obsecrate, Petition, Plead, Pray

Imply, Implied Hint, Insinuate, Intimate, Involve, Predicate, Signify, → **SUGGEST**, Tacit, Unstated, Unwritten

Impolite Ill-bred, Ripe, Rude, Uncivil

Import(s) Convey, Denote, Drift, Invisible, Mean, Moment, Parallel, Sense, Signify, Spell, Visible

Importance, Important (person) Account, Big, Big cheese, Big pot, Big wheel, Billing, Calibre, Cardinal, Central, Cheese, Cob, Coming, Consequence, Considerable, Core, Cornerstone, Count, Critical, Crucial, Crux, Earth-shaking, Earth-shattering, Ego-trip, Eminent, Epochal, Flagship, Grave, Gravitas, Gravity, Greatness, Heavy, High, High-muck-a-muck, High-profile, His nibs, Historic, Honcho, Hotshot, Huzoor, Key, Keystone, Leading, Life and death, Macher, Magnitude, Main, Major, Material, Matters, Megastar, Mighty, Milestone, Moment(ous), Nabob, Nawab, Nib, Note, Numero uno, Obbligato, Outbalance, Overriding, Paramount, Personage, Pivotal, Pot, Preponderate, Prime, Principal, Red-carpet, Red-letter, Salient, Seminal, Senior, Serious, Signal, Significant, Something, Special, Stature, Status, Stress, Substantive, Tuft, Urgent, VIP, Visiting fireman, Vital, Weight, Weighty, Worth

Importune, Importunate Beg, Coax, Flagitate, Press(ing), Prig, Solicit, Urgent

Impose(r), Imposing, Imposition Allocate, Assess, August, Burden, Charge, Cheat, Diktat, Dread, Enforce, Enjoin, Epic, Fine, Flam, Foist, Fraud, Grand(iose), Handsome, Hidage, Homeric, Hum, Impot, Inflict, Kid, Lay, Levy, Lumber, Majestic, Noble, Obtrude, Penance, Pensum, Pole, Scot, Sponge, Stately, Statuesque, Stonehand, Sublime, Titan, Try-on, Whillywhaw

Impossible Can't, Hopeless, Inconceivable, Incorrigible, Insoluble, Insurmountable, Irreparable, No-go, No-no, Unacceptable

Impost Excise, Levy, Tax, Toll

Imposter, Impostor Bunyip, Charlatan, Disaster, Faitor, Faitour, → **FAKE**, Fraud, Idol, Phantasm, Pretender, Ringer, Sham, Triumph, Warbeck

Impotent Barren, Helpless, Spado, Sterile, Weak

Impound(er) Appropriate, Bond, Confiscate, Intern, Pen, Pinder, Poind

Impoverish(ed) Bankrupt, Bare, Beggar, Exhaust, Indigent, Needy, Poor, Straiten

Impractical Absurd, Academic, Blue-sky, Chim(a)era, Idealist, Inoperable, Laputan, Non-starter, Not on, Other-worldly, Quixotic, Theoretic, Useless

Imprecation Drat, Oath, Pize, Rat(s), 'Slife

Imprecise Approximate, Inaccurate, Indeterminate, Intangible, Loose, Nebulous, Rough, Sloppy, Vague

Impregnable, Impregnate Conceive, Embalm, Enwomb, Imbue, Inexpugnable, Inseminate, Milt, Permeate, Resinate, Watertight

Impresario Maestro, Manager, Producer, Showman

Impress(ive), Impression(able) Air, Appearance, Astonish, Awe, Blur, Blurb, Bowl over, Brand, Class act, Cliché, Commanding, Conscript, Crimp, Deboss, Dent, Description, Dramatic, Edition, Effect, Engrain, Engram(ma), Engrave, Enstamp, Epic, Etch, Feel(ing), Fingerprint, Fossil, Frank, Gas, Glorious, Grab, Grandiose, Greeking, Heroic, Homeric, Idea, Idée, Imitation, Impinge, Imposing, Imprint, Incuse, Indent, Intaglio, Kick ass, Knock, Let, Majestic, Mould, Name-drop, Niello, Noble, Note, Palimpsest, Plastic, Plate, Pliable, Powerful, Prent, Presence, Press(gang), Print, Prodigious, Proof, Recruit, Register, Repute, Resplendent, Responsive, Ripsnorter, Rotund, Seal, Seize, Sense, Shanghai, Slay, Smite, Soft, Spectacular, Stamp, Stereotype, Strike, Stunning, Susceptible, Sway, Tableau, Take, Touch, Type, Vibrant, Watermark, Weal, Weighty, Whale, Woodcut, Wow

Impressionist Caxton, Cézanne, Impersonator, Liebermann, Lumin(ar)ist, Manet, Matisse, Monet, Morisot, Renoir

Imprint Edition, Engrave, Etch, Stamp

Imprison(ment) Cage, Cape, Committal, Confine, Constrain, Custody, Durance, Emmew, False, Gherao, Immure, Incarcerate, Inside, Intern, Jail, Lock-up, Penal servitude, Quad, Quod, Stretch, Time

Improbable Buckley's chance, Buckley's hope, Dubious, Far-fetched, Unlikely

Impromptu Ad lib(itum), Extempore, Improvised, Offhand, Pong, Spontaneous, Sudden, Unrehearsed

Improper, Impropriety Abnormal, Blue, Demirep, False, Illegitimate, Indecent, Indecorum, Naughty, Outré, Prurient, Solecism, Undue, Unmeet, Unseemly, Untoward

▷ **Improperly** may indicate an anagram

Improve(ment), Improver, Improving Advance, Ameliorate, Beat, Benefit, Bete, Better, Boost, Break, Buck, Cap, Chasten, Conditioner, Convalesce, Cultivate, Détente, Didactic, Ease, Edify, Edutainment, Embellish, Embroider, Emend, Enhance, Enrich, Eugenic, Euthenics, File, Gentrify, Kaizen, Meliorate, Mend, Modernise, Potentiate, Promote, Rally, Refine, Reform, Resipiscence, Retouch, Revamp, Sarvodaya, Slim, Streamline, Surpass, Tart, Tatt, Titivate, Top, Touch-up, Turn round, Tweak, Upswing, Uptrend, Upturn

Improvident Feckless, Micawber, Poor-white, Wasteful

Improvise(d), Improvisation Ad hoc, Adlib, Break, Busk it, Devise, Drumhead, Extemporise, Gorgia, Invent, Jury-rig, Knock-up, Lash-up, Noodle, On the fly, Pong, Ride, Scratch, Sodain, Sudden, Tweedle, Vamp, Wing it

Imprudent Foolhardy, Foolish, Impetuous, Impolitic, Indiscreet, Injudicious, Rash, Reckless, Unadvised, Unguarded, Unwary, Unwise

Impudence, Impudent Audacious, Backchat, Bardy, Bold, Brash, Brassy, Brazen, Cheeky, Cool, Crust, Effrontery, Forward, Gall, Gallus, Hussy, Impertinent, Insolent, Jackanapes, Jack-sauce, Lip, Malapert, Neck, → **NERVE**, Pert, Sass(y), Sauce, Saucebox, Saucy, Skipjack, Slack-jaw, Temerity, Whippersnapper, Yankie

Impugn Censure, Challenge, Defame, Impeach, Malign

Impulse, Impulsive Acte gratuit, Beat, Compelling, Conatus, Dictate, Drive, Efferent, Foolhardy, Headlong, Horme, Ideopraxist, Impetus, Instigation, → **INSTINCT**, Libido,

Madcap, Nerve, Nisus, Precipitant, Premature, Premotion, Send, Signal, Snap, Specific, Spontaneous, Tearaway, Tendency, Thrust, Tic, Urge, Whim

Impure, Impurity Adulterated, Contaminated, Donor, Faints, Feints, Indecent, Lees, Lewd, Regulus, Scum, Unchaste, Unclean

Imputation, Impute Ascribe, Attribute, Charge, Scandal, Slander, Slur

In A, Amid, Amidst, At, Batting, Chic, Current, Hip, Home, Hostel, I', Indium, Inn, Intil, Occupying, On, Pop(ular), Pub, Trendy, Within

Inability Agnosia, Anosmia, Aphagia, Aphasia, Apraxia, Ataxy, Prosopagnosia

Inaccessible Abaton, Eyrie, Impervious, Remote, Unattainable, Uncom(e)atable

Inaccurate Distorted, Erroneous, Faulty, Imprecise, Inexact, Misquote, Out, Overestimate, Rough, Slipshod, Unfaithful

Inactive, Inaction, Inactivity Acedia, Anestrum, Anoestrus, Cabbage, Comatose, Dead, Dormant, Extinct, Fallow, Hibernate, Idle, Inert, Languor, Lotus-eater, Masterly, Moratorium, Passive, Quiescent, Racemic, Recess, Rusty, Sedentary, Sluggish, Stagnation, Stasis, Torpid, Vacancy, Veg(etate)

In addition Eke, Else, Further, Moreover, Plus, Thereto, To boot, Too, Yet

Inadequate Derisory, Feeble, Hopeless, Inapt, Inferior, Joke, Measly, Pathetic, Poor, Ropy, Scanty, Slight, Thin, Unable, Unequal

Inadvertent(ly) Accidental, Careless, Chance, Unwitting

▷ **In a flap** *may indicate* an anagram

In a high degree So

In a hundred Percent

Inane Empty, Fatuous, Foolish, Imbecile, Silly, Vacant

Inanimate Abiotic, Lifeless

Inappropriate Amiss, Incongrous, Infelicitous, Malapropos, Off-key, Out of place, Pretentious, Unapt, Unbecoming, Undue, Unmeet, Unsuitable, Untoward

Inapt Maladroit, Unsuitable

Inarticulate(ness) Indistinct, Mumbling, Psellism

Inartistic Artless, Crude

Inattentive, Inattention Absent, Asleep, Careless, Deaf, Distrait, Dwaal, Dwa(l)m, Dwaum, Heedless, Loose, Slack, Unheeding, Unobservant

Inaudible Infrasonic, Silent, Superhet

Inaugurate Han(d)sel, Initiate, Install, Introduce, Swear in

Inauspicious Adverse, Ominous, Sinister

▷ **In a whirl** *may indicate* an anagram

▷ **In a word** *may indicate* two clue words linked to form one

Inborn, Inbred Homogamy, Inherent, Innate, Native, Selfed, Sib

Inca Quechua, Quichua

Incalculable Endless, Unpredictable, Untold

Incandescent Alight, Bright, Brilliant, Excited, Radiant

Incantation Chant, Charm, Magic, Mantra, Spell

Incapable Blotto, Can't, Downa-do, Powerless, Unable, Useless

Incapacitate Paralyse

Incarcerate Intern

Incarnation Advent, Avatar, Embodiment, Fleshing, Hyperion, Krishna, Rama, Ramachandra

In case Lest, So

Incautious Cavalier, Foolhardy, Rash, Reckless, Unwary

Incendiary Arsonist, Combustible, Firebug, Fire-lighter, Fireship, Napalm, Thermite

Incense(d), Incenser Anger, Aroma, Elemi, Enfelon, Enrage, Homage, Hot, → **INFLAME**, Joss-stick, Mosquito coil, Navicula, Onycha, Outrage, Pastil(le), Provoke, Stacte, Thurible, Thus, Vex, Wrathful

Incentive Carrot, Carrot and stick, Feather-bed, Fillip, Impetus, Inducement, Motive, Premium, Spur, Stakhanovism, Stimulus, Wage

Incessant Constant, Endless, Unremitting
Incest Backcross, Spiritual
Inch(es) Ait, Column, Edge, Isle(t), Mil, Miner's, Sidle, Tenpenny, Uncial
Inchoate Formless, Immature, Incipient
Incident(al) Affair, Baur, Bawr, Carry-on, Case, Chance, Circumstance, Episode, Event, Facultative, Handbags, Negligible, Occasion, Occurrent, Page, Peripheral, Scene, Throwaway
Incinerate, Incinerator Burn, Combust, Cremate, Destructor
Incipient Beginning, Germinal, Inchoate, Nascent
Incise, Incision, Incisive(ness) Bite, Cut, Edge, Engrave, Episiotomy, Incavo, Lobotomy, McBurney's, Mordant, Notch, Phlebotomy, Pleurotomy, Punchy, Rhizotamy, Scarf, Scribe, Slit, Surgical, Thoracotomy, Tracheotomy, Trenchant
Incisor Foretooth
Incite(ment) Abet, Agitate, Drive, Egg, Fillip, Goad, Hortative, Hoy, Impassion, Inflame, Instigate, Kindle, Motivate, Onsetting, Prod, Prompt, Provoke, Put, Rouse, Sa sa, Sedition, Set, Sic(k), Sool, → **SPUR**, Stimulus, Sting, Suborn, Suggest, Tar, Urge
Incline(d), Inclination Acclivity, Angle, Aslant, Aslope, Atilt, Bank, Batter, Bent, Bevel, Bias, Bow, Camber, Clinamen, Cock, Crossfall, Declivity, Dip, Disposed, Drift, Enclitic, Escarpment, Glacis, → **GRADIENT**, Grain, Habitus, Hade, Heel, Hill, Italic, Kant, Kip, Lean, Liable, Liking, List, Maw, Minded, Nod, On, Partial, Peck, Penchant, Proclivity, Prone, Propensity, Rake, Ramp, Ready, Rollway, Set, Shelve, Slant, → **SLOPE**, Steep, Steeve, Stomach, Supine, Sway, Tend, Tilt, Tip, Trend, Upgrade, Uptilt, Velleity, Verge, Weathering, Will
Include(d), Inclusion, Inclusive Add, All-told, Bracket, Compass, Comprise, Connotate, Contain, Cover, Embody, Embrace, Enclose, Involve, Short-list, Social, Subsume, Therein
Incognito Anonymous, Disguised, Faceless, Secret, Unnamed, Unobserved
Incoherent Confused, Delirious, Disconnected, Disjointed, Gabbling, Garbled, Inarticulate, Rambling, Skimble-skamble, Spluttering
Incombustible Clinker
Income Annuity, Benefice, Discretionary, Disposable, Dividend, Earned, Entry, Fixed, Franked, Livelihood, Living, Meal-ticket, Milch cow, National, Notional, OTE, Penny-rent, Prebend, Primitiae, Private, Proceeds, Rent, Rente, Rent-roll, Returns, Revenue, Salary, Stipend, Take, Unearned, Unfranked, Wages
Incomeless E
Incommunicado Isolated, Silent
Incomparable Par excellence, Supreme, Unequalled, Unique, Unmatched
Incompatible, Incompatibility Clashing, Contradictory, Dyspathy, Incongruous, Inconsistent, Mismatched, Unsuited
Incompetent(ly) Blind Freddie, Bungler, Deadhead, Helpless, Hopeless, Ill, Inefficient, Inept, Not for nuts, Palooka, Shlepper, Shower, Slouch, Unable, Unfit, Useless
Incomplete Broadbrush, Cagmag, Catalectic, Deficient, Inchoate, Lacking, Partial, Pendent, Rough, Sketchy, Unfinished
Incomprehensible, Incomprehension Acatalepsy, Acatamathesia, Double Dutch, Hard, Obscure, Unbelievable
Inconceivable Impossible, Incredible
▷ **In confusion** *may indicate* an anagram
Incongruous, Incongruity Absurd, Discordant, Heterogenous, Irish, Ironic, Sharawadgi, Sharawaggi, Solecism
In connection with Re
Inconsequential Light
Inconsiderable Light, Slight
Inconsiderate Asocial, High-handed, Hog, Light-minded, Petty, Presumptuous, Roughshod, Thoughtless, Unkind, Unthinking

Inconsistency, Inconsistent Alien, Anacoluthon, Anomaly, Contradictory, Discrepant, Oxymoronic, Paradoxical, Patchy, Unequal, Unsteady, Variance

Inconsolable Heartbroken, Niobe

Inconspicuous Background, Obscure, Small, Unobtrusive

Inconstant Chameleon, Desultory, Fickle, Light, Mutable, → **VARIABLE**

Inconvenience, Inconvenient Awkward, Bother, Discommode, Fleabite, Incommodious, Inopportune, Put out, → **TROUBLE**, Ungain(ly), Unseemly, Untoward

Incorporate(d), Incorporation Absorb, Embody, Hard wire, Inc, Inorb, Integrate, Introgression, Introject, Join, Merge, Subsume

Incorporeal Aery, Airy, Spiritual

Incorrect Catachresis, False, Improper, Invalid, Naughty, Wrong

Incorrigible Hopeless, Obstinate

Incorruptible Copper-bottomed, Honest, Immortal, Pure, Robespierre, Sea-green

Increase(s), Increasing Accelerando, Accelerate, Accession, Accretion, Accrew, Accrue, Add, Additur, Aggrandise, Amplify, Amp up, Appreciate, Approve, Augment, Auxetic, Bolster, Boost, Build up, Bulge, Burgeon, Charge, Crank up, Crescendo, Crescent, Crescive, Deepen, Dilate, Double, Ech(e), Eech, Eik, Eke, Enhance, Enlarge, Escalate, → **EXPAND**, Explosion, Extend, Gain, Greaten, → **GROW**, Heighten, Hike, Ich, Increment, Interbreed, Jack, Jack up, Joseph, Lift, Magnify, Mark up, Mount, Multiply, Plus, Proliferate, Prolong, Propagate, Ramp up, Redshift, Reflation, Regrate, Resurgence, Rise, Snowball, Speed up, Supercharger, Surge, Swell, Thrive, Up, Upsize, Upswell, Upswing, Wax, Write up

Incredible Amazing, Astonishing, Cockamamie, Extraordinary, Fantastic, Steep, Stey, Tall, Unreal

Incredulity, Incredulous As if, Distrust, Infidel, Sceptic, Suspicion, Thunderstruck, Unbelief

Increment Accrual, Augment, Growth, Increase, Unearned

Incriminate Accuse, Implicate, Inculpate, Stitch up

Incubate, Incubator Brooder, Develop, Eccaleobion, Hatch

Incubus Demon, Load, Nightmare

Inculcate Implant, Infuse

Incumbent Lying, Obligatory, Occupier, Official, Resident

Incur Assume, Earn, Involve

Incursion Foray, Inroad, Invasion, Raid, Razzia

Indecent Bare, Blue, Fescennine, Free, Immodest, Immoral, Improper, Lewd, Obscene, Rabelaisian, Racy, Scurril(e), Sotadic, Spicy, Sultry, Uncomely, Unnatural, Unproper, Unseem(ly), X-rated

Indecision, Indecisive Demur, Dithery, Doubt, Hamlet, Havering, Hesitation, Hung jury, Inconclusive, Shilly-shally, Suspense, Swither, Weakkneed, Wishy-washy

Indeclinable Aptote

Indecorous Graceless, Immodest, Outré, Unbecoming, Unseemly

Indeed Absolutely, Atweel, Ay, Aye, Begorra(h), Da, Een, Even, Faith, Haith, I, Insooth, Ja wohl, La, Marry, Quotha, Soothly, Truly, Verily, Yah, Yea

Indefensible Implausible, Inexcusable, Untenable, Vincible

Indefinable Je ne sais quoi

Indefinite(ly) A, An, Any, Evermore, Hazy, Nth, Some, Undecided, Vague

Indelible Fast, Permanent

Indelicate Broad, Coarse, Improper, Sultry, Vulgar, Warm

Indemnify, Indemnification, Indemnity Assythement, Compensation, Double, Insurance, Voetstoots

Indent(ed), Indentation Apprentice, Contract, Crenellate, Dancetty, Dimple, Impress, Niche, Notch, Order, Philtrum, Prophet's thumbmarks, Subentire

Independence, Independent Apart, Autocephalous, Autogenous, Autonomy, Crossbencher, Detached, Extraneous, Free(dom), Free-lance, Free spirit, Freethinker,

I, Individual, Liberty, Mana motuhake, Maverick, Mugwump, Perseity, Self-contained, Self-sufficient, Separate, Separatist, Sui juris, Swaraj, Udal, UDI, Uhuru, Viscosity

Indescribable Incredible, Ineffable

Indestructible Enduring, Impenetrable, Inextirpable

Indeterminate Borderline, Formless, Incalculable, Open-ended, Unknown

Index Alidad(e), All-Ordinaries, Catalogue, Cephalic, Colour, Cranial, Cross, DAX, Dial, Dow Jones, Exponent, Facial, Finger, Fist, Fog, Footsie, Forefinger, Gazetteer, Glycaemic, Hang Seng, Kwic, Librorum Prohibitorum, Margin, Misery, Mitotic, Nasal, Nikkei, Opsonic, Power, Price, Refractive, → **REGISTER**, Rotary, Share, Stroke, Table, Therapeutic, Thumb, TPI, UV, Verborum, Zonal

India(n) Adivisi, Asian, Assamese, Ayah, Baboo, Babu, Bharat(i), Bihari, Canarese, Carib, Chin, Dard, Dravidian, East, File, Gandhi, Goanese, Gond(wanaland), Gujarati, Harijan, Harsha, Hindu, .in, Indic, Ink, Jain, Jat, Jemadar, Kafir, Kanarese, Kannada, Khalsa, Kisan, Kolarian, Kshatriyas, Lepcha, Maratha, Ma(h)ratta, Maya, Mazhbi, → **MEXICAN**, Mishmi, Mission, Mofussil, Mogul, Mulki, Munda, Munshi, Naga, Nagari, Nair, Nasik, Nation, Nayar, → **NORTH AMERICAN**, Nuri, Ocean, Oriya, Pali, Panjabi, Pargana, Parsee, Parsi, Pathan, Peshwa, Plains, Poppadom, Prakrit, Punja(u)bee, Punjabi, Red, Redskin, Sanskrit, Sepoy, Shri, Sikh, Sind(h), → **SOUTH AMERICAN**, Sowar, Summer, Swadeshi, Taino, Tamil, Telegu, Treaty, Vakeel, Vakil, West, Ynd

Indiaman Clive

Indiana, Indianian Hoosier

Indicate, Indication, Indicative, Indicator Adumbrate, Allude, Argue, Barcode, Bespeak, Betoken, Blinker, Cite, Clue, Convey, Cursor, → **DENOTE**, Design, Designate, Desine, Dial, Dial gauge, Endeixis, Evidence, Evince, Fluorescein, Gesture, Gnomon, Hint, Litmus, Manifest, Mean, Mood, Nod, Notation, Performance, Pinpoint, Plan-position, Point, Portend, Proof, Ray, Register, Remarque, Representative, Reveal, Show, → **SIGN**, Signify, Specify, Speedo, Symptom, Tip, Token, Trace, Trafficator, Trait, Winker

Indictment Accusation, Arraign, Caption, Charge, Dittay, Reproach, Trounce

Indifference, Indifferent Adiaphoron, Aloof, Apathetic, Apathy, Blasé, Blithe, Callous, Cavalier, Cold, Cool(th), Dead, Deaf, Detached, Disdain, Easy-osy, Empty, Fico, Incurious, Insouciant, Jack easy, Lax, Lukewarm, Mediocre, Neutral, Nonchalant, Perfunctory, Phlegm, Pococurante, Sangfroid, So-so, Stoical, Supercilious, Supine, Tepid, Thick-skinned, Unconcerned

Indigence, Indigent Need, Pauper, Penury, Poverty, Want

Indigenous Aboriginal, Endemic, Native

▷ **Indi-gent** *may indicate* Baboo or Babu

Indigestion Apepsia, Apepsy, Dyspepsia, Heartburn

Indignant, Indignation Anger, Annoyed, Bridling, Incensed, Irate, Outrage, Pique, Resentful, Steamed up, Umbrage, Wrathful

Indignity Affront, Outrage

Indigo Anil, Blue, Bunting, Carmine, Indole, Isatin(e), Wild

Indirect Aside, Back-handed, By(e), Circumlocution, Devious, Implicit, Mediate, Oblique, Remote, Roundabout, Second-hand, Sidelong, Subtle, Vicarious, Zig-zag

Indiscreet, Indiscretion Blabbermouth, Folly, Gaffe, Imprudence, Indelicate, Injudicious, Loose cannon, Rash, Unguarded, Wild oats

Indiscriminate Haphazard, Random, Scattershot, Sweeping, Wholesale

Indispensable Basic, Essential, King-pin, Linch-pin, Necessary, Requisite, Sine qua non, Vital

Indispose(d), Indisposition Adverse, Disincline, Ill, Incapacitate, Reluctant, Sick, Unwell

Indisputable Evident

Indistinct Ambiguous, Bleary, Blur, Bumble, Bummle, Faint, Filmy, Fuzzy, Grainy, Hazy, Misty, Mumbling, Mush-mouthed, Nebulous, Neutral, Nondescript, Pale, Sfumato,

S(c)hwa, Slurred, Smudged, → **VAGUE**

Indistinguishable Nondescript

▷ **In distress** *may indicate* an anagram

Indite Compose, Pen, Write

Indium In

Individual(ist), Individuality Apiece, Being, Discrete, Exclusive, Free spirit, Gemma, Haecceity, Identity, Ka, Libertarian, Loner, Man, Man-jack, Morph, One-to-one, Own, Particular, Person, Poll, Respective, Seity, Separate, Single, Singular, Solo, Soul, Special, Unit, Zoon

Indoctrinate Brainwash, Discipline, Instruct

Indo-European Aryan, Jat(s)

Indolence, Indolent Bone idle, Fainéance, Inactive, Languid, Lazy, Lentor, Otiose, Purposeless, Shiftless, Sloth, Sluggish, Supine

Indomitable Brave, Dauntless, Invincible

Indonesia(n) Batavian, .id, Nesiot, RI

Indoor(s) Within

Indubitably Certainly, Certes, Manifestly, Surely

Induce(ment) Bribe, Carrot, Cause, Coax, Draw, Encourage, Evoke, Get, Inveigle, Lead, Motivate, → **PERSUADE**, Prevail, Suasion, Suborn, Tempt

Induct(ion), Inductance Epagoge, Henry, Inaugurate, Initiate, Install, L, Logic, Mutual, Ordain, Prelude, Remanence

Indulge(nce), Indulgent Absolution, Aristippus, Binge, Coddle, Cosset, Dissipation, Drink, Favour, Gratify, Humour, Law, Lie-in, Luxuriate, Oblige, Orgy, Pamper, Pander, Pardon, Partake, Permissive, Pet, Pettle, Pig-out, Please, Plenary, → **SATISFY**, Splurge, Spoil, Spoonfeed, Spree, Surfeit, Sybarite, Tolerant, Venery, Voluptuous, Wallow

Industrial, Industrious, Industry Appliance, Application, Basic, Business, Busy, Cottage, Deedy, Diligence, Eident, Energetic, Growth, Heavy, Heritage, Labour, Legwork, Millicent, Ocnus, Operose, Process, Ruhr, Service, Smokestack, Sunrise, Technical, Technics, Tertiary, Tourism, Zaibatsu

▶ **Inebriate** *see* **INTOXICATE(D)**

Inedible Inesculent, Noisome, Rotten

Ineffective, Ineffectual Chinless wonder, Clumsy, Deadhead, Drippy, Droob, Dud, Empty, Eunuch, Fainéant, Feeble, Fruitless, Futile, Idle, Ill, Impotent, Lame, Mickey Mouse, Neuter, Neutralised, Null, Otiose, Powerless, Resty, Sterile, Stumbledown, Toothless, → **USELESS**, Void, Weak, Wet, Wimp

Inefficient Clumsy, Incompetent, Lame, Shiftless, Slack, Slouch

Inelegant Awkward, Inconcinnity, Stiff, Turgid, Unneat

Ineligible Unqualified

Inept Absurd, Amateurish, Anorak, Cack-handed, Farouche, Fumbler, Galoot, Loser, Maladjusted, Nerd, Otaku, Plonker, Sad sack, Schlimazel, Schmo, Unskilled, Wet

Inequality Anomaly, Chebyshev's, Disparity, Evection, Imparity, Injustice, Odds, Tchebyshev's

Inert(ia) Catatonia, Comatose, Dead, Dull, Excipient, Inactive, Krypton, Languid, Leaden, Mollusc, Motionless, Neon, Oblomovism, Potato, Rigor, Sluggish, Stagnant, Stagnation, Thowless, Torpid

Inescapable Act of God

Inestimable Incalculable, Invaluable, Priceless

Inevitable, Inevitably Automatic, Certain, Fateful, Inescapable, Inexorable, Infallible, Necessary, Needs, Perforce, TINA, Unavoidable

Inexact(itude) Cretism, Incorrect, Terminological, Wrong

Inexhaustible Infinite, Tireless

Inexorable Relentless

Inexpedient Impolitic, Imprudent, Unwise

Inexpensive Bargain, Cheap, Dirt-cheap, Economic

Inexperience(d), Inexpert Amateur, Awkward, Callow, Colt, Crude, Fledgling, Fresh, → **GREEN**, Greenhorn, Ham, Ingénue, Jejune, Put(t), Raw, Rookie, Rude, Tender, Unconversant, Unseasoned, Unseen, Unversed, Waister, Wide-eyed, Yardbird, Youthful

Inexplicable Magical, Mysterious, Paranormal, Unaccountable

In fact Insooth

Infallible Foolproof, Right, Sure-fire, Unerring

Infamous, Infamy Base, Ignominious, Notorious, Opprobrium, Shameful, Villainy

Infant, Infancy Babe, Baby, Innocent, Lamb, Minor, Nurseling, Oral, Rug rat, The cradle

▷ **Infantry** *may refer to* babies

Infantry(man) Buff, Foot, Grunt, Jaeger, Phalanx, Pultan, Pulto(o)n, Pultun, → **SOLDIER**, Tercio, Turco, Twenty, Voetganger, Zouave

Infatuate(d), Infatuating, Infatuation Assot, Besot, Circean, Crush, Enamoured, Engou(e)ment, Entêté, Epris, Fanatic, Foolish, Lovesick, Mash, → **OBSESSION**, Pash, Rave, Turn

Infect(ed), Infecting, Infection, Infectious Adenoviral, Angina, Anthrax, Babesiasis, Babesiosis, Candidiasis, Canker, Carrier, Catching, Catchy, Cholera, Communicable, Contagious, Contaminate, Corrupt, Cowpox, Cryptococcosis, Cryptosporidiosis, Dermatophytosis, Diseased, E-coli, Fascioliasis, Fester, Focal, Fomes, Giardiasis, Gonorrhoea, Herpes, Impetigo, Leishmaniasis, Listeria, Lockjaw, Mycetoma, NSU, Opportunistic, Orf, Overrun, Poison, Polio(myelitis), → **POLLUTE**, Py(a)emia, Pyoderma, Quittor, Rife, Ringworm, Roup, Salmonella, Sarcoid, SARS, Scabies, Secondary, Septic, Shingles, Smit(tle), Strep throat, Strongyloidiasis, Strongylosis, Taint, Taking, Tetanus, Thrush, Tinea, Toxocariasis, Toxoplasmosis, Transfection, Trichuriasis, Typhoid, Typhus, Varroa, Vincent's angina, Viral pneumonia, Virion, Virulent, Whitlow, Wog, Yersiniosis, Zoonosis, Zymosis

Infeftment Sasine, Seisin

Infer(ence), Inferred Conclude, Conjecture, Deduce, Divine, Educe, Extrapolate, Generalise, Guess, Illation, Imply, Judge, Obversion, Putative, Surmise, Syllogism

▷ **Infer** *may indicate* 'fer' around another word

Inferior Base, Bodgier, Cheap-jack, Cheesy, Coarse, Crummy, Degenerate, Dog, Epigon, Ersatz, Gimcrack, Grody, Grub-Street, Impair, Indifferent, Infra, Jerkwater, Less, Lo-fi, Lower, Low-grade, Mediocre, Minor, Naff, Nether, One-horse, Ornery, Paravail, Petty, Poor, Rop(e)y, Schlock, Second, Second-best, Shilpit, Shlock, Shoddy, Shonky, Slopwork, Sprew, Sprue, Subjacent, Subordinate, Substandard, Surat, Tatty, Tinpot, Trashy, Under(man), Underdog, Underneath, Understrapper, Untermensch, Waste, Worse

Infernal All-fired, Cotton-picking, Demogorgon, Diabolic, Hellish, Phitonian, Tartarean, Unholy

Infertile Barren, Farrow, Sterile

Infest(ed), Infestation Acariasis, Acrawl, Beset, Blight, Dog, Hoatching, Overrun, Pediculosis, Phthiriasis, → **PLAGUE**, Stylopised, Swamp, Swarm, Taeniasis, Torment, Trombiculiasis, Trombidiasis, Trypanosomiasis, Uncinariasis

Infidel Atheist, Caffre, Giaour, Heathen, Heretic, Kafir, Miscreant, Pagan, Paynim, Saracen

Infield Intown

Infiltrate(d), Infiltrator Encroach, Enter, Fifth columnist, Gatecrash, Instil, Intrude, Mole, Pervade, Trojan horse

Infinite, Infinity Cosmic, Endless, Eternal, N

Infinitive Split

Infirm Decrepit, Doddery, Feeble, Frail, Lame, Shaky, Sick

▷ **Infirm** *may indicate* 'co' around another word

Infirmary Hospital, Sick bay

Inflame(d), Inflammable, Inflammation Afire, Anger, → **AROUSE**, Bloodshot, Enamoured, Enchafe, Enfire, Enkindle, Fever, Fire, Founder, Gleet, Ignite, Impassion,

Incense, Infection, Ire, Kindle, Methane, Napalm, Naphtha, → **RED**, Stimulate, Swelling, Touchwood

INFLAMMATIONS

3 letters:
Sty

4 letters:
Acne
Gout
Noma
Stye

5 letters:
Croup
Felon

6 letters:
Ancome
Angina
Bunion
Canker
Coryza
Eczema
Garget
Iritis
Otitis
Quinsy
Thrush
Ulitis

7 letters:
Bubonic
Catarrh
Colitis
Ecthyma
Ignatis
Ileitis
Onychia
Pinkeye
Prurigo
Rosacea
Sunburn
Sycosis
Tylosis
Uveitis
Whitlow

8 letters:
Adenitis
Aortisis
Bursitis
Carditis

Colpitis
Cystisis
Fibrosis
Hyalitis
Mastitis
Metritis
Mycetoma
Myelitis
Myositis
Neuritis
Orchitis
Osteitis
Ovaritis
Phlegmon
Pleurisy
Pyelitis
Rachitis
Rectitis
Rhinitis
Thylosis
Uvulitis
Vulvitis
Windburn

9 letters:
Arteritis
Arthritis
Balanitis
Barotitis
Carbuncle
Cheilitis
Chilblain
Cloacitis
Dysentery
Enteritis
Fasciitis
Frostbite
Gastritis
Glossitis
Keratitis
Laminitis
Nephritis
Onychitis
Parotitis
Phlebitis
Phrenitis
Pneumonia
Proctitis
Pyorrhoea

Retinitis
Scleritis
Sinusitis
Splenitis
Strumitis
Synovitis
Typhlitis
Vaginitis
Vent gleet

10 letters:
Asbestosis
Bronchitis
Cellulitis
Cephalitis
Cerebritis
Cervicitis
Dermatitis
Duodenitis
Erysipelas
Fibrositis
Gingivitis
Hepatitis A
Hepatitis B
Hysteritis
Intertrigo
Laryngitis
Meningitis
Oophoritis
Ophthalmia
Papillitis
Paronychia
Phlegmasia
Phlogistic
Stomatitis
Tendinitis
Tendonitis
Thrombosis
Tracheitis
Tympanitis
Urethritis
Valvulitis
Vasculitis

11 letters:
Blepharitis
Farmer's lung
Mad staggers
Mastoiditis

Myocarditis
Parotiditis
Peritonitis
Pharyngitis
Pneumonitis
Prostatitis
Salpingitis
Sandy blight
Sclerotitis
Shin splints
Spondylitis
Staphylitis
Tennis elbow
Thoroughpin
Thyroiditis
Tonsillitis
Trenchmouth
Utriculitis
Woody-tongue

12 letters:
Appendicitis
Crystallitis
Encephalitis
Endocarditis
Endometritis
Folliculitis
Golfer's elbow
Lymphangitis
Lympodenitis
Mesenteritis
Ophthalmitis
Osteoporosis
Panarthritis
Pancreatitis
Pericarditis
Polymyositis
Polyneuritis
Sacroillitis
Swimmer's itch
Vestibulitis

13 letters:
Cholecystitis
Enterocolitis
Epicondylitis
Jogger's nipple
Labyrinthitis
Lymphadenitis

Osteomyelitis
Perihepatitis
Perinephritis
Periodontisis
Perityphlitis
Tenosynovitis
Tenovaginitis
Thrombophilia

14 letters:
Clergyman's knee
Conjunctivitis
Diverticulitis
Osteoarthritis
Pyelonephritis
Sleepy staggers
Tendovaginitis
Trichomoniasis

Vincent's angina

15 letters:
Gastroenteritis
Pachymeningitis
Panophthalmitis

16 letters:
Bronchopneumonia

Rhinopharyngitis
Thrombophlebitis

17 letters:
Encephalomyelitis
Meningocephalitis

19 letters:
St Louis encephalitis

Inflate(d), Inflation Aerate, Aggrandise, Bloat, Bombastic, Bracket-creep, Cost-push, Demand-pull, Dilate, Distend, Distent, Exaggerate, Grade, Increase, Pneumatic, Pompous, Pump, Raise, Remonetise, RPI, Spiral, Stagflation, Stagnation, Swell, Wage-push

Inflect(ion) Accidence, Cadence, Conjugation, Tone

Inflexible, Inflexibility Adamant(ine), Byzantine, Doctrinaire, Hard-ass, Hard-liner, Iron, Obstinate, Ossified, Ramrod, Relentless, Resolute, Rigid, Rigour, Set, Staid, Stubborn, Unbending

Inflict(ion) Deal, Force, Give, Impose, Subject, Trouble, Visit, Wreak

Inflorescence Bostryx, Catkin, Ci(n)cinnus, Drepanium, Glomerule, Panicle, Pleiochasium, Polychasium, Raceme, R(h)achis, Umbel, Verticillaster

Inflow Affluence, Influx

Influence(d), Influential Act, Affect, After, Amenable, Backstairs, Brainwash, Catalyse, Charm, Clamour, Clout, Colour, Credit, Determine, Dominant, Drag, Earwig, Eclectic, Embracery, Éminence grise, Factor, Force, Get at, Govern, Guide, Hold, Hypnotise, Impact, Impinge, Impress, Incubus, Inspire, Interfere, Lead, Leverage, Lobby, Macher, Mastery, Militate, Mogul, Mould, Nobble, Octopus, Operation, Outreach, Panjandrum, Power, Preponderant, Pressure, Prestige, → **PULL**, Push, Reach, Rust, Say, Securocrat, Seminal, Significant, Star, Star-blasting, Stimulus, Suggest, Svengali, Sway, Swing, Telegony, Thrall, Undue, Weigh with, Will, Work, Wull

Influenza Asian, Equine, Flu, Gastric, Grippe, Lurgi, Spanish, Wog, Yuppie

Influx Inbreak

Infold(ing) Invagination

Inform(ation), Informant, Informed, Informer Acquaint, Advise, Agitprop, Apprise, Au fait, Aware, Beagle, Bit, Blow, Burst, Callboard, Canary, Ceefax®, Clype, Contact, Cookie, Datum, Deep throat, Delate, Dicker, Dob(ber), Dobber-in, Dope, Education, Exposition, Facts, Fact sheet, Feedback, Fink, Fisgig, Fiz(z)gig, Gen, Genome, Good oil, Grapevine, Grass, Griff, Gunsel, Hep, Immersive, Input, Inside, Instruct, Izvesti(y)a, Light, Lowdown, Media, Metadata, Microdot, Moiser, Nark, Nepit, Nit, Nose, Notify, Occasion, Oracle®, Peach, Pem(m)ican, Pentito, Pimp, Poop, Prestel®, Prime, Printout, Promoter, Propaganda, Prospectus, Rat, Read-out, Report, Revelation, Rheme, Rumble, Shelf, Shop, Sidelight, Sing, Sneak, Snitch, Squeak, Squeal, Stag, Stoolie, Stool-pigeon, Supergrass, Sycophant, Teletext®, Tell, Throughput, Tidings, Tip-off, Up, Videotext®, Viewdata®, Whistle(-blower), Wire, Witting

Informal Casual, Intimate, Irregular, Outgoing, Rough and ready, Unofficial

Infra Under

Infra dig Ignominious

Infrequent Casual, Occasional, Rare, Scant, Seldom, Sparse

Infringe(ment) Contravene, Piracy, Violate

Infuriate Anger, Bemad, Bepester, Enrage, Exasperate, Incense, Madden, Pester, Provoke

Infuse(r), Infusion Brew, Distill, Gallise, Instil, Mash, Ooze, Saloop, Saturate, Steep, Tea, Tea-ball, Tea-egg, Tisane, Toddy, Uva-ursi

Ingenious, Ingenuity Acumen, Adept, Adroit, Art, Artificial, Clever, Cunning, Cute,

Inventive, Natty, Neat, Resourceful, Smart, Subtle, Trick(s)y, Wit

Ingenuous Artless, Candid, Green, Innocent, Naive, Open, Transparent

Ingest Eat, Endue, Incept, Indue, Swallow

Ingle Bardash, Hearth, Nook

In good condition Fit, Shipshape, Taut, Trim

Ingot Bar, Billet, Bullion, Lingot, Sycee, Wedge

Ingrain(ed) Deep-seated, Fix, Impregnate, Train

Ingrate Thankless, Viper

Ingratiate, Ingratiating Bootlick, Butter, Court, Flatter, Greasy, Oily, Pick-thank, Silken, Smarm(y)

Ingredient(s) Additive, Admixture, Asafoetida, Basis, Content, Element, Factor, Formula, Makings, Mincemeat, Staple

Ingrowing, Ingrowth Onychocryptosis, T(h)ylosis

Inhabit(ant), Inhabitants Affect, Children, Denizen, Dweller, Inholder, Inmate, Live, Native, Occupant, People, Populate, Population, Populous, Resident, Towny

Inhale(r), Inhalation Aspirate, Breath(e), Draw, Gas, Inspire, Intal, Sniff, Snort, Snuff, Take, Toot, Tout

Inharmonious Out, Patchy

Inherent Characteristic, Essential, Immanent, Inbred, Innate, Native

Inherit(ance), Inherited, Inheritor Accede, Birthright, Borough-English, Congenital, Esnecy, Feoffee, Gene, Genom, Heirloom, Heritage, Inborn, Legacy, Legitim, Meek, Mendelism, Particulate, Patrimony, Portion, Reversion, Succeed, Tichborne, Ultimogenitive

Inhibit(ing), Inhibition, Inhibitor ACE, Antihistamine, Anuria, Captopril, Chalone, Chalonic, Deter, Donepezil, Enalapril, Etanercept, Feedback, Finasteride, Forbid, Hang-up, Protease, Restrain, Retard, Retroactive, Stunt, Suppress, Tightass

Inhuman Barbarous, Brutal, Merciless

Inimical Adverse, Harmful, Hostile

Iniquity, Iniquitous Diabolical, Evil, Offence, Sin, Vice

Initial Acronym, First, Letter, Monogram, Paraph, Prelim(inary), Primary, Rubric

▷ **Initially** *may indicate* first letters

Initiate(d), Initiating, Initiation, Initiative Baptism, Begin, Bejesuit, Blood, Bora, Bring, Ceremony, Debut, Démarche, Enter, Enterprise, Epopt, Esoteric, Gumption, Induct, Instigate, Instruct, → **LAUNCH**, Neophyte, Nous, Onset, Proactive, Spark, → **START**

Inject(or), Injection Antiserum, Bang, Blast, Bolus, Booster, Collagen, Direct, Enema, Epidural, Epipen®, Fuel, Hypo, Immit, Implant, Innerve, Inoculation, Instil, Introduce, Jab, Jack up, Jag, Lidocaine, Mainline, Pop, Reheat, Serum, Shoot, Shoot up, Skin-pop, Solid, Spike, Syringe, Transfuse, Venipuncture

Injunction Command, Embargo, Freezing, Mandate, Mareva, Quia timet, Swear, Writ

Injure(d), Injury, Injurious, Injustice ABH, Abuse, Accloy, Aggrieve, Bale, Barotrauma, Bled, Bruise, Casualty, Concuss, Contrecoup, Contuse, Damage, De(a)re, Disservice, Forslack, Frostbite, Gash, GBH, Harm, → **HURT**, Ill-turn, Impair, Industrial, Iniquity, Lesion, Malign, Mar, Mayhem, Mistreat, Mutilate, NAI, Needlestick, Nobble, Nocuous, Non-accidental, Noxal, Nuisance, Occupational, Oppression, Outrage, Packet, Paire, Prejudice, Rifle, RSI, Scaith, Scald, Scath(e), Scotch, Shend, Sore, Sprain, Teen(e), Tene, Tort, Trauma, Umbrage, Whiplash, Wound, Wrong

▶ **Injury** *see* **AFTER INJURY**

Ink(y) Atramental, Black, Bray, China, Chinese, Copying, Cyan, Gall, Gold, Indian, Invisible, Magnetic, Marking, Monk, Printer's, Printing, Sepia, Stained, Sympathetic, Toner, Tusche

Inkling Clue, Glimpse, Hint, Idea

Inkpot Standish

Inlaid, Inlay(er) Boulle, Buhl, Clear, Compurgation, Crustae, Damascene, Emblemata,

Empaestic, Enamel, Enchase, Incrust, Intarsia, Intarsio, Koftgar(i), Marquetrie, Marquetry, Pietra-dura, Piqué, Set, Tarsia, Unsuspecting, Veneer

Inland Hinterland, Interior, Up

Inlet Arm, Bay, Bohai, Cook, Cove, Creek, Entry, Estuary, Fiord, Firth, Fjord, Fleet, Flow, Geo, Gio, Golden Horn, Gulf, Gusset, Hope, Infall, Ingate, Jervis Bay, Loch, McMurdo Sound, Moray Firth, Pamlico Sound, Pearl Harbor, Plymouth Sound, Pohai, Port Jackson, Port Phillip Bay, Puget Sound, Rio de la Plata, Sogne Fjord, Solway Firth, Strait, Sullom Voe, Table Bay, The Wash, Tor Bay, Zuyder Zee

▷ **Inlet** *may indicate* 'let' around another word

Inmate Intern(e), Lodger, Patient, Prisoner, Resident

Inn(s), Innkeeper Albergo, Alehouse, Auberge, Barnard's, Boniface, Caravanserai, Chancery, Change-house, Coaching, Court, Gray's, Halfway-house, Host(ry), Hostelry, Hotel, House, Imaret, In, Inner Temple, Jamaica, Khan, Kneipe, Ladin(ity), Law, Licensee, Lincoln's, Lodging, Luckie, Lucky, Maypole, Middle Temple, Motel, Padrone, Parador, Patron, Porterhouse, Posada, Posthouse, Pothouse, Publican, Roadhouse, Ryokan, Serai, Stabler, Tabard, Taphouse, Tavern(er), Victualler

▷ **Inn** *may refer to* the law

Innards Entrails, Giblets, Gizzard, Guts, Harigals, Harslet, Haslet, Omasa, Rein, Viscera

Innate Congenital, Essential, Inborn, Inbred, Inbuilt, Ingenerate, Instinctive, Natural, Original

Inner(most) Bencher, Esoteric, Internal, Intima, Intimate, Lining, Man, Marrow, Medulla, Private, Red, Woman

Innings Chance, Knock, Turn

▸ **Innkeeper** *see* **INN(S)**

Innocent Absolved, Angelic, Arcadian, Babe, Blameless, Canny, Chaste, Cherub, Childlike, Clean, Clear, Compurgation, Dewy-eyed, Doddypoll, Dodipoll, Dove, Encyclical, Green, Guileless, Idyllic, Ingenue, Lamb, Lily-white, Maiden, Naive, Opsimath, Pope, → **PURE**, Sackless, Seely, Simple, St, Unsuspecting, Unwitting, White

Innocuous Harmless, Innocent

Innovate, Innovative, Innovation, Innovator Alteration, Cutting edge, Departure, Ground-breaking, Modernise, Newell, Novelty, Novity, Pioneer, Promethean, Radical, Wrinkle

Inn-sign Bush

Innu Naskapi

Innumerable Countless, Infinite, Myriad, N

Inoculate, Inoculation Engraft, Immunise, Jab, Protect, Vaccine, Variolate

Inoffensive Anodyne, Mild, Neutral, Pleasant

Inoperative Futile, Nugatory, Silent, Void

Inopportune Disadvantageous, Inconvenient, Intempestive, Untimely

Inordinate Excessive, Irregular, Undue

▷ **Inordinately** *may indicate* an anagram

In place of For, Qua, Vice, With

Input Direct, OCR

Inquest Debriefing, Hearing, Inquiry, Investigation

Inquire, Inquiring, Inquiry Ask, Demand, Investigation, Maieutic, Nose, Organon, Probe, Public, Query, Question, See, Speer, Speir

Inquisition, Inquisitive, Inquisitor Curious, Interrogation, Meddlesome, Nosy, Prying, Rubberneck, Snooper, Spanish, Stickybeak, Torquemada

▷ **In revolt, In revolution** *may indicate* an anagram

Inroad(s) Breach, Encroachment, Honeycomb, Infall, Invasion

Insane, Insanity Absurd, Batty, Berserk, Crack-brained, Crazy, Dementia, Deranged, Headcase, Hebephrenia, Loco, Looniness, Lune, Mad, Manic, Mattoid, Mental, Nutso, Paranoia, Pellagra, Psycho, Schizo, Troppo, Yarra

Insatiable Greedy, Ravenous, Voracious

Insatiate child Killcrop
Inscribe(d), Inscription Chisel, Chronogram, Colophon, Dedicate, Emblazon, Endoss, Engrave, Enter, Epigraph, Epitaph, Exergue, Graffiti, Hic jacet, Hierograph, Lapidary, Legend, Lettering, Neum(e), Ogham, Posy, Writ
Inscrutable Deadpan, Esoteric, Mysterious, Sphinx
Insect(s) Entomic, Nonentity, Non-person, Stridulator, Wax

INSECTS

3 letters:
Ant
Bee
Bot
Bug
Fly
Ked
Lac
Nit
Wog

4 letters:
Flea
Gnat
Grig
Lice
Mite
Moth
Pium
Pupa
Tick
Wasp
Weta
Zimb

5 letters:
Aphis
Borer
Brise
Cimex
Culex
Emmet
Gogga
Imago
Louse
Midge
Nymph
Ox-bot
Roach
Scale
Stick
Zebub

6 letters:
Acarid

Botfly
Breese
Breeze
Capsid
Chigoe
Cicada
Cicala
Coccid
Day-fly
Earwig
Elater
Gadfly
Hopper
Hornet
Instar
Locust
Maggot
Mantid
Mantis
Mayfly
Medfly
Noctua
Phasma
Podura
Psocid
Psylla
Punkie
Redbug
Sawfly
Scarab
Slater
Spider
Tettix
Thrips
Vespid
Walker
Weevil

7 letters:
Aeschna
Antlion
Bee moth
Bristle
Bushfly
Buzzard

Carabid
Chalcid
Chigger
Corixid
Cornfly
Cricket
Culicid
Cutworm
Daphnid
Ergates
Firefly
Gallfly
Girdler
Gordius
Goutfly
Grayfly
Hexapod
Hive-bee
Humbuzz
Katydid
Ladybug
Ladycow
Ladyfly
Odonata
Oestrus
Oniscus
Phasmid
Pill-bug
Pyralis
Sandfly
Spectre
Spittle
Stylops
Tabanus
Termite

8 letters:
Alderfly
Blackfly
Bookworm
Cercopid
Circutio
Coccidae
Crane-fly
Dipteras

Dust mite
Firebrat
Fruit fly
Gall-wasp
Glossina
Goatmoth
Greenfly
Horntail
Horsefly
Isoptera
Itchmite
Lacewing
Ladybird
Lygus bug
Mealybug
Metabola
Milliped
Mosquito
Myriapod
Oak-egged
Onion-fly
Pauropod
Pillworm
Puss-moth
Reduviid
Ruby-tail
Scarabee
Silkworm
Snowflea
Stinkbug
Stonefly
Symphile
Waterbug
Wheelbug
Whitefly
Wireworm
Woodworm

9 letters:
Ametabola
Booklouse
Butterfly
Caddis-fly
Campodeid
Centipede

Cochineal
Cockroach
Damselfly
Dobsonfly
Dor-beetle
Dragonfly
Ephemerid
Ergataner
Hawstreak
Hemiptera
Homoptera
Leaf-miner
Mecoptera
Millepede
Millipede
Notonecta
Oil beetle
Rearhorse
Robber-fly
Songololo
Squash bug
Synoekete
Tabanidae
Thysanura
Tiger-moth
Woodlouse
Xylophage

10 letters:
Apterygota
Bark mantis
Bluebottle
Casebearer
Cecidomyia
Chironomid
Cockchafer
Coleoptera
Collembola
Fan-cricket
Fen-cricket
Froghopper
Greendrake
Harvestman
Leaf-cutter
Leafhopper
Mallophaga
Orthoptera
Phylloxera
Plant-louse
Plecoptera
Pond-skater
Psocoptera
Rhipiptera
Rice weevil
Silverfish

Spider-mite
Spittlebug
Springtail
Thysanuran
Treehopper
Waterstick
Web spinner

11 letters:
Bristletail
Collembolan
Dermapteran
Grasshopper
Greenbottle
Heteroptera
Hymenoptera
Mole-cricket
Neuropteran
Plectoptera
Rhopalocera
Tiger-beetle
Trichoptera
Vine-fretter

12 letters:
Bishop's mitre
Creepy-crawly

Dictyopteran
Groundhopper
Heteropteran
Neuropterous
Orthopterous
Rhipidoptera
San Jose scale
Strepsiptera
Thousand-legs
Thysanoptera
Water boatman

13 letters:
Cotton stainer
Daddy-long-legs
Jenny-longlegs
Leatherjacket
Pine-leaf scale
Praying mantis
Staphylinidae
Water scorpion

14 letters:
Strepsipterous

19 letters:
Cottony-cushion scale

Insecticide Aldrin, Allethrin, Aphicide, Carbaryl, Carbofuran, Chromene, Cube, DDT, Deet, Derris, Diazinon, Dieldrin, Endosulfan, Endrin, Flycatcher, Gammexane®, Ivermectin, Lindane®, Malathion®, Menazon, Methoxychlor, Miticide, Naphthalene, Parathion, Paris green, Piperazine, Pulicide, Pyrethrin, Pyrethrum, Repellent, Rotenone, Spray, Systemic, Timbo, Toxaphene, Zineb

Insectivore Agouta, Desman, Donaea, Drongo, Drosera, Hedgehog, Jacamar, Nepenthaceae, Otter-shrew, Sarracenia, Tanrec, Tenrec(idae), Tupaia, Venus flytrap, Zalambdodont

Insecure Infirm, → **LOOSE**, Needy, Precarious, Shaky, Unsafe, Unstable, Unsteady, Vulnerable

Insensible Iron-witted

Insensitive, Insensitivity Analgesia, Blunt, Callous, Crass, Dead, Indurate, Log, Numb, Obtuse, Pachyderm, Stolid, Tactless, Thick-skinned

Inseparable Indiscrete, One, United

Insert(ed), Insertion, Inset Anaptyxis, Cue, Empiecement, Enchase, Enter, Entry, Epenthesis, Foist, Fudge, Godet, Gore, Graft, Gusset, Immit, Imp, Implant, Inchase, Inject, Inlay, Input, Intercalar, Interject, Interpolate, Interpose, Intersperse, Introduce, Intromit, Intubate, Lexical, Mitre, Pin, Punctuate, Sandwich

Inside(r) Content, Core, Entrails, Gaol, Giblets, Heart, Indoors, Interior, Internal, Interne, Inward, Inwith, Mole, Tum, → **WITHIN**

Insidious Artful, Crafty, Sly

Insight Acumen, Anagoge, Aperçu, Enlightenment, Hunch, Inkling, Intuition, → **PERCEPTION**, Profundity, Tais(c)h

Insignia Armour, Arms, Badger, Charge, Chevron, Mark, Order, Regalia, Ribbon, Roundel, Tab

Insignificant (person) Bobkes, Bubkis, Bupkes, Bupkis, Chickenfeed, Dandiprat, Fico,

Fiddling, Flea-bite, Fractional, Gnat, Inconsiderable, Insect, Jerkwater, Mickey Mouse, Minimus, Miniscule, Minnow, Nebbich, Nobody, Nominal, Nondescript, Nonentity, Non-event, Non-person, One-eyed, Paltry, Peanuts, Petit, Petty, Piddling, Pipsqueak, Pissant, Quat, Rabbit, Scoot, Scout, Scrub, Shrimp, Slight, Small potatoes, Small-time, Squirt, Squit, Tenuous, Trifling, Trivial, Two-bit, Unimportant, Venial, Warb, Whiffet, Whippersnapper, Wind

Insincere, Insincerity Affected, Artificial, Barmecide, Cant, Double, Double-faced, Duplicity, Empty, Factitious, Faithless, False, Forced, Glib, Greenwash, Hollow, Janus-faced, Lip service, Mealy-mouthed, Meretricious, Mouth-made, Pseudo, Shallow, Synthetic, Tongue-in-cheek, Two-faced, Unnatural

Insinuate, Insinuating, Insinuation Allude, Foist, Hint, Imply, Innuendo, Intimate, Sleek, Slur, Sneck-draw

Insipid Banal, Blab, Bland, Drippy, Fade, Flat, Insulse, Jejune, Lash, Mawkish, Milk and water, Shilpit, Spiritless, Tame, Tasteless, Vapid, Weak, Wearish, Wersh

Insist(ent) Adamant, Assert, Demand, Dogmatic, Exact, Inhale, Pig's whisper, Press, Require, Stickler, → **STIPULATE**, Stoke, Stress, Swear, Threap, Threep, Urge

Insolence, Insolent Audacity, Bardy, Brassy, Cheek, Contumely, Cub, Effrontery, Gum, Hectoring, Hubris, Hybris, Impudence, Lip, Rude, Snash, Stroppy, Wanton

Insoluble Cerasin, Hard, Irresolvable, Mysterious

Insolvent Bankrupt, Broke, Destitute, Penniless

Insomnia Agrypnotic, Sleeplessness, Wakefulness, White night

Insouciant Carefree, Careless, Cavalier

Inspect(ion), Inspector Ale-conner, Alnage(r), Auditor, Case, Comb, Conner, Cook's tour, Darogha, Examine, Exarch, Go-over, Government, Investigator, Jerque, Keeker, Lestrade, Look over, Look-see, Maigret, Morse, Muster, Once-over, Peep, Perlustrate, Provector, Rag-fair, Recce, Review, Sanitary, School, Scrutinise, Searcher, Spot check, Supervisor, Survey, Test, Vet, Vidimus, Visitation

Inspire(d), Inspiration, Inspiring Actuate, Aerate, Afflatus, Aganippe, Animate, Brainstorm, Brainwave, Breath(e), Castalian, Draw, Duende, Elate, Exalt, Fire, Flash, Geist, Hearten, Hunch, Hwyl, Idea, Illuminate, Imbue, Impress, Impulse, Induce, Inflatus, Infuse, Inhale, Kindle, Motivate, Move, Muse, Pegasus, Plenary, Prompt, Prophetic, Satori, Sniff(le), Stimulus, Stoke, Taghairm, Theopnautic, Theopneust(y), Uplift, Vatic, Verbal

In spite of Malgrado, Malgré, Maugre, Maulgre

Instability Anomie, Anomy

Install(ation) Elect, Enchase, Enthrone, Inaugurate, Induction, Infrastructure, Insert, Invest, Put (in)

Instalment Call, Episode, Fascicle, Fascicule, Heft, Insert, Livraison, Never-never, Part, Serial, Tranche

Instance, Instant As, Case, Chronon, Example, Flash, Jiffy, Moment, Pig's whisper, Present, Say, Shake, Spur, Tick, Trice, Twinkling, Urgent

Instead (of) Deputy, For, Lieu, Locum, Vice

Instigate, Instigating Arouse, Foment, Impel, Incite, Proactive, Prompt, Spur

Instil(l) Implant, Inculcate, Infuse, Inspire, Teach, Transfuse

Instinct(ive) Automatic, Conation, Flair, Gut, Herd, Id, Impulse, Inbred, Innate, Intuition, Knee-jerk, Life, Nature, Nose, Pleasure principle, Prim(a)eval, Reflex, Second nature, Talent, Tendency, Visceral

Institute, Institution Academy, Activate, Asylum, Bank, Begin, Bring, Broadmoor, Charity, College, Collegiate, Create, Erect, Found(ation), Halls of ivy, I, Inaugurate, Mechanical, Mechanics, MORI, Organise, Orphanage, Poorhouse, Protectory, Raise, Redbrick, Retraict, Retrait(e), Retreat, Royal, Smithsonian, Start, Technical, University, Varsity, WI, Women's, Workhouse

Instruct(ed), Instruction, Instructor ADI, Advice, Algorithm, Apprenticeship, Brief, CAI, Catechism, Chautauquan, Clinic, Coach, Course, Didactic, Direct(ive), Document, Edify, Educate, Enjoin, Ground(ing), Guide, How-to, Inform, Lesson, Loop,

Macro, Maharishi, Manual, Master class, Mystagogue, Mystagogus, Notify, Order, Patch, Pedagogue, Precept, Prescription, Program, RE, Recipe, RI, Rubric, Script, Sensei, Statement, Swami, → **TEACH**, Train, Tutelage, Tutorial, Up

Instrument(al) Ablative, Act, Agent, Dash(board), Helpful, Kit, Mean(s), Measure, Mechanical, → **MUSICAL INSTRUMENT**, Negotiable, → **RESPONSIBLE**, → **TOOL**, Transit, Transposing, → **UTENSIL**, Weapon

INSTRUMENTS

3 letters:
Fan
Gad

4 letters:
Celt
Clam
Dupe
Fork
Mike
Prog
Rasp
Rote
Tram

5 letters:
Brake
Chuck
Curet
Fleam
Float
Gadge
Groma
Lance
Meter
Miser
Organ
Probe
Sonde
Tongs
Wecht

6 letters:
Bougie
Broach
Etalon
Grater
Megger®
Octant
Opener
Pallet
Peeler
Pestle
Reamer
Ripple

Scythe
Sector
Seeker
Speedo
Spline
Strobe
Trocar
Wimble
Xyster

7 letters:
Alidade
Cadrans
Caliper
Caltrop
Cautery
Compass
Curette
Dilator
Diopter
Flesher
Forceps
Grapple
Monitor
Organic
Pelican
Plogger
Plotter
Pointel
Pricker
Probang
Scalpel
Scanner
Scriber
Scummer
Sextant
Shuttle
Snuffer
Sounder
Spatula
Stapler
Strigil
Swatter
Swazzle
Swingle

Swozzle
Syringe
Trammel
Trimmer
Vocoder
Walkman

8 letters:
Barnacle
Boothook
Burdizzo
Calutron
Diagraph
Dividers
Ecraseur
Enlarger
Geophone
Iriscope
Luxmeter
Myograph
Nailfile
Odometer
Ohmmeter
Otoscope
Oximeter
Picklock
Quadrant
Repeater
Rheostat
Scalprum
Scissors
Snuffler
Speculum
Stiletto
Strickle
Trephine
Tweezers
Viameter
Vuvuzela
Waywiser

9 letters:
Algometer
Alphonsin
Arcograph

Areometer
Astrolabe
Atmometer
Auriscope
Auxometer
Barometer
Baryscope
Bolometer
Cauterant
Coelostat
Crows-bill
Cryoprobe
Cryoscope
Cymograph
Depressor
Dermatome
Dip-circle
Dosemeter
Dosimeter
Dropsonde
Eidograph
Endoscope
Ergograph
Ergometer
Eriometer
Extractor
Fadometer
Fetoscope
Flowmeter
Fluxmeter
Focimeter
Graduator
Haemostat
Heliostat
Hodometer
Hourglass
Konimeter
Kymograph
Lysimeter
Machmeter
Manometer
Marigraph
Megaphone
Megascope
Metronome

Microlith
Microtome
Milometer
Monochord
Nocturnal
Nut-wrench
Oedometer
Oncometer
Ondograph
Optometer
Optophone
Osmometer
Osteotome
Pedometer
Periscope
Pintadera
Polygraph
Potometer
Pyrometer
Pyroscope
Raspatory
Repositor
Retractor
Rheometer
Salometer
Scalprium
Set square
Skiascope
Somascope
Sonograph
Tasimeter
Telemeter
Telescope
Tellurian
Tellurion
Tenaculum
Tonometer
Toothpick
Tripmeter
Try square
Voltmeter
Volumeter
Wattmeter
Wavemeter
Xylometer
Zymometer

10 letters:
Acidimeter
Almacantar
Almucantar
Altazimuth
Anemograph
Anemometer

Araeometer
Buttonhook
Ceilometer
Clinometer
Colposcope
Comparator
Cross-staff
Cryophorus
Cultivator
Cyanometer
Cyclograph
Cystoscope
Declinator
Densimeter
Dictograph
Drosometer
Eudiometer
Fibrescope
Gaussmeter
Geodimeter®
Goniometer
Gonioscope
Gradienter
Gravimeter
Heliograph
Heliometer
Hydrometer
Hydroscope
Hygrograph
Hygrometer
Hygroscope
Hypsometer
Iconometer
Integrator
Lactometer
Lactoscope
Light organ
Lithoclast
Micrograph
Micrometer
Microphone
Microscope
Mileometer
Milliprobe
Multimeter
Nephograph
Nephoscope
Nitrometer
Opisometer
Orthoscope
Oscillator
Osteoclast
Pachymeter
Pantograph

Photometer
Piezometer
Pilliwinks
Plane table
Planigraph
Planimeter
Protractor
Pulsimeter
Pulsometer
Pycnometer
Radiometer
Radiophone
Radioscope
Radiosonde
Rhinoscope
Scotometer
Siderostat
Spirograph®
Spirometer
Tachograph
Tachometer
Telewriter
Tensimeter
Theodolite
Thermopile
Tintometer
Transputer
Trommeter
Tuning fork
Urinometer
Variometer
Viscometer
Voltameter

11 letters:
Actinometer
Auxanometer
Cardiograph
Chronograph
Chronometer
Chronoscope
Coercimeter
Colonoscope
Colorimeter
Coronagraph
Craniometer
Crescograph
Dendrometer
Dilatometer
Fluorometer
Fluoroscope
Fugitometer
Gastroscope
Gradiometer

Helicograph
Intoximeter
Jacob's staff
Keratometer
Laparoscope
Nephroscope
Odontograph
Opeidoscope
Pinnywinkle
Pitchometer
Planetarium
Plastometer
Plessimeter
Polarimeter
Polariscope
Proctoscope
Psychograph
Pyranometer
Pyrgeometer
Quantometer
Ragman Rolls
Rangefinder
Retinoscope
Rocketsonde
Salinometer
Sclerometer
Screwdriver
Seismograph
Seismometer
Seismoscope
Solarimeter
Spherometer
Stactometer
Stadiometer
Stauroscope
Stereometer
Stereoscope
Stethoscope
Stroboscope
Synthesizer
Tacheometer
Tensiometer
Thermograph
Thermometer
Thermoscope
Torsiograph
Trochometer
Vaporimeter
Vectorscope
Velocimeter
Voltammeter
Volumometer

12 letters:
Aethrioscope
Astrocompass
Averruncator
Bronchoscope
Camera lucide
Cathetometer
Cephalometer
Declinometer
Densitometer
Electrometer
Electroscope
Ellipsograph
Extensimeter
Extensometer
Galactometer
Galvanometer
Galvanoscope
Harmonograph
Harmonometer
Inclinometer
Isoteniscope
Kaleidoscope
Katharometer
Keraunograph
Laryngoscope
Magnetograph

Meteorograph
Methanometer
Monkey wrench
Myringoscope
Nephelometer
Oscilloscope
Penetrometer
Pinniewinkle
Psychrometer
Resectoscope
Respirometer
Scarificator
Scintillator
Sensitometer
Snooperscope
Spectrometer
Spectroscope
Sphygmograph
Sphygmometer
Sphygmophone
Sphygmoscope
Synchroscope
Tellurometer
Thoracoscope
Turbidimeter
Urethroscope
Zenith-sector

13 letters:
Accelerometer
Alcoholometer
Diaphanometer
Dipleidoscope
Electrophorus
Inclinatorium
Opthalmometer
Perpendicular
Pharyngoscope
Phonendoscope
Pneumatograph
Pneumatometer
Potentiometer
Pyrheliometer
Reflectometer
Refractometer
Saccharometer
Scatterometer
Sigmoidoscope
Stalagmometer
Tachistoscope
Weatherometer

14 letters:
Circumferentor
Diffractometer

Dividing engine
Interferometer
Kinetheodolite
Oesophagoscope
Ophthalmometer
Ophthalmoscope
Phosphoroscope
Pyrophotometer
Scintillascope
Scintilloscope
Spinthariscope
Synchronoscope

15 letters:
Electromyograph
Phenakestoscope
Radiogoniometer
Telestereoscope

16 letters:
Photopolarimeter
Sphygmomanometer
Telespectroscope

17 letters:
Spectrophotometer
Transit theodolite

Insubordinate Contumacious, Faction, Mutinous, Rebel, Refractory

Insubstantial Airy, Brief, Flimsy, Frothy, Illusory, Jackstraw, Scotch mist, Slender, Slight, Syllabub, Thin, Wispy, Ye(a)sty

Insufferable Egregious

Insufficient Exiguous, Inadequate, Poor, Scant, Shortfall

Insular Isolated, Little Englander, Moated, Narrow, Sectarian, Xenophobe

Insulate, Insulation, Insulator Biotite, Bushing, Corkboard, Dielectric, Electret, Enwind, Fibrefill, Grommet, Haybox, Inwind, Lagging, Mica, Non-conductor, Padding, Pugging, Sleeving, Standoff, Tog

Insult(ing) Abuse, Affront, Aspersion, Barb, Becall, Charientism, Contumely, Cut, Derogatory, Dyslogistic, Effrontery, Embarrass, Facer, Fig, Injurious, Lese-majesty, Mud, Mud-pie, Offend, Opprobrious, Rip on, Scurrilous, Skit, Slagging, Sledge, Slight, Slur, Snub, Trample, Trauma, Uncomplimentary, Verbal, Wazzock, Yenta, Yente

Insure(r), Insurance Abandonee, Accident, Comprehensive, Cover, Death futures, Endowment, Fidelity, Fire, Group, Guarantee, Hedge, Indemnity, Knock-for-knock, Life, Lloyds, Marine, Medibank, Medicaid, Medicare, Mutual, National, Participating, Pluvius, Policy, Public liability, Reversion, Safety net, Security, Social, Term, Third party, Tontine, Travel, Underwrite, Whole-life

Insurgent, Insurrection Cade, Jacquerie, Mutiny, Outbreak, Pandy, Rebel, Revolt, Sedition, Terrorist, Uprising, Whisky

▷ **Insurgent** *may indicate* 'reversed'

Intact Complete, Entire, Inviolate, Unused, Whole

Intaglio, Intagliate Diaglyph, Incavo

Intake Absorption, Entry, Fuel

Integer, Integral Component, Definite, Entire, Improper, Inbuilt, Indefinite, Needful, Number, Organic, Unital, Unitary

Integrate(d), Integration Amalgamate, Assimilate, Combine, Coordinate, Fuse, Harmonious, Holistic, Large-scale, Mainstream, Merge, Postural, Synergism, Tightknit, Vertical

Integrity Honesty, Principle, Probity, Rectitude, Strength, Uprightness, Whole, Worth

Integument Coat, Primine, Secundine, Sheath, Skin, Velum

Intellect, Intellectual(s) Academic, Aptitude, Belligerati, Brain, Cerebral, Chattering class, Cultural, Dianoetic, Egghead, Eggmass, Far-out, Genius, Grey matter, Highbrow, Intelligent, Intelligentsia, -ist, Learned, Literati, Luminary, Mastermind, Mental(ity), Mind, Noesis, Noetic, Noology, Nous, Pointy-headed, Profound, Reason, Sublime, Titan

Intelligence, Intelligent Advice, Artificial, Boss, Brainiac, Brains, Bright, CIA, Discerning, Dope, Eggmass, Emotional, Esprit, G, Grey matter, GRU, Guile, Humint, Info, Ingenious, IQ, Knowledgeable, Machiavellian, Machine, MI, Mossad, Mother wit, News, Pate, Perspicacity, Pointy-headed, Rational, Sconce, Sense, Sharp(-witted), Shrewd, Smart, Spetsnaz, Spetznaz, Tidings, Wit

Intelligible Exoteric

Intemperance Acrasia, Crapulent, Excess, Gluttony, Immoderation

Intend(ed), Intending Allot, Betrothed, Contemplate, Deliberate, Design, Destine, Ettle, Fiancé(e), Going, → **MEAN**, Meditate, Planned, Propose, Purpose, Think

Intense, Intensify, Intensity Acute, Aggravate, Ardent, Compound, Crash, Crescendo, Deep, Depth, Earnest, Earthquake, Emotional, Enhance, Escalate, Estro, Excess, Extreme, Fervent, Hot up, Keen, Luminous, Might, Profound, Radiant, Redouble, Saturation, Sharpen, Strong, Towering, Vehement, Vivid, Warmth

Intent, Intention(al) À dessein, Aim, Animus, Deliberate, Design, Dole, Earmark, Earnest, Ettle, Hellbent, Manifesto, Mens rea, Mind, Paradoxical, Prepense, Purpose, Rapt, Resolute, Set, Special, Studious, Systematic, Thought, Tire, Wilful, Witting, Yrapt

Inter Amid, Bury, Entomb

Interaction Chemistry, Enantiodromia, Solvation, Synergy

Interbreed(ing) Cross, Miscegenation

Intercalation Embolism

Intercede, Intercession Mediate, Negotiate, Plead, Prayer

Intercept Absciss(a), Abscisse, Check, Hack, Meet, Tackle, Waylay

Interchange(d) Altercation, Alternate, Clover-leaf, Crossing, Equivalent, Junction, Mutual, Permute, Reciprocate, Substitute, Transpose

Intercom Entryphone®

Intercourse Arse, Ball, Bang, Bed, Blow job, Boff, Bone, Bonk, Buggery, Bukkake, Bump, Coition, Coitus, Commerce, Commixture, Congress, Connection, Consummation, Converse, Copulation, Cottaging, Coupling, Cover, Cunnilingus, Deflowering, Diddling, Enjoy, Fluff, Fornication, Gam, Gamahuche, Gamaruche, Gangbang, Greens, Hochmagandy, Houghmagandie, How's your father, Hump, Incest, Jass, Jazz, Jiggy, Jiggy-jiggy, Jig(-a)-jig, Jump, Knee-trembler, Knock, Know(ledge), Koap, Laying, Leg-over, Lie with, Make, Marriage bed, Mell, Mix, Nail, Naughty, Necrophilia, Nookie, Nooky, Nooner, Oats, One-night-stand, On the job, Plough, Poke, Poontang, Pussy, Quickie, Ride, Rim, Roger, Roll, Root, Rump, Rumpy(-pumpy), Satyriasis, Score, Screw, Sexual, Shaft, Shag, Shtup, Sixty-nine, Sociality, Sodomy, Soixante-neuf, Stuff, Swive, Tail, Teledildonics, The other, Tie, Trade, Tribadism, Trock, Troilism, Truck, Tumble, Venereal, Whoredom

Interdict Ban, Forbid, Prohibit, Taboo

Interest(ed), Interesting Amusive, APR, Attention, Behalf, Benefit, Care, Clou, Compound, Concern, Contango, Controlling, Coupon, Dividend, Double-bubble, Ear-grabbing, Engage, Engross, Enthusiasm, Fad, Fascinate, Fee-simple, Fee-tail, Grab, Hot, Human, Import, Income, Insurable, Int(o), Intrigue, Juicy, Landed, Life, Line, Negative, Part, Partisan, Percentage, Public, Readable, Rente, Respect, Revenue, Reversion, Riba, Riding, Scene, Sepid, Share, Side, Sideline, Simple, Spice, Stake, Tasty, Tickle, Topical, Usage, Usance, Use, Usure, Usury, Vested, Vig(orish), Warm

Interface Centronics, Spigot
Interfere(r), Interference Atmospherics, Busybody, Clutter, Disrupt, Disturb, Hamper, Hinder, Hiss, Intrude, Mar, → **MEDDLE**, Molest, Noise, Nose, Officious, Pry, Radio, Shash, Shot noise, Static, Tamper, Teratogen
Interferometer Etalon
Intergrowth Perthite
Interim Break, Meantime, Meanwhile, Temporary
Interior Backblocks, Cyclorama, Domestic, Innards, Innate, Inner, Inside, Outback, Plain, Up-country, Vitals
Interject(ion) Ahem, Begorra(h), Chime-in, Doh, Duh, Gertcha, Haith, Hoo-oo, Interpolate, Lackaday, Lumme, Nation, Sese(y), Sessa, 'Sheart, 'Slid, Tarnation, Tush
Interlace Mingle, Pleach, Weave, Wreathe
Interlock Dovetail, Engage, Knit, Mesh, Tangle
Interlocutor Elihu, MC, Questioner
Interloper Cowan, Gate-crasher, Intruder, Trespasser
Interlude Antimask, Antimasque, Divertimento, Entr'acte, Interruption, Kyogen, Lunch-hour, Meantime, Pause, Verset
Intermediary, Intermediate, Intermediatory Agent, Bardo, Between, Bytownite, Comprador(e), Contact man, Go-between, In-between, Instar, Mean, Medial, Mesne, Mezzanine, Middleman, Middle-of-the-road, Negotiant, Thirdsman, Transitional
Interminable Endless, Infinite, Unending
Intermission Apyrexia, Break, Interval, Pause, Recess
Intermittent Broken, Fitful, Off-on, Periodic, Random, Spasmic, Spasmodic, Sporadic
Intermix, Intermingle Lace, Melting pot
Intern(e) Confine, Doctor, Impound, Restrict, Trainee
Internal Domestic, Inner, Internecine, Inward, Within
International Cap, Cosmopolitan, Fourth, Lion, Second, Test, Trotskyist, UN, Universal
Internet Dotco(m), e(-), Infobahn, URL, Web, WWW
Interpolate(r), Interpolation Diaskeuast, Insert, Intercalate, Interrupt, Spatchcock, Tmesis
Interpose Butt in, Horn in, Interject, Interlay, Interprone, Intervene, Spatchcock, Stickle
Interpret(er) Aread, Ar(r)e(e)de, Conster, Construe, Decipher, Decode, Dobhash, Dragoman, Exegete, Explain, Exponent, Expositor, Expound, Glossator, Hermeneutist, Hierophant, Jehovist, Latiner, Lingster, Linguistic, Linkster, Medium, Moonshee, Moonshi, Moralise, Munshi, Oneirocritic, Oneiroscopist, Origenist, Polyglot, Prophet, Rabbi, Rationalise, Read, Rede, Reed(e), Render, Represent, Spokesman, Subjectivity, Textualist, → **TRANSLATE**, Truchman, Ulema
Interpretation Anagoge, Anagogy, Analysis, Cabbala(h), Construction, Copenhagen, Dittology, Eisegesis, Euhemerism, Exegesis, Exegete, Gematria, Gloss(ary), Gospel, Halacha(h), Halakah, Hermeneutics, Kabbala(h), Midrash, Oneirocriticism, Portray, Reading, Rede, Rendition, Spin, Targum, Translation, Tropology, Zohar
Interrogate, Interrogation Catechism, Corkscrew, Cross-question, Debrief(ing), Enquire, Examine, Grill, Inquisitor, Maieutic, Pump, → **QUESTION**, Quiz
Interrupt(ion), Interrupter Ahem, Aposiopesis, Blip, Break, Butt, Chequer, Chip in, Cut in, Disturb, Entr'acte, Heckle, Hiatus, Intercept, Interfere, Interject, Interlard, Interpellate, Interpolate, Interpose, Interregnum, Intrusion, Overtalk, Pause, Portage, Punctuate, Rheotome, Stop, Suspend, Time-out, Tmesis
Intersect(ion), Intersecting Carfax, Carfox, Carrefour, Chiasm(a), Clover-leaf, Compital, Cross, Crunode, Cut, Decussate, Divide, Groin, Metacentre, Node, Orthocentre, Quadrivium, Trace
Intersperse Dot, Interlard, Interpose, Scatter, Sprinkle
Interstice Areole, Interlude, Pore, Space
Intertwine Braid, Impleach, Knit, Lace, Plait, Splice, Twist, Wreathe, Writhe
Interval Between, Break, Breather, Class, Closed, Comma, Confidence, Contour,

Diapente, Diastaltic, Diatesseron, Diesis, Distance, Ditone, Duodecimo, Entr'acte, Fifth, Gap, Half-time, Harmonic, Hiatus, Hourly, Imperfect, Interim, Interlude, Interregnum, Interruption, Interspace, Interstice, Leap, Limma, Lucid, Lull, Lunitidal, Meantime, Meantone, Meanwhile, Melodic, Microtone, Minor third, Ninth, Octave, Open, Ottava, Parenthesis, Perfect, Pycnon, QT, Respite, Rest, Schisma, Semitone, Seventh, Sixth, Space, Span, Spell, Third, Thirteenth, Time lag, Tritone, Twelfth, Unison, Wait

Intervene, Intervening, Intervention Agency, Arbitrate, Expromission, Hypothetical, Interfere, Interjacent, Interrupt, Intromit, Mediate, Mesne, Step in, Theurgy, Up

Interview Audience, Audition, Beeper, Conference, Debriefing, Doorstep, Examine, Hearing, Oral, Press conference, See, Vox pop

Interweave, Interwoven, Interwove Complect, Entwine, Interlace, Monogram, Pirnit, Plait, Plash, Pleach, Raddle, Splice, Wreathed

Intestate Heirless, Unwilling

Intestinal, Intestine(s) Bowel, Chit(ter)lings, Derma, Duodenum, Enteric, Entrails, Guts, Harigals, Innards, Jejunum, Kishke, Large, Mesenteron, Omenta, Rectum, Small, Splanchnic, Thairm, Tripes, Viscera

In the club Gravid, Pregnant, Up the spout

Intimacy, Intimate(ly) Achates, À deux, Boon, Bosom, Close, Communion, Confidante, Connote, Familiar, Far ben, Friend, Heart-to-heart, Hint, Inmost, Innuendo, Intrigue, Nearness, Opine, Pack, Private, Signal, Special, Thick, Throng, Warm, Well

Intimation Clue, Hint, Implication, Inkling, Innuendo, Si quis

Intimidate, Intimidating Awe, Browbeat, Bulldoze, Bully, Cow, Daunt, Dragon, Hector, Menace, Niramiai, Overawe, Psych, Scare, Threaten, Tyrannise, Unnerve

Into At, Intil, Within

Intolerant, Intolerable Allergic, Bigotry, Egregious, Excessive, Illiberal, Impatient, Impossible, Insupportable, Ombrophobe, Redneck, Self-righteous

Intone, Intonation Cadence, Just, Twang

In touch Au fait

Intoxicate(d), Intoxicant, Intoxicating, Intoxication Alcoholic, Areca-nut, Benj, Bhang, Coca, Corn, Crink, Cup, Disguise, Fuddle, Ganja, Half-cut, Heady, → **HIGH**, Hocus, Hou high, Inebriate, Jag, Krunk, La-la land, Merry, Mescal, Methystic, Narcotise, Nitrogen narcosis, Peyote, Pixil(l)ated, Potent, Rapture of the deep, Rumbullion, Shroom, Slewed, Soma, Sozzle, Spirituous, Swacked, Temulent, The narks, Whiskeyfied, Whiskified, Zonked

Intractable Disobedient, Kittle, Mulish, Obdurate, Perverse, Surly, Unruly, Wilful

Intransigent Adamant, Inflexible, Rigid, Uncompromising

Intransitive Neuter, Objectless

Intravenous IV

Intrepid(ity) Aweless, Bold, Bottle, Brave, Dauntless, Doughty, Fearless, Firm, Gallant, → **RESOLUTE**, Stout, Unafraid, Undaunted, Valiant

Intricate Complex, Crinkum-crankum, Daedal(ian), Daedale, Dedal, Gordian, Intrince, Involute, Knotty, Parquetry, Pernickety, Sinuous, Tirlie-wirlie, Tricky, Vitruvian

Intrigue(r), Intriguing Affaire, Artifice, Brigue, Cabal, Camarilla, Cloak and dagger, Collogue, Conspiracy, Fascinate, Hotbed, Ignatian, Interest, Jesuit, Jobbery, Liaison, Machinate, Plot, Politic, Rat, → **SCHEME**, Stairwork, Strategy, Traffic, Trinketer, Web

Intrinsic(ally) Basically, Essential, Genuine, Inherent, Innate, Inner, Per se

▷ **Intrinsically** *may indicate* something within a word

Introduce(r), Introduction, Introductory Acquaint, Alap, Anacrusis, Code name, Curtain-raiser, Debut, Emcee, Enseam, Entrée, Exordial, Foreword, Immit, Import, Induct, Initiate, Inject, Insert, Instil(l), Institutes, Intercalate, Interpolate, Intrada, Introit, Isagogic, Lead-in, Lead up, Opening, Phase in, Plant, Preamble, Preface, Preliminary, Prelude, Prelusory, Preparatory, Present, Presentment, Proem, Prolegomena, Prolegomenon, Prolog, Prologue, Prooemium, Proponent, Referral, Standfirst, Start, Usher

▷ **Introduction** *may indicate* a first letter
Intromission Vicious
Introspective Indrawn, Musing, Reflex, Ruminant, Thoughtful
▷ **In trouble** *may indicate* an anagram
Introvert(ed) Cerebrotonic, Ingrow, In-toed, Invaginate, Reserved, Shy, Withdrawn
Intrude(r), Intrusion, Intrusive Abate, Aggress, Annoy, Bother, Burglar, Derby dog, Disturb, → **ENCROACH**, Gatecrash, Hacker, Inroad, Interloper, Invade, Lopolith, Meddle, Nosey, Personal, Porlocking, Presume, Raid, Sorn, Trespass
In truth En verite
Intuition, Intuitive Belief, ESP, Hunch, Insight, Instinct, Inwit, Noumenon, Premonition, Presentiment, Seat-of-the-pants, Telepathy, Theosophy, Visceral
Inturn(ing) Trichiasis
▷ **In two words** *may indicate* a word to be split
Inuit Caribou, Eskimo, Inuk, Inupiat, Yupik
Inundate, Inundation Engulf, Flood, Overflow, Overwhelm, Submerge, Swamp
Inure Acclimatise, Accustom, Harden, Season, Steel
Invade(r), Invasion Angle, Attack, Attila, Dane, Descent, Encroach, Goth, Hacker, Hengist, Horsa, Hun, Incursion, Infest, Inroad, Intruder, Irrupt, Jute, Lombard, Martian, Norman, Norsemen, Occupation, Ostrogoth, Overlord, Overrun, Permeate, Raid, Trespass, Vandal, Viking, Visigoth
In vain No go
Invalid(ate), Invalidation Bad, Bogus, Bunbury, Cancel, Chronic, Clinic, Defunct, Diriment, Erroneous, Expired, False, Inauthentic, Inform, Inoperative, Irritate, Lapsed, Nugatory, Null, Nullify, Overturn, Quash, Refute, Shut-in, Terminate, Valetudinarian, Vitiate, Void
Invaluable Essential, Excellent, Precious, Useful
Invariable, Invariably Always, Constant, Eternal, Habitual, Perpetual, Steady, Uniform
Invective Abuse, Billingsgate, Diatribe, Philippic, Reproach, Ribaldry, Tirade
Inveigh Declaim, Denounce, Marprelate, Protest, Rail
Inveigle Charm, Coax, Entice, Persuade, Subtrude
Invent(ion), Inventive Adroit, Babe, Baby, Brainchild, Chimera, Coin, Concept, Contrive, Cook up, → **CREATE**, Creed, Daedal, Design, Device, Dream up, Embroider, Excogitate, Fabricate, Fain, Fantasia, Feign, Fiction, Figment, Imaginary, Improvise, Independent, Ingenuity, Make up, Mint, Myth, Originate, Patent, Plateau, Pretence, Resourceful, Synectics, Whittle, Wit
Inventor Artificer, Author, Coiner, Creator, Engineer, Idea-hamster, Mint-master, Patentee

INVENTORS

3 letters:	Watt	*6 letters:*	Sutton
Kay		Bramah	Wright
Sax	*5 letters:*	Dunlop	
	Baird	Duryea	*7 letters:*
4 letters:	Jubal	Edison	Babbage
Bell	Maxim	Geiger	Celsius
Biro	Mills	Hansom	Daimler
Boys	Minié	McAdam	Eastman
Brix	Morse	Nernst	Galileo
Hero	Nobel	Pearse	Hartley
Moon	Tesla	Savery	Marconi
Otis		Singer	Pullman
Tull		Solvay	Schmidt

Siemens
Unaipon
Whitney

Newcomen
Sinclair
Zworykin

10 letters:
Archimedes
Cartwright
Hargreaves
Lilienthal
Torricelli
Trevithick
Wheatstone

11 letters:
Montgolfier

12 letters:
Frankenstein
Prince Rupert

8 letters:
Crompton
Daedalus
Goodyear
Mercator

9 letters:
Arkwright
Cockerell
Macintosh

Inventory Account, Index, Itemise, List, Perpetual, Personality, Register, Steelbow, Stock, Terrier

Inverse, Inversion, Invert(ed) Anastrophe, Antimetabole, Antimetathesis, Arch, Back to front, Capsize, Chiasmus, Entropion, Entropium, First, Homosexuality, Lid, Opposite, Overset, Reciprocal, Resupinate, Retrograde, Reverse, Second, Tête-bêche, Turn, Upset, Upside down

Invertebrate Acanthocephalan, Annelida, Anthozoan, Arrowworm, Arthropod, Brachiopod, Chaetognath, Cnidarian, Coelenterate, Crinoid, Ctenophore, Decapod, Echinoderm, Echinoid, Entoprocta, Euripterid, Feather star, Gast(e)ropod, Globigerina, Holothurian, Hydrozoan, Lobopod, Mollusc, Nacre, Onychophoran, Parazoan, Pauropod, Peritrich, Platyhelminth, Polyp, Poriferan, Protostome, Rotifer, Roundworm, Scyphozoan, Sea-cucumber, Sea-lily, → **SHELLFISH**, Slug, Spineless, Sponge, Spoonworm, Starfish, Tardigrade, Trepang, Trochelminth, Trochophore, Unio, Water bear, Worm, Zoophyte

Invest(or), Investment Agamemnon, Ambient, Angel, Bate, Beleaguer, Besiege, Bet, Blockade, Blue-chip, Bond, Bottom-fisher, Capitalist, Clothe, Collins Street farmer, Contrarian, Dignify, Dub, Embark, Empanoply, Enclothe, Endow, Enrobe, Ethical, Financier, Flutter, Gilt, Girt, Gross, Holding, Infeft, Install, Inward, On, Pannicle, Panniculus, Parlay, Place, Portfolio, Put, Retiracy, Ring, Robe, Saver, Share, Siege, Sink, Smart money, Spec, Speculation, Stag, Stake, Stock, Surround, Tessa, Tie up, Trochophore, Trojan War, Trust, Trustee, Venture, Zaitech

▷ **Invest** *may indicate* one word surrounding another

Investigate, Investigator, Investigation Analyse, Audit, Canvass, Case, Chart, CID, Delve, DI, Enquire, Examine, Explore, Fact-find, Fed, Ferret, Fieldwork, Going over, Go into, Gumshoe, Hunt, Inquest, Inquirendo, Inquiry, Inquisition, McCarthyism, Nose, Organon, Organum, Probe, Prodnose, Pry, Quester, Rapporteur, Research, Scan, Scout, Screen, Scrutinise, Search, Sleuth, Snoop, Study, Suss, Tec, Test, T-man, Track, Try, Zetetic

Investiture Award, Inauguration

Inveterate Chronic, Double-dyed, Dyed-in-the-wool, Engrained, Habitual, Hardened

Invidious Harmful, Hostile, Malign

Invigilator Proctor

Invigorate, Invigorating, Invigoration Analeptic, Animate, Brace, Brisk, Cheer, Crispy, Elixir, Energise, Enliven, Fortify, Insinew, Pep, Refresh, Renew, Stimulate, Tonic, Vital

Invincible Almighty, Brave, Stalwart, Valiant

Inviolatable, Inviolate, Inviolable Intemerate, Sacred, Sacrosanct

Invisible Blind, Hidden, Imageless, Infra-red, Secret, Tusche, Unseen

Invite, Invitation, Inviting Ask, Attract, Bid, Call, Card, Overture, → **REQUEST**, Solicit, Stiffie, Summons, Tempt, Toothsome, Woo

Invocation, Invoke Appeal, Begorra, Call, Conjure, Curse, Entreat, Epiclesis, Solicit, White rabbits

Invoice Account, Bill, Docket, Itemise, Manifest, Pro forma

Involuntary Automatic, Instinctive, Unwitting

Involve(d), Involvement Active, Close knit, Commitment, Complicate, Complicit, Concern, Deep, Embroil, Engage, Enlace, Entail, Entangle, Envelop, Imbroglio, Immerse, → **IMPLICATE**, Include, Intricate, Knee-deep, Meet, Necessitate, Participate, Tangle, Tortuous, Tricksy

▷ **Involved** *may indicate* an anagram

Inward(s) Afferent, Centripuntal, Homefelt, Introrse, Mental, Private, Varus, Within

Iodine I, Kelp, Thyroxin(e)

Iolanthe Peri

Ion Ammonium, Anion, Carbanion, Carborium, Hydrogen, Hydronium, Hydroxyl, Isomer, Onium, Zwitterion

Ionian Iastic, Te(i)an

Iota Atom, Jot, Subscript, Whit

IOU Cedula, Market, PN, Shinplaster, Vowels

IOW Vectis

IRA Provisional, Provo

Iran(ian) Babist, Kurd, Mede, Osset, Pahlavi, Parsee, Pehlevi, Persic, Tadzhik, Ta(d)jik

Irascible Choleric, Crusty, Fiery, Grouchy, Peevish, Quick-tempered, Snappy, Tetchy, Toustie

Irate Angry, Cross, Infuriated, Wrathful

Ire Anger, Bait, Cholera, Fury, Rage, Wrath

Ireland Blarney-land, Composer, Deirdre, Gaeltacht, Hibernia, .ie, Innisfail, Irena, IRL, Iverna, Ould Sod, ROI, Twenty-six counties

Irenic Peaceful

Iridescence, Iridescent Chatoyant, Flambé, Opaline, Reflet, Shimmering, Shot, Water-gall

Iridium Ir

Iris Areola, Eye, Flag, Fleur-de-lis, Florence, Gladdon, Gladioli, Ixia, Lily, Lis, Orris, Rainbow, Roast-beef plant, Sedge, Seg, Stinking, Sunbow, Triandria, Uvea, Water flag

Irish(man) Bark, Bog-trotter, Boy, Bucko, Celt(ic), Clan-na-gael, Declan, Defender, Dermot, Dubliner, Eamon(n), Eirann, Eoin, Erse, Fenian, Gael, Gaeltacht, Goidel, Greek, Hibernian, Jackeen, Keltic, Kern(e), Mick(e)(y), Middle, Milesian, Mulligan, Ogamic, Orange(man), Ostmen, Paddy(-whack), Partholon, Pat(rick), Rapparee, Redshank, Reilly, Riley, Rory, Ryan, Sean, Shoneen, Teague, Temper, Ultonian, Whiteboy, Wildgeese

Irk(some) Annoy, Bother, Irritate, Needle, Tedious

Iron(s), Ironstone, Ironwork(s) Airn, Alpha, Angle, Beta, Bloom, Branding, Carron, Cast, Cautery, Chains, Chalybeate, Chancellor, Channel, Climbing, Coquimbite, Corrugated, Cramp(on), Crimp, Cross, Curling, Curtain, Delta, Derringer, Dogger, Dogs, Driving, Eagle-stone, Even, Fayalite, Fe, Ferredoxin, Ferrite, Fetter, Fiddley, Flip-dog, Galvanised, Gamma, Gem, Golfclub, Goose, Grappling, Grim, Grozing, → **GUN**, Gyve, Horse, Ingot, Italian, Kamacite, Laterite, Lily, Lofty, Long, Maiden, Malleable, Marcasite, Mars, Martensite, Mashie, Mashy, Merchant, Meteoric, Mitis (metal), Pea, Pig, Pinking, → **PRESS**, Pro-metal, Rabble, Rations, Rod, Sad, Scrap, Shooting, Short, Smoother, Soft, Soldering, Spathic, Specular, Speeler, Spiegeleisen, Steam, Stirrup, Stretching, Strong, Taconite, Taggers, Terne, Tin terne, Toggle, Tow, Turfing, Wafer, Waffle, Wear, Wedge, White, Wrought

Iron age Latene, Villanovan

Ironic, Irony Antiphrasis, Asteism, Dramatic, Meiosis, Metal, Ridicule, Sarcasm, Satire, Socratic, Tongue-in-cheek, Tragic, Trope, Wry

Ironside Edmund

Ironwood Pyengadu

▶ **Ironwork(s)** *see* **IRON(S)**

Irrational Absurd, Brute, Delirious, Doolally, Foolish, Illogical, Number, Squirrelly, Superstitious, Surd, Wild, Zany

Irreconcilable Poles apart

Irrefutable Cast-iron, Evident, Positive, Undeniable
▷ **Irregular** *may indicate* an anagram
Irregular(ity) Abnormal, Alloiostrophus, Anomaly, Aperiodic, A salti, Asymmetric, Atypical, Bashi-bazouk, Blotchy, Carlylean, Casual, Crazy, Eccentric, Ectopic, Episodic, Erratic, Evection, Fitful, Flawed, Formless, Free-form, Glitch, Guerilla, Heteroclitic, Incondite, Inordinate, Intermittent, Jitter, Kink, Occasional, Orthotone, Para-military, Partisan, Patchy, Rambling, Random, Rough, Scalene, Scraggy, Scrawl, Sebundy, Sharawadgi, Sharawaggi, Snatchy, Solecism, Sporadic, Strange, TA, Uneven, Unorthodox, Unsteady, Unwonted, Variable, Wayward, Zigzag
Irrelevant Academic, Digression, Extraneous, Gratuitous, Immaterial, Inapplicable, Inconsequent, Inept, Non sequitur, Pointless, Ungermane, Unrelated
Irreligious Antinomian, Heathen, Impious, Pagan, Profane, Secular
Irremedial Hopeless, Incurable, Laches
Irrepressible Resilient
Irreproachable Blameless, Spotless, Stainless
Irresistible Almighty, Endearing, Inevitable, Mesmeric, Overwhelming
Irresolute, Irresolution Aboulia, Doubtful, Hesitant, Timid, Unsure, Wavery, Weak-willed
Irresponsible Capricious, Feckless, Flighty, Fly-by-night, Free spirit, Gallio, Reckless, Skittish, Slap-happy, Strawen, Trigger-happy, Wanton, Wildcat
Irreverent Blasphemous, Disrespectful, Godless, Impious, Profane
Irrigate, Irrigation Canalise, Colonic, Douche, Drip, Enema, Flood, Get, Water
Irritable, Irritability, Irritant, Irritate(d), Irritation Acerbate, Anger, Annoy, Bête noire, Bile, Blister, Bother, Bug, Chafe, Chauff, Chippy, Chocker, Choleric, Crabbit, Crabby, Cross-grained, Crosspatch, Crotchety, Crusty, Dod, Dyspeptic, Eat, Eczema, Edgy, Emboil, Enchafe, Erethism, Ewk, Exasperate, Eyestrain, Fantod, Feverish, Fiery, Fleabite, Frabbit, Fractious, Fraught, Fretful, Gall, Get, Gnat, Goad, Grate, Gravel, Hasty, Heck, Hoots, Humpy, Impatience, Intertrigo, Irk, Itch, Jangle, Livery, Mardy, Narky, Needle, Nerk, Nettle, Niggly, Ornery, Peckish, Peevish, Peppery, Pesky, Pestilent(ial), Pet, Petulance, Pinprick, Pique, Prickly, Provoke, Rag'd, Ragde, Rankle, Rasp, Rattle, Ratty, Rile, Riley, Roil, Rub, Ruffle, Savin(e), Scratchy, Shirty, Snappy, Snit, Snitchy, Sore, Splenetic, Sting, Tease, Techy, Testy, Tetchy, Thorn, Tickle, Tiresome, Toey, Touchy, Uptight, → **VEX**, Waxy, Windburn, Yuke
▷ **Irritated** *may indicate* an anagram
Irving Actor, Berlin
Is Est, Exists, Ist
Isaiah Is
Isinglass Carlock, Fish-glue, Mica, Sturgeon
Islam(ic) Al Q(u)aeda, Crescent, Druse, Druz(e), Hamas, Kurd(ish), Pillars, Salafism, Sanusi, Senus(si), Sheriat, Shia(h), Shiite, Sunni(te), Taleban, Taliban, Wah(h)abi
Island, Isle(t) Ait, Archipelago, Atoll, Cay, Char, Desert, Eyot, Floating, Heat, Holm, I, Inch, Is, Key, Lagoon, Motu, Refuge, Traffic

ISLANDS

2 letters:	3 letters:		4 letters:	
TT	Aru	Kos	Amoy	Cebu
	Cos	Man	Aran	Coll
	Diu	May	Arru	Cook
	Fyn	Rat	Attu	Cuba
	Hoy	Rum	Bali	Dogs
		Sea	Biak	Dunk
		Yap	Bute	Eigg
			Calf	Elba
				Erin

Fair
Fiji
Goat
Gozo
Guam
Herm
Holy
Hova
Idse
Iona
Java
Jolo
Jura
Keos
King
Line
Long
Mahe
Maui
Mazu
Mona
Muck
Mull
Niue
Oahu
Rona
Ross
Saba
Sark
Skye
Soay
Spud
Thas
Truk
Uist
Unst
Wake
Yell

5 letters:
Aland
Apple
Arran
Aruba
Banka
Banks
Barra
Batan
Belle
Bioko
Bohol
Bonin
Canna
Capri

Ceram
Cheju
Chios
Clare
Cocos
Coney
Coral
Corfu
Crete
Delos
Disko
Ellis
Faial
Farne
Faroe
Fayal
Funen
Haiti
Hondo
Ibiza
Islay
Isola
Iviza
Jerba
Kauai
Kiska
Koror
Kuril
Kyoto
Lanai
Lewis
Leyte
Lundy
Luzon
Maewo
Malta
Matsu
Melos
Nauru
Naxos
Nevis
North
Ocean
Oland
Ormuz
Palau
Panay
Papua
Paros
Pelew
Pemba
Pines
Qeshm
Qishm

Reil's
Rhode
Samar
Samoa
Samos
Saria
Seram
South
Spice
Sumba
Sunda
Thass
Thera
Thule
Timor
Tiree
Tonga
Union
Upolu
Whale
White
Wight
Youth
Zante

6 letters:
Achill
Aegean
Aegina
Amager
Andros
Aurora
Avalon
Azores
Baffin
Banaba
Bangka
Barrow
Bedloe
Bequia
Bikini
Borneo
Bounty
Butung
Caicos
Caldey
Cancun
Canvey
Cayman
Ceylon
Chiloe
Cyprus
Devil's
Diomed

Djerba
Easter
Eelpie
Ellice
Euboea
Flores
Fraser
Hainan
Harris
Hawaii
Hobart
Honshu
Hormuz
Icaria
Imbros
Indies
Insula
Ionian
Ischia
Ithaca
Jersey
Kodiak
Kurile
Kvaley
Kyushu
Labuan
Laputa
Lemnos
Lesbos
Leucas
Leukas
Levkas
Lipari
Lizard
Lombok
Madura
Majuro
Marajo
Mercer
Midway
Negros
Ogygia
Orkney
Paphos
Patmos
Penang
Pharos
Philae
Phuket
Pladdy
Quemoy
Ramsey
Rhodes
Rialto

Robben
Royale
Ryukyu
Safety
Saipan
Savage
Savaii
Scilly
Sicily
Skerry
Skomer
Skyros
Snares
Soemba
Soenda
Staffa
Staten
Tahiti
Taiwan
Thanet
Thasos
Tobago
Tresco
Tubuai
Tuvalu
Unimak
Ushant
Veneti
Virgin

7 letters:
Aeolian
Aldabra
Amboina
Andaman
Antigua
Ashmore
Austral
Bahamas
Baranof
Barbuda
Basilan
Batavia
Battery
Bedloe's
Bermuda
Bonaire
Cartier
Celebes
Channel
Chatham
Cipango
Corsica
Crannog

Curacao
Cythera
Diomede
Eivissa
Emerald
Eriskay
Falster
Frisian
Fur Seal
Gambier
Gilbert
Gotland
Grenada
Hawaiki
Howland
Ireland
Iwo Jima
Jamaica
Keeling
Laaland
Ladrone
La Palma
Leeward
Liberty
Lofoten
Lolland
Madeira
Majorca
Mariana
Masbate
Mayotte
Mindoro
Minicoy
Minorca
Molokai
Moreton
Mykonos
Nicobar
Norfolk
Oceania
Okinawa
Orcades
Orkneys
Pacific
Palawan
Palmyra
Paracel
Phoenix
Purbeck
Rathlin
Reunion
Roanoke
Rockall
Salamis

San Juan
Sheppey
Shikoku
Society
Socotra
Sokotra
Solomon
Spratly
St Croix
Stewart
St Kilda
St Kitts
St Lucia
Sumatra
Sumbawa
Suqutra
Surtsey
Tenedos
Tokelau
Tortola
Tortuga
Tutuila
Vanuatu
Visayan
Volcano
Waihake
Watling
Western
Wrangel
Zealand
Zetland

8 letters:
Alcatraz
Alderney
Aleutian
Amindiva
Anglesey
Anguilla
Antilles
Atlantis
Auckland
Balearic
Barbados
Bass Rock
Bathurst
Billiton
Blefuscu
Bora-Bora
Bornholm
Brownsea
Campbell
Canaries
Canounan

Caroline
Catalina
Choiseul
Colonsay
Cyclades
Dominica
Falkland
Farquhar
Flinders
Foulness
Friendly
Gothland
Gottland
Guernsey
Hamilton
Hatteras
Hebrides
Hokkaido
Holyhead
Hong Kong
Jan Mayen
Kangaroo
Kermadec
Key Largo
Kiribati
Ladrones
Lilliput
Lord Howe
Luggnagg
Mackinac
Mainland
Maldives
Mallorca
Malvinas
Marianas
Marquesa
Marshall
Mauna Loa
Melville
Mindanao
Miquelon
Moluccas
Mustique
Njazidja
Northern
Pelagian
Pitcairn
Pleasant
Portland
Pribilof
Principe
Sakhalin
Sandwich
Sardinia

Schouten
Shetland
Soembawa
Somerset
South Sea
Sporades
Sri Lanka
St Helena
St Helier
St Martin
St Thomas
Sulawesi
Svalbard
Sverdrup
Tasmania
Tenerife
Terceira
Thousand
Thursday
Trinidad
Tsushima
Unalaska
Venetian
Victoria
Viti Levu
Windward
Zanzibar

9 letters:
Admiralty
Alexander
Andreanof
Anticosti
Antipodes
Ascension
Barataria
Belle Isle
Benbecula
Chichagof
Christmas
Elephanta
Ellesmere
Falklands
Fortunate
Galapagos
Governors
Greenland
Guadalupe
Hainan Tao
Halmahera
Innisfree
Jamestown

Kerguelen
Laccadive
Lampedusa
Lanzarote
Macquarie
Manhattan
Margarita
Marquesas
Mascarene
Mauritius
Melanesia
Nantucket
New Guinea
Polynesia
Rangitoto
Rarotonga
Runnymede
Saghalien
Santorini
Sao Miguel
Shetlands
Sjaelland
Stromboli
St Vincent
Teneriffe
Three Mile
Tongatapu
Trobriand
Vancouver
Vanua Levu
Walcheren
Zakinthos

10 letters:
Ailsa Craig
Basse-Terre
Bermoothes
Campobello
Cape Barren
Cape Breton
Cephalonia
Corregidor
Dirk Hartog
Dodecanese
Formentera
Grand Manan
Grenadines
Heligoland
Hispaniola
Isle Royale
Kiritimati
Langerhans

Madagascar
Manitoulin
Marinduque
Martinique
Micronesia
Montserrat
Mornington
New Britain
New Georgia
New Ireland
Pescadores
Puerto Rico
Sahghalien
Samothrace
Sandalwood
Seychelles
Three Kings
Vesteralen
West Indies
Whitsunday

11 letters:
Austronesia
Dry Tortugas
Florida Keys
Glubdubdrib
Gran Canaria
Grand Bahama
Grand Canary
Grande-Terre
Guadalcanal
Lakshadweep
Lesser Sunda
Lindisfarne
Mount Desert
New Siberian
Pantelleria
Philippines
Poor Knights
San Salvador
Southampton
South Orkney
Spitsbergen

12 letters:
Bougainville
Cassiterides
Ellef Ringnes
Glubbdubdrib
Greater Sunda
Hinchinbrook
Marie Galante

New Caledonia
Newfoundland
Nusa Tenggara
Prince Edward
San Cristobal
Santa Barbara
Seringapatam
South Georgia
Torres Strait

13 letters:
Espiritu Santo
Fuerteventura
Furneaux Group
Groote Eylandt
Juan Fernandez
Little Barrier
New Providence
Outer Hebrides
Prince Charles
Prince of Wales
Santa Catalina
South Shetland

14 letters:
Amboina oceanic
D'Entrecasteaux
Lesser Antilles
Papua New Guinea
Queen Charlotte
Queen Elizabeth
Tristan da Cunha
Turks and Caicos
Vestmannaeyjar

15 letters:
Greater Antilles
Martha's Vineyard
Mont-Saint-Michel
Northern Mariana
North Stradbroke
Wallis and Futuna

16 letters:
Heard and McDonald

17 letters:
British West Indies
Fernando de Noronha

19 letters:
Netherlands Antilles

Islander Bermudan, Chian, Cretan, D(a)yak, Filipino, Kanaka, Kelper, Laputan,

Madeiran, Maltese, Mauritian, Native, Nesiot, Newfie, Orcadian, Parian, Rhodian, Samiot, Scillonian, Sican, Singalese, Taiwanese

Isle of Wight Vectis

Isn't Aint, Nis, Nys

Isolate(d) Alienate, Ancress, Apart, Backwater, Cleidoic, Cut off, Desolate, Enclave, Enisle, Exclude, Incommunicado, Inisle, In vacuo, Island, Lone, Lonely, Maroon, Outlying, Pocket, Quarantine, Sea-girt, Seclude, Secret, Segregate, Separate, Sequester, Sequestration, Set apart, Six-finger country, Solitary, Sporadic, Stray

Isomer(ic) Carotene, Carotin, Carvacrol, Geranial, Neral, Octane, Pinene, Pyran, Theophylline, Tolidine

Isopod Gribble

Isosceles Triangle

Isotope Actinon, Cobalt-60, Deuterium, Iodine-131, Muonium, Protium, Radiothorium, Strontium-90, Thoron, Tritium

Israel(i) Beulah, IL, Meir, Sabra, Zion

Issue(s) Bonus, Capitalization, Children, Come, Crux, Debouch, Denouement, Derive, Disclose, Dispense, Edition, Effluence, Egress, → EMANATE, Emerge, Emit, Escape, Exit, Exodus, Family, Feigned, Fiduciary, Flotation, Fungible, General, Government, Gush, Handout, Immaterial, Ish, Litter, Material, Matter, Mise, Number, Offspring, Outcome, Outflow, Part, Privatization, Proof, Publish, Release, Result, Rights, Sally, Scion, Scrip, Seed, Side, Son, Spawn, Special, Spring, Stream, Subject, Topic, Turn, Utter

Istanbul Byzantium, Constantinople

Isthmus Darien, Karelian, Kra, Neck, Panama, San Blas, Suez, Tehuantepec

It A, Chic, Hep, Hip, Id, Italian, Oomph, SA, Same, Sex appeal, 't, Vermouth

Italian, Italy Alpini, Ausonian, Bolognese, Calabrian, Chian, Dago, Ding, Este, Etnean, Etrurian, Etruscan, Eyeti(e), Eytie, Faliscan, Florentine, Genoese, Ghibelline, Guelf, Guelph, Hesperia, Irredentist, It, Latian, Latin, Lombard, Medici, Mezzogiorno, Milanese, Moro, Oscan, Paduan, Patarin(e), Rocco, Roman, Sabine, Samnite, Sicel, Sienese, Signor(i), Sikel, Spag, Tuscan, Umbrian, Venetian, Vermouth, Volscian, Wop

Italic Swash

Itch(ing), Itchiness Acariasis, Annoy, Burn, Cacoethes, Dhobi, Euk, Ewk, Hanker, Heat rash, Hives, Jock, Miliaria, Photopsy, Prickle, Prickly heat, Prurience, Prurigo, Pruritis, Psora, Scabies, Scrapie, Seven-year, Swimmer's, Tickle, → URGE, Urtication, Yen, Yeuk, Youk, Yuck, Yuke

Item(ise) Also, Article, Bulletin, Couple, Detail, Entry, Equipment, Flash, Line, List, Note, Number, Pair, Piece, Point, Spot, Talking point, Too, Topic, Twosome, Unit

Iterate Repeat

Itinerant, Itinerary Ambulant, Didakai, Didakei, Did(d)icoy, Dusty Feet, Gipsy, Gypsy, Hobo, Journey, Log, Pedlar, Peripatetic, Pie-powder, Roadman, Roamer, Romany, Rootless, Route, Stroller, Traveller, Vagrom, Wayfarer

Itself Aseity, In se, Ipso, Per se, Sui

Ivan Russian, Terrible

Ivory (tower) Black, Bone, Chryselephantine, Dentine, Distant, Eburnean, Impractical, Incisor, Key, Solitude, Teeth, Tower, Tusk, Vegetable, Whale's bone

Ivy Ale-hoof, Angelica-tree, Aralia, Boston, Bush, Cat's-foot, Climber, Creeper, Evergreen, Gill, Grape, Ground, Hedera, Helix, Japanese, Panax, Poison, Rhoicissus, Shield, Sweetheart, Udo, Weeping

Izzard Z

Jj

J Curve, Juliet, Pen

Jab(ber) Chatter, Foin, Gabble, Immunise, Immunologist, Inject, Jaw, Jook, Nudge, One-two, Peck, Poke, Prattle, Prod, Proke, Punch, Puncture, Sook, Sputter, Stab, Stick, Venepuncture, Yak

Jack(s) AB, Apple, Artocarpus, Ass, Ball, Boot, Bower, Bowl(s), Boy, Cade, Card, Cheap, Coatcard, Crevalle, Deckhand, Dibs(tones), Five stones, Flag, Frost, Giant-killer, Hoist, Honour, Hopper, Horner, Hydraulic, Idle, J, Jock, Jumping, Ketch, Kitty, Knave, Knucklebones, Lazy, London, Loord, Lout, Lumber, Maker, Mark, Matlow, Mistress, Nob, Noddy, Pilot, Point, Pot, Pur, Rabbit, Raise, Rating, Ripper, Roasting, Robinson, Russell, Sailor, Salt, Screw, Seafarer, Seaman, Shaun, Sprat, Spring-heeled, Springtail, Steeple, Sticker, Straw, Tar, Tee, Tradesman, Turnspit, Union, Uplift, Wood, Yellow

Jackal Anubis, Dieb, Hack, Lion's provider, Stooge

Jackass Aliboron, Goburra, Kookaburra, Stupid

Jackdaw Bird, Chawk, Chough, Daw, Kae, Raven, Rheims, Thief

Jacket Acton, Afghanistan, Air, Amauti(k), Anorak, Atigi, Bainin, Baju, Bania(n), Banyan, Barbour®, Basque, Battle, Bawneen, Bed, Bellhop, Biker, Blazer, Blouse, Blouson, Body-warmer, Bolero, Bomber, Brigandine, Bumfreezer, Bush, Cagoul(e), Camisole, Can, Caraco, Cardigan, Carmagnole, Casing, → **COAT**, Combat, Cover, Dinner, Dolman, Donkey, Drape, Dressing, Dressing-sack, Duffel coat, Duffle coat, Dust-cover, Dustwrapper, Duvet, Fearnought, Flak, Fleece, Gambeson, Gendarme, Grego, Habergeon, Hacking, Half-kirtle, Ha(c)queton, Hug-me-tight, Jerkin, Jupon, Kagool, Kaross, Life, Life preserver, Lumber, Mackinaw, Mae West, Mandarin, Mandilion, Mao, Matinée, Mess, Monkey, Nehru, Newmarket, Norfolk, Parka, Pea, Petenlair, Pierrot, Pilot, Polka, Potato, Pyjama, Railly, Reefer, Roundabout, Sackcoat, Safari, Sayon, Shearling, Shell, Shooting, Shortgown, Simar(re), Sleeve, Slip-cover, Smoking, Spencer, Sports, Steam, Strait, Sweatshirt, Tabard, Tailcoat, Toreador, Tunic, Tux(edo), Tweed, Vareuse, Waistcoat, Wampus, Wam(m)us, Water, Waxed, Windbreaker®, Windcheater, Windjammer, Wrapper, Zouave

Jackknife Dive, Fold, Jockteleg, Pike

Jackpot Cornucopia, Kitty, Pool

Jackson Stonewall

Jackstraw Spellican, Spil(l)ikin

Jacob Epstein, Ladder, Sheep

Jacobite(s) Non-compounder, Non juror, Wild Geese

Jacquard Matelasse

Ja(c)ques Melancholy, Tati

Jade(d) Axe-stone, Bidet, Cayuse, Cloy, Crock, Disjaskit, Exhaust, Fatigue, Greenstone, Hack, Hag, Horse, Hussy, Limmer, Minx, Nag, Nephrite, Pounamu, Rip, Rosinante, Sate, Screw, Slut, Spleenstone, Stale, Tired, Trite, Weary, Yaud, Yu(-stone)

Jaeger Skua

Jag(ged) Barbed, Cart, Drinking, Erose, Gimp, Hackly, Injection, Laciniate, Ragde, Ragged, Serrate, Snag, Spree, Spur, Tooth

Jagger Mick, Pedlar

Jaguar American tiger, Car, Caracal, Cat, E-type, Ounce, Tiger

Jail(er) Adam, Alcaide, Alcatraz, Bastille, Bedford, Bin, Bridewell, Can, Clink, Commit, Cooler, Gaol, Hoosegow, Imprison, Incarcerate, Jug, Keeper, Kitty, Limbo, Lockup,

Marshalsea, Newgate, Nick, Pen, Pokey, Porridge, → **PRISON**, Screw, Shop, Slammer, Spandau, Strangeways, Tronk, Turnkey, Warder

Jailbird Con, Lag, Lifer, Trusty

Jain(ism) Mahavira

Jakarta Batavia

Jake Honest, Hunkydory, OK, Rube

Jalopy Banger, Boneshaker, Buggy, Car, Crate, Heap, Shandry(dan), Stock-car

Jam(my) Apple butter, Block, Choke, Clog, Confiture, Crowd, Crush, Cushy, Damson, Dilemma, Extra, Fix, Gridlock, Hold-up, Hole, How d'ye do, Improvise, Jeelie, Jeely, Lock, Log, Pack, Paper, Plight, → **PREDICAMENT**, Preserve, Press, Quince, Rat run, Rush hour, Seize, Snarl-up, Spot, Squeeze, Stall, Standstill, Stick, Tailback, Tangle, Traffic, Vice, Vise, Wedge

Jamaica(n) Inn, Rasta(farian), Rastaman, Yardie

Jamb Doorpost, Durn, Sconcheon, Scontion, Scuncheon, Upright

James Agee, Bond, Bothwell, Henry, Jacobite, Jemmy, Jesse, Jim, Joyce, Pretender, Screw, Seamus, Seumas, Sid, Watt

Jane Austen, Calamity, Eyre, Seymour, Shore, Sian

Jangle Clank, Clapperclaw, Clash, Rattle, Wrangle

Janitor Concierge, Doorman, Porter, Servitor, Sweeper, Tiler

Jankers KP

Jansky Jy

Janus Two-faced

Japan(ese), Japanese drama Ainu, Burakumin, Daimio, Eta, Finish, Geisha, Genro, Gloss, Gook, Haiku, Heian, Hondo, Honshu, Issei, Japlish, Kabuki, Kami, Kana, Kirimon, Lacquer, Mandarin, Meiji, Mikado, Mousmé, Mousmee, Nihon, Nip, Nippon, Nisei, No(h), Resin, Sansei, Satsuma, Shinto, Shogun, Taisho, Togo, Tycoon, Yamato, Yellow peril

Jape Jeer, Joke, Prank, Trick

Jar(ring) Albarello, Amphora, Bell, Canopus, Churr, Clash, Crock, Cruet, Din, Dissonant, Distune, Dolium, Enrough, Gallipot, Gas, Grate, Greybeard, Gride, Grind, Gryde, Humidor, Hydria, → **JOLT**, Kalpis, Kang, Kilner®, Leyden, Mason, Monkey, Off-key, Olla, Pint, Pithos, Pot(iche), Quarrel, Rasp, Rock, Screwtop, Shake, Shelta, Shock, Stamnos, Start, Stave, Stean, Steen, Stein, Tankard, Terrarium, Tinaja, Turn, Vessel, Water-monkey

Jargon Argot, Baragouin, Beach-la-mar, Buzzword, Cant, Chinese, Chinook, Cyberspeak, Eurobabble, Eurospeak, Geekspeak, Gobbledegook, Gobbledygook, Jive, Kennick, Legalese, Lingo, Lingoa geral, Lingua franca, Mumbo-jumbo, Netspeak, Newspeak, Officialese, Parlance, Patois, Patter, Patter-flash, Psychobabble, Shelta, Shoptalk, → **SLANG**, Sociologese, Technobabble, Technospeak, Vernacular

Jargoon Chinook

Jasmine Cape, Frangipani, Gelsemine, Gelsemium, Gessamine, Jessamy, Madagascar, Olea, Red

Jasper Basanite, Bloodstone, Egyptian, Porcelain, Touchstone

Jaundice(d) Cholestasis, Cynical, Icterus, Prejudiced, Sallow, Yellow

Jaunt Journey, Outing, Sally, Stroll, Swan, Trip

Jaunty Airy, Akimbo, Chipper, Debonair, Perky, Rakish

▷ **Jaunty** *may indicate* an anagram

Java(man) Pithecanthropus, Sundanese

Javelin Dart, Gavelock, Harpoon, Jereed, Jerid, Pile, Pilum, Spear

Jaw(s), Jawbone Blab, Chaft, Chap, Chat, Chaw, Cheek, Chide, Chin, Confab, Entry, Gills, Glass, Gnathic, Gnathite, Gonion, Hypognathous, Jabber, Jobe, Kype, Lantern, Lumpy, Mandible, Masseter, Maxilla, Mesial, Muzzle, Mylohyoid, Natter, Opisthognathous, Overbite, Overshot, Phossy, Pi, Premaxillary, Prognathous, Ramus, Rubber, Shark, Stylet, Underhung, Undershot, Wapper-jaw, Ya(c)kety-Ya(c)k

Jay Bird, Grey, J, Sirgang, Whisky-jack, Whisky-john

Jazz(er), Jazzman Acid, Afro-Cuban, Barber, Barrelhouse, Basie, Bebop, Blues, Boogie, Boogie-woogie, Bop, Cat, Coleman, Cool, Dixieland, Enliven, Free, Funky, Gig, Gutbucket, Hardbop, High life, Hipster, Jam, Jive, Kansas City, Latin, Lick, Mainstream, Modern, New Orleans, New Wave, Nouvelle Vague, Progressive, Ragtime, Riff, Scat, Skiffle, Slap base, Stomp, Stride, Swinger, Tailgate, Trad, Traditional, West Coast

Jealous(y) Envious, Green(-eyed), Green-eyed monster, Grudging, Zelotypia

Jean(s) Chinos, Denims, Levis®, Pants, Trousers, Wranglers®

Jeer(ing) Ballyrag, Barrack, Belittle, Birl, Boo, Burl, Digs, Fleer, Flout, Frump, Gird, Heckle, Hoot, Jape, Jibe, → **MOCK**, Rail, Razz, Ridicule, Scoff, Sling off, Sneer, Taunt, Twit, Yah

Jeeves Valet

Jehovah God, Lord, Yahve(h), Yahwe(h)

Jehovah's Witness Russellite

Jehu Charioteer, Driver

Jejune Arid, Barren, Dry, Insipid, Juvenile

Jelly Acaleph(a), Acalephe, Agar(-agar), Aspic, Brawn, Calf's foot, Chaudfroid, Comb, Cow-heel, Cranberry, → **EXPLOSIVE**, Flummery, Gel, Isinglass, Jam, Kanten, K-Y®, Liquid paraffin, Macedoine, Meat, Medusa, Mineral, Mould, Napalm, Neat's foot, Petrolatum, Petroleum, Quiddany, Royal, Shape, Sterno®, Tunicin, Vaseline®, Vitreous humour

▷ **Jelly** *may indicate* an anagram

Jellyfish Acaleph(a), Acalephe, Aurelia, Blubber, Box, Cnidaria, Discomedusae, Discophora, Hydromedusa, Hydrozoa, Irukandji, Medusa, Mesogloea, Nettlefish, Physalia, Planoblast, Portuguese man-of-war, Quarl, Scyphistoma, Scyphozoan, Sea-blubber, Sea-nettle, Sea-wasp, Strobila

Jemmy Betty, Crowbar, Lever

Jenkins Ear, Roy, Up

Jenny Ass, Lind, Long, Mule, Short, Spinner, Spinning, Spinster, Wren

Jeopardise, Jeopardy Danger, Double, Expose, Hazard, Peril, Risk

Jerboa Desert rat

Jeremiad Lament, Tragedy, Woe

Jeremy Fisher, Irons, Jerry

Jerk(y), Jerkily, Jerking, Jerks Aerobics, A salti, Bob, Braid, Cant, Diddle, Ebrillade, Flirt, Flounce, Gym(nastics), Hike, Hitch, Hoi(c)k, Idiot, Jigger, Jut, Kant, Knee, PE, Peck, Physical, Saccade, Shove, Shrug, Spasm, Start, Strobe, Surge, Switch, Sydenham's chorea, Tic, Toss(en), Tweak, → **TWITCH**, Wrench, Yank

Jerkin Body warmer, Jacket, Tabard

Jerome Kern, Vulgate

Jerry, Jerry-built Boche, Flimsy, Fritz, Hun, Kraut, Lego, Mouse, Po(t), Slop-built

Jersey(s) Bailiwick, CI, Cow, Football, Frock, Gansey, Guernsey, Kine, Lily, Maillot, Polo, Potato, Roll-neck, Singlet, → **SWEATER**, Sweatshirt, V-neck, Yellow, Zephyr

Jerusalem Ariel, Hierosolymitan, Sion, Zion

Jess(e) James, Strap

Jest(er), Jesting Badinage, Barm, Baur, Bawr, Bourd(er), Buffoon, Clown, Cod, Comic, Droll, Gleek, Goliard, Humorist, Inficete, Jape, Jig, Joculator, Joker, Josh, Merryman, Miller, Mot, Motley, Patch, Quip, Raillery, Ribaldry, Ribaudry, Rigoletto, Scogan, Scoggin, Sport, Toy, Trinculo, Wag, Waggery, Wit, Yorick

Jesuit Bollandist, Ignatius, Loyola, Scholastic, SJ

Jesus → **CHRIST**, Emmanuel, IHS, Immanuel, INRI, Isa, Jabers, Lord

Jet, Jet lag Airbus®, Aircraft, Beadblast, Black, Burner, Chirt, Douche, Executive, Fountain, Geat, Harrier, Ink, Jumbo, Plane, Pump, Sable, Sandblast, Sloe, Soffione, Spirt, Spout, Spray, Spurt, Squirt, Stream, Time-zone disease, Time-zone fatigue, Turbine, Turbo, Vapour, Water

Jettison Discard, Dump, Flotsam, Jetsam, Lagan, Ligan

Jetty Groin, Mole, Pier, Wharf

Jew(ish), Jews Ashkenazi, Chas(s)id, Diaspora, Essene, Falasha, Grecian, Greek, Has(s)id, Haskala(h), Hebrew, Hellenist, Hemerobaptist, Kahal, Karaite, Kike, Ladino, Landsman, Levite, Lubavitch, Maccabee, Marrano, Misnaged, Mitnag(g)ed, Nazarite, Neturei Karta, Nicodemus, Peculiar People, Pharisee, Refusenik, Sabra, Sadducee, Semite, Sephardim, Sheeny, Shemite, Shtetl, Smouch, Smouse, Tobit, Wandering, Yid(dish), Zealot

Jeweller(y), Jewel(s) Agate, Aigrette, Almandine, Artwear, Beryl, Bijouterie, Bling(-bling), Brilliant, Cameo, Chrysoprase, Cloisonné, Coral, Cornelian, Costume, Crown, Diamond, Earbob, Ear-drop, Emerald, Ewe-lamb, Fabergé, Fashion, Ferron(n)ière, Finery, Garnet, → **GEM**, Girandole, Gracchi, Jade, Junk, Lherzolite, Locket, Marcasite, Navette, Olivine, Opal, Parure, Paste, Pavé, Pearl, Pendant, Peridot, Rivière, Rock, Rubin(e), Ruby, Sapphire, Sard, Scarab, Smaragd, Solitaire, Stone, Sunburst, Taonga, Tiara, Tiffany, Tom, Tomfoolery, Topaz, Torc, Treasure, Trinket

Jezebel Harlot, Loose, Whore

Jib Ba(u)lk, Boggle, Boom, → **DEMUR**, Face, Flying, Foresail, Genoa, Milk, Reest, Reist, Sideswipe, Stay-sail, Storm

Jibe Barb, Bob, Correspond, Crack, Dig, Fling, Gleek, → **JEER**, Mock, Quip, Sarcasm, Slant, Taunt

Jiffy Mo, Pronto, Twinkling, Whiff

Jig(gle) Bob, Bounce, Dance, Fling, Frisk, Hornpipe, Jog, Juggle, Morris

Jigger(ed) Beat, Chigoe, Jolley, Ruin

Jill Ferret

Jilt(ed) Discard, Lorn, Reject, Shed, Throw-over

Jim(my) Diamond, Dismal, Jas, Lucky, Pee, Piddle, Riddle

Jingle(r) Clerihew, Clink, Ditty, Doggerel, Rhyme, Tambourine, Tinkle

Jingo(ism), Jingoist Chauvin, Flag waver, Odzooks, Patriot, Sabre-rattling, War-rant

Jink Elude

Jinn(i) Afreet, Eblis, Genie, Jann, Marid, Spirit

Jinx Curse, Hex, Jonah, Kibosh, Moz(z), Spoil, Voodoo, Whammy

Jitter(s), Jittery Coggly, DT, Fidgets, Funk, Jumpy, Nervous, Willies

▷ **Jitter(s)** *may indicate* an anagram

Jo → **LOVER**, Sweetheart

▷ **Job** *may indicate* the biblical character

Job(bing), Jobs Agiotage, Appointment, Assignment, Berth, Career, Chore, Comforter, Crib, Darg, Desk, Duty, Earner, Errand, Gig, Gut, Hatchet, Homer, Inside, Métier, Mission, Nixer, Occupation, Oratorio, Paint, Parergon, Patient, Pensum, Place(ment), Plum, Position, Post, Problem, Pursuit, Put-up, Sinecure, Snow, Spot, Steady, → **TASK**, Ticket, Trotter, Truck, Undertaking, Work

Jock Deejay, DJ, Mac, Sawn(e)y, Scot

Jockey Carr, Cheat, Diddle, Disc, Eddery, Horseman, Jostle, Jump, Lester, Manoeuvre, Mouse, Piggott, Rider, Steve, Suicide, Swindle, Trick, Video, Vie, Winter

▷ **Jockey** *may indicate* an anagram

Jocose, Jocular, Jocund Cheerful, Debonair, Facete, Facetious, Jesting, Lepid, Scurril(e), Waggish

Joe(y), Joseph Addison, Dogsbody, GI, Kangaroo, Pal, Roo, Sloppy, Stalin, Surface, Trey

Jog(ger), Joggle, Jog-trot Arouse, Canter, Dog-trot, Dunch, Dunsh, Heich-how, Heigh-ho, Hod, Jiggle, Jolt, Jostle, Memo, Mnemonic, Mosey, Nudge, Piaffe, Prompt, Ranke, Refresh, Remind, Run, Shake, Shog, Tickle, Trot, Whig

Johannesburg Jozi

John(ny) Ajax, Augustus, Barleycorn, Beatle, Bog, Bright, Brown, Bull, Bunyan, Can, Cloaca, Collins, Dee, Doc, Doree, Dory, Elsan®, Elton, Evan, Gaunt, Gents, Gilpin, Groats, Halifax, Ia(i)n, Ivan, Lackland, Lat(rine), Latecomer, Lav, Lennon, Little, Loo, Peel, Po(t), Prester, Privy, Stage-door, Throne, Toot, Tout, WC

Johnny-come-lately Upstart

Johnson Cham, Doctor, Idler

Join(er), Joined, Joining About, Accede, Accompany, Add, Affix, Alligate, Ally, Amalgamate, And, Annex, Associate, Attach, Bond, Brad, Braze, Butt-end, Cabinet-maker, Cement, Cleave, Club, Cold-well, Combine, Conflate, Confluent, Conglutinate, Conjugate, Conjunct, Connect, Cope, → COUPLE, Dovetail, Engraft, Enlist, Enrol, Enter, Entrant, Entrist, Fay, Federate, Fuse, Glue, Graft, Hasp, Hitch, Hyphen, Include, Inosculate, Interconnect, Jugate, Knit, Link, Marry, Meet, Member, Menuisier, Merge, Mix, Mortar, Mortise, Oop, Oup, Overlaunch, Piece, Piecen, Pin, Push fit, Rabbet, Rebate, Regelation, Rivet, Scarf, Seam, Se-tenant, Sew, Siamize, Snug, Solder, Splice, Spot-weld, Squirrel, Staple, Stick, Stylolite, Tack-weld, Tenon, Toenail, Together, Unite, Wed, Weld, Wire, Yoke

Joint(ed) Ancon, Ankle, Arthrosis, Articular, Ball and socket, Bar, Baron, Butt, Capillary, Cardan, Carpus, Chine, Clip, Co, Cogging, Collar, Colonial goose, Commissure, Compression, Conjunction, Coursing, Cuit, Cup and ball, Cut, Dive, Dovetail, Drumstick, Elbow, Enarthrosis, Entrecôte, Expansion, False, First, Fish, Gambrel, Genu, Gimmal, Gimmer, Ginglymus, Hainch, Haunch, Heel, Hinge, Hip, Hough, Housing, Huck, Hunker, J, Joggle, Jolly, Junction, Knee, Knuckle, Lap(ped), Lith, Loin, Marijuana, Meat, Mitre, Mortise, Mouse (buttock), Mouse-piece, Mutton, Mutual, Phalange, Phalanx, Pin, Popliteal, Psoas, Push-fit, Rabbet, Rack, Raphe, Reducer, Reefer, Rhaphe, Ribroast, Roast, Saddle, Scarf, Schindylesis, Seam, Second, Shoulder, Silverside, Sirloin, Soaker, Splice, Spliff, Stifle, Straight, Strip, Symphysis, Synchondrosis, Syndesmosis, T, Tarsus, T-bone, Temperomandibular, Tenon, Together, Toggle, Tongue and groove, Topside, Trochanter, Trochite, Undercut, Union, Universal, Vertebra, Water, Wedging, Weld, Wrist

Joist Accouplement, Bar, Beam, Dormant, Ground plate, Groundsill, H-beam, I-beam, Rib, Rolled-steel, Sleeper, Solive, String, Trimmer

Joke(r), Joke-book, Joking Banter, Bar, Baur, Bawr, Boff, Booby-trap, Bourdon, Card, Chaff, Chestnut, → CLOWN, Cod, Comedian, Comic, Crack, Cut-up, Facete, Farceur, Farceuse, Fool, Fun, Funster, Gab, Gag, Glike, Guy, Have-on, Hazer, Hoax, Hum, Humorist, In fun, Jape, Jest, Jig, Jocular, Josh, Knock-knock, Lark, Legpull, Merry-andrew, Merryman, Mistigris, One, One-liner, Pleasantry, Practical, Prank(ster), Pun, Punchline, Pundigrion, Quip, Rag, Rib-tickler, Rot, Sally, Scherzo, Scogan, Scoggin, Sick, Skylark, Sottisier, Squib, Standing, Throwaway, Tongue-in-cheek, Wag, Wheeze, Wild, Wisecrack, Wit

Jollity, Jolly, Jollification 'Arryish, Bally, Beano, Bright, Cheerful, Convivial, Cordial, Do, Festive, Galoot, Gaucie, Gaucy, Gawcy, Gawsy, Gay, Hilarious, Jocose, Jovial, Marine, Mirth, Rag, Revel, RM, Roger, Sandboy, Sight, Tar, Trip, Very

Jolt(ing) Bump, Jar, Jig-a jig, Jog(gle), Jostle, Jounce, Jumble, Shake, Shog, Start

Jonah Hoodoo, Jinx, Moz(z)

Jones Davy, Dow, Emperor, Inigo

Jordan(ian) Moabite, Pot, Urinal

Joris Horseman

▶ **Joseph** *see* JOE(Y)

Josh Chaff, Kid, Rib, Tease

Josiah Stamp, Wedgewood

Joss Incense, Luck, Stick

Jostle Barge, Bump, Compete, Elbow, Hog-shouther, Hustle, Jockey, Push, Shoulder, → SHOVE, Throng

Jot(ter), Jotting(s) Ace, Fig, Iota, Memo, Mite, Note, Notelet, Pad, Stime, Styme, Tittle, Whit

Journal Band(e), Blog, Chronicle, Daily, Daybook, Diary, Ephemeris, E-zine, Gazette, Hansard, Lancet, Log, Mag, Noctuary, Organ, Paper, Periodical, Pictorial, Punch, Rag, Record, Reuter, TES, TLS, Trade, Waste book, Weblog, Webzine

Journalism, Journalist Cheque-book, Columnist, Commentariat, Contributor, Diarist, Diurnalist, Ed, Fleet St, Freelance, (GA) Sala, Gazetteer, Gonzo, Hack, Hackery, Hackette, Hatchetman, Inkslinger, Interviewer, Investigative, Keyhole, Leader-writer, Lobby, Marat, Muckraker, Newshound, Newsman, Northcliffe, NUJ, Penny-a-liner, Pepys, Press(man), Reporter, Reviewer, Scribe, Sob sister, Stead, Stringer, Wireman, → **WRITER**, Yellow

Journey Bummel, Circuit, Cruise, Errand, Expedition, Eyre, Foray, Grand Tour, Hadj, Hop, Jaunce, Jaunse, Jaunt, Lift, Long haul, Mush, Odyssey, Passage, Peregrination, Periegesis, Ply, Raik, Rake, Red-eye, Ride, Round trip, Run, Sabbath-day's, Sentimental, Soup run, Step, Swag, Tour, Travel, Trek, Trip, Viatical, Voyage, Walkabout

Journeyman Artisan, Commuter, Craftsman, Sterne, Trekker, Yeoman

Joust Giust, Pas d'armes, Tilt, Tiltyard, Tournament, Tourney

Jove Egad, Gad, Igad, Jupiter, Thunderbearer, Thunderer

Jovial Bacchic, Boon, Convivial, Cordial, Festive, Genial, Jolly

Jowl(s) Cheek, Chollers, Chops, Jaw

Joy(ful), Joyous Ah, Bliss, Blithe, Charmian, Cheer, → **DELIGHT**, Dream, Ecstasy, Elation, Exulting, Fain, Felicity, Festal, Frabjous, Glad, Glee, Gloat, Groove, Hah, Hey, Jubilant, Nirvana, Rapture, Schadenfreude, Sele, Tra-la, Transport, Treat, Yahoo, Yay, Yippee

Joyce Haw Haw, Traitor

Joyrider Twoccer

JP Beak, Queer cuffin, Quorum

Jubilant, Jubilation, Jubilee Celebration, Cock-a-hoop, Diamond, Ecstatic, Elated, Exultant, Holiday, Joy, Triumphant

Judaism Semitism

Judas Double-crosser, Iscariot, Traitor, Tree

Judder Put-put, Shake, Vibrate

Jude Obscure

Judge(ment), Judges Absolute, Addoom, Adjudicator, Agonothetes, Alacus, Alcalde, Arbiter, Areopagite, Aret(t), Arrêt, Assess, Assize, Auto-da-fé, Avizandum, Award, Banc, Believe, Brehon, Cadi, Calculate, Censure, Centumvirus, Chancellor, Chief Justice, Circuit(eer), Common Serjeant, Comparative, Connoisseur, Consider, Coroner, Court, Critic(ise), Daniel, Dayan, Daysman, Deborah, Decern(e), Decide, Decision, Decreet, Deem(ster), Dempster, Dicast, Dies irae, Dies non, Differential, Dikast, Discern(ment), District, Ephor, Ermined, Estimate, Evaluate, Faisal, Faysal, Gauge, Gesse, Gideon, Good-sense, Guess, Hakeem, Hakim, Hearing, Hold, Honour, Inky-smudge, Interlocutor, J, Jeffreys, Jephthah, Justice, Justiciar, Kadi, Last, Line, Lord Chief Justice, Lud, Lynch, Minos, Mufti, Non prosequitur, Nonsuit, Official Referee, Old Fury, Opine, Opinion, Ordinary, Outfangthief, Panel, Paris, Podesta, Providence, Provisional, Puisne, Puny, Ragnarok, Reckon(ing), Recorder, Ref(eree), Regard, Rhadamanthus, Ruler, Samson, Samuel, Sapience, Scan, Second guess, See, Sentence, Sentiment, Shallow, Sheriff, Sizer, Sober, Solomon, Sound, Suppose, Surrogate, Syndic, Tact, Think, Touch, Trior, Try, Umpire, Value, Verdict, Ween, Weigh up, Wig, Wik, Wine-taster, Wisdom, Worship

Judicious Critical, Discreet, Politic, Rational, Sage, Sensible, Shrewd, Sound

Judo, Judo costume Dojo, Gi(e), Kyu, Shiai, Waza-ari

Jug(s) Amphora, Aquamanale, Aquamanile, Bellarmine, Bird, Blackjack, Bombard, Breasts, Can, Cooler, Cream(er), Crock, Enghalskrug, Ewer, Flagon, Gaol, Gotch, Greybeard, Growler, John Roberts, Malling, Measuring, Olpe, Pitcher, Pound, Pourer, Pourie, → **PRISON**, Quad, Quod, Sauceboat, Shop, Slammer, Stir, Tits, Toby, Urceolus

Juggle(r), Jugglery Conjuror, Cook, Escamotage, Fake, Fire-eater, Hocus-pocus

Juice, Juicy Aloe vera, Bacca, Cassareep, Cassaripe, Cremor, Current, Fluid, Fruity, Gastric, Hypocist, Ichor, Jungle, La(b)danum, Laser, Latex, Lush, Moist, Must, Oil, Pancreatic, Perry, Petrol, Ptisan, Rare, Sap, Snake, Soma, Spanish, Stum, Succulent, Succ(o)us, Tarantula, Thridace, Vril, Walnut, Zest

Juju Charm, Fetish

Jujube Christ's thorn, Lotus, Nabk, Padma, Sweet
Jukebox Nickelodeon
Julian Apostate
Juliet J
July Dogdays
Jumble Cast offs, Chaos, Conglomeration, Farrago, Garble, Hodge-podge, Huddle, Jabble, Lumber, Mass, Medley, Mingle-mangle, Mish-mash, Mixter-maxter, Mixtie-maxtie, Mixture, Mix(t)y-max(t)y, Pasticcio, Pastiche, Praiseach, Printer's pie, Raffle, Ragbag, Scramble, Shuffle, Wuzzle
▷ **Jumbled** *may indicate* an anagram
Jumbo Aircraft, Colossal, Elephant, Jet, Large-scale, Mammoth, OS, Plane, Vast
Jump(er), Jumping, Jumpy Aran, Assemble, Axel, Base, Batterie, Bean, Boomer, Bound, Bungee, Bungy, Bunny-hop, Caper, Capriole, Cicada, Cicata, Crew-neck, Cricket, Croupade, Daffy, Desultory, Entrechat, Euro, Eventer, Flea, Fosbury flop, Frog, Gansey, Gazump, Gelande(sprung), Grasshopper, Guernsey, Halma, Helicopter, High, Hurdle, Impala, Itchy, Jersey, Joey, Jolly, Kangaroo, Katydid, Kickflip, Knight, Lammie, Lammy, Leap(frog), Lep, Long, Lope, Lutz, Nervous, Nervy, Ollie, Para, Parachute, Pig, Pogo, Polo-neck, Pounce, Prance, Prank, Pronking, Puissance, Quantum, Quersprung, Rap, Roo, Salchow, Saltatory, Saltigrade, Saltus, Scissors, Scoup, Scowp, Shy, Skip, Skipjack, Skydiver, → **SPRING**, Star, Start, Steeplechaser, Straddle, Sweater, Toe(-loop), Trampoline, Triple, Turtle-neck, Vau(l)t, V-neck, Water, Western roll
Jumping jack Pantine
Junction Abutment, Alloyed, Angle, Box, Bregma, Carfax, Circus, Clapham, Close, Clover-leaf, Connection, Crewe, Crossroads, Diffused, Gap, Intersection, Joint, Josephson, Knitting, Meeting, Node, P-n, Point, Raphe, Rhaphe, Roundabout, Spaghetti, Stage, Suture, T, Tight, Turn off, Union
Juneberry Saskatoon, Shadbush
Jungle Asphalt, Blackboard, Boondocks, Bush, Concrete, Forest, Maze, Shola, Tangle
Junior Cadet, Chota, Cion, Dogsbody, Filius, Fils, Gofer, Minor, Name-son, Office, Petty, Puisne, Scion, Second fiddle, Sub(ordinate), Underling, Understrapper, Younger
Juniper Cade, Pencil-cedar, Red-cedar, Savin(e)
Junk(ie), Junkshop Addict, Bric-à-brac, Chuck in, Jettison, Litter, Lorcha, Lumber, Refuse, Schmeck, Ship, Shmek, Spam, Tagareen, Tatt, Trash, Tripe, User
▷ **Junk** *may indicate* an anagram
Junker Aristo, Prussian
Junket(ing) Beano, Creel, Custard, Feast, Picnic, Rennet, Spree
Juno Lucina, Moneta
Junta Cabal, Council
Jupiter Jove, Newspaper, Zeus
Jurassic Bajocian, Lias, R(h)aetic
Jurisdiction Authority, Bailiwick, Domain, Pashalic, Pashalik, Province, Soke(n), Sucken, Verge
Juror(s), Jury Array, Assize, Blue-ribbon, Dicast, Grand, Hung, Inquest, Judges, Man, Mickleton, Old Fury, Pais, Panel, Panellist, Party, Petit, Petty, Sail, Special, Strike, Tales, Talesman, Tribunal, Venire, Venireman, Venue
Just(ice) Adeel, Adil, Alcalde, All, Aristides, Astraea, Balanced, Barely, By a nose, Condign, Cupar, Deserved, E(v)en, Equal, Equity, Fair, Fair-minded, Forensic, Honest, Impartial, J, Jasper, Jeddart, Jethart, Jurat, Kangaroo, Mere, Moral, Natural, Nemesis, Newly, Nice, Only, Palm-tree, Piso, Poetic, Precisely, Provost, Puisne, Pure and simple, Quorum, Recent, Restorative, Right(ful), Righteous, Rightness, Rough, Shallow, Silence, Simply, Solely, Sommer, Street, Themis, Tilt, Upright
Justifiable, Justification, Justify Apology, Autotelic, Avenge, Aver, Avowry, Clear, Darraign(e), Darrain(e), Darrayn, Defend, Deraign, Deserve, Excusable, Explain, Grounds, Pay off, Raison d'etre, Rationale, Reason, Vindicate, Warrant

Just so Exactly, Sic, Stories
Jut Beetle, Bulge, Overhang, Project, Protrude, Sail
Jute Burlap, China, Corchorus, Gunny, Hengist, Hessian, Horsa, Jew's mallow, Urena, Wool bale
Juvenile Childish, Pupa, Teenage(r), Yonkers, Young, Younkers, Youth
Juxtaposition Parataxis

Kk

K Kelvin, Kilo, King, Kirkpatrick
K2 Dapsang, Godwin Austen
Kaffir Shares, Xosa
Kail, Kale Borecole, Cabbage, Cole, Curly-greens, Ninepins
Kaiser Doorn, Wilhelm
Kaleidoscope Dappled, Motley, Myrioscope, Various
Kangaroo Bettong, Boodie-rat, Boomer, Boongary, Bounder, Brush, Cus-cus, Diprotodont, Euro, Forester, Joey, Macropodidae, Nototherium, Old man, Potoroo, Rat, Red, Steamer, Tree, Troop, Wallaby, Wallaroo
Kansas Sunflower
Kaolin Lithomarge
Karate (costume) Gi(e), Kung Fu, Shotokan, Wushu
Karma Destiny, Fate, Predestination
Kate Greenaway, Shrew
Kayak Bidarka
Kebab Cevapcici, Doner, Gyro, Satay, Sate, Shashli(c)k, Sosatie, Souvlakia
Keel Bilge, Bottom, Carina, Centreboard, Cheesecutter, Daggerboard, Even, Faint, False, Fin, List, Overturn, Skeg(g), Sliding
Keen(ness), Keener Acid, Acuity, Acute, Agog, Ardent, Argute, Aspiring, Astute, Athirst, Avid, Aygre, Bemoan, Bewail, Breem, Breme, Cheap, Coronach, Cutting, Dash, Devotee, Dirge, Eager, Elegy, Enthusiastic, Fanatical, Fell, Game, Greet, Grieve, Hone, Hot, Howl, Into, Itching, Lament, Mourn, Mustard, Mute, Narrow, Ochone, Ohone, Overfond, Partial, Peachy, Perceant, Persant, Pie, Raring, Razor, Ready, Red-hot, Rhapsodic, Sharp, Shrewd, Shrill, Snell, Thirsting, Threnodic, Thrillant, Trenchant, Ululate, Wail, Whet, Zeal(ous)
Keep(er), Keeping, Kept Ames, Armature, Austringer, Castellan, Castle, Celebrate, Chatelain(e), Citadel, Conceal, Conserve, Curator, Custodian, Custody, Custos, Depositary, Depository, Detain, Donjon, Escot, Fastness, Finder, Fort, Gaoler, Goalie, Guardian, Harbour, Have, Hoard, → **HOLD**, Maintain, Nab, Net, Observe, On ice, Ostreger, Own, Park, Pickle, Preserve, Retain, Safe, Safeguard, Save, Stay, Stet, Stock, Store, Stow, Stronghold, Stumper, Support, Sustain, Tower, Warden, Withhold
Keep back Detain, Recoup, Reserve, Retard, Stave
Keepsake Memento, Relic, Souvenir, Token
Keep under Cow, Subdue, Submerge
Keep up Float
Keg(s) Barrel, Cask, Ks, Powder, Tub, Tun, Vat
Kelly('s) Eye, Gene, Ned
Kelp Varec
Kelvin Absolute, K
Ken Eyeshot, Know(ledge), Purview, Range
Kennel(s) Guard, Home, House, Shelter
Kent Lathe, SE, Superman
Kentuckian, Kentucky Chicken, Corn-cracker, Derby, KY
Kenya(n) EAK, .ke, Luo, Masai, Mau Mau
Kerala Nair, Nayar
Kerb Edge, Gutter, Roadside

Kerchief Babushka, Bandan(n)a, Headcloth, Romal, Scarf
Kernel Copra, Core, Corn, Grain, Nucleus, Pine, Pistachio, Praline, Prawlin
Kestrel Bird, Hawk, Keelie, Stallion, Staniel, Stannel, Stanyel, Windhover
Ket Carrion, Wool
Ketch Jack
Ketchup Relish, Sauce, Tomato
Kettle Boiler, Caldron, Cauldron, Dixie, Dixy, Drum, Fanny, Pot, Tea, Turpin, War, Whistling
Keuper Trias
Key(s), Keyhole A, Ait, Allen, Alt, Ash, Atoll, B, Backspace, Basic, C, Cardinal, Cay, Central, Chip, Church, Cipher, Claver, Clavis, Clew, Clink, Clue, Command, Control, Crib, Cryptographer, D, Del(ete), Dichotomous, Digital, Dital, Dominant, E, Enter, Esc(ape), Essential, F, Flat, Florida, Fruit, Function, G, Grecque, Greek, High, Holm, Hot, Ignition, Important, Inch, Index, INS, Instrumental, Isle(t), Ivory, Kaie, King-pin, Largo, Latch, Legend, Linchpin, Locker, Low, Main, Major, Master, Minor, Note, Nut, Octachord, Opener, Oustiti, Outsiders, Pass(word), Passe-partout, Piano, Pipe, Pivot, Pony, Prong, Reef, Return, Semibreve, Shift, Signature, Skeleton, Spanner, Spline, Stimulate, Subdominant, Supertonic, Swipecard, Tab, Table, Tipsy, Tonal, Turning, USB, Vital, Watch, Water, Wedge, West, Woodruff, Yale®
Keyboard, Keypad Azerty, Console, Digitorium, Dvorak, Electronic, Manual, Martenot, Numeric(al), Piano, Pianola®, Qwerty, Spinet
Keyholder Chatelaine, Occupant, Resident, Tenant, Warder
Key man Islander, Kingpin
Keynote Line, Mese, Theme, Tonic
Keystone Cops, Crux, PA, Pennsylvania, Quoin, Sagitta, Voussoir
Keyword Kwic, Sesame
Khan Aga, Chagan, Cham, Serai, Shere
Kibbutz Collective
Kick(ing) Abandon, Back-heel, Banana, Bicycle, Boot, Buzz, Corner, Dribble, Drop, Fling, Flutter, Fly, Free, Frog, Garryowen, Goal, Grub, Hack, Heel, High, Hitch, Hoof, Lash, Nutmeg, Pause, Penalty, Pile, Place, Punce, Punt, Recalcitrate, Recoil, Recoyle, Renounce, Savate, Scissors, Shin, Sixpence, Speculator, Spot, Spur, Spurn, Squib, Stab, Tanner, Tap, Thrill, Toe, Up and under, Vigour, Volley, Wince, Yerk, Zip
Kid(s) Arab, Bamboozle, Befool, Billy, Brood, Chaff, Cheverel, Cheveril, Chevrette, Child, Chit, Cisco, Con, Delude, Fox, Giles, Goat, Hircosity, Hoax, Hocus, Hoodwink, Hum, Joke, Josh, Leather, Mag, Minor, Misguide, Nappe, Nipper, Offspring, Outwit, Pretend, Rag, Rib, Small fry, Spoof, Sprig, Suede, Sundance, → **TEASE**, Tot, Trick, Whiz(z), Wiz
Kidnap(per) Abduct, Captor, Hijack, Plagium, Shanghai, Snatch, Spirit, Steal
Kidney(-shaped) Character, Mettle, Nature, Pronephros, Reins, Renal, Reniform, Sort, Type
Kildare Dr
Kill(ed), Killer, Killing Asp, Assassin, Attrit, Axeman, Bag, Battue, Behead, Biocidal, Boojum, Booth, Bump off, Butcher, Carnage, Carnifex, Category, Chance-medley, Choke, Comical, Coup de grâce, Croak, Crucify, Cull, Deep six, Despatch, Destroy, Do in, Electrocute, Eradicate, Euthanasia, Execute, Exhibition, Exterminate, Extirpate, Fallen, For(e)do, Frag, Garotte, Germicide, Gun(man), Handsel, Hatchet man, Hilarious, Homicide, Honour, Humane, Ice, Immolate, Infanticide, Jugulate, K, Knacker, Knock off, Liquidate, Lynch, Mactation, Matador(e), Mercy, Misadventure, Misdo, Mortify, Murder, Napoo, Necklace, Ninja, NK, Off, Orc(a), Penalty, Pesticide, -phage, Pick off, Pip, Predator, Prolicide, Put down, Quell, Quietus, Regrate, Sacrifice, Serial, Settle, Shochet, Shoot up, Slaughter, Slay(er), Slew, Smite, Snuff, Spike, Stifle, Stonker, Strangle, Swat, Tailor, Take out, Thagi, Thug(gee), Top, Toreador, Total, Vandal, Vaticide, Veto, Waste, Written off, Zap
Killjoy Crab, Puritan, Sourpuss, Spoilsport, Trouble-mirth, Wowser

Kiln Lime, Oast, Oven, Queen's tobacco pipe
Kilometre K, Km, Verst
Kilt Drape, Filabeg, Fil(l)ibeg, Fustanella, Phil(l)abeg, Phil(l)ibeg, Plaid, Tartan
Kimono Yukata
Kin(ship), Kin(sman) Ally, Family, Kith, Like, Nearest, Phratry, Relation, Sib(b), Sybbe
Kind(ly) Akin, Amiable, Avuncular, Benefic, Benevolent, Benign, Boon, Breed, Brood,
    Brotherly, Category, Class, Clement, Considerate, Doucely, Favourable, Gender, Generic,
    Generous, Genre, Gentle, Genus, Good, Gracious, Human, Humane, Ilk, Indulgent,
    Kidney, Kin, Lenient, Manner, Merciful, Modal, Nature, Nice, Sisterly, → **SORT**, Species,
    Strain, Strene, Thoughtful, Trine, Type, Understanding, Variety, Well-disposed, Ylke
Kindle, Kindling Accend, Fire, Ignite, Incense, Incite, Inflame, Kitten, → **LIGHT**, Litter,
    Lunt, Spark, Stimulate, Teend, Tind, Tine, Touchwood, Tynd(e)
Kindness Aloha, Benevolence, Clemency, Favour, Humanity, Mitzvah, Ubuntu
Kindred Allied, Blood, Like, Related
King(s), Kingly Ard-ri(gh), Butcher, Coatcard, Cobra, Csar, Elvis, English, ER, Evil,
    Face card, Highness, Hyksos, Kong, Ksar, Majesty, Monarch, Negus, Pearly, Peishwa(h),
    Penguin, Peshwa, Pharaoh, Philosopher, Potentate, R, Raja, Ransom, Reigner, Rex, Rial,
    Roi, Royalet, Ruler, Ryal, Sailor, Seven, Shah, Shepherd, Shilling, Sophy, Sovereign, Stork,
    Tsar, Tzar

KINGS

2 letters:	Offa	Mpret	Farouk
GR	Olaf	Ninus	Fergus
Og	Otto	Oscar	Harold
Re	Rama	Osric	Hassan
	Saul	Penda	Hellen
3 letters:	Zeus	Prial	Josiah
Asa		Priam	Lucomo
Erl	5 letters:	Rufus	Ludwig
Ine	Apple	Uther	Lycaon
Lir	Asoka		Memnon
Log	Balak	6 letters:	Miledh
Lud	Basil	Acetes	Nestor
Zog	Brute	Aegeus	Oberon
	Creon	Alaric	Ogyges
4 letters:	Cyrus	Alfred	Oswald
Agag	David	Alonso	Paphos
Agis	Edgar	Amasis	Peleus
Ahab	Edwin	Arthur	Philip
Atli	Etzel	Atreus	Ramses
Brut	Gwern	Attila	Rhesus
Ceyx	Gyges	Baliol	Robert
Cnut	Herod	Brutus	Rudolf
Cole	Hiram	Canute	Utgard
Edwy	Idris	Casper	Xerxes
Fahd	Ixion	Cheops	
Inca	James	Clovis	7 letters:
Jehu	Laius	Daneus	Acestes
Knut	Lludd	Darius	Admetus
Lear	Louis	Duncan	Athamas
Loki	Mesha	Edmund	Baldwin
Nudd	Midas	Egbert	Balliol
Numa	Minos	Faisal	Beowulf

Busiris
Caradoc
Casimir
Cecrops
Cepheus
Croesus
Danaiis
Diomede
Elidure
Evander
Gentius
Gordius
Gunther
Jupiter
Kenneth
Macbeth
Malcolm
Oedipus
Porsena
Ptolemy
Pyrrhus
Rameses
Regulus
Servius
Sigmund
Solomon
Stephen
Tarquin
Umberto

Alberich
Alcinous
Alphonso
Cambyses
Cophetua
Diomedes
Endymion
Ethelred
Hezekiah
Jereboam
Jonathan
Leonidas
Melchior
Menander
Menelaus
Milesius
Nehemiah
Odysseus
Pentheus
Porsenna
Rehoboam
Sarpedon
Siegmund
Sisyphus
Tantalus
Thutmose
Thyestes
Tigranes
Waldener
Zedekiah

Alexander
Atahualpa
Athelstan
Balthazar
Bretwalda
Brian Boru
Conchobar
Cunobelin
Cymbeline
Ethelbert
Ferdinand
Florestan
Frederick
Gambrinus
Gargantua
Gilgamesh
Idomeneus
Lionheart
Lobengula
Nabonidus
Pygmalion
Ras Tafari
Rodomonte
Sigismund
Theodoric
Tyndareus
Vortigern
Wenceslas

Erechtheus
Maximilian
Ozymandias
Tarquinius
Wenceslaus

11 letters:
Charlemagne
Hardicanute
Jehoshaphat
John Balliol
Melchizedek
Mithridates
Prester John
Sennacherib
Tutenkhamen

12 letters:
Ashurbanipal
Wayland Smith

13 letters:
Chulalongkorn

14 letters:
Harold Harefoot
Nebuchadnezzar
Servius Tullius
Sweyn Forkbeard
Tigrath-pileser
Uther Pendragon

10 letters:
Artaxerxes
Belshazzar
Cadwaladar
Caractacus

8 letters:
Abdullah
Adrastus
Aegyptus

9 letters:
Agamemnon
Ahasuerus

Kingdom, Kingship An(n)am, Animal, Aragon, Arles, Armenia, Ashanti, Assyria, Austrasia, Babylonia, Barataria, Belgium, Bhutan, Bohemia, Brandenburg, Brunel, Buganda, Burgundy, Castile, Cilicia, Connacht, Connaught, Dahomey, Dalriada, Darfur, Denmark, Dominion, Edom, Elam, Fes, Fez, Fife, Galicia, Granada, He(d)jaz, Heptarchy, Hijaz, Jordan, Kongo, Latin, Leon, Lesotho, Lydia, Lyonnesse, Macedon(ia), Media, Mercia, Meroe, Middle, Mineral, Moab, Morocco, Murcia, Naples, Navarre, Nepal, Netherlands, Neustria, Noricum, Northumbria, Norway, Nubia, Numidia, Parthia, Phyla, Plant, Pontic, Protista, Pruce, Rayne, Realm, Reame, Reich, Reign, Royalty, Ruritania, Saba, Samaria, Sardinia, Saudi Arabia, Saul, Sennar, Sheba, Siam, Spain, Sphere, Swaziland, Sweden, Sweyn, Thailand, Throne, Tonga, Two Sicilies, Ulster, Vegetable, Wessex, Westphalia, World

Kingfisher Alcyone, Halcyon, Kookaburra, Laughing jackass

Kingmaker Neville, Warwick

King-of-arms Clarenc(i)eux, Garter, Lyon, Norroy (and Ulster)

King's evil Crewels, Cruels, Scrofula

Kingsley Amis, Charles

King's son Dauphin, Delphin, P, Prince

Kink(y) Bent, Buckle, Crapy, Curl, Enmeshed, Flaw, Gasp, Knurl, Null, Nurl, Odd, Perm, Perverted, Quirk, SM, Twist, Wavy

▷ **Kink(y)** *may indicate* an anagram
Kinkajou Honey-bear, Potto
Kiosk Booth, Call-box
Kip(per) At, Cure, Dosser, Doze, Limey, Nap, → **SLEEPER**, Smoke, → **TIE**
Kipling Beetle
Kirkpatrick K
Kish Rubbish, Scum, Tat
Kismet Destiny, Fate, Karma, Predestination
Kiss(er), Kissing Air, Baisemain, Buss, Butterfly, Caress, Contrecoup, Cross, Deep,
    French, Graze, Lip, Mouth, Mwah, Neck, Osculate, Pax(-board), Pax-brede, Peck, Pet,
    Plonker, Pree, Salue, Salute, Smack(er), Smooch, Smouch, Snog, Spoon, Suck face,
    Thimble, Tonsil hockey, Tonsil tennis, Trap, X, Yap
Kit Accoutrement, Amenity, Apparatus, Apparel, Christopher, Clobber, Clothes, Dress,
    Housewife, Jack, Layette, Marlowe, Mess, → **OUTFIT**, Press, Rig, Set, Slops, Sportswear,
    Strip, Tackle, Toolbag, Uniform
Kitchen Caboose, Chuck-wagon, Cookhouse, Cuisine, Dinette, Galley, Percussion,
    Scullery, Soup, Thieves
Kite Belly, Bird, Box, Chil, Crate, Dragon, Elanet, Forktail, Gled(e), Hawk, Milvus, Paunch,
    Puttock, Rokkaku
Kitsch Naff
Kitten(ish) Cute, Kindle, Sexy
Kittiwake Bird, Gull, Hacklet, Haglet
Kitty Ante, Cat, Fisher, Float, Fund, Jackpot, Pool, Pot, Puss, Tronc
Kiwi Apteryx, Chinese gooseberry, Enzed, Erk, NZ, Ratitae
Klu-Klux-Klan Nightrider
Knack Art, Faculty, Flair, Forte, Gift, Hang, Instinct, → **TALENT**, Technique, Trick
Knacker Castanet, Exhaust
Knapsack Kitbag, Musette
Knapweed Matfelon
Knave(ry) Bezonian, Bower, Boy, Cad, Card, Coatcard, Coistril, Coystril, Custrel, Dog,
    Drôle, Fripon, Jack(-a-napes), Jock, Loon, Makar, Maker, Nob, Noddy, One for his nob,
    Pam, Pur, Rapscallion, → **RASCAL**, Recreant, Ropery, Scoundrel, Skelm, Taroc, Tarot,
    Tom, Treachery, Two for his heels, Varlet, Villain
Knead Conche, Malax(ate), Massage, Mould, Pug, Pummel, Work
Knee(s), Knee-cap, Knee-pan Genicular, Genu, Hock, Housemaid's, Lap,
    Marrowbones, Patella, Poleyn, Popliteal, Punch, Rotula, Stifle, Whirl bone
Knee-jerk Unthinking
Kneel(er) Defer, Genuflect, Hassock, Kowtow, Prie-dieu, Truckle
Knell Bell, Curfew, Dirge, Peal, Ring, Toll
Knicker(bockers), Knickers Bloomers, Culottes, Directoire, Irving, Panties,
    Plus-fours, Rational dress, Shorts, Trousers
Knick-knack Bagatelle, Bibelot, Bric-à-brac, Gewgaw, Pretty(-pretty), Quip, Smytrie,
    Toy, Trangam, Trifle, Victoriana
Knife Anelace, Athame, Barlow, Barong, Bistoury, Blade, Boline, Bolo, Bolster, Bowie,
    Bread, Bush, Butterfly, Canelle, Carver, Carving, Case, Catling, Chakra, Chiv, Clasp,
    Cleaver, Couteau, Cradle, Cuttle, Cutto(e), Da(h), Dagger, Dirk, Fleam, Flick, Fruit,
    Gamma, Gulley, Gully, Hay, Hunting, Jockteleg, Kard, Keratome, Kukri, Lance(t),
    Machete, Matchet, Moon, Oyster, Palette, Panga, Paper, Parang, Paring, Peeler, Pen,
    Pigsticker, Pocket, Putty, Scalpel, Scalping, Sgian-dhu, Sgian-dubh, Sheath, Shiv, Simi,
    Skean-dhu, Slash, Snee, Snickersnee, Spade, Stab, Stanley, Steak, Sticker, Stiletto, Swiss
    army, Switchblade, Table, Toothpick, Tranchet, Trench
Knight(hood) Accolon, Aguecheek, Alphagus, Amfortas, Artegal, Balan, Banneret,
    Bayard, Bedivere, Black, Bliant, Bors, Britomart, Caballero, Calidore, Cambel, Caradoc,
    Carpet, Cavalier, Chevalier, Companion, Crusader, Douceper, Douzeper, Dub, Equites,

Errant, Galahad, Gallant, Gareth, Garter, Gawain, Geraint, Giltspurs, Gladys, Grey, Guyon, Hospitaller, Jedi, Kay, KB, KBE, Kemper, KG, Lamorack, La(u)ncelot, Launfal, Lionel, Lochinvar, Lohengrin, Maecenas, Malta, Mark, Medjidie, Melius, Modred, Mordred, N, Noble, Orlando, Paladin, Palmerin, Palomides, Papal, Paper, Parsifal, Perceforest, Perceval, Percival, Pharamond, Pinel, Precaptory, Preux chevalier, Red Cross, Ritter, Round Table, St Columba, Samurai, Sir, Tannhauser, Templar, Teutonic, Tor, Trencher, Tristan, Tristram, Valvassor, Vavasour, White

Knit(ting), Knitter, Knitwear Aran, Cardigan, Contract, Crochet, Double, Entwine, Fair Isle, Hosiery, Intarsia, Interlock, Intertwine, Jersey, Jumper, K, Marry, Mesh, Porosis, Pullover, Purl, Seam, Set, Stockinet, Sweater, Tricoteuse, Weave, Woolly, Wrinkle

Knob(by) Berry, Boll, Boss, Botoné, Bottony, Bouton, Bur(r), Cam, Caput, Cascabel, Croche, Gear, Handle, Hill, Inion, Knub, Knur(r), Mouse, Mousing, Node, Noop, Pellet, Pommel, Protuberance, Pulvinar, Push-button, Snib, Snub, Snuff, Stud, Torose, Trochanter, Tuber, Tuner, Wildfowl

Knobless Enodal

Knock(er), Knocked, Knock(ed) down, (off, out), Knockout Bang, Beaut, Biff, Blow, Bonk, Bump, Ca(a), Chap, Chloroform, Clash, Clour, Collide, Con, Criticise, Dad, Daud, Dawd, Degrade, Denigrate, Dent, Deride, Dev(v)el, Ding, Dinnyhauser, Dod, Etherise, Eyeful, Floor, Grace-stroke, → **HIT**, Innings, KD, King-hit, Knap, KO, Lowse, Lowsit, Mickey Finn, Opportunity, Pan, Pink, Quietus, Rap, Rat-tat, Semi-final, Six, Skittle, Socko, Spat, Steal, Stop, Stoun, Strike, Stun(ner), Sucker punch, Tap, Technical, Thump, Tonk, Wow

Knock-kneed In-kneed, Valgus

Knot(ted), Knotty Apollo, Baff, Band, Bend, Bind, Blackwall hitch, Bow, Bowline, Bur(r), Burl, Carrick-bend, Cat's paw, Clinch, Clove hitch, Cluster, Crochet, Diamond hitch, Englishman's, Entangle, Figure of eight, Fisherman's (bend), Flat, French, Geniculate, Gnar, → **GNARL**, Gordian, Granny, Half-hitch, Harness hitch, Hawser-bend, Herculean, Hitch, Interlace, Knag, Knap, Knar, Knob, Knur(r), Loop, Love(r's), Macramé, Macrami, Magnus hitch, Marriage-favour, Matthew Walker, Mouse, Nirl, Node, Nowed, Nub, Nur(r), Overhand, Peppercorn, Picot, Porter's, Problem, Prusik, Quipu, Reef, Rolling hitch, Root, Rosette, Running, Seizing, Sheepshank, Sheetbend, Shoulder, Shroud, Sleave, Slip, Slub, Spurr(e)y, Square, Stevedore's, Surgeon's, Sword, Tangle, Tat, Thumb, Tie, Timberhitch, Torose, Truelove, True lover's, Tubercle, Turk's head, Virgin, Wale, Wall, Weaver's (hitch), Windsor, Witch

Know(how), Knowing(ly), Knowledge(able), Known Acquaintance, Au fait, Autodidactic, Aware, Carnal, Cognition, Common, Compleat, Comprehend, Cred, Epistemics, Erudite, Experience, Expertise, Famous, Fly, Gnosis, Gnostic, Have, Hep, Hip, Info, Information, Insight, Intentional, Intuition, Jnana, Ken, Kith, Kydst, Lare, Light, Lore, Mindful, Omniscience, On, On to, Pansophy, Paragnosis, Party, Polymath, Positivism, Privity, Realise, Recherché, → **RECOGNISE**, Resound, Sapient, Savvy, Science, Scienter, Scilicet, Sciolism, Sciosophy, Shrewd, Smartarse, Smattering, Suss, Technology, Telegnosis, Understand(ing), Up, Versed, Wat(e), Weet(e), Well-informed, Well-read, Wis(dom), Wise(acre), Wist, Wit, Wonk, Wost, Wot

Know-all Arrogant, Besserwisser, Bumptious, Cognoscenti, Pansophist, Polymath, Poseur, Smart alec(k), Smart-arse, Smart-ass, Wiseacre

Knuckle (bone) Apply, Dolos, Fist, Joint, Ossein, Submit

Koko List

Kookaburra Laughing jackass, Settler's clock

Kop Berg, Spion

Koran Scripture, Sura(h)

Korea(n) Chosen, ROK

Kosher Approved, Genuine, Legitimate, Real

Kremlin Citadel, Fortress

Kri Masora

Krypton Kr
Kudos Credit, Glory, Praise
Ku Klux Klan Nightrider
Kurd Yezidi
Kyanite Disthene

L Latitude, League, Learner, Left, Length, Liberal, Lima, Litre, Long, Luxembourg, Pound
La Indeed, My
Label Badge, Band, Book-plate, Brand, Care, Crowner, Designer, Docket, File, Identifier, Indie, Mark, Name tag, Own, Seal, Sticker, Style, Tab, Tag, Tally, Ticket, Trace
Labiate Catmint, Hoarhound, Horehound
Laboratory Lab, Language, Skunkworks, Skylab, Space-lab, Studio, Workshop
Labour(er), Laboured, Laborious Aesthetic, Agonise, Arduous, Begar, Birth, Bohunk, Carl, Casual, Childbirth, Chore, Churl, Confinement, Coolie, Cooly, Corvée, Cottager, Cottar, Culchie, Dataller, Day, Direct, Docker, Dwell, Effort, Emotional, Farmhand, Forced, Gandy-dancer, Ganger, Gibeonite, Grecian, Grind, Grunt, Hard, Hercules, Hod carrier, Hodge, Hodman, Ida, Indirect, Job, Journeyman, Kanaka, Katorga, Leaden, Manpower, Militant tendency, Moil, Navvy, New, Okie, Operose, Opposition, Pain, Peon, Pioneer, Prole, Redneck, Roll, Rouseabout, Roustabout, Rouster, Seagull, Serf, Sisyphean, Slave, Spalpeen, Statute, Stertorous, Stint, Strive, Sudra, Swagman, Sweated, Task, Tedious, The grip, The lump, → **TOIL(S)**, Toss, Travail, Uphill, Vineyard, Wetback, → **WORK(ER)**, Workforce, Workmen, Yakka
Labrador Innu, Retriever, Tea
Laburnum Golden chain
Labyrinth Daedalus, Maze, Mizmaze, Warren, Web
▷ **Labyrinthine** *may indicate an anagram*
Lac Lacquer, Lakh, Resin, Shellac, Tomans
Lace, Lacy Alençon, Babiche, Beat, Blonde, Bobbin, Bone, Bourdon, Brussels, Chantilly, Cluny, Colbertine, Dash, Dentelle, Duchesse, Embraid, Entwine, Filet, Galloon, Guipure, Honiton, Inweave, Irish, Jabot, Lash, Macramé, Malines, Mechlin, Mignonette, Mode, Net, Orris, Pearlin, Picot, Pillow, Point, Queen Anne's, Reseau, Reticella, Ricrac, Rosaline, Seaming, Shoestring, Shoe-tie, Spiderwork, Spike, Stay, Tat(ting), Tawdry, Thrash, Thread, Tie, Torchon, Trim, Troll(e)y, Truss, Tucker, Valenciennes, Venise, Weave, Welt, Window-bar
Lacerate(d) Ganch, Gash, Gaunch, Maul, Rent, Rip, Slash, Tear
Lachrymose Maudlin, Niobe, Tearful, Water-standing, → **WEEPY**
Lack(ing), Lacks Absence, Ab(o)ulia, Aplasia, Bereft, Catalexis, Dearth, Decadent, Famine, Gap, Ha'n't, Insufficiency, Manqué, Meagre, Minus, → **NEED**, Paucity, Poor, Poverty, Privation, Remiss, Sans, Shortage, Shortfall, Shy, Void, Want
Lackadaisical Languid, Listless, Torpid
Lackaday Haro
Lackey Boots, Flunkey, Moth, Page, Poodle, Satellite, Skip-kennel, Underling
Lacklustre Dull, Insipid, Matt
Lack of confidence Doubt, Scepsis
Laconic Blunt, Close-mouthed, Curt, Dry, Spartan, Succinct, Terse
Lacquer Coromandel, Enamel, Hair(spray), Japan, Shellac, → **VARNISH**
Lad Boy(o), Bucko, Callan(t), Chiel(d), Child, Geit, Gyte, Knight, Loonie, Master, Nipper, Shaver, Stableman, Stripling, Tad, Whipper-snapper
Ladder(y) Accommodation, Aerial, Bucket, Companion, Companionway, Etrier, Extension, Fish, Jack, Jacob's, Pompier, Potence, Rope, Run, Salmon, Scalado, Scalar, Scaling, Sea, Squash, Step, Stie, Sty, Stye, Trap, Turntable
▶ **Lade** *see* **LOAD(ED)**

Ladle Bail, Dipper, Divider, Punch, Scoop, Shank, Toddy

Lady, Ladies Baroness, Bevy, Bountiful, Burd, Dame, Dark, Dinner, Don(n)a, Duenna, Female, First, Frau, Frow, Gemma, Godiva, Hen, Khanum, Lavatory, Leading, Loo, Luck, Maam, Madam(e), Martha, Memsahib, Muck, Nicotine, Peeress, Powder room, Señ(h)ora, Shopping bag, Signora, Slate, Tea, WC, White, Windermere

▷ **Lady** *may indicate* an '-ess' ending

Ladybird Cushcow, Hen, Vedalia

▷ **Ladybird** *may indicate* a female of a bird family

Ladykiller, Ladies' man Bluebeard, Lothario, Masher, Poodle-faker, Wolf

Lady of the Lake Vivian

Lady's fingers Gumbo, Okra

Lady's maid Abigail

Laevorotatory L, Left

Lag(gard) Culture, Dawdle, Delay, Drag, Flag, Hysteresis, Inmate, Jailbird, Jet, Leng,
→ **LINGER**, Loiter, Prisoner, Retard, Slowcoach, Slowpoke, Time, Tortoise, Trail

Lager Pils(e)ner

Lagoon Alexandrina, Aveiro, Barachois, Coorong, Haff, Pontchartrain, Pool, Salina,
Saline, Vistula

▶ **Laic, Laid** *see* **LAY(ING)**

Lair Couch, Den, Earth, Haunt, Hideaway, Holt, Kennel, Lodge, Warren

Lake(s) Alkali, Basin, Bayou, Carmine, Cirque, Cowal, Crater, Crimson, Cut off, L,
Lacustrine, Lagoon, Lagune, Limnology, → **LOCH**, Lochan, Lode, Lough, Madder, Meer,
Mere, Natron, Nyanza, Ox-bow, Poets, Pool, Pothole, Red, Reservoir, Salina, Salt, Shott,
Soda, Tank, Tarn, Turlough, Vlei, Wine, Zee

LAKES

2 letters:	Chott	Taupo	Monona
No	Cowan	Tsana	Nakuru
	Frome	Urmia	Nam Tso
3 letters:	Garda	Volta	Nyassa
Ewe	Gatun		Oneida
Van	Great	*6 letters:*	Peipus
	Huron	Albert	Poyang
4 letters:	Ilmen	Argyle	Rudolf
Amin	Leman	Averno	Saimaa
Bala	Leven	Baikal	St John
Biel	Lherz	Barlee	Te Anau
Bled	Lower	Bienne	Tekapo
Chad	Malar	Bitter	Vanern
Como	Morar	Broads	Varese
Erie	Mungo	Cayuga	Wanaka
Erne	Mweru	Corrib	Zurich
Eyre	Myall	Edward	
Kivu	Nam Co	Finger	*7 letters:*
Mead	Neagh	Geneva	Amadeus
Nyos	Nyasa	George	Aral Sea
Pink	Onega	Kariba	Avernus
Taal	Pitch	Kittle	Axolotl
Tana	Playa	Ladoga	Balaton
Thun	Poopo	Lugano	Balqash
	Pskov	Malawi	Bizerte
5 letters:	Sevan	Miveru	Dead Sea
Atlin	Tahoe	Mobutu	Iliamna

Kara Kul
Katrine
Koko Nor
Lucerne
Managua
Mendota
Nipigon
Ontario
Red Deer
Rotorua
Sempach
Shkoder
St Clair
Toronto
Torrens
Turkana
Vattern

8 letters:
Balkhash
Bodensee
Carnegie
Dongting
Gairdner
Grasmere
Issyk-kul
Kinneret
Maggiore
Manitoba
Masurian

Menindee
Michigan
Naumachy
Okanagan
Onondaga
Regillus
Reindeer
Rosebery
Schwerin
Superior
Tiberias
Titicaca
Tonle Sap
Tungting
Veronica
Victoria
Wakatipu
Wanawaka
Winnipeg

9 letters:
Athabasca
Bangweulu
Champlain
Constance
Ennerdale
Everglade
Genfersee
Great Bear
Great Salt

Innisfree
Killarney
Macquarie
Manapouri
Maracaibo
Naumachia
Neuchatel
Nicaragua
Nipissing
Qinghai Hu
Serbonian
Thirlmere
Trasimeno
Ullswater
Wairarapa
Wast Water
Winnebago
Ysselmeer

10 letters:
Buttermere
Caspian Sea
Chautawqua
Clearwater
Great Slave
Hawes Water
Ijsselmeer
Malabo Pool
Miraflores
Mistassini

Of the Woods
Okeechobee
Okefenokee
Serpentine
Tanganyika
Washington
Windermere

11 letters:
Lesser Slave
Paralimnion
Stanley Pool

12 letters:
Derwentwater
Memphremagog
Waikaremoana
Winnipegosis

13 letters:
Bassenthwaite
Coniston Water
Crummock Water
Pontchartrain

14 letters:
Chiputneticook
Disappointment
Ennerdale Water

Lake-dwelling Crannog
Lakeland Cumbria
Lam Flee, Scram
Lama Dalai, Karmapa, Panchen, Tashi
Lamb(skin) Baa, Barometz, Beaver, Budge, Bummer, Cade, Canterbury, Caracul, Cosset, Ean(ling), Elia, Fat, Fell, Grit, Innocent, Keb, Larry, Noisette, Paschal, Persian, Poddy, Rack, Shearling, Target, Yean(ling)
Lambent Flickering, Glowing, Licking
Lambert Constant, L
Lame(ness) Accloy, Claude, Cripple, Crock, Game, Gammy, Gimp(y), Halt, Hamstring, Hirple, Hors de combat, Maim, Main, Spavined, Springhalt, Stringhalt, Useless, Weak
Lament(able), Lamentation, Lamenter Bemoan, Bewail, Beweep, Boo-hoo, Complain, Croon, Cry, Deplore, Dirge, Dumka, Dump, Elegy, Funest, Jeremiad, Jeremiah, Keen, Meane, Mein, Mene, Moon, Mourn, Ochone, Paltry, Piteous, Plain, Repine, Sigh, Sorry, Threne, Threnody, Ululate, → **WAIL**, Wel(l)away, Welladay, Yammer
Lamia Deadnettle
Lamina(te), Laminated Film, Flake, Folium, Formica®, Lamella, Layer, Plate, Scale, Table, Tabular, Veneer
Lamp(s) Aladdin's, Aldis, Anglepoise, Arc-light, Argand, Blow, Bowat, Bowet, Buat, Cru(i)sie, Crusy, Cru(i)zie, Davy, Daylight, Discharge, Diya, Eye, Eyne, Flame, Fluorescent, Fog, Gas, Geordie, Glow, Head, Hurricane, Incandescent, Induction, Kudlik, Lampion, Lantern, Lava, Lucigen, Mercury vapour, Miner's, Moderator, Neon, Nernst, Nightlight, Padella, Pendant, Photoflood, Pilot, Platinum, Quartz, Reading, Riding, Safety,

Sanctuary, Scamper, Searchlight, Signal, Sodium, Sodium-vapour, Spirit, Standard, Street, Stride, Striplight, Strobe, Stroboscope, Sun, Tail, Tantalum, Tiffany, Tilley, Torch, Torchier(e), Tungsten, Uplight(er), Veilleuse, Xenon

Lampblack Soot

Lamplighter Leerie, Spill

Lampoon Caricature, Parody, Pasquil, Pasquin(ade), Satire, Skit, Squib

Lamprey Hag, Lampern, Sandpride

Lancaster Burt, Osbert, Red rose

Lance Dart, Harpoon, Impale, Morne, Pesade, Pike, Prisade, Prisado, Rejôn, Spear, Speisade, Thermic, White arm

Lancelet Amphioxus

Lancer Bengal, Picador, Uhlan

Lancet Fleam

Land(s), Landed Acreage, Aina, Alight, Alluvion, Arpent, Bag, Beach, Bigha, Bovate, Brownfield, Byrd, Carse, Carucate, Cavel, Conacre, Corridor, Country, Croft, Crown, Curtilage, Debatable, Demain, Demesne, Disbark, Disembark, Ditch, Doab, Dock, Earth, Edom, Enderby, Estate, Fallow, Farren, Farthingland, Fee, Feod, Feoff, Feud, Fief, Freeboard, Gair, Glebe, Gondwanaland, Gore, Graham, Greenfield, Ground, Hide, Holding, Holm, Holy, Horst, Ind, Innings, Isthmus, Kingdom, La-la, Laurasia, Lea, Leal, Ley, Light, Link, Machair, Maidan, Manor, Marginal, Marie Byrd, Mesnalty, Métairie, Moose pasture, Morgen, Mortmain, Nation, Net, Never-never, Nod, No man's, Odal, Onshore, Oxgang, Oxgate, Pakahi, Palmer, Pangaea, Panhandle, Parcel, Pasture, Peneplain, Peneplane, Peninsula, Piste, Plot, Ploughgate, Point, Polder, Pr(a)edial, Premises, Private, Promised, Property, Public, Purlieu, Queen Maud, Real estate, Realm, Realty, Reservation, Roman candle, Run, Rundale, Runrig, Rupert's, Savanna(h), Seigniory, Set-aside, Settle, Several, Smallholding, Soil, Spit, Splash down, Swidden, Tack, Taluk, Tenement, Terra(e), Terra-firma, Terrain, Territory, Thwaite, Tie, Tir na n'Og, Touchdown, Turbary, Tye, Udal, Unship, Ure, Van Diemen's, Veld(t), Victoria, Wainage, Waste, Whenua, Wilkes, Yird

▸ **Landfall** *see* **LANDSLIDE**

Landing (craft, stair, system) Autoflare, Crash, Duck, Forced, Gallipoli, Gha(u)t, Half, Halfpace, Hard, Instrument, LEM, Module, Pancake, Pier, Quay, Quayside, Roman candle, Soft, Solar, Sol(l)er, Sollar, Splashdown, Three-point, Three-pricker, Touchdown, Undercarriage

Landless Dispossessed

Landlock Embay

Landlord, Land owner Absentee, Balt, Boniface, Bonnet laird, Copyholder, Eupatrid, Fiar, Franklin, Herself, Host, Innkeeper, Junker, Laird, Lessor, Letter, Licensee, Patron, Patroon, Proprietor, Publican, Rachman, Rentier, Squatter, Squattocracy, Squire, Squirearchy, Squireen, Thane, Zamindar(i), Zemindar

Landmark Cairn, Meith, Watershed

Landmass Angaraland, Laurasia

Land right Emphyteusis

Landscape Karst, Paysage, Picture, Saikei, Scene, Stoss and lee, Vista

Landslide, Landfall Avalanche, Earthfall, Éboulement, Lahar, Scree, Slip

Landsman Lubber

Land tenure Frankalmoign, Raiyatwari, Rundale, Runrig, Ryotwari

Lane Alley, Bikeway, Boreen, Bus, Corridor, Crawler, Drangway, Drury, Express, Fast, Fetter, Gut, Inside, La, Loan, Lois, Loke, Lovers', Memory, Middle, Mincing, Nearside, Offside, Outside, Overtaking, Passage, Passing, Petticoat, Pudding, Ruelle, Sea-road, Slow, Twitten, Twitting, Vennel, Wynd

Langerhans Insulin, Islets

Language(s) Argot, Armoric, Artificial, Assembly, Auxiliary, Basic, Body, Cant, Centum, Clinic, Command, Community, Comparative, Computer, ➔ **COMPUTER**

LANGUAGE, Dead, Demotic, Descriptive, Dialect, Estem, Formal, Georgian, Gothic, Heritage, High-level, Hobson-Jobson, Humanities, Idioglossia, Idiolect, Idiom, Inclusive, Jargon, Langue, Ledden, Legalese, Lingo, Lingua franca, Macaronic, Machine code, Median, Mellowspeak, Meta-, Mixed, Mobspeak, Modern, Mother tongue, Native, Natural, Neutral, Newspeak, Novelese, Object, Officialese, Page description, Parlance, Patois, Penutian, PERL, Philology, Pidgin, Plain, Polysynthetic, Pragmatics, Private, Procedural, Programming, Prose, Query, Rabbinic, Register, Relay, Rhetoric, Satem, Sea-speak, Second, Semitic, Sign, Slanguage, Sociolect, → **SPEECH**, Strong, Style, Symbolic, Synthetic, Target, Technobabble, Telegraphese, Tone, → **TONGUE**, Tropology, Tushery, Union, Vedic, Verbiage, Vernacular, Vocabulary, Wawa, Words, World

LANGUAGES

3 letters:	Nupe	Hindi	Shuar
Ada	Pali	Hokan	Sindi
Bat	Pedi	Incan	Sinha
Edo	Pict	Indic	Sintu
Fur	Shan	Joual	Sioux
Giz	Sulu	Kafri	Sotho
Gur	Susu	Koine	Suomi
Ibo	Taal	Kriol	Swazi
Ido	Thai	Kuo-yu	Taino
Kwa	Tshi	Kwadi	Tajik
Lao	Tupi	Ladin	Tamil
Mam	Urdu	Lamba	Temne
Mon	Veps	Lamut	Te reo
Neo	Xosa	Latin	Tigre
San	Zulu	Lubon	Tonga
Tai	Zuni	Lunda	Turki
Tiv		Lyele	Ugric
Twi	*5 letters:*	Makah	Uzbeg
	Aleut	Malay	Uzbek
4 letters:	Aryan	Mande	Venda
Ainu	Azeri	Maori	Vogul
Avar	Balti	Masai	Welsh
Cham	Bantu	Mayan	Wolof
Dani	Batak	Munda	Xhosa
Erse	Cajun	Ngoni	Yakut
Geez	Carib	Nguni	Yuman
Hopi	Chewa	Norse	Yupik
Igbo	Cobol	Oriya	
Inca	Dogon	Oscan	*6 letters:*
Innu	Doric	Palau	Adyahe
Komi	Dutch	Papua	Adygei
Krio	Dyula	P-Celt	Adyghe
Lozi	Fanti	Ponca	Altaic
Manx	Farsi	Ponka	Arabic
Mari	Galla	Punic	Aranda
Maya	Ganda	Sakai	Asante
Motu	Gondi	Sango	Aymara
Naga	Greek	Saxon	Bahasa
Nakh	Gumbo	Shona	Baluch
Nuba	Hausa	Shono	Basque

Basutu	Pakhti	Chaldee	Ottoman
Berber	Panoan	Chechen	Pahlavi
Bihari	Papuan	Chinook	P-Celtic
Bokmal	Pashto	Chuvash	Pehlevi
Brahui	Pashtu	Cushite	Persian
Breton	Polish	Dhivehi	Pictish
Buryat	Pushto	Dzongka	Prakrit
Celtic	Pushtu	Elamite	Punjabi
Chadic	Quapaw	Euskara	Pushtoo
Coptic	Romany	Faroese	Quechua
Creole	Rwanda	Flemish	Riksmal
Cymric	Salish	Frisian	Romance
Danish	Samoan	Gagauzi	Romanes
Dardic	Shelta	Gaulish	Romansh
Divehi	Sherpa	Guajiro	Saharan
Eskimo	Sindhi	Guarani	Sahrawi
Evenki	Siouan	Hamitic	Samnite
Fantee	Slovak	Hittite	Samoyed
Fijian	Somali	Hokkien	Serbian
Finnic	Strine	Ingrian	Servian
French	Svanan	Inupiaq	Sesotho
Fulani	Syriac	Italian	Shawnee
Gaelic	Tanoan	Janlish	Sinhala
Gagauz	Tartar	Japlish	Sinitic
Galibi	Telegu	Judezmo	Slovene
German	Telugu	Kannada	Sogdian
Gullah	Tigray	Khoisan	Sorbian
Hebrew	Tongan	Kikapoo	Spanish
Herero	Tsonga	Kirundi	Sudanic
Inupik	Tswana	Kurdish	Swahili
Italic	Tuareg	Kushite	Swedish
Jivaro	Tungus	Lallans	Tagalog
Kafiri	Turkic	Laotian	Tahitan
Ladino	Udmurt	Lingala	Tibetan
Lahnda	Ugrian	Luganda	Tlingit
Lakota	Uralic	Malayan	Turkish
Lepcha	Yakama	Maleate	Turkmen
Lu-wian	Yoruba	Malinke	Umbrian
Lycian	Zyrian	Marathi	Uralian
Lydian		Mashona	Venetic
Macush	***7 letters:***	Miao-Yao	Volapuk
Macusi	Adamawa	Mingrel	Voltaic
Manchu	Amboina	Miskito	Walloon
Micmac	Amerind	Mordvin	Wendish
Mishmi	Amharic	Moriori	Wergaia
Mixtec	Aramaic	Nahuatl	Yerkish
Na-Dene	Ashanti	Nauruan	Yiddish
Nepali	Austric	Ndebele	
Novial	Baluchi	Nilotic	***8 letters:***
Nubian	Bengali	Nynorsk	Akkadian
Nyanja	Bislama	Nyungar	Albanian
Ostyak	Cabiric	Occitan	Arawakan
Pahari	Caddoan	Oceanic	Assamese
Paiute	Catalan	Ossetic	Balinese

Bulgaric
Cheremis
Cherkess
Chibchan
Chichewa
Creolian
Croatian
Cushitic
Dzongkha
Ethiopic
Etrurian
Etruscan
Faliscan
Fanagalo
Filipino
Frankish
Friesian
Goidelic
Gujarati
Gujerati
Gurkhali
Hiri-Motu
Illyrian
Japanese
Japhetic
Javanese
Judezono
Jugoslav
Kashmiri
Khoikhoi
Kickapoo
Kingwana
Kolarian
Kwakiutl
Landsmal
Lusatian
Makyalam
Malagasy
Mampruli
Mandarin
Mikasuki
Moldovan
Mongolic
Mon-Khmer
Mordvine
Netspeak
Nez Perce
Ossetian
Phrygian
Pilipino
Polabian
Rhaetian
Romanian
Romansch

Rumansch
Rumonsch
Salishan
Sanscrit
Sanskrit
Scythian
Setswana
Shemitic
Shoshone
Slavonic
Sumatran
Sumerian
Tahitian
Teutonic
Thracian
Tigrinya
Tshiluba
Tucanoan
Tungusic
Turanian
Turkoman
Tuvaluan
Ugaritic
Volscian
Wakashan
Warlpiri
Yanomani
Yugoslav

9 letters:

Abkhazian
Afrikaans
Algonkian
Algonquin
Anatolian
Brittonic
Brythonic
Cantonese
Chari-Nile
Cheremiss
Cingalese
Diglossia
Dravidian
Esperanto
Esthonian
Euskarian
Franglais
Goidhelic
Gujarathi
Gujerathi
Hottentot
Hungarian
Inuktitut
Iroquoian

Kabardian
Kamilaroi
Kiswahili
Landsmaal
Langue d'oc
Leizghian
Makyaalam
Malayalam
Marquesan
Messapian
Mongolian
Muskogean
Nostratic
Onondagan
Provençal
Putonghua
Roumanian
Roumansch
Sabellian
Sardinian
Semi-Bantu
Sinhalese
Tocharian
Tokharian
Tokharish
Tungurian
Ukrainian
Ursprache
Varangian
Winnebago

10 letters:

Algonquian
Araucanian
Athabascan
Athapaskan
Azerbayani
Bêche-la-Mar
Beach-la-Mar
Caprolalia
Circassian
Diachronic
Eteocretan
Finno-Ugric
Gallo-Roman
Halkomelom
Himyaritic
Hindustani
Indonesian
Kartvelian
Langue d'oil
Langue d'oui
Lithuanian
Macedonian

Malayalaam
Melanesian
Mingrelian
Montagnais
Muskhogean
Niger-Congo
Papiamento
Phoenician
Pima-pipogo
Police Motu
Portuguese
Proto-Norse
Rajasthani
Serbo-Croat
Singhalese
Synchronic
Ugro-Finnic
Union Shona
Ural-Altaic
Uto-Aztecan
Vietnamese
Wemba-Wemba

11 letters:

Azerbaijani
Belarussian
Celtiberean
Dagestanian
Finno-Ugrian
Hokan-Siouan
Interglossa
Interlingua
Kordofanian
Langobardic
Micronesian
Moeso-gothic
Nilo-Saharan
Old Prussian
Osco-Umbrian
Oto-Manquean
Pama-Nyungan
Potawatomic
Sino-Tibetan
Sranantongo
Tessaraglot
Tupi-Guarani
Yuwaalaraay

12 letters:

Billingsgate
Gallo-Romance
Idiom neutral
Indo-European
Platt-deutsch

Proto-Romance	**13 letters:**	**14 letters:**	**15 letters:**
Sprachgefuhl	Neo-Melanesian	Palaeo-Siberian	Sahaptin-Chinook
Tibeto-Burman	Semito-Hamitic	Thraco-Phrygian	
Volga-Baltaic	Serbo-Croatian		**16 letters:**
			Malayo-Polynesian

Languid, Languish Die, Divine, Droop, Feeble, Flagging, Listless, Lukewarm, Lydia, Melancholy, Quail, Torpid, Wilt

Languor Lassitude

Langur Simpai, Wanderoo

Lanky Beanpole, Gangly, Gawky, Lean(y), Spindleshanks, Windlestraw

Lanolin Woolfat, Wool oil, Yolk

Lantern Aristotle's, Bowat, Bowet, Buat, Bull's eye, Chinese, Dark(e)y, Epidiascope, Episcope, Friar's, Glim, Japanese, Jaw, Lanthorn, Magic, Sconce, Stereopticon, Storm, Turnip

Lanthanum La

Laodicean Lukewarm

Lap Circuit, Drink, Gremial, Leg, Lick, Lip, Luxury, Override, Pace, Sypher

Lapdog Messan, Shough, Showghe

▷ **Lapdog** *may indicate* 'greyhound'

Lapel Revers

Laplander, Lapp Saam(e), Sabme, Sabmi, Sami

Lappet Infula, Jardiniere

Lapse Backslide, Drop, Error, Expire, Fa', Fall, Nod, Sliding, Trip

Lapwing Hornywink, Teru-tero

Larceny Compound, Grand, Petty, Simple

Larch Hackmatack, Tamarack

Lard Enarm, Leaf, Saim, Seam(e)

Larder Buttery, Pantry, Spence, Springhouse

Large(ness), Largest Ample, Astronomical, Big, Boomer, Bulky, Bumper, Buster, Colossus, Commodious, Considerable, Decuman, Enormous, Epical, Extensive, Gargantuan, → **GIGANTIC**, Ginormous, Gog, Great, Grit, Gross, Handsome, Hefty, Helluva, Huge, Hulking, Humdinger, Humongous, Humungous, Kingsize, L, Labour intensive, Lg, Lunker, Macrocephaly, Magog, Man-sized, Massive, Maximin, Maximum, Outsize, Plethora, Prodigious, Rounceval, Rouncival, Scrouger, Skookum, Slew, Slue, Snorter, Sollicker, Spacious, Spanking, Stonker, Stout, Swingeing, Tidy, Titanic, Vast, Voluminous, Well-endowed, Whopping

Large number Centillion, Fermi, Gazillion, Giga, Gillion, Googol, Googolplex, Grillion, Infinitude, Jillion, Lac, Lakh, Legion, Mille, Myriad, Nation, Nonillion, Nth, Octillion, Quadrillion, Quintillion, Raft, Regiment, Ruck, Scads, Sea, Septillion, Sextillion, Shitload, Slather, Slew, Slue, Squillion, Toman, Trillion, Zillion

Largess Alms, Charity, Frumentation, Generosity

Lariat Lasso, Reata, Riata

Lark Adventure, Aunter, Caper, Dido, Dunstable, Exaltation, Fool, Gammock, Giggle, Guy, Laverock, Magpie, Mud, Pipit, Prank, Spree

Larkspur Stavesacre

Larva Ammacoete, Amphibiotic, Amphiblastule, Aphid lion, Army-worm, Augerworm, Axolotl, Bagworm, Bipinnaria, Bloodworm, Bookworm, Bot(t), Budworm, Cabbage worm, Caddice, Caddis(-worm), Cankerworm, Caterpillar, Cercaria, Chigger, Chigoe, Coenurus, Corn borer, Corn earworm, Cysticercoid, Doodlebug, Glass-crab, Grub, Hellgram(m)ite, Hydatid, Indusium, Instar, Jigger, Jointworm, Leather-jacket, Leptocephalus, Maggot, Mealworm, Measle, Microfilaria, Miracidium, Muckworm, Mudeye, Naiad, Nauplius, Neoteny, Nigger, Nymph, Ox-bot, Planula, Pluteus, Polypod, Porina, Redia, Screwworm, Shade, Silkworm, Spat, Strawworm, Tadpole, Trochophore, Trochosphere, Veliger, Warble,

Water penny, Wireworm, Witchetty, Witchetty grub, Woodworm, Xylophage, Zoea

Larynx, Laryngitis Cricoid, Croup, Hives, Voice box

Lascar Seacunny, Tindal

Lascivious(ness) Crude, Drooling, Goaty, Horny, Lewd, Lubric, Paphian, Raunch(y), Satyric, Sotadic, Tentigo, Wanton

Laser Argon

Lash(ed), Lashing(s) Cat, Cilium, Firk, Flagellum, Flog, Frap, Gammon, Gripe, Knout, Mastigophora, Mousing, Oodles, Oup, Quirt, Riem, Rope's end, Scourge, Secure, Sjambok, Stripe, Swinge, Tether, Thong, Trice, Whang, → **WHIP**, Wire

Lass(ie) Colleen, Damsel, Maid, Quean, Queyn, Quin(i)e

Lassitude Accidie, Acedie, Languor, Lethargy

Lasso Lariat, Lazo, Reata, Rope

Last(ing) Abide, Abye, Aft(er)most, → **AT LAST**, Boot-tree, Bottom, Cargo, Chronic, Coda, Dernier, Dure, Dying, Eleventh, Endmost, Endurance, Endure, Extend, Extreme, → **FINAL**, Hinder, Hindmost, Hold out, In extremis, Latest, Latter, Linger, Live, Load, Long-life, Model, Nightcap, Outstay, Perdure, Permanent, Perpetuate, Persist, Rearmost, Spin, Stable, Stamina, Stand, Stay, Supper, Survive, Swan-song, Thiller, Thule, Tree, Trump, Ult(imate), Ultima, Ultimo, Utmost, Wear, Weight, Whipper-in, Yester, Z

Last drop Supernaculum

Last resort Pis aller

Last syllable Ultima

Last word(s) Amen, Envoi, Farewell, Ultimatum, Zythum

Latch Bar, Clicket, Clink, Espagnolette, Lock, Night, Sneck, Thumb, Tirling-pin

Late(r), Latest After(wards), Afterthought, Anon, Behindhand, Chit-chat, Dead, Deid, Delayed, Ex, Former, Gen, Infra, Lag, Lamented, New(s), Overdue, Overrunning, Owl-car, Past, PM, Recent, Serotine, Sine, Slow, State-of-the-art, Stop-press, Syne, Tardive, Tardy, Top shelf, Trendy, Umquhile, Update

Late-learner Opsimath

Latent Concealed, Delitescent, Dormant, Maieutic, Potential

Lateral Askant, Edgeways, Sideways

Latex Antiar, Dental dam, Gutta-percha, Jelutong, Ule

Lath Lag, Splat

Lathe Capstan, Mandrel, Mandril, Turret

Lather Flap, Foam, Froth, Sapples, Suds, Tan

Latin(ist) Biblical, Classical, Criollo, Dago, Dog, Erasmus, Eyeti, Greaseball, High, Humanity, Italiot, L, Late, Law, Low, Medieval, Mexican, Middle, Modern, Neapolitan, New, Pig, Quarter, Rogues', Romanic, Romish, Scattermouch, Silver, Spic, Thieves', Uruguayan, Vulgar, Wop

Latin-American Criollo, Tico

Latitude Breadth, Celestial, Ecliptic, Free hand, Horse, L, Leeway, Liberty, Licence, Meridian, Parallel, Play, Roaring forties, Scope, Tropic, Width, Wiggle room

Latrine Ablutions, Benchhole, Bog, Cloaca, Furphy, Garderobe, Loo, Privy, Rear

Latter Last, Previous

Latter-day Recent, Saints, Young

Lattice Bravais, Cancelli, Clathrate, Crystal, Espalier, Grille, Matrix, Pergola, Red, Space, Treillage, Treille, Trellis

Lattice-leaf Ouvirandra

Latvian Lett

Laud(able), Lauder Commend, Eulogist, Extol, Harry, Hery, Praise, Worthily

Lauderdale Caballer

Laugh(ing), Laughable, Laughter Belly, Boff, Cachinnate, Cackle, Canned, Chortle, Chuckle, Cod, Corpse, Democritus, Deride, Derision, Fit, Fou rire, Gas, Gelastic, Giggle, Goster, Guffaw, Ha, He-he, Ho-ho, Homeric, Hoot, Horse, Hout, Howl, Irrision, Isaac, Jackass, Last, Lauch, Leuch, Levity, Ludicrous, → **MIRTH**, Mock, Nicker, Peal, Present,

Riancy, Riant, Rich, Rident, Ridicule, Risus, Scream, Snigger, Snirt(le), Snort, Tehee, Titter, Yo(c)k

Laughing-stock Outspeckle, Sport

Launcelot Gobbo

Launch(ing), Launch pad Begin, Blast-off, Catapult, Chuck, Cosmodrome, Debut, ELV, Fire, Float, Hurl, Initiate, Lift-off, Moonshot, Motoscalp, Opening, Pioneer, Presentation, Release, Rolling, Roll out, Send, Shipway, Shot, Slipway, Start, Steam, → **TOSS**, Unstock, Upsend, VTO

Launder, Laund(e)rette, Laundress, Laundry Bagwash, Blanchisseuse, Clean, Coin-op, Lav, Linen, Steamie, Tramp, Transfer, Wash(ery), Washhouse, Whites

Laurel(s) Aucuba, Bay, Camphor, Cherry, Daphne, Japan, Kalmia, Kudos, Mountain, Pichurim, Rose (bay), Sassafras, Spicebush, Spotted, Spurge, Stan, Sweet-bay, True

Laurence Sterne

Lava Aa, Block, Bomb, Coulée, Cysticercus, Dacite, Flood basalt, Lahar, Lapilli, Magma, Mud, Nuée ardente, Pahoehoe, Palagonite, Pillow, Pitchstone, Plug, Pumice, Pyroclast, Scoria, Tephra, Toadstone

Lavatory Ajax, Bogger, Brasco, Can, Carsey, Carzey, Cludgie, Comfort station, Convenience, Cottage, Dike, Draught, Dunnakin, Dunny, Dyke, Earth closet, Elsan®, Facilities, Forica, Furphey, Gents, Heads, Jakes, Jane, John, Kars(e)y, Karzy, K(h)azi, Kleinhuisie, Kybo, Ladies, Lat(rine), Loo, Necessary, Netty, Office, Outhouse, Pissoir, Portaloo®, Privy, Rear(s), Reredorter, Shithouse, Shouse, Siege, Smallest room, Superloo, Throne, Thunderbox, Toilet, Toot, Tout, Urinal, Washroom, WC

Lave Lip, Wash

Lavender Aspic, Sea, Spike

Lavengro Borrow

Laver Moabite, Nori, Ore-weed

Lavish Barmecidal, Copious, Excessive, Extravagant, Exuberant, Flush, Free, Fulsome, Generous, Liberal, Lucullan, Lush, Palatial, Prodigal, Shower, Slap-up, Sumptuous, Wanton, Waste

Law(ful), Laws Abingdon, Act, Agrarian, Anti-trust, Ass, Association, Avogadro's, Babo's, Bar, Barratry, Bernoulli's, → **BILL**, Biogenetic, Blue-sky, Bode's, Bonar, Bourlaw, Boyle's, Bragg's, Brehon, Brewster's, Brocard, Buys Ballot's, Byelaw, Byrlaw, Cain, Canon, Capitulary, Case, Chancery, Charles's, Civil, Code, Common, Constitution, Corn, Coulomb's, Criminal, Cupar, Curie's, Curie-Weiss, Cy pres, Dalton's, Dead-letter, Decree, Decretals, Decretum, De Morgan's, Deodand, Dharma, Dictate, Digest, Din, Distributive, Dry, Edict, Einstein's, Enact, Excise, Fiqh, Forensic, Forest, Fuero, Fundamental, Fuzz, Game, Gas, Gay-Lussac's, Graham's, Gresham's, Grimm's, Grotian, Haeckel's, Halal, Halifax, Hardy-Weinberg, Henry's, Hess's, Homestead, Hooke's, Hubble's, Hudud, Hume's, International, Irade, Iure, Joule's, Jura, Jure, Jus, Kain, Kashrut(h), Kepler's, Kirchhoff's, Labour, Land, Lay, Legal, Leibniz's, Lemon, Lenz's, Licit, Lien, Liquor, Lor(d), Losh, Lydford, Lynch, Magdeburg, Mariotte's, Martial, May, Megan's, Mendel's, Mercantile, Military, Mishna(h), Mishnic, Moral, Mosaic, Murphy's, Natural, Newton's, Noahide, Nomistic, Nomothetic, Octave, Ohm's, Oral, Ordinance, Pandect, Parity, Parkinson's, Pass, Penal, Periodic, Planck's, Plebiscite, Poor, Principle, Private, Public, Rape shield, Regulation, Rhodian, Roman, Rubric, Rule, Salic, Salique, Scout, Sharia(h), Sheria(t), Shield, Shulchan Aruch, Snell's, Sod's, → **STATUTE**, Stefan's, Stokes, Sumptuary, Sunna, Sus(s), Sword, Table, Talmud, Tenet, The (long) robe, Thorah, Thorndike's, Torah, Tort, Tradition, Twelve Tables, Ulema, Unwritten, Use, Valid, Verner's, Vigilante, Written

Lawless(ness) Anarchy, Anomie, Anomy, Antinomian, Bushranger, Piratical, Rowdy, Wild and woolly

Lawmaker, Lawman, Lawyer Alfaqui, Ambulance chaser, Att(orney), AV, Avocat, Avvogadore, Barrack room, Barrister, Bencher, BL, Bluebottle, Bramble, Bush, Cadi, Canon, Coke, Counsel, DA, Decemvir, Deemster, Defence, Dempster, Doge, Draco,

Eagle(t), Earp, Enactor, Fiscal, Greenbag, Grotius, Hammurabi, Jurisconsult, Jurist, Juvenal, Legal eagle, Legist, Mooktar, Moses, MP, Mufti, Mukhtar, Nomothete, Notary, Penang, Pettifoggers, Philadelphia, Proctor, Procurator fiscal, Prosecutor, Rabbi, Shirra, Shyster, Silk, Solicitor, Spenlow, Stratopause, Talmudist, Templar, Thesmothete, Vakil, Writer, WS

Lawn Cambric, Cloth, Grass, Green, Linen, Ruche, Sward, Turf

Lawrence DH, Ross, Shaw, TE

Lawrencium Lr

Lawsuit Case, Cause, Plea, Trover

▶ **Lawyer(s), Lawman** *see* **LAWMAKER**

Lax(ity) Freedom, Inexact, Laissez-aller, Latitude, Lenience, Loose, Remiss, → **SLACK**, Wide, Wide-open

▷ **Lax** *may indicate* an anagram

Laxative Aloin, Aperitive, Cascara, Cassia, Cathartic, Eccoprotic, Elaterin, Elaterium, Glauber's salt, Gregory (powder), Hydragogue, Loosener, Magnesia, Physic, Purgative, → **PURGE**, Saline, Senna-pod, Taraxacum

Lay(ing), Layman, Laic, Laid, Laity Air, Amateur, Antepost, Aria, Ballad, Bed, Bet, Blow, Chant, Christian Brothers, Civil, Ditty, Drop, Earthly, Egg, Embed, Fit, Impose, Lied, Lodge, Man, Minstrel, Oat, Oblate, Ode, Ordinary, Outsider, Oviparous, Oviposit, Parabolanus, Pose, Secular, Set, Sirvente, → **SONG**, Songsmith, Sypher, Temporalty, Tertiary, Tribal, Untrained, Wager, Warp

Layabout Corner boy, Idler, Loafer, Lotophagus, Ne'er-do-well, Oaf, Slob

Lay-by Rest stop

Layer(s) Abscission, Aeuron(e), Ancona, Appleton, Battery, Bed, Boundary, Cake, Caliche, Cambium, Canopy, Chromosphere, Cladding, Coating, Crust, D, Depletion, E, Ectoplasm, Ectosarc, Ekman, Epiblast, Epilimnion, Epitaxial, Epitheca, Epithelium, Erathem, E-region, Exine, Exocarp, F, Film, Flake, Friction, Ganoin, Germ, Gossan, Gozzan, Granum, Ground, Heaviside, → **HEN**, Herb, Hypotheca, Intima, Inversion, Kennelly(-Heaviside), Kerf, Lamella, Lamina, Lap, Leghorn, Lenticle, Lie, Malpighian, Media, Miocene, Ozone, Palisade, Pan, Patina, Paviour, Photosphere, Ply, Retina, Reversing, Rind, Scale, Scattering, Sclerite, Screed, Shrub, Skim, Skin, Skiver, Sliver, Spathic, Stratify, Stratopause, Stratum, Substratum, Tabular, Tapetum, Tier, Tremie, Trophoblast, Trophoderm, Uvea, Varve, Vein, Velamen, Veneer

Lay-off Dismiss, Hedge, Redundance, Suspend

Lay-out Ante, Design, Expend, Fell, Format, Map, Mise, Pattern, Spend, Straucht, Straught, Streak, Streek, Stretch

Laze, Laziness, Lazy (person), Lazybones Bed-presser, Bone idle, Bummer, Cabbage, Couch potato, Faineant, Grunge, Hallian, Hallion, Hallyon, Indolent, Inert, Lackadaisical, Laesie, Languid, Layabout, Lie-abed, Lig(ger), Lime, Lither, Loaf, Lotus-eater, Lusk, Mollusc, Ne'er-do-well, Oblomovism, Resty, Shiftless, Sleepyhead, Sloth, Slouch, Slug(-a-bed), Sluggard, Susan, Sweer, Sweir, Timeserver, Veg, Workshy

▷ **Lazily** *may indicate* an anagram

Lea Grass, Meadow

Leach(ing) Cheluviation, Lixivial, Ooze

Lead(er), Leading, Leadership Ag(h)a, Ahead, Akela, Amakosi, Anglesite, Arch, Article, Atabeg, Atabek, Ayatollah, Bab, Bellwether, Black, Bluey, Bodhisattva, Bonaparte, Brand, Cable, Cade, Calif, Caliph, Came, Capitano, Capo, Captain, Castro, Caudillo, Causal, Centre, Ceruse, Cheer, Chief, Chieftain, Chiliarch, Chin, China white, Choragus, Choregus, CO, Codder, Concert-master, Condottiere, Conducive, Conduct, Corporal, Coryphaeus, Coryphee, Czar, Dalai Lama, De Gaulle, Demagogue, Dictator, Dominant, Drail, Duce, Dux, Editorial, Escort, Ethnarch, Extension, Figurehead, First, Flake-white, Floor, Foreman, Foremost, Frontrunner, Fugleman, Fu(e)hrer, Gaffer, Gandhi, Garibaldi, General, Gerent, Go, Graphite, Guide(r), Halter, Hand, Headman, Headmost, Headnote, Hegemony, Heresiarch, Hero, Hetman, Hiawatha, Hierarch, Honcho, Idi, Imam, Imaum,

Induna, Ink(h)osi, Inveigle, Jason, Jefe, Jeune premier(e), Jump, Juve(nile), Kabir, Kame, King, Ksar, Leam, Litharge, Livid, Loss, Lost, Lyam, Lym(e), Mahatma, Mahdi, Main, Market, Marshal, Massicot, Masticot, Mayor, Meer, Mehdi, Minium, Mir, Nanak, No 1, Nomarch, Nose, Numero uno, Omrah, Open, Pacemaker, Pacesetter, Padishah, Panchen Lama, Patriarch, Pb, Petain, Pilot, Pioneer, Pit, Plumb(um), Plummet, PM, Pointer, Precede, Precentor, Premier(e), President, Price, Primo, Rangitara, Ratoo, Rebbe, Rebecca, Red, Role, Ruler, Sachem, Sagamore, Saturn, Saturn's tree, Scotlandite, Scout, Scuddaler, Scudler, Senior, Shaper, Sharif, Sheik(h), Sixer, Skipper, Skudler, Soaker, Soul, Sounding, Spearhead, Stalin, Staple, Star, Start, Sultan, Supremo, Taoiseach, Tecumseh, Tetraethyl, Top banana, Top dog, Trail(blazer), Tribune, Tsaddik, Tsaddiq, Tsar, Tzaddik, Up, Usher, Vaivode, Van(guard), Vanadinite, Va(u)nt, Vaunt-courier, Voivode, Vozhd, Waivode, Wali, Warlord, White, Whitechapel, Wulfenite, Yeltsin, Youth, Zaddik, Zia

▷ **Lead(s), Leaders** *may indicate* first letters of words

Leaden Flat, Plumbeous, Saturnine

Lead-glance Galena

Leading to Pre

Leaf(y), Leaves Acanthus, Acrospire, Amphigastrium, Amplexicaul, Ascidia, At(t)ap, Baccy, Betel, Blade, Bract, Carpel, Cataphyll, Cladode, Coca, Compound, Consent, Corolla, Costate, Cotyledon, Crocket, Dolma, Drop, Duff, Fig, Finial, Foil, Foliage, Foliar, Folio(se), Folium, Frond, Frondose, Glume, Gold, Green, Holiday, Induviae, Jugum, K(h)at, Lattice, Lilypad, Lobe, Lobulus, Maple, Megaphyll, Microphyll, Needle, Nervate, Out, P, Pad, Page, Pan, Paper, Phyllid, Phyllode, Phyllome, Pot, Qat, Repair, Riffle, Rosula, Salad, Scale, Sclerophyll, Secede, Sepal, Sheet, Siri(h), Skim, Skip, Spathe, Sporophyll, Stipule, Succubus, Tea, Title, Tobacco, TTL, Valve, Vert, Vine, Withdraw

Leafhopper Thrip

Leafless Ebracteate, Nudicaul, Scape

Leaflet At(t)ap, Bill, Bracteole, Circular, Dodger, Fly-sheet, Foliolose, Handbill, Hand-out, Pinna, Pinnula, Prophyll, Stipel, → **TRACT**

League Achaean, Alliance, Amphictyony, Arab, Band, Bund, Compact, Decapolis, Delian, Denominal, Entente, Federation, Gueux, Guild, Hanse(atic), Holy, Ivy, L, Land, Little, Major, Minor, Muslim, Nations, Parasang, Primrose, Redheaded, Rugby, Solemn, Super, Union, Ypres, Zollverein, Zupa

Leak(y) Bilge, Drip, Escape, Extravasate, Gizzen, Holed, Holey, Ooze, Pee, Porous, Run, Seepage, Sype, Trickle, Wee, Weep, Wee-wee

Leak-proof Airtight

Leamington Spa

Lean(ing) Abut, Aslope, Barren, Batter, Bend, Careen, Carneous, Carnose, Griskin, Heel, Hike out, → **INCLINE**, Lie, Lig(ge), List, Minceur, Partiality, Prop, Propend, Rake, Rawboned, Rely, Rest, Scraggy, Scrawny, Skinny, Spare, Stoop, Taste, Tend, Thin, Tilt, Tip, Walty, Wiry

Leander Abydos

Lean-to Skillion

Leap(ing), Leapt Assemblé, Bound, Brisé, Cabriole, Caper, Capriole, Cavort, Clear, Croupade, Curvet, Echappé, Entrechat, Falcade, Fishdive, Flying, Frisk, Galumph, Gambade, Gambado, Gambol, Jeté, Jump, Loup, Luppen, Ollie, Over, Pigeon-wing, Pounce, Pronk, Quantum, Sally, Salto, Somersa(u)lt, Somerset, → **SPRING**, Stag, Transilient, Vault, Volte

Leap year Bissextile, Penteteric

Lear Edward, King, Nonsense

Learn(ed), Learner Associative, Beginner, Blended, Blue, Bluestocking, Chela, Classical, Con, Culture, Discipline, Discover, Discrimination, Distance, Doctor, Don, Erudite, Erudition, Gather, Get, Glean, Hear, Index, Insight, Instrumental, Kond, L, Latent, Lear(e), Leir, Lere, Lifelong, Literate, Literati, Literato, Lore, Lucubrate, Machine, Master, Memorise, Mirza, Mug up, New, → **NOVICE**, Open, Opsimath(y), Pandit,

Polymath, Programmed, Pundit, Pupil, Rep, Rookie, Savant, Scan, Scholar(ship), Scient, See, Sleep, Starter, Student, → **STUDY**, Tiro, Trainee, Tutee, Tyro, Visile, Wise, Wit

Lease(-holder) Charter, Farm, Feu, Gavel, Hire, Let, Long, Novated, → **RENT**, Set(t), Subtack, Tack, Tacksman

Leash Lead, Lune, Lyam, Lym(e), Slip, Three, Trash, Triplet

Least Minimum, Rap

Leather(s), Leather-worker, Leathery Aqualeather, Artificial, Bouilli, Bouilly, Box-calf, Brail, Buckskin, Buff, Cabretta, Calf, Capeskin, Chammy, Chamois, Chaps, Checklaton, Cheverel, Chevrette, Chrome, Cordovan, Cordwain, Corium, Counter, Cowhide, Crispin, Crocodile, Cuir(-bouilli), Currier, Deacon, Deerskin, Diphthera, Doeskin, Dogskin, Durant, Fair, Foxing, Goatskin, Grain, Hide, Hog-skin, Horsehide, Japanned, Kid, Kip(-skin), Labretta, Lacquered, Lamp, Levant, Marocain, Maroquin, Mocha, Morocco, Mountain, Nap(p)a, Neat, Nubuck®, Oak, Ooze, Oxhide, Paste-grain, Patent, Pigskin, Plate, Rand, Rawhide, Rexine®, Riem(pie), Roan, Rock, Rough-out, Russet, Russia, Saffian, Shagreen, Shammy, Sharkskin, Shecklaton, Sheepskin, Shoe, Skiver, Slinkskin, Snakeskin, Spetch, Split, Spruce, Spur, Spur-whang, Stirrup, Strand, Strap, Strop, Suede, Tan, Taw, Thong, Upper, Wallop, Wash, Waxed, White, Whitleather, Yuft

Leatherneck Marine, RM

Leave(r), Leaving(s), Leave off Abandon, Abiturient, Abscond, Absit, Absquatulate, Acquittal, Adieu, Annual, Avoid, Bequeath, Betake, Blessing, Blow, Broken meats, Bug, Compassionate, Congé, Congee, Days off, Decamp, Depart, Desert, Desist, Devisal, Devise, Ditch, Evacuate, Except, Exeat, Exit, Exodus, Extrude, Forego, Forgo, Forsake, French, Furlough, Gardening, Garlandage, Get out, → **GO**, Inspan, Ish, Legate, Liberty, Licence, Log off, Maroon, Mass, Maternity, Mizzle, Omit, Orts, Pace, Parental, Park, Part, Paternity, → **PERMISSION**, Permit, → **QUIT**, Residue, Resign, Sabbatical, Scapa, Scat, Scram, Shore, Sick, Skedaddle, Skidoo®, Stick, Strand, Vacate, Vade, Vamo(o)se, Will, Withdraw

Leaven Barm, Ferment, Yeast

Lebanese, Lebanon Druse, RL

Lecher(ous), Lechery Gate, Goaty, Lascivious, Libertine, Lickerish, Lustful, Profligate, Rake, Randy, Roué, Salaciousness, Satirisk, Satyr, Silen, Whoremonger, Wolf

Lectern Ambo, Bookstand, Desk, Eagle, Oratory

Lecture(r), Lectures, Lecturing Address, Aristotelian, Chalktalk, Creed, Curtain, Dissert(ator), Docent, Don, Earful, Erasmus, Expound, Harangue, Homily, Hulsean, Jaw, Jawbation, Jobe, L, Lantern, Lector, Orate, Pi-jaw, Prelect, Privatdocent, Prone, Rate, Read(er), Rede, Reith, Roasting, Rubber chicken circuit, Scold, Sententious, → **SERMON**, Spout, Take to task, Talk, Teacher, Teach-in, Tongue-lashing, Wigging, Yaff

Ledge Altar, Berm, Buttery-bar, Channel, Fillet, Gradin(e), Linch, Miserere, Misericord(e), Nut, Rake, Scarcement, Settle, → **SHELF**, Subsellium, Window (sill)

Ledger Book, General, Purchase, Register

Lee(s) Dregs, Dunder, Grout, Heeltaps, Sediment, Shelter, Ullage

Leech Annelid, Bleeder, Gnathobdellida, Horse, Medicinal, Parasite, Rhynchobdellida

Leek Allium, Fouat, Fouet, Porraceous, Rocambole, Sengreen

Leer Eliad, Fleer, Oeillade, Ogle, Perv

Leeway Drift

Left (hand), Left-handed, Left-hander, Left-winger Abandoned, Adrift, Avoided, Balance, Bolshy, Corrie-fisted, Dolly-push, Fellow traveller, Forsaken, Gallock, Haw, Hie, High, Inherited, L, Laeotropic, Laevorotation, Larboard, Links, Loony, Lorn, Militant, Near, New, Other, Over, Pink, Pinko, Port, Portsider, Quit, Rad, Red (Brigade), Relic, Residuum, Resigned, Secondo, Sinister, Soc(ialist), Southpaw, Split, Thin, Titoism, Trot, Unused, Verso, Vo, Went, West, Wind, Yet

Left-over Astatki, Dregs, End, Gone, Lave, Oddment, Offcut, Orra, Remains, Remanet, → **REMNANT**, Residue, Rest, Waste

Leg(s), Leggings, Leggy, Leg-wear Antigropelo(e)s, Bandy, Barbados, Barley-sugar, Bow, Breeches, Cabriole, Cannon, Chaparajos, Chaparejos, Chaps, Crural, Crus, Cuisse, Cush, Dib, Drumstick, Fine, Fly-sail, Gaiter, Galligaskins, Gam(b), Gamash, Gambado, Garter, Gaskin, Giambeux, Gigot, Gramash, Gramosh, Ham, Haunch, Hest, Hock, Jamb, Jambeau, Jambeaux, Knock-knee(d), Limb, Long, Member, Milk, Myriapod, Oleo, On(side), Peg, Peraeopod, Periopod, Peroneal, Pestle, Pin, Podite, Proleg, Puttees, Pylon, Relay, Section, Shanks, Shanks's pony, Shaps, Shin, Short, Spats, Spatterdash, Spider, Spindleshanks, Square, Stage, Start up, Stifle, Stump, Thigh, Tights, White

Legacy Bequest, Cumulative, Demonstrative, Dowry, Entail, General, Heirloom, Residuary, Specific, Substitutional

Legal(ism), Legally, Legitimate Above board, Bencher, Decriminalised, De regle, Forensic, Halacha, Halaka(h), Halakha, Lawful, Licit, Nomism, Scienter, Statutory

Legal book Halacha, Halaka(h), Halakha, Talmud

Leg-armour, Leg-covering Cootikin, Cu(i)tikin, Gambado, Jamb(e), Pad

Legate, Legator A latere, Ambassador, Consul, Devisor, Emissary, Envoy, Nuncio

Legato Slur

Legend(ary) Arthurian, Caption, Edda, Fable, Folklore, Hadith, Motto, Myth, Saga, Story, Urban, Yowie

▷ **Legend** *may indicate* leg-end e.g. foot, talus

Leger Swindler

Leghorn Livorno

Legible Clear, Lucid, Plain

Legion(ary), Legionnaire Alauda, American, Army, British, Cohort, Countless, Deserter, Foreign, Geste, Honour, → **HOST**, Maniple, Many, Throng, Thundering, Zillions

Legislate, Legislation, Legislator, Legislature Assemblyman, Congress, Decemvir, Decree, Delegated, MP, Nomothete, Oireachtas, → **PARLIAMENT**, Persian, Senator, Solon, Supreme soviet, Thesmothete, Zemstvo

Legitimate Kosher, Loyal, Proper, Rightful, Valid

Legless Amelia, Blotto, Boozy, Caecilia, Drunk, Mermaid, Paralytic, Psyche

Leg-pull Chaff, Joke, Rise, Rot

Legume, Leguminous Bean, Guar, Lentil, Lomentum, Pea, Peanut, Pipi, Pod, Pulse

Leibniz Monadism

Leicester Sheep

Leigh Amyas

Leisure(ly) Adagio, Bytime, Ease, Lento, Liberty, Moderato, Off day, Otium, Respite, Rest, Vacation

Lemming Morkin

Lemon Answer, Cedrate, Citron, Citrus, Dud, Smear-dab, Sole, Twist, Yellow

Lemonade Pop

Lemur Angwantibo, Aye-aye, Babacoote, Bush-baby, Colugo, Cynocephalus, Galago, Half-ape, Indri(s), Loris, Macaco, Malmag, Mongoose, → **MONKEY**, Nagapie, Potto, Ringtail, Sifaka, Spectre, Tana, Tarsier

Lend(er) Advance, Library, Loan, Prest, Sub, Vaunce

Length(y), Lengthen(ing), Lengthwise Archine, Arsheen, Arshin(e), Aune, Barleycorn, Braccio, Cable, Chain, Cubit, Distance, Eke, Ell, → **ELONGATE**, Endways, Ennage, Epenthetic, Expand, Extensive, Focal, Foot, Footage, Furlong, Inch, Ley, Mile, Nail, Passus, Perch, Piece, Plethron, Pole, Prolate, Prolix, Prolong, Protract, Reach, Remen, Rigmarole, Rod, Rope, Slow, Span, Stadium, Toise, Vara, Verbose, Yard

Lenient, Leniency Clement, Exurable, Lax, Mild, Permissive, Soft, Soft line, Tolerant

Lens Achromatic, Acoustic, Anamorphic, Anastigmat, Aplanatic, Apochromat(ic), Bifocal, Bull's eye, Compound, Contact, Corneal, Crookes, Crown, Crystalline, Dielectric, Diopter, Dioptre, Diverging, Electron, Electrostatic, Eye, Eyeglass, Eye-piece, Facet, Field, Fish-eye, Fresnel, Gas-permeable, Gravitational, Hard, Immersion, Lentil, Macro, Magnetic, Metallic, Mirror, Object(ive), Object-glass, Optic, Pantoscope, Phacoid,

Piano-concave, Piano-convex, Soft, Soft-focus, Stanhope, Sunglass, Telephoto, Toric, Trifocal, Varifocal, Water, Wide-angle, Zoom

Lent Carême, Fast, Laetare, Out, Quadragesimal, Term

Lentil(s) D(h)al, Dholl, Ervalenta, Lens, Phacoid, Pulse, Puy, Revalenta

Leonora Overture

Leopard Catamountain, Clouded, Cougar, Hunting, Jaguar, Leap, Libbard, Oceloid, Ounce, Panther, Pard, Snow, Spots, Tiger

Leopold Bloom

Leotard Maillot

Leper, Leprosy, Leprous Gehazi, Hansen's disease, Lazar, Leontiasis, Lionism, Meazel, Mesel, Outcast, Pariah

Lepidopterist Aurelian, Moth-er, Pendleton, Treacler

Leprechaun Elf, Gremlin, Imp

Lepton Muon

Lesbian Boi, Bull dyke, Crunchie, Diesel, Dike, Dyke, Homophile, Lipstick, Sapphist, Tribade

Lese-majesty Treason

Lesion Cut, Gash, Pannus, Scar, Serpiginous, Sore, Wheal, Whelk

Less(en), Lesser, Lessening Abate, Alaiment, Bate, Comedown, Contract, Deaden, Decline, Deplete, Derogate, Dilute, → **DWINDLE**, Extenuate, Fewer, Junior, Littler, Meno, Minus, Play down, Reduce, Relax, Remission, Sen, Shrink, Subordinate, Subsidiary, Tail, Under

Lesson Class, Example, Lear(e), Lection, Leir, Lere, Life, Liripipe, Masterclass, Moral, Object, Parashah, Period, Sermon, Shiur, Tutorial

Let (go, off, out), Letting Allow, Cap, Charter, Conacre, Displode, Divulge, Enable, Entitle, Explode, Hire, Impediment, Indulge, Leak, Lease, Litten, Loot(en), Luit(en), Lutten, Net, Obstacle, Obstruct, → **PERMIT**, Rent, Reprieve, Sett, Tenancy, Unhand, Warrant

Let down Abseil, Betray, Lower, Sell, Vail

Let-down Disappointment, Non-event

Lethal Deadly, Fatal, Fell, Mortal

Lethargic, Lethargy Accidie, Apathy, Coma, Drowsy, Ennui, Hebetude, Inactive, Inertia, Lassitude, Listless, Logy, Passive, Sleepy, Sluggish, Stagnant, Stupor, Supine, Torpid, Turgid, Weariness

Letter(s) Ache, Aerogram, Aesc, A(y)in, Airgraph, Aleph, Alif, Alpha, Ascender, Aspirate, Bayer, Begging, Beta, Beth, Block, Breve, Cadmean, Canine, Caph, Capital, Capon, Casket, Chain, Cheth, Chi, Chitty, Circular, Col, Collins, Consonant, Covering, Cue, Cuneiform, Daled, Daleth, Dead, Dear John, Delta, Digamma, Digraph, Dispatch, Dominical, Edh, Ef(f), Emma, Encyclical, Ep(isemon), Epistle, Epsilon, Eta, Eth, Fan, Favour, Form, Fraktur, French, Gamma, Gimel, Grapheme, He, Heth, Hieratic, Initial, Iota, Izzard, Jerusalem, Kaph, Kappa, Koppa, Kufic, Labda, Lambda, Lamed(h), Landlady, Landlord, Lessee, Lessor, Literal, Love, Mail, Mail-shot, Majuscule, Mem, Memo, Message, Miniscule, Minuscule, Missive, Monogram, Mu, Nasal, Night, Note, Notelet, Nu, Nun, Og(h)am, Omega, Omicron, Open, Ou, Pacifical, Pahlavi, Paragoge, Paston, Pastoral, Patent, Pe, Pehlevi, Phi, Pi, Plosive, Poison-pen, Polyphone, Postbag, Psi, Pythagorean, Qof, Qoph, Resh, Rho, Rhyme, Rom, Runestave, Sad(h)e, Samekh, Samian, Sampi, San, Scarlet, Screed, Screeve, Screwtape, Script, See, Shin, Ship, Siglum, Sigma, Sign, Signal, Sin, Sort, Stiff, Swash, Tau, Tav, Taw, Teth, Theta, Thorn, Toc, Tsade, Typo, Uncial, Upsilon, Vau, Vav, Versal, Vowel, Waw, Wen, Wyn, Wynn, Xi, Yod(h), Yogh, Ypsilon, Zayin, Zed, Zeta

Lettering Cufic, Kufic

Lettuce Batavia, Butterhead, Cabbage, Chicon, Corn-salad, Cos, Frog's, Iceberg, Lactuca, Lamb's, Lollo rosso, Mache, Mizuna, Radicchio, Romaine, Salad, Sea, Thridace

Leucoma Albugo

Levant(ine) Coptic, Go, Israelite, Jew, Ottamite, Ottomite

Levee Bank, Dyke, Embankment, Party

Level(ler) A, Abney, Abreast, Aclinic, Ad eundum, Aim, Awash, Bargaining, Base, Break even, Bulldoze, Champaign, Confidence, Countersink, Degree, Dumpy, Echelon, Energy, Equal, → **EVEN**, Extent, Eye, Flat, Flight, Flush, Fog, Grade, Horizontal, Impurity, Infill, Logic, Meet, O, Occupational, Ordinary, Par, Plane, Plat(eau), Point, Price, Race, Rank, Rase, Raze, Reduced, Savanna, Sea, Spirit, Split, Springing, → **SQUARE**, Status, Stor(e)y, Stratum, Street, Strew, Strickle, Subsistence, Summit, Support, Surveyor's, Tear-down, Tier, Top, Trophic, True, Water, Wye, Y

Lever(age) Backfall, Bell-crank, Brake, Cock, Crampon, Crowbar, Dues, Gear, Handspike, Jaw, Jemmy, Joystick, Key, Knee-stop, Landsturm, Pawl, Peav(e)y, Pedal, Pinch, Prise, Prize, Pry, Purchase, Stick, Sweep, Swipe, Tappet, Throttle, Tiller, Treadle, Treddle, Tremolo arm, Trigger, Tumbler, Typebar, Whipstaff

Leviathan Whale

Levitate, Levitation Float, Hover, Magnetic, Rise, Yogic flying

Levity Flippancy, Glee, Humour, Jollity

Levy Capital, Estreat, Impose, Imposition, Leave, Militia, Octroi, Raise, Scutage, Stent, Talliate, Tax, Tithe, Toll

Lewd(ness) Bawd(r)y, Blue, Cyprian, Debauchee, Impure, Libidinous, Lubricity, Obscene, Priapism, Prurient, Raunchy, Silen(us), Tentigo, Unclean

Lewis Carroll, Tenon

Lexicographer, Lexicon Compiler, Craigie, Drudge, Etymologist, Florio, Fowler, Glossarist, Grove, Johnson(ian), Larousse, Liddell, Mental, Murray, OED, Thesaurus, Vocabulist, Webster, Words-man

Liability, Liable Anme, Apt, Current, Debt, Employer's, Incur, Limited, Open, Product, Prone, Subject, Susceptible, White elephant

Liaison Affair, Amour, Contact, Link

Liana Guarana

Libel(lous) Blasphemous, Defamatory, Malign, Sclaunder, Slander, Smear, Sully, Vilify

Liberal(ity) Abundant, Adullamites, Ample, Besant, Bounteous, Bountiful, Breadth, Bright, Broad, Catholic, Enlightened, Free(hander), Free-hearted, → **GENEROUS**, Giver, Grey, Grimond, Grit, Handsome, Indulgent, L, Largesse, Latitudinarian, Lavish, Limousine, Munificent, Octobrist, Open, Permissive, → **PROFUSE**, Rad(ical), Samuelite, Simonite, Spender, Steel, Tolerant, Trivium, Unstinted, Verlig, Verligte, Whig

Liberate(d), Liberation, Liberator Bolivar, Deliver, Dissimure, Emancipate, Fatah, → **FREE**, Gay, Inkatha, Intolerant, Messiah, Nick, PLO, Release, Risorgimento, Save, Steal, Sucre, Unfetter, UNITA, Women's

Liberian Kroo, Kru

Libertarian, Libertine Chartered, Corinthian, Debauchee, Don Juan, Laxist, Lecher, Lothario, Lovelace, Orgiast, Playboy, Rake, Rip, Roué, Wencher, Wolf

Liberty Bail, Civil, Discretion, Franchise, Freedom, Hall, Latitude, Licence, Mill, Sauce

Libra L

Library, Librarian Bibliothecary, BL, Bodleian, Bookmobile, British, Chartered, Circulating, Copyright, Cottonian, Dewey, Film, Gene, Genomic, Harleian, Laurentian, Lending, Mazarin, Mobile, Morgue, PL, Public, Radcliffe, Reference, Rental, Subscription, Tauchnitz

Librettist Boito, Gilbert, Hammerstein, Lyricist

▶ **Lice** *see* **LOUSE**

Licence, License Abandon, Allow, Authorisation, Carnet, Charter, Dispensation, Driving, Enable, Exequatur, Fling, Franchise, Free(dom), Gale, Import, Imprimatur, Indult, → **LATITUDE**, Let, Marriage, Occasional, Passport, → **PERMIT**, Poetic, Pratique, Provisional, Road-fund, Rope, Slang, Special, Table, Ticket of leave

Licentious Artistic, Corinthian, Debauchee, Hot, Immoral, Large, Lax, Liberal, Loose, Orgiastic, Prurient, Ribald, Sensual, Wanton

Lichen Apothecia, Archil, Corkir, Crotal, Crottle, Cup, Epiphyte, Epiphytic, Graphis, Korkir, Lecanora, Litmus, Moss, Oakmoss, Orchel, Orchil(la), Orcine, Orseille, Parella, Parelle, Roccella, Rock tripe, Sea-ivory, Soredium, Stone-rag, Stone-raw, Tree-moss, Usnea, Wartwort

Lick(ing) Bat, Beat, Deer, Felch, Lambent, Lap, Leather, Rate, Salt, Slake, Speed, Tongue, Whip

▶ **Licorice** *see* **LIQUORICE**

Lid Cover, Hat, Kid, Maximum, Opercula, Screwtop, Twist-off

Liddell Alice

Lido Beach, Pool

Lie(s), Liar, Lying Abed, Accubation, Accumbent, Ananias, Bam, Bare-faced, Bask, Billy, Bounce(r), Braide, Cau(l)ker, Cellier, Clipe, Clype, Concoction, Contour, Couch(ant), Cracker, Cram(mer), Cretism, Cumbent, Deception, Decubitous, Decumbent, Direct, Doggo, Fable, False(r), Falsehood, Falsify, Falsity, Fib, Fiction, Figment, Flam, Gag, Gonk, Hori, Incumbent, Invention, Inveracity, Kip, Lair, Leasing, Lee(ar), Lig(ge), Lurk, Mythomania, Nestle, Obreption, Oner, Perjury, Plumper, Porky (pie), Procumbent, Prone, Prostrate, Pseudologia, Recline, Recumbent, Repent, Repose, Reptant, Ride, Romance(r), Sham, Sleep, Strapper, Stretcher, Supine, Swinger, Tale, Tappice, Tar(r)adiddle, Thumper, Tissue, Try, Untruth, Whacker, Whid, White, Whopper, Yanker

Lied Art-song, Song

Lie-detector Polygraph

Lien Mortgage, Title

Lieu Locus, Place

Lieutenant Cassio, Flag, Loot, Lt, No 1, Sub(altern)

Life Age, Animation, Being, Bio, Biog(raphy), Breath, Brian, Brio, C'est la vie, Chaim, Clerihew, CV, Energy, Esse, Eva, Eve, Existence, Good, Heart, High, Mean, Memoir, Mortal coil, Nellie, Nelly, Night, Non-fiction, Pep, Plasma, Private, Public, Quick, Real, Riley, Shelf, Span, Spirit, Still, Subsistence, Time, True, Useful, Vita, Vitality, Zoe

Life-blood Essence, Lethee

Lifeboat(man) Ark, Noah

Life-cell Energid

Life-cycle Redia

Life-force, Life-style Chi, Mana, Od, Orgone, Port, Qi

Lifeless(ness) Abiosis, Algidity, Amort, Arid, Azoic, Barren, Catatonic, Cauldrife, → **DEAD**, Dull, Flat, Inanimate, Inert, Key-cold, Log, Mineral, Possum, Sterile, Stonen, Wooden

Lifelike Breathing, Speaking

Lifeline Umbilicus

Life-rent Usufruct

Life-saver Cheesemonger, Lineman, Mae West, Preserver, Raft, Reelman

Lift(ed), Lifter, Lifting Araise, Arayse, Arsis, Attollent, Bone, Cable-car, Camel, Chair, Cly, Copy, Crane, Davit, Dead, Dumb waiter, Elate, Elevator, Enhance, Extol, Filch, Fillip, Fireman's, Heave, Heeze, Heezie, Heft(e), Heist, Hitch, Hoise, Hoist, Hove, Jack, Jigger, Kleptomania, Leaven, Lefte, Lever, Lewis, Nab, Nap, Nim, Otis®, Paternoster, Pilfer, Press, Pulley, → **RAISE**, Ride, Rotor, Scoop, Service, Shearlegs, Ski, Sky, Snatch, Sneak, Spout, Stair, Steal, Surface, T-bar, Teagle, Theft, Thumb, Topping, Up, Winch, Windlass

Ligament Annular, Cruciate, Fr(a)enum, Paxwax, Peacock-stone, Spring, Suspensory, Tendon, Urachus

Ligation, Ligature Ae(sc), Ash, Bandage, Bind, Funicle, Tubal

▷ **Light** *may indicate* an anagram

Light(en), Lighting, Lighter, Lights Aerate, Afterglow, Airglow, Airy, Albedo, Ale, Alow, Alpenglow, Amber, Ancient, Ans(wer), Arc, Aurora, Back-up, Barge, Batement, Batswing, Beacon, Beam, Bengal, Beshine, Bezel, Birlinn, Black, Bleach, Blond(e), Brake, Breezy, Bude, Bulb, Calcium, Candle, Cannel, Canstick, Casco, Casement, Chiaroscuro,

Cierge, Clue, Courtesy, Day, Dewali, Diffused, Direct, Diwali, Dormer, Dream-hole, Drop, Drummond, Earth-shine, Eddystone, Electrolier, Ethereal, Fairy, Fall, Fan, Fantastic, Fastnet, Feathery, Fetch-candle, Fidibus, Fill, Filter, Fire, First, Fixed, Flambeau, Flame, Flare, Flax(y), Flicker, Flimsy, Flippant, Flit(t), Floating, Flood, Fluorescent, Fog (lamp), Frothy, Fuffy, Gas-poker, Gegenschein, Glare, Gleam, Glim(mer), Glow, Gossamer, Green, Guiding, Gurney, Haggis, Halation, Hazard, Head, House, Idiot, Ignite, Illum(in)e, Incandescence, Indirect, Induction, Inner, Irradiate, Junior, Keel, Key, Kindle, Kiran, Klieg, Lamp, Lampion, Land, Lantern, Lanthorn, Laser, Leading, LED, Leerie, Leggiero, Levigate, Lime, Link, Linstock, Loadstar, Lobuli, Lodestar, Lozen, Lucarne, Lucigen, Luminaire, Lumine, Luminescence, Luminous, Lunt, Lustre, Lux, Mandorla, Match, Menorah, Mercurial, Merry-dancers, Mithra(s), Moon, Naphtha, Navigate, Navigation, Neon, New, Nit, Northern, Obstruction, Od(yl), Offal, Optics, Pale, Pane, Parhelion, Pavement, Pennyweight, Phosphene, Phosphorescence, Phot(ic), Photon, Photosphere, Pilot, Pipe, Polar, Pontoon, Portable, Pra(a)m, Producer-gas, Range, Rear, Red, Reflex, Relieve, Relume, Rembrandt, Reversing, Riding, Robot, Rocket, Running, Rush, Safe(ty), Satori, Scoop, Sea-dog, Sea fire, Search, Shine, Shy, Solid-state, Southern, Southern-vigil, Spill, Spot, Spry, Steaming, Strip, Strobe, Stroboscope, Subtle, Sun, Sunshine, Suttle, Svelte, Tail, Tally, Taper, Taps, Tead, Threshold, Tind, Tine, Torch, Torchère, Touchpaper, Track, Traffic, Trivial, Ultraviolet, Unchaste, Unoppressive, UV, Ver(e)y, Vesica, Vesta, Vigil, Watch, Wax, Welsbach burner, White, Windock, Window, Winker, Winnock, Zippo, Zodiacal

Light-headed Dizzy

Light-hearted Captious, Gay, Kicksin

Lighthouse Beacon, Caisson, Eddystone, Fanal, Fastnet, Phare, Pharos, Sea-mark, Signal

Lightless Aphotic, Dark, Obscure, Unlit

Lightness Buoyancy, Galant, Levity, Pallor

Lightning Ball, Bolt, Catequil, Chain, Dry, Éclair, Enfouldered, Fireball, Fire flag, Forked, Fulmination, Heat, Levin, Sheet, Thunderbolt, Wildfire, Zigzag

Lightship Floating beacon, Nore

Lightweight Jack straw, Nobody, Oz, Trivial

Lignite Jet, Surtarbrand, Surturbrand

Like(ness), Liking À la, Analogon, As, Assimilate, Attachment, Broo, Care, Corpse, Dig, Duplicate, Effigy, Eg, Egally, Enjoy, Equal, Fancy, Fellow, Guise, Lich, Palate, Parallel, Peas, Penchant, -philus, Please, Predilection, Resemblance, Semblant, Shine, Similar, Simile, Simulacrum, Smaak, Sort, Speaking, Taste, Tiki, Uniformity

Likely, Likelihood Apt, Fair, Liable, Maximum, Odds-on, Offchance, On, Plausible, Possible, Probable, Probit, Prone, Prospective

Likewise Also, Ditto, Do, Egally, Eke, Item, So, Too, Tu quoque

Lilac French, Laylock, Mauve, Pipe-tree, Syringa

Lilliputian Minute

Lilt Swing

Lily African, Agapanthus, Aloe, Amaryllis, Annunciation, Arum, Asphodel, Aspidistra, Belladonna, Blackberry, Calla, Camas(h), Camass, Canada, Candock, Chincherinchee, Colchicum, Colocasia, Convallaria, Corn, Crinum, Dale, Day, Easter, Elaine, Endogen, Fawn, Fleur de lys, Fritillary, Funkia, Galtonia, Guernsey, Haemanthus, Hellebore, Hemerocallis, Herb-Paris, Jacobean, Jacob's, Jersey, Kniphofia, Laguna, Lent, Leopard, Lote, Lotos, Lotus, Madonna, Mariposa, Martagon, Meadow, Moorva, Mount Cook, Nelumbo, Nenuphar, Nerine, Nuphar, Nymphaea, Orange, Padma, Phormium, Pig, Plantain, Pond, Quamash, Regal, Richardia, Sabadilla, Sansevieria, Sarsa, Scilla, Sego, Skunk cabbage, Smilax, Solomon's seal, Spider, Star of Bethlehem, Stone, Sword, Tiger, Trillium, Tritoma, Tuberose, Turk's cap, Vellozia, Victoria, Water, Water maize, Yucca, Zephyr

Lily-maid Elaine

Lima L, Sugar bean

Limb Arm, Bough, Branch, Crural, Exapod, Flipper, Forearm, Hindleg, Imp, Leg, Leg-end, Member, Phantom, Proleg, Pterygium, Ramus, Scion, Shin, Spald, Spall, Spaul(d), Wing

Limbless Amelia

Limbo Bardo, Isolation, Oblivion

Lime Bass(wood), Beton, Calc, Calcicolous, Caustic, Lind(en), Malm, Mortar, Slaked, Soda, Teil, Tilia, Trap, Unslaked, Viscum, Whitewash

Limerick Doggerel, Twiner, Verse

Limestone Burren, Calc-sinter, Calm, Calp, Ca(u)m, Clint, Coquina, Coral Rag, Cornbrash, Cornstone, Dolostone, Forest Marble, Grike, Karst, Kentish rag, Kunkar, Kunkur, Landscape marble, Magnesian, Malm, Marble, Muschelkalk, Nero-antico, Oolite, Pisolite, Rottenstone, Scaglia, Stalagma, Stinkstone, Travertin(e)

Limey Rooinek

Limit(ation), Limited, Limiting Ambit, Asymptote, Bind, Border, Borné, Bound, Bourn(e), Brink, Cap, Cash, Ceiling, Chandrasekhar, Circumscribe, Climax, Compass, Confine, Constrict, Curb, Deadline, Define, Demark, Determine, Earshot, Eddington, Edge, Edition, End, Entail, Esoteric, → **EXTENT**, Extreme, Finite, Fraenum, Frontier, Gate, Goal, Gole, Hourlong, Impound, Induciae, Insular, Limes, Line, Lite, Lynchet, March, Maximum, Meare, Mete, Minimum, Nth, Outedge, Pale, Parameter, Perimeter, Periphery, Predetermine, Qualify, Range, Rate-cap, Ration, Reservation, Restrict, Rim, Roche, Roof, Scant, Shoestring, Sky, Somedeal, Somedele, Speed, Stint, String, Sumptuary, Tail(lie), Tailye, Tailzie, Term(inus), Tether, Three-mile, Threshold, Thule, Tie, Time, Tramline, Tropic, Twelve-mile, Utmost, Utter, Verge

▷ **Limit** *may indicate* 'surrounding'

Limner RA

Limousine Daimler, Rolls, Stretch, Zil

Limp Claudication, Dot, Droopy, Flabby, Flaccid, Flaggy, Flimsy, Floppy, Gimp, Hamble, Hilch, Hirple, Hitch, Hobble, Hop, Lank, Lifeless, Spancel, Tangle, Wilting

Limpet Keyhole, Patella, Slipper, Streptoneura

Limpid Clear, Lucid, Pure

Linch Terrace

Lincoln(shire) Abe, Poacher, Yellow-belly

Linden Baucis, Lime, Tilia

Line(d), Lines, Lining Abreast, Aclinic, Agate, Agonic, Allan, Anacreontic, → **ANCESTRY**, Anent, Angle, Apothem, Arew, Asclepiadean, Assembly, Asymptote, Attention, Axis, Babbitt, Bakerloo, Bar, Barcode, Baton, Battle, Baulk, Becket, Bikini, Bluebell, Bob, Body, Bombast, Bottom, Boundary, BR, Brail, Branch, Bread, Building, Bush, By, Canal, Carolingian, Carriage, Casing, Cathetus, Ceil, Cento, Ceriph, Chord, Ciel, Clew, Club, Coach, Coffle, Colour, Column, Command, Contour, Cord(on), Coseismal, Course, Crease, Credit, Crib, Crocodile, Crowfoot, Crow's feet, Cunard, Curve, Cushion, Dancette, Danger, Date, Datum, Dead-ball, Decidua, Delay, Descent, DEW, Diagonal, Diameter, Diffusion, Directrix, Distaff, Dochmiachal, Dotted, Doublure, Downhaul, Downrigger, Dress, Dynasty, Earing, El, E-la-mi, Encase, End, Equator, Equinoctial, Equinox, Faint, Fall(s), Fathom, Fault, Feint, Fess(e), Fettle, File, Finishing, Firing, Firn, Fixed, Flex, Flight, Frame, Fraunhofer, Front, Frontier, Frost, Furr(ow), Geodesic, Geotherm, Germ, Gimp, Giron, Goal, Graph, Grass, Green, Gridiron, Gymp, Gyron, Hachure, Halyard, Hard, Hatching, Hawser, Header, Hemistich, Heptameter, Hexameter, Hexapody, High-watermark, Hindenburg, Hockey, Hogscore, Hot, House, Impot, Inbounds, Inbred, Incase, Inhaul(er), Insole, Interfluve, Intima, Isallobar, Isentrope, Isobar, Isobath, Isobront, Isocheim, Isochime, Isochron(e), Isoclinic, Isoclude, Isocryme, Isogloss, Isogonal, Isogonic, Isogram, Isohel, Isohyet, Isolex, Isomagnetic, Isometric, Isonome, Isopach(yte), Isophone, Isophote, Isopiestic, Isopleth, Isopyenal, Isotach, Isothere, Isotherm, Kill, Knittle, L, Land, Lane, Lansker, Lap, Lariat, Lateral, Latitude, Lead, Leash, Le(d)ger, Length, Ley, Lie, Ling, LMS, Load, Log, Longitude, Lossy, Loxodrome, Lubber, Lugger, Lye, Macron, Maginot, Main, Mainsheet, Mark, Marriage,

Mason-Dixon, Median, Meridian, Mesal, Metropolitan, Miurus, Monorail, Multiplet, Nacre, Naman, Nazca, Nidation, Noose, Norsel, Northern, Number, Oche, Octastichon, Ode, Oder-Neisse, Og(h)am, Omentum, Onedin, Ordinate, Orphan, Orthostichy, Painter, Panty, Parallel, Parameter, Parastichy, Party, Paternoster, Path, Penalty, Pencil, Phalanx, Picket, Pinstripe, Plasterboard, Pleuron, Plimsoll, Plumb, Poetastery, Polar, Police, Policy, Popping-crease, Poverty, Power, Princess, Product(ion), Profession, Punch, Pure, Queue, Race, Radial, Radius, Rail, Rank, Raster, Ratlin(e), Ratling, Rattlin, Ray, Receiving, Red, Reticle, Retinue, Rew, Rhumb, Ripcord, Rope, Route, Row, Rugose, Rugous, Rule, Ry, Sarking, Scazon, Score, Scotch, Scratch, Scrimmage, Script, Secant, Seperatrix, Serif, Seriph, Service, Set, Shielded, Shore, Shout, Shroud, Siding, Siegfried, Sield, Sight, Silver, Six-yard, Slur, Snood, Snow, Soft, Solidus, Sounding, Specialty, Spectral, Spider, Spilling, Spring, Spunyarn, Squall, SR, Staff, Stance, Stanza, Starting, Static, Stave, Stean, Steen, Stein, Stem, Stich(os), Stock, Story, Strain, Strap, Streak, Strene, Striate, String, Stripe, Stuff, Subject, Subtense, Swap, Swifter, Symphysis, Syzygy, Tag, Tailback, Talweg, Tangent, Teagle, Tea lead, Terminator, Tetrameter, Thalweg, Thin blue, Thin red, Thread, Throwaway, Tidemark, Tie, Tier, Tiercet, Timber, Touch, Trade, Transmission, Transoceanic, Transversal, Tree, Trimeter, Tropic, Trot, Trunk, Try, Tudor, Twenty-five, Twenty-two, Upstroke, Variety, Verse, Vinculum, Virgule, Wad, Wallace's, Washing, Water(shed), White, Widow, Wire, World, Wrinkle, Yellow, Z, Zag, Zip, Zollner's

Lineage Ancestry, Descent, Extraction, Filiation, Parage, Pedigree

Linen Amice, Amis, Barb, Bed, Byssus, Cambric, Crash, Damask, Dornick, Dowlas, Duck, Ecru, Flax, Harn, Huckaback, Inkle, Lawn, Line, Lint, Lockram, Moygashel, Napery, Percale, Seersucker, Sendal, Silesia, Snow, Table, Toile, Undies

Liner Artist, Bin-bag, Eye, Ocean greyhound, RMS, Rule(r), Ship, Sleeve, Steamer, Steen, Titanic

Linesman Beeching, Parodist, → **POET**, Touch-judge

Linger(ing) Chronic, Dawdle, Dwell, Hang, Hove(r), Lag, Loaf, → **LOITER**, Straggle, Taigle, Tarry, Tie

Lingerie Bra, Drawers, Undies

Lingo Argot, Bat, Cant, Jargon, Polglish, Speech

Linguist(ic), Linguistics Clitic, Comparative, Descriptive, Glottic, Historical, Onomastics, Philological, Phonemics, Polyglot, Pragmatics, Semantics, Structural, Stylistics, Syntax, Tagmemics, Taxeme

Liniment Balm, Camphor, Carron-oil, Embrocation, Ointment, Opodeldoc, Salve

Link(ed), Linking, Links Associate, Between, Bond, Bridge, Chain, Cleek, Close knit, Colligate, Concatenation, Connect, Copula, Couple, Course, Cross-reference, Cuff, Desmid, Drag, Draw-gear, Ess, Flambeau, Golf, Hookup, Hot, Hotline, Incatenation, Index, Interconnect, Interface, Internet, Interrelation, Intertwine, Karabiner, Krab, Liaise, Machair, Missing, Modem, Nexus, On-line, Pons, Preposition, Reciprocal, Relate, Ring, Tead(e), Terrestrial, → **TIE**, Tie-in, Tie-line, Torch, Unite, Weakest, Wormhole, Yoke

Linkman Lamplighter, Mediator

Linnet Finch, Lintie, Lintwhite, Twite

Linoleum Waxcloth

Lint Charpie, Dossil

Lintel Summer, Transom

Lion(ess) Androcles, Aphid, Aslan, Chindit, Elsa, Glitterati, Hero, Leo, Maned, Mountain, Nemean, Opinicus, Personage, Pride, Simba

Lionel Trilling

Lion-tamer Androcles, Dan(iel)

Lip(py), Lips Beestung, Cheek, Cupid's bow, Fat, Fipple, Flews, Hare, Helmet, Jib, Labellum, Labial, Labiate, Labret, Labrum, Ligula, Muffle, Philtrum, → **RIM**, Rubies, Sass, Sauce, Slack-jaw, Spout, Submentum

Lipase Steapsin

Lipid Ganglioside, Inositol, Sphingarine
Lipstick Chapstick
Liquefy Deliquesce, Dissolve, Fuse, Melt
Liqueur, Liquor Bree, Brew, Broo, Broth, Creature, Elixir, Fumet, Hard stuff, Hooch, Lap, Mother, Ooze, Pot, Potation, Stock, Stuff, Vat

LIQUORS

3 letters:	*6 letters:*	*8 letters:*	Limoncello
Ale	Cassis	Abisante	Maraschino
Kir	Cerise	Absinthe	Mickey Finn
Rum	Chasse	Advokaat	Pousse-café
	Chicha	Amaretto	
4 letters:	Enzian	Anisette	*11 letters:*
Apry	Kahlua®	Calvados	Aguardiente
Feni	Kummel	Choclair	Benedictine
Malt	Mastic	Cocoribe	Jungle juice
Ouzo	Midori®	Drambuie®	Kirshwasser
Raki	Mobbie	Galliano	Tickle-brain
Rose	Pastis	Geropiga	
Tape	Pernod®	Kaoliang	*12 letters:*
Tiff	Rakija	Prunelle	Cherry brandy
Wine	Roiano	Rum shrub	Crème de cacao
Wort	Rotgut	Schnapps	Grand Marnier®
	Shypoo	Sciarada	Kirschwasser
5 letters:	Stingo	Tia Maria®	Supernaculum
Anise	Strega®	Witblits	
Crème	Strunt		*13 letters:*
Fenny		*9 letters:*	Cherry Marnier®
Hogan	*7 letters:*	Cointreau®	Crème de menthe
Hogen	Chococo	Framboise	Eau des creoles
Kirsh	Curaçao	Metheglin	Parfait d'amour
Lager	Fraises	Mirabelle	
Mobby	Fustian	Triple sec	*14 letters:*
Noyau	Persico	Van der Hum®	John Barleycorn
Pasha	Ratafia		White lightning
Rakee	Roncoco	*10 letters:*	
Sabra	Sambuca	Almondrado	
Skink	Samshoo	Chartreuse	
Stout	Taplash	Cher-suisse	
Toddy	Tequila	Hogan-mogen	

Liquid(ate), Liquidity, Liquids, Liquefaction Acetal, Amortise, Annihilate, Apprize, Aqua-regia, Azeotrope, Bittern, Bouillon, Bromine, Butanal, Butanol, Butyraldehide, Butyrin, Cacodyl, Cadaverine, Cash, Cash flow, Chloramine, Cinerin, Clyster, Court-bouillon, Creosol, Creosote, Decoction, Dispersant, Dope, Eluate, Erase, Ethanol, Ether, Eucalyptol, Eugenol, Flow, Fluid, Fural, Furfural, Furol, Guaiacol, Halothene, Indisputable, Ink, Isoprene, Jaw, Kakodyl, Lewisite, Limonene, Linalool, Lye, Massacre, Mess, Minim, Mouillé, Nebula, Picamar, Pipe, Potion, Protoplasm, PSL, Ptisan, Pyrrole, Pyrrolidine, Quinoline, Raffinate, Rhigolene, Safrole, Semen, Serum, Smectic, Solution, Solvent, Syrup, Terebene, Thinner, Thixotropy, Titer, Titre, Triptane, Tuberculin, Tusche, Ullage, Verjuice, Washing-up, Whey, Wind up, Wort
Liquorice Indian, Jequirity, Nail, Nail-rod, Pomfret, Pontefract-cake, Spanish juice, Sugarallie, Sugarally, Wild

Lis Iris, Lily
Lisa Mona
Lisp(er) Ephraimite, Sibilance
Lissom(e) Agile, Lithe, Nimble, Supple, Svelte
List(s), Listing A, Active, Agenda, Antibarbarus, Appendix, Army, Atilt, B, Barocco, Barrace, Bead-roll, Bibliography, Border, British, Canon, Cant, Catalog(ue), Categorise, Catelog, Cause, Check, Choice, Civil, Class, Compile, Credits, Danger, Debrett, Docket, Empanel, Entry, Enumerate, Front, Glossary, Hark, Hearken, Heel, Hit, Hit-parade, Honours, Index, Indian, Interdiction, Inventory, Itemise, Laundry, Lean, Leet, Line-up, Linked, Litany, Lloyds, Mailing, Manifest, Menu, Navy, Notitia, Official, Panel, Paradigm, Party, Price, Prize, Register, Repertoire, Reserved, Retired, Roin, Roll, Roon, Roster, Rota, Rund, Schedule, Script, Short, Sick, Slate, Slope, Strip, Syllabary, Syllabus (of Errors), Table, Tariff, Tick, Ticket, Tilt, Timetable, Tip, To-do, Transfer, Union, Waiting, Waybill, White, Wine, Wish
▷ **List** *may indicate* 'listen'
Listen(er) Attend, Auditor, Auscultate, Bug, Ear, Eavesdropper, Gobemouche, Hark, → **HEED**, List, Lithe, Lug, Monitor, Oyez, Simon, Sithee, Tune-in, Wire-tap, Yo-ho(-ho)
▷ **Listen to** *may indicate* a word sounding like another
Lister Plough, Surgeon
Listless(ness) Abulia, Accidie, Acedia, Apathetic, Atony, Dawney, Draggy, Inanition, Indolent, Lackadaisical, Languor, Mooning, Mope, Mopus, Sloth, Thowless, Torpor, Upsitting, Waff
Lit Alight, Landed
▷ **Lit** *may indicate* an anagram
Litany Eirenicon, Lesser, Procession, Synapte
Literacy Emotional
Literal(ly), Literal sense Etymon, Misprint, Simply, Typo, Verbatim, Word for word
Literary Academic, Bas bleu, Booksie, Erudite, Lettered
Literary girls Althea, Jenny, Maud, Pippa
Literature Agitprop, Belles lettres, Comparative, Corpus, Fiction, Gongorism, Hagiology, Midrash, Musar, Page, Picaresque, Polite, Prose, Responsa, Samizdat, Sci-fi, Splatterpunk, Sturm und Drang, Wisdom
Lithe Flexible, Limber, Pliant, Sinuous, Souple, → **SUPPLE**, Svelte, Willowy
Lithium Li
Litigant Barrator, John-a-Nokes, John-a-Stiles, John Doe, Party, Richard Roe, Suer, Suitor
Litmus Indicator, Lacmus, Lichen, Turnsole
Litre L
Litter Bed, Brancard, Brood, Cacolet, Cat, Cubs, Debris, Deep, Doolie, Duff, Emu-bob, Farrow, Jampan, Kago, Kajawah, Kindle, Mahmal, Mor, Nest, Norimon, Palankeen, Palanquin, Palkee, Palki, Pup, → **REFUSE**, Scrap, Sedan, Stretcher, Sweepings, Team, Whelp
Little Bagatelle, Beans, Billee, Brief, Chota, Curn, Diddy, Dorrit, Drib, Drop, Fewtrils, Fraction, Haet, Hait, Hate, Ickle, Insect, Iota, John, Jot, Leet, Lilliputian, Limited, Lite, Lyte, Means, Mini, Miniscule, Minnow, Minuscule, → **MINUTE**, Modicum, Morceau, Nell, Paltry, Paucity, Paul, Petite, Pink, Pittance, Ronte, Runt, Scant, Scut, Shade, Shoestring, Short, Shred, Shrimp, Slight, Sma', → **SMALL**, Smattering, Smidge(o)n, Smidgin, Smout, Smowt, Some, Soupçon, Spot, Tad, Teensy(-weensy), Tich, Tiddly, Tine, Titch, Touch, Tyne, Vestige, Wee, Weedy, Whit, Women
Littoral Coast(al)
Liturgical, Liturgy Divine, Doxology, Hallel, Rite, Shacharis, Versicle
Live(d), Livelihood, Living, Liveliness, Lively, Lives Active, Alert, Allegretto, Allegro, Am, Animated, Animation, Animato, Are, AV, Awake, Be, Birkie, Bouncy, Breezy, Brio, Brisk, Cant(y), Capriccio(so), Cheery, Chipper, Chirpy, Cohabit, Con moto,

Con spirito, Crouse, Dash, Durante vita, → **DWELL**, Dynamic, Ebullient, Entrain, Exist, Extant, Exuberant, Feisty, Frisky, Galliard, Gamy, Gay, Giocoso, Gracious, Grig, Hang-out, Hard, High jinks, Hijinks, Hot, Is, Jazz, Kedge, Lad, Lead, Mercurial, Merry, Mouvementé, Outgo, Pacey, Peart, Pep, Piert, Quicksilver, Rackety, Racy, Reside, Rousing, Salt, Saut, Scherzo, Skittish, Smacking, Spanking, Sparky, Spiritoso, Spirituel(le), Sprack, Sprightly, Spry, Spunky, Sustenance, Swinging, Thrive, Unrecorded, Up tempo, Vibrant, Vigoroso, Vital, Vitality, Vivace, Vive, Vivo, → **VOLATILE**, Vyvyan, Wick, Zappy, Zingy, Zippy, Zoe

▶ **Livelihood** see **LIVED**

Liver(ish) Foie gras, Hepar, Hepatic(al), Pate, Porta, Puce, Resident, Tomalley

Liverpool, Liverpudlian Scouse(r)

Liverwort Gemma-cup, Hepatica, Riccia

Livery(man) Ermine, Flunkeydom, Goldsmith, Skinner, Tiger, Uniform

Livid Blae, Bruised, Cross, → **FURIOUS**, Pale

Living Advowson, Benefice, Biont, Bread, Canonry, Crust, Glebe, Inquiline, Lodging, Quick, Resident, Simony, Subsistence, Symbiotic, Vicarage, Vital

Livingstone Doctor, Ken

Liza, Lizzie Bess, Betty, Flivver, Hexam, Tin

Lizard Abas, Agama, American chameleon, Amphisbaena, Anguis, Anole, Basilisk, Bearded, Bearded-dragon, Blindworm, Blue-tongued, Brontosaurus, Chameleon, Chuckwalla, Dinosaur, Draco, Dragon, Eft, Evet, Fence, Flying, Frilled, Frill-necked, Galliwasp, Gecko(ne), Gila, Gila monster, Glass snake, Goanna, Gotcha, Guana, Hatteria, Hellbender, Horned, Iguana, Jew, Kabaragoya, Komodo (dragon), Lacerta, Legua(a)n, Lounge, Malayan monitor, Mastigure, Menopome, Mokomoko, Moloch, Monitor, Mosasaur(us), Mountain devil, Newt, Ngarara, Perentie, Perenty, Reptile, Rock, Sand, Sauria, Scincoid, Seps, Skink, Slow-worm, Snake, Sphenodon, Stellio(n), Sungazer, Swift, Tegu(exin), Teiid, Thorny devil, Tokay, Tuatara, Tuatera, Varan, Wall, Whiptail, Worm, Worral, Worrel, Zandoli, Zonure

Llama Alpaca, Alpaco, Cria, Guanaco, Huanaco, Paco, Vicuña

Load(ed), Loader, Loading, Loads Accommodation, Affluent, Back-end, Ballast, Base, Biased, Boot-strap, Boozy, Burden, Cargo, Charge, Cobblers, Dead weight, Disc, Dope, Drunk, Dummy, Fardel, Fother, Frau(gh)tage, Freight, Front-end, Fulham, Full, Gestant, Glyc(a)emic, Heap, Input, Jag, Lade, Lard, Last, Live, Onus, Pack, Packet, Pay, Peak, Power, Prime, Raft, Rich, Scads, Seam, Shipment, Shoal, Some, Span, Super, Surcharge, → **TIGHT**, Tipsy, Tod, Traction, Ultimate, Useful, Wealthy, Weight, Wharfinger, Wing

Loaf(er), Loaves Baguette, Bannock, Barmbrack, Batch, Baton, Beachbum, Beachcomber, Bloomer, Bludge, Bonce, Boule, Bread, Brick, Bum, Bu(r)ster, Cad, Cob, Coburg, Cottage, Currant, Danish, Farmhouse, French stick, Hawm, Head, Hoe-cake, Idle, Layabout, → **LAZE**, Long tin, Lusk, Manchet, Meat, Miche, Milk, Mooch, Mouch, Pan, Pan(h)agia, Plain, Plait, Quartern, Roll, Roti, Shewbread, Showbread, Slosh, Split tin, Square tin, Stollen, Stotty, Sugar, Tin, Vantage, Vienna, Yob

Loam Clay, Loess, Loss, Malm

Loan(s) Advance, Balloon, Benevolence, Bottomry, Bridging, Call, Consolidation, Debenture, Demand, Droplock, Imprest, Lane, Mutuum, Omnium, Out, Prest, Respondentia, Roll-over, Soft, Start-up, Student, Sub, Time, Top-up, War

Loathe, Loathing, Loathsome Abhor(rent), Abominate, Carrion, Detest, Execrate, Hate, Keck, Nauseate, Odious, Reptilian, Scunner, Ug(h)

Lob Fungo, Loft, Sky, Underarm

Lobby Demo, Division, Entry, Foyer, Gun, Hall, Press, Urge

Lobe(d) Anisocercal, Fluke, Frontal, Glossa, Insula, Jugum, Lacinia, Lap, Occipital, Optic, Palmate, Parietal, Pinnule, Prostomium, Runcinate, Segment, Temporal, Uvula, Vermis

Lobster Cock, Crawfish, Crayfish, Crustacean, Decapoda, Langouste, Macrura, Newburg, Norway, Pereion, Pot, Rock, Scampo, Spiny, Squat, Thermidor, Tomalley

Local(ity) Area, Bro, Close, Des(h)i, Endemic, Home, Inn, Insider, Landlord, Native,

Near, Nearby, Neighbourhood, Number, Parochial, Pub, Regional, Resident, Swadishi, Tavern, Topical, Vernacular, Vicinal

▷ **Local** *may indicate* a dialect word

Locale Scene, Site

Locate(d), Location Address, Connect, Echo, Emplacement, Find, Fix, Lay, Milieu, Node, Pinpoint, Place, Placement, Plant, Put, Recess, Sat, Set-up, Site, Situate, Situation, Sofar, Spot, Theatre, Trace, Ubiety, Website, Where(abouts), Workplace, Zone

Loch, Lough Allen, Ashie, Awe, Derg, Earn, Eil, Erne, Etive, Fine, Gare, Garten, Glen Lyon, Holy, Hourn, Katrine, → **LAKE**, Larne, Leven, Linnhe, Lomond, Long, Moidart, Morar, More, Na Keal, Neagh, Ness, Rannoch, Ryan, Sea, Shiel, Strangford, Tay, Torridon

Lock(ing), Locker, Locks, Lock up Bar, Barnet, Bolt, Canal, Central, Chain, Chubb®, Clap-sill, Clinch, Combination, Cowlick, Curlicue, Davy Jones, Deadbolt, Detent, Drop, Fastener, Fermentation, Foretop, Gate, Haffet, Haffit, Handcuff, Hasp, Hold, Intern, Key, Latch, Lazaretto, Man, Mane, Mortise, Percussion, Prison, Quiff, Ragbolt, Rim, Ringlet, Safety, Sasse, Scalp, Scissors, → **SECURE**, Sluice, Snap, Spring, Staircase, Sta(u)nch, Stock, Strand, Tag, Talon, Tetanus, Time, Trap, Tress, Tuft, Tumbler, Vapour, Villus, Ward, Wheel, Wrestle, Yale®

Locket Lucy

Lockjaw Tetanus, Trismus

Locksmith Garret-master, Hairdresser

Locomotive Banker, Bogie, Bul(l)gine, Engine, Iron horse, Mobile, Mogul, Rocket, Steam, Steamer, Train

Locum Deputy, Relief, Stand-in, Stopgap

Locus Centrode, Horopter, Lemniscate, Place, Spot

Locust, Locust tree Acacia, Anime, Carob, Cicada, Hopper, Nymph, Robinia, Seventeen-year, Voetganger

Lode Comstock, Lodge, Mother, Reef, Vein

Lodestone Magnes, Magnet

Lodge(r) Billet, Board(er), Box, Cosher, Deposit, Dig, Doss, Encamp, Entertain, Freemason, Grange, Grove, Guest, Harbour, Host, Hunting, Inmate, Inquiline, Layer, Lie, Masonic, Nest, Orange, Parasite, PG, Porter's, Put up, Quarter, Rancho, Resident, Room(er), Roomie, Stay, Storehouse, Stow, Sweat, Tenant, Tepee, Wigwam

Lodging(s) Abode, B and B, Chummage, Dharms(h)ala, Diggings, Digs, Dosshouse, Ferm, Grange, Grove, Hospitium, Hostel, Inquiline, Kip, Minshuku, Pad, Padding-ken, Pension, Pied-à-terre, Quarters, Resiant, Rooms, Singleen, Sponging-house, Spunging-house, YHA

Loft(iness), Lofty Aerial, Airy, Arrogant, Attic, Celsitude, Chip, Choir, Exalted, Garret, Garryowen, Grand, Haymow, High, Jube, Lordly, Magniloquent, Noble, Olympian, Organ, Pulpitum, Rarefied, Rigging, Rood, Roost, Sky, Sublime, Tallat, Tallet, Tallot

Log(ging) Billet, Black box, Cabin, Chip, Chock, Deadhead, Diarise, Diary, Enter, Hack, Key(stroke), Ln, Mantissa, Nap(i)erian, Neper, Patent, Poling, → **RECORD**, Stock, Tachograph, Yule

Logarithm Common, Lod, Mantissa, Nap(i)erian, Natural

Logic(al) Alethic, Analytical, Aristotelian, Boolean, Chop, Cogent, Deontic, Dialectic(s), Digital, Distributed, Doxastic, Elench(us), Epistemics, Formal, Fuzzy, Hardhead(ed), Heuristics, Iff, Mathematical, Modal, Organon, Philosophical, Premise, Pusser's, Ramism, Ratiocinate, Rational(e), Reason, Sane, Sequacious, Shared, Sorites, Syllogism, Symbolic, Tense, Trivium, Vienna circle

Logo Brand, Colophon, Motif

Loin(s) Flank, Inguinal, Lisk, Lungie, Lunyie, Reins

Loincloth Dhoti, Lungi, Pareu, Waist-cloth

Loiter(ing) Dally, Dare, Dawdle, Dilatory, Dilly-dally, Idle, Lag, Lallygag, Leng, Lime,

→ **LINGER**, Loaf, Lollygag, Mike, Mooch, Mouch, Potter, Saunter, Scamp, Suss, Taigle, Tarry

Lola Dolores

Loll Hawm, Lounge, Sprawl

Lollipop, Lolly Ice pole, Lulibub, Sucker

Lolly Money, Popsicle®, Sweetmeat

London(er) 'Arry, Big Smoke, Cockaigne, Cockney, Co(c)kayne, East-ender, Flat-cap, Jack, Port, Roseland, Smoke, Town, Troynovant, Wen

London pride None-so-pretty

Lone(r), Lonely Bereft, Isolated, Recluse, Remote, Rogue, Saddo, Secluded, Sole, Solitary, Unked, Unket, Unkid

Long(er), Longing, Longs Ache, Aitch, Ake, Appetent, Aspire, Brame, Covet, Desire, Die, Earn, Erne, Eternal, Far, Greed, Green, Grein, → **HANKER**, Huey, Hunger, Inveterate, Island, Itch, L, Lanky, Large, Lengthy, Longa, Lust, Macron, Miss, More, → **NO LONGER**, Nostalgia, Option, Pant, Parsec, → **PINE**, Prolix, Sesquipedalian, Side, Sigh, Tall, Thirst, Trews, Wearisome, Weary, Wish, Wist, Yearn, Yen

Long-eared Spicate

Longitude Celestial, Ecliptic, Meridian

Long-lashed Mastigophora(n)

Long live(d) Banzai, Macrobian, Viva, Vive, Zindabad

Longshoreman Hobbler, Hoveller, Wharfinger

Long-sighted(ness) Hypermetropia

Long-suffering Job, Patient, Stoical

Long-tailed Macrural

Long-winded Prolix, Rambling, Verbose, Wordy

Loo Ajax, Bog, Can, Chapel, Dike, Game, Gents, Jakes, John, Latrine, Privy, Toilet

Loofah Towel gourd

Look(s), Look at After-eye, Air, Aspect, Await, Behold, Belgard, Bonne-mine, Browse, Busk, Butcher's, Butcher's hook, Case, Clock, Close-up, Crane, Daggers, Decko, Deek, Dekko, Ecce, Ecco, Expression, Eye, Eye-glance, Face, Facies, Gander, Gawp, Gaze, Geek, Glad-eye, Glance, Glare, Gleam, Gledge, Glimpse, Glom, Glower, Goggle, Good, Grin, Hallo, Hangdog, Hey, Hippocratic, Iliad, Inspect, Keek, La, Leer, Lo, Mien, New, Ogle, Old-fashioned, Peek, Peep, Prospect, Ray, Recce, Refer, → **REGARD**, Scan, Scrutinise, Search, See, Seek, Shade, Sheep's eyes, Shufti, Shufty, Spy, Squint, Squiz, Stare, Survey, Toot, V, Vista, Wet

Look-out (man) Cockatoo, Crow's nest, Dixie, Huer, Mirador, Nit, Pas op, Picket, Prospect, Sangar, Sentinel, Sentry, Spotter, Sungar, Tentie, Toot(er), Watch, Watchtower

▷ **Look silly** *may indicate* an anagram

Loom Beamer, Dobby, Emerge, Impend, Jacquard, Lathe, Lease-rod, Menace, Picker, Temple, Threaten, Tower

Loon(y) Airhead, Diver, Nutter

Loop(ed), Loophole, Loopy Articulatory, Becket, Bight, Billabong, Bouclé, Carriage, Chink, Closed, Coil, Eyelet, Eyesplice, Fake, Feedback, Frog, Frontlet, Grom(m)et, Ground, Grummet, Hank, Heddle-eye, Henle's, Hysteresis, Infinite, Kink, Knop, Lasket, Lippes, Local, Lug, Noose, Oillet, Parral, Parrel, Pearl(-edge), Picot, Prusik, Purl, Scrunchie, Squiggle, Staple, Stirrup, Swag, Tab, Terry, Toe, Twist

Loos Anita

Loose(n), Loose woman Absolve, Abstrict, Adrift, Afloat, Anonyma, Baggage, Bail, Besom, Bike, Bunter, Chippie, Chippy, Clatch, Cocotte, Cutty, Demi-mondaine, Demirep, Demivierge, Desultory, Dissolute, Dissolve, Doxy, Draggletail, Dratchell, Drazel, Ease, Emit, Flabby, Flipperty-flopperty, Flirt-gill, Floosie, Floozie, Floozy, Floppy, Franion, Free, Gangling, Gay, Geisha, Hussy, Insecure, Jade, Jay, Jezebel, Lax, Light-heeled, Limp, Loast, Loon, Loste, Mob, Mort, Naughty pack, Painted, Pinnace, Profligate, Promiscuous, Quail, Ramp, → **RELAX**, Sandy, Scrubber, Skanky-ho, Slag, Slapper, Slipshod, Slut,

Streel, Strumpet, Tart, Tramp, Trull, Ungyve, Unhasp, Unhitch, Unknit, Unknot, Unlace, Unlash, Unleash, Unpin, Unreined, Unscrew, Unstuck, Unthread, Untie, Vague, Waistcoateer, Wappend, Whore

Loot Boodle, Booty, Cragh, Creach, Foray, Haul, Mainour, Peel, Pluck, → **PLUNDER**, Ransack, Rape, Reave, Reif, Rieve, Rob, Sack, Smug, Spoils, Spoliate, Stouth(e)rie, Swag, Treasure, Waif

Lop Behead, Clip, Clop, Curtail, Detruncate, Droop, Shroud, Sned, Trash

Lope Stride

Loquacious Chatty, Gabby, Garrulous, Rambling

Lord(s), Lordship, Lordly Adonai, Ahura Mazda, Anaxandron, Arrogant, Boss, Byron, Cardigan, Cripes, Cyril, Dieu, Domineer, Dominical, Drug, Duc, Earl, Elgin, Gad, Gilded Chamber, God, Haw-haw, Herr, Idris, Imperious, Jim, Justice, Kami, Kitchener, Land, Landgrave, Law, Ld, Liege, Lonsdale, Losh, Lud, MCC, Meneer, Mesne, Misrule, Mynheer, Naik, Oda Nobunaga, Omrah, Ordinary, Ormazd, Ormuzd, Palsgrave, Peer, Sea, Seigneur, Seignior, Shaftesbury, Sire, Spiritual, Taverner, Temporal, Tuan, Ullin

Lords and ladies Wake-robin

Lore Cab(b)ala, Edda, Lair, Lare, Riem, Upanis(h)ad

Lorelei Siren

Lorgnette Starers

Lorna Doone

Lorry Artic(ulated), Camion, Carrier, Crummy, Double-bottom, Drag, Drawbar outfit, Dropsided, Flatbed, Juggernaut, Low-loader, Rig, Tipper, Tonner, → **TRUCK**, Wagon

Lose(r) Also-ran, Decrease, Drop, Elude, Forfeit, Hesitater, Leese, Misère, Mislay, Misplace, Nowhere, Spread, Tank, Throw, Tine(r), Tyne, Underdog, Unsuccessful, Waste, Weeper

Loss, Lost Angel's share, Anosmia, Aphesis, Aphonia, Apocope, Apraxia, Astray, Attainder, Boohai, Chord, Cost, Dead, Decrease, Depreciation, Detriment, Disadvantage, Elision, Extinction, Foredamned, Forfeited, Forgotten, Forlorn, Gone, Hurtful, Lore, Lorn, Lurch, Missing, Omission, Outage, Pentimento, Perdition, Perdu, Perished, Preoccupied, Privation, Psilosis, Reliance, Tine, Tinsel, Tint, Toll, Traik, Tribes, Tyne(d), Ullage, Unredeemed, Wastage, Wasted, Will, Write-off, Wull

Loss of memory Amnesia, Black-out, Fugue, Infonesia, Paramnesia

▷ **Lost** *may indicate* an anagram or an obsolete word

Lot(s) Abundant, Amount, Aret(t), Badly, Batch, Boatload, Bomb, Caboodle, Cavel, Chance, Deal, Dole, Doom, Drove, Due, → **FATE**, Fortune, Group, Hantle, Hap, Heaps, Horde, Host, Item, Job, Kevel, Kismet, Lank, Lashings, Legion, Loads, Loadsa, Luck, Manifold, Many, Mass, Moh, Moira, Mony, Mort, Myriad, Oceans, Omnibus, Oodles, Oodlins, Pack, Parcel, Parking, Plenitude, Plenty, Portion, Power, Purim, Raft, Rich, Scads, Set, Sight, Slather, Slew, Slue, Sortilege, Sortition, Stack, Sum, Tall order, The works, Tons, Vole, Wagonload, Weird

Loth Averse, Circumspect, Sweer(t), Sweir(t), Unwilling

Lothario Lady-killer, Libertine, Poodle-faker, Rake, Womaniser

Lotion After-shave, Blackwash, Calamine, Collyrium, Cream, Emollient, Eye-wash, Humectant, Setting, Suntan, Unguent, Wash, Yellow wash

Lottery, Lotto Art union, Ballot, Bingo, Cavel, Draw, Gamble, National, Pakapoo, Pools, Postcode, Punchboard, Raffle, Rollover, Scratchcard, Sweepstake, Tattersall's, Tombola

Lotus (eater), Lotus land Asana, Djerba, Lotophagus, Padmasana, White

Louche Rip

Loud(ness), Loudly Bel, Big, Blaring, Booming, Brassy, Decibel, Ear-splitting, F, FF, Flashy, Forte, Fracas, Full-mouthed, Garish, Gaudy, Glaring, Hammerklavier, High, Lumpkin, Noisy, Orotund, Plangent, Raucous, Roarie, Siren, Sone, Stentor(ian), Strident, Tarty, Vocal, Vociferous, Vulgar

Loudspeaker Action, Boanerges, Bullhorn, Hailer, Megaphone, PA, Squawk box, Stentor, Subwoofer, Tannoy®, Tweeter, Woofer

▶ **Lough** *see* LOCH

Louis Baker, Roi

Louisianian Cajun

Lounge(r) Cocktail, Daiker, Da(c)ker, Departure, Doze, Executive, Hawm, Idle, Laze, Lie, Lizard, Loaf, Loll, Lollop, Parlour, Paul's man, Settee, Sitkamer, Slouch, Sun, Sunbed, Transit, Transitive

Louse (up), Lousy, Lice Acrawl, Argulus, Bolix, Bollocks, Chat, Chicken, Cootie, Crab, Crummy, Fish, Head, Isopod(a), Kutu, Mallophaga, Nit, Oniscus, Pedicular, Phthiriasis, Plant, Psocid, Psocoptera, Psylla, Pubic, Slater, Snot, Sowbug, Sucking, Vermin, Whale

Lout Auf, Clod(hopper), Coof, Cuif, Galere, Hallian, Hallion, Hallyon, Hick, Hob, Hobbledehoy, Hooligan, Hoon, Jack, Jake, Keelie, Lager, Larrikin, Litter, Lob(lolly), Loord, Lubber, Lumpkin, Lycra, Oaf, Oik, Rube, Swad, Tout, Tripper, Yahoo, Yob(bo)

Louvre Shutter

Love(d), Lovable, Lover Abelard, Admire, Adore, Adulator, Affection, Agape, Alma, Amabel, Amanda, Amant, Amateur, Ami(e), Amoret, Amoroso, Amour, Angharad, Antony, Ardour, Ariadne, Aroha, Aucassin, Beau, Bidie-in, Blob, Calf, Care, Casanova, Chamberer, Cicisbeo, Concubine, Coquet, Court, Courtly, Cupboard, Cupid, Dear, Dona(h), Dotard, Dote, Doxy, Duck(s), Ducky, Dulcinea, Eloise, Eloper, Emotion, Enamorado, Eros, Esme, Fan(boy), Fancy man, Flame, Frauendienst, Free, Gal(l)ant, Goose-egg, Greek, Hon(ey), Idolise, Inamorata, Inamorato, Iseult, Isolde, Item, Jo, Kama, Lad, Lancelot, Leander, Leman, Like, Lochinvar, Loe, Loo, Lurve, Man, Nada, Nihility, Nil, Nothing, Nought, Nut, O, Pairs, Paramour, Pash, Passion, Pet, Philander, -phile, Philtre, Platonic, Precious, Protestant, Psychodelic, Puppy, Revere, Rhanja, Romance, Romeo, Sapphism, Spark, Spooner, Stale, Storge, Suitor, Swain, Thisbe, Tough, Toyboy, Treasure, Tristan, Troilus, True, Turtle(-dove), Valentine, Venus, Virtu, Woman, Worship, Zeal, Zero

Love-apple Tomato, Wolf's-peach

Love-bite Hickey

Love-child By-blow, Come-by-chance

Love-in-a-mist Nigella

Love letter Capon

Lovely Adorable, Belle, Cute, Dishy, Dreamy, Exquisite, Fair, Gorgeous, Nasty, Super

Love-making → INTERCOURSE, Kama Sutra, Sex, Snog

Love-sick Smit(ten), Strephon

Loving(ly) Amoroso, Amorous, Fond, Tender

Low(est), Low-born, Low-cut, Lower(ing), Low-key Abase, Abate, Abysmal, Amort, Area, Avail(e), Avale, B, Basal, Base(-born), Bass(o), Beneath, Blue, Caddish, Canaille, Cartoonist, Cheap, Church, Cocktail, Condescend, Contralto, Couch, Cow, Crestfallen, Croon, Crude, Darken, Debase, Declass, Décolleté, Deepen, Deepmost, Degrade, Demean, Demit, Demote, Depress, Despicable, Devalue, Dim, Dip, Dispirited, Doldrums, Drawdown, Drop, Early, Embase, Flat, Foot, Frown, Gazunder, Glare, Guernsey, Gurly, Gutterblood, Hedge, Hidalgo, Humble, Ignoble, Imbase, Inferior, Jersey, Laigh, Lallan, Law, Light, Lite, Mass, Mean(born), Menial, Moo, Mopus, Morose, Nadir, Net, Nether, Nett, Non-U, Ornery, Ostinato, Paravail, Plebeianise, Profound, Prole, Relegate, Ribald, Rock-bottom, Sad, Scoundrel, Scowl, Secondo, Settle, Shabby, Short, Soft, Stoop, Subordinate, Sudra, Sunken, Undermost, Unnoble, Unobtrusive, Vail, Vulgar, Weak, Wretched

Lowbrow Essex man, Philistine

Low country Flanders

Lowdown Dirt, Gen, Info, Stats

▷ **Lower** *may refer to* cattle

Lowland(er) Carse, Fen, Gallovidian, Glen, Laigh, Lallans, Merse, Mudflat, Plain, Polder, Sassenach, Vlei

Low-lying Callow, Epigeous, Fens, Inferior, Sump

Low person Boor, Bunter, Cad, Caitiff, Cocktail, Demirep, Ratfink, Snot

Lowry LS

Loyal(ty) Adherence, Allegiant, Brand, Brick, Dependable, Diehard, Esprit de corps, Faithful, Fast, Fealty, Fidelity, Firm, Gungho, Leal, Liegedom, Patriotic, Pia, Stalwart, Staunch, Tribalism, Troth, → TRUE, True blue, Trusty

Loyalist Hard core, Paisley, Patriot, Tory

Lozenge Cachou, Catechu, Coughdrop, Fusil, Jujube, Mascle, Pastille, Pill, Rhomb, Rustre, Tablet, Troche, Voided

LSD Acid, Money

Lubber(ly), Lubbers Booby, Clod, Clumsy, Gawky, Hulk, Landsman, Lob, Looby, Oaf, Slowback, Swab, Swads

Lubricant, Lubricate, Lubrication Carap-oil, Coolant, Derv, Fluid, Force-feed, Grease, Oil, Petrolatum, Sebum, Unguent, Vaseline®, Wool-oil

Luce Ged

Lucerne Alfalfa, Medick, Nonsuch

Lucia Mimi

Lucid Bright, Clear, Perspicuous, Sane

Lucifer Devil, Match, Proud, Satan, Venus

Luck(y) Amulet, Auspicious, Beginner's, Bonanza, Break, Caduac, Canny, Cess, Chance, Charmed, Chaunce, Daikoku, Dip, Fat, Fate, Fluke, → FORTUNE, Godsend, Hap, Heather, Hit, Jam(my), Jim, Joss, Lady, Lot, Mascot, Mercy, Mozzle, Pot, Prosit, Providential, Pudding-bag, Purple passage, Purple patch, Seal, Seel, Sele, Serendipity, Sess, Sonsie, Sonsy, Spawny, Star(s), Streak, Success, Talisman, Tinny, Tough, Turn-up, White rabbits, Windfall, Worse

Luckless Hapless, Wight

Lucrative Earner

Lucre Money, Pelf, Tin

Lucy Locket

Lud Gad

Luddite Rioter, Saboteur, Wrecker

Ludicrous Absurd, Bathetic, Bathos, Crackpot, Farcical, Fiasco, Inane, Irish, Jest, Laughable, Risible

Ludo Uckers

Luff Derrick

Lug Ear, Earflap, Haul, Sea-worm, Sowle, Tote, Tow

Luggage Bags, Carryon, Cases, Dunnage, Excess, Grip, Hand, Kit, Petara, Samsonite®, Suiter, Traps, Trunk

Luggage-carrier Grid

Lugubrious Dismal, Drear

Luke-warm Laodicean, Lew, Tepid

Lull, Lullaby Berceuse, Calm, Cradlesong, Hushaby, Respite, Rock, Sitzkreig, Soothe, Sopite

Lulu Honey, Stunner

Lumbar Hip

Lumber(ing) Clump, Galumph, Jumble, Pawn, Ponderous, Raffle, Saddle, Scamble, Timber

Lumberjack Bushwhacker, Feller, Logger, Logman, Rafter

Luminance, Luminous, Luminosity, Luminescence Aglow, Arc, Candela, Dayglo, Foxfire, Glow, Hero, Ignis-fatuus, L, Light, Meteor, Nit, Phosphorescent, Scintillon, Sea-dog, Wildfire, Will o' the wisp

Lumme Coo, Lor

Lummox Galoot

Lump(ectomy), Lump(s), Lump(y) Aggregate, Bolus, Bubo, Bud, Bulge, Bur(r), Caruncle, Chuck, Chunk, Clat, Claut, Clod, Clot, Cob, Combine, Da(u)d, Dallop, Dollop,

Enhydros, Epulis, Flocculate, Ganglion, Geode, Gnarl, Gob(bet), Goiter, Goitre, Goop, Grape, Grip, Grumose, Hunch, Hunk, Inium, Knarl, Knob, Knub, Knur(r), Knurl, Lob, Lunch, Malleolus, Mass, Moss-litter, Mote, Mott, Myxoma, Neuroma, Nibble, Nirl, Node, Nodule, Nodulus, Nub(bin), Nubble, Nugget, Nur(r), Nurl, Osteophyte, Plook, Plouk, Quinsy, Raguly, Sarcoma, Scybalum, Sitfast, Slub, Strophiole, Tragus, Tuber(cle), Tumour, Tylectomy, Wart, Wodge

Lumpsucker Sea-owl

Lunacy, Lunatic Bedlam, Dementia, Demonomania, Folly, Insanity, Mad(ness), Madman, Maniac, Moonstruck, Nutter, Psychosis

Lunar Evection, Mascon, Selenological

▷ **Lunatic** *may indicate* an anagram

Lunch(time) Bait, Box, Crib, Dejeune, Déjeuner, Fork, L, Liquid, Nacket, Nocket, Nuncheon, Packed, Piece, Ploughman, Pm, Power, Tiff(in), Working

Lung(s) Alveoli, Bellows, Book, Coalminer's, Farmer's, Green, Iron, Lights, Pulmo, Pulmonary, Soul

Lung disease Anthracosis, Atelectasis, Byssinosis, Emphysema, Farmer's lung, Pneumoconiosis, Siderosis, Silicosis, Tuberculosis

Lunge Breenge, Breinge, Dive, Stab, Thrust, Venue

Lungfish Dipnoi(an)

Lupin Arsene

Lurch Reel, Slew, Stoit, Stumble, Swee, Toss

Lure Bait, Bribe, Carrot, Decoy, Devon minnow, Entice, Horn, Inveigle, Jig, Judas, Plug, Roper, Spinner, Spoon, Spoonbait, Spoonhook, Squid, Stale, Temptation, Tice, Tole, Toll, Train, Trepan, Wormfly

Lurgi Illness

Lurid Gruesome, Purple, Sensational

Lurk(ing) Dare, Latitant, Skulk, Slink, Snoke, Snook, Snowk

Lusatia(n) Wend(ic), Wendish

Luscious Succulent

Lush Alcoholic, Alkie, Alky, Dipso(maniac), Drunk, Fertile, Green, Juicy, Lydian, Soak, Sot, Succulent, Toper, Tosspot, Verdant

Lust(ful), Lusty Cama, Concupiscence, Corflambo, Desire, Eros, Frack, Greed, Kama, Lech(ery), Lewd, Megalomania, Obidicut, Prurience, Radge, Randy, Rank, Raunchy, Salacious, Venereous

Lustre, Lustrous Brilliance, Census, Chatoyant, Galena, Gaum, Gilt, Gloss, Gorm, Inaurate, Lead-glance, Lovelight, Pearlescent, Pearly, Pentad, Reflet, Satiny, Schiller, → **SHEEN**, Water

Lute, Lutist Amphion, Chitarrone, Cither, Dichord, Orpharion, Pandora, Pandore, Pipa, Theorbo, Vielle

Lutetium Lu

Lutheran Adiaphorist, Calixtin(e), Pietist, Protestant, Ubiquitarian

Lux Lx

Luxemburg L

Luxuriant, Luxuriate, Luxurious, Luxury (lover) Apician, Bask, Clover, Cockaigne, Cockayne, Comfort, Copious, Delicate, Deluxe, Dolce vita, Extravagant, Exuberant, Fleshpots, Lavish, Lucullan, Lush, Mollitious, Ornate, Palatial, Pie, Plush, Posh, Rank, → **RICH**, Ritzy, Sumptuous, Sybarite, Wallow

Lycanthropist Werewolf

Lydia Languish

Lye Buck

▶ **Lying** *see* **LIE(S)**

Lymph Chyle

Lymphoma Burkett's

Lynch(ing), Lyncher Dewitt, Hang, Necktie party, Nightrider

Lynx Bay, Bobcat, Caracal, Desert, Rooikat
Lyre Box, Cithern, Harp, Psaltery, Testudo, Trigon
Lyric(s), Lyrical, Lyricist, Lyrist Awdl, Cavalier, Dit(t), Epode, Gilbert, Hammerstein, Melic, Ode, Orphean, Paean, Pean, Poem, Rhapsodic, Song, Spinto, Words

Mm

M Married, Member, Metre, Mike, Mile, Thousand
Mac Bo, Mino, Scot, Waterproof
Macabre Gothic, Grotesque, Morbid, Sick
Macaroni Beau, Blood, Cat, Dandy, Elbow, Exquisite, Fop, Jack-a-dandy, Olio, Pasta, Petitmaitre
Macaroon Biscuit, Signal
Macaulay Layman
Mace Club, Nutmeg, Sceptre, Spice
Mace-bearer Beadle, Bedel, Poker
Macedonian Alexander, Philip, Stagirite, Stagyrite
Machete Bolo
Machiavellian Savvy
Machine(ry) Apparat(us), Appliance, Bathing, → DEVICE, Facsimile, Fax, Fruit, Infernal, Instrument, Life-support, Party, Plant, Propaganda, Rowing, Sausage, Sewing, Slot, Spin, Tape, Teaching, Time, Vending, Virtual, War, Washing, Weighing

---

MACHINES

3 letters:	Linter	Enginery	Stamp-mill
Gin	Ludlow	Filatory	Stenotype®
	Planer	Hot-press	Treadmill
4 letters:	Pulper	Linotype®	Wimshurst
Drum	Seeder	Moulinet	
Haik	Slicer	Nintendo®	10 letters:
Heck	Tedder	Pulsator	Centrifuge
Loom	Turing	Shredder	Clobbering
Mule	Willow	Symatron	Earth-mover
Wind		Thresher	Emi-scanner®
	7 letters:	Throstle	Jawbreaker
5 letters:	Burster	Transfer	Liquidiser
Churn	Dredger	Windlass	Passimeter
Cycle	Hawk-Eye®	Windmill	Pile-driver
Lathe	Jukebox		Roadroller
Poker	Milling	9 letters:	Rototiller
Pokie	Moviola®	Air-engine	Typewriter
Press	Potcher	Answering	Watersnail
Robot	Slasher	Automaton	
Rover	Tumbler	Bulldozer	11 letters:
Stamp	Turbine	Dynamotor	Comptometer®
	Twin tub	Excavator	Fourdrinier
6 letters:	Wringer	Hummeller	Weighbridge
Dredge	Zamboni®	Osmometer	
Engine		Perfector	12 letters:
Enigma	8 letters:	Processor	Lithotripter
Grader	Calender	Rotavator®	Muckspreader
Hopper	Dialyser	Separator	

Macho Jock, Laddish, Rambo
Mackerel Albacore, Amber-fish, Brack, Dory, Fish, Horse, Pacific, Pimp, Scad, Scomber, Sky, Spanish, Spotted, Tinker, Trevally
Mackintosh Burberry®, Mac, Mino, Oilskin, Slicker, Waterproof
Macropus Euro, Wallaroo
Mad(den), Madman, Madness Angry, Balmy, Bananas, Barking, Barmy, Bedlam, Besotted, Bonkers, Crackbrained, Crackpot, Crazy, Cuckoo, Cupcake, Daffy, Delirious, Dement, Détraqué, Distract, Dotty, Enrage, Fay, Fey, Folie, Folly, Frantic, Frenetic(al), Fruitcake, Furioso, Fury, Gelt, Gyte, Harpic, Hatter, Idiotic, Incense, Insane, Insanie, Insanity, Into, Irate, Ireful, Irritate, Kook, Livid, Loco, Lunatic, Lycanthropy, Madbrained, Maenad, Mango, Mania, Mattoid, Mental, Meshug(g)a, Metric, Midsummer, Moonstruck, Motorway, Mullah, Nuts, Porangi, Psycho, Rabid, Rasputin, Raving, Redwood, Redwud, Scatty, Screwy, Short-witted, Starkers, Tonto, Touched, Troppo, Unhinged, Wacko, Wood, Wowf, Wrath, Wud, Xenomania, Yond, Zany
▷ **Mad(den)** *may indicate* an anagram
Madagascan, Madagascar Aye-aye, Hova, Indri, Lemur, Malagash, Malagasy, RM
Madam(e) Baggage, Bawd, Lady, M, Memsahib, Proprietress
Madcap Cake, Impulsive, Tearaway
Madder Alizari, Alyari, Chay(a), Gardenia, Genipap, Rose, Rubia, Shaya
Made (it) Built, Did, Fec(it), Ff, Gart, Invented
Made (up) Synthesized
Madeira Cake
Madge Pie
▷ **Madly** *may indicate* an anagram
Madonna Lady, Lily, Mary, Pietà, Sistine, Virgin
Madras Chennai
Madrigal Ballet, Fala, Song
Maelstrom Voraginous, Vortex, Whirlpool
Maenad Devotee, Fan
Maestro Artist, Toscanini, Virtuoso
Mafia, Mafioso Camorra, Capo, Cosa Nostra, Godfather, Goombah, Mob, Ndrangheta, Omerta, Padrone, Pentito, Sicilian, The Mob
Mag Mail
Magazine Arsenal, Clip, Colliers, Contact, Cornhill, Cosmopolitan, Digizine, Economist, E-zine, Field, Girlie, Glossy, Granta, House organ, Jazz mag, Ladmag, Lady, Lancet, Life, Listener, Little, Magnet, New Yorker, Organ, Paper, Part work, Periodical, Pictorial, Playboy, Powder, Private Eye, Pulp, Punch, She, Skin, Slick, Spectator, Store, Strand, Tatler, Time, Vogue, Warehouse, Weekly, Yoof, Zine
Magdalene St Mary
Maggie Rita
Maggot Bot, Flyblow, Gentiles, Gentle, Grub, Larva, Mawk, Myiasis, Whim, Worm
Magi Balthazar, Gaspar, Melchior
Magic(al), Magician, Magic square Alchemy, Archimage, Art, Baetyl, Black, Black art, Charm, Circle, Conjury, Diablerie, Diablery, Druid, Enchanting, Fabulous, Faust, Faustus, Fetish, Genie, Goetic, Goety, Gramary(e), Grimoire, Hermetic, Houdini, Illusionist, Incantation, Makuto, Math, Medea, Medicine man, Merlin, Mojo, Moly, Morgan le Fay, Myal, Nasik, Natural, Necromancer, Obeah, Pawaw, Powwow, Prospero, Reim-kenner, Rhombus, Shamanism, Sorcery, Sortilege, Spell, Speller, Supernatural, Sympathetic, Talisman, Thaumaturgics, Theurgy, Voodoo, Warlock, White, Wizard, Zendik

Magistracy, Magistrate Aedile, Amman, Amtman, Archon, Avoyer, Bailie, Bailiff, Bailli(e), Beak, Bench, Boma, Burgess, Burgomaster, Cadi, Censor, Consul, Corregidor, Curule, Decemvirate, Demiurge, Doge(ate), Draco, Edile, Effendi, Ephor, Field cornet, Finer, Foud, Gonfalonier, JP, Judiciary, Jurat, Justice, Kotwal, Landamman(n), Landdrost, Lord Provost, Maire, Mayor, Mittimus, Novus homo, Pilate, Podesta, Portreeve, Pr(a)efect, Pr(a)etor, Prior, Proconsul, Propraetor, Provost, Qadi, Quaestor, Recorder, Reeve, Shereef, Sherif, Stad(t)holder, Stipendiary, Syndic, Tribune, Worship

Magnanimity, Magnanimous Altruistic, Big, Charitable, → **GENEROUS**, Largeness, Lofty, Noble

Magnate Baron, Beaverbrook, Bigwig, Industrialist, Mogul, Onassis, Randlord, Tycoon, Vanderbilt, VIP

Magnesia, Magnesium Bitter-earth, Epsomite, Humite, Kainite, Mg, Periclase

Magnet(ic), Magnetism Animal, Artificial, Attraction, Bar, Charisma, Field, Gauss, Horseshoe, Induction, It, Loadstone, Lodestone, Maxwell, Od, Oersted, Oomph, Permanent, Personal, Polar, Pole, Pole piece, Poloidal, Pull, Remanence, Retentivity, Slug, Solenoid, Terrella, Terrestrial, Tesla, Tole, Weber

Magnificence, Magnificent Fine, Gorgeous, Grandeur, Imperial, Laurentian, Lordly, Noble, Pride, Regal, Royal, Splendid, Splendo(u)r, State, Sumptuous, Superb

Magnifier, Magnify(ing) Aggrandise, Augment, Binocle, → **ENLARGE**, Exaggerate, Increase, Loupe, Megaphone, Microscope, Praise, Teinoscope, Telescope

Magniloquent Bombastic, Orotund

Magnitude Absolute, Abundance, Amplitude, Apparent, Earthquake, Extent, First, Modulus, Muchness, Photoelectric, Photographic, Scalar, Size, Visual

Magnolia An(n)ona, Beaver-tree, Champac, Champak, Mississippi, Sweet bay, Umbrella-tree, Yulan

Magpie Bell, Bird, Bishop, Chatterer, Hoarder, Madge, Mag, Margaret, Outer, Pica, Piet, Pyat, Pyet, Pyot

Magus Artist

Magyar Hungarian, Szekei, Szekel(y), Szekler, Ugrian, Ugric

Mahogany Acajou, African, Carapa, Cedrela, Philippine, Toon, Wood

Mahommedan Dervish, Shiah

Maid(en) Abigail, Aia, Amah, Biddy, Bonibell, Bonne, Bonnibell, Burd, Chamber, Chloe, Clothes-horse, Dam(o)sel, Debut, Dell, Dey, Dresser, Femme de chambre, First, Girl, Guillotine, Ignis-fatuus, Imago, Inaugural, Io, Iras, Iron, Lorelei, M, Marian, May, Miss, Nerissa, Nymph, Opening, Over, Parlour, Pucelle, Racehorse, Rhian, Rhine, Skivvy, Soubrette, Stillroom, Suivante, Table, Thestylis, Tirewoman, Tweeny, Valkyrie, Virgin, Walkyrie, Wench, Wicket

Maidenhair Fern, Ginkgo

Mail Air, → **ARMOUR**, Byrnie, Cataphract, Chain, Da(w)k, Direct, E(lectronic), Express, Fan, Gusset, Habergeon, Hate, Hauberk, Helm, Junk, Letter, Media, Metered, Panoply, Pony express, Post, Ring, Send, Snail, Spam, Surface, Tuille(tte), Voice

Mailbag Pouch

Mailboat Packet

Maim Cripple, Impair, Lame, Main, Mayhem, Mutilate, Vuln

Main(s) Atlantic, Brine, Briny, Bulk, → **CENTRAL**, Chief, Cockfight, Conduit, Essential, Foremost, Gala, Gas, Generally, Grid, Gross, Head, → **KEY**, Lead(ing), Major, Pacific, Palmary, Predominant, Prime, Principal, Ring, → **SEA**, Sheer, Spanish, Staple, Water

Mainland Continent, Pomona

Mainstay Backbone, Bastion, Pillar, Support

Maintain(er), Maintenance Alimony, Allege, Ap(p)anage, Argue, Assert, Aver, Avouch, Avoure, Avow, Claim, Contend, Continue, Defend, Escot, Insist, Keep (up), Lengthman, Preserve, Run, Serve, Service, Sustain, Upbear, Uphold, Upkeep

Maize Corn, Hominy, Indian, Indian corn, Mealie, Milo, Polenta, Popcorn, Samp, Silk, Stamp, Zea

Majestic, Majesty August, Britannic, Dignity, Eagle, Grandeur, Imperial, Maestoso, Olympian, Regal, Royal, SM, Sovereign, Stately, Sublime, Tuanku

Major (domo) Barbara, Drum, → **IMPORTANT**, Momentous, Pipe, PM, Read, Seneschal, Senior, Sergeant, Star, Trumpet, Wig

Majority Absolute, Age, Body, Eighteen, Landslide, Latchkey, Maturity, Moral, Most, Preponderance, Relative, Silent, Working

Make(r), Make do, Making Amass, Brand, Build, Cause, Clear, Coerce, Coin, Compel, Compulse, Concoct, Creant, Create, Devise, Earn, Execute, Fabricate, Factive, Fashion, Faute de mieux, Fet(t), Forge, Form, Gar(re), God, Halfpenny, Increate, Mail(e), Manage, Marque, Meg, Prepare, Production, Reach, Render, Shape, Sort, Temporise, Turn, Wright

▷ **Make** *may indicate* an anagram

Make believe Fantasy, Fictitious, Pretend, Pseudo

Make good Abet, Compensate, Remedy, Succeed, Ulling

Make hay Ted

Make off Bolt, Leg it, Mosey, Run, Scarper

Makeover Redo

Makeshift Bandaid, Crude, Cutcha, Expedient, Jury, Jury-rigged, Kacha, Kachcha, Kludge, Kutcha, Lash-up, Mackle, Pis-aller, Rude, Stopgap, Timenoguy

Make up, Make-up artist Ad lib, Compensate, Compose, Concealer, Constitution, Cosmetics, Fucus, Gaud, Gawd, Gene, Genotype, Greasepaint, Identikit®, Kohl, Liner, Lipstick, Maquillage, Mascara, Metabolism, Orchel, Paint, Pancake, Panstick, Powder, Prime, Reconcile, Rouge, Slap, Tidivate, Titivate, Toiletry, Visagiste, War paint, White-face

Maladroit Awkward, Clumsy, Gauche, Graceless, Inapt, Inelegant, Unperfect

Malady Disease, Illness, Sickness

Malagas(e)y Hova, RM

Malaise Affluenza

Malapropism Catachresis, Slipslop

Malaria Ague, Falciparum, Marsh-fever, Paludism, Tap, Vivax

Malawi(an) Nyanja, Nyasa

Malay(an), Malaysia(n) Austronesian, Bahasa, Bajou, Brunei, Datin, Datuk, D(a)yak, Jawi, Madurese, Moro, .my, Sabahan, Sakai, Tagalog, Tokay, Tuan

Male Alpha, Arrhenotoky, Buck, Bull, Butch, Dog, Ephebe, Ephebus, Gent, Hob, John Doe, Macho, Mansize, Masculine, Patroclinous, Ram, Rogue, Spear(side), Stag, Stamened, Telamon, Tom, Worthiest of the blood

Malediction Curse, Cuss, Oath, Slander

Malefactor Criminal, Felon, Villain

Malevolent, Malevolence Evil, Fell, Malign, Pernicious, Venomous

Malformation Parrot-mouth, Teratogenesis

Malfunction Glitch, Hiccup

Mali RMM

Malice, Malicious Bitchy, Catty, Cruel, Despiteous, Envy, Hatchet job, Malevolent, Malign, Mudslinger, Narquois, Prepense, Schadenfreude, Serpent, Snide, Spite, Spleen, Venom, Viperish, Virulent, Vitriol

Malign(ant), Malignity Asperse, Backbite, Baleful, Bespatter, Defame, Denigrate, Evil, Gall, Harm, Hate-rent, Hatred, Libel, Poor-mouth, Sinister, Slander, Spiteful, Swart(h)y, Toxin, Traduce, Vicious, Vilify, Vilipend, Viperous, Virulent

Malinger(er) Dodge, Leadswinger, Scrimshank, Shirk, Skrimshank, Truant

Mall Parade

Mallard Duck, Sord

Malleable Clay, Ductile, Fictile, Pliable

▷ **Malleable** *may indicate* an anagram

Mallet Beetle, Club, Gavel, Hammer, Mace, Maul, Serving, Stick, Tenderizer

Mallow Abutilon, Dwarf, Musk, Sida, Urena

Malodorous Mephitic, Stenchy
Malpractice(s) Sculduggery, Simony, Skulduggery
Malt Brewer's grain, Diastase, Grains, Grist, Single, Stingo, Straik, Wort
Maltese (cross) Falcon, GC
Maltreat Abuse, Harm, Maul, Mishandle, Misuse
Mammal Animal, Primate

MAMMALS

3 letters:	6 letters:	Manatee	Musteline
Bat	Bobcat	Meerkat	Pachyderm
	Cervid	Peccary	Pronghorn
4 letters:	Colugo	Polecat	Solenodon
Anta	Cuscus	Raccoon	Stegodont
Arna	Dugong	Rhytina	Wolverine
Bear	Fisher	Sea-lung	
Hare	Glires	Tamandu	10 letters:
Lynx	Grison	Therian	Cacomistle
Peba	Hydrax	Tylopod	Chevrotain
Pika	Margay	Zorilla	Dermoptera
Pudu	Marten		Jaguarondi
Seal	Numbat	8 letters:	Jaguarundi
Tahr	Olingo	Cetacean	Pine marten
Titi	Sea-ape	Creodont	Springhaas
	Sealch	Eutheria	Uintathere
5 letters:	Sealgh	Kinkajou	
Coati	Serval	Mongoose	11 letters:
Dhole	Taguan	Pangolin	Artiodactyl
Hyrax	Tanrec	Pinniped	Chiropteran
Indri	Tee-tee	Platypus	Metatherian
Lemur	Teledu	Porpoise	Monodelphia
Loris	Tenrec	Sirenian	Pipistrelle
Otter	Theria	Stegodon	Titanothere
Pekan	Vicuña	Tamandua	
Rasse	Weasel	Viverrid	12 letters:
Ratel			Chalicothere
Sable	7 letters:	9 letters:	Prototherian
Saola	Caracal	Armadillo	
Shrew	Dolphin	Binturong	13 letters:
Skunk	Echidna	Cacomixle	Notocingulate
Sloth	Giraffe	Charronia	Perissodactyl
Takin	Glutton	Dinothere	
Tapir	Guanaco	Glyptodon	
Tayra	Leporid	Lagomorph	
Whale	Linsang	Monotreme	

Mammon Money, Riches, Wealth
Mammoth Epic, Gigantic, Huge, Jumbo, Mastodon, Whopping, Woolly
Man(kind), Manly, Manliness Adam, Advance, Andrew, Ask(r), Belt, Best, Betty,
  Bimana(l), Biped, Bloke, Bo, Boxgrove, Boy, Boyo, Bozo, Cad, Cairn, Calf, Castle,
  Cat, Chal, Chap, Checker, Chequer, Chiel, Cockey, Cod, Contact, Continuity, Crew,
  Cro-Magnon, Cuffin, Cully, Dog, Don, Draught, Dude, Emmanuel, Essex, Everyman,
  Family, Fancy, Fella, Feller, Fellow, Folsom, Friday, Front, G, Gayomart, Geezer, Gent,
  Gingerbread, Grimaldi, Guy, He, Heidelberg, Himbo, Hombre, Hominid, Homme,

Homo, Homo sapiens, Inner, IOM, Iron, Isle, It, Jack, Java, Joe (Bloggs), Joe Blow, Joe Sixpack, Joe Soap, John(nie), John Doe, Josser, Limit, Link, Lollipop, M, Mac, Male, Medicine, Microcosm, Mister, Mon, Mondeo, Mr, Muffin, Mun, Neanderthal, Numbers, Nutcracker, Oreopithecus, Organisation, Ou, Paleolithic, Party, Pawn, Peking, Person, Piece, Piltdown, Pin, Pithecanthropus, Property, Raff, Ray, Remittance, Renaissance, Resurrection, Rhodesian, Right-hand, Rook, Sandwich, Servant, Servitor, Ship, Sinanthropus, Sodor, Soldier, Solo, Spear, Staff, Stag, Standover, Straw, Terran, Third, Thursday, Trinil, Twelfth, Tyke, Type, Utility, Valet, Vir, Vitality, White van, Wight

Man-about-town Boulevardier

Manacle Fetter, Handcuff, Iron, Shackle

Manage(r), Manageable, Management, Managing Adhocracy, Administer, Agent, Amildar, Attain, Aumil, Behave, Board, Boss, Chief, Come by, Conduct, Contrive, Control, Cope, Crisis, Darogha, Direct, Docile, Eke, Exec(utive), Fare, Fend, Find, Floor, Fund, Gerent, Get by, Govern, Grieve, Handle, Head bummer, Honcho, IC, Impresario, Intendant, Line, Logistical, MacReady, Maître d('hotel), Make do, Manipulate, Manoeuvre, Middle, Nomenklatura, Organise, Proctor, Procurator, Régisseur, Rig, Roadie, → **RUN**, Scrape, Shift, Steward, Strategy, Subsist, Succeed, Suit, Superintend, Supervisor, Swing, Sysop, Tawie, Top, Tractable, Transact, Treatment, Trustee, Wangle, Webmaster, Wield(y), Yare

Manatee Lamantum, Mermaid, Sea-ape

Manchu Fu

Mandala Kalachakra

Mandarin Bureaucrat, Chinaman, Kuo-Yu, Nodding, Satsuma, Yamen

Mandate Authority, Decree, Fiat, Order

Mandela Madiba, Nelson

Mandrake Springwort

Mandrel Triblet

Mane(d), Manes Crest, Encolure, Jubate, Larva(e), Shades

Manège Horseplay, Train

Manganese Diagolite, Mn, Synadelphite, Wadd

Mange, Mangy Sarcoptic, Scabby

Manger Cratch, Crib, Hack, Stall

Mangle Agrise, Butcher, Distort, Garble, Hack, Hackle, Haggle, Mammock, Wring(er)

▷ **Mangle** *may indicate* an anagram

Mango Dika

Manhandle Frogmarch, Maul, Mousle, Rough

Manhater Misanthrope

Manhattan Bowery

Mania Cacoethes, Craze, Frenzy, Lunacy, Paranoia, Passion, Rage

Manichaean Albi

Manifest(ation), Manifestly Apparent, Attest, Avatar, Epiphany, Evident, Evince, Exhibit, Extravert, Extrovert, Feat, List, Marked, Mode, Notably, Obvious, Open, Overt, Schizothymia, Show, Undisguised

Manifesto Communist, Plank, Platform, Policy, Pronunciamento

Manifold(ness) Many, Multeity, Multiple

Manila Abaca, Cheroot

Manioc Cassava

Maniple Fannel, Fanon

Manipulate, Manipulative, Manipulator, Manipulation Bend, Chiropractor, Cog, Control, Cook, Demagogic, Diddle, Fashion, Finagle, Finesse, Gerrymander, Handle, Hellerwork, Jerrymander, Juggle, Legerdemain, Logodaedalus, Massage, Masseuse, Master-slave, McTimoney chiropractic, Milk, Osteopath, Play off, Ply, Rig, Spin, Svengali, Swing, Tong, Tweeze, Use, Wangle, → **WIELD**

▷ **Manipulate** *may indicate* an anagram

Manna Alhagi, Briancon, Food, Trehala, Turkish

Manner(ism), Mannerly, Manners Accent, Airs, À la, Appearance, Attitude, Bedside, Behaved, Behaviour, Bon ton, Breeding, Carriage, Conduct, Couth, Crew, Custom, Deportment, Ethos, Etiquette, Farand, Farrand, Farrant, Guise, Habit, How, Mien, Mister, Mode, Mood, Morality, Mores, Of, Ostent, Panache, Politesse, Presence, Presentation, P's & Q's, Quirk, Rate, Rhetoric, Sort, Style, Table, Thew(s), Thewe(s), Trick, Upsee, Upsey, Upsy, Urbanity, Way, Wise

▷ **Manoeuvre** *may indicate* an anagram

Manoeuvre(s) Alley-oop, Campaign, Castle, Christie, Christy, Démarche, Ebrillade, Engineer, Exercise, Faena, Fianchetto, Fork, Gambit, Grey mail, Half-board, Heimlich, Hot-dog, Jink(s), Jockey, Loop, Manipulate, Op(eration), Pendule, Pesade, Ploy, Pull out, Renversement, Ruse, Short cut, Skewer, Steer, Stickhandle, Tactic, Takeover, Telemark, Use, U-turn, Valsalva, Wear, Wheel(ie), Whipstall, Wile, Wingover, Zigzag

Man-of-war Armada, Bluebottle, Destroyer, Ironclad, Portuguese

Manor (house) Area, Demain, Demesne, Estate, Hall, Kelmscott, Schloss, Vill(a), Waddesdon

Mansion Broadlands, Burghley House, Casa, Castle Howard, Chatworth House, Cliveden, Knole, Luton Hoo, Mentmore, Penshurst Place, Pile, Queen's House, Seat, Stourhead, Stowe, Waddesdon Manor, Woburn Abbey

Mantle Asthenosphere, Authority, Burnous(e), Capote, Caracalla, Chlamydate, Cloak, Dolman, Elijah, Gas, Lithosphere, Pall, Pallium, Paludament, Pelisse, Rochet, Shawl, Sima, Toga, Tunic, Vakas, Veil

Mantuan Maro, Virgil

Manual Blue collar, Bradshaw, Cambist, Console, Enchiridion, Great (organ), Guide, Hand, Handbook, How-to, Portolan(o), Positif, Sign

Manufacture(r), Manufacturing Assemble, Fabricate, Industrial, Kanban, Make, Produce

Manure Compost, Dressing, Dung, → **FERTILISER**, Green, Guano, Hen-pen, Lime, Muck, Sha(i)rn, Tath

Manuscript(s) Book of Kells, Codex, Codicology, Folio, Hand, Holograph, Longhand, Miniscule, MS, Opisthograph, Palimpsest, Papyrus, Parchment, Script, Scroll, Scrowl(e), Slush-pile, Uncial, Vellum

Manx(man) Cat, IOM, Kelly, Kelt

▷ **Manx** *may indicate* a last letter missing

Many C, CD, Countless, Crew(e), D, Hantle, Herd, Horde, Host, L, Lot, M, Manifold, Mony, Multi(tude), Myriad, Numerous, Oodles, Power, Scad, Sight, Slew, Stacks, Tons, Umpteen, Untold

▷ **Many** *may indicate* the use of a Roman numeral letter

Maoist Naxalite, Red Guard

Maori (house) Hapu, Hauhau, Hori, Jikanga, Kaumatua, Mallowpuff, Moa hunter, Tangata whenua, Te reo, Wahine, Whare

Map(s), Mapping Atlas, A-Z, Bijection, Card, Cartogram, Chart, Chorography, Choropleth, Chromosome, Cognitive, Contour, Digital, Face, Genetic, Image, Inset, Key, Loxodromic, Mappemond, Mental, Mosaic, Moving, Mud, OS, Perceptual, Plan(isphere), Plat, Plot, Portolano, Relief, Road, Sea-card, Sea-chart, Site, Star, Strip, Topography, Weather

Maple Acer, Bird's-eye, Box elder, Flowering, Japanese, Manitoba, Mazer, Norway, Plane, Silver, Sugar, Sycamore, Syrup

Map-maker Cartographer, OS, Speed

Maquis Queach, Underground

Mar Blight, Blot, Damage, Denature, Dere, Impair, Poison, Soil, Spoil, Taint

Marabout Sofi, Sufi

Marathon Comrades, Huge, London, Long, Race, Two Oceans

Maraud(er) Amalekite, Attacker, Bandit, Hun, Pillager, Pirate, Predator, Prowler, Raid

Marble(s), Marbling Aeginetan, Agate, All(e)y, Arch, Arundelian, Bonce, Bonduc, Bool, Boondoggle, Bowl, Calcite, Carrara, Chequer, Cipollino, Commoney, Devil's, Dump, Elgin, Forest, Humite, Hymettus, Knicker, Languedoc, Lucullite, Marl, Marmarosis, Marmoreal, Marver, Mosaic, Mottle, Nero-antico, Nickar, Nicker, Onychite, Onyx, Ophicalcite, Paragon, Parian, Pavonazzo, Pentelic(an), Petworth, Phigalian, Plonker, Plunker, Purbeck, Rance, Ringer, Ring-taw, Ruin, Sanity, Scagliola, Spangcockle, Taw, Tolley, Variegate, Verd antique, Wits, Xanthian

Marcel Proust

March(ing), Marcher Abut, Adjoin, Advance, Anabasis, Border(er), Borderland, Boundary, Colonel Bogey, Dead, Defile, Demo(nstration), Étape, File, Footslog, Forced, Freedom, Fringe, Galumph, Go, Goosestep, Grand, Hikoi, Hunger, Ides, Jarrow, Lide, Limes, Lockstep, Long, Meare, Music, → **PARADE**, Paso doble, Procession, Progress, Protest, Quick, Rogue's, Route, Saint, Slow time, Step, Strunt, Strut, Tramp, Trio, Tromp, Troop, Wedding, Yomp

▷ **March** *may indicate* 'Little Women' character, Amy, Beth, Jo, Meg

Marco Il Milione, Polo

Mardi Gras J'ouvert

Mare Dam, Flanders, Horse, M, MacCurdle's, Shanks's, Spanish, Yaud

Margaret Anjou, Meg, Peg, Rita

Margarine Oleo

Marge, Margin(al) Andean, Annotate, Bank, Border, Borderline, Brim, Brink, Constructive, Convergent, Curb, Edge, Fimbria, Gross, Hair's breadth, Kerb, Lean, Leeway, Limit, Lip, Littoral, Neck, Nose, Peristome, Profit, Rand, Repand, → **RIM**, Selvedge, Sideline, Spread, Tail, Term

Marginal note Apostil(le), K'ri, Postil

Margosa Melia, Nim

Maria(nne) France, Tia

Marie Dressler, Tempest

Marigold Calendula, Gool, Gule, Kingcup, Tagetes

Marijuana Alfalfa, Bhang, Camberwell carrot, Dagga, Gage, Ganja, Grass, Greens, Gungeon, Ha-ha, Hay, Hemp, Herb, J, Jimson weed, Jive, Joint, Kaif, Kef, Kif, Leaf, Lid, Locoweed, Mary-Jane, Pot, Roach, Rope, Shit, Sinsemilla, Splay, Spliff, Tea, Toke, Weed

Marina Wharf

Marinade Chermoula, Escabeche

Marine (animal) Aquatic, Bootie, Bootneck, Cephalopod, Chaetognath, Cnidarian, Coelenterate, Comatulid, Ctenophora, Cunjevoi, Enteropneusta, Flustra, Foram(inifer), Galoot, Graptolite, Harumfrodite, Hemichorda, Holothurian, Horse, Hydrocoral, Hydroid, Hydromedusa, Jarhead, Jolly, Lancelet, Leatherneck, Lobster, Mercantile, Mere-swine, Mistress Roper, Oceanic, Otarine, Physalia, Pogonophoron, Pollywag, Pollywog, Salpa, Sea(-soldier), Seston, Thalassian, Ultra, Venus's girdle

Mariner AB, Ancient, MN, Noah, RM, Sailor, Salt, Seafarer, Spacecraft, Tar

Marionette(s) Fantoccini, Puppet

Marjoram Amaracus, Origan, Pot, Sweet, Wild, Winter-sweet

Mark(ing), Marked, Marks, Marker Accent, Aesc, Annotate, Anoint, Antony, Apostrophe, Asterisk, Astrobleme, Badge, Banker, Bethumb, Biological, Birth, Blaze, Blot, Blotch, Bollard, Brand, Bruise, Buck, Bull, Buoy, Butt, Cachet, Cairn, Calibrate, Caract, Caret, Caste, CE, Cedilla, Chatter, Chequer, Cicatrix, Class, Clout, Colon, Comma, Coronis, Crease, Criss-cross, Cross(let), Cup (and ring), Dash, Denote, Dent, Diacritic, Diaeresis, Dieresis, Distinction, Ditto, DM, Dot, Duckfoot quote, Dupe, Emblem, Enseam, Ensign, Enstamp, Exclamation, Expression, Fanion, Feer, Flag, Flash, Fleck, Fox(ing), Freckle, Genetic, Glyph, Gnomon, Gospel, Grade, Guillemet, Gybe, Hacek, Haemangioma, Hair-line, Hash, Hatch, Heed, Hickey, High water, Hoofprint, Hyphen, Impress(ion), Imprint, Indicium, Infinitive, Ink, Inscribe, Insignia, Interrogation, Inukshuk, Keel, Kite, Kumkum, Label, Lentigo, Line, Ling, Livedo, Logo, Lovebite,

Low water, M, Macron, Matchmark, MB, Medical, Merk, Mint, Minute, Mottle, NB, Nick, Nota bene, Notal, Note, Notice, Obelisk, Observe, Oche, Paginate, Paragraph, Paraph, Peg, Period, Pilcrow, Pin, Pit, Plage, Pling, Pock, Point(ille), Popinjay, Port wine, Post, Presa, Printer's, Proof, Punctuation, Question, Quotation, Record, Reference, Register, Regulo, Remarque, Rillmark, Ripple, Roundel, Sanction, Scar, Scorch, Score(r), Scratch, Section, See, Service, Shadow, Shelf, Shilling, Shoal, Sigil, Sign(ature), Smit, Smut, Smutch, Soft touch, Speck, Splodge, Splotch, Spot, Stain, Stamp, Stencil, Stigma(ta), Strawberry, Stress, Stretch, Stroke, Sucker, Swan-upping, Symbol, Tag, Target, Tarnish, Tatow, Tattoo, Tee, Theta, Thread, Tick, Tide, Tie, Tika, Tikka, Tilak, Tilde, Tittle, Token, Touchmark, Trace, Track, Trema, Trout, Tug(h)ra, Twain, Umlaut, Ure, Victim, Wand, Warchalking, Watch, Weal, Welt, Whelk

Market(ing), Market day, Market place Advergaming, Agora, Alcaiceria, Available, Baltic, Bazaar, Bear, Billingsgate, Black, Black stump, Borgo, Bull, Buyers', Capital, Captive, Cattle, Change, Chowk, Cinema, Circular, Cluster, Commodity, Common, Covent Garden, Demo, Denet, Direct, Discount, Dragon, EC, Emerging, Emporium, Errand, Exchange, Exhibition, Fair, Farmers', Feeing, Flea, Forum, Forward, Free, Grey, Growth, Insert, Internal, Kerb, Lloyds, Main, Mandi, Mart, Mass, Meat, Mercat, Money, Niche, Nundine, Obigosony, Oligopoly, Open, Order-driven, Outlet, Overt, Pamphlet, Perfect, Piazza, Poster, Press, Publicity, Radio, Reach, Relationship, Rialto, Sale, Sellers', Servqual, Share, Shop, Single, Social, Societal, Sook, Souk, Spot, Stance, Staple, Stock, Stock Exchange, Tattersall's, TECHMARK®, Terminal, Test, Third, Tiger, Trade, Tron, Tryst, USP, Vent, Viral, Wall Street, Yard sale

Market garden Truck-farm

Marksman Sharpshooter, Shootist, Shot, Sniper, Tell

Marlborough Blenheim, Churchill

Marlene Lilli

Marmalade Cat, Mammee-sapota, Preserve, Squish

Marmoset Jacchus, Mico, Midas, Monkey, Wistiti

Marmot Bobac, Bobak, Dassie, Groundhog, Hoary, Hyrax, Rodent, Whistler, Woodchuck

Maroon Brown, Castaway, Enisle, Firework, Inisle, Isolate, Strand

Marquee Pavilion, Tent, Top

Marquess, Marquis Granby, Lorne, Sade

Marquetry Boul(l)e, Buhl, Inlay

Marriage, Marry, Married → **ALLIANCE**, Ally, Amate, Arranged, Bed, Beenah, Bigamy, Bridal, Buckle, Buckle-beggar, Civil, Cleek(it), Coemption, Combine, Common law, Commuter, Companionate, Confarreation, Conjugal, Connubial, Couple, Coverture, Digamy, Endogamy, Espousal, Espouse, Exogamy, Feme covert, Forsooth, Fuse, Gandharva, Genial, Goody, Group, Hedge, Hetaerism, Hetairism, Hitch, Hymen(eal), Indeed, Join, Jugal, Ketubah, Knit, Knot, Lavender, Levirate, M, Match, Mating, Matrilocal, Matrimony, Matron, Memsahib, Mésalliance, Ming, Missis, Missus, Mixed, Monandry, Monogamy, Morganatic, Nikah, Noose, Nuptial, Open, Pair, Pantagamy, Pardie, Patrilocal, Polygamy, Punalua, Putative, Quotha, Sacrament, Sannup, Shidduch, Shotgun, Splice, Tie, Tie the knot, Trial, Troggs, Troth, Umfazi, → **UNION**, Unite, W, Wed, Wedding, Wedlock, Wive

Marriageable Marrow, Nubile, Parti

Marriage-broker Shadchan

Marrow Courgette, Friend, Gist, Kamokamo, Medulla, Myeloid, Pith, Pumpkin, Spinal, Squash, Vegetable

Mars Areography, Ares, Red (planet), Syrtis major, Tharsis

Marsh(y) Bayou, Bog, Chott, Corcass, Emys, Everglades, Fen(land), Hackney, Maremma, Merse, Mire, Morass, Ngaio, Paludal, Palustrine, Plashy, Pontine, Pripet, Quagmire, Rann of Kutch, Romney, Salina, Salt, Shott, Slade, Slough, Sog, Spew, Spue, Swale, Swamp, Taiga, Terai, Vlei, Wetlands

Marshal Arrange, Array, Commander, Earp, Foch, French, Hickok, MacMahon, Muster,

Neil, Ney, Order, Pétain, Provost, Shepherd, Sky, Steward, Tedder, Usher, Vauban, Yardman

Marshmallow Althaea, Mallowpuff

Marsupial Bandicoot, Bilby, Cuscus, Dasyure, Dibbler, Didelphia, Diprotodon(t), Dunnart, Euro, Honey mouse, Honey possum, Kangaroo, Koala, Macropod, Metatheria, Notoryctes, Nototherium, Numbat, Opossum, Pademelon, Pad(d)ymelon, Petaurist, Phalanger, Pig-rat, Polyprodont, Possum, Potoroo, Pouched mouse, Pygmy glider, Quokka, Quoll, Roo, Tammar, Tasmanian devil, Theria, Thylacine, Tuan, Wallaby, Wambenger, Wombat, Yapo(c)k

Marten Fisher, Mustela, Pekan, Pine, Sable, Woodshock

Martensite Sorbite

Martha Vineyard

Martial (arts) Bellicose, Budo, Capoeira, Capuera, Chopsocky, Dojo, Iai-do, Judo, Ju-jitsu, Karate, Kata, Kendo, Kick boxing, Krav Maga, Kumite, Kung fu, Militant, Muay thai, Ninjitsu, Ninjutsu, Sensei, Shintaido, Tae Bo®, Tae kwon do, T'ai chi (chuan), Warlike, Wushu

Martin Bird, Dean, Luther, Swallow

Martinet Captious, Ramrod, Stickler, Tyrant

Martini® Cocktail, Henry

Martyr(dom), Martyrs Alban, Alphege, Campion, Colosseum, Cranmer, Donatist, Justin, Lara, Latimer, Metric, MM, Passional, Persecute, Ridley, Sebastian, Shaheed, Shahid, Stephen, Suffer, Tolpuddle, Wishart

Marvel(lous) Bodacious, Brilliant, Bully, Épatant, Fab, Fantabulous, Lulu, Magic, Marl, Miracle, Mirific, Phenomenon, Prodigious, Selcouth, Superb, Super-duper, Swell, Terrific, Wonder

Marx(ism), Marxist Aspheterism, Chico, Comintern, Commie, Groucho, Gummo, Harpo, Karl, Lenin, Mao, Menshevik, Revisionism, Tanky, Tipamaro, Zeppo

Mary Bloody, Celeste, Contrary, Madonna, Magdalene, Moll, Morison, Our Lady, Tum(my), Typhoid, Virgin

Marylebone Station

Marzipan Marchpane

Mascara Eye-black

Mascot Charm, Four-leaf clover, → **TALISMAN**, Telesm, Token

Masculine, Masculinity He, He-man, Linga(m), M, Machismo, Macho, Male, Manly, Virile, Yang

Maser Laser

Mash(er) Beat, Beau, Beetle, Brew, Lady-killer, Pap, Pestle, Pound, Puree, Sour, Squash

Mask(ed) Bird cage, Camouflage, Cloak, Cokuloris, Death, Disguise, Dissemble, Domino, Face pack, False face, Front, Gas, Hide, Larvated, Life, Loo, Loup, Mascaron, Matte, Oxygen, Persona, Respirator, Screen, Semblance, Shadow, Ski, Stalking-horse, Stocking, Stop out, Template, Visor, Vizard

Mason(ry) Ashlar, Ashler, Brother, Builder, Cowan, Emplecton, Isodoma, Isodomon, Isodomum, Jude, Lodge, Moellon, Monumental, Nogging, Opus, Perry, Random, Rubblework, Squinch, Stylobate

Masque(rade), Masquerader Comus, Domino, Guisard, Mum(m), Pose, Pretend

Mass(es) Aggregate, Agnus Dei, Anniversary, Atomic, Banket, Bezoar, Bike, Blob, Body, Bulk, Cake, Canon, Chaos, Clot, Compound, Congeries, Conglomeration, Consecration, Core, Crith, Critical, Crowd, Demos, Density, Dozens, Flake, Floc, Flysch, Folk, Geepound, Gramme, Gravitational, Great, Herd, High, Horde, Hulk, Inertial, Isobare, Jud, Kermesse, Kermis, Kilo(gram), Kirmess, Low, Lump, M, Magma, Majority, Missa, Missa solemnis, Mob, Month's mind, Mop, Nelson, Nest, Phalanx, Pile, Plebs, Plumb, Pontifical, Populace, Proper, Raft, Red, Requiem, Rest, Ruck, Salamon, Salmon, Scrum, Sea, Serac, Service, Shock, Sicilian, Size, Slub, Slug, Solar, Solemn, Solid, Stack, Stroma, Sursum Corda, Te Igitur, Tektite, Trental, Vesper, Vigil, Volume, Wad, Weight, Welter

Massacre Amritsar, Battue, Beziers, Blood-bath, Butcher, Carnage, Glencoe, Havock, Kanpur, Lidice, Manchester, Peterloo, Pogrom, Purge, St Bartholomew's Day, Scullabogue, Scupper, September, Sicilian vespers, Slaughter, Slay, Trounce, Wounded Knee

Massage, Masseur An mo, Cardiac, Chafer, Chavutti thirumal, Do-in, Effleurage, Hellerwork, → KNEAD, Malax, Manipulate, Palp, Petrissage, Physio, Reiki, Rolf(ing), Rubber, Shampoo, Shiatsu, Stone, Stroke, Swedish, Tapotement, Thai, Tripsis, Tui na

Massif Makalu

Massive Big, Bull, Colossal, Gang, Gargantuan, Heavy, Herculean, Huge, Monolithic, Monumental, Ponderous, Strong, Titan

Mast(ed), Masthead Acorn, Banner, Captain's, Crosstree, Flag, Foretop, Foreyard, High top, Hounds, Jigger, Jury, M, Mizzen, Mooring, Pannage, Pole, Racahout, Royal, Ship-rigged, Spar, Top-gallant, Truck, Venetian

Master(ly), Mastery Artful, Baalebos, Baas, Beak, Beat, Boss, Buddha, Bwana, Careers, Checkmate, Choir, Chorus, Conquer, Control, Dan, Dominate, Dominie, Employer, Enslave, Exarch, Expert, Genius, Gov, Grand, Grip, Harbour, Herr, Himself, International, Learn, Lord, MA, Maestro, Magistral, Mas(s), Massa, Maulana, Mes(s), Nkosi, Old, Ollamh, Ollav, Oner, Oppress, Original, Overcome, Overlord, Overpower, Overseer, Passed, Past, Pedant, Question, Rabboni, Schoolman, Seed, Seigneur, Seignior, Signorino, Sir(e), Skipper, → SUBDUE, Subjugate, Superate, Surmount, Swami, Tame, Task, Teach, Thakin, Towkay, Tuan, Usher, Vanquish, Virtuoso

Mastermind Brain, Conceive, Direct

Masterpiece Chef d'oeuvre, Creation

Mastersinger Sachs

Master-stroke Coup, Triumph

Mastic Sealant

Masturbate, Masturbation Abuse, Blow, Frig, Gratify, Jerk off, Jock, Onanism, Self-pollution, Toss off, Tribady, Wank, Whack off

Mat(ted), Matting Bast, Capillary, Coaster, Doily, Dojo, Doyley, Dutch mattress, Felt, Inlace, Pad, Paunch, Place, Plat, Prayer, Rug, Rush, Surf, Table, Taggy, → TANGLE, Tat(ami), Tatty, Taut, Tautit, Tawt, Tomentose, Web, Welcome, Zarf

Matador Card, Espada, Ordonez, Theseus, Torero

Match(ed) Agree, Alliance, Amate, Balance, Besort, Bonspiel, Bout, Carousel, Compare, Compeer, Congreve, Consolation, Contest, Cope, Correlate, Correspond, Counterpane, Cup tie, Doubles, Emulate, Engagement, Equal(ise), Equate, Even, Exhibition, Fellow, Fit, Fixture, Four-ball, Foursome, Friction, Friendly, Fusee, Fuzee, Game, Go, Greensome, Grudge, International, Joust, Light, Locofoco, Love, Lucifer, Main, Marrow, Marry, Meet, Mouse, Needle, Pair(s), Paragon, Parallel, Parti, Pit, Play-off, Prizefight, Promethean, Quick, Replica, Reproduce, Return, Rival, Road game, Roland, Rubber, Safety, Semifinal, Sevens, Shield, Shoo-in, Shooting, Shouting, Singles, Slanging, Slow, Slugfest, Spunk, Striker, Suit, Sync(h), → TALLY, Team, Test, Texas scramble, Tie, Twin, Twosome, Union, Venue, Vesta, Vesuvian, Wedding

Matchbox label (collecting) Phillumeny

Match girl Bride

Match-holder Lin(t)stock

Matchless Non(e)such, Orinda

Matchmaker Blackfoot, Broker, Pairer, Promoter, Shadchan

Mate, Mating Achates, Adam, Amigo, Amplexus, Assistant, Assortative, Bedfellow, Bo, Breed, Buddy, Buffer, Butty, Check, Chess, China, Chum, Cobber, Cock, Comrade, Consort, Crony, Cully, Digger, Eve, Feare, Feer, Fellow, Fere, Fiere, First, Fool's, Helper, Husband, Ilex, Inbreed, Maik, Make, Marrow, Marry, Match, Mister, Mucker, Nick, Nickar, Oldster, Oppo, → PAIR, Pal, Pangamy, Panmixia, Panmixis, Paragon, Partner, Pheer(e), Pirrauru, Running, Scholar's, Second, Serve, Sex, Skaines, Smothered, Soul, Sport, → SPOUSE, Tea, Tup, Wack, Wacker, Wife, Wus(s)

Material(ism) Agitprop, Appropriate, Apt, → CLOTH, Compo, Composite, Copy,

Corporeal, Data, Documentation, Earthling, Earthy, → **FABRIC**, Factual, Fallout, Fertile, Fuel, Germane, Historical, Hylic, Illusion, Infill, Leading, Matter, Pertinent, Physical, Positive, Raw, Real, Reify, Relevant, Repertoire, Substance, Tangible, Thingy, Worldly

MATERIALS

3 *letters:*	6 *letters:*	8 *letters:*	Towelling
Cob	Armure	Blastema	
Pug	Borsic	Concrete	10 *letters:*
	Byssus	Fettling	Fibreboard
4 *letters:*	Cermet	Graphite	Fibreglass
Bole	Corfam®	Illuvium	Protoplasm
Frit	Fablon®	Lambskin	Thermolite®
Gang	Gangue	Oilcloth	
Moxa	Gypsum	Regolith	11 *letters:*
Tape	Sporex®	Silicone	Fibrocement
Ylem	Tartan®	Skirting	Interfacing
	Tusser		Papier-maché
5 *letters:*		9 *letters:*	Polystyrene
Fibro	7 *letters:*	Aggregate	
Fines	Ballast	Austenite	12 *letters:*
Flong	Ceramic	Celluloid	Agalmatolite
Fomes	Matting	Cellulose	Plasterboard
Fritt	Oilskin	Fibrefill	Plasterstone
Metal	Phantom	Macintosh	
Oasis®	Protore	Micromesh	13 *letters:*
Staff	Pugging	Pina-cloth	Wattle and daub
Stuff	Sagathy	Polythene	
	Textile	Sackcloth	
	Tinfoil	Samsonite®	

Materialise Appear, Apport, Click, Reify
Materialist(ic) Banausian, Earthling, Hylist, Hyloist, Philistine, Somatist
Mathematician Optime, Statistician, Wrangler

MATHEMATICIANS

4 *letters:*	Bessel	7 *letters:*	Goldbach
Hero	Briggs	Fourier	Hamilton
Zeno	Cantor	Hawking	Lagrange
	Cocker	Hilbert	Mercator
5 *letters:*	Euclid	Laplace	Playfair
Bayes	Fermat	Leibniz	Poincare
Boole	Gunter	Neumann	
Euler	Jacobi	Penrose	9 *letters:*
Frege	Jevons	Poisson	Bernoulli
Gauss	Kaluza	Ptolemy	Descartes
Godel	Napier	Pytheas	Dunstable
Julia	Newton	Riemann	Fibonacci
Klein	Pascal		Friedmann
Pitts	Turing	8 *letters:*	Minkowski
	Walker	Archytas	Whitehead
6 *letters:*	Wiener	Bourbaki	
Agnesi		De Morgan	

10 letters:	Mandelbrot	**11 letters:**	**12 letters:**
Apollonius	Pythagoras	Von Leibnitz	Eratosthenes
Archimedes	Torricelli		
Diophantus	Von Neumann		

Mathematics, Mathematical, Maths Algebra, Applied, Arithmetic, Arsmetrick, Calculus, Combinatorics, Exact science, Geometry, Haversine, Higher, Logarithms, Mechanics, New, Numbers, Porism, Pure, Topology, Trig, Trigonometry

Matilda Liar, Swag, Untruthful, Waltzing

Matinee Coat, Idol, Show

Mating Pangamy

Matins Nocturn

Matricide Orestes

Matrimony Bed, Conjugal, Marriage, Sacrament, Spousal, Wedlock

Matrix Active, Array, Boston, Hermitian, Jacobian, Mould, Orthogonal, Pattern, Scattering, Square, Symmetric, Transpose, Uterus

Matron Dame, Hausfrau, Lucretia, Nurse, Warden

Matt(e) Dense, Dingy, Dull

Matter Affair, Alluvium, Bioblast, Biogen, Body, Business, Concern, Condensed, Consequence, Count, Dark, Degenerate, Empyema, Epithelium, Front, Gear, Gluon, Go, Grey, Hyle, Ichor, Impost(h)ume, Issue, Mass, Material, Molecule, Multiverse, Phlegm, Pith, Plasma, Point, Positron, Premise, Protoplasm, Pulp, Pus, Quark, Reading, Reck, Reke, Scum, Shebang, Signify, Solid, Sputum, Stereome, Stuff, Subject, → **SUBSTANCE**, Theme, Thing, Topic, Tousle, Touzle, Vinyl, White, Ylem

Matter of fact Pragmatic

Matthew Arnold

Mattress Bed(ding), Biscuit, Dutch, Featherbed, Foam, Futon, Lilo®, Pallet, Pa(i)lliasse, Spring, Tick

Mature, Maturity Adult, Age, Auld, Blossom, Bold, Concoct, Develop, Fully-fledged, Grow (up), Mellow, Metaplasis, Old, Puberty, Ripe(n), Rounded, Seasoned, Upgrow(n)

Maudlin Fuddled, Mawkish, Sentimental, Slip-slop, Sloppy, Too-too

Maul Hammer, Manhandle, Paw, Rough, Savage, Tear

Maundy Money, Nipter, Thursday

Mauretanian, Mauritania(n) Moor, RIM

Mauritius MS

Mausoleum Halicarnassus, Mole, Sepulchre, Taj Mahal, Tomb

Mauve Lavender, Lilac, Mallow, Perkin's

Maverick Misfit, Nonconformist, Rogue, Unconventional

Mavis Throstle

Maw Crop, Gorge, Gull(et), Mouth, Oesophagus

Mawkish Sentimental, Sickly

Max Ernst

Maxim Adage, Aphorism, Apo(ph)thegm, Axiom, Byword, Dictum, Gnome, Gorki, Gun, Hiram, Moral, Motto, Precept, Proverb, Restaurateur, → **RULE**, Saw, Saying, Sentence, Sentiment, Watchword

Maximum All-out, Full, Highest, Most, Peak, Utmost

May Blossom, Can, Hawthorn, Merry, Might, Month, Mote(n), Quickthorn, Shall, Whitethorn

Maybe Happen, Mebbe, Peradventure, Percase, Perchance, Perhaps, Possibly

▷ **May become** *may indicate* an anagram

May day Beltane, SOS

Mayfair WI

Mayfly Ephemera, Ephemeroptera, Green-drake, Sedge

Mayhem Chaos, Crime, Damage, Havoc, Pandemonium

Mayonnaise Aioli, Rémoulade

Mayor Alcaide, Burgomaster, Casterbridge, Charter, Councilman, Portreeve, Provost, Syndic, Whittington, Worship

Maze Honeycomb, Labyrinth, Meander, Network, Theseus, Warren, Wilderness

MC Compere, Host, Ringmaster

MD Doctor, Healer

ME Yuppie flu

Me I, Mi, One, Sel(f), Us

Mead(ow) Flood, Grass(land), Haugh, Hydromel, Inch, Ing, Lea(se), Ley, Meath(e), Metheglin, → PASTURE, Runnymede, Saeter, Salting, Water

Meadowsweet Dropwort

Meagre Arid, Bar, Bare, Exiguous, Measly, Mingy, Paltry, Pittance, Scant, Scrannel, Scranny, Scrawny, Skimpy, Skinny, Spare, Sparse, Stingy, Thin

Meal(s), Mealie, Mealy Allseed, Banquet, Barbecue, Barium, Beanfeast, Blow-out, Board, Breakfast, Brunch, Buffet, Carry out, Cassava, Cereal, Chilled, Cholent, Chota-hazri, Collation, Corn, Cornflour, Cottoncake, Cottonseed, Cou-cou, Cribble, Dejeune(r), Deskfast, Dinner, Drammock, Ear, Ervalenta, Fare, Farina, Feast, Flour, Food, Glacier, Grits, Grout, Hangi, High tea, Iftar, Indian, Italian, Kai, Lock, Lunch, Mandioc, Mandioc(c)a, Mani(h)oc, Matzo, Melder, Meltith, Mensal, Mess, Morning, Mush, No-cake, Nosh, Nuncheon, Obento, Ordinary, Picnic, Piece, Plate, Poi, Polenta, Porridge, Prandial, Prix fixe, Rac(c)ahout, Refection, Repast, Revalenta, Rijst(t)afel, Salep, Scambling, Scoff, Seder, Sehri, Smorgasbord, Snack, Sohur, Spread, Square, Suhur, Supper, Table d'hôte, Takeaway, Tea, Thali, Tiffin, Tightener, Tousy tea, Twalhours, Undern

Meal-ticket LV

Mean(ing), Meant Aim, Arithmetic(al), Average, Base, Betoken, Bowsie, Caitiff, Cheap, Connotation, Curmudgeon, Definition, Denotate, Denote, Design, Dirty, Drift, Essence, Ettle, Feck, Footy, Foul, Geometric(al), Gist, Golden, Hang, Harmonic, Humble, Hunks, Ignoble, Illiberal, Imply, Import, Inferior, Insect, Intend, Intermediate, Kunjoos, Lexical, Low(down), Mang(e)y, Marrow, Medium, Mesquin, Message, Method, Mid, Miserly, Narrow, Near, Norm, Nothing, One-horse, Ornery, Paltry, Par, Penny-pinching, Petty, Piker, Pinch-penny, Pith, Point, Purport, → PURPOSE, Quadratic, Ratfink, Revenue, Ribald, Roinish, Roynish, Scall, Scrub, Scurvy, Semanteme, Semantic(s), Sememe, Sense, Shabby, Signify, Slight, Slink, Small, Sneaky, Snoep, Snot, Sordid, Sparing, Spell, Stingy, Stink(ard), Stinty, Substance, Symbol, Thin, Threepenny, Tight-lipped, Tightwad, Two-bit, Value, Vile, Whoreson

Meander Fret, Ring, Sinuate, Stray, Wander, Weave, Wind

Meaningless Ducdame, Empty, Flummery, Hollow, Hot air, Insignificant, Nonny, Rumbelow

Means Agency, Dint, Income, Instrumental, Media, Method, Mode, Opulence, Organ, Private, Resources, Staple, Substance, Tactics, Visible, Ways, Wherewithal

Meantime, Meanwhile Among, Emong, Greenwich, Interim, Whilst

Measles Morbilli, Roseola, Rose-rash, Rubella, Rubeola, Sheep

Measure(d), Measuring, Measure(ment) By(e)law, Calibre, Centile, Circular, Crackdown, Customise, → DANCE, Démarche, → DIMENSION, Distance, Dose, Dry, → GAUGE, Gavotte, Gross, Imperial, → INSTRUMENT, Limit, Linear, Liter, Litre, Meed, Metage, Moratorium, Of, Offset, Precaution, Prophylactic, Quickstep, Ration, Remen, Sanction, Share, Short, → SIZE, Standard, Statute, Step, Stichometry, Strike, Struck, Survey, Tachymetry, Token, Triangulate, → UNIT, Wine

MEASUREMENTS

2 letters:	Mu	Bel	Ell
As		Cab	Erg
Em	3 letters:	Cor	Fat
En	Are	DIN	Hin

Lay
Lea
Ley
Log
Lug
Mil
Rod
Tot
Tsp
Wey

4 letters:
Acre
Aune
Bath
Boll
Bolt
Comb
Cord
Coss
Cran
Culm
Dram
Epha
Foot
Gage
Gill
Hank
Hide
Inch
Koss
Last
Line
Link
Maze
Mete
Mile
Mole
Mott
Muid
Nail
Omer
Pace
Peck
Pint
Pipe
Pole
Pond
Pood
Ream
Reau
Rood
Rope
Rotl

Shot
Span
Tape
Thou
Unit
Vara
Volt
Warp
Yard

5 letters:
Anker
Ardeb
Barye
Bekah
Bigha
Caneh
Carat
Chain
Clove
Combe
Coomb
Crore
Cubit
Cumec
Cusec
Depth
Ephah
Fermi
Float
Gauge
Grain
Groma
Hanap
Homer
Joule
Kaneh
Lento
Liang
Ligne
Lippy
Loure
Mease
Meter
Metre
Middy
Noddy
Optic®
Perch
Plumb
Quart
Romer
Ruler
Scale

Skein
Sound
Stade
Stere
Tesla
Therm
Toise
Verst
Wecht
Yojan

6 letters:
Albedo
Alnage
Arpent
Arshin
Barrel
Barren
Beegah
Bovate
Bushel
Chenix
Chopin
Cicero
Cubage
Denier
Double
Etalon
Exergy
Fathom
Firkin
Firlot
Gallon
Height
Hemina
Jigger
Kelvin
Kilerg
League
Lippie
Liquid
Modius
Morgan
Mutton
Noggin
Oxgang
Parsec
Pascal
Pottle
Radius
Rotolo
Runlet
Sazhen
Second

Stadia
Thread
Tierce
Yojana

7 letters:
Aneroid
Arshine
Braccio
Breadth
Burette
Caliper
Candela
Chalder
Choenix
Conguis
Coulomb
Cyathus
Decibel
Drastic
Entropy
Furlong
Geodesy
Lambert
Leaguer
Pelorus
Quarter
Refract
Rundlet
Sleever
Spindle
Spondee
Venturi
Virgate

8 letters:
Angstrom
Calipers
Calliper
Carucate
Chaldron
Crannock
Desyatin
Diameter
Exitance
Fistmele
Foot rule
Hogshead
Kilogray
Luxmeter
Mutchkin
Odometer
Oximeter
Parasang

Poulter's
Puncheon
Tape-line
Teraflop
Viameter
Waywiser

9 letters:
Astrolabe
Atmometer
Bolometer
Callipers
Cryometer
Decalitre
Decastere
Dosimeter
Ergometer
Eriometer
Flowmeter
Hodometer
Kilometre
Konimeter
Lysimeter
Machmeter
Manometer
Mekometer
Nipperkin
Octameter

Oenometer
Pedometer
Pentapody
Potometer
Salimeter
Steradian
Tappet-hen
Tasimeter
Telemeter
Titration
Tonometer
Yardstick

10 letters:
Acidometer
Amphimacer
Anemometer
Barleycorn
Bathometer
Centimetre
Chronotron
Coulometer
Cyclometer
Densimeter
Dessiatine
Dessyatine
Drosometer
Eudiometer

Geodimeter
Goniometer
Gravimeter
Humidistat
Hydrometer
Hygrometer
Lactometer
Mileometer
Micrometer
Millimetre
Opisometer
Photometer
Piezometer
Pychometer
Resistance
Touchstone
Tromometer
Winchester

11 letters:
Actinometer
Auxanometer
Calorimeter
Dioptometer
Dynamometer
Gradiometer
Intoximeter
Jacob's staff

Long Hundred
Stereometer
Tacheometry
Venturi tube
Weighbridge

12 letters:
Breathalyzer
Cathetometer
Coulombmeter
Densitometer
Electrometer
Electronvolt
Extensimeter
Extensometer
Galactometer
Gravitometer
Katharometer
Nephelometer
Permittivity
Tellurometer
Viscosimeter

13 letters:
Saccharometer

15 letters:
Katathermometer

Meat(s) Aitchbone, Bacon, Bard, Beef, Beefsteak, Biltong, Brawn, Brisket, Brown, Burger, Cabob, Carbonado, Carrion, Charcuterie, Chop, Collop, Confit, Croquette, Cut, Dark, Devon, Dog-roll, Easy, Edgebone, Entrecôte, Escalope, Essence, Fanny Adams, Fatback, Fleishig, Fleishik, Flesh, Flitch, Force, Galantine, Gigot, Gobbet, Gosht, Griskin, Ham, Haslet, Jerky, Joint, Junk, Kabab, Kabob, Kebab, Kebob, Lamb, Loin, Luncheon, Mart, Medaillon, Medallion, Mince, Mutton, Noisette, Offal, Olive, Oyster, Pastrami, Paupiette, Pem(m)ican, Piccata, Pith, Pope's eye, Pork, Processed, Prosciutto, Rack, Red, Rillettes, Roast, Saddle, Sasatie, Satay, Scaloppino, Schnitzel, Scran, Scrapple, Sey, Shank, Shashlik, Shishkebab, Short ribs, Side, Sirloin, Sosatie, Spam®, Spare rib, Spatchcock, Spaul(d), Steak, Strong, Tenderloin, Tiring, Tongue, Variety, Veal, Venison, Vifda, Virgate, Vivda, White, Wiener schnitzel, Wurst

Meatball(s) Cecils, Croquette, Faggot, Falafel, Felafel, Fricadel, Frikkadell, Goujon, Knish, Kofta, Kromesky, Quenelle, Rissole

Meat extract Brawn, Gravy, Juice, Stock

Meatless Banian, Lent, Maigre, Vegetarian

Mecca Centre, Honeypot, Kaaba, Keblah, Kibla(h), Omayyad, Qibla, Umayyad

▷ **Mechanic(al)** *may indicate* characters from 'A Midsummer Night's Dream'

Mechanic(s) Apron-man, Artificer, Artisan, Banausic, Barodynamics, Bottom, Card, Celestial, Classical, Dynamics, Engineer, Fitter, Fluid, Fundi, Grease monkey, Greaser, Hand, Journeyman, Kinematics, Kinesiology, Kinetics, Newtonian, Operative, Quantum, Rock, Soil, Statics, Statistical, Technician, Wave

Mechanical, Mechanism Action, Apparatus, Auto, Autodestruct, Banausic, Clockwork, Defence, Dérailleur, Escape, Escapement, Foul-safe, Gimmal, Gust-lock, Instrument, Machinery, Movement, Organical, Pulley, Pushback, Rackwork, Regulator, Robotic, Servo, Synchroflash, Synchromesh, Traveller, Trippet, Works

Medal(lion)(s) Award, Bar, Bronze, Congressional, Croix de guerre, Decoration, Dickin, DSM, GC, George, Gold, Gong, Gorget, Military, MM, Numismatic, Pan(h)agia, Purple Heart, Putty, Roundel, Silver, Tony, Touchpiece, VC, Vernicle

Meddle(r), Meddlesome, Meddling Busybody, Dabble, Finger, Hen-hussy, → **INTERFERE**, Interloper, Marplot, Mell, Monkey, Officious, Pantopragmatic, Potter, Pragmatic, Pry, Snooper, Spoilsport, Tamper, Tinker, Trifle

Media Fibre, Mass, Mixed, New, PR

Mediate, Mediator ACAS, Arbitrate, Intercede, Interpose, Intervene, Liaison, Muti, Referee, Stickler, Thirdsman, Trouble-shooter

Medic(k) Corpsman, Extern, Lucern(e), Nonesuch, Snail

Medical, Medicine (chest), Medicament, Medication Aesculapian, Algology, Allopathy, Aloetic, Alternative, Amulet, Andrology, Anodyne, Antacid, Antibiotic, Antidote, Antisepsis, Antiseptic, Arnica, Arrowroot, Asafetida, Aurum potabile, Aviation, Ayurveda, Bariatrics, Bi, Bismuth, Blister, Brunonian, Buchu, Bucku, Calumba, Carminative, Charm, Chinese, Chiropody, Chlorodyne, Chrysarobin, Clinician, Complementary, Cordial, Corpsman, Cubeb, Curative, Defensive, Demulcent, Diapente, Diascordium, Diatessaron, Discutient, Doctor's stuff, Dose, Draught, Drops, → **DRUG**, Dutch drops, Eardrop, Electuary, Elixir, Emetic, Emmenagogue, Empirics, Enema, Epulotic, Excipient, Expectorant, Fall-trank, Febrifuge, Feldsher, Folk, Forensic, Fringe, Functional, Galen, Galenism, Gelcap, Genitourinary, Gripe water®, Gutta, Haematinic, Haematology, Herb, Herbal, Hesperidin, Holistic, Hom(o)eopathy, Horse-drench, Iatric(al), Imhotep, Indian, Industrial, Inhalant, Inro, Internal, Iodine, Ipecac(uanha), Iron, Ko cycle, Lariam®, Laxative, L-dopa, Leechcraft, Legal, Loblolly, Lotion, Magnesia, Maqui, Menthol, Microbubbles, Mishmi, Mixture, Moxar, Muti, Natural, Naturopathy, Nephritic, Nephrology, Nervine, Neurology, Nosology, Nostrum, Nuclear, Nux vomica, Ob-gyn, Occupational, Officinal, Oncology, Oporice, Orthopoedics, Osteopath, Palliative, Panacea, Paregoric, Patent, Pathology, Pectoral, P(a)ediatrics, Pharmacy, Phlegmagogue, Physic, Physical, Pill, Placebo, Polychrest, Polypill, Posology, Potion, Poultice, Preparation, Preventive, Proctology, Prosthetics, Psionic, Psychiatry, Ptisan, Purgative, Quin(quin)a, Quinacrine, Quinine, Radiology, Reborant, Red Crescent, Red Cross, Relaxative, → **REMEDY**, Salve, Sanative, Sanguinaria, Sebesten, Senna, Serology, Simple, Snake-oil, Space, Specific, Sports, Steel, Stomachic, Stomatology, Stramonium, Stupe, Suppository, Synergast, Syrup, Tabasheer, Tabashir, Tablet, Tar-water, Tetracycline, Therapeutics, Thimerosal, TIM, Tisane, Tocology, Tonic, Totaquine, Trade, Traditional Chinese, Traumatology, Treatment, Trichology, Troche, Valerian, Veronal, Veterinary, Virology

Medicine man, Medico Bone-setter, Koradji

Medieval Archaic, Feudal, Gothic, Med, Old, Trecento

Mediocre Average, Fair, Indifferent, Middle-of-the-road, Middling, Ordinary, Pap, Respectable, Run-of-the-mill, Second-class, So-So, Undistinguished

Meditate, Meditation, Meditator, Meditative Brood, Chew, Cogitate, Contemplate, Falun gong, Fifteen o's, Gymnosophy, Hesychast, Insight, Muse, Mystic, Pensive, Ponder, Reflect, Reverie, Revery, Ruminate, Samadhi, Tantric, Thanatopsis, Transcendental, Vipassana, Weigh, Yoga, Yogic flying, Zazen

Mediterranean Great Sea, Levant, Med, Midi, Scattermouch

Medium (A)ether, Agency, Air, Average, Channel, Clairvoyant, Contrast, Culture, Dispersive, Earth, Element, Ether, Even, Fire, Happy, Home, Intermediary, Interstellar, M, Magilp, Mean, Megilp, Midsize, Midway, Milieu, Oils, Organ, Ouija, Planchette, Press, Radio, Regular, Shaman, Spiritist, Spiritualist, Television, Telly, TV, Vehicle, Water

Medley Charivari, Collection, Gallimaufry, Individual, Jumble, Macedoine, Melange, Mishmash, Mix, Pastiche, Patchwork, Pi(e), Pot-pourri, Quodlibet, Ragbag, Salad, Salmagundi, Series, Tat

▷ **Medley** *may indicate* an anagram

Medusa Jellyfish, Planoblast

Meek Docile, Griselda, Humble, Milquetoast, Patient, Sheepy, Tame
Meerkat Suricate
Meerschaum Sepiolite
Meet(ing), Meeting place Abide, Abutment, AGM, Appointment, Apropos, Ascot,
Assemblage, Assemble, Assembly, Assignation, Audience, Baraza, Bosberaad, Briefing,
Camporee, Caucus, Chapterhouse, Chautauqua, Clash, Commissure, Conclave,
Concourse, Concur, Confluence, Confrontation, Congress, Connivance, Conseil d'etat,
Consistory, Consulta, Contact, Conterminous, Convene, Convent(icle), Convention,
Converge, Conversazione, Convocation, Correspond, Cybercafé, Defray, Demo, EGM,
Encounter, Ends, Experience, Face, Find, Fit, For(e)gather, Forum, Fulfil, Gemot, General,
Giron, Gorsedd, Greeting, Guild, Gyeld, Gymkhana, Gyron, Hall, Howf(f), Hunt, Hustings,
Imbizo, Indaba, Infall, Interface, Interview, Join, Junction, Kgotla, Korero, Lekgotla,
Liaise, Marae, Moot, Mother's, Obviate, Occlusion, Occur, Oppose, Overflow, Partenariat,
Pay, Plenary, Plenum, Pnyx, Pow-wow, Prayer, Prosper, Quadrivial, Quaker, Quorate,
Quorum, Race, Races, Rally(ing point), Rencontre, Rencounter, Rendezvous, Reunion,
Sabbat(h), Satisfy, Séance, See, Seminar, Session, Sit, Social, Sports, Suitable, Summit,
Swap, Symposium, Synastry, Synaxis, Synod, Tackle, Talkfest, Talk-in, Talking-shop,
Think-in, Town, Track, Tryst, Venery, Venue, Vestry, Wapinshaw, Wardmote, Wharenui,
Wharepuni, Workshop
Megalith(ic) Sarsen, Skara Brae, Stonehenge
Megalomaniac Monarcho
Megaphone Bull-horn, Loudhailer
Megapode Mound-bird, Talegalla
Meiosis Understatement
Melancholy, Melancholic Adust, Allicholy, Allycholly, Anatomy, Atrabilious,
Cafard, Despond(ency), Dreary, Dump(s), Gloom, Heart-sore, Hipped, Hump, Hyp,
Hypochondria, Jaques, Lienal, Lugubrious, Moper, Panophobia, Pensieroso, Pensive,
Saturnine, Sombre, Spleen, Splenetic, Triste, Tristesse, Weltschmerz
Melanese, Melanesian Kanak, Motu
Mêlée Brawl, Commotion, Dogfight, Fracas, Rally, Salmagundi, Scrum
Melia Margosa, Neem, Nim
Mellifluent, Mellifluous Cantabile, Melodic
Mellow Age, Fruity, Genial, Mature, Ripe, Smooth
Melodrama(tic) Bathos, Histrionic, Sensation, Transpontine
Melody, Melodious Air, Arioso, Cabaletta, Canorous, Cantabile, Cantilena, Canto
(fermo), Cantus, Cavatina, Chant, Chopsticks, Conductus, Counterpoint, Descant, Dulcet,
Euphonic, Fading, Musical, Orphean, Part-song, Plainsong, Ranz-des-vaches, Refrain,
Songful, Strain, Sweet, Theme, Tunable, → **TUNE(S)**
Melon(like) Cantaloup(e), Cas(s)aba, Charentais, Galia, Gourd, Honeydew, Mango,
Musk, Nar(r)as, Ogen, Pepo, Persian, Rock, Spanspek, Winter
Melt(ed), Melting Ablate, Colliquate, → **DISSOLVE**, Eutectic, Eutexia, Flux, Found,
Fuse, Fusil(e), Liquescent, Liquid, Run, Smectic, Syntexis, Thaw, Touch
Member Adherent, Arm, Branch, Bro(ther), Charter, Chin, Confrère, Cornice, Coulisse,
Crossbeam, Crypto, Direction, Felibre, Fellow, Forearm, Forelimb, Founder, Gremial,
Harpin(g)s, Insider, Keel, Leg, Limb, Lintel, Longeron, M, MBE, Montant, MP, Organ,
Part, Partisan, Peer, Politicaster, Politician, Private, Rood-beam, Soroptomist, Stile,
Stringer, Strut, Syndic, Tie, Toe
Membrane, Membranous Amnion, Arachnoid, Axilemma, Bilayer, Caul, Cell,
Chorioallantois, Chorion, Choroid (plexus), Chromoplast, Conjunctiva, Cornea,
Cyst, Decidua, Dissepiment, Dura (mater), Eardrum, Endocardium, Endometrium,
Endosteum, Ependyma, Exine, Extine, Fell, Film, Foetal, Frenulum, Fr(a)enum, Haw,
Head, Hyaloid, Hymen, Indusium, Intima, Intine, Involucre, Kell, Mater, Mediastinum,
Meninx, Mesentery, Mucosa, Mucous, Neurolemma, Nictitating, Nuclear, Parchment,
Patagium, Pellicle, Pericardium, Pericarp, Perichondrium, Pericranium, Periost(eum),

Periton(a)eum, Pia mater, Plasma, Plasmalemma, Pleura, Putamen, Retina, Rim, Sarcolemma, Scarious, Schneiderian, Sclera, Serosa, Serous, Skin, Synovial, Tectorial, Tela, Third eyelid, Tissue, Tonoplast, Trophoblast, Tunic, Tympan(ic), Vacuolar, Velamen, Velum, Vitelline, Web, Yolk-sac

Memento, Memoir Keepsake, Locket, Relic, Remembrancer, Souvenir, Token, Trophy

Memo(randum) Bordereau, Cahier, Chit, IOU, Jot, Jurat, Minute, Note, Notepad, → REMINDER, Slip

Memoirist Casanova

Memorable, Memorise, Memory Associative, ATLAS, Bubble, Cache, Catchy, Collective, → COMPUTER MEMORY, Con, Core, DRAM, Dynamic, Echoic, Engram(ma), Extended, Flash (bulb), Folk, Get, Highlight, Historic, Hypermnesia, Iconic, Immortal, Immunological, Learn, Living, Long-term, Main, Mainstore, Memoriter, Mind, Mneme, Mnemonic, Mnemosyne, Non-volatile, Noosphere, Notable, Pelmanism, Photographic, Race, Read-write, Recall, Recollection, Recovered, Red-letter day, → REMEMBER, Retention, Retrospection, ROM, Ro(a)te, Samskara, Screen, Semantic, Short-term, SIMM, Souvenir, Sovenance, Static, Study, Video, Virtual, Volatile, Word, Working

Memorial Albert, Altar tomb, Cenotaph, Cromlech, Ebenezer, Gravestone, Hatchment, Headstone, Marker, Martyr's, Monument, Mount Rushmore, Obelisk, Plaque, Relic, Relique, Statue, Tomb, Trophy, War, Wreath

▶ **Memory loss** *see* LOSS OF MEMORY

Men(folk) Amadoda, Chaps, Chess, Cuffins, Male, Messrs, Mortals, OR, People, Race, Troops

Menace, Menacing Danger, Dennis, Endanger, Foreboding, Intimidate, Jeopardise, Minatory, Ominous, Peril, Pest, Scowl, Sinister, Threat(en)

Menagerie Ark, Circus, Zoo

Mend Beet, Bete, Bushel, Cobble, Correct, Cure, Darn, Fix, Heal, Improved, Mackle, Patch, Piece, Recover, Remedy, → REPAIR, Set, Sew, Solder, Trouble-shoot

Mendelevium Md

Mendicant Beggar, Calender, Fakir, Franciscan, Frater, Servite

Menial Bottlewasher, Drudge, Drug, Eta, Fag, Flunkey, Lackey, Lowly, Scullion, Servile, Toady, Underling, Wood-and-water joey

Meninx (D)jerba

Menopause Andropause, Climacteric

Menstruation Curse, Menarche, Menorrh(o)ea, Menses, Monthly, Period

Mental (condition), Mental disorder, Mentality Alienism, Bunker, Doolally, Eject, Hallucinosis, Insane, Noetic, Nut job, Nutty, Paranoia, Psychic, Siege

▷ **Mental** *may indicate* the chin

Mention(ed) Advert, Allusion, Bename, Benempt, Broach, Bynempt, Citation, Hint, Honourable, Instance, Name(-check), Notice, Quote, Refer, Same, Speech, State, Suggest, Touch

Mentor Advisor, Guru, Rebbe, Tutor

Menu Agenda, Card, Carte, Carte du jour, Cascading, Drop-down, Fare, List, Option, Table d'hôte, Tariff

Mercantile Commercial, Trade

Mercator Cartographer

Mercenary Arnaout, Condottiere, Freelance, Greedy, Hack, Hessian, Hired gun, Hireling, Landsknecht, Legionnaire, Pindaree, Pindari, Rutter, Sordid, Spoilsman, Swiss Guard, Switzer, Venal, Warmonger, Wildgeese

Merchandise Cargo, Goods, Line, Produce, Ware(s)

Merchant(man) Abbas, Abudah, Antonio, Argosy, Broker, Bun(n)ia, Burgher, Chandler, Chap, Commission, Crare, Crayer, Dealer, Factor, Flota, Gossip, Hoastman, Importer, Jobber, Law, Magnate, Marcantant, Mercer, Monger, Négociant, Pedlar, Polo, Provision, Retailer, Seller, Shipper, Speed, Squeegee, Stapler, Sutler, Trader, Vintner, Wholesaler

Mercia Offa

Merciful, Mercy Amnesty, Charity, Clement, Compassionate, Corporal, Grace, Humane, Kind, Kyrie, Lenient, Lenity, Miserere, Misericord(e), Pacable, Pity, Quarter, Ruth, Sparing, Spiritual

Merciless Cruel, Hard, Hard-hearted, Inclement, Pitiless

Mercurial, Mercuric sulphide, Mercury Azoth, Cyllenius, Dog's, Freddie, Fulminating, Herald, Hermes, Hg, Horn, Hydrargyrum, Messenger, Proteus, Quicksilver, Red, Red-man, Spurge, Thimerosal, Tiemannite, Torr, Volatile

Mere(ly) Allenarly, Bare, Common, Lake, Pond, Pool, Poor, Pure, Sheer, Tarn, Ullswater, Very

Merge(r), Merging Amalgamate, Blend, Coalesce, Coalise, Composite, Conflate, Consolidate, Die, Elide, Fusion, Incorporate, Interflow, Interpenetrate, Liquesce, Meld, Melt, Mingle, Symphysis, Syncretism, Synergy, Unify, Unite

Meridian Magnetic, Noonday, Prime

Meringue Pavlova

Merit(ed) CL, Condign, Deserve, Due, Earn, Found, Meed, Rate, Virtue, Worth(iness)

Mermaid Dugong, Halicore, Merrow, Siren, Tavern, Undine

Merriment, Merry Andrew, Blithe(some), Bonny, Boon, Cant, Cherry, Chirpy, Crank, Cricket, Elated, Full, Gaudy, Gay, Gean, Glad, Gleesome, Greek, Jocose, Jocular, Jocund, Jolly, Joyous, L'allegro, Lively, Nitid, On, Page, Riant, Sportive, Sunny, Vogie, Waggery, Wassail

Merry-andrew Clown, Jack-pudding, Pickle-herring

Merry-go-round Carousel, Galloper, Whirligig

Merry-making Cakes and ale, Carnival, Festivity, Gaiety, Gaud, Gawd, Revel, Wassail

Merrythought Clavicle, Collarbone, Wishbone

Mesh Cancellate, Chain, Entangle, Mantle, Net, Reseau, Screen

Mesmer(ise) Hypnotise

Mess(y), Mess up Anteroom, Balls-up, Bedraggled, Boob, Boss, Botch, Canteen, Caudle, Chaos, Clamper, Clutter, Cock-up, Dining-room, Dog's dinner, Failure, Farrago, Fiasco, Flub, Garboil, Glop, G(l)oop, Gory, Guddle, Gunge, Gunk, Gun-room, Hash, Horlicks, Hotch-potch, Hugger-mugger, Imbroglio, Lash-up, Louse, Mash, Meal, Mismanage, Mix, Mixter-maxter, Modge, Muck, Muddle, Muff, Mullock, Muss, Mux, Pi(e), Piss-up, Plight, Pollute, Pottage, Screw-up, Scungy, Shambles, Shambolic, Shemozzle, Sight, Slaister, Smudge, Snafu, Soss, Sty, Sully, Tousle, Trifle, Untidy, Wardroom, Whoopsie, Yuck(y)

Message(s), Messaging Aerogram, Bull, Bulletin, Cable, Caption, Contraplex, Dépêche, Despatch, Dispatch, Email, Epistle, Errand, Error, Flame, Inscription, Kissagram, Kissogram, Letter, Marconigram, Missive, News, Note, Pager, Ping, Posting, Postscript, Radiogram, Radio telegraph, Read-out, Rumour, Signal, Slogan, SOS, Stripagram, Strippergram, Subtext, Telco, Telegram, Telepheme, Telephone, Teletype®, Telex, Text, Tidings, Toothing, Tweet, Valentine, Voice mail, Wire, → **WORD**

Messenger Angel, Angela, Apostle, Azrael, Beadle, Caddie, Caddy, Carrier pigeon, Chaprassi, Chuprassy, Corbie, Courier, Culver, Despatch-rider, Emissary, Envoy, Forerunner, Gaga, Gillie-wetfoot, Gillie whitefoot, Hatta, Herald, Hermes, Internuncio, Iris, Ladas, Mercury, Nuncio, Page, Peon, Post, Pursuivant, Runner, Send, Seraph, Shellycoat, Valet de place, Valkyrie

Messiah Christ, Emmanuel, Immanuel, Mahdi, Mashiach, Prince of peace, Saviour, Shiloh, Son of man, Southcott

Met Constabulary, Faced, Old Bill, Opera, Weather, Weatherman

Metabolism Basal, Cryptobiotic

Metal(s), Metallic, Metalware, Metalwork Aeneous, Antifriction, Base, Death, Expanded, Filler, Fine, Fusible, Heavy, Hot, Jangling, Leaf, Mercuric, Mineral, Noble, Nonferrous, Ore, Perfect, Planchet, Precious, Prince's, Road, Scrap, Sheet(-iron), Sprue, Stannic, Thrash, Tramp, Transition, Type, White, Yellow

METALS

2 letters:	Invar®	*7 letters:*	Platinum
Ag	Misch	Babbitt	Samarium
Al	Monel	Cadmium	Speculum
Er	Muntz	Gallium	Tantalum
Sm	Steel	Iridium	Thallium
Sn	Terne	Lithium	Titanium
		Natrium	
3 letters:	*6 letters:*	Protore	*9 letters:*
Gib	Aiglet	Regulus	Aluminium
Tin	Alkali	Rhenium	Beryllium
	Billon	Taggers	Britannia
4 letters:	Chrome	Terbium	Germanium
Bell	Cobalt	Thorium	Manganese
Foil	Copper	Tutania	Ruthenium
Gold	Erbium	Tutenag	Strontium
Iron	Monell	Wolfram	Toreutics
Slug	Nickel	Zorgite	
Tole	Niello		*10 letters:*
Zinc	Ormolu	*8 letters:*	Dysprosium
	Osmium	Actinium	
5 letters:	Silver	Antimony	*11 letters:*
Aglet	Sodium	Chromium	Aiguillette
Brass	Speiss	Europium	
Ingot	Terbic	Kamacite	

Metallurgy Powder
Metal-worker Blacksmith, Founder, Goldsmith, Lorimer, Silversmith, Smith, Spurrier, Tinsmith, Tubal Cain, Whitesmith
Metamorphose, Metamorphosis, Metamorphism Regional, Transfiguration, Transmogrify
▷ **Metamorphosing** *may indicate* an anagram
Metaphor Conceit, Figure, Image, Kenning, Malonym, Mixed, Symbol, Trope, Tropical
Metaphysics Ontology, Scotism
Mete Inflict
Meteor(ic), Meteorite Achondrite, Aerolite, Aerosiderite, Bolide, Chondrite, Comet, Drake, Falling star, Fireball, Geminid, Iron, Leonid, Perseid, Quadrantid, Siderite, Siderolite, Star(dust), Stony(-iron), Tektite
Meter Alidad(e), Electric, Exposure, Flow, Gas, Light, Orifice, Parking, Postage, Postal, Torque, Torsion, Water, White
Methamphetamine Chalk, Ice
Methane, Methanol Alkane, Synthesis gas
Methedrine® Speed
Method(ology), Methodical Art, Billings, Buteyko, Direct, Feldenkrais, Formal, Formula, Gram's, Historical, Hi-tec(h), How, Kenny, Kumon, Line, Manner, Mode, Modus, Modus operandi, Monte Carlo, Montessori, Neat, Orderly, Organised, Organon, Organum, Ovulation, Painstaking, Phonic, Plan, Ploy, Procedure, Process, Q, Rhythm, Schafer's, Scientific, Socratic, Stanislavski, Systematic, Tactics, Technique, Way, Withdrawal
Methodism, Methodist Huntingdonian, Itinerant, Jumper, Methody, Primitive, Ranter, Scientism, Sim, Soper, Southcottian, Swaddler, Wesley
Meths White Lady
Methuselah Bottle, Macrobiote

Meticulous Careful, Diligent, → **EXACT**, Finicky, Minute, Precise, Punctilious, Quiddler, Scrupulous, Thorough

Métier Line, Trade, Vocation

Metre, Metrical Alexandrine, Amphibrach, Amphimacer, Anapaest, Antispast, Arsis, Ballad, Cadence, Choliamb, Choree, Choriamb, Common, Dipody, Galliambic, Iambic, Ithyphallic, Long, M, Penthemimer, Prosody, Pyrrhic, Rhythm, Sapphic, Scansion, Scazon, Semeion, Service, Short, Spondee, Strophe, Tribrach, Tripody, Trochee

Metric (system) MKS

Metroland Subtopia

Metropolis, Metropolitan Big Apple, Eparch

Metrosexual Epicene

Mettle Ardour, Bravery, Courage, Ginger, Guts, Pith, → **PLUCK**, Pride, Smeddum, Spirit, Spunk, Steel

Mew Caterwaul, Cry, Miaou, Miaow, Pen, Purr, Seagull, Shed, Waul, Wrawl

Mews Meuse, Muse(t), Musit, Stables, Yard

Mexican (Indian) Atlalt, Aztec, Carib, Chicano, Chichibec, Cuna, Diaz, Greaser, Gringo, Hairless, Hispanic, Kuna, Latino, Maya, Mixe-Zoque, Mixtec, Montezuma, Nahuatl, Nortéño, Olmec, Otomi, Pachuco, Spic, Spik, Taino, Tewa, Toltec, Wetback, Zapotec, Zuni

Mezzanine Entresol

Mezzo-soprano Tessa

Mica Biotite, Daze, Fuchsite, Glimmer, Isinglass, Lepidolite, Lepidomelane, Muscovite, Paragonite, Phlogopite, Rubellan, Sericite, Talc, Verdite, Vermiculite

Micawber Wilkins

Michael Mick(e)y

Mick(ey) Greek, Mouse

Micro Mu

Microbe, Microorganism Extremophile, Germ, Lactobacillus, Nanobe, Organism

Microbiologist Fleming, Salk

Microphone Bug, Carbon, Crystal, Directional, Lavaliere, Lip, Mike, Phonic Ear®, Radio, Ribbon, Throat

Microscope Acoustic, Compound, Confocal, Darkfield, Dissecting, Electron, Engyscope, Field-ion, Lens, Optical, Phase-contrast, Phase-difference, Polarizing, Proton, Reading, Reflecting, SEM, Simple, Solar, TEM, Ultraviolet

Microwave Nuke

Mid(st) Amongst, Mongst

Midas Goldinger, Tamarin

Midday Meridian, N, Noon, Noon-tide, Noon-time

Middle, Middling, Midpoint Active, Ariston metron, Basion, Centre, Core, Crown, Enteron, Epitasis, Excluded, Eye, Girth, Heart, Innermost, Internal, Loins, Median, Mediocre, Meridian, Meseraic, Mesial, Mesne, Meso, Midriff, Moderate, Nasion, Noon, Passive, Turn, Twixt, Undistributed, Via media, Wa(i)st

Middle age(d) Grey, Menopause

Middle-Cambrian Menevian

Middle class Bourgeois, Hova, Mondeo Man

Middle East(ern) Arab, Iraqi, Kurdish, Omani, Persic

Middle European Magyar

Middleman Broker, Comprador(e), Diaphragm, Interlocutor, Intermediary, Jobber, Median, Navel, Regrater, Regrator

Middlesex Hermaphrodite

Midge Gall, Gnat

Midget Dwarf, Homunculus, Lilliputian, Pygmy, Shrimp

Midianite Prowler

Midlander Brummie

Midlands Mercia
Midnight G, O Am
▶ **Midnight** *see* **PAST MIDNIGHT**
Midriff Phrenic, Skirt, Waist
Midshipman Brass-bounder, Easy, Middy, Oldster, Reefer, Snottie, Snotty
▶ **Midst** *see* **MID(ST)**
Midsummer Solstice
Mid-Westerner Indianan
Midwife Accoucheur, Doula, Gran(nie), Granny, Howdie, Howdy, Lucina, Mab, Maieutic,
 Obstetric
Midwinter Solstice
Mien Air, Bearing, Demean, Manner
Might(iness), Mighty Force, Main, Maud, Mote, Nibs, Oak, Potence, → **POWER**,
 Prowess, Puissant, Should, Strength
Mignon(ette) Dyer's rocket, Fillet, Reseda, Wald, Weld
Migraine Megrim, Scotodinia, Teichopsia
Migrant Economic, Externe, Gastarbeiter, Lemming, Snowbird, Traveller
Migrate, Migration, Migratory Colonise, Diapedesis, Diaspora, Drift, Eelfare,
 Exodus, Fleet, Great Trek, Run, Tre(c)k, Volk(er)wanderung
Mikado Emperor, Kami, Teno
Mike Bug, M, Stentorphone
Milanese Patarine
Mild(ly) Balmy, Benign, Bland, Clement, Euphemism, Genial, Gentle, Lenient, Litotes,
 Mansuete, Meek, → **MODERATE**, Pacific, Patient, Pussycat, Sarcenet, Sars(e)net,
 Temperate
Mildew Downy, Foxing, Fungus, Mould, Oidium, Powdery, Vine, Wheat
Mile(r), Miles Admiralty, Coss, Coverdale, Food, Geographical, Hour, Irish, Knot, Kos,
 League, Li, Mi, Milliary, Nautical, Passenger, Roman, Royal, Scots, Sea, Soldier, Square,
 Standish, Statute, Swedish, Train
Milesian Teague
Milestone Milliary, MS
Milfoil Yarrow
Militancy, Militant, Military Activist, Aggressive, Battailous, Black Panther, Black
 Power, Commando, Fortinbras, Hawkish, Hezbollah, Hizbollah, Hizbullah, Hostile,
 Ireton, Janjaweed, Janjawid, Junta, Kshatriya, Landsturm, Landwehr, Leftist, Logistics,
 Lumper, Mameluke, Martial, Presidio, Provisional, Provo, Soldatesque, Stratocracy,
 Tactical, War machine, War paint, West Point
Militia(-man) Band, Fyrd, Guard, Haganah, Milice, Minuteman, Peshmerga, Reserve,
 Tanzim, Trainband, Yeomanry
Milk(er), Milky Acidophilus, Beestings, Bland, Bleed, Bonny-clabber, Bristol, Butter,
 Casein, Certified, Churn, Colostrum, Condensed, Creamer, Crud, Curd, Dairy, Emulge,
 Evaporated, Exploit, Galactic, Glacier, Goat's, Homogenised, Jib, Kefir, Kephir,
 K(o)umiss, Lactation, Lacteal, Latex, Maas, Madafu, Madzoon, Magnesia, Malted,
 Mamma, Matzoon, Mess, Moo-juice, Opaline, Pasteurised, Pigeon's, Pinta, Posset, Raw,
 Rice, Sap, Semi-skimmed, Shedder, Skim(med), Soya, Squeeze, Strip(pings), Stroke,
 Suckle, Town, UHT, Use, Whig, Whole, Yaourt, Yogh(o)urt
Milking-machine, Milking parlour Loan, Tapper
Milking-pail Leglan, Leglen, Leglin
Milkless Agalactic, Dry, Eild
Milkmaid, Milkman Chalker, Dey, Emulge, Kefir, Kephir, Radha, Rounder,
 Roundsman, Skimmed
Milksop Coward, Meacock, Namby-pamby, Nance, Pance, Weakling
Milk-vetch Loco
Milkweed Asclepias

Milkwort Senega

Milky Way Via Lactea

Mill(ing), Mills Aswarm, Ball, Barker's, Boxing, Coffee, Crazing, Economist, Flour, Gang, Gastric, Gig, Grind(er), Hayley, Kibble, Knurl, Lumber, Malt, Mano, Melder, Molar, Nurl, Oil, Paper, Pepper, Plunge-cut, Post, Powder, Press, Pug, Pulp, Quartz, Quern, Reave, Rob, Rolling, Rumour, Satanic, Scutcher, Smock, Spinning, Stamp, Stamping, Strip, Sucken, Sugar, Surge, Thou, Tide, Tower, Tuck, Water, Wool(len), Works

Miller Dusty, Glen, Grinder, Jester, Joe, Molendinar, Multurer

Millet Bajra, Bajree, Bajrii, Couscous, Dari, Dhurra, Doura, Dur(r)a, Grain, Miliary, Negro-corn, Pearl, Proso, Ragee, Raggee, Ragi, Whisk

Milliner Hatter, Modiste

Millionaire Astor, Carnegie, MOP, Rockefeller, Rothschild, Vanderbilt

Millions, Millionth Crore, Femto-, Milliard, Muckle, Pico-

Millipede Diplopod, Songololo

Millstone Ligger, Rind, Rynd

Mim Perjink

Mime, Mimic(ry) Ape, Batesian, Copycat, Echo, Farce, Imitate, Impersonate, Lipsync, Marceau, Mina, Mock, Mullerian, Mummer, Parody, Sturnine, Take-off

Mimosa Cacoon, Raintree, Saman

Mince, Mincing Cecils, Chop, Dice, Grate, Grind, Keema, Nipperty-tipperty, Prance, Rice

Mind(er) Aide, Beware, Bodyguard, Brain, Gaum, Genius, Grasshopper, Handler, Head, → HEED, Herd, Id, Intellect, Mentality, Month's, Noology, Noosphere, Nous, One-track, Open, Phrenic, Psyche, Psychogenic, Resent, Sensorium, Tabula rasa, Tend, Thinker, View, Wit, Woundwort, Year's

Mine, Mining Acoustic, Antenna, Appalachia, Biomining, Bomb, Bonanza, Bord and pillar, Bottom, Bouquet, Burrow, Camouflet, Chemical, Claymore, Colliery, Contact, Creeping, Dane-hole, Data, Dig(gings), Drifting, Egg, Eldorado, Excavate, Explosive, Fiery, Floating, Flooder, Fougade, Fougasse, Gallery, Gob, Golconda, Gold, Gopher, Grass, Homing, Land, Limpet, Magnetic, Microbiological, Naked-light, Nostromo, Open-cast, Open-cut, Ophir, Pit, Placer, Pressure, Prospect, Rising, Sap, Set(t), Show, Sonic, Stannary, Stope, Strike, Strip, Undercut, Wheal, Win, Workings

Mine-deflector Otter, Paravane

Mine-owner Operator

Miner, Mine-worker, Mine-working Bevin boy, Butty-gang, Collier, Continuous, Corporal, Cutter, Digger, Faceworker, Forty-niner, Geordie, Leaf, Molly Maguire, Noisy, NUM, Oncost(man), Pitman, Shot-firer, Stall, Tippler, Tributer, Tunneler, UDM

Mineral(s) Accessory, Essential, Index, Ore, Owre

MINERALS

3 letters:	5 letters:	Umber	Hauyne
YAG	Balas		Illite
	Borax	6 letters:	Iolite
4 letters:	Chert	Acmite	Jargon
Clay	Emery	Albite	Kermes
Foid	Flint	Augite	Lithia
Gang	Fluor	Blende	Natron
Mica	Macle	Cerite	Nosean
Sard	Mafic	Galena	Pinite
Spar	Nitre	Gangue	Pyrite
Talc	Prase	Garnet	Quartz
Trap	Topaz	Glance	Rutile
Urao	Trona	Gypsum	Schorl

Silica
Sphene
Spinel
Tincal
Zircon

7 letters:
Alunite
Anatase
Apatite
Axinite
Azurite
Barytes
Biotite
Bornite
Brucite
Calcite
Calomel
Catseye
Cuprite
Cyanite
Diamond
Dysodil
Epidote
Euclase
Eucrite
Fahlore
Felspar
Gahnite
Göthite
Gummite
Hessite
Ice spar
Jadeite
Jargoon
Kainite
Kernite
Kyanite
Leucite
Mellite
Mullite
Nacrite
Niobite
Olivine
Pennine
Peridot
Pyrites
Realgar
Rosaker
Sylvine
Sylvite
Thorite
Thulite
Tripoli

Turgite
Ulexite
Uralite
Uranite
Uranium
Zeolite
Zeuxite
Zincite
Zoisite
Zorgite

8 letters:
Adularia
Allanite
Analcime
Analcite
Andesine
Ankerite
Antimony
Aphanite
Asbestos
Autunite
Blue john
Boehmite
Boracite
Braunite
Bronzite
Brookite
Calamine
Cerusite
Chlorite
Chromite
Cinnabar
Cleveite
Corundum
Crocoite
Cryolite
Datolite
Dendrite
Diallage
Diaspore
Diopside
Disthene
Dolomite
Dysodile
Dysodyle
Enargite
Epsomite
Erionite
Euxenite
Fayalite
Feldspar
Flinkite
Fluorite

Galenite
Gibbsite
Goethite
Gyrolite
Hematite
Idocrase
Ilmenite
Iodyrite
Jarosite
Lazulite
Lazurite
Lewisite
Limonite
Liparite
Massicot
Meionite
Melilite
Mimetite
Monazite
Nephrite
Noselite
Orpiment
Petuntse
Picotite
Prehnite
Pyroxene
Resalgar
Rock-salt
Sanidine
Saponite
Sardonyx
Siderite
Smaltite
Smectite
Sodalite
Stannite
Stibnite
Stilbite
Sunstone
Taconite
Tenorite
Titanite
Troilite
Vesuvian
Xenotime
Zaratite

9 letters:
Alabaster
Allophane
Amazonite
Amphibole
Anglesite
Anhydrite

Anorthite
Aragonite
Argentite
Atacamite
Blackjack
Blacklead
Carnelian
Carnotite
Celestine
Celestite
Cerussite
Chabazite
Chalybite
Cheralite
Chondrule
Cobaltine
Cobaltite
Coccolite
Columbate
Columbite
Covellite
Cystolith
Dolomitic
Elaeolite
Endomorph
Enhydrite
Enstatite
Erythrite
Fibrolite®
Flowstone
Fluorspar
Gehlenite
Germanite
Geyserite
Gmelinite
Goslarite
Haematite
Harmotome
Hercynite
Hiddenite
Hornstone
Kaolinite
Kermesite
Kieserite
Magnesite
Magnetite
Malachite
Manganite
Marcasite
Margarite
Marialite
Microlite
Microlith
Millerite

Mispickel
Mizzonite
Moonstone
Muscovite
Natrolite
Nepheline
Nephelite
Niccolite
Nitratine
Olivenite
Ottrelite
Paramorph
Pargasite
Pectolite
Penninite
Periclase
Pericline
Perimorph
Phenacite
Pigeonite
Pleonaste
Polianite
Pollucite
Powellite
Proustite
Rhodonite
Rubellite
Scapolite
Scheelite
Scolecite
Sepiolite
Septarium
Spodumene
Sylvanite
Tantalite
Tremolite
Troostite
Tungstite
Uraninite
Uvarovite
Variscite
Vulpinite
Wavellite
Wernerite
Willemite
Witherite
Wulfenite

Zinkenite

10 letters:
Actinolite
Alabandine
Alabandite
Andalusite
Bastnasite
Calaverite
Carnallite
Chalcocite
Chessylite
Chrysolite
Colemanite
Cordierite
Crocoisite
Dyscrasite
Forsterite
Gadolinite
Garnierite
Glauconite
Halloysite
Heulandite
Honey-stone
Hornblende
Indicolite
Indigolite
Jamesonite
Laurdalite
Meerschaum
Microcline
Mirabilite
Oligoclase
Oomphacite
Orthoclase
Paragonite
Perovskite
Phosgenite
Piemontite
Polybasite
Polyhalite
Pyrolusite
Pyrrhotine
Pyrrhotite
Redruthite
Riebeckite
Ripidolite

Samarskite
Saphir d'eau
Sapphirine
Saussurite
Serpentine
Smaragdite
Sperrylite
Sphalerite
Staurolite
Tennantite
Thaumasite
Thenardite
Thorianite
Tiemannite
Torbernite
Tourmaline
Triphylite
Vanadinite
Wolframite

11 letters:
Alexandrite
Amblygonite
Annabergite
Apophyllite
Baddeleyite
Bastnaesite
Cassiterite
Chiastolite
Chloanthite
Chrysoberyl
Clinochlore
Crocidolite
Dendrachate
Franklinite
Greenockite
Hypersthene
Idiomorphic
Josephinite
Labradorite
Molybdenite
Pentlandite
Philogopite
Phosphorite
Piedmontite
Pitchblende
Plagioclase

Pseudomorph
Psilomelane
Pyrargyrite
Pyrrhotiner
Sal ammoniac
Sillimanite
Smithsonite
Tabular spar
Tetradymite
Vermiculite
Vesuvianite
Ythro-cerite

12 letters:
Adularescent
Arfvedsonite
Arsenopyrite
Babingtonite
Chalcanthite
Chalcopyrite
Cristobalite
Dumortierite
Feldspathoid
Fluorapatite
Hemimorphite
Pyromorphite
Pyrophyllite
Senarmontite
Skutterudite
Strontianite
Synadelphite
Tetrahedrite
Wollastonite

13 letters:
Cummingtonite
Rhodochrosite

14 letters:
Yttro-tantalite

15 letters:
Gooseberry-stone
Montmorillonite

Mineralogy, Mineralogist Haüy, Heuland, Miller-Smithson, Oryctology
Mineral water Apollinaris, Tonic
Minesweeper Oropesa, Unity
Mingle, Mingling Blend, Circulate, Commix, Consort, Interfuse, Mell, Merge, → **MIX**,
    Participate, Socialise, Theocrasy, Unite
Mini Cab, Car, Skirt, Teen(s)y, Teeny-weeny

Miniature, Miniaturist Cosway, Lilliputian, Microcosm, Midget, Model, Toy, Young

Minimise, Minimum (range) Bare, Downplay, Fewest, Floor, Gloze, Least, Neap, Pittance, Scant, Shoestring, Stime, Styme, Threshold, Undervalue

▷ **Minimum of** *may indicate* the first letter

Minion Flunkey, Lackey, Pet, Subordinate, Tool, Vassal

Minister Ambassador, Attend, Buckle-beggar, Cabinet, Chancellor, Chaplain, Cleric, Coarb, Commissar, Deacon, Dewan, Diplomat, Divine, Dominee, Dominie, D(i)wan, Envoy, First, Foreign, Holy Joe, Mas(s)john, Mes(s)john, Moderator, Nurse, Officiant, Ordinand, Ordinee, Padre, Parson, Pastor, Peshwa, Preacher, Predikant, Presbyter, Priest, Prime, Rector, Richelieu, Secretary, Seraskier, → **SERVE**, Stick, Stickit, Subdeacon, Tanaiste, Tend, Visier, Vizier, Wazir, Wizier

Ministry Defence, Department, Dept, DoE, MOD, MOT, Orders, Service, Treasury

▷ **Ministry** *may indicate* some government department

Mink Kolinsky, Mutation, Vison

Minnow Devon, Penk, Pink, Tiddler

Minoan Knossus

Minor(ity) Child, Comprimario, Ethnic, Faction, Few, Fractional, Incidental, Infant, Junior, Less, Marginal, Minutia, Nonage, One-horse, Peripheral, Petty, Pupillage, Signed, Slight, Small-time, Sub(sidiary), Trivial, Ward, Weeny

Minotaur Bull-headed, Cretan

Minstrel Allan-a-Dale, Bard, Blondel, Bones, Busker, Cantabank, Christy, Cornerman, Gleeman, Hamfatter, Joculator, Jongleur, Minnesinger, Nigger, Pierrot, Scop, Singer, Taillefer

Mint Aim, Bugle-weed, Bull's eye, Catnip, Coin, Ettle, Fortune, Herb, Horse, Humbug, Labiate, Monarda, Monetise, Nep, New, Penny-royal, Pepper, Pile, Polo®, Poly, Rock, Royal, Selfheal, Spear, Stamp, Stone, Strike, Unused, Utter, Water

Minus Less, Nonplus

Minute(s), Minutiae Acta, Alto, Degree, Detailed, Diatom, Entry, Infinitesimal, Little, Mere, Micron, Mo, Mu, Nano-, New York, Pinpoint, Resume, Small, Teen(t)sy, Teeny, Tine, Tiny, Trivia, Tyne, Wee

Minx Hellion

Miracle(s), Miraculous, Miracle worker Cana, Marvel, Merel(l), Meril, Morris, Mystery, Mythism, Phenomenon, Saluter, Supernatural, Thaumatology, Thaumaturgic, Theurgy, Wirtschaftswunder, Wonder, Wonderwork

Mirage Fata morgana, Illusion, Loom, Northern lights

Mire Bog, Glaur, Lair(y), Latch, Lerna, Lerne, Loblolly, Marsh, Mud, Mudge, Quag, Sludge, Soil

Mirky Dark, Dirk(e)

Mirror(s), Mirrored Alasnam, Antidazzle, Busybody, Cambuscan, Catoptric, Cheval, Claude Lorraine glass, Coelostat, Conde, Conjugate, Dare, Driving, Enantiomorph, Glass, Image, Imitate, Keeking-glass, Lao, Magnetic, Merlin, One-way, Pierglass, Primary, Psyche, Rearview, → **REFLECT**, Reynard, Shisha, Siderostat, Sign, Specular, Speculum, Stone, Tiring-glass, Two-way, Vulcan, Wing

Mirror-image Perversion

Mirth(ful) Cheer, Dream, Festive, Hilarity, Joy, Laughter, Spleen

▷ **Misalliance** *may indicate* an anagram

Misanthrope Cynic, Timon

Misapplication Catachresis, Misuse

Misappropriate, Misappropriation Asport, Detinue, Embezzle, Purloin, Steal

Miscarry Abort, Backfire, Fail, Slink, Warp

Miscegenation Allocarpy

Miscellaneous, Miscellany Ana, Assortment, Chow, Collectanea, Diverse, Etceteras, Job lot, Misc, Odds and ends, Odds and sods, Olio, Omnium-gatherum, Pie, Potpourri, Raft, Ragbag, Sundry, Varia, Variety, Various

Mischance Misfare
Mischief(-maker), Mischievous Ate, Bale, Bane, Cantrip, Cloots, Devilment, Diablerie, Dido, Disservice, Gallus, Gremlin, Hanky-panky, Harm, Hellery, Hellion, Hob, Imp, Injury, Jinks, Larky, Larrikin, Limb, Litherly, Make-bate, Malicho, Mallecho, Monkeyshines, Monkey-tricks, Nickum, Owl-spiegle, Pestilent, Pickle, Prank, Puckish, Rascal, Scally(wag), Scamp, Scapegrace, Shenanigans, Spalpeen, Spriteful, Tricksy, Varmint, Wag, Wicked, Widgie
Misconception Delusion, Idol(on), Idolum, Mirage, Misunderstanding
Misconduct Impropriety, Malfeasance, Malversation
Miscreant Reprobate, Sinner, Tortfeasor
Misdeed Offence, Peccadillo, Trespass, Wrong
▷ **Misdelivered** *may indicate* an anagram
Misdemeanour Delict, Offence, Peccadillo, Tort, Wrongdoing
Miser(ly) Carl, Cheapskate, Cheese-parer, Close, Curmudgeon, Flay-flint, Gare, Grasping, Harpagon, Hunks, Marner, Meanie, Mingy, Muckworm, Niggard, Nipcheese, Nipcurn, Nipfarthing, Pennyfather, Pinch-commons, Puckfist, Runt, Save-all, Scrape-good, Scrape-penny, Screw, Scrimping, Scrooge, Shylock, Skinflint, Snudge, Storer, Tightwad, Timon
Miserable, Misery, Miserably Abject, Angashore, Bale, Cat-lap, Crummy, Cut up, Distress, Dole, Face-ache, Forlorn, Gloom, Grief, Heartache, Hell, Joyless, Killjoy, Lousy, Mean, Measly, Perdition, Punk, Sad, Scungy, Sorry, Sourpuss, Tragic, Triste, → **UNHAPPY**, Wet blanket, Woe(begone), Wretched
Misfire Dud, Pink
Misfit Black sheep, Drop-out, Geek, Loner, Maverick, Sad sack
Misfortune Accident, Affliction, Bale, Calamity, Curse, Disaster, Distress, Dole, Hex, Ill, Ill-luck, Kicker, Reverse, Rewth, Ruth, Wroath
Misgiving(s) Anxiety, Doubt, Dubiety, Qualms, Scruples
Misguide(d) Impolitic, Off-beam
▷ **Misguided** *may indicate* an anagram
Mishandle Abuse
Mishap Accident, Contretemps, Drere, Misaunter, Misfortune, Pile-up, Wroath
Misheard Mondegreen
Mishit, Misstroke Crab, Draw, Edge, Fluff, Muff, Sclaff, Shank, Slice, Thin, Toe, Top
Misinformation Bum steer
Misinterpret(ation) Mondegreen, Warp, Wrest
Misjudge Misween, Overrate
Mislay Leese, Lose
Mislead(ing) Blind, Bum steer, Con, Cover-up, Deceive, Delude, Dupe, Equivocate, Fallacious, False, Gag, Half-truth, Red herring, Runaround, Smoke and mirrors, Snow job
▷ **Misled** *may indicate* an anagram
Mismanage Blunder, Bungle, Muddle
Mismatch Kludge
Misplace(ment) Anachorism, Ectopia
Misplay Fluff, Whitechapel
Misprint Error, Literal, Literal error, Slip, Typo
Mispronunciation Cacoepy, Lallation, Lambdacism
Misrepresent(ation) Abuse, Belie, Calumny, Caricature, Colour, Distort, Falsify, Garble, Lie, Slander, Subreption, Traduce, Travesty
Miss(ing) Abord, Air, Astray, Avoid, AWOL, Colleen, Desiderate, Dodge, Drib, Err(or), Fail, Forego, Gal, → **GIRL**, Kumari, Lack, Lass, Link, Lose, Mademoiselle, Maid, Maiden, Mile, Muff(et), Near, Neglect, Negligence, Omit, Otis, Overlook, Señorita, Shy, Skip, Spinster, Stoke, Unmeet, Wanting, Whiff
▷ **Miss** *may refer to* Missouri
Missal Breviary, Te igitur, Triodion

Misshapen Crooked, Deformed, Dysmelia, Gnarled

Missile Air-to-air, ALCM, Ammo, Anti-ballistic, Arrow, Artillery, Atlas, Ball, Ballistic, Beam Rider, Blue streak, Bolas, Bolt, Bomb, Boomerang, Brickbat, Bullet, Condor, Cruise, Dart, Death star, Dingbat, Doodlebug, Dum-dum, Exocet®, Falcon, Fléchette, Genie, Grenade, Guided, HARM, Harpoon, Hawk, Hellfire, Hound Dog, ICBM, Interceptor, Jired, Kiley, Kyley, Kylie, Lance, Mace, MARV, Maverick, Minuteman, MIRV, Missive, Mx, Onion, Patriot, Pellet, Pershing, Phoenix, Polaris, Poseidon, Qual, Quarrel, Rocket, SAM, Scud, Sea Skimmer, Sergeant, Shell, Shillelagh, Shot, Shrike, Side-winder, Smart bomb, Snowball, Sparrow, Spartan, Spear, Sprint, SSM, Standard Arm, Standoff, Styx, Subroc, Surface to air, Surface to surface, Talos, Tartar, Terrier, Thor, Titan, Tomahawk, Torpedo, Tracer, Trident, UAM, Warhead

Mission(ary) Aidan, Alamo, Antioch, Apostle, Assignment, Augustine, Barnabas, Bethel, Boniface, Caravan, Charge, Columba, Cuthbert, Cyril, Delegation, Embassage, Embassy, Errand, Evangelist, Foreign, Happy-clappy, Iona, Legation, Livingstone, LMS, Message, Missiology, NASA, Neurolab, Ninian, Op, Paul, Pr(a)efect, Quest, Reclaimer, Redemptorist, Schweitzer, Silas, Task, Vocation, Xavier

Missis, Missus, Mrs Devi, Maam, Mrs, Wife

Missive Dispatch, Epistle, Letter, Message, Note

Missouri Mo

▶ **Misstroke** *see* **MISHIT**

Mist(y) Aerosol, Australian, Blur, Brume, Cloud, Dew, Drow, Dry-ice, Film, Fog, Fret, Haar, Haze, Hoar, Miasma, Moch, Nebular, Niflheim, Rack, Red, Roke, Scotch, Sea-fret, Sfumato, Smir(r), Smog, Smur, Spotted, Vapour, Veil

Mistake(n) Aberration, Barry (Crocker), Bish, Bloomer, Blooper, Blue, Blunder, Boner, Boob, Booboo, Boss, Botch, Bull, Category, Clanger, Clinker, Confound, Deluded, Domino, Erratum, Error, Fault, Floater, Flub, Fluff, Folly, Gaffe, Goof, Hash, Horlicks, Howler, Identity, Incorrect, Lapse, Malapropism, Misprision, Miss, Muff, Mutual, Nod, Off-beam, Oops, Oversight, Own goal, Plonker, Pratfall, Ricket, Screw-up, → **SLIP**, Slip-up, Solecism, Stumer, Trip, Typo, Wrongdoing

▷ **Mistake(n)** *may indicate* an anagram

Mister Babu, Effendi, Lala, Mr, Reb, Sahib, Señor, Shri, Sir, Sri, U

Mistletoe Album, Hemiparasite, Missel, Parasite, Sinker, Viscum

Mistreat Abuse, Attrite, Manhandle, Violate

Mistress Amie, Aspasia, Canary-bird, Chatelaine, Concubine, Courtesan, Demimondaine, Devi, Doxy, Goodwife, Herself, Hussif, Inamorata, Instructress, Kept woman, Lady, Leman, Maintenon, Martha, Montespan, Mrs, Natural, Paramour, Querida, Stepney, Teacher, Wardrobe, Wife

Mistrust(ful) Askant, Doubt, Gaingiving, Suspect, Suspicion

Misunderstand(ing) Disagreement, Discord, Generation gap, Mistake

Misuse Abuse, Catachresis, Defalcate, Malappropriate, Malapropism, Maltreat, Perversion, Torment

Mite Acaridian, Acarus, Berry bug, Bit, Bulb, Cheese, Child, Dust, Flour, Forage, Fowl, Gall, Harvest, Itch, Lepton, Little, (Red) spider, Rust, Sarcoptes, Speck, Sugar, Trombiculid, Tyroglyphid, Varroa, Widow's

Mitigate, Mitigating Abate, Allay, Allieve, Ameliorate, Assuage, Excuse, Extenuating, Lenitive, Lessen, Mease, Palliate, Quell, Relief, Relieve

Mitosis Anaphase

Mitre Hat, Tiar(a)

Mitt(en), Mittens Fist, Glove, Hand, Paw, Pockies

Mix(ed), Mixer, Mixture, Mix-up Allay, Alloy, Amalgam, Ambivalent, Associate, Assortment, Attemper, Balderdash, Bigener, Bittersweet, Bland, Blend, Blunge, Bombay, Bordeaux, Brew, Carburet, Card, Caudle, Chichi, Chow, Cocktail, Co-meddle, Compo, Compound, Conché, Conglomerate, Consort, Cross, Cut, Disperse, Diversity, Dolly, Drammock, Embroil, Emulsion, Eutectic, Farrago, Fold-in, Freezing, Friar's balsam,

Garble, Grill, Griqua, Half-breed, Heather, Hobnob, Hodge-podge, Hotchpotch, Hybrid, Imbroglio, Immingle, Interlace, Intermingle, Isomorphous, Jumble, Lace, Lard, Lignin, Linctus, Load, Macedoine, Marketing, Matissé, Meddle, Medley, Melange, Mell, Meng(e), Ment, Mess, Mestizo, Métis, Ming(le), Miscellaneous, Miscellany, Mishmash, Mong, Motley, Muddle, Muss(e), Neapolitan, Octaroon, Octoroon, Olio, Olla, Pi(e), Potin, Pousowdie, Powsowdy, Praiseach, Preparation, Promiscuous, Raggle-taggle, Ragtag, Salad, Scramble, Shuffle, Soda, Spatula, Stew, Stir, Temper, Through-other, Tonic, Trail, Vision, Witches' brew, Yblent

▷ **Mixed** *may indicate* an anagram

Mixed marriage Miscegenation

Mizzle Decamp, Scapa, Scarper

Mnemonic(s) Fleming's rules, Mafic, Memoria technica, Quipo, Quipu, Reminder

Moab(ite) Balak, Ruth, Wash-pot

Moan(ing) Beef, Bewail, Bleat, Complain, Groan, Grouse, Grumble, Hone, Keen, → **LAMENT**, Meane, Plangent, Sigh, Snivel, Sough, Wail, W(h)inge

Moat Dike, Ditch, Foss(e)

Mob(ster) Army, Assail, Canaille, Crew, Crowd, Doggery, Faex populi, Flash, Gaggle, Gang, Herd, Hoi-polloi, Hoodlum, Horde, Lynch, Many-headed beast, Ochlocrat, Press, Rabble, Rabble rout, Raft, Ragtag, Ribble-rabble, Riff-raff, Rout, Scar-face

Mobile, Mobilise, Mobility Agile, Donna, Downward, Fluid, Horizontal, Intergenerational, Movable, Plastic, Rally, Social, Thin, Upward(ly), Vagile, Vertical

Mob-rule Ochlocracy

Mocassin Larrigan, Shoe, Snake

Mock(ery), Mocking Ape, Banter, Catcall, Chaff, Chyack, Cod, Cynical, Deride, Derisory, Dor, Ersatz, False, Farce, Fleer, Flout, Gab, Geck, Gibe, Gird, Guy, Imitation, Ironise, Irony, Irrisory, Jape, → **JEER**, Jibe, Lampoon, Laugh, Mimic, Narquois, Parody, Paste, Pillorise, Piss-taking, Rail(lery), Rally, Ridicule, Sacrilege, Sardonic, Satirise, Scorn, Scout, Send up, Serve, Sham, Simulate, Slag, Sneer, Snide, Sport, Tease, Travesty, Twit, Wry

Mocking-bird Mimus, Sage-thrasher

Mode Aeolian, Authentic, Church, Convention, Dorian, Ecclesiastical, Fashion, Form, Formal, Greek, Gregorian, Hyperdorian, Hypo(dorian), Hypolydian, Iastic, Insert, Ionian, Locrian, Lydian, Major, Manner, Material, Medieval, Minor, Mixolydian, Phrygian, Plagal, Rate, Real-time, Sleep, Step, Style, Ton

Model(ler), Modelling Archetype, Bozzetto, Cast, Copy, Cutaway, Demonstration, Diorama, Doll, Dress-form, Dummy, Ecorché, Effigy, Epitome, Example, Exemplar, Exemplary, Fashionist, Fictor, Figure, Figurine, Icon, Ideal, Image, Instar, Jig, Last, Lay-figure, Layman, Madame Tussaud, Manakin, Manikin, Mannequin, Maquette, Mark, Matchstick, Mirror, Mock-up, Moulage, → **MOULD**, Norm, Original, Orrery, Papier-mâché, Parade, Paradigm, Paragon, Pattern, Phelloplastic, Pilot, Plasticine, Plastilina, Play-Doh®, Pose(r), Posture-maker, Precedent, Prototype, Replica, Role, Scale, Schema, Sedulous, Sitter, Specimen, Standard, Superwaif, T, Tellurion, Template, Templet, Terrella, Toy, Trilby, Twiggy, Type, Typify, Waif, Waxwork, Working

▷ **Model(s)** *may indicate* an anagram

Modem Subset

Moderate(ly), Moderation Abate, Allay, Alleviate, Assuage, Attemper, Average, Ca'canny, Centre, Chasten, Continent, Decent, Diminish, Discretion, Ease, Gentle, Girondist, Ho, Lessen, Lukewarm, Measure, Mediocre, Medium, Menshevik, Mezzo, Middling, Mild, Mitigate, Muscadin, OK, Politique, Realo, Reason(able), Restraint, RR, Slake, So-so, Sparing, Sumptuary, Temper(ate), Temperance, Tolerant, Tone, Via media, Wet

Modern(ise) AD, Aggiornamento, Contemporary, Fresh, Latter(-day), Milly, Neonomian, Neoterical, → **NEW**, New-fangled, Present-day, Progressive, Recent, Retrofit, Space age, State-of-the-art, Swinger, Trendy, Update, Up-to-date

Modest(y) Aidos, Blaise, Chaste, Coy, Decent, Demure, Discreet, Fair, Humble, Humility, Ladylike, Low-key, Lowly, Maidenly, Mim, Mussorgsky, Propriety, Prudish, Pudency, Pudicity, Pure, Reserved, Reticent, Shame, Shamefaced, Shy, Simple, Unassuming, Unpretending, Unpretentious, Verecund

Modicum Dash

Modifiable, Modification, Modified, Modifier, Modify Adapt, Adjust, Adverb, Alter, Backpedal, Change, Enhance, Extenuate, Genetically, H, Hotrod, Leaven, Misplaced, Plastic, Qualify, Restyle, Retrofit, Sandhi, Scumble, Soup, Streamline, Temper, Top, Trim, Vary

Modulation, Module, Modulus Accent, Amplitude, Bulk, Cadence, Command, Distance, Excursion, Frequency, Habitat, Inflexion, Lem, Lunar, Mitigate, Phase, Pulse, Service, Shear, Tune, Unit, Vary, Velocity, Young's

Mogul Bigwig, Magnate, Nawab, Padishah, Plutocrat, Potentate, Taipan, VIP

Mohair Moire

Mohammed, Mohammedan (era) Hadith, Hegira, Hejira, Hejra, Hijra, Islamite, Mahdi, Mahoun(d), Moslem, Muezzin, Mussulman, Prophet, Said, Shiite, Sunna(h)

Moist(en), Moisture Baste, Bedew, Damp, Dank, De(a)w, Dewy, Humect, Imbue, Latch, Love-in-a-mist, Madefy, Mesarch, Mesic, Moil, Nigella, Oozy, Precipitation, Slake, Slocken, Soggy, Sponge, Wet

▷ **Moither** *may indicate* an anagram

Molar Cheek tooth, Grinder, Mill-tooth, Secodont, Tooth, Wang

Molasses Blackstrap, Sorghum, Treacle

Mole(hill) Beauty spot, Breakwater, Fen-cricket, Golden, Groyne, Hydatidiform, Insider, Jetty, Marsupial, Miner, Mo(u)diewart, Moudi(e)wart, Mouldiwarp, Naeve, Notoryctes, Orology, Pier, Sea-wall, Shrew, Sleeper, Spot, Spy, Star-nose(d), Talpa, Want(hill), Want knap, Warp

Molecule, Molecular Acceptor, Achiral, Aptameter, Atom, Buckyball, Carbene, Cavitand, Chimera, Chiral, Chromophore, Closed chain, Cobalamin, Codon, Coenzyme, Cofactor, Dimer, DNA, Electrogen, Enantiomorph, Footballene, Fullerene, Gram, Hapten, Iota, Isomer, Kinin, Kisspeptin, Ligand, Long-chain, Metabolite, Metameric, Monomer, Nanotube, Peptide, Polymer, Polysaccharide, Quark, Replicon, Ribozyme, Semantide, Stereoisomer, Synthon, Triatonic, Trimer, Uridine, Vector

Molendinar Mill

Molest(er) Annoy, Bother, Disturb, Harass, Nonce, Scour, Touch up

Moll(y), Mollie Bloom, Bonnie, Carousal, Cutpurse, Flanders, Girl, Maguire, Malone, May, Sissy

Mollify Appease, Fob, Mease, Mitigate, Pacify, Placate, Relax, Soften, Temper

Mollusc(s) Bivalve, Malacology, Opisthobranch, → **SHELLFISH**, Tectibranch, Univalve

MOLLUSCS

3 letters:	Chank	Solen	Loligo
Mya	Conch	Spoot	Mussel
	Cowry	Squid	Nerita
4 letters:	Doris	Turbo	Oyster
Arca	Gaper	Venus	Pecten
Clam	Helix	Whelk	Pholas
Slug	Idler		Poulpe
Spat	Murex	*6 letters:*	Quahog
Unio	Olive	Chiton	Tellen
	Pinna	Cockle	Tellin
5 letters:	Polyp	Cowrie	Teredo
Bulla	Sepia	Cuttle	Triton
Capiz	Snail	Limpet	Winkle

7 letters:
Abalone
Octopod
Octopus
Pandore
Piddock
Quahaug
Scallop
Sea-hare
Sea-slug
Spirula
Toheroa
Trochus
Veliger
Vitrina

8 letters:
Ammonite
Argonaut
Ark-shell

Auricula
Nautilus
Pteropod
Saxicava
Sea-lemon
Shipworm
Strombus
Top-shell

9 letters:
Belemnite
Cone-shell
Dentalium
Gastropod
Goniatite
Nautiloid
Neopilina
Razor-clam
Razor-fish
Rock borer

Tusk-shell
Wing-shell
Wood-borer

10 letters:
Amphineura
Cephalopod
Cuttlefish
Gasteropod
Heart-shell
Money cowry
Pelecypoda
Protostome
Razorshell
Scaphopoda
Venus shell
Wentletrap

11 letters:
Horse mussel

Marine boxer
Paper-sailor
Trochophore
Trough-shell

12 letters:
Heart-cockler
Pelican's-foot

13 letters:
Lamellibranch
Paper nautilus
Slipper limpet

14 letters:
Monoplacophora
Pearly nautilus
Polyplacophora

Mollycoddle Indulge, Nanny, Pamper

Moloch Thorn-devil

Molten Dissolved, Fusil, Melted

Molybdenum Mo

Moment(s), Momentous Aha, Bending, Bit, Blonde, Dipole, Electromagnetic, Eureka, Eventful, Flash(point), Gliffing, Hogging, Import, Instant, Jiffy, Magnetic, → MINUTE, Mo, Nonce, Point, Psychological, Pun(c)to, Sagging, Sands, Sec, Senior, Shake, Stound, Stownd, Tick, Time, Trice, Twinkling, Two-ticks, Weighty, Wink

Momentum Angular, Impetus, L, Speed, Steam, Thrust

Mona(s) I, IOM

Monaco Grimaldi

Mona Lisa La Gioconda

Monarch(y) Absolute, Autocrat, Butterfly, Caesar, Constitutional, Crown, Dual, Emperor, HM, K, Karling, King, Kuwait, Limited, Merry, Netherlands, Norway, Potentate, Q, Queen, R, Raine, Realm, Reign, Ruler, Saudi Arabia, Swaziland, Sweden, Tonga, Tsar

Monarchist Cavalier

Monastery, Monastic Abbey, Abthane, Celibate, Charterhouse, Chartreuse, Cloister, Community, Gompa, Holy, Hospice, Iona, Lamaserai, Lamasery, La Trappe, Laura, Monkish, Oblate, Priory, Sangha, Secluded, Tashi, Vihara, Wat

Monday Black, Collop, Handsel, J'ouvert, Meal, Oatmeal, Plough, Whit

Mondrian Piet

Money, Monetary Ackers, Akkas, Allowance, Annat, Ante, Appearance, Archer, Assignat, Banco, Batta, Blood, Blue, Blunt, Boodle, Bottle, Brass, Bread, Bread and honey, Broad, Bull's eye, Bunce, Cabbage, Capital, Cash, Caution, Century, Change, Chink, Circulating medium, Cob, Cock, → COIN, Collateral, Confetti, Conscience, Crackle, Cranborne, Crinkly, Crust, Currency, Danger, Dib(s), Dingbat, Dollar, Dosh, Dough, Dump, Dust, Earnest, Easy, Escrow, Even, Fat, Fee, Fiat, Finance, Float, Folding, Fonds, Found, Fund, Funny, Gate, Gelt, Gilt, Godiva, Gold, Grand, Grant, Gravy, Greens, Gross, Hard, Head, Heavy sugar, Hello, Hoot, Hot, Housekeeping, Hush, Husk, Idle, Ingots, Investment, Jack, Kale, Kembla, Key, Knife, L, Legal tender, Lolly, Loot, Lucre, M, Mammon, Maundy, Mazuma, Means, Mint, Monkey, Monopoly, Moola(h), Narrow, Near, Necessary, Needful, Nest-egg, Note, Nugger, Numismatic, Nummary, Oaker, Ocher, Ochre, Offertory, Oof, Option, Outlay, P, Packet, Paper, Passage, Pavarotti, Payroll,

Peanuts, Pecuniary, Pelf, Petrodollar, Pin, Pine-tree, Pink, Pittance, Plastic, Plum, Pocket, Pony, Posh, Press, Prize, Proceeds, Profit, Protection, Purse, Push, Quid, Ration, Ready, Reap silver, Rebate, Remuneration, Resources, Revenue, Rhino, Ring, Risk, Rogue, Rowdy, Salt(s), Score, Scratch, Scrip, Seed, Shekels, Shell, Shin-plaster, Ship, Short, Siller, Silly, Silver, Sinews of war, Slush, Smart, Soap, Soft, Spending, Spondulicks, Stake, Sterling, Stipend, Stuff, Subsidy, Subsistence, Sugar, Sum, Surety, Table, Take, Takings, Tea, Tender, Tin, Toea, Token, Tranche, Treaty, Tribute, Turnover, Viaticum, Wad, Wealth, Windfall, Wonga

Money-box Penny-pig, Piggy bank

Moneylender Gombeen, Scrivener, Shroff, Shylock, Usurer

Moneymaking Earner, Profitable, Quaestuary

Mongol(ian) Bashkir, Buriat, Buryat, Calmuck, Chuvash, Epicanthic, Evenski, Genghis Khan, Golden Horde, Kalmuck, Kara-Kalpak, Kazak(h), Khalifa(h), Khalkha, Kubla(i) Khan, Kyrgyz, Lapp, Lepcha, Manchoo, Manchu, Mishmi, Mogul, Pareoean, Samoyed, Shan, Sherpa, Tamerlane, Tatar, Tungus(ic), Uig(h)ur, Ural-altaic, Uzbek

Mongoose Herpestes, Ichneumon, Mangouste, Meerkat, Suricate, Urva

Mongrel Bitser, Cross(bred), → **DOG**, Goorie, Goory, Hybrid, Kuri, Lurcher, Mutt, Quadroon, Tyke, Underbred, Zo

Monitor(ing) Dataveillance, Detect, Goanna, Iguana, Komodo dragon, Lizard, Observe, Offer, Ofgas, Ofgem, Oflot, Ofsted, Oftel, Ofwat, Oversee, Prefect, Preview, Record, Regulator, Screen, Ship, Sniffer, Sphygmophone, Surveillance, Tag, Track, Warship, Watchdog, Whole-body, Worral, Worrel

Monk(s) Bodhidharma, Bro, Brother, Frere, General, Order, Provincial, Religieux, Thelonious, Votary

MONKS

3 letters:	Jerome	Rakehell	Savonarola
Dan	Oblate	Rasputin	
Dom	Palmer	Salesian	*11 letters:*
Fra	Sangha	Sub-prior	Abbey-lubber
		Talapoin	Augustinian
4 letters:	*7 letters:*	Theatine	Benedictine
Bede	Beghard	Trappist	Bonaventura
Lama	Caedmon		Camaldolite
	Caloyer	*9 letters:*	Ignorantine
5 letters:	Cluniac	Celestine	Mekhitarist
Abbot	Dervish	Cellarist	Tironensian
Aidan	Félibre	Coenobite	
Black	Hegumen	Dominican	*12 letters:*
Bonze	Jacobin	Feuillant	Bethlehemite
Bruno	Maurist	Gyrovague	Mechitharist
Frati	Recluse	Hesychast	Obedientiary
Friar		Recollect	
Minor	*8 letters:*	Thelemite	*13 letters:*
Prior	Acoemeti		Archimandrite
Roshi	Angelico	*10 letters:*	Crutched Friar
	Basilian	Bernardine	Possessionate
6 letters:	Cenobite	Carthusian	Thomas à Kempis
Austin	Jacobite	Cistercian	
Bhikhu	Minorite	Fraticelli	*14 letters:*
Culdee	Olivetan	Hildebrand	Simeon Stylites
Hermit	Pelagian	Norbertine	

Monkey Anger, Ape, Aye-aye, Baboon, Bandar, Bobbejaan, Bonnet, Bushbaby, Capuchin, Catar(r)hine, Cebidae, Cebus, Chacma, Coaita, Colobus, Cynomolgus, Diana, Douc, Douroucouli, Drill, Durukuli, Entellus, Galago, Gelada, Gibbon, Gorilla, Grease, Green, Grison, Grivet, Guenon, Guereza, Hanuman, Hoolock, Howler, Hylobates, Imp, Indri, Jacchus, Jackey, Jocko, Kippage, Kipunji, Langur, Leaf, Lemur, Loris, Macaco, Macaque, Magot, Malmag, Mandrill, Mangabey, Marmoset, Meddle, Meerkat, Mico, Midas, Mona, Mycetes, Nala, Nasalis, New World, Old World, Orang-utang, Ouakari, Ouistiti, Phalanger, Platyrrhine, Pongo, Powder, → **PRIMATE**, Proboscis, Pug, Puzzle, Rage, Ram, Rapscallion, Rascal, Rhesus, Sago(u)in, Saguin, Sai(miri), Sajou, Saki, Sapajou, Satan, Scamp, Semnopithecus, Siamang, Sifaka, Silen(us), Silverback, Simian, Simpai, Slender loris, Spider, Squirrel, Talapoin, Tamarin, Tamper, Tana, Tarsier, Tee-tee, Titi, Toque, Trip-hammer, Troop, Tup, Uakari, Urchin, Vervet, Wanderoo, White-eyelid, Wistiti, Wou-wou, Wow-wow, Wrath, Zati
Monkey-nut Earth-pea
Monkey-puzzle Araucaria, Bunya-bunya
Monkshood Aconite
Monocle Eye-glass, Gig-lamp, Lorgnon, Quiz(zing-glass)
Monocot(yledon) Araceae, Endogen, Tradescantia
Monodon Narwhal
Monogram, Monograph Chi-rho, Cipher, Study, Treatise, Tug(h)ra
Monolith Ayers Rock, Cenotaph, Chambers Pillar, Uluru
Monologue Dramatic, Interior, Patter, Rap, Recitation, Soliloquy, Speech
Monopolise, Monopoly Absolute, Appalto, Bloc, Bogart, Cartel, Coemption, Corner, Engross, Octroi, Régie, Trust
Monorail Aerobus
Monosyllable Proclitic
Monotone, Monotonous, Monotony Boring, Dull, → **FLAT**, Grey, Humdrum, Same(y), Sing-song, Tedious, Thrum
Monsoon Dry, Hurricane, Typhoon, Wet, → **WIND**
▷ **Monsoon** *may indicate* weekend Mon soon
Monster, Monstrous Alecto, Apollyon, Asmodeus, Bandersnatch, Behemoth, Bunyip, Caliban, Cerberus, Cete, Charybdis, Chichevache, Chim(a)era, Cockatrice, Colossal, Cyclops, Dabbat, Dalek, Deform, Dinoceras, Dismayd, Div, Dragon, Echidna, Enormous, Erebus, Erinys, Erl-king, Eten, Ettin, Evil-one, Fiend, Fire-drake, Frankenstein, Freak, Geryon, Ghost, Giant, Gila, Goblin, Godzilla, Golem, Gorgon, Green-eyed, Grendel, Harpy, Hippocampus, Hippogriff, Hippogryph, Huge, Hydra, Jabberwock, Kraken, Lamia, Leviathan, Lilith, Lusus naturae, Mastodon, Medusa, Minotaur, Misbegotten, Moloch, Mooncalf, Mylodont, Nessie, Nicker, Nightmare, Ogopogo, Ogre, Ogr(e)ish, Opinicus, Orc, Outrageous, Pongo, Prodigy, Sasquatch, Satyral, Scylla, Serra, Shadow, Simorg, Simurg(h), Siren, Skull, Snark, Spectre, Sphinx, Spook, Stegodon, Stegosaur, Succubus, Taniwha, Teras, Teratism, Teratoid, Triceratops, Triffid, Troll, Typhoeus, Typhon, Unnatural, Vampire, Vast, Wasserman, Wendego, Wendigo, Wer(e)wolf, Wyvern, Xiphopagus, Yowie, Ziffius
Monstrance Ostensory
Month(ly) Ab, Abib, Adar, Anomalistic, April, Asadha, Asvina, August, Bhadrapada, Brumaire, Bul, Caitra, Calendar, Cheshvan, Chislev, December, Dhu-al-Hijjah, Dhu-al-Qadah, Draconic, Elul, February, Floréal, Frimaire, Fructidor, Gander, Germinal, Hes(h)van, Iy(y)ar, January, July, Jumada, June, Jyaistha, Karttika, Kisleu, Kislev, Lide, Lunar, Lunation, Magha, March, Margasirsa, May, Messidor, Mo, Moharram, Moon, Muharram, Muharrem, Nisan, Nivôse, Nodical, November, October, Periodical, Phalguna, Pluviôse, Prairial, Rabi(a), Rajab, Ramadan, Ramazon, Rhamadhan, Safar, Saphar, S(h)ebat, September, Sha(a)ban, Shawwal, Sidereal, Sivan, Solar, Stellar, Synodic, Tammuz, Tebeth, Thermidor, Tishri, Tisri, Tropical, Vaisakha, Veadar, Vendémiaire, Ventôse
Monument Ancient, Arch, Archive, Cairn, Cenotaph, Charminar, Column, Cromlech,

Cross, Dolmen, Eugubine, Henge, Megalith, Memorial, Menhir, Monolith, National, Pantheon, Pyramid, Sacellum, Stele(ne), Stone, Stonehenge, Stupa, Talayot, Tombstone, Trilith, Trilithon, Urn

Mood(y) Active, Anger, Atmosphere, Attitude, Capricious, Conjunctive, Dudgeon, Emoticon, Enallage, Fettle, Fit, Foulie, Glum, Grammar, Humour, Hump, Imperative, Indicative, Infinitive, Mercurial, Miff, Morale, Optative, Passive, Peat, Pet, Revivalist, Sankey, Spleen, Strop, Subjunctive, Sulky, Temper, Temperamental, Tid, Tone, Tune, Vein, Vinegar, Whim

Moon(light), Moony Aah, Adrastea, Alignak, Amalthea, Aningan, Apogee, Artemis, Astarte, Blue, Callisto, Calypso, Chandra, Cheese, Cynthia, Diana, Epact, Europa, Eye, Flit, Full, Gander, Ganymede, Gibbous, Glimmer, Grimaldi, Harvest, Hecate, Hunter's, Hyperion, Iapetus, Inconstant, Io, Juliet, Leda, Lucina, Luna(r), Mani, Mascon, McFarlane's Buat, Midsummer, Mock, Month, Mooch, Mope, New, Nimbus, Nocturne, Octant, Oliver, Orb, Paddy's lantern, Paraselene, Paschal, Pasiphaë, Phobos, Phoebe, Plenilune, Proteus, Raker, Rear-view, Satellite, Selene, Set, Shepherd, Shot, Sickle, Sideline, Silvery, Sonata, Stargaze, Stone, Syzygy, Thebe, Thoth, Titan, Triton, Umbriel, Wander

Moon god Thoth, Trismegistus

Moonraker Astrogeologist, Gothamite

Moonshine(r) Balderdash, Hootch, Poteen, Rot, Shebeener, Starveling, Tosh

Moor(ing), Moorish, Moorland Berth, Bodmin, Culloden, Dock, Fen, Fern land, Flow country, Grouse, Heath, Iago, Ilkley, Makefast, Marina, Marston, Moresque, Moroccan, Mudéjar, Othello, Otter, Palustrine, Roadstead, Ry(e)peck, Saracen, Secure, Sternfast, Tether, → **TIE**, Wharf, Wold

Mop(ping) Dwile, Flibbertigibbet, Girn, Glib, Malkin, Shag, Squeegee, Squilgee, Swab, Swob, Thatch, → **WIPE**

Mope Boody, Brood, Peak, Sulk

Mor Humus

Moral(ity), Morals Apologue, Austere, Deontic, Ethic(al), Ethos, Everyman, Fable, Gnomic, High-minded, Integrity, Laxity, Message, Parable, Precept, Principled, Probity, Puritanic, Righteous, Sittlichkeit, Tag, Upright, Virtuous, Well-thewed

Morale Ego, Mood, Spirit, Zeal

Moralise, Moralising Preach, Sententious

Moralist Prig, Prude, Puritan, Whitecap

Morass Bog, Fen, Flow, Marsh, Moss, Quagmire, Slough

Morbid(ity) Anasarca, Ascites, Cachaemia, Dropsy, Ectopia, Ghoul(ish), Gruesome, Pathological, Plethora, Prurient, Religiose, Sick, Sombre, Unhealthy

Mordant Base, Biting, Caustic, Critic(al), Sarcastic, Tooth

Mordent Inverted, Lower, Pralltriller, Upper

More Added, Additional, Else, Extra, Increase, Intense, Less, Mae, Merrier, Mo(e), → **NO MORE**, Over, Piu, Plus, Rather, Seconds, Stump, Utopia

Moreover Also, Besides, Eft, Either, Eke, Further, Too, Yet

Morgan Buccaneer, Pirate

Moribund Dying, Stagnant, Withered

Mormon Danite, Latter-day Saint, Salt Lake City, Utah, Young

Morning Ack-emma, Am, Antemeridian, Dawn, Daybreak, Early, Forenoon, Levée, Matin(al), Morrow, Sparrowfart

Morning-glory Bindweed, Ipomoea, Turbith, Turpeth

Morning-star Morgenstern, Phosphor(us), Threshel, Venus

Moroccan, Morocco Agadir, French, Leather, Levant, MA, Mo(o)r, Persian, Riff, Tangerine, Venus

Moron Fool, Idiot, Imbecile, Schmuck, → **STUPID**

Morose Acid, Boody, Churlish, Crabby, Cynical, Disgruntled, Gloomy, Glum, Grum, Moody, Sour-eyed, Sullen, Surly

Morph Phase
Morris Car, Dance, Fivepenny, Merel(l), Meril, Nine Men's, Ninepenny
Morrow Future
Morse Code, Endeavour, Iddy-umpty, Tusker, Walrus
Morsel Bit, Bite, Bouche, Canape, Crumb, Dainty, Morceau, Ort, Scrap, Sippet, Sop, Tidbit, Titbit
Mortal(ity) Averr(h)oism, Being, Deathly, → **FATAL**, Grave, Human, Lethal, Yama
Mortar, Mortar-board Bowl, Cannon, Cement, Co(e)horn, Compo, Grout, Gunite, Hawk, Life, Metate, Mine-thrower, Minnie, Moaning (Minnie), Parget, Plaster, Pot gun, Screed, Square, Squid, Toc emma, Trench(er)
Mortgage(e) Balloon, Bond, Cap and collar, Cedula, Chattel, Debt, Dip, Encumbrance, Endowment, First, Hypothecator, Loan, Pension, Pledge, Repayment, Reverse, Wadset(t)
Mortification, Mortified, Mortify Abash, Ashame, Chagrin, Crucify, Crush, Gangrene, Humble, Humiliate, Infarct, Necrose, Penance, Sick, Sphacelus, Wormwood
Mortuary Deadhouse
Mosaic Buhl, Cosmati, Impave, Inlay, Intarsia, Musive, Opus musivum, Pietra dura, Screen, Tarsia, Terrazzo, Tessella(te), Tessera, Tobacco, Venetian
Moscow Dynamo
Moses Grandma
▸ **Moslem** *see* **MUSLIM**
Mosque Dome of the Rock, El Aqsa, Jami, Masjid, Medina, Musjid
Mosquito Aedes, Anopheles, Culex, Culicine, Gnat, Parasite, Stegomyia
Moss(y) Acrogen, Agate, Bryology, Bur(r), Carrag(h)een, Ceylon, Club, Fairy, Fog, Fontinalis, Hag(g), Hypnum, Iceland, Irish, Lecanoram, Lichen, Litmus, Liverwort, Long, Lycopod, Marsh, Musci, Muscoid, Parella, Peat, Polytrichum, Protonema, Reindeer, Rose, Scale, Selaginella, Spanish, Sphagnum, Staghorn, Tree, Usnea, Wall, Wolf's claw
Most(ly) Basically, Largest, Major, Maxi(mum), Optimum
Mot Quip, Saying
Mote Atom, Particle, Speck

MOTHS

2 letters:	*5 letters:*	Y-moth	Sphinx
Io	Atlas	Yucca	Turnip
	Eggar		Veneer
3 letters:	Egger	*6 letters:*	Winter
Bag	Flour	Antler	
Bee	Ghost	Bogong	*7 letters:*
Fox	Gipsy	Bugong	Abraxas
Nun	Grass	Burnet	Buff-tip
Owl	Gypsy	Carpet	Cabbage
Wax	House	Codlin	Clothes
	Imago	Dagger	Codling
4 letters:	Owlet	Ermine	Emerald
Arch	Plane	Herald	Emperor
Bell	Plume	Kitten	Hook-tip
Corn	Snout	Lackey	Leopard
Goat	Swift	Lappet	Lobster
Hawk	Thorn	Lichen	Noctuid
Luna	Tiger	Magpie	Old-lady
Meal	Tinea	Muslin	Pug-moth
Puss	Umber	Noctua	Silver-Y
Wave	Wheat	Psyche	Tortrix

Tussock
Unicorn
Zygaena

8 letters:
Bobowler
Bombycid
Cecropia
Cinnabar
Dart-moth
Drepanid
Geometer
Goldtail
Night-fly
Oak-egger
Peppered
Saturnia
Silkworm
Sphingid
Tapestry

Tineidae
Vapourer
Wainscot

9 letters:
Arctiidae
Brown-tail
Carpenter
Clearwing
Corn -borer
Geometrid
Honeycomb
Notodonta
Pyralidae
Saturniid
Scavenger
Underwing
Woodborer

10 letters:
Death's head
Gooseberry
Leafroller
Peach-bloom
Peppercorn
Pine-beauty
Pine-carpet
Polyphemus
Privet hawk

11 letters:
Diamondback
Hummingbird
Lepidoptera

12 letters:
Cactoblastis
Giant peacock
Kentish glory

Large emerald
Lymantriidae
Red underwing
Sallow-kitten

13 letters:
Lasiocampidae
Mother of pearl
Mother Shipton
Processionary
Purple emperor

15 letters:
Yellow underwing

16 letters:
Clifden nonpareil
Macrolepidoptera
Microlepidoptera

Mothball(s) Abeyance, Camphor, Naphtha, Preserver

Mother Abbess, Bearer, Church, Cognate, Cosset, Courage, Dam(e), Den, Dregs, Ean, Earth, Eoan, Eve, Foster, Generatrix, Genetrix, Genitrix, Goose, Hubbard, Lees, Ma, Machree, Madre, Mam(a), Mamma, Mater, Matroclinic, Maya, Minnie, Mollycoddle, Mom, Multipara, Mum, Mummy, Native, Nature, Nourish, Nursing, Parent, Parity, Pourer, Primipara, Progenitress, Reverend, Shipton, Slime, Superior, Surrogate, Theotokos, Venter, Wit

▷ **Mother** *may indicate* a lepidopterist; moth-er

Mother-in-law Naomi

Motherless Adam, Orphan

Motif Anthemion, Design, Gist, Idée, Theme

Motion Angular, Blocking, Composite, Contrary, Direct, Diurnal, Early day, Fast, Free-fall, Gesture, Harmonic, Impulse, Kepler, Kinematics, Kinetic, Kipp, Link, Move, Oblique, Offer, Parallactic, Parallel, Peculiar, Perpetual, PL, Precession, Proper, Proposal, Rack and pinion, Rider, Sewel, Similar, Slow, Spasm, Wave

Motionless Doggo, Frozen, Immobile, Inert, Quiescent, Stagnant, Stasis, Still, Stock-still

Motive, Motivate, Motivation Actuate, Cause, Drive, Ideal, Impel, Incentive, Intention, Mainspring, Mobile, Object, → **PURPOSE**, Reason, Spur, Ulterior

Motley Jaspé, Medley, Piebald, Pied, Variegated

Motor(boat) Auto, Benz, Car, Dynamo, Electric, Engine, Hot rod, Hydroplane, Inboard, Induction, Jato, Linear, Mini, Outboard, Paint job, Rocket, Scooter, Series-wound, Stator, Supermini, Sustainer, Synchronous, Thruster, Turbine, Turbo, Universal, Vaporetto, Water

Motorcycle, Motorcyclist Bambi, Beemer, Bikie, Chookchaser, Chopper, Combination, Cyma recta, Farm-bike, Greaser, Harley Davidson, Hell's Angel, Minimoto, Moped, Pipsqueak, Scooter, Scramble, Tourist Trophy, Trail bike, TT, Yamaha®

Motorist(s) AA, Driver, Petrolhead, RAC, Road hog, Tripper

Motorman Austin, Benz, Ford, Morris

Motor race, Motor sport F1, Formula One, Rally, Scramble, TT

Motorway Autobahn, Autopista, Autoput, Autoroute, Autostrada, Expressway, M(1), Orbital, Superhighway, Throughway, Thruway

Mottle(d) Brindled, Chiné, Jaspé, Marbled, Marly, Mirly, Pinto, Poikilitic, Tabby

Motto Device, Epigraph, Excelsior, Gnome, Impresa, Imprese, Impress(e), Legend, Maxim, Mot, Poesy, Posy, Saw, Slogan

Mou(e) Grimace, Mim

Mould(ed), Moulder, Mouldable, Moulding, Mouldy Accolade, Architrave, Archivolt, Astragal, Baguette, Balection, Bandelet, Beading, Bend, Black, Blow, Blue, Bolection, Bread, Briquet(te), Cabling, Casement, Cast(ing), Cavetto, Chain, Chessel, Chill, Cold, Cornice, Coving, Cyma, Cymatium, Dancette, Dariole, Die, Die-cast, Dogtooth, Doucine, Dripstone, Ductile, Echinus, Egg and dart, Emboss, Flong, → **FORM**, Foughty, Fousty, Fungose, Fungus, Fusarol(e), Fust, Gadroon, Geat, Godroon, Gorgerin, Green, Hood-mould, Hore, Humus, Injection, Iron, Jelly, Leaf, Machine, Matrix, Mildew, Model, Mool, Moulage, Mucedinous, Mucid, Mucor, Must, Mycetozoan, Myxomycete, Nebule, Necking, Noble rot, Ogee, Ovolo, Palmette, Papier-mâché, Penicillin, Phycomycete, Picture, Pig, Plasm(a), Plaster, Plastic, Plastisol, Plat, Platband, Plate, Prototype, Prunt, Quarter-round, Reeding, Reglet, Rhizopus, Rib, Rot, Rust, Sandbox, Scotia, Shape, Slime, Smut, Soil, Soot(y), Spindle, Storiated, Stringcourse, Stucco, Surbase, Tailor, Talon, Template, Templet, Timbale, Tondino, Torus, Trochilus, Vinew, Water table

Moult(ing) Cast, Metecdysis, Mew, Shed

Mound Agger, Bank, Barp, Barrow, Berm, Cahokia, Cone, Dike, Dun, Embankment, Heap, Hog, Knoll, Kurgan, Mogul, Molehill, Monticule, Mote, Motte, Orb, Pile, Pingo, Pome, Rampart, Rampire, Remblai, Tel(l), Teocalli, Teopan, Tuffet, Tumulus, Tussock

Mound-bird Leipoa, Megapode

Mount(ed), Mounting, Mountain (peak), Mountains Air, → **ALPINE**, Ascend, Back, Barp, Ben, Berg, Board, Breast, Butter, Chain, Charger, → **CLIMB**, Colt, Cordillera, Cradle, Dew, Display, Djebel, Dolly, Eminence, Escalade, Frame, Hinge, Horse, Inselberg, Jebel, Massif, Monture, Mt, Nunatak, Orography, Orology, Passe-partout, Peak, Pike, Pile, Pin, Pownie, Quad, → **RANGE**, Ride, Saddlehorse, Saddle up, Scalado, Scale, Sclim, Set, Soar, Stage, → **STEED**, Stie, Strideways, Tel, Tier, Topo, Tor, Turret, Upgo, Volcano

MOUNTAINS

2 letters:	Rigi	Green	Tyrol
K2	Ubac	Guyot	Uinta
	Zeil	Hekla	Urals
3 letters:		Horeb	Welsh
Apo	*5 letters:*	Idris	White
Ida	Abora	Kamet	
Kaf	Adams	Kenya	*6 letters:*
Ore	Aldan	Logan	Ala Dag
	Altai	Munro	Alaska
4 letters:	Amara	Ozark	Amhara
Alai	Andes	Pelée	Anadyr
Blue	Aneto	Rocky	Arafat
Bona	Athos	Rydal	Ararat
Cook	Atlas	Sayan	Averno
Etna	Badon	Serra	Balkan
Fuji	Black	Sinai	Bogong
Harz	Blanc	Siple	Carmel
Hoss	Coast	Smoky	Cho Oyu
Jaya	Djaja	Snowy	Dragon
Jura	Eiger	Table	Egmont
Meru	Ellis	Tabor	Elbert
Nebo	Er Rif	Tatra	Elberz
Oeta	Evans	Tirol	Elbrus
Ossa	Ghats	Tyree	Erebus

Gilead
Gimbal
Hermon
Hoggar
Hoosac
Katmai
Kazbek
Kunlun
Lhotse
Makalu
Mourne
Olives
Ortles
Pamirs
Pelion
Pindus
Pisgah
Pocono
Robson
Scopus
Sintra
Sorata
Steele
Tasman
Taunus
Taurus
Umbria
Vernon
Vosges
Zagros

7 letters:
Aetolia
Ala Dagh
Aorangi
Aragats
Arcadia
Bernina
Brocken
Buffalo
Calvary
Cariboo
Cascade
Chianti
Corbett
Dapsang
Estreia
Everest
Helicon
Kaufman
Kennedy
Khingan
Kuenlun
Lebanon

Lucania
Manaslu
Markham
Nan Shan
Olympic
Olympus
Orontes
Palomar
Perdido
Pilatus
Rainier
Rhodope
San Juan
Scafell
Selkirk
Skiddaw
Snowdon
Sperrin
Stanley
St Elias
Sudeten
Tibesti
Travers
Troglav
Whitney
Wicklow

8 letters:
Anapurna
Arcadian
Aspiring
Ben Nevis
Cambrian
Carstenz
Catskill
Caucasus
Cevennes
Cumbrian
Damavand
Demavend
Fujiyama
Grampian
Guerrero
Hymettus
Illimani
Jungfrau
Katahdin
Kinabalu
King Peak
Leibnitz
McKinley
Mulhacen
Ngaliema
Ouachita

Pennines
Pinatubo
Pyrenees
Rushmore
Seamount
St Helen's
Taraniki
Tian Shan
Tien Shan
Vesuvius
Victoria
Wrangell

9 letters:
Aconcagua
Allegheny
Annapurna
Apennines
Ben Lomond
Blackburn
Blue Ridge
Cairngorm
Carstensz
Catskills
Caucasian
Connemara
Demavrand
Dhaulagir
Dolomites
El Capitan
Grampians
Guadalupe
Helvellyn
Hercynian
Highlands
High Tatra
Himalayas
Hindu Kush
Jebel Musa
Karakoram
Lenin Peak
Longs Peak
Marmolada
Mont Blanc
Monte Rosa
Nanda Devi
Parnassus
Pikes Peak
Ruwenzori
Shivering
Sugar Loaf
Tirich Mir
Tongariro
Trans Alai

Tupungato
Vancouver
Venusberg
Voralberg
Weisshorn
Woodroffe
Yablonovy
Zugspitze

10 letters:
Altazimuth
Arakan Yoma
Armageddon
Black Hills
Cantabrian
Carpathian
Delectable
Dhaulagiri
Equatorial
Erymanthus
Erzgebirge
Great Gable
Great Smoky
Harney Peak
Horselberg
Kongur Shan
Kosciuszko
Laurentian
Masharbrum
Masherbrum
Matterhorn
Monte Corno
Montserrat
Pentelicus
Pentelikon
Puncak Jaya
Puy de Sancy
Qomolangma
Sagarmatha
St Michael's
Tengri Khan
Teton Range
Vorarlberg
Washington
Waziristan
Wellington
Wetterhorn

11 letters:
Adirondacks
Alaska Range
Anti-Lebanon
Appalachian
Bartle Frere

Bimberi Peak
Brooks Range
Coast Ranges
Drakensberg
Fairweather
Gerlachovka
Kilimanjaro
Kirkpatrick
Kolyma Range
Machu Picchu
Nanga Parbat
Pico de Aneto
Pico de Teide
Salmon River
Scafell Pike
Sierra Madre

12 letters:
Albert Edward
Cascade Range
Eastern Ghats
Godwin Austen
Gran Paradiso
Ingleborough
Kanchenjunga

Monte Perdido
Ruahine Range
Sierra Morena
Sierra Nevada
Slieve Donard
Southern Alps
Tararua Range
Victoria Peak
Vindhya Range
Vinson Massif
Wasatch Range
Western Ghats

13 letters:
Carrantuohill
Croagh Patrick
Flinders Range
Frenchman's Cap
Great Dividing
Grossglockner
Humphrey's Peak
Kangchenjunga
Massif Central
Mount Klinovec
Petermann Peak

San Bernardino
Stanovoi Range
Tibesti Massif

14 letters:
Admiralty Range
Bohemian Forest
Carnarvon Range
Finsteraarhorn
Hamersley Range
Kaikoura Ranges
Kommunizma Peak
Liverpool Range
Musgrove Ranges
Queen Maud Range
Ruwenzori Range
Sangre de Cristo
Stirling Ranges
Stzelecki Range
Thadentsonyane
Wind River Range

15 letters:
New England Range
Teutoburger Wald

16 letters:
Emperor Seamounts
Macdonnell Ranges
Owen Stanley Range
Thabana-Ntlenyana

17 letters:
Continental Divide
Transylvanian Alps
Warrumbungle
Range

18 letters:
Great Dividing Range

19 letters:
Macgillicuddy's
Reeks

20 letters:
Salmon River
Mountains

Mountain-building Orogenesis
Mountaineer(ing) Aaron, Abseil, Alpinist, Arnaut, Climber, Hunt, Sherpa, Smythe, Upleader
Mountebank Antic(ke), Baladin(e), Charlatan, Jongleur, Quack, Saltimbanco
Mourn(er), Mournful, Mourning Adonia, Black, Cypress, Dirge, Dole, Elegiac, Grieve, Grone, Half-mast, Hatchment, Jamie Duff, Keen, Lament, Mute, Niobe, Omer, Ovel, Plangent, Saulie, Shibah, Shivah, Shloshim, Sorrow, Tangi, Threnetic, Threnodial, Weeds, Weep, Willow
Mouse(like), Mousy Black eye, Bus, Church, Deer, Dormouse, Dun(nart), Fat, Field, Flitter, Harvest, Honey, House, Icon, Jerry, Jumping, Kangaroo, Marsupial, Meadow, Mechanical, Mickey, Minnie, Muridae, Murine, Optical, Pocket, Pouched, Rodent, Shiner, Shrew, Vermin, Waltzer, White-footed
Mousetrap Samson's post
Mousse Styling
Moustache(d) Algernon, Boxcar, Burnside, Charley, Charlie, Chevron, Excrement, Fu Manchu, Handlebar, Hindenburg, Horseshoe, Kaiser, Mistletoe, Pencil, Pyramid, Regent, Roman T, Ronnie, Soupstrainer, Toothbrush, Walrus, Waxed, Wings, Zapata
Mouth(piece) Aboral, Bazoo, Bocca, Brag, Buccal, Cakehole, Chapper, Check, Crater, Debouchure, Delta, Embouchure, Estuary, Fauces, Fipple, Gab, Gam, Geggie, Gills, Gob, Gub, Gum, Hard, Horn, Kisser, Labret, Laughing gear, Lawyer, Lip, Manubrium, Maw, Neb, Orifex, Orifice, Os, Oscule, Ostium, Outfall, Outlet, Peristome, Port, Potato trap, Rattle-trap, Speaker, Spokesman, Spout, Stoma, Swazzle, Swozzle, Teat, Trap, Trench, Uvula
Mouthful Bite, Gob, Gobbet, Morceau, Morsel, Sip, Sup, Taste
Mouthless Astomatous
Mouth-organ Harmonica, Harp, Palp, Sang
Mouth-watering Sialogogue
Move(d), Mover, Movable, Moving Act, Actuate, Affect, Andante, Astir, Aswarm,

Budge, Career, Carry, Castle, Catapult, Chattel, Claw off, Coast, Counter-measure, Coup, Decant, Démarche, Deploy, Displace, Disturb, Ease, Eddy, Edge, Evoke, Extrapose, False, Fidget, Flit, Flounce, Fluctuate, Forge, Fork, Frogmarch, Gambit, Gee, Give and go, Go, Gravitate, Haulier, Hustle, Inch, Inspire, Instigate, Jee, Jink, Jump, Kedge, Kinetic, Knight's progress, Link, Lunge, March, Mill, Mobile, Mosey, Motivate, Motor, Nip, Opening, Outwin, Overcome, Pan, People, Poignant, Prime, Proceed, Progress, Progressional, Prompt, Propel, Propose, Qui(t)ch, Quinche, Quicken, Rearrange, Redeploy, Relocate, Remuage, Retrocede, Roll, Rollaway, Rouse, Roust, Sashay, Scoot, Scramble, Scroll, Scurry, Scuttle, Sealed, Sell, Shift, Shog, Shoo, Shunt, Sidle, Skelp, Skitter, Slide, Soulful, Spank, Steal, Steer, Step, Stir, Styre, Surf, Swarm, Sway, Swish, Tack, Tactic, Taxi, Teleport, Touch, Transfer, Translate, Translocate, Transplant, Transport, Travel, Troll, Trundle, Turn, Unstep, Up, Up sticks, Vacillate, Vagile, Veronica, Vire, Volt(e), Waft, Wag, Wapper, Whirry, Whish, Whisk, Whiz, Whoosh, Wuther, Yank, Zoom, Zwischenzug

Movement(s) Action, Advection, Aerotaxis, Akathisia, Al Fatah, Allegro, Allemande, Almain, Andantino, Antic, Antistrophe, Arts and crafts, Azapo, Badinerie, Bandwagon, Brownian, Buchmanism, Cadence, Capoeira, Cell, Charismatic, Chartism, Chemonasty, Constructivism, Course, Crusade, Dadaism, Diaspora, Diastole, Ecumenical, Enlightenment, Eoka, Epeirogeny, Eurhythmics, Expressionism, Faction, Feint, Fianchetto, Fris(ka), Gait, Gallicanism, Geneva, Gesture, Groundswell, Heliotaxis, Hip-hop, Honde, Imagism, Indraught, Inkatha, Intermezzo, Jhala, Jor, Kata, Keplarian, Kinematics, Kinesis, Kin(a)esthetic, Kinetic, Kipp, Larghetto, Largo, Lassu, Ligne, Logistics, Maltese cross, Manoeuvre, Men's, Migration, Motion, Mudra, Nastic, Naturalism, Naziism, Neofascism, Neorealism, New Age, New Urbanism, New Wave, Nihilism, Official, Operation, Orchesis, Overspill, Oxford, Oxford Group, Panislamism, Pan-Slavism, Pantalon, Parallax, Pase, Passade, Passage, Pedesis, Photokinesis, Photonasty, Piaffer, Pincer, Plastique, Play, Populist, Port de bras, Poule, Poulette, Procession, Progress, Provisional, Punk, Puseyism, Reconstructionism, Reformation, Regression, REM, Renaissance, Resistance, Revivalism, Ribbonism, Risorgimento, Romantic, Rondo, Saccade, Scherzo, Scissors, Seiche, Seismic, Sinn Fein, Solifluction, Solifluxion, Spuddle, Stir(e), Sturm und Drang, Subsidence, Swadeshi, Swing, Symbolist, Tachism, Tamil Tigers, Tantrism, Taphrogenesis, Taxis, Tectonic, Telekinesis, Thermotaxis, Thigmotaxis, Tic, Tide, Tractarianism, Transhumance, Trend, Trenise, Ultramontanism, UNITA, Verismo, Veronica, Wave, Wheel, White flight, Women's, Zionism

Movie Bioscope, Buddy, Cine(ma), Disaster, Film, Flick, Nudie, Popcorn, Road, Slasher, Snuff, Splatter, Star Wars, Talkie

Mow(er), Mowing Aftermath, Cut, Grimace, Lattermath, Lawn, Math, Rawing, Rawn, Reap, Rowan, Rowen, Rowing, Scytheman, Shear, Sickle, Strimmer®, Tass, Trim

MP Backbencher, Commoner, Gendarme, Knight of the Shire, Member, Oncer, Politico, Provost, Redcap, Retread, Snowdrop, Stannator, Statist, TD

▶ **Mr** *see* MISTER

▶ **Mrs** *see* MISSIS

Mrs Brown VR

Mrs Copperfield Agnes, Dora

Mrs Siddons Tragic muse

Mrs Simpson Marge, Wallis

Much Abundant, Ever so, Far, Glut, Great, Lots, Mickle, Rotten, Scad, Sore, Viel

Mucilage Gum, → MUC(O)US, Putty, Resin

Muck (up), Mucky Bungle, Dirt, Dung, Grime, Island, Lady, Leep, Manure, Midden, Mire, Rot, Sludge, Slush, Soil, Sordid, Spoil, Stercoral

Mucker Fall, Pal, Purler

Muc(o)us Blennorrhoea, Booger, Catarrh, Gleet, Operculum, Phlegm, Pituate, Pituita, Salt rheum, Sleep, Snivel, Snot, Snotter, Sputum

Mud(dy) Adobe, Clabber, Clart, Clay, Cutcha, Dirt, Drilling, Dubs, Fango, Glaur, Glob, Gutter, Kacha, Lahar, Lairy, Limous, Lumicolous, → **MIRE**, Moya, Mudge, Ooze, Peloid, Pise, Poach, Red, Riley, Roily, Salse, Silt, Slab, Slake, Sleech, Slime, Slob, Slobland, Slough, Sludge, Slur(ry), Slush, Slutch, Tocky, Trouble, Turbid, Volcanic

Muddle(d) Befog, Bemuse, Botch, Cock up, Confuse, Disorder, Embrangle, Fluster, Gump, Higgledy-piggledy, Jumble, Mash, Mêlée, Mess, Mess up, Mix, Mull, Pickle, Puddle, Screw up, Shemozzle, Snarl-up, Stupefy, Tangle, Ta(i)vert, Tiert

▷ **Muddled** *may indicate* an anagram

Mudfish Lepidosiren

Mudguard Splashboard, Wing

Mudlark Ragamuffin, Urchin

Muesli Granola

Muff Blunder, Boob, Botch, Bungle, Drop, Snoskyn

Muffin Bun, Mule, Popover

Muffle(d), Muffler Baffle, Damp, Deaden, Envelop, Hollow, Mob(b)le, Mute, Scarf, Silencer, Sourdine, Stifle

Mug(ger), Muggy Assault, Attack, Bash, Beaker, Bock, Can, Club, Con, Croc(odile), Cup, Dial, Do over, Dupe, Enghalskrug, Face, Fool, Footpad, Gob, Humid, Idiot, Latron, Learn, Mou, Noggin, Pan, Pot, Puss, Rob, Roll, Sandbag, Sap, Sconce, Simpleton, Steamer, Stein, Sucker, Swot, Tankard, Tax, Thief, Thug(gee), Tinnie, Tinny, Toby, Trap, Ugly, Visage, Yap

Mulatto Griff(e)

Mulberry Artocarpus, Breadfruit, Cecropia, Contrayerva, Cow-tree, Indian, Jack, Morat, Morus, Murrey, Osage orange, Overlord, Paper, Sycamine

Mulch Compost

Mulct Fine

Mule, Mulish Ass, Bab(o)uche, Barren, Donkey, Funnel, Hemionus, Hybrid, Mocassin, Moccasin, Moyl(e), Muffin, Muil, Obdurate, Pack, Rake, Shoe, Slipper, Spinning, Sumpter

Muleteer Arriero

Mull Brood, Chew, Kintyre, Ponder, Promontory, Study

Mullein Aaron's rod

Mullet Goatfish, Hairpiece, Wig

Mullion Monial, Trumeau

Multi-coloured Scroddled

Multiform Allotropic, Diverse, Manifold

Multiple, Multiplication, Multiplied, Multiplier, Multiply Augment, Breed, Chorisis, Common, Double, Elixir, → **INCREASE**, Manifold, Modulus, Populate, Product, Proliferate, Propagate, Raise, Scalar, Severalfold

Multi-purpose Polychrest

Multitude Army, Crowd, Hirsel, Horde, Host, Legion, Populace, Shoal, Sight, Throng, Zillion

Mum(my) Boutonné, Carton(n)age, Corpse, Egyptian, Embalm, Mamma, Mine, Mute, Peace(ful), Pharaoh, Quiet, Sh, Shtum, Silent, Tacit, Whisht, Wordless

Mumble Grumble, Moop, Moup, Mouth, Mump, Mushmouth, Mutter, Royne, Slur

Mumbo jumbo Hocus pocus, Mammet, Maumet, Mawmet, Mommet

Mummer(y) Actor, Guising, Mime, Scuddaler, Scudler, Skudler

Mumps Parotitis

Munch Champ, Chew, Chomp, Expressionist, Moop, Moup, Scranch

Mundane Banal, Common, Earthly, Nondescript, Ordinary, Prosaic, Quotidian, Routine, Secular, Subcelestial, Trite, Workaday, Worldly

Mungo Park

Municipal(ity) Civic, Nasik

Munificent, Munificence Bounteous, Generous, Largesse, Liberal, Profuse

Munition(s) Arms, Arsenal, Artillery, Matériel, Ordnance

Munro Saki

Mural(s) Fresco, Graffiti

Murder(er), Murderess, Murderous Abort, Aram, Assassin, Blue, Bluebeard, Bravo, Burke, Butcher, Butler, Cain, Cathedral, Crackhalter, Crippen, Crows, Cutthroat, Danaid(e)s, Do in, Eliminate, End, Filicide, First degree, Fratricide, Genocide, Hare, Hatchet man, Hit, Hitman, Homicide, Hyde, Internecine, Judicial, → **KILL**, Liquidate, Locusta, Made man, Man-queller, Massacre, Matricide, Modo, Mullah, Muller, Parricide, Patricide, Petty treason, Poison, Red, Regicide, Removal, Ripper, Ritual, Ritz, Rub out, Second degree, Sikes, Slaughter, Slay, Stiff, Strangle(r), Sweeney Todd, Take out, Thagi, Throttle, Thug(gee), Ugly man, Vaticide, Whodun(n)it

Murk(y) Black, Dirk(e), Gloom, Obscure, Rookish, Stygian

Murmur(ing) Babble, Brool, Bruit, Bur(r), Burble, Coo, Croodle, Croon, Grudge, Heart, Hum, → **MUTTER**, Purr, Repine, Rhubarb, Rumble, Rumour, Souffle, Sowf(f), Sowth, Sturnoid, Syllable, Undertone, Whisper

Murphy Chat, Potato, Pratie, Spud, Tater

Muscle, Muscleman, Muscular Abductor, Abs, Accelerator, Accessorius, Adductor, Agonist, Anconeus, Aristotle's lantern, Aryepiglottic, Arytaenoid, Athletic, Attollens, Azygous, Beef(y), Beefcake, Biceps, Bowr, Brachialus, Brawn, Buccinator, Buff, Cardiac, Ciliary, Clout, Complexus, Corrugator, Creature, Cremaster, Delt(oid), Depressor, Diaphragm, Digastric, Dilat(at)or, Duvaricator, Écorché, Effector, Elevator, Erecter, Erector, Evertor, Extensor, Eye-string, Flexor, Force, Gastrocnemius, Gemellus, Glute, Glut(a)eus, Gluteus maximus, Gracilis, Hamstring, Heavy, Hiacus, Hunky, Iliacus, Intrinsic, Involuntary, Kreatine, Lat, Latissimus dorsi, Laxator, Levator, Lumbricalis, Masseter, Mesomorph, Might, Motor, Mouse, Myalgia, Mylohyoid, Myology, Myotome, Myotonia, Nasalis, Obicularis, Oblique, Occlusor, Omohyoid, Opponent, Orbicularis, Pathos, Pec(s), Pectoral, Perforans, Perforatus, Peroneus, Plantaris, Platysma, Popliteus, → **POWER**, Pronator, Protractor, Psoas, Pylorus, Quad(riceps), Quadratus, Rambo, Rectus, Retractor, Rhomboid, Rhomboideus, Ripped, Risorius, Rotator cuff, Sarcolemma, Sarcous, Sartorius, Scalene, Scalenus, Serratus, Sinew, Six-pack, Smooth, Soleus, Sphincter, Spinalis, Splenial, Sthenic, Striated, Striped, Supinator, Suspensory, Temporal, Tenaculum, Tendon, Tensor, Teres, Thenar, Thew, Tibialis, Toned, Tonus, Trapezius, Triceps, Vastus, Voluntary, Xiphihumeralis, Zygomatic

Muscovite Mica, Talc

Muse(s), Muse's home, Musing Aglaia, Aonia(n), Attic, Calliope, Clio, Cogitate, Consider, Dream, Erato, Euphrosyne, Euterpe, Goddess, Helicon, Inspiration, IX, Laura, Melpomene, Mull, Nine, Nonet, Pensée, Pierides, Poly(hy)mnia, Ponder, → **REFLECT**, Ruminate, Study, Teian, Terpsichore, Thalia, Tragic, Urania, Wonder

Museum Alte-Pinakothek, Ashmolean, BM, British, Fitzwilliam, Gallery, Getty, Guggenheim, Heritage centre, Hermitage, Hunterian, Louvre, Metropolitan, National Gallery, Parnassus, Prado, Repository, Rijksmuseum, Science, Smithsonian, Tate, Te papa Tongarewa, Uffizi, VA, V and A, Waxworks

Mush Cree, Glop, Goo, Mess, Pop, Porridge, Puree, Schmaltz, Slop

Mushroom Aecidium, Aedium, Agaric, Ascomycetes, Blewits, Boletus, Burgeon, Button, Cep, Champignon, Chanterelle, Darning, Destroying angel, Enoki, Escalate, Expand, Field, Fly agaric, → **FUNGUS**, Girolle, Grisette, Gyromitra, Honey fungus, Horse, Hypha(l), Ink-cap, Liberty cap, Magic, Matsutake, Meadow, Morel, Oyster, Parasol, Penny-bun, Pixy-stool, Porcino, Reishi, Russula, Sacred, St George's, Scotch bonnet, Shaggy cap, Shaggymane, Shiitake, Shroom, Sickener, Spread, Start-up, Straw, Truffle, Upstart, Velvet shank, Waxcap

Music Absolute, A-side, B-side, Classical, Colour, Electro, Indeterminate, Lesson, Light, Lounge, Medieval, Minstrelsy, Mood, Morceau, → **MUSICAL INSTRUMENTS**, Passage work, Phase, Piece, Popular, Programme, Quotation, Recital, Score, Sound, Table, Tremolando

MUSIC

2 letters:
Oi

3 letters:
Air
AOR
Art
Dub
EMI
Emo
Gat
Jor
Mas
MOR
Pop
Rag
Rai
Rap
Rug
Ska
Son

4 letters:
Alap
Chin
Coda
Duet
Folk
Funk
Go-go
Jazz
Loco
Meno
Note
Opus
Prom
Raga
Rave
Riff
Rock
Romo
Roxy
Soca
Soul
Surf
Tala
Trad
Trio
Tune
Zouk

5 letters:
Alaap
Alapa
Bebop
Benga
Canon
Chant
Cliff
Conga
Crunk
Cu-bop
Disco
Dream
Dumka
Early
Etude
Fugue
Funky
Gabba
House
Indie
Jhala
Krunk
Kwela
Largo
March
Motet
Muzak®
Neume
Nonet
Outro
Piped
Ragga
Rondo
Roots
Rough
Salon
Salsa
Salve
Sheet
Sokah
Staff
Suite
Swing
Thema
Tonal
Trash
Truth
Vocal
World
Zoppo

6 letters:
Arioso
Aubade
Bebung
Bouree
Decani
Doo-wop
Enigma
Equali
Façade
Fugato
Fusion
Gagaku
Galant
Garage
Gospel
Gothic
Grunge
Hip-hop
Jungle
Khayal
Kirtan
Kwaito
Lydian
Mantra
Marabi
Mashup
Melody
Motown®
New Age
Organa
Plagal
Popera
Pycnon
Ragini
Redowa
Reggae
Rhythm
Rootsy
Sextet
Skronk
Sonata
Strain
Techno
Tenuto
Thrash
Trance
Verset
Zydeco

7 letters:
Afropop

Allegro
Andante
Ars nova
Ballade
Baroque
Bhangra
Bluette
Bourree
Britpop
Cadenza
Calypso
Cantata
Ceilidh
Chamber
Chorale
Country
Dad rock
Europop
Euterpe
Fanfare
Gangsta
Hardbag
Introit
Klezmer
Landler
Marcato
Melisma
Messiah
Mordent
New Wave
Numbers
Nu-metal
Organum
Orphean
Partita
Passion
Pecking
Pibroch
Prelude
Qawwali
Quartet
Quintet
Ragtime
Rastrum
Requiem
Reverse
Romanza
Rondeau
Rondino
Rosalia
Roulade
Sanctus

Scherzo
Secondo
Setting
Skiffle
Soukous
Stretto
Toccata
Trip hop
Ziganka

8 letters:
Acid rock
Aleatory
Berceuse
Blue beat
Chaconne
Cock rock
Concerto
Concrete
Continuo
Coranach
Coronach
Elevator
Entracte
Fantasia
Flamenco
Folk rock
Glam rock
Hard core
Hard rock
High life
In nomine
Janizary
Karnatak
Lollipop
Madrigal
Maggiore
Mariachi
Mbaqanga
Modality
Nocturne
Notation
Old-skool
Oratorio
Parlando
Partitur
Pastiche
Postlude

Post-rock
Preludio
Psalmody
Punk rock
Rhapsody
Ricercar
Romantic
Saraband
Serenade
Serenata
Sinfonia
Symphony
Synth-pop
Waltzian
Warhorse

9 letters:
Acid-house
Allemande
Antiphony
Arabesque
Bagatelle
Bluegrass
Breakbeat
Cantilena
Capriccio
Dixieland
Drum'n'bass
Fioritura
Goa trance
Grandioso
Hardhouse
Hillbilly
Honky-tonk
Interlude
Klezmorim
Obbligato
Partitura
Pastorale
Pastorali
Pitchbend
Plainsong
Polonaise
Polyphony
Portabeul
Prick-song
Queercore
Quodlibet

Reggaeton
Ricercare
Rock'n'roll
Septimole
Serialist
Slow march
Spiritual
Swingbeat
Tambourin
Technopop
Toccatina
Voluntary
Warehouse

10 letters:
Albumblatt
Anacrustic
Chopsticks
Coloratura
Death metal
Desert rock
Electronic
Gangsta rap
Gothic rock
Heavy metal
Hindustani
Humoresque
Incidental
Intermezzo
Jam session
Lovers' rock
Martellato
Mersey beat
Minimalist
New Country
Percussion
Polyhymnia
Polyrhythm
Portamento
Quadrivium
Ragamuffin
Rare groove
Ritornello
Rockabilly
Rocksteady
Seguidilla
Shoegazing
Toccatella

Twelve-tone
Urban blues

11 letters:
Boeremusiek
Concertante
Country rock
Motor rhythm
Passacaglia
Psychobilly
Raggamuffin
Renaissance
Rogues' march
Sinfonietta
Solmisation
Stadium rock
Third stream
Thrash metal
Tin Pan Alley

12 letters:
Blue-eyed soul
Boogie-woogie
Concertstück
Contrapuntal
Divertimento
Electroclash
Late medieval
Neoclassical
Nunc Dimittis
Pralltriller
Western swing

13 letters:
Choral prelude
Detroit techno
Early medieval
Progressional

14 letters:
Durchkomponirt
Rhythm and blues

15 letters:
Durchkomponiert
Musique concrete
Progressive rock

Musical Annie, Arcadian, Azione, Brigadoon, Canorous, Carousel, Cats, Chess, Euphonic, Evergreen, Evita, Gigi, Grease, Hair, Half a Sixpence, Harmonious, Kabuki, Kismet, Lyric, Mame, Melodic, My Fair Lady, Oliver, Opera, Operetta, Oratorio, Orphean, Revue, Showboat, South Pacific, West Side Story

Musical box Juke-box, Polyphon(e), Stereo

MUSICAL INSTRUMENTS

2 letters:
Ax
Gu

3 letters:
Axe
Gue
Kit
Oud
Qin
Saz
Uke
Zel

4 letters:
Buva
Chyn
Crwd
Drum
Erhu
Fife
Gong
Harp
Horn
Kora
Koto
Lure
Lute
Lyre
Moog®
Oboe
Pipa
Rate
Reed
Rote
Sang
Tuba
Vina
Viol
Whip
Zeze

5 letters:
Aulos
Banjo
Bugle
Cello
Clave
Cobza
Corno

Crowd
Crwth
Esraj
Flute
Gaita
Gazog
Guiro
Guqin
Gusla
Gusle
Gusli
Kaval
Kazoo
Labia
Mbira
Naker
Nebel
Organ
Piano
Quena
Rebec
Regal
Sanko
Sansa
Sarod
Shalm
Shawm
Sitar
Stick
Tabla
Tabor
Tenor
Tibia
Veena
Viola
Zanze
Zinke

6 letters:
Antara
Atabal
Biniou
Bisser
Bongos
Citole
Cornet
Cymbal
Euphon
Flugel
Guitar

Kanoon
Maraca
Poogye
Racket
Rebeck
Relish
Ribibe
Sancho
Santir
Santur
Shalme
Shofar
Sittar
Spinet
Syrinx
Tom-tom
Trigon
Vielle
Violin
Yidaki
Zither
Zufolo

7 letters:
Alphorn
Anklong
Bagpipe
Bandore
Bandura
Baryton
Bassoon
Bazooka
Celesta
Celeste
Cembalo
Ceol mor
Chikara
Cithara
Cittern
Clarino
Clarion
Clavier
Clogbox
Console
Cornett
Dichord
Dulcian
Fagotto
Flutina
Gamelan

Gazogka
Gittern
Hautboy
Helicon
High-hat
Kalimba
Kantela
Kantele
Kithara
Klavier
Lyricon
Mandola
Marimba
Musette
Ocarina
Pandora
Pandore
Pandura
Pianola®
Piccolo
Poogyee
Posaune
Rackett
Rellish
Ribible
Sackbut
Sambuca
Samisen
Santour
Sarangi
Saxhorn
Saxtuba
Serpent
Tambour
Tambura
Theorbo
Timbrel
Timpano
Trumpet
Tympany
Ukelele
Ukulele
Vihuela
Violone
Whistle
Zuffolo

8 letters:
Angklung
Archlute

Autoharp®
Barytone
Berimbau
Bombarde
Bouzouki
Calliope
Canorous
Carillon
Charango
Cimbalom
Clarinet
Clarsach
Clavecin
Cornetto
Cornpipe
Cromorna
Cromorne
Crumhorn
Dulcimer
Gemshorn
Guarneri
Guimbard
Handbell
Hautbois
Humstrum
Jew's harp
Key-bugle
Langspel
Lyra-viol
Mandolin
Manzello
Martenot
Melodeon
Melodica
Melodion
Mirliton
Oliphant
Ottavino
Pan pipes
Phorminx
Pianette
Polyphon
Psaltery
Recorder
Reco-reco
Slughorn
Sourdine
Spinette
Squiffer
Sticcado
Sticcato
Surbahar

Tamboura
Tamburin
Tenoroon
Theremin
Triangle
Trichord
Trombone
Virginal
Vocalion
Zambomba
Zampogna

9 letters:
Accordion
Aerophone
Alpenhorn
Balalaika
Bandoneon
Bandurria
Banjulele
Bombardon
Chalumeau
Clarionet
Cornemuse
Decachord
Dulcitone®
Euphonium
Flageolet
Flexatone
Flute-à-bec
Gittarone
Gutbucket
Harmonica
Harmonium
Idiophone
Kent-bugle
Krummhorn
Langspiel
Mandoline
Mellotron®
Monochord
Mouth-harp
Nose flute
Orpharion
Pantaleon
Pastorale
Polyphone
Saxophone
Seraphine
Slughorne
Snare-drum
Sonometer

Sopranino
Steel drum
Stockhorn
Trompette
Vibraharp
Washboard
Welsh harp
Xylophone
Xylorimba

10 letters:
Arpeggione
Bullroarer
Chitarrone
Clavichord
Colascione
Concertina
Cor anglais
Cornettini
Didgeridoo
Flugelhorn
Fortepiano
French horn
Gramophone
Hurdy-gurdy
Kettledrum
Lagerphone
Light organ
Mellophone
Nun's fiddle
Ophicleide
Orpheoreon
Pentachord
Shakuhachi
Small pipes
Sousaphone
Squeeze-box
Stylophone®
Symphonium
Tambourine
Thumb piano
Tin whistle
Vibraphone
Wokka board

11 letters:
Chordophone
Clairschach
Contrabasso
Harmoniphon
Harpsichord
Heckelphone

Nickelodeon
Octave flute
Orchestrina
Orchestrion
Phonofiddle
Player piano
Stock-in-horn
Straduarius
Synthesizer
Trump-marine
Viola d'amore
Violoncello
Wobble-board

12 letters:
Chapman stick®
Chinese block
Clavicembalo
Glockenspiel
Harmonichord
Harmoniphone
Metallophone
Penny-whistle
Sarrusophone
Stock and horn
Stradivarius
Tromba-marina
Tubular bells
Viola da gamba

13 letters:
Contrabassoon
Contrafagotto
Ondes Martenot
Panharmonicon
Physharmonica

14 letters:
Clavicytherium
Glass harmonica
Hawaiian guitar
Jingling Johnny
Ondes musicales
Piano accordion
Swannee whistle
Viola da braccio

15 letters:
Moog synthesiser

18 letters:
Chinese temple block

Music-hall Alhambra, Disco, Empire, Odeon

Musician(s), Musicologist Accompanist, Arion, Arist, Armstrong, Bassist, Beiderbecke, Boy band, Brain, Buononcini, Carmichael, Casals, Chanter, Clapton, Combo, → **COMPOSER**, Conductor, Crowder, Duet, Ensemble, Executant, Flautist, Gate, Group, Grove, Guido d'Arezzo, Guslar, Handel, Jazzer, Jazzman, Joplin, Keyboardist, Klezmer, Labelmate, Lyrist, Maestro, Mahler, Mariachi, Menuhin, Minstrel, Muso, Noisenik, Nonet, Octet, Orphean, Percussionist, Pianist, Pied Piper, Quartet, Quintet, Rapper, Reed(s)man, Répétiteur, Rubinstein, Satchmo, Schonberg, Septet, Session, Sextet, Sideman, Spohr, String, Techno, Tortelier, Troubador, Trouvère, Violinist, Waits

Musk Civet, Mimulus, Must

Musket Brown Bess, Caliver, Carabine, Eyas, Flintlock, Fusil, Gingal(l), Hawk, Jezail, Jingal, Nyas, Queen's-arm, Weapon

Musketeer Aramis, Athos, D'Artagnan, Fusilier, Ja(e)ger, Porthos, Rifleman, Sam

Muslim (ritual), Moslem Alaouite, Alawite, Ali, Almohad(e), Balochi, Baluchi, Berber, Black, Caliph, Dato, Dervish, Druse, Fatimid, Ghazi, Hadji, Hafiz, Hajji, Hamas, Hezbollah, Hizbollah, Hizbullah, Iranian, Islamic, Ismaili, Karmathian, Khotbah, Khotbeh, Khutbah, Mahometan, Mawlawi, Meivievi, Mog(h)ul, Mohammedan, Moor, Morisco, Moro, Muezzin, Mufti, Mughal, Mus(s)ulman, Mutazilite, Nawab, Panislam, Paynim, Pomak, Said, Saracen, Say(y)id, Senus(s)i, Shafiite, Shia(h), Shiite, Sofi, Sonnite, Sufi, Sulu, Sunna, Sunni(te), Tajik, Turk, Umma(h), Wahabee, Wahabi(te), Wahhabi, Whirling Dervish

Muslin Butter, Cloth, Coteline, Gurrah, Jamdani, Leno, Mousseline, Mull, Nainsook, Organdie, Persienne, Swiss, Tarlatan, Tiffany

Musquash Ondatra

Mussel(s) Bearded, Bivalve, Clabby-doo, Clam, Clappy-doo, Deerhorn, Duck, Edible, Horse, Modiolus, Moules marinières, Mytilus, Naiad, Niggerhead, Pearl, Scalp, Swan, Unio, Unionidae, Zebra

Mussolini Benini, Il Duce

Mussorgsky Modest

Must(y) Amok, Essential, Foughty, Fousty, Froughy, Frowsty, Frowy, Funky, Fust, Gotta, Man, Maun(na), Mote, Mould, Mucid, Mun, Need(s)-be, Shall, Should, Stum, Vinew, Wine

▷ **Must** *may indicate* an anagram

Mustard Black, Brown, Charlock, Cress, English, Erysimum, French, Garlic, Gas, Nitrogen, Praiseach, Quinacrine, Runch, Sarepta, Sauce-alone, Senvy, Treacle, Wall, White, Wild, Wintercress

Mustard plaster Sinapism

Musteline Atoc, Atok, Skunk

Muster Array, Assemble, Bangtail, Call up, Mass, Peacock, Raise, Rally, Really, Recruit, Round-up, Wappenshaw

Mutability Wheel

Mutate, Mutant, Mutation Auxotroph(ic), Change, Heterogenesis, Polybasic, Saltation, Somatic, Sport, Suppressor, Terata, Transform, Vowel

▷ **Mutation** *may indicate* an anagram

Mute(d) Deaden, Dumb, Harpo, Noiseless, Saulie, Silent, Sorda, Sordino, Sordo, Sourdine, Stifle, Stop

Mutilate(d), Mutilation Castrate, Concise, Deface, Dismember, Distort, Garble, Hamble, Injure, Maim, Mangle, Mayhem, Obtruncate, Riglin, Tear

▷ **Mutilate(d)** *may indicate* an anagram

Mutineer, Mutiny Bounty, Caine, Christian, Curragh, Indian, Insurrection, Jhansi, Meerut, Nore, Pandy, → **REVOLT**, Rising, Sepoy

Mutter(ing) Chunter, Fremescent, Grumble, Maunder, Mumble, Mump, Murmur, Mussitate, Rhubarb, Roin, Royne, Rumble, Sotto voce, Whittie-whattie, Witter

Mutton Braxy, Colonial goose, Em, Ewes, Fanny Adams, Gigot, Macon, Rack, Saddle, Sheep, Theave, Traik

Mutual (aid) Common, Complementary, Interplay, Log-roll, Reciprocal, Symbiosis
Muzzle Decorticate, Gag, Jaw, Mouth, Restrain, Snout
My Begorra, Blimey, By Jove, Christ, Coo, Gad, Gee, Gemini, Golly, Gorblimey, Gosh, Great
Scott, Ha, Lor, Lumme, M, Musha, Odso, Oh, Our, Tush
Myna(h) Hill, Stare, Starling
Mynheer Stadholder
Myopia, Myopic Hidebound, Mouse-sight, Narrow, Short-sighted, Thick-eyed
Myriad Host, Zillion
Myristic Nutmeg
Myrrh Stacte
Myrtle Bog, Callistemon, Crape, Creeping, Crepe, Eucalyptus, Gale, Jambolana,
Tasmanian, Tooart, Trailing, Tuart
Mysterious, Mystery Abdabs, Abdals, Acroamatic, Arcane, Arcanum, Cabbala, Closed
book, Craft, Creepy, Cryptic, Dark, Deep, Delphic, Eleusinian, Enigma, Esoteric, G(u)ild,
Grocer, Incarnation, Inscrutable, Miracle, Mystagogue, Numinous, Occult, Original sin,
Orphic, Penetralia, Recondite, Riddle, Sacrament, → SECRET, Shady, Telestic, Trinity,
UFO, Uncanny, Unearthly, Unexplained, Whodunit
▷ **Mysterious(ly)** *may indicate* an anagram
Mystic (word), Mystical Abraxas, Agnostic, Cab(e)iri, Eckhart, Epopt, Fakir, Familist,
Gnostic, Hesychast, Mahatma, New Age, Occultist, Quietism, Rasputin, Secret, Seer,
Sofi, Sufi, Swami, Tantrist, Theosophy, Transcendental, Zohar
Mystify Baffle, Bamboozle, Bewilder, Metagrabolise, Metagrobolise, Perplex, Puzzle
Myth(ology), Mythological, Mythical (beast) Allegory, Atlantis, Behemoth,
Bunyip, Centaur, Cockatrice, Dragon, Dreamtime, Euhemerism, Fable, Fantasy,
Fictitious, Folklore, Garuda, Geryon, Griffin, Hippocampus, Impundulu, Kelpie, Kylin,
Legend, Leviathan, Lore, Lyonnesse, Otnit, Pantheon, Pegasus, Phoenix, Sasquatch,
Sea horse, Sea serpent, Selkie, Solar, Speewah, Sphinx, Sun, Tarand, Therianthropic,
Thunderbird, Tokoloshe, Tragelaph, Unicorn, Urban, Wivern, Wyvern, Yale, Yeti

Nn

N Name, Nitrogen, Noon, North, November
Nab Arrest, Capture, Collar, Confiscate, Grab, Seize
Nabob Deputy, Nawab, Wealthy
Nadir Bottom, Depths, Dregs, Minimum
Nag(ging) Badger, Bidet, Brimstone, Callet, Cap, Captious, Complain, Fret, Fuss, Harangue, Harp, Henpeck, Horse, Jade, Jaw, Keffel, Peck, Pester, Pick on, Plague, Rosinante, Rouncy, → SCOLD, Tit, Xant(h)ippe, Yaff
Nail(ed) Brad, Brod, Catch, Clinker, Clout, Coffin, Fasten, Frost, Hob, Horse, Keratin, Onyx, Pin, Rivet, Screw, Secure, Seize, Shoe, Sisera, Sixpenny, Sparable, Sparrow-bill, Spick, Spike, Sprig, Staple, Stub, Stud, Tack(et), Talon, Tenpenny, Tenterhook, Thumb, Tingle, Toe, Unguis, Wire
Naive(té) Artless, Dewy-eyed, Green(horn), Guileless, Gullible, Ingenuous, Innocence, Open, Pollyanna, Simpliste, Simplistic, Starry-eyed, Trusting, Unsophisticated, Wide-eyed
Naked(ness) Adamical, Artless, Bare, Blunt, Buff, Clear, Cuerpo, Defenceless, Encuerpo, Exposed, Gymno-, Kaal gat, Nature, Nuddy, Nude, Querpo, Raw, Scud, Simple, Skyclad, Stark(ers), Uncovered
Namby-pamby Milksop, Nance, Sissy, Weak, Weakling, White-shoe
Name(d), Names Agnomen, Alias, Allonym, Anonym, Appellation, Appoint, Attribute, Baptise, Behight, Byline, Call, Celeb(rity), Christen, Cite, Cleep, Clepe, Cognomen, Day, Designate, Dinges, Dingus, Dit, Domain, Dub, Entitle, Epithet, Eponym, Exonym, Family, First, Font, Generic, Given, Handle, Hete, Hight, Hypocorism, Identify, Identity, Label, Maiden, Marque, Masthead, Mention, Metronymic, Middle, Moni(c)ker, Mud, N, Nap, Nemn, Nempt, Nom, Nomen(clature), Noun, Onomastics, Onymous, Patronymic, Pennant, Personage, Pet, Place, Praenomen, Proper, Proprietary, Pseudonym, Quote, Red(d), Repute, Scilicet, Sign, Signature, Sir, Specify, Stage, Street, Subdomain, Substantive, Tag, Tautonym, Teknonymy, Term, → TITLE, Titular, Titule, Toponymy, Trade, Trivial
Name-dropper Eponym
Nameless Anon, Unchrisom
Namely Ie, Sc, Scilicet, To-wit, Videlicet, Viz
Namesake Homonym
Name unknown Anon, A N Other, NU
Namibian Herero
Nancy Coddle, Effeminate, Milksop
Nanny Ayah, Foster, Goat, Nurse, Wet-nurse
Naos Cell(a)
Nap(py) Ale, Bonaparte, Diaper, Doze, Drowse, Fluff, Frieze(d), Fuzz, Game, Happen, Hippin(g), Kip, Moze, Nod, Oose, Ooze, Oozy, Power, Put(t), Shag, Siesta, → SLEEP, Slumber, Snooze, Tease, Teasel, Teaze, Terry, Tipsy, Tuft
Nape Niddick, Noddle, Nucha, Scrag, Scruff, Scuff, Scuft
Napier Logarithm
Napkin Cloth, Diaper, Doily, Doyley, Linen, Muckender, Paper, Sanitary, Serviette, Table
Napless Threadbare
Napoleon Badinguet, Bonaparte, Boustrapa, Cognac, Coin, Consul, Corporal Violet, Corsican, December, Little Corporal, Nantz, Nap, Pig, Rantipole, Solo

▷ **Napoleon** *may indicate* a pig
Napper Bonce, Shearman
Narcissus Echo, Egocentric, Jonquil
Narcotic Ava, B(h)ang, Benj, Charas, Churrus, Coca, Codeine, Dagga, Datura, Dope,
→ DRUG, Heroin, Hop, Kava, Laudanum, Mandrake, Marijuana, Meconium, Methadone,
Morphia, Narceen, Narceine, Nicotine, Opiate, Opium, Pituri, Sedative, Tea, Tobacco,
Trional
Nark Grass, Inform, Irritate, Nose, Pique, Roil, Squealer, Stag
Narrate, Narration, Narrative, Narrator Allegory, Anecdote, Cantata, Describe,
Diegesis, Fable, History, Ishmael, Oblique, Periplus, Plot, Raconteur, Récit, Recite,
Recount, Saga, Sagaman, Scheherazade, Splatterpunk, Story, Tell, Thanatography,
Voice-over
Narrow(ing), Narrow-minded Alf, Babbitt, Bigoted, Borné, Bottleneck, Constringe,
Cramp, Ensiform, Grundy(ism), Hairline, Hidebound, Illiberal, Insular, Kyle, Limited,
Meagre, Nary, One-idead, Parochial, Phimosis, Pinch, Pinch-point, Provincial, Prudish,
Puritan, Scant, Sectarian, Shrink, Slender, Slit, Specialise, Squeak, Stenosed, Strait,
Straiten, Strait-laced, Strict, Suburban, Verkramp, Wafer-thin, Waist
Narwhal Monodon
Nasal Adenoidal, Rhinolalia, Sonorant, Twang
Nash Beau
Nashville Bath
Nastiness, Nasty Disagreeable, Drevill, Filth, Fink, Ghastly, Lemon, Lo(a)th,
Malign(ant), Noisome, Noxious, Obscene, Odious, Offensive, Ogreish, Ribby, Scummy,
Sif, Sordid, Unholy, Vile, Virose
Nat(haniel) Hawthorne, Winkle
Natal Inborn, Native, Patrial
Natant Afloat, Swimming
Nation(s), National(ist), Nationalism Anthem, Baathist, Broederbond, Casement,
Chetnik, Country, Cuban, Debt, De Valera, Eta, Federal, Five, Folk, Grand, Hindutva,
Indian, IRA, Israeli, Jingoist, Kuomintang, Land, Malcolm X, Mexican, Oman, Pamyat,
Parnell, Patriot, → PEOPLE, Plaid Cymru, Polonia, Race, Rainbow, Risorgimento,
Scottish, Shiv Sena, Six, SNP, Subject, Swadeshi, Timor-Leste, Tonga, Tribespeople,
Turk, United, Vanuatu, Vatican City, Verkrampte, Vietminh, Wafd, Yemini, Young
Ireland, Young Turk, Zionist
Native(s) Abo(rigin), Aborigine, African, Amerind, Annamese, Arab, Ascian, Australian,
Autochthon, Aztec, Basuto, Belonging, Bengali, Boy, Bushman, Cairene, Carib, Carioca,
Chaldean, Citizen, Colchester, Conch, Creole, Criollo, Domestic, Dyak, Edo, Enchorial,
Eskimo, Fleming, Fuzzy-wuzzy, Genuine, Habitual, Home-bred, Inborn, Inca, Indigene,
Indigenous, Inhabitant, Intuitive, John Chinaman, Kaffir, Libyan, Local, Malay, Maori,
Mary, Micronesian, Moroccan, Norwegian, Oyster, Polack, Portuguese, Scythian, Son,
Spaniard, Te(i)an, Thai, Tibetan, Uzbeg, Uzbek, Whitstable, Yugoslav
Nativity Birth, Jataka, Putz
Natron Urao
Natter Chat, Gossip, Jack, Prate
Natty Bumppo, Chic, Dapper, Leatherstocking, Smart, Spruce
Natural(ly), Naturalise(d), Naturalism Altogether, Artless, Ass, Denizen, Easy,
Endenizen, Genuine, Green, Gut, Homely, Idiot, Illegitimate, Inborn, Inbred, Indigenous,
Ingenerate, Inherent, Innate, Instinctive, Moron, Native, Nidget, Nitwit, Nude, Ordinary,
Organic, Prat, Real, Simpleton, Simpliciter, Sincere, True, Undyed, Untaught, Verism
Naturalist Banks, Bates, Buffon, Darwin, De Lamarck, Durrell, Wallace, White
Nature Adam, Akin, Character, Disposition, Esse(nce), Ethos, Haecceity, Human,
Hypostasis, Inbeing, Inscape, Manhood, Mould, Quiddity, Quintessence, Root, Second,
SN, Temperament
Naught Cypher, Failure, Nil, Nothing, Zero

Naughty Bad, Disobedient, Girly, Improper, Indecorous, Light, Marietta, Nonny, Offender, Rascal, Remiss, Spright, Sprite, Wayward

Nausea, Nauseous Disgust, Fulsome, Malaise, Queasy, Sickness, Squeamish, Wamble, Wambly

Nave Aisle, Apse, Centre, Hub, Modiolus, Nef

Navel Belly-button, Jaffa, Naff, Nave, Omphalos, Orange, Tummy button, Umbilicus

Navigate, Navigator Albuquerque, Baffin, Bering, Bougainville, Cabot, Cartier, Columbus, Control, Cook, Da Gama, Davis, Dias, Direct, Drake, Franklin, Frobisher, Gilbert, Hartog, Haul, Henry, Hudson, Keel, Magellan, Navvy, Orienteer, Pilot, Raleigh, Sail, Star-read, → **STEER**, Tasman, Traverse, Vancouver, Vespucci, Weddell

Navigation (aid, system) Asdic, Cabotage, Celestial, Decca, Dectra, Echosounder, Fido, Gee, Inertial, Inland, Loran, Loxodromics, Navarho, Omnirange, Portolan(o), Portulan, Radar, Satnav, Seamark, Shoran, Tacan, Teleran®, Vor

Navvy Workhorse

Navy, Naval AB, Armada, Blue, Fleet, French, Maritime, Merchant, N, Red, RN, Senior Service, Wavy, White squadron, Wren

Nawab Huzoor, Nabob, Viceroy

Nazi Brownshirt, Gauleiter, Hess, Hitler, Jackboot, SS, Stormtrooper, Third Reich, Wer(e)wolf

NB Niobium, Nota bene

NCO Bombardier, Corp(oral), Havildar, Noncom, Orderly, Pipe-major, Sergeant, SM

Neanderthal Mousterian

Neap Low, Tide

Neapolitan Ice

Near(er), Nearest, Nearby, Nearly, Nearness About, Adjacent, All-but, Almost, Anigh, Approach, Approximate, Beside, By, Close, Cy pres, Degree, Even, Ewest, Feckly, Forby, Gain, Handy, Hither, Imminent, Inby(e), Mean, Miserly, Most, Narre, Neist, Next, Nie, Niggardly, Nigh, Oncoming, Outby, Propinquity, Proximity, Short-range, Stingy, Thereabout(s), To, Upon, Warm, Well-nigh

Neat(ly), Neatness Bandbox, Cattle, Clean-cut, Clever, Dainty, Dapper, Deft, Dink(y), Doddy, Donsie, Elegant, Featly, Feat(e)ous, Featuous, Gayal, Genty, Gyal, Intact, Jemmy, Jimpy, Lower, Nett, Nifty, Ninepence, Orderly, Ox(en), Perjink, Preppy, Pretty, Rother, Saola, Shipshape, Short(horn), Smug, Snod, Spick and span, Spruce, Straight, → **TIDY**, Trig, Trim, Uncluttered, Unwatered, Well-groomed

Neb Beak, Bill, Nose, Snout

Nebula, Nebulous Aeriform, Celestial, Cloudy, Dark, Emission, Gum, Hazy, Horsehead, Obscure, Planetary, Reflection, Shadowy, Vague

Necessary, Necessarily Bog, Cash, De rigueur, → **ESSENTIAL**, Estovers, Imperative, Important, Indispensable, Intrinsic, Loo, Money, Moolah, Needful, Ought, Perforce, Prerequisite, Requisite, Vital, Wherewithal

Necessitate, Necessity Ananke, Compel, Constrain, Cost, Emergency, Entail, Exigent, Fate, Indigence, Logical, Mathematical, Moral, Must, Natural, Need, Need-be, Oblige, Perforce, Require, Requisite, Staple

Neck(ed) Bottle, Brass, Canoodle, Cervical, Cervix, Channel, Col, Crag, Craig, Crew, Crop, Cuff, Embrace, Ewe, Gall, Gorgerin, Halse, Hause, Hawse, Inarm, Inclip, Isthmus, Kiss, Mash, Nape, Pet, Polo, Rack, Rubber, Scoop, Scrag, Scruff, Smooch, Snog, Stiff, Strait, Surgical, Swan, Swire, Theorbo, Torticollis, Trachelate, Vee, Volcanic

▷ **Necking** *may indicate* one word around another

Necklace Afro-chain, Anodyne, Bib, Brisingamen, Chain, Choker, Collar, Corals, Laval(l)ière, Lunula, Mangalsutra, Negligee, Pearls, Rope, Sautoir, String, Torc, Torque

Neckline Boat, Collar, Cowl, Crew, Décolletage, Lanyard, Palter, Plunging, Scoop, Sweetheart, Turtle, Vee

Neckwear Ascot, Barcelona, Boa, Bow, Collar, Cravat, Fur, Rail, Steenkirk, Stock, Tie

Necromancer Goetic, Magician, Ormandine, Osmand, Witch, Wizard

Necrosis Infarct, Sphacelus
Nectar Ambrosia, Amrita, Honey, Mead
Ned(dy) Donkey, Kelly, Ludd
Need(ed), Needy Beggarly, Call, Demand, Desiderata, Egence, Egency, Exigency, Gap, Gerundive, Impecunious, Indigent, → LACK, Mister, Prerequisite, Pressing, PRN, Require, Special, Strait, Strapped, Want
Needle(s) Acerose, Acicular, Aciform, Acupuncture, Anger, Between, Bodkin, Cleopatra's, Darner, Darning, Dip, Dipping, Dry-point, Electric, Etching, Goad, Gramophone, Hagedorn, Hype, Hypodermic, Ice, Icicle, Inoculate, Knitting, Leucotome, Magnetic, Miff, Monolith, Neeld, Neele, Netting, Obelisk, Packing, Pine, Pinnacle, Pique, Pointer, Prick, R(h)aphis, Sew, Sharp, Spanish, Spicule, Spike, Spine, Spud, Stylus, Tattoo, Tease, Thorn, Wire
Needlewoman Cleopatra, Seamstress
Needlework Applique, Baste, Crewel, Drawn(-thread), Embroidery, Fag(g)oting, Fancy work, Gros point, Lacet, Mola, Patchwork, Petit point, Piqué, Plainwork, Rivière, Sampler, Smocking, Spanish, Tapestry, Tattoo, White-seam, Woolwork, Worsted-work
Ne'er-do-well Badmash, Budmash, Bum, Good-for-nothing, Scallywag, Scullion, Shiftless, Skellum, Waster, Wastrel
Negation, Negative Ambrotype, Anion, Apophatic, Cathode, Denial, Double, Downside, Enantiosis, False, Infinitant, Ne, No, Non, Nope, Nullify, Pejorative, Photograph, Refusal, Resinous, Unresponsive, Veto, Yin
Neglect(ed), Neglectful, Negligence, Negligent Careless, Casual, Cinderella, Contributory, Cuff, Default, Dereliction, Disregard, Disuse, Failure, Forget, Forlorn, For(e)slack, G-devant, Heedless, Inadvertence, Inattention, Incivism, Laches, Malpractice, Misprision, Omission, Oversight, Pass, Pass-up, Rack and ruin, → REMISS, Scamp, Shirk, Slight, Slipshod, Undone, Unilateral, Unnoticed, Waif, Wanton
▷ **Neglected** *may indicate* an anagram
Negligee Déshabillé, Manteau, Mob, Nightgown, Peignoir, Robe
Negligible Fig, Minimal
Negotiate, Negotiator Arbitrate, Arrange, Bargain, Barter, Clear, Confer, Deal, Diplomat, Haggle, Intercede, Interdeal, Intermediary, Liaise, Manoeuvre, Mediator, Parley, Petition, Talk, Trade, Transact, Treat(y), Tret, Weather
Negro(id) → AFRICAN, Baganda, Bambara, Barotse, Bemba, Bergdama, Bini, Black, Blackamoor, Buck, Chewa, Creole, Cuffee, Cuffy, Damara, Dinge, Duala, Dyula, Ebon(y), Edo, Efik, Ethiop, Ewe, Fang, Ga, Ganda, Gullah, Hausa, Hottentot, Hutu, Ibibio, Ibo, Igbo, Igorot, Jim Crow, Kikuyu, Kongo, Luba, Luganda, Malinke, Maninke, Mestee, Moke, Moor, Mossi, Mustee, Ndebele, Nilote, Nupe, Nyanja, Nyoro, Ovambo, Pondo, Quashee, Quashie, Sambo, Snowball, Sotho, Spade, Susu, Temne, Thick-lips, Tiv, Tonga, Tsonga, Tswana, Twi, Uncle Tom, Venda, Watu(t)si, Wolof, Xhosa, Yoruba, Zambo, Zulu
Negus Emperor, Rumfruction, Selassie
Nehru Pandit
Neigh Bray, Hinny, Nicker, Whicker, Whinny
Neighbour(ly), Neighbouring, Neighbours Abut(ter), Adjoin, Alongside, Amicable, Bor, Border, But, Friendly, Joneses, Nearby, Next-door, Vicinal
Neighbourhood(s) Acorn®, Area, Community, District, Environs, Locality, Precinct, Vicinage, Vicinity
Neither Nor
Nell(ie), Nelly Bly, Dean, Trent
Nelson Columnist, Eddy, Horatio
Nemesis Alastor, Avenger, Deserts, Downfall, Fate, Retribution, Revenge
Neodymium Nd
Neolithic Avebury, Halafian, Skara Brae, Stonehenge
Neon Ne
Nepalese Gurkha

Neper N
Nephrite Yu
Nepotism Kin, Partisan, Patronage
Neptune God, Planet, Poseidon
Neptunium Np
Nerd Anorak, Geek, Otaku
Nereid Cymodoce, Nymph, Panope
Nerve(s), Nervous(ness), Nervure, Nerve centre, Nervy Abdabs, Abducens, Accessory, Acoustic, Afferent, Aflutter, Afraid, Alveolar, Antsy, Appestat, Auditory, Autonomic, Axon, Baroreceptor, Bottle, Bouton, Brass neck, Buccal, Butterflies, Chord, Chutzpah, Collywobbles, Column, Commissure, Cones, Courage, Cranial, Cyton, Dendron, Depressor, Edgy, Effector, Efferent, Electrotonus, Epicritic, Excitor, Facial, Fearful, Fidgety, Gall, Ganglion, Glossopharyngeal, Grit, Guts, Habdabs, Heart-string, High, Highly-strung, Hyp, Hypoglossal, Impudence, Jitters, Jittery, Jumpy, Median, Mid-rib, Motor, Moxie, Myelon, Nappy, Neck, Neurological, Nidus, Oculomotor, Olfactory, On edge, Optic, Pavid, Perikaryon, Pons, Proprioceptor, Protopathic, Rad, Radial, Receptor, Restiform, Restless, Sacral, Sangfroid, Sass, Sauce, Sciatic, Screaming abdabs, Screaming meemies, Sensory, Shaky, Shpilkes, Solar plexus, Somatic, Splanchnic, Spunk, Squirrel(l)y, Stage fright, Steel, Strung-up, Sympathetic, Synapse, Tense, Timorous, Tizzy, Toey, Tongue-tied, Trembler, Tremulous, Trigeminal, Trochlear, Twitchy, Ulnar, Uptight, Vagus, Vapours, Vasodilator, Vestibular, Vestibulocochlear, Wandering, Willies, Windy, Wired, Wittery, Yips
Nervous disease, Nervous disorder Chorea, Epilepsy, Neuritis, Tarantism, Tetany
▷ **Nervously** *may indicate* an anagram
Ness Cape, Headland, Ras
Nessus Centaur
Nest Aerie, Aery, Aiery, Ayrie, Bike, Bink, Brood, Byke, Cabinet, Cage, Caliology, Clutch, Dray, Drey, Eyrie, Eyry, Guns, Hive, Lodge, Love, Nid, Nide, Nidify, Nidus, Norwegian, Sett, Termitarium, Turkey, Wurley
Nestle Burrow, Coorie, Cose, Courie, Cuddle, Nuzzle, Rest, Snug(gle)
Nestor Counsellor, Kea, King, Parrot, Sage
Net(ting), Nets, Network(ing), Networker Anastomosis, Bamboo, BR, Bunt, Bus, Butterfly, Cast, Casting, Catch, Caul, Clap, Clathrate, Clear, Co-ax(ial), Cobweb, → **COMPUTER NETWORK**, Craquelure, Crinoline, Criss-cross, Crossover, Diane, Drift, Earn, Eel-set, Enmesh, Equaliser, Fetch, File server, Filet, Final, Fish, Fisherman, Flew, Flue, Fret, Fyke, Gain, Gill, → **GRID**, Hammock, Heliscoop, Honeycomb, Hose, Insect, Kiddle, Lace, LAN, Land, Landing, Lattice, Leap, Line, Linin, Mains, Malines, Mattress, Maze, → **MESH**, Mist, Mosquito, Mycelium, Nerve, Neural, Neuropil, Old boys', PCN, Plexus, Portal system, Pound, Pout, Purse-seine, Quadripole, Reseau, Rete, Retiary, Reticle, Reticulate, Reticulum, Ring, Safety, Sagene, Scoop, Screen, Sean, Seine, Senior, Set(t), Shark, Skype®, Snood, Speed, Stake, Sweep-seine, Symplast, System, Tangle, Tela, Telex, Tissue, Toil, Torpedo, Trammel, Trap, Trawl, Trepan, Tulle, Tunnel, Wire
Netball Let
Nether Below, Inferior, Infernal, Lower, Under
Nettle(rash) Anger, Annoy, Day, Dead, Hemp, Hives, Horse, Irritate, Labiate, Nark, Ongaonga, Pellitory, Pique, Ramee, Rami, Ramie, Rhea, Rile, Roman, Ruffle, Sting, Urtica(ceae), Urticaria
Neuralgia, Neuritis Migraine, Pleurodynia, Sciatica, Tic
Neurosis Combat, Compulsion, Hang up, Obsessive-compulsive, Shellshock, Trichotillomania
Neuter Castrate, Gib, Impartial, Neutral, Sexless, Spay
Neutral(ise) Alkalify, Angel gear, Buffer zone, Counteract, Degauss, Grey, Impartial, Inactive, Schwa, Sheva, Shiva, Unbiased
Neutron(s) Delayed, Fast, Nucleon, Prompt, Slow, Thermal, Virgin

Never(more) As if, Nary, Nathemo(re), No more, Nowise, St Tibb's Eve

Never-ending Age-long

Never mind Nix my dolly

Nevertheless Algate, All the same, Anyhow, But, Even, Howbeit, However, Quand même, Still, Tout de même, Yet

New(s), Newborn, News agency Avant garde, Bulletin, Communique, Copy, Coranto, Dope, Euphobia, Evangel, Flash, Forest, Fresh, Fudge, Gen, Green, Griff, Info, Initiate, Innovation, Intake, Intelligence, Itar Tass, Item, Kerygma, Latest, Mint, Modern, N, Novel, Oil(s), Original, PA, Paragraph, Pastures, Pristine, Propaganda, Raw, Reborn, Recent, Report, Reuter, Scoop, Sidebar, Snippet, Span, Splash, Split, Stranger, Tass, Teletext®, Tidings, Ultramodern, Unco, Update, Usenet, Wire service, Word, Young

▷ **New** *may indicate* an anagram

New boy Gyte

Newcomer Dog, Freshman, Griffin, Immigrant, Jackaroo, Jackeroo, Jillaroo, Johnny-come-lately, L, Learner, Newbie, Novice, Parvenu, Pilgrim, Settler, Tenderfoot, Upstart

Newfoundland Dog, Nana, Vinland

Newgate Calendar

Newly wed Benedick, Benedict, Bride, Groom, Honeymooner, Neogamist

Newman Cardinal, Noggs, Paul

New moon Rosh Chodesh

New Orleans Big easy

Newsman, News-reader Announcer, Editor, Journalist, Legman, Press, Reporter, Sub, Sysop

Newsmonger, News-vendor Butcher, Gossip, Quidnunc

Newspaper Beast, Big Issue, Blat(t), Broadsheet, Compact, Courier, Daily, Express, Fanzine, Feuilleton, Freesheet, Gazette, Guardian, Heavy, Herald, Intelligencer, Izvestia, Journal, Jupiter, Le Monde, Mercury, National, Organ, Patent inside, Patent outside, Post, Pravda, Press, Print, Rag, Red-top, Scandal sheet, Scotsman, Sheet, Spoiler, Squeak, Sun, Tabloid, Today, Yellow Press

Newsreel Actualities

Newsworthy Topical

Newt(s) Ask(er), Eft, Evet, Swift, Triton, Urodela

Newton N

New World USA

New Year Hogmanay, Ne'er-day, Rosh Hashana(h), Tet

New York(er) Big Apple, Bronx, Coney Island, Gotham, Knickerbocker, Manhattan, Queens

New Zealand(er) Aotearoa, Diggers, Enzed, Jafa, Kiwi, Maori, Mooloo, Moriori, .nz, Pakeha, Pig Island, Ronz(er), Shagroon, Zelanian

Next Adjacent, Adjoining, After, Alongside, Beside, By, Following, Immediate, Later, Nearest, Neighbour, Neist, Proximate, Proximo, Sine, Subsequent, Syne, Then, Thereafter

Nib(s) Cocoa, J, Pen, Point, Tip

Nibble Bite, Brouse, Browse, Byte, Canapé, Crop, Eat, Gnaw, Knap(ple), Moop, Moup, Munch, Nag, Nepit, Nosh, Peck, Pick, Snack

Niblick Wedge

Nice(ly), Nicety Accurate, Amene, Appealing, Cool, Dainty, Fastidious, Fine, Finical, Genteel, Lepid, Mooi, Ninepence, Pat, Pleasant, Precise, Quaint, Rare, Refined, Subtil(e), Subtle, Sweet, T, To a t

Niche Alcove, Almehrahb, Almery, Ambry, Apse, Aumbry, Awmrie, Awmry, Columbarium, Cranny, Exedra, Fenestella, Mihrab, Recess, Slot

Nicholas Santa

Nick(ed) Appropriate, Arrest, Bin, Blag, Can, Chip, Cly, Colin, Copshop, Crib, Cut, Denay,

Dent, Deny, → **DEVIL**, Erose, Groove, Hoosegow, Kitty, Knock, Nab, Nap, Nim, Nock, Notch, Pinch, Pocket, Pook, Pouk, Prison, Run in, Scratch, Serrate, Sneak, → **STEAL**, Steek, Swan-upping, Swipe, Thieve, Whip, Wirricow, Worricow, Worrycow

Nickel (silver) Coin, Garnierite, Jitney, Millerite, Ni, Packfong, Paktong, Zaratite

Nicker Bonduc, Neigh, Whinny

Nickname Alias, Byname, Byword, Cognomen, Monicker, So(u)briquet, To-name

Nicotine Tobacco, Weed

Nifty Smart, Stylish

Niger RN

Nigeria(n) Biafran, Cross River, Efik, Hausa, Ibibio, Ibo, Igbo, .ng, Nupe, Tiv, WAN, Yoruba

Niggard(ly) Dry-fist, Illiberal, Mean, Miser, Near-(be)gaun, Nippy, Nirlie, Nirlit, Parsimonious, Penny wise, Pinchcommons, Pinchgut, Pinchpenny, Scrunt, Skinflint, Tightwad

Niggle Carp, Gripe, Nag, Potter, Trifle

Night(s), Nightfall Acronical, Acronychal, Arabian, Burns, Darkling, Darkmans, First, Gaudy, Guest, Guy Fawkes, Hen, Leila, Nacht, Nicka-nan, Nutcrack, Nyx, Opening, School, Sleepover, Stag, Twelfth, Twilight, Walpurgis, Watch, White

Night-blindness Day-sight, Nyctalopia

Night-cap Biggin, Cocoa, Kilmarnock cowl, Nip, Pirnie, Sundowner

Nightclub Boite de nuit, Clip joint, Dive, Honkytonk, Hot spot

Night-dew Serein, Serene

Nightdress Baby doll, Wylie-coat

Nightingale Bulbul, Florence, Frog, Jugger, Lind, Philomel, Philomena, Scutari, Swedish, Watch

Nightjar Chuck-will's-widow, Churn-owl, Evejar, Fern-owl, Goatsucker, Poorwill, Potoo

Night-light Moonbeam

Nightmare, Nightmarish Cacod(a)emon, Ephialtes, Incubus, Kafkaesque, Oneirodynia, Phantasmagoria

Night-rider Revere

Nightshade Atropin(e), Belladonna, Bittersweet, Black, Circaea, Deadly, Dwale, Enchanter's, Henbane, Morel, Solanum, Woody

Nightwatchman Charley, Charlie, Rug-gown

Nightwork Lucubrate

Nihilist Anarchist, Red, Sceptic

Nil Nothing, Nought, Zero

Nile Albert, Blue, Luvironza, Victoria, White

Nimble(ness), Nimbly Active, → **AGILE**, Alert, Deft, Deliver, Fleet, Legerity, Light, Light-footed, Lissom(e), Lithe, Quiver, Sciolto, Springe, Spry, Supple, Sure-footed, Swack, Wan(d)le, Wannel, Wight, Ya(u)ld

Nimbus Aura, Aureole, Cloud, Gloriole, Halo

Nimrod Hunter

Nincompoop Ass, Fool, Imbecile, Moron, Ninny, Stupid

Nine, Ninth Choral, Ennead, Muses, Nonary, Nonet, Novenary, Pins, Sancho, Skittles, Tailors, Worthies

Nine hundred Sampi

Nine of diamonds Curse of Scotland

Nineteen(th) Bar, Decennoval

Ninetieth, Ninety N, Nonagesimal

Ninevite Assyrian

Ninny (hammer) Fool, Goose, Idiot, Stupid, Tony

Ninon Nan

Niobium Nb

Nip(per), Nippers Bite, Brat, Check, Chela, Chill, Claw, Cutpurse, Dip, Dram, Fang, Foil,

Gook, Jack Frost, Jap, Lad, Lop, Nep, Nirl, Outsiders, Peck, Pickpocket, Pincers, Pinch, Pook, Pop, Scotch, Sneap, Susan, Tad, Talon, Taste, Tot, Tweak, Urchin, Vice, Vise

Nipa At(t)ap, Palm

Nipple Dug, Grease, Jogger's, Mastoid, Pap, Teat

Nis Brownie, Goblin, Kobold, Sprite

Nit Egg, Insect, Louse

Nit-picking Carping, Pedantry, Quibble

Nitre Saltpetre

Nitric, Nitrogen Azote, Azotic, Gas, N, Quinoline

Nitroglycerine Glonoin, Soup

Nitwit Ass, Flat, Fool, Scatterbrain, Simpleton, → STUPID

No Aikona, Denial, Na(e), Nah, Naw, Negative, Nix, Nope, Nyet, O, Refusal

Noah Arkite, Beery, Utnapishtim

Nob(by) Grandee, Parage, Prince, Swell, Toff

Nobble Dope, Hilch, Injure, Interfere

▷ **Nobbled** *may indicate* an anagram

Nobelium No

Noble(man), Noblewoman, Nobility, Nobly Adela, Adele, Adeline, Aneurin, Aristocrat, Atheling, Baron(et), Baroness, Baronet(ess), Baronne, Bart, Blue blood, Boyar, Brave, Bt, Burgrave, Childe, Contessa, Count, County, Cousin, Daimio, Datuk, Dauphine, Dom, Don, Doucepere, Douzeper(s), Duc, Duke, Duniwassal, Earl, Empress, Eorl, Ethel, Eupatrid, Fine, Galahad, Gent, Glorious, Graf, Grandee, Grandeur, Great, Heroic, Hidalgo, Highborn, Illustrious, Infant, Jarl, Junker, King, Landgrave, Lofty, Lord, Maestoso, Magnate, Magnificent, Magnifico, Manly, Margrave, Marquis, Mona, Nair, Nawab, Nayar, Palatine, Patrician, Patrick, Peer, Rank, Ritter, Rose, Seigneur, Seignior, Sheik(h), Stately, Sublime, Thane, Thegn, Titled, Toiseach, Toisech, Vavasour, Vicomte, Vidame, Viscount, Waldgrave

Noble gas(es) Argon, Helium, Krypton, Neon, Radon, Xenon

Nobody Diarist, Gnatling, Jack-straw, Nebbish, Nemo, None, Nonentity, Nyaff, Pipsqueak, Pooter, Quat, Schlepp, Scoot, Shlep, Zero

Nocturnal (creature) Bat, Galago, Moth, Night, Owl

Nod(ding) Agree, Assent, Beck(on), Bob, Browse, Catnap, Cernuous, Dip, Doze, Drowsy, Headbang, Mandarin, Nutant, Somnolent

Node, Nodular, Nodule Ascending, Boss, Descending, Enhydros, Geode, Knot, Lump, Lymph, Milium, Pea-iron, Ranvier, Root, Septarium, Swelling, Thorn, Tophus, Tubercle

No doubt Iwis, Ywis

Noel Christmas, Coward, Yule

Nog(gin) Ale, Cup, → DRINK, Peg

No go Anergia

No good Dud, NG, Ropy

No-hoper Drongo, Gone goose, Goner

Noise, Noisy Ambient, Babel, Bedlam, Big, Blare, Blat(t), Bleep, Blip, Blue murder, Bobbery, Boing, Boink, Bray, Bruit, Cangle, Charm, Cheep, Chellup, Clam, Clamant, Clamour, Clangour, Clash, Clatter, Clitter, Clutter, Coil, Crackle, Creak, Deen, Din, Dirdum, Discord, Euphonia, Euphony, F, Flicker, Fuss, Hewgh, Howlround, Hubbub, Hue, Hullabaloo, Hum, Hurly-burly, Knocking, Loud, Mush, Obstreperous, Phut, Ping, Pink, Plangent, Quonk, Racket, Raucous, Report, Risp, Roar, Roarie, Roary, Robustious, Rorie, Rort, Rory, Row(dow-dow), Rowdedow, Rowdy(dow)(dy), Rucous, Rumble, Schottky, Schottky-Utis, Scream, Screech, Shindig, Shindy, Shot, Shreek, Shreik, Shriech, Shriek, Slosh, Solar, Sone, Sonorous, Sound, Strepent, Strepitation, Strepitoso, Stridor, Surface, Thermal, Thunder, Tinnitus, Top, Trumpet, Tumult, → UPROAR, VIP, Visual, Vociferous, Whinny, White, Whoomph, Zoom

Noisome Fetid, Invidious, Noxious, Offensive, Rank

No longer Ex, Past

Nomad(ic) Amalekite, Ammonites, Bedawin, Bedu, Bed(o)uin, Berber, Chal, Drifter, Edom(ite), Errant, Fula(h), Gypsy, Hottentot, Hun, Hunter-gatherer, Hyksos, Itinerant, Kurd, Kyrgyz, Lapp, Rom, Rootless, Rover, Saracen, Sarmatian, Strayer, Tsigane, Tsigany, Tuareg, Turk(o)man, Unsettled, Vagabond, Vagrant, Wanderer, Zigan

Noman Ta(r)tar

No man's land Tom Tiddler's ground

Nome Province

Nomenclature Term

Nominal Formal, Onomastic, Titular, Token, Trifling

Nominate, Nomination Appoint, Baptism, Designate, Elect, Postulate, Present, → **PROPOSE**, Slate, Specify, Term

Nomogram Abac

No more Gone, Napoo

Nomothete Enactor, Legislator

Non-Aboriginal Wudjula

Non-attachment Limbo

Non-attender Absentee, Recusant

Non-attribute Ens

Non-believer Atheist, Cynic, Infidel, Sceptic

Non-catalyst Zymogen

Nonchalance, Nonchalant Blasé, Casual, Cool, Debonair, Insouciant, Jaunty, Poco

Non-Christian New-age, Saracen

Noncommittal Pussyfoot, Trimmer

Non-communist West

Non-conductor Insulatro

Non-conformist, Non-conformity Beatnik, Bohemian, Chapel, Deviant, Dissent(er), Dissident, Drop-out, Ebenezer, Enfant terrible, Heresiarch, Heretic, Maverick, Odd-ball, Outlaw, Pantile, Patarine, Rebel, Recusant, Renegade, Renegate, Sectarian, Wesleyan

Nondescript Dull, Grey, Insipid, Neutral, Nyaff

Non-directional Scalar

Non-drip Thixotropic

None Nada, Nary, Nil, Nought, Zero

Nonentity Cipher, Nebbich, Nebbish(er), Nebish, Nobody, Pipsqueak, Quat

Non-essential Adiaphoron, Disposable, Extrinsic, Incidental

Nonesuch Model, Nonpareil, Paradigm, Paragon, Rarity

Nonetheless Mind you

▷ **Nonetheless** *may indicate* an 'o' to be omitted

Non-existent Unbeing, Virtual

Non-finite Verbid

Non-Gypsy Gajo, Gorgio

Non-interference Laissez faire

Non-Jewish Goy, Shegetz, Shi(c)ksa, Shkotzim, Sho(y)getz

Non-juror Usager

Non-Maori Tangata tiriti, Tauiwi

Non-Muslim Raia, Rayah

No-nonsense Hardball, Strict

Non-orthodox Progressive

Nonpareil Nonesuch, Pearl, Peerless, Type, Unequal, Unique

Nonplus(sed) Baffle, Bewilder, Blank, Perplex, Stump

Non-professional Amateur, Laic

Non-radiative Auger

Non-resident Extern, Outlier

Non-runner Scratched, Solid

Nonsense Absurdity, Amphigon, Amphigory, Balderdash, Baloney, Bilge, Bizzo, Blague,

Blah, Blarney, Blat(her), Blatherskite, Blether, Bollocks, Boloney, Bora(c)k, Borax, Bosh, Bs, Bull, Bulldust, Bullshit, Bull's wool, Buncombe, Bunk, Bunkum, Clamjamfr(a)y, Clamjamphrie, Claptrap, Cobblers, Cock, Cockamamie, Cod, Codswallop, Crap, Crapola, Drivel, Dust, Eyewash, Faddle, Falderal, Fandangle, Fiddlededee, Fiddle-faddle, Fiddlesticks, Flannel, Flapdoodle, Flim-flam, Folderol, Footling, Fudge, Gaff, Galimatias, Gammon, Gas and gaiters, Get away, Gibberish, Gobbledygook, Guff, Gum, Hanky-panky, Haver, Hogwash, Hokum, Hooey, Hoop-la, Horsefeathers, Humbug, Jabberwocky, Jazz, Jive, Kibosh, Kidstakes, Malark(e)y, Moonshine, Mouthwash, Mumbo-jumbo, My eye, Niaiserie, Phooey, Piffle, Pishogue, Pshaw, Pulp, Ratbaggery, Rats, Rawmaish, Rhubarb, Rigmarole, Rot, Rubbish, Scat, Shenanigans, Shit(e), Squit, Stuff, Taradiddle, Tom(foolery), Tommy-rot, Tosh, Trash, Tripe, Tush, Twaddle, Unreason, Waffle
Non-sequitur Anacoluthia, Irish bull, Irrelevant
Non-specialist User-friendly
Non-standard Anomalous
Non-starter No-no
Non-stick PTFE, Teflon®, Tusche
Non-stop Through
Non-transferable Adiabatic
Non-U Naff
Non-Unionist Freerider
Non-violence Ahimsa, Pacificism, Satyagraha
Non-white Coloured, Yolk
Noodle(s) Capellini, Crispy, Daw, Fool, Head, Laksa, Lokshen, Manicotti, Mee, Moony, Ninny, Pasta, Sammy, Simpleton, Soba, Udon
Nook Alcove, Angle, Corner, Cranny, Niche, Recess, Rookery
Noon Am end, M, Midday, N, Narrowdale
No one Nemo, None
Noose Fank, Halter, Hempen caudle, Lanyard, Loop, Necktie, Rebecca, Rope, Rope's end, Snare, Twitch
▸ **Nor** *see* **NOT**
Nordic, Norse(man) Icelander, Norn, → **NORWEGIAN**, Scandinavian, Viking
Norm Canon, Criterion, Rule, Standard
Normal Average, Conventional, Customary, Everyday, General, Natural, Norm, Ordinary, Orthodox, Par, Perpendicular, Regular, Standard, Straight, Unexceptional, Usu(al)
Normal eyes Emmetropia
Norman French, Mailer, Rufus
North(ern), Northerner Arctic, Boreal, Cispontine, Copperhead, Dalesman, Doughface, Eskimo, Geographic, Hyperborean, Magnetic, N, Norland, Runic, Scotia, Sea, Septentrion, True, Up
North American (Indian) Injun, Papoose, Red(skin), Scalper, Totemist, Tribe

NORTH AMERICAN INDIANS

3 letters:		*5 letters:*	Ponca
Fox	Innu	Brave	Sioux
Sao	Pima	Cajun	Taino
Ute	Pomo	Creek	Teton
	Sauk	Haida	
	Tewa	Huron	*6 letters:*
4 letters:	Tiwa	Miwok	Abnaki
Crow	Yana	Omaha	Apache
Dene	Yuma	Osage	Cayuga
Erie	Zuni	Piute	Galibi
Hopi			

Klooch
Lakota
Micmac
Mixtec
Mohave
Mohawk
Navaho
Nootka
Oglala
Ojibwa
Oneida
Paiute
Papago
Pawnee
Pequot
Plains
Pueblo
Quapaw
Sachem
Salish
Sannup
Shasta
Siwash
Yanqui

7 letters:
Abenaki
Arapaho
Caddoan
Chibcha
Chinook
Choctaw
Gwich'in
Hidatsa
Kikapoo
Klootch
Kutenai
Mahican

Miskito
Mission
Mohegan
Mohican
Mugwump
Natchez
Norteno
Ojibway
Palouse
Pontiac
Senecan
Serrano
Shawnee
Shuswap
Tahitan
Tlingit
Wichita
Wyandot
Yalkama
Zapotec

8 letters:
Algonkin
Angeleno
Cahuilla
Cherokee
Cheyenne
Chippewa
Comanche
Delaware
Flathead
Geronimo
Hiawatha
Iroquois
Kickapoo
Kootenai
Kootenay
Kwakiutl

Menomini
Mikasuki
Mogollon
Muskogee
Nez Percé
Okanagon
Okinagan
Onondaga
Sagamore
Sahaptan
Sahaptin
Seminole
Shoshone

9 letters:
Algonkian
Algonquin
Blackfoot
Chichimec
Chickasaw
Chipewyan
Manhattan
Melungeon
Menominee
Mescalero
Muskogean
Potawatom
Sahaptian
Shahaptin
Suquamish
Tsimshian
Tuscarora
Wampanoag
Winnebago
Wyandotte
Yawelmani

10 letters:
Algonquian
Copperskin
Crazy Horse
Halkomelem
Miniconjou
Montagnais
Montagnard
Muskhogean
Pocahontas
Six Nations
Tarahumara
Uto-Aztecan

11 letters:
Assiniboine
Basket Maker
Five Nations
Kiowa Apache
Massachuset
Minneconjou
Narraganset
Sitting Bull

12 letters:
Mound Builder

13 letters:
Massachusetts
Northern Piute
Southern Piute
Susquehannock

14 letters:
Northern Paiute
Southern Paiute

Northern Ireland NI, Six Counties
North star Tyrian cynosure
Northwestern Aeolis
Norway, Norwegian Bokmal, Fortinbras, Landsma(a)l, N, Nordic, Norweyan, Nynorsk, Rollo, Scandinavian
Nose, Nosy A(d)jutage, Aquiline, Beak, Bergerac, Boko, Bouquet, Breather, Catarrhine, Conk, Copper, Cromwell, Curious, Desman, Droop, Fink, Flair, Gnomon, Grass, Grecian, Greek, Grog-blossom, Honker, Hooknose, Hooter, Index, Informer, Leptorrhine, Meddle, Muffle, Muzzle, Nark, Neb, Nozzle, Nuzzle, Parker, Platyrrhine, Proboscis, Prying, Pug, Red, Rhinal, Roman, Schnozzle, Shove, Smelly, Sneb, Sniff, Snoot, Snout, Snub, Squeal, Stag, Stickybeak, Toffee
Noseband Barnacle, Cavesson, Musrol
Nose-bleed Epistaxis
Nosh Eat, Food, Nibble, Snack
Nostalgia Longing, Memory lane, Oldie, Retrophilia, Wistfulness, Yearning

Nostril(s) Blowhole, Cere, Choana, Nare

Nostrum Elixir, Medicine, Remede, Remedy

Not, Nor Aikona, Dis-, Na(e), Narrow A, Ne, Neither, Never, No, Pas, Polled, Taint

Notable, Notability Conspicuous, Dignitary, Distinguished, Eminent, Especial, Landmark, Large, Lion, Memorable, Personage, Signal, Striking, Unco, VIP, Worthy

Not allowed NL

▷ **Not allowed** *may indicate* a word to be omitted

Notary Apostolical, Ecclesiastical, Escribano, Scrivener

Not at all Au contraire

Notation(al) Benesh, Cantillation, Descriptive, Entry, Formalism, Hexadecimal, Infix, Memo, Octal, Polish, Positional, Postfix, Romic, Scientific, Staff, Tablature

Notch(ed) Crena(l), Crenel, Cut, Dent, Erode, Erose, Gain, Gap, Gimp, Indent, Insection, Jag, Kerf, Mush, Nick, Nock, Raffle, Score, Serrate, Serrulation, Sinus, Snick, Tally, Vandyke

Not clear Blocked, NL, Obscure, Opaque, Pearl

Note(s), Notebook, Noted A, Acciaccatura, Accidental, Advance, Adversaria, Advice, Agogic, Apostil(le), Apparatus, Appoggiatura, Arpeggio, Auxiliary, B, Bill(et), Bradbury, Bread and butter letter, Breve, C, Cedula, Chit(ty), Chord, Cob, Comment, Conceit, Continental, Cover, Credit, Crotchet, Currency, D, Debit, Delivery, Demand, Dig, Dispatch, Do(h), Dominant, Double-dotted, E, E-la, F, Fa(h), False, Fame, Fiver, Five-spot, Flat, Flim, G, Gamut, Gloss(ary), Gold, Grace, Greenback, Gruppetto, Heed, Hemiole, Hypate, Identic, Index rerum, IOU, Iron man, Item(ise), Jot(tings), Jug(-jug), Key, Kudos, La, Large, Leading, Letter, Lichanos, Line(r), Log, Long, Longa, Lower mordent, Marginalia, Mark, Masora(h), Masoretic, Me, Mediant, Melisma, Melody, Memo(randum), Mese, Message, Mi, Minim, Minute, Missive, → **MONEY**, Mordent, Music, Muzak®, Nachschlag, Natural, NB, Nete, Neum(e), Oblong, Observe, Octave, Oncer, On record, Open, Ostmark, Outline, Parhypate, Passing, Postal, Post-it®, Pound, Promissory, Prompt, Proslambanomenos, Protocol, PS, Quarter, Quaver, Rag-money, Re, Reciting, Record, Remark, Renown, Request, Right, Root, Scholion, Scholium, Scotch catch, Scotch snap, Semibreve, Semiquaver, Semitone, Sensible, Septimole, Sextolet, Sharp, Shinplaster, Shoulder, Si, Sick, Sixteenth, Sixty-fourth, Sleeve, Smacker, Snuff-paper, So(h), Sol, Some, Stem, Strike, Subdominant, Submediant, Subtonic, Supertonic, Te, Ten(ner), Third, Thirty-second, Tierce, Tonic, Treasury, Treble, Two-spot, Undecimole, Ut, Variorum, Verbal, Wad, Warison, Whole, Wolf, Wood

Note-case Pochette, Purse, Wallet

▷ **Notes** *may indicate* the use of letters A-G

Noteworthy Eminent, Extraordinary, Memorable, Particular, Signal, Special

Nothing, Nought Buckshee, Bugger-all, Cipher, Damn-all, Devoid, Diddlysquat, Emptiness, FA, Gratis, Jack, Love, Nada, Napoo, Naught, Nihil, Niks-nie, Nil, Nix(-nie), Noumenon, Nowt, Nuffin, Nullity, O, Ought, Rap, Rien, Small beer, Sweet FA, Void, Z, Zero, Zilch, Zip(po)

Notice(able) Ad(vertisement), Advance, Advice, Affiche, Apprise, Attention, Avis(o), Banns, Bill, Blurb, Bold, Bulletin, Caveat, Circular, Clock, Cognisance, Crit, D, DA, Descry, Detect, Discern, Dismissal, Enforcement, Evident, Gaum, Get, Gorm, Handbill, → **HEED**, Intimation, Marked, Mensh, Mention, NB, No(t)chel, Obit, Observe, Oyez, Perceptible, Placard, Plaque, Playbill, Poster, Press, Proclamation, Prominent, Pronounced, → **REMARK**, Review, See, Short, Si quis, Spot, Spy, Sticker, Tent, Warning, Whip

Notify, Notification Acquaint, Advise, Apprise, Aviso, Awarn, Inform, Payslip, → **TELL**, Warn

Notion(al) Academic, Conceit, → **CONCEPT**, Crotchet, Fancy, Hunch, Idea, Idée, Idolum, Inkling, Opinion, Reverie, Vapour, Whim

Notoriety, Notorious Arrant, Byword, Crying, Egregious, Esclandre, Fame, Flagrant, Infamous, Infamy, Legendary, Notour, Proverbial, Réclame, → **RENOWN**, Repute

No trump Laical, Lay, NT

Notwithstanding Albe(e), Although, Despite, Even, For, Howbeit, However, Mau(l)gre, Natheless(e), Nath(e)less, Naythles, Nevertheless, Spite

Nougat Montelimar, Sundae

▸ **Nought** *see* NOTHING

Noughts and crosses Tic(k)-tac(k)-to(e)

Noumenon Thing-in-itself

Noun Abstract, Agent, Agentive, Aptote, Collective, Common, Concrete, Count, Gerund, Mass, N, Proper, Seg(h)olate, Substantive, Tetraptote, Verbal, Vocative

Nourish(ing), Nourishment Aliment, Battill, Cherish, Cultivate, Feed, Ingesta, Manna, Meat, Nurse, Nurture, Nutrient, Promote, Repast, Replenish, Sustenance, Trophic

Nous Intellect, Intelligence, Reason, Sense

Nova Scotia(n) Acadia, Blue-nose

Novel(ty) Aga-saga, Airport, Bildungsroman, Bonkbuster, Book, Campus, Change, Clarissa, Different, Dime, Dissimilar, Emma, Epistolary, Erewhon, Fad, Fiction, Fresh, Gimmick, Gothic, Graphic, Historical, Horror, Idiot, Innovation, Ivanhoe, Kenilworth, Kidnapped, Kim, Middlemarch, → NEW, Newfangled, Novation, Original, Outside, Page-turner, Pamela, Paperback, Pendennis, Penny dreadful, Persuasion, Picaresque, Pot-boiler, Primeur, Pulp, Rebecca, River, Roman-à-clef, Romance, Roman fleuve, Saga, Scoop, Sex and shopping, She, Shilling-dreadful, Shilling-shocker, Terror, Thesis, Ulysses, Unusual, Weepie, Whodun(n)it, Yellowback

▹ **Novel** *may indicate* an anagram

▸ **Novelist** *see* WRITER

November N, Nov

Novice Acolyte, Apprentice, Beginner, Cadet, Chela, Colt, Cub, Green(horn), Griffin, Jackaroo, Jillaroo, Johnny-raw, Kyu, L, Learner, Neophyte, New chum, Noob, Patzer, Postulant, Prentice, Rabbit, Rookie, Tenderfoot, Tyro(ne), Unweaned

Now(adays) AD, Alate, Anymore, Current, Here, Immediate, Instantaneously, Instanter, Interim, Nonce, Nunc, Present, Pro tem, This

Nowhere Limbo

No-win Dead heat

Nowt Cattle, Cows, Ky(e), Neat, Nothing

Noxious Harmful, Noisome, Offensive, Poisonous, Toxic, Toxin, Venomous

Nozzle Aerospike, A(d)jutage, Fishtail, Nose, Nose-piece, Rose, Spout, Stroup, Syringe, Tewel, Tuyere, Tweer, Twier, Twire, Twyer(e)

Nuance Gradation, Nicety, Overtone, Shade

Nub Crux, Gist, Knob, Lump, Point

Nubile Beddable, Marriageable, Parti

Nuclear, Nucl(e)ide, Nucleus Cadre, Calandria, Centre, Core, Crux, Daughter, Deuteron, Eukaryon, Euratom, Even-even, Even-odd, Heartlet, Hub, Isomer, Isotone, Karyon, Kernel, Linin, Mesic, Mesonic, Mushroom, Nuke, Organelle, Pith, Prokaryon, Recoil, Synkaryon, Triton

▹ **Nucleus** *may indicate* the heart of a word

Nude, Nudism, Nudist, Nudity Adamite, Altogether, Aphylly, Bare, Buff, Eve, Exposed, Full-frontal, Gymnosophy, → NAKED, Nuddy, Scud, Stark, Stripped, Undress

Nudge Dunch, Dunsh, Elbow, Jostle, Knee, Poke, Prod

Nudibranch Sea-slug

Nugget Chunk, Cob, Gold, Lump

Nuisance Bore, Bot, Bugbear, Chiz(z), Drag, Impediment, Inconvenience, Mischief, Pest, Plague, Public, Terror, Trial

Null(ification), Nullify Abate, Cancel, Counteract, Defeasance, Destroy, Diriment, Disarm, Invalid(ate), Negate, Neutralise, Overturn, Recant, Terminate, Undo, Veto, Void

Numb(ness) Asleep, Blunt, Dead(en), Stun, Stupor, Torpefy, Torpescent, Torpid, Unfeeling

Number(s) Abscissa, Abundant, Access(ion), Air, Aleph-null, Aleph-zero, Algebraic,

Algorithm, Aliquant, Aliquot, Amiable, Amicable, Anaesthetic, Analgesic, Antilog, Apocalyptic, Apostrophus, Army, Atomic, Augend, Avogadro, Babylonian, Binary, Box, Brinell, Calculate, Cardinal, Cetane, Chromosome, Class, Cocaine, Coefficient, Cofactor, Complex, Composite, Concrete, Constant, Coordination, Count, Cyclic, Decillion, Deficient, Deficit, Diapason, Digit, DIN, Drove, E, Edition, Epidural, Ether, Eucaine, Ex-directory, F, Feck, Figurate, Figure, Folio, Folksong, Fraction, Friendly, Frost(bite), Froude, Gas, Gobar, Golden, Googol, Handful, Hantle, Hash(mark), Hemlock, Host, Hyperreal, Imaginary, Include, Incomposite, Index, Infimum, Integer, Irrational, Isospin, Isotopic, Item, Lac, Lakh, Legion(s), Lepton, Livraison, Local, Mach, Magazine, Magic, Mantissa, Mass, Melodic, Milliard, Minuend, Minyan, Mixed, Mort, Muckle, Multiple, Multiplex, Multiplicity, Multitude, Myriadth, Nasik, Natural, Neutron, No(s), Nonillion, Nth, Nuclear, Nucleon, Num, Numerator, Numerical, Octane, Octillion, Opiate, Opium, Opposite, Opus, Ordinal, OT, Paginate, Par, Paucal, Peck, Perfect, Pile, PIN, Plural, Polygonal, Prime, Procaine, Production, Proton, Quantum, Quarternion, Quorum, Quota, Quotient, Radix, Raft, Random, Rational, Real, Reckon, Registration, Regulo®, Repunit, Reynold's, Root, Sampi, Scads, Serial, Show-stopper, Sight, Slew, Slue, Some, Square, Strangeness, Strength, Subtrahend, Summand, Surd, T, Tale, Telephone, Tell, Thr(e)ave, Totient, Totitive, Transcendental, Transfinite, Troop, Turn-out, Umpteen, Umpty, Urethan(e), Verse, Wave, Whole, Wrong, Zeroth

▷ **Number** *may indicate* a drug

Numeral(s) Arabic, Chapter, Figure, Ghubar, Gobar, Integer, Number, Roman, Sheep-scoring

Numerous(ness) Divers, Galore, Legion, Lots, Many, Multeity, Myriad, Teeming

Numskull Blockhead, Booby, Dunce, Stupid

Nun Basilian, Beguine, Bhikkhuni, Clare, Cloistress, Cluniac, Conceptionist, Dame, Deaconess, Gilbertine, Minim, Minoress, Mother Superior, Outsister, Pigeon, Poor Clare, Prioress, Religeuse, Salesian, Sister, Sister of Mercy, Top, Trappistine, Ursuline, Vestal, Visitant, Vowess, Zelator, Zelatrice, Zelatrix

▷ **Nun** *may indicate* a biblical character, father of Joshua

Nuptial (chamber) Bridal, Marital, Marriage, Thalamus

Nurse(ry), Nursing Aia, Alice, Amah, Angel, Ant, Ayah, Barrier, Bonne, Caledonia, Candy-striper, Care(r), Cavell, Charge, Cherish, Consultant, Cradle, Crèche, Day, Deborah, District, Dry, EN, Flo(rence), Foster, Gamp, Glumdalclitch, Harbour, Health visitor, Karitane, Mammy, Midwife, Minister, Mother, Mrs Gamp, Nan(n)a, Nanny, Night, Nightingale, Norland, Nourice, Nourish, Parabolanus, Phytotron, Playroom, Playschool, Plunket, Practical, Probationer, RN, School, Scrub, Seminary, SEN, Sister, Staff, Suckle, Tend, VAD, Visiting, Wet

Nursery(man) Conservatory, Crèche, Garden, Hothouse, Rhyme, Seedsman, Slope

▷ **Nursing** *may indicate* one word within another

Nurture Cherish, Cradle, Cultivate, Educate, Feed, Foster, Suckle, Tend

Nut *may refer to* Egyptian god, father of Osiris

Nut(s), Nutcase, Nutshell, Nutter, Nut tree, Nutty Acajou, Acorn, Almond, Amygdalus, Anacardium, Aphorism, Arachis, Areca, Arnut, Babassu, Barcelona, Barking, Barmy, Bats, Beech-mast, Bertholletia, Betel, Bonce, Brazil, Briefly, Buffalo, Butterfly, Butternut, Cashew, Castle, Chock, Coal, Cob, Coco-de-mer, Coffee, Cohune, Coke, Cola, Conker, Coquilla, Coquina, Core, Cranium, Crank, Cream, Cuckoo, Dukka(h), En, Filberd, Filbert, Frog, Gelt, Gilbert, Gland, Glans, Goober, Goober-pea, Gum, Hard, Hazel, Head, Helmet, Hickory, Illipe, Ivory, Kachang puteh, Kernel, Kola, Kooky, Lichee, Li(t)chi, Litchi, Loaf, Lug, Lunatic, Lychee, Macadamia, Macahuba, Macaw-palm, Macoya, Manic, Marking, Mast, Mockernut, Monkey, Noisette, Noodle, Nucule, Oak, Oil, Pakan, Palmyra, Para, Pate, Pecan, Pekan, Philippina, Philippine, Philopoena, Physic, Pili, Pine, Pin(y)on, Pistachio, Poison, Praline, Prawlin, Quandang, Quantong, Queensland, Rhus, Sapucaia, Sassafras, Scrotum, Shell, Skull, Slack, Sleeve, Stuffing, Supari, Testicles, Thumb, Tiger, Tough, Walnut, Weirdo, Wing, Zany, Zealot

▸ **Nutcase, Nutshell** *see* NUT(S)

Nutcracker Cosh

Nutmeg Calabash, Connecticut, CT, Mace, Myristica

Nutrient, Nutriment, Nutrition Betacarotene, Eutrophy, Food, Ingesta, Protein, Sitology, Sustenance, Trace element, Trophic, Vitamin

▷ **Nuts** *may indicate* an anagram

Nuzzle Snoozle

Nyasaland Malawi

Nymph(et) Aegina, Aegle, Amalthea, Arethusa, Callisto, Calypso, Camenae, Carme, Clytie, Constant, Cymodoce, Daphne, Doris, Dryad, Echo, Egeria, Eurydice, Galatea, Hamadryad, Hesperides, Houri, Hyades, Ida, Insect, Larva, Liberty, Lolita, Maelid, Maia, Maiden, Mermaid, Naiad, Nereid, Oceanid, Oenone, Oread, Pupa, Rusalka, Sabrina, Satyra, Scylla, Siren, Sylph, Syrinx, Tessa, Tethys, Thetis, Water, Wood

Oo

O Blob, Duck, Nought, Omega, Omicron, Oscar, Oxygen, Spangle, Tan, Zero

Oaf Auf, Changeling, Dolt, Fool, Mou, Ocker, Ouph(e), Stupid, Twit, Yahoo

Oak(s) Bog, Bur, Cerris, Classic, Cork, Desert, Dumbarton, Durmast, Flittern, Fumed, Gabriel, Herne, Holly, Holm, Honour, Ilex, Jerusalem, Kermes, Live, Major, Native, Parliament, Pedunculate, Philemon, Poison, Quercus, Red, Roble, Royal, Scrub, Sessile, Silky, Swamp, Swilcar, → **TREE**, Turkey, Valonia, Watch, White

Oakley Annie

Oar(s), Oarsmen Blade, Ctene, Eight, Galley slave, Leander, Organ, Paddle, Palm, Propel, Rower, Scull, Spoon, Stroke, Sweep

Oasis Biskra, Buraimi, Haven, Hotan, Hotien, Refuge, Spring, Tafilalet, Tafilelt

Oat(meal), Oats Ait, Athole brose, Avena, Brome-grass, Fodder, Grain, Grits, Groats, Gruel, Haver, Loblolly, Parritch, Pilcorn, Pipe, Porridge, Quaker®, Rolled, Wild

Oatcake Bannock, Clapbread, Farle, Flapjack, Jannock

Oath Affidavit, Begorrah, Blast, Blimey, Bribery, Burgess, Curse, Damn, Dang, Dash, Demme, Doggone, Drat, Ecod, Egad, Expletive, God-so, Gospel, Halidom, Hell, Hippocratic, Igad, Imprecation, Jabers, Jesus, Keech, Lumme, Lummy, Nouns, Oons, Promise, Rats, Sacrament, Sal(a)mon, Sapperment, Saucer, 'sbodikins, Sbud(dikins), Sdeath, Sfoot, Sheart, Shoot, Slid, 'slife, 'slight, Snails, Sonties, Strewth, Stygian, Swear, Tarnation, Tennis-court, Voir dire, Vow, Zbud, Zounds

Obdurate Adamant, Cruel, Flinty, Hard, Intransigent, Stony, Stubborn, Tenacious

Obedient, Obedience, Obey Bent, Biddable, Bridlewise, Canonical, Comply, Dutiful, Follow, Good, Hear, Mindful, Obsequious, Observe, Obtemper, Passive, Perform, Pliant, Servant, Yielding

Obeisance → **BOW**, Salaam

Obelisk, Obelus Aguilla, Column, Dagger, Monument, Needle, Pillar

Oberon King, Merle

Obese, Obesity Bariatrics, Corpulent, Fat, Stout

Object(s), Objection(able), Objective(ness), Objector Ah, Aim, Ambition, Argue, Artefact, Article, Artifact, Bar, Beef, But, Case, Cavil, Challenge, Clinical, Cognate, Complain(t), Conchy, Conscientious, Cow, Demur, Detached, Direct, Dissent, Doodah, End, Exception, Fetish, Found, Fuss, → **GOAL**, Her, Him, Ifs and buts, Impersonal, Improper, Indifferent, Indirect, Intensional, Intention, It, Item, Jib, Lion, Loathe, Mind, Moral, Near-earth, Niggle, Nitpick, Non-ego, Non-partisan, Noumenon, Ob, Obnoxious, Offensive, Oppose, Outness, Percept, Perspective, Plan, Plot, Point, Protest, Proximate, Quasi-stellar, Question, Quibble, Quiddity, Rank, Rebarbative, Recuse, Refuse, Relation, Resist, Retained, Sake, Scruple, Sex, Subject, Sublime, Target, Thing, Transitive, Tut, Ultimate, Unbiased, Virtu, Wart

▷ **Object** *may indicate* a grammatical variant

Objectless Intransitive

Objet d'art Curio

Oblate, Oblation Gift, Monk, Offering, Offertory, Prothesis, Sacrifice

Oblige, Obliging, Obligation, Obligatory Accommodate, Affable, Behold, Binding, Burden, Charge, Coerce, Compel, Complaisant, Compliant, Contract, Corvée, Debt, De rigueur, Duty, Easy, Encumbent, Force, Giri, Gratify, Impel, Incumbent, IOU, Mandatory, Must, Necessitate, Novation, Obruk, Obstriction, Peremptory, Promise, Recognisance, Responsibility, Sonties, Synallagmatic, Tie, Wattle

Oblique(ly) Askance, Askew, Asklent, Asquint, Athwart, Awry, Cross, Diagonal, Indirect, Perverse, Plagio-, Separatrix, Sidelong, Skew, Skewwhiff, Slanting, Solidus, Squint, Virgule

▷ **Oblique** *may indicate* an anagram

Obliterate(d) Annul, Black out, Blot, Dele(te), Efface, Eradicate, Expunge, Exterminate, Rase, Rast, Raze, Wash away, Wipe, Zap

Oblivion, Oblivious Forgetful, Lethe, Limbo, Nirvana, Obscurity, Unaware

Oblong Rectangular

Obloquy Opprobrium

Obnoxious Eyesore, Foul, Horrid, Offensive, Pestilent, Repugnant, Septic, Sod, Unpleasant, Wart

Oboe Piffero

Obscene(ly), Obscenity Bawdy, Blue, Fescennine, Filth, Gross, Hard-core, Indecent, Lewd, Lubricious, Paw(paw), Porn(o), Profane, Raunchy, Ribald, Salacious, Scatology, Smut, Vulgar

Obscure, Obscurity Abstruse, Anheires, Becloud, Befog, Blear, Blend, Blot out, Blur, Break, Cloud, Cobweb, Conceal, Cover, Cryptic, Darken, Deep, Dim, Disguise, Eclipse, Elliptic, Encrypt, Engloom, Envelop, Esoteric, Filmy, Fog, Hermetic, Hide, Indistinct, Jude, Mantle, Mist, Murk, Nebular, Night, Nubecula, Obfuscate, Obnubilate, Opaque, Oracular, Overcloud, Overshade, Overshadow, Recherché, Recondite, Shadowy, Tenebrific, Twilit, Unclear, Unobvious, → **VAGUE**, Veil, Vele, Wrap

▷ **Obscure(d)** *may indicate* an anagram

Obsequious(ness) Bootlicker, Brown nose, Creeping Jesus, Fawn, Fulsome, Grovelling, Kowtowing, Menial, Parasitic, Pig, Servile, Slavish, Sleeveen, Slimy, Subservient, Suck-hole, Suck up, Sycophantic, Tantony, Toady

Observance, Observant, Observation Adherence, Alert, Attention, Comment, Custom, Empirical, Espial, Experience, Eyeful, Holy, Honour, Hour-angle, Lectisternium, Mass, → **NOTICE**, Obiter dicta, Perceptive, Percipient, Practice, Quip, Ready-eyed, Recce, Remark, Right, Rite, Ritual, Use, Vising

Observatory Arecibo, Atalaya, Greenwich, Herstmonceux, Hide, Hurstmonceux, Jodrell Bank, Lookout, Mount Palomar, Tower

Observe(d), Observer Behold, Bystander, Celebrate, Commentator, Detect, Espy, Eye, Fly-on-the-wall, Heed, Keep, Mark, NB, Note, Notice, Obey, Onlooker, Optic, Pharisee, Regard(er), Remark, Rite, Scry, See, Seer, Sight, Spectator, Spial, Spot, Spy, Study, Take, Twig, View, Voyeur, Watch, Witness

Obsess(ed), Obsession, Obsessive Anal, Anorak, Besot, Bug, Bugbear, Complex, Craze, Dominate, Fetish, Fixation, Hang-up, Haunt, Hobbyhorse, Hooked, Idée fixe, Infatuation, Mania, Monomania, Necrophilia, Nerd, Neurotic, One-track, Preoccupy, Smitten, Thing, Wonk

Obsidian Pe(a)rlite

Obsolete, Obsolescence, Obsolescent Abandoned, Antique, Archaic, Dated, Dead, Defunct, Disused, Extinct, Latescent, Obs, Outdated, Outworn, Passé, Planned

Obstacle Barrage, Barrier, Boyg, Cheval de frise, Chicane, Dam, Drag, Dragon's teeth, Drawback, Gate, Handicap, Hazard, Hindrance, Hitch, Hurdle, Node, Oxer, Remora, Rock, Sandbank, Snag, Stimie, Stumbling-block, Stymie, Tank-trap

Obstetrics Gynaecology, Midwifery, Tocology, Tokology

Obstinacy, Obstinate Asinine, Bigoted, Bitter-ender, Buckie, Bullheaded, Bullish, Contrarian, Contumacious, Cussed, Die-hard, Dour, Entêté, Froward, Headstrong, High-stomached, Inflexible, Intractable, Intransigent, Mule, Persistent, Perverse, Pervicacious, Piggish, Pig-headed, Recalcitrant, Refractory, Restive, Rusty, Self-will, Stiff(-necked), Strure, Stubborn, Thraward, Thrawart, Wilful

Obstreperous Defiant, Noisy, Stroppy, Truculent, Unruly

Obstruct(ion) Bar, Barricade, Barrier, Block, Bottleneck, Caltrop, Chicane, Clog, Crab, Cross, Cumber, Dam, Embolus, Fil(l)ibuster, Gridlock, Hamper, Hand-off, Hedge, Hinder,

Hurdle, Ileus, Impede, Let, Obstacle, Occlude, Sab(otage), Sandbag, Snarl-up, Snooker, Stall, Stap, Stonewall, Stop, Stymie, Sudd, Thwart, Trammel, Trump

Obtain Achieve, Acquire, Buy, Cop, Derive, Exist, Gain, Get, Land, Pan, Prevail, Procure, Realise, Secure, Succeed, Wangle, Win

Obtrude, Obtruding, Obtrusive Expel, Impose, King Charles' head, Loud, Prominent, Push, Sorn, Thrust

Obtuse Blunt, Dense, Dull, Purblind, Stupid, Thick

Obverse, Obversion Complement, Cross, Equipollence, Face, Front, Head, Permutation

Obviate Forestall, Preclude, Prevent

Obvious Apparent, Axiom, Bald, Blatant, Brobdingnag, Clear, Distinct, Evident, Flagrant, Frank, Inescapable, Kenspeck(le), Manifest, Marked, Needless, Open(ness), Open and shut, Overt, Palpable, Patent, Pikestaff, Plain, Pronounced, Salient, Self-evident, Staring, Stark, Transparent, Truism, Visible

Occasion Call, Cause, Ceremony, Do, Encheason, Engender, Event, Fête, Field day, Nonce, → **OPPORTUNITY**, Reason, Ride, Sometime, Tide, Time, Treat, Whet

Occasional(ly) At times, Casual, Chance, Daimen, Ever and anon, Intermittent, Irregular, Motive, Orra, Periodic, Scattered, Sometimes, Sporadic, While

Occident(al) West, Western(er)

Occlude, Occlusion Absorb, Clog, Coronary, Embolism, Obstruct

Occult(ist) Angekkok, Arcane, Art, Esoteric, I-Ching, Magic, Mysterious, Mystic, Supernatural

Occupant, Occupation, Occupy(ing) Absorb, Activity, Avocation, Beset, Business, Busy, Career, Denizen, Dwell, Embusy, Employ, Engage, Engross, Fill, Hold, In, Incumbent, Indwell, Inhabitant, Inmate, Invade, Involve, Line, Man, Métier, Overrun, People, Profession, Pursuit, Reserved, Residency, Resident, Runrig, Sideline, Squat, Stay, Tenancy, Tenant, Tenure, Thrift, Trade, Upon, Use, Vocation, Walk of life

Occur(rence) Arise, Be, Betide, Betime, Case, Contingency, Crop up, Event, Fall, Happen, Incident, Instance, Outbreak, Outcrop, Pass, Phenomenon

Ocean(ic), Oceania Abundance, Abyssal, Antarctic, Arctic, Atlantic, Blue, Deep, German, Hadal, Herring-pond, High seas, Indian, Melanesia, Micronesia, Pacific, Panthalassa, Pelagic, Polynesia, Pond, Sea(way), Southern, Thalassic, Waves, Western

Och aye Troggs

Ochre Burnt, Keel, Lemnian ruddle, Rubric, Ruddle, Sienna

Octave Diapason, Diminished, Eight, Great, Ottava, Perfect, Small, Utas

Octopus Blue-ringed, Cephalopod, Cuero, Devilfish, Paper nautilus, Polyact, Polyp, Poulp(e), Scuttle, Squid

Octoroon Mestee, Mestizo, Mustee

Od Energy, Force

Odd (person), Oddity Abnormal, Anomaly, Bizarre, Card, Cure, Curio, Droll, Eccentric, Eery, Erratic, Fishy, Freaky, Gink, Gonzo, Impair, Imparity, Jimjam, Offbeat, Original, Orra, Outré, Paradox, Parity, Peculiar, Queer, Quirky, Quiz, Random, Rare, Remote, Rum, Screwball, Singular, Spooky, → **STRANGE**, Unequal, Uneven, Unmatched, Unpaired, Unusual, Weird, Whims(e)y, Zany

▷ **Odd(s)** *may indicate* an anagram or the odd letters in words

Oddfellow OF

Odd job man Joey, Loppy, Orraman, Rouster, Smoot, Thronner

Odds, Oddments Bits, Carpet, Chance, Gubbins, Handicap, Line, Long, Price, Short, SP, Tails, Variance

Ode Awdl, Dit, Epicede, Epicedium, Epinicion, Epinikion, Genethliacon, Horatian, Hymn, Lay, Lyric, Monody, Paeon, Pindaric, Poem, Sapphic, Song, Stasimon, Strophe, Threne, Threnody, Verse

Odin One-eyed, Woden

Odium, Odious Comparison, Disestimation, Disgrace, Foul, Hatred, Heinous, Invidious, Ponce, Repellent, Repugnant, Stigma

Odorous, Odour Air, Aroma, Bad, BO, Flavour, Funk, Good, Hum, Opopanax, Perfume, Quality, Redolence, Sanctity, Scent, Smell, Stench, Waff, Waft, Whiff

Odourless Silent

Odyssey Epic, Journey, Wandering

Oedipus Complex, Parricide

Oeillade Glance, Leer, Ogle, Wink

Oesophagus Crop

Oestrogen, Oestrus Daidzein, Frenzy, Genistein®, Heat, Isoflavone, Mestranol, Must, Rut, Stilb(o)estrol

Of (me) About, Among, Aus, By, De, From, In, My, Re

▷ **Of** *may indicate* an anagram

Of course Certainly, Natch, Yes

Off Absent, Agee, Ajee, Away, Discount, Distance, Far, From, High, Inexact, Licence, Odd, Rancid, Reasty, Reesty, Relâche, Start

▷ **Off** *may indicate* an anagram

Offal Cagmag, Carrion, Chidlings, Chitterling, Entrails, Fry, Giblets, Gralloch, Gurry, Haggis, Ha(r)slet, Heart, Innards, Kidney, Lamb's fry, Lights, Liver, Numbles, Pig's fry, Pluck, Sweetbread, Tripe, Variety meat

Off-beat Zoppo

Off-colour Pale, Seedy, Wan

▷ **Off-colour** *may indicate* an anagram

Offence Attack, Crime, Delict, Delinquency, Distaste, Fault, Huff, Hurt, Indictable, Lapse, Lese majesty, Miff, Misdemeanour, Misprision, Odium, Outrage, Peccadillo, Pip, Pique, Piracy, Praemunire, Regrate, Sedition, → **SIN**, Summary, Trespass, Umbrage, Violation

Offend(ed), Offender Affront, Anger, Annoy, Boobhead, Bridles, Criminal, Culprit, Default, Delinquent, Disoblige, Displease, Distaste, Hip, Huff, Hurt, Hyp, Infringe, Inveigh, Miffy, Miscreant, Nettle, Nonce, Nuisance, Peeve, Perp, Provoke, Serial, Sin(ner), Sledge, Sting, Stray, Transgress, Twoccer, Umbrage, Violate, Wrongdoer

Offensive(ness) Affront, Aggressive, Alien, Attack, Bombardment, Campaign, Charm, Cruel, Derisatory, Derogatory, Dysphemism, Embracery, Euphemism, Execrable, Eyesore, Foul, Gobby, Hedgehog, Hedgepig, Indecent, Indelicate, Inroad, Insulting, Invidious, Miasmic, Nasty, Noisome, Obnoxious, Obscene, Odious, Peccant, Personal, Push, Putrid, Rank, Repugnant, → **RUDE**, Scandalous, Scurrilous, Sortie, Storm, Ugly, Unbecoming, Unsavoury, War

Offer(ing) Alms, Altarage, Anaphora, Approach, Bargain, Bid, Bode, Bouchée, Cadeau, Corban, Deodate, Dolly, Epanophora, Extend, Ex voto, Gift, Give, Godfather, Heave, Hold, Inferiae, Introduce, Invitation, Libation, Oblation, Overture, Peace, Peddle, Plead, Pose, Potla(t)ch, Present, Propine, → **PROPOSE**, Propound, Sacrifice, Shewbread, Shore, Special, S(h)raddha, Stamp, Stand, Submit, Suggestion, Tender, Utter, Volunteer, Votive, Wave, Xenium

Offhand Airy, Banana, Brevi manu, Brusque, Casual, Cavalier, Currente calamo, Curt, Extempore, Impromptu, Indifferent, Snappy

Office(s) Abbacy, Agency, Bedelship, Booking, Box, Branch, Broo, Bucket shop, Bureau, Buroo, Caliphate, Chair, Chancery, Circumlocution, Clerical, Colonial, Commonwealth, Complin(e), Consulate, Crown, Cube farm, Cutcher(r)y, Daftar, Dataria, Dead-letter, Deanery, Decemvirate, Den, Divine, Dogate, Drostdy, Employment, Evensong, Foreign, Front, Function, Holy, Home, Job, Land, Last, Lav(atory), Left luggage, Lieutenancy, Little, Little hours, Loan, Lost property, Mayoralty, Met(eorological), Ministry, Missa, Mistery, Mudiria, Mutessarifat, Mystery, Nocturn, Nones, Obit, Oval, Palatinate, Papacy, Patent, Patriarchate, Penitentiary, Personnel, Petty Bag, Pipe, Place, Plum, Portfolio, Position, Post, Prefecture, Prelacy, Press, Prime, Printing, Provosty, Record, Regency, Register, Registry, Rite, Satrapy, Scottish, Secretarial, Secretariat, See, Seraskierate, Shogunate, Sinecure, Situation, Sorting, Stamp, Stationery, Sultanate,

Tariff, Tenebrae, Terce, Ticket, Tierce, Tol(l)booth, Tribunate, Vespers, Vicary, War, Yamen
Officer(s) Branch, Compliance, Counter-round, Customs, Duty, Engineer, Executive, First, Flag, Flying, Gal(l)ant, Gazetted, Group, Incumbent, Liaison, Non-commissioned, Nursing, Orderly, Peace, Petty, PO, Police, Presiding, Press, Prison, Probation, Radio, Relieving, Returning, Rodent, Safety, Scene-of-crime, Staff, Treasurer, Wardroom, Warrant, Watch

OFFICERS

2 letters:
Lt
SL
SM

3 letters:
Aga
CEO
Cop
Gen
GOC
NCO
Sub

4 letters:
Agha
Aide
Bosn
Capt
CIGS
Exon
Imam
Mate

5 letters:
Blimp
Bosun
Gager
Imaum
Janty
Jonty
Jurat
Major
Pacha
Pasha
Pilot
Posse
Sewer

6 letters:
Acater
Beatty
Copper
Cornet

Datary
Deacon
Ensign
Gauger
Gunner
Hetman
Jaunty
Lictor
Purser
Pusser
Rector
Rosser
Sbirro
Schout
Serang
Sexton
Tindal
Varlet
Warden
Warder
Yeoman

7 letters:
Admiral
Agistor
Bailiff
Blue Rod
Captain
Colonel
Co-pilot
Coroner
Darogha
Dragoon
Equerry
Filacer
Filazer
General
Hayward
Jamadar
Jauntie
Jemadar
Jemidar
Marshal
Pantler

Prefect
Proctor
Provost
Samurai
Sea Lord
Sheriff
Skipper
Speaker
Striper
Subadar
Tribune

8 letters:
Adjutant
Bimbashi
Black Rod
Brass-hat
Cursitor
Decurion
Familiar
Havildar
Phylarch
Subahdar
Tipstaff
Woodward

9 letters:
Ale-conner
Apparitor
Brigadier
Catchpole
Catchpoll
Cellarist
Centurion
Commander
Commodore
Constable
Exciseman
First mate
Messenger
Moderator
Number one
Pipe major
President

Prorector
Select-man
Subaltern
Tahsildar
Tarpaulin
Waldgrave

10 letters:
Air-marshal
Bluebottle
Bombardier
Bumbailiff
Chancellor
Pursuivant
Second mate
Securocrat
Subchanter
Supercargo
Tidewaiter

11 letters:
Chamberlain
Earl Marshal
Grand Vizier
Infirmarian
Silver-stick

12 letters:
Commissioned
Commissioner
Field Marshal
Group captain
Remembrancer

13 letters:
Drill-sergeant
Lance-sergeant
Quartermaster
Sergeant-major
Sublieutenant

14 letters:
Air vice-marshal
Provost-marshal

	16 letters:	**17 letters:**	**21 letters:**
Superintendent	Procurator fiscal	Official Solicitor	Quartermaster-sergeant
15 letters:			
Lord High Steward			

Office-worker Clerk, Peon, Temp, Typist
Official(s), Officiate, Officious Aga, Agent, Aleconner, Amban, Amtman, Apparatchik, Atabeg, Atabek, Attaché, Authorised, Beadle, Borough-reeve, Bossy, Bumble, Bureaucrat, Catchpole, Censor, Chamberlain, Chancellor, Chinovnik, Claviger, Commissar, Commissioner, Consul, Convenor, Coroner, Count, Count palatine, Dean, Dignitary, Diplomat, Dockmaster, Dogberry, Ealdorman, Ephor, Equerry, Escheater, Eurocrat, Executive, Factotum, Fonctionnaire, → **FORMAL**, Fourth, Functionary, Gauleiter, Governor, Gymnasiarch, Handicapper, Hayward, Hazzan, Incumbent, Inspector, Intendant, Jack-in-office, Jobsworth, Keeper, Landdrost, Lictor, Line judge, Linesman, Macer, Mandarin, Marplot, Marshal, Mayor, MC, Meddlesome, Mirza, Mueddin, Muezzin, Mukhtar, Nazir, Notary, Notary public, Ombudsman, Omlah, Overbusy, Palatine, Panjandrum, Paymaster, Placeman, Pleaseman, Plenipotentiary, Polemarch, Pontificate, Poohbah, Postmaster, Postulator, Praefect, Pragmatic, Prefect, Proconsul, Proctor, Procurator, Prog, Proveditor, Provedor(e), Providor, Provost, Purveyor, Reeve, Ref(eree), Régisseur, Registrar, Remembrancer, Sachem, Scrutineer, Secretary, Shammash, Shammes, Sherpa, Silentiary, Souldan, Spoffish, Stadtholder, Staff, Standard, Steward, Subdean, Suffete, Suit, Summoner, Surveyor, Syndic, Timekeeper, Tipstaff, Touch judge, Tribune, Trier, Trior, Triumvir, Turncock, Valid, Valuer General, Veep, Verderer, Verger, Vicar-general, Viscount, Vizier, Walla(h), Whiffler, Whip, Woodward, Yamen, Yeoman
Offprint Separate
Off-putting Dehortative, Discouraging, Mañana, Negative, Procrastination, Rebarbative, Repellent, Yips
Offset Balance, Cancel, Compensate, Counter(act), Counterbalance
Offshoot Bough, Branch, Cion, Limb, Lye, Member, Outgrowth, Plant, Scion, Sien, Sient, Swarm, Syen
Offspring Boy, Brood, Burd, Chick, Children, Daughter, Descendant, Family, Fruit, Fry, Get, Girl, Heir, Litter, Procreation, Product, Progeny, Seed, Sient, Son, Spawn
Offstage Wings
Off-the-cuff Improv(isation)
Off-white Cream, Ecru
Often Frequent, Habitual, Repeated
▷ **Often** *may indicate* 'of ten'
Ogee Cyma, Moulding, Talon
Ogle Astare, Drake, Eliad, Eye, Glad eye, Glance, Leer, Oeillade, Wodewose
Ogre(ss) Baba Yaga, Boyg, Brute, Eten, Etten, Fiend, Giant, Monster, Orc, Shrek
Ohio Buckeye
Oil(s), Oily, Oil producer Anele, Anoint, Balm, Black gold, Bribe, Crude, Derv, Diesel, Drying, Essence, Essential, Ethereal, Fatty, Fish, Fixed, Frying, Fuel, Good, Grease, Hair, Heavy, Joint, Lamp, Lipid, Long, Lube, Lubricant, Macaw-tree, Midnight, Mineral, Monounsaturated, Multigrade, Oint, Oleaginous, Pellitory, Polyunsaturated, Pomade, Residual, Seed, Short, Sleek, Slick, Smalmy, Smarmy, Smeary, Sweet, Topped crude, Unction, Zest

---

OILS

2 letters:	**3 letters:**		**4 letters:**
BP®	Ben	Nim	Baby
	Emu	Nut	Bath
	Gas		Bone

Cade
Coal
Corn
Musk
Nard
Neem
Nimb
Oleo
Otto
Palm
Poon
Rape
Rock
Rose
Rusa
Slum
Tall
Tolu
Tung
Wood
Wool
Yolk

5 letters:
Ajwan
Argan
Attar
Benne
Benni
Clove
Colza
Copra
Fusel
Grass
Maize
Niger
Olein
Olive
Ottar
Poppy
Pulza
Rosin
Savin
Sebum
Shale
Shark
Snake
Sperm
Spike
Stand
Thyme
Train
Ulyie

Ulzie
Whale

6 letters:
Ajowan
Almond
Balsam
Banana
Butter
Canola
Carapa
Carron
Castor
Chrism
Cineol
Cloves
Cohune
Croton
Elaeis
Illipe
Jojoba
Magilp
Megilp
Monola®
Neroli
Oleine
Peanut
Ramtil
Savine
Semsem
Seneca
Sesame
Shamoy
Tallow
Virgin
Walnut

7 letters:
Aniline
Apiezon®
Arachis
Bittern
Cajeput
Cajuput
Camphor
Cineole
Coconut
Dittany
Eugenol
Gingili
Jinjili
Linalol
Linseed

Lumbang
Menthol
Mirbane
Moringa
Mustard
Myrbane
Myrrhol
Naphtha
Picamar
Pyrrole
Retinol
Ricinus
Rocktar
Saffron
Safrole
Spindle
Verbena
Vitriol
Wallaba

8 letters:
Bergamot
Camphire
Cod-liver
Creasote
Creosote
Flaxseed
Gingelli
Gingelly
Hazelnut
Hempseed
Kerosene
Kerosine
Lavender
Linalool
Macassar
North Sea
Oiticica
Pachouli
Paraffin
Photogen
Pristane
Rapeseed
Rosewood
Volatile

9 letters:
Aleuritis
Beech-mast
Candlenut
Carvacrol
Eleoptene
Golomynka

Grapeseed
Groundnut
Neat's-foot
Parathion
Patchouli
Patchouly
Petroleum
Photogene
Quinoline
Safflower
Sassafras
Spearmint
Spikenard
Star-anise
Sunflower
Terpineol
Vanaspati
Vegetable

10 letters:
Chaulmugra
Citronella
Cotton-seed
Elaeoptene
Eucalyptus
Guttiferae
Juniper tar
Peppermint
Petit grain
Sandalwood
Turpentine
Ylang-ylang

11 letters:
Camphorated
Chaulmoogra
Chinese wood
Extra virgin
Stearoptene
Wintergreen

12 letters:
Benzaldehyde
Benzonitrile
Brilliantine
Hungary water

14 letters:
Glutaraldehyde
Parnassus grass

15 letters:
Evening primrose

Oilcake Poonac
Oilcan Pourie
Oilcloth American, Lino
Oilman Driller, Prospector, Rigger, Texan
Oil painting Master, Titian
Ointment Balm, Basilicon, Boracic, Boric, Cerate, Collyrium, Cream, Liniment, Lipsalve, Nard, Pomade, Pomatum, Rub, Salve, Spikenard, Theriac, Tiger balm®, Unction, Unguent, Vaseline®, Zinc
OK Agree(d), Approve, Authorise, Clearance, Copacetic, Copesettic, Go-head, Green light, Hunky-dory, Initial, Kosher, Mooi, No sweat, Respectable, Right(o), Roger, Sanction, Sound, U, Vet
Okra Bhindi, Gumbo, Lady's fingers
Old(er), Oldie Ae(t), Aged, Aine(e), Ancient, Antique, Auld, Bean, Decrepit, Dutch, Earlier, Elderly, Fogram, Former, Gaffer, Geriatric, Glory, Golden, Gray, Grey, Hills, Hoary, Immemorial, Major, Mature, Methusaleh, Moore, Nestor, Nick, O, OAP, Obsolete, Off, Ogygian, One-time, Outworn, Palae-, Passé, Primeval, Ripe, Rugose, Sen(escent), Senile, Senior, Shot, Signeur, Stager, Stale, Trite, Venerable, Veteran, Victorian(a), Worn
Old boy, Old girl Alumnae, Alumnus, Fossil, OB
Old days Once, Past, Yore
Old English OE
Old-fashioned Aging, Ancient, Antediluvian, Antwackie, Arch(aic), Arriéré, Back number, Bygone, Corn(y), Dated, Dodo, Dowdy, Fogey, Fuddy-duddy, Fusty, Hidebound, Medieval, Museum piece, Neanderthal, No tech, Obsolete, Ogygian, Oldfangled, Outdated, Outmoded, Outre, Outworn, Passé, Podunk, Primeval, Quaint, Relic, Retro, Rinky-dink, Schmaltzy, Shot, Square, Square-toes, Steam, Stick-in-the-mud, Traditional, Uncool, Victorian, Vieux jeu, Vintage, Worm-eaten
Old hat Clichéd
Old maid Biddy, Spinster
Old man, Old woman Anile, Aunty, Bodach, Buda, Budi, Burd, Cailleach, Carlin(e), Codger, Crinkly, Crow, Crumbly, Faggot, Fantad, Fantod, Fogey, Fogramite, Fogy, Fussy, Gammer, Geezer, Gramps, Grandam, Grannam, Greybeard, Greyhen, Husband, Kangaroo, Koro, Kuia, Luckie, Lucky, Matriarch, Methuselah, Mort, Mzee, OAP, Oom, Pantaloon, Patriarch, Presbyte, Roo, Rudas, Southernwood, Tripod, Trot, Trout, Whitebeard, Wife, Wight, Woopie, Wrinkly
Old-timer Hourglass, Sundial, Veteran
Oleander Nerium, Rhododaphne
Olid Fetid, Foul, High, Rancid, Rank
Olio Hash, Medley, Mess, Potpourri, Stew
Olive (grove), Olivine Calamata, Cerulein, Drupe, Dunite, Gethsemane, Kalamata, Lilac, Olea(ster), Peridot, Queen, Russian
Oliver Bath, Cromwell, Goldsmith, Hardy, Noll, Protector, Twist
Olympian, Olympics, Olympus Asgard, Athlete, Celestial, Coe, Demeter, Elis, Hera, Pantheon, Quadrennium, Summer, Winter, Zeus
Ombudsman Trouble shooter
Omelette Crêpe, Foo yong, Foo yung, Frittata, Fu yung, Pancake, Spanish, Tortilla
Omen Abodement, Absit, Augury, Auspice, Foreboding, Forewarning, Freet, Freit, Portent, Presage, Prodrome, Sign, Token, Warning
Omentum Caul, Epiploon
Ominous Alarming, Baleful, Bodeful, Dire, Dour, Forbidding, Grim, Inauspicious, Menacing, Oracular, Portentous, Sinister, Threatening
Omission, Omit Aph(a)eresis, Apocope, Apospory, Apostrophe, Asyndeton, Caret, Disregard, Drop, Elide, Elision, Ellipse, Ellipsis, Failure, Haplography, Haplology, Lipography, Loophole, Miss, Neglect, Nonfeasance, Non-user, Oversight, Paral(e)ipomenon, Pass, Pretermit, Senza, Skip

Omnibus Anthology, Coach, Collection
Omniscient, Omniscience Encyclopedia, Pansophy
Omnivorous Pantophagous
On (it) Aboard, About, Agreed, An, An't, At, Atop, By, Game, Half-cut, In, Leg, O', Of, Oiled, Over, Pon, Re, Tipsy, Up(on), Viable
▷ **On** *may indicate* an anagram
On account of Over
▷ **On board** *may indicate* chess, draughts, or 'SS' around another word
Once(r) Ance, As was, → **AT ONCE**, Bradbury, Earst, Erst(while), Ever, Ex, Fore, Former, Jadis, Oner, Onst, Secular, Sole, Sometime, Whilom
One(self) A, Ace, Ae, Alike, An(e), Any, Body, Chosen, Eeny, Ego, Ein, Formula, I, Individual, Integer, Me, Monad, Per se, Person, Single(ton), Singular, Solo, Tane, Un, Unify, Unit(y), Unitary, United, Us, We, Yin, You
One-act-er Playlet
One-eared Monaural
One-eyed Arimasp(ian), Cyclops
One-man band Moke
One o'clock 1 am, NNE
One-off Ad hoc, Sui generis
One-rayed Monact
Onerous Arduous, Exacting, Taxing, Tedious, Weighty
Ongoing Continual
Onion(s) Allium, Bengi, Bonce, Bulb, Chibol, Chive, Cibol, Cive, Eschalot, Green, Head, Ingan, Jibbons, Leek, Lyonnaise, Moly, Pate, Pearl, Ramp, Ramson, Rocambole, Ropes, Scallion, Scilla, Shal(l)ot, Soubise, Spanish, Spring, Squill, Sybo(e), Sybow, Tree, Welsh
Onlooker Beholder, Bystander, Kibitzer, Observer, Rubberneck, Spectator, Witness
Only Allenarly, Anerly, But, Except, Just, Meer, Merely, Nobbut, Seul, Singly, Sole, Sommer, Unique
Onset Affret, Attack, Beginning, Charge, Dash, Ending, Rush, → **START**, Thrust
Onslaught Attack, Barrage, Cannonade, Dead-set, Onset, Raid, Spreagh, Storm, Swoop
On the way Agate
On this side Cis
On time Pat, Prompt, Punctual
Onus Burden, Charge, → **DUTY**, Responsibility
Onward Advance, Ahead, Away, Forth, Forward, Progress
Oodles Heaps, Lashings, Lots, Slather
Oolite Peastone, Pisolite, Roestone
Oomph Energy, It, SA, Verve
Ooze, Oozy Drip, Exhale, Exude, Gleet, Globigerena, Ichorous, Mud, Percolate, Pteropod(a), Radiolarian, Seep, Sew, Sipe, Slime, Slob, Spew, Spue, Sweat, Sype, Transude, Uliginose, Uliginous
Opal(escent) Black, Cymophanous, Fire, Gem, Girasol, Girosol, Hyalite, Hydrophane, Liver, Menilite, Noble, Potch, Wood
Opaque, Opacity Dense, Dull, Intense, Leucoma, Milky, Obscure, Obtuse, Onycha, Onyx, Roil, Thick, Turbid
Open(er), Opening, Openness Adit, Aedicule, Agape, Airhole, Ajar, Antithesis, Anus, Apert(ure), Apparent, Apse, Armhole, Autopsy, Bald, Bare, Bat, Bay, Begin, Bole, Breach, Break, Broach, Buttonhole, Candid, Cardia, Cavity, Champaign, Chance, Chasm, Chink, Circumscissile, Clear, Crevasse, Crowbar, Dehisce, Deploy, Dispark, Door, Dup, Embrasure, Exordium, Expansive, Explicit, Eyelet, Fair, Fenestra, Fissure, Fistula, Flue, Fontanel(le), Foramen, Frank, Free, Free-for-all, Gambit, Gap, Gaping, Gat, Gate, Give, Glasnost, Glottis, Guichet, Gullwing, Hagioscope, Hatch, Hatchback, Hatchway, Hiatus, Hilus, → **HOLE**, Inaugural, Intake, Interstice, Intro, Key, Lacy, Lance, Lead, Loid, Loophole, Loose, Machicolation, Manhole, Meatus, Micropyle, Mofette, Moongate,

Mouth, Naked, Nare, Oillet, Orifice, Os, Oscule, Osculum, Ostiole, Ostium, Overt, Overture, Pandora, Patent, Peephole, Pert, Pervious, Pick(lock), Placket, Plughole, Pop, Pore, Port(age), Porta, Porthole, Preliminary, Premiere, Prise, Pro-am, Public, Pylorus, Receptive, Relaxed, Rent, Ring-pull, Riva, Room, Scuttle, Scye, Sesame, Sicilian, Sincere, Slit, Slot, Spare, Spirant, Squint, Start, Stenopaic, Stokehole, Stoma, Stulm, Syrinx, Thereout, Thirl, Touchhole, Transparent, Trapdoor, Trema, Trou, Truthful, Unbar, Unbolt, Unbutton, Uncope, Uncork, Undo, Unfurl, Unhasp, Unlatch, Unreserved, Unscrew, Unstop, Unsubtle, Untie, Unzip, Upfront, Vent, Vulnerable, Wide, Window, Yawning

Open air Alfresco, Sub divo, Sub Jove

Opera(tic), Opera house, Operetta Aida, Ariadne, Ballad, Boris Godunov, Bouffe, Buffo, Burletta, Carmen, Comic, Comique, Die Fledermaus, Don Carlos, Don Giovanni, Dramma giocoso, Electra, ENO, Ernani, Falstaff, Faust, Fedora, Fidelio, Glyndebourne, Grand, Hansel and Gretel, Horse, Idomeneo, Iolanthe, I Puritani, Kirov, La Bohème, La Donna e Mobile, La Scala, Light, Lohengrin, Lulu, Macbeth, Magic Flute, Met, Musical, Nabucco, Norma, Oater, Oberon, Onegin, Orfeo, Otello, Owen Wingrave, Pag, Parsifal, Pastorale, Patience, Peter Grimes, Pinafore, Rienzi, Rigoletto, Ring, Ruddigore, Rusalka, Salome, Savoy, Seria, Simon Boccanegra, Singspiel, Soap, Space, Sudsen, Tell, The Met, Threepenny, Tosca, Turandot, Verismo, Werther, Work, Zarzuela

Opera-glasses Jumelle, Starers

Opera-lover Wagnerite

Opera-singer Baritone, Bass, Contralto, Diva, Savoyard, Soprano

Operate, Operation(s), Operative Act(ion), Activate, Actuate, Agent, Artisan, Attuition, Barbarossa, Bypass, Caesarean, Campaign, Combined, Conduct, Couching, Current, Desert Storm, Detective, Doffer, Exercise, Function, Game, Hobday, Holding, Hysterectomy, Jejunostomy, Keystroke, Laparotomy, Leucotomy, Liposuction, Lithotomy, Lithotripsy, Lobotomy, Logical, Manipulate, Mechanic, Mules, Nip and tuck, Nose job, Oner, Overlord, Plastic, Practice, Rhytidectomy, Run, Sealion, Shirodkar's, Sortie, Splenectomy, Sting, Strabotomy, Surgery, Titration, Unit, Ure, Valid, Wertheim, Work

Operator Agent, Conductor, Dealer, Laplace, Manipulator, Nabla, Sawbones, Sparks, Surgeon, Sysop, System

Opiate, Opium Buprenorphine, Dope, Drug, Hop, Laudanum, Meconin, Meconite, Meconium, Morphine, Narcotic, Paregoric, Religion, Soporific, Thebaine

Opinion, Opinionative Attitude, Belief, Bet, Bias, Conjecture, Consensus, Cri, Deem, Diagnosis, Dictum, Dogma, Doxy, Editorial, Entêté, Esteem, Fatwa(h), Feeling, Groundswell, Guess, Heresy, Impression, Judgement, Mind, Mumpsimus, Parti pris, Pious, Prejudice, Private, Public, Pulse, Say, Second, Sense, Sentence, Sentiment, SO, Stand, Syndrome, Take, Tenet, Thought, Utterance, View, Viewpoint, Voice, Vote, Vox pop, Vox populi

Opossum Lie, Marmose, Phalanger, Tarsipes, Vulpine, Water, Yapo(c)k

Oppidan Cit, Townsman, Urban

Opponent(s) Adversary, Antagonist, Anti, Denier, E-N, Enemy, E-S, Foe, Gainsayer, Mitnaged, N-E, N-W, S-E, Straw-man, S-W, Tiger, W-N, W-S

Opportune, Opportunist, Opportunity Appropriate, Apropos, Break, Buccaneer, Carpetbagger, → **CHANCE**, Day, Equal, Facility, Favourable, Ganef, Ganev, Ganof, Godsend, Go-go, Golden, Gonif, Gonof, Heaven-sent, Occasion, Opening, Pat, Photo, Providential, Room, Scope, Seal, Seel, Sele, Snatcher, Sneak thief, Tabula rasa, Tide, Timely, Timous, Vantage, Well-timed, Window

Oppose(d), Opposer, Opposing, Opposite, Opposition Against, Agin, Anti, Antipathy, Antipodes, Antiscian, Antithesis, Antithetic, Antitype, Antonym, Argue, At, Au contraire, Averse, Battle, Beard, Black, Breast, Collision, Colluctation, Combat, Confront, Contradict, Contrary, Converse, Counter(part), Diametric, Dis(en)courage, Disfavour, Dissent, Dissident, Distance, E contrario, Face, Foreanent, Fornen(s)t, Hinder, Hostile, Impugn, Inimical, Inverse, Ironic, Meet, Militate, Mugwump, Noes, Object, Obscurant,

Overthwart, Polar, Reactance, Reaction, Recalcitrate, Reluct, Repugn, Resist, Retroact, Reverse, Rival, Shadow, Subtend, Syzygy, Teeth, Terr, Thereagainst, They, Thwart, Toe to toe, Toto caelo, Traverse, V, Versus, Vice versa, Vis-à-vis, Withstand

Oppress(ion), Oppressive Airless, Bind, Burden, Close, Crush, Dead hand, Despotic, Holy cruel, Incubus, Jackboot, Laden, Onerous, Overbear, Overpower, Persecute, Ride, Snool, Stifling, Sultry, Totalitarian, Tyrannise

Opprobrium Disgrace, Envy, Odium, Scandal

Oppugn Attack, Criticise

Opt, Option(al) Alternative, Call, → CHOICE, Choose, Crown-jewel, Decide, Default, Double zero, Elect, Facultative, Fine, Leipzig, Local, Menu, Naked, Omissible, Pick, Plump, Put, Select, Share, Soft, Swap(tion), Trade(d), Traditional, Voluntary, Votive, Wale, Zero(-zero)

Optic(al), Optics Active, Adaptive, Electron, Fibre, Fire, Lens, Photics, Prism, Reticle, Visual

Optimism, Optimist(ic) Bull, Chiliast, Elated, Expectant, Feelgood, Hopeful, Micawber, Morale, Pangloss, Pollyanna, Rosy, Sanguine, Starry-eyed, Upbeat, Utopiast, Yea-sayer

Opulent Abundant, Affluent, Moneyed, Rich, Wealthy

Opus Piece, Study, Work

Or Au, Either, Ere, Gold, Ossia, Otherwise, Sol

Oracle(s), Oracular Delphi, Dodonian, Mirror, Prophet, Pythian, Pythoness, Sage, Seer, Sibyl(line), Thummim, Trophonius, Urim, Vatic

Oral Acroamatic, Noncupative, Sonant, Spoken, Unwritten, Verbal, Viva, Viva voce, Vocal

Orange Agent, An(n)atta, An(n)atto, Arnotto, Aurora, Bergamot, Bigarade, Bilirubin, Bitter, Blenheim, Blood, Blossom, Calamondin, Chica, Claybank, Clockwork, Croceate, Flame, Flamingo, Fulvous, Genip(ap), Jaffa, Kamala, Kamela, Kamila, Karaka, Kumquat, Mandarin, Methyl, Mock, Naartje, Nacarat, Nartjie, Navel, Ochre, Osage, Petit grain, Pig, Roucou, Ruta, Satsuma, Seville, Shaddock, Sour, Sweet, Tangerine, Tenné, Ugli®, Ulsterman

Orang-utan Ape, Monkey, Satyr

Orate, Oration Address, Declaim, Eloge, Elogium, Elogy, Eulogy, Harangue, Panegyric, Philippics, Speech

Oratorio, Orator(y) Boanerges, Brompton, Brougham, Cantata, Cicero, Creation, Demagogue, Demosthenes, Diction, Elijah, Hwyl, Isocrates, Lectern, Morin, Nestor, Prevaricator, Proseucha, Proseuche, Rant, Rhetor, Samson, Spellbinder, Stump, Tub-thumper, Windbag, Yarra-banker

Orb Ball, Eyeball, Firmament, Globe, Mound, Ocellus, Pome, Sphere

Orbit(al) Apolune, Apse, Apsis, Circuit, Dump, Eccentric, Ellipse, Eye, Graveyard, Lunar, Osculating, Parking, Path, Periastron, Perigee, Perihelion, Perilune, Periselenium, Polar, Revolution, Stationary, Subshell, Synchronous

Orcadian Hoy

Orchard Arbour, Grove, Holt

Orchestra(te), Orchestration Chamber, Charanga, Concertgebouw, Concerto, ECO, Ensemble, Gamelan, Hallé, Instrumentation, LPO, LSO, Palm Court, Pit, Ripieno, Score, Sinfonietta, SNO, String, Symphony

Orchid Adam and Eve, Adder's mouth, Arethusa, Babe-in-a-cradle, Bee, Bee-orchis, Bird's nest, Bog, Burnt-tip, Butterfly, Calanthe, Calypso, Cattleya, Cooktown, Coralroot, Coral wort, Cymbidium, Cypripedium, Disa, Epidendrum, Fly, Fly orchis, Fragrant, Fringed orchis, Frog, Helleborine, Hyacinth, Lady, Lady's slipper, Lady's tresses, Lizard, Man, Marsh, Military, Miltonia, Moccasin-flower, Monkey, Musk, Naked lady, Odontoglossum, Oncidium, Phalaenopsis, Pogonia, Purple-fringed, Puttyroot, Pyramidal, Rattlesnake plantain, Salep, Scented, Slipper, Snakemouth, Soldier, Spider, Spotted, Swamp pink, Swan, Twayblade, Vanda, Vanilla

Ord Beginning, Point

Ordain Arrange, Command, Decree, Destine, Enact, Induct, Japan, Priest
Ordeal Corsned, Disaster, Preeve, Test, → **TRIAL**, Via Dolorosa
Order(ed), Orderly, Orders Acoemeti, Adjust, Administration, Affiliation,
Alphabetical, Anton Piller, Apollonian, Apple-pie, Arrange, Array, ASBO, Attachment,
Attendant, Attention, Attic, Augustine, Avast, Bade, Banker's, Bankruptcy, Bath,
Batman, Battalia, Bed, Behest, Benedictine, Bernardine, Bespoke, Bid, Book, Boss, Call,
Camaldolite, Canon, Category, Caveat, CB, Chaprassi, Charter, Cheque, Chit, Chuprassy,
Class, Coherent, Command(ment), Committal, Compensation, Composite, Corinthian,
Cosmo, Cosmos, Court, Decorum, Decree, Demand, Dictate, Diktat, Direct(ion),
Directive, Dispone, Distringas, Dominican, Doric, DSO, Edict, Embargo, Enclosed,
Enjoin, En règle, Errand, Established, Establishment, Eutaxy, Eviction, Exclusion,
Feldsher, Fiat, Fiaunt, Firing, Firman, Form(ation), Franciscan, Fraternity, Freemason,
Full, Gagging, Garnishee, Garter, Gilbertine, Ginkgo, Good, Grade, Group, Habeas corpus,
Heast(e), Hecht, Hest, Holy, Hospitaller, Indent, Injunction, Instruct, Interdict, Ionic,
Irade, Khalsa, Kilter, Knights Hospitallers, Kosmos, Language, Large, Lexical, Loblolly
boy, Loblolly man, Loose, Mail, Major, Mandamus, Mandate, Marching, Marist, Market,
Marshal, Masonic, Medjidie, Merit, Methodical, Minor, Mittimus, Monastic, Money,
Monitor, Moose, Natural, Neatness, Nunnery, OBE, Oddfellows, Official, OM, Open,
Orange, Ord, Ordain, Organic, Organised, Pecking, Plot, Possession, Postal, Precedence,
Precept, Premonstrant, Prescribe, Preservation, Prioritise, Provisional, Pyragyrite,
Rank, Receiving, Reception, Règle, Regular, Religious, Requisition, Restraining, Return,
Right, Rule, Ruly, Sailing, Sarvodaya, Sealed, Search, Sequence, Seraphic, Series, Settle,
Shipshape, Short, Side, Standing, Starter's, State, Statutory, Stop(-loss), Straight,
Subpoena, Summons, Supersedere, Supervision, System, Tabulate, Tall, Taxis, Tell,
Templar, Teutonic, Third, Thistle, Tidy, Trim, Tuscan, Ukase, Uniformity, Warison,
Warrant, Word, Working, Writ
▷ **Ordering** *may indicate* an anagram
Ordinal Book, Number, Second, Sequence
Ordinance Byelaw, Capitulary, Decree, Edict, Law, Prescript, Rescript, Rite, Statute
Ordinary Average, Banal, Bog standard, Canton, Chevron, Comely, Common (or garden),
Commonplace, Cot(t)ise, Everyday, Everyman, Exoteric, Fess(e), Flanch, Flange, Folksy,
Grassroots, Hackneyed, Humdrum, Mass, Mediocre, Middling, Mundane, → **NORMAL**, O,
OR, Pedestrian, Plain, Prosy, Pub, Rank and file, Routine, Ruck, Run-of-the-mill, Saltier,
Saltire, Scarp, Simple, So-so, Tressure, Trite, Trivial, Undistinguished, Unexceptional,
Uninspired, Usual, Vanilla, Workaday, Your
Ordnance Artillery, Cannon, Guns, Pelican, Supply
Ordure Cess, Dung, Fertiliser, Manure
Ore Alga, Babingtonite, Bauxite, Bornite, Braunite, Breunnerite, Calamine, Calaverite,
Cerusite, Chalcocite, Chalcopyrite, Chloanthite, Coffinite, Coin, Coltan, Copper, Crocoite,
Dry-bone, Element, Enargite, Galenite, Glance, Haematite, Hedyphane, Horseflesh,
Ilmenite, Iridosmine, Ironstone, Kidney, Limonite, Magnetite, Mat, Melaconite,
Middlings, Millhead, Milling grade, Mineral, Minestone, Morass, Niobite, Oligist, Owre,
Peacock, Pencil, Phacolite, Pipe, Pitchblende, Proustite, Psilomelane, Pyrargyrite,
Pyromorphite, Realgar, Red-lead, Ruby silver, Schlich, Seaweed, Siderite, Sinoptite, Slime,
Slug, Smaltite, Speiss, Sphalerite, Stephanite, Stilpnosiderite, Stockwork, Stream-tin,
Taconite, Tailing, Tenorite, Tetrahedrite, Tin, Wad(d), White-lead, Yellow cake
Organ(s), Organic Adjustor, Adnexa, American, Anlage, Antimere, Apollonicon,
Appendix, Archegonium, Barrel, Biogenic, Biotic, Bursa, Calliope, Carbon, Carpel,
Carpogonium, Cercus, Chamber, Chemoreceptor, Choir, Chord, Claspers, Clave,
Colour, Conch(a), Console, Corti's, Cribellum, Ctene, Ear, Echo, Electric, Electronic,
Electroreceptor, Emunctory, End, Epinastic, Essential, Exteroceptor, Eyeball, Feeler,
Fin, Flabellum, Fundus, Gametangium, Gill, Glairin, Gonad, Hammond®, Hand,
Hapteron, Harmonica, Harmonium, Haustorium, House, Hydathode, Hydraulos,
Imine, Isomere, Kerogen, Kidney, Lien, Light, Liver, Lung-book, Lyriform, Mag(azine),

Means, Mechanoreceptor, Media, Medulla, Melodion, Ministry, Modiolus, Nasal, Natural, Nectary, Nematocyst, Nephridium, Newspaper, Olfactory, Oogonia, Ovary, Ovipositor, Ovotestis, Palp, Pancreas, Parapodium, Part, Pedal, Photogen, Photophore, Photoreceptor, Physharmonics, Pipe, Pipeless, Placenta, Plastid, Portative, Positive, Procarp, Prothallus, Pudenda, Pulmones, Purtenance, Pyrophone, Radula, Receptor, Recit, Reed, Regal, Relict, Rhizoid, Sang, Saprobe, Scent, Sense, Sensillum, Serinette, Serra, Siphon, Spinneret, Spleen, Sporangium, Sporocarp, Sporophore, Stamen, Statocyst, Steam, Swell, Syrinx, Systaltic, Tentacle, Textual, Theatre, Theca, Thymus, Tongue, Tonsil, Tool, Trichocyst, Tympanum, Uterus, Vegetative, Velum, Verset, Viscera, Viscus, Vitals, Voice, Voluntary, Wing, Womb, Wurlitzer®

Organelle Peroxisome

Organise(d), Organisation, Organiser Activate, Administer, Agency, Aggregator, Amnesty, Anatomy, Apparat, → **ARRANGE**, Association, Body, Brigade, Broederbond, Caucus, Class(ify), Codify, Collect, Comecon, Company, Constitution, Coordinate, Design, Direct, Edifice, Embody, Entrepreneur, Eoka, Fascio, Fatah, Firm, Group, Guild, Hierarchy, Impresario, Infrastructure, Jaycee, Krewe, Ku Klux Klan, Logistics, Machine, Mafia, Marshal, Mastermind, Mobilise, Movement, NATO, Octopus, Opus Dei, Orchestrate, Outfit, Personal, PLO, Promotor, Quango, Rally, Red Crescent, Red Cross, Regiment, Resistance, Rosicrucian, Run, Setup, Sharpbender, Social, Soroptimist, Sort, Stage, Stage manage, Stahlhelm, Steward, Sysop, System, Tidy, Together, UN, UNESCO, Viet Minh

▷ **Organise(d)** *may indicate* an anagram

Organism(s) Aerobe, Agamic, Alga, Archaea, Asymmetron, Auxotroph, Being, Biometric, Biont, Biotic, Cell, Chimeric, Chlamydia, Ciliate, Clade, Coral, Detritivore, Diplont, Ecad, Endogenous, Endosymbiont, Entity, Eozoon, Epibenthos, Epizoite, Epizoon, Eucaryote, Euglena, Eukaryote, Eurytherm, Extremophile, Germ, Halobiont, Halophile, Haplont, Hemiparasite, Holophyte, Holoplankton, Homeotherm, Incross, Infauna, Infusoria(n), Lichen, Macrobiote, Medusa, Meiosis, Meroplankton, Metamale, Microaerophile, Microbe, Moneron, Morphology, Nekton, Neuston, Osmoconformer, Paramecium, Pathogen, Periphyton, Phenetics, Ph(a)enology, Plankter, Plankton, Pleuston, Poikilotherm, Prokaryote, Protist, Protista, Protozoan, Radiolarian, Saprobe, Saprotroph, Schizomycete, Seaslater, Sea spider, Sea squirt, Streptococcus, Symbion(t), Teratogen, Thermophile, Torula, Trypanosome, Virino, Volvox, Vorticella, Zoarium

Organ-part, Organ-stop Bourdon, Clarabella, Diapason, Gamba, Montre, Nasard, Principal, Pyramidon, Quint, Salicet, Stop

Organ-tuner Reed-knife

Orgasm Climax, Come

Orgy Bacchanalia(n), Binge, Blinder, Bust, Carousal, Dionysian, Feast, Revel, Saturnalia, Spree, Wassail

Orient(al) Adjust, Annamite, Attune, Chinoiserie, Dawn, Dayak, E, East(ern), Fu Manchu, Hindu, Laotian, Levant, Leyton, Malay, Mongol, Mongolian, Pareoean, Shan, Sunrise, Tatar, Thai, Tibetan, Turk(o)man

Orientation Tropism

Orifice Aperture, Blastosphere, Gap, Hole, Micropyle, Nare, Opening, Pore, Spiracle, Trema, Vent

Origen's work Tetrapla

Origin(al), Originate, Originating Abiogenesis, Abo, Adam, Arise, As per, Beginning, Big bang, Birth, Come, Cradle, Creation, Derive, Editio princeps, Elemental, Emanate, Epicentre, Etymon, Extraction, First, Firsthand, Focus, Found, Generic, Genesis, Genetical, Germ, Grow, Hatch, Incunabula, Ingenious, Initial, Innovate, Invent, Master, Mother, Nascence, Natality, New, Novel, Ord, Parentage, Precedent, Primal, Primary, Primigenial, Primordial, Pristine, Promethean, Protoplast, Prototype, Provenance, Provenience, Rise, Root, Seed, Seminal, Source, Spring, Start, Unborrowed, Ur, Urtext, Ylem, Zoism

Oriole Firebird, Hangbird

Orion Alnilam, Alnitak, Ballatrix, Betelgeuse, Hatsya, Lambda, Meissa, Mintaka, Rigel, Saiph

Orison Blessing, Prayer

Ormer Abalone, Haliotis

Ornament(al), Ornamentation Acroter(ia), Additament, Adorn, Aglet, Aiguillette, Anaglyph, Antefix, Anthemion, Aplustre, Arabesque, Bahuti, Ball-flower, Barbola, Baroque, Barrette, Bead, Bedeck, Bez(z)ant, Billet, Blister, Boss, Bracelet, Breloque, Broider, Brooch, Bugle, Bulla, Cartouche, Charm, Chase, Clock, Cockade, Conceit, Corbeil(le), Cornice, Coromandel work, Crocket, Cross-quarters, Curin, Curlicue, Decor, Decorate, Decoration, Diamanté, Die-work, Diglyph, Dog's-tooth, Doodad, Dreamcatcher, Egg and anchor, Egg and dart, Egg and tongue, Embellish, Emblem(a), Enrich, Epaulet(te), Epergne, Fallal, Fandangle, Festoon, Fiddlehead, Figuration, Figurine, Filagree, Filigrain, Filigree, Fillagree, Fleur de lis, Fleuret, Fleurette, Fleuron, Florid, Fret, Fretwork, Frill, Frounce, Furbelow, Furnish, Gadroon, Gaud, Gingerbread, Gorget, Griff(e), Guilloche, Gutta, Headwork, Hei-tiki, Helix, Hip-knob, Honeysuckle, Illustrate, Inlay, Knotwork, Labret, Lambrequin, Leglet, Lotus, Lunette, Lunula, Macramé, Mantling, Mense, Millefleurs, Mordent, Moresque, Motif, Nail-head, Necklet, Netsuke, Nicknackery, Niello, Nose-ring, O, Okimono, Ouch, Ovolo, Palmette, Parure, Patera, Paternoster, Paua, Pawa, Pectoral, Pendant, Picot, Pipe, Piping, Pompom, Pompo(o)n, Poppyhead, Pounce, Pralltriller, Prettify, Prunt, Purfle, Quatrefoil, Rel(l)ish, Rocaille, Rococo, Rosette, Scalework, Scrollwork, Shell, Shoulder-knot, Snowdome, Snowglobe, Spangle, Spar, Tassel, Tettix, Tiki, Tool, Torc, Torque, Torsade, Tracery, Trappings, Trill, Trimming, Trinket, Triquetra, Tsuba, Turn, Twiddle, Versal, Wally, Water-leaf, Whigmaleerie, Whigmaleery, Whim-wham

Ornate Baroque, Churrigueresque, Dressy, Elaborate, Fancy, Florid, Flowery

▷ **Ornate** *may indicate* an anagram

Ornithologist Audubon, Birdman

Orotund Bombastic, Grandiose, Pompous, Rhetorical, Sonant

Orphan Annie, Foundling, Topsy, Ward

Orpiment Arsenic, Zarnec, Zarnich

Orpington Buff, Hen

Ort Bit, Crumb, Morsel, Remnant

Orthodox Bien-pensant, Cocker, Conventional, Hardshell, Proper, Sound, Standard

Orthorhombic Enstatite

Ortolan Bird, Bunting, Rail

Oscar Award, O, Statue, Wilde

Oscillate, Oscillation, Oscillator Dynatron, Excitor, Fluctuate, Librate, Local, Parasitic, Relaxation, Ripple, Rock, Seesaw, Seiche, Squeg, Surge, Swing(swang), Vibrate, Waver

Osier Red, Reed, Sallow, Willow

Osmium Os

Osmosis Reverse

Osprey Fish-hawk, Lammergeier, Ossifrage, Pandion

Osseous Bony, Hard, Skeletal, Spiny

Ostensibly Apparent, External, Seeming

Ostentation, Ostentatious Camp, Dash, Display, Dog, Éclat, Epideictical, Extravagant, Fantoosh, Fastuous, Flamboyant, Flash(y), Flaunt, Florid, Flourish, Garish, Gaudy, Ghetto fabulous, Highfalutin(g), Large, Parade, Pomp, Ponc(e)y, Pretence, Puff, → **SHOW(ING)**, Side, Splash, Swank, Tacky, Tulip

Osteoporosis Sudeck's atrophy

Ostler Stabler

Ostracise, Ostracism Banish, Blackball, Blacklist, Boycott, Cut, Exclude, Exile, Petalism, Potsherd, Snub, Taboo, Tabu

Ostrich Em(e)u, Estrich, Estridge, Nandoo, Nandu, Ratite, Rhea, Struthio(nes), Titanis
Othello Moor, Morisco
Other(s), Otherwise Additional, Aka, Alia, Alias, Allo-, Alternative, Besides, Different, Distinct, Else, Et al, Et alli, Etc, Excluding, Former, Further, It, Rest, Significant, Unlike
Other things Alia
▷ **Otherwise** *may indicate* an anagram
Otiose Idle, Indolent, Ineffective, Lazy, Needless, Superfluous, Useless
Otis Bustard
Otologist Aurist
Ottawa Bytown
Otter Edal, Paravane, Sea, Tarka, Waterdog
Otto Attar, Chypre, Mahratta
Ottoman Osmanli, Porte, Rayah, Rumelia, Turk
Oubliette Dungeon, Pit, Prison
Ouch Brooch, Ornament, Ow
Ought All, Should
Ouida Ramée
Ouija Board, Planchette
Ounce Cat, Fluid, Liang, Oz, Panther, Snow leopard, Tael, Uncial
Our(selves) Us, We
▶ **Ousel** *see* **OUZEL**
Oust Depose, Dislodge, Eject, Evict, Expel, Fire, Supplant, Unnest, Unseat
Out (of) Absent, Aglee, Agley, Al fresco, Asleep, Aus, Away, Begone, Bowl, Dated, En ville, Exposed, External, Forth, From, Furth, Haro, Harrow, Hence, Hors, Lent, Oust, Skittle, Striking, Stump, Taboo, Uit, Unfashionable, Up, York
▷ **Out** *may indicate* an anagram
Out and out Absolute, Arrant, Rank, Sheer, Stark, Teetotal, Thorough, Totally, Utter
Outback Backblocks, Bundu, Never-never, The mulga
Outbreak Ebullition, Epidemic, Eruption, Explosion, Flare-up, Plague, Putsch, Rash, Recrudescence
Outburst Access, Blurt, Bluster, Boutade, Evoe, Explosion, Fit, Flaw, Furore, Fusillade, Gale, Gush, Gust, Paroxysm, Passion, Philippic, Salvo, Storm, Tantrum, Torrent, Tumult, Volley
Outcast Cagot, Discard, Eta, Exile, Exul, Ishmael, Leper, Mesel, Pariah, Robinson, Rogue
Outcome Aftermath, Consequence, Dénouement, Effect, Emergence, End, Event, Issue, → **RESULT**, Sequel, Upshot, Wash-up
Outcrop Basset, Blossom, Crag, Creston, Inlier, Mesa, Rognon, Spur, Tarpit
Outcry Alew, Blue murder, Bray, → **CLAMOUR**, Halloa, Halloo, Howl, Hue, Humdudgeon, Protest, Racket, Shright, Steven, Uproar, Utas
Outdated, Out of date Archaic, Dinosaur, Effete, Feudal, Fossil, Horse and buggy, Obsolete, Old hat, Outmoded, Passé, Square
Outdo Beat, Best, Cap, Picnic, Superate, Surpass, Top, Trump, Worst
Outdoor(s) Alfresco, External, Garden, Open air, Outbye, Plein-air
Outer External, Extrogenous, Magpie, Superficial, Top
Outfit(ter) Accoutrement, Catsuit, Drawbar, Ensemble, Equipage, Fitout, Furnish, Get-up, Haberdasher, Habit, Kit, Rig, Samfoo, Samfu, Strip, Suit, Team, Trousseau, Turnout, Weed(s), Whites
Outflank Overlap
Outflow Anticyclone, Discharge, Effluence, Eruption, Exodus, Gorge, Issue, Surge
Outgoing Egression, Exiting, Extrovert, Migration, Open, Retiring
Outgrowth Ala(te), Aril, Bud, Caruncle, Enation, Epiphenomenon, Exostosis, Flagellum, Ligule, Offshoot, Osteophyte, Propagulum, Root-hair, Sequel, Strophiole, Trichome
Outhouse Lean to, Privy, Shed, Skilling, Skillion, Skipper, Stable
Outing Excursion, Hike, Jaunt, Junket, Picnic, Sortie, Spin, Spree, Treat, Trip, Wayzgoose

Outlandish Barbarous, Bizarre, Exotic, Foreign, Peregrine, Rum

Outlaw Allan-a-Dale, Attaint, Badman, Ban, Bandit(ti), Banish, Broken man, Bushranger, Exile, Friar Tuck, Fugitive, Hereward, Horn, Jesse James, Klepht, Ned Kelly, Proscribe, Put to the horn, Robin Hood, Rob Roy, Ronin, Tory, Waive

Outlay Cost, Expense, Mise

Outlet Débouché, Egress, Escape, Estuary, Exit, Femerall, Market, Opening, Orifice, Outfall, Overflow, Sluice, Socket, Spout, Tuyere, Tweer, Twier, Twire, Twyer(e), Vent

Outline Adumbration, Aperçu, Circumscribe, Configuration, Contorno, Contour, Delineate, Digest, → **DRAFT**, Draught, Esquisse, Footprint, Layout, Note, Perimeter, Plan, Profile, Projet, Prospectus, Relief, Scenario, Schematic, Shape, Silhouette, Skeletal, Skeleton, Sketch, Summary, Syllabus, Synopsis, T(h)alweg, Trace

Outlook Aspect, Casement, Perspective, Prospect, View, Vista, Weltanschauung

Outmoded Wasm

▷ **Out of** *may indicate* an anagram

Out of date Corny, Obs, Passé, Scrap, Square, Worn

Out of form Amorphous, Awry

Out of order Fritz, Kaput

Out of sorts Cachectic, Nohow, Peevish, Poorly

▷ **Out of sorts** *may indicate* an anagram

Out of tune Discordant, Flat, Scordato, Scordatura

Outpatient Externe

Outpost Colony, Picquet

Outpour(ing) Bavardage, Effuse, Flood, Flow, Gush, Libation, Stream, Torrent

Output Data, Emanation, Get, Gross, Produce, Production, Turnout, Yield

▷ **Output** *may indicate* an anagram

Outrage(ous) Affront, Apoplectic, Appal, Atrocity, Desecrate, Disgust, Egregious, Enorm(ity), Flagitious, Flagrant, Insult, OTT, Rich, Sacrilege, Scandal, Shocking, Ungodly, Unholy, Violate

▷ **Outrageously** *may indicate* an anagram

Outright Clean, Complete, Entire, Point-blank, Utter

Outrun Spreadeagle

Outset Ab initio, Beginning, Start

Outshine Eclipse, Excel, Overshadow, Surpass, Upstage

Outside Ab extra, Crust, Derma, Exterior, External, Extramural, Front, Furth, Hors, Periphery, Plein-air, Rim, Rind, Rine, Shell, Surface

Outsider Alien, Bolter, Bounder, Cad, Extern, Extremist, Foreigner, Incomer, Oustiti, Palagi, Pariah, Ring-in, Roughie, Stranger, Stumer, Unseeded, Upstart

Outsize Capacious, Giant, Gigantic, Huge, OS

Outskirts Edge, Fringe, Periphery, Purlieu

Outspoken Bluff, Blunt, Broad, Candid, Explicit, Forthright, Frank, Plain, Rabelaisian, Round, Vocal, Vociferous

Outstand(ing) Ace, Beaut(y), Belter, Billowing, Bulge, Chief, Crackerjack, Debt, Egregious, Eminent, Especial, Exceptional, Extant, Extraordinaire, First, Fugleman, Highlight, Humdinger, Impasto, Jut, Lulu, Marked, Matchless, Oner, Overdue, Owing, Paragon, Peerless, Phenom(enal), Pièce de résistance, Prince, Prize, Prominent, Promontory, Prosilient, Protrude, Protuberant, Proud, Purler, Relief, Relievo, Salient, Signal, Special, Squarrose, Star, Stellar, Strout, Super(b), Tour de force, Unpaid, Unsettled, Vocal

Outstrip Best, Cap, Cote, Distance, Exceed, Overtake

Outward Efferent, Extern(e), External, Extrinsic, Extrorse, Extrovert, Posticous, Postliminary, Superficial

Outweigh Preponderate

Outwit Baffle, Best, Circumvent, Crossbite, Dish, Euchre, Fox, Outthink, Over-reach, → **THWART**, Trick

Outwork Demilune, Jetty, Moon, Tenail(le), Tenaillon

Outworn Decrepit, Obsolete, Used

Ouzel Merle, Ring, Water

Oval(s) Cartouche, Cassini, Ellipse, Henge, Mandorla, Navette, Obovate, Ooidal

Ovary Oophoron

Ovation Applause, Cheer, Standing

Oven(-like) Aga®, Calcar, Camp, Combination, Convection, Cul-de-four, Dutch, Electric, Fan, Furnace, Gas, Hangi, Haybox, Horn(it)o, Kiln, Lear, Leer, Lehr, Lime kiln, Maori, Microwave, Muffle, Norwegian, Oast, Oon, Stove, Umu

Over Above, Across, Again, Atop, C, Clear, Done, Finished, Hexad, Left, Maiden, Of, On, Ore, Ort, Owre, Past, Sopra, Spare, Superior, Surplus, Through, Uber, Wicket maiden, Yon

Overact Burlesque, Emote, Ham, Hell, Hoke

Overactive Hyper

Overall(s) Boiler suit, Chaps, Denims, Dungarees, Dust-coat, Fatigues, Generally, Jumper, Siren suit, Smicket, Smock, Tablier, Workwear

Overbalance Outweigh

Overbear(ing) Arrogant, Dogmatic, Domineering, High-muck-a-muck, Imperious, Insolent, Lordly, Macher, Supercilious, Weigh down

Overbid Gazump

Overcast Cloudy, Lowering, Sew, Sombre

Overcharge Clip, Extort, Fleece, Gyp, OC, Rack-rent, Rook, Rush, Soak, Sting

Overcoat Balmacaan, Benjamin, Benny, British warm, Chesterfield, → **COAT**, Crombie, Dolman, Grego, Inverness, Jemmy, Joseph, Paletot, Pea-jacket, Petersham, Pos(h)teen, Prince Albert, Raglan, Redingote, Spencer, Surtout, Tabard, Taglioni, Ulster, Warm, Wooden, Wrap-rascal

Overcome Beat, Bested, Conquer, Convince, Dead-beat, Defeat, Expugn, Hit for six, Kill, Master, Mither, Moider, Moither, Prevail, Quell, Speechless, Stun, Subdue, Subjugate, Superate, Surmount, Survive, Swampt, Underfong, Vanquish, Win

Overconfident, Overconfidence Besserwisser

Overcrowd Congest, Jam, Pack

Overdo(ne) Exceed, Ham, Hokey, Hokum, OTT, Percoct, Tire

Overdose OD, Surfeit

Overdraft Red

▷ **Overdrawn** *may indicate* 'red' outside another word

Overdress(ing) Dudism, Flossy, Overall

Overdue Behindhand, Belated, Excessive, Late, Unpaid

Overeat(ing) Binge, Gorge, Hypertrophy, Pig out, Satiate

Overemphasize Rub in, Stress

Overfeed(ing) Glut, Gorge, Sate, Stuff

Overflow(ing) Abrim, Lip, Nappe, Ooze, Outpour, Ream, Redound, Spillage, Surfeit, Teem

Overfull Brimming, Hept

Overground Subaerial

Overgrow(n) Ivy'd, Jungle, Ramp(ant), Rank, Rhinophyma

Overhang(ing) Beetle, Bulge, Cornice, → **JUT**, Loom, Project, Shelvy

Overhasty Rash

Overhaul Bump, Catch, Overtake, Recondition, Revision, Service, Strip

Overhead(s) Above, Aloft, Ceiling, Cost, Exes, Hair(s), Headgear, Oncost, Rafter, Upkeep, Zenith

Overhear Catch, Eavesdrop, Tap

Overheat Enrage

Overindulge(nt) Crapulent, Crass, Dissipated, Dissolute, Pig

Overjoy Elate, Thrill

Overland Portage
Overlap(ping) Correspond, Equitant, Imbricate, Incubous, Kern(e), Limbous, Obvolute, Stretto, Tace, Tasse
Overlay Ceil, Smother, Stucco, Superimpose, Veneer
Overlearned Pedantic
Overload Burden, Plaster, Strain, Surcharge, Tax
Overlook(ed) Condone, Disregard, Excuse, Forget, Miss, Neglect, Omit, Pretermit, Superintend, Unnoticed, Waive
Overlord Edwin, Excess, Invasion
Overlying Incumbent, Jessant, Pressing
Overmuch Excessive, Surplus, Too, Undue
Overplay Ham, Hoke
Overpower(ing) Crush, Evince, Mighty, Onerous, Oppress, Overwhelm, Profound, Subdue, Surmount, Swelter, Whelm
Overpraise Adulate
Overprotective Nannyish
Over-refined Dainty, Nice, Pernickety, Precious
Override, Overrule Abrogate, Disallow, Outvote, Outweigh, Paramount, Preponderant, Reverse, Talk down, Veto
Overrun Exceed, Extra, Infest, Inundate, Invade, Lip, Swarm, Teem
Overseas Abroad, Colonial, Foreign, Outremer, Transmarine, Ultramarine
Oversee(r) Baas, Banksman, Boss, Captain, Care, Deputy, Direct, Eyebrow, Foreman, Forewoman, Grieve, Handle, Induna, Mediate, Moderator, Periscope, Steward, Supercargo, Superintend, Survey(or)
Oversentimental Byronic, Slushy
Overshadow(ed) Cloud, Dominate, Dwarf, Eclipse, Obscure, Outclass, Umbraculate
Overshoe Arctic, Galosh, Sandal, Snowboot
Oversight Blunder, Care, Error, Gaffe, Inadvertence, Lapse, Neglect, Parablepsis
Overstate(ment) Embroider, Exaggerate, Hyperbole
Overstrained Epitonic
Overt Manifest, Patent, Plain, Public
Overtake Catch, For(e)hent, Lap, Leapfrog, Overget, Overhaul, → **PASS**, Supersede, Usurp
Overthrow Dash, Defeat, Demolish, Depose, Dethrone, Down, Labefact(at)ion, Putsch, Ruin, Smite, Stonker, Subvert, Supplant, Topple, Unhorse, Usurp, Vanquish, Whemmle, Whommle, Whummle, Worst
Overture Advance, Carnival, Concert, Egmont, French, Hebrides, Intro, Italian, Leonora, Offer, → **OPENING**, Prelude, Propose, Sinfonia, Toccata, Toccatella, Toccatina
Overturn(ing) Capsize, Catastrophe, Coup, Cowp, Engulf, Quash, Reverse, Tip, Topple, Up(set), Upend, Whemmle, Whomble, Whommle, Whummle
Overuse(d) Hackney(ed), RSI
Overvalue Exaggerate, Salt
Overweening Bashaw, Cocky, Excessive, Imperious, Presumptuous
Overweight Heavy, Obese, Pursy, Sunk
Overwhelm(ed), Overwhelming Accablé, Assail, Banging, → **CRUSH**, Dearth, Defeat, Deluge, Engulf, Flabbergast, Foudroyant, Inundate, KO, Mind-boggling, Oppress, Overcome, Plough under, Scupper, Smother, Snow, Submerge, Swamp, Whup
Overwork(ed) Fag, Hackneyed, Ornament, Slog, Stale, Supererogation, Tax, Tire, Toil, Travail
Overwritten Palimpsest
Overwrought Frantic, Hysterical, Ore-rested, Ornate, Rococo
Ovid Naso
Ovum Egg, Oosphere, Seed, Zygote
Owe(d), Owing Attribute, Due, OD
Owen Glendower

Owl(s) African, Barn, Barred, Blinker, Boobook, Brown, Bubo, Bunter, Chinese, Eagle, Elegant, English, Fish, Glimmergowk, Grey, Hawk, Hoo(ter), Horned, Howlet, Jenny, Little, Long-eared, Longhorn, Madge, Moper, Mopoke, Mopus, Night, Ogle, Parliament, Ruru, Saw-whet, Scops, Screech, Sea, Snowy, Spotted, Strich, Striges, Strigiformes, Tawny, Wood

Own(er), Owning, Ownership Admit, Agnise, Confess, Domain, Dominium, Fess, Have, Hold, Mortmain, Nain, Of, Personal, Possess, Proper, Proprietor, Recognise, Reputed, Title, Tod, Use

Own way More suo

Ox(en) Anoa, Aquinas, Aurochs, Banteng, Banting, Bison, Bonas(s)us, Buffalo, Bugle, Bullock, Cat(t)alo, Fee, Gaur, Gayal, Gyal, Kouprey, Mart, Musk, Musk-sheep, Neat, Ovibos, Rother, Saola, Sapi-utan, S(e)ladang, Steare, Steer, Stirk, Taurus, Ure, Urus, Vu quang, Water, Water buffalo, Yak, Yoke, Zebu, Z(h)o

Oxford (group) Blue, Buchmanism, OU, Puseyism, Shoe

Oxhead Aleph

Oxidation, Oxide Alumina, Anatase, Ceria, Erbium, Eremacausis, Gothite, Gummite, Holmia, Kernite, Lithia, Magnesia, Nitrous, Psilomelane, Quicklime, Red lead, Rutile, Samarskite, Strontia, Thoria, Zaffer, Zaffre

▷ **Oxtail** *may indicate* 'x'

Oxygen (and lack of) Anoxia, Epoxy, Liquid, Lox, Loxygen, O, Vital air

Oyer Hearing, Trial

Oyster (bed), Oyster disease, Oyster-eater Avicula, Bivalve, Bonamia, Bush, Cul(t)ch, Kentish, Lay, Mollusc, Native, Ostrea, Ostreophage, Pandore, Pearl, Plant, Prairie, Salsify, Scallop, Scalp, Scaup, Seed(ling), Spat, Spondyl, Stew, Vegetable

Oyster-catcher Sea-pie

Oyster-plant Gromwell, Salsify

Oz Amos, Australia

Ozone Air, Atmosphere, Oxygen

Pp

P Papa, Parking, Penny, Piano, Prince

PA Aide, Tannoy

Pabulum Aliment, Cheer, Food, Fuel, Nourishment

Pace, Pacemaker Canter, Clip, Cracking, Dog-trot, Easter, Footstep, Gait, Geometric, Heel and toe, Jog-trot, Lope, Measure, Military, Pari passu, Pioneer, Rack, → **RATE**, Roman, Scout's, Single-foot, Snail's, Spank, Speed, Step, Stride, Stroll, Tempo, Tramp, Tread, Trot

Pachyderm Armadillo, Elephant, Hippo, Mastodon, Rhino

Pacific, Pacify Appease, Bromide, Calm, Conciliate, Dove, Ease, Eirenic, Imperturbable, Irenic, Lull, Mild, Moderate, Ocean, Placate, Placid, Quiet, Serene, Soothe, Subdue, Sweeten, Tranquil

Pacifist CO, Conciliator, Dove, D(o)ukhobor, Peacenik

Pack(age), Packed, Packing, Pack in Back, Bale, Blister, Bobbery, Box, Bubble, Bundle, Can, Cards, Cold, Compress, Congest, Cram, Crate, Crowd, Cry, Deck, Dense, Dunnage, Embox, Entity, Everest, Excelsior, Face, Fardel, Floe, Forswear, Gasket, Gaskin, Glut, Hamper, Hooker, Hunt, Ice, Jam, Kennel, Knapsack, Lies, Load, Matilda, Naughty, Pair, → **PARCEL**, Pikau, Power, Pun, Ram, Rat, Rout, Ruck, Rucksack, Set, Shiralee, Shrink-wrap, Steeve, Stow, Suits, Sumpter, Tamp, Team, Tread, Troop, Truss, Wad, Wet, Wolf, Wrap

Packet Bindle, Boat, Bomb, Bundle, Deck, Liner, Mailboat, Mailer, Mint, Parcel, Pay, Red, Roll, Sachet, Steam, Steamboat, Wage

Pack-horse Sumpter

Packman Chapman, Hawker, Hiker, Pedlar, Tinker

Pact Agreement, Alliance, Bargain, Bilateral, Cartel, Contract, Covenant, Locarno, Munich, Stability, Suicide, → **TREATY**, Warsaw

Pad(ding) Batting, Bombast, Brake, Bustle, Compress, Condo, Crash, Cushion, Dabber, Damper, Dossil, Enswathe, Expand, Falsies, Filler, Flat, Frog, Gumshield, Hard, Hassock, Horse, Ink, Jotter, Knee, Launch, Leg-guard, Lily, Nag, Note, Numnah, Patch, Paw, Ped, Pillow, Pincushion, Plastron, Pledget, Plumper, Porters' knot, Pouf(fe), Protract, Pudding, Puff, Pulvillus, Pulvinar, Scratch, Shoulder, Stamp, Stuff, Sunk, Swab, Tablet, Thief, Touch, Tournure, Tylopod, Tympan, Velour(s), Velure, Wad, Wase, Writing

Paddington Bear, Station

Paddle, Paddle boat, Paddle-foot Canoe, Dabble, Doggy, Oar, Pinniped, Row, Seal, Side-wheel, Spank, Splash, Stern-wheeler, Wade

Paddock Enclosure, Field, Frog, Holding, Meadow, Park, Parrock, Sacrifice

Paddy, Paddy field Fury, Ire, Irishman, Mick, Pat(rick), Pet, Rag, Rage, Sawah, Tantrum, Temper, Wax

Padre Chaplain, Cleric, Father, Monk, Priest

Paean Eulogy, Hymn, Ode, Praise, Psalm

Paediatrician Rett

Paedophile Nonce

Pagan(ism) Animist, Atheist, Gentile, Gentoo, Godless, Heathen, Idolater, Infidel, Lectisternium, Odinist, Paynim, Saracen, Sun cult

Page(s), Pageboy Back, Beep, Bellboy, Bellhop, Bleep, Boy, Buttons, Callboy, Centrefold, Flyleaf, Fold out, Folio, Foolscap, Front, Gate-fold, Groom, Haircut, Hairdo, Home, Hornbook, Leaf, Master, Messenger, Moth, Octavo, Op-ed, P, Pane, PP, Problem, Quarto,

Ream, Recto, Ro, Servant, Sheet, Side, Splash, Squire, Tear sheet, Thirty-twomo, Tiger, Title, Varlet, Verso, Web, Yellow

Pageant Antic, Antique, Cavalcade, Pomp, Spectacle, Tattoo, Triumph

Pagoda Anking, Anqing, Temple, To

Pah Pish, Tush, Umph

▶ **Paid** *see* **PAY(MASTER)**

Pail Bucket, Kettle, Leglan, Leglen, Leglin, Piggin, Slop

Pain(ful), Pains Ache, Aggrieve, Agony, Ake, Algesis, Angina, Anguish, A(a)rgh, Arthralgia, Bad, Bale, Bedsore, Bitter, Bore, Bot(t), Bother, Burn, Causalgia, Colic, Cramp, Crick, CTS, Distress, Dole, Doleur, Dolour, Dool(e), Dysmenorrhoea, Dysury, Eina, Excruciating, Fash, Felon, Fibrositis, Gastralgia, Gip, Grief, Gripe, Growing, Gyp, Harrow, Heartburn, Hemialgia, → **HURT**, Ill, Kink, Laborious, Lancination, Lumbago, Mal, Mastalgia, Mastodynia, Metralgia, Migraine, Misery, Molimen, Mulligrubs, Myalgia, Neuralgia, Nociceptive, Pang, Persuant, Pest, Phantom, Pleurodynia, Prick, Pungent, Rack, Raw, Referred, Rick, Sair, Sciatica, Smart, Sore, Sorrow, Splitting, Sten(d), Sternalgia, Sting, Stitch, Strangury, Stung, Tarsalgia, Teen(e), Tene, Throe, Topalgia, Torment, Tormina, Torture, Travail, Twinge, Wo(e), Wrench, Wring

▷ **Pain** *may indicate* bread French

Painkiller Aminobutene, Analgesic, Bute, Celecoxib, Cocaine, Coxib, Distalgesic, Endorphin, Enkephalin, Jadeite, Meperidine, Metopon, Morphine, Number, Pethidine

Painless(ness) Analgesia, Easy

Painstaking Assiduous, Careful, Diligent, Elaborate, Exacting, Meticulous, Sedulous, Studious, Thorough

Paint(ed), Painting Abstract, Abstract expressionism, Acrylic, Action, Airbrush, Alla prima, Aquarelle, Arcimboldo, Art autre, Art deco, Artificial, Art nouveau, Ash Can School, Barbizon, Baroque, Battlepiece, Bice, Blottesque, Brushwork, Byzantine, Camaieu, Canvas, Cellulose, Cerograph, Chiaroscuro, Clair-obscure, Clobber, Coat, Colour, Cubism, Dadaism, Daub, Dayglo, Decorate, Depict, Describe, Diptych, Distemper, Duco, Eggshell, Emulsion, Enamel, Encaustic, Expressionist, Fard, Fauvism, Finery, Finger, Flatting, Flemish, Fore-edge, Fresco, Fucus, Genre, Gild, Gloss, Gothic, Gouache, Graining, Gravure, Grease, Grisaille, Guernica, Hard-edge, Historical, Icon, Impasto, Impressionism, Intimism(e), Intonaco, Intumescent, Lead, Limn, Lithochromy, Luminous, Magilp, Mannerist, Maquillage, Matt, Megilp, Mehndi, Miniate, Miniature, Modello, Mona Lisa, Monotint, Mural, Naive, Neoclassical, Neo-expressionist, Neo-Impressionism, Neo-Plasticism, Nightpiece, Nihonga, Nocturne, Non-drip, Oaker, Ochre, Oil, Old Master, Oleo(graph), Op art, Orphism, Paysage, Pentimento, Pict, Picture, Pigment, Pinxit, Plein air, Pointillism(e), Polyptych, Pop art, Portray, Poster, Post-Impressionism, Predella, Pre-Raphaelite, Primavera, Primitive, Quadratura, Raddle, Rag-rolling, Realist, Renaissance, Rococo, Romantic, Rosemaling, Roughstuff, Sand, Scenography, Scumble, Secco, Semi-gloss, Sfumato, Sien(n)ese, Skyscape, Spray, Stencil, Stereochrome, Still life, Stipple, Suprematism, Surrealist, Tablature, Tachism(e), Tag, Tall-oil, Tanka, Tempera, Tenebrism, Thangka, Tondo, Townscape, Ukiyo-e, Umber, Umbrian, Undercoat, Underglaze, Vanitas, Veduta, Vorticism, War, Wax

Painted woman Courtesan, Harlot, Pict, Tart

Painter(s) Animalier, Aquarellist, → **ARTIST**, Ash Can School, Colourist, Cubist, Decorator, Gilder, Illusionist, Impressionist, Limner, Little Master, Luminarist, Miniaturist, Muralist, Old Master, Paysagist, Plein-airist, Primitive, Sien(n)ese, Soutine, Sunday, Vedutista

Pair(ing) Brace, Cooper, Couple(t), Doublet, Duad, Duo, Dyad(ic), Exciton, Fellows, Geminate, Item, Jugate, Jumelle, King, Link, Lone, Match, Mate, Minimal, Ocrea, Pigeon Pr, Span, Spouses, Synapsis, Syndyasmian, Syzygy, Tandem, Thummim, Twa(e), Tway, Two, Urim, Yoke

Paisley Ian, Orange, Shawl

Pakistan(i) Jat, Pathan, .pk, Punjabi, Sind(h)i

Pal Ally, Amigo, Bud(dy), China, Chum, Comrade, Crony, Cully, Friend, Mate, Playmate, Wus(s)

Palace Alcazar, Alhambra, Basilica, Blenheim, Buckingham, Court, Crystal, Edo, Élysée, Escorial, Escurial, Fontainebleau, Forbidden City, Fulham, Gin, Goslar, Hampton Court, Holyrood, Holyroodhouse, Hotel, Istana, Lambeth, Lateran, Linlithgow, Louvre, Mansion, Nonsuch, Palatine, Picture, Pitti, Pushkin, Quirinal, St James's, Sans Souci, Schloss, Seraglio, Serail, Shushan, Topkapi, Trianon, Tuileries, Valhalla, Vatican, Versailles, Winter

Paladin Champion, Charlemagne, Defender, Douzeper, Fièrabras, Ganelon, → **KNIGHT**, Ogier, Oliver, Orlando, Rinaldo, Roland

Palanquin Doolie, Kago, Litter, Palkee, Palki, Sedan

Palatable, Palatalized, Palate Cleft, Dainty, Hard, Mouille, Relish, Roof, Sapid, Savoury, Soft, Taste, Toothsome, Uranic, Uraniscus, Uvula, Velum

Palatial Ornate, Splendid

Palatinate, Palatine Officer, Pfalz

Palaver Chatter, Debate, Parley, Powwow, → **TALK**

Pale, Paling Ashen, Blanch, Bleach, Cere, Dim, English, Etiolate(d), Fade, → **FAINT**, Fence, Ghostly, Haggard, Insipid, Jewish, Lily (white), Livid, Mealy, Ox-fence, Pallescent, Pastel, Pasty-faced, Peaky, Peelie-wally, Picket, Sallow, Shilpit, Stang, Verge, Wan, Whey-faced, White, Wishy-washy

Paleography Diplomatics

Pal(a)eolithic Acheulean, Acheulian, Azilian, Capsian, Chellean, Clactonian, Gravettian, Levallois(ian), Lower, Madelenian, Magdalenian, Middle, Neanderthal, Perigordian, Solutrean, Strepyan, Upper

Paleozoic Hercynian, Permian, Silurian

Palestine, Palestinian Amorite, Fatah, Gadarene, Gaza, Hamas, Holy Land, Intifada, Israel, Pal, Per(a)ea, Philistine, PLO, Samaria

Palette Board, Cokuloris

Palindrome, Palindromic Cancrine, Sotadic

Palisade Barrier, Fence, Fraise, Stacket, Stockade

Pall Bore, Cloy, Curtain, Damper, Glut, Hearse-cloth, Mantle, Mortcloth, Satiate, Shroud

Palladium Defence, Pd, Safeguard

Pallas Athene

Pallet Bed, Cot, Couch, Mattress, Tick

Palliate, Palliative Alleviate, Anetic, Ease, Extenuate, Lessen, Mitigate, Reduce, Relieve, Sedative

Pallid Anaemic, Ashen, Insipid, Pale, Wan, Waxy

Palm Accolade, Areca, Assai, Atap, Babassu, Bangalow, Betel, Buriti, Burrawang, Bussu, Cabbage, Calamus, Carna(h)uba, Carpentaria, Chamaerops, Chiqui-chiqui, Coco, Cohune, Conceal, Coquito, Corozo, Corypha, Cycad, Date (tree), Doom, Doum, Elaeis, Euterpe, Fan, Feather, Fob, Foist, Gomuti, Gomuto, Groo-groo, Gru-gru, Hand, Hemp, Ita, Itching, Ivory, Jip(p)i-Jap(p)a, Jipyapa, Jupati, Kentia, Kittul, Laurels, Loof, Looves, Macahuba, Macaw, Macoya, Miriti, Moriche, Nikau, Nipa, Oil, Palmyra, Paxiuba, Peach, Pupunha, Raffia, Raphia, Rat(t)an, Royal, Sabal, Sago, Saw palmetto, Sugar, Talipat, Talipot, Thatch, Thenar, Toddy, Triumph, Troelie, Troolie, Trooly, Trophy, Vola, Washingtonia, Wax, Wine, Zamia

Palmer Lilli, Pilgrim

Palmerston Pam

Palmistry Ch(e)irognomy

Palm-leaf Frond

Palm-oil Bribe, Payola

Palpable Evident, Gross, Manifest, Patent, Plain, Tangible

Palpitate, Palpitation Flutter, Pitpat, Pulsate, Throb, Twitter, Vibrate

Palsy Bell's, Cerebral, Paralysis, Scrivener's, Shakes, Shaking, Spastic paralysis

Paltry Bald, Cheap, Exiguous, Mean, Measly, Mere, Peanuts, Pelting, Petty, Pimping, Poor, Puny, Scald, Scalled, Shabby, Shoestring, Sorry, Tin(-pot), Tinny, Trashy, Trifling, Two-bit, Vile, Waff, Whiffet

Pamper(ed) Baby, Cocker, Coddle, Cosher, Cosset, Cuiter, Feather-bed, Gratify, High-fed, → INDULGE, Mollycoddle, Overfeed, Pet, Pompey, Spoon-fed

Pamphlet Brochure, Catalogue, Chapbook, Leaflet, Notice, Sheet, Tract

Pan Agree, Auld Hornie, Bainmarie, Balit, Basin, Betel(-pepper), Braincase, Chafer, Dent, Dial, Drip, Dripping, Drub, Goat-god, Goblet, God, Hard, Ice-floe, Iron, Jelly, Karahi, Knee, Ladle, Lavatory, Muffin, Nature-god, Non-stick, Oil, Pancheon, Panchion, Patella, Patina, Peter, Poacher, Preserving, Prospect, Roast, Salt, Search, Skid, Skillet, Slag, Slate, Spider, Sweep, Tube, Vacuum, Vessel, Warming, Wo(c)k, Work

Panacea All-heal, Azoth, Catholicon, Cure(-all), Diacatholicon, Elixir, Ginseng, Heal-all, Parkleaves, Remedy, Tutsan

Panache Bravura, Crest, Dash, Elan, Flair, Paz(z)azz, Piz(z)azz, Plume, Pzazz, Show, Style, Talent

Panama Isthmus

Pancake Blin(i), Blintz(e), Burrito, Crêpe (suzette), Crumpet, Drop(ped)-scone, Flam(m), Flapjack, Flaune, Flawn, Fraise, Fritter, Froise, Latke, Pikelet, Poppadum, Potato, Quesadilla, Ro(e)sti, Scotch, Slapjack, Spring roll, Suzette, Taco, Tortilla, Tostada, Waffle

Pancreas Isles of Langerhans, Sweetbread

Panda Bear-cat, Car, Chi-chi, Chitwah, Common, Giant, Lesser, Red, Squad car

Pandarus Go-between

Pandemonium Bedlam, Inferno, Mayhem, Uproar

Pander Broker, Indulge, Minister, Pimp, Procurer, Toady

Pane Glass, Light, Panel, Quarrel, Quarry, Sheet

Panegyric Encomium, Eulogy, Laudation, Praise, Tribute

Panel(ling) Adoption, Array, Board, Cartouche, Children's, Console, Control, Dashboard, Fa(s)cia, Gore, Hatchment, Inset, Instrument, Jury, Lacunar, Mandorla, Mimic, Mola, Orb, Patch(board), People's, Reredorse, Reredos(se), Rocker, Screen, Skreen, Solar, Stile, Stomacher, Table, Tablet, Valance, Volet, Wainscot

Pang Achage, Ache, Crick, Qualm, Spasm, Stab, Stound, Travail, Twinge, Wrench

Pangloss Optimist

Pangolin Ant-eater, Manis

Panhandle(r) Beggar, W. Virginia

Panic Alar(u)m, Amaze, Blue funk, Consternation, Fear, Flap, Flat-spin, Flip, Fright, Funk, Guinea-grass, Hysteria, Lather, Millet, Raggee, Raggy, Ragi, Sauve qui peut, → SCARE, Scaremonger, Scarre, Stampede, Stampedo, State, Stew, Tailspin, → TERROR

Panicle Thyrse

Panjandrum Bashaw

Pannier Basket, Cacolet, Corbeil, Dosser, Saddlebag, Skip, Whisket

Panoply Armour, Array, Pomp

Panorama, Panoramic Cyclorama, Range, Scenery, Veduta, View, Vista

Pansy Gay, Heart's-ease, Herb-trinity, Kiss-me-quick, Love-in-idleness, Nance, Powder-puff, Queer, Viola

Pant(s) Bags, Breeches, Capri, Cargo, Chaps, Chinos, Culottes, Deck, Dhoti, Drawers, Fatigues, Flaff, Gasp, Gaucho, Harem, Hot, Knickers, Long johns, Longs, Parachute, Pech, Pedal-pushers, Pegh, Puff, Rot, Ski, Slacks, Smalls, Stirrup, Stovepipe, Sweat, The pits, Throb, Toreador, Training, Trews, Trousers, Trunks, Wheeze, Yearn

Pantaloon Columbine, Dupe, Pants

Pantheism Idolatry, Immanency

Panther Bagheera, Black, Cat, Cougar, Grey, Jaguar, Leopard, Pink

Panties Briefs, Knickers, Scanties, Step-ins, Undies

Pantomime, Pantomime character Aladdin, Charade, Cheironomy, Dumb-show, Farce, Galanty, Harlequinade, Pierrot, Play

Pantry Buttery, Closet, Larder, Spence, Stillroom

Pap Dug, Mealie, Mush, Nipple, Teat, Udder

Papa Dad, Father, P

Papal, Papist, Papistry Catholic, Clementine, Concordat, Guelf, Guelph, Holy See, Legation, Pontifical, RC, Roman, Vatican

Paper(s), Paperwork, Papery Admin, Allonge, Antiquarian, Art, Atlas, Ballot, Baryta, Bible, Blotting, Bond, Brief, Broadsheet, Broadside, Bromide, Brown, Building, Bumf, Bumph, Butter, Cap, Carbon, Cartridge, Cellophane®, Chad, Chinese, Chiyogami, Cigarette, Colombier, Command, Commercial, Confetti, Corrugated, Cream-laid, Cream-wove, Credentials, Crêpe, Crown, Curl, Cutch, Daily, Deckle-edge, Decorate, Demy, Document, Dossier, Eggshell, Elephant, Emery, Emperor, Essay, Exam, File, Filter, Final, Flock, Folio, Foolscap, Form(s), Fourdrinier, FT, Funny, Furnish, Galley, Garnet, Gazette, Gem, Glass(ine), Glumaceous, Government, Grand eagle, Grand Jesus, Graph, Greaseproof, Green, Guardian, Hieratica, ID, Imperial, India, Japanese, Jesus, Journal, Kent cap, Kraft, Kutch, Lace, Laid, Lavatory, Legal cap, Linen, Litmus, Loo-roll, Manifold, Manil(l)a, Marble, Mercantile, Mirror, MS, Munimenti, Music(-demy), Needle, News(print), → **NEWSPAPER**, Note, Notelet, Oil, Onion-skin, Order, Origami, Packing, Pad, Page, Papillote, Papyrus, Parchment, Pickwick, Plotting, Position, Post, Pot(t), Pravda, Press, Print, Printing, Quair, Quarto, Quire, Rag, Ramee, Rami(e), Ream, Red top, Retree, Rhea, Rice, Rolled, Rolling, Royal, Safety, Satin, Saxe, Scent, Scotsman, Scrip, Script, Scroll, Scrowl, Sheaf, Sheet, Ship's, Silver, Skin, Slipsheet, Spoilt, Stamp, Starch, State, Steamer, Sugar, Sun, Super-royal, Tabloid, Taffeta, Tap(p)a, Tar, Term, Ternion, TES, Test, Thesis, Thread, Tiger, Tissue, Today, Toilet, Torchon, Touch, Tracing, Trade, Transfer, Treatise, Treeware, Tri-chad, Turmeric, Two-name, Vellum, Velvet, Voucher, Walking, Wall, Waste, Watch, Wax(ed), Web, Whatman®, White, Willesden, Wirewove, Wood(chip), Woodfree, Worksheet, Wove, Wrapping, Writing, Zine

Paperback Limp(back)

Paper-cutting, Paper-folding Decoupage, Kirigami, Origami, Psaligraphy

Papier-mâché Carton-pierre, Flong

Paprika Spanish

Par Average, Equate, Equivalent, → **NORMAL**, Scratch

Parable Allegory, Fable, Proverb

Parabola Arc, Curve, Hyperbola

Parachute, Parachutist Aeroshell, Aigrette, Brake, Drag, Drogue, Extraction, Float, Freefall, Golden, Jump, Pack, Pappus, Para, Parabrake, Parapente, Red Devil, Ribbon, Silk, Sky-diving, Skyman, Thistledown, Umbrella

Parade (ground) Air, Arcade, Catwalk, Cavalcade, Ceremony, Church, Concours d'élégance, Display, Dress, Drill, Easter, Emu, Flaunt, Gala, Hit, Identification, Identity, Line-up, Maidan, March-past, Monkey-run, Pageantry, Passing-out, Pomp, Prance, Procession, Prom(enade), Sashay, Show, Sick, Sowarry, Stand-to, Ticker tape, Troop

Paradise Arcadia, Avalon, Bliss, Eden, Elysium, Fool's, Garden, Happy-hunting-ground, Heaven, Lost, Malaguetta, Nirvana, Park, Regained, Shangri-la, Svarga, Swarga, Swerga, → **UTOPIA**

Paradox(ical) Absurdity, Cantor's, Contradiction, Dilemma, Electra, Epimenides, French, Gilbertian, Hydrostatic, Irony, Koan, Liar, Olber's, Puzzle, Russell's, Sorites, Twin, Zeno's

Paraffin Earthwax, Kerosene, Kerosine, Liquid, Ozocerite, Ozokerite, Photogen(e), Propane

Paragon Model, Non(e)such, Pattern, Pearl, Phoenix, Role model, Rose

Paragraph (mark) Balaam, Causerie, Note, Passage, Piece, Pilcrow

Paraguay PY

Parakeet Parrot, Popinjay, Rosella

Parallax Annual, Daily, Diurnal, Geocentric, Heliocentric

Parallel Analog, Arctic circle, Collateral, Collimate, Corresponding, Equal, Even,

Forty-ninth, Like, Pattern

Parallelogram Rhomb

Paralysis, Paralyse Apoplexy, Cataplexy, Catatonia, Cramp, Curarise, Cycloplegia, Diplegia, Halt, Hemiplegia, Infantile, Lithyrism, Monoplegia, Numbness, Ophthalmoplegia, Palsy, Paraplegia, Paresis, Polio, Quadriplegia, Radial, Scram, Shock, Shut, Spastic, Spina bifida, Stun, Torpefy, Transfix

Paramedic Ambulance-man

Paramilitary Inkatha, Phalangist, SAS, Sena, UDA

Paramount Chief, Dominant, Greatest, Overall, Premier, → **SUPREME**, Topless, Utmost

Paramour Beau, Franion, Gallant, Leman, Lover, Mistress, Thais

Paranoid Tweak

Paranormal Clairvoyant, ESP, Psionics, Psychic, Spiritual, Telekinesis

Parapet (space) Barbette, Bartisan, Bartizan, Battlement, Breastwork, Brisure, Bulwark, Crenel, Flèche, Machicolation, Merlon, Rampart, Redan, Surtout, Terreplein, Top, Wall

Paraphernalia Armamentarium, Belongings, Equipment, Gear, Trappings

Parasite, Parasitic Ascarid, Autoecious, Aweto, Babesiasis, Beech-drops, Bilharzia, Biogenous, Biotroph, Bladder-worm, Bloodsucker, Bonamia, Bot, Candida, Chalcid, Coccus, Conk, Copepod, Cosher, Crab-louse, Cryptosporidium, Cryptozoite, Dodder, Ectogenous, Ectophyte, Endamoeba, Endophyte, Entophyte, Entozoon, Epiphyte, Epizoon, Facultative, Filarium, Flatworm, Flea, Freeloader, Gapeworm, Giardia, Gregarinida, Haematozoon, Hair-eel, Heartworm, Heteroecious, Hook-worm, Ichneumon, Inquiline, Isopod, Kade, Ked, Lackey, Lamprey, Leech, Leishmania, Licktrencher, Liverfluke, Louse, Lungworm, Macdonald, Mallophagous, Measle, Mistletoe, Monogenean, Necrotroph, Nematode, Nit, Obligate, Orobanche, Phytosis, Pinworm, Plasmodium, Puccinia, Pulix, Quandong, Rafflesia, Redia, Rhipidoptera, Rickettsia, Root, Roundworm, Schistosoma, Scrounger, Shark, Smut-fungus, Sponge(r), Sporozoa(n), Strangleweed, Strepsiptera, Strongyle, Strongyloid, Stylops, Sucker, Symphile, Tachinid, Tapeworm, Tick, Toady, Toxoplasma, Trematode, Trencher-friend, Trencher-knight, Trichina, Trichomonad, Tryp(anosoma), Vampire, Viscum, Wheatworm, Whipworm, Witchweed, Worms

Parasol Awning, Brolly, En tout cas, Marquise, Sunshade, Umbrella

Paratrooper Red Devil, Skyman, Stick leader

Parcel Allocate, Allot, Aret, Bale, Bundle, Dak, Holding, Lot, Package, Packet, Plot, Sort, Wrap

Parch(ed), Parching Arid, Bake, Dry, Graddan, Hot coppers, Roast, Scorched, Sere, Thirsty, Toast, Torrefied, Torrid, Xerotes

Parchment Diploma, Forel, Mezuzah, Panel, Papyrus, Pell, Pergameneous, Roll, Roule, Scroll, Scrow, Sheepskin, Vegetable, Vellum, Virgin

Pard Leopard, Pal, Partner

Pardon(able), Pardoner Absolution, Absolve, Amnesty, Anan, Assoil, Clear, Condone, Eh, Excuse, → **FORGIVE**, Grace, Mercy, Quaestionary, Quaestuary, Qu(a)estor, Release, Remission, Remit, Reprieve, Venial, What

Pare Flaught, Flay, Peel, Shave, Skive, Sliver, Strip, Whittle

Parent(al) Ancestral, Father, Forebear, Generant, Genitor, Maternal, Mother, Paternal, Single, Solo, Storge

Parenthesis Aside, Brackets, Innuendo

Parhelion Sun-dog

Pariah Ishmael, Leper, Outcast, Pi(e)dog, Pyedog

Paris(ian), Parisienne Abductor, Athene, Elle, Gai, Gay, Grisette, Lutetia (Parisiorum), Lutetian, Maillotin, Midinette, Trojan

Parish Charge, District, Flock, Kirkto(w)n, Parischan(e), Parishen, Parochin(e), Peculiar, Province, Title

Parity Equalness, Smithsonian

Park(ing) Amusement, Business, Car, Caravan, Common, Country, Domain, Enclosure,

Forest, Fun, Game, Garage, Grounds, Hardstand, Industrial, Lung, Motor, National, Off-street, P, Petrified Forest, Pitch, Preserve, Rec, Safari, Sanctuary, Science, Siding, Stand, Stop, Technology, Terrain, Theme, Trailer, Valet, Water, Wildlife, Wind, Yard

PARKS

4 letters:
Hyde

5 letters:
Dales
Green
Ibrox
Mungo
Tsavo

6 letters:
Etosha
Exmoor
Hwange
Jasper
Kakadu
Katmai
Kruger
Oyster
Tivoli

7 letters:
Central
Gardens
Nairobi
Phoenix

Regent's
Sandown

8 letters:
Daintree
Dartmoor
Jurassic
Osterley
Paradise
St James's
Yosemite

9 letters:
Algonquin
Battersea
Fiordland
Grampians
Green lung
Lamington
Mansfield
Mesa Verde
Serengeti
Snowdonia

10 letters:
Disneyland

Everglades
Kejimkujik
Pittie-ward

11 letters:
Alton Towers
Death Valley
Grand Canyon
Kobuk Valley
Mammoth Cave
Wood Buffalo
Yellowstone

12 letters:
Lake District
Mount Rainier
Peak District
Quttinirpaaq

13 letters:
Banff National
Brecon Beacons
Mount Aspiring
Mount McKinley

14 letters:
Egmont National
Jasper National
Lassen Volcanic
Northumberland
North York Moors
Riding Mountain
Yorkshire Dales

15 letters:
Kalahari Gemsbok
Nahanni National
Sequoia National

16 letters:
Gates of the Arctic

18 letters:
Mount Kenya
  National
Prince Edward Island
Shenandoah National

19 letters:
Great Smoky
  Mountains

Parka Atigi
Parker Dorothy, Nos(e)y
Parkleaves Tutsan
Parley Confer, Discourse, Palaver, Speak, Tret
Parliament Addled, Althing, Barebones, Black, Boule, Bundestag, Chamber, Commons, Congress, Cortes, Council, Cross-bench, Dail, Diet, Drunken, D(o)uma, Eduskunta, European, Folketing, House, Imperial, Knesset, Lack-learning, Lagt(h)ing, Landst(h)ing, Lawless, Legislature, Lok Sabha, Long, Lords, Majlis, Merciless, Mongrel, Odelst(h)ing, Political, Rajya Sabha, Reichsrat, Reichstag, Riksdag, Rump, St Stephens, Sanhedrin, Seanad, Seanad Éireann, Sejm, Short, Stannary, States-general, Stirthing, Stormont, Stort(h)ing, The Beehive, Thing, Tynwald (Court), Unicameral, Unlearned, Useless, Vidhan Sabha, Volkskammer, Volksraad, Westminster
Parliamentarian Cabinet, De Montfort, Fairfax, Ireton, Leveller, Member, MP, Politico, Roundhead, Whip
Parlour Beauty, Funeral, Ice-cream, Lounge, Massage, Milking, Salon, Snug, Spence
Parnassus Museum, Verse
Parochial Insular, Narrow-minded
Parody Burlesque, Cod, Lampoon, Mock, Piss-take, Satire, Send-up, Skit, Spoof, Travesty
Parole Pledge, Promise, Trust, Word
Paronychia Agnail, Felon, Whitlow
Paroxysm Fit, Frenzy, Rapture, Spasm, Subintrant, Throe

Parricide Cenci

Parrot Amazon, Ape, Cockatoo, Conure, Copy, Echo, Flint, Green leek, Grey, Imitate, Kaka(po), Kea, Lorikeet, Lory, Lovebird, Macaw, Mimic, Nestor, Owl, Parakeet, Paroquet, Poll(y), Popinjay, Psittacine, Quarrion, Repeat, Rosella, Rote, Shell, Stri(n)gops, T(o)uraco

Parrot-bill Glory-pea

Parry Block, Counter, Defend, Dodge, Forestall, Parade, Riposte, Sixte, Tac-au-tac, Thwart, Ward

Parsee Zoroastrian

Parsimonious, Parsimony Aberdonian, Cheese-paring, Mean, Narrow, Near(ness), Niggardly, Scanty, Stingy, Thrift, Tight

Parsley Apiol, Cicely, Dog, Kecks, Kex, Persillade, Pot-herb

Parsnip Buttered, Buttery, Dill, Masterwort, Sium, Skirret

Parson Clergyman, Cleric, Holy Joe, Minister, Non juror, Pastor, Priest, Rector, Rev, Sky-pilot, Soul-curer, Yorick

Parsonage Glebe, Manse, Rectory, Vicarage

Part(s), Parting Accession, Aliquot, Antimere, Area, Aught, Bad, Behalf, Bit, Bulk, Bye, Cameo, Character, Chunk, Cog, Component, Constituent, Crack, Cue, Dislink, Diverge, Dole, Element, Episode, Escapement, Farewell, Fascicle, Fork, Fraction, Good, Goodbye, Great, Half, Ill, Imaginary, Ingredient, Instalment, Into, Lathe, Lead, Leave, Leg, Lill, Lilt, Lines, List, Livraison, Member, Meronym, Moiety, Organ, Parcel, Passus, → **PIECE**, Portion, Primo, Principal, Private, Proportion, Pt, Quit, Quota, Rape, Ratio, Real, Region, Rive, Role, Scena, Scene, Secondo, Section, Sector, Segment, Segregate, Separate, Serial, Sever, Shade, Share, Shed, Sleave, Sle(i)ded, Small, → **SOME**, Spare, Split, Stator, Sunder, Synthon, Tithe, Tranche, Twin(e), Unit, Vaunt, Voice, Walking, Walk on, Wrench

Partake(r) Allottee, Eat, Participate, Share

Parthenogenesis Deuterotoky, Thelytoky

Partial(ity), Partially Biased, Ex-parte, Fan, Favour, Halflins, Imbalance, Incomplete, One-sided, Predilection, Prejudiced, Slightly, Unequal, Weakness

Participate, Participant, Participation Audience, Engage, Field, Join, Muck-in, Panellist, Partake, Share, Symposiast, Traceur

Participle Dangling, Misrelated, Past, Perfect, Present

Particle(s) Alpha, Anion, Antielectron, Antineutron, Antiproton, Atom, Baryon, Beta, Bit, Boson, Charmonium, Corpuscle, Curn, Dander, Delta, Deuteron, Effluvium, Electron, Elementary, Episome, Exchange, Fermion, Fleck, Floccule, Fragment, Fundamental, Gauge boson, Gemmule, Globule, Gluon, Grain, Granule, Graviton, Hadron, Heavy, Higgs, Hyperon, Ion, J, Jot, J/psi, Kaon, Lambda, Lemail, Lemel, Lepton, Lipoplast, Liposome, Meson, Micelle, Microsome, Mite, Molecule, Monopole, Mote, Muon, Negatron, Neutralino, Neutretto, Neutrino, Neutron, Nibs, Nobiliary, Nucleon, Omega-minus, Parton, Pentaquark, Photon, Pion, Plasmagene, Plastisol, Platelet, Positon, Positron, Preon, Proton, Psi(on), Quark, Radioactivity, Shives, Shower, Sigma, Singlet, Sinter, Smithereen, Spark, Speck, Strange, Subatom, Submicron, Subnuclear, Tachyon, Tardyon, Tau neutrino, Tauon, Thermion, Tittle, Virion, W, Whit, WIMP, X-hyperon, XI, Z

Parti-coloured Fancy, Motley, Piebald, Pied, Variegated

Particular Choosy, Dainty, → **DETAIL**, Endemic, Especial, Essential, Express, Fiky, Fog, Fussy, Item, Itself, London fog, Minute, Nice, Niffy-naffy, Nipperty-tipperty, Nitpicker, Old-maidish, Own, Pea-souper, Peculiar, Pedant, Pernickety, Pet, Point, Prim, Proper, → **RESPECT**, Special, Specific, Stickler, Strict, Stripe

Partisan Adherent, Axe, Biased, Carlist, Champion, Devotee, Factional, Fan, Irregular, Partial, Provo, Queenite, Sider, Spear, Stalwart, Supporter, Tendentious, Yorkist, Zealot

Partition(ed) Abjoint, Bail, Barrier, Brattice, Bretasche, Bulkhead, Cloison, Cubicle, Diaphragm, Dissepiment, Divider, Division, Hallan, Mediastinum, Parpane, Parpen(d), Parpent, Parpoint, Perpend, Perpent, Replum, → **SCREEN**, Scriene, Septum, Skreen, Tabula, Wall, With

Partlet Hen, Overlaid

Partner(ship) Accomplice, Alliance, Ally, Associate, Bidie-in, Butty, Cahoot(s), Coachfellow, Cohab(itee), Cohabitor, Colleague, Comrade, Confederate, Consort, Copemate, Couple, Date, Dutch, Escort, E-W, Firm, Gigolo, Husband, Limited, Mate, N-S, Offsider, Oppo, Other half, Pair, Pal, Pard, Rival, Sidekick, Significant other, Silent, Sleeping, SOP, Sparring, Spouse, Stablemate, Stand, Symbiosis, Wag, Wife

▷ **Part of** *may indicate* a hidden word

Partridge Bird, Chik(h)or, Chukar, Chukor, Covey, Flapper, Quail, Red-legged, Tinamou, Ynambu

Party Acid house, Advance, Aftershow, Alliance, ANC, Apparat, Assembly, At-home, Ba'ath, Bake, Ball, Band, Barbecue, Bash, Beano, Bee, Bloc, Blowout, Body, Bottle, Buck's, Bunfight, Bust, Caboodle, Camp, Carousal, Carouse, Caucus, Celebration, Clambake, Coach, Cocktail, Colour, Commando, Communist, Concert, Congress, Conservative, Contingent, Cookie-shine, Cooperative, Coterie, Cult, Democratic, Detail, Ding, Dinner, Discotheque, Do, Drum, DUP, Faction, Falange, Federalist, Fest, Fête champêtre, Fête Galante, Fianna Fáil, Fiesta, Fine Gael, Firing, Foy, Function, Funfest, Gala, Galravage, Gang, Garden, Ghibel(l)ine, Green, Greenback, Grumbletonian, Guelf, Guelph, Guilty, Hen, High heels, Hoedown, Hooley, Hootenannie, Hootenanny, Hoot(a)nannie, Hoot(a)nanny, House, Housewarming, Hurricane, Inkatha, Irredentist, Jana Sangh, Janata, Jol(lities), Junket, Junto, Kettledrum, Kitchen tea, Klat(s)ch, Knees-up, Kuomintang, L, Labour, Launch, Lawn, Levee, Lib, Liberal, Lig, Love-in, Low heels, Luau, Mallemaroking, Mollie, Movement, Musicale, National, Necking, Neck-tie, Octobrist, Opposition, Orgy, Peace, People's, Person, Petting, Plaid, Populist, Posse, Progressive, Prohibition, Pyjama, Radical, Rage, Rave, Rave-up, Razzle(-dazzle), Reception, Republican, Reunion, Revel, Ridotto, Roast, Rocking, Roister, Rort, Rout, Scottish Nationalist, SDP, Search, Sect, Set, Shindig, Shindy, Shine, Shivoo, Shooting, Shower, Shower tea, Side, Sinn Fein, Slumber, Small and early, Smoker, SNP, Soc(ialist), Social, Social Credit, Social Democratic, Socialise, Soirée, Spree, Squad(rone), Squadrone volante, Stag, Symposium, Tailgate, Tea, Teafight, Third, Thrash, Tory, Treat, Ultramontane, Unionist, United, Wafd, Wake, Warehouse, Whig, Whoop-de-do(o), Wine, Wingding, Working, Wrap

Partygoer Rager, Raver, Reveller, Socialite

Party-piece Solo

Parvenu Arriviste, Upstart

Pascal Blaise, Pa, Pressure

Pash Crush, Devotion

Pasha Achmed, Dey, Emir, Ismet

Pass(ed), Passing, Pass on, Past Absit, Aforetime, Ago, Agon, Annie Oakley, Aorist, Approve, Arise, Arlberg, Before, Behind, Bernina, Beyond, Boarding, Bolan, Botte, Brenner, Brief, Burgess, By (the by), Bygone, Caudine Forks, Centre, Cerro Gordo, Chal(l)an, Chilkoot, Chine, Chit(ty), Cicilian Gates, Clear, Col, Cote, Cross, Cursory, Death, Dee, Defile, Delate, Demise, Diadrom, Die, Disappear, Double, Dummy, Dunno, Elapse, Emit, Enact, End, Ensue, Ephemeral, Exceed, Exeat, Faena, Flashback, Fleeting, Foist, Forby, Forgone, Former, Forward, Gap, Gate, Gha(u)t, Give, Glencoe, Glide, Go, Go by, Gorge, Great St Bernard, Gulch, Halse, Hand, Happen, Hause, Hospital, ID, Impart, Impermanent, Interrail, Interval, In transit, Jark, Jump, Khyber, Killiecrankie, Kloof, La Cumbre, Lap, Late, Lead, Live, Long syne, Mesmerism, Migrate, Mont Cenis, Moravian Gate, Nek, Nine days' wonder, No bid, Nod through, Notch, Nutmeg, Nye, Occur, Oer, O grade, OK, Okay, Oke, Omit, One-time, Overhaul, Overshoot, Overslaugh, Overtake, Pa, Palm, Parade, Participle, Perish, Permeate, Permit, Perpetuate, Poll, Poort, Predicament, Preterit(e), Pretty, Proceed, Propagate, Pun(c)to, Qualify, Railcard, Reach, Reeve, Refer, Relay, Retro, Retroactive, Retrospect, Reverse, Roncesvalles, Run, Safe conduct, St Bernard, St Gotthard, San Bernardino, Sanitation, Scissors, Sea-letter, Senile, Serve, Shangri-la, Shipka, Simplon, Since, Skim, Skip, Skirt, Slap, Sling, Small and early, Snap, Spend, Stab, State, Temporal, Thermopylae, Thread, Through, Ticket,

Time immemorial, Tip, Transient, Transilient, Transitory, Transmit, Transude, Travel,
Triptyque, Troop, Uspallata, Veronica, Vet, Visa, Visé, Wall, Wayleave, Weather, While,
Wrynose, Yesterday, Yesteryear, Ygoe

Passable, Passible Adequate, Fair, Navigable, Tolerable

Passage(way) Abature, Adit, Airway, Aisle, Alley(way), Alure, Apostrophe, Arcade,
Archway, Areaway, Arterial, Atresia, Avenue, Bank, Breezeway, Bridge, Bylane, Cadenza,
Caponier(e), Career, Catwalk, Channel, Chute, Citation, Clarino, Clause, Close, Coda,
Condie, Conduit, Corridor, Creep, Crossing, Crush, Cundy, Dead-end, Deambulatory,
Defile, Drake, Drift, Duct, Eel-fare, Episode, Excerpt, Extract, Fare, Fat, Fauces, Fistula,
Flat, Flight, Flue, Fogou, Gallery, Gangway, Gap, Gat, Gate, Ghat, Ginnel, Gully-hole,
Gut, Hall, Head, Inlet, Journey, Kyle, Labyrinth, Lane, Lapse, Larynx, Lick, Lientery,
Loan, Lobby, Locus, Meatus, Melisma, Meridian, Middle, Mona, Moto perpetuo,
Movement, Northeast, Northwest, Para(graph), Parashah, Path, Pend, Pericope, Phrase,
Pore, Port, Portion, Prelude, Presto, Prose, Purple, Race, Retournelle, Ride, Ripieno,
Rite, Ritornell(o), Road, Rough, Route, Sailing, Screed, Shaft, Shunt, Sinus, Skybridge,
Skywalk, Slap, Slype, Snicket, Solus, Spillway, Sprue, Strait, Street, Stretta, Stretto,
Subway, Sump, Text, Thirl, Thorough(fare), Throat, Tour, Trachea, Trance, Transe,
Transit(ion), Travel, Tunnel, Tutti, Undercast, Unseen, Ureter, Voyage, Walkway, Way,
Windpipe, Windway

▷ **Passage of arms** *may indicate* 'sleeve'

Passé Corny, Dated, Ex, Obsolete, Old-fashioned

Passenger(s) Cad, Commuter, Fare, Parasite, Pax, Payload, Pillion, Rider, Slacker,
Steerage, Straphanger, Transit, Traveller, Voyager, Way, Wayfarer

Passible Patible

▶ **Passible** *see* BAULK

Passion(ate), Passionately Anger, Appetite, Ardour, Con calore, Con fuoco, Crush,
Duende, Emotion, Fervour, Fire, Flame, Frampold, Fury, Gust, Gutsy, Hate, Heat, Hot,
Hunger, Hwyl, Ileac, Iliac, Infatuation, Intense, Ire, Irish, Kama, Love, Lust, Mania,
Messianic, Metromania, Obsession, Oestrus, Polemic, Rage, Reverent, Sizzling, Stormy,
Sultry, Torrid, Vehement, Violent, Warm, Wax, Wrath, Yen, Zeal, Zoolatria

Passion-fruit Water-lemon

Passion play Oberammergau

Passive (stage) Apathetic, Dormant, Drifter, Inert, Pathic, Patient, Pupa, Stolid, Supine,
Yielding

Pass out Faint, Graduate, Swarf, Swarve, Swoon

Passover Agadah, Haggada, Omer, Pesach

Passport Access, Clearance, Congé(e), E, ID, Key, Laissez-passer, Nansen, Navicert,
Sea-letter, Visa, Visitors'

Password Code, Countersign, Logon, Nayword, Parole, Sesame, Shibboleth, Sign,
Tessera, Watchword

▶ **Past** *see* PASS(ED)

Pasta Agnolotti, Anelli, Angel hair, Bucatini, Cannelloni, Cappelletti, Cellentani,
Conchiglie, Durum, Eliche, Farfal, Farfalle, Farfel, Fedelini, Fettuc(c)ine, Fusilli,
Gnocch(ett)i, Lasagna, Lasagne, Linguini, Macaroni, Maccheroncini, Manicotti, Noodles,
Orecchietti, Orzo, Pappardelle, Penne, Perciatelli, Ravioli, Rigatoni, Ruote, Spaghetti,
Spaghettina, Tagliarini, Tagliatelle, Tortelli(ni), Vermicelli, Ziti

Paste, Pasty Almond, Ashen, Batter, Beat, Berbere, Botargo, Boule, Bridie, Cerate,
Clobber, Cornish, Dentifrice, Dough, E, Electuary, Fake, Filler, Fondant, Frangipane,
Gentleman's Relish®, Glue, Guarana, Hard, Harissa, Knish, Lute, Magma, Marchpane,
Marzipan, Masala, Mastic, Meat, Miso, Mountant, Pale, Pallid, Panada, Pâté, Patty,
Pearl-essence, Pie, Piroshki, Pirozhki, Poonac, Pulp, Punch, Putty, Rhinestone, Rillettes,
Rout, Samosa, Sham, Slip, Slurry, Soft, Spread, Strass, Tahina, Tahini, Tapenade,
Taramasalata, Trounce, Wan, Wasabi

Pastern Hobble, Knee, Tether

Pastiche Cento, Collage, Medley, Patchwork, Potpourri

Pastille Jujube, Lozenge

Pastime Diversion, Game, Hobby, Recreation, Seesaw, Sport

Past master Champion, Expert, Historian, Pro

Past midnight 1 am

Pastor(al) Arcadia, Bucolic, Curé, Eclogue, Endymion, Idyl(l), Minister, Priest, Rector, Rural, Shepherd, Simple

Pastry Apfelstrudel, Baclava, Bakemeat, Baklava, Beignet, Bouchée, Bridie, Brik, Calzone, Cannoli, Chausson, Cheese straw, Choux, Clafoutis, Coquile, Creamhorn, Cream puff, Croustade, Cruller, Crust, Danish, Dariole, Dough, Eclair, Empanada, Feuilleté, Filo, Flaky, Flan, Frangipane, French, Gougère, Hamantasch, Millefeuille, Muffin, Phyllo, Pie, Pie-crust, Pirog, Piroshki, Pirozhki, Profiterole, Puff, Quiche, Raised, Rough-puff, Rug(g)elach, Samosa, Shortcrust, Strudel, Tart, Turnover, Vol-au-vent

Pasture Alp, Eadish, Eddish, Feed, Fell, Fodder, Grassland, Graze, Herbage, Kar(r)oo, Lair, Lare, Lay, Lea, Lease, Leasow(e), Leaze, Lee, Ley, Machair, Mead(ow), Moose, Pannage, Pascual, Potrero, Raik, Rake, Sheal(ing), Shiel(ing), Soum, Sowm, Tie, Transhume, Tye

▶ **Pasty** *see* **PASTE**

Pat Apt, Bog-trotter, Butter, Chuck, Clap, Dab, Glib, Lump, On cue, Postman, Print, Prompt, Rap, Slap, Stroke, Tap

Patch(work) Cento, Fleck, Miscellany, Mosaic, Motley, Piecing, Pocket, Sexton, Speculum, Turf

Patch(y) Bed, Bit, Blotchy, Cabbage, Chloasma, Clout, Coalsack, Cobble, Cooper, Court plaster, Cover, Friar, Fudge, → **MEND**, Mosaic, Mottled, Nicotine, Pasty, Piebald, Piece, Plage, Plaque, Plaster, Pot, Purple, Shinplaster, Shoulder, Solder, Sunspot, Tingle, Tinker, Transdermal, Turf, Vamp, Variegated

Pate, Pâté Crown, Paste, Rillettes, Taramasalata, Terrine

Patent(ed) Brevet d'invention, Breveté, Clear, Copyright, Evident, Letters, Licence, License, Obvious, Overt, Plain, Rolls

Pater(nity) Father, Filiation, Walter

Paterfamilias Coarb, Master

Path(way) Aisle, Allée, Alley, Arc, Berm, Berme, Boreen, Borstal(l), Bridle, Bridleway, Byroad, Catwalk, Causeway, Causey, Clickstream, Corridor, Course, Downlink, Eclipse, Ecliptic, Eightfold, Embden-Meyerhof, Flare, Flight, Garden, Gate, Gennel, Ginnel, Glide, Lane, Ley, Lichwake, Lichway, Locus, Lykewake, Mean-free, Metabolic, Orbit, Packway, Pad, Parabola, Pavement, Peritrack, Primrose, Ride, Ridgeway, Route, Run, Runway, Sidewalk, Slipway, Spurway, Stie, Sty(e), Swath(e), Taxiway, Tow, Track, Trail, Trajectory, Trod, Walkway, → **WAY**, Xystus

Pathan Pakhto, Pakhtu, Pashto, Pashtu, Pushto(o), Pushtu

Pathetic(ally) Abysmal, Derisory, Doloroso, Drip, Forlorn, Piss-poor, Piteous, Poignant, Sad, Saddo, Schlub, Schnook, Touching

Pathfinder Compass, Explorer, Guide, Pioneer, Scout

Pathogen Virus

Pathological Diseased, Gangrene, Morbid, Septic

Pathos Bathos, Pity, Sadness, Sob-stuff

Patience Calm, Endurance, Forbearance, Fortitude, Indulgence, Klondike, Klondyke, Longanimity, Monument, Operetta, Solitaire, Stoicism, Virtue

Patient(s) Calm, Case, Clinic, Cot-case, Forbearing, Grisel(da), Grisilda, Invalid, Job, Long-suffering, Passive, Private, Resigned, Stoic, Subject, Walking case, Ward

Patois Argot, Cant, Dialect, Gumbo, Jargon, Jive, Lingo, Scouse

Patriarch Aaron, Abraham, Abuna, Asher, Catholicos, Ecumenical, Elder, Enoch, Isaac, Job, Levi, Maron, Methuselah, Nestor, Noah, Pope, Simeon, Venerable

Patrician Aristocrat, Noble, Senator

Patrick Mick, Paddy, Pat, Spens

Patrimony Ancestry, Estate, Heritage

Patriot(ic), Patriotism Cavour, Chauvinist, DAR, Emmet, Flag-waving, Flamingant, Garibaldi, Hereward, Irredentist, Jingoism, Loyalist, Maquis, Nationalist, Revere, Tell, Wallace, Zionist

Patrol Armilla, Beat, Guard, Outguard, Picket, Piquet, Prowl-car, Reconnaissance, Round, Scout, Sentinel, Sentry-go, Shark, Shore, Turm

Patron(age), Patroness, Patronise(d), Patronising Advowson, Aegis, Athena, Auspices, Backer, Benefactor, Business, Champion, Client, Customer, Donator, Egis, Fautor, Friend, Lady Bountiful, Maecenas, Nepotic, Protector, Protégé, Provider, Shopper, → **SPONSOR**, Stoop, Stoup

Patsy Dupe, Hendren, Scapegoat, Stooge

Patter Backchat, Cant, Jargon, Lingo, Mag, Pitch, Rap, Sales talk, S(c)htick, Spiel

Pattern(ed) Agouti, Agouty, Aguti, Archetype, Argyle, Bird's eye, Blueprint, Branchwork, Broché, Candy stripe, Check, Chequer, Chiné, Chladni figure, Clock, Crisscross, Design, Dévoré, Diaper, Diffraction, Dog's tooth, Draft, Egg and dart, Epitome, Example, Exemplar, Faconné, Fiddle, Figuration, Format, Fractal, Fret, Gestalt, Grain, Grammadion, Greek key, Greque, Herringbone, Holding, Hound's tooth, Ideal, Imprint, Intarsia, Intonation, Koru, Kowhaiwhai, Matel(l)asse, Matrix, Meander, → **MODEL**, Moire, Moko, Mosaic, Norm, Paisley, Paradigm, Paragon, Pinstripe, Plan, Polka-dot, Pompadour, Precedent, Prototype, Queenstitch, Quincunx, Radiation, Raster, Rat-tail, Rhythm, Ribbing, Scansion, Shawl, Starburst, Stencil, Structure, Symmetry, Syndrome, Tala, Talea, Tangram, Tarsia, Tattersall, Template, Tessella, Tessera, Test, Tracery, Traffic, Tread, Type, Veneration, Vol, Whorl, Willow

Patty Bitok, Bouchée, Fishcake, Hoecake, Pie

Paul Jones, Oom, Pry, Revere, Robeson, S, St

Pauline Day-boy, Perils

Paunch Belly, Corporation, Gut, Kite, Kyte, Pod, Rumen, Tripe, Tum

Pauper Bankrupt, Beggar, Have-not, Mendicant, Penniless

Pause Break, Breakpoint, Breather, Caesura, Cessation, Cesura, Comma, Desist, Er, Fermata, Hesitate, Hiatus, Interkinesis, Intermission, Interregnum, Interval, Limma, Lull, Pitstop, Pregnant, → **RESPITE**, Rest, Selah, Semi-colon, Stop, Tacet, Time out, Whistle-stop

Pave(d), Pavement, Paving Causeway, Causey, Clint, Cobble, Corsey, Crazy, Desert, Diaper, Flagging, Granolith, Limestone, Moving, Path, Plainstanes, Plainstones, Roadside, Set(t), Sidewalk, Tessellate, Travolator, Trottoir

Pavilion Chinese, Ear, Gazebo, Jingling Johnny, Kiosk, Marquee, Tent

Paw Kangaroo, Maul, Mitt, Pad, Pat, Pud, Pug, Pussyfoot

Pawky Dry, Humorous, Shrewd, Sly

Pawn(shop), Pawnbroker, Pawnee Agent, Betel, Chessman, Counter, Derby, Dip, Gage, Gallery, Hanging, Hock, Hockshop, Hostage, Isolated, Leaving-shop, Lumber, Lumberer, Moneylender, Monte-de-piété, Monti di pietà, Nunky, Pan, Passed, Peacock, Piece, Pignerate, Pignorate, Pledge, Pledgee, Pop, Security, Sheeny, Siri, Spout, Stalking horse, Three balls, Tiddleywink, Tool, Tribulation, Uncle, Usurer, Wadset, Weed

Pax Peace, Truce

Pay(master), Payment, Paid, Pay off, Pay out Aby, Advertise, Agterskot, Amortise, Annat, Annuity, Ante, Arles, Atone, Balloon, Bank draft, Basic, Batta, Blench, Bonus, Bukshee, Bukshi, Cain, Cashier, Cens, Cheque, COD, Commute, Compensate, Consideration, Damage, Defray, Disburse, Discharge, Dividend, Down, Dub, E, Emolument, Endow, Equalisation, Eric, Escot, Farm, Fee, Feu-duty, Finance, Foot, Fork out, Fund, Gale, Gate, Give, Grassum, Grave, Greenmail, Guarantee, Han(d)sel, Hazard, Hire, Honorarium, Hoot(oo), HP, Imburse, Intown multure, Kain, Kickback, Leads and lags, Lobola, Lobolo, Lump sum, Mail, Meet, Merchet, Métayage, Mise, Modus, Mortuary, Overtime, Payola, Pension, Pittance, Pony, Posho, Prebendal, Premium, Primage, Pro, Pro forma, Progress, Purser, Quarterage, Quit(-rent), Ransom, Reap-silver,

Rebuttal, Redundancy, Refund, Remittance, Remuneration, Rent, Requite, Residual, Respects, Royalty, Salary, Satisfaction, Scot, Screw, Scutage, Settle, Severance, Shell, Shell out, Shot, Sick, Sink, SO, Sold(e), Soul-scat, Soul-scot, Soul-shot, → **SPEND**, Square, Stipend, Strike, Stump, Sub, Subscribe, Sweetener, Table, Take-home, Tar, Tender, Token, Tommy, Transfer, Treasure, Treat, Tribute, Truck, Unpurse, Usance, Veer, Wage, Wardcorn, X-factor

PC Constable, Right on

PE Aerobics, Gym

Pea(s) Carling, Chaparral, Chickling, D(h)al, Desert, Dholl, Egyptian, Garbanzo, Goober, Hastings, Legume, Mangetout, Marrow, Marrowfat, Passiform, Petit pois, Pigeon, Pulse, Rounceval, Snow, Split, String, Sturt's desert, Sugar, Sugar snap

Peace(ful), Peaceable, Peace-keeper, Peace organisation, Peace symbol Ahimsa, Antiwar, Ataraxy, Calm, Ease, Frieda, Frith, Halcyon, Hush, Interceder, Irenic(on), King's, Lee, Lull, Nirvana, Olive, Order, Pacific, Pax, Pbuh, Queen's, Quiet, Repose, Rest, Rose, Roskilde, Salem, Serene, Sh, Shalom, Siegfried, Siesta, Silence, Solomon, Soothing, Still, Tranquil, Truce, UN

Peacemaker ACAS, Arbitrator, Conciliator, Mediator, Trouble-shooter, Wilfred

Peach Blab, Cling, Clingstone, Dish, Dob, Freestone, Humdinger, Inform, Laetrile, Malakatoone, Melba, Melocoto(o)n, Nectarine, Oner, Quandang, Shop, Sing, Sneak, Split, Squeak, Stunner, Tattle, Tell, Victorine

Peachum Polly

Peacock Coxcomb, Dandy, Fop, Junonian, Muster, Paiock(e), Pajock(e), Pavo(ne), Pawn, Payock(e), Pown, Sashay

Peak(y) Acme, Aiguille, Alp, Ancohuma, Apex, Ben, Cap, Chimborazo, Climax, Comble, Communism, Cone, Crag, Crest, Darien, Drawn, Eiger, Flower, Gable, Gannett, Garmo, Harney, Horn, Ismail Samani, Kazbek, Matterhorn, Meridian, Mons, → **MOUNTAIN**, Nevis, Nib, Nunatak, Optimum, Pale, Petermann, Pikes, Pin, Pinnacle, Piton, Pyramidal, Rainier, Sallow, Snowcap, Snowdon, Spire, Stalin, Sukarno, Top, Tor, Visor, Widow's, Zenith

Peal Carillon, Change, Chime, Clap, Toll, Triple

Peanut(s) Arnut, Chickenfeed, Goober, Groundnut, Monkey-nut, Pittance

Pear Aguacate, Alligator, Anchovy, Anjou, Asian, Asparagus, Avocado, Bartlett, Bergamot, Beurré, Blanquet, Carmelite, Catherine, Choke, Colmar, Comice, Conference, Cuisse-madame, Dutch admiral, Jargonelle, Muscadel, Muscatel, Musk, Nashi, Neli(e)s, Nelis, Perry, Poperin, Poppering, Poprin, Prickly, Pyrus, Queez-maddam, Sabra, Seckel, Seckle, Taylor's Gold, Warden, William

Pearl(s), Pearly Barocco, Barock, Baroque, Cultured, False, Gem, Imitated, Jewel, Mabe, Margaret, Margaric, Nacrous, Olivet, Onion, Orient, Prize, Rope, Seed, Simulated, String, Sulphur, Unio(n)

Pear-shaped Obconic, Obovate, Pyriform

Peasant Bogtrotter, Bonhomme, Boor, Bumpkin, Carlot, Chouan, Churl, Clodhopper, Contadino, Cossack, Cottar, Cott(i)er, Fellah(s), Fellahin, Hick, Jungli, Kern(e), Kisan, Kulak, M(o)ujik, Muzhik, Prole, Quashi(e), Raiyat, Roturier, Rustic, Ryot, Swain, Tyrolean, Volost, Whiteboy, Yokel

Pea-shaped Pisiform

Peat(y) Moss-litter, Sod, Turbary, Turbinacious, Turf, Yarfa, Yarpha

Pebble(s), Pebbly Banket, Bibble, Calculus, Chuck, Cobblestone, Dornick, Dreikanter, Gallet, Gooley, Gravel, Psephism, Pumie, Pumy, Scotch, Scree, Shingle, Ventifact

Peccadillo Mischief, Misdemeanour, Offence

Peccary Mexican hog, Tayassuid

Peck Bill, Bushel, Dab, Forpet, Forpit, Gregory, Job, Kiss, Lip, Lippie, Modius, Nibble, Pickle, Tap

Pecksniff Charity

Peculiar(ity) Appropriate, Bizarre, Characteristic, Curiosity, Curious, Distinct, Eccentric,

Eery, Especial, Exclusive, Ferly, Funny, Idiosyncratic, Kink, Kooky, Odd, Original, Own, Proper, Queer, Quirk, Royal, Singular, → **SPECIAL**, Specific, Strange, Unusual

▷ **Peculiar** *may indicate* an anagram

Pedagogue Academic, B.Ed, Teacher

Pedal Accelerator, Bike, Brake, Chorus, Clutch, Cycle, Damper, Lever, P, Rat-trap, Soft, Sostenuto, Sustaining, Treadle, Treddle, Wah-wah

Pedal-coupler Tirasse

Pedant(ic) Casaubon, Chop logic, Dogmatic, Don, Dryasdust, Elucubrate, Inkhorn, Intellectual, Jobsworth, Lucubrate, Nit-picking, Pedagogue, Pernickety, Pompous, Precisian, Quibbler, Scholastic, Sesquipedalian, Stickler

Peddle, Pedlar Bodger, Boxwallah, Camelot, Chapman, Cheapjack, Colporteur, Crier, Drummer, Duffer, Hawk, Huckster, Jagger, Packman, Pedder, Pether, Sell, Smouch, Smouse(r), Sutler, Tallyman, Tink(er), Yagger

▷ **Peddling** *may indicate* an anagram

Pedestal Acroter(ion), Axle guard, Dado, Die, Footstall, Pillar, Support

Pedestrian Banal, Commonplace, Dull, Earth-bound, Ganger, Hack, Hike, Itinerant, Jaywalker, Laborious, Mediocre, Mundane, Trite, Voetganger, Walker

Pedigree(s) Ancestry, Blood, Breeding, Descent, Family tree, Genealogy, House, Lineage, Phylogeny, Stemma(ta), Stirp(s), Studbook, Thoroughbred, Whakapapa

Pediment Fronton

Peduncle Scape, Stalk

Peek Eye, Glance, Glimpse, Peep

Peel(er) Bark, Bobby, Candied, Decorticate, Desquamate, Exfoliate, Flype, Grilse, Orange, Pare, PC, Pill, Rind, Rine, Rumbler, Scale, Sewen, Shell, Skin, → **STRIP**, Tirr, Zest

▷ **Peeled** *may indicate* outside letters to be removed from a word

Peep(er), Peephole Cheep, Cook, Crow, Glance, Gledge, Judas, Keek, Kook, Lamp, Nose, Peek, Pink, Pry, Snoop, Spy, Squeak, Squint, Stime, Styme, Voyeur

Peer(age), Peers Archduke, Aristocrat, Backwoodsman, Baron(et), Burke, Coeval, Counterpart, Daimio, Debrett, Doucepere, Douzeper(s), Duke, Earl, Egal, Elevation, Equal, Eyeball, Gynt, Hereditary, Life, Lord, Match, Noble, Paladin, Peregal, Pink, Rank, Representative, Scry, Spiritual, Squint, Stare, Stime, Styme, Temporal, Toot, Tweer, Twire

Peerless Best, Matchless, Nonpareil, Supreme

Peevish(ness) Capernoited, Captious, Crabby, Cross, Doddy, Frabbit, Frampal, Frampold, Franzy, Fretful, Girner, Hipped, Lienal, Meldrew, Moody, Nattered, Pet, Petulant, Pindling, Protervity, Querulous, Shirty, Sour, Spleen, Teachie, Te(t)chy, Testy

Peewit Lapwing, Peewee

Peg(gy) Cheville, Cleat, Clothespin, Cotter-pin, Crawling, Die, Drift-pin, Fix, Freeze, Knag, Lee, Leg, Margaret, Nail, Nog, Odontoid, Pin(-leg), Piton, Shoe, Snort, Spigot, Spile, Square, Stengah, Stinger, Support, Tap, Tee, Thole, Tholepin, Thowel, Toggle, Tot, Tuning, Vent, Woffington

Pegboard Solitaire

Pegleg Timber-toes

Peking man Pithecanthropus, Sinanthropus

Pelagic Deep-sea, Marine, Oceanic

Pelf Lucre, Mammon, Money, Notes, Riches

Pelican Alcatras, Bird, Crossing, Golden Hind, LA, Louisiana, Steganopode

Pellagra Maidism

Pellet Birdshot, Bolus, Buckshot, Bullet, Pill, Pithball, Prill, Slug, Snow

Pelmet Valance

Pelt Assail, Clod, Fleece, Fur, Hail, Hide, Hie, Lam, Pepper, Random, Sealskin, Shower, Skin, Squail, Stone

Peltast Soldier, Targeteer

Pelvis Ilium, Pubis, Renal

Pen Author, Ballpoint, Bamboo, Bic®, Biro®, Cage, Calamus, Can, Cartridge, Catching,

Confine, Coop, Corral, Crawl, Crib, Crow-quill, Cru(i)ve, Cub, Cyclostyle, Dabber, Data, Enclosure, Epi®, Fank, Farm, Felt(-tipped), Fold, Fountain, Gaol, Gladius, Hen, Highlighter, Hoosegow, J, → JAIL, Keddah, Kraal, Lair, Laser, Light, Magic marker, Marker, Mew, Mure, Music, Piggery, Poison, Pound, Quill(-nib), Rastrum, Ree, Reed, Ring, Rollerball, Scribe, Sheepfold, Stell, Stie, Stir, Sty(e), Stylet, Stylo, Stylograph, Stylus, Submarine, Swan, Sweatbox, Tank, Weir, Write, → WRITER

▷ **Pen** *may indicate* a writer

Penal(ize) Cost, Fine, Gate, Handicap, Huff, Mulct, Punitive, Servitude

Penalty Abye, Amende, Card, Cost, Death, Endorsement, Eriach, Eric, Fine, Fixed, Forfeit, Han(d)sel, Huff, Keltie, Kelty, Levy, Major, Pain, Price, Punishment, Rubicon, Sanction, Tap, Ticket, Wide

Penance Atonement, Expiation, Shrift

Penates Lares

Pence D, P, Peter's

Penchant Predilection

Pencil Beam, Ca(l)m, Caum, Charcoal, Chinagraph®, Crayon, Draft, Draw, Eyebrow, Fusain, Grease, Harmonic, Ink, Keelivine, Keelyvine, Lead, Outline, Propelling, Slate, Stump, Styptic, Tortillon

Pendant Albert, Chandelier, Drop, Earring, Girandole, Laval(l)ière, Medallion, Necklace, Poffle, Sautoir, Stalactite

Pending Imminent, In fieri, Unresolved, Until

Pendragon Uther

Pendule Poffle

Pendulous, Pendulum Compensation, Dewlap, Foucault's, Metronome, Noddy, One-way, Seconds, Swing, Wavering

Penetrate, Penetrating, Penetration Acumen, Acuminate, Bite, Bore, Bridgehead, Cut, Enpierce, Enter, Imbue, Impale, Incisive, Indent, Indepth, Infiltrate, Insight, Into, Intrant, Lance, Permeate, Pierce, Probe, Sagacious, Shear, Strike, Thrust, Touch, X-ray

Penguin Adélie, Aeroplane, Anana, Auk, Blue, Emperor, Fairy, Gentoo, King, Korora, Little, Macaroni, Rock-hopper

Penicillin Cloxacillon, Fleming

Peninsula Arm, Neck, Promontory, Spit, Spur

PENINSULAS

4 letters:	Yorke	Boothia	Delmarva
Alte		Cape Bon	East Cape
Ards	*6 letters:*	Cape Cod	Galloway
Cape	Alaska	Chukchi	Hispania
Eyre	Avalon	Florida	Labrador
Kola	Balkan	Furness	Liaodong
	Bataan	Iberian	Liaotung
5 letters:	Crimea	Jutland	Malaysia
Banks	Iberia	Kintyre	Melville
Fylde	Istria	Kowloon	Portland
Gaspé	Palmer	Leizhou	Quiberon
Gower	Seward	Luichow	S. Jutland
Kerch	Taimyr	Olympic	
Korea	Tasman	S.W. Malay	*9 letters:*
Lleyn	Taymyr	Yucatan	Antarctic
Malay	Wirral		Black Isle
Otago		*8 letters:*	Cape Verde
Sinai	*7 letters:*	Brittany	Freycinet
Upper	Arabian	Cape York	Gallipoli

		11 letters:	16 letters:
Indo-China	Chalcidice	Peloponnese	Rhinns of Galloway
Kamchatka	Chersonese		
Kathiawar	Coromandel		
Northland	Dunnet Head	12 letters:	17 letters:
The Lizard	Graham Land	Scandinavian	Wilson's Promontory
	Mornington		
10 letters:	Nova Scotia	14 letters:	
Cape Blanco		Baja California	

Penis Archie, Chopper, Cock, Cor(e)y, Dick, Dildo(e), Dipstick, Dong, Ferret, Giggle(stick), Horn, Jack, John Thomas, Knob, Langer, Member, Membrum virile, Mojo, Organ, Pecker, Peezle, Percy, Peter, Phallus, Pillicock, Pintle, Pisser, Pizzle, Plonker, Prick, Putz, Rod, Roger, Schlong, Schmock, Shaft, Shmock, Shmuck, Stiffy, Tallywhacker, Tockley, Todger, Tonk, Tool, W(h)ang, Weenie, Weeny, Willie, Willy, Winkle, Yard, Zeppelin

Penitent(iary) Calaboose, Cilice, Clink, Contrite, Gaol, Jail, Jug, Prison, Repenter, Rosary, Rueful, Stir

Pennant, Pennon Banner, Broad, Bunting, Fane, Flag, Guidon, Streamer

Penniless Bankrupt, Boracic, Broke, Bust, Impecunious, Poor, Skint, Strapped

Penny Bean, Cartwheel, Cent, Copper, D, Dreadful, Gild, Honest, New, P, Pretty, Sen, Sou, Sterling, Stiver, Win(n), Wing

Penny-farthing Bicycle, Ordinary

Penpusher Plumassier

Pension(er) Allowance, Ann(at), Annuitant, Board, Chelsea, Cod, Cor(r)ody, Full board, Gasthaus, Gratuity, Guest-house, Half-board, Hostel, Hotel, Non-contributory, Occupational, Old-age, Oldster, Payment, Personal, Retire(e), Serps, SIPP, Stakeholder, Stipend, Superannuation

Pensive Dreamy, Moody, Musing, Thoughtful, Triste, Wistful

Pentameter Elegiac, Iambic

Pentateuch T(h)orah

Pentecost Whit(sun)

Penthouse Cat, Lean-to, Roof, Skyhome

Penultimate Y

Peon Peasant, Serf, Slave, Ticca

Peony Moutan

People(s) Beings, Bods, Body, Chosen, Commonalty, Commons, Demos, Ecology, Electorate, Enchorial, Flower, Folk, Fraim, Gens, Grass roots, Guild, Human(kind), Inca, Indigenous, Inhabit, Janata, Kin, Land, Lapith, Lay, Man(kind), Masses, Men, Mob, Nair, Nation(s), Nayar, One, Peculiar, Personalities, Phalange, Populace, Proletariat(e), Public, Punters, Quorum, Rabble, Race, Raffle, September, Settle, Society, Souls, They, Tribe, Tuath, Tungus, Volk

Pep Buck, Dash, Enliven, Gism, Go, Jism, Jissom, Stamina, Verve, Vim

Pepper(y) Alligator, All-spice, Ancho, Ava, Betel, Bird, Black, Caper, Capsicum, Cayenne, Cherry, Chilli, Chipotle, Condiment, Cubeb, Devil, Dittander, Dittany, Ethiopian, Green, Guinea, Habanero, Jalapeno, Jamaica, Kava, Long, Malaguetta, Matico, Negro, Paprika, Pelt, Pim(i)ento, Piper, Piperine, Piquillo, Red, Riddle, Sambal, Scotch bonnet, Spice, Sprinkle, Sweet, Szechuan, Szechwan, Tabasco®, Techy, Wall, Water, White, Yaqona, Yellow

Peppercorn Nominal, → **PAYMENT**, → **RENT**

Peppermint Bull's Eye, Humbug, Pandrop

Peptide Cecropin, Substance P

Per By, Each, Through, Thru

Perambulate, Perambulator Buggy, Expatiate, Pedestrian, Pram, Stroller, Wagon, Walker

Perceive, Perception, Perceptive Acumen, Alert, Anschauung, Apprehend,

Astute, Clairvoyance, Clear-eyed, Cryptaesthetic, Descry, Dianoia, Discern, Divine, ESP, Extrasensory, Feel, Image, Insight, Intelligence, Intuit(ion), Kinaesthesia, Noesis, Notice, Observe, Pan(a)esthesia, Remark, → **SEE**, Sense, Sensitive, Sentience, Shrewd, Sixth sense, Subjective, Subliminal, Tact, Taste, Telegnosis, Tel(a)esthesia, Understanding

Percentage Agio, Commission, Contango, Cut, Mark-up, Proportion, Rake off, Royalty, Scalage, Share, Vigorish

Perch(ing) Aerie, Alight, Anabis, Bass, Comber, Eyrie, Fish, Fogash, Gaper, Insessorial, Lug, Miserere, Ocean, Perca, Pole, Roost, Ruff(e), Seat, Serranid, → **SIT**, Wall-eye, Zingel

Percolate, Percolation Filter, Infiltrate, Leach, Lixiviate, Ooze, Osmosis, Permeate, Seep, Sipe, Soak, Strain, Sype

Percussion (cap) Amorce, Battery, Chinese temple block, Gong, Idiophone, Impact, Knee, Knock, Spoons, Thump, Timbrel, Traps

Percy Harry Hotspur, Shelley

Perdition Ades, Hades

Peremptory Absolute, Decisive, Haughty, Imperative, Imperious

Perennial Continual, Enduring, Flower, Livelong, Perpetual, Recurrent

Perfect(ly), Perfection(ist) Absolute, Accomplish, Accurate, Acme, Apple-pie, Bloom, Complete, Consummation, Cross-question, Dead, Develop, Edenic, Fare-thee-well, Finish, Flawless, Fulfil, Full, Holy, Hone, Ideal(ist), Impeccable, Intact, It, Matchless, Mature, Mint, Mr Right, Par, Paradisal, Paragon, Past, Pat, Peace, Pedant, Point-device, Practice, Present, Pure, Quintessential, Refine, Salome, Siddha, Soma, Sound, Spot-on, Stainless, Stickler, Sublime, The nines, Thorough, Three-pricker, To a t(ee), Unblemished, Unflawed, Unqualified, Utopian, Utter, Whole, Witeless

Perfidy Betrayal, Falsehood, Treachery, Treason

Perforate(d), Perforation, Perforator Cribrate, Cribrose, Drill, Eyelet, Hole, → **PIERCE**, Prick, Punch, Puncture, Riddle, Trephine, Trocar

Perforce Necessarily, Needs

Perform(ed), Performer, Performing Achieve, Acrobat, Act(or), Action, Aerialist, Appear, Artist(e), Barnstorming, Basoche, Busk, Carry out, Chansonnier, Comedian, Contortionist, Discharge, Do, Duo, Enact, Entertainer, Execute, Exert, Exhibit, Fancy Dan, Fire-eater, Fulfil, Function, Geek, Hand, Headliner, Hersall, Hot dog, Houdini, Implement, Interlocutor, Majorette, Make, Mime, Moke, Nonet, Octet, Officiate, On, Operant, Perpetrate, Player, Praxis, Quartet(te), Quintet, Rap artist, Recite, Render, Ripieno, Scene-stealer, Septet, Sextet, Showstopper, Strongman, Supererogate, Sword-swallower, Throw, Trio, Vaudevillian, Virtuoso, Wire-dancer

Performance Accomplishment, Achievement, Act(ion), Auto, Blinder, Bravura, Broadcast, Chevisance, Command, Concert, Dare, Deed, Demonstration, Discharge, Division, Double act, Enactment, Entr'acte, Execution, Floorshow, Gas, Gig, Hierurgy, Holdover, Hootenanny, House, Masque, Master-class, Masterstroke, Matinee, Mime, Monodrama, Monologue, One-night stand, Operation, Perpetration, Practice, Première, Production, Programme, Recital, Rehearsal, Rendering, Rendition, Repeat, Repertoire, Rigmarole, Scene, Show (stopper), Showing, Simul, Sketch, Sneak preview, Solo, Specific, Spectacle, Stunt, Theatricals, Track record, Turn, Unicycle

Perfume (box) Abir, Ambergris, Angel water, Aroma, Attar, Bergamot, Cassolette, Chypre, Civet, Cologne, C(o)umarin, Eau de cologne, Eau de toilette, Enfleurage, Essence, Fragrance, Frangipani, Incense, Ionone, Lavender (water), Linalool, Millefleurs, Muscone, Muskone, Myrrh, Nose, Opopanax, Orris, Orrisroot, Otto, Patchouli, Patchouly, Pomander, Potpourri, Redolence, → **SCENT**, Smellies, Terpineol, Toilet water, Tonka bean

Perfunctory Apathetic, Careless, Cursory, Indifferent, Token

Perhaps A(i)blins, Belike, Haply, Happen, May(be), Peradventure, Percase, Perchance, Possibly, Relative, Say, Yibbles

▷ **Perhaps** *may indicate* an anagram

Perigee Apsis, Epigeum

Peril(ous) → DANGER, Hazard, Jeopardy, Precarious, Risk, Threat, Yellow
Perimeter Boundary, Circuit, Circumference, Limits
Period(ic) Abbevillian, Acheulian, AD, Age, Alcher(ing)a, Andropause, Annual, Archaean, Aurignacian, Azilian, Base, Bi-weekly, Bout, Cal(l)ippic, Cambrian, Carboniferous, Chalcolithic, Chukka, Chukker, Climacteric, Comanchean, Cooling off, Cretaceous, Critical, Curse, Cycle, Day, Decad(e), Devonian, Diapause, Dot, Down, Dreamtime, → DURATION, Eocene, Epoch, Excerpt, Floruit, Full-stop, Glacial, Grace, Great schism, Haute époque, Hercynian, Heyday, Holocene, Horal, Incubation, Indiction, Innings, Interregnum, Jurassic, Kalpa, Latency, Latent, Lesson, Liassic, Limit, Meantime, Meanwhile, Menopause, Menses, Mesolithic, Mesozoic, Middle Kingdom, Miocene, Mississippian, Monthly, Moratorium, Neocomian, Neolithic, Neozoic, Octave, Olde-worlde, Oligocene, Ordovician, Palaeogene, Paleolithic, Payback, Pennsylvanian, Permian, Phanerozoic, Phase, Phoenix, Pleistocene, Pliocene, Pre-Cambrian, Proterozoic, Protohistory, QT, Quarter, Quaternary, Recurrent, Reformation, Refractory, Regency, Rent, Riss, Romantic, Saeculum, Safe, Saros, Season, Session, Sidereal, Silurian, Span, Spasm, Spell, Stage, Stop, Stretch, Synodic, Teens, Term, Tertiary, Trecento, Triassic, Triduum, Trimester, Tri-weekly, Usance, Weekly, Window
Periodic(al) Bi-weekly, Catamenia, Comic, Digest, Economist, Etesian, Journal, Liassic, Listener, Mag, New Yorker, Organ, Paper, Phase, Publication, Punch, Rambler, Regency, Review, Scandal sheet, Solutrean, Solutrian, Spectator, Strand, Stretch, Tatter, Tract
Peripatetic Ambulatory, Gadabout, Itinerant, Promenader, Travelling
Periphery Ambit, Bounds, Exurb, Fringe, Outskirts, Surface
Periscope Eye(-stalk)
Perish(able), Perished, Perishing Brittle, → DIE, End, Ephemeral, Expire, Fade, Forfair, Fungibles, Icy, Tine, Tint, Transitory, Tyne, Vanish
Periwinkle Apocynum, Blue, Madagascar, Myrtle
Perjure(d) Forswear, Lie, Mansworn
Perk(s), Perky, Perk up Brighten, Chipper, Deadhead, Enliven, Freebie, Freshen, Jaunty, LV, → PERQUISITE, Tronc
Perm(anent) Abiding, Durable, Enduring, Eternal, Everlasting, Fixed, For keeps, Full-time, Indelible, → LASTING, Marcel, Stable, Standing, Stative, Wave
Permeable, Permeability, Permeate Infiltrate, Leaven, Magnetic, Osmosis, Penetrate, Pervade, Poromeric, Porous, Seep, Transfuse
Permission, Permit(ted) Allow, Authorise, By-your-leave, Carnet, Chop, Clearance, Congé(e), Consent, Copyright, Enable, Give, Grant, Green light, Indult, Lacet, Laisser-passer, Latitude, Leave, Legal, Let, Liberty, Licence, License, Lief, Loan, Luit, Nihil obstat, Ok(e), Pace, Pass, Placet, Planning, Power, Pratique, Privilege, Remedy, Safe-conduct, Sanction, Stamp-note, Suffer, Ticket, Triptyque, Visa, Vouchsafe, Warrant, Way-leave, Wear
Pernicious Damnable, Evil, Harmful, Lethal, Noisome, Pestilent, Wicked
Pernickety Fikish, Niggly
Peroration Pirlicue, Purlicue
Peroxide Bleach, Blonde, Colcothar
Perpendicular Aplomb, Apothem, Atrip, Cathetus, Erect, Normal, Orthogonal, Plumb, Sheer, Sine, → UPRIGHT, Vertical
Perpetrate Commit, Effect, Execute
Perpetual Constant, Eternal, Incessant, Sempiternal
Perplex(ed), Perplexity Anan, Baffle, Bamboozle, Bemuse, Beset, Bewilder, Bother, Buffalo, Bumbaze, Cap, Confound, Confuse, Embarrass, Feague, Floor, Flummox, Knotty, Meander, Mystify, Nonplus, Obfuscate, Out, Pother, Pudder, Puzzle, Quizzical, Stump, Tangle, Throw, Tickle, Tostication
Perquisite Ap(p)anage, Emolument, Extra, Gratuity, → PERK, Tip
Perrier Stoner

Perry Mason

Persecute, Persecution Afflict, Annoy, Badger, Bully, Crucify, Dragon(n)ades, Harass, Haze, Intolerant, McCarthyism, Oppress, Pogrom, Ride, Torment, Torture, Witch hunt

Persevere, Perseverance Assiduity, Continue, Fortitude, Hold on, Insist, Jusqu'auboutisme, Patience, Persist, Plug, Soldier on, Stamina, Steadfastness, Stick, Stickability, Tenacity

Persia(n) Achaemenid, Babee, Babi, Bahai, Cyrus, Dari, Farsi, Iran(ian), Mazdean, Mede, Middle, Pahlavi, Parasang, Parsee, Pehlevi, Pushtu, Samanid, Sassanid, Sohrab, Xerxes, Zoroaster

Persimmon Kaki, Sharon fruit

Persist(ence), Persistent Adhere, Assiduity, Chronic, Constant, Continual, Diligent, Doggedness, Endure, Hang-on, Importunate, Incessant, Labour, Longeval, Lusting, Nag, Persevere, Press, Sedulous, Sneaking, Stick, Tenacity, Urgent

Person(s), Personal(ly) Alter, Artificial, Aymaran, Being, Bird, Bod(y), Chai, Chal, Character, Chav, Chi, Cookie, Displaced, Entity, Everyman, Figure, First, Fish, Flesh, Ga(u)dgie, Gadje, Gauje, Gut, Head, Human, Individual, In propria persona, Nabs, Natural, Nibs, One, Own, Party, Passer-by, Pod, Private, Quidam, Second, Selfhood, Skate, Sod, Soul, Specimen, Tales, Third, Walla(h), Wight

Personage, Personality Anima, Celeb(rity), Character, Charisma, Dignitary, Ego, Godhead, Grandee, Identity, Jekyll and Hyde, Megastar, Multiple, Noble, Notability, Panjandrum, Presence, Psychopath, Sama, Schizoid, Seity, Sel, Self, Sell, Somatotonia, Split, Star, Temperament, Tycoon, Viscerotonia

Personified, Personification, Personify Embody, Incarnate, Prosopop(o)eia, Represent

Personnel Employees, Hands, Liveware, Manpower, Staff

Perspective Aerial, Atmosphere, Attitude, Distance, Linear, Point of view, Proportion, Scenography, Slant, Take, View, Vista

Perspicacious, Perspicacity Astute, Clear-sighted, Discerning, Insight, Keen, Shrewd

Perspiration, Perspire, Perspiring Aglow, Forswatt, Glow, Hidrosis, Sudor, Suint, Sweat, Swelter

Persuade(d), Persuasion, Persuasive Cajole, Carrot and stick, Coax, Cogent, Conviction, Convince, Disarm, Eloquent, Faith, Feel, Forcible, Geed, Get, Induce, Inveigle, Lead on, Move, Plausible, → **PREVAIL**, Religion, Rhetoric, Seduce, Smooth-talking, Soft sell, Suborn, Sweet-talk, Truckled, Wheedle, Winning

Pert(ness) Bold, Brisk, Cocky, Dicacity, Flippant, Forward, Fresh, Impertinent, Insolent, Jackanapes, Minx, Quean, Saucy, Tossy

Pertain Apply, Belong, Concern, Effeir, Effere, Relate, Touch

Pertinacious Dogged, Obstinate, Persistent, Stickler, Stubborn

Pertinent Ad rem, Apropos, Apt, Fit, Germane, Relevant, Timely

Perturb(ation) Aerate, Confuse, Dismay, Disturb, Dither, Faze, Pheese, State, Trouble, Upset, Worry

Peru(vian) Inca, PE, Quechua(n), Quichua(n)

Peruse, Perusal Examine, Inspect, Read, Scan, Scrutiny, → **STUDY**

Pervade, Pervasion, Pervasive(ness) Atmosphere, Diffuse, Drench, Immanence, Permeate, Saturate

Perverse, Perversion, Pervert(ed), Perversity Aberrant, Abnormal, Algolagnia, Awkward, Awry, Balky, Cam(stairy), Camsteary, Camsteerie, Cantankerous, → **CONTRARY**, Corrupt, Crabbed, Cussed, Decadent, Deviate, Distort, Donsie, False, Froward, Gee, Kam(me), Kinky, Licentious, Misinterpret, Misuse, Nonce, Paraphilia, Protervity, Refractory, Sadist, Sicko, Stubborn, Thrawn, Traduce, Twist, Unnatural, Untoward, Uranism, Warp(ed), Wayward, Wilful, Wrest, Wry

▷ **Perverted** *may indicate* an anagram

Pessimism, Pessimist(ic) Alarmist, Bear, Cassandra, Crapehanger, Crepehanger, Cynic, Defeatist, Dismal Jimmy, Doom merchant, Doomwatch, Doomy, Doubter,

Downbeat, Fatalist, Glumbum, Jeremiah, Killjoy, Negative

Pest(er) Aggravate, Badger, Bedbug, Beleaguer, Blight, Bot, → **BOTHER**, Brat, Breese, Bug, Dim, Disagreeable, Earbash, Fly, Fowl, Gapeworm, Greenfly, Harass, Hassle, Irritate, Microbe, Mither, Molest, Mouse, Nag, Nudnik, Nuisance, Nun, Pize, Plague, Rotter, Scourge, Tease, Terror, Thysanoptera, Vermin, Weevil

Pesticide Benomyl, Botanic(al), DDT, Derris, Dichlorvos, Endrin, Glucosinolate, Heptachlor, Mouser, Permethrin, Synergist, Warfarin

Pestilence, Pestilent Curse, Epidemic, Evil, Lues, Murrain, Murren, Noxious, Outbreak, Pernicious, Plague

Pet Aversion, Cade, Canoodle, Caress, Chou, Coax, Coddle, Cosset, Cuddle, Dandle, Darling, Daut(ie), Dawt(ie), Dod, Dort, Ducky, Favourite, Fondle, Glumps, Hamster, Huff, Hump, Indulge, Ire, Jarta, Jo, Lallygag, Lapdog, Miff, Mouse, Neck, Pique, Rabbit, Smooch, Snog, Spat, Strum, Sulk(s), Tantrum, Teacher's, Temper, Tiff, Tout, Towt, Umbrage, Virtual, Yarta

Petal Ala, Keels, Labellum, Leaf, Standard, Vexillum

Petard Firework, Squib

Peter (out) Aumbry, Bell, Diminish, Dwindle, Grimes, Hermit, Pan, Pears, Principle, Quince, Quint, Rabbit, Safe, Saint, Sellers, Simon, Simple, Wane, Weaken

Petite Dainty, Mignon, Small

Petition(er) Appeal, Beg, Boon, Crave, Entreaty, Litany, Millenary, Orison, Plaintiff, Postulant, Prayer, Representation, Request, Round robin, Solicit, Sue, Suit(or), Suppli(c)ant, Supplicat, Vesper

Pet-name Hypocorisma, Nickname, So(u)briquet

Petrel Bird, Mother Carey's chicken, Nelly, Prion, Procellaria, Stormbird, Stormy, Wilton's

Petrify(ing) Fossilise, Frighten, Lapidescent, Niobe, Numb, Ossify, Scare, Terrify

Petrol(eum) Cetane, Cutting, Diesel, Esso®, Ethyl, Fuel, Gas, High-octane, High-test, Leaded, Ligroin, Maz(o)ut, Octane, Oilstone, Olein, Platforming, Refinery, Rock oil, Rock-tar, STP, Unleaded, Vaseline®

Petticoat Balmoral, Basquine, Crinoline, Female, Filabeg, Fil(l)ibeg, Jupon, Kilt, Kirtle, Phil(l)abeg, Phil(l)ibeg, Placket, Sarong, Shift, Underskirt, Wylie-coat

Pettifogger Lawmonger

Petty, Pettiness Baubling, Bumbledom, Childish, Little, Mean, Minor, Narrow, Niggling, Nyaff, One-horse, Parvanimity, Picayunish, Piffling, Pimping, Puisne, Shoestring, Small, Small-minded, Small town, Stingy, Tin, Trivial, Two-bit

Petty officer Cox, CPO, PO

Petulance, Petulant Fretful, Huff, Mardy, Moody, Peevish, Perverse, Procacity, Querulous, Sullen, Toutie, Waspish

Pew Box, Carrel, Chair, Seat, Stall

Pewter Trifle, Tutenag

Phaeton Spider

Phalanger Cus-cus, Honey-mouse, Honey possum, Opossum, Petaurist, Phascogale, Possum, Sugar glider, Tait, Tarsipes, Tuan, Wambenger

Phalanx Cohort, Coterie, Legion

Phalarope Lobe-foot

Phallus Linga(m), Penis, Priapus

Phantasist, Phantasm Apparition, Chimera, Spectre, Werewolf

Phantom Apparition, Bogey, Bugbear, Eidolon, Feature, Idol, Incubus, Maya, Pepper's ghost, Shade, Spectre, Tut, Wild hunt, Wraith

Pharaoh Akhenaton, Amenhotep, Cheops, Egyptian, Rameses, River-dragon, Thutmose, Tut, Tutankhamen, Tutankhamun, Tyrant

Pharisee Formalist, Humbug, Hypocrite, Nicodemus

Pharmacist, Pharmacologist → **CHEMIST**, Dispenser, Druggist, Loewi, MPS, Officinal, Preparator

Phase Climacteric, Coacervate, Colour, Cycle, Form, Nematic, Period, Post-boost, Primary, Quarter, REM, Schizont, Stage, State, Synchronise, Transition

Pheasant Argus, Bird, Fireback, Junglefowl, Mona(u)l, Nide, Nye, Peacock, Ring-necked, Silver, Tragopan

Phenol Orcine, Orcinol, Resorcinol, Xylenol

Phenomenon Autokinetic, Blip, Eclipse, Effect, Event, Figure ground, Flying saucer, Flysch, Geohazard, Heterography, Hormesis, Marvel, Meteor, Miracle, Mirage, Paranormal, Parascience, Phenology, Phi, Psi, Rankshift, Raynaud's, Synergy

Phial Bologna, Bottle, Flask

Phil, Philip Fluter, Macedonia, Pip

Philander(er) Flirt, Keeper, Libertine, Lothario, Playboy, Toyer, → **TRIFLE**, Wolf, Womaniser

Philanthropist, Philanthropy Altruist, Barnardo, Benefactor, Carnegie, Charity, Chisholm, Coram, Donor, Freemason, Geldof, Guggenheim, Hammer, Humanist, Humanitarian, Lever, Mayer, Nobel, Nuffield, Peabody, Rockefeller, Rowntree, Samaritan, Shaftesbury, Tate, Wilberforce

Philately Timbromania

Phileas Fogg

▸ **Philip** *see* **PHIL**

Philippic Diatribe, Invective, Tirade

Philippine(s) Bisayan, Igorot, Moro, Pangasinian, PI, RP, Tagalog, Visayan

Philistine, Philistinism Artless, Ashdod, Barbarian, Foe, Gath, Gaza, Gigman, Goliath, Goth, Lowbrow, Podsnappery, Vandal

Philology Linguistics, Semantics, Speechcraft

Philosopher, Philosophy Academist, Activism, Ahimsa, Analytical, Animism, Anthrosophy, Antinomianism, Antiochian, Atomic, Atomist, Attitude, Averr(h)oism, Cartesian, Casuist, Comtism, Conceptualism, Conservatism, Cracker-barrel, Critical, Cynic, Deipnosophist, Deontology, Eclectic, Eleatic, Empiricism, Enlightenment, Epistemology, Ethics, Existentialism, Fatalism, Gnostic, Gymnosophist, Hedonism, Hermeneutics, Hobbism, Holist, Humanism, I Ching, Idealism, Ideology, Instrumentalism, Ionic, -ism, Kaizen, Linguistic, Logical atomism, Logicism, Logos, Maieutic, Marxism, Materialism, Mechanism, Megarian, Metaphysician, Metaphysics, Metempiricism, Monism, Moral(ist), Natural, Neoplatonism, Neoteric, Nihilism, Nominalism, Occamist, Occam's razor, Ockhamist, Opinion, Panhellenism, Peripatetic, Phenomenology, Platonism, Populism, Positivism, Rationalism, Realism, Rosminian, Sage, Sankhya, Sceptic, Schoolman, Scientology, Scotism, Secular-humanism, Sensist, Shankara(-charya), Solipsism, Sophist, Stoic, Synthetic, Taoism, Theism, Theosophy, Thomist, Thought, Transcendentalism, Ultraism, Utilitarianism, Utopianism, Vedanta, Voluntarism, Weltanschauung, Whitehead, Yoga, Yogi

PHILOSOPHERS

4 *letters:*	5 *letters:*		
Ayer	Amiel	Moore	Arendt
Hume	Bacon	Paine	Carnap
Jedi	Bayle	Pater	Cicero
Kant	Bruno	Plato	Cousin
Mach	Buber	Quine	Engels
Mill	Comte	Renan	Farabi
Ryle	Croce	Smith	Godwin
Weil	Dewey	Sorel	Herder
Wolf	Hegel	Taine	Hobbes
Zeno	James		Lao-tzu
	Locke	6 *letters:*	Ockham
		Agnesi	Olbers

Ortega
Pascal
Peirce
Popper
Pyrrho
Sartre
Scotus
Seneca
Tagore
Thales

7 letters:
Abelard
Aquinas
Barthes
Bentham
Bergson
Bradley
Buridan
Derrida
Diderot
Eckhart
Emerson
Erasmus
Erigena
Haldane
Herbart
Hypatia
Leibniz
Malthus
Marcion

Marcuse
Mencius
Meng-tse
Ptolemy
Rosmini
Russell
Schlick
Serbati
Sheffer
Spencer
Spinoza
Steiner
Tillich

8 letters:
Alembert
Anderson
Avicenna
Berkeley
Boethius
Cyreniac
Diogenes
Epicurus
Foucault
Hamilton
Harrison
Maritain
Menippus
Old Moore
Passmore
Plotinus

Plutarch
Rousseau
Schiller
Socrates
Xenophon

9 letters:
Antiochus
Aristotle
Bosanquet
Cleanthes
Confucius
Descartes
Euhemerus
Heidegger
Helvetius
Leucippus
Lucretius
Nietzsche
Santayana
Schelling

10 letters:
Anacharsis
Anaxagoras
Anaximenes
Antiochene
Apemanthus
Apollonius
Aristippus
Campanella

Chrysippus
Democritus
Empedocles
Heraclitus
Hutchinson
Maimonides
Paracelsus
Parmenides
Protagoras
Pythagoras
Saint Simon
Swedenborg
Von Leibniz
Xenocrates
Xenophanes

11 letters:
Anaximander
Antisthenes
Kierkegaard
Machiavelli
Montesquieu

12 letters:
Callisthenes
Merleau-Ponty
Schopenhauer
Theophrastus
Wittgenstein

Philosophic(al) Rational, Resigned, Thoughtful, Tranquil

Philtre Aphrodisiac, Charm, Drug, Hippomanes, Potion

Phlegm(atic) Calm, Composed, Pituita(ry), Pituite, Stolid, Unperturbed, Unruffled

Phloem Leptome, Liber

Phobia Aversion, Dread, Fear, Neurosis, Thing

Phoebe, Phoebus Apollo, Artemis, Day-star, Deaconess, Moon, Selene, Sol, Sun

Phoenician Tripolitania

Phoenix Bird-of-wonder, Fum, Fung, Paragon, Self-begotten

Phone Bell, Blower, Call, Cellular, Clamshell, Dial, Dual band, Flip, Intercom, Mob(i)e, Mobile, Moby, Pay, Picture, Ring, Roam, Satellite, Smart, Talkback, Tel, → **TELEPHONE**, Text

Phonetic(s) Acoustic, Articulatory, Auditory, Interdental, Mouille, Oral, Palaeotype, Palatal, Palato-alveolar, Plosion, Spoken, Symbol, Synaeresis

▷ **Phonetically** *may indicate* a word sounding like another

Phon(e)y Bogus, Charlatan, Counterfeit, Faitor, Fake, Hokey, Impostor, Poseur, Quack, → **SHAM**, Specious, Spurious

▷ **Phony** *may indicate* an anagram

Phosphate Apatite, Monazite, Sphaerite, Torbernite, Vivianite, Wavellite, Xenotime

Phosphor(escent), Phosphorescence, Phosphorus Bologna, Briming, Cephalin, Foxfire, Friar's lantern, Ignis fatuus, Jack o'lantern, Luminescent, Malathion®, Noctilucent, P, Pyrosome, Sarin, Sea-fire, Tabun, Will o' the wisp

Photo(copy), Photograph(y), Photographic, Photo finish Ambrotype,

Anaglyph, Angiogram, Beefcake, Black and white, Blow-up, Cabinet, Calotype, Clog, Close-up, Composite, Contre-jour, Daguerrotype, Diazo, Digicam, Duplicate, Dyeline, Enprint, Exposure, Ferroprint, Ferrotype, Film, Flash, Half-tone, Headshot, Heliochrome®, Heliotype, Hologram, Infra-red, Kallitype, Karyogram, Kirlian, Kodak®, Microdot, Microfilm, Microgram, Micrograph, Microprint, Monochrome, Montage, Mugshot, Negative, Nephogram, Opaline, Panel, Picture, Pinhole, Platinotype, Polaroid®, Positive, Print, Resorcin, Rotograph, Rotogravure, Schlieren, Sepia, Shoot, Shot, Shutterbug, Slide, Snap, Spirit, Still, Take, Talbotype, Time-lapse, Tintype, Tomography, Topo, Trimetrogon, Vignette, Wire, Woodburytype, Xerography, X-ray

Photographer Bailey, Beaton, Brandt, Brassai, Cameraman, Cameron, Capa, Cartier-Bresson, Daguerre, Fox Talbot, Man Ray, Mapplethorpe, Pap(arazzo), Schlierin, Shutterbug, Snowdon, Stalkerazzi, Stannotype

Phrase Abject, Actant, Asyndeton, Buzzword, Cadence, Catch(word), Catchcry, Cliché, Climacteric, Comma, Expression, Hapax legomenon, Heroic, Hook, Idiophone, Laconism, Leitmotiv, Lemma, Locution, Mantra, Motto, Noun, Phr, Prepositional, Refrain, Riff, Set, Slogan, Soundbite, Tag, Term, Trope, Verb

Phrygian Midas

Phthisis Decay, TB

Phylactery Amulet, Talisman, Tefillin, Tephillin

Phyllopod Brine-shrimp

Physic(s) Cluster, Cryogenics, Culver's, Cure, Dose, Electrostatics, Geostatics, Health, High-energy, Kinematics, Medicine, Nuclear, Nucleonics, Particle, Photometry, Purge, Remedy, Rheology, Science, Solid-state, Sonics, Spintronics, Thermodynamics, Ultrasonics

Physical Bodily, Carnal, Corpor(e)al, Material, Natural, Tangible

Physician Addison, Allopath, Bach, Buteyko, Chagas, Doctor, Erastus, Eustachio, Galen, Gilbert, Graves, Guillotin, Hakim, Hansen, Harvey, Hippocrates, Internist, Jenner, Lamaze, Leech, Linacre, Lister, Medic(o), Menière, Mesmer, Mindererus, Paean, Paian, Paracelsus, Practitioner, Preceptor, Quack, Ranvier, Roget, Russell, Salk, Sézary, Spiegel, Stahl, Still, Therapist, Time, Vaidya, Wavell

Physicist → SCIENTIST

PHYSICISTS

3 letters:	Curie	Weber	Planck
Ohm	Debye	Young	Powell
	Dicke	Zener	Skyrme
4 letters:	Dirac		Teller
Bohr	Fermi	6 letters:	Wilson
Born	Gamow	Alfven	
Bose	Gauss	Ampère	7 letters:
Gold	Henry	Carnot	Alhazen
Hahn	Hertz	Dalton	Alvarez
Kerv	Hooke	Davies	Bardeen
Lawe	Hoyle	Geiger	Broglie
Mach	Joule	Giorgi	Charles
Rabi	Lodge	Kelvin	Coulomb
Vafa	Nambu	Landau	Crookes
	Pauli	Morley	Doppler
5 letters:	Penny	Nernst	Faraday
Adams	Popov	Newton	Feynman
Auger	Raman	Peirce	Fresnel
Bondi	Stark	Penney	Galileo
Bragg	Volta	Picard	Gilbert

Hawking	Tyndall	Oliphant	Robertson
Huygens	Wheeler	Rayleigh	
Laplace		Roentgen	*10 letters:*
Lorentz	*8 letters:*	Schottky	Archimedes
Marconi	Anderson	Susskind	Bernouilli
Maxwell	Angstrom	Van Allen	Heisenberg
Meitner	Appleton		Rutherford
Moseley	Avogadro	*9 letters:*	Torricelli
Nielsen	Blackett	Alanasoff	Watson-Watt
Oersted	Brattain	Becquerel	
Peebles	Brewster	Cockcroft	*11 letters:*
Penzias	Bridgman	Friedmann	Chamberlain
Piccard	Cerenkov	Heaviside	Joliot-Curie
Rankine	Davisson	Josephson	Oppenheimer
Reaumur	Einstein	Kirchhoff	Schrödinger
Rontgen	Foucault	Michelson	Van der Waals
Sievert	Millikan	Ovshinsky	

Physiognomist, Physiognomy Face, Features, Lavater
Physiology, Physiologist Bernard, Bordet, Dale, Eccles, Einthoven, Loeb, Malpighi, Pavlov, Purkinje, Schafer, Wagner, Zoonomia
Physiotherapist Masseur
Physique Body, Build, Figure, Pyknic, Set-up, Somatotype
Pi, Pious Breast-beater, Craw-thumper, Devotional, Devout, Fraud, Gallio, God-fearing, Godly, Holy, Holy Willie, Mid-Victorian, Religiose, Reverent, Sanctimonious, Savoury, Smug, Wise, Zaddik
Pi(ous) Orant, Reverent, Saintly
Piaffe Spanish-walk
Pianist Anda, Arrau, Hambourg, Hess, Hofmann, Liszt, Mingus, Morton, Ogdon, Pachmann, Paderewski, Peterson, Répétiteur, Schnabel, Tatum, Vamper, Virtuoso
Piano Baby grand, Bechstein, Boudoir grand, Broadwood, Celesta, Celeste, Concert grand, Cottage, Dumb, Flugel, Forte, Grand, Hammerklavier, Honkytonk, Keyboard, Mbira, Overstrung, P, Player, Prepared, Semi-grand, Softly, Steinway, Stride, Thumb, Upright
Piano-maker Erard
Picaresque Roman à tiroirs
Picaroon Brigand, Corsair, Pirate, Rogue
Piccadilly Whist
Piccolo Ottavino
Pick(er), Pickaxe, Picking, Pick out, Pick up Break, Choice, → CHOOSE, Contract, Cream, Cull, Elite, Evulse, Flower, Gather, Glean, Gurlet, Hack, Holing, Hopper, Mattock, Nap, Nibble, Oakum, Plectrum, Pluck, Plum, Select, Single, Sort, Steal, Strum, Tong, Wale
▷ **Picked** *may indicate* an anagram
Picket Demonstrate, Fence, Flying, Pale, Palisade, Protester, Riata, Stake, Tether, Tie
Pickings Harvest, Profits, Scrounging, Spoils
Pickle(r) Achar, Brine, Cabbage, Caper, Chow-chow, Chutney, Corn, Corner, Cucumber, Cure, Dilemma, Dill, Eisel, Esile, Gherkin, Girkin, Imp, Jam, Kimchi, Marinade, Marinate, Mess, Mull, Olive, Onion, Peculate, Peregrine, Piccalilli, → PLIGHT, Relish, Rod, Samp(h)ire, Scrape, Souse, Trouble, Vinegar, Wolly
Picklock Oustiti, Peterman
Pick-me-up Bracer, Drink, Restorer, Reviver, Tonic
Pickpocket(s) Adept, Bung, Cly-faker, Cutpurse, Dip, Diver, Fagin, File, Nipper, Swell mob, Swellmobsman, Whizzer, Wire
Pick-up Arrest, Light o'love, Truck, Ute

Picnic Alfresco, Braaivleis, Burgoo, Clambake, Fun, Junketing, Outing, Push-over, Spread, Tailgate, Valium, Wase-goose, Wayzgoose

Picture(s) Anaglyph, Arpillera, Art, Bambocciades, Bitmap, B-movie, Canvas, Cinema, Cloudscape, Collage, Cutaway, Cyclorama, Decoupage, Depict, Describe, Diptych, Drawing, Drypoint, Emblem, Envisage, Epitome, Etching, Film, Flick, Fresco, Gouache, Graphic, Histogram, Icon, Identikit®, Imagery, Inset, Kakemono, Landscape, Lenticular, Likeness, Lithograph, Montage, Mosaic, Motion, Movie, Moving, Movy, Mugshot, Myriorama, Oil, Painture, Photo, Photofit®, Photogram, Photomontage, Photomosaic, Photomural, Pin-up, Pix, Plate, Polyptych, Portrait, Predella, Prent, Presentment, Print, Represent, Retraitt, Retrate, Rhyparography, Scene, Semble, Shadowgraph, Shot, Slide, Snapshot, Stereochrome, Stereogram, Stereograph, Stevengraph, Still-life, Table(au), Talkie, Thermogram, Tone, Topo, Transfer, Transparency, Vanitas, Vectograph, Vision, Votive, Vraisemblance, Word, Zincograph

Picturesque Idyllic, Scenic

Pidgin Bislama, Chinook jargon, Creole, Fanagalo, Fanakalo, Hiri Motu, Japlish, Kamtok, Mobilian, New Guinea, Police Motu, Solomon Islands, Tok Pisin

Pie(s) Anna, Banoffee, Battalia, Bird, Bridie, Camp, Chewet, Cinch, Cobbler, Cottage, Coulibiac, Curry puff, Custard, Deep-dish, Easy, Flan, Floater, Florentine, Hash, Humble, Koulibiaca, Madge, Meat, Mess, Mince(meat), Mud, Mystery bag, Pandowdy, Pastry, Pasty, Patty, Périgord, Pica, Piet, Pirog, Pizza, Printer's, Pyat, Pyet, Pyot, Quiche, Rappe, Resurrection, Shepherd's, Shoofly, Shred, Spoil, Squab, Stargaz(e)y, Star(ry)-gazy, Sugar, Tart, Tarte tatin, Torte, Tourtière, Turnover, Tyropitta, Umble, Vol-au-vent, Warden

▷ **Pie** *may indicate* an anagram

Piebald Calico, Dappled, Lacuna, Motley, Paint, Pied, Pinto, Skewbald, Tangun

Piece(s) Adagio, Add, Arioso, Bagatelle, Bishop, Bit, Blot, Cameo, Cannon, Cent, Charm, → **CHESSMAN**, Chip, Chunk, Coin, Companion, Component, Concerto, Conversation, Counter, Crumb, Domino, End, Episode, Extract, Firearm, Fit, Flake, Flitters, Fragment, Frust, Gat, Goring, → **GUN**, Haet, Hait, Hunk, Item, Join, Mammock, Médaillons, Mite, Money, Morceau, Morsel, Museum, Nip, Novelette, Oddment, Off-cut, Ort, Part, Party, Pastiche, Patch, Pawn, Pce, Period, Peso, Pin, Pistareen, Pole, → **PORTION**, Recital, Scliff, Scrap, Section, Sector, Set, Shard, Sherd, Skliff, Slice, Slip, Sliver, Snatch, Sou, Spare part, Speck, String, Stub, Swatch, Tad, Tait, Tate, Tile, Toccata, Truncheon, Wedge, Wodge

Pièce de résistance Star-turn

Piecemeal, Piecework Gradually, Intermittent, Jigsaw, Serial, Task, Tut

Pie-crust Coffin, Lid, Pastry

Pied-à-terre Nest, Pad

Pieman Pastrycook, Shepherd

Pier(s) Anta, Chain, Groyne, Jetty, Jutty, Landing, Mole, Plowman, Quay, Slipway, Swiss roll, Wharf, Wigan

Pierce(d), Piercer, Piercing Accloy, Awl, Bore, Broach, Cleave, Cribrose, Dart, Drill, Endart, Fenestrate(d), Fulminant, Gimlet, Gore, Gride, Gryde, Hull, Impale, Jag, Keen, Lance, Lancinate, Lobe, Move, Needle, Penetrate, Perforate, Pertusate, Pike, Pink, Poignant, Prince Albert, Punch, Puncture, Riddle, Rive, Shrill, Skewer, Slap, Sleeper, Spear, Spike, Spit, Stab, Steek, Stilet(to), Sting, Tap, Thirl, Thrill(ant)

Piety Devotion, Godliness, Purity, Sanctity

Piffle Bilge, Codswallop, Hogwash, Poppycock, Tommy-rot, Twaddle

Pig(s), Piggy, Pigmeat, Pigskin Anthony, Babe, Babirusa, Baconer, Barrow, Bartholomew, Bessemer, Bland, Boar, Bonham, British Lop, Bush, Captain Cooker, Cutter, Doll, Duroc, Elt, Farrow, Fastback, Football, Gadarene, Gilt, Gloucester, Gloucester Old Spot, Glutton, Grice, Grumphie, Gryce, Guffie, Guinea, Gus, Gutzer, Ham, Hampshire, Hog, Ingot, Iron, Javelina, Kentledge, Kintledge, Kunekune, Lacombe, Landrace, Land-shark, Lard, Large Black, Large White, Lingot, Long, Middle White, Napoleon, Old Spot, Peccary, Policeman, Porchetta, Pork(er), Raven, Razorback, Rosser,

Runt, Saddleback, Shoat, Shot(e), Shott, Slip, Snowball, Sounder, Sow, Squealer, Sucking, Suid(ae), Tamworth, Tayassuid, Tithe, Toe, Tootsie, Truffle, Vietnamese potbellied, Warthog, Welsh, Yelt

Pig-disease Bullnose

Pigeon Archangel, Barb, Bird, Bronze-winged, Cape, Capuchin, Carrier, Clay, Cropper, Culver, Cumulet, Danzig, Dove, Fairy Swallow, Fantail, Goura, Ground, Gull, Homer, Homing, Horseman, Jacobin, Kereru, Kuku, Manumea, Mourning dove, New Zealand, Nun, Owl, Passenger, Peristeronic, Piwakawaka, Pouter, Ringdove, Rock(er), Roller, Ront(e), Ruff, Runt, Scandaroon, Solitaire, Spot, Squab, Squealer, Stale, Stock-dove, Stool, Stork, Swift, Talkie-talkee, Tippler, Tooth-billed, Trumpeter, Tumbler, Turbit, Wonga(-wonga), Zoozoo

Pigeonhole Classify, Compartment, File, Label, Postpone, Shelve, Slot, Stereotype

Pigeon-house Columbary, Cote, Dovecot(e)

Pig-food Mast, Slop, Swill

Pig-headed Self-willed

Pig-iron Kentledge, Kintledge

Pigment(s), Pigmentation Accessory, Anthoclore, Anthocyan(in), Argyria, Betacyanin, Bilirubin, Biliverdin, Bister, Bistre, Bronzing, Cappagh-brown, Carmine, Carotene, Carotenoid, Carotin, Carotinoid, Chloasma, Chlorophyll, Chrome, Chromogen, Cobalt, Colcothar, Colour, Crocus, Curcumin, Dye, Etiolin, Eumelanin, Flake-white, Flavin(e), Fucoxanthin, Gamboge, Gossypol, Green earth, Haem, Hem(e), H(a)ematin, H(a)emocyanin, H(a)emoglobin, Iodopsin, King's yellow, Lake, Lamp-black, Lipochrome, Lithopone, Liverspot, Lutein, Luteolin, Lycopene, Madder, Madder lake, Melanin, Monastral®, Naevus, Naples yellow, Nigrosine, Ochre, Opsin, Orpiment, Paris-green, Phthalocyanine, Phycobilin, Phycocyan, Phycoerythrin, Phycophaein, Phycoxanthin, Phytochrome, Porphyrin, Porphyropsin, Pterin, Puccoon, Quercetin, Realgar, Red lead, Respiratory, Retinene, Rhiboflavin, Rhodophane, Rhodopsin, Saffron, Scheele's green, Sepia, Sienna, Sinopia, Sinopsis, Smalt, Tapetum, Tempera, Terre-verte, Tincture, Toner, Turacoverdin, Ultramarine, Umber, Urobilin, Urochrome, Verditer, Vermilion, Viridian, Whitewash, Xanthophyll, Xanthopterin(e), Yellow ochre, Zinc white

Pigtail Braid, Cue, Plait, Queue

Pi jaw Cant

Pike Assegai, Crag, Dory, Fogash, Gar(fish), Ged, Gisarme, Glaive, Hie, Holostei, Javelin, Lance, Luce, Partisan, Pickerel, Ravensbill, Scafell, Snoek, Spear, Speed, Spontoon, Vouge, Walleyed

▶ **Pilaster** *see* **PILLAR(ED)**

Pilchard Sardine

Pile(d), Piles, Piling Agger, Amass, Atomic, Bing, Bomb, Bubkes, Camp-sheathing, Camp-shedding, Camp-sheeting, Camp-shot, Clamp, Cock, Column, Crowd, Deal, Dolphin, Down, Emerods, Farmers, Fender, Fig, Floccus, Fortune, Galvanic, Hair, Haycock, Heap, Hept, Historic, Hoard, Load, Lot, Mansion, Marleys, Mass, Moquette, Nap, Pier, Post, Pyre, Raft, Reactor, Ream(s), Rouleau, Screw, Shag, Sheet, Slush, → **STACK**, Starling, Stilt, Toorie, Trichome, Upheap, Velvet, Voltaic, Wealth, Windrow, Wodge

Pile-driver Tup

Pilfer(ing) Crib, Filch, Finger, Maraud, Miche, Nick, Peculate, Pickery, Pickle, Pinch, Plagiarise, Plunder, Purloin, Snitch, → **STEAL**

Pilgrim(age) Aske, Childe Harold, Expedition, Fatima, Gaya, Hadj(i), Haji, Hajj(i), Karbala, Kerbela, Kum, Loreto, Lourdes, Mathura, Mecca, Nasik, Nikko, Palmer, Pardoner, Qom, Questor, Qum, Reeve, Scallop-shell, Shrine, Umra(h), Voyage, Yatra

Pill(s) Abortion, Ball, Beverley, Bitter, Bolus, Cachou, Caplet, Capsule, Chill, Dex, Doll, Dose, Globule, Golfball, Goofball, Lob, Medication, Medicine, Number nine, Peace, Peel, Pellet, Pep, Pilula, Pilule, Placebo, Poison, Protoplasmal, Radio, Sleeping, Spansule, Tablet, Troche, Trochisk, Upper

Pillage Booty, Devastate, Plunder, Ransack, Rapine, Ravage, Razzia, Robbery, Sack, Spoil

Pillar(ed), Pillars Anta, Apostle, Atlantes, Baluster, Balustrade, Boaz, Canton, Caryatides, Chambers, Cippus, Columel, Column, Earth, Eustyle, Gendarme, Goal, Hercules, Herm, Impost, Islam, Jachin, Lat, Man, Modiolus, Monolith, Newel, Nilometer, Obelisk, Pedestal, Peristyle, Pier, Post, Respond, Saddle, Serac, Stack, Stalactite, Stalagmite, Stoop, Telamon, Tetrastyle, Trumeau

Pill-box Hat, Inro

Pillion Cushion, Pad, Rear

Pillory Cang(ue), Cippus, Crucify, Jougs, Little-ease, Pelt, Satirise, Slam

Pillow(case) Bear, Beer, Bere, Bolster, Cod, Cow, Cushion, Headrest, Hop, Lace, Pad, Pulvinar, Throw

Pilot Ace, Airman, Auto(matic), Aviator, Biggles, Branch, Bush, Captain, → **CONDUCT**, Experimental, Flier, George, Govern, Guide, Hobbler, Lead, Lodesman, Lodestar, Palinure, Palinurus, Pitt, Prune, Shipman, Steer, Test, Tiphys, Trial, Usher, Wingman

Pimento Allspice

Pimp Apple-squire, Bludger, Fancyman, Fleshmonger, Hoon, Lecher, Mack, Pandarus, Pander, Ponce, Procurer, Solicit, Souteneur

Pimpernel Bastard, Bog, Poor man's weatherglass, Scarlet, Water, Wincopipe, Wink-a-peep, Yellow

Pimple, Pimply Blackhead, Botch, Bubukle, Button, Goosebump, Gooseflesh, Grog-blossom, Hickey, Horripilation, Milium, Papilla, Papula, Papule, Plook, Plouk, Pock, Pustule, Quat, Rumblossom, Rum-bud, Spot, Tetter, Uredinial, Wen, Whelk, Whitehead, Zit

Pin Bayonet, Belaying, Bolt, Brooch, Candle, Cask, Corking, Cotter, Curling, Dowel, Drawing, Drift, End, Fasten, Fid, Firing, Fix, Gam, Gnomon, Gudgeon, Hair, Hairgrip, Hob, Hook, Joggle, Kevel, King, Leg, Nail, Needle, Nog, Panel, Peg, Pintle, Pivot, Preen, Rivet, Rolling, Saddle, Safety, Scarf, SCART, Scatter, Shear, Shirt, Skewer, Skittle, Skiver, Spike, Spindle, Split, Staple, Stick, Stump, Swivel, Taper, Tertial, Thole, Thumbtack, Tie, Tietac(k), Tre(e)nail, Trunnion, U-bolt, Woolder, Wrest, Wrist

Pinafore Apron, Brat, HMS, Overall, Pinny, Save-all, Tire

Pinball Pachinko

Pince-nez Nose-nippers

Pincers Chela, Claw, Forceps, Forfex, Nipper, Nips, Tweezers

Pinch(ed) Arrest, Bit, Bone, Chack, Constrict, Cramp, Crimp, Crisis, Emergency, Gaunt, Misappropriate, Nab, Nick, Nim, Nip, Nirlit, Peculate, Peel, Pilfer, Pocket, Pook(it), Pouk, Prig, Pugil, Raft, Raw, Rob, Save, Scrimp, Scrounge, Skimp, Smatch, Snabble, Snaffle, Sneak, Sneap, Sneeshing, Snuff, Squeeze, → **STEAL**, Swipe, Tate, Trace, Tweak, Twinge

Pine(s), Pining Arolla, Bristlecone, Celery, Cembra, Chile, Cluster, Cone, Conifer, Cypress, Droop, Dwine, Earn, Erne, Fret, Green, Ground, Hone, Hoop, Huon, Jack, Japanese umbrella, Jeffrey, Kauri, Knotty, Languish, Languor, Loblolly, Lodgepole, Long, Longleaf, Lovesick, Monkey-puzzle, Monterey, Moon, Norfolk Island, Norway, Nut, Oregon, Parana, Picea, Pinaster, Pitch, Ponderosa, Radiata, Red, Scotch, Scots, Screw, Slash, Softwood, Spruce, Starve, Stone, Sugar, Tree, Umbrella, Urman, Waste, White, Yearn, Yellow

Pineapple Anana, Bomb, Bromelia, Grenade, Piña, Poll, Sorosis, Tillandsia

Ping Knock, Whir(r)

Pinguin Anana(s)

Pinion Fetter, Lantern, Penne, Pinnoed, Secure, Shackle, Wing

Pink Blush, Carnation, Carolina, Castory, Cheddar, Clove, Colour, Coral, Cyclamen, Dianthus, Dutch, Emperce, FT, Fuchsia, Gillyflower, Indian, Knock, Kook, Lake, Lily, Lychnis, Maiden, Moss, Mushroom, Old rose, Oyster, Peach-blow, Peak, Perce, Pierce, Pompadour, Pounce, Rose(ate), Rose-hued, Ruddy, Salmon, Scallop, Sea, Shell, Shocking, Shrimp, Spigelia, Spit, Stab, Tiny

Pinnacle Acme, Apex, Apogee, Crest, Crown, Gendarme, Height, Needle, Pinnet, Summit

Pinniped Seal

Pin-point Focus, Highlight, Identify, Isolate, Localise

Pint(s) Cab, Jar, Log, Reputed

Pintail Duck, Smeath, Smee(th)

Pin-up Bimbo, Cheesecake, Dish, Star, Sweater girl

Pioneer Avant garde, Babbage, Baird, Bandeirante, Blaze, Boone, Colonist, Emigrant, Explore, Fargo, Fawkner, Fleming, Frontiersman, Harbinger, Herodotus, Innovator, Lead, Marconi, Oecist, Pathfinder, Planter, Rochdale, Sandgroper, Settler, Spearhead, Stopes, Trail-blazer, Trekker, Turing, Voortrekker, Waymaker, Wells, Yeager

▶ **Pious** *see* **PI**

Pip Ace, Acinus, Blackball, Bleep, Distemper, Hip, Hump, Phil, Pyrene, Seed, Star

Pipe(s), Piper, Pipeline, Piping Ait, Antara, Aorta, Aulos, Balance, Barrel, Blub, Boatswain's, Bong, Briar, Briarroot, Bronchus, Broseley, Bubble, Calabash, Call, Calumet, Chanter, Cheep, Cherrywood, Chibouk, Chibouque, Chillum, Churchwarden, Clay, Cob, Conduit, Corncob, Crane, Cutty, Dip, Division, Down, Downcomer, Drain, Drill, Drillstring, Drone, Dry riser, Duct, Dudeen, Dudheen, Ell, Escape, Exhaust, Faucet, Feed, Fistula, Flue, Flute, Gage, Gas main, Gedact, Gedeckt, Hawse, Hod, Hogger, Hooka(h), Hose, Hubble-bubble, Hydrant, Indian, Injection string, Irish, Jet, Kalian, Kelly, Mains, Manifold, Marsyas, Meerschaum, Mirliton, Montre, Narghile, Nargile(h), Narg(h)il(l)y, Oat(en), Oboe, Organ, Ottavino, Outlet, Pan, Peace, Pepper, Pibroch, Piccolo, Pied, Pifferaro, Pitch, Poverty, Principal, Pule, Qanat, Quill, Rainwater, Recorder, Ree(d), Rise, Riser, Sack-doudling, Salicional, Sennit, Serpent, Service, Sewer, Shalm, Shawm, Sheesha, Shisha, Shoe, Shrike, Sing, Siphon, Skirl, Sluice, Soil, Spout, Squeak, Stack, Standpipe, Stopcock, Stummel, Sucker, Syrinx, Tail, Tee, Throttle, Tibia, Tootle, Trachea, Tremie, Tube, Tubule, Tweet, U-bend, Uillean(n), Union, Uptake, U-trap, U-tube, Vent, Ventiduct, Volcanic, Waste, Water(-spout), Watermain, Weasand, Whiss, Whistle, Woodcock's head, Woodnote, Worm

Pipefish Sea-adder

Pipe-laying Graft

Pipit Bird, Skylark, Titlark

Pippin Apple, Orange, Ribston

Pipsqueak Nobody

Piquancy, Piquant Pungent, Racy, Relish, Salt, Savoury, Sharp, Spicy, Tangy

Pique Dod, Huff, Resentment, Titillate

Piranha Caribe, Characinoid, Piraya

Pirate(s), Pirated, Piratical, Piracy Algerine, Barbarossa, Blackbeard, Boarder, Bootleg, Brigand, Buccaneer, Buccanier, Cateran, Condottier, Conrad, Corsair, Crib, Dampier, Fil(l)ibuster, Flint, Gunn, Hijack, Hook, Kidd, Lift, Loot, Morgan, Penzance, Picaro(on), Pickaroon, Plagiarise, Plunder, Rakish, Rover, Sallee-man, Sallee-rover, Sea-dog, Sea-king, Sea-rat, Sea-robber, Sea-wolf, Silver, Skull and crossbones, Smee, Steal, Teach, Thief, Unauthorised, Viking, Water-rat, Water-thief

Pistillate Female

Pistol Air, Ancient, Automatic, Barker, Barking-iron, Captive bolt, Colt®, Dag, Derringer, Gat, → **GUN**, Hackbut, Horse, Iron, Luger®, Pepperbox, Petronel, Pocket, Puffer, Revolver, Rod, Saloon, Shooter, Sidearm, Starter, Starting, Very, Water, Weapon, Zip gun

Piston Four-stroke, Plunger, Ram, Trunk

Pit(ted), Pitting Abyss, Alveolus, Antrum, Bed, Bottomless, Catch, Cave, Cesspool, Chasm, Cissing, Cloaca, Colliery, Crater, Den, Depression, Depth, Dungmere, Ensile, Fossa, Fougasse, Fovea, Foxhole, Gehenna, Hangi, Heapstead, Heartspoon, Hell, Hillhole, Hole, Hollow, Inferno, Inspection, Khud, Lacunose, Lime, Mark, Match, Measure, → **MINE**, Mosh, Orchestra, Parterre, Pip, Plague, Play, Pock-mark, Potato, Punctate, Putamen, Pyrene, Ravine, Rifle, Salt, Scrobicule, Silo, Slime, Soakaway, Solar plexus, Stone, Sump, Tar, Tear, Trap, Trous-de-loup, Underarm

Pitch(ed) Absolute, Asphalt, Atilt, Attune, Bitumen, Burgundy, Coal-tar, Concert, Crease, Diamond, Diesis, Dive, Ela, Elect, Elevator, Encamp, Erect, Establish, Fever, Fling, Fork(ball), French, Ground, Height, International, Intonation, Key, Knuckleball, Labour, Length, Level, Lurch, Maltha, Mineral, Nets, Neume, Outfield, Patter, Peck, Perfect, Philharmonic, Philosophical, Piceous, Pight, Pin, Plong(e), Plunge, Pop, Purl, Relative, Resin, Rock, Ruff(e), Sales, Scend, Seel, Send, Shape, Sling, Slope, Soprarino, Spiel, Spitball, Stoit, Tar, Tessitura, Tilt, Tone, Tonemic, Tonus, Tremolo, Tune, Unison, Vibrato, Wicket, Wild, Wood

Pitchblende Cleveite

Pitcher(-shaped) Aryt(a)enoid, Ascidium, Baseballer, Bowler, Cruse, Ewer, Jug, Steen, Urceolus

Pitchfork Hurl, Toss

Pitchstone Retinite

Pitfall Ambush, Danger, Hazard, Snare, Trap

Pith(y) Ambatch, Aphorism, Apo(ph)thegm, Core, Down, Essence, Gnomic, Hat-plant, Heart, Laconic, Marrow, Meaty, Medulla, Moxa, Nucleus, Rag, Sententious, Succinct, Terse

Pithead Broo, Brow, Minehead

Pithless Thowless

Pitiless Flint-hearted, Hard, Hard-headed, Ruthless

Piton Rurp

Pitt Chatham

Pity, Piteous, Pitiful, Pitiable Ah, Alack, Alas, Commiseration, → **COMPASSION**, Hapless, Mercy, Pathos, Pilgarlic, Poor, Quarter, Red-leg, Rue, Ruth(ful), Seely, Shame, Sin, Sympathy

Pivot(al) Ax(i)le, Central, Focal, Fulcrum, Gooseneck, Gudgeon, Kingbolt, Marker, Revolve, Rotate, Slue, → **SWIVEL**, Trunnion, Turn, Wheel

Pixie Brownie, Elf, Fairy, Gremlin, Sprite

Pizza Calzone, Pepperoni

Placard Affiche, Bill, Playbill, Poster

Placate Appease, Calm, Conciliate, Mollify, Pacify, Placate, Propitiate, Soothe

Place(ment) Ad loc, Aim, Allocate, Area, Arena, Assisted, Berth, Bro, Decimal, Deploy, Deposit, Dispose, First, Fix, Habitat, Haunt, Hither, Howf, Identify, Impose, → **IN PLACE OF**, Insert, Install, Job, Joint, Juxtapose, Lay, Lieu, Locality, Locate, Locus, Parking, Pitch, Plat, Plaza, Point, Posit, → **POSITION**, Post, Product, Put, Realm, Region, Repose, Resting, Room, Rowme, Scene, Second, Set, Sit, Site, Situate, Situation, Slot, Spot, Stead, Sted(e), Stedd(e), Stratify, Third, Toponym, Town, Vendôme

Placebo Snake-oil

Placid Cool, Easy, Easy-osy, Even-tempered, Quiet, Tame, Tranquil

Plagiarise, Plagiarist Copy, Crib, Lift, Pirate, Steal

Plague (spot) Annoy, Bane, Bedevil, Black death, Boil, Bubonic, Burden, Cattle, Curse, Death, Dog, Dun, Frogs, Gay, Goodyear, Goujeers, Harry, Infestation, Locusts, Lues, Molest, Murrain, Murran, Murrin, Murrion, Nag, Pest, Pester, Pox, Press, Scourge, Tease, Token, Torment, Torture, Try, Vex

Plaid Maud, Roon, Shepherd's, Tartan, Wales

Plain(s) Abraham, Archimedes, Artless, Ascetic, Au naturel, Bald, Banat, Bare, Blatant, Broad, Campagna, Campo, Campus Martius, Candid, Carse, Ceará, Chryse, Clavius, Clear, Cook, Dowdy, Downright, Dry, Esdraelon, Evident, Explicit, Flat, Flood, Girondist, Gran Chaco, Great, Homely, Homespun, Inornate, Jezreel, Kar(r)oo, Lande, Langrenus, Liverpool, Llano, Lombardy, Lowland, Maidan, Manifest, Marathon, Mare, Monochrome, Nullarbor, Obvious, Ocean of Storms, Oceanus Procellarum, Olympia, → **ORDINARY**, Outspoken, Overt, Packstaff, Pampa(s), Paramo, Patent, Pikestaff, Plateau, Playa, Polje, Prairie, Prose, Ptolemaeus, Purbach, Sabkha(h), Sabkha(t), Sailing, Salisbury, Savanna(h), Secco, Serengeti, Sharon, Simple, Sodom, Spoken, Staked, Steppe, Tableland, Thessaly,

Tundra, Unremarkable, Vanilla, Vega, Veldt, Visible, Walled

Plainchant Canto fermo

Plainsman Llanero

Plainsong Alternatim, Ambrosian, Chant

Plaint(ive) Complaint, Dirge, Lacrimoso, Lagrimoso, Lament, Melancholy, Sad, Whiny

Plaintiff Doe, Impeacher, Litigant, Suer

Plait Braid, Crimp, Cue, Frounce, Furbelow, Goffer, Intertwine, Pigtail, Plica, Plight, Queue, Ruche, Sennit, Sinnet, Splice

Plan(s), Planned, Planner, Planning Aim, American, Angle, Architect, Arrange, Atlas, Axonometric, Battle, Blueprint, Brew, Budget, Care, Chart, Commission, Complot, Contingency, Contrive, Dalton, Dart, Deep-laid, Deliberate, Delors, Design, Desyne, Device, Devise, Diagram, Draft, Drawing, Elevation, Engineer, European, Family, Figure on, Five-Year, Flight, Floor, Format, Galveston, Game, Ground, Hang, Ichnography, Idea, Idée, Instal(l)ment, Intent, Lay(out), Leicester, Leicestershire, Machinate, Map, Marshall, Master, Mastermind, Mean, Meditate, Nominal, Open, Outline, Pattern, Pipe-dream, Plat, Plot, Ploy, Policy, Premeditate, Prepense, Procedure, Programme, Project, Projet, Proposal, Prospectus, Protraction, Rapacki, Road map, Scenario, Schedule, Scheme, Schlieffen, Shape, Spec(ification), Stratagem, Strategy, Subterfuge, System, Tactician, Town, Trace, View, Wallchart, Wheeze

Plane(s) Aero(dyne), Air, → **AIRCRAFT**, Airliner, Airship, Axial, Bandit, Basal, Block, Boeing, Bomber, Bus, Buttock, Camel, Canard, Cartesian, Cessna, Chenar, Chinar, Comet, Concorde, Crate, Dakota, Datum, Delta-wing, Even, Facet, Fault, Fillister, Flat, Float, Focal, Galactic, Glider, Gliding, Gotha, Homaloid, Hurricane, Icosahedron, Icosohedra, Inclined, Jack, Jet, Jointer, Jumbo, Level, London, Main, MIG, Mirage, Mosquito, Moth, Octagon, Perspective, Platan(us), Polygon, Prop-jet, Pursuit, Rocket, Router, Shackleton, Shave, Smooth, Sole, Spitfire, Spokeshave, Spy, Stealth (bomber), STOL, Surface, Sycamore, Tail, Taube, Thrust, Tow, Trainer, Tree, Trident, Tropopause, Trying, Two-seater, Viscount

Plane figure Endecagon, Hendecagon

Planet(s), Planetary Alphonsine, Ariel, Asteroid, Body, Cabiri, Ceres, Chiron, Constellation, Dispositor, Earth, Eros, Extrasolar, Gas giant, Georgian, Giant, House, Hyleg, Inferior, Inner, Jovian, Jupiter, Lucifer, Major, Mars, Mercury, Minor, Moon, Neptune, Outer, Pallas, Pluto, Primary, Psyche, Quartile, Red, Satellitium, Saturn, Sedna, Significator, Sphere, Starry, Sun, Superior, Terra, Terrestrial, Uranus, Venus, Vista, Vulcan, World, Zog

Plangent Mournful

Plank Board, Chess, Deal, Duckboard, Garboard, Plonk, Sarking, Slab, Spirketting, Straik, Strake, Stringer, Weatherboard, Wood, Wrest

Plankton Nekton, Neuston, Noctiluca, Pelagic, Red tide, Seston, Spatfall

Plant(s), Plant part Acrogen, Amphidiploid, Anemochore, Annual, Anther, Aphotoic, Autophyte, Bed, Biennial, Biota, Bloomer, Bonsai, Bryophyte, CAM, Chamaephyte, Chomophyte, Cotyledon, Cropper, Cultigen, Cultivar, Dayflower, Dibble, Ecad, Eccremocarpus, Embed, Endogen, Enrace, Epilithic, Epiphyllous, Epiphyte, Establish, Factory, Fix, Flora, Forb, Geophyte, G(u)ild, Growth, Gymnosperm, Halophyte, Halosere, Herbage, Herbarium, House, Humicole, Hydrastus, Hydrophyte, Hygrophyte, Hylophyte, Incross, Insert, Instil, Inter, Labiate, Land, Lathe, Legume, Lithophyte, Livelong, Longday, Machinery, Mill, Monocotyledon, Ornamental, Perennial, Phanerogam, Phloem, Pilot, Pitcher, Power, Protophyte, Psilophyte, Ramet, Resurrection, Root, Rosin, Saprophyte, Schizophyte, Sciophyte, Sclerophyll, Scrambler, Sensitive, Sere, Shortday, Shrub, Simple, Sow, Spermatophyte, Sponge, Steelworks, Stickseed, Sticktight, Strangler, Streptocarpus, Succulent, Superweed, Thallophyte, Therophyte, Thickleaf, Trailer, → **TREE**, Trifolium, Trillium, Tropophyte, Twining, Vascular, Vegetal, Vegetation, Washery, Wilding, Works, Zoophyte

PLANTS

3 letters:
Dal
Hom
Hop
Ivy
Kex
Meu
Nep
Pia
Rue
Set
Soy
Til
Udo
Urd
Yam

4 letters:
Alga
Aloe
Anil
Arum
Beet
Bixa
Chay
Cube
Daal
Dahl
Deme
Dhal
Dill
Fern
Flag
Flax
Geum
Grex
Guar
Hebe
Herb
Hioi
Homa
Hoya
Ixia
Kaki
Kali
Kava
Khat
Lily
Loco
Mate
Mint
More

Moss
Musk
Nard
Noni
Ombu
Pink
Pita
Poly
Rape
Reed
Rhus
Rose
Rush
Sage
Sego
Sida
Snow
Sola
Soma
Sunn
Tare
Taro
Thea
Vine
Weld
Woad
Wort
Yarr

5 letters:
Abaca
Agave
Ajwan
Anise
Anona
Arnut
Aroid
Aster
Basil
Benni
Betel
Blite
Bluet
Boree
Broom
Buchu
Bucku
Bugle
Calla
Camas
Canna
Carex

Chara
Chaya
Chufa
Clary
Clote
Cress
Cubeb
Cumin
Daisy
Erica
Ficus
Fitch
Fouat
Fouet
Fucus
Gemma
Glaux
Gorse
Guaco
Hosta
Hovea
Inula
Jalap
Kenaf
Knawe
Kudzu
Laser
Ledum
Liana
Linum
Loofa
Lotus
Luffa
Lupin
Lurgi
Medic
Morel
Murva
Musci
Naiad
Orach
Orpin
Orris
Orval
Oshac
Osier
Oxeye
Oxlip
Panax
Pansy
Peony
Phlox

Pilea
Poppy
Sedge
Sedum
Senna
Shaya
Sotol
Spart
Spink
Stock
Tansy
Tetra
Timbo
Tulip
Urali
Urari
Urena
Vetch
Vinca
Viola
Vitex
Vitis
Xyris
Yucca
Yulan
Zamia

6 letters:
Abelia
Acacia
Acorus
Ajowan
Alisma
Allium
Alpine
Althea
Ambari
Ambary
Amomum
Annona
Arabis
Aralia
Arnica
Aucuba
Azalea
Bablah
Balsam
Bamboo
Bauera
Betony
Borage
Briony

Bryony
Burnet
Cactus
Caltha
Camash
Camass
Cassia
Catnep
Catnip
Celery
Cicely
Cicuta
Cissus
Cistus
Cleome
Clivia
Clover
Clusia
Cnicus
Cockle
Cohage
Cohosh
Coleus
Conium
Coonty
Cornel
Cosmea
Cosmos
Cotton
Cowpea
Crinum
Crocus
Croton
Cummin
Dahlia
Daphne
Darnel
Datura
Derris
Dodder
Echium
Endive
Erinus
Erynga
Exacum
Exogen
Fat hen
Fennel
Ferula
Funkia
Garlic
Gnetum
Henbit
Hoodia

Hyssop
Iberis
Jojoba
Juncus
Kentia
Kerria
Kie-kie
Knawel
Kochia
Korari
Kumara
Kumera
Lentil
Lichen
Lolium
Loofah
Lovage
Lunary
Lupine
Luzula
Madder
Maguey
Mallow
Manioc
Manoao
Medick
Mimosa
Moorva
Nerine
Nerium
Nettle
Nuphar
Orache
Orchid
Orchis
Orpine
Ourali
Ourari
Oxalis
Oxslip
Oyster
Pachak
Paeony
Peanut
Pepino
Pepper
Pieris
Protea
Radish
Ramtil
Rattle
Reseda
Retama
Rubber

Ruscus
Salvia
Savory
Scilla
Senega
Sesame
Seseli
Silene
Smilax
Sorbus
Sorrel
Spider
Spirea
Spurge
Spurry
Squill
Styrax
Sundew
Teasel
Teazle
Thrash
Thrift
Tomato
Tulipa
Turnip
Tutsan
Violet
Viscum
Wasabi
Yacona
Yarrow
Yautia
Zinnia

7 letters:
Absinth
Aconite
Alkanet
All-good
Allheal
Allseed
Alyssum
Anchusa
Anemone
Arachis
Astilbe
Awlwort
Barilla
Bartsia
Bee-balm
Begonia
Bogbeam
Boneset
Brinjal

Bugbean
Bugloss
Burdock
Burweed
Calluna
Caltrap
Caltrop
Campion
Caraway
Cardoon
Carduus
Carline
Cascara
Cassava
Catechu
Catmint
Cat's ear
Celosia
Century
Chayote
Chelone
Chervil
Chicory
Clarkia
Clivers
Cocoyam
Comfrey
Compass
Coontie
Cowbane
Cowbird
Cowhage
Cowherb
Cowitch
Cowslip
Cudweed
Cumquat
Curcuma
Cushion
Dasheen
Deutzia
Diascia
Dioecia
Dittany
Dogbane
Dogwood
Drosera
Epacris
Ephedra
Erodium
Eugenia
Felicia
Felwort
Filaree

Fly-trap
Freesia
Frogbit
Fuchsia
Gazania
Genista
Gentian
Gerbera
Ginseng
Godetia
Gunnera
Haemony
Hawkbit
Heather
Hemlock
Henbane
Hogweed
Ipomoea
Isoetes
Jasmine
Jonquil
Juniper
Kingcup
Kumquat
Lantana
Lettuce
Liatris
Lobelia
Logania
Lucerne
Lychnis
Lythrum
Madwort
Mahonia
Manihot
Maranta
Matweed
Mayweed
Melilot
Mercury
Milfoil
Mimulus
Monarda
Mudwort
Mugwort
Mullein
Mustard
Nelumbo
Nemesia
Nigella
Nonsuch
Olearia
Opuntia
Palmiet

Pareira
Parella
Parelle
Parsley
Parsnip
Penthia
Petunia
Pigface
Pinesap
Pinguin
Potherb
Primula
Puccoon
Pumpkin
Ragwort
Rampion
Raoulia
Redroot
Rhatany
Rhodora
Rhubarb
Ribwort
Ricinus
Robinia
Romneya
Rosebay
Ruellia
Saffron
Salfern
Salsify
Salsola
Sampire
Sanicle
Sawwort
Scandix
Seakale
Sea pink
Senecio
Setwall
Skirret
Solanum
Spignel
Spinach
Spiraea
Spurrey
Squilla
Stachys
Stapela
Statice
Syringa
Tagetes
Thallus
Tobacco
Trefoil

Triffid
Tritoma
Turbith
Turpeth
Vanilla
Verbena
Vervain
Vetiver
Weigela
Woorali
Woorara
Wourali
Yaquona
Zebrina
Zedoary

8 letters:
Abelmosk
Absinthe
Abutilon
Acanthus
Achillea
Ageratum
Agrimony
Agueweed
Alocasia
Alumroot
Angelica
Apocynum
Arenaria
Argemone
Asphodel
Barometz
Bauhinia
Bear's ear
Bedstraw
Beetroot
Bellwort
Bergamot
Bergenia
Bignonia
Bindi-eye
Bindweed
Bird's eye
Bluebell
Bottonia
Boxberry
Brassica
Buckbean
Buddleia
Bull-hoof
Buplever
Caladium
Calamint

Calamite
Calathea
Calthrop
Camellia
Camomile
Canaigre
Cannabis
Capsicum
Cardamom
Cardamum
Carl-hemp
Catchfly
Cat's foot
Centaury
Charlock
Chayroot
Chenopod
Chickpea
Cilantro
Cleavers
Clematis
Clubrush
Coltwood
Costmary
Cow-wheat
Crowfoot
Crucifer
Cucurbit
Cumbungi
Cunjevoi
Cyclamen
Daffodil
Damewort
Dentaria
Diandria
Dianthus
Dicentra
Dielytra
Dogberry
Dog daisy
Dog's bone
Dracaena
Dropwort
Duckweed
Dumbcane
Earthnut
Eelgrass
Erigeron
Eucharis
Euonymus
Feverfew
Fireweed
Flax-lily
Fleabane

Fleawort
Fluellin
Foxglove
Fumitory
Furcraea
Galangol
Galtonia
Gardenia
Geranium
Gesneria
Gladioli
Gloriosa
Glory pea
Gloxinia
Glyceria
Gnetales
Goutweed
Grape ivy
Gromwell
Hag-taper
Harakeke
Hardhack
Harebell
Hawkweed
Helenium
Henequen
Hepatica
Hesperis
Heuchera
Hibiscus
Hippuris
Honewort
Hornwort
Horokaka
Hyacinth
Hydrilla
Hyperium
Japonica
Khuskhus
Knapweed
Knotweed
Kohlrabi
Krameria
Lad's love
Larkspur
Lathyris
Lavatera
Lavender
Licorice
Locoweed
Lonicera
Lungwort
Macleaya
Mandrake

Marigold
Mariposa
Marjoram
Martagon
Milkweed
Milkwort
Miltonia
Monstera
Moonseed
Moonwort
Mosspink
Mouse-ear
Myosotis
Navicula
Nenuphar
Nepenthe
Nymphaea
Oleander
Oleaster
Oncidium
Opopanax
Origanum
Oxtongue
Pandanus
Paspalum
Phacelia
Phormium
Physalis
Pinkroot
Pipewort
Plantain
Plumbago
Pokeroot
Pokeweed
Polygata
Pondweed
Primrose
Prunella
Psilotum
Psoralea
Psyllium
Purslane
Putchock
Queencup
Ratooner
Ratsbane
Redshank
Rock rose
Roly-poly
Rosemary
Sainfoin
Saltwort
Salvinia
Samphire

Sandwort
Scabious
Scammony
Sea-blite
Sea-holly
Self-heal
Sept-foil
Shamrock
Shinleaf
Sidalcea
Silkweed
Silphium
Snowdrop
Soapwort
Solidago
Sowbread
Sparaxis
Spergula
Stapelia
Staragen
Starwort
Suckling
Sunberry
Sundrops
Sweet pea
Tamarisk
Tarragon
Tayberry
Tickseed
Tigridia
Tree-lily
Trigynia
Tritonia
Trollius
Tuberose
Tuckahoe
Turmeric
Turnsole
Valerian
Venidium
Veratrum
Veronica
Viburnum
Viscaria
Wait-a-bit
Wallwort
Water yam
Wistaria
Wisteria
Withwind
Woodroof
Woodruff
Woodrush
Wormseed

Wormwood
Xanthium

9 letters:
Aaron's rod
Achimenes
Adderwort
Alfilaria
Alfileria
Amaryllis
Anacharis
Andromeda
Anthurium
Aquilegia
Archangel
Arracacha
Arrowhead
Arrowroot
Artemisia
Artichoke
Artillery
Asclepias
Asparagus
Astrantia
Aubrietia
Ayabuasca
Bald-money
Baneberry
Bear's foot
Beech fern
Bee-orchid
Birthroot
Birthwort
Bloodroot
Bog myrtle
Breadroot
Bromeliad
Brooklime
Brookweed
Broom-rape
Browallia
Buckwheat
Buglewood
Burrawang
Butterbur
Buttercup
Calcicole
Calcifuge
Calendula
Calla lily
Campanula
Candytuft
Cardamine
Carnation

Catchweed
Ceanothus
Celandine
Centaurea
Chamomile
Cherry pie
Cineraria
Claytonia
Clianthus
Clintonia
Clove pink
Cocklebur
Cock's comb
Colchicum
Colicroot
Colicweed
Collinsia
Colocasia
Colocynth
Coltsfoot
Columbine
Cordaites
Coreopsis
Coriander
Corydalis
Creamcups
Crocosnia
Crosswort
Crowberry
Crowsfoot
Dandelion
Day nettle
Desert pea
Desmodium
Devil's bit
Didynanua
Digitalis
Dittander
Dock-cress
Dog fennel
Dog violet
Doronicum
Dulcamara
Dutch rush
Dyer's weed
Echeveria
Echinacea
Edelweiss
Eglantine
Equisetum
Erythrina
Euphorbia
Eyebright
Fatshedra

Fenugreek
Feverwort
Flame tree
Forsythia
Fourcroya
Friar's cap
Galingale
Gelsemium
Germander
Gessamino
Gladiolus
Glasswort
Goldenrod
Goosefoot
Grass tree
Greenweed
Grindelia
Groundnut
Groundsel
Gypsywort
Hardheads
Heliconia
Hellebore
Helophyte
Herb-Paris
Herb Peter
Hieracium
Hoarhound
Hollyhock
Horehound
Horsemint
Horse-tail
House leek
Houstonia
Hydrangea
Hypericum
Impatiens
Jacaranda
Job's tears
Judas tree
Kalanchoe
Kniphofia
Ladysmock
Lamb's ears
Laserwort
Lespedeza
Liquorice
Lithodora
Liver-wort
Lousewort
Mare's-tail
Marijuana
Marshwort
Meadow-rue

Mistletoe
Mitrewort
Monandria
Moneywort
Monkshood
Monogynia
Monotropa
Moon daisy
Moschatel
Moss plant
Mousetail
Muscadine
Myristica
Naked lady
Narcissus
Navelwort
Nemophila
Nicotiana
Oenothera
Ouviranda
Parrot jaw
Patchouli
Pearlwort
Pellitory
Pennywort
Penstemon
Peperomia
Pimpernel
Pineapple
Pokeberry
Polygonum
Portulaca
Pyrethrum
Quillwort
Rafflesia
Rattlebox
Riverweed
Rocambole
Rosinweed
Rudbeckia
Sabadilla
Safflower
Sagebrush
Santoline
Santonica
Saponaria
Saxifrage
Screwpine
Sea-rocket
Shoreweed
Sinningia
Snakeroot
Snakeweed
Spearmint

Spearwort
Speedwell
Spikenard
Spikerush
Sprekalia
Stargrass
Stickweed
Stinkweed
Stone-crop
Strapwort
Sunflower
Sweet flag
Sweet-gale
Taraxacum
Telegraph
Thorow-wax
Tiger lily
Titan arum
Tomatillo
Toothwort
Tormentil
Twinberry
Vaccinium
Verbascum
Vetchling
Wake-robin
Waterleaf
Water vine
Wincopipe
Witchweed
Withywind
Wolf's bane
Wood avens
Woundwort
Xanthoxyl

10 letters:
Adder's wort
Agapanthus
Alexanders
Ampelopsis
Anacardium
Angiosperm
Artocarpus
Asarabacca
Aspidistra
Astralagus
Barrenwort
Beggarweed
Biddy-biddy
Bitter-king
Bitterweed
Bladder-nut
Bluebottle

Brugmansia
Busy Lizzie
Butterdock
Butterwort
Buttonbush
Calico-bush
Canada-lily
Candelilla
Catananche
Cat-cracker
China aster
Chionodoxa
Cinquefoil
Cloudberry
Commiphora
Coneflower
Coralberry
Corncockle
Cornflower
Cottonweed
Cow parsley
Cow parsnip
Crakeberry
Cranesbill
Crown vetch
Cuckoopint
Cupid's dart
Day-neutral
Deadnettle
Delphinium
Dog's-fennel
Dog's-tongue
Dragonhead
Dragonroot
Dyer's-broom
Earth-smoke
Easter lily
Elecampane
Escallonia
Eupatorium
Fatshedera
Five-finger
Flamboyant
Fleur-de-lis
Foamflower
Four o'clock
Frangipani
Fraxinella
Friar's cowl
Fritillary
Frog's mouth
Gaillardia
Gaultheria
Glycophate

Gnaphalium
Goat-sallow
Goatsbeard
Goat's-thorn
Goat-willow
Goldenseal
Goldilocks
Goldthread
Goose grass
Gypsophila
Hawksbeard
Heart's-ease
Heathberry
Helianthus
Heliotrope
Herb-bennet
Herb-Robert
Hobble-bush
Hop-trefoil
Hyoscyamus
Icosandria
Illecebrum
Immortelle
Indian pink
Indian pipe
Indian poke
Indian shot
Jew's mallow
Jew's-myrtle
Jimsonweed
Joe-pye weed
Joshua-tree
Lemon grass
Loganberry
Maidenhair
Marchantia
Marguerite
Masterwort
Meconopsis
Mexican-tea
Mignonette
Montbretia
Moonflower
Motherwort
Nasturtium
Nightshade
Nipplewort
Ouvirandra
Ox-eye daisy
Painted cup
Parkleaves
Parrot-beak
Parrot-bill
Passiflora

Pennycress
Pennyroyal
Pentagynia
Pentandria
Pentstemon
Peppermint
Pepperwort
Periwinkle
Pimpinella
Pipsissewa
Plume poppy
Poinsettia
Polemonium
Polianthes
Polyanthus
Potentilla
Puschkinia
Ragged lady
Ranunculus
Rest-harrow
Rhoicissus
Rock violet
Rose laurel
Rose mallow
Salicornia
Sarracenia
Sauce-alone
Scindapsus
Scorzonera
Setterwort
Silverweed
Sinsemilla
Snake's-head
Snapdragon
Sneezewort
Spiderwort
Stavesacre
Stitchwort
Stonebreak
Storksbill
Strelitzia
Sweetbriar
Thalictrum
Thunbergia
Tibouchina
Tillandsia
Touch-me-not
Tragacanth
Tree mallow
Tropaeolum
Tropaesium
Tumbleweed
Turtlehead
Twinflower

Venus's comb
Wallflower
Watercress
Water lemon
Windflower
Woodsorrel
Yellowroot
Yellowweed
Yellowwort

11 letters:
Aaron's beard
Acidanthera
Adam's needle
Antirrhinum
Baby's breath
Bastard balm
Bear's-breech
Beggar's lice
Biscuit-root
Bishop's weed
Bittercress
Bittersweet
Bitter vetch
Bladderwort
Blazing star
Blood-flower
Bog asphodel
Bottlebrush
Brankursine
Bristle-fern
Bur-marigold
Burning bush
Calceolaria
Callitriche
Cheddar pink
Cheese plant
Convolvulus
Corn spurrey
Cotoneaster
Crape-myrtle
Crepe-myrtle
Dragon's head
Dusty-miller
Dyer's rocket
Erythronium
Fingergrass
Flamboyante
Forget-me-not
Fothergilla
Gentianella
Gillyflower
Globeflower
Gobe-mouches

Greendragon
Hart's tongue
Helichrysum
Herb of grace
Herb-trinity
Hippeastrum
Honeysuckle
Horseradish
Hurtleberry
Incarvillea
Kangaroo paw
Kiss-me-quick
Labrador tea
Lady's finger
Lady's mantle
Lamb's tongue
Lattice-leaf
Lithotripsy
London pride
Loosestrife
Love-in-a-mist
Madonna lily
Marsh mallow
Meadowsweet
Menispermum
Monadelphia
Mountain tea
Nancy-pretty
Oysterplant
Pachysandra
Paritaniwha
Parma violet
Parrot's bill
Pelargonium
Potamogeton
Proletarian
Ragged robin
Rupturewort
Saintpaulia
Sansevieria
Schizanthus
Scurvy grass
Sea lavender
Sea milkwort
Selaginella
Shrimp plant
Slipperwort
Spanish moss
Sparaganium
Steeplebush
Stephanotis
St John's wort
Strawflower
Sulphurwort

Sweet cicely
Sweet sultan
Swiss cheese
Thimbleweed
Thoroughwax
Tiger flower
Tous-les-mois
Trumpetweed
Vallisneria
Water purple
Water violet
Welwitschia
White bryony
Wild mustard
Wintercress
Wintergreen
Xeranthemum

12 letters:

Adam's flannel
Adder's tongue
Alstroemeria
American aloe
Aristolochia
Autumn crocus
Bacon and eggs
Beggar's ticks
Brandy bottle
Cactus dahlia
Calico flower
Cape hyacinth
Cape primrose
Carolina pink
Checkerbloom
Cheese-rennet
Christophene
Christ's thorn
Cobblers' pegs
Corn marigold
Cuckoo flower
Cucumber tree
Darlingtonia
Devil-in-a-bush
Dragoon's head
Elephant's ear
Epacridaceae
Eschscholzia
Fennelflower
Flower delice
Flower deluce
Globe-thistle
Grapple-plant
Helianthemum
Hemp-agrimony

Hound's tongue
Iceland poppy
Indian turnip
Jacob's ladder
Lady's fingers
Lady's slipper
Lady's thistle
Lady's tresses
Lemon verbena
Leopard's bane
Lithospermum
Mariposa lily
Marvel of Peru
Midsummermen
Monkey flower
Morning glory
Mountain flax
None-so-pretty
Old man's beard
Ornithogalum
Parsley-piert
Pasqueflower
Philadelphus
Philodendron
Phytobenthos
Pickerelweed
Pitcher plant
Plantain lily
Pleurisy root
Prickly poppy
Pteridosperm
Pterydophyte
Rhododendron
Rose geranium
Rose of Sharon
Salpiglossis
Sarsaparilla
Scouring rush
Scrophularia
Sea buckthorn
Sempervivium
Service berry
Shepherd's rod
Shirley poppy
Snow-in-summer
Solomon's seal
Southernwood
Spring beauty
Stone bramble
Stone parsley
Strophanthus
Sweet alyssum
Sweet William
Tradescantia

Venus flytrap
Virgin's bower
Wandering Jew
Water-soldier
Weatherglass
Wild hyacinth
Wild williams
Zantedeschia

13 letters:

African violet
Alligator pear
Asparagus fern
Barbados pride
Black bindweed
Bladder cherry
Bleeding heart
Bougainvillea
Butcher's broom
Butterfly bush
Carrion-flower
Christmas rose
Cranberry bush
Creeping jenny
Creosote plant
Crown imperial
Dieffenbachia
Dutchman's pipe
Elephant's ears
Elephant's foot
Eschscholtzia
Flannel flower
Grape hyacinth
Greek valerian
Indian tobacco
Mariposa tulip
Marsh marigold
Marsh samphire
Meadow saffron
Mountain avens
Noli-me-tangere
Paschal flower
Passionflower
Rose of Jericho
Shepherd's club
Slipper orchid
Spathyphyllum
Summer cypress
Sweet woodruff
Swine's succory
Tortoise plant
Townhall clock
Traveller's joy
Venus's flytrap

Viper's bugloss
Virginia stock
Water chestnut
Water dropwort
Water hyacinth
Water plantain
Winter aconite

14 letters:
Alder-buckthorn
Barberton daisy
Belladonna lily
Bird of paradise
Black-eyed Susan
Bladder campion
Bougainvillaea
Canterbury bell
Cape gooseberry
Cardinal flower
Castor-oil plane
Chincherinchee
Chinese cabbage
Chinese lantern
Gold-of-pleasure
Hen and chickens

Lords and ladies
Love-in-idleness
Partridgeberry
Prince's feather
Queen Anne's lace
Shepherd's glass
Shepherd's purse
Spanish bayonet
Star-of-the-earth
Sweet horsemint
Treacle mustard
Vegetable sheep
Witches' thimble

15 letters:
Bird's nest orchid
Burnet saxifrage
Christmas cactus
Creeping thistle
Dog's tooth violet
Evening primrose
Golden saxifrage
Jack-in-the-pulpit
Lily-of-the-valley
Meadow saxifrage

Michaelmas daisy
Shepherd's myrtle
Star of Bethlehem
Virginia creeper
Wandering sailor

16 letters:
Annunciation lily
Barren strawberry
Bird's foot trefoil
Carolina allspice
Clove gillyflower
Clowgillie-flower
Deadly nightshade
Herb of repentance
Indian paintbrush
Livingstone daisy
Love-lies-bleeding
Mesembrianthemum
Poached-egg flower
Queen-of-the-
  meadow
Swiss cheese plant

17 letters:
Devil's bit scabious
Dutchman's breeches
Mother-of-thousands
Queen of the prairie
Sheep's bit scabious
Snow-on-the-
  mountain
Squarrose knapweed
St Patrick's cabbage

18 letters:
Mother-in-law's
  tongue
Venus's looking glass

19 letters:
Ploughman's
  spikenard

20 letters:
Chickweed
  wintergreen
Enchanter's
  nightshade

Plantagenet Angevin, Broom

Plantain Mato(o)ke, Ribwort, Waybread

Plantation Arboretum, Bosket, Bosquet, Estate, Grove, Hacienda, Pen, Pinetum, Ranch, Tara, Tope, Veticetum, Vineyard

Plant disease Anthracnose, Blight, Bunt, Club-root, Curlytop, Ear-cockle, Eyespot, Frogeye, Leaf curl, Leaf-roll, Leaf-spot, Psyllid yellows, Rosette, Shanking, Smut, Sooty mould, Streak

Planted In, Under

Planter Dibber, Farmer, Settler, Trowel

Plaque Calculus, Dental, Plateau, Scale

Plasm Germ

Plasma Dextran, Sigmond

Plaster(ed), Plaster board Artex®, Bandage, Blister, Blotto, Butterfly clip, Cake, Cataplasm, Clam, Clatch, Compo, Court, Daub, Diachylon, Diachylum, Dressing, Drunk, Emplastrum, Fresco, Gesso, Grout, Gyprock®, Gypsum, Intonaco, Laying, Leep, Lit, Mud, Mustard, Oiled, Parge(t), Polyfilla®, Porous, Poultice, Render, Roughcast, Scratch-coat, Screed, Secco, Shellac, Sinapism, Smalm, Smarm, Smear, Sowsed, Staff, Sticking, Stookie, Stucco, Teer, Wattle and daub

Plastic Bakelite®, Bubblewrap, Cel(luloid), Cling film, Ductile, Fablon®, Fibreglass, Fictile, Fluon, Formica®, Ionomer, Laminate, Loid, Lucite®, Melamine, Mylar®, Perspex®, Plexiglass®, Pliant, Polyethylene, Polystyrene, Polythene, Polyvinyl, PVC, Reinforced, Styrene, Styrofoam®, Teflon®, Urea-formaldehyde, Vinyl, Wet-look, Xylonite, Yielding

▷ **Plastic** *may indicate* an anagram

Plasticine Morph

Plastic surgeon McIndoe

Plastic surgery Neoplasty, Nose job, Otoplasty, Rhinoplasty

Plate(s), Plated, Platelet, Plating Acierage, Ailette, Anchor, Angle, Anode,

Armadillo, Armour, Ashet, Baffle, Bakestone, Baleen, Base, Batten, Brass, Butt, Chamfrain, Chape, Charger, Chrome, Coat, Coccolith, Communion, Copper, Cramper, Cribellum, Ctene, Dasypus, Deadman, Denture, Diaphragm, Dinner, Disc, Dish, Echo, Electro, Electrotype, Elytron, Elytrum, Enamel, Entoplastron, Equatorial, Escutcheon, Face, Fashion, Feet, Fine, Fish, Flatware, Foil, Frog, Frons, Futtock, Glacis, Gold, Graal, Gravure, Ground, Gula, Half, Hasp, Home, Horseshoe, Hot, Hypoplastron, Illustration, Kick, L, Lame, Lamella, Lamina, Lanx, Latten, Lead, Licence, Madreporic, Mascle, Mazarine, Nail, Nef, Neural, Nickel, Notum, Number, Ortho, Osteoderm, P, Paten, Patin(e), Patina, Pauldron, Peba, Petri, Phototype, Planometer, Plaque, Plastron, Platter, Pleximeter, Poitrel, Prescutum, Print, Pygal, Quarter, Race, Registration, Riza, Roof, Rove, Salamander, Scale, Screw, Scrim, Scutcheon, Scute, Scutum, Seg, Selling, Sheffield, Shield, Shoe, Side, Sieve, Silver, Slab, Soup, Spacer, Spoiler, Squama, Stall, Steel, Stencil, Stereo(type), Sternite, Strake, Surface, Swash, T, Tablet, Tace, Tasse(l), Tea, Tectonic, Tergite, Terne, Thali, Theoretical, Tin(ware), Torsel, Touch, Trade, Tramp, Trencher, Trivet, Trophy, Tsuba, Tuill(ett)e, Tymp, Urostegite, Vane, Vanity, Vassail, Vessail, Vessel, Wall, Water, Web, Wet, Whirtle, Whole, Wobble, Workload, Wortle, Wrap(a)round, Zincograph

Plateau Altiplano, Anatolian, Barkly Tableland, Central Karoo, Chota Nagpur, Darling Downs, Dartmoor, Deccan, Durango, Eifel, Ellesworth Land, Field, Fjeld, Fouta Djallon, Had(h)ramaut, Highland, Highveld, Horst, Kalahari, Kar(r)oo, Kimberleys, Kurdestan, Kurdistan, La Mancha, Lamington, Langres, Laurentian, Mat(t)o Grosso, Mesa Verde, Meseta, Najd, Nilgiris, Ozark, Paramo, Piedmont, Puna, Shan, Shillong, Shire Highlands, Tableland, The Kimberleys, Ust Urt, Ustyurt

Platform Accommodation, Almemar, Balcony, Bandstand, Barbette, Base, Bay, Bema, Bench, Bier, Bridge, Catafalque, Catwalk, Crane, Crow's nest, Dais, Deck, Dolly, Drilling, Emplacement, Entablement, Estrade, Exedra, Exhedra, Fighting top, Flake, Footpace, Footplate, Foretop, Gangplank, Gantry, Gauntree, Gauntry, Gravity, Hustings, Kang, Landing stage, Launch-pad, Machan, Manifesto, Monkeyboard, Oil, Oil-rig, Pad, Paint-bridge, Pallet, Perron, Plank, Podium, Predella, Production, Programme, Pulpit, Quay, Raft, Rig, Rostrum, Round-top, Scaffold, Shoe, Skidway, Skylab, Soapbox, Space, Sponson, → **STAGE**, Stand, Stereobate, Stoep, Strandflat, Stylobate, Tee, Terminal, Thrall, Ticket, Top, Traverser, Tribunal, Tribune, Turntable, Wave-cut, Wharf

Platinum Pt, Ruthenium, Sperrylite, Spongy

Platitude Bromide, Cliché, Commonplace, Phrase, Truism

Platocephalus Flat-headed

Platonic, Platonist Academician, Ideal, Spiritual

Platoon Company, Squad, Team

Platter Dish, EP, Graal, Grail, Lanx, LP, Plate, Record, Salver, Trencher

Platypus Duckbill, Duck-mole, Water mole

Plausible, Plausibility Cogent, Credible, Fair, Glib, Likely, Logical, Oil, Probable, Proball, Sleek, Smooth, Specious

Play(s), Playing Accompany, Active, Amusement, Antic, Antigone, Assist, Brand, Busk, Candida, Caper, Charm, Chronicle, Clearance, Closet, Coriolanus, Crucible, Curtain-raiser, Daff, Dandle, Docudrama, Doodle, Drama, Echo, Endgame, Epitasis, Equus, Escapade, Everyman, Extended, Fair, Finesse, Foul, Freedom, Frisk, Frolic, Fun, Gamble, Gambol, Game, Ghosts, Grand Guignol, Hamlet, Harlequinade, Harp, History, Holiday, Inside, Interlude, Jam, Jape, Jest, Jeu, Kinderspiel, Kitchen-sink, Laik, Lake, Lark, Latitude, Lear, Leeway, Licence, Lilt, Long, Loot, Macbeth, Mask, Masque, Match, May, Medal, Melodrama, Miracle, Monodrama, Morality, Mousetrap, Mummers, Mysteries, Nativity, Noh, Nurse, Oberammergau, On, One-acter, Orestaia, Othello, Parallel, Passion, Pastorale, Perform, Personate, Peter, Portray, Power, Prank, Pretend, Puppet, Recreation, Represent, Riff, Role, Rollick, Romp, Room, Rope, RUR, Satyr, Saw, Screen, Shadow, Shoot, Show, Shuffle, Sketch, Sport, Squeeze, Stage, Straight, Strain, Strike up, Stroke, Strum, Summerstock, Thrum, Tolerance, Tonguing, Touchback,

Toy, Tragedy, Tragicomedy, Trifle, Triple, Tweedle, Twiddle, Two-hander, Vamp, Vent, Whitechapel, Word

▷ **Play** *may indicate* an anagram

Playback Echo, Repeat, Replay

Playboy Casanova, Don Juan, Hedonist, Rake, Roué

Player(s) Actor, Athlete, Back, Backstop, Black, Brass, Bugler, Busker, Cast, CD, Centre, Centre forward, Centre-half, Colt, Contestant, Cornerback, Cover point, Dealer, Defenceman, Disc, DVD, E, East, ENSA, Equity, Fetcher, Fiddle, Flanker, Fly-half, Flying wing, Fly-slip, Franchise, Fullback, Gary, Ghetto-blaster, Goalie, Gramophone, Grand master, Gridder, Half, Half-back, Half-forward, Harlequin, Hooker, Infielder, iPod®, It, Juke-box, Keg(e)ler, Kest, Kicker, Linebacker, Lineman, Lion, Lock, Long-leg, Longstop, Loose-head, Lutanist, Lutenist, Man, Marquee, Midfield, Mid-on, Mime, Muffin, Musician(er), N, Nero, Nickelback, Nightwatchman, North, Nose guard, Nose tackle, Ombre, Onside, Orpheus, Outfielder, Out(side)-half, Pagliacci, Participant, Pianola®, Pitcher, Pocket, Pone, Pro, Prop, Quarterback, Receiver, Record, Red shirt, Reliever, Reserve, Rover, S, Safetyman, Scrape, Scratch, Scrum half, Seagull, Secondo, Seed, Shamateur, Short-leg, Shortstop, Side, South, Split end, Stand-off, Stand-off half, Stereo, Striker, Strings, Strolling, Substitute, Super, Sweeper, Tabrere, Target man, Team, Thesp(ian), Tight end, Troubador, Troupe, Upright, Utility, Virtuosi, W, Walker-on, Walkman®, West, White, Wide receiver, Wing(back), Winger, Wingman

Playfair Code

Playfellow Actor, Chum, Companion

Playful Arch, Coy, Frisky, Humorous, Impish, Jocose, Kittenish, Ludic, Merry, Piacevole, Scherzo, Skittish, Sportive, Wanton

Playgirl Actress, Electra

Playgoer Groundling

Playground Adventure, Close, Garden, Park, Rec(reational), Rectangle, Theatre, Tot lot, Yard

Playhouse Amphitheatre, Cinema, Theatre, Wendy

Playsuit Rompers

Playwright → **DRAMATIST**, Dramaturge, Dramaturgist, Scriptwriter

---

PLAYWRIGHTS

3 letters:	Genet	Miller	Garrick
Fry	Gorky	Morton	Goldoni
Hay	Ibsen	O'Casey	Harwood
Kyd	Leigh	O'Neill	Hellman
	Odets	Pinero	Ionesco
4 letters:	Orton	Pinter	Kaufman
Bolt	Simon	Racine	Marlowe
Bond	Synge	Sherry	Marston
Gems	Wilde	Storey	Mauriac
Hare		Toller	Molière
Inge	*6 letters:*	Wesker	Osborne
Shaw	Barrie		Plautus
Tate	Bellow	*7 letters:*	Rostand
	Besier	Anouilh	Simpson
5 letters:	Brecht	Beckett	Terence
Albee	Coward	Bennett	Thespis
Arden	Dekker	Chekhov	Travers
Barry	Dryden	Delaney	Webster
Behan	Jonson	Doggett	
Frayn	Lerner	Feydeau	

8 letters:	Sheridan	Euripides	Williamson
Beaumont	Stoppard	Massinger	
Congreve	Vanbrugh	Priestley	**11 letters:**
Etherege	Wedekind	Sophocles	Maeterlinck
Fletcher	Williams	Wycherley	
MacNeice			**12 letters:**
Marivaux	**9 letters:**	**10 letters:**	Beaumarchais
Menander	Aeschylus	Drinkwater	
Mortimer	Ayckbourn	Pirandello	
Rattigan	Corneille	Strindberg	

Plea(s) Alford, Appeal, Claim, Common, Defence, Entreaty, Essoin, Excuse, Exoration, Nolo contendere, Orison, Placit(um), Prayer, Rebuttal, Rebutter, Rogation, Suit

Plead(er), Pleading Answer, Argue, Beg, Entreat, → **IMPLORE**, Intercede, Litigate, Moot, Placitory, Special, Supplicant, Urge, Vakeel, Vakil

Please(d), Pleasant, Pleasing, Pleasure(-seeker), Pleasurable Affable, Aggrate, Agreeable, Alcina, Algolagnia, Amenable, Amene, Amiable, Amuse, Apolaustic, Arride, Benign, Bitte, Braw, Cheerful, Chuffed, Comely, Comfort, Content, Cordial, Cute, Delectation, Delice, Delight, Divine, Do, Euphonic, Eye candy, Fair, Felicitous, Fit, Flatter, Fun, Genial, Glad, Gladness, Gratify, Harmonious, Hedonism, Jammy, Joy, Kama, Kindly, Lekker, Lepid, List, Naomi, Oblige, Piacevole, Primrose path, Prithee, Prythee, Purr, Queme, Regale, Sapid, Satisfy, Sightly, Suit, Tasty, Thrill, Tickle, Tickle pink, Treat, Vanity, Voluptuary, Wally, Will, Winsome, Wrapped, Xanadu List

Pleasure-garden, Pleasure-ground Lung, Oasis, Park, Policy, Ranelagh, Tivoli

Pleat Accordion, Box, Crimp, Crystal, Fold, French, Frill, Goffer, Gusset, Inverted, Kick, Kilt, Knife, Plait, Pranck(e), Prank, Ruff(le), Sunburst, Sunray

Pleb(eian) Common, Essex Man, Homely, Laic, Ordinary, Popular, Roturier

Pledge Affidavit, Arlene, Arles, Band, Betroth, Bond, Borrow, Bottomry, Collateral, Commitment, Dedicate, Deposit, Earnest(-penny), Engage, Fine, Frithborn, Gage, Gilbert, Giselle, Guarantee, Hand, Hock, Hypothecate, Impignorate, Mortgage, Oath, Pass, Pawn, Pignerate, Pignorate, Plight, Pop, Promise, Propine, Sacrament, Security, Sponsorship, Stake, Surety, Teetotal, Toast, Troth, Undertake, Vow, Wad, Wage(r), Wed

Pleiades Alcyone, Celaeno, Electra, Maia, Merope, Sterope, Taygete

Plenitude Stouth and routh

Plentiful, Plenty Abounding, Abundance, Abundant, Ample, Bags, Copious, Copy, Easy, Excess, Foison, Fouth, Ful(l)ness, Fushion, Galore, Goshen, Lashings, Loads, Lots, Oodles, Pleroma, Profusion, Quantity, Riches, Rife, Routh, Rowth, Scouth, Scowth, Slue, Sonce, Sonse, Teeming, Umpteen

Plenum Spaceless

Pliable, Pliant Amenable, Flexible, Limber, Limp, Lithe, Malleable, Plastic, Sequacious, Supple, Swack, Swank, Wanle

▶ **Pliers** *see* **PLY**

Plight Betrothal, Case, Misdight, Peril, Pickle, Pledge, State, Troth

Plimsoll(s) Dap, Gutty, Gym-shoe, Line, Mutton-dummies, Sandshoe, Tacky

Plinth Acroter, Base, Block, Socle, Stand, Zocco, Zoccolo

Plod(der) Drudge, Ploughman, Traipse, Tramp, Trog, Trudge

Plonk Rotgut, Wine

Plop Cloop, Drop, Fall, Plap, Plump

Plot(s) Allotment, Area, Babington, Bed, Brew, Carpet, Chart, Cliché, Collude, Connive, Conspiracy, Conspire, Covin, Covyne, Device, Engineer, Erf, Erven, Frame-up, Graden, Graph, Gunpowder, Imbroglio, Intrigue, Locus, Lot, Machination, Map, Meal-tub, Odograph, Pack, Parcel, Patch, Plan, Plat, Popish, Rye-house, Scenario, → **SCHEME**, Sect(ion), Seedbed, Shot, Site, Story, Storyline, Taluk, Terf, Turf, Web

Plotter Artist, Box (and whisker), Brutus, Cabal, Camarilla, Casca, Catesby, Conspirator,

Device, Digital, Engineer, Incremental, Intrigant, Microfilm, Oates, Rosary, Schemer

Plough(man), Ploughed, Ploughing Arable, Ard, Arval, Big Dipper, Breaker, Bull tongue, Chamfer, Charles's Wain, Contour, Dipper, Disc, Drail, Drill, Ear, Earth-board, Ere, Fail, Fallow, Farmer, Feer, Flunk, Gadsman, Gang, Great bear, Harrow, Lister, Middlebreaker, Middlebuster, Mouldboard, Piers, Pip, Pleuch, Pleugh, Plodder, Push, Rafter, Rib, Ridger, Rive, Rotary, Rove, Sand, Scooter, Septentrion(e)s, Sill, Sodbuster, Sow, Stump-jump, Swing, The Wagon, Till(er), Tractor, Trench, Triones, Wheel

Plough-cleaner Pattle, Pettle

Ploughshare Co(u)lter, Sock

Ploughwise Boustrophedon

Plover Bud, Dott(e)rel, Lapwing, Pratincole, Prostitute, Stand, Tewit, Wing

Plowman Piers

Ploy Brinkmanship, Dodge, Finesse, Gambit, Manoeuvre, M(a)cGuffin, Stratagem, Strike, Tactic, Wile

Pluck(ing), Plucky Avulse, Bare, Carphology, Cock, Courage, Deplume, Epilate, Evulse, Floccillation, Gallus, Game, → **GRIT**, Guts, Loot, Mettle, Pick, Pinch, Pip, Pizzicato, Plectron, Plectrum, Ploat, Plot, Plumassier, Plunk, Pook(it), Pouk(it), Pull, Race, Scrappy, Snatch, Spin, Spirit, Spunk, Summon, Tug, Twang, Tweak, Tweeze, Vellicate, Yank

Plug Access eye, Ad, Advocate, Banana, Block, Bung, Caulk, Chaw, Chew, Commercial, Dam, DIN, Dook, Dossil, Dottle, Douk, Fipple, Fother, Gang, Glow, Go-devil, Heater, Hype, Jack, Lam, Operculum, Pessary, Phono, Prod, Promote, Publicity, Ram, Rawlplug®, Recommendation, Safety, Salt, Scart, Spark(ing), Spigot, Spile, Spiling, Stop(per), Stopple, Strobili, Suppository, Tampion, Tap, Tent, Tompion, Vent, Volcanic, Wage, Wall, Wander, Wedge

Plum Beach, Bullace, Cherry, Choice, Damask, Damson, Gage, Greengage, Ground, Jamaica, Japanese, Java, Kaki, Mammee-sapota, Marmalade, Maroon, Mirabelle, Musk, Mussel, Myrobalan, Naseberry, Neesberry, Peach, Persimmon, Proin(e), Pruin(e), Prune(llo), Quetsch, Raisin, Sapodilla, Sebesten, Victoria, Wodehouse

Plumage, Plume Aigrette, Crest, Eclipse, Egret, Feather, Hackle, Mantle, Panache, Preen, Ptilosis, Quill

Plumb(er), Plumbing Bullet, Dredge, Fathom(eter), Lead(sman), Perpendicular, Plummet, Sheer, Sound, Test, True, U-trap, Vertical

Plumbago Graphite, Leadwort, Wad(d), Wadt

Plummet Dive, Drop, Lead, → **PLUNGE**

Plump(er) Bold, Bonnie, Bonny, Buxom, Choose, Chopping, Chubbed, Chubby, Cubby, Cuddly, Dumpy, Embonpoint, Endomorph, Fat, Fleshy, Flop, Fubsy, Full, Lie, Matronly, Opt, Plank, Plonk, Plop, Podgy, Portly, Pudgy, Roll-about, Rolypoly, Rotund, Round(about), Rubenesque, Sonsie, Sonsy, Soss, Souse, Squab, Squat, Stout, Swap, Swop, Tidy, Well-covered, Well-fed, Well-padded, Well-upholstered, Zaftig, Zoftig

Plunder(er) Berob, Booty, Brigand, Depredate, Despoil, Devastate, Escheat, Fleece, Forage, Freebooter, Gut, Harry, Haul, Herriment, Herryment, Hership, Loot, Maraud, Peel, Pill(age), Predation, Prey, Privateer, → **RANSACK**, Rape, Rapparee, Raven, Ravin, Ravine, Reave, Reif, Reive, Rieve, Rifle, Rob, Rummage, Sack, Scoff, Shave, Skoff, Spoil(s), Spoliate, Sprechery, Spuilzie, Spuly(i)e, Spulzie, Swag

Plunge(r) Dasher, Demerge, Dive, Douse, Dowse, Duck, Enew, Immerge, Immerse, La(u)nch, Nose-dive, Plummet, Plump, Raker, Send, Sink, Souse, Swoop, Thrust

Plural Multiply, Pl

Plus Addition, And, Gain, More, Positive

Plush(ed) Die, Luxurious, Rich, Smart, Tint, Velour, Velvet

Pluto(crat), Plutonic Abyssal, Dis, Dog, Hades, Hypogene, Magnate, Nob, Pipeline, Underground

Plutonium Pu

Ply, Plier(s) Bend, Birl, Cab, Exercise, Exert, Gondoliers, Importune, Layer, Practise, Run, Trade, Wield

▷ **Plying** *may indicate* an anagram
Plymouth Brethren Darbyite
PM Addington, Afternoon, Arvo, Asquith, Attlee, Autopsy, Bute, Cabinet-maker,
  Callaghan, Chamberlain, Chatham, De Valera, Disraeli, Gladstone, Major, Melbourne,
  Peel, Pitt, Portland, Premier, → **PRIME MINISTER**, Salisbury, Taoiseach
Pneumonia Lobar, Lobular, Visna
Poach Burn-the-water, Cook, Encroach, Filch, Lag, Steal, Trespass
Pochard Duck, Scaup
Pocket Air, Appropriate, Bag, Bin, Breast, Cargo, Cavity, Cly, Cup, Enclave, Fob, Glom,
  Hideaway, Hip, Jenny, Misappropriate, Patch, Placket, Plaid-neuk, Pot, Pouch, Purloin,
  Purse, Sac, Sky, Slash, Sling, Slit, Steal, Take, Trouser, Vest, Watch, Whitechapel
Pocketbook Reader
Pod(s) Babul, Bean, Belly, Carob, Chilli, Dividivi, Engine, Gumbo, Lablab, Lomentum,
  Neb-neb, Okra, Pipi, Pregnant, Pudding-pipe, Seed, Siliqua, Tamarind, Vanilla, Vine
Podgy Roly-poly
Poem(s), Poetry Acmeism, Acrostic, Aeneid, Alcaic, Anthology, A Shropshire Lad,
  Awdl, Ballad(e), Beowulf, Bestiary, Bucolic, Byliny, Caccia, Canzone, Cargoes, Cento,
  Choliamb, Choriamb, Cicada, Cinquain, Complaint, Concrete, Decastich, Dit(t),
  Dithyramb, Divan, Dizain, Doggerel, Duan, Dub, Dunciad, Eclogue, Elegy, Elene,
  Endymion, Epic(ede), Epigram, Epilogue, Epithalamium, Epode, Epopee, Epopoeia, Epos,
  Epyllion, Erotic, Fifteener, Finlandia, Gauchesco, Georgic, Ghazal, Graveyard, Haikai,
  Haiku, Heptastich, Heroic, Hexastich, Hokku, Hull, Hypermeter, Idyll, If, Iliad, Imagism,
  Inferno, Jazz, Kyrielle, Lay, Limerick, Logaoedic, London, Madrigal, Mahabharata(m),
  Mahabharatum, Meliboean, Melic, Metaphysical, Metre, Mock-heroic, Monostich,
  Monostrophe, Nostos, Ode, Odyssey, Palinode, Paracrostic, Parnassus, Pastoral,
  Penill(ion), Pentameter, Pentastich, Performance, Poesy, Prelude, Prose, Prothalamion,
  Punk, Purana, Qasida, Quatorzain, Quatrain, Quire, Ramayana, Rat-rhyme, Renga,
  Rhapsody, Rig-Veda, Rime, Rime riche, Rondeau, Rondel(et), Rubai(yat), Rune, Scazon
  (iambus), Senryu, Sestina, Sijo, Sirvente, Sixain, Song, Sonnet, Sound, Spondee, Stanza,
  Stornello, Symphonic, Tanka, Telestich, Temora, Tercet, Tetrastich, Thebaid, Title, Tone,
  Triolet, Tristich, Vers(e), Versicle, Villanelle, Völuspá, Voluspe, Waka
Poet(s), Poetic Amorist, Bard(ling), Beatnik, Cavalier, Cumberland, Cyclic, Elegist,
  Georgian, Iambist, Idyllist, Imagist, Lake, Laureate, Layman, Liner, Lyrist, Makar, Maker,
  Meistersinger, Metaphysical, Metrist, Minnesinger, Minor, Minstrel, Mistral, Monodist,
  Odist, Parnassian, Performance, PL, Pleiad(e), Poetaster, Rhymer, Rhymester, Rhymist,
  Rymer, Scald, Scop, Skald, Smart, Sonneteer, Sound, Spasmodic, Spasmodic School,
  Thespis, Tragic, Trench, Troubadour, Trouvère, Trouveur, Verse-monger, Verse-smith,
  Versifier, Vers librist(e), Water

POETS

2 *letters:*	Dyer	Pope	Blair
AE	Gray	Rowe	Blake
	Gunn	Rumi	Burns
3 *letters:*	Hogg	Tate	Byron
Gay	Hood	Vega	Cadou
Poe	Hope		Carew
	Hugo	5 *letters:*	Cinna
4 *letters:*	Hunt	Alley	Clare
Abse	Lang	Arion	Crane
Baif	Lear	Auden	Dante
Bemi	Omar	Ayres	Donne
Blok	Ovid	Basho	Eliot
Cory	Owen	Bemia	Flint

Frost
Gower
Griot
Heine
Hesse
Homer
Horne
Hulme
Iqbal
Jarry
Keats
Keyes
Lewis
Logue
Lorca
Lucan
Marot
Meyer
Moore
Nashe
Noyes
Plath
Pound
Prior
Rilke
Rishi
Sachs
Smith
Tasso
Theon
Tzara
Vazor
Wyatt
Yeats
Young

6 letters:
Adamov
Alonso
Arnold
Austin
Barham
Barnes
Belloc
Binyon
Borges
Brecht
Brooke
Butler
Cibber
Clarke
Clough
Cowley
Cowper

Crabbe
Curnow
Daniel
Daurat
Davies
Domett
Dowson
Dryden
Dunbar
Ennius
Fuller
George
Glycon
Goethe
Graves
Harpur
Heaney
Hemans
Hesiod
Horace
Hughes
Jensen
Jonson
Landor
Larkin
Lawman
Lowell
Marini
Milton
Morris
Motion
Neruda
Newman
Ossian
Pindar
Porter
Racine
Sappho
Seaman
Shanks
Sidney
Tagore
Thomas
Valery
Vergil
Villon
Virgil
Waller
Warton

7 letters:
Addison
Alcaeus
Alfieri

Aneirin
Aretino
Ariosto
Beddoes
Belleau
Bridges
Bunting
Caedmon
Campion
Chapman
Chaucer
Collins
Corinna
Cynwulf
Doughty
Douglas
Drayton
Emerson
Enright
Flaccus
Flecker
Herbert
Heredia
Herrick
Hopkins
Housman
Juvenal
Layamon
Martial
Marvell
Meynell
Montale
Newbolt
Orpheus
Patmore
Pushkin
Rimbaud
Ronsard
Russell
Sassoon
Service
Shelley
Sitwell
Skelton
Sotades
Southey
Spender
Spenser
Statius
Terence
Thomson
Vaughan
Whitman
Woolner

8 letters:
Anacreon
Banville
Beranger
Berryman
Betjeman
Brentano
Browning
Campbell
Catullus
Cummings
Cynewulf
Davenant
Day Lewis
De la Mare
De Musset
Drummond
Du Bellay
Ginsberg
Hamilton
Harrison
Hausmann
Kynewulf
Laforgue
Langland
Lawrence
Leopardi
Lovelace
Macaulay
Mallarmé
Menander
Meredith
Petrarch
Rossetti
Sandberg
Schiller
Shadwell
Stephens
Suckling
Taliesin
Tennyson
Thompson
Traherne
Tyrtaeus
Verlaine
Voltaire
Whittier

9 letters:
Aeschylus
Alexander
Bunthorne
Coleridge
Deschamps

Dickinson
Euripides
Goldsmith
Henderson
Lamartine
Lucretius
Marinetti
Masefield
Quasimodo
Shenstone
Simonides
Sophocles

Stevenson
Swinburne
Wergeland

10 letters:
Baudelaire
Chatterton
Drinkwater
Fitzgerald
Longfellow
McGonagall
Propertius

Tannhauser
Theocritus
Wordsworth

11 letters:
Apollinaire
Archilochus
Asclepiades
Bildermeier
Castiglione
Maeterlinck
Pherecrates

12 letters:
Archilochian
Aristophanes

14 letters:
Dante Alighieri

15 letters:
Ettrick Shepherd

Poetaster Della-Cruscan
Poetess Ingelow, Orinda
Poet laureate Motion, PL
▶ **Poetry** *see* POEM(S)
Po-faced Stolid
Poignant Acute, Biting, Haunting, Keen, Moving, Pungent, Stirring, Touching
Point(ed), Pointer, Points Accumulation, Ace, Acerose, Acnode, Acro-, Aculeate, Aim, Angular, Antinode, Antler, Apex, Aphelion, Apogee, Appui, Apse, Apsis, Arrowhead, Ascendant, Bar, Barb, Barrow, Base, Basis, Bisque, Boiling, Break(ing), Brownie, Burble, Burbling, Calk, Cape, Cardinal, Cash, Catch, Centre, Choke, Clou, Clovis, Clue, Colon, Comma, Compass, Compensation, Cone, Conic, Corner, Cover, Crag, Crisis, Critical, Crux, Culmination, Cultrate, Curie, Cursor, Cusp, Cuss, Cutting, Danger, Dead, Decimal, Deflater, Deflator, Degree, Descendant, Detail, Dew, Diamond, Di(a)eresis, Direct, Dot, Dry, E, Ear, End, Entry, Epanodos, Épée, Equant, Equinoctial, Eutectic, Exclamation, Extremity, Fang, Fastigiate, Feature, Fescue, Fesse, Fielder, Firing, Fitch(e), Five, Fixed, Flash, Focal, Focus, Foreland, Fourteen, Freezing, Fulcrum, Gallinas, Game, Germane, Gist, Gnomon, Gold, Hastate, Head, High, Hinge, Hint, Home-thrust, Horn, Hour hand, Icicle, Ideal, Index, Indicate, Indicator, Intercept, Ippon, Isoelectric, Jag, Jester, Jog, Juncture, Keblah, Kiblah, Kip(p), Knub, Lace, Lagrangian, Lance, Lanceolar, Lead, Limit, Lizard, Locate, Locus, Low, Mandelbrot set, Mark, Match, Melting, Metacentre, Microdot, Moot, Mucro, Mull, Muricate, N, Nail, Nasion, Near, Neb, Needle, Neel, Ness, Nib, Nocking, Node, Nodus, Nombril, Now, Nub, Obconic, Obelion, Obelisk, Objective, Opinion, Ord, Organ, Oscillation, Particle, Peak, Pedal, Penalty, Periapsis, Periastron, Perigee, Perihelion, Perilune, Pin, Pinch, Pinnacle, Pixel, Place, Pour, Power, Pressure, Promontory, Prong, Prow, Punchline, Punctilio, Punctual, Punctum, Purpose, Radix, Rallying, Ras, Reef, Respect, Rhumb, Rhumbline, S, Sample, Saturation, Scribe, Seg(h)ol, Selling, Set, Setter, Shaft, Sharpener, Sheva, Show, Shy, Silly, Socket, Sore, Spearhead, Specie, Spicate, Spick, Spike, Spinode, Spinulose, Stage, Stagnation, Starting, Stationary, Steam, Sticking, Stigme, Stiletto, Sting, Stipule, Strong, Sum, Suspension, Synapse, Tacnode, Talking, Tang, Taper, Tax, Technicality, Tine, → TIP, Tongue, Trafficator, Train, Transition, Trig, Trigger, Triple, Turning, Urde(e), Urdy, Use, Vane, Vanishing, Vantage, Verge, Verse, Vertex, Vowel, Voxel, W, Weak, Yad, Yield, Yuko, Zenith
Pointless Blunt, Curtana, Flat, Futile, Idle, Inane, Inutile, Muticous, Otiose, Stupid, Vain
Point of honour Pundonor
Poise Aplomb, Balance, Composure, P, Serenity
Poison(er), Poisoning, Poisonous Bane, Botulism, Contact, Deleterious, Envenom, Ergotise, Food, Malevolent, Miasma, Noxious, Phalloidin, Plumbism, Rot, Sausage, Systemic, Taint, Toxic, Toxicology, Toxicosis, Toxin, Toxoid, Venom(ous), Viperous, Virose, Virous, Virulent

POISONS

4 letters:
Cube
Fugu
Gila
Lead
Loco
Tutu
Upas

5 letters:
Abron
Algae
Aspic
Ricin
Sarin
Soman
Timbo
Urali
Venin

6 letters:
Aldrin
Antiar
Borgia
Cicuta
Curara
Curare
Curari
Datura
Dioxin
Durban
Emetin
Endrin
Hebona
Iodism
Obeism
Ourali
Ourari
Phenol
Pyemia
Septic
Uremia
V-agent
Wabain

7 letters:
Aconite
Amanita
Arsenic
Atropia
Atropin

Boletus
Bromism
Brucine
Cacodyl
Coniine
Cowbane
Cyanide
Emetine
Flybane
Hebenon
Hemlock
Henbane
Lindane
Mineral
Neurine
Neutron
Ouabain
Oxalate
Phallin
Pyaemia
Safrole
Solpuga
Stibine
Stibium
Surinam
Tanghin
Tropine
Venefic
Woorali
Woorara
Wourali

8 letters:
Acrolein
Adamsite
Apocynum
Atropine
Barbasco
Cannabin
Cyanuret
Daturine
Dumbcane
Embolism
Exotoxin
Flypaper
Gossypol
Lewisite
Litharge
Lobeline
Locoweed
Mephitic

Methanol
Mezereon
Miticide
Nerve gas
Nicotine
Paraquat®
Ptomaine
Pulicide
Raphania
Ratsbane
Rhodanic
Samnitis
Santonin
Solanine
Thebaine
Toxaemia
Trembles
Urushiol
Veratrin
Warfarin

9 letters:
Aflatoxin
Benzidine
Brominism
Bufotalin
Ciguatera
Coyotillo
Digitalin
Echidnine
Fluorosis
Gelsemine
Monkshood
Muscarine
Mycotoxin
Parathion
Sapraemia
Sassy wood
Saturnism
Saxitoxin
Sparteine
Stonefish
Tanghinin
Toxaphene
Veratrine
Wolfsbane
Yohimbine

10 letters:
Aqua-tofana
Belladonna

Bufotenine
Cadaverine
Colchicine
Hydrastine
Jimson weed
Limberneck
Manchineal
Mandragora
Molybdosis
Neurotoxin
Paris green
Phylotoxin
Picrotoxin
Salicylism
Salmonella
Strychnine
Tetrotoxin
Thorn-apple

11 letters:
Calabar-bean
Dog's mercury
Gelseminine
Gila monster
Hyoscyamine
Listeriosis
Phosphorism
Pilocarpine
Scopolamine
Septicaemia
Sugar of lead
Sulphur tuft
Veratridine

12 letters:
Fool's parsley
Formaldehyde
Hydrargyrism
Nitromethane
Noogoora burr
Strophanthus
Tetrodotoxin

13 letters:
Scheele's green
Silver nitrate

16 letters:
Deadly nightshade

Poke, Poky Bonnet, Broddle, Chook, Dig, Garget, Itchweed, Jab, Jook, Meddle, Mock, Nousle, Nudge, Nuzzle, Ombu, Peg, Pick, Poach, Pote, Pouch, Powter, → **PRISON**, → **PROD**, Prog, Proke, Punch, Root(le), Rout, Rowt, Sporran, Stab, Thrust

Poker (work) Bugbear, Curate, Draw, Game, Gas, High-low, Lowball, Mistigris, Penny ante, Pyrography, Red-hot, Salamander, Strip, Stud(-horse), Texas hold'em, Tickler, Tine, Toe

Poland, Polish Cracovian, PL, Polack, Pomeranian, Racovian, Sarmatia, Sejm, Slav, Stefan

Polar, Pole(s), Poler Animal, Anode, Antarctic, Arctic, Boathook, Boom, Bowsprit, Bum(p)kin, Caber, Celestial, Clothes, Copernicus, Cowl-staff, Crossbar, Electret, Extremity, Fishgig, Fizgy, Flagstaff, Flagstick, Furlong, Gaff, Galactic, Gas, Geomagnetic, Icy, Janker, Kent, Liberty, Lug, Magnetic, Mast, May, N, Nadir, Negative, Nib, North, Oar, Periscian, Po, Polack, Positive, Punt, Quant, Quarterstaff, Range, Ricker, Ripeck, Rood, Roost, Ry(e)peck, S, Shaft, South, Spar, Spindle, Sprit, Staff, Stake, Stanchion, Stang, Starosta, Stilt, Sting, Stobie, Telegraph, Terrestrial, Thyrsos, Thyrsus, Tongue, Topmast, Totem, Utility, Vegetal, Zenith

▷ **Polar** *may indicate* with a pole

Polaris Lodestar, Rhodanic, Rocket, Star

Polecat Ferret, Fitch, Fitchet, Foulmart, Foumart, Quail, Weasel

Polemic(al) Argument, Controversy, Debate, Eristic(al)

Police(man), Policewoman Babylon, Bear, Beast, Beria, Bill, Bizzy, Black and Tans, Blue, Bluebottle, Blue heeler, Bobby, Bog(e)y, Boss, Boys in blue, Bull, Busy, Carabinero, Carabiniere, Catchpole, Centenier, Cheka, Chekist, CID, Constable, Cop(per), Cotwal, Crusher, Darogha, Detective, DI, Dibble, Druzhinnik, Europol, Filth, Flatfoot, Flattie, Flic, Flying Squad, Force, Fuzz, Garda, Garda Siochana, Gendarme, Gestapo, Gill, G-man, Guard, Gumshoe, Harmanbeck, Heat, Hermandad, Inspector, Interpol, Jamadar, Jawan, Jemadar, John Hop, Keystone, KGB, Kitchen, Kotwal, Lawman, Limb, Mata-mata, Met(ropolitan), Military, Mobile, Morse, Mountie, MP, Mulligan, Nabman, Nark, Ochrana, Officer, OGPU, Ovra, Patrolman, PC, Peeler, Peon, Pig, Pointsman, Polis, Polizei, Porn squad, Posse (comitatus), Prefect, Provincial, Provost, Puppy-walker, Ranger, Redbreast, Redcap, Regulate, RIC, Riot, Robert, Rosser, Roundsman, Rozzer, RUC, Sbirro, SC, Secret, Securitate, Securocrat, Sepoy, Shamus, Sleeping, Slop, Smokey, Snatch squad, Sowar(ry), Special, Special Branch, Stasi, State Trooper, Super, Superintendent, Sureté, Sweeney, T(h)anadar, Texas Rangers, The Bill, The Law, Thirdborough, Thought, Traffic, Traps, Vice squad, Vigilante, Walloper, Wolly, Woodentop, Yardie squad, Zabtieh, Zaptiah, Zaptieh, Zomo

Police car Black Maria, Panda, Patrol, Prowl

Police station Copshop, Lock-up, Tana, Tanna(h), Thana(h), Thanna(h), Watchhouse

Policy Assurance, Ballon d'essai, CAP, Comprehensive, Course, Demesne, Endowment, Expedience, First-loss, Floating, Good neighbour, Gradualism, Insurance, Keystone, Knock for knock, Laisser-faire, Lend-lease, Line, Manifesto, Method, Open(-sky), Open door, Perestroika, Plank, Platform, Pork-barrel, Practice, Programme, Reaganism, Reaganomics, Revanchism, Scorched earth, Socred, Stop-go, Tack, Tactics, Ticket, Traditional, Valued, White Australia

Polish(ed), Polisher Beeswax, Black, Blacklead, Bob, Bruter, Buff, Bull, Burnish, Chamois, Complaisant, Edit, Elaborate, Elegant, Emery, Enamel, Finish, French, Furbish, Gentlemanly, Glass, Gloss, Heelball, Hone, Inland, Jeweller's rouge, Lap, Lustre, Nail, Perfect, Pewter-mill, Planish, Polite, Polverine, Pumice, Refinement, Refurbish, Rottenstone, Rub, Sand, Sandblast, Sandpaper, Sheen, Shellac, Shine, Sleekstone, Slick, Slickenside, Sophistication, Supercalender, Svelte, Tutty, Urbane, Veneer, Wax

Polite(ness) Cabinet, Civil, Courteous, Genteel, Grandisonian, Mannered, Suave, Urbane, Well-bred

Politic(al), Politics Apparat, Azapo, Body, Chartism, Civic, Diplomacy, Discreet, Dog-whistle, Expedient, Falange, Fascism, Gesture, Leftism, Neoliberalism, Party,

Poujadism, Power, Practical, Public, Radicalism, Rightism, State, Statecraft, Tactful, Wise, Yuppie, Yuppy

Politician(s) Bright, Carpet-bagger, Catiline, Centrist, Chesterfield, Christian Democrat, Congressman, Coningsby, Delegate, Demagogue, Demo(crat), Diehard, Disraeli, DUP, Eden, Euro-MP, Eurosceptic, Evita, Gladstone, Green, Hardie, Hardliner, Incumbent, Independent, Ins, Isolationist, Laski, Left, Legislator, Liberal, Log-roller, MEP, Minister, Moderate, MP, Nationalist, Nazi, Obstructionist, Octobrist, Parliamentarian, Parnell, Politico, Pollie, Polly, Poujade, Powell, Puppet, Rad, Rep, Richelieu, Senator, Socialist, Statesman, Statist, Tadpole, Taper, TD, Thatcherite, Tory, Trotsky, Unionist, Veep, Warhorse, Whig, Whip, Wilberforce

Poll(ing) Advance, Ballot, Bean, Canvass, Count, Cut, Deed, Dod, Election, Exit, Gallup, Head, Humlie, Hummel, Lory, MORI, Nestor, Not(t), Opinion, Parrot, Pineapple, Pow, Push, Referendum, Scrutiny, Sondage, Straw, Votes

▷ **Poll** *may indicate* a first letter

Pollack Coalfish, Coley, Fish, Lob, Lythe, Saith(e)

Pollard Doddered

Pollen, Pollinate(d), Pollination Anemophilous, Beebread, Dust, Entomophilous, Errhine, Farina, Fertilised, Geitonogamy, Intine, My(i)ophily, Palynology, Sternotribe, Witch-meal, Xenia

Pollenbrush Scopa

Pollex Thumb

Pollster Psephologist

Pollute(d), Pollutant, Pollution Acid rain, Adulterate, Atmosphere, Besmear, Contaminate, Defile, Dirty, Feculent, File, Foul, Impure, Infect, Light, Miasma, Noise, Nox, Oil slick, Rainout, Smog, Soil, Soilure, Stain, Sully, Taint, Thermal, Violate, Waldsterben

Polly Flinders, Parrot, Peachum

Polo Bicycle, Chukka, Marco, Mint, Navigator, Rink, Water

Polonium Po

Poltergeist Apport, Ghost, Spirit, Trouble-house

Poltroon Coward, Craven, Dastard, Scald, Scaramouch

Polyandry Nair

Polygraph Lie-detector

Polymath Knowall, Toynbee

Polymer Elastomer, Fructans, Isotactic, Lignin, Oligomer, Paraldehyde, Resin, Seloxane, Silicone, Sporopollenin, Tetramer, Trimer

Polymorphic Multiform, Proteus, Variform

Polynesian Moriori, Niuean, Tahitian, Tongan

Polyp(s) Alcyonaria, Cormidium, Gonophore, Hydra, Hydranth, Nematophore, Obelia, Sea-anemone, Tumour

Polyphemus Cyclops

Polyphony Counterpoint

Polystyrene Expanded

Polyzoan Sea-mat

Pom Choom

Pomander Pounce(t)-box

Pome Apple

Pomegranate Punica, Punic apple

Pommel Beat, Knob, Pound, Pummel

Pomp(ous) Big, Bloviate, Bombastic, Budge, Ceremonial, Display, Dogberry, Euphuistic, Fustian, Grandiloquent, Grandiose, Heavy, Highfalutin(g), High-flown, High-muck-a-muck, High-sounding, Hogen-mogen, Holier than thou, Inflated, Orotund, Ostentatious, Pageantry, Panjandrum, Parade, Pretentious, Self-important, Sententious, Solemn, Splendour, Starchy, State, Stilted, Stuffed shirt, Stuffy, Turgid

Pom-pom Ball, Tassel
Ponce Pander, Pimp, Solicit, Souteneur
Poncho Ruana
Pond(s) Curling, Dew, Dub, Flash, Hampstead, Lakelet, Lentic, Mill, Oceanarium, Pool, Pound, Puddle, Settling, Shield(ing), Slough, Stank, Stew, Tank, Turlough, Vivarium, Viver
Ponder(ous) Brood, Cogitate, Contemplate, Deliberate, Heavy, Laboured, Mull, Muse, Perpend, Poise, Pore, Reflect, Ruminate, → **THINK**, Vise, Volve, Weigh, Weight(y), Wonder
Poniard Bodkin, → **DAGGER**, Dirk, Stiletto
Pontiff, Pontifical, Pontificate Aaron, Aaronic, Antipope, Dogmatise, Papal
Pontoon Blackjack, Bridge, Caisson, Chess, Game, Twenty one, Vingt-et-un
Pony Bidet, Canuck, Cayuse, Cow, Dales, Dartmoor, Eriskay, Exmoor, Fell, Garran, Garron, Gen(n)et, GG, Griffin, Griffon, Gryfon, Gryphon, Jennet, Jerusalem, Mustang, New Forest, One-trick, Pit, Polo, Pownie, Sable Island, Shanks', Sheltie, Shetland, Show, Tangun, Tat(too), Timor, Welsh, Welsh Mountain, Western Isles
Ponytail Queue
Poodle Barbet, Swan
Pooh Bah, Bear, Pish, Pugh, Winnie, Yah
Pool Backwater, Bank, Bethesda, Billabong, Birthing, Bogey hole, Cenote, Cess, Collect, Combine, Dub, Dump, Flash, Flow, Gene, Hag, Hot, Infinity, Jackpot, Jacuzzi®, Kitty, Lasher, Lido, Lin(n), Malebo, Meer, Mere, Mickery, Mikvah, Mikveh, Millpond, Moon, Natatorium, Paddling, Piscina, Piscine, Plash, Plesh, Plunge, → **POND**, Reserve, Share, Siloam, Snooker, Spa, Stank, Stanley, Sump, Tank, Tarn, Wading, Water(ing) hole, Wave
Poor(ly) Bad, Bare, Base, Bijwoner, Breadline, Buckeen, Bywoner, Catchpenny, Cheapo, Churchmouse, Conch, Cronk, Destitute, Desuetude, Dirt, Gens de peu, Gritty, Half-pie, Hard-up, Have-nots, Hopeless, Humble, Hungry, Ill(-off), Impecunious, Indigent, Lazarus, Lean, Lo-fi, Lousy, Low, Low-downer, Low-fi, Low-paid, Lumpen, Meagre, Mean, Needy, Obolary, One-horse, Pauper, Peaky, Poxy, Redleg, Roinish, Rop(e)y, Roynish, Sad, Scrub, Shabby, Shitty, Sober, Sorry, Sub, Tacky, Tatty, Thin, Third-rate, Tinpot, Trashy, Undeserving, Unwell, Wattle, Wishy-washy
▷ **Poor** *may indicate* an anagram
Poorhouse Union, Workhouse
Pooter Nobody, Nonentity
Pop (off), Popper, Popping Bang, Brit, Burst, Cloop, Crease, Daddy, Die, → **DRUG**, Father, Fr, Ginger ale, Gingerbeer, Hip-hop, Hock, Iggy, Insert, Lemonade, Lumber, Mineral, Nip, Parent, Party, Pater, Pawn, Pledge, Population, Press-stud, Punk, Scoosh, Sherbet, Soda, Splutter, Sputter, Weasel
▷ **Pop** *may indicate* an anagram
Pope(s) Adrian, Alexander, Atticus, Benedict, Black, Boniface, Borgia, Clement, Dunciad, Eminence, Fish, Great Schism, Gregory, Hildebrand, Holiness, Innocent, Joan, Leo, Papa, Pius, Pontiff, Ruff(e), Schism, Sixtius, Theocrat, Tiara, Urban, Vatican, Vicar-general of Christ, Vicar of Christ
Pop-gun Bourtree-gun
Popinjay Barbermonger, Coxcomb, Dandy, Fop, Macaroni, Parrot, Prig, Skipjack
Poplar Abele, Aspen, Balsam, Cottonwood, Lombardy, Trembling, Tulip, White, Yellow
Poppet Cutie pie, Valve
Poppy Argemone, Bloodroot, Blue, California, Chicalote, Coquelicot, Corn, Diacodin, Eschscholtzia, Field, Flanders, Horned, Iceland, Matilija, Mawseed, Opium, Papaver, Plume, Ponceau, Prickly, Puccoon, Rhoeadales, Shirley, Tall, Welsh
Poppycock Bosh, Nonsense, Rubbish
Popular(ity), Popularly Best-seller, Common, Crowd-pleaser, Cult, Democratic, Demotic, Enchorial, Fashionable, General, Grass roots, Heyday, Hit, Hot ticket, In, Laic, Lay, Mass, Plebeian, Prevalent, Public, Sell-out, Street cred, Successful, Tipped, Trendy,

Vogue, Vulgo

Population, Populace Catchment, Census, Closed, Deme, Demography, Inhabitants, Malthusian, Mass, Mob, Optimum, → **PEOPLE**, Public, Universe

Porcelain Arita, Artificial, Bamboo, Belleek®, Blanc-de-chine, Celadon, Chantilly, Chelsea, China, Coalport, Crackle(ware), Crouch-ware, Crown Derby, Derby, Dresden, Eggshell, Famille, Famille jaune, Famille noir, Famille rose, Famille verte, Frit, Goss, Hard-paste, Hizen, Imari, Ivory, Jasp(er), Jasper(ware), Kakiemon, Limoges, Lithophane, Meissen, Minton, Parian, Petuntse, Petuntze, Sèvres, Softpaste, Spode, Sung, Yuan

Porch Galilee, Lanai, Stoa, Stoep, Veranda(h)

Porcupine Hedgehog, Urson

Pore Browse, Hole, Hydrathode, Lenticel, Muse, Ostiole, Ostium, Outlet, Ponder, Stoma, Study

Porgy Braise, Scup(paug)

Pork(y) Bacon, Boar, Brawn, Chap, Char sui, Crackling, Cracknel, Flitch, Griskin, Ham, Lie, Pancetta, Salt, Scrapple, Scruncheon, Scrunchion, Spare-rib, Spek, Tenderloin

Porn(ography), Pornographic Curiosa, Erotica, Hard, Hard-core, Jazz mag, Rhyparography, Snuff-film, Soft, Soft-core, Video nasty

Porous Cellular, Permeable, Pumice, Sponge

Porpoise Bucker, Dolphin, Mereswine, Pellach, Pellack, Pellock, Phocaena, Sea pig, Sea swine

Porridge Berry, Bird, Brochan, Brose, Burgoo, Busera, Crowdie, Drammach, Drammock, Gaol, Grits, Grouts, Gruel, Hominy, Kasha, Mabela, Mahewu, Mealie pap, Mielie pap, Oaten, Oatmeal, Parritch, Pease-brose, Polenta, Pottage, Praiseach, Sadza, Samp, Sentence, Skilly, Stirabout, Stretch, Sup(p)awn, Time, Ugali

Porridge stick Thible, Thivel

Port(s) Beeswing, Carry, Cinque, Container (terminal), Entrepot, Free, Gate, Gateway, Geropiga, → **HARBOUR**, Haven, Hinterland, Induction, Larboard, Left, Manner, Mien, Outport, Parallel, Row, Ruby, Serial, Tawny, Treaty, USB, Wine

PORTS

3 letters:	Eisk	Oulu	Anzio
Abo	Elat	Perm	Aqaba
Ayr	Faro	Pori	Arhus
Gao	Gary	Pula	Arica
Hué	Gaza	Puri	Aulis
Rio	Gyor	Ruse	Bahia
Rye	Hilo	Safi	Bahru
Tyr	Hull	Said	Banff
	Icel	Salé	Barry
4 letters:	I-pin	Sfax	Basra
Acre	Kiel	Suez	Batum
Aden	Kiev	Susa	Beira
Akko	Kobe	Suva	Belem
Amoy	Kure	Tang	Bharu
Apia	Lima	Tema	Blyth
Baku	Linz	Tvev	Brest
Bari	Lomé	Tyre	Cadiz
Boma	Luda	Vigo	Cairo
Cobh	Naha	Wick	Canea
Cork	Oban	Wuhu	Colon
Deal	Omsk		Dakar
Dill	Oran	*5 letters:*	Davao
Doha	Oslo	Akaba	Derry

Dilli
Dover
Duala
Dubai
Eilat
Elath
Emden
Fowey
Gabes
Galle
Gavie
Genoa
Ghent
Gijon
Goole
Haifa
Hania
Hithe
Horta
Hythe
Imari
Izmir
Jaffa
Jambi
Jedda
Jidda
Joppa
Kerch
Kochi
Larne
Leith
Lulea
Mainz
Malmo
Masan
Merca
Miami
Mocha
Mokpo
Narva
Newry
Omaha
Ophir
Osaka
Ostia
Palma
Palos
Pisco
Ponce
Poole
Pusan
Pylos
Rabat
Rouen

Saida
Sakai
Salto
Selby
Sidon
Skien
Split
Surat
Susah
Tajik
Tampa
Tanga
Tunis
Turku
Vaasa
Varna
Visby
Vlore
Volos
Yalta
Yeisk
Yeysk
Yibin

6 letters:
Aarhus
Abadan
Agadir
Albany
Alborg
Amalfi
Ancona
Andong
Annaba
Aveiro
Balboa
Bastia
Batumi
Bergen
Bilbao
Bissao
Bissau
Blanca
Bombay
Bootle
Boston
Braila
Bremen
Bukavu
Burgas
Cairns
Calais
Callao
Candia

Cannes
Canton
Cavite
Chania
Chi-lin
Cochin
Cuiaba
Cuyaba
Dalian
Da Nang
Danzig
Darwin
Dieppe
Djambi
Douala
Duluth
Dunbar
Dundee
Durban
Durres
Elblag
Galata
Galati
Gdansk
Gdynia
Harbin
Havana
Hobart
Ichang
Iligan
Iloilo
Inchon
Jaffna
Jarrow
Juneau
Kalmar
Khulna
Kisumu
Lepaya
Lisbon
Lobito
Lubeck
Lushun
Macelo
Mackay
Madras
Malabo
Malaga
Manado
Manama
Manaos
Manaus
Manila
Maputo

Matadi
Melaka
Menado
Mersin
Mobile
Mumbai
Muscat
Nagano
Namibe
Nantes
Napier
Naples
Narvik
Nassau
Nelson
Newark
Ningbo
Ningpo
Nizhni
Oamaru
Odense
Odessa
Oporto
Ostend
Padang
Patras
Peoria
Pesaro
Quebec
Quincy
Rabaul
Ragusa
Recife
Rijeka
Rimini
Romney
Roseau
Rostov
Samara
Samsun
Santos
Sarnia
Sasebo
Savona
Skikda
Smyrna
Sousse
Speyer
Spires
St John
St Malo
St Paul
Suakin
Sydney

Syzran
Szeged
Tacoma
Tajiki
Thurso
Timaru
Tobruk
Toledo
Toulon
Tromso
Tyumen
Velsen
Venice
Vyborg
Weihai
Whitby
Wismar
Wonsan
Xiamen
Yangon
Yantai

7 letters:
Aalborg
Abidjan
Ajaccio
Alesund
Almeria
Antalya
Antibes
Antwerp
Aracaju
Astoria
Augusta
Averiro
Bamberg
Bangkok
Bayonne
Bengasi
Berbera
Bizerta
Bizerte
Bristol
Buffalo
Bushehr
Bushire
Calabar
Cam Ranh
Canopus
Cantala
Cardiff
Catania
Changde
Changte

Chicago
Chilung
Cologne
Colombo
Conakry
Corinth
Corunna
Cotonou
Derbent
Detroit
Drammen
Dunedin
Dunkirk
El Minya
Ephesus
Esbjerg
Foochow
Fukuoka
Funchal
Gauhati
Geelong
Gosport
Grimsby
Halifax
Hamburg
Hampton
Harwich
Heysham
Hodeida
Horsens
Houston
Hungnam
Incheon
Iquique
Iquitos
Kaolack
Karachi
Karumba
Kavalla
Kenitra
Kherson
Kinsale
Kolding
Konakri
Kowloon
Kuching
La Plata
Latakia
Legaspi
Le Havre
Lepanto
Liepaja
Livorno
Lorient

Makurdi
Marsala
Masbate
Massaua
Massawa
Maulman
Melilla
Memphis
Messina
Milazzo
Mits'twa
Mombasa
Moulman
Munster
Nanjing
Nanking
Nanning
Neusatz
Newport
Niigata
Niteroi
Novi Sad
Oakland
Okayama
Onitsha
Otranto
Pahsien
Palermo
Pelotas
Phocaea
Piraeus
Qingdao
Qiqihar
Randers
Rangoon
Rapallo
Ravenna
Rosario
Rostock
Runcorn
Salerno
San Remo
Sao Luis
Seattle
Sekondi
Setubal
Seville
Shantou
Shantow
Sinuiju
Stettin
St John's
St Louis
Sukhumi

Swansea
Tadzhik
Tampico
Tangier
Taranto
Trabzon
Trapani
Trieste
Tripoli
Ulan-Ude
Ushuaia
Vitebsk
Vitoria
Wanxian
Wenchou
Wenchow
Wenzhou
Whyalla
Yakutsk
Yichang
Yingkou
Yingkow

8 letters:
Aalesund
Abeokuta
Aberdeen
Acapulco
Alicante
Alleppey
Arbroath
Auckland
Badalona
Barletta
Batangas
Bathurst
Benghazi
Benguela
Bobruisk
Bobryusk
Bordeaux
Boulogne
Brindisi
Brisbane
Bromberg
Caesarea
Cagliari
Calcutta
Castries
Changsha
Changteh
Chaochow
Cheribon
Chimbote

Chingtao
Chongjin
Cuxhaven
Dortmund
Drogheda
Duisburg
Dunleary
El Ferrol
Elsinore
Falmouth
Flushing
Freetown
Gisborne
Gonaives
Goteborg
Greenock
Haiphong
Hakodate
Halmstad
Hamilton
Hangchow
Hangzhou
Harfleur
Hartford
Hastings
Helsinki
Holyhead
Honolulu
Iraklion
Istanbul
Jayapura
Jinjiang
Kanazawa
Kawasaki
Keflavik
Kingston
Klaipeda
La Coruna
La Guaira
La Guyara
La Spezia
Lattakia
Les Cayes
Limassol
Limerick
Luderitz
Mariupol
Matanzas
Maulmain
Mayaguez
Mazatlan
Monrovia
Montreal
Moulmein

Murmansk
Mytilene
Nagasaki
Nan-ching
Newhaven
Nha Trang
Novgorod
Nykøbing
Pago Pago
Paramibo
Pavlodar
Paysandu
Peiraeus
Penzance
Pevensey
Plymouth
Pnom Penh
Port Said
Pozzuoli
Qui Nhong
Ramsgate
Rio Bravo
Salvador
Samarang
Sanarang
Sandakan
San Diego
Sandwich
Santarem
Santiago
Savannah
Schiedam
Selencia
Semarang
Shanghai
Sorrento
St Helier
Stockton
Surabaja
Surabaya
Syracuse
Szczecin
Tadzhiki
Taganrog
Takoradi
Tangiers
Tarshish
Tauranga
Teresina
Tjirebon
Tsingtao
Valdivia
Valencia
Veracruz

Victoria
Wakayama
Wanganui
Weymouth
Yarmouth
Yokohama
Yokosuka
Zaanstad

9 letters:
Anchorage
Angostura
Annapolis
Antserana
Archangel
Balaclava
Balaklava
Baltimore
Barcelona
Bass-Terre
Bhavnagar
Bujumbura
Bydgoszcz
Carnarvon
Cartagena
Cherbourg
Chisimaio
Chongqing
Chungking
Cleveland
Constanta
Dartmouth
Den Helder
Djajapura
Dordrecht
Dubrovnik
Ellesmere
Epidaurus
Esperance
Esquimalt
Essaouira
Europoort
Famagusta
Fishguard
Fleetwood
Flensburg
Fortaleza
Fremantle
Gallipoli
Gateshead
Geraldton
Gravesend
Guayaquil
Hangchoio

Helsinger
Heraklion
Hiroshima
Immingham
Inhambane
Jasselton
Kagoshima
Kaohsiung
King's Lynn
Kingstown
Kirkcaldy
Kota Bahru
Kozhikode
Krasnodar
Kronstadt
Las Palmas
Lowestoft
Magdeburg
Mahajanga
Mangalore
Maracaibo
Mariehamn
Marseille
Matamoros
Matsuyama
Melbourne
Milwaukee
Morecambe
Newcastle
Nuku'alofa
Palembang
Peterhead
Phnom Penh
Pontianak
Port Blair
Port Louis
Port Sudan
Reykjavik
Rotterdam
Santa Cruz
Santander
Schleswig
Sheerness
Singapore
Soerabaja
Stavanger
St George's
St Nazaire
Stornoway
Stralsund
Stranraer
Sundsvall
Takamatsu
Tarragona

Toamasina
Trebizond
Trondheim
Tynemouth
Volgograd
Walvis Bay
Waterford
Weihaiwei
Whangarei
Zamboanga
Zeebrugge

10 letters:
Alexandria
Balikpapan
Belize City
Birkenhead
Bratislava
Bridgeport
Bridgetown
Caernarvon
Cap-Haitien
Casablanca
Charleston
Cheboksary
Chittagong
Cienfuegos
Copenhagen
Corrientes
Dzerzhinsk
East London
Felixstowe
Folkestone
Fray Bentos
Fredericia
Georgetown
Gothenburg
Hammerfest
Hartlepool
Herakleion
Iskenderun
Joao Pessoa
Karlskrona
Khabarovsk
Khota Bharu
Kitakyushu
La Rochelle

Launceston
Libreville
Los Angelos
Louisville
Matozinhos
Montevideo
Mostaganem
New Bedford
New Orleans
Norrkoping
Paramaribo
Pittsburgh
Pontevedra
Port Gentil
Portobello
Portsmouth
Port Talbot
Providence
Queenstown
Sacramento
Santa Marta
Sebastopol
Sevastopol
Strasbourg
Sunderland
Talcahuano
Thunder Bay
Townsville
Valparaiso
Whitstable
Willemstad
Wilmington
Winchelsea

11 letters:
Antofagusta
Antseranana
Bahia Blanca
Banjarmasin
Banjermasin
Baranquilla
Bremerhaven
Cheng-chiang
Dares Salaam
Fredrikstad
Grangemouth
Helsingborg

Hermoupolis
Kaliningrad
Makhachkala
Maryborough
New Plymouth
Newport News
Nuevo Laredo
Pointe-Noire
Port Moresby
Porto Alegre
Port of Spain
Punta Arenas
Rockhampton
San Fernando
Scarborough
Shimonoseki
Southampton
Telukbetong
Trincomalee
Vizagapatam
Vlaardingen
Vladivostok

12 letters:
Angtofagasta
Bandjarmasin
Bandjermasin
Barranquilla
Buenaventura
Chandemagore
Dun Laoghaire
Ho Chi Min City
Jacksonville
Kota Kinabalu
Kristiansand
Milford Haven
Philadelphia
Pointe-à-Pitre
Ponta Delgada
Port Adelaide
Port-au-Prince
Port Harcourt
Prince Rupert
Rio de Janeiro
San Francisco
San Sebastian
Santo Domingo

South Shields
St Petersburg
Tanjungpriok
Thessaloniki
Ujung Pandang
Usti nad Labem

13 letters:
Chandernagore
Charlottetown
Ciudad Bolivar
Corpus Christi
Florianopolis
Great Yarmouth
Ho Chi Minh City
Hook of Holland
Middlesbrough
Port Elizabeth
Tandjungpriok
Teloekbetoeng
Trois Rivières
Visakhapatnam
Wilhelmshaven

14 letters:
Burnie-Somerset
Mina Hassen Tani
Nizhni Novgorod
Santiago de Cuba
Vishakhapatnam

15 letters:
Alexandroupolis
Angra-de-Heroismo
Blagoveshchensk
Charlotte-Amalie
Forster-Tuncurry
Sault Saint Marie

16 letters:
Reggio di Calabria
Sault Sainte Marie

18 letters:
Castellon de la Plana

Portable Lapheld, Laptop, Palmtop
Portend, Portent(ous) Augur, Awesome, Bode, Dire, Omen, Ostent, Phenomenon,
Presage, → **WARN(ING)**
Porter Ale, Bearer, Bellboy, Bellhop, Bummaree, Caddie, Caddy, Cole, Concierge, Coolie,
Door-keeper, Doorman, Dvornik, Entire, Gatekeeper, Ham(m)al, Hamaul, Humper,
Janitor, October, Ostiary, Plain, Red-cap, Skycap, Stout, Ticket

Portfolio Holding

Portico Colonnade, Decastyle, Distyle, Dodecastyle, Exedra, Loggia, Narthex, Parvis(e), Porch, Propylaeum, Prostyle, Stoa, Veranda(h), Xyst(us)

Portion Aliquot, Ann(at), Bit, Deal, Distribute, Dole, Dose, Dotation, Fraction, Fragment, Helping, Heritage, Hunk, Instalment, Jointure, Lot, Lump, Measure, Meed, Mess, Modicum, Moiety, Nutlet, Ounce, Parcel, → **PART**, Piece, Ratio, Sample, Scantle, Scantling, Section, Segment, Serving, Share, Size, Slice, Something, Spoonful, Tait, Taste, Tate, Tittle, Tranche, Wodge

Portland Bill, Cement, Stone

Portly Ample, Corpulent, Gaucie, Gaucy, Gawcy, Gawsy, Stout

Portmanteau, Portmanteau word Avoision, Bag, Combination, Holdall, Valise

Portrait(ist) Carte de visite, Composite, Depiction, Drawing, Eikon, Icon, Identikit®, Ikon, Image, Kit-cat, Lely, Likeness, Painting, Pin-up, Retraitt, Retrate, Sketch, Vignette

Portray(al) Caricature, Depict, Describe, Feature, Image, Limn, Notate, Paint, Personate, Render, Represent, → **SHOW**

Portsmouth Pompey

Portugal, Portuguese Lusitania(n), Luso-, Macanese, Senhor

Pose(r), Poseur Aesthete, Affect(ation), Arabesque, Asana, Ask, Contrapposto, Drape, Enigma, Lotus, Man(n)ikin, Mannequin, Masquerade, Model, Place, Plastique, Posture, Pretend, Problem, Propound, Pseud, Puzzle, Sit, Stance, Sticker, Tableau vivant, Tickler

Poseidon Earthshaker

Posh Chic, Classy, Grand, Lah-di-dah, Ornate, Ritzy, Swanky, Swish, Toff, U

Position Arrange, Asana, Attitude, Bearing(s), Brace, Bridgehead, Case, Close, Codille, Delta, Ecarte, Emplacement, Enfilade, False, F(o)etal, Fixure, Foothold, Fowler's, Grade, Instal, Lay, Lie, Location, Locus, Lodg(e)ment, Lotus, Missionary, Mudra, Office, Open, Pass, Peak, Place, Plant, Point, Pole, Port, Possie, Post, Pozzy, Put, Rank, Recovery, Recumbent, Root, Seat, Set(ting), Sextile, Sims, Sinecure, Site, Situ, Situs, Stance, Standing, Standpoint, Station, Status, Strategic, Syzygy, Tagmeme, Thesis, Tierce, Trendelenburg's, Tuck, Viewpoint

Positive, Positivist Absolute, Actual, Anode, Assertive, Categorical, → **CERTAIN**, Comte, Definite, Emphatic, False, Plus, Print, Rave, Sure, Thetic, Upbeat, Upside, Veritable, Yang, Yes

Posse Band, Mob, Vigilantes

Possess(ed), Possession(s), Possessive Adverse, Apostrophe, Asset, Aver, Bedevil, Belonging(s), Demonic, Driven, Energumen, Estate, Ewe lamb, Have, Haveour, Haviour, Heirloom, His, Hogging, Know, Lares (et) penates, Mad, Obsessed, Occupation, → **OWN**, Proprietorial, Sasine, Seisin, Sprechery, Substance, Tenancy, Usucap(t)ion, Vacant, Worth

Possible, Possibility, Possibly Able, Contingency, Feasible, Imaginable, Likely, Maybe, Mayhap, Off-chance, On, Oyster, Peradventure, Perchance, Perhaps, Posse, Potential, Prospect, Resort, Viable, Well, Will

▷ **Possibly** *may indicate* an anagram

Possum Burramys, Cataplexy, Opossum, Pygmy, Rigo(u)r, Ringtail, Sugar glider, Sugar squirrel, Tait

Post(s), Postage Affix, After, Assign, Bitt, Bollard, Carrick bitt, Command, Correspondence, Cossack, Dak, Dawk, Delivery, Dragon's teeth, Durn, Emily, Excess, Finger, First, Flagpole, Fly, Goal, Graded, Gradient, Guardhose, Heel, Hitching, Hovel, Hurter, Jamb, Joggle, Junk, King, Last, Laureate, Listening, Log, Mail, Mast, Newel, Observation, Outstation, Pale, Paling, Parcel, Pendant, Penny, Picket, Pigeon, Pile, Piling, Piquet, Placard, Place, Plant, Plum, Pole, Position, Presidio, Puncheon, Pylon, Queen, Quintain, Quoin, Registered, Remit, Residency, RM, Rubbing, Samson's, Seat, Send, Sheriff's, Snubbing, Sound, Spile, Staff, Staging, Stake, Stanchion, Starting, Station, Stell, Stoop, Stoup, Stud, Studdle, Tana, Tee, Term(inal), Thanna(h), Tom, Tool, Totem pole, Trading, Upright, Vacancy, Waymark, Winning

Postcard(s) Deltiology, Picture

Poster Advertisement, Affiche, Bill, Broadsheet, Pin-up, Placard, Playbill, Sender, Showbill, Solus

Posterior Behind, Bottom, Jacksie, Jacksy, Later, Lumbar, Pygal, Rear, Tail

Post-free Franco

Postman, Postmaster, Postwoman Carrier, Courier, Emily, Hill, Messenger, Nasby, Pat, Portionist, Sorter

Postmark Frank

Post-modern Po-mo

Post mortem Autopsy, Enquiry, Necropsy

Postpone(ment), Postponed Adjourn, Backburner, Carryover, Contango, Defer, Delay, Frist, Hold over, Lay over, Long-finger, Moratorium, Mothball, Offput, On ice, Pigeon-hole, Postdate, Prorogue, Put over, Remanet, Reprieve, Respite, Roll back, Shelve, Spike, Stay, Suspend, Withhold

Postulant Candidate, Noumenon, Novice

Postulate(s) Assert, Assume, Claim, Koch's, Propound

Posture(r), Posturing Affectation, Asana, Attitude, Birkie, Camp, Carriage, Counter-view, Decubitus, Deportment, Gesture, Mudra, Pose, Pretence, Site, Stance, Swank, Vorlage, Yoga

Post-war Post-bellum

Posy Bouquet, Buttonhole, Corsage, Nosegay, Tussiemussie, Tussle-mussle, Tuzzi-muzzy, Tuzzy-muzzy

Pot(s), Potting, Potty Abridge, Aludel, Ante, Bankroll, Basil, Belly, Billycan, Cafetière, Ca(u)ldron, Cannabis, Cannikin, Casserole, Ceramic, Chamber, Chanty, Chatti, Chatty, Chimney, Close-stool, Cocotte, Coil, Commode, Crewe, Crock(ery), Crucible, Cruse(t), Cupel, Delf(t), Dixie, Ewer, Flesh, Gage, Gallipot, Ganja, Gazunder, Grass, Hash(ish), Helmet, Hemp, Hooped, In off, Inurn, Jardinière, Jordan, Kaif, Kef, Kettle, Kitty, Livery, Lobster, Loco, Lota(h), Maiolica, Majolica, Marijuana, Marmite, Melting, Ming, Monkey, Olla, Olpe, Pan, Papper, Pat, Piñata, Pint, Pipkin, Planter, Po, Pocket, Poot, Posnet, → **POTTERY**, Pottle, Pounce, Pout, Prize, Quart, Samovar, Shoot, Sink, Skeet, Skillet, Smudge, Steamer, Steane, Stomach, Tajine, Tea, Test, Throw, Togine, Trivet, Tureen, Urn, Vial, Ware, Wash, Whitechapel, Wok

Potash Kalinite, Polverine, Potassa, Sylvine, Sylvite

Potassium K, Kalium, Pearl ash, Saleratus, Saltpetre

Potation Dram, Drink

Potato(es) African, Aloo, Alu, Batata, Chat, Clean, Couch, Datura, Duchesse, Early, Fluke, Hashbrowns, Hog, Hole, Hot, Irish, Jacket, Jersey, Kidney, Kumara, Lyonnaise, Maris piper, Mash, Murphy, Parmentier, Peel-and-eat, Pratie, Praty, Roesti, Rumbledethump(s), Seed, Small, Solanum, Stovies, Sweet, Tatie, Tattie, Teddy, Tuber, Ware, White, Yam

Pot-bearer Trivet

Pot-bellied Kedge, Kedgy, Kidge, Paunchy, Portly, Stout

Potboiler Hob

Pot-boy Basil, Ganymede, Scullion

Potent(ate) Cogent, Dynamic, Emeer, Emir, Emperor, Huzoor, Imaum, Influential, Kinglet, Mogul, Nawab, Panjandrum, Powerful, Ras, Ruler, Satrap, Squirearch, Sultan, Virile

Potential(ly) Action, Capability, Capacity, Chemical, Electric, Electrode, In posse, Ionization, Latent, Making(s), Manqué, Possible, Promise, Resting, Scope, Viable

▷ **Potentially** *may indicate* an anagram

Pothole(r) Chuckhole, Giant's kettle, Spelunker

Pot-house Shebeen, Tavern

Potion Dose, Draught, Drink, Dwale, Love, Mixture, Philtre, Tincture

Pot-pourri Hotchpotch, Medley, Miscellany, Pasticcio, Salmi

Potsherd Ostracon, Ostrakon

Pottage Berry

Potter Cue, Dabbity, Dabble, Dacker, Daidle, Daiker, Daker, Dibble, Dilly-dally, Dodder, Etruscan, Fettle, Fictor, Fiddle, Footer, Footle, Fouter, Gamesmanship, Harry, Idle, Mess, Minton, Muck, Niggle, One-upmanship, Plouter, Plowter, Poke, Spode, Thrower, Tiddle, Tink(er), Troke, Truck, Wedgewood, Wedgwood

▷ **Potter** *may indicate* a snooker-player

Pottery Agatewear, Bank, Basalt, Bisque, Cameo ware, Celadon, Ceramet, Ceramic, China, Creamware, Crock, Crouch-ware, Dabbity, Delf(t), Earthenware, Encaustic, Etruria(n), Faience, Flatback, Gombroon, Granitewear, Hollowware, Ironstone, Jomon, Lustreware, Maiolica, Majolica, Ming, Minton, Pebbleware, Raku, Red-figured, Satsuma, Scroddled, Sgraffito, Slab, Slipware, Smalto, Spode, Spongeware, Stoneware, Studio, Sung, Terra sigillata, Ware, Wedgwood®, Wemyss, Whieldon, Whiteware

Pouch(ed) Bag, Brood, Bum-bag, Bursa, Caecum, Cheek, Cisterna, Codpiece, Cyst, Diverticulum, Fanny pack, Gill, Jockstrap, Marsupial, Marsupium, Papoose, Poke, Posing, Purse, Sac, Scrip, Scrotum, Snood, Spleuchan, Sporran, Tobacco

Pouffe Humpty

Poultice Application, Cataplasm, Embrocation, Emollient, Epithem(a), Lenient, Plaster

Poultry Dorking, Fowl, Gallinaceous, Plymouth Rock, Poot, Pout, Welsummer

Poultry disease Keel, Scaly-leg, Vent gleet

Pounce Claw, Jump, Lunge, Powder, Sere, Souse, Sprinkle, Swoop, Talon

Pound(er) Ache, As, Bar, Bash, Batter, Beat, Bombard, Bradbury, Bray, Broadpiece, Bruise, Catty, Clomp, Contund, Coop, Drub, Embale, Enclosure, Ezra, Fold, Green, Greenie, Greeny, Hammer, Hatter, Imagist, Intern, Iron man, Jail, Jimmy o'goblin, Kiddle, Kidel, Kin, Knevell, L, Lam, Lb, Lock, Mash, Nevel, Nicker, Oncer, One-er, Oner, Pale, Pen, Penfold, Pestle, Pin, Pindar, Pinfold, Pink, Powder, Pulverise, Pun, Quid, Quop, Rint, Scots, Smacker, Sov(ereign), Squid, Stamp, Sterling, Strum, Tenderise, Throb, Thump, Tower, Troy, Weight

Pour(ing) Affusion, Be mother, Birl(e), Bucket, Cascade, Circumfuse, Decant, Diffuse, Disgorge, Flood, Flow, Jaw, Jirble, Libate, Rain, Seil, Shed, Sile, Skink, Spew, Stream, Teem, Trill, Turn, Vent, Weep, Well

Pout Bib, Blain, Brassy, Eel, Fish, Horn(ed), Mope, Mou(e), Scowl, Sulk, Tout, Towt, Whiting

Poverty Beggary, Dearth, Deprivation, Illth, Indigence, → **LACK**, Locust years, Necessity, Need, Paucity, Penury, Poortith, Puirtith, Squalor, Tobacco Road, Want

Powder(ed), Powdery Allantoin, Alumina, Amberite, Araroba, Baking, Ballistite, Bleaching, Boracic, Calamine, Calomel, Chalk, Chilli, Colcothar, Cosmetic, Crocus, Culm, Curry, Custard, Cuttlefish, Dentifrice, Dover's, Dust, Dusting, Eupad, Explosive, Face, Flea, Floury, Fly, Fulminating, Giant, Glaucous, Goa, Gregory, Grind, Gun, Hair, Insect, Itching, Kohl, Levigate, Lithia, Litmus, Lupulin, Magnesia, Meal, Mepacrine, Mould-facing, Moust, Mu(i)st, Pearl, Pemoline, Percussion, Persian, Plaster of Paris, Plate, Polishing, Pollen, Pounce, Priming, Prismatic, Projecting, Pruinose, Pulver, Pulvil, Putty, Rachel, Rochelle, Rottenstone, Rouge, Saleratus, Seidlitz, Seme(e), Sherbet, Silver iodide, Sitosterol, Smeddum, Smokeless, Snuff, Soap, Spode, Spodium, Talc(um), Talcose, Thimerosal, Toner, Tooth, Triturate, Tutty, Washing, Zedoary, Zein

Power(ful), Powers Ability, Able, Aeon, Aggrandisement, Air, Almighty, Alpha, Amandla, Arm, Arnold, Athletic, Atomic, Attorney, Audrey, Autarchy, Authority, Axis, Beef, Big, Capability, Chakra, Cham, Charisma, Clairvoyance, Clout, Cogency, Colossus, Command, Corridor, Cube, Danger, Despotic, Diadem, Dioptre, Dominion, Effective, Electricity, Eminence, Éminence grise, Empathy, Empery, Energy, Eon, Exponent, Facility, Faculty, Fire, Flower, Force, Force majeure, Gaddi, Gas, Geothermal, Grey, Grip, Gutty, Hands, Hefty, Hegemony, Herculean, High, Hildebrandic, Horse, Hot, Hp, Hydroelectric, Imperium, Influence, Kami, Kick, Kilowatt, Leccy, Log, Logarithm, Lusty, Mana, Mandate, Mastery, Megalomania, Might, Mogul, Motive, Motor, Movers and shakers,

Muscle, Natural, Nature, Nth, Nuclear, Od-force, Oligarch, Omnificent, Omnipotent, Option, P, Panjandrum, People, Pester, Plenary, Plenipotency, Posse, Potency, Prepollence, Prepotent, Puissant, Punch, Purchasing, Regime, Resolving, Say-so, Sea, Siddhi, Sinew, Solar, Soup, Stamina, Staying, Steam, Steel, Stiff, Stopping, Stranglehold, Strength, → **STRONG**, Supercharge, Supreme, Suzerain, Teeth, Telling, Throne, Tidal, Tycoon, Tyranny, Tyrone, Ulric, Valency, Vertu(e), Vigour, Vis, Volt, Vroom, Water, Watt, Wattage, Wave, Weight, Welly, Wheel and axle, Whiphand, Wind, World, Yeast

Powerless Diriment, Downa-do, Failing, Freewheel, Hamstrung, Helpless, Impotent, Impuissant, Incapable, Inert, Unable, Unarmed, Weak

Powwow Confab, Conference, Council, Meeting

Pox Chicken, Cow, French, Great, Orf, Pize, Small, Spanish

Practical, Practicable, Practicalities Active, Applied, Brass tacks, Doable, Easy-care, Feasible, Hands on, Hard-boiled, Joker, Logistics, Nitty-gritty, No-nonsense, Nuts and bolts, On, Pragmatic, Realist(ic), Realpolitik, Rule of thumb, Sensible, Shrewd, Technical, Useful, Utilitarian, Viable, Virtual

Practice, Practise, Practitioner, Practised Abuse, Adept, Custom, Distributed, Do, Drill, Dry run, Enure, Exercise, Fire, General, Graft, Group, Habit, Inure, Ism, Keep, Knock-up, Massed, Meme, Mock, Nets, Operate, Order, Ordinance, Pipe opener, Ply, Policy, Praxis, Private, Prosecution, Pursuit, Rehearsal, Rehearse, Restrictive, Rite, Rule, Rut, Sadhana, Sharp, Sighter, Spanish, System, Target, Teaching, Test-run, Trade, Tradition, Train, Trial, Ure, Usage, Use, Wage

Pragmatic, Pragmatist Ad hoc, Busy, Dogmatic, Humanist, Meddling, Officious, Realist, Trimmer, Unholy

Prairie IL, Illinois, Llano, Plain, Savanna, Steppe, Tundra, Veldt

Prairie dog Whippoorwill, Wishtonwish

Praise(worthy) Acclaim, Adulation, Alleluia, Allow, Anthem, Applause, Beatify, Belaud, Bepuff, Bless, Blurb, Bouquet, Butter, Carol, Citation, CL, Commend(ation), Compliment, Congratulate, Cry up, Dulia, Ego boost, Encomium, Envy, Eulogise, Eulogium, Eulogy, Exalt, Exemplary, Extol, Gloria, Glory, Hero-worship, Herry, Hery(e), Hosanna, Hymn, Hype, Incense, Kudos, Laud, Lip service, Lo(o)s, Meritorious, Palmary, Panegyric, Puff(ery), Rap, Rave, Roose, Talk-up, Tout, Tribute

Pram Carriage, Cart, Dinghy, Pram, Scow

Prance Brank, Canary, Caper, Cavort, Galumph, Gambol, Jaunce, Jaunse, Prank(le), Swagger, Tittup, Trounce

Prang Accident, Crash, Smash, Whale

Prank(s) Attrap, Bedeck, Bedizen, Caper, Dido, Escapade, Fredaine, Frolic, Gaud, Jape, Lark, Mischief, Pliskie, Rag, Reak, Reik, Rex, Rig, Spoof, Trick, Vagary, Wedgie

Praseodymium Pr

Prat Bottom, → **STUPID PERSON**

Prate Babble, Boast, Haver, Talk

Prattle Babble, Blat(her), Chatter, Gab(nash), Gas, Gibber, Gossip, Gup, Lalage, Patter, Smatter, Yap

Prawn Banana, Crevette, Dublin Bay, King, Scampi, School, Shrimp, Tiger

Pray(ing) Appeal, Bed, Beg, Beseech, Bid, Daven, → **ENTREAT**, Impetrate, Intone, Invoke, Kneel, Mantis, Patter, Solicit, Wrestle

▷ **Prayer** *may indicate* one who begs

Prayer(s), Prayer book Acoemeti, Act, Amidah, Angelus, Ardas, Ave (Maria), Bead, Beadswoman, Bede, Bene, Bidding, Breviary, Collect, Commination, Common, Confiteor, Cry, Cursus, Daven, Deus det, Devotion, Eleison, Embolism, Entreaty, Epiclesis, Euchologion, Evensong, Geullah, Grace, Habdalah, Hail Mary, Hallan-shaker, Imam, Intercession, Invocation, Kaddish, Khotbah, Khotbeh, Khutbah, Kol Nidre, Kyrie, Kyrie eleison, Lauds, Litany, Lord's, Loulat-ul-qadr, Lychnapsia, Ma'ariv, Ma(c)hzor, Mantis, Mat(t)ins, Mincha(h), Missal, Morning, Musaf, Novena, Opus dei, Orant, Orarium, Orison, Our Father, Paternoster, Patter, Petition, Phylactery, Placebo, Plea, Preces,

Proseucha, Proseuche, Puja, Requiem, Requiescat, Responses, Rogation, Rosary, Salat, Secret, Shema, Siddur, State, Stations of the Cross, Suffrage, Te igitur, Tenebrae, Terce, Triduum, Venite, Vesper, Vigils, Yajur-Veda, Yizkor

Preach(er) Ainger, Boanerges, Circuit rider, Dawah, Devil-dodger, Dominican, Donne, Ecclesiastes, Evangelist, Exhort, Gospeller, Graham, Holy Roller, Itinerant, Kerygma, Knox, Lecture, Local, Mar-text, Minister, Moody, → **MORALISE**, Patercove, Pontificate, Postillate, Predicant, Predicate, Predikant, Priest, Prophet, Pulpiteer, Rant, Revivalist, Sermonise, Soper, Spintext, Spurgeon, Teach, Televangelist

Preamble Introduction, Lead-in, Preface, Proem, Prologue

Prearrange(d) Book, Stitch up

Pre-Cambrian Torridonian

Precarious Dangerous, Knife edge, Parlous, Perilous, Risky, Touch and go, Trickle, Uncertain, Unsteady, Unsure

Precaution Care, Fail-safe, Guard, In case, Prophylaxis, Safeguard, Safety net

Precede(nce), Precedent Antedate, Example, Forego, Forerun, Head, Herald, Pas, Predate, Preface, Prepotent, Priority, Protocol, Zeroth

Precept(s) Adage, Canon, Commandment, Maxim, Mishna, Motto, Saw

Precession Larmor

Precinct(s) Ambit, Area, Banlieue, Close, Courtyard, District, Environs, Pedestrian, Peribolos, Region, Shopping, Temenos, Verge, Vihara

Precious Adored, Chary, Chichi, Costly, Dear, Dearbought, Ewe-lamb, La-di-da, Murr(h)a, Nice, Owre, Precise, Priceless, Prissy, Rare, Valuable

Precipice Bluff, Cliff, Crag, Krans, Kran(t)z, Sheer

Precipitate, Precipitation, Precipitous, Precipitator Abrupt, Accelerate, Catalyst, Cause, Deposit, Hailstone, Hasty, Headlong, Impetuous, Launch, Lees, Pellmell, Pitchfork, Rash, Sca(u)r, Sheer, Shoot, Sleet, Snowflake, Start, → **STEEP**, White

Précis Abstract, Aperçu, Epitome, Résumé, Summary

Precise(ly), Precisian, Precision Absolute, Accurate, Dry, Exact, Explicit, Fine-drawn, Literal, Minute, Nice(ty), Niminy-piminy, Overnice, Particular, Perfect, Pernickety, Plumb, Point-device, Prig, Prim, Punctilious, Razor, Sharpness, Spang, Specific, Starchy, Stringent, Succinct, Surgical, Tight, Very

Preclude Bar, Debar, Estop, Foreclose, Hinder, Impede, Prevent

Precocious(ness) Advanced, Bratpack, Forward, Madam, Premature, Protogyny

Preconception Ideating

Precursor Avant-courier, Forerunner, Harbinger

Predator(y) Carnivore, Eagle, Fox, Glede, Harpy-eagle, Honey badger, Jackal, Kestrel, Kite, Lycosa, Mantis, Marauder, Predacious, Prey, Puma, Skua, Tanrec, Tarantula, Tenrec, Trapper

Pre-dawn Antelucan, Ante lucem

Predecessor Ancestor, Forebear, Foregoer

Predestined Doomed, Fated, Tramway

Predetermine(d) Set

Predicament Box, Dilemma, Embarrassment, Embroglio, Hobble, Hole, In chancery, Jam, Pass, Peril, Pickle, Plight, Quandary, Scrape, Spot

Predict(ion), Predictable, Predictor Astrologer, Augur, Belomancy, Bet, Damn, Divination, Doomsayer, Doomster, Doomwatch, Ex ante, Far-seeing, Forecast, Foreordain, Foreread, Foresay, Foresee, Foreshadow, Foreshow, Forespeak, Foretell, Formulaic, Forsay, Futurist, Geomancy, Horoscope, Jeremiah, Nap, Necromancy, Portend, Presage, Previse, Prognosis, Project, Prophecy, Prophesy, Quant, Regular, Second-guess, Soothsayer, Spae

Predilection Fancy, Liking, Prejudice, Taste, Tendency

Predisposition Aptitude, Inclination, Parti-pris, Tendency

Predominate Abound, Govern, Overshadow, Prevail, Reign

Pre-eminence, Pre-eminent Arch, Foremost, Palm(ary), Paramount, Primacy,

Supreme, Topnotch, Unique

Pre-empt(ive) Enter

Preen Perk, Primp, Prink, Prune, Titivate

Prefab(ricated) Quonset, Terrapin®

Preface Avant-propos, Foreword, Herald, Intro, Preamble, Precede, Proem, Prolegomenon, Prolepsis, Usher

Prefect Haussmann, Pilate, Prepositor, Pr(a)eposter

Prefer(ence), Preferred Advance, Better, Choose, Discriminate, Druthers, Elect, Faard, Faurd, Favour, Imperial, Incline, Lean, Liquidity, Predilect(ion), Prefard, Priority, Proclivity, Promote, Rather, Select, Sooner, Stocks, Taste, Will

Prefix Eka, Introduce, Name

Pregnancy, Pregnant Big, Clucky, Cyesis, Due (to), Ectopic, Enceinte, Extrauterine, Fertile, F(o)etation, Gestation, Gravid(a), Great, Great-bellied, Heavy, Hysterical, In foal, In pig, In pup, Knocked-up, Molar, Phantom, Pseudocyesis, Pudding-club, Retirement, Stomack, Teem, Up the duff, Up the pole, Up the spout, Up the stick, With child

Prehistoric Ancient, Azilian, Beaker Folk, Boskop, Brontosaurus, Cambrian, Clovis, Cro-Magnon, Eocene, Folsom, Mound Builder, Ogygian, Primeval, Primitive, Pteranodon, Pterodactyl(e), Pterosaur, Saurian, Sinanthropus, Stonehenge, Titanis, Titanosaurus, Trilith(on)

Prejudice(d) Ageism, Bias, Bigotry, Derry, Discrimination, Down, Illiberal, Impede, Inequity, Injure, Insular, Intolerance, Partiality, Parti pris, Preoccupy, Prepossession, Racism, Sexism, Slant, Unfair

Prelate Archiepiscopal, Cardinal, Churchman, Exarch, Monsignor, Odo, Priest

Preliminary Curtain-raiser, Draft, Exploration, Heat, Initial, Introductory, Precursory, Preparatory, Previous, Prodrome, Proem, Prolusion, Propaedeutic, Rough, Title-sheet

Prelude Entrée, Forerunner, Intrada, Overture, Proem(ial), Ritornell(e), Ritornello, Verset

Premature Early, Precocious, Pre(e)mie, Premy, Pre term, Previous, Slink, Untimely, Untimeous

Premedication Atropia

Premeditate Anticipate, Foresee, Plan

Premier Chief, Leader, Main, PM, → **PRIME MINISTER**, Tojo, Top drawer

Premise(s) Assumption, Datum, Epicheirema, Ground, Hypothesis, Inference, Lemma, Licensed, Major, Postulate, Property, Proposition, Reason, Syllogism, Unlicensed

Premium Ap, Bond, Bonus, Discount, Grassum, Pm, Reward, Scarce, Share

Premonition Hunch, Omen, Presentiment, Prodromal, Specter, Spectre, Warning

Preoccupation, Preoccupied, Preoccupy Absorb, Abstracted, Distrait, Engross, Hang-up, Intent, Obsess, Self-centred, Thing

Prepaid Pro-forma, Sae

Prepare(d), Preparation Address, À la, Arrange, Attire, Boun, Bowne, Brilliantine, Busk, Calver, Cock, Concoct, Cook, Cooper, Countdown, Decoct, Did, Do, Dress, Edit, Extract, Forearm, Game, Gear (up), Groom, Ground, Groundwork, Inspan, Key, Lay, Legwork, Lotion, Measure, Mobilise, Organise, Parasceve, Paste up, Pomade, Preliminary, Prime, Procinct, Prothesis, Provide, Psych, → **READY**, Redact, Rehearsal, Ripe, Rustle up, Set, Spadework, Stand-to, Suborn, Train, Trim, Truss, Type, Up to, Warm-up, Whip up, Yare

▷ **Prepare(d)** *may indicate* an anagram

Preponderance, Preponderant, Preponderate Important, Majority, Outweigh, Paramount, Prevalence, Sway

Preposition Lemma, Premise

Prepossessing, Prepossession Attractive, Fetching, Predilection, Winsome

Preposterous Absurd, Chimeric, Foolish, Grotesque, Rich, Tall order, Unreasonable

▷ **Preposterous** *may indicate* a word reversed

Pre-Raphaelite Rossetti, Waterhouse

Prerequisite Condition, Essential, Necessity, Sine qua non

Prerogative Faculty, Franchise, Liberty, Privilege, Right, Royal

Presage Abode, Foresight, Omen, Portend, Presentiment, Prophesy

Presbyter(ian) Berean, Blue, Cameronian, Classic, Classis, Covenanter, Elder, Knox, Macmillanite, Moderator, Sacrarium, Seceder, Secesher, Secession Church, Wee Free, Whig(gamore)

Prescient Clairvoyant, Fly

Prescribe, Prescription Appoint, Assign, Dictate, Enjoin, Impose, Negative, Ordain, Positive, Rule, Scrip, Set

Prescription Cipher, Decree, Direction, Formula, Medicine, Placebo, R, Rec, Receipt, Ritual, Specific

Presence Aspect, Bearing, Closeness, Company, Debut, Face, Hereness, Mien, Real, Shechinah, Shekinah, Spirit

Present(ation), Presented, Presenter, Presently Ad sum, Advowson, Anchorman, Anon, Assists, Autocutie, Award, Befaba, Bestow, Bonsela, Boon, Bounty, Box, Breech, By, By and by, Cadeau, Congiary, Coram, Current, Debut, Dee-jay, Demo, Deodate, DJ, Donate, Dotal, Douceur, Dower, Emcee, Endew, Endow, Endue, Enow, Étrenne, Exhibit, Existent, Exposition, Fairing, Feature, Format, Free-loader, Front-man, Gie, → **GIFT**, Give, Going, Grant, Gratuity, Hand, Here, Historical, Hodiernal, Host, Immediate, Inbuilt, Inst, Introduce, Jock(ey), Largess(e), Linkman, MC, Mod, Nonce, Now, Nuzzer, Offering, On hand, Porrect, Potlach, Pr, Prevailing, Produce, Proffer, Pro-tem, Put, Render, Serve-up, Show, Slice, Stage, Study, Submit, The now, There, Tip, Today, Trojan horse, Vee-jay, Window dressing, Xenium, Yeven

Preserve(d), Preservative, Preserver Bottle, Burnettize, Can, Chill, Chow-chow, Cocoon, Confect, Confiture, Corn, Creosote, Cure, Dehydrate, Dry, Eisel, Embalm, Enshield, Enshrine, Fixative, Formaldehyde, Formalin, Freeze, Guard, Hain, Hesperides, Index link, Jam, Jerk, Keep, Kinin, Kipper, Konfyt, Kyanise, Lay up, Life, Lifebelt, → **MAINTAIN**, Marmalade, Mothball, Mummify, On ice, Paraben, Pectin, Peculiar, Piccalilli, Pickle, Pot, Powellise, Quince, Quinoline, Salt(petre), Salve, Saut, Season, Souse, Store, Stratify, Stuff, Tanalith, Tanalized, Tar, Tin, Vinegar, Waterglass

Preshrunk Sanforized®

Preside(nt) Abe, Adams, Arthur, Ataturk, Banda, Botha, Buchanan, Bush, Carter, Chair, Chief Barker, Childers, Chirac, Cleveland, Clinton, Coolidge, Coty, Dean, De Gaulle, Director, Eisenhower, Fillmore, Ford, Garfield, Grand Pensionary, Grant, Harding, Harrison, Hayes, Hoover, Ike, Jackson, Jefferson, Johnson, Kennedy, Kruger, Lead, Lincoln, Madison, Mitterand, Moderator, Monroe, Mugabe, Nixon, Old Hickory, P, Peron, Polk, Pompidou, Pr(a)eses, Prexy, Reagan, Roosevelt, Sa(a)dat, Speaker, Superintendent, Supervisor, Taft, Taylor, Tito, Truman, Tyler, Van Buren, Vasquez, Veep, Washington, Wilson

Press(ed), Pressing, Pressure Acute, Aldine, Armoire, Atmospheric, Bar, Bench, Blackmail, Blood, Bramah, Button, Cabinet, Chivvy, Cider, Clarendon, Click, Closet, Clothes, Coerce, Compact, Compression, Copying, Cram, Crease, Crimp, Critical, Crowd, Crush, Cupboard, Cylinder, Dragoon, Drill, Dun, Durable, Duress, Duresse, Enforcement, Enslave, Exigent, Filter, Flat-bed, Fleet St, Fluid, Fly, Folding, Force, Fourth estate, Full-court, Goad, Greenmail, Gutter, Hasten, Head, Heat, Herd, Hie, High, Hug, Hurry, Hustle, Hydraulic, Hydrostatic, Impact, Important, Importune, Inarm, Intense, Iron, Isobar, Jam, Jostle, Knead, Leverage, Lie, Lobby, Low, Mangle, Megabar, Microbar, Mill, Minerva, Newspapers, Obligate, Oil, Onus, Osmotic, PA, Partial, Pascal, Peer, Permanent, Persist, Piezo-, Ply, Prease, Printing, Private, Psi, Pump, → **PUSH**, Racket, Ram, Ratpack, Record, Recruit, Reportage, Reporter, Ridge, Roll, Root, Rotary, Rounce, Rub, Rush, Samizdat, Sandwich, Screw, Scrooge, Scrouge, Scrowdge, Scrum, Serr(e), Sit, Speed, Spur, Squash, Squeeze, Stanhope, Static, Stop, Strain(t), Stress, Tension, Thlipsis, Threap, Three-line-whip, Threep, Throng, Throttle, Thrutch, Torr, Tourniquet, Turgor, → **URGE**, Urgence, Urgency, Vanity, Vapour, Vice, Waid(e), Wardrobe, Weight, Wine, Wring, Yellow

Press agent Flack, Spin doctor

Press-gang Crimp, Force, Impress, Shanghai

Pressman Ed, Journalist, Journo, PRO, Reporter, Twicer

Prestidigitate(r) Conjure, Juggle, Legerdemain, Magician, Palm

Prestige, Prestigious Asma, Cachet, Credit, Distinguished, Fame, Influence, Izzat, Kudos, Mana, Notable, Status

Presume, Presumably, Presumption, Presumptuous Allege, Arrogant, Audacity, Believe, Bold, Brass, Cocksure, Cocky, Doubtless, → **EXPECT**, Familiar, Forward, Gall, Impertinent, Insolent, Liberty, Outrecuidance, Overweening, Pert, Probably, Put upon, Suppose, Uppish, Upstart, Whipper-snapper

Pretence, Pretend(er), Pretext Act, Affect(ation), Afflict, Assume, Blind, Bluff, Charade, Charlatan, Claim, Claimant, Cover, Cram, Dauber(y), Dissemble, Dissimulate, Dive, Excuse, False, Feign, Feint, Gondolier, Guise, Hokum, Humbug, Hypocrisy, Impersonation, Impostor, Jactitation, Kid(stakes), Lambert Simnel, Let-on, Make-believe, Malinger, Masquerade, Obreption, Old, Parolles, Perkin Warbeck, Plea, Pose, Pretension, Profess, Pseud(o), Quack, Sham, Simulate, Stale, Stalking-horse, Subterfuge, Suppose, Swanking, Warbeck, Would-be, Young

Pretentious(ness), Pretension Arty, Bombast, Chi-chi, Fantoosh, Fustian, Gaudy, Grandiose, High-falutin(g), Kitsch, La-di-da, Orotund, Ostentatious, Overblown, Paraf(f)le, Pompous, Ponc(e)y, Pseud(o), Sciolism, Showy, Snob, Snobbish, Squirt, Tat, Tattie-peelin, Tinhorn, Toffee-nosed, Uppity, Upstart, Vulgar, Wanky, Whippersnapper

Pretty Attractive, Becoming, Bobby-dazzler, Chocolate-box, Comely, Cute, Dear, Decorate, Dish, Elegant, Fair(ish), Fairway, Inconie, Incony, Keepsaky, Looker, Moderately, Pass, Peach, Personable, Picturesque, Primp, Pulchritudinous, Purty, Quite, Sweet, Twee, Winsome

Prevail(ing) Dominate, Endure, Go, Induce, Outweigh, Persist, Persuade, Predominant, Preponderate, Reign, Ring, Triumph, Victor, Win

Prevalent Catholic, Common, Dominant, Endemic, Epidemic, Obtaining, Rife, Set in, Widespread

Prevaricate, Prevarication Equivocate, Hedge, Lie, Runaround, Stall, Whiffle, Whittie-whattie

Prevent(ion), Prevent(at)ive Avert, Bar, Block, Daidzein, Debar, Deter, Disallow, Disenable, Dissuade, Embar, Estop, Foreclose, Forfend, Hamper, Help, Hinder, Hold back, Impound, Inhibit, Keep, Let, Nobble, Obstruct, Obturation, Obviate, Preclude, Prophylactic, Save, Sideline, Stop, Theriac, Thwart, Trammel

Preview Foretaste, Sneak, Taster, Trailer, Vernissage

Previous(ly) Afore, Already, Before, Earlier, Ere(-now), Fore, Foreran, Former, Hitherto, Once, Prior, Whilom

Prey Booty, Currie, Curry, Feed, Kill, Pelt, Plunder, Predate, Proul, Prowl, Quarry, Raven, Ravin(e), Soyle, Spreagh, Victim

Price(d), Pricing, Price-raising Appraise, Asking, Assess, Bride, Charge, Consequence, Contango, → **COST**, Cost-plus, Dearth, Due, Evens, Exercise, Expense, Factory-gate, Fee, Fiars, Hammer, Hire, Intervention, Issue, Limit, List, Lobola, Loco, Market, Mark up, Offer, Packet, Perverse, Predatory, Prestige, Quotation, Quote, Rack, Ransom, Rate, Regrate, Reserve, Sale, Selling, Shadow, Song, Spot, Starting, Street value, Striking, Subscription, Toll, Trade, Unit, Upset, Valorise, Value, Vincent, Weregild, Wergeld, Wergild, Worth, Yardage

Priceless Comic, Invaluable, Killing, Unique

Prick(ed), Prickle, Prickly Acanaceous, Acanthus, Accloy, Argemone, Arrect, Bearded, Brakier, Bramble, Brog, Bunya, Cactus, Cloy, Cnicus, Echinate, Goad, Gore, Gorse, Hedgehog, Hedgepig, Impel, Inject, Jab, Jag, Jaggy, Jook, Juk, Kali, Penis, Perse, Pierce, Prod, Prog, Puncture, Rowel, Rubus, Ruellia, Seta, Setose, Smart, Spicula, Spinate, Stab, Star-thistle, Stimulus, Sting, Tattoo, Tatu, Teasel, Thistle, Thorn, Tingle, Urge

Prickly heat Miliaria
Prickly-pear Opuntia, Tuna
Pride Bombast, Brag, Conceit, Elation, Esprit de corps, Glory, Hauteur, Hubris, Inordinate, Lions, London, Machismo, Plume, Preen, Purge, Triumphalism, Vainglory, Vanity
Priest(ess), Priests Aaron, Abaris, Abbess, Abbot, Ananias, Annas, Archimandrite, Bacchae, Bacchantes, Baptes, Becket, Bonze, Brahmin, Caiaphas, Cardinal, Celebrant, Clergyman, Cleric, Cohen, Concelebrant, Corybant(es), Curé, Dalai Lama, Druid, Eli, Elisha, Exorcist, Father, Fetial, Flamen, Fr, Habacuc, Habakkuk, Hero, Hieratic, Hierophant, High, H(o)ungan, Io, Jethro, John, Kohen, Lack-Latin, Lama, Laocoon, Lazarist, Levite, Lucumo, Mage, Magus, Mallet, Mambo, Marabout, Mass, Mess, Metropolitan, Minister, Missionary, Monsignor, Mufti, Norma, Oratorian, Ordinand, P, Padre, Papa, Parish, Parson, Pastor, Patercove, Patrico, Pawaw, Père, Pontifex, Pontiff, Pope, Pope's knight, Powwow, Pr, Preacher, Prelate, Presbyter, Prior(ess), Pujari, Pythia, Pythoness, Rabbi, Rebbe, Rector, Rev, Sacerdotal, Salian, Savonarola, Seminarian, Shaman, Shaveling, Sir John Lack-Latin, Sky pilot, Spoiled, Tohunga, Turbulent, Vicar, Vivaldi, Worker, Zadok, Zymite
Prig(gish) Dandy, Fop, Humbug, Nimmer, Pilfer, Prim, Prude, Puritan
Prim Demure, Governessy, Mun, Neat, Old-maidish, Perjink, Preceese, Precise, Proper, Starchy
Primacy, Primate Angwantibo, Ape, Australopithecus, Aye-aye, Bandar, Bigfoot, Biped, Bishop, Bush baby, Cardinal, Catar(r)hine, Colobus, Ebor, Gibbon, Hanuman, Hominid, Jackanapes, King Kong, Lemur, Loris, Macaque, Magot, Mammal, Marmoset, → **MONKEY**, Orang, Pongid, Potto, Prosimian, Protohuman, Quadruman, Ramapithecus, Rhesus, Sifaka, Slender loris, Tarsier, Wanderoo, Zinjanthropus
Prima donna Diva, Patti, Star
Prime(r), Primary, Priming Arm, Basic, Bloom, Cardinal, Charging, Chief, Choice, Claircolle, Clearcole, Clerecole, Closed, Detonator, Direct, Donat, Donet, Election, Enarm, Fang, First, Flower, Heyday, Mature, Open, Original, Paint, Paramount, Peak, Radical, Remex, Sell-by-date, Supreme, Thirteen, Tip-top, Totient, Totitive, Valuable, Windac, Windas, Ylem
Prim(a)eval Ancient, Prehistoric, Primitive
Prime Minister Aberdeen, Asquith, Attlee, Baldwin, Balfour, Begin, Bute, Callaghan, Canning, Chamberlain, Chatham, Dewan, Diefenbaker, Disraeli, Diwan, Eden, Gladstone, Grafton, Grand Vizier, Grey, Home, Iron Duke, Leaderene, Liverpool, Lloyd George, Macdonald, Macmillan, Major, North, Number Ten, Palmerston, Peel, Perceval, Pitt, PM, Premier, Shastri, Tanaiste, Taoiseach, Thatcher, Trudeau, Walpole, Wilson, Winston
Primitive Aborigine, Amoeba, Antediluvian, Arabic, Archaic, Atavistic, Barbaric, Caveman, Crude, Early, Eozoon, Evolué, Fundamental, Hunter-gatherer, Medi(a)eval, Naive, Neanderthal, Neolithic, Oidia, Old, Persian, Prim(a)eval, Primordial, Pro, Prothyl(e), Protomorphic, Protyl(e), Radical, Rudimentary, Savage, Subman, Turkish, Uncivilised, Ur
Primordial Blastema, Fundamental, Original
Primrose, Primula Auricula, Bear's ear, Bird's eye, Cape, Evening, League, Oenothera, Onagra, Ox-lip, Pa(i)gle, Rosebery, Vicar, Yellow
Prince(ly) Ahmed, Albert, Ameer, Amir, Amphitryon, Anchises, Arjuna, Atheling, Barmecide, Black, Cadmus, Caliph, Chagan, Charming, Crown, Czarevich, Donalbain, Elector, Emir, Equerry, Eugene, Florizel, Fortinbras, Gaekwar, Ganymede, Gospodar, Guicowar, Hal, Hamlet, Highness, Hospodar, Huzoor, Igor, Inca, Infante, Jason, Khan, Ksar, Lavish, Lucumo, Maharaja, Margrave, Meleager, Merchant, Mir, Mirza, Nawab, Nizam, Noble, Orange, Otto, P, Pantagruel, Paris, Pendragon, Pirithous, Porphyrogenite, Potentate, Rainier, Rajah, Rana, Ras, Rasselas, Ratoo, Ratu, Regal, RH, Rudolph, Rupert, Serene, Sharif, Shereef, Sherif, Siegfried, Student, Tengku, Tereus, Tsar(evich), Tunku, Upper Roger

Princess Anastasia, Andromache, Andromeda, Anne, Ariadne, Begum, Creusa, Czarevna, Czarista, Danae, Di(ana), Electra, Electress, Eudocia, Europa, Grace, Helle, Hermione, Hesione, Ida, Imogen, Infanta, Isabella, Iseult, Isolde, Jezebel, Maharanee, Maharani, Medea, Palatine, Philomela, Pocahontas, Procne, Rani, Regan, Sadie, Sara(h), Tou Wan, Tsarevna, Tsarista, Turandot, Yseult

Principal Arch, Capital, Central, → CHIEF, Decuman, Especial, First, Foremost, Grand, Head, Headmaster, Leading, Lion's share, Main(stay), Major, Mass, Mistress, Protagonist, Ringleader, Special, Staple, Star, Top banana

Principality Andorra, Flanders, Liechtenstein, Moldavia, Moldova, Monaco, Muscovy, Orange, Wal(l)achia, Wales

Principle(s), Principled Accelerator, Animistic, Anthropic, Archimedes, Aufbau, Axiom, Basis, Bernouilli, Brocard, Canon, Carnot, Code, Contradiction, Correspondence, Cosmological, Criterion, Cui bono, Cy pres, D'Alembert's, Doctrine, Dogma, Element, Entelechy, Equivalence, Essential, Estoppel, Exclusion, Fermat's, First, Fourier, Gause's, Geist, Generale, Germ, Greatest happiness, Ground rule, Guideline, Hard line, Heisenberg uncertainty, Honourable, Huygen's, Ideal, Indeterminacy, Key, Law, Least time, Le Chatelier's, Lights, Logos, Methodology, Modus, Object soul, Occam's razor, Organon, Ormazd, Ormuzd, Pauli-exclusion, Peter, Plank, Platform, Pleasure, Precautionary, Precept, Prescript, Psyche, Purseyism, Rationale, Reality, Reason, Reciprocity, Relativity, Remonstrance, Right-thinking, Rudiment, Rule, Sakti, Sanction, Scrupulous, Seed, Shakti, Spirit, Summum bonum, Tenet, Theorem, Ticket, Uncertainty, Uti possidetis, Verification, Vital, Weismannism, Word, Yang, Yin

Prink Beautify, Bedeck, Dress

Print(er), Printing A la poupée, Baskerville, Batik, Benday, Bromide, Calotype, Caveman, Caxton, Chain, Chapel, Chromo, Cibachrome, Cicero, Collotype, Compositor, Contact, Copperplate, Counter, Creed, Cyclostyle, Dab, Dot matrix, Duotone, Electrostatic, Electrothermal, Electrotint, Electrotype, Elzevir, Engrave, Etching, Ferrotype, Film set, Fine, Flexography, Font, Gravure, Gurmukhi, Gutenberg, Half-tone, Hard copy, Hectograph, Heliotype, HMSO, Image, Impact, Impress, Incunabula, India, Ink-jet, Intaglio, Italic, Jobbing, Laser, Letterpress, Letterset, Line, Line-engraving, Lino-cut, Lithograph, Logotype, Lower-case, Matrix, Metallographer, Mezzotint, Mimeograph®, Monotype®, Moon, Non-impact, Off-line, Offset, Offset litho, Old-face, Oleo, Oleograph, Opaline, Perfector, Perfect proof, Phototype, Plate, Platinotype, Positive, Press, Process, Publish, Release, Remarque, Report, Reproduction, Retroussage, Reverse, Rotogravure, Samizdat, Screen, Serigraph, Ship, Shout, Silk-screen, Small, Smoot, Splash, Spore, Stamp, Stenochrome, Stereotype, Stonehand, Strike, Thermal, Three-colour, Thumb, Thumb mark, Trichromatic, Typesetter, Typewriter, Typography, Typothetae, Whorl, Woodburytype, Woodcut, Xerography, Xylograph, Zincograph

Printing-press Rounce

Print out Hard copy

Prior(ity) Abbot, Afore, Antecedent, Anterior, Aperture, Earlier, Former, Grand, Hitherto, Monk, Overslaugh, Pre-, Precedence, Prefard, Preference, Previous, Privilege, Shutter, Triage, Until

▶ **Prise** *see* PRIZE(S)

Prism(s), Prismatic Catadioptric, Iriscope, Nicol, Periaktos, Rhombohedron, Spectrum, Teinoscope, Wollaston

Prison Albany, Alcatraz, Bagnio, Barracoon, Bastille, Belmarsh, Big house, Bin, Bird, Boob, Bridewell, Brig, Brixton, Bullpen, Cage, Can, Carceral, Cell, Chillon, Chok(e)y, Clink, Club, College, Confine, Cooler, Coop, Counter, Dartmoor, Dispersal, Dungeon, Durance, Encage, Fleet, Fotheringhay, Gaol, Glass-house, Guardhouse, Guardroom, Gulag, Hokey, Holloway, Hoos(e)gow, Hulk(s), Internment, → JAIL, Jug, Kitty, Labour camp, Limbo, Little-ease, Lob's pound, Lock-up, Logs, Lumber, Marshalsea, Massymore, Mattamore, Maze, Newgate, Nick, Oflag, On ice, Open, Panopticon, Parkhurst, Pen, Penitentiary,

Pentonville, Pit, Pok(e)y, Porridge, Pound, Princetown, Quad, Quod, Rasp-house, Reformatory, Roundhouse, Scrubs, Shop, Sing-Sing, Slammer, Spandau, Stalag, State, Stir, Strangeways, Supermax, The Leads, Tol(l)booth, Tower, Tronk, Wandsworth, Wormwood Scrubs

Prisoner Canary-bird, Captive, Collegian, Collegiate, Con(vict), Detainee, Detenu, Hostage, Inmate, Internee, Jailbird, Lag, Lifer, Parolee, Passman, Political, POW, Rule 43, Trustee, Trusty, Yardbird, Zek

Pristine Fire-new, Fresh, New, Original, Unmarked, Unspoiled

Private(ly) Ain, Apart, Aside, Atkins, Auricular, Buccaneer, Byroom, Clandestine, Close, Closet, Conclave, Confidential, Enisle(d), Esoteric, Homefelt, Hush-hush, In camera, Individual, Inmost, Inner, Intimate, Inward, Non-com, Non-governmental, Own, Personal, Piou-piou, Poilu, Postern, Proprietary, Pte, Rank(er), Retired, Sanctum, Sapper, Secluded, Secret, Sequestered, Several, Single soldier, → **SOLDIER**, Squaddie, Sub rosa, Tommy, Under the rose

Privateer(s) Buccaneer, Corsair, Freebooter, Marque(s), Pirate

Privation Hardship, Penury, Want

Privilege(d) Birthright, Blest, Charter, Curule, Enviable, Exempt, Favour, Franchise, Freedom, Indulgence, Insider, Liberty, Mozarab, Nomenklatura, Octroi, Palatine, Parliamentary, Patent, Prerogative, Pryse, Regale, Regalia, Right, Sac, Sloane

Privy Apprised, Can, Closet, In on, Intimate, Jakes, John, Loo, Necessary, Reredorter, Secret, Sedge, Siege

Prize(s), Prizewinner, Prized Acquest, Apple, Archibald, Assess, Award, Best, Booby, Booker, Bravie, Bronze, Capture, Champion, Cherish, Consolation, Creach, Cup, Dux, Efforce, → **ESTEEM**, Force, Garland, Gold, Goncourt, Grice, Honour, Jackpot, Jemmy, Lever, Lot, Man Booker, Money, Nobel, Palm, Pearl, Pewter, Pie, Plum, Plunder, Pot, Premium, Prix Goncourt, Pulitzer, Purse, Ram, Reprisal, → **REWARD**, Rollover, Rosette, Scalp, Ship, Silver, Spreaghery, Sprechery, Stakes, Sweepstake, Taonga, Tern, Treasure, Trophy, Turner, Value, Win, Wooden spoon

Pro Aye, Coach, For, Harlot, Moll, Paid, Tramp, Yea, Yes

▶ **Pro** *see* **PROSTITUTE**

Probable, Probability Apparent, Belike, Classical, Conditional, Ergodic, Feasible, Likely, Marginal, Mathematical, Possible, Posterior, Prior, Proball, Verisimilar

Probation(er) Cadet, Novice, Novitiate, Stibbler, Test, Trainee, Trial

Probe Antenna, Bore, Bougie, Canopus, Cassini, Corot, Delve, Dredge, Explore, Fathom, Feeler, Fossick, Galileo, Gene(tic), Giotto, Inquire, Investigate, Magellan, Mariner, Mars Surveyor, Pelican, Pioneer, Poke, Pump, Ranger, → **SEARCH**, Seeker, Sonde, Sound, Space, Stardust, Stylet, Tent, Thrust, Tracer, Venera

Probity Honour, Integrity, Justice

Problem(s), Problematic Acrostic, BO, Boyg, Brainteaser, Business, Can of worms, Catch, Crisis, Crux, Difficulty, Dilemma, Egma, Enigma, Facer, Glitch, Handful, Hang-up, Headache, Hiccup, Hitch, How d'ye do, Hurdle, Indaba, Issue, Knot(ty), Koan, Mind-body, Miniature, Musive, Net, Nuisance, Obstacle, Pons asinorum, Poser, Predicament, Quandary, Question, Re, Rebus, Retractor, Riddle, Rider, Snag, Sorites, Sum, Teaser, Teething, Thing, Thorny, Tickler, Toughie, Trilemma, Trouble, Tsuris, Weed, Yips

Problem-solving Synectics

Proboscis Haustellum, Promuscis, Snout, Trunk

Proceed(s), Proceeding, Procedure Acta, Afoot, Algorithm, Assets, Continue, Course, Derive, Do, Drill, Emanate, Fand, Flow, Fond, Goes, Haul, Issue, Machinery, March, Mechanics, Method, Mine, MO, Modal, Move, On (course), Paracentesis, Pass, Point of order, Practice, Praxis, Process, Profit, Protocol, Punctilio, Pursue, Put, Rake, Return, Rigmarole, Rite, Ritual, Routine, Sap, Steps, Subroutine, System, Take, Tootle, Use, Yead(s), Yede, Yeed

Process(ing), Procession, Processor Acromion, Action, Additive, Ala, Ambarvalia, Anger, Axon, Ben Day, Bessemer, Bosch, Calcination, Castner, Catalysis, Cavalcade,

Cibation, Coction, Concoction, Congelation, Conjunction, Corso, Cortège, Cyanide, Demo, Diagonal, Dissolution, Double, Exaltation, Fermentation, Frack(ing), Front-end, Haber(-Bosch), Handle, Managing, Markov, Method, Moharram, Mond, Motorcade, Muharram, Multiple pounding, Multiplication, Odontoid, Open hearth, -osis, Pageant, Parade, Parallel, Paseo, Photosynthesis, Pipeline, Planar, Pomp, Primary, Projection, Pterygoid, Puddling, Pultrusion, Purex, Putrefaction, Recycle, Ritual, Screen, Secondary, Separation, Series, Silkscreen, Single, Skimmington, Solvay, Speciation, Spinous, Sterygoid, String, Sublimation, Subtractive, Thermite, Thought, Tie and dye, Torchlight, Train, Transaction, Transverse, Treat, Trial, Turn(a)round, Unit, Vermiform, Xiphoid, Zygomatic

Proclaim, Proclamation Announce, Annunciate, Ban, Blaze, Blazon, Boast, Broadsheet, Cry, Edict, Enounce, Enunciate, Herald, Indiction, Kerygma, Oyez, Preconise, Predicate, Profess, Publish, Ring, Shout, Trumpet, Ukase

Proconsul Ape, Hominid

Procrastinate, Procrastinating, Procrastinator Cunctator, Defer, Delay, Dilatory, Dilly-dally, Linger, Pettifog, Postpone, Shelve, Temporise, Vacillate

Procreate Beget, Engender, Generate, Initiate

Procrustean Conformity, Stretcher

Proctor Agent, King's, Monitor, Prog, Proggins, Proxy, Queen's

Procurator, Procure(r) Achieve, Acquire, Aunt, Crimp, Earn, Get, Induce, Naunt, Obtain, Pander, Pilate, Pimp, Sort, Suborn

Prod Cattle, Egg, Goad, Impel, Jab, Job, Jog, Nudge, Poke, Pote, Powter

Prodigal Costly, Lavish, Profligate, Scattergood, Spendall, Unthrift, Wanton, Wasteful, Waster

Prodigious, Prodigy Abnormal, Amazing, Huge, Immense, Infant, Monster, Monument, Mozart, Phenomenal, Portentous, Tremendous, Wonder, Wonderwork, Wunderkind

Produce(r), Producing Afford, Bear, Beget, Breed, Cause, Create, Crop, Disney, D'oyly Carte, Dramaturg, Ean, Edit, Effect, Engender, Evoke, Exhibit, Extend, Fabricate, Fruit, Generate, Get, Giulini, Goldwyn, Grow, Home-grown, Impresario, Ingenerate, Issue, Kind, Make, Offspring, Onstream, Originate, Output, Propage, Propound, Puttnam, Raise, Roach, Selznick, Sloganeer, Son, Spawn, Spielberg, Stage, Supply, Teem, Throw, Tree, Trot out, Upcome, Wares, Whelp, Yield, Ziegfeld

▷ **Produces** *may indicate* an anagram

Product(ion), Productive(ness), Productivity Actualities, Apport, Artefact, Ashtareth, Ashtaroth, Astarte, Autogeny, Bore, Cartesian, Coefficient, Commodity, Cross, Depside, Dot, Drama, Effectual, End, Factorial, Fecund, Fertile, Fruit, Genesis, Global, Handiwork, Harvest, Inner, Line, Net domestic, Net national, Output, Outturn, Pair, Partial, Power(house), Primary, Profilic, Result, Rich, Scalar, Secondary, Set, Show, Speiss, Substitution, Uberous, Uberty, Vector, Waste, Work, Yield

▷ **Production** *may indicate* an anagram

Proem Foreword, Overture, Pre, Preface

Profane, Profanation, Profanity Blaspheming, Coarse, Coprolalia, Desecrate, Impious, Irreverent, Sacrilege, Unholy, Violate

Profess(ed), Professor Absent-minded, Academic, Adjoint, Admit, Artist, Aspro, Asset, Assistant, Associate, Avow, Challenger, Claim, Declare, Disney, Emeritus, Full, Higgins, Hodja, Kho(d)ja, Know-all, Ostensible, Own, Practise, Pundit, Regent, Regius, RP, STP, Visiting

Profession(al) Admission, Assurance, Avowal, Buppy, Business, Career, Creed, Expert, Métier, Practice, Practitioner, Pretence, Pursuit, Regular, Salaried, Skilled, Trade, Vocation, Yuppie

Proffer Give, Present, Proposition, Tender

Proficiency, Proficient Able, Adept, Alert, Dan, Expert, Forte, Past master, Practised, Skill, Technique

Profile Analysis, Contour, Cross, Half-cheek, Half-face, High, Long, Loral, Low, Market, Outline, Silhouette, Sketch, Statant, T(h)alweg, Vignette

Profit(able), Profiteer, Profits Advantage, Arbitrage, Asset, Avail, Benefit, Bestead, Boon, Boot, Bunce, Cash cow, Cere, Clear, Divi(dend), Earn, Economic, Edge, Emblements, Emoluments, Exploit, Extortionist, Fat, Gain, Gelt, Graft, Gravy, Grist, Gross, Income, Increase, Increment, Issue, Jobbery, Juicy, Landshark, Leech, Lucrative, Makings, Margin, Melon, Mesne, Milch cow, Mileage, Moneymaker, Negative, Net, Overcharge, Pay(ing), Perk, Pickings, Preacquisition, Productive, Quids in, Rake-off, Return, Reward, Royalty, Scalp, Spoils, Tout, Use, Usufruct, Utile, Utility, Vail

Profligate Corinthian, Corrupt, Degenerate, Dissolute, Extravagant, Lech(er), Libertine, Lorel, Losel(l), Oatmeal, Rakehell, Reprobate, Roué, Spend-all, Spendthrift, Unprincipled, Wastrel

Profound Altum, Bottomless, Complete, Deep, Intense, Recondite

Profuse, Profusion Abounding, Abundant, Copious, Excess, Free, Galore, Lavish, Liberal, Lush, Quantity, Rank, Rich, Two-a-penny

Progenitor, Progenitrix Ancestor, Ma, Predecessor, Sire, Stock

Progeny Burd, Children, Descendants, Fruit, Issue, Offspring, Seed

Prognosis Forecast, Prediction

Prognosticate, Prognostication Augur, Foretell, Omen, Predict, Presage, Prophesy

▶ **Program(ming), Programming language, Programmer** *see* COMPUTER PROGRAMS

Programme(s) Agenda, Broadcast, Card, Chat show, Code, Community, Corrida, Countdown, Docudrama, Documentary, Docusoap, Docutainment, Double-header, Dramedy, Entitlement, Est, Event, Faction, Feature, Fly-on-the-wall, Format, Infotainment, Linear, Medicaid, Mockumentary, Neurolinguistic, Newscast, Newsreel, PDL, Phone-in, Pilot, Plan, Playbill, Prank, Race card, Radiothon, RECHAR, Regimen, Report, Schedule, Scheme, Sepmag, Serial, Shockumentary, Show, Simulcast, Sitcom, Sked, Soap, Software, Sportscast, Sustaining, Syllabus, System, Telecast, Teleplay, Telethon, Timetable, Twelve step, Webcast, YPO

Progress(ive), Progression → ADVANCE, Afoot, Arithmetic, Arpeggio, Avant garde, Course, Endosmometric, Fabian, Flow, Forge, Forward, Forward-looking, Gain, Geometric, Get along, Go, Growth, Harmonic, Headway, Incede, Knight's, Left, Liberal, Move, Onwards, Paraphonia, Periegesis, Pilgrim's, Prosper, Rack, Radical, Rake's, Reformer, Roll, Run, Sequence, Series, Step, Stepping stone, Vaunce, Way, Yead, Yede, Yeed

Prohibit(ed), Prohibition(ist) Ban, Block, Debar, Dry, Embargo, Enjoin, Estop, Forbid, Hinder, Index, Injunct, Interdict, Noli-me-tangere, Off-limits, Prevent, Pussyfoot, Rahui, Suppress, Taboo, Tabu, Verboten, Veto

Project(ile), Projecting, Projection, Projector Aim, Ammo, Antitragus, Assignment, Astral, Astrut, Axonometric, Azimuthal, Ball, Ballistic, Beetle, Bullet, Butt, Buttress, Cam, Canopy, Carina, Cast, Catapult, Channel, Cinerama®, Cog, Conceive, Condyle, Conic, Conical, Console, Corbel, Coving, Cremaster, Crossette, Cutwater, Dendron, Denticle, Diascope, Discus, Ear, Eaves, Echinus, Elance, Enterprise, Episcope, Excrescence, Exsert, Extrapolate, Extrude, Fet(ter)lock, Flange, Gair, Gore, Guess, Halter(e), Hangover, Helicity, Hoe, Homolosine, Housing, Human genome, Hurtle, Inion, Jut, Kern, Kinetoscope, Knob, Ledge, Lobe, Lug, Magic lantern, Malleolus, Manhattan, Map, Mercator, Mitraille, Mohole, Mollweide, Mucro, Mutule, Nab, Nose, Nunatak(er), Oblique, Olecranon, Opaque, Orillion, Orthogonal, Orthographic, Outcrop, Outjet, Outjut, Outrigger, Outshot, Overhang, Overhead, Oversail, Palmation, Peak, Peters', Pitch, Planetarium, Planisphere, Polyconic, Pork barrel, Prickle, Promontory, → PROTRUDE, Proud(er), Prow, Pseudopod, Quillon, Raguly, Roach, Rocket, Sail, Salient, Sally, Sanson-Flamsteed, Scaw, Scheme, Scrag, Screen, Shelf, Shot, Shrapnel, Sinusoidal, Skaw, Skeg, Slide, Snag, Snout, Spline, Sponson, Sprocket, Spur, Squarrose, Stand out, Stereopticon, Stick out, Stud, Tang, Tappet, Tenon, Throw, Toe, Tongue,

Tracer, Trimetric, Trippet, Trunnion, Turnkey, Turtleback, Tusk, Umbo, Underhung, Undertaking, Villiform, Villus, Vitascope, Whizzbang, Zenithal

Prolapse Procidence

Proletarian, Proletariat Jamahiriya, People, Plebeian, Popular

Proliferate Expand, Increase, Multiply, Propagate, Snowball, Teem

Prolific Abounding, Fecund, Fertile, Fruitful, Profuse, Teeming

Prolix(ity) Lengthy, Prosaic, Rambling, Rigmarole, Verbose, Wire-draw, Wordy

Prologue Introduce, Preface

Prolong(ed) Continue, Drag out, Extend, Lengthen, Protract, Sostenuto, Spin, Sustain

Prom(enade) Alameda, Boulevard, Cakewalk, Catwalk, Crush-room, Esplanade, Front, Mall, Parade, Paseo, Pier, Sea-front, Stroll, → **WALK**

Prometheus Fire

Promethium Pm

Prominence, Prominent Antitragus, Blatant, Bold, Colliculus, Condyle, Conspicuous, Egregious, Emphasis, Featured, Gonion, High profile, Important, Insistent, Luminary, Manifest, Marked, Mastoid, Obtrusive, Outstanding, Salient, Signal, Solar, Spotlight, Tall poppy, Teat, Toot, Tragus

Promiscuous, Promiscuity Casual, Chippie, Chippy, Demivierge, Fast, Free, Goer, Hornbag, Horny, Indiscriminate, Licentious, Light, Loose, Loslyf, Mixed, Motley, Pell-mell, Skanky(-ho), Slapper, Trollop, Whoredom

Promise, Promising Accept, Assure, Augur, Auspicious, Avoure, Behest, Behight, Behote, Bode, Coming, Commit, Compact, Covenant, Earnest, Engagement, Foreshadow, Foretaste, Gratuitous, Guarantee, Hecht, Hest, Hete, Hight, IOU, Likely, Manifest, Oath, Parole, Pledge, Plight, Pollicitation, Potential, Pregnant, Recognisance, Recognizance, Rosy, Sign, Sponsor, Swear, Tile, Troth, Undertake, Upbeat, Vow, Warranty, Word

Promised land Beulah, Canaan, Israel

Promissory note IOU, PN

Promontory Bill, Cape Sable, Cliff, Flamborough Head, Foreland, Giant's Causeway, Hatteras, → **HEADLAND**, Hoe, Hogh, Land's End, Mull, Mull of Galloway, Naze, Ness, Nose, Peak, Pillars of Hercules, Ras, Spit, The Lizard, Tintagel Head

Promote(r), Promotion Ad, Adman, Advance, Advancement, → **ADVERTISE**, Advocate, Aggrandise, Aid, Assist, Back, Banner ad, Blurb, Boost, Breed, Buggin's turn, Campaign, Churn, Dog and pony show, Elevate, Encourage, Eulogy, Exponent, Foment, Foster, Further, Help, Hype, Incite, Increase, Kick upstairs, Leaflet, Lord of Misrule, Mailshot, Make, Market, Pracharak, Prefer, Prelation, Promulgate, Provoke, Push, Queen, Raise, Rear, Remove, Roadshow, Run, Salutary, Sell, Sponsor, Spruik, Stage, Step (up), Subserve, Tendencious, Tendentious, Tout, Upgrade, Uplead, Uprate

Prompt(er), Promptly, Promptness Actuate, Alacrity, Autocue®, Believe, Cause, Celerity, Chop-chop, Cue, Early, Egg, Expeditious, Feed, Frack, Idiot-board, Immediate, Incite, Inspire, Instigate, Move, On-the-nail, Opposite, Pernicious, Premove, Punctual, Quick, Ready, Sharp, Speed(y), Spur, Stage right, Stimulate, Sudden, Swift, Tight, Tit(e), Titely, Trigger, Tyte, Urgent

Promulgate Preach, Proclaim, Publish, Spread

Prone Apt, Groof, Grouf, Grovel, Laid back, Liable, Lying, Prostrate, Recumbent, Subject, Susceptible

Prong Fang, Fork, Grain, Peg, Tang, Tine

Pronghorn Cabrie, Cabrit

Pronoun Impersonal, Oneself, Personal, Reciprocal, Relative

Pronounce(d), Pronouncement Adjudicate, Affirm, Agrapha, Articulate, Assert, Asseveration, Clear, Conspicuous, Declare, Definite, Dictum, Emphatic, Enunciate, Fatwa, Fiat, Indefinite, Marked, Opinion, Palatalise, Pontificate, Predication, Recite, Utter, Velarise, Vocal, Voice, Vote

Pronto PDQ

Pronunciation Betacism, Cacoepy, Delivery, Diction, Etacism, Itacism, Labiodental, Labionasal, Labiovelar, Lallation, Localism, Orthoepy, Phonetics, Plateasm, Proclitic, Received, Rhotacism, Sound, Syllabic, Tense

Proof(s) Apagoge, Argument, Artist's, Assay, Bona fides, Confirmation, Direct, Evidence, Firm, Foundry, Galley, Godel's, India, Indirect, Justification, Lemma, Positive, Preif(e), Probate, Pull, Quality, Refutation, Remarque, Reproduction, Resistant, Revision, Secure, Slip, Smoking gun, Strength, Test, Tight, Token, Trial, Upmake, Validity

Prop Airscrew, Becket, Bolster, Buttress, Clothes, Crutch, Dog-shore, Fulcrum, Leg, Loosehead, Misericord(e), Pit, Point d'appui, Punch(eon), Rance, Rest, Scotch, Shore, Sprag, Spur, Staff, Stay, Stempel, Stemple, Stilt, Stoop, Stoup, Strut, Studdle, Stull, → **SUPPORT**, Tighthead, Trig, Underpin

Propaganda, Propagandist Agitprop, Ballyhoo, Black, Brainwashing, Chevalier, Doctrine, Exponent, Goebbels, Grey, Promotion, Psyop, Psywar, Publicity, Slogan, Spin doctor, White

Propagate, Propagator, Propagation Breed, Clone, Dispread, Generate, Graft, Hatch, Hotbed, Hothouse, Increase, Layering, Populate, Produce, Promulgate, Provine, Spread, Tan-bed

Propel(ler) Airscrew, Ca', Drive, Fin, Frogmarch, Launch, Leg, Lox, → **MOVE**, Oar(sman), Paddle, Pedal, Pole, Project, Push, Rotor, Row, Screw, Send, Tail rotor, Throw, Thruster, Tilt-rotor, Twin-screw, Vane

Propensity Aptness, Bent, Inclination, Penchant, Tendency

Proper(ly) Ain, Convenance, Correct, Decent, Decorous, Due, Eigen, En règle, Ethical, → **FIT**, Genteel, Governessy, Kosher, Legitimate, Nimity-pimity, Noun, Ought, Own, Pakka, Pathan, Prim, Pucka, Pukka, Puritanic, Real, Rightful, Seemly, Strait-laced, Suitable, Tao, Trew, True, Veritable, Well

Property, Properties Assets, Attribute, Aver, Belongings, Capacitance, Chattel, Chirality, Chose, Contenement, Dead-hand, Demesne, Des res, Dowry, Effects, Enclave, Enthalpy, Escheat, Escrow, Essence, Estate, Fee, Feu, Flavour, Fonds, Freehold, Goods, Haecceity, Hereditament, Heritable, Holding, Hot, Hotchpot, Immoveable, Inertia, In rem, Intellectual, Jointure, Land, Leasehold, Living, Means, Mortmain, Paraphernalia, Peculium, Personal, Personalty, Pertinent, Predicate, Premises, Private, Projective, Public, Quale, Quality, Real, Stock, Stolen, Theft, Thixotropy, Time-share, Timocracy, Trait, Usucapion, Usucaption

Prophesy, Prophecy, Prophet(s), Prophetess, Prophetic Amos, Augur, Bab, Balaam, Calchas, Cassandra, Daniel, Deborah, Divine, Druid, Elias, Elijah, Elisha, Ezekiel, Ezra, Fatal, Fatidical, Forecast, Foretell, Former, Geomancer, Habakkuk, Haggai, Hosea, Is, Isa, Is(a)iah, Jeremiah, Joel, Jonah, Latter, Mahdi, Mahound, Major, Malachi, Mani, Mantic, Micah, Minor, Mohamet, Mohammed, Mopsus, Mormon, Moses, Mother Shipton, Nahum, Nathan, Nostradamus, Obadiah, Old Mother Shipton, Ominous, Oracle, Portend, Predictor, Prognosticate, Pythoness, Samuel, Second sight, Seer, Sibyl, Tipster, Tiresias, Vatic, Vaticinate, Völuspá, Zachariah, Zarathustra, Zechariah, Zephaniah, Zoroaster, Zwickau

Prophylactic, Prophylaxis Inoculation, Preventive, Serum, Vaccine, Variolation

Propitiate Appease, Atone, Pacify, Reconcile, Sop

Propitious Benign, Favourable, Lucky

Proponent Advocate, Backer, Partisan

Proportion(ate) Commensurable, Cotangent, Dimension, Harmonic, Inverse, Portion, Pro rata, Quantity, Quota, Ratio, Reason, Regulate, Relation, Sine, Size, Soum, Sowm, Symmetry, Tenor

Propose(r), Proposal Advance, Aim at, Ask, Bid, Bill, Canvass, Eirenicon, Feeler, Fiancé, Idea, Irenicon, Mean, Motion, Move, Nominate, Offer, Overture, Plan, Pop, Premise, Proffer, Propound, Recommend, Resolution, Scheme, Slate, Submission, → **SUGGEST**, Table, Tender, Toast, Volunteer, Woot, Would

Proposition Asses' bridge, Axiom, Convertend, Corollary, Deal, Disjunction, Ergo,

Hypothesis, Identical, Implicature, Lemma, Overture, Pons asinorum, Porism, Premise, Premiss, Rider, Sorites, Spec, Superaltern, Theorem, Thesis

Propound Advocate, Purpose, State

Proprietor, Propriety Bienséance, Convenance, Correctitude, Decorum, Etiquette, Grundy, Keeper, Lord, Master, Owner, Patron, Rectitude

Prosaic Common, Drab, Everyday, Flat, Humdrum, Tedious, Workaday

Proscenium Forestage

Proscribe(d) Exile, Forbid, Outlaw, Prohibit, Taboo, Tabu

Prose, Prosy Euphuism, Haikai, Polyphonic, Purple, Purple patch, Saga, Stich, Verbose, Version, Writing

Prosecute, Prosecutor, Prosecution Allege, Avvogadore, Charge, Crown, Do, Double jeopardy, Fiscal, Furtherance, Impeach, Indict, Lord Advocate, Practise, Public, Pursue, Sue, Wage

Proselytise(r), Proselytism Convert, Indoctrination, Propagandism, Souper

Prospect(or), Prospecting Bellevue, Costean, Dowser, Explore, Forty-niner, Fossick, Look-out, Mine, Opportunity, → **OUTLOOK**, Panorama, Perspective, Pleases, Possibility, Reefer, Scenery, Search, Sourdough, Street, Sweep-washer, View, Vista, Visto, Wildcatter

Prospectus Menu, Pathfinder

Prosper(ity), Prospering, Prosperous Aisha, Ay(e)sha, Blessed, Blossom, Boom, Fair, Fat cat, Flourish, Get ahead, Heyday, Mérimée, Palmy, Sleek, → **SUCCEED**, Thee, Thrift, Thrive, Up, Warison, Wealth, Welfare, Well-heeled, Well-to-do, Well-to-live

Prosthetic Fals(i)e

Prostitute, Prostitution Brass, Broad, Bulker, Callet, Catamite, Chippie, Cockatrice, Cocotte, Comfort woman, Convertite, Debase, Dell, Demi-mondaine, Dolly-mop, Doxy, Drab, Fancy woman, Fille de joie, Floozie, Floozy, Grande cocotte, Harlot, Hetaera, Hetaira, Hierodule, Ho, Hooker, Hustler, Jailbait, Laced mutton, Lady of the night, Loon, Loose-fish, Loose woman, Lowne, Madam, Magdalen(e), Moll, Mutton, Night-walker, Pict, Plover, Pole-cat, Poule, Pro, Public woman, Pug, Punk, Quail, Quiff, Rent-boy, Road, Rough trade, Scrubber, Shippie, Slap, Social evil, Stale, Stew, Streetwalker, Strumpet, Tart, Tramp, Trull, Venture, Wench, Whore, Working girl

Prostrate, Prostration Collapse, Exhausted, Fell, Flat, Flatling, Ko(w)tow, Laid, Obeisance, Overcome, Procumbent, Prone, Repent, Throw

Protactinium Pa

Protagonist Anti-hero

Protean Amoebic, Fusible, Variable

Protect(ed), Protection, Protector Adonise, Aegis, Aircover, Alexin, Amulet, Antigropelo(e)s, Arm, Armour, Asylum, Auspice, Barbican, Bastion, Bestride, Bield, Buckler, Bullet-proof, Cathodic, Chaffron, Chain mail, Chamfrain, Chamfron, Charm, Cherish, Cloche, Coat, Cocoon, Coleor(r)hiza, Conserve, Copyright, Cosset, Cover, Covert, Cromwell, Curb, Cushion, Danegeld, Data, Defend, Defilade, Degauss, Diaper, Egis, Enamel, Entrenchment, Escort, Estacade, Faun, Fence, Firewall, Flank, Gobo, Groundsheet, Guard(ian), Gumshield, Hedge, House, Hurter, Immune, Inalienable, Indemnify, Indusium, Insure, Integument, Keckle, Keep, Kickback, Klendusic, Lee, Listed, Mac(k)intosh, Mail, Male, Mentor, Mollycoddle, Mother, Mothproof, Mouthpiece, Mudguard, Muniment, Napkin, Nappy, Noddy suit, Noll, Nosey, Oliver, Ombrella, Orillion, Overall, Palladium, Parados, Parapet, Patent, Patron, Pelta, Penthouse, Police, Polytunnel, Pomander, Preserve, Procrypsis, Rabbit's foot, Radome, Rampart, Raymond, Reserve, Revetment, Ride shotgun, Safeguard, Sandbag, Save, Schanse, Schan(t)ze, Screen, Scug, Security, Shadow, Sheathing, Sheeting, Shelter, → **SHIELD**, Skug, Souteneur, Splashback, Splashboard, Splasher, Starling, Sunscreen, Supermax, Talisman, Telomere, Testa, Thimble, Thumbstall, Tribute, Tutelar, Twilled, Umbrella, Underlay, Underseal, Vaccine, Waist-cloth, Ward(ship), Warhead, Warrant, Weatherboard, Weatherstrip, Windbreaker, Windshield, Wing, Winterweight, Write

Protectorate Qatar

Protégé Godson, Pupil, Tutee, Ward, Whiteheaded boy
Protein Complement, Conjugated, Repressor, Simple

PROTEINS

3 letters:
PSA
RNA
TSP
TVP

4 letters:
CREB
Meat
Soya
Zein

5 letters:
Abrin
Actin
Lysin
Mucin
Opsin
Pharm
Porin
Prion
Quorn®
Renin
Ricin

6 letters:
Alexin
Avidin
Capsid
Cyclin
Enzyme
Fibrin
Globin
Gluten
Lectin
Leptin
Leucin
Myogen

Myosin
Ossein
Pepsin
Tempeh

7 letters:
Adipsin
Alanine
Albumen
Albumin
Aleuron
Elastin
Fibroin
Gelatin
Gliadin
Histone
Hordein
Legumin
Leucine
Nuclein
Opsonin
Pepsine
Peptone
Sarcode
Sericin
Spongin
Tubulin

8 letters:
Aleurone
Allergen
Amandine
Analogon
Antibody
Collagen
Copaxone®
Cytokine
Ferritin

Gliadine
Globulin
Glutelin
Integrin
Pellicle
Permease
Prolamin
Proteose
Pyrenoid
Ribosome
Spectrin
Troponin
Vitellin

9 letters:
Apoenzyme
Aquaporin
Capsomere
Fibrillin
Filaggrin
Flagellin
Luciferin
Myoglobin
Ovalbumin
Phaseolin
Prolamine
Properdin
Protamine
Sclerotin
Spirulina
Ubiquitin

10 letters:
Actomyosin
Bradykinin
Calmodulin
Caseinogen
Conchiolin

Dystrophin
Factor VIII
Ferredoxin
Fibrinogen
Huntingtin
Incaparina
Interferon
Lewy bodies
Lymphokine
Single-cell
Thrombogen
Toxalbumin

11 letters:
Angiostatin
Angiotensin
Haemoglobin
Haptoglobin
Interleukin
Lactalbumin
Prothrombin
Transferrin
Tropomyosin

12 letters:
Fibronectina
Neurotrophin
Serum albumin

13 letters:
Ceruloplasmin
Lactoglobulin
Macroglobulin
Serum globulin

14 letters:
Immunoglobulin

Protest(er) Abhor, Andolan, Aver, Avouch, Black Bloc(k), Boycott, Clamour, Come,
Complaint, Démarche, Demo, Demonstrate, Demur, Deprecate, Dharna, Dhurna,
Dissent, Expostulate, Gherao, Go-slow, Gripe, Hartal, Inveigh, I say, Lock-out, Luddite,
March, Moonlighter, Nimby, Object, Outcry, Peenge, Picket, Plea, Rail, Refus(e)nik,
Remonstrate, Representation, Sit-in, Squawk, Squeak, Squeal, Stand, Suffragette,
Work-to-rule
Protestant Amish, Anabaptist, Anglo, Arminian, Calvin, Congregationalism,
Covenanter, Cranmer, Dissenter, Evangelic, Gospeller, Huguenot, Independent, Lady,
Loyalist, Lutheran, Mennonite, Methodist, Moravian, Neo-Orthodoxy, Nonconformist,
Oak-boy, Orangeman, Peep o' day Boys, Pentecostal, Pietism, Prod(die), Puritan,

Reformed, Religioner, Right-footer, Sacramentarian, Seventh Day Adventist, Stundist, Swaddler, Waldensian, Wasp, Wesleyan

Protocol Agreement, Code, Convention, Etiquette, Geneva, Kyoto, Point-to-Point

Proton Nucleon, Quark

Protoplasm(ic) Coenocyte, Coenosarc, Cytode, Plasmodium, Sarcode, Somatoplasm

Prototype Blueprint, Exemplar, Model, Original, Pattern, Pilot

Protozoa(n) Am(o)eba, Foraminifer, Giardia, Globigerina, Gregarine, Heliozoan, Infusoria, Leishmania, Mastigophoran, Merozoite, Moner(a), Moneron, Paramecium, Peritricha, Phagocyte, Radiolaria, Rhizopod, Sarcodinian, Sea-mat, Toxoplasm, Trichomonad, Trophozoite, Trypanosome, Volvox, Vorticella

Protract(ed) Delay, → EXTEND, Lengthen, Livelong, Long, Prolong

Protrude, Protrusion Bulge, Eventration, Exsert, Hernia, Jut, Pop, Pout, Project, Pseudopodium, Rectocele, Strout, Tel

Protuberance, Protuberant Apophysis, Bulge, Bump, Burl, Condyle, Crankle, Ergot, Gibbous, Hump, Inia, Knap, Knob, Malleolus, Node, Papillose, Papule, Spadix, Styloid, Swelling, Tragus, Tuber, Tuberosity, Venter

Proud Arrogant, Boaster, Cocky, Conceited, Dic(k)ty, Egotistic, Elated, Flush, Haughty, Haut, Level, Lordly, Orgulous, Protruding, Superb, Vain

Prove(d), Proving Apod(e)ictic, Argue, Ascertain, Assay, Attest, Attribution, Authenticate, Aver, Confirm, Convince, Deictic, Establish, Evince, Justify, Probative, → PROOF, Quote, → SHOW, Substantiate, Test, Trie, Try

Proverb Adage, Axiom, Byword, Gnome, Maxim, Paroemia, Saw

▷ **Proverbial** *may refer to* the biblical Proverbs

Provide(d), Provident(ial) Afford, Allow, Arrange, Besee, Bring, Cater, Compare, Conditional, Endow, Endue, Equip, Far-seeing, Feed, Fend, Find, Furnish, Generate, Give, Grubstake, Heaven sent, If, Lay on, Lend, Maintain, Offer, Plenish, Proviso, Purvey, Quote, Serve, So, Sobeit, → SUPPLY, Suttle

Province, Provincial(ism) Area, Circar, District, Eparchy, Exclave, Eyalet, Forte, Insular, Land, Mofussil, Narrow, Nomarchy, Nome, Nomos, Oblast, Palatinate, Pale, Petrographic, Realm, Regional, Rural, Sircar, Sirkar, Small-town, Subah, Suburban, Territory, Vilayet

---

PROVINCES

2 letters:	Honan	*6 letters:*	Shensi
NI	Hopeh	Acadia	Sikang
	Hopei	Anhwei	Tabasa
4 letters:	Hubei	Artois	Ulster
Gaul	Hunan	Basque	Yunnan
Ifni	Irian	Bengal	
Jaen	Jehol	Fujian	*7 letters:*
Jaya	Jilin	Fukien	Alberta
Shoa	Kansu	Gansul	Almeria
Sind	Kirin	Hainan	Antwerp
	Liege	Kosovo	Bohemia
5 letters:	Namur	Marche	Brabant
Anhui	Natal	Poitou	Drenthe
Anjou	Otago	Pontus	Eritrea
Anwei	Skane	Punjab	Galilee
Coorg	Tigre	Quebec	Gascony
Gansu	Tirol	Raetia	Gauteng
Hebei	Tyrol	Sanjak	Granada
Hejaz		Shansi	Guienne
Henan		Shanxi	Guizhou

Guyenne
Hainaut
Jiangsu
Jiangxi
Jiazhou
Kiangsi
Kiangsu
Kwazulu
Limpopo
Livonia
Munster
Ningsia
Ontario
Picardy
Prairie
Qinghai
Rhaetia
Satrapy
Shaanxi
Sichuan
Suiyuan
Tucuman
Utrecht
Western
Zeeland

Hainault
Helvetia
Illyrian
Kiaochow
Leinster
Liaoning
Limousin
Lorraine
Lyonnais
Manitoba
Maritime
Ninghsia
Normandy
Northern
Nuristan
Pashalic
Pashalik
Provence
Shandong
Shantung
Szechuan
Touraine
Tsinghai
Zhejiang

Free State
Friesland
Groningen
Guangdong
Hainan Tao
Illyricum
Kurdistan
Languedoc
Lusitania
Nivernais
North West
Orleanais
Santa Cruz
Sungkiang
Transvaal

Hesse-Nassau
Kaliningrad
Paphlagonia
Western Cape
West Prussia

12 letters:
Heilongjiang
New Brunswick
North Brabant
North Holland
Saskatchewan
South Holland

13 letters:
Syrophoenicia

10 letters:
Gelderland
Mpumalanga
New Castile
Nova Scotia
Overijssel
Patavinity
Roussillon
Wellington
Westphalia

14 letters:
Eastern Rumelia
Flemish Brabant
Walloon Brabant

15 letters:
British Columbia
Orange Free State

8 letters:
Atlantic
Chekiang
Chinghai
Connacht
Dauphine

9 letters:
Apeldoorn
Aquitaine
Bubalidar
Connaught
Flevoland

11 letters:
Balochistan
Baluchistan
Eastern Cape
Guelderland

17 letters:
North West Frontier

23 letters:
Newfoundland and
    Labrador

Provision(s), Provisional Acates, Ap(p)anage, Board, Entrenched, Fodder, Foresight, Insolvency, Jointure, Larder, Lend-lease, Proggins, Scran, Skran, Stock, Stuff, Supply, Suttle, Viands, Viaticum, Victuals

Proviso, Provisional Caution, Caveat, Clause, Condition, Interim, IRA, Makeshift, Nisi, On trial, Reservation, Salvo, Stipulation, Temporary, Tentative

Provocation, Provocative, Provoke Agacant, Aggro, Alluring, Challenge, Egg, Elicit, Erotic, Exacerbate, Excite, Flirty, Gar, Harass, Incense, Induce, Inflame, Instigate, Irk, Irritate, Kindle, Needle, Nettle, Occasion, Pique, Prompt, Raise, Red rag, Sedition, Sound, Spark, Stimulate, Stir, Tar, Tarty, Tease, Urge, Vex, Wind up

Provost Dean, Keeper, Marshal, Warden

Prow Bow, Cutwater, Fore, Nose, Prore, Stem

Pro-war Hawk

Prowess Ability, Bravery, Forte, Fortitude

Prowl(er) Hunt, Lurch, Lurk, Mooch, Prog, Prole, Rache, Ramble, Ratch, Roam, Rove, Snoke, Snook, Snowk, Tenebrio, Tom

Proxime accessit Next best

Proximity Handiness

Proxy Agent, Attorn, Deputy, PP, Regent, Sub, Surrogate, Vicar, Vice

Prude(nce), Prudent, Prudery Bluenose, Canny, Caution, Circumspect, Comstocker, Conservative, Discreet, Discretion, Far-sighted, Foresight, Frugal, Grundyism, Judicious, Metis, Mrs Grundy, Politic, Prig, Prissy, Provident, Sage, Sensible, Sparing, Strait-laced,

Strait-lacer, Thrifty, Tight-laced, Vice-nelly, Victorian, Ware, Wary, Well-advised, Wise

Prune(r) Bill-hook, Clip, Dehorn, Lop, Plum, Proign, Proin(e), Reduce, Reform, Secateur, Shred, Slash, Sned, Snip, Thin, Trim

Prunella Hedge-sparrow, Self-heal

Prurient Avaricious, Itchy, Lewd, Obscene

Prussia(n) Blue, Junker, Pruce, Spruce, Westphalian

Pry Ferret, Force, Lever, Meddle, Nose, Paul, Peep, Question, Search, Snoop, Stickyback, Toot

Psalm Anthem, Cantate, Chant, Chorale, Hallel, Hymn, Introit, Jubilate, Metrical, Miserere, Neck-verse, Paean, Penitential, Proper, Ps, Song, Tone, Tract, Tractus, Venite

Pseud(o) Bogus, Mock, Posy, Pretentious, Sham, Spurious

Pseudonym Aka, Alias, Allonym, Anonym, Pen-name, Stage-name

Pshaw Chut, Pooh, Tilley-valley, Tilly-fally, Tilly-vally

Psyche Anima, Ego, Self, Soul, Spirit, Superego

Psychiatrist, Psychologist Adler, Alienist, Asperger, Clare, Coué, Ellis, Freud, Headshrinker, Jung, Kraft-Ebing, Laing, Müller-Lyer, Rat-tamer, Reich, Shrink, Skinner, Trick-cyclist

Psychic, Psychosis Clairvoyant, ESP, Fey, Korsakoff's, Lodge, Medium, Mind-reader, Seer, Telekinesis, Telepathic

Psychological, Psychology, Psychologist Analytical, Behaviourism, Clinical, Comparative, Constitutional, De Bono, Depth, Development, Dynamic, Educational, Experimental, Eysenck, Gestalt, Hedonics, Humanistic, Industrial, James, Latah, Occupational, Organisational, Piaget, Skinner, Social, Structural, Windt

Psychosis, Psychotic Korsakoff's, Manic-depressive, Organic, Schizophrenia

Psychotherapist, Psychotherapy Coué, Laing, Rebirthing, Shen

Ptarmigan Rype

Ptomaine Neurine

Pub Bar, Beerhall, Beverage room, Boozer, Chequers, Free-house, Gin-palace, Groggery, Houf(f), House, Howf(f), Inn, Jerry-shop, Joint, Local, Lush-house, Mughouse, Pothouse, Potshop, Rubbidy, Rubbity, Shanty, Tavern, Tiddlywink, Tied house

Puberty, Pubic Adolescence, Beaver, Bush, Hebetic, Teens

Pubescence Tomentum

Pubis Sharebone

Public (house) Apert, Bar, Brew, Civil, Common, Demos, Estate, General, Great unwashed, Hostelry, Inn, Janata, Lay, Limelight, National, Open, Out, Overt, PH, Populace, Roadhouse, State, Vulgar, World

Publican Ale-keeper, Bung, Host, Landlord, Licensee, Tapster, Taverner

Publication Announcement, Bluebook, Book, Booklet, Broadsheet, Edition, Ephemera, Exposé, Festschrift, Issue, → **JOURNAL**, Lady, Mag, Magazine, Organ, Pamphlet, Pictorial, Samizdat, Tabloid, Tatler, Tract, Tribune, Yearbook

Publicise, Publicist, Publicity Ad(vert), Airing, Announce, Ballyhoo, Billing, Build up, Coverage, Exposure, Flack, Glare, Headline, Hype, Leakage, Limelight, Notoriety, Plug, PR(O), Promo(te), Promotion, Promulgate, Propaganda, Réclame, Spin-doctor, Splash

Publish(er), Published, Publishing, Publicise Air, Blaze, Cape, Copyleft, Delator, Desktop, Disclose, Edit, Electronic, Evulgate, Gollancz, Issue, Larousse, Noise, OUP, Out, Pirate, Plug, Post, Print(er), Proclaim, Propagate, Put about, Release, Ren, Run, Stationer, Vanity, Vent, Ventilate

Puck Disc, Elf, Lob, Sprite, Squid

Pucker(ed) Bullate, Cockle, Contract, Gather, Plissé, Purse, Ruck, Shir(r), Wrinkle

Pud Fin, Neafe, Nief, Nieve, Paw

Pudding Afters, Baked Alaska, Bakewell, Black, Blancmange, Blood, Bread (and butter), Brown Betty, Cabinet, Charlotte, Christmas, Clootie dumpling, College, Crumble, Custard, → **DESSERT**, Dog's body, Drisheen, Duff, Dumpling, Eve's, Flummery, Fritter,

Fromenty, Frumenty, Furme(n)ty, Furmity, Haggis, Hasty, Hodge, Hog's, Ice-cream, Kugel, Lokshen, Mealie, Milk, Nesselrode, Panada, Pandowdy, Parfait, Pease, Plum, Plum-duff, Pockmanky, Pockmantic, Pock-pudding, Popover, Portmanteau, Queen's, Rice, Roly-poly, Sago, Savarin, Semolina, Sowens, Sponge, Spotted dick, Spotted dog, Stickjaw, Stodge, Suet, Summer, Sundae, Sweet, Tansy, Tapioca, Umbles, White, White hass, White hause, White hawse, Yorkshire, Zabaglione

Puddle Collect, Dub, Flush, Pant, Plash, Plouter, Plowter, Pool, Sop

Pueblo Aldea, Zuni

Puff(ed), Puffer, Puffy Advertise, Blouse, Blow, Blowfish, Blurb, Bouffant, Breath, Chuff, Chug, Cream, Drag, Encomist, Eulogy, Exsufflicate, Fag, Flaff, Flatus, Fluffy, Fuff, Globe-fish, Grampus, Gust, Hype, Lunt, Pech, Pegh, Pluffy, Plug, Powder, Quilt, Recommend, Skiff, Slogan, Smoke, Steam, Swell, Toke, Twilt, Waff, Waft, Waif, Whiff, Whiffle

Puffin Fratercula, Rockbird, Sea-parrot, Tammie Norie, Tam Noddy

Pug(ilist), Pugilism Belcher, Boxer, Bruiser, Carlin, Fancy, Fistic, Monkey, Ring

Pugnacious Aggressive, Belligerent, Combative, Scrappy

Puke Retch, Sick, Vomit

Pukka Authentic, Genuine, Real, True, Valid

Pulchritude Beauty, Cheese-cake, Grace

Pull (up), Pull out Adduce, Attraction, Charm, Crane, Cry off, Demand, Drag, Draw, Earn, Force, Haul, Heave, Heeze, Hook, → **INFLUENCE**, Lug, Mousle, Pluck, Pop-top, Rein, Ring, Rove, Rug, Saccade, Sally, Seduce, Sole, Sool(e), Sowl(e), Stop, Tit, Touse, Touze, Tow, Towse, Towze, Traction, Trice, Tug, Undertow, Wrest, Yank

Pulley Block, Capstan, Idle(r), Jack-block, Swig, Trice, Trochlea, Truckle

Pullover Jersey, Jumper, Sweater, Sweatshirt, Tank-top, Windcheater

Pullulate Teem

▶ **Pull up** *see* **PULL**

Pulp Cellulose, Chyme, Chymify, Crush, Flong, Gloop, Kenaf, Marrow, Mash, Mush, Pap, Paste, Pomace, Pound, Puree, Rot, Rubbish, Squeeze, Squidge, Wood

Pulpit Ambo(nes), Bully, Lectern, Mimbar, Minbar, Pew, Rostrum, Tent, Tub, Wood

Pulsar Geminga

Pulsate, Pulsatory Beat, Palpitate, Quiver, Systaltic, Throb, Vibrate

Pulse Adsuki, Adzuki, Alfalfa, → **BEAN**, Beat, Calavance, Caravance, Chickpea, Daal, D(h)al, Dholl, Dicrotic, Fava (bean), Flageolet, Garbanzo, Gram, Groundnut, Ictus, Lentil, Lucerne, Pea, Rhythm, Sain(t)foin, Soy beans, Sphygmic, Sync, Systaltic, Systole, Throb

Pulverise Calcine, Comminute, Contriturate, Demolish, Grind, → **POUND**, Powder

Puma Catamount, Cougar, Mountain lion, Panther

Pummel(ling) Batter, Beat, Drub, Fib, Knead, Massage, Nevel, Pound, Tapotement, Thump

▷ **Pummelled** *may indicate* an anagram

Pump(ing) Aerator, Air, Bellows, Bicycle, Bilge, Bowser, Breast, Centrifugal, Chain, Compressor, Cross-examine, Cross-question, Diaphragm, Donkey, Drive, Electromagnetic, Elicit, Feed, Filter, Foot, Force, Fork, Geissler, Grease-gun, Grill, Heart, Heat, Hydropult, Inflate, Interrogate, Knee-swell, Lift, Monkey, Mud, Nodding-donkey, Optical, Parish, Petrol, Piston, Pulsometer, Question, Rotary, Scavenge, Shoe, Sodium, Stirrup, Stomach, Suction, Turbine, Vacuum, Water, Wind

Pumpernickel Rye (bread)

Pumphandle Sweep

Pumpkin Butternut, Cashaw, Gourd, Pampoen, Quash, Queensland blue, Squash

Pun Calembour, Clinch, Equivoque, Jeu de mots, Paragram, Paronomasia, Quibble, Quip, Ram, Wordplay

Punch(ed) Antic, Bell, Biff, Blow, Boff, Bolo, Box, Bradawl, Bumbo, Card, Centre, Chad, Check, Chop, Clip, Cobbler's, Conk, Dry-beat, Fib, Fid, Fist(ic), Fourpenny one, Gang, Glogg, Haymaker, Hit, Hook, Horse, Jab, Key, Kidney, Knevell, Knobble, Knubble,

KO, Lam, Lander, Mat, Milk, Nail set, Nevel, Nubble, One-er, One-two, Overhand, Perforate, Pertuse, Planter's, Plug, Poke, Polt, Pommel, Pounce, Prod, Pummel, Rabbit, Roundhouse, Rum, Rumbo, Sangria, Slosh, Sock, Steed, Sting(o), Stoush, Sucker, Suffolk, Sunday, Swop, Tape, Upper-cut, Wap, Wind, Zest

Punctilious Exact, Formal, Nice, Particular, Picked, Precise, Prim, Stickler

Punctual(ly), Punctual(ity) Politesse, Prompt, Regular, Sharp

Punctuate, Punctuation (mark) Apostrophe, Bracket, Close, Colon, Comma, Duckfoot quote, Emphasize, Guillemet, Interabang, Interrobang, Interrupt, Mark, Semicolon, Tittle

Puncture(d) Bore, Centesis, Criblé, Cribrate, Deflate, Drill, Flat, Hole, Lance, Lumbar, Pearse, Perforate, Pierce, Pounce, Prick, Scarify, Thoracocentesis

Pundit Egghead, Erudite, Expert, Guru, Maven, Oracle, Sage, Savant, Swami, Teacher

Pungency, Pungent Acid, Acrid, Acrolein, Alum, Ammonia, Bite, Bitter, Caustic, Hot, Mordant, Nidorous, Piquant, Poignant, Point, Racy, Sair, Salt, Spice, Sting, Tangy, Witty

Punish(ment), Punished, Punishing Algates, Amerce, Attainder, Baculine, Baffle, Bastinado, Beat, Birch, Brasero, Bum rap, Cane, Cang, Capital, Cart, Castigate, Chasten, Chastise, Come-uppance, Commination, Corporal, Correct, Cucking-stool, Dam(nation), Defrock, Desert(s), Detention, → **DISCIPLINE**, Fatigue, Fine, Flog, Gantlope, Gate, Gauntlet, Gruel, Hellfire, Hiding, High jump, Horsing, Hot seat, Imposition, Impot, Interdict, Jankers, Jougs, Kang, Keelhaul, Knee-capping, Knout, Laldie, Laldy, Lambast(e), Leathering, Lines, Log, Marmalise, Necklace, Nemesis, Pack-drill, Padre Pio, Pandy, Pay out, Peine forte et dure, Penalise, Penance, Penology, Pensum, Perdition, Picket, Pillory, Pine, Rap, Red card, Reprisal, Retribution, Ruler, Scaffold, Scath, Scourge, Sentence, Serve out, Six of the best, Smack, Smite, Spank, Spif(f)licate, Stocks, Strafe, Straff, Strap, Strappado, Swinge(ing), Talion, Tar and feather, Toco, Toko, Tophet, Torture, Treadmill, Trim, Tron(e), Trounce, Tumbrel, Tumbril, Vice anglais, Visit, War(r)ison, What for, Whip, Whirligig, Wild mare, Ywrake, Ywroke

▷ **Punish** *may indicate* an anagram

Punk Goop, Inferior, Ne'er-do-well, Nobody, Touchwood, Worthless

Punnet Basket, Pottle, Thug

Punt(er), Punting Antepost, Back, Bet, Gamble, Kent, Kick, Pound, Quant, Turfite, Wager

Puny Frail, Inferior, Petty, Reckling, Runtish, Scram, Shilpit, Sickly, Small, Weak

Pup(py) Cub, Nurseling, Whelp

Pupa Chrysalis, Exarate, Neanic, Nymph, Obtect

Pupil Abiturient, Academical, Adie's, Apple, Apprentice, Boarder, Cadet, Catechumen, Dayboy, Daygirl, Disciple, Etonian, Exit, Eyeball, Fag, Follower, Greycoat, Gyte, Intake, Junior, L, Monitor, Prefect, Preppy, Protégé(e), Scholar, Senior, Student, Tiro, Tutee, Ward, Wykehamist

▷ **Pupil** *may refer to* an eye

Puppet(s), Puppeteer Bunraku, Creature, Doll, Dummy, Fainéant, Fantoccini, Finger, Galanty show, Glove, Guignol, Jack-a-lent, Judy, Mammet, Marionette, Mawmet, Mommet, Motion(-man), Motion generative, Pageant, Pawn, Pinocchio, Promotion, Punch(inello), Quisling, Rod, Thunderbird, Tool

Purchase(r), Purchasing Acquisition, Bargain, Buy, Coff, Compulsory, Earn, Emption, Gadsden, Get, Grip, Halliard, Halyard, Hold, Layaway, → **LEVERAGE**, Louisiana, Money, Offshore, Oligopsony, Parbuckle, Perquisitor, Repeat, Secure, Shop, Toehold

Pure, Purist, Purity Absolute, Angelic, Cando(u)r, Cathy, Chaste, Chiarezza, Clean(ly), Cleanness, Cosher, Fine, Glenys, Good, Holy, Immaculate, Incorrupt, Innocent, Intemerate, Inviolate, Kathy, Kosher, Lily, Lilywhite, Maidenhood, Meer, Me(a)re, Net(t), Precisionist, Pristine, Quintessence, Sanctity, Sheer, Simon, Simple, Sincere, Snow-white, Stainless, True, Unalloyed, Unapplied, Undrossy, Vertue, Virgin, Virtue, White

Puree Baba ghanoush, Coulis, Dahl, Dal, Dhal, Fool

Purgative, Purge Aloes, Aloetic, Araroba, Aryanise, Cacoon, Calomel, Cascara, Cassia, Castor-oil, Catharsis, Cholagogue, Colquintida, Comstockery, Croton, Delete, Diacatholicon, Diarrh(o)ea, Drastic, Elaterin, Elaterium, Eliminate, Eluant, Emetic, Enos®, Erase, Evacuant, Exonerate, Expiate, Flux, Gleichschaltung, Hiera-picra, Hydragogue, Ipecacuanha, Ipomoea, Jalap, Jalop, Laxative, McCarthyism, Number nine, Physic, Picra, Pride's, Relaxant, Scour, Scur, Senna, Soil, Turbith, Turpeth, Wahoo

Purgatory Cacatopia

Purification, Purifier, Purify(ing) Absolve, Bowdlerise, Catharsis, Clay, Clean(se), Depurate, Despumate, Dialysis, Distil, Edulcorate, Eluent, Elution, Exalt, Expurgate, Filter, Fine, Gas-lime, Green vitriol, Lustre, Lustrum, Niyama, Osmosis, Refine, Retort, Reverse osmosis, Samskara, Sanctify, Sanitise, Scorify, Scrub, Smudging, Sublime, Try, Whiten

Puritan(ical) Ascetic, Bible belt, Bluenose, Browne, Cromwell, Digger(s), Ireton, Ironsides, Killjoy, Pi, Pilgrim, Plymouth Colony, Precisian, Prig, Prude, Prynne, Roundhead, Seeker, Strait-laced, Traskite, Waldenses, Wowser, Zealot

Purl(er) Cropper, Eddy, Fall, Knit, Ripple, Stream

Purloin Abstract, Annex, Appropriate, Lift, Nab, Pilfer, Snaffle, Sneak, Steal

Purple Amaranthine, Amarantin(e), Amethyst, Assai, Aubergine, Burgundy, Cassius, Chlamys, Claret, Corkir, Cudbear, Dubonnet, Eminence, Fuchsia, Golp(e), Heather, Heliotrope, Hyacinthine, Imperial, Indigo, Korkir, Lavender, Lilac, Magenta, Mallow, Mauvin(e), Mulberry, Murrey, Orcein, Orcin(e), Orcinol, Pance, Pansy, Plum, Pompadour, Pontiff, Porporate, Proin(e), Prune, Puce, Puke, Punic, Purpure, Rhodopsin, Royal, Solferino, Tyrian, Violet, Visual

Purport Bear, Claim, Drift, Feck, Mean, Tenor

Purpose(ful) Advertent, Aim, Avail, Calculated, Cause, Cautel, Design, Errand, Ettle, Function, Goal, Here-to, Idea, → **INTENT**, Marrow, Mean(ing), Meant, Mint, Mission, Motive, Object, Plan, Point, Raison d'être, → **REASON**, Resolution, Resolve, Sake, Telic, Telos, Tenor, Use, View

Purposeless Dysteleology, Futile, Indiscriminate, Otiose

Purr Curr, Rumble

Purse Ad crumenam, Bag, Bung, Caba, Clutch, Contract, Crease, Crumenal, Egg, Embouchure, Fisc, Fisk, Long Melford, Mermaid's, Pocket, Prim, Privy, Prize, Public, Pucker, Spleuchan, Sporran, Wallet, Whistle

▷ **Pursed** *may indicate* one word within another

Purser Mud-clerk

Purslane Sea, Water

Pursue(r), Pursuit Alecto, Business, Chase, Chivvy, Course, Dog, Follow, Follow up, Harry, Hobby, Hot-trod, Hound, Hue and cry, Hunt, Line, Pastime, Practice, Practise, Proceed, Prosecute, Quest, Scouring, Stalk, Trivial

Pursuivant Blue Mantle

Purulent Mattery

Purvey(or) Cater, Provide, Provisor, Sell, Supply

Pus Empyema, Matter, Purulence, Pyuria, Quitter, Quittor

Push(er), Push in, Push out Airscrew, Astrut, Barge, Birr, Boost, Bunt, Butt, Ca', Detrude, Drive, Edge, Effort, Elbow, Fire, Horn, Hustle, Impulse, Invaginate, Jostle, Motivation, Nose, Nudge, Nurdle, Obtrude, Onrush, Pitchfork, Plod, Ply, Press, Promote, Propel, Railroad, Ram, Rush, Sell, Shog, Shoulder, → **SHOVE**, Snoozle, Subtrude, Thrust, Urge

Pushchair Baby Buggy®, Buggy, Stroller, Trundler

Pushover Doddle, Soda

Pusillanimous Coward, Timid, Weak, Weak-kneed, Wimp, Yellow

Puss(y) Amentum, → **CAT**, Catkins, Face, Feline, Galore, Hare, Malkin, Mouth, Rabbit, Septic

Pussyfoot Dry, Equivocate, Inch, Paw, Steal, TT

Pustule Blotch, Pimple, Pock

Put (off; on; out; up) Accommodate, Add, Alienate, Bet, Board, Cup, Daff, Defer, Dish, Do, Don, Douse, Implant, Impose, Incommode, Inn, Lade, Launch, Lay, Locate, Lodge, Lump, Oust, Pit, Pitch, Place(d), Plonk, Set, Smore, Snuff, Station, Stow, Temporise

Put away, Put by Distance, Save, Sheathe, Store, Stow

Put down Abase, Degrade, Demean, Disparage, Floor, Humiliate, Land, Relegate, Repress, Reprime, Snuff, Write

▷ **Put off** *may indicate* an anagram

Putrefaction, Putrefy(ing), Putrid Addle, Bitter, Corrupt, Decay, Fester, Mephitic, Olid, Rot, Sepsis, Septic

Putsch Revolution

Putt(ing) Gimme, Gobble, Green, Hash, Pigeon, Sink, → STUPID PERSON

Putter Chug, Club

Put together Assemble, Compile, Synthesize

Putty Glaziers', Jewellers', Painters', Plasterers', Polishers'

Puzzle(r) Acrostic, Baffle, Bemuse, Bewilder, Brainteaser, Chinese, Confound, Confuse, Conundrum, Crossword, Crux, Crux medicorum, Egma, Elude, Enigma, Fox, Get, Glaik, Gravel, Intrigue, Jigsaw, Kakuro, Kittle, Logograph, Magic pyramid, Maze, Mind-bender, Monkey, Mystery, Mystify, Nonplus, Perplex, Ponder, Pose(r), Rebus, Riddle, Rubik's Cube®, Sorites, Sphinx, Stick(l)er, Stump, Sudoku, Tangram, Teaser, Thematic, Tickler, Wordsearch, Wordsquare

Pygmalion Centennial brown

Pygmy Atomy, Dwarf, Hop o'my thumb, Negrillo, Negrito, Pyknic, Thumbling

Pyjamas Baby-doll, Churidars, Jimjams

Pyramid Cheops, Chephren, Frustum, Magic, Population, Stack, Teocalli

Pyre Bale(-fire), Bonfire, Brasero, Darga, Gha(u)t

Pyrenean Basque

Pyrites Arsenical, Cockscomb, Copper, Fool's gold, Iron, Magnetic, Mispickel, Mundic, Spear, White

Pyrotechnics Arson, Fireworks

Pyroxene Aegirine, Aegirite, Diopside

Pyrus Service-tree

Pythagoras Samian

Pythian (seat) Delphic, Tripod

Python Anaconda, Diamond, Kaa, Monty, → SNAKE, Zombi(e)

Q Koppa, Quebec, Question
Qatar Emirate
Q-boat Mystery ship
QC Silk
Qua As
Quack Charlatan, Crocus, Dulcamara, Empiric, Fake, Homeopath, → **IMPOSTOR**, Katerfelto, Mountebank, Pretender, Saltimbanco
Quad(rangle) Close, Complete, Compluvium, Court, Em, En, Horse, Oblong, Pane
Quadrilateral Lambeth, Tetragon, Trapezium, Trapezoid
Quadrille Dance, Lancers, Matador(e), Pantalon
Quaff Carouse, Drink, Imbibe
Quagmire Bog, Fen, Imbroglio, Marsh, Morass, Swamp, Wagmoire
Quahog Clam
Quail Asteria, Bevy, Bird, Blench, Bob-white, Button, Caille, Colin, Flinch, Harlot, Hen, Quake, Shrink, Tremble
Quaint Cute, Far(r)and, Farrant, Fie, Naive, Odd, Old-world, Picturesque, Strange, Twee, Wham, Whim(sy)
Quake(r), Quaking Aminadab, Broad-brim, Didder, Dither, Dodder, Fox, Friend, Fry, Hicksite, Obadiah, Penn, Quail, Seism, Shake(r), Shiver, → **TREMBLE**, Tremor, Trepid
Qualification, Qualified, Qualify Able, Adapt, Adverb, Capacitate, Caveat, Competent, Condition, Credential, Degree, Diplomatic, Eligible, Entitle, Fit, Graduate, Habilitate, Higher Still, Meet, Modifier, Nisi, Parenthetical, Pass, Past-master, Proviso, Quantify, Restrict, Temper, Versed
Quality Aroma, Attribute, Body, Calibre, Cast, Charisma, Esse, Essence, Fabric, Fame, First water, Five-star, Flavour, Grade, Inscape, Insight, It, Kite-mark, Letter, Long suit, Mystique, Nature, Phat, Pitch, Plus, Premium, Primary, Property, Q, Quale, Reception, Sanctitude, Savour, Sort, Standard, Stature, Style, Substance, Suchness, Terroir, Texture, Thew, Thisness, Timbre, Tone, Tophole, Top notch, Total, Up-market, Vein, Vinosity, Virgin, Virtu(e), Water, Worth
Qualm Compunction, Misgiving, Scruple
Quandary Dilemma, Fix, Predicament, Trilemma
Quantity → **AMOUNT**, Analog(ue), Batch, Bundle, Capacity, Deal, Dose, Feck, Fother, Hank, Heaps, Hundredweight, Idempotent, Intake, Jag, Loads, Lock, Lot, Mass, Measure, Melder, Multitude, Myriad, Niblet, Nonillion, Number, Ocean(s), Omnium, Operand, Parameter, Parcel, Peck, Plenty, Posology, Pottle, Qs, Qt, Quire, Quota, Quotient, Radicand, Ream, Scalar, Slather, Slew, Slue, Sum, Surd, Tret, Unknown, Vector, Wad, Warp, Whips
Quantum Graviton, Isospin, Magnon, Phonon, Photon, Roton
Quarantine Isolate, Lazarette
Quark Bottom, Charm(ed), Down, Flavo(u)r, Particle, Strange, Top up
Quarrel(some) Affray, Aggress, Altercate, Argue, Arrow, Barney, Barratry, Barretry, Bate, Bicker, Brabble, Brattle, Brawl, Breach, Breeze, Broil, Brulyie, Brulzie, Bust-up, Cagmag, Cantankerous, Carnaptious, Cat and dog, Caterwaul, Chance-medley, Chide, Clash, Combative, Contentious, Contretemps, Difference, Disagree, Dispute, Domestic, Dust-up, Eristic, Estrangement, Exchange, Fall out, Feisty, Feud, Fracas, Fractious, Fratch(et)y, Fray, Hassle, Issue, Jar, Loggerheads, Miff, Outcast, Outfall, Pugnacious,

Ragbolt, Row, Ruction, Spat, Squabble, Tangle, Tiff, Tile, Tink, Vendetta, Vitilitigation, Wap, Whid, Wrangle

Quarry, Quarry face Chalkpit, Chase, Currie, Curry, Game, Heuch, Mark, Mine, Pit, Prey, Scabble, Scent, Stone pit, Victim

Quart Winchester

Quarter(ing), Quarters Airt, Barrio, Billet, Camp, Canton(ment), Casbah, Casern(e), Chinatown, Chum, Clemency, Close, Coshery, District, Dorm, E, Empty, Enclave, Fardel, Farl, First, Fo'c'sle, Forecastle, Forpet, Forpit, Fourth, Ghetto, Ham(s), Harbour, Haunch, Last, Latin, Medina, → **MERCY**, N, Note, Oda, Pity, Point, Principium, Quadrant, Region, S, Season, Sector, Tail, Trimester, Two bits, W, Wardroom, Warp, Winter

Quarter-day LD

▷ **Quarterdeck** *may indicate* a suit of cards

Quartermaster Seacunny

Quartet Foursome, Mess, String, Tetrad

Quarto Crown, Demy, Foolscap, Imperial, Medium, Royal, Small

Quartz Adventurine, Agate, Amethyst, Bristol diamond, Buhrstone, Cacholong, Cairngorm, Chalcedony, Chert, Citrine, Flint, Granophyre, Granulite, Itacolumite, Jasp(er), Morion, Onyx, Plasma, Prase, Rainbow, Rose, Rubasse, Sapphire, Silex, Silica, Smoky, Spanish topaz, Stishovite, Tiger-eye, Tonalite, Whin Sill

Quash Abrogate, Annul, Nullify, Quell, Rebut, Recant, Scotch, Subdue, Suppress, Terminate, Void

Quasimodo Bellringer, Gibbose, Hunchback

Quaver(ing) Shake, Tremulous, Trill, Vibrate, Warble

Quay Bund, Jetty, Landing, Levee, Staithe, Wharf

Queasy Delicate, Nauseous, Squeamish

Quebec Q

Queen(ly) Adelaide, African, Alcestis, Alexandra, Anna, Anne, Artemesia, Atossa, Balkis, Beauty, Bee, Begum, Bess, Boadicea, Boudicca, Brun(n)hild(e), Camilla, Candace, Card, Caroline, Cat, Christina, Cleopatra, Closet, Clytemnestra, Coatcard, Dido, Drag, Drama, Eleanor(a), Ellery, Ena, ER, Esther, FD, Gertrude, Guinevere, Harvest, Hatshepset, Hatshepsut, Hecuba, Helen, Henrietta Maria, Hera, Here, Hermione, Hippolyta, HM, Isabel, Isabella, Ishtar, Isolde, Jocasta, Juliana, Juno, King, Leda, Maam, Mab, Maeve, Margaret, Marie Antoinette, Mary, Matilda, May, Medb, Mobled, Monarch, Nance, Nefertiti, Omphale, Pance, Pansy, Parr, Paunce, Pawnce, Pearly, Penelope, Persephone, Phaedra, Prince, Prom, Proserpina, Qu, R, Ranee, Rani, Regal, Regina(l), Sara, Semiramis, Sheba, Sultana, Titania, Vashti, Victoria, Virgin, Warrior

Queen Anne Mrs Morley

Queer(ness) Abnormal, Berdash, Bizarre, Crazy, Cure, Curious, Fey, Fie, Fifish, Fishy, Gay, Nance, Nancy, → **ODD**, Outlandish, Peculiar, Pervert, Poorly, Quaint, Rum, Spoil, Uranism, Vert

Quell Alegge, Allay, Calm, Quiet, Repress, Subdue, Suppress

Quench Assuage, Cool, Extinguish, Satisfy, Slake, Slo(c)ken, Sta(u)nch, Yslake

▸ **Query** *see* **QUESTION(ING)**

Quest Goal, Graal, Grail, Hunt, Pursuit, Search, Venture, Vision

Question(ing), Questionnaire Appose, Ask, Bi-lateral, Burning, Catechise, Chin, Consult, Contest, Conundrum, Cross-examine, Debrief, Dichotomous, Direct, Dispute, Dorothy Dixer, Doubt, Erotema, Eroteme, Erotesis, Examine, Fiscal, Good, Grill, Heckle, Homeric, Impeach, Impugn, Indirect, Information, Innit, Interpellation, Interrogate, Interview, Investigate, Issue, Koan, Leading, Loaded, Maieutic, Matter, Open, Oppugn, Peradventure, Point of order, Pop, Pose, Previous, Probe, Problem, Pump, Q, Qu, Quaere, Quiz, Rapid-fire, Refute, Rhetorical, Riddle, Socratic method, Sound, Speer, Speir, Survey, Suspect, Tag, Teaser, Tickler, Vexed, West Lothian, WH, What, Worksheet

Questionable Ambiguous, Dubious, Fishy, Socratic

Question-master Interrogator, Socrates, Torquemada, Ximenes

Queue Braid, Breadline, Cercus, Crocodile, Cue, Dog, File, Kale, → **LINE**, Line up, Pigtail, Plait, Plat, Stack, Tail(back), Track

Quibble(r), Quibbling Balk, Carp, Carriwitchet, Casuist, Cavil, Chicaner, Dodge, Elenchus, Equivocate, Hairsplitting, Nitpick, Pedantry, Pettifoggery, Prevaricate, Pun, Quiddity, Quillet, Quirk, Sophist

Quiche Flan, Tart

Quick(en), Quickening, Quicker, Quickie, Quickly, Quickness Accelerate, Acumen, Adroit, Agile, Alive, Allegr(ett)o, Animate, Apace, Breakneck, Breathing, Bright, Brisk, Celerity, Chop-chop, Citigrade, Cito, Con moto, Core, Cracking, Cuticle, Dapper, Deft, Enliven, Existent, Expeditious, Express, Fastness, Festination, Fleet, Foothot, Gleg, Hasten, Hie, High-speed, Hotfoot, Impetuous, Impulsive, Intelligent, Jiffy, Keen, Lickety-split, Living, Mercurial, Meteoric, Mistress, Mosso, Nailbed, Nimble, Nippy, Nooner, Pdq, Piercing, Piu mosso, Post-haste, Prestissimo, Presto, Prompt, Pronto, Rapid, Rath(e), Ready, Rough and ready, Schnell, Sharp, Skin, Slippy, Smart, Snappy, Snort, Sodain(e), Soon, Spry, Streamline, Stretta, Stretto, Sudden, Swift, Swith, Tout de suite, Trice, Up tempo, Veloce, Vital, Vite, Vivify, Wikiwiki, Yare

Quicksand Flow, Syrtis

Quicksilver Mercury

Quid Chaw, Chew, L, Nicker, Oner, Plug, Pound, Quo, Sov, Tertium, Tobacco

Quid pro quo Mutuum, Tit-for-tat

Quiescence, Quiescent Calm, Di(o)estrus, Inactive, Inert, Latent, Still

Quiet(en), Quieter, Quietly Accoy, Allay, Appease, Barnacle, Calm, Clam, Compose, Conticent, Decrescendo, Doggo, Ease, Easeful, Easy, Encalm, Entame, Gag, Grave, Kail, Laconic, Loun(d), Low, Lown(d), Low-profile, Lull, Meek, Mezzo voce, Mp, Muffle, Mute, Orderly, P, Pacify, Pastel, Pauciloquent, Pause, Peace, Piano, Pipe down, Plateau, QT, Reserved, Reticent, Sedate, Settle, Sh, Shtoom, Shtum, Silence, Sitzkrieg, Sly, Sober, Soothe, Sotto voce, Still, Stum(m), Subact, Subdued, Tace, Taciturn, Tranquil, Wheesht, Whish, Whisht, Whist

Quill Calamus, Feather, Float, Plectre, Plectron, Plectrum, Plume, Remex

Quillwort Isoetes

Quilt(ed), Quilting Comfort(er), Continental, Counterpane, Cover, Crazy, Doona®, Duvet, Echo, Eiderdown, Futon, Kantha, Matel(l)asse, Patch(work), Puff, Trapunto

Quince Bael, Bel, Bengal, Bhel, Flowering, Japanese, Japonica

Quinine China, Crown-bark, Kina, Quina, Tonic

Quinsy Angina, Cynanche, Garget, Squinancy

Quintessence, Quintessential Classic, Heart, Pith

Quintet Pentad, Trout

Quip Carriwitchet, Crack, Epigram, Gibe, Jest, Jibe, Joke, Taunt, Zinger

Quirk Concert, Foible, Idiosyncrasy, Irony, Kink, Mannerism, Twist

Quisling Collaborator, Traitor

Quit(s) Abandon, Absolve, Ap(p)ay, Cease, Desert, Desist, Even(s), Go, Leave, Meet, Part, Resign, Rid, Stash, → **STOP**, Vacate, Yield

Quite Actually, All, Ap(p)ay, Clean, Dead, Enough, Enow, Fairly, Fully, Mezzo, Precisely, Rather, Real, Right, Sheer, Very, Yes

Quiver(ing) Aspen, Quake, Shake, Sheaf, Sheath, The yips, Tremble, Tremolo, Tremor, Tremulate, Trepid, Vibrant, Vibrate, Wobble

Qui vive Go-go

Quixote, Quixotic Don, Errant, Impractical

Quiz Bandalore, Banter, Bee, Catechism, Examine, Hoax, Interrogate, I-spy, Mastermind, Mockery, Oddity, Probe, Pump, Question, Smoke, Third degree, Trail, Yo-yo

Quizzical Askance, Curious, Derisive, Odd, Queer, Socratic

Quod Can, Clink, Jail, Prison

Quoit Disc(us), Disk, Ring

Quondam Once, Sometime, Whilom

Quorum Minyan
Quota Numerus clausus, Proportion, Ration, Share
Quotation, Quote(d), Quote Adduce, Citation, Cite, Co(a)te, Duckfoot, Epigraph, Evens, Extract, Forward, Instance, Name, Price, Recite, Reference, Say, Scare, Soundbite, Tag, Verbatim, Wordbite
Quoth Co, Said
Quotient Achievement, Intelligence, Kerma, Quaternion, Ratio, Respiratory

Rr

R Arithmetic, Canine letter, Dog letter, King, Queen, Reading, Recipe, Right, Romeo, Run, Writing

RA Academy, Argentina

Rabbi Dayan, Mashgiah, Rav, Rebbe

Rabbit Angora, Astrex, Blather, Brer, British Lop, Buck, Bun(ny), Chat, Chitchat, Con(e)y, Cottontail, Daman, Dassie, Doe, Duffer, Earbash, Harp, Haver, Hyrax, Jabber, Jack, Jaw, Klipdas, Long White, Lop-eared, Marmot, Muff, Natter, Nest, Novice, Oarlap, Palaver, Patzer, Prate, Rack, Rattle, Rex, Rock, Sage, Snowshoe, Tapeti, Terricole, Waffle, Welsh, White, Witter, Yak, Yap, Yatter

Rabble, Rabble-rousing Canaille, Clamjamphrie, Clanjamfray, Colluvies, Crowd, Demagoguery, Doggery, Galère, Herd, Hoi-polloi, Horde, Legge, Meinie, Mein(e)y, Menyie, Mob, Raffle, Rag-tag, Rascaille, Rascal, Riff-raff, Rout, Scaff-raff, Shower, Tag, Tagrag

Rabelaisian Pantagruel, Panurge

Rabid, Rabies Extreme, Frenzied, Hydrophobia, Lyssa, Mad, Raging, Virulent

Raccoon Coati(-mondi), Coati-mundi, Olingo, Panda, Procyon

Race, Racing Alpine, Autocross, Autopoint, Bathtub, Boat, Boskop, Broose, Brouze, Bumping, Car rally, Caucus, Chantilly, Chase, Claiming, Classic, Comrades, Cone, Consolation, Corso, Country, Criterium, Cursus, Cyclo-cross, Dogs, Double sculls, Drag, Egg and spoon, Enduro, F1, Flapping, Flat, Formula One, Fun-run, Half-marathon, Handicap, Hare and hounds, Harness, Hialeah, High hurdles, Hurdles, Indy car, Keiren, Keirin, Kentucky Derby, Kermesse, Lampadedromy, Lampadephoria, Leat, Leet, Marathon, Meets, Mile, Monza, Motocross, Nascar, National Hunt, Nursery, Nursery stakes, Obstacle, One-horse, Palio, Paper chase, Pattern, Picnic, Plate, Point-to-point, Potato, Prep, Rallycross, Rallying, Rapids, Rat, Regatta, Relay, Rill, Road, Rod, Roost, Run-off, Sack, Scramble, Scratch, Selling(-plate), Shan, Sheep, Slalom, Slot-car, Smock, Speedway, Steeplechase, Supermoto, Sweepstake, Tail, Three-legged, Torch, Trotting, TT, Turf, Two-horse, Volsungs, Walking, Wetherby

Race Ancestry, Arms, Aztec, Belt, Breed, Career, Contest, Course, Current, Dash, Event, Fastnet, Flow, Generation, Ginger, Herrenvolk, Human(kind), Hurry, Inca, Kind, Lick, Lignage, Line(age), Man, Master, Mediterranean, Nation, → **NATIONAL**, Pluck, Pre-Dravidian, Pursuit, Ronne, Scud, Scurry, Seed, Slipstream, Sloot, Sluit, Sprint, Stakes, Stem, Stirp(s), Stirpes, Stock, Strain, Streak, Strene, Taste, Tear, Tide, Torpids, Tribe, Walk-over, Waterway, Welter, Whid, White

Racehorse, Racer Arkle, Dragster, Eclipse, Filly, Go-kart, Hare, Maiden, Mudder, Neddy, Novice, Plater, Red Rum, Shergar, Snake, Steeplechaser, Trotter

Raceme Bunch, Corymb, Panicle

Race meeting, Racetrack Aintree, Ascot, Cambridgeshire, Catadrome, Catterick, Cesarewitch, Derby, Doggett's Coat and Badge, Doncaster, Dromical, Dromos, Epsom, Goodwood, Grand National, Grand Prix, Guineas, Hippodrome, Imola, Indy, Kentucky Derby, Leger, Le Mans, Longchamps, Madison, National Hunt, Newmarket, Oaks, Paceway, Racino, Redcar, St Leger, Super G, Thousand Guineas, Towcester, Two Thousand Guineas, Velodrome, Wincanton

Racial (area), Racialist Apartheid, Colour, Ethnic, Ghetto, National Front, Quarter

Rack Agonise, Bin, Cloud, Cratch, Drier, Flake, Frame, Hack, Hake, Heck, Pipe, Plate, Pulley, Roof, Stretcher, Toast, Torment, Torture, Touse, Towse

Racket(eer) Bassoon, → **BAT**, Battledore, Bloop, Blue murder, Brattle, Caterwaul, Chirm,

Clamour, Con, Crime, Deen, Din, Discord, Earner, → **FIDDLE**, Gyp, Hubbub, Hullaballoo, Hustle, → **NOISE**, Noisiness, Protection, Ramp, Rattle, Rort, Sokaiya, Stridor, Swindle, Tirrivee, Tumult, Uproar, Utis

Racy Ethnic, Piquant, Pungent, Ribald, Salty, Spicy, Spirited

Rad Rem

Radar Acronym, Angel, AWACS, Beacon, DEW line, Doppler, Gadget, Gee, Gull, Lidar, Loran, Monopulse, Navar, Rebecca-eureka, Shoran, Surveillance, Teleran®, Tracking

Raddle Hurdle, Ochre, Red

Radial Osteal, Quadrant, Rotula, Spoke, Tire, Tyre

Radiance, Radiant Actinic, Aglow, Aureola, Beamish, Brilliant, Gleam(y), Glory, Glow, Happy, Lustre, Refulgent, Shechina, Sheen, Shekinah

Radiate, Radiating, Radiation, Radiator Actinal, Adaptive, Air-colour, Annihilation, Beam, Black body, Bremsstrahlung, Cavity, C(h)erenkov, Characteristic, Disseminate, Dosimetry, Effulgence, Effuse, Emanate, Emit, Exitance, Fluorescence, Gamma, Glow, Hawking, Heater, Infrared, Insolation, Ionizing, Isohel, Laser, Microwave, Millirem, Non-ionizing, Pentact, Photon, Picowave, Pulsar, Quasar, Rem(s), Rep, Roentgen, → **SHINE**, Sievert, Soft, Spherics, Spoke, Stellate, Stray, SU, Sun, Synchrotron, Terrestrial, Ultra violet, UVA, UVB, Van Allen, Visible

Radical Acetyl, Alkyl, Allyl, Amide, Ammonium, Amyl, Aryl, Benzil, Benzoyl, Bolshevist, Bolshie, Butyl, Calumba, Carbene, Cetyl, Chartist, Dibutyl, Drastic, Dyad, Elemental, Ester, Ethynyl, Extreme, Free, Fundamental, Gauchist, Genre-busting, Glyceryl, Glycosyl, Hexyl, Hydroxy, Innate, Isopropyl, Jacobin, Leftist, Leveller, Ligand, Maximalist, Methyl, Montagnard, Nitryl, Oxonium, Parsnip, Phenyl, Phosphonium, Pink, Propyl, Red, Revolutionary, Rhizocaul, Root, Rudiment, Sulfone, Sulphone, Taliban, Taproot, Trot(sky), Uranyl, Vinyl, Vinylidene, Whig, Xylyl, Yippie, Yippy

Radio Beatbox, Blooper, Bluetooth, Boom-box, Cat's whisker, CB, Cellular, Citizen's band, Cognitive, Community, Crystal set, Digital, Ether, Gee, Ghetto-blaster, Ham, Local, Loudspeaker, Marconigraph, Pirate, Receiver, Receiving-set, Rediffusion®, Reflex, Rig, Set, Simplex, Sound, Steam, Talk, Talkback, Tranny, Transceiver, Transistor, Transmitter, Transponder, Walkie-talkie, Walkman®, Walky-talky, Wireless

Radioactive, Radioactivity Actinide, Americium, Astatine, Autinite, Bohrium, Cheralite, Cobalt 60, Curie, Emanation, Fall-out, Hot, Megacurie, Niton, Nucleonics, Plutonium, Radon, Steam, Thorianite, Thorite, Thorium, Torbernite, Uranite

Radiogram, Radiograph(y) Cable, Telegram, Venography, Ventriculography, Wire

Radiology Interventional

Radish Charlock, Daikon, Mooli, Runch

Radium Ra

Radius Bone, Long, Schwarzschild, Short, Turning

Radon Rn

Raffia Rabanna

Raffle(s) Burglar, Draw, Lottery, Sweepstake

Raft(ing) Balsa, Carley float, Catamaran, Float, Kon-Tiki, Life, Log, Mohiki, Pontoon, Slew, Whitewater

Rafter Barge-couple, Beam, Chevron, Jack, Joist, Principal, Ridge, Spar, Timber

Rag(ged), Rags Bait, Bate, Clout, Coral, Daily, Deckle, Dud(s), Duddery, Duddie, Duster, Fent, Figleaf, Glad, Gutter press, Guyed, Haze, Kid, Lap(pie), Lapje, Mop, Moth-eaten, → **NEWSPAPER**, Nose, Paper, Red(top), Remnant, Revel, Rivlins, Roast, Rot, Scabrous, Scold, Scrap, S(c)hmatte, → **SHRED**, Slate, Slut, Splore, Tack, Tat(t), Tatter(demalion), Tatty, Taunt, → **TEASE**, Tiger, Tongue, Uneven

▷ **Rag(ged)** *may indicate* an anagram

Rage, Raging Amok, → **ANGER**, Ardour, Bait, Bate, Bayt, Boil, Chafe, Conniption, Explode, Fad, Fashion, Fierce, Fit, Fiz(z), Fume, Furibund, Furore, Fury, Gibber, Go, Irate, Ire, Mode, Monkey, Paddy(-whack), Passion, Pelt, Pet, Pique, Rabid, Rail, Ramp, Rant, Road, 'roid, See red, Snit, Storm, Tear, Temper, Ton, Trolley, Utis, Wax, Wrath

Raglan Sleeve
Ragout Blanquette, Compot, Goulash, Haricot, Stew
Rag-picker Bunter
Raid(er) Assault, Attack, Baedeker, Bear, Bodrag, Bust, Camisado, Chappow, Commando, Corporate, Dawn, Do, Forage, For(r)ay, Imburst, Incursion, Inroad, Inrush, Invade, Jameson, Maraud, March-treason, Mosstrooper, Pict, Pillage, Plunder, Ram, Ransel, Razzia, Reive, Rob, Sack, Scrump, Skrimp, Skrump, Smash-and-grab, Sortie, Spreagh, Storm, Swoop, Viking
Rail(er), Railing Abuse, Amtrack, Arm(rest), Arris, Balustrade, Ban, Banister, → **BAR**, Barre, Barrier, Bird, Bullhead, Cloak, Communion, Conductor, Coot, Corncrake, Crake, Criticise, Dado, Fender, Fiddle, Fife, Flanged, Flat-bottomed, Flite, Flow, Fulminate, Grab, Grinding, Guide, Gush, Insult, Inveigh, Light, Limpkin, Live, Metal, Monkey, Neckerchief, Notornis, Parclose, Picture, Pin, Plate, Post, Pulpit, Pushpit, Rack, Rag, Rate, Rave, Rung, Scold, Slang-whang, Slate, Slip, Snash, Sneer, Sora, Soree, Spar, T, Taffrail, Takahe, Taunt, Thersites, Third, Towel, Train, Vituperation, Weka
Raillery Badinage, Banter, Chaff, Persiflage, Sport
Railroad, Railway Aerial, Amtrak, BR, Bulldoze, Cable, Cash, Coerce, Cog, Crémaillère, Dragoon, El, Elevated, Funicular, Gantlet, GWR, Inclined, L, Light, Lines, LMS, LNER, Loop-line, Maglev, Marine, Metro, Monorail, Mountain, Narrow-gauge, Press, Rack, Rack and pinion, Rly, Road, Rollercoaster, Ropeway, ROSCO, Ry, Scenic, Ship, Siding, SR, Stockton-Darlington, Switchback, Telpher-line, Track, Train, Tramline, Tramway, Trans-Siberian, Tube, Underground
Railwayman Driver, Fettler, Footplateman, Gandy dancer, Guard, Length(s)man, Locoman, NUR, Plate layer, Stephenson, Stoker, Tracklayer
Raiment Apparel, Clothes, Garb, Ihram
Rain(y), Rainstorm Acid, Blash, Deluge, Downpour, Drizzle, Flood, Hyad(e)s, Hyetal, Mistle, Mizzle, Oncome, Onding, Onfall, Pelt, Pelter, Piss, Plump, Pluviose, Pluvious, Pour, Precipitation, Right, Roke, Scat, Seil, Serein, Serene, Shell, Shower, Sile, Silver thaw, Skiffle, Skit, Smir(r), Smur, Soft, Spat, Spet, Spit, Storm, Thunder-plump, Virga, Water, Weep, Wet, Yellow
Rainbow(-maker) Arc, Arc-en-ciel, Bifrost, Bruise, Dew-bow, Iridescence, Iris, Moon-bow, Spectroscope, Sunbow, Sundog, Torrent-bow, Water-gall, Weather-gall, White
Raincoat, Rainproof Burberry®, Cagoule, Gaberdine, Mac, Mino, Oils(kins), Slicker, Waterproof, Weatherboard
Raingauge Ombrometer, Udometer
Rain-maker Indra
Rain tree Saman
Raise(d), Raising Advance, Aggrade, Attollent, Boost, Bouse, Bowse, Build, Buoy up, Cat, Coaming, Cock, Collect, Elate, → **ELEVATE**, Emboss, Enhance, Ennoble, Erect, Escalate, Exalt, Extol, Fledge, Grow, Heave, Heezie, Heft, High(er), Hike, Hoick, Hoist, Increase, Jack, Key, Leaven, Lift, Mention, Overcall, Perk, Prise, Rear, Regrate, Repoussé, Revie, Rouse, Saleratus, Siege, Sky, Snarl, Step-up, Sublimate, Take up, Up, Upgrade, Weigh
Rake, Raker, Rakish Bag of bones, Bed-hopper, Buckrake, Casanova, Comb, Corinthian, Croupier, Dapper, Dissolute, Don Giovanni, Don Juan, Enfilade, Gay dog, Jaunty, Lecher, Libertine, Lothario, Raff, Reprobate, Rip, Roam, Roué, Scan, Scour, Scowerer, Scrape, Scratch, Strafe, Straff, Stubble, Swash-buckler, Swinge-buckler, Wagons, Wolf, Womaniser
Rale Crepitus, Rattle
Rally, Rallying-point Autocross, Autopoint, Badinage, Banter, Demo, Gather, Jamboree, Meeting, Mobilise, Monte Carlo, Morcha, Muster, Oriflamme, Persiflage, Raise, Recover, Regroup, Rely, Rest, Reunion, Revive, Risorgimento, Roast, Rouse, Scramble, Spirit, Treasure hunt

Ralph Imp, Nader, Rackstraw

Ram Aries, Battering, Buck, Bunt, Butt, Butter, Corvus, Crash, Drive, Hidder, Hydraulic, Mendes, Pound, Pun, Sheep, Stem, Tamp, Thrust, Tup, Wether

Ramble(r), Rambling Aberrant, Aimless, Digress, Incoherent, Liana, Liane, Maunder, Meander, Rabbit, Rigmarole, Roam, Rose, Rove, Skimble-skamble, Sprawl, Stray, Stroll, Vagabond, Wander

Rameses Pharaoh

Ramp Bank, Gradient, Helicline, Incline, Linkspan, Runway, Slipway, Slope, Speed, Vert

Rampage Fury, Riot, Spree, Storm, Warpath

Rampant Lionel, Predominant, Profuse, Rearing, Rife

▷ **Rampant** *may indicate* an anagram or a reversed word

Rampart Abat(t)is, Brisure, Butt, Defence, Fortification, Parapet, Terreplein, Vallum, Wall

Ramrod Gunstick

Ramshackle Decrepit, Heath Robinson, Rickety, Rickle

Ranch Bowery, Corral, Dude, Estancia, Farm, Fazenda, Hacienda, Spread, Stump

Rancid Frowy, Rafty, Reast(y), Reest(y), Reist(y), Sour, Turned

Rancour Bad blood, Gall, Hate, Malgré, Malice, Resentment, Spite

Rand Border, R, Roon

Random Accidental, Aleatoric, Arbitrary, → **AT RANDOM**, Blind, Casual, Desultory, Fitful, → **HAPHAZARD**, Harvest, Hit-or-miss, Hobnob, Indiscriminate, Lucky dip, Scattershot, Sporadic, Stochastic, Stray

▷ **Random(ly)** *may indicate* an anagram

Range(r), Rangy Admiralty, Aga, Align, Ambit, Andes, Atlas, AZ, Ballpark, Band, Bowshot, Bushwhack, Capsule, Carry, Cascade, Chain, Cheviot, Compass, Cotswolds, Course, Dandenong, Darling, Diapason, Dispace, Dolomites, Dynamic, Err, → **EXTENT**, Eye-shot, Flinders, Forest, Game warden, Gamme, Gamut, Glasgow, Grade, Great Dividing, Gunshot, Hamersley, Harmonic, Helicon, Himalayas, Home, Interquartile, Kaikoura, Karakoram, Ken(ning), Kolyma, Ladakh, Leggy, Limit, Line, Locus, Long, MacDonnell, Massif, Middleback, → **MOUNT**, Musgrave, New England, Orbit, Otway, Oven, Owen Stanley, Palette, Pennine Hills, Point-blank, Prairie, Purview, Pyrenees, Radius, Rake, Reach, Register, Repertoire, Rifle, Roam, Rocket, Rove, Ruivenzori, Run, Saga, Scale, Scope, Sc(o)ur, Selection, Serra, Shooting, Short, Sierra, Sloane, Spectrum, Sphere, Stanovoi, Stanovoy, Stove, Strzelecki, Sweep, Tape, Tessitura, Teton, Texas, The Wolds, Tier, Urals, Waldgrave, Wasatch, Waveband, Woomera

Range-finder Telemeter

Rank(s), Ranking Arrant, Assort, Ayatollah, Begum, Brevet, Caste, Category, Cense, Classify, Cornet, Curule, Degree, Dignity, Downright, Earldom, Echelon, Estate, État(s), Flag, Flight sergeant, Grade, Graveolent, Gree, Gross, High, Hojatoleslam, Hojatolislam, Majority, Malodorous, Olid, Parage, Percentile, Petty Officer, Place, Rammish, Range, Rate, Reist, Rooty, Row, Seed, Seigniorage, Sergeant, Serried, Sheer, Shoulder-strap, Sort, Stance, Stand(ing), → **STATION**, Status, Substantive, Table, Taxi, Tier, → **TITLE**, Titule, Top drawer, Utter, Viscount

Rankle Chafe, Fester, Gall, Grate, Irritate, Nag

Ransack Fish, Loot, Pillage, Plunder, Rifle, Ripe, Rob, Rummage, Tot(ter)

Ransom King's, Redeem, Release, Rescue

Rant(er), Ranting Bluster, Bombast, Declaim, Fustian, Ham, Harangue, Rail, Rodomontade, Scold, Slang-whang, Spout, Spruik, Stump, Thunder, Tirade, Tub-thump

Rap(ped) Blame, Censure, Chat, Clour, Gangsta, Halfpenny, Knock, Ratatat, Shand, Strike, Swapt, Tack, Tap

Rapacious Accipitrine, Esurient, Exorbitant, Greedy, Harpy, Kite, Predatory, Ravenous, Ravine

Rape Abuse, Assault, Belinda, Cole-seed, Colza, Creach, Creagh, Date, Deflower, Despoil,

Gangbang, Grass(line), Hundred, Lock, Lucretia, Navew, Oilseed, Plunder, Ravish, Statutory, Stuprate, Thack, Tow, Violate, Vitiate

Rapid(ity), Rapidly Chute, Dalle, Double-quick, Express, Fast, Fleet, Meteoric, Mosso, Presto, Pronto, Quick-fire, Riffle, Sault, Shoot, Skyrocket, Speedy, Stickle, Swift, Tantivy, Veloce, Vibrato, Whiz(zing), Wildfire

Rapier Sword, Tuck

Rappel Abseil

Rapport Accord, Affinity, Agreement, Harmony

Rapprochement Détente, Reconciliation

Rapt Riveted

Raptor Eagle, Kestrel, Osprey, Standgale, Staniel, Stannel, Stanyel, Stooper

Rapture, Rapturous Bliss, → **DELIGHT**, Ecstasy, Elation, Joy, Trance

Rare, Rarity Blue moon, Curio, Earth, Geason, Infrequent, Intemerate, Oddity, One-off, Rear, Recherché, Scarce, Seeld, Seld(om), Singular, Surpassing, Thin, → **UNCOMMON**, Uncooked, Underdone, Unusual

Rare earth Lu(tetium)

Rarefied Thin

Rascal(ly) Arrant, Bad hat, Cad, Cullion, Cur, Deer, Devil, Gamin, Hallian, Hallion, Hallyon, → **KNAVE**, Limner, Loon, Lorel, Losel(l), Low, Lozel(l), Nointer, Rip, Rogue, Scallywag, Scamp, Scapegrace, Schelm, Skeesicks, Skellum, Skelm, Smaik, Spalpeen, Tinker, Toe-rag, Varlet, Varmint, Villain

Rash(ness), Rasher Acne, Bacon, Barber's, Brash, Collop, Daredevil, Eczema, Eruption, Erysipelas, Exanthem(a), Fast, Foolhardy, Gum, Harum-scarum, → **HASTY**, Headlong, Heat, Hives, Hotspur, Ill-advised, Impetigo, Impetuous, Imprudent, Impulsive, Indiscreet, Lardo(o)n, Lichen, Madbrain, Madcap, Miliaria, Morphew, Nappy, Nettle, Outbreak, Overhasty, Pox, Precipitate, Purpura, Reckless, Road, Roseola, Rubella, St Anthony's fire, Sapego, Scarlatina, Serpigo, Spots, Temerity, Tetter, Thoughtless, Unheeding, Unthinking, Unwise, Urticaria

Rasp(er) File, Grate, Odontophore, Radula, Risp, Rub, Scrape, Scroop, Xyster

Raspberry Berate, Black(cap), Boo, Bronx-cheer, Etaerio, Hindberry, Razz, Wineberry

Rastafarian Dread

Rat(s), Ratty Agouta, Bandicoot, Blackleg, Blackneb, Boodie, Brown, Bug-out, Cad, Camass, Cane, Cur, Cutting grass, Defect, Desert, Fink, Footra, Foutra, Geomyoid, Gym, Heck, Heel, Hood, Hydromys, Informer, Kangaroo, Malabar, Mall, Maori, Mole, Moon, Norway, Pack, Pig, Poppycock, Potoroo, Pouched, Pshaw, Pup(py), Renegade, Renegate, Rice, Rink, Rodent, Roland, Rot(ten), Scab, Sewer, Shirty, Squeal, Stinker, Tell, Turncoat, Vole, Wharf, Whiskers, White, Wood

Rat-catcher Cat, Ichneumon, Mongoose, Pied Piper

Rate(s), Rating A, Able, Able-bodied, Apgar, Appraise, Appreciate, Assess, Base, Basic, Birth, Bit, Carpet, Castigate, Cess, Cetane, Chide, Classify, Click, Conception, Conversion, Cost, Count, Credit, Deserve, Effective, ELO, Erk, Estimate, Evaluate, Exchange, Grade, Headline, Hearty, Horsepower, Hurdle, Incidence, Interest, ISO, Lapse, Leading, Mate's, Merit, Mortality, Mortgage, MPH, Mutation, Octane, Ordinary, OS, Pace, Penalty, Percentage, PG, Piece, Poor, Prime (lending), Rag, Rank, Rebuke, Red, Refresh, Reproof, Rocket, Row, Sailor, Scold, Sea-dog, → **SET**, Slew, → **SPEED**, Standing, Starting, Steerageway, Surtax, Take-up, TAM, Tariff, Tax, Tempo, Tog, U, Upbraid, Value, Water, Wig, World-scale, X

Rather Affirmative, Assez, Degree, Fairly, Gay, Gey, Instead, Lief, Liever, Loor, More, Prefer, Pretty, Some(what), Somedele, Sooner, Yes

Ratify Amen, Approve, Confirm, Homologate, Pass, Sanction, Seal, Validate

Ratio Advance, Albedo, Aspect, Bypass, Cash, Compound, Compression, Cosine, Distinctiveness, Duplicate, Focal, Fraction, Gear, Golden, Gyromagnetic, Inverse, Liquidity, Loss, Mark space, Mass, Neper, PE, Pi, Picture, Pogson, Poisson's, Position, Price-dividend, Prise-earnings, Proportion, Protection, Quotient, Reserve, Savings,

Signal-to-noise, Sin(e), Slip, Space, Tensor, Trigonometric

Ration(s) Allocate, Allot, Apportion, Compo, Dole, Étape, Iron, K, Quota, Restrict, Scran, Share, Short commons, Size, Whack

Rational(ism), Rationalisation, Rationalize A posteriori, Descartes, Dianoetic, Dispassionate, Humanistic, Level-headed, Logical, Lucid, Matter-of-fact, Pragmatic, Reasonable, Sane, Sapient, Sensible, Sine, Sober, Tenable, Wice

Rationale Motive

Ratten Sabotage

Rattle (box), Rattling, Rattle on Alarm, Blather, Chatter, Clack, Clank, Clap, Clatter, Clitter, Conductor, Crescelle, Crotalaria, Death, Demoralise, Discombobulate, Discomfort, Disconcert, Gas-bag, Hurtle, Jabber, Jangle, Jar, Maraca, Natter, Nonplus, Rale, Rap, Red, Reel, Rhonchus, Ruckle, Sabre, Shake, Sistrum, Sunn, Tirl, Upset, Vuvuzela, Yellow

Raucous Discordant, Guttural, Hoarse, Loud, Strident

Ravage Depredation, Desecrate, Despoil, Havoc, Pillage, Prey, Ruin, Sack, Waste

Rave, Raving Adulate, Boil, Doiled, Enthuse, Praise, Redwood, Redwud, Storm, Ta(i)ver, Tear

Ravel Disentangle, Entrammel, Explain, Fray, Involve, Snarl, Tangle

Raven(ous) Black, Corbel, Corbie, Corvine, Croaker, Daw, Grip, Hugin, Munin, Prey, Unkindness, Wolfish

Ravine Arroyo, Barranca, Barranco, Canada, Canyon, Chasm, Chine, Clough, Coulée, Couloir, Dip, Flume, Ghyll, Gorge, Goyle, Grike, Gulch, Gully, Kedron, Khor, Khud, Kidron, Kloof, Lin(n), Nal(l)a, Nallah, Nulla(h), Pit, Purgatory, Wadi

Ravish Abduct, Constuprate, Debauch, Defile, Devour, Outrage, Rape, Stuprate, Transport, Violate

Raw Brut, Chill, Coarse, Crude, Crudy, Damp, Fresh, Green(horn), Natural, New, Recruit, Rude, Uncooked, Wersh

Raw-boned Gaunt, Lanky, Lean, Randle-tree

Ray(s), Rayed Actinic, Alpha, Beam, Beta, Bivium, Canal, Cathode, Cosmic, Cramp-fish, Death, Delta, Devil, Devilfish, Diactine, Dun-cow, Eagle, Electric, Extraordinary, Fish, Gamma, Grenz, Guitarfish, Homelyn, Manta, Medullary, Monactine, Numbfish, Ordinary, Polyact, Positive, R, Radius, Re, Roentgen, Roker, Röntgen, Sawfish, Sea-devil, Sea-vampire, Sephen, Shaft, Skate, Starburst, Stick, Sting, Stingaree, T, Tetract, Thornback, Torpedo, Vascular

Rayon Acetate, Faille, Viscose

Raze Annihilate, Bulldoze, Demolish, Destroy, Level, Slight

Razor(-maker) Cut-throat, Occam, Safety, Shaver, Straight

Razorbill Murre

Razor-fish Solen

Razz Raspberry

RE Sappers

Re About, Rhenium, Touching

Reach(ed) Ar(rive), Attain, Boak, Boke, Carry, Come, Extend, Gain, Get at, Get out, Grasp, Hent, Hit, Key-bugle, Lode, Octave, Peak, Raught, Rax, Retch, Ryke, Seize, Stretch, Touch, Win

Reach-me-downs Slop-clothing

React(or), Reaction(ary) Addition, Allergy, Anaphylaxis, Answer, Backlash, Backwash, Behave, Blimp, Blowback, Boiling water, Bourbon, Breeder, Bristle, Bummer, Calendria, CANDU, Cannizzaro, Catalysis, Chain, Chemical, Converter, Convertor, Core, Counterblast, Dark, Dibasic, Diehard, Diels-Adler, Dinosaur, Double-take, Dounreay, Emotion, Endergonic, Exoergic, Falange, Fast(-breeder), Feedback, Fission, Flareback, Flehmen, Flinch, Friedel–Crafts, Furnace, Fusion, Gas-cooled, Graphite, Gut, Heavy-water, Hydrolysis, Imine, Incomplete, Insulin, Interplay, Inulase, Junker, Kickback, Knee-jerk, Light, Lightwater, Magnox, Molten salt, Neanderthal, Nuclear,

Outcry, Oxidation, Pebble-bed, Photolysis, Pile, Polymerization, Poujade, Pressure-tube, Pressurized water, Reciprocate, Recoil, Redox, Reflex, Repercussion, Respond, Reversible, Rigid, Sensitive, Solvolysis, Spallation, Sprocket, Stereotaxis, Swing-back, Thermal, Thermonuclear, Tokamak, Topochemistry, Ultraconservative, Vaccinia, Wassermann, Water

▷ **Reactionary** *may indicate* reversed or an anagram

Read(ing) Abomasum, Bearing, Browse, Decipher, Decode, Exegesis, First, Grind, Grounden, Haftarah, Haphtarah, Haphtorah, Interpret, Learn, Lection, Lesson, Lu, Maftir, Maw, Paired, Pericope, Peruse, Pore, Rad, Rennet-bag, Say, Scan, Second, See, Sight, Skim, Solve, Speed, Stomach, → **STUDY**, Third, Uni(versity), Vell, Version, Ycond

Reader(s) ABC, Academic, Alidad(e), Bookworm, Document, Editor, Epistoler, Gentle, Homeridae, Lay, Lector, Microfilm, Primer, Silas Wegg, Softa, Tape, Taster

Readiest, Readily, Readiness, Ready Alacrity, Alamain, Alert, Amber, Amenability, Apt, Atrip, Available, Boun, Bound, Braced, Brass, Cash, Conditional, Dough, Eager, Early, Eftest, Fettle, Fit, Fiver, Forward, Game, Geared-up, Gelt, Go, Keyed, Latent, Lolly, Masterman, Money, On (call), Predy, Prepared, Present, Prest, Primed, Procinct, Prompt, Promptitude, Ransom, Reckoner, Ripe, Running costs, Set, Soon, Spot, Tenner, To hand, Turnkey, Unhesitant, Usable, Wherewithal, Willing, Yare, Yark

Readjust Mend, Regulate, Retrue

Readymade Bought, Precast, Prepared, Prêt-à-porter, Slops, Stock, Store

Reagent Analytical, Benedict's, Grignard, Ninhydrin, Reactor, Schiff's, Titrant, Tollens

Real, Reality, Realities, Really Actual, Ah, Augmented, Bona-fide, Brass tacks, Coin, Deed, De facto, Dinkum, Dinky-di(e), Earnest, Echt, Ens, Entia, Entity, Essence, Fact(ion), → **GENUINE**, Hard, Honest, Indeed, Mackay, McCoy, McKoy, Naive, Ontic, Positive, Quite, Royal, Simon Pure, Sooth, Sterling, Straight up, Substantial, Tangible, Tennis, The case, Thingliness, True, Verismo, Verity, Very, Virtual

Realgar Rosaker, Zarnec, Zarnich

Realise, Realisation, Realism, Realistic Achieve, Attain, Attuite, Cash, Dirty, Down-to-earth, Embody, Encash, Entelechy, Fetch, Fruition, Fulfil, Hard-edged, Learn, Lifelike, Magic, Naive, Naturalism, Practical, Pragmatism, See, Sell, Sense, Social, Socialist, Suss, Understand, Verisimilitude, Verismo, Verité

▶ **Realities, Reality** *see* **REAL**

Realm Domain, Dominion, Field, Kingdom, Land, Notogaea, Region, Special(i)ty, UK

Ream Bore, Foam, Froth, Paper, Printer's, Rime, Screed

Reap(er) Binder, Crop, Death, Earn, Gather, Glean, Harvest, Scythe, Shear, Sickleman, Solitary, Stibbler

Reappear(ance) Emersion, Materialise, Recrudesce

Rear(ing) Aft, Back(side), Background, Baft, Behind, Bottom, Breeches, Bring-up, Bunt, Butt, Cabré, Catastrophe, Derrière, Empennage, Foster, Haunch, Hind, Hindquarters, Loo, Natch, Nousell, Nurture, Podex, Poop, Prat(t), → **RAISE**, Retral, Rump, Serafile, Serrefile, Stern, Sternward, Tonneau

Rearmament Moral

Rearrange(ment) Adjust, Anagram, Ectopia, Permute, Reorder, Shuffle

Reason(able), Reasoning A fortiori, Agenda, Analytical, Apagoge, A priori, Argue, Argument, Basis, Call, Casuistry, Cause, Colour, Consideration, Deduce, Economical, Expostulate, Fair, Ground(s), Hypophora, Ijtihad, Inductive, Intelligent, Ipso facto, Justification, Logic, Logical, Logistics, Logos, Metamathematics, Mind, Moderate, Motive, Noesis, Petitio principii, Plausible, Point, Practical, Pretext, Pro, Proof, Pure, Purpose, Ratiocinate, Rational(e), Sanity, Sense, Sensible, Settler, Somewhy, Sophism, Syllogism, Synthesis, Temperate, Think, Viable, What for, Why, Wit

Reave Despoil, Reif, Rob, Spoil

Rebate Diminish, Lessen, Refund, Repayment

Rebecca Sharp

Rebel(s), Rebellion, Rebellious Aginner, Apostate, Arian, Beatnik, Blouson noir,

Bolshy, Bounty, Boxer, Cade, Contra, Croppy, Danton, Defiance, Diehard, Disobedient, Dissident, Drop out, Emeute, Fifteen, Forty-five, Frondeur, Glendower, Green Mountain Boys, Hampden, Hereward the Wake, Hippy, Iconoclast, Insubordinate, Insurgent, Insurrection, IRA, Jacobite, Jacquerie, Kick, Luddite, Maccabee, Malignant, Mutine(er), Mutiny, Oates, Pilgrimage of Grace, Putsch, Rebecca, Recalcitrant, Recusant, Reluct, Resist, → **REVOLT**, Rise, Rum, Scofflaw, Sedition, Sepoy, Spartacus, Steelboy, Straw, Taiping, Ted, Titanism, Tyler, Unruly, Venner, Warbeck, Wat Tyler, Whiteboy, Young Turk, Zealot

▷ **Rebellious** *may indicate* a word reversed

Rebirth Palingenesis, Reincarnation, Renaissance, Revival, Samsara

Rebound Backfire, Bounce, Cannon, Carom, Elastic, Recoil, Repercussion, Ricochet, Snapback

Rebuff Check, Cold-shoulder, Noser, Quelch, Repulse, Retort, Rubber, Setdown, Sneb, Snib, Snub

Rebuild Haussmannize

Rebuke Admonish, Berate, Check, Chide, Earful, Lecture, Neb, Objurgate, Rap, Rate, Razz, Reprimand, Reproof, Reprove, Rollick, Scold, Score, Slap, Slate, Snib, Snub, Strop, Threap, Threep, Tick off, Trim, Tut, Upbraid, Wig

Rebut Disprove, Elide, Refute, Repulse, Retreat

Recalcitrant Mulish, Obstinate, Renitent, Unruly, Wilful

Recall(ing) Annul, Echo, Eidetic, Encore, Evocative, Flashback, Go over, Memory, Partial, Reclaim, Recollect, Redolent, Remember, Remind, Reminisce, Repeal, Retrace, Revoke, Total, Unsay, Withdraw

Recant(ation) Disclaim, Palinode, Retract, Revoke

Recap(itulate), Recapitulation Epanodos, Palingenesis, Summarise

Recapture Rescue

▷ **Recast** *may indicate* an anagram

▶ **Recce** *see* **RECONNAISSANCE**

Recede Decline, Ebb, Lessen, Regress, Retrograde, Shrink, Withdraw

Receipt(s) Acknowledge, Chit, Docket, Gate, Quittance, Recipe, Revenue, Take, Voucher

Receive(d), Receiver Accept, Accoil, Acquire, Admit, Aerial, Antenna, Assignee, Bailee, Bleeper, Dipole, Dish, Donee, Ear, Earphone, Fence, Get, Grantee, Greet, Hydrophone, Inherit, Intercom, Official, Pernancy, Phone, Pocket, Radio, Radiopager, Remit, Reset, Responser, Responsor, Roger, Set, Sounder, Take, Tap, Transistor, Transponder, Tuner, Wide, Wireless

Recent(ly) Alate, Current, Fresh, Hot, Just, Late, Low, Modern, New, New-found, Yesterday, Yestereve, Yesterweek

Receptacle Ash-tray, Basket, Bin, Bowl, Box, Chrismatory, Ciborium, Container, Cyst, Hell-box, Locket, Loom, Monstrance, Muffle, Receiver, Reliquary, Relique, Reservatory, Sacculus, Spermatheca, Spittoon, Tank, Thalamus, Tidy, Tore, Torus, Trash can

Reception, Receptive Accoil, At home, Bel-accoyle, Couchée, Court, Durbar, Entertainment, First-class, Ghost, Greeting, Helpdesk, Infare, Kursaal, Levée, Open, Ovation, Pervious, Ruelle, Saloon, Sensory, Soirée, Superheterodyne, Teleasthetic, Warm, Welcome

Receptor(s) Metabotropic, Steroid

Recess(ion) Alcove, Antrum, Apse, Apsidal, Apsis, Bay, Bole, Bower, Break, Breaktime, Bunk, Closet, Columbarium, Corner, Corrie, Cove, Croze, Dinette, Ebb, Embrasure, Exedra, Fireplace, Grotto, Hitch, Indent, Inglenook, Interval, Loculus, Mortise, → **NICHE**, Nook, Oriel, Outshot, Pigeonhole, Rabbet, Rebate, Respite, Rest, Slump, Withdrawal

▷ **Recess** *may indicate* 'reversed'

Rechabite TT

Réchauffé Hachis, Hash, Salmi

Recidivist Relapser

▷ **Recidivist** *may indicate* 'reversed'

Recipe Dish, Formula, Prescription, R, Receipt, Take

Recipient Assignee, Beneficiary, Disponee, Donee, Grantee, Heir, Legatee, Receiver, Suscipient

Reciprocal, Reciprocate Corresponding, Elastance, Exchange, Inter(act), Mutual, Repay, Return, Two-way

Recite(r), Recital, Recitation(ist) Ave, Concert, Declaim, Diseuse, Enumerate, Incantation, Litany, Monologue, Mystic, Parlando, Quote, Reading, Reel, Relate, Rhapsode, Say, Sing, Tell

▷ **Reckless** *may indicate* an anagram

Reckless(ness) Bayard, Blindfold, Careless, Catiline, Desperado, Desperate, Devil-may-care, Gadarene, Harum-scarum, Hasty, Headfirst, Headlong, Hell-bent, Irresponsible, Jaywalker, Madcap, Perdu(e), Ramstam, Rantipole, → **RASH**, Slapdash, Temerity, Ton-up, Wanton, Wildcat

Reckon(ed), Reckoning Assess, Bet, Calculate, Cast, Census, Computer, Consider, Count, Date, Doomsday, Estimate, Fancy, Figure, Guess, Impute, Number, Rate, Reputed, Settlement, Shot, Tab

Reclaim(ed), Reclamation Assart, Empolder, Impolder, Innings, Novalia, Polder, Recover, Redeem, Restore, Salvage, Swidden, Tame, Thwaite

Recline, Reclining Accubation, Accumbent, Lean, Lie, Lounge, Rest

Recluse, Reclusive Anchor(et), Anchorite, Ancress, Eremite, Essene, Hermit, Lone wolf, Low-profile, Solitaire

Recognise(d), Recognition Accept, Accredit, Acknow(ledge), Admit, Anagnorisis, Appreciate, Ascetic, Character, Cit(ation), Discern, Exequatur, Gaydar, Identify, Isolated, Ken, → **KNOW**, Nod, Notice, Oust, Own, Perception, Resipiscence, Reward, Salute, Scent, Standard, Sung, Voice, Weet, Wot

Recoil Backlash, Bounce, Kick(back), Quail, Rebound, Redound, Repercussion, Resile, Reverberate, Shrink, Shy, Spring, Start, Whiplash

Recollect(ion) Anamnesis, Memory, Pelmanism, Recall, → **REMEMBER**, Reminisce

▷ **Recollection** *may indicate* an anagram

Recommend(ation) Advise, Advocate, Counsel, Direct, Encourage, Endorse, Exhort, Move, Nap, Praise, Precatory, Promote, Rider, Suggest, Testimonial, Tip, Tout, Urge

Recompense Cognisance, Deodand, Deserts, Eric, Expiate, Guerdon, Pay, Remunerate, Repayment, Requite, Restitution, Reward

Reconcile(d) Accord, Adapt, Adjust, Affrended, Atone, Harmonise, Henotic, Make up, Mend

Recondite Difficult, Esoteric, Mystic, Obscure, Occult, Profound

Reconnaissance, Reconnoitre Case, Investigate, Patrol, Recce, Scout, Survey

Reconstitute, Reconstitution Diagenesis

Reconstruction Perestroika, Telophase

Record(er), Recording (company) All-time, Book, Chart, Chronicle, Clock, Coat(e), Enter, Entry, Ever, Fact, File, Itemise, Log, Mark, Memorise, Mind, Notate, Note, Previous, Quote, Release, Remember, Set down, Sunshine, Take, Tally, Tallyman, Trace, Trip, Vote, Weigh, Write

RECORDS

2 *letters:*	Rec	Gram	Wire
CD	Vid	List	
EP	Wax	Memo	5 *letters:*
LP		Mono	Album
	4 *letters:*	Roll	Ampex
3 *letters:*	Disc	Tape	Annal
Can	Film	TiVo®	A-side
EMI	Form	VERA	Aulos

B-side
Crash
Decca
Diary
Eloge
Elpee
Flute
Indie
Meter
Notch
Quipo
Quipu
Score
Track
Video

6 letters:
Flight
Ledger
Memoir
Minute
Public
Regest
Single
Wisden

7 letters:
Acetate
Archive
Daybook
Digital
Dossier

Estreat
Filater
Hansard
History
Journal
Logbook
Memento
Platter
Practic
Shellac

8 letters:
Analogue
Annalist
Black box
Bookmark
Casebook
Document
Herstory
Hologram
Lap-chart
Marigram
Memorial
Miniment
Noctuary
Odometer
Open-seel
Pass book
Playback
Practick
Pratique
Pressing

Protocol
Rapsheet
Register
Studbook
Travelog

9 letters:
Archivist
Bench-mark
Cartulary
Ephemeris
Forty-five
Seven-inch
Spirogram
Stenotype®
Time sheet
Videotape
Worksheet

10 letters:
Audit trail
Blue Riband
Dictaphone®
Dictograph®
Gramophone
Maxi-single
Memorandum
Provenance
Quadruplex
Reel-to-reel
Scoreboard
Spectogram

Tachograph
Transcript
Twelve-inch

11 letters:
Cardiograph
Case history
Clickstream
Clog-almanac
Electrogram
Endorsement
Helical scan
Hill and dale
Incremental
Oscillogram
Sphygmogram
Thirty-three

12 letters:
English flute
Hierogrammat
Remembrancer
Seventy-eight

13 letters:
Congressional
Ghetto blaster
Quadrophonics

14 letters:
Campbell-Stokes

Record-holder Champion, Sleeve

Record-player DJ, Stereo

Recount Describe, Enumerate, → **NARRATE**, Relate, Tell

Recourse Access, Resort

Recover(y) Amend, Clawback, Comeback, Common, Convalescence, Cure, Dead cat bounce, Get over, Lysis, Over, Perk, Pull through, Rally, Rebound, Reclaim, Recoup, Redeem, Regain, Rehab, Repaint, Replevin, Replevy, Repo(ssess), Rescript, Rescue, Resile, → **RETRIEVE**, Revanche, Salvage, Salve, Second-wind, Spontaneous, Upswing, Upturn

Recreate, Recreation Diversion, Hobby, Palingenesia, Pastime, Play, Pleasure, Revive, Sport

Recriminate, Recrimination Ruction

Recruit(s) Attestor, Bezonian, Choco, Conscript, Crimp, Draft, Employ, Engage, Enlist, Enrol, Headhunt, Intake, Muster, New blood, Nignog, Nozzer, Press, Rookie, Sprog, Volunteer, Wart, Yardbird, Yobbo

Rectangle, Rectangular Dimetric, Golden, Matrix, Oblong, Quad, Quadrate, Square

Rectifier, Rectify Adjust, Amend, Dephlegmate, Redress, Regulate, → **REMEDY**, Right, Silicon

Recto Ro

Rector R

Rectum Tewel

Recumbent Prone

Recuperate Convalesce, Rally, Recover

Recur(rent), Recurring Chronic, Quartan, Quintan, Recrudesce, Repeated, Repetend, Return

▷ **Recurrent** *may indicate* 'reversed'

Recycle(r), Recycling Freegan, Pulp

Red(den), Redness Admiral, Alizarin, Anarch(ist), Angry, Archil, Arun, Ashamed, Auburn, Bashful, Beet, Bilirubin, Bloodshot, Blush, Bolshevik, Brick, Burgundy, C, Cain-coloured, Carmine, Carrot-top, Carroty, Castory, Cent, Cerise, Cherry, Chica, Chinese, Choy-root, Chrome, Cinnabar, Claret, Coccineous, Commie, Commo, Communist, Congo, Copper, Coquelicot, Coral, Corallin(e), Corkir, Cramesy, Cremosin, Crimson, Crocoite, Cuprite, Cyanin, Damask, Debit, Dubonnet, Duster, Embarrassed, Eosin, Eric, Erik, Erythema, Ffion, Flame, Flaming, Florid, Flush, Foxy, Garnet, Geranium, Ginger, Gory, Grog-blossom, Gule(s), Guly, Hat, Henna, Herring, Incarnadine, Indian, Indigo, Inflamed, Infra, Inner, Intertrigo, Iron, Jacqueminot, Judas-coloured, Keel, Kermes, Korkir, Lac-lake, Lake, Lateritious, Left(y), Lenin, Letter, Magenta, Maoist, Maroon, Marxist, McIntosh, Medoc, Menshevik, Miniate, Minium, Modena, Mulberry, Murrey, Neaten, Orchel, Orchilla-weed, Orseille, Oxblood, Phenol, Pillar-box, Pinko, Plethoric, Plum, Pompeian, Ponceau, Poppy, Pyrrhous, Raddle, Radical, Raspberry, Raw, Realgar, Rhodamine, Rhodopsin, Ridinghood, Roan, Rosaker, Rose, Rot, Rouge, Roy, Rubefaction, Rubefy, Rubella, Rubescent, Rubicund, Rubric, Ruby, Ruddle, Ruddy, Rufescent, Rufus, Russ(e), Russet, Russian, Russky, Rust(y), Rutilant, Safranin(e), Sang-de-boeuf, Sanguine, Santalin, Sard, Scarlet, Sea, Sericon, Setter, Solferino, Stammel, Tape, Tidy, Tile, Titian, Trot, Trotsky, Turacin, Turkey, Tyrian, Venetian, Vermeil, Vermilion, Vermily, Vinaceous, Wallflower, Wax, Wine

▷ **Red** *may indicate* an anagram

Redcoat Rust, Soldier

Redeem(er), Redemption Cross, Liberate, Lowse, Mathurin, Messiah, Ransom, Retrieve, Salvation, Save

Red-faced Coaita, Florid, Flushed, Rubicund

Red-handed Bang to rights

Redhead Auburn, Bashful, Blue(y), Carrot-top, Carroty, Commie, Commissar, Ginger, Mao, Medoc, Rufus, Safranin(e), Sea

Red herring Norfolk capon, Soldier

▶ **Red Indian** *see* **NORTH AMERICAN INDIAN**

Redirect Reset, Sublimate

▷ **Rediscovered** *may indicate* an anagram

Redistil Cohobate

Redolent Aromatic, Fragrant, Reeking, Suggestive

Redoubtable Stalwart

Redress Amends, Offset, Recompense, Rectify, Regrate, Remedy, Right

Redshank Gambet, Totanus

Redskin Indian, Tomato

Red spot Tika

Reduce(d), Reducer, Reduction Abatement, Allay, Alleviate, Amortize, Asyndeton, Attenuate, Bate, Beggar, Beneficiate, Calcine, Clip, Commutation, Commute, Concession, Condense, Contract, Cull, Cut, Cutback, Damping, Debase, Decimate, Decrease, Decrement, De-escalate, Demote, Deoxidate, Deplete, Depreciation, Detract, Devalue, Diminish, Diminuendo, Discount, Downgrade, Downscale, Downsize, Draw-down, Drop, Emasculate, Epitomise, Foreshorten, Grate, Grind, Hatchet job, Jeff, Kinone, → **LESSEN**, Lite, Markdown, Miniature, Mitigate, Moderate, Palliate, Pot, Proclitic, Pulp, Put, Quinol, Rarefaction, Razee, Regression, Remission, Retrench, Rundown, Scant, Shade, Shorten, Shrinkage, Slash, Strain, Supersaver, Taper, Telescope, Thin, Weaken, Whittle, Write-off

Redundancy, Redundant Frill, Futile, Lay-off, Needless, Otiose, Pink slip, Pleonasm, Retrenchment, Superfluous, Surplus

Redwood Amboyna, Mahogany, Sanders, Wellingtonia

Reed Arundinaceous, Broken, Calamus, Double, Free, Oboe, Papyrus, Pipe, Quill, Raupo, Rush, Sedge, Seg, Sley, Spear, Sudd, Syrinx, Thatch, Twill, Whistle

Reef Atoll, Barrier, Bioherm, Bombora, Bommie, Cay, Coral, Fringing, Great Barrier, Key, Knot, Lido, Motu, Saddle, Sca(u)r, Skerry, Witwatersrand

Reefer Cigarette, Jacket, Joint

Reek Emit, Exude, Stink

Reel Bobbin, Dance, Eightsome, Hoolachan, Hoolican, Inertia, Lurch, Multiplier, News, Pirn, Spin, Spool, Stagger, Strathspey, Sway, Swift, Swim, Tirl, Totter, Virginia, Wheel, Whirl, Wince, Wintle

Re-enlist Re-up

Reestablish Redintegrate, Transplant

Refectory Frater

Refer Advert, Allude, Assign, Cite, Direct, Mention, Pertain, Relate, Remit, Renvoi, Renvoy, See, Submit, Touch, Trade

Referee Arbiter, Commissaire, Linesman, Mediate, Oddsman, Official, Ref, Umpire, Voucher, Whistler, Zebra

Reference, Reference room Allusion, Apropos, Autocue, Biaxal, Chapter and verse, Character, Coat, Grid, Guidebook, Index, Innuendo, Lexicon, Mention, Morgue, Passion, Promptuary, Quote, Regard, Renvoi, Respect, Retrospect, Testimonial, Thesaurus, Vide

Referendum Mandate, Plebiscite, Vox populi

Refill Replenish, Top up

Refine(d), Refinement, Refiner(y) Alembicated, Attic, Catcracker, Couth, Cultivate, Culture, Cupellation, Cut-glass, Distil, Distinction, Elaborate, Elegance, Ethereal, Exility, Exquisite, Genteel, Grace, Ladify, Nice, Nicety, Polish(ed), Polite, Précieuse, Preciosity, Pure, Rare(fy), Recherché, Saltern, Sieve, Sift, Smelt, Sophisticated, Spiritualize, Spirituel, Sublimate, Subtilise, Subtlety, Tasteful, Try, U, Urbane, Veneer

Reflect(ing), Reflection, Reflective, Reflector Albedo, Apotheosis, Blame, Catoptric, Cat's eye®, Chaff, Chew, Cogitate, → **consider**, Echo, Glass, Glint, Glisten, Image, Meditate, Mirror, Muse, Nonspecular, Ponder, Redound, Repercuss, Ricochet, Ruminate, Spectacular, Speculum, Symmetrical, Tapetum, Thought

Reflex(ive) Achilles, Babinski, Bent, Cancrizans, Diving, In, Knee-jerk, Patellar, Pavlovian, Reciprocal, Re-entrant, Single-lens, Tic, Twin-lens

Reflux Acid

Reform(er), Reforming, Reformist Agrarian, Amend, Apostle, Besant, Beveridge, Bloomer, Calvin, Chartism, Chastise, Convert, Correct, Counter-Reformation, Enrage, Fourier, Fry, Gandhi, Gradualism, Howard, Hussite, Improve, Knox, Lafayette, Land, Lollard, Luther, Meiji, Melanchthon, Mend, Modify, Mucker, New Deal, Owenite, Penn, Pietism, PR, Progressionist, Protestant, Proudhon, Puritan, Rad(ical), Really, Recast, Reclaim, Reconstruction, Rectify, Regenerate, Resipiscence, Ruskin, Satyagraha, Savonarola, Simons, Stanton, Syncretise, Tariff, Transmute, Tyndale, Wilberforce, Wilkes, Wycliffe, Young Turk, Zinzendorf, Zwingli

▷ **Reform(ed)** *may indicate an anagram*

Reformatory Borstal, Magdalen(e)

Refract(ion), Refractive, Refractor(y) Anaclastic, Double, Firestone, Obstinate, Perverse, Prism, Recalcitrant, Refringe, Restive, Stubborn, Sullen, Wayward

Refrain Abstain, Alay, Avoid, Bob, Burden, Chorus, Desist, Epistrophe, Faburden, Fa-la, Forbear, Hemistich, Mantra, O(v)erword, Owreword, Repetend, Ritornello, Rumbelow, Rum(p)ti-iddity, Rum-ti-tum, Spare, Tag, Tirra-lirra, Tirra-lyra, Tra-la, Turn again, Undersong, Waive, Wheel

Refresh(ment), Refresher Air, Bait, Be(a)vers, Buffet, Cheer, Coffee, Elevenses, Enliven, Exhilarate, Food, Four-hours, Milk shake, Nap, New, Nourishment, Purvey, Refection, Reflect, Refocillate, Reinvigorate, Renew, Repast, Restore, Revive, Seltzer, Shire, Slake, Tea, Water

Refrigerator Chill, Chiller, Cooler, Deep freeze, Esky®, Freezer, Freon, Fridge, Ice-box, Minibar, Reefer

Refuge Abri, Ark, Asylum, Bolthole, Bothie, Bothy, Burrow, Caravanserai, Dive, Fastness, Funkhole, Girth, Grith, Harbour, Haven, Hideaway, Hole, Holt, Home, Hospice, Oasis, Port, Reefer, Resort, Retreat, Sanctuary, Sheet-anchor, → **SHELTER**, Soil, Stronghold, Women's

Refugee(s) Boat people, DP, Economic, Escapist, Fugitive, Grenzganger, Huguenot, Reffo

Refund Clawback, Repayment, Surcharge

Refurbish New, Renew

▷ **Refurbished** *may indicate* an anagram

Refusal, Refuse Attle, Bagasse, Ba(u)lk, Bilge, Bin, Black, Blackball, Boycott, Bran, Brash, Breeze, Brock, Bull, Bunkum, Cane-trash, Chaff, Cinder, Clap-trap, Contumacy, Crane, Crap, Cul(t)ch, Debris, Decline, Denay, Deny, Disown, Draff, Drivel, Dross, Dunder, Dung, Eighty-six, Fag-end, Fenks, Fiddlesticks, Finks, First, Flock, Frass, Garbage, Gob, Guff, Hards, Hogwash, Hold-out, Hurds, Husk, Interdict, Jews' houses, Jews' leavings, Jib, Junk, Knickknackery, Knub, Lay-stall, Leavings, Litter, Lumber, Mahmal, Marc, Megass(e), Midden, Mother, Mullock, Mush, Nay(-say), Nill, No (dice), Noser, Nould(e), Nub, Offal, Off-scum, Orts, Pellet, Pigwash, Potale, Punk, Radwaste, Raffle, Rags, Rape(cake), Rat(s), Rebuff, Recrement, Recusance, Red(d), Redargue, Redline, Reest, Regret, Reject, Reneg(u)e, Renig, Repudiate, Resist, Rot, → **RUBBISH**, Ruderal, Scaff, Scrap, Scree, Screenings, Scum, Sewage, Shant, Shell heap, Slag, Sordes, Spurn, Sullage, Sweepings, Swill, Tailings, Tinpot, Tip, Toom, Tosh, Trade, Trash, Tripe, Trock, Troke, Trumpery, Turndown, Twaddle, Unsay, Utter, Wash, Waste, Waste paper, Wastrel

▷ **Re-fused** *may indicate* an anagram

Refutation, Refute Deny, Disprove, Elench(us), Rebut, Rebuttal, Redargue, Refel

Regain Recoup, Recover, Revanche

Regal Maeve, Organ

▶ **Regal** *see* **ROYAL(TY)**

Regalia → **CIGAR**, Mound, Orb, Sceptre

Regard(ing) Anent, Apropos, As to, Attention, Care, Consider, → **ESTEEM**, Eye, Gaum, Look, Observe, Odour, Pace, Rate, Re, Repute, Respect, Revere, Sake, Steem, Value, Vis-à-vis

Regardless Anyway, Despite, Heedless, In any event, Irrespective, No matter, Notwithstanding, Rash, Though, Uncaring, Unmindful, Willy-nilly

Regatta Head of the river, Henley

Regenerate Restore

Regent Interrex, Ruler, Viceroy

Regent's Park Zoo

Reggae Ska

Regicide Ireton, Macbeth

Regime(n) Administration, Control, Diet(etics), Method, Regency, Reich, Tyrannus

Regiment Black Watch, Buffs, Colour(s), Discipline, Foot, Greys, Ironsides, Life Guards, Marching, Monstrous, Nutcrackers, Organise, RA, RE, REME, Rifle, Royals, → **SAS**, Scots Greys, Tercio, Tertia

▷ **Regiment** *may indicate* an anagram

Region(s) → **AREA**, Belt, Central, Climate, Climature, Clime, Critical, District, Domain, End, Heaviside layer, Offing, Part, Province, Quart(er), Realm, Sector, Side, Territory, Thermosphere, Tract, Variable, Zone

REGIONS

1 letter:	*4 letters:*		*5 letters:*
D	Aceh	Midi	Bundu
E	Ards	Nejd	Caria
F	Asir	Oudh	Dacia
	Brie	Vaud	Ionia

Lycia
Lydia
Macao
Mysia
Negeb
Negev
Nubia
Opher
Segou
Sumer
Tagma
Thule
Tibet
Tigré
Troas
Weald

6 letters:
Alsace
Amhara
Canaan
Guiana
Mallee
Mascon
Molise
Murcia
Ogaden
Persis
Sparta
Thrace
Tigray
Tundra
Umbria
Ungava
Valois
Veneto

7 letters:
Algarve
Alsatia
Bavaria

Bohemia
Borders
Cariboo
Chaldea
Chiasma
Cilicia
Elysium
Hundred
Illyria
Kashmir
Katanga
Lapland
Lothian
Lusatia
Maghreb
Masuria
Moravia
Navarre
Neogaea
Ossetia
Pargana
Scythia
Siberia
Tayside
Tuscany

8 letters:
Asturias
Brittany
Calabria
Camargue
Carnatic
Carniola
Caucasia
Chaldaea
Dust bowl
Ethiopia
Hebrides
La Mancha
Lorraine
Nuristan

Oriental
Pannonia
Piedmont
Provence
Refugium
Ruthenia
Sarmatia
Slavonia
Sogdiana
Stannery
Subtopia
Taymiria
Teesside
Thessaly
Walachia
Zululand

9 letters:
Andalusia
Aquitaine
Arctogaea
Bantustan
Catalonia
Circassia
Cleveland
Ecosphere
Holarctic
Lusitania
Macedonia
Manchuria
Molossian
Mordvinia
New Quebec
Palestine
Patagonia
Pergunnah
Rhineland
Turkestan
Turkistan
Val d'Aosta
Vojvodina

10 letters:
Appalachia
Bessarabia
Cappadocia
Constantia
Hinterland
Lacustrine
Mauretania
New Castile
Old Castile
Westphalia

11 letters:
Austronesia
Mecklenburg
Mesopotamia
Namaqualand
Rhizosphere
Spanish Main
Strathclyde
Tetrarchate
Ultima Thule
Vuelta Abajo

12 letters:
Low Countries
Matabeleland
Transylvania

13 letters:
Transcaucasia

14 letters:
Transdniestria

16 letters:
Champagne-Ardenne

Register(ing), Registration, Registry Actuarial, Almanac, Annal, Cadastral, Cadastre, Calendar, Cartulary, Cash, Census, Check-in, Child abuse, Dawn, Diptych, Docket, Enlist, Enrol, Enter, Flag out, Gross, Handicap, Index, Indicate, Inscribe, Inventory, Land, Ledger, List, Lloyd's, Log, Matricula, Menology, NAI, Net, Note, Notitia, Obituary, Parish, Park, Patent, Patent Rolls, Poll, Quotation, Read, Reception, Record, Reg(g)o, Rent-roll, Roll, Roule, Score, Shift(ing), Ship's, Sink in, Soprano, Terrier, Voice

Registrar Actuary, Greffier, Medical, Protocolist, Recorder, Specialist, Surgical

Regress(ion) Backslide, Recidivism, Revert

Regret(ful), Regrettable Alack, Alas, Apologise, Bemoan, Deplore, Deprecate, Ewhow, Forthwink, Ichabod, Lackaday, Lament, Mourn, Otis, Penitent, Pity, Remorse, Repentance, Repine, Resent, Rew, → **RUE**, Ruth, Sorrow, Tragic

Regular(ity), Regularly By turn, Clockwork, Constant, Custom, Daily, Episodic,

Even, Giusto, Goer, Habitual, Habitude, Habitué, Hourly, Insider, Methodic, Nightly, Nine-to-five, Normal, Often, Orderly, Orthodox, Patron, Peloria, Periodic, Rhythmic, Routine, Set, Smooth, → **STANDARD**, Stated, Statutory, Steady, Strict, Symmetric, Uniform, Usual, Yearly

Regulate, Regulation, Regulator Adjust, Appestat, Ballcock, Bye-law, Code, Control, Correction, Curfew, Customary, Direct, Dispensation, Gibberellin, Governor, Guide, King's, Logistics, Metrostyle, Order, Ordinance, Police, Prescriptive, Protocol, Queen's, Rule, Snail, Square, Standard, Statute, Stickle, Stopcock, Sumptuary, Thermostat, Valve

Regulus Matte

Regurgitation Merycism, Trophallaxis

Rehab(ilitate), Rehabilitation AA, Cure, Orthotics, Physio(therapy), Repone

Rehearsal, Rehearse Band-call, Dress, Drill, Dry-block, Dry-run, Dummy-run, Practice, Practise, Preview, Recite, Repeat, Run through, Technical, Trial, Walk through

Reichenbach Falls, Od

Reign Era, Govern, Meiji, Prevail, Raine, Realm, Restoration, → **RULE**, Sway

Reimburse(ment) Compensate, Indemnity, Recoup, Redress, Repay

Rein(s) Bearing, Caribou, Check, Control, Curb, Deer, Free, Gag, Leading strings, Long, Lumbar, Restrain, Ribbons, Safety, Stop, Tame, Tight, Walking

Reincarnation Palingenesis

Reindeer Blitzen, Caribou, Comet, Cupid, Dancer, Dasher, Donner, Moss, Prancer, Rudolf, Tarand, Vixen

Reinforce(ment) Aid, Augment, Beef up, Bolster, Boost, Brace, Buttress, Cleat, Counterfort, Line, Negative, Partial, Plash, Pleach, Positive, Re-bar, Recruit, Reserve, Ripieno, → **STRENGTHEN**, Support, Tenaiile, Tenaillon, Tetrapod, Underline, Welt

Reinstate Repone, Restore

Reinvigorate Recruit

Reiterate(d), Reiteration Battology, Ding, Emphasize, Ostinato, Plug, → **REPEAT**

Reject(ion) Abhor, Abjure, Athetise, Bin, Blackball, Brush off, Cast, Cast off, Deny, Dice, Disallow, Discard, Disclaim, Discount, Disdain, Disown, Diss, Elbow, Eliminate, Export, Flout, Frass, Heave-ho, Iconoclasm, Jettison, Jilt, Kest, Kill, Knock-back, Ostracise, Oust, Outcast, Outtake, Pip, Plough, Quash, Rebuff, Recuse, Refuse, Reny, Repel, Reprobate, Repudiate, Repulse, Retree, Scout, Scrub, Spet, Spike, Spin, Spit, → **SPURN**, Sputum, Thumbs-down, Trash, Turndown, Veto

Rejoice, Rejoicing Celebrate, Exult, Festivity, Gaude, Glory, Joy, Maffick, Sing

Rejoin(der), Rejoined Answer, Comeback, Counter, Relide, Reply, Response, Retort, Reunite

Rejuvenation Shunamitism

Rekindle Relume

Relapse Backslide, Deteriorate, Hypostrophe, Recidivism, Regress, Revert, Sink

Relate(d), Relation(ship), Relations, Relative About, Account, Affair, Affine, Affinity, Agnate, Akin, Allied, Antibiosis, Appertain, Apposition, Associate, Blood, Blude, Bluid, Brer, Brisure, Causality, Cognate, Commensal, Commune, Concern, Connection, Connexion, Consanguinity, Coosen, Cousin(-german), Coz, Deixis, Dependent, Dispersion, Eme, Enate, Equation, Equivalence, External, False, Formula, German(e), Granny, Guanxi, Heterogeneous, Homologous, Impart, Industrial, In-law, Internal, International, Item, Kin, Kinsman, Labour, Liaison, Link, Love-hate, Mater, Material, Matrix, Mutualism, Nan(n)a, Narrative, Naunt, Nooky, Object, One-to-one, Osculant, Pertain, Phratry, Pi, Plutonic, Poor, Predation, Privity, → **PROPORTION**, Pro rata, Proxemics, Public, Race, Rapport, Rapprochement, Ratio, Reciprocity, Recite, Recount, Rede, Refer(ence), Relevant, Respect(s), Saga, Sib(b), Sibbe, Sibling, Sine, Sybbe, Symbiosis, Syntax, Tale, Tell, Truck, Who

Relating to Of

Relax(ation), Relaxant, Relaxed Abate, Atony, Autogenics, Calm, Casual, Chalone,

Chill out, Com(m)odo, Contrapposto, Dégagé, Délassement, Détente, Diversion, Downbeat, Ease, Easy-going, Flaccid, Gallamine, Icebreaker, Informal, Laid-back, Laze, Leisured, Lesh states, Let-up, Lighten, → **LOOSEN**, Mellow out, Mitigate, Outspan, Peace, Relent, Relief, Remit, Rest, Settle, Sit down, Slacken, Sleep, Slump, Soma, Toneless, Unbend, Unknit, Unrein, Untie, Unwind, Veg out

▷ **Relaxed** *may indicate* an anagram

Relay(er) Convey, Medley, OB, Race, Shift, Tell, Telstar, Torch-race, Webcast

▷ **Relay(ing)** *may indicate* an anagram

Release Abreact, Abrogation, Announcement, Bail, Block, Cable, Catharsis, Clear, Day, Death, Deliver(y), Desorb, Disburden, Discharge, Disclose, Disengage, Disimprison, Dismiss, Disorb, Emancipate, Enfree, Excuse, Exeem, Exeme, Exonerate, Extricate, Exude, Free, Handout, Happy, → **LIBERATE**, Manumit, Merciful, Moksa, Nirvana, Outrush, Parole, Press, Quietus, Quitclaim, Quittance, Relinquish, Remission, Ripcord, Soft, Spring, Tre corde, Unconfine, Uncouple, Undo, Unhand, Unleash, Unlock, Unloose, Unpen, Unshackle, Unsnap, Unteam, Untie

Relegate Banish, Consign, Demote, Exile, Marginalise, Sideline, Stellenbosch

Relent Bend, Mollify, Soften, Weaken, Yield

Relentless Cruel, Hard, Hardface, Indefatigable, Inexorable, Pitiless, Rigorous, Stern

Relevance, Relevant Ad rem, Applicable, Apposite, Apropos, Apt, Bearing, Germane, Material, Pertinent, Point, Real world, Valid

▶ **Reliable, Reliance** *see* **RELY**

Relic Antique, Ark, Artefact, Fly-in-amber, Fossil, Leftover, Memento, Neolith, Remains, Sangraal, Sangrail, Sangreal, Souvenir, Survival, Vestige

Relict Survivor, Widow

Relief, Relieve(d) Aid, Air-lift, Allay, Allegeance, Alleviate, Alms, Anaglyph, Anastatic, Anodyne, Assistance, Assuage, Bas, Beet, Beste(a)d, Bete, Cameo, Catharsis, Cavo-relievo, Comfort, Cure, Détente, Ease(ment), Emboss, Emollient, Exempt, Free, Grisaille, Help, High, Indoor, Let-up, Lighten, Linocut, Low, Lucknow, Mafeking, MIRAS, On the parish, Outdoor, Palliate, Phew, Photo, Pog(e)y, Reassure, Redress, Refection, Remedy, Remission, Replacement, Repoussé, Reprieve, → **RESCUE**, Respite, Retirement, Rid, Spare, Spell, Stand-in, Stiacciato, Succour, Taper, Tax, Thermoform, Tondo, Toreutics, Wheugh, Whew, Woodcut

Religion, Religious (sect) Congregant, Creed, Cult, Denomination, Devout, Doctrine, Faith, God-squad, Hieratic, Hospital(l)er, Messeigneurs, Missionary, Missioner, Monastic, Monseigneur, Nun, Oblate, Opium, Pagan, Pi, Russellite, Serious, Spiritual, State, Theology, Whore, Zealous

---

RELIGIONS

3 *letters:*	Moony	Maoism	Bogomil
MAM	Pietà	Sabian	Ismaili
	Spike	Shaker	Judaism
4 *letters:*	Sunna	Shango	Lamaism
Druz	Wicca	Shiism	Macumba
Jain		Shinto	Mahatma
	6 *letters:*	Taoism	Orphism
5 *letters:*	Culdee	The Way	Parsism
Baha'i	Gueber	Yezidi	Piarist
Druse	Guebre	Zabian	Sikhism
Druze	Hadith		Tsabian
Hasid	Hassid	7 *letters:*	
Islam	Jesuit	Aaronic	8 *letters:*
Jaina	Khalsa	Animism	Buddhism
Jewry	Loyola	Biblist	Druidism

Familist	Jansenism	Heathenism	**12 letters:**
Lutheran	Mithraism	Manicheism	Christianity
Manichee	Mormonism	Revivalism	Confucianism
Mathurin	Pantheist	Solifidian	Zarathustric
Mazdaism	Parseeism	Triphysite	
Mazdeism	Postulant	Zend-Avesta	**13 letters:**
New Light	Sectarian		Redemptionist
Revealed	Shamanism	**11 letters:**	Sons of Freedom
Salesian	Shintoism	Camaldolite	Swedenborgian
Santeria	Utraquist	Hare Krishna	Tractarianism
Sodality	Voodooism	Ignorantine	
Stundism	Zoroaster	Manichaeism	**14 letters:**
Theatine	Zwinglian	Progressive	Sacramentarian
		Rastafarian	
9 letters:	**10 letters:**	Reformation	**15 letters:**
Arya Samaj	Albigenses	Rosicrucian	Christadelphian
Candomble	Brahmanism	Ryobu Shinto	Jehovah's Witness
Cargo cult	Carthusian	Sabbatarian	Resurrectionist
Celestine	Cistercian	Scientology®	
Coenobite	Gilbertine	Trinitarian	**17 letters:**
Falun Gong	Gnosticism		Premonstratensian

Religious book Bible, Koran, Missal, NT, OT, Sefer, Sifrei, Tantra, Targum, T(h)orah

Relinquish Abdicate, Cede, Demit, Discard, Drop, Forgo, Forlend, Remise, Surrender, Waive(r), Yield

Reliquary Chef, Encolpion, Encolpium, Simonious, Tope

Relish(ing) Aspic, Botargo, Caponata, Catsup, Chakalaka, Chow-chow, Condiment, Embellishment, Enjoy, Flavour, Gentleman's, Gout, Gust(o), Ketchup, Lap(-up), Lust, Opsonium, Palate, Pesto, Piccalilli, Pickle, Sapid, Sar, Sauce, Savour, Seasoning, Tang, Tooth, Worcester sauce, Zest

Reluctant Averse, Backward, Chary, Circumspect, Cockshy, Grudging, Half-hearted, Laith, Loath, Loth, Nolition, Renitent, Shy, Under protest, Unwilling

Rely, Reliance, Reliant, Reliable Addiction, Authentic, Bank, Bread and butter, Brick, Confidence, Constant, Copper-bottomed, → **COUNT**, Dependent, Found, Honest, Hope, Inerrant, Jeeves, Leal, Lean, Loyal, Mensch, Presume, Pukka, Rest, Robin, Safe, Secure, Solid, Sound, Sponge, Stalwart, Stand-by, Staunch, Steady, Sure, Trade on, Trump, Trustworthy, Trusty, Unfailing

Remain(s), Remainder, Remaining Abide, Ash(es), Balance, Bide, Continue, Corse, Dreg(s), Dwell, Embers, Estate, Extant, Exuviae, Fag-end, Fossils, Kreng, Last, Late, Lave, Left, Lie, Locorestive, Manet, Nose, Oddment, Orts, Other, Outstand, Persist, Relic(ts), Reliquae, → **REMNANT**, Residue, Rest, Ruins, Rump, Scourings, Scraps, Stand, Stay, Stick, Stub, Stump, Surplus, Survive, Tag-end, Talon, Tarry, Wait, Wreck(age)

Remark Aside, Barb, Bromide, Comment(ary), Descry, Dig, Epigram, Generalise, Mention, Noise, → **NOTE**, Notice, Obiter dictum, Observe, Platitude, Pleasantry, Reason, Sally, Say, Shot, State

Remarkable, Remarkably A1, Amazing, A one, Arresting, Beauty, Bodacious, Come-on, Conspicuous, Dilly, Egregious, Eminent, Extraordinary, Heliozoan, Legendary, Lulu, Mirable, Notable, Notendum, Noteworthy, Personal, Phenomenal, Rattling, → **SIGNAL**, Singular, Some, Striking, Tall, Unco, Uncommon, Visible

Remedial, Remedy Adaptogen, Aid, An mo, Antacid, Antibiotic, Antidote, Antiodontalgic, Antispasmodic, Arcanum, Arnica, Azoth, Bach®, Bach Flower®, Basilicon, Bicarb, Boneset, Calomel, Catholicon, Corrective, Cortisone, → **CURE**, Decongestant, Dinic, Drug, Elixir, Febrifuge, Femiter, Feverfew, Fumitory, Ginseng, Heal, Ipecac, Leechdom, Medicate, Medicine, Moxa, Nosode, Nostrum, Palliative,

Panacea, Panpharmacon, Paregoric, Poultice, Provisional, Rectify, Redress, Repair, Rescue®, Salutory, Salve, Simillimum, Simple, Specific, Taraxacum, Therapeutic, Tonga, Treatment, Tutsan

Remember(ed), Remembering, Remembrance Bethink, Catchy, Commemorate, Con, Mem, Memorial, Memorise, Mention, Mneme, Poppy, Recall, Recollect, Remind, Reminisce, Retain, Rosemary, Souvenir

▷ **Remember** *may indicate* RE-member, viz. Sapper

Remind(er) Aftertaste, Aide-memoire, Bell ringer, Bethought, Bookmark, Evocatory, Evoke, Jog, Keepsake, Mark, Memento, Memo, Mnemonic, Mnemotechnic, Monition, Nudge, Phylactery, Prod, Prompt, Shades of, Souvenir, Throwback, Token

Reminiscence(s), Reminiscent Ana, Evocative, Memory, Recall, Recollect, Remember, Retrospect

Remiss Careless, Derelict, Lax, Lazy, Negligent, Slack-handed, Tardy

Remission Abatement, Absolution, Acceptilation, Indulgence, Pardon, Pause, Spontaneous

Remit Excuse, Forgive, Forward, Pardon, Postpone

Remnant Butt, End, Fent, Heeltap, Leavings, Left-over, Odd-come-short, Offcut, Relic, Relict, → **REMAINDER**, Rump, Stub, Sweepings, Trace, Vestige, Witness

Remonstrate Argue, Complain, Expostulate, Protest, Reproach

Remorse Angst, Ayenbite, Breast-beating, Compunction, Contrition, Had-i-wist, Pity, → **REGRET**, Repentance, Rue, Ruing, Ruth, Sorrow, Worm

Remote(ness) Aloof, Aphelion, Back blocks, Backveld, Backwater, Backwood, Boondocks, Bullamakanka, Bundu, Bush, → **DISTANT**, Far flung, Forane, Foreign, Inapproachable, Insular, Irrelevant, Jericho, Lonely, Long(inquity), Mystique, Out(part), Outback, Out of the way, Scrub, Secluded, Shut-out, Slightest, Surrealistic, Unlikely, Withdrawn, Woop Woop, Wop-wops

Remount(s) Remuda

Removal, Remove(d) Abduct, Ablation, Abstract, Airbrush, Apocope, Asport, Banish, Blot, Circumcision, Clear, Couch, Deaccession, Debridement, Declassify, Dele(te), Depilate, Depose, Deracinate, Detach, Dethrone, Detract, Dishelm, Dislodge, Disloign, Dismiss, Dispel, Displace, Doff, Efface, Eject, Eliminate, Eloi(g)n, Emend, Eradicate, Erase, Esloin, Esloyne, Estrange, Evacuate, Evict, Exalt, Excise, Expunge, Extirpate, Extradite, Extricate, Far, Flit, Huff, Nick, Obviation, Ouster, Raise, Raze, Razee, Recuse, Redline, Remble, Rid, Scratch, Sequester, Shift, Sideline, Spirit, Strip, Sublate, Subtract, Supplant, Swipe, Transfer, Transport, Unbelt, Unload, Unperson, Unseat, Unstep, Uproot

Remuneration Pay, Return, Reward, Salary, Solde

Remus Uncle

Renaissance Awakening, Cinquecento, Early, High, Quattrocento, Revival

Rend Cleave, Harrow, Lacerate, Rip, Rive, Rupture, Tear

Render(ing) Construe, Deliver, Do, Gie, Give, Interpretation, Make, Melt, Pebble-dash, Plaster, Provide, Recite, Represent, Restore, Setting, Submit, Tallow, Try, Yeve, Yield

Rendezvous Date, Meeting, Philippi, Tryst, Venue

Rendition Account, Delivery, Interpretation, Translation, Version

René Descartes

Renegade, Renege, Renegue Apostate, Default, Defector, Deserter, Pike, Rat(ton), Recreant, Traitor, Turncoat, Weasel out

▷ **Renegade** *may indicate* a word reversal

Renew(al) Instauration, Neogenesis, Palingenesis, Refresh, Replace, Resumption, Retrace, Revival, Urban

Rennet Steep, Vell

Renounce, Renunciation Abandon, Abdicate, Abjure, Abnegate, Disclaim, Disown, Forfeit, For(e)go, Forisfamiliate, Forsake, For(e)say, Forswear, Kenosis, Outclaim, Pass up, Quitclaim, Recede, Recuse, Relinquish, Renay, Retract, Sacrifice

Renovate(d), Renovation Duff, Face-lift, Instauration, Makeover, Refurbish, Renew, Repair, Restore, Revamp, Touch up, Translate

Renown(ed) Fame, Glory, Illustrious, Kudos, Lustre, Notoriety, Prestige, Stardom

Rent(er), Rented, Renting Asunder, Broken, Charge, Cornage, Cost, Crack, Cranny, Cuddeehih, Cuddy, Division, Economic, Fair, Farm, Fee, Fissure, Gale, Gavel, Ground, → **HIRE**, Lease, Let, List, Mail, Market, Occupy, Pendicle, Penny(-mail), Peppercorn, Quit-rent, Rack, Rip, Rived, Riven, Screed, Seat, Slit, Split, Stallage, Subtenant, Tare, Tenant, Tithe, Tore, Torn, Tythe, White

Reorganise Rationalise

▷ **Reorganised** *may indicate* an anagram

Reorientate Rabat

Repair(s), Repairer, Reparation Amend(s), Anaplasty, Assythment, Botch, Cobble, Damages, Darn, DIY, Doctor, Excision, Expiation, Fettle, Fitter, Fix, Garage, Go, Haro, Harrow, Heel, Jury rig, → **MEND**, Neoplasty, Overhaul, Patch, Piece, Point, Recompense, Redress, Refit, Reheel, Remedy, Renew, Renovate, Repoint, Resort, Restore, Retouch, Revamp, Roadworks, Running, Satisfaction, Service, Stitch, Tenorrhaphy, Ulling, Vamp, Volery

Repartee Backchat, Badinage, Banter, Persiflage, Rejoinder, Retort, Riposte, Wit, Wordplay

Repast Bever, Collection, Food, Meal, Tea, Treat

Repay(ment) Avenge, Compensate, Perseverate, Quit, Reassert, Refund, Requite, Retaliate, Revenge, Reward, Satisfaction

Repeal Abrogate, Annul, Cancel, Rescind, Revoke

Repeat(ed), Repeatedly, Repetition, Repetitive Again, Alliteration, Anadiplosis, Anaphora, Ancora, Battology, Belch, Bis, Burden, Burp, Copy, Cycle, Ditto(graphy), Do, Duplicate, → **ECHO**, Echolalia, Encore, Epanalepsis, Epistrophe, Epizeuxis, Eruct, Facsimile, Habitual, Harp, Image, Imitate, Ingeminate, Iterate, Iterum, Leit-motiv, Merism, Ostinato, Palillogy, Parrot, Parrot-fashion, Passion, Perpetuate, Perseverate, Playback, Polysyndeton, Reassert, Recapitulate, Recite(r), Redo, Refrain, Regurgitate, Reiterate, Renew, Rep, Repetend, Reprise, Rerun, Retail, Rondo, Rosalia, Rote, Same(y), Screed, Segno, Symploce, Tautology, Tautophony, Thrum, Trite, Verbigerate

Repel(lent) Aversive, Camphor, Deet, Estrange, Harsh, Offensive, Rebarbative, Reject, Repulse, Revolt, Shoo, Squalid, Turn-off, Ug(h), Ward

Repent(ant), Repentance Metanoia, Penitent, Regret, Rue, Sackcloth, Yamim Nora'im

Repercussion Backlash, Backwash, Echo, Effect, Impact, Recoil

Repertoire, Repertory Company, Depot, Rep, Store

▶ **Repetition** *see* **REPEAT(ED)**

Replace(ment), Replaceable, Replacing Change, Deputise, Diadochy, Euphorism, For, Instead, Novation, Pinch-hit, Pre-empt, Prosthesis, Raincheck, Refill, Reinstate, Relief, Renew, Replenish, Restore, Spare part, Stand-in, Substitute, Supersede, Supplant, Surrogate, Taxis, Transform, Transliterate, Understudy, Usurp

Replay Action, Instant, Iso(lated), Segno, Slo-mo

Replenish Refill, Refresh, Revictual, Stock, Supply, Top

Replete, Repletion Awash, Full, Gorged, Plenitude, Plethora, Sated, Satiation

Replica Clone, Copy, Duplicate, Facsimile, Image, Repetition, Spit

Reply Accept, Answer, Churlish, Duply, Echo, Over, Rejoinder, Replication, Repost, Rescript, Response, Retort, Roger, Surrebut, Surrebutter, Surrejoinder, Triply

Report(s), Reporter Account, Announce, Annual, Auricular, Bang, Beveridge, Blacksmith, Bruit, Bulletin, Cahier, Clap, Columnist, Comment, Commentator, Compte rendu, Correspondent, Court, Court circular, Cover, Crack, Crump, Cub, Debrief, Describe, Despatch, Disclose, Dispatch, Dissertation, Explosion, Fame, Fireman, Grapevine, Hansard, Hearsay, Informant, Item, Jenkins, Journalist, Legman, Libel,

Narrative, News, Newsflash, Newshawk, Newshound, Newsman, Noise, Notify, Paper, Pop, Powwow, Pressman, Protocol, Rapporteur, Recount, Relate, Relay, Representation, Repute, Return, Roorback, Rumour, Sitrep, Sound(bite), Staffer, State(ment), Stringer, Tale, → **TELL**, Thesis, Transactions, Transcribe, Tripehound, Troop, Update, Weather, Whang, White paper, Wolfenden, Write up

▷ **Reported** *may indicate* the sound of a letter or word

Repose Ease, Kaif, Kef, Kif, Lie, Lig, Peace, Relax, → **REST**, Serenity

Repository Archive, Ark, Cabinet, Cinerarium, Container, Genizah, Reservoir, Sepulchre, Vault

Repossess(ion) Distringas

Reprehend, Reprehensible Base, Blame, Blameworthy, Censure, Criticise, Ill, Paper, Rebuke, Shameful, Warn

Represent(ation), Representative, Represented Agent, Ambassador, Anaconic, Archetypal, Caricature, Client, Commercial, Commissary, Commissioner, Cross-section, Delegate, Depict, Deputation, Describe, Display, Drawing, Drummer, Effigy, Elchee, Eltchi, Emblem, Embody, Emissary, Epitomise, Example, Figurative, Histogram, Ikon, Image, Instantiate, John Bull, Legate, Limn, Lobby, Map, Mimesis, Mouthpiece, MP, Personate, Personify, Piechart, Portray, Proportional, Quintessence, Rep, Resemble, Salesman, Senator, Shop steward, Simulacrum, Spokesman, Stand-in, Statua, Status, Steward, Symbolic, Syndic, Tableau, Tableau vivant, Tiki, Transcription, Traveller, Typical, Vakeel, Vakil, Vernicle, Vice-consul, Visitor-general

▷ **Represented** *may indicate* an anagram

Repress(ed) Bottle, Check, Curb, Pent, Quell, Reprime, Sneap, Stifle, Stultify, Subjugate, Withhold

Reprieve Delay, Mercy, Postpone, Relief, Respite

Reprimand Admonish, Blast, Bounce, Carpet, Castigate, → **CENSURE**, Chastise, Chew out, Chide, Dressing-down, Earful, Jobe, Lace, Lambast, Lecture, Rark up, Rating, Rebuke, Reproof, Rocket, Rollicking, Scold, Slate, Strafe, Targe, Tick off, Tongue-lashing, Wig

Reprint Copy, Paperback, Replica

Reprisal(s) Marque, Recaption, Retaliation, Revenge

Reproach Besom, Bisom, Blame, Braid, Byword, Cataian, Catayan, Chide, Discredit, Dispraise, Exprobate, Gib, Mispraise, Odium, Opprobrium, Rebuke, Ronyon, Runnion, Scold, Shend, Sloan, Stigma, Taunt, Truant, Twat, Twit, Upbraid, Upcast, Yshend

Reprobate Cur, Lost soul, Outcast, Rascal, Scallywag, Scamp

Reprocess Re-make

Reproduce(r), Reproduction, Reproductive (organ) Amphimixis, Ape, Apomixis, Archegonium, Arrhenotoky, Carpel, Clone, Copy, Counterfeit, Depict, Ectype, Edition, Etch, Eugenics, Gamogenesis, Gemmate, Homogenesis, Isospory, Loins, Megaspore, Meristematic, Mono, Monogenesis, Monogony, Multiply, Oogamy, Ozalid®, Parthenogenesis, Phon(e)y, Pirate, Playback, Proliferate, Propagate, Pullulation, Refer, Replica, Roneo®, S(h)akti, Schizogony, Seminal, Simulate, Spermatia, Stereo, Strobilation, Syngamy, Syngenesis, Vegetative, Viviparism

▷ **Reproduce** *may indicate* an anagram

Reproof, Reprove Admonish, Berate, Censure, Chide, Correction, Corruption, Lecture, Rate, Rebuff, Rebuke, Reprehension, Scold, Sloan, Take to task, Tut, Upbraid

Reptile, Reptilian Agamid, Alligarta, Alligator, Base, Basilisk, Caiman, Cayman, Chameleon, Chelonian, Creeper, Crocodile, Cynodont, Diapsid, Dicynodont, Dinosaur, Galliwasp, Goanna, Herpetology, Lacertine, Lizard, Mamba, Pelycosaur, Pit viper, Pteranodon, Pterodactyl, Rhynchocephalian, Sauroid, → **SNAKE**, Sphenodon, Squamata, Synapsid, Tegu(exin), Thecodont, Therapsid, Theriodontia, Tortoise, Tuatara, Tuatera, Turtle, Worm

Republic(an) Abkhazid, Antimonarchist, Belarussian, Cyprus, Democrat, Fenian, Fianna Fáil, Girondist, GOP, International Brigade, IRA, Iraqi, Khakhassa, Leveller,

Montagnard, Mugwump, Plato, Provisional, Provo, Red, Russia, Sansculotte,
Sansculottic, Sinn Fein, Tatarstan, Udmurtia, United Arab, Weimar, Whig, Young Italy
Republic(s) Banana, Federal, Fifth, First, Fourth, People's, Second, State, Third, Weimar

REPUBLICS

1 letter:
R

3 letters:
RMM
UAR
USA

4 letters:
Chad
Cuba
Eire
Fiji
Iran
Iraq
Komi
Laos
Mali
Peru
Togo
Tuva

5 letters:
Adhar
Altai
Belau
Benin
Chile
China
Congo
Czech
Egypt
Gabon
Ghana
Haiti
India
Italy
Kenya
Khmer
Libya
Malta
Nauru
Nepal
Niger
Palau
Sakha
Sudan
Syria

Tatar
Yakut
Yemen
Zaire

6 letters:
Adygai
Adygei
Angola
Bharat
Biafra
Brazil
Bukavu
Buryat
Cyprus
France
Gambia
Greece
Guinea
Guyana
Ingush
Israel
Kalmyk
Latvia
Malawi
Mari-El
Mexico
Myanma
Panama
Poland
Russia
Rwanda
Serbia
Somali
Turkey
Udmurt
Uganda
Venice
Weimar
Zambia

7 letters:
Adharca
Albania
Algeria
Andorra
Armenia
Austria

Bashkir
Belarus
Bolivia
Burkina
Burundi
Chechen
Chuvash
Comoros
Croatia
Ecuador
Estonia
Finland
Georgia
Germany
Hungary
Iceland
Ireland
Jibouti
Kalmuck
Kalmyck
Khakass
Lebanon
Liberia
Moldova
Myanmar
Namibia
Nigeria
Romania
Senegal
Somalia
Surinam
Tunisia
Ukraine
Uruguay
Vanuatu
Vietnam
Yakutia

8 letters:
Abkhazid
Botswana
Bulgaria
Buryatia
Cambodia
Cameroon
Chechnya
Colombia
Dagestan

Djibouti
Dominica
Esthonia
Honduras
Karelian
Kiribati
Malagasy
Maldives
Moldavia
Mongolia
Pakistan
Paraguay
Portugal
Roumania
Sinn Fein
Slovakia
Slovenia
Sri Lanka
Suriname
Tanzania
Udmurtia
Zimbabwe

9 letters:
Argentina
Badakshan
Cape Verde
Costa Rica
Dominican
Guatemala
Indonesia
Kazakstan
Lithuania
Macedonia
Mauritius
Nicaragua
San Marino
Singapore
Tatarstan
Venezuela

10 letters:
Azerbaijan
Bangladesh
Belarussia
El Salvador
Gorno-Altai
Kara-Kalpak

Kazakhstan	Uzbekistan	*12 letters:*	United Provinces
Khakhassia	Yugoslavia	Guinea-Bissau	
Kyrgyzstan		South Vietnam	*16 letters:*
Madagascar	*11 letters:*	Turkmenistan	Congo-Brazzaville
Mauritania	Afghanistan		Equatorial Guinea
Montenegro	Burkina-Faso	*13 letters:*	Karachai-Cherkess
Mordvinian	Byelorussia	Bashkortostan	São Tomé e Príncipe
Mozambique	Cote d'Ivoire	North Ossetian	
North Korea	Nakhichevan		*17 letters:*
North Yemen	Philippines	*14 letters:*	Bosnia-Herzegovina
Seychelles	Sierra Leone	Czechoslovakia	Mari El-Nakhichevan
South Korea	South Africa		Trinidad and Tobago
South Yemen	Soviet Union	*15 letters:*	
Tajikistan	Switzerland	Gorno-Badakhshan	
Ubang-Shari	Tadjikistan	Kabardino-Balkar	
United Arab	West Germany	Marshall Islands	

Repudiate Abjure, Deny, Disaffirm, Discard, Disclaim, Disown, Ignore, Recant, Reject, Renounce, Repel, Retract

Repugnance, Repugnant Abhorrent, Alien, Disgust, Distaste, Fulsome, Horror, Loathing, Nastiness, Obscene, Odious, Revulsion

Repulsive, Repulse Creepy, Grooly, Icky, Lo(a)th, Odious, Off-putting, Rebuff, Rebut, Refel, Refuse, Repel, Repugnant, Slimy, Squalid, Ugly, Vile

Reputable, Reputation, Repute(d) Bubble, Credit, Dit, Estimate, Fame, Good, Izzat, Loos, Los, Name, Note, Notoriety, Odour, Opinion, Prestige, Putative, Regard, Renown, Said, Sar, → **STANDING**, Stature, Status, Stink, Stock, Trustworthy

Request Adjure, Appeal, Apply, Ask, Beg, Desire, D-notice, Entreaty, Invite, Petition, Plea, Prayer, Precatory, Solicit, Supplication, Touch

Requiem Agnus Dei, Mass

Require(d), Requirement Charge, Crave, De rigueur, Desideratum, Desire, Enjoin, Entail, Essential, Exact, Expect, Incumbent, Lack, Mandatory, Necessity, Need, Prerequisite, Priority, Sine qua non, Stipulate, Then

Requisite, Requisition Commandeer, Due, Embargo, Essential, Indent, Necessary, Needful, Order, Press, Simplement

Rescind Abrogate, Annul, Recant, Remove, Repeal

Rescue(r) Aid, Air-sea, Deliver, Free, Liberate, Lifeline, Lifesave, Mountain, Ransom, Reclaim, Recover, Recower, Redeem, Regain, Relieve, Repatriate, Reprieve, Retrieve, Salvage, Salvation, → **SAVE**, White knight

Research(er) Audience, Boffin, Delve, Dig, Enquiry, Explore, Fieldwork, Indagator, Investigate, Legwork, Market, MORI, Motivation(al), Near-market, Operational, Opposition, Pioneer, Post-doctoral, Psychical, Quest, Res, Scientist, Sus(s), Test, Think-tank

Resell Scalp

Resemblance, Resemble, Resembling Affinity, Apatetic, Approach, Assonant, Dead ringer, Homophyly, Likeness, -oid, -opsis, Quasi, Replica, Similitude, Simulacrum, Simulate

Resent(ful), Resentment Anger, Bitter(ness), Bridle, Chippy, Choler, Cross, Derry, Dudgeon, Embittered, Grudge, Indignation, Ire, Jaundiced, Malign, Miff, Mind, Pique, Rancour, Rankle, Smart, Snarling, Spite, Umbrage

Reservation, Reserve(d), Reservist(s) Aloof, Arrière-pensée, Aside, Backlog, Bank, Bashful, Book, But, By, Capital, Caveat, Central, Cold, Condition, Coy, Demiss, Detachment, Distant, Earmark, Engage, Ersatz, Except, Fall-back, Federal, Fort Knox, Fund, General, Gold, Hold, Husband, Ice, Indian, Introvert, Landwehr, Layby, Locum, Median strip, Mental, Militiaman, Modesty, Nature, Nest-egg, Nineteenth man, Proviso, Qualification, Reddendum, Res, Rest, Restraint, Retain, Reticence, Retiring,

Rez, Salvo, Sanctuary, Save, Scenic, Scruple, Serengeti, Set aside, Special, Spoken for, Stand-by, Stand-offishness, Starch, Stash, Stock(pile), Substitute, TA (men), Twelfth man, Uncommunicate, Understudy, Warren, Waves, Withhold

Reservoir Basin, Cistern, Font, G(h)ilgai, Gilgie, Header tank, Oilcup, Repository, Rybinsk, Service, Stock, Sump, Tank, Water tower, Well

Reset Taxis

Reside(nce), Resident(s), Residential Abode, Address, Amban, Chequers, Commorant, Consulate, Denizen, Domicile, Dwell, Embassy, Establishment, Expatriate, Exurb(anite), Gaff, Gremial, Guest, Home, In, Indweller, Inholder, Inmate, Intern, Ledger, Lei(d)ger, Lieger, Liveyer(e), Lodger, Masonry, Metic, Occupant, Pad, Parietal, Permanent, Resiant, Settle, Settlement, Sojourn, Squat, Stay, Tenant, Tenement, Up, Uptown, Vicinage, Villager, Yamen

Residual, Residue Ash, Astatki, Boneblack, Calx, Caput, Chaff, Cinders, Coke, Crud, Dottle, Draff, Dregs, Expellers, Greaves, Heeltap, Leavings, Mazout, Mortuum, Prefecture, Raffinate, Remainder, Remanent, Remnant, Scourings, Sediment, Slag, Slurry, Snuff, Vinasse

Resign(ed), Resignation Abandon, Abdicate, Demit, Fatalism, Heigh-ho, Leave, Meek, Philosophical, → **QUIT**, Reconcile, Step down, Stoic, Submit

Resilience, Resilient Bounce, Buoyant, Elastic, Flexible, Recoil, Rugged, Springy, Stamina

Resin Acaroid, Acrylic, Agila, Alkyd, Amber, Amine, Amino, Anime, Arar, Asaf(o)etida, Bakelite®, Bal(sa)m of Gilead, Balsam, Benjamin, Benzoin, Burgundy pitch, Bursera, Cachou, Cannabin, Cannabis, Caranna, Carauna, Catechu, Charas, Cholestyramine, Churrus, Colophony, Conima, Copai(ba), Copaiva, Copal(m), Coumarone, Courbaril, Cutch, Cymene, Dam(m)ar, Dammer, Dragon's blood, Elaterite, Elemi, Epoxy, Frankincense, Galbanum, Galipot, Gambi(e)r, Gamboge, Glyptal, Guaiacum, Gum, Hasheesh, Hashish, Hing, Jalapic, Jalapin, Kino, Labdanum, Lac, Ladanum, Lignaloes, Limonene, Lupulin, Mastic, Melamine, Methacrylate, Myrrh, Natural, Olibanum, Opopanax, Perspex®, Phenolic, Phenoxy, Plastisol, Podophyl(l)in, Polycarbonate, Polyester, Polymer, Polypropylene, Polysterene, Polyvinyl, Propolis, Retinite, Roset, Rosin, Rosit, Rozet, Rozit, Sagapenum, Sandarac(h), Saran®, Scammony, Shellac, Silicone, Storax, Styrene, Synthetic, Tacamahac, Tacmahack, Takamaka, Taxin, Thus, Urea, Vinyl, Xylenol

Resist, Resistance, Resistant, Resistor All-weather, Anti, Antibiotic, Barretter, Bleeder, Bristle, Buck, Ceramal, Cermet, Chetnik, Coccidiostat, Combat, Consumer, Contest, Defiance, Defy, Drag, Element, Face, Fend, Friction, Gainstrive, Grapo, Hostile, Immunity, Impede, Impediment, Internal, Intifada, Invar, Klendusic, Klepht, Maquis, Maraging, Market, Megohm, Microhm, Negative, Obstacle, Ohm, Omega, Oppose, Partisan, Passive, Pat, Pull, R, Radiation, Redound, Reluct, Reluctance, Renitent, Resilient, Rheostat, Sales, Satyagraha, Shockproof, Soul-force, Specific, Stability, Stand (pat), Stonde, Stubborn, Tamil Tiger, Tough, Toughen, Voltage divider, → **WITHSTAND**

Resolute, Resolution Adamant, Analysis, Bold, Cast-iron, Casuistry, Closure, Courage, Decided, Decision, Denouement, Determined, Dogged, Doughty, → **FIRM**, Fortitude, Granite, Grim, Grit, Hardiness, Insist, Joint, Motion, New Year, Pertinacity, Promotion, Rede, Reed(e), Resolve, Stable, Stalwart, Staunch, Stout, Strength, Strong-willed, Sturdy, Telic, Tenacity, Unbending, Valiant, Willpower

Resolve(d), Resolver Analyse, Calculate, Conation, Decide, Declare, → **DETERMINE**, Deus ex machina, Factorise, Fix, Grit, Hellbent, Intent, Nerve, Pecker, → **PURPOSE**, Right, Settle, Sort out, Steadfast, Tenacity, Vow, Will

▷ **Resolved** *may indicate* an anagram

Resonance, Resonant, Resonator Canorous, Cavity, Electromer, Morphic, Orotund, Parallel, Rhumbatron, Ringing, Sonorous, Timbre, Vibrant

Resort Acapulco, Aspen, Benidorm, Biarritz, Bognor, Cancun, Centre, Chamonix, Clacton, Copacabana, Davos, Dive, Étaples, Expedient, Frame, Frequent, Gstaad, Haunt, Health, Herne Bay, Hove, Hydro, Invoke, Klosters, Lair, Last, Las Vegas, Locarno, Lowestoft,

Malibu, Miami, Morecambe, Nassau, Nice, Paignton, Palm Beach, Pau, Penzance, Pis
aller, Poole, Rapallo, Recourse, Redcar, Repair, Riviera, St Ives, Seaside, Skegness,
Southend, Spa(w), Stand by, Thredbo, Torremolinos, Troon, Use, Utilise, Waikiki,
Watering place, Weston-super-Mare, Weymouth, Whitby, Worthing, Yalta, Zermatt

▷ **Resort(ing)** *may indicate* an anagram

Resound(ing) Echo, Plangent, Reboant, Reboation, Reverberate, Ring, Sonorous

Resource(s), Resourceful Assets, Beans, Bottom, Chevisance, Clever, Enterprise,
Faculty, Funds, Gumption, Human, Ingenious, Input, Inventive, Manpower, Means, Natural,
Renewable, Shared, Sharp, Smeddum, Stock-in-trade, → **VERSATILE**, Wealth, Webliography

Respect(ed), Respectable, Respectful Admire, Ahimsa, Aspect, Behalf, Clean cut,
Consecrate, Consider, Cred(it), Decent, Deference, Devoir, Doyen, Duty, Eminent, Esteem,
Fear, Genteel, Gigman, Homage, → **HONOUR**, Intent, Kempt, Kowtowing, Latria, Obeisant,
Officious, Pace, Particular, Preppy, Prestige, Proper, Reference, Regard, Relation, Reputable,
Revere, Sir, S(t)irrah, U, Venerate, Way, Wellborn, Well-thought-of, Wise, Worthy

Respirator, Respire, Respiration Artificial, Blow, Breathe, Exhale, External,
Gasmask, Inhale, Iron lung, Mouth-to-mouth, Pant, Snorkel

Respite Break, Breather, Frist, Interval, Leisure, Let up, Pause, Reprieve, Rest, Stay, Truce

Respond, Response, Responsive Amenable, Answer, Antiphon, Autoreply,
Backlash, Bi, Comeback, Conditioned, Counteroffer, Duh, Echo, Feedback, Flechman,
Grunt, Immune, Kneejerk, Kyrie, Litany, Nastic, Pavlovian, Photonasty, Plea, Prebuttal,
Psychogalvanic, React(ion), Reagency, Rebutter, Reflex, Reply, Repost, Retort, Rheotaxis,
Rheotropism, Rise, Sensitive, Stayman, Synapte, Syntonic, Tender, Thigmotropic, Tic,
Tropism, Unconditioned, Voice, Warm, Wilco

Responsibility, Responsible Accountable, Anchor, Answerable, Baby, Behind,
Blame, Buck, Charge, Collective, Culpable, Dependable, Diminished, Duty, Frankpledge,
Guilty, Hot seat, Incumbent, Instrumental, Liable, Mantle, Mea culpa, Millstone, Onus,
Perpetrate, Pigeon, Sane, Solid, Stayman, Trust

Rest(ing), Rest day Alt, Anchor, Avocation, Balance, Bed, Beulah, Break, Breather,
Calm, Catnap, Cetera, Comma, Depend, Dwell, Ease, Easel, Etc, Fermata, Feutre,
Fewter, Gallows, Gite, Half-time, Halt, Inaction, Jigger, Lance, Lave, Lay to, Lean, Lie,
Lie-in, Light, Lodge, Loll, Lound, Lull, Lyte, Minim, Nap, Noah, Nooning, Oasis, Others,
Outspan, Overlie, Pause, Quiescence, Quiet, Relâche, Relax, Rely, Remainder, Repose,
Requiem, Reserve, Residue, Respite, Sabbath, Shut-eye, Sick leave, Siesta, Silence,
→ **SLEEP**, Slide, Sloom, Slumber, Spell, Spider, Static, Stopover, Support, Surplus,
Teabreak, Time out, Waypoint, Y-level

Re-start Da capo, Reboot

Restaurant, Restaurateur Automat, Beanery, Bistro, Brasserie, British, Cabaret, Café,
Canteen, Carvery, Chew'n'spew, Chinkie, Chinky, Chip-shop, Chophouse, Commissary,
Cook shop, Creperie, Diner, Eatery, Eating-house, Estaminet, Gastropub, Greasy spoon,
Grill, Grillroom, Grub shop, Luncheonette, Maxim's, Naafi, Noshery, Padrone, Pizzeria,
Porter-house, Rathskeller, Ratskeller, Raw bar, Roadhouse, Rotisserie, Slap-bang,
Steakhouse, Takeaway, Taqueria, Taverna, Tea garden, Teahouse, Tearoom, Teashop,
Trat(toria)

Rest-home Aggie, Hospice

Resting-place Bed, Couch, Dharmsala, Gite, Grave, Inn, Khan, Serai, She'ol, Stage

Restitute, Restitution Amends, Apocatastasis, Reparation, Restore, Return

Restive, Restless(ness) Agitato, Chafing, Chorea, Fidgety, Fikish, Free-arm, Itchy,
Jactitation, Spring fever, Toey, Unsettled

▷ **Restless** *may indicate* an anagram

Restoration, Restorative, Restore(d) Bring to, Cure, Descramble, Heal, Mend,
New, Pentimento, Pick-me-up, Postliminy, Rally, Recondition, Redeem, Redintegrate,
Redux, Refresh, Refurbish, Regenerate, Rehabilitate, Reintegrate, Rejuvenate, Remedial,
Renew, Renovate, Replenish, Replevy, Repone, Restitute, Resuscitate, Retouch, Revamp,
Revive, Righten, Stet, Tonic, Undelete, Whole

Restrain(ed), Restraint Abstinence, Ban, Bate, Bit, Bottle, Branks, Bridle, Cage, Chain, Chasten, → **CHECK**, Checks and balances, Chokehold, Coerce, Cohibit, Compesce, Confinement, Contain, Control, Cramp, Curb, Dam, Decorum, Detent, Dry, Duress, Embargo, Enfetter, Estoppel, Fetter, Freeze, Gag-rein, Gyve, Halt, Hamshackle, Handcuffs, Harness, Heft, Hinder, Hopple, Immanacle, Impound, Inhibit, Jess, Leg-iron, Lid, Low-key, Manacle, Measure, Mince, Moderation, Muzzle, Patient, Quiet, Rein, Repress, Restrict, Ritenuto, Shackle, Sober, Sobriety, Squeeze, Stay, Stent, Stint, Straitjacket, Strait-waistcoat, Tabu, Temper, Tether, Tie, Tieback, Trash, Underplay

Restrict(ed), Restriction Band, Bar, Bind, Bit, Block, Burden, Cage, Catch, Censorship, Chain, Circumscribe, Closet, Condition, Cord, Corset, Cramp, Curb, Curfew, DORA, Fence, Fetter, Fold, Gate, Ground, Guard, Hamper, Hidebound, Hobble, Inhibit, Intern, Kennel, Let, → **LIMIT**, Localise, Lock, Mere, Narrow, Net, Nick, No-go, Oche, Pale, Parochial, Pen, Pent, Pier, Pin, Poky, Pot-bound, Private, Proscribed, Qualify, Regulate, Rein, Rent, Repression, Rope, Safety belt, Scant, Seal, Section, Selected, Shackle, Snare, Squeeze, Stenopaic, Stent, Stint, Stop, Straiten, Stunt, Swaddle, Tether, Tie

Restructure, Restructuring Perestroika

Result(s) After-effect, Aftermath, Ans(wer), Arise, Bring, Causal, Consequence, Effect, Emanate, End, End-product, Ensue, Entail, Event, Eventuate, Finding, Fruict, Fruition, Fruits, Issue, Karmic, Knock-on, Lattermath, → **OUTCOME**, Outturn, Pan, Pay off, Proceeds, Product, Quotient, Sequel, Side-effect, Sum, Therefore, Upshot, Verdict, Wale

Resume, Résumé Continue, Pirlicue, Purlicue, Summary

Resurrect(ion) Anabiosis, Anastasia, Rebirth, Revive, Zomb(ie)

Resuscitate(d), Resuscitation Mouth-to-mouth, Quicken, Redivivus, Restore, Revive

Retail(er) Category killer, Chandler, Dealer, → **NARRATE**, Regrate, Sell, Shopkeeper, Shopman, Stockist, Superstore, Symbol, Tell

Retain(er), Retains, Retention, Retentive Brief, Contain, Deposit, Fee, Hold, Hold-all, Keep, Long, Panter, Pantler, Reserve, Retinue, Servant, Ur(a)emia, Vassal

Retaliate, Retaliation Avenge, Carousel, Counter, Lex talionis, Pay back, Pay home, Quid pro quo, Quit(e), Redress, Repay, Reprisal, Requite, Retort, Revenge, Talion

Retard(ed), Retardation Arrest, Belate, Brake, Cretin, Encumber, Hinder, Hysteresis, Slow, Stunt

Retch Boak, Bock, Boke, Cowk, Gap, Heave, Keck, Reach, Vomit

Reticence, Reticent Clam, Cowardly, Coy, Dark, Guarded, Reserve, Restraint, Secretive, Shy, Taciturn

Reticule, Reticulum Bag, Carryall, Dragnet, Handbag, Lattice, Net

Retina Detached, Fovea, Macula lutea

Retinue Comitatus, Company, Cortège, Equipage, Following, Meiney, Meinie, Meiny, Menyie, Sowarry, Suite

Retire(d), Retiree, Retirement, Retiring Abed, Aloof, Asocial, Baccare, Backare, Backpedal, Blate, Bowler-hat, Bow out, Cede, Coy, Demob, Demure, Depart, Ebb, Emeritus, Essene, Former, Leave, Lonely, Modest, Mothball, Nun, Outgoing, Pension, Perfing, Private, Put out, Quit, Recede, Recluse, Reserved, Resign, Retract, Retread, Retreat, Retrocedent, Roost, Rusticate, Scratch, Sequester, Shy, Superannuate, Timid, Unassertive, Withdraw

▷ **Retirement** *may indicate* 'bed' around another word, or word reversed

Retort Alembic, Comeback, Courteous, Floorer, Quip, Repartee, → **REPLY**, Retaliate, Riposte, Still, Tu quoque

Retract(ion) Backpedal, Backtrack, Disavow, Epanorthosis, Palinode, Recall, Recant, Renounce, Revoke

Retread Recap

Retreat Abbey, Arbour, Ashram(a), Asylum, Backpedal, Backwater, Berchtesgaden, Bower, Bug, Camp David, Cell, Cloister, Convent, Crawfish, Dacha, Departure, Donjon, Funkhole, Girth, Grith, Hermitage, Hibernaculum, Hideaway, Hide-out, Hole,

Interstadial, Ivory-tower, Katabasis, Lair, Lama(sery), Mew, Monastery, Nest, Neuk, Nook, Pullback, Recede, Recoil, Recu(i)le, Redoubt, Reduit, Refuge, Retire, Retraite, Right-about, Rout, Shangri-La, Shelter, Skedaddle, Stronghold, Withdraw

Retribution Come-uppance, Deserts, Nemesis, Revenge, Reward, Utu, Vengeance

Retrieve(r), Retrieval Access, Bird-dog, Chesapeake Bay, Field, Gundog, Labrador, Read-out, Recall, Reclaim, Recoup, Recover, Redeem, Rescue, Salvage

Retroflex Cacuminal

Retrograde Backward, Deasi(u)l, Deasoil, Decadent, Decline, Hindward, Rearward, Regrede

Retrospect(ive) Contemplative, Ex post facto, Hindsight, Regardant

Return(s) Agen, Answer, Bricole, Census, Comeback, Day, Diminishing, Dividend, Earnings, Elect, Er, Extradite, Gain, Homecoming, Nil, Pay, Payback, Proceeds, Profit, Rebate, Rebound, Recur, Redound, Regress, Reject, Rejoin, Render, Rent, Repair, Repay, Replace, Reply, Requital, Respond, Rest, Restitution, Restoration, Restore, Retort, Retour, Revenue, Reverse, Revert, Riposte, Takings, Tax, Tit for tat, Traffic, → **YIELD**

Reuse Cannibalise

Rev(ving) Gun, Minister, Vroom

Reveal(ing), Revelation Acute, Admit, Advertise, Air, Apocalyptic, Bar, Bare, Betray, Bewray, Confess, Descry, Disclose, Discover, Discure, → **DIVULGE**, Epiphany, Exhibit, Explain, Expose, Eye-opener, Giveaway, Hierophantic, Impart, Indicate, Indiscreet, Ingo, Kythe, Leak, Let on, Low-cut, Manifest, Open, Out, Parade, Pentimento, Satori, Scry, → **SHOW**, Skimpy, Spill, Tell-tale, Unclose, Uncover, Unfold, Unheal, Unmask, Unveil

Reveille Raise

Revel(ling), Revelry Ariot, Bacchanalia, Bend, Carnival, Carouse, Comus, Dionysian, Feast, Gloat, Glory, Joy, Maffick, Merriment, On the tiles, Orgy, Rant, Rejoice, Riot, Roister, Rollicks, Rout, Royst, Saturnalia, Splore, Swig, Upsee, Ups(e)y, Wallow, Wassail, Whoopee

Reveller Bacchant, Birler, Corybant, Guisard, Guiser, Maenad, Merrymaker, Orgiast, Silenus

Revenant Fetch, Ghost, Spectre

Revenge(r), Revengeful Aftergame, Avenge, Commination, Goel, Grenville, Montezuma's, Nightrider, Payback, Reprise, Requite, Retaliation, Revanche, Settlement, Tit for tat, Ultion, Utu, Vigilante, Vindictive

Revenue Capital, Finance, Fisc(al), Fisk, Income, Inland, Internal, Jaghire, Jag(h)ir, Prebend, Primitiae, Rent, Taille, Tax, Turnover, Zamindar, Zemindar

Reverberate Echo, Recoil, Reflect, Repercuss, Resound

Revere(nce) Admire, Adoration, Awe, Bostonian, Dread, Dulia, Esteem, Fear, Hallow, Hery, Homage, → **HONOUR**, Hyperdulia, Idolise, Latria, Obeisance, Paul, Respect, Venerate

Reverie Brown study, Daydream, Dream(iness), Fantasy, Memento

Revers Lap(p)el

Reversal, Reverse, Reversing, Reversion, Reversible Anatropy, Antithesis, Antonym, Arsy-versy, Atavism, Back(slide), B-side, Change-over, Chiasmus, Commutate, Counter(mand), Escheat, Evaginate, Exergue, Flip, Flip side, Inversion, Mirror image, Misfortune, → **OPPOSITE**, Overturn, Palindrome, Pile, Regress, Repeal, Retrograde, Revoke, Rheotropic, Setback, Switchback, Tails, Throwback, Transit, Turn, Turnabout, Two-faced, Un-, Undo, Upend, U-turn, Verso, Vice versa, Volte-face, Woman

Revert Annul, Backslide, Regress, Relapse, Resort, Retrogress, Return

Review(er) Appeal, Censor, Credit, Critic, Critique, Editor, Encomium, Feuilleton, Footlights, Glimpse, Inspect, Iso-, Judicial, Magazine, March-past, Notice, Pan, Peer, Recapitulate, Repeat, Revise, Rundown, Run over, Slate, Spithead, Summary, Summing-up, Survey, Write-up

▷ **Review** *may indicate* an anagram or a reversed word

Revile, Reviling Abuse, Execrate, Inveigh, Rail, Rayle, Vilify, Vituperate

Revise(r) | 650

Revise(r), Revision(ist) Alter, Amend, Change, Correct, Diaskeuast, Diorthosis, Edit, Emend, Heretic, Peruse, Reappraise, Reassess, Recense, Reform, Rev, Update

▷ **Revise(d)** *may indicate* an anagram

Revive, Revival, Revivify, Reviving Araise, Classical, Enliven, Gothic, Greek, Kiss of life, Rake up, Rally, Reanimate, Reawake(n), Rebirth, Redintegrate, Redux, Refresh, Rekindle, Relive, Renaissance, Renascent, Renew, Renovate, Restore, Resurrect, Resuscitate, Risorgimento, Romantic, Romo, Rouse, Wake

Revoke Abrogate, Cancel, Countermand, Negate, → **RECALL**, Repeal, Rescind

Revolt(ing), Revolution(ary) Agitator, Agitprop, American, Anarchist, Apostasy, Appal, Barrel roll, Bloodless, Bolivar, Bolshevik, Bolshevist, Boxer, Bukharin, Bulldog, Cade, Castro, Chartist, Che, Chinese, Circle, Commune, Coup d'état, Cultural, Cycle, Danton, Defection, Dervish, Desmoulins, De Valera, Disgust, Emeute, Emmet, Engels, Enragé, February, Fenian, Foul, French, Girondin, Girondist, Glorious, Green, Grody, Guevara, Gyration, Ho Chi Minh, Icky, Industrial, Inqilab, → **IN REVOLT**, Insurgent, Insurrection, Intifada, IRA, Jacobin, Jacquerie, Komitaji, Lap, Lenin, Leninist, Mao, Marat, Marti, Marx, Marxist, Maximalist, Maypole, Minimalist, Montagnard, Mutiny, Nauseating, Nihilist, October, Orbit, Outbreak, Paine, Palace, Paris Commune, Peasants, Poujadist, Putsch, Radical, → **REBEL**, Red, Red Guard, Red Shirt, Reformation, Reign of terror, Riot, Rise, Robespierre, Roll, Rotation, Round, Run, Russian, Sandinista, Sansculotte(rie), Savimbi, Sedition, Septembrist, Sicilian Vespers, Spartacist, Spartacus, Syndicalism, The Mountain, Thermidor, Titanomachy, Trot(sky), Twist, Ugly, Up(rise), → **UPRISING**, Upryst, Velvet, Villa, Wat Tyler, Weatherman, Whirl, Wolfe Tone, Young Turk, Zapata

▷ **Revolutionary** *may indicate* 'reversed'

Revolve(r), Revolving Carrier, Catherine wheel, Centrifuge, Colt®, Gat, Girandole, Grindstone, → **GUN**, Gyrate, Iron, Klinostat, Lathe, Maelstrom, Peristrephic, Pistol, Pivot, Planet, Roller, Rotate, Rotifer, Rotor, Roundabout, Run, Six-shooter, Spin, Swivel, Tone, Turn(stile), Turntable, Turret, Wheel, Whirl(igig), Whirlpool

Revue Follies

Revulsion Abhorrence, Loathing, Repugnance, The creeps, Ugh

Reward(ing) Albricias, Bonus, Bounty, Compensate, Consideration, Desert, Emolument, Fee, Guerdon, Head money, Medal, Meed, Payment, Premium, Price, Prize, Profit, Purse, Push money, Reap, Recognise, Recompense, Reguerdon, Remuneration, Repay, Requital, Requite, S, Shilling, Tanti, Tribute, Wage, War(r)ison

Reword Edit, Paraphrase

Reworking Rifacimento

Rex Cornish, Devon, Priam, R

Reynolds Joshua, PRA

Rhapsodic, Rhapsody Ecstasy, Epic, Music, Unconnected

Rhea Em(e)u, Nandoo, Nandu, Nhandu, Ostrich, Ramee, Rami, Ramie

Rhenium Re

Rheostat Potentiometer

Rhesus Bandar, Macaque, Monkey

Rhetoric(al) Alliteration, Anaphora, Anastrophe, Antimetabole, Antithesis, Antostrophe, Apophasis, Aposiopesis, Assonance, Asteism, Asyndeton, Aureate, Bombast, Brachylogia, Cacophony, Catachresis, Chiasmus, Ecbole, Eloquence, Enantiosis, Epanadiplosis, Epanados, Epanalepsis, Epanorthosis, Epexegesis, Epistrophe, Epizeuxis, Erotema, Eroteme, Erotesis, Euphemism, Hendiadys, Hypallage, Hyperbole, Litotes, Metonymy, Oratory, Oxymoron, Paradox, Paral(e)ipsis, Periphrasis, Peroration, Platform, Pleonasm, Scesisonomaton, Speechcraft, Syllepsis, Synoeciosis, Trivial, Trivium, Zeugma

Rhino Blunt, Bread, Cash, Lolly, Loot, → **MONEY**, Tin

Rhinoceros Baluchitherium, Keitloa, Square-lipped, Sumatran, White

Rhodes, Rhodesia(n) Cecil, Colossus, Ridgeback, Scholar, Zimbabwe

Rhodium Rh
Rhomboid Fusil
Rhubarb Fiddlesticks, Forced, Monk's, Pie-plant, Rhapontic, Rheum, Rot, Spat, Tripe
Rhyme(s), Rhymer, Rhyming Assonance, Clerihew, Closed couplet, Counting out,
Couplet, Crambo, Cynghanedd, Doggerel, Double, Eye, Feminine, Head, Identical, Internal,
Jingle, Macaronic, Male, Masculine, Measure, Mother Goose, Near, Nursery, Pararhyme,
Perfect, Poetry, Poulter's measure, Rich, Riding, Rime riche, Rondel, Royal, Runic, Sight,
Slang, Slant, Tail(ed), Tercet, Terza-rima, Thomas, Triple, → **VERSE**, Virelay, Vowel
Rhythm(ic) Agoge, Alpha, Asynartete, Backbeat, Beat, Beta, Bo Diddley beat, Breakbeat,
Cadence, Circadian, Clave, Dolichurus, Dotted, Duple, Euouae, Evovae, Four-four,
Hemiol(i)a, Ictic, In-step, Meter, Movement, Oompah, Ostinato, Prosody, Pulse, Pyrrhic,
Rising, Rove-over, Rubato, Scotch catch, Scotch snap, Sdrucciola, Sesquialtera, Singsong,
Sprung, Stride piano, Swing, Syncopation, Tala, Talea, → **TEMPO**, Theta, Three-four,
Time, Two-four, Voltinism
Rib(bed), Ribbing, Rib-joint Bar, Chaff, Chiack, Chip, Chyack, Cod, Cord, Costa,
Cross-springer, Dutch, Eve, False, Fin, Floating, Futtock, Groin, Intercostal, Lierne,
Nervate, Nervular, Nervure, Ogive, Persiflage, Rack, Rag, Rally, Short, Spare, Springer,
Subcosta, Taunt, Tease, Tierceron, Tracery, True, Wife
Ribald(ry) Balderdash, Bawdy, Coarse, Scurrilous, Smut, Sotadic, Vulgar
Ribbon Band, Bandeau, Blue, Bow, Braid, Caddis, Caddyss, Cordon, Fattrels, Ferret, Fillet,
Grosgrain, Hatband, Infula, Multistrike, Pad, Petersham, Radina, Red, Rein, Riband,
Rosette, Rouleau, Soutache, Taenia, Tape, Teniate, Tie, Topknot, Torsade, Yellow
Ribless Ecostate
Rice (cake) Arborio, Basmati, Bir(i)yani, Brown, Canada, Carnaroli, Elmer, Entertainer,
Golden, Idli, Indian, Kedgeree, Miracle, Paddy, Patna, Pilaf, Pilau, Pilaw, Pillau, Reis,
Risotto, Spanish, Sushi, Twigs, Vialone nano, Water, Wild, Zizania
Rich(es) Abounding, Abundant, Affluent, Amusing, Bonanza, Buttery, Comic, Copious,
Croesus, Dives, Edmund, Edwin, Fat, Feast, Fertile, Filthy, Flamboyant, Flush, Fruity,
Full, Golconda, Haves, Heeled, High, Larney, Loaded, Luscious, Lush, Luxurious,
Mammon, Moneybags, Moneyed, Nabob, New, Oberous, Oofy, → **OPULENT**, Plenteous,
Plush, Plutocrat, Resonant, Rolling, Silvertail, Sumptuous, Toff, Treasure, Vulgarian,
→ **WEALTHY**, Well-heeled, Well off, Well-to-do
Richard Angevin, Burbage, Dick(y), Lionheart, Nixon, Rick, Roe
Richthofen Red Baron
Rick (burning) Goaf, Sprain, Swingism, Wrench
Rickets, Rickety Dilapidated, Rachitis, Ramshackle, Rattletrap, Shaky, Unsound
▷ **Rickety** *may indicate* an anagram
Rickshaw Pedicab, Tuktuk
Ricochet Boomerang, Glance, Rebound
Rid Clear, Deliver, Ditch, Eliminate, Eradicate, Expulse, Expunge, Free, Obviate, Offload,
Purge, Scrap, Scrub, Shot
Riddle(r) Boulter, Charade, Colander, Dilemma, Enigma, Koan, Logogriph, Pepper,
Perforate, Permeate, Puzzle, Screen, Searce, Search, Seil, Sieve, Sift, Sile, Siler, Sorites,
Sphinx, Strain, Tems(e), Trommel
Ride, Riding Annoy, Aquaplane, Bareback, Bestride, Big dipper, Bruise, Burn, Canter,
Coast, Crog(gy), Cycle, District, Division, Draisene, Draisine, Drive, Equitation, Field,
Free, Hack, Harass, Haute école, Hitchhike, Lift, Merry-go-round, Mount, Pick(-a-)back,
Pickpack, Piggyback, Postil(l)ion, Rape, Revere's, Roadstead, Rollercoaster, Rural,
Sit, Spin, Stang, Surf, Switchback, Third, Trot, Weather, Welter, Wheelie, Whip,
White-knuckle
Rider(s) Addendum, Adjunct, Appendage, Attachment, Boundary, Bucket, Cavalier,
Charioteer, Circuit, Clause, Codicil, Condition, Corollary, Dispatch, Equestrian, Eventer,
Freedom, Gaucho, Godiva, Guidon, Haggard, Horseman, Jockey, Lochinvar, Messenger,
Peloton, Postil(l)ion, Proviso, PS, Revere, Scrub, Spurrer, Transport, Walkyrie

Ridge(pole) Alveolar, Anthelix, Antihelix, Arête, Arris, As(ar), Aseismic, Balk, Bank, Baulk, Berm, Bur(r), Carina, Chine, Clint, Costa, Coteau, Crease, Crest, Crista, Cuesta, Culmen, Darling Range, Drill, Drum(lin), Dune, Eskar, Esker, Fret, Gonys, Gyrus, Hammock, Hoe, Hogback, Hog's back, Horst, Hummock, Interfluve, Kaim, Kame, Keel, Knur(l), Ledge, Linch, List(er), Lynchet, Mid-Atlantic, Middleback, Mid-ocean, Missionary, Moraine, Nek, Nut, Oceanic, Offset, Pressure, Promontory, Ramp, Rand, Raphe, Razor-back, Reef, Rib, Riblet, Rig, Rim, Roof-tree, Sastruga, Screw-thread, Serac, Serpentine, Shoulder, Sowback, Torus, Varix, Verumontanum, Vimy, Wale, Weal, Whelp, Whorl, Windrow, Withers, Witwatersrand, Wrinkle, Yardang, Zastruga

Ridicule, Ridiculous Absurd, Badinage, Bathos, Chaff, Cockamamie, Deride, Derisory, Egregious, Foolish, Gibbet, Gibe, Gird, Goad, Guy, Haze, Jibe, Josh, Lampoon, Laughable, Ludicrous, Mimic, Mock, Paradox, Pasquin, Pillory, Pish, Pooh-pooh, Rag, Raillery, Rally, Rib, Rich, Risible, Roast, Satire, Scoff, Scout, Screwy, Send up, Sight, Silly, Skimmington, Taunt, Travesty

Ridinghood Nithsdale, Red, Trot-cos(e)y

Riding-master RM

Riding-school Manège

Rife Abundant, Manifest, Numerous, Prevalent

Riffle Rapid

Riff-raff Canaille, Hoi polloi, Mob, Populace, Rag-tag, Rag, tag and bobtail, Scaff, Scum, Trash

Rifle Air, Armalite®, Assault, Bone, Browning, Bundook, Burgle, Calic, Carbine, Chassepot, Enfield, Enfield musket, Escopette, Express, Garand, → **GUN**, Kalashnikov, Lee Enfield, Loot, Magazine, Martini®, Martini-Henry, Mauser®, MI, Minié, Pea, Petronel, Pick, Pilfer, Pillage, Raid, Ransack, Reave, Reive, Remington, Repeater, Rieve, Rob, Ruger, Saloon, Shiloh, Springfield, Winchester®

Rift Altercation, Canyon, Chasm, Chink, Cleft, Crevasse, Fault, Fissure, Gap, Gulf, Split

Rig(ging), Rigger Accoutre, Attire, Bermuda, Drilling, Equip, Feer, Frolic, Gaff, Get-up, Gunter, Hoax, Jack-up, Mainbrace, Manipulate, Marconi, Martingale, Oil(man), Outfit, Panoply, Platform, Ratline, Ropes, Roughneck, Schooner, Semisubmersible, Slant, Sport, Stack, Standing, Strip, Swindle, Tackle, Togs, Top hamper, Trull, Wanton

▷ **Rigged** *may indicate* an anagram

Right(s), Righten, Rightness Accurate, Advowson, Affirmative, Ancient lights, Angary, Animal, Appropriate, Appurtenance, Ay, Bang, Befit, Blue-pencil, BNP, Bote, Cabotage, Champart, Civil, Claim, Competence, Conjugal, Conservative, Copyhold, Cor(r)ody, → **CORRECT**, Coshery, Cuddy, Cure, Curtesy, Customer, Dead on, De jure, Dexter, Direct, Divine, Doctor, Droit, Due, Easement, Eminent domain, Emphyteusis, Entitlement, Equity, Esnecy, Estover, Ethical, Exactly, Faldage, Farren, Fascist, Feu, Fire-bote, Fitting, Forestage, Franchise, Free-bench, Freedom, Gay, Germane, Gunter, Haybote, Hedge-bote, Human, Infangthief, Interest, Isonomy, Iure, Junior, Jural, Jure, Jus (mariti), Leet, Legal, Legit, Letters patent, Liberty, Lien, Maritage, Maternity, Meet, Merit, Miner's, Miranda, Moral, Naam, New, Ninepence, Off, Offhand, Offside, OK, Okay, Oke, Okey-dokey, Option, Ortho-, Oughtness, Paine, Pannage, Passant, Pasturage, Pat, Patent, Paternity, Performing, Pit and gallows, Ploughbote, Pose, Postliminy, Pre-emption, Prerogative, Primogeniture, Priority, Prisage, Privilege, Proper, Property, Pukka, R, Rain, Reason, Recourse, Rectify, Rectitude, Redress, Remainder, Remedy, Repair, Ripe, Rt, Sac, Sake, Serial, Side, Slap, So, Soc, Spot-on, Squatter's, Stage, Starboard, Stillicide, Substantive, Suo jure, Suo loco, Tao, Tenants', Terce, Ticket, Tickety-boo, Title, Tory, Trivet, Trover, True, Turbary, User, Usucap(t)ion, Usufruct, Venville, Vert, Warren, Water, Women's

Right-angle(d) Orthogonal

Righteous(ness) Devout, Good, Just, Moral, Pharisee, Prig, Rectitude, Sanctimonious, Tzaddik, Virtuous

Right-hand Dexter, E, Far, Recto, RH, Ro

Right-winger Dry, Falangist, Neocon, Neo-fascist

Rigid(ity) Acierated, Catalepsy, Craton, Extreme, Fixed, Formal, Hard and fast, Hard-set, Hard-shell, Hidebound, Inflexible, Lignin, Renitent, Rigor, Set, Slavish, Starch(y), Stern, Stiff, Stretchless, Strict, Stringent, Tense, Turgor

Rigmarole Jazz, Nonsense, Palaver, Paraphernalia, Protocol, Ragman, Ragment, Riddlemeree, Screed

Rigorous, Rigour Accurate, Austere, Cruel, Exact, Firm, Hard, Inclement, Iron-bound, Stern, Strait, Strict, Stringent, Thorough

Rile Anger, Annoy, Harry, Irritate, Needle, → **NETTLE**, Vex

▷ **Rile(y)** *may indicate* an anagram

Rill Purl, Sike

Rim Atlantic, Border, Chimb, Chime, Edge, Felloe, Felly, Flange, Girdle, Kelyphitic, → **LIP**, Margin, Pacific, Strake, Verge

Rime Crust, Frost, Hoar, Rhyme, Rhythm

Rind Bark, Crackling, Crust, Peel, Skin

Ring(ed), Ringer, Ringing, Rings Anchor, Angelus, Annual, Annulus, Anthelion, Arcus, Arena, Band, Bangle, Bayreuth, Bell, Benzine, Betrothal, Boom-iron, Broch, Brogh, Call, Cambridge, Carabiner, Cartel, Cartouche, Change, Chime, Circinate, Circle, Circlet, Circlip, Circus, Claddagh, Clam, Clang, Clink, Coil, Collet, Cordon, Cornice, Corona, Corral, Corrida, Cramp, Crawl, Cricoid, Cringle, Cromlech, Cycle, Cyclic, Dead, Death's head, Dial, Dicyclic, Diffraction, Ding, Disc, Dohyo, Dong, Donut, Draupnir, D(o)uar, Echo, Encircle, Enclosure, Encompass, Engagement, Enhalo, Enlace, Envelop, Environ, Enzone, Eternity, Extension, Eyelet, Fainne, Fairlead(er), Fairy, Ferrule, Fisherman, Fisti(cuffs), Gas, Gimmal, Gimmer, Gird(le), Girr, Gloriole, Groin, Grom(m)et, Growth, Grummet, Guard, Gyges, Gymmal, Gyre, Halo, Hank, Hob, → **HOOP**, Hoop-la, Hula-hoop, Ideal, Image, Inner, Inorb, Involucre, Jougs, Jow, Karabiner, Kartell, Keeper, Key, Knell, Knock-out, Kraal, Lactam, Laer, Lifebelt, Link, Loop, Luned, Lute, Magpie, Manacle, Manilla, Marquise, Mourning, Napkin, Newton's, Nibelung, Nimbus, Nose, O, Oil-control, Orb, Outer, Pappus, Parral, Parrel, Peal, Pele, Pen, Phone, Ping, Piston, Potato, Price, Prize, Puteal, Quoit, Re-echo, Resonant, Resound, Retaining, Reverberate, Round, Rove, Rowel, Rundle, Runner, Rush, Sale, Scarf, Scraper, Scrunchy, Seal, Signet, Slinger, Slip, Snap-link, Solomon, Sound, Spell, Split, Stemma, Stemme, Stonehenge, Surround, Swivel, Syndicate, Tang, Tattersall, Teething, Terret, Territ, Thimble, Thumb, Timbre, Ting, Tingle, Tink, Tinnitus, Tintinnabulate, Toe, Token, Toll, Toplady, Tore, Torquate, Torques, Torret, Torus, Travelling, Tree, Trochus, Troth, Turret, Tweed, Varvel, Vervel, Vice, Vortex, Wagnerian, Washer, Wedding, Welkin, Withe, Woggle, Zero

Ring-dance Carol

Ring-leader Bell-wether, Fugleman, Instigator

Ringlet Curl(icue), Lock, Tendril, Tress

Ringmaster Wagner

Ringworm Serpigo, Tinea

Rink Ice, Roller, Skating

Rinse Bathe, Blue, Cleanse, Douche, Sind, Sine, Sluice, Swill, Synd, Syne, Tint, Wash

Riot(er), Riotous(ly), Riots Anarchy, Brawl, Clamour, Demo, Deray, Gordon, Hilarious, Hubbub, Luddite, Medley, Mêlée, Nicker, Orgy, Pandemonium, Peterloo, Petroleur, Porteous, Profusion, Quorum, Race, Rag, Ragmatical, Rebecca, Rebel, Roaring, Roister, Rout, Rowdy, Ruction, Ruffianly, Scream, Swing, Tumult

▷ **Rioters, Riotous** *may indicate* an anagram

Rip(per), Ripping, Rip off Avulse, Basket, Buller, Cur, Dilacerate, Fleece, Grand, Handful, Horse, Jack, Lacerate, Rent, Rep, Roué, Splendid, Tear, Tide, Topnotch, To-rend, Unseam

Ripe, Ripen(ing) Auspicious, Full, Geocarpy, Mature, Mellow, Rathe, Ready

Riposte Countermove, Repartee, Retaliate, Retort

Ripple Bradyseism, Fret, Overlap, Popple, Purl, Ruffle, Undulation, Wave, Wavelet, Wimple, Wrinkle

▷ **Rippling** *may indicate* an anagram

Rise(r), Rising Advance, Appreciate, Ascend, Aspire, Assurgent, Bull, Butte, Cause, Dry, Dutch, Easter, Eger, Elevation, Emerge, Émeute, Eminence, Erect, Escalate, Get up, Hance, Hauriant, Haurient, Heave, Heliacal, Hike, Hill, Hummock, Hunt's up, Improve, Increase, Incremental, Insurgent, Intifada, Intumesce, Jibe, Knap, Knoll, Lark, Levee, Levitate, Lift, Molehill, Motte, Mount, Mutiny, Orient, Origin, Peripety, Point, Prove, Putsch, Rear, Resurgent, Resurrection, → **REVOLT**, Rocket, Saleratus, Scarp, Sklim, Sky-rocket, Soar, Spiral, Stand, Stie, Sty, Stye, Surface, Surge, The Fifteen, Tor, Tower, Transcend, Up, Upbrast, Upburst, Upcurl, Upgo, Uprest, Upshoot, Upspear, Upsurge, Upswarm, Upturn, Well

Risk(y) Actuarial, Adventure, Apperil, Back, Calculated, Chance, Compromise, Counterparty, → **DANGER**, Daring, Dice, Dicy, Emprise, Endanger, Fear, Gamble, Game, Hairy, Hazard, High-wire, Imperil, Impetuous, Jeopardy, Liability, Morass, Nap, Peril, Precarious, Security, Shoot the works, Spec, Stake, Throw, Touch and go, Touchy, Unsafe, Venture

Risorgimento Renaissance

Risqué Blue, Racy, Salty, Saucy, Scabrous, Spicy

Rissole(s) Cecils, Chillada, Croquette, Faggot, Falafel, Felafel, Paupiette, Quennelle, Veggieburger

Rite(s) Asperges, Bora, Ceremony, Eastern, Exequies, Initiation, Last offices, Liturgy, Mystery, Nagmaal, Obsequies, Powwow, Ritual, Sacrament, Sarum use, Superstition, York

Ritual Agadah, Arti, Ceremony, Chanoyu, Cultus, Customary, Formality, Haggada, Lavabo, Liturgy, Mumbo-jumbo, Puja, Rite, Sacring, Seder, Social, Tantric, Telestic, Use

Rival(ry), Rivals Absolute, Acres, Aemule, Binocular, Compete, Contender, Emulate, Emule, Envy, Fo(n)e, → **MATCH**, Needle, Opponent, Retinal, Touch, Vie

River(s) Bayou, Creek, Dalles, Ea, Eau, Estuary, Flood, Flower, Fluvial, Potamic, Potamology, R, Riverain, Runner, Stream, Tide(-way), Tributary, Waterway

---

RIVERS

2 letters:	Fox	Yeo	Culm
Ay	Han		Dart
Ob	Hsi	***4 letters:***	Deva
Po	Hué	Abus	Doon
Si	Inn	Abzu	Dove
Xi	Lee	Acis	Drin
	Lot	Adda	Earn
3 letters:	Luo	Adur	East
Aar	Lys	Aire	Ebbw
Aln	Mur	Alma	Ebro
Axe	Nar	Alph	Eden
Ayr	Oil	Amur	Eder
Bug	Oka	Aran	Elbe
Cam	Ord	Aras	Erne
Dee	Red	Arno	Esla
Don	San	Aude	Eure
Ems	Tay	Avon	Gila
Esk	Tet	Back	Gota
Exe	Ure	Beni	Huon
Fal	Usk	Bomu	Idle
Fly	Wye	Cher	Isar

Iser
Isis
Isla
Jiul
Juba
Kama
Kill
Kura
Kwai
Lahn
Lech
Lena
Liao
Luan
Lune
Maas
Main
Meta
Milk
Mino
Mole
Nene
Neva
Nile
Nith
Oder
Ohio
Oise
Ouse
Oxus
Prut
Rock
Ruhr
Saar
Sava
Soar
Spey
Styx
Swan
Swat
Tadi
Taff
Tana
Tarn
Tees
Teme
Test
Tone
Tyne
Uele
Ural
Uvod
Vaal
Waal

Wear
Xero
Yalu
Yare
Yate
Yser
Yuan
Yuen

5 letters:
Abana
Acton
Adige
Afton
Agate
Aisne
Aldan
Apure
Argun
Avoca
Benue
Boyne
Broad
Cauca
Chari
Clwyd
Clyde
Clyst
Colne
Congo
Conwy
Cross
Culbá
Dasht
Desna
Doubs
Douro
Drava
Drave
Duero
Dvina
Eblis
Ebola
Firth
Fleet
Forth
Ganga
Gogra
Green
Havel
Hotan
Indre
Indus
Isere

Ishim
James
Jumna
Juruá
Kasai
Kaven
Kefue
Kenga
Kuban
Lethe
Liard
Limay
Loire
Marne
Mbomu
Meuse
Minho
Mosel
Mulla
Mures
Namoi
Negro
Neman
Niger
Ogowe
Onega
Oreti
Peace
Pearl
Pecos
Pelly
Piave
Pison
Plate
Purus
Rainy
Rance
Rhône
Rhine
Rogue
Roper
Saône
Seine
Shari
Shire
Siang
Siret
Skien
Slave
Snake
Snowy
Somme
Spree
Staff

Stour
Swale
Tagus
Tamar
Tapti
Tarim
Teign
Terek
Tiber
Tisza
Tobol
Trent
Tweed
Volga
Volta
Warta
Weser
Xiang
Xingu
Yaqui
Yarra
Yonne
Yssel
Yukon

6 letters:
Allier
Amazon
Anadyr
Angara
Arzina
Atbara
Barcoo
Barrow
Bio-Bio
Broads
Buller
Calder
Canton
Chenab
Clutha
Colima
Croton
Crouch
Cydnus
Danube
Dawson
Donets
Duddon
Durack
Escaut
Finlay
Fraser
Gambia

Ganges	Ribble	Dubglas	St Croix
Glomma	Riffle	Durance	St Johns
Granta	Rother	Ettrick	St Mary's
Harlem	Sabine	Fitzroy	Swannee
Hodder	Saluda	Garonne	Tapajos
Hsiang	Sambre	Genesee	Thomson
Hudson	Santee	Gironde	Tugaloo
Humber	Seneca	Guapore	Ucayali
Iguacu	Severn	Hari Rud	Uruguay
Ijssel	St John	Helmand	Vistula
Irtish	Struma	Hooghly	Waikato
Irtysh	Sutlej	Huang He	Waitaki
Irwell	Swanee	Hwangho	Washita
Isonzo	Tanana	Iguassu	Wateree
Itchen	Tarsus	Irawadi	Welland
Japura	Tevere	Kanawha	Xi Jiang
Javari	Teviot	Klamath	Yangtse
Javary	Thames	Krishna	Yenisei
Jhelum	Ticino	Lachlan	Yenisey
Jordan	Tigris	Limpopo	Zambese
Kaduna	Tugela	Lualaba	Zambezi
Kagera	Tyburn	Madeira	
Kaveri	Ubangi	Manning	**8 letters:**
Kennet	Ussuri	Maranon	Amu Darya
Kistna	Vardar	Maritsa	Anderson
Kolyma	Vienne	Mataura	Apurimac
Komati	Vltava	Meander	Araguaia
Liffey	Vyatka	Moselle	Araguaya
Loiret	Wabash	Narbada	Arkansas
Mamoré	Wairau	Narmada	Berezina
Medway	Wensum	Neuquén	Blue Nile
Mekong	Wharfe	Niagara	Burdekin
Mersey	Wupper	Nipigon	Canadian
Mindel	Yarrow	Oceanus	Charente
Mohawk	Yellow	Orinoco	Cherwell
Molopo		Orontes	Cheyenne
Morava	**7 letters:**	Parrett	Chindwin
Moskva	Acheron	Pechora	Chu Kiang
Murray	Aruwimi	Pharpar	Clarence
Neckar	Bassein	Potomac	Colorado
Neisse	Berbice	Red Deer	Columbia
Nelson	Berezua	Rubicon	Congaree
Nyeman	Bermejo	Sabrina	Daintree
Ogooue	Buffalo	Salinas	Demerara
Orange	Burnett	Salween	Dneister
Orwell	Caqueta	Salzach	Dordogne
Ottawa	Cauvery	Sanders	Flinders
Pahang	Chagres	San Juan	Franklin
Parana	Cocytus	Scheldt	Gascoyne
Peneus	Damodar	Senegal	Godavari
Platte	Darling	Shannon	Granicus
Pripet	Derwent	Songhua	Guadiana
Prosna	Detroit	Spokane	Hamilton
Rakaia	Dnieper	St Clair	Han Jiang

Illinois
Kennebec
Kentucky
Klondike
Kootenay
Maeander
Mahanadi
Manawatu
Menderes
Missouri
Mitchell
Ob 'Irtysh
Ocmulgee
Okanagan
Okavango
Okovango
Ouachita
Pactolus
Paraguay
Parnaiba
Putumayo
Rio Negro
Safid Rud
Saguenay
Savannah
Suwannee
Syr Darya
Thompson
Tonle Sap
Torridge
Toulouse
Tunguska

Van Hades
Veronezh
Victoria
Volturno
Wanganui
Windrush
Zhu Jiang

9 letters:
Allegheny
Ashburton
Athabasca
Billabong
Churchill
Crocodile
Des Moines
Essequibo
Euphrates
Irrawaddy
Kuskokwim
Mackenzie
Magdalena
Murchison
Parnahiba
Perihonca
Pilcomayo
Porcupine
Qu'Appelle
Rangitata
Richelieu
Rio Branco
Rio Grande

Salambria
Santa Cruz
St George's
White Nile
Wisconsin

10 letters:
Black Volta
Blackwater
Chao Phraya
Courantyne
Cumberland
Great Slave
Hawkesbury
Housatonic
Kizil Irmak
Phlegethon
Rangitaiki
Rangitikei
Sacramento
San Joaquin
Schuylkill
St Lawrence
White Volta
Yesil Irmak

11 letters:
Aegospotami
Assiniboine
Brahmaputra
Castlereagh
Connecticut

Cooper Creek
Delaguadero
Guadalentin
Lesser Slave
Madre de Dios
Mississauga
Mississippi
Monongahela
Montmorency
Shatt-al-Arab
Susquehanna
Yellowstone

12 letters:
Guadalquivir
Murrumbidgee
Saõ Francisco
Saskatchewan
Victoria Nile

13 letters:
Little Bighorn

14 letters:
Jacques Cartier

17 letters:
North Saskatchewan
South Saskatchewan

River-bank, Riverside Brim, Carse, Riparian
River-bed T(h)alweg
River-mouth Firth, Frith
Rivet(ing) Bolt, Clinch, Clink, Concentrate, Explosive, Fasten, Fix, Pean, Peen, Stud, Transfix, Unputdownable
Rivulet Beck, Brook, Burn, Gill, Rill, Runnel, Strand
RMA The Shop
RNA Antisense, → **DNA**, Initiator codon, Messenger, Molecule, M-RNA, Retrotransposon, Ribosomal, Ribosome, Ribozyme, Soluble, Transcribe, Transfer, Uracil, Viroid
Roach Arch(ie), Fish, Red-eye
Road(s), Roadside, Road surface A, A1, Access, Anchorage, Arterial, Asphalt, Autobahn, Autopista, Autostrada, Ave(nue), B, Beltway, Blacktop, Boulevard, Burma, Bypass, Carriageway, Causeway, Clay, Clearway, Close, Cloverleaf, Coach, Concession, Corduroy, Corniche, Course, Crossover, Cul-de-sac, Dirt, Drift-way, Driveway, Drove, Dunstable, Escape, Exit, Expressway, Fairway, Feeder, Fly-over, Fly-under, Foss(e) Way, Freeway, Frontage, Grid, Hampton, Hard, Highway, Horseway, Interstate, Kerb, Lane, Loan, Loke, M1, Mall, Metal, Motorway, Off-ramp, Orbital, Overpass, Parkway, Path, Pike, Post, Private, Rat-run, Rd, Relief, Ride, Ridgeway, Ring, → **ROUTE**, Royal, Service, Shoulder, Shunpike, Side, Silk, Skid, Slip, Speedway, Spur(way), St(reet), Superhighway, Switchback, Tarmac, Tar-seal, Terrace, Thoroughfare, Throughway, Tobacco, Toby, Tollway, Track(way), Trunk, Turning, Turnpike, Unadopted, Underpass, Unmade, Verge, Via, Viaduct, Way

Roadblock Barrier, Cone, Jam, Sleeping policeman, Thank-you-ma'am, Toll
Road-keeper Way-warden
Road-maker Drunkard, Macadam, Navigator, Telford, Wade
Roadstead La Hogue
Roam Enrange, Extravagate, Peregrinate, Rake, Ramble, Rove, Stray, Wander, Wheel
Roan Barbary, Bay, Horse, Leather, Schimmel, Strawberry
Roar(ing) Bawl, Bell(ow), Bluster, Boom, Boys, Cry, Forties, Guffaw, Laugh, Leonine, Roin, Rote, Rout, Royne, Thunder, Tumult, Vroom, Wuther, Zoom
Roast Bake, Barbecue, Baste, Birsle, Brent, Cabob, Cook, Crab, Crown, Decrepitate, Excoriate, Grill, Kabob, Pan, Pot, Ridicule, Scald, Scathe, Sear, Slate, Spit, Tan, Torrefy
Rob(bed), Robber(y) Abactor, Abduct, Bandalero, Bandit, Barabbas, Bereave, Blag, Bonnie, Brigand, Burgle, Bust, Cabbage, Cacus, Cateran, Clyde, Dacoit, Dakoit, Daylight, Depredation, Despoil, Do, Drawlatch, Fake, Filch, Fleece, Flimp, Footpad, Gilderoy, Heist, Hership, Highjack, High toby, Highwayman, Hijack, Hold-up, Hustle, Job, Kondo, Ladrone, Land-pirate, Larceny, Latrocinium, Latron, Loot, Mill, Moskonfyt, Mosstrooper, Pad, Pandoor, Pandour, Pillage, Pinch, Piracy, Pluck, Plunder, Procrustes, Ramraid, Rapine, Reave, Reft, Reive, Rieve, Rifle, Roberdsman, Robertsman, Roll, Rover, Roy, Rubbet, Rustler, Sack, Sciron, Score, Screw, Sheppard, Short change, Sinis, Sirup, Skinner, Smash and grab, Snaphaunch, Spoiler, Spoliation, Spring-heeled Jack, → **STEAL**, Steaming, Stick-up, Sting, Swindle, Syrup, Thief, Thug(gee), Toby, Turn-over, Turpin
Robe(s) Alb, Amice, Amis, Attrap, Buffalo, Camis, Camus, Canonicals, Cassock, Chimer, Chrisom(-cloth), Christom, Dalmatic, Dolman, → **DRESS**, Gown, Habit, Ihram, Jilbab, Kanga, Kanzu, Khalat, Khilat, Kill(a)ut, Kimono, Mantle, Night, Parament, Parliament, Pedro, Peplos, Pontificals, Purple, Regalia, Rochet, Saccos, Sanbenito, Soutane, Sticharion, Stola, Stole, Talar, Tire, Vestment, Yukata
Robert Bob(by), Bridges, Browning, Burns, Cop, Flic, Peel, Rab, Rob
Robin Adair, American, Bird, Cock, Day, Goodfellow, Hob, Hood, Puck(-hairy), Ragged, Redbreast, Reliant, Round, Ruddock, Starveling, Wake
Robot Android, Automaton, Cyborg, Dalek, Golem, Nanobot, Puppet, RUR, Telechir
Robust Hale, Hardy, Healthy, Hearty, Iron, Lusty, Muscular, Rude, Sound, Stalwart, Sthenic, Stout, Strapping, Sturdy, Vigorous
Roc Bird, Ruc, Rukh
Rock(s), Rocker, Rocking, Rocky Acid, Ages, Agitate, Astound, Ayers, Cap, Cock, Country, Cradle, Destabilise, Edinburgh, Erratic, Extrusive, Garage, Gem, Gib(raltar), Goth, Heavy metal, Hybrid, Jounce, Jow, Lithology, Mantle, Marciano, Marlstone, Matrix, Native, Nunatak(kr), Permafrost, Petrology, Petrous, Platform, Plymouth, Progressive, Punk, Quake, Reel, Reggae, Reservoir, Rimrock, Rip-rap, Rudaceous, Sally, Scare, Scaur, Sclate, → **SHAKE**, Shoogle, Showd, Soft, Stonehenge, Stun, Sway, Swee, Swing, Ted, Teeter, Totter, Tremble, Ultrabasic, Ultramafic, Uluru, Unstable, Unsteady, Wall, Weeping, Whin, Wind, Windsor

ROCKS

2 letters:	Crag	Trap	Chalk
Aa	Gang	Tufa	Chert
	Glam	Tuff	Cliff
3 letters:	Jura	Zoic	Clint
Ice	Lava		Craig
Tor	Lias	*5 letters:*	Elvan
	Noup	Arête	Emery
4 letters:	Reef	Brash	Flint
Bell	Sill	Calpe	Geode
Coal	Sima	Chair	Glass

Krans
Loess
Mafic
Magma
Nappe
Olgas
Peter
Scalp
Scrae
Scree
Shale
Slate
Solid
Stone
Trass
Wacke

6 letters:
Albite
Aplite
Arkose
Banket
Basalt
Dacite
Desert
Diapir
Dogger
Dunite
Felsic
Flaser
Flysch
Fossil
Gabbro
Gangue
Garnet
Gibber
Gneiss
Gossan
Gozzan
Inlier
Kingle
Living
Marble
Masada
Norite
Oolite
Oolith
Ophite
Pelite
Pluton
Pumice
Rognon
Sarsen
Schist

Sinter
Skerry
Sklate
S. Peter
Stonen
Synroc
Tephra

7 letters:
Aquifer
Archean
Arenite
Boulder
Breccia
Clastic
Cuprite
Cyanean
Diamond
Diorite
Erathem
Eucrite
Fastnet
Felsite
Geofact
Granite
Greisen
Haplite
Igneous
Lignite
Lorelei
Marlite
Minette
Molasse
Moraine
Needles
Olivine
Ophites
Outcrop
Outlier
Pennant
Peridot
Picrite
Remanie
Rhaetic
Sinking
Spilite
Stadium
Syenite
Terrane
Thulite
Tripoli
Wenlock

8 letters:
Adularia
Aegirine
Aiguille
Andesite
Aphanite
Archaean
Asbestos
Basanite
Brockram
Burstone
Calcrete
Calc-tufa
Calc-tuff
Ciminite
Diabasic
Dolerite
Dolomite
Eclogite
Eklogite
Elvanite
Eutaxite
Fahlband
Felstone
Footwall
Ganister
Hepatite
Hornfels
Idocrase
Inchcape
Isocline
Laterite
Lenticle
Lopolith
Mesolite
Mudstone
Mylonite
Obsidian
Oil shale
Peperino
Petuntse
Phyllite
Pisolite
Plutonic
Porphyry
Psammite
Psephite
Ragstone
Regolith
Rhyolite
Rocaille
Roe-stone
Saxatile
Saxonite

Scorpion
Sunstone
Taconite
Tarpeian
Tephrite
The Olgas
Tonalite
Trachyte
Trappean
Volcanic
Whin sill
Xenolith

9 letters:
Anticline
Argillite
Batholite
Batholith
Bentonite
Bluestone
Buhrstone
Caenstone
Claystone
Cockhorse
Colluvium
Cornstone
Dalradian
Diatomite
Dinantian
Dolostone
Eddystone
Evaporite
Firestone
Flagstone
Flowstone
Gannister
Goslarite
Granulite
Greensand
Greystone
Greywacke
Gritstone
Hornstone
Impactite
Intrusion
Ironstone
Laccolite
Laccolith
Lardalite
Larvikite
Limestone
Meteorite
Mica-slate
Migmatite

Monadnock
Monocline
Monzonite
Mortstone
Mugearite
Natrolite
Neocomian
Ophiolite
Ottrelite
Pegmatite
Phonolite
Phosphate
Pleonaste
Propylite
Protogine
Quartzite
Sandstone
Saprolite
Scablands
Schistose
Siltstone
Soapstone
Tachylyte
Theralite
Tinguaite
Toadstone
Travertin
Underclay
Uriconian
Variolite

Veinstone
Veinstuff
Ventifact
Vulcanite
Whinstone
White Lias
Whunstane
Zechstein

10 letters:
Ailsa Craig
Amygdaloid
Camptonite
Epidiorite
Foundation
Granophyre
Greenstone
Grey-wether
Hypabyssal
Ignimbrite
Kersantite
Kimberlite
Laurdalite
Laurvikite
Lherzolite
Limburgite
Mica-schist
Novaculite
Orthophyre
Palagonite

Peridotite
Phenocryst
Pitchstone
Pyroxenite
Rupestrian
Schalstein
Serpentine
Sparagmite
Stinkstone
Stonebrash
Syntagmata
Teschenite
Touchstone
Travertine
Troctolite

11 letters:
Agglomerate
Amphibolite
Annabergite
Anorthosite
Carbonatite
Geanticline
Halleflinta
Lamprophyre
Metamorphic
Monchiquite
Napoleonite
Nephelinite
Phillipsite

Pyroclastic
Sedimentary
Slickenside
Symplegades

12 letters:
Babingtonite
Baltic Shield
Coal Measures
Granodiorite
Grossularite
Serpentinite
Straticulate
Stromatolite
Syntagmatite
Thunderstone

13 letters:
Hypersthenite

14 letters:
Giant's Causeway
Knotenschiefer
Rhombenporphyr
Roche moutonnée

18 letters:
Scandinavian Shield

Rock-boring Pholas
Rock-cress Arabis
Rocket Arugula, Blue, Booster, Capsule, Carpet, Carrier, Congreve, Dame's, Delta, Drake, Dressing down, Dyer's, Earful, Engine, Eruca, Flare, Ion, Jato, Life, London, Missile, Multistage, Onion, Payload, Posigrade, Reprimand, Reproof, Retro, Rockoon, Rucola, Salad, SAM, Sea, Skylark, Soar, Sonde, Sounding, Space probe, Step, Stephenson, Take-off, Thruster, Tourbillion, Ullage, Upshoot, V1, Vernier, Von Braun, Wall, Warhead, Weld, Yellow, Zero stage
Rock-living Rupicoline, Saxatile, Saxicoline, Saxicolous
Rock-pipit Sea-lark
▷ **Rocky** *may indicate* an anagram
Rococo Baroque, Fancy, Ornate, Quaint
Rod(-shaped), Rodlike, Rods Aaron's, Angler, Axle, Baculiform, Bar, Barbel(l), Barre, Birch, Caduceus, Caim, Came, Can, Cane, Centre, Connecting, Control, Cue, Cuisenaire®, Dipstick, Divining, Dopper, Dowser, Drain, Ellwand, Fasces, Filler, Fin-ray, Firearm, Fisher, Fishing, Fly, Fuel, Gauging, Gold stick, Gun, Handspike, Jacob's staff, Kame, King, Laver, Lightning, Linchpin, Lug, Mapstick, Mopstick, Moses, Napier's bones, Nervure, Newel, Notochord, Perch, Pin, Pistol, Piston, Pitman, Pointer, Poker, Poking-stick, Pole, Pontie, Pontil, Ponty, Probang, Puntee, Punty, Push, Raddle, Range, Regulating, Rhabdoid, Rhabdus, Riding, Rood, Scollop, Shaft, Sounding, Spindle, Spit, Stadia, Stair, Stanchion, Staple, Stave, Stay-bolt, Stick, Sticker, Strickle, Switch, Tension, Tie, Track, Triblet, Tringle, Trocar, Twig, Urochord, Ventifact, Verge, Virgate, Virgulate, Wand, Welding, Withe

Rod-bearer Lictor
Rode Raid
Rodent Acouchi, Acouchy, Agouty, Ag(o)uti, Bandicoot, Bangsring, Banxring, Beaver, Biscacha, Bizcacha, Bobac, Bobak, Boomer, Capybara, Cavy, Chickaree, Chincha, Chinchilla, Chipmunk, Civet, Coypu, Cricetus, Dassie, Deer-mouse, Degu, Delundung, Dormouse, Fieldmouse, Gerbil(le), Glires, Glutton, Gnawer, Gopher, Groundhog, Guinea pig, Ham(p)ster, Hedgehog, Hog-rat, Hutia, Hyrax, Hystricomorph, Jerboa, Jird, Lemming, Loir, Mara, Marmot, Mole rat, Mouse, Murid, Mus, Musk-rat, Musquash, Nutria, Ochotona, Ondatra, Paca, Porcupine, Potoroo, Prairie dog, Rat, Ratel, Ratton, Renegade, Runagate, Sciurine, Sewellel, Shrew, Simplicidentate, Spermophile, Springhaas, Springhase, Squirrel, S(o)uslik, Taguan, Taira, Tuco-tuco, Tucu-tuco, Vermin, Viscacha, Vole, Woodchuck, Woodmouse
Roderick Random, Usher
Rodomontade Bluster, Boast, Bombast, Brag, Gas
Roe Avruga, Botargo, Bottarga, Caviar(e), Coral, Fry, Hard, Melt, Milt(z), Pea, Raun, Rawn, Soft
Roger Ascham, Bacon, Jolly, OK, Rights
Rogue, Roguish(ness) Aberrant, Arch, Bounder, Charlatan, Chiseller, Drole, Dummerer, Elephant, Espiègle(rie), Ganef, Ganev, Ganof, Gonif, Gonof, Greek, Gypsy, Hedge-creeper, Heel, Hempy, Herries, Imp, Knave, Latin, Limmer, Monkey, Palliard, Panurge, Picaresque, Picaroon, Pollard, Poniard, Rapparee, Ra(p)scal(l)ion, Reprobate, Riderhood, Rotter, Savage, Scallywag, Scamp, Schellum, Schelm, Scoundrel, Skellum, Sleeveen, Slip-string, Sly, Swindler, Terror, Varlet, Villain, Wrong 'un
Roil Agitate, Annoy, Churn, Provoke, Vex
Roin Roar
Roister(er) Blister, Carouse, Ephesian, Revel, Rollick, Scourer, Scowrer, Skylark, Swashbuckler, Swinge-buckler
Role Bit, Cameo, Capacity, Function, Gender, Hat, Métier, → **PART**, Persona, Prima-donna, Stead, Title, Travesty
Roll(ed), Roller, Roll-call, Rolling, Rolls Absence, Bagel, Bap, Barrel, Beigel, Billow, Birmingham, Bolt, Bridge, Brioche, Bun, Butterie, Calender, Cambridge, Chamade, Comber, Convolv(ut)e, Cop, Couch, Court, Croissant, Cylinder, Dandy, Drum, Dutch, Electoral, Enswathe, Enwallow, Eskimo, Even, Fardel, Fardle, Finger, Flatten, Forward, Furl, Go, Goggle, Holy, Hotdog, Inker, Involute, Labour, List, Loaded, Lurch, Makimono, Mangle, Mano, Marver, Matricula, Morning, Motmot, Moving, Music, Muster, Notitia, Opulent, Pain au chocolat, Paradiddle, Patent, Paupiette, Pay, Petit-pain, Piano, Pigeon, Pipe, Platen, Porteous, Rafale, Ragman, Record, Reef, Reel, Register, Ren, Rent, Revolute, Revolve, Rhotacism, Rich, Ring, Road, Rob, Rolag, Roster, Rota, Rotate, Rotifer, Roul(e), Roulade, Rouleau, Row, RR, Rub-a-dub, Rumble, Run, Sausage, Schnecke(n), Skin up, Snap, Somersault, Souter's clod, Spool, Spring, Summar, Sway, Swell, Swiss, Table, Tandem, Taxi, Temple, Tent, Terrier, Thread, Toilet, Tommy, Toss, Trill, Trindle, Trundle, Upfurl, Valuation, Victory, Volume, Volutation, Wad, Wallow, Wamble, Waul, Wave, Wawl, Weather, Web, Welter, Western, Wince, Wrap, Yaw, Zorbing
Rollick(ing) Frolic, Gambol, Romp, Sport
▷ **Rollicking** *may indicate* an anagram
Roly-poly Chubby
Roman Agricola, Agrippa, Aurelius, Calpurnia, Candle, Catholic, Cato, Consul, CR, Crassus, Dago, Decemviri, Decurion, Empire, Flavian, Galba, Holiday, Italian, Jebusite, Latin, Maecenas, Papist, Patrician, PR, Quirites, Raetic, RC, Retarius, Rhaetia, Road, Scipio, Seneca, Sulla, Tarquin, Tiberius, Trebonius, Type, Uriconian, Veneti, Volsci
Romance, Romantic (talk) Affair, Amoroso, Amorous, Byronic, Casanova, Catalan, Dreamy, Fancy, Fantasise, Fib, Fiction, Gest(e), Gothic, Historical, Invention, Ladin(o), Ladinity, Langue d'oc(ian), Langue d'oil, Langue d'oui, Liaison, Lie, Neo-Latin, New,

Novelette, Poetic, Quixotic, R(o)uman, Ruritania, Stardust, Sweet nothings, Tale, Tear-jerker

Ro(u)manian, Rumanian Ro, RO, R(o)uman, Transylvanian, Vlach, Wal(l)achian

Romanov Nicholas

▶ **Romany** *see* GYPSY

Rome Holy See, Imperial City

Romeo Casanova, Montagu, R, Swain

Romp(ing) Carouse, Escapade, Fisgig, Fizgig, Frisk, Frolic, Hoyden, Jaunce, Randy, Rig, Rollick, Skylark, Sport, Spree

Ron Glum, Moody

Rondo Rota

Ronnie Biggs

Röntgen R, X-ray

Roo Joey

Roof (edge), Roofing Belfast, Bell, Broach, Ceil, Cl(e)ithral, Cover, Curb, Divot, Dome, Drip, Eaves, French, Gable, Gambrel, Hardtop, Hip(ped), Home, Housetop, Hypostyle, Imperial, Jerkin-head, Leads, M, Mansard, Monopitch, Onion dome, Palate, Pavilion, Pent, Pitched, Pop-top, Porte-cochère, Rag top, Rigging, Saddle, Saddleback, Shingle, Skillion, Skirt, Span, Sun(shine), Targa top, Tectiform, Tectum, Tegula, Thatch, Thetch, Tiling, Top, Uraniscus, Vaulting

Roof-climber Stegopholist

Roofless Hypaethral, Upaithric

Rook Bird, Builder, Castle, Cheat, Crow, Fleece, Fool, Overcharge, R, Swindle

Rookie Beginner, Colt, Galoot, Greenhorn, Learner, Nignog, Novice, Recruit, Tenderfoot, Tyro

Room(y) Capacity, Ceiling, Clearance, Commodious, Elbow, Family, Latitude, Leeway, Margin, Place, Scope, Smoke-filled, → SPACE, Spacious, Standing, Wiggle

ROOMS

2 *letters:*	Digs	Divan	6 *letters:*
CC	Dojo	Foyer	Boiler
Rm	Hall	Green	Camera
	Kiva	Grill	Cellar
3 *letters:*	Loft	Lanai	Closet
Ben	Long	Laura	Common
But	Pump	Lavra	Durbar
Day	Rest	Lodge	Engine
End	Sale	Music	Exedra
Gap	Snug	Oriel	Garret
Gun	Tool	Panic	Hostel
Lab	Twin	Press	Living
Leg	Ward	Rangy	Locker
Loo	Wash	Sales	Lounge
Oda	Work	Salle	Lumber
Pad	Zeta	Salon	Parvis
Sun		Solar	Powder
Tap	5 *letters:*	Spare	Public
Tea	Attic	Staff	Robing
	Berth	Steam	Rubber
4 *letters:*	Bibby	Still	Rumpus
Cell	Bower	Stock	School
Chat	Cabin	Study	Serdab
Dark	Cuddy	Suite	Single

Spence
Street
Strong
Studio
Tardis
Throne
Tiring
Ullage
Vestry

7 letters:
Apadana
Boudoir
Cabinet
Cenacle
Chamber
Chaumer
Control
Cubicle
Cutting
Dinette
Drawing
Exhedra
Genizah
Kursaal
Library

Megaron
Oratory
Orderly
Parlour
Pentice
Pentise
Private
Reading
Sanctum
Servery
Service
Shebang
Sitting
Smoking
Stowage
Two-pair
Utility
Waiting

8 letters:
Anteroom
Assembly
Casemate
Changing
Cockloft
Conclave

Delivery
Dressing
Incident
Property
Recovery
Sacristy
Scullery
Sitkamer
Solarium
Vestiary

9 letters:
Apartment
Boardroom
Camarilla
Composing
Extension
Herbarium
Mould-loft
Palm Court
Receiving
Reception
Single-end
Voorkamer

10 letters:
Commercial
Consulting
Dissecting
Lebensraum
Misericord
Operations
Penetralia
Priesthole
Projection
Recitation
Recreation

11 letters:
Antechamber
Calefactory
Chancellery
Combination
Compartment
Misericorde
Scriptorium

13 letters:
Spheristerion

Roost(er) Cock, Perch, Siskin, Sit

Root(s), Rooted, Rooting Aruhe, Asarum, Beet, Buttress, Calamus, Calumba, Cassava, Cheer, Cocco, Contrayerva, Costus, Couscous, Cube, Culver's, Cuscus, Dasheen, Delve, Deracinate, Derivation, Derris, Dig, Eddo, Elecampane, Eradicate, Eringo, Eryngo, Etymic, Etymon, Extirpate, Fern, Fibrous, Foundation, Gelseminine, Ginseng, Grass, Grout, Grub, Heritage, Horseradish, Hurrah, Immobile, Implant, Incorrigible, Insane, Irradicate, Jalap, Jicama, Khuskhus, Knee, Lateral, Licorice, Mallee, Mandrake, Mangold, Mishmee, Mishmi, Mooli, More, Myall, Navew, Nousle, Nuzzle, Origins, Orris, Pachak, Pleurisy, Pneumatophore, Poke, Prop, Pry, Putchock, Putchuk, Race, Radical, Radish, Radix, Repent, Rhatany, Rhizic, Rhizoid, Rhizome, Scorzonera, Senega, Sessile, Setwall, Skirret, Snuzzle, Source, Spur, Square, Stilt, Stock, Strike, Tap, Taro, Tuber, Tuberous, Tulip, Turbith, Turnip, Turpeth, Ventral, Vetiver, Yam, Zedoary

Rootless Psilotum

Rope(s) Abaca, Backstay, Ba(u)lk, Becket, Bind, Bobstay, Boltrope, Bracer, Brail, Breeching, Bunt-line, Cable, Cablet, Colt, Cord, Cordage, Cordon, Cringle, Downhaul, Drag, Earing, Fake, Fall, Flake, Flemish coil, Foot, Fore-brace, Foresheet, Forestay, Funicular, Futtock-shroud, Gantline, Garland, Grass line, Grist, Guest, Guide, Guy, Halliard, Halser, Halter, Halyard, Hawser, Hawser-laid, Headfast, Inhaul, Jack-stay, Jeff, Jib-sheet, Jump, Kernmantel, Kickling, Knittle, Ladder, Lanyard, Lasher, Lashing, Lasso, Lazo, Leg, Lifeline, Line, Longe, Lunge, Mainbrace, Mainsheet, Manil(l)a, Marlin(e), Match-cord, Messenger, Monkey, Mooring, Nettle, Nip, Noose, Oakum, Outhaul, Painter, Parbuckle, Pastern, Prolonge, Prusik, Pudding, Rawhide, Reef point, Riata, Ridge, Ringstopper, Roband, Robbin, Rode, Runner, St Johnston's ribbon, St Johnston's tippet, Sally, Salt-eel, Seal, Selvagee, Sennit, Sheet, Shroud, Sinnet, Span, Spancel, Spun-yarn, Stay, Sternfast, Stirrup, String, Strop, Sugan, Swifter, Tackle, Tail, Tether, Tie, Timenoguy, Tippet, Tow(line), Trace, Trail, Triatic, Triatic stay, Vang, Wanty, Warp, Widdy, Wire, Yarn

Rosalind Ganymede
Rosary Beads, Mala, Paternoster
Rose(-red), Rosie, Rosy Albertine, Alexandra, Amelanchier, Aurorean, Avens, Bear's-foot, Blooming, Bourbon, Breare, Briar, Brier, Burnet, Cabbage, Canker, Ceiling, Cherokee, China, Christmas, Compass, Corn, Crampbark, Damask, Dog, Eglantine, Eglatère, England, English, Floribunda, G(u)elder, Geum, Golden, Hellebore, Hybrid, Jack, Jacque, Jacqueminot, Lal(age), Lancaster, Lee, Monthling, Moss, Multiflora, Musk, Noisette, Opulus, Peace, Petra, Pink, Potentilla, Promising, Provence, Province, Provincial, Provins, Pyrus, Quillaia, Quillaja, Rambler, Red(dish), Remontant, Rhoda, Rhodo-, Rock, Rugosa, Scotch, Snowball, Sprinkler, Standard, Sweetbrier, Tea, Tokyo, Tudor, White, Whitethorn, York
Rose-apple Jamboo, Jambu
Rose-bay Oleander
Roseland SE
Rosemary Rosmarine
Rosette Buttonhole, Chou, Cockade, Favour, Patera, Rosula
Rosin Colophony, Resin, Roset, Rosit, Rozet, Rozit
Rosinante Jade
Roster List, Register, Scroll, Table
Rostrum Ambo, Bema, Lectern, Podium, Pulpit, Tribune
Rot(ten), Rotting Addle, Baloney, Boo, Bosh, Botrytis, Brown, Bull, Caries, Carious, Corrode, Corrupt, Crown, Daddock, Decadent, → **DECAY**, Decompose, Decrepitude, Degradable, Dotage, Dricksie, Druxy, Dry, Eat, Erode, Fester, Foot, Foul, Gangrene, Kibosh, Manky, Mildew, Noble, Nonsense, Off, Poppycock, Poxy, Punk, Putid, Putrefy, Putrescent, Putrid, Rail, Rancid, Rank, Rat, Red, Ret, Rhubarb, Ring, Rust, Sapropel, Septic, Soft, Sour, Squish, Twaddle, Vrot, Wet
Rotate, Rotating, Rotation, Rotator Backspin, Crankshaft, Crop, Feather, Gyrate, Laevorotation, Lay-farming, Optical, Pivot, Pronate, Rabat(te), Reamer, Revolve, Roll, Selsyn, Succession, Teres, Topspin, Trochilic, Trundle, Turn, Turntable, Twiddle, Vortex, Vorticose, Wheel, Windmill
Rote Heart, Memory, Recite, Routine
Rotor Auxiliary, Flywheel, Impeller, Squirrel cage, Tilt
▶ **Rotten** *see* **ROT(TEN)**
▷ **Rotten** *may indicate* an anagram
Rotter Cad, Heel, Knave, Stinker, Swine
Rotund Chubby, Corpulent, Plump, Round, Stout, Tubby
Rotunda Pantheon
Roué Debauchee, Decadent, Libertine, Lothario, Profligate, Rake(-shame), Rip
Rouge Blush, Gild, Jeweller's, Raddle, Redden, Reddle, Ruddle, Ruddy
Rough(en), Roughly, Roughness About, Abrasive, Approximate, Asper(ate), Broad, Broad brush, Burr, C, Ca, Choppy, Circa, Coarse, Craggy, Craig, Crude, Exasperate, Frampler, Grained, Gross, Gruff, Guestimate, Gurly, Gusty, Hard, Harsh, Hispid, Hoarse, Hoodlum, Hooligan, Ill, Impolite, Imprecise, Incondite, Inexact, Irregular, Jagged, Karst, Keelie, Kokobeh, Muricate, Obstreperous, Of sorts, Or so, Push, Ragged, Ramgunshoch, Raspy, Raucle, Rip, Risp, Robust, Row, Rude, Rugged, Rusticate, Rusty, Sandblast, Scabrid, Scabrous, Scratchy, Sea, Shaggy, Sketchy, Some, Spray, Spreathe, Squarrose, Stab, Strong-arm, Stubbly, Swab, Tartar, Tearaway, Ted, Textured, Tiger country, Tousy, Touzy, Towsy, Towzy, Uncut, Violent, Yahoo
Roughage Ballast, Bran, Fodder
Rough breathing Asper, Rale, Wheeze
Roughcast Harl
▷ **Roughly** *may indicate* an anagram
Roulette Russian
Round(ed), Roundness About, Ammo, Ball, Beat, Bombe, Bout, Cartridge, Catch,

Circle, Complete, Cycle, Dome, Doorstep, Fat, Figure, Full, Geoidal, Global, Globate, Hand, Heat, Jump-off, Lap, Leg, Milk, O, Oblate, Orb, Orbicular, Orbit, Orby, Ought, Patrol, Peri-, Pirouette, Plump, Pudsy, Qualifying, Quarter, Quarter-final, Rev, Ring, Robin, Roly-poly, Ronde, Rondure, Rota, Rotund, Route, Routine, Rundle, Rung, Salvo, Sandwich, Sarnie, Sellinger's, Semi-final, Shot, Skirt, Slice, Sphaer, Sphere, Spherical, Spiral, Step, Table, Tour, Tubby, Tune, U-turn, Walk

▷ **Round** *may indicate* a word reversed

Roundabout Ambages, Approximately, Bypass, Carousel, Circle, Circuit, Circumambient, Circumbendibus, Circus, Devious, Eddy, → **INDIRECT**, Merry-go-round, Peripheral, Rotary, Tortuous, Traffic circle, Turntable, Waltzer, Whirligig, Windlass

▷ **Roundabout** *may indicate* an anagram

Round building Tholos, Tholus

Rounders Patball

Round-mouth Hag

Round up Bang-tail muster, Collate, Corner, Corral, Gather, Herd, Muster, Rodeo, Spiral

Roup Auction, Croak, Pip, Roop

Rouse(r), Rousing Abrade, Abraid, Abray, Amo(o)ve, Animate, Beat, Bestir, Cheerleader, Emotive, Enkindle, Excite, Firk, Flush, Hearten, Heat, Innate, Kindle, Knock up, Rear, Send, Shake up, Stimulate, Suscitate, Unbed, Waken, Whip

Rousseau Émile

Rout Clamour, Debacle, Defeat, Drub, Fleme, Flight, Hubbub, Hurricane, Rabble, Retreat, Rhonchal, Snore, Thiasus, Upsee, Upsey, Upsy, Vanquish, Whoobub

Route(s) Arterial, Autobahn, Avenue, Byroad, Camino real, Causeway, Course, Direction, Itinerary, I-way, Line, Ling, M-way, Path, Red, Road, Sea-lane, Stock, Topo, Track, Trade, Transit, Via, Via Dolorosa, Walk, Waterway, Way

Routine Automatic, Day-to-day, Drill, Everyday, Grind, Groove, Habitual, Heigh-ho, Helch-how, Ho-hum, Jogtrot, Journeywork, Monotony, Pattern, Perfunctory, Pipe-clay, Red tape, Rota, Rote, Round, Run-of-the-mill, Rut, Schtik, S(c)htick, SOP, Treadmill, Workaday

Rove(r), Roving Car, Discursive, Enrange, Errant, Freebooter, Gad, Globetrotter, Marauder, Nomad, Proler, Prowl, Ralph, Range, → **ROAM**, Slub(b), Stray, Vagabond, Varangarian, Viking, Wander

Row(er) Align, Altercation, Arew, Argue, Argument, Bank, Barney, Bedlam, Bobbery, Bow, Brattle, Cannery, Colonnade, Death, Debate, Deen, Din, Dispute, Dust-up, Feud, File, Fireworks, Food, Fyle, Hoo-ha, Hullabaloo, Leander, Line(-up), Noise, Note, Oar, Octastich, Orthostichy, Paddle, Parade, Peripteral, Pluriserial, Ply, Pull, Quarrel, Rammy, Range, Rank, Raunge, Remigate, Reproach, Rew, Rhubarb, Rotten, Ruction, Rumpus, Savile, Scene, Scrap, Scull, Series, Set, Shindig, Shindy, Shine, Skid, Spat, Splore, Stern, Stound, Street, Stridor, Stroke, Stushie, Sweep, Terrace, Tier, Tiff, Tone, Torpid, Twelve-tone, Wetbob, Wherryman

Rowan Ash, Quicken, Sorb

Rowdy, Rowdiness Bovver, Cougan, Hoo, Hooligan, Loud, Noisy, Rorty, Rough, Roughhouse, Ruffian, Scourer, Scozza, Skinhead, Stroppy, Unruly, Uproarious

Roy Rob

Royal(ty), Royalist Academy, Angevin, Basilical, Battle, Bourbon, Crowned, Emigré, Exchange, Fee, Hanoverian, HR(H), Imperial, Imposing, Inca, Kingly, King's man, Majestic, Malignant, Palatine, Payment, Pharaoh, Plantagenet, Prince, Princess, Purple, Queenly, Real, Regal, Regis, Regius, Regnal, Sail, Sceptred, Society, Tsarista

Rub(bing), Rubber(y), Rub out Abrade, Attrition, Balata, Buff, Buna®, Bungie, Bungy, Bunje(e), Bunjie, Bunjy, Butyl, Calk, Calque, Camelback, Caoutchouc, Chafe, Cold, Condom, Corrade, Corrode, Cow gum®, Crepe, Cul(t)ch, Delete, Destroy, Dunlop®, Ebonite, Efface, Elastic, Elastomer, Elaterite, Embrocate, Emery, Eradicator, Erase, Factice, Factis, Fawn, Foam, Fray, Fret, Friction, Fridge, Frottage, Frotteur, Fudge, Funtumia, Gall, Galoch, Goodyear®, Grate, Graze, Grind, Guayule, Gum elastic,

Gutta-percha, Hale, Hard, Hevea, High-hysteresis, Hule, India, Inunction, Irritate, Isoprene, Jelutong, Johnnie, Lagos, Latex, Leather, Masseur, Negrohead, Neoprene, Nuzzle, Obstacle, Para, Polish, Pontianac, Pontianak, Root, Safe, Sandpaper, Scour, Scrub, Scuff, Seringa, Silastic®, Smoked, Sorbo®, Sponge, Stroke, Synthetic, Towel, Trace, Ule, Vulcanite, Wild, Wipe, Xerotripsis

▷ **Rubbed** *may indicate* an anagram

Rubbish Bad mouth, Balls, Bilge, Brash, Brock, Bull, Bunkum, Cack, Clap-trap, Cobblers, Codswallop, Culch, Debris, Detritus, Dirt, Discredit, Dre(c)k, Drivel, Dross, Eyewash, Fiddlesticks, Garbage, Grot, Grunge, Guff, Hogwash, Kack, Kak, Landfill, Leavings, Litter, Mullock, Nonsense, Phooey, Piffle, Pish, Raff, Raffle, Red(d), → **REFUSE**, Riff-raff, Scrap, Sewage, Spam, Stuff, Tinpot, Tinware, Tip, Tom(fool), Tosh, Totting, Trade, Tripe, Trouch, Truck, Trumpery, Twaddle, Urethra

Rubbish heap Coup, Cowp, Dump, Lay-stall, Sweepings, Toom

Rubble Brash, Debris, Detritus, Hard-core, Moellon, Random, Remains, Riprap, Talus

Rubidium Rb

Ruby Agate, Balas, Brazilian, Colorado, Cuprite, Oriental, Pigeon's blood, Port, Red, Spinel, Star, Starstone, Type

Ruck Furrow, Scrum, Wrinkle

Rucksack Backpack, Bergen, Pickapack, Pikau

Ruction Ado, Fuss, Quarrel

Rudder Budget, Helm, Steerer

Ruddle Lemnian

Ruddy Bally, Bloody, Flashy, Florid, Raddled, Red, Roseate, Rubicund, Rufous, Sanguine

Rude(ness) Abusive, Barbaric, Bear, Bestial, Bumpkin, Callow, Carlish, Churlish, Coarse, Discourteous, Disrespect, Elemental, Goustrous, Green, Ill-bred, Impolite, Indecorous, Indelicate, Inficete, Ingram, Ingrum, Insolent, Ocker, Offensive, Peasant, Profane, Raw, Ribald, Risqué, Rough, Simple, Surly, Unbred, Uncivil, Uncomplimentary, Uncourtly, Unlettered, Unmannered, Vulgar, Yobbish

Rudiment(ary), Rudiments ABC, Absey, Anlage, Beginning, Element, Embryo, Foundation, Germ(en), Germinal, Inchoate, Primordial, Seminal, Vestige

Rudolph Hess, Reindeer

Rue(ful) Boulevard, Dittany, Goat's, Harmala, Harmel, Herb of grace, Meadow, Mourn, Poignant, Regret, Repent, Rew, Ruta, Sorry, Wall

Ruff Collar, Crest, Fraise, Frill, Mane, Partlet, Pope, Rabato, Rebato, Ree, Trump

Ruffian Apache, Bashi-bazouk, Brute, Bully, Cut-throat, Desperado, Goon(da), Highbinder, Hoodlum, Hooligan, Keelie, Larrikin, Lout, Miscreant, Mohock, Myrmidon, Ned, Phansigar, Plug-ugly, Raff, Rowdy, Skinhead, Sweater, Tearaway, Thug, Toe-ragger, Trailbaston, Tumbler

Ruffle(d) Bait, Dishevel, Falbala, Flounce, Fluster, Fret, → **FRILL**, Gather, Irritate, Jabot, Peplum, Rouse, Ruche, Rumple, Shirty, Tousle

▷ **Ruffle** *may indicate* an anagram

Rug Afghan, Bearskin, Bergama, Buffalo-robe, Carpet, Drugget, Ensi, Flokati, Gabbeh, Hearth, Herez, Heriz, Kelim, K(h)ilim, Kirman, Lap robe, Mat, Maud, Numdah, Oriental, Pilch, Prayer, Rag, Runner, Rya, Scatter, Steamer, Tatami, Throw, Travelling, Wig

Rugby (player) Back, Fifteen, Forward, Harlequin, League, Lion, Pack, Quin, RU, Scrum, Sevens, Threequarter, Touch, Union, Wing

Rugged Craggy, Gnarled, Harsh, Knaggy, Rough, Strong

Ruin(ed), Ruins, Ruinous Annihilate, Banjax, Bankrupt, Blast, Blight, Blue, Butcher, Carcase, Collapse, Corrupt, Crash, Crock, Damn, Decay, Defeat, Demolish, Despoil, Destroy, Devastate, Dilapidation, Disaster, Disfigure, Dish, Disrepair, Dogs, Do in, Doom, Downcome, Downfall, End, Fine, Fordo, Hamstring, Heap, Hell, Insolvent, Inure, Kaput(t), Kibosh, Loss, Mar, Mocers, Mockers, Mother's, Overthrow, Perdition, Perish, Petra, Pigs and whistles, Pot, Puckerood, Ravage, Reck, Relic, Scotch, Screw, Scupper, Scuttle, Shatter, Sink, Smash, Spill, → **SPOIL**, Stramash, Subvert, Undo, Unmade, Ur,

Violate, Vitiate, Whelm, Woe, Wrack, Write off
▷ **Ruined** *may indicate* an anagram
Rule(r), Rules, Ruling Advantage, Algorithm, Align, Aristocrat, Arrêt, Article,
Bosman, Bylaw, Caesar, Calliper, Canon, Chain, Club-law, Code, Condominium,
Constitution, Control, Criterion, Decree, Domineer, Dominion, Em, Empire, En,
Establishment, Estoppel, Etiquette, Fatwa, Feint, Fetwa, Fleming's, Formation, Formula,
Gag, Global, Golden, Govern, Govern-all, Ground, Gynocracy, Home, In, Institutes,
Jackboot, Law, Leibniz's, Lesbian, Lex, Lindley, Liner, Majority, Markownikoff's,
Mastery, Matriarchy, Maxim, McNa(u)ghten, Measure, Mede, Meteyard, Method,
Ministrate, Mistress, Mobocracy, Motto, Naismith's, Netiquette, Norm(a),
Oppress, Ordinal, Organon, Organum, Pantocrator, Parallel, Parallelogram, Phase,
Phrase-structure, Pie, Placitum, Plumb, Precedent, Precept, Prescript, Prevail,
Principle, Protocol, Ptochocracy, Pye, Rafferty's, Raine, Realm, Reciprocity, Rector,
Regal, Regnant, Regula, Reign, Rewrite, Ring, Routine, Rubric, Scammozzi's, Selection,
Setting, Slide, Standard, Statute, Straight edge, Stylebook, Sutra, Sway, System,
Ten-minute, Ten-yard, Theorem, Three, Thumb, Transformation(al), Trapezoid,
T-square, Tycoon, Tyrant, Uti possidetis, Wield

RULERS

1 letter:	*5 letters:*	Cheops	*7 letters:*
K	Ameer	Dergue	Abbasid
R	Ardri	Despot	Ardrigh
	Creon	Dynast	Autarch
3 letters:	Dewan	Exarch	Bajayet
Ban	Diwan	Führer	Bajazet
Bey	Henry	Franco	Bodicea
Dey	Herod	Gerent	Catapan
Mir	Hoyle	Harold	Chogyal
Oba	Hyleg	Hitler	Elector
Raj	Judge	Judges	Emperor
Rex	Mogul	Kabaka	Gaekwar
	Mpret	Kaiser	Gaikwar
4 letters:	Mudir	Mamluk	Jamshid
Amir	Nawab	Manchu	Jamshyd
Cham	Negus	Mikado	Khedive
Czar	Nizam	Peshwa	Miranda
Doge	Octet	Prince	Monarch
Duce	Pasha	Rajput	Omayyad
Emir	Queen	Regent	Pharaoh
Imam	Rajah	Ronald	Podesta
Inca	Ratoo	Sachem	Rajpoot
Khan	Shaka	Satrap	Richard
King	Sheik	Sheikh	Saladin
Nero	Sophi	Sherif	Serkali
Pope	Sophy	Shogun	Souldan
Rana	Tenno	Sirdar	Toparch
Ratu		Sovran	Umayyad
Shah	*6 letters:*	Squier	Viceroy
Tsar	Atabeg	Squire	Zamorin
Vali	Atabek	Stalin	
Wali	Caliph	Sultan	*8 letters:*
	Castro	Swaraj	Archduke
	Chagan	Walter	Autocrat

Bismarck
Boudicca
Burgrave
Caligula
Caudillo
Cromwell
Dictator
Ethnarch
Frederic
Heptarch
Hespodar
Hierarch
Maharaja
Mamaluke
Mameluke
Napoleon
Oligarch
Overlord

Padishah
Pentarch
Pericles
Reginald
Roderick
Sagamore
Sassanid
Suleiman
Suzerain
Synarchy
Tetrarch
Thearchy
Theocrat

9 letters:
Alexander
Amenhotep
Bretwalda

Britannia
Cleopatra
Cosmocrat
Frederick
Montezuma
Ochlocrat
Pendragon
Plutocrat
Potentate
President
Sovereign
Tamerlane

10 letters:
Caractacus
Plantocrat
Principate
Rajpramukh

Stratocrat

11 letters:
Charlemagne
Genghis Khan
Prester John
Queensberry
Stadtholder
Tutankhamun

12 letters:
Chandragupta

13 letters:
Haile Selassie

Rule-book Code, Pie, Pye

Rum(mer) Abnormal, Baba, Bacardi, Bay, Cachaca, Curious, Daiquiri, Dark, Demerara, Droll, Eerie, Eery, Glass, Grog, Island, Jamaica, Kooky, Odd(er), Peculiar, Quaint, Queer, Screech, Strange, Tafia, Weird

▶ **Rumanian** *see* RO(U)MANIAN

Rumble, Rumbling Borborygmus, Brool, Curmurring, Drum-roll, Groan, Growl, Guess, Lumber, Mutter, Roll, Rumour, Thunder, Tonneau, Twig

Ruminant, Ruminate Antelope, Cabrie, Camel, Cavicornia, Cervid, Champ, Chew, Contemplate, Cow, Eland, Gemsbok, Gnu, Goat, Ibex, Llama, Meditate, Merycism, Nilgai, Nyala, Okapi, Oorial, Oryx, Palebuck, Pecora, Pronghorn, Reindeer, Saola, Serow

Rummage Delve, Ferret, Fish, Foray, Fossick, Jumble, Powter, Ransack, Rifle, Root, Rootle, Scavenge, Search, Tot

Rummy Canasta, Cooncan, Game, Gin, Queer

Rumour Breeze, Bruit, Buzz, Canard, Cry, Fame, Furphy, → GOSSIP, Grapevine, Hearsay, Kite, Kite-flying, Mail, Noise, On-dit, Pig's-whisper, Report, Repute, Say-so, Smear, Tale, Talk, Underbreath, Unfounded, Vine, Voice, Whisper, Word

Rump Arse, Bottom, Buttocks, Croup(e), Croupon, Crupper, Curpel, Derrière, Nates, Parliament, Podex, Pygal, Steak, Uropygium

Rumple Corrugate, Crease, Mess, Muss, Touse, Tousle, Touze, Towse, Towze, Wrinkle

Rumpus Bagarre, Commotion, Din, Noise, Rhubarb, Riot, Row, Ruction, Shemozzle, Shindig, Shindy, Shine, Storm, Stushie, Tirrivee, Uproar

Run(ning), Run away, Run into, Run off, Runny, Runs Admin(ister), Arpeggio, Black, Bleed, Blue, Bolt, Break, Bunk, Bye, Canter, Career, Chase, Chicken, Clip, Coop, Corso, Course, Cresta, Cross-country, Current, Cursive, Cursorial, Cut, Dart, Dash, Decamp, Diarrhoea, Dinger, Direct, Double, Dribble, Drive, Dry, Dummy, Enter, Escape, Execute, Extra, Fartlek, Flee, Flit, Flow, Fly, Follow, Fun, Fuse, Gad, Gallop, Gauntlet, Go, Green, Ground, Hare, Haste(n), Hennery, Hie, Hightail, Home, Idle, Jog, Jump bail, Ladder, Lam, Lauf, Leg, Leg bye, Lienteric, Liquid, Lope, Manage, Marathon, Melt, Milk, Mizzle, Mole, Molt, Monkey, Neume, Now, On, On-line, Operate, Pace, Pacific, Paper chase, Parkour, Pelt, Pilot, Ply, Pour, Print, Purulent, R, Race, Range, Rear end, Red, Renne, Rin, Roadwork, Romp, Root, Roulade, Rounder, Ruck, Scamper, Scapa, Scarpa, Scarper, School, Schuss, Scud, Scuddle, Scutter, Scuttle, See, Sequence, Shoot, Single, Skate, Skedaddle, Ski, Skid, Skirr, Skitter, Slalom, Slide, Smuggle, Spew, Split, Spread, Sprint, Sprue, Squitters, Stampede, Straight, Streak, Stream, Taxi, Tear, Tenor, Tick over, Tie-breaker, Tirade, Trial, Trickle, Trill, Trot, Well

Runaway Drain, Easy, Escapee, Fugie, Fugitive, Refugee

Run down Asperse, Belie, Belittle, Calumniate, Decry, Denigrate, Derelict, Detract, Dilapidated, Infame, Knock, Low, Obsolesce(nt), Poorly, Rack, Résumé, Scud, Seedy, Tirade, Traduce

Rune, Runic Ash, Futhark, Futhorc, Futhork, Kri, Ogham, Spell, Thorn, Wen, Wyn(n)

Rung Crossbar, Roundel, Rundle, Stave, Step, Tolled, Tread

Runner(s) Atalanta, Bean, Blade, Bow Street, Carpet, Coe, Courser, Dak, Deserter, Drug, Emu, Field, Geat, Gentleman, Gillie-wetfoot, Harrier, Hatta, Hencourt, Internuncio, Lampadist, Leg bye, Legman, Messenger, Miler, Milk, Mohr, Mousetrap, Nurmi, Oribi, Ovett, Owler, Policeman, Racehorse, Rhea, → **RIVER**, Rug, Rum, → **RUN(NING)**, Sarmentum, Scarlet, Scud, Series, Slipe, Smuggler, Stolon, Stream, Tailskid, Trial

▷ **Running, Runny** *may indicate* an anagram

Run of the mill Mediocre

Runt Anthony, Dilling, Oobit, Oubit, Reckling, Scalawag, Scrog, Smallest, Tantony, Titman, Woobut, Woubit

Run through Impale, Pierce, Rehearsal

Runway Airstrip, Drive, Slipway, Strip, Tarmac®

Run wild Lamp, Rampage

Rupee(s) Lac, Lakh, Re

Rupert Bear

Rupture Breach, Burst, Crack, Enterocele, Hernia, Rend, Rhexis, Rift, Scissure, Split

Rural Agrarian, Agrestic, Backwoodsman, Boo(h)ai, Booay, Boondocks, Bucolic, Country, Cracker-barrel, Forane, Georgic, Hick, Mofussil, Platteland, Praedial, Predial, Redneck, Rustic, Sticks, The Shires, Ulu, Upland, Wop-wops

Ruse Artifice, Decoy, Dodge, Engine, Hoax, Pawk, Stratagem, → **TRICK**

Rush(ed) Accelerate, Barge, Bolt, Bustle, Career, Charge, Dart, Dash, Dutch, Eriocaulon, Expedite, Fall, Faze, Feese, Feeze, Feeze, Feze, Fly, Forty-nine, Frail, Friar, Gad, Gold, Gust, Hare, Hasten, High-tail, Horsetail, → **HURRY**, Hurry and scurry, Hurtle, Jet, Juncus, Lance, Lash, Leap, Luzula, Moses, Odd-man, Onset, Palmiet, Pellmell, Phase, Pheese, Pheeze, Phese, Plunge, Pochard, Precipitate, Railroad, Rampa(u)ge, Rash, Rayle, Reed, Rip, Scamp(er), Scirpus, Scour(ing), Scramble, Scud, Scurry, Sedge, Shave-grass, Spate, Speed, Stampede, Star(r), Streak, Streek, Surge, Swoop, Swoosh, Tantivy, Tear, Thrash, Thresh, Tilt, Torrent, Tule, Viretot, Whoosh, Zap, Zoom

Rusk Zwieback

Russell AE, Bertrand, Jack

Russet Rutile

Russia(n), Russian headman, Russian villagers Apparatchik, Ataman, Bashkir, Belorussian, Beria, Bolshevik, Boris, Boyar, Buryat, Byelorussian, Cesarevitch, Chechen, Chukchee, Chukchi, Circassian, Cossack, Dressing, D(o)ukhobor, Esth, Evenki, Ewenki, Igor, Ingush, Ivan, Kabardian, Kalmuk, Kalmyck, Leather, Leonid, Lett, Mari, Menshevik, Mingrel(ian), Minimalist, Mir, Misha, Muscovy, Octobrist, Osset(e), Red, Romanov, Rus, Russ(niak), Russki, Ruthene, Salad, Serge, Sergei, Slav, Stakhanovite, SU, Tatar, The Bear, Thistle, Udmurt, Uzbeg, Uzbek, Vladimir, Vogul, White, Yakut, Yuri, Zyrian

Rust(y) Aeci(di)um, Blister, Brown, Corrode, Cor(ro)sive, Eat, Erode, Etch, Ferrugo, Goethite, Iron oxide, Iron-stick, Laterite, Maderise, Oxidise, Puccinia, Rubiginous, Soare, Stem, Teleutospore, Telium, Uredine, Uredo, Verdigris, Wheat, Yellow

Rust-fungus Aecidiospore

Rustic Arcady, Bacon, Bor(r)el(l), Bucolic, Bumpkin, Carl, Carlot, Chawbacon, Churl, Clodhopper, Clown, Corydon, Cracker-barrel, Crackle, Culchie, Damon, Doric, Forest, Georgic, Hayseed, Hick, Hillbilly, Hind, Hob, Hobbinoll, Hodge, Homespun, Idyl(l), Pastorale, Peasant, Pr(a)edial, Put(t), Rube, Rural, Silk, Strephon, Swain, Sylvan, Uplandish, Villager, Villatic, Yokel

▷ **Rustic** *may indicate* an anagram

Rusticate Banish, Seclude

Rustle(r), Rustling Abactor, Crackle, Crinkle, Duff, Fissle, Frou-frou, Gully-raker, Poach, Silk, Speagh(ery), Sprechery, Steal, Stir, Susurration, Swish, Thief, Whig
Rust-proof Zinced
Rut Channel, Furrow, Groove, Heat, Routine, Sulcus, Track
Ruth Babe, Compassion, Mercy, Pity, Remorse, Rewth
Ruthenium Ru
Rutherfordium Rf
Ruthless Brutal, Cruel, Dog eat dog, Fell, Hard, Hardball, Hard-bitten, Indomitable
Rwanda(n) Tutsi
Rye Gentleman, Grain, Grass, Spelt, Whisky

S Ogee, Saint, Second, Sierra, Society, South, Square

SA It, Lure

Sabbatarian Wee Free

Sabbath Juma, Lord's Day, Rest-day, Shabbat, Sunday, Witches'

Sabbatical Leave, Year off

Sabine Horace, Women

Sable American, Black, Jet, Negro, Pean, Zibel(l)ine

Sabotage, Saboteur Cripple, Destroy, Frame-breaker, Hacktivism, Ratten, Spoil, Treachery, Undermine, Vandalise, Worm, Wrecker

Sabre, Sabre rattler Jingo, Sword, Tulwar

Sabrina Severn

Sac Air, Allantois, Amnion, Aneurism, Aneurysm, Bag, Bladder, Bursa, Caecum, Castoreum, Cisterna, Cyst, Diverticulum, Embryo, Follicle, Ink, Pericardium, Peritoneum, Pneumatophore, Pod, Pollen, Scrotum, Spermatheca, Tylose, Tylosis, Utricle, Vesica, Vocal, Yolk

Saccharine Dulcite, Dulcose

Sack(cloth), Sacking Axe, Bag, Bed, Boot, Bounce, Budget, Burlap, Can, Cashier, Chasse, Chop, Coal, Compression, Congé, Congee, Dash, Depose, Depredate, Despoil, Discharge, Dismissal, Doss, Fire, Growbag, Gunny, Havoc, Hessian, Hop-pocket, Jute, Knap, Lay waste, Loot, Mailbag, Maraud, Marching orders, Mat, Mitten, Pillage, Plunder, Poke, Postbag, Push, Raid, Rapine, Ravage, Reave, Replace, Rieve, Road, Rob, Sad, Sanbenito, Sherris, Sherry, Spoliate, Vandalise, Walking papers

▷ **Sacks** *may indicate* an anagram

Sacrament Baptism, Christening, Communion, Confirmation, Eucharist, Extreme unction, Housel, Lord's Supper, Matrimony, Nagmaal, Orders, Penance, Promise, Reconciliation, Ritual, Unction, Viaticum

Sacred (object), Sacred place Adytum, Churinga, Delphi, Divine, Hallowed, Hareem, Harem, Harim, Heart, Hierurgy, → **HOLY**, Ineffable, Inner sanctum, Manito(u), Nine, Omphalos, Padma, Pietà, Sacrosanct, Sanctum, Taboo, Tapu, Temenos

Sacrifice Alcestic, Cenote, Corban, Cost, Forego, Gambit, Gehenna, Hecatomb, Holocaust, Immolate, Iphigenia, Isaac, Lay down, Molech, Moloch, Molochize, Oblation, → **OFFERING**, Peace offering, Relinquish, Sati, Suovetaurilia, Supreme, Surrender, Suttee, Taurobolium, Tophet, Vicarious, Victim

Sacrilege, Sacrilegious Blaspheme, Impiety, Profane, Violation

Sacristan, Sacristy Diaconicon, Sceuophylax, Sexton

Sacrosanct Inviolable

Sad(den), Sadly, Sadness Alas, Attrist, Blue, Con dolore, Dejected, Depressed, Desolate, Disconsolate, Dismal, Doleful, Dolour, Downcast, Drear, Dull, Dumpy, Fadeur, Forlorn, Heartache, Lovelorn, Low, Lugubrious, Mesto, Mournful, Niobe, Oh, Plaintive, Plangent, Poignancy, Proplastid, Sorrowful, Sorry, Tabanca, Tearful, Tear-jerker, Threnody, Tragic, Triste, Tristesse, Unhappy, Wan, Weltschmerz, Wo(e)begone

Saddle (bag, cloth, flap, girth, pad), Saddled Alforja, Aparejo, Arson, Bicycle, Burden, Cantle, Cinch, Col, Crupper, Demipique, Kajawah, Lumber, Numnah, Oppress, Pack, Pad, Panel, Pigskin, Pilch, Pillion, Seat, Sell(e), Shabrack, Shabracque, Side, Skirt, Stock, Tree, Unicycle, Western

Saddle-bow Arson

Saddler Whittaw(er)
Sadie Thompson
Sadism, Sadist(ic) Algolagnia, Cruel, Dominator
▷ **Sadly** *may indicate* an anagram
Safari Expedition, Hunt
Safe(ty) Active, All right, Almery, Ambry, Awmrie, Coolgardie, Copper-bottomed, Delouse, Deposit, GRAS, Harmless, Hunk, Immunity, Impunity, Inviolate, Keister, Meat, Night, Passive, Peter, Proof, Reliable, Roadworthy, Sanctuary, Secure, Sheltered, Sound, Strong-box, Strongroom, Sure, Whole-skinned, Worthy
Safebreaker Yegg
Safeguard Bulwark, Caution, Ensure, Fail-safe, Frithborh, Fuse, Hedge, Palladium, Protection, Register, Ward
Saffron Bastard, Crocus, False, Meadow, Mock, Yellow
Sag(gy) Decline, Dip, Droop, Hang, Hogged, Lop, Slump, Swayback, Wilt
Saga Aga, Chronicle, Edda, Epic, Forsyte, Icelandic, Laxdale, Legend, Odyssey, Volsunga
Sagacity, Sagacious Astute, Commonsense, Depth, Elephant, Judgement, Sapience, Wisdom
Sage(s) Abaris, Aquinian, Bactrian, Bias, Carlyle, Cheronian, Chilo(n), Clary, Cleobulus, Confucius, Counsellor, Egghead, Greybeard, Hakam, Herb, Imhotep, Jerusalem, Maharishi, Mahatma, Malmesbury, Manu, Mirza, Moolvie, Orval, Pandit, Periander, Philosopher, Pittacus, Rishi, Salvia, Savant, Seer, Seven, Solomon, Solon, Tagore, Thales, Wiseacre, Wood
Sage-brush Nevada
Sago Portland
Saharan Hassaniya, Sahrawi
Sahelian Chad, Mali, Mauritinia, Niger
Sahib Burra, Pukka
Said Above-named, Co, Emir, Port, Quo(th), Related, Reputed, Spoken, Stated
▷ **Said** *may indicate* 'sounding like'
Sail(s), Sailing Balloon, Bunt, Canvas, Circumnavigate, Cloth, Coast, Course, Cross-jack, Cruise, Drag, Drift, Fan, Fore(course), Fore-and-aft, Full, Gaff(-topsail), Gennaker, Genoa, Goose-wing, Head, Jib, Jigger, Jut, Land, Lateen, Leech, Luff, Lug, Moon, Moonraker, Muslin, Navigate, Orthodromy, Parachute spinnaker, Peak, Plain, Plane, Ply, Rag, Reef, Rig, Ring-tail, Royal, Sheet, Shoulder-of-mutton, Smoke, Solar, Spanker, Spencer, Spinnaker, Spritsail, Square, Staysail, Steer, Storm-jib, Studding, Stun, Stuns'l, Suit, Top(-gallant), Top-hamper, Van, Vela, Wardrobe, Water, Yard
Sailor(s) AB, Admiral, Anson, Argonaut, Blue-jacket, Boatman, Boatswain, Bos'n, Bos(u)n, Budd, Canvas-climber, Commodore, Crew, Deckhand, Drake, Evans, Foremastman, Freshwater, Galiongee, Gob, Greenhand, Grommet, Hand, Hat, Hearties, Helmsman, Hornblower, Hydronaut, Jack, Janty, Jauntie, Jaunty, Jonty, Khalasi, Killick, Killock, Kroo(boy), Krooman, Kru(boy), Kruman, Lascar, Leadsman, Liberty man, Limey, Loblolly (boy), Lt, Lubber, Mariner, Matelot, Matlo(w), Middy, MN, Nelson, Noah, NUS, Oceaner, Oldster, OS, Petty Officer, Polliwog, Pollywog, Popeye, Powder monkey, Privateer, Rating, Reefer, RN, Salt, Seabee, Seacunny, Sea-dog, Seafarer, Sea-lord, → **SEAMAN**, Serang, Shellback, Sin(d)bad, Steward, Stowaway, Submariner, Swabber, Swabby, Tar, Tarp(aulin), Tarry-breeks, Tindal, Topman, Triton, Waister, Wandering, Water-dog, Wave, Wren, Yachtsman
Saint(ly) Canonise, Canonize, Hagiology, Hallowed, Holy, Latterday, Leger, Patron, Pi, Pillar, Plaster, St, Sunday, Templar, Thaumaturgus

SAINTS

1 letter:	2 letters:	3 letters:	4 letters:
S	SS	Cyr	Bede
			Bees

Chad	Peter	Birinus	Cuthbert
Elmo	Ronan	Brandan	Dorothea
Eloi	Roque	Brendan	Gertrude
Hugh	Simon	Bridget	Hilarion
John	Vitus	Cecilia	Ignatius
Jude		Clement	Lawrence
Just	*6 letters:*	Columba	Margaret
Lucy	Agatha	Crispin	Nicholas
Luke	Alexis	Dominic	Paulinus
Malo	Andrew	Dunstan	Polycarp
Mark	Anselm	Dymphna	Veronica
Odyl	Audrey	Eulalie	Vladimir
Olaf	Brigid	Francis	Winifred
Paul	George	Isidore	
Ride	Helena	Leonard	*9 letters:*
Roch	Hilary	Matthew	Augustine
Rule	Jerome	Michael	Catharine
	Joseph	Pancras	Genevieve
5 letters:	Loyola	Patrick	Hildegard
Agnes	Magnus	Quentin	Kentigern
Aidan	Martha	Regulus	Sebastian
Alban	Martin	Rosalie	Valentine
Alvis	Monica	Severus	
Asaph	Ninian	Stephen	*10 letters:*
Basil	Oswald	Swithin	Crispinian
David	Simeon	Theresa	Stanislaus
Denis	Teresa	Vincent	
Denys	Thecia	Walstan	*11 letters:*
Diego	Thomas	Wilfred	Bartholomew
Elvis	Tobias	William	Bernardette
Enoch	Ursula		Christopher
Giles		*8 letters:*	
Hilda	*7 letters:*	Aloysius	*12 letters:*
James	Alphege	Barnabas	Simon Zelotes
Kevin	Ambrose	Benedict	
Kilda	Anthony	Boniface	*13 letters:*
Linus	Barbara	Columban	Francis Xavier
Mungo	Bernard	Crispian	

Sake Account, Behalf, Cause, Drink, Mirin
Sal Nitre, Salt, Volatile
Salacious, Salacity Fruity, Lewd, Lust, Obscene, Scabrous
Salad Beetroot, Burnet, Caesar, Calaloo, Calalu, Chef's, Chicon, Coleslaw, Corn, Cos, Cress, Cucumber, Days, Endive, Escarole, Fennel, Finnochio, Finoc(c)hio, Frisée, Fruit, Greek, Guacamole, Horiatiki, Lactuca, Lamb's lettuce, Lettuce, Lovage, Mache, Mesclum, Mesclun, Mixture, Mizuna, Niçoise, Purslane, Radicchio, Radish, Rampion, Rocket, Rojak, Roquette, Russian, Salmagundi, Salmagundy, Slaw, Tabbouleh, Tabbouli, Tomato, Waldorf, Watercress, Word
▷ **Salad** *may indicate* an anagram
Salamander Axolotl, Congo eel, Ewt, Hellbender, Lizard, Menopome, Mole, Mudpuppy, Olm, Proteus, Siren, Snake, Spring-keeper, Tiger
Salami, Salami technique Fraud, Peperoni
Salary Emolument, Fee, Hire, Pay, Prebend, Screw, Stipend, → **WAGE**
Sale(s) Attic, Auction, Boot, Breeze up, Cant, Car-boot, Clearance, Farm-gate, Fire,

Garage, Jumble, Market, Outroop, Outrope, Pitch, Raffle, Retail, Roup, Rummage, Subhastation, Trade, Turnover, Upmarket, Venal, Vend, Vendue, Vent, Voetstoets, Voetstoots, Warrant, Wash, White, Wholesale, Yard

Saleroom Pantechnicon

Salesman, Saleswoman Agent, Assistant, Bagman, Banian, Banyan, Broker, Buccaneer, Bummaree, Counterhand, Counter jumper, Drummer, Huckster, Loman, Pedlar, Rep, Retailer, Tallyman, Tout, Traveller, Vendeuse

Salient Coign, Jut, Projection, Prominent, Redan, Spur

Salisbury Cecil, Sarum

Saliva Dribble, Drool, Parotid, Ptyalism, Sial(oid), Slobber, Spawl, Spit(tle), Sputum

Sallow Adust, Pallid, Pasty, Sale, Sauch, Saugh, Wan

Sally Aunt, Boutade, Charge, Dash, Escape, Excursion, Flight, Foray, Issue, Jest, Mot, Pleasantry, Quip, Retort, Ride, Sarah, Sortie, Wisecrack, Witticism

Salmagundi Mess

Salmon Alevin, Atlantic, Australian, Baggit, Blueback, Blue-cap, Boaz, Burnett, Chinook, Chum, Cock, Coho(e), Dog, Dorado, Grav(ad)lax, Grayling, Grilse, Humpback, Kelt, Keta, King, Kipper, Kokanee, Lax, Ligger, Lox, Masu, Mort, Nerka, Oncorhynchus, Ouananiche, Par(r), Peal, Pink, Quinnat, Red, Redfish, Rock, Samlet, Shedder, Silver, Skegger, Slat, Smelt, Smolt, Smout, Smowt, Sockeye, Sparling, Spirling, Springer, Sprod, Umber

Salon, Saloon Barrel-house, Car, Hall, Honkytonk, Last chance, Lounge, Nail bar, Pullman, Sedan, Shebang, Tavern

Salt(s), Salty AB, Acid, Alginate, Aluminate, Andalusite, Antimonite, Arseniate, Arsenite, Aspartite, Attic, Aurate, Azide, Base, Bath, Benzoate, Bicarbonate, Bichromate, Borate, Borax, Brackish, Brine, Bromate, Bromide, Capr(o)ate, Caprylate, Carbamate, Carbonate, Carboxylate, Celery, Cerusite, Chlorate, Chlorite, Chromate, Citrate, Columbate, Complex, Corn, Cure(d), Cyanate, Cyclamate, Datolite, Deer lick, Diazonium, Dichromate, Dioptase, Dithionate, Double, Enos, Eosin, Epsom, Ferricyanide, Formate, Glauber, Glutamate, Halite, Halo-, Health, Hydrochloride, Hygroscopic, Iodide, Ioduret, Isocyanide, Kosher, Lactate, Lake-basin, Linoleate, Lithate, Liver, Magnesium, Malate, Malonate, Manganate, Mariner, Matelot, Mersalyl, Microcosmic, Monohydrate, Mucate, Muriate, NaCl, Niobate, Nitrate, Nitrite, Oleate, Orthoborate, Orthosilicate, Osm(i)ate, Oxalate, Palmitate, Pandermite, Perborate, Perchlorate, Periodate, Phosphate, Phosphite, Phthalate, Picrate, Piquancy, Plumbate, Plumbite, Potassium, Powder, Propionate, Pyruvate, Rating, Reh, Resinate, Rochelle, Rock, Rosinate, Sailor, Sal ammoniac, Salicylate, Salify, Sal volatile, Saut, Sea-dog, Seafarer, Seasoned, Sebate, Selenate, Smelling, Soap, Sodium, Solar, Sorbate, Sorrel, Stannate, Stearate, Suberate, Succinate, Sulfite, Sulphate, Sulphite, Sulphonate, Table, Tannate, Tantalate, Tartrate, Tellurate, Tellurite, Thiocyanate, Thiosulphate, Titanate, Tungstate, Uranin, Urao, Urate, Vanadate, Volatile, Water-dog, White, Wit(ty), Xanthate

Salt meat Mart

Saltpetre Caliche, Chile, Cubic, Nitre, Norway

Salt-water Sea

Salubrious Healthy, Sanitary, Wholesome

Salutary Beneficial, Good, Wholesome

Salutation, Salute Address, Asalam-wa-leikum, Australian, Ave, Banzai, Barcoo, Bid, Cap, Cheer, Command, Coupé(e), Curtsey, Embrace, Feu de joie, Fly-past, Genuflect, Greet, Hail, Hallo, Halse, Homage, Honour, Jambo, Kiss, Middle finger, Namas kar, Namaste, Present, Salaam, Salvo, Sieg Heil, Toast, Tribute, Wassail

Salvador Dali

Salvage Dredge, Lagan, Ligan, Reclaim, Recover, Recycle, Rescue, Retrieve, Tot

Salvation(ist) Booth, Redemption, Rescue, Socinian, Soterial, Yeo

Salve Anele, Anoint, Assuage, Ave, Lanolin(e), Lotion, Ointment, Remedy, Saw, Tolu, Unguent, Weapon

Salver Dish, Platter, Tray, Waiter

Salvo Fusillade, Salute, Volley
Sal volatile Hartshorn
Sam Browse, Soapy, Uncle, Weller
Samara Ash-key
Samaritan Good
Samarium Sm
Same(ness) Ae, Agnatic, Congruent, Contemporaneous, Do, Egal, Ejusd(en), Equal, Equivalent, Ib(id), Ibidem, Id, Idem, Identical, Identity, Ilk, Iq, Like, One, Thick(y), Thilk, Uniform, Ylke
Samovar Urn
Samoyed Dog, Uralian, Uralic
Sample, Sampling Amniocentesis, Biopsy, Blad, Browse, Example, Fare, Foretaste, Handout, Matched, Muster, Pattern, Pree, Prospect, Quadrat, Quota, Random, Scantling, Smear, Snip, Specimen, Spread, Stratified, Swatch, Switch, → **TASTE**, Taster, Transect, Try
Samuel Pepys, Smiles
Samurai Ronin
▷ **Sam Weller** *may indicate* the use of 'v' for 'w' or vice versa
Sanctify Consecrate, Enhalo, Purify, Saint
Sanctimonious Banbury, Creeping Jesus, Devout, Goody-goody, Holy, Pi, Preachy, Religiose, Righteous, Saintly
Sanction(s), Sanctioned Allow, Appro, Approbate, Approof, Approve, Assent, Authorise, Bar, Countenance, Economic, Endorse, Fatwa(h), Fetwa, Fiat, Green light, Homologate, Imprimatur, Legitimate, Mandate, OK, Pass, Pragmatic, Ratify, Smart, Sustain, Upstay, Warrant
Sanctities, Sanctity Enhab, Halidom, Holiness, Hollidam, Sonties
Sanctuary, Sanctum Adytum, Ark, Asylum, By-room, Cella, Ch, Church, Delubrum, Frithsoken, Frithstool, Girth, Grith, Holy, JCR, Kaaba, Lair, Naos, Oracle, Penetralia, Preserve, Refuge, Sacellum, Sacrarium, Salvation, SCR, → **SHELTER**, Shrine, Tabernacle, Temple
Sand(bank), Sandbar, Sands, Sandy Alec, Alex, Alexander, Areg, Arena(ceous), Arenose, Arkose, As, Atoll, Bar, Barchan(e), Bark(h)an, Beach, Beige, Caliche, Dene, Desert, Dogger Bank, Down, Dudevant, Dune, Dupin, Ecru, Eremic, Erg, Esker, Foundry, Gat, George, Ginger, Goodwin, Grain, Granulose, Hazard, Hurst, Light, Loess, Machair, Nore, Oil, Outwash, Overslaugh, Podsol, Podzol, Portlandian, Psammite, Ridge, River, Sabulous, Saburra, Sawney, Seif dune, Shelf, Shoal, Shore, Singing, Tar, Tee, Time, Tombolo
Sandal(s) Alpargata, Buskin, Calceamentum, Chappal, Espadrille, Flip-flop, Ganymede, Geta, Huarache, Jelly, Patten, Pump, Slip-slop, Talaria, Thong, Zori
Sandalwood Algum, Almug, Chypre, Pride, Santal
Sandarac Arar
Sander Pike-perch
Sandgroper Pioneer
Sandhopper Amphipod
Sandhurst RMA
Sand-loving Ammophilous, Psammophil(e)
Sandpiper Bird, Dunlin, Knot, Oxbird, Peetweet, Ree, Ruff, Sandpeep, Stint, Terek, Turnstone
Sandstone Arkose, Calciferous, Cat's brains, Dogger, Fa(i)kes, Flysch, Grey-wether, Grit, Hassock, Holystone, Itacolumite, Kingle, Molasse, New Red, Old Red, Psammite, Quartzite, Red, Sarsen, Silica
Sandstorm Haboob, Tebbad
Sandwich(es) Bruschetta, Butty, Club, Clubhouse, Croque-monsieur, Cuban, Doorstep, Earl, Hamburger, Hoagie, Island, Jeely piece, Open, Panini, Piece, Roti, Round, Sanger, Sango, Sarmie, Sarney, Sarnie, Smørbrød, Smörgåsbord, Smørrebrød, Stottie, Sub,

Submarine, Tartine, Thumber, Toastie, Toebie, Triple-decker, Twitcher, Victoria, Wad, Western, Zak(o)uski

▷ **Sandwich(es)** *may indicate* a hidden word

Sane, Sanity Compos mentis, Formal, Healthy, Judgement, Rational, Reason, Right-minded, Sensible, Wice

Sangfroid Aplomb, Cool, Poise

Sanguine Confident, Haemic, Hopeful, Optimistic, Roseate, Ruddy

Sanitary Hygienic, Salubrious, Sterile

Sanskrit Bhagavad-Gita, Panchatantra, Purana, Ramayana, Sutra, Upanishad, Vedic

Santa (Claus) Abonde, Kriss Kringle, Secret

Sap Benzoin, Bleed, Cremor, Drain, Enervate, Entrench, Ichor, Juice, Laser, Latex, Lymph, Mine, Mug, Nuclear, Pulque, Ratten, Resin, Roset, Rosin, Rozet, Rozit, Secretion, Soma, Sura, Swot, Undermine, Weaken

Sapid Flavoursome, Savoury, Tasty

Sapience, Sapient Discernment, Sage, Wisdom

Sapling Ash-plant, Flittern, Ground-ash, Plant, Tellar, Teller, Tiller, Youth

Sapper(s) Miner, RE

Sapphire Star, Water, White

Sappho Lesbian

Sapwood Alburnum

Sarah Battle, Gamp, Sal

Sarcasm, Sarcastic Acidity, Antiphrasis, Biting, Cutting, Cynical, Derision, Irony, Mordacious, Mordant, Pungent, Quip, Quotha, Sarky, Satire, Sharp, Sharp-tongued, Smartmouth, Snide, Sting, Wisecrack

Sardine Fish, Sard

Sardonic Cutting, Cynical, Ironical, Scornful, Wry

Sargasso Ore, Sea(weed)

Sark Chemise, CI, Shirt

Sarong Sulu

SAS Red Devils

Sash Baldric(k), Band, Belt, Burdash, Cummerbund, Fillister, Lungi, Obi, Scarf, Window

Saskatchewan .sk

Sassaby Tsessebe

Sassenach English, Lowlander, Pock-pudding

Satan Adversary, Apollyon, Arch-enemy, Arch-foe, Cram, → **DEVIL**, Eblis, Evil One, Lucifer, Prince of darkness, Shaitan, Tempter, The old serpent

Satchel Bag, Postbag, Scrip

Sate(d), Satiate Cloy, Glut, Replete, Sad, Surfeit

Satellite Adrastea, Ananke, Ariel, Artificial, Astra, Atlas, Attendant, Aussat, Belinda, Bianca, Bird, Callisto, Calypso, Camenae, Carme, Charon, Communications, Comsat®, Cordelia, Cosmos, Cressida, Deimos, Desdemona, Despina, Dione, Disciple, Early bird, Earth, Echo, Elara, Enceladus, Europa, Explorer, Fixed, Follower, Galatea, Galilean, Ganymede, Geostationary, Helene, Henchman, Himalia, Hipparchus, Hyperion, Iapetus, Intelsat, Io, Janus, Lackey, Larissa, Leda, Lysithea, Meteorological, Metis, Mimas, Miranda, Moon, Mouse, Naiad, Navigation, Nereid, Oberon, Ophelia, Orbiter, Pan, Pandora, Pasiphae, Phobos, Phoebe, Planet, Portia, Prometheus, Puck, Rhea, Rosalind, Sinope, Smallset, Space probe, SPOT, Sputnik, Syncom, Telesto, Telstar, Tethys, Thalassa, Thebe, Tiros, Titan, Titania, Triton, Umbriel, Weather

▸ **Satin** *see* **SILK(Y)**

Satire, Satirical, Satirist Arbuthnot, Archilochus, Burlesque, Butler, Candide, Chaldee, Dryden, Horace, Iambographer, Juvenal, Lampoon, Lash, Lucian, Mazarinade, Menippean, Menippos, Mockery, Pantagruel, Parody, Pasquil, Pasquin(ade), Pope, Raillery, Sarky, Sotadic, Spoof, Squib, Swift, Travesty, Wasps

Satisfaction, Satisfactory, Satisfy(ing), Satisfied, Satisfactorily Adequate,

Agree, Ah, Ap(p)ay, Appease, Assuage, Atone, Change, Compensation, Complacent, → **CONTENT**, Defrayment, Enough, Feed, Fill, Fulfil, Glut, Gratify, Happy camper, Indulge, Jake, Job, Liking, Meet, Nice, OK, Okey-dokey, Pacation, Palatable, Pay, Please, Pride, Propitiate, Qualify, Redress, Relish, Repay, Replete, Revenge, Sate, Satiate, Sensual, Serve, Settlement, Slake, Smug, Square, Suffice, Supply, Tickety-boo, Well

Saturate(d) Drench, Glut, Imbue, Impregnate, Infuse, Permeate, → **SOAK**, Sodden, Steep, Surcharge, Waterlog

Saturday Holy, Sabbatine

Saturn God, Kronos, Lead, Planet, Rocket

Satyr Faun, Lecher, Leshy, Lesiy, Libertine, Marsyas, Pan, Silen(us), Woodhouse, Woodwose

Sauce, Saucy Agrodolce, Alfredo, Allemanse, Apple, Arch, Baggage, Barbecue, Béarnaise, Béchamel, Bigarade, Bold(-faced), Bolognese, Bordelaise, Bourguignonne, Bread, Brown, Caper, Carbonara, Catchup, Catsup, Chasseur, Chaudfroid, Cheek, Chilli, Chutney, Condiment, Coulis, Cranberry, Cream, Creme anglaise, Cumberland, Custard, Dapper, Dip, Dressing, Enchilada, Espagnole, Fenberry, Fondue, Fricassee, Fudge, Fu yong, Fu yung, Gall, Garum, Gravy, Hard, Hoisin, Hollandaise, Horseradish, HP®, Impudence, Jus, Ketchup, Lip, Malapert, Marinade, Marinara, Matelote, Mayo(nnaise), Melba, Meunière, Mint, Mirepoix, Mole, Monkeygland, Mornay, Mousseline, Mouth, Nam pla, Nerve, Newburg, Nuoc mam, Oxymal, Oyster, Panada, Parsley, Passata, Peart, Peking, Pert, Pesto, Piert, Piri-piri, Pistou, Pizzaiola, Ponzu, Portugaise, Puttanesca, Ragu, Ravigote, Relish, Remoulade, Rouille, Roux, Sabayon, Sal, Salad cream, Salpicon, Salsa, Salsa verde, Sambal, Sass, Satay, Shoyu, Soja, Soubise, Soy, Soya, Stroganoff, Sue, Sugo, Supreme, Sweet and sour, Tabasco®, Tamari, Tartar(e), Tomato, Topping, Tossy, Trimmings, Velouté, Vinaigrette, Vindaloo, White, Wine, Worcester, Worcestershire, Yakitori

Sauceboat-shaped Scaphocephalate

Saucepan Chafer, Goblet, Skillet, Steamer, Stockpot

Saucer Ashtray, Discobolus, Flying, Pannikin, UFO

Sauna Banya, Bath, Steam room, Sudatorium, Sudorific

Saunter Amble, Dacker, Da(i)ker, Dander, Lag, Mosey, Promenade, Roam, Shool, Stroll, Toddle

Sausage(s) Andouille, Andouillette, Banger, Black pudding, Blood, Boerewors, Bologna, Boudin, Bratwurst, Cervelat, Cheerio, Chipolata, Chorizo, Corn dog, Cumberland, Devon, Drisheen, Frankfurter, Garlic, Hot dog, Kielbasa, Kishke, Knackwurst, Knockwurst, Liver(wurst), Lorne, Mortadella, Mystery bag, Pep(p)eroni, Polony, Pudding, Salami, Sav(eloy), Snag(s), Snarler, Square, String, Vienna, Weenie, Weeny, White pudding, Wiener(wurst), Wienie, Wurst, Zampone

Sausage-shaped Allantoid

Sauté Fry

Savage Ape, Barbarian, Boor, Brute, Cannibal, Cruel, Feral, Fierce, Frightful, Grim, Gubbins, Immane, Inhuman, Maul, Noble, Sadistic, Truculent, Vitriolic, Wild

Savanna Cerrado, Plain, Sahel

Savant Expert, Mahatma, Sage, Scholar

Save, Saving(s) Bank, Bar, Besides, But, Capital, Conserve, Cut-rate, Deposit, Economy, Except, Hain, Hoard, Husband, ISA, Keep, Layby, National, Nest egg, Nirlie, Nirly, Not, PEPS, Post office, Preserve, Put by, Reclaim, Recycle, Redeem, Relieve, Reprieve, → **RESCUE**, Reskew, Sa', Salt (away), Salvage, SAYE, Scrape, Scrimp, Shortcut, Slate club, Soak away, Sock away, Sou-sou, Spare, Stokvel, Succour, Susu, TESSA, Unless

Saviour Deliverer, Jesu(s), Lifeline, Messiah, Redeemer

Savour(ed), Savoury Aigrette, Bouchée, Canapé, Devils-on-horseback, Essence, Fag(g)ot, Flavour, Olent, Ramekin, Relish, Resent, Sair, Sapid, Sar, Smack, Starter, Tang, → **TASTE**, Umami, Vol au vent

Savoy Cabbage, Opera

Savvy Sense

Saw Adage, Aphorism, Apothegm, Azebiki, Back, Band, Beheld, Bucksaw, Buzz, Chain, Circular, Cliché, Compass, Coping, Cross-cut, Crown, Cut, Dictum, Double-ender, Dovetail, Dozuki, Flooring, Frame, Fret, Gang, Glimpsed, Gnome, Grooving, Hack, Hand, Jig, Keyhole, Legend, Log, Maxim, Met, Motto, Pad, Panel, Paroemia, Pitsaw, Proverb, Pruning, Quarter, Rabbeting, Rack, Ribbon, Rip, Ryoba, Sash, Saying, Scroll, Serra, Skil®, Skip-tooth, Slasher, Slogan, Span, Spied, Stadda, Stone, Sweep, Tenon, Trepan, Trephine, Whip, Witnessed

Sawbill Merganser

Sawbones Surgeon

Saw-toothed Runcinate

Sawyer Logger, Tom

Saxifrage Astilbe, Bishop's cap, Burnet, Golden, Heuchera, London pride, Mitre-wort, St Patrick's cabbage

Saxon Cedric, Hengist, Hereward, Wend

Saxophone Axe

Say, Saying(s) Adage, Agrapha, Allege, Aphorism, Apophthegm, Apostrophise, Articulate, Axiom, Beatitude, Bon mot, Bromide, Byword, Cant, Catchphrase, Cliché, Declare, Dict(um), Eg, Enunciate, Epigram, Expatiate, Express, Fadaise, For instance, Gnome, Impute, Input, Logia, Logion, → **MAXIM**, Mean, Mot, Mouth, Observe, Predicate, Pronounce, Proverb, Put, Quip, Recite, Rede, Relate, Remark, Report, Saine, Saw, Sc, Sententia, → **SPEAK**, Suppose, Sutra, Talk, Utter, Voice, Word

▷ **Say, Saying(s)** *may indicate* a word sounding like another

Scab(by) Blackleg, Crust, Eschar, Leggism, Leprose, Mangy, Rat, Scald, Scall, Sore, Strike-breaker

Scabbard Frog, Pitcher, Sheath, Tsuba

Scabies Itch, Psora, Scotch fiddle

Scabrous Harsh, Rough, Thersites

Scaffold(ing), Scaffolder Gallows, Gantry, Hoarding, Putlock, Putlog, Rig, Spiderman, Stage, Staging

Scald Blanch, Burn, Leep, Ploat, Plot

Scale(s), Scaly Analemma, API gravity, Ascend, Balance, Baumé, Beaufort, Binet-Simon, Bismar, Brix, Bud, Burnham, Celsius, Centigrade, Ceterach, Chromatic, → **CLIMB**, Cottony-cushion, Dander, Dandruff, Desquamate, Diagonal, Diatonic, Douglas, Elo, Enharmonic(al), Escalade, Fahrenheit, Flake, Fujita, Full, Furfur, Gamme, Gamut, Ganoid, Gapped, Gauge, Gravity, Gray, Gunter's, Heptatonic, Hexachord, Humidex, Indusium, Interval, Kelvin, Krab, Ladder, Lamina, Layer, Leaf, Lepid, Lepidote, Leprose, Libra, Ligule, Likert, Lodicule, Loricate, Magnitude, Major, Mercalli, Mesel, Minor, Mohs, Munsell, Natural, Nominal, Octad, Ordinal, Oyster shell, Palea, Palet, Patagium, Peel, Pentatonic, Pholidosis, Placoid, Plate, Platform, Proportion, Ramentum, → **RANGE**, Rankine, Ratio, Réau(mur), Regulo, Richter, San Jose, Scalade, Scan, Scarious, Scent, Scincoid, Scurf, Scutellate, Shin, Skink, Sliding, Speel, Spring, Squama, Squame(lla), Submediant, Tegmentum, Tegula, Tonal, Tridymite, Tron(e), Unified, Vernier, Wage, Weighbridge, Wentworth, Whole-tome, Wind

▷ **Scale(d)** *may indicate* a fish

Scallion Leek

Scallop(ed) Bivalve, Clam, Coquille, Crenate, Crenulate, Escalop, Frill, Gimp, Mush, Pecten, Queenie, Seashell, Vandyke

Scallywag Rascal, Scamp, Skeesicks, Whippersnapper

Scalp Cut, Scrape, Skin, Trophy

Scalpel Bistoury, Knife

Scam Con, Fast and loose, Ramp, Strap game

Scamp Fripon, Imp, Limb, Lorel, Lorrell, Losel, Lozell, Neglect, → **RASCAL**, Reprobate, Rip, Rogue, Scallywag, Skeesicks, Toerag

Scamper Gambol, Lamp, Run, Scurry, Scutter, Skedaddle, Skelter, Skitter

Scan(ning), Scanner Barcode, CAT, CT, EEG, Examine, Flat-bed, Helical, Inspect, Interlaced, Iris, OCR, Optical, Oversee, Peruse, PET, Rake, Raster, Scrutinise, Sector, SEM, Sequential, SPET, Study, Survey, Tomography, Ultrasound, Vertical, Vet

Scandal(ous), Scandalise Belie, Canard, Commesse, Disgrace, Exposé, Gamy, -gate, Hearsay, Muck-raking, Opprobrium, Outrage, Shame, Slander, Stigma, Stink, Watergate

Scandalmonger Muckraker

Scandinavian Dane, Finn, Gotland, Icelander, Laplander, Lapp, Nordic, Norman, Norseland, Northman, Olaf, Runic, Squarehead, Swede, Varangian, Viking

Scandium Sc

Scant(y), Scantness Bare, Brief, Exiguous, Jejune, Jimp, Low, Meagre, Oligotrophy, Poor, Scrimpy, Short, Shy, Skimpy, Slender, Spare, Sparse, Stingy

Scapegoat, Scapegrace Butt, Fall-guy, Hazazel, Joe Soap, Patsy, Skainesmate, Stooge, Target, Victim, Whipping-boy

Scapula Blade, Omoplate

Scar(face) Al, Blemish, Cheloid, Cicatrix, Cliff, Craig, Epulotic, Hilum, Keloid, Leucoma, Leukoma, Mark, Pockmark, Stigma, Ulosis, Wipe

Scarab Beetle, Gem

Scarce(ly), Scarcity Barely, Dear, Dearth, Famine, Few, Hardly, Ill, Lack, Paucity, Rare, Scanty, Seldom, Short, Strap, Uncommon, Want

Scare(d), Scaring, Scaremongering, Scary Adaw, Afraid, Alarmist, Alert, Amaze, Fleg, Fright, Gally, Gliff, Glift, Hair-raising, Hairy, Panic, Petrify, Skeer, Spook, Startle, Tattie-bogle

Scarecrow Bogle, Bugaboo, Dudder, Dudsman, Gallibagger, Gallibeggar, Gallicrow, Gallybagger, Gallybeggar, Gallycrow, Malkin, Mawkin, Potato-bogle, Ragman, S(h)ewel, Tattie-bogle

Scarf Babushka, Belcher, Cataract, Comforter, Cravat, Curch, Doek, Dupatta, Fascinator, Fichu, Hai(c)k, Haique, Headsquare, Hyke, Lambrequin, Madras, Mantilla, Muffettee, Muffler, Neckatee, Neckcloth, Neckerchief, Neckgear, Neckpiece, Necktie, Neckwear, Nightingale, Orarium, Pagri, Palatine, Pashmina, Patka, Pugg(a)ree, Rail, Rebozo, Sash, Screen, Shash, Stock, Stole, Tallith, Tippet, Trot-cosy, Trot-cozy, Vexillum

Scarifier Scuffler

Scarlet Cinnabar, Cochineal, Crimson, Pimpernel, Pink, Ponceau, Red, Vermilion

Scarper Abscond, Absquatulate, Bunk, Hightail, Run, Shoo, Welsh

Scat Aroint, Dropping, Vamo(o)se

Scathe, Scathing Caustic, Mordant, Sarcastic, Savage, Severe, Vitriolic

Scatter(ed), Scattering Bestrew, Broadcast, Diaspora, Disgregation, Disject, Dispel, → **DISPERSE**, Dissipate, Flurr, Inelastic, Interspace, Litter, Rayleigh, Rout, Scail, Skail, Sow, Sparge, Sparse, Splutter, Sporadic, Sprad, Spread, Sprinkle, Squander, Straw, Strew, Strinkle

Scatterbrain(ed) Dippy, Ditsy, Ditz(y), Tête folie

Scavenge(r) Ant, Dieb, Forage, Hunt, Hy(a)ena, Jackal, Rake, Ratton, Rotten, Scaffie, Sweeper, Totter

Scenario Outline, Plot, Script, Worst case

Scene(ry) Arena, Boscage, Cameo, Coulisse, Decor, Flat(s), Landscape, Locale, Periaktos, Phantasmagoria, Prop, Prospect, Riverscape, Set, Set piece, Sight, Site, Sketch, Stage, Tableau, Take, Tormenter, Tormentor, Transformation, Venue, View, Wing

Scent Aroma, Attar, Chypre, Civet, Cologne, Eau de cologne, Essence, Fragrance, Frangipani, Fumet(te), Gale, Moschatel, Musk, Nose, Odour, Orris, Ottar, Otto, Perfume, Sachet, Smell, Spoor, Vent, Waft, Wind

Scentless Anosmia

Sceptic, Sceptical(ly), Scepticism Agnostic, Askant, Cynic, Doubter, Europhobe, Incredulous, Infidel, Jaundiced, Nihilistic, Nullifidian, Pyrrho(nic), Sadducee, Solipsism, Thomas

Schedule Agenda, Calendar, Classification, Itinerary, Prioritise, Programme, Register, Slot, Table, Timescale, Timetable

Scheme, Schemer, Scheming Angle, CATS, Colour, Concoct, Conspire, Crafty, Cunning, Dare, Darien, Dart, Decoct, Design, Devisal, Diagram, Dodge, Draft, Gin, Honeytrap, Housing, Intrigue, Jezebel, Machiavellian, Machinate, Manoeuvre, Master plan, Nostrum, Pilot, → **PLAN**, Plat, Plot, Ponzi, Project, Proposition, Purpose, Put-up job, Racket, Rhyme, Ruse, Scam, Set-aside, Stratagem, System, Table, Top-hat, Wangle, Wheeler-dealer, Wheeze

Schism(atic) Break, Disunion, Division, Eastern, Great, Greek, Heterodox, Rent, Secession, Split, Western

Schizo(phrenia) Catatonic, Dementia praecox, Hebephrenia, LSD

Schmaltz(y) Goo, Mush, Slush, Tear-jerker

Schmieder S

Schmook Drip

Schmuck Gunsel

Schnapps Enzian

Scholar, Scholiast Abelard, Academic, Alcuin, Alumni, Atticus, BA, Bookman, Boursier, Catachumen, Classicist, Clergy, Clerisy, Clerk, Commoner, Demy, Disciple, Don, Erasmus, Erudite, Etonian, Exhibitioner, Extern(e), Externat, Faculty, Goliard, Graduate, Grecian, Hafiz, Hebraist, Inkhorn, Jowett, Literate, Littérateur, MA, Mal(l)am, Masorete, Maulana, Noter, Occam Ulama, Ollamh, Ollav, Pauline, Plutarch, Polymath, Pupil, Rhodes, Sap, Savant, Saxonist, Schoolboy, Sizar, Soph, → **STUDENT**, Tabardar, Taberdar, Taberder, Tom Brown, Varro

Scholarship Bursary, Closed, Education, Erudition, Exhibition, Grant, Grant-in-aid, Learning, Lore, Mass, Rhodes

School Business, Discipline, Drill, Educate, Exercise, Feeder, Institute, Integrated, Madrasa, Peripatetic, Sciences, Scul, Scull(e), Teach, → **TRAIN**, Tutor

---

SCHOOLS

3 letters:	Play	Lycée	Lyceum
Day	Poly	Night	Magnet
Gam	Prep	Perse	Middle
LSE	RADA	Piano	Normal
Old	Real	Rydal	Oundle
Pod	Sect	Shoal	Public
RAM	Sink	Slade	Ragged
Ski	Song	State	Ramean
	Tech	Stowe	Repton
		Style	Summer
4 letters:		Trade	Sunday
Coed	*5 letters:*	Upper	Whales
Cool	Board		
Cult	Charm		
Dada	Choir	*6 letters:*	*7 letters:*
Dame	Drama	Ash Can	Academy
Dojo	Faith	Beacon	Alleyn's
Dual	First	Cheder	Bauhaus
Eton	Grade	Church	Cockney
Free	Group	Fettes	Council
High	Heder	Harrow	Crammer
Home	Hedge	Honour	Driving
Kant	Ionic	Hostel	Essenes
Lake	List D	Infant	Flemish
Life	Lower	Junior	Grammar

Jim Crow
Lancing
Loretto
Nursery
Primary
Private
Rhodian
Roedean
Rossall
Sabbath
Satanic
Special
Writing
Yeshiva

8 letters:
Approved
Barbizon
Benenden
Bluecoat
Boarding
Cranwell
Downside
Externat
Graduate
Hospital
Kailyard
Kaleyard

Language
Mahayana
Mannheim
National
Provided
Sadducee
Seminary
Separate
Tenebrum

9 letters:
Chartreux
Classical
Community
Composite
Finishing
Frankfurt
Gymnasien
Gymnasium
Madrassah
Palaestra
Parochial
Porpoises
Sandhurst
Secondary
Single-sex
Spasmodic
Tonbridge

Voluntary

10 letters:
Ampleforth
Chautauqua
Elementary
Foundation
Grant-aided
Greyfriars
Historical
Industrial
Maintained
Manchester
Parnassian
Pensionnat
Scandalous
Sole charge
Stonyhurst
St Trinian's
Wellington
Winchester

11 letters:
Direct grant
Giggleswick
Gordonstoun
Hypermodern
Independent

Maintaining
Marlborough
Preparatory
Reformatory
Residential

12 letters:
Charterhouse
Conservative
Conservatory
Intermediate
Kindergarten
Progymnasium

13 letters:
Comprehensive
Conservatoire

14 letters:
Correspondence
Voluntary-aided

15 letters:
Grant-maintained
Secondary-modern

19 letters:
Voluntary-controlled

Schoolboy, Schoolgirl Alumna, Carthusian, Coed, Colleger, East, Etonian, Fag, Gait, Geit, Gyte, Miss, Monitor, Oppidan, Petty, Stalky, Wykehamist

School-leaver Abiturient

Schoolma'am, Schoolman, Schoolmaster, Schoolmistress Aram, Beak, Dominie, Duns, Holofernes, Miss, Occam, Orbilius, Pedagogue, Pedant, Servitor, Sir, Squeers, Teacher, Tutress, Ursuline

Schooner Glass, Hesperus, Hispaniola, Prairie, Ship, Tern

Sciatica Hip-gout

Science Anatomy, Anthropology, Applied, Art, Astrodynamics, Astrophysics, Atmology, Avionics, Axiology, Behavioural, Biology, Biotech, Botany, Chemistry, Christian, Cognitive, Computer, Crystallography, Cybernetics, Dismal, Domestic, Earth, Ekistics, Electrodynamics, Entomology, Eth(n)ology, Euphenics, Exact, Forensic, Gay, Geodesy, Geology, Hard, Information, Life, Lithology, Macrobiotics, Materia medica, Mechanics, Metallurgy, Military, Mineralogy, Natural, Noble, Nomology, Noology, Nosology, Occult, Ology, Ontology, Optics, Optometry, Pedagogy, Penology, Phrenology, Physical, Physics, Policy, Political, Psychics, Pure, Rocket, Rural, Semiology, Serology, Skill, Social, Soft, Soil, Sonics, Stinks, Stylistics, Tactics, Technics, Technology, Tectonics, Telematics, Thremmatology, Toxicology, Tribology, Typhlology, Zootechnics

Science fiction Cyberpunk

Scientist Alchemist, Anatomist, Archimedes, Aston, Astronomer, Atomist, Bacteriologist, Bell, → **BIOLOGIST**, Boffin, BSc, Cavendish, → **CHEMIST**, Climatologist, Copernicus, Curie, Dalton, Darwin, Davy, Dopper, Egghead, Einstein, Experimenter, Expert, Faraday, Fourier, FRS, Galileo, Gay-Lussac, Geodesist, Harvey, Heaviside, Herschel, Hooke, Hubble, Kennelly, Lodge, Lovell, Mach, Magnetist, Medawar, Mendeleev, Newton, Oersted, Pascal, Pasteur, Pauli, → **PHYSICIST**, Piccard,

Potamologist, Réaumur, Researcher, Rocket, Technocrat, Theremin, Van der Waals, Volta

Scimitar Acinaciform, Sword

Scintillate Dazzle, Emicate, Gleam, Glitter, → **SPARKLE**

Scion Cion, Graft, Imp, Offspring, Sien(t), Slip, Sprig, Sprout, Syen

Scissors Clippers, Criss-cross, Cutters, Forfex, Nail, Probe, Shears

Scoff Belittle, Boo, Chaff, Deride, Dor, Eat, Feast, Flout, Food, Gall, Geck, Gibe, Gird, Gobble, → **JEER**, Jest, Mock, Rail, Rib, Ridicule, Roast, Scaff, Scorn, Send up, Sneer, Taunt

Scold(ing) Admonish, Berate, Callet, Catamaran, Chastise, Chide, Clapperclaw, Cotquean, Do, Earful, Earwig, Flite, Flyte, Fuss, Jaw(bation), Jobation, Lecture, Nag, Objurgate, Philippic, Rag, Rant, Rate, → **REBUKE**, Reprimand, Reprove, Revile, Rollick, Rollock, Rouse on, Row, Sas(s)arara, Sis(s)erary, Slang, Slate, Termagant, Threap, Threep, Through-going, Tick-off, Tongue-lash, Trimmer, Upbraid, Virago, Wig, Xant(h)ippe, Yaff, Yankie, Yap

Sconce Candlestick, Crown, Forfeit, Head, Ice, Nole

Scone Drop, Girdle

Scoop Bale, Dipper, Exclusive, Gouge, Grab, Hollow, Ladle, Lap, Pale, Rout, Shovel, Spoon, Story, Trowel

Scooter Vespa®

Scope Ambit, Bargaining, Breadth, Compass, Diapason, Domain, Elbow-room, Extent, Freedom, Gamut, Indulgence, Ken, Latitude, Leeway, Play, Purview, Range, Remit, Room, Rope, Scouth, Scowth, Size, Sphere

Scorch(er) Adust, Birsle, Blister, Brasero, → **BURN**, Char, Destroy, Frizzle, Fry, Parch, Scouther, Scowder, Scowther, Sear, Singe, Soar, Speed, Swale, Swayl, Sweal, Sweel, Torrefy, Torrid, Wither

Score(s), Scoring Apgar, Behind, Bill, Birdie, Bradford, Bye, Capot, Chalk up, Chase, Clock up, Conversion, Count, Crena, Debt, Dunk, Eagle, Etch, Full, Gash, Groove, Hail, Honours, Incise, Ingroove, Ippon, Koka, Law, Leaderboard, Lots, Magpie, Make, Mark, Music, Net, Nick, Notation, Notch, Nurdle, Open, Orchestrate, Partitur(a), Peg, Pique, Point, Record, Repique, Rit(t), Rouge, Run, Rut, Scotch, Scrat, Scratch, Scribe, Scrive, Set, Sheet music, Single, Spare, Stableford, Stria, String, Sum, Tablature, → **TALLY**, TE, Try, Twenty, Vocal, Waza-ari, Win, Yuko

Score-board, Score-sheet Card, Telegraph

▷ **Scorer** *may indicate* a composer

▷ **Scoring** *may indicate* an anagram

Scorn(ful) Arrogant, Bah, Contemn, Contempt, Contumely, Deride, Despise, Dis(s), Disdain, Dislike, Disparagement, Flout, Geck, Haughty, Insult, Meprise, Mock, Opprobrium, Phooey, Putdown, Rebuff, Ridicule, Sarcastic, Sardonic, Sarky, Scoff, Scout, Sdaine, Sdeigne, Sneer, Sniffy, Spurn, Wither

Scorpion Arachnid, Book, Chelifer, False, Father-lasher, Pedipalp(us), Rock, Vinegarroon, Water, Whip

Scot(sman), Scots(woman), Scottish Alistair, Angus, Antenati, Berean, Blue-bonnet, Bluecap, Caledonian, Celt, Clansman, Covenanter, Duni(e)wassal, Dunniewassal, Erse, Fingal, Gael, Highland, Ian, Jock, Kelt, Kelvinside, Kiltie, Kitty, Knox, Laird, Lallan(s), Lot, Lowland, Luckie, Lucky, Mac, Mon, Morningside, Peght, Pict, Ross, Sandy, Sawn(e)y, Shetlander, Stuart, Tartan, Tax, Teuchter, Torridonian

Scotch(man) Censor, Dish, Distiller, Glenlivet®, Notch, Score, Scratch, Stop, Thwart, Usquebaugh, Whisky

Scot-free Wreakless

Scotland Alban(y), Albion, Caledonia, Gaeltacht, Gaidhealtachd, Lallans, Lothian, NB, Norland, Scotia

Scoundrel Cad, Cur, Dog, Fink, Heel, Hound, Knave, Miscreant, Rat, Reprobate, Scab, Smaik, Varlet, → **VILLAIN**, Wretch

Scour(er) Beat, Depurate, Full, Holystone, Lant, Purge, Quarter, Scrub

▷ **Scour** *may indicate* an anagram

Scourge Bible-thumper, Cat, Disciplinarium, Discipline, Flagellate, Flog, Knout, Lash, Pest, → **PLAGUE**, Scorpion, Whip, Wire

Scouse Liver bird, Wacker

Scout Akela, Beaver, Bedmaker, Bird dog, Colony, Disdain, Emissary, Explorer, Flout, Guide, King's, Outrider, Pathfinder, Pickeer, Pioneer, Queen's, Reconnoitre, Rover, Runner, Scoff, Scorn, Scourer, Scurrier, Scurriour, Sea, Sixer, Spial, Spyal, Talent, Tenderfoot, Tonto, Track, Vedette, Venture

Scowl(ing) Frown, Glower, Gnar, Lour, Lower, Sullen

Scrabble Paw

Scrag(gy) Bony, Dewitt, Ewe-necked, Neck, Scrawny

Scram Begone, Hence, Scat, Shoo

Scramble Addle, Clamber, Encode, Grubble, Hurry, Mêlée, Mix, Motocross, Muss(e), Scamble, Sprattle, Sprawl, Swerve, Texas

Scrap(s), Scrappy Abandon, Abolish, Abrogate, Bin, → **BIT**, Brock, Cancel, Conflict, Cutting, Discard, Dump, → **FIGHT**, Fisticuffs, Fragment, Fray, Iota, Jot, Junk, Mêlée, Mellay, Morceau, Morsel, Odd, Off-cut, Ort, Ounce, Papier collé, Patch, Piece, Pig's-wash, Rag, Rase, Raze, Remnant, Rescind, Scarmoge, Scissel, Scissil, Scroddled, Scrub, Set-to, Shard, Sherd, Shred, Skerrick, Skirmish, Snap, Snippet, Spall, Stoush, Tait, Tate, Tatter, Titbit, Trash, Truculent, Tussle, Whit

Scrap book Album, Grangerism

Scrap box Tidy

Scrape(r) Abrade, Agar, Bark, Clat, Claw, Comb, Curette, D and C, Erase, Escapade, Grate, Graze, Gride, Harl, Hoe, Hole, Jar, Kowtow, Lesion, Lute, Pick, Predicament, Racloir, Rake, Rasorial, Rasp, Rasure, Raze, Razure, Saw, Scalp, Scart, Scrat(ch), Scroop, Scuff, Shave, Skimp, Skin, Skive, Squeegee, Strake, Stridulate, Strigil, Xyster

Scraping noise Curr, Scroop

Scrap merchant Didakai, Didakei, Diddicoi, Diddicoy, Didicoi, Didicoy, Gold-end-man, Totter

Scratch(es), Scratched, Scratching Annul, Cancel, Cla(u)t, Claw, Cracked heels, Curry, Devil, Efface, Eradicate, Erase, Etch, Grabble, Graze, Key, Mar, Nick, Par, Periwig, Pork, Quit, Race, Rase, Rasp, Rast, Ritt, Root, Satan, Scarify, Scart, Score, Scrab(ble), Scram(b), Scrape, Scrattle, Scrawm, Scrawp, Scrooch, Scrorp, Scrub, Spag, Streak, Striation, Tease, Teaze, Wig, Withdraw

▷ **Scratch(ed)** *may indicate* an anagram

Scrawl Doodle, Scratch, Scribble, Squiggle

Scream(er) Bellow, Cariama, Caterwaul, Comedian, Comic, Cry, Eek, Headline, Hern, Hoot, Kamichi, Laugh, Priceless, Primal, Riot, Scare-line, Screech, Seriema, Shriek, Skirl, Squall, Sutch, Yell

Scree Bahada, Bajada, Eluvium, Talus

Screech(ing) Cry, Screak, Screich, Screigh, Scriech, Scritch, Skreigh, Skriech, Skriegh, Ululant, Whoot

Screed Blaud, Megillah, Ms, Plastered, Rat-rhyme, Tirade

Screen(s), Screening Abat-jour, Air, Arras, Back projection, Backstop, Blind(age), Block, Blue, Boss, Brise-soleil, Camouflage, Cervical, Chancel, Check, Chick, Cinerama®, Cloak, Cornea, Coromandel, Cover, Cribble, Curtain, Divider, Dodger, Eyelid, Festoon-blind, Fight, Fire, Flat, Fluorescent, Glib, Gobo, Grid, Grille, Hallan, Help, Hide, Hoard, Hoarding, Iconostas(is), Intensifying, Jube, Lattice, Long-persistence, Mantelet, Mask, Monitor, Net, Nintendo®, Nonny, Obscure, Organ, Over-cover, Overhead, Parclose, Partition, Part-off, Pella, Plasma, Pulpitum, Purdah, Radar, Radarscope, Reardos, Reredorse, Reredos(se), Retable, Riddle, Rood, Scog, Sconce, Scope, → **SHADE**, Shelter, Shield, Shoji, Show, Sift, Sight, Silver, Skug, Small, Smoke, Split, Sunblock, Televise, Tems, Test, Testudo, TFT, Touch, Transenna, Traverse, Umbrella, VDU, Vet, Wide, Windbreak, Window, Windshield, Winnow

Screw Adam, Allen, Archimedes, Blot, Butterfly, Cap, Cheat, Coach, Coitus, Countersunk, Double-threaded, Dungeoner, Extort, Female, Fleece, Grub, Guard, Gyp, Ice, Interrupted, Jailer, Jailor, Lag, Lead, Levelling, Lug, Machine, Male, Mar, Micrometer, Miser, Monkey-wrench, Niggard, Pay, Perpetual, Phillips®, Prop(ellor), Pucker, Raised head, Robertson, Rotate, Ruin, Salary, Screweye, Scrunch, Skinflint, Spiral, Squinch, Swiz(zle), Thumb(i)kins, Twin, Twist, Vice, Wages, Whitworth, Worm, Wreck

Screwdriver Cocktail, Phillips®, Pozidriv®, Ratchet, Scrum, Stubby, Tweaker

Scribble Doodle, Pen, Scrawl

Scribe Clerk, Ezra, Mallam, Scrivener, Sopherim, Tabellion, Writer, WS

Scrimmage Bully, Maul, Mêlée, Rouge, Scrap, Skirmish, Struggle

Scrimp Economise, Pinch, Save, Scrape, Skrimp

Script (reader) Book, Calligraphy, Demotist, Devanagari, Gurmukhi, Hand, Hieratic, Hiragana, Italic, Jawi, Kana, Kufic, Libretto, Linear A, Linear B, Lines, Lombardic, Longhand, Miniscule, Nagari, Nastalik, Nastaliq, Ogam, Prompt book, Ronde, Scenario, Screenplay, Shooting, Writing

Scripture(s), Scriptural version Adi Granth, Agadah, Alcoran, Antilegomena, Avesta, Bible, Gemara, Gematria, Gospel, Granth (Sahib), Guru Granth, Haggada(h), Hermeneutics, Hexapla, Holy book, Holy writ, Koran, K'thibh, Lesson, Lotus Sutra, Mishna(h), OT, Rig-veda, Smriti, Tantra, Targum, Testament, Upanishad, Veda, Vedic, Verse, Vulgate

Scrivener Tabellion

Scrofula Crewels, Cruel(l)s, King's evil, Struma

Scroll(-work) Cartouche, Dead Sea, Gohonzon, Makimono, Megillah, Mezuza(h), Monkeytail, Parchment, Pell, Roll, Roul(e), Scrow, Sefer Torah, Stemma, Torah, Turbinate, Upcurl, Vitruvian, Volume, Volute

Scrooge Blagueur, Miser

Scrotum Oscheal

Scrounge(r) Beg, Blag, Bludge(r), Borrow, Bot, Cadge, Forage, Freeload, Layabout, Ligger, Scunge, Sponge

Scrub(ber), Scrubland, Scrubs Abandon, Cancel, Chaparral, Cleanse, Dele(te), Exfoliate, Facial, Fynbos, Gar(r)igue, Hog, Holystone, Horizontal, Loofa(h), Luffa, Mallee, Masseur, Negate, Pro, Rescind, Rub, Scour, Sticks, Strim, Tart, Wormwood

▷ **Scrub** *may indicate* 'delete'

Scruff(y) Dog(-eared), Fleabag, Grubby, Mangy, Nape, Raddled, Tatty, Uncombed, Untidy

Scrum(mage) Bajada, Maul, Melée, Mob, Pack, Rouge, Ruck

Scrummy, Scrumptious Delectable, Delicious, Toothy, Yum-yum

Scrunt Carl

Scruple(s), Scrupulous Compunction, Conscience, Doubt, Meticulous, Nicety, Precise, Punctilious, Qualm, Queasy, Righteous, Stickle

Scrutinize, Scrutiny Check, Docimasy, Examine, Inspect, Observe, Peruse, Pore, Pry, → SCAN, Size up, Study

Scud East, Scoot, Spark, Spindrift, Spoom, Spoon, Spray

Scuff Brush, Nape, Shuffle

Scuffle Bagarre, Brawl, Melee, Scarmage, Skirmish, Struggle, Tussle

▷ **Scuffle** *may indicate* an anagram

Scull Oar, Row

Sculpt(ure) Acrolith, Aeginetan, Bas-relief, Boast, Bronze, Bust, Calvary, Canephor(a), Canephore, Canephorus, Carve, Chryselephantine, Della-robbia, Figure, Glyptics, High-relief, Kore, Kouros, Mezzo-relievo, Mezzo-rilievo, Mobile, Nude, Pergamene, Pietà, Relief, Relievo, Sc, Scabble, Scapple, Shape, Stabile, → STATUARY, Topiary

Sculptor Arp, Artist, Bartholdi, Bernini, Brancusi, Butler, Calder, Canova, Cellini, Daedalus, Della Robbia, Donatello, Dubuffet, Epstein, Flaxman, Giacometti, Gibbons, Gill, Hepworth, Klippel, Landseer, Michelangelo, Moore, Myron, Nicholson, Noguchi,

Nollekens, Paolozzi, Pevsner, Phidias, Picasso, Pisano, Praxiteles, Pygmalion, Rodin, Scopas, Stevens, Tatlin, Wheeler, Woolner

Scum, Scumbag Confervoid, Dregs, Dross, Epistasis, Film, Glass-gall, Kish, Legge, Louse, Mantle, Mother, Pellicle, Pond, Rabble, Rat, Sandiver, Scorious, Scruff, Slag, Slime, Spume, Sullage, Vermin

Scupper Drain, Ruin, Scuttle, Sink

Scurf, Scurvy Dander, Dandriff, Dandruff, Furfur, Horson, Lepidote, Lepra, Leprose, Scabrous, Scall, Scorbutic, Whoreson, Yaws, Yaw(e)y

Scurrilous Cur, Fescennine, Profane, Ribald, Sotadic, Thersites, Vulgar

Scurry Beetle, Hurry, Scamper, Scutter, Skedaddle, Skelter

Scut Fud, Tail

Scute Plate

Scuttle Abandon, Dan, Dash, Hod, Purdonium, Scamper, Scoop, Scrattle, Scupper, Scurry, Sink, Wreck

Scythe Bushwhacker, Cradle, Cut, Hook, Sickle, Sieth, Snath(e), Snead, Sneath, Sned

Sea(s), Seawards Beam, Billow, Brine, Briny, Cortes, Ditch, Drink, Electron, Euphotic, Euxine, Foam, Herring-pond, Main, Mare, Mare clausum, Mare liberum, Molten, Narrow, → OCEAN, Offing, Offshore, Open, Out, Quantity, Strand, Tide, Tide-rip, Water

---

SEAS

3 letters:	Japan	Benthos	*9 letters:*
Ler	North	Caspian	Bosphorus
Med	Oggin	Celebes	Caribbean
Red	Seven	Channel	East China
Zee	Short	Chukchi	E. Siberian
	South	Euripus	Greenland
4 letters:	Timor	Galilee	Hudson Bay
Aral	White	Icarian	Norwegian
Azov		Marmara	Skagerrak
Blue	*6 letters:*	Marmora	Thalassic
Dead	Aegean	Okhotsk	Waddenzee
Four	Baltic	Pelagic	
Head	Bering	Polynya	*10 letters:*
High	Biscay	Solomon	Philippine
Java	Celtic	Weddell	South China
Kara	Flores		Tyrrhenian
Ross	Inland	*8 letters:*	
Sulu	Ionian	Adriatic	*11 letters:*
	Laptev	Amundsen	Spanish Main
5 letters:	Tasman	Beaufort	
Banda	Tethys	Bismarck	*12 letters:*
Black	Yellow	Bosporus	Nordenskjold
Ceram		Hwang Hai	
China	*7 letters:*	Kattegat	*13 letters:*
Coral	Andaman	Labrador	Mediterranean
Cross	Arabian	Ligurian	
Great	Arafura	Sargasso	*14 letters:*
Irish	Barents	Tiberias	Bellingshausen

Sea-anemone Actinia, Zoantharia
Sea-bear Fur-seal, Otary, Seal, Seecatchie
Sea-beast Ellops, Lamp-shell, Loriciferan, Manatee
Sea-bream Carp, Fish, Porgie, Porgy, Tai

Sea-cow Dugong, Lamantin, Manatee, Rhytina, Sirenian
Sea-cucumber Bêche-de-mer, Trepang
Sea-dog Salt, Seal, Tar
Sea-ear Abalone, Paua
Sea-fight Naumachy
Seafood Crab, Crevette, → FISH, Lobster, Prawn, Shrimp, Whelk, Zooplankton
Seafront, Seashore, Seaside Beach, Coast(line), Esplanade, Littoral, Orarian, Prom(enade), Seaboard, Waterfront
Sea-god Neptune, Nereus, Triton
Sea-green Glaucous, Incorruptible, Robespierre
Sea-horse Hippocampus, Hippodame, Lophobranchiate, Morse, Pipefish, Tangie
Seal(ant), Seal box, Sealed, Seals Airtight, Appose, Atlantic, Bachelor, Bladdernose, Block(ade), Bull(a), Cachet, Cap, Caulk, Chesterfield, Chop, Clinch, Close, Cocket, Common, Consign, Cork, Crab-eater, Cylinder, Eared, Earless, Elephant, Emblem, Fisherman's ring, Fob, Fur, Gasket, Great, Greenland, Grey, Hair, Harbour, Harp, Hermetic, Hooded, Hudson, Impress, Jark, Lemnian, Leopard, Lute, Mastic, Monk, Obsign, Operculum, O-ring, Otary, Phoca, Pinnipedia, Pintadera, Plug, Pod, Privy, Proof, Putty, Quarter, Ribbon, Ringed, Ronan, Rookery, Saddleback, Sea-bear, Sealch, Sea-leopard, Sealgh, Seecatch(ie), Selkie, Sigil, Signet, Silkie, Silky, Size, Skippet, Solomon's, Sphragistics, Stamp, SWALK, Tar, Vacuum-packed, Wafer, Washer, Water, Weddell, Whitecoat, Womb, Zalophus, Ziplock
Sea-legs Balance, Pleons
Sea-level Geoid
Sea-lily Crinoid, Palmatozoa
Seam, Seamstress Channel, Commissure, Dorsal suture, Fell, Felled, French, Furrow, Join, Layer, Middle-stitching, Midinette, Monk's, Sew, Suture, Thread, Welt, Zawster
Seaman, Seamen AB, Crew, Jack, Lascar, Lubber, Mariner, OD, Ordinary, PO, Rating, RN, → SAILOR, Salt, Swabby, Tar
Sea-mat Flustra, Hornwrack
Sea-matiness Gam
Sea-monster Kraken, Merman, Wasserman, Ziffius
Sea-mouse Bristle-worm
Séance Communication, Levitation, Session, Sitting
Sea-parrot Puffin
Sear Brand, Burn, Catch, Cauterise, Char, Frizzle, Parch, Scath(e), Scorch, Singe, Wither
Search(ing) Beat, Body, Comb, Delve, Dragnet, Examine, Ferret, Fingertip, Fish, → FORAGE, Fossick, Frisk, Global, Google(-whack), Grope, Home, Hunt, Indagate, Inquire, Jerk, Jerque, Kemb, Manhunt, Perquisition, Perscrutation, Probe, Proll, Prospect, Proul, Prowl, Pursue, Quest, Rake, Rancel, Ransack, Ransel, Ranzel, Ravel, Ripe, Root, Rootle, Rummage, Scan, Scavenge, Scour, Scout, Scur, Sker, Skirr, Snoop, Strip, Surf, Sweep, Thumb, Trace, Trawl, Zotetic
Sea-rover Norseman, Viking
Sea-serpent, Sea-snake Ellops, Hydrophidae, Phoca
▶ **Seaside** _see_ SEAFRONT
Sea-slug Bêche-de-mer, Trepang
Sea-snail Neritidae
Season(able), Seasonal, Seasoned, Seasoning Accustom, Age, Aggrace, Autumn, Betimes, Christmas, Close, Condiment, Devil, Dress, Duxelles, Easter, Enure, Etesian, Fall, Fennel, Festive, Fines herbes, Flavour, Garlic, G(h)omasco, Growing, Heat, Hiems, High, In, Inure, Lent, Marjoram, Master, Mature, Noel, Nutmeg, Open, Paprika, Peak, Pepper, Powellise, Practised, Ripen, Salt, Sar, Seal, Seel, Seil, Sele, Silly, Solstice, Spice, Spring, Summer(y), Tahini, Ticket, Tide, Time, Timeous, Weather-beaten, Whit, Winter, Xmas
Sea-squirt Ascidian, Cunjevoi, Salpa(e)

Seat(ing) Arthur's, Backside, Banc, Banquette, Barstool, Beanbag, Behind, Bench, Bleachers, Booster, Borne, Bosun's chair, Bottom, Box, Bucket, Bum, Bunker, Buttocks, Canapé, Catbird, Centre, Chair, Chaise longue, Coit, Couch, Country, Creepie, Croup(e), Croupon, Cushion, Davenport, Deckchair, Derrière, Dick(e)y, Dicky, Divan, Ejector, Epicentre, Faldistory, Faldstool, Foundation, Fud, Fundament, Gradin, Hall, Hassock, Home, Hot, Houdah, Howdah, Humpty, Hurdies, Judgement, Jump, Knifeboard, Love, Marginal, Marquise, Mercy, Misericord, Natch, Nates, Ottoman, Palanquin, Palfrey, Passenger, Perch, Pew, Pillion, Pit, Pouffe, Ringside, Rumble, Rumble-tumble, Rump, Saddle, Safe, Sagbag, Sedes, Sedile, Sedilium, See, Sell, Selle, Settee, Settle, Sidesaddle, Siege, Siege Perilous, Sliding, Sofa, Squab, Stool, Strapontin, Subsellium, Sunk(ie), Sunlounger, Synthronus, Tabo(u)ret, Throne, Tonneau, Upholstery, Window, Woolsack

Sea-urchin Asterias, Echinus, Pluteus, Whore's egg

Sea-vampire Manta

Sea-wall Bulwark, Dyke, Groyne

Seaweed Agar, Alga(e), Arame, Badderlock, Bladderwort, Bladderwrack, Carrag(h)een, Ceylon moss, Chondrus, Conferva, Coralline, Cystocarp, Desmid, Devil's apron, Diatom, Driftweed, Dulse, Enteromorpha, Florideae, Fucus, Gulfweed, Heterocontae, Hijiki, Hornwrack, Karengo, Kelp, Kilp, Kombu, Konbu, Laminaria, Laver, Lemon-weed, Maerl, Nori, Nullipore, Oarweed, Ore, Peacock's tail, Phyco-, Porphyra, Purple laver, Redware, Rockweed, Sargasso, Seabottle, Sea-furbelow, Sea-girdle, Sea-lace, Sea-lettuce, Sea-mat, Sea-moss, Sea-tangle, Seaware, Sea-whistle, Sea-wrack, Tang, Tetraspore, Ulva, Varec(h), Vraic, Wakame, Ware, Wrack

Sea-wolf Pirate

Sea-worm Palolo, Spunculid

Sebastian Coe

Sec Dry, Instant

Secede(r), Secession(ist) Adullamite, Antiburgher, Cave, Defy, Desert, Dissident, Flamingant, Separatist, Sever, Splinter, UDI

Seclude(d), Seclusion Cloister, Incommunicado, Isolate, Ivory tower, Maroon, Nook, Pleasance, Poke(y), Privacy, Purdah, Quarantine, Retiracy, Retreat, Secret, Sequester, Shyness, Solitude

Second(ary), Seconds Abet, Alternative, Another (guess), Appurtenance, Assist, Atomic, Back(er), Beta, Byplay, Chaser, Collateral, Coming, Comprimario, Congener, Cornerman, Deuteragonist, Ephemeris, Fiddle, Flash, Friend, Handler, Imperfect, Indirect, Inferior, Instant, Jiffy, Latter, Leap, Lesser, Minor, Mo(ment), Nature, Other, Pig's-whisper, Red ribbon, Redwood, Runner-up, Saybolt-Universal, Sec, Shake, Share, Side(r), Sideline, Sight, Silver, Split, Subsidiary, Subtype, Support, Tick, Tone, Trice, Twinkling, Universal, Wind

Second-best Worsted

▶ **Second-class** *see* SECOND-RATE

Second coming Parousia

Second earth Antichthon

Second-hand Hand-me-down, Hearsay, Preloved, Reach-me-down, Re-paint, Tralaticious, Used, Vicarious

Second-rate, Second-class B, Inferior, Mediocre

Second-sight Deuteroscopy, Divination, Tais(c)h

Second tine Bay, Bez

Second-year student Semi(e)(-bajan), Sophomore

Secrecy, Secret(s), Secretive Apocrypha, Arcana, Arcane, Arcanum, Backstairs, Cabbalistic, Cagey, Clam, Clandestine, Classified, Closet, Code, Conference, Confidence, Conventicle, Couvert, Covert, Cranny, Cryptadia, Cryptic, Crypto, Dark, Dearn, Deep, Deep-laid, Dern, Devious, Esoteric, Hidden, Hidling, Hidlin(g)s, Hole and corner, Hugger-mugger, Hush-hush, Hushy, Inly, Inmost, Inner, In pectore, In petto, Know-nothing, Latent, Mysterious, Mystical, Mystique, Open, Oyster, Password,

Penetralia, Petto, → **PRIVATE**, Privity, Privy, QT, Rune, Scytale, Seal, Sensitive, Shelta, Silent, Slee, Sly, State, Stealth, Sub rosa, Tight-lipped, Top, Trade, Unbeknown, Underboard, Undercover, Underhand, Undescried, Unknown, Unre(a)d, Unrevealed, Untold

Secretary Aide, Amanuensis, Chancellor, Chronicler, CIS, Desk, Desse, Famulus, Home, Minuteman, Moonshee, Munshi, Notary, Parliamentary, Permanent, Private, Prot(h)onotary, Scrive, Social, Steno(grapher), Stenotyper, Temp

Secretary-bird Messenger, Serpent-eater

Secrete, Secretion Aequorin, Aldosterone, Allomone, Apocrine, Autacoid, Cache, Castor, Chalone, Colostrum, Cuckoo-spit, Discharge, Emanation, Exude, Hide, Honeydew, Hormone, Juice, Lac, Lactate, Lerp, Melatonin, Mucus, Musk, Nectar, Osmidrosis, Phlegm, Pruina, Ptyalin, Recrement, Renin, Resin, Rheum, Saliva, Sebum, Secern, Smegma, Spit(tle), Succus, Trypsin

Sect(arian), Secret society Abelite, Adamite, Ahmadiy(y)ah, Albigenses, Amish, Anabaptist, Assassin, Babee, Babi, Bahai, Bigendian, Brahmin, Cabal, Cainite, Calixtin(e), Camorra, Campbellite, Cathar, Clan, Clapham, Covenantes, Crypto, Cult, Cynic, Danite, Darbyite, Disciples of Christ, Dissenter, Docate(s), Donatist, Druse, Druze, Dunkard, Dunker, Ebionite, Encratite, Essene, Familist, Fifth monarchy, Gabar, Gheber, Ghebre, Giaour, Glassite, Gnostic, Group, Gueber, Guebre, Gymnosophist, Harmonist, Harmonite, Hassid, Hauhau, Hemerobaptist, Hesychast, Hillmen, Holy Roller, Hutterite, Illuminati, Ismaili, Jacobite, Jansenist, Jehovah's Witness, Jodo, Karaite, Karmathian, Little-endian, Lollard, Macedonian, Macmillanite, Mandaean, Marcionite, Maronite, Mendaites, Monothelite, Montanist, Moonie, Mormon, Mucker, Muggletonian, Nasorean, Nazarine, Noetian, Ophites, Order, Partisan, Patripassian, Paulician, Perfectation, Perfectionist, Pharisee, Philadelphian, Phrygian, Picard, Pietist, Plymouth Brethren, Plymouthite, Porch, Pure Land, Ranter, Rappist, Ribbonism, Russellite, Sabbatian, Sabian, Sadducee, S(h)aiva, Saktas, Sandeman, School, Schwenkfelder, Seekers, Senus(s)i, Seventh Day Adventist, Sex, Shafiite, Shaker, Shembe, Shia(h), Soka Gakkai, Sons of Freedom, Taliban, Therapeutae, Tunker, Unitarian, Utraquist, Vaishnava, Valdenses, Vaudois, Wahabee, Wahabi(i)te, Waldenses, Yezdi, Yezidee, Yezidi, Zealot, Zen, Zezidee

Section, Sector Area, Balkanize, Caesarian, Chapter, Classify, Conic, Cross, Cut, Department, Division, Ellipse, Empennage, Episode, Eyalet, Gan, Golden, Gore, Hyperbola, Length, Lith, Lune, Meridian, Metamere, Mortice, Movement, Octant, Outlier, Panel, Passus, → **PIECE**, Platoon, Private, Public, Pull-out, Quarter, Rhythm, Rib, S, Segment, Severy, Shard, Sherd, Slice, Stage, Ungula, Unit, Warm, Wing, Zenith, Zone

Secular(ise) Earthly, Laic, Non-CE, Profane, Temporal, Ungod, Worldly

Secure(d), Security Anchor, Assurance, Bag, Bail, Band, Bar, → **BASIC**, Batten, Belay, Bellwether, Belt and braces, Bolt, Bond, Bottomry, Buck Rogers, Calm, Cash ratio, Catch, Cement, Chain, Cheka, Cinch, Clamp, Clasp, Clench, Clinch, Close, Cocoon, Collateral, Collective, Come by, Consolidate, Consols, Cosy, Counterseal, Cushy, Debenture, Deposit, Disreputable, Doorman, Dunnage, Earthwork, Engage, Enlock, Ensure, Equity, Establishment, Fasten, Fastness, Firm, Fortify, Frap, Fungibles, Gain, Gilt, Gilt-edged, Grith, Guarantee, Guy, Heritable, Hypothec, Immune, Impregnable, Indemnity, Inlock, Invest(ment), Knot, Lace, Land, Lash, Latch, Lien, Listed, Lock, Lockaway, Lockdown, Lockfast, Long-dated, Longs, Medium-dated, Mortgage, Nail, National, Obtain, Padlock, Patte, Pin, Pledge, Pot, Pre-empt, Preference, Procure, Protect, Quad, Rope, Rug, → **SAFE**, Safety, Screw, Seal, Settle, Shutter, Snell, Snug, Social, Sound, Stable, Stanchion, Staple, Staylace, Stock, Strap, Sure(ty), Tack, Take, Tie, Tight, Trap, Trice, Tyde, Vest, Warrant, Watertight, Wedge, Win

Sedan Battle, Brougham, Chair, Jampan(i), Jampanee, Litter, Palanquin, Palkee, Palki, Saloon

Sedate Calm, Cool, Decorous, Demure, Dope, Douce, Drug, Sad, Serene, Sober(sides), Staid, Stand

Sedative Amytal®, Anodyne, Aspirin, Barbitone, Bromal, Bromide, Chloral, Depressant, Deserpidine, Hypnic, Laurel water, Lenitive, Lupulin, Meprobamate, Metopryl, Miltown, Morphia, Narcotic, Nembutal®, Opiate, Paraldehyde, Pethidine, Phenobarbitone, Premed(ication), Rohypnol®, Roofie, Scopolamine, Seconal®, Soothing, Temazepam, Thridace, Valerian, Veronal®

Sedentary Inactive, Sessile, Stationary

Sedge Carex, Chufa, Cinnamon, Clubrush, Grey, Seg, Xyris

Sediment Alluvium, Chalk, Deposit, Dregs, F(a)eces, Fecula, Flysch, Foots, Graded, Grounds, Grouts, Incrustation, Lees, Molasse, Placer, Residue, Salt, Sapropel, Silt, Sludge, Terrigenous, Till, Turbidite, Varve, Warp

Sedition, Seditious Incitement, Insurrection, Leasing-maker, Revolt, Riot, Treason

Seduce(r), Seduction, Seductive Allure, Bed, Beguilement, Betray, Bewitch, Bribe, Come-hither, Cuckold-maker, Debauch, Dishonour, Entice, Honeyed, Honied, Jape, Lothario, Luring, Mislead, Pull, Siren, Slinky, Tempt, Trepan, Undo, Vamp, Wrong

▷ **Seduce** *may indicate* one word inside another

See(ing) Acknow, Apostolic, Barchester, Behold, Bishopric, C, Carlisle, Consider, Date, Deek, Descry, Diocesan, Discern, Durham, Ebor, Ecce, Ely, Episcopal, Exeter, Eye, Get, Glimpse, Holy, In as much as, La, Lo, Meet, Norwich, Notice, Observe, Papal, Perceive, Realise, Remark, Ripon, Rochester, Rubberneck, Rumble, St David's, Salisbury, Sight, Since, Sodor and Man, Spae, Spot, Spy, Truro, Twig, Understand, V, Vatican, Vid(e), View, Vision, Visit, Voilà, Witness, York

Seed(s), Seedy Achene, Apiol, Argan, Arilli, Arillode, Ash-key, Bean, Ben, Best, Blue, Bonduc, Cacoon, Caraway, Cardamom, Carvy, Cebadilla, Cevadilla, Chickpea, Cocoa, Colza, Coriander, Corn, Crabstone, Cum(m)in, Dragon's teeth, Embryo, Endosperm, Ergot, Favourite, Fern, Germ, Grain, Gritty, Inseminate, Issue, Ivory-nut, Kernel, Lentil, Lima, Lomentum, Mangy, Mawseed, Miliary, Mote, Nickar, Nicker, Niger, Nucellous, Nut, Oat, Offspring, Ovule, Pea, Pinon, Pip, Poorly, Poppy, Pyxis, Sabadilla, Samariform, Scuzz, Semen, Seminal, Senvy, Sesame, Shabby, Shea-nut, Silique, Sorus, Sow, Sperm, Spore, Stane, Stone, Terminator, Thistledown, Zoosperm

Seed-case Aril, Bur(r), Endopleura, Husk, Pea(s)cod, Pod, Testa, Theca

Seed-leaf Cotyledon

Seedsman Driller, Nurseryman, Sower

Seek(er), Seeking Ask, Beg, Busk, Cap-in-hand, Chase, Court, Endeavour, Ferret out, Fish, Gun for, Pursue, Quest, Scur, Search, Skirr, Solicit, Suitor, Try

Seem(ing), Seemingly Apparent, Appear, As if, Look, Ostensible, Purport, Quasi, Think

Seemly Apt, Comely, Decent, Decorous, Fit, Suitable

Seep(age) Angel's share, Dribble, Exude, Leak, Ooze, Osmose, Percolate, Permeate

Seer Augur, Auspex, Balaam, Eye, Melampus, Nahum, Observer, Oculiform, Onlooker, Oracle, Prescience, Prophet, Sage, Sibyl, Soothsayer, T(e)iresias, Witness, Zoroaster

Seesaw Bascule, Boom and bust, Teeter(-totter), Teeter-board, Tilt, Vacillate, Wild mare

Seethe(d) Boil, Bubble, Churn, Ferment, Simmer, Smoulder, Sod

Segment(ation) Antimere, Arthromere, Cut, Division, Gironny, Gyronny, Intron, Lacinate, Lith, Lobe, Merogenesis, Merome, Merosome, Metamere, Metathorax, Part, Piece, Pig, Proglottis, Propodeon, Prothorax, Scliff, Section, Share, Shie, Skliff, Somite, Split, Sternite, Syllable, Tagma, Telson, Trochanter, Urite, Uromere

Segregate, Segregation Apartheid, Exile, Insulate, Intern, → **ISOLATE**, Jim Crow, Seclude, Separate

Seidlitz Powder, Rochelle

Seismic, Seismography Richter, Terremotive

Seismograph Tromometer

Seize, Seizure Angary, Apprehend, Appropriate, Areach, Arrest, Assume, Attach(ment), Bag, Bone, Capture, Catch, Claw, Cleek, Cly, Collar, Commandeer, Confiscate, Distrain, Distress, Extent, For(e)hent, → **GRAB**, Grip, Hend, Ictus, Impound, Impress, Maverick,

Nab, Na(a)m, Nap, Nim, Poind, Possess, Pot, Raid, Ravin, Replevy, Rifle, Sease, Sequestrate, Smug, Snag, Snatch, Tackle, Trover, Usurp, Wingding, Wrest

Seldom Infrequent, Rare, Unoften

Select(ion), Selecting, Selector Adopt, Artificial, Assortment, Bla(u)d, Cap, Casting, Choice, Choose, Classy, Clonal, Cull, Darwinism, Discriminate, Draft, Draw, Eclectic, Edit, Elite, Excerpt, Exclusive, Extract, Favour, Garble, Inside, K, Kin, Nap, Natural, Pericope, → **PICK**, Pot-pourri, Prefer, Recherché, Redline, Sample, Seed, Sex, Single, Sort, Stream, Tipster, Triage, UCCA, Vote

Selenium Se, Zorgite

Self Atman, Auto, Character, Ego, Person, Psyche, Seity, Sel, Soul

Self-concern Dog-eat-dog

Self-confident, Self-confidence, Self-willed Aplomb, Ego, Headstrong, Jaunty

Self-conscious Guilty

Self-contained Absolute, Reticent, SC, Taciturn

Self-contradictory Absurd, Irish

Self-control, Self-discipline Abstinence, Ascesis, Encraty, Modesty, Patience, Restraint, Stiff upper lip, Temper(ance), Willpower

▶ **Self-defence** *see* **MARTIAL ARTS**

Self-destructive Lemming

Self-esteem Amour-propre, Conceit, Confidence, Egoism, Pride, Vainglory

Self-evident Axiom, Ipso facto, Manifest, Obvious, Patent, Truism, Truth

Self-existence Solipsism

Self-fertilisation, Self-origination Aseity, Autogamy

Self-governing Autonomy, Idior(r)hythmic, Kabele, Kebel, Puritanism, Swaraj

Self-help Smiles

Self-important, Self-indulgent, Self-interested Aristippus, Arrogant, Bumptious, Chesty, Cocky, Conceited, Egocentric, Immoderate, Jack-in-office, Licentious, Narcissistic, Pompous, Pooterish, Pragmatic, Primadonna, Profligate, Solipsist, Sybarite

Selfish(ness) Avaricious, Egocentric, Egoist, Grabby, Greedy, Hedonist, Mean, Solipsism

Selfless(ness) Non-ego, Tuism

Self-limiting Kenotic

▶ **Self-origination** *see* **SELF-FERTILISATION**

Self-pollinating Cl(e)istogamic

Self-possession Aplomb, Assurance, Composure, Cool, Nonchalant, Phlegm

Self-satisfied, Self-satisfaction Complacent, Narcissism, Smug, Tranquil

Self-service Automat, Buffet, Cafeteria, Supermarket

Self-styled Soi-disant

Self-sufficient, Self-sufficiency Absolute, Autarky, Complete, Hunter-gatherer

Self-taught Autodidact

Sell(er), Selling Apprize, Auction, Barter, Bear, Betray, Blackmail, Blockbuster, Cant, Catch, Chant, Chaunt, Cold-call, Cope, Costermonger, Direct, Dispose, Divest, Do, Eggler, Fancier, Fellmonger, Flog, Go, Hard, Have, Hawk, Huckster, Hustle, Inertia, Knock down, Market, Marketeer, Ménage, Merchant, Missionary, Oligopoly, Pardoner, Party, Peddle, Peddler, Pick-your-own, Purvey, Push, Pyramid, Rabbito(h), Realise, Rep, Retail, Ruse, Scalp, Short, Simony, Soft, Stall-man, Sugging, Switch, Tout, → **TRADE**, Trick, Vend, Vent

Selvage Border, Edge, Roon, Rund

Semantics General, Generative, Interpretive, Notional, Onomasiology, Semasiology, Sematology

Semaphore Signal, Tic-tac, Wigwag

Semblance Appearance, Aspect, Guise, Likeness, Sign, Verisimilitude

Semen Jis(so)m, Milt, Spoof, Spunk

Semi-circular D, Hemicycle

Semi-conductor Germanium, LED, Thryristor

Seminar(y) Class, → **COLLEGE**, Colloquium, Group, Theologate, Tutorial, Webinar, Workshop, Yeshiva

Semiotics Syntactics

Semi-paralysis Dyaesthesia

Semitic Accadian, Akkadian, Ammonite, Amorite, Arab, Aramaic, Canaanite, Chaldean, Geez, Jewish, Phoenician

Semitone Pycnon

Semolina Couscous

Senate Council, Curia, Seanad (Eireann)

Senator Antiani, Cicero, Concept father, Elder, Legislator, Patrician, Shadow, Solon

Send, Sent Consign, → **DESPATCH**, Disperse, Emanate, Emit, Entrance, Extradite, Issue, Launch, Mail, Order, Post, Rapt, Remit, Ship, Transmit, Transport

Send back Refer, Remand, Remit, Return

Send down Demit, Lower, Refer, Rusticate

Send up Chal(l)an, Lampoon, Promote

Senegal SN

Senescence Age

Senile, Senility Caducity, Dementia, Disoriented, Doddery, Doited, Doitit, Dotage, Eild, Eld, Gaga, Nostology, Twichild

Senior(ity) Aîné, Doyen, Elder, Father, Grecian, Major, Majorat, Old(er), Oubaas, Père, Primus, Superior, Upper

Senna Bladder, Cassia

Señor(a) Caballero, Don(a), Hidalga, Hidalgo

Sensation(al) Acolouthite, Anoesis, Aura, Blood, Blood and thunder, Commotion, Drop-dead, Emotion, Empfindung, Feeling, Gas, Impression, Lurid, Melodrama, Organic, Par(a)esthesia, Phosphene, Photism, Pyrotechnic, Rush, Shocker, Shock-horror, Showstopper, Splash, Stir, Styre, Synaesthesia, Thrill, Tingle, Vibes, Wow, Yellow

Sense, Sensual(ist), Sensing Acumen, Attuite, Aura, Carnal, Coherence, Common, Dress, Ear, ESP, Faculty, Feel, Gaydar, Gross, Gumption, Gustation, Hearing, Horse, Idea, Import, Instinct, Intelligence, Intuition, Lewd, Loaf, Logic, Marbles, Meaning, Moral, Nous, Olfactory, Palate, Perceptual, Proprioceptive, Rational, Receptor, Remote, Rumble-gumption, Rum(m)el-gumption, Rumgumption, Rum(m)le-gumption, Sanity, Satyr, Sight, Sixth, Slinky, Smell, Spirituality, Sybarite, Synesis, Taste, Taste bud, Touch, Voluptuary, Voluptuous, Wisdom, Wit

Senseless Absurd, Anosmia, Asinine, Illogical, Inane, Lean-witted, Mad, Numb, Stupid, Stupor, Unconscious, Unwise, Vegetal

Sensible Aware, Clear-headed, Dianoetic, Down to earth, No-nonsense, Prudent, Raisonné, Rational, Realistic, Sane, Solid, Together, Well-balanced

Sensitive, Sensitivity Aesthete, Algesia, Alive, Allergic, Atopy, Dainty, Delicate, Discreet, Erethism, Erogenous, Hypaesthesia, Keen, Nesh, Nociceptive, Orthochromatic, Passible, Quick, Radiesthesia, Sympathetic, Tactful, Tender, Thermaesthesia, Thin-skinned, Ticklish, Touchy(-feely), Vulnerable

Sensor(y) Cercus, Detector, Exteroceptor, Interoceptor, Palpi, Proprioceptor, Remote

Sentence(s) Antiphon, Assize, Bird, Carpet, Clause, Closed, Commit, Complex, Compound, Condemn, Custodial, Death, Decree(t), Deferred, Doom, Fatwah, Indeterminate, Judgement, Life, Matrix, Open, Pangram, Paragraph, Period(ic), Porridge, Predicate, Punish, Rap, Rheme, Rune, Send up, Simple, Stretch, Suspended, Swy, Tagmene, Time, Topic, Verdict, Versicle, Weigh off

Sententious Concise, Gnomic, Laconic, Pithy, Pompous, Terse

Sentiment(al), Sentimentality Byronism, Corn, Cornball, Drip, Feeling, Goo, Govey, Gucky, Gush, Hokey, Icky, Lovey-dovey, Maudlin, Mawkish, Mind, Mush, Namby-pamby, Nationalism, Nostalgia, Opinion, Posy, Romantic, Rose-pink, Rosewater, Saccharin, Schmaltzy, Sloppy, Slushy, Smoochy, Soppy, Spoony, Sugary, Swoony, Syrupy, Tear-jerker, Too-too, Traveller, Treacly, Twee, View, Weepy, Wertherian, Yucky

Sentry Cordon sanitaire, Custodian, Guard, Jaga, Look-out, Picket, Sentinel, Vedette, Vidette, Watch

Separate(d), Separation, Separately, Separatist Abscise, Abstract, Apart, Asunder, Atmolysis, Avulsion, Bust up, Comma, Compartmentalise, Cull, Cut, Decollate, Decompose, Decouple, Deduct, Deglutinate, Demarcate, Demerge, Detach, Dialyse, Diastasis, Diazeuxis, Diremption, Disaggregate, Disally, Discerp, Disconnect, Discrete, Disjunction, Dissociate, Distance, Distinct, Disunite, Divide, Division, Divorce, Eloi(g)n, Elute, Elutriate, Esloin, Estrange, ETA, Filter, Grade, Gulf, Heckle, Hive, Hyphenate, Insulate, Intervene, Isolate, Judicial, Laminate, Lease, Legal, Monosy, Part, Particle, Partition, Partitive, Peel off, Piece, Prescind, Prism, Ramify, Red(d), Rift, Sashing, Scatter, Schism, Screen, Scutch, Secern, Segregate, Sever, Several, Shear, Shed, Shore, Shorn, Sift, Sleave, Sle(i)ded, Solitary, Sort, → **SPLIT**, Spread, Steam-trap, Stream, Sunder, Sundry, Tems(e), Tmesis, Try, Twin(e), Unclasp, Unhitch, Unravel, Winnow, Wrench, Yandy

Sepia Cuttle, Ink

Seppuku Hara-kiri, Hari-kari

Septic Festering, Poisonous, Rotting

Septimus Small

Septum Cloison, Mediastinum

Sepulchral, Sepulchre Bier, Cenotaph, Charnel, Crypt, Easter, Funeral, Monument, Pyramid, Tomb, Vault, Whited

Sequel After-clap, Aftermath, Consequence, Effect, Offshoot, Outcome, Suite

Sequence, Sequential Agoge, Algorithm, Byte, Cadence, Chronological, Consecution, Consensus, Continuity, Continuum, Escape, Fibonacci, Gene, Intervening, Intron, Line, Linear, Main, Montage, Order, Peptide, Polar, Program(me), Routine, Run, Seriatim, Series, Shot, Signal, Sonnet, Storyboard, String, Succession, Suit, Suite, Train, Vector

Sequester, Sequestrate Confiscate, Esloin, Esloyne, Impound, Isolate, Retire, Seclude, Separate

Sequin Paillette, Zecchino, Zechin

Sequoia Redwood, Wellingtonia

Seraph Abdiel, → **ANGEL**

Serb(ian) Chetnik

Sere Arid, → **DRY**, Scorch, Wither

Serenade(r) Aubade, Charivari, Horning, Love song, Minstrel, Nocturne, Shivaree, Sing-song, Wait, Wake

Serene, Serenity Calm, Composed, Impassive, Placid, Quietude, Repose, Sangfroid, Sedate, Seraphic, Smooth, → **TRANQUIL**

Serf(dom) Adscript, Bondman, Ceorl, Churl, Helot, Manred, → **SLAVE**, Thete, Thrall, Vassal, Velle(i)nage, Villein

Serge Russian, Say

Sergeant Buzfuz, Chippy, Chips, Colour, Cuff, Drill, Flight, Halberdier, Havildar, Kite, Lance, Master, → **NCO**, Pepper, Platoon, RSM, Sarge, SL, SM, Staff, Technical, Troy

Serial(ism) Episode, Feuilleton, Heft, Livraison, Total

Series Actinide, Actinium, Arithmetical, Balmer, Battery, Catena, Chain, Concatenation, Consecution, Continuum, Course, Cycle, Cyclus, Docusoap, Electromotive, Enfilade, Engrenage, En suite, Episode, Epos, Ethylene, Exponential, Fibonacci, Fourier, Geometric, Gradation, Harmonic, Homologous, Lanthanide, Line, Links, Loop, Maclaurin's, Methane, Molasse, Neptunium, Partwork, Pedigree, Power, Process, → **PROGRESSION**, Radioactive, Rally, Random walk, Ranks, Rest, Rosalia, Rosary, Routine, Rubber, Run, Sequence, Ser, Set, Sitcom, String, Succession, Suit, Taylor's, Thorium, Time, Tone, Tournament, Train, Uranium, World

Serious(ly) Critical, Earnest, For real, Grave, Gravitas, Harsh, Heavy, Important, In earnest, Intense, Major, Momentous, Pensive, Radical, Real, Sad, Serpentine, Sober, Solemn, Sombre, Staid, Straight(-faced), Very

Sermon Address, Discourse, Gatha, Homily, Khutbah, Lecture, Preachment, Prone, Ser, Spital

Serow Goral, Thar

Serpent(ine) Adder, Amphisbaena, Anguine, Apepi, Apophis, Asp, Aspic(k), Basilisk, Boa, Caduceus, Cockatrice, Dipsas, Firedrake, Midgard, Nagas, Ophiolite, Ouroboros, Peridotite, Pharaoh's, Retinalite, Sea-snake, Shesha, → **SNAKE**, Traitor, Uraeus, Verd-antique, Verde-antico, Viper, Wyvern

Serrate(d) Diprionidian, Saw, Scallop, Serried

Serum Albumin, Antiglobulin, Antilymphocyte, Antitoxin, ATS, Fluid, Globulin, Humoral, Opsonin, Senega

Serval Bush-cat

Servant, Server Aid(e), Attendant, Ayah, Batman, Bearer, Bedder, Bedmaker, Between-maid, Boot-catcher, Boots, Boy, Busboy, Butler, Caddie, Chaprassi, Chokra, Chuprassy, Civil, Columbine, Cook, Cook-general, Daily, Dogsbody, Domestic, Dromio, Drudge, Employee, Factotum, Famulus, File, Flunkey, Footboy, Footman, Friday, Gehazi, General, G(h)illie, Gip, Gully, Gyp, Haiduk, Handmaid, Helot, Henchman, Heyduck, Hind, Hireling, Iras, Jack, Jack-slave, Jeames, Khansama(h), Khidmutgar, Khitmutgar, Kitchen-knave, Kitchen-maid, Knave, Lackey, Lady's maid, Lazy Susan, Leroy, Maid, Major-domo, Man, Man Friday, Menial, Minion, Mixologist, Muchacha, Muchacho, Myrmidon, Nethinim, Obedient, Page, Pantler, Parlourmaid, Person, Pistol, Postman, Public, Pug, Retainer, Retinue, Scout, Scrub, Scullion, Servitor, Sewer, Skip, Slavey, Soldier, Soubrette, Steward, Tablespoon, Tapsman, Tendance, Theow, Thete, Tiger, Trotter, Turnspit, Tweeny, Underling, Vails, Vales, Valet, Valkyrie, Varlet, Vassal, Waiter, Wash-rag, Weller

Serve(r), Service(s) Acas, Ace, Act, Active, All-up, Amenity, Answer, Army, Arriage, Asperges, Assist, ATS, Attendance, Avail, Baptism, Barista, Barman, Barperson, Benediction, Breakfast, Campaign, Candlemas, Cannonball, Ceefax®, China, Christingle, Civil, Communion, Community, Compline, Conception(e), Conscription, Corvée, Credo, Devotional, Dien, Dinnerset, Diplomatic, Dish, Divine, Do, Dollop, Dow, Drumhead, Dry, Duty, Ecosystem, Emergency, Employ, Evensong, Facility, Fault, Fee, Feudal, Fish, Foreign, Forensic, Forward, → **FUNCTION**, Funeral, Further, Go, Help, Helpline, Hour, Ibadat, Jury, Ka(e), Kol Nidre, Ladle, Let, Line, Ling, Lip, Litany, Liturgy, Ma'ariv, Marriage, Mass, Mat(t)ins, Memorial, Mincha, Minister, Ministration, Ministry, Missa, National, Navy, Nocturn, Nones, Oblige, Offertory, Office, Oracle, Overarm, Overhaul, Pass, Pay, Personal, Pit stop, Possum, Pottery, Pour, Prime, Proper, Public, Radio, RAF, Regular, Requiem, Rite, RN, Room, Sacrament, SAS, Satisfy, SBS, Secret, Selective, Senior, Sext, Shacharis, Shaharith, Shuttle, Silver, Skeleton, Social, Sorb(us), Stead, Sted, Sue, Tableware, Tea, Tenebrae, Tierce, Trental, Uncork, Under-arm, Use, Utility, Vespers, Wait, Waiterage, Waitron, Waitstaff, Watch-night, Wild, Worship, Yeoman('s)

Service-book Hymnal, Hymnary, Missal, Triodion

▷ **Serviceman** *may indicate* a churchman

Servile, Servility Abasement, Base, Crawling, Knee, Kowtowing, Lickspittle, Menial, Minion, Obsequious, Slavish, Slimy, Submissive, Suck-hole, Sycophantic, Tintookie, Truckle

Serving Helping, Heuristic, Portion

Servitude Bondage, Domination, Penal, Peonage, Peonism, Slavery, Thirlage, Thrall, Vassalry, Yoke

Sesame Beni, Benne, Gingelly, Gingili, Grapple-plant, Jinjilli, Semsem, Tahini, Til

Session(s) All-nighter, Bout, Executive, Galah, Hearing, Jam, Kirk, Meeting, Nightshift, Petty, Poster, Quarter, Rap, Round, Séance, Sederunt, Settle, Sitting, Special, Term

Set(ting) (about; aside; down; in; off; out; up) Activate, Adjust, Apply, Appoint, Arrange, Array, Assiege, Batch, Bent, Bezel, Boun, Brooch, Cabal, Cake, Case, Cast, Chaton, Class, Claw, Clique, Cliveden, Closed, Coagulate, Cock, Cockshy, Codomain, Collection, Collet, Comp(ositor), Companion, Compose, Congeal, Context, Coterie,

Couvert, Crew, Crystal, Cyclorama, Data, Dead, Decline, Decor, Detonate, Diorama, Direct, Dispose, Duchesse, Earmark, Earnest, Earth, Enchase, Ensky, Environment, Establish, Explode, Film, Firm, Fit, Flagstone, Flash, Flat(s), Found, Garniture, Geal, Gel, Gelatinise, Genome, Group, Hairdo, Harden, Heliacal, Ilk, Inchase, Incrowd, Incut, Infinite, Inlay, Jee, Jeel, Jell(y), Jet, Julia, Kit, Knit, Laid, Land, Lay, Leg, Locale, Locate, Lot, Mandelbrot, Mental, Milieu, Mise en scène, Miserere, Monture, Mournival, Nail, Nest, Occident, Open, Ordain, Ordered, Ordinate, Ouch, Pair, Parure, Pavé, Permanent, Physique, Pitch, Place(ment), Plant, Plaste, Ply, Point, Posed, Posit, Power, Put, Radio, Rate, Ready, Receiver, Relay, Rig, Rigid, Rooted, Rouse, Rubber, Saw, Scenery, Series, Settle(d), Showcase, Sink, Slate, Smart, Solidify, Solution, Squad, Stand, Stationed, Stede, Stell, Stick, Stiffen, Still, Stream, Stud, Subscriber, Suit, Suite, Surround, Synchronize, Tar, Tea, Team, Teeth, Televisor, Telly, The four hundred, Theme, Tiffany, Till, Toilet, Trannie, Transistor, Trigger, Truth, Tube, TV, Union, Universal, Venn (diagram), Weather, Wide-screen, Yplast

Setback Bodyblow, Checkmate, Downturn, Glitch, Hiccough, Hiccup, Jolt, Knock, Relapse, Retard, Retreat, Reversal, Scarcement, Sickener, Tes, Vicissitude, Whammy

Setter Cement, Comp, Dog, English, Gelatin(e), Gordon, Gundog, Hairspray, Irish, Pectin, Red, Smoot, Sphinx, Trend

Settle(d), Settlement, Settler Adjust, Agree, Alight, Ante, Appoint, Arrange, Ascertain, Ausgleich, Avenge, Balance, Bandobast, Bed, Bench, Boer, Borghetto, Botany Bay, Bundobust, Bustee, Camp, Clear, Clench, Clinch, Colonial, Colonise, Colony, Compose, Compound, Compromise, Crannog, Decide, Defray, Determine, Diktat, Discharge, Dispose, Dorp, Dowry, Ekistics, Encamp, Endow, Ensconce, Entail, Establish, Expat, Faze, Feeze, Finalise, Fix, Foot, Foreclose, Gravitate, Gridironer, Guilder, Habitant, Hama, Hyannis, Illegitimate, Informal, Jamestown, Jointure, Kibbutz, Land, Ledge, Light, Lull, Lyte, Manyat(t)a, Meet, Merino, Mise, Mission, Moreton Bay, Moshav, Nahal, Nest, Nestle, New Amsterdam, Oecist, Oikist, Opt, Outpost, Over, Pa(h), Pakka, Pale, Patroon, Pay, Payment, Peise, Penal, People, Perch, Pheazar, Pheese, Pheeze, Phese, Pilgrim, Pioneer, Placate, Planter, Populate, Port Arthur, Port Nicholson, Presidio, Pucka, Pueblo, Pukka, Rancheria, Rancherie, Readjust, Reduction, Reimburse, Remit, Reside, Resolve, Rest, Roofie, Roost, Sate, Satisfaction, Seal, Seat, Secure, Sedimentary, Set fair, Shagroon, Shtetl, Silt, Smoot, Snuggle, Sofa, Soldier, Solve, Soweto, Square, Square up, State, Still, Straits, Subside, Taurus, Township, Ujamaa, Undertaker, Utu, Vest(ed), Viatical, Voortrekker, Wrap up

▷ **Settlement** *may indicate* an anagram

▷ **Settler** *may indicate* a coin

Set upon Assail, Attack, Sick

Seven(th), Seven-sided Ages, Days, Dials, Great Bear, Hebdomad, Hepta-, Hills, Magnificent, Nones, Pleiad(es), S, Sages, Seas, Septenary, Septilateral, Septimal, Sins, Sisters, Sleepers, Stars, Wonders, Zeta

Seventy S

Seven-week Omer

Sever Amputate, Cut, Detach, Divide, Sunder

Several Divers, Many, Multiple, Plural, Some, Sundry, Various

Severe(ly), Severity Acute, Astringent, Austere, Bad, Caustic, Chronic, Cruel, Dour, Draconian, Drastic, Eager, Extreme, Grave, Grievous, Gruel(ling), Hard, → **HARSH**, Ill, Inclement, Morose, Penal, Rhadamanthine, Rigo(u)r, Roaming, Roundly, Ruthless, Serious, Sharp, Snell(y), Sore, Spartan, Stark, Stern, Strict, Swingeing

Sew(ing), Sew up Baste, Clinch, Cope, Darn, Embroider, Fell, Fine-draw, Machine, Mitre, Overcast, Overlock, Run up, Seam, Seel, Stitch, Tack, Whip

Sewage, Sewer Cesspool, Cloaca, Culvert, Dorcas, → **DRAIN**, Effluence, Jaw-box, Jaw-hole, Mimi, Needle, Privy, Seamster, Shore, Soil, Sough, Soughing-tile, Sure, Waste

Sex(ist), Sexual, Sexy Bed-hopping, Carnal, Congress, Cottaging, Coupling, Cunnilingus, Cybersex, Erotic, Fair, Favours, Fellatio, Female, Foreplay, Fornication,

French, Gam(ic), Gamahuche, Gamaruche, Gender, Greek love, Hanky-panky, Hump, Incest, Intercourse, Intimacy, Jailbait, Kind, Knee-trembler, Libidinous, Libido, Lingam, Lumber, Male, Mate, Non-penetrative, Nookie, Oomph, Opposite, Oral, Outercourse, Paedophilia, Paraphilia, Pederasty, Phallocratic, Phat, Phone, Priapean, Prurient, Race, Randy, Raunchy, Rough trade, Rut(ish), Safe, Salacious, Screw, Sect, Six, Slinky, SM, Steamy, Sultry, Tantric, Teledildonics, Troilism, Unprotected, Unsafe, Venereal, Venery, VI, Voluptuous, Weaker

Sex appeal It, Oomph, SA

Sexcentenarian Shem

Sexless Agamogenetic, Atoke, N, Neuter, Platonic

Sextet Over, Six

Sexton Blake, Fossor, Patch, Sacristan, Shammes, Warden

Seychelles SY

Sh P, Quiet

Shabby Base, Buckeen, Dog-eared, Down-at-heel, Fleapit, Fusc(ous), Grotty, Grungy, Low-lived, Mangy, Mean, Moth-eaten, Old hat, Oobit, Oorie, Oubit, Ourie, Outworn, Owrie, Raunch, Scaly, Scarecrow, Scruffy, Seedy, Shoddy, Squalid, Tacky, Tatty, Tawdry, Threadbare, Unkempt, Worn, Woubit

Shack Fibro, Heap, Hideout, Hovel, Hut, Sheal

Shackle(s) Bilboes, Bind, Bracelet, Chain, Darbies, Entrammel, Fetter(lock), Gyve, Hamper, Irons, Manacle, Restrict, Tie, Trammel, Yoke

Shad Allice, Allis, Fish, Twait(e)

Shaddock Grapefruit, Pomelo

Shade(d), Shades, Shading, Shadow, Shady Adumbrate, Arbour, Arcade, Awning, Blend, Blind, Bongrace, Bowery, Brise-soleil, Brocken spectre, Buff, Cast, Chiaroscuro, Chroma, Cloche, Cloud, Cross-hatch, Degree, Demirep, Dis, Dog, Dubious, Eclipse, Eye, Five o'clock, Galanty, Gamp, Ghost, Gnomon, Gradate, Gray, Hachure, Hatch, Hell, Herbar, Hint, Hue, Inumbrate, Larva, Lee, Magnolia, Melt, Mezzotint, Modena, Nuance, Opaque, Overtone, Parasol, Pastel, Phantom, Presence, Rain, Ray-Bans®, Satellite, Screen, Shroud, Sienna, Silhouette, Silvan, Skia-, Soften, Sound, Spectre, Spirit, Stag, Sunglasses, Swale, Swaly, Tail, Tenebrious, Tinge, Tint, Titian, Tone, Track, Trail, Ugly, Umbra(tile), Umbrage(ous), Underhand, Velamen, Velar(ium), Velum, Visitant, Visor

Shadowless Ascian

Shaft(ed), Shafting Arbor, Arrow, Axle tree, Barb, Barrow-train, Beam, Befool, Capstan, Cardan, Chimney, Collet, Column, Crank, Cue, Diaphysis, Disselboom, Dolly, Downcast, Drive, Escape, Fil(l), Fust, Gleam, Idler, Incline, Journal, Lamphole, Lay, Limber, Loom, Mandrel, Mandril, Manhole, Moon pool, Moulin, Parthian, Passage, Pile, Pit, Pitbrow, Pitch, Pole, Propeller, Quill (drive), Ray, Rib, Rise, Scape, Scapus, Shank, Snead, Spindle, Staff, Stairwell, Stale, Steal(e), Steel, Steen, Stele, Stem, Stulm, Sunbeam, Telescopic, Thill, Tige, Tomo, Trave, Truncheon, Upcast, Well, Winning, Winze

Shag Cronet, Hair, Intercourse, Nap, Pile, Scart(h), Skart(h), Tire, Tobacco

Shaggy Ainu, Beetle-browed, Bushy, Comate, Hairy, Hearie, Hirsute, Horrid, Horror, Maned, Nappy, Rough, Rugged, Shock, Shough, Tatty, Tousy, Touzy, Towsy, Towzy, Untidy

Shah Abbas, Pahlavi, Ruler, Sophi, Sophy

Shake(n), Shake off, Shakes, Shaky Agitate, Ague(-fit), Astonish, Bebung, Brandish, Coggle, Concuss, Dabble, Dick(e)y, Didder, Diddle, Disconcert, Dither, Dodder, → **DT'S**, Feeble, Groggy, Hod, Hotch, Ictal, Jar, Jiggle, Joggle, Jolt, Jounce, Judder, Jumble, Lose, Milk, Mo, Nid-nod, Press flesh, Quake, Quiver, Quooke, Rattle, Rickety, Rickle, → **ROCK**, Rouse, Shimmer, Shiver, Shock, Shog, Shoogle, Shudder, Succuss(ation), Sweat, Swish, Tremble, Tremolo, Tremor, Tremulous, Trill(o), Tumbledown, Undulate, Unsteady, Vibrate, Vibrato, Wag, Waggle, Wind, Wobble, Wonky

▷ **Shake** *may indicate* an anagram

Shakedown Blackmail, Chantage, Pallet

Shakespeare Bard, Will, WS
Shale Blaes, Fa(i)kes, Kerogen, Kupferschiefer, Oil, Rock, Till, Torbanite
Shall Sal
Shallot C(h)ibol, Onion, Scallion, Sybo(e), Sybow
Shallow(s) Ebb, Flat, Fleet, Flew, Flue, Justice, Neritic, Rattlebrain, Riffle, Sandbank, Sandbar, Shoal, Slight, Superficial
Sham Apocryphal, Bluff, Bogus, Braide, Charade, Counterfeit, Deceit, Fake, → **FALSE**, Hoax, Idol, Impostor, Mimic, Mock, Phony, Pinchbeck, Postiche, Potemkin, Pretence, Pseudo, Repro, Simulated, Snide, Spurious, Straw man
Shaman Angek(k)ok, Sorcerer
Shamble(s) Abattoir, Bauchle, Butchery, Mess, Scamble, Shuffle, Totter, Tripple
Shame(ful), Shame-faced Abash, Aidos, Atimy, Chagrin, Confusion, Contempt, Crying, Degrade, Discredit, Disgrace, Dishonour, Disrepute, Embarrass, Fi donc, Fie, Gross, Hangdog, Honi, Humiliate, Ignominy, Infamy, Inglorious, Modesty, Mortify, Ohone, Pity, Pudency, Pudor, Pugh, Sad, Shend, Sin, Slander, Stain, Stigma, Yshend
Shameless Audacious, Barefaced, Brash, Brazen, Flagrant, Immodest, Ithyphallic, Jezebel
Shampoo(ing) Massage, Tripsis, Wash
Shandy Drink, Sterne, Tristram
Shanghai Abduct, Kidnap, Trick
Shank Leg, Shaft, Steal(e), Steel, Steil, Stele, Strike
Shanty, Shanty town Bidonville, Boatsong, Bothy, Bustee, Cabin, Chant, Dog-hole, Favela, Forebitter, Hutment, Lean-to, Pondok, Sea, Shack, Shypoo, Song
Shape(d), Shapely, Shaping Blancmange, Boast, Bruting, Cast, Contour, Cuneiform, Die-cast, Face, Fashion, Figure, Form, Format, Fractal, Geoid, Geometrical, Gnomon, Headquarters, Hew, Holohedron, Jello, Model, Morph, Morphology, → **MOULD**, Net, Pendentive, Polyomine, Ream, Rhomb(us), Roughcast, Scabble, Sculpt, Spile, Step-cut, Tromino, Turn, Voluptuous, Whittle, Wrought, Zaftig, Zoftig
Shapeless Amorphous, Chaos, Dumpy, Indigest, Vague
Shard Fragment, Sliver, Splinter
Share(d), Shares, Sharing Allocation, Allotment, Angels' cost, Apportion, Blue-chip, Bovate, Cahoots, Chop, Co, Cohabit, Coho(e), Common, Communal, Contango, Co-portion, Co-tenant, Culter, Cut, Deferred, Divi(dend), Divide, Divvy, Dole, Dutch, Equity, Finger, Flatmate, Founders, Golden, Grubstake, Impart, Interest, Job, Kaffer, Kaf(f)ir, Kangaroo, Law, Lion's, Market, Moiety, Mutual, Odd lot, OFEX, Ordinary, Oxgang, Oxgate, Oxland, Parcener, → **PART**, Partake, Participate, Penny, PIBS, Plough, Plough-iron, Portfolio, Portion, Prebend, Pref(erred), Preference, Pro rata, Prorate, Quarter, Quota, Rake off, Ration, Rug, Rundale, Scrip, Security, Shr, Slice, Snack, Snap, Sock, Split, Stock, Taurus, Teene, Time, Tranche, Two-way, Whack
Shareholder Plough, Stag
Shark Angel, Basking, Beagle, Blue, Bluepointer, Bonnethead, Bronze-whaler, Bull, Carpet, Cestracion, Cow, Demoiselle, Dog(fish), Flake, Fox, Great white, Gummy, Hammerhead, Houndfish, Huss, Lemonfish, Leopard catshark, Loan, Mackerel, Mako, Miller's dog, Monkfish, Noah, Nurse, Penny-dog, Plagiostomi, Porbeagle, Requiem, Reremai, Rhin(e)odon, Rigg, Rook, Sail-fish, Sand, Saw, School, Sea-ape, Sea-fox, Sea-lawyer, Sevengill, Sharp, Shortfin mako, Shovelhead, Smoothhound, Soupfin, Spotted ragged-tooth, Squaloid, Swindler, Thrasher, Thresher, Tiger, Tope, Usurer, Whale, Whaler, Wobbegong, Zygaena
Sharkskin Shagreen
Sharp(er), Sharpen(er), Sharpness Abrupt, Accidental, Acerose, Acidulous, Acrid, Aculeus, Acumen, Acuminate, Acute, Alert, Angular, Arris, Astringent, Bateless, Becky, Benchstone, Bitter, Brisk, Cacuminous, Cheat, Clear, Coticular, Cutting, Dital, Edge(r), Fine, Fly, Gleg, Grind, Hone, Hot, Keen, Kurtosis, Massé, Mordant, Oilstone, Penetrant, Peracute, Piquant, Poignant, Pronto, Pungent, Quick-witted, Razor, Rogue, Rook,

Saw doctor, Set, Shrewd, Snap, Snell, Sour, Spicate, Strop, Swindler, Tart, Testy, Tomium, Twenty-twenty, Varment, Vivid, Volable, Vorpal, Whet

Sharpshooter Bersaglier, Franc-tireur, Sniper, Tirailleur, Voltigeur

Sharp-sighted Lynx-eyed

Shatter(ing) Astone, Astound, Break, Brisance, Bust, Craze, Dash, Explode, Shiver, Smash, Smithereen, Splinter, Unnerve

Shave(r), Shaving(s) Barb(er), Depilation, Electric, Excelsior, Filings, Flake, Grain, Moslings, Pare, Plane, Pogonotomy, Poll, Raze, Scrape, Skive, Sliver, Splinter, Swarf, Todd, Tonsure, Turnings, Whittle

Shaw Artie, Green, Spinn(e)y, Wood

Shawl Afghan, Buibui, Cashmere, Chuddah, Chuddar, Dopatta, Dupatta, Fichu, India, Kaffiyeh, Kashmir, Manta, Mantilla, Maud, Paisley, Partlet, Pashmina, Prayer, Serape, Sha(h)toosh, Stole, Tallis, Tallit(ot), Tallith, Tonnag, Tozie, Tribon, Whittle, Wrap(per), Zephyr

She A, Hoo

Sheaf, Sheave Aplustre, Bee, Bundle, Clevis, Dorlach, Folder, Gait, Garb(e), Gerbe, Mow, Shock, Thr(e)ave

Shear(er), Shearing, Shears Clip, Cut, Fleece, Greasy, Jaws of life, Mulesing, Pinking, Poll, Pruning, Ring(er), Shave, Snips, Tinsnips, Trim, Wind

Sheath Axolemma, Capsule, Case, Cocoon, Coleoptile, Coleorhiza, Condom, Cover, Epineurium, Extine, Fingerstall, Glume, Medullary, Myelin, Neurilemma, Neurolemma, Node of Ranvier, Oc(h)rea, Perineurium, Periosteum, Quiver, Rhinotheca, Root, Scabbard, Spathe, Thecal, Thumbstall, Urceolus, Vagina, Volva, Wing

Shed(ding), Shedder Autotomy, Barn, Byre, Cast, Cho(u)ltry, Coducity, Cootch, Cwtch, Depot, Discard, Doff, Downsize, Drop, Ecdysis, Effuse, Emit, Exuviate, Hangar, Hovel, Hut, Infuse, Lair, Lean-to, Linhay, Linn(e)y, Mew, Milking, Moult, Outhouse, Pent, Potting, Salmon, Shearing, Shippen, Shippon, Shuck, Skeo, Skillion, Skio, Slough, Sow, Spend, Spent, Spill, Spit, Tilt, Tool

Sheen Glaze, Gloss, Luminance, Lustre, Patina, Schiller, Shine

Sheep(ish) Ammon, Ancon(es), Aoudad, Argali, Ashamed, Barbary, Bell(wether), Bharal, Bident, Bighorn, Black, Blackface, Blate, Border Leicester, Broadtail, Burhel, Burrel(l), Caracul, Charollais, Cheviots, Coopworth, Corriedale, Cotswold, Cotswold lion, Coy, Crone, Dall('s), Dinmont, Domestic, Dorset Down, Dorset Horn, Down, Drysdale, Embarrassed, Ewe, Exmoor, Fank, Fat-tailed, Flock, Fold, Hair, Hampshire, Hampshire Down, Hangdog, Herdwick, Hidder, Hirsel, Hog(g), Hogget, Jacob, Jemmy, Jumbuck, Karakul, Kent, Kerry Hill, Lamb, Lanigerous, Leicester, Lincoln, Lo(a)ghtan, Loghtyn, Long, Lonk, Marco Polo, Masham, Merino, Mor(t)ling, Mouf(f)lon, Mountain, Muflon, Mug, Mus(i)mon, Mutton, Oorial, Ovine, Oxford Down, Perendale, Portland, Ram, Rambouillet, Romeldale, Romney Marsh, Rosella, Ryeland, Scottish Blackface, Shearling, Shetland, Shidder, Short, Shorthorn, → **SHY**, Soay, Southdown, Spanish, Stone('s), Suffolk, Sumph, Swaledale, Teeswater, Teg(g), Texel, Theave, Trip, Tup, Twinter, Two-tooth, Udad, Urial, Vegetable, Welsh Mountain, Wensleydale, Wether, Wiltshire Horn, Woollyback, Yow(e), Yowie

Sheep disease, Sheep problem Black, Blue tongue, Braxy, Dunt, Gid, Hoove, Louping-ill, Orf, Ringwomb, Rubbers, Scabby mouth, Scrapie, Staggers, Sturdy, Swayback, Variola, Water-brain, Wildfire, Wind

Sheepdog Collie, Huntaway, Maremma, Polish Lowland, Puli

Sheepfold Fank, Pen

Sheepskin Basan, Caracul, Karakul, Mouton, Parchment, Roan, Wool

Sheeptrack Terracette

Sheer Absolute, Clear, Main, Mere, Peekaboo, Plumb, Precipitous, Pure, Simple, Stark, Steep, Swerve, Thin, Utter

Sheet(ing), Sheets Balance, Cel, Cellophane, Cere-cloth, Cerement, Charge, Chart, Clean, Crime, Cutch, Dope, Expanse, Film, Flow, Fly, Folio, Foolscap, Heft, Ice, Inset,

Intrusive, Lasagne, Leaf, Membrane, Nappe, Out-hauler, Page, Pane, Pot(t), Pour, Proof, Prospectus, Rap, Ream, Rope, Sail, Scandal, Scratch, Shroud, Stern, Stratus, Taggers, Tarpaulin(g), Tear, Tentorium, Terne, Thunder, Time, Title, Web, White, Winding

Sheet-anchor Letter-weight, Paperweight

Sheet-iron Taggers, Terne(plate)

Sheik(dom) Abu Dhabi, Bahrein, Dubai

Shekel Mina, Sickle

Sheldrake Bergander

Shelf, Shelve(d), Shelves Bank, Bar, Bracket, Continental, Counter, Credence, Delay, Dresser, Étagère, Gondola, Grand Banks, Hob, Ice, Ledge, Leeboard, Mantelpiece, Mantle, On ice, Overmantel, Parcel, Postpone, Rack, Retable, Rick, Ross Ice, Shunt, Sidetrack, Sill, Spinsterhood, Whatnot, Windowsill

Shell(ed), Shellfish, Shellwork Abalone, Acorn-shell, Admiral, Ambulacrum, Ammo, Argonaut, Balamnite, Balanus, Balmain bug, Belemnite, Bivalve, Blitz, Boat, Bodywork, Bombard, Buckie, Camera, Capiz, Capsid, Carapace, Cartridge, Casing, Chank, Chelonia, Chitin, Clam, Cleidoic, Clio, Coat-of-mail, Cochlea, Cockle, Cohog, Conch, Cone, Copepoda, Cover, Cowrie, Cowry, Crab, Cracked, Crustacea, Cuttlebone, Dariole, Deerhorn, Dentalium, Dop, Drill, Electron, Escallop, Eugarie, Foraminifer, Framework, Frustule, Gas, Geoduck, Globigerina, Haliotis, Hull, Husk, Hyoplastron, Isopoda, Kernel, Lamp, Langouste, Limacel, Limpet, Live, Lobster, Lorica, Lyre, Malacostraca, Midas's ear, Mitre, Mollusc, Money, Monocoque, Moon, Moreton Bay bug, Mother-of-pearl, Murex, Music, Mussel, Nacre, Nautilus, Olive, Ormer, Ostracod, Ostrea, Otter, Oyster, Paua, Pawa, Pea(s)cod, Peag, Peak, Pecten, Peel, Pereia, Periostracum, Periwinkle, Pilgrim's, Pipi, Pipsqueak, Plastron, Pod, Prawn, Projectile, Purple, Putamen, Quahaug, Quahog, Razor, Rocaille, Sal, Scalarium, Scallop, Scollop, Sea-ear, Sea-pen, Shale, Shard, Sheal, Sheel, Shiel, Shill, Shock, Shot, Shrapnel, Shrimp, Shuck, Sial, Smoke-ball, Spat, Spend, Spindle, Star, Stomatopod, Stonk, Straddle, Strafe, Stromb(us), Swan-mussel, Tear, Tellen, Tellin, Test(a), Thermidor, Toheroa, Tooth, Top, Torpedo, Tracer, Trivalve, Trough, Trumpet, Turbo, Turritella, Tusk, Univalve, Valency, Venus, Wakiki, Wampum, Whelk, Whiz(z)bang, Winkle, Xenophya, Yabbie, Yabby, Zimbi

▷ **Shelled** *may indicate* an anagram

Shell money Wakiki, Wampum, Zimbi

Shelter(ed) Abri, A l'abri, Anderson, Arbour, Asylum, Awn, Awning, Barn, Bay, Belee, Bender, Bield, Billet, Blind, Blockhouse, Booth, Bunker, Burladero, Butt, Cab, Carport, Casemate, Coop, Cot(e), Cove, Covert, Coverture, Defence, Dodger, Donga, Dovecote, Dripstone, Dug-out, Fall-out, Garage, Gunhouse, Gunyah, Harbour, Haven, Hithe, Hospice, Hostel, House, Hovel, Humpy, Hut, Hutchie, Igloo, Imbosom, Kipsie, Lee, Lee-gage, Loun, Lound, Lown, Lownd, Mai mai, Mission, Morrison, Nissen, Nodehouse, Palapa, Pilothouse, → **REFUGE**, Retreat, Roadstead, Roof, Sanctuary, Scog, Sconce, Scoog, Scoug, Screen, Scug, Secluded, Shed, Shiel(ing), Shroud, Skug, Snowhole, Snowshed, Stell, Storm-cellar, Succah, Sukkah, Summerhouse, Suntrap, Tax, Tent, Tepee, Testudo, Tortoise, Tupik, Twigloo, Umbrage, Weather, Wheelhouse, Wickyup, Wi(c)kiup, Wil(t)ja, Windbreak, Windscreen, Windshield

Shemozzle Debacle

Shenanigan Antic

Shepherd(ess) Abel, Acis, Amaryllis, Amos, Bergère, Bo-peep, Bucolic, Chloe, Clorin, Conduct, Corin, Corydon, Cuddy, Daphnis, Dorcas, Drover, Endymion, Escort, Ettrick, Feeder, Flock-master, German, Good, Grubbinol, Gyges, Herdsman, Hobbinol, Lindor, Marshal, Menalcas, Padre, Pastor(al), Pastorella, Phebe, Pilot, Sheepo, Strephon, Tar-box, Thenot, Thyrsis, Tityrus

Sherbet Beer, Soda

Sheriff Bailiff, Deputy, Earp, Grieve, Land-dros(t), Lawman, Process-server, Shireman, Shire-reeve, Shirra, Shrievalty, Viscount

Sherry Amoroso, Bristol milk, Cobbler, Cream, Cyprus, Doctor, Dry, Fino, Gladstone,

Jerez, Manzanilla, Oloroso, Palo cortado, Sack, Solera, Sweet, Whitewash, Xeres

Sherwood Anderson, Forest

Shiah Ismaili

Shibboleth Password

Shield(s), Shield-shaped Ablator, Achievement, Aegis, Ancile, Armour, Arms, Baltic, Biological, Bodyguard, Box, Brolly, Buckler, Canadian, Cartouche, Clypeus, Defend, Dress, Escutcheon, Fence, Gobo, Guard, Gumshield, Gyron, Hatchment, Heat, Hielaman, Human, Inescutcheon, Insulate, Laurentian, Lozenge, Mant(e)let, Mask, Pavis(e), Pelta, Plastron, Protect, Randolph, Ranfurly, Riot, Rondache, Scandinavian, Screen, Scute, Scutum, Sheffield, Splashboard, Sternite, Targe(t), Thyroid, Toecap, Vair, Visor, Water

Shift(er), Shifty Amove, Astatic, Back, Blue, Budge, Change, Chemise, Core, Cymar, Day, Devious, Displace, Dogwatch, Doppler, Dress, Dying, Einstein, Evasive, Expedient, Fend, Function, Graveyard, Great Vowel, Hedging, Lamb, Landslide, Lateral, Linen, Louche, Meve, Move, Night, Nighty, Paradigm, Red, Relay, Remove, Rota, Ruse, Scorch, Sell, Shirt, Shovel, Shunt, Simar(re), Slicker, Slip(pery), Sound, Spell, Split, Stagehand, Steal, Stick, Stint, Swing, Switch, Tergiversate, Tour, Transfer, Tunic, Turn, Turnabout, Vary, Veer, Warp

▷ **Shift(ing)** *may indicate* an anagram

Shilling Bob, Deaner, Falkiner, Hog, King's, Queen's, S, Teston

Shilly-shally Whittie-whattie

Shimmer(ing) Avanturine, Aventurine, Chatoyant, Glint, Glitter, Iridescence, Mona(u)l, Opalescence, Shine

▷ **Shimmering** *may indicate* an anagram

Shin Clamber, Climb, Cnemial, Leg, Shank, Skink, Swarm

Shindig, Shindy Bobbery, Row, Rumpus, Shivoo, Uproar

Shine(r), Shining, Shiny Aglitter, Aglow, Beam, Bright, Buff, Burnish, Deneb, Effulge, Excel, Flash, Gleam, Glimmer, Glisten, Glitzy, Gloss, → **GLOW**, Irradiant, Japan, → **LAMP**, Leam, Leme, Lucent, Luminous, Lustre, Mouse, Nitid, Nugget, Phoebe, Phosphoresce, Polish, Radiant, Radiator, Refulgent, Relucent, Resplend, Rutilant, Shimmer, Skyre, Sleek, Twinkle, Varnish

Shingle(s), Shingly Beach, Chesil, Cut, Dartre, Dartrous, Gravel, Herpes, Herpes Zoster, Herpetic, Loose metal, Shake, Shale, Stone, Zona, Zoster

Shinpad Greave

Shinty Caman, Camanachd

▷ **Shiny** *may indicate* a star

Ship(ping), Ships Boat, Container, Convoy, Cruiser, → **DISPATCH**, Embark, Export, Flagship, Flatboat, Flota, Her, Hulk, Jolly, Keel, Man, Marine, MV, Nautical, Post, Privateer, Prize, Prow, Raft, Ram, Sail, Saique, She, Smack, SS, Tall, Transport, Tub, Vessel, Victualling, Weather

SHIPS

1 letter:	Hoy	Dory	Prau
Q	Kit	Duck	Proa
	Red	Fire	Ro-ro
2 letters:		Flat	Saic
PT	*4 letters:*	Grab	Scow
	Argo	Isis	Snow
3 letters:	Bark	Koff	Tern
Ark	Brig	Long	Trow
Cat	Buss	Nina	Yare
Cog	Cock	Pink	Yawl
Dow	Cott	Pont	Zulu
Fly	Dhow	Pram	

Ships | 700

5 letters:
Aviso
Barge
Broke
Camel
Canoe
Cargo
Coble
Coper
Crare
Dandy
Dingy
Drake
Ferry
Funny
Ketch
Laker
Liner
Moses
Oiler
Pinky
Pinto
Plate
Praam
Prahu
Prore
Pucan
Q-boat
Razee
Rover
Sabot
Saick
Scoot
Screw
Scull
Shell
Skiff
Slave
Sloop
Tramp
Troop
U-boat
Umiak
Wager
Whiff
Xebec
Yacht
Zabra
Zebec

6 letters:
Argosy
Banker
Barque

Bateau
Bawley
Beagle
Bethel
Bireme
Borley
Bottom
Bounty
Caique
Carack
Carvel
Castle
Coaler
Cobble
Codder
Cooper
Crayer
Curagh
Cutter
Decker
Dingey
Dinghy
Dogger
Droger
Dromon
Drover
Dugout
Escort
Flying
Frigot
Galiot
Galley
Gay-you
Goldie
Hooker
Howker
Jigger
Launch
Lorcha
Lugger
Masula
Monkey
Mother
Nuggar
Packet
Pedalo
Pequod
Pinkie
Pirate
Pitpan
Pulwar
Puteli
Randan
Reefer

Sampan
Sandal
School
Schuit
Schuyt
Settee
Slaver
Tanker
Tartan
Tender
Tonner
Torpid
Trader
Trek-ox
Triton
Turret
Whaler
Wherry
Zebeck

7 letters:
Belfast
Bidarka
Bumboat
Capital
Caravel
Carrack
Carract
Carrect
Catboat
Clipper
Coaster
Collier
Consort
Coracle
Counter
Currach
Curragh
Dredger
Drifter
Drogher
Dromond
Factory
Felucca
Flattop
Flyboat
Frigate
Gabbard
Gabbart
Galleon
Galliot
Galloon
Geordie
Gondola

Gunboat
Jetfoil
Kontiki
Liberty
Lymphad
Masoola
Mistico
Monitor
Mudscow
Mystery
Oomiack
Patamar
Pelican
Pinnace
Piragua
Pirogue
Polacca
Polacre
Pontoon
Repulse
Revenge
Sculler
Shallop
Sharpie
Steamer
Stew-can
Tartane
Titanic
Trawler
Trireme
Tugboat
Vedette
Victory
Vidette

8 letters:
Acapulco
Bilander
Billyboy
Bylander
Cabotage
Corocore
Corocoro
Corvette
Dahabieh
Faldboat
Foldboat
Galleass
Galliass
Gallivat
Hospital
Hoveller
Indiaman
Ironclad

Longboat	Freighter	*10 letters:*	Side-wheeler
Longship	Frigatoon	Brigantine	Skidbladnir
Mackinaw	Hydrofoil	Fourmaster	Submersible
Mary Rose	Klondiker	Golden Hind	Supertanker
Masoolah	Klondyker	Hydroplane	Three-decker
Merchant	Lapstrake	Icebreaker	Three-master
Monohull	Lapstreak	Knockabout	Torpedo boat
Mosquito	Leviathan	Mine-hunter	
Pinafore	Lightship	Paddleboat	*12 letters:*
Sallyman	Lusitania	Quadrireme	Deepwaterman
Savannah	Mayflower	Sandsucker	East Indiaman
Schooner	Minelayer	Santa Maria	Fore-and-after
Shanghai	Monoxylon	Trekschuit	Great Eastern
Showboat	Multihull	Triaconter	Marie Celeste
Training	Outrigger	Windjammer	Stern-wheeler
	Peter-boat		Tangle-netter
9 letters:	Sallee-man	*11 letters:*	
Bucentaur	Shear-hulk	Barquentine	*13 letters:*
Catamaran	Sheer-hulk	Bellerophon	Paddle steamer
Cutty Sark	Steamboat	Berthon-boat	
Dahabeeah	Submarine	Cockleshell	*14 letters:*
Dahabiyah	Temeraire	Dreadnought	Flying Dutchman
Dahabiyeh	Vaporetto	Merchantman	Ocean greyhound
Discovery	Whale-back	Minesweeper	
Dromedary	Whaleboat	Penteconter	
First-rate		Quinquereme	

Shipmate Crew, Hearty, Sailor
Shipment Cargo
Shipping line P and O
Ship's biscuit Dandyfunk, Dunderfunk
Shipshape Apple-pie, Neat, Orderly, Tidy, Trim
Shipwreck Split
Shire Comitatus, County
Shirk(er) Bludge, Cuthbert, Dodge, Embusqué, Evade, Funk, Gold brick, Malinger, Mike, Pike, Poler, Scrimshank, Skive, Skrimshank, Slack, Soldier
Shirt Aloha, Black, Boiled, Brown, Bush, Calypso, Camese, Camise, Chemise, Choli, Cilice, Dasheki, Dashiki, Dick(e)y, Dress, Fiesta, Garibaldi, Grandad, Hair, Hawaiian, Hoodie, Jacky Howe, Kaftan, Kaross, K(h)urta, Muscle, Nessus, Non-iron, Parka, Partlet, Polo, Rash, Red, Rugby, Safari, Sark, Serk, Set, Shift, Smock, Sports, Stuffed, Subucula, Swan(n)dri®, Sweat, T
Shiva Destroyer
▷ **Shiver(ed)** *may indicate* an anagram
Shiver(ing), Shivers, Shivery Aguish, Atingle, Break, Brrr, Chitter, Crumble, Dash, Dither, Fragile, Frisson, Gooseflesh, Grew, Grue, Malaria, Matchwood, Nither, Oorie, Ourie, Owrie, Quake, Quiver, → **SHAKE**, Shatter, Shrug, Shudder, Smash, Smither, Smithereens, Splinter, Timbers, Tremble
Shoal Bar, Fish, Quantity, Reef, Run, Sand-bar, School, Shallows, Shelf, Tail
Shock(ed), Shocker, Shocking Acoustic, Aghast, Agitate, Amaze, Anaphylactic, Appal, Astone, Astony, Astound, Astun, Awful, Awhape, Bombshell, Brunt, Bunch, Consternate, Criminal, Culture, Defibrillate, Disgust, Dorlach, Dreadful, Drop, Dumbfound, Earthquake, ECT, Egregious, Electric, Electrocute, Epiphenomenon, EST, Eye-opener, Fleg, Floccus, Forelock, Gait, Galvanism, Gobsmack, Hair, Haycock, Haystack, Horrify, Horror, Impact, Infamous, Insulin, Isoseismic, Jar, Jolt, Knock cold, Live, Mane,

Mop, Numb, Obscene, Outrage, Poleaxe, Putrid, Recoil, Return, Revolt, Rick(er), Rigor, Scandal(ise), Seismic, Septic, Shaghaired, Shake, Sheaf, Shell, Shilling, Shog, Shook, Stagger, Start(le), Stitch, Stook, Stound, Stun, Surgical, Tangle, Thermal, Trauma, Turn

Shock-absorber Buffer, Oleo, Snubber

▷ **Shocked** *may indicate* an anagram

Shod Calced

Shoddy Cagmag, Catchpenny, Cheap, Cheapjack, Cheapo, Cloth, Cowboy, Drecky, Gimcrack, Imitation, Oorie, Ourie, Owrie, Poor, Rag-wool, Ropy, Schlock, → **SHABBY**, Slapdash, Slopwork, Tatty, Tawdry, Tinny

Shoe(s) Accessory, Arctic, Athletic, Ballet, Balmoral, Bauchle, Birkenstock, Blocked, Boat, Boot, Bootee, Brake, Brogan, Brogue, Brothel creepers, Buskin, Calceate, Calk(er), Calkin, Carpet slipper, Casuals, Caulker, Cawker, Charlier, Chaussures, Chopin(e), Clodhopper, Clog, Co-respondent, Court, Creeper, Dap, Deck, Espadrille, Flattie, Flip-flops, Galoche, Galosh, Gatty, Geta, Ghillie, Golosh, Gumboot, Gumshoe, Gym, High-low, High tops, Hot, Hush-puppies®, Jandal®, Jellies, Kletterschue, Kurdaitcha, Lace up, Launch(ing), Loafer, Mary-Janes®, Mocassin, Moccasin, Muil, Mule, Open-toe, Oxford, Oxonian, Panton, Patten, Peeptoe, Pennyloafer, Pile, Plate, Plimsole, Plimsoll, Poulaine, Pump, Rivlin, Rope-soled, Rubbers, Rullion, Runner, Sabaton, Sabot, Saddle, Safety, Sandal, Sandshoe, Sannie, Scarpetto, Shauchle, Skid, Skimmer, Slingback, Slip-on, Slipper, Slip-slop, Sneaker, Snow, Sock, Soft, Solleret, Spike, Stoga, Stogy, Suede, Tackies, Takkies, Tennis, Tie, Topboot, Track, Trainer, T-strap, Upper, Vamp(er), Veld-schoen, Veldskoen, Velskoen, Vibram®, Vibs, Wagon lock, Wedgie, Welt, Winkle-picker, Zori

Shoeless Barefoot, Discalced

Shoemaker Blacksmith, Clogger, Cobbler, Cordiner, Cordwainer, Cosier, Cozier, Crispi(a)n, Farrier, Gentle craft, Leprechaun, Sachs, Smith, Snob, Soutar, Souter, Sowter, Sutor

Shoe-string Cheap, Lace, Pittance

Shoe-toe Poulaine

Shoo Away, Begone, Hoosh, Off, Scat(ter), Voetsek

Shoot(er), Shooting Ack-ack, Airgun, Arrow, Bine, Bostryx, Braird, Breer, Bud, Bulbil, Camera, Catapult, Chit, Cion, Cyme, Dart(le), Delope, Discharge, Drib, Elance, Enate, Eradiate, Film, Fire, Flagellum, Germ, Germain(e), Germen, Germin(ate), Glorious twelfth, → **GUN**, Gunsel, Head-reach, Hurl, Imp, Jet, Lateral, Layer, Lens, Limb, Loose, Marksmanship, Offset, Osier, Photocall, Photograph, Pip, Plink, Pluff, Plug, Poot, Pop, Pot, Pout, Ramulus, Rapids, Ratoon, Riddle, Rod, Rough, Rove, Runner, Scion, Septembriser, Sien(t), Skeet, Snap, Snipe, Spire, Spirt, Spout, Spray, Sprout, Spurt, Spyre, Start, Stole, Stolon, Strafe, Sucker, Syen, Tellar, Teller, Tendril, Tendron, Tiller, Trap, Turion, Twelfth, Twig, Udo, Vimen, Wand, Weapon, Whiz(z), Wildfowler, Zap

Shop(per), Shopping, Shops Agency, Arcade, Assembly, Atelier, Automat, Bag, Betray, Body, Boutique, Bucket, Buy, Chain, Charity, Chippy, Chop, Closed, Coffee, Commissary, Cook, Co-op, Cop, Corner, Cut-price, Dairy, Delicatessen, Denounce, Dobbin, Dolly, Duddery, Duka, Duty-free, Emporium, Factory, Five and dime, Food court, Galleria, Gift, Grass, In bond, Inform, Junk, Luckenbooth, Machine, Mall, Mall crawl, Mall-rat, Market, Megastore, Mercat, Messages, Minimart, Muffler, Office, Officinal, Off-licence, Off-sales, Op(portunity), Open, Outlet, Parlour, Patisserie, Personal, Pharmacy, Precinct, Print, PX, Rat on, Report, Retail, RMA, Salon, Sex, Shambles, Share, Shebang, Spaza, Squat, → **STORE**, Strip mall, Studio, Sundry, Superette, Supermarket, Superstore, Swap, Talking, Tally, Tea (room), Thrift, Tick, Tommy, Trade, Truck, Tuck, Union, Vintry, Warehouse, Whistle-blow, Works

Shopkeeper British, Butcher, Chemist, Clothier, Gombeen-man, Greengrocer, Grocer, Haberdasher, Hosier, Ironmonger, Merchant, Newsagent, Provisioner, Retailer, Stationer, Tradesman

Shoplift(er) Boost, Heist

Shore Bank, Beach, Buttress, Coast, Coastline, Coste, Eustatic, Foreside, Landfall, Lee,

Littoral, Machair, Offing, Prop, Rance, Rivage, Saxon, Seaboard, Strand, Strandline, Support

Short(en), Shortly Abbreviate, Abridge, Abrupt, Anon, Apocope, Brief, Brusque, Close-in, Commons, Compendious, Concise, Contract, Crisp, Cross, Curt, Curtail, Curtal, Cutty, Digest, Diminish, Drink, Eftsoons, Epitomise, Ere-long, Flying, Fubsy, Fuse, Impolite, Inadequate, In a while, Lacking, Laconical, Light, Limited, Low, Mini, Near, Nip, Nutshell, Offing, Pithy, Pudsey, Punch, Pyknic, Reduce, Reef, Retrench, Scantle, Scanty, Scarce, Shrift, Shy, Soon, Sparse, Spirit, Squab, Squat(ty), Staccato, Stint, Stocky, Strapped, Stubby, Succinct, Syncopate, Systole, Taciturn, Teen(s)y, Telescope, Temporal, Temporaneous, Terse, Tight, Tot, Towards, Transient, Wee

Shortage Brevity, Dearth, Deficiency, Deficit, Drought, Famine, Lack, Need, Paucity, Scarcity, Sparsity, Ullage, Wantage

Short circuit Varistor

Shortcoming Sin, Weakness

Shortfall Deficit

Shorthand Diphone, Gregg, Outline, Phonographic, Phraseogram, Pitman, Speedwriting®, Stenography, Stenotypy, Tachygraphy, Tironian, Tironian notes, Triphone, Weblish

Short-headed Brachycephal

Short-lived, Short-term Day to day, Ephemeral, Fragile, Meson, Transitory

Shorts Bermuda, Board, Boxer, Briefs, Culottes, Cycling, Hot pants, Kaccha, Lederhosen, Plus-fours, Skort, Stubbies®, Trunks

Short-sight Myopia, Myosis

Short-winded Breathless, Concise, Puffed, Purfled, Pursy, Succinct

Shot(s) Aim, All-in, Ammo, Approach, Attempt, Backhand, Ball, Bank, Barrage, Bisque, Blank, Blast, Bricole, Bull, Bullet, Burl, Canna, Cannonball, Cartridge, Case, Chain, Chatoyant, Chip, Close up, Corner, Cover, Crab, Crack, Daisy cutter, Dink, Dolly, Dram, Draw, Drop, Duckhook, Dum dum, Dunk, Elt, Essay, Exhausted, Explosion, Flew, Forehand, Fusillade, Gesse, Get, Glance, Go, Grape, Guess, Gun-stone, Hazard, Hook, In-off, Iridescent, Jump, Kill, Langrage, Langrel, Langridge, Lay-up, Longjenny, Magpie, Marksman, Maroon, Massé, Matte, Mitraille, Money, Moon-ball, Mulligan, Multi-coloured, Musket, Noddy, Pack, Parthian, Parting, Passing, Pelican, Pellet, Penalty, Photo, Pitch, Plant, Pluff, Pop, Pot, Puff, Push, Rake, Rid, Round, Safety, Salvo, Scratch, Shy, Sighter, Silk, Six, Slam-dunk, Slap, Slice, Slug, Slung, Snap, Snifter, Sped, Spell, Spent, Square cut, Stab, Still, Streaked, Tap in, Tee, Throw, Toepoke, Tonic, Tot, Tracking, Trial, Try, Turn, Volley, Warning, Wrist, Yahoo

Should Ought

Shoulder(-blade) Carry, Cold, Crossette, Epaule, Frozen, Hard, Hump, Joggle, Omohyoid, Omoplate, Pick-a-back, Roadside, Scapula, Shouther, Soft, Spald, Spall, Spaul(d), Speal, Spule, Tote, Withers

Shout(er), Shouting Alley-oop, Barrack, Bawl, Bellock, Bellow, Boanerges, Call, Claim, Clamour, Conclamation, Cry, Din, Exclaim, Geronimo, Heckle, Hey, Hoi(cks), Holla, Holla-ho(a), Holler, Hollo, Holloa, Hooch, Hosanna, Howzat, Hue, Oi, Oy, Parnell, Rah, Rant, Roar, Root, Round, Sa sa, Treat, Trumpet, Vociferate, Whoop, Yammer, Yell(och), Yippee, Yodel, Yoohoo, Yorp

Shove Barge, Birr, Elbow, Jostle, Push, Ram, Spoon, Thrust

Shovel Backhoe, Dustpan, Hat, Loy, Main, Peel, Power, Scoop, Shool, Spade, Steam, Trowel, Van

Show(ing), Shown, Showy Anonyma, Appearance, Aquacade, Bad, Bench, Betray, Branky, Broadcast, Brummagem, Burlesque, Cabaret, Cattle, Chat, Circus, Come, Con, Cruft's, Demo(nstrate), Depict, Describe, Dime museum, Diorama, Display, Do, Dramedy, Dressy, Dumb, Effeir, Effere, Endeictic, Entertainment, Epideictic, Establish, Evince, → **EXHIBIT**, Expo, Express, Extravaganza, Exude, Facade, Fair, Fangled, Farce, Flamboyant, Flash, Flaunt, Floor, Folies Bergere, Galanty, Game, Garish, Gaudy, Gay, Gig, Give, Glitter, Glitz(y), Gloss, Good, Horse, Indicate, Jazzy, Kismet, Light, Loud,

Manifest, Matinée, Meretricious, Minstrel, Moon, Musical, Naumachy, One-man, Ostensible, Ostentatious, Pageant, Panel game, Pantomime, Parade, Patience, Peacock, Performance, Phen(o), Phone-in, Point, Pomp, Portray, Presentation, Pretence, Pride, Procession, Prog(ramme), Project, Prominence, Prove, Pseudery, Puff, Puppet, Quiz, Raree, Razzmatazz, Reality, Register, Represent, Reveal, Revue, Road, Rodeo, Roll-out, Ruddigore, Rushes, Screen, Shaw, Sight, Singspiel, Sitcom, Slang, Soap, Son et lumière, Specious, Spectacle, Splash, Splay, Stage, Stunt, Talk, Tamasha, Tattoo, Tawdry, Telecast, Telethon, Theatrical, Three-man, Tinhorn, Tinsel(ly), Tulip, Unbare, Uncover, Usher, Vain, Variety, Vaudeville, Veneer, Viewy, Wear, Wild west, Zarzuela

Showdown Confrontation, Crunch

Shower Douche, Exhibitor, Flurry, Hail, Indicant, Indicator, Kitchen tea, Lavish, Lot, Meteor, Party, Pelt, Pepper, Precipitation, Rain, Scat, Scouther, Scowther, Scud, Skatt, Skit, Snow, Spat, Spet, Spit, Splatter, Spray, Sprinkle, Ticker tape, Volley

▷ **Showers** *may indicate* an anagram

Showgirl Evita, Nanette

▷ **Showing, Shown in** *may indicate* a hidden word

Showman Bailey, Barnum, Buffalo Bill, Entertainer, Goon, Impresario, Lord Mayor, MC, Ringmaster, Todd

Show-off Coxcomb, Exhibitionist, Extrovert, Flash Harry, Jack the lad, Peacock, Piss artist, Poseur, Sport, Swagger, Swank, Tulip, Wiseacre

Showpiece Flagship

Show-place Exhibition, Olympia, Pavilion, Theatre

Shrapnel Fragment, Shell, Splinter

Shred Clout, Filament, Grate, Julienne, Mammock, Mince, Mummock, Rag, Screed, Swarf, Tag, Tatter, Ta(i)ver, Tear up, Thread, To-tear, Wisp

Shrew Bangsring, Banxring, Callet, Catamaran, Elephant, Fury, Hellcat, Kate, Marabunta, Musk, Nag, Otter, Pygmy, Show, Solenodon, Sondeli, Sorex, Spitfire, Squirrel, Tana, Termagant, Tree, Trull, Tupaia, Virago, Vixen, Water, Xant(h)ippe, Yankie, Yenta

Shrewd(ness) Acumen, Acute, Arch, Argute, Artful, Astucious, Astute, Callid, Canny, Clued-up, Cute, Far-sighted, File, Gnostic, Gumptious, Hard-nosed, Judicious, Knowing, Pawky, Politic, Prudent(ial), Sagacious, Sapient(al), Savvy, Sharp-sighted, Wide boy, Wily, Wise

Shriek Cry, Scream, Scrike, Shright, Shrike, Shrill, Shritch, Skirl, Yell

Shrift Attention, Penance, Short

Shrike Bird, Boubou, Butcher-bird

Shrill Argute, High, Keen, Piping, Reedy, Scraich, Screech, Sharp, Skirl, Squeaky, Treble

Shrimp(s) Brine, Crevette, Fairy, Freshwater, Krill, Mantis, Midge, Opossum, Potted, Prawn, Runt, Sand, Skeleton, Small, Spectre, Squill(a), Stomatopod, Tiger

Shrine Adytum, Altar, Dagaba, Dagoba, Dargah, Delphi, Fatima, Feretory, Harem, Holy, Joss house, Kaaba, Lourdes, Marabout, Martyry, Memorial, Naos, Pagoda, Pilgrimage, Reliquary, Scrine, Scryne, Stupa, Tabernacle, Temple, Tope, Vimana, Walsingham

Shrink(age), Shrink from, Shrinking, Shrunk Abhor, Alienist, Analyst, Blanch, Blench, Boggle, Cling, Compress, Constringe, Contract, Cour, Cower, Creep, Crine, Cringe, Dare, Decrew, Depreciate, Dread, Dwindle, Flinch, Funk, Gizzen, Less, Nirl, → **PSYCHIATRIST**, Pycnosis, Quail, Recoil, Reduce, Retract, Sanforised, Shrivel, Shrug, Shy, Sphacelate, Timid, Violet, Wane, Waste, Wince, Wizened

Shrivel(led) Cling, Crine, Desiccate, Dry, Gizzen, Nirl, Parch, Scorch, Scrump, Sear, Shrink, Skrimp, Skrump, Tabid, Welk, Wither, Wizened, Writhled

Shropshire Salop

Shroud(s) Cerecloth, Chadri, Chuddah, Chuddar, Cloak, Cloud, Conceal, Cover, Futtock, Grave-cloth, Pall, Rigging, Screen, Sheet, Sindon, Turin, Veil, Winding-sheet, Wrap

Shrove Tuesday Fastens, J'ouvert, Pancake

Shrub(bery) Arboret, Brush, → **BUSH**, Dead-finish, Horizontal, Petty whin, Plant, Undergrowth, Wintergreen

SHRUBS

3 letters:
Kat
Qat
Rue

4 letters:
Acer
Coca
Cola
Dita
Grex
Hebe
Kava
Nabk
Olea
Rhus
Ruta
Sunn
Titi
Tutu
Ulex

5 letters:
Aalii
Bosky
Brere
Buaze
Buazi
Buchu
Caper
Gorse
Hakea
Hazel
Henna
Holly
Ledum
Maqui
Monte
Mulga
Nebek
Peony
Pyxie
Ramee
Ramie
Salal
Savin
Senna
Sumac
Thyme
Toyon
Wahoo
Yapon

Yupon
Zamia

6 letters:
Acacia
Alhagi
Ambach
Aucuba
Azalea
Bauera
Cobaea
Correa
Croton
Crowea
Daphne
Fatsia
Feijoa
Frutex
Fustet
Fynbos
Garrya
Jojoba
Kalmia
Laurel
Lignum
Manoao
Manuka
Maquis
Matico
Mimosa
Myrica
Myrtle
Nebbuk
Nebeck
Neinei
Paeony
Pituri
Privet
Protea
Prunus
Savine
Smilax
Sorbus
Storax
Sumach
Tutsan
Wandoo
Yaupon

7 letters:
Acerola
Akiharo

Ambatch
Arbutus
Bauhini
Boronia
Bullace
Cascara
Chamise
Chamiso
Cytisus
Deutzia
Dogwood
Emubush
Epacris
Ephedra
Filbert
Fuchsia
Guayule
Hop-tree
Jasmine
Juniper
Lantana
Mahonia
Mesquit
Muntrie
Oleacea
Olearia
Phlomis
Rhatany
Romneya
Rosebay
Savanna
Shallon
Skimmia
Syringa
Tea-tree
Waratah
Weigela

8 letters:
Abutilon
Allspice
Balisier
Barberry
Bayberry
Berberis
Bignonia
Bilberry
Bluebush
Buddleia
Camellia
Caragana
Coprosma

Cowberry
Danewort
Euonymus
Gardenia
Hardhack
Heketara
Hibiscus
Horopito
Inkberry
Japonica
Jetbread
Koromiko
Krameria
Lavender
Leadwort
Magnolia
Mairehau
Mezereon
Ninebark
Ocotillo
Oleander
Oleaster
Photinia
Rangiora
Rock rose
Rosemary
Saltbush
Savannah
Shadbush
Snowbush
Sorbaria
Spekboom
Sweetsop
Tamarisk
Viburnum
Waxplant

9 letters:
Andromeda
Bearberry
Buckthorn
Ceanothus
Clianthus
Cordyline
Coreopsis
Coyotillo
Croqberry
Eucryphia
Firethorn
Forsythia
Gelsemium
Grevillia

Hamamelis	**10 letters:**	Parkleaves	Postanthera
Hydrangea	Aphelandra	Pilocarpus	Sheep laurel
Jaborandi	Callicarpa	Poinsettia	Silverberry
Jessamine	Cascarilla	Potentilla	Staggerbush
Kumarahou	Coralberry	Pyracantha	Steeplebush
Manzanita	Crossandra	Schefflera	Stephanotis
Melaleuca	Embothrium	Supplejack	Wintersweet
Mistletoe	Eriostemon	Twinflower	Wortleberry
Patchouli	Escallonia		
Pernettya	Fatshedera	**11 letters:**	**12 letters:**
Perovskia	Frangipani	Beautybrush	Phanerophyte
Phillyria	Fringe tree	Bottlebrush	Philadelphus
Rauwolfia	Gaultheria	Carpenteria	Rhododendron
Screw bean	Goat's thorn	Chaenomeles	Serviceberry
Snowberry	Gooseberry	Cotoneaster	Southernwood
Spicebush	Greasewood	Farkleberry	Streptosolen
Sterculia	Holodiscus	Honeysuckle	Strophanthus
Tree peony	Joshua tree	Huckleberry	
Twinberry	Laurustine	Japan laurel	**13 letters:**
Widow wail	Marcgravia	Leatherwood	Wayfaring tree
Wolfberry	Mock orange	Mustard tree	Winter jasmine
	Mock privet	Pittosporum	

Shrug Discard, Toss

Shuck Peel

Shudder(ing) Abhor, Ashake, Frisson, Grew, Grise, Grue, Horror, Jerk, Quake, Shake, Spasm, Tremble, Tremor

Shuffle(d) Dodge, Drag, Hedge, Make, Mix, Palter, Permute, Randomise, Rearrange, Redeployment, Riffle, Scuff, Shamble, Shauchle, Soft-shoe, Stack

▷ **Shuffle(d)** *may indicate* an anagram

Shun Attention, Avoid, Eschew, Evade, Forbear, Ignore, Ostracise, Secede, → **SPURN**

Shunt Move, Shelve, Shuttle, Side-track

Shut(down; in; out; up), Shut(s) Bar, Cage, Close, Closet, Confined, Coop, Debar, Embar, Emure, Fasten, Fend, Impale, Impound, Latch, Lay-off, Lock, Occlude, Rid, Scram, Seal, Shet, Slam, Spar, Steek, Telescope, Tine, To

Shutter(s) Blind, B-setting, Damper, Dead-lights, Douser, Focal-plane, Jalousie, Louvre, Persiennes, Shade

Shuttle Alternate, Challenger, Commute, Drawer, Flute, Go-between, Navette, Orbiter, Shoot, Shunt, Space, Tat(t), Weave

Shy Bashful, Blate, Blench, Cast, Catapult, Chary, Coconut, Coy, Deficient, Demure, Farouche, Flinch, Funk, Heave, Introvert, Jerk, Jib, Laithfu', Leery, Lob, Mim, Mims(e)y, Modest, Mousy, Rear, Recoil, Reserved, Reticent, Retiring, Sheepish, Shrinking violet, Skeigh, Start, Thraw, Throw, Timid, Tongue-tied, Toss, Try, Verecund, Wallflower, Willyard, Willyart, Withdrawn

Shyster Ambulance chaser

Siamese, Siamese twins Chang, Eng, Parabiosis, Seal-point, T(h)ai

Siberia(n) Chukchi, Evenki, Ostiak, Ostyak, Samo(y)ed, Tungus, Vogul, Yakut, Yupik

Sibilant Hissing, Whistling

Sibling Brother, German, Kin, Sister

Sibyl Oracle, Prophetess, Seer, Seeress, Soothsayer, Voluspa, Witch

Sicilian Sicanian, Trinacrian

Sick(en), Sickening, Sickliness, Sickly, Sickness Aegrotat, Affection, Ague, Ail, Altitude, Anaemic, Bad, Bends, Bilious, Cat, Chalky, Chunder, Colic, Crapulence, Cringeworthy, Crook, Decompression, Delicate, Disorder, Donsie, Emetine, Gag,

Green, Hacked off, Hangover, Icky, Ill, Infection, Leisure, Maid-pale, Mal, Mawkish, Milk, Morbid, Morning, Motion, Mountain, Nauseous, Pale, Peaky, Peelie-wallie, Peely-wally, Pestilent, Pindling, Plague, Poorly, Puly, Puna, Queachy, Queasy, Queechy, Radiation, Regorge, Repulsive, Retch, Serum, Shilpit, Sleeping, Sleepy, Soroche, Space, Spue, Squeamish, Sweating, Travel, Twee, Uncle Dick, Valetudinarian, Virus, Vomit, Wamble-cropped, Wan

Sick bay San

Sickle(-shaped) Badging-hook, Baging-hook, Falcate, Falx, Grasshook, Hook, Scythe, Shear

Side, Sidepiece Abeam, Airs, Ally, B, Beam, Blind, Border, Branch, Camp, Cis-, Distaff, Division, Edge, Effect, Eleven, English, Epistle, Ex intraque parte, Facet, Flank, Flip, Gospel, Gunnel, Hand, Heavy, Hypotenuse, Iliac, Lateral, Lee(ward), Left, Long, Lore, Obverse, Off, On, OP, Pane, Part, Partisan, Party, Pleura, Port, Pretension, Profile, Prompt, Rave, Reveal, Reverse, Right, Rink, Short, Silver, Slip, Spear, Spindle, Starboard, Swank, → **TEAM**, Tight, Weak, West, Wind, Windward, Wing, XI

Sideboard(s) Beauf(f)et, Buffet, Cellaret, Commode, Credence, Credenza, Dinner-wagon, Dresser, Whiskers

Side-effect, Side-issue Fall-out, Logograph, Logogriph, Offshoot, Secondary, Spin-off

Sidekick Right-hand man, Satellite

Side-line Hobby, Lye, Siding, Spur

Sidepost Cheek

Side-step Crab, Dodge, Evade, Hedge, Maori, Volt

Side-track Distract, Divert, Shunt

Sidewalk Crab, Footpath, Pavement

Sideways Askance, End-on, Indirect, Laterally, Laterigrade, Oblique

Siding Alliance, Byway, Lie, Lye, Spur, Turnout

Sidle Edge, Passage

Siege (work), Siege engine Alamo, Antioch, Antwerp, Beleaguer, Beset, Blockade, Bog, Charleston, Gherao, Investment, Khartoum, Ladysmith, Leaguer, Mafeking, Masada, Metz, Obsidional, Perilous, Pleven, Plevna, Poliorcetic, Ravelin, Sarajevo, Surround, Verdun, Vicksburg, Warsaw, Warwolf

Sienese Tuscan

Sienna Burnt, Raw

Sierra Range, S

Sierra Leone Mende

Siesta Nap, Noonday, Nooning

Sieve, Sift(ing) Analyse, Bolt(er), Boult(er), Bunting, Colander, Coliform, Cribble, Cribrate, Cribrose, Cullender, Eratosthenes, Ethmoid, Filter, Molecular, Rice, Riddle, Screen, Searce, Search, Separate, Siler, Strain, Sye, Tamis, Tammy, Tems(e), Trommel, Try, Winnow

Sigh Exhale, Heave, Lackaday, Long, Moan, Sithe, Sough, Suspire, Welladay

Sight(ed) Aim, Barleycorn, Bead, Conspectuity, Eye(ful), Eyesore, Glimpse, Ken, Long, Oculated, Panoramic, Peep, Prospect, Range, Rear, Riflescope, Scene, Scotopia, Second, See, Short, Spectacle, Taish, Telescopic, Vane, → **VIEW**, Visie, Vision, Vista, Vizy, Vizzie

Sight-screen Eyelid

Sightsee(ing), Sightseer Do, Lionise, Observer, Rubberneck, Tourist, Tripper, Viewer

Sign(ing), Signpost, Signs Accidental, Ache, Addition, Air, Ale-pole, Ale-stake, Ampassy, Ampersand, Aquarius, Archer, Aries, Arrow, Auspice, Autograph, Badge, Balance, Beck, Beckon, Birth, Board, Brand, Bull, Bush, Call, Cancer, Capricorn, Caract, Caret, Character, Chevron, Clue, Coronis, Crab, Cross, Cue, Dactylology, Dele, Denote, Diacritic, Di(a)eresis, Diphone, Division, Dollar, DS, Earmark, Earth, Emblem, Endeixis, Endorse, Endoss, Enlist, Enrol(l), Evidence, Exit, Fascia, Fire, Fish, Gemini, Gesture, Goat, Grammalogue, Hallmark, Hamza(h), Harbinger, Harvey Smith, Hash, Hex, Hieroglyphic, Hint, Ideogram, Indian, Indicate, Indication, Indicium, Initial,

INRI, Inscribe, Ivy-bush, Leo, Lexigram, Libra, Local, Logogram, Milepost, Milestone, Minus, Motion, Mudra, Multiplication, Negative, Neume, Nod, Notice, Obelisk, Obelus, Omen, Peace, Phraseogram, Pisces, Plus, Positive, Pound, Presa, Presage, Prodrome, Prodromus, Radical, Ram, Ratify, Red lattice, Rest, Rune, Sacrament, Sagittarius, Sain, Scorpio, Segno, Semeion, Semiotics, Shingle, Show, Sigil, Sigla, Signal, Star, Subscribe, Subtraction, Superscribe, Symbol, Symptom, Syndrome, Tag, Taurus, Tic(k)tac(k), Tilde, Titulus, Token, Trace, Triphone, Twins, Umlaut, V, Vestige, Virgo, Vital, Warison, Warning, Water, Waymark, Word, Zodiac

Signal(ler) Alarm, Aldis lamp, Alert, Amber, Assemble, Baud, Beacon, Beckon, Bell, Bleep, Bugle, Busy, Buzz, Call, Chamade, Code, Compander, Compandor, Cone, Cue, Detonator, Diaphone, Distant, Distress, Duplex, Earcon, Emit, Flag, Flagman, Flare, Flash, Fog, Gantry, Gesticulate, Gong, Griffin, Gun, Harmonic, Heliograph, Heliostat, Herald, Heterodyne, High sign, Hooter, Horse and hattock, Icon, Important, Indicator, Interrupt, Interval, Knell, Luminance, Mark, Mase, Megafog, Message, Modem, Morse, Navar, NICAM, Notation, Noted, Output, Password, Peter, Pheromone, Pinger, Pip, Pollice verso, Prod, Pulsar, Radio, Renowned, Reveille, Robot, Salient, Semaphore, Semiology, Simplex, Singular, Smoke, Sonogram, SOS, Spoiler, Squawk, Taps, Target, Tattoo, Tchick, Telegraph, Teles(e)me, Thumb, Tic(k)-tac(k), Time, Token, Traffic, Transmit, Troop, Vehicle-actuated, Very, Video, V-sign, Waff, Waft, Wave, Wave-off, Wigwag, Word, Yeoman

Signature Alla breve, Allograph, Autograph, By-line, Digital, Hand, John Hancock, John Henry, Key, Mark, Onomastic, Per pro, Sheet, Specimen, Subscription, Thermal, Time

Signet Ring, Seal, Sigil, Sphragistics

Significance, Significant Cardinal, Consequence, Cosmic, Emblem, Ethos, Great, Impact, Important, Indicative, Key, Landmark, Magnitude, Major, Material, Matter, M(a)cGuffin, Meaningful, Milestone, Moment(ous), Notable, Noted, Noteworthy, Operative, Other, Paramount, Pith, Pregnant, Salient, Special, Telling

Signify Bemean, Denote, Imply, Indicate, Intimate, Matter, → **MEAN**, Represent

Sign language Ameslan, Finger spelling, Makaton, Semaphore, Tic(k)tac(k)

Sikh(ism) Granth, Kaccha, Kangha, Kara, Kesh, Khalsa, Kirpan, Mazhbi, Mechanised, Nanak, (Ranjit) Singh

Silage Haylage

Silas Uncle, Wegg

Silence(r), Silent Amyclaean, Choke-pear, Clam, Clamour, Conticent, Creepmouse, Dead air, Dumbstruck, Earplug, Gag, Hesychastic, Hist, Hush, Hushkit, Mim(budget), Muffler, Mum(p), Mumchance, Mute, Obmutescent, Omertà, Quench, Quiesce, → **QUIET**, Reticence, Shtoom, Shtum, Shush, Speechless, Squelch, Still, Sulky, Tace(t), Tacit(urn), Throttle, Tight-lipped, Tongue-tied, Unvoiced, Wheesh(t), Whis(h)t

Silhouette Contour, Outline, Planform, Profile, Shadow figure, Shadowgraph, Shape, Skyline

Silica(te) Albite, Analcite, Andalusite, Chabazite, Chert, Cristobalite, Datolite, Diopside, Dioptase, Fayalite, Float-stone, Gadolinite, Garnierite, Harmotome, Heulandite, Hiddenite, Humite, Iolite, Kieselguhr, Kyanite, Monticellite, Montmorillonite, Natrolite, Olivine, Opal, Pectolite, Penninite, Phillipsite, Pinite, Quartz, Rhodonite, Riebeckite, Saponite, Sard, Scapolite, Silex, Spodumene, Staurolite, Stishovite, Tridymite, Tripoli, Ultrabasic, Vermiculite, Vitreosil®, Vitreous, Zeolite

Silicon Chip, Moore's law, Si

Silk(y), Silk screen Alamode, Artificial, Atlas, Barathea, Blonde-lace, Brocade, Bur(r), Charmeuse®, Chenille, Chiffon, Cocoon, Corn, Crape, Crepe, Duchesse, Dupion, Faille, Fibroin, Filature, Filoselle, Florence, Florentine, Flosh, Floss, Flox, Foulard, Gazar, Gazzatum, Georgette, Gimp, Glossy, Grosgrain, Honan, KC, Kente, Kincob, Lustrine, Lustring, Lutestring, Madras, Makimono, Malines, Marabou(t), Matelasse, Mercery, Milanese, Moiré, Near, Ninon, Oiled, Organza, Ottoman, Paduasoy, Parachute, Peau de soie, Pongee, Prunella, Prunelle, Prunello, Pulu, QC, Raw, Samite, Sars(e)net,

Satin, Schappe, Seal(ch), Sendal, Seric, Sericeous, Sericite, Serigraph, Shalli, Shantung, Sien-tsan, Sleave, Sle(i)ded, Sleek, Slipper satin, Smooth, Soft, Spun, Surah, Tabaret, Tabby, Taffeta, Tasar, Thistledown, Thrown, Tiffany, Tram, Tulle, Tussah, Tusseh, Tusser, Tussore, Vegetable, Velvet, Wild

Silkworm (eggs), Silkworm disease Bombyx, Eria, Graine, Multivoltine, Muscardine, Sericulture, Tussore

Sill Ledge, Straining, Threshold, Whin

Silly, Silliness Absurd, Anserine, Apish, Brainless, Buffer, Childish, Crass, Cuckoo, Daffy, Daft, Dandy, Ditsy, Divvy, Dotish, Drippy, Dumb, Dunce, Fatuous, Fluffy, Folly, Fool, Foolery, Footling, Frivolous, Goopy, Goosey, Gormless, Hen-witted, Idiotic, Imbecile, Inane, Inept, Infield(er), Liminal, Mid-off, Mid-on, Mopoke, Prune, Puerile, Season, Simple, Soft(y), Spoony, → **STUPID**, Tomfoolery, Tripe, Wacky

▷ **Silly** *may indicate* relating to a sill

Silt Alluvium, Deposit, Dregs, Land, Lees, Loess, Residue, Sullage, Varve

Silver(skin) Ag, Albata, Alpac(c)a, Arg(ent), Argyria, British plate, Cardecue, Cat, Cerargyrite, Diana's tree, Electroplate, Free, Fulminating, German, Grey, Horn, Luna, Nickel, One-legged, Pa(c)kfong, Pakt(h)ong, Parcel-gilt, Pegleg, Piastre, Plate, Plateresque, Ruby, Stephanite, Sterling, Sycee, Thaler

▷ **Silver** *may indicate* a coin

Silversmith Demetrius, Lamerie, Plater

Simian Apelike, Catar(r)hine

Similar(ity) Akin, Analog(ue), Analogical, Corresponding, Equivalent, Etc, Homoeoneric, Homogeneous, Homoiousian, Homologous, Homonym, Isomorphism, Kindred, → **LIKE**, Likeness, Parallel, Patristic, Resemblance, Samey, Suchlike

Simile Epic, Homeric

Similitude Parable

Simmer Bubble, Poach, Seethe, Stew

Simon Bolivar, Cellarer, Magus, Peter, Pure, Simple

Simper Bridle, Giggle, Smirk

Simple(r), Simplicity, Simplify, Simply Aefa(u)ld, Afa(w)ld, Arcadian, Artless, Austere, Bald, Bare, Basic, Bog-standard, Breeze, Crude, Daw, Doddle, Doric, → **EASY**, Eath(e), Elegant, Elemental, ESN, Ethe, Facile, Fee, Folksy, Gomeral, Gotham, Green, Gullish, Herb(alist), Herborist, Homespun, Idyllic, Incomposite, Inornate, Jaap, Japie, Mere, Moner(on), Naive(té), Naked, Niaiserie, No brainer, Noddy, One-fold, Open and shut, Ordinary, Paraphrase, Pastoral, Peter, Plain, Pleon, Provincial, Pure, Reduce, Renormalise, Rustic, Saikless, Sapid, Semplice, Sheer, Silly, Simon, Spartan, Straight, Stupid, Suave, Tout court, Uncluttered, Understated, Unicellular, Unsophisticated, Woollen

Simpleton Abderite, Airhead, Cokes, Cuckoo, Daw, Duffer, Flat, Fool, Gaby, Galah, Gomeral, Gomeril, Greenhorn, Johnny, Juggins, Natural, Shot-clog, Spoon, → **STUPID PERSON**, Wiseacre, Zany

Simulate(d), Simulating Affect, Anti, Feign, Pretend, VR

Simultaneous Coincidental, Coinstantaneous, Contemporaneous, Synchronous, Together, Unison

Sin(ful) Aberrant, Accidie, Acedia, Actual, Anger, Avarice, Besetting, Bigamy, Capital, Cardinal, Covetousness, Crime, Deadly, Debt, Depravity, Envy, Err, Evil, Folly, Gluttony, Hamartiology, Harm, Hate, Impious, Impure, Lapse, Lust, Misdeed, Misdoing, Mortal, → **OFFENCE**, Original, Peccadillo, Piacular, Pride, Scape, Scarlet, Shirk, Sine, Sloth, Transgress, Trespass, Unrighteous, Venial, Vice, Wicked, Wrath, Wrong

Sinai Horeb, Mount

Since Ago, As, For, Meantime, Seeing, Sens, Sine, Sinsyne, Sith(en), Syne, Whereas, Ygo(e)

Sincere(ly), Sincerity Bona-fide, Candour, Earnest, Entire, Frank, Genuine, Heartfelt, Heartwhole, Honest, Open, Real(ly), Realtie, Simple-hearted, True, Verity, Whole-hearted

Sinclair Lewis, Upton

Sine Coversed, Versed

Sinecure Bludge, Commendam

Sinew(y) Fibre, Ligament, Nerve, String, Tendinous, Tendon

▶ **Sinful** *see* SIN(FUL)

Sing(ing) Antiphony, Barbershop, Bel canto, Belt out, Bhajan, Carol, Chant, Cheep, Chorus, Coloratura, Community, Cough, Croon, Crow, Diaphony, Diddle, Doo-wop, Glee club, Gorgia, Gregorian, Hum, Incant, Inform, Intone, Karaoke, Kirtan, La-la, Lilt, Lyricism, Melic, Parlando, Peach, Pen(n)illion, Pipe, Plainchant, Rand, Rant, Rap, Record, Render, Scat, Second(o), Serenade, Solmization, Sprechgesang, Sprechstimme, Squeal, Tell, Thrum, Trill, Troll, Vocalese, Warble, Woodshedding, Yodel

Singapore .sg

Singe Burn, Char, Scorch, Swale, Swayl, Sweal, Sweel

Singer(s) Alto, Baillie, Baker, Balladeer, Bard, Baritone, Bass, Beatle, Bing, → BIRD, Blondel, Bono, Brel, Buffo, Callas, Canary, Cantabank, Cantatrice, Cantor, Car, Carreras, Caruso, Castrato, Chaliapin, Chanteur, Chanteuse, Chantor, Chauntress, Chazan, Cher, Chorister, Coloratura, Comprimario, Countertenor, Crooner, Dawson, Diva, Dylan, Ella, Falsetto, Folk, Gigli, Glee club, Gleemaiden, Gleeman, Grass, Griot, Hammond, Haz(z)an, Heldentenor, Isaac, Kettle, Lark, Lauder, Lay clerk, Lead, Lind, Lorelei, Lulu, Mathis, Melba, Melodist, Mezzo, Minstrel, Opera, Orbison, Oscine, Patti, Piaf, Pitti, Precentor, Prima donna, Qawwal, Rapper, Robeson, Semi-chorus, Session, Shrike, Sinatra, Siren, Snitch, Songman, Songstress, Soprano, Soubrette, Stoolie, Succentor, Swan, Tatiana, Tenor, Tenure, Torch, Treble, Troubador, Vocalist, Voice, Wait, Warbler

Single, Singly Ace, Aefa(u)ld, Aefawld, Alone, Azygous, Bachelor, Celibate, Discriminate, EP, Exclusive, Feme sole, Haplo-, Individual, Lone, Matchless, Monact, Mono, Odd, One-off, One-shot, Only, Pick, Run, Seriatim, Sole, Solitary, Solo, Spinster, Unary, Unattached, Uncoupled, Uniparous, Unique, Unwed, Versal, Yin

Single-cell Protista

Single-chambered Monothalamous

Singlestick Sword

Singlet Tunic, Vest

Singular(ity) Curious, Especial, Exceptional, Extraordinary, Ferly, Naked, Odd, Once, One, Peculiar, Queer(er), Rare, S, → UNIQUE, Unusual

Singultus Hiccup

Sinister Bend, Dark, Dirke, Evil, L, Left, Lh, Louche, → OMINOUS, Port, Spooky, Svengali

Sink(ing), Sunken Abandon, Basin, Bidet, Bog, Cadence, Carbon, Cower, Delapse, Depress, Descend, Devall, Dip, Down, Drain, Draught-house, Drink, Drop, Drown, Ebb, Embog, Flag, Founder, Gravitate, Heat, Hole, Immerse, Invest, Jarbox, Kitchen, Lagan, Laigh, Lapse, Ligan, Merger, Pad, Poach, Pot, Prolapse, Put(t), Relapse, Sag, Scupper, Scuttle, Set, Settle, Shipwreck, Slump, Steep-to, Stoop, Sty, Submerge, Subside, Swag, Swamp

Sinner Evildoer, Malefactor, Offender, Reprobate, Trespasser

Sinuous Curvy, Eely, Ogee, Slinky, Snaky, Wavy, Winding

Sinus Cavity, Ethmoidal, Frontal, Maxillary, Recess, Sphenoidal

Sioux Sitting Bull

Sip(ping) Delibate, Hap'orth, Libant, Sample, Sowp, Sup, Taste, Tiff(ing)

Siphon Draw, Rack, Soda, Suck, Transfer

Sir Dan, Dom, K, Knight, Kt, Lord(ing), Sahib, Signor, Sirrah, Stir, Stirra(h), Towkay, Tuan

Sire Ancestor, Beget, Father, Get

Siren Alarm, Alert, Charmer, Delilah, Diaphone, Enchanter, Femme fatale, Hooter, Houri, Leucosia, Ligea, Lorelei, Mermaid, Oceanides, Parthenope, Salamander, Shark, Teaser, Temptress, Vamp

Sirenian Dugong, Lamantin, Manatee, Manati, Sea-cow

Sirius Sothic

Sirloin Backsey

Sirree Bo

Sisal Agave

Siskin Aberdevine, Bird, Finch

Sister(s) Anne, Beguine, Carmelite, Fatal, Lay, Minim, → **NUN**, Nurse, Out, Religeuse, Sib, Sibling, Sis, Sob, Soul, Swallow, Theatre, Titty, Ugly, Ursuline, Verse, Ward, Weak, Weird

Sistine Chapel, Sextus

Sisyphean Uphill

Sit(ter), Sitting Bestride, Clutch, Dharna, Duck, Gaper, Gimme, Incubate, Lime, Lit de justice, Model, MP, Perch, Pose, Reign, Represent, Roost, Séance, Sederunt, Sejeant, Sesh, Session, Squat

Site, Siting Area, Arpa, Brochure, Brownfield, Building, Camp, Caravan, Chat room, Cobweb, Feng shui, Gap, Greenfield, Home-page, Location, Lot, Mirror, Orphan, Pad, Place, Plot, Ramsar, Rogue, Sacred, Silo, Spot, Stance, World Heritage

Situation Affair, Ballpark, Berth, Cart, Case, Catch, Catch-22, Chicken and egg, Cliff-hanger, Contretemps, Cow, Dilemma, Drama, Galère, Hole, Hornet's nest, Hot seat, Job, Knife-edge, Lie, Location, Lurch, Matrix, Mire, Nail-biter, Niche, No-win, Office, Place, Plight, Position, Post, Scenario, Scene, Schmear, Schmeer, Set-up, Shebang, Showdown, State of play, Status quo, Sticky wicket, Strait, Stringalong, Where, Worst case

Six(th) Digamma, French, German, Half(-a)dozen, Hexad, Italian, Neapolitan, Prime, Sax, Senary, Sestett(e), Sextet, Sice, Size, Vau, VI

Six counties NI

Six days Hexa(e)meron

Six feet, Six-footer Fathom, Insect, Miurus

Sixpence Bender, Kick, Slipper, Tanner, Tester(n), Testril(l), Tizzy, VID, VIP, Zack

Sixteen Hexadecimal, Sweet

Sixty Degree, Sexagesimal, Shock, Threescore

Size(able) Amplitude, Area, Bulk, Calibre, Clearcole, Countess, Demy, Displacement, → **EXTENT**, Format, Girth, Glair, Glue, Guar, Gum, Imperial, Measure, Particle, Party, Physique, Plus, Pot(t), Princess, Proportion, Tempera, Tidy, Trim

Sizzle Fry, Hiss, Scorch

Skate(r), Skateboard(er), Skateboarding, Skating Blade, Bob, Cheap, Choctaw, Cousins, Curry, Dean, Fakie, Figure, Fish, Free, Grommet, Half-pipe, Hot dog, In-line, Maid, Mohawk, Ollie, Overacid, Rink, Rock(er), Roller, Rollerblade®, Runner, Short-track, Sit spin, Speed, Torvill

Skedaddle Beat it, Scarper, Scram, Shoo, Vamoose

Skein Hank, Hasp

Skeleton, Skeletal Anatomy, Atomy, Axial, Bones, Cadaverous, Cadre, Cage, Coenosteum, Coral, Corallite, Corallum, Family, Framework, Hydrostatic, Key, Ossify, Outline, Scenario, Sclere, Tentorium

Sketch(y) Bozzetto, Cameo, Character, Charade, Croquis, Delineate, Diagram, Doodle, Draft, → **DRAW**, Ébauche, Esquisse, Illustration, Limn, Line, Maquette, Modello, Outline, Pencilling, Playlet, Pochade, Précis, Profile, Rough, Skit, Summary, Tenuous, Thumbnail, Trick, Vignette, Visual

Skew Agee, Ajee, Oblique, Sheer, Squint, Swerve, Veer

Skewer Brochette, En brochette, Prong, Spit, Transfix

Ski(er), Skiing Aquaplane, Carving, Free ride, Glide, Glissade, Hot-dog, Langlauf, Mogul, Nordic, Schuss, Schussboomer, Super G, Telemark, Vorlage, Wedeln

Skid Aquaplane, Drift, Jackknife, Side-slip, Slew, Slide, Slip, Slither, Spinout

▷ **Skidding** *may indicate* an anagram

Skiff Canoe, Dinghy, Outrigger

Skilful, Skill(ed) Ability, Able, Accomplished, Ace, Address, Adept, Adroit, Art,

Bravura, Canny, Chic, Competence, Craft, Deacon, Deft, Demon, Dextrous, Enoch, Expertise, Facility, Feat, Finesse, Flair, Gleg, Habile, Hand, Handicraft, Handy, Hend, Hot, Ingenious, Keepy-uppy, Knack, Know-how, Knowing, Lear(e), Leir, Lere, Masterly, Masterpiece, Mastery, Mean, Métier, Mistery, Mystery, Mystique, Practised, Proficient, Prowess, Quant, Resource, Savvy, Science, Skeely, Sleight, Soft, Speciality, Tactics, Talent, Technic, Technique, Touch, Trade, Transferable, Trick, Versed, Virtuoso, Wise, Workmanship

Skim Cream, Despumate, Flit, Glide, Graze, Plane, Ream, Scan, Scud, Scum, Skiff, Skitter

Skimp Restrict, Scamp, Scrimp, Stint

Skin(s) Ablate, Agnail, Armour, Bark, Basan, Basil, Bingo wing, Box-calf, Bronzed, Calf, Callus, Case, Cere, Chevrette, Coat, Corium, Cortex, Crackling, Cutaneous, Cuticle, Cutis, Deacon, Deer, Derm(a), Dermatome, Dermis, Dewlap, Disbark, Ectoderm, Enderon, Epicanthus, Epicarp, Epidermis, Eschar, Excoriate, Exterior, Fell, Film, Flaught, Flay, Flench, Flense, Flinch, Forel, Fourchette, Goldbeater's, Hangnail, Hide, Integra®, Jacket, Kip, Kirbeh, Leather, Membrane, Muktuk, Nebris, Nympha, Pachyderm, Parfleche, Patagium, Peau, Peel, Pell, Pellicle, Pelt, Perinychium, Plew, Plu(e), Prepuce, Pteryla, Rack, Rape, Rind, Scalp, Scarfskin, Serosa, Shagreen, Shell, Shoder, Spetch, Strip, Swindle, Tegument, Tulchan, Veneer, Water-bouget, Wattle, Woolfell

Skin disease, Skin problem, Skin trouble Boba, Boil, Buba, Causalgia, Chloasma, Chloracne, Cowpox, Cradle cap, Cyanosis, Dartre, Dermatitis, Dermatosis, Dyschroa, EB, Ecthyma, Eczema, Erysipelas, Exanthem(a), Favus, Flay, Framboesia, Gum rash, Herpes, Hives, Ichthyosis, Impetigo, Leishmaniasis, Leucodermia, Lichen, Livedo, Lupus vulgaris, Maidism, Mal del pinto, Mange, Miliaria, Morphew, Morula, Patagium, Pellagra, Pemphigus, Pinta, Pityriasis, Prurigo, Pseudofolliculitis, Psoriasis, Pyoderma, Rash, Red-gum, Ringworm, Rosacea, Rose-rash, St Anthony's fire, Sapego, Scabies, Sclerodermia, Scurvy, Seborrhoea, Serpigo, Strophulus, Telangiectasia, Tetter, Tinea, Vaccinia, Verruca, Verruga, Vitiligo, Xanthoma, Xerodermia, Xerosis, Yaws, Yawy

Skinflint Cheapo, Dryfist, Miser, Niggard, Pinch-gut, Scrooge, Tightwad

Skinful Drunk, Sausage

Skinhead Not, Punk, Scalp

Skink Seps

Skinless Ecorché

Skinny Angular, Barebone, Bony, Cutaneous, Dermal, Emaciate, Lean, Scraggy, Thin, Underweight, Weed

Skint Broke, Ghat, Penniless, Stony

Skip(ped), Skipper Boss, Caper, Captain, Cavort, Drakestone, Dumpster, Elater, Frisk, Hesperian, Jump, Jumping-mouse, Lamb, Luppen, Miss, Omit, Patroon, Ricochet, Saury, Scombresox, Spring, Tittup, Trip, Trounce(r)

Skirl Humdudgeon, Pibroch, Pipe, Screigh

Skirmish(er) Brawl, Brush, Dispute, Escarmouche, Fray, Pickeer, Spar, Tirailleur, Velitation, Voltigeur

Skirt(ing) Bases, Bell, Border, Bouffant, Bypass, Cheongsam, Circle, Coat, Crinoline, Culotte(s), Dado, Dirndl, Edge, Fil(l)ibeg, Fringe, Fustanella, Fustanelle, Girl, Gore, Grass, Harem, Hobble, Hoop, Hug, Hula, Kilt, Lamboys, Lava-lava, Marge, Mini, Mopboard, Pareo, Pareu, Pencil, Peplum, Petticoat, Philibeg, Pinafore, Piu-piu, Plinth, Puffball, Ra-ra, Rim, Sarong, Sidestep, Stringboard, Tace, Tail, Taslet, Tasse(t), Tonlet, Tube, Tutu, Valance, Washboard, Wrapover, Wrap(a)round

Skit Lampoon, Parody, Sketch

Skittish Coy, Curvetting, Frisky, Restless, Skeigh

Skittle(s) Bayle, Bowl, Cheese, Kail(s), Kayle, Kingpin, Ninepin, Pin, Spare

Skive(r) Absentee, Laik, Malinger, Scrimshank, Shirk, Skewer

Skivvy Drudge, Slave

Skrimshank Bludge, Skive

Skua Boatswain, Bos'n

Skulk Loiter, Lurk, Mooch, Shool

Skull Brainpan, Bregma(ta), Calvaria, Cranium, Death's head, Fontanel, Harnpan, Head, Malar, Maz(z)ard, Obelion, Occiput, Pannikell, Phrenology, Scalp, Sinciput, Vault, Yorick

Skullcap Ya(r)mulka, Yarmulke, Zucchetto

Skunk Atoc, Atok, Hognosed, Polecat, Pot, Striped, Teledu, Zoril(lo), Zorino

Sky(-high), Sky-tinctured, Skywards Air, Azure, Blue, Canopy, Carry, El Al, E-layer, Element, Empyrean, Ether, Firmament, Heaven, Lift, Lob, Loft, Mackerel, Occident, Octa, Okta, Raise, Rangi, Uranus, Welkin

Sky-diver Para

Skylark Aerobatics, Bird

Skylight Abat-jour, Aurora, Comet, Companion, Lunette, Star

Skyline Horizon, Rooftops

Sky-pilot Chaplain, Vicar

Slab(s) Briquette, Bunk(er), Cake, Cap(e)stone, Chunk, Dalle, Hawk, Ledger, Marver, Metope, Mihrab, Mud, Paver, Paving-stone, Planch, Plank, Sclate, Sheave, Slate, Slice, Stela, Stelene, Tab, Tablet, Tile, Wood-wool

Slack(en), Slacker, Slackness Abate, Careless, Crank, Dilatory, Dross, Ease (off), Easy-going, Glen, Idle, Lax(ity), Lazybones, Let-up, Loose, Malinger, Nerveless, Off-peak, Off-season, Relax, Release, Remiss, Shirk, Skive, Slatch, Slow, Surge, Unscrew, Unwind, Veer

Slag Badmouth, Basic, Calx, Cinder, Dross, Foamed, Lava, Scoria, Scum, Sinter, Tap cinder, Tart

Slake Abate, Cool, Quench, Refresh, Satisfy

Slalom Super-G

Slam Crash, Criticise, Dad, Grand, Little, Pan(dy), Poetry, Small, Sock, Swap, Swop, Vole, Wap

Slander(ous) Asperse, Backbite, Calumny, Defame, Derogatory, Detraction, Disparage, Insult, Libel, Malediction, Malign, Missay, Mud, Mudslinging, Obloquy, Sclaunder, Smear, Traduce, Vilify, Vilipend

Slang Abuse, Argot, Back, Berate, Blinglish, Cant, Colloquial, Ebonics, Flash, Jargon, Lingo, Nadsat, Parlyaree, Polari, Rhyming, Slate, Tsotsitaal, Verlan, Vernacular, Zowie

Slant(ed), Slanting Angle, Asklent, Atilt, Bevel, Bias, Brae, Cant, Careen, Chamfer, Clinamen, Diagonal, Escarp, Oblique, Prejudice, Slew, → SLOPE, Splay, Squint, Talus, Tilt, Virgule

Slap(ping) Clatch, Clout, Cuff, Daub, Happy, Make-up, Pandy, Piston, Sclaff, Scud, Skelp, Smack, Spat, Tape, Twank, Warpaint

Slapdash Careless, Hurried, Random

Slash(ed) Chive, Cut, Diagonal, Gash, Hack, Jag, Lacerate, Laciniate, Leak, Oblique, Rash, Rast, Reduce, Scorch, Scotch, Separatrix, Slice, Slit, Solidus, Stroke, Virgule, Wee

Slat(s) Fish, Jalousie, Louvre, Stave

Slate, Slaty, Slating Alum, Berate, Calm, Cam, Caum, Countess, Credit, Criticise, Decry, Diatribe, Double, Duchess, Duchy, Enter, Flak, Griseous, Imperial, Killas, Knotenschiefer, Lady, List, Log, Marchioness, Ottrelite, Pan, Peggy, Polishing, Princess, Queen, Rag(g), Roof, Run down, Schalstein, Shingle, Slat, Small, Small lady, Tabula, Tomahawk, Viscountess

Slater Hellier, Insect

Slattern Bag, Besom, Bisom, Drab, Drazel, Frump, Mopsy, Ragbag, Ragdoll, Slammakin, Slammerkin, Sloven, Slummock, Sozzle, Traipse, Trapes, Trollop

Slaughter(house), Slaughterer Abattoir, Behead, Bleed, Bloodshed, Butcher, Carnage, Decimate, Hal(l)al, Holocaust, Immolation, Jhatka, Kill, Mactation, → MASSACRE, Scupper, Shambles, S(c)hechita(h), Shochet, Smite

Slav, Slavonic Bohunk, Bulgar, Croat, Czech, Czechic, Jack, Kulak, Lusatia, Polabian, Russian, Serb, Sorb, Toil, Wend(ic)

Slave(ry), Slaves, Slavish Addict, Aesop, Aida, Androcles, Barracoon, Blackbird, Bond,

Bond(s)man, Bondwoman, Bordar, Boy, Caliban, Coffle, Contraband, Dogsbody, Drudge, Drug, Dulocracy, Dulosis, Esne, Galley, Gibeonite, Helot, Hierodule, Jack, Mameluke, Mamluk, Marmaluke, Maroon, Minion, Nativity, Odali(s)que, Odalisk, Peasant, Pr(a)edial, Rhodope, Serf, Servitude, Spartacus, Terence, Theow, Thersites, Thete, Thrall, Toil, Topsy, Vassal, Villein, Wage, Wendic, White, Yoke

Slave-driver, Slave-owner Assam, Sweater, Task-master

Slaver Bespit, Dribble, Drivel, Drool, Slabber, Slobber, Spawl, Spit

Slay(er), Slaying Destroy, Execute, Ghazi, → **KILL**, Mactation, Murder, Quell, Saul, Slaughter, Transport

Sleazy, Sleaze Flimsy, Red-light, Scuzzy, Seamy, Sordid, Squalid, Tack, Thin

Sled(ge), Sleigh(-ride) Bob, Dog train, Dray, Hurdle, Hurley-hacket, Kibitka, Komatic, Komatik, Lauf, Luge, Mud-boat, Mush, Polack, Pulk(h)(a), Pung, Rocket, Skeleton bob(sleigh), Skidoo®, Slipe, Stoneboat, Tarboggin, Toboggan, Train, Travois

Sleek Bright, Shine, Silky, Smarm, Smooth, Smug

Sleep, Sleeper(s), Sleepiness, Sleeping, Sleepy Beauty, Bed, Bivouac, Blet, Bundle, Bye-byes, Car, Catnap, Coma, Couchette, Crash, Cross-sill, Cross-tie, Dormant, Dormient, Dormouse, Doss, Doze, Drop off, Drowse, Earring, Endymion, Epimenides, Flop, Gowl, Gum, Hibernate, Hypnology, Hypnos, Kip, Land of Nod, Lassitude, Lethargic, Lie, Morpheus, Nap, Narcolepsy, Narcosis, Nod, Oscitation, Over, Paradoxical, Petal, Pop off, Psychopannychism, REM, Repast, Repose, Rest, Rip Van Winkle, Rough, Sandman, Seven, Shuteye, Siesta, Skipper, Sleepover, Sloom, Slumber, Snooz(l)e, Somnolent, Sopor(ose), Sownd, Spine bashing, Swone, Tie, Torpid, Twilight, Wink, Zeds, Zizz

Sleeping place Bed, Cot, Dormitory, Kang, Roost

Sleeping sickness Trypanosomiasis

Sleepless Wake-rife, Wauk-rife

Sleep-walking Noctambulation, Somnambulism

Sleet Graupel, Hail, Virga

Sleeve (opening) Arm(hole), Balloon, Batwing, Bishop's, Bush, Cap, Collet, Cover, Dolman, Gatefold, Gigot, Gland, Kimono, Lawn, Leg-o'-mutton, Liner, Magyar, Manche, Pagoda, Pudding, Querpo, Raglan, Record, Sabot, Scye, Slashed, Trunk, Turnbuckle, Wind

Sleeveless Exomis

▶ **Sleigh** *see* **SLED(GE)**

Sleight Artifice, Conjury, Cunning, Dodge, Legerdemain, Trick

Slender(ness) Asthenic, Ectomorph, Elongate, Exiguity, Exility, Fine, Flagelliform, Flimsy, Gracile, Jimp, Leptosome, Loris, Narrow, Rangy, Skinny, Slight, Slim, Small, Spindly, Stalky, Styloid, Svelte, Swank, Sylph, Tenuous, Trim, Waif

Sleuth Bloodhound, Detective, Dick, Eye, Lime-hound, Lyam(-hound), Lyme(-hound), Wimsey

Slew Number, Skid, Slide, Twist

Slice Cantle, Chip, Collop, Cut, Doorstep, Fade, Frustrum, Lop, Piece, Rasure, Round, Sector, Segment, Share, Sheave, Shive, Slab, Sliver, Spoon, Tranche, Wafer, Whang

▷ **Slice of** *may indicate* a hidden word

Slick Adroit, Glim, Mealy-mouthed, Oil, Sheen, Sleeveen, Smooth, Suave

Slide Barrette, Chute, Cursor, Diapositive, Drift, Ease, Fader, Glissando, Hair, Helter-skelter, Hirsle, Hollow-ground, Ice-run, Illapse, Lantern, Mount, Pulka, Schuss, Scoop, Ski, Skid, Skite, Slip, Slippery dip, Slither, Snowboard, Telescope, Transparency, Volplane

Slight(ly) Affront, Belittle, Cold shoulder, Cut, Detract, Disparage, Disregard, Disrespect, Facer, Flimsy, Halfway, Insult, Minor, Misprise, Neglect, Nominal, Pet, Petty, Puny, Rebuff, Remote, → **SLENDER**, Slim, Slimsy, Slur, Small, Smattering, Sneaking, Snub, Sparse, Stent, Subtle, Superficial, Sylphine, Tenuous, Thin, Tiny, Trivial, Wee, Wispy

Slim(mer) Bant, Cut, Jimp, Macerate, Reduce, Slender, Slight, Svelte, Sylph, Tenuous, Thin, Trim, Weight-watcher

Slime, Slimy Glair, Glareous, Glit, Gorydew, Guck, Gunk, Mother, Muc(o)us, Myxomycete, Oily, Ooze, Sapropel, Slabbery, Slake, Sludge, Uliginous

Sling Balista, Catapult, Drink, Fling, Hang, Parbuckle, Prusik, Shy, Singapore, Support, Toss, Trebuchet

Slink Lurk, Proll, Prowl, Skulk, Slope

Slip(ped), Slipping, Slips Avalanche, Boner, Come home, Coupon, Cover, Cutting, Disc, Docket, Drift, EE, Elapse, Elt, Engobe, Error, Escape, Faux pas, Fielder, Form, Freudian, Glide, Glissade, Infielder, Label, Landslide, Lapse, Lapsus linguae, Lath, Lauwine, Leash, Lingerie, Lingual, Mistake, Muff, Nod, Oversight, Parapraxis, Peccadillo, Petticoat, Pink, Plant, Prolapse, Ptosis, Quickset, Rejection, Relapse, Run, Scape, Sc(h)edule, Scoot, Set, Shim, Sin, Ski, Skid, Skin, Skite, Slade, Slidder, Slide, Slither, Slive, Spellican, Spillican, Stumble, Surge, Ticket, Trip, Tunicle, Underskirt, Unleash, Wage(s)

Slipper(s) Baboosh, Babouche, Babuche, Baffies, Calceolate, Carpet, Eel, Errorist, Japanese, Mocassin, Moccasin, Moyl, Muil, Mule, Pabouche, Pampootie, Pantable, Pantof(f)le, Panton, Pantoufle, Pump, Rullion, Runner, Ski, Sledge, Sneaker, Sock

Slippery Eely, Elusive, Errorist, Foxy, Glid, Icy, Lubric, Shady, Shifty, Skidpan, Slick, Slimy

Slipshod Careless, Haphazard, Hurried, Jerry, Lax, Slapdash, Slatternly, Sloppy, Slovenly, Toboggan

▷ **Slipshod** *may indicate* an anagram

Slit Buttonhole, Cranny, Cut, Fent, Fissure, Fitchet, Gash, Gill, Loop, Pertus(at)e, Placket, Placket-hole, Race, Rit, Scissure, Spare, Speld(er), Vent

Slithy Tove

Sliver Flake, Fragment, Moslings, Rove, Shaving, Slice, Splinter, Trace

Sloan Snib, Snub

Slob(ber) Couch potato, Drool, Lout, Slaver, Smarm, Wet

Sloe(thorn) Blackthorn, Slae

Slog(ger) Drag, Logwork, Strike, Swink, Swot, Traipse, Tramp, Trape, Trauchle, Trudge, Yacker, Yakka, Yakker

Slogan Amandla, Byword, Catchword, Chant, Jai Hind, Jingle, Masakhane, Mot(to), Murdabad, Nayword, Phrase, Rallying-cry, Slughorn(e), Splash, Street cry, Tapline, Warcry, Watchword

Sloop Cutter, Hoy, Ship

Slop(pily), Slops, Sloppy Cop(per), Gardyloo, Jordeloo, Lagrimoso, Lowse, Madid, Muck, Mushy, Policeman, Remiss, Rossers, Rozzers, Schmaltz, Schmaltzy, Shower, Slapdash, Slipshod, Sloven, Slushy, Sop, Sozzly, Spill, Swill, Unmethodical, Untidy, Weepie

Slope(s), Sloping Acclivity, Angle, Anticline, Bahada, Bajada, Bank, Batter, Bevel, Borrow, Borstal(l), Brae, Breast, Camber, Chamfer, Cle(e)ve, Cuesta, Declivity, Delve, Diagonal, Dip, Dry, Escarp, Escarpment, Fastigiate, Fla(u)nch, Foothill, Geanticline, Glacis, Grade, Gradient, Heel, Hill, Hipped, Incline, Isoclinical, Kant, Lean, Natural, Nursery, Oblique, Pediment, Pent, Periclinal, Pitch, Rake, Ramp, Rollway, Scarp, Schuss, Scrae, Scree, Shelve, Sideling, Skewback, Slade, Slant, Slippery, Slipway, Splay, Steep, Stoss, Talus, Tilt, Verge, Versant, Weather

▷ **Sloppy** *may indicate* an anagram

Slosh(y) Dowse, Fist, Splash, Wet

Slot(ted) Expansion, God, Graveyard, Groove, Hasp, Hesp, Hole, Key, Keyway, Mortice, Mortise, Niche, Seat, Slit, Swanmark, Time

Sloth(ful) Accidie, Acedia, Ai, Bradypus, Edentate, Ground, Idle, Inaction, Indolent, Inertia, Lazy, Lie-abed, Megatherium, Mylodon, Slugabed, Sweer(t), Sweered, Sweir(t), Three-toed, Torpor, Unau

Slot machine One-armed bandit, Pokey, Pokie

Slouch Lop, Mooch, Mope, Slump

Slough(ing) Cast, Despond, Ecdysis, Eschar, Exfoliate, Exuviae, Lerna, Marish, Marsh, Mire, Morass, Paludine, Shed, Shuck, Swamp

Slovakia .sk

Sloven(ly) Careless, Dag(gy), D(r)aggle-tail, Dishevelled, Down-at-heel, Frowsy, Grobian, Jack-hasty, Mawkin, Rag-doll, Ratbag, Slaister, Slammakin, Slammerkin, Slattern, Sleazy, Slipshod, Slubberdegullion, Slubberingly, Slummock, Slut, Streel, Untidy

Slow(er), Slowing, Slowly, Slow-witted Adagio, Allargando, Andante, Andantino, Brady, Brake, Broad, Calando, Calf, Crawl, Dawdle, Decelerate, Deliberate, Dilatory, Draggy, Dull, Dumka, ESN, Flag, Gradual, Halting, Inchmeal, Lag, Langram, Larghetto, Largo, Lash, Lassu, Late, Lean-witted, Leisurely, Lentamente, Lentando, Lento, Lifeless, Loiter, Losing, Meno mosso, Obtuse, Pedetentous, Rall(entando), Rein, Reluctant, Retard, Ribattuta, Rit, Ritardando, Ritenuto, Roll-out, Slack, Slug, Sluggish, Snail's pace, Snaily, Solid, Stem, Tardigrade, Tardive, Tardy, Tardy-gaited, Thick

Slowcoach Slowpoke, Slug

Slow-match Portfire

Sludge Activated, Gunge, Mire, Muck, Sapropel, Slob

Slug(s) Ammo, Bêche-de-mer, Blow, Brain, Bullet, Cosh, Drink, Grapeshot, Knuckle sandwich, Limaces, Limax, Linotype®, Mollusc, Nerita, Pellet, Shot, Snail, Trepang

Sluggard Drone, Lazy, Lie-abed, Lusk, Unau

Sluggish Dilatory, Drumble, Idler, Inactive, Inert, Jacent, Lacklustre, Laesie, Languid, Lazy, Lentor, Lethargic, Lug, Phlegmatic, Saturnine, Sleepy, → **SLOW**, Stagnant, Tardy, Torpid, Unalive

Sluice Aboideau, Aboiteau, Drain, Floodgate, Gutter, Koker, Penstock, Rinse, Sasse

Slum Basti, Bustee, Busti, Cabbagetown, Cardboard city, Favela, Ghetto, Rookery, Shanty, Shantytown, Slurb, Warren

Slumber Doze, Drowse, Nap, Nod, Sleep, Sloom, Snooze

Slump Decrease, Depression, Deteriorate, Dip, Flop, Recession, Sag, Sink, Slouch, Sprawl

Slur(ring) Defame, Drawl, Innuendo, Libel, Opprobrium, Slight, Smear, Synaeresis, Tie

Slush(y) Bathos, Boodle, Bribe, Drip, Money, Mush, Pap, Slop, Snow-broth, Sposh, Swash, Swashy

Slut Candle, Dollymop, Draggle-tail, Dratchell, Drazel, Floosie, Harlot, Pucelle, Puzzle, Slattern, Sow, Tart, Traipse, Trapes, Trollop

Sly Christopher, Clandestine, Coon, Covert, Cunning, Foxy, Furtive, Leery, Peery, Reynard, Secretive, Shifty, Slee, Sleekit, Sleeveen, Slicker, Sneaky, Stallone, Stealthy, Subtle, Surreptitious, Tinker, Tod, Tricky, Weasel, Wily

▷ **Slyly** *may indicate* an anagram

Smack(er) Aftertaste, Buss, Cuff, Flavour, Foretaste, Fragrance, Hooker, Kiss, Klap, Lander, Lips, Pra(h)u, Relish, Salt, Saut, Skelp, Slap, Slat, Smatch, Smell, Smouch, Soupçon, Spank, Spice, Splat, Tack, → **TANG**, Taste, Thwack, Tincture, Trace, Twang, X, Yawl

Small (thing), Smallest amount Ateleiosis, Atom, Bantam, Beer, Bijou, Bittie, Bitty, Centesimal, Chickenfeed, Chotta, Curn, Denier, Diddy, Diminutive, Dinky, Dreg, Drib, Driblet, Elfin, Elfish, Few, Fry, Grain, Haet, Ha'it, Half-pint, Handful, Hint, Hobbit, Holding, Hole-in-the-wall, Hyperosmia, Insect, Ion, Itsy-bitsy, Knurl, Leet, Leetle, Lepton, Lilliputian, Limited, Lite, → **LITTLE**, Lock, Low, Meagre, Mean, Measly, Microscopic, Midget, Mignon, Miniature, Minikin, Minority, Minute, Mite, Modest, Modicum, Neap, Nurl, Peerie, Peewee, Petit(e), Petty, Pickle, Pigmean, Pigmy, Pink(ie), Pinky, Pint-size, Pittance, Pocket, Poky, Poujadist, Puckle, Rap, Reduction, Runt, S, Santilla, Scantling, Scattering, Scrump, Scrunt, Scruple, Scut, Shoebox, Shortarse, Shrimp, Single, Skerrick, Slight, Slim, Smattering, Smidge(o)n, Smidgin, Smithereen, Smout, Snippet, Soupçon, Sprinkling, Spud, Squirt, Stim, Stunted, Tad, Teenty, Thin, Tidd(l)y, Tiny, Titch(y), Tittle, Tot(tie), Totty, Trace, Trivial, Unheroic, Wee, Weedy, Whit

Smallest Least, Minimal, Runt

Smallholder, Smallholding Croft, Nursery, Rundale, Share-cropper, Stead

Small-minded(ness) Parvanimity, Petty
Smallness Exiguity, Exility, Paucity
Smallpox Alastrim, Variola
Smarm(y) Oil, Smoothie, Unctuous
Smart(en), Smartest, Smartness Ache, Acute, Alec, Astute, Best, Bite, Burn, Chic,
Classy, Clever, Cute, Dandy, Dapper, Dressy, Elegant, Flash, Flip, Fly, Groom, Gussy up,
Jemmy, Kookie, Kooky, Larnery, Natty, Neat, New pin, Nifty, Nip, Nobby, Pac(e)y, Pacy,
Posh, Preen, Primp, Prink, Pusser, Raffish, Rattling, Ritzy, Saucy, Slick, Sly, Smoke,
Smug, Snappy, Snazzy, Soigné(e), Spiff, Sprauncy, Sprightly, Spruce, Sprush, Spry, Sting,
Street cred, Stylish, Swagger, Sweat, Swish, Tiddley, Tippy, Titivate, Toff, Trendy, U,
Well-groomed, Wiseacre, Zippy
Smash(ed), Smasher, Smashing Atom, Bingle, Brain, Break, Cannon, Corker, Crush,
Demolish, Devastate, Dish, Drunk, Forearm, High, Jarp, Jaup, Kaput, Kill, Lulu, Shatter,
Shiver, Slam, Squabash, Stave, Super, Terrific, Tight, To-brake, → **WRECK**
▷ **Smash(ed)** *may indicate* an anagram
Smear Anoint, Assoil, Bedaub, Besmirch, Blur, Borm, Calumniate, Cervical, Clam, Daub,
Defile, Denigrate, Discredit, Drabble, Enarm, Gaum, Gild, Gorm, Lick, Mud, Oil, Oint,
Pap(anicolaou), Pay, Plaster, Slairg, Slaister, Slake, Slander, Slather, Slime, Slubber, Slur,
Smalm, Smarm, Smudge, Spredd, Sully, Swipe, Teer, Traduce, Wax
Smell(ing), Smelly Aroma, Asafoetida, BO, Cacodyl, Caproate, Effluvium, Empyreuma,
Exhale, F(o)etid, Fetor, Fug, Gale, Gamy, Graveolent, Guff, Hing, Honk, Hum, Ionone,
Mephitis, Miasm(a), Ming, Musk, Nidor, Niff, Nose, Odour, Olent, Olfact(ory), Osmatic,
Osmic, Perfume, Pong, Ponk, Pooh, Rank, Redolent, Reech, Reek, Sar, Savour, → **SCENT**,
Sensory, Sniff, Snifty, Snook, Snuff, Steam, Stench, Stifle, Stink, Tang, Whiff
Smelling salts Sal volatile
Smelt(ing) Atherinidae, Melt, Salmon, Scoria, Sparling, Speiss, Sperling, Spirling
Smile(s), Smiling, Smily Agrin, Beam, Cheese, Emoticon, Favour, Gioconda, Grin,
Rictus, Samuel, Self-help, Simper, Smirk, Watch the birdie
Smirk Grimace, Simper
Smite, Smitten Assail, Enamoured, Epris(e), Hit, Strike, Strook
Smith Adam, Artisan, Farrier, FE, Forger, Hammerman, Mighty, Stan, Vulcan, Wayland
Smithy Forge, Smiddy, Stithy, Studdie
Smock Blouse, Chemise, Drabbet, Gather, Shift, Slop, Smicket
Smog Electronic, Photochemical
Smoke(r), Smoking, Smoky Blast, Bloat, Censer, Chain, Chillum, → **CIGAR(ETTE),**
Cure, Drag, Exhaust, Fog, Fuliginous, Fume, Fumigate, Funk, Gasper, Hemp, Incense,
Indian hemp, Inhale, Kipper, Latakia, London ivy, Lum, Lunt, Mainstream, Manil(l)a,
Nicotian, Passive, Peat reek, Peaty, Pother, Pudder, Puff, Reech, Reek, Reest, Roke,
Secondary, Sidestream, Smeech, Smeek, Smirting, Smoor, Smother, Smoulder, Smudge,
Snout, Tear, Tobacconalian, Toke, Vapour, Viper, Water, Whiff, Wreath
Smoke-hating Misocapnic
Smoking-room Divan
Smollett Tobias
▶ **Smooch** *see* **SMOUCH**
Smooth(e), Smoother, Smoothly Alabaster, Bald, Bland, Brent, Buff, Cantabile,
Chamfer, Clean, Clockwork, Dress, Dub, Easy, Even, Fettle, File, Flat, Fluent,
Fretless, Glabrous, Glare, Glassy, Glib, Goose, Iron, Legato, Level, Levigate, Linish,
Mealy-mouthed, Mellifluous, Mellow, Millpond, Oil, Plane, Planish, Plaster, Pumice,
Rake, Roll, Rub, Sad-iron, Sand(er), Satiny, Scrape, Shiny, Sleek, Slick, Slickenslide,
Slithery, Slur, Smug, Snod, Sostenuto, Straighten, Streamlined, Suave, Swimmingly,
Terete, Trim, Unwrinkled, Urbane
Smooth-haired Lissotrichous
Smother Burke, Choke, Dampen, Muffle, Oppress, Overlie, Smoor, Smore, Smoulder,
Stifle, Suppress

Smouch Cheat, Kiss, Lallygag, Lollygag, Neck

Smoulder Burn, Seethe

Smudge Blur, Dab, Offset, Slur, Smear, Smooch, Stain

Smug Complacent, Conceited, Goody-goody, Goody-two-shoes, Neat, Oily, Pi, Sanctimonious, Self-satisfied, Trim

Smuggle(d), Smuggler, Smuggling Body-packer, Bootleg, Contraband, Contrabandist, Coyote, Donkey, Fair trade, Free trader, Gunrunning, Moonshine, Mule, Owler, Rum-runner, Run, Secrete, Steal, Traffic

Smut(ty) Bawdy, Blight, Blue, Brand, Burnt-ear, Coom, Crock, Filth, Grime, Racy, Soot, Speck, Stinking

Smut-fungus Basidia, Ustilago

Snack Bever, Bhelpuri, Bite, Blintz, Bombay mix, Breadstick, Breakfast bar, Brunch, Burger, Butty, Canapé, Chack, Churro, Crisps, Croque monsieur, Crudités, Doner kebab, Elevenses, Entremets, Four-by-two, Gorp, Hoagie, Hors (d'oeuvres), Hot dog, Knish, Meze, Munchies, Nacho, Nacket, Nibble, Nigiri, Nocket, Nooning, Nuncheon, Padkos, Pie, Piece, Ploughman's lunch, Popcorn, Rarebit, Refreshment, Samo(o)sa, Sandwich, Sarnie, Savoury, Scroggin, Sloppy joe, Small chop, Spring roll, Tapa, Taste, Toast(y), Trail mix, Vada, Voidee, Wada, Wrap, Zakuska

Snaffle Bit, Bridoon, Grab, Purloin

Snag Aggro, Anoint, Contretemps, Drawback, Hindrance, Hitch, Impediment, Knob, Nog, Obstacle, Remora, Rub, Snubbe, Stub, Tear

Snail(s) Brian, Cowrie, Cowry, Dew, Dodman, Escargot, Garden, Gasteropod, Giant African, Heliculture, Helix, Hodmandod, Limnaea, Lymnaea, Nautilus, Nerite, Planorbis, Pond, Ramshorn, Roman, Slow, Slug, Strombus, Unicorn-shell, Univalve, Wallfish, Whelk, Wing

Snake, Snaking Drag, Meander, → **SERPENT**, Slither, Wind

SNAKES

3 letters:	Worm	Carpet	Diamond
Asp		Clotho	Hognose
Boa	5 letters:	Daboia	Langaha
Kaa	Adder	Dipsas	Rattler
Rat	Apode	Dugite	Reptile
Sea	Blind	Elaeis	
	Brown	Ellops	8 letters:
4 letters:	Cobra	Flying	Anaconda
Apod	Congo	Garter	Cerastes
Boma	Coral	Gopher	Jararaca
Bull	Cribo	Indigo	Jararaka
Corn	Elaps	Karait	Joe Blake
Habu	Glass	Python	Lachesis
Hoop	Grass	Ratbag	Mocassin
King	Hydra	Ribbon	Moccasin
Milk	Krait	Smooth	Ophidian
Naga	Mamba	Taipan	Pit-viper
Naia	Mulga	Thread	Plumber's
Naja	Racer	Uraeus	Ringhals
Pine	Tiger	Vasuki	Ringneck
Pipe	Viper		Rinkhals
Rock	Water	7 letters:	Slowworm
Seps		Anguine	Spitting
Tree	6 letters:	Camoodi	Squamata
Whip	Anguis	Coluber	Sucurujú

Surucucu	Puff-adder	Dendrophis	Diamond-back
Takshaka	River jack	Fer-de-lance	Horned viper
	Sand viper	Homorelaps	Massasauger
9 letters:		Massasauga	
Berg-adder	*10 letters:*	Sidewinder	*13 letters:*
Blue-racer	Bandy-bandy		Russell's viper
Boomslang	Blacksnake	*11 letters:*	Water moccasin
Coachwhip	Bush-master	Aesculapian	
Hamadryad	Copperhead	Amphisbaena	*17 letters:*
Horsewhip	Crotalidae	Constrictor	Timber rattlesnake
King cobra	Death-adder	Cottonmouth	

Snake-charmer Lamia
Snake-in-the-grass Peacher, Rat, Traitor
Snake-root Bistort, Senega, Snakeweed, Virginia, White
Snap(per), Snappy, Snap up Abrupt, Alligator, Autolycus, Bite, Break, Brittle, Camera, Click, Cold, Cold wave, Crack, Crocodile, Cross, Curt, Edgy, Fillip, Girnie, Glitch, Glom, Gnash, Grab, Hanch, Knacker, Knap, Livery, Mugshot, Photo, Photogene, Scotch, Snack, Snatch, Spell, Still, Tetchy, Vigour
Snare Bait, Benet, Engine, Enmesh, Entrap, Gin, Grin, Honeytrap, Hook, Illaqueate, Inveigle, Mantrap, Net, Noose, Rat-trap, Springe, Springle, Toil, → **TRAP**, Trapen, Trepan, Web, Weel, Wire
Snarl(ing) Chide, Complicate, Cynic, Enmesh, Girn, Gnar(l), Gnarr, Growl, Grumble, Knar, Knot, Snap, Tangle, Yirr
Snatch Claucht, Claught, Excerpt, Fragment, Glom, Grab, Kidnap, Nip, Pluck, Race, Ramp, Rap, Rase, Raunch, Refrain, Snippet, Song, Spell, Steal, Strain, Take, Tweak, Wheech, Whip up, Wrap, Wrest
▷ **Snatch** *may indicate* the first letter of a word
Snazzy Cat
Snead Snath
Sneak(y) Area, Carry-tale, Clipe, Clype, Creep, Furtive, Infiltrate, Inform, Lurk, Mumblenews, Nim, Peak, Scunge, Skulk, Slink, Slip, Slyboots, Snitch, Snoop, Split, Steal, Stoolie, Surreptitious, Tell(-tale), Underhand
Sneer(ing) Barb, Critic, Cynical, Fleer, Gibe, Jeer, Scoff, Smirk, Snide, Twitch
Sneeze (at), Sneezing Atishoo, Errhine, Neese, Neeze, Ptarmic, Scorn, Sternutation
Snick Click, Cut, Edge, Glance
Snicker Snigger, Titter, Whinny
Snide Bitchy, Shand
Sniff Inhale, Nose, Nursle, Nuzzle, Scent, Smell, Snivel, Snort, Snuffle, Vent, Whiff
Snigger Giggle, Laugh, Snicker, Snirtle, Titter, Whicker
Snip(pet) Bargain, Cert, Clip, Cut, Doddle, Piece, Sartor, Snatch, Snick, Tailor
Snipe(r) Bird, Bushwhacker, Criticise, Dunlin, Franc-tireur, Gunman, Gutter, Heather-bleat(er), Heather-bluiter, Heather-blutter, Pick off, Potshot, Scape, Shoot, Walk, Wisp
Snitch Conk, Konk, Nose
Snivel Blubber, Snotter, Snuffle, Weep, Whine
Snob(bery), Snobbish Cobbler, Crachach, Crispin, Dic(k)ty, High-hat, Inverted, Prudish, Pseud, Scab, Side, Sloane, Snooty, Snow, Soutar, Souter, Sowter, Toffee-nose, Vain, Vamp
Snooker Crucible, Pool, Stimie, Stimy, Stym(i)e
Snoop(er) Curtain-twitcher, Meddle, Nose, Pry, Tec
Snooty Bashaw, Snob(bish)
Snooze Calk, Caulk, Dove, Dover, Doze, Nap, Nod, Siesta, Sleep
Snore, Snoring Rhonchus, Rout, Snort, Snuffle, Stertorous, Zz

Snort(er) Dram, Drink, Grunt, Nare, Nasal, Roncador, Snore, Toot
Snot(ty) Mucoid
Snout Bill, Boko, Cigar, Gasper, Gruntie, Informer, Muzzle, Nose, Nozzle, Proboscis, Schnozzle, Tinker, Tobacco, Wall
Snow(y), Snowdrift, Snowstorm Brig, Buran, Cocaine, Coke, Corn, Cornice, Crud, Firn, Flake, Flurry, Graupel, Half-pipe, Heroin, Marine, Mogul, Neve, Nival, Niveous, Nivose, Noise, Oncome, Onding, Powder, Red, Sastruga, Sleet, Spotless, Stall, Virga, White-out, Wintry, Wreath, Yellow, Zastruga
Snowball Accelerate, Cramp-bark, Cumulative, Guelder-rose, Increase, Magnify, Opulus, Pelt, Rose
Snowdrop Avalanche, Eirlys
Snowflake(s) Graupel, Leucojum, St Agnes' flower
Snow-goose Wav(e)y
Snowman Abominable, Eskimo, Junkie, Sherpa, Yeti
Snowmobile Sno-cat
Snowshoe Bear paw, Racket, Racquet, Ski
Snub Cut, Diss, Go-by, Lop, Pug, Put-down, Quelch, Rebuff, Reproof, Retroussé, Set-down, Short, Slap, Slight, Sloan, Sneap, Snool, Wither
Snuff(le) Asarabacca, Douse, Dout, Errhine, Extinguish, Maccabaw, Maccaboy, Maccoboy, Ptarmic, Pulvil, Rappee, Smother, Snaste, Sneesh(an), Sniff, Snift, Snotter, Snush, Tobacco, Vent
Snuffbox Anatomical, Mill, Mull, Ram's horn
Snug(gery), Snuggle Burrow, Comfy, Cose, → **cosy**, Couthie, Couthy, Croodle, Cubby(hole), Cuddle, Embrace, Intime, Lion, Neat, Nestle, Nuzzle, Rug, Snod, Tight, Trim
So Argal, Ergo, Forthy, Hence, Sae, Sic(h), Sol, Such, Therefore, This, Thus, True, Very, Yes
Soak(ed) Bate, Bath(e), Beath, Bewet, Bloat, Blot, Buck, Cree, Deluge, Drench, Drent, Drink, Drook, Drouk, Drown, Drunk, Duck, Dunk, Embay, Embrue, Fleece, Grog, Imbrue, Impregnate, Infuse, Lush, Macerate, Marinate, Mop, Oncome, Permeate, Plastered, Rait, Rate, Ret(t), Rinse, Rob, Saturate, Seep, Sipe, Sog, Sop, Sorb, Souce, Souse, Sows(s)e, Steep, Sype, Thwaite, Toper, Waterlog, Wet, Wino
Soap(y), Soap opera Cake, Carbolic, Castile, Coronation St, Eluate, Flake, Flannel, Flattery, Glass, Green, Hard, Joe, Lather, Lux®, Marine, Metallic, Moody, Mountain, Pears®, Pinguid, Saddle, Safrole, Saponaceous, Saponin, Sawder, Shaving, Slime, Soft, Spanish, Suds, Sudser, Sugar, Syndet, Tablet, Tall-oil, Tallow, The Bill, Toheroa, Toilet, Washball, Windsor, Yellow
Soapstone French chalk, Spanish chalk, Steatite, Talc
Soar(ing) Ascend, Essorant, Fly, Glide, Hilum, Plane, Rise, Tower, Zoom
Sob (stuff) Blub(ber), Boohoo, Goo, Gulp, Lament, Singult, Singultus, Snotter, Wail, Weep, Yoop
Sober(sides), Sobriety Abstemious, Calm, Demure, Pensive, Sedate, Staid, Staidness, Steady, Steddy, TT
Sobriquet Byname, Cognomen, Nickname, To-name
So-called Alleged, Nominal, Soi-disant
Soccer Footer, Footie
Sociable, Sociability Affable, Cameraderie, Chummy, Clubby, Cosy, Couthie, Extravert, Extrovert, Folksy, Friendly, Genial, Gregarious, Mixer, Phatic
Social(ise) Barn dance, Convivial, Hobnob, Hui, Mingle, Mix, Musicale, Phatic, Tea-dance, Thé dansant, Yancha
Socialism, Socialist Ba'(a)th, Champagne, Chartist, Dergue, Engels, Fabian, Fourierism, Guild, Hardie, ILP, International, Karmathian, Lansbury, Left(y), Marxism, Menchevik, Menchevist, National, Nihilism, Owen(ist), Owenite, Parlour pink, Pasok, Pinko, Red, Revisionist, St Simonist, Sandinista, Second international, Spartacist, Utopian, Webb

Socialite Deb, It girl, Jet set, Mingler, Silvertail, Sloane

Society Affluent, Alternative, Association, Band of Hope, Beau monde, Benefit, Black Hand, Body, Boxer, Brahma, Brahmo, Broederbond, Building, Camorra, Carbonari, Casino, Choral, Class, Club, College, Company, Conger, Consumer, Co-op, Cooperative, Culture, Danite, Debating, Defenders, Dorcas, Duddieweans, Eleutheri, Elite, Elks, Fabian, Fashion, Fellowship, Foresters, Freemans, Freemasons, Friendly, Friends, Glee club, Grand monde, Grotian, Group, Guarantee, Guilds, Haut monde, Hetairia, High, High life, Humane, Illuminati, Institute, Invincibles, John Birch, Ku-Klux-Klan, Kyrle, Law, Linnean, Lodge, Mafia, Malone, Masonic, Mass, Mau-Mau, Ménage, Molly Maguire, National, Oddfellows, Open, Oral, Orangemen, Oratory, Order, Permissive, Phi Beta Kappa, Plunket, Plural, Pop, Provident, Repertory, Ribbonism, Risk, Rosicrucian, Rotary, Royal, S, Samaj, School, Secret, Soc, Sodality, Somaj, Soroptomist, Sorority, Stakeholder, Surveillance, Tammany, Theosophical, Toc H, Ton, Tong, Triad, U, Whiteboy, World

Sociologist Weber

Sock(s) Argyle, Argyll, Biff, Bobby, Bootee, Digital, Hose(n), Lam, Leg warmer, Punch, Rock, Slipper, Slosh, Strike, Tabi, Trainer, Walk, Wind

Socket Acetabulum, Alveole, Budget, Eyepit, Gudgeon, Hollow, Hosel, Hot shoe, Jack, Keeper, Lampholder, Nave, Nozzle, Orbit, Ouch, Outlet, Plug, Pod, Point, Port, Power-point, Serial port, Shoe, Strike, Torulus, Whip

Sock-eye Nerka, Salmon

Socle Tube, Zocco(lo)

Socrates, Socratic Ironist, Maieutics, Sage

Sod Clump, Delf, Delph, Divot, Fail, Gazo(o)n, Mool, Mould, Mouls, Scraw, Sward, Turf

Soda, Sodium Acmite, Arfvedsonite, Baking, Barilla, Bicarb, Caustic, Club, Cream, La(u)rvikite, Na, Natrium, Natron, Reh, Saleratus, Splash, Thenardite, Trona, Washing

Sodomy Vice anglais

Sofa Canapé, Chaise longue, Chesterfield, Couch, Daybed, Divan, Dos-à-dos, Dosi-do, Lounge, Ottoman, Settee, Squab, Tête-à-tête

So far (as) As, As yet, Quoad, Until, Yonder

Soft(en), Softener, Softening, Softly Amalgam, Anneal, Assuage, B, BB, Blet, Boodle, Calm, Casefy, Cedilla, Cottony, Cree, Cushion, Dim, Dolcemente, Doughy, Ease, Emolliate, Emollient, Flabby, Furry, Gentle, Hooly, Humanise, Intenerate, Lash, Lax, Lenient, Lenition, Limp, Low, Macerate, Malacia, Malax(ate), Malleable, Mardarse, Mardie, Mease, Mellow, Melt, Mild, Milksop, Mitigate, Modulate, Mollify, Mollities, Morendo, Mulch, Mush(y), Mute, Neale, Nesh, Option, P, Palliate, Pastel, Piano, Plushy, Porous, Propitiate, Rait, Rate, Relent, Scumble, Sentimental, Silly, Slack, Spongy, Squashy, Squidgy, Squishy, Sumph, Talcose, Temper, → TENDER, Tone, Velvet, Weak

Softness Lenity

▶ **Software** *see* COMPUTER SOFTWARE

Sog(gy) Goop, Sodden

Soil(ed), Soily Acid, Adscript, Agrology, Agronomy, Alkali(ne), Alluvium, Azonal, Backfill, Bedraggle, Bemire, Beray, Besmirch, Chernozem, Clay, Cohesive, Contaminate, Defile, Desecrate, Desert, Dinge, Dirt(y), Discolour, Earth, Edaphic, Edaphology, Frictional, Gault, Glebe, Grey, Grimy, Ground, Gumbo, Hotbed, Humus, Illuvium, Intrazonal, Lair, Land, Latosol, Lithosol, Loam, Loess, Lome, Loss, Marl, Mire, Mo(u)ld, Mool, Mud, Mulch, Mull, Night, Ordure, Peat, Ped, Pedalfer, Pedocal, Pedogenic, Pedology, Phreatic, Planosol, Podsol, Podzol, Prairie, Pure, Regar, Regolith, Regosol, Regur, Rendzina, Rhizosphere, Root-ball, Sal, Sedentary, Smudge, Smut, Solonchak, Solonetz, Solum, Soot, Stain, Stonebrash, Sub, Sully, Tarnish, Tash, Terrain, Terricolous, Tilth, Top, Tschernosem, Udal, Umber, Virgin, Yarfa, Yarpha, Zonal

Soirée Drum, Levee, Musicale

Sojourn Abide, Respite, Stay, Tabernacle, Tarry

Sol G, Soh, Sun

Solace Cheer, Comfort

Solar(ium) Heliacal, Tannery
Sold Had
Solder Braze, Join, Spelter, Tin, Weld
Soldier(s) Ant, Chocolate, Detachment, Fighter, Gyrene, Insect, Old Bill, Persevere,
Regular, Unknown, Warmonger

SOLDIERS

2 letters:
GI
OR

3 letters:
ATS
Bod
Ded
Inf
Joe
NCO
POW
Reb
SAS
Tin
Toy
Vet

4 letters:
Army
Corp
Foot
Fyrd
Impi
Jock
Kern
Levy
Line
Naik
Peon
Post
Rank
Swad

5 letters:
Anzac
Bluff
Botha
Brave
Cadet
Choco
Corps
El Cid
Emmet
Fagot
GI Joe

Gippo
Grunt
Gyppo
Jawan
Kerne
Miles
Miner
Nahal
Nizam
Pandy
Perdu
Poilu
Pongo
Sabre
Sammy
Sepoy
Soger
Sowar
Sweat
Tommy
Turco
Uhlan
Wagon

6 letters:
Alpini
Amazon
Arnaut
Askari
Atkins
Banner
Caimac
Chocko
Cohort
Cornet
Detail
Digger
Dugout
Evzone
Faggot
Galoot
Gurkha
Hussar
Knight
Lancer
Nasute

Non-com
Perdue
Rajput
Ranger
Ranker
Reiter
Rutter
Sodger
Swaddy
Tercio
Troops
Yeoman
Zouave

7 letters:
Arnaout
Brigade
Bullman
Chindit
Colonel
Colours
Cossack
Dog-face
Draftee
Dragoon
Enomoty
Federal
Flanker
General
Goorkha
Grim dig
Guardee
Hobbler
Hoplite
Jackman
Lashkar
Lobster
Maniple
Man o' war
Orderly
Palikar
Pandoor
Pandour
Peltast
Phalanx
Pikeman

Platoon
Private
Rat-tail
Redcoat
Retread
Saddler
Samurai
Sebundy
Snarler
Soldado
Sowaree
Sowarry
Squaddy
Tarheel
Templar
Terrier
Trooper
Vedette
Velites
Veteran
Warrior

8 letters:
Achilles
Bluecoat
Borderer
Buff-coat
Caimacam
Centinel
Centonel
Chasseur
Commando
Crusader
Doughboy
Engineer
Fugleman
Fusilier
Greycoat
Guerilla
Immortal
Infantry
Iron Duke
Ironside
Janizary
Kaimakam
Linesman

Martinet	Carbinier	Targeteer	Stalhelmer
Palatine	Centinell	Train-band	
Partisan	Centonell	Turcopole	**11 letters:**
Piou-piou	Centurion	Voltigeur	Bashi-Bazouk
Point man	Desert rat	Volunteer	Bersagliere
Regiment	Fencibles	Whitecoat	Confederate
Rifleman	Field-gray	Wild Geese	Continental
Sentinel	Field-grey		Forlorn-hope
Serafile	Gregarian	**10 letters:**	Gallowglass
Silladar	Grenadier	Bersaglier	Imperialist
Spearman	Guardsman	Bombardier	Johnny Rebel
Squaddie	Irregular	Buff-jerkin	Landsknecht
Stalhelm	Janissary	Cameronian	Leatherneck
Strelitz	Johnny Reb	Campaigner	Legionnaire
Timariot	Kitchener	Carabineer	Rank and file
Trencher	Legionary	Carabinier	Territorial
Warhorse	Men-at-arms	Cataphract	
Woodbind	Minuteman	Contingent	**12 letters:**
Woodbine	Missileer	Cuirassier	Cannon-fodder
Yardbird	Musketeer	Foederatus	Old moustache
	Paratroop	Fuzzy-wuzzy	Stormtrooper
9 letters:	Pistoleer	Galloglass	
Battalion	Rapparree	Green beret	**14 letters:**
Blue beret	Reformado	Hackbuteer	Miles gloriosus
Butter-nut	Reservist	Lansquenet	
Cannoneer	Signaller	Militiaman	**16 letters:**
Carbineer	Subaltern	Serviceman	Old Contemptibles

▷ **Soldiers** *may indicate* bread for boiled eggs

Sole, Solitaire, Solitary Alone, Anchoret, Anchorite, Antisocial, Asocial, Clump, Convex, Corporation, Dover, Dropped, Eremite, Fish, Friendless, Incommunicado, Inner, Lemon, Lonesome, Megrim, Merl, Meunière, Monastical, Monkish, On ice, Only, Pad, Palm, Patience, Pelma, Planta(r), Plantigrade, Platform, Recluse, Sand, Scaldfish, Single(ton), Skate, Slip, Smear-dab, Tap, Thenar, Tread, Unique, Vibram®, Vola

Solemn Agelast, Austere, Devout, Earnest, Grave, Gravitas, Impressive, Majestic, Owlish, Po-faced, Sacred, Sedate, Serious, Sober, Sobersides, Sombre

Solent Lee

Solicit Accost, Approach, Ask, Attract, Bash, → **BEG**, Canvass, Commission, Cottage, Drum up, Importun(at)e, Plead, Ply, Proposition, Speer, Speir, Touch, Tout, Woo

Solicitor(s) Advocate, Attorney, Avoué, Beggar, Canvasser, Crown agent, Hallanshaker, Law-agent, Lawyer, Moll, Notary, Official, Side-bar, SL, Tout, Trull, Writer to the Signet, WS

Solid(arity), Solidify, Solidity Cake, Chunky, Clot, Clunky, Compact, Comradeship, Concrete, Cone, Congeal, Consolidate, Cube, Cylinder, Dense, Dilitancy, Enneahedron, Esprit de corps, Ethan, Firm, Foursquare, Freeze, Frustrum, Fuchsin(e), Gel, Hard, Holosteric, Impervious, Kotahitanga, Masakhane, Merbromin, Octahedron, Pakka, Parallelepiped, Petrarchan, Platonic, Polyhedron, Prism, Pucka, Pukka, Purin(e), Robust, Set, Skatole, Square, Squatly, Stilbene, Sturdy, Sublimate, Substantial, Tetrahedron, Thick, Trusty, Unanimous

Solipsism Egotism, Panegoism

▸ **Solitary** *see* **SOLE**

Solitude Privacy, Seclusion

Solo Aria, Cadenza, Cavatine, Concertante, Lone, Monodrama, Monody, Ombre, One-man, Recit, Scena, Unaided, Variation

Solon Sage
So long Cheerio, Ciao, Goodbye, Tata
Solstice Summer, Tropic, Winter
Soluble Alkaline, Consolute, Poristic, Surfactant
Solution Acetone, Alkali, Ammonia, Amrit, → **ANSWER**, Austenite, Benedict's, Collodion, Colloidal, Dakin's, Dobell's, Éclaircissement, Electrolyte, Elixir, Emulsion, Eusol, Fehling's, Final, Hairspray, Key, Leachate, Limewater, Lixivium, Lye, Normal, Oleoresin, Oleum, Rationale, Reducer, Remedy, Ringer's, Rinse, Rubber, Saline, Solid, Solvent, Soup, Standard, Suspensoid, Tincture, Titrate, Tone, Viscose
▷ **Solution** *may indicate* an anagram
Solve(d), Solver Absolve, Assoil, Calculate, Casuist, Clear, Crack, Decode, Holmes, Loast, Loose, Read(er), Suss out, Troubleshoot, Unclew, Undo, Unriddle, Work
Solvent Above water, Acetaldehyde, Acetone, Afloat, Alcahest, Aldol, Alkahest, Anisole, Aqua-regia, Banana oil, Benzene, Chloroform, Cleanser, Cyclohexane, Cyclopentane, Cymene, Decalin, Denaturant, Diluent, Dioxan(e), Eleunt, Eluant, Ether, Funded, Furan, Heptane, Hexane, Ligroin, Megilp, Menstruum, Methanol, Methylal, Naphtha, Paraldehyde, Picoline, Protomic, Pyridine, Sound, Stripper, Terebene, Terpineol, Terts, Tetrachloromethane, Thinner, Thiophen, Toluene, Toluol, Trike, Trilene, Turpentine, White spirit
Somalia .so
Sombre Dark, Drab, Drear, Dull, Funereal, Gloomy, Grave, Morne, Morose, Subfusc, Subfusk, Sullen, Triste
Some Any, Arrow, Ary, Certain, Divers, Few, One, Part, Portion, Quota, Sundry, These, They, Wheen
▷ **Some** *may indicate* a hidden word
Somebody Dignitary, Name, Notable, One, Person, Quidam, Someone, Tuft, → **VIP**
Somehow Somegate
▷ **Somehow** *may indicate* an anagram
Somersault Back-flip, Barani, Catherine wheel, Deltcher, Flip(-flap), Flip-flop, Handspring, Pitchpole, Pitchpoll
Somerset Protector
Something Aliquid, Article, Chattel, Item, Matter, Object, Summat, What, Whatnot
Sometime(s) Erstwhile, Ex, Former, Occasional, Off and on, Otherwhiles, Quondam
Somewhat Bit, -ish, Mite, Partly, Quasi, Quite, Rather, Relatively, Slightly, Summat, Wheen
Somewhere Somegate
Somnolence Drowsiness
Son Boy, Descendant, Disciple, Epigon(e), Fils, Fitz, Lad, Lewis, M(a)c, Native, Offspring, Prodigal, Progeny, Scion
Sonata Moonlight
Song Air, Amoret, Anthem, Antistrophe, Aria, Ariette, Art, Aubade, Ayre, Ballad, Ballant, Ballata, Barcarol(l)e, Belter, Berceuse, Bhajan, Blues, Brindisi, Burden, Burthen, Cabaletta, Calypso, Cancionero, Cante hondo, Cante joudo, Canticle, Cantilena, Cantion, Canzona, Canzone, Canzonet(ta), Carmagnole, Carol, Catch, Cavatina, Chanson, Cha(u)nt, Chantey, Come-all-ye, Conductus, Corn-kister, Corroboree, Cycle, Descant, Dirge, Dithyramb, Ditty, Elegy, Epithalamion, Epithalamium, Fado, Fit, Fitt, Flamenco, Folk, Forebitter, Gaudeamus, Gita, Glee, Gorgia, Gradual, Hillbilly, Hum, Hymeneal, Hymn, Internationale, Jug(-jug), Lament, Lay, Lied(er), Lilt, Lullaby, Lyric, Madrigal, Magnificat, Marseillaise, Matin, Melic, Melisma, Melody, Mento, Minnesang, Negro spiritual, Noel, Number, Nunc dimittis, Oat, Paean, Pane, Part, Patter, Penillion, Plain, Plaint, Plantation, Pop, Prick, Prothalamion, Prothalamium, Psalm, Qawwali, Rap, Recitativo, Red Flag, Relish, Rhapsody, Rispetto, Roulade, Roundelay, Rune, Scat, Scolion, Sea-shanty, Secular, Serenade, Shanty, Shosholoza, Siren, Sirvente, Skolion, Sososholoza, Spiritual, Stave, Stomper, Strain, Strophe, Swan, Taps, Tenebrae, Theme,

Torch, Trill, Tune, Tyrolienne, Villanella, Volkslied, Waiata, War, Warble, Wassail, Waulking, Yodel, Yodle

Songbook Cancionero, Hymnal, Kommersbuch, Libretto, Psalter

Songsmith, Songwriter Carmichael, Dowland, Espla, Foster, Kern, Minot, Waitz, Zappa

Sonnet Amoret, Elizabethan, English, Italian, Miltonic, Petrarch(i)an, Shakespearean, Shakespearian, Spenserian

Sonometer Monochord

Soon(er) Anon, Directly, Enow, Erelong, Imminent, Lief, OK, Oklahoma, Presently, Shortly, Tight, Timely, Tit(ely), Tite, Tyte

Soot(y) Colly, Coom, Crock, Fuliginous, Gas black, Grime, Lampblack, Smut, Speck

Soothe(r), Soothing Accoy, Allay, Anetic, Anodyne, Appease, Assuage, Bucku, Calm, Compose, Demulcent, Dulcet, Ease, Emollient, Irenic, Lenitive, Lull, Mellifluous, Mollify, Obtundent, Pacific, Paregoric, Poultice, Quell, Rock, Stroke

Soothsayer Astrologer, Augur, Calchas, Chaldee, Divine, Forecaster, Haruspex, Melampus, Oracle, Picus, Prophet, Pythoness, → **SEER**, Shipton, Tiresias

Sop(py) Appease, Berry, Douceur, Rait, Ret, Salvo, Sashy, Sponge

Sophist(ic) Casuist, Elenchic, Quibbler

Sophisticate(d) Blasé, Boulevardier, City slicker, Civilised, Classy, Cosmopolitan, Couth, Doctor, High-end, Hitec, Patrician, Polished, Sative, Slicker, Suave, Svelte, Urbane, Worldly

▷ **Sophoclean** *may indicate* Greek alphabet, etc

Sophomore Semie

Soporific Barbiturate, Bromide, Drowsy, Halothane, Hypnotic, Lullaby, Narcotic, Opiate, Sedative, Tedious

Soppiness, Soppy Maudlin, Salvo, Sashy, Schwärmerei, Sloppy, Slushy, Wet

Soprano Caballé, Castrato, Crespin, Descant, Lind, Patti, Treble

Sorb Wend

Sorbet Glacé, Water ice

Sorcerer, Sorceress, Sorcery Angekok, Ashipu, Circe, Conjury, Diablerie, Diabolist, Hoodoo, Kadaitcha, Kurdaitcha, Lamia, Mage, Magian, Magic(ian), Magus, Medea, Merlin, Morgan le Fay, Mother Shipton, Necromancer, Obi, Pishogue, Shaman, Sortilege, Venefic(ious), Voodoo, Warlock, Witch, Witch knot, Wizard

Sordid Base, Low-life, Miserable, Rhyparography, Scungy, Seamy, Seedy, Sleazy, Squalid, Vile

Sore(ly), Sores Abrasion, Anthrax, Bitter, Blain, Boil, Canker, Chancre, Chap, Chilblain, Cold, Dearnly, Felon, Gall, Impost(h)ume, Ireful, Kibe, Nasty, Pressure, Quitter, Quittor, Raw, Running, Rupia(s), Saddle, Sair, Sensitive, Shiver, Sitfast, Soft, Surbate, Tassell, Tercel, Ulcer(s), Whitlow, Wound

Sore throat Garget, Prunella, Quinsy, Tonsillitis

Sorghum Kaoliang, Mabela, Milo

Sorrel Common, French, Hetty, Mountain, Oca, Roman, Sheep, Soar(e), Sore, Sourock

Sorrow(ful) Affliction, Attrition, Deplore, Distress, Dole, Dolente, Doloroso, Dolour, Emotion, Fee-grief, → **GRIEF**, Lament, Misery, Nepenthe, Ochone, Penance, Pietà, Remorse, Rue, Triste, Wae, Waugh, Wirra, Woe, Yoop

Sorry Apologetic, Ashamed, Contrite, Miserable, Oops, Penitent, Pitiful, Poor, Regretful, Relent, Rueful, Simple, Wan, Wretched

▷ **Sorry** *may indicate* an anagram

Sort(ing) Arrange, Brand, Breed, Category, Character, Classify, Collate, Drive, Grade, → **KIND**, Nature, Pranck(e), Prank, Sift, Species, Stamp, Stripe, Systemise, Tidy, Triage, Type, Variety

Sortie Attack, Foray, Mission, Outfall, Raid, Sally

▶ **Sorts** *see* **OUT OF SORTS**

So-so Average, Indifferent, Mediocre, Middling

So to speak Quasi

▷ **So to speak** *may indicate* 'sound of'
Sotto voce Murmur, Whisper
▶ **Soubriquet** *see* SOBRIQUET
Sough Rustle, Sigh
Soul(ful) Alma, Ame, Anima, Animist, Atman, Ba, Bardo, Brevity, Deep, Entelechy, Eschatology, Essence, Expressive, Heart, Inscape, Ka, Larvae, Lost, Manes, Motown, Object, Person, Pneuma, Psyche, Saul, Shade, Spirit, Traducian, Universal
Sound(ed), Sounding, Soundness, Sound system Accurate, Ach-laut, Acoustic, Affricate, Albemarle, Allophone, All there, Alveolar, Amphoric, Audio, Bay, Bleep, Blip, Bloop, Blow, Boing, Bong, Bray, Breathed, Cacophony, Chime, Chirl, Chirr(e), Chord, Chug, Clam, Clang, Clank, Clink, Cloop, Clop, Clunk, Compos, Consistent, Continuant, Copper-bottomed, Dah, Dental, Diphthong, Dit, Dive, Dolby®, Dream, Dusky, Echo, Eek, Euphony, Fast, Fathom, Fere, Fettle, Fit, Flow, Foley, Glide, Good, Hale, Harmonics, Healthy, Hearty, Hi-fi, Ich-laut, Inlet, Islay, Jura, Kalmar, Knell, Kyle, Labiodental, Lo-fi, Long Island, Low, Lucid, Mach, Madrilene, McMurdo, Mersey, Milford, Monophthong, Mouillé, Murmur, Musak, Music, Muzak®, Narrow, Nicam, → NOISE, Off-glide, Onomatopaeia, Oompah, Optical, Orate, Orinasal, Orthodox, Palatal, Palato-alveolar, Pamlico, Paragog(u)e, Peal, Pectoriloquy, Phone(me), Phonetic, Phonic, Phonology, Pitter(-patter), Plap, Plink, Plonk, Plop, Plosion, Plosive, Plumb, Plummet, Plunk, Plymouth, Probe, Pronounce, Puget, Put-put, Quadraphonic(s), Quadrophonic(s), Rale, Rational, Rat-tat, Real, Reasonable, Reliable, Ring, Roach, Robust, Rong, Rumble, Rustle, Sabin, Safe, Sandhi, Sane, Scoresby, Sensurround®, S(c)hwa, Skirl, Solid, Sonance, Sondage, Sone, Souffle, Sough, Sowne, Speech, Splat, Stereo, Stereophony, Strait, Surround, Swish, Tamber, Tannoy®, Tchick, Tenable, Thorough, Timbre, Ting, Tone, Toneme, Trig, Trill, Triphthong, Trumpet, Twang, Ultrasonic(s), Unharmed, Uvular, Valid, Viable, Voice, Vowel, Wah-wah, Watertight, Well, Whine, Whinny, Whistle, Whole(some), Whoosh, Whump, Wolf
Sounder Echo, Lead(sman)
Sounding board Abat-voix
Soundproof Deaden
Sound-track Dubbing, Movietone®, Stripe
Soup Alphabet, Avgolemono, Bird's nest, Bisk, Bisque, Borsch, Bouillabaisse, Bouillon, Brewis, Broth, Burgoo, Cal(l)aloo, Chowder, Cioppino, Cock-a-leekie, Cockieleekie, Cockyleeky, Consommé, Crab chowder, Duck, Garbure, Gazpacho, Gomb(r)o, Gruel, Gumbo, Harira, Hoosh, Julienne, Kail, Kale, Lokshen, Madrilene, Marmite, Mess, Minestrone, Mock turtle, Mulligatawny, Oxtail, Palestine, Pea(se), Pho, Pot(t)age, Pot-au-feu, Primordial, Puree, Ramen, Rice, Rubaboo, Sancoche, Scoosh, Scotch broth, Shchi, Shtchi, Skilligalee, Skilligolee, Skilly, Skink, Stock, Tattie-claw, Toheroa, Turtle, Vichyssoise
▷ **Soup** *may indicate* an anagram
Soupçon Thought, Touch
Sour(puss) Acerb, Acescent, Acid, Acidulate, Aigre-deux, Alegar, Bitter, Citric, Crab, Eager, Esile, Ferment, Moody, Stingy, Subacid, → TART, Turn, Unamiable, Verjuice, Vinegarish
Source Authority, Basis, Bottom, Centre, Closed, Database, Derivation, Egg, Fons, Font, Fount, Fountain-head, Germ, Head-stream, Leak, Literary, Mine, Mother, Neutron, Origin, Parent, Pi, Pion, Point, Principle, Prot(h)yle, Provenance, Quarry, Reference, Rise, Riverhead, Root, Seat, Seed, Spring, Springhead, Stock, Supply, Urn, Well, Wellhead, Wellspring, Widow's cruse, Ylem
Sour milk Curds, Smetana, Whey, Whig, Yogh(o)urt
Souse Beath, Duck, Immerse, Pickle, Plunge, Soak, Spree, Steep
South(ern), Southerner Austral, Confederacy, Dago, Decanal, Decani, Deep, Dixieland, Meridian, Meridional, S, Scal(l)awag, Scallywag
South Africa(n) Azania, Bantu, Caper, Ciskei, Grikwa, Griqua, Hottentot, Kaf(f)ir,

Lebowa, Qwaqwa, SA, Soutie, Soutpiel, Springbok, Swahili, Xhosa, ZA, Zulu

South American Araucanian, Arawak, Argentino, Aymara, Bolivian, Carib, Chibcha, Chilean, Galibi, Guarani, Inca, Jivaro, Kechua, Latin, Llanero, Mam, Mapuchi, Mayan, Mixe-Zogue, Mixtac, Mochica, Quechua, SA, Shuar, Tapuyan, Tupi

South-east Roseland, SE

Southwark Boro'

Souvenir Goss, Keepsake, Memento, Relic, Remembrance, Scalp, Token, Trophy

Sou'wester Cornishman

Sovereign(ty), Sovereign remedy Anne, Autocrat, Bar, Condominium, Couter, Dominant, Emperor, ER, Goblin, Haemony, Harlequin, Imperial, Imperium, James, King, L, Liege, Napoleon, Nizam, Pound, Quid, Rangatiratanga, Royalty, Ruler, Shiner, Supreme, Swaraj, Synarchy, Thick' un, Thin' un

Soviet Circassian, Council, Estonian, Russian, Stalin, Supreme, Volost

Sow(ing) Catchcrop, Elt, Foment, Gilt, Inseminate, Plant, Scatter, Seed, Sprue, Strew, Yelt

Soya Sitosterol, Tempe(h)

Spa Aachen, Baden, Baden-Baden, Bath, Buxton, Evian, Fat farm, Godesberg, Harrogate, Hydro, Kurhaus, Kursaal, Leamington, Malvern, Vichy

Space, Spaced (out), Spaceman, Spacing, Spacious, Spatial Abyss, Acre, Alley, Area, Areola, Bay, Bolthole, Bracket, Breathing, Bronchus, Cellule, C(o)elom, Cislunar, Clearing, Coelome, Cofferdam, Compluvium, Concourse, Contline, Crawl, Crookes, Cubbyhole, Daylight, Deducted, Deep, Diastema, Distal, Distance, Elbow-room, Elliptic, Em, En, Esplanade, Ether, Exergue, Expanse, Extent, Flies, Footprint, Forecourt, Freeband, Gagarin, Gap, Glade, Glenn, Goaf, Gob, Gutter, Hair, Hash(mark), Headroom, Hell, Homaloid, Indention, Inner, Intergalactic, Interim, Interlinear, Interplanetary, Interstellar, Interstice, Invader, Kerning, Killogie, Kneehole, Lacuna, Lair, Leading, Lebensraum, Legroom, Life, Lobby, Logie, Lumen, Lunar, Lung, Machicolation, Maidan, Manifold, Manorial, Metope, Mihrab, Minkowski, Mosh pit, MUD, Muset, Musit, Orbit, Outer, Palatial, Parking, Parvis(e), Peridrome, Personal, Plenum, Polemics, Pomoerium, Priest hole, Proportional, Proxemics, Quad, Retrochoir, Riemannian, → **ROOM**, Ruelle, Sample, Sheets, Shelf room, Slot, Spandrel, Spandril, Sparse, Step, Steric, Storage, Third, Topological, Tympanum, Ullage, Uncluttered, Vacua, Vacuole, Vacuum, Vast, Vector, Virtual, Void, Volume, Well

Spacecraft, Space agency, Space object, Spaceship, Space station Apollo, Capsule, Columbia, Columbus, Deep Space, Explorer, Galileo, Gemini, Genesis, Giotto, Lander, LEM, Luna, Lunik, Mariner, Mercury, MIR, Module, NASA, Orbiter, Pioneer, Probe, Quasar, Ranger, Salyut, Shuttle, Skylab, Soyuz, Space lab, Sputnik, Starship, Tardis, Viking, Voskhod, Vostok, Voyager, Zond

Spacer (plate) Bead(s)

Space walk EVA

Spade Breastplough, Caschrom, Cas crom, Castrato, Detective, Flaughter, Graft, Loy, Negro, Paddle, Paddle staff, Pattle, Peat, Pettle, Pick, S, Shovel, Slane, Spit, Suit, Turf, Tus(h)kar, Tus(h)ker, Twiscar

Spain E, Hesperia, Iberia, Wean

Spalpeen Sinner

Span Age, Arch, Attention, Bestride, Bridge, Chip, Ctesiphon, Extent, Life, Memory, Range, Timescale

Spangle(d) Avanturine, Aventurine, Glitter, Instar, O, Paillette, Sequin

Spaniard, Spanish Alguacil, Alguazil, Andalusian, Asturian, Balearic, Barrio, Basque, Cab, Caballero, Carlist, Castilian, Catalan, Chicano, Dago, Diego, Don, Fly, Grandee, Hidalgo, Hispanic, José, Main, Mestizo, Mozarab, Pablo, Papiamento, Señor, Spic(k), Spik

Spaniel Blenheim, Cavalier, Clumber, Cocker, Crawler, Creep, Dog, Fawner, Field, Irish water, King Charles, Maltese, Papillon, Placebo, Skip-kennel, Springer, Sussex, Tibetan, Toad-eater, Toady, Toy, Water, Welsh springer

Spank(ing) Cob, Paddywhack, Rapid, Scud, Slap, Slipper, Sprack

Spanner Arc, Box, Bridge, Clapper, Key, Monkey wrench, Ring, Shifter, Shifting, Socket, Spider, Torque, Wrench

Spar Barite, Barytes, Blue John, Boom, Bowsprit, Box, Cauk, Cawk, Derbyshire, Fight, Gaff, Heavy, Iceland, Icestone, Jib-boom, Mainyard, Manganese, Martingale, Mast, Nail-head, Outrigger, Rafter, Rail, Ricker, Satin, Schiller, Shearleg, Sheerleg, Snotter, Spathic, Sprit, Steeve, Stile, Tabular, Triatic, Whiskerboom, Whiskerpole, Yard

Spare, Sparing(ly) Angular, Cast-off, Dup(licate), Economical, Fifth wheel, Free, Frugal, Galore, Gash, Gaunt, Hain, Lean, Lenten, Narrow, Other, Pardon, Reserve, Rib, Save, Scant, Skimp, Skinny, Slender, Stint, Subsecive, Tape, Thin

Spark Animate, Arc, Beau, Blade, Bluette, Dandy, Flash, Flaught, Flicker, Flint, Funk, Ignescent, Ignite, Kindle, Life, Muriel, Quenched, Scintilla, Smoulder, Spunk, Trigger, Vital, Zest

Sparkle(r), Sparkling Aerated, Aventurine, Bling, Burnish, Coruscate, Crémant, Diamanté, Effervesce, Élan, Emicate, Fire, Fizz, Flicker, Frizzante, Gem, Glamour, Glint, Glisten, Glitter, Life, Pétillant, Scintillate, Seltzer, Seltzogene, Spangle, Spritzig, Spumante, Twinkle, Verve, Witty, Zap

Sparrow Bird, Cape, Chipping, Hedge, Isaac, Java, Junco, Mah-jong(g), Mossie, Passerine, Piaf, Prunella, Savanna, Song, Spadger, Speug, Sprug(gy), Titling, Tree, Vesper

Sparrow-grass Asparagus, Sprue

Sparse Meagre, Rare, Scant, Thin

Spartan(s) Ascetic, Austere, Basic, Enomoty, Hardy, Helot, Heraclid, Lacedaemonian, Laconian, Lysander, Menelaus, Severe, Valiant

Spasm(s), Spasmodic Ataxic, Blepharism, Chorea, Clonus, Convulsive, Cramp, Crick, Fit(ful), Hiccup, Hippus, Hyperkinesis, Intermittent, Irregular, → **JERK**, Kink, Laryngismus, Nystagmus, Paroxysm, Periodical, Start, Strangury, Tetany, Throe, Tonic, Tonus, Trismus, Twinge, Twitch, Vaginismus, Writer's cramp

▷ **Spasmodic** *may indicate* an anagram

Spastic Athetoid, Clonic, Jerky

Spat(s) Altercation, Bicker, Brattle, Gaiters, Legging, Quarrel, Set to, Shower, Tiff

Spate Flood, Sluice, Torrent

▸ **Spatial** *see* **SPACE**

Spatter Disject, Ja(u)p, Scatter, Splash, Splosh, Spot, Sprinkle

▷ **Spattered** *may indicate* an anagram

Spatula Applicator, Tongue depressor

Spawn(ed), Spawning (place) Anadromous, Blot, Eelfare, Fry, Progeny, Propagate, Redd, Roud, Seed, Shotten, Spat, Spet, Spit

Speak(er), Speaking Address, Articulate, Bang on, Broach, Chat, Cicero, Collocuter, Communicate, Converse, Coo, Declaim, Diction, Dilate, Discourse, Diseur, Dwell, Effable, Elocution, Eloquent, Expatiate, Express, Extemporise, Filibuster, Intercom, Intone, Inveigh, Jabber, Jaw, Lip, Loq, Loquitur, Management, Mang, Mention, Mike, Mina, Mouth, Mouthpiece, Nark, Native, Open, Orate, Orator, Palaver, Parlance, Parley, Perorate, Pontificate, Prate, Preach, Prelector, Public, Rhetor, → **SAY**, Sayne, Soliloquize, Spout, Spruik, Squawk box, Stump, Talk, Tannoy®, Tongue, Trap, Tub-thumper, Tweeter, Utter, Voice, Waffle, Wibble, Witter, Word

Speakeasy Fluent, Shebeen

Spear Ash, Asparagus, Assagai, Assegai, Barry, Dart, Demi-lance, Engore, Fishgig, Fizgig, Gad, Gavelock, Gig, Glaive, Gleave, Gum digger's, Gungnir, Hastate, Impale, Javelin, Lance(gay), Launcegaye, Leister, Morris-pike, Partisan, Pierce, Pike, Pilum, Prong, Skewer, Spike, Trident, Trisul(a), Waster

Spearhead Lead

Spear-rest Feutre, Fewter

Special(ly) Ad hoc, Constable, Designer, Disparate, Distinctive, Extra, Important, Notable, Notanda, Particular, Peculiar, Red-letter, S, Specific, Strong suit, Vestigial

Specialise, Specialist(s) Allergist, Authority, Concentrate, Connoisseur, Consultant, ENT, Esoteric, Expert, Illuminati, Internist, Maestro, Major, Quant, Recondite, Technician

Species Biotype, Class, Ecotype, Endangered, Genera, Genre, Genus, Indicator, Infima, Kind, Opportunistic, Pioneer, Strain, Taxa

Specific(ally), Specification, Specified, Specify Adduce, As, Ascribe, Assign, Concretize, Cure, Define, Detail, Explicit, Formula, Full-blown, Itemise, Medicine, Namely, Precise, Quantify, Remedy, Sp, Special, Spell out, State, Stipulate, Stylesheet, The, To wit, Trivial, Vide licit

Specimen(s) Assay, Example, Exemplar, Imago, Model, Museum piece, Sample, Slide, Swab, Topotype, Type

Specious False, Glib, Hollow, Pageant, Plausible, Spurious

Speck, Speckle(d) Atom, Bit, Dot, Fleck, Floater, Freckle, Gay, Mealy, Muscae volitantes, Particle, Peep(e), Pip, Spot, Spreckle, Stud

Spectacle(s), Spectacled, Spectacular Arresting, Barnacles, Bifocals, Blazers, Blinks, Bossers, Cheaters, Colourful, Epic, Escolar, Giglamps, → **GLASSES**, Goggles, Horn-rims, Lorgnette, Lorgnon, Meteoric, Nose-nippers, Oo, Optical, Outspeckle, Pageant, Pebble glasses, Pince-nez, Pomp, Preserves, Raree-show, Scene, Show, Sight, Son et lumière, Staggering, Sunglasses, Tamasha, Tattoo, Trifocal, Varifocals

Spectate, Spectator(s) Audience, Bystander, Dedans, Etagère, Eyer, Gallery, Gate, Groundling, Kibitzer, Observer, Onlooker, Ringsider, Standerby, Wallflower, Witness

Spectograph, Spectometer Aston, Calutron

Spectral, Spectre Apparition, Bogle, Bogy, Brocken, Eidolon, Empusa, Ghost, Idola, Iridal, Larva, Malmag, Phantasm, Phantom, Phasma, Spirit, Spook, Tarsier, Walking-straw, Wraith

Spectrum Absorption, Band, Continuous, Emission, Fission, Iris, Mass, Optical, Radio, Rainbow, Sunbow, Sundog, Visible, X-ray

Speculate, Speculative, Speculator, Speculation Agiotage, Arb(itrage), Bear, Better, Boursier, Bull, Conjecture, Flier, Flyer, Gamble, Guess, Ideology, If, Imagine, Meditate, Notional, Operate, Pinhooker, Raider, Shark, Stag, Theoretical, Theorise, Theory, Thought, Trade, Wonder

Speech, Speech element Accents, Address, Argot, Articulation, Bunkum, Burr, Curtain, Delivery, Dialect, Diatribe, Diction, Direct, Discourse, Dithyramb, Drawl, Éloge, English, Epilogue, Eulogy, Filibuster, Free, Gab, Glossolalia, Grandiloquence, Guttural, Harangue, Helium, Idiolect, Idiom, Inaugural, Indirect, Jargon, Keynote, King's, Lallation, → **LANGUAGE**, Lingua franca, Litany, Logopaedics, Maiden, Monologue, Morph(eme), Motherese, Musar, Oblique, Occlusive, Oral, Oration, Parabasis, Parle, Peroration, Phasis, Philippic, Phonetics, Prolocution, Prolog(ue), Queen's, Reported, Rhetoric, RP, Sandhi, Scanning, Screed, Sermon, Set, Side, Slang, Soliloquy, Stemwinder, Stump, Tagmeme, Talk, Taxeme, Tirade, Tongue, Uptalk, Vach, Verbal, Visible, Voice, Wawa, Whaikorero, Whistle-stop, Xenoglossia

Speech defect, Speech disease Alalia, Alogia, Aposiopesis, Dysarthria, Dysphasia, Dysphoria, Echolalia, Halt, Idioglossia, Lallation, Lisp, Palilalia, Paralalia, Paraphasia, Pararthria, Phonasthenia, Psellism, Rhinolalia, Stammer, Stutter

Speechless Alogia, Dumb, Dumbstruck, Inarticulate, Mute, Silent, Tongue-tied

Speech-writer Logographer

Speed(ily), Speedy Accelerate, Alacrity, Amain, Amphetamine, ANSI, Apace, ASA, Average, Bat, Belive, Belt, Benzedrine, Breakneck, Burn, Cast, Celerity, Clip, Dart, Despatch, DIN, Dispatch, Expedite, Fang, Fast, Film, Fleet, Further, Gait, Gallop, Goer, Group, Gun, Hare, Haste, Hie, Hotfoot, Hypersonic, Induce, Instantaneous, Knot, Landing, Lick, Mach, Merchant, MPH, → **PACE**, Pelt, Phase, Pike, Post-haste, Prompt, Pronto, Race, Rapidity, Rate, RPS, Rush, Scorch, Scud, Scurr, Skirr, Soon, Spank, Split, Stringendo, Supersonic, Swift, Tach, Tear, Tempo, Teraflop, Ton up, V, Velocity, Ventre à terre, Vroom, Wave, Whid, Wing, Zoom

Speedwell Bird's eye, Brooklime, Fluellin, Germander, Veronica
Spelaean Troglodyte
Spelk Skelf, Splinter
Spell(ing) Abracadabra, Bewitch, Bout, Cantrip, Charm, Conjuration, Do, Elf-shoot,
  Enchantment, Entrance, Fit, Go, Gri(s)-gri(s), Hex, Incantation, Innings, Jettatura, Juju,
  Knock, Knur, → **MAGIC**, Mojo, Need-fire, Nomic, Open sesame, Orthography, Period,
  Phase, Philter, Philtre, Phonetic, Pinyin, Relieve, Ride, Romaji, Run, Rune, Scat, Shift,
  Shot, Signify, Sitting, Snap, Snatch, Sorcery, Sp, Span, Spasm, Splinter, Stint, Stretch,
  Tack, Time, Tour, Trick, Turn, Weird, Whammy, Wicca, Witchcraft
Spelling-book ABC, Grimoire
Spencer Bodice, Topcoat, Tracy, Vest
Spend(er), Spending Anticipate, Birl, Blow, Blue, Boondoggling, Consume, Deficit,
  Deplete, Disburse, Exhaust, Fritter, Lash out, Lay out, Live, Outlay, Pass, Pay, Shopaholic,
  Splash, Splash out, Splurge, Squander, Squandermania, Ware
Spendthrift Essex Man, High-roller, Prodigal, Profligate, Profuser, Scattergood, Wastrel
Spent All-in, Consumed, Dead, Done, Expended, Gone, Stale, Tired, Used, Weak, Weary,
  Zonked
Sperm Gossypol, Seed, Semen
Spew Eject, Emit, Gush, Spit, Vomit
Sphagnum Moss, Peat
Sphere, Spherical Armillary, Attraction, Ball, Benthoscope, Celestial, Discipline, Earth,
  Element, Field, Firmament, Globe, Magic, Mound, Orb(it), Planet, Primum mobile,
  Prolate, Province, Realm, Schwarzschild, Theatre, Wheel
Sphincter Pylorus
Sphinx Criosphinx, Hawk-moth, Oracle, Riddler
Spice, Spicy Amomum, Anise, Aniseed, Aryl, Baltic, Caraway, Cardamom, Cardamon,
  Cardamum, Cassareep, Cassaripe, Cayenne, Chili powder, Cinnamon, Clove, Clow,
  Coriander, Cough drop, Cubeb, Cum(m)in, Dash, Devil, Garam masala, Ginger, Green
  ginger, Mace, Malaguetta, Marjoram, Masala, Myrrh, Nutmeg, Oregano, Paprika,
  Peppercorn, Picante, Pimento, Piperic, Piquant, Root ginger, Saffron, Salsa verde,
  Season, Sexed up, Stacte, Staragen, Tamal(e), Tamara, Tansy, Tarragon, Taste, Turmeric,
  Vanilla, Variety, Za'atar
Spick Dink, Neat, Spike, Tidy
Spicule Sclere, Tetract
Spider(s) Anancy, Ananse, Arachnid, Aranea, Araneida, Arthrapodal, Attercop, Bird,
  Black widow, Bobbejaan, Bolas, Cardinal, Cheesemite, Chelicerate, Citigrade, Diadem,
  Epeira, Epeirid, Ethercap, Ettercap, Funnel-web, Harvester, Harvestman, House,
  Hunting, Huntsman, Jumping, Katipo, Lycosa, Mite, Money, Mygale, Orb-weaver, Pan,
  Phalangid, Podogona, Program, Pycnogonid, Red, Redback, Rest, Ricinulei, Saltigrade,
  Scorpion, Solifugae, Solpuga, Spinner, Strap, Tarantula, Telary, Trapdoor, Violin, Water,
  Wolf, Zebra
Spiderwort Tradescantia
Spiel Patter, Pitch, Spruik
Spignel Baldmoney, Meu
Spigot Bung, Plug, Tap
Spike(d) Barb, Brod, Calk, Calt(h)rop, Chape, Cloy, Crampon, Doctor, Ear, Fid,
  Filopodium, Foil, Gad, Gadling, Goad, Grama, Herissé, Icicle, Impale, Kebab, Lace,
  Locusta, Marlin(e), Nail, Needle, → **PIERCE**, Piton, Point, Pricket, Prong, Puseyite, Rod,
  Sharp, Shod, Skewer, Spadix, Spear, Spicate, Spicule, Spire, Strobiloid, Tang, Thorn, Tine
Spill(age) Divulge, Drop, Fidibus, Jackstraw, Lamplighter, Leakage, Let, Overflow,
  Overset, Reveal, Scail, Scale, Shed, Skail, Slart, Slop, Stillicide, Taper, Tumble
Spin(ner), Spinning (wheel) Aeroplane, Arabian, Arachne, Aswirl, Bielmann, Birl,
  Camel, Centrifuge, Chark(h)a, Cribellum, Cut, Dance, Day trip, Dextrorse, DJ, Flat, Flip,
  Gimp, Googly, Gymp, Gyrate, Gyre, Gyroscope, Hurl, Isobaric, Isotopic, Jenny, Lachesis,

Mole, Nun, Peg-top, Piecener, Piecer, Pirouette, Pivot, PR, Precess, Prolong, Purl, Reel, Rev(olve), Ride, Rotate, Royal, Screw, Side, Sinistrorse, Slant, Slide, Somersault, Spider, Stator, Strobic, Swirl, Swivel, Throstle, Tirl, Toss, Trill, Trundle, Turntable, Twirl, Twist, Wheel, Whirl, Whirligig, Work

Spinach Florentine, Orach(e), Popeye, Sa(a)g

Spinal (chord), Spine(d), Spiny Acanthoid, Acerose, Acicular, Acromion, Aculeus, Areole, Arête, Backbone, Barb, Chine, Coccyx, Column, Doorn, Dorsal, Epidural, Muricate, Myelon, Notochord, Ocotillo, Prickle, Quill, Rachial, R(h)achis, Ray, Ridge bone, Thorn, Torso, Tragacanth

Spindle(-shanks), Spindly Arbor, Axle, Bobbin, Capstan, Fusee, Fusiform, Fusil, Mandrel, Mandril, Pin, Scrag, Staff, Triblet

▶ **Spine** *see* SPINAL

Spinel Balas, Picotite

Spineless(ness) Cowardice, Inerm, Invertebrate, Muticous, Timid, Weak, Wimp

Spinning-wheel Chark(h)a

Spinn(e)y Coppice, Shaw, Thicket

Spin-off By-product

Spinster Discovert, Feme sole, Old maid, Tabby

Spiral Archimedes, Caracol, Chalaza, Cochlea, Coil, Curl, Dexiotropic, Dextrorse, Ekman, Genetic, Gyrate, Gyre, Helical, Helix, Hyperbolic, Inflationary, Logarithmic, Loxodromical, Parastichy, Screw, Scroll, Sinistrorse, Spin, Tailspin, Turbinate, Turnpike, Vibrio, Volute, Vortex, Whorl, Wind

Spire(-shaped) Broach, Flèche, Peak, Shaft, Steeple, Thyrsoid

Spirit, Spirited Animal, Animation, Animus, Ardent, Blithe, Dash, → DRINK, Élan, Element(al), Emit, Entrain, Essence, Etheric, Ethos, Feisty, Fettle, Fight, Free, Geist, Ginger, Gism, Go, Grit, Gumption, Heart, Holy, Hugh, Kindred, → LIQUOR, Lively, Mettle, Morale, Mystique, Nobody, Panache, Pecker, Pep, Presence, Pride, Racy, Scientology, Soul, Spunk, Steam, Stomach, Team, Ton, Verve, Vigour, Vim, Zing

SPIRITS

2 *letters:*	Jinn	Fenny	Shade
Ka	Jism	Genie	She'ol
	Loki	→ GHOST	Short
3 *letters:*	Mare	Ghoul	Sylph
Div	Peri	Huaca	Tafia
Imp	Puck	Jinni	Turps
Nis	Raki	Jumby	Vodka
Nix	Ruin	Kehua	White
Rum	Salt	Larva	
Rye	Saul	Lemur	6 *letters:*
	Wili	Manes	Arrack
4 *letters:*	Wine	Marid	Astral
Arak	Wood	Metal	Brandy
Bogy		Meths	Buggan
Brio	5 *letters:*	Mobby	Buggin
Cant	Angel	Numen	Cherub
Deev	Ariel	Party	Cognac
Deva	Bogie	Peart	Crouse
Feni	Bogle	Pluck	Daemon
Gamy	Djinn	Pooka	Djinni
Ginn	Dryad	Proof	Duende
Grog	Duppy	Rakee	Dybbuk
Jann	Eblis	Satyr	Empusa

Esprit
Fachan
Faints
Feints
Fetich
Fetish
Geneva
Genius
Grappa
Jinnee
Jumbie
Kelpie
Kirsch
Kobold
Lemure
Manito
Manitu
Methyl
Mobbie
Numina
Ondine
Orenda
Pernod®
Petrol
Plucky
Pneuma
Potato
Poteen
Psyche
Python
Samshu
Seraph

Shadow
Sprite
Strunt
Tangie
Undine
Voodoo
Wairua
Wraith
Zephon
Zombie

7 letters:
Ahriman
Akvavit
Alcohol
Ammonia
Apsaral
Aquavit
Archeus
Asmoday
Banshee
Bitters
Boggart
Bravura
Buggane
Courage
Eidolon
Erl king
Eudemon
Fetiche
Glastig
Gremlin

Gytrash
Incubus
Indwelt
Kachina
Manitou
Mineral
Neutral
Phantom
Rakshas
Samshoo
Shaitan
Smeddum
Spectre
Spright
Taniwha
Tequila

8 letters:
Archaeus
Creature
Erdgeist
Familiar
Hollands
Rakshasa
Schnapps
Surgical
Witblits

9 letters:
Applejack
Aqua vitae
Domdaniel

Firewater
Hartshorn
Nain rouge
Paraclete
Rectified
Tokoloshe
Weltgeist
Zeitgeist

10 letters:
Brollachan
Glendoveer
Methylated
Mindererus
Rumbullion
Turpentine
Water horse

11 letters:
Poltergeist
Rosicrucian

12 letters:
Apathodaimon
Distillation

13 letters:
Crème de menthe

Spiritless Craven, Dowf, Insipid, Languid, Meek, Milksop, Poor, Tame, Vapid
Spirit-level Vial
Spiritual(ism), Spiritualist, Spirituality Aerie, Aery, Channelling, Coon-song,
Ecclesiastic, Ethereous, Eyrie, Eyry, Incorporeal, Inwardness, Mystic, Negro, Planchette,
Platonic, Psychic, Slate-writing, Swedenborg, Table-rapping, Table-turning, Yogi
Spirt Gush, Jet, Rush, → SPURT, Squirt
Spit(ting), Spittle Bar, Barbecue, Broach, Brochette, Chersonese, Dead ringer, Dribble,
Drool, Emptysis, Eructate, Expectorate, Fuff, Gob, Golly, Gooby, Goss, Grill, Hawk,
Hockle, Impale, Jack, Lookalike, Peninsula, Phlegm, Ras, Ringer, Rotisserie, Saliva,
Skewer, Slag, Spade(ful), Spawl, Spear, Sputter, Sputum, Tombolo, → TONGUE, Yesk,
Yex
Spite(ful) Backbite, Bitchy, Catty, Grimalkin, Harridan, Irrespective, Malevolent,
Malgrado, Malgré, Malice, Mau(l)gre, Mean, Nasty, Petty, Pique, Rancour, Spleen,
Venom, Viperish, Waspish
Spitfire Cacafogo, Cacafuego, Wildcat
Spittoon Cuspidor(e)
Spiv Lair, Rorter
Splash Befoam, Blash, Blue, Dabble, Dash, Dog, Drip, Feature, Flouse, Fl(o)ush,
Gardyloo, Jabble, Ja(u)p, Jirble, Paddle, Plap, Plop, Plowter, Sket, Slosh, Slush, Soda,
Soss, Sozzle, Spairge, Spat(ter), Spectacle, Splat(ch), Splatter, Splodge, Splosh, Splotch,
Spray, Spree, Squatter, Swash, Swatter, Water, Wet

▷ **Splash** *may indicate* an anagram

Splay(ed) Curl, Flew, Flue, Patté(e), Spread

Spleen Acrimony, Bite, Lien, Melt, Milt(z), Pip, Stomach, Vitriol, Wrath

Splendid, Splendour Ah, Braw, Brilliant, Bully, Capital, Champion, Clinker, Dandy, Divine, Éclat, Effulgent, Excellent, Fine, Finery, Fulgor, Gallant, Garish, Glitterand, Glittering, Glorious, Glory, Gorgeous, Grand(eur), Grandiose, Ha, Heroic, Hunky-dory, Lustrous, Majestic, Mooi, Noble, Palatial, Panache, Pomp, Proud, Radiant, Rich, Ripping, Royal, Stunning, Super(b), Superduper, Wally, Zia

Splice(d) Braid, Eye, Join, Knit, Mainbrace, Married, Wed

▷ **Spliced** *may indicate* an anagram

Splint Airplane, Banjo, Brace, Cal(l)iper, Splenial, Stent, T

Splinter(s) Bone-setter, Breakaway, Flinder, Fragment, Matchwood, Shatter, Shiver, Skelf, Sliver, Spale, Spall, Speel, Spelk, Spell, Spicula, Spill

Split(ting) Areolate, Axe, Banana, Bifid, Bifurcate, Bisect, Breach, Break, Broach, Burst, Chasm, Chine, Chop, Chorism, Cleave, Clint, Clove(n), Crack, Crevasse, Cut, Decamp, Departmentalise, Disjoin, Distrix, → **DIVIDE**, Division, Divorce, End, Fissile, Fissure, Flake, Fork(ed), Fragment, Grass, Lacerate, Left, Partition, Red(d), Rift(e), Rip, Rive, Rupture, Russian, Ryve, Schism, Scissor, Segment, Segregate, Separate, Septemfid, Sever, Share, Skive, Slit, Sliver, Spall, Spalt, Speld, Spring, Tattle, Tmesis, Told, To-rend, To-tear, Trifurcate, Wedge

▷ **Split** *may indicate* a word to become two; one word inside another; or a connection with Croatia or the former Yugoslavia

Splodge, Splotch Blot, Drop, Splash

Splurge Binge, Indulge, Lavish, Spend, Splash, Spree

Splutter Chug, Expectorate, Fizz, Gutter, Spray, Stammer

Spode Roderick

Spoil(s), Spoiler, Spoilt Addle, Agrise, Agrize, Agryze, Air dam, Blight, Blunk, Booty, Botch, Bribe, Coddle, Corrupt, Crool, → **DAMAGE**, Dampen, Deface, Defect, Deform, Disfigure, Dish, Fairing, Foul, Gum, Hames, Harm, Impair(ed), Impoverish, Indulge, Loot, Maderise, Maltreat, Mar, Mardy, Mollycoddle, Muck, Mutilate, Mux, Pamper, Party pooper, Pet, Pickings, Pie, Plunder, Prejudicate, Prize, Queer, Rait, Rate, Ravage, Ret, Rot, Ruin, Screw up, Scupper, Spuly(i)e, Swag, Taint, Tarnish, Vitiate, Wanton, Winnings, Wreck

▷ **Spoil(ed), Spoilt** *may indicate* an anagram

Spoilsport Damper, Killjoy, Marsport, Meddler, Party pooper, Wet blanket, Wowser

Spoke(s) Concentric, Radius, Ray, Rung, Said, Sed, Strut

Spoken Dixi

▷ **Spoken** *may indicate* the sound of a word or letter

Spokesman Foreman, Mouthpiece, Orator, Prophet, Representative

Spoliation, Spoliative Devastation, Pillage, Plunder, Predatory, Reif

Sponge(r), Spongy Alcoholic, Ambatch, Angel cake, Argentine, Battenburg, Bum, Cadge, → **CAKE**, Cleanse, Diact, Diploe, Fozy, Free-loader, Glass-rope, Hexact, Hyalonema, Leech, Lig, Lithistid(a), Loofa(h), Madeira, Madeleine, Mermaid's glove, Mooch, Mop, Mouch, Mump, Parasite, Parazoa, Pentact, Platinum, Poachy, Porifera(n), Porous, Quandong, Rhabdus, Sarcenchyme, Scambler, Schnorrer, Scrounge, Shark, Shool(e), Shule, Siphonophora, Smell-feast, Sooner, Sop, Sucker, Swab, Sweetbriar, Sycophant, Tectratine, Tetract, Tetraxon, Tiramisu, Tylote, Vegetable, Velamen, Venus's flowerbasket, Wangle, Wipe, Zimocca, Zoophyte

Spongewood Sola

Sponsor(ship) Aegis, Angel, Auspice, Backer, Bankroll, Egis, Finance, Godfather, Godparent, Gossip, Guarantor, Lyceum, Patron, Surety, Undertaker

Spontaneous Aleatoric, Autonomic, Exergonic, Free, Gratuitous, Immediate, Impromptu, Improvised, Impulsive, Instant, Intuitive, Natural, Off-the-cuff, Ultroneus, Unasked, Unpremeditated, Unprompted, Unrehearsed, Untaught

Spoof Chouse, Cozenage, Deception, Delusion, Fallacy, → **HOAX**, Imposture, Ramp, Swindle, Trick

Spook(s), Spooky CIA, Eerie, Fantom, Frightening, Ghost, Haunted, Phantom, Shade

Spool Bobbin, Capstan, Pirn, Reel, Spit, Trundle

Spoon(ful), Spoon-shaped Apostle, Canoodle, Cochlear, Deflagrating, Dollop, Dose, Eucharistic, Gibby, Greasy, Horn, Labis, Ladle, Mote, Neck, Rat-tail, Runcible, Salt, Scoop, Scud, Server, Snuff, Spatula, Sucket, Trolling, Trout, Woo, Wooden

Spoonerism Marrowsky, Metathesis

Spoor Trace, Track, Trail

Sporadic Fitful, Isolated, Occasional, Patchy

Spore(s), Spore case Asexual, Conidium, Ex(t)ine, Fungus, Glomerule, Lenticel, Palynology, Resting, Seed, Sexual, Sorus, Spreathed, Telium, Uredinium

Sporran Pock

Sport(ing), Sportive, Sports, Sporty Amusement, Bet, Blood, Breakaway, Brick, By-form, Contact, Daff, Dalliance, Dally, Demonstration, Deviant, Extreme, Field, Freak, Frisky, Frolic, Fun, → **GAME**, Gent, In, Joke, Laik, Lake, Lark, Merimake, Merry, Morph, Mutagen, Pal, Pastime, Recreate, Rogue, Rules, Spectator, Tournament, Tourney, Toy, Wear, Winter

---

SPORTS

2 letters:	Netball	Motocross	Kite-surfing
PE	Parkour	Potholing	Paragliding
RU	Putting	Skijoring	Paralympics
	Rafting	Ski-kiting	Parapenting
3 letters:	Shot put	Ski-towing	Parasailing
Gig	Skating	Skydiving	Race-walking
	Snooker	Speedball	Scuba-diving
4 letters:	Surfing	Twitching	Showjumping
Polo	Tailing	Wargaming	Snorkelling
Sumo		Water polo	Table tennis
	8 letters:	Wrestling	Tent-pegging
5 letters:	Aquatics		Truck racing
Basho	Ballgame	**10 letters:**	Water-skiing
Fives	Bonspiel	Cyclo-cross	Windsurfing
Kendo	Climbing	Drag-racing	
	Eventing	Heli-skiing	**12 letters:**
6 letters:	Korfball	Kickboxing	Bar billiards
Aikido	Lacrosse	Monoskiing	Boardsailing
Diving	Langlauf	Pancratium	Cross country
Hockey	Natation	Parakiting	Heli-boarding
Karate	Octopush	Paraskiing	Kite-boarding
Shinny	Ringette	Rallycross	Orienteering
Shinty	Skipping	Real tennis	Parascending
Squash	Softball	Sky-jumping	River bugging
Tennis	Speedway	Sky-surfing	Sailboarding
	Swoffing	Street luge	Snowboarding
7 letters:		Volleyball	Speed-skating
Angling	**9 letters:**		Steeplechase
Archery	Abseiling	**11 letters:**	Tag-wrestling
Camogie	Athletics	Coasteering	Trampolining
Curling	Autocross	Fell walking	Trapshooting
Fencing	Autopoint	Free running	Wakeboarding
Hurling	Canyoning	Hang-gliding	

13 letters:	Weightlifting	*16 letters:*	*18 letters:*
Bungee-jumping		Ultimate fighting	White-water
Prizefighting	*15 letters:*		canoeing
Skeet Shooting	Extreme fighting	*17 letters:*	
Ten-pin bowling		Whitewater rafting	

▷ **Sport(s)** *may indicate* an anagram

Sportsground Rec

Sportsman, Sportsmen All-rounder, Athlete, Blue, Corinthian, Half-blue, Hunter, Nimrod, Pentathlete, Pitcher, Shamateur, Shikaree, Shikari, Shot putter, Showjumper, Varment, Varmint

Sportswear Gie, Wet suit

Spot(s), Spotted, Spotting, Spotty Ace, Acne, Area, Areola, Areole, Baily's beads, Bausond, Bead, Beauty, Befoul, Bespatter, Blackhead, Blain, Blemish, Blind, Blip, Blister, Blob, Blot, Blotch(ed), Blur, Brind(l)ed, Café-au-lait, Carbuncle, Caruncle, Cash, Check, Cloud, Colon, Comedo, Corner, Curn, Cyst, Dance, Dapple(-bay), Defect, Descry, Detect, Dick, Dilemma, Discern, Discover, Dot, Drop, Eruption, Espy, Eye, Facula, Flat, Flaw, Fleck, Floater, Fogdog, Foxed, Freak, Freckle, Furuncle, G, Gay, Glimpse, Gout, Gräfenberg, Gricer, Guttate, High, Hot, Identify, Jam, Leaf, Lentago, Light, Little, Liver, Locale, Location, Loran, Mackle, Macle, Macul(at)e, Mail, Meal, Measly, Microdot, Milium, Moil, Mole, Morbilli, Mote, Motty, Muscae volitantes, Naevoid, Naevus, Note, Notice, Ocellar, Ocellus, Paca, Papule, Paraselene, Pardal, Parhelion, Patch, Peep(e), Penalty, Perceive, Performance, Petechia, Pied, Pimple, Pin, Pip, Place, Plague, Plight, Plook, Plot, Plouk, Pock, Point, Poxy, Predicament, Punctuate, Pupil, Pustule, Quat, Radar, Rash, Recognise, Red, Rose-drop, Scene, Scotoma, Situation, Skewbald, Smut, Soft, Speck(le), Speculum, Splodge, Spoil, Spy, Stigma, Sully, Sun, Sweet, Taint, Tar, Tight, Touch, Trace, Trouble, Venue, Weak, Whelk, Whitehead, Witness, X, Yellow, Zit

Spotless Clean, Immaculate, Pristine, Spick and span, Virginal

Spotlight Ace, Baby, Bon-bon, Brute, Maxi-brute

Spot on To a t

Spouse Companion, Consort, Dutch, Feare, Feer, F(i)ere, Hubby, Husband, Mate, Oppo, Partner, Pheer, Pirrauru, Significant other, Wife, Xant(h)ippe

Spout(er) Adjutage, Erupt, Gargoyle, Geyser, Grampus, Gush, Impawn, Jet, Mouth, Nozzle, Orate, Pawn, Pourer, Raile, Rote, Spurt, Stream, Stroup, Talk, Tap, Vent

Sprain(ed) Crick, Rax, Reckan, Rick, Stave, Strain, Wrench, Wrick

Sprat Brit, Fish, Garvie, Garvock

Sprawl Grabble, Loll, Scamble, Spraddle, Sprangle, Spread, Stretch, Urban

Spray Aerosol, Aigrette, Airbrush, Antiperspirant, Atomiser, Bespatter, Blanket, Buttonhole, Corsage, Cyme, Egret, Fly, Hair, Mace®, Nasal, Nebuliser, Pesticide, Posy, Rose, Rosula, Scatter, Shower, Sparge, Spindrift, Splash, Spoondrift, Sprent, Sprig, Sprinkle, Spritz, Strinkle, Syringe, Twig, Wet

▷ **Spray** *may indicate* an anagram

Spread(ing), Spreader Air, Apply, Banquet, Bestrew, Beurre, Bid offer, Blow-out, Branch, Bush, Butter, Carpet, Centre, Circumfuse, Contagious, Couch, Coverlet, Coverlid, Deploy, Diffract, Diffuse, Dilate, Disperse, Dissemination, Distribute, Divulge, Double, Double-page, Drape, Dripping, Elongate, Emanate, Engarland, Expand, Extend, Fan, Feast, Flare, Guac(h)amole, Honeycomb, Jam, Lay, Mantle, Marge, Marmite®, Meal, Metastasis, Middle-age(d), Multiply, Mushroom, Nutter, Oleo, Open, Overgrow, Paste, Pâté, Patent, Patté, Patulous, Perfuse, Pervade, Picnic, Pour, Proliferate, Propagate, Radiant, Radiate, Rampant, Ran, Ranch, Run, Scale, Scatter, Sea-floor, Set, Sheet, Slather, Smear, Smörgåsbord, Sow, Span, Speld, Spelder, Spillover, Splay, Sprawl, Spray, Straddle, Straw, Stretch, Strew, Strow, Suffuse, Systemic, Tath, Teer, Unfold, Unfurl, Unguent, Unroll, Vegemite®, Widen, Wildfire

▷ **Spread** *may indicate* an anagram

Spree Bat, Batter, Beano, Bender, Binge, Bum, Bust, Buster, Carousal, Frolic, Gilravage, Jag, Jamboree, Juncate, Junket, Lark, Loose, Orgy, Randan, Rantan, Razzle(-dazzle), Revel, Rouse, Splore, Tear, Ups(e)y

Sprig Brad, Branch, Cion, Cyme, Nail, Scion, Sien, Sient, Spray, Syen, Twig, Youth

Sprightly, Sprightliness Agile, Airy, Chipper, Esprit, Jaunty, Mercurial

Spring(s), Springtime, Springy Aganippe, Air, Alice, Arise, Black smoker, Bolt, Bounce, Bound, Box, Bunt, Cabriole, Caper, Capriole, Castalian, Cavort, Cee, Coil, Dance, Elastic, Eye, Fount(ain), Free, Gambado, Germinate, Geyser, Grass, Hair, Helix, Hippocrene, Hop, Hot, Jeté, Jump, Leaf, Leap, Lent, Lep, Litt, Low-water, May, Mineral, Originate, Persephone, Pierian, Pounce, Prance, Primavera, Prime, Resilient, Ribbon, Rise, Saddle, Season, Skip, Snap, Source, Spa, Spang, Spaw, Start, Stem, Stot, Submarine, Sulphur, Summer, Suspension, Teal, Thermae, Thermal, Trampoline, Valve, Vault, Vaute, Vawte, Vernal, Voar, Ware, Watch, Waterhole, Weeping, Well(-head), Whip, Winterbourne

▷ **Spring(y)** *may indicate* an anagram

Springbok Amabokoboko

Springless Telega

Springtail Apterygota

Sprinkle(r), Sprinkling Asperge, Aspergill(um), Bedash, Bedew, Bedrop, Bescatter, Caster, Disponge, Dispunge, Dredge, Dust, Hyssop, Lard, Pouncet, Powder, Rose, Scatter, Scouthering, Shower, Sow, Spa(i)rge, Spatter, Splash, Spray, Spritz, Strinkle

Sprint(er) Burst, Dash, Race, Rash, Run, Rush, Scurry, Wells

Sprite Apsaras, Banshee, Croquemitaine, Dobbie, Dobby, Echo, Elf, Fairy, Fiend, Genie, Gnome, Goblin, Gremlin, Hobgoblin, Icon, Kelpie, Kelpy, Nickel, Nis(se), Ondine, Puck, Pug, Spirit, Troll, Trow, Umbriel, Undine

Sprocket Whelp

Sprout Braird, Breer, Brussels, Bud, Burgeon, Chit, Crop, Eye, Germ(inate), Grow, Pullulate, Shoot, Spire, Tendron, Vegetate

Spruce Balsam, Dapper, Engelmann, Hemlock, Natty, Neat, Norway, Picea, Pitch-tree, Prink, Shipshape, Sitka, Smart, Spiff, Tidy, Tree, Trim, Tsuga, White

Spry Active, Agile, Constance, Dapper, Nimble, Volable

Spud Murphy, Potato, Spade, Tater, Tatie

Spume Eject, Foam, Froth, Lather, Spet, Spit

Spunk Courage, Grit, Pluck, Spark, Tinder

Spur(s) Accourage, Activate, Aphrodisiac, Calcar(ate), Encourage, Fame, Fire, Fuel, Galvanise, Gee, Gilded, Goad, Groyne, Heel, Incite, Limb, Lye, Needle, Offset, Prick, Prong, Rippon, Rowel, Shoot, Spica, Stimulus, Strut, Stud, Tar, Urge

Spurge (tree) Candelilla, Croton, Euphorbia, Kamala, Manihot, Poinsettia, Ricinus

Spurious Adulterine, All-to, Al-to, Apocryphal, Bogus, Counterfeit, Dog, Fake, False, Phoney, Pseudo, Sciolism, Untrue

▷ **Spurious** *may indicate* an anagram

Spurn Despise, Disdain, Eschew, Ignore, Jilt, Leper, Rebuff, Reject, → **SCORN**, Sdayn, Shun, Snub

Spurrey Yarr

Spurt Burst, Forge, Geyser, Jet, Outburst, Pump, Spout, Start

Sputter Fizzle, Spit, Splutter, Stutter

Spy(ing), Spies Agent, Beagle, Blunt, Burgess, Caleb, CIA, Cicero, Curtain-twitcher, Descry, Dicker, Double agent, Eavesdrop, Emissary, Espionage, Fink, Fuchs, Infiltrate, Informer, Keeker, Maclean, Mata Hari, MI, Mole, Mossad, Mouchard, Nark, Ninja, Nose, Operative, Pickeer, Pimp, Plant, Pry, Recce, Scout, See, Setter, Shadow, Sinon, Sleeper, Snoop, Spetsnaz, Spook, Tachometer, Tout, Wait

Spyhole Eyelet, Judas-hole, Oillet, Peephole

Squab Chubby, Cushion, Obese

Squabble Argue, Bicker, Brabble, Quarrel, Rhubarb, Row, Scene, Scrap

Squad(ron) Awkward, Band, Blue, Company, Crew, Death, Drugs, Escadrille, Fifteen, Firing, Flying, Force, Fraud, Hit, Nahal, Platoon, Porn, Red, Snatch, Vice, White, Wing

Squalid, Squalor Abject, Colluvies, Dickensian, Dinge, Dingy, Filth, Frowsy, Grungy, Mean, Poverty, Scuzzy, Seedy, Skid Row, Sleazy, Slum(my), Slurb, Sordid

Squall Blast, Blow, Chubasco, Commotion, Cry, Drow, Flaw, Flurry, Gust, Line, Rainstorm, Sumatra, Wail, White, Williwaw, Yell, Yowl

Squander Blow, Blue, Dissipate, Fritter, Frivol, Lash, Mucker, Slather, Splash, Splurge, Ware, → **WASTE**

Square(d), Squares Agree, Anta, Arrière, Ashlar, Ashler, Bang, Barrack, Belgrave, Berkeley, Bevel, Block, Bribe, Chequer, Compone, Compony, Corny, Deal, Dinkum, Even(s), Fair, Fog(e)y, Forty-nine, Fossil, Four, Gobony, Grey, Grosvenor, Latin, Least, Leicester, Level, Magic, Market, Meal, Mean, Mitre, Nasik, Neandert(h)aler, Nine, Norma, Old-fashioned, Out, Palm, Passé, Pay, Perfect, Piazza, Place, Platz, Plaza, Quad(rangle), Quadrate, Quarry, Quits, Red, Rhomboid, Rood, S, Set(t), Sloane, Solid, Squier, Squire, Stick-in-the-mud, Straight, T, Tee, Tiananmen, Times, Traditionalist, Trafalgar, Try, Unhip

Squash(y) Adpress, Butternut, Conglomerate, Crush, Flatten, Gourd, Kia-ora®, Knead, Marrow, Mash, Obcompress, Oblate, Pattypan, Press, Pulp, Pumpkin, Shoehorn, Silence, Slay, Slew, Slue, Soft, Squeeze, Squidge, Squidgy, Summer, Suppress, Torpedo, Winter

Squat(ter), Squatting Bywoner, Caganer, Crouch, Croup(e), Cubby, Dumpy, Fubby, Fubsy, Hunker, Inquilinism, Occupy, Pudsey, Pyknic, Rook, Ruck, Sawed off, Sit, Spud, Stubby, Stumpy, Swatter, Tubby, Usucaption

Squaw Kloo(t)chman

Squawk Cackle, Complain, Cry, Scrauch, Scraugh

Squeak(er) Cheep, Creak, Narrow, Near, Peep, Pip, Scroop, Shoat, Squeal

Squeal(er) Blow, Creak, Eek, Howl, Inform, Pig, Screech, Sing, Sneak, Tell, Wee, Yelp

Squeamish(ness) Delicate, Disgust, Missish, Nervous, Prudish, Queasy, Reluctant

Squeeze(r) Bleed, Chirt, Coll, Compress, Concertina, Constrict, Cram, Cramp, Credit, Crowd, Crush, Dispunge, Exact, Express, Extort, Extrude, Hug, Jam, Mangle, Milk, Pack, Preace, Press, Reamer, Sandwich, Sap, Scrooge, Scrouge, Scrowdge, Scruze, Shoehorn, Squash, Squish, Sweat, Thrutch, Thumbscrew, Vice, Wring

Squelch Gurgle, Squash, Squish, Subdue

Squib Banger, Damp, Firework, Lampoon

Squid Calamari, Calamary, Cephalopod, Cuttlefish, Ink-fish, Loligo, Mortar, Nautilus, Octopus, Sleeve fish

Squiffy Drunk, Lit, Tiddley, Tipsy

▷ **Squiggle** *may indicate* an anagram

Squill Sea, Spring

Squint(ing) Boss-eyed, Cast, Cock-eye, Cross-eye, Glance, Gledge, Glee, Gley, Hagioscope, Heterophoria, Louche, Opening, Proptosis, Skellie, Skelly, Sken, Squin(n)y, Strabism, Swivel-eye, Vergence, Wall-eye

Squire Armiger(o), Beau, Donzel, Escort, Hardcastle, Headlong, Land-owner, Sancho Panza, Scutiger, Swain, Western, White

Squirm(ing) Fidget, Reptation, Twist, Worm, Wriggle, Writhe

Squirrel, Squirrel's nest Aye-aye, Boomer, Bun, Cage, Chickaree, Chipmuck, Chipmunk, Dray, Drey, Flickertail, Flying (-fox), Gopher, Grey, Ground, Hackee, Hoard(er), Marmot, Meerkat, Petaurist, Phalanger, Prairie dog, Red, Richardson's ground, Sciuroid, Sewellel, Skug, Spermophile, S(o)uslik, Taguan, Vair, Zizel

Squirt(er) Chirt, Cockalorum, Douche, Jet, Scoosh, Scoot, Skoosh, Spirt, Spout, Spritz, Urochorda, Wet, Whiffet, Whippersnapper

Sri Lanka(n) Ceylon, Cingalese, CL, .lk, Serendip, Sinhalese, Tamil, Vedda

St Saint, Street

Stab Bayonet, Chib, Chiv, Crease, Creese, Dag, Effort, Go, Gore, Guess, Jab, Knife, Kreese, Kris, Lancinate, Pang, Pierce, Pink, Poniard, Prick, Prong, Punch, Stick, Stiletto, Turk, Wound

Stabilise(r), Stability Aileron, Balance, Balloonet, Emulsifier, Even, Fin, Fixure, Gyroscope, Maintain, Pax Romana, Peg, Permanence, Plateau, Poise, Steady, Tail panel

Stable(s) Augean, Balanced, Barn, Byre, Certain, Consistent, Constant, Durable, Equerry, Equilibrium, Firm, Livery, Loose box, Manger, Mews, Permanent, Poise, Secure, Solid, Sound, Stall, Static(al), Steadfast, Steady, Stud, Sure, Together, Well-adjusted

Stableman Groom, Lad, Ostler

Stachys Betony

Stack(s) Accumulate, À gogo, Chimney, Clamp, Cock, End, Funnel, Heap, Lum, → **PILE**, Reckan, Rick, Shock, Sight, Smoke, Staddle

Stadium Arena, Astrodome, Ballpark, Bowl, Circus, Circus Maximus, Coliseum, Headingley, Hippodrome, Murrayfield, Speedway, Velodrome, Wembley

Staff Aesculapius, Alpenstock, Ash-plant, Bato(o)n, Bouche, Bourdon, Burden, Caduceus, Cane, Crew, Crook, Crosier, Cross(e), Crozier, Crutch, Cudgel, Entourage, Equerry, Establishment, État-major, Faculty, Ferula, Ferule, Flagpole, General, Ground, Jacob's, Jeddart, Linstock, Lituus, Mace, Man, Office, Omlah, Pastoral, Personnel, Pike, Pole, Ragged, Rod, Rung, Runic, Sceptre, Seniority, Skeleton, Stave, Stick, Supernumerary, Taiaha, Tapsmen, Tau, Thyrsus, Token, Truncheon, Verge, Wand, Workers, Workforce, Wring

Stag Actaeon, Brocket, Buck, Deer, For men, Hummel, Imperial, Knobber, Line, Male, Party, Royal, Rutter, Shadow, Ten-pointer, Wapiti

Stage Act, Anaphase, Apron, Arena, Ashrama, Bandstand, Bardo, Bema, Boards, Catasta, Centre, Chrysalis, Committee, Diligence, Dog-leg, Estrade, Fare, Fargo, Fit-up, Grade, Hop, Imago, Instar, Juncture, Key, Landing, Leg, Level, Metaphase, Milestone, Moment, Mount, Napron, Oidium, Orbital, Perform, Phase, Phasis, Pier, Pin, Platform, Podium, Point, Postscenium, Prophase, Proscenium, PS, Puberty, Report, Resting, Rostrum, Scene, Sensorimotor, Sound, Stadium, Step, Stepping stone, Stor(e)y, Subimago, Theatre, Theatrical, Thrust, Transition, Trek, Wells Fargo, Yuga, Zoea

Stage-coach Diligence, Thoroughbrace

Stagecraft Pinafore

Stagehand Flyman, Grip

Stagger(ed) Alternate, Amaze, Astichous, Astonish, Astound, Awhape, Daidle, Dodder, Falter, Floor, Lurch, Recoil, Reel, Rock, Shock, Stoiter, Stot(ter), Stumble, Sway, Teeter, Thunderstricken, Thunderstruck, Titubate, Tolter, Totter, Wamble, Wintle

▷ **Staggered** *may indicate* an anagram

Stagirite, Stagyrite Aristotle

Stagnant, Stagnation Cholestasis, Foul, Inert, Moribund, Scummy, Stasis, Static

Staid Decorous, Demure, Formal, Grave, Matronly, Prim, Prudish, Sad, Seemly, Sober, Stick-in-the-mud

Stain(er) Aniline, Bedye, Besmirch, Blemish, Blob, Blot, Blotch, Chica, Discolour, Dishonour, Dye, Embrue, Ensanguine, Eosin, Fox, Gram-negative, Gram-positive, Gram's, Grime, Imbrue, Inkspot, Iodophile, Keel, Maculate, Mail, Meal, Mote, Portwine, Slur, Smirch, Smit, Soil, Splodge, Splotch, Stigma, Sully, Taint, Tarnish, Tinge, Tint, Vital, Woad

Stair(case), Stairs Apples, Apples and pears, Caracol(e), Cochlea, Companionway, Escalator, Flight, Moving, Perron, Rung, Scale (and platt), Spiral, Step, Tread, Turnpike, Vice, Wapping, Winding

Stake(s) Ante, Bet, Claim, Deposit, Extracade, Gage, Go, Holding, Impale, Impone, Interest, Lay, Loggat, Mark, Mise, Nursery, Paal, Pale, Paliform, Paling, Palisade, Peel, Peg, Pele, Picket, Pile, Play, Post, Pot, Punt, Put, Rest, Revie, Risk, Septleva, Set, Spike, Spile, Stang, Stob, Straddle, Sweep, Tether, Vie, Wager, Weir, Welter

Stalactite Dripstone, Dropstone, Helictite, Lansfordite, Soda straw

Stalagmite Onyx marble

Stale Aged, Banal, Flat, Fozy, Frowsty, Fusty, Hackneyed, Handle, Hoary, Mouldy, Musty, Old, Pretext, Rancid, Urine, Worn

▷ **Stale** *may indicate* an obsolete word

Stalemate Deadlock, Dilemma, Draw, Hindrance, Impasse, Mexican standoff, Saw-off, Standoff, Tie, Zugswang

Stalinist Kirov

Stalk(er), Stalks Anthophore, Bennet, Bun, Cane, Caulicle, Follow, Funicle, Garb(e), Gynophore, Ha(u)lm, Keck(s), Kecksey, Keksye, Kex, Ommatophore, Pedicel, Pedicle, Peduncle, Petiole, Petiolule, Phyllode, Prowler, Pursue, Reed, Rush, Scape, Seta, Shaw, Spear, Spire, Stem, Sterigma, Still-hunter, Stipe(s), Strae, Straw, Stride, Strig, Strut, Stubble, Stump, Trail, Yolk

Stalking-horse Stale

Stall(s) Arrest, Bay, Booth, Box, Bulk, Crib, → **DELAY**, Floor, Flypitch, Hedge, Horse-box, Kiosk, Loose-box, Orchestra, Pen, Pew, Prebendal, Seat, Shamble, Sideshow, Stable, Stand, Starting, Stasidion, Sty, Sutlery, Temporise, Trap, Traverse, Travis, Trevis(s), Whip, Whipstall

Stallion Cooser, Cuisser, Cusser, Entire, → **HORSE**, Stag, Staig, Stonehorse, Stud

Stalwart Anchor-man, Buirdly, Firm, Manful, Robust, Sturdy, Trusty, Valiant

Stamen(ed) Androecium, Octandria, Polyandria, Synandrium

Stamina Endurance, Fibre, Fortitude, Guts, Last, Stamen, Stay, Steel, Vigour

Stammer(ing) Balbutient, Er, Hesitate, Hum, Psellism, Sputter, Stumble, → **STUTTER**, Waffle

Stamp(s), Stamped Albino, Appel, Cast, Character, Coin, Date(r), Die, Dry print, Enface, Enseal, Fiscal, Frank, Gutter-pair, Health, Imperforate, Impress, Imprint, Incuse, Kind, Label, Matchmark, Mint, Mintage, Obsign, Pane, Penny black, Perfin, Philately, Pintadera, Postage, Press(ion), Rubber, Seal, Seebeck, Se-tenant, Signet, Spif, Strike, Swage, Tête-bêche, Touch, Touchmark, Trading, Trample, Tread, Tromp, Type

Stamp-collecting Philately, Timbrology, Timbrophily

Stampede Debacle, Flight, Panic, Rampage, → **RUSH**, Sauve qui peut

Stance Attitude, Ecarté, Pose, Position, Posture, Quinte

Stand(ing), Stand for, Stand up Apron, Arraign, Attitude, Base, Bay, Be, Bear, Bide, Bier, Binnacle, Bipod, Bristle, Brook, Canterbury, Caste, Confrontation, Cradle, Crease, Dais, Degree, Desk, Dock, Dree, Dumb-waiter, Easel, Epergne, Étagère, Face, Foothold, Freeze, Gantry, Gueridon, Hard, Hob, Importance, Insulator, Klinostat, Last, Lazy Susan, Lectern, Leg, Lime, Music, Nef, Odour, One-night, Ovation, Pedestal, Place, Plant, Podium, Pose, Position, Pou sto, Predella, Prestige, Promenade, Protest, Qua, Rack, Rank, Regent, Remain, Represent, Repute, Rise, Rouse, Stall, Statant, Station, → **STATUS**, Stay, Stillage, Stock, Stomach, Stool, Straddle, Straphang, Striddle, Stroddle, Strut, Table, Tantalus, Taxi, Teapoy, Terrace, Toe, → **TREAT**, Tree, Tripod, Trivet, Umbrella, Upright, Whatnot, Witness

Standard(s) Banner, Base, Baseline, Basic, Benchmark, Bog, Bogey, British, Canon, CAT, Classic(al), Cocker, Code, Colour(s), Copybook, Criterion, Double, Eagle, English, Ethics, Etiquette, Examplar, Example, Exemplar, Fiducial, Flag, Ga(u)ge, Gold, Gonfalon, Grade, Guidon, Horsetail, Ideal, Jolly Roger, Kite-marker, Labarum, Level, Living, Model, Netiquette, Norm(a), Normal, Numeraire, Old Glory, Oriflamme, Par, Parker Morris, Pennon, Principle, Rate, Regular, Rod, Rose, Routine, Royal, → **RULE**, Scruples, Silver, Spec(ification), Staple, Sterling, Stock, Time, Touchstone, Tricolour, Troy, Two-power, Usual, Valuta, Vexillum, Yardstick

Standard-bearer Alferez, Cornet, Ensign, Vexillary

Stand-by Adminicle, Reserve, Substitute, Support, Twelfth man, Understudy

Stand-in Double, Locum, Stunt man, Sub(stitute), Surrogate, Temp, Understudy

Standish Miles

Stand-off(ish) Aloof, Number ten, Remote, Reserved, Stalemate, Upstage

Standpoint Angle, Slant, View

Standstill Deadset, Halt, Jam

Stanley Baldwin, Knife, Rupert

Stannic Tin
St Anthony's fire Ergotism, Erysipelas
Stanza Antistrophe, Ballad, Elegiac, Envoi, Envoy, Heroic, Matoke, Ottava, Ottava rima, Poem, Quatrain, Sixaine, Spasm, Spenserian, Staff, Stave, Tantum ergo, Tetrastich, Troparion, Verse
Staple Basic, Bread, Chief, Maize, Matoke, Oats, Pin, Rice, Stock, Wool
Star(s) Adept, Aster(isk), Binary, Body, Celebrity, Champ, Companion, Constant, Constellation, Cushion, Cynosure, Dark, Death, Double, Esther, Exploding, Falling, Fate, Feather, Feature, Film, Fixed, Flare, Giant, Headline, Hero, Hester, Hexagram, Idol, Late type, Lead, Lion, Main sequence, Mogen David, Movie, Mullet, Multiple, Pentacle, Personality, Phad, Pip, Plerion, Pointer, Principal, Pulsating, Seven, Shell, Shine, Shooting, Sidereal, Solomon's seal, Spangle, Starn(ie), Stellar, Stern, Swart, (The) Pointers, Top banana, Top-liner, Ultraviolet, Valentine, Variable, Vedette

STARS

3 letters:
Dog
Sol

4 letters:
Argo
Beta
Grus
Lode
Lyra
Mira
Nova
Pavo
Pole
Ursa
Vega
Vela
Zeta

5 letters:
Acrux
Agena
Algol
Alpha
Ceres
Comet
Delta
Deneb
Draco
Dubhe
Dwarf
Gamma
Hyads
Indus
Lupus
Mensa
Merak
Mizar

Norma
North
Polar
Radio
Rigel
Rigil
Saiph
Spica
Theta
Venus
Virgo
Wagon
Whale

6 letters:
Alioth
Alkaid
Altair
Aquila
Étoile
Auriga
Boötes
Carbon
Carina
Castor
Cygnus
Dorado
Fornax
Galaxy
Hatsya
Hyades
Lambda
Lizard
Megrez
Meissa
Merope
Meteor
Octans

Phecda
Plough
Pollux
Psyche
Pulsar
Puppis
Quasar
Saturn
Sirius
Sothis
Uranus
Vesper
Volans

7 letters:
Alnilam
Alnitak
Antares
Éstoile
Calaeno
Canopus
Capella
Cepheus
Chamber
Columba
Dolphin
Epsilon
Evening
Gemingo
Lucifer
Mintaka
Morning
Neutron
Perseus
Phoenix
Polaris
Procyon
Proxima

Regulus
Sabaism
Serpens
Sterope
Triones
Wagoner

8 letters:
Achernar
Arcturus
Barnard's
Circinus
Denebola
Equuleus
Eridanus
Hesperus
Magnetar
Mira Ceti
Pegasean
Phosphor
Pleiades
Praesepe
Red dwarf
Red giant
Scorpius
Synastry
Waggoner

9 letters:
Aldebaran
Andromeda
Bellatrix
Big Dipper
Black hole
Centaurus
Collapsar
Delphinus
Fire-drake

Fomalhaut	**10 letters:**	White dwarf	**13 letters:**
Meteorite	Betacrucis		Grande vedette
Ophiuchus	Betelgeuse	**11 letters:**	Southern Cross
Pentagram	Betelgeuze	Circumpolar	
Rigil-Kent	Brown dwarf		**14 letters:**
Supernova	Cassiopeia	**12 letters:**	Camelopardalis
Wolf-Rayet	Orion's Belt	Little Dipper	
	Phosphorus	Septentrione	**15 letters:**
	Supergiant		Proxima Centauri

Starboard Right

Starch(y), Starch producer Amyloid, Amylum, Animal, Arrowroot, Cassava, Ceremony, Congee, Conjee, Coontie, Coonty, Cycad, Farina, Fecula, Formal, Glycogen, Lichenin, Manioc, Maranta, Pentosan, Pyrene, Pyroid, Sago, Stamina, Statolith, Stiff, Tapioca, Tous-les-mois

Stare Eyeball, Fisheye, Gape, Gapeseed, Gawp, Gaze, Geek, Glare, Goggle, Gorp, Look, Ogle, Outface, Peer, Rubberneck, Scowl

Starfish Ambulacra, Asterid, Asteroid(ea), Bipinnaria, Brittlestar, Ophiurid, Radiata

Star-gaze(r), Star-gazing Astrodome, Astronomy, Copernicus

Stark Apparent, Austere, Bald, Bare, Gaunt, Harsh, Naked, Nude, Sheer, Stiff, Utterly

Starling Bird, Gippy, Hill mynah, Murmuration, Pastor, Rosy pastor, Stare, Stuckie

Star of Bethlehem Chincherinchee, Chinkerinchee

▷ **Start** *may indicate* an anagram or first letters

Start(ed), Starter, Starting-point Ab ovo, Abrade, Abraid, Abray, Activate, Actuate, Begin, Bhajee, Boggle, Boot-up, Bot, Broach, Bug, Bully off, Bump, Chance, Commence, Consommé, Course, Crank, Create, Crudités, Dart, Debut, Ean, Embryo, Entrée, Face-off, False, Fire, Flinch, Float, Flush, Flying, Found, Gambit, Gan, Generate, Genesis, Getaway, Gun, Handicap, Head, Hors-d'oeuvres, Hot-wire, Impetus, Imprimis, Incept(ion), Initiate, Instigate, Institute, Intro(duce), Jar, Jerk, Judder, Jump, Jump lead, Jump-off, Kick-off, L, Lag, Launch, Lead, Melon, Nidus, Novice, Off, Offset, Onset, Ope(n), Ord, Origin, Outset, Poppadom, Potage, Preliminary, Prelude, Proband, Push, Put-up, Reboot, Resume, Roll, Roul, Rouse, Scare, Set off, Shy, Slip, Snail, Soup, Spark, Spring, Springboard, Spud, String, Tee-off, Terminus a quo, Toehold, Wince

Startle(d), Startling Agape, Alarm, Bewilder, Disturb, Eye-opener, Flush, Frighten, Lurid, Magical, Rock, Scare

Starvation, Starve(d), Starving Anorexia, Anoxic, Bant, Clem, Cold, Deprive, Diet, Famish, Foodless, Inanition, Macerate, Perish, Pine, Undernourished

▷ **Starving** *may indicate* an 'o' in the middle of a word

Stash Hide, Hoard, Secrete

State(s), Stateside Affirm, Alle(d)ge, Aread, Arrede, Assert, Assever, Attest, Aver, Avow, Buffer, Case, Circar, Cite, Client, Commonwealth, Condition, Confederate, Construct, Country, Critical, Cutch, Declare, Dependency, Dirigisme, Emirate, Empire, État, Express, Federal, Fettle, Flap, Formulate, Free, Going, Habitus, Humour, Kingdom, Land, Lesh, Limbo, Mess, Metastable, Mode, Name, Nanny, Nation, Native, Palatinate, Papal, Para, Plateau, Plight, Police, Posit, Power, Predicament, Predicate, Premise, Profess, Pronounce, Protectorate, Puppet, Quantum, Realm, Republic, Rogue, Samadhi, Sanctitude, Satellite, Say, Sircar, Sirkar, Slave, Sorry, Standard, Standing, Steady, Succession, Threeness, Thusness, Uncle Sam, Union, United, Welfare, Yap

STATES

2 letters:	Md	NC	RI
Ga	Me	NY	UK
Ia	Mi	Pa	US

Ut
Va

3 letters:
Ark
Del
Fla
Goa
NSW
Oyo
USA
Wis

4 letters:
Abia
Acre
Chad
Conn
Gulf
Iowa
Kano
Kogi
Laos
Mass
Ogun
Ohio
Oman
Ondo
Osun
Shan
Swat
Togo
Utah

5 letters:
Amapa
Assam
Bahia
Benin
Benue
Bihar
Ceará
Dixie
Dubai
Gabon
Ghana
Hesse
Idaho
Jammu
Kalat
Kedah
Kutch
Kwara
Lippe

Maine
Malay
Mewar
Nepal
Oshun
Perak
Piaui
Qatar
Reich
Sabah
Samoa
Texas
Tibet
Tyrol

6 letters:
Alaska
Balkan
Baltic
Baroda
Bauchi
Belize
Bremen
Brunei
Cochin
Colima
Dakota
Hawaii
Indore
Jigawa
Johore
Kaduna
Kansas
Kerala
Khelat
Kuwait
Madras
Malawi
Mysore
Nevada
Oaxaca
Oregon
Orissa
Pahang
Parana
Penang
Perlis
Puebla
Punjab
Rivers
Saxony
Serbia
Sikkim
Sokoto

Sonora
Sparta
Styria
Tassie
Tonkin

7 letters:
Alabama
Alagoas
Anambra
Andorra
Arizona
Barbary
Bavaria
Belarus
Buffalo
Chiapas
Comoros
Croatia
Durango
Florida
Georgia
Grenada
Gujarat
Gujerat
Haryana
Hidalgo
Indiana
Ireland
Jalisco
Jamaica
Jodhpur
Kashmir
Malacca
Manipur
Mizoram
Montana
Morelos
Nayarit
New York
Nirvana
Paraiba
Pradesh
Prussia
Roraima
Sarawak
Sergipe
Sinaloa
Tabasco
Tongkin
Tonking
Tripura
Trucial
Udaipur

Vermont
Vietnam
Wyoming
Yucatan

8 letters:
Abu Dhabi
Amazonas
Arkansas
Botswana
Campeche
Carolina
Coahuila
Colorado
Delaware
Ethiopia
Honduras
Illinois
Jharkand
Kelantan
Kentucky
Kiribati
Maranhao
Maryland
Michigan
Missouri
Nagaland
Nebraska
Oklahoma
Paraguay
Rondonia
Saarland
Sao Paulo
Selangor
Tanzania
Tasmania
Tiaxcala
Tongking
Transkei
Veracruz
Victoria
Virginia

9 letters:
Chihuahua
Costa Rica
Dixieland
Guatemala
Hyderabad
Karnataka
Louisiana
Manchukuo
Meghalaya
Michoacán

Minnesota
Nassarawa
New Jersey
New Mexico
Nuevo Léon
Queretaro
Rajasthan
Rajputana
Singapore
St Vincent
Tamil Nadu
Tennessee
Thuringia
Tocantins
Trengganu
Venezuela
Wisconsin
Zacatecas

10 letters:
California
Guanajuato
Jamahiriya

Jumhouriya
Manchoukuo
Orange Free
Pernambuco
Queensland
Tamaulipas
Tanganyika
Terengganu
Travancore
Washington
West Bengal

11 letters:
Brandenberg
Connecticut
Jamahouriya
Maharashtra
Mecklenburg
Minas Gerais
Mississippi
North Dakota
Quintana Roo
South Dakota

Uttaranchal
Vatican City

12 letters:
Chhattisgarh
Madhya Bharat
New Hampshire
Pennsylvania
Saxony-Anholt
Uttar Pradesh
West Virginia

13 letters:
Andhra Pradesh
Madhya Pradesh
Massachusetts
Negri Sembilan
New South Wales
San Luis Potosi
Santa Catarina
South Carolina

14 letters:
Aguascalientes
Rio Grande do Sul
South Australia
Vindhya Pradesh

15 letters:
Himachal Pradesh
Schaumburg-Lippe
St Kitts and Nevis

16 letters:
Rio Grande do Norte

17 letters:
Schleswig-Holstein

19 letters:
Rhineland-Palatinate

20 letters:
North Rhine-
    Westphalia

▷ **Stated** *may indicate* a similar sounding word

Stately, Stately home August, Dome, Grand, Imposing, Junoesque, Majestic, Mansion, Noble, Regal, Solemn

Statement Accompt, Account, Affidavit, Aphorism, Assertion, Asseveration, Attestation, Avowal, Axiom, Bill, Bulletin, Case, Communiqué, Deposition, Dictum, Diktat, Encyclical, Enigma, Evidence, Expose, Factoid, Generalisation, Grand Remonstrance, Impact, Indictment, Invoice, Jurat, Manifesto, Mission, Non sequitur, Outline, Paraphrase, Pleading, Press release, Profession, Pronouncement, Pronunciamento, Proposition, Protocol, Quotation, Release, Report, Sentence, Shema, Shout out, Soundbite, Sweeping, Testament, Testimony, Theologoumenon, Truism, Utterance, Verbal

Stateroom Bibby, Cabin

Statesman American, Attlee, Augustus, Botha, Briand, Bright, Canning, Castlereagh, Cato, Chesterfield, Chirac, Cicero, Clarendon, Clemenceau, Cosgrave, De Valera, De Witt, Diefenbaker, Diplomat, Disraeli, Dollfuss, Draco, Dulles, Elder, Flaminius, Franklin, Gandhi, Genro, Georgian, Gladstone, Gracchi, Grotius, Guy, Kissinger, Kruger, Lafayette, Lie, Mitterand, Molotov, Nasser, North, Palmerston, Peel, Perceval, Pericles, Peron, Pitt, Politician, Politico, Pompidou, Pretorius, Rockingham, Seneca, Smuts, Stein, Talleyrand, Tasmanian, Texan, Thiers, Tito, Verwoerd, Vorster, Walesa, Walpole, Walsingham, Wealsman, Yankee

Static Atmospherics, Becalmed, Electricity, Inert, Maginot-minded, Motionless, Sferics, Stagnant, Stationary

Station(s) Action, Aid, Air, Base, Berth, Birth, Camp, Caste, CCS, Coaling, Comfort, Crewe, Deploy, Depot, Docking, Dressing, Earth, Euston, Filling, Fire, Garrison, Gas, Generation, Halt, Head, Hill, Hilversum, Ice, Lay, Location, Marylebone, Meridian, Mir, Nick, Outpost, Paddington, Panic, Pay, Petrol, Pitch, Place, Plant, Point, Police, Polling, Post, Power, Powerhouse, Quarter, Radio, Rank, Relay, Rowme, Seat, Service, Sheep, Sit, Space, Stance, Stand, Star, Status, Stond, Subscriber, Tana, Tanna(h), Terminus, Testing, Thana(h), Thanna(h), Tracking, Transfer, Triangulation, Vauxhall, Victoria, Waterloo, Waverley, Way, Weather, Whistlestop, Wind farm, Wireless, Work

Stationary At rest, Fasten, Fixed, Immobile, Parked, Sessile, Stable, Static

Stationer(y), Stationery-case Continuous, Multi-part, Papeterie

Statistic(ian), Statistics Actuary, Bose-Einstein, Descriptive, ERA, Fermi-Dirac, Figure, Gallup, Gradgrind, Graph, Inferential, Isotype, Lod, Nonparametric, Number, Parametric, Percentage, Quant(um), Sampling, Student's t, Vital

Statuary, Statue(tte) Acrolith, Bronze, Bust, Colossus (of Rhodes), Discobolus, Effigy, Figure, Figurine, Galatea, Idol, Image, Kore, Kouros, Liberty, Memnon, Monolith, Monument, Oscar, Palladium, Pietà, Sculpture, Sphinx, Stonework, Stookie, Tanagra, Torso, Xoanon

Stature Growth, Height, Inches, Rank

Status Amateur, Beacon, Caste, Class, Curule, Pecking-order, Political, → **POSITION**, Prestige, Professional, Quo, Rank, Standing

Statute Act, Capitular, Chapter 11, Chapter 7, Decree, Edict, Law, Limitations, Novels, Provisors, Westminster

Staunch Amadou, Leal, Resolute, Steady, Stem, Stout, Styptic, Watertight

Stave Break, Dali, Forestall, Lag, Slat, Stanza, Ward

Stay(ing), Stays Abide, Alt, Avast, Bide, Board, Bolster, Cohab(it), Corselet, Corset, Embar, Endure, Fulcrum, Gest, Guy, Hawser, Hold, Indwell, Jump, Lie, Lig, Linger, Lodge, Manet, Moratorium, Pause, Piers, Postpone, Prop, → **REMAIN**, Reprieve, Restrain, Settle, Sist, Sleepover, Sojourn, Stamina, Stem, Stop off, Stop-over, Strut, Sustain, Tarry, Triatic, Villeggiatura

Stay-at-home Indoor, Tortoise

STD Aids, Herpes, Telephone, VD

Steadfast Abiding, Changeless, Constance, Constant, Dilwyn, Firm, Implacable, Perseverant, Resolute, Sad, Stable

Steadier, Steady Andantino, Ballast, Beau, Boyfriend, Changeless, Composer, Consistent, Constant, Even, Faithful, Firm, Girlfriend, Level-headed, Malstick, Measured, Regular, Rock, Rock-solid, Stabilise, Stable, Unswerving

Steak Carpet-bag, Chateaubriand, Chuck, Diane, Entrecote, Fillet, Flitch, Garni, Mignon, Minute, Pepper, Pope's eye, Porterhouse, Ribeye, Rump, Slice, Tartare, T-bone, Tenderloin, Tournedos, Vienna

Steal(ing), Steal away Abstract, Bag, Bandicoot, Bone, Boost, Cabbage, Cly, Condiddle, Convey, Creep, Crib, Duff, Edge, Elope, Embezzle, Filch, Glom, Grab, Half-inch, Heist, Hotting, Joyride, Kidnap, Knap, Knock down, Knock off, Lag, Liberate, Lift, Loot, Mag(g), Mahu, Mill, Misappropriate, Naam, Nam, Nap, Nick, Nim, Nip, Nobble, Nym, Peculate, Phone-jack, Pilfer, Pillage, Pinch, Piracy, Plagiarise, Plunder, Poach, Pocket, Prig, Proll, Purloin, Purse, Ram-raid, Remove, Rifle, Rip-off, Rob, Rustle, Scrump, Skrimp, Smug, Snaffle, Snatch, Sneak, Snitch, Souvenir, Swipe, Take, Theft, Thieve, Tiptoe, TWOC, Whip

Stealth(y) Art, Catlike, Covert, Cunning, Furtive, Obreption, Stolenwise, Surreptitious, Tiptoe

Steam(ed), Steaming, Steamy Boil, Condensation, Cushion, Dry, Fume, Gaseous, Het, Humid, Live, Livid, Mist, Porn, Radio, Roke, Sauna, Spout, Vapor, Vapour, Wet

Steamer, Steamboat Hummum, Kettle, Ocean tramp, Paddle, Showboat, Side-wheeler, SS, Str, Tramp, Turbine

Steam-hammer, Steamroller Crush, Ram

Steed Avenger, Charger, Horse, Mount, Pownie

Steel(y) Acierate, Adamant, Bainite, Bethlehem, Blade, Blister, Bloom, Brace, Carbon, Cast, Chrome, Chromium, Cold, Concrete, Crucible, Damascus, Damask, High-carbon, High-speed, Low-carbon, Magnet, Manganese, Maraging, Martensite, Metal, Mild, Nickel, Pearlite, Pedal, Ripon, Rolled, Shear, Silver, Sorbite, Spray, Stainless, Structural, Sword, Taggers, Terne plate, Toledo, Tool, Tungsten, Vanadium, Wootz

Steelyard Bismar

Steep(ening) Abrupt, Arduous, Bold, Brent, Buck, Cliff-face, Costly, Embay, Expensive,

High-pitched, Hilly, Immerse, Krans, Krantz, Kranz, Macerate, Marinade, Marinate, Mask, Monocline, Plo(a)t, Precipice, Precipitous, Rait, Rapid, Rate, Ret, Saturate, Scarp, → **SHEER**, Soak, Sog, Sop, Souse, Stey, Stickle, Tan

Steeple(jack) Spiderman, Spire, Turret

Steer(er), Steering Ackerman, Airt, Buffalo, Bullock, Bum, Cann, Castor, Con(n), Cox, Direct, → **GUIDE**, Helm, Navaid, Navigate, Ox, Pilot, Ply, Power, Rudder, Stot, Whipstaff, Zebu

St Elmo's fire Corona discharge, Corposant

Stem Alexanders, Arrow, Axial, Biller, Bind, Bine, Bole, Caudex, Caulicle, Caulome, Check, Cladode, Cladophyll, Confront, Corm, Culm, Dam, Eddo, Epicotyl, Floricane, Ha(u)lm, Kex, Pedicle, Peduncle, Pin, Pseudaxis, R(h)achilla, Rachis, Rhachis, Rhizome, Rise, Rod, Sarment, Scapus, Seta, Shaft, Shank, Sobole(s), Spring, Stalk, Staunch, Stipe, Stolon, Stopple, Straw, Sympodium, Tail, Tamp, Terete

Stench F(o)etor, Funk, Miasma, Odour, Pong, Reek, Smell, Stink, Whiff

Stencil Copy, Duplicate, Mimeograph®, Pochoir

Stenographer, Stenography Amanuensis, Secretary, Shorthand, Typist

Step(s) Act, Apples and pears, Balancé, Chassé, Choctaw, Corbel, Corbie, Curtail, Dance, Degree, Démarche, Echelon, Escalate, False, Flight, Fouetté, Gain, Gait, Glissade, Goose, Grade, Grapevine, Grecian, Greece, Grees(e), Greesing, Grese, Gressing, Grice, Griece, Grise, Grize, Halfpace, Increment, Lavolt, Lock, Measure, Move, Notch, Pace, Pas, Pas de souris, Phase, Pigeon('s) wing, Quantal, Raiser, Ratlin(e), Rattlin(e), Rattling, Roundel, Roundle, Rung, Sashay, Shuffle, Slip, Stage, Stair, Stalk, Stile, Stope, Stride, Sugarfoot, Toddle, Trap, Tread, Trip, Unison, Waddle, Walk, Whole, Winder

Stephen Martyr, Stainless

Stepmother Novercal

Stepney Spare

Steppe Kyrgyz, Llano, Plain

Stereo iPod®, Personal

Stereoscope Pseudoscope

Stereotype(d) Hackney, Ritual, Spammy

Sterile, Sterilise(r), Sterilisation, Sterility Acarpous, Aseptic, Atocia, Autoclave, Barren, Clean, Dead, Fruitless, Impotent, Infertile, Neuter, Pasteurise, Spay, Tubal ligation, Vasectomy

Sterling Excellent, Genuine, Pound, Silver, Sound

Stern Aft, Austere, Back, Counter, Dour, Flinty, Grim, Hard, Implacable, Iron, Isaac, Nates, Poop, Rear, Relentless, Rugged, Stark, Strict, Tailpiece, Transom

Steroid Anabolic, Androsterone, Calciferol, Cortisone, Dexamethasone, Ergosterol, Fusidic, Lipid, Lumisterol, Mifepristone, Nandrolone, Predniso(lo)ne, Spironolactone, Stanozolol, Testosterone, Tetrahydrogestrinone

Sterol Stigmasterol

Stertorous Snore

Stet Restore

Stevedore Docker, Dockhand, Lighterman, Loader, Longshoreman, Stower, Wharfinger

Stevenson RLS, Tusitala

Stew(ed), Stews Bagnio, Bath, Blanquette, Boil, Bordel(lo), Bouillabaisse, Bouilli, Bourguignon, Braise, Bredie, Brothel, Burgoo, Carbonade, Carbonnade, Casserole, Cassoulet, Cholent, Chowder, Coddle, Colcannon, Compot(e), Daube, Flap, Fume, Fuss, Goulash, Haricot, Hash, Hell, Hot(ch)pot(ch), Irish, Jug, Lather, Lobscouse, Maconochie, Matapan, Matelote, Mulligan, Navarin, Olla podrida, Osso bucco, Oyster, Paddy, Paella, Pepperpot, Pot-au-feu, Pot-pourri, Ragout, Ratatouille, Rubaboo, Salmi, Sass, Scouse, Seethe, Simmer, Slumgullion, Squiffy, Stie, Stove, Stovies, Sty, Succotash, Sweat, Swelter, Tajine, Tatahash, Tzimmes, Zamzawed, Zarzuela

Steward(ess) Butler, Cellarer, Chamberlain, Chiltern Hundreds, Dewan, Factor, Flight

attendant, Hind, Keeper, Major domo, Malvolio, Manciple, Maormor, Mormaor, Official, Oswald, Panter, Purser, Reeve, Seneschal, Sewer, Shop, Smallboy, Sommelier, Waiter
▷ **Stewed** *may indicate* an anagram
St Francis Seraphic Father
Stibnite Antimony, Kohl
Stick(ing) (out), Sticks, Stuck, Sticky Adhere, Affix, Agglutinant, Aground, Ash, Ashplant, Atlatl, Attach, Bamboo, Bastinado, Bat, Baton, Bauble, Bayonet, Beanpole, Blackthorn, Bludgeon, Bond, Boondocks, Broadside, Caman, Cambrel, Cammock, Cane, Celery, Cement, Chalk, Chapman, Clag, Clam(my), Clarty, Clave, Cleave, Cleft, Cling, Clog, Club, Cocktail, Cohere, Coinhere, Composing, Control, Crab, Crayon, Crosier, Cross(e), Crotch, Crozier, Crummock, Cue, Distaff, Divining-rod, Dog, Dure, Endure, Execration, Exsert, Fag(g)ot, Firewood, Fix, Flak, Founder, Fuse, Gad(e), Gaid, Gambrel, Gelatine, Glair, Gliadin, Glit, Gloopy, Glue, Goad, Gold, Goo, Gore, Ground-ash, Gum, Gunge, Gunk, Harpoon, Hob, Hold on, Hurley, Immobile, Impale, Inhere, Isinglass, Jab, Jam, Joss, Jut, Kebbie, Kid, Kierie, Kindling, Kip, Kiri, Knife, Knitch, Knobkerrie, Ko, Lance, Lath(i), Lathee, Lentisk, Limy, Lug, Mallet, Message, Minder, Molinet, Needle, Orange, Parasitic, Paste, Penang-lawyer, Persist, Phasmid, Piceous, Pierce, Piolet, Plaster, Pogo, Pole, Posser, Pot, Protrude, Protuberant, Pugil, Q-tip, Quarterstaff, Rash, Ratten, Rhubarb, Rhythm, Rod, Ropy, Rural, Scouring, Seat, Shillela(g)h, Shooting, Size, Ski, Smeary, Smudge, Spanish windlass, Spear, Spillikin, Spurtle, Squail(er), Stab, Staff, Stand, Stang, Stob, Stodgy, Stubborn, Supplejack, Swagger, Switch, Swizzle, Swordstick, Tacamahac, Tack(y), Tally, Tar, Thick, Throwing, Toddy, Tokotoko, Truncheon, Trunnion, Twig, Vare, Viscid, Viscose, Viscous, Waddy, Wait, Walking, Wand, Wedge, White, Woolder, Woomera(ng), Yardwand
Sticker Araldite®, Barnacle, Bumper, Bur, Burr, Flash, Gaum, Glue, Label, Limpet, Partisan, Pin, Poster, Post-it®, Slogan, Viscose
Stickler Pedant, Poser, Problem, Purist, Rigid, Rigorist, Tapist
Stickybeak Nosy Parker, Paul Pry
Stiff, Stiffen(er), Stiffening, Stiffness Anchylosis, Angular, Ankylosis, Baleen, Bandoline, Body, Brace, Buckram, Budge, Cadaver, Corpse, Corpus, Dear, Defunct, Dilate, Expensive, Fibrositis, Formal, Frore(n), Frorn(e), Gammy, Goner, Gromet, Grommet, Grummet, Gut, Hard, Inelastic, Lignin, Mort, Myotonia, Petrify, Pokerish, Prim, Ramrod, Rheumatic(ky), Rigid, Rigor, Rigor mortis, Sad, Set, Shank-iron, Size, Solid, Starch, Stark, Stay, Steeve, Stieve, Stilted, Stoor, Stour, Stowre, Sture, Tensive, Trubenize®, Unbending, Unyielding, Upper lip, Whalebone, Wigan, Wooden
Stifle Crush, Dampen, Depress, Funk, Muffle, Scomfish, Smore, Smother, Stive, Strangle
Stigma(tise) Blemish, Brand, Carpel, Discredit, Note, Slur, Smear, Spot, → **STAIN**, Wound
Stile Gate, Slamming, Steps, Sty
Stiletto Bodkin, Heel, Knife
Still Accoy, Airless, Alembic, Assuage, At rest, Becalm, Breathless, Calm, Check, Current, Doggo, Ene, Even(ness), Freeze-frame, Higher, Howbe, However, Hush, Illicit, Inactive, Inanimate, Inert, Kill, Languid, Limbec(k), Lull, Motionless, Nevertheless, Nonetheless, Patent, Peaceful, Photograph, Placate, Placid, Polaroid, Posé, Pot, Quiescent, Quiet, Resting, Silent, Snapshot, Soothe, Stagnant, Static, Stationary, Stock, Stone, Though, Tranquil, Windless, Yet
Stilt Avocet, Bird, Poaka, Prop, Scatch
Stilted Formal, Mannered, Pedantic, Stiff, Unruffled, Wooden
Stimulate, Stimulus, Stimulant, Stimulation Activate, Adrenaline, Anilingus, Ankus, Antigen, Aperitif, Aphrodisiac, Arak, Arouse, Auxin, Benny, Brace, Caffeine, Cardiac, Cinder, Clomiphene, Coca, Conditioned, Coramine, Cue, Dart, Dex(edrine)®, Digitalin, Digoxin, Doxapram, Egg, Energise, Erotogenic, Evoke, Excitant, Fillip, Foreplay, Fuel, Galvanize, Ginger, Goad, Grains of Paradise, G-spot, Guinea grains, Hop up, Hormone, Incentive, Incitant, Incite, Innerve, Inspire, Irritate, Jog, K(h)at, Key, Kick, L-dopa, Mneme, Motivate, Nikethamide, Oestrus, Oxytocin, Pa(a)n, Paraphilia,

Paratonic, Pemoline, Pep, Pep pill, Peyote, Philtre, Pick-me-up, Piquant, Pituitrin, Potentiate, Prod, Promote, Provoke, Psych, Qat, Rim, Ritalin®, Roborant, → **ROUSE**, Rowel, Rub, Sassafras, Sensuous, Somatosensory, Spark, Spur, Sting, Stir, Suggestive, Tannin, Tar, Theine, Tickle, Tik-tik, Titillate, Tone, Tonic, Tropism, Unconditioned, Upper, Urge, Whet(stone), Wintergreen, Winter's bark

Sting(er), Stinging Aculeate, Barb, Bite, Cheat, Cnida, Con, Goad, Nematocyst, Nettle(tree), Overcharge, Perceant, Piercer, Poignant, Prick, Provoke, Pungent, Rile, Scorcher, Scorpion, Sea anemone, Sephen, Smart, Spice, Stang, Stimulus, Surcharge, Tang, Tingle, Trichocyst, Urent, Urtica, Venom

Sting-ray Sephen, Trygon

Stingy Cheeseparing, Chintzy, Close, Costive, Hard, Illiberal, Mean, Miserly, Narrow, Near, Niggardly, Nippy, Parsimonious, Save-all, Skimpy, Snippy, Snudge, Tight(wad), Tight-arse

▷ **Stingy** *may indicate* something that stings

Stink(er), Stinking, Stinks Abroma, Atoc, Atok, Brock, Cacodyl, Cad, Crepitate, Desman, Fetor, Foumart, Guff, Heel, Hellebore, Malodour, Mephitis, Miasma, Ming, Niff, Noisome, Polecat, Pong, Ponk, Rasse, Reek, Rich, Science, → **SMELL**, Sondeli, Stench, Teledu

Stinkbird Hoa(c)tzin

Stint Allot, Chore, Economise, Limit, Scamp, Scantle, Scrimp, Session, Share, Skimp, Spell

Stipend Ann(at), Annexure, Pay, Prebend, Remuneration, Salary, Wages

Stipulate, Stipulation Clause, Condition, Covenant, Insist, Provision, Proviso, Rider, Specify

Stipule Ocrea

Stir(red), Stirrer, Stirring Accite, Admix, Ado, Afoot, Agitate, Amo(o)ve, Animate, Annoy, Araise, Arouse, Awaken, Bird, Bother, Bustle, Buzz, Can, Churn, Cooler, Evocative, Excite, Foment, Furore, Fuss, Gaol, Hectic, Impassion, Incense, Incite, Inflame, Instigate, Insurrection, Intermix, Jee, Jog, Jug, Kitty, Limbo, Live, Makebate, → **MIX**, Molinet, Move, Newgate, Nick, Noy, Paddle, Penitentiary, Poach, Poss, Pother, → **PRISON**, Prod, Provoke, Quad, Quatch, Quetch, Qui(t)ch, Quinche, Quod, Rabble, Rear, Roil, Rouse, Roust, Rummage, Rustle, Sod, Steer, Styre, Swizzle, To-do, Touch, Upset, Upstart, Wake

▷ **Stir(red), Stirring** *may indicate* an anagram

Stirrup (guard) Bone, Footrest, Footstall, Gambado, Iron, Stapes, Tapadera, Tapadero

Stitch(ing), Stitch up Bargello, Bar tack, Basket, Baste, Blanket, Blind, Box, Buttonhole, Cable, Chain, Couching, Crewel, Crochet, Cross, Daisy, Embroider, Fancy, Feather, Fell, Flemish, Florentine, Garter, Gathering, Grospoint, Hem, Herringbone, Honeycomb, Insertion, Kettle, Knit, Lazy daisy, Lock, Middle, Monk's seam, Moss, Needle, Open, Overcast, Overlock, Pearl, Petit point, Pinwork, Plain, Purl, Queen, Rag, Railway, Rib, Rope, Running, Saddle, Satin, Screw, Sew, Slip, Smocking, Spider, Split, Stab, Stay, Steek, Stem, Stockinette, Stocking, Straight, Sutile, Suture, Tack, Tailor's tack, Tent, Topstitch, Vandyke, Wheat-ear, Whip, Whole, Zigzag

St James Scallop-shell

St Jerome Hieronymic

St John's bread Carob

St Lucia WL

Stock(ed), Stocks, Stocky Aerie, Aery, Alpha, Ambulance, Amplosome, Arsenal, Barometer, Blue-chip, Bouillon, Bree, Breech, Brompton, Buffer, But(t), Capital, Cards, Carry, Cattle, Choker, Cippus, Common, Congee, Conjee, Court-bouillon, Cravat, Dashi, Debenture, Delta, Die, Endomorph, Equip, Evening, Fumet, Fund, Gamma, Gear(e), Government, Graft, Growth, Gun, Hackneyed, Handpiece, He(a)rd, Hilt, Hoosh, Industrial, Intervention, Inventory, Joint, Just-in-time, Kin, Larder, Laughing, Line, Little-ease, Locuplete, Log, Night-scented, Omnium, Pigeonhole, Preferred, Pycnic,

Race, Ranch, Recovery, Rep(ertory), Replenish, Reserve, Resource, Rolling, Root, Scrip, Seed, Shorts, Soup, Squat, Staple, Stash, Steale, Steelbow, Stirp(e)s, → **STORE**, Strain, Stubby, Supply, Surplus, Talon, Tap, Taurus, Team, Tie, Trite, Trust(ee), Utility, Virginian, Water

Stockade Barrier, Eureka, Zare(e)ba, Zereba, Zeriba

Stock Exchange Big Board

Stocking(s) Bas, Body, Boot-hose, Fishnet, Hogger, Hose, Leather, Legwarmer, Legwear, Moggan, Netherlings, Netherstocking, Nylons, Popsock, Seamless, Sheer, Silk, Sock, Spattee, Support, Surgical, Tights

Stockman, Stockbroker Broker, Jobber, Neatherd

Stodge, Stodgy Dull, Filling, Heavy

Stoic(al) Impassive, Job, Logos, Patient, Philosophical, Plato, Porch, Seneca(n), Spartan, Stolid, Zeno

Stoke(r), Stokes Bram, Chain grate, Coal-trimmer, Fire(man), Fuel, S, Shovel

Stole(n) Bent, Boa, Epitrachelion, Hot, Maino(u)r, Manner, Manor, Nam, Orarion, Orarium, Reft, Scarf, Screen, Soup, Staw, Tippet, Tweedle, Waif, Wrap

Stolid Beefy, Deadpan, Dour, Dull, Impassive, Phlegmatic, Po(-faced), Thickset, Wooden

Stomach(ic) Abdomen, Abomasum, Accept, Alvine, Appetite, Belly, Bible, Bingy, Bonnet, Bread-basket, Brook, C(o)eliac, Corporation, Craw, Epigastrium, Epiploon, Face, Fardel-bag, Gaster, Gizzard, Gut, Heart, Inner man, Jejunum, King's-hood, Kite, Kyte, Little Mary, Manyplies, Mary, Maw, Mesaraic, Midriff, Omasum, Opisthosoma, Paunch, Potbelly, Propodon, Proventriculus, Psalterium, Puku, Pylorus, Read, Rennet, Reticulum, Rumen, Stand, Stick, Swagbelly, → **SWALLOW**, Tripe, Tum, Tun-belly, Urite, Vell, Venter, Wame, Washboard, Wem, Zingiber

Stomach-ache Colic, Colitis, Collywobbles, Gastralgia, Giardiasis, Gripe, Gutrot, Mulligrubs

Stone(s), Stone age, Stoned, Stony Blotto, Cast, Drunk, Foundation, → **GEM**, Henge, Imposing, Ink, Inukshuk, Lapideous, Lucky, Lydian, Masonry, Mort, Niobe(an), Pelt, Precious, Putting, Rolling, Roughcast, Seeing, Sermon, Shingle, Standing, Step(ping), Through, Touch, Tusking

STONES

2 letters:	Kerb	Chalk	Quoit
St	Lias	Chert	Rubin
	Lime	Coade	Rufus
3 letters:	Lode	Culch	Rybat
Gem	Onyx	Drupe	Satin
Hog	Opal	Flint	Scone
Pip	Plum	Gooly	Scree
Pit	Ragg	Grape	Slate
Rag	Sard	Jewel	Slick
Tin	Skew	Kenne	Sneck
	Slab	Lapis	Stela
4 letters:	Soap	Logan	Stele
Bath	Tile	Menah	Topaz
Blue	Trap	Metal	Wacke
Celt		Mocha	Wyman
Door	*5 letters:*	Paste	
Flag	Agate	Penny	*6 letters:*
Hone	Amber	Prase	Amazon
Horn	Balas	Pumie	Arthur
Iron	Beryl	Quern	Ashlar
Jasp	Black	Quoin	Ashler

Baetyl
Bezoar
Brinny
Chesil
Chisel
Cobble
Coping
Cultch
Dolmen
Flusch
Fossil
Gibber
Gooley
Goolie
Gravel
Humite
Iolite
Jargon
Jasper
Kernel
Kidney
Kingle
Ligure
Lithic
Menhir
Metate
Mihrab
Mosaic
Muller
Nutlet
Oamaru
Paving
Pebble
Pencil
Pot-lid
Pumice
Pyrene
Rip-rap
Samian
Sarsen
Scarab
Summer
Tanist
Yonnie

7 letters:
Asteria
Avebury
Azurite

Blarney
Bologna
Boulder
Breccia
Callais
Cat's eye
Chuckie
Clinker
Curling
Girasol
Granite
Hyacine
Hyalite
Jargoon
Lia-fail
Lithoid
Moabite
Olivine
Parpane
Parpend
Parpent
Peacock
Pennant
Peridot
Perpend
Perpent
Petrous
Pudding
Purbeck
Putamen
Rocking
Rosetta
Rubbing
Sardine
Sardius
Sarsden
Scaglia
Schanse
Schanze
Smaragd
Staddle
Tektite
Telamon
Thunder
Trilith
Tripoli
Urolith
Zauxite

8 letters:
Aerolite
Aerolith
Amethyst
Asteroid
Baguette
Cabochon
Calculus
Cinnamon
Corundum
Cromlech
Cryolite
Ebenezer
Elf-arrow
Endocarp
Essonite
Ganister
Girasole
Lapidate
Megalith
Menamber
Monolith
Nephrite
Omphalos
Onychite
Parpoint
Peastone
Petrosal
Phengite
Pisolite
Portland
Potstone
Rollrich
Sapphire
Sardonyx
Scalpins
Schantze
Specular
Tonalite
Traprock
Voussoir

9 letters:
Alabaster
Almandine
Asparagus
Cairngorm
Carnelian
Cholelith

Chondrite
Cornelian
Crossette
Dichroite
Firestone
Gannister
Greensand
Hessonite
Hoarstone
Lithiasis
Meteorite
Paleolith
Pipestone
Rubicelle
Scagliola
Trilithon
Turquoise
Ventifact

10 letters:
Adamantine
Alectorian
Aragonites
Chalcedony
Draconites
Enhydritic
Fieldstone
Gastrolith
Grey-wether
Kimberlite
Lherzolite
Lithophyte
Pearlstone
Penny-stone
Rhinestone
Sleekstone
Slickstone

11 letters:
Meteorolite
Pencil-stone
Peristalith

12 letters:
Carton-pierre
Philosopher's

Stone-crop Orpin(e), Sedum, Succulent
Stone-pusher Sisyphus
Stone-thrower Bal(lista), Catapult, David, Mangonel, Onager, Perrier, Sling, Trebuchet
Stone-wall(er) Block, Jackson, Mule, Revet

Stoneware Crouch-ware

Stone-worker Jeweller, Knapper, Sculptor

Stooge Butt, Cat's-paw, Feed, Joe Soap, Straight man

Stook(s) Sheaf, Stack, Thr(e)ave

Stool Bar, Buffet, Coppy, Cracket, Creepie, Cricket, Cucking, Curule, Cutty, Ducking, Faeces, Foot, Hassock, Litany, Milking, Music, Piano, Pouf(fe), Repentance, Ruckseat, Seat, Sir-reverence, Step, Stercoral, Sunkie, Taboret, Tripod, Tripos, Turd

Stoop(ed) Bend, Condescend, Cringe, Crouch, C(o)urb, Daine, Deign, Incline, Lout, Lowt, Porch, Round-shouldered, Slouch

Stop(page), Stopcock, Stopper, Stopping Abort, Adeem, Anchor, An(n)icut, Aperture, Arrest, Aspirate, Avast, Bait, Ba(u)lk, Belay, Bide, Blin, Block, Brake, Buffer, Bung, Canting-coin, Carillon, → **CEASE**, Cessation, Chapter, Check, Checkpoint, Cheese, Cholestasis, Clarabella, Clarino, Clarion, Clog, Close, Cog, Colon, Comfort, Comma, Conclude, Conversation, Cork, Coupler, Cremo(r)na, Cremorne, Cromorna, Cut, Cut out, Deactivate, Debar, Demurral, Desist, Deter, Devall, Diapason, Diaphone, Discontinue, Discourage, Dit, Dock, Dolce, Dot, Dulciana, Echo, Embargo, End, Enough, Expression, Extinguish, F, Fagotto, Fare stage, Field, Fifteenth, Flag, Flue, Flute, Forbid, Foreclose, Forestall, Foundation, Freeze, Fr(a)enum, Frustrate, Full, Full point, Gag, Gamba, Gemshorn, Glottal, Gong, Halt, Hamza(h), Hartal, Heave to, Hinder, Hitch, Ho, Hoa, Hoh, Hold, Hoy, Inhibit, Intermit, Ischuria, Jam, Kibosh, Lay to, Let-up, Lill, Lin, Lute, Media, Mutation, Nasard, Oboe, Obstruent, Obturate, Occlude, Oppilate, Organ, Outage, Outspan, Pack in, Pause, Period, Piccolo, Pit, Plug, Point, Poop, Preclude, Prevent, Principal, Prop, Prorogue, Pull-in, Pull over, Pull-up, Punctuate, Pyramidon, Quash, Quint, Quit, Racket, Red, Reed, Refrain, Register, Rein, Remain, Request, Rest, Salicet, Salicional, Scotch, Screw-top, Semi-colon, Sese, Sesqualtera, Sext, Sist, Sneb, Snub, Snuff out, Sojourn, Solo, Spigot, Stall, Stanch, Standstill, Stap, Stash, Stasis, Station, Staunch, Stay, Stent, Stive, Strike, Subbase, Subbass, Suction, Supersede, Suppress, Suspend, T, Tab, Tamp(ion), Tap, Tea break, Tenuis, Terminate, Thwart, Toby, Toho, Truck, Trumpet, Twelfth, Voix celeste, Vox angelica, Vox humana, Waldflute, Waldhorn, Waypoint, When, Whistle, Whoa

Stopgap Caretaker, Gasket, Gaskin, Interim, Makeshift, Pis aller, Temporary

Stopwatch Chronograph

Storage, Store(house) Accumulate, Archive, Armoury, Arsenal, Associative, Backing, Barn, Big box, Bin, Bottle, Bottom drawer, Boxroom, Buffer, Bunker, Buttery, Byte, Cache, Capacitance, Catacomb, Cell, Cellar(et), Chain, Cheek pouch, Clamp, Clipboard, Coffer, Convenience, Co-op(erative), Cootch, Core, Corn-crib, Cupboard, Cutch, Database, Deep freeze, Deli, Dene-hole, Dépanneur, Department(al), Depository, Depot, Dime, Discount, Dolia, Dolly-shop, Elevator, Emporium, Ensile, Entrepot, Étape, External, Freezer, Fridge, Fund, Galleria, Garner, Gasholder, Genizah, Girnal, Glory hole, Go-down, Granary, Groceteria, Hive, → **HOARD**, Hog, Hold, Honeycomb, Hope chest, House, Houseroom, Humidor, Husband, Hypermarket, Imbarn, Larder, Lastage, Lazaretto, Liquor, Locker, Lumber room, Magazine, Main, Mart, Mattamore, Meat safe, Memory, Mine, Minimart, Morgue, Mothball, Mow, Multiple, Nest-egg, Off-licence, One-step, Package, Pantechnicon, Pantry, Pithos, Provision, Pumped, Rack(ing), RAM, Reel, Repertory, Reposit, ROM, Root house, Save, Sector, Shed, → **SHOP**, Silage, Silo, Spence, Spooling, Springhouse, Squirrel, Stack, Stash, Stock, Stockpile, Stockroom, Stow, Superbaza(a)r, Superette, Supermarket, Supply, Tack-room, Tank, Thesaurus, Tithe-barn, Tommy-shop, Trading post, Vestiary, Vestry, Virtual, Volutin, Warehouse, Woodshed, Woodyard, Wool (shed), WORM

▶ **Storey** *see* **STORY**

Stork Adjutant, Antigone, Argala, Bird, Jabiru, Marabou(t), Marg, Saddlebill, Shoebill, Wader, Whale-headed, Wood, Wood ibis

Stork's bill Erodium

Storm(y) Ablow, Adad, Assail, Assault, Attack, Baguio, Blizzard, Bluster, Bourasque,

Brouhaha, Buran, Calima, Charge, Cockeye(d) bob, Cyclone, Devil, Dirty, Dust, Electric, Enlil, Expugn, Furore, Gale, Gusty, Haboob, Hurricane, Ice, Line, Magnetic, Monsoon, Onset, Oragious, Pelter, Rage(ful), Raid, Rain, Rampage, Rant, Rate, Rave, Red spot, Rugged, Rush, Shaitan, Snorter, Squall, Sumatra, Tea-cup, Tebbad, Tempest, Tornade, Tornado, Tropical, Unruly, Violent, Weather, White squall, Willy-willy, Wroth, Zu

▷ **Stormy** *may indicate* an anagram

Story, Storyline, Stories Account, Allegory, Anecdote, Apocrypha, Arthuriana, Bar, Basement, Baur, Bawr, Biog, Blood and thunder, Chestnut, Cock and bull, Conte, Cover, Decameron, Edda, Epic, Episode, Exclusive, Exemplum, Fable, Fabliau, Falsehood, Feature, Fib, Fiction, Folk-lore, Folk-tale, Gag, Geste, Ghost, Glurge, Hair-raiser, Hard-luck, Heptameron, Hitopadesa, Horror, Idyll, Iliad, Jataka, Lee, Legend, Lie, Mabinogion, Märchen, Myth(os), Mythus, Narrative, Nouvelle, Novel(la), Oratorio, Parable, Passus, Pentameron, Photo, Plot, Rede, Report, Roman a clef, Romance, Rumour, Saga, Scoop, Script, Serial, SF, Shaggy dog, Shocker, Short, Smoke-room, Sob, Spiel, Spine-chiller, Splash, Spoiler, Success, Tale, Tall, Thread, Thriller, Version, Whodun(n)it, Yarn

Storyteller Aesop, Fibber, Griot, Liar, Miller, Munchausen, Narrator, Raconteur, Sagaman, Shannachie, Tusitala, Uncle Remus

Stoup Benitier, Bucket, Vessel

Stout(ness) Ale, Beer, Black velvet, Burly, Chopping, Chubby, Cobby, Corpulent, Doughty, Embonpoint, Endomorph, Entire, Fat, Fubsy, Hardy, Humpty-dumpty, Lusty, Manful, Milk, Obese, Overweight, Porter, Portly, Potbelly, Robust, Stalwart, Stalworth, Sta(u)nch, Strong, Stuggy, Sturdy, Substantial, Tall, Velvet

Stove Aga, Baseburner, Break, Calefactor, Chauf(f)er, Chiminea, Cockle, Cooker, Cooktop, Furnace, Gasfire, Oven, Potbelly, Primus®, Range, Salamander

Stow Cram, Flemish (down), Load, Pack, Rummage, Stack, Stash, Steeve

St Paul's Wren-ch

Strabismus Squint

Straddle, Straddling Bestride, Enjamb(e)ment, Strodle

Strafe Bombard, Shell, Shoot

Straggle(r), Straggly Estray, Gad, Meander, Ramble, Rat-tail, Spidery, Sprawl, Stray, Wander

Straight(en), Straightness Align, Bald, Beeline, Boning, Correct, Die, Direct, Downright, Dress, Frank, Gain, Het(ero), Home, Honest, Lank, Legit, Level, Line, Neat, Normal, Ortho-, Orthotropous, Rectilineal, Rectitude, Righten, Sheer, Slap, Tidy, True, Unbowed, Uncurl, Unlay, Upright, Veracious, Virgate

Straight edge Lute, Ruler

Straightfaced Agelast

Straightforward Candid, Direct, Downright, Easy, Even, Forthright, Honest, Jannock, Level, Plain sailing, Pointblank, Simple, Uncomplicated

Straight-haired Leiotrichous

Strain(ed), Strainer, Straining Agonistic, Ancestry, Aria, Breed, Bulk, Carol, Charleyhorse, Clarify, Colander, Distend, Drawn, Effort, Exert, Filter, Filtrate, Fit, Fitt(e), Force, Fray, Fytt(e), Intense, Kind, Melody, Milsey, Minus, Molimen, Music, Nervy, Note, Overstretch, Overtask, Passus, Percolate, Plus, Pressure, Pull, Purebred, Rack, Raring, Reck(an), Repetitive, Retch, Rick, Seep, Seil(e), Set, Shear, Sieve, Sift, Sile, Stape, Start, Stirps, Stock, Streak, Stress, Stretch, Sye, Tamis, Tammy, Tax, Tems(e), Tenesmus, Tense, Tension, Threnody, Try, Tune, Unease, Vein, Vice, Work, Wrick

Strait(s) Bab el Mandeb, Basilan, Bass, Bering, Bosp(h)orus, Canso, Channel, Condition, Cook, Crisis, Cut, Dardanelles, Davis, Denmark, Desperate, Dover, Drake Passage, East River, Euripus, Florida, Formosa, Foveaux, Gat, Gibraltar, Golden Gate, Great Belt, Gut, Hainan, Hormuz, Hudson, Johore, Juan de Fuca, Kattegat, Kerch, Korea, Kyle, Little Belt, Lombok, Mackinac, Magellan, Malacca, Menai, Messina, Mona Passage, Narrow,

North Channel, Oresund, Otranto, Palk, Predicament, Soenda, Solent, Sound, St, Sumba, Sunda, Taiwan, Tatar, Tiran, Torres, Tsugaru, Windward Passage

Straiten(ed) Impecunious, Impoverish, Poor, Restrict

Strait-laced Blue-nosed, Narrow, Prig, Primsie, Prudish, Puritan, Stuffy

Strand(ed) Abandon, Aground, Bank, Beach, Desert, Enisle, Fibre, Haugh, Hexarch, Isolate, Lock, Maroon, Neaped, Ply, Rice, Rope, Shore, Sliver, Thread, Three-ply, Tress, Twist, Wisp

Strange(ness), Stranger Alien, Aloof, Amphitryon, Bizarre, Curious, Dougal, Eccentric, Eerie, Exotic, Ferly, Foreign, Fraim, Freaky, Frem(d), Fremit, Frenne, Funny, Guest, Jimmy, Malihini, New, Novel, Odd(ball), Outlandish, Outsider, Quare, Quark, Queer, Rum, S, Screwy, Selcouth, Singular, Surreal, Tea-leaf, Uncanny, Unco, Uncommon, Unfamiliar, Unked, Unket, Unkid, Unused, Unusual, Wacky, Weird, Weyard, Wondrous

▷ **Strange** *may indicate* an anagram

Strangle(r) Anaconda, Bindweed, Choke, Garotte, Jugulate, Suffocate, Suppress, Throttle, Thug(gee)

Strap(ping) Able-bodied, Band, Barber, Beat, Bowyangs, Braces, Brail, Braw, Breeching, Browband, Cheekpiece, Crownpiece, Crupper, Cuir-bouilli, Curb, Deckle, Girth, Halter, Harness, Holdback, Jess, Jock(ey), Kicking, Larrup, Lash, Leather, Ligule, Lorate, Lore, Manly, Martingale, Nicky-tam, Octopus, Overcheck, Palmie, Pandy, Rand, Rein, Robust, Shoulder, Sling, Spaghetti, Spider, Strop, Surcingle, Suspender, T, Tab, Taws(e), T-bar, Thong, Thoroughbrace, Throatlash, Throatlatch, Trace, Tump-line, Wallop, Watch, Watchband

Stratagem, Strategist, Strategy Artifice, Clausewitz, Contrivance, Coup, Deceit, Device, Dodge, Exit, Fetch, Finesse, Fraud, Game plan, Guile, Heresthetic, Kaupapa, Lady Macbeth, Manoeuvre, Maskirovka, Masterstroke, Maximum, Minimax, Plan, Realpolitik, Rope-a-dope, → **RUSE**, Salami, Scheme, Scorched earth, Sleight, Subterfuge, Tack, Tactic(s), Tactician, Trick, Wheeze, Wile

Stratum, Strata Bed, Coal Measures, Kar(r)oo, Layer, Neogene, Permian, Schlieren, Seam, Syncline

Straw(s), Strawy Balibuntal, Boater, Buntal, Chaff, Cheese, Crosswort, Halm, Hat, Haulm, Hay, Insubstantial, Kemple, Last, Leghorn, Monkey-pump, Nugae, Oaten, Panama, Parabuntal, Pea(se), Pedal, Rush, Short, Sipper, Stalk, Strae, Stramineous, Strammel, Strummel, Stubble, Trifles, Truss, Wisp, Ye(a)lm

Strawberry Alpine, Barren, Birthmark, Fragaria, Fraise, Garden, Hautbois, Hautboy, Potentilla, Wild

Stray(ing) Abandoned, Aberrant, Alleycat, Chance, Depart, Deviate, Digress, Err, Forwander, Foundling, Gamin, Maverick, Meander, Misgo, Pye-dog, Ramble, Roam, Sin, Straggle, Streel, Traik, Unowned, Waff, Waif, Wander, Wilder

Streak(ed), Streaker, Streaky Archimedes, Bended, Blue, Brindle, Comet, Flambé, Flaser, Flash, Fleck, Freak, Hawked, Hawkit, Highlights, Lace, Layer, Leonid, Lowlight, Marble, Mark, Merle, Mottle, Primitive, Race, Ra(t)ch, Run, Schlieren, Seam, Shot, Striate, Striga, Strip(e), Vein, Venose, Vibex, Waif, Wake, Wale, Yellow

Stream Acheron, Anabranch, Arroyo, Beam, Beck, Blast, Bogan, Bourne, Brook, Burn, Consequent, Course, Current, Driblet, Fast, Flow, Flower, Freshet, Ghyll, Gill, Gulf, Gush, Headwater, Influent, Jet, Kill, Lade, Lane, Leet, Logan, Meteor, Nala, Nalla(h), Nulla(h), Obsequent, Pokelogan, Pour, Pow, Riffle, Rill, River, Rivulet, Rubicon, Run, Runnel, Sike, Slough, Spill, Spruit, Squirt, Star, Strand, Streel, Subsequent, Syke, The Fleet, Third, Thrutch, Tide-race, Torrent, Tributary, Trickle, Trout, Watercourse, Water-splash, Winterbourne

Streamer Banderol(e), Bandrol, Banner(all), Bannerol, Pennon, Pinnet, Ribbon, Tape, Tippet, Vane

Streamline(d), Streamliner Clean, Fair, Fairing, Simplify, Sleek, Slim

Street Alley, Ave(nue), Bay, Boulevard, Bowery, Broad, Carey, Carnaby, Cato, Causey,

Champs Elysées, Cheapside, Civvy, Close, Corso, Court, Crescent, Downing, Drive, Easy, Ermine, Fleet, Gate, Grub, Harley, High(way), Kármán vortex, Lane, Lombard, Main, Main drag, Meuse, Mews, One-way, Parade, Paseo, Poultry, Queer, Road, Sesame, Side, Sinister, St, Strand, Terrace, Thoroughfare, Threadneedle, Throgmorton, Two-way, Vortex, Wall, Wardour, Watling, Way, Whitehall

Street arab Mudlark

Streetcar Desire, Tram

Strength(en), Strengthened, Strengthening Afforce, Anneal, Arm, Asset, Augment, Ausforming, Bant, Beef, Brace, Brawn, Build, Confirm, Consolidate, Edify, Embattle, Enable, Energy, Field, Fish, Foison, Force, Force majeure, Forte, Fortify, Fortitude, Freshen, Fus(h)ion, Grit, Heart, Herculean, Horn, Intensity, Invigorate, Iron, Lace, Line, Main, Man, Might, Munite, Muscle, Neal, Nerve, → **POWER**, Prepotence, Pre-stress, Proof, Reinforce, Roborant, Shear, Sinew, Spike, Spine, Stamina, Steel, Sthenia, Stoutness, → **STRONG**, Tensile, Thews, Titration, Ultimate, Unity, Vim, Willpower, Yield

Strenuous Arduous, Effort, Exhausting, Hard, Laborious, Vehement

Strephon Rustic, Wooer

Stress(ed), Stressful Accent, Actuate, Arsis, Birr, Brunt, Careworn, Creep, Drive home, Emphasis, Ictus, Impress, Italicise, Marcato, Orthotonesis, Oxidative, Oxytone, Paroxytone, Post-traumatic, Primary, Proclitic, Proof, PTSD, Rack, Ram, Rhythm, RSI, Secondary, Sentence, Sforzando, Shear, Strain, Taut, Tense, → **TENSION**, Testing, Thetic, Tonic, Try, Underline, Underscore, Urge, Wind shear, Word, Yield (point)

Stretch(able), Stretched, Stretcher, Stretching Alength, Belt, Brick, Crane, Distend, Doolie, Draw, Ectasis, Eke, Elastic, Elongate, Exaggerate, Expanse, Extend, Extensile, Farthingale, Fib, Frame, Give, Gurney, Home, Lengthen, Lie, Limo, Litter, Narrows, Outreach, Pallet, Pandiculation, Porrect, Procrustes, Prolong, Protend, Pull, Rack, Rax, → **REACH**, Sentence, Shiner, Span, Spell, Spread, Spreadeagle, Strain, Streak, Taut, Tend, Tense, Tensile, Tenter, Term, Time, Tract, Tractile, Traction, Tree, Trolley

Stretcher-bearer Fuzzy-wuzzy angel

Striate Lineolate, Vein

Stricken Beset, Hurt, Overcome, Shattered

Strict(ly) De rigueur, Dour, Exacting, Harsh, Literal, Medic, Narrow, Orthodox, Penal, Proper, Puritanical, Religious, Rigid, Rigorous, Severe, Spartan, Stern, Strait(-laced), Stringent

Stride(s) Gal(l)umph, Jeans, Leg, Lope, March, Pace, Piano, Stalk, Sten, Stend, Straddle, Stroam, Strut, Stump

Strident Brassy, Discordant, Grinding, Harsh, Raucous, Screech, Shrill

Strife Bargain, Barrat, Bate(-breeding), Brigue, Colluctation, Conflict, Conteck, Contest, Discord, Disharmony, Dissension, Feud, Food, Friction, Ignoble, Scrap(ping), Sturt

Strike(r), Striker, Striking, Strike out Affrap, Air, Alight, Annul, Appulse, Arresting, Astonishing, Attitude, Backhander, Baff, Band, Bandh, Bang, Bash, Bat, Baton, Batsman, Batter, Beat, Belabour, Better, Biff, Black, Bla(u)d, Bonanza, Bop, British disease, Buff, Buffet, Bund(h), Butt, Cane, Catch, Chime, Chip, Clap, Clash, Clatch, Clip, Clock, Clout, Club, Cob, Collide, Conk, Constitutional, Coup, Cue, Cuff, Dad, Dent, Dev(v)el, Ding, Dint, Dismantle, Distingué, Douse, Dowse, Dramatic, Drive, Dush, Éclat, Effective, Emphatic, Especial, Événement, Fat, Fet(ch), Fillip, Firk, Fist, Flail, Flog, Frap, General, Get, Gnash, Go-slow, Gowf, Hail, Handsome, Hartal, Head-butt, → **HIT**, Horn, Hour, Hunger, Ictus, Illision, Impact, Impinge, Impress, Jarp, Jaup, Jole, Joll, Joule, Jowl, Knock, Lam, Lambast, Laser, Lay(-off), Lightning, Match, Middle, Mint, Notable, Noticeable, Official, Out, Pash, Pat(ter), Pat, Pean, Peen, Pein, Pene, Percuss, Picket, Pize, Plectrum, Pronounced, Pummel, Punch, Quarter-jack, Rag-out, Ram, Rap, Remarkable, Rolling, Roquet, Salient, Scrub, Scutch, Shank, Sick out, Sideswipe, Signal, Sitdown, Sit-in, Sizzling, Slam, Slap, Slat, Slog, Slosh, Smack, Smash, Smite, Sock, Souse, Sowce, Sowse, Spank, Stayaway, Stop(page), Stub, Swap, Swat, Swinge, Swipe, Swop, Sympathy,

Tan, Tangent, Tapotement, Tat, Thump, Thwack, Tip, Token, Tonk, Tripper, Twat, Unconstitutional, Unofficial, Walk-out, Wallop, Wap, Whack, Whale, Whang, Whap, Wherret, Who does what, Whomp, Whop, Wick, Wildcat, Wipe, Wondrous, Zap

Strike-breaker Blackleg, Fink, Rat, Scab

String(s), Stringy Anchor, Band, Bant, Beads, Bootlace, Bow, Bowyang, Cello, Chalaza, Chanterelle, Cord, Cosmic, Creance, Cremaster, Drill, Enfilade, Fiddle, Fillis, First, G, Glass, Gut, Henequin, Heniquin, Hypate, Idiot, Injection, Keyed, Kill, Lace, Lag, Leading, Lichanos, Macramé, Mese, Necklace, Nete, Nicky-tam, Oil, Paramese, Paranete, Pledget, Production, Proviso, Purse, Quint, Ripcord, Rope, Rosary, Rough, Second, Series, Shoe(-tie), Silly®, Sinewy, Snare, Spit, Stable, Straggle, Strand, Sultana, Sympathetic, Team, Tendon, Thairm, Tie, Tough, Train, Trite, Twiddling-line, Viola, Violin, Worry-beads, Wreathed

String-course Moulding, Table

Stringent Exacting, Extreme, Rigid, Severe, Strict, Urgent

Strip(ped), Stripper, Striptease Airfield, Armband, Band, Bare, Bark, Batten, Belt, Bereave, Bimetallic, Blowtorch, Caprivi, Casparian, Chippendale, Comic, Cote, Defoliate, Denude, Deprive, Derobe, Despoil, Devest, Disbark, Dismantle, Dismask, Disrobe, Divest, Doab, Dosing, Drag, Ecdysiast, Ecdysis, Écorché, Fannel(l), Fiche, Film, Flashing, Flaught, Flay, Fleece, Flench, Flense, Flight, Flinch, Flounce, Flype, Furring, Gaza, Goujon, Hatband, Infula, Jib, Label, Landing, Lap-dancer, Lardon, Lath, Ledge, Linter, List, Littoral, Loading, Locust, Magnetic, Mail-rod, Maniple, Median, Möbius, Paint, Panhandle, Parting, Peel, Pillage, Pluck, Pull, Puttee, Puttie, Rand, Raunch, Raw, Reglet, Reservation, Riband, Ribbon, Ring-bark, Roon, Royne, Rumble, Rund, Runway, Scent, Screed, Scrow, Shear, Shed, Shim, Shred, Shuck, Skin, Slat, Slit, Sliver, Spellican, Spilikin, Spill(ikin), Splat, Splent, Spline, Splint, Splinter, Spoil, Straik, Strake, Strap, Streak, Strop, Sugar soap, Swath, Sweatband, Tack, Tear, Tear-off, Tee, Thong, Tirl, Tirr, Tombolo, Tongue, Trash, Unbark, Uncase, Unclothe, Undeck, Undress, Unfrock, Unrig, Unrip, Unrobe, Unvaile, Valance, Weather, Widow, Zona, Zone

Stripe(d) Band, Bausond, Candy, Chevron, Cingulum, Cove, Endorse, Go-faster, Lance-jack, Laticlave, Line, List, Magnetic, → **NCO**, Ombré, Pale, Paly, Pin, Pirnie, Pirnit, Slash, Snip, Straik, Strake, Streak, Striation, Stroke, Tabaret, Tabby, Tiger, Tragelaph(us), Vitta, Weal, Zebroid

Stripling Lad

Strive, Striving Aim, Aspire, → **ATTEMPT**, Contend, Endeavour, Enter, Kemp, Labour, Nisus, Persevere, Pingle, Press, Strain, Struggle, Toil, Try, Vie

Stroke Apoplex(y), Backhander, Bat, Bisque, Blow, Boast, Breast, Butterfly, Caress, Carom, Chip, Chop, Counterbuff, Coup, Coy, Crawl, Dab, Dash, Dint, Dog(gy)-paddle, Down-bow, Drear(e), Drere, Dropshot, Effleurage, Estrarnazone, Exhaust, Feat, Flick, Fondle, Foozle, Forehand, Glance, Ground, Hairline, Hand(er), Ictus, Inwick, Jenny, Jole, Joll, Joule, Jowl, Knell, Knock, Lash, Lightning, Like, Line, Loft, Long jenny, Loser, Massé, Oarsman, Oblique, Odd, Off-drive, Outlash, Palp, Paw, Pot-hook, Pull, Punto reverso, Put(t), Reverso, Ridding straik, Roquet, Rub, Scart, Scavenge, Sclaff, Scoop, Seizure, Sheffer's, Short jenny, Sider, Sixte, Slash, Smooth, Solidus, Spot, Strike, Stripe, Sweep, Swipe, Tact, Tittle, Touch, Touk, Trait, Trudgen, Trudgeon, Tuck, Upbow, Virgule, Wale, Whang, Wrist shot

Stroll(er), Strolling Amble, Ambulate, Bummel, Dander, Daun(d)er, Dawner, Flânerie, Flâneur, Frescade, Idle, Lounge, Perambulate, Ramble, Saunter, Stravaig, Stray, Toddle, Walk, Walkabout, Wander

Strong(est) Able, Boofy, Brawny, Buff, Cast-iron, Doughty, Durable, F, Fat, Fierce, Firm, Fit, Forceful, Forcible, Forte, Full-blown, Hale, Heady, Hercules, High-powered, Humming, Husky, Intense, Ironside, Marrowy, Mighty, Nappy, Ox, Pithy, Pollent, Potent, Powerful, Pronounced, Pungent, Racy, Rank, Robust, Samson, Solid, Sour, Stale, Stalwart, Stark, Steely, Sthenic, Stiff, Stout, Str, Strapping, → **STRENGTH**, Sturdy, Substantial, Suit, Tarzan, Tenable, Thesis, Thewy, Thickset, Tough, Trusty, Valid, Vegete,

Vehement, Vigorous, Violent, Virile, Well-built, Well-set, Wight, Ya(u)ld

Stronghold Acropolis, Aerie, Bastion, Castle, Citadel, Eyrie, Eyry, Fastness, Fortalice, Fortress, Keep, Kremlin, Redoubt, Tower

Strongroom Genizah, Safe

Strontium Sr

Strop(py) Cantankerous, Leather, Sharpen, Strap

Struck Aghast, Raught, Smitten

Structural, Structure Acrosome, Allotrope, Analysis, Anatomy, Armature, Atomic, Building, Catafalque, Centriole, Chromosome, Cold frame, Compage(s), Conus, Data, Database, Deep, Edifice, Erection, Fabric, Fairing, Flaser, Format(ion), Formwork, Frame, Galea, Gantry, Heterarchy, Hut, Hyperbolic, Hyperfine, Ice-apron, Idant, Kekulé, Lantern, Lattice, Macrocosm, Malpighian, Manubrium, Mole, Organic, Ossature, Palmation, Parawalker, Pediment, Pergola, Phloem, Physique, Pod, Power, Protein, Retinaculum, Set-up, Shape, Shell, Shoring, Skeleton, Sponson, Sporocarp, Squinch, Staging, Stand, Starling, Stylobate, Surface, Syntax, System, Tectonic, Telomere, Texas, Texture, Thylakoid, Trabecula, Trilithon, Trochlea, Undercarriage

Struggle, Struggling Agon(ise), Agonistes, Amelia, Buckle, Camp, Chore, Class, Conflict, Contend, Contest, Cope, Debatement, Duel, Effort, Encounter, Endeavour, Fight, Flounder, Grabble, Grapple, Hassle, Jockey, Kampf, Labour, Luctation, Maul, Mill, Pingle, Rat-race, Reluct, Resist, Scrabble, Scramble, Scrape, Scrimmage, Scrum, Scrummage, Scuffle, Slugfest, Sprangle, Strain, → **STRIVE**, Toil, Tug, Tuilyie, Tussle, Up a tree, Uphill, Vie, War(sle), Warfare, Work, Wrestle

▷ **Struggle** *may indicate* an anagram

Strum Thrum, Twang, Tweedle, Vamp

Strumpet Cocotte, Harlot, Hiren, Lorette, Paramour, Succubus, Waistcoateer, Wench

Strut(ter), Strutting Bracket, Brank, Bridging, Cock, Dolphin striker, Flounce, Haught(y), Jet, Kingrod, Longeron, Martingale boom, Member, Nervure, Peacock, Pown, Prance, Pronk, Prop, Scotch, Shore, Spur, Stalk, Stretcher, Strunt, Swagger, Swank, Tail-boom, Tie-beam

Stuart Anne, James, Pretender

Stub(by) Butt, Counterfoil, Dout, Dowt, Dumpy, Squat, Stob, Stocky

Stubble Ar(r)ish, Bristle, Designer, Hair, Ill-shaven, Stump

Stubborn(ness) Adamant, Bigoted, Bull-headed, Contumacious, Cross-grained, Cussed, Diehard, Dogged, Entêté, Hard(-nosed), Hidebound, Intransigent, Inveterate, Moyl(e), Mulish, Mumpsimus, Obdurate, Obstinate, Opinionated, Ornery, Ortus, Pertinacious, Perverse, Recalcitrant, Reesty, Refractory, Rigwiddie, Rigwoodie, Self-willed, Stiff, Stoor, Stout, Tenacious, Thrawn, Tough, Wrong-headed

Stucco Cement

Stuck Fast, Glued, Jammed, Lodged, Set, Stopped, Wedged

Stuck-up Chesty, Highty-tighty, Hoity-toity, La(h)-di-da(h), Proud, Sealed, Toffee-nosed, Vain

Stud(ded) Boss, Cooser, Cripple, Cu(i)sser, Doornail, Entire, Farm, Frost, He-man, Knob, · Nail, Press, Race, Rivet, Seg, Set, Shear, Shirt, Sire, Stop

Student(s) Abiturient, Alphabetarian, Alumnus, Apprentice, Bajan, Bejant, Bursar, Bursch(en), Cadet, Candle-waiter, Catechumen, Class, Coed, Commoner, Dan, Dig, Disciple, Dresser, Dux, Exchange, Exhibitioner, Extensionist, External, Form, Fresher, Freshman, Gownsman, Graduand, Green welly, Gyte, Hafiz, Ikey, Internal, Junior, Kommers, Kyu, → **LEARNER**, Magistrand, Matie, Mature, Medical, Nomologist, NUS, Opsimath, Ordinand, Oxonian, Peking duck, Pennal, Plebe, Poll, Postgraduate, Preppy, Pupil, Reader, Rushee, Sap, → **SCHOLAR**, Self-taught, Semi, Seminar, Seminarian, Senior, Shark, Sixth former, Sizar, Sizer, Smug, Softa, Soph(omore), Sophister, Spod, Subsizar, Swot, Talibe, Templar, Tiro, Tosher, Trainee, Tuft, Tukkie, Tutee, Underclassman, Undergraduate, Wedge, Welly, Witsie, Wonk, Wooden spoon, Wooden wedge, Wrangler, Year

Studio(s) Atelier, Bottega, Elstree, Gallery, Lot, Pinewood, Workshop

Study, Studies, Studied, Studious, Studying Analyse, Bionics, Bone, Brown, Carol, Case, Classics, Comparability, Con(ne), Conscious, Consider, Course, Cram, Den, Dig, Étude, Examine, Eye, Feasibility, Field, Gen up, Intramural, Isagogics, Lair, Learn, Liberal, Lucubrate, Media, Motion, Mug up, Mull, Muse, Nature, Perusal, Peruse, Pilot, Pore, Post-doctoral, Prep(aration), Probe, Read, Recce, Reconnoitre, Research, Reverie, Revise, Sanctum, Sap, Scan, Science, Scrutinise, Shiur, Sketch, Specialize, Stew, Swat, Swot, Take, Time and motion, Trade-off, Train, Tutorial, Typto, Voulu, Work

Stuff(iness), Stuffing, Stuffy Airless, Bloat, Bombast, Canvas, Close, Cloth, Codswallop, Cram, Crap, Dimity, Farce, Feast, Fiddlesticks, Fill, Force, Forcemeat, Frows(t)y, Frowzy, Fug, Gear, Glut, Gobble, Gorge, Guff, Hair, Havers, Hooey, Horsehair, Hot, Inlay, Kapok, Lard, Line, Linen, → **MATERIAL**, Matter, Musty, No-meaning, Nonsense, Overeat, Pad, Pang, Panne, Pompous, Ram, Replete, Rot, Salpicon, Sate, Satiate, Scrap, Sob, Stap, Steeve, Stew, Stifling, Taxidermy, Trig, Upholster, Wad, Youth

Stultify Repress, Ridicule, Smother

Stumble Blunder, Bobble, Daddle, Err, Falter, Flounder, Founder, Lurch, Peck, Snapper, Stoit, Titubate, Trip

Stump(ed), Stumps, Stumpy At sea, Bamboozle, Black, Bobtail, Butt, Clump, Fag-end, Floor, More, Nog, Nonplus, Orate, Runt, Scrag, Snag, Snooker, Squab, St, Staddle, Stob, Stock, Stool, Stub(ble), Stud, Tortillon, Tramp, Truncate, Wicket

Stun(ned), Stunning Astonish, Astound, Awhape, Bludgeon, Concuss, Cosh, Daze, Dazzle, Deafen, Donnard, Donnert, Dove(r), Drop-dead, Eclectic, Glam, Gobsmack, KO, Numb, Poleaxe, Shell-shocked, Shock, Stoun, Stupefy, Taser®

Stunner Belle, Bobby-dazzler, Cheese, Cosh, Doozy, KO, Peach, Plastic bullet, Taser®

Stunt(ed) Aerobatics, Confine, Droichy, Dwarf, Escapade, Exploit, Feat, Gimmick, Hot-dog, Hype, Jehad, Jihad, Loop, Nirl, Puny, Ront(e), Runt, Ruse, Scroggy, Scrub(by), Scrunt(y), Stub, Trick, Wanthriven, Wheelie

Stupefaction, Stupefy(ing), Stupefied Ag(h)ast, Amaze(ment), Assot, Astonishment, Awesome, Benumb, Catatonic, Dozen, Dumbfound, Etherise, Fuddle, Hocus, Moider, Moither, Mull, Narcoses, Numb, Stonne, Stun

Stupid, Stupid person Anserine, Asinine, Besotted, Blithering, Blockish, Braindead, Clay-brained, Crass, Daft, Datal, Dense, Desipient, Dim(wit), Donner(e)d, Dozy, Dull(ard), Fatuous, Flat, Foolish, Gross, Half-arsed, Half-baked, Hammerheaded, Hare-brained, Hen-witted, Inane, Insensate, Insipient, Lamming, Mindless, Natural, Obtuse, Senseless, Silly, Thick, Thick-witted, Torpid, Vacuous, Wooden(head)

STUPID PERSON

3 letters:		Cony	Gaga
Ass	Put	Coof	Geck
Auf	Sap	Coot	Gelt
Bev	Sot	Dill	Goat
Bob	Wof	Ditz	Goof
Cod	Yap	Doat	Goon
Daw		Dodo	Goop
Div	4 letters:	Does	Gorm
Fon	Berk	Dolt	Gouk
Git	Bete	Dorb	Gowk
Jay	Bobb	Dork	Gull
Lob	Bozo	Dote	Gump
Log	Burk	Fogy	Hash
Nit	Cake	Fool	Jaap
Oaf	Calf	Fozy	Jerk
Owl	Clod	Gaby	Lown
	Clot		

Lunk
Meff
Mome
Mong
Mook
Mutt
Nana
Nerd
Nerk
Nong
Nurd
Ouph
Poon
Poop
Prat
Putt
Putz
Rook
Simp
Slow
Stot
Tony
Tube
Twit
Warb
Yo-yo
Zany

5 letters:
Bevan
Blent
Bobby
Booby
Brute
Bumbo
Chick
Chump
Clunk
Cokes
Cuddy
Cully
Dicky
Diddy
Divvy
Dorba
Dorky
Dubbo
Dumbo
Dummy
Dunce
Dweeb
Eejit
Fogey
Galah

Golem
Goofy
Goose
Hoser
Idiot
Kerky
Klutz
Looby
Loony
Lowne
Moron
Neddy
Ninny
Nitty
Noddy
Ocker
Ouphe
Patch
Plank
Prune
Quo-he
Schmo
Simon
Snipe
Spoon
Stock
Stupe
Sumph
Tonto
Twerp
Waldo
Wally
Yampy

6 letters:
Bampot
Barren
Bauble
Boodle
Buffer
Cretin
Cuckoo
Cuddie
Dawney
Dickey
Dodkin
Donkey
Doofus
Dottle
Drongo
Gander
Gaupus
Gunsel
Ignaro

Ingram
Ingrum
Johnny
Josser
Loonie
Lummox
Lurdan
Lurden
Muppet
Newfie
Nidget
Nig-nog
Nincum
Nitwit
Noodle
Nudnik
Numpty
Obfusc
Oxhead
Sawney
Schlep
Schmoe
Scogan
Shmock
Shmuck
Simple
Sucker
Tavert
Thicko
Tosser
Tumphy
Turkey
Turnip
Wigeon
Wommit
Zombie

7 letters:
Airhead
Asinico
Barmpot
Becasse
Buffoon
Charlie
Cupcake
Damfool
Dawbake
Dawcock
Dim bulb
Dipshit
Dizzard
Donnard
Donnart
Donnert

Fuckwit
Gomeral
Gomeril
Gubbins
Half-wit
Haverel
Insulse
Jackass
Johnnie
Juggins
Jughead
Lurdane
Mafflin
Mampara
Muggins
Palooka
Pampven
Pillock
Pinhead
Plonker
Pot-head
Saphead
Schmock
Schmuck
Schnook
Scoggin
Taivert
Thickie
Tosspot
Twinkle
Want-wit
Wazzock

8 letters:
Abderian
Abderite
Baeotian
Boeotian
Bonehead
Boofhead
Bullhead
Clodpate
Clodpole
Clodpoll
Clueless
Crackpot
Deadhead
Dickhead
Dipstick
Dodipoll
Dotterel
Dottrell
Dumbbell
Flathead

Gobshite
Goofball
Goose-cap
Gormless
Imbecile
Knobhead
Liripipe
Liripoop
Lunkhead
Maffling
Meathead
Moon-calf
Numskull
Omadhaun
Pea-brain
Shithead
Shot-clog
Softhead
Tom-noddy
Wiseacre

Woodcock

9 letters:
Beccaccia
Birdbrain
Blockhead
Capocchia
Chipochia
Clarthead
Cornflake
Doddipoll
Doddypoll
Dottipoll
Dumb-cluck
Gothamite
Ignoramus
Jobernowl
Lamebrain
Malt-horse
Nicompoop

No brainer
Numbskull
Pigsconce
Schlemiel
Schlemihl
Simpleton
Thickhead
Thick-skin
Woodentop

10 letters:
Analphabet
Changeling
Dummelhead
Dunderhead
Dunderpate
Headbanger
Hoddy-doddy
Loggerhead
Muttonhead

Nickumpoop
Nincompoop
Sheepshead
Thickskull
Thimblewit
Touchstone

11 letters:
Chowderhead
Featherhead
Knucklehead
Leather-head
Ninny-hammer
Simple Simon
Van der Merwe

12 letters:
Featherbrain
Shatterbrain

Stupidity Betise, Goosery, Hebetude, Oscitancy, Thickness, Torpor

Stupor Catatony, Coma, Daze, Dwa(u)m, Fog, Lethargy, Narcosis, Trance

Sturdy Burly, Dunt, Gid, Hardy, Hefty, Lubbard, Lubber, Lusty, Robust, Rugged, Solid, Stalwart, Staunch, Steeve, Stieve, Strapping, Strong, Stuffy, Thickset, Turnsick, Vigorous

Sturgeon Beluga, Ellops, Fish, Huso, Osseter, Sevruga, Sterlet

Stutter(ing) Blaise, Hesitate, Stammer

St Vincent WV

Sty Frank, Hogpen, Hovel, Pen

Stye Eyesore, Hordeolum

Style(s), Stylish, Stylist Adam, À la, A-line, Anime, Band, Barocco, Barock, Baroque, Biedermeier, Blocked, Blow-dry, Brachylogy, Burin, Call, Cantilena, Carry-on, Chic, Chinoiserie, Chippendale, Class, Cultism, Cursive, Cut, Dapper, Dash, Decor, Decorated, Demotic, Diction, Directoire, Dress sense, Dub, Élan, Elegance, Empire, Entitle, Euphuism, Execution, Face, Farand, → **FASHION**, Fetching, Finesse, Flamboyant, Flava, Flossy, Fly, Font, Form(at), Free, Friseur, Galant, Genre, Ghetto fabulous, Gnomon, Gongorism, Gothic, Grace, Grand, Gr(a)ecism, Groovy, Hair-do, Hand, Hepplewhite, Heuristic, Hip, Homeric, House, International (Gothic), Intitule, Katharev(o)usa, Lapidary, Locution, Manner, Marivaudage, Metrosexual, Mod(e), Modernism, Modish, Natty, New, New Look, Nib, Nifty, Novelese, Old, Panache, Pattern, Pen, Perm, Perpendicular, Personal, Phrase, Picturesque, Pistil, Plateresque, Pointel, Port, Posh, Post-modernism, Preponderant, Probe, Prose, Queen Anne, Rakish, Rank, Regency, Retro, Ritzy, Rococo, Romanesque, Rudie, Sheraton, Silk, Slap-up, Smart, Snappy, Snazzy, Soigné, Spiffy, Sporty, Street, Surname, Swish, Taste, Term, Title, Ton, Tone, Tony, Touch, Traditional, Tuscan, Uncial, Vain, Va-va-voom, Verismo, Vogue, Way

Stymie Baulk, Frustrate, Thwart

Styptic Alum, Amadou, Matico, Sta(u)nch

Suave Bland, Debonair, Oily, Smooth, Unctuous, Urbane

Sub Advance, Due, Fee, Lieu, Submarine, Subordinate, U-boat, Under

Subaltern Lt

Subarea Talooka

Sub-atomic Mesic

Subconscious Inner, Instinctive, Not-I, Subliminal, Suppressed

Sub-continent India(n)

Subcontract Outsource

Subdivision Arm, Branch, Commot(e), Cotyledon, Oblast, Sanjak, Senonian, Sheading, Tepal, Wapentake

Subdominant Fah

Subdue(d) Abate, Adaw, Allay, Chasten, Conquer, Cow, Crush, Dant(on), Daunt(on), Dominate, Entame, Lick, Low-key, Master, Mate, Mute, Overbear, Overpower, Quail, → QUELL, Quieten, Reduce, Refrain, Repress, Slow, Sober, Soft pedal, Subact, Suppress, Tame, Under

Subfusc, Subfusk Dim, Dressy, Dusky, Evening, Sombre

Subheading Strapline

Subhuman Apeman, Bestial

Subject(ed), Subjection, Subjects, Subject to Amenable, Art, Bethrall, Caitive, Case, Citizen, Contingent, Core, Cow, Dhimmi, Donné(e), Enthrall, Foundation, Gist, Hobby, Hobby-horse, Inflict, Liable, Liege(man), Matter, Metic, National, On, Oppress, Overpower, PE, People, Poser, Rayah, RE, RI, Serf, Servient, Servitude, Sitter, Slavery, Snool, Submit, Suit, Syllabus, → THEME, Thirl, Thrall, Topic, Under, Undergo, Vassal, Villein

Subjugate Enslave, Master, Oppress, Overcome, Reduce, Repress, Suppress

Sublieutenant Cornet

Sub-lieutenant Cornet

Sublimate(r) Aludel, Cleanse, Suppress, Transfer

Sublime Ali, Alice, August, Empyreal, Grand, Great, Holy, Lofty, Majestic, Outstanding, Perfect, Porte, Splendid

Submarine Boomer, Diver, Innerspace, Nautilus, Pig-boat, Polaris, Sub, U-boat, Undersea, X-craft

▷ **Submarine** *may indicate* a fish

Submerge(d) Dip, Dive, Drown, Embathe, Engulf, Imbathe, Impinge, Lemuria, Overwhelm, Ria, Sink, Take, Whelm

Submissive, Submission, Submit Acquiesce, Bow, Capitulate, Comply, Defer, Docile, File, Folio, Gimp, Knuckle, Lapdog, Meek, Obedient, Obtemperate, Passive, Pathetic, Refer, Render, Resign, Snool, Stepford, Stoop, Succumb, Truckle, → YIELD

Subordinate Adjunct, Dependent, Flunky, Inferior, Junior, Minion, Myrmidon, Offsider, Postpone, Secondary, Second banana, Servient, Stooge, Subject, Subservient, Subsidiary, Surrender, Under(ling), Underman, Under-strapper, Vassal

Subscribe(r), Subscription Abonnement, Approve, Assent, Conform, Due, Pay, Pay TV, Sign(atory), Signature, Undersign, Underwrite

Subsequent(ly) Anon, Consequential, Future, Later, Next, Postliminary, Since, Then, Ulterior

Subservient Kneel, Obedient, Obsequious, Tame cat

Subside, Subsidence, Subsidy Abate, Adaw, Aid, Assuage, Bonus, Cauldron, Diminish, Ebb, Grant, Headage, Sink, Sit, Swag

Subsidiary, Subsidise Anglesey, Auxiliar(y), By(e), By-end, Feather-bed, Junior, Secondary, Second banana, Side, Sideline, Spin-off, Succursal

Subsist(ence) Batta, Bread-line, Dole, Keep, Live, Maintain, Rely, Survive

Substance, Substantial Ambergris, Anethole, Antithrombin, Antitoxin, Apiol, Blanco, Blocky, Body, Calyx, Castoreum, Cermet, Chalone, Chemzyne, Chitin, Chromatin, Cofactor, Colloid, Considerable, Content, Cosmin(e), Creatine, Cytochalasin, Ectocrine, Ectoplasm, Elemi, Endorphin, Enzyme, Essential, Ethambutol, Excipient, Extender, Exudate, Fabric, Fixative, Flavanone, Getter, Gist, Gluten, Gossypol, Gravamen, Growth, Guanazolo, Gutta-percha, Hearty, Hefty, Hirudin, Imine, Indol, Inhibitor, Iodoform, Iodophor, Isatin(e), Isomer, Kryptonite, Lase, Lecithin, Lectin, Leucotriene, Linin, Luciferin, Material, Matter, Meaning, Meat(y), Metabolite, Metol, Mineral, Misoprostol, Mitogen, Mole, Morphactin, Morphogen, Mucigen, Murr(h)ine, Mutagen, Myelin, Naloxone, Neotoxin, Neurotoxin, Noselite, Nutrient, Orgone, P, Papier mâché,

Particulate, Pepsinogen, Perforine, Phlogiston, Phosphor, Pith, Polymer, Proinsulin, Promoter, Prostaglandin, Protyl(e), Purin(e), Queen (bee), Quid, Reality, Resin, Salacin(e), Secretagogue, Sense, Sequestrant, Smeclic, Solid, Sorbitol, Stramonium, Stuff, Suint, Sum, Sunblock, Surfactant, Sympathin, Synergist, Syntonin, Tabasheer, Tabashir, Taeniafuge, Tangible, Terra alba, Thermoplastic, Thiouracil, Thiourea, Tocopherol, Tusche, Viricide, Volutin, Weighty, Ylem

Substandard Inferior, Infra dig, Off, Poor, Schlo(c)k, Second, Small

▶ **Substantial** *see* SUBSTANCE

Substantiate Confirm, Flesh, Prove, Strengthen, Support

Substantive Direct, Noun

Substitute, Substitution Acting, Carborundum®, Change, Changeling, Commute, Creamer, Deputy, Dextran, Double, Dub, Emergency, Ersatz, -ette, Euphemism, Eusystolism, Exchange, Fill-in, Imitation, Improvise, Instead, Lieu(tenant), Locum, Makeshift, Metonymy, Nominee, Novation, Pinch-hit, Proxy, Regent, Relieve, Replace, Represent, Reserve, Resolution, Ringer, Sentence, Seth, Simulacrum, Soya, Stalking-horse, Stand-in, Stead, Step in, Stopgap, Subrogate, Succedaneum, Supernumerary, Supply, Surrogate, Switch, Swop, Synthetic, Twelfth man, Twentieth man, Understudy, Vicar(ial), Vicarious

Substructure Base, Foundation, Keelson, Platform, Podium

Subterfuge Artifice, Chicane, Evasion, Hole, Manoeuvre, Off-come, Ruse, Strategy, Trick

Subterranean Concealed, Mattamore, Sunken, Underground, Weem

Subtle(ty) Abstruse, Alchemist, Crafty, Fine(spun), Finesse, Ingenious, Nice(ty), Nuance, Overtone, Refinement, Sly, Suttle, Thin, Wily

Subtle difference Nuance

Subtract(ion) Commission, Deduct, Discount, Sum, Take, Tithe, Withdraw

Suburb(s) Banlieue, Dormitory, Environs, Exurbia, Faubourg, Garden, Metroland, Outskirts, Purlieu, Subtopia

Subverse, Subversion, Subversive, Subvert Agitprop, Fifth column, Overthrow, Reverse, Sabotage, Sedition, Treasonous, Undermine, Upset

Subway Dive, Metro, Passage, Tube, Underground

Succeed, Success(ful) Accomplish, Achieve, Answer, Arrive, Big-hitter, Bingo, Blockbuster, Boffo, Breakthrough, Chartbuster, Coast, Contrive, Coup, Do well, Éclat, Effective, Efficacious, Ensue, Fadge, Fare, Felicity, Flourish, Follow, Fortune, Gangbuster, Get, Go, Hit, Hotshot, Inherit, Killing, Landslide, Luck, Made, Make good, Make it, Manage, Masterstroke, Mega, Midas touch, Offcome, Parlay, Pass, Prevail, Procure, Prosper, Purple patch, Pyrrhic, Reach, Replace, Result, Riot, Score, Seal, Seel, Sele, Sell out, Soaraway, Socko, Speed, Stardom, Superstar, Sure thing, Take, Tanistry, The bitch goddess, Thumbs up, Triumph, Up, Up and coming, Upstart, Vault, Victory, Weather, Win, Winnitude, W(h)iz(z)kid, Wow, Wunderkind

Succession Apostolic, Chain, Cognate, Dead men's shoes, Ecological, Indian file, Line, Mesarch, Neum(e), Order, Parlay, Result, Reversion, Sequence, Seriatim, Series, String, Suite

Successor Co(m)arb, Deluge, Descendant, Ensuite, Epigon(e), Heir, Incomer, Inheritor, Khalifa, Next, Syen

Succinct Brief, Cereus, Compact, Concise, Houseleek, Laconic, Pithy, Short

Succour Aid, Assist, Help, Minister, Relieve, Rescue, Sustain

Succulent Agave, Aloe, Cactus, Echeveria, Hoodia, Juicy, Lush, Rich, Saguaro, Sappy, Spekboom, Tender, Toothy

Succumb Capitulate, Fall, Go under, Surrender, Yield

Such Like, Sae, Sike, Similar, So, That

Suck(er), Sucking Absorb, Acetabular, Acetabulum, Amphistomous, Antlia, Aphis, Aspirator, Ass, Bull's eye, Culicidae, Dracula, Drink, Dupe, Fawn, Felch, Fellatio, Gnat, Gobstopper, Graff, Graft, Gull, Haustellum, Haustorium, Hoove, Lamia, Lamprey, Leech,

Liquorice, Lollipop, Mammal, Monotremata, Mouth, Mug, Muggins, Osculum, Patsy, Plunger, Remora, Rook, Shoot, Siphon, Slurp, Smarm, Spire, Spyre, Straw, Surculus, Sweetmeat, Swig, Sycophant, Tellar, Teller, Tick, Tiller, Toad-eater, Turion, Vampire

Suckle Feed, Mother, Nourish, Nurse, Nurture

Suction Adhere, Pump, Siphon

Sud(s) Foam, Lather, Sapples

Sudanese Dinka, Mahdi, Nigritian, Nuba

Sudden(ly) Abrupt, Astart, Astert, Extempore, Ferly, Flash, Fleeting, Foudroyant, Fulminant, Hasty, Headlong, Impulsive, Overnight, Precipitate, Rapid, Slap, Sodain, Subitaneous, Subito, Swap, Swop, Unexpected

Sue Apply, Ask, Beseech, Dun, Entreat, Implead, Implore, Litigate, Petition, Pray, Process, Prosecute, Woo

Suede Split

Suffer(er), Suffering Abide, Aby(e), Ache, Affliction, Agonise, Auto, Be, → **BEAR**, Brook, Calvary, Cop, Die, Distress, Dree, Dukkha, Endurance, Endure, Feel, Gethsemane, Golgotha, Grief, Hardship, Have, Hell, Incur, Languish, Let, Luit, Mafted, Martyr, Pain, Passible, Passion, Passive, Patible, Patience, Pay, Pellagrin, Permit, Pine, Plague, Purgatory, Stand, Stomach, Stress, Sustain, Thole, Tolerate, Toll, Torment, Torture, Trial, Tribulation, Undergo, Use, Victim

Suffering remnant Macmillanite

Suffice, Sufficient Adequate, Ample, Basta, Do, Due, Enough, Enow, Experimental, Nuff, Run to, Satisfy, Serve

Suffix Enclitic

Suffocate Asphyxiate, Choke, Smoor, Smore, Smother, Stifle, Stive, Strangle, Throttle

Suffrage(tte) Ballot, Davison, Feminist, Franchise, Manhood, Pankhurst, Vote

Suffuse Colour, Glow, Imbue, Saturate, Spread

Sugar(y), Sugar cane Aldohexose, Aldose, Amygdalin, Arabinose, Barley, Beet, Blood, Brown, Candy, Cane, Caramel, Carn(e), Cassonade, Caster, Cellobiose, Cellose, Chaptalise, Confectioner's, Cube, Daddy, Demerara, Deoxyribose, Dextrose, Disaccharide, Flattery, Fructose, Fucose, Furanose, Galactose, Gallise, Glucose, Glucosoric, Glycosuria, Goo(r), Granulated, Granulose, Grape, Gur, Heptose, Heroin, Hexose, Honeydew, Hundreds and thousands, Iced, Icing, Inulin, Invert, Jaggary, Jaggery, Jagghery, Ketose, Lactose, Laevulose, Loaf, Lump, Maltose, Manna, Mannose, Maple, Milk, Money, Monosaccharide, Muscovado, Nectar, Nucleoside, Palm, Panocha, Pentose, Penuche, Pyranose, Raffinose, Rhamnose, Ribose, Saccharine, Saccharoid, Simple, Sis, Sorbose, Sorghum, Sorg(h)o, Sparrow, Spun, Sweet, Tetrose, Trehalose, Triose, White, Wood, Xylose

Sugar-daddy Lyle, Tate

Suggest(ion), Suggestive Advance, Advice, Advise, Breath, Connote, Counter-proposal, Cue, Float, Hint, Hypnotic, Idea, Imply, Innuendo, Insinuate, Intimate, Kite, Mention, Modicum, Moot, Nominate, Posit, Posthypnotic, Postulate, Prompt, Proposal, Propound, Provocative, Racy, Raise, Recommend, Redolent, Reminiscent, Risqué, Savour, Scenario, Smacks, Soft core, Suspicion, Threat, Touch, Trace, Twang, Undertone, Vote, Wind, Wrinkle

Suicide Felo-de-se, Hara-kiri, Hari-kari, Kamikaze, Lemming, Lethal, Sati, Seppuku, Shinju, Suttee

Suit Action, Adapt, Adjust, Agree, Answer, Anti-G, Apply, Appropriate, Become, Befit, Beho(o)ve, Bequest, Beseem, Besit, Birthday, Boiler, Cards, Case, Cat, Clubs, Conform, Courtship, Demob, Diamonds, Dittos, Diving, Do, Drapes, Dress, Dry, Effeir, Effere, Etons, Exec(utive), Fadge, Fashion, Fit, G, Garb, Gee, Gree, Hearts, Hit, Jump, Lis pendens, Long, Lounge, Major, Mao, Match, Minor, Monkey, NBC, Noddy, Orison, Outcome, Paternity, Penguin, Petition, Plaint, Play, Plea, Please, Point, Prayer, Pressure, Process, Pyjama, Quarterdeck, Queme, Romper(s), Safari, Sailor, Salopettes, Samfoo, Samfu, Satisfy, Serve, Shell, Siren, Skeleton, Slack, Space, Spades, Strong, Sun, Sunday,

Supplicat, Sweat, Swim, Swords, Tailleur, Three-piece, Track, Trouser, Trumps, Tsotsi, Tweeds, Twin, Two-piece, Uniform, Union, Wet, Wingsuit, Zoot

Suitable Apposite, Appropriate, Apropos, Apt, Becoming, Capable, Competent, Congenial, Consonant, Convenance, Convenient, Decorous, Due, Expedient, → **FIT**, Giusto, Habile, Keeping, Meet, Opportune, Relevant, Seasonal, Seemly, Sittlichkeit, Very, Worthy

Suite Allemande, Apartment, Chambers, Court, Dolly, Edit, Ensemble, Entourage, Hospitality, Lounge, Nutcracker, Partita, Retinue, Rooms, Serenade, Set, Skybox, Tail, Three-piece, Train, Two-piece

Suitor Beau, Gallant, John Doe, Lover, Petitioner, Pretendant, Pretender, Suppli(c)ant, Swain, Wooer

Sulk(y), Sulkiness B(r)oody, Disgruntled, Dod, Dort, Gee, Glout(s), Glower, Glum, Grouchy, Grouty, Grumps, Gumple-foisted, Huff, Hump, Jinker, Mardy, Maungy, Mope, Mulligrubs, Mump, Pet, Petulant, Pique, Pout, Snit, Spider, Strunt, Stuffy, Stunkard, Sullen, Tout(ie), Towt, Umbrage

Sullen Black, Brooding, Dorty, Dour, Farouche, Glum(pish), Grim, Grumpy, Moody, Mumpish, Peevish, Stunkard, Sulky, Sumph, Surly, Truculent

Sully Assoil, Bedye, Besmirch, Blot, Deface, Defile, Glaur(y), Smear, Smirch, Smutch, Soil(ure), Tarnish, Tar-wash

Sulphate, Sulphide Alum, Alunite, Blende, Bluestone, Bornite, Copperas, Coquimbite, Glance, Melanterite, Pyrites, Zarnec, Zarnich

Sulphur Baregine, Brimstone, Cysteine, Hepar, Oleum, S, Stannite, Thionic

Sultan(a), Sultanate Brunei, Caliph, Emir, Grand Seignoir, Grand Turk, Hen, Kalif, Murad, Nejd, Oman, Osman, Padishah, Roxane, Saladin, Soldan, Suleiman, Tippoo, Tipu, Vizier, Wadai

Sultry Houri, Humid, Sexy, Smouldering, Steamy, Tropical

Sum(s), Sum up Add(end), Aggregate, All (told), Amount, Arsmetric, Bomb, Connumerate, Encapsulate, Foot, Logical, Lump, Number, Perorate, Plumule, → **QUANTITY**, Re-cap, Refund, Remittance, Reversion, Slump, Solidum, Total, Vector

Summarize, Summary Abridge, Abstract, Aperçu, Bird's eye, Breviate, Brief, Coda, Compendium, Condense, Conspectus, Digest, Docket, Epanodos, Epitome, Gist, Instant, Memo, Minute, Offhand, Outline, Overview, Pirlicue, Précis, Purlicue, Recap, Resume, Résumé, Round-up, Rundown, Short (shrift), Sitrep, Syllabus, Synopsis, Tabloid, Tabulate, Tabulation, Wrap-up

Summer(time) Aestival, August, BST, Computer, Estival, Heyday, Indian, Lintel, Luke, Prime, St Luke's, St Martin's, Season, Solstice, Totter

Summerhouse Belvedere, Chalet, Conservatory, Folly, Gazebo, Pavilion

Summit Acme, Acro-, Apex, Braeheid, Brow, Climax, Conference, → **CREST**, Crown, Eminence, Height, Hillcrest, Jole, Mont Blanc, Peak, Pike, Pinnacle, Spire, Vertex, Vertical, Yalta

Summon(s) Accite, Arraign, Arrière-ban, Azan, Beck(on), Bleep, Call, Call in, Cist, Cital, Citation, Command, Conjure, Convene, Convent, Drum, Evoke, Garnishment, Gong, Hail, Invocation, Muster, Order, Originating, Page, Post, Preconise, Rechate, Recheat, Reveille, Signal, Sist, Subpoena, Ticket, Warn, Warrant, What-ho, Whoop, Writ

Sumo (wrestling) Makunouchi, Niramial, → **WRESTLING**, Yokozuna

Sump Bilge, Drain, Pool, Sink

Sumpter Led horse, Pack-horse

Sumptuous Expensive, Lavish, Luxurious, Opulent, Palatial, Rich(ly), Superb

Sun(-god), Sunlight, Sunny, Sunshine Albedo, Amen-Ra, Amon-Ra, Apollo, Ashine, Aten, Bright, Cheer, Combust, Daily, Day(star), Dry, Earthshine, Eye of the day, Glory, Heater, Helio(s), Helius, Horus, Mean, Midnight, Mock, New Mexico, Nova, Orb, Paper, Paranthelion, Parhelion, Pet-day, Phoebean, Photosphere, Ra, Radiant, Rays, Re, Rising, Shamash, Sol(ar), Soleil, Sonne, Surya, Svastika, Swastika, Tabloid, Tan, Titan, UV

Sunbathe Apricate, Bask, Brown, Tan
Sunbeam Car, Ray
Sunblock Parasol
Sunburn Bronze, Combust, Peeling, Tan
Sunday Advent, Best, Cantate, Care, Carle, Carling, Dominical, Easter, Fig, Jubilate, Judica, Laetare, Lord's Day, Lost, Low, Mid-Lent, Mothering, Orthodox, Palm, Passion, Quadragesima, Quasimodo, Quinquagesima, Refection, Refreshment, Remembrance, Rogation, Rose, Rush-bearing, S, Septuagesima, Sexagesima, Stir-up, Tap-up, Trinity, Whit
Sunday school SS
Sunder Divide, Divorce, Part, Separate, Sever, Split
Sundew Drosera, Eyebright
Sundial Analemma, Gnomon, Solarium
Sundry Divers, Several, Various
Sunflower Kansas, KS
Sunglasses Ray-Bans®, Shades
▶ **Sun-god** *see* SUN(-GOD)
▶ **Sunken** *see* SINK(ING)
Sunrise, Sun-up Aurora, Cosmical, Dawn, East
Sunset Acronical, Evening
Sunshade Awning, Bongrace, Brise-soleil, Canopy, Chi(c)k, Cloud, Parasol, Umbrella
Sunspot Facula, Freckle, Macula
Sunstroke Heliosis, Siriasis
Sunwise Deasi(u)l, Deasoil, Deis(h)eal, Eutropic
Sun-worshipper Heliolater
Sup Dine, Eat, Feast, Sample, Sip, Swallow
Super A1, Actor, Arch, Extra, Fab(ulous), Great, Grouse, Ideal, Lulu, Paramount, Superb, Terrific, Tip-top, Top-notch, Tops, Walker-on, Wizard
Superadded Advene
Superb A1, Concours, Fine, Gorgeous, Grand, Great, Majestic, Peerless, Phat, Splendid, Top-notch
Supercilious Aloof, Arrogant, Bashaw, Cavalier, Haughty, Lordly, Snide, Sniffy, Snooty, Snotty, Snouty, Superior, Toffee-nosed, Upstage, Withering
Supercontinent Pangaea
Superficial Cosmetic, Cursenary, Cursory, Dilettante, Exterior, Facile, Glib, Outside, Outward, Overlying, Perfunctory, Shallow, Sketchy, Skindeep, Smattering, Veneer
▷ **Superficial(ly)** *may indicate* a word outside another
Superfluous, Superfluity Cheville, De trop, Extra, Lake, Mountain, Needless, Otiose, Pleonastic, Plethora, Redundant, Spare, Unnecessary
Superhuman Bionic, Herculean, Heroic, Supernatural
Superintend(ent) Boss, Curator, Director, Foreman, Guide, Janitor, Oversee(r), Preside, Provost, Sewer, Supercargo, Surveillant, Warden, Zanjero
Superior(ity) Abbess, Abbot, Abeigh, Above, Advantage, Ahead, Aloof, Ascendant, Atop, Better, Brahmin, Choice, Condescending, Custos, De luxe, Dinger, Elite, Eminent, Excellent, Exceptional, Feuar, Finer, Forinsec, Gree, Herrenvolk, High-class, High-grade, Jethro, Lake, Liege, Master race, Mastery, Morgue, Mother, Nob, Outstanding, Over, Overlord, Paramount, Pooh-Bah, Posh, Predominance, Premium, Prestige, Pretentious, Prevalent, Prior, Smug, Snooty, Speciesism, Superordinate, Supremacy, Swell, Top(-loftical), Transcendent(al), U, Udal, Upmarket, Upper(most), Upper crust, Uppish, Upstage
Superlative Best, Exaggerated, Peerless, Smasheroo, Supreme, Utmost
Superman Batman, Bionic, Titan, Übermensch
Supermarket ASDA, Co-op, Fund, GUM, Self service, Store
Supernatural Divine, Eerie, Endemon, Fay, Fey, Fie, Fly, Gothic, Kachina, Mana,

Manito(u), Metaphysical, Paranormal, Selky, Sharp, Siddhi, Tokoloshe, Uncanny, Unearthly, Wargod, Wight

Supernova Plerion

Supernumerary Additional, Corollary, Extra, Mute, Orra

Supersede Replace, Stellenbosch, Supplant

Superstition Aberglaube, Abessa, Fable, Folk-lore, Freet, Myth, Pisheog, Pishogue, Uncertainty

Superstructure Mastaba(h)

Supertonic Ray

Supervise(d), Supervision, Supervisor Administer, Chaperone, Check, Direct, Engineer, Floorwalker, Foreman, Gaffer, Grieve, Handle, Honcho, Invigilate, Key grip, Manager, Monitor, Officiate, Organise, Overman, Oversee(r), Probation, Proctor, Regulate, Seneschal, Shopwalker, Stage-manage, Steward, Symposiarch, Targe, Tool pusher, Under, Walla(h)

Supine Inactive, Inert, Lying, Passive, Protract

Supper Bar, Burns, Dinner, → **DRINK(ER)**, Fork, Hawkey, Hockey, Horkey, Last, Meal, Nagmaal, Repast, Soirée

Supplant Displace, Exchange, Oust, Overthrow, Pre-empt, Replace, Substitute, Supersede

Supple Compliant, Leish, Limber, Lissom(e), → **LITHE**, Loose, Loose-limbed, Lythe, Pliable, Sinuous, Souple, Wan(d)le, Wannel, Whippy

Supplement(ary), Supplementing Addend(um), Addition, Adjunct, And, Annex(e), Appendix, As well as, Augment, Auxiliary, Bolt-on, Codicil, Colour, Eche, Eik, Eke, Extra, Glucosamine, Incaparina, Inset, Paralipomena, Postscript, Practicum, PS, Relay, Ripienist, Ripieno, Rutin, Sports, TES, Weighting

Supplicant, Supplicate Beg, Entreat, Importune, Invoke, Petition, Plead, Pray, Request, Schnorr, Sue

Supply, Supplies, Supplier Accommodate, Advance, Afford, Amount, Cache, Cater, Commissariat, Contribute, Crop, Deal, Endue, Equip, Excess, Exempt, Feed, Fill, Find, Fit, Foison, Fund, Furnish, Give, Grist, Grubstake, Heel, Holp(en), Indew, Indue, Issue, Lay on, Lend, Lithely, Mains, Matériel, Pipeline, Plenish, Ply, → **PROVIDE**, Provision, Purvey, Push, RASC, Replenishment, Reservoir, Resource, Retailer, Serve, Source, Stake, Stock, → **STORE**, Viands, Vintner, Water, Widow's cruse, Yield

Support(er), Supporting Abacus, Abet, Abutment, Adherent, Adminicle, Advocate, Aegis, Affirm, Aficionado, Aftercare, Aid, Aidance, Aide, Aliment(ative), Ally, Ammunition, Anchor, Ancillary, Andiron, Anta, Appui, Arch, Arm, Assistant, Athletic, Axle, Back(bone), Back-up, Baculum, Baluster, Banister, Bankroll, Barrack, Barre, Base, Basis, Batten, Beam, Bear, Befriend, Behind, Belt, Benefactor, Bibb, Bier, Bolster, Boom, Bouclée, Bra, Brace, Bracket, Brassiere, Breadwinner, Breast-summer, Bridge, Bridgeboard, Buttress, Carlist, Chair, Champion, Chaptrel, Cherish, Circumstantiate, Clientele, Clipboard, Colonnade, Column, Confirm, Console, Corbel, Corbel-table, Cornerstone, Countenance, Cradle, Cripple, Cross-beam, Cruck, Crutch, C(ee)-spring, Dado, Diagrid, Dog-shore, Doula, Easel, Encourage, Endorse, Endoss, Endow, Engager, Enlist, Enthusiast, Espouse, Family, Fan, Favour, Fid, Finance, Flying buttress, Fly-rail, Footrest, Footstool, For, Friend, Gamb, Gantry, Garter, Girder, Glia, Grass roots, Groundswell, Handrail, Hanger, Harpin(g)s, Headrest, Help, Henchman, Hold with, Home help, Horse, Hound, I-beam, Idealogue, Impost, Income, Indorse, Instantiate, Ite, Jack, Jackstay, Jockstrap, Joist, Keep, Kingpost, Knee, Knife rest, Knighthead, Lath, Learning, Lectern, Leg, Lierne, Lifebelt, Lifebuoy, Lobby, Loper, Loyalist, Mahlstick, Mainbrace, Mainstay, Maintain, Makefast, Mill-rind, Miserere, Misericord(e), Monial, Moral, Mortsafe, Mount, Neck, Nervure, Neuroglia, -nik, Nourish, Pack, Pack-frame, Packstaff, Paranymph, Parawalker, Partisan, Partizan, Partners, Patronage, Pedestal, Peronist, Pessary, Phalanx, Pier, Pile(-cap), Pillar, Pin, Plinth, Poppet, Post, Potent, Price, Prop, Proponent, Prop-root, PTA, Pull-for, Puncheon, Purlin(e), Purlins, Pylon, Raft,

Rally round, Rebato, Regular, Reinforce, Relieve, Respond, Rest, Rind, Rod, Roof-plate, Root, Royalist, Rynd, Samaritan, Sanction, Sarking, Sawhorse, Scaffolding, Second, Shoetree, Shore, Skeg, Skeleton, Skewput, Skid, Sleeper, Sling, Snotter, Socle, Solidarity, Spectator, Splat, Splint, Sponson, Sponsor, Sprag, Spud, Squinch, Staddle, Staddlestone, Staff, Staging, Stake, Stalwart, Stanchion, Stand(-by), Stay, Steady, Stem(pel), Step, Stick, Stirrup, Stool, Stringer, Strut, Stull, Stylobate, Subscribe, Subsidy, Succour, Suffragist, Summer, Suppedaneum, Suspender, Sustain, Sustentacular, Sustentaculum, Sustentation, Tailskid, Tartan army, Technical, Tee, Telamon, Tendril, Third, Tie, Tige, Torsel, Trabecula, Tress(el), Trestle, Tripod, Trivet, Truss, Tumpline, Underlay, Underpin, Understand, Unipod, Uphold, Upkeep, Verify, Viva, Walker, Waterwings, Welfare, Well-wisher, Y-level, Yorkist, Zealot

Suppose(d), Supposition An, Assume, Believe, Conjecture, Daresay, Expect, Guess, Hypothetical, Idea, If, Imagine, Imply, Infer, Opine, Presume, Putative, Said, Sepad, Theory, What if

Suppository Pessary

Suppress(ion), Suppressed Abolish, Adaw, Burke, Cancel, Censor, Check, Clampdown, Conditioned, Crackdown, Crush, Cushion, Ecthlipsis, Elide, Elision, Epistasis, Gag, Gleichschaltung, Hide, Hush-up, Mob(b)le, Quash, Quell, Quench, Restrain, Silence, Sit on, Smother, Squash, Squelch, Stifle, Strangle, Submerge, Subreption, Throttle, Under

Suppurate, Suppuration Diapyesis, Discharge, Exude, Fester, Maturate, Ooze, Pus, Pyorrhoea, Rankle

Supreme, Supremacy, Supremo Apical, Baaskap, Best, Caudillo, Consummate, Dominant, Kronos, Leader, Napoleon, Overlord, Paramount, Peerless, Pre-eminent, Regnant, Sovereign, Sublime, Sudder, Superlative, Top, Utmost, White

Surcharge Addition, Extra, Tax

Surd Voiceless

Sure(ly) Assured, Ay, Bound, Cert(ain), Certes, Confident, Definite, Doubtless, Firm, Indeed, Infallible, Know, Pardi(e), Pardy, Perdie, Positive, Poz, Safe, Secure, Shoo-in, Sicker, Syker, Uh-huh, Unerring, Yeah, Yep, Yes

Surety Bail, Frithborth, Guarantee, Mainprise, Security, Sponsional

Surf(er), Surfing Breach, Breaker, Browse, Corndogging, Grommet, Internet, Lurk, Rollers, Rote, Sea, Waxhead

Surface Aerofoil, Appear, Area, Arise, Astroturf®, Brane, Camber, Carpet, Caustic, Control, Crust, Cutis, Day, Dermal, Dermis, Emerge, Epigene, Exterior, External, Face, Facet, Finish, Flock, Interface, Linish, Macadam, Meniscus, Nanograss, Notaeum, Out, Outcrop, Outward, Overglaze, Paintwork, Patina, Pave, Plane, Reveal, Rise, Salband, Scarfskin, Side, Skim, Skin, Soffit, Spandrel, Superficial, Superficies, Tarmac®, Tar-seal, Texture, Top, Topping, Toroid, Veneer, Wearing course, Worktop

Surf-boat, Surfboard(er), Surfboard(ing) Goofy-footer, Masoola(h), Masula, Shredder

Surfeit(ed) Blasé, Cloy, Excess, Glut, Overcloy, Plethora, Satiate, Stall, Staw

▷ **Surfer** *may indicate* programming

Surge Billow, Boom, Drive, Gush, Onrush, Seethe, S(c)end, Storm, Sway, Swell, Wind

Surgeon Abernethy, Barber, BCh, BS, CHB, CM, Doctor, DS, Dupuytren, House, Hunter, Lister, Medic, Operator, Orthopod, Plastic, Sawbones, Staff, Tang, Vet(erinary)

Surgery Anaplasty, Bypass, Cordotomy, Cosmetic, Facelift, Hobday, Keyhole, Knife, Laparotomy, Laser, LASIK, Mammoplasty, Medicine, Nip and tuck, Nose job, Op, Open-heart, Orthop(a)edics, Osteoplasty, Plastic, Prosthetics, Reconstructive, Repair, Spare-part, Stereotaxis, Ta(g)liacotian, Thoracoplasty, Tuboplasty, Zolatrics

Surly Bluff, Cantankerous, Chough, Chuffy, Churl(ish), Crabby, Crusty, Cynic, Glum, Gruff, Grum, Grumpy, Rough, Snarling, Sullen, Truculent

Surmise Extrapolate, Guess, Imagine, Infer, Presume, Suppose

Surmount Beat, Climb, Conquer, Crest, Master, Overcome, Scan, Superate, Tide, Transcend

Surname Cognomen, Patronymic

Surpass(ing) Bang, Beat, Best, Cap, Cote, Ding, Eclipse, Efface, Exceed, Excel, Frabjous, Outdo, Outgo, Outgun, Out-Herod, Outman, Outreach, Outshine, Outstrip, Overshadow, Overtop, Transcend, Trump

Surplice Cotta, Ephod, Rochet, Sark, Serk, Vakass

Surplus De trop, Excess, Extra, Glut, Lake, Mountain, Offcut, Out-over, Over, Overabundance, Overage, Overcome, Remainder, Residue, Rest, Spare, Superplus, Surfeit

Surprise(d), Surprising Ag, Alert, Amaze, Ambush, Arrah, Astonish, Aykhona wena, Bewilder, Blimey, Boilover, Bombshell, By Jove, Caramba, Catch, Confound, Coo, Cor, Crick(e)y, Crikey, Criminé, Cripes, Criv(v)ens, Crumbs, Dear, Eye-opener, Gadso, Gee, Geewhiz, Gemini, Geminy, Gemony, Gobsmacked, Godsend, Golly, Good-lack, Gorblimey, Gordon Bennett, Gosh, Great Scott, Ha, Hah, Hallo, Heavens, Hech, Heck, Heh, Hello, Hey, Hit for six, Ho, Holy cow, Hullo, Jeepers, Jeepers creepers, Jeez(e), Jinne, Jirre, Law, Lawks, Lor, Lordy, Lumme, Lummy, Man alive, Marry, Musha, My, Nooit, Obreption, Och, Odso, Omigod, Oops, Open-mouthed, Overtake, Phew, Pop-eyed, Really, Sheesh, Shock, Singular, Sjoe, Spot, Stagger, Startle, Strewth, Struth, Stun, Sudden, Treat, Turn-up, Uh, Whew, Whoops, Whoops-a-daisy, Wide-eyed, Wonderment, Wow, Wrongfoot, Yikes, Yipes, Yow, Zart, Zinger, Zowie

Surrealist Bizarre, Dali, Ernst, Grotesque, Magritte, Man Ray, Miró

Surrender Capitulate, Cave-in, Cessio honorum, Cession, Enfeoff, Extradite, Fall, Forego, Forfeit, Handover, Hulled, Kamerad, Naam, Recreant, Release, Relinquish, Remise, Rendition, Roll over, Strike, Submit, Succumb, Waive, → **YIELD**, Yorktown

Surreptitious Clandestine, Covert, Fly, Furtive, Secret, Slee, Sly, Stealthy, Underhand

Surrey Carriage, Sy

Surrogate Agent, Depute, Deputy, Locum, Proxy

Surround(ed), Surrounding(s) Ambient, Amid, Amongst, Architrave, Background, Bathe, Bego, Beset, Bundwall, Cinct, Circumvallate, Circumvent, Compass, Doughnutting, Ecology, Embail, Encase, → **ENCIRCLE**, Enclave, Enclose, Encompass, Enfold, Entomb, Envelop, Environ, Enwrap, Fence, Gherao, Gird, Girt, Hedge, Hem in, Impale, Inorb, Invest, Mid, Orb, Orle, Outflank, Outside, Perimeter, Setting, Wall

Surtees Jorrocks, Sponge

Surveillance, Survey(ing), Surveyor Behold, Browse, Cadastre, Case, Census, Chartered, Conspectus, Dialler, Domesday, Doomwatch, Espial, Examination, Eye, Geodesy, Geological, Groma, Look-see, Map, Once-over, Ordnance, Overeye, Patrol, Poll, Prospect, Quantity, Recce, Reconnaissance, Regard, Review, Rodman, Scan, Scrutiny, Staffman, Stakeout, Straw poll, Supervision, Terrier, Theodolite, Triangulate, Trilateration, Vigil, Watch

Survival, Survive, Surviving, Survivor Castaway, Cope, Die hard, Endure, Exist(ence), Extant, Finalist, Hibakusha, Last, Leftover, Live, Outdure, Outlast, Outlive, Outwear, Overlive, Persist, Pull through, Relic(t), Ride, Street-wise, Viability, Warhorse, Weather

Susan Lazy

Susceptible, Susceptibility Anaphylaxis, Electrical, Impressionable, Liable, Receptive, Vulnerable

Suspect, Suspicion, Suspicious Askance, Assume, Breath, Cagey, Dodgy, Doubt, Dubious, Equivocal, Fishy, Grain, Grey list, Guess, Hinky, Hint, Hunch, Hunky, Imagine, Inkling, Jalouse, Jealous, Leery, Misdeem, Misdoubt, Misgiving, Mislippen, Mistrust, Modicum, Notion, Paranoia, Queer, Scent, Sense, Smatch, Soupçon, Thought, Tinge, Whiff

▷ **Suspect, Suspicious** *may indicate* an anagram

Suspend(ed), Suspender, Suspense, Suspension Abate, Abeyance, Adjourn, Anabiosis, Anti-shock, Cliffhanger, Colloid, Dangle, Defer, Delay, Dormant, Freeze, Garter, Ground, → **HANG**, Hydraulic, Independent, Intermit, Lay off, Mist, Moratorium, Nailbiter, Pensile, Poise, Prorogue, Put on ice, Reprieve, Respite, Rub out, Rusticate,

Sideline, Sol, Stand off, Stay, Swing, Tension, Tenterhooks, Truce, Underslung, Withhold

▷ **Suspended** *may indicate* 'ice' on ice at the end of a down light

Sussex Rape

Sustain(ed), Sustaining, Sustenance Abide, Afford, Aliment, Bear, Constant, Depend, Endure, Food, Keep, Last, Maintain, Nourish, Nutrient, Nutriment, Nutrition, Pedal, Prolong, Sostenuto, Succour, Support, Ten(uto), Upbear

Sutler Vivandière

Suture Button, Catgut, Cobbler, Coronal, Lambda, Pterion, Purse-string, Sagittal, Stitch

Suzanne, Suzie Lenglen, Wong

Svelte Lithe, Slender, Slim

Swab Dossil, Dry, Mop, Pledget, Scour, Sponge, Squeegee, Stupe, Tampon, Tompon, Wipe

Swaddle, Swaddling Bind, Envelop, Incunabula, Swathe, Wrap

Swag Booty, Bundle, Encarpus, Festoon, Haul, Loot, Maino(u)r, Manner, Matilda, Shiralee, Toran(a)

Swagger(er), Swaggering Birkie, Bluster, Boast, Brag, Bragadisme, Bravado, Bucko, Cock, Cockiness, Crow, Jaunty, Matamore, Nounce, Panache, Pra(u)nce, Roist, Roll, Rollick, Roul, Royster, Ruffle, Sashay, Side, Strive, Swagman, Swank, Swash(-buckler), Tigerism

Swain Amoretti, Beau, Churl, Corin, Damon, Hind, Lover, Rustic, Shepherd, Strephon, Wooer

Swallow(able), Swallowing Absorb, Accept, Aerophagia, Ariel, Barn, Bird, Bolt, Bredit, Cliff, Consume, Credit, Deglutition, Devour, Down, Drink, Eat, Endue, Englut, Engulf, Engulph, Esculent, Glug, Gobble, Gula, Gulch, Gulp, Hirundine, Incept, Ingest, Ingulf, Ingurgitate, Itys, Lap, Martin, Martlet, Neck, Progne, Quaff, Shift, Sister, Slug, Stomach, Swig, Take, Take off

Swamp(y) Bog, Bunyip, Cowal, Cypress, Deluge, Dismal, Drown, Engulf, Everglade, Flood, Great Dismal, Inundate, Lentic, Lerna, Lerne, Loblolly, Mar(i)sh, Morass, Muskeg, Okavango, Okefenokee, Overrun, Overwhelm, Pakihi, Paludal, Poles'ye, Pripet Marshes, Purgatory, Quagmire, Slash, Slough, Sudd, Uliginous, Urman, Vlei, Vly, Wetland

Swan(s) Avon, Bewick's, Bird, Black, Cob, Cygnet, Cygnus, Game, Leda, Lindor, Mute, Pen, Seven, Seward, Song, Stroll, Trumpeter, Whistling, Whooper, Whooping

Swank(y) Boast, Lugs, Pretentious, Side, Style

Swansong Finale, Last air, Last hurrah

Swap, Swop → **BARTER**, Chop, Commute, Exchange, Scorse, Switch, Trade, Transpose, Truck

▷ **Swap(ped)** *may indicate* an anagram

Sward Grass, Green, Lawn, Sod, Turf

Swarm(ing) Abound, Alive, Bike, Bink, Byke, Cast, Clamber, Cloud, Crowd, Flood, Geminid, Hoatching, Host, Hotch, Hotter, Infest, Meteor, Overrun, Pullulate, Rife, Shin, Shoal, Teem, Throng

Swarthy Black-à-vised, Dark, Dusky, Melanotic

Swash Send, Swig, Swill

Swash-buckler Adventurer, Boaster, Braggart, Gascon, Swordsman

Swastika Filfot, Fylfot, Gamma(dion), Hakenkreuz

▶ **Swat** *see* **SWOT**

Swath(e) Bind, Enfold, Enroll, Envelop, Swaddle, Swipe, Wrap

Sway(ing) Careen, Carry, Command, Diadrom, Domain, Dominion, Flap, Fluctuate, Govern, Hegemony, Influence, Lilt, Oscillate, Prevail, Reel, Reign, Rock, Roll, Rule, Sally, Shog, Shoogie, Shoogle, Swag, Swale, Swee, Swing(e), Teeter, Titter, Totter, Vacillate

Swear(ing), Swear word Attest, Avow, Billingsgate, Coprolalia, Curse, Cuss, Depose, Execrate, Expletive, Invective, Jurant, Juratory, Oath, Objure, Pledge, Plight, Rail, Sessa, Tarnal, Tarnation, Verify, Vow

Sweat(ing), Sweaty Apocrine, Beads, Clammy, Cold, Dank, Diaphoresis, Eccrine,

Egest, English, Excrete, Exude, Flop, Forswatt, Glow, Hidrosis, Lather, Muck, Ooze, Osmidrosis, → **PERSPIRE**, Secretion, Slave, Stew, Sudament, Sudamina, Sudate, Suint, Swelter, Toil

Sweater Aran, Argyle, Circassian, Circassienne, Cowichan, Fair Isle, Gansey, Guernsey, Indian, Jersey, Polo, Pullover, Roll-neck, Siwash, Skinny-rib, Skivvy, Slip-on, Slop-pouch, Sloppy Joe, Turtleneck, Woolly

Swede Inga, Nordic, Olaf, Rutabaga, Scandinavian, Sven, Turnip

Sweeney Police, Todd

Sweep(er), Sweeping(s) Besom, Broad, Broom, Brush, Chimney, Chummy, Clean, Curve, Debris, Detritus, Expanse, Extensive, Generalisation, Lash, Libero, Lottery, Net, Oars, Pan, Phasing, Police-manure, Range, Scavenger, Scud, Sling, Snowball, Soop, Sooterkin, Street, Stroke, Surge, Swathe, Sway, Vacuum, Waft, Well, Wide, Widespread

Sweepstake Draw, Gamble, Lottery, Raffle, Tattersall's, Tombola

Sweet, Sweeten(er), Sweetmeat, Sweetness Afters, Baclava, Baklava, Bonus, Bribe, Bung, Cachou, Chaptalise, Charity, Charming, Cherubic, Cloying, Confect(ion), Conserve, Crème, Cute, → **DESSERT**, Douce(t), Dowset, Drop, Dulcet, Dulcie, Dulcitude, Edulcorate, Flummery, Fool, Fragrant, Fresh, Glucose, Glycerin, Goody, Honey(ed), Icky, Indican, Kiss, Lavender, Liqueur, Luscious, Melodious, Nectared, Nonpareil, Nothing, Pea, Pet, Pie, Pontefract cake, Pud(ding), Redolent, Romic, Seventeen, Sillabub, Sixteen, Solanine, Soot(e), Sop, Sorbet, Spice, Split, Sucrose, Sugar, Sugary, Syllabub, Syrupy, Tart(let), Thaumatin, Torte, Trifle, Twee, Uses, William, Winsome, Xylitol, Zabaglione

SWEETS

3 letters:	Eryngo	Cracknel	Confiserie
Gum	Halvah	Licorice	Elecampane
Ice	Humbug	Lollipop	Fairy floss
	Jujube	Marzipan	Gob-stopper
4 letters:	Mousse	Noisette	Nanaimo Bar
Choc	Nougat	Pastille	Saccharine
Jube	Sucker	Peardrop	
Mint	Tablet	Pick'n'mix	*11 letters:*
Rock	Toffee	Scroggin	Barley sugar
		Stickjaw	Marshmallow
5 letters:	*7 letters:*		
Bombe	Adeline	*9 letters:*	*12 letters:*
Candy	Alcorza	Aspartame	Acesulflame-K
Dolce	Amabile	Bubble gum	Burnt-almonds
Dolly	Caramel	Chocolate	Butterscotch
Fudge	Fondant	Cyclamate	Dolly mixture
Gundy	Gumdrop	Jelly baby	
Halva	Halavah	Jelly bean	*14 letters:*
Lolly	Lozenge	Lemon drop	Peppermint drop
Taffy	Pandrop	Liquorice	Turkish delight
	Praline	Marchpane	
6 letters:	Swedger	Muscavado	*15 letters:*
Aldose	Truffle	Saccharin	Peppermint cream
Bonbon	Wine-gum	Sugarplum	
Choccy			*20 letters:*
Comfit	*8 letters:*	*10 letters:*	Hundreds and
Confit	Acid drop	Brandyball	thousands
Dragée	Bull's eye	Candyfloss	
Eringo	Confetti	Coconut ice	

Sweetbread Bur(r), Inchpin, Pancreas, Thymus

Sweetheart Amoret, Amour, Beau, Boyfriend, Darling, Dona(h), Dowsabel(l), Doxy, Dulcinea, Flame, Follower, Girlfriend, Honey(bunch), Honeybun, Jarta, Jo(e), Lass, Leman, Lover, Masher, Neaera, Peat, Romeo, Steady, Toots(y), True-love, Valentine, Yarta, Yarto

Sweet-seller Butcher, Confectioner

Sweet talk Taffy

Swell(ing) Adenomata, Ague-cake, Anasarca, Aneurysm, Apophysis, Bag, Balloon, Bellying, Berry, Billow, Blab, Blister, Bloat, Blow, Boil, Boll, Bolster, Botch, Braw, Bubo, Bulb, Bulge, Bump, Bunion, Burgeon, Capellet, Carnosity, Cat, Chancre, Chilblain, Clour, Cratches, Curb, Cyst, Dandy, Desmoid, Diapason, Dilate, → **DISTEND**, Dom, Don, Eche, Ectasia, Eger, Elephantiasis, Encanthis, Enhance, Entasis, Epulis, Excellent, Farcy-bud, Frog, Gall, Gathering, Gent, Goiter, Goitre, Gout, Grandee, Ground, Heave, Heighten, H(a)ematoma, Hove, Hydrocele, Hydroma, Hygroma, Increase, Inflate, Intumesce, Kibe, L, Lampas(se), Lampers, Louden, Lump, Macaroni, Milk leg, Mouse, Nodule, Odontoma, Oedema, OK, Onco-, Ox-warble, Parotitis, Plim, Plump, Protrude, Protuberance, Proud, Pulvinus, Rise, Roil, Scirrhus, Scleriasis, Sea, Shinsplints, Splenomegaly, Strout, Struma, Stye, Stylopodium, Sudamina, Surge, Teratoma, Toff, Torose, Torulose, Tragus, Tuber(cle), Tumefaction, Tumescence, Tumour, Tympanites, Tympany, Upsurge, Varicocele, Varicose, Venter, Vesicle, Vulvitis, Vulvovaginitis, Wallow, Warble, Wen, Whelk, Windgall, Xanthoma

▷ **Swelling** *may indicate* a word reversed

Swelter(ing) Perspire, Roast, Stew, Sweat, Tropical

Swerve, Swerving Bias, Broach, Careen, Deflect, Deviate, Lean, Sheer, Shy, Stray, Sway, Swee, Swing, Veer, Warp, Wheel

Swift(ly) Apace, Bird, Dean, Dromond, Fleet, Flock, Hasty, Martlet, Newt, Nimble, Presto, Prompt, Pronto, Quick, → **RAPID**, Reel, Slick, Spanking, Velocipede, Wight

Swig Drink, Gulp, Nip, Scour, Swill, Tighten

Swill Guzzle, Leavings, Rubbish, Slosh, Swash

▷ **Swilling** *may indicate* an anagram

Swim(ming) Bathe, Bogey, Bogie, Crawl, Dip, Float, Freestyle, Naiant, Natant, Natatorial, Paddle, Reel, Run, Skinny-dip, Soom, Synchro(nized), Trudgen, Whim, Whirl

▷ **Swim** *may indicate* an anagram

Swimmer Bather, Cichlid, Copepod(a), Ctene, Duckbill, Duckmole, Dugong, Frogman, Leander, Mermaid, Pad(d)le, Paidle, Planula, Pleopod, Pobble, Terrapin, Trudgen, Webb

▷ **Swimmer** *may indicate* a fish

Swimming costume Bathers, Bikini, Cossie, Maillot, Monokini, One-piece, Tanga, Tankini, Tog, Trunks

Swindle(r) Beat, Bite, Bucket(-shop), Bunco, Bunkosteerer, Cajole, Champerty, → **CHEAT**, Chiz(z), Chouse, Con, Concoct, Crimp, Defraud, Diddle, Do, Escroc, Fake, Fiddle, Finagle, Fineer, Fleece, Fraud, Gazump, Gip, Gold brick, Goose-trap, Graft, Grifter, Gyp, Hocus, Hoser, Hustler, Leg, Leger, Long-firm, Magsman, Mountebank, Mulct, Nobble, Peter Funk, Plant, Ponzi scheme, Racket, Ramp, Rig, Rogue, Scam, Sell, Shaft, Shakedown, Shark, Sharper, Shicer, Shyster, Skelder, Skin, Skin game, Slicker, Sting, Stitch-up, Stumer, Suck, Swiz(z), Take, Trick, Tweedle, Twist, Two-time

Swine(herd) Boar, Brute, Cad, Eumaeus, Gadarene, Heel, Hog, Peccary, Pig, Porcine, Pork, Rat, Rotter, Sounder, Sow, Sybotic

Swing(er), Swinging Colt, Dangle, Flail, Gate, Hang, Hep, Hip, Kip(p), Lilt, Metronome, Mod, Music, Oscillate, Pendulate, Pendulum, Reverse, Rock, Rope, Shog, Shoogie, Shuggy, Slew, Swale, Sway, Swee, Swerve, Swey, Swipe, Trapeze, Vibratile, Voop, Wave, Western, Wheel, Whirl, Yaw

Swipe(s) Backhander, Beer, Haymaker, Seize, Steal, Strike, Tap-lash

Swirl Eddy, Purl, Swoosh, Tourbill(i)on, Twist, Whirl

▷ **Swirling** *may indicate* an anagram
Swish Cane, Frou-frou, Rustle, Smart, Whir, Whisper
Swiss Genevese, Ladin, Roll, Tell, Vaudois
Switch(ed), Switches, Switching Birch, Change, Churn, Convert, Crossbar,
Cryotron, Dead man's handle, Dimmer, Dip, Dolly, Exchange, Gang, Hairpiece, Knife,
Legerdemain, Master, Mercury, Mercury tilt, Message, Pear, Point, Relay, Replace,
Retama, Rocker, Rod, Scutch, Thyristor, Time, Toggle, Tress, Trip, Tumbler, Twig,
Wave, Zap
Switchback Rollercoaster
▷ **Switched** *may indicate* an anagram
Switzerland CH, Helvetia
Swivel Caster, Pivot, Root, Rotate, Spin, Terret, Territ, Torret, Turret, Wedein
Swiz Chiz(z)
Swollen Blown, Bollen, Bombe, Bulbous, Full, Gourdy, Gouty, Incrassate, Nodose, Puffy,
Tumid, Turgescent, Turgid, Varicose, Ventricose, Vesiculate
Swoon Blackout, Collapse, Deliquium, Dover, Dwa(l)m, Dwaum, Faint, Swarf, Swerf
Swoop Descend, Dive, Glide, Plummet, Souse
▶ **Swop** *see* **SWAP**
Sword(-like), Swordplay Andrew Ferrara, Anelace, Angurvadel, Anlace, Arondight,
Assegai, Balisarda, Balmunc, Balmung, Bilbo, Blade, Brand, Brandiron, Broad(sword),
Brondyron, Caliburn, Cemitare, Claymore, Colada, Cold steel, Court, Curtal-ax, Curtana,
Curtax, Cutlass, Daisho, Damascene, Damaskin, Damocles, Dance, Dirk, Duranda(l),
Durindana, Ensate, Ensiform, Epée, Espada, Estoc, Excalibur, Falchion, Faulchi(o)n,
Firangi, Foil, Forte, Fox, Gladius, Glaive, Glamdring, Gleave, Glorious, Hanger, Iai-do,
Jacob's staff, Joyeuse, Katana, Kendo, Khanda, Kirpan, Kreese, Kris, Kukri, Kusanagi,
Machete, Mandau, Merveilleuse, Mimming, Montanto, Morglay, Nothung, Parang,
Philippan, Rapier, Reverso, Rosse, Sabre, Samurai, Schiavone, Schläger, Scimitar,
Semita(u)r, Shabble, Shamshir, Sharp, Sigh, Simi, Skene-dhu, Smallsword, Spadroon,
Spirtle, Spit, Spurtle(blade), Steel, Toasting-iron, Toledo, Tuck, Tulwar, Two-edged,
Waster, Whinger, Whiniard, Whinyard, White-arm, Xiphoid, Yatag(h)an
Sword-bearer, Swordsman(ship), Swordswoman Aramis, Athos, Baldric,
Blade, Brenda(n), D'Artagnan, Fencer, Frog, Gladiator, Matador, Porthos, Sai-do, Selictar,
Spadassin, Spadroon, Spartacus, Swashbuckler, Zorro
Sword-dancer Matachin
Swordfish Espada, Istiophorus, Xiphias
Sword-swallower Samite
Swot Dig, Grind, Kill, Mug, Read up, Smug, Stew, Strike, Swat, Wonk
Sybarite, Sybaritic Aristippus, Decadent, Epicure, Hedonist, Voluptuary
▶ **Sybil** *see* **SIBYL**
Sycamore Acer, Maple, Plane, Tree
Sycophant(ic) Apple polisher, Brown-nose, Claqueur, Crawler, Creeper, Damocles,
Fawner, Gnathonic, Groveller, Hanger-on, Lickspittle, Parasite, Pickthank, Placebo,
Servile, Toad-eater, Toady, Yesman
Syllabary Hiragana, Kana, Katakana
Syllable(s) Acatalectic, Anacrusis, Aretinian, Nonsense, Om, Outride, Thesis, Tonic,
Ultima
Syllabus Program(me), Prospectus, Résumé, Summary, Table, Timetable
Syllogism Argument, Conclusion, Deduction, Enthymeme, Epicheirema, Sorites
Sylph Ariel, Nymph
Symbiotic Adnascent
Symbol(ic), Symbolism, Symbolist Allegory, Character, Charactery, Decadent, Del,
Descriptor, Diesis, Iconography, Metaphor, Minus, Moral, Mystical, Nominal, Notation,
Operator, Placeholder, Plus, Quantifier, Semicolon, Semiotic, Sex, Shadowy, Shamrock,
Slur, Status, Syllabary, Syllabogram, Synthetism, Type, Weather

SYMBOLS

2 letters:
Om
Pi

3 letters:
Edh
Eng
One
Tag

4 letters:
Agma
Ankh
Clef
Hash
Icon
Logo
Mark
Neum
Rose
Rune
Sign
Tiki
Yoni

5 letters:
Badge
Caret
Chord
Colon
Crest
Eagle
Equal
Index

Kanji
Motif
Nabla
Neume
Omega
Presa
Redon
Segno
Sigla
Tilde
Token
Totem

6 letters:
Cachet
Cipher
Emblem
Filfot
Fylfot
Letter
Obelus
Smiley
Uraeus
Wreath

7 letters:
Algebra
Cedilla
Dingbat
Heitiki
Ichthus
Ichthys
Mandala
Menorah

Mezuzah
Thistle
Waymark

8 letters:
Aniconic
Aramanth
Asterisk
Caduceus
Daffodil
Emoticon
Grapheme
Hashmark
Hiragana
Ideogram
Kitemark
Lexigram
Logogram
Pentacle
Phonetic
Svastika
Swastika
Talisman
Triskele
Wild card

9 letters:
Acrophony
Ampersand
Double-axe
Fertility
Hierogram
Ideograph
Logograph

Ouroborus
Paragraph
Phonogram
Pictogram
Sacrament
Trademark

10 letters:
Choropleth
Hieroglyph
Kalachakra
Length mark
Mogen David
Pictograph
Triskelion

11 letters:
Apostrophus
Christogram
Grammalogue
Liberty Bell
Phraseogram
Punctuation
Spread eagle
Star of David

12 letters:
Metalanguage

14 letters:
Tetragrammaton

Symmetric(al), Symmetry Balance, Bilateral, Digonal, Diphycercal, Even, Harmony, Isobilateral, Mirror, Pseudocubic, Radial, Regular, Skew

Sympathetic, Sympathise(r), Sympathy Affinity, Approval, Commiserate, Commiseration, Compassion, Condole(nce), Condone, Congenial, Crypto, Dear-dear, Empathy, Fellow-traveller, Humane, Kind, Mediagenic, Par, Pathos, Pity, Rapport, Ruth, Side, Understanding, Vicarious, Well-disposed

Symphony Alpine, Antar, Babi Yar, Bear, Clock, Concert, Drum-roll, Echo, Eroica, Farewell, Feuer, Fifth, Haffner, Horn-signal, Hunt, Ilya Murometz, Jupiter, Laudon, London, Manfred, Matin, Midi, Miracle, Music, New World, Ninth, Opus, Oxford, Pastoral, Queen, Resurrection, Rhenish, Sinfonia, Sinfonietta, Surprise, Tragic, Unfinished

Symposium Assembly, Conference, Synod

Symptom(s) Epiphenomenon, Feature, Indicia, Merycism, Mimesis, Prodrome, Semiotic, Sign, Syndrome, Token, Trait, Withdrawal

Synagogue Beit Knesset, Beth Knesseth, Shul, Temple

Synchronise(r) Coincide, Genlock, Tune

Synclinal Basin

Syncopated, Syncopation, Syncope Abridged, Breakbeat, Revamp, Vasovagal, Zoppa, Zoppo

Syndicate Associate, Cartel, Combine, Mafioso, Pool, Ring, Stokvel

Syndrome Adams-Stokes, Alport's, Asperger's, Carpal tunnel, Cerebellar, Characteristic, China, Chinese restaurant, Chronic fatigue, Compartment, Couvade, Cri du chat, Crush, Cushing's, De Clerambault's, Down's, Economy-class, Empty nest, Erotomania, False memory, Fetal alcohol, Fragile X, Goldenhar's, Gorlin, Guillain-Barré, Gulf War, Hughes, Hutchinson-Gilford, Irritable-bowel, Jerusalem, Klinefelter's, Korsakoff's, Locked-in, Long QT, Marfan, ME, Menières, Metabolic, Munch(h)ausen's, Nonne's, Overuse, Parkinson's, Pattern, POS, Postviral, Prader-Willi, Premenstrual, Proteus, Reiter's, Rett's, Revolving door, Reye's, SADS, SARS, Savant, Sezary, Shaken baby, Sick building, SIDS, Sjogren's, Stevens-Johnson, Stockholm, Stokes-Adams, Sturge-Weber, Tall-poppy, Temperomandibular, TMJ, Total allergy, Tourette's, Toxic shock, Turner's, Wag the dog, Wernicke-Korsakoff, Williams, Wobbler, XYY

Synod Assembly, Conference, Convocation, General, Robber, Whitby

Synonym(ous) Comparison, Reciprocal

Synopsis Abstract, Blurb, Conspectus, Digest, Outline, Résumé, Schema, → SUMMARY

Syntax Grammar

Synthesis Amalgam, Aperture, Fusion, Merger

Synthesizer Moog®, Vocoder, Wind

Synthetic Empirical, Ersatz, Fake, False, Mock, Neoprene, Plastic, Polyamide, Silicone, Spencerian, Urea

Syphilis Chancre, French pox, Lues, Pip, Pox, Secondary, Tertiary

Syrian Aramaean, Aramaic, Druse, Druz(e), Hittite, Hurrian, Levantine, Phoenician

Syringe(s) Douche, Flutes, Harpoon, Hypo, Hypodermic, Needle, Reeds, Spray, Squirt, Wash, Works

Syrphid Hoverfly

Syrup(y) Capillaire, Cassareep, Cassis, Cocky's joy, Coquito, Corn, Diacodion, Diacodium, Flattery, Glycerol, Golden, Goo, Grenadine, Linctus, Maple, Molasses, Moskonfyt, Orgeat, Quiddany, Rob, Sorghum, Starch, Sugar, Treacle, Viscous

System(s), Systematic ABO, Alpha, An mo, Apartheid, Auditory, BACS, Beam, Bertillon, Binary, Black, Bordereau, Braille, Brunonian, Carboniferous, Ceefax, Centauri, Circulatory, Closed loop, Code, Colloidal, Colonial, Compander, Complexus, Continental, Copernican, Cosmos, Course, Crystal, Cybernetics, Decimal, Delsarte, Dewey (Decimal), Dianetics, Distributed, Dolby®, Early warning, Economy, Eocene, Ergodic, Establishment, Expert, Feng Shui, Feudal, Fixed, Folksonomy, Formal, Fourierism, Froebel, Front-end, Giorgi, Grading, Harvard, Haversian, Hexagonal, HLA, Holist, Honour, Hub and spoke, Iastic, I Ching, Immune, Imperial, Imprest, Imputation, Induction loop, Inertial, ISA, Ism, Kalamazoo, Kanban, Life-support, Limbic, Lobby, Long wall, Loop, Lymphatic, Madras, Mercantile, Mereology, Merit, → METHOD, Metric, Microcosm, Midi, Minitel, Miocene, MKSA, Movable, Muschelkalk, Natural, Navigational, Neat, Nervous, Network, Nicam, Notation, Number, Octal, Operating, Order, Organon, Orphism, Orrery, Panel, Periodic, Permian, Pleiocene, Plenum, Points, Portal, Process, Ptolemaic, Public address, Purchase, Quota, Quote-driven, Raisonné, Regime, Regular, Reproductive, Respiratory, Root, Run-time, Scheme, Schmitt, Scientific, Selsyn, Servo, Sexual, SI, Sofar, Solar, Solmisation, Sonar, Sound, Spoils, Sprinkler, Squish lip, Stack(ing), Staff, Stakhanovism, Stand-alone, Stanislavski, Star, STOL, Structure, Studio, Support, Sweating, Tactic, Talk-down, Tally, Ternary, Theory, Third-rail, Tommy, Totalitarianism, Touch, Trias(sic), Truck, Turnkey, Tutorial, Two-party, Universe, Unix, Urogenital, Vestibular, VOIP, Warehousing, Water, Water vascular, Weapon, Windows

Tt

T Bone, Junction, Potence, Tango, Tau-cross, Tee, Time, Toc(k)

Tab Bill, Check, Cig(arette), Decimal, Flap, → **LABEL**, Ring-pull, Slate, Stay-on, Tally, Trim, Trimming

Tabby Blabbermouth, Brindled, → **CAT**, Gossip, Mottled, Spinster, Striped, Trout

Tabernacle Niche

Tabitha Gazelle

Table(-like) Alphonsine, Altar, Board, Bradshaw, Breakfast, Calendar, Capstan, → **CHART**, Coffee, Communion, Console, Contingency, Corbel, Counter, Credence, Credenza, Cricket, Decision, Desk, Diagram, Dinner, Dissecting, Dolmen, Draw-leaf, Draw-top, Dressing, Drop-leaf, Drum, Ephemeris, Experience, Food, Gateleg, Gate-legged, Glacier, Graph, Green-cloth, Gueridon, High, Imposing, Index, Key, Ladder, League, Life, Light, → **LIST**, Log, Lord's, Lowboy, Mahogany, Matrix, Mensa(l), Mesa, Monopode, Mortality, Multiplication, Occasional, Operating, Orientation, Pembroke, Periodic, Piecrust, Pier, Plane, Plateau, Platen, Pool, Prothesis, Pythagoras, Ready-reckoner, Reckoner, Refectory, Roll, Round, Rudolphine, Sand, Schedule, Scheme, Slab, Sofa, Spoon, Stall, Statistical, Stone, Suggest, Taboret, Tabular, Tariff, Tea, Te(a)poy, Throwing, Tide, Times, Toilet, Toning, Top, Tray(mobile), Trestle, Trolley, Truth, Twelve, Washstand, Water, Whirling, Wool, Workbench, Writing

Tableau Semantic

Tablecloth Damask, Linen

Table-land Barkly, Kar(r)oo, Mesa, Plateau, Puna

Table-list Memo, Menu

Tablet Abacus, Album, Aspirin, Caplet, Cartouche, E, Eugebine, Graphics, Hatch, Medallion, Opisthograph, Osculatory, Ostracon, Ostrakon, → **PAD**, → **PILL**, Pilule, Plaque, Slate, Stele, Stone, Tabula, Tombstone, Torah, Triglyph, Triptych, Troche, Trochisk, Ugarit, Votive, Wax

Table-talker Deipnosophist

Table-turner Tartar

Table-ware China, Cutlery, Silver

Taboo, Tabu Ban(ned), Bar, Blackball, Forbidden, Incest, Non dit, No-no, Tapu, Unclean

Tachograph Spy-in-the-cab

Tacit, Taciturn(ity) Implicit, Laconic, Mumps, Oyster, Reticent, Silent, Understood

Tack(y) Bar, Baste, Beat, Boxhaul, Brass, Cheesy, Cinch, Clubhaul, Cobble, Gybe, Leg, Martingale, Nail, Saddlery, Salt-horse, → **SEW**, Sprig, Stirrup, Tailor's, Tasteless, Veer, Wear, White-seam, Yaw, Zigzag

Tackle Accost, Approach, Attempt, Beard, Bobstay, Burton, Cat, Chin, Claucht, Claught, Clevis, Clew-garnet, Collar, Dead-eye, Fishing, Garnet, Gear, Haliard, Halyard, Harness, Jury-rig, Ledger, Nose, Rig, Rigging, Sack, Scrag, Spear, Stick, Straight-arm, Topping-lift, Undertake

Tact, Tactful Delicacy, Diplomacy, Diplomatic, Discreet, Discretion, Kidglove, Politic, Savoir-faire

Tactic(s) Audible, Carrot and stick, Crossruff, Finesse, Hardball, Manoeuvre, Masterstroke, Plan, Ploy, Ruse, Salami, Scare, Shock, Smear, → **STRATEGY**, Strong-arm, Zwischenzug

Tactless(ness) Blundering, Brash, Crass, Gaffe, Gauche, Indelicate, Indiscreet, Loud mouth, Maladroit

Tadpole Ascidian, Polliwig, Polliwog, Pollywig, Pollywog, Porwiggle

Taffy Thief, Toffee, Welshman

Tag Aglet, Aiguillette, Cliché, Dog, Electronic, End, Epithet, → **FOLLOW**, Kabaddi, Kimball, Label, Meta, Price, Question, Quotation, Quote, Remnant, Tab, Tail end, → **TICKET**, Treasury

Tail, Tailpiece, Tailboard All-flying, Amentum, Apocopate, → **APPENDAGE**, Bob, Brush, Bun, Caudal, Cercal, Cercus, Coda, Codetta, Colophon, Cue, Dock, Empennage, Endgate, Fan, Fee, Flag, Floccus, → **FOLLOW**, Fud, Liripoop, Parson's nose, Point, Pole, Pope's nose, PS, Queue, Rumple-bane, Scut, Seat, Shirt, Stag, Stern, Telson, → **TIP**, Train, Uro(some), Uropod, Uropygium, Women

Tailless Acaudal, An(o)urous, Fee-simple

Tail-lobes Anisocercal

Tailor(ed) Adapt, Bespoke, Bushel, Cabbager, Couturier, Cutter, Darzi, Draper, Durzi, Epicene, Feeble, Flint, Form, Merchant, Nine, Outfitter, Pick-the-louse, Pricklouse, Sartor, Seamster, Snip, Starveling, Style, Whipcat, Whipstitch

▷ **Tailor** *may indicate* an anagram

Taint(ed) Besmirch, Blemish, Fly-blown, Foughty, High, Infect, Leper, Off, Poison, → **SPOIL**, Stain, Stale, Stigma, Tinge, Trace, Unwholesome

Taiwan RC

Take(n), Take in, Taking(s), Take over, Takeover Absorb, → **ACCEPT**, Adopt, Appropriate, Assume, Attract, Bag, Beg, Bewitch, Bite, Bone, Borrow, Bottle, → **CAPTURE**, Catch, Charming, Claim, Cop, Coup (d'etat), Detract, Dishy, Distrain, Eat, Entr(y)ism, Epris, Exact, Expropriate, Film, Get, Grab, Greenmail, Handle, Haul, Hent, House, Howe, Huff, Incept, Ingest, Leveraged buy out, Mess, Misappropriate, Nationalise, Nick, Occupy, On, Pocket, Poison pill, Quote, R, Rec, Receipt, Receive, Recipe, Reverse, Rob, Seise, Sequester, Ship, Smitten, Snaffle, Snatch, Sneak, → **STEAL**, Stomach, Subsume, Swallow, Sweet, Swipe, Toll, Trump, Turnover, Usher, Usurp, Wan, Winsome, Wrest

Take away, Take-away, Take off Aph(a)eresis, Asport, Carry-out, Deduct, Destruct, Dock, Doff, Doggy bag, Dot, Esloin, Exenterate, Expropriate, Indian, Jato, Minus, Parody, Parrot, Press-gang, Recaption, Shanghai, Skit, Spoof, Subtract, Vertical, VTO(L)

Take care Guard, See, Tend, Watch

Take down, Take up Appropriate, Cap, Choose, Osmose, Shot, Snaffle, Unhook

▷ **Taken up** *may indicate* reversed

Take part Act, Engage, Side

Talbot House Toc H

Talc Potstone, Rensselaerite, Soapstone, Steatite, Venice

Tale(s) Aga-saga, Allegory, Anecdote, Blood, Boccaccio, Cautionary, Conte, Decameron, Edda, Fable, Fabliau, Fairy, Fairy story, Fiction, Folk, Gag, Geste, Hadith, Iliad, Jataka, Jeremiad, Legend, Lie, Mabinogion, Maise, Märchen, Ma(i)ze, Mease, Milesian, Narrative, Odyssey, Old wives', Pentameron, Rede, Saga, Sandabar, Score, Sinbad, Sind(a)bad, Sob-story, Spiel, → **STORY**, Tradition, Traveller's, Weird, Yarn

Tale-bearer, Tale-teller Gossip, Grass, Informer, Sneak, Tattler, Tusitala

Talent(ed) Ability, Accomplishment, Aptitude, Beefcake, Bent, Budding, Dower, Endowment, Faculty, Flair, Forte, Genius, Gift, Idiot savant, Ingenium, Knack, Long suit, Nous, Obol, Prodigy, Schtick, Strong point, Versatile, Virtuoso, Whiz-kid, W(h)iz(z)

Talion Reprisal

Talisman Amulet, Charm, Mascot, Saladin, Sampo, Scarab, Telesm

Talk(ing), Talking point, Talker, Talks Address, Ana, Articulate, Babble, Bibble-babble, Blab, Blague(er), Blat, Blather, Blether-skate, Cant, Chalk, Chat, Chew the fat, Chinwag, Chirp, Circumlocution, Colloquy, Commune, Confabulate, Confer, Converse, Coo, Cross, Descant, Dialog(ue), Diatribe, Dilate, Discourse, Diseur, Dissert, Double, Earbash, Earful, Expatiate, Express, Fast, Filibuster, Froth, Gab, Gabble, Gabnash, Gas, Gibber, Gossip, Grandiloquence, Guff, Harp, High-level, Hobnob, Hot air, Imparl, Jabber, Jargon, Jaw, Jazz, Korero, Lalage, Lalla, Lip, Logorrhoea, Macrology,

Mang, Maunder, Mince, Monologue, Motormouth, Nashgab, Natter, Noise, Omniana, Palabra, Palaver, Parlance, Parley, Patter, Pawaw, Pep, Perorate, Phraser, Pidgin, Pillow, Pitch, Potter, Powwow, Prate, Prattle, Presentation, Prose, Proximity, Ramble, Rap, Rigmarole, Rote, Sales, SALT, Shop, Slang(-whang), Small, Soliloquy, → **SPEAK**, Spiel, Spout, Straight, Sweet, Table, Tachylogia, Topic, Turkey, Twaddle, Twitter, Unbosom, Up(s), Utter, Vocal, Waffle, Wibble, Witter, Wongi, Wrangle, Yabber, Yack, Yad(d)a-yad(d)a-yad(d)a, Yak, Yalta, Yammer, Yap, Yatter

Talkative Chatty, Expansive, Fluent, Gabby, Garrulous, Gash, Glib, Loquacious, Vocular, Voluble, Windbag

Tall Etiolated, Exaggerated, Far-fetched, Hie, High, Hye, Lanky, Lathy, Leggy, Lofty, Long, Order, Procerity, Randle-tree, Rantle-tree, Tangle, Taunt, Tower, Towery

Tallboy Chest, Dresser

Tallow Greaves, Hatchettite, Lead-arming, Mineral, Vegetable, Wax

Tally Accord, → **AGREE**, Census, Correspond, Count, Match, Nickstick, Notch, Record, → **SCORE**, Stick, Stock, Tab, Tag

Talmud Gemara, Mishna(h)

Talon Claw, Ogee, Single

Talus Scree

Tamarind Assam

Tamasha Fuss, To-do

Tame Amenage, Break, Docile, Domesticate, Lapdog, Mail, Mansuete, Meek, Mild, Safe, Snool, Subdue

Tammany Hall, Sachem

Tamp, Tampon Plug

Tamper(ing) Bishop, Cook, Doctor, Fake, Fiddle, Meddle, Medicate, Monkey, Nobble, Phreaking

Tam-tam Gong

Tan(ned), Tanned skin, Tanning Adust, Bablah, Babul, Bark, Basil, Beige, Bisque, Boarding, Bronze, → **BROWN**, Canaigre, Catechu, Furan, Furfuran(e), Insolate, Lambast, Leather, Neb-neb, Paste, Pipi, Puer, Pure, Spank, Sun, Sunbathe, Tenné, Umber, Valonea, Val(l)onia, Ybet

Tandem Duo, Randem

Tang Relish, Smack, Taste

Tangent Ratio, Slope, Touching

Tangible Concrete, Palpable, Plain, Solid, Tactual

Tangle Alga, Badderlock, Burble, Driftweed, Dulse, Embroil, Enmesh, Entwine, Fank, Fankle, Heap, Hole, Implication, Ket, → **KNOT**, Labyrinth, Laminaria, Lutin, Mat, Mess, Mix, Nest, Oarweed, Ore, Perplex, Pleach, Raffle, → **RAVEL**, Sea-girdle, Seaweed, Skean, Skein, Snarl, Taigle, Taut(it), Tawt, Thicket, Tousle, Varec

▷ **Tangled** *may indicate* an anagram

Tango Dance, T

Tank(ed) Abrams, Alligator, Amphibian, Aquarium, Back boiler, Belly, Bosh, Casspir, Centurion, Cesspool, Challenger, Chieftain, Cistern, Crusader, Dracone, Drop, Drunk, Fail, Feedhead, Float, Flotation, Fuel, Gasholder, Gasometer, Header, Keir, Kier, Mouse, Panzer, Pod, Quiescent, → **RESERVOIR**, Ripple, Sedimentation, Septic, Sherman, Shield pond, Sponson, Sump, Surge, Think, Tiger, Valentine, Vat, Venter, Ventral, Vivarium, Whippet

Tankard Blackjack, Jug, Peg, Pewter, Pot, Stein, Tappit-hen

Tanker Bowser, Crude carrier, Lorry, Oiler, VLCC

Tanner(y) Bender, Currier, Kick, Solarium, Sunbather, Sunshine, Tawery, Tester(n), 'VId', Zack

Tannin Catechu

Tantalise Entice, Tease, Tempt, Torture

Tantalum Ta

Tantivy Alew, Halloo

Tantrum Hissy fit, Paddy, Pet, Rage, Scene, Snit, Tirrivee, Tirrivie, Wobbly

Tanzania(n) EAT, Sandawe

Tap(ping), Taps Accolade, Ague, Bibcock, Blip, Bob, Broach, Bug, Cock, Col legno, Dip into, Drum, Eavesdrop, Faucet, Fever, Fillip, Flick, Hack, H and C, Listen, Mag, Milk, Mixer, Monitor, Paracentesis, Pat, Patter, Percuss, Petcock, → **RAP**, Screw, Spigot, Spinal, Stopcock, Stroup, Tack, Tat, Tit, Touk, Tuck, Water

Tape Chrome, DAT, Demo, → **DRINK**, Duct, Ferret, Finish, Friction, Gaffer, Grip, Idiot, Incle, Inkle, Insulating, Magnetic, Masking, Measure, Metal, Narrowcast, Paper, Passe-partout, Perforated, Punched, Record, Red, Reel to reel, Scotch, Sellotape®, Shape, Stay, Sticky, Ticker, Tit, Video, Welding

Taper(ed), Tapering Candle, Diminish, Fastigiate, Featheredge, Flagelliform, Fusiform, Lanceolate, Morse, Narrow, Nose, Subulate, Tail

Tapestry Alentous, Arras(ene), Aubusson, Bayeux, Bergamot, Crewel-work, Dosser, Gobelin, Hanging, Mural, Oudenarde, Petit point, Sewing, Tapet, Weaving

Tapeworm Coenurus, Echinococcus, Hydatid, Measle, Scolex, Strobila, Taenia, Teniasis

Tapioca Cassava, Pearl, Yuca, Yucca

Tapir Anta, S(e)ladang

Tar, Tar product AB, Aniline, Bitumen, Carbazole, Coal, Creosote, Egg, Furan, Gas, Gladwellise, Gob, Indene, Juniper, Maltha, Matelot, Matlo, Mineral, Naphtha, Needle, OS, Parcel, Pay, Picamar, Picene, Pine, Pitch, Rating, Retene, Sailor, Salt, Uintahite, Uintaite, Wood, Wood pitch, Wren, Xylol

Tardy Behindhand, Dilatory, Late, → **SLOW**

Tare T, Tine, Vetch

Target Admass, → **AIM**, Attainment, Blank, Butt, Clay, Clout, Cockshy, Dart, Drogue, End, Ettle, Hit, Home, Hub, Inner, Magpie, Mark, Mark-white, Motty, Nick, → **OBJECT**, Object ball, Outer, Peg, Pelta, Pin, Popinjay, Prey, Prick, Quintain, Sitter, Sitting (duck), Tee, Victim, Wand, Zero in, Zero on

Tariff List, Menu, Preferential, Protective, Rate, Revenue, Zabeta

Tarnish Defile, Discolour, Soil, Stain, Sully, Taint

Taro Arum, Coc(c)o, Dasheen, Eddo

Tarot Arcana

Tarpaulin Weathercloth

Tarragon Staragen

Tarry Bide, Dally, Leng, → **LINGER**, Stay, Sticky

Tarsier Malmag

Tarsus Saul

Tart Acetic, Acid, Bakewell, Broad, Charlotte, Cheesecake, Cocotte, Croquante, Cupid, Custard, Dariole, Deck, Doxy, Duff, Flam(m), Flan, Flawn, Frock, Harlot, Hussy, Jade, Lemony, Mirliton, Moll, Mort, Nana, Painted woman, → **PIE**, Pinnace, Piquant, Pro, Quean, Quiche, Quine, Rate, → **SHARP**, Slag, Slapper, Slut, Snappy, Sour, Stew, Strumpet, Tatin, Tom, Tramp, Treacle, Trollop, Trull, Unsweet

Tartan Argyle, Argyll, Maud, Plaid, Set(t), Trews

Tartar Argal, Argol, Beeswing, Calculus, Crust, Hell, Plaque, Rough, Scale, Tam(b)erlane, Zenocrate

Tarzan Greystoke

Tashkent Uzbek

Task Assignment, Aufgabe, → **CHORE**, Clat, Duty, Emprise, Errand, Exercise, Fag, Imposition, Legwork, Mission, Onus, Ordeal, Pensum, Stint, Thankless, Vulgus

Tasmania Apple Isle, Van Diemen's Land

Tassel Pompom, Toorie, Tourie, Tsutsith, Tuft

Taste(ful), Taster, Tasty Acquired, Aesthetic, Appetite, Assay, Degust, Delibate, Delicious, Discrimination, → **EAT**, Elegant, Excerpt, Fad, Fashion, Flavour, Form, Gout, Gust, Gustatory, Hint, Lekker, Lick, Liking, Palate, Penchant, Pica, Pree, Refinement,

Relish, → **SAMPLE**, Sapor, Sar, Savour, Seemly, Sensation, S(c)hme(c)k, Sip, Smack, Smatch, Smattering, Snack, Soupçon, Stomach, Succulent, Tang, Titbit, Toothsome, → **TRY**, Umami, Vertu, Virtu, Waft, Wine

Tasteless Appal, Brassy, Fade, Flat, Indelicate, Insipid, Insulse, Kitsch, Stale, Tacky, Vapid, Vulgar, Watery, Wearish, Wersh

Tat, Tatter, Tatty Flitter, Grot, Rag, Ribbon, Roon, Schlock, Scrap, Shred, Tag, Tan, Ta(i)ver, Untidy

Tattie-bogle Scarecrow

Tattle(r) Blab, Chatter, Gash, → **GOSSIP**, Prate, Rumour, Sneak, Snitch, Totanus, Willet

Tattoo Devil's, Drum, Edinburgh, Moko, Rataplan, Row-dow, Tat

Tatum Art

Taught Up

Taunt Dig, Fling, Gibe, Gird, → **JEER**, Jest, Rag, Ridicule, Twight, Twit

Taut Stiff, Strained, Tense

Tavern Bar, Bodega, Bousing-ken, Bush, Fonda, → **INN**, Kiddleywink, Kneipe, Mermaid, Mitre, Mughouse, Night-house, Pothouse, Shebeen, Taphouse

Taw Alley, Ally, Marble

Tawdry Brash, Catchpenny, → **CHEAP**, Flashy, Gaudy, Gingerbread, Raffish, Sleazy, Tatty, Tinsey

Tawny Brindle, Dusky, Fawn, Fulvous, Mulatto, Port, Tan

Tawse Cat, Lash, Thong, Whip

Tax(ation), Taxing ACT, Agist, Aid, Alms-fee, Arduous, Assess, Capital gains, Capitation, Carbon, Carucage, Cense, Cess, → **CHARGE**, Corporation, Council, CRT, Custom, Danegeld, Death duty, Deferred, Direct, Duty, Energy, EPT, Escot, Escuage, Eurotax, Exact, Excise, Exercise, EZT, Fat, Gabelle, Geld, Gelt, Gift, Green, Head, Head money, Hearth money, Hidage, Hidden, Impose, Imposition, Impost, Impute, Indirect, Inheritance, IR, Jaghir(e), Jagir, Keelage, Land, Levy, Likin, Lot, Murage, Negative, Octroi, Operose, Overtask, Overwork, Pavage, PAYE, Peter's-pence, Poll, Poundage, Precept, Primage, Property, Proportional, PT, Punish, Purchase, Rate, Regressive, Road, Rome-pence, Sales, Scat(t), Scot (and lot), Scutage, Sess, SET, Ship money, Sin, Single, Skat, Stealth, Stent, Streetage, Stretch, Stumpage, Super, Taille, Tallage, Talliate, Tariff, Tartan, Task, Teind, Tithe, Tobin, Toilsome, Toll, Tonnage, Tribute, Try, Turnover, Unitary, Value-added, VAT, Wattle, Wealth, Weary, White rent, Windfall, Window, Withholding, Zakat

Tax area Tahsil, Talooka, Taluk(a)

Tax-collector, Taxman Amildar, Cheater, Exciseman, Farmer, Gabeller, Ghostbuster, Inspector, IR(S), Publican, Stento(u)r, Tidesman, Tithe-proctor, Tollman, Undertaker, Vatman, Zemindar

Taxi(s), Taxi driver Cab, Coast, Gharri, Gharry, Hackie, Hackney, Joe baxi, Minicab, Samlor, System, Zola Budd

Taxidermist Venus

Taxiway Peritrack

▶ **Taxman** *see* **TAX-COLLECTOR**

TB Scrofula

TE Lawrence, Ross, Shaw

Tea Afternoon, Assam, Beef, Black, Bohea, Brew, Brew-up, Brick, Bubble, Bush, Cambric, Camomile, Caper, Ceylon, Cha, Chai, Chamomile, Chanoyu, Char, China, Chirping-cup, Congo(u), Cream, Cuppa, Darjeeling, Earl Grey, Grass, Green, Gunfire, Gunpowder, Herb(al), High, Hyson, Ice(d), Indian, Jasmine, K(h)at, Kitchen, Labrador, Lapsang, Lapsang Souchong, Leaves, Ledum, Lemon, Malt, Manuka, Marijuana, Maté, Mexican, Mint, Morning, Mountain, New Jersey, Oolong, Orange pekoe, Oulong, Paraguay, Pekoe, Post and rail, Pot, Qat, Red-root, Rooibos, Rosie Lee, Russian, Sage, Senna, Souchong, Stroupach, Stroupan, Switchel, Tay, Thea, Theophylline, Tousy, Twankay, White, Yerba (de Maté)

Teach(er), Teaching (material), Teachings Acharya, Adjoint, Advisory, Agrege, AMMA, Anthroposophy, Apostle, Aristotle, AUT, Barbe, Beale, BEd, Bhagwan, Buss, Catechist, Chalk and talk, Chalkface, → **COACH**, Con(ne), Didactic, Didascalic, Docent, Doctrine, Dogma, Dominie, Dressage, Edify, → **EDUCATE**, Educationalist, Edutainment, EIS, ELT, Explain, Faculty, Froebel, Gerund-grinder, Gooroo, Gospel, Governess, Guru, Head, Heuristic, Hodja, Inculcate, Indoctrinate, Inform, Instil, Instruct, Ism, Kho(d)ja, Kindergart(e)ner, Kumon (Method), Lair, Lancasterian, Larn, Lear(e), Lecturer, Leir, Lere, Maam, Maggid, Magister, Maharishi, Mahavira, Mallam, Marker, Marm, Master, Maulvi, Mentor, Message, Miss, Mistress, Molla(h), Monitor, Montessorian, Moola(h), Moolvi(e), Mufti, Mullah, Munshi, Mwalimu, Mystagogue, Nuffield, NUT, Paedotribe, PAT, Pedagogue, Pedant, Peripatetic, Phonic method, Posture-master, Preceptor, Pr(a)efect, Privat-docent, Proctor, Prof, Prog, PT, Pupil, Rabbetzin, Rabbi, Rav, Realia, Rebbe, Remedial, Rhetor, Scholastic, Schoolie, Schoolman, Scribe, Sensei, Show, Sir, Smriti, Socrates, Sophist, Specialist, Staff, Starets, Staretz, Stinks, Substitute, Sunna, Supply, Swami, Tantra, Team, Tonic sol-fa, Train(er), Tuition, Tutelage, Tutor, Tutress, Tutrix, Usher

Teach-in Seminar
Teahouse Sukiya
Teak African, Bastard, White
Teal Spring
Team Argyll, Bafana Bafana, Colts, Crew, Dream, Écurie, Eleven, Équipe, Farm, Fifteen, Hearts, Nine, Outfit, Oxen, Panel, Possibles, Probables, Proto, Relay, Scrub, Set, → **SIDE**, Span, Special, Spurs, Squad, Squadron, Staff, Syndicate, Tiger, Troupe, Turnout, Unicorn, Unit, United, XI
Tea-party Boston, Bunfight, Cookie-shine, Drum, Kettledrum, Shine
Teapot Billycan, Cadogan, Samovar
Tear(s), Tearable, Tearful, Tearing Beano, Claw, Crocodile, Divulsion, Drop(let), Eye-drop, Eye-water, Greeting, Hurry, Lacerate, Lachrymose, Laniary, Mammock, Pelt, Ranch, Rash, Reave, → **REND**, Rheum, Rip, Rive, Rume, Scag, Screed, Shred, Snag, Split, Spree, Tire, Vale, Waterworks, Wet, Worry, Wrench, Wrest
Tearaway Get, Hothead, Ned
Tear-jerker Melodrama, Onion
Tear-pit Crumen, Larmier
Tease, Teaser, Teasing Arch, Backcomb, Badinage, Bait, Ballyrag, Banter, Card, Chaff, Chap, Chiack, Chip, Chyack, Cod, Coquet, Enigma, Grig, Guy, Hank, Imp, Ironic, Itch, Josh, Kemb, Kid, Mag, Mamaguy, Nark, Persiflage, → **RAG**, Raillery, Rally, Razz, Rib, Rip on, Rot, Strip, → **TANTALISE**, Toaze, Torment(or), Touse, Touze, Towse, Towze, Twilly, Twit, Worrit
Teasel Dipsacus, Valerian
Teat Dug, Dummy, Mamilla, Mastoid, Nipple, Pap, Soother, Tit
Tea-time Chat
Teaze Gig, Moze
Technetium Tc
Technical, Technician, Technique Adept, Alexander, Artisan, Brushwork, Campimetry, College, Cusum, Delphi, Execution, Foley artist, Footsteps editor, Harmolodics, Honey-trap, Junior, Kiwi, Know-how, Layback, Manner, Metamorphic, → **METHOD**, Operative, Phasing, Pixil(l)ation, Reflectography, Salami, Sandwich, Science, Senior, Serial, Split-screen, Stop-motion, Toe and heel, Touch, Western blotting, Work around
Technology, Technological Blue tooth, Electronics, High, Information, Intermediate, IT, Pull, Push, State of the art, Stealth, Telescience, Thickfilm, Thinfilm
Ted(dy) Bodgie, Dexter, Ducktail, Moult, Roosevelt, Underwear, Widgie, Yob
Tedium, Tedious Boring, Chore, Deadly, Doldrums, Drag, Dreariness, Dreich, Dull, Ennui, Foozle, Heaviness, Ho-hum, Langueur, Long, Longspun, Longueur, Monotony,

Operose, Prosy, Soul-destroying, Tiresome, → **TIRING**, Twaddle, Wearisome, Yawn

Tee Hub, Umbrella, Wind

Teem(ing) Abound, Bustling, Empty, Great, Heaving, Pullulate, Swarm

Teenager Adolescent, Bobbysoxer, Junior, Juvenile, Minor, Mod, Rocker, Sharpie, Skinhead, Youth

▶ **Teeth** *see* **TOOTH(ED)**

Teething ring Coral

Teetotal(ler) Abdar, Abstainer, Blue Ribbon, Nephalist, Rechabite, Sober, Temperate, TT, Water-drinker, Wowser

Tegument Seed coat

Telecommunications Cellnet®, Vodafone®

Telegram, Telegraph Bush, Cable, Ems, Facsimile, Fax, Grapevine, Greetings, International, Marconi, Message, Moccasin, Mulga wire, Overseas, Quadruplex, Radiogram, Singing, Telautograph®, Telex, Wire

Telepathy, Telepathic Clairvoyance, ESP, Psychic, Seer

Telephone Ameche, ATLAS, Bell, Blackberry, Blower, BT, Call, Cellphone, Centrex, Cordless, Detectophone, Dial, Dog and bone, Freephone®, GRACE, Handset, Horn, Hotline, Intercom, Line, Lo-call®, Mercury, Mobile, Noki, Patchboard, Payphone, Pay-station, Pdq, → **PHONE**, POTS, Ring, Snitch line, Speakerphone, Squawk box, STD, Telebridge, Textphone, Tie line, Touch-tone, Utility, Vodafone®, Wire

Teleprinter Creed

Telescope Altazimuth, Astronomical, Binocle, Cassegrain(ian), Collimator, Comet finder, Coronagraph, Coronograph, Coudé, Electron, Equatorial, Finder, Galilean, Gemini, Glass, Gregorian, Heliometer, Hubble, Interferometer, Intussuscept, Meniscus, Newtonian, Night-glass, Optical, Palomar, Perspective, Prospect(ive)-glass, Radio, Reading, Reflecting, Reflector, Refractor, Schmidt, Shorten, Sniperscope, Snooperscope, Speculum, Spyglass, Stadia, Terrestrial, Tube, X-ray, Zenith

Teletext® Ceefax®, Oracle®

Television, Telly Appointment, Box, Breakfast, Cable, Closed-circuit, Confessional, Digibox®, Digital, Diorama, Docu-soap, Event, Flatscreen, Goggle box, Iconoscope, Image orthicon, Interactive, ITV, MAC, Narrowcast, PAL, Pay, Plumbicon®, Projection, RTE, Satellite, SECAM, Set, Small screen, Subscription, Tree and branch, Tube, → **TV**, Video

Tell(ing), Teller, Telltale Acquaint, Announce, Apprise, Archer, Beads, Blab, Break, Cashier, Clipe, Clype, Compt, Confess, Direct, → **DISCLOSE**, Divulge, Effective, Fess, Give, Grass, Impart, Influential, Inform(er), → **NARRATE**, Noise, Nose, Notify, Number, Rat, Recite, Recount, Relate, Report, Retail, Rumour, Scunge, Sneak, Snitch, Spin, Teach, Unbosom, William

Tellurium Te

Temerity Cheek, Gall, Impertinence, Imprudence, Impudence, Incaution, Rashness, Recklessness

Temper, Temperate Abstemious, Abstinent, Allay, Alloy, Anneal, Assuage, Attune, Balmy, Bate, Bile, Blood, Calm, Cantankerous, Choler, Comeddle, Continent, Dander, Delay, Ease, Fireworks, Flaky, Inure, Irish, Leaven, → **MILD**, Mitigate, Moderate, Modify, → **MOOD**, Neal, Paddy, Paddywhack, Pet, Radge, Rage, Season, Short fuse, Snit, Sober, Soften, Spitfire, Spleen, Strop, Swage, Tantrum, Techy, Teen, Teetotal, Tetchy, Tiff, Tone, Trim, Tune, Wax

Temperament(al) Bent, Blood, Choleric, Crasis, Cyclothymia, Disposition, Equal, Just, Kidney, Mean-tone, Melancholy, Mettle, Moody, → **NATURE**, Neel, Over-sensitive, Phlegmatic, Prima donna, Sanguine, Unstable, Up and down, Viscerotonia

Temperance Good Templar, Moderation, Pledge, Rechabite

Temperature Absolute, Black body, Celsius, Centigrade, Chambré, Colour, Core, Critical, Curie, Dew point, Eutectic, Fahrenheit, Fever, Flashpoint, Heat, Heterothermal, Hyperthermia, Ignition, Kelvin, Melting, Néel, Permissive, Regulo, Restrictive, Room, Supercritical, T, Thermodynamic, Transition, Weed, Weid

Tempest(uous) Bourasque, Euraquilo, Euroclydon, Gale, High, Marie, → **STORM(Y)**, Wrathy

Template Stencil

Temple, Temple gate Abu Simbel, Abydos, Adytum, Amphiprostyle, Artemis, Capitol, Cella, Chapel, Church, Delphi, Delubrum, Ephesus, Erechtheum, Erechthion, Fane, Gompa, Gurdwara, Haffet, Haffit, Heroon, Inner, Josshouse, Mandir(a), Masjid, Middle, Monopteron, Monopteros, Mosque, Museum, Naos, Nymphaeum, Pagod(a), Pantheon, Parthenon, Sacellum, Serapeum, → **SHRINE**, Shul(n), Teocalli, Teopan, Torii, Vihara, Wat

Tempo Agoge, Lento, Rate, → **RHYTHM**, Rubato

Temporal Petrosal, Petrous

Temporary Acting, Caretaker, Casual, Cutcha, Ephemeral, Fleeting, Hobjob, Impermanent, Interim, Jury-rigged, Kutcha, Lash-up, Locum, Makeshift, Pro tem, Provisional, Quick-fix, Short-term, Stopgap, Temp, Transient, Transitional

Temporise(r) Politique

Tempt(ation), Tempting, Tempter, Temptress Allure, Apple, Bait, Beguile, Beset, Circe, Dalilah, Dangle, Decoy, Delilah, → **ENTICE**, Eve, Femme fatale, Groundbait, Impulse, Lure, Mephistopheles, Peccable, Providence, Satan, Seduce, Serpent, Sexy, Siren, Snare, Tantalise, Test, Tice, Trial

Ten 10, Commandments, Decad, Dectet, Decury, Denary, Googol, Iota, Long, Tera-, Tribes, X

Tenacious, Tenacity Clayey, Determined, Dogged, Fast, Guts, Hold, Intransigent, Persevering, Persistent, Resolute, Retentive, Sticky

Tenancy, Tenant(s) Boarder, Censuarius, Cosherer, Cottager, Cottar, Cotter, Cottier, Dreng, Feuar, Feudatory, Gavelman, Homage, Ingo, Inhabit, Kindly, Leaseholder, Lessee, Liege, → **LODGER**, Mailer, Metayer, Occupier, Pendicler, Periodic, Regulated, Rentaller, Renter, Secure, Shorthold, Sitting, Socager, Socman, Sokeman, Suckener, Tacksman, Valvassor, Vassal, Vavasour, Villein, Visit

Tend(ing) Apt, Care, Dress, Herd, Incline, Keep, Lean, Liable, Mind, Nurse, Prone, Run, Shepherd, Verge

Tendency Apt, Bent, Bias, Central, Conatus, Disposition, Drift, Genius, Idiosyncrasy, Import, Inclination, Leaning, Militant, Orientation, Penchant, Proclivity, Propensity, Trend

Tender(iser), Tenderly, Tenderness Affettuoso, Amoroso, Bid, Bill, Coin, Con amore, Crank, Dingey, Ding(h)y, Fond, Frail, Gentle, Green, Humane, Jolly-boat, Legal, Nesh, Nurse, → **OFFER**, Painful, Papain, Pinnace, Pra(a)m, Prefer, Present, Proffer, Proposal, Quotation, Red Cross, Sair, Shepherd, → **SOFT**, Sore, SRN, Submit, Sweet, Swineherd, Sympathy, Tendre

Tenderfoot Babe, Chechacho, Chechako, Cub, Greenhorn, Innocent

Tenderloin Psoas, Undercut

Tendon Achilles, Aponeurosis, Hamstring, Kangaroo, Leader, Paxwax, Sinew, String, Vinculum, Whitleather

Tendril(led) Capreolate, Cirrose, Cirrus, Tentacle

Tenement(s) Dominant, Land, Rook, Rookery, Tack

Tenet Adiaphoron, Creed, → **DOCTRINE**, Dogma

Tenfold Decuple

Tennis Close, Court, Deck, Jeu de paume, Lawn, LTA, Real, Royal, Set, Short, Sphairistike, Squash, Table, Wimbledon

Tenon Cog, Dovetail, Lewis, Lewisson, Tusk

Tenor Caruso, Course, Direction, Domingo, → **DRIFT**, Effect, Ferreras, Gigli, Gist, Heldentenor, Heroic, Pavarotti, Purport, Sense, Singer, T, Tide, Timbre, Trial, Vein

Tense Agitato, Aor, Aorist, Case, Clench, Cliffhanger, Conditional, Drawn, Edgy, Electric, Essive, Flex, Fraught, Imperfect, Keyed up, Knife-edge, Laconic, Mood(y), Nervy, Overstrung, Past, Perfect, Pluperfect, Preterit, Preterite, Rigid, Simple, Stiff, Strained, Stressed(-out), Strict, T, → **TAUT**, Tighten, Uptight

Tensing Sherpa
Tension Creative, Dialectic, High, Isometrics, Isotonic, Meniscus, Nail-biting, Nerviness, Premenstrual, → **STRAIN**, Stress, Stretch, Surface, Tone, Tonicity, Tonus, Yips
Tent Bell, Bivvy, Cabana, Douar, Dowar, Duar, Ger, Gur, Kedar, Kibitka, Marquee, Oxygen, Pavilion, Probe, Pup, Red wine, Ridge, Shamiana(h), Shamiyanah, Shelter, Tabernacle, Teepee, Tepee, Tilt, Tipi, Top, Topek, Trailer, Tupek, Tupik, Wigwam, Wine, Y(o)urt
Tentacle Actinal, Cirrate, Feeler, Hectocotylus, Horn, Limb, Lophophore
Tentative Empirical, Experimental, Gingerly, Peirastic
Tent-dweller, Tent-maker Camper, Indian, Kedar, Omar, St Paul
Tenth Disme, Submerged, Teind, Tithe
Ten Thousand Toman
Tenuous Frail, Slender, Slight, Thin, Vague
Tenure Blench, Burgage, Copyhold, Cottier(ism), Drengage, Fee, Fee-farm, Feu, Frankalmoi(g)n(e), Frank-fee, Gavelkind, Leasehold, Manorial, Occupation, Raiyatwari, Rundale, Runrig, Ryotwari, Socage, → **TERM**, Vavasory, Venville, Zemindar
Tepid Laodicean, Lew, Lukewarm
Terbium Tb
Terete Centric(al)
Term(s), Terminal, Termly Air, Anode, Boundary, Buffer, Buzzword, Cathode, Coast, Container, Coste, Designate, Desinent(ial), Distal, Distributed, Dub, Dumb, Easy, → **EPITHET**, Euphemism, Expression, Final, Gnomon, Goal, Half, Hilary, Inkhorn, Intelligent, Law, Lent, Major, Michaelmas, Middle, Minor, Misnomer, → **PERIOD**, Point-of-sale, Rail(head), Real, Removal, Sabbatical, School, Semester, Session, Smart, Stint, Stretch, Trimester, Trimestrial, Trinity, Ultimatum, Verb, Waterloo, → **WORD**, Work station, Zeroth
Termagant Jade, Shrew, Shrow, Spitfire, Virago, Vixen
Terminate, Termination, Terminus Abolish, Abort, Axe, Cease, Conclude, Depot, Desinent, Earth, → **END**, Expiry, → **FINISH**, Goal, Liquidate, Naricorn, Railhead, Suffix
Terminology Jargon
Termite Duck-ant, White ant
Tern Egg-bird, Noddy, Scray(e), Sooty, Three, Trio
Terpene Squalene
Terrace Barbette, Beach, Bench, Crescent, Kop, Linch, Lynchet, Offset, Patio, Perron, River, Row house, Shelf, Stoep, Tarras, Undercliff, Veranda(h)
Terra-cotta Della-Robbia, Tanagra
Terrain Area, Hinterland, Landscape, Scablands, Tract
Terrapin Diamondback, Emydes, Emys, Slider, Turtle
Terrible, Terribly Appalling, Atrocity, Awful, Deadly, Dire, Fearsome, Fell, Fiendish, Frightful, Ghastly, Hellacious, Horrible, Humgruffi(a)n, Ivan, Much, Odious, Very
Terrible person Humgruffi(a)n, Ivan, Ogre
Terrier Aberdeen, Airedale, Apsos, Australian, Australian silky, Bedlington, Black and tan, Border, Boston, Bull, Catalogue, Cesky, Dandie Dinmont, Fox, Glen of Imaal, Griffon, Irish, Jack Russell, Kerry blue, Lakeland, Maltese, Manchester, Norfolk, Norwich, Pinscher, Pit bull, Ratter, Register, Schauzer, Scotch, Scottie, Scottish, Sealyham, Silky, Skye, Soft-coated wheaten, Staffordshire bull, Sydney silky, TA, Tibetan, Welsh, West Highland, West Highland white, Westie, Wheaten, Wire-haired, Yorkshire
Terrific, Terrified, Terrify(ing) Affright, Aghast, Agrise, Agrize, Agryze, Appal, Awe, Blood-curdling, Enorm, Fear, Fine, Fley, Gast, Helluva, Huge, Mega, Overawe, → **PETRIFY**, Scare, Superb, Unman, Yippee
Territory, Territorialist Abthane, Ap(p)anage, Area, Colony, Coral Sea Islands, Doab, Domain, Dominion, Duchy, Emirate, Enclave, Exclave, Goa, Indian, Irredentist, Latium, Lebensraum, Mandated, Manor, Margravate, No-man's-land, Northern, Northwest, Nunavut, Palatinate, Panhandle, Papua, Patch, Petsamo, Princedom, Principality,

Principate, Protectorate, Province, Realm, → **REGION**, Rupert's Land, Scheduled, Sphere, Stamping ground, Sultanate, Swazi, Ter(r), Trieste, Trust, Tuath, Union, Yukon

Terror(s) Blue funk, Bugaboo, Bugbear, Eek, → **FEAR**, Fright, Holy, Imp, Night, Panic, Skrik

Terrorism, Terrorist Alarmist, Al Fatah, Anarchist, Black Hand, Bogeyman, Bomber, Bully, Cagoulard, Consumer, Death squad, Desperado, Dynamitard, Eta, Grapo, Hijacker, Ku Klux Klan, Mau-mau, Maximalist, Mountain, Nightrider, Nihilist, OAS, Pirate, Player, PLO, Provo, Red Brigade, Robespierre, Ustashi

Terry Ellen, Towel

Terse Abrupt, Brief, Brusque, Curt, Laconic, Pithy, Precise, Succinct

Tertiary Cainozoic, Eocene, Miocene, Neogene, Oligocene, Palaeogene, Pliocene

Tessellation Mosaic

Test(er), Testing Achievement, Acid, Alpha, Ames, Amnio(centesis), Analyse, Apgar, Appro, Aptitude, Assay, Audition, Barany, Bench, Bender, Benedict, Beta, Bioassay, Blood, Breath, Breathalyser®, Brinell, Burn-in, Candle, Canopy, Check, Chi-square, Cis-trans, Cloze, Conn(er), Coomb's, Crash, Criterion, Cross-match, Crucial, Crucible, Crunch, Dick, Docimastic, Driving, Drop, Dummy-run, Éprouvette, Esda, Essay, Exacting, Examine, Exercise, Experiment, Fehling's, Field, Finals, Flame, Frog, Hagberg, Ink-blot, Intelligence, International, Litmus, Lydian stone, Mann-Whitney, Mantoux, Match, Mazzin, Means, Medical, Mom, MOT, Mug, Neckverse, Needs, Objective, Oral, Ordalian, → **ORDEAL**, Pale, Pap, Papanicolaou, Paraffin, Patch, Paternity, Performance, Personality, PH, Pilot, Pons asinorum, Pree, Preeve, Preif, Preve, Prieve, Probative, Probe, Projective, Proof, Prove, Proving-ground, PSA, Pyx, Q-sort, Qualification, Quiz, Rally, Reagent, Reliability, Road, Rorschach, SAT, Scalogram, Scan, Schick's, Schilling, Schutz-Charlton, Scientise, Scratch, Screen, Shadow, Shibboleth, Showdown, Shroff, Sign, Signed-ranks, Significance, Sixpence, Skin, Slump, Smear, Smoke, Snellen, Soap, Sound, Sounding, Spinal, Stanford-Binet, Stress, Task, Tempt, Tensile, Thematic apperception, Tongue-twister, Touch, Touchstone, Trial, Trier, Trior, Try, Turing, Ultrasonic, Viva, Wassermann's, Weigh, Wilcoxon, Zack, Zohar

Testament Bible, Covenant, Hagographa, Heptateuch, Hexateuch, Hornolog(o)umena, Midrash, New, Old, Pentateuch, Scripture, Septuagint, Tanach, Targum, Will

Test-drive Trial run

Testicle(s) Ballocks, Balls, Bollix, Bollocks, Bush oyster, Cobblers, Cojones, Cruet, Doucets, Dowsets, Family jewels, Goolie, Gool(e)y, Knackers, Monkey-gland, Monorchid, Nads, Nuts, Orchis, Pills, Prairie oyster, Ridgel, Ridgil, Rig(gald), Rocks, Stone

Testify(ing), Testimonial, Testimony Attestation, Character, Chit, Declare, Depone, Deposition, → **EVIDENCE**, Hard, Rap, Reference, Scroll, Tribute, Viva voce, Vouch, Witness

Testy, Tetchy Cross, Narky, Peevish, Ratty

Tetanus Lockjaw

Tête-à-tête A quattr' occhi, Collogue, Confab, Hobnob, Twosome

Tether Cord, Endurance, Hitch, Knot, Lariat, Leash, Noose, Picket, Seal, Stringhalt, → **TIE**

Tetrahedrite Fahlerz, Fahlore

Tetrarchy Iturea

Tetrasyllabic Paeon

Tetrode Resnatron

Teuton(ic) Erl-king, German, Goth, Herren, Vandal

Texas Lone Star, Ranger

Text(s), Textbook, Texting ABC, Apocrypha, Body, Brahmana, Church, Codex, Copy, Corpus, Donat, Ennage, Greeked, Harmony, Letterpress, Libretto, Mandaean, Mantra(m), Masoretic, Mezuzah, Minitel, Nynorsk, Octapla, Op-cit, Philology, Plain, Proof, Purana, Pyramid, Quran, Responsa, Rubric, S(h)astra, Script, Shema, SMS, → **SUBJECT**, Sura, Sutra, Tao Te Ching, Tefillin, Tephillin, Tetrapla, Thesis, Topic, Tripitaka, Typography, Upanis(h)ad, Urtext, Variorum, Viewdata, Vulgate, Writing, Zohar

Textile Cloth, Fabric, Mercy

Texture Constitution, Feel, Fiber, Fibre, Grain, Open, Set(t), Wale, Weave, Woof
Thai(land) Karen, Lao(s), Mon, Shan, Siam
Thalamus Optic
Thallium Tl
Thames Father, Tamesis
Than And
Thane Banquo, Ross
Thank(s), Thankful, Thanksgiving Appreciate, Collins, Deo gratias, Gloria, Grace, Gramercy, Grateful, Gratitude, Kaddish, Mercy, Roofer
Thankless Ingrate, Vain
That (is), That one As, By, Cestui, Das heisst, Dh, Exists, How, Id est, Ie, Ille, Namely, Que, Sc, Such, Thence, Thon(der), What, Which, Yon, Yonder, Yt
Thatch(er), Thatching At(t)ap, Daych, Hair, Heard, Hear(i)e, Hele, Hell, Lath, Mane, PM, Reed, Straw, Sway, Thack, Theek, Wig, Ye(a)lm
Thaw Debacle, Defreeze, Defrost, Detente, Freeze, → **MELT**, Melt-water, Relax, Silver
▷ **Thaw** *may indicate* 'ice' to be removed from a word
The Der, Die, El, Il, La, Le, Los, T', That, Ye, Ze
Theatre(s), Theatrical(ity) Abbey, Absurd, Adelphi, Aldwych, Arena, Auditorium, Balcony, Broadway, Camp, Cinema, Circle, Coliseum, Criterion, Crucible, Drama, Drury Lane, Epic, Event, Everyman, Field, Folies Bergere, Fourth-wall, Fringe, Gaff, Gaiety, Globe, Grand Guignol, Great White Way, Hall, Haymarket, Hippodrome, Histrionic, House, Kabuki, La Scala, Legitimate, Little, Living, Lyceum, Melodramatic, Mermaid, Music-hall, National, News, Nickelodeon, Noh, Odeon, Odeum, Off-Broadway, Off-off-Broadway, Old Vic, Operating, OUDS, Palladium, Panache, Pennygaff, Pit, Playhouse, Political, Rep(ertory), Sadler's Wells, Shaftesbury, Sheldonian, Shop, Stage, Stalls, Stoll, Straw-hat, Street, Summer stock, Tivoli, Total, Touring, Vic, Windmill, Zarzuela
Theatregoer Circle, Gallery, Gods, Pit, Pittite, Stalls
Theft, Thieving Appropriation, Bluesnarfing, Burglary, Heist, Identity, Kinchinlay, Larceny, Maino(u)r, Manner, Petty larceny, Pilfery, Pillage, Plagiarism, Plunder, Pugging, Ram-raid, Rip off, Robbery, Shrinkage, Stealth, Stouth(rief), → **THIEF**, Touch, TWOC, Walk-in
Their Her
Theist Believer, Unitarian
Them 'Em, Hem, Tho
Theme Burden, Crab canon, Donnée, Fugue, Idea, Leitmotiv, Lemma, Lemmata, → **MELODY**, Motif, Mythos, Mythus, Peg, Question, → **SUBJECT**, Subtext, Text, Topic, Topos
Then(ce) Already, Away, Next, Since, Sine, So, Syne, Thereupon, Tho
▷ **The northern** *may indicate* t'
Theodolite Diopter, Dioptre, Groma, Tacheometer, Tachymeter, Transit
Theologian, Theologist, Theology Abelard, Ambrose, Aquinas, Arminius, Barth, Baur, Calvin, Christology, Colet, DD, Divine, Eckhart, Erastus, Eschatology, Eusebius, Exegetics, Faustus, Fideism, Genevan, Harnack, Hase, Infralapsarian, Irenics, Isidore, Jansen, Kierkegaard, Knox, Laelius, Liberation, Luther, Moral, Mullah, Natural, Newman, Niebuhr, Origen, Paley, Pastoral, Patristics, Pectoral, Pelagius, Peritus, Pusey, Rabbi, Religious, Sacramentarian, Schoolman, Schwenkfeld, Scotus, Socinus, Softa, STP, Supralapsarian, Swedenborg, Tertullian, Thomas à Kempis, Tirso de Molina, Ulema, Universalist
Theory, Theorem, Theoretical, Theorist Abstract, Academic, Atomic, Attachment, Attribution, Auteur, Automata, Band, Bayes(ian), Bernouilli's, Big bang, Binomial, Bohr, Boo-hurrah, Boolean, Calorific, Catastrophe, Chaos, Communications, Complexity, Connectionism, Conspiracy, Corpuscular, Cosmogony, Creationism, Darwinian, Decision, Deduction, Dependency, Dictum, Doctrinaire, Domino, Double aspect, Dow, Einstein, Emboîtement, Empiricism, Epigenesist, Euhemerism, Exponential, Fermat's

(last), Fortuitism, Gaia, Galois, Game, Gauge, Germ, Gödel's, Grand Unified, Grotian, Group, Guess, Holism, Hormic, Hypothesis, Ideal, Identity, Ideology, Information, Ism(y), James-Lange, Jordan curve, Kinetic, Kock's, Laingian, Lamarckism, Lemma, Lunar, MAD, Metaphysical, Milankovitch, Model, Monism, Mythical, Nebular, Neo-Lamarckism, Neovitalism, Nernst heat, Notion, Number, Object relations, Pancosmism, Pantologism, Perturbation, Petrinism, Pluralism, Positivism, Poynting, Probability, Proof, Pure, Pythagoras, Quantity, Quantum, Quantum field, Queueing, Random walk, Rational choice, Reception, Relativism, Relativity, Satisfaction, Set, Solipsism, Speculative, Steady state, String, Superdense, Superstring, Supersymmetry, System, Tachyon, TOE, Traducianism, Trickle-down, Twistor, Tychism, Unified Field, Utilitarianism, Voluntarism, Vortex, Vulcanist, Wages fund, Wasm, Wave, Wholism, Wolfian

Therapy, Therapeutic, Therapist Analyst, Family, Fever, Insight, Non directive, Past life, → TREATMENT

THERAPIES

3 letters:
Art
CST
ECT
HRT
MLD
ORT
Sex

4 letters:
Deep
Gene
Germ
SHEN
TENS
X-ray
Zone

5 letters:
Bowen
Drama
Group
Light
Music
Narco
Natal
Radio
Reiki
Serum
Shock
Sound
Touch

6 letters:
Colour
Gerson
Larval

Oxygen
Primal
Radium
Retail
Scream
Speech

7 letters:
Crystal
Gestalt
Natural
Pattern
Rainbow
Rolfing
Shiatsu
Shiatzu

8 letters:
Aura-Soma
Aversion
Cellular
Curative
Faradism
Gemstone
Germ-line
Hypnosis
Live cell
Magnetic
Movement
Physical
Polarity
Pressure
Reichian
Rogerian
Sanatory
Sitz-bath

9 letters:
Auricular
Behaviour
Chelation
Cognitive
Dianetics
Flotation
Implosive
Radiation
Root-canal
Theriacal
Water cure

10 letters:
Hellerwork
Logopedics
Looyenwork
Osteopathy
Regression
Relaxation
Supportive

11 letters:
Acupressure
Acupuncture
Combination
Gate control
Logopaedics
Psychodrama
Reflexology
Scientology®

12 letters:
Chemotherapy
Craniosacral
Curietherapy
Electroshock

Heliotherapy
Narcotherapy
Occupational
Phototherapy
Primal scream

13 letters:
Arsenotherapy
Brachytherapy
Client-centred
Electric shock
Immunotherapy
Speleotherapy
Thermotherapy

14 letters:
Crystal healing
Electrotherapy

15 letters:
Minimal invasive
Oral rehydration
Psychosynthesis
Röntgenotherapy
Thalassotherapy

16 letters:
Chavuttithirumal

17 letters:
Electroconvulsive

20 letters:
Cognitive-
  behavioural
Metamorphic
  technique

There(after), Thereby, Thereupon Attending, Holla, Ipso facto, Present, Thither, Thon, Upon, With that, Y, Yonder

Therefore Argal, Ergo, Forthy, Hence, So, Why

Thermodynamic Enthalpy, Entropy

Thermometer Aethrioscope, Centesimal, Clinical, Cryometer, Gas, Glass, Katathermometer, Maximum and minimum, Psychrometer, Pyrometer, Resistance, Thermograph, Water, Wet and dry bulb, Wet bulb

Thermoplastic Cel(luloid), Resin

Thesaurus Dictionary, Lexicon, Roget, Treasury, Word-finder

These Thir

Theseus Champion

Thesis Argument, Dissertation, Doctorial, Theme

Thespian → ACTOR, Ham, Olivier, Performer, Theatrical

Thessalonian Lapith

They A

Thick(en), Thickening, Thickener, Thickness, Thickset Abundant, Algin, Burly, Bushy, Callosity, Callus, Clavate, Cloddy, Cruddle, Curdle, Dense, Dextrin(e), Dumb, Dumose, Engross, Fat, Grist, Grouty, Grume, Guar, Gum, Hyperostosis, In cahoots, Incrassate, Inspissate, Kuzu, Liaison, Lush, Luxuriant, Nuggety, Pally, Panada, Ply, Reduce, Roux, Sclerosis, → SOLID, Soupy, Spissitude, Squat, Stocky, Stumpy, → STUPID, Thieves, This, Thixotropic, Turbid, Viscous, Waulk, Wooden, Xantham

Thick-coated Atheromatous

Thicket Bosk, Brake, Brush, Cane-brake, Chamisal, Chapparal, Coppice, Copse, Covert, Dead-finish, Fernshaw, Greve, Grove, Macchia, Maquis, Queach, Reedrand, Reedrond, Salicetum, Shola

Thick-lipped Labrose

Thick-skinned Armadillo, Call(o)us, Pachyderm, Tough

Thief, Thieves, Thievish Abactor, Area sneak, Autolycus, Blood, Bulker, Chummy, Coon, Corsair, Cracksman, Cutpurse, Dip, Dismas, Dysmas, Filcher, Flood, Footpad, Freebooter, Furacious, Ganef, Gestas, Gully-raker, Heist, Hotter, Huaquero, Ice-man, Jackdaw, Joyrider, Kiddy, Kondo, Larcener, Lifter, Light-fingered, Limmer, Looter, Mag, Magpie, Montith, Nip(per), Nuthook, Pad, Peculator, Pickpocket, Pilferer, Pirate, Plagiarist, Poacher, Poddy-dodger, Prig, Raffles, River-rat, → ROBBER, Rustler, Safeblower, Safebreaker, Safecracker, St Nicholas's clerks, Scrump, Shark, Shop-lifter, Sneak, Snowdropper, Sticky fingers, Taffy, Taker, Tarry-fingered, Tea-leaf, Thick, Twoccer

Thigh Femoral, Gaskin, Ham, Haunch, Hock, Meros

Thin(ner), Thinness Acetone, Atomy, Attenuate, Bald, Beanpole, Bony, Cadaverous, Cornstalk, Cull, Diluent, Dilute, Ectomorph, Emaciated, Enseam, Fine, Fine-drawn, Flimsy, Gaunt, Hair('s-)breadth, Hairline, Inseam, Lanky, Lean, Matchstick, Mawger, Puny, Rackabones, Rangy, Rare, Rarefied, Reedy, Scant, Scraggy, Scrannel, Scrawny, Sheer, Sieve, Skeletal, Skelf, Skimpy, Skinking, Slender, Slim, Slimline, Slink, → SPARE, Sparse, Spindly, Stilty, Stringy, Subtle, Taper, Tenuous, Threadbare, Turpentine, Turps, Wafer, Washy, Waste, Watch, Water(y), → WEAK, Weedy, Whirtle, Wiry, Wispy, Wortle, Wraith

Thing(s) Alia, Article, Chattel, Chose, Craze, Doodah, Doofer, Entia, Fetish, First, Fixation, It, Item, Jingbang, Job, Last, Material, Matter, Near, Noumenon, → OBJECT, Obsession, Paraphernalia, Phobia, Res, Tool, Vision, Whatnot

Thingumabob, Thingummy Dingbat, Dinges, Dingus, Doodad, Doodah, Doofer, Doohickey, Gubbins, Hootenanny, Hoot(a)nanny, Jigamaree, Oojamaflip, Whatsit, Yoke

Think(er), Thinking Associate, Audile, Believe, Brain, Brainstorm, Brood, Casuistry, Chew over, Cogitate, Cognition, Conjecture, Consider, Contemplant, → CONTEMPLATE, Deem, Deliberate, Descartes, Devise, Dianoetic, Divergent, Esteem, Fancy, Fear, Feel, Fogramite, Ghesse, Gnostic, Guess, Hegel, Hold, → IMAGINE, Judge, Lateral, Meditate, Mentation, Mindset, Mull, Muse, Opine, Pensive, Philosopher, Phrontistery, Ponder,

Pore, Presume, Ratiocinate, Rational, Reckon, Reflect, Reminisce, Ruminate, Speculate, Synectics, Trow, Vertical, Ween, Wishful

Thin-skinned Sensitive

Third, Third rate Bronze, C, Eroica, Gamma, Gooseberry, Interval, Major, Mediant, Minor, Picardy, Quartan, Tertiary, Tertius, Tierce, Trisect

Third man Abel, Lime

Thirst(y) Adry, → CRAVE, Dives, Drought, Drouth, Dry, Hydropic, Nadors, Pant, Polydipsia, Thrist

Thirteen Baker's dozen, Devil's dozen, Long dozen, Riddle, Triskaidekaphobia, Unlucky

Thirty Lambda

Thirty nine books All-OT, OT

This Hic, Hoc, The, Thick, Thilk, Thir

Thistle Canada, Carduus, Carline, Cnicus, Creeping, Dayshell, Echinops, Milk, Musk, Rauriki, Russian, Safflower, Scotch, Sow, Spear, Star, Thrissel, Thristle

This year Ha

Thomas Aquinas, Arnold, Christadelphian, De Quincey, Didymus, Doubting, Dylan, Erastus, Hardy, Loco, Parr, Rhymer, Tompion, True, Turbulent

Thomas Aquinas Angelic Doctor

Thong Babiche, Jandal®, Lash, Latchet, Leather, Lore, Riem, Riempie, Shoe-latchet, → STRAP, Strop, Taws(e), Whang, Whip

Thor Thunderer

Thorax Chest, Peraeon, Pereion, Scutellum, Throat

Thorium Th

Thorn(y) Acantha, Aculeus, Bael, Bel, Bhel, Bramble, Briar, Coyotillo, Doom, Edh, Eth, Irritation, Jerusalem, Jew's, Mahonia, Mayflower, Nabk, Nar(r)as, Nebbuk, Nebe(c)k, → NEEDLE, Paloverde, Pricker, Prickle, Slae, Spine, Spinescent, Spinulate, Trial, Wagn'bietjie, Y, Ye, Zare(e)ba, Zariba, Zeriba

Thorn-apple Jimpson-weed

Thornless Inerm

Thorough(ly) À fond, Complete, Deep, Even-down, Firm, Fully, In depth, Ingrained, Inly, Intensive, Not half, Out, Out and out, Painstaking, Pakka, Pucka, Pukka, Radical, Rigorous, Ripe, Root and branch, Searching, Sound, Strict, Total, Tout à fait, Up

Thoroughbred Arab, Bloodstock, Pedigree, Post-vintage, Pursang

Thoroughfare Avenue, Broadway, Causeway, Freeway, Highway, Parkway, → ROAD, Street

Those Thae, Thaim, Them, Tho, Yon

Thou M, Mil

Though Albe, Albeit, All-be, Ever, Tho, Whenas

Thought(s), Thoughtful(ness) Avisandum, Broody, Censed, Cerebration, Charitable, Cogitation, Concept, Considerate, Contemplation, Dianoetic, Felt, Idea, Imagination, Indrawn, Innate, Kind, Maieutic, Mind, Musing, Notion, Opinion, Pansy, Pensée, Pensive, Philosophy, Reason, Reflection, Rumination, Second

Thoughtless Blindfold, Careless, Goop, Heedless, Improvident, Incogitant, Inconsiderate, Pillock, → RASH, Reckless, Reflexive, Remiss, Scatter-brained, Stupid, Unintentional, Unkind, Vacant, Vain

Thousand(s) Chiliad, G, Gorilla, Grand, K, Lac, Lakh, M, Millenary, Millennium, Myriad, Octillion, Plum, Sextillion, Toman

Thracian Spartacus

Thrall Captive, Esne, Serf, Slave

Thrash(ing) → BEAT, Belabour, Belt, Bepelt, Binge, Bless, Cane, Dress, Drub, Flail, Flog, Jole, Joll, Joule, Jowl, Lace, Laidie, Laidy, Lambast, Larrup, Lather, Leather, Lick, Marmelise, Onceover, Paste, Ploat, Quilt, Slog, Smoke, Strap-oil, Swaddle, Swat, Tank, Targe, Thraiping, Towel, Trim, Trounce, Wallop, Whale, Whap, Work over, Writhe

Thread(ed), Threadlike Acme screw, Addenda, Ariadne, Bar, Bottom, Bride, Buttress,

Chalaza, Chromatid, Chromatin, Chromosome, Clew, Clue, Cop(pin), Cord, Coventry blue, Eel-worm, End, Female, Fibre, Filament, File, Filiform, Filose, Filoselle, Float, Floss, Flourishing®, Gist, Gold, Gossamer, Heddle, Ixtle, Lace, Lap, Lingel, Lingle, Link, Lisle, Lurex®, Male, Meander, Microfibre, Mycellum, Needle, Nematode, Nematoid, Organzine, Pack, Pearlin(g), Pick, Plasmodesm, Ravel, Reeve, Roon, Rope-yarn, Rove, Sacred, Screw, Sellers screw, Seton, Shoot, Silver, Single, Spider line, Spireme, Sporangiophore, Stamen, → **STRAND**, Stroma, Suture, Tassel, Tendril, Theme, Thrid, Thrum, Trace, Tram, Trundle, Tussore, Twine, Twist, Two-start, Warp, Watap, Wax(ed) end, Weft, Whitworth, Whitworth screw, Wick, → **WIND**, Wisp, Worm, Zari

Threadbare Hackneyed, Motheaten, Napless, Shabby, Worn

Threadworm Nemathelminth, Strongyl, Vinegar-eel

Threat(en), Threatened, Threatening Baleful, Black(en), Blackmail, Bluster, Brew, Brutum fulmen, Bully, Coerce, Comminate, Discovered check, Duress, Extort, Face, Fatwa, Fraught, Greenmail, Greymail, Hazard, Impend, Imperil, Intimidate, Jeopardise, Loom, → **MENACE**, Minacious, Minatory, Mint, Omen, Ominous, Or else, Overcast, Overhang, Parlous, Peril, Portent, Ramp, Sabre-rattling, Shore, Strongarm, Ugly, Veiled, Warning, Yellow peril

Three, Threefold, Three-wheeler, Thrice Cheers, Graces, Har, Harpies, Jafenhar, Leash, Muses, Musketeers, Pairial, Pair-royal, Parial, Prial, Ter, Tercet, Tern, Terzetta, Thridi, Tid, T.i.d, Tierce, Tray, Trey, Triad, Trial, Tricar, Triennial, Trifid, Trigon, Trilogy, Trinal, Trine, Trinity, Trio, Triple, Triptote, Troika

Three-D(imensional) Cinerama, Lenticular, Stereopsis, Vectograph

Three-day Triduan, Triduum

Threehalfpence Dandiprat, Dandyprat

Three-handed Cutthroat

Three-headed Cerberus, Geryon

Three hundred B, Carpet

Three-legged IOM, Triskele, Triskelion

Threepence, Threepenny bit Tickey, Tray, Trey, Treybit

Three-quarter Wing

Three-year old Staggard

Threnody Dirge, Epicede, → **LAMENT**

Thresh Beat, Flail, Separate

Threshold Absolute, Brink, Cill, Difference, Doorstep, Limen, Liminal, Nuclear, Sill, Tax, Verge

▸ **Thrice** *see* **THREE**

Thrift(y) Economy, Frugal, Husbandry, Oeconomy, Scrimping, Sea-grass, Sea-pink, Virtue, Wary

Thrill(er), Thrilling Atingle, Buzz, Charge, Delight, Dindle, Dinnle, Dirl, Dread, Dynamite, Electric, Emotive, → **ENCHANT**, Enliven, Excite, Film noir, Frisson, Gas, Jag, Kick, Page-turner, Perceant, Plangent, Pulsate, Pulse, Quiver, Sensation, Thirl, Tinglish, Tremor, Vibrant, Whodunit, Wow

Thrive Batten, Blossom, Boom, Do, Fl, → **FLOURISH**, Flower, Grow, Mushroom, → **PROSPER**, Succeed, Thee

Throat(y) Craw, Crop, Deep, Dewlap, Fauces, Gorge, Gular, Gullet, Guttural, Hot coppers, Jugular, Laryngeal, Maw, Oropharynx, Pereion, Pharynx, Prunella, Quailpipe, Red lane, Roopit, Roopy, Strep, Swallet, Thrapple, Thropple, Throttle, Weasand, Wesand, Whistle, Windpipe

Throb(bing) Beat, Palpitate, Pant, Pit-a-pat, Pound, Pulsate, Quop, Stang, Tingle, Vibrato

▷ **Throbbing** *may indicate* an anagram

Throe(s) Agony, Pang, Paroxysm

Thrombosis Deep-vein

Throne Bed-of-justice, Cathedra, Episcopal, Gadi, → **LAVATORY**, Mercy-seat, Peacock, Rule, Seat, See, Siege, Stool, Tribune

Throng(ing) Crowd, Flock, Horde, Host, Multitude, Press, Resort, Swarm

Throttle → **CHOKE**, Gar(r)otte, Gun, Mug, Regulator, Scrag, Silence, Stifle, Strangle, Strangulate, Thrapple, We(a)sand

Through, Throughout Along, Ana, By, Dia-, During, Everywhere, Over, Passim, Per, Pr, Sempre, Sic passim, To, Trans, Via, Yont

▶ **Throw(n)** *see* **TOSS(ING)**

Throw (up), Thrower, Throw-out Bin, Cast-off, Chunder, Discobolus, Egesta, Eject, Emesis, Estrapade, Floor, Flummox, Flying mare, Go, Jettison, Mangonel, Pash, Puke, Reject, Slam-drunk, Spatter, Spew, Squirt, Squit, → **TOSS**, Ventriloquism

Throwback Atavism, Echo

Thrush Antbird, Aphtha, Bird, Chat, Fieldfare, Hermit, Homescreetch, Mavis, Missel, Mistle, Olive-back, Pitta, Prunella, Redwing, Sprue, Turdine, Veery

Thrust(er) Abdominal, Aventre, Bear, Boost, Botte, Burn, Burpee, Detrude, Dig, Drive, Elbow, Engine, Exert, Extrude, Flanconade, Foin, → **FORCE**, Gist, Hay, Hustle, Imbroc(c)ata, Impulse, Jet, Job, Lift-off, Lunge, Montant(o), Muscle, Obtrude, Oust, Pass, Passado, Peg, Perk, Pitchfork, Poach, Poke, Potch(e), Pote, Probe, Prog, Propel, Pun, Punto, → **PUSH**, Put, Ram, Remise, Repost, Run, Shoulder, Shove, Single-stock, Sock, Sorn, Squat, Stap, Stick, Stoccado, Stoccata, Stock, Stuck, Thrutch, Tilt, Tuck, Venue

Thud Bounce, Drum, Dump, Flump, Phut, Plod, Thump, Thunk, Whump

Thug(s) Brute, Gangster, Goon(da), Gorilla, Gurrier, Hood(lum), Keelie, Loord, Ninja, Ockers, Phansigar, Plug-ugly, Rough(neck), SS, Strangler, Ted, Tityre-tu, Tsotsi, Yahoo

Thule Ultima

Thulium Tm

Thumb Bally, Green, Hitch, Midget, Ovolo, Pollex, Scan, Sore, Tom

Thump(ing) Blow, Bonk, Clobber, Cob, Crump, Da(u)d, Dawd, Ding, Dod, Drub, Dub, Hammer, Knevell, Knock, Lamp, Nevel, Oner, Paik, Percuss, → **POUND**, Pummel, Ribroast, Slam, Slosh, Souse, Swat, Swingeing, Thud, Trounce, Tund, Whud, Whump

Thunder(ing), Thunderstorm Astrophobia, Bolt, Boom, Clap, Coup de foudre, Donnerwetter, Foudroyant, Foulder, Fulminate, Intonate, Lei-king, Microburst, Pil(l)an, Raiden, → **ROAR**, Rumble, Summanus, Tempest, Thor, Tonant

Thunderbolt Ward

Thursday Chare, Holy, Maundy, Sheer, Shere

Thus Accordingly, Ergo, Sic, So, Therefore

Thwart Baffle, Balk, → **CROSS**, Dash, Dish, Foil, Frustrate, Hamstring, Hogtie, Obstruct, Outwit, Pip, Prevent, Scotch, Scupper, Snooker, Spike, Spite, Stonker, Stymie, Transverse

Thy Yourn

Thyme Basil, Lemon, Water

Thyroid Goitre, Myxodema

Tiara Cidaris, Crownet, Triple crown

Tiberius Gracchus

Tibetan Ladakhi, Lamaist, Naga, Sherpa, Sitsang

Tic Spasm, Synkinesis, Vocal

Tick, Tick off Acarida, Acarus, Beat, Bloodsucker, Check, → **CHIDE**, Click, Cr, → **CREDIT**, Deer, HP, Idle, Instant, Jar, Ked, Mattress, Mile, Mo, Moment, Ricinulei, Second, Seed, Sheep, Soft, Strap, Worm

Ticket(s) Billet, Bone, Brief, Carnet, Commutation, Complimentary, Coupon, Day, Docket, Dream, E(lectronic), Excursion, Hot, Kangaroo, Label, Meal, One-day, One-way, Open-jaw, Parking, Pass, Pass-out, Pasteboard, Pawn, Platform, Raffle, Raincheck, Return, Round-trip, Rover, Saver, Scratchcard, Season, Single, Soup, Split, Straight, Stub, Supersaver, → **TAG**, Tempest, Tessera(l), Through, Tix, Transfer, Tyburn, Unity, Voucher, Walking, Zone

Ticket-seller Scalper

Tickle, Ticklish Amuse, Delicate, Divert, Excite, Gratify, Gump, → **ITCH**, Kittle, Queasy,

Thrill, Titillate

Tiddler Brit, Tom

Tide, Tidal Current, Drift, Eagre, Easter, Eger, Estuary, Flood, High, High water, Lee, Low, Marigram, Neap, Red, Rising, River, Roost, Sea, Seiche, Slack water, Spring, Surge, Trend, Wave

Tide-gate Aboideau, Aboiteau, Weir

Tidings Gospel, → **NEWS**, Rumour, Word

Tidy Big, Comb, Considerable, Curry, Do, Fair, Fettle, Groom, Kempt, Large, Neat, Neaten, → **ORDER**, Pachyderm, Predy, Preen, Primp, Red(d), Slick, Snug, Sort, Spruce, Trim, Valet

Tie, Tied, Tying Ascot, Attach, Barcelona, Berth, Bind, Black, Bolo, → **BOND**, Bootlace, Bow, Bowyang, Cable, Clip-on, Cope, Cord, Cravat, Cup, Dead-heat, Drag, Draw, Fetter, Four-in-hand, Frap, Halter, Handicap, Harness, Hitch, Holdfast, Kipper, → **KNOT**, Lace, Lash, Level, Ligament, Ligate, Ligature, Link, Marry, Match, Moor, Neck and neck, Oblige, Obstriction, Old School, Oop, Oup, Overlay, Raffia, Restrain, Rod, Rope, Scarf, School, Score draw, Scrunchie, Semifinal, Shackle, Sheave, Shoelace, Shoestring, Sleeper, Slur, Solitaire, Soubise, Splice, Stake, Standoff, Strap, String, Tawdry-lace, Tether, Together, Trice, Truss, Unite, White, Windsor

Tier Apron, Bank, Gradin(e), Knotter, Layer, Range, Rank, Row, Stage, Storey

Tierce Leash, Tc

Tiff Bicker, Contretemps, Difference, Dispute, Exchange, Feed, Feud, Huff, Miff, Skirmish, Spat, Squabble

Tiffany Gauze

Tiger Bengal, → **CAT**, Clemenceau, Demoiselle, Lily, Machairodont, Machairodus, Man-eater, Margay, Paper, Sabre-tooth, Shere Khan, Smilodon, Stripes, Tamil, Tasmanian, Woods

Tight(en), Tightness, Tights Boozy, Bosky, Brace, Canny, Cinch, Close(-hauled), Constriction, Cote-hardie, → **DRUNK**, Fishnet, Fleshings, High, Hose, Jam, Leggings, Leotards, Lit, Loaded, Maillot, Mean, Merry, Niggardly, Oiled, Pang, Pantihose, Phimosis, Pickled, Pinch(penny), Plastered, Prompt, Proof, Rigour, Snug, Squiffy, Stenosis, → **STINGY**, Stinko, Strict, Stringent, Swift, Swig, Taut, Tense, Tipsy, Trig, Woozy

Tight-lipped Shtum

Tightrope(-walker) Aerialist, Blondin, Equilibrist, Funambulist, High wire, Petauriste

Tightwad Cheapskate, → **MISER**, Scrooge

Tile(s), Tiled Antefix, Arris, Azulejo, Carpet, Chapeau, Dalle, Derby, Dutch, Encaustic, Field, → **HAT**, Hung, Imbrex, Imbricate, Lid, Lino, Mahjong(g), Ostracon, Ostrakon, Peever, Quarrel, Quarry, Rag(g), Ridge, Rooftop, Sclate, Shingle, Slat, → **SLATE**, Tegular, Tessella, Tessera, Titfer, Topper, Wall, Wally

Till Cashbox, Checkout, Coffer, Ear, Eulenspiegel, Farm, Hasta, Hoe, Husband, Lob, Peter, → **PLOUGH**, Rotavate, Set, Unto, Up to

Tiller Gardener, Helm, Ploughman, Rotavator, Wheel

Tilt(ed) Awning, Bank, Camber, Cant, Careen, Cock, Dip, Heel, Hut, Joust, Just, → **LIST**, Quintain, Rock, Tip, Trip, Unbalance, Version

Timber Apron, Ashlaring, Balk, Batten, Beam, Bolster, Bond, Bowsprit, Bridging, Cant-rail, Carapa, Cedarwood, Chess, Clapboard, Compass, Coulisse, Cross-tree, Cruck, Dogshores, Driftwood, Druxy, Dwang, Elmwood, Flitch, Float, Four-by-two, Futchel, Futtock, Greenheart, Groundsell, Hardwood, Harewood, Intertie, Iroko, Ironwood, Joist, Knee, Knighthead, Lauan, Ligger, Lignum, Lintel, Log, Lumber, Nogging, Nothofagus, Plank-sheer, Purlin(e), Putlock, Putlog, Pyengadu, Radiata, Ramin, Rib, Ridgepole, Roseweed, Roundwood, Rung, Sandalwood, Sapele, Sapodilla, Satinwood, Scantling, Shook, Shorts, Sissoo, Skeg, Sneezewood, Softwood, Souari, Stemson, Stere, Sternpost, Sternson, Straddle, Stud, Stull, Stumpage, Summer, Swing-stock, Tilting fillet, Towing-bitts, Transom, Trestletree, Two-by-four, Wale, Wall plate, Weatherboard, Whitewood, → **WOOD**, Yang

Timbre Clang, Klang(farbe), Register, → **TENOR**, Tone, Tone colour
Time(s), Timer Access, African, Agoge, Apparent, Assymetric, Astronomical, Atlantic,
Atomic, Autumn, Awhile, Bird, BST, By, Central, Chronaxy, Chronic, Chronometer,
Chronon, Clock, Closing, Common, Compound, Connect, Core, Counter, Cryptozoic,
Date, Day, Dead, Decade, Dimension, Double, Duple, Duration, Early, Eastern,
Eastern Standard, Egg-glass, Enemy, Eon, Ephemeris, Epoch, Epocha, Equinox, Era,
EST, European, Eve(ning), Extra, Father, Flexitime, Fold, Forelock, Four-four, Fourth
dimension, Free, Full, Geological, Gest, Glide, Half, Healer, High, Horologe, Hour,
Hourglass, Hr, Idle, Imprisonment, Injury, Innings, Instant, Interim, Interlude, Jiff,
Juncture, Kalpa, Killing, Latent, Lay-day, Lead, Lean, Leisure, Life, Lighting-up, Lilac,
Local, Lowsing, Man-day, Mean, Menopause, Metronome, Mountain standard, Multiple,
Needle, Nonce, Nones, Normal, Occasion, Oft, → **ON TIME**, Opening, Pacific, Paralysis,
Part, Peak, Period, Phanerozoic, Pinger, Porridge, Post, Precambrian, Prelapsarian,
Prime, Proper, Quadruple, Quality, Question, Quick, Reaction, Real, Reaper, Recovery,
Released, Response, Responsum, Reverberation, Rhythm, Run(ning), Sandglass, Sands,
Schedule, Seal, → **SEASON**, Seel, Seil, Semeion, Serial, Session, Shelf-life, Sidereal,
Sight, Simple, Sith(e), Slow, Solar, Solstice, Space, Spacious, Span, Spare, Spell, Spin,
Split, Spring, Squeaky-bum, Standard, Stoppage, Stopwatch, Stound, Stownd, Stretch,
Summer, Sundial, Sundown, Sythe, T, Tem, Tempo, Tempore, Tense, Thief, Three-four,
Thunderer, Tick, Tid, Tide, Trice, Triple, True, Turnaround, Two-four, Universal, Usance,
What, While, Winter, X, Yonks, Yukon, Zero
Timebomb Demographic
Time-keeper, Timepiece Ben, Chronometer, Clock, Hourglass, Ref, Sand-glass,
Sundial, Ticker, Tompion, Watch
Timeless Eternal, Nd, Undying
Timely Appropriate, Apropos, Happy, Heaven-sent, Opportune, Pat, Prompt, Punctual
Timescale Geological
Time-server Fence-sitter, Prisoner, Trimmer, Vicar of Bray
Timeshare Box and cox
Timetable ABC(ee), Absee, Bradshaw, → **CHART**, Schedule
Timid, Timorous Afraid, Aspen, Bashful, Blate, Chicken, Cowardly, Eerie, Eery,
Faint-hearted, Fearful, Hare, Hen-hearted, Meticulous, Milquetoast, Mouse, Mous(e)y,
Pavid, Pigeon-hearted, Pusillanimous, Pussy, Quaking, Schnok, Shrinking, → **SHY**,
Skeary, Sook, Tremulous, Wuss, Yellow
Timothy Cat's-tail, Grass, Phleum
Tin(ned), Tinfoil, Tinny Argentine, Block, Britannia metal, Can, Cash, Debe, Dixie,
Maconochie, Mess, → **MONEY**, Moola(h), Ochre, Plate, Rhino, Sn, Stannary, Stannic,
Stream, Tain, Tole
Tincture Arnica, Brown, Bufo, Chroma, Elixir, Fur, Infusion, Laudanum, Metal, Or,
Sericon, Sol, Spice, Taint, Tenné, Vert
Tinder Amadou, Faggot, Fuel, Funk, Punk, Spark, Spunk, Touchwood
Tine Antler, Bay, Cusp, Grain, Prong, Snag, Spire, Surroyal, Trey
Tinge(d) Cast, Dye, Eye, Flavour, Gild, → **HUE**, Infuscate, Taint, Tincture, Tone, Touch
Tingle, Tingling Dinnle, Dirl, Paraesthesia, Pins and needles, Prickle, Thrill, Throb,
Tinkle
Tinker Bell, Caird, Coster, Didakai, Didakei, Diddicoy, Didicoy, Didikoi, → **FIDDLE**, Gypsy,
Meddle, Mender, Pedlar, Potter, Prig, Putter, Repair, Sly, Smouse, Snout, Tamper, Tramp,
Traveller, Tweak
Tinkle, Tinkling Pink, Thin
Tinsel(ly) Clinquant, Gaudy, Glitter, O, Spangle, Turkey
Tint Colour, Henna, Hue, Pigment, → **STAIN**, Tinct, Tinge, Tone, Woad
Tiny Atto-, Baby, Diddy, Dwarf, Ha'it, Infinitesimal, Itsy-bitsy, Lilliputian, Midget,
Minikin, Minim, Mite, Negligible, Petite, Pint-sized, Pitiful, Pittance, Small, Smidge(o)n,
Smidgin, Stime, Teeny, Tiddl(e)y, Tiddy, Tim, Tine, Tottie, Totty, Toy, Wee

Tip (off), Tipping Apex, Arrowhead, Ash-heap, Asparagus, Backshish, Baksheesh, Batta, Beer-money, B(u)onamono, Bonsel(l)a, Bonus, Cant, Cert, Chape, Counsel, Coup, Cowp, Crown, Cue, Cumshaw, Douceur, Dump, Extremity, Fee, Felt, Ferrule, Filter, Forecast, Glans, Gratillity, Gratuity, Heel, → **HINT**, Hunch, Inkle, Iridise, Lagniappe, Largess(e), List, Mag(g), Mess, Middenstead, Nap, Nib, Noop, Ord, Perk, Perquisite, Point, Pointer, Pour, Pourboire, Previse, Prong, Straight, Suggestion, Summit, Tag, Tail, Tilt, Toom, Touch, Tronc, Upset, Vail, Vales, Warn, Whisper, Wink, Wrinkle

Tipper Ale

Tippet Cape, Fur, Scarf

Tipple Bib, Booze, → **DRINK**, Paint, Pot, Poteen

Tipster Prophet, Tout

Tipsy Bleary, Boozy, Bosky, → **DRUNK**, Elevated, Merry, Moony, Nappy, Oiled, On, Rocky, Screwed, Slewed, Slued, Squiffy, Tight, Wet

▷ **Tipsy** *may indicate* an anagram

Tiptoe Digitigrade, Spanish, Walk

Tirade Diatribe, Invective, Jobation, Laisse, Philippic, Rand, Rant, Screed, Slang

Tire(d), Tiredness, Tiring All-in, Aweary, Beat, Bejade, Bleary-eyed, Bore, Brain fag, Bushed, Caparison, Cooked, Deadbeat, Dress, Drowsy, → **EXHAUST**, Fag, Fagged out, Fatigue, Flag, Footsore, Fordid, Fordod, Forjeskit, Frazzle, Gruel, Irk, Jack, Jade, Languor, Lassitude, Limp, ME, Overspent, Pall, Poop, Puggled, → **ROBE**, Rubber, Sap, Shagged, Sicken, Sleepry, Sleepy, Snoozy, Spent, Swinkt, Tax, Tedious, Trying, Tucker, Wabbit, Wappend, Weary, World-weary, Wrecked

Tiresome Boring, Exhausting, Humdrum, Pill, Tedious, Trying, Vexing

Tirl Rattle, Risp, Strip, Turn

▶ **Tiro** *see* **TYRO**

Tissue Adenoid, Adhesion, Adipose, Aerenchyma, Aponeurosis, Archesporium, Bast, Callus, Carbon, Cartilage, C(o)elom, Cementum, Chalaza, Cheloid, Chlorenchyma, Coenosarc, Collagen, Collenchyma, Commissure, Conducting, Connective, Corpus luteum, Corpus Striatum, Cortex, Dentine, Diploe, Elastic, Elastin, Endarch, Endosperm, Endosteum, Epigenesis, Epimysium, Epineurium, Epithelium, Eschar, Evocator, Fabric, Fascia, Fibroid, Filament, Flesh, Gamgee, Gauze, Gleba, Glia, Granulation, Granuloma, Gum, Handkerchief, Hankie, Heteroplasia, Histogen, Histoid, Hypoderm(is), Infarct, Interlay, Junk, Keloid, Kleenex®, Lamina, Liber, Lies, Ligament, Luteal, Lymphate, Lymphoid, Macroglia, Marrow, Matrix, Mechanical, Medulla, → **MEMBRANE**, Meristem, Mesenchyme, Mesophyll, Mestom(e), Mole, Muscle, Myelin(e), Myocardium, Neoplasia, Neoplasm, Neuroglia, Nucellus, Olivary, Pack, Palisade, Pannus, Paper, Papilla, Parenchyma, Periblem, Perichylous, Pericycle, Peridesmium, Perimysium, Perinephrium, Perineurium, Perisperm, Phellogen, Phloem, Pith, Placenta, Plerome, Polyarch, Pons, Primordium, Procambium, Prosenchyma, Prothallis, Pterygium, Pulp, Radula, Retina, Sarcenet, Sars(e)net, Scar, Sclerenchyma, Scleroma, Sequestrum, Sinew, Siphonostele, Siphuncle, Soft, Somatopleure, Stereome, Stroma, Submucosa, Suet, Tarsus, Tela, Tendon, Toilet, Tonsil, Trace, Tunica, Vascular, Velum, Web, Wound, Xylem, Zoograft

Tit, Tit-bit(s) Analecta, Canapé, Crested, Currie, Curry, Delicacy, Dug, Nag, Nipple, Nun, Pap, Quarry, Sample, Scrap, Snack, Teat, Tug, Twitch, Willow, Wren, Zakuska

Titan(ic), Titaness Atlas, Colossus, Cronos, Cronus, Drone, Enormous, Giant, Ginormous, Huge, Hyperion, Kronos, Large, Leviathan, Liner, Oceanus, Phoebe, Prometheus, Rhea, Superman, Themis, Vast

Titanium, Titanite Rutin, Sagenite, Sphene, Ti

Tit for tat Deserts, Revenge, Talion

Tithe Disme, Dyzemas, Frankpledge, Teind, Tenth

Titian Abram, Auburn

Titillate(r), Titillating Delight, Excite, Fluffer, Naughty, Tickle

Titivate Preen, Primp

Title Abbé, → **ADDRESS**, Ag(h)a, Agname, Antonomasia, Appellative, Bab, Bahadur, Baroness, Baronet, Bart, Bastard, Bhai, Bretwalda, Burra sahib, Calif, Caliph, Caption, Charta, Chogyal, Claim, Conveyance, Count(ess), Courtesy, Credit, Dan, Datin, Datuk, Dauphin, Dayan, Deeds, Denominative, Devi, Dom, Don, Don(n)a, Dowager, Dub, Duchess, Duke, Earl, Effendi, Eminence, Epithet, Esquire, Excellency, Fra, Frau(lein), Ghazi, Gospodin, Grand Master, Great Mogul, Gyani, Hafiz, Handle, Header, Heading, Headline, Highness, Hojatoleslam, Hon, Honour, Imperator, Interest, Kabaka, Kalif, Kaliph, Kaur, Khan, King, Kumari, Lady, Lala, Lemma, → **LIEN**, Lord, Mal(l)am, Marchesa, Marchese, Marquess, Marquis, Master, Masthead, Maulana, Memsahib, Meneer, Mevrou, Miladi, Milady, Milord, Mirza, Mr(s), Name, Native, Negus, Nemn, Nizam, Nomen, Padishah, Pasha, Peerage, Pir, Polemarch, Prefix, Prince(ss), Queen, → **RANK**, Reb, Reverence, Reverend, → **RIGHT**, Rubric, Running, Sahib, Sama, San, Sardar, Sayid, Senhor(a), Señor(a), Shri, Singh, Sir, Sirdar, Son, Sowbhagyawati, Sri, Stratum, Tannie, Tenno, Titule, Torrens, Tuanku, Tycoon, U, Voivode, Worship

Title-holder Cartouche, Champion, Landlord, Noble

Titmouse Bird, Hickymal, Mag, Reedling, Tit

Titter Giggle, Snigger, Tehee

Tittle Jot

Titus Oates

Tizz(y) Pother, Spin, State, Tanner, Testril, VId

TNT Explosive, Trotyl

To(wards) At, Beside, Inby, Intil, Oncoming, Onto, Prone, Shet, Shut, Till, Until

Toad(y) Bootlicker, Bufo, Bumsucker, Cane, Clawback, Cocksucker, Crapaud, Crawler, Fawn, Frog, Hanger-on, Horned, Jackal, Jenkins, Knot, Lackey, Lick-platter, Lickspittle, Midwife, Minion, Natterjack, Nototrema, Paddock, Parasite, Pick-thank, Pipa, Placebo, Platanna, Poodle, Puddock, Queensland cane, Sook, Spade-foot, Squit, Surinam, Sycophant, Tree, Tuft-hunter, Walking, Warty, Xenopus, Yesman

Toadstone Lava

Toadstool Amanita, Death-cap, Death-cup, Destroying angel, Fly agaric, → **FUNGUS**, Grisette, Horsehair, Marasmus, Paddock-stool, Parrot, Saffron milk cap, Sickener, Sulphur tuft, Verdigris, Wax cap

Toast(er) Bacchus, Bell, Birsle, Brindisi, → **BROWN**, Bruschetta, Bumper, Cheers, Chin-chin, Crostini, Crouton, Drink-hail, French, Gesundheit, Grace-cup, Grill, Health, Heat, Iechyd da, Immortal memory, Kia-ora, L'chaim, Lechayim, Loyal, Melba, Pledge, Pop up, Propose, Prosit, Round, Salute, Scouther, Scowder, Scowther, Sentiment, Sippet, Skoal, Slainte, Slainte mha(i)th, Soldier, Sunbathe, Wassail, Zwieback

Toastmaster MC, Symposiarch

Tobacco, Tobacco-field Alfalfa, Bacchi, Baccy, Bird's eye, Broadleaf, Burley, Burn, Canaster, Capa, Caporal, Cavendish, Chew, Dottle, Filler, Honeydew, Indian, Killikinnick, Kinnikinick, Latakia, Mundungus, Nailrod, Navy-cut, Negro-head, Nicotian, Nicotine, Niggerhead, Perique, Pigtail, Pipe, Plug, Quid, Rapper, Régie, Returns, Shag, Sneesh, Snout, Snuff, Straight cut, Stripleaf, Turkish, Twist, Vega, Virginia, Weed, Wrapper

To be arranged TBA

Toboggan Sled(ge), Sleigh

To boot Furthermore

Toby Dog, High, Highwayman, Jug, Low

Tocsin Alarm, Siren

Today Hodiernal, Now, Present

Toddle(r) Baim, Gangrel, Mite, Tot, Totter, Trot, Waddle

Toddy Arrack, → **DRINK**, Sura, Whisky

To-do Sensation, Stir

Toe(s) Dactyl, Digit, Fissiped, Hallux, Hammer, Piggy, Pinky, Pointe, Poulaine, Prehallux, Tootsie

Toff Gent, Nob, Nut, Snob, Swell

Toffee Banket, Butterscotch, Caramel, Cracknel, Gundy, Hard-bake, Hokey-pokey, Humbug, Tom-trot

Toga Palla

Together Among, At-one, Atone, Attone, Col, En bloc, En masse, Gathered, Hand-in-glove, Hand-in-hand, In concert, Infere, → **JOINT**, Pari-passu, Sam, Simultaneous, Unison, Wed, Y, Yfere, Ysame

Toggle Fastener, Netsuke

Togs Clothes, Gear, Rig, Strip

Toil(s) Drudge, Fag, Industry, → **LABOUR**, Mesh, Net, Seine, Sisyphus, Slog, Sweat, Swink, Tela, Tew, Trap, Trauchle, Travail, Tug, Web, → **WORK**, Wrest, Yacker, Yakka, Yakker

Toilet Can, Chemical, Coiffure, Garderobe, Head(s), John, Lat(rine), Lavabo, → **LAVATORY**, Loo, Necessary house, Necessary place, Pot, Powder room, Toot, WC

Token Abbey-piece, Buck, Check, Chip, Counter, Coupon, Disc, Double-axe, Emblem, Gift, Indication, Mark, → **MEMENTO**, Monument, Nominal, Omen, Portend, Seal, Sign, Signal, Slug, Symbol, Symptom, Tessella, Tessera, Valentine, Voucher

Tolerable Acceptable, Bearable, Mediocre, Passable, So-so

Tolerance, Tolerant, Tolerate(d) Abear, Abide, Accept, → **ALLOW**, Bear, Broadminded, Brook, Countenance, Endure, Enlightened, Good-natured, Hack, Had, Immunological, Latitude, → **LENIENT**, Liberal, Lump, Mercy, Permit, Stand, Stick, Stomach, Studden, Suffer, Support, Thole, Wear, Zero

Toll Chime, Chok(e)y, Customs, Due, Duty, Excise, Jole, Joll, Joule, Jow, Light-dues, Octroi, Pierage, Pike, Pontage, Rates, → **RING**, Scavage, Streetage, Tariff, Tax

Toll-breaker Rebecca

Tom(my) Atkins, Bell, Bowling, Bread, Brown, → **CAT**, Collins, Edgar, Gib, Grub, Gun, He-cat, Jerry, Jones, Mog(gy), Nosh, Peeping, Private, Pro(stitute), Pte, Puss, Ram-cat, Sawyer, Snout, Soldier, Stout, Thos, Thumb, Tiddler, Tucker

Tomato Beef(steak), Cherry, Gooseberry, Husk, Love-apple, Plum, Portuguese, Strawberry, Tamarillo, Tree, Wolf's peach

Tomb(stone) Burial, Catacomb, Catafalque, Cenotaph, Cist, Coffin, Dargah, Durgah, Grave, Hypogeum, Inurn, Kistvaen, Marmoreal, Mastaba, Mausoleum, Megalithic, Monument, Pyramid, Repository, → **SEPULCHRE**, Sepulture, Serdab, Shrine, Speos, Tell el Amarna, Tholos, Tholus, Through-stane, Through-stone, Treasury, Vault

Tombola Draw, Lottery, Raffle

Tomboy Gamine, Gilpey, Gilpy, Hoyden, Ladette, Ramp, Romp

Tome → **BOOK**, Volume

Tomfoolery Caper, Fandangle, Shenanigan

Tomorrow Future, Manana, Morrow, The morn

Tompion Watchman

Tom Snout Tinker

Ton(nage) C, Century, Chic, Displacement, Freight, Gross, Hundred, Long, Measurement, Metric, Net register, Register, Shipping, Short, T

Tone, Tonality Aeolian, Brace, Combination, Compound, Dialling, Difference, Differential, Engaged, Fifth, Gregorian, Harmonic, Hum, Hypate, Inflection, Key, Klang, Mediant, Minor, Ninth, Partial, Passing, Pure, Qualify, Quarter, Real, Resultant, Ring, Ringing, Side, → **SOUND**, Strain, Summational, Temper, Tenor, Timbre, Touch, Trite, Whole

Tong(s) Curling, Lazy, Sugar, Wafer

Tongue, Tonguing Brogue, Burr, Chape, Clack, Clapper, Doab, Double, Final, Flutter, Forked, Glossa, Glossolalia, Glottal, Isthmus, Jinglet, → **LANGUAGE**, Languet(te), Lap, Ligula, Lill, Lingo, Lingual, Lingulate, Lytta, Mother, Organ, Radula, Ranine, Rasp, Red rag, Single, Spit, Tab, Triple, Voice, Vulgar

Tongue-tied Mush-mouthed, See a wolf

Tongue-twister Jaw-breaker, Shibboleth

Tonic Booster, Bracer, C(h)amomile, Cascara, Doh, Elixir, Key, Keynote, Mease, Medicinal, Mishmee, Mishmi, Myrica, Oporice, Pareira brava, Pick-me-up, Quassia, Refresher, Roborant, Sage tea, Sarsaparilla, Solfa

▷ **Tonic** *may indicate* a musical note

Tonsil, Tonsillitis Amygdala, Antiaditis, Pharyngeal, Quinsy

Tonsure(d) Epilate, Haircut, Peel, Pield

Tony Bête, Chic, Classy, Fool, Smart, U

Too Als(o), As well, Besides, Eke, Excessive, Item, Likewise, Moreover, Oer, Over, Overly, Plus, Troppo

Took Naam, Nam, Set, Stole, Wan, Won

Tool(s) Flatter, → IMPLEMENT, → INSTRUMENT, Maker, Palaeolith, Penis, Percussion, Power, Property, Utensil

TOOLS

2 letters:	Burin	Gouger	Grapnel
Ax	Croze	Graver	Icepick
	Dolly	Hammer	Insculp
3 letters:	Drift	Hopdog	Jim Crow
Awl	Drill	Husker	Jointer
Axe	Drove	Jackal	Machine
Bit	Edger	Jumper	Nail gun
Bur	Elsin	Laster	Nail set
Die	Facer	Mallet	Nippers
Fid	Float	Muller	Oustiti
Gad	Graip	Pattle	Pickaxe
Hob	Hardy	Pestle	Plunger
Hoe	Jemmy	Pliers	Pointer
Saw	Lewis	Rabble	Pricker
Set	Miser	Rammer	Rocking
	Piton	Reamer	Rounder
4 letters:	Plane	Ripple	Scalpel
Adze	Prunt	Roller	Scalper
Brog	Punch	Router	Scauper
Burr	Snake	Sander	Scorper
File	Spade	Saw set	Scraper
Froe	Swage	Scutch	Scriber
Frow		Scythe	Seamset
Iron	*6 letters:*	Shoder	Slasher
Loom	Beetle	Sickle	Sleeker
Lute	Bodkin	Slater	Spanner
Pawn	Broach	Strike	Spudder
Pick	Chaser	Switch	Swingle
Rasp	Chisel	Trowel	Swipple
Rirp	Dibber	Wimble	Terebra
Roll	Dibble	Wrench	Triblet
Rurp	Eatche		T-square
Snap	Eolith	*7 letters:*	Twibill
Tint	Firmer	Bradawl	Upright
Vice	Former	Carbide	
	Fraise	Catspaw	*8 letters:*
5 letters:	Fuller	Chopper	Aiguille
Auger	Gimlet	Fretsaw	Airbrush
Bevel	Gnomon	Go-devil	Billhook

Calipers
Chainsaw
Clippers
Driftpin
Findings
Grattoir
Hardware
Picklock
Pitching
Puncheon
Scissors
Strickle
Strimmer®
Tjanting
Tranchet
Tweezers

Vibrator

9 letters:
Centre bit
Come-along
Corkscrew
Drawknife
Drawshave
Microlith
Moon-knife
Outsiders
Pitchfork
Secateurs
Toothpick
Try square

10 letters:
Float-stone
Fore-hammer
Jackhammer
Loggerhead
Spokeshave

11 letters:
Bagging-hook
Glass-cutter
Marlinspike
Mitre square
Plough-staff
Screwdriver
Spirit-level
Spitsticker

Steam hammer

12 letters:
Hedge-trimmer
Marlinespike
Monkey wrench
Sledge-hammer
Spell-checker
Wire-stripper

13 letters:
Microkeratome
Shooting stick

Toot(er) Blow, Horn, Parp, Trumpet
Tooth(ed), Toothy, Teeth Baby, Bicuspid, Bit, Buck, Bunodont, Cadmean, Canine,
Carnassial, Chactodon, Cheek tooth, Chisel, Choppers, Cog, Comb, Comer, Cott's,
Crena(te), Ctenoid, Cusp, Deciduous, Denticle, Dentin(e), Dentures, Egg, Eye, False,
Fang, Gam, Gap, Gat, Gnashers, Grinder, Heterodont, Impacted, Incisor, Ivory, Joggle,
Laniary, Milk, Mill, Molar, Nipper, Odontoid, Orthodontics, Overbite, Pawl, Pearly gates,
Pectinate, Periodontics, Peristome, Permanent, Phang, Plate, Poison-fang, Pre-molar,
Prong, Radula, Ratch, Ratchet, Scissor, Secodont, Sectorial, Selenodont, Serration, Set,
Snaggle, Sprocket, Stomach, Store, Sweet, Trophi, Tush, Tusk, Uncinus, Upper, Wallies,
Wang, Wiper, Wisdom, Wolf, Zalambdodont, Zygodont
Toothache, Tooth troubles Caries, Odontalgia, Odontoma, Tartar
Toothless(ness) Anodontia, Edentate, Gummy, Pangolin
Toothpaste Dentifrice
Top (drawer; hole; line; notcher), Topmost, Topper 1st, A1, Ace, Acme,
Altissimo, Apex, Apical, Behead, Best, Better, Big, Blouse, Blouson, Boob tube, Brow,
Bustier, Cacumen, Cap, Capstone, Ceiling, Coma, Cop, Coping, Corking, Cream, → **CREST**,
Crista, Crop, Crown, Culmen, De capo, Decollate, Diabolo, Dog, Dome, Double, Drawer,
Dreid(e)l, Dux, Elite, Execute, Fighting, Finial, Flip, Gentry, Gyroscope, Halterneck, Hard,
Hat, → **HEAD**, Height, Hummer, Humming, Imperial, Impost, Jumper, Lid, Maillot, Nun,
One-er, Optimate, Orb, Parish, → **PEAK**, Peerie, Peery, Peg, Peplos, Peplus, Pinnacle,
Pitch, Quark, Replenish, Ridge, Roof, Sawyer, Screw, Secret, Shaw, Shirt, Skim, Sky, Slay,
Soft, Spinning, Star, Summit, Superate, Superb, Supernal, Supreme, Supremo, Surface,
Sweater, Table, Tambour, Targa, Teetotum, Texas, Tile, Trash, Trump, T-shirt, Turbinate,
Up(most), Uppermost, V, Vertex, Whipping, Whirligig, Winner
▷ **Top** *may indicate* first letter
Topaz Citrine, Colorado, Occidental, Oriental, Pycnite, Rose, Scottish, Spanish
Topcoat Finish, Overcoat, Ulster
Tope(r) Boozer, Bouser, Dagaba, Dagoba, → **DRUNK**, Sot, Tosspot
Topic(al) Head, Hobbyhorse, Item, Local, Motion, Place, Shop, Subject, Text, → **THEME**
Top-knot Tuft
Topping Grand, Icing, Meringue, Pepperoni, Piecrust, Streusel
Topple Dethrone, Oust, Overbalance, Overturn, Tip, Upend, → **UPSET**
Topsy Parentless
Topsy-turvy Careen, Cockeyed, Inverted, Summerset, Tapsalteerie, Tapsleteerie
Torah Maftir
Torch Blow, Brand, Cresset, Fire, Flambeau, Hards, Hurds, Lamp, Lampad, Link,
Olympic, Penlight, Plasma, Roughie, Tead(e), Weld, Wisp

Torch-bearer Usherette
Toreador Escamillo, Matador, Picador, Torero
Torment(ed), Tormentor Agony, Anguish, Bait, Ballyrag, Bedevil, Butt, Cruciate,
Crucify, Curse, Distress, Excruciate, Frab, Gehenna, Grill, Hag-ridden, Harass, Harry,
Hell, Martyrdom, Molest, Nag, Nettle, Pang, Pine, Plague, → **RACK**, Sadist, Tantalise,
Tease, Wrack
Tornado Cyclone, Twister, Waterspout
Toronto Hogtown
Torpedo Bangalore, Bomb, Fish, Missile, Ray, Subroc, Tin fish, Weapon
Torpedo-guard Crinoline
Torpid, Torpor Accidie, Acedia, Comatose, Dormant, Gouch, Inertia, Languid,
Lethargic, Sluggish, Slumbering
Torrent Flood, Spate
Torrid Amphiscian, Fiery, Hot, Sultry, Tropical
Torsk Cusk
Torso Body, Midriff, Trunk
Tortilla Pancake, Quesadilla, Taco, Tostada
Tortoise Chelonia, Emydes, Emys, Galapagos, Giant, Hic(c)atee, Kurma, Pancake,
Snapping-turtle, Terrapin, Testudo, Timothy, Turtle, Water
Tortoiseshell Epiplastra, Hawksbill, Testudo
Tortuous Ambagious, Twisty, Winding
▷ **Tortuous** *may indicate* an anagram
Torture, Torture chamber, Torture instrument Agonise, Auto-da-fé,
Bastinade, Bastinado, Boot, Bootikin, Catasta, Chinese burn, Chinese water, Crucify,
Devil-on-the-neck, Engine, Excruciate, Flageolet, Fry, Gadge, Gauntlet, Gyp, Hell, Iron
maiden, Knee-cap, Naraka, Peine forte et dur, Persecute, Pilliwinks, Pine, Pinniewinkle,
Pinnywinkle, → **RACK**, Sadism, Scaphism, Scarpines, Scavenger, Scavenger's daughter,
Scourge, Skeffington's daughter, Skevington's daughter, Strappado, Tantalise, Third
degree, Thumb(i)kins, Thumbscrew, Torment, Treadmill, Triphook, Tumbrel, Tumbril,
Water, Wheel, Wrack
▷ **Tortured** *may indicate* an anagram
Torturer Torquemada
Torus Disc, Stellarator
Tory Abhorrer, Blimp, Blue, C, Catholic, Opposition, Right, Taig, Tantivy, Unionist, Young
England
Tosh Old bean
Toss(ing), Throw(n) Abject, Bandy, Birl, Bounce, Buck, Bung, Buttock, Cant, Canvass,
Cast, Catapult, → **CHUCK**, Cottabus, Crabs, Crap, Cross-buttock, Dad, Daud, Dawd, Deal,
Dink, Discomfit, Disconcert, Dod, Elance, Estrapade, Falcade, Faze, → **FLING**, Flip, Floor,
Flump, Flutter, Flying (head)-mare, Free, Full, Gollum, Hanch, Haunch, Heave, Hipt,
Hoy, → **HURL**, Jack, Jact(it)ation, Jaculation, Jeff, Juggle, Jump, Lance, Launch, Lob, Loft,
Nick, Pash, Pick, Pitch, Purl, Put(t), Round-arm, Salad, Seamer, Shy, Slat, Sling, Squail,
Unhorse, Unseat, Upcast, Wheech, Yuko
Toss-up Cross and pile, Heads or tails
Tot Add, Babe, Bairn, → **CHILD**, Dop, Dram, Infant, Mite, Moppet, Nightcap, Nip(per),
Nipperkin, Slug, Snifter, Snort, Tad
Total(ity), Toto Absolute, Aggregate, All(-out), All told, Amount, Balance, Be-all,
→ **COMPLETE**, Entire, Gross, Lot, Mass, Ouroboros, Overall, Sum(mate), Tale, Tally,
Unqualified, Uroborus, Utter, Whole
Totalitarian Autocrat, Despot, Étatiste, Fascist
Tote Bear, → **CARRY**, Yomp
Totem Fetish, Icon, Image, Pole
To the point Ad rem
Tottenham Hotspur

Totter Abacus, Daddle, Daidle, Didakai, Didakei, Didicoi, Did(d)icoy, Halt, Lurch, Ragman, Reel, Rock, Shamble, → **STAGGER**, Swag, Sway, Topple, Waver

Toucan Ariel, Ramphastos

Touch(ed), Touching, Touchy Abut, Accolade, Adjoin, Affect, Against, Anent, Apropos, Badass, Barmy, Cadge, Captious, Carambole, Caress, Carom, Common, Concern, Connivent, Contact, Contiguous, Dash, Easy, Emove, → **FEEL**, Feisty, Finger, Finishing, Flick, Fondle, Haptic, Heart-warming, Huffish, Huffy, → **IN TOUCH**, Iracund, Irascible, Irritable, J'adoube, Liaison, Libant, Loan, Loco, Meet, Midas, Miffy, Near, Nie, Nigh, Nudge, Palp, Pathetic, Paw, Potty, Re, Sense, Shade, Skiff, Soft, Sore, Spice, → **SPOT**, Tactile, Tactual, Tag, Tangible, Tap, Taste, Tat, Tetchy, Tickle, Tig, Tinderbox, Tinge, Titivate, Trace, Trait, Trifle, Tuck, Vestige

Touchdown Rouge

Touchline Tangent

Touchstone Basanite, Criterion, Norm, Standard

Touch wood Unberufen

Touchwood Absit omen, Monk, Punk, Spunk, Tinder

Tough(en) Adamantine, Anneal, Apache, Arduous, Ballsy, Bruiser, Burly, Chewy, → **HARD**, Hardball, Hard-boiled, Hard-nosed, Hard nut, Hardy, Heavy duty, He-man, Hood, Hoodlum, Husky, Indurate, Keelie, Knotty, Leathern, Leathery, Nut, Pesky, Rambo, Resilient, Rigwiddie, Rigwoodie, Robust, Roughneck, Sinewy, Skinhead, Spartan, Steely, Stiff, Strict, String, Sturdy, Teuch, Thewed, Tityre-tu, Virile, Withy, Yob

Toupee Hairpiece, Rug, Tour, → **WIG**

Tour(er), Tourism, Tourist Adventure, Barnstorm, Benefit, Circuit, Conducted, Cook's, Emmet, Excursion, Gig, Grand, Grockle, GT, Holiday-maker, Itinerate, → **JOURNEY**, Lionise, Mystery, Outing, Package, Parra, Posting, Pub crawl, Reality, Roadie, Road show, Rubberneck, Safari, Sightsee, Spin, Swing, Tiki, → **TRAVEL**, Trip(per), Viator, Weather, Whistle-stop

Tourmaline Indicolite, Indigolite, Schorl, Zeuxite

Tournament American, Basho, Bonspiel, Bridge drive, Carousel, Drive, Event, Jereed, Jerid, Joust, Just, Ladder, Plate, Pro-am, Pro-celebrity, Round robin, Royal, Spear-running, Super Twelve, Swiss, Tilt, Tourney, Whist drive, Wimbledon

Tourniquet Garrot(e), Throttle, Torcular

Tousle Dishevel, Rumple

Tout Barker, Laud, Ply, Praise, Runner, Solicit, Spruik, Toot, Work-watcher

Tow(ing), Towpath Aquaplane, Button, Fibre, → **HAUL**, Pull, → **ROPE**, Ski, Skijoring, Stupe, Track road

▶ **Towards** *see* **TO(WARDS)**

Towel Dry, Jack, Nappy, Pantyliner, Roller, Rub, Sanitary, Tea, Tea-cloth, Terry, Turkish

Tower AA, Aspire, Atalaya, Babel, Barbican, Bastille, Bastion, Belfry, Bell, Bloody, Brattice, Brettice, Brogh, Campanile, Clock, Conning, Control, Cooling, Donjon, Dungeon, Edifice, Eiffel, Fly, Fortress, Gantry, Garret, Gate, Giralda, Gopura(m), Guérite, Hawser, Horologium, Husky, Ivory, Keep, Leaning, Loom, Maiden, Martello, Minar(et), Monument, Mooring, Mouse, Nuraghe, Nurhag, Overtop, Peel, Pinnacle, Pisa, Pound, Pylon, Rear, Rise, Rolandseck, Rood, Round, Sail, Sears, Shot, Signal, Sikhara, Silo, Ski-lift, Space Needle, Specula, Spire, Stealth, Steeple, Swiss Re, Tête-de-pont, Texas, Tractor, Tugboat, → **TURRET**, Victoria, Watch, Water, Yagura, Ziggurat, Zikkurat

Town, Township Boom, Borgo, Borough, Bourg, Burg(h), City, Company, Conurbation, County, Deme, Dormitory, Dorp, Favella, Five, Garrison, Ghost, Ham(let), Intraurban, Market, Municipal, Nasik, One-horse, Open, Place, Podunk, Pueblo, Satellite, Shanty, Shire, Soweto, Staple, Tinsel, Tp, Twin, Urban, Whistle stop, Wick

Townee, Townsman Cad, Cit(izen), Dude, Freeman, Oppidan, Philister, Resident, Snob

Town hall Prytaneum

Toxaemia Eclampsia

Toxic(ity), Toxin Abrin, Aflatoxin, Antigen, Botox®, Botulin, Cadaverine, Cadmium, Chlorin(e), Coumarin, Curare, Deadly, Dioxan, Dioxin, Eclampsia, Fluorin(e), Lethal, Melittin, Muscarine, Nicotine, Phalloidin, Phenol, Phenothiazine, Pre-eclampsia, Psoralen, Ricin, Sepsis, Serology, Venin, Venomous, Virulence, Yellow rain, Zootoxin

Toy Babyhouse, Bauble, Bottle-imp, Bull-roarer, Cartesian devil, Cockhorse, Coral, Cyberpet, Dally, Dandle, Dinky®, Doll, Doll's house, Dreid(e)l, Executive, Faddle, Finger, Flirt, Frisbee®, Gewgaw, Golly, Gonk, Jack-in-the-box, Jumping-jack, Kaleidoscope, Kickshaw, Knack, Lego®, Meccano®, Newton's cradle, Noah's ark, Novelty, Paddle, Pantine, Peashooter, Pinwheel, Plaything, Pogo stick, Popgun, Praxinoscope, Quiz, Rattle, Russian doll, Scooter, Shoofly, Skipjack, Stroboscope, Tantalus-cup, Taste, Teddy, Thaumatrope, Top, → **TRIFLE**, Trinket, Tu(r)ndun, Wheel of life, Whirligig, Windmill, Yoyo, Zoetrope

Trace Atom, Cast, Derive, Describe, Draft, Draw, Dreg, Echo, Footprint, Ghost, Gleam, → **HINT**, Leaf, Limn, Mark, Memory, Outline, Relic, Relict, Remnant, Scan, Scintilla, Semblance, Sign, Smack, Soupçon, Strap, Tinge, → **TOUCH**, Track, Vestige, Whiff, Whit

Tracery Filigree, Frostwork

Track(s), Tracker, Tracking, Trackman Aintree, Aisle, Band, B-road, Caterpillar®, Cinder, Circuit, Course, Crawler, Cycleway, Dirt, Dog, DOVAP, Drag strip, Drift, Ecliptic, El, Fast, Fettler, Flap(ping), Footing, Gandy dancer, Green road, Greenway, Groove, Hunt, Ichnite, Ichnolite, Icknield Way, Inside, Lane, Ley, Line, Loipe, Loopline, Mommy, Monitor, Monza, Pad, → **PATH**, Persue, Piste, Pitlane, Pug, Pursue, Race, Raceway, Rail, Railway, Rake, Ridgeway, Riding, Route, Run, Rut, Scent, Siding, Sign, Skidway, Sleuth, Slot, Sonar, Speedway, Spoor, Tan, Tan-ride, Taxiway, Tenure, Tideway, Title, Trace, → **TRAIL**, Trajectory, Tram, Tramline, Tramroad, Tramway, Tread, Trode, Tug(boat), Twin, Wake, Wallaby, Way, Y

Tract(able), Tracts Area, Belt, Bench, Clime, Colporteur, Common, Dene, Digestive, Enclave, Enteral, Flysheet, Lande, Leaflet, Monte, Moor, Olfactory, → **PAMPHLET**, Park, Prairie, Province, Purlieu, Pusey, Pyramidal, Region, Scabland, Screed, Taluk, Tawie, Terrain, Wold

Tractarian(ism) Newman, Oxford movement, Pusey(ism)

Tractor Back hoe, Bombardier®, Bulldozer, Cat, Caterpillar®, Chelsea, Fendalton, Pedrail, Remuera, Skidder, Tower

Tracy Dick, Spencer

Trade(r), Tradesman, Trading Arb(itrageur), Art, Banian, Banyan, Bargain, Barter, Bear, Bilateral, Bricks and clicks, Bull, Bun(n)ia, Burgher, Business, Cabotage, Calling, Carriage, Chaffer, Chandler, Chapman, Cheapjack, Cheesemonger, Clicks and mortar, Coaster, Comanchero, → **COMMERCE**, Coster, Costermonger, Crare, Crayer, Deal(er), Dicker, Easterling, Errand, Exchange, Exporter, Factor, Fair, Floor, Free, Galleon, Handle, Horse, Hosier, Hot, Importer, Indiaman, Industry, Insider, Ironmonger, Jobber, Kidder, Line, Logrolling, Matrix, Mercantile, Mercer, Merchant, Mercosur, Métier, Middleman, Mister, Monger, Mystery, Occupy, Outfitter, Paralleling, Pitchman, Ply, Program(me), Rag, Retailer, Roaring, Rough, Roundtripping, Salesman, Scalp, Screen, Sell, Shrivijaya, Simony, Slave, Stallenger, Stallholder, Stallinger, Stationer, Sutler, Suttle, → **SWAP**, Traffic, Transit, Trant, Truck, Union, Vaisya, Vend, Wholesaler, Wind

Trademark, Trade name Brand, Chop, Idiograph, Label, Logo, Tm, TN

Trade union Amicus, ASLEF, COHSE, Local, Samiti, Solidarity, Syndicalism, UNISON, USDAW

Trading money, Trading post Cabotage, Fort, Wampum

Tradition(s), Traditional(ist) Ancestral, Classical, Convention, Custom(ary), Eastern, Folksy, Folkway, Hadith, Heritage, Legend, Lore, Mahayana, Misoneist, Old guard, Old-line, Old-school, Orthodox, Pharisee, Pompier, Practice, Purist, Square, Suburban, Time-honoured, Trad, Tralaticious, Tralatitious, Unwritten

Traduce Abuse, Asperse, Defame, Impugn, Malign, Smear, Vilify

Traffic(ker), Traffic pattern Air, Barter, Broke, Cabotage, Clover-leaf, Commerce,

Contraflow, Coyote, Deal, Export, Negotiate, Passage, Run, Slave trade, Smuggle, Tailback, Through, Trade, Truck, Vehicular, Way

Tragedian, Tragedy, Tragic Aeschylus, Antigone, Buskin, Calamity, Cenci, Corneille, Dire, → **DRAMA**, Euripides, Lear, Macready, Melpomene, Oedipean, Oresteia, Otway, Pathetic, Seneca, Sophoclean, Thespian, Thespis

Trail(er), Trailing Abature, Advert, Appalachian, Audit, Bedraggle, Caravan, Condensation, Creep, Dissipation, Drag, Draggle, Fire, Follow, Horsebox, Ipomaea, Ivy, Lag, Liana, Liane, Nature, Oregon, Paper, Path, Persue, Preview, Prevue, Promo(tion), Pursue, Repent, Runway, Santa Fe, Scent, Shadow, Sickle-cell, Sign, Sleuth, Slot, Spoor, Straggle, Stream, Streel, Tag, Tow, Trace, → **TRACK**, Trade, Traipse, Trape, Trauchle, Trayne, Troad, Vapour, Vine, Virga, Wake

Train(er), Training Accommodation, Advanced, APT, Autogenic, Baggage, Boot camp, BR, Breed, Brighton Belle, Bullet, Caravan, Cat, Cavalcade, Choo-choo, Circuit, Coach, Commuter, Condition, Cortège, Day release, Diesel, Direct, Discipline, Dog, Double-header, Dressage, Drill, Drive, Educate, Entourage, Enure, Epicyclic, Eurostar®, Excursion, Exercise, Express, Fartlek, Field, Flier, Flight simulator, Freightliner®, Fuse, Gear, Ghan, Ghost, Gravy, Grounding, GWR, Handle(r), HST, → **INSET**, Instruct, Intercity®, Interval, Jerkwater, Journey, Liner, Link, LMS, LNER, Loco, Longe, Lunge, Maglev, Mailcar, Manège, Manrider, Meinie, Mein(e)y, Mentor, Milk, Mixed, Multiple unit, Nopo, Nurture, Nuzzle, Omnibus, Orient Express, Outward Bound®, Owl, Pack, Paddy, Parliamentary, PE, Pendolino, Personal, Potty, Power, Practise, → **PREPARE**, Procession, PT, Puffer, Puff-puff, Push-pull, Q, Queue, Rattler, Rehearse, Retinue, Road, Roadwork, Rocket, Roughrider, Royal Scot, Ry, Sack, Sacque, → **SCHOOL**, Series, Shoe, Shuttle service, Siege, Simulator, Sinkansen, Skill centre, Sloid, Sloyd, Sowarree, Sowarry, Special, Square-bashing, SR, Steer, String, Suite, Tail, Tame, → **TEACH**, Through, Tire, Tirocinium, Track shoe, Trail, Trellis, Tube, Twin bill, Wage, Wagon, Wave, Way, Whale oil

▷ **Train(ed)** *may indicate* an anagram

Trainee → **APPRENTICE**, AT, Cadet, Cub, Intern, Jackaroo, Jackeroo, Learner, Ordinand, Pupil, Rookie, Rooky, T

Train-spotter Gricer

Traipse Gad

Trait Characteristic, Feature, Knack, Peculiarity, Ph(a)enotype, Sickle-cell, Strain, Thew, Trick, Vein

Traitor Benedict Arnold, Betrayer, Casement, Dobber-in, Fifth column, Joyce, Judas, Judas Maccabaeus, Nid(d)ering, Nid(d)erling, Nithing, Proditor, Quisling, Renegade, Reptile, Snake, Tarpeian, Traditor, Treachetour, Turncoat, Viper, Wallydraigle, Weasel

Trajectory Parabola, Track

Tram, Tramcar Tip, Trolley

▷ **Trammel** *may indicate* an anagram

Tramp, Trample Bog-trotter, Bum, Caird, Clochard, Clump, Crush, Deadbeat, Derelict, Derro, Dingbat, Dosser, Down and out, Estragon, Footslog, Freighter, Gadling, Gangrel, Gook, Hike, Hobo, Knight of the road, Lumber, Meff, Override, Overrun, Pad, Piepowder, Piker, Plod, Poach, Potch(e), Prostitute, Rover, Scorn, Ship, Slut, Splodge, Sundowner, Swagman, → **TINKER**, Toe-rag(ger), Tom, Track, Traipse, Tread, Trek, Trog, Tromp, Truant, Trudge, Tub, Vagabond, Vagrant, Weary Willie, Whore

Trampoline Trampet(te)

Trance Aisling, Catalepsy, Cataplexy, Goa, Narcolepsy, Somnambulism

Tranche Gold, Reserve

Tranquil(lity) Ataraxy, Calm, Compose, Composure, Easy, Halcyon, Lee, Peace(ful), Placid, Quietude, Restful, Sedate, → **SERENE**, Still

Tranquillise(r) Appease, Ataractic, Ataraxic, → **CALM**, Diazepam, Downer, Hypnone, Hypnotic, Largactil®, Librium®, Nervine, Nitrazepam, Oxazepam, Placate, Satisfy, Soothe, Still, Valium®

Transact, Transaction(s) Affair, Agio, Brokerage, Deal, Deed, Escrow, Ex-div, Fasti, Leaseback, Passage, Put through, Retour, Tr

Transcend(ent), Transcendental(ist), Transcendentalism Emerson, Excel, Mystic, Overtop, Surpass, Thoreau

Transcribe, Transcript(ion) Copy, Inclusive, Rescore, Tenor, → **TRANSLATE**, Transume

Transfer(ence), Transferance Alien, Alienate, → **ASSIGN**, Attorn, Bosman, Calk, Calque, Carryover, Cede, Chargeable, Communize, Consign, Convey(ance), Credit, Crosstalk, Cutover, Dabbity, Decal(comania), Deed, Demise, Devolve, Download, Embryo, Exchange, Explant, Extradite, Flit, Gene, Hive off, Letraset®, Make over, Mancipation, Metathesis, Mortmain, Nuclear, On-lend, Pass, Photomechanical, Print through, Provection, Reassign, Redeploy, Remit, Remove, Render, Repot, Second, Settlement, Slam, Spool, Thought, Transcribe, Transduction, Transfection, Transhume, Translocation, Uproot, Vire, Virement

▷ **Transferred** *may indicate* an anagram

Transfix Gore, Impale, Rivet, → **SKEWER**, Spear, Spit

Transform(ation), Transformer Affine, Alchemist, Alter, Apotheosis, Balun, Change, Fourier, Linear, Lorentz, Metamorphism, Metamorphose, Metamorphosis, Metaplasia, Metastasis, Morphallaxis, Morphing, Permute, Rectifier, Sea change, Sepalody, Tinct, Toroid, Toupee, Transfigure, Transmogrify, Variation, Wig

▷ **Transform(ed)** *may indicate* an anagram

Transfusion Apheresis

Transgress(ion) Encroach, Err, Infraction, Infringe, Offend, Overstep, Peccancy, → **SIN**, Violate

Transient, Transit(ion), Transitory Brief, Caducity, Ecotone, Ephemeral, Evanescent, Fleeting, Fly-by-night, Forbidden, Fugacious, Hobo, Metabasis, Passage, Passing, Provisional, Rapid, Seque, Sfumato, T, Temporary

Transistor Drift, Emitter, Epitaxial, Field-effect, Junction

Translate, Translation, Translator Calque, Construe, Convert, Coverdale, Crib, Decode, Decrypt, Encode, Explain, Free, Horse, Interpret, In vitro, Jerome, Key, Linguist, Loan, Machine, Metaphrase, Nick, Paraphrase, Pinyin, Polyglot, Pony, Reduce, Render, Rendition, Rhemist, Septuagint, Simultaneous, Targum, Tr, Transcribe, Transform, Trot, Tyndale, Unseen, Version(al), Vulgate, Wycliffe

▷ **Translate(d)** *may indicate* an anagram

Transmigrate, Transmigration Exodus, Metempsychosis, Passage, Trek

Transmit(ter), Transmitted, Transmission Aerial, Air, Aldis lamp, Allele, Analogue, Automatic, Band, Baseband, Beacon, Broadband, → **BROADCAST**, Cable, Carry, CB, Communicate, Compander, Compandor, Conduct, Consign, Contagion, Convection, Convey, Digital, Diplex, Facsimile, Filler, Forward, Gearbox, Gene, Heredity, Impart, Intelsat, Localizer, Manual, Mast, Mic(rophone), Modem, Nicol, Permittivity, Pipe, Propagate, Racon, Radiate, Radio, Receiver, Responser, Send, Simplex, Simulcast, Sonabuoy, Spark, Synchronous, Tappet, Telautograph®, Telecast, Telegony, Telematics, Telemetry, Telepathy, Teleprinter, Teletex, Televise, Telex, Tiptronic®, Tiros, Traduce, Traject, Tralaticious, Tralatitious, UART, Ultrawideband, Uplink, Upload, Walkie-talkie, WAP, Webcam, Wi-Fi®

Transom Reverse, Traverse

Transparent, Transparency Adularia, Clarity, Clear, Crystal(line), Diaphanous, Dioptric, Glassy, Glazed, Hyaloid, Iolite, Leno, Limpid, Lucid, Luminous, Patent, Pellucid, Porcelain, Sheer, Slide, Tiffany, Transpicuous

Transpire Happen, Occur

Transplant Allograft, Anaplasty, Graft, Repot, Reset, Shift

Transport(ed), Transporter, Transportation Active, Aerotrain, Air-lift, Ar(a)ba, Argo, Bathorse, Bear, Bike, Broomstick, BRS, Buggy, Bus, Cargo, Carract, → **CARRY**, Cart, Casevac, Cat-train, Charabanc, Charm, Conductor, Convey, Cycle, Delight, Deliver,

Ecstasy, Elation, Electron, Eloin, Enrapt, Enravish, Entrain, Esloin, Estro, Exalt, Ferriage, Ferry, Fishyback, Freight, Haul(age), Hearse, Helicopter, Jerrican, Joy, Kart, Kurvey, Lift, Lug, Maglev, Mambrane, Matatu, Medevac, Minicab, Monorail, Overjoy, Pack animal, Palanquin, Pantechnicon, Park and ride, Paytrain, Public, Put, Rape, Rapine, Rapture, Roadster, Ship, Shorthaul, Shuttle, Sidecar, Skateboard, Sledge, Sno-Cat, Snowmobile, Supersonic, Tandem, Tanker, Tape, Tardis, Tote, Train, Tramway, Trap, Troopship, Tuktuk, Ubiquinone, Waft, Waterbus, Wheels, Wireway

Transpose, Transposition Anagram, Commute, Convert, Invert, Metathesis, Shift, Spoonerism, Switch, Tr

▷ **Transposed** *may indicate* an anagram

Transsexual Invert

Transubstantiate, Transubstantiation Capernaite

Transverse Across, Crosscut, Diagonal, Obliquid, Thwart

Transvest(it)ism, Transvestite Berdache, Berdash, Cross-dressing, Eonist

Tranter Dolly

Trap(s), Trapdoor, Trapped, Trappings Ambush, → **BAGGAGE**, Bags, Belongings, Birdlime, Booby, Buckboard, Bunker, Carriage, Catch, Catch-pit, Clapnet, Cobweb, Corner, Cru(i)ve, Deadfall, Death, Decoy, Dip, Dogcart, Downfall, Drain, Eelset, Emergent, Ensnare, Entoil, Entrain, Fall, Fit-up, Fly, Flypaper, Frame-up, Fyke, Geel, Gig, Gin, Gob, Gravel, Grin, Hatch, Housings, Ice-bound, Illaqueate, Jinri(c)ksha(w), Keddah, Kettle, Kheda, Kiddle, Kidel, Kipe, Kisser, Knur(r), Light, Lime, Live, Lobster pot, → **LUGGAGE**, Lure, Mesh, Mouth, Net, Nur(r), Oil, Paraphernalia, Pitfall, Plant, Polaron, Police, Pot, Poverty, Putcheon, Putcher, Quicksand, Radar, Regalia, Sand, Scruto, Scuttle, → **SNARE**, Speed, Spell, Spider, Springe, Stake-net, Star, Steam, Stench, Sting, Stink, Sun, Tangle, Tank, Teagle, Toil, Tonga, Tourist, Trapfall, Tripwire, Trojan horse, Trou-de-loup, Two-wheeler, U, U-bend, Vampire, Waterseal, Web, Weel, Weir, Wire

Trapezist Leotard

Trapper Carson, Voyageur

Trash(y) Bosh, Deface, Desecrate, Dre(c)k, Garbage, Junk, Kitsch, Pulp, → **RUBBISH**, Schlock, Scum, Tinpot, Trailer, Vandalise, White, Worthless

Trauma Insult, Shell-shock, Shock

Travel(ler), Travelling Aeneas, Backpack, Bagman, Bushwhacker, Columbus, Commercial, Commute, Crustie, Crusty, Drive, Drummer, Explorer, Fare, Fellow, Fly, Fogg, Geoffrey, Gipsen, Gipsy, Gitano, Globe-trotter, Go, Gulliver, Gypsy, Hike, Hitchhiker, Interrail, Itinerant, Jet-setter, Journey, Locomotion, Long-haul, Marco Polo, Meve, Migrant, Motor, Move, Mush, New Age, Nomad, Odysseus, Passenger, Passepartout, Peregrination, Peripatetic, Pilgrim, Ply, Polo, Pootle, Range, Rep, Ride, Road, Roam, Rom(any), Rove, Safari, Sail, Salesman, Samaritan, Sinbad, Space, Teleport, Tool, → **TOUR**, Tourist, Trek, Tripper, Tsigane, Viator, Voyage, Wanderjahr, Wayfarer, Wend, Wildfire, Zigan

Traverse Cross, Girdle, Measure, Quest, Trace

Travesty Burlesque, Charade, Distortion, Parody, Show, Skit

Trawl Beam, Drag-net, Hose-net, Net

Tray Antler, Bottle-slide, Carrier, Case, Charger, Coaster, Gallery, In, Joe, Lazy Susan, Mould, Out, Plateau, → **SALVER**, Shower, Tea, Trencher, Typecase, Voider, Waiter

Treacherous, Treachery Bad faith, Betrayal, Deceit, Delilah, Fickle, Ganelon, Guile, Insidious, Judas-kiss, Knife, Mala fide, Medism, Perfidious, Punic, Punic faith, Quicksands, Sedition, Serpentine, Sleeky, Snaky, Sneaky, Trahison, Traitor, Trappy, → **TREASON**, Two-faced, Viper, Weasel

Treacle Black(jack), Butter, Molasses, Venice

Tread Clamp, Clump, Dance, Pad, Step, Stramp, Track, Trample

Treadle Footboard

Treason Betrayal, Constructive, High, Insurrection, Lèse-majesté, Lese-majesty, Perduellion, Petty, Sedition, → **TREACHERY**

Treasure(r), Treasury Banker, Bursar, Cache, Camera, Camerlengo, Camerlingo, Cherish, Chest, Cimelia, Coffer, Ewe-lamb, Exchequer, Fisc(al), Fisk, Godolphin, Golden, Heritage, Hoard, Hon(ey), Montana, Palgrave, Pork barrel, → **PRIZE**, Procurator, Purser, Quaestor, Relic, Riches, Steward, Taonga, Thesaurus, Trove

Treat, Treatment Actinotherapy, Action, Acupressure, Acupuncture, Allopathy, Antidote, Apitherapy, Archilowe, Arenation, Aromatherapy, Balneotherapy, Beano, Beneficiate, Besee, Body wrap, Botox®, Capitulate, Care, Chemotherapy, Chiropractic, Condition, Course, Coverage, Crymotherapy, Cryotherapy, Cupping, Cure, Deal, Detox(ification), Dialysis, Do, → **DOCTOR**, Dose, Dress, Dutch, Electrotherapy, Enantiopathy, Entertain, EST, Facial, Faith-healing, Fango, Faradism, Figuration, Foment, Frawzey, Handle, Heliotherapy, Hellerwork, Holistic, Homeopathy, HRT, Hydrotherapy, Hypnotherapy, Immunotherapy, Intermediate, Jin shin do, Kenny, Laser, Manage, Massotherapy, Mechanotherapy, Medicament, Medicate, Mercerise, Mesotherapy, Moxibustion, Narcotherapy, Naturopathy, Negotiate, Opotherapy, Organotherapy, Orthoptics, Osteopathy, → **OUTING**, Pasteur, Pedicure, Pelotherapy, Phototherapy, Physiatrics, Physic, Physiotherapy, Pie, Poultice, Probiotics, Process, Prophylaxis, Psychoanalysis, Psychodrama, Psychotherapy, Radiotherapy, Regale, Rehab(ilitation), Rest cure, Root, Secretage, Serotherapy, Setter, Shout, Shrift, Sironise, Smile, Softener, Speleotherapy, → **STAND**, Tablet, Tebilise®, TENS, Thalassotherapy, → **THERAPY**, Thermotherapy, Titbit, Traction, Turkish bath, Twelve-step, UHT, Usance, Use, Vet

▷ **Treated** *may indicate* an anagram

Treatise Almagest, Bestiary, Commentary, Cybele, Didache, Discourse, Dissertation, Essay, Monograph, Pandect, Prodrome, Profound, Summa, Tract(ate), Upanishad, Vedanta

Treaty Agreement, Alliance, Assiento, Concordat, Covenant, Entente, GATT, Jay's, Lateran, Locarno, Lunéville, Maastricht, Nijmegen, North Atlantic, → **PACT**, Paris, Private, Protocol, Rapallo, Rijswijk, Ryswick, San Stefano, Sovetsk, Test-ban, Utrecht, Verdun, Versailles, Yorktown

Treble Castrato, Choirboy, Chorist(er), Pairial, Soprano, → **TRIPLE**, Triune, Voice

Tree(s) Actor, → **ANCESTRY**, Axle, Beam, Bluff, Boom, Bosk, Clump, Conifer, Coppice, Corner, Cross, Daddock, Deciduous, Decision, Dendrology, Descent, Family, Fault, Fringe, Gallows, Genealogical, Grove, Hang, Hardwood, Jesse, Nurse, Pedigree, Phanerophyte, Pole, Rood, Roof, Sawyer, Shoe, Silviculture, Softwood, Staddle, Stemma, Summer, Thicket, Timber, Tyburn, Ulmaceous, Vista, Wicopy, → **WOOD**

TREES

2 letters:	Ita	Aloe	Jack
Bo	Jak	Amla	Kaki
Ti	Koa	Arar	Karo
	Mot	Atap	Kiri
3 letters:	Nim	Bael	Kola
Ake	Oak	Bhel	Lead
Ash	Oil	Bito	Lime
Asp	Sal	Cade	Lote
Bay	Tea	Coco	Mako
Bel	Til	Cola	Meal
Ben	Ule	Dali	Milk
Box	Wax	Dhak	Ming
Cow	Yew	Dika	Mira
Elm		Dita	Mott
Fig	4 letters:	Eugh	Mowa
Fir	Acer	Gean	Neem
Gum	Akee	Hule	Nipa

Noni	Bunya	Mugga	Akeake
Olea	Butea	Mulga	Alerce
Ombu	Cacao	Mvule	Angico
Palm	Carap	Myall	Annona
Pine	Cedar	Ngaio	Antiar
Pipe	Ceiba	Nikau	Arbute
Pith	China	Nyssa	Arolla
Plum	Clove	Olive	Babaco
Poon	Cocoa	Opepe	Bablah
Puka	Cocus	Osier	Balsam
Rain	Coral	Palas	Banyan
Rata	Ebony	Palay	Baobab
Rhus	Elder	Panax	Bilian
Rimu	Fagus	Peach	Bombax
Sack	Fever	Pecan	Bonsai
Shea	Flame	Pinon	Bo-tree
Silk	Fruit	Pipal	Bottle
Sloe	Gauze	Pipul	Buriti
Soap	Genip	Pitch	Cadaga
Sorb	Grass	Plane	Cadagi
Tawa	Guava	Quina	Carapa
Teak	Hakea	Ramin	Carica
Teil	Hazel	Roble	Cashew
Titi	Hevea	Rowan	Cembra
Toon	Holly	Sabal	Cercis
Tung	Iroko	Saman	Cerris
Tutu	Ivory	Sassy	Chaste
Upas	Jambu	Scrog	Chenar
Wych	Jarul	Silva	Cherry
Yang	Judas	Smoke	Chinar
Yuzu	Kapok	Sumac	Citron
	Karri	Tawai	Coffee
5 letters:	Kauri	Taxus	Cordon
Abele	Khaya	Thorn	Cornel
Abies	Kiaat	Thuja	Cornus
Ackee	Kokum	Thuya	Damson
Afara	Larch	Tilia	Deodar
Agila	Lemon	Tsuga	Diana's
Alamo	Lichi	Tuart	Dragon
Alder	Lilac	Tulip	Durian
Alnus	Lotus	Vitex	Durion
Anona	Mahoe	Wahoo	Emblic
Areca	Mahua	Wenge	Eumong
Argan	Mahwa	Wilga	Eumung
Aspen	Maire	Withy	Feijoa
Babul	Mamey	Xylem	Fustet
Banak	Mango	Yacca	Fustic
Bania	Mapau	Yulan	Gallus
Beech	Maple	Zaman	Garjan
Belah	Marri	Zamia	Gidgee
Birch	Matai		Gidjee
Bodhi	Melia	**6 letters:**	Gingko
Boree	Motte	Abroma	Ginkgo
Bread	Mowra	Acacia	Glinap

Gnetum
Gopher
Guango
Gurjun
Gympie
Hupiro
Illipe
Illipi
Illupi
Jarool
Jarrah
Joshua
Jujube
Jupati
Kamahi
Kamala
Kamela
Kapuka
Karaka
Karamu
Karite
Kentia
Kowhai
Laurel
Lebbek
Linden
Locust
Longan
Loquat
Lucuma
Lungah
Macoya
Mallee
Manuka
Mastic
Mazard
Medlar
Mimosa
Missel
Mopane
Mopani
Myrtle
Nutmeg
Obeche
Orange
Orihou
Padauk
Padouk
Pagoda
Papaya
Pawpaw
Peepul
Pepper
Platan

Pomelo
Poplar
Popple
Protea
Pumelo
Puriri
Quince
Red-bud
Red gum
Ricker
Roucou
Rubber
Sabicu
Sallow
Samaan
Sapele
Sapium
Sapota
Saxaul
She-oak
Sinder
Sissoo
Sorrel
Souari
Spruce
Styrax
Sumach
Sunder
Sundra
Sundri
Tallow
Tamanu
Tawhai
Tewart
Thyine
Titoki
Tooart
Totara
Tupelo
Waboom
Wandoo
Wicken
Willow
Witgat
Yarran
Zamang

7 letters:
Ailanto
Ambatch
Amboina
Apricot
Araroba
Arbutus

Avodire
Bebeeru
Bilimbi
Bilsted
Bubinga
Buck-eye
Bursera
Cajeput
Cajuput
Calamus
Camphor
Camwood
Canella
Carbeen
Cascara
Cassava
Catalpa
Cedrela
Champac
Champak
Chayote
Chesnut
Coquito
Corylus
Corypha
Cumquat
Cypress
Dagwood
Dogwood
Dryades
Durmast
Geebung
Genipap
Gluinap
Gumtree
Hickory
Hog-plum
Holm-oak
Houhere
Jipyapa
Kumquat
Lacquer
Lagetto
Lentisk
Logwood
Lumbang
Madrono
Mahaleb
Manjack
Marasca
Margosa
Mazzard
Meranti
Mesquit

Moringa
Morrell
Mustard
Papauma
Pereira
Pilinut
Pimento
Platane
Pollard
Populus
Pukatea
Quassia
Quicken
Quillai
Quinain
Radiata
Rampick
Rampike
Redwood
Rock elm
Saksaul
Sandbox
Saouari
Sapling
Saturn's
Sausage
Sequoia
Seringa
Service
Shittah
Sourgum
Soursop
Spindle
Sundari
Talipat
Talipot
Taraire
Taupata
Tawhiri
Trumpet
Varnish
Wallaba
Wirilda
Witchen
Wych-elm
Xylopia
Zelkova

8 letters:
Aguacate
Algaroba
Aquillia
Bangalay
Bangalow

Basswood
Benjamin
Bergamot
Berrigan
Blackboy
Blimbing
Bountree
Bourtree
Breadnut
Brigalow
Calabash
Chestnut
Cinchona
Cinnamon
Cocoplum
Coolabah
Coolibah
Corkwood
Crabwood
Cucumber
Cudgerie
Dendroid
Dracaena
Espalier
Flittern
Fraxinus
Garcinia
Ghost-gum
Gnetales
Guaiacum
Hagberry
Hawthorn
Hinahina
Hornbeam
Huon-pine
Igdrasil
Inkberry
Ironbark
Ironwood
Jelutong
Kawakawa
Kingwood
Laburnum
Lacebark
Lecythis
Loblolly
Magnolia
Mahogany
Makomako
Mangrove
Manna-ash
Mesquite
Mulberry
Ocotillo

Oiticica
Oleaceae
Oleaster
Pachouli
Palmetto
Pandanus
Parapara
Pichurim
Pinaster
Pithtree
Pyinkado
Quandang
Quandong
Quantong
Quillaia
Quillaja
Raintree
Rambutan
Rangiora
Rewa-rewa
Sago-palm
Sandarac
Santalum
Sapindus
Sapucaia
Sasswood
Sea grape
Shaddock
Shagbark
Simaruba
Snowball
Snowdrop
Soapbark
Sourwood
Standard
Stinging
Sugar gum
Sweet gum
Sweetsop
Sycamine
Sycamore
Sycomore
Tamarack
Tamarind
Tamarisk
Taxodium
Umbrella
Whitegum
Wine-palm
Ygdrasil

9 letters:
Agila-wood
Ailantous

Albespine
Angophora
Araucaria
Azedarach
Bilimbing
Bitternut
Blackbutt
Blackjack
Blackwood
Bloodwood
Bolletrie
Boobialla
Broadleaf
Bulletrie
Bully-tree
Bulwaddee
Burrawary
Butternut
Caliatour
Caliature
Candlenut
Canoewood
Carambola
Casuarina
Chempaduk
Cherimoya
Chincapin
Chinkapin
Coachwood
Coco-de-mer
Cordyline
Courbaril
Crab apple
Cupressus
Curryleaf
Eaglewood
Evergreen
Firewheel
Flame-leaf
Greengage
Greenwood
Grevillea
Hackberry
Ivory palm
Jacaranda
Jackfruit
Kahikatea
Krummholz
Kurrajong
Lancewood
Lemonwood
Leylandii
Macadamia
Marmalade

Melaleuca
Mirabelle
Mockernut
Monkeypot
Naseberry
Nectarine
Nux vomica
Paloverde
Paperbark
Patchouli
Patchouly
Paulownia
Persimmon
Pistachio
Pitch-pine
Poinciana
Ponderosa
Pontianac
Prickwood
Pricky ash
Primavera
Quebracho
Rauwolfia
Rose-apple
Sapodilla
Saskatoon
Sassafras
Satinwood
Shellbark
Simarouba
Soapberry
Star-anise
Star-apple
Sterculia
Stinkwood
Stone pine
Sweetwood
Tacamahac
Tamarillo
Terebinth
Toothache
Torchwood
Wagenboom
Wayfaring
Whitebeam
Whitewood
Wineberry
Wych-hazel
Yggdrasil
Zebrawood

10 letters:
Arbor Vitae
Axe-breaker

Bitterbark	Kaffirboom	Witgatboom	Maceranduba
Blackbully	Kotokutuku	Woollybutt	Metasequoia
Breadfruit	Letter-wood	Yellowwood	Osage orange
Bulletwood	Lilly-pilly	Ylang-ylang	Pomegranate
Bunya-bunya	Macrocarpa		Purpleheart
Buttonball	Manchineel	**11 *letters:***	Retinispora
Buttonwood	Mangabeira	Anchovy-pear	River red gum
Calamondin	Mangosteen	Appleringie	Shittimwood
Calliature	Marblewood	Bladderwort	Sitka spruce
Candle-wood	Nithofagus	Bristlecone	Stringybark
Cannonball	Palisander	Bristlepine	
Chamaerops	Paper birch	Cabbage-palm	**12 *letters:***
Chaulmugra	Pepperidge	Chaulmoogra	African tulip
Cheesewood	Pohutukawa	Chokecherry	Haemotoxylon
Chinaberry	Prickly ash	Copperbeech	Hercules' club
Chinquapin	Quercitron	Cryptomeria	Liriodendron
Cottonwood	Ribbonwood	Dipterocarp	Mammee-sapota
Cowrie-pine	Sandalwood	Eriodendron	Masseranduba
Eucalyptus	Sappanwood	Flamboyante	Monkey-puzzle
Fiddlewood	Schefflera	Fothergilla	Raspberry jam
Flamboyant	Silk-cotton	Gingerbread	Washingtonia
Flindersia	Silverbell	Guttapercha	Wellingtonia
Frangipani	Sneezewood	Honey locust	
Ginkgoales	Spotted gum	Horseradish	**13 *letters:***
Green-heart	Strawberry	Jesuit's bark	Paper-mulberry
Hackmatack	Tawheowheo	Leatherwood	
Ilang-ilang	Traveller's	Lignum vitae	**14 *letters:***
Jaboticaba	Turpentine	Liquidambar	Western hemlock
Jippi-jappa	Witch-hazel	Loblolly bay	

Tree-climber, Tree-dweller Monkey, Opossum, Sciurus, Squirrel, Unau
Tree disease Dutch elm, Oak wilt, Waldsterben
Tree-man Ent
Tree-moss Usnea
Tree-paeony Moutan
Tree-pecker Picus
Tree-shrew Tana
Trefoil Bird's foot, Clover, Hop, Lotos, Lotus
Trek(ker) Afrikaner, Hike, Journey, Leg, Odyssey, Safari, Yomp
Trellis Espalier, Lattice, Pergola, Treillage, Treille
Tremble, Trembling, Tremor Aftershock, Ashake, Ashiver, Butterfly, Dither, Dodder, Foreshock, Hotter, Intention, Judder, Marsquake, Milk sickness, Moonquake, Palpitate, Quail, Quake, Quaver, Quiver, Seismal, → **SHAKE**, Shiver, Shock, Shudder, Stound, Temblor, Titubation, Trepid, Twitchy, Vibrant, Vibrate, Vibration, Vibratiuncle, Vibrato, Wobble, Wuther, Yips
Tremendous Big, Enormous, Gargantuan, Howling, Immense, Marvellous, Thundering
Tremolo Bebung, Quaver, Trill(o)
▶ **Tremor** *see* **TREMBLE**
Tremulous Cranky, Dithering, Hirrient, Quaking, Shaky, Timorous
Trench(er) Boyau, Cunette, Cuvette, Delf, Delph, Dike(r), → **DITCH**, Dyke(r), Encroach, Fleet, Foss(e), Foxhole, Fur(r), Furrow, Grip, Gullet, Gutter, Leat, Line, Mariana, Moat, Oceanic, Outwork, Rill, Rille, Ring-dyke, Robber, Salient, Sap, Shott, Slidder, Slit, Sod, Sondage

Trenchant Acid, Cutting

Trend(y), Trendsetter Bellwether, Bent, Bias, Chic, Climate, Drift, Fashion, Hep, Hip, Hipster, In, Mainstream, New Age(r), Newfangled, Pacemaker, Pop, Poserish, Posey, Rage, Right-on, Smart, Style, Swim, Tendency, Tendenz, Tenor, Tide, Tonnish

Trepidation Butterflies

Trespass(ing) Aggravated, Encroach, Errant, Hack, Impinge, Infringe, Offend, Peccancy, Sin, Trench, Wrong

Tress(es) Curl, Lock, Ringlet, Switch, Tallent

Trestle Sawhorse

Triad Chord, Ternion, Three, Trey, Trimurti, Trinity

Trial Acid test, Adversity, Affliction, Appro, Approbation, Approval, Assize, Attempt, Bane, Bernoulli, Bout, Burden, Case, Clinical, Compurgation, Corsned, Court-martial, Cow, Cross, Dock, Drumhead, Empirical, Essay, → **EXPERIMENT**, Field, Fitting, Go, Hearing, Jeddart justice, Jethart justice, Lydford law, Nuremberg, Ordeal, Pest, Pilot, Pree, Probation, Proof, Race, Rehearsal, Salem, Scramble, Sheepdog, Show, State, Taste, Test, Test bed, Time

Triangle(d), Triangular Acute, Bermuda, Circular, Cosec, Deltoid, Equilateral, Eternal, Gair, Golden, Gore, Gyronny, Isosceles, Obtuse, Pascal's, Pedimental, Pendentive, Pyramid, Rack, Right-angled, Scalene, Similar, Spherical, Trigon, Triquetral, Tromino, Warning

Trias(sic) Bunter, Keuper, Muschelkalk, Rhaetic

Tribe(s), Tribal, Tribesman Amalekite, Ammonites, Ashanti, Asher, Benjamin, Celt, Cherokee, Cimmerii, Clan(nish), Cree, Creek, Crow, Dan, Dinka, D(a)yak, Dynasty, Edomites, Ephraim, Family, Gad, Gens, Gentes, Gentilic, Gond, Goth, Guarani, Hapu, Helvetii, Hittite, Horde, Hottentot, Ibo, Iceni, Israelite, Issachar, Iwi, Jat, Judah, Kaffir, Kenite, Kurd, Lashkar, Levi, Levite, Longobardi, Lost, Manasseh, Masai, Moabite, Mongol, Moro, Naga, Naphtali, Nation, Nervii, Ngati, Ordovices, Ostrogoths, Pathan, Phyle, Picts, → **RACE**, Reuben, Riff, Rod, Sakai, Salian, Schedule, Senones, Senussi, Sept, Shawnee, Silures, Simeon, Strandloper, Tasaday, Teuton, Trinobantes, Ute, Vandals, Wolof, Wyandot(te), X(h)osa, Zebulun

Tribune, Tribunal Aeropagus, Bema, Bench, → **COURT**, Divan, Employment, Forum, Hague, Industrial, Leader, Platform, Rienzi, Rota, Star-chamber, Waitangi

Tributary Affluent, Bogan, Branch, Creek, Fork

Tribute Cain, Capelline, Citation, Commemoration, Compliment, Crants, Dedication, Deodate, → **DUE**, Encomium, Epitaph, Festschrift, Floral, Gavel, Heriot, Homage, Kain, Memento, Ode, Panegyric, Peter's pence, → **PRAISE**, Rome-penny, Rome-scot, Scat(t), Tax, Testimonial, Toast, Toll, Wreath, Wroth

Trice Flash, Instant

Trichosanthin Q

Trick(ed), Trickery, Tricks(ter), Tricky Antic, Art, Artifice, Attrap, Awkward, Bamboozle, Begunk, Book, Bunco, Bunko, Cantrip, Capot, Catch, Charley pitcher, Cheat, Chicane(ry), Chouse, Claptrap, Cod(-act), Cog, Con(fidence), Coyote, Crook, Davenport, Deception, Deck, Delicate, Delude, Device, Dirty, → **DO**, → **DODGE**, Double, Dupe, Elf, Elfin, Elvan, Elven, Fard, Feat, Fetch, Fiddle, Finesse, Finicky, Flam, Flim-flam, Fob, Fox, Fraud, Fun, Gambit, Game, Gammon, Gaud, Gimmick, Gleek, Glike, Gowk, Guile, Had, Hanky-panky, Hey presto, Hoax, Hocus(-pocus), Hoodwink, Hornswoggle, Hot potato, Hum, Illude, Illusion, Illywhacker, Imposture, Jadery, Jape, Jockey, John, Kittle, Knack, Lark, Leg pull, Magsman, Mislead, Monkey, Monkey-shine, Murphy's game, Nap, Nasruddin, Palter, Parlour, Pass, Pawk, Phish, Pleasantry, Pliskie, Prank, Prestige, Put-on, Quick, Ramp, Raven, Reak, Reik, Rex, Rig, Rope, Ropery, Roughie, Ruse, Scam, Sell, Set-up, Shanghai, Shavie, Shenanigan, Shifty, Shill, Skin-game, Skite, Skul(l)duggery, Skylark, Skyte, Slam, Sleight, Slight, Slinter, Sophism, Spoof, Stall, Stealth, Stint, Stunt, Subterfuge, Sug, Swiftie, Thimble-rig, Three-card, Ticklish, Tip, Trait, Trap, Tregetour, Trump, Turn, Tweedler, Undercraft, Underplot, Vole, Wangle, Wheeze, Wile, Wrinkle

▷ **Trick** *may indicate* an anagram

Trickle Drib(ble), Driblet, Dropple, Gutter, Leak, Ooze, Rill, Seep

Trickless Misère

Triclinic Anorthic

Tricycle Pedicab

Trident Fork, Plane, Trisul(a)

Trifle(s), Trifling Bagatelle, Banal, Baubee, Bauble, Bibelot, Birdseed, Bit, Bric-a-brac, Bubkas, Cent, Chickenfeed, Coquette, Dabble, Dalliance, → **DALLY**, Denier, Desipient, Dessert, Do, Doit, Faddle, Falderal, Falderol, Fallal, Fattrell, Feather, Fewtril, Fiddle, Fiddle-faddle, Fig, Fingle-fangle, Fizgig, Flamfew, Fleabite, Flirt, Folderol, Fool, Footle, Fribble, Frippery, Fritter, Frivol, Gewgaw, Idle, Insignificant, Iota, Kickshaw, Knick-knack, Luck-penny, Mess, Mite, Nick-nacket, Niff-naff, Nothing, Nugae, Nugatory, Nyaff, Old song, Palter, Paltry, Peanuts, Peddle, Peppercorn, Petty, Philander, Picayune, Piddle, Piffle, Pin, Pingle, Pittance, Play, Potty, Quelquechose, Quiddity, Quiddle, Slight, Small beer, Small wares, Smatter, Song, Sport, Stiver, Strae, Straw, Sundry, Sweet Fanny Adams, Tiddle, Tom, Toy, Trinket, Trivia, Whifflery, Whim-wham, Whit

Trig(onometry) Neat, Sech, Spherical, Tosh, Trim

Trigger Activate, Detent, Hair, Instigate, Krytron, Pawl, Precipitate, Schmitt, Set off, Spark, Start, Switch on, Touch off, Tripwire

Trill(ed), Triller, Trilling Burr, Churr, Hirrient, Quaver, Ribattuta, Roll, Staphyle, Trim, Twitter, Warble

Trilobite Olenellus, Olenus, Paradoxide

Trim(med), Trimmer, Trimming Abridge, Ballast, Barb, Bleed, Braid, Bray, Chipper, Clip, Dapper, Defat, Dinky, Dress, Ermine, Face, Falbala, Fettle, File, Froufrou, Garni, Garnish, Garniture, Gimp, Guimpe, Hog, Macramé, Macrami, Marabou, Neat, Net(t), Ornament, Pare, Passament, Passement(erie), Pipe, Plight, Posh, Preen, Proign, Proyn(e), Pruin(e), Prune, Roach, Robin, Ruche, Sax, Sett, Shear, Shipshape, Smirk, Smug, Sned, Snod, Soutache, → **SPRUCE**, Straddle, Stroddle, Strodle, Stylist, Svelte, Tiddley, → **TIDY**, Time-server, Top, Torsade, Trick, Whippersnipper, Wig

Trinidadian Carib

Trinity, Trinitarian Mathurin(e), Prosopon, Triad, Trimurti, Triune, Word

Trinket(s) Bauble, Bibelot, Bijou(terie), Charm, Falderal, Fallal, Folderol, Nicknack, Toy, Trankum, Trumpery

Trio Catch, Graces, Magi, Randan, Random, Skat, Terzetto, Threesome

Trip(per) Awayday, Cruise, Dance, Day, Druggie, Ego, Errand, Expedition, → **FALL**, Field, Flight, Flip, Guilt, Head, High, Joint, Jolly, Journey, Junket, Kilt, Link, Outing, Passage, Pleasure, Ply, Power, Ride, Round, Run, Sail, Sashay, Spin, Spurn, → **STUMBLE**, Tootle, Tour, Trek, Trial, Voyage

▷ **Trip** *may indicate* an anagram

Tripe Abracadabra, Bosh, Bull, Caen, Entrails, Honeycomb, Offal, Plain, Rot

Triple, Triplet Codon, Hemiol(i)a, Perfect, Sdrucciola, Ternal, Tiercet, Treble, Trifecta, Trilling, Trin(e), Tripling

Tripod Cat, Cortina, Highhat, Oracle, Triangle, Trippet, Trivet

Triptych Volet

Trishaw Cycle

Trite Banal, Boilerplate, Cornball, Corny, Hackneyed, Hoary, Laughable, Mickey Mouse, Novelettish, Pabulum, Platitude, Rinky-dink, Stale, Stock, Time-worn, Worn

Triton Eft, Evet, Ewt, Newt, Trumpet-shell

Triumph(ant) Cock-a-hoop, Codille, Cowabunga, Crow, Eureka, Exult, Glory, Impostor, Killing, Oho, Olé, Ovation, Palm, Prevail, Victorious, → **WIN**

Triumvir Caesar, Crassus, Pompey

Trivet Brandise, Tripod, Trippet

Trivia(l), Triviality Adiaphoron, Bagatelle, Balaam, Bald, → **BANAL**, Bathos, Footling, Frippery, Frothy, Futile, Idle, Inconsequential, Light, Minutiae, Nitpicking, No-brainer,

Nothingism, Paltry, Pap, Peppercorn, Pettifoggery, Petty, Picayune, Piddling, Piffling, Puerile, Shallow, Small, Small beer, Small fry, Snippety, Squirt, Squit, Toy(s), Twaddle, Vegie

Trixie Bea

Trochee Choree

Troglodyte Ape, Caveman, Hermit, Spelean, Wren

Trojan Aeneas, Agamemnon, Dardan(ian), Iliac, Paris, Priam, Teucrian, Troic

Troll → FISH, Gnome, Rove, Spoon, Trawl, Warble

Trolley Brute, Cart, Crane, Dinner-wagon, Dolly, Gurney, Hostess, Shopping, Tea, Teacart, Traymobile, Truck, Trundler

▶ **Trollop** *see* LOOSE(N)

Trombone Bass, Posaune, Sackbut, Tenor

Trompe l'oeil Quadratura, Quadratura

Troop(s), Trooper Alpini, Anzac, Band, BEF, Brigade, Cohort, Company, Depot, Detachment, Garrison, Guard, Horde, Household, Logistics, Midianite, Militia, Monkeys, Pultan, Pulton, Pultoon, Pultun, SAS, School, Shock, → SOLDIER, Sowar, State, Storm, Subsidiary, Tp, Turm(e), Velites

Troopship Transport

Trope Euouae, Evovae

Trophy Adward, Ashes, → AWARD, Bag, Belt, Cup, Emmy, Memento, Palm, Plate, → PRIZE, Scalp, Schneider, Shield, Silverware, Spoils, Tourist, Triple crown, TT

Tropic(al) Cancer, Capricorn, Derris, Jungle, Neogaea, Sultry

Trot(ter), Trot out Air, Clip, Crib, Crubeen, Hag, Job, Jog, Passage, Pettitoes, Piaffe, Pony, Ranke, Red(-shirt), Rising, Tootsie, Trotskyist

Troth Perfay, Troggs

Trotsky(ist) Entr(y)ism, Leon, Militant Tendency

Troubador Blondel, Griot, Manrico, Minstrel, Singer, Sordello

Trouble(s), Troublemaker, Troublesome Ache, Ado, Affliction, Aggro, Agitate, Ail, Alarm, Annoy, Bale, Barrat, Bedevil, Beset, → BOTHER, Bovver, Brickle, Burden, Care, Coil, Concern, Debate, Disaster, Dismay, Disquiet, Distress, Disturb, Dog, Dolour, Eat, Esclandre, Exercise, Fash, Fashious, Finger, Firebrand, Fossick, Frondeur, Gram(e), Grief, Hag-ride, Harass, Harry, Hassle, Hatter, Heat, Heist, Hellion, Hot water, Howdyedo, Hydra, Incommode, Inconvenience, Infest, → IN TROUBLE, Irk, Jam, Kaugh, Kiaugh, Malcontent, Mayhem, Mess, Mixer, Moil, Molest, Noy, Onerous, Perturb, Pester, Pestiferous, Picnic, Plague, Play up, Poke, Reck, Rub, Scamp, Scrape, Shake, Shtook, Shtuck, Soup, Spiny, Stir, Stirrer, Storm, Sturt, Tartar, Teen, Teething, Thorny, Tine, Toil, Trial, Tsouris, Tsuris, Turn-up, Tyne, Typhoid Mary, Unpleasant, Unrest, Unsettle, Vex, → WORRY

Trouble-free Gallio

Trouble-shooter Ombudsman

▷ **Troublesome** *may indicate* an anagram

Trough Back, Backet, Bed, Buddle, Channel, Chute, Culvert, Graben, Gutter, Hod, Hutch, Langmuir, Launder, Leachtub, Manger, Pneumatic, Puerto Rico, Stock, Straik, Strake, Syncline, Troffer, Tundish, Tye, Watering

Trounce → BEAT, Hammer, Thrash, Thump

Trouser(s) Bags, Bell-bottoms, Bloomers, Breeches, Bumsters, Capri pants, Cargo pants, Chinos, Churidars, Clam-diggers, Combat, Continuations, Cords, Corduroys, Cossacks, Culottes, Daks, Denims, Drainpipe, Drawers, Ducks, Dungarees, Eel-skins, Flannels, Flares, Galligaskins, Gaskins, Gauchos, Hip-huggers, Hipsters, Indescribables, Inexpressibles, Innominables, Jazzpants, Jeans, Jodhpurs, Jog-pants, Kaccha, Ke(c)ks, Knee cords, Lederhosen, Levis, Longs, Loon-pants, Loons, Moleskins, Overalls, Oxford bags, Palazzo (pants), Palazzos, Pantalet(te)s, Pantaloons, Pants, Pedal pushers, Pegtops, Plus-fours, Plus-twos, Pyjamas, Rammies, Reach-me-downs, Salopettes, Shalwar, Ski pants, Slacks, Stirrup pants, Stovepipes, Strides, Strossers, Sweatpants, Thornproofs, Trews, Trouse, Trunk-breeches, Unmentionables, Unutterables, Utterless

Trout Aurora, Brook, Brown, Bull, Coral, Cutthroat, Finnac(k), Finnock, Fish, Gillaroo, Hag(fish), Herling, Hirling, Kamloops, Peal, Peel, Phinnock, Pogies, Quintet, Rainbow, Salmon, Sewen, Sewin, Speckled, Splake, Steelhead, Togue, Whitling

Trow Faith, Meseems

Trowel Float, Slicker

Troy Ilium, Laomedon, Sergeant, T, Weight

Truant Absentee, AWOL, Bunk off, Dodge, Hooky, Idler, Kip, Mich(e), Mitch, Mooch, Mouch, Wag

Truce Armistice, Barley, Ceasefire, Fainites, Fains, Hudna, Interlude, Keys, Pax, Stillstand, Treague, Treaty

Truck Bakkie, Bogie, Breakdown, Business, Cabover, Cattle, Cocopan, Dealings, Dolly, Dumper, Flatbed, Forklift, Haul, Hopper, Journey, → LORRY, Low-loader, Monster, Pallet, Panel, Pick-up, Road-train, Semi, Sound, Stacking, Tipper, Tommy, Tow(ie), Traffic, Tram, Trolley, Trundle, Ute, Utility, Van, Wrecker

Trudge Footslog, Jog, Lumber, Pad, Plod, Stodge, Stramp, Taigle, Traipse, Trash, Trauchle, Trog, Vamp

True Accurate, Actual, Apodictic, Axiomatic, Candid, Constant, Correct, Exact, Factual, Faithful, Genuine, Honest, Indubitable, Leal, Literal, Loyal, Platitude, Plumb, Pure, Real, Realistic, Richt, Right, Sooth, Vera, Very

Truffle Tartuffe, Tuber, Tuberaceae

Trug Basket, Wisket

Truly Certainly, Certes, Fegs, Forsooth, Honestly, Indeed, Insooth, Surely, Verily, Yea

Trump(s), Trumpet(er) Agami, Alchemy, Alchymy, Armstrong, Bach, Blare, Blast, Bray, Buccina, Bugle(r), Call, Card, Clang, Clarion, Conch, Cornet, Corona, Crossruff, Crow, Daffodil, Ear, Elephant, Extol, Fanfare, Hallali, Honours, → HORN, Invent, Jew's, Last, Lituus, Long ten, Lur(e), Lurist, Manille, Marine, Megaphone, → NO TRUMP, Overruff, Pedro, Proclaim, Ram's-horn, Rant, Resurrect, Ruff, Salpingian, Salpinx, Sancho, Satchmo, Sennet, Shell, Shofar, Shophar, Slug-horn, Speaking, Splash, Surpass, Tantara, Tantarara, Tar(at)antara, Theodomas, Tiddy, Triton, Triumph

Trumpery Fattrels, Jimcrack, Paltry, Trashy

Truncate(d) Abrupt, Cut, Dock, Shorten, Snub

Truncheon Billie, Billy, Blackjack, Cosh, Night-stick, Warder

Trundle Hump, Roll, Trill, Troll, Wheel

Trunk(s) Aorta(l), A-road, Body, Bole, Box, Bulk, Bus, But(t), Caber, Cabin, Carcase, Chest, Coffer, Hose, Imperial, Log, Nerve, Peduncle, Pollard, Portmanteau, Portmantle, Proboscis, Puncheon, Ricker, Road, Saratoga, Shorts, STD, Steamer, Stock, Stud, Synangium, Togs, Torso, Valise, Wardrobe

Truss → BIND, Ligate, Oop, Oup, Sheaf, Tie, Upbind

Trust(y), Trusting, Trustworthy Active, Affy, Apex, Authentic, Belief, Bet on, Blind, Box, Camaraderie, Care, Cartel, Charge, Charitable, Combine, Confide, Count on, Credit, Dependable, Dewy-eyed, Discretionary, → FAITH, Fidelity, Fiduciary, Foundation, Gullible, Honest, Hope, Hospital, Investment, Leal, Lippen, Loyal, Naif, National, NT, Reliable, Reliance, Rely, Repose, Reputable, Responsible, Sound, Special, Split, Staunch, Tick, Trojan, Trow, True, Trump, Unit

Trustee Agent, Executor, Fiduciary, Judicial, Pensioneer, Public, Tr

Truth(ful), Truism Accuracy, Alethic, Axiom, Bromide, Cliché, Cold turkey, Dharma, Dialectic, → FACT, Facticity, Forsooth, Gospel, Griff, Home, Honesty, Idea(l), Logical, Maxim, Naked, Necessary, Pravda, Principle, Reality, Sooth, Soothfast, Strength, Troggs, Veracity, Veridical, Verisimilitude, Verity, Vraisemblance

Try(ing) Aim, Approof, Assay, Attempt, Audition, Bash, Bate, Bid, Birl, Burden, Burl, Conative, Contend, Court martial, Crack, Effort, Empiric(utic), → ENDEAVOUR, Essay, Examine, Experiment, Fand, Fish, Fling, Foretaste, Go, Gun for, Harass, Hard, Hear, Impeach, Importunate, Irk, Noy, Offer, Ordalium, Penalty, Pop, Practise, Pree, Prieve, Prove, Push-over, → SAMPLE, Seek, Shot, Sip, Stab, Strain, Strive, Taste, Tax, Tempt,

Test, Touchdown, → **TRIAL**, Whirl
Tryst Date, Rendezvous
Tsar(ist) Alexis, Boris, Drug, Emperor, Godunov, Ivan the Terrible, Octobrist, Peter the Great, Romanov, Ruler, Tyrant
TT Dry, Race, Rechabite
Tub(by), Tubbiness, Tubman, Tub-thumper Ash-leach, Back, Bath, Boanerges, Bran, Bucket, Cooper, Corf, Cowl, Dan, Diogenes, Dolly, Endomorph, Firkin, Hip bath, Keeve, Kid, Kieve, Kit, Luckydip, Mashing, Meat, Pin, Podge, Pot-bellied, Powdering, Pudge, Pulpit, Rolypoly, Seasoning, Stand, Swill, Tun, Twin, Vat, Wash, Whey
Tuba Bombardon, Euphonium, Helicon
Tube, Tubing, Tubular Acorn, Arteriole, Artery, Barrel, Blowpipe, Bronchus, Buckyball, Buckytube, Burette, Calamus, Camera, Canaliculus, Can(n)ula, Capillary, Casing, Catheter, Cathode-ray, Cave, Conduit, Crookes, Digitron, Diode, Discharge, Drain, Draw, Drift, Dropper, Duct, Electron, Endiometer, Epididymis, Eustachian, Extension, Fallopian, Fistula, Flash, Fluorescent, Fulgurite, Geissler, Germ, Glowstick, Grommet, Hawsepipe, Hose, Iconoscope, Idiot box, Image (orthicon), Inner, Kinescope, Klystron, Macaroni, Malpighian, Matrass, Metro, Morris, Nasogastric, Neural, Nixie, Optic, Orthicon, Oval, Oviduct, Pastille, Peashooter, Pentode, Picture, → **PIPE**, Pipette, Piping, Pitot(-static), Pneumatic, Pollen, Postal, Salpinx, Saticon®, Saucisse, Saucisson, Schnorkel, Shadow-mask, Shock, Sieve, Siphon, Siphonet, Siphonostele, Siphuncle, Skelp, Skiatron, Sleeve, Slide, Snorkel, Spaghetti, Speaking, Spout, Staple, Static, Stent, Stone canal, Storage, Strae, Straw, Strip light, Strobotron, Subway, Sucker, Swallet, Syringe, Tele, Telescope, Teletron, Television, Telly, Terete, Test, Tetrode, Thermionic, Thyratron, Tile, Torpedo, Torricellian, Trachea, Travelling-wave, Triniscope, Trocar, Trochotron, Trunk, Tunnel, Tuppenny, TV, U, Underground, Ureter, Urethra, Vacuum, Vas, VDU, Vein, Vena, Venturi, Video, Vidicon®, Worm, X-ray
Tuber(s) Arnut, Arracacha, Bulb, Chufa, Coc(c)o, Dahlia, Dasheen, Earth-nut, Eddoes, Ginseng, Jicama, Mashua, Oca, Pignut, Potato, Salep, Taproot, Taro, Tuckahoe, Yam, Yautia
Tuberculosis Consumption, Crewels, Cruel(l)s, Decline, King's evil, Lupus, Lupus vulgaris, Phthisis, Scrofula, White plague
Tuck Dart, Friar, Gather, Grub, Hospital corner, Kilt, Pin, Pleat, Scran, Truss, Tummy
Tudor Stockbrokers'
Tuesday Hock, Pancake, Shrove, Super
Tuff Schalstein
Tuft(ed) Aigrette, Amentum, Beard, Candlewick, Catkin, C(a)espitose, Cluster, Coma, Comb, Cowlick, Crest, Dollop, Ear, Flaught, Floccus, Flock, Goatee, Hank, Hassock, Knop, Lock, Pappus, Penicillate, Pledget, Quiff, Scopate, Shola, Tait, Tassel, Tate, Toorie, Topknot, Toupee, Tourie, Tussock, Tuzz, Whisk
Tug Chain, Drag, Haul, Jerk, Lug, Pug, → **PULL**, Rive, Rug, Saccade, Ship, Sole, Soole, Sowl(e), Tit, Tow, Towboat, Yank
Tui Poebird
Tuition Grind, Masterclass, Seminal
Tully Cicero
Tumble, Tumbler Acrobat, Cartwheel, Drier, Fall, → **GLASS**, Header, Jack, Jill, Lock, Pitch, Popple, Purl, Realise, Spill, Stumble, Tailer, Topple, Touser, Towser, Trip, Twig, Voltigeur, Welter
▷ **Tumble** *may indicate* an anagram
Tumbledown Decrepit, Dilapidated, Ramshackle, Rickle, Ruinous
Tumbril Caisson
Tummy Belly, Colon, Mary, Paunch, Pod
Tummy-ache Colic, Gripe, Tormina
Tumour Adenoma, Anbury, Angioma, Angiosarcoma, Astroblastoma, Astrocytoma, Burkitt('s) lymphoma, Cancer, Carcinoid, Carcinoma, Carcinosarcoma, Chondroma,

Condyloma, Crab(-yaws), Craniopharyngioma, Dermoid, Encanthis, Encephaloma, Enchondroma, Endothelioma, Epulis, Exostosis, Fibroid, Fibroma, Ganglion, Germinoma, Gioblastoma, Glioma, Granuloma, Grape, → **GROWTH**, Gumma, Haemangioma, Haematoma, Hepatoma, Lipoma, Lymphoma, Medulloblastoma, Melanoma, Meningioma, Mesothelioma, Metastasis, Mole, Myeloma, Myoma, Myxoma, Neoplasm, Nephroblastoma, Neuroblastoma, Neurofibroma, Neuroma, Odontoma, -oma, Oncogenesis, Oncology, Osteoclastoma, Osteoma, Osteosarcoma, Papilloma, Polypus, Retinoblastoma, Rhabdomyoma, Rous sarcoma, Sarcoma, Scirrhous, Secondary, Seminoma, Steatoma, Struma, Syphiloma, Talpa, Teratocarcinoma, Teratoma, Thymoma, Wart, Warthin's, Wen, Wilms', Windgall, Wolf, Xanthoma, Yaw

Tumult Brattle, Brawl, Coil, Deray, Ferment, Fracas, Hirdy-girdy, Hubbub, Hurly-burly, Reird, Riot, → **ROAR**, Romage, Rore, Stoor, Stour, Stowre, Stramash, Tew, Tristan, Tristram, → **UPROAR**

Tumulus Barrow, How(e), Mote, Motte

Tun Cask, Keg

Tuna Ahi, Pear, Skipjack, Yellowfin

Tundra Barren Grounds, Barren Lands

Tune(s), Tuneful, Tuner, Tuning Adjust, Air, Aria, Ayre, Canorous, Carillon, Catch, Choral(e), Dump, Earworm, Étude, Fine, Fork, Gingle, Harmony, Hornpipe, Hunt's up, Jingle, Key, Maggot, Measure, Melisma, → **MELODY**, Morrice, Morris, Old Hundred, → **OUT OF TUNE**, Peg, Planxty, Port, Potpourri, Raga, Rant, Ranz-des-vaches, Reel, Signature, Snatch, Song, Spring, Strain, Sweet, Syntonise, Syntony, Temper, Temperament, Theme, Tone, Toy, Tweak

Tungstate, Tungsten Scheelite, W, Wolfram

Tunic Ao dai, Caftan, Chiton, Choroid, Cote-hardie, Dalmatic, Dashiki, Gymslip, Hauberk, Kabaya, Kaftan, Kameez, K(h)urta, Salwar kameez, → **SINGLET**, Surcoat, Tabard, Toga

Tunicate Pyrosoma, Salpa

Tunnel(ler) Blackwall, Bore, Channel, Chunnel, Condie, Countermine, Culvert, Cundy, Earthworm, Euro, Gallery, Head, Mine, Mole, Qanat, Rotherhithe, Sewer, Simplon, Smoke, Stope, Subway, Sure, Syrinx, Transmanche, Tube, Underpass, Water, Wind, Wormhole

Tunny Bonito, Tuna

Turban Bandanna, Hat, Mitral, Pagri, Puggaree, Puggery, Puggree, Sash, Scarf, Tulipant

Turbid Cloudy, Dense, Drumly, Roily

Turbine Francis, Gas, Impulse, Ram air, Reaction, Steam, Water, Wind

Turbulence, Turbulent Atmospheric, Becket, Bellicose, Buller, Factious, Fierce, Overfall, Rapids, Roil, Stormy, Unruly

▷ **Turbulent, Turbulence** *may indicate* an anagram

Tureen Terreen

Turf Caespitose, Clod, Divot, Earth, Fail, Feal, Flaught, Gazo(o)n, → **GRASS**, Greensward, Kerf, Peat, Racing, Scraw, → **SOD**, Sward

Turk(ish) Anatolian, Bashaw, Bashkir, Bey, Bimbashi, Bostangi, Byzantine, Caimac(am), Crescent, Effendi, Golden Horde, Grand, Gregory, Horse(tail), Irade, Kaimakam, Kazak(h), Kurd, Mameluke, Mutessarif(at), Omar, Osman(li), Ottamite, Ottoman, Ottomite, Rayah, Scanderbeg, Selim, Seljuk(ian), Seraskier, Spahi, Tartar, Tatar, Timariot, Usak, Uzbeg, Uzbek, Yakut, Young

Turkey, Turkey-like Anatolia, Antioch, Brush, Bubbly(-jock), Cold, Curassow, Eyalet, Flop, Gobbler, Lame brain, Norfolk, Plain, Scrub, Sultanate, Talegalla, Talk, TR, Trabzon, Vulturn

Turkish delight Rahat lacoum, Trehala

Turmeric Curcumin(e)

Turmoil Ariot, Chaos, Confusion, Din, Dust, Ferment, Mess, Pother, Pudder, Stoor, Stour, Tornado, Tracasserie, Tumult, → **UPROAR**, Welter

▷ **Turn(ing)** *may indicate* an anagram

Turn(ing), Turn(ed) away, Turn(ed) up, Turns Acescent, Act, Adapt, Addle, Advert, Antrorse, Apostrophe, Apotropaic, Avert, Bad, Bank, Become, Bend, Blow in, Buggins, Bump, Canceleer, Cancelier, Caracol(e), Careen, Cartwheel, Cast, Chainé, Chandelle, Change, Char(e), Chore, Christiana, Christie, Christy, Churn, Cock, Coil, Corotate, Crank(le), Cuff, Curd(le), Curve, Defect, Deflect, Demi-volt(e), Detour, Deviate, Dig, Digress, Divert, Ear, Earn, Elbow, Evert, Fadge, Ferment, Flip, Forfend, Go, Good, Gruppetto, Gyrate, Hairpin, Handbrake, Head-off, Hie, High, Hinge, Hup, Immelmann, Influence, Innings, Intussuscept, Invert, Jar, Jink, Jump, Keel, Kick, Laeotropic, Lodging, Lot, Luff, Mohawk, Nip, Number, Obvert, Parallel, Parry, Penchant, Pivot, Plough, Pronate, Prove, PTO, Quarter, Quersprung, Rebut, Refer, Refract, Remuage, Retroflex, Retroussé, Retrovert, Rev, Revolt, Ride, Riffle, Rocker, Roll, Root, → **ROTATE**, Rote, Roulade, Rout, Routine, Screw, Secund, Sheer, → **SHOT**, Shout, Sicken, Skit, Slew, Slue, Solstice, Sour, → **SPELL**, Spin, Spot, Sprain, Star, Start, Stem, Step, Stunt, Swash, Swerve, Swing, Swivel, Telemark, Thigmotropism, Three-point, Throw, Tiptilt, Tirl, T-junction, Torque, Transpose, Trend, Trick, Trie, Trochilic, Turtle, Twiddle, Twist, Twizzle, U, Uey, U-ie, Up, Veer, Versed, Version, Vertigo, Volta, Volte-face, Volutation, Wap, Warp, Wedeln, Wend, Went, → **WHEEL**, Whelm, Whirl, Whorl, Wimple, Wind, Wrast, Wrest, Wriggle, Zigzag
Turn-coat Apostate, Cato, Defector, Quisling, Rat, Renegade, Tergiversate, Traitor
Turner Axle, Capstan, Lana, Lathe, Painter, Pivot, Rose-engine, Spanner, Tina, Worm, Wrench
Turning point Crisis, Crossroads, Landmark, Watershed
Turnip(-shaped) Baggy, Bagie, Hunter, Indian, Jicama, Napiform, Navew, Neep, Prairie, Rutabaga, Shaw, → **STUPID PERSON**, Swede, Tumshie
Turnkey Gaoler, Jailer, Locksman
Turn on Boot
Turn-out Eventuate, Gathering, Product, Rig, Splay, Style, Team
Turn over Capsize, Careen, Flip, Inversion, Mull, Production, PTO, Somersault, TO, Up-end
Turnpike Highway, Toll
Turnstile Tourniquet
Turntable Racer, Rota, Rotator
Turpentine Galipot, Rosin, Thinner, Turps, Venice
Turquoise Bone, Fossil, Ligure, Occidental, Odontolite, Oriental, Turkey stone
Turret(ed) Barmkin, Bartisan, Garret, Louver, Louvre, Mirador, Pepperbox, Sponson, Tank top, → **TOWER**, Turriculate
Turtle, Turtle head Bale, Box, Calipash, Calipee, Chelone, Cooter, Diamondback, Emys, Floor, Green, Hawk(s)bill, Inverted, Leatherback, Loggerhead, Matamata, Mossback, Mud, Musk, Painted, Ridley, Screen, Snapper, Snapping, Soft-shelled, Stinkpot, Terrapin, Thalassian
Tuscany Chiantishire
Tusk Gam, Horn, Ivory, Tooth, Tush
Tusker Dicynodont, Elephant, Mastodon
Tussle Giust, Joust, Mêlée, Scrimmage, Scrum, Scuffle, Skirmish, Touse, Touze, Towse, Towze, Tuilyie, Wrestle
Tussock Hassock, Niggerhead, Tuft
Tut(-tut) Mummy, Och, Pooh
Tutelary Guardian, Protector
Tutor Abbé, Aristotle, Ascham, Bear, → **COACH**, Crammer, Don, Edify, Instruct, Leader, Mentor, Preceptor, Répétiteur, Supervisor, Teacher, Train
Tuxedo DJ
TV Baird, Box, Breakfast, Cable, Digibox®, Digital, Docudrama, Docusoap, Flat screen, Idiot-box, Lime Grove, Monitor, NICAM, PAL, Pay, Reality, SECAM, Sitcom, Sky, Tele, → **TELEVISION**, Telly, Tie-in, Triniscope, Tube, Video

Twaddle Blether, Drivel, Fadaise, Rot, Slipslop, Tripe
Twang Nasal, Pluck, Plunk, Rhinolalia
Tweak Pinch, Pluck, Primp, Twiddle, Twist, Twitch
Tweed(y) Donegal, Harris®, Homespun, Lovat, Raploch
Tweet Chirrup
Twelfth, Twelve Apostles, Dozen, Epiphany, Glorious, Grouse, Midday, Midnight, N, Night, Noon(tide), Ternion, Twal
Twenty, Twenty-sided Icosahedron, Score, Vicenary, Vicennial, Vicesimal, Vigesimal
Twenty-five, Twentyfifth Pony, Quartern, Semi-jubilee
Twenty-four Thr(e)ave
Twerp Pipsqueak
▶ **Twice** *see* **TWO(SOME)**
Twice-yearly Biennial, Equinox
Twiddle Fidget, Twirl
Twig(s) Besom, Birch, Brushwood, Cotton, Cow, Dig, Grasp, Kow, Osier, Realise, Reis, Rice, Rod, Rumble, Sarment, See, Sprig, Sticklac, Switch, Understand, Walking, Wand, Wattle, Whip, Wicker, Withe
Twilight Astronomical, Civil, Cockshut, Crepuscular, Demi-jour, Dimpsy, Dusk, Gloam(ing), Götterdämmerung, Nautical, Ragnarok, Summerdim
Twill Cavalry, Chino, Serge
Twin(s) Asvins, Castor, Coetaneous, Conjoined, Couplet, Didymous, Dioscuri, Ditokous, Dizygotic, Double, Fraternal, Gemel, Geminate, Gemini, Hemitrope, Identical, Isogeny, Juxtaposition, Kindred, Kray, Look-alike, Macle, Monozygotic, Parabiotic, Pigeon-pair, Pollux, Siamese, Thomas, Tweedledee, Tweedledum
Twine Binder, Braid, Coil, Cord, Inosculate, Packthread, Sisal, Snake, String, Twist, Wreathe
Twinge Pang, Scruple, Stab, Twang
Twinkle, Twinkling Glimmer, Glint, Mo(ment), → **SPARKLE**, Starnie, Trice
Twirl Spin, Swivel, Tirl, Tirlie-wirlie, Trill, Trundle, Twiddle, Twizzle, Whirl
▷ **Twirling** *may indicate* an anagram
Twist(ed), Twister, Twisting, Twisty Anfractuous, Askant, Askew, Baccy, Becurl, Bought, Braid, Buckle, Card-sharper, Chisel, Coil, Contort, Convolution, Corkscrew, Crinkle, Crinkum-crankum, Crisp, Cue, Curl(icue), Curliewurlie, Cyclone, Deform, Detort, Dishonest, Distort, → **DODGE**, Eddy, Embraid, Entrail, Entwine, Garrot, Helix, Imposture, Kink, Lemon peel, Loop, Mangulate, Mat, Möbius strip, Oliver, Pandanaceous, Plait, Quirk, Raddle, Ravel, Rick, Rogue, Rotate, Rove, Serpent, Skew, Slew, Slub(b), Slue, Snake, Snarl, Spin, Spiral, Sprain, Squiggle, Squirm, Strand, Swivel, Tendril, Thraw(n), Torc, Tornado, Torque, Torsade, Torsion, Torticollis, Tortile, Turn, Tweak, Twiddle, Twine, Twirl, Twizzle, Typhoon, Valgus, Volvulus, Wamble, Warp, Welkt, Wigwag, Wind, Wound-wrap, Wrast, Wreathe, Wrench, Wrest, Wrethe, Wrick, Wriggle, Wring, Writhe, Wry, Zigzag
▷ **Twisted, Twisting** *may indicate* an anagram
Twit, Twitter Birdbrain, Chaff, Cherup, Chirrup, Dotterel, Gear(e), Giber, → **JEER**, Rag, Stupid, Taunt, Tweet, Warble
Twitch(ing), Twitchy Athetosis, Clonic, Fibrillation, Grass, Jerk, Life-blood, Saccadic, Sneer, Spasm, Start, Subsultive, Tic, Tig, Tippet, Tit, Tweak, Twinge, Vellicate, Yips
Two(some), Twofold, Twice Bice, Bis, Bisp, Both, Brace, Couple(t), Deuce, Double, Duad, Dual, Duet, Duo, Duple, Dyad, Item, → **PAIR**, Swy, Tête-à-tête, Twain, Twins, Twister
Two-edged Ancipitous
Two-faced Dihedral, Dorsiventral, Hypocritical, Janus, Redan
Two-gallon Peck
Two-headed Amphisbaenic, Dicephalous, Orthos
Two hundred H

Two hundred and fifty E, K
Two-master Brig
Two-pronged Bidental
Two-rayed Diactinal
Two-sided Bilateral, Equivocatory
Two thousand Z
Two-tone Shot
Two-up Kip, Swy
Two-wheeler Bicycle, Scooter
Tycoon Baron, Empire-builder, Fat cat, Magnate, Mogul, Murdoch, Nabob, Onassis,
Plutocrat, Shogun
Tyke Geit, RC
Tympany Castanets, Cymbal, Drum, Kitchen, Triangle, Xylophone
Type(s), Typing A, Agate, Aldine, Antimony, Antique, B, Balaam, Baskerville, Bastard,
Batter, Beard, Bembo, Black-letter, Block, Blood, Bodoni, Body, Bold face, Bourgeois,
Braille, Brand, Brevier, Brilliant, Canon, Caslon, Category, Character, Chase, Cicero,
Clarendon, Class, Columbian, Condensed, Cut, Egyptian, Elite, Elzevir, Em, Emblem,
Emerald, En(nage), English, Face, Font, Footer, Form(e), Founder's, Fount, Fraktur,
Fudge, Garamond, Gem, Genre, Gent, Gothic, Great primer, Gutenberg, Hair, Hot metal,
Ilk, Image, Kern(e), Key, Keyboard, Kidney, Kind, Late-star, Ligature, Light-faced,
Logotype, Longprimer, Ludlow, Make, Mating, Melanochroi, Minion, Modern,
Monospaced, Moon, Mould, Non-pareil, Norm, Old English, Old-face, Old Style,
Paragon, Pattern, Pearl, Peculiar, Personality, Pi, Pica, Pie, Plantin, Point, Primer, Print,
Quad(rat), Roman, Ronde, Ruby, Sanserif, Secretary, Semibold, Serif, Serological, Slug,
→ **SORT**, Sp, Species, Spectral, Stanhope, Style, Times, Tissue, Touch, Version
▷ **Type of** *may indicate* an anagram
Typesetting Hot metal
Typewriter Golfball, Portable, Stenograph, Stenotype®, Varityper®
Typhoid, Typhus Camp-fever, Murine, Putrid fever, Scrub, Tick-borne
Typhoon Cyclone, Hurricane, Monsoon, Tornado, Wind
Typical Average, Characteristic, Classic, Echt, Everyman, Normal, Representative,
Standard, Symbolic, True-bred, Usual
Typist Audio, Copy, Printer, Steno(grapher), Temp
Tyrannise(d) Domineer, Lord, Under
Tyrant, Tyranny, Tyrannical Absolutism, Autocrat, Caligula, Czar, Despot, Dictator,
Drawcansir, Gelon, Herod, Ivan the Terrible, Lordly, Nero, Oppressor, Pharaoh,
Pisistratus, Sardanapalus, Satrap, Stalin, Totalitarian, Tsar, Yoke
Tyre(s) Balloon, Cross-ply, Cushion, Earthing, Flat, Michelin®, Pericles, Pneumatic,
Radial(-ply), Recap, Remould, Retread, Shoe, Sidewall, Slick, Snow, Spare, Stepney, Toe
in, Tread, Tubeless, Whitewall
Tyro Beginner, Ham, → **NOVICE**, Rabbit, Rookie, Rooky, Starter
Tyrolese R(h)aetian

Uu

U, U-type Gent, Unicorn, Universal, Uranium
U-bend Airtrap
Ubiquitous Everywhere, Inescapable, Omnipresent
Udder Bag, Dug
UFO Roswell
Uganda(n) Obote, .ug
Ugly Butters, Cow, Crow, Customer, Eyesore, Faceache, Foul, Gorgon, Gruesome,
  Hideous, Homely, Huckery, Jolie laide, Loath, Loth, Mean, Ominous, Plain, Sight
Ugrian Ostiak, Ostyak, Samo(y)ed, Vogul
UK GB
Ukase Decree
Ukraine, Ukrainian Russniak, Ruthene, UA
Ulcer(ous) Abscess, Aphtha, Bedsore, Canker, Chancre, Chancroid, Decubitus,
  Duodenal, Enanthema, Gastric, Helcoid, Imposthume, Mouth, Noli-me-tangere, Noma,
  Peptic, Phagedaena, Plague-sore, Rodent, Rupia, Sore, Varicose, Wolf
Ulster NI, Overcoat, Raincoat, Ulad
Ulterior External, Hidden
Ultimate(ly) Absolute, Basic, Deterrent, Eventual, Final, Furthest, Last, Maximum,
  Mostest, Omega, So, Supreme, Thule, Ult
Ultimatum Threat
Ultra Drastic, Extreme, Radical
Ultra-modern Space age
Ultra-republican Leveller
Ultrasound Lithotripsy
Ululate Wail
Ulysses Bloom, Grant, Odysseus
Umbellifer(ous) Angelica, Arnut, Car(r)away, Dill, Honewort, Narthex, Pig-nut, Seseli
Umber Burnt, Mottled, Raw, Waved
Umbrage Offence, Pique, Resentment, Shade
Umbrella(-shaped) Brolly, Bubble, Bumbershoot, Chatta, Gamp, Gingham, Gloria,
  Mush(room), Nuclear, Parasol, Sunshade, Tee
Umbria Eugubine, Iguvine
Umpire Arb(iter), Byrlawman, Daysman, Decider, Judge, Mediate, Oddjobman,
  Odd(s)man, Overseer, Oversman, Referee, Rule, Stickler, Thirdsman
Unabashed Bare-faced, Brazen, Shameless
Unable Can't, Downa-do, Incapable
Unaccented Atonic, Proclitic
Unacceptable Beyond the pale, Non-U, Not on, Out, Repugnant, Stigmatic, Taboo
Unaccompanied A cappella, Alone, High-lone, Secco, Single, Solo, Solus
Unaccustomed Desuetude, Inusitate, New, Unwonted, Usedn't
Unacknowledged Covert
Unadorned Au naturel, Bald, Plain, Stark
Unadulterated Sincere
Unaffected Artless, Genuine, Homely, Insusceptible, Natural, Plain, Sincere,
  Unattached
Unaided Single-handed, Solo

Unaltered Constant, Same
Unambiguous Categorical, Univocal
Unanimous Accord, Nem con, Per curiam
Unanswerable Erotema, Irrefragable, Irrefutable
Unappealing Distasteful, Grim, Offensive, Rank
Unappreciated, Unappreciative Ingrate, Thankless
Unapproachable Remote
Unarguable Erotema
Unarmed Inerm, → **MARTIAL ARTS**, Naked, Vulnerable
Unashamed Blatant, Brazen, Open
Unassigned Adespota, Anonymous, Vacant
Unassisted Naked eye
Unassuming Lowly, Modest
Unattached Fancy free, Freelance, Loose
Unattractive Demagnetised, Drac(k), Hideous, Lemon, Minger, Munter, Plain,
  Plug-ugly, Rebarbative, Scungy, Seamy, Skanky, Ugly
Unattributable Anon
Unauthentic Plagal
▷ **Unauthentic** *may indicate* an anagram
Unavail(able), Unavailing Bootless, Futile, Ineluctable, Lost, NA, No use, Off,
  Useless, Vain
Unavoidable Ineluctable, Inevitable, Necessary, Perforce
Unaware(ness) Blind-side, Cloistered, Coma, Heedless, Ignorant, Incognisant,
  Innocent, Oblivious, Stupor
Unbalanced Asymmetric, Deranged, Doolalli, Doolally, Loco, Lopsided, Nutty, Out to
  lunch, Twisted, Uneven
Unbearable Bassington, Intolerable
Unbeaten, Unbeatable All-time, Perfect
Unbecoming, Unbefitting Improper, Indecent, Infra dig, Shabby, Unfitting,
  Unseemly, Unsuitable, Unworthy
Unbelievable, Unbeliever Agnostic, Atheist, Cassandra, Doubter, Giaour, Heathen,
  Heretic, Incredible, Infidel, Pagan, Painim, Paynim, Sceptic, Tall, Zendik
Unbend(ing) Relent, Strict
Unbent Relaxed
Unbiased Fair, Impartial, Just, Neutral, Objective, Unattainted
Unblemished Clean, Intact, Spotless, Vestal
Unblinking Alert, Astare, Fearless
Unblock(ing) Free, Recanalization
Unborn Future, Unbred
Unbounded Infinite
Unbowed In-kneed, Resolute
Unbranded Cleanskin
Unbreakable Infrangible, Inviolate
Unbridled Fancy free, Footloose, Lawless, Uncurbed, Unrestricted, Unshackled,
  Untramelled
Unburden Confide, Offload, Relieve, Unload
Uncanny Eerie, Eldritch, Extraordinary, Geason, Rum, Spooky, Wanchancie, Wanchancy,
  Weird
Uncastrated Stone
Unceasing Continuous
Uncertain(ty) Acatalepsy, Agnostic, Blate, Broken, Chancy, Chary, Contingent, Delicate,
  Dicey, Dither, Dodgy, Doubtful, Dubiety, Grey, Heisenberg, Hesitant, Iffy, Indeterminate,
  Indistinct, Irresolute, Obscure, Parlous, Peradventure, Precarious, Queasy, Risky,
  Slippery, Suspense, Tentative, Vor, Wide open

▷ **Uncertain** *may indicate* an anagram

Unchallengeable, Unchallenge(d) Inerrant, Irrecusable, Sackless

Unchangeable, Unchanged, Unchanging As is, Enduring, Eternal, Idempotent, Immutable, Monotonous, Perennial, Pristine, Read only, Stable, Standpat, Timeless

Uncharacteristic Atypical

Uncharged Neutral, Neutron

Unchaste Corrupt, Immodest, Immoral, Impure, Lewd, Light-heeled, Wanton

Unchecked Rampant, Raw, Unrestrained

Uncivil(ised) Barbaric, Benighted, Boondocks, Brutish, Discourteous, Disrespectful, Giant-rude, Goth, Heathen, Impolite, Liberty, Military, Rude, Rudesby, Short, Unmannerly

Uncle Abbas, Afrikaner, Arly, Bob, Dutch, Eme, Nunky, Oom, Pawnbroker, Pledgee, Pop-shop, Remus, Sam, Silas, Tio, Tom, U, Usurer, Vanya

Unclean Defiled, Dirty, Impure, Obscene, Ordure, Squalid, Tabu, T(e)refa(h)

Unclear Ambitty, Blurred, Cloudy, Grey area, Hazy, Nebulous, Obscure, Opaque, Sketchy, Slurred

Unclothed Bald, Nude

Uncloven Soliped

Uncoded En clair

Uncomfortable Awkward, Mean, Uneasy

Uncommitted Evasive, Free-floating, Laodicean

Uncommon Rara avis, Rare, Sparse, Strange, Unusual

▷ **Uncommon(ly)** *may indicate* an anagram

Uncommunicative Reserved, Tight-lipped

Uncompanionable Threesome

Uncomplimentary Blunt

Uncomprehending Anan, Ignorant

Uncompromising Cutthroat, Hardline, Hardshell, Intransigent, Relentless, Rigid, Strict, Ultra

Unconcealed Open, Pert

Unconcerned Bland, Careless, Casual, Cold, Indifferent, Insouciant, Nonchalant, Strange

Unconditional Absolute, Free, No strings, Pure

Uncongenial Icy

Unconnected Asyndetic, Detached, Disjointed, Enodal, Off-line

Unconscionable Ordinate, Ungodly

Unconscious(ness) Asleep, Catalepsy, Cold, Comatose, Instinctive, Non-ego, Not-I, Subliminal, Syncope, Trance, Unaware, Under, Zonked out

Unconsidered Impetuous, Rash

Unconsummated Mariage blanc

Uncontrolled Adrift, Anarchic, Atactic, Free, Incontinent, Intemperate, Loose, Loose cannon, Rampant, Wild

Uncontroversial Anodyne

Unconventional Anti-hero, Avant garde, Beatnik, Bohemian, Divergent, Drop-out, Eccentric, Far-out, Freeform, Gonzo, Heretic, Heterodox, Hippy, Informal, Irregular, Offbeat, Off-the-wall, Original, Outlandish, Outré, Out there, Raffish, Rebel, Screwball, Spac(e)y, Swinger, Unorthodox, Way-out, Wild

▷ **Unconventional** *may indicate* an anagram

Unconverted Neat

Unconvinced, Unconvincing Farfet(ched), High-flown, Humph, Lame, Thin, Wafer-thin

Uncooked Rare, Raw

Uncooperative Bolshie, Recalcitrant

Uncoordinated Asynergia, Ataxic, Awkward, Clumsy

Uncorrect Stet

Uncouth(ness) Backwoodsman, Bear, Boorish, Churlish, Crude, Gothic, Inelegant, Rough, Rube, Rude, Rugged, Slob, Sloven, Uncivil

Uncover(ed) Bare, Denude, Disclose, Dismask, Expose, Inoperculate, Open, Overt, Peel, Reveal, Shave, Shill, Shuck, Uncap, Unveil

Uncritical Indiscriminate

Unction, Unctuous(ness) Anele, Balm, Chrism, Extreme, Oil(y), Ointment, Oleaginous, Ooze, Smarm, Soapy

Uncultivated, Uncultured Artless, Bundu, Fallow, Ignorant, Incult, Philistine, Rude, Tramontane, Wild, Wildland, Wildwood

Undamaged Intact, Sound, Whole

Undated Sine die

Undecided Aboulia, Double-minded, Doubtful, Moot, Non-committal, Open-ended, Pending, Pendulous, Torn, Uncertain, Wavering

Undefiled Chaste, Clean, Pure, Virgin

Undeniable Fact, Incontestable, Irrefutable

Under(neath) Aneath, Below, Beneath, Hypnotized, Hypo-, Infra, Sotto, Sub-, Unconscious, Unneath

Underarm Axilla, Lob

Underburnt Samel

Under-butler Bread-chipper

Undercarriage Bogie, Chassis

Undercoat Base, Primer

Undercooked Rare, Raw, Samel

Undercover Espionage, Secret, Veiled

Undercurrent Acheron, Undertone, Undertow

Underdeveloped, Underdevelopment Ateleiosis, Retarded

Underdog Cerberus, Loser, Victim

▶ **Undergarment** *see* UNDERWEAR

Undergo Bear, Dree, Endure, Solvate, Sustain

Undergraduate Commoner, Fresher, L, Pup, Questionist, Sizar, Sophomore, Student, Subsizar, Tuft

Underground (group) Basement, Catacomb, Cellar, Clandestine, Fogou, Hell, Hypogaeous, Infernal, Irgun, Kiva, Macchie, Maquis, Mattamore, Metro, Phreatic, Pict, Plutonia, Pothole, Secret, Souterrain, Subsoil, Subterranean, Subway, Tube

Undergrowth Brush, Chaparral, Firth, Frith, Scrub

Underhand Backstair, Dirty, Haunch, Insidious, Lob, Oblique, Scullduggery, Secret, Shady, Sinister, Sly, Sneaky, Surreptitious

Underlease Subtack

Underlie, Underlying Subjacent, Subtend

Underline Emphasise, Insist, Sublineation

Underling Bottle-washer, Cog, Inferior, Jack, Menial, Minion, Munchkin, Subordinate

Undermine Destabilise, Erode, Fossick, Handbag, Sap, Subvert, Tunnel, Weaken

Undernourished Puny, Starveling

Underpaid Rat

Underpass Simplon, Subway

Underside Bed, Soffit

Understand(able), Understanding, Understood Accept, Acumen, Agreement, Apprehend, Capeesh, Clear, Cognisable, Comprehend, Conceive, Concept, Connivance, Cotton-on, Deal, Dig, Digest, Empathy, Enlighten, Entente, Exoteric, Fathom, Follow, Gather, Gauge, Gaum, Geddit, Get it, Gorm, Grasp, Grok, Have, Head, Heels, Hindsight, Implicit, Insight, Intelligible, Intuit, Ken, Kind, Knowhow, Learn, Light(s), Lucid, OK, Omniscient, Pact, Perspicuous, Plumb, Prajna, Rapport, Rapprochement, Realise, Roger, Savey, Savvy, See, Sense, Sole, Subintelligitur, Substance, Tacit, Take, Tolerance, Treaty, Tumble, Twig, Unspoken, Unstated, Uptak(e), Wisdom, Wit

Understate(d), Understatement Litotes, Minify, M(e)iosis, Subtle

▶ **Understood** *see* **UNDERSTAND(ABLE)**

Understudy Deputy, Double, Stand-in, Sub

Undertake, Undertaking Attempt, Commitment, Contract, Covenant, Emprise, Endeavour, Enterprise, Essay, Feat, Guarantee, Misere, Pledge, Promise, Scheme, Shoulder, Task, Venture, Warranty

Undertaker Editor, Entrepreneur, Mortician, Obligor, Sponsor, Upholder

Under-ten Unit, Yarborough

Undertone Murmur, Rhubarb, Sotto voce

Underwater Demersal

Underwear Alb, Balbriggan, Balconette, Bloomers, Bodice, Body, Bodyshaper, Body stocking, Body suit, Bra(ssiere), Briefs, Broekies, Butt bra, Camiknickers, Camisole, Chemise, Chemisette, Chuddies, Combinations, Combs, Corselet, Corset, Dainties, Drawers, (French) knickers, Frillies, Girdle, Grundies, G-string, Hosiery, Innerwear, Jump, Linen, Lingerie, Linings, Long johns, Pantalets, Pantaloons, Panties, Pantihose, Panty girdle, Petticoat, Scanties, Semmit, Shift, Shimmy, Shorts, Singlet, Skivvy, Slip, Smalls, Stammel, Stays, Step-ins, Subucula, Suspender-belt, Suspenders, Tanga, Teddy, Thermal, Trunks, Underdaks, Undergarments, Underlinen, Underpants, Underset, Undershirt, Underthings, Undies, Unmentionables, Vest, Wyliecoat, Y-fronts®

Underworld All-fired, Avernus, Chthonic, Criminal, Hades, Hell, Lowlife, Mafia, Pluto, Shades, Tartar(e), Tartarus, Tartary

Underwrite, Underwritten Assure, Endorse, Guarantee, Insure, Lloyds, PS

Undeserving Immeritous

Undesirable Kibitzer, Riff-raff

Undeveloped Ament, Backward, Depauperate, Green, Inchoate, Latent, Nubbin, Ridgel, Ridgil, Ridgling, Rig, Riggald, Riglin(g), Rudimentary, Seminal

Undifferentiated Thalliform, Thallus

Undigested Crude

Undignified (end) Disaster, Foot, Improper, Infra dig, Unseemly

Undiluted Neat, Pure, Sheer, Straight

Undiminished Entire, Intact, Whole

Undiplomatic Brusque, Tactless

Undisciplined Hothead, Rule-less, Rulesse, Sloppy, Unruly, Wanton

Undisclosed Hidden, In petto

Undisguised Apert, Clear, Plain

Undistinguished Nameless, Plebeian, Run of the mill

Undisturbed Halcyon

Undivided Aseptate, Complete, Entire, Indiscrete, One

Undo(ing) Annul, Defeat, Destroy, Disconnect, Downfall, Dup, Poop, Poupe, Release, Rescind, Ruin, Unravel

Undoctored Neat

Undone Arrears, Left, Postponed, Ran, Ruined, Unlast

Undoubtedly Ay, Certes, Ipso facto, Positively, Sure, To be sure

Undress(ed) Bare, Disarray, Disrobe, En cuerpo, Expose, Négligé, Nude, Nue, Peel, Querpo, Raw, Rough, Self-faced, Spar, Strip, Unapparelled

Undue Premature

Undulate, Undulating Billow, Nebule, Ripple, Roll, Swell, Wave

▷ **Unduly** *may indicate* an anagram

Undyed Greige

Undying Amaranthine, Eternal

Unearth(ly) Astral, Dig, Discover, Disentomb, Exhumate, Indagate

Unease, Uneasiness, Uneasy Angst, Anxious, Creeps, Disquiet, Inquietude, Itchy, Malaise, Queasy, Restive, Shy, Tense, The willies, Trepidation, Uptight, Windy, Womble-cropped

Unedifying Idle

Unembarrassed Blasé, Dégagé

Unemotional Bland, Clinical, Cool, Iceberg, Matter-of-fact, Phlegmatic, Poker-face, Sober, Stolid

Unemployed, Unemployment Drone, Idle, Jobless, Laik, Lake, Latent, Lay-off, Redundant, Residual, Stalko, Surfie

Unending Chronic, Eternal, Lasting, Sempiternal

Unenlightened Ignorant, Nighted, Obscure

Unenthusiastic Cool, Damp, Lackadaisical, Tepid

Unenveloped Achlamydeous

Unequal(led) Aniso-, Disparate, Non(e)such, Scalene, Unjust

Unerring Dead, Exact, Precise

Unestablished Free

Unethical Amoral, Corrupt, Immoral, Sharp, Shyster

Uneven(ness) Accident, Blotchy, Bumpy, Erose, Erratic, Irregular, Jaggy, Patchy, Ragged, Rough, Scratchy, Streaky

▷ **Unevenly** *may indicate* an anagram

Unexceptional Ordinary, Run of the mill, Workaday

Unexciting Flat, Mundane, Staid, Tame

Unexpected(ly) Abrupt, Accidental, Adventitious, Fortuitous, Infra dig, Inopinate, Ironic, Snap, Sodain(e), Sudden, Turn-up, Unawares, Unforeseen, Untoward, Unware, Unwary, Windfall

Unexperienced Strange

Unexplained Mystery, Obscure

Unexploded Live

Unfading Evergreen, Immarcescible

Unfailing Sure

Unfair Bias(s)ed, Crook, Dirty, Discriminatory, Inclement, Iniquitous, Invidious, Mean, Partial, Raw deal, Thick, Unsportsmanlike

Unfaithful Disloyal, Godless, Infidel, Traitor, Two-timing

Unfamiliar Alien, Disinure, Foreign, New, Quaint, Strange

Unfashionable Cube, Daggy, Demode, Dowdy, Lame, Mumsy, Out(moded), Out-of-date, Passé, Square, Vieux jeu

▷ **Unfashionable** *may indicate* 'in' to be removed

Unfasten Undo, Untie, Untruss

Unfathomable Abysmal, Bottomless, Deep

Unfavourable Adverse, Ill, Inimical, Poor, Untoward

Unfeeling Adamant, Callous, Cold, Cruel, Dead, Hard, Inhuman(e), Insensate, Iron-witted, Robotic, Stony-hearted

Unfinished, Unfinishable Crude, Inchoate, Incondite, Raw, Scabble, Scapple, Sisyphean, Stickit

Unfit(ting) Cronk, Disabled, Faulty, Ill, Impair, Inept, Outré, Stiffie, Tre(i)f, Trefa, Unable

▷ **Unfit** *may indicate* an anagram

Unfixed Indeterminate, Isotropic, Loose

Unflappable Stoic

Unfledged Gull

Unflinching Fast, Staunch

Unfocused Glazed

Unfold Deploy, Display, Divulge, Evolve, Interpret, Open, Relate, Spread

Unforced Voluntary

Unforeseen Accident, Sudden, Surprising

Unfortunate(ly) Accursed, Alack, Alas, Catastrophic, Devil, Hapless, Ill-starred, Indecorous, Luckless, Shameless, Sorry, Star-crossed, Unlucky, Worse luck

Unfounded Baseless, Groundless

Unfrequented Lonely
Unfriendly Aloof, Antagonistic, Asocial, Chill(y), Cold, Cold fish, Fraim, Fremd, Fremit, Hostile, Icy, Inhospitable, Remote, Standoffish, Surly, Wintry
Unfruitful Abortive, Barren, Sterile
Unfulfilled Frustrated, Manqué
Ungainly Awkward, Gawkish, Uncouth, Weedy
Ungenerous Cheapskate, Illiberal, Small
Ungodliness, Ungodly Impiety, Pagan, Perfidious, Profane, World
Ungracious Cold, Mesquin(e), Offhand, Rough, Rude
Ungrammatical Anacoluthia
Ungrateful Ingrate, Snaky
Unguent Nard, Pomade, Salve
Ungulate Anta, Antelope, Dinoceras, Eland, Equidae, Hoofed, Moose, Pachydermata, Rhino, Ruminantia, Takin, Tapir, Tylopoda
Unhappily, Unhappy, Unhappiness Blue, Depressed, Disconsolate, Dismal, Distress, Doleful, Downcast, Down-hearted, Dysphoria, Glumpish, Love-lorn, Lovesick, Miserable, Sad, Sore, Tearful, Unlief, Upset
▷ **Unhappily** *may indicate* an anagram
Unharmed Safe, Scatheless, Spared
Unharness Outspan
Unhealthy Bad, Clinic, Diseased, Epinosic, Insalubrious, Morbid, Noxious, Peaky, Poxy, Prurient, Sickly, Twisted
Unholy Profane, Wicked
Unhurried Deliberate, Gradual, Patient
Unhurt Whole-skinned
Unhygienic Grubby
Uniat Maronite, Melchite
Unicorn Ch'i-lin, Coin, Monoceros, Moth, Myth, Narwhal, U
Unidentified Anon, Anonym(ous), Incognito, Ligure
Unification, Unify(ing) Esemplastic, Henotic, Integrate, Risorgimento, Unite
Uniform Abolla, Alike, Battledress, Consistent, Doublet, Dress, Equable, Equal, Even, Flat, Forage-cap, Homogeneous, Homomorphic, Identical, Khaki, Kit, Level, Livery, Monkey suit, Regimentals, Regular, Rig, Robe, Same, Sole, Standard, Steady, Strip, Suit, U, Unvaried
Unimaginative Banausic, Literalistic, Meagre, Pedestrian, Pooter, Short-sighted, Slavish
Unimpaired Entire, Intact, Sound
Unimportant Academic, Cog, Down-the-line, Expendable, Fiddling, Folderol, Footling, Frivolous, Hot air, Idle, Immaterial, Inconsequent, Inconsiderable, Insignificant, Junior, MacGuffin, Makeweight, Miniscule, Minnow, Minutiae, Negligible, Nonentity, Nugatory, Peddling, Peripheral, Petty, Piddling, Small beer, Small-time, Trifling, Trivia(l)
Unimpressible Cynical
Uninformed Ingram
Uninhabited Bundu, Deserted, Lonely
Uninhibited Bold, Free spirit, Raunchy
Uninjured Inviolate
Uninspired, Uninspiring Barren, Bored, Flat, Humdrum, Pedestrian, Pompier, Stereotyped, Tame
Unintelligent Dull, Dumb, Fuckwit, Obtuse, Quo-he, Stupid, Witless
Unintelligible Arcane, Code, Double Dutch, Greek, Inarticulate
Unintentional Inadvertent, Unwitting
Uninterested, Uninteresting Apathetic, Bland, Drab, Dreary, Dry, Dull, Grey, Incurious, Nondescript
Uninterrupted Constant, Continuous, Incessant, Running, Steady

Uninvited Gatecrasher, Interloper, Intruder, Sorner, Trespasser, Umbra
Union(ist) Affiance, African, Agreement, Allegiance, Alliance, Anschluss, Art,
Association, Bed, Benelux, Bond, Brotherhood, Civil, Close, Combination, Company,
Concert, Confederacy, Covalency, Craft, Credit, Customs, Diphthong, Economic, Enosis,
Ensemble, Equity, EU, European, Fasciation, Federal, Federation, French, Frithgild,
Fusion, Group, Guild, Heterogamy, Horizontal, Impanation, Industrial, Integration,
Isogamy, Knight of labour, Latin, Liaison, Liberal, Link-up, Management, Marriage,
Match, Merger, NUM, Nuptials, NUR, NUS, NUT, OILC, Pan-American, Parabiosis,
Pearl, Postal, Print, RU, Rugby, Samiti, Sex, Sherman, Solidarity, Soviet, Splice, Sponsal,
Student, Symphysis, Syngamy, Synizesis, Synostosis, Synthesis, Syssarcosis, Teamsters,
Tenorrhaphy, → **TRADE UNION**, TU, U, UNISON, USDAW, Uxorial, Verein, Vertical,
Vienna, Wedding, Wedlock, Western European, Wield, Yoke, ZANU, Zollverein, Zygosis
Unique(ness) Alone, A-per-se, Farid, Hacceity, Inimitable, Irreplaceable, Lone,
Matchless, Nonesuch, Nonpareil, Nonsuch, One-off, One(-to)-one, Onliest, Only,
Peerless, Rare, Singular, Sole, Sui generis
Unisex(ual) Epicene, Hermaphrodite
Unison Chorus, Harmony, One, Sync
Unit(s) Bargaining, Board of Trade, Brigade, Cadre, Cell, Cohort, Commune, Control,
Corps, Derived, Detachment, Division, Ecosystem, Element, Ensuite, Feedlot, Flight,
Fundamental, Home, Hub, Income, Item, Last, Measure, Message, Module, Monetary,
Panzer, Patrol, Peninsular, Period, Peripheral, Practical, Sealed, Secure, Segment, Shed,
Squad, Stock, Syllable, Team, Terminal, Theme, Timocracy, Tower

---

UNITS

1 letter:	Mol	Nest	Field
K	Nit	Octa	Gauss
X	Ohm	Okta	Henry
	Ped	Phot	Hertz
2 letters:	Rem	Pica	Holon
AU	Rep	Pint	Joule
Em	Tex	Pond	Katal
En	Tod	Rood	Litre
RA	Tog	Sink	Lumen
SI	Var	Slug	Metre
TA		Sone	Monad
	4 letters:	Torr	Mongo
3 letters:	Acre	Vara	Neper
Ace	Barn	Volt	Nepit
Amp	Base	Wall	Ounce
Bar	Baud	Watt	Pixel
Bit	Byte	Wing	Point
BTU	DALY	Yard	Poise
DIN	Dyne		Pound
Dol	Gram	*5 letters:*	Power
EMU	Grav	Codon	Quart
Erg	Gray	Crith	Qubit
Fps	Hank	Cusec	Remen
Gal	Hapu	Daraf	Sabin
GeV	Hide	Darcy	Stere
Ion	Hour	Debye	Stilb
Lux	Inch	Ephah	Stoke
Mho	Mile	Farad	Stone
Mil	Mole	Fermi	Tesla

Therm
Token
Voxel
Weber
Yrneh

6 letters:
Biogen
Bushel
Calory
Dalton
Degree
Denier
Dobson
Emdash
Erlang
Gallon
Jansky
Kelvin
Kilerg
League
Lexeme
Megohm
Micron
Minute
Mongoe
Morgan
Morgen
Newton
Pascal
Phyton
Probit
Radian
Reverb
Second
Sememe
Stokes
Vanity

7 letters:
Archine

Biophor
Calorie
Candela
Centare
Chronon
Congius
Coulomb
Dioptre
Echelon
Energid
Episome
Foot-ton
Fresnel
Gestalt
Gigabit
Gilbert
Hartree
Lambert
Langley
Maceral
Man-hour
Maxwell
Megaton
Micella
Micelle
Milline
Nephron
Oersted
Phoneme
Poundal
Rontgen
Semeion
Siemens
Sievert
Syntagm
Tagmeme
Tripody

8 letters:
Abampere
Absolute

Acre-foot
Angstrom
Bioblast
Biophore
Centiare
Chaldron
Electron
Gigaflop
Gigawatt
Glosseme
Hogshead
Kilowatt
Magneton
Megabyte
Megaflop
Megawatt
Morpheme
Mutchkin
Parasang
Petaflop
Roentgen
Syntagma
Terabyte
Teraflop
Therblig
Vanitory
Watt-hour

9 letters:
Becquerel
Degree day
Foot-pound
Gigahertz
Kilderkin
Kilometre
Light-year
Megahertz
Microinch
Microvolt
Organelle
Singleton

Steradian
Strontium
Tetrapody
Yottabyte
Zettabyte

10 letters:
Centimetre
Centipoise
Dessiatine
Foot-candle
Hoppus-foot
Microcurie
Millilitre
Millimetre
Nanosecond
Person-hour
Picosecond
Ploughgate
Protoplast
Rutherford

11 letters:
Centimorgan
Foot-lambert
Pennyweight

12 letters:
Archiphoneme
Astronomical
Bohr magneton

13 letters:
Electrostatic

15 letters:
Electromagnetic

Unitarian Arian, Paulian, Racovian, Socinian
Unite(d), Uniting, Unity Accrete, Bind, Cement, Coalesce, Combine, Concordant, Connate, Connect, Consolidate, Consubstantiate, Covalent, Ecumenical, Fay, Federal, Federalise, Federate, Fuse, Gene, Graft, Injoint, Inosculate, Join, Joinder, Kingdom, Knit, Lap, Link, Marry, Meint, Meng, Ment, Merge, Meynt, Ming, Nations, Oop, Oup, Piece, Siamese, Solid, States, Tie, Tightknit, Unify, → **WED**, Weld, Yoke
United Ireland Fine Gael
United Kingdom Old Dart, UK
Unity Cohesion, Harmony, One, Solidarity, Sympathy, Togetherness
Univalent Monatomic
Universal, Universe All, Catholic, Cosmogony, Cosmos, Creation, Ecumenic(al), Emma, Expanding, General, Global, Infinite, Inflationary, Island, Macrocosm, Mandala,

Microcosm, Omnify, Oscillating, Sphere, U, Via Lactea, World(wide)

University Academe, Academy, Alma mater, Aston, Bath, Berkeley, Bonn, Brown, Campus, Civic, College, Columbia, Cornell, Dartmouth, Exeter, Gown, Harvard, Heidelberg, Ivy League, Keele, Open, OU, Oxbridge, Pennsylvania, Princeton, Reading, Redbrick, St Andrews, Sorbonne, Stamford, Syracuse, Varsity, Whare wananga, Wittenberg, Witwatersrand, Yale

Unjust(ified) Groundless, Inequitable, Inequity, Iniquitous, Invalid, Tyrannical

Unkempt Bedraggled, Bushy, Dishevelled, Greaseball, Greebo, Mal soigné, Raddled, Ragged, Raggle-taggle, Scody, Scraggy, Scuzzy, Shaggy, Tousy, Touzy, Towsy, Towzy

Unknot Burl

Unknown, Unknowable Acamprosate, Agnostic, Anon, A.N. Other, Hidden, Ign, Incog(nito), Inconnu, N, Nobody, Noumenon, Occult, Quantity, Secret, Soldier, Strange, Symbolic, Tertium quid, Unchartered, Untold, Warrior, X, Y

Unlawful Illegal, Non-licit

Unleavened Azymous

Unless Nisi, Save, Without

Unliable Exempt

Unlicensed Illicit

Unlike(ly) As if, Difform, Disparate, Dubious, Far-fetched, Implausible, Improbable, Inauspicious, Last, Long shot, Outsider, Remote, Tall, Unlich

Unlimited Almighty, Boundless, Indefinite, Measureless, Nth, Open-ended, Pure, Universal, Vast

Unlisted Ex-directory

Unload Disburden, Discharge, Drop, Dump, Jettison, Land, Strip, Unship

Unlock(ed) Bald

Unlucky Donsie, Hapless, Ill(-starred), Ill-omened, Inauspicious, Infaust, Jonah, Misadventure, Misfallen, S(c)hlimazel, Sinister, Stiff, Thirteen, Untoward, Wanchancie, Wanchancy, Wanion

Unman Castrate

Unmannerly Crude, Discourteous, Impolite, Low bred, Rude, Solecism

Unmarried Bachelor, Celibate, Common-law, Single, Spinster

Unmask Expose, Rumble

Unmatched Bye, Champion, Orra, Unique

Unmentionable(s) Bra, Foul, No-no, Secret, → **UNDERWEAR**, Undies

Unmindful Heedless, Oblivious

Unmistakable Clear, Manifest, Plain

Unmitigated Absolute, Arrant, Sheer, Ultra

Unmixed Meer, Me(a)re, Neat, Nett, Pure, Raw, Sincere, Straight

Unmoved, Unmoving Adamant, Doggo, Firm, Serene, Static, Stolid

Unnamed Anon

Unnatural Abnormal, Absonant, Affected, Artificial, Cataphysical, Contrived, Eerie, Far-fetched, Flat, Geep, Irregular, Man-made, Strange, Studied, Transuranian

▷ **Unnaturally** *may indicate* an anagram

Unnecessary De trop, Extra, Gash, Gratuitous, Needless, Otiose, Redundant, Superfluous

Unnerve, Unnerving Creepy, Discouraging, Eerie, Faze, Rattle

Unobserved Backstage, Sly, Unseen

Unobtainable Nemesis

Unobtrusive Discreet, Low profile, Stealthy

Unoccupied Désouvré, Empty, Idle, Inactive, Otiose, Vacant, Void

Unofficial Disestablish, Fringe, Wildcat

Unopened Sealed

Unoriginal Banal, Copy, Derivative, Imitation, Plagiarised, Slavish, Trite

Unorthodox Heretic, Heterodox, Maverick, Off-beat, Off-the-wall, Outré, Stagyrite, Unconventional

▷ **Unorthodox** *may indicate* an anagram

Unpaid Amateur, Brevet, Hon(orary), Outstanding, Voluntary

Unpaired Azygous, Bye

Unpalatable Acid, Bitter, Unsavoury

Unparalleled Sublime, Supreme, Unique

Unpartitioned Aseptate

Unperturbed Bland, Calm, Serene

Unpigmented Albino

Unplanned Disorganised, Impromptu, Improvised, Spontaneous

Unpleasant, Unpleasant person Cow, Creep, Drastic, Fink, Foul, God-awful, Grim, Grotty, Gruesome, Harsh, Hoor, Horrible, Icky, Insalubrious, Invidious, Nasty, Obnoxious, Odious, Offensive, Painful, Pejorative, Poxy, Rank, Rebarbative, Reptile, Scrote, Shady, Shitty, Shocker, Skanky, Snarky, Snot, Sour, Sticky, Thorny, Toerag, Wart

Unploughed Lea-rig

Unpolluted Sterile

Unpopular Avant garde, Detested, Friendless, Hat(e)able

Unpractical Futile, Orra

Unpredictable Aleatory, Capricious, Dicy, Erratic, Maverick, Scatty, Vagary, Wayward, Wild card

Unprepared Ad lib, Cold, Extempore, Impromptu, Last minute, Raw, Unready

Unpretentious Comely, Down home, Hole in the wall, Honest, Modest, Quiet

Unprincipled Amoral, Dishonest, Irregular, Opportunist, Reprobate, Unscrupulous

Unproductive Arid, Atokal, Atokous, Barren, Dead-head, Eild, Fallow, Futile, Infertile, Lean, Poor, Shy, Sterile, Yeld, Yell

Unprofessional Laic, Malpractice

Unprofitable Bootless, Fruitless, Lean, Thankless, Wasted

Unprogressive Inert, Square

Unproportionate Incommensurate

Unprotected Exposed, Nude, Vulnerable

Unpublished Inedited

Unpunctual Tardy

Unqualified Absolute, Arrant, Categoric, Entire, Outright, Perfect, Profound, Pure, Quack, Sheer, Straight, Thorough, Total, Tout court, Utter

Unquestionably, Unquestioning, Unquestioned Absolute, Axiomatic, Certain, Doubtless, Implicit

Unravel(ling) Construe, Denouement, Disentangle, Feaze, Fray, Solve

Unreadable Poker-faced

Unready Unripe

Unreal(istic) Alice-in-Wonderland, Cockamamie, Eidetic, En l'air, Escapist, Fake, Fancied, Illusory, Insubstantial, Mirage, Oneiric, Phantom, Phon(e)y, Planet Zog, Pseudo, Romantic, Sham, Spurious, Virtual

Unreasonable, Unreasoning Absurd, Bigot, Exorbitant, Extreme, Illogical, Irrational, Misguided, Perverse, Rabid, Steep, Tall order

Unrecognised Incognito, Inconnu, Invalid, Thankless, Unsung

Unrefined Bestial, Coarse, Common, Crude, Earthy, Gur, Impure, Natural, Rude, Slob, Vul(g), Vulgar

Unreformed Impenitent

Unregistered Flapping

Unrehearsed Extempore, Impromptu

Unrelenting Implacable, Remorseless, Severe, Stern

Unreliable Broken reed, Chequered, Dodgy, Dubious, Erratic, Fair-weather, Fickle, Flibbertigibbet, Flighty, Fly-by-night, Insincere, Kludge, Shonky, Skitter, Unstable, Wankle, Weak sister, Wonky

Unremarkable Nondescript

Unremitting Dogged, Intensive

Unreserved Implicit

Unresponsive Aloof, Blank, Catatonic, Cold, Frigid, Nastic, Rigor

Unrest Discontent, Ferment, The Troubles

Unrestrained Ariot, Effusive, Extravagant, Free, Freewheeling, Hearty, Homeric, Immoderate, Incontinent, Lax, Lowsit, Rampant, Wanton, Wild

Unreturnable Ace

Unrighteousness Adharma

Unrivalled Nonesuch, Supreme

Unromantic Classic(al), Mundane, Prosaic

Unruffled Calm, Placid, Serene, Smooth, Tranquil

Unruly Anarchic, Bodgie, Buckie, Camstairy, Camsteary, Camsteerie, Coltish, Disruptive, Exception, Fractious, Lawless, Obstreperous, Obstropalous, Ragd(e), Raged, Ragged, Rambunctious, Rampageous, Rattlebag, Refractory, Riotous, Tartar, Torn-down, Turbulent, Turk, Wanton, Wayward, Zoo

▷ **Unruly** *may indicate* an anagram

Unsafe Deathtrap, Fishy, Insecure, Perilous, Precarious, Unsound, Vulnerable

Unsatisfactory, Unsatisfying Bad, Lame, Lemon, Lousy, Meagre, Rocky, Thin, Wanting

Unsavoury Epinosic, On the nose

Unscramble Decode, Decrypt

Unscripted Ad lib

Unscrupulous Chancer, Immoral, Rascally, Sharp, Shyster, Slippery

Unseasonable, Unseasoned Green, Hors de saison, Murken, Raw, Untimely

Unseat Depose, Dethrone, Oust, Overset, Overthrow, Throw

Unseemly Coarse, Improper, Incivil, Indecent, Indecorous, Indign, Risque, Seedy, Untoward

Unseen Masked

Unselfish Altruist, Generous

Unsent Square

Unsentimental Gradgrindery, Hard-nosed

Unsettle(d) Faze, Homeless, Hunky, Indecisive, Nervous, Open, Outstanding, Overdue, Queasy, Restive, Restless, Troublous

▷ **Unsettled** *may indicate* an anagram

Unsexy N, Neuter

Unsheltered Bleak, Exposed, Homeless

Unsight(ed), Unsightly Eyeless, Hideous, Repulsive, Ugly

Unsinning Impeccable, Pure

Unskilled, Unskilful Awkward, Dilutee, Gauche, Green, Hunky, Inexpert, Menial, Raw, Rude, Stumblebum, Talentless, Whitechapel

Unsmiling Agelastic

Unsociable Anchoretic, Grouchy, Solitary, Stay-at-home

Unsolicited Sponte sua

Unsophisticated Alf, Boondocks, Boonies, Bushie, Cornball, Corny, Cracker-barrel, Direct, Down-home, Faux-naïf, Hick, Hillbilly, Homebred, Homespun, Inurbane, Jaap, Jay, Naive, Natural, Primitive, Provincial, Rube, Rustic, Verdant

Unsound Barmy, Infirm, Invalid, Shaky, Wildcat, Wonky

▷ **Unsound** *may indicate* an anagram

Unsparing Severe

Unspeakable Dreadful, Ineffable, Nefandous

Unspecific, Unspecified Broad, General, Generic, Somehow, Such, Vague

Unspoiled, Unspoilt Innocent, Natural, Perfect, Pristine, Pure, Virgin

Unspoken Silent, Tacit

Unspotted Innocent

Unstable, Unsteady Anomic, Astatic, Bockedy, Casual, Crank(y), Dicky, Erratic, Fitful, Flexuose, Flexuous, Flit(ting), Fluidal, Giddy, Groggy, Infirm, Insecure, Labile, Minute-jack, Quicksand, Rickety, Shaky, Shifty, Skittish, Slippy, Tickle, Top-heavy, Tottery, Totty, Variable, Volatile, Walty, Wambling, Wankle, Warby, Wobbly, Wonky

Unstated Concordat, Tacit, Unknown

▸ **Unsteady** *see* UNSTABLE

Unstressed Enclitic

▷ **Unstuck** *may indicate* an anagram

Unsubstantial Aeriform, Airy, Flimsy, Paltry, Shadowy, Slight, Thin, Yeasty

Unsubtle Overt, Sledgehammer

Unsuccessful Abortive, Disastrous, Duff, Futile, Joyless, Manqué, Vain

Unsuitable Amiss, Ill-timed, Impair, Improper, Inapt, Incongruous, Inexpedient, Malapropos, Misbecoming, Unbecoming, Unfit

Unsupported, Unsupportable Astylar, Floating, Stroppy, Unfounded

Unsure Hesitant, Tentative

Unsurpassed All-time, Best, State-of-the-art, Supreme

Unsuspecting Credulous, Innocent, Naive

Unsweetened Brut, Natural

Unsymmetrical Heterauxesis(m), Irregular, Lopsided

Unsympathetic Short shrift

Unsystematic Piecemeal

Unthinking Inadvertent, Mechanical, Not-I, Robotic

Untidy Daggy, Dishevelled, Dog's breakfast, Dog's dinner, Dowd(y), Frowzy, Frump, Guddle, Litterbug, Ragged, Ragtag, Raunchy, Scruff(y), Slipshod, Slovenly, Slut, Straggly, Tatty

▷ **Untidy** *may indicate* an anagram

Untie Free, Undo, Unlace

Until Hasta

Untilled Fallow

Untiring Assiduous

Unto Intil, Until

Untold Secret, Umpteen, Unread, Unred, Vast

Untouchable Burakumin, Dalit, Harijan, Immune, Sacrosanct, Sealed

Untouched Intact, Inviolate, Pristine, Virgin

▷ **Untrained** *may indicate* 'BR' to be removed

Untreated Raw

Untried New, Potential, Virgin

Untroubled Carefree, Insouciant

Untrue, Untruth Apocryphal, Eccentric, Fable, Fabrication, Faithless, False(hood), Lie, Prefabrication, Unleal

Untrustworthy Dishonest, Eel, Fickle, Fly-by-night, Mamzer, Momzer, Shifty, Sleeky, Slippery, Tricky

Untypical Anomalous, Etypic(al), Foreign, Isolated, Unusual

Unused, Unusable Impracticable, New, Over, Wasted

Unusual(ly) Aberration, Abnormal, Atypical, Departure, Different, Exceptional, Extra(ordinary), Eye-popping, Freak, Gonzo, Kinky, New, Novel, Odd, Offbeat, Out-of-the-way, Outré, Particular, Quaint, Queer, Rare (bird), Remarkable, Singular, Special, → STRANGE, Unco, Unique, Untypical, Unwonted, Variant, Wacko

▷ **Unusual** *may indicate* an anagram

Unutterable Ineffable

Unvarying Constant, Eternal, Monotonous, Repetitive, Stable, Static, Uniform

Unveil Expose, Honour, Roll up

Unvoiced Surd

Unwanted De trop, Exile, Gooseberry, Nimby, Outcast, Pidog, Sorn

Unwashed Grubby

Unwavering Steadfast, Steady, Thick and thin

Unwed Celibate, Single

Unwelcome, Unwelcoming Frosty, Hostile, Icy, Lulu, Obtrusive, (Persona) Non grata

Unwell Ailing, Crook, Dicky, Ill, Impure, Indisposed, Poorly, Quazzy, Queasy, Rop(e)y, Rough, Seedy, Shouse, Toxic

Unwholesome Insalutary, Miasmous, Morbid, Noxious, Stinkpot

Unwieldy Cumbersome, Elephantine

Unwilling(ness) Averse, Disinclined, Intestate, Laith, Loath, Loth, Nolition, Nolo, Obdurate, Perforce, Reluctant, Tarrow

Unwind Relax, Straighten, Unclew, Undo, Unreave, Unreeve

▷ **Unwind** *may indicate* an anagram

Unwinnable Catch 22

Unwise(ly) Foolish, Ill-advised, Ill-judged, Impolitic, Imprudent, Inexpedient, Injudicious, Insipient, Rash

Unwitting Accidental, Nescient

Unwonted Inusitate

Unworkable Impossible, Inoperable

Unworldly Naif, Naive

Unworried Carefree

Unworthy Below, Beneath, Golden calf, Indign, Inferior, Infra dig, Substandard, Undeserving

Unwritten Verbal

Unyielding Adamant, Eild, Firm, Granite, Hardline, Inexorable, Inextensible, Intransigent, Obdurate, Relentless, Rigid, Steely, Stern, Stolid, Stubborn, Tough, Unalterable

Unyoke Outspan

Up(on), Upturned, Upper, Uppish, Uppity A, Acockbill, Afoot, Ahead, Antidepressant, Arrogant, Astir, Astray, Astride, Cloud-kissing, Erect, Euphoric, Heavenward, Hep, Horsed, Incitant, Off, On, Overhead, Primo, Quark, Range, Ride, Riding, Risen, Senior, Skyward, Speed, → **UPPER CLASS**, Vamp, Ventral, Wart

Up-anchor Atrip, Weigh

Upbeat Anacrusis, Arsis

Upbraid Abuse, Rebuke, Reproach, Reprove, Scold, Storm, Twit

Upcountry Anabasis, Inland

Update Brief, Refresh, Renew, Report, Sitrep

Upfront Open

Upheaval Cataclysm, Chaos, Eruption, Rummage, Seismic, Shake out, Stir, Upturn, Volcano

▷ **Upheld** *may indicate* 'up' in another word

Uphill Arduous, Borstal, Sisyphean

Uphold Assert, Defend, Maintain, Sustain

Upholster(ed), Upholstery Fleshy, Lampas, Moquette, Tabaret, Trim

Upkeep Support

Upland(s) Alps, Dartmoor, Downs, Hilly, Moor, Wold

Uplift Boost, Edify, Elate, Elevation, Exalt, Hoist, Levitation, Sky

Upmarket Smart

Upper class, Upper crust Aristocrat, County, Crachach, Nobility, Patrician, Posh, Sial, Top-hat, Tweedy, U

Upright(s), Uprightness Aclinic, Anend, Apeak, Apeek, Aplomb, Arrect, Atrip, Erect, Goalpost, Honest, Incorrupt, Jamb, Joanna, Merlon, Moral, Mr Clean, Mullion, Orthograde, Perpendicular, Piano, Pilaster(s), Post, Probity, Rectitude, Roman, Splat, Stanchion, Stares, Stile, Stud, Vertical, Virtuous, White

Uprising Incline, Insurrection, Intifada, Meerut, Naxalbari, Rebellion, Revolt, Tumulus

Uproar(ious) Ballyhoo, Bedlam, Blatancy, Brouhaha, Charivari, Clamour, Clangour, Collieshangie, Commotion, Cry, Din, Dirdam, Dirdum, Durdum, Emeute, Ferment, Flaw, Fracas, Furore, Garboil, Hell, Hooha, Hoopla, Hubbub(oo), Hullabaloo, Hurly(-burly), Imbroglio, Katzenjammer, Madhouse, Noise, Noyes, Outcry, Pandemonium, Racket, Raird, Randan, Razzmatazz, Reird, Riotous, Roister, Romage, Rough music, Rowdedow, Rowdydow(dy), Ruckus, Ruction, Rumpus, Shemozzle, Stramash, Tumult, Turmoil, Utis, Whoobub

Uproot Averruncate, Deracinate, Dislodge, Eradicate, Evict, Outweed, Supplant, Weed

Upset(ting) Aerate, Aggrieve, Alarm, Applecart, Ate, Bother, Capsize, Catastrophe, Choked, Coup, Cowp, Crank, Derail, Derange, Dip, Discomboberate, Discombobulate, Discomfit, Discomfort, Discommode, Disconcert, Dismay, Disquiet, Distraught, Disturb, Dod, Eat, Fuss, Gutted, Heart-rending, Inversion, Keel, Miff, Nauseative, Offend, Overthrow, Overtip, Overturn, Peeve, Perturb, Pip, Pother, Purl, Rattle, Renverse, Rile, Ruffle, Rumple, Sad, Seel, Shake, Shatter, Shook up, Sore, Spill, Tapsalteerie, Teary, Tip, Topple, Trauma, Undo, Unsettled

▷ **Upset** *may indicate* an anagram; a word upside down; or 'tes'

Upshot Outcome, Result, Sequel

Upside down Inverted, Resupinate, Tapsie-teerie, Topsy-turvy

Upsilon Hyoid

Upstart Buckeen, Jumped-up, Mushroom, Parvenu, Vulgarian

▷ **Upstart** *may indicate* 'u'

Upstream Thermal

Upsurge Thrust, Waste

Uptake Shrewdness, Understanding, Wit

Up to Till, Until

Up-to-date Abreast, Advanced, Contemporary, Current, Hip, Mod, New-fashioned, Rad, Right-on, State-of-the-art, Swinging, Topical, Trendy

Upwards Acclivious, Aloft, Antrorse, Cabré

Uranium Depleted, Pitchblende, U, Yellowcake

Urban Civic, Megalopolis, Municipal, Town

Urbane, Urbanity Civil, Debonair, Eutrapelia, Refined, Smooth, Townly

Urchin Arab, Asterias, Brat, Crinoid, Crossfish, Cystoid, Echinoderm, Echinoidea, Echinus, Gamin, Guttersnipe, Gutty, Heart, Mudlark, Nipper, Pedicellaria, Pluteus, Ragamuffin, Sand-dollar, Sea, Sea-egg, Spatangoidea, Spatangus, Street-arab, Townskip

Urge, Urgency, Urgent Acute, Admonish, Ca, Coax, Coerce, Constrain, Crying, Dire, Drive, Egg, Enjoin, Exhort, Exigent, Goad, Hard, Haste, Hie, Hoick, Hunger, Hurry, Id, Immediate, Impel, Imperative, Impulse, Incense, Incite, Insist(ent), Instance, Instigate, Itch, Kick, Libido, Nag, Orexis, Peremptory, Persuade, Press(ing), Prod, Push, Scrub, Set on, Sore, Spur, Stat, Strenuous, Strident, Strong, Threapit, Threepit, Vehement, Wanderlust, Whig, Whim, Yen

▷ **Urgent** *may indicate* 'Ur-gent', viz. Iraqi

Uriah Hittite, Humble, Umble

Urinal Bog, John, Jordan, → **LAVATORY**, Loo, Pissoir

Urinate(d), Urine Chamber-lye, Emiction, Enuresis, Lant, Leak, Micturition, Number one, Oliguria, Pee, Piddle, Piss, Planuria, Relieve, Slash, Stale, Strangury, Tiddle, Uresis, Werris (Creek), Whiz(z), Widdle

Urn(s), Urn-shaped Canopic, Cinerarium, Ewer, Grecian, Lachrymal, Olla, Ossuary, Samovar, Storied, Tea, Urceolate, Vase

Us 's, UK, Uns, We

Usage, Use(r), Used, Utilise Accustomed, Application, Apply, Avail, Boot, Consume, Custom, Deploy, Dow, → **EMPLOY**, End, Enure, Ex, Exercise, Exert, Expend, Exploit, Flesh, Function, Habit, Hand-me-down, Inured, Manner, Milk, Ply, Practice, Sarum, Snorter, Spare, Spent, Sport, Stock, Take, Tradition, Treat, Try, Ure, Utilisation, Wield, With, Wont

Useful Asset, Availing, Commodity, Dow, Expedient, Invaluable, Practical

Useless Appendix, Base, Bung, Cumber, Cumber-ground, Dead duck, Dead-wood, Dud, Empty, Futile, Gewgaw, Grotty, Ground, Idle, Inane, Incapable, Ineffective, Inutile, Lame, Lemon, Nonstarter, Nugatory, Otiose, Plug, Pointless, Sculpin, Sterile, Swap, US, Vain, Void, Wet

Usher Black Rod, Blue Rod, Chobdar, Commissionaire, Conduct(or), Doorman, Escort, Gentleman, Guide, Herald, Huissier, Macer, Rod, Show, Steward

Usual Common, Customary, Habit(ual), Most, Natural, Normal, Ordinary, Routine, Rule, Solito, Standard, Stock, Tipple, Typical, Vanilla, Wont

Usurer, Usury Gombeen, Gripe, Lender, Loanshark, Moneylender, Note-shaver, Shark, Uncle

Usurp(er) Abator, Arrogate, Encroach, Invade

Ut As, Doh, Utah

Utah Ut

Utensil(s) Batterie, Battery, Ca(u)ldron, Canteen, Chopsticks, Colander, Cookware, Corer, Double boiler, Egg-slice, Fish-kettle, Fork, Funnel, Gadget, Grater, Gridiron, Holloware, Implement, Instrument, Jagger, Knife, Mandolin(e), Ricer, Scoop, Sieve, Skillet, Spatula, Spoon, Things, Tool, Whisk, Zester

▶ **Utilise** *see* USAGE

Utilitarian Benthamite, Mill, Practical, Useful

Utility Elec(tricity), Expected, Gas, Public, Water

Utmost Best, Extreme, Farthest, Maximum, Nth

Utopia(n) Adland, Cloud-cuckoo-land, Ideal, More, Pantisocracy, Paradise, Perfect, Shangri-la

Utter(ance), Uttered, Utterly Absolute, Accent, Agrapha, Agraphon, Aread, Arrant, Cry, Dead, Deliver, Dictum, Dog, Downright, Ejaculate, Emit, Enunciate, Express, Extreme, Glossolalia, Issue, Judgement, Lenes, Lenis, Locution, Mint, Most, Oracle, Pass, Phonate, Pronounce, Pure, Quo(th), Rank, Rap, Rattle, Remark, Saw, → SAY, Sheer, Speak, Spout, Stark, State, Syllable, Tell, Thorough, Tongue, Unmitigated, Vend, Vent, Very, Voice

Uvula Staphyle

Vv

V Anti, Bomb, Del, Five, Nabla, See, Sign, Verb, Verse, Versus, Victor(y), Volt, Volume

Vacancy, Vacant Blank, Empty, Glassy, Goaf, Hole, Hollow, Inane, Place, Space, Vacuum

Vacation Holiday, Leave, Long, Non-term, Outing, Recess, Trip, Voidance, Volunteer

Vaccination, Vaccine Antigen, Antiserum, Attenuated, Bacterin, Booster, Cure, HIB, Jenner, MMR, Sabin, Salk, Serum, Subunit

Vacillate, Vacillating Chop, Dither, Feeble, Halt, Hesitate, Shilly-shally, Trimmer, Wabble, Wave(r), Whiffle

Vacuous, Vacuity Blank, Empty, Inane, Toom, Vacant, Void

Vacuum Blank, Cleaner, Dewar, Emptiness, Magnetron, Nothing, Nothingness, Plenum, Thermos®, Torricellian, Ultra-high, Void

Vade-mecum Ench(e)iridion, Notebook

Vagabond Bergie, Gadling, → **GYPSY**, Hobo, Landlo(u)per, Outcast, Picaresque, Rapparee, Romany, Rover, Runabout, Runagate, Tramp

Vagina Box, Crack

Vagrant Beachcomber, Bum, Bummer, Caird, Crusty, Derro, Dosser, Drifter, Flotsam, Gangrel, Gang-there-out, Goliard, Gypsy, Hobo, Landlo(u)per, Lazzarone, Nomad, Patercove, Pikey, Rinthereout, Rogue, Romany, Scatterling, Strag, Straggle, Stroller, Swagman, Tinker, Tinkler, → **TRAMP**, Truant, Vagabond, Walker

Vague(ness) Amorphous, Bleary, Blur, Confused, Dim, Dreamy, Equivocal, General, Hazy, Ill-defined, Ill-headed, Imprecise, Indecisive, Indefinite, Indeterminate, Indistinct, Loose, Mist, Nebulous, Obscure, Shadowy, Woolly-minded

▷ **Vaguely** *may indicate* an anagram

Vain Bootless, Conceited, Coxcomb, Coxcomical, Dandyish, Egoistic, Empty, Fruitless, → **FUTILE**, Hollow, Idle, Peacock, Pompous, Profitless, Proud, Strutting, Unuseful, Useless, Vogie

Vainglory Panache

Valance Pand, Pelmet

Vale Addio, Adieu, Cheerio, Coomb, Dean, Dedham, Dene, Ebbw, Enna, Evesham, Glamorgan, Glen, Tara, Ta-ta, Tempé, Valley

Valediction, Valedictory Apopemptic, Cheerio, Farewell, Tata

Valentine Card, Sweetheart

Valerian All-heal, Cetywall, Greek, Red, Setuale, Setwale, Setwall, Spur

Valet Aid, Andrew, Gentleman's gentleman, Jeames, Jeeves, Man, Passepartout, Quint, Servant, Skip-kennel

Valetudinarian Hypochondriac, Invalid

Valiant Brave, Doughty, Heroic, Redoubtable, Resolute, Stalwart, Stouthearted, Wight

Valid(ity), Validate Confirm, Establish, Just, Legal, Legitimate, Probate, Rational, Right, Sound

Valise Bag, Case, Dorlach, Satchel

Valkyrie Brynhild

Valley Ajalon, Aosta, Argolis, Baca, Barossa, Bekaa, Beqaa, Bolson, Cleavage, Cleugh, Clough, Comb(e), Coomb, Cwm, Dale, Dargle, Dean, Death, Defile, Dell, Den, Dene, Dingle, Dip, Drowned, Dry, Emmental, Gehenna, Ghyll, Glen, Glencoe, Gleneagles, Glyn, Gorge, Graben, Great Glen, Great Rift, Griff(e), Grindelwald, Gulch, Hanging, Haugh, Heuch, Hollow, Hope, Humiliation, Hutt, Imperial, Indus, Ladin, Lagan, Lallan,

Monument, Napa, Nemea, Olympia, Po, Ravine, Rhondda, Ria, Rift, Ruhr, San Fernando, Seaton, Silicon, Slack, Slade, Sonoma, Strath(spey), Strathmore, Tempe, Tophet, Trossachs, Umbria, U-shaped, Valdarno, Vale, Vallambrosa, Vallis Alpes, Water, Water gap, Yosemite

Valour Bravery, Courage, Gallantry, Heroism, Merit, Prowess

Valuable, Valuation, Value(s) Absolute, Acid, Appraise, Appreciate, Apprize, Assess(ment), Asset, Attention, Bargain, Book, Break up, Calibrate, Calorific, Carbon, Checksum, Cherish, CIF, Cop, Cost, Crossover, Datum, Dear, Denomination, Entry, Equity, Esteem, Estimate, Exit, Expected, Face, Feck, Hagberg, Intrinsic, Jew's eye, Limit, Market, Merit, Modulus, Museum piece, Net present, Net realizable, Nominal, Nuisance, Omnium, Par, PH, Place, Prairie, Precious, Premium, Present, Price, Prize, Prys, Q, Quartile, Rarity, Rate, Rateable, Rating, Regard, Residual, Respect, Rogue, Salt, Sentimental, Set, Snob, Steem, Stent, Store, Street, Surplus, Surrender, Taonga, Time, Treasure, Tristimulus, Truth, Valuta, → **WORTH**

Valueless Bum, Fig, Mare's nest, Orra, Trivial, Useless, Worthless

Valve Acorn, Air, Aortic, Ball, Bicuspid, Bleed, Blow, Butterfly, Check, Clack, Cock, Diode, Drawgate, Dynatron, Escape, Eustachian, Exhaust, Flip-flop, Foot, Gate, Induction, Inlet, Magnetron, Mitral, Mixing, Needle, Non-return, Outlet, Pallet, Pentode, Petcock, Piston, Poppet, Pulmonary, Puppet, Radio, Resnatron, Safety, Seacock, Semilunar, Shut-off, Side, Sleeve, Slide, Sluice, Sluicegate, Snifter, Snifting, Stopcock, Suction, Tap, Tetrode, Thermionic, Throttle, Thyratron, Tricuspid, Triode, Turncock, Vacuum, Ventil, Vibrotron

Vamoose Abscond, Decamp, Scarper, Scat, Scram

Vamp Adlib, Charm, Improvise, Maneater, Rehash, Seduce, Siren, Strum, Twiddle

Vampire Bat, Dracula, False, Ghoul, Lamia, Lilith, Nosferatu, Pontianak, Stringes

Van(guard) Advance, Box-car, Brake, Breakdown, Camper, Cart, Cube, Delivery, Dormobile®, Forefront, Foremost, Freight-car, Front, Furniture, Guard's, Head, Kombi®, Lead, Leader(s), Lorry, Loudspeaker, Luggage, Meat wagon, Panel, Panel-truck, Pantechnicon, Patrol-wagon, Prison, Removal, Spearhead, Tartana, Truck, Ute, Wagon

Vanadium V

Vandal(ise), Vandalism Desecrate, Freebooter, Hooligan, Hun, Loot, Pillage, Ravage, Rough, Sab(oteur), Sack, Saracen, Skinhead, Slash, Smash, Trash, Wrecker

Vandyke Beard, Painter

Vane(s) Dog, Fan, Guide, Rudder, Swirl, Telltale, Vexillum, Weather(cock), Web, Wind (tee), Wing

Vanessa Butterfly

Vanilla Pinole

Vanish(ed), Vanishing Cease, Disappear, Disperse, Dissolve, Evanesce(nt), Evaporate, Extinct, Faint(ed), Mizzle, Slope, Transitory, Unbe

Vanity Amour-propre, Arrogance, Ego, Ego-trip, Esteem, Futility, Pomp, Pretension, Pride, Self-conceit, Self-esteem

Vanquish Beat, Conquer, Floor, Master, Overcome, Overwhelm, Rout

Vantage (point) Ascendancy, Coign(e), Height

Vaporise, Vapour Boil, Cloud, Contrail, Effluent, Fog, Fume, Halitus, Inhalant, Iodine, Miasma, Mist, Reek, Roke, Skywriting, → **STEAM**, Steme, Water

▸ **Variable, Variance, Variant, Variation** *see* **VARY(ING)**

Varicose Haemorrhoids

▸ **Varied, Variety** *see* **VARY(ING)**

▹ **Varied** *may indicate* an anagram

Variegate(d) Calico, Dappled, Flecked, Fretted, Harlequin, Motley, Mottle, Pied, Rainbow, Skewbald, Tissue

▹ **Variety of** *may indicate* an anagram

Various Divers(e), Manifold, Multifarious, Separate, Several, Sundry

Various years Vy

Varlet Cad, Knave, Page, Rascal, Rogue

Varnish(ing) Arar, Bee-glue, Copal, Cowdie-gum, Dam(m)ar, Desert, Dope, Dragon's-blood, French polish, Glair, Japan, Lacquer, Lentisk, Mastic, Nail, Nibs, Oil, Resin, Sandarac, Shellac, Spirit, Tung-oil, Tung-tree, Vernis martin, Vernissage

Vary(ing), Variable, Variance, Variant, Variation, Varied, Variety Ablaut, Aelotropy, Alter, Amphoteric, Assorted, Assortment, Breed, Brew, Cepheid, Change, Chequered, Colour, Contrapuntal, Counterpoint, Daedal(e), Dedal, Dependent, Differ, Discrepancy, Diverse, Diversity, Dummy, Eclectic, Eclipsing, Enigma, Farraginous, Fickle, Fluctuating, Form, Grid, Heterodox, Iid, Inconsistent, Inconstant, Independent, Intervening, Isochor, Isopleth, Isotopy, Line, Local, Medley, Mix, Morph, Morphosis, Multifarious, Multiplicity, Music hall, Mutable, Nimrod, Nuance, Nutation, Olio, Omniform, Orthogenesis, Parametric, Partita, Protean, Random, Remedy, Response, Smörgåsbord, Sort, Species, Spice, Sport, Stirps, Stochastic, Strain, String, Timeserver, Tolerance, Twistor, Var, Varicellar-zoster, Vaudeville, Versatile, Versiform, Version, Vicissitude, Vl, Wane, Wax, X, Y, Z

Vase Bronteum, Canopus, Cornucopia, Diota, Hydria, Jardinière, Kalpis, Lachrymal, Lecythus, Lekythos, Lustre, Moon flask, Murr(h)a, Portland, Pot, Potiche, Stamnos, Urn, Vessel

Vasectomy Desexing

Vassal Client, Daimio, Dependant, Feoffee, Lackey, Liege, Liegeman, Man, Manred, Servant, Vavaso(u)r

Vast(ness) Big, Cosmic, Cyclopic, Enormous, Epic, Extensive, Googol, Huge(ous), Immeasurable, Immense, Mighty, Monumental, Ocean, Prodigious

Vat Back, Barrel, Bath, Blunger, Chessel, Copper, Cowl, Cuvée, Fat, Girnel, Keir, Kier, Pressfat, Stand, Tank, Tan-pit, Tub, Tun, Winefat

Vatican Rome, V

Vaudeville Zarzuela

Vaughan Silurist

Vault(ed), Vaulting Arch, Barrel, Cavern, Cellar, Chamber, Charnel house, Clear, Cross, Crypt, Cul-de-four, Cupola, Dome, Dungeon, Fan, Firmament, Fornicate, Groin, Hypogeum, Jump, Kiva, Leap(frog), Lierne, Mausoleum, Ossuary, Palm, Pend, Pendentive, Pole, Rib, Safe, Sepulchre, Serdab, Severy, Shade, Souterrain, Tholus, Tomb, Tunnel, Undercroft, Underpitch, Vaut, Wagon, Weem, Wine

▷ **Vault** *may indicate* an anagram

Vaunt Boast, Brag, Crow

Veal Escalope, Fricandeau, Galantine, Scallop, Schnitzel, Vituline, Wiener schnitzel

Vector, Vector operator Del, Dyad, Expression, Nabla, Phasor, Polar, Radius

Veda Yajurveda

Veer Bag, Boxhaul, Broach, Clubhaul, Deviate, Draw, Gybe, Splay, Swerve, Tack, Turn, Wear, Yaw

Veg(etate), Vegetator, Vegetation Alga, Biome, Brush, Cover, Flora, Fynbos, Gar(r)igue, Greenery, Herb, Laze, Lemna, Maquis, Quadrat, Scrub, Stagnate, Sudd, Transect

Vegan Parev(e), Parve

Vegetable(s) Flora, Hastings, Inert, Jardinière, Plant, Root, Salad, Sauce, Truck

---

VEGETABLES

3 *letters:*	4 *letters:*		5 *letters:*
Alu	Aloo	Okra	Beans
Oca	Beet	Okro	Chana
Pea	Cole	Sium	Chard
Udo	Guar	Spud	Chive
Yam	Kale	Taro	Choko
	Leek	Wort	Chufa
	Neep		Crout

Ingan	Pomato	Salsify	Radicchio
Mooli	Potato	Shallot	Rocambole
Navew	Pratie	Skirret	Romanesco
Onion	Quinoa	Spinach	Succotash
Orach	Radish	Spinage	Sweet corn
Pease	Rapini	Sprouts	Tonka-bean
Pulse	Sorrel	Succory	Turnip top
Sabji	Squash	Triffid	
Savoy	Tomato	Witloof	**10 letters:**
Sibol	Turnip		Alexanders
Swede	Wakame	**8 letters:**	Cavalo nero
		Beetroot	Chiffonade
6 letters:	**7 letters:**	Borecole	Runner bean
Allium	Brinjal	Brassica	Sauerkraut
Batata	Cabbage	Broccoli	Scorzonera
Calalu	Calaloo	Celeriac	String bean
Camote	Cardoon	Chick pea	Swiss chard
Carrot	Castock	Cucumber	Tuscan kale
Catalu	Cataloo	Escarole	
Celery	Chayote	Eschalot	**11 letters:**
Coulis	Chicory	Kohlrabi	Bamboo shoot
Daikon	Cocoyam	Leaf-beet	Cauliflower
Endive	Collard	Mirepoix	Chinese leaf
Fennel	Custock	Rutabaga	Ratatouille
Frisée	Filasse	Samphire	Spinach-beet
Garlic	Gherkin	Zucchini	Spring onion
Greens	Legumen		Sweet potato
Jicama	Lettuce	**9 letters:**	
Kumara	Mangold	Artichoke	**12 letters:**
Lablab	Matooke	Asparagus	Corn-on-the-cob
Legume	Olitory	Aubergine	Mangel-wurzel
Mangel	Pak-choi	Calabrese	Marrow-squash
Marrow	Parsnip	Colcannon	
Matoke	Pimento	Courgette	**18 letters:**
Mibuna	Pot herb	Finocchio	Jerusalem artichoke
Mizuna	Pottage	Macedoine	
Orache	Pumpkin	Mangetout	
Pepper	Rampion	Primavera	

Vegetable extract Solanine
Vegetarian Herbivore, Lactarian, Maigre, Meatless, Parev(e), Parve, Pythagorean, Vegan, Veggie
Vehemence, Vehement(ly) Amain, Ardent, Fervid, Forcible, Frenzy, Heat, Hot, Intense, Violent
Vehicle Agent, Artic, Articulated, Base, Commercial, Conveyance, Half-track, High occupancy, Hybrid, Machine, Means, Medium, Multipurpose, Offroad, Oil, Recovery, Recreational, Re-entry, Space, Superload, Tempera, Tracked, Ute, Utility, Wheels, Wrecker

VEHICLES

3 letters:	Car	**4 letters:**	Duck
ATV	Fly	Biga	Jeep®
Bus	LEM	Cart	Kago
Cab	SUV	Dray	Kart

Limo
MIRV
Quad
Rego
Scow
Shay
Sled
Taxi
Tram
Trap

5 letters:
Brake
Buggy
Crate
Cycle
Delta
Float
Go-Ped®
Lorry
Motor
Reggo
Rover
Soyuz
Sulky
Tip-up
Tonga
Truck
Turbo
Vespa®
Wagon

6 letters:
Boxcar
Camper
Dennet
Estate
Fiacre
Gharri
Gharry
Go-cart
Go-kart
Hansom
Hearse
Hummer
Humvee®
Jet-Ski
Jingle

Jinker
Jitney
Koneke
Landau
Launch
Limber
Litter
Matatu
Pick-up
Put-put
Samlor
Skibob
Skidoo®
Sledge
Sleigh
Sno-Cat®
Spider
Surrey
Tardis
Tricar
Troika
Tuk tuk
Vahana
Weasel

7 letters:
Air taxi
Amtrack
Blokart
Capsule
Caravan
Casspir
Channel
Chariot
Crew cab
Dog-cart
Gritter
Growler
Jeepney
Minibus
Minicab
Minivan
Norimon
Pedicab
Phaeton
Rail bus
Ricksha
Shebang

Shuttle
Sidecar
Taxi cab
Tipcart
Tractor
Trailer
Trishaw
Trolley
Tumbril
Volante

8 letters:
Brancard
Cable car
Carry-all
Curricle
Dragster
Rickshaw
Runabout
Sport ute
Stanhope
Steam-car
Tarantas
Tricycle
Trimotor
Unicycle

9 letters:
Ambulance
Autocycle
Battlebus
Buckboard
Dormobile®
Dune buggy
Estate car
Gladstone
Hatchback
Land Rover®
Motorhome
Sand-yacht
Tarantass
Tumble-car
Two-seater
Wagonette
Winnebago

10 letters:
All-terrain

Earth-mover
Four-by-four
Four-seater
Gas-guzzler
Hovercraft
Juggernaut
Load-lugger
Mammy wagon
Roadroller
Rust-bucket
Snowmobile
Snowplough
Trolleybus
Tumble-cart
Two-wheeler
Velocipede

11 letters:
People-mover
Semitrailer
Transporter
Wheelbarrow

12 letters:
Autorickshaw
Double-decker
Micro-scooter
Pantechnicon
Perambulator
Single-decker
Space shuttle
Station wagon
Three-wheeler

13 letters:
Paddock-basher
Penny-farthing
People carrier

14 letters:
Chelsea tractor

16 letters:
Personnel carrier

Veil Burk(h)a, Calyptra, Chad(d)ar, Chador, Chuddah, Chuddar, Cloud, Cover, Curtain, Envelop, Eucharistic, Hejab, Hide, Hijab, Humeral, Kalyptra, Khimar, Kiss-me, Lambrequin, Mantilla, Mist, Nikab, Niqab, Obscure, Purdah, Sacramental, Scene, Sudarium, Veale, Volet, Weeper, Wimple, Yashmak

Vein Artery, Azygas, Basilic, Brachiocephalic, Coronary, Costa, Diploic, Epithermal,

Fahlband, Gate, Hemiazygous, H(a)emorrhoid, Innominate, Jugular, Ledge, Lode, Mainline, Media, Midrib, Mood, Naevus, Nervure, Organic, Outcrop, Percurrent, Pipe, Portal, Postcava, Precava, Pulmonary, Radius, Rake, Reef, Rib, Saphena, Sectorial, Spur, Stockwork, Stringer, Style, Thread, Varicose, Varix, Vena, Venule, Vorticose

Vellum Cutch, Japanese, Kutch, Parchment

Velocity Angular, Circular, Escape, Mustard, Muzzle, Orbital, Parabolic, Radial, Rate, Speed, Terminal, V

Velvet(y) Bagheera, Chenille, Moleskin, National, Panne, Pile, Three-pile, Velour, Velure, Villose, Villous

Venal Corruptible, Mercenary, Sale

Vend(or), Vending Auctor, Automat, Hawk, Peddle, Pedlar, Rep, Sammy, Sell, Sutler

Vendetta Feud

Veneer Facade, Gloss, Varnish

Venerable Aged, August, Augustus, Bede, Guru, Hoary, Iconic, Sacred, Sage, Vintage

Venerate, Veneration Adore, Awe, Douleia, Dulia, Filiopietistic, GOM, Hallow, Homage, Honour, Hyperdulia, Idolise, Latria, Respect, Revere, Worship

Venereal NSU, VD

Venery Chase

Venetian Aldine, Blind, Doge, Gobbo, Polo

Vengeance, Vengeful Commination, Erinyes, Reprisal, Ultion, Vindictive, Wan(n)ion, Wrack, Wreak

Venial Base, Excusable

Venice La Serenissima

Venison Cervena, Deer

Venom(ous) Gall, Gila, Jamestown-weed, Jim(p)son-weed, Poison, Rancour, Solpuga, Spite, Toxic, Virus, Zootoxin

Vent Airway, Aperture, Belch, Chimney, Emit, Express, Fumarole, Hornito, Issue, Louver, Louvre, Ostiole, Outlet, Smoker, Solfatara, Spiracle, Undercast, Wreak

Venter Uterus

Ventilate, Ventilator Air, Air-brick, Air-hole, Discuss, Draught, Express, Louvre, Plenum, Shaft, Voice, Windsail, Windway, Winze

Venture(d) Ante, Assay, Bet, Callet, Chance, Dare, Daur, Durst, Enterprise, Flutter, Foray, Handsel, Hazard, Jump, Opine, Presume, Promotion, Prostitute, Risk, Spec, Strive, Throw

Venue Bout, Locale, Place, Showground, Stadium, Stateroom, Tryst, Visne

Venus Clam, Cohog, Cytherean, Hesper(us), Love, Lucifer, Morning-star, Phosphorus, Primavera, Quahaug, Quahog, Rokeby, Vesper

Venus fly-trap Dionaea

Veracity, Veracious Accurate, Factual, Sincere, Truth(ful)

Veranda(h) Balcony, Gallery, Lanai, Patio, Piazza, Porch, Sleep-out, Stoep, Stoop, Terrace

Verb(al), Verbs Active, Argy-bargy, Auxiliary, Causative, Conative, Copula, Ergative, Factitive, Finite, Infinitive, Intransitive, Irregular, Modal, Passive, Perfective, Performative, Phrasal, Preterite, Stative, Transitive, Vb, Word-of-mouth

Verbascum Mullein

Verbatim Literally

Verbena Vervain

Verbose, Verbosity Gassy, Padding, Prolix, Talkative, Wordy

Verdant Lush

Verdict Decision, Fatwah, Formal, Judg(e)ment, Majority, Narrative, Open, Opinion, Pronouncement, Resolution, Ruling, Special

Verdigris Aeruginous, Patina

Verge Border, Brink, → EDGE, Hard shoulder, Incline, Long paddock, Rim, Threshold

Verger Beadle, Pew-opener

Verify, Verification Affirm, Ascertain, Check, Confirm, Constatation, Control, Crosscheck, Prove, Validate
Verily Yea
Verisimilitude Artistic, Authenticity, Credibility
Verity Fact, Sooth, Truth
Vermifuge Cow(h)age, Cowitch
Vermilion Cinnabar, Minium, Red
Vermin(ous) Carrion, Catawampus, Lice, Mice, Pest, Ratty, → **RODENT**, Scum
Vermouth Absinthiated, French, It(alian), Martini®
Vernacular Common, Dialect, Idiom, Jargon, Lingo, Native, Patois, Slang, Vulgate
Veronica Hebe, Hen-bit, Speedwell
Verruca Plantar wart, Wart
Versatile Adaptable, All-rounder, Flexible, Handy, Many-sided, Multipurpose, Protean, Resourceful
Verse(s), Versed Dactyl, Free, Linked, Logaoedic, Passus, Poetry, Political, Reported, → **RHYME**, System

---

VERSES

1 letter:
V

3 letters:
Fit

4 letters:
Awdl
Blad
Duan
Epic
Epos
Fitt
Hymn
Line
Neck
Poem
Rime
Sijo
Song
Vers

5 letters:
Blank
Blaud
Canto
Comus
Epode
Fitte
Fytte
Gazal
Haiku
Hokku
Ionic
Lyric

Meter
Poesy
Renga
Rubai
Spasm
Stave
Tanka
Tract
Triad

6 letters:
Adonic
Ballad
Burden
Ghazal
Ghazel
Gnomic
Haikai
Heroic
Jingle
Laisse
Miurus
Octave
Pantun
Rondel
Scazon
Senary
Sonnet
Stanza
Strain
Tenson
Tercet
Vulgus

7 letters:
Alcaics
Couplet
Dimeter
Elegiac
Epigram
Fabliau
Huitain
Leonine
Pantoum
Pennill
Prosody
Pythian
Rondeau
Sapphic
Sestina
Sestine
Sixaine
Stiches
Strophe
Tiercet
Triolet
Tripody

8 letters:
Cinquain
Clerihew
Doggerel
Glyconic
Hexapody
Kyrielle
Madrigal
Nonsense
Pindaric
Quatrain

Rhopalic
Rove-over
Rubaiyat
Scansion
Senarius
Sing-song
Sirvente
Syllabic
Terzetta
Trimeter
Tristich
Versicle

9 letters:
Amphigory
Asclepiad
Beatitude
Dithyramb
Ditrochee
Goliardic
Hexameter
Macaronic
Monometer
Monorhyme
Monostich
Octameter
Octastich
Saturnian
Stornello
Terza rima
Vers libre

10 letters:
Asynartete
Catalectic

Cynghanedd	Serpentine	Hudibrastic	Hudibrastics
Fescennine	Tetrameter	Octastichon	Octosyllabic
Hypermeter	Tetrastich	Riding-rhyme	
Mock-heroic	Villanelle	Septenarius	*14 letters:*
Ottava rima			Longs and shorts
Pennillion	*11 letters:*	*12 letters:*	
Pentameter	Acatalectic	Archilochian	*15 letters:*
Rhyme-royal	Alexandrine	Asclepiadean	Poulter's measure

▷ **Versed** *may indicate* reversed
Versed sine Sagitta
Versifier, Versification Lyricist, Poetaster, Prosody, Rhymer, Rhymester
Version Account, Adaptation, Authorised, Cephalic, Cover, Edition, Form, Paraphrase, Rede, Remake, Rendering, Rendition, Revised, Revision, Rhemish, Standard, Summary, Translation, Urtext, Variorum
Vertebra(e), Vertebrate Agnathan, Amniote, Amphioxus, Ascidian, Atlas, Axis, Bone, Centrum, Cervical, Chordae, Coccyx, Cyclostome, Dorsal, Foetus, Gnathostome, Ichthyopsida, Lamprey, Lumbar, Placoderm, Reptile, Sacral, Sauropsida, Spondyl, Tetrapod, Tunicata, Vermis
Vertex Apex, Crest, Crown, Summit, Zenith
Vertical Apeak, Apeek, Atrip, Erect, Lapse, Montant, Muntin(g), Ordinate, Perpendicular, Plumb, Prime, Sheer, Standing, Stemmed, Stile, Upright
Vertigo Dinic, Dizziness, Fainting, Giddiness, Megrim, Nausea, Staggers, Whirling
Vertue Visne
Verve Dash, Energy, Go, Gusto, Panache, Vigour
Very (good, well) A1, Ae, Assai, Awfully, Boffo, Bonzer, Boshta, Boshter, Dashed, Dead, Def, Ever, Extreme(ly), Fell, Frightfully, Full, Gey, Grouse, Heap, Hellova, Helluva, Highly, Hugely, Jolly, Keen, Light, Mighty, Molto, Much, OK, Opt, Precious, Precise, Purler, Real, Right, Self same, So, Sore, Stinking, Très, Unco, Utter, V, VG, Way
Vesicle Ampul, Bladder
Vespers Evensong, Lychnic, Placebo, Sicilian
Vessel → **BOAT**, Capillary, Container, Craft, Dish, Lacteal, Logistics, Motor, Pressure, Receptacle, Seed, → **SHIP**, Tomentum, Utensil, Vascular, Weaker

VESSELS

3 letters:	Brig	Zulu	Mazer
Bin	Buss		Oiler
Cog	Cask	*5 letters:*	Phial
Cup	Cowl	Aorta	Pokal
Dow	Dhow	Blood	Quart
Fat	Etna	Cogue	Round
Obo	Font	Crare	Scoop
Pan	Grab	Crewe	Shell
Pig	Horn	Crock	Sloop
Pyx	Lota	Cruet	Stean
Tub	Olpe	Cruse	Steen
Urn	Raft	Cupel	Stoop
Vas	Skin	Dandy	Stoup
Vat	Snow	Dixie	Tazza
	Vase	Gourd	Varix
4 letters:	Vein	Ketch	Xebec
Back	Vena	Laver	Zabra
Bowl	Vial	Lotah	

6 letters:
Aludel
Argyle
Argyll
Artery
Banker
Beaker
Bicker
Bouget
Bucket
Carafe
Carboy
Chatty
Copper
Crayer
Dinghy
Dogger
Dolium
Elutor
Flagon
Frigot
Galiot
Galley
Goblet
Goglet
Guglet
Humpen
Jam jar
Jet-ski
Kettle
Lorcha
Mortar
Noggin
Retort
Rumkin
Sailer
Sampan
Sconce

Settee
Shippo
Situla
Steane
Tassie
Trough
Tureen
Urinal
Venule
Wherry

7 letters:
Amphora
Ampoule
Ampulla
Canteen
Chalice
Cistern
Coaster
Costrel
Creamer
Cresset
Cuvette
Cyathus
Dredger
Drifter
Felucca
Firepan
Four oar
Frigate
Gaff-rig
Galleon
Galliot
Gunship
Gurglet
Jugular
Mudscow
Patamar

Pinnace
Pirogue
Pitcher
Polacca
Precava
Sharpie
Steamer
Stewpot
Tankard
Terreen
Vedette
Washpot

8 letters:
Billycan
Calabash
Cauldron
Ciborium
Colander
Coolamon
Crucible
Cucurbit
Decanter
Figuline
Flatboat
Galleass
Galliass
Gallipot
Gallivat
Hoveller
Hydroski
Jerrican
Longboat
Monteith
Pancheon
Panchion
Pannikin
Schooner

Showboat
Sinusoid
Trimaran
Workboat

9 letters:
Alcarraza
Autoclave
Bucentaur
Calandria
Casserole
Cullender
Destroyer
Hydrofoil
Privateer
Tappit-hen
Whaleback
Whaleboat

10 letters:
Bathyscaph
Deep-sinker
Jardinière
Triaconter

11 letters:
Aspersorium
Bathyscaphe
Side-wheeler

12 letters:
Fore-and-after
Lachrymatory
Stern-wheeler
Sternwheeler

Vest Beset, Confer, Crop top, Gilet, Modesty, Rash, Semmit, Singlet, Skivvy, Spencer, Sticharion, String, Undercoat, Undershirt, Waistcoat

Vestibule Anteroom, Atrium, Entry, Exedra, Foyer, Hall, Lobby, Narthex, Oeil-de-boeuf, Porch, Portico, Pronaos, Tambour

Vestige Hint, Mark, Mention, Shadow, Sign, Trace

Vestment Alb, Breastplate, Canonicals, Chasuble, Chimar, Chimer(e), Cotta, Dalmatic, Ephod, Fannel, Fanon, Garb, → **GARMENT**, Maniple, Mantelletta, Omophorion, Pallium, Parament, Ph(a)elonian, Pontificals, Raiment, Rational, Rochet, Rocquet, Sakkos, Sticharion, Stole, Superhumeral, Surplice, Tunic(le)

Vestry Common, Sacristy, Select

Vet(ting), Veterinary, Vets Censor, Check, Doc(tor), Examine, Ex-serviceman, Herriot, Horse-doctor, Inspect, OK, Positive, Screen, Veteran, Zoiatria, Zootherapy

Vetch Bitter, Ers, Fitch, Kidney, Locoweed, Milk, Tare, Tine

Veteran BL, Expert, GAR, Master, Old-stager, Oldster, Old sweat, Old-timer, Old 'un, Retread, Seasoned, Soldier, Stager, Stalwart, Stalworth, Vet, War-horse, Warrior

▷ **Veteran** *may indicate* 'obsolete'

Veto Ban, Bar, Blackball, Debar, Item, Line-item, Local, Negative, Pocket, Reject, Taboo, Tabu

Vex(ing), Vexatious, Vexed Ail, Anger, Annoy, Bepester, Bother, Chagrin, Debate, Fret, Gall, Grieve, Harass, Haze, Irritate, Madden, Mortify, Noy, Peeve, Pester, Rankle, Rile, Sore, Spite, Tease, Torment, Trouble, Trying, Worrisome

Vexation(s) Barrator, Chagrin, Drat, Fashery, Grief, Humph, Nuisance, Pique, Spite, Trouble, Try, Umph

Vexillum Web

Via By, Per, Through

Viable Economic, Going, Healthy, Possible

Vial Spirit-level

Viand Cate

Vibrate, Vibration(s), Vibrant Atmosphere, Chatter, Diadrom, Dinnle, Dirl, Energetic, Flutter, Free, Fremitus, Harmonogram, Hotter, Jar, Judder, Oscillate, Plangent, Pulse, Purr, Quake, Resonance, Resonant, Rumble, Seiche, Shimmy, Shudder, Thrill, Throb, Tingle, Tremble, Tremor, Trill, Trillo, Twinkle, Uvular, Wag, Whir(r)

Viburnum Opulus

Vicar Apostolic, Bray, Choral, Elton, Forane, General, Incumbent, Lay, Pastoral, Plenarty, Primrose, Rector, Rev(erend), Trimmer

Vice Clamp, Cramp, Crime, Deputy, Eale, Evil, Foible, Greed, Iniquity, Instead, Jaws, Regent, Second (in command), → **SIN**, Stair

Vice-president Croupier, Veep

Viceroy Khedive, Nawab, Provost, Satrap, Willingdon

Vichy (water) Eau, Milice

Vicinity Area, Environs, Hereabouts, Locality, Neighbourhood, Region, Round about

Vicious Brutal, Cruel, Flagitious, Hotbed, Lethal, Vitriolic

Victim(s) Abel, Angel, Butt, Casualty, Currie, Curry, Dupe, Easy meat, Fall guy, Fashion, Frame, Hitlist, Host, Lay-down, Mark, Martyr, Nebbich, Neb(b)ish, Pathic, Patsy, Pigeon, Prey, Quarry, Sacrifice, Scapegoat, Sitting duck, Target

Victor(y) Bangster, Banzai, Beater, Cadmean, Cannae, Captor, Champ(ion), Conqueror, Conquest, Epinicion, Epinikion, Eunice, Flagship, Fool's mate, Gree, Gris, Hallelujah, Hugo, Jai, Jai Hind, Kobe, Landslide, Lepanto, Ludorum, Mature, Moral, Nike, Palm, Philippi, Pyrrhic, Romper, Runaway, Scalp, Shut-out, Signal, Squeaker, Triumph, V, VE (day), Vee, Vic, Walk-away, Walkover, Win(ner)

Victoria(n) Aussie, Empress, Plum, Prig, Prude(nt), Station, Terminus

Victualler Caterer, Grocer, Licensed, Purveyor, Supplier, Vivandière

Video(-tape) Betacam®, Cassette, Digital, Full-motion, Interactive, Laser vision, Minitel, Pixelation, Promo, Quadruplex, Reverse, Scratch, Still, Vera

Vie Compete, Contend, Emulate, Strive

Vienna Wien

Vietcong Charley, Charlie

Vietnam(ese) Cham, Tonkin, VN

View(er) Aim, Angle, Aspect, Attitude, Behold, Belief, Bird's eye, Cineaste, Consensus, Consider, Cosmorama, Cutaway, Dekko, Dogma, Doxy, Endoscope, Exploded, Eye, Facet, Gander, Glimpse, Grandstand, Helicopter, Heresy, Idea, Introspect, Kaleidoscope, Landscape, Line, Notion, Observe, Opinion, Optic®, Outlook, Pan, Panorama, Parallax, Perspective, Point, Private, Profile, → **PROSPECT**, Scan, Scape, Scene(ry), Scope, See, Sight, Sightlined, Skyscape, Slant, Snapshot, Specular, Spyglass, Standpoint, Stereoscope, Strain, Survey, Synop(sis), Tenet, Terrain, Thanatopsis, Theory, Vantage-point, Veduta, Vista, Visto, Watch, Witness, Worm's eye

Viewpoint Angle, Attitude, Belvedere, Conspectus, Eyeshot, Grandstand, Instance, Observatory, Perspective, Sight, Sightline, Tendentious, Voxpop, Watch tower

Vigil, Vigilant(e) Awake, Aware, Baseej, Basij, Deathwatch, Eve, Guardian angel,

Hawk-eyed, Lyke-wake, Pernoctate, Wake, Wake-rife, Wary, Watch, Waukrife, Whitecap

Vignette Print, Profile, Sketch

Vigorous(ly), Vigour Aggressive, Athletic, Bant, Bellona, Billy-o, Billy-oh, Birr, Blooming, Bouncing, Brio, Brisk, Con brio, Cracking, Drastic, Élan, Emphatic, Energetic, Flame, Forceful, Full-blooded, Furioso, Go, Green, Heart(y), Heterosis, Hybrid, Lush, Lustihood, Lustique, Lusty, Moxie, P, Pep, Pith, Potency, Punchy, Pzazz, Racy, Rank, Raucle, Robust, Round, Rude, Smeddum, Spirit, Sprack, Sprag, Steam, Sthenic, Stingo, Strength, Strenuous, Strong, Thews, Tireless, Tone, Tooth and nail, Trenchant, Two-fisted, Up, Vegete, Vim, Vinegar, Vitality, Vivid, Vivo, Voema, Zip

▷ **Vigorously** *may indicate* an anagram

Viking Dane, Norseman, Raider, Rollo, R(y)urik, Sea king, Sea wolf, Varangian

Vile(ness) Base, Corrupt, Depraved, Dregs, Durance, Earthly, Infamy, Mean, Offensive, Scurvy, Vicious

Vilify, Vilification Slander, Smear

Villa Bastide, Chalet, Dacha, House

Village Aldea, Auburn, Borghetto, Burg, Clachan, Corporate, Dorp, Endship, Global, Gram, Greenwich, Hamlet, Kaik, Kainga, Kampong, Kirkton, Kraal, Legoland, Manyat(t)a, Mir, Outlet, Outport, Pit, Pueblo, Rancheria, Rancherie, Shtetl, Skara Brae, Thorp(e), Ujamaa, Vill, Wick

Villain(y) Baddy, Bluebeard, Bravo, Crim(inal), Crime, Dastard, Dog, Fagin, Heavy, Iago, Knave, Lawbreaker, Macaire, Miscreant, Mohock, Nefarious, Ogre, Reprobate, Rogue, Scab, Scelerat, Scoundrel, Skelm, Tearaway, Traitor

Villein Bordar, Churl, Serf

Vim Go, Vigour, Vitality, Zing

Vincent Van Gogh

Vindicate, Vindication Absolve, Acquit, Apologia, Avenge, Clear, Compurgation, Darraign(e), Darrain(e), Darrayn, Defend, Deraign, Exculpate, Justify

Vindictive Bunny-boiler, Hostile, Malevolent, Repay(ing), Spiteful, Vengeful

Vine(yard) Akatea, Ampelopsis, Ayahuasco, Balloon, Balsam apple, Bine, Bush rope, Château, Clinging, Clos, Colocynth, Cross, Cru, Cubeb, Cypress, Dodder, Domaine, Grapery, Hop, Idaean, Ivy, Kangaroo, Kudzu, Lawyer, Liana, Martha's, Matrimony, Muskmelon, Naboth's, Potato, Puncture, Quinta, Russian, Sarsaparilla, Stephanotis, Supplejack, Swallowwort, Trumpet, Turpeth, Vitis, Winery, Wonga-wonga, Yam, Yquem

Vinegar Acetic, Acetum, Alegar, Balsam, Balsamic, Eisel(l), Esile, Malt, Oxymel, Tarragon, Wine, Wood

Vintage Classic, Crack, Cru, Old, Quality

Viol(a), Violet African, Alto, Amethyst, Archil, Crystal, Dame's, Dog, Dog's tooth, Gamba, Garden, Gentian, Gridelin, Heart's ease, Hesperis, Ianthine, Indole, Ionone, Kiss-me, Lyra, Mauve, Methyl, Neapolitan, Orchil, Pansy, Parma, Prater, Quint(e), Rock, Saintpaulia, Shrinking, Sweet, Tenor, Visual, Water

Violate, Violating, Violation Abuse, Breach, Contravene, Defile, Desecrate, Fract, Infraction, → **INFRINGE**, March-treason, Outrage, Peccant, Rape, Ravish, Solecism, Stuprate, Transgress, Trespass

Violence, Violent(ly) Acquaintance, Amain, Attentat, Bangster, Berserk, Bloody, Brutal, Brute force, Cataclysmic, Crude, Drastic, Droog, Extreme, Fierce, Flagrant, Force, Frenzied, Furious, Heady, Het, High, Hot, Inbreak, Mighty, Onset, Rage, Rampage, Rampant, Riot, Rough, Rough stuff, Rude, Rumbustious, Savage, Severe, Slap, Stormy, Strongarm, Ta(r)tar, Tearaway, Terrorism, Thuggery, Tinderbox, Tub-thumping, Vehement, Vie, Wrath

Violet Crystal, Ianthine, Iodine, Lilac, Shrinking, → **VIOLA**

Violin(ist), Violin-maker, Violin-shaped Alto, Amati, Cremona, Fiddle, Griddle, Gu(e), Guarneri(us), Guarnieri, Kennedy, Kit, Kubelik, Leader, Luthier, Menuhin, Nero, Oistrakh, Paganini, Pandurate, Rebeck, Rote, Stradivarius

VIP Bashaw, Bigshot, Bigwig, Brass, Cheese, Cob, Effendi, Envoy, Grandee, Imago, Kingpin, Magnate, Magnifico, Mugwump, Nabob, Nib, Nob, Pot, Snob, Someone, Swell, Tuft, Tycoon, Worthy

Viper Asp, Cerastes, Gaboon, Horned, Judas, Pit, Rattlesnake, River-jack, Russell's, Sand, Saw-scaled, → **SNAKE**, Traitor, Villain

Virago Amazon, Battle-axe, Beldam(e), Harpy, Randy, Shrew, Termagant

Virgil Maro

Virgin(al), Virginity, Virgin Mary Airline, Blessed, Celibate, Chaste, Cherry, Extra, Intact, Ladykin, Madonna, Maiden, Maidenhead, Maidenhood, Marian, May, New, Our lady, Pan(h)agia, Parthenos, Pietà, Pucel(l)age, Pucelle, Pure, Queen, Snood, Tarpeia, Theotokos, Untainted, Vestal, Zodiacal

Virginia(n) Creeper, Old Dominion, Tuckahoe, Va, Wade

Virile, Virility Energetic, Machismo, Macho, Male, Manly, Red-blooded

Virtu Curio

Virtue(s), Virtuous, Virtual Angelic, Aret(h)a, Assay-piece, Attribute, Cardinal, Caritas, Charity, Chastity, Continent, Cyber, Dharma, Efficacy, Ethical, Excellent, Faith, Foison, Fortitude, Fus(h)ion, Good, Goody-goody, Grace, Hope, Justice, Moral(ity), Natural, Patience, Plaster-saint, Practical, Principal, Prudence, Pure, Qua, Say-piece, Squeaky-clean, Straight and narrow, Temperance, Theological, Upright, Worth

Virtuosity, Virtuoso Artist, Bravura, Brilliance, Excellence, Executant, Maestro, Paganini, Savant

Virulent Acrimonious, Deadly, Hostile, Malign, Noxious, Toxic, Vitriolic, Waspish

Virus AIDS, Antigen, Arbovirus, Bacteriophage, Boot, Capsid, Chikungunya, Computer, Contagium, Coronavirus, Coxsackie, Defective, DNA, EB, Ebola, Echo, Enterovirus, Epstein-Barr, Filovirus, Filterable, Fowlpest, Germ, Granulosis, Hantavirus, Hendra, Herpes, HIV, HIV negative, HIV positive, Lassa, Latent, Leaf-mosaic, Lentivirus, Michelangelo, Microbe, Microorganism, Norwalk, Oncogen, Oncornavirus, Parainfluenza, Parvo(virus), Pathogen, Peach-yellow, Picornavirus, Polyoma, Prophage, Reovirus, Retrovirus, Rhabdovirus, Rhinovirus, Ross River, Rotavirus, SARS, Shingles, Slow, Street, SV40, Swine flu, Tobacco mosaic, Varicella, Virino, Virion, West Nile, Zoster

Visa Transit

Viscera Bowels, Entrails, Giblets, Guts, Harigal(d)s, Haslet, Innards, Omentum, Splanchnic, Umbles, Vitals

Viscount Vis

Viscous (liquid), Viscosity Absolute, Glaireous, Gleety, Gluey, Gummy, Kinematic, Slab, Specific, Sticky, Stoke, Tacky, Tar, Thick, Thixotropic

Visible, Visibility Clear, Conspicuous, Evident, Explicit, In sight, Obvious, Zero-zero

Visigoth Asaric

Vision(ary) Abstraction, Aery, Aisling, Apparition, Awareness, Beatific, Binocular, Bourignian, Day-dreamer, Double, Dream(er), Emmetropia, Fancy, Fantast, Fey, Foresight, Idealist, Ideologist, Illusionist, Image, Kef, Moonshine, Mouse-sight, Mystic, Ocular, Phantasm(a), Phantom, Pholism, Photism, Photopia, Rainbow-chaser, Romantic, Seeing, Seer, Sight, Sightline, Stereo, Stereopsis, Sweven, Tunnel, Twenty-twenty, Viewy

Visit(or) Affliction, Alien, Caller, Day-tripper, Domiciliary, ET, Event, First-foot, Frequent, Gam, Guest, Habitué, Haunt, Health, Hit, Inflict, Kursaal, Look up, Manuhiri, Pop in, Prison, See, Sightseer, Sojourn, State, Stay, Stranger, Take, Wait upon

Visor, Vizor Eyeshade, Face-saver, Mesail, Mezail, Umbrel, Umbr(i)ere, Umbril, Vent(ayle)

Vista Enfilade, Outlook, Scene, View

Visual(ise) Envisage, Imagine, Ocular, Optical, See, Visible

Vital(ity) Alive, Bounce, Central, Critical, Crucial, Energy, Esprit, Essential, Existent, Foison, Gusto, Indispensable, Juice, Key, Kick, Life-blood, Linchpin, Lung, Mites,

Momentous, Necessary, Oomph, Organ, Pizzazz, Pulse, Salvation, Sap, Verve, Viable, Vigour, Zing, Zoetic

Vitals Numbles, Umbles, Viscera

Vitamin(s) A, Adermin, Aneurin, Axerophthol, B, Bioflavonoid, Biotin, C, Calciferol, Calcitriol, Citrin, Cobalamin, D, E, Ergocalciferol, Folacin, G, H, Inositol, K, Linoleic, Menadione, Menaquinone, Niacin, Niacinamide, P, Pan(to)thenol, Phylloquinone, Phytonadione, Pyridoxine, Retinene, Retinol, Riboflavin, Ribose, Thiamin(e), Tocopherol, Torulin, Tretinoin

Vitiate(d) Flaw(ed)

Vitreous Glassy, Hyaline

Vitriol(ic) Acid, Acrimonious, Biting, Blue, Caustic, Green, Mordant, White

Vituperate Abuse, Berate, Castigate, Censure, Defame, Inveigh, Lash, Rail, Scold

Viva Oral

Vivacity, Vivacious Animation, Brio, Esprit, Exuberant, Sparkle, Spirit, Sprightly, Verve

Vivid Bright, Brilliant, Colourful, Dramatic, Eidetic, Fresh, Graphic, Keen, Live, Pictorial, Picturesque, Sharp, Violent

Vivien Leigh

Vixen Catamaran, Harridan, Shrew, Virago

Viz Sc, Videlicet

Vizier Pheazar, Wazir

▶ **Vizor** *see* **VISOR**

Vocabulary Active, Glottochronology, Idiolect, Idioticon, Jargon, (Kata)kana, Lexicon, Lexis, Meta-language, Nomenclator, Passive, Wordbook

Vocal(isation), Vocalist Articulate, Cantilena, Doo-wop, Eloquent, Minstrel, Oral, Schwa, Singer, Songster, Sprechgesang

Vocation Call, Career, Métier, Mission, Priesthood, Profession, Pursuit, Shop

Vociferous(ly) Clamant, Loud, Loud-mouth(ed), Ore rotundo, Strident

Vogue Chic, Day, → **FASHION**, Groovy, It, Mode, Rage, Style, Ton, Trend

Vogul Ugrian, Ugric

Voice(d) Active, Air, Alto, Ancestral, Bass, Chest, Contralto, Countertenor, Descant, Edh, Emit, Eth, Express, Falsetto, Glottis, Harp, Head, Inner, Intonate, Lyric, Mastersinger, Meistersinger, Mezzo-soprano, Middle, Mouth, Opinion, Passive, Phonic, Pipe, Presa, Quill, Say, Sonant, Soprano, Speak, Spinto, Sprechstimme, Steven, Syrinx, Tais(c)h, Tenor, Throat, Tone, → **TONGUE**, Treble, Utter, White

Voiceless Aphonia, Aphony, Dumb, Edh, Eth, Mute, Silent, Tacit

Void Abyss, Annul, Belch, Blank, Chasm, Counter, Defeasance, Defecate, Diriment, Empty, Evacuate, Gape, Hollow, Inane, Inoperative, Invalid, Irritate, Lapse, Negate, Nullify, Quash, Space, Vacuum

Volatile Excitable, Explosive, Inconsistent, Latin, Live(ly), Mercurial, Skittish, Tear gas, Temperamental, Terpene, Tinderbox

Volcano(es), Volcanic Agglomerate, Black smoker, Burning mountain, Composite, Cone, Conic, Fumarole, Greystone, Hornito, Ice, Idocrase, Igneous, Ignimbrite, Monticule, Mud, Obsidian, Pele, Pelée, Plinian, Pozz(u)olana, Pumice, Puzzolana, Sandblow, Shield, Soffioni, Solfatara, Stratovolcano, Tephra, Trass, Tuff

VOLCANOES

2 letters:	*4 letters:*	*5 letters:*	
Aa	Etna	Askja	Salse
	Fuji	Hekla	Thera
3 letters:	Maui	Kauai	*6 letters:*
Aso	Taal	Mayon	Ararat
Puy		Misti	Asosan
		Okmok	Azores

Egmont
Erebus
Ischia
Katmai
Kazbek
Lipari
Semeru
Tolima

7 letters:
Aragats
Comoros
El Misti
Huascan
Iliamna
Iwo Jima
Kilauea
Mofette
Rotorua
Ruapehu
Semeroe
St Kilda
Tambora

8 letters:
Amygdale

Andesite
Antisana
Cameroon
Cotopaxi
Jan Mayan
Krakatoa
Mauna Kea
Mauna Loa
St Helena
St Helens
Taranaki
Unalaska
Vesuvius

9 letters:
Aniakchak
Corcovado
Haleakala
Helgafell
Huascaran
Mount Fuji
Nevis Peak
Paricutin
Scablands
Stromboli
Tangariro

10 letters:
Chimborazo
Lassen Peak
Montserrat
Mount Eigon
Mount Kenya
Mount Pelée
Nyiragongo

11 letters:
Erciyas Dagi
Kilimanjaro
Mount Egmont
Mount Erebus
Mount Katmai
Mount Kazbek
Mount Shasta
Nyamuragira
Olympus Mons
Pico de Teide
Pico de Teyde

12 letters:
Citlaltépetl
Ixtaccahuatl
Iztaccahuatl

National Park
Popocatepetl

13 letters:
Mount Demavend
Mount Pinatubo
Mount St Helens

14 letters:
Mount Suribachi
Nevada de Colima
Nevada de Toluca
Soufrière Hills

17 letters:
Fernando de
  Noronha
Warrumbungle
  Range

20 letters:
D'Entrecasteau
  Islands

Vole Arvicola, Meadow mouse, Muskrat, Musquash, Ondatra
Volition Velleity, Will
Volley Barrage, Boom, Broadside, Platoon, Salvo, Tirade, Tire
Volt(age) BeV, Bias, Grid bias, HT
Voltaire Arouet
Volte face U-turn, Zig
Voluble Fluent, Glib
Volume Atomic, Band, Bande, Barrel, Book, Bushel, Capacity, CC, Code(x), Content, Critical, Cubage, Gallon, Hin, Loudness, Mass, Ml, Molecular, Omnibus, Peck, Pint, Quart(o), Roll, Roul(e), Size, Space, Specific, Stere, Swept, Tidal, Tom, Tome, Ullage, Vol
Voluntary, Volunteer Docent, Enlist, Fencible, Free, Free-will, Honorary, Offer, Postlude, Reformado, Spontaneous, Tender, Tennessee, Terrier, TN, Ultroneous, Yeoman
Voluptuary, Voluptuous Carnal, Hedonist, Houri, Luscious, Sensuist, Sensuous, Sybarite
Volute Helix, Roll
Vomit(ing) Anacatharsis, Barf, Black, Boak, Boke, Cascade, Cat, Chuck up, Chunder, Disgorge, Egest, Egurgitate, Emesis, Fetch-up, Haematemesis, Honk, Keck, Kotch, Parbreak, Posset, Puke, Ralph, Regorge, Regurgitate, Retch, Rolf, Spew, Technicolour yawn, Throw up, Upchuck
Voodoo Charm, Jettatura, Kurdaitcha, Macumba, Mambo, Obeah, Sorcery, Zombi(e)
Voracious, Voracity Bulimia, Edacity, Gluttony, Greed, Ravenous, Serrasalmo
Vortex Charybdis, Eddy, Gyre, Trailing, Whirlpool
Votary Adherent, Cenobite, Devotee, Disciple, Fan, Nun, Swinger, Zealot
Vote(r), Votes, Voting Alternative, Assentor, Aye, Ballot, Ballotee, Block, Card, Casting, Choose, Colonist, Constituent, Coopt, Cross, Crossover, Cumulative, Division, Donkey, Fag(g)ot, Floating, Franchise, Free, Grey, Informal, Mandate, Nay, Negative,

No, Opt, People, Placet, Plebiscite, Plump, Plural, Poll, Postal, Pot-wabbler, Pot-waller, Pot-walloner, Pot-walloper, Pot-wobbler, PR, Preferential, Proportional representation, Protest, Qualified majority, Referendum, Return, Scrutin de liste, Scrutiny, Show of hands, Side, Single transferable, Straw(-poll), Suffrage, Swinging, Sympathy, Tactical, Ten-pounder, The stump, Theta, Ticket, Token, Transferable, Voice, X, Yea, Yes

Vote-catcher Pork

Vouch(er), Vouchsafe Accredit, Assure, Attest, Beteem(e), Book token, Chit, Coupon, Endorse, Gift, Guarantee, Luncheon, Meal-ticket, Promise, Receipt, Slip, Ticket, Token, Warrant

Voussoir Quoin, Wedge

Vow Affirm, Baptismal, Behight, Behot(e), Earnest, Ex voto, Hecht, Hest, I do, Nuncupate, → **OATH**, Obedience, Pledge, Plight, Promise, Simple, Solemn, Swear, Troth, Vum

Vowel(s) Ablaut, Anaptyxis, Aphesis, Breve, Cardinal, Diphthong, Gradation, Indeterminate, Monophthong, Murmur, Mutation, Point, Rhyme, Seg(h)ol, S(c)hwa, Svarabhakti, Triphthong

Voyage(r) Anson, Columbus, Course, Cruise, Launch, Maiden, Passage, Peregrinate, Sinbad, Travel

Voyeur Peeping Tom, Scopophiliac

VTOL Convertiplane

Vulcan(ite) Blacksmith, Ebonite, Fire, Mulciber, Spock, Wayland

Vulgar(ian) Banausic, Barbaric, Base, Blatant, Blue, Brassy, Buffoon, Canaille, Cheap, Cit, Coarse, Common, Crude, Demotic, Filthy, Flash, Forward, Gaudy, General, Gent, Gorblim(e)y, Gross, Heel, Hussy, Ignorant, Indecent, Kitsch, Laddish, Lavatorial, Lewd, Low(-life), Naff, Obscene, Ostentatious, Pandemian, Plebby, Plebeian, Popular, Proletarian, Raffish, Ribald, Riff-raff, Rude, Scaff, Scurrilous, Slag, Snob, Tacky, Tarty, Tawdry, Threepenny, Tiger, Tink, Upstart, Vulg

Vulnerable Defenceless, Exposed, Open, Pregnable, Susceptible, Unguarded, Weak, Wide-open

Vulture Aasvogel, Bearded, Bird, Buzzard, California (condor), Condor, Culture, Falcon, Gallinazo, Gier, Griffon, Gripe, Grype, King, Lammergeier, Lammergeyer, Ossifrage, Predator, Turkey, Urubu, Zopilote

Ww

W Watt, West, Whisky, Women

Wad(ding) Batt(ing), Lump, Pad, Pledget, Roll, Swab, Wodge

Waddle Toddle, Waggle

Waddy Club, Cowboy, Stick

Wade(r), Wading Antigropelo(e)s, Ardea, Crane, Curlew, Dikkop, Egret, Flamingo, Ford, Gallae, Godwit, Grallatorial, Greenshank, Gumboot, Heron, Ibis, Jacksnipe, Lapwing, Limpkin, Oyster-catcher, Paddle, Phalarope, Plodge, Plover, Ree, Sandpiper, Sarus, Seriema, Shoebill, Snipe, Splodge, Stilt(bird), Terek, Virginia

Waesucks Ewhow, O(c)hone

Wafer Biscuit, Cracker, Crisp, Gaufer, Gaufre, Gofer, Gopher, Host, Papad, Seal

Waff Flap, Flutter, Wave

Waffle Adlib, Blather, Cake, Equivocate, Fudge, Gas, Gaufer, Gaufre, Gofer, Gopher, Hedge, Poppycock, Prate, Rabbit, Wibble

Waft(ing) Airborne, Aura, Blow, Drift, Float

Wag(gish), Waggle Arch, Card, Comedian, Facetious, Joker, Lick, Niddle-noddle, Nod, Rogue, Shake, Sway, Wit(snapper), Wobble

Wage(s) Ante, Award, Fee, Hire, Income, Living, Meed, Minimum, Nominal, Pay, Portage, Practise, Prosecute, Rate, Salary, Screw, Subsistence

Wage-earner Breadwinner, Employee, Proletariat(e)

Wager Ante, Back, → **BET**, Gamble, Lay, Pascal's, Stake, Wed

Wagon(er) Ar(a)ba, Aroba, Boötes, Boxcar, Brake, Break, Buck, Buckboard, Buggy, Caisson, Carriage, Cart, Cattle truck, Chuck, Coachman, Cocopan, Conestoga, Corf, Covered, Democrat, Drag, Dray, Flatcar, Fourgon, Freight-car, Gambo, Go-cart, Hopper, Hutch, Low-loader, Mammy, Paddy, Palabra, Patrol, Plaustral, Police, Prairie schooner, Rave, Reefer, Rubberneck, Shandry, Stage, Station, Tank, Tartana, Telega, Tender, Trap, Trekker, Truck, Van, Victoria, Wain, Water

Waif Arab, Foundling, Gamin, Jetsam, Stray, Urchin, Victoria, Wastrel, Water, Weft

Wail(er) Banshee, Bawl, Blubber, Howl, Keen, Lament, Moan, Skirl, Threnody, Threnos, Ululate, Vagitus, Wah-wah, Yammer

Wain Cart, Dray, Wagon

Waist(band) Belt, Cummerbund, Girdlestead, Girth, Hour-glass, Middle, Midship, Obi, Sash, Shash, Wasp, Zoster

Waistcoat Gilet, Jerkin, Lorica, MB, Pressure, Sayon, Shawl, Sleeve(d), Stabvest, Vest, Weskit

Wait(er), Waiting Abid(e), Ambush, Attend, Barista, Bide, Busboy, Butler, Buttle, Carhop, Commis, Cupbearer, Dally, Delay, Estragon, Expect, Flunkey, Frist, Garçon, Hang on, Hesitate, Hover, Interval, Khidmutgar, Lead time, Lime, Linger, Lurch, Maître d', Maître d'hôtel, Minority, Omnibus, Pannier, Pause, Penelope, Pozzo, Queue, Remain, Serve(r), Sommelier, Stacking, Stay, Steward, Suspense, Taihoa, Tarry, Tend(ance), Tray, Vladimir, Wine, Won

Waitress Bunny girl, Hebe, Miss, Mousme(e), Nippy, Server

Waive Abandon, Defer, Forgo, Overlook, Postpone, Relinquish, Renounce, Suspend

Wake(n) Abrade, Abraid, Abray, Aftermath, Alert, American, Animate, Arouse, Astern, Deathwatch, Excite, Hereward, Keen, Knock-up, Like, Lyke, Prod, Rear, → **ROUSE**, Surface, Trail, Train, Wash

Waldo Emerson

Wale(r) Prop, Ridge, Weal

Wales Cambria, Cymru, Dyfed, Principality

Walk(er), Walking, Walkabout, Walkway Alameda, Alley, Alure, Amble, Ambulate, Arcade, Berceau, Birdcage, Charity, Cloister, Clump, Constitutional, Daddle, Dander, Dauner, Emu, Esplanade, EVA, Expatiate, Festination, Flânerie, Frescade, Gait, Gallery, Ghost, Go, Gradient, Gressorial, Heel and toe, Hike, Hookey, Hump, Lambeth, Leg, Lumber, Mainstreeting, Mall, March, Mince, Mosey, Nordic, Pace, Pad, Paddle, Pasear, Paseo, Passage, Passerby, Path, Pavement, Ped(estrianism), Perambulate, Pergola, Perp, Piaffe, Piazza, Pipe-opener, Pole, Pound, Power, Prance, Prom(enade), Rack, Ramble, Rampart, Random, Ring, Routemarch, Sashay, Scamble, Schlep, Shamble, Sidle, Slommock, Space, Spanish, Sponsored, Stalk, Step, Stoa, Striddle, Stride, Stroll, Strut, Stump, Taligrade, Terrace, Toddle, Tramp, Trash, Travolator, Tread, Trog, Truck, Trudge, Turn, Wade, Wander, Wayfare, Wend, Widow's, Xyst

Walk-over Doddle, Pie, Scratch

Wall Antonine, Bail, Bailey, Barrier, Berlin, Berm, Cavity, Cell, Chinese, Climbing, Countermure, Crib, Curtain, Dado, Dam, Dike, Dry-stone, Enceinte, Epispore, Exine, Fail-dike, Fourth, Fronton, Frustule, Gable, Great, Groyne, Hadrian's, Hanging, Hangman, Head, Immure, Intine, Mahjongg, Mani, Merlon, Mutual, Myocardium, Non-bearing, Parapet, Parie(te)s, Parietal, Parpane, Parpen(d), Parpent, Parpoint, Partition, Party, Peribolos, Pericarp, Perpend, Perpent, Pleuron, Podium, Puteal, Qibla, Retaining, Reveal, Revet(ment), Ring, River, Roman, Roughcast, Screen, Sea, Septum, Severus, Side, Somatopleure, Spandrel, Spandril, Street, Studding, Tambour, Tariff, Trumeau, Vallation, Vallum, Video, Wa', Wailing, Western, Withe, Zooecia

Wallaby Brusher, Dama, Kangaroo, Pademelon, Pad(d)ymelon, Quokka, Tammar, Whiptail

Wallah Competition

Wallaroo Euro

Wall-covering, Wallpaper Anaglypta®, Arras, Burlap, Flock, Lincrusta, Paper, Tapestry, Tapet

Waller Fats, Mason

Wallet Billfold, Case, Flybook, Folder, Notecase, Pochette, Pocket-book, Purse, Scrip

Wallflower Crucifer, Dowd(y), Pariah

Wall-game Eton, Mahjongg

Wallop Bash, Baste, Batter, Beat, Biff, Clout, Cob, Gigantic, → **HIT**, Lam, Lounder, Oner, Polt, Pound, Slog, Strap, Swinge, Tan, Tat, Thud, Trounce

Wallow(ing) Bask, Flounder, Luxuriate, Revel, Roll, Slubber, Splash, Swelter, Tolter, Volutation, Welter

Wall-painting Fresco, Graffiti, Grisaille

Wallpaper → **WALL-COVERING**, Woodchip

Wall-plate Tassel, Torsel

Wall-support Beam, Foundation, Pier, Rear-arch, Rere-arch

Wally Dipstick, Moron, Nincompoop, Prat

Walnut Black, Butternut, Hickory, Juglans, Satin, White

Walrus Morse, Moustache, Pinniped, Rosmarine, Sea-horse, Tash

Walter Bruno, Mitty, Pater, Raleigh, Scott

Waltz Anniversary, Blue Danube, Boston, Concert, Dance, Hesitation, Rotate, Valse

Wampum Peag(e), Shell-money

Wan Lurid, Pale, Pallid, Pasty, Sanguine, Sorry

Wanchancy Unlucky

Wand Baton, Caduceus, Rod, Runic, Stick, Thyrse, Thyrsus, Vara, Vare

Wander(er), Wandering Aberrance, Amble, Bedouin, Berber, Bum, Caird, Daiker, Delirious, Desultory, Deviate, Digress, Divagate, Drift, Errant, Estray, Evagation, Excursive, Expatiate, Extravagate, Gad(about), Grope, Hobo, Itinerant, Jew, Landloper, Maunder, Meander, Meandrian, Mill, Mither, Moider, Moither, Moon, Nomad(e),

Odysseus, Pedder, Peregrine, Peripatetic, Polar, Prodigal, Rache, Ramble, Range, Ratch, Roamer, Romany, Room, Rove, Solivagant, Stooge, Straggle, Stravaig, Stray, Strayve, Streel, Stroam, Stroll, Swan, Ta(i)ver, Tramp, Troll, Truant, Tuareg, Vagabond, Vagile, Vagrant, Vague, Waif, Wend, Wheel, Wilder, Wolves

▷ **Wandering** *may indicate* an anagram

Wane Decline, Decrease, Diminish, Ebb

Wangle Arrange, Finagle, Trick

Want(ing), Wants Absence, Conative, Covet, Crave, Dearth, Defect, Deficient, Derth, Desiderata, → **DESIRE**, Destitution, Envy, For, Hardship, Indigent, Itch, Lack, Like, Long, Mental, Moldwarp, Mole, Need, Penury, Require, Scarceness, Scarcity, Shortfall, Shy, Void, Wish, Yen

Wanton(ness) Bona-roba, Cadgy, Chamber, Cocotte, Colt's tooth, Deliberate, Demirep, Filly, Flirt-gill, Gammerstang, Giglet, Giglot, Gillflirt, Hussy, Jay, Jezebel, Jillflirt, Lewd, Licentious, Light o' love, Loose, Nice, Protervity, Rig, Roué, Slut, Smicker, Sportive, Sybarite, Toyish, Twigger, Unchaste, Wayward

Wap Blow, Knock, Strike

War(fare), Wars American Civil, American Independence, Ares, Armageddon, Arms, Asymmetrical, Attrition, Bacteriological, Barons', Bate, Battle, Biological, Bishop, Chemical, Civil, Clash, Class, Cod, Cold, Combat, Conflict, Crescentade, Crimean, Crusade, Culture, Electronic, Emergency, Feud, → **FIGHT**, Flagrante bello, Flame, Food, Franco-Prussian, Fray, Germ, Gigantomachy, Great, Guer(r)illa, Gulf, Holy, Hostilities, Hot, Hundred Years', Information, Internecine, Jehad, Jenkins' ear, Jihad, Jugurthine, Korean, Krieg, Limited, Mars, Mexican, Napoleonic, Nuclear, Opium, Peasants', Peloponnesian, Peninsular, Phony, Price, Private, Propaganda, Psychological, Punic, Push-button, Queen Anne's, Rebellion, Revolutionary, Roses, Russo-Japanese, Secession, Seven against Thebes, Seven Years', Shooting, Six Day, Social, Spam, Spanish-American, Spanish Civil, Star, Stoush, Sword, Terrapin, Theomachy, Thirty Years', Total, Trench, Trojan, Turf, Vietnam, Winter, World, Yom Kippur

Warble(r) Carol, Cetti's, Chiff-chaff, Chirl, Fauvette, Peggy, Record, Rel(l)ish, Trill, Vibrate, Yodel, Yodle

War-chant, War-cry Alalagmos, Haka, Slogan

Ward (off) Artemus, Averruncate, Avert, Care, Casual, Casualty, Charge, Defend, District, Fend, Guard, Hand-off, Inner, Marginal, Maternity, Minor, Nightingale, Oppose, Outer, Parry, Protégé, Pupil, Soc, Soken, Thunderbolt, Vintry, Wear, Weir

Warden Caretaker, Church, Concierge, Constable, Crossing, Curator, Custodian, Game, Guardian, Keeper, Maori, Meter maid, Pear, Provost, Ranger, Septimus, Sidesman, Spooner, Steward, Traffic, Way

Warder, Wardress Beefeater, Gaoler, Guardian, Keeper, Matron, Provost, Screw, Turnkey, Twirl

Wardrobe Almirah, Armoire, Breakfront, Capsule, Closet, Clothes, Garderobe, Outfit, Vestuary

Ware(s) Arretine, Basalt, Beware, Biscuit, Cameo, Canton, Chelsea, China, Etruria, Fabergé, Faience, Goods, Hollow(w)are, Jasper, Lapis lazuli, Lustre, Merchandise, Palissy, Plate(d), Queen's, Samian, Sanitary, Satsuma, Shippo, Truck, Wemyss

Warehouse Bonded, Data, Depository, Entrepôt, Freight-shed, Go-down, Hong, Store

▶ **Warfare** *see* **WAR(FARE)**

War-game Kriegs(s)piel

War-god Ares, Mars, Tiu, Tiw, Tyr

Warhead Atomic, Supremo

Warhorse Charger, Destrier, Fighter

Wariness, Wary Ca'canny, Cagey, Careful, Cautel, Caution, Chary, Discreet, Distrust, Gingerly, Guarded, Leery, Mealy-mouthed, Prudent, Sceptical, Suspicious, Tentie, Tenty, Vigilant

Warlike Battailous, Bellicose, Gung-ho, Lachlan, Martial, Militant

Warlord Haw-haw, Kitchener, Shogun, Tuchun

Warm(er), Warming, Warmth Abask, Admonish, Air, Ardour, Atingle, Balmy, Bonhomie, British, Calefacient, Calid(ity), Cardigan, Chambré, Cordial, Eager, El Nino, Empressement, Enchafe, Fervour, Flame, Foment, Gemütlich, Genial, Global, Glow, → **HEAT**, Hot, Incalescent, Kang, Kindly, Lew, Logic, Loving, Muff, Muggy, Mull, Nuke, Radiator, Tepid, Thermal, Toast, Toasty

Warm-blooded Endothermic, Homothermal, Homothermic, Homothermous, Idiothermous

Warmonger Hawk

Warn(ing) Admonish, Alarum, Alert, Amber, Aposematic, Apprise, Beacon, Bell, Beware, Bleep, Buoy, Caution, Cave, Caveat, Caveat emptor, Commination, Cone, Counsel, Cowbell, Detector, DEW, Document, Early, En garde, Example, Foghorn, Fore, Foretoken, Gardyloo, Garnishment, Griffin, Harbinger, Hazchem, Heads up, Hoot, Horn, Illocution, Klaxon, Knell, Larum, Lesson, Light, Maroon, Minatory, Monition, Nix, Noli-me-tangere, Nota bene, Notice, Notification, Omen, Pi-jaw, Portent, Premonish, Premonitory, Presage, Prodromal, Profit, Protevangelium, Red alert, Red flag, Red light, Remind, Riot Act, Rumble strip, Scaldings, Scarborough, Sematic, Shore, Signal, Spindle, Storm, Tattler, Threat, Timber, Tip-off, Token, Toot, Vigla, Vor, Yellow card

Warner Alarm, Fore, Plum, Siren

Warp(ed) Bent, Bias, Buckle, Cast, Contort, Distort, Hog, Kam, Kedge, Pandation, Spring, Time, Twist, Weft, Zag

Warpath Rampage

▷ **Warped** *may indicate* an anagram

Warrant(y), Warrant officer Able, Authorise, Behight, Behote, Bench, Bosun, Capias, Caption, Certificate, Death, Deserve, Detainer, Distress, Dividend, Fiat, Fiaunt, Fugle, General, Guarantee, Justify, Merit, Mittimus, Peace, Permit, Precept, Reprieve, Royal, Search, Sepad, Special, Swear, Transire, Vouch, Warn, Writ

Warren Burrow, Colony, Hastings, Rabbit

Warrior Achilles, Agamemnon, Ajax, Amazon, Anzac, Attila, Berserk(er), Brave, Cold, Cossack, Crusader, Eorl, Fianna, Fighter, Finlay, Finley, Geronimo, Ghazi, Haiduk, Heimdall, Heyduck, Housecarl, Impi, Jihadi, Lewis, Louis, Myrmidon, Nestor, Rainbow, Rajput, Roger, Samurai, Soldier, Tatar, Unknown, Wardog, Warhorse, Warwolf, Zulu

Warship Battleship, Blockship, Castle, Cog, Corvette, Cruiser, Destroyer, Drake, Dromon(d), Frigate, Galleass, Galliass, Invincible, Man-o-war, Mine-layer, Monitor, Privateer, Ram, Repulse, Wooden Walls

Wart(y) Anbury, Angleberry, Blemish, Genital, Keratose, Lump, Muricate, Plantar, Tuberous, Verruca, Wen

Warwick Kingmaker

▶ **Wary** *see* **WARINESS**

Was Erat, Existed, Lived, Past

Wash(ed), Washer, Washing (up), Wash out Ablution, Affusion, Alluvion, Bath, Bay(e), Bidet, Bubble-dancing, Bur(r), Calcimine, Circlip, Clean(se), Cradle, D, Dashwheel, Dele(te), Dip, Edulcorate, Elute, Elutriate, Enema, Erode, Fen, Flush, Freshen, Front-loader, Gargle, Grom(m)et, Grummet, Hose, Hush, Irrigate, Kalsomine, Lap, → **LAUNDER**, Lavabo, Lave, Leather, Lip, Lotion, Marsh, Maundy, Mop, Nipter, Pan, Pigswill, Poss, Purify, Rinse, Sapple, Scrub, Shampoo, Shim, Sind, Sloosh, Sluice, Soogee, Soojee, Soojey, Squeegie, Stream, Sujee, Swab, Synd, Syne, Tie, Toilette, Top and tail, Twin tub, Tye, Wake, Wudu, Yellow

Washbasin, Washing machine, Washtub, Washhouse Copper, Dash-wheel, Lavabo, Steamie

Washerman, Washerwoman Dhobi, Laundress

Washington Dinah, Wa

Wasn't Nas, Wasna

Wasp(ish) Appledrain, Bembex, Bink, Bite, Chalcid, Cuckoo-fly, Cynipidae, Cynips, Digger, European, Fig, Fretful, Gall(-fly), Gold, Hornet, Horntail, Hoverfly, Irritable, Marabunta, Mason, Miffy, Muddauber, Paper, Peevish, Pompilid, Potter, Ruby-tail, Sand, Seed, Solitary, Spider, Syrphus, Velvet ant, Vespa, Wood, Yellow jacket

▷ **Wasp** *may indicate* a rugby player

Wasp's nest Bike, Bink, Byke

Wassail Carouse, Pledge, Toast

Wast Wert

Wastage, Waste(d), Wasting, Wasteful, Wasteland, Waster, Wastrel
Amyotrophy, Atrophy, Blow, Blue, Bluer, Boondoggle(r), Cesspit, Cirrhosis, Colliquative, Consume, Contabescent, Coom(b), Cotton, Crud, Culm, Decay, Dejecta, Desert, Detritus, Devastate, Dilapidate, Dissipate, Dross, Dung, Dwindle, Dwine, Dystrophy, Effluent, Egesta, Emaciate, Erode, Estrepe, Excrement, Exhaust, Expend, Exudate, Faeces, Flue, Forpine, Fribble, Fritter, Garbage, Gash, Gob, Grog, Gunge, Haggard, Half-cut, Havoc, Hazardous, High-level, Hi(r)stie, Husk, Idler, Knub, Landfill, Lavish, Lean, Loose, Lose, Loss, Low-level, Marasmus, Merino, Misspent, Moor, Moulder, Muir, Mullock, Mungo, Natural, Novalia, Nub, Nuclear, Offal, Offcut, Oller, Ordure, Pellagra, Perish, Phthisis, Pigswill, Pine, Prodigalise, Profligate, Rack and manger, Radioactive, Rammel, Ravage, Recrement, Red mud, Red tape, → **REFUSE**, Reif, Rubble, Ruderal, Ruin, Scant o' grace, Scattergood, Schappe, Scissel, Scoria, Scrap, Scum, Sewage, Slag, Slurry, Spend, Spend-all, Spendthrift, Spill, Spoil(age), Squander, Stalko, Sullage, Swarf, Syntexis, Tabes, Tailing, Thin, Thwaite, Ureal, Urine, Uropoiesis, Vagabond, Vast, Wanze, Wear, Wilderness, Yearn

▷ **Wasted** *may indicate* an anagram

Watch(er) Accutron®, Analog(ue), Analogon, Argus, Await, Bark, Behold, Big brother, Bird-dog, Black, Case, Chronograph, Clock, Coastguard, Cock-crow, Digital, Dog, Eryl, Espy, Eyeball, Fob, Glom, Gregory, Guard, Half-hunter, Huer, Hunter, Kettle, Latewake, Lever, Lo, Look, Look-out, Middle, Monitor, Morning, Nark, Neighbourhood, Night, Nit, Note, Nuremberg egg, Observe, Overeye, Patrol, Pernoctation, Posse, Quartz, Regard, Repeater, Rolex®, Scout, Sentinel, Sentry, Shadow, Snoop, Spectate, Spie, Spotter, Spy, Stemwinder, Suicide, Surveillance, Tend, Ticker, Timekeeper, Timepiece, Timer, Tompion, Tout, Vedette, → **VIGIL**, Voyeur, Wait, Wake, Weather eye, Wrist(let)

Watch-chain Albert, Slang

Watch-control Escapement

Watchful(ness) Alert, Aware, Care, Dragon, Ira, Jealous, Vigilant, Wakerife, Wary, Waukrife, Weather eye

Watchman Argus, Bellman, Charley, Charlie, Cho(w)kidar, Chok(e)y, Guard, Huer, Sentinel, Sentry, Speculator, Tompion, Viewer

Watch-tower Atalaya, Barbican, Beacon, Garret, Mirador, Sentry-go, Turret

Watchword Cry, Password, Shibboleth, Slogan

Water(ed), Waters, Watery Adam's ale, Adam's wine, Aerated, Amrit, Apollinaris, Aq(ua), Aquatic, Aqueous, Ascites, Barley, Bayou, Bedabble, Bilge, Bound, Branch, Brine, Broads, Brook, Burn, Canal, Cancer, Chresard, Chuck, Cold, Cologne, Compensation, Conductivity, Connate, Dead, Deaw, Deg, Demersal, Dew, Dill, Dilute, Dribble, Drinking, Eau, Ebb, Echard, Element, Ennerdale, Epilimnion, Euphotic, Evian®, First, Flood, Ford, Fossil, Functional, Gallise, Gallize, Ganga jal, Grey, Gripe, Ground, Hard, Heavy, Hectum, Hellespont, High, Holy, Hot, Hungary, Hydatoid, Irrigate, Javel(le), Kuroshio, Kyle, Lagoon, Lagune, Lake, Lant, Laurel, Lavender, Leachate, Lentic, Light, Lime, Limnology, Lithia, Loch(an), Lode, Lotic, Lough, Low, Lubricated, Lymph, Melt, Meteoric, Mineral, Miner's inch, Moiré, Mother, Nappe, North, Oasis®, Oedema, Orange-flower, Overfall, Pani, Pawnee, Pee, Perrier®, Phreatic, Pisces, Polly, Polynia, Polynya, Poppy, Potash, Potass, Pump, Purest, Quarry, Quick, Quinine, Rain, Rapids, Rate, Reach, Rheumy, Rice, Rip, Riverine, Rose, Running, Runny, Rydal, Saltchuck, Scorpio, Sea, Seltzer, Sera, Serous, Serum, Shoal, Shower, Simpson, Skinkling, Slack, Slick, Sluice, Soda, Sodden,

Soft, Solent, Sound, Souse, Southampton, Sprinkle, Steam, Stream, Surface, Tabby, Table, Tam, Tap, Tar, Temper, Territorial, Thermocline, Thin, Tide, Toilet, Tonic, Urine, Utility, Vadose, Vichy, Viscous, Vlei, Vly, Wai, Wake, Wash(y), Weak, Wee, Whey, White, White coal, Wild, Wishy-washy

Waterbaby Moses, Tom

Water-boa Anaconda

Water-boatman Notonecta

Water-brash Pyrosis

Waterbuck Kob

Water-buckets Noria

Water-carrier Aqueduct, Bheestie, Bheesty, Bhistee, Bhisti, Bucket, Carafe, Chatty, Drain, Furphy, Hose, Hydra, Hydria, Kirbeh, Pail, Pitcher, Rigol

Water-chestnut Saligot

Water-colour Aquarelle, Painting, Pastel, RI

Water-course Arroyo, Billabong, Canal, Ditch, Dyke, Falaj, Furrow, Gutter, Khor, Lead, Leat, Nala, Nalla(h), Nulla, Nullah, Rean, Rhine, Rill, River(et), Riverway, Serpentine, Shott, Spruit, Wadi, Whelm

Watercress Nasturtium

Water-device Shadoof, Shaduf

Water-diviner Dowser, Hydrostat

Waterfall Angel (Falls), Cataract, Churchill, Chute, Cuquenan, Espelands, → **FALL(S)**, Force, Foss, Iguaçú, Kahiwa, Kaieteur, Kile, Lasher, Lin(n), Lower Mar Valley, Mardel, Montmorency, Mtarazi, Niagara, Overfall, Rapid, Salmon leap, Sault, Sutherland, Takakkaw, Tugela, Tyssestrengene, Utigord, Victoria, Yellowstone, Yosemite

Water-fern Marsilea, Salvinia

Water-gate Penstock, Sluice, Sluse

Water-god Aleion, Aleyin, Alpheus

Water-hen Gallinule

Water-hole, Watering place Bore, Gilgai, Mickery, Oasis, Wiesbaden

Water-lily Candock, Lotus, Nenuphar, Nuphar, Spatterdock, Victoria

Waterloo Rout

Waterman Aquarius, Bargee, Ferryman, Oarsman

Water-monster Nicker

Water-nymph Kelpie, Kelpy, Naiad, Ondine, Rusalka

Water-parsnip Sium, Skirret

Water-plant Alisma, Aquatic, Cress, Crowfoot, Elodea, Gulfweed, Lace-leaf, Lattice-leaf, Nelumbo, Nenuphar, Nuphar, Ouvirandra, Pontederia, Quillwort, Reate, Rush, Sea-lace, Sea-mat, Sedge, Seg, Stratiotes, Urtricularia, Vallisneria

Waterproof, Water-tight Caisson, Camlet, Caulk, Cerecloth, Cofferdam, Corfam®, Curry, Dampcourse, Dubbin(g), Groundsheet, Loden, Mac, Mino, Oilers, Oilskin, Pay, Sealant, Seaworthy, Sta(u)nch, Stank, Suberin, Tarp, Tar-paper, Tarpaulin, Waders

Water pump Ee, Eye

Water-rat Arvicola, Musk-rat, Ratty, Vole

Watershed Divide, Height of land, Hilltop

Water-spout Gargoyle, Geyser, Hurricano

Water-sprite Kelpie, Kelpy, Nix(ie), Nixy, Tangie, Undine, Water-nymph

Water supply Dewpond, H, Hydrant, Spring, Tank, Tap

Waterway Aqueduct, Billabong, Canal, Channel, Creek, Culvert, Ditch, Igarapé, Illinois, Intracoastal, Lode, River, St Lawrence Seaway, Sny(e), Sound, Straight, Suez

Water-wheel Noria, Overshot, Pelton, Sakia, Saki(y)eh, Tympanum, Undershot

Wattle(s) Acacia, Boobialla, Boree, Dewlap, Gills, Golden, Mimosa, Mulga, Sallow, Savanna, Snot, Snotter

Wave(s), Waved, Waveform, Wavelength, Wavy Alfven, Alpha, Beachcomber, Beam, Beck, Beta, Billow, Bore, Bow, Brain, Brandish, Breaker, Carrier, Circular polarisation, Clapotis, Cold, Comber, Complex, Compression, Continuous, Crenulate, Crest, Crime, Crimp, Crispate, Cymotrichous, De Broglie, Decuman, Delta, Dominant, Dumper, Elastic, Electromagnetic, Feather, Finger, Flap, Flaunt, Float, Flote, Flourish, Fourier series, Gesticulate, Gesture, Gravitational, Gravity, Graybeard, Ground, Groundswell, Gyrose, Harmonic, Haystack, Head sea, Heat, Hertzian, Internal, Ionospheric, Lee, Long, Longitudinal, Marcel, Matter, Medium, Mexican, Nebule, New, Oundy, Peristalsis, Perm(anent), Plunger, Primary, Pulse, Radar, Radiation, Radio, Rayleigh, Repand, Rip, Ripple, Roller, Rooster, Sastrugi, Scrub, Sea, Secondary, Seiche, Seismic, Shake, Shock, Short, Signal, Sine, Sinuate, Skipper's daughter, Sky, Skyrmion, Snaky, Soliton, Sound, Spiller, Square, Squiggle, Standing, Stationary, Stern, Stream, Supplementary, Surf, Surge, Sway, Tabby, Theta, Third, Thought, Tidal, Tidal bore, Tide, Tide rip, Train, Transverse, Travelling, Tsunami, Ultrasonic, Undate, Unde, Undulate, Vermicular, Waffle, Waft, Wag, Waive, Wash, Waw, Wawe, Whelm, Whitecap, White-horse, Wigwag

▷ **Wave(s)** *may indicate* an anagram

Wave-band Channel

Wave-detector Coherer

Wavelength Band, Complementary, De Broglie, Ultrashort

Waver(ing), Waverer Dither, Double-minded, Falter, Flag, Gutter, Halt, Hesitate, Indecision, Oscillate, Reel, Stagger, Sway, Swither, Teeter, Trimmer, Vacillate, Waffle, Wet, Wobble, Wow

Wax(ed), Waxing, Waxy Adipocere, Ambergris, Appal, Bate, Bees, Bone, Brazilian, Candelilla, Carna(h)uba, Cere, Ceresin, Cerumen, Chinese, Cobbler's, Cutin, Earth, Effuse, Enseam, Enthuse, Ethal, Fury, Geraldton, Grave, Greaves, Grow, Heelball, Honeycomb, Increase, Increscent, Inseam, Ire, Japan, Kiss, Lecithin, Lipide, Livid, Lost, Lyrical, Mineral, Montan, Mummy, Myrtle, Ozocerite, Ozokerite, Paraffin, Parmacitie, Pela, Petroleum, Propolis, Pruina, Rage, Rise, Seal, Sealing, Spermaceti, Suberin, Tallow, Tantrum, Temper, Toxaphene, Vegetable, White, Yielding

Waxwing Cedar-bird, Icarus

Way(s), Wayside Access, Agate, Appian, Autobahn, Avenue, Boardwalk, Borstal(l), Budo, Bypass, Companion, Course, Crescent, Defile, Direction, Door, Draw, E, Each, Entrance, Family, Fashion, Flaminian, Foss(e), Four-foot, Gate, Habit, Hatch, Hedge, High, Hither, How, Icknield, Lane, Manner, Means, Method, Milky, MO, Mode, Modus, N, Pass, Path, Pennine, Permanent, Pilgrim's, Procedure, Railroad, Regimen, Ridge, → **ROAD**, Route, S, Sallypost, St(reet), Style, System, Taoism, Technique, Third, Thoroughfare, Thus, Trace, Trail, Troade, Turnpike, Underpass, Untrodden, Via, W, Wise

Wayfarer Commuter, Piepowder, Pilgrim, Traveller, Voyager

Waylay Accost, Ambuscade, Ambush, Beset, Bushwhack, Buttonhole, Molest, Obstruct, Stick up

Way-out Advanced, Bizarre, Egress, Esoteric, Exit, Exotic, Extreme, Offbeat, Trendy

Wayward Capricious, Disobedient, Errant, Erratic, Loup-the-dyke, Obstreperous, Perverse, Scapegrace, Stray, Unruly, Wilful

WC Gents, Ladies, Lav, Loo

We I and I, Oo, Royal, Us

Weak(er), Weaken(ing), Weakest, Weakness Achilles' heel, Acrasia, Adynamia, Antimnemonic, Aphesis, Appair, Appal, Arsis, Asthenia, Attenuate, Blot, Brickle, Brittle, Cachexia, Cataplexy, Chink, Cissy, Cripple(d), Debile, Debilitate, Decimate, Decrease, Delay, Delicate, Deplete, Dilling, Dilute, Disable, Drip, Effete, Emasculate, Embrittle, Enervate, Enfeeble, Entender, Fade, Faible, Failing, Faint, Fatigue, Feeble, Fissile, Flag, Flaw, Flimsy, Foible, Fragile, Frail(tee), Frailty, Frontolysis, Give, Glass chin, Gone, Groggy, Ham, Hamartia, Helpless, Honeycomb, Impair, Impotence, Infirm, Knock-kneed, Labefaction, Lame, Languishing, Lassitude, Leptosomatic, Loophole, Low, Low ebb, Meagre, Mild, Milk and water, Myasthenia, Namby-pamby, Pale, Pall, Paraparesis,

Paresis, Penchant, Puny, Push-over, Pusillanimous, Reckling, Reduce, Sap, Simp, Slack, Softie, Softling, Soft spot, Spineless, Tenuous, Thesis, Thin, Thready, Tottery, Unable, Underdog, Undermine, Unman, Unnerve, Unstable, Vapid, Velleity, Vessel, Vulnerability, W, Wane, Washy, Water(y), Weed, Weenie, Wimp, Wish(y)-wash(y), Wuss(y)

Weakling Dilling, Drip, Milksop, Nerd, Nisgul, Reed, Softie, Wuss

Weal Ridge, Stripe, Urticant, Wealth, Welfare, Welt, Whelk

Wealth(y) Abundance, Affluence, Bullion, Capital, Croesus, Digerati, Ease, Fat-cat, Fortune, Golconda, Jet-set, Klondike, Klondyke, Load(sa), Loaded, Loadsamoney, Lolly, Magnate, Mammon, Means, Mine, Mint, Moneyed, Nabob, Opulence, Ore, Pelf, Plutocrat, Reich, Rich, Ritzy, Solid, Substance, Treasure, Trustafarian, Untold, Well-heeled, Well-off, Well-to-do

Wean Ablactation, Bairn, Spain, Spane, Spean

Weapon(s) Ammo, Antitank, Arm, Arsenal, Assault, Binary, Cultural, Deterrent, Greek fire, → **GUN**, Hoplology, Long-range, Missile, Munition, Nuclear, Nuke, Ordnance, Piece, → **PISTOL**, → **SWORD**, Theatre, Tool, Traditional

WEAPONS

2 letters:	*4 letters:* (cont.)	*6 letters:* (cont.)	*7 letters:* (cont.)
Da	Beam	Airgun	Halberd
V1	Bill	Archie	Halbert
	Bolo	Cestus	Harpoon
3 letters:	Bomb	Cohorn	Hatchet
Axe	Club	Creese	Javelin
Bow	Cosh	Cudgel	Longbow
Dag	Dart	Dagger	Machete
Gad	Gade	Dragon	Matchet
Gat	Gaid	Duster	Petrary
Rod	Kris	Gingal	Poleaxe
SAM	Mere	Glaive	Poniard
Uzi	Mine	Jingal	Sandbag
	Pike		Shotgun
Blade	Spat	*Blade*	Sidearm
Brand	Sten	Katana	Sjambok
Estoc	Tank	Lathee	Sticker
Flail	Tuck	Mauser®	Swatter
Knife		Mortar	Torpedo
Kukri	*5 letters:*	Musket	Trident
Lance	Arrow	Onager	Warhead
Lathi	Baton	Rapier	
Maxim		Sparke	*8 letters:*
Orgue		Sparth	Alderman
Panga		Sumpit	Arbalest
Pilum		Taiaha	Armalite®
Rifle		Tomboc	Arquebus
Sabre		Voulge	Ballista
Saker			Blowpipe
Slung		*7 letters:*	Bludgeon
Spear		Arblast	Calthrop
Staff		Assegai	Catapult
Stick		Ataghan	Culverin
Sting		Bayonet	Elf-arrow
Taser®		Bazooka	Fougasse
Vouge		Blowgun	Howitzer
		Bondook	Mangonel
		Caliver	Nunchaku
		Caltrap	
		Caltrop	
		Carbine	
		Chopper	
		Coehorn	
		Cutlass	
		Dragoon	
		Enfield	
		Fougade	
		Gingall	
		Gisarme	
		Grenade	

Partisan	**9 letters:**	Sword cane	Singlestick
Petronel	Arquebuse	Tormentum	Snickersnee
Repeater	Backsword	Trebuchet	Switchblade
Revolver	Battleaxe	Truncheon	
Scimitar	Boomerang	Welsh hook	**12 letters:**
Scorpion	Catchpole		Dagger of lath
Shuriken	Chainshot	**10 letters:**	Flamethrower
Skean-dhu	Derringer	Broadsword	Jeddart staff
Skene-dhu	Doodlebug	Knobkerrie	Quarterstaff
Spontoon	Escopette	Pea-shooter	
Stiletto	Excalibur	Shillelagh	**13 letters:**
Stinkpot	Flintlock	Smallsword	Knuckleduster
Tomahawk	Forty-five	Swordstick	Life-preserver
Whirl-bat	Harquebus	Throw-stick	Manrikigusari
Whorl-bat	Nunchucks		
Yataghan	Sarbacane	**11 letters:**	**14 letters:**
	Slingshot	Morgenstern	Nunchaku sticks
	Slungshot	Morning star	

Wear(ing), Wear Out Abate, Ablative, Abrade, Air, Attrition, Chafe, Clothing, Corrade, Corrode, Deteriorate, Detrition, Efface, Erode, Erosion, Fashion, For(e)spend, Fray, Frazzle, Fret, Garb, Garni, Impair, In, Mush, Pack, Sap, Scuff, Sport, Stand, Tedy, Tolerate, Utility

▷ **Wear** *may indicate* the NE eg Sunderland

Weariness, Wearisome, Weary(ing) Beat, Bejade, Blethered, Bore, Cloy, Deave, Dog-tired, Ennui, Ennuyé, Exhaust, Fag, Fatigate, Fatigue, Flag(ging), Harass, Hech, Heigh-ho, Irk, Jade, Lacklustre, Lassitude, Pall, Puny, Ramfeezle, Sate, Sick, Sleepy, Spent, Tire, Tiresome, Trash, Try, Tucker, Wabbit, Worn

Weasel Beech-marten, Cane, Delundung, Ermine, Ferret, Glutton, Grison, Kolinsky, Marten, Mink, Mustela, Pekan, Pine-marten, Polecat, Stoat, Taira, Tayra, Vermin, Whit(t)ret, Whitterick, Whittrick, Wolverine, Woodshock, Zorilla

Weather, Weather forecast Atmosphere, Climate, Cyclone, Discolour, Dreich, Ecoclimate, Elements, El Niño, Endure, Hail, La Nina, Met, Monkey's wedding, Rain, Sky, Snow, Sprat, Stand, Survive, Synoptic, Tiros, Undergo, Withstand

Weatherboard Rusticating

Weathercock Barometer, Fane, Vane

Weave(r), Weaves, Weaving Arachne, Basket, Broché, Cane, Complect, Contexture, Entwine, Finch, Fishnet, Folk, Heald, Heddle, Interlace, Jacquard, Knotwork, Lace, Lease, Leno, Lion, Loom, Marner, Osiery, Penelope, Pick, Plain, Plait, Raddle, Ripstop, Rya, Satin, Shuttle, Sparrow, Spider, Splice, Stevengraph, Taha, Textorial, Texture, Throstle, Throwster, Tissue, Tweel, Twill, Twine, Wabster, Waggle, Wattle, Webster, Zigzag

Weaver-bird Amadavat, Avadavat, Quelea, Rice-bird, Taha

Web(bed), Webbing, Web-footed, Web-site Aranea, Fissipalmate, Food, Fourchette, Hit, Infomediary, Internet, Mat, Maze, Mesh(work), Network, Offset, Palama, Palmate, Palmiped, Patagium, Pinnatiped, Portal, Retiary, Skein, Snare, Spider, Tear, Tela, Tissue, Toil, Totipalmate, Vane, World Wide

Webster Spider, Weaver

Wed(ding), Wedlock Alliance, Bet, Destination, Diamond, Espousal, Golden, Hymen, Join, Knobstick, Liaison, Link, Marriage, Marry, Mate, Matrimony, Meng(e), Me(i)nt, Meynt, Ming, Monkey's, Nuptials, Pair, Penny, Ruby, Sacrament, Shotgun, Silver, Spousage, Spousal, → **UNION**, Unite, White, Y

Wedge(d) Accretionary, Canting-coin, Chock, Chunk, Cleat, Cotter, Cuneal, Doorstop, Feather, Forelock, Gad, Gagger, Gib, Impacted, Jack, Jam, Key, Niblick, Pitching, Prop,

Quoin, Sand, Scotch, Shim, Spaceband, Sphenic, Stick, Texas, Trig, Vomerine, Voussoir, Whipstock

Wedgwood Benn, China

Wednesday Ash, Midweek, Pulver, Spy

Wee Leak, Little, Pee, Slash, Sma(ll), Tinkle, Tiny, → **URINATE**, Widdle

Weed(y) Adderwort, Agrestal, Alga, Allseed, Anacharis, Arenaria, Bedstraw, Bell-bind, Blinks, Burdock, Buttercup, Carpetweed, Catch, Charlock, Chickweed, Chlorella, Cigar(ette), Cissy, Clotbur, Clover, Cobbler's pegs, Cockle, Cocklebur, Colonist, Coltsfoot, Corncockle, Couch, Daisy, Dallop, Dandelion, Darnel, Dock, Dollop, Dulse, Elder, Elodea, Ers, Fag, Fat hen, Femitar, Fenitar, Fluellen, Fluellin, Fork, Fucoid, Fumitory, Gangly, Goutweed, Goutwort, Ground elder, Groundsel, Helodea, Hoe, Indian, Joe-pye, Knapweed, Knawel, Knot-grass, Lanky, Lemna, Mare's-tail, Marijuana, Matfelon, Mayweed, Nard, Nettle, Nipplewort, Nostoc, Onion, Oxygen, Paterson's curse, Pearlwort, Pilewort, Pineapple, Piri-piri, Plantain, Potamogeton, Purslane, Ragi, Ragwort, Reate, Rest-harrow, Ribbon, Rib-grass, Ribwort, Ruderal, Runch, Sagittaria, Sargasso, Scal(l)awag, Scallywag, Senecio, Softy, Sorrel, Speedwell, Spurge, Spurrey, Sudd, Sun-spurge, Swine's-cress, Tab, Tansy, Tare, Thistle, Tine, Tobacco, Tormentil, Twitch, Ulotrichale, Ulva, Vetch, Viper's bugloss, Wartcress, Widow's, Winnow, Yarr

▷ **Weed** *may indicate* 'urinated'

Weedkiller Arsenic, Atrazine, Dalapon, Diquat, Diuron, Herbicide, Hoe, Paraquat®, Selective, Simazine

Week(s), Weekly Ember, Expectation, Great, Hebdomadary, Holy, Omer, Orientation, Ouk, Oulk, Passion, Periodical, Prophetic, Rag, Rogation, Schoolies, Sennight, Working

Weekday Feria

Weekend K, Sat, Sun

Weep(er), Weeping, Weepy, Wept Bawl, Blubber, Cry, Grat, Greet, Lachrymose, Lament, Loser, Maudlin, Niobe, Ooze, Pipe, Screet, Seep, Sob, Wail, Waterworks

Weevil Anthonomous, Bean, Boll, Bug, Cornworm, Curculio, Diamond-beetle, Grain, Insect, Nut, Pea, Rice, Seed, Snout beetle

Weft Roon, Shot, Texture, Warp, Woof

Weigh(ing), Weigh down, Weight(y) All-up, Apothecaries', Atomic, Avoirdupois, Balance, Bantam, Baric, Bob, Bow, Bulk, Burden, Clout, Consider, Count, Counterpoise, Cruiser, Dead, Deliberate, Drail, Dumbbell, Emphasis, Equivalent, Feather, Formula, Grammage, Great, Gross, Handicap, Heft, Import, Importance, Impost, Incumbent, Journey, Kerb, Live, Load, Mark, Massive, Matter, Metage, Metrology, Minimum, Molecular, Moment, Mouse, Nett, Onerous, One-sided, Oppress, Overpoise, Perpend, Plumb-bob, Plummet, Poise, Ponderal, Pregnant, Preponderance, Prey, Rate, Sash, Sinker, Slang, Slung-shot, Stress, Tare, Throw, Ton(nage), Tophamper, Tron(e), Troy, Trutinate, Unmoor, Welter, Wey

WEIGHTS

1 letter:	Kin	Gram	Tola
G	Kip	Kati	Unce
K	Mna	Khat	
	Oke	Last	*5 letters:*
2 letters:	Pud	Mina	Artal
As	Rod	Nail	Candy
Ct	Ser	Obol	Carat
Oz	Sit	Peck	Catty
Wt	Tod	Pood	Clove
		Rotl	Gerah
3 letters:	*4 letters:*	Seer	Grain
Kat	Dram	Tael	Kandy

Katti	Stone	Firkin	**8 letters:**
Liang	Tical	Fother	Decagram
Libra	Tonne	Kantar	Lispound
Maund	Truss	Rotolo	Semuncia
Ounce		Talent	
Pease	**6 letters:**		**9 letters:**
Peaze	Arroba	**7 letters:**	Micromole
Peise	Candie	Centner	Shippound
Peize	Cantar	Drachma	
Peyse	Cental	Kiloton	**10 letters:**
Pikul	Derham	Lispund	Decagramme
Pound	Dirham	Pesante	
Pudge	Dirhem	Quintal	
Recul	Drachm	Scruple	

Weighing machine Bismar, Scales, Steelyard, Tron(e)
Weightless Agravic
Weight-lifter Crane, Lewis, Windlass
Weir Cauld, Dam, Garth, Kiddle, Kidel, Lasher, Pen, Watergate
Weird Bizarre, Curious, Dree, Eerie, Eery, Eldritch, Far out, Kookie, Odd, Offbeat,
    Spectral, Strange, Supernatural, Taisch, Uncanny, Unearthly, Zany
Welch, Welsh Abscond, Cheat, Default, Embezzle, Levant, Rat, Reneg(u)e, Renig,
    Skedaddle, Weasel
Welcome, Welcoming Aloha, Ave, Bel-accoyle, Ciao, Embrace, Entertain, Glad-hand,
    Godsend, Greet, Haeremai, Hail, Hallo, Halse, Heil, Hello, Hi, Hospitable, How,
    Hullo, Karanga, Open-armed, Open house, Powhiri, Receive, Reception, Salute, Snug,
    Ticker-tape, Yellow-ribbon
Weld(ing) Arc, Butt, Cold, Explosion, Fillet, Friction, Fuse, Gas, Join, Merge, MIG,
    Resistance, Seam, Sinter, Stud, Tack, TIG, Ultrasonic, Unite
Welfare Advantage, Alms, Benison, Common weal, Ha(y)le, Heal, Health, Sarvodaya,
    Social, Weal
Welkin Firmament, Sky
Well (done) Artesian, Atweel, Ave, Aweel, Bien, Bore(hole), Bravo, Carbon, Casinghead,
    Cenote, Chipper, Development, Discovery, Downhole, Dropping, Dry hole, Easily, Euge,
    Famously, Fine, Fit, Foot, Gas, Gasser, Good, Gosh, Gusher, Hale, → **HEALTHY**, Hot,
    Inkpot, Ka pai, Law, Mickery, My, Namma hole, Odso, Oh, Oil(er), Phreatic, Potential,
    Pour, Pump, So, Source, Spa, Spouter, Spring, Sump, Surge, Teek, Tube, Um, Upflow,
    Wildcat, Worthily, Zemzem
Wellbeing Atweel, Bien-être, Comfort, Euphoria, Euphory, Good, Health, Oomph, Welfare
Well-born Eugene
Well-bred Genteel
Well-built Sturdy, Tight
Well-covered Chubby, Padded
Well-curb Puteal
Welles Orson
Wellington, Welly Accelerate, Boot, Green, Gumboot, Iron Duke, Nosey
Well-known Famous, Illustrious, Notorious, Notour, Prominent
Well-off Affluent, Far, Rich, Wealthy
Well part Bucket, Shadoof, Shaduf
Wells Bombardier, Fargo, HG, Llandrindod, Sadler's
Well-wisher Friend
▶ **Welsh** *see* **WELCH**
Welsh(man), Welshwoman Aled, Briton, Brittonic, Brython, Cake, Cambrian, Celtic,
    Cog, Crachach, Cym(ric), Cymry, Dafydd, Dai, Ebbw, Emlyn, Enid, Evan, Fluellen, Gareth,

Harp, Idris, Ifor, Ivor, Keltic, Megan, P-Celtic, P-Keltic, Rabbit, Rarebit, Rees, Rhys, Sion, Taff(y), Tudor, W, Walian

Wen Cyst, Talpa, Tumour, Wart

Wench Blowze, Court, Girl, Gouge, Hussy, Maid, Ramp, Rig, Smock, Strumpet

Wend Meander, Sorb, Steer

Wendy Darling, House

Went Left, Peed, Sold, Yode

Werewolf Loup-garou, Lycanthrope, Nazi, Turnskin, Vampire

Wesleyan Epworth, Methodist

West(ern), Westerly Ang mo, Far, Favonian, Film, Hesperian, Mae, Middle, Movie, Oater, Occidental, Ponent, Spaghetti, Sunset, True Grit, W, Westlin, Wild

West African Fantee, Fanti, Kroo, Mandingo, Wolof

▷ **West end** *may indicate* 't' or 'W1'

West Indian Carib, Creole, Jamaican, Quashee, Quashie, Taino

Westminster SW1

Wet(ting), Wetland Bedabble, Bedraggled, Clammy, Daggle, Damp, Dank, Dew, Dip, Douse, Dowse, Drench, Drip(ping), Drook, Drouk, Embrue, Enuresis, Feeble, Humect, Humid, Hyetal, Imbrue, Imbue, Irrigate, Irriguous, Madefy, Madid, Marshy, Moil, Moist(en), Molly, Namby-pamby, Pee, Piddle, Pouring, Rainy, Ramsar site, Ret(t), Rheumy, Roral, Roric, Runny, Saturate, Shower, Simp(leton), Sipe, Sissy, Sluice, → **SOAK**, Sodden, Sopping, Sour, Steep, Tiddle, Tipsy, Urinate, Wat, Wee, Widdle, Wimpy, Wringing

Wetsuit Steamer

Whack(ed), Whacking Astronomic, Belt, Bemaul, Biff, Deadbeat, Jiggered, Joll, Joule, Jowl, Lambast, Lounder, Share, Swat, Swish, Thump

Whale(meat), Whaling Baleen, Beaked, Beluga, Black, Blower, Blubber, Blue, Bottlehead, Bottlenose, Bowhead, Bull, Cachalot, Calf, Cetacea(n), Cete, Cetology, Cow, Cowfish, Dolphin, Dorado, Fall, Fin(back), Finner, Gam, Glutton, Grampus, Greenland (right), Grey, Greyback, Humpback, Ishmael, Killer, Kreng, Leviathan, Manatee, Minke, Monodon, Mysticeti, Narwhal, Odontoceti, Orc(a), Paste, Physeter, Pilot, Pod, Porpoise, Right, River dolphin, Rorqual, School, Scrag, Sea-canary, Sea-unicorn, Sei, Social, Sperm, Spouter, Sulphur-bottom, Thrasher, Toothed, Toothless, White, Zeuglodon(t), Ziphius

▷ **Whale** *may indicate* an anagram

Whalebone Busk

Whaler Ahab, Harpooner, Ship, Specksioneer, Specktioneer, Waister

Whales' meat Clio

Wham Bang, Collide

Whang Blow, Flog, Thrash, Whack

Wharf(inger) Dock(er), Jetty, Key, Landing, Pier, Quay, Roustabout, Rouster, Staith(e)

What, Whatever Anan, Eh, How, Pardon, Que, Regardless, Siccan, Sorry, Such, That, Which

Whatnot, What's-its-name Dinges, Dingus, Doings, Doobrey, Doobrie, Étagère, Gismo, Jigamaree, Jiggumbob, Thingamy, Thingumajig, Thingumbob, Thingummy, Timenoguy

Wheat Allergen, Amber, Amelcorn, Bald, Beard(ed), Beardless, Blé, Bulg(h)ur, Cone, Couscous, Cracked, Durum, Einkorn, Emmer, Federation, Fromenty, Frumenty, Furme(n)ty, Furmity, Grain, Hard, Mummy, Red, Rivet, Sarrasin, Sarrazin, Seiten, Semolina, Sharps, Soft, Spelt, Spring, Summer, Triticum, White, Winter

Wheatsheaf Bale, Gerbe, Stook

Wheedle Banter, Barney, Blandish, Butter up, Cajole, Coax, Cog, Cuiter, Cuittle, Flatter, Inveigle, Tweedle, Whilly(whaw)

Wheel(er) Balance, Bedel, Bevel, Bicycle, Big, Bogy, Breast, Bucket, Buff(ing), Caracol(e), Cart's tail, Caster, Castor, Catherine, Chain, Chark(h)a, Circle, Cistern, Count, Crown,

Cycle, Daisy, Diamond, Disc, Driving, Emery, Epicycloidal, Escape, Fan, Felloe, Felly, Ferris, Fifth, Fortune, Gear, Grinding, Gyrate, Helm, Hurl, Idle(r), Jagger, Jigger, Jolley, Joy, Kick, Lantern, Magnate, Master, Medicine, Mitre, Monkey, Mortimer, Nabob, Nave, Nose, Paddle, Pattern, Pedal, Pelton, Perambulator, Persian, Pin, Pinion, Pitch, Pivot, Planet, Potter's, Prayer, Pulley, Rag, Ratchet, Rhomb, Roll, Roller, Rotate, Roulette, Rowel, Sheave, Snail, Spare, Spider, Spinning, Sprocket, Spur, Star, Steering, Stepney, Stitch, Swing, Tail, Throwing-table, Training, Tread, Treadmill, Trindle, Trochus, Trolley, Truckle, Trundle, → **TURN**, Tympan(um), Water, Web, Wharve, Whirling-table, Wire, Worm, Zoetrope

Wheelbarrow Hurlbarrow, Monotroch

Wheelhouse Caravan, Paddle-box

Wheel-hub Axle, Nave

Wheelman Cyclist, Ixion

Wheelwright Spokesman

Wheeze Asthma, Breathe, Jape, Joke, Pant, Pech, Ploy, Rale, Reak, Reik, Rhonchus, Ruse, Stridor, Trick, Whaisle, Whaizle

Whelk Buckie, Limpet, Shellfish, Stromb, Triton

Whelm Nalla(h), Nulla(h)

Whelp Bear, Bra(t)chet, Pup

When(ever) Although, As, If, Once, Though, Time

Where(abouts) Location, Neighbourhood, Place, Site, Vicinity, Whaur, Whither

Wherefore Cause, Reason, Why

Whereupon So, When

Wherewithal Finance, Means, Money, Needful, Resources

Wherry Barge, Rowboat

Whet(stone) Coticular, Excite, Hone, Oilstone, Rubstone, Sharpen, Stimulate, Stroke

Whether Conditional, If

Whey Plasma, Serum, Whig

Which(ever), Which is Anyway, As, QE, Whatna, Whilk, Who

Whiff Breath, Cigarette, Gust, Hum, Puff, Redolence, Smatch, Sniff, Trace, Waft

Whig Adullamite, Jig, Rascal, Tory, Whey

While Although, As, Interim, Since, Space, Span, Spell, Though, Throw, Time, When, Whenas, Whereas, Yet

Whim(s), Whimsical, Whimsy Bizarre, Caprice, Conceit, Crotchet, Fad, Fancy, Fantastic, Fay, Fey, Fie, Flisk, Impulse, Kicksy-wicksy, Kink, Maggot, Notion, Quaint, Quirk, Tick, Toy, Vagary

Whimper Cry, Grizzle, Mewl, Pule, Snivel, Whine

Whin Furze, Gorse, Ulex

Whine, Whinge(r) Cant, Carp, Complain, Cry, Grumble, Kvetch, Mewl, Miaow, Moan, Peenge, Pule, Snivel, Sword, Whimper, Yammer

Whinny Neigh, Nicker, Whicker

Whip(ped), Whip out, Whipping Beat, Braid, Brede, Bullwhack, Bullwhip, Cat, Cat o' nine tails, Chabouk, Chantilly, Chastise, Chief, Cilium, Colt, Crop, Drive, Feague, Firk, Five-line, Flagellate, Flagellum, Flay, Gad, Hide, Jambok, Knout, K(o)urbash, Larrup, → **LASH**, Leather, Limber, Lunge, Quirt, Rawhide, Riem, Scourge, Sjambok, Slash, Steal, Stock, Strap-oil, Swinge, Swish, Switch, Taw, Thong, Three-line, Thresh, Trounce, Welt, West Country, Whap, Whop

Whippersnapper Dandiprat, Dandyprat, Pup, Squirt

Whippoorwill Wishtonwish

Whirl(er), Whirling Bullroarer, Circumgyrate, Dervish, Eddy, Gyrate, → **IN A WHIRL**, Maelstrom, Pivot, Reel, Spin, Swing, Swirl, Vortex, Vortical, Vorticose, Vortiginous, Whirry

Whirlpool Eddy, Gulf, Gurge, Maelstrom, Moulin, Sea purse, Swelchie, Vorago, Vortex, Weel, Wiel

Whirlwind Cyclone, Dust devil, Eddy, Sand-devil, Tornado, Tourbillion, Typho(o)n, Vortex, Willy-willy

Whirr Birr

Whisk Balloon, Chowri, Chowry, Fly, Swish, Switch, Whid, Whip

Whisker(s) Beard, Beater, Bristles, Burnsides, Cat's, Dundreary, Excrement, Face fungus, Hackle, Hair, Moustache, Mutton-chop, Samuel, Satyric tuft, Side(-boards), Side-burns, Sidelevers, Stibble, Stubble, Vibrissa

Whisk(e)y Alcohol, Barley-bree, Barley-broo, Barley-broth, Bond, Bourbon, Canadian, Cape smoke, Chain lighting, Corn, Cratur, Crayther, Creature, Fife, Fire-water, Grain, Hard stuff, Hard tack, Highball, Hokonui, Hoo(t)ch, Irish, Malt, Monongahela, Moonshine, Morning, Mountain dew, Nip, Peat-reek, Pot(h)een, Ragwater, Red eye, Rye, Scotch, Sourmash, Southern Comfort®, Spunkie, Tanglefoot, Tarantula juice, Tun, Usquebaugh, W, Wheech, Whiss

▷ **Whisky** *may indicate* an anagram

Whisper Breath(e), Bur(r), Hark, Hint, Innuendo, Murmur, Pig's, Round, Rumour, Rustle, Sigh, Stage, Susurrus, Tittle, Undertone, Whittie-whattie

Whist Dummy, Hush, Long, Progressive, Quiet, Sh, Short, Solo, Whisk and swabbers

Whistle(r) Blow, Boatswain's, Calliope, Catcall, Feedback, Flageolet, Flute, Hewgh, Hiss, Marmot, Pedro, Penny, Phew, Ping, Pipe, Quail-pipe, Ref, Siffle(ur), Sowf(f), Sowth, Steam, Stop, Stridor, Swab(ber), Swanee, Tin, Toot, Tweedle, Tweet, Warbler, Wheeple, Wheugh, Whew, Whiffle, Wolf

Whistle-blower Informer, Nark, Ref

Whit Atom, Doit, Figo, Haet, Hait, Hate, Iota, Jot, Particle, Pentecost, Point, Red cent, Snap, Straw

White(n), Whitener, Whiteness, White-faced Agene, Agenise, Alabaster, Albedo, Albescent, Albino, Albugineous, Albumen, Argent, Ashen, Au lit, Bakra, Blameless, Blanch, Blanche, Blanco, Bleach, Buckra, Cabbage, Calm, Cam, Camstone, Candid, Candida, Candour, Canescent, Canities, Caucasian, Caum, Chalk(y), Chardonnay, Chaste, China, Chinese, Christmas, Cliffs, Collar, Company, Cream, Cue ball, Dealbate, Egg, Elephant, Ermine, European, Fang, Fard, Feather, Flag, Flake, French, Glair, Gwen(da), Gwendolen, Gwyn, Hawked, Hoar(y), Hock, Honorary, Hore, House, Innocent, Ivory, Large, Leucoma, Lie, Lily, Livid, Man, Marbled, Mealy, Niveous, Opal, Oyster, Pakeha, Pale(face), Pallor, Paper, Paris, Pearl, Poor, Pure, Redleg, Russian, Sclerotic, Selborne, Sheep, Silver, Small, Snow(y), Spanish, Taw, Vitiligo, Wan, Wedding, Wyn, Zinc

Whitefish Menominee

Whitefriars Alsatia

Whitehall Ministry

Whitehead Milium

White horse(s) Skipper's daughters, Wave

White man Anglo, Ba(c)kra, Buckra, Caucasian, Corn-cracker, Cracka, Gora, Gub(bah), Haole, Honkie, Honky, Kabloona, Larney, Mzungu, Norteno, Occidental, Ofay, Pakeha, Paleface, Redleg, Redneck, Umlungu, WASP, Wigga, Wigger

Whitewash Calcimine, Excuse, Kalsomine, Lime, Skunk, Trounce

Whitlow Ancome, Felon, Panaritium, Paronychia

Whitsun Pentecost, Pinkster, Pinxter

Whittle Carve, Pare, Sharpen

Whizz Wheech

Who As, Doctor, Qui

Whodunit Mystery

Who knows Quien sabe

Whole, Wholehearted, Wholeness, Wholly All, Cosmos, Eager, Entire(ty), Entity, Every inch, Fully, Hale, Indiscrete, Intact, Integer, Integrity, Largely, Lot, Shebang, Sum, Systemic, Thoroughly, Total, Tout à fait, Unbroken, Uncut

Wholesale(r) Cutprice, En bloc, Engrosser, Ingross, Jobber, Root and branch,

Stockjobber, Supplier, Sweeping

Wholesome Clean, Good, Healthy, Physical, Pure, Salubrious, Salutary, Sound

Whoop(er), Whooping cough Alew, Celebrate, Chincough, Crane, Cry, Excite, Kink(cough), Kink-host, Pertussis, Swan, War

Whoopee Carouse, Evoe, Hey-go-mad, Roister

Whoosh Birr, Swish

Whopper, Whopping Barn, Crammer, Huge, Immense, Jumbo, Lie, Lig, Oner, Out and outer, Plumper, Scrouger, Slapper, Slockdolager, Soc(k)dalager, Soc(k)dolager, Soc(k)doliger, Soc(k)dologer, Sogdolager, Sogdoliger, Sogdologer, Stonker, Tale, Taradiddle

Whore Drab, Harlot, Loose woman, Pinnace, Pro, Prostitute, Quail, Road, Strumpet, Tart

Whorl Corolla, Eucyclic, Spiral, Swirl, Verticil, Volute, Volution

Why How come, Raison d'être, Reason, Yogh

Wick Farm, Rush, Snaste, Snuff, Vill(age)

Wicked(ness) Adharma, Atrocity, → **BAD**, Candle, Criminal, Cru(i)sie, Crusy, Depravity, Devilish, Evil, Facinorous, Flagitious, Goaty, Godless, Heinous, High-viced, Immoral, Impious, Improbity, Iniquity, Lantern, Miscreant, Naughty, Nefarious, Night-light, Pernicious, Perverse, Ponerology, Pravity, Rush, Satanic, Scelerate, Sin(ful), Taper, Turpitude, Unholy, Vile

▷ **Wicked** *may indicate* containing a wick

Wicker(work) Basketry, Sale, Seal, Wattlework

Wicket Gate, Hatch, Infield, Maiden, Pitch, Square, Sticky, Stool, Stump, W, Yate

Wicket-keeper Stumper

Wide, Widen(ing), Width Abroad, Ample, Bay, Braid, Broad, Comprehensive, Dilate, Drib, Eclectic, Expand, Extend, Far, Flanch, Flange, Flare, Flaunch, Ga(u)ge, General, Latitude, Miss, Prevalent, Roomy, Set, Spacious, Span, Spread, Sundry, Sweeping, Vast

Wide-awake Alert, Fly, Hat, Wary, Watchful

Widespread Catholic, Diffuse, Epidemic, Extensive, General, Pandemic, Panoramic, Pervasive, Prevalent, Prolate, Rife, Routh(ie), Sweeping, Universal

Widow(ed) Bereft, Black, Dame, Discovert, Dowager, Golf, Grass, Hempen, Jointress, Relict, Sati, Sneerwell, Suttee, Vidual, Viduous, Whydah-bird, Widdy

Wield Brandish, Control, Exercise, Handle, → **MANIPULATE**, Ply, Sound

Wife, Wives Ball and chain, Better half, Bride, Concubine, Consort, Devi, Dutch, Enid, Evadne, Feme, Feme covert, Fiere, Frau, Goody, Haram, Harem, Harim, Helpmate, Helpmeet, Hen, Her indoors, Kali, Kickie-wickie, Kicksy-wicksy, Kloo(t)chman, Lakshmi, Little woman, Mate, Memsahib, Missis, Missus, Mrs, Mummer's, Partner, Penelope, Pirrauru, Potiphar's, Rib, Seraglio, Spouse, Squaw, Stepford, Trophy, Trouble and strife, Umfazi, Ux(or), Vrou, W, Wag

Wig Adonis, Bagwig, Bob(wig), Brigadier, Brutus, Buzz-wig, Cadogan, Campaign, Carpet, Cauliflower, Caxon, Chevelure, Chide, Cockernony, Dalmahoy, Fright, Full-bottomed, Gizz, Gooseberry, Gorgone, Gregorian, Hair(piece), Heare, Jas(e)y, Jazy, Jiz, Macaroni, Major, Periwig, Peruke, Postiche, Ramil(l)ie(s), Rate, Reprimand, Rug, Scold, Scratch, Sheitel, Spencer, Syrup, Targe, Tie, Toupee, Toupet, Tour

Wiggle, Wiggly Jiggle, Scoleciform, Wobble, Wriggle

Wight Man, Vectis

Wigwam Te(e)pee

Wild(er) Aberrant, Agitato, Agrestal, Amok, Angry, Barbarous, Berserk, Bundu, Bush, Chimeric, Crazy, Demented, Dionysian, Earl, Enthusiastic, Errant, Erratic, Extravagant, Farouche, Feral, Frantic, Frenetic, Gene, Haggard, Hectic, Lawless, Mad(cap), Manic, Meshugge, Myall, Natural, Outlaw, Rampant, Raver, Riotous, Romantic, → **SAVAGE**, Skimble-skamble, Tearaway, Unmanageable, Unruly, Violent, Warrigal, West, Woolly

▷ **Wild(ly)** *may indicate* an anagram

Wild beast Eyra, Sapi-utan, Scrubber

Wildcat Lion, Manul, Ocelot, Strike, Tiger

Wilde Marty, Oscar

Wilderness Bush, Desert, Negev, Ruderal, Sinai, Solitude, Waste, Wasteland
Wild goose Chase, Greylag
Wild oats Haver
Wile, Wily Art, Artful, Artifice, Astute, Braide, → **CUNNING**, Deceit, Foxy, Peery, Ruse,
   Shifty, Shrewd, Slee, → **SLY**, Spider, Stratagem, Streetwise, Subtle, Trick, Versute, Wide
Wilful Deliberate, Headstrong, Heady, Obstinate, Recalcitrant, Wayward
Will, Willing(ly) Alsoon, Amenable, Bard, Bequeath, Bewildered, Biddable, Bill(y),
   Can do, Complaisant, Compliant, Conation, Content, Desire, Devise, Fain, Force, Free,
   Game, General, Hay, Holographic, Leave, Legator, Leve, Lief, Lieve, Living, Mind, Nerve,
   Noncupative, Obedient, On, Open, Pacable, Please, Prone, Purpose, Raring, Rather,
   Ready, Receptive, Resolution, Scarlet, Soon, Spirit, Swan, Testament, Testate, Thelma,
   Volens, Volition, Voluntary, Volunteer, Way, Wimble, Woot
▷ **Will** *may indicate* an anagram
William(s) Bill(y), Conqueror, Occam, Orange, Pear, Rufus, Silent, Sweet, Tell,
   Tennessee
Will o' the wisp Fatuous fire, Fen-fire, Friar's lantern, Ignis-fatuus, Jack o'lantern, Min
   min, Nightfire, Rush, Spunkie
Willow(ing), Willowy Arctic, Crack, Diamond, Lissom(e), Lithe, Osier, Poplar, Port
   Jackson, Pussy, Sale, Salix, Sallow, Sauch, Saugh, Seal, Supple, Twilly, Weeping, Withy
Willpower Ab(o)uha, Determination, Resolve, Strength
Willy-nilly Nolens volens, Perforce
Wilt Decline, Droop, Fade, Flag, Sap, Shalt, Wither
Wiltshireman Moonraker
▶ **Wily** *see* **WILE**
Wimp(ish) Drip, Mouse, Namby-pamby, Pantywaist, Saddo, Weed
Wimple Gorget, Meander, Ripple, Turn, Veil
▷ **Wimple** *may indicate* an anagram
Win(ner), Winning Achieve, Acquire, Adorable, Ahead, Appealing, Backgammon,
   Bangster, Banker, → **BEAT**, Capot, Carry off, Cert, Champion, Conciliate, Conquer, Cup,
   Cute, Decider, Disarming, Dividend, Dormie, Dormy, Earn, Effect, Endearing, Engaging,
   First, Gain, Gammon, Grand slam, Hit, Jackpot, Land, Laureate, Lead, Luck out, Medallist,
   Motser, Motza, Nap hand, Nice, On a roll, Pile, Pot, Prevail, Profit, Purler, Reap, Repique,
   Result, Rubicon, Scoop, Shoo-in, Slam, Snip, Success, Sweet, Take, Top dog, → **TRIUMPH**,
   Up, Vellet, Velvet, Victor(y), Vole, Walk over, Wrest, Yellow jersey, Yokozuna
Wince Blench, Cringe, Flinch, Recoil
Winch Crab, Crane, Jack, Windlass
Winchester® Rifle, Wykehamist
Wind(er), Winding(s), Windy Air, Airstream, Anabatic, Anfractuous, Backing,
   Bend, Blow, Bottom, Brass, Burp, Capstan, Carminative, Chill, Coil, Colic, Crank, Creeky,
   Curl, Curve, Draught, Draw, Entwist, Evagation, Fearful, Flatulence, Flatus, Flaw, Gas,
   Gust, Katabatic, Meander, Nervous, Periodic, Ponent, Poop, Prevailing, Purl, Quarter,
   Quill, Reeds, Reel, Roll, Screw, Sea, Second, Series, Serpentine, Serpentize, Sinuous,
   Slant, Snake, Spiral, Spool, Surface, Swirl, Tail, Thread, Throw, Tortuous, Trade, Trend,
   Turn, Twaddle, Twine, Twisty, Veer, Veering, Ventose, Waffle, Weave, Wiggle, Winch,
   Windle, Winnle, Woold, Wrap, Wreathe, Wrest, Wuthering

WINDS

4 *letters:*		5 *letters:*	
Berg	Gale	Blore	Foehn
Bise	Libs	Buran	Gibli
Bora	Link	Chili	Greco
Firn	Puna	Corus	Noser
Fohn	Vayu	Eurus	Notus
			Ostro

Solar
Sough
Zonda

6 letters:
Aquilo
Auster
Baguio
Boreas
Breeze
Buster
Ghibli
Haboob
Heaves
Kamsin
Levant
Samiel
Sciroc
Shamal
Simoom
Simoon
Solano
Squall
Typhon
Wester
Zephyr

7 letters:
Aeolian
Ambages
Aquilon
Bluster
Chinook
Cyclone
Etesian
Gregale
Kamseen
Khamsin
Maestro
Meltemi
Mistral
Monsoon
Muzzler
Noreast
Norther
Pampero
Shimaal
Sirocco
Snifter
Snorter
Souther
Sumatra
Tornado
Twister
Typhoon

8 letters:
Apparent
Argestes
Downwash
Easterly
Favonian
Favonius
Levanter
Libeccio
Scirocco
Taranaki
Westerly
Williwaw
Zephyrus

9 letters:
Anti-trade
Bourasque
Cordonazo
Dust devil
Euraquilo
Harmattan
Hurricane
Hurricano
Jet stream
Knee-swell
Libecchio
Norwester

Volturnus

10 letters:
Cape doctor
Euroclydon
Rip-snorter
Tourbillon
Tramontana
Whirlblast
Willy-willy

11 letters:
Northwester
Norwesterly
White squall

12 letters:
Brickfielder

13 letters:
Northwesterly
Tehuantepecer

15 letters:
Southerly buster

Windbag Balloon, Bore, Drogue, Prattler, Whoopee cushion, Zeppelin
Windfall Bonanza, Buckshee, Caduac, Fortune, Godsend, Manna
Windflower Anemone
Windlass Differential, Spanish, Whim, Winch
Windmill Pinwheel, Post, Smock, Whirligig
Window(s) Atmosphere, Bay, Bow, Casement, Catherine-wheel, Companion, Compass, Day, Deadlight, Dormer, Double-hung, Dream-hole, Entry, Eye, Eyelids, Fanlight, Fenestella, Fenestra, French, Gable, Garret, Glaze, Guichet, Jalousie, Jesse, Judas, Jut, Lancet, Lattice, Launch, Loop-light, Louver, Louvre, Lozen, Lucarne, Lunette, Luthern, Lychnoscope, Marigold, Mezzanine, Mirador, Monial, Mullion, Oculus, Oeil-de-boeuf, Ogive, Opportunity, Orb, Oriel, Ox-eye, Pane, Pede, Picture, Pop-under, Pop-up, Porthole, Program, Quarterlight, Radio, Re-entry, Rosace, Rose, Round, Sash, Sexfoil, Shed dormer, Shop, Shot, Spyhole, Storm, Transom, Trellis, Ventana, Weather, Wheel, Wicket, Windock, Windore, Winnock
Window-bar, Window-fastening Astragal, Espagnolette
Windpipe Bronchus, Gular, Throat, Trachea, Weasand
Windscale Beaufort
Windsock Drogue, Sleeve
Windsor Castle, Knot
Windswept Scud
Wind-up End, Fright, Liquidate, Miff, Span
Windward Ahold, Aloof, A-weather, Laveer, Luff, Up
Wine Bin, Blush, Cabinet, Case, Cup, Cuvée, Doc, Espumoso, Essence, Fortified, Grand cru, Low, Must, Piece, Pigment, Premier cru, Prisage, Rotgut, Rouge, Semi-dry, Sparkling, Steen, Tannin, Terroir, The grape, Tirage, Unoaked, Varietal, Vat, Vintage, Zymurgy

WINES

2 letters:
It

3 letters:
Dao
Red
Sec
Tun
Vin

4 letters:
Asti
Brut
Cava
Hock
Mull
Palm
Pipe
Port
Race
Rosé
Rosy
Sack
Sekt
Stum
Tent
Tutu
Vino

5 letters:
Anjou
Anker
Biddy
Blanc
Bombo
Comet
Gallo
Gamay
Macon
Médoc
Maqui
Mirin
Mosel
Negus
Pinot
Plonk
Rhine
Rioja
Soave
Straw
Syrah
Table

Tavel
Toddy
Tokay
White
Xeres

6 letters:
Alsace
Barley
Barolo
Barsac
Beaune
Bishop
Bubbly
Canary
Claret
Ginger
Graves
Lisbon
Malaga
Malbec
Merlot
Muscat
Piment
Plotty
Red Ned
Sherry
Shiraz
Solera

7 letters:
Alicant
Amoroso
Auslese
Bastard
Catawba
Chablis
Château
Chianti
Cowslip
Currant
Demi-sec
Dessert
Eiswein
Fendant
Icewine
Madeira
Malmsey
Margaux
Marsala
Moselle
Oenomel

Orvieto
Pomerol
Pommard
Retsina
Rhenish
Sangria
Sherris
Vouvray

8 letters:
Bordeaux
Bucellas
Buckfast®
Burgundy
Cabernet
Champers
Charneco
Dubonnet®
Essencia
Frascati
Gluhwein
Jerepigo
Kabinett
Log-juice
Malvasia
Malvesie
Montilla
Mountain
Muscadel
Muscadet
Muscatel
Nebbiolo
Oenology
Pinotage
Pradikat
Prosecco
Red biddy
Resinata
Rheingau
Riesling
Sémillon
Sancerre
Sangaree
Sauterne
Spätlese
Spumante
St Julien
Sylvaner
Verdelho
Vermouth
Vinsanti

9 letters:
Bacharach
Bardolino
Carmenère
Champagne
Dandelion
En primeur
Falernian
Gladstone
Hermitage
Hippocras
Hoccamore
Inglenook
Lambrusco
Languedoc
Loll-shrob
Malvoisie
Meersault
Minervois
Muscadine
Ordinaire
Pinot noir
Sauvignon
St Emilion
Tafelwein
Tarragona
Vin-du-pays
Zinfandel

10 letters:
Beaujolais
Bull's blood
Chambertin
Chardonnay
Constantia
Elderberry
Genevrette
Hochheimer
Loll-shraub
Manzanilla
Montrachet
Muscadelle
Napa Valley
Peter-see-me
Piesporter
Sangiovese
Vinho verde

11 letters:
Amontillado
Dom Perignon
Niersteiner

Petite Sirah
Pouilly-Fumé
Rudesheimer
Scuppernong
Steinberger

12 letters:
Johannisberg
Marcobrunner
Supernaculum

Valpolicella
Vin ordinaire

13 letters:
Beerenauslese
Entre-Deux-Mers
Liebfraumilch
Montepulciano
Pouilly-Fuissé

14 letters:
Gewürztraminer
Johannisberger

15 letters:
Lachryma Christi
Liebfrauenmilch

16 letters:
London particular

17 letters:
Cabernet Sauvignon
Châteaux cardboard
Nuits Saint Georges

20 letters:
Trockenbeeren-
auslese

Wine-cellar, Wine-shop Bistro, Bodega, Vault, Vaut(e)
Wine-glass Flute
Wine-making Gallising, Remuage
Wing(s), Winged, Winger, Wing-like Aerofoil, Ala(r), Alula, Annexe, Appendage, Arm, Bastard, → **BIRD**, Branch, Buffalo, Canard, Cellar, Corium, Coulisse, Delta, Dipteral, El(l), Elevon, Elytral, Elytriform, Elytron, Elytrum, Fan, Fender, Flap, Flew, Flex, Flipper, Flying, Forward, Gull, Halteres, Hurt, Left, Limb, Offstage, Parascenia, Parascenium, Patagium, Pennate, Pennon, Pinero, Pinion, Pip, Pterygoid, Putto, Right, Rogallo, Sail, Samariform, Satyrid, Scent-scale, Segreant, Seraphim, Split, Standard, Sweepback, Sweptback, Sweptwing, Swift, Swingwing, Tailplane, Tectrix, Tegmen, Tormentor, Transept, Van, Vol(et), Water, Wound(ed)
Winged sandals Talaria
▷ **Winger** *may indicate* a bird
Wing-footed Aliped, Fleet, Swift
Wingless Apteral
Wink (at) Atone, Bat, Condone, Connive, Eyelid, Flicker, Ignore, Instant, Nap, Nictitate, Pink, Twinkle
Winnie Pooh
Winnow Fan, Riddle, Separate, Sift, Van, Wecht
Winsome Bonny, Engaging, Gay, Pleasant
Winter, Wintry Blackthorn, Bleak, Brumal, Cold, Dec, Fimbul, Frigid, Frore, Hibernate, Hiemal, Hiems, Hodiernal, Jack Frost, Jasmine, Nuclear, Shrovetide, Snowy, Subniveal, W
Winter cherry Chinese lantern
Wintergreen Chickweed, Pyrola, Sarcodes
Winter pear Nelis
Winter-sport Ski
Wipe (out), Wiping Abolish, Abrogate, Absterge, Amortise, Cancel, Cleanse, Demolish, Destroy, Deterge, Dicht, Dight, Efface, Eradicate, Erase, Expunge, Forget, Hanky, Mop, Nose-rag, Null, Purge, Raze, Retroussage, Slorm, Sponge, Tersion, Tissue
Wire(s), Wiry Aerial, Barb(ed), Cable, Cat's whiskers, Chicken, Coil, Earth, Element, Fencing, Filament, Filar, File, Heald, Heddle, High, In on, Kirschner, Lead, Lean, Lecher, Live, Marconigram, Messenger, Mil, Nichrome®, Nipper, Number eight, Piano, Pickpocket, Razor, Sevice, Shroud, Sinewy, Snake, Solenoid, Spit, Staple, Stilet, Strand, String, Stylet, Telegram, Telegraph, Thoth, Thread, Trace, Trip
Wireless (operator), Wireless part Baffle, Set, Sparks, Tranny, Valve
Wise(acre), Wisdom Advisedly, Ancient, Astute, Athena, Athene, Canny, Conventional, Cracker barrel, Depth, Ernie, Ganesa, Gothamite, Gudrun, Hep, Hindsight, Judgement, Judicious, Learned, Long-headed, Lore, Manner, Mimir, Minerva, Norman, Oracle, Owl, Pearl, Penny, Philosopher, Philosophy, Politic, Polymath, Prajna, Profound, Prudence, Sagacity, Sage, Salomonic, Sapience, Savvy, Shrewd, Smartie, Solomon, Solon, Sophia, Tooth, Wice

Wisecrack Dig, One-liner, Quip

Wise man Balthazar, Caspar, Gaspar, Hakam, Heptad, Melchior, Nestor, Pandit, Sage, Sapient, Seer, Solomon, Swami, Thales, Tohunga, Worldly

Wish(es), Wishing Ache, Ake, Covet, Crave, Death, Desiderate, → **DESIRE**, Envy, For, Hope, Itch, List, Long, Nill, Pant, Pleasure, Pray, Precatory, Regards, RIP, Velleity, Want, Yearn

Wishbone Furcula, Marriage-bone, Merrythought, Skipjack

Wishy-washy Bland, Feeble, Insipid, Irresolute, Milksop, Weak, Wheyey

Wisp(y) Cirrate, Cirrose, Frail, Scrap, Shred, Virga, Wase

Wistful Elegiac

Wit(s), Witticism, Witty Acumen, Attic, Badinage, Banter, Bon mot, Brevity, Commonsense, Concetto, Cunning, Dry, Epigram, Esprit, Estimation, Eutrapelia, Eutrapely, Facetious, Fantasy, Gnome, Hartford, Horse sense, Humour, Imagination, Intelligence, Irony, Jest, Jeu d'esprit, Joke, Marbles, Marinism, Memory, Mind, Mot, Mother, Native, Nous, Oscar Wilde, Pawky, Pun, Quipster, Repartee, Rogue, Sally, Salt, Saut, Sconce, → **SENSE**, Shaft, Smart, Sparkle, Videlicet, Viz, Wag, Weet, Wisecrack, Word-play

Witch(craft) Beldam(e), Besom-rider, Broomstick, Cantrip, Carline, Circe, Coven, Craigfluke, Crone, Cutty Sark, Diabolism, Enchantress, Ensorcell, Galdragon, Glamour, Goety, Gramary(e), Gyre-carlin, Hag, Hecat(e), Hex, Invultuation, Lamia, Magic, Medea, Myal(ism), Necromancy, Night-hag, Obeahism, Obia, Obiism, Pishogue, Pythoness, Salem, Selim, Sibyl, Sieve, Sorceress, Speller, Sycorax, Trout, Valkyrie, Vaudoo, Vilia, Voodoo, Water, Weird, Wicca, Wise woman

Witch-doctor Animist, Boyla, Medicine man, Mganga, Obi, Pawaw, Powwow, Sangoma, Shaman

Witch-hazel Fothergilla, Platan(e), Winter-bloom

Witch-hunter McCarthy

With And, By, Con, Cum, Hereby, In, Mit, Of, Plus, W

Withdraw(al), Withdrawn Abdicate, Alienate, Aloof, Back out, Breakaway, Cloistered, Cold turkey, Cry off, Detach, Disengage, Distrait, Enshell, Evacuate, Hive off, Inshell, Introvert, Leave, Offish, Palinode, Phantom, Precede, Preserve, Recant, Recoil, Repair, Rescind, Resile, Reticent, Retire, Retract(ion), Retreat, Revoke, Revulsion, Scratch, Secede, Secesh, Sequester, Shrink, Shy, Stand down, Subduce, Subduct, Unreeve, Unsay

Wither(ed), Withering, Withers Arefy, Atrophy, Blight, Burn, Corky, Die, Droop, Dry, Evanish, Fade, Forpine, Gizzen, Googie, Languish, Marcescent, Miff, Nose, Scram, Sere, Shrink, Shrivel, Welk, Welt

Withershins Eastlin(g)s

▷ **With gaucherie** *may indicate* an anagram

Withhold(ing), Withheld Abstain, Conceal, Curt, Deny, Detain, Detinue, Hide, Keep, → **RESERVE**, Ritenuto, Trover

Within Enclosed, Endo-, Immanent, Indoors, Inside, Interior, Intra

With it Hep, Hip, Syn, Trendy, W

Without Bar, Beyond, Ex, Lack(ing), Less, Minus, Orb, Outdoors, Outside, Sans, Save, Sen, Senza, Sine, X

▷ **Without** *may indicate* one word surrounding another

▷ **Without restraint** *may indicate* an anagram

Without stimulus Nastic

Withstand Blight, Brave, Contest, Defy, Endure, Oppose, Resist, Weather

Witless Crass, → **STUPID PERSON**

Witness Attend, Attest, Bystander, Catch, Character, Compurgator, Confirm, Crown, Deponent, Depose, Endorse, Evidence, Experience, Expert, Eye, Glimpse, Hostile, Jehovah's, Mark, Martyr, Material, Muggletonian, Note, Notice, Observe, Obtest, Onlooker, Perceive, Proof, → **SEE**, Show, Sight, Sign, Spy, Stander-by, Survey, Testament,

Teste, Testify, Testimony, View, Vouchee, Watch

Witness-box Peter, Stand

▸ **Witticism** *see* WIT(S)

Wizard (priest) Archimage, Awesome, Carpathian, Conjuror, Demon, Expert, Gandalf, Hex, Mage, Magician, Merlin, Obiman, Oz, Prospero, Shaman, Sorcerer, Super, Warlock, → WITCH-DOCTOR

Wizen(ed) Dehydrate, Dry, Sere, Shrivel, Sphacelate, Wither

Woad Anil, Dye, Indigo, Isatis, Pastel, Pastil

Wobble, Wobbling, Wobbly Chandler's, Coggle, Hissy fit, Precess, Quaver, Reel, Rock, Shimmy, Shoggle, Shoogle, Teeter, Totter, Tremble, Trillo, Unstable, Wag, Waggle, Walty, Waver, Wibble

Wodehouse Plum

Woe(ful), Woebegone Agony, Alack, Alas, Bale, Bane, Distress, Dool(e), Dule, Ewhow, Execrable, Gram, Grief, Hurt, Jeremiad, Lack-a-day, Misery, Pain, Plague, → SORROW, Torment, Tribulation, Triste, Unhappy, Wailful

Wolds Lincoln(shire), Yorkshire

Wolf(ish), Wolf-like Akela, Assyrian, Bolt, Cancer, Carcajou, Casanova, Coyote, Cram, Dangler, Dasyure, Dire, Earth, Engorge, Fenrir, Fenris, Gorge, Grey, Ise(n)grim, Lobo, Lone, Lothario, Lupine, Luster, Lycanthrope, MI, Michigan, Pack, Prairie, Rake, Ravenous, Red, Rip, Roué, Rout, Rudolph, Rye, Scoff, Sea, Seducer, Strand, Tasmanian, Thylacine, Tiger, Timber, Wanderer, Were, Whistler

Wolfram Tungsten

Wolf's bane Aconite, Friar's-cap

Wolseley Sir Garnet

Woman(hood), Women Aguna(h), Anile, Beldam(e), Bellibone, Besom, Biddy, Bimbo, Bint, Bit, Boiler, Broad, Cailleach, Callet, Chai, Chapess, Chook, Citess, Cotquean, Crone, Crumpet, Cummer, Dame, Daughter, Distaff, Doe, Dona(h), Dorcas, Doris, Drab, Duenna, Eve, F, Fair, Fair sex, → FEMALE, Feme, Femme fatale, Flapper, Floozy, Frail, Frow, Gammer(stang), Gimmer, Gin, Girl, Gyno-, -gyny, Harpy, Harridan, Hausfrau, Hen, Her, Ho, Housewife, Inner, It, Jade, Jane, Kloo(t)chman, Lady, Liberated, Lilith, Lorette, Madam(e), Mademoiselle, Maenad, Mary, Miladi, Milady, Millie, Minge, Mob, Mort, Ms, Muliebrity, Painted, Pandora, Peat, Pict, Piece, Piece of goods, Placket, Point, Popsy, Puna(a)ni, Puna(a)ny, Pussy, Quean, Queen, Ramp, Rib, Ribibe, Ronyon, Rudas, Runnion, Sabine, Sakti, Scarlet, Shakti, Shawlay, Shawlie, She, Skirt, Sloane Ranger, Sort, Squaw, Tail, Tedesca, Tib, Tiring, Tit, Tottie, Totty, Trot, Umfazi, Vahine, Wahine, Weaker sex, Wifie, Zena

Womaniser Casanova, Lady-killer, Poodle-faker, Wolf

Womb Belly, Matrix, Metritis, Side, Uterus, Ventricle

Women's club, Women's lib S(h)akti, Soroptimist

Won Chon, W

Wonder(s) Admire, Agape, Amazement, AR, Arkansas, Arrah, Awe, Chinless, Colossus, Ferly, Grape-seed, Hanging Gardens, Marle, → MARVEL, Mausoleum, Meteor, Mirabilia, Miracle, Muse, Nine-day, Pharos, Phenomenon, Prodigy, Pyramids, Seven, Speculate, Statue of Zeus, Stupor, Suppose, Surprise, Temple of Artemis, Thaumatrope, Wheugh, Whew, Wow(ee)

Wonderful(ly) Amazing, Bees' knees, Bitchin(g), Chinless, Divine, Épatant, Fantastic, Far-out, Ferly, Geason, Gee-whiz, Glorious, Gramercy, Great, Heavenly, Keen, Lal(l)apalooza, Magic, Mirable, Must-see, Old, Purely, Ripping, Smashing, Stellar, Sublime, Superb, Wicked

Wonder-worker Fakir, Thaumaturgist, Thaumaturgus

Wonky Cockeyed, Lopsided

Wont(ed) Accustomed, Apt, Custom, Habit, Shan't, Used, Winna

Woo(er) Address, Beau, Carve, Court, Frog, Seduce, Serenade, Suitor, Swain

Wood(s), Wooden, Woodland, Woody Arboretum, Batten, Beam, Birken,

Board, Boord(e), Bough, Brake, Cask, Channel, Chipboard, Chuck, Chump, Clapboard, Conductor, Dead, Deadpan, Expressionless, Fardage, Fathom, Fire, Fish, Funk, Furious, Gantry, Gauntree, Guthrie, Hanger, Hard, Hyle, Kindling, Knee, Krummholz, Late, Lath, Lumber, Mad, Magnetic, Miombo, Nemoral, Nemorous, Offcut, Pallet, Plastic, Pulp(wood), Punk, Silvan, Slat, Spinney, Splat, Spline, Splint, Stolid, Sylvan, Tenon, Three-ply, Timber, Tinder, Touch, Treen, Trees, Twiggy, Vert, Xylem, Xyloid

WOODS

3 letters:
Ash
Box
Cam
Elm
Log
Red

4 letters:
Beef
Bent
Bowl
Carr
Cord
Cork
Deal
Eugh
Gapó
Holt
Iron
King
Lana
Lima
Lime
Pine
Rata
Rock
Shaw
Soft
Spar
Teak
Wild
Yang

5 letters:
Afara
Agila
Algum
Almug
Balsa
Bavin
Beech
Cedar
Copse
Drive

Ebony
Elfin
Firth
Frith
Green
Grove
Heben
Hurst
Igapó
Iroko
Jarul
Joist
Klaat
Kokra
Lance
Maple
Mazer
Myall
Opepe
Peach
Plane
Ramin
Rowan
Sapan
Spoon
Stink
Taiga
Thorn
Tiger
Tulip
Wenge
Zante
Zebra

6 letters:
Alerce
Bamboo
Beaver
Birnam
Bocage
Brazil
Calico
Canary
Carapa
Cheese

Citron
Citrus
Deodar
Dingle
Forest
Fustet
Fustic
Fustoc
Gaboon
Gopher
Herman
Jarool
Jarrah
Letter
Lignum
Loggat
Manuka
Muntin
Obeche
Orache
Orange
Paddle
Poplar
Raddle
Sabele
Sabicu
Sandal
Sapele
Sappan
Sissoo
Sponge
Tallow
Tupelo
Violet
Waboom
Walnut
Wandoo
Yellow

7 letters:
Amboina
Barwood
Boscage
Brassie
Cambium

Cerrado®
Coppice
Dudgeon
Dunnage
Duramen
Gambrel
Gumwood
Hadrome
Hickory
Leopard
Meranti
Mesquit
Nutwood
Palmyra
Paranym
Pimento
Sanders
Sapwood
Shawnee
Shittim
Trumpet
Wallaba

8 letters:
Agalloch
Alburnum
Basswood
Bushveld
Caatinga
Coulisse
Harewood
Hornbeam
Kingwood
Laburnum
Ligneous
Mahogany
Masonite®
Mesquite
Mountain
Ovenwood
Pyengadu
Pyinkado
Rosewood
Sapucaia
Shagbark

Southern	Heartwood	Blockboard	Palisander
Tamarack	Ivorywood	Bulletwood	Scaleboard
	Matchwood	Calamander	Sneezewood
9 letters:	Partridge	Candlewood	Springwood
Briarwood	Porcupine	Cheesewood	Summerwood
Butternut	Primavera	Chittagong	
Caliature	Quebracho	Coromandel	**11 letters:**
Campeachy	Satinwood	Fiddlewood	Lignum-vitae
Coachwood	Snakewood	Greenheart	Sanderswood
Cocuswood	Torchwood	Hackmatack	Slippery elm
Driftwood		Marblewood	
Eaglewood	**10 letters:**	Nettle-tree	**13 letters:**
Fruitwood	Afrormosia	Orangewood	Savanna-wattle

▷ **Wood** *may indicate* an anagram in sense of mad
Wood-carver Bodger, Gibbons, Whittler
Woodchuck Bobac, Marmot
Woodcock Becasse, Beccaccia, Snipe
Woodlouse Isopod, Oniscus, Slater
Woodman Ali (Baba), Coureur de bois, Feller, Forester, Hewer, Logger, Lumberjack, Sawyer
Woodpecker Bird, Flicker, Hairy, Hickwall, Picalet, Picarian, Pileated, Rainbird, Sapsucker, Saurognathae, Witwall, Woodspite, Woodwale, Woody, Yaffle
Wood-pigeon Bird, Cushat, Que(e)st, Qu(o)ist, Torquate
Wood-sorrel Oca
Wood-tar Furan, Furfuran
Woodwind Bassoon, Clarinet, Cornet, Flute, Oboe, Piccolo, Pipe, Recorder, Reed
Woodwork(er) Carpentry, Ebonist, Forestry, Intarsia, Joinery, Marquetrie, Marquetry, Sloid, Sloyd, Tarsia, Termite
Woodworm Gribble, Termes
Wookey Stalactite
Wool(len), Woolly (haired) Alpaca, Angora, Aran, Ardil, Bainin, Barège, Beige, Berlin, Botany, Bouclé, Calamanco, Cardi(gan), Cashmere, Cas(s)imere, Clean, Clip, Combings, Cotton, Crutchings, Daglock, Delaine, Doeskin, Dog, Doily, Down, Doyley, Drugget, Duffel, Fadge, Fingering, Fleece, Flock, Frib, Frieze, Fuzz, Glass, Greasy, Guernsey, Hank, Hause-lock, Heather mixture, Hogget, Indumentum, Jaeger, Jersey, Kashmir, Ket, Lanate, Laniferous, Lanigerous, Lanose, Lock, Loden, Merino, Mineral, Mortling, Moul, Mullein, New, Noil(s), Nun's-veiling, Offsorts, Oo, Paco, Pashm, Pelage, Persian, Pine, Qiviut, Rock, Rolag, Sagathy, Saxon, Say, Shahtoosh, Shalloon, Shamina, Shetland, Shoddy, Skein, Skin, Slag, Slipe, Slip-on, Slub, Smart, Spencer, Staple, Steel, Strouding, Stuff, Swansdown, Tamise, Tammy, Telltale, Thibet, Three-ply, Tod, Tricot, Tweed, Twin set, Ulotrichous, Vicuña, Virgin, Wire, Wood, Worcester, Yarn, Zephyr, Zibel(l)ine
Wool-gather(er), Woolgathering Argo, Dreamer, Reverie
Wool-holder, Woolsack Bale, Distaff
Woolly-bear Tiger-moth, Woubit
Wool-oil Yolk
Wooster Bertie
Woozy Drunk, Faint, Vague, Woolly
Worcester Wigorn
Word(s), Wording, Wordy Al(l)-to, Appellative, Aside, Bahuvrihi, Buzz, Cataphor(a), Catch, Cheville, Claptrap, Clipped, Clitic, Code, Comment, Content, Dick, Dit(t), Echoic, Effable, Embolalia, Enclitic, Epitaph, Epithet, Epos, Etymon, Faith, Four-letter, Function, Functor, Ghost, Grace, Hapax legomenon, Hard, Heteronym, Hint, Holophrase,

Homograph, Homonym, Horseman's, Household, Hyponym, → IN A WORD, → IN
TWO WORDS, Janus, Jonah, Key, Last, Lexeme, Lexicon, Lexis, Loan, Logia, Logos,
Long-winded, Lyrics, Mantra, Meronym, Message, Morpheme, Mot, Neologism, News,
Nonce, Nonsense, Noun, Om, Operative, Oracle, Order, Palabra, Paragram, Paranym,
Parenthesis, Parlance, Parole, Paronym, Paroxytone, Particle, Perissology, Peristomenon,
Phrase, Piano, Pledge, Pleonasm, Polysemen, Portmanteau, Preposition, Prolix,
Promise, Pronoun, Reserved, Rhematic, Rhyme, Rumbelow, Rumour, Saying, Selah,
Semantics, Signal, Soundbite, Subtitle, Surtitle, Syntagma, Talkative, Tatpurusha, Term,
Tetragram, Text, Trigger, Trope, Typewriter, Verb, Verbiage, Verbose, Vocab(ulary),
Vogue, Warcry, Weasel, Winged, Wort, Written

Word-blindness Alexia, Dyslexia
Word-play Charade, Paronomasia, Pun
Wordsmith Logodaedalus
▷ **Work** *may indicate* a book or play, etc
Workable Feasible, Practical
Workaholic, Work(er), Working(-class), Workmen, Works,
Workman(ship) Act(ivate), Aga saga, Ant, Application, Appliqué, Apronman,
Artefact, Artel, Artifact, Artificer, Artisan, At it, At task, Barmaid, Beamer, Beaver, Bee,
Blue-collar, Blue-singlet, Bohunk, Boon(er), Boondoggle, Brief, Bull, Business, Busy,
Careerist, Casual, Char, Chare, Chargehand, Chigga, Chippy, Chore, Claim, Clock, Colon,
Community, Contingent, Coolie, Cooly, Corvée, Craftsman, Crew, Cultivate, Darg, Dig,
Do, Dog, Dogsbody, Donkey, Draft-mule, Droil, Drudge, Drug, Dung, Earn, Effect, Effort,
Em, Erg(ataner), Ergatoid, Erg-nine, Ergon, Ergonomics, Erg-ten, Eta, Everything,
Evince, Exercise, Exergy, Exploit, Factotum, Facture, Fast, Fat, Fettler, Field, Flex(i)time,
Floruit, Fret, Fuller, → FUNCTION, Gae, Gastarbeiter, Gel, Girl Friday, Go, Graft, Grass,
Grind, Grisette, Grunt, Guest, Hand, Harness, Hat, Hobo, Horse, Hot-desking, Hunky,
Indian, Industry, Innards, Jackal, Job, Journeyman, Key, Knead, Knowledge, Kolhoznik,
Labour, Laid, Leave, Luddite, Lump, Machinist, Maid, Man, Manipulate, Manpower,
McJob, Mechanic(ian), Meng, Menge, Menial, Midinette, Mine, Ming, MO, Moider, Moil,
Moonlight, Movement, Navvy, Neuter, Number, Oeuvre, On, Op, Opera(tion), Operative,
Operator, Opus, Opusc(u)le, Outreach, Outside, Ouvrier, Ox, Parergon, Part, Passage,
Peasant, Peg, Pensum, Peon, Pink-collar, Plasterer, Ply, Poker, Portfolio, Postlude,
Potboiler, Practicum, Practise, Production, Prole(tariat), Prud'homme, Public, Pursuit,
Red-neck, Reduction, Rep, Ride, Robot, Rotovate, Roughneck, Round, Rouseabout,
Roustabout, Run, Salaryman, Samiti, Sandhog, Satisfactory, Scabble, Scapple, Serve,
Service, Servile, Seven, Sewage, Shift, Shop (floor), Situation, Skanger, Slogger, Smithy,
Social, Soldier, Spiderman, Staff, Stagehand, Stakhanovite, Stevedore, Stint, Strap, Straw,
Strive, Support, Surface, Swaggie, Swagman, Sweat, Swink, Take, Tamper, Task, Team,
Technician, Telecommuter, Temp, Tenail(le), Tenaillon, Termite, Tew, Text, Tick, Till,
Toccata, Toil, Toreutic, Travail, Treatise, Trojan, TU, TUC, Turk, Tut, Tutman, Typto,
Uphill, Wage plug, Walla(h), Wark, Welfare, White-collar, Wobblies, Yacker, Yakka,
Yakker, Yarco

Work-basket, Workbox Caba(s), Nécessaire
Workbench Banker, Siege
Workhouse Casual ward, Spike, Union
▷ **Working** *may indicate* an anagram
Working-party Bee, Quilting-bee, Sewing-bee, Squad
Workmate Yokefellow
Work out Deduce
Works, Workplace, Workshop Atelier, Engine, Factory, Forge, Foundry, Garage,
Hacienda, Hangar, Innards, Lab, Mill, Passage, Plant, Public, Shed, Sheltered, Shipyard,
Shop, Skylab, Smithy, Studio, Study, Sweatshop, Telecottage, Time, Tin, Turnery, Upper
Workshy Indolent, Lazy, Sweer(ed), Sweert, Sweir(t)
World(ly), Worldwide Adland, Carnal, Chthonic, Cosmopolitan, Cosmos, Cyberspace,

Dream, Earth, First, Fleshly, Fourth, Free, Ge, Global village, Globe, Kingdom, Lay, Lower, Mappemond, Meatspace, Microcosm, Midgard, Mondaine, Mondial, Mould, Mundane, Natural, Nether, New, Old, Orb, Other, Oyster, Planet, Possible, Second, Secular, Sensual, Small, Society, Sphere, Spirit, Temporal, Terra, Terrene, Terrestrial, Third, Universe, Vale, Web, Welt, Whole

Worm(-like), Worms, Wormy Acorn, Angle, Anguillula, Annelid, Annulata, Apod(e), Apodous, Army, Arrow, Articulata, Ascarid, Bilharzia, Bladder, Blind, Blood, Bob, Bootlace, Brandling, Bristle, Caddis, Capeworm, Caseworm, Catworm, Cercaria, Cestode, Cestoid, Chaetopod, Clamworm, Copper, Dew, Diet, Diplozoon, Dracunculus, Edge, Enteropneust, Fan, Filander, Filaria, Flag, Flat, Flesh, Fluke, Galley, Gape, Gilt-tail, Gordius, Gourd, Gru-gru, Guinea, Hair, Hair-eel, Hairworm, Heartworm, Helminth, Hemichordata, Hookworm, Horsehair, Idle, Inchworm, Leech, Liver-fluke, Lob, Lumbricus, Lytta, Maw, Measuring, Merosome, Miner's, Mopani, Muck, Nemathelminthes, Nematoda, Nematode, Nematodirus, Nematomorpha, Nemertean, Nemertina, Nereid, Night-crawler, Oligochaete, Onychophoran, Paddle, Palmer, Palolo, Paste-eel, Peripatus, Phoronid, Pile, Pin, Piper, Planarian, Platyhelminth, Polychaete, Ragworm, Redia, Ribbon, Rootworm, Roundworm, Sabella, Sand mason, Schistosome, Scoleciform, Scolex, Screw, Seamouse, Serpula, Servile, Ship, Sipunculacea, Sipunculoidea, Spiny-headed, Stomach, Strawworm, Strongyl(e), Taenia, Tag-tail, Taint, Tapeworm, Tenioid, Teredo, Termite, Threadworm, Tiger, Tiger tail, Tongue, Toxocara, Trematode, Trichin(ell)a, Trichinosed, Triclad, Tube, Tubifex, Turbellaria, Vermiform, Vinegar, Vinegar eel, Wheat-eel, Wheatworm, Whipworm

Wormkiller Anthelmintic, Santonin

Wormwood Absinth, Appleringie, Artemisia, Moxa, Mugwort, Santonica, Southernwood

Worn (out) Attrite, Bare, Decrepit, Detrition, Effete, Épuisé, Exhausted, Forfairn, Forfoughten, Forjaskit, Forjeskit, Frazzled, Gnawn, Knackered, Old, On, Passé, Raddled, Rag, Seedy, Shabby, Shopsoiled, Shot, Spent, Stale, Tatty, Threadbare, Tired, Traikit, Trite, Used, Weathered, Whacked

Worried, Worrier, Worry Agonise, Angst, Annoy, Anxiety, Badger, Bait, Beset, Bother, Brood, Burden, Care(worn), Cark, Chafe, Concern, Consternate, Deave, Deeve, Distress, Disturb, Dog, Eat, Exercise, Faze, Feeze, Frab, Fret, Fuss, Gnaw, Harass, Harry, Headache, Hyp, Inquietude, Knag, Nag, Niggle, Perturb, Pester, Pheese, Pheeze, Phese, Pingle, Pium, Preoccupy, Rattle, Rile, Sool, Stew, Tew, Touse, Towse, Trouble, Unease, Unnerve, Vex, Wherrit, Worn

▷ **Worried** *may indicate* an anagram

Worse(n) Adversely, Compound, Degenerate, Deteriorate, Exacerbate, Impair, Inflame, Pejorate, Regress, Relapse, War(re), Waur, Well away

Worship(per) Adore, Adulation, Ancestor, Angelolatry, Aniconism, Animist, Autolatry, Bardolatry, Bless, Churchgoer, Cosmolatry, Cult, Deify, Devotion, Dote, Douleia, Doxology, Dulia, Epeolatry, Exalt, Exercise, Fetish, Glorify, Gurdwara, Happy-clappy, Henotheism, Hero, Ibadah, Iconology, Idolatry, Idolise, Latria, Lauds, Lionise, Liturgics, Lordolatry, Mariolatry, Meeting-house, Monolatry, Oncer, Orant, Praise, Puja, Revere, Sabaism, Sakta, Service, Shacharis, Shakta, Sun, Synaxis, Thiasus, Vaishnava, Venerate, Votary, Wodenism

Worst Beat, Best, Defeat, Get, Less, Nadir, Outdo, Overpower, Pessimum, Rock-bottom, Scum, Severest, The pits, Throw, Trounce

Worsted Caddis, Caddyss, Challis, Coburg, Crewel, Genappe, Lea, Ley, Serge, Shalli, Tamin(e), Whipcord

▷ **Worsted** *may indicate* an anagram

Wort Hopped, Laser, Parkleaves, Plant, Sweet, Tutsan

Worth(while), Worthy, Worthies Admirable, Asset, Be, Cop, Cost, Cost effective, Deserving, Eligible, Estimable, Face value, Feck, → **MERIT**, Nine, Notable, Substance, Tanti, Use, Value, Venerable, Vertu, Virtu(e), Virtuous, Wealth

Worthless (person) Average, Base, Beggarly, Bilge, Blown, Bodger, Bootless, Bum, Candy floss, Catchpenny, Cheapjack, Crumb, Cypher, Damn, Despicable, Docken, Dodkin, Doit, Doitkin, Draffish, Draffy, Dreck, Dross, Duff, Ephemeron, Fallal, Footra, Fouter, Foutre, Frippery, Gimcrack, Gingerbread, Glop, Gubbins, Hilding, Javel, Jimcrack, Knick-knack, Left, Light, Lorel, Lorrell, Losel, Lozell, Manky, Mare's nest, Mauvais sujet, Mud, Nugatory, Nyaff, Obol, Ornery, Orra, Otiose, Pabulum, Paltry, Pin, Poxy, Punk, Raca, Rag, Rap, Razoo, Riffraff, Rubbishy, Scabby, Scrote, Scum, Shinkin, Shotten, Siwash, Sorry, Straw, Tawdry, Tinhorn, Tinpot, Tinsel, Tittle, Toerag, Trangam, Trashy, Tripy, Trumpery, Tuppenny, Twat, Two-bit, Twopenny, Useless, Vain, Vile, Waff, Wanworthy, Wauff, Zero

Wotchermean Anan

Would be Assumed, Pseudo, Soi-disant

Wouldn't Nould(e)

Wound(ed) Battery, Bite, Bless, Blighty, Bruise, Chagrin, Coiled, Crepance, Cut, Dere, Dunt, Engore, Entry, Exit, Flesh, Ganch, Gash, Gaunch, Gore, Harm, Hurt, Injury, Knee, Lacerate, Lesion, Maim, Maul, Molest, Mortify, Offend, Pip, Sabre-cut, Scab, Scar, Scath, Scotch, Scratch, Shoot, Snaked, Snub, Sore, Stab, Sting, Trauma, Twined, Umbrage, Vuln, Vulnerary, Walking, Wing, Wint

Woundwort Clown's, Marsh

Woven Faconne, Inwrought, Knitted, Pirnit, Textile, Wattle

Wow Amaze, Howl, Impress, My, Success

Wrack Destroy, Downfall, Kelp, Ore, Torment, Varec(h), Vengeance

Wraith Apparition, Fetch, Ghost, Phantom, Shadow, Spectre

Wrangle(r), Wrangling Altercate, Argie-bargie, → **ARGUE**, Bandy, Bicker, Brangle, Broil, Cample, Controvert, Dispute, Haggle, Horse, Mathematical, Rag, Second, Senior, Vitilitigation

Wrap(per), Wrapped, Wrapping, Wraparound, Wrap up Amice, Amis, Bag, Bathrobe, Bind, Boa, Body, Bubble, Bundle, Carton(age), Cellophane®, Cere, Clingfilm, Cloak, Clothe, Cocoon, Conclude, Cover-up, Drape, Emboss, Enfold, Enrol(l), Ensheath(e), Envelop(e), Enwind, Foil, Folio, Furl, Gladwrap®, Hap, Hem, Infold, Kimono, Kraft, Lag, Lap, Mail, Mob, Muffle, Negligee, Nori, Outsert, Package, Parcel, Plastic, Roll, Rug, Shawl, Sheath(e), Sheet, Shrink, Shroud, Stole, Swaddle, Swathe, Throw, Tinfoil, Tsutsumu, Velamen, Wap, Wimple

Wrasse Conner, Cunner, Parrot-fish, Scar

Wrath Anger, Cape, Fury, Ire, Passion, Vengeance

Wreak Avenge, Indulge, Inflict

Wreath(e) Adorn, Anadem, Bridal, Chaplet, Civic crown, Coronal, Crown, Entwine, Festoon, Garland, Laurel, Lei, Steven, Torse, Tortile, Twist

Wreathe(d) Hederated

Wreck(age), Wrecked, Wrecker Banjax, Blight, Blotto, Crab, Debris, Demolish, Devastate, Flotsam, Founder, Goner, Hesperus, Hulk, Lagan, Ligan, Loss, Luddite, Mutilate, Nervous, Ruin(ate), Sabotage, Saboteur, Shambles, Shatter, Sink, Smash, Spif(f)licate, Stramash, Subvert, Torpedo, Trash, Vandalise, Wrack

▷ **Wrecked** *may indicate* an anagram

Wren Architect, Bird, Fairy, Fire-crested, Golden-crested, Hannah, Heath, Jenny, Kinglet, Rifleman-bird, Sailor, Superb blue, Willow

Wrench Allen, Bobbejaan, Box, Fit, Jerk, Lug, Mole, Monkey, Nut, Pin, Pipe, Pull, Screw, Socket, Spanner, Spider, Sprain, Stillson®, Strain, Strap, T-bar, Tear, Torque, Twist, Windlass, Wrest

Wrestle(r), Wrestling All-in, Antaeus, Arm, Backbreaker, Basho, Bearhug, Bodycheck, Boston crab, Catch-as-catch-can, Catchweight, Clinch, Clothes line, Cross buttock, Cross press, Featherweight, Flying mare, Folding-press, Forearm smash, Freestyle, Full-nelson, Grapple, Gr(a)eco-Roman, Grovet, Half-nelson, Hammerlock, Haystacks, Headlock, Hip-lock, → **HOLD**, Indian, Judo, Knee-drop, Makunouchi, Milo, Monkey climb, Mud,

Nelson, Niramiai, Ozeki, Palaestral, Pancratium, Pinfall, Posting, Rikishi, Sambo, Stable, Straight arm lift, Stranglehold, Struggle, Sumo, Sumotori, Suplex, Tag (team), Toehold, Tussle, Whip, Wraxle, Wristlock, Writhe, Yokozuna

Wretch(ed) Abject, Bally, Blackguard, Blue, Caitiff, Chap-fallen, Crumb, Cullion, Cur, Darned, Donder, Forlorn, Git, Goddamned, Hapless, Ignoble, Lorn, Low, Measly, Miscreant, Miser, Miserable, Peelgarlic, Pilgarlick, Pipsqueak, Pitiable, Poltroon, Poor, Punk, Rakeshame, Rascal, Rat, Scoundrel, Scroyle, Seely, Snake, Sorry, Toerag, Unblest, Waeful, Wo(e), Woeful

▷ **Wretched** *may indicate* an anagram

Wriggle Hirsle, Shimmy, Squirm, Twine, Wiggle, Writhe

Wring(er) Drain, Extort, Mangle, Screw, Squeeze, Twist

Wrinkle(d), Wrinkly Clue, Cockle, Corrugate, Crankle, Crease, Crepy, Crimple, Crimpy, Crinkle, Crow's-foot, Crumple, Fold, Frounce, Frown, Frumple, Furrow, Gen, Groove, Headline, Hint, Idea, Knit, Line, Lirk, Plissé, Plough, Pucker, Purse, Ridge, Rimple, Rivel, Rop(e)y, Ruck(le), Rugose, Rumple, Runkle, Seamy, Shrivel, Sulcus, Time-worn, Tip, Whelk, Wizened, Wrizled

Wrist Carpus, Radialia, Shackle-bone

Writ(s) Attachment, Audita querela, Capias, Certiorari, Cursitor, Dedimus, Devastatit, Distringas, Elegit, Fieri facias, Filacer, Habeas corpus, Holy, Injunction, Jury process, Latitat, Law-burrows, Mandamus, Mise, Mittimus, Noverint, Praemunire, Process, Quare impedit, Quo warranto, Replevin, Scirefacias, Significat, Subpoena, Summons, Supersedeas, Supplicavit, Tolt, Venire, Venire facias, Warrant

Write(r), Writing Allograph, Amphigory, Annotator, Apocrypha, → **AUTHOR**, Automatic, Ballpoint, Bellet(t)rist, BIC®, Biographer, Biro®, Blog, Bloomsbury Group, Book-hand, Boustrophedon, Calligraphy, Causerie, Cento, Charactery, Clerk, Clinquant, Collectanea, Columnist, Continuity, Copperplate, Creative, Cuneiform, Cursive, Diarist, Dissertation, Dite, Draft, → **DRAMATIST**, Elohist, Endorse, Endoss, Engross, Enrol, Epigrammatise, Epistle, → **ESSAYIST**, Expatiate, Farceur, Festschrift, Feudist, Fist, Form, Formulary, Freelance, Ghost, Gongorism, Graffiti, Grammatology, Graphite, Hack, Hairline, Hand, Haplography, Hieratic, Hieroglyphics, Hierology, Hiragana, Homiletics, Indite, Ink, Inkhorn-mate, Ink-jerker, Inkslinger, Inscribe, Join-hand, Jot(tings), Journalese, Journalist, Journo, Kaleyard School, Kana, Kanji, Katakana, Keelivine, Keelyvine, Leader, Leetspeak, Lexigraphy, Lexis, Linear A, Lipogram, Littérateur, Longhand, Lucubrate, Marivaudage, Memoirist, Mimographer, Minoan, Mirror, Miscellany, Monodist, Ms(s), Nesk(h), Nib, Notary, Notate, Novelese, → **NOVELIST**, Palaeography, Pamphleteer, Paragraphia, Pasigraphy, Pen, Pencil, Penmanship, Penne, Penny-a-liner, Pentel®, Phrasemonger, Picture, Pinyin, Planchette, → **POET**, Polemic, Polygraphy, Pot-hook, Prosaist, Proser, Pseudepigrapha, Psychogram, Psychography, Purana, Purple patch, Quill, Rhymer, Roundhand, Samizdat, Sanskrit, Scenarist, Sci-fi, Scissorer, Score, Scratch, Scrawl, Screed, Screeve, Scribble, Scribe, Scrip(t), Scripture, Scrivener, Scrow, Scytale, Secretary, Shaster, Shastra, Sign, Sing, Sling-ink, Small-hand, Space, Spirit, Stichometry, Style, Stylography, Subscript, Superscribe, Sutra, Syllabary, Syllabic, Syllabism, Syngraph, Tantra, Text, Tractarian, Transcribe, Treatise, Tushery, Type, Uncial, Varityper®, Wisdom, Wordsmith, Zend-Avesta

WRITERS

3 letters:	Roy	Behn	Grey
APH		Bolt	Hope
Eco	*4 letters:*	Buck	Hugo
Lee	Amis	Cary	Hunt
Paz	Asch	Dahl	King
Poe	Aymé	Elia	Lamb
RLS	Bede	Gide	Lang

Lear
Loos
Loti
Lyly
Mahy
Mann
More
Nash
Opie
Ovid
Pope
Roth
Rudd
Saki
Sand
Seth
Shaw
Snow
Ward
West
Zola

5 letters:
Acton
Adams
Aesop
Albee
Alger
Auden
Awdry
Ayres
Bates
Benet
Blair
Blake
Byatt
Caine
Camus
Capek
Corvo
Crane
Crump
Dante
Defoe
Doyle
Dumas
Duras
Eliot
Ellis
Genet
Gogol
Gorki
Gorky
Gosse

Greer
Grimm
Hardy
Harte
Henry
Henty
Hesse
Heyer
Homer
Hoyle
Ibsen
Innes
James
Joyce
Kafka
Lewis
Lodge
Lorca
Marsh
Mason
Milne
Munro
Musil
Nashe
Orczy
Ouida
Paine
Pater
Paton
Pliny
Pound
Powys
Reade
Renan
Rilke
Sagan
Scott
Seuss
Shute
Spark
Stark
Stead
Stein
Stowe
Swift
Synge
Twain
Verne
Vidal
Waugh
Wells
White
Wilde
Woolf

Yates
Yonge

6 letters:
Alcott
Ambler
Arnold
Artaud
Asimov
Atwood
Austen
Balzac
Baring
Barrie
Belloc
Bellow
Bierce
Blyton
Borges
Borrow
Braine
Bronte
Buchan
Bunyan
Butler
Capote
Cardus
Cather
Cicero
Clancy
Clarke
Conrad
Cooper
Cowper
Cronin
Daudet
De Sade
Dryden
Duggan
Engels
Ennius
Fowles
France
Gibbon
Goethe
Graves
Greene
Harris
Heller
Hobbes
Hoberg
Hughes
Huxley
Jekyll

Jerome
Jonson
Le Fanu
London
Lucian
Lytton
Mailer
Malory
Mannin
Masoch
Miller
Milton
Morgan
Nerval
Nesbit
O'Brien
Onions
Orwell
Powell
Proust
Racine
Romaji
Runyon
Ruskin
Sapper
Sappho
Sartre
Sayers
Sendac
Sewell
Singer
Smiles
Sontag
Spring
Steele
Sterne
Stoker
Storey
Tagore
Thiele
Thomas
Updike
Virgil
Walker
Walton
Wilder

7 letters:
Addison
Aldrich
Allston
Angelou
Aretino
Bagehot

Bagnold
Balchin
Baldwin
Ballard
Beckett
Bennett
Bentley
Boileau
Boswell
Burgess
Burnett
Carlyle
Chaucer
Chekhov
Claudel
Cobbett
Cocteau
Coetzee
Colette
Collins
Cookson
Coppard
Corelli
Cranmer
Deeping
Dickens
Dinesen
Dodgson
Douglas
Drabble
Dreiser
Duhamel
Durrell
Emerson
Fenelon
Feydeau
Fleming
Forster
Fuentes
Gardner
Gaskell
Gissing
Golding
Grahame
Grisham
Haggard
Hammett
Hazlitt
Hazzard
Herbert
Herriot
Hichens
Holberg
Johnson

Kerouac
Kipling
Lardner
Leacock
Le Carre
Lessing
Malamud
Mallory
Mérimée
Marryat
Maugham
Mauriac
Mitford
Moravia
Murdoch
Nabokov
Naipaul
Narayan
Peacock
Pushkin
Pynchon
Ransome
Rendell
Richter
Robbins
Rostand
Rowling
Rushdie
Saroyan
Sassoon
Shelley
Simenon
Sitwell
Spender
Surtees
Tennant
Terence
Theroux
Thoreau
Tolkien
Tolstoy
Travers
Ustinov
Wallace
Walpole
Wharton
Whitman
Wyndham

8 letters:

Anacreon
Andersen
Beaumont
Beerbohm

Bradbury
Brittain
Brookner
Browning
Caldwell
Cartland
Chandler
Childers
Christie
Constant
Crompton
Deighton
De la Mare
Disraeli
Donleavy
Faulkner
Fielding
Flaubert
Forester
Goncourt
Gordimer
Ishiguro
Kingsley
Koestler
Langland
Lawrence
Mannheim
McCarthy
Melville
Meredith
Mitchell
Ondaatje
Perrault
Plutarch
Proudhon
Rabelais
Rattigan
Remarque
Rousseau
Salinger
Schiller
Shadbolt
Sheridan
Sillitoe
Smollett
Spillane
Stendhal
Strachey
Taffrail
Traherne
Trollope
Turgenev
Voltaire
Vonnegut

Williams
Xenophon

9 letters:

Aeschylus
Ainsworth
Aldington
Allingham
Blackmore
Boccaccio
Burroughs
Cervantes
Charteris
Corneille
Courtenay
De Quincey
Dos Passos
Du Maurier
Edgeworth
Goldsmith
Hawthorne
Hemingway
Isherwood
La Bruyère
Lermontov
Linklater
Lovecraft
Mackenzie
Madariaga
Mansfield
Martineau
O'Flaherty
Oppenheim
Pasternak
Priestley
Santayana
Sholokhov
Steinbeck
Stevenson
Thackeray
Wodehouse

10 letters:

Ballantyne
Chesterton
De Beauvoir
Dostoevsky
Fitzgerald
Galsworthy
Mandeville
Maupassant
Pirandello
Richardson
Williamson

11 letters:	12 letters:	Solzhenitsyn	14 letters:
Dostoyevsky	Aristophanes		Compton-Burnett
Machiavelli	Quiller-Couch	13 letters:	
Maeterlinck	Robbe-Grillet	Chateaubriand	15 letters:
Shakespeare	Saint-Exupéry	Sackville-West	Somerset Maugham

Write-off Amortise, Annul, Cancel, Scrap

Writhe, Writhing Athetosis, Contort, Curl, Scriggle, Squirm, Thraw, Twist, Wriggle

▷ **Writhing** *may indicate* an anagram

Writing-case Kalamdan

Writing-room Scriptorium

Wrong(ful), Wrongdoer, Wrongdoing Aggrieve, Agley, Amiss, Astray, Awry, Bad, Bum, Chout, Delict, Disservice, Err, Fallacious, False, Falsism, Harm, Ill, Immoral, Improper, Incorrect, Injury, Mischief, Misconduct, Misfaring, Misintelligence, Misled, Mistake(n), Misuse, Nocent, Offbase, Offend, Pear-shaped, Peccadillo, Perpetrator, Perverse, Private, Public, Sin(ful), Sinner, Tort, Tortious, Transgress, Unethical, Unright, Unsuitable, Withershins, Wryly, X

▷ **Wrong** *may indicate* an anagram

Wrong opinion Cacodoxy

Wrought (up) Agitated, Beaten, Carved, Created, Excited, Filigree, Freestone, Shaped

Wrung Twisted, Withers

Wry Askew, Contrary, Devious, Distort, Droll, Grimace, Ironic

Wryneck Iynx, Jynx, Torticollis, Yunx

Wycliffian Lollard

Wyoming Wy

X(-shaped) Buss, By, Chi, Christ, Cross, Decussate, Drawn, Generation, Kiss, Ten, Times, Unknown, X-ray

Xant(h)ippe Battle-axe, Dragon

Xenon Xe

Xenophobia Insularism

Xerophyte, Xerophytic Cactus, Cereus, Mesquite, Tamaricaceae, Tamarisk

Xhosan Caffre, Kaf(f)ir

Ximenes Cardinal

▶ **Xmas** *see* CHRISTMAS(TIME)

X-ray Angiogram, Anticathode, Arthrogram, Characteristic, Cholangiography, C(A)T-scanner, Emi-Scanner, Encephalogram, Encephalograph, Fermi, Grenz, Mammogram, Plate, Pyelogram, Radiogram, Radioscopy, Rem, Roentgen, Sciagram, Screening, Skiagram, Tomography, Venogram, X, Xeroradiography

Xylophone Marimba, Semantra, Sticcado, Sticcato

Y Samian, Unknown, Yankee, Yard, Year, Yen, Yttrium

Yacht Britannia, Dragon, Ice, Keelboat, Ketch, Knockabout, Land, Maxi, Sailboat, Sand, Yngling

Yachtsman, Yachtsmen Chichester, Heath, RYS

Yak Gup, Talk

Yale® Key, Lock

Yam Adjigo, Batata, Breadroot, Camote, Dioscorea, Diosgenin, Kumara

Yank(ee) Bet, Carpetbagger, Hitch, Jerk, Jonathan, Lug, Northerner, Pluck, Pull, Rug, Schlep(p), So(o)le, Sowl(e), → **TUG**, Tweak, Twitch, Wrench, Wrest, Y

▷ **Yank** *may indicate* an anagram

Yap Bark, Yelp

Yard(s) Area, CID, Close, Court, Farm-toun, Garden, Hard, Haw, Hof, Junk, Kail, Knacker's, Main, Marshalling, Mast, Measure, Met, Navy, Patio, Poultry, Prison, Ree(d), Sail, Scotland, Show, Spar, Sprit, Steel, Stick, Stockyard, Stride, Switch, Tilt, Timber, Victualling, Y, Yd

Yarn(s) Abb, Berlin, Bouclé, Caddice, Caddis, Chenille, Clew, Clue, Cop, Cord, Crewel, Fib, Fibroline, Fingering, Genappe, Gimp, Gingham, Guimp(e), Gymp, Homespun, Jaw, Knittle, Knot, Lay, Lea, Ley, Line, Lisle, Lurex®, Marl, Merino, Mohair, Nylon, Organzine, Orlon®, Ply, Rigmarole, Ripping, Rogue's, Rope, Saxony, Schappe, Sennit, Sinnet, Skein, Small stuff, Spun, Story, Strand, Tale, Taradiddle, Thread, Thrid, Thrum(my), Tram, Twice-laid, Warp, Water twist, Weft, Woof, Wool, Worsted, Zephyr

Yarrow Milfoil

Yashmak Veil

Yaw(s) Boba, Buba, Deviate, Framboesia, Lean, Morula, Tack, Veer

Yawn(ing) Boredom, Chasmy, Fissure, Gant, Gape, Gaunt, Greys, Hiant, Oscitation, Pandiculation, Rictus

Yea Certainly, Surely, Truly, Verily, Yes

Year(ly), Years A, Age, Anno, Annual, Anomalistic, Astronomical, AUC, Autumn, Calendar, Canicular, Civil, Common, Cosmic, Decennium, Donkey's, Dot, Ecclesiastical, Egyptian, Embolismic, Equinoctial, Financial, Fiscal, Gap, Grade, Great, Hebrew, Holy, Indiction, Julian, Leap, Legal, Light, Locust, Lunar, Lunisolar, Natural, PA, Perfect, Platonic, Prophetic week, Riper, Sabbatical, School, Sidereal, Solar, Sothic, Spring, Summer, Sun, Tax, Theban, Time, Towmon(d), Towmont, Tropical, Twelvemonth, Vintage, Wander(j)ahr), Winter, Zodiac

Yearbook Almanac, Annual

Yearling Colt, Hogget, Stirk, Teg

Yearn(ing) Ache, Ake, Aspire, Brame, Burn, Covet, Crave, Curdle, Desire, Erne, Greed, Green, Grein, Hanker, Hone, → **LONG**, Lust, Nostalgia, Pant, Pine, Sigh

▷ **Yearning** *may indicate* an anagram

Year's end Dec

Yeast Barm, Bees, Brewer's, Ferment, Flor, Leaven, Saccharomycete, Torula, Vegemite®

Yell Cry, Hue, Rebel, Shout, Skelloch, Squall, Thunder, Tiger, Ululate, Waul, Yoick

Yellow(ish) Abram, Amber, Anthoclore, Auburn, Back, Beige, Bisque, Bistre, Buff, Butternut, Cadmium, Canary, Chartreuse, Chicken, Chrome, Citrine, Clay-bank, Cowardly, Craven, Curcumin(e), Daffadowndilly, Daffodil, Eggshell, Etiolin, Fallow, Fever, Filemot, Flavescent, Flavin(e), Flavon, Flaxen, Fulvous, Gamboge, Gold, Icteric, Isabel(le),

Isabella, Jack, Jaundiced, King's, Lammer, Lemon(y), Lupulin, Lurid, Lutein, Luteous, Lutescent, Maize, Mustard, Nankeen, Naples, Oaker, Ochery, Ochre(y), Ochroid, Or(eide), Oroide, Pages, Peach, Peril, Pink, Primrose, Queen's, River, Saffron, Sallow, Sand, Sear, Sherry, Spineless, Strae, Straw, Sulfur, Sulphur, Tawny, Topaz, Tow, Vitelline, Weld, Xanthous, Yolk

Yellowhammer Bunting, Yeldring, Yeldrock, Yite, Yoldring

Yellow-wood Gopher

Yelp Cry, Squeal, Whee, Ya(w)p

Yemeni Adeni, Saba, Sabean, Sheba

Yen Desire, Itch, Longing, Urge, Y, Yearn

Yeoman Beefeater, Exon, Goodman, Goodwife, Salvation

Yep OK, Yes

Yerd Inter

Yes Agreed, Ay(e), Da, I, Indeed, Ja, Jokol, Nod, OK, Oke, Quite, Sure, Truly, Uh-huh, Whoopee, Wilco, Yah, Yea, Yokul, Yup

Yesterday Démodé, Eve, Hesternal, Pridian

Yet But, Even, How-be, Moreover, Nay, Nevertheless, Now, Still, Though

Yeti Abominable snowman, Sasquatch

Yew Podocarp(us), Taxus, Yvonne

Yibbles A(i)blins

Yield(ing), Yielded Abandon, Afford, Bear, Bend, Bow, Breed, Capitulate, Catch, Cede, Come, Comply, Concede, Crack, Crop, Defer, Dividend, Docile, Ductile, Easy, Elastic, Exert, Facile, Flaccid, Flexible, Give, Harvest, Interest, Knock under, Knuckle, Knuckle under, Meek, Meltith, Mess, Obtemper, Output, Pan, Pay, Pliant, Produce, Quantum, Redemption, Relent, Render, Return, Sag, Soft, Squashy, → **SUBMIT**, Succumb, Supple, Surrender, Susceptible, Sustained, Temporise, Truckle, Weak-kneed, Yold

Yob Lager lout, Lout, Oaf, Ted

Yodel Song, Warble

Yoga, Yogi As(h)tanga (vinyasa), Bear, Bhakti, Bikram, Fakir, Hatha, Hot, Maha, Power, Raja, Sid(d)ha, Sivananda

Yog(h)urt Dahi, Madzoon, Matzoon, Tzatziki

Yoke Bow, Cang(ue), Collar, Couple, Harness, Inspan, Jugal, Oxbow, Pair, Span, Square, Tucker

Yokel Boor, Bumpkin, Chaw(-bacon), Clumperton, Culchie, Hayseed, Hick, Jake, Jock, Peasant, Rustic

Yolk Parablast, Vitellicle, Vitelline, Vitellus, Yelk, Yellow

Yon(der) Distant, Further, O'erby, Thae, There, Thether, Thither

Yore Agone, Olden, Past

Yorick Sterne

York(shire), Yorkshireman Batter, Bowl, Dales, Ebor, Pudding, Ridings, See, Tyke, White rose

Yorker Tice

You One, Sie, Thee, Thou, Usted, Wena, Ye

Young (person), Youngster, Youth(ful) Adolescent, Ageless, Amorino, Bairn, Bev(an), Bit, Bodgie, Boy, Boyhood, Brigham, Bub, Buckeen, Buckie, Buppie, Calf-time, Ch, Charver, Chick, Chicken, Chiel, Child, Chile, Cion, Cock(erel), Cockle, Colt, Comsomol, Cornstalk, Cub, Day-old, Dell, Dilling, DJ, Early, Ephebe, Ephebus, Esquire, Flapper, Fledgling, Foetus, Fox, Fry, Gigolo, Gilded, Gillet, Girl, Gunsel, Halfling, Hebe, Hobbledehoy, Immature, Imp, Infant, Issue, Jeunesse d'orée, Junior, Juvenal, Juvenesce, Juvenile, Keral, Kid, Kiddo, Kiddy, Kipper, Knave-bairn, Komsomol, Lad, Lamb, Latter-day, Leaping-time, Less, Litter, Little, Loretta, Middle, Minor, Misspent, Mod, Mormon, Mot, Muchacha, Nance, Narcissus, Neanic, Ned(ette), Neophyte, Nestling, New, New Romantic, Nipper, Nurs(e)ling, Nymph, Plant, Popsy, (Pre-)pubescent, Progeny, Protégé(e), Punk, Pup, Rude boy, Salad days, Sapling, Scent, Scion, Screenager,

Shaveling, Shaver, Sien(t), Skinhead, Slip, Small, Son, Spark, Spawn, Spide, Sprig, Springal(d), Stripling, Subteen, Swain, Syen, Ted, Teenager, Teens, Teenybopper, Tir na n'Og, Tit, Toyboy, Vernal, Waif, Well-preserved, Whelp, Whippersnapper, Widge, Wigga, Wigger, Wimp, Yippy, Yoof, Yopper, Younker, Yumpie, Yuppie

Younger, Youngest Baby, Benjamin, Cadet, Last born, Less, Minimus, Seneca, Wallydrag, Wallydraigle, Yr

Your(s) Thee, Thine, Thy

▶ **Youth** *see* YOUNG PERSON

Yo-yo Bandalore

Ytterbium Yb

Yttrium Y

Yucatan Maya

Yucca Adam's needle

Yuck(y) Gooey, Grooly, Gross, Sickly, Sticky

Yugoslav Croat(ian), Serb, Slovene, Ustashi

Yukon YT

Yuletide Advent, Dec, Noel, Xmas

Zz

Z Izzard, Izzet, Zambia, Zebra
Zambia .zm
Zamenhof Esperanto
Zander Fogash, Sander
Zany Bor(r)el, Comic, Cuckoo, Idiotic, Mad, Offbeat
Zanzibar Swahili
Zap Nuke
Zeal(ous) Ardour, Bigotry, Devotion, Eager, Earnest, Enthusiasm, Evangelic, Fanatical, Fanaticism, Fervour, Fire, Hamas, Perfervid, Rabid, Study, Zest
Zealot Bigot, Crusader, Devotee, Essene, Fan(atic), St Simon, Votary
Zebra Convict, Quagga
Zebu Brahmin bull, Brahmin cow
Zenith Acme, Apogee, Height, Pole, Summit, Vertex
Zeno Colonnade, Elea, Stoic
Zeolite Analcime, Analcite, Gmelinite
Zephyr Breeze, Wind
Zeppelin Airship, Balloon, Dirigible
Zero Absolute, Blob, Cipher, Circle, Donut, Double, Ground, Nil, None, Nothing, Nought, O, Status, Year, Z
Zest Condiment, Crave, Élan, Enthusiasm, Gusto, Peel, Pep, Piquancy, Relish, Spark, Spice, Tang, Taste, Zap, Zing
Ziegfeld Flo
Zigzag Crémaillère, Crinkle-crankle, Dancette, Feather-stitch, Indent, Major Mitchell, Ric-rac, Slalom, Stagger, Switchback, Tack, Traverse, Vandyke, Yaw
Zimbabwe .zw
Zinc Blende, Gahnite, Mossy, Sherardise, Spelter, Sphalerite, Tutenag, Tutty, Willemite, Wurtzite, Zn
Zip(per) Dart, Dash, Energy, Fastener, Fly, Go, Nada, O, Oomph, Presto, Slide fastener, Stingo, Verve, Vim, Vivacity, Whirry, Zero
Zircon Hyacinth, Jacinth, Jargo(o)n
Zirconium Baddeleyite, Zr
Zither Autoharp, Cithara, Kantela, Kantele, Koto
Zodiac(al) Aquarius, Archer, Aries, Bull, Cancer, Capricorn, Counter-glow, Crab, Fish, Gegenschein, Gemini, Goat, Horoscope, Leo, Libra, Lion, Ophiuchus, Pisces, Ram, Sagittarius, Scales, Scorpio(n), Taurus, Twins, Virgin, Virgo, Watercarrier
Zola Budd, Emile, Nana, Realism
Zombie Catatonic, Dolt, Robot, Undead
Zone(s) Abyssal, Anacoustic, Area, Arid, Auroral, Band, Bathyal, Belt, Benioff, Buffer, Canal, Climate, Collision, Comfort, Convergence, Crumple, Dead, Demilitarized, District, Drop, Economic, Ecotone, End, Enterprise, Erogenous, Eruv, Euro, Exclusion, Exclusive, F layer, Fracture, Free(-fire), Fresnel, Frigid, Hadal, Home, Hot, Impact, Ionopause, Krumhole, Low velocity, Mix, Neutral, No-fly, Nuclear-free, Precinct, → REGION, Rift, Ring, Russian, Sahel, Saturation, Schlieren, Sector, Shear, Skip, Smokeless, Soviet, Stratopause, Strike, Subduction, T, Temperate, Time, Tolerance, Torrid, Tundra, Twilight, Vadose, Z
Zoo Bedlam, Circus, Menagerie, Vivarium, Whipsnade

Zoologist, Zoology Biologist, Botanist, Cetology, Naturalist, Primatology, Schneider
Zoom Close-up, Speed
Zoroastrian Fire-worshipper, Gabar, Gheber, Ghebre, Gueber, Guebre, Magus, Mazdaist, Mazdean, Ormazd, Ormuzd, Parsee, Parsi
Zulu Chaka, Impi, Inkatha, Matabele, Niger, Shaka, Warrior
Zut Crimini
Zygote Oospore